2002

ESPN®
Information Please®

Sports Almanac

Edited by

Gerry Brown
Michael Morrison

John Gettings
Associate Editor

Information Please
www.infoplease.com
Part of LEARNING NETWORK

HYPERION

ESPN®
BOOKS

Editors
Gerry Brown, Michael Morrison

Associate Editor
John Gettings

Reporter
Joe Lurie

Production Editor & Graphics
Phyllis McKee

Database/Production Manager
Susan Hyde

Technical Support
Karl DeBisschop

Thanks to . . .

John Hassan, Rick Sommers, Gretchen Young, Mike Meserole, Liz Kubik, Borgna Brunner, Sean Dessureau, Natalie Kaire, Rick Campbell, Gary Johnson, Barbara Zidovsky, David Lott, Carolyn McMahon, Jim Jenks, Craig Wachs, Steve Rutkowski, Paul Kinney, Todd Snyder, Jeff Bennett, Matt Wilansky, Jim Samia, Chris Fallica, Sanford Appell, Michael Freer

---

Comments and suggestions from readers are invited. Because of the many letters received, however, it is not possible to respond personally to every correspondent. Nevertheless, all letters are welcome and each will be carefully considered. The **2002 ESPN Information Please Sports Almanac** does not rule on bets or wagers. Address all correspondence to: Sports, Information Please, 20 Park Plaza, Boston, MA 02116.
Email: ipsa@infoplease.com.

ISBN 0-7868-8534-3

FIRST EDITION

10 9 8 7 6 5 4 3 2 1

CONTENTS

WHO PLAYS WHERE 7

UPDATES........................8

THE YEAR IN REVIEW—2000-01
Top 20 Personalities by Dan Patrick
and Linda Cohn 11
Top 20 Moments by Rich Eisen
and Stuart Scott.........................19
Month by Month Calendar.................27
Coming Attractions 52

BASEBALL
Year in Review by Karl Ravech.............53
2001 Statistics...............................59
Final Major League Standings 59
Regular Season Leaders....................60
2001 All-Star Game.......................66
Team by Team Statistics 67
World Series and Playoffs.................75
College Baseball 84
College Baseball by Dave Ryan 87
Through the Years 89
The World Series 89
Reg. Season League & Div. Winners 94
The All-Star Game 96
Major League Franchise Origins..........98
Annual Leaders 100
No Hitters 111
All-Time Leaders 113
All-Time Winningest Managers..........121
Annual Awards 122
College Baseball........................126

COLLEGE FOOTBALL
Year in Review by Chris Fowler
and Lee Corso............................129
2000 Season Statistics 135
Final AP Top 25 Poll 135
NCAA Division 1-A Final Standings.....140
NCAA Division 1-A Leaders..............141
NCAA Div. 1-AA Final Standings 145
NCAA Division 1-AA Leaders 147
Through the Years..........................150
National Champions, 1869-2000 150
AP Final Polls, 1936-2000 154
Bowl Games 171
All-Time Winningest Div. 1-A Teams 179
Major Conference Champions 180
Annual NCAA Division 1-A Leaders ...186
All-Time NCAA Division 1-A Leaders....189
Annual Awards 192
All-Time Winningest Div. 1-A Coaches ..197
All-Time NCAA Div. 1-AA Leaders 199

PRO FOOTBALL
Year in Review by Chris Berman
and John Clayton.........................203
2000 Season Statistics 209
Final NFL Standings 209
Regular Season Individual Leaders......210
Team by Team Results and Statistics 214
NFL Playoffs and Super Bowl XXXV 225
2001 NFL Draft...........................230

PRO FOOTBALL (CONT.)
NFL Europe...............................231
Canadian Football League 232
Arena League and XFL...................233
Through the Years.........................234
The Super Bowl 234
Super Bowl Playoffs, 1966-2000 238
NFL-NFC Championship Game 244
AFL-AFC Championship Game 245
NFL Divisional Champions..............246
NFL Franchise Origins 250
Annual NFL Leaders 252
All-Time NFL Leaders.....................256
All-Time Winningest NFL Coaches 263
Annual Awards 264
Canadian Football League 268

COLLEGE BASKETBALL
Year in Review by Chris Fowler
and Dick Vitale 271
2000-01 Statistics 277
Final Regular Season AP Men's Top 25 .277
2001 NCAA Men's Div. 1 Tournament .278
Final NCAA Men's Div. 1 Standings 281
Women's College Basketball
by Nancy Lieberman 291
2001 NCAA Women's Div. 1 Tourn....293
Through the Years..........................296
National Champions, 1901-2001 296
All-Time NCAA Div. 1 Tourn. Leaders ..300
AP Final Polls, 1949-2001 304
Annual NCAA Div. 1 Leaders 318
All-Time NCAA Div. 1 Indiv. Leaders ...319
Annual Awards 322
All-Time Winningest Div. 1 Coaches ...324
Women's Basketball 328

PRO BASKETBALL
Year in Review by Ric Bucher............335
2000-01 Statistics 341
Final NBA Standings......................341
Regular Season Individual Leaders 343
Team by Team Statistics..................345
NBA Playoffs..............................351
Annual Awards 355
NBA Draft 357
Through the Years..........................361
The NBA Finals, 1947-2001 361
NBA Franchise Origins 365
Annual NBA Leaders 367
All-Time NBA Regular Season Leaders ..369
All-Time Winningest NBA Coaches 372
Annual Awards 373
Number One Draft Choices 374
American Basketball Association........377

HOCKEY
Year in Review by Steve Levy.............379
2000-01 Statistics 385
Final NHL Standings 385
Regular Season Individual Leaders......387
Team by Team Statistics..................389
Stanley Cup Playoffs.....................397

HOCKEY (CONT.)

2001 NHL Draft 402
College Hockey 402
Through the Years 407
   Stanley Cup Champions, 1893-2001...407
   All-Time Playoff Leaders.................409
   NHL Franchise Origins 413
   Annual NHL Leaders....................415
   All-Time NHL Regular Season Leaders...418
   All-Time Winningest NHL Coaches.....421
   Annual Awards 422
   Number One Draft Choices 426
   World Hockey Association 427
   College Hockey..........................430

COLLEGE SPORTS

Year in Review by Steve Cyphers 433
   Div. 1-A Football Schools 439
   Div. 1-AA Football Schools 441
   Div. 1 Basketball Schools 443
   2000-01 NCAA Team Champions......452
   Annual NCAA Div. 1 Team Champions.457

HALLS OF FAME & AWARDS

Halls of Fame 465
Retired Numbers 497
Awards...................................501
Trophy Case 509

WHO'S WHO

Sports Personalities 513

BALLPARKS & ARENAS

Coming Attractions 545
Sport by Sport 548

BUSINESS

Year in Review by Bob Stevens...........569
   Media Statistics and Awards 575
   Directory of Organizations 586

INTERNATIONAL SPORTS

Year in Review by Jack Edwards 613
   2001 Statistics 619
   Track & Field World Records 620
   Swimming World Records 627
Through the Years 636

OLYMPIC GAMES

Winter Games Through the Years 655
   Winter Games Recaps...................657
   Event by Event 683
   All-Time Leading Medal Winners........692
Summer Games Through the Years 695
   Event by Event 696
   All-Time Leading Medal Winners.......716

SOCCER

Year in Review by Jack Edwards 721
   2001 International Results...............728
   2001 Major League Soccer 735
   College Soccer..........................741
Through the Years 744
   The World Cup, 1930-98 744
   Other Competition 749

BOWLING

Year in Review by Dick Evans 759
2000-01 Statistics 765
Through the Years.........................768

HORSE RACING

Year in Review by Steve Cyphers 773
2000-01 Statistics 779
   Thoroughbred Racing...................779
   Harness Racing 783
Through the Years 785
   Thoroughbred Racing...................785
   Harness Racing 801

TENNIS

Year in Review by Sal Paolantonio 805
2000-01 Statistics 811
   Men's and Women's Tournaments.......811
   Singles Rankings........................815
Through the Years 817
   Grand Slam Championships 817
   Annual Number One Players...........826
   Annual Top 10 World Rankings 827
   Year-end Tournaments...................831
   Colleges................................833

GOLF

Year in Review by Karl Ravech 835
2000-01 Statistics 841
   PGA, Seniors and LPGA Tournaments...841
   2001 Statistics 848
Through the Years 851
   Major Championships 851
   Annual Money Leaders 868
   National Team Competition 872
   Colleges................................873

AUTO RACING

Year in Review by John Kernan..........875
2000-01 Statistics 881
   NASCAR Results 881
   CART Results 884
   Indy Racing League Results 886
   Formula One Results 887
   NHRA Results 889
Through the Years 890
   NASCAR Circuit 890
   CART Circuit 893
   IRL Circuit 894
   Formula One 896
   NHRA 900

BOXING

Year in Review by Al Bernstein 901
   Current Champions 907
   Major Bouts, 2000-01 908
Through the Years 913
   Major Hvywgt. Championship Fights ...913
   Major Titleholders......................919

MISCELLANEOUS SPORTS

Little League Baseball
   by Dave Ryan 931
2000-01 Statistics 934

DEATHS 949

BIBLIOGRAPHY 957

Major League Cities & Teams

As of Oct. 31, 2001, there were 133 major league teams playing or scheduled to play men's baseball, men's basketball, NFL football, hockey and men's soccer in 51 cities in the United States and Canada. Listed below are the cities and the teams that play there.

Anaheim
AL   Angels
NHL   Mighty Ducks of Anaheim

Atlanta
NL   Braves
NBA   Hawks
NFL   Falcons
NHL   Thrashers

Baltimore
AL   Orioles
NFL   Ravens

Boston
AL   Red Sox
NBA   Celtics
NFL   N.E. Patriots (Foxboro)
NHL   Bruins
MLS   N.E. Revolution (Foxboro)

Buffalo
NFL   Bills (Orchard Park)
NHL   Sabres

Calgary
NHL   Flames

Charlotte
NBA   Hornets
NFL   Carolina Panthers

Chicago
AL   White Sox
NL   Cubs
NBA   Bulls
NFL   Bears
NHL   Blackhawks
MLS   Fire

Cincinnati
NL   Reds
NFL   Bengals

Cleveland
AL   Indians
NBA   Cavaliers
NFL   Browns

Columbus
NHL   Blue Jackets
MLS   Crew

Dallas
AL   Texas Rangers (Arlington)
NBA   Mavericks
NFL   Cowboys (Irving)
NHL   Stars
MLS   Burn

Denver
NL   Colorado Rockies
NBA   Nuggets
NFL   Broncos
NHL   Colorado Avalanche
MLS   Colorado Rapids

Detroit
AL   Tigers
NBA   Pistons (Auburn Hills)
NFL   Lions (Pontiac)
NHL   Red Wings

East Rutherford
NBA   New Jersey Nets
NFL   New York Giants
NFL   New York Jets
NHL   New Jersey Devils
MLS   NY/NJ Metrostars

Edmonton
NHL   Oilers

Green Bay
NFL   Packers

Houston
NL   Astros
NBA   Rockets
NFL   Texans

Indianapolis
NBA   Indiana Pacers
NFL   Colts

Jacksonville
NFL   Jaguars

Kansas City
AL   Royals
NFL   Chiefs
MLS   Wizards

Los Angeles
NL   Dodgers
NBA   Clippers
NBA   Lakers
NHL   Kings
MLS   Galaxy

Memphis
NBA   Grizzlies

Miami
NL   Florida Marlins
NBA   Heat
NFL   Dolphins
NHL   Florida Panthers (Sunrise)
MLS   Fusion (Ft. Lauderdale)

Milwaukee
NL   Brewers
NBA   Bucks

Minneapolis
AL   Minn. Twins
NBA   Minn. Timberwolves
NFL   Minn. Vikings

Montreal
NL   Expos
NHL   Canadiens

Nashville
NFL   Tennessee Titans
NHL   Predators

New Orleans
NFL   Saints

New York
AL   Yankees
NL   Mets (Flushing)
NBA   Knicks
NHL   Rangers
NHL   Islanders (Uniondale)

Oakland
AL   Athletics
NBA   Golden St. Warriors
NFL   Raiders

Orlando
NBA   Magic

Ottawa
NHL   Senators (Kanata)

Philadelphia
NL   Phillies
NBA   76ers
NFL   Eagles
NHL   Flyers

Phoenix
NL   Arizona Diamondbacks
NBA   Suns
NFL   Arizona Cardinals (Tempe)
NHL   Coyotes

Pittsburgh
NL   Pirates
NFL   Steelers
NHL   Penguins

Portland
NBA   Trail Blazers

Raleigh
NHL   Carolina Hurricanes

Sacramento
NBA   Kings

St. Louis
NL   Cardinals
NFL   Rams
NHL   Blues

St. Paul
NHL   Minnesota Wild

Salt Lake City
NBA   Utah Jazz

San Antonio
NBA   Spurs

San Diego
NL   Padres
NFL   Chargers

San Francisco
NL   Giants
NFL   49ers

San Jose
NHL   Sharks
MLS   Earthquakes

Seattle
AL   Mariners
NBA   SuperSonics
NFL   Seahawks

Tampa
AL   T.B. Devil Rays (St. Petersburg)
NFL   T.B. Buccaneers
NHL   T.B. Lightning
MLS   T.B. Mutiny

Toronto
AL   Blue Jays
NBA   Raptors
NHL   Maple Leafs

Vancouver
NHL   Canucks

Washington
NBA   Wizards
NFL   Redskins (Raljon, Md.)
NHL   Capitals
MLS   D.C. United

GOLF

Late 2001 Tournament Results
PGA Tour

Last Rd	Tournament	Winner	Earnings	Runner-Up
Oct. 21	National Car Rental Classic at WDW Resort	Jose Coceres (265)	$612,000	D. Love III (266)
Oct. 28	Buick Challenge	Chris DiMarco (267)*	612,000	D. Duval (267)

Remaining Events (6): The Tour Championship (Nov. 1-4); Southern Farm Bureau Classic (Nov. 1-4); Franklin Templeton Shootout (Nov. 8-11); World Golf Championships: EMC World Cup (Nov. 15-18); Hyundai Team Matches (Dec. 7-9); Williams World Challenge (Dec. 10-16).
*Playoff: DiMarco won on the first hole.
Note: The EMC World Cup (Nov. 15-18) is the final official PGA Tour event of 2001.

European PGA Tour

Last Rd	Tournament	Winner	Earnings	Runner-Up
Oct. 21	Dunhill Links Championship	Paul Lawrie (270)	€881,250	E. Els (271)
Oct. 28	Madrid Masters	Retief Goosen (264)*	233,330	S. Webster (264)

Remaining Events (3): Italian Open (Nov. 1-4) Volvo Masters (Nov. 9-11); World Golf Championships: EMC World Cup (Nov. 15-18).
*Playoff: Goosen won on the third hole.

Senior PGA Tour

Last Rd	Tournament	Winner	Earnings	Runner-Up
Oct. 21	SBC Championship	Larry Nelson (199)	$210,000	B. Gilder & G. McCord (201)
Oct. 28	Senior Tour Championship	Bob Gilder (277)	440,000	D. Tewell (278)

Remaining Events (4): Senior Slam (Nov. 5-11); Office Depot Father-Son Challenge (Nov. 26-Dec. 2); Hyundai Team Matches (Dec. 7-9); Wendy's Three-Tour Challenge (Dec. 22-23).

LPGA Tour

Last Rd	Tournament	Winner	Earnings	Runner-Up
Oct. 21	Sports Today Classic	cancelled		
Oct. 28	Cisco World Ladies Match Play Championship	Annika Sorenstam (1-up)	$144,000	S. Ri Pak

Remaining Events (4): Mizuno Classic (Nov. 2-4); Tyco/ADT Championship (Nov. 15-18); Hyundai Team Matches (Dec. 7-9); Wendy's Three-Tour Challenge (Dec. 22-23).

TENNIS

Late 2001 Tournament Results
Men's Tour

Finals	Tournament	Winner	Earnings	Loser	Score
Sept. 23	Heineken Open (Shanghai)	Rainer Schuettler	$54,000	M. Kratochvil	63 64
Sept. 30	Salem Open (Hong Kong)	Marcelo Rios	54,000	R. Schuettler	76 62
Sept. 30	International Championship of Sicily (Palermo)	Felix Mantilla	54,000	D. Nalbandian	76 64
Oct. 7	Japan Open (Tokyo)	Lleyton Hewitt	115,000	M. Kratochvil	64 62
Oct. 7	Kremlin Cup (Moscow)	Yevgeny Kafelnikov	137,000	N. Kiefer	64 75
Oct. 14	CA Tennis Trophy (Vienna)	Tommy Haas	130,000	G. Canas	62 76 64
Oct. 14	Grand Prix of Tennis (Lyon)	Ivan Ljubicic	109,000	Y. El Aynaoui	63 62
Oct. 21	TMS—Stuttgart	Tommy Haas	434,000	M. Mirnyi	62 62 62
Oct. 28	St. Petersburg Open	Marat Safin	109,000	R. Schuettler	36 63 63
Oct. 28	Stockholm Open	Sjeng Schalken	109,000	J. Nieminen	36 63 63 46 63
Oct. 28	Swiss Indoors (Basel)	Tim Henman	137,000	R. Federer	63 64 62

Remaining Events (3): Tennis Masters Series-Paris (Nov. 4); ATP Tour World Doubles Championship (Nov. 11); Tennis Masters Cup (Nov. 18).

Women's Tour

Finals	Tournament	Winner	Earnings	Loser	Score
Sept. 23	Princess Cup (Tokyo)	Jelena Dokic	$90,000	A. Sanchez Vicario	64 62
Sept. 30	Sparkassen Cup (Leipzig)	Kim Clijsters	90,000	M. Maleeva	61 61
Sept. 30	Wismilak International (Bali)	Angelique Widjaja	27,000	J. Kruger	76 76
Oct. 7	Kremlin Cup (Moscow)	Jelena Dokic	175,000	E. Dementieva	63 63
Oct. 7	Japan Open (Tokyo)	Monica Seles	27,000	T. Tanasugarn	63 62
Oct. 14	Porsche Tennis Grand Prix (Filderstadt)	Lindsay Davenport	90,000	J. Henin	75 64
Oct. 14	Kiwi Open (Shanghai)	Monica Seles	22,000	N. Pratt	62 63
Oct. 21	Swisscom Challenge (Zurich)	Lindsay Davenport	175,000	J. Dokic	63 61
Oct. 21	Slovak Indoor (Bratislava)	Rita Grande	16,000	M. Sucha	61 61
Oct. 28	Generali Open (Linz)	Lindsay Davenport	90,000	J. Dokic	61 64
Oct. 28	Seat Open (Luxembourg)	Kim Clijsters	27,000	L. Raymond	62 62

Remaining Events (4): Sanex WTA Tour Championships (Nov. 4); Wismilak International (Nov. 4); Volvo Open (Nov. 11); Fed Cup Final (Nov. 11).

THOROUGHBRED RACING

Late 2001 Major Stakes Races

Date	Race	Location	Miles	Winner	Jockey	Purse
Sept. 29	Gallant Bloom Handicap	Belmont	6 ½ F	Finder's Fee	John Velazquez	$129,225
Sept. 29	Flower Bowl Invitational	Belmont	1 ¼ (T)	Lailani (GBR)	Jerry Bailey	750,000
Sept. 29	Turf Classic Invitational	Belmont	1 ½	Timboroa (GBR)	Edgar Prado	750,000
Sept. 29	Lady's Secret BC Handicap	Santa Anita	1 1⁄16	Queenie Belle	Brice Blanc	209,400
Sept. 29	Nofolk Stakes	Santa Anita	1	Essence of Dubai	Alex Solis	250,000
Sept. 29	Yellow Ribbon Stakes	Santa Anita	1 ¼ (T)	Janet (GBR)	David Flores	500,000
Sept. 30	E.P. Taylor Stakes	Woodbine	1 ¼ (T)	Choc Ice (IRE)	John Murtagh	500,000
Sept. 30	Canadian International	Woodbine	1 ½ (T)	Mutamam (GBR)	Richard Hills	1,500,000
Sept. 30	Clement L. Hirsch Turf Championship Stakes	Santa Anita	1 ¼ (T)	Senure	Alex Solis	300,000
Sept. 30	Oak Leaf Stakes	Santa Anita	1	Tali'sluckybusride	Jose Valdivia Jr.	250,000
Oct. 6	Frizette Stakes	Belmont	1 1⁄16	You	Edgar Prado	500,000
Oct. 6	Champagne Stakes	Belmont	1 1⁄16	Officer	Victor Espinoza	500,000
Oct. 6	Beldame Stakes	Belmont	1 ⅛	Exogenous	Javier Castellano	750,000
Oct. 6	Kelso Handicap	Belmont	1	Forbidden Apple	Jose Santos	250,000
Oct. 6	Jockey Gold Cup	Belmont	1 ¼	Aptitude	Jerry Bailey	1,000,000
Oct. 6	Lane's End Breeders' Futurity Stakes	Keeneland	1 1⁄16	Siphonic	Chris McCarron	454,400
Oct. 6	Ancient Title B.C. Handicap	Santa Anita	6 F	Swept Overboard	Eddie Delahoussaye	207,100
Oct. 7	Shadwell Keeneland Turf Mile	Keeneland	1 (T)	Hap	Jerry Bailey	558,500
Oct. 7	Overbrook Spinster Stakes	Keeneland	1 ⅛	Miss Linda (ARG)	Richard Migliore	562,000
Oct. 7	Oak Tree B.C. Mile	Santa Anita	1 (T)	Val Royal (FRA)	Jose Valdivia Jr.	219,000
Oct. 7	Goodwood B.C. Handicap	Santa Anita	1 ⅛	Freedom Crest	Kent Desormeaux	488,000
Oct. 13	My Dear Girl	Calder	1 1⁄16	Blissful Kiss	Cornelio Velasquez	400,000
Oct. 13	Smile Sprint Handicap	Calder	6 F	Fappie's Notebook	Jorge Chavez	200,000
Oct. 13	Calder Oaks	Calder	1 ⅛ T	Sara's Success	Cornelio Velasquez	200,000
Oct. 13	In Reality Stakes	Calder	1 1⁄16	Booklet	Eibar Coa	400,000
Oct. 13	QE II Challenge Cup	Keeneland	1 ⅛ (T)	Affluent	Eddie Delahoussaye	500,000
Oct. 13	Oak Tree Derby	Santa Anita	1 ⅛	No Slip (FRA)	Kent Desormeaux	150,000
Oct. 27	Breeders' Cup Distaff	Belmont	1 ⅛	Unbridled Elaine	Pat Day	2,161,760
Oct. 27	Breeders' Cup Juvenile Fillies	Belmont	1 1⁄16	Tempera	David Flores	916,000
Oct. 27	Breeders' Cup Mile	Belmont	1	Val Royal (FRA)	Jose Valdivia Jr.	1,044,240
Oct. 27	Breeders' Cup Sprint	Belmont	6 F	Squirtle Squirt	Jerry Bailey	916,000
Oct. 27	Breeders' Cup F&M	Belmont	1 ¼ (T)	Banks Hill (GBR)	Olivier Peslier	1,273,240
Oct. 27	Breeders' Cup Juvenile	Belmont	1 1⁄16	Johannesburg	Michael Kinane	916,000
Oct. 27	Breeders' Cup Turf	Belmont	1 ½	Fantastic Light	Frankie Dettori	1,960,240
Oct. 27	Breeders' Cup Classic	Belmont	1 ¼	Tiznow	Chris McCarron	3,664,000

HARNESS RACING

Late 2001 Major Stakes Races

Date	Race	Raceway	Winner	Driver	Purse
Sept. 29	**Kentucky Futurity**	Lexington	Chasing Tail	John Campbell	$460,000
Oct. 27	**Messenger Stakes**	Ladbroke	Bagel Beach Boy	Luc Ouellette	254,385

BOWLING

2001 Fall Tour Results

PBA

Final	Event	Winner	Earnings	Final	Runner-Up
Sept. 18	Columbia 300 Open	postponed			
Sept. 25	Peoria Open	Kurt Pilon	$40,000	202-182	Paul Koehler
Oct. 2	Greater Nashville Open	Chris Barnes	40,000	234-195	Mike Scroggins
Oct. 9	Miller High Life Open	Dave Arnold	40,000	222-160	Roger Bowker
Oct. 16	Great Lakes Classic	Pete Weber	40,000	235-201	Parker Bohn III
Oct. 23	Greater Detroit Open	Patrick Allen	40,000	236-204	Robert Smith

Remaining Events: See PBA fall schedule on page 766.

Senior PBA

Final	Event	Winner	Earnings	Final	Runner-Up
Sept. 27	Senior Tarheel Open	Bob Chamberlain	$12,000	233-196	Bob Glass
Oct. 18	Senior National Championship	Dale Eagle	12,000	237-205	Gene Stus
Oct. 26	Senior Hammond Open	Bob Glass	8,000	233-232	Charlie Tapp

Bowling (Cont.)

PWBA

Final	Event	Winner	Earnings	Final	Runner-Up
Sept. 6	Foundation Games V	Liz Johnson	$9,000	183-181	Wendy Macpherson
Sept. 13	Paula Carter Classic	Liz Johnson	9,000	300-226	Carolyn Dorin-Ballard
Sept. 21	Storm Challenge	Leanne Barrette	11,000	224-156	Cara Honeychurch
Sept. 28	Jacksonville Open	Carolyn Dorin-Ballard	9,000	234-191	Leanne Barrette
Oct. 4	North Myrtle Beach Classic	Cara Honeychurch	9,000	184-179	Wendy Macpherson
Oct. 11	Columbia 300 Open	Wendy Macpherson	11,000	257-169	Leanne Barrette
Oct. 18	Three Rivers Open	Michelle Feldman	9,000	206-191	Tammy Turner
Oct. 24	Hammer Players Championship . . .	Liz Johnson	13,000	205-202	Michelle Feldman

Remaining Events See PWBA fall schedule on page 766.

RUGBY

Six Nations Tournament

	W	T	L	PF	PA	PD	Pts
England	4	0	1	229	74	155	8
Ireland	4	0	1	129	89	40	8
Scotland	2	1	2	92	116	–24	5
Wales	2	1	2	125	166	–41	5
France	2	0	3	115	138	–23	4
Italy	0	0	5	106	207	–101	0

Note: England wins 2001 Six Nations Tournament on points differential, despite losing 20-16 to Ireland.
Results (home team listed first): Feb 3–Italy 22, Ireland 41; Wales 15, England 44. Feb. 4–France 16, Scotland 6; Feb. 17–Scotland 28, Wales 28; England 80, Italy 23; Ireland 22, France 15; Mar. 3–Italy 30, France 19; England 43, Scotland 3; Mar. 17– France 35, Wales 43; Scotland 23, Italy 19; Apr. 7–England 48, France 19; Apr. 8–Italy 23, Wales 33. Sept. 22–Scotland 32, Ireland 10; Oct. 13–Wales 6, Ireland 36; Oct. 20–Ireland 20, England 16.

SOCCER

MLS Playoffs

Semifinals

Teams earn three points for a win and one point for a tie; first team to earn five points advances.

Date	Result	Date	Result
Oct. 10	at Miami 1, San Jose 0	Oct. 10	Los Angeles 1, at Chicago 1
Oct. 14	at San Jose 4, Miami 0	Oct. 13	at Los Angeles 1, Chicago 0 (OT)
Oct. 17	San Jose 1, at Miami 0	Oct. 17	Los Angeles 2, at Chicago 0
	(San Jose wins series, 6 points to 3)		(Los Angeles wins series, 7 points to 1)

MLS Cup 2001
San Jose Earthquakes, 2-1 (OT)
Oct. 21 at Crew Stadium, Columbus, Ohio
Attendance: 21,626

	1	2	OT	—F
San Jose	1	0	1	—2
Los Angeles	1	0	0	—1

First Half: LA-Luis Hernandez (Greg Vanney, Kevin Hartman), 21st minute; SJ-Landon Donovan (Ian Russell, Richard Mulrooney), 43rd.
Overtime: SJ-Dwayne DeRosario (Ronnie Ekelund, Zak Ibsen), 96th.
MVP: Dwayne DeRosario, San Jose, Forward

2001 U.S. Open Cup Final
Los Angeles Galaxy, 2-1 (OT)
Oct. 27 at Titan Stadium, Fullerton, Calif.
Attendance: 4,195

	1	2	OT	—F
New England	1	0	0	—1
Los Angeles	0	1	1	—2

First Half: NE-Wolde Harris (unassisted), 30th minute.
Second Half: LA-Ezra Hendrickson (Greg Vanney), 70th.
Overtime: LA-Danny Califf (Cobi Jones), 92nd.

Personalities

AP/Wide World Photos

After launching his 73rd homer, **Barry Bonds** does his best Michael Jordan impression.

Top 20 Sports Personalities of 2001

Dan and Linda salute their top newsmakers of the year.

by **Dan Patrick** and **Linda Cohn**

My top personalities of the year are, as always, in no particular order. But I'll kick this year off with a man that needs no introduction.

Barry Bonds

It was probably the greatest offensive season ever but it won't change a thing. Bonds doesn't need to be loved. He never asked to be loved. He probably wouldn't believe it if we said we did love him. At most, we probably saw something likable (not lovable) in him that we didn't see before. Not as a hitter but as a man. Bonds' 2001 season was probably harder than Mark McGwire's in 1998. He was in a pennant race until the end. Teams pitched around him. His teammates ripped him in the press. He still hit 73 homers.

Dan Patrick is a co-anchor on ESPN's SportsCenter and hosts The Dan Patrick Show from 1-4 p.m. EST, Monday through Friday on ESPN Radio.

Jennifer Capriati

Hers was a story out of Hollywood, more befitting a child actress than a tennis prodigy. Initial success, instant fame, instant riches, stage parents—and it all led to an early flameout. But she came back to win the Australian Open and French Open this year. She is now the top-ranked player in the world. And there is no one who can utter an honest "I told you so." Except maybe for Capriati herself.

Shane Battier

He let the world and the game come to him. Battier enjoyed being a college student and had no serious intention of leaving early. He was in no rush and it paid off as he led his Duke Blue Devils to the NCAA title. He may not lead the NBA in anything but the Memphis Grizzlies have a player who will contribute right now while all the high schoolers "develop."

Todd Warshaw/Allsport

He Hate Me became the most well-known player in the short-lived XFL era. By the way, his real name is Rod Smart.

Rod Smart

Not a familiar name? You know him as "He Hate Me" from the ill-fated NBC-WWF project known as the XFL. Despite a strong opening weekend of ratings, the XFL quickly fell victim to its hybrid nature: the football wasn't good enough for football fans and the freak show wasn't wild enough for wrestling fans. We hated it.

Paul Tagliabue

When the sports world was looking for the right response to the terrorist attacks of Sept. 11, Tagliabue and the NFL stood tall. MLB was mum about when its games would resume. College football was divided. But when Tagliabue announced that there would be no NFL games on Sept. 16, everyone else fell in line. That weekend would be for mourning and remembrance. The games would wait.

David Duval

As with Barry Bonds, the breakthrough for Duval this year means much more to us than to him. He won't change. Duval won't lean over a twisting 10-footer at Augusta next April and think "This will go in. I won the 2001 British Open." But we'll expect it to go in. Because he won the 2001 British Open.

AP/Wide World Photos

Dale Earnhardt Jr. made his first trip to Daytona since his father was killed a victorious one.

Kobe Bryant

Kobe and Shaq had so many run-ins early in the season, it seemed even guru Phil Jackson wouldn't be able to mend the wounds. But somewhere along the line, Kobe grew up. He said the right things. He did the right things. He even got married. And when it came time to really go to work in the playoffs, the Lakers went on a 15-1 run. Kobe's best move this year was accepting his role, and in the process making the Lakers a great team.

Dale Earnhardt Jr.

When he got in his car at Daytona and won the Pepsi 400 on the track where his father died, there were murmurs that a fix was in. Preposterous. The story was that Little E was every bit the man and driver his dad was. The bloodlines were real. Along with Jeff Gordon, Earnhardt Jr.'s season shows that NASCAR is still in very good hands.

Danny Almonte

In the end, it was consumer fraud. Obviously, the grownups who orchestrated the charade are to blame. But Almonte let himself be used. And we got taken for a ride. I certainly hope that Almonte is allowed to move on from this with a lesson learned. Unfortunately though, this won't be a one-year problem for the rest of us. The next time we see a kid in the Little League World Series who is a cut above the rest, we'll just say "Is he another Danny Almonte?"

Ichiro Suzuki

Though it seemed impossible, Ichiro was better than advertised. The Japanese batting champion came over to the American League and didn't miss a beat. He ignited the Mariners to a record-setting 116-win season and was the first man to lead the majors in batting average and stolen bases since Jackie Robinson: 242 hits, 127 runs scored, 56 stolen bases. Make that much better than advertised.

Thanks Dan. Could it be? A Top 20 list of personalities that doesn't include Tiger? Amazing. Here are my top 10.

Ray Bourque

Sometimes sports stories really do work out exactly the way you want them to. When Bourque joined the Avalanche in 2000 after toiling with the Bruins for close to 21 seasons, he had just one mission—his first Stanley Cup. Boston fans understood this.

And while his new teammates wanted nothing more than to win one for Ray, make no mistake—this wasn't Willie Mays on the New York Mets or Babe Ruth on the Boston Braves. This was a veteran player with the talent to make a serious contribution on the ice and a work ethic that had a rippling effect on every Colorado player—young and old.

Seeing captain Joe Sakic receive the Cup from commissioner Gary Bettman after Game 7 then immediately turn and hand it to Bourque, should tell you all you need to know about how Bourque was viewed by his teammates.

Derek Jeter

Sure you've seen his numerous spectacular highlight plays—like the ones where he ranges deep in the hole and throws a runner out by a step, or when he dives into the stands for a pop fly, or when he races over to the first base line to flip a relay throw to his catcher to nail a runner at the plate.

But it's all the things you don't see that made Jeter one of my choices this year. You don't have to be a Yankee fan to respect and appreciate Derek Jeter. He quietly leads by example. Like Magic Johnson and Larry Bird, he makes the biggest games his best. He puts Joe Torre's mind and the mind of every Yankee fan at ease. All of this has made him the posterboy for the latest Yankees dynasty.

Michael Jordan

Will he or won't he? Will he or won't he? Even as Kobe and Shaq were putting the finishing touches on the Lakers' second straight title, NBA fans and media seemed to be every bit as enthralled with the doings of the Washington Wizards president.

At first it was just the ever-candid Charles Barkley leaking the possibility of the return of His Airness. Then Jordan, himself, started dropping hints and participating in more offseason practices. And finally he made it official. The greatest basketball player in the history of the NBA would be returning to the league—again. Sure he's 38 now, but he's still fit and he still has his competitive nature. And if season ticket sales are any indication, returning to

Linda Cohn *is a co-anchor on ESPN's SportsCenter.*

AP/Wide World Photos

New York mayor **Rudy Giuliani** is surrounded by the Yankees
during a ceremony honoring the victims of the Sept. 11 attacks.

the court is far and away his best executive move as Wizards president.

Mario Lemieux

When Michael Jordan ultimately made his decision to return to the NBA, one deciding factor was the immensely successful return to the NHL by his good friend and owner of the Pittsburgh Penguins.

When Lemieux was originally drafted in 1984, he brought new life to a struggling Penguins franchise that had won just 16 games that season. He saved the team again in 1999 by purchasing the financially-strapped team, rescuing them from bankruptcy. And finally in December 2000, with his club wallowing around the .500 mark, it was Super Mario to the rescue again.

He wasted no time, scoring two goals and dishing out an assist against Toronto in front of a standing-room-only crowd in his first game back. And he took his team deep into the Stanley Cup playoffs.

Rudy Giuliani

The New York City mayor earned praise around the globe for his actions after the Sept. 11 attacks on New York and Washington. With two icons of his city lying in ruin, he remained a voice of

AP/Wide World Photos

Lance Armstrong flashes the victory sign on the Champs Elysees in Paris after winning his third straight Tour de France.

calm and bravery, boosting spirits and providing comfort to those in need.

After the sports world was rightfully put on hold for several days, Giuliani pleaded with U.S. citizens to return to doing the things they loved. And he backed up his words. One of the Yankees' most ardent fans, the mayor was a fixture on the first base line during Yankee playoff games—right where he should have been.

Ian Thorpe

"The Thorpedo" could have suffered a bit of a hangover after his five-medal performance at the Sydney Games in 2000. But he didn't. At the 2001 FINA Swimming and Diving World Championships in Japan, the 18-year-old phenom set three world records and became the first swimmer, male or female, to win six gold medals at one world championships.

And if there was any part of him that took his accomplishments for granted, that all changed on the morning of Sept. 11. Thorpe was on his way to the World Trade Center moments before the plane struck the first tower, but forgot his camera and had to return to his hotel.

Karrie Webb

With her victories at the U.S. Open and the LPGA Championship this year, Webb became the fifth, and youngest, woman to win the career Grand Slam. She's now won five of the last nine majors.

None were tougher than the LPGA Championship in June when Webb learned after the third round that her grandfather had suffered a stroke and was gravely ill in Australia. Convinced by her family to stay and finish the event, Webb built up an insurmountable six-stroke lead and fought off her tears until just after her winning putt. Webb arrived at the hospital just hours after Mick Collinson died at age 71.

Venus Williams

Richard Williams certainly has his critics, and many times they're justified. His methods as a coach and father are at times unconventional, and his statements to the press are usually baffling.

But one thing's for sure—he raised two wonderful daughters. Over the past two years we've seen the maturation of Venus Williams. She's become a beautiful, young woman off the court and an intimidating, dominant player on it. She won her second straight Wimbledon in 2001 and capped off her season with a primetime win over sister, Serena, in front of a packed house at the U.S. Open. And yet she remains humble.

Allen Iverson

It appeared as though Iverson finally "got it" in 2001. His squabbles with coach Larry Brown became a thing of the past, as the two developed a mutual respect. He put his rap career on hold, shed his "selfish" label and proved with his words and, more importantly, his actions, that winning the NBA championship was more important than winning the scoring championship.

Iverson spent much of the season and the playoffs acting like a human pinball, getting knocked around by players sometimes 10 inches taller and 80 pounds heavier. Anyone who watched the 76ers playoff run saw this relatively little man, playing hurt, carry his team on his back.

Lance Armstrong

Just when you think Armstrong's legacy can't get any larger, it does. Never underestimate what this man has done. He fought back from cancer and so thoroughly dominated the Tour de France three years in a row, that organizers were forced to change their race to give other riders a chance to win.

Given the current state of the world, it seems silly to think of athletes as heroes. But that's precisely what he is. He's an inspiration. When Montreal Canadiens captain Saku Koivu was diagnosed with cancer, one of his first requests was a copy of Armstrong's book.

Moments

Perhaps the most anticipated kiss in NHL history took place in 2001 when **Ray Bourque** lifted his first Stanley Cup.

Top 20 Sports Moments of 2001

Stuart Scott and Rich Eisen give us their picks for the biggest moments of the year in sports.

by **Stuart Scott** and **Rich Eisen**

It was as emotional a calender year as any in our lifetime. Rich and I could easily make a list of the top 20 sports moments of the year and they'd all focus on our nation's response to the Sept. 11 terrorists attacks—the way our athletes proved that they're really not the heroes but still they were first in line at ground zero in New York and Washington, D.C. thanking, hugging and gushing over the *real* heroes. In retrospect, shouldn't the response of our athletes still be considered a little bit heroic? All of these moments won't focus on the aftermath of Sept. 11, 2001...but they could.

The NFL shuts down

Save for a players' strike, the National Football League hadn't shut down before.

Stuart Scott is an anchor/reporter on ESPN's SportsCenter.

Maybe the closest it came was the weekend after President John F. Kennedy was assassinated. But then NFL Commissioner Pete Rozelle decided the games would go on. Rozelle would later say it was the biggest mistake he would ever make. Paul Tagliabue won't have the same regret. After consulting with the NFLPA's Gene Upshaw, who consulted with the players, he cancelled the weekend's games after the attack. It turned out that almost all of them felt like playing was not the thing to do. A few, mostly guys that played for the Giants and Jets, who play at Giants Stadium, from where you could see the smoking ruins of the World Trade Center, said even if the league hadn't postponed the games they wouldn't have played.

MJ Returns, Again

It was Michael Jordan's first real NBA game since hitting the game-winning shot to win the 1998 NBA title. This would have made the list anyway, but because of what happened in New York; because of Jordan's history at Madison Square Garden; because MJ

AP/Wide World Photos

The smoldering ruins of the World Trade Center, *clearly visible from across the river at Giants Stadium in the Meadowlands, put sports in perspective.*

donated his entire year's salary to the relief effort; in effect, Jordan was playing the game and the season for the home crowd at the Garden. It was magical before MJ even took the court.

A Ravens' Tale

Steve Young, the highest-rated passer in NFL history, and the man who lost in a game of HORSE to me in that Sunday NFL Countdown commercial, says football as we know it is over when a team like the Baltimore Ravens wins a Super Bowl—a team with an offense that was non-existent at one point in the season, going five games without a TD. Baltimore's defense was so good, so nasty, so vicious, so unrelenting, they set an NFL record for fewest points allowed in a season. Their success rested on the shoulders of Ray Lewis, the best middle linebacker in football, period. Ray Lew went from being charged with double-murder at a Super Bowl after-party in 2000 to being the Super Bowl MVP in 2001. As for Trent Dilfer, he won his last 11 starts. Then he said he was going to Disney World and then had all the time in the world to go, because the Ravens let him go.

Tiger Woods' double three-peat

The last time a golfer won the same tournament three straight years was 1980. So all Tiger Woods does is pull of that feat TWICE this year. First at The Memorial in June, then later in August, he pulled a three-peat at the NEC

Invitational with a seven-hole playoff win over Jim Furyk. If he had won the PGA Championship, it would have been a triple three-peat.

Dale Departs

It was a track he owned, so to speak. Dale Earnhardt had won more races at the Daytona International Speedway than any other man, ever. And after being denied the big one at Daytona, the Daytona 500, for so long, he finally got it three years ago. It was fitting then, that if Earnhardt was to die on a race track it was on this track. Turn three, the last lap of The 500, slamming into a wall, headfirst at about 180 mph, his death was the biggest blow NASCAR had ever felt. Earnhardt was arguably, the best driver ever. He was unquestionably the man who changed the way drivers raced. He was, and will always be, "The Intimidator."

Shane is Able

As a Tarheel alum, it used to pain me to even act like I was giving Duke some props. I say this begrudgingly…but I can't help but respect Duke University's basketball program. Coach K is all class. And Michael Jordan agrees with me. So there. In winning the school's third national title in the previous 10 years, Duke showed why it's the second best program in the nation (I won't give them #1…that's still UNC). Shane Battier had everything you could want in a student athlete: smarts, heart, courage and will…a true leader. Plus, he wants to be president of the United States someday.

Lakers Repeat

With all due respect to Allen Iverson—and he deserves more than his due—was there really any doubt? To actually watch "The Answer" up close and personal, to see him give everything every second he's on the court is awe-inspiring. Still, if Iverson is one of the three best players in the NBA, there's no defense against the team that has the other two. It's simple: too much Shaq, too much Kobe. They don't have to love each other. They just have to respect and admire what the other does. They did.

Webb out of sight

For those football-basketball-baseball-only sports junkies, you wouldn't get it. But that doesn't mean it's too late to learn. On May 27, Alan Webb made history. The high schooler, yes, high schooler, as in proms, prep days, crushes on cheerleaders and "Dad, can I borrow the car?" Webb ran a mile in 3:53.43. Did I mention he's in high school? A high schooler hadn't broken the four-minute barrier in 34 years, let alone break Jim Ryun's 36-year-old high school record of 3:55.3.

Big Drive

Since we're on a youth kick, I was at the Hootie and the Blowfish celebrity golf tournament in April. It was down in Kiawah Island, S.C.—windy Kiawah Island. During the long-drive competition my turn came up. I turned to my friend and caddy for the weekend, Mallory Hetzel, and told her I was gonna put her on the spot. I had seen her play the year before, as a 14-year-old. She's one of the top junior golfers in the state. It's her cool, collected state of mind that's as impressive as her game. She stepped up...with my driver...in tennis shoes ...with no warm-up...and a gallery watching...into the wind...uphill...14-years old...261 yards. I asked her later if she blocked out the crowd. She calmly replied, "No. I *like* the crowd."

Barry!

A funny thing happened on the way to breaking a record most people thought was unbreakable. Barry Bonds became somewhat of a likeable guy to the media...somewhat. Now, I'm not one of those writers who thinks Barry oughta be this or that. Barry Bonds can be whomever and whatever he wants. There's no doctrine that says he has to make himself available to the media. But to do what he did—not just 70 homers but 71, then 72 in the same game and then 73 to end it, all in a season where he was walked more times than any man ever. His slugging percentage was better than anyone's, even Ruth's. He hit a home run every 12 swings—not at bats—SWINGS. None of his team-mates may have been at home plate to greet him when he hit 500—but they were all there for his record breakers.

Rich...I defer to you.

And I'll take my crack at it...

Sept. 21, 2001

Ten days after the attacks on the World Trade Center, the city still burning, feelings of fear still palpable, 41,235 people congregated in Shea Stadium—the largest public gathering since the disaster—for a baseball game. But it was far more than just a game. The night began with an emotional ceremony honoring the dead and the city's uniformed services. The Mets, like they had all week, wore hats bearing the logos of those services. And to make matters more special, the Mets hadn't lost the whole week, creeping to within 5½ games of the Braves. As for the game, it was a taut, well-played affair and entered the bottom of the 8th with Atlanta leading 2-1. That is, until Mike Piazza strode to the plate and belted a game-winning, two-run homer off of Queens native Steve Karsay. As the ball left the park, every person there, even if they had just lost a loved one, forgot about misery for a split second. We learned where sports fit into the country, post-Sept. 11.

Agassi-Sampras, again

Twenty combined grand slam titles after their first U.S. Open matchup 11 years before, Andre Agassi and Pete Sampras represented the oldest U.S. Open quarterfinals pairing since 32-year-old Jimmy

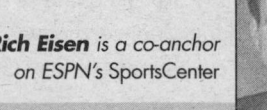

Rich Eisen is a co-anchor on ESPN's SportsCenter

AP/Wide World Photos

Yankees catcher **Jorge Posada** puts the tag on **Jeremy Giambi** following **Derek Jeter**'s improbable relay toss to the plate in Game 3 of the ALDS.

Connors knocked off 30-year-old John Lloyd in 1984. And Agassi and Sampras did not disappoint. In fact, the only disappointing matter about the match is that it didn't go five sets. Just four intense sets, all ending in tiebreaks. Sampras won, and eventually made the finals, but everything after this night and this match proved to be anti-climactic.

The Play

Game 3. AL Divisional Series. Oakland up on the Yankees two games to none. Seventh inning. Two-out base hit down the right-field line by Terrence Long. Shane Spencer heaves the ball past two cut-off men. Jeremy Giambi is sure to tie the score, 1-1. And like the blur of Superman's cape, in flies Derek Jeter. Why was Jeter on the first base line in the first place? How did he know the ball would wind up there and then require a backhanded, shovel toss to Jorge Posada in order to nail Giambi at the plate? Why didn't Giambi slide? How did Posada hold on to the ball? Who knew at the time it would turn the tide and send the Yankees on a fourth straight World Series run? Actually, many folks sensed that at the time, as Jeter, who later became the all-time postseason hit king, proved that defense wins championships.

Final All-Star moment for Cal

The crowd at Safeco Field in Seattle went nuts for Cal Ripken Jr., who was playing his 18th and final All-Star Game. Ripken stepped out of the batter's box and acknowledged the raucous cheers by waving his helmet to all points of the ballpark. Now came time for the at-bat. The Dodgers' Chan Ho Park no doubt thought Ripken, having received such an ovation, would not be focused for the first pitch. Or perhaps, he felt the Ironman deserved a cookie. Either way, with flashbulbs popping from all points, Park delivered and so did Ripken. Home run. Bedlam. A true goosebump moment.

Duval's Deliverance

The Greatest Player to Not Win a Major. Perhaps the worst tag any professional golfer can wear. And with the Tiger Slam completed three months before, David Duval no doubt felt the pressure taking the tee at Royal Lytham and Saint Anne's on the final Sunday of the British Open. Sure, he had shot a 65 in round three, but he was a final-round contender the previous year and (paired with Tiger), collapsed. But, on this Sunday, at the 130th British Open, Duval was rock steady. A closing-round 67 to capture the Open, remove the monkey from his back and place his name, fittingly, next to Tiger's on the Claret Jug.

Almost Perfect

With the Yankees eight games in front, the division had already been decided. Still, 33,734 rabid fans filled Fenway Park for a game that delivered on every front. Mike Mussina faced David Cone, who though now with Boston is the last man to pitch a perfect game for the Yanks. This time it was Mussina approaching perfection while Cone pitched into the ninth himself, the first time he had done so since his perfecto in 1999. The tension built with each pitch. Finally, in the top of the ninth, the Yankees broke through on Cone after 120 pitches. But, with just one run. Mussina strode to the mound. One out. Two outs. Then, the mercurial Carl Everett appeared as a pinch-hitter. Clean base hit to left-center on a 1-2 pitch. Mussina had come within one strike of the first perfect game in the 89-year history of Fenway Park. But, by virtually matching him pitch for pitch, Cone made it all the more memorable.

Everybody Loves Raymond

Born Dec. 28, 1960 in Montreal Quebec, he was the eighth pick in the 1979 NHL Entry Draft. The next 20 years he captured the hearts and minds of Boston hockey fans, only to leave March 6, 2000 in a trade to Colorado. After a season and a half there, he led all defensemen in career goals, assists and points. And then, finally, in his 21st NHL postseason, surpassing Gordie Howe and Larry Robinson for most all-time, Raymond Bourque finally got to lift Lord Stanley's Cup. As testament to his popularity, Bourque not only paraded with the Cup in Denver, but did so in Boston, too.

What a Comeback!

When working at SportsCenter, following any live sporting event, you want the game over quickly and you would like it to remain competitive. That way, you get more people watching the end of the game and the beginning of SportsCenter. On Aug. 5, the prospect of a large carry-over audience from our Sunday Night Baseball game seemed remote, with the Mariners taking a 14-2 lead over the Indians into the seventh inning. What happened next boggled the mind, and hopefully, got some remotes clicking. Three Cleveland runs in the seventh, four in the eighth and five in the ninth tied the ball game—all against the Seattle bullpen, one of the best in the business. And then, in the 11th, Jolbert Cabrera singled off Jose Paniagua, the sixth Mariner reliever of the night, and plated Kenny Lofton, completing the biggest comeback in 76 years. When it was 14-2, one of our producers, sitting at home, decided to order "Castaway" on pay-per-view. As soon as the movie ended, he flipped over to ESPN just in time to watch Lofton slide past home plate and touch off the celebration. He said he felt like Tom Hanks, wondering: "What in the world happened when I was gone?"

The 2001 World Series

This World Series could have produced all the moments required for this space. From the outstanding pitching performances of the Series co-MVPs, Curt Schilling (the first to start three games of a Series since Jack Morris 10 years before) and Randy Johnson (three wins in the Series and the first pitcher to win Games 6 and 7 in 56 years) to the

improbable finishes of Games 4 and 5: the first-ever instances of World Series games won by a team that trailed by two runs with two outs in the 9th inning...and it happened on back-to-back nights! Then there's the improbable conclusion to a scintillating Game 7, in which the Yankees got dethroned with their best, Mariano Rivera, on the mound. But, for me, the most memorable moment came prior to Game 3. With 57,000 fans on hand at Yankee Stadium and the flag recovered from the World Trade Center flying overhead, the President of the United States was there to throw out the first ball. With the entire world watching via satellite, it probably represented the single juiciest terrorist target since Sept. 11 and despite that the president strolled to the mound, right in the middle of it all, gave the thumbs up as if to say, "take your best shot." And he does, throwing a perfect strike. God Bless America.

Lance, once again

How does this guy do it? Everyone in Europe wants to know. They poke and prod his body. Test his blood over and over again. But all they have to do is measure Lance Armstrong's heart and they'll find out all they have to know about why he keeps winning the Tour de France. Once again, Armstrong was behind heading into the mountains. Once again, Armstrong made his move and made his competition look as if they were going backwards. It was his third straight Tour win and it was truly remarkable.

Calendar

He's baaaaaack. **Michael Jordan** *announced his return to the NBA in September.*

NOVEMBER 2000

Sun	Mon	Tue	Wed	Thu	Fri	Sat
			1	2	3	4
5	6	7	8	9	10	11
12	13	14	15	16	17	18
19	20	21	22	23	24	25
26	27	28	29	30		

Quote of the Month

"Kids today are kids. I probably was a smart aleck too when I was 18 in 1885. I think the only people who should get booed [are] the officials."

Joe Paterno, Penn State's ageless football coach, on how hard it will be to enforce a new school policy against "negative cheering" in the stadium.

Bad Boys

Boston Bruins defenseman Marty McSorley's 82-game suspension—levied this month by the NHL—is the longest in NHL history. The following is a list of the longest NHL suspensions ever.

82 games—Marty McSorley, Boston, 2000-01, for knocking out Vancouver's Donald Brashear with a slash to the head.

23 games—Gordie Dwyer, Tampa Bay, 2000, for abusing officials and for leaving the penalty box to fight.

21 games—Dale Hunter, Washington, 1993, for a blind-side check of the Islanders' Pierre Turgeon after a goal.

20 games—Brad May, Phoenix, 2000, for a slash to the face of Columbus' Steve Heinze; Tom Lysiak, Chicago 1983, for intentionally tripping a linesman.

Divas of Dunk

Only three women in college basketball history have successfully dunked during a game. Here is a closer look at those women and their remarkable dunks.

Michelle Snow—Tennessee; 6-5, Jr. C; dunked on Nov. 25, 2000 during a victory over Illinois in the inaugural Maui Invitational championship game. The two-handed dunk at the end of the first half was the first to be televised. (Snow dunked again on January 23, 2001)

Charlotte Smith—North Carolina; 6-1, Sr. F; dunked on Dec. 4, 1994 during a victory over North Carolina A&T State. The dunk came on UNC's first possession 17 seconds into the game.

Georgeann Wells—West Virginia; 6-7, Jr. C; recorded the first dunk in women's basketball history on Dec. 21, 1984 during a victory over the University of Charleston. After taking a full-court pass, Wells threw down a one-handed dunk early in the second half. Three games later Wells dunked again during a victory over Xavier.

1 **Alabama football coach Mike DuBose** announces that he will resign at the end of the season, bringing an end to four turbulent seasons with the school.

Boston Bruins GM Harry Sinden steps down after 28 seasons in that role with the team. He remains as team president.

Miami Heat coach Pat Riley earns his 1,000th career victory in a 105-79 trouncing of the Orlando Magic.

2 **St. Louis Cardinals 1B Will Clark** announces his retirement after 15 major league seasons.

Former Baltimore Orioles manager Earl Weaver lashes back at Hall of Fame pitcher Jim Palmer—accusing him of faking injuries that cost the team games—and turns the otherwise amicable roast in his honor into an angry confrontation in front of a crowd of 1,100 people.

3 **Former K.C. Royals manager Bob Boone** is named manager of the Cincinnati Reds, agreeing to a two-year contract with a club option for a third.

4 **West Virginia football coach Don Nehlen** announces his retirement (effective at the end of the season) after a 31-27 loss to Syracuse, bringing an end to his 21-year tenure with the school.

Jockey Chris McCarron rides Tiznow to a surprising victory in the $4.77 million Breeders' Cup Classic at Churchill Downs.

5 **Golfer Phil Mickelson defeats** Tiger Woods at the Tour Championship, handing Woods his first defeat in 20 tournaments in which he held or shared the lead going into the final round.

Runner Abdelkhader El Mouaziz breaks away after the 12-mile mark and easily wins the New York City Marathon, becoming the first Moroccan champion. On the women's side, Ludmila Petrova becomes the race's first Russian champion.

California native Norton Davey, 82, becomes the oldest person ever to complete the Ironman Triathlon, finishing in 18 hours, 20 minutes.

6 **Detroit Lions coach Bobby Ross** unexpectedly resigns a day after a 23-8 loss to Miami, admitting he is burned out. He is replaced by assistant Gary Moeller.

Baseball Hall of Famer Ted Williams, 82, has a pacemaker surgically implanted into his chest at a Florida hospital.

7 **Boston Bruins D Marty McSorley** has his NHL suspension extended through Feb. 20, making it a full-year banishment for his notorious slash/assault of Vancouver forward Donald Brashear.

8 **Seattle center Patrick Ewing** tells the media he will donate a kidney to ailing fellow Georgetown alum Alonzo Mourning if he should need one.

9 **An arbitrator upholds** the penalties against Timberwolves forward Joe Smith by NBA Commissioner David Stern, voiding his final two contract years with Minnesota.

Tampa Bay assistant coach Wendell Avery, whose mysterious disappearance (since Nov. 4) has made newspaper headlines, is fired after a meeting with head coach Tony Dungy who wanted to know why Avery was not at Sunday's Buccaneers game.

10 **Golfer Tiger Woods expresses** his irritations about the unfair control of his marketing rights by the PGA Tour and commissioner Tim Finchem in an interview published in today's *Golf World* magazine.

11 **Heavyweight champion Lennox Lewis** fends off David Tua in a unanimous decision victory and retains his title at Mandalay Bay Resort and Casino in Las Vegas.

AP/Wide World Photos

These enthusiastic Duke fans with "Krzyzewski 500" painted on their chests aren't advertising a new NASCAR event, rather it's in recognition of basketball coach **Mike Krzyzewski** *whose 500th victory at the school came on Nov. 17 against Villanova.*

12 **Winston Cup driver Bobby Labonte** finishes fourth in the Pennzoil 400 in Miami and secures his first series championship.

14 **Indiana basketball coach Mike Davis** leads the Hoosiers to an 80-68 victory over Pepperdine in his debut, the school's first game without Bobby Knight in 29 years.

15 **Phoenix Coyotes winger Brad May** is suspended 20 games by the NHL for a slash of Columbus' Steve Heinze in a game Nov. 11.

The U.S. men's national soccer team scores four times in the second half and beats Barbados 4-0 in a must-win game to move on to the final round of World Cup qualifying for North America, Central America and the Caribbean.

16 **Minnesota governor Jesse Ventura**, a former WWF employee of Vince McMahon, is introduced as the XFL's superstar television analyst. He will help broadcast 12 games on NBC beginning Feb. 3.

18 **Japan's top hitter Ichiro Suzuki** is signed to a three-year deal by the Seattle Mariners, making him the first Japanese position player to reach the major leagues.

19 **Golfer Tiger Woods wins** his 10th tournament of the calendar year, carding a three-stroke victory at the Johnnie Walker Classic in Bangkok.

20 **Jurors hear Cherica Adams'** recorded 911 call and opening statements during the first day of the trial of Carolina Panthers receiver Rae Carruth, who's charged with the murder of his then-pregnant girlfriend (Adams).

Former Minnesota forward Joe Smith, whose contract with the Timberwolves was voided by NBA Commissioner David Stern, signs a one-year, $2.25 million contract with the Detroit Pistons.

Winston Cup veteran Darrell Waltrip finishes 34th at the rain-delayed NAPA 500, ending his 29-year career behind the wheel.

A survey released today shows the graduation rate for football players at NCAA Division I-A schools at 48 percent, the lowest since 1985.

22 **Charlotte forward Elden Campbell** scores 22 points and Allen Iverson is held to seven, as the Hornets halt Philadelphia's franchise-best, season-opening winning streak at 10 games.

Dallas Mavericks owner Mark Cuban is fined $25,000 by the NBA for publicly criticizing referees. It is the third time in the last eight days he's been fined for similar offenses.

24 **Detroit Red Wings coach Scotty Bowman** leads his team to a 3-2 victory over Vancouver at home, representing his NHL-record 2,000th regular season game as a head coach.

25 **Tennessee junior Michelle Snow** shocks the crowd at the inaugural women's Maui Invitational tournament in Hawaii by finishing a breakaway with the fourth slam dunk in the history of women's college basketball.

27 **Seattle Supersonics coach Paul Westphal** is fired after his team's 6-9 start and is replaced by assistant Nate McMillan.

Former Flyers captain Eric Lindros, who is a restricted free-agent, is cleared to play hockey again by doctors monitoring the effects of his last concussion.

28 **NASCAR officials announce shifts** in upper-management with Bill France Jr. becoming chairman of a newly formed board of directors and Mike Helton given the title of president in charge of day-to-day operations.

The plane crash that killed golfer Payne Stewart was caused by a loss of cabin pressure and the crews' failure to obtain oxygen, a yearlong investigation by the National Transportation Safety Board reveals today.

29 **PGA Tour Commissioner Tim Finchem** and Tiger Woods meet privately in Thousand Oaks, Calif. and reach a compromise on almost all of the issues concerning control of Woods' marketing rights.

30 **Baltimore Orioles ace Mike Mussina** signs a six-year, $88.5 million free-agent contract to join the world champion N.Y. Yankees' pitching staff.

DECEMBER 2000

Sun	Mon	Tue	Wed	Thu	Fri	Sat
					1	2
3	4	5	6	7	8	9
10	11	12	13	14	15	16
17	18	19	20	21	22	23
24	25	26	27	28	29	30
31						

Quote of the Month

"Cars are out. No more cars. He's not allowed to buy a car unless he wins a Grand Slam—that's the deal we have. It hasn't stopped him from buying motorbikes. I think we'll have to put the deal on motorbikes as well."

Peter McNamara, tennis coach of Mark Philippoussis, explaining the new deal with his star pupil who has a stable of almost 20 sports cars including several Ferraris.

Going the Distance

Florida State quarterback Chris Weinke won the 2000 Heisman Trophy in one of the closest races in the trophy's 65-year history. Here are the 10 closest.

Year	Winner	Runner-up	Margin
1985	Bo Jackson	Chuck Long	45 pts
1961	Ernie Davis	Bob Ferguson	53 pts
1935	Jay Berwanger	Monk Meyer	55 pts
1953	John Lattner	Paul Giel	56 pts
1989	Andre Ware	Anthony Thompson	70 pts
1956	Paul Hornung	John Majors	72 pts
1964	John Huarte	Jerry Rhome	74 pts
2000	**Chris Weinke**	**Josh Heupel**	**76 pts**
1978	Billy Sims	Chuck Fusina	77 pts
1962	Terry Baker	Jerry Stovall	89 pts

Sharing the Spotlight 50/50

On Dec. 6, Golden State Warriors forward Antawn Jamison and Los Angeles Lakers guard Kobe Bryant became the first pair of NBA players to score 50 points in the same game in almost 40 years.

Date	Players, team	Pts.	Result
Dec. 6 2000	Antawn Jamison, Warriors	51	Warriors, 125-122 (OT)
	Kobe Bryant, Lakers	51	
Dec. 14 1962	Wilt Chamberlain, Warriors	63	Lakers, 120-118
	Elgin Baylor, Lakers	50	
Feb. 25 1962	Wilt Chamberlain, Warriors	67	Knicks, 149-135
	Richie Guerin, Knicks	50	

Source: The Boston Globe

1 **N.Y. Mets reliever Turk Wendell** signs another unusual contract. This time it's a three-year deal with the team worth a penny short of $9.4 million.

2 **Thoroughbred jockey Chris Antley**, 34, is found dead from severe trauma to the head in his Pasadena, Calif. home in what, according to police, appears to be a homicide.

WBA junior middleweight champion Felix Trinidad knocks down opponent Fernando Vargas twice in the first round and three times in the 12th, halting the bout and improving his record to 39-0.

3 **Former English professor Sandra Baldwin** is elected the first female president of the 106-year-old U.S. Olympic Committee.

WNBA coach Cheryl Miller resigns from the Phoenix Mercury after four seasons, explaining that her work schedule has taken a serious physical and emotional toll on her.

4 **Redskins coach Norv Turner** is fired after a 9-7 loss to the N.Y. Giants, ending a season of high expectations and missed opportunities for Washington.

Georgia football coach Jim Donnan is fired after a 7-4 season and three losses in the team's final four games.

5 **Utah Jazz forward Karl Malone** moves past Wilt Chamberlain for second place on the NBA's career scoring list, finishing with 31 points (31,443) in a 98-84 victory over Toronto at home.

6 **Golden State's Antawn Jamison** and the Lakers' Kobe Bryant score 51 points apiece in the first NBA game to feature two 50-point scorers since 1962. The Warriors win the game 125-122 in overtime.

U.S. skier Picabo Street finishes 34th in a super-G race at her first World Cup event in three years.

Two-time CART champion Alex Zanardi announces he'll return to the series in 2001, ending his year-long retirement from racing.

Chicago Bears offensive coordinator Gary Crowton is named to replace LaVell Edwards as head coach at BYU.

7 **Newspapers break the news** that Pittsburgh Penguins owner Mario Lemieux is planning a comeback to the team within the next 30 days.

San Diego Padres OF Tony Gwynn removes his name from the list of baseball free agents, re-signing with the team to an incentive-laden $2 million deal.

8 **L.A. Lakers center Shaquille O'Neal** misses all 11 of his free-throw attempts in a game against Seattle, breaking Wilt Chamberlain's record (10) for missed attempts in a game.

Free agent pitcher Mike Hampton signs an eight-year, $123.8 million deal with the Colorado Rockies.

9 **Florida State quarterback Chris Weinke**, 28, wins the Heisman Trophy over Oklahoma's Josh Heupel by a mere 76 points, the eighth-closest race in award history.

10 **Spain's Juan Carlos Ferrero** defeats Australia's Lleyton Hewitt to earn Spain its first Davis Cup title.

Philadelphia Flyers coach Craig Ramsay is fired and replaced by assistant Bill Barber after GM Bob Clarke told him the team seemed to lack intensity.

Cowboy Joe Beaver wins his third career all-around title at the National Finals Rodeo in Las Vegas.

11 **Free agent Alex Rodriguez** signs a whopping 10-year, $252 million deal with the Texas Rangers, the biggest contract in sports history.

Denver Nuggets players boycott practice today purportedly because of anger over the coaching of Dan Issel.

AP/Wide World Photos

*Spain's Davis Cup captain **Javier Duarte** (left), and players **Albert Costa**, **Alex Corretja**, **Juan Carlos Ferrero**, and **Juan Balcells** celebrate after beating defending champion Australia to capture Spain's first Davis Cup title in 79 years of competition.*

Virginia football coach George McCloud retires after 19 seasons with the Cavaliers.

12 Cleveland slugger Manny Ramirez, the final top-shelf free agent, signs an eight-year, $160 million deal to play outfield for the Boston Red Sox.

Denver Nuggets captain George McCloud denies that the team boycotted practice and threatened to boycott a game, instead calling the team's decision not to show up for practice (Dec. 11) a "miscommunication" with the coaches.

13 U.S. tennis player Patrick McEnroe is appointed by the U.S. Tennis Association to succeed his brother as the 38th U.S. Davis Cup captain.

14 Mighty Ducks coach Craig Hartsburg is fired after the team had lost 12 of its last 21 games and is replaced by assistant Guy Charron.

15 Lakers star Shaquille O'Neal misses a game against Vancouver when he travels to his alma mater LSU to receive his bachelor of arts degree in general studies.

Former NFL coach Pete Carroll signs a deal to succeed Paul Hackett as coach of the USC Trojans.

Virginia Tech QB Michael Vick tells the media at the Gator Bowl he'll return to school next season for his junior year.

17 San Francisco WR Terrell Owens hauls in an NFL-record 20 receptions in a 17-0 victory over Chicago, stealing the spotlight from former All-Pro Jerry Rice who plays in his final home game as a 49er.

19 Hall of Famer Mario Lemieux practices with the Pittsburgh Penguins for the first time since 1997.

20 Philadelphia 76ers coach Larry Brown returns to the team after a two-day absence for personal reasons and denies it had anything to do with a rift with Allen Iverson.

21 Tennis star Venus Williams announces that she's signed a five-year contract extension with Reebok worth more than $40 million, the most lucrative endorsement deal ever for a female athlete. She also endorses her father's controversial idea of paying top tennis stars appearance fees.

23 Nashville center David Legwand scores the first goal on an overtime penalty shot (against Kirk McLean) in NHL history, leading the visiting Predators to a 3-2 victory over the N.Y. Rangers.

24 Referee Johnny Grier orders the New England Patriots and Miami Dolphins back out on to the field for one final play 35 minutes after the officials incorrectly called the game's final play a fumble rather than an incomplete pass with three seconds remaining.

25 Baseball commissioner Bud Selig will propose a "competitive balance draft" to owners at their meetings next month, the Associated Press reports today.

27 Pittsburgh Penguins owner Mario Lemieux returns to the ice, scoring a goal and registering two assists in a 5-0 victory over Toronto in front of a standing-room-only crowd of 17,148 at home.

Orlando Magic forward Grant Hill learns the ankle injury he sustained last season needs more surgery and he will miss the entire 2000-01 season.

28 Florida Panthers president Bill Torrey fires brothers Bryan Murray (GM) and Terry Murray (coach) and hires Duane Sutter (coach) and himself (interim GM).

Miami and Florida football players are reportedly involved in a scuffle on Bourbon Street in New Orleans the first night the teams were in town for the Sugar Bowl.

30 N.Y. Jets coach Al Groh accepts a multi-year deal to coach his alma mater, the University of Virginia, leaving the Jets after one season as head coach.

JANUARY 2001

Sun	Mon	Tue	Wed	Thu	Fri	Sat
	1	2	3	4	5	6
7	8	9	10	11	12	13
14	15	16	17	18	19	20
21	22	23	24	25	26	27
28	29	30	31			

Quote of the Month

"It was the first putt Tom made all day."

Rusty Uresti, caddie for Gary Nicklaus, who watched a ball driven by Andrew Magee bounce off Tom Byrum's putter and roll into the cup for the first hole-in-one on a par-4 in PGA Tour history.

Inductions With No Introductions

The Baseball Writers' Association of America voted to induct Kirby Puckett and Dave Winfield to the Baseball Hall of Fame in 2001. It marked the fifth time in history the BWAA selections were former teammates.

Class	Inductees	Teammates
1947	Lefty Grove & Mickey Cochrane	Philadelphia-AL (1925-33)
1974	Mickey Mantle & Whitey Ford	New York-AL (1953-67)
1991	Ferguson Jenkins & Gaylord Perry	Texas-AL (1975, 1980)
2000	Carlton Fisk & Tony Perez	Boston-AL (1980)
2001	Kirby Puckett & Dave Winfield	Minnesota-AL (1993-94)

Note: The occasions in which Veterans' Committee selections and BWAA selections have been teammates are not shown.

Not-So Uniform Careers

When journeyman Chucky Brown signed with the Golden State Warriors on Jan. 13 he set an NBA record by suiting up for his 11th team. No player in basketball history has played for more teams in a career. But who is the all-time leader in the big four pro sports? Look below.

League	Player (pos.)	Teams
MLB	Mike Morgan, P	12
NBA	Chucky Brown, F	11
NHL	(tie) J.J. Daigneault, D & Michel Petit, D	10
NFL	Walter Voss, DE/T	10

Note: All but the NHL's Petit and NFL's Voss are still active.

1 **Arizona basketball coach Lute Olson's wife** and unofficial "team mom," Bobbi, dies of ovarian cancer while her husband is on a leave of absence from the team.

2 **Ohio State football coach John Cooper** is fired one day after an Outback Bowl loss to South Carolina.

Montreal Canadiens goalie Jose Theodore becomes the sixth goalie in NHL history to score a goal, connecting on an empty-netter with nine seconds left in a 3-0 shutout of the N.Y. Islanders.

3 **Former Chiefs coach Marty Schottenheimer** is hired to coach the Washington Redskins.

Assistant coach Donnie Nelson replaces his father, Don, as head coach of the Dallas Mavericks on the eve of his father's prostate cancer surgery.

4 **Oklahoma RB Quentin Griffin's** fourth-quarter touchdown seals a 13-2 victory over Florida State in the Orange Bowl and earns the undefeated Sooners their seventh national title.

5 **Retired Harlem Globetrotters** Meadowlark Lemon (#36) and Marques Haynes (#20) have their numbers retired by the team, joining the late Wilt Chamberlain (#13) as the only three to earn that distinction.

6 **Tampa Bay Lightning coach Steve Ludzik** is fired and replaced by assistant John Tortorella, who was the N.Y. Rangers' interim coach at the end of last season.

7 **Cuban boxing legend Felix Savon**, a three-time Olympic heavyweight champion, announces his retirement to become coach of Cuba's national team.

8 **Boston Celtics president-coach Rick Pitino** resigns after 3½ seasons and no playoff appearances. He is replaced by assistant Jim O'Brien.

Kansas City outfielder Johnny Damon is traded to Oakland, highlighting a three-team, nine-player deal that also involves Tampa Bay.

Buffalo Bills coach Wade Phillips is fired for refusing to fire assistant Ronnie Jones, the special-teams coach Phillips hired after the "Music City Miracle."

Former WNBA star Cynthia Cooper is given a three-year contract to replace Cheryl Miller as coach of the Phoenix Mercury.

9 **FOX broadcaster Matt Millen** is named president and CEO of the Detroit Lions.

Utah men's basketball coach Rick Majerus announces he is leaving the team to be with his ailing mother and to recover from health problems that resulted in heart surgery in December.

10 **NFL Commissioner Paul Tagliabue rules** that should Kansas City hire retired St. Louis coach Dick Vermeil the Chiefs must give a second-round draft pick in 2001 and a third-round pick in 2002, plus $500,000 to the Rams.

4 **Jockey Chris Antley died of an overdose** of multiple drugs, and injuries found on his body probably were the result of a fall while under the influence, the L.A. coroner's office reveals today.

Cleveland Browns coach Chris Palmer is fired by the team after five wins over two seasons.

Virginia Tech QB Michael Vick reverses his previous decision and announces he will forgo his final two seasons of college eligibility to apply for the NFL draft.

12 **Former St. Louis Rams coach Dick Vermeil** is lured out of retirement for a second time, this time agreeing to a reported three-year deal to coach the Kansas City Chiefs.

14 **Toronto Blue Jays ace David Wells** and Chicago White Sox pitcher Mike Sirotka highlight a six-player trade inked by the teams today.

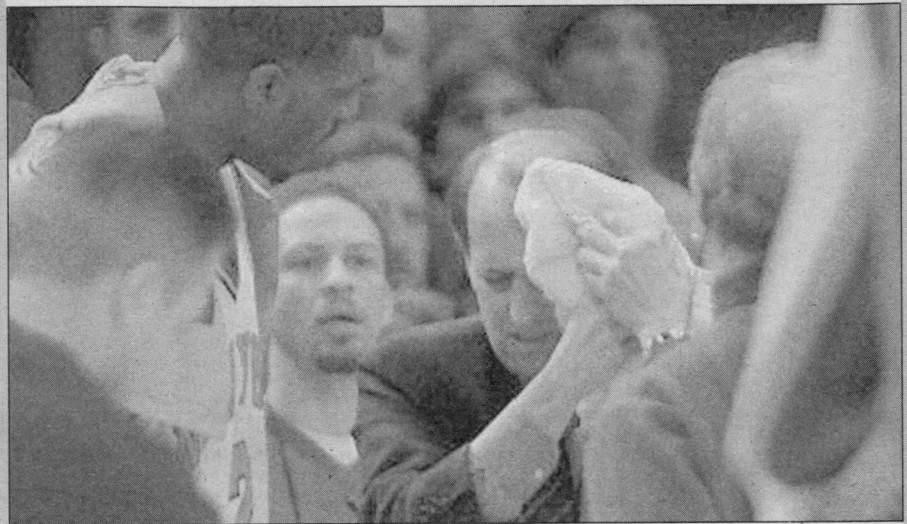

AP/Wide World Photos

*N.Y. Knicks coach **Jeff Van Gundy**, who seems to have made a second career out of breaking up on-court brawls, is led off the court at Madison Square Garden on Jan. 15 after butting heads with Knicks center Marcus Camby who was trying to land a punch on San Antonio Spurs forward Danny Ferry when Van Gundy got in the way.*

15 **University of Tennessee's Tamika Catchings** is lost for the season after tearing a knee ligament in a 66-59 victory over Mississippi State.

16 **Fan favorite Kirby Puckett** and former Twins teammate Dave Winfield are elected to the Baseball Hall of Fame.

17 **Golfer Casey Martin's disability-rights** case against the PGA Tour is heard by the U.S. Supreme Court. A decision isn't expected until July.

18 **Phoenix Suns guard Jason Kidd** is arrested on suspicion of domestic violence, a misdemeanor, after his wife calls 911 to report Kidd struck her.

19 **Former Carolina Panthers WR Rae Carruth** is convicted of three charges in relation to the shooting of his pregnant girlfriend in November 1999, but is cleared of first-degree murder, therefore avoiding the death penalty.

20 **Iowa State wrestler Cael Sanderson** wins his 101st consecutive match, surpassing the disputed mark set by Dan Gable between 1967-70, which statisticians disagree is either 98 or 100.

22 **Former Carolina Panthers WR Rae Carruth** is sentenced to spend a minimum of 18 years, 11 months in prison as a result of his conviction on Jan. 19.

Notre Dame's women's basketball team takes over the number-one ranking in the AP Top-25 Poll, ending UConn's 30-week reign at the top.

Hawaiian-born sumo legend Akebono, the most successful foreigner in the sport's history, announces his retirement at the age of 31.

23 **Tennessee's Michelle Snow becomes** the second woman in college basketball history to dunk twice in one season, slamming home a dunk during a 70-64 victory over Vanderbilt in Nashville.

Boxing referee Richard Steele, 57, retires after working 167 title fights in a career that spanned 30 years.

24 **San Francisco offensive coordinator** Marty Mornhinweg is named head coach of the Detroit Lions, inking a reported five-year, $5 million deal.

27 **Two Oklahoma State basketball players** and six staffers and broadcasters are among 10 people killed in a plane crash in Colorado.

Jennifer Capriati upsets three-time Australian Open champion Martina Hingis in the finals at Melbourne to win her first career Grand Slam title.

28 **Game MVP Ray Lewis leads** the Baltimore Ravens defense to a decisive 34-7 victory over the N.Y. Giants in Super Bowl XXXV.

Defending champ Andre Agassi beats Arnaud Clement for his third career Australian Open title.

30 **American skier Daron Rahlves** shocks the host Austrians and wins the super-G championship at the World Alpine Ski Championships, becoming just the third U.S. world champion ever.

University of Miami coach Butch Davis is hired to coach the Cleveland Browns, signing a reported five-year, $15 million deal.

31 **American businessman George Gillett Jr.** buys the Montreal Canadiens and the Molson Centre, becoming the first American to own Canada's beloved hockey franchise.

FEBRUARY 2001

Sun	Mon	Tue	Wed	Thu	Fri	Sat
				1	2	3
4	5	6	7	8	9	10
11	12	13	14	15	16	17
18	19	20	21	22	23	24
25	26	27	28			

Quote of the Month

"It is sometimes hard to get all the information on boxers, and we obviously missed the fact that Darrin was dead. It is regrettable."

Francisco Valcarcel, WBO president explaining how boxer Darrin Morris could have posthumously appeared in his organization's rankings (and moved up two spots!) for four months.

Racing's Fallen Stars

On Feb. 18, Dale Earnhardt joined this pantheon of revered drivers who were still very competitive and wildly popular when they were fatally injured while racing. The drivers are listed chronologically by the year in which their death occurred.

Rex Mays (1949) Mays became the first driver to win four poles at the Indianapolis 500 in 1948. Although he never won the race in 12 attempts, Mays won every other major race of his day and was well respected by other drivers. He was killed on the 13th lap at a Del Mar, Calif. event when a wheel got caught in a rut in the dirt track, flipping the car and throwing Mays to his tragic death at age 36.

Bill Vukovich (1955) Vukovich, 36, was attempting to become the first driver to win three consecutive Indy 500s. He died from injuries sustained after his car was thrown from the track in a horrific crash on the 57th lap of the Indianapolis 500 in 1955.

Fireball Roberts (1964) Although he never won a series title, Roberts, won 32 Winston Cup races, including the Daytona 500 in 1962. He sustained serious burns in a fiery crash on the seventh lap of the World 600 at Charlotte Motor Speedway. He was rescued by Ned Jarrett but died two months later of complications from the burns.

Jim Clark (1968) Despite just eight years on the Formula One racing circuit, Clark had won 25 races, two world championships and the Indy 500 in 1965. His life ended at age 32 on Germany's Hockenheim course when his car slid off the track at around 150 mph and crashed into a wooded area.

Ayrton Senna (1994) A three-time Formula One world champion and possibly the world's most popular driver at the time of his death. Senna, 34, was fatally injured when his car slid off the track at Imola, Italy during the San Marino Grand Prix and smashed into a concrete wall at 186 mph. Senna was a national hero in his native Brazil, and President Itamar Franco declared three days of national mourning and closed schools on the day of his funeral.

1 **Tennessee Titans defensive** coordinator Greg Williams is hired to coach the Buffalo Bills.

Green Bay Packers GM Ron Wolf announces his retirement effective June 1, with head coach Mike Sherman taking on double duty.

3 **Opening night for the XFL** is a success, as ratings on NBC more than double expectations (9.5/17 share), and create a buzz about the newest pro football league to challenge the NFL.

Former NFL tight end Mark Chmura is acquitted of charges of child enticement and sexual assault.

4 **Boston's Bill Guerin** scores three goals, overshadowing the return of Mario Lemieux and leading North America to a 14-12 victory at the NHL All-Star Game.

Raiders QB Rich Gannon throws two touchdown passes in the game's first 11 minutes, leading the AFC to a 38-17 victory over the NFC in the NFL Pro Bowl.

NBA referee Joe Forte ejects singer Jimmy Buffett from his courtside seat during the fourth quarter of the Knicks-Heat game for using profanity. The bizarre confrontation delays the game for several minutes.

Pole vaulter Sergei Bubka, 37, retires after a meet in his hometown of Donetsk, Ukraine.

UCLA men's volleyball coach Al Scates records his 1,000th career victory, after his team defeats Pepperdine 3-1. No volleyball coach in the nation has more victories.

5 **Oklahoma State's men's basketball** team beats Missouri 69-66 in its first game since a plane crash killed two players and eight other people associated with the team nine days ago.

6 **Anaheim Angels 1B Mo Vaughn** has surgery to repair a ruptured tendon in his left arm and is expected to miss all of the 2001 season.

7 **Minnesota Vikings RB Robert Smith,** 28, the NFC's leading rusher in 2000, retires from the NFL.

The IOC rejects Olympics organizers' proposal to alter the opening and closing ceremonies in Salt Lake City by having an athlete from each nation greet the world in his/her native language and to have athletes march together by sport rather than by country.

8 **NBA Hall of Famer Isiah Thomas,** owner of the Continental Basketball Association (which is mired in heavy debt), suspends play after failing to find a new buyer.

11 **New team captain Patrick McEnroe** watches the United States fall 3-2 to Switzerland in the first round, eliminating it from Davis Cup competition. Defending champion Spain is eliminated by the Netherlands.

Game MVP Allen Iverson scores 15 of his game-high 25 points in the fourth quarter to lead the Eastern Conference to a 111-110 come-from-behind victory over the West at the NBA All-Star Game.

12 **NBA Commissioner David Stern** gives the Vancouver Grizzlies franchise, which will lose at least $40 million this year, permission to look for a new home.

Golfer Tiger Woods wins a record four ESPY Awards in Las Vegas, including the award for Male Athlete of the Year.

Fox network officials and NASCAR executives meet to discuss the network's coverage of the Bud Shootout on Feb. 10-11, where Fox graphics of cars with non-network sponsors had ads missing.

14 **International Boxing Federation founder** Robert Lee is sentenced to 22 months in prison for money laundering and tax evasion. He settles a related government suit by paying a $50,000 fine to the IBF and agreeing to a lifetime ban from boxing.

AP/Wide World Photos

On opening night of the XFL, Feb. 3, this scramble—the league's attempt to make the coin toss more exciting—results in a separated left shoulder for Orlando Rage's **Hassan Shamsid-Deen** (right). And the rest, as they say, was history.

15 **Mavericks owner Mark Cuban runs** on the court at Reunion Arena during a shoving match between Dallas and Cleveland players that begins after Dallas is accused of running its score up over 100 so the fans could win a fast food promotion with Taco Bell. The media dubs it the "Chalupa Caper."

16 **N.Y. Yankees closer Mariano Rivera** becomes the highest paid reliever in baseball, agreeing to a four-year, $39.99 million contract.

18 **NASCAR legend Dale Earnhardt**, 49, is killed in a last-lap crash at the Daytona 500, overshadowing veteran Michael Waltrip's first career Winston Cup victory.

Distance runner Marla Runyan, who is legally blind, sets a new American indoor record in the 5000-meter race, finishing in 15:07.33.

20 **Dallas Mavericks coach Don Nelson returns** to the sideline after a 52-day, 21-game absence for cancer treatment, but the Mavs lose to the Lakers 119-109 at home.

21 **The immediate family of Dale Earnhardt** holds a private funeral service and buries the deceased Winston Cup star in an unspecified plot somewhere in his hometown of Kannapolis, N.C.

L.A. Kings defenseman Rob Blake is acquired by the Colorado Avalanche.

Duke forward Shane Battier becomes the 10th Blue Devil to have his number (#31) retired by the school.

22 **Deceased racing star** Dale Earnhardt is honored in a memorial attended by 3,000 mourners, and televised live, at the Calvary Church in Charlotte, N.C.

University of Hawaii football coach June Jones is critically injured in a one-car accident on the H-1 Freeway near the Honolulu Airport.

Atlanta center Dikembe Mutombo is acquired by the Philadelphia 76ers in a six-player deal made hours before the NBA's trade deadline.

25 **Winston Cup driver Dale Earnhardt Jr.** crashes on the first lap of the DuraLube 400 at North Carolina Speedway (the first race since his father was killed), but limps away OK before the race is suspended by rain.

Finnish police confirm that a medicine bag belonging to the Finnish Ski Association contained banned substances and bloody syringes, widening a cross-country team drug scandal that began when Jari Isometsa failed a drug test (Feb. 15) at the Nordic world championships.

Phoenix Suns forward Shawn Marion sustains a serious concussion and leaves on a stretcher after a scary fall in the final minute of a 90-80 victory over Utah.

26 **Winston Cup driver Steve Park** holds off Bobby Labonte to win an emotional rain-delayed DuraLube 400 in a car owned by Dale Earnhardt, Inc. Earnhardt's replacement, Kevin Harvick, finishes 14th.

St. Louis defenseman Chris Pronger suffers a broken left forearm after being hit by a puck in a victory over San Jose and will miss the remainder of the regular season.

Toronto's Bryan Berard, 24, ends his comeback from serious eye trauma after failing to meet the NHL's minimum sight requirements.

27 **Seattle center Patrick Ewing receives** a three-minute standing ovation upon his return to Madison Square Garden for the first time since being traded in the offseason after 15 years with the N.Y. Knicks. Seattle loses to the Knicks 101-92.

28 **Buffalo Bills QB Doug Flutie** is released by the team, ending the team's much-publicized quarterback dilemma.

N.Y. Rangers winger Theo Fleury voluntarily enters the league's substance-abuse program and is out indefinitely.

St. Louis slugger Mark McGwire agrees to a two-year, $30 million contract extension with the Cardinals.

MARCH 2001

Sun	Mon	Tue	Wed	Thu	Fri	Sat
				1	2	3
4	5	6	7	8	9	10
11	12	13	14	15	16	17
18	19	20	21	22	23	24
25	26	27	28	29	30	31

Quote of the Month

"I said a lot of things in the heat of the moment, I'm sorry. It was all meant to promote the fight."

Muhammad Ali, former heavyweight boxing champion, apologizing during an interview with the New York Times for disparaging remarks he made about Joe Frazier in 1971 before the first of their three legendary fights.

March Madness

Three-time LPGA Player of the Year Annika Sorenstam set or tied six LPGA records, including the record for lowest 18-hole score (59) on Mar. 16 during the second round of the Standard Register Ping at the Moon Valley Country Club in Phoenix, Ariz. Here is a look at her scorecard from that record-setting round.

Moon Valley CC (6,435 yards, par 72)

Hole	1	2	3	4	5	6	7	8	9	OUT
Par	4	3	4	5	3	4	4	5	4	36
Rd. 2	2	3	4	3	4	4	4	4	3	31

Hole	10	11	12	13	14	15	16	17	18	IN
Par	5	3	4	5	4	3	4	4	4	36
Rd. 2	4	2	3	4	3	2	3	3	4	28

Notes: Sorenstam started on the back nine. Her playing partners were Charlotta Sorenstam (her sister) and Meg Mallon.

Olympic Preview?

American figure skater Michelle Kwan may have improved her chances at winning her first Olympic gold medal by winning the last world championship title before the 2002 Winter Games. The last four women to do that went on to win Olympic gold.

Year	Worlds	Olympics
1987	Katarina Witt	Katarina Witt (1988)
1991	Kristi Yamaguchi	Kristi Yamaguchi (1992)
1993	Oksana Baiul	Oksana Baiul (1994)
1997	Tara Lipinski	Tara Lipinski (1998)
2001	Michelle Kwan	???? (2002)

1 **SW Missouri St. senior Jackie Stiles** hits a three-pointer early in the second half and becomes the NCAA Div. I women's basketball career scoring leader.

Carolina defensive end Reggie White retires (again) from the NFL as the league's all-time sack leader.

F1 world champion Michael Schumacher tops Forbes magazine's list of the highest-paid athletes of 2000 with $59 million in earnings.

2 **Louisville coach Denny Crum** announces his retirement, ending his 30-year coaching career that closed with weeks of public jabbing with AD Tom Jurich.

3 **Boxer John Ruiz upsets** Evander Holyfield at Mandalay Bay in Las Vegas with a 12-round unanimous-decision victory to become the first Hispanic heavyweight champion of the world.

Free agent defensive tackle John Randle signs a contract reportedly worth $25 million over five years to play for the Seattle Seahawks.

5 **Orioles slugger Albert Belle admits** in an interview that it will take "a miracle" for him to return from his degenerative and inoperable hip condition.

San Jose Sharks acquire Teemu Selanne from Anaheim, sending forward Jeff Friesen and backup goalie Steve Shields to the Ducks.

N.Y. Islanders coach Butch Goring is fired and replaced by assistant Lorne Henning.

6 **Free agent Elvis Grbac signs** a five-year, $30 million deal to play quarterback for the defending Super Bowl champion Baltimore Ravens.

7 **Dallas Cowboys QB Troy Aikman**, 34, is released by the team after 12 seasons.

New England Patriots QB Drew Bledsoe agrees to the biggest contract in NFL history, a 10-year, $103 million deal.

Baseball commissioner Bud Selig rules that a disputed trade that sent pitchers David Wells to Chicago and Mike Sirotka to Toronto (among others) will stand despite an injury to Sirotka and protests from Jays' fans.

8 **Shot put world champion C.J. Hunter** announces that he has dropped his appeal of the drug test he failed last year, and he confirms his retirement.

9 **Quarterback Doug Flutie signs** a six-year deal with the San Diego Chargers, his fourth NFL team.

10 **Defending champion Michigan State**, Stanford, Duke and Illinois are handed No. 1 seeds for the men's NCAA basketball tournament.

11 **NASCAR rookie Kevin Harvick** is victorious in the car Dale Earnhardt would have driven at the Cracker Barrel 500 in Hampton, Ga. three weeks after the legend's death.

13 **Phoenix Coyotes forward Keith Tkachuk** is sent to the St. Louis Blues for three players and a first-round draft pick hours before today's NHL trade deadline.

Freshman reserve D'or Fischer and senior Chris Thompson lead Northwestern State to a 71-67 victory over Winthrop in the first play-in game for the 64th and 65th teams in NCAA tournament history.

Houston Rockets center Hakeem Olajuwon is suffering from a blood condition that may end his career, the team announces today.

14 **ABC officials announce** that actor Jason Priestly will be an analyst for Indy Racing League broadcasts this season.

Three-time champion Doug Swingley wins the 2001 Iditarod Sled Dog Race, pulling him into a tie for career wins with Susan Butcher and one short of five-time winner Rick Swenson.

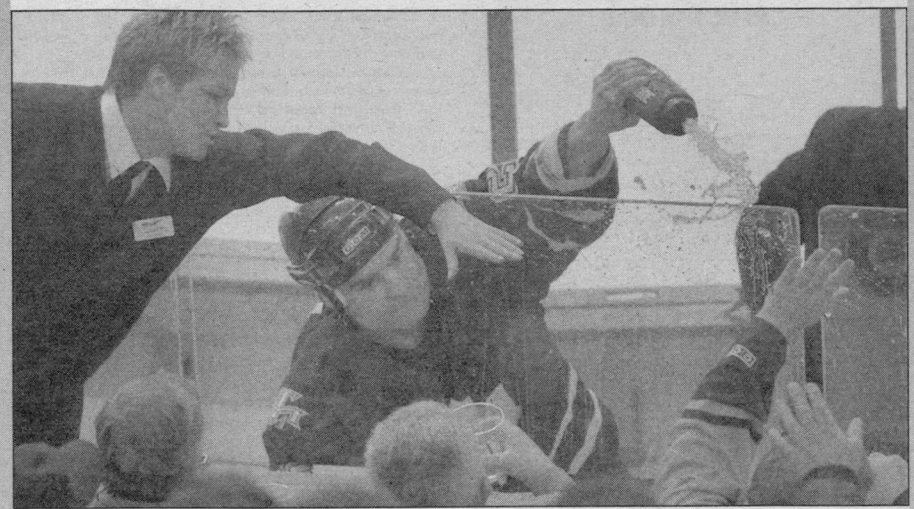

AP/Wide World Photos

*Toronto Maple Leafs right wing **Tie Domi** squirts water on taunting Flyers fans in Philadelphia during the third period of a game on March 29, causing one soaked fan to go "Cup Crazy" and dive into the penalty box to wrestle with one of the NHL's top goons.*

15 Tennis star Venus Williams pulls out of a semifinal match against her sister, Serena, at Indian Wells, Calif., citing knee tendonitis. The announcement draws boos from the crowd and afterward, Venus denies speculation that her father, Richard, made her duck the match to help Serena, who has beaten Venus once in five matches.

16 LPGA star Annika Sorenstam makes 13 birdies, including eight in a row, en route to shooting a tour-record 59 at Moon Valley CC in Phoenix during the second round of the Standard Register Ping.

Cubs outfielder Sammy Sosa signs a four-year, $72 million contract extension with the team.

19 Dallas Mavericks center Wang Zhizhi becomes the first Chinese player in an NBA game and scores six points in Dallas' 108-94 victory over Atlanta.

21 Former Celtics coach Rick Pitino returns to the NCAA coaching ranks (and the state of Kentucky), signing a six-year deal to be the next head coach at Louisville.

22 Former Olympic champion Bill Johnson is critically injured with serious head trauma and comatose after crashing during a downhill skiing run in Whitefish, Mont., ending his comeback hopes.

Russia's Evgeni Plushenko ends the three-year reign of countryman Alexei Yagudin, winning his first world figure skating championship in front of a sellout crowd at General Motors Place in Vancouver.

Duke associate professor and crash expert Barry Myers is chosen to view autopsy photos of Dale Earnhardt and will submit a report to the *Orlando Sentinel* per a settlement worked out between the newspaper and Earnhardt's widow, Teresa.

23 Ousted Indiana coach Bob Knight is announced as the new head coach at Texas Tech, signing a five-year, $1.25 million deal.

American skater Michelle Kwan wins her fourth world figure skating title, becoming the first woman to do so since Katarina Witt in 1988.

24 Colorado defenseman Ray Bourque returns to Boston to play the Bruins for the first time since being traded last year. He records two assists in a 4-2 Avs victory.

25 Sophomore wing Maria Rooth scores a goal and adds one assist to lead Minnesota-Duluth past St. Lawrence 4-2 in the inaugural women's NCAA Div. I Ice Hockey National Championship Game.

27 Miami Heat center Alonzo Mourning, out all season with a kidney disorder, returns to the lineup six months sooner than expected, logging 18 minutes, nine points and seven rebounds in a 101-92 loss to Toronto.

28 The NFL bars players from wearing bandanas and stocking caps, citing the need to tighten its uniform code.

Rockies first baseman Todd Helton signs the fourth-largest deal in sports history, an 11-year, $151 million deal to stay in Colorado.

Milwaukee Bucks coach George Karl becomes the highest-paid pro coach without executive duties, agreeing to a two-year contract extension worth $14 million.

Former Browns tackle Orlando Brown sues the NFL for $200 million, claiming his career was ended by an eye injury sustained when a penalty flag hit him.

29 Florida Gov. Jeb Bush signs a bill making it a felony to improperly release autopsy records, a measure inspired by Teresa Earnhardt's battle with the *Orlando Sentinel* over her husband Dale's records.

APRIL 2001

Sun	Mon	Tue	Wed	Thu	Fri	Sat
1	2	3	4	5	6	7
8	9	10	11	12	13	14
15	16	17	18	19	20	21
22	23	24	25	26	27	28
29	30					

Quote of the Month

"I might have a special engagement in Saudi Arabia."

Art Modell, Baltimore Ravens owner, when asked if he will be attending his team's Oct. 21, 2001 road game in Cleveland, the city he pulled his 49-year-old NFL franchise out of in 1995 to relocate to Baltimore..

The World's Game

According to Major League Baseball, more than a quarter of the players on opening day rosters were born outside of the U.S. Out of 815 players (including those on the DL), 216, or 25.3% come from 16 foreign countries and Puerto Rico. Here is the breakdown.

	Players
Dominican Republic	79
Puerto Rico	37
Venezuela	33
Mexico	14
Canada	11
Cuba	10
Panama	9
Japan	8
Australia	3
Colombia	3
Nicaragua	2
South Korea	2

Note: Aruba, Curacao, England, Jamaica and Virgin Islands, 1 each.

World Domination

Until California native Rosie Jones won the Harvey Penick Invitational on Apr. 29, foreign-born players had won every LPGA tournament in 2001. The 10-tournament winning streak established a new LPGA record. Here are the ladies who claimed titles and the country in which they were born.

Titles	Player	Country
4	Annika Sorenstam	Sweden
2	Se Ri Pak	South Korea
1	Sophie Gustafson	Sweden
1	Lorie Kane	Canada
1	Grace Park	South Korea
1	Catriona Matthew	Scotland

1 **Senior Ruth Riley's** two free throws with 5.8 seconds left leads Notre Dame to a 68-66 victory over Purdue and earn the Irish their first women's basketball national title.

Major League Baseball opens the 2001 regular season in Puerto Rico. Toronto defeats Texas 8-1.

Portland forward Rasheed Wallace breaks his own NBA record for technical fouls in a season, notching fouls #39 and #40 in a 99-95 loss to Minnesota.

2 **Sophomore Mike Dunleavy Jr.** scores 18 of his 21 points in the second half, leading Duke to an 82-72 victory over Arizona in the men's college basketball National Championship Game.

Former Yankees OF Darryl Strawberry is admitted to a Tampa hospital and arrested for violation of a probation warrant, ending his four-day disappearance that was rumored to be a kidnapping.

N.Y. Yankees pitcher Roger Clemens strikes out Royals 3B Joe Randa in the ninth inning and moves ahead of Walter Johnson to become the American League's all-time strikeout leader with 3,509.

3 **Croatian-born naval architect** Dubravko Rajcevic, from Australia, is found guilty of stalking tennis star Martina Hingis and faces four years in prison.

Philadelphia 76ers owner Pat Croce reveals that the team's physical conditioning coach, John Croce, his brother, was fired on Jan. 12 after being videotaped stealing money from 76ers star Allen Iverson's pants in the team locker room.

4 **Red Sox pitcher Hideo Nomo** throws the second no-hitter of his career and the first at Camden Yards, mowing down the Orioles 3-0.

5 **Admitted gunman Van Brett Watkins** is sentenced to 40 years and five months for the death of the pregnant girlfriend of former Carolina receiver Rae Carruth.

Cleveland Indians GM John Hart says he will step down at the end of this season.

6 **Portland forward Shawn Kemp** voluntarily enters a drug rehab program to be treated for cocaine abuse and will miss the remainder of the season.

7 **Boston College sophomore Krys Kolanos'** overtime goal earns the Eagles a 3-2 victory over North Dakota and the team's first men's hockey national championship since 1949.

8 **Tiger Woods shoots a final-round 68** and wins the Masters by two strokes, completing the "Tiger Slam" by becoming the first golfer to ever hold all four major tournament crowns simultaneously.

9 **Former Dallas QB Troy Aikman** announces his retirement at a news conference at Texas Stadium.

Anaheim Mighty Ducks coach Guy Charron is fired for leading the team to the second-worst record in franchise history since taking over on Dec. 14.

10 **Duke professor Barry Myers** issues his findings on the Dale Earnhardt autopsy photos (See March 22), reporting that he died of a skull fracture caused by the violent whipping motion of his head, not a broken seatbelt.

11 **Disaster strikes during a soccer game** featuring South Africa's two most popular clubs. Forty-three people are killed and 160 more injured when thousands of ticketless fans storm the fences at the Ellis Park Oval stadium in Johannesburg.

12 **The NBA's board of governors** approves the elimination of the illegal defense, clearing the way for zone defenses to return to the NBA in 2001-02.

Boston Bruins coach Mike Keenan is fired for failing to get the team into the playoffs after taking over for Pat Burns last October.

AP/Wide World Photos

A little Buddhist monk lines up an extraordinary penalty kick attempt during a festival to celebrate the birthday of Buddha in Seoul Stadium in South Korea on April 29. It's a clear sign the country is getting everybody prepared for its **2002 World Cup** *co-hosting duties.*

14 **Middleweight Bernard Hopkins** wins a 12-round unanimous decision over Keith Holmes, qualifying him for the finals of promoter Don King's three-fight Middleweight World Championship Series.

Golfer Annika Sorenstam wins her fourth tournament in a row, The Office Depot at Los Angeles, tying an LPGA record for consecutive tournament victories.

Brazilian soccer star Pretinha nets a penalty shot in the game's 70th minute to lead the host Washington Freedom past the Bay Area CyberRays 1-0 in the inaugural game of the first women's pro soccer league in U.S. history.

16 **South Korean runner Lee Bong-Ju** wins the 105th Boston Marathon, ending a 10-year streak of Kenyan victories in the men's division.

17 **San Francisco Giants OF Barry Bonds** hits career home run #500, a two-run blast in the eighth inning off Dodgers reliever Terry Adams that lands in the bay outside Pac Bell Park and leads the Giants to a 3-2 victory.

18 **Devil Rays manager Larry Rothschild** is fired and replaced by bench coach Hal McRae.

Wizards coach Leonard Hamilton resigns following Washington's season-ending loss to Toronto.

19 **Wizards president Michael Jordan** signs former coach Doug Collins to a five-year, $20 million deal.

Dodgers GM Kevin Malone resigns from his post, citing the distraction he caused when he challenged a heckling fan to a fight on Apr. 14 in San Diego.

20 **Australia's Lauren Jackson** is selected first overall at the WNBA draft by the Seattle Storm.

21 **Baltimore native Hasim Rahman** knocks out heavyweight champion Lennox Lewis in the fifth round of their fight in South Africa to capture the WBC and IBF titles in one of the biggest upsets in heavyweight history.

Virginia Tech QB Michael Vick is the first overall selection of the Atlanta Falcons at the NFL draft, which traded with San Diego for the pick the day before.

League MVP Tommy Maddox quarterbacks the Los Angeles Extreme to a 38-6 victory over the San Francisco Demons in the first XFL title game dubbed "The Million Dollar Game."

23 **N.Y. Knicks center Marcus Camby's** arrival in South Windsor, Conn. ends an eight-hour standoff with a knife-wielding man who held Camby's mother and two sisters hostage in their home.

24 **San Diego OF Rickey Henderson** ties Babe Ruth's career record of 2,062 walks in the sixth inning, drawing a free pass off Philadelphia reliever Chris Brock.

Houston Comets star Sheryl Swoopes suffers a season-ending knee injury during a pickup game at the team's practice facility.

25 **New heavyweight champ Hasim Rahman** and his family suffer minor injuries in Baltimore when the car they are traveling in collides with two others after a ceremony to award the boxer with the keys to his home city.

29 **CART race officials** call off today's inaugural race at Texas Motor Speedway after discovering G-forces in turns are almost twice as high on the high-banked track compared to other CART tracks.

MAY 2001

Sun	Mon	Tue	Wed	Thu	Fri	Sat
		1	2	3	4	5
6	7	8	9	10	11	12
13	14	15	16	17	18	19
20	21	22	23	24	25	26
27	28	29	30	31		

Quote of the Month

"Wake up the damn Bambino and have him face me. Maybe I'll drill him in the ass."

Pedro Martinez, Boston Red Sox pitcher, tired of fielding questions about the N.Y. Yankees and the supposed curse put on the Red Sox for selling "The Bambino," Babe Ruth, to the Yankees in 1919.

Walk This Way

On May 12, Florida pitcher A.J. Burnett threw one of the wildest no-hitters ever—literally. He walked nine batters, which was the most ever for a nine-inning, no-hit game but one short of the all-time record.

10	Jim Maloney, Cin	at Chi-NL*	Aug. 19, 1965
9	A.J. Burnett, Fla	at SD	May 12, 2001
8	Johnny Vander Meer, Cin	at Bklyn	June 15, 1938
8	Cliff Chambers, Pit	at Bos†	May 6, 1951
8	Doc Ellis, Pit	at SD	June 12, 1970
8	Nolan Ryan, Cal	at Minn	Sept. 28, 1974

*10 innings
†Boston Braves (now Atlanta Braves)

In a Class of Their Own

On May 27, Alan Webb, an 18-year-old senior from South Lakes High School in Reston, Va. broke Jim Ryun's seemingly unbreakable, nearly 36-year-old record for the high school mile. Ryun, who became the first high-schooler to run a sub-four-minute mile in 1964, set the record four times between 1964-65. Here is a look at the fastest mile times ever recorded by American high school runners.

Time	Runner (Home state)	Year Set
3:53.43	Alan Webb (Va.)	2001
3:55.30	Jim Ryun (Kan.)	1965
3:59.40	Tim Danielson (Calif.)	1966
3:59.80	Marty Liquori (N.J.)	1967

Source: *Runner's World*

1 Cincinnati Reds OF Deion Sanders returns to Major League Baseball, smacking a home run and going 3-for-3 in a 7-6 victory over the Dodgers—his first game in four years.

2 Yankees OF Chuck Knoblauch, a former Minnesota Twins 2B, is pelted by objects thrown by fans in the Metrodome's left-field stands. The game is delayed twice and almost forfeited by the Twins.

3 NHL coaching veteran Brian Sutter is named head coach of the Chicago Blackhawks, his fourth team in the last 13 years.

Minnesota Vikings WR Cris Carter announces that he will retire after the 2001-02 NFL season.

4 UCLA runner Meb Keflezighi breaks Mark Nenow's nearly 15-year-old American record in the 10,000-meter run, recording a 27:13.98 at the Cardinal Invitational in Palo Alto, Calif.

Toronto Maple Leafs winger Tie Domi is suspended for the remainder of the Stanley Cup playoffs and possibly the first eight games of next season for his flagrant knockout elbow of Scott Niedermayer in the final seconds of New Jersey's 3-1 victory a night earlier.

Texas Rangers manager Johnny Oates resigns, saying he was unable to turn around a team off to its worst start since 1985 despite the addition of superstar shortstop Alex Rodriguez.

5 Thoroughbred Monarchos is the surprising winner of the 127th Kentucky Derby, threatening Secretariat's 28-year-old track record in the process and becoming only the second horse to finish in under two minutes.

6 CART rookie Scott Dixon, 20, becomes the youngest driver to claim an open-wheel racing title, when he holds off Kenny Brack to capture the Lehigh Valley Grand Prix in Nazareth, Penn.

8 Arizona pitcher Randy Johnson strikes out 20 Reds in a 4-3 victory that goes 11 innings, making Johnson one strikeout short of the extra-inning record.

Texas Motor Speedway officials file a lawsuit against CART for the last-minute postponement of the Firestone Firehawk 600 on April 29.

Portland Trail Blazers coach Mike Dunleavy is fired after his team was swept by the Lakers in the first round of the NBA playoffs.

9 Top draft pick Michael Vick signs a six-year, $62 million contract with the Atlanta Falcons.

Veteran NHL coach Robbie Ftorek is named head coach of the Boston Bruins.

A soccer match in Ghana ends in tragedy when at least 100 people are reported killed in a stampede after police fired tear gas to subdue riotous fans.

10 XFL founder Vince McMahon announces the cancellation of the renegade WWF-and-NBC-funded football league after just one season.

Colorado Avalanche center Peter Forsberg undergoes emergency surgery to remove his ruptured spleen, causing him to miss the rest of the playoffs.

11 Cincinnati RB Corey Dillon signs a five-year contract extension with the Bengals that reportedly makes him the highest-paid player in franchise history. Terms were not disclosed.

St. Louis Cardinals pitcher Rick Ankiel is sent to the minors after his latest wild pitching performance, a three-inning, 76-pitch outing against the Pittsburgh Pirates a day earlier.

Chinese basketball star Yao Ming's quest for NBA eligibility status ends when the Shanghai Sharks refuse to release his rights.

AP/Wide World Photos

President George W. Bush *and his wife,* **Laura,** *listen to the national anthem on May 6 before the first game of the president's new tee-ball initiative, a series of games to be played on the South Lawn of the White House to help pay tribute to America's national pastime.*

12 **Florida Marlins pitcher A.J. Burnett** walks nine batters and throws just 65 of 128 pitches for strikes, but still manages to throw the third no-hitter in team history—a 3-0 victory over the Padres.

WBA middleweight champ Felix Trinidad stops William Joppy in the fifth round at Madison Square Garden in the second fight of Don King's Middleweight World Championship Series.

13 **U.S. Olympian Coralie Simmons** scores her second goal with 1:28 remaining to lift UCLA to a 5-4 upset of previously undefeated Stanford in the first NCAA Div. I Women's Water Polo Championship Game.

14 **Young golfer Morgan Pressel**, 12, shoots a 2-under 70 and becomes the youngest woman since 10-year-old Beverly Klass (1967) to qualify for the U.S. Women's Open.

15 **Sonics forward Ruben Patterson** is sentenced to a year in jail for attempting to rape the family's nanny last September.

Philadelphia 76ers guard Allen Iverson wins the NBA MVP Award, becoming the shortest (6-0) and lightest (165 pounds) in league history to do so.

16 **Chicago Cubs OF Sammy Sosa** hits his 400th career home run, blasting a two-run shot off Houston's Shane Reynolds.

17 **Former N.Y. Yankees OF Darryl Strawberry** avoids another stint in prison when a judge sends him to rehab instead for his four-day drug binge last month.

19 **Jockey Gary Stevens guides** Point Given to victory at the 126th running of the Preakness Stakes, ending Monarchos' bid for the Triple Crown.

20 **Toronto Raptors star Vince Carter** returns to the University of North Carolina to receive his undergraduate degree and then flies to Toronto to play in a Game 7 loss to Philadelphia in the conference semifinals.

21 **A Los Angeles jury hands** the Oakland Raiders two defeats in its $1.2 billion lawsuit against the NFL, claiming the NFL did not sabotage the team's efforts to build a stadium in 1995, and it does not still own rights to the L.A. market.

22 **NFL owners unanimously approve** plan A-1, the simplest of seven proposed realignment options for 2002.

24 **Vikings all-pro receiver Randy Moss** makes his pro basketball debut, scoring seven points for the U.S. Basketball League's Pennsylvania ValleyDawgs in their 113-112 victory over the Long Island Surf.

25 **Former Panthers GM Bryan Murray** is named head coach of the Mighty Ducks of Anaheim.

Canadian sprinter Donovan Bailey, a former world record holder, announces that he will retire at the end of the outdoor season.

27 **Brazilian driver Helio Castroneves** becomes the second rookie driver, and second CART series driver, in as many years to win the Indianapolis 500.

NASCAR driver Tony Stewart finishes sixth in the Indianapolis 500 and helicopters to the Coca-Cola 600 in North Carolina where he finishes third.

High school senior Alan Webb, 18, breaks the 36-year-old high school record in the mile by nearly two seconds at the Prefontaine Classic in Eugene, Ore.

28 **Marlins manager John Boles** is fired after his team's 22-26 start and is replaced, on an interim basis, by Hall of Famer Tony Perez.

29 **Golfer Casey Martin** has his legal right to use a golf cart during PGA Tour events defended by the Supreme Court in a 7-2 decision handed down today.

31 **Montreal Expos skipper Felipe Alou** is fired and replaced by Jeff Torborg.

JUNE 2001

Sun	Mon	Tue	Wed	Thu	Fri	Sat
					1	2
3	4	5	6	7	8	9
10	11	12	13	14	15	16
17	18	19	20	21	22	23
24	25	26	27	28	29	30

Quote of the Month

"She said, 'You can't walk over the hole,' I was like, 'whatever.'"

Morgan Pressel, 13-year-old amateur golfer, describing a confrontation about golf etiquette with her U.S. Open playing partner Heather Daly-Donofrio, who scolded the teen-ager for stepping in her putting line.

L.A. Sweeps Weeks

The 2001 Los Angeles Lakers put together the best postseason run in NBA history, setting the tone with sweeps over Portland, Sacramento and San Antonio. Their only blemish was a six-point overtime loss to the 76ers in Game 1 of the NBA Finals. Here is a list of the best postseason winning percentages in league history.

Year	Team	W-L	Pct.
2001	L.A. Lakers	15-1	.938
1983	Philadelphia	12-1	.923
1999	San Antonio	15-2	.882
1989	Detroit	15-2	.882
1991	Chicago	15-2	.882
1971	Milwaukee	12-2	.857
1982	L.A. Lakers	12-2	.857

Who's Next?

After 22 seasons and 1,612 regular season games Colorado Avalanche defenseman Ray Bourque finally won his first Stanley Cup championship on June 9. Here are the active leaders in games played in each of the four major pro sports who have yet to be on a league-championship winning team.

NHL	Dave Andreychuk	1361 games
NBA	John Stockton	1340 games
NFL	Gary Anderson	293 games
MLB	Harold Baines	2798 games

Note: Games played totals are through the 2000-01 NBA and NHL regular seasons; and 2000 NFL and Major League Baseball seasons.

3 **League MVP Allen Iverson** scores 44 points to lead Philadelphia to a 108-91 Game 7 victory over Milwaukee in the NBA Eastern Conference Finals.

4 **Strip club manager** Thomas "Ziggy" Sicignano begins naming several professional athletes who were set up with sex shows by Gold Club owner Steve Kaplan during his testimony in a federal racketeering trial.

The American Hockey League announces its expansion to 30 teams after adding six from the defunct International Hockey League.

Giants slugger Barry Bonds reaches the 30 home run mark in the 57th game of the season, surpassing the record set by Babe Ruth (63 games) in 1928.

5 **All-Pro WR Jerry Rice signs** a deal to play for the Oakland Raiders one day after the 16-year veteran was released by San Francisco 49ers.

Former NFL QB Bernie Kosar and seven other South Florida investors purchase the NHL's Florida Panthers.

8 **Boxer Laila Ali punches** her way to an eight-round decision victory over Jacqui Frazier-Lyde in front of 6,500 fans at Turning Stone Casino in Verona, N.Y.

9 **Colorado defenseman Ray Bourque** ends his 22-year quest for the Stanley Cup as the Avalanche beat the N.J. Devils 3-1 in just the 11th Game 7 in finals history.

Australian Open champ Jennifer Capriati continues her amazing comeback by capturing her second Grand Slam title of the year, beating Kim Clijisters in the French Open finals.

Senator Hillary Clinton and her husband present Point Given owner Ahmed bin Salman the winner's trophy for the thoroughbred's romp in the 133rd Belmont Stakes.

10 **Brazil's Gustavo Kuerten** successfully defends his French Open men's singles crown, defeating Spain's Alex Corretja in four sets.

11 **Grand Slam tennis officials** announce that next year all four major tournaments will double their number of seeded players to 32.

12 **The surprising Seattle Mariners** continue their torrid start to the season, sporting a 49-13 record through the season's first 62 games. Only the 1912 N.Y. Giants (51-11) had a better record.

13 **Dale Earnhardt's widow,** Teresa, celebrates a Daytona Beach judge's decision to refuse release of autopsy photos of her husband to the public, citing the pain it would cause the family.

NBA referee Hugh Evans works his 35th, and final, NBA Finals game, concluding a 28-year officiating career that began in 1972.

14 **Five-time Olympic champion** Michael Johnson announces he will retire after the Goodwill Games conclude in September.

15 **NBA Finals MVP Shaquille O'Neal** scores 29 points to lead the L.A. Lakers to a 108-96 victory over the Philadelphia 76ers in Game 5 of the NBA Finals, capping a 15-1 playoff record and the team's second consecutive league championship.

16 **Center fielder Charlton Jimerson** sparks the Miami Hurricanes to a 12-1 victory over Stanford in the final game of the College World Series, making it two national titles in the last three seasons for the 'Canes.

17 **Golfer Mark Brooks watches** Retief Goosen three-put the 72nd hole of the U.S. Open, forcing a 18-hole playoff between himself and Goosen scheduled for the next day.

Defending champ Tiger Woods finishes tied for 12th at the U.S. Open with a 3-over-par 283, bringing to an end his streak of major tournament victories at four.

Al Bello /Allsport

Professional baseball returned to **Brooklyn, N.Y.** *on June 25 when the Cyclones, a Class-A affiliate of the N.Y. Mets, beat the Mahoning Valley Scrappers 3-2 in the first pro baseball game played in the New York City borough since the Dodgers last game in 1957. The Cyclones were named after the 74-year-old Cyclone roller coaster at Coney Island's amusement park, seen here behind the left-field fence.*

Thoroughbred trainer Bob Baffert is suspended 60 days (June 25 to Aug. 24) by Santa Anita racing officials because of a positive morphine test on one of his horses.

18 South African Retief Goosen shoots an even-par 70 to beat Mark Brooks by two strokes in an 18-hole playoff to decide the winner of the U.S. Open.

Baltimore Orioles 3B Cal Ripken announces his plans to retire at the end of the season.

The Michigan-Michigan State rivalry will attempt to break the world record for attendance at an ice hockey game, as the schools announce today that their game on Oct. 6 will be played outdoors on a temporary ice rink in 72,027-seat Spartan Stadium in East Lansing.

19 Utah Jazz guard DeShawn Stevenson, 20, is charged with statutory rape in Fresno, Calif. for allegedly having sex with a 14-year-old girl.

20 Giants slugger Barry Bonds hits his 38th home run of the season in his 71st game, which sets a new major league record for homers hit before the All-Star break and makes him the quickest to reach 38 (passing Babe Ruth who needed 88 games).

21 Former Cowboys WR Michael Irvin is indicted by a Texas grand jury on drug possession charges stemming from an incident in August 2000.

Judge Miriam Goldman Cedarbaum rules that heavyweight champ Hasim Rahman breached his contract with Lennox Lewis when he denied Lewis a rematch, ruling that he can either fight Lewis next or sit idle for 18 months.

22 Braves xenophobe John Rocker is traded from Atlanta to the Cleveland Indians for pitchers Steve Karsay and Steve Reed.

23 Islanders GM Mike Milbury follows up Atlanta's first overall pick, Russian Ilya Kovalchuk, by trading his team's second overall pick to Ottawa for the talented, but frequently disgruntled, Alexei Yashin.

24 Australian golfer Karrie Webb, 26, wins her first LPGA Championship tournament by two strokes over Laura Diaz and becomes the fifth LPGA golfer—and youngest—in history to complete a career Grand Slam.

25 Former Toronto 3B Tony Batista, who hit 41 home runs for the Jays last season, is claimed off waivers by the Baltimore Orioles.

26 Colorado defenseman Ray Bourque announces his retirement 17 days after winning his first Stanley Cup championship.

27 Wizards president Michael Jordan selects Georgia high school star Kwame Brown with the first pick overall, sparking a run of four high school players among the first eight picks of the NBA draft.

Grizzlies star Shareef Abdur-Rahim is sent to Atlanta for Spain's Pau Gastol (the #3 pick in the draft), F/C Lorenzen Wright and guard Brevin Knight.

Chicago's Elton Brand is sent to the L.A. Clippers for the rights to 18-year-old center Tyson Chandler and forward Brian Skinner.

Sacramento Kings guard Jason Williams is dealt to the Grizzlies for guard Mike Bibby.

28 Padres legend Tony Gwynn confirms that he will retire at season's end and campaign for the vacant coaching job at his alma mater San Diego State.

Phoenix guard Jason Kidd is traded to the New Jersey Nets for point guard Stephon Marbury.

Boston relief pitcher Bryce Florie makes his first appearance since being hit in the face by a line drive in September 2000 that nearly ended his career and left him with impaired vision.

29 Denver Broncos LB Bill Romanowski is acquitted on charges of illegally obtaining diet pills prescribed to his wife and two other people during the 1998 season.

JULY 2001

Sun	Mon	Tue	Wed	Thu	Fri	Sat
1	2	3	4	5	6	7
8	9	10	11	12	13	14
15	16	17	18	19	20	21
22	23	24	25	26	27	28
29	30	31				

Quote of the Month

"I've got a hundred bucks that says my baby beats Pete's baby."

Andre Agassi, ATP Tour tennis star, boasting that the child he and retired women's tennis great Steffi Graf are expecting will have superior tennis skills to that of any offspring longtime Agassi-rival Pete Sampras and his actress wife Bridgette Wilson could produce. Incidentally, Sampras and Wilson have yet to start a family.

Armstrong Makes His Move

Defending champion Lance Armstrong continued his mastery of the Tour de France's mountain stages in 2001. Here is a look at his four-day move from 23rd place to first that will go down in history as one of the event's greatest performances.

Date	Stage	Miles	Margin	Overall Place
July 16	#9	115.0	−35:19	23rd
July 17	#10	129.9	−20:07	4th
July 18	#11	19.9	−13:07	3rd
July 20	#12	103.5	−9:10	3rd
July 21	#13	120.6	+3:54	1st

Note: Armstrong's finish in each of the above stages: #9 (32nd); #10 (1st); #11 (1st); #12 (3rd); #13 (1st).

Not-So Hostile Takeover

International Olympic Committee President Juan Antonio Samaranch handed his successor, Jacques Rogge, an Olympic torch this month that—despite the Salt Lake City scandal—is burning a lot brighter than when he took over. Look at how the nations of the world, or National Olympic Committees, have come together at the Summer Games during Samaranch's 21-year term.

Year	Host	Total NOC's	NOC's at Games	NOC's Absent (%)
1980	Moscow	142	81	42.96
1984	Los Angeles	154	140	9.09
1988	Seoul	167	159	4.79
1992	Barcelona	172	169	1.74
1996	Atlanta	197	197	0
2000	Sydney	199	199	0

2 **Nineteen-year-old Roger Federer** upsets defending and seven-time champion Pete Sampras in a five-set, fourth-round match at Wimbledon.

Seattle Mariners OF Ichiro Suzuki becomes the first rookie to be the leading vote-getter for the Major League Baseball All-Star Game.

4 **Marlins outfielder Cliff Floyd** and N.Y. Mets manager Bobby Valentine spat through the media after Valentine doesn't include Floyd on the N.L. All-Star team after assuring him he would.

7 **NASCAR driver Dale Earnhardt Jr.** makes a late charge from sixth place to win the Pepsi 400, the first Winston Cup event at Daytona International Speedway since his father's fatal accident during the Daytona 500.

8 **Tennis star Venus Williams** defends her Wimbledon women's singles title, defeating Justine Henin in three sets.

9 **Croatian Goran Ivanisevic** becomes the first wild card to win a Wimbledon singles title, defeating Australia's Patrick Rafter in a five-set thriller that was delayed one day due to rain.

Arizona outfielder Luis Gonzalez defeats Cubs slugger Sammy Sosa 6-2 in the finals of the annual Home Run Derby at Safeco Field in Seattle.

Louisiana officials announce they have agreed on a financial package with the NFL's poorest franchise, the Saints, that will keep the team in New Orleans.

10 **Orioles All-Star Cal Ripken Jr.** hits a home run during his first plate appearance of his 19th and final All-Star Game, sparking the American League to a 4-1 victory in Seattle. Ripken also wins MVP honors.

11 **Pittsburgh Penguins star Jaromir Jagr** and defenseman Frantisek Kucera are traded to the Washington Capitals for three prospects and future considerations.

Detroit Red Wings goalie Dominik Hasek has been hospitalized since July 5 in the Czech Republic with a mysterious illness, a friend tells the media today.

13 **The International Olympic Committee** chooses Beijing to host the 2008 Summer Games.

Wizards president Michael Jordan makes a surprise appearance at the team's practice, adding fuel to rumors of his NBA comeback.

16 **Belgian surgeon Jacques Rogge** is elected the eighth president of the International Olympic Committee.

17 **Two-time champ Lance Armstrong** makes his move at the Tour de France, winning the mountainous 10th stage and improving from 23rd place to fourth overall.

18 **County prosecutors drop charges** against the wife of Broncos LB Bill Romanowski who was suspected of illegally obtaining diet pills for her husband, who was acquitted last month on similar charges.

Veteran NBA center Patrick Ewing signs a two-year deal to play with the Orlando Magic.

19 **Arizona pitcher Randy Johnson sets** a major league record by striking out 16 batters in a relief appearance and comes four pitches from throwing a combined no-hitter with Curt Schilling. Johnson throws seven innings after the game Schilling started was suspended after two innings a night earlier.

20 **Marathoner Tegla Laroupe** vows never to run again for her country after she's dismissed from Kenya's world championship team because she trains in Germany.

21 **Sacramento Kings star Chris Webber,** one of the summer's biggest NBA free agents, signs the second-largest contract in league history, a seven-year, $122.7 million deal to stay with the team.

Michael Thompson/Allsport

*Moments after the start of the German Grand Prix on July 29, the car of Brazilian Formula One driver **Luciano Burti** rear-ends the car of defending F1 champion Michael Schumacher and launches into the air, causing this spectacular accident in which, incredibly, nobody was seriously hurt.*

22 **PGA Tour golfer David Duval** captures his first major tournament title, holding off Sweden's Niclas Fasth for a three-stroke victory at the 130th British Open.

Final round co-leader Ian Woosnam is penalized two strokes and throws an extra driver in disgust on the second hole after his caddie, Myles Byrne, notices Woosnam's bag has 15 clubs, one more than the limit.

Aussie swimmer Ian Thorpe breaks his own world record in the 400-meter freestyle and then anchors Australia's 400-meter freestyle relay team to gold at the first day of the FINA World Swimming Championships.

23 **Retired tennis star Steffi Graf** reveals that she and Andre Agassi are expecting the birth of a baby boy in December.

24 **Controversies surface** at the swimming world championships after the apparent winner of the women's 4x200-meter relay, Australia, is disqualified for a premature celebration, and then the second-place squad, the United States, is disqualified for an illegal exchange.

25 **Vikings receiver Randy Moss** hauls in an eight-year, $75 million contract extension that includes an NFL-record $18 million signing bonus, making him the highest-paid player at his position.

K.C. Royals outfielder Jermaine Dye winds up in Oakland as part of a five-player, three-team trade that also involves Colorado.

Philadelphia 76ers coach Larry Brown announces that he will return to the team next season, but team president Pat Croce announces he will step down and become a consultant to the team.

Florida freshman Eraste Autin dies six days after he collapsed at the football team's voluntary conditioning workout because of heat stroke.

Free agent Joe Smith signs a contract to play with the Minnesota Timberwolves, the NBA team that illegally signed him and was penalized for doing so last year.

27 **Former IOC president** Juan Antonio Samaranch is released from a Swiss hospital after being admitted for "extreme fatigue" shortly after leaving the IOC's 102nd session in Moscow last week.

Redskins cornerback Deion Sanders, 33, quietly retires from football, releasing a statement that was read by Redskins coach Marty Schottenheimer.

Devil Rays 1B Fred McGriff, who turned down a trade to Chicago earlier this year, is acquired by Cubs for pitcher Manny Aybar and a player to be named.

28 **Light heavyweight champ Roy Jones Jr.** wins a unanimous decision over Julio Gonzalez at the Staples Center in Los Angeles, and says he's rooting for a September bout with Felix Trinidad.

San Jose rookie Landon Donovan scores four goals and takes home MVP honors at the Major League Soccer All-Star Game in San Jose, which ends in a 6-6 tie.

Tournament promoters announce that three men's college basketball tournaments to be held at Las Vegas casinos later this year will be switched to different venues due to pressure from NCAA officials, administrators and coaches.

29 **Cyclist Lance Armstrong wins** the Tour de France by 3 minutes, 44 seconds over Germany's Jan Ullrich and becomes the first American to win three consecutive races.

30 **LPGA star Annika Sorenstam** teams with Tiger Woods and defeats Karrie Webb and David Duval in a primetime golf match-up on ABC.

Grand Rapids owner Joel Langlois agrees to purchase the name and logo of the defunct Continental Basketball Association for $16,000. He and other owners plan to start a new pro basketball minor league.

31 **Montreal Expos closer Ugueth Urbina** goes to the Red Sox and Colorado pitcher Pedro Astacio is sent to the Astros, highlighting the final handful of trades made hours before baseball's trading deadline.

AUGUST 2001

Sun	Mon	Tue	Wed	Thu	Fri	Sat
			1	2	3	4
5	6	7	8	9	10	11
12	13	14	15	16	17	18
19	20	21	22	23	24	25
26	27	28	29	30	31	

Quote of the Month

"He has been eating—and he has been playing baseball."

Felipe de Jesus Almonte, father of 14-year-old Little League baseball pitcher Danny Almonte, explaining to the *New York Daily News* what his son has been doing in the United States the past 18 months since he never enrolled his son in P.S. 70 in the Bronx, the public elementary school he told Little League officials his son attended.

Schumacher Races to 51

On Aug. 19, Ferrari's Michael Schumacher won the Hungarian Grand Prix. It was his 51st career Formula One victory, which ties him with the all-time leader, Alain Prost. Here is a quick look at each driver's statistics en route to his 51st victory.

	Schumacher (1991-present)	Prost (1980-93)*
Seasons	11	13
Wins	51	51
Races	158	202
Win Pct.	32.3%	25.2%
Points	772.0	798.5

*Prost sat out the 1992 F1 season.

Note: Schumacher's stats are through Aug. 19, 2001.

Zebra Lockouts

On August 30, The NFL became the last of the four major men's professional sports organizations to experience a lockout of its officials. Here is a timeline of those lockouts.

Year	League
2001	National Football League
1995	Major League Baseball & National Basketball Association
1993	National Hockey League
1984	Major League Baseball
1982	National Basketball Association
1979	Major League Baseball
1977	National Basketball Association

1 **Minnesota Vikings lineman Korey Stringer**, 27, suffers heat stroke at the team's training camp and dies in the early hours at a local hospital.

Houston Rockets center Hakeem Olajuwon is traded to the Toronto Raptors for two draft picks.

2 **Atlanta Gold Club owner Steve Kaplan** pleads guilty to racketeering charges, ending the much-publicized trial that featured professional athletes testifying about sexual favors they received at the glitzy strip bar.

3 **Northwestern safety Rashidi Wheeler**, 22, suffers an asthma attack during conditioning drills and dies shortly thereafter.

New England WR Terry Glenn is suspended four games by the NFL for violating the league's substance abuse policy.

Super Bowl-winning QB Trent Dilfer signs a contract to backup Matt Hasselbeck in Seattle.

5 **World record holder Maurice Greene** wins his third consecutive 100-meter world championship race, recording the third fastest time in history (9.82).

6 **U.S. sprinter Marion Jones** has a four-year, 42-race finals unbeaten streak end at the World Track and Field Championships, losing to Ukraine's Zhanna Pintusevich-Block in the 100-meter race by .03 seconds.

7 **Mayor Anthony Williams** announces that Washington D.C. will host an endurance-type auto race in the parking lot of RFK Stadium beginning in July 2002.

8 **Baltimore Ravens RB Jamal Lewis** tears a ligament in his left knee which will keep him out of the entire 2001 NFL season.

10 **N.Y. Knicks All-Star Glen Rice** is dealt to the Houston Rockets as part of a four-player, three-team trade that also involves the Dallas Mavericks.

Royals 1B Mike Sweeney sparks a brawl after asking the umpire to check a ball thrown by Tigers starter Jeff Weaver. The game is delayed 12 minutes and three people are ejected.

The NCAA executive committee approves a two-year moratorium against scheduling championship events in South Carolina because the Confederate flag is displayed on the Statehouse grounds.

12 **Scotland's Marc Warren defeats** James Driscoll on the par-3, 17th hole, clinching a 12½-11½ victory over the United States in amateur golf's Walker Cup tournament.

Atlanta pitcher Greg Maddux ends his N.L.-record streak of consecutive innings pitched without a walk (72⅓) by intentionally walking Arizona's Steve Finley in the third inning of a 9-1 loss to the Diamondbacks.

Driver Jeff Gordon sets a Winston Cup record by winning the seventh road race of his career, and third straight at Watkins Glen (N.Y.) International.

13 **Veterans Stadium officials** cancel an NFL preseason game between Philadelphia and Baltimore because of problems with the turf.

15 **Cardinals slugger Mark McGwire** ends his remarkable streak of 11 straight hits for home runs (which began July 18) when he singles off the Reds' Chris Reitsma leading off the fifth inning.

Patriots head coach Bill Belichick issues a season-long suspension of Terry Glenn after the wide receiver's training camp absence reaches 11 days.

16 **Red Sox manager Jimy Williams** is fired and replaced by pitching coach Joe Kerrigan in a pennant-race shake-up in Beantown.

AP/Wide World Photos

What looks like a normal extra-point attempt is actually quite extraordinary. Jacksonville State sophomore kicker **Ashley Martin** *kicked three extra points in a 72-10 victory on Aug. 30, making her the first woman to play and score in a NCAA Division I football game.*

Coppin State assistant coach Stephanie Ready is introduced as the assistant coach of the Greenville (S.C.) Groove of the NBDL (the NBA's new minor league), making her the first woman to coach a men's professional team.

18 Bronx, N.Y. pitcher Danny Almonte throws the first perfect game in 44 years at the Little League World Series, striking out 16 of 18 batters in a 1-0 victory.

19 Formula One driver Michael Schumacher secures his fourth world championship and matches Alain Prost's all-time victories record (51) by winning the Hungarian Grand Prix over teammate Rubens Barrichello.

Quarterback Clint Dolezel throws seven touchdowns to lead the host Grand Rapids Rampage to a 64-42 victory over the Nashville Kats in Arena Bowl XV.

20 Six-time NHL All-Star Eric Lindros, a restricted free agent with the Flyers, is dealt to the N.Y. Rangers for three players and a third-round pick in the 2003 draft.

21 NASCAR releases a report of its six-month investigation into the death of Dale Earnhardt, admitting his broken seat belt was one of many factors that contributed to his death at the Daytona 500 in February.

Expos minor leaguer Tim Raines plays in a Triple-A double-header against his son, Tim Jr., which is believed to be the first time in modern professional baseball history a father and son played against each other.

22 NHL free agent Brett Hull signs a contract with the Detroit Red Wings.

23 Arizona ace Randy Johnson passes the 300-strikeout mark for the season, becoming the first pitcher in the major leagues to reach that plateau four consecutive seasons.

24 Austrian skier Hermann Maier is involved in a motorcycle accident and suffers a severely broken right leg that is expected to keep him out of the 2002 Salt Lake City Winter Games.

25 Game MVP Julie Murray leads the Bay Area CyberRays to victory over the Atlanta Beat, capturing the first Women's United Soccer Association league championship on penalty kicks (4-2) after a 3-3 tie in regulation.

26 Golfer Tiger Woods beats Jim Furyk on the seventh sudden-death playoff hole at the NEC Invitational, the longest playoff on the PGA Tour in 10 years.

27 Little League officials begin an investigation into whether or not Bronx pitcher Danny Almonte is 14 years old and should have been ineligible to play the past two seasons and during this year's World Series.

Talks between the NFL Referees Association and the league breakdown in Dallas. And with no resolution to speak of, the first labor stoppage among NFL officials will begin on Aug. 30.

28 Indians manager Charlie Manuel undergoes abdominal surgery to have scar tissue removed from his colon after being hospitalized twice within the last week.

30 Replacement NFL officials work six NFL exhibition games on the schedule tonight.

Heavyweight champ Hasim Rahman and Lennox Lewis brawl during a taping of ESPN's Up Close, making for some memorable TV. Nobody was hurt in the fracas.

31 Little League pitcher Danny Almonte is ruled ineligible after government records experts determine that he is 14 years old.

SEPTEMBER 2001

Sun	Mon	Tue	Wed	Thu	Fri	Sat
						1
2	3	4	5	6	7	8
9	10	11	12	13	14	15
16	17	18	19	20	21	22
23	24	25	26	27	28	29
30						

Quote of the Month

"Things will be back to normal when I hear boos at Shea Stadium. I'm a Yankees fan."

Rudolph Giuliani, New York City mayor, taking in the city's first baseball game since the Sept. 11 attacks and responding to the crowd's ovation upon his arrival.

Baseball Becomes Secondary

On Sept. 11, Commissioner Bud Selig postponed a full slate of regular-season Major League Baseball games for just the third time in history. Here is a closer look at those instances.

Aug. 2, 1923—President Warren G. Harding, 57, who fell ill while returning from a trip across the country and into Alaska, dies at a hotel in San Francisco. Commissioner Kenesaw Mountain Landis cancels all games to mourn the sudden and unexpected loss of the country's 29th president.

June 6, 1944—D-Day. Allied forces invade Western Europe in World War II. Commissioner Landis cancels all games scheduled for that day.

Sept. 11-16, 2001—New York City and Washington D.C. are attacked. With just 2½ weeks remaining in the pennant races, Bud Selig cancels all games on Sept. 11. He eventually postpones all games from Sept 11-16. An extra week is added to the regular season and all games are made up the first week in October.

Pistol Pete: Past His Peak

With his loss in the U.S. Open finals, tennis star Pete Sampras fell to 0-4 in singles finals in 2001 and is on his way to completing his first season without a singles title since 1989. It's also the first time since 1992 Sampras didn't capture at least one Grand Slam title. Here is a look at his annual singles titles totals since 1990 (Grand Slam titles are in parentheses).

Year		Year	
1990	4 (1)	1996	8 (1)
1991	4	1997	8 (2)
1992	5	1998	4 (1)
1993	8 (2)	1999	5 (1)
1994	10 (2)	2000	2 (1)
1995	5 (2)	2001	0

2 **N.Y. Yankees pitcher Mike Mussina** comes one strike away from pitching the first perfect game at Fenway Park when Boston's Carl Everett connects on a ninth-inning single in a 1-0 Yankees victory.

3 **St. Louis Cardinals pitcher Bud Smith** throws a no-hitter against the host San Diego Padres, becoming the first rookie to throw a no-no since 1999.

Tampa Bay QB Ryan Leaf is waived by the team after the free-agent pickup was unable to beat third-stringer Joe Hamilton in training camp.

4 **Redskins cornerback Darrell Green** announces that he will retire after the 2001-02 NFL season, his 19th with the Skins.

5 **N.Y. Islanders center Alexei Yashin** agrees to the richest contract in NHL history, a 10-year, $87.5 million deal.

7 **Track star Michael Johnson wins** his final race, anchoring the United States' 1,600-meter relay team at the Goodwill Games.

8 **Tennis star Venus Williams** defeats her sister, Serena, in the women's final of the U.S. Open in front of a record crowd at Arthur Ashe Stadium.

9 **Giants' slugger Barry Bonds** hits three home runs to give him 63 for the season, passing Roger Maris' once-magical mark and moving him closer to Mark McGwire's record.

Australian Lleyton Hewitt defeats Pete Sampras in the men's final of the U.S. Open.

11 **Sports comes to a standstill** in the wake of terrorist attacks on New York City and Washington D.C., with Major League Baseball postponing its full slate of regular-season games for the first time since 1944.

Olympic officials in Salt Lake City announce that security for the 2002 Winter Games will be completely re-evaluated but vow the games will go on.

12 **New England WR Terry Glenn** has his team-issued, season-long suspension lifted by an arbitrator, meaning he only has to honor the NFL's four game suspension for violating the league's substance-abuse policy.

13 **NFL commissioner Paul Tagliabue** postpones Week 2 of the NFL season due to the effect of the Sept. 11 attack on the league's players. The decision sets off a chain reaction of unprecedented cancellations, with Major League Baseball, the NHL, college football, NASCAR and almost every other major sports' organization suspending play through the weekend.

Tennessee-Martin athletic director Phil Dane, hoping to create a business-as-usual atmosphere, orders the football game between Div. I-AA Tenn.-Martin and Div. II Ky. Wesleyan to go on as scheduled.

14 **CART officials announce** that the name of the German 500 will be changed to the American Memorial 500. On Sept. 13 officials announced that the race would continue as scheduled, but its broadcast on U.S. television will be postponed a week.

15 **Two-time CART champion Alex Zanardi** loses both legs in a serious accident during the American Memorial 500 that occurred when he exited pit lane and was struck broadside by Alex Tagliani's car.

16 **Eight University of Wyoming cross-country** athletes are killed when the SUV they were driving in collides with a pickup driven by another Wyoming student at 1:30 a.m. on U.S. 287, about 17 miles south of Laramie, Wyo.

The PGA of America tells the European Ryder Cup board that "last Tuesday's tragedy is so overwhelming that it would be impossible" for the U.S. team and officials to take part in the matches, postponing the biennial event until 2002.

Ezra Shaw/Allsport

The way we go "out to the ballgame" changed in the wake of the Sept. 11 attacks. Here, a massive line forms behind a wall of security guards at **Foxboro Stadium***, as football fans are greeted with unprecedented security checks before the Patriots-Jets game on Sept. 23.*

17 N.Y. Mets players and coaches sport New York City police and fire department caps, and fans in all six National League stadiums chant "U-S-A, U-S-A" as baseball returns after a six-day break.

Team president Michael Jordan has his name accidentally appear on the Washington Wizards roster on NBA.com for about 90 minutes. The NBA said later it was a "clerical error."

18 NFL officials ratify a new contract, meaning the two-week lockout is over and replacement officials will be, uh, replaced this Sunday by the regular crews.

19 The Seattle Mariners clinch the American League West Division title by virtue of second-place Oakland's loss to Texas.

N.Y. Yankees pitcher Roger Clemens wins his 20th game of the season, improving his record this season to an unprecedented 20-1.

The Federal Aviation Administration grants requests for "no-fly zones" above several schools, including Clemson, Michigan and Penn State, barring flights within a mile radius of their stadiums.

20 San Diego Padres star Tony Gwynn is hired by his alma mater, San Diego State, to replace baseball coach Jim Dietz following the 2002 season.

22 U.S. Open champion Lleyton Hewitt beats Thomas Johansson as Australia clinches its semifinal against Sweden 3-1 to advance to its third consecutive Davis Cup final. France also qualifies for the final.

23 L.A. Dodgers ace Kevin Brown, who has made his last five starts with a torn flexor muscle in his pitching elbow, announces he will undergo surgery and miss the rest of the season.

25 Wizards president Michael Jordan ends a year-long media saga when he reveals he is returning to the NBA to play with the Wizards. He also says he'll play for two seasons and donate his first-year salary to the Sept. 11 victims.

N.Y. Yankees ace Roger Clemens strikes out Tampa Bay's Toby Hall to lead off the fourth inning and moves into third place on Major League Baseball's all-time strikeouts list.

26 New IOC president Jacques Rogge warns the Greek government that it must begin building nearly a dozen long-delayed sports venues and facilities, saying the country had no time to spare in meeting the "unparalleled" construction task.

27 Utah Jazz guard John Stockton signs a two-year contract extension with the team that will keep him in Utah past his 41st birthday.

Tennis star Anna Kournikova returns to the WTA Tour after being sidelined for more than three months with a stress fracture in her left foot.

29 "The Executioner" Bernard Hopkins knocks out favored Felix Trinidad in the 12th round to become the undisputed middleweight champion of the world.

Mariners leadoff star Ichiro Suzuki sets a major league rookie record when he gets his 234th hit, a single to center off Oakland's Erik Hiljus.

Mariners shortstop Carlos Guillen is diagnosed with pulmonary tuberculosis and is hospitalized, threatening the remainder of his season.

30 Finnish driver Mika Hakkinen overcomes a penalty that dropped him from second to fourth in the starting grid to win the U.S. Grand Prix at Indianapolis Motor Speedway.

OCTOBER 2001

Sun	Mon	Tue	Wed	Thu	Fri	Sat
	1	2	3	4	5	6
7	8	9	10	11	12	13
14	15	16	17	18	19	20
21	22	23	24	25	26	27
28	29	30	31			

Quote of the Month

"When you use words like 'mystique' and 'aura,' those are dancers in a night-club, not things we concern ourselves with on the ball field."

Curt Schilling, Arizona Diamondbacks pitcher, downplaying the implied intangibles the three-time defending world champion N.Y. Yankees bring to the World Series.

Roaring to the Top

With Penn State's win over Ohio State on Oct. 29, football coach Joe Paterno earned his 324th career victory, surpassing the legendary Bear Bryant. Here is a look at how Paterno, in his 36th season with the Nittany Lions, has fared against some of the sport's top programs.

Alabama	4-8	Nebraska	2-3
Brigham Young	2-1	Notre Dame	8-5
Florida State	0-1-1	Ohio State	6-7
Miami (Fla.)	7-5	Texas	3-2
Florida	0-1	UCLA	1-2
Michigan	3-6	USC	4-3

Padres Fans: Save Your Stubs

Although the San Diego Padres finished 13 games back in the NL West Division, Qualcomm Stadium seemed to be *the* stadium for baseball history in 2001:

April 25—Rickey Henderson passes Babe Ruth to become baseball's all-time walks leader.

May 12—A.J. Burnett, of the Florida Marlins, hurls a no-hitter against the Padres.

June 19—Barry Bonds hits his 37th home run of the season, tying Babe Ruth's record for most home runs hit before the all-star break.

July 19—When the game on July 18 is stopped after the second inning because of malfunctioning lights, Randy Johnson comes on "in relief" and sets a Major League Baseball record for strikeouts by a reliever, fanning 17 in Arizona's 3-0 victory.

Sept. 3—Bud Smith, of the St. Louis Cardinals, hurls the second no-hitter against the Padres at Qualcomm Stadium this season.

Oct. 4—Rickey Henderson scores on a solo home run and breaks Ty Cobb's major league record for career runs scored.

Oct. 7—Rickey Henderson gets his 3,000th hit and Tony Gwynn is honored in his last game.

2 **Cubs slugger Sammy Sosa** becomes the first player to hit 60 home runs in three major league seasons, connecting on a solo shot in the first inning off Cincinnati's Lance Davis at Wrigley Field.

Promoter Don King and HBO announce that plans for a third fight between heavyweights John Ruiz and Evander Holyfield in Beijing on Nov. 24, will be changed, citing a State Department advisory about international travel since Sept. 11.

The NCAA hands the University of Wisconsin a five-year probation sentence and takes away some football and basketball scholarships after an investigation revealed that a shoe store gave athletes discounts.

3 **Giants slugger Barry Bonds** draws a walk, his third of the game, off Astros reliever Mike Williams, breaking Babe Ruth's record for walks in a season with 171.

NFL commissioner Paul Tagliabue announces an agreement with auto dealers that will allow the Super Bowl to be held at the Louisiana Superdome but be pushed back a week to Feb. 3, 2002—the same date on which an auto convention had been scheduled.

Montreal OF Tim Raines is traded to Baltimore and joins his son (Tim Jr.) in the Orioles dugout, making them the second father-son teammates in major league history (Griffeys).

Defenseman Paul Coffey retires from the NHL after 21 years, eight teams and four Stanley Cups.

4 **Giants slugger Barry Bonds** hits his 70th home run of the season, a ninth-inning blast off Houston rookie Wilfredo Rodriguez, tying Mark McGwire's record.

San Diego's Rickey Henderson passes Ty Cobb's major league record of 2,245 career runs by hitting a solo home run then sliding into home plate to celebrate.

5 **Giants slugger Barry Bonds** hits two home runs (his 71st and 72nd) in a game against the Los Angeles Dodgers, setting a new single-season home run record.

7 **President Bush announces** the start of "Operation Enduring Freedom," which is the American-led military action in Afghanistan, just before the start of the day's Sunday sports schedule. Some stadiums broadcast the announcement on scoreboard video screens.

Giants slugger Barry Bonds hits home run #73 off the Dodgers' Dennis Springer, setting a new single-season record for home runs and slugging percentage (.863).

San Diego OF Ricky Henderson smacks a double off Rockies pitcher John Thomson, becoming the 25th player in major league history to reach 3,000 career hits.

USA midfielder Joe-Max Moore scores both goals in a 2-1 United States victory over Jamaica in CONCACAF regional qualifying, which (after help from other teams) gets the U.S. into the 2002 World Cup tournament.

8 **New England Patriots WR Terry Glenn** returns to the team after serving his league-imposed four game suspension for violating the NFL's substance abuse policy.

11 **Wizards team president Michael Jordan** appears in his first NBA game in more than two years, playing 17 first-half minutes in a 95-85 preseason loss to Detroit.

13 **N.Y. Yankees SS Derek Jeter** single handedly preserves a 1-0 victory over Oakland in Game 3 of the ALDS with an uncanny defensive play when he flips an errant relay throw to catcher Jorge Posada, who tags the potential game-tying run at the plate.

15 **WTA Tour star Jennifer Capriati** claims the world's #1 ranking in women's tennis, succeeding Martina Hingis and becoming just the ninth woman to hold that title.

Pittsburgh Penguins coach Ivan Hlinka is fired after a 0-4 start and is replaced by assistant Rick Kehoe.

*College hockey fans in East Lansing, Mich. broke a 41-year-old world record for hockey game attendance on Oct. 6 when 74,554 fans filled **Spartan Stadium** to watch host Michigan State and Michigan skate to a 3-3 tie on an ice rink set up in the school's football stadium.*

Cuban high jumper Javier Sotomayor announces his retirement after a successful and controversial 23-year career.

16 Texas Motor Speedway's lawsuit against CART over a race cancelled two hours before its start on April 29 is settled for an undisclosed amount.

N.Y. Jets safety Damien Robinson is fined a week's pay by the NFL after being charged with taking an assault rifle into a Giants Stadium parking lot before his game on Oct. 14. Robinson said he inadvertently left it in his car after visiting a shooting range.

17 Seattle Mariners SS Carlos Guillen returns to the starting lineup for Game 1 of the ALCS after a battle with tuberculosis.

18 Seattle Mariners skipper Lou Piniella tells the media "We will be back here for Game 6—print it," following a loss at Safeco Field which gives the Yankees a 2-0 advantage in the ALCS.

Houston Astros manager Larry Dierker resigns after losing in the first round of the playoffs for the fourth time in five postseason appearances.

19 Officials at the Downtown Athletic Club in lower Manhattan announce that the 2001 Heisman Trophy presentation will be moved for the first time in 67 years due to repairs on the building's elevators, which suffered damage during the Sept. 11 attacks.

21 Arizona ace Randy Johnson leads Arizona to a 3-2 victory over the Atlanta Braves in Game 5 of the NLCS, securing the Diamondbacks' first-ever trip to the World Series.

San Jose substitute Dwayne DeRosario scores six minutes into overtime as the Earthquakes beat the Los Angeles Galaxy, 2-1, to win their first MLS Cup.

22 ALCS MVP Andy Pettitte pitches seven shutout innings and helps contain the Seattle Mariners in a 12-3, Game 5 victory, earning the Bronx Bombers their fourth straight American League pennant.

24 Boston Bruins holdout Jason Allison and winger Mikko Eloranta are dealt to the L.A. Kings for former Bruins Jozef Stumpel and Glen Murray.

25 U.S. Tennis Association officials announce that the United States is pulling out of the Fed Cup finals in Madrid, citing worries about the safety of its players.

27 Penn State football coach Joe Paterno earns career victory No. 324, which moves him past Bear Bryant atop the all-time list.

Defending champion Tiznow becomes the first horse to win consecutive Breeders' Cup Classics, holding off Sakhee to win the $4 million purse.

Tennis stars Steffi Graf and Andre Agassi confirm the birth of their son, Jaden Gil, in a Las Vegas hospital.

28 Pittsburgh Penguins' Mario Lemieux undergoes arthroscopic surgery on a sore hip that will keep him sidelined for at least a month.

30 President Bush throws out the ceremonial opening pitch of Game 3 of the World Series at Yankee Stadium.

Team president Michael Jordan scores 19 points in his regular-season debut with the Wizards, a 93-91 loss to the N.Y. Knicks at Madison Square Garden.

Olympics
Winter Games

Year	No.	Host City	Dates
2002	XIX	Salt Lake City, Utah	Feb. 8-24
2006	XX	Turin, Italy.	Feb. 4-19

Summer Games

Year	No.	Host City	Dates
2004	XXVIII	Athens, Greece	Aug. 13-29
2008	XXIX	Beijing, China	TBA

All-Star Games
Baseball

Year	Site	Date
2002	Miller Park, Milwaukee	July 9
2003	Comiskey Park, Chicago	July 8

NBA Basketball

Year	Site	Date
2002	First Union Center, Philadelphia	Feb. 10
2003	Philips Arena, Atlanta	Feb. 9

NFL Pro Bowl

Year	Site	Date
2002	Aloha Stadium, Honolulu	Feb. 9
2003	Aloha Stadium, Honolulu	Feb. 2
2004	Aloha Stadium, Honolulu	Feb. 8

NHL Hockey

Year	Site	Date
2002	Staples Center, Los Angeles	Feb. 2
2003	National Car Rental Center, Sunrise, Fla.	Feb. 2

Auto Racing

The Daytona 500 stock car race is usually held on the Sunday before the third Monday in February, while the Indianapolis 500 is usually held on the Sunday of Memorial Day weekend in May. The following dates are tentative.

Year	Daytona 500	Indianapolis 500
2002	Feb. 17	May 26
2003	Feb. 16	May 25
2004	Feb. 15	May 30

NCAA Basketball
Men's Final Four

Year	Site	Dates
2002	Georgia Dome, Atlanta	Mar. 30-Apr. 1
2003	Louisiana Superdome, New Orleans	April 5-7
2004	Alamodome, San Antonio	April 3-5
2005	The Dome at America's Center, St. Louis	April 2-4

Women's Final Four

Year	Site	Dates
2002	Alamodome, San Antonio	March 29-31
2003	Georgia Dome, Atlanta	April 4-6
2004	New Orleans Sports Arena	April 2-4
2005	Indianapolis (TBA)	April 1-3
2006	FleetCenter, Boston	March 31-April 2
2007	Gund Arena, Cleveland	March 30-April 1

NFL Football
Super Bowl

No.	Site	Date
XXXVI	Louisiana Superdome, New Orleans	Feb. 3, 2002
XXXVII	Qualcomm Stadium, San Diego	Jan. 26, 2003
XXXVIII	Reliant Stadium, Houston	Feb. 1, 2004
XXXIX	ALLTEL Stadium, Jacksonville	Feb. 6, 2005
XL	Ford Field, Detroit	Feb. 5, 2006

Golf
The Masters

Year	Site	Dates
2002	Augusta (Ga.) National GC	April 11-14
2003	Augusta (Ga.) National GC	April 10-13

U.S. Open

Year	Site	Dates
2002	Bethpage State Park, Farmingdale, N.Y.	June 13-16
2003	Olympia Fields (Ill.) Country Club	June 12-15
2004	Shinnecock Hills GC, Southampton, N.Y.	June 17-20

U.S. Women's Open

Year	Site	Dates
2002	Prairie Dunes CC, Hutchinson, Kan.	July 4-7
2003	Lake Merced GC, Daly City, Calif.	TBA

U.S. Senior Open

Year	Site	Dates
2002	Caves Valley GC, Owings Mills, Md.	June 27-30
2003	Inverness Club, Toledo, Ohio	TBA

PGA Championship

Year	Site	Dates
2002	Hazeltine National CC, Chaska, Minn.	Aug. 15-18
2003	Oak Hill CC, Rochester, N.Y.	Aug. 14-17

British Open

Year	Site	Dates
2002	Muirfield, Scotland	July 18-21
2003	Royal St. George GC, Sandwich, England	July 17-20

Ryder Cup

Year	Site	Date
2002	The Belfry, Sutton Coldfield, England	Sept. 27-29
2004	Oakland Hills CC, Bloomfield Hills, Mich.	TBA
2006	Kildare Hotel and CC, Dublin, Ireland	TBA

Horse Racing
Triple Crown

The Kentucky Derby is always held at Churchill Downs in Louisville on the first Saturday in May, followed two weeks later by the Preakness Stakes at Pimlico Race Course in Baltimore and three weeks after that by the Belmont Stakes at Belmont Park in Elmont, N.Y.

Year	Ky Derby	Preakness	Belmont
2002	May 4	May 18	June 8
2003	May 3	May 17	June 7
2004	May 1	May 15	June 5

Soccer
World Cup

Year	Site	Dates
2002	Japan/South Korea	May 31-June 30
2006	Germany	TBA

Women's World Cup

Year	Site	Date
2003	China	TBA

Tennis
U.S. Open

Usually held from the last Monday in August through the second Sunday in September, with Labor Day weekend the midway point in the tournament.

Year	Site	Dates
2002	Arthur Ashe Stadium, NYC	Aug. 26-Sept. 8
2003	Arthur Ashe Stadium, NYC	Aug. 25-Sept. 7

Baseball

Ichiro Suzuki set a rookie record for hits (242) in 2001 and led the Mariners to 116 wins.

Aces High

Schilling and Johnson pitch the Diamondbacks to victory over the Yankees in a stunning World Series.

Karl Ravech
is an analyst for ESPN's baseball coverage.

Simply put, 2001 was the best baseball season of all time. Powerful stuff for a game whose roots run back into the late 1800's. However, when you combine the power, the pitching, the pennant races and the postseason with the pulse of the nation, one can make a particularly compelling case that this season stands above all others.

Sept. 11, 2001 will be a date marked in history. Its significance may not ultimately be determined for years, decades or, perhaps, even centuries. A terrorist attack on America. Thousands of Americans killed. And in the White House sat a president who once owned the Texas Rangers.

Immediately following the attacks, baseball, like everything in the country, shut down. A period of shock, followed by grief, followed by a need for relief led President Bush to plead with the people of the nation to "try to return to normal." For baseball that meant getting the players back on the field and the fans back in the seats. The game

had the potential, as it had during World War II, of assisting the healing process. The president knew it, and his intuition served him well.

When play resumed on Sept. 17, Barry Bonds was seven home runs short of tying Mark McGwire's record of 70. Sammy Sosa had already hit 54 and Luis Gonzalez had belted 51. Never before had the game witnessed power like this. In the National League, nine teams were still battling for a playoff spot. In Seattle, the Mariners were on pace to break the all-time record for regular season wins. In New York, the Yankees were in the midst of another playoff run. On Sept. 19 their ace pitcher Roger Clemens won in Chicago to raise his record to 20-1. Never before had a pitcher had such a successful start to the season.

The final month of the season saw attendance steadily climb like Bonds' home run total. There were also emotional goodbyes on both coasts for two sure-fire first-ballot hall of famers—Cal Ripken Jr. and Tony Gwynn. Their contributions on and off the

*The jubilant **Arizona Diamondbacks** celebrate their come-from-behind victory in Game 7 of the World Series.*

field were legendary. Their legacies will resonate for generations to come. Ripken's parting shot came during the All-Star game in Seattle, when he hit a home run on the first pitch he saw.

On Oct. 4, in Houston, one night after setting a major league record for walks in a season, Bonds hit #70. He and his team would go home with three games to play. Bonds hit #71 and #72 against archrival Los Angeles, but his personal achievements were overshadowed by his team's disappointing loss. Bonds broke the record. The loss broke the Giants. He ended the year with 73 homers and a new single season slugging percentage mark. It was an offensive season like no other.

The first two rounds of the playoffs hardly went according to the script. The Yankees scraped by Oakland in five games, despite losing the first two. They then took care of the Mariners, whose record-tying 116 regular-season wins proved to mean nothing in the playoffs. The Arizona Diamondbacks rode the arms of their two 20-game winners, Randy Johnson and Curt Schilling, all the way to the World Series. The Fall Classic was set. The Yankees with all their tradition and 26 World Series titles would face a team that was only 4 years old.

The cleanup of the World Trade Towers continued as the Yankees flew west with the "responsibility," according to manager

AP/Wide World Photos

*Giants slugger **Barry Bonds** put on an offensive show in 2001, walking a record 177 times and blasting 73 homers. This particular one happens to be #66.*

Joe Torre, of trying to lift the spirits of New York City—and in some eyes—the country.

Games 1 and 2 were dominated by Schilling and Johnson. Combined they allowed one earned run in 16 innings. The Yankees went home for games 3, 4 and 5 knowing they would likely face Schilling again, but aware of the fact that he would be performing in one of the most hostile and exciting places in all of sports.

The Yankees won Game 3 behind Roger Clemens, the tireless workhorse of the staff. Mariano Rivera closed it out, as he always did. It was his 22nd straight postseason save. However, neither of those men threw the most important pitch of the night. That happened before the game.

President Bush was on hand to remind the nation that it was okay to go out to a ball game, to live and to laugh. Fittingly, his ceremonial first pitch was a perfect strike.

Games 4 and 5 deserve their own place in baseball history. On consecutive nights the Yankees trailed by two runs in the bottom of the ninth. Twice they were down to their final out and twice they hit game-tying home runs. Tino Martinez in Game 4. Scott Brosius in Game 5. Both times the Yankees won in extra innings. Both times the losing pitcher was 22-year-old closer Byung-Hyun Kim. Arizona needed to get the heck out of New York.

continued on page 58 ▶

Karl Ravech's Ten Biggest Stories of the Year in Baseball

10   Recent league doormats, the Twins, Cubs and Phillies reverse their downward spirals to go a combined 32 games over .500 for the season. Despite the turnaround, none of the three advance to the postseason.

9   Given the latest offensive explosion in baseball, no lead is safe—even if it's 12 runs. On Aug. 5, the Indians tie a major league record and become the first team in 76 years to erase a 12-run deficit, storming back to beat the Mariners, 15-14, in 11 innings.

8   The Rangers ink standout shortstop Alex Rodriguez to a 10-year, $252 million contract in the offseason. Rodriguez performs as expected, leading the AL in home runs and runs...and the Rangers finish exactly two games better in 2001 than in 2000.

7   Future hall-of-famers Cal Ripken Jr. and Tony Gwynn hang up their cleats after the season. Ripken provides one last thrilling moment, depositing Chan Ho Park's first pitch into the left field seats at Safeco Field and becoming the 2001 All-Star game MVP.

6   The Oakland A's appear to be lost after a 2-10 start, but behind the offensive production of Jason Giambi and tremendous starting pitching from Tim Hudson, Barry Zito and Mark Mulder, they roll to a 102-win season and a wild card berth. The A's go 58-17 (.773 pct.) after the all-star break.

5   Baseball is rightfully shut down following the Sept. 11 attacks on America. Games are postponed for almost a week, which ultimately pushes the World Series into November.

4   Seven-time Japanese batting champ Ichiro Suzuki leads the American League in hitting and steals to vault the Seattle Mariners to a 116-win season, tying the all-time mark set by the Chicago Cubs in 1906.

3   Barry Bonds has an offensive season even Babe Ruth would envy, setting a new standard for homers in a season with 73. The Giants left fielder also walks 177 times and records an astounding .863 slugging percentage, breaking two of Ruth's single-season records.

2   The three-time defending champion Yankees prove they won't give up their crown without a fight. Their gripping postseason run is highlighted by Derek Jeter's series-saving relay flip home against Oakland, and then *two* ninth-inning, two-out, game-tying home runs in the World Series.

1   The Arizona Diamondbacks give the Yankees a taste of their own medicine in Game 7 of the World Series, scoring two runs in the ninth inning off ace reliever Mariano Rivera to win one of the most enthralling World Series ever. Pitchers Curt Schilling and Randy Johnson go a combined 4-0 and are named Series co-MVPs.

As close as the previous two games were, Game 6 was as lopsided as any in Yankees' World Series history. Arizona knew Johnson would keep New York down, and the offense gave him a huge lift by scoring 15 runs.

In Game 7 Schilling would once again pitch on three days rest, this time against Roger Clemens, the man who had once sat him down in a gym and told him if he didn't shape up, he'd waste his career.

Now it was the Diamondbacks who were desperate late in the game. Yankees second baseman Alfonso Soriano's home run off Schilling in the eighth had given the Yankees a 2-1 lead. The prevailing thought everywhere except in the Diamondbacks' dugout was that this game was now over. Rivera pitched a perfect bottom-half and was three outs away from his 23rd straight postseason save. It never came.

Rivera contributed to his own demise by throwing a sacrifice bunt attempt into center field. Tony Womack's double tied the game, 2-2, and Gonzalez, Arizona's offensive MVP of the year, delivered a game-ending, Series-winning single over a drawn-in infield. It was pandemonium.

Four of the seven games were decided by one run. Three were decided in the final at bat. Baseball had done its part. The players and teams delivered to the nation a combination of energy and excitement unlike any it had presented before. Statistically the season was unprecedented. Emotionally it was unmatched.

Given all the circumstances, this was indeed baseball's best season ever.

Whiff of Success

Arizona aces Randy Johnson and Curt Schilling, World Series co-MVPs, dominated in the regular season as well, registering the most strikeouts by two teammates since 1900.

Year	Pitchers (strikeouts)	Total
2001	Johnson 372/Schilling 293	665
1973	Ryan 383/Singer 241	624
1965	Koufax 382/Drysdale 210	592
1976	Ryan 327/Tanana 261	588
1963	Koufax 306/Drysdale 251	557

Season for the Ages

The home run record is the one that grabs all the headlines, but it sure wasn't the only single-season mark set by Barry Bonds in 2001. Here are just some of the records Bonds set, along with the former record holders (post-1900).

Category	Record (former)
HR (ML)	73 (McGwire, 70, '98)
Slug % (ML)	.863 (Ruth, .847, '20)
Walks (ML)	177 (Ruth, 170, '23)
AB/HR (ML)	6.5 (McGwire, 7.3, '98)
OBP (NL)	.515 (Hornsby, .507, '24)

Note: The major league record for OBP (on base pct.) is .551 by Ted Williams in 1941. The pre-1900 NL mark is .547, set by John McGraw in 1899.

2001 Season in Review

Final Major League Standings

Division champions (*) and Wild Card (†) winners are noted. Number of seasons listed after each manager refers to current tenure with club.

American League

East Division

	W	L	Pct	GB	Home	Road
*New York	95	65	.594	–	51-28	44-37
Boston	82	79	.509	13½	41-40	41-39
Toronto	80	82	.494	16	40-42	40-40
Baltimore	63	98	.391	32½	30-50	33-48
Tampa Bay	62	100	.383	34	37-44	25-56

2001 Managers: NY–Joe Torre (6th season); **Bos**–Jimy Williams (5th, 65-53) was fired on Aug. 16 and replaced by pitching coach Joe Kerrigan (17-26); **Tor**–Buck Martinez (1st); **Bal**–Mike Hargrove (2nd); **TB**–Larry Rothschild (4th, 4-10) was fired on Apr. 18 and replaced by bench coach Hal McRae (58-90).

2000 Standings: 1. New York (87-74); 2. Boston (85-77); 3. Toronto (83-79); 4. Baltimore (74-88); 5. Tampa Bay (69-92).

Central Division

	W	L	Pct	GB	Home	Road
*Cleveland	91	71	.562	–	44-36	47-35
Minnesota	85	77	.525	6	47-34	38-43
Chicago	83	79	.512	8	46-35	37-44
Detroit	66	96	.407	25	37-44	29-52
Kansas City	65	97	.401	26	35-46	30-51

2001 Managers: Cle–Charlie Manuel (2nd season); **Min**–Tom Kelly (16th); **Chi**–Jerry Manuel (4th); **Det**–Phil Garner (2nd); **KC**–Tony Muser (5th).

2000 Standings: 1. Chicago (95-67); 2. Cleveland (90-72); 3. Detroit (79-83); 4. Kansas City (77-85); 5. Minnesota (69-93).

West Division

	W	L	Pct	GB	Home	Road
*Seattle	116	46	.716	–	57-24	59-22
†Oakland	102	60	.630	14	53-28	49-32
Anaheim	75	87	.463	41	39-42	36-45
Texas	73	89	.451	43	41-41	32-48

2001 Managers: Sea–Lou Piniella (9th season); **Oak**–Art Howe (6th); **Ana**–Mike Scioscia (2nd); **Tex**–Johnny Oates (7th, 11-17) resigned and third base coach Jerry Narron (62-72) took over on May 4.

2000 Standings: 1. Oakland (91-70); 2. Seattle (91-71); 3. Anaheim (82-80); 4. Texas (71-91).

National League

East Division

	W	L	Pct	GB	Home	Road
*Atlanta	88	74	.543	–	40-41	48-33
Philadelphia	86	76	.531	2	47-34	39-42
New York	82	80	.506	6	44-37	38-43
Florida	76	86	.469	12	46-34	30-52
Montreal	68	94	.420	20	34-47	34-47

2001 Managers: Atl–Bobby Cox (12th season); **Phi**–Larry Bowa (1st); **NY**–Bobby Valentine (6th); **Fla**–John Boles (3rd, 22-26) was fired on May 28 and replaced by Tony Perez (54-60); **Mon**–Felipe Alou (10th, 21-32) was fired on May 31 and replaced by Jeff Torborg (47-62).

2000 Standings: 1. Atlanta (95-67); 2. New York (94-68); 3. Florida (79-82); 4. Montreal (67-95); 5. Philadelphia (65-97).

Central Division

	W	L	Pct	GB	Home	Road
*Houston	93	69	.574	–	44-37	49-32
†St. Louis	93	69	.574	–	54-28	39-41
Chicago	88	74	.543	5	48-33	40-41
Milwaukee	68	94	.420	25	36-45	32-49
Cincinnati	66	96	.407	27	27-54	39-42
Pittsburgh	62	100	.383	31	38-43	24-57

Note: Houston won the division over St. Louis due to a better head-to-head record.

2001 Managers: Hou–Larry Dierker (5th season); **St.L**–Tony La Russa (6th); **Chi**–Don Baylor (2nd); **Mil**–Dave Lopes (2nd); **Cin**–Bob Boone (1st); **Pit**–Lloyd McClendon (1st).

2000 Standings: 1. St. Louis (95-67); 2. Cincinnati (85-77); 3. Milwaukee (73-89); 4. Houston (72-90); 5. Pittsburgh (69-93); 6. Chicago (65-97).

West Division

	W	L	Pct	GB	Home	Road
*Arizona	92	70	.568	–	48-33	44-37
San Francisco	90	72	.556	2	49-32	41-40
Los Angeles	86	76	.531	6	44-37	42-39
San Diego	79	83	.488	13	35-46	44-37
Colorado	73	89	.451	19	41-40	32-49

2001 Managers: Ari–Bob Brenly (1st season); **SF**–Dusty Baker (9th); **LA**–Jim Tracy (1st); **SD**–Bruce Bochy (7th); **Col**–Buddy Bell (2nd).

2000 Standings: 1. San Francisco (97-65); 2. Los Angeles (86-76); 3. Arizona (85-77); 4. Colorado (82-80); 5. San Diego (76-86).

Interleague Play Standings

American League

	W-L	Pct		W-L	Pct
Chicago	12-6	.667	Minnesota	9-9	.500
Oakland	12-6	.667	Kansas City	8-10	.444
Seattle	12-6	.667	Texas	8-10	.444
Anaheim	10-8	.556	Toronto	8-10	.444
Boston	10-8	.556	Cleveland	7-11	.389
Detroit	10-8	.556	Baltimore	6-12	.333
New York	10-8	.556	**Totals**	**132-120**	**.524**
Tampa Bay	10-8	.556			

National League

	W-L	Pct		W-L	Pct
Florida	12-6	.667	Montreal	8-10	.444
San Francisco	10-5	.667	Los Angeles	6-9	.400
Chicago	9-6	.600	San Diego	6-9	.400
Houston	9-6	.600	Philadelphia	7-11	.389
New York	10-8	.556	Milwaukee	5-10	.333
Pittsburgh	8-7	.533	Cincinnati	4-11	.267
St. Louis	8-7	.533	Colorado	2-10	.167
Atlanta	9-9	.500	**Totals**	**120-132**	**.476**
Arizona	7-8	.467			

Seattle Mariners	Oakland A's	Texas Rangers	Seattle Mariners
Ichiro Suzuki	**Jason Giambi**	**Alex Rodriguez**	**Freddy Garcia**
BA, Stolen Bases, Hits	OBP, SLG, Walks, Doubles	Home Runs, Runs, Total Bases	ERA, Innings, Opp. BA

American League Leaders
(*) indicates rookie.

Batting

	Bat	Gm	AB	R	H	Avg	TB	2B	3B	HR	RBI	BB	SO	SB	Slg Pct	OBP
Ichiro Suzuki*, Sea	L	157	692	127	242	**.350**	316	34	8	8	69	30	53	56	.457	.381
Jason Giambi, Oak	L	154	520	109	178	**.342**	343	47	2	38	120	129	83	2	.660	.477
Roberto Alomar, Cle	S	157	575	113	193	**.336**	311	34	12	20	100	80	71	30	.541	.415
Bret Boone, Sea	R	158	623	118	206	**.331**	360	37	3	37	141	40	110	5	.578	.372
Frank Catalanotto, Tex	L	133	463	77	153	**.330**	227	31	5	11	54	39	55	15	.490	.391
Juan Gonzalez, Cle	R	140	532	97	173	**.325**	314	34	1	35	140	41	94	1	.590	.370
Alex Rodriguez, Tex	R	162	632	133	201	**.318**	393	34	1	52	135	75	131	18	.622	.399
Shannon Stewart, Tor	R	155	640	103	202	**.316**	296	44	7	12	60	46	72	27	.463	.371
Derek Jeter, NY	R	150	614	110	191	**.311**	295	35	3	21	74	56	99	27	.480	.377
Jeff Conine, Bal	R	139	524	75	163	**.311**	232	23	2	14	97	64	75	12	.443	.386
Bernie Williams, NY	S	146	540	102	166	**.307**	282	38	0	26	94	78	67	11	.522	.395
Edgar Martinez, Sea	R	132	470	80	144	**.306**	255	40	1	23	116	93	90	4	.543	.423
Carlos Beltran, KC	S	155	617	106	189	**.306**	317	32	12	24	101	52	120	31	.514	.362
Manny Ramirez, Bos	R	142	529	93	162	**.306**	322	33	2	41	125	81	147	0	.609	.405
Doug Mientkiewicz, Min	L	151	543	77	166	**.306**	252	39	1	15	74	67	92	2	.464	.387

Note: Batters must have 3.1 plate appearances per their team's games played to qualify.

Home Runs
Rodriguez, Tex	52
Thome, Cle	49
Palmeiro, Tex	47
Glaus, Ana	41
Ramirez, Bos	41
Delgado, Tor	39
Ja. Giambi, Oak	38
Boone, Sea	37
Gonzalez, Cle	35

Triples
Guzman, Min	14
Alomar, Cle	12
Beltran, KC	12
Cedeno, Det	11
Durham, Chi	10
McLemore, Sea	9
Suzuki*, Sea	8
Vizquel, Cle	8

On Base Pct.
Ja. Giambi, Oak	.477
Martinez, Sea	.423
Thome, Cle	.416
Alomar, Cle	.415
Delgado, Tor	.408
Ramirez, Bos	.405
Olerud, Sea	.401
Rodriguez, Tex	.399

Runs Batted In
Boone, Sea	141
Gonzalez, Cle	140
Rodriguez, Tex	135
Ramirez, Bos	125
Thome, Cle	124
Anderson, Ana	123
Palmeiro, Tex	123
Ja. Giambi, Oak	120
Martinez, Sea	116
Chavez, Oak	114

Doubles
Ja. Giambi, Oak	47
Sweeney, KC	46
Stewart, Tor	44
Chavez, Oak	43
Durham, Chi	42
Martinez, Sea	40
Ordonez, Chi	40

Slugging Pct.
Ja. Giambi, Oak	.660
Thome, Cle	.624
Rodriguez, Tex	.622
Ramirez, Bos	.609
Gonzalez, Cle	.590
Boone, Sea	.578
Palmeiro, Tex	.563

Hits
Suzuki*, Sea	242
Boone, Sea	206
Stewart, Tor	202
Rodriguez, Tex	201
Anderson, Ana	194
Alomar, Cle	193
Jeter, NY	191
Beltran, KC	189
Ordonez, Chi	181

Runs
Rodriguez, Tex	133
Suzuki*, Sea	127
Boone, Sea	118
Alomar, Cle	113
Jeter, NY	110
Ja. Giambi, Oak	109
Damon, Oak	108
Tejada, Oak	107
Beltran, KC	106

Walks
Ja. Giambi, Oak	129
Delgado, Tor	111
Thome, Cle	111
Glaus, Ana	107
Palmeiro, Tex	101
Salmon, Ana	96
Olerud, Sea	94

Stolen Bases
	SB	CS
Suzuki*, Sea	56	14
Cedeno, Det	55	15
Soriano*, NY	43	14
McLemore, Sea	39	7
Knoblauch, NY	38	9
Cameron, Sea	34	5
Cruz, Tor	32	5

Total Bases
Rodriguez, Tex	393
Boone, Sea	360
Ja. Giambi, Oak	343
Palmeiro, Tex	338
Thome, Cle	328
Ramirez, Bos	322
Anderson, Ana	321
Beltran, KC	317

Strikeouts
Thome, Cle	185
Grieve, TB	159
Glaus, Ana	158
Cameron, Sea	155
Gonzalez, Tor	149
Ramirez, Bos	147
Cruz, Tor	138
Delgado, Tor	136

Pitching

	Arm	W	L	ERA	Gm	GS	CG	ShO	Sv	IP	H	R	ER	HR	HB	BB	SO	WP
Freddy Garcia, Sea	R	18	6	3.05	34	34	4	3	0	238.2	199	88	81	16	5	69	163	3
Mike Mussina, NY	R	17	11	3.15	34	34	4	3	0	228.2	202	87	80	20	4	42	214	6
Joe Mays, Min	R	17	13	3.16	34	34	4	2	0	233.2	205	87	82	25	5	64	123	11
Mark Buehrle, Chi	L	16	8	3.29	32	32	4	1	0	221.1	188	89	81	24	8	48	126	1
Tim Hudson, Oak	R	18	9	3.37	35	35	3	0	0	235.0	216	100	88	20	6	71	181	9
Jamie Moyer, Sea	L	20	6	3.43	33	33	1	0	0	209.2	187	84	80	24	10	44	119	1
Mark Mulder, Oak	L	21	8	3.45	34	34	6	4	0	229.1	214	92	88	16	5	51	153	4
Barry Zito, Oak	L	17	8	3.49	35	35	3	2	0	214.1	184	92	83	18	13	80	205	6
Roger Clemens, NY	R	20	3	3.51	33	33	0	0	0	220.1	205	94	86	19	5	72	213	14
Cory Lidle, Oak	R	13	6	3.59	29	29	1	0	0	188.0	170	84	75	23	10	47	118	5
Aaron Sele, Sea	R	15	5	3.60	34	33	1	1	0	215.0	216	93	86	25	7	51	114	1
Steve Sparks, Det	R	14	9	3.65	35	33	8	1	0	232.0	244	110	94	22	6	64	116	8
Jarrod Washburn, Ana	L	11	10	3.77	30	30	1	0	0	193.1	196	89	81	25	7	54	126	3
Tim Wakefield, Bos	R	9	12	3.90	45	17	0	0	3	168.2	156	84	73	13	18	73	148	5
Brad Radke, Min	R	15	11	3.94	33	33	6	2	0	226.0	235	105	99	24	10	26	137	4

Note: Pitchers must have 1 inning pitched per their team's games played to qualify.

Wins

Mulder, Oak	21-8
Clemens, NY	20-3
Moyer, Sea	20-6
Garcia, Sea	18-6
Hudson, Oak	18-9
Abbott, Sea	17-4
Sabathia*, Cle	17-5
Zito, Oak	17-8
Mussina, NY	17-11
Mays, Min	17-13

Losses

Mercedes, Bal	8-17
Durbin, KC	9-16
Weaver, Det	13-16
Suppan, KC	10-14
Rekar, TB	3-13
Valdes, Ana	9-13
Mays, Min	17-13
Seven tied with 12 each.	

Walks

Nomo, Bos	96
Sabathia*, Cle	95
Colon, Cle	90
Abbott, Sea	87
Zito, Oak	80
Stein, Bal	79
Sturtze, TB	79
Johnson, Bal	77
Schoeneweis, Ana	77
Ortiz, Ana	76

Strikeouts

Nomo, Bos	220
Mussina, NY	214
Clemens, NY	213
Zito, Oak	205
Colon, Cle	201
Hudson, Oak	181
Sabathia*, Cle	171
Pettitte, NY	164
Garcia, Sea	163
Martínez, Bos	163

Appearances

Quantrill, Tor	80
Stanton, NY	76
Grimsley, KC	73
Foulke, Chi	72
Borbon, Tor	71
Rhodes, Sea	71
Rivera, NY	71

Innings

Garcia, Sea	238.2
Hudson, Oak	235.0
Mays, Min	233.2
Sparks, Det	232.0
Mulder, Oak	229.1
Weaver, Det	229.1
Mussina, NY	228.2
Radke, Min	226.0
Colon, Cle	222.1
Buehrle, Chi	221.1

HRs Allowed

Helling, Tex	38
Milton, Min	35
Rupe, TB	30
Carpenter, Tor	29
Johnson, Bal	28
Heredia, Oak	27
Loaiza, Tor	27

Opp. Batting Average

Garcia, Sea	.225
Sabathia*, Cle	.228
Buehrle, Chi	.230
Zito, Oak	.230
Nomo, Bos	.231
Mays, Min	.235
Mussina, NY	.237
Abbott, Sea	.238
Moyer, Sea	.239
Lidle, Oak	.242

Complete Games

Sparks, Det	8
Mulder, Oak	6
Radke, Min	6
Weaver, Det	5
Buehrle, Chi	4
Garcia, Sea	4
Mays, Min	4
Mussina, NY	4

Saves

	SV	BS
Rivera, NY	50	7
Sasaki, Sea	45	7
Foulke, Chi	42	3
Percival, Ana	39	3
Koch, Tor	36	8
Isringhausen, Oak	34	9
Wickman, Cle	32	3
Hawkins, Min	28	9
Hernandez, KC	28	6
Zimmerman, Tex	28	3

Wild Pitches

Clemens, NY	14
K. Wells, Chi	14
Reichert, KC	12
Abbott, Sea	11
Mays, Min	11
Sturtze, TB	11
Stein, Bal	10

SB Allowed

Nomo, Bos	52
Clemens, NY	34
Johnson, Bal	34
Wakefield, Bos	32
Castillo, Bos	27
Sabathia*, Cle	27
Hudson, Oak	24

WHIP

(Walks + Hits/IP)

Buehrle, Chi	1.07
Mussina, NY	1.07
Moyer, Sea	1.10
Garcia, Sea	1.12
Mays, Min	1.15
Lidle, Oak	1.15
Radke, Min	1.15
Mulder, Oak	1.16
Hudson, Oak	1.22
Zito, Oak	1.23

Shutouts

Mulder, Oak	4
Garcia, Sea	3
Mussina, NY	3
Six tied with 2 each.	

Fielding

Put Outs

Delgado, Tor	1519
Konerko, Chi	1276
Mientkiewicz, Min	1263
Ja. Giambi, Oak	1224
Olerud, Sea	1211
Thome, Cle	1177
Martinez, NY	1144
Posada, NY	1003
Diaz, Cle	959
Sweeney, KC	945

Assists

Gonzalez, Tor	509
Easley, Det	496
Tejada, Oak	473
Hairston, Bal	458
Rodriguez, Tex	452
Durham, Chi	446
Alomar, Cle	423
Vizquel, Cle	414
Boone, Sea	410
Menechino, Oak	407

OF Assists

Mondesi, Tor	18
Beltran, KC	14
Hunter, Min	14
Salmon, Ana	13
Winn, TB	12
Dye, KC-Oak	12
Ordonez, Chi	11
Higginson, Det	10
Erstad, Ana	10
Gonzalez, Cle	10

Errors

Halter, Det	26
Brosius, NY	22
Valentin, Chi	22
Guzman, Min	21
Huff*, TB	20
Tejada, Oak	20
Glaus, Ana	19
Hairston, Bal	19
Soriano*, NY	19
Four tied with 18 each.	

Colorado Rockies
Larry Walker
Batting Average

San Francisco Giants
Barry Bonds
Home Runs, SLG, OBP, Walks

Chicago Cubs
Sammy Sosa
RBI, Runs, TB

Arizona Diamondbacks
Curt Schilling
Wins, Innings, Complete Games

National League Leaders
(*) indicates rookie.

Batting

	Bat	Gm	AB	R	H	Avg	TB	2B	3B	HR	RBI	BB	SO	SB	Slg Pct	OBP
Larry Walker, Col	L	142	497	107	174	**.350**	329	35	3	38	123	82	103	14	.662	.449
Todd Helton, Col	L	159	587	132	197	**.336**	402	54	2	49	146	98	104	7	.685	.432
Moises Alou, Hou	R	136	513	79	170	**.331**	284	31	1	27	108	57	57	5	.554	.396
Lance Berkman, Hou	S	157	577	110	191	**.331**	358	55	5	34	126	92	121	7	.620	.430
Chipper Jones, Atl	S	159	572	113	189	**.330**	346	33	5	38	102	98	82	9	.605	.427
Albert Pujols*, St.L	R	161	590	112	194	**.329**	360	47	4	37	130	69	93	1	.610	.403
Barry Bonds, SF	L	153	476	129	156	**.328**	411	32	2	73	137	177	93	13	.863	.515
Sammy Sosa, Chi	R	160	577	146	189	**.328**	425	34	5	64	160	116	153	0	.737	.437
Juan Pierre, Col	L	156	617	108	202	**.327**	256	26	11	2	55	41	29	46	.415	.378
Luis Gonzalez, Ari	L	162	609	128	198	**.325**	419	36	7	57	142	100	83	1	.688	.429
Rich Aurilia, SF	R	156	636	114	206	**.324**	364	37	5	37	97	47	83	1	.572	.369
Paul Lo Duca, LA	R	125	460	71	147	**.320**	250	28	0	25	90	39	30	2	.543	.374
Jose Vidro, Mon	S	124	486	82	155	**.319**	236	34	1	15	59	31	49	4	.486	.371
Cliff Floyd, Fla	L	149	555	123	176	**.317**	321	44	4	31	103	59	101	18	.578	.390
Jeff Cirillo, Col	R	138	528	72	165	**.313**	250	26	4	17	83	43	63	12	.473	.364

Note: Batters must have 3.1 plate appearances per their team's games played to qualify.

Home Runs

Bonds, SF	.73
Sosa, Chi	.64
Gonzalez, Ari	.57
Green, LA	.49
Helton, Col	.49
Sexson, Mil	.45
Nevin, SD	.41
Bagwell, Hou	.39
C. Jones, Atl	.38
L. Walker, Col	.38

Runs Batted In

Sosa, Chi	.160
Helton, Col	.146
Gonzalez, Ari	.142
Bonds, SF	.137
Bagwell, Hou	.130
Pujols*, St.L	.130
Berkman, Hou	.126
Nevin, SD	.126
Green, LA	.125
Sexson, Mil	.125

Hits

Aurilia, SF	.206
Pierre, Col	.202
Gonzalez, Ari	.198
Helton, Col	.197
Pujols*, St.L	.194
Berkman, Hou	.191
Vina, St.L	.191
C. Jones, Atl	.189
Sosa, Chi	.189

Stolen Bases

	SB	CS
Rollins*, Phi	.46	8
Pierre, Col	.46	17
Guerrero, Mon	.37	16
Abreu, Phi	.36	14
Castillo, Fla	.33	16
Young, Chi	.31	14
Glanville, Phi	.28	6
Womack, Ari	.28	7

Triples

Rollins*, Phi	.12
Pierre, Col	.11
Uribe*, Col	.11
Castillo, Fla	.10
Perez, Col	.8
Tucker, Cin-Chi	.8
Vina, St.L	.8

Doubles

Berkman, Hou	.55
Helton, Col	.54
Kent, SF	.49
Abreu, Phi	.48
Pujols*, St.L	.47
Guerrero, Mon	.45
Floyd, Fla	.44

Runs

Sosa, Chi	.146
Helton, Col	.132
Bonds, SF	.129
Gonzalez, Ari	.128
Bagwell, Hou	.126
Floyd, Fla	.123
Green, LA	.121
Abreu, Phi	.118
Biggio, Hou	.118

Total Bases

Sosa, Chi	.425
Gonzalez, Ari	.419
Bonds, SF	.411
Helton, Col	.402
Green, LA	.370
Aurilia, SF	.364
Pujols*, St.L	.360
Berkman, Hou	.358

On Base Pct.

Bonds, SF	.515
L. Walker, Col	.449
Sosa, Chi	.437
Helton, Col	.432
Berkman, Hou	.430
Gonzalez, Ari	.429
C. Jones, Atl	.427
Sheffield, LA	.417

Slugging Pct.

Bonds, SF	.863
Sosa, Chi	.737
Gonzalez, Ari	.688
Helton, Col	.685
L. Walker, Col	.662
Berkman, Hou	.620
Pujols*, St.L	.610

Walks

Bonds, SF	.177
Sosa, Chi	.116
Abreu, Phi	.106
Bagwell, Hou	.106
Gonzalez, Ari	.100
Helton, Ari	.98
C. Jones, Atl	.98

Strikeouts

Hernandez, Mil	.185
Sexson, Mil	.178
Burrell, Phi	.162
Stevens, Mon	.157
Sosa, Chi	.153
Burnitz, Mil	.150
Nevin, SD	.147
Lankford, St.L-SD	.145

Pitching

	Arm	W	L	ERA	Gm	GS	CG	ShO	Sv	IP	H	R	ER	HR	HB	BB	SO	WP
Randy Johnson, Ari	L	21	6	2.49	35	34	3	2	0	249.2	181	74	69	19	18	71	372	8
Curt Schilling, Ari	R	22	6	2.98	35	35	6	1	0	256.2	237	86	85	37	1	39	293	4
John Burkett, Atl	R	12	12	3.04	34	34	1	1	0	219.1	187	83	74	17	6	70	187	5
Greg Maddux, Atl	R	17	11	3.05	34	34	3	3	0	233.0	220	86	79	20	7	27	173	2
Darryl Kile, St.L	R	16	11	3.09	34	34	2	1	0	227.1	228	83	78	22	11	65	179	6
Matt Morris, St.L	R	22	8	3.16	34	34	2	1	0	216.1	218	86	76	13	13	54	185	5
Russ Ortiz, SF	R	17	9	3.29	33	33	1	1	0	218.2	187	90	80	13	0	91	169	8
Al Leiter, NY	L	11	11	3.31	29	29	0	0	0	187.1	178	81	69	18	4	46	142	5
Kerry Wood, Chi	R	12	6	3.36	28	28	1	1	0	174.1	127	70	65	16	10	92	217	9
Wade Miller, Hou	R	16	8	3.40	32	32	1	0	0	212.0	183	91	80	31	4	76	183	8
Javier Vazquez, Mon	R	16	11	3.42	32	32	5	3	0	223.2	197	92	85	24	3	44	208	3
Chan Ho Park, LA	R	15	11	3.50	36	35	2	1	0	234.0	183	98	91	23	20	91	218	3
Tom Glavine, Atl	L	16	7	3.57	35	35	1	1	0	219.1	213	92	87	24	2	97	116	2
Kevin Appier, NY	R	11	10	3.57	33	33	1	1	0	206.2	181	89	82	22	15	64	172	12
Brad Penny, Fla	R	10	10	3.69	31	31	1	1	0	205.0	183	92	84	15	7	54	154	2

Note: Pitchers must have 1 inning pitched per their team's games played to qualify.

Wins

Schilling, Ari 22-6
Morris, St.L 22-8
Johnson, Ari 21-6
Lieber, Chi 20-6
Ortiz, SF 17-9
Maddux, Atl 17-11
Glavine, Atl 16-7
Miller, Hou 16-8
Kile, St.L 16-11
Vazquez, Mon 16-11

Appearances

Kline, St.L 89
Lloyd, Mon 84
Fassero, Chi 82
King, Mil 82
Rodriguez, SF 80
Weathers, Mil-Chi 80
Nen, SF 79
Sullivan, Cin 79
Kim, Ari 78

Complete Games

Schilling, Ari 6
Lieber, Chi 5
Vazquez, Mon 5
Astacio, Col-Hou 4
Ritchie, Pit 4
Wolf, Phi 4

Shutouts

Maddux, Atl 3
Vazquez, Mon 3
Johnson, Ari 2
Lopez, Ari 2
Ritchie, Pit 2
Wolf, Phi 2

Losses

Jones, SD 8-19
Haynes, Mil 8-17
Anderson, Pit 9-17
Reitsma*, Cin 7-15
Ritchie, Pit. 11-15
Hernandez, SF 13-15
Astacio, Col-Hou 8-14
Armas, Mon 9-14
Tapani, Chi 9-14
Dessens, Cin 10-14

Innings

Schilling, Ari 256.2
Johnson, Ari 249.2
Park, LA 234.0
Maddux, Atl 233.0
Lieber, Chi 232.1
Kile, St.L 227.1
Hernandez, SF 226.2
Vazquez, Mon 223.2
Williams, SD-St.L . . .220.0

Saves

	SV	BS
Nen, SF	.45	7
Benitez, NY	.43	3
Hoffman, SD	.43	3
Shaw, LA	.43	9
Mesa, Phi	.42	4
Wagner, Hou	.39	2
Graves, Cin	.32	7
Alfonseca, Fla	.28	6
Gordon, Chi	.28	4
Williams, Pit-Hou	.22	3

Walks

Dempster, Fla 112
Wright, Mil 98
Glavine, Atl 97
Wood, Chi 92
Armas, Mon 91
Ortiz, SF 91
Park, LA 91
Chacon*, Col 87

HR Allowed

Jarvis, SD 37
Jones, SD 37
Schilling, Ari 37
Williams, SD-St.L 35
Elarton, Hou-Col 34
Hermanson, St.L 34
Person, Phi 34
Dessens, Cin 32

Wild Pitches

Clement, Fla 15
Appier, NY 12
Dreifort, LA 10
Estes, SF 10
Person, Phi 10
Suzuki, Col-Mil 10
Armas, Mon 9
Wood, Chi 9

SB Allowed

Anderson, Pit 33
Batista, Ari 24
Maddux, Atl 24
Appier, NY 22
Jones, SD 22
Trachsel, NY 22
Wood, Chi 21

Strikeouts

Johnson, Ari 372
Schilling, Ari 293
Park, LA 218
Wood, Chi 217
Vazquez, Mon 208
Burkett, Atl 187
Morris, St.L 185
Miller, Hou 183
Person, Phi 183
Kile, St.L 179

Opp. Batting Average

Wood, Chi 202
Johnson, Ari 203
Park, LA 216
Burkett, Atl 230
Burnett, Fla 231
Ortiz, SF 232
Miller, Hou 234
Person, Phi 234
Vazquez, Mon 235
Appier, NY 237

WHIP

Walks + Hits/Innings

Johnson, Ari 1.01
Maddux, Atl 1.06
Schilling, Ari 1.08
Vazquez, Mon 1.08
Lieber, Chi 1.15
Penny, Fla 1.16
Park, LA 1.17
Burkett, Atl 1.17

Fielding

Put Outs

Sexson, Mil 1356
Lee, Phi 1332
Helton, Col 1303
Bagwell, Hou 1291
Stevens, Mon 1287
Lee, Fla 1271
Zeile, NY 1184
Young, Pit 1154
Casey, Cin 1145
Klesko, SD 1135

Assists

Cabrera, Mon 514
Sanchez, Atl 479
Hernandez, Mil 427
Rollins*, Phi 426
Aurilia, SF 423
Kent, SF 404
Gonzalez, Fla 396
Renteria, St.L 390
Biggio, Hou 389
Anderson, Phi 387

OF Assists

Burrell, Phi 18
Sheffield, LA 17
Guerrero, Mon 14
Burnitz, Mil 13
Edmonds, St.L 12
Ochoa, Cin-Col 12
Wilson, Fla 12
Shinjo*, NY 12
Abreu, Phi 11
Jordan, Atl 11
Hidalgo, Hou 11

Errors

Nevin, SD 27
Gonzalez, Fla 26
Ramirez, Pit 25
Renteria, St.L 24
Lugo, Hou 22
Womack, Ari 22
Jimenez*, SD 21
Pujols*, St.L 20
Cora, LA 20
Boone, Cin 19
Stevens, Mon 19

Team Batting Statistics

American League

Team	Avg	AB	R	H	HR	RBI	SB
Seattle	.288	5680	927	1637	169	881	174
Cleveland	.278	5600	897	1559	212	868	79
Texas	.275	5685	890	1566	246	844	97
Minnesota	.272	5560	771	1514	164	717	146
Chicago	.268	5464	798	1463	214	770	123
New York	.267	5577	804	1488	203	774	161
Boston	.266	5605	772	1493	198	739	46
Kansas City	.266	5643	729	1503	152	691	100
Oakland	.264	5573	884	1469	199	835	68
Toronto	.263	5663	767	1489	195	728	156
Anaheim	.261	5551	691	1447	158	662	116
Detroit	.260	5537	724	1439	139	691	133
Tampa Bay	.258	5524	672	1426	121	645	115
Baltimore	.248	5472	687	1359	136	663	133

National League

Team	Avg	AB	R	H	HR	RBI	SB
Colorado	.292	5690	923	1663	213	874	132
Houston	.271	5528	847	1500	208	805	64
St. Louis	.270	5450	814	1469	199	768	91
Arizona	.267	5595	818	1494	208	776	71
San Fran.	.266	5612	799	1493	235	775	57
Florida	.264	5542	742	1461	166	713	89
Cincinnati	.262	5583	735	1464	176	690	103
Chicago	.261	5406	777	1409	194	748	67
Atlanta	.260	5498	729	1432	174	696	85
Philadelphia	.260	5497	746	1431	164	708	153
Los Angeles	.255	5493	758	1399	206	714	89
Montreal	.253	5379	670	1361	131	622	101
San Diego	.252	5482	789	1379	161	753	129
Milwaukee	.251	5488	740	1378	209	712	66
New York	.249	5459	642	1361	147	608	66
Pittsburgh	.247	5398	657	1333	161	618	93

Team Pitching Statistics

American League

Team	ERA	W	Sv	CG	ShO	HR	BB	SO
Seattle	3.54	116	56	8	14	160	465	1051
Oakland	3.59	102	44	13	9	153	440	1117
New York	4.02	95	57	7	9	158	465	1266
Boston	4.15	82	48	3	9	146	544	1259
Anaheim	4.20	75	43	6	1	168	525	947
Toronto	4.28	80	41	7	10	165	490	1041
Minnesota	4.51	85	45	12	8	192	445	965
Chicago	4.55	83	51	8	7	181	500	921
Cleveland	4.64	91	42	3	4	148	573	1218
Baltimore	4.67	63	31	10	6	194	528	938
Kansas City	4.87	65	30	5	1	209	576	911
Tampa Bay	4.94	62	30	1	6	207	569	1030
Detroit	5.01	66	34	16	2	180	553	859
Texas	5.71	73	37	4	3	222	596	951

National League

Team	ERA	W	Sv	CG	ShO	HR	BB	SO
Atlanta	3.59	88	41	5	13	153	499	1133
Arizona	3.87	92	34	12	13	195	461	1297
St. Louis	3.93	93	38	8	11	196	526	1083
Chicago	4.03	88	41	6	6	164	550	1344
New York	4.07	82	48	6	14	186	438	1191
Philadelphia	4.15	86	47	8	7	170	527	1086
San Fran.	4.18	90	47	3	8	145	579	1080
Los Angeles	4.25	86	46	3	5	184	524	1212
Florida	4.32	76	32	5	11	151	617	1119
Houston	4.37	93	48	7	6	221	486	1228
San Diego	4.52	79	46	5	6	219	476	1088
Milwaukee	4.64	68	28	3	8	197	667	1057
Montreal	4.68	68	28	5	11	190	525	1103
Cincinnati	4.77	66	35	2	2	198	515	943
Pittsburgh	5.05	62	36	8	9	167	549	908
Colorado	5.29	73	26	8	8	239	598	1058

Home Attendance

Overall 2001 regular season attendance in Major League Baseball was 72,566,416 in 2,413 games for an average per game crowd of 30,073; numbers in parentheses indicate ranking in 2000; HD indicates home dates; Attendance is based on tickets sold.

American League

	Attendance	HD	Average
1 Seattle (4)	3,512,326	81	43,362
2 New York (3)	3,264,552	80	40,807
3 Cleveland (1)	3,182,523	80	39,782
4 Baltimore (2)	3,094,841	80	38,686
5 Texas (5)	2,831,111	81	34,952
6 Boston (6)	2,625,333	81	32,412
7 Oakland (11)	2,133,477	81	26,339
8 Anaheim (8)	2,001,319	81	24,708
9 Detroit (7)	1,920,995	80	24,012
10 Toronto (10)	1,895,236	80	23,690
11 Minnesota (14)	1,782,926	80	22,287
12 Chicago (9)	1,766,172	80	22,077
13 Kansas City (12)	1,536,101	81	18,964
14 Tampa Bay (13)	1,298,075	81	16,026
TOTALS	32,844,987	1127	29,144

National League

	Attendance	HD	Average
1 San Francisco (2)	3,311,000	81	40,877
2 Colorado (3)	3,168,579	81	39,118
3 St. Louis (1)	3,109,578	81	38,390
4 Los Angeles (6)	3,017,143	81	37,249
5 Houston (5)	2,906,277	81	35,880
6 Chicago (9)	2,780,465	79	35,196
7 Atlanta (4)	2,823,530	81	34,858
8 Milwaukee (14)	2,811,040	81	34,704
9 Arizona (7)	2,735,821	81	33,776
10 New York (8)	2,658,330	81	32,819
11 Pittsburgh (12)	2,435,867	79	30,834
12 San Diego (11)	2,378,128	80	29,727
13 Cincinnati (10)	1,879,757	79	23,794
14 Philadelphia (13)	1,782,054	78	22,847
15 Florida (15)	1,261,226	80	15,765
16 Montreal (16)	642,743	81	7,935
TOTALS	39,701,538	1285	30,896

Note: Not included in the above table is the April 1 game played between Texas and Toronto in San Juan, P.R. The attendance for that game was 19,891.

Bonds Breaks HR Record

In 2001 Barry Bonds swatted 73 home runs to break Mark McGwire's single-season record of 70 set in 1998. Below is a chronological list of his home runs, which includes the opposing team and pitcher and the number of men on base.

No.	Date	Opponent	On Base	No.	Date	Opponent	On Base
1	Apr. 2	vs. San Diego (Williams)	0	39	June 23	at St. Louis (Kile)	1
2	Apr. 12	at San Diego (Eaton)	0				
3	Apr. 13	at Milwaukee (Wright)	1	40	July 12	at Seattle (Abbott)	0
4	Apr. 14	at Milwaukee (Haynes)	2	41	July 18	vs. Colorado (Hampton)	0
5	Apr. 15	at Milwaukee (Weathers)	0	42	July 18	vs. Colorado (Hampton)	1
6	Apr. 17	vs. Los Angeles (Adams)	1	43	July 26	at Arizona (Schilling)	0
7	Apr. 18	vs. Los Angeles (Park)	0	44	July 26	at Arizona (Schilling)	3
8	Apr. 20	vs. Milwaukee (Haynes)	1	45	July 27	at Arizona (Anderson)	0
9	Apr. 24	vs. Cincinnati (Brower)	1				
10	Apr. 26	vs. Cincinnati (Sullivan)	1	46	Aug. 1	vs. Pittsburgh (Beimel)	0
11	Apr. 29	vs. Chi-NL (Aybar)	0	47	Aug. 4	vs. Philadelphia (Figueroa)	1
				48	Aug. 7	at Cincinnati (Graves)	0
12	May 2	at Pittsburgh (Ritchie)	1	49	Aug. 9	at Cincinnati (Winchester)	0
13	May 3	at Pittsburgh (Anderson)	1	50	Aug. 11	at Chi-NL (Borowski)	2
14	May 4	at Philadelphia (Chen)	1	51	Aug. 14	vs. Florida (Bones)	3
15	May 11	vs. NY-NL (Trachsel))	0	52	Aug. 16	vs. Florida (Burnett)	0
16	May 17	at Florida (Smith)	1	53	Aug. 16	vs. Florida (Darensbourg)	2
17	May 18	at Atlanta (Remlinger)	0	54	Aug. 18	at Atlanta (Marquis)	0
18	May 18	at Atlanta (Remlinger)	0	55	Aug. 23	at Montreal (Lloyd)	0
19	May 19	at Atlanta (Cabrera)	0	56	Aug. 27	at NY-NL (Appier)	0
20	May 19	at Atlanta (Marquis)	0	57	Aug. 31	vs. Colorado (Thomson)	1
21	May 20	at Atlanta (Burkett)	0				
22	May 20	at Atlanta (Remlinger)	0	58	Sept. 3	vs. Colorado (Jennings)	0
23	May 21	at Arizona (Schilling)	0	59	Sept. 4	vs. Arizona (Batista)	0
24	May 22	at Arizona (Springer)	1	60	Sept. 6	vs. Arizona (Lopez)	0
25	May 24	vs. Colorado (Thomson)	0	61	Sept. 9	at Colorado (Elarton)	0
26	May 27	vs. Colorado (Neagle)	1	62	Sept. 9	at Colorado (Elarton)	0
27	May 30	vs. Arizona (Ellis)	0	63	Sept. 9	at Colorado (Belitz)	2
28	May 30	vs. Arizona (Ellis)	1	64	Sept. 20	vs. Houston (Miller)	1
				65	Sept. 23	at San Diego (Middlebrook)	0
29	June 1	at Colorado (Chacon)	1	66	Sept. 23	at San Diego (Middlebrook)	0
30	June 4	vs. San Diego (Jones)	0	67	Sept. 24	at Los Angeles (Baldwin)	0
31	June 5	vs. San Diego (Serrano)	0	68	Sept. 28	vs. San Diego (Middlebrook)	0
32	June 7	vs. San Diego (Lawrence)	1	69	Sept. 29	vs. San Diego (McElroy)	0
33	June 12	vs. Anaheim (Rapp)	0				
34	June 14	vs. Anaheim (Pote)	0	70	Oct. 4	at Houston (Rodriguez)	0
35	June 15	vs. Oakland (Mulder)	0	71	Oct. 5	vs. Los Angeles (Park)	0
36	June 15	vs. Oakland (Mulder)	0	72	Oct. 5	vs. Los Angeles (Park)	0
37	June 19	at San Diego (Eaton)	0	73	Oct. 7	vs. Los Angeles (Springer)	0
38	June 20	at San Diego (Myers)	1				

Bonds By the Numbers

Most victimized team:	San Diego (11)	Grand Slams: ... 2
Most victimized pitchers:	Remlinger, Atl. (3)	Two men on base: ... 4
	Park, LA (3)	One man on base: ... 21
	Schilling, Ari. (3)	Solo home runs: ... 46
	Middlebrook, SD (3)	Home: ... 37
vs. lefties: ... 17		Away: ... 36
vs. righties: ... 56		Longest ... 480 feet

Baseball's Eight Work Stoppages

The expiration of Major League Baseball's labor contract after the 2001 World Series brings the threat of yet another work stoppage. Below is a breakdown of the previous eight work stoppages.

Year	Work Stoppage	Games Missed	Length	Dates	Issue
1972	Strike	86	13 days	April 1-13	Pensions
1973	Lockout	0	17 days	February 8-25	Salary arbitration
1976	Lockout	0	17 days	March 1-17	Free agency
1980	Strike	0	8 days	April 1-8	Free-agent compensation
1981	Strike	712	50 days	June 12-July 31	Free-agent compensation
1985	Strike	0	2 days	August 6-7	Salary arbitration
1990	Lockout	0	32 days	Feb. 15-March 18	Salary arbitration and salary cap
1994	Strike	920	232 days	Aug. 12-March 31	Salary cap and revenue sharing

2001 All-Star Game

72nd Baseball All-Star Game. Date: July 10 at Safeco Field, Seattle, Wash.; **Managers:** Bobby Valentine, New York (NL) and Joe Torre, New York (AL); **Most Valuable Player:** SS-3B Cal Ripken Jr., Baltimore: 1-for-2 with a home run.

National League

	AB	R	H	BI	BB	SO	Avg
Luis Gonzalez, Ari, cf	2	0	1	0	0	0	.500
Lance Berkman, Hou, cf	2	0	1	0	0	0	.500
Todd Helton, Col, 1b	2	0	0	0	0	1	.000
Ryan Klesko, SD, 1b	1	0	1	0	0	1	.000
Barry Bonds, SF, lf	2	0	0	0	0	1	.000
Vladimir Guerrero, ph-rf	1	0	0	0	0	0	.000
Brian Giles, Pit, ph	1	0	0	0	0	0	.000
Sammy Sosa, Chi, rf	2	0	0	0	0	0	.000
Moises Alou, Hou, rf-lf	1	0	0	0	0	1	.000
Sean Casey, Cin, ph	1	0	0	0	0	1	.000
Larry Walker, Col, dh	2	0	0	0	0	0	.000
Cliff Floyd, Fla, ph	2	0	0	0	0	0	.000
Mike Piazza, NY, c	2	0	0	0	0	0	.000
Albert Pujols, St.L, 3b-2b	0	0	0	0	1	0	.000
Chipper Jones, Atl, 3b	2	0	1	0	0	0	.000
Charles Johnson, Fla, c	1	0	0	0	0	0	.000
Jeff Kent, SF, 2b	2	1	1	0	0	0	.500
Phil Nevin, SD, ph-3b	1	0	0	0	0	0	.000
Rich Aurilia, SF, ss	2	0	0	0	0	0	.000
Jimmy Rollins, Phi, ss	0	0	0	0	1	0	.000
TOTALS	29	1	3	1	2	5	.103

American League

	AB	R	H	BI	BB	SO	Avg
Ichiro Suzuki, Sea, cf-rf	3	0	1	0	0	0	.333
Bernie Williams, NY, cf	1	0	0	0	0	0	.000
Alex Rodriguez, Tex, 3b-ss	2	0	0	0	0	2	.000
Derek Giambi, Oak, pr-rf	1	1	1	0	0	1	1.000
Cristian Guzman, Min, ph-ss	1	0	0	0	0	1	.000
Manny Ramirez, Bos, lf	1	0	0	0	0	1	.000
Magglio Ordonez, Chi, lf	3	1	2	1	0	0	.667
Bret Boone, Sea, 2b	2	0	0	0	0	0	.000
Roberto Alomar, Cle, 2b	2	0	0	0	0	0	.000
Juan Gonzalez, Cle, rf	2	0	0	0	0	0	.000
Mike Cameron, Sea, cf-rf	3	0	1	0	0	1	.333
John Olerud, Sea, 1b	2	0	0	0	0	0	.000
Jason Giambi, Oak, pr-1b	1	0	0	0	0	0	.000
Mike Sweeney, KC, 1b	1	0	0	0	0	0	.000
Edgar Martinez, Sea, dh	2	0	0	0	0	1	.000
Tony Clark, Det, ph	1	0	0	0	0	1	.000
Cal Ripken Jr., Bal, ss-3b	2	1	1	1	0	0	.500
Troy Glaus, Ana, 3b	1	0	0	0	0	0	.000
Ivan Rodriguez, Tex, c	2	0	1	1	0	0	.500
Jorge Posada, NY, c	1	0	1	0	0	1	1.000
TOTALS	33	4	8	4	0	7	.242

	1	2	3	4	5	6	7	8	9	R	H	E
National League	0	0	0	0	0	1	0	0	0	–	1	3	1
American League	0	0	1	0	1	2	0	0	x	–	4	8	0

E—Kent (NL, throw). **LOB**— National 4, American 5. **2B**—Kent (NL), Cameron and Posada (AL). **HR**—Ripken (AL, off Park, 0 on), Jeter (AL, off Lieber, 0 on), Ordonez (AL, off Lieber, 0 on). **SB**—Rollins (NL, 2nd base off Percival/Posada), Suzuki (AL, 2nd base off Johnson/Piazza). **SF**—Klesko (NL). **GIDP**—none.

NL Pitching	IP	H	R	ER	BB	SO
Randy Johnson, Ari	2.0	1	0	0	0	3
Chan Ho Park, LA (L)	1.0	1	1	1	0	1
John Burkett, Atl	1.0	0	0	0	0	1
Mike Hampton, Col	1.0	1	1	0	0	1
Jon Lieber, Chi	1.0	3	2	2	0	1
Matt Morris, St.L	1.0	1	0	0	0	1
Jeff Shaw, LA	0.1	1	0	0	0	0
Billy Wagner, Hou	0.1	0	0	0	0	0
Ben Sheets, Mil	0.1	0	0	0	0	0
TOTALS	8.0	8	4	3	0	7

AL Pitching	IP	H	R	ER	BB	SO
Roger Clemens, NY	2.0	0	0	0	0	1
Freddy Garcia, Sea (W)	1.0	0	0	0	0	0
Andy Pettitte, NY	1.0	1	0	0	0	1
Joe Mays, Min	1.0	0	0	0	0	0
Paul Quantrill, Tor	0.1	2	1	1	0	0
Mike Stanton, NY	0.2	0	0	0	0	0
Jeff Nelson, Sea	1.0	0	0	0	1	1
Troy Percival, Ana	1.0	0	0	0	1	1
Kazuhiro Sasaki, Sea (S)	1.0	0	0	0	0	1
TOTALS	9.0	3	1	1	2	5

Umpires—Dana DeMuth (plate); Dale Scott (1b); Jim Joyce (2b); Jerry Layne (3b); Ron Kulpa (lf); Tony Randazzo (rf). **Attendance**—47,364 (47,116 capacity). **Time**—2:48 (Ripken/Gwynn ceremony delay for six minutes in 6th). **TV Rating**—11.0/19 share (FOX).

Home Run Derby

Results of the All-Star Home Run Derby at Safeco Field, Seattle, Wash. on July 9.

First Round

	No.	Long (feet)
Jason Giambi, Oakland	14	460
Barry Bonds, San Francisco	7	476
Luis Gonzalez, Arizona	5	440
Sammy Sosa, Chi. Cubs	3	467
Bret Boone, Seattle	3	406
Alex Rodriguez, Texas	2	415
Todd Helton, Colorado	2	425
Troy Glaus, Anaheim	0	—

Semifinals

Gonzalez def. Bonds, 5-3
Sosa def. Giambi, 8-6

Finals

Gonzalez def. Sosa, 6-2

AL Team by Team Statistics

At least 135 at bats or 40 innings pitched during the regular season, unless otherwise indicated. Players who competed for more than one AL team are listed with their final club. Players traded from the NL are listed with AL team only if they have 135 AB or 40 IP. Note that (*) indicates rookie and PTBN indicates player to be named.

Anaheim Angels

Batting (135 AB)	Avg	AB	R	H	HR	RBI	SB
Shawn Wooten*	.312	221	24	69	8	32	2
Benji Gil	.296	260	33	77	8	39	3
Garret Anderson	.289	672	83	194	28	123	13
David Eckstein*	.285	582	82	166	4	41	29
Scott Spiezio	.271	457	57	124	13	54	5
Adam Kennedy	.270	478	48	129	6	40	12
Ben Molina	.262	325	31	85	6	40	0
Darin Erstad	.258	631	89	163	9	63	24
Troy Glaus	.250	588	100	147	41	108	10
Orlando Palmeiro	.243	230	29	56	2	23	6
Wally Joyner	.243	148	14	36	3	14	1
Tim Salmon	.227	475	63	108	17	49	-9
Jorge Fabregas	.223	148	9	33	2	16	0

Pitching (40 IP)	ERA	W-L	Gm	IP	BB	SO
Al Levine	2.38	8-10	64	75.2	28	40
Troy Percival	2.65	4-2	57	57.2	18	71
Ben Weber*	3.42	6-2	56	68.1	31	40
Jarrod Washburn	3.77	11-10	30	193.1	54	126
Shigetoshi Hasegawa	4.04	5-6	46	55.2	20	41
Lou Pote	4.15	2-0	44	86.2	32	66
Ramon Ortiz	4.36	13-11	32	208.2	76	135
Matt Wise*	4.38	1-4	11	49.1	18	50
Ismael Valdes	4.45	9-13	27	163.2	50	100
Pat Rapp	4.76	5-12	31	170.0	71	82
Scott Schoeneweis	5.08	10-11	32	205.1	77	104

Saves: Percival (39); Levine and Pote (2). **Complete games:** Ortiz (2); Washburn, Valdes, Rapp and Schoeneweis (1). **Shutouts:** none.

Baltimore Orioles

Batting (135 AB)	Avg	AB	R	H	HR	RBI	SB
Joff Conine	.311	524	75	163	14	97	12
David Segui	.301	292	48	88	10	46	1
Mike Kinkade	.275	160	19	44	4	16	2
Chris Richard	.265	483	74	128	15	61	11
Brian Roberts*	.253	273	42	69	2	17	12
Melvin Mora	.250	436	49	109	7	48	11
Mike Bordick	.249	229	32	57	7	30	9
Fernando Lunar*	.246	167	8	41	0	16	0
Cal Ripken Jr.	.239	477	43	114	14	68	0
Tony Batista	.238	579	70	138	25	87	5
Jay Gibbons*	.236	225	27	53	15	36	0
Jerry Hairston Jr.	.233	532	63	124	8	47	29
Brook Fordyce	.209	292	30	61	5	19	1
Brady Anderson	.202	430	50	87	8	45	12
Delino DeShields	.197	188	29	37	3	21	11

Signed: IF Batista off waivers from Tor. (June 25). **Released:** OF DeShields (June 25). **Traded:** P Trombley to LA for P Kris Foster and C Geronimo Gil (July 31).

Pitching (50 IP)	ERA	W-L	Gm	IP	BB	SO
Mike Trombley	3.46	3-4	50	54.2	27	45
Pat Hentgen	3.47	2-3	9	62.1	19	33
Buddy Groom	3.55	1-4	70	66.0	9	54
Jason Johnson	4.09	10-12	32	196.0	77	114
Calvin Maduro	4.23	5-6	22	93.2	36	51
B.J. Ryan	4.25	2-4	61	53.0	30	54
Josh Towers*	4.49	8-10	24	140.1	16	58
Willis Roberts*	4.91	9-10	46	132.0	55	95
Sidney Ponson	4.94	5-10	23	138.1	37	84
Jose Mercedes	5.82	8-17	33	184.0	63	123

Saves: Groom (11); Trombley, Roberts and Ryan Kohlmeier (6); Ryan (2). **Complete games:** Ponson (3); Johnson and Mercedes (2); Hentgen, Towers and Roberts (1). **Shutouts:** Towers and Ponson (1).

Boston Red Sox

Batting (190 AB)	Avg	AB	R	H	HR	RBI	SB
Manny Ramirez	.306	529	93	162	41	125	0
Dante Bichette	.286	391	45	112	12	49	2
Trot Nixon	.280	535	100	150	27	88	7
Chris Stynes	.280	361	52	101	8	33	4
Jose Offerman	.267	524	76	140	9	49	5
Brian Daubach	.263	407	54	107	22	71	1
Shea Hillenbrand*	.263	468	52	123	12	49	1
Carl Everett	.257	409	61	105	14	58	9
Mike Lansing	.250	352	45	88	8	34	3
Scott Hatteberg	.245	278	34	68	3	25	1
Troy O'Leary	.240	341	50	82	13	50	1
Doug Mirabelli	.226	190	20	43	11	29	0

Acquired: C Mirabelli from Tex. for P Justin Duchscherer (June 12).
Traded: P Ohka and P Rich Rundles to Mon. for P Ugueth Urbina (July 31).

Pitching (40 IP)	ERA	W-L	Gm	IP	BB	SO
Pedro Martinez	2.39	7-3	18	116.2	25	163
Rolando Arrojo	3.48	5-4	41	103.1	35	78
Derek Lowe	3.53	5-10	67	91.2	29	82
Tim Wakefield	3.90	9-12	45	168.2	73	148
Rich Garces	3.90	6-1	62	67.0	25	51
Rod Beck	3.90	6-4	68	80.2	28	63
Frank Castillo	4.21	10-9	26	136.2	35	89
David Cone	4.31	9-7	25	135.2	57	115
Hideo Nomo	4.50	13-10	33	198.0	96	220
Casey Fossum*	4.87	3-2	13	44.1	20	26
Sun-Woo Kim*	5.83	0-2	20	41.2	21	27
Tomokazu Ohka	6.19	2-5	12	52.1	19	37

Saves: Lowe (24); Ugueth Urbina (9); Beck (6); Arrojo (5); Wakefield (3); Garces (1). **Complete games:** Nomo (2); Martinez (1). **Shutouts:** Nomo (2).

Chicago White Sox

Batting (150 AB)	Avg	AB	R	H	HR	RBI	SB
Magglio Ordonez	.305	593	97	181	31	113	25
Chris Singleton	.298	392	57	117	7	45	12
Paul Konerko	.282	582	92	164	32	99	1
Carlos Lee	.269	558	75	150	24	84	17
Ray Durham	.267	611	104	163	20	65	23
Royce Clayton	.263	433	62	114	9	60	10
Jose Valentin	.258	438	74	113	28	68	9
Jose Canseco	.258	256	46	66	16	49	2
Herbert Perry	.256	285	38	73	7	32	2
Jeff Liefer	.256	254	36	65	18	39	0
Mark Johnson	.249	173	21	43	5	18	2
Sandy Alomar Jr.	.245	220	17	54	4	21	1

Signed: free agent OF Canseco (June 20).
Traded: P Baldwin to LA for P Onan Masaoka, P Gary Majewski and OF Jeff Barry (July 26).

Pitching (40 IP)	ERA	W-L	Gm	IP	BB	SO
Keith Foulke	2.33	4-9	72	81.0	22	75
Mark Buehrle	3.29	16-8	32	221.1	48	126
Sean Lowe	3.61	9-4	45	127.0	32	71
Jon Garland	3.69	6-7	35	117.0	55	61
David Wells	4.47	5-7	16	100.2	21	59
James Baldwin	4.61	7-5	17	95.2	38	42
Bob Howry	4.69	4-5	69	78.2	30	64
Kip Wells	4.79	10-11	40	133.1	61	99
Gary Glover*	4.93	5-5	46	100.1	32	63
Rocky Biddle*	5.39	7-8	30	128.2	52	85
Dan Wright*	5.70	5-3	13	66.1	39	36

Saves: Foulke (42); Howry (5); Lowe (3); Garland (1). **Complete games:** Buehrle (4); Baldwin (2); Jim Parque and D. Wells (1). **Shutouts:** Buehrle (2); Baldwin (1).

Cleveland Indians

Batting (135 AB)	Avg	AB	R	H	HR	RBI	SB
Roberto Alomar	.336	575	113	193	20	100	30
Juan Gonzalez	.325	532	97	173	35	140	1
Marty Cordova	.301	409	61	123	20	69	0
Jim Thome	.291	526	101	153	49	124	0
Ellis Burks	.280	439	83	123	28	74	5
Einar Diaz	.277	437	54	121	4	56	1
Travis Fryman	.263	334	34	88	3	38	1
Jolbert Cabrera	.261	287	50	75	1	38	10
Kenny Lofton	.261	517	91	135	14	66	16
Omar Vizquel	.255	611	84	156	2	50	13
Wil Cordero	.250	268	30	67	4	21	0
Russell Branyan	.232	315	48	73	20	54	1

Traded: P Karsay, P Steve Reed and cash to Atl. for P John Rocker and IF Troy Cameron (June 22).

Pitching (40 IP)	ERA	W-L	Gm	IP	BB	SO
Steve Karsay	1.25	0-1	31	43.1	8	44
Bob Wickman	2.39	5-0	70	67.2	14	46
Danys Baez*	2.50	5-3	43	50.1	20	52
Paul Shuey	2.82	5-3	47	54.1	26	70
Ricardo Rincon	2.83	2-1	67	54.0	21	50
Bartolo Colon	4.09	14-12	34	222.1	90	201
C.C. Sabathia*	4.39	17-5	33	180.1	95	171
Steve Woodard	5.20	3-3	29	97.0	17	52
Chuck Finley	5.54	8-7	22	113.2	35	96
Jake Westbrook*	5.85	4-4	23	64.2	22	48
Dave Burba	6.21	10-10	32	150.2	54	118
Charles Nagy	6.40	5-6	15	70.1	20	29

Saves: Wickman (32); John Rocker (4); Shuey and Rincon (2); Karsay and David Riske (1). **Complete games:** Colon, Finley and Burba (1). **Shutouts:** none.

Detroit Tigers

Batting (135 AB)	Avg	AB	R	H	HR	RBI	SB
Randall Simon	.305	256	28	78	6	37	0
Roger Cedeno	.293	523	79	153	6	48	55
Tony Clark	.287	428	67	123	16	75	0
Shane Halter	.284	450	53	128	12	65	3
Bobby Higginson	.277	541	84	150	17	71	20
Robert Fick	.272	401	62	109	19	61	0
Jose Macias	.268	488	62	131	8	51	21
Deivi Cruz	.256	414	39	106	7	52	4
Damion Easley	.250	585	77	146	11	65	10
Juan Encarnacion	.242	417	52	101	12	52	9
Dean Palmer	.222	216	34	48	11	40	4
Wendell Magee	.213	207	26	44	5	17	3
Brandon Inge*	.180	189	13	34	0	15	1

Acquired: P Lima and cash from Hou. for P Mlicki (June 23); P Redman from Min. for P Todd Jones (July 28).
Traded: P Nitkowski to NYM for PTBN (Sept. 2).

Pitching (40 IP)	ERA	W-L	Gm	IP	BB	SO
Danny Patterson	3.06	5-4	60	64.2	12	47
Victor Santos*	3.30	2-2	33	76.1	49	52
Steve Sparks	3.65	14-9	35	232.0	64	116
Jeff Weaver	4.08	13-16	33	229.1	68	152
Mark Redman	4.50	2-6	11	58.0	23	33
Jose Lima	4.71	5-10	18	112.2	22	43
Matt Anderson	4.82	3-1	62	56.0	18	52
C.J. Nitkowski	5.96	0-3	56	45.1	31	38
Chris Holt	5.77	7-9	30	151.1	57	80
Adam Pettyjohn*	5.82	1-6	16	65.0	21	40
Heath Murray	6.54	1-7	40	63.1	40	42
Dave Mlicki	7.33	4-8	15	81.0	41	48
Nate Cornejo*	7.38	4-4	10	42.2	28	22

Saves: Anderson (22); Patterson (1). **Complete games:** Sparks (8); Weaver (5); Lima (2); Holt (1). **Shutouts:** Sparks (1).

Kansas City Royals

Batting (160 AB)	Avg	AB	R	H	HR	RBI	SB
Carlos Beltran	.306	617	106	189	24	101	31
Mike Sweeney	.304	559	97	170	29	99	10
Rey Sanchez	.303	390	46	118	0	28	9
Raul Ibanez	.280	279	44	78	13	54	0
Luis Alicea	.274	387	44	106	4	32	8
Mark Quinn	.269	453	57	122	17	60	9
Joe Randa	.253	581	59	147	13	83	3
Dave McCarty	.250	200	26	50	7	26	0
Dee Brown*	.245	380	39	93	7	40	5
Neifi Perez	.241	199	18	48	1	12	3
Brent Mayne	.241	166	13	40	2	20	1
Carlos Febles	.236	292	45	69	8	25	5

Acquired: P Byrd from Phi. for P Jose Santiago (June 5); C Mayne from Col. for C Sal Fasano and P Suzuki (June 24); IF Perez in a three-team deal that sent OF Jermaine Dye from KC to Oak. and IF Jose Ortiz, OF Mario Encarnacion and P Todd Belitz from Oak. to Col. (July 25).
Traded: IF Sanchez to Atl. for P Brad Voyles and IF Alexander Machado (July 31).

Pitching (55 IP)	ERA	W-L	Gm	IP	BB	SO
Jason Grimsley	3.02	1-5	73	80.1	28	61
Cory Bailey	3.48	1-1	53	67.1	33	61
Paul Byrd	4.05	6-6	16	93.1	22	49
Roberto Hernandez	4.12	5-6	63	67.2	26	46
Jeff Suppan	4.37	10-14	34	218.1	74	120
Blake Stein	4.74	7-8	36	131.0	79	113
Chad Durbin	4.93	9-16	29	179.0	58	93
Kris Wilson	5.19	6-5	29	109.1	32	67
Mac Suzuki	5.30	2-5	15	56.0	25	37
Chris George*	5.59	4-8	13	74.0	18	32
Dan Reichert	5.63	8-8	27	123.0	67	77
Doug Henry	6.07	2-2	53	75.2	45	57

Saves: Hernandez (28); Stein and Wilson (1). **Complete games:** Durbin (2); Byrd, Suppan and George (1). **Shutouts:** none.

Minnesota Twins

Batting (135 AB)	Avg	AB	R	H	HR	RBI	SB
Doug Mientkiewicz	.306	543	77	166	15	74	2
Cristian Guzman	.302	493	80	149	10	51	25
Matt Lawton	.293	376	71	110	10	51	19
A.J. Pierzynski	.289	381	51	110	7	55	1
Corey Koskie	.276	562	100	155	26	103	27
Jacque Jones	.276	475	57	131	14	49	12
Brian Buchanan	.274	197	28	54	10	32	1
Luis Rivas*	.266	563	70	150	7	47	31
Chad Allen	.263	175	20	46	4	20	1
Torii Hunter	.261	564	82	147	27	92	9
Denny Hocking	.251	327	34	82	3	25	6
David Ortiz	.234	303	46	71	18	48	1
Tom Prince	.219	196	19	43	7	23	3

Acquired: P Jones from Det. for P Mark Redman (July 28); P Reed from NYM for OF Lawton (July 30).

Pitching (50 IP)	ERA	W-L	Gm	IP	BB	SO
Joe Mays	3.16	17-13	34	233.2	64	123
Eddie Guardado	3.51	7-1	67	66.2	23	67
Jack Cressend*	3.67	3-2	44	56.1	16	40
Brad Radke	3.94	15-11	33	226.0	26	137
Todd Jones	4.24	5-5	69	68.0	29	54
Eric Milton	4.32	15-7	35	220.2	61	157
Hector Carrasco	4.64	4-3	56	73.2	30	70
Bob Wells	5.11	8-5	65	68.2	18	49
Rick Reed	5.19	4-6	12	67.2	14	43
Kyle Lohse*	5.68	4-7	19	90.1	29	64
LaTroy Hawkins	5.96	1-5	62	51.1	39	36
J.C. Romero	6.23	1-4	14	65.0	24	39

Saves: Hawkins (28); Jones (13); Guardado (12); Wells (2); Carrasco (1). **Complete games:** Radke (6); Mays (4); Milton (2). **Shutouts:** Mays and Radke (2); Milton (1).

New York Yankees

Batting (135 AB)	Avg	AB	R	H	HR	RBI	SB
Derek Jeter	.311	614	110	191	21	74	27
Bernie Williams	.307	540	102	166	26	94	11
Scott Brosius	.287	428	57	123	13	49	3
Tino Martinez	.280	589	89	165	34	113	1
Randy Velarde	.278	342	50	95	9	32	6
Jorge Posada	.277	484	59	134	22	95	2
Alfonso Soriano*	.268	574	77	154	18	73	43
Paul O'Neill	.267	510	77	136	21	70	22
Shane Spencer	.258	283	40	73	10	46	4
Chuck Knoblauch	.250	521	66	130	9	44	38
David Justice	.241	381	58	92	18	51	1
Gerald Williams	.201	279	42	56	4	19	13

Acquired: P Witasick from SD for IF D'Angelo Jimenez (June 23); P Hitchcock from SD for P Brett Jodie and OF Darren Blakely (July 30); IF Velarde from Tex. for two PTBN (Aug. 31).
Signed: OF G. Williams off waivers from TB (June 28).

Pitching (40 IP)	ERA	W-L	Gm	IP	BB	SO
Mariano Rivera	2.34	4-6	71	80.2	12	83
Mike Stanton	2.58	9-4	76	80.1	29	78
Mike Mussina	3.15	17-11	34	228.2	42	214
Randy Choate*	3.35	3-1	37	48.1	27	35
Roger Clemens	3.51	20-3	33	220.1	72	213
Ramiro Mendoza	3.75	8-4	56	100.2	23	70
Andy Pettitte	3.99	15-10	31	200.2	41	164
Jay Witasick	4.69	3-0	32	40.1	18	53
Orlando Hernandez	4.85	4-7	17	94.2	42	77
Ted Lilly*	5.37	5-6	26	120.2	51	112
Randy Keisler*	6.22	1-2	10	50.2	34	36
Sterling Hitchcock	6.49	4-4	10	51.1	18	28

Saves: Rivera (50); Mendoza (6); Brian Boehringer (1). **Complete games:** Mussina (4); Pettitte (2); Hitchcock (1). **Shutouts:** Mussina (3).

Oakland Athletics

Batting (135 AB)	Avg	AB	R	H	HR	RBI	SB
Jason Giambi	.342	520	109	178	38	120	2
Eric Chavez	.288	552	91	159	32	114	8
Jeremy Giambi	.283	371	64	105	12	57	0
Terrence Long	.283	629	90	178	12	85	9
Jermaine Dye	.282	599	91	169	26	106	9
Miguel Tejada	.267	622	107	166	31	113	11
Johnny Damon	.256	644	108	165	9	49	27
Ramon Hernandez	.254	453	55	115	15	60	1
Frank Menechino	.242	471	82	114	12	60	2
Greg Myers	.224	161	24	36	11	31	0
Olmedo Saenz	.220	305	33	67	9	32	0

Acquired: OF Dye in a three-team deal that sent IF Neifi Perez from KC to Col. and IF Jose Ortiz, OF Mario Encarnacion and P Todd Belitz from Oak. to Col. (July 25).
Signed: C Myers off waivers from Bal. (June 25).

Pitching (40 IP)	ERA	W-L	Gm	IP	BB	SO
Jason Isringhausen	2.65	4-3	65	71.1	23	74
Mike Magnante	2.77	3-1	65	55.1	13	23
Jeff Tam	3.01	2-4	70	74.2	29	44
Tim Hudson	3.37	18-9	35	235.0	71	181
Erik Hiljus*	3.41	5-0	16	66.0	21	67
Jim Mecir	3.43	2-8	54	63.0	26	61
Mark Mulder	3.45	21-8	34	229.1	51	153
Barry Zito	3.49	17-8	35	214.1	80	205
Cory Lidle	3.59	13-6	29	188.0	47	118
Mark Gynthie	4.47	6-2	54	52.1	20	52
Gil Heredia	5.58	7-8	24	109.2	29	48

Saves: Isringhausen (34); Tam and Mecir (3); Guthrie, Chad Bradford, T.J. Mathews and Luis Vizcaino (1). **Complete games:** Mulder (6); Hudson and Zito (3); Lidle (1). **Shutouts:** Mulder (4); Zito (2).

Seattle Mariners

Batting (135 AB)	Avg	AB	R	H	HR	RBI	SB
Ichiro Suzuki*	.350	692	127	242	8	69	56
Bret Boone	.331	623	118	206	37	141	5
Edgar Martinez	.306	470	80	144	23	116	4
John Olerud	.302	572	91	173	21	95	3
Stan Javier	.292	281	44	82	4	33	11
Mark McLemore	.286	409	78	117	5	57	39
Mike Cameron	.267	540	99	144	25	110	34
Dan Wilson	.265	377	44	100	10	42	3
David Bell	.260	470	62	122	15	64	2
Carlos Guillen	.259	456	72	118	5	53	4
Al Martin	.240	283	41	68	7	42	9
Tom Lampkin	.225	204	28	46	5	22	1

Pitching (40 IP)	ERA	W-L	Gm	IP	BB	SO
Arthur Rhodes	1.72	8-0	71	68.0	12	83
Joel Pineiro*	2.03	6-2	17	75.1	21	56
Jeff Nelson	2.76	4-3	69	65.1	44	88
Norm Charlton	3.02	4-2	44	47.2	11	48
Freddy Garcia	3.05	18-6	34	238.2	69	163
Kazuhiro Sasaki	3.24	0-4	69	66.2	11	62
Jamie Moyer	3.43	20-6	33	209.2	44	119
Ryan Franklin*	3.56	5-1	38	78.1	24	60
Aaron Sele	3.60	15-5	34	215.0	51	114
Paul Abbott	4.25	17-4	28	163.0	87	118
Jose Paniagua	4.36	4-3	60	66.0	38	46
John Halama	4.73	10-7	31	110.1	26	50

Saves: Sasaki (45); Nelson (4); Rhodes and Paniagua (3); Charlton (1). **Complete games:** Garcia (4); Sele (2); Moyer and Abbott (1). **Shutouts:** Garcia (3); Sele (1).

Tampa Bay Devil Rays

Batting (160 AB)	Avg	AB	R	H	HR	RBI	SB
Fred McGriff	.318	343	40	109	19	61	1
Chris Gomez	.302	189	31	57	8	36	3
Toby Hall*	.298	188	28	56	4	30	2
Russ Johnson	.294	248	32	73	4	33	2
Jason Tyner	.280	396	51	111	0	21	31
Randy Winn	.273	429	54	117	6	50	12
Brent Abernathy*	.270	304	43	82	5	33	8
Ben Grieve	.264	542	72	143	11	72	7
Damian Rolls*	.262	237	33	62	2	12	12
Steve Cox	.257	342	37	88	12	51	2
Aubrey Huff*	.248	411	42	102	8	45	1
Felix Martinez	.247	219	24	54	1	14	6
John Flaherty	.238	248	20	59	4	29	1
Greg Vaughn	.233	485	74	113	24	82	11

Acquired: P Bierbrodt, OF Jason Conti and cash from Ari. for P Lopez and C Mike DeFelice (July 25).
Signed: IF Gomez off waivers from SD (June 27).
Traded: IF McGriff to ChC for P Manny Aybar and IF Jason Smith (July 27).

Pitching (40 IP)	ERA	W-L	Gm	IP	BB	SO
Victor Zambrano*	3.16	6-2	36	51.1	18	58
Jesus Colome*	3.33	2-3	30	48.2	25	31
Jeff Wallace	3.40	0-3	29	50.1	37	38
Travis Phelps*	3.48	2-2	49	62.0	24	54
Esteban Yan	3.90	4-6	54	62.1	11	64
Doug Creek	4.31	2-5	66	62.2	49	66
Tanyon Sturtze	4.42	11-12	39	195.1	79	110
Joe Kennedy*	4.44	7-8	20	117.2	34	78
Nick Bierbrodt*	4.55	3-4	11	61.1	27	56
Paul Wilson	4.88	8-9	37	151.1	52	119
Albie Lopez	5.34	5-12	20	124.2	51	67
Bryan Rekar	5.89	3-13	25	140.2	45	87
Ryan Rupe	6.59	5-12	28	143.1	48	123

Saves: Yan (22); Phelps (5); Zambrano (2); Sturtze (1). **Complete games:** Lopez (1). **Shutouts:** Lopez (1).

Texas Rangers

Batting (200 AB)	Avg	AB	R	H	HR	RBI	SB
Frank Catalanotto	.330	463	77	153	11	54	15
Alex Rodriguez	.318	632	133	201	52	135	18
Ivan Rodriguez	.308	442	.70	136	25	65	10
Mike Lamb	.306	284	42	87	4	35	2
Ruben Sierra	.291	344	55	100	23	67	2
Rusty Greer	.273	245	38	67	7	29	1
Rafael Palmeiro	.273	600	98	164	47	123	1
Gabe Kapler	.267	483	77	129	17	72	23
Michael Young*	.249	386	57	96	11	49	3
Andres Galarraga ..	.235	243	33	57	10	34	1
Ken Caminiti	.232	185	24	43	9	25	0
Ricky Ledee	.231	242	33	56	2	36	3

Acquired: P Bell from Cin. for OF Ruben Mateo and IF Edwin Encarnacion (June 15).
Claimed: P Michalak off waivers from Tor. (Aug. 22). **Signed:** free agent OF Sierra (May 1). **Traded:** IF Galarraga to SF for three minor leaguers (July 24). **Released:** IF Caminiti (July 2).

Pitching (50 IP)	ERA	W-L	Gm	IP	BB	SO
Jeff Zimmerman	2.40	4-4	66	71.1	16	72
Chris Michalak*	4.41	8-9	35	136.2	55	67
Doug Davis	4.45	11-10	30	186.0	69	115
Mike Venafro	4.80	5-5	70	60.0	28	29
Rick Helling	5.17	12-11	34	215.2	63	154
Pat Mahomes........	5.70	7-6	56	107.1	55	61
Darren Oliver	6.02	11-11	28	154.0	65	104
Kenny Rogers	6.19	5-7	20	120.2	49	74
Mark Petkovsek	6.69	1-2	55	76.2	28	42
Aaron Myette*	7.14	4-5	19	80.2	37	67
Rob Bell	7.18	5-5	18	105.1	47	64

Saves: Zimmerman (28); Venafro and Tim Crabtree (4); Michalak (1). **Complete games:** Helling (2); Davis and Oliver (1). **Shutouts:** Helling (1).

Toronto Blue Jays

Batting (135 AB)	Avg	AB	R	H	HR	RBI	SB
Shannon Stewart......	.316	640	103	202	12	60	27
Homer Bush	.306	271	32	83	3	27	13
Carlos Delgado	.279	574	102	160	39	102	3
Brad Fullmer........	.274	522	71	143	18	83	5
Jose Cruz Jr........	.274	577	92	158	34	88	32
Felipe Lopez*	.260	177	21	46	5	23	4
Alex Gonzalez	.253	636	79	161	17	76	18
Raul Mondesi	.252	572	88	144	27	84	30
Jeff Frye	.246	175	24	43	2	15	2
Darrin Fletcher........	.226	416	36	94	11	56	0

Pitching (40 IP)	ERA	W-L	Gm	IP	BB	SO
Paul Quantrill........	3.04	11-2	80	83.0	12	58
Roy Halladay........	3.16	5-3	17	105.1	25	96
Bob File*	3.27	5-3	60	74.1	29	38
Kelvim Escobar	3.50	6-8	59	126.0	52	121
Dan Plesac..........	3.57	4-5	62	45.1	24	68
Pedro Borbon........	3.71	2-4	71	53.1	12	45
Chris Carpenter	4.09	11-11	34	215.2	75	157
Brandon Lyon*	4.29	5-4	11	63.0	15	35
Steve Parris	4.60	4-6	19	105.2	41	49
Billy Koch	4.80	2-5	69	69.1	33	55
Esteban Loaiza......	5.02	11-11	36	190.0	40	110
Joey Hamilton	5.89	5-8	22	122.1	38	82

Saves: Koch (36); Quantrill and Scott Eyre (1); Plesac (1). **Complete games:** Carpenter (3); Halladay, Escobar, Parris and Loaiza (1). **Shutouts:** Carpenter (2); Halladay, Escobar and Loaiza (1).

Players Who Played in Both Leagues in 2001

While all individual major league statistics count on career records, players cannot transfer their stats from one league to the other if they are traded during the regular season. Here are the combined stats for batters with 350 at bats and pitchers with 120 innings pitched, who played in both leagues in 2001.

Batters (350 AB)

	Avg	AB	R	H	HR	RBI	SB		Avg	AB	R	H	HR	RBI	SB
Ken Caminiti	.228	356	36	81	15	41	0	Matt Lawton	.277	559	95	155	13	64	29
TEX	.232	185	24	43	9	25	0	MIN........	.293	376	71	110	10	51	19
ATL	.222	171	12	38	6	16	0	NYM	.246	183	24	45	3	13	10
Vinny Castilla........	.260	538	69	140	25	91	1	Fred McGriff........	.306	513	67	157	31	102	1
TB	.215	93	7	20	2	9	0	TB........	.318	343	40	109	19	61	1
HOU	.270	445	62	120	23	82	1	CHC	.282	170	27	48	12	41	0
Delino DeShields......	.234	351	55	82	5	37	23	Neifi Perez	.279	581	83	162	8	59	9
BAL	.197	188	29	37	3	21	11	COL........	.298	382	65	114	7	47	6
CHC	.276	163	26	45	2	16	12	KC	.241	199	18	48	1	12	3
Andres Galarraga....	.256	399	50	102	17	69	1	Rey Sanchez	.281	544	56	153	0	37	11
TEX	.235	243	33	57	10	34	1	KC........	.303	390	46	118	0	28	9
SF	.288	156	17.	45	7	35	0	ATL........	.227	154	10	35	0	9	2

Pitchers (120 IP)

	ERA	W-L	Gm	IP	BB	SO		ERA	W-L	Gm	IP	BB	SO
James Baldwin........	4.42	10-11	29	175.0	63	95	Albie Lopez	4.81	9-19	33	205.2	75	136
CHW	4.61	7-5	17	95.2	38	42	TB	5.34	5-12	20	124.2	51	67
LA	4.20	3-6	12	79.1	25	53	ARI........	4.00	4-7	13	81.0	24	69
Rob Bell	6.67	5-10	27	149.2	64	97	Dave Mlicki	6.17	11-11	34	167.2	74	97
CIN	5.48	0-5	9	44.1	17	33	DET	7.33	4-8	15	81.0	41	48
TEX	7.18	5-5	18	105.1	47	64	HOU	5.09	7-3	19	86.2	33	49
Jose Lima	5.54	6-12	32	165.2	38	84	Rick Reed	4.05	12-12	32	202.1	31	142
HOU	7.30	1-2	14	53.0	16	41	NYM	3.48	8-6	20	134.2	17	99
DET	4.71	5-10	18	112.2	22	43	MIN........	5.19	4-6	12	67.2	14	43

NL Team by Team Statistics

At least 135 at bats or 40 innings pitched during the regular season unless otherwise indicated. Players who competed for more than one NL team are listed with their final club. Players traded from the AL are listed with NL team only if they have 135 AB or 40 IP. Note that (*) indicates rookie and PTBN indicates player to be named.

Arizona Diamondbacks

Batting (170 AB)

	Avg	AB	R	H	HR	RBI	SB
Luis Gonzalez	.325	609	128	198	57	142	1
Danny Bautista	.302	222	26	67	5	26	3
Mark Grace	.298	476	66	142	15	78	1
David Dellucci	.276	217	28	60	10	40	2
Craig Counsell	.275	458	76	126	4	38	6
Steve Finley	.275	495	66	136	14	73	11
Matt Williams	.275	408	58	112	16	65	1
Damian Miller	.271	380	45	103	13	47	0
Erubiel Durazo	.269	175	34	47	12	38	0
Tony Womack	.266	481	66	128	3	30	28
Reggie Sanders	.263	441	84	116	33	90	14
Jay Bell	.248	428	59	106	13	46	0

Acquired: P Lopez and C Mike DeFelice from TB for P Nick Bierbrodt, OF Jason Conti and cash (July 25).

Pitching (45 IP)

	ERA	W-L	Gm	IP	BB	SO
Randy Johnson	2.49	21-6	35	249.2	71	372
Byung-Hyun Kim	2.94	5-6	78	98.0	44	113
Curt Schilling	2.98	22-6	35	256.2	39	293
Miguel Batista	3.36	11-8	48	139.1	60	90
Albie Lopez	4.00	4-7	13	81.0	24	69
Erik Sabel*	4.38	3-2	42	51.1	12	25
Greg Swindell	4.53	2-6	64	53.2	8	42
Troy Brohawn*	4.93	2-3	59	49.1	23	30
Brian Anderson	5.20	4-9	29	133.1	30	55
Robert Ellis*	5.77	6-5	19	92.0	34	41
Armando Reynoso	5.98	1-6	9	46.2	13	15

Saves: Kim (19); Bret Prinz (9); Swindell and Matt Mantei (2); Brohawn and Russ Springer (1). **Complete games:** Schilling (6); Johnson (3); Lopez (2); Anderson (1). **Shutouts:** Johnson and Lopez (2); Schilling (1).

Atlanta Braves

Batting (180 AB)

	Avg	AB	R	H	HR	RBI	SB
Chipper Jones	.330	572	113	189	38	102	9
Brian Jordan	.295	560	82	165	25	97	3
Dave Martinez	.287	237	33	68	2	20	3
Rafael Furcal	.275	324	39	89	4	30	22
B.J. Surhoff	.271	484	68	131	10	58	9
Javy Lopez	.267	438	45	117	17	66	1
Marcus Giles*	.262	244	36	64	9	31	2
Quilvio Veras	.252	258	39	65	3	25	7
Andruw Jones	.251	625	104	157	34	104	11
Rico Brogna	.248	206	15	51	3	21	3
Wes Helms*	.222	158	28	48	10	36	1

Acquired: P Karsay, P Steve Reed and cash from Cle. for P John Rocker and IF Troy Cameron (June 22).
Signed: P Cabrera off waivers from Hou. (April 12).
Released: IF Veras (July 31).

Pitching (40 IP)

	ERA	W-L	Gm	IP	BB	SO
Mike Remlinger	2.76	3-3	74	75.0	23	93
Jose Cabrera	2.88	7-4	55	59.1	25	43
Kerry Ligtenberg	3.02	3-3	53	59.2	30	56
John Burkett	3.04	12-12	34	219.1	70	187
Greg Maddux	3.05	17-11	34	233.0	27	173
John Smoltz	3.36	3-3	36	59.0	10	57
Steve Karsay	3.43	3-4	43	44.2	17	39
Jason Marquis*	3.48	5-6	38	129.1	59	98
Tom Glavine	3.57	16-7	35	219.1	97	116
Kevin Millwood	4.31	7-7	21	121.0	40	84
Odalis Perez	4.91	7-8	24	95.1	39	71

Saves: John Rocker (19); Smoltz (10); Karsay (7); Cabrera (2); Ligtenberg, Remlinger, Steve Reed and Rudy Seanez (1). **Complete games:** Maddux (3); Burkett and Glavine (1). **Shutouts:** Maddux (3); Burkett and Glavine (1).

Chicago Cubs

Batting (150 AB)

	Avg	AB	R	H	HR	RBI	SB
Sammy Sosa	.328	577	146	189	64	160	0
Rondell White	.307	323	43	99	17	50	1
Bill Mueller	.295	210	38	62	6	23	1
Ricky Gutierrez	.290	528	76	153	10	66	4
Fred McGriff	.282	170	27	48	12	41	0
Eric Young	.279	603	98	168	6	42	31
Delino DeShields	.276	163	26	45	2	16	12
Ron Coomer	.261	349	25	91	8	53	0
Joe Girardi	.253	229	22	58	3	25	0
Michael Tucker	.252	436	62	110	12	61	16
Matt Stairs	.250	340	48	85	17	61	2
Todd Hundley	.187	246	23	46	12	31	0

Acquired: OF Tucker from Cin. for two minor leaguers (July 20); IF McGriff from TB for P Manny Aybar and IF Jason Smith (July 27); P Weathers and P Roberto Miniel from Mil. for P Ruben Quevedo and OF Peter Zoccolillo (July 25).
Signed: OF DeShields off waivers from Bal. (July 6).

Pitching (40 IP)

	ERA	W-L	Gm	IP	BB	SO
Dave Weathers	2.41	4-5	80	86.0	34	66
Todd Van Poppel	2.52	4-1	59	75.0	38	90
Kyle Farnsworth	2.74	4-6	76	82.0	29	107
Juan Cruz*	3.22	3-1	8	44.2	17	39
Kerry Wood	3.36	12-6	28	174.1	92	217
Tom Gordon	3.38	1-2	47	45.1	16	67
Jeff Fassero	3.42	4-4	82	73.2	23	79
Jon Lieber	3.80	20-6	34	232.1	41	148
Jason Bere	4.31	11-11	32	188.0	77	175
Kevin Tapani	4.49	9-14	29	168.1	40	149
Julian Tavarez	4.52	10-9	34	161.1	69	107
Courtney Duncan*	5.06	3-3	36	42.2	25	49

Saves: Gordon (27); Fassero (12); Weathers (3); Farnsworth (2). **Complete games:** Lieber (5); Bere (2); Wood (1). **Shutouts:** Wood and Lieber (1).

Cincinnati Reds

Batting (135 AB)

	Avg	AB	R	H	HR	RBI	SB
Wilton Guerrero	.338	142	16	48	1	8	5
Sean Casey	.310	533	69	165	13	89	3
Dmitri Young	.302	540	68	163	21	69	8
Todd Walker	.296	551	93	163	17	75	1
Aaron Boone	.294	381	54	112	14	62	6
Ken Griffey Jr.	.286	364	57	104	22	65	2
Adam Dunn*	.262	244	54	64	19	43	4
Kelly Stinnett	.257	187	27	48	9	25	2
Barry Larkin	.256	156	29	40	2	17	3
Ruben Rivera	.255	263	37	67	10	34	6
Jason LaRue	.236	364	39	86	12	43	3
Pokey Reese	.224	428	50	96	9	40	25
Juan Castro	.223	242	27	54	3	13	0

Acquired: IF Walker and a minor leaguer from Col. for OF Alex Ochoa (July 19).

Pitching (45 IP)

	ERA	W-L	Gm	IP	BB	SO
Scott Sullivan	3.31	7-1	79	103.1	36	82
Jim Brower	3.97	7-10	46	129.1	60	94
Hector Mercado*	4.08	3-2	56	53.0	30	59
Danny Graves	4.15	6-6	60	80.1	18	49
Elmer Dessens	4.48	10-14	34	205.0	56	128
Lance Davis*	4.74	8-4	20	106.1	34	53
Dennys Reyes	4.92	2-6	35	53.0	35	52
Chris Reitsma*	5.29	7-15	36	182.0	49	96
Jose Acevedo*	5.44	5-7	18	96.0	34	68
Osvaldo Fernandez	6.92	5-6	20	79.1	33	35

Saves: Graves (32); Brower and John Riedling (1). **Complete games:** Dessens and Davis (1). **Shutouts:** Dessens (1).

Colorado Rockies

Batting (175 AB)	Avg	AB	R	H	HR	RBI	SB
Larry Walker	.350	497	107	174	38	123	14
Todd Helton	.336	587	132	197	49	146	7
Juan Pierre	.327	617	108	202	2	55	46
Jeff Cirillo*	.312	528	72	165	17	83	12
Juan Uribe*	.300	273	32	82	8	53	3
Neifi Perez	.298	382	65	114	7	47	6
Terry Shumpert	.289	242	37	70	4	24	14
Alex Ochoa	.276	536	73	148	8	52	17
Greg Norton	.267	225	30	60	13	40	1
Jose Ortiz*	.255	204	38	52	13	35	3
Ben Petrick	.238	244	41	58	11	39	3

Acquired: P Davis, P Juan Acevedo and IF Jose Flores from Mil. for P Mike DeJean, P Mark Leiter and IF Elvis Pena (April 4); P Powell from Hou. for P Ron Villone and cash (June 27); OF Ochoa from Cin. for IF Todd Walker and a minor leaguer (July 20); IF Ortiz, OF Mario Encarnacion and P Todd Belitz in a three-team deal that sent IF Perez from Col. to KC and OF Jermaine Dye from KC to Oak. (July 25); P Elarton and PTBN from Hou. for P Pedro Astacio and cash (July 31).
Claimed: P Speier off waivers from NYM (May 30).
Signed: Free agent P Miceli (July 2).

Pitching (45 IP)	ERA	W-L	Gm	IP	BB	SO
Jay Powell	3.24	5-3	74	75.0	31	54
Justin Speier	3.70	4-3	42	56.0	12	47
John Thomson	4.04	4-5	14	93.2	25	68
Jose Jimenez	4.09	6-1	56	55.0	22	37
Kane Davis*	4.35	2-4	57	68.1	32	47
Dan Miceli	4.80	2-5	51	45.0	16	48
Shawn Chacon*	5.06	6-10	27	160.0	87	134
Denny Neagle	5.38	9-8	30	170.2	60	139
Mike Hampton	5.41	14-13	32	203.0	85	122
Gabe White	6.25	1-7	69	67.2	26	47
Scott Elarton	7.06	4-10	24	132.2	59	87
Brian Bohanon	7.14	5-8	20	97.0	47	47

Saves: Jimenez (17); Powell (7); Miceli, Chris Nichting and Craig Dingman (1). **Complete games:** Hampton (2); Thomson and Jason Jennings (1). **Shutouts:** Thomson, Jennings and Hampton (1).

Florida Marlins

Batting (135 AB)	Avg	AB	R	H	HR	RBI	SB
Cliff Floyd	.317	555	123	176	31	103	18
Kevin Millar	.314	449	62	141	20	85	0
Mike Redmond	.312	141	19	44	4	14	0
Mike Lowell	.283	551	65	156	18	100	1
Derrek Lee	.282	561	83	158	21	75	4
Preston Wilson	.274	468	70	128	23	71	20
Luis Castillo	.263	537	76	141	2	45	33
Charles Johnson	.259	451	51	117	18	75	0
Eric Owens	.252	400	51	101	5	28	8
Alex Gonzalez	.250	515	57	129	9	48	2
Dave Berg	.242	215	26	52	4	16	0
John Mabry	.208	154	14	32	6	20	1

Acquired: IF Mabry from St.L for cash (April 9); P Acevedo from Col. for IF Josue Espada (Aug. 6).

Pitching (40 IP)	ERA	W-L	Gm	IP	BB	SO
Vladimir Nunez	2.74	4-5	52	92.0	30	64
Antonio Alfonseca	3.06	4-4	58	61.2	15	40
Braden Looper	3.55	3-3	71	71.0	30	52
Brad Penny	3.69	10-10	31	205.0	54	154
A.J. Burnett	4.05	11-12	27	173.1	83	128
Juan Acevedo	4.18	2-5	59	60.1	35	47
Vic Darensbourg	4.25	1-2	58	48.2	10	33
Chuck Smith	4.70	5-5	15	88.0	35	71
Jesus Sanchez	4.74	2-4	16	62.2	31	46
Armando Almanza	4.83	2-2	52	41.0	26	45
Ryan Dempster	4.94	15-12	34	211.1	112	171
Matt Clement	5.05	9-10	31	169.1	85	134
Ricky Bones	5.06	4-4	61	64.0	33	41

Saves: Alfonseca (28); Looper (3); Darensbourg (1). **Complete games:** Burnett and Dempster (2); Penny (1). **Shutouts:** Penny, Burnett and Dempster (1).

Houston Astros

Batting (135 AB)	Avg	AB	R	H	HR	RBI	SB
Moises Alou	.331	513	79	170	27	108	5
Lance Berkman	.331	577	110	191	34	126	7
Craig Biggio	.292	617	118	180	20	70	7
Jeff Bagwell	.288	600	126	173	39	130	11
Jose Vizcaino	.277	256	38	71	1	14	3
Richard Hidalgo	.275	512	70	141	19	80	3
Vinny Castilla	.270	445	62	120	23	82	1
Julio Lugo	.263	513	93	135	10	37	12
Daryle Ward	.263	213	21	56	9	39	0
Orlando Merced	.263	137	19	36	6	29	5
Tony Eusebio	.253	154	16	39	5	14	0
Brad Ausmus	.232	422	45	98	5	34	4
Chris Truby	.206	136	11	28	8	23	1

Acquired: P Mlicki from Det. for P Lima and cash (June 23); P Villone and cash from Col. for P Jay Powell (June 27); P Astacio and cash from Col. for P Scott Elarton and PTBN (July 31); P Williams from Pit. for P Tony McKnight (July 31).
Signed: IF Castilla off waivers from TB (May 15).

Pitchers (40 IP)	ERA	W-L	Gm	IP	BB	SO
Octavio Dotel	2.66	7-5	61	105.0	47	145
Billy Wagner	2.73	2-5	64	62.2	20	79
Roy Oswalt*	2.73	14-3	28	141.2	24	144
Wade Miller	3.40	16-8	32	212.0	76	183
Mike Williams	3.80	6-4	65	64.0	35	59
Nelson Cruz	4.15	3-3	66	82.1	24	75
Shane Reynolds	4.34	14-11	28	182.2	36	102
Mike Jackson	4.70	5-3	67	69.0	22	46
Dave Mlicki	5.09	7-3	19	86.2	33	49
Pedro Astacio	5.09	8-14	26	169.2	54	144
Tim Redding*	5.50	3-1	13	55.2	24	55
Ron Villone	5.89	6-10	53	114.2	53	113
Kent Bottenfield	6.40	2-5	13	52.0	16	39
Jose Lima	7.30	1-2	14	53.0	16	41

Saves: Wagner (39); Williams (22); Jackson (4); Dotel and Cruz (2); Bottenfield (1). **Complete games:** Astacio (4); Oswalt and Reynolds (3); Miller (1). **Shutouts:** Oswalt and Astacio (1).

Los Angeles Dodgers

Batting (135 AB)	Avg	AB	R	H	HR	RBI	SB
Paul Lo Duca	.320	460	71	147	25	90	2
Gary Sheffield	.311	515	98	160	36	100	10
Shawn Green	.297	619	121	184	49	125	20
Mark Grudzielanek	.271	539	83	146	13	55	4
Jeff Reboulet	.266	214	35	57	3	22	0
Adrian Beltre	.265	475	59	126	13	60	13
Dave Hansen	.236	140	13	36	2	20	0
Eric Karros	.235	438	42	103	15	63	3
Tom Goodwin	.231	286	51	66	4	22	22
Marquis Grissom	.221	448	56	99	21	60	7
Alex Cora	.217	405	38	88	4	29	0
Chad Kreuter	.215	191	21	41	6	17	0

Acquired: P Baldwin from ChW for P Onan Masaoka, P Gary Majewski and OF Jeff Barry (July 26); P Mulholland from Pit. for P Mike Fetters and P Adrian Burnside (July 31).

Pitching (40 IP)	ERA	W-L	Gm	IP	BB	SO
Kevin Brown	2.65	10-4	20	115.2	38	104
Giovanni Carrara	3.16	6-1	47	85.1	24	70
Matt Herges	3.44	9-8	75	99.1	46	76
Chan Ho Park	3.50	15-11	36	234.0	91	218
Jeff Shaw	3.62	3-5	77	74.2	18	58
James Baldwin	4.20	3-6	12	79.1	25	53
Terry Adams	4.33	12-8	43	166.1	54	141
Terry Mulholland	4.66	1-1	41	65.2	17	42
Eric Gagne	4.75	6-7	33	151.2	46	130
Luke Prokopec*	4.88	8-7	29	138.1	40	91
Darren Dreifort	5.13	4-7	16	94.2	47	91

Saves: Shaw (43); Herges and Al Reyes (1). **Complete games:** Park (2); Brown (1). **Shutouts:** Park (1).

Milwaukee Brewers

Batting (135 AB)	Avg	AB	R	H	HR	RBI	SB
Tyler Houston	.289	235	36	68	12	38	0
Mark Loretta	.289	384	40	111	2	29	1
Devon White	.277	390	52	108	14	47	18
Richie Sexson	.271	598	94	162	45	125	2
Luis Lopez	.270	222	22	60	4	18	0
Geoff Jenkins	.264	397	60	105	20	63	4
Ron Belliard	.264	364	69	96	11	36	5
Raul Casanova	.260	192	21	50	11	33	0
Jeromy Burnitz	.251	562	104	141	34	100	0
Jose Hernandez	.249	542	67	135	25	78	5
Jeffrey Hammonds	.247	174	20	43	6	21	5
James Mouton	.246	138	20	34	2	10	7
Henry Blanco	.210	314	33	66	6	31	3

Acquired: P DeJean, P Mark Leiter and IF Elvis Pena from Col. for P Juan Acevedo, P Kane Davis and IF Jose Flores (April 4); P Quevedo and OF Peter Zoccolillo from ChC for P Dave Weathers and P Roberto Miniel (July 30).
Claimed: P Suzuki off waivers from Col. (July 12).

Pitching (40 IP)	ERA	W-L	Gm	IP	BB	SO
Chad Fox	1.89	5-2	65	66.2	36	80
Mike DeJean	2.77	4-2	75	84.1	39	68
Ray King	3.60	0-4	82	55.0	25	49
Curtis Leskanic	3.63	2-6	70	69.1	31	64
Mike Buddie	3.89	0-1	31	41.2	17	22
Ruben Quevedo	4.61	4-5	10	56.2	30	60
Ben Sheets*	4.76	11-10	25	151.1	48	94
Jimmy Haynes	4.85	8-17	31	172.2	78	112
Jamey Wright	4.90	11-12	33	194.2	98	129
Will Cunnane	5.40	0-3	31	51.2	22	37
Paul Rigdon	5.79	3-5	15	79.1	46	49
Allen Levrault*	6.06	6-10	32	130.2	59	80
Jeff D'Amico	6.08	2-4	10	47.1	16	32
Mac Suzuki	6.35	3-7	18	62.1	48	52

Saves: Leskanic (17); Fox, DeJean and Buddie (2); King (1).
Complete games: Sheets, Wright and Levrault (1). **Shutouts:** Sheets and Wright (1).

Montreal Expos

Batting (135 AB)	Avg	AB	R	H	HR	RBI	SB
Jose Vidro	.319	486	82	155	15	59	4
Vladimir Guerrero	.307	599	107	184	34	108	37
Mike Mordecai	.280	254	28	71	3	32	2
Orlando Cabrera	.276	626	64	173	14	96	19
Fernando Tatis	.255	145	20	37	2	11	0
Michael Barrett	.250	472	42	118	6	38	2
Lee Stevens	.245	542	77	133	25	95	2
Mark Smith	.242	194	28	47	6	18	0
Geoff Blum	.236	453	57	107	9	50	9
Milton Bradley	.223	220	19	49	1	19	7
Peter Bergeron	.211	375	53	79	3	16	10

Acquired: P Ohka and P Rich Rundles from Bos. for P Urbina (July 31).
Traded: OF Bradley to Cle. for P Zach Day (July 31).

Pitching (40 IP)	ERA	W-L	Gm	IP	BB	SO
Scott Strickland	3.21	2-6	77	81.1	41	85
Javier Vazquez	3.42	16-11	32	223.2	44	208
Scott Stewart	3.78	3-1	62	47.2	13	39
Tony Armas Jr.	4.03	9-14	34	196.2	91	176
Ugueth Urbina	4.24	2-1	45	46.2	21	57
Graeme Lloyd	4.35	9-5	84	70.1	21	44
Tomokazu Ohka	4.77	1-4	10	54.2	10	31
Masato Yoshii	4.78	4-7	42	113.0	26	63
Bobby Munoz*	5.14	0-4	15	42.0	21	21
Guillermo Mota	5.26	1-3	53	49.2	18	31
Mike Thurman	5.53	9-11	28	147.0	50	96
Britt Reames*	5.59	4-8	41	95.0	48	86
Troy Mattes	6.00	3-3	8	45.0	21	26
Carl Pavano	6.33	1-6	8	42.2	16	36

Saves: Urbina (15); Strickland (9); Stewart (3); Lloyd (1). **Complete games:** Vazquez (5). **Shutouts:** Vazquez (3).

New York Mets

Batting (135 AB)	Avg	AB	R	H	HR	RBI	SB
Desi Relaford	.302	301	43	91	8	36	13
Mike Piazza	.300	503	81	151	36	94	0
Joe McEwing	.283	283	41	80	8	30	8
Benny Agbayani	.277	296	28	82	6	27	4
Tsuyoshi Shinjo*	.267	400	46	107	10	56	4
Todd Zeile	.266	531	66	141	10	62	1
Jay Payton	.255	361	44	92	8	34	4
Rey Ordonez	.247	461	31	114	3	44	3
Timo Perez*	.247	239	26	59	5	22	1
Matt Lawton	.246	183	24	45	3	13	10
Edgardo Alfonzo	.243	457	64	111	17	49	5
Robin Ventura	.237	456	70	108	21	61	2
Lenny Harris	.222	135	12	30	0	9	3

Acquired: P Chen and P Adam Walker from Phi. for P Turk Wendell and P Dennis Cook (July 27); OF Lawton from Min. for P Reed (July 30).

Pitching (40 IP)	ERA	W-L	Gm	IP	BB	SO
Al Leiter	3.31	11-11	29	187.1	46	142
Jerrod Riggan*	3.40	3-3	35	47.2	24	41
Rick Reed	3.48	8-6	20	134.2	17	99
Kevin Appier	3.57	11-10	33	206.2	64	172
Armando Benitez	3.77	6-4	73	76.1	40	93
Rick White	3.88	4-5	55	69.2	17	51
John Franco	4.05	6-2	58	53.1	19	50
Steve Trachsel	4.46	11-13	28	173.2	47	144
Glendon Rusch	4.63	8-12	33	179.0	43	156
Donne Wall	4.85	0-4	32	42.2	17	31
Bruce Chen	4.87	7-7	27	146.0	59	126
Dicky Gonzalez*	4.88	3-2	16	59.0	17	31

Saves: Benitez (43); White and Franco (2). **Complete games:** Reed (3); Appier, Trachsel and Rusch (1). **Shutouts:** Reed, Appier and Trachsel (1).

Philadelphia Phillies

Batting (135 AB)	Avg	AB	R	H	HR	RBI	SB
Tomas Perez	.304	135	11	41	3	19	0
Marlon Anderson	.293	522	69	153	11	61	8
Bobby Abreu	.289	588	118	170	31	110	36
Scott Rolen	.289	554	96	160	25	107	16
Brian L. Hunter	.276	145	22	40	2	16	14
Jimmy Rollins*	.274	656	97	180	14	54	46
Doug Glanville	.262	634	74	166	14	55	28
Pat Burrell	.258	539	70	139	27	89	2
Travis Lee	.258	555	75	143	20	90	3
Johnny Estrada*	.228	298	26	68	8	37	0
Todd Pratt	.185	173	18	32	4	11	1

Acquired: P Santiago from KC for P Paul Byrd (June 5); C Pratt from NYM for C Gary Bennett (July 22); P Wendell and Cook from NYM for P Bruce Chen and P Adam Walker (July 27).

Pitchers (40 IP)	ERA	W-L	Gm	IP	BB	SO
Jose Mesa	2.34	3-3	71	69.1	20	59
Brandon Duckworth*	3.52	3-2	11	69.0	29	40
Jose Santiago	3.61	2-4	53	62.1	13	28
Randy Wolf	3.70	10-11	28	163.0	51	152
Ricky Bottalico	3.90	3-4	66	67.0	25	57
Nelson Figueroa*	3.94	4-5	19	89.0	37	61
Dave Coggin*	4.17	6-7	17	95.0	39	62
Robert Person	4.19	15-7	33	208.1	80	183
Rheal Cormier	4.21	5-6	60	51.1	17	37
Turk Wendell	4.43	4-5	70	67.0	34	56
Omar Daal	4.46	13-7	32	185.2	56	107
Dennis Cook	4.53	1-1	62	45.2	14	38
Amaury Telemaco	5.54	5-5	24	89.1	32	59

Saves: Mesa (42); Bottalico (3); Cormier and Wendell (1). **Complete games:** Wolf (4); Person (3); Telemaco (1). **Shutouts:** Wolf (2); Person (1).

Pittsburgh Pirates

Batting (135 AB)	Avg	AB	R	H	HR	RBI	SB
Craig Wilson*	.310	158	27	49	13	32	3
Brian Giles	.309	576	116	178	37	95	13
Aramis Ramirez	.300	603	83	181	34	112	5
Rob Mackowiak*	.266	214	30	57	4	21	4
Jason Kendall	.266	606	84	161	10	53	13
Abraham Nunez	.262	301	30	79	1	21	8
Armando Rios	.260	319	38	83	14	50	3
Kevin Young	.232	449	53	104	14	65	15
Gary Matthews Jr.	.227	405	63	92	14	44	8
Jack Wilson*	.223	390	44	87	3	25	1
Pat Meares	.211	270	27	57	4	25	0
Derek Bell	.173	156	14	27	5	13	0

Acquired: OF Rios and P Ryan Vogelsong from SF for P Jason Schmidt and OF John Vander Wal (July 30); P McKnight from Hou. for P Mike Williams (July 31); P Fetters and P Adrian Burnside from LA for P Terry Mulholland (July 31).
Claimed: OF Matthews Jr. off waivers from ChC (Aug. 10).

Pitching (40 IP)	ERA	W-L	Gm	IP	BB	SO
Mike Lincoln	2.68	2-1	31	40.1	11	24
Josias Manzanillo	3.39	3-2	71	79.2	26	80
Dave Williams*	3.71	3-7	22	114.0	45	57
Todd Ritchie	4.47	11-15	33	207.1	52	124
Tony McKnight*	4.95	3-6	15	87.1	24	46
Bronson Arroyo	5.09	5-7	24	88.1	34	39
Jimmy Anderson	5.10	9-17	34	206.1	83	89
Joe Beimel*	5.23	7-11	42	115.1	49	58
Mike Fetters	5.51	3-2	54	47.1	26	37
Scott Sauerbeck	5.60	2-2	70	62.2	40	79
Omar Olivares	6.55	6-9	45	110.0	42	69

Saves: Fetters (9); Manzanillo and Sauerbeck (2); Olivares and Rich Loiselle (1). **Complete games:** Ritchie (4); Arroyo, Anderson and Olivares (1). **Shutouts:** Ritchie (2).

St. Louis Cardinals

Batting (135 AB)	Avg	AB	R	H	HR	RBI	SB
Albert Pujols*	.329	590	112	194	37	130	1
J.D. Drew	.323	375	80	121	27	73	13
Placido Polanco	.307	564	87	173	3	38	12
Jim Edmonds	.304	500	95	152	30	110	5
Fernando Vina	.303	631	95	191	9	56	17
Miguel Cairo	.295	156	25	46	3	16	2
Kerry Robinson*	.285	186	34	53	1	15	11
Craig Paquette	.282	340	47	96	15	64	3
Eli Marrero	.266	203	37	54	6	23	6
Edgar Renteria	.260	493	54	128	10	57	17
Mike Matheny	.218	381	40	83	7	42	0
Bobby Bonilla	.213	174	17	37	5	21	1
Mark McGwire	.187	299	48	56	29	64	0

Acquired: P Williams from SD for OF Ray Lankford and cash (Aug. 2).
Claimed: IF Cairo off waivers from ChC (Aug. 10).

Pitching (40 IP)	ERA	W-L	Gm	IP	BB	SO
Steve Kline	1.80	3-3	89	75.0	29	54
Darryl Kile	3.09	16-11	34	227.1	65	179
Matt Morris	3.16	22-8	34	216.1	54	185
Mike Matthews*	3.24	3-4	51	89.0	33	72
Dave Veres	3.70	3-2	71	65.2	28	61
Bud Smith*	3.83	6-3	16	84.2	24	59
Gene Stechschulte*	3.86	1-5	67	70.0	30	51
Woody Williams	4.05	15-9	34	220.0	56	154
Mike Timlin	4.09	4-5	67	72.2	19	47
Dustin Hermanson	4.45	14-13	33	192.1	73	123
Andy Benes	7.38	7-7	27	107.1	61	78

Saves: Veres (15); Kline (9); Stechschulte (3); Timlin (3) Matthews and Luther Hackman (1). **Complete games:** Williams (3); Kile and Morris (2), Smith (1). **Shutouts:** Kile, Morris, Smith and Williams (1).

San Diego Padres

Batting (135 AB)	Avg	AB	R	H	HR	RBI	SB
Phil Nevin	.306	546	97	167	41	126	4
Mark Kotsay	.291	406	67	118	10	58	13
Ryan Klesko	.286	538	105	154	30	113	23
Mike Darr	.277	289	36	80	2	34	6
D'Angelo Jimenez*	.276	308	45	85	3	33	2
Wiki Gonzalez	.275	160	16	44	8	27	2
Bubba Trammell	.261	490	66	128	25	92	2
Ray Lankford	.252	389	58	98	19	58	10
Damian Jackson	.241	440	67	106	4	38	23
Ben Davis	.239	448	56	107	11	57	4
Rickey Henderson	.227	379	70	86	8	42	25
Alex Arias	.226	137	19	31	2	12	1
Cesar Crespo*	.209	153	27	32	4	12	6
Emil Brown	.190	137	21	26	3	13	12

Acquired: IF Jimenez from NYY for P Jay Witasick (June 23); OF Brown from Pit. for 2 minor leaguers (July 10); OF Lankford and cash from St.L for P Woody Williams (Aug. 2).
Claimed: P Nunez off waivers from LA (May 11).

Pitching (40 IP)	ERA	W-L	Gm	IP	BB	SO
Trevor Hoffman	3.43	3-4	62	60.1	21	63
Brian Lawrence*	3.45	5-5	27	114.2	34	84
David Lee	3.70	1-0	41	48.2	27	42
Brian Tollberg	4.30	10-4	19	117.1	25	71
Adam Eaton	4.32	8-5	17	116.2	40	109
Jose Nunez*	4.58	4-2	62	59.0	25	60
Kevin Jarvis	4.79	12-11	32	193.1	49	133
Bobby J. Jones	5.12	8-19	33	195.0	38	113
Rodney Myers	5.32	1-2	37	47.1	20	29
Junior Herndon*	6.33	2-6	12	42.2	25	14
Wascar Serrano*	6.56	3-3	20	46.2	21	39

Saves: Hoffman (43); Myers and Jay Witasick (1). **Complete games:** Eaton (2); Lawrence, Jarvis and Jones (1). **Shutouts:** Jarvis (1).

San Francisco Giants

Batting (135 AB)	Avg	AB	R	H	HR	RBI	SB
Barry Bonds	.328	476	129	156	73	137	13
Rich Aurilia	.324	636	114	206	37	97	1
Jeff Kent	.298	607	84	181	22	106	7
Andres Galarraga	.288	156	17	45	7	35	0
Shawon Dunston	.280	186	26	52	9	25	3
John Vander Wal	.270	452	58	122	14	70	8
Marvin Benard	.265	392	70	104	15	44	10
Benito Santiago	.262	477	39	125	6	45	5
Russ Davis	.257	167	16	43	7	17	1
Ramon Martinez	.253	391	48	99	5	37	1
J.T. Snow	.246	285	43	70	8	34	0
Calvin Murray	.245	326	54	80	6	25	8
Pedro Feliz*	.227	220	23	50	7	22	2
Eric Davis	.205	156	17	32	4	22	1

Acquired: P Gomes from Phi. for IF Felipe Crespo (July 27); IF Galarraga from Tex. for 3 minor leaguers (July 24); P Schmidt and OF Vander Wal from Pit. for OF Armando Rios and P Ryan Vogelsong (July 30).

Pitching (40 IP)	ERA	W-L	Gm	IP	BB	SO
Felix Rodriguez	1.68	9-1	80	80.1	27	91
Robb Nen	3.01	4-5	79	77.2	22	93
Russ Ortiz	3.29	17-9	33	218.2	91	169
Tim Worrell	3.45	2-5	73	78.1	33	63
Shawn Estes	4.02	9-8	27	159.0	77	109
Jason Schmidt	4.07	13-7	25	150.1	61	142
Ryan Jensen*	4.25	1-2	10	42.1	25	26
Kirk Rueter	4.42	14-12	34	195.1	66	83
Aaron Fultz	4.56	3-1	66	71.0	21	67
Livan Hernandez	5.24	13-15	34	226.2	85	138
Wayne Gomes	5.29	6-3	55	63.0	29	52
Mark Gardner	5.40	5-5	23	91.2	34	53

Saves: Nen (45); Jason Christiansen (3); Fultz, Gomes and Brian Boehringer (1). **Complete games:** Hernandez (2); Ortiz and Schmidt (1). **Shutouts:** Ortiz (1).

Divisional Series Summaries
AMERICAN LEAGUE

Yankees, 3-2

Date	Winner	Home Field
Oct. 10	Athletics, 5-3	at New York
Oct. 11	Athletics, 2-0	at New York
Oct. 13	Yankees, 1-0	at Oakland
Oct. 14	Yankees, 9-2	at Oakland
Oct. 15	Yankees, 5-3	at New York

Game 1
Wednesday, Oct. 10, at New York

	1 2 3	4 5 6	7 8 9	R H E
Oakland	1 0 0	1 0 0	1 2 0	5 10 1
New York	0 0 0	0 1 0	0 2 0	3 10 1

Win: Mulder, Oak. (1-0). **Loss:** Clemens, NY (0-1). **Save:** Isringhausen, Oak. (1).
2B: Oakland—Je. Giambi, Dye; New York—Posada. **HR:** Oakland—Long 2 (2), Ja. Giambi (1); New York—Martinez (1). **RBI:** Oakland—Ja. Giambi 2 (2), Long 2 (2), Tejada (1); New York—Knoblauch (1), Martinez 2 (2). **SB:** Oakland—Damon 2 (2); New York—Soriano (1). **CS:** New York—Soriano. **E:** Oakland—Menechino; New York—Knoblauch.
Attendance: 56,697. **Time:** 3:45.

Game 2
Thursday, Oct. 11, at New York

	1 2 3	4 5 6	7 8 9	R H E
Oakland	0 0 0	1 0 0	0 0 1	2 9 0
New York	0 0 0	0 0 0	0 0 0	0 7 1

Win: Hudson, Oak. (1-0). **Loss:** Pettitte, NY (0-1). **Save:** Isringhausen, Oak. (2).
2B: Oakland—Tejada 2, Long, Damon; New York—B. Williams. **3B:** Oakland—Damon. **HR:** Oakland—Gant (1). **RBI:** Oakland—Gant (1). **CS:** New York—B. Williams. **E:** New York—Brosius.
Attendance: 56,684. **Time:** 3:24.

Game 3
Saturday, Oct. 13, at Oakland

	1 2 3	4 5 6	7 8 9	R H E
New York	0 0 0	0 1 0	0 0 0	1 2 0
Oakland	0 0 0	0 0 0	0 0 0	0 6 1

Win: Mussina, NY (1-0). **Loss:** Zito, Oak. (0-1). **Save:** Rivera, NY (1).
2B: New York—Spencer; Oakland—Long, Dye. **HR:** New York—Posada (1). **RBI:** New York—Posada (1).
E: Oakland—Tejada.
Attendance: 55,861. **Time:** 2:42.

Game 4
Sunday, Oct. 14, at Oakland

	1 2 3	4 5 6	7 8 9	R H E
New York	0 2 2	3 0 0	0 0 2	9 11 1
Oakland	0 0 2	0 0 0	0 0 0	2 11 1

Win: Hernandez, NY (1-0). **Loss:** Lidle, Oak. (0-1).
2B: New York—B. Williams 2, O'Neill; Oakland—Tejada, Santangelo, Chavez. **3B:** New York—Justice. **RBI:** New York—Brosius (1), B. Williams 5 (5), Soriano (1), Posada (2); Oakland—Long (3), Je. Giambi (1). **SB:** New York—Soriano (2). **CS:** New York—Jeter. **E:** New York—Brosius; Oakland—Santangelo.
Attendance: 56,915. **Time:** 3:42.

Game 5
Monday, Oct. 15, at New York

	1 2 3	4 5 6	7 8 9	R H E
Oakland	1 1 0	0 1 0	0 0 0	3 7 3
New York	0 2 1	1 0 1	0 0 x	5 10 1

Win: Stanton, NY (1-0). **Loss:** Mulder, Oak. (1-1). **Save:** Rivera, NY (2).
2B: Oakland—Damon, Long; New York—Jeter. **HR:** New York—Justice (1). **RBI:** Oakland—Ja Giambi 2 (2), Je. Giambi (2); New York—Soriano 2 (3), Jeter (1), Justice (1). **SB:** Oakland—Je. Giambi (1); New York—Posada (1), Knoblauch (1). **CS:** New York—Knoblauch, B. Williams. **E:** Oakland—Myers, Chavez, Ja. Giambi; New York—Brosius.
Attendance: 56,642. **Time:** 3:23.

Mariners, 3-2

Date	Winner	Home Field
Oct. 9	Indians, 5-0	at Seattle
Oct. 11	Mariners, 5-1	at Seattle
Oct. 13	Indians, 17-2	at Cleveland
Oct. 14	Mariners, 6-2	at Cleveland
Oct. 15	Mariners, 3-1	at Seattle

Game 1
Tuesday, Oct. 9, at Seattle

	1 2 3	4 5 6	7 8 9	R H E
Cleveland	0 0 0	3 0 1	0 1 0	5 11 1
Seattle	0 0 0	0 0 0	0 0 0	0 6 1

Win: Colon, Cle. (1-0). **Loss:** Garcia, Sea. (0-1).
2B: Cleveland—Burks, Alomar; Seattle—Javier, Suzuki; **HR:** Cleveland—Burks (1). **RBI:** Cleveland—Gonzalez (1), Fryman (1), Cordova (1), Diaz (1), Burks (1). **SB:** Seattle—Martinez (1). **CS:** Seattle—Suzuki. **E:** Cleveland—Diaz; Seattle—Garcia.
Attendance: 48,033. **Time:** 3:05.

Game 2
Thursday, Oct. 11, at Seattle

	1 2 3	4 5 6	7 8 9	R H E
Cleveland	0 0 0	0 0 0	1 0 0	1 6 0
Seattle	4 0 0	0 1 0	0 0 x	5 6 0

Win: Moyer, Sea. (1-0). **Loss:** Finley, Cle. (0-1).
HR: Seattle—Cameron (1), Martinez (1), Bell (1). **RBI:** Seattle—Cameron 2 (2), Martinez 2 (2), Bell (1). **SB:** Seattle—Suzuki (1).
Attendance: 48,052. **Time:** 2:41.

Game 3
Saturday, Oct. 13, at Cleveland

	1 2 3	4 5 6	7 8 9	R H E
Seattle	1 0 0	0 0 0	1 0 0	2 9 3
Cleveland	2 2 4	0 1 3	0 5 x	17 19 0

Win: Sabathia, Cle. (1-0). **Loss:** Sele, Sea. (0-1).
2B: Seattle—Cameron 2, Wilson, Bell; Cleveland—Alomar 2, Gonzalez 2, Vizquel. **3B:** Cleveland—Vizquel. **HR:** Cleveland—Gonzalez (1), Lofton (1), Thome (1). **RBI:** Seattle—Olerud (1), Suzuki (1); Cleveland—Alomar 3 (3), Gonzalez 3 (4), Vizquel 6 (6), Diaz (2), Lofton 2 (2), Thome (1), Cabrera (1). **E:** Seattle—Suzuki, Boone, Buhner.
Attendance: 45,069. **Time:** 3:24.

Game 4
Sunday, Oct. 14, at Cleveland

	1 2 3	4 5 6	7 8 9	R H E
Seattle	0 0 0	0 0 0	3 1 2	6 11 0
Cleveland	0 1 0	0 0 0	1 0 0	2 5 2

Win: Garcia, Sea. (1-1). **Loss:** Colon, Cle. (1-1).
2B: Seattle—Martinez; Cleveland—Gonzalez. **HR:** Seattle—Martinez (2); Cleveland—Gonzalez (2). **RBI:** Seattle—Bell (2), Suzuki (2), McLemore (1), Cameron (3), Martinez 2 (4); Cleveland—Gonzalez (5), Fryman (2). **SB:** Seattle—Boone (1); Cleveland—Vizquel (1). **E:** Cleveland—Vizquel.
Attendance: 45,025. **Time:** 3:16.

Game 5
Monday, Oct. 15, at Seattle

	1 2 3	4 5 6	7 8 9	R H E
Cleveland	0 0 1	0 0 0	0 0 0	1 4 0
Seattle	0 2 0	0 0 1	0 x	3 9 1

Win: Moyer, Sea. (2-0). **Loss:** Finley, Cle. (0-2). **Save:** Sasaki (1).
2B: Cleveland—Fryman. **RBI:** Cleveland—Lofton (3); Seattle—McLemore 2 (3), Martinez (5). **CS:** Seattle—Suzuki, Cameron. **E:** Seattle—McLemore.
Attendance: 47,867. **Time:** 3:18.

Divisional Series Summaries (Cont.)
NATIONAL LEAGUE

Diamondbacks, 3-2

Date	Winner	Home Field
Oct. 9	Diamondbacks, 1-0	at Arizona
Oct. 10	Cardinals, 4-1	at Arizona
Oct. 12	Diamondbacks, 5-3	at St. Louis
Oct. 13	Cardinals, 4-1	at St. Louis
Oct. 14	Diamondbacks, 2-1	at Arizona

Game 1
Tuesday, Oct. 9, at Arizona

	1 2 3	4 5 6	7 8 9	R H E
St. Louis	0 0 0	0 0 0	0 0 0 -	0 3 1
Arizona	0 0 0	0 1 0	0 0 x -	1 8 1

Win: Schilling, Ari. (1-0). **Loss:** Morris, St. L (0-1).
2B: St. Louis—Renteria, Edmonds; Arizona—Finley, Sanders, Grace. **RBI:** Arizona—Finley (1). **E:** St. Louis—Pujols; Arizona—Womack.
Attendance: 42,251. **Time:** 2:36.

Game 2
Wednesday, Oct. 10, at Arizona

	1 2 3	4 5 6	7 8 9	R H E
St. Louis	2 0 1	0 0 0	0 0 1 -	4 7 0
Arizona	0 0 0	0 0 0	0 1 0 -	1 5 2

Win: Williams, St. L (1-0). **Loss:** Johnson, Ari. (0-1). **Save:** Kline, St. L (1).
2B: St. Louis—Williams. **HR:** St. Louis—Pujols (1). **RBI:** St. Louis—Pujols 2 (2), Polanco (1), Robinson (1); Arizona—Bautista (1). **E:** Arizona—Williams, Batista.
Attendance: 41,793. **Time:** 3:15.

Game 3
Friday, Oct. 12, at St. Louis

	1 2 3	4 5 6	7 8 9	R H E
Arizona	0 0 0	0 0 1	4 0 0 -	5 9 0
St. Louis	0 0 0	2 0 0	1 0 0 -	3 6 0

Win: Batista, Ari. (1-0). **Loss:** Matthews, St. L (0-1). **Save:** Kim, Ari. (1)
HR: Arizona—Gonzalez (1), Counsell (1); St. Louis—Edmonds (1), Renteria (1). **RBI:** Arizona—Gonzalez (1), Colbrunn (1), Counsell 3 (3); St. Louis—Edmonds 2 (2), Renteria (1); **SB:** St. Louis—Polanco (1), Cairo (1). **CS:** Arizona—Womack.
Attendance: 52,273. **Time:** 3:36.

Game 4
Saturday, Oct. 13, at St. Louis

	1 2 3	4 5 6	7 8 9	R H E
Arizona	1 0 0	0 0 0	0 0 0 -	1 6 0
St. Louis	0 0 0	0 0 0	0 0 x -	4 7 1

Win: Smith, St. L (1-0). **Loss:** Lopez, Ari. (0-1). **Save:** Kline, St. L (2)
2B: Arizona—Womack. **HR:** St. Louis—Edmonds (2), Vina (1). **RBI:** Arizona—Finley (2); St. Louis—Drew (1), Edmonds (3), Vina 2 (2). **SB:** Arizona—Sanders (1); St. Louis—Vina (1). **E:** St. Louis—Polanco.
Attendance: 52,194. **Time:** 2:47.

Game 5
Sunday, Oct. 14, at Arizona

	1 2 3	4 5 6	7 8 9	R H E
St. Louis	0 0 0	0 0 0	0 1 0 -	1 6 1
Arizona	0 0 0	1 0 0	0 0 1 -	2 9 1

Win: Schilling, Ari. (1-0). **Loss:** Kline, St. L (0-1).
2B: Arizona—Williams. **HR:** St. Louis—Drew (1); Arizona—Sanders (1). **RBI:** St. Louis—Drew (2); Arizona—Sanders (1), Womack (1). **CS:** Arizona—Cummings. **E:** St. Louis—Renteria; Arizona—Womack.
Attendance: 42,810. **Time:** 3:05.

Braves, 3-0

Date	Winner	Home Field
Oct. 9	Braves, 7-4	at Houston
Oct. 10	Braves, 1-0	at Houston
Oct. 12	Braves, 6-2	at Atlanta

Game 1
Tuesday, Oct. 9, at Houston

	1 2 3	4 5 6	7 8 9	R H E
Atlanta	1 0 0	1 0 0	0 4 1 -	7 13 1
Houston	0 0 0	0 2 1	0 0 1 -	4 6 1

Win: Seanez, Atl. (1-0). **Loss:** Jackson, Hou. (0-1). **Save:** Smoltz, Atl. (1).
2B: Atlanta—Lockhart, Torrealba. **HR:** Atlanta—Jordan (1), C. Jones (1), A. Jones (1); Houston—Ausmus (1), Castilla (1). **RBI:** Atlanta—B Jordan 2 (2), Giles (1), C. Jones 3 (3), A. Jones (1); Houston—Ausmus 2 (2), Alou (1), Castilla (1). **CS:** Atlanta—C. Jones, Franco. **E:** Atlanta—Sanchez; Houston—Lugo.
Attendance: 35,553. **Time:** 2:51.

Game 2
Wednesday, Oct. 10, at Houston

	1 2 3	4 5 6	7 8 9	R H E
Atlanta	0 1 0	0 0 0	0 0 0 -	1 7 0
Houston	0 0 0	0 0 0	0 0 0 -	0 7 2

Win: Glavine, Atl. (1-0). **Loss:** Mlicki, Hou. (0-1). **Save:** Smoltz, Atl. (2).
2B: Atlanta—Surhoff, Giles. **SB:** Atlanta—Surhoff (1). **CS:** Houston—Bagwell. **E:** Houston—Lugo 2.
Attendance: 35,704. **Time:** 2:41.

Game 3
Friday, Oct. 12, at Atlanta

	1 2 3	4 5 6	7 8 9	R H E
Houston	0 0 0	0 0 0	2 0 0 -	2 6 0
Atlanta	0 2 1	1 0 0	0 2 x -	6 10 0

Win: Burkett, Atl. (1-0). **Loss:** Reynolds, Hou. (0-1).
2B: Houston—Eusebio, Alou; Atlanta—Sanchez, Bako. **HR:** Houston—Ward (1); Atlanta—Bako (1), Franco (1), C. Jones (2). **RBI:** Houston—Ward 2 (2); Atlanta—Bako 3 (3), Franco (1), C. Jones 2 (5). **CS:** Atlanta—Jordan.
Attendance: 39,923. **Time:** 2:33.

American League Championship Series

Yankees, 4-1

Date	Winner	Home Field
Oct. 17	Yankees, 4-2	at Seattle
Oct. 18	Yankees, 3-2	at Seattle
Oct. 20	Mariners, 14-3	at New York
Oct. 21	Yankees, 3-1	at New York
Oct. 22	Yankees, 12-3	at New York

Most Valuable Player
Andy Pettitte, New York, P

ERA	W-L	IP	H	R	ER	BB	K
2.51	2-0	14.1	11	4	4	2	8

Game 1

Wednesday, Oct. 17, at Seattle

	1 2 3	4 5 6	7 8 9	R	H	E
New York	0 1 0	2 0 0	0 0 1	4	9	0
Seattle	0 0 0	0 0 1	0 0 1	2	4	0

Win: Pettitte, NY (1-1). **Loss:** Sele, Sea. (0-2). **Save:** Rivera, NY (3).
2B: New York—Posada, Knoblauch; Seattle—Cameron, Suzuki. **HR:** New York—O'Neill (1). **RBI:** New York—O'Neill 2 (2), Knoblauch (2), Justice (2); Seattle—Olerud (2). **SB:** New York—Soriano (3).
Attendance: 47,644. **Time:** 3:06.

Game 2

Thursday, Oct. 18, at Seattle

	1 2 3	4 5 6	7 8 9	R	H	E
New York	0 3 0	0 0 0	0 0 0	3	9	1
Seattle	0 0 0	2 0 0	0 0 0	2	6	0

Win: Mussina, NY (2-0). **Loss:** Garcia, Sea. (1-2). **Save:** Rivera, NY (4).
2B: New York—Brosius, Spencer. **HR:** Seattle—Javier (1). **RBI:** New York—Brosius 2 (3), Knoblauch (3); Seattle—Javier 2 (2). **SB:** New York—Spencer (1). **CS:** New York—Knoblauch, Martinez. **E:** New York—B. Williams.
Attendance: 47,791. **Time:** 3:25.

Game 3

Saturday, Oct. 20, at New York

	1 2 3	4 5 6	7 8 9	R	H	E
Seattle	0 0 0	0 2 7	2 1 2	14	15	0
New York	2 0 0	0 0 0	0 1 0	3	7	2

Win: Moyer, Sea. (3-0). **Loss:** Hernandez, NY (1-1).

Game 4

Sunday, Oct. 21, at New York

	1 2 3	4 5 6	7 8 9	R	H	E
Seattle	0 0 0	0 0 0	0 1 0	1	2	0
New York	0 0 0	0 0 0	0 1 2	3	4	0

Win: Rivera, NY (1-0). **Loss:** Sasaki, Sea. (0-1).
2B: New York—Martinez. **HR:** Seattle—Boone (2); New York—B. Williams (3), Soriano (1). **RBI:** Seattle—Boone (6); New York—Soriano 2 (5), B. Williams (8). **SB:** Seattle—Suzuki (3); New York—Soriano (4). **CS:** New York—B. Williams.
Attendance: 56,375. **Time:** 3:24.

Game 5

Monday, Oct. 22, at New York

	1 2 3	4 5 6	7 8 9	R	H	E
Seattle	0 0 0	0 0 0	3 0 0	3	9	1
New York	1 0 4	1 0 4	0 3 x	12	13	1

Win: Pettitte, NY (2-1). **Loss:** Sele, Sea. (0-3).
2B: Seattle—Cameron; New York—Justice, Brosius. **HR:** New York—B. Williams (4), O'Neill (2), Martinez (2). **RBI:** Seattle—Bell 2 (6), Suzuki (3); New York—Martinez 3 (5), Jeter 2 (3), Justice 2 (5), B. Williams 2 (10), O'Neill (3), Knoblauch (4). **E:** Seattle—Bell; New York—Soriano.
Attendance: 56,370. **Time:** 3:18.

Top-right continuation:
2B: Seattle—Martinez. **3B:** Seattle—McLemore, Martin. **HR:** Seattle—Olerud (1), Boone (1), Buhner (1); New York—B. Williams (1). **RBI:** Seattle—Boone 5 (5), McLemore 3 (6), Olerud 2 (4), Bell 2 (4), Buhner (1); New York—B. Williams 2 (7), Justice (3). **SB:** Seattle—Suzuki (2), Javier (1). **E:** New York—Stanton, Wohlers.
Attendance: 56,517. **Time:** 3:49.

ALCS Composite Box Score
New York Yankees

Batting		LCS vs. Seattle								Overall AL Playoffs						
	Avg	AB	R	H	HR	RBI	BB	SO	Avg	AB	R	H	HR	RBI	BB	SO
Enrique Wilson	1.000	1	0	1	0	0	0	0	1.000	1	0	1	0	0	0	0
Paul O'Neill	.417	12	2	5	2	3	1	0	.261	23	3	6	2	3	1	0
Alfonso Soriano	.400	15	5	6	1	2	3	3	.303	33	7	10	1	5	4	8
Chuck Knoblauch	.333	18	0	6	0	3	2	3	.300	40	1	12	0	4	2	3
Shane Spencer	.286	7	1	2	0	0	1	1	.267	15	2	4	0	0	2	5
David Justice	.278	18	3	5	0	4	3	1	.258	31	6	8	1	5	5	6
Tino Martinez	.250	20	3	5	1	3	0	4	.184	38	4	7	2	5	1	10
Bernie Williams	.235	17	4	4	3	5	4	3	.229	35	8	8	3	10	8	7
Jorge Posada	.214	14	4	3	0	0	6	7	.344	32	7	11	1	2	8	9
Scott Brosius	.188	16	3	3	0	2	0	6	.121	33	3	4	0	3	0	9
Derek Jeter	.118	17	0	2	0	2	2	2	.286	35	2	10	0	3	3	2
Clay Bellinger	.000	1	0	0	0	0	0	0	.000	1	0	0	0	0	0	0
Randy Velarde	.000	1	0	0	0	0	0	1	.167	6	0	1	0	0	0	1
Todd Greene	.000	1	0	0	0	0	0	0	.000	1	0	0	0	0	0	0
Luis Sojo	.000	1	0	0	0	0	0	0	.000	1	0	0	0	0	0	0
TOTALS	.264	159	25	42	7	24	23	31	.252	325	43	82	10	40	34	60

Pitching	ERA	W-L	SV	Gm	IP	H	BB	SO	ERA	W-L	Sv	Gm	IP	H	BB	SO
Roger Clemens	0.00	0-0	0	1	5.0	1	4	7	3.38	0-1	0	3	13.1	10	8	13
Ramiro Mendoza	1.69	0-0	0	3	5.1	3	2	4	0.98	0-0	0	6	9.2	5	3	9
Mariano Rivera	1.93	1-0	2	4	4.2	2	1	3	0.98	1-0	4	7	9.2	6	1	7
Andy Pettitte	2.51	2-0	0	2	14.1	11	2	8	2.18	2-1	0	3	20.2	18	4	12
Mike Mussina	3.00	1-0	0	1	6.0	4	1	3	1.38	2-0	0	2	13.0	8	2	7
Orlando Hernandez	7.20	0-1	0	1	5.0	5	5	7	5.06	1-1	0	2	10.2	13	7	12
Jay Witasick	9.00	0-0	0	1	3.0	6	0	2	9.82	0-0	0	2	3.2	7	1	2
Mark Wohlers	13.50	0-0	0	1	0.2	3	1	1	13.50	0-0	0	1	0.2	3	1	1
Mike Stanton	27.00	0-0	0	2	1.0	1	2	0	4.76	0-0	0	5	5.2	4	2	1
Sterling Hitchcock	—	0-0	0	0	0.0	0	0	0	6.00	0-0	0	1	3.0	5	0	2
TOTALS	3.80	4-1	2	5	45.0	36	18	35	3.00	7-3	4	10	90.0	79	29	66

Wild Pitches— LCS (Rivera 2, Clemens); OVERALL (Rivera 2, Clemens 2, Hernandez). **Hit Batters—** LCS (Mussina); OVERALL (Clemens 2, Hernandez, Mussina).

ALCS Composite Box Score (Cont.)
Seattle Mariners

Batting		LCS vs New York								Overall AL Playoffs						
	Avg	AB	R	H	HR	RBI	BB	SO	Avg	AB	R	H	HR	RBI	BB	SO
Al Martin	.500	2	1	1	0	0	0	0	.250	4	2	1	0	0	0	0
Jay Buhner	.333	6	2	2	1	1	1	3	.222	9	2	2	1	1	3	4
Bret Boone	.316	19	2	6	2	6	2	2	.200	40	3	8	2	6	3	13
Tom Lampkin	.250	4	0	1	0	0	1	2	.167	6	0	1	0	0	1	4
Carlos Guillen	.250	8	1	2	0	0	0	1	.250	8	1	2	0	0	0	1
Ichiro Suzuki	.222	18	3	4	0	1	4	4	.421	38	7	16	0	3	5	4
Stan Javier	.214	14	2	3	1	2	1	3	.227	22	4	5	1	2	3	4
John Olerud	.211	19	2	4	1	3	2	4	.194	36	3	7	1	4	5	9
David Bell	.188	16	1	3	0	4	0	3	.250	32	3	8	1	6	1	9
Mike Cameron	.176	17	3	3	0	0	4	4	.200	35	5	7	1	3	6	11
Dan Wilson	.154	13	2	2	0	0	0	1	.179	28	2	5	0	0	0	6
Edgar Martinez	.150	20	1	3	0	0	1	6	.222	36	4	8	2	5	6	8
Mark McLemore	.143	14	1	2	0	3	2	2	.156	32	1	5	0	6	3	10
Charles Gipson	.000	1	1	0	0	0	0	0	.000	2	1	0	0	0	0	0
Ed Sprague	—	0	0	0	0	0	0	0	.000	1	0	0	0	0	0	0
Ramon Vazquez	—	0	0	0	0	0	0	0	.000	0	0	0	0	0	0	0
TOTALS	.211	171	22	36	5	20	18	35	.228	329	38	75	9	36	36	83

Pitching																
	ERA	W-L	Sv	Gm	IP	H	BB	SO	ERA	W-L	Sv	Gm	IP	H	BB	SO
Norm Charlton	0.00	0-0	0	2	1.2	1	2	2	0.00	0-0	0	3	3.1	1	2	4
Paul Abbott	0.00	0-0	0	1	5.0	0	8	2	9.00	0-0	0	2	8.0	9	3	13
Jeff Nelson	0.00	0-0	0	2	2.1	1	1	3	0.00	0-0	0	5	5.1	2	2	8
Jamie Moyer	2.57	1-0	0	1	7.0	4	1	5	1.89	3-0	0	3	19.0	12	3	15
Aaron Sele	3.60	0-2	0	2	10.0	11	4	5	4.50	0-3	0	3	12.0	16	4	5
Freddy Garcia	3.68	0-1	0	1	7.1	7	4	6	3.79	1-2	0	3	19.0	20	7	19
Arthur Rhodes	4.50	0-0	0	2	2.0	2	0	2	1.93	0-0	0	4	4.2	3	0	3
Joel Pineiro	4.50	0-0	0	1	2.0	4	2	5	4.50	0-0	0	1	2.0	4	2	5
Jose Paniagua	12.27	0-0	0	3	3.2	7	1	1	17.47	0-0	0	5	5.2	11	3	2
John Halama	13.50	0-0	0	2	2.0	3	0	0	5.40	0-0	0	4	5.0	6	0	3
Kazuhiro Sasaki	54.00	0-1	0	1	0.1	2	0	0	5.40	0-1	1	4	3.1	3	0	5
TOTALS	4.36	1-4	0	5	43.1	42	23	31	4.53	4-6	1	10	87.1	87	36	74

Wild Pitches— LCS (Pineiro, Paniagua); OVERALL (Pineiro, Paniagua, Rhodes). **Hit Batters—**LCS (Moyer, Sele); OVERALL (Moyer, Sele, Paniagua).

Score by Innings

	1	2	3	4	5	6	7	8	9		R	H	E
New York	2	4	4	3	0	4	0	5	3	—	25	42	4
Seattle	0	0	0	2	3	7	5	2	3	—	22	36	1

E: New York— Soriano, Stanton, B. Williams, Wohlers; Seattle— Bell. **DP:** New York 4, Seattle 5. **2B:** New York— Brosius 2, Justice, Knoblauch, T. Martinez, Posada, Spencer; Seattle— Cameron 2, E. Martinez, Suzuki. **3B:** Seattle— Martin, McLemore. **SB:** New York— Soriano 2, Spencer; Seattle— Suzuki 2, Javier. **CS:** New York— Knoblauch, T. Martinez, B. Williams. **S:** New York— Brosius 2, Jeter, Knoblauch; Seattle— Bell. **SF:** New York— Jeter. **HBP:** by Mussina (Cameron), by Moyer (Justice), by Sele (Soriano). **LOB:** New York— 34; Seattle— 34.
Umpires: Ed Montague, Wally Bell, Gary Cederstrom, Charlie Reliford, John Shulock, Tim Welke.

National League Championship Series

Diamondbacks, 4-1

Date	Winner	Home Field
Oct. 16	Diamondbacks, 2-0	at Arizona
Oct. 17	Braves, 8-1	at Arizona
Oct. 19	Diamondbacks, 5-1	at Atlanta
Oct. 20	Diamondbacks, 11-4	at Atlanta
Oct. 21	Diamondbacks, 3-2	at Atlanta

Most Valuable Player
Craig Counsell, Arizona, 2B

AVG	AB	R	H	HR	RBI	SB
.381	21	5	8	0	4	1

Game 1
Tuesday, Oct. 16, at Arizona

	1 2 3	4 5 6	7 8 9	R H E
Atlanta	0 0 0	0 0 0	0 0 0	- 0 3 1
Arizona	1 0 0	0 1 0	0 0 0	- 2 8 0

Win: Johnson, Ari. (1-1). **Loss:** Maddux, Atl. (1-1).
2B: Arizona—Counsell. **RBI:** Arizona—Sanders (2), Gonzalez (2). **E:** Atlanta—Giles.
Attendance: 37,729. **Time:** 2:44.

Game 2
Wednesday, Oct. 17, at Arizona

	1 2 3	4 5 6	7 8 9	R H E
Atlanta	1 0 0	0 0 0	2 5 0	- 8 8 0
Arizona	0 0 0	0 0 1	0 0 0	- 1 5 1

Win: Glavine, Atl. (2-0). **Loss:** Batista, Ari. (1-1).
2B: Atlanta—Jordan. **HR:** Atlanta—Giles (1), Lopez (1), Surhoff (1). **RBI:** Atlanta—Lopez 2 (2), Jordan 2 (4), Surhoff 2 (2), Giles (2), Sanchez (1); Arizona—Williams (1). **E:** Arizona—Williams.
Attendance: 49,334. **Time:** 2:54.

Game 3
Friday, Oct. 19, at Atlanta

	1 2 3	4 5 6	7 8 9	R H E
Arizona	0 0 2	0 3 0	0 0 0 -	5 9 1
Atlanta	0 0 0	1 0 0	0 0 0 -	1 4 1

Win: Schilling, Ari. (3-0). **Loss:** Burkett, Atl. (1-1).
2B: Arizona—Williams, Finley; Atlanta—Giles, Jordan.
RBI: Arizona—Finley 3 (5); Atlanta—C. Jones (6). **SB:** Arizona—Counsell (1). **CS:** Atlanta—Surhoff. **E:** Arizona—Williams; Atlanta—Lopez.
Attendance: 41,624. **Time:** 2:59.

Game 4
Saturday, Oct. 20, at Atlanta

	1 2 3	4 5 6	7 8 9	R H E
Arizona	0 0 4	2 0 0	0 1 4 -	11 12 0
Atlanta	1 1 0	0 0 0	1 1 0 -	4 13 4

Win: Anderson, Ari. (1-0). **Loss:** Maddux, Atl. (0-2). **Save:** Kim, Ari. (2).

2B: Arizona—Counsell 2, Womack; Atlanta—C. Jones, Maddux, Sanchez. **HR:** Arizona—Gonzalez (2); Atlanta—A. Jones (2). **RBI:** Arizona—Counsell 4 (7), Gonzalez 3 (5), Finley (6), Williams (2), Grace (1); Atlanta—C. Jones (7), A. Jones (2), Jordan (5). **SB:** Arizona—Sanders (2), Finley (1). **CS:** Arizona—Womack. **E:** Atlanta—Sanchez 2, C. Jones, Maddux.
Attendance: 42,291. **Time:** 3:47.

Game 5
Sunday, Oct. 21, at Atlanta

	1 2 3	4 5 6	7 8 9	R H E
Arizona	0 0 0	1 2 0	0 0 0 -	3 6 1
Atlanta	0 0 0	1 0 0	1 0 0 -	2 7 1

Win: Johnson, Ari. (2-1). **Loss:** Glavine, Atl. (2-1). **Save:** Kim, Ari. (3).
HR: Arizona—Durazo (1); Atlanta—Franco (2). **RBI:** Arizona—Durazo 2 (2), Bautista (2); Atlanta—Franco 2 (3). **E:** Arizona—Williams; Atlanta—Giles.
Attendance: 35,652. **Time:** 3:13.

NLCS Composite Box Score
Atlanta Braves

Batting		LCS vs Arizona							Overall NL Playoffs						
	Avg	AB	R	H	HR	RBI	BB	SO	Avg	AB	R	H	HR	RBI	BB	SO
Greg Maddux	.333	3	0	1	0	0	0	2	.200	5	0	1	0	0	0	3
Rey Sanchez	.294	17	1	5	0	1	0	4	.269	26	2	7	0	1	0	6
Chipper Jones	.263	19	1	5	0	2	3	6	.321	28	3	9	2	7	6	7
Julio Franco	.261	23	2	6	1	2	0	2	.278	36	5	10	2	3	0	3
B.J. Surhoff	.231	13	1	3	1	2	0	1	.250	24	2	6	1	2	0	1
Dave Martinez	.200	5	0	1	0	0	0	1	.167	6	0	1	0	0	0	1
Bernard Gilkey	.200	5	0	1	0	0	2	1	.200	5	0	1	0	0	2	1
Marcus Giles	.200	20	4	4	1	1	3	4	.219	32	6	7	1	2	3	7
Brian Jordan	.190	21	1	4	0	3	1	6	.188	32	2	6	1	5	0	11
Andruw Jones	.176	17	4	3	1	1	1	5	.310	29	6	9	2	2	1	8
Javy Lopez	.143	14	1	2	1	2	1	4	.143	14	1	2	1	2	1	4
John Burkett	.000	1	0	0	0	0	0	0	.000	3	0	0	0	0	0	2
Keith Lockhart	.000	1	0	0	0	0	1	0	.333	3	1	1	0	0	1	0
Paul Bako	.000	3	0	0	0	0	0	0	.200	10	1	2	1	3	1	0
Tom Glavine	.000	3	0	0	0	0	0	0	.167	6	0	1	0	0	0	2
Mark DeRosa	.000	4	0	0	0	0	0	0	.200	5	0	1	0	0	0	0
Steve Torrealba	—	0	0	0	0	0	0	0	1.000	1	0	1	0	0	0	0
John Smoltz	—	0	0	0	0	0	0	0	.000	1	0	0	0	0	0	0
Ken Caminiti	—	0	0	0	0	0	0	0	.000	2	0	0	0	0	0	1
TOTALS	.207	169	15	35	5	14	11	39	.243	268	29	65	11	27	15	57

Pitching	ERA	W-L	Sv	Gm	IP	H	BB	SO	ERA	W-L	Sv	Gm	IP	H	BB	SO
John Smoltz	0.00	0-0	0	2	3.0	0	0	1	1.29	0-0	2	5	7.0	3	0	4
Rudy Seanez	0.00	0-0	0	2	2.0	1	3	3	0.00	1-0	0	3	3.0	1	4	3
Mike Remlinger	0.00	0-0	0	3	2.1	3	2	2	0.00	0-0	0	4	2.2	3	2	2
Steve Reed	0.00	0-0	0	1	0.0	0	0	0	0.00	0-0	0	2	0.1	0	0	0
Kevin Millwood	0.00	0-0	0	1	1.0	0	0	1	0.00	0-0	0	1	1.0	0	0	1
Kerry Ligtenberg	0.00	0-0	0	2	3.0	0	1	2	0.00	0-0	0	2	3.0	0	1	2
Jason Marquis	0.00	0-0	0	2	2.0	2	3	3	0.00	0-0	0	2	2.0	2	3	3
Tom Glavine	1.50	1-1	0	2	12.0	10	5	5	0.90	2-1	0	3	20.0	16	7	8
Steve Karsay	2.08	0-0	0	4	4.1	3	1	6	1.69	0-0	0	5	5.1	3	1	7
Greg Maddux	5.40	0-2	0	2	10.0	14	2	7	4.50	0-2	0	3	16.0	18	5	12
John Burkett	8.31	0-1	0	1	4.1	7	2	2	5.06	1-1	0	2	10.2	13	4	6
TOTALS	2.66	1-4	0	5	44.0	40	18	32	2.28	4-4	2	8	71.0	59	26	48

Wild Pitches—LCS (Karsay, Glavine); OVERALL (Karsay, Glavine). **Hit Batters**—LCS (Maddux); OVERALL (Maddux).

NLCS Composite Box Score (Cont.)
Arizona Diamondbacks

Batting	Avg	AB	R	H	HR	RBI	BB	SO	Avg	AB	R	H	HR	RBI	BB	SO
									Overall NL Playoffs							
		LCS vs Atlanta														
David Dellucci	.500	2	1	1	0	0	0	0	.500	2	1	1	0	0	0	0
Craig Counsell	.381	21	5	8	0	4	0	3	.297	37	7	11	1	7	2	5
Mark Grace	.375	16	1	6	0	1	2	1	.300	30	1	9	0	1	4	4
Erubiel Durazo	.333	3	1	1	1	2	0	1	.250	4	1	1	1	2	0	1
Steve Finley	.286	14	1	4	0	4	3	1	.364	33	2	12	0	6	3	3
Matt Williams	.278	18	1	5	0	2	2	3	.176	34	1	6	0	2	6	7
Curt Schilling	.250	4	1	1	0	0	0	2	.111	9	1	1	0	0	0	4
Danny Bautista	.250	4	1	1	0	1	1	1	.100	10	2	1	0	2	1	2
Luis Gonzalez	.211	19	4	4	1	4	3	3	.237	38	5	9	2	5	5	7
Tony Womack	.200	20	4	4	0	0	0	2	.243	37	5	9	0	1	3	4
Damian Miller	.176	17	0	3	0	0	2	5	.219	32	1	7	0	0	3	8
Reggie Sanders	.118	17	2	2	0	1	5	5	.226	31	4	7	1	2	8	8
Randy Johnson	.000	6	0	0	0	0	0	0	.000	8	0	0	0	0	0	4
Miguel Batista	.000	2	0	0	0	0	0	1	.000	3	0	0	0	0	0	1
Albie Lopez	.000	1	0	0	0	0	0	1	.000	1	0	0	0	0	0	1
Brian Anderson	.000	1	0	0	0	0	0	0	.000	1	0	0	0	0	0	0
Midre Cummings	.000	1	0	0	0	0	0	0	.000	1	1	0	0	0	0	0
Jay Bell	.000	4	0	0	0	0	0	0	.125	8	0	1	0	0	0	1
Greg Colbrunn	.000	1	0	0	0	0	0	0	.286	7	0	2	0	1	1	0
Byung-Hyun Kim	.000	1	0	0	0	0	0	0	.000	1	0	0	0	0	0	0
TOTALS	.233	172	22	40	2	19	18	32	.235	328	32	77	5	29	36	61

Pitching	ERA	W-L	Sv	Gm	IP	H	BB	SO	ERA	W-L	Sv	Gm	IP	H	BB	SO
Byung-Hyun Kim	0.00	0-0	2	3	5.0	0	1	3	0.00	0-0	3	4	6.1	1	3	4
Curt Schilling	1.00	1-0	0	1	9.0	4	2	12	0.67	3-0	0	3	27.0	13	4	30
Randy Johnson	1.12	2-0	0	2	16.0	10	3	19	1.88	2-1	0	3	24.0	16	5	28
Brian Anderson	2.70	1-0	0	1	3.1	4	1	0	2.45	1-0	0	3	7.1	7	1	3
Miguel Batista	5.14	0-1	0	2	7.0	5	2	3	3.95	1-1	0	4	13.2	8	3	7
Albie Lopez	6.00	0-0	0	1	3.0	5	1	1	9.00	0-1	0	2	6.0	9	4	1
Mike Morgan	27.00	0-0	0	2	1.0	3	1	1	15.43	0-0	0	5	2.1	5	3	2
Bobby Witt	27.00	0-0	0	1	0.1	3	0	0	27.00	0-0	0	1	0.1	3	0	0
Greg Swindell	27.00	0-0	0	2	0.1	1	0	0	4.50	0-0	0	4	2.0	2	0	2
TOTALS	3.00	4-1	2	5	45.0	35	11	39	2.73	7-3	3	10	89.0	64	23	77

Wild Pitches—LCS (none); OVERALL (Kim). **Hit Batters**—LCS (none); OVERALL (Anderson).

Score by Innings

	1	2	3	4	5	6	7	8	9		R	H	E
Atlanta	2	1	0	2	0	0	4	6	0	–	15	35	7
Arizona	1	0	6	3	6	1	0	1	4	–	22	40	3

E: Atlanta—Giles 2, Sanchez 2, C. Jones, Lopez, Maddux; Arizona—Williams 3. **DP:** Atlanta 5, Arizona 3. **2B:** Atlanta—Jordan 2, Giles, C. Jones, Maddux, Sanchez; Arizona—Counsell 3, Finley, Williams, Womack. **SB:** Arizona—Counsell, Finley, Sanders. **CS:** Atlanta— Surhoff; Arizona—Womack. **S:** Arizona—Counsell 2. **PB:** Atlanta—Bako. **HBP:** by Maddux (Gonzalez). **LOB:** Atlanta—30; Arizona—39.
Umpires: Jerry Crawford, Jeff Kellogg, Angel Hernandez, Mike Reilly, Gerry Davis, Tim McClelland.

WORLD SERIES

Diamondbacks, 4-3

Date	Winner	Home Field
Oct. 27	Diamondbacks, 9-1	at Arizona
Oct. 28	Diamondbacks, 4-0	at Arizona
Oct. 30	Yankees, 2-1	at New York
Oct. 31	Yankees, 4-3 (10 inn.)	at New York
Nov. 1	Yankees, 3-2 (12 inn.)	at New York
Nov. 3	Diamondbacks, 15-2	at Arizona
Nov. 4	Diamondbacks, 3-2	at Arizona

Game 1
Saturday, Oct. 27, at Bank One Ballpark

	1	2	3	4	5	6	7	8	9		R	H	E
New York	1	0	0	0	0	0	0	0	0	–	1	3	2
Arizona	1	0	4	4	0	0	0	0	x	–	9	10	0

Win: Schilling, Ari. (1-0). **Loss:** Mussina, NY (0-1).
2B: New York—B. Williams, Brosius; Arizona—Miller, Gonzalez, Grace. **HR:** Arizona—Counsell (1), Gonzalez (1). **RBI:** New York—B. Williams (1); Arizona—Counsell (1), Gonzalez 2 (2), Williams (1), Miller (1), Finley (1), Grace 2 (2). **S:** Arizona—Counsell. **SF:** Arizona—Williams. **HBP:** by Schilling (Jeter), by Mussina (Womack). **E:** New York—Justice, Brosius.
Attendance: 49,646. **Time:** 2:44.

Co-Most Valuable Players
Randy Johnson, Arizona, P

ERA	W-L	IP	H	R	ER	BB	K
1.04	3-0	17.1	9	2	2	3	19

Curt Schilling, Arizona, P

ERA	W-L	IP	H	R	ER	BB	K
1.69	1-0	21.1	12	4	4	2	26

Game 2
Sunday, Oct. 28, at Bank One Ballpark

```
                1 2 3  4 5 6  7 8 9    R H E
New York.....0 0 0  0 0 0  0 0 0 – 0 3 0
Arizona.......0 1 0  0 0 0  3 0 x – 4 5 0
```

Win: Johnson, Ari. (1-0). **Loss:** Pettitte, NY (0-1).
2B: Arizona—Bautista. **HR:** Arizona—Williams (1). **RBI:** Arizona—Bautista (1), Williams 3 (4). **BB:** New York—Velarde. **HBP:** by Pettitte (Gonzalez).
Attendance: 49,646. **Time:** 2:35.

Game 3
Tuesday, Oct. 30 at Yankee Stadium

```
                1 2 3  4 5 6  7 8 9    R H E
Arizona.......0 0 0  1 0 0  0 0 0 – 1 3 3
New York.....0 1 0  0 0 1  0 0 x – 2 7 1
```

Win: Clemens, NY (1-0). **Loss:** Anderson, Ari. (0-1). **Save:** Rivera, NY (1).
HR: New York—Posada (1). **RBI:** Arizona—Williams (5); New York—Posada (1), Brosius (1). **BB:** Arizona—Finley 2, Durazo; New York—B. Williams, Posada, Spencer. **SF:** Arizona—Williams. **SB:** Arizona—Sanders (1); New York—O'Neill (1). **CS:** Arizona—Finley. **Picked Off:** Arizona—Counsell. **E:** Arizona—Womack, Miller, Grace; New York—Soriano. **HBP:** by Clemens (Sanders).
Attendance: 55,820. **Time:** 3:26.

Game 4
Wednesday, Oct. 31, at Yankee Stadium

```
                1 2 3  4 5 6  7 8 9 10    R H E
Arizona.....0 0 0  1 0 0  0 2 0 0 – 3 6 0
New York...0 0 1  0 0 0  0 0 2 1 – 4 7 0
```

Win: Rivera, NY (1-0). **Loss:** Kim, Ari. (0-1).
2B: Arizona—Womack, Durazo; New York—Brosius. **HR:** Arizona—Grace (1); New York—Spencer (1), Martinez (1), Jeter (1). **RBI:** Arizona—Grace (3), Durazo (1), Williams (6); New York—Spencer (1), Martinez 2 (2), Jeter (1). **BB:** Arizona—Womack, Gonzalez, Durazo, Grace; New York—Martinez, Posada. **S:** Arizona—Counsell 3. **HBP:** by Hernandez (Gonzalez, Miller).
Attendance: 55,863. **Time:** 3:31.

Game 5
Thursday, Nov. 1, at Yankee Stadium

```
              1 2 3 4 5 6 7 8 9 10 11 12    R H E
Arizona....0 0 0 0 2 0 0 0 0  0  0 – 2 8 0
New York...0 0 0 0 0 0 0 0 2  0  0  1 – 3 9 1
```

Win: Hitchcock, NY (1-0). **Loss:** Lopez, Ari. (0-1).
2B: New York—Posada. **HR:** Arizona—Finley (1), Barajas (1); New York—Brosius (1). **RBI:** Arizona—Finley (2), Barajas (1); New York—Brosius 2 (3), Soriano (1). **S:** Arizona—Williams; New York—Brosius. **BB:** Arizona—Grace 2, Durazo, Finley; New York—O'Neill 2, B. Williams, Spencer, Justice. **SB:** Arizona—Womack (1). **CS:** New York—Soriano. **E:** New York—Posada.
Attendance: 56,018. **Time:** 4:15.

Game 6
Saturday, Nov. 3, at Bank One Ballpark

```
                1 2 3  4 5 6  7 8 9    R H E
New York.....0 0 0  0 0 2  0 0 0 – 2 7 1
Arizona.......1 3 8  3 0 0  0 0 x – 15 22 0
```

Win: Johnson, Ari. (2-0). **Loss:** Pettitte, NY (0-2).
2B: New York—Greene; Arizona—Womack, Sanders, Williams 2, Gonzalez, Miller. **RBI:** New York—Spencer (2), Sojo (1); Arizona—Bautista 5 (6), Womack 2 (2), Sanders (1), Bell (1), Johnson (1), Gonzalez 2 (4), Colbrunn (1), Williams (7), Miller (1). **BB:** New York—B. Williams 2, Knoblauch; Arizona—Finley, Colbrunn, Miller. **E:** New York—Soriano.
Attendance: 49,707. **Time:** 3:33.

Game 7
Sunday, Nov. 4, at Bank One Ballpark

```
                1 2 3  4 5 6  7 8 9    R H E
New York.....0 0 0  0 0 0  1 1 0 – 2 6 3
Arizona.......0 0 0  0 0 1  0 0 2 – 3 11 0
```

Win: Johnson, Ari. (3-0). **Loss:** Rivera, NY (1-1).
2B: New York—O'Neill; Arizona—Bautista, Womack. **HR:** New York—Soriano (1). **RBI:** New York—Martinez (3), Soriano (2); Arizona—Bautista (7), Womack (3), Gonzalez (5). **BB:** Arizona—Bautista. **CS:** Arizona—Womack. **E:** New York—Clemens, Soriano, Rivera. **HBP:** by Rivera (Counsell).
Attendance: 49,589. **Time:** 3:20.

World Series Composite Box Score
New York Yankees

| Batting | WS vs Arizona | | | | | | | Overall Playoffs | | | | | | |
	Avg	AB	R	H	HR	RBI	BB	SO	Avg	AB	R	H	HR	RBI	BB	SO
Todd Greene.............	.500	2	1	1	0	0	0	0	.333	3	1	1	0	0	0	0
Andy Pettitte.............	.333	3	0	1	0	0	0	1	.333	3	0	1	0	0	0	1
Paul O'Neill.............	.333	15	1	5	0	0	2	2	.289	38	4	11	2	3	3	2
Luis Sojo..............	.333	3	0	1	0	1	0	0	.250	4	0	1	0	1	0	0
Alfonso Soriano..........	.240	25	1	6	1	2	0	7	.276	58	8	16	2	7	4	15
Bernie Williams..........	.208	24	2	5	0	1	4	6	.220	59	10	13	3	11	12	13
Shane Spencer..........	.200	20	1	4	1	2	2	6	.229	35	3	8	1	2	4	11
Tino Martinez..........	.190	21	1	4	1	3	2	2	.186	59	5	11	3	8	3	12
Jorge Posada..........	.174	23	2	4	1	1	3	8	.273	55	9	15	2	3	11	17
Scott Brosius..........	.167	24	1	4	1	3	0	8	.140	57	4	8	1	6	0	17
David Justice..........	.167	12	0	2	0	0	1	4	.233	43	6	10	1	5	6	15
Derek Jeter..........	.148	27	3	4	1	1	0	6	.226	62	5	14	1	4	3	8
Chuck Knoblauch........	.056	18	1	1	0	1	2	2	.224	58	2	13	0	4	3	5
Mike Mussina..........	.000	1	0	0	0	0	0	1	.000	1	0	0	0	0	0	1
Clay Bellinger..........	.000	2	0	0	0	0	0	2	.000	3	0	0	0	0	0	2
Roger Clemens..........	.000	2	0	0	0	0	0	1	.000	2	0	0	0	0	0	1
Randy Choate..........	.000	1	0	0	0	0	0	1	.000	1	0	0	0	0	0	1
Randy Velarde..........	.000	3	0	0	0	1	1	1	.111	9	0	1	0	1	2	1
Enrique Wilson..........	—	0	0	0	0	0	0	0	.250	4	0	1	0	0	0	0
TOTALS..................	.183	229	14	42	6	14	16	63	.224	554	57	124	16	54	50	123

Pitching	ERA	W-L	Sv	Gm	IP	H	BB	SO	ERA	W-L	Sv	Gm	IP	H	BB	SO
Sterling Hitchcock	0.00	1-0	0	2	4.0	1	0	6	2.57	1-0	0	3	7.0	6	0	8
Ramiro Mendoza	0.00	0-0	0	2	2.2	1	0	1	0.73	0-0	0	8	12.1	6	3	10
Roger Clemens	1.35	1-0	0	2	13.1	10	4	19	2.36	1-1	0	5	26.2	20	12	32
Orlando Hernandez	1.42	0-0	0	1	6.1	4	4	5	3.71	1-1	0	3	17.0	17	11	17
Mariano Rivera	1.42	1-1	1	4	6.1	6	1	7	1.69	2-1	5	11	16.0	12	2	14
Randy Choate	2.45	0-0	0	2	3.2	7	1	2	2.45	0-0	0	2	3.2	7	1	2
Mike Stanton	3.18	0-0	0	5	5.2	3	1	3	3.97	1-0	0	10	11.1	7	3	4
Mike Mussina	4.09	0-1	0	2	11.0	11	4	14	2.62	2-1	0	4	24.0	19	6	21
Andy Pettitte	10.00	0-2	0	2	9.0	12	2	9	4.55	2-3	0	5	29.2	30	6	21
Jay Witasick	54.00	0-0	0	1	1.1	10	0	4	21.60	0-0	0	3	5.0	17	1	6
Mark Wohlers	—	0-0	0	0	0.0	0	0	0	13.50	0-0	0	1	0.2	3	1	1
TOTALS	4.29	3-4	1	7	63.1	65	17	70	3.58	10-7	5	17	153.1	144	46	136

Wild Pitches—WS (Mussina, Witasick); OVERALL (Rivera 2, Clemens, Mussina, Witasick). **Hit Batters**—WS (Hernandez 2, Clemens, Mussina, Pettitte, Rivera); OVERALL (Clemens 3, Hernandez 3, Mussina 2, Pettitte, Rivera).

Arizona Diamondbacks

	WS vs New York								Overall Playoffs							
Batting	Avg	AB	R	H	HR	RBI	BB	SO	Avg	AB	R	H	HR	RBI	BB	SO
Danny Bautista	.583	12	1	7	0	7	1	1	.364	22	3	8	0	9	2	3
David Dellucci	.500	2	0	1	0	0	0	0	.500	4	1	2	0	0	0	0
Rod Barajas	.400	5	1	2	1	1	0	0	.400	5	1	2	1	1	0	0
Greg Colbrunn	.400	5	2	2	0	1	1	1	.333	12	2	4	0	2	2	1
Steve Finley	.368	19	5	7	1	2	4	5	.365	52	7	19	1	8	7	8
Erubiel Durazo	.364	11	0	4	0	1	3	4	.333	15	1	5	1	3	3	5
Reggie Sanders	.304	23	6	7	0	1	1	7	.259	54	10	14	1	3	9	15
Matt Williams	.269	26	3	7	1	7	0	6	.217	60	4	13	1	7	0	5
Mark Grace	.263	19	1	5	1	3	4	1	.286	49	2	14	1	4	8	5
Luis Gonzalez	.259	27	4	7	1	5	1	11	.246	65	9	16	3	10	6	18
Tony Womack	.250	32	3	8	0	3	1	7	.246	69	8	17	0	4	4	11
Damian Miller	.190	21	3	4	0	2	1	11	.208	53	4	11	0	2	4	19
Randy Johnson	.143	7	2	1	0	1	0	2	.067	15	2	1	0	1	0	6
Jay Bell	.143	7	3	1	0	1	0	2	.133	15	3	2	0	1	0	3
Craig Counsell	.083	24	1	2	1	1	0	7	.213	61	8	13	2	8	2	12
Curt Schilling	.000	6	0	0	0	0	0	5	.067	15	1	1	0	0	0	9
Midre Cummings	—	0	2	0	0	0	0	0	.000	1	2	0	0	0	0	0
Brian Anderson	—	0	0	0	0	0	0	0	.000	1	0	0	0	0	0	1
Mike Morgan	—	0	0	0	0	0	0	0	.000	5	0	0	0	0	0	1
Greg Swindell	—	3	0	0	0	0	0	0	.000	5	0	0	0	0	0	0
Byung-Hyun Kim	—	0	0	0	0	0	0	0	.000	1	0	0	0	0	0	0
Miguel Batista	—	0	0	0	0	0	0	0	.000	3	0	0	0	0	0	1
Albie Lopez	—	0	0	0	0	0	0	0	.000	2	0	0	0	0	0	0
Troy Brohawn	—	0	0	0	0	0	0	0	.000	1	0	0	0	0	0	0
TOTALS	.265	245	37	65	6	36	17	70	.247	574	68	142	11	65	53	131

Pitching	ERA	W-L	Sv	Gm	IP	H	BB	SO	ERA	W-L	Sv	Gm	IP	H	BB	SO
Miguel Batista	0.00	0-0	0	2	8.0	5	5	6	2.49	1-1	0	6	21.2	13	8	13
Troy Brohawn	0.00	0-0	0	1	1.0	1	0	1	0.00	0-0	0	1	1.0	1	0	1
Mike Morgan	0.00	0-0	0	3	4.2	1	0	1	5.14	0-0	0	8	7.0	6	3	0
Greg Swindell	0.00	0-0	0	3	2.2	1	1	2	1.93	0-0	0	7	4.2	3	1	4
Bobby Witt	0.00	0-0	0	1	1.0	0	1	1	6.75	0-0	0	2	1.1	3	1	1
Randy Johnson	1.04	3-0	0	3	17.1	9	3	19	1.52	5-1	0	6	41.1	25	8	47
Curt Schilling	1.69	1-0	0	3	21.1	12	2	26	1.12	4-0	0	6	48.1	25	6	56
Brian Anderson	3.38	0-0	0	3	5.1	5	3	1	2.84	1-1	0	4	12.2	12	4	4
Byung-Hyun Kim	13.50	0-1	0	2	3.1	6	1	6	4.66	0-1	3	6	9.2	7	4	10
Albie Lopez	27.00	0-1	0	1	0.1	2	0	0	9.95	0-2	0	3	6.1	11	4	1
TOTALS	1.93	4-3	0	7	65.0	42	16	63	2.40	11-6	3	17	154.0	106	39	140

Wild Pitches—WS (Anderson, Batista, Morgan, Swindell); OVERALL (Anderson, Batista, Kim, Morgan, Swindell). **Hit Batters**—WS (Schilling); OVERALL (Anderson, Schilling).

Score by Innings

	1	2	3	4	5	6	7	8	9	10	11	12		R	H	E
New York	1		0	0	3	1	1	4	1	0	1		–	14	42	8
Arizona	2	4	12	9	2	1	3	2	2	0	0		–	37	65	3

E: New York—Soriano 3, Brosius, Clemens, Justice, Posada, Rivera; Arizona—Grace, Miller, Womack. **GIDP:** New York—O'Neill 2, Posada 2, Sojo; Arizona—Gonzalez, Grace, Sanders, Womack. **LOB:** New York 38, Arizona 49. **2B:** New York—Brosius 2, Greene, O'Neill, Posada, B. Williams; Arizona—Womack 3, Bautista 2, Gonzalez 2, Miller 2, Williams 2, Durazo, Grace, Sanders. **HR:** New York—Brosius, Jeter, Martinez, Posada, Soriano, Spencer; Arizona—Barajas, Counsell, Finley, Gonzalez, Grace, Williams. **SB:** New York—O'Neill; Arizona—Sanders, Womack. **CS:** New York—Soriano; Arizona—Finley, Womack. **Picked Off:** Arizona—Counsell. **S:** New York—Brosius; Arizona—Counsell 4, Williams. **SF:** Arizona—Williams 2.
Umpires: Dana Demuth, Mark Hirschbeck, Jim Joyce, Ed Rapuano, Steve Rippley, Dale Scott.

AP/Wide World Photos

World Series co-MVPs **Randy Johnson** *and* **Curt Schilling** *went a combined 9-1 for Arizona in the 2001 postseason.*

2001 Postseason Leaders

Batting
(Minimum 10 AB)

	Gm	AB	R	H	Avg	HR	RBI
Ichiro Suzuki, Sea	10	38	7	16	**.421**	0	3
Johnny Damon, Oak	5	22	3	9	**.409**	0	0
Omar Vizquel, Cle	5	22	2	9	**.409**	0	6
Terrence Long, Oak	5	18	3	7	**.389**	2	3
Steve Finley, Ari	17	52	7	19	**.365**	1	8
Danny Bautista, Ari	10	22	3	8	**.364**	0	9
Jason Giambi, Oak	5	17	2	6	**.353**	1	4
Juan Gonzalez, Cle	5	23	4	8	**.348**	2	5
Erubiel Durazo, Ari	7	15	1	5	**.333**	1	3
Greg Colbrunn, Ari	6	12	2	4	**.333**	0	2
Chipper Jones, Atl	8	28	3	9	**.321**	2	7
Ellis Burks, Cle	5	19	4	6	**.316**	1	1
Fernando Vina, St.L	5	19	2	6	**.316**	1	2
Einar Diaz, Cle	5	16	3	5	**.313**	0	2
Andruw Jones, Atl	8	29	6	9	**.310**	2	2

Pitching
(Minimum 10 IP)

	Gm	IP	W-L	ERA	BB	SO
Ramiro Mendoza, NY	8	12.1	0-0	**0.73**	3	10
Tom Glavine, Atl	3	20.0	2-1	**0.90**	7	8
Curt Schilling, Ari	6	48.1	4-0	**1.12**	6	56
Matt Morris, St.L	2	15.0	0-1	**1.20**	5	12
Randy Johnson, Ari	6	41.1	5-1	**1.52**	8	47
Mariano Rivera, NY	11	16.0	2-1	**1.69**	2	14
Bartolo Colon, Cle	2	14.2	1-1	**1.84**	6	13
Jamie Moyer, Sea	3	19.0	3-0	**1.89**	3	15
Roger Clemens, NY	5	26.2	1-1	**2.36**	12	32
Mark Mulder, Oak	2	11.0	1-1	**2.45**	2	7
Miguel Batista, Ari	6	21.2	1-1	**2.49**	8	13
Brian Anderson, Ari	4	12.2	1-1	**2.84**	4	4
Mike Mussina, NY	4	24.0	2-1	**2.62**	6	21
Orlando Hernandez, NY	3	17.0	1-1	**3.71**	11	17
Freddy Garcia, Sea	3	19.0	1-2	**3.79**	7	19

Home Runs
Gonzalez, Ari 3
Martinez, NY 3
B. Williams, NY 3
Twelve tied with 2 each.

Runs
Sanders, Ari 10
B. Williams, NY 10
Gonzalez, Ari 9
Posada, NY 9
Counsell, Ari 8
Soriano, Ari 8
Womack, Ari 8
Finley, Ari 7
Suzuki, Sea 7

Runs Batted In
B. Williams, NY 11
Gonzalez, Ari 10
Bautista, Ari 9
Williams, Ari 9
Counsell, Ari 8
Finley, Ari 8
Martinez, NY 8
C. Jones, Atl 7
Soriano, NY 7

Stolen Bases
	SB	CS
Soriano, NY	4	2
Sanders, Ari	3	0
Suzuki, Sea	3	2
Damon, Oak	2	0
Sixteen tied with 1 each.

Wins
Johnson, Ari 5-1
Schilling, Ari 4-0
Moyer, Sea 3-0
Glavine, Atl.......... 2-1
Mussina, NY 2-1
Rivera, NY 2-1
Pettitte, NY 2-3
Fifteen tied with 1 each.

Innings
Schilling, Ari 48.1
Johnson, Ari 41.1
Pettitte, NY 29.2
Clemens, NY 26.2
Mussina, NY 24.0
Batista, Ari 21.2
Glavine, Atl 20.0

Strikeouts
Schilling, Ari 56
Johnson, Ari 47
Clemens, NY 32
Mussina, NY 21
Pettitte, NY 21
Garcia, Sea 19
Hernandez, NY 17
Moyer, Sea 15

Saves
Rivera, NY 5
Kim, Ari 3
Isringhausen, Oak 2
Kline, St.L 2
Smoltz, Atl 2
Sasaki, Sea 1

COLLEGE

Final *Baseball America* Top 25

Final 2001 Division I Top 25, voted on by the editors of *Baseball America* and released after the NCAA College World Series. Given are final records (excluding ties) and winning percentage (including all postseason games); records in College World Series and team eliminated by (DNP indicates team did not play in tourney); head coach (career years and four-year college record including 2001 postseason); preseason ranking and rank before start of CWS.

		Record	Pct	CWS Recap	Head Coach	Preseason Rank	Rank before CWS
1	Miami-FL	53-12	.815	4-0	Jim Morris (20 yrs: 897-363-2)	4	1
2	Stanford	51-17	.750	3-1 (Miami)	Mark Marquess (25 yrs: 1046-515-5)	14	6
3	CS-Fullerton	48-18	.727	2-2 (Stanford)	George Horton (5 yrs: 222-94-1)	15	4
4	USC	45-19	.703	1-2 (Tennessee)	Mike Gillespie (15 yrs: 608-332-2)	2	2
5	Tulane	56-13	.812	1-2 (CS-Fullerton)	Rick Jones (13 yrs: 520-220-1)	19	5
6	Nebraska	50-16	.758	0-2 (Tulane)	Dave Van Horn (8 yrs: 324-147)	5	3
7	Georgia	47-22	.681	0-2 (Tennessee)	Ron Polk (28 yrs: 1123-534)	16	7
8	Tennessee	48-20	.706	2-2 (Miami)	Rod Delmonico (12 yrs: 492-250)	NR	8
9	Louisiana St.	44-22	.667	DNP	Skip Bertman (18 yrs: 870-330-3)	3	9
10	Florida State	47-19	.712	DNP	Mike Martin (22 yrs: 1179-402-3)	7	10
11	East Carolina	47-13	.783	DNP	Keith LeClair (10 yrs: 398-211-2)	23	11
12	South Carolina	49-20	.710	DNP	Ray Tanner (14 yrs: 612-268-3)	8	12
13	Rice	47-20	.701	DNP	Wayne Graham (10 yrs: 426-198)	12	13
14	Central Florida	51-14	.785	DNP	Jay Bergman (25 yrs: 972-540-3)	17	14
15	Notre Dame	49-13	.790	DNP	Paul Mainieri (13 yrs: 456-282)	9	15
16	Pepperdine	42-18	.700	DNP	Frank Sanchez (5 yrs: 190-104)	18	16
17	Clemson	41-22	.651	DNP	Jack Leggett (22 yrs: 757-445)	10	17
18	Wake Forest	44-18	.710	DNP	George Greer (20 yrs: 621-434-7)	NR	18
19	Mississippi St.	39-24	.619	DNP	Pat McMahon (9 yrs: 353-174)	21	19
20	Florida International	43-21	.672	DNP	Danny Price (22 yrs: 880-447)	NR	20
21	Texas Tech	43-20	.683	DNP	Larry Hays (31 yrs: 1278-686-2)	NR	21
22	Arizona St.	37-20	.649	DNP	Pat Murphy (17 yrs: 640-316-3)	6	22
23	South Alabama	45-19	.703	DNP	Steve Kittrell (19 yrs: 746-412-1)	NR	23
24	Winthrop	47-16	.746	DNP	Joe Hudak (9 yrs: 302-220-4)	NR	24
25	Rutgers	42-17	.712	DNP	Fred Hill (25 yrs: 730-441-6)	NR	25

College World Series

CWS Participants: Tulane (55-11); Miami-FL (49-12); Stanford (48-16); Nebraska (50-14); Cal. State-Fullerton (46-16); Tennessee (46-18); Georgia (47-20); USC (44-17).

Bracket One

June 8—Stanford 13	Tulane 11
June 8—CS-Fullerton 5	Nebraska 4
June 10—Stanford 5	CS-Fullerton 2
June 10—Tulane 6	Nebraska 5 (out)
June 12—CS-Fullerton 11	Tulane 2 (out)
June 13—Stanford 4	CS-Fullerton 1 (out)

Bracket Two

June 9—USC 11	Georgia 5
June 9—Miami-FL 21	Tennessee 13
June 11—Miami-FL 4	USC 3
June 11—Tennessee 19	Georgia 12 (out)
June 12—Tennessee 10	USC 2 (out)
June 14—Miami-FL 12	Tennessee 6 (out)

CWS Championship Game

Saturday, June 16, at Rosenblatt Stadium in Omaha, Neb.

	1 2 3	4 5 6	7 8 9	R H E
Stanford	0 0 0	0 0 1	0 0 0	1 5 2
Miami-FL	0 0 4	0 5 2	0 1 x	12 13 0

Win: MIA–Tom Farmer (15-2). **Loss:** STAN–Mike Gosling (7-3). **Save:** None. **Strikeouts:** STAN–Gosling 2, Ryan McCally and J.D. Willcox 1; MIA–Farmer 3, Luke DeBold 2. **2B:** STAN–Ryan Garko; MIA–Javy Rodriguez, Danny Matienzo, Kevin Mannix, Kevin Brown. **HR:** MIA–Brown (15). **SB:** MIA–Mike Rodriguez (53). **Attendance:** 24,070. **Time** 3:09.

Most Outstanding Player

Charlton Jimerson, Miami-FL, CF

AB	R	H	HR	RBI	SB	Avg.
18	5	6	2	2	7	.333

All-Tournament Team

C– Ryan Garko, Stanford; **1B**–Kevin Brown, Miami-FL; **2B**–David Bacani, CS-Fullerton; **3B**–Kris Bennett, Tennessee; **SS**–Chris Burke, Tennessee; **OF**–Jeff Christensen, Tennessee; Sam Fuld, Stanford; Charlton Jimerson, Miami-FL; **DH**–Danny Matienzo, Miami-FL; **P**–Jeff Bruksch, Stanford; Tom Farmer, Miami-FL.

Annual Awards

Chosen by *Baseball America*, *Collegiate Baseball*, National Collegiate Baseball Writers Association and the American Baseball Coaches Association. The Rotary Smith award is chosen by college sports information directors.

Player of the Year

Mark Prior, P, USC .....*BA*, *CB*, Dick Howser (NCBWA), ABCA, Smith

Coaches of the Year

Jim Morris, Miami ....ABCA, *CB*
Dave Van Horn, Nebraska ....*BA*

Consensus All-America Team

NCAA Division I players cited most frequently by the following four selectors: the American Baseball Coaches Assn. (ABCA), *Baseball America*, *Collegiate Baseball* and the National Collegiate Baseball Writers Assn. (NCBWA).

First Team

Pos		Cl	Avg	HR	RBI
C	Kelly Shoppach, Baylor	Jr.	.397	12	69
1B	John VanBenschoten, Kent St...	Jr.	.440	31	84
2B	Michael Woods, Southern	Jr.	.453	14	54
SS	Chris Burke, Tennessee	Jr.	.435	20	60
3B	Jeff Baker, Clemson	So.	.369	23	75
OF	John Cole, Nebraska	Jr.	.418	11	61
OF	Shelley Duncan, Arizona	Jr.	.338	24	78
OF	John Ford-Griffin, Florida St....	Jr.	.450	19	75
DH	Jake Gautreau, Tulane	Jr.	.355	21	96
UT	Cory Sullivan, Wake Forest....	Jr.	.390	13	67

Pos		Cl	W-L	Sv	ERA
P	Dewon Brazelton, Mid. Tenn. St.	Jr.	13-2	0	1.42
P	Aaron Heilman, Notre Dame	Sr.	15-0	0	1.74
P	Mark Prior, USC	Jr.	15-1	0	1.69
P	Kirk Saarloos, CS-Fullerton....	Sr.	15-2	4	2.18
P	Lee Gronkiewicz, S. Carolina	Sr.	2-1	19	1.31

Second Team

Pos		Cl	Avg	HR	RBI
C	Casey Myers, Arizona S.	Sr.	.395	7	69
1B	Dan Johnson, Nebraska	Sr.	.361	25	86
2B	Chris O'Riordan, Stanford	Jr.	.359	12	68
SS	Javy Rodriguez, Miami-FL	Jr.	.382	5	60
3B	Kevin Youkilis, Cincinnati	Sr.	.405	18	61
OF	Matt Davis, Va. Commonwealth.	Jr.	.396	3	26
OF	Greg Dobbs, Oklahoma	Jr.	.428	10	62
OF	Jason Knoedler, Miami-OH	Jr.	.402	17	50
DH	Ryan Brunner, Northern Iowa	Sr.	.377	25	82
UT	Dan Haren, Pepperdine	Jr.	.308	5	47

Pos		Cl	W-L	Sv	ERA
P	Kenny Baugh, Rice	Sr.	13-2	0	2.17
P	Nate Fernley, Brigham Young	Sr.	16-3	0	3.12
P	Shane Komine, Nebraska	Jr.	14-2	0	3.35
P	Justin Pope, Central Florida	Jr.	15-1	0	1.68
P	Noah Lowry, Pepperdine	Jr.	14-2	1	1.71

NCAA Division I Leaders

Batting

Average

(At least 75 AB)	Cl	Gm	AB	H	Avg
Chris Tuttle, Wright St.	So.	54	203	97	.478
Chris May, Pennsylvania	Jr.	39	143	65	.455
Michael Woods, Southern	Jr.	47	170	77	.453
John-Ford Griffin, Florida St.	Jr.	65	251	113	.450
Mitch Maier, Toledo	Fr.	44	160	71	.444
Brian Baron, UCLA	Sr.	56	237	105	.443
John VanBenschoten, Kent St.	Jr.	61	225	99	.440
Jason Law, Monmouth	Jr.	53	204	89	.436
Chris Burke, Tennessee	Jr.	67	271	118	.435
Phil Pilewski, Toledo	So.	47	171	74	.433

Home Runs (per game)

(At least 10 HR)	Cl	Gm	HR	Avg
John VanBenschoten, Kent St.	Jr.	61	31	0.51
Jason Brooks, Marshall	Sr.	49	23	0.47
Alex Trezza, Stony Brook	Jr.	51	23	0.45
Shelley Duncan, Arizona	Jr.	56	24	0.43
Dan Johnson, Nebraska	Sr.	62	25	0.40
Ryan Brunner, Northern Iowa	Sr.	63	25	0.40
Jeff Baker, Clemson	So.	60	23	0.38
Mike Bohlander, Pace	Jr.	45	17	0.38
Kevin Mitchell, McNeese St.	Sr.	51	19	0.37
Aaron Clark, Alabama	Sr.	55	20	0.36
Scott Martin, Delaware St.	So.	44	16	0.36

Runs Batted In (per game)

(At least 50 RBI)	Cl	Gm	RBI	Avg
Scott Martin, Delaware St.	So.	44	77	1.75
Jason Brooks, Marshall	Sr.	49	73	1.49
Jake Gautreau, Tulane	Jr.	65	96	1.48
Chris May, Pennsylvania	Sr.	39	55	1.41
Shelley Duncan, Arizona	Jr.	56	78	1.39
Dan Johnson, Nebraska	Sr.	62	86	1.39
John VanBenschoten, Kent St.	Jr.	61	84	1.38
Andrew See, Ohio	Sr.	51	70	1.37
Scott Henley, Ga. Southern	Sr.	62	84	1.35
Alex Trezza, Stony Brook	Jr.	51	68	1.33

Stolen Bases (per game)

(At least 25)	Cl	Gm	SB	SBA	Avg
Javy Rodriguez, Miami-FL	Jr.	63	66	82	1.05
Matt Lemanczyk, Sacred Heart	Jr.	45	40	44	0.89
Christopher Graziano, Villanova	So.	42	37	41	0.88
Mike Rodriguez, Miami-FL	Jr.	64	53	55	0.83
Matt Davis, Va. Commonwealth.	Jr.	60	49	59	0.82
Marcus Nettles, Miami-FL	Sr.	54	44	54	0.81
Bartowski Cowan, Alabama St.	Jr.	47	37	41	0.79
Sean Hill, Mississippi Valley St.	Jr.	46	36	42	0.78
Dwaine Bacon, Florida A&M	Jr.	44	34	41	0.77
Rick Lynn, Brown	Jr.	42	32	35	0.76

Pitching

Earned Run Avg.

(At least 50 inn.)	Cl	Gm	IP	ERA
Todd Pennington, SE Missouri	Jr.	18	95.0	1.33
Dewon Brazelton, Mid. Tenn. St.	Jr.	15	127.0	1.42
Justin Pope, Central Florida	Jr.	17	123.1	1.68
Mark Prior, USC	Jr.	20	138.2	1.69
Noah Lowry, Pepperdine	Jr.	18	121.1	1.71
Aaron Heilman, Notre Dame	Sr.	15	114.0	1.74
Kyle Johnson, St. Bonaventure	So.	13	72.0	1.88
Casey Shumaker, Jacksonville	So.	33	75.1	1.91
Jonathon Stern, Brown	Jr.	9	61.0	1.92
Joe Engel, Pittsburgh	Fr.	10	70.1	1.92

Wins

	Cl	Gm	IP	W-L
Nate Fernley, Brigham Young	Sr.	21	152.2	16-3
Aaron Heilman, Notre Dame	Sr.	15	114.0	15-0
Justin Pope, Central Florida	Jr.	17	123.1	15-1
Mark Prior, USC	Jr.	20	138.2	15-1
Kirk Saarloos, CS-Fullerton	Sr.	25	153.0	15-2
Tom Farmer, Miami-FL	Sr.	20	114.1	15-2
Michael Rogers, Oral Roberts	Jr.	18	121.1	14-1
Noah Lowry, Pepperdine	Jr.	18	121.1	14-2
Shane Komine, Nebraska	Jr.	18	131.2	14-2
Ben Thurmond, Winthrop	So.	20	150.0	14-3
Jason Arnold, Central Florida	Sr.	19	118.2	14-3

Strikeouts (per 9 inn.)

(At least 50 inn.)

	Cl	IP	SO	Avg
Casey Shumaker, Jacksonville	So.	75.1	117	14.0
Mark Prior, USC	Jr.	138.2	202	13.1
Brad Hennessey, Youngstown St.	Jr.	88.2	126	12.8
Pat Neshek, Butler	So.	85.0	118	12.5
Chris Flinn, Stony Brook	Jr.	88.2	121	12.3
Brandon Woodward, Mt. St. Mary's	So.	61.0	82	12.1
Neal Cotts, Illinois St.	Jr.	87.1	113	11.6
Marcos Mendoza, San Diego St.	Jr.	91.1	118	11.6
Justin Pope, Central Florida	Jr.	123.1	158	11.5
Brian Houdek, Western Ky.	Sr.	79.0	101	11.5

Saves

	Cl	IP	ERA	Saves
Lee Gronkiewicz, S. Carolina	Sr.	61.2	1.31	19
Dave Bush, Wake Forest	Jr.	74.2	2.65	16
Chad Cordero, CS-Fullerton	Fr.	64.0	1.83	14
George Huguet, Miami-FL	Fr.	44.1	2.03	14
Casey Shumaker, Jacksonville	So.	75.1	1.91	12
Randy Corn, Citadel	Jr.	57.2	2.50	12
Andy Hutchings, Col. of Charleston	Fr.	27.2	3.25	12
Justin Craker, Valparaiso	Sr.	31.1	4.02	12
Four tied with 11 each.				

Other College World Series

Participants' final records in parentheses.

NCAA Div. II

at Montgomery, Ala. (May 26-June 2)

Participants: Southern Ill.-Edwardsville (40-25); Tampa, Fla. (49-8); North Florida (45-15); Delta State, Miss. (47-9); Kutztown, Penn. (38-17); St. Mary's, Texas (46-12); UMass-Lowell (38-17), Central Missouri St. (49-8).

Championship: St. Mary's def. Central Missouri St., 11-3.

NAIA

at Lewiston, Idaho (May 25-June 1)

Participants: Western Oregon (38-18); Warner Southern, Fla. (51-14); Birmingham-Southern, Ala. (50-10); Ohio Dominican (36-17); Biola, Calif. (45-11); Bellevue, Neb. (46-16); Mobile, Ala. (40-18); Lewis-Clark St., Idaho (50-12).

Championship: Birmingham-Southern def. Lewis-Clark, 8-3.

NCAA Div. III

at Appleton, Wis. (May 25-29)

Participants: Montclair St., N.J. (35-9); Chapman, Calif. (37-9); Salisbury St., Md. (31-11); Marietta, Ohio (44-7-1); St. Thomas, Minn. (35-9); Illinois Wesleyan (37-13-1); Southern Maine (36-12); Cortland St., N.Y. (33-9).

Championship: St. Thomas def. Marietta, 8-4.

NJCAA Div. I

at Grand Junction, Colo. (May 26-June 1)

Participants: Cowley County CC, Kan. (46-14); Middle Georgia (38-23); Miami-Dade CC, Fla. (45-10); Texarkana, Texas (39-19); Central Alabama CC (35-20); North Central Texas (47-14); Dixie St., Utah (48-12); Spartanburg Methodist, S.C. (49-10).

Championship: North Central Texas def. Dixie St., 7-6.

MLB First-Year Player Draft

First round selections at the 37th First-Year Player Draft held June 5-7, 2001 in New York. Clubs select in reverse order of their standing from the preceding season. The worst National League team selects first in even years and the worst American League team goes first in odd years. Leagues then alternate picks throughout the rounds.

First Round

No			Pos
1	Minnesota	Joe Mauer, Cretin-Durham HS St. Paul, Minn.	C
2	Chicago-NL	Mark Prior, USC	RHP
3	Tampa Bay	Dewon Brazelton, Mid. Tenn. St.	RHP
4	Philadelphia	Gavin Floyd, Mt. St. Joseph's HS Severna Park, Md.	RHP
5	Texas	Mark Teixeira, Georgia Tech	3B
6	Montreal	Josh Karp, UCLA	RHP
7	Baltimore	Chris Smith, Cumberland Univ.	LHP
8	Pittsburgh	John VanBenschoten, Kent. St.	1B
9	Kansas City	Colt Griffin, Marshall (Tex.) HS	RHP
10	Houston	Chris Burke, Tennessee	SS
11	Detroit	Kenneth Baugh, Rice	RHP
12	Milwaukee	Michael Jones, Thunderbird HS Phoenix, Ariz.	RHP
13	Anaheim	Casey Kotchman, Seminole (Fla.) HS	1B
14	San Diego	Jake Gautreau, Tulane	1B
15	Toronto	Gabriel Gross, Auburn	OF
16	**a**-Chicago-AL	Kris Honel, Providence Catholic HS, New Lenox, Ill.	RHP

No			Pos
17	**b**-Cleveland	Dan Denham, Deer Valley HS Antioch, Calif.	RHP
18	**c**-New York-NL	Aaron Heilman, Notre Dame	RHP
19	**d**-Baltimore	Michael Fontenot, LSU	2B
20	Cincinnati	Jeremy Sowers, Ballard HS Louisville, Ky.	LHP
21	**e**-San Francisco	Brad Hennessey, Youngstown St.	RHP
22	Arizona	Jason Bulger, Valdosta St.	RHP
23	**f**-New York-AL	John Ford-Griffin, Florida St.	OF
24	**g**-Atlanta	Joseph McBride, Screven County HS Sylvania, Ga.	LHP
25	Oakland	Robert Crosby, Long Beach St.	SS
26	**h**-Oakland	Jeremy Bonderman, Pasco (Wash.) HS	RHP
27	**i**-Cleveland	William Horne, Marianna (Fla.) HS	RHP
28	St. Louis	Justin Pope, Central Florida	RHP
29	Atlanta	Joshua Burrus, Wheeler HS Marietta, Ga.	SS
30	San Francisco	Noah Lowry, Pepperdine	LHP

Acquired picks: a–from Florida for signing Charles Johnson; **b**–from Boston for signing Manny Ramirez; **c**–from Colorado for signing Mike Hampton; **d**–from NY Yankees for signing Mike Mussina; **e**–from Cleveland for signing Ellis Burks; **f**–from Seattle for signing Jeff Nelson; **g**–from Los Angeles for signing Andy Ashby; **h**–from NY Mets for signing Kevin Appier; **i**–from Chicago-AL for signing Sandy Alomar Jr.

Unsung Hero
by Dave Ryan

The 2001 Miami Hurricanes were, by far, the deepest and most talented team I've seen in my four years covering the College World Series in Omaha. Head Coach Jim Morris' team had it all—power hitting, superior pitching, great team speed and solid defense. The lineup and pitching staff were loaded with players on their way to minor league ball, some destined for the majors.

The Hurricanes won their final 17 games, culminating in a 12-1 shellacking of Stanford in the championship game, for their fourth NCAA title. Along the way, the team set numerous school and College World Series records. But it was one player's sister who may still emerge as the real Hurricane hero.

Miami center fielder Charlton Jimerson was the paramount talent in Omaha. He electrified the crowds with his game-saving catches, laser-beam throws from the outfield and blazing speed on the basepaths. He is the type of player fans always watch closely. No matter how good the hot dogs at Rosenblatt Stadium were, fans would always stop eating and talking just to see what Jimerson would do next. His .333 batting average, seven steals and handful of acrobatic catches made him the College World Series Most Outstanding Player. His talent and ability to take over a game went unmatched. But that's only part of his story.

The fact that Jimerson made it to Omaha, or even Miami, is nothing short of a miracle. Growing up in California's Bay Area, his parents ran into repeated personal problems. Jimerson's older sister Lanette took over, raising Charlton and his younger brother Terrance. Lanette juggled several low-paying jobs to keep the household afloat while she earned her teaching degree.

When it came time for Charlton to pick a college, Lanette provided valuable counsel. Jimerson had always dreamed of playing for Miami, but he was relatively unknown to schools on the East Coast. Lanette recommended her younger brother put together a scrapbook of his high school accomplishments, complete with an essay

AP/Wide World Photos

Miami's **Charlton Jimerson** stole the show at the College World Series in Omaha.

introducing himself to Morris. Jimerson was selected in the 24th round of the draft by the Houston Astros, but again Lanette made the right decision. She advised Charlton, who had received an academic scholarship, to go to Miami as a walk-on and turn down the relatively low contract value a 24th-round pick commands. Charlton took his sister's advice and became the first man in his family to earn a college degree. He also went from a 24th-round pick to a 5th-round selection of the Astros in 2001.

Lanette is still working her magic. Younger brother Terrance carries a 3.75 grade point average, is an honor student and a great basketball player.

There always seems to be a strong family behind great athletes. She won't show up in any College World Series record book, or earn millions some day in the majors, but Lanette may have been the most important member of the Hurricane family in 2001. Just having a conversation with Charlton tells the whole story. He's intelligent, well spoken, focused and determined. Best of all he's thankful, and truly appreciative of what his big sister has done for him. ∎

Dave Ryan is an in-the-stands reporter for ESPN's college baseball coverage.

Minor League Triple-A Final Standings

Division champions (*) and Wild Card (†) winners are noted.

International League

North Division	W	L	Pct	GB
*Buffalo (Indians)	91	51	.641	—
†Scranton-WB (Phillies)	78	65	.545	13½
Syracuse (Blue Jays)	71	73	.493	21
Ottawa (Expos)	68	76	.472	24
Pawtucket (Red Sox)	60	82	.423	31
Rochester (Orioles)	60	84	.417	32

South Division	W	L	Pct	GB
*Norfolk (Mets)	85	57	.599	—
Durham (Devil Rays)	74	70	.514	12
Richmond (Braves)	68	76	.472	18
Charlotte (White Sox)	67	77	.465	19

West Division	W	L	Pct	GB
*Louisville (Reds)	84	60	.583	—
Columbus (Yankees)	67	76	.469	16½
Indianapolis (Brewers)	66	78	.458	18
Toledo (Tigers)	65	79	.451	19

Playoffs

Division Finals (Best-of-Five)

Louisville 3	Norfolk 2
Scranton-WB 3	Buffalo 2

Championship (Best-of-Five)

Scranton-WB vs. Louisville

Sept. 10	Louisville, 2-1	at Louisville

Note: The remaining Governors' Cup finals games were cancelled due to the Sept. 11 attacks on America. Due to its 1-0 series advantage at the time of the tragedy, Louisville was crowned champion of the International League.

Pacific Coast League

American Conference

Eastern Division	W	L	Pct	GB
*New Orleans (Astros)	82	57	.590	—
Oklahoma (Rangers)	74	69	.517	10
Nashville (Pirates)	64	77	.454	19
Memphis (Cardinals)	62	81	.434	22

Central Division	W	L	Pct	GB
*Iowa (Cubs)	83	60	.580	—
Salt Lake (Angels)	79	64	.552	4
Omaha (Royals)	70	74	.486	13½
Colorado Springs (Rockies)	62	79	.440	20

Pacific Conference

Northern Division	W	L	Pct	GB
*Tacoma (Mariners)	85	59	.590	—
Calgary (Marlins)	72	71	.503	12½
Portland (Padres)	71	73	.493	14
Edmonton (Twins)	60	83	.420	24½

Southern Division	W	L	Pct	GB
*Sacramento (A's)	75	69	.521	—
Fresno (Giants)	68	71	.489	4½
Las Vegas (Dodgers)	68	76	.472	7
Tucson (D'Backs)	65	77	.458	9

Playoffs

Division Finals (Best-of-Five)

Tacoma 3	Sacramento 2
New Orleans 3	Iowa 0

Championship (Best-of-Five)

Tacoma vs. New Orleans

Note: The 2001 Pacific Coast League Championship series was cancelled due to the Sept. 11 attacks on America. As a result, Tacoma and New Orleans were named Pacific Coast League co-champions.

2001 International League All-Star Team

As selected by the league's managers, coaches, media and club representatives.

Pos. Name, Team (Affiliate)

C	Toby Hall, Durham (Devil Rays)
1B	Calvin Pickering, Rochester (Orioles)
2B	P.J. Forbes, Scranton-WB (Phillies)
3B	Kevin Orie, Scranton-WB (Phillies)
SS	Cesar Izturis, Syracuse (Blue Jays)
OF	Karim Garcia, Buffalo (Indians)
OF	Eric Valent, Scranton-WB (Phillies)
OF	Chris Wakeland, Toledo (Tigers)
DH	Izzy Alcantara, Pawtucket (Red Sox)
UT	Brian Rios, Toledo (Tigers)
SP	Brandon Duckworth, Scranton-WB (Phillies)
RP	Matt DeWitt, Syracuse (Blue Jays)

Awards

MVP	Toby Hall, C, Durham
Pitcher of the Year	Brandon Duckworth, Scranton-WB
Rookie of the Year	Brandon Duckworth, Scranton-WB
Manager of the Year	Eric Wedge, Buffalo

2001 Pacific Coast League All-Star Team

As selected by the league's managers and media representatives.

Pos. Name, Team (Affiliate)

C	Ramon Castro, Calgary (Marlins)
1B	Todd Betts, Tacoma (Mariners)
2B	Chad Meyers, Iowa (Cubs)
3B	Jose Fernandez, Salt Lake (Angels)
SS	Ramon Vazquez, Tacoma (Mariners)
OF	Roosevelt Brown, Iowa (Cubs)
OF	Jason Conti, Tucson (D'Backs)
OF	Jack Cust, Tucson (D'Backs)
DH	Phil Hiatt, Las Vegas (Dodgers)
SP	Dennis Stark, Tacoma (Mariners)
SP	Bud Smith, Memphis (Cardinals)
RP	Jim Mann, New Orleans (Astros)

Awards

MVP	Phil Hiatt, 3B/DH, Las Vegas
Pitcher of the Year	Dennis Stark, Tacoma
Rookie of the Year	Sean Burroughs, 3B, Portland
Manager of the Year	Dan Rohn, Tacoma

1876-2001 Through the Years

ESPN information please® SPORTS ALMANAC

The World Series

The World Series began in 1903 when Pittsburgh of the older National League (founded in 1876) invited Boston of the American League (founded in 1901) to play a best-of-9 game series to determine which of the two league champions was the best. Boston was the surprise winner, 5 games to 3. The 1904 NL champion New York Giants refused to play Boston the following year, so there was no Series. Giants' owner John T. Brush and his manager John McGraw both despised AL president Ban Johnson and considered the junior circuit to be a minor league. By the following year, however, Brush and Johnson had smoothed out their differences and the Giants agreed to play Philadelphia in a best-of-7 game series. Since then the World Series has been a best-of-7 format, except from 1919-21 when it returned to best-of-9.

After surviving two world wars and an earthquake in 1989, the World Series was cancelled for only the second time in 1994 due to the players' strike.

In the chart below, the National League teams are listed in CAPITAL letters. Also, each World Series champion's wins and losses are noted in parentheses after the Series score in games.

Multiple champions: New York Yankees (26); Philadelphia-Oakland A's and St. Louis Cardinals (9); Brooklyn-Los Angeles Dodgers (6); Boston Red Sox, Cincinnati Reds, New York-San Francisco Giants and Pittsburgh Pirates (5); Detroit Tigers (4); Baltimore Orioles, Boston-Milwaukee-Atlanta Braves and Washington Senators-Minnesota Twins (3); Chicago Cubs, Chicago White Sox, Cleveland Indians, New York Mets and Toronto Blue Jays (2).

Year	Winner	Manager	Series	Loser	Manager
1903	Boston Red Sox	Jimmy Collins	5-3 (LWLLWWWW)	PITTSBURGH	Fred Clarke
1904	Not held				
1905	NY GIANTS	John McGraw	4-1 (WLWWW)	Philadelphia A's	Connie Mack
1906	Chicago White Sox	Fielder Jones	4-2 (WLWLWW)	CHICAGO CUBS	Frank Chance
1907	CHICAGO CUBS	Frank Chance	4-0-1 (TWWWW)	Detroit	Hughie Jennings
1908	CHICAGO CUBS	Frank Chance	4-1 (WWLWW)	Detroit	Hughie Jennings
1909	PITTSBURGH	Fred Clarke	4-3 (WLWLWLW)	Detroit	Hughie Jennings
1910	Philadelphia A's	Connie Mack	4-1 (WWWLW)	CHICAGO CUBS	Frank Chance
1911	Philadelphia A's	Connie Mack	4-2 (LWWWLW)	NY GIANTS	John McGraw
1912	Boston Red Sox	Jake Stahl	4-3-1 (WTLWWLLW)	NY GIANTS	John McGraw
1913	Philadelphia A's	Connie Mack	4-1 (WLWWW)	NY GIANTS	John McGraw
1914	BOSTON BRAVES	George Stallings	4-0	Philadelphia A's	Connie Mack
1915	Boston Red Sox	Bill Carrigan	4-1 (LWWWW)	PHILA. PHILLIES	Pat Moran
1916	Boston Red Sox	Bill Carrigan	4-1 (WWLWW)	BROOKLYN	Wilbert Robinson
1917	Chicago White Sox	Pants Rowland	4-2 (WWLLWW)	NY GIANTS	John McGraw
1918	Boston Red Sox	Ed Barrow	4-2 (WLWWLW)	CHICAGO CUBS	Fred Mitchell
1919	CINCINNATI	Pat Moran	5-3 (WWLWWLLW)	Chicago White Sox	Kid Gleason
1920	Cleveland	Tris Speaker	5-2 (WLLWWWW)	BROOKLYN	Wilbert Robinson
1921	NY GIANTS	John McGraw	5-3 (LLWWLWWW)	NY Yankees	Miller Huggins
1922	NY GIANTS	John McGraw	4-0-1 (WTWWW)	NY Yankees	Miller Huggins
1923	NY Yankees	Miller Huggins	4-2 (LWLWWW)	NY GIANTS	John McGraw
1924	Washington	Bucky Harris	4-3 (LWLWLWW)	NY GIANTS	John McGraw
1925	PITTSBURGH	Bill McKechnie	4-3 (LWLLWW)	Washington	Bucky Harris
1926	ST.L. CARDINALS	Rogers Hornsby	4-3 (LWWLLWW)	NY Yankees	Miller Huggins
1927	NY Yankees	Miller Huggins	4-0	PITTSBURGH	Donie Bush
1928	NY Yankees	Miller Huggins	4-0	ST.L. CARDINALS	Bill McKechnie
1929	Philadelphia A's	Connie Mack	4-1 (WWLWW)	CHICAGO CUBS	Joe McCarthy
1930	Philadelphia A's	Connie Mack	4-2 (WWLLWW)	ST.L. CARDINALS	Gabby Street
1931	ST.L. CARDINALS	Gabby Street	4-3 (LWWLWLW)	Philadelphia A's	Connie Mack
1932	NY Yankees	Joe McCarthy	4-0	CHICAGO CUBS	Charlie Grimm
1933	NY GIANTS	Bill Terry	4-1 (WWWLW)	Washington	Joe Cronin
1934	ST.L. CARDINALS	Frankie Frisch	4-3 (WLWLLWW)	Detroit	Mickey Cochrane
1935	Detroit	Mickey Cochrane	4-2 (LWWWLW)	CHICAGO CUBS	Charlie Grimm
1936	NY Yankees	Joe McCarthy	4-2 (WLWWLW)	NY GIANTS	Bill Terry
1937	NY Yankees	Joe McCarthy	4-1 (WWWLW)	NY GIANTS	Bill Terry
1938	NY Yankees	Joe McCarthy	4-0	CHICAGO CUBS	Gabby Hartnett
1939	NY Yankees	Joe McCarthy	4-0	CINCINNATI	Bill McKechnie
1940	CINCINNATI	Bill McKechnie	4-3 (LWLWLWW)	Detroit	Del Baker
1941	NY Yankees	Joe McCarthy	4-1 (WLWWW)	BKLN. DODGERS	Leo Durocher
1942	ST.L. CARDINALS	Billy Southworth	4-1 (LWWWW)	NY Yankees	Joe McCarthy
1943	NY Yankees	Joe McCarthy	4-1 (WLWWW)	ST.L. CARDINALS	Billy Southworth
1944	ST.L. CARDINALS	Billy Southworth	4-2 (LWLWWW)	St. Louis Browns	Luke Sewell
1945	Detroit	Steve O'Neill	4-3 (LWLWWLW)	CHICAGO CUBS	Charlie Grimm
1946	ST.L. CARDINALS	Eddie Dyer	4-3 (LWLWLW)	Boston Red Sox	Joe Cronin
1947	NY Yankees	Bucky Harris	4-3 (WWLLLWW)	BKLN. DODGERS	Burt Shotton

Year	Winner	Manager	Series	Loser	Manager
1948	Cleveland	Lou Boudreau	4-2 (LWWWLW)	BOSTON BRAVES	Billy Southworth
1949	NY Yankees	Casey Stengel	4-1 (WLWWW)	BKLN. DODGERS	Burt Shotton
1950	NY Yankees	Casey Stengel	4-0	PHILA. PHILLIES	Eddie Sawyer
1951	NY Yankees	Casey Stengel	4-2 (LWLWWW)	NY GIANTS	Leo Durocher
1952	NY Yankees	Casey Stengel	4-3 (LWLWLWW)	BKLN. DODGERS	Charlie Dressen
1953	NY Yankees	Casey Stengel	4-2 (WWLLWW)	BKLN. DODGERS	Charlie Dressen
1954	NY GIANTS	Leo Durocher	4-0	Cleveland	Al Lopez
1955	BKLN. DODGERS	Walter Alston	4-3 (LLWWWLW)	NY Yankees	Casey Stengel
1956	NY Yankees	Casey Stengel	4-3 (LLWWWLW)	BKLN. DODGERS	Walter Alston
1957	MILW. BRAVES	Fred Haney	4-3 (WLWLWW)	NY Yankees	Casey Stengel
1958	NY Yankees	Casey Stengel	4-3 (LLWLWWW)	MILW. BRAVES	Fred Haney
1959	LA DODGERS	Walter Alston	4-2 (LWWWLW)	Chicago White Sox	Al Lopez
1960	PITTSBURGH	Danny Murtaugh	4-3 (WLLWWLW)	NY Yankees	Casey Stengel
1961	NY Yankees	Ralph Houk	4-1 (WLWWW)	CINCINNATI	Fred Hutchinson
1962	NY Yankees	Ralph Houk	4-3 (WLWLWLW)	SF GIANTS	Alvin Dark
1963	LA DODGERS	Walter Alston	4-0	NY Yankees	Ralph Houk
1964	ST.L. CARDINALS	Johnny Keane	4-3 (WLLWLWW)	NY Yankees	Yogi Berra
1965	LA DODGERS	Walter Alston	4-3 (LLWWWLW)	Minnesota	Sam Mele
1966	Baltimore	Hank Bauer	4-0	LA DODGERS	Walter Alston
1967	ST.L. CARDINALS	Red Schoendienst	4-3 (WLWWLLW)	Boston Red Sox	Dick Williams
1968	Detroit	Mayo Smith	4-3 (LWLWWW)	ST.L. CARDINALS	Red Schoendienst
1969	NY METS	Gil Hodges	4-1 (LWWWW)	Baltimore	Earl Weaver
1970	Baltimore	Earl Weaver	4-1 (WWWLW)	CINCINNATI	Sparky Anderson
1971	PITTSBURGH	Danny Murtaugh	4-3 (LLWWWLW)	Baltimore	Earl Weaver
1972	Oakland A's	Dick Williams	4-3 (WWLWLLW)	CINCINNATI	Sparky Anderson
1973	Oakland A's	Dick Williams	4-3 (LWLWLWW)	NY METS	Yogi Berra
1974	Oakland A's	Alvin Dark	4-1 (WLWWW)	LA DODGERS	Walter Alston
1975	CINCINNATI	Sparky Anderson	4-3 (LWWLWLW)	Boston Red Sox	Darrell Johnson
1976	CINCINNATI	Sparky Anderson	4-0	NY Yankees	Billy Martin
1977	NY Yankees	Billy Martin	4-2 (WLWWLW)	LA DODGERS	Tommy Lasorda
1978	NY Yankees	Bob Lemon	4-2 (LLWWWW)	LA DODGERS	Tommy Lasorda
1979	PITTSBURGH	Chuck Tanner	4-3 (LWLLWWW)	Baltimore	Earl Weaver
1980	PHILA. PHILLIES	Dallas Green	4-2 (WWLLWW)	Kansas City	Jim Frey
1981	LA DODGERS	Tommy Lasorda	4-2 (LLWWWW)	NY Yankees	Bob Lemon
1982	ST.L. CARDINALS	Whitey Herzog	4-3 (LWWLLWW)	Milwaukee Brewers	Harvey Kuenn
1983	Baltimore	Joe Altobelli	4-1 (LWWWW)	PHILA. PHILLIES	Paul Owens
1984	Detroit	Sparky Anderson	4-1 (WLWWW)	SAN DIEGO	Dick Williams
1985	Kansas City	Dick Howser	4-3 (LLWLWWW)	ST.L. CARDINALS	Whitey Herzog
1986	NY METS	Davey Johnson	4-3 (LLWLWWW)	Boston Red Sox	John McNamara
1987	Minnesota	Tom Kelly	4-3 (WWLLLWW)	ST.L. CARDINALS	Whitey Herzog
1988	LA DODGERS	Tommy Lasorda	4-1 (WWLWW)	Oakland A's	Tony La Russa
1989	Oakland A's	Tony La Russa	4-0	SF GIANTS	Roger Craig
1990	CINCINNATI	Lou Piniella	4-0	Oakland A's	Tony La Russa
1991	Minnesota	Tom Kelly	4-3 (WWLLLWW)	ATLANTA BRAVES	Bobby Cox
1992	Toronto	Cito Gaston	4-2 (LWWWLW)	ATLANTA BRAVES	Bobby Cox
1993	Toronto	Cito Gaston	4-2 (WLWWLW)	PHILA. PHILLIES	Jim Fregosi
1994	Not held				
1995	ATLANTA BRAVES	Bobby Cox	4-2 (WWLLWW)	Cleveland	Mike Hargrove
1996	NY Yankees	Joe Torre	4-2 (LLWWWW)	ATLANTA BRAVES	Bobby Cox
1997	FLORIDA	Jim Leyland	4-3 (WLWLWLW)	Cleveland	Mike Hargrove
1998	NY Yankees	Joe Torre	4-0	SAN DIEGO	Bruce Bochy
1999	NY Yankees	Joe Torre	4-0	ATLANTA BRAVES	Bobby Cox
2000	NY Yankees	Joe Torre	4-1 (WWLWW)	NY METS	Bobby Valentine
2001	ARIZONA	Bob Brenly	4-3 (WWLLLWW)	NY Yankees	Joe Torre

Most Valuable Players

Currently selected by media panel and World Series official scorers. Presented by *Sport* magazine from 1955-88 and by Major League Baseball since 1989. Winner who did not play for World Series champions is in **bold** type.

Multiple winners: Bob Gibson, Reggie Jackson and Sandy Koufax (2).

Year	Year	Year
1955 Johnny Podres, Bklyn, P	1966 Frank Robinson, Bal., OF	1977 Reggie Jackson, NY, OF
1956 Don Larsen, NY, P	1967 Bob Gibson, St.L., P	1978 Bucky Dent, NY, SS
1957 Lew Burdette, Mil., P	1968 Mickey Lolich, Det., P	1979 Willie Stargell, Pit., 1B
1958 Bob Turley, NY, P	1969 Donn Clendenon, NY, 1B	1980 Mike Schmidt, Phi., 3B
1959 Larry Sherry, LA, P	1970 Brooks Robinson, Bal., 3B	1981 Pedro Guerrero, LA, OF;
1960 **Bobby Richardson**, NY, 2B	1971 Roberto Clemente, Pit., OF	Ron Cey, LA, 3B;
1961 Whitey Ford, NY, P	1972 Gene Tenace, Oak., C	& Steve Yeager, LA, C
1962 Ralph Terry, NY, P	1973 Reggie Jackson, Oak., OF	1982 Darrell Porter, St.L., C
1963 Sandy Koufax, LA, P	1974 Rollie Fingers, Oak., P	1983 Rick Dempsey, Bal., C
1964 Bob Gibson, St.L., P	1975 Pete Rose, Cin., 3B	1984 Alan Trammell, Det., SS
1965 Sandy Koufax, LA, P	1976 Johnny Bench, Cin., C	1985 Bret Saberhagen, KC, P

Year
1986 Ray Knight, NY, 3B
1987 Frank Viola, Min., P
1988 Orel Hershiser, LA, P
1989 Dave Stewart, Oak., P
1990 Jose Rijo, Cin., P
1991 Jack Morris, Min., P

Year
1992 Pat Borders, Tor., C
1993 Paul Molitor, Tor., DH/1B/3B
1994 Series not held.
1995 Tom Glavine, Atl., P
1996 John Wetteland, NY, P
1997 Livan Hernandez, Fla., P

Year
1998 Scott Brosius, NY, 3B
1999 Mariano Rivera, NY, P
2000 Derek Jeter, NY, SS
2001 Curt Schilling, Ari., P
    & Randy Johnson, Ari., P

All-Time World Series Leaders
CAREER

World Series leaders through 2001. Years listed indicate number of World Series appearances.

Hitting

Games

	Yrs	Gm
Yogi Berra, NY Yankees	14	75
Mickey Mantle, NY Yankees	12	65
Elston Howard, NY Yankees-Boston	10	54
Hank Bauer, NY Yankees	9	53
Gil McDougald, NY Yankees	8	53

At Bats

	Yrs	AB
Yogi Berra, NY Yankees	14	259
Mickey Mantle, NY Yankees	12	230
Joe DiMaggio, NY Yankees	10	199
Frankie Frisch, NY Giants-St.L. Cards	8	197
Gil McDougald, NY Yankees	8	190

Batting Avg. (minimum 50 AB)

	AB	H	Avg
Pepper Martin, St.L. Cards	55	23	.418
Paul Molitor, Mil. Brewers-Tor. Blue Jays	55	23	.418
Lou Brock, St. Louis	87	34	.391
Marquis Grissom, Atl-Cle	77	30	.390
Thurman Munson, NY Yankees	67	25	.373
George Brett, Kansas City	51	19	.373
Hank Aaron, Milw. Braves	55	20	.364

Hits

	AB	H	Avg
Yogi Berra, NY Yankees	259	71	.274
Mickey Mantle, NY Yankees	230	59	.257
Frankie Frisch, NYG-St.L. Cards	197	58	.294
Joe DiMaggio, NY Yankees	199	54	.271
Hank Bauer, NY Yankees	188	46	.245
Pee Wee Reese, Brooklyn	169	46	.272

Runs

	Gm	R
Mickey Mantle, NY Yankees	65	42
Yogi Berra, NY Yankees	75	41
Babe Ruth, Boston Red Sox-NY Yankees	41	37
Lou Gehrig, NY Yankees	34	30
Joe DiMaggio, NY Yankees	51	27

Home Runs

	AB	HR
Mickey Mantle, NY Yankees	230	18
Babe Ruth, Boston Red Sox-NY Yankees	129	15
Yogi Berra, NY Yankees	259	12
Duke Snider, Brooklyn-LA	133	11
Lou Gehrig, NY Yankees	119	10
Reggie Jackson, Oakland-NY Yankees	98	10

Runs Batted In

	Gm	RBI
Mickey Mantle, NY Yankees	65	40
Yogi Berra, NY Yankees	75	39
Lou Gehrig, NY Yankees	34	35
Babe Ruth, Boston Red Sox-NY Yankees	41	33
Joe DiMaggio, NY Yankees	51	30

World Series Appearances

In the 97 years that the World Series has been contested, American League teams have won 57 championships while National League teams have won 40.

The following teams are ranked by number of appearances through the 2001 World Series; (*) indicates AL teams.

	App	W	L	Pct.	Last Series	Last Title
NY Yankees*	38	26	12	.684	2001	2000
Bklyn/LA Dodgers	18	6	12	.333	1988	1988
NY/SF Giants	16	5	11	.313	1989	1954
St.L. Cardinals	15	9	6	.600	1987	1982
Phi/KC/Oak.A's*	14	9	5	.643	1990	1989
Chicago Cubs	10	2	8	.200	1945	1908
Boston Red Sox*	9	5	4	.556	1986	1918
Cincinnati Reds	9	5	4	.556	1990	1990
Detroit Tigers*	9	4	5	.444	1984	1984
Bos/Mil/Atl.Braves	9	3	6	.333	1999	1995
Pittsburgh Pirates	7	5	2	.714	1979	1979
St.L/Bal.Orioles*	7	3	4	.429	1983	1983
Wash/Min.Twins*	6	3	3	.500	1991	1991
Cle. Indians*	5	2	3	.400	1997	1948
Phi. Phillies	5	1	4	.200	1993	1980
Chi. White Sox*	4	2	2	.500	1959	1917
NY Mets	4	2	2	.500	2000	1986
Tor. Blue Jays*	2	2	0	1.000	1993	1993
KC Royals*	2	1	1	.500	1985	1985
SD Padres	2	0	2	.000	1998	—
Ari. Diamondbacks	1	1	0	1.000	2001	2001
Fla. Marlins	1	1	0	1.000	1997	1997
Sea/Mil.Brewers*	1	0	1	.000	1982	—

Stolen Bases

	Gm	SB
Lou Brock, St. Louis	21	14
Eddie Collins, Phi. A's-Chisox	34	14
Frank Chance, Chi. Cubs	20	10
Davey Lopes, Los Angeles	23	10
Phil Rizzuto, NY Yankees	52	10

Total Bases

	Gm	TB
Mickey Mantle, NY Yankees	65	123
Yogi Berra, NY Yankees	75	117
Babe Ruth, Boston Red Sox-NY Yankees	41	96
Lou Gehrig, NY Yankees	34	87
Joe DiMaggio, NY Yankees	51	84

Slugging Pct. (minimum 50 AB)

	AB	Pct
Reggie Jackson, Oakland-NY Yankees	98	.755
Babe Ruth, Boston Red Sox-NY Yankees	129	.744
Lou Gehrig, NY Yankees	119	.731
Al Simmons, Phi. A's-Cincinnati	73	.658
Lou Brock, St. Louis	87	.655

Pitching

Games

	Yrs	Gm
Whitey Ford, NY Yankees	11	22
Mike Stanton, Atlanta-NY Yankees	6	20
Mariano Rivera, NY Yankees	5	18
Rollie Fingers, Oakland	3	16
Allie Reynolds, NY Yankees	6	15
Bob Turley, NY Yankees	5	15
Clay Carroll, Cincinnati	3	14

Wins

	Gm	W-L
Whitey Ford, NY Yankees	22	10-8
Bob Gibson, St. Louis	9	7-2
Allie Reynolds, NY Yankees	15	7-2
Red Ruffing, NY Yankees	10	7-2
Lefty Gomez, NY Yankees	7	6-0
Chief Bender, Philadelphia A's	10	6-4
Waite Hoyt, NY Yankees-Phi. A's	12	6-4

ERA (minimum 25 IP)

	Gm	IP	ERA
Jack Billingham, Cincinnati	7	25.1	0.36
Harry Brecheen, St. Louis	7	32.2	0.83
Babe Ruth, Boston Red Sox	3	31.0	0.87
Sherry Smith, Brooklyn	3	30.1	0.89
Sandy Koufax, Los Angeles	8	57.0	0.95

Saves

	Gm	IP	Sv
Mariano Rivera, NY Yankees	18	27.0	8
Rollie Fingers, Oakland	16	33.1	6
Allie Reynolds, NY Yankees	15	77.1	4
Johnny Murphy, NY Yankees	8	16.1	4
John Wetteland, NY Yankees	5	4.1	4
Eight pitchers tied with 3 each.			

Shutouts

	GS	CG	ShO
Christy Mathewson, NY Giants	11	10	4
Three Finger Brown, Chi. Cubs	7	5	3
Whitey Ford, NY Yankees	22	7	3
Seven pitchers tied with 2 each.			

Innings Pitched

	Gm	IP
Whitey Ford, NY Yankees	22	146.0
Christy Mathewson, NY Giants	11	101.2
Red Ruffing, NY Yankees	10	85.2
Chief Bender, Philadelphia A's	10	85.0
Waite Hoyt, NY Yankees-Phi. A's	12	83.2

Complete Games

	GS	CG	W-L
Christy Mathewson, NY Giants	11	10	5-5
Chief Bender, Philadelphia A's	10	9	6-4
Bob Gibson, St. Louis	9	8	7-2
Whitey Ford, NY Yankees	22	7	10-8
Red Ruffing, NY Yankees	10	7	7-2

Strikeouts

	Gm	IP	SO
Whitey Ford, NY Yankees	22	146.0	94
Bob Gibson, St. Louis	9	81.0	92
Allie Reynolds, NY Yankees	15	77.1	62
Sandy Koufax, Los Angeles	8	57.0	61
Red Ruffing, NY Yankees	10	85.2	61

Losses

	Gm	W-L
Whitey Ford, NY Yankees	22	10-8
Christy Mathewson, NY Giants	11	5-5
Joe Bush, Phi. A's-Bosox-NY Yankees	9	2-5
Rube Marquard, NY Giants-Brooklyn	11	2-5
Eddie Plank, Philadelphia A's	7	2-5
Schoolboy Rowe, Detroit	8	2-5

League Championship Series

Division play came to the major leagues in 1969 when both the American and National Leagues expanded to 12 teams. With an East and West Division in each league, League Championship Series (LCS) became necessary to determine the NL and AL pennant winners. In 1994, teams were realigned into three divisions, the East, Central, and West with division winners and one wildcard team playing a best of five series to determine the LCS competitors. In the charts below, the East Division champions are noted by the letter E, the Central division champions by C and the West Division champions by W. A wildcard winner is noted by WC. Also, each playoff winner's wins and losses are noted in parentheses after the series score. The LCS changed from best-of-5 to best-of-7 in 1985. Each league's LCS was cancelled in 1994 due to the players' strike.

National League

Multiple champions: Atlanta, Cincinnati and LA Dodgers (5); NY Mets (4); Philadelphia and St. Louis (3); Pittsburgh and San Diego (2).

Year	Winner	Manager	Series		Loser	Manager
1969	E- New York	Gil Hodges	3-0		W- Atlanta	Lum Harris
1970	W- Cincinnati	Sparky Anderson	3-0		E- Pittsburgh	Danny Murtaugh
1971	E- Pittsburgh	Danny Murtaugh	3-1 (LWWW)		W- San Francisco	Charlie Fox
1972	W- Cincinnati	Sparky Anderson	3-2 (LWLWW)		E- Pittsburgh	Bill Virdon
1973	E- New York	Yogi Berra	3-2 (LWLWW)		W- Cincinnati	Sparky Anderson
1974	W- Los Angeles	Walter Alston	3-1 (WWLW)		E- Pittsburgh	Danny Murtaugh
1975	W- Cincinnati	Sparky Anderson	3-0		E- Pittsburgh	Danny Murtaugh
1976	W- Cincinnati	Sparky Anderson	3-0		E- Philadelphia	Danny Ozark
1977	W- Los Angeles	Tommy Lasorda	3-1 (LWWW)		E- Philadelphia	Danny Ozark
1978	W- Los Angeles	Tommy Lasorda	3-1 (WWLW)		E- Philadelphia	Danny Ozark
1979	E- Pittsburgh	Chuck Tanner	3-0		W- Cincinnati	John McNamara
1980	E- Philadelphia	Dallas Green	3-2 (WLLWW)		W- Houston	Bill Virdon
1981	W- Los Angeles	Tommy Lasorda	3-2 (WLLWW)		E- Montreal	Jim Fanning
1982	E- St. Louis	Whitey Herzog	3-0		W- Atlanta	Joe Torre
1983	E- Philadelphia	Paul Owens	3-1 (WLWW)		W- Los Angeles	Tommy Lasorda
1984	W- San Diego	Dick Williams	3-2 (LLWWW)		E- Chicago	Jim Frey
1985	E- St. Louis	Whitey Herzog	4-2 (LLWWWW)		W- Los Angeles	Tommy Lasorda
1986	E- New York	Davey Johnson	4-2 (LWWLWW)		W- Houston	Hal Lanier
1987	E- St. Louis	Whitey Herzog	4-3 (WWLLWLW)		W- San Francisco	Roger Craig
1988	W- Los Angeles	Tommy Lasorda	4-3 (LWLWWLW)		E- New York	Davey Johnson
1989	W- San Francisco	Roger Craig	4-1 (WLWWW)		E- Chicago	Don Zimmer
1990	W- Cincinnati	Lou Piniella	4-2 (LWWLWW)		E- Pittsburgh	Jim Leyland
1991	W- Atlanta	Bobby Cox	4-3 (LWWLLWW)		E- Pittsburgh	Jim Leyland

Year	Winner	Manager	Series	Loser	Manager
1992	W- Atlanta	Bobby Cox	4-3 (WWLWLLW)	E- Pittsburgh	Jim Leyland
1993	E- Philadelphia	Jim Fregosi	4-2 (WLLWWW)	W- Atlanta	Bobby Cox
1994	Not held				
1995	E- Atlanta	Bobby Cox	4-0	C- Cincinnati	Davey Johnson
1996	E- Atlanta	Bobby Cox	4-3 (WLLLWWW)	C- St. Louis	Tony La Russa
1997	WC-Florida	Jim Leyland	4-2 (WLWLWW)	E-Atlanta	Bobby Cox
1998	W-San Diego	Bruce Bochy	4-2 (WWWLLW)	E-Atlanta	Bobby Cox
1999	E-Atlanta	Bobby Cox	4-2 (WWWLLW)	WC-New York	Bobby Valentine
2000	WC-New York	Bobby Valentine	4-1 (WWLWW)	C- St. Louis	Tony La Russa
2001	W-Arizona	Bob Brenly	4-1 (WLWWW)	E-Atlanta	Bobby Cox

NLCS Most Valuable Players

Winners who did not play for NLCS champions are in **bold** type.

Multiple winner: Steve Garvey (2).

Year	Year	Year
1977 Dusty Baker, LA, OF	1986 **Mike Scott,** Hou., P	1994 LCS not held.
1978 Steve Garvey, LA, 1B	1987 **Jeff Leonard,** SF, OF	1995 Mike Devereaux, Atl., OF
1979 Willie Stargell, Pit., 1B	1988 Orel Hershiser, LA, P	1996 Javy Lopez, Atl., C
1980 Manny Trillo, Phi., 2B	1989 Will Clark, SF, 1B	1997 Livan Hernandez, Fla., P
1981 Burt Hooton, LA, P	1990 Rob Dibble, Cin., P	1998 Sterling Hitchcock, SD, P
1982 Darrell Porter, St.L., C	& Randy Myers, Cin., P	1999 Eddie Perez, Atl., C
1983 Gary Matthews, Phi., OF	1991 Steve Avery, Atl., P	2000 Mike Hampton, NY, P
1984 Steve Garvey, SD, 1B	1992 John Smoltz, Atl., P	2001 Craig Counsell, Ari., 2B
1985 Ozzie Smith, St.L., SS	1993 Curt Schilling, Phi., P	

American League

Multiple champions: NY Yankees (9); Oakland (6); Baltimore (5); Boston, Cleveland, Kansas City, Minnesota and Toronto (2).

Year	Winner	Manager	Series	Loser	Manager
1969	E- Baltimore	Earl Weaver	3-0	W- Minnesota	Billy Martin
1970	E- Baltimore	Earl Weaver	3-0	W- Minnesota	Bill Rigney
1971	E- Baltimore	Earl Weaver	3-0	W- Oakland	Dick Williams
1972	W- Oakland	Dick Williams	3-2 (WWLLW)	E- Detroit	Billy Martin
1973	W- Oakland	Dick Williams	3-2 (LWWLW)	E- Baltimore	Earl Weaver
1974	W- Oakland	Alvin Dark	3-1 (LWWW)	E- Baltimore	Earl Weaver
1975	E- Boston	Darrell Johnson	3-0	W- Oakland	Alvin Dark
1976	E- New York	Billy Martin	3-2 (WLWLW)	W- Kansas City	Whitey Herzog
1977	E- New York	Billy Martin	3-2 (LWLWW)	W- Kansas City	Whitey Herzog
1978	E- New York	Bob Lemon	3-1 (WLWW)	W- Kansas City	Whitey Herzog
1979	E- Baltimore	Earl Weaver	3-1 (WWLW)	W- California	Jim Fregosi
1980	W- Kansas City	Jim Frey	3-0	E- New York	Dick Howser
1981	E- New York	Bob Lemon	3-0	W- Oakland	Billy Martin
1982	E- Milwaukee	Harvey Kuenn	3-2 (LLWWW)	W- California	Gene Mauch
1983	E- Baltimore	Joe Altobelli	3-1 (LWWW)	W- Chicago	Tony La Russa
1984	E- Detroit	Sparky Anderson	3-0	W- Kansas City	Dick Howser
1985	W- Kansas City	Dick Howser	4-3 (LLWLWWW)	E- Toronto	Bobby Cox
1986	E- Boston	John McNamara	4-3 (LWLLWWW)	W- California	Gene Mauch
1987	W- Minnesota	Tom Kelly	4-1 (WWLWW)	E- Detroit	Sparky Anderson
1988	W- Oakland	Tony La Russa	4-0	E- Boston	Joe Morgan
1989	W- Oakland	Tony La Russa	4-1 (WWLWW)	E- Toronto	Cito Gaston
1990	W- Oakland	Tony La Russa	4-0	E- Boston	Joe Morgan
1991	W- Minnesota	Tom Kelly	4-1 (WLWLW)	E- Toronto	Cito Gaston
1992	E- Toronto	Cito Gaston	4-2 (LWWWLW)	W- Oakland	Tony La Russa
1993	E- Toronto	Cito Gaston	4-2 (WWLLWW)	W- Chicago	Gene Lamont
1994	Not held				
1995	C- Cleveland	Mike Hargrove	4-2 (LWLWWW)	W- Seattle	Lou Piniella
1996	E- New York	Joe Torre	4-1 (WLWWW)	WC- Baltimore	Davey Johnson
1997	C- Cleveland	Mike Hargrove	4-2 (LWWWLW)	E- Baltimore	Davey Johnson
1998	E- New York	Joe Torre	4-2 (WLLWWW)	C- Cleveland	Mike Hargrove
1999	E- New York	Joe Torre	4-1 (WLWWW)	WC- Boston	Jimy Williams
2000	E- New York	Joe Torre	4-2 (LWWWLW)	WC- Seattle	Lou Piniella
2001	E- New York	Joe Torre	4-1 (WWLWW)	W- Seattle	Lou Piniella

ALCS Most Valuable Players

Winner who did not play for ALCS champions is in **bold** type.

Multiple winner: Dave Stewart (2).

Year	Year	Year
1980 Frank White, KC, 2B	1988 Dennis Eckersley, Oak., P	1996 Bernie Williams, NY, OF
1981 Graig Nettles, NY, 3B	1989 Rickey Henderson, Oak., OF	1997 Marquis Grissom, Cle., OF
1982 **Fred Lynn,** Cal., OF	1990 Dave Stewart, Oak., P	1998 David Wells, NY, P
1983 Mike Boddicker, Bal., P	1991 Kirby Puckett, Min., OF	1999 Orlando Hernandez, NY, P
1984 Kirk Gibson, Det., OF	1992 Roberto Alomar, Tor., 2B	2000 Dave Justice, NY, OF
1985 George Brett, KC, 3B	1993 Dave Stewart, Tor., P	2001 Andy Pettitte, NY, P
1986 Marty Barrett, Bos., 2B	1994 LCS not held.	
1987 Gary Gaetti, Min., 3B	1995 Orel Hershiser, Cle., P	

Other Playoffs

Ten times since 1946, playoffs have been necessary to decide league or division championships or wild card berths when two teams were tied at the end of the regular season. Additionally, in the strike year of 1981 there were playoffs between the first and second half-season champions in both leagues.

National League

Year	NL	W	L	Manager
1946	Brooklyn	96	58	Leo Durocher
	St. Louis	96	58	Eddie Dyer
	Playoff: (Best-of-3) St. Louis, 2-0			

	NL	W	L	Manager
1951	Brooklyn	96	58	Charlie Dressen
	New York	96	58	Leo Durocher
	Playoff: (Best-of-3) New York, 2-1 (WLW)			

	NL	W	L	Manager
1959	Milwaukee	86	68	Fred Haney
	Los Angeles	86	68	Walter Alston
	Playoff: (Best-of-3) Los Angeles, 2-0			

	NL	W	L	Manager
1962	Los Angeles	101	61	Walter Alston
	San Francisco	101	61	Alvin Dark
	Playoff: (Best-of-3) San Francisco, 2-1 (WLW)			

	NL West	W	L	Manager
1980	Houston	92	70	Bill Virdon
	Los Angeles	92	70	Tommy Lasorda
	Playoff: (1 game) Houston, 7-1 (at LA)			

Year	NL East	W	L	Manager
1981	(1st Half) Philadelphia	34	21	Dallas Green
	(2nd Half) Montreal	30	23	Jim Fanning
	Playoff: (Best-of-5) Montreal, 3-2 (WWLLW)			

	NL West	W	L	Manager
1981	(1st Half) Los Angeles	36	21	Tommy Lasorda
	(2nd Half) Houston	33	20	Bill Virdon
	Playoff: (Best-of-5) Los Angeles, 3-2 (LLWWW)			

	NL Wild Card	W	L	Manager
1998	Chicago	89	73	Jim Riggleman
	San Francisco	89	73	Dusty Baker
	Playoff: (1 game) Chicago, 5-3 (at Chicago)			

	NL Wild Card	W	L	Manager
1999	Cincinnati	96	66	Jack McKeon
	New York	96	66	Bobby Valentine
	Playoff: (1 game) New York, 5-0 (at Cincinnati)			

American League

Year	AL	W	L	Manager
1948	Boston	96	58	Joe McCarthy
	Cleveland	96	58	Lou Boudreau
	Playoff: (1 game) Cleveland, 8-3 (at Boston)			

	AL East	W	L	Manager
1978	Boston	99	63	Don Zimmer
	New York	99	63	Bob Lemon
	Playoff: (1 game) New York, 5-4 (at Boston)			

	AL East	W	L	Manager
1981	(1st Half) N.Y.	34	22	Bob Lemon
	(2nd Half) Milw.	31	22	Buck Rodgers
	Playoff: (Best-of-5) New York, 3-2 (WWLLW)			

Year	AL West	W	L	Manager
1981	(1st Half) Oakland	37	23	Billy Martin
	(2nd Half) Kan. City	30	23	Jim Frey
	Playoff: (Best-of-5), Oakland, 3-0			

	AL West	W	L	Manager
1995	Seattle	78	66	Lou Piniella
	California	78	66	M. Lachemann
	Playoff: (1 game) Seattle, 9-1 (at Seattle)			

Regular Season League & Division Winners

Regular season National and American League pennant winners from 1900-68, as well as West and East divisional champions from 1969-93. In 1994, both leagues went to three divisions, West, Central and East, and each league also sent a wild card (WC) team to the playoffs. Note that (*) indicates 1994 divisional champion is unofficial (due to the players' strike). Note that **GA** column indicates games ahead of the second place club.

National League

Year		W	L	Pct	GA	Year		W	L	Pct	GA
1900	Brooklyn	82	54	.603	4½	1926	St. Louis	89	65	.578	2
1901	Pittsburgh	90	49	.647	7½	1927	Pittsburgh	94	60	.610	1½
1902	Pittsburgh	103	36	.741	27½	1928	St. Louis	95	59	.617	2
1903	Pittsburgh	91	49	.650	6½	1929	Chicago	98	54	.645	10½
1904	New York	106	47	.693	13	1930	St. Louis	92	62	.597	2
1905	New York	105	48	.686	9	1931	St. Louis	101	53	.656	13
1906	Chicago	116	36	.763	20	1932	Chicago	90	64	.584	4
1907	Chicago	107	45	.704	17	1933	New York	91	61	.599	5
1908	Chicago	99	55	.643	1	1934	St. Louis	95	58	.621	2
1909	Pittsburgh	110	42	.724	6½	1935	Chicago	100	54	.649	4
1910	Chicago	104	50	.675	13	1936	New York	92	62	.597	5
1911	New York	99	54	.647	7½	1937	New York	95	57	.625	3
1912	New York	103	48	.682	10	1938	Chicago	89	63	.586	2
1913	New York	101	51	.664	12½	1939	Cincinnati	97	57	.630	4½
1914	Boston	94	59	.614	10½	1940	Cincinnati	100	53	.654	12
1915	Philadelphia	90	62	.592	7	1941	Brooklyn	100	54	.649	2½
1916	Brooklyn	94	60	.610	2½	1942	St. Louis	106	48	.688	2
1917	New York	98	56	.636	10	1943	St. Louis	105	49	.682	18
1918	Chicago	84	45	.651	10½	1944	St. Louis	105	49	.682	14½
1919	Cincinnati	96	44	.686	9	1945	Chicago	98	56	.636	3
1920	Brooklyn	93	61	.604	7	1946	St. Louis†	98	58	.628	2
1921	New York	94	59	.614	4	1947	Brooklyn	94	60	.610	5
1922	New York	93	61	.604	7	1948	Boston	91	62	.595	6½
1923	New York	95	58	.621	4½	1949	Brooklyn	97	57	.630	1
1924	New York	93	60	.608	1½	1950	Philadelphia	91	63	.591	2
1925	Pittsburgh	95	58	.621	8½	1951	New York†	98	59	.624	1

Year		W	L	Pct	GA	Year		W	L	Pct	GA
1952	Brooklyn	96	57	.627	4½	1985	West—Los Angeles	95	67	.586	5½
1953	Brooklyn	105	49	.682	13		East—St. Louis	101	61	.623	3
1954	New York	97	57	.630	5	1986	West—Houston	96	66	.593	10
1955	Brooklyn	98	55	.641	13½		East—N.Y. Mets	108	54	.667	21½
1956	Brooklyn	93	61	.604	1	1987	West—San Francisco	90	72	.556	6
1957	Milwaukee	95	59	.617	8		East—St. Louis	95	67	.586	3
1958	Milwaukee	92	62	.597	8	1988	West—Los Angeles	94	67	.584	7
1959	Los Angeles†	88	68	.564	2		East—N.Y. Mets	100	60	.625	15
1960	Pittsburgh	95	59	.617	7	1989	West—San Francisco	92	70	.568	3
1961	Cincinnati	93	61	.604	4		East—Chicago	93	69	.574	6
1962	San Francisco†	103	62	.624	1	1990	West—Cincinnati	91	71	.562	5
1963	Los Angeles	99	63	.611	6		East—Pittsburgh	95	67	.586	4
1964	St. Louis	93	69	.574	1	1991	West—Atlanta	94	68	.580	1
1965	Los Angeles	97	65	.599	2		East—Pittsburgh	98	64	.605	14
1966	Los Angeles	95	67	.586	1½	1992	West—Atlanta	98	64	.605	8
1967	St. Louis	101	60	.627	10½		East—Pittsburgh	96	66	.593	9
1968	St. Louis	97	65	.599	9	1993	West—Atlanta	104	58	.642	1
1969	West—Atlanta	93	69	.574	3		East—Philadelphia	97	65	.599	3
	East—N.Y. Mets	100	62	.617	8	1994	West—Los Angeles*	58	56	.509	3½
1970	West—Cincinnati	102	60	.630	14½		Central—Cincinnati*	66	48	.579	½
	East—Pittsburgh	89	73	.549	5		East—Montreal*	74	40	.649	6
1971	West—San Francisco	90	72	.556	1	1995	West—Los Angeles	78	66	.542	1
	East—Pittsburgh	97	65	.599	7		Central—Cincinnati	85	59	.590	9
1972	West—Cincinnati	95	59	.617	10½		East—Atlanta	90	54	.625	21
	East—Pittsburgh	96	59	.619	11		WC—Colorado	77	67	.535	—
1973	West—Cincinnati	99	63	.611	3½	1996	West—San Diego	91	71	.562	1
	East—N.Y. Mets	82	79	.509	1½		Central—St. Louis	88	74	.543	6
1974	West—Los Angeles	102	60	.630	4		East—Atlanta	96	66	.593	8
	East—Pittsburgh	88	74	.543	1½		WC—Los Angeles	90	72	.556	—
1975	West—Cincinnati	108	54	.667	20	1997	West—San Francisco	90	72	.556	2
	East—Pittsburgh	92	69	.571	6½		Central—Houston	84	78	.519	5
1976	West—Cincinnati	102	60	.630	10		East—Atlanta	101	61	.623	9
	East—Philadelphia	101	61	.623	9		WC—Florida	92	70	.568	—
1977	West—Los Angeles	98	64	.605	10	1998	West—San Diego	98	64	.605	9½
	East—Philadelphia	101	61	.623	5		Central—Houston	102	60	.630	12½
1978	West—Los Angeles	95	67	.586	2½		East—Atlanta	106	56	.654	18
	East—Philadelphia	90	72	.556	1½		WC—Chicago†	90	73	.552	—
1979	West—Cincinnati	90	71	.559	1½	1999	West—Arizona	100	62	.617	14
	East—Pittsburgh	98	64	.605	2		Central—Houston	97	65	.599	1½
1980	West—Houston †	93	70	.571	1		East—Atlanta	103	59	.636	6½
	East—Philadelphia	91	71	.562	1		WC—N.Y. Mets†	97	66	.595	—
1981	West—Los Angeles$	63	47	.573	—	2000	West—San Francisco	97	65	.599	11
	East—Montreal$	60	48	.556	—		Central—St. Louis	95	67	.586	10
1982	West—Atlanta	89	73	.549	1		East—Atlanta	95	67	.586	1
	East—St. Louis	92	70	.568	3		WC—N.Y. Mets	94	68	.580	—
1983	West—Los Angeles	91	71	.562	3	2001	West—Arizona	92	70	.568	2
	East—Philadelphia	90	72	.556	6		Central—Houston@	93	69	.574	—
1984	West—San Diego	92	70	.568	12		East—Atlanta	88	74	.543	2
	East—Chicago	96	65	.596	6½		WC—St. Louis	93	69	.574	—

†**Regular season playoffs:** See "Other Playoffs" on page 94 for details.
$**Divisional playoffs:** See "Other Playoffs" on page 94 for details.
@Houston (93-69) won the division over St. Louis (93-69) due to a better head-to-head record.

American League

Year		W	L	Pct	GA	Year		W	L	Pct	GA
1901	Chicago	83	53	.610	4	1919	Chicago	88	52	.629	3½
1902	Philadelphia	83	53	.610	5	1920	Cleveland	98	56	.636	2
1903	Boston	91	47	.659	14½	1921	New York	98	55	.641	4½
1904	Boston	95	59	.617	1½	1922	New York	94	60	.610	1
1905	Philadelphia	92	56	.622	2	1923	New York	98	54	.645	16
1906	Chicago	93	58	.616	3	1924	Washington	92	62	.597	2
1907	Detroit	92	58	.613	1½	1925	Washington	96	55	.636	8½
1908	Detroit	90	63	.588	½	1926	New York	91	63	.591	3
1909	Detroit	98	54	.645	3½	1927	New York	110	44	.714	19
1910	Philadelphia	102	48	.680	14½	1928	New York	101	53	.656	2½
1911	Philadelphia	101	50	.669	13½	1929	Philadelphia	104	46	.693	18
1912	Boston	105	47	.691	14	1930	Philadelphia	102	52	.662	8
1913	Philadelphia	96	57	.627	6½	1931	Philadelphia	107	45	.704	13½
1914	Philadelphia	99	53	.651	8½	1932	New York	107	47	.695	13
1915	Boston	101	50	.669	2½	1933	Washington	99	53	.651	7
1916	Boston	91	63	.591	2	1934	Detroit	101	53	.656	7
1917	Chicago	100	54	.649	9	1935	Detroit	93	58	.616	3
1918	Boston	75	51	.595	2½	1936	New York	102	51	.667	19½

Year		W	L	Pct	GA
1937	New York	102	52	.662	13
1938	New York	99	53	.651	9½
1939	New York	106	45	.702	17
1940	Detroit	90	64	.584	1
1941	New York	101	53	.656	17
1942	New York	103	51	.669	9
1943	New York	98	56	.636	13½
1944	St. Louis	89	65	.578	1
1945	Detroit	88	65	.575	1½
1946	Boston	104	50	.675	12
1947	New York	97	57	.630	12
1948	Cleveland†	97	58	.626	1
1949	New York	97	57	.630	1
1950	New York	98	56	.636	3
1951	New York	98	56	.636	5
1952	New York	95	59	.617	2
1953	New York	99	52	.656	8½
1954	Cleveland	111	43	.721	8
1955	New York	96	58	.623	3
1956	New York	97	57	.630	9
1957	New York	98	56	.636	8
1958	New York	92	62	.597	10
1959	Chicago	94	60	.610	5
1960	New York	97	57	.630	8
1961	New York	109	53	.673	8
1962	New York	96	66	.593	5
1963	New York	104	57	.646	10½
1964	New York	99	63	.611	1
1965	Minnesota	102	60	.630	7
1966	Baltimore	97	63	.606	9
1967	Boston	92	70	.568	1
1968	Detroit	103	59	.636	12
1969	West—Minnesota	97	65	.599	9
	East—Baltimore	109	53	.673	19
1970	West—Minnesota	98	64	.605	9
	East—Baltimore	108	54	.667	15
1971	West—Oakland	101	60	.627	16
	East—Baltimore	101	57	.639	12
1972	West—Oakland	93	62	.600	5½
	East—Detroit	86	70	.551	½
1973	West—Oakland	94	68	.580	6
	East—Baltimore	97	65	.599	8
1974	West—Oakland	90	72	.556	5
	East—Baltimore	91	71	.562	2
1975	West—Oakland	98	64	.605	7
	East—Boston	95	65	.594	4½
1976	West—Kansas City	90	72	.556	2½
	East—New York	97	62	.610	10½
1977	West—Kansas City	102	60	.630	8
	East—New York	100	62	.617	2½
1978	West—Kansas City	92	70	.568	5
	East—New York†	100	63	.613	1
1979	West—California	88	74	.543	3
	East—Baltimore	102	57	.642	8
1980	West—Kansas City	97	65	.599	14
	East—New York	103	59	.636	3
1981	West—Oakland$	64	45	.587	—

Year		W	L	Pct	GA
	East—New York$	59	48	.551	—
1982	West—California	93	69	.574	3
	East—Milwaukee	95	67	.586	1
1983	West—Chicago	99	63	.611	20
	East—Baltimore	98	64	.605	6
1984	West—Kansas City	84	78	.519	3
	East—Detroit	104	58	.642	15
1985	West—Kansas City	91	71	.562	1
	East—Toronto	99	62	.615	2
1986	West—California	92	70	.568	5
	East—Boston	95	66	.590	5½
1987	West—Minnesota	85	77	.525	2
	East—Detroit	98	64	.605	2
1988	West—Oakland	104	58	.642	13
	East—Boston	89	73	.549	1
1989	West—Oakland	99	63	.611	7
	East—Toronto	89	73	.549	2
1990	West—Oakland	103	59	.636	9
	East—Boston	88	74	.543	2
1991	West—Minnesota	95	67	.586	8
	East—Toronto	91	71	.562	7
1992	West—Oakland	96	66	.593	6
	East—Toronto	96	66	.593	4
1993	West—Chicago	94	68	.580	8
	East—Toronto	95	67	.586	7
1994	West—Texas*	52	62	.456	1
	Central—Chicago*	67	46	.593	1
	East—New York*	70	43	.619	6½
1995	West—Seattle†	79	66	.545	1
	Central—Cleveland	100	44	.694	30
	East—Boston	86	58	.597	7
	WC—New York	79	65	.549	—
1996	West—Texas	90	72	.556	4½
	Central—Cleveland	99	62	.615	14½
	East—New York	92	70	.568	4
	WC—Baltimore	88	74	.543	—
1997	West—Seattle	90	72	.556	6
	Central—Cleveland	86	75	.534	6
	East—Baltimore	98	64	.605	2
	WC—New York	96	66	.593	—
1998	West—Texas	88	74	.543	3
	Central—Chicago	89	73	.549	9
	East—New York	114	48	.704	22
	WC—Boston	92	70	.568	—
1999	West—Texas	95	67	.586	8
	Central—Cleveland	97	65	.599	21½
	East—New York	98	64	.605	4
	WC—Boston	94	68	.580	—
2000	West—Oakland	91	70	.565	½
	Central—Chicago	95	67	.586	5
	East—New York	87	74	.540	2½
	WC—Seattle	91	71	.562	—
2001	West—Seattle	116	46	.716	14
	Central—Cleveland	91	71	.562	6
	East—New York	95	65	.594	13½
	WC—Oakland	102	60	.630	—

†**Regular season playoffs:** See "Other Playoffs" on page 94 for details.
$**Divisional playoffs:** See "Other Playoffs" on page 94 for details.

The All-Star Game

Baseball's first All-Star Game was held on July 6, 1933, before 47,595 at Comiskey Park in Chicago. From that year on, the All-Star Game has matched the best players in the American League against the best in the National. From 1959-62, two All-Star Games were played. The only year an All-Star Game wasn't played was 1945, when World War II travel restrictions made it necessary to cancel the meeting. The NL leads the series, 40-31-1. In the chart below, the American League is listed in **bold** type.

MVP Multiple winners: Gary Carter, Steve Garvey, Willie Mays and Cal Ripken Jr. (2).

Year		Host	AL Manager	NL Manager	MVP
1933	**American,** 4-2	Chicago (AL)	Connie Mack	John McGraw	No award
1934	**American,** 9-7	New York (NL)	Joe Cronin	Bill Terry	No award
1935	**American,** 4-1	Cleveland	Mickey Cochrane	Frankie Frisch	No award
1936	National, 4-3	Boston (NL)	Joe McCarthy	Charlie Grimm	No award
1937	**American,** 8-3	Washington	Joe McCarthy	Bill Terry	No award

Year		Host	AL Manager	NL Manager	MVP
1938	National, 4-1	Cincinnati	Joe McCarthy	Bill Terry	No award
1939	**American**, 3-1	New York (AL)	Joe McCarthy	Gabby Hartnett	No award
1940	National, 4-0	St. Louis (NL)	Joe Cronin	Bill McKechnie	No award
1941	**American**, 7-5	Detroit	Del Baker	Bill McKechnie	No award
1942	**American**, 3-1	New York (NL)	Joe McCarthy	Leo Durocher	No award
1943	**American**, 5-3	Philadelphia (AL)	Joe McCarthy	Billy Southworth	No award
1944	National, 7-1	Pittsburgh	Joe McCarthy	Billy Southworth	No award
1945	Not held				
1946	**American**, 12-0	Boston (AL)	Steve O'Neill	Charlie Grimm	No award
1947	**American**, 2-1	Chicago (NL)	Joe Cronin	Eddie Dyer	No award
1948	**American**, 5-2	St. Louis (AL)	Bucky Harris	Leo Durocher	No award
1949	**American**, 11-7	Brooklyn	Lou Boudreau	Billy Southworth	No award
1950	National, 4-3 (14)	Chicago (AL)	Casey Stengel	Burt Shotton	No award
1951	National, 8-3	Detroit	Casey Stengel	Eddie Sawyer	No award
1952	National, 3-2 (5, rain)	Philadelphia (NL)	Casey Stengel	Leo Durocher	No award
1953	National, 5-1	Cincinnati	Casey Stengel	Charlie Dressen	No award
1954	**American**, 11-9	Cleveland	Casey Stengel	Walter Alston	No award
1955	National, 6-5 (12)	Milwaukee	Al Lopez	Leo Durocher	No award
1956	National, 7-3	Washington	Casey Stengel	Walter Alston	No award
1957	**American**, 6-5	St. Louis	Casey Stengel	Walter Alston	No award
1958	**American**, 4-3	Baltimore	Casey Stengel	Fred Haney	No award
1959-a	National, 5-4	Pittsburgh	Casey Stengel	Fred Haney	No award
1959-b	**American**, 5-3	Los Angeles	Casey Stengel	Fred Haney	No award
1960-a	National, 5-3	Kansas City	Al Lopez	Walter Alston	No award
1960-b	National, 6-0	New York	Al Lopez	Walter Alston	No award
1961-a	National, 5-4 (10)	San Francisco	Paul Richards	Danny Murtaugh	No award
1961-b	TIE, 1-1 (9, rain)	Boston	Paul Richards	Danny Murtaugh	No award
1962-a	National, 3-1	Washington	Ralph Houk	Fred Hutchinson	Maury Wills, LA (NL), SS
1962-b	**American**, 9-4	Chicago (NL)	Ralph Houk	Fred Hutchinson	Leon Wagner, LA (AL), OF
1963	National, 5-3	Cleveland	Ralph Houk	Alvin Dark	Willie Mays, SF, OF
1964	National, 7-4	New York (NL)	Al Lopez	Walter Alston	Johnny Callison, Phi., OF
1965	National, 6-5	Minnesota	Al Lopez	Gene Mauch	Juan Marichal, SF, P
1966	National, 2-1 (10)	St. Louis	Sam Mele	Walter Alston	Brooks Robinson, Bal., 3B
1967	National, 2-1 (15)	California	Hank Bauer	Walter Alston	Tony Perez, Cin., 3B
1968	National, 1-0	Houston	Dick Williams	Red Schoendienst	Willie Mays, SF, OF
1969	National, 9-3	Washington	Mayo Smith	Red Schoendienst	Willie McCovey, SF, 1B
1970	National, 5-4 (12)	Cincinnati	Earl Weaver	Gil Hodges	Carl Yastrzemski, Bos., OF-1B
1971	**American**, 6-4	Detroit	Earl Weaver	Sparky Anderson	Frank Robinson, Bal., OF
1972	National, 4-3 (10)	Atlanta	Earl Weaver	Danny Murtaugh	Joe Morgan, Con., 2B
1973	National, 7-1	Kansas	Dick Williams	Sparky Anderson	Bobby Bonds, SF, OF
1974	National, 7-2	Pittsburgh	Dick Williams	Yogi Berra	Steve Garvey, LA, 1B
1975	National, 6-3	Milwaukee	Alvin Dark	Walter Alston	Bill Madlock, Chi. (NL), 3B & Jon Matlack, NY (NL), P
1976	National, 7-1	Philadelphia	Darrell Johnson	Sparky Anderson	George Foster, Cin., OF
1977	National, 7-5	New York (AL)	Billy Martin	Sparky Anderson	Don Sutton, LA, P
1978	National, 7-3	San Diego	Billy Martin	Tommy Lasorda	Steve Garvey, LA, 1B
1979	National, 7-6	Seattle	Bob Lemon	Tommy Lasorda	Dave Parker, Pit, OF
1980	National, 4-2	Los Angeles	Earl Weaver	Chuck Tanner	Ken Griffey, Cin., OF
1981	National, 5-4	Cleveland	Jim Frey	Dallas Green	Gary Carter, Mon., C
1982	National, 4-1	Montreal	Billy Martin	Tommy Lasorda	Dave Concepcion, Cin., SS
1983	**American**, 13-3	Chicago (AL)	Harvey Kuenn	Whitey Herzog	Fred Lynn, Cal., OF
1984	National, 3-1	San Francisco	Joe Altobelli	Paul Owens	Gary Carter, Mon., C
1985	National, 6-1	Minnesota	Sparky Anderson	Dick Williams	LaMarr Hoyt, SD, P
1986	**American**, 3-2	Houston	Dick Howser	Whitey Herzog	Roger Clemens, Bos., P
1987	National, 2-0 (13)	Oakland	John McNamara	Davey Johnson	Tim Raines, Mon., OF
1988	**American**, 2-1	Cincinnati	Tom Kelly	Whitey Herzog	Terry Steinbach, Oak., C
1989	**American**, 5-3	California	Tony La Russa	Tommy Lasorda	Bo Jackson, KC, OF
1990	**American**, 2-0	Chicago (NL)	Tony La Russa	Roger Craig	Julio Franco, Tex., 2B
1991	**American**, 4-2	Toronto	Tony La Russa	Lou Piniella	Cal Ripken Jr., Bal., SS
1992	**American**, 13-6	San Diego	Tom Kelly	Bobby Cox	Ken Griffey Jr., Sea., OF
1993	**American**, 9-3	Baltimore	Cito Gaston	Bobby Cox	Kirby Puckett, Min., OF
1994	National, 8-7 (10)	Pittsburgh	Cito Gaston	Jim Fregosi	Fred McGriff, Atl., 1B
1995	National, 3-2	Texas	Buck Showalter	Felipe Alou	Jeff Conine, Fla., PH
1996	National, 6-0	Philadelphia	Mike Hargrove	Bobby Cox	Mike Piazza, LA, C
1997	**American**, 3-1	Cleveland	Joe Torre	Bobby Cox	Sandy Alomar Jr., Cle., C
1998	**American**, 13-8	Colorado	Mike Hargrove	Jim Leyland	Roberto Alomar, Bal., 2B
1999	**American**, 4-1	Boston	Joe Torre	Bruce Bochy	Pedro Martinez, Bos., P
2000	**American**, 6-3	Atlanta	Joe Torre	Bobby Cox	Derek Jeter, NY (AL), SS
2001	**American**, 4-1	Seattle	Joe Torre	Bobby Valentine	Cal Ripken Jr., Bal., SS-3B

Major League Franchise Origins

Here is what the current 30 teams in Major League Baseball have to show for the years they have put in as members of the National League (NL) and American League (AL). Pennants and World Series championships are since 1901.

National League

	1st Year	Pennants & World Series	Franchise Stops
Arizona Diamondbacks	1998	1 NL (2001) 1 WS (2001)	• Phoenix (1998–)

Atlanta Braves	1876	9 NL (1914,48,57-58,91-92,95,96,99)
		3 WS (1914,57,95)
			• Boston (1876–1952)
			  Milwaukee (1953–65)
			  Atlanta (1966–)

Chicago Cubs	1876	10 NL (1906-08,10,18,29,32,35,38,45) 2 WS (1907-08)	• Chicago (1876–)
Cincinnati Reds	1876	9 NL (1919,39-40,61,70,72,75-76,90) 5 WS (1919,40,75-76,90)	• Cincinnati (1876–80) Cincinnati (1890–)
Colorado Rockies	1993	None	• Denver (1993–)
Florida Marlins	1993	1 NL (1997) 1 WS (1997)	• Miami (1993–)
Houston Astros	1962	None	• Houston (1962–)
Los Angeles Dodgers	1890	18 NL (1916,20,41,47,49,52-53,55-56, 59,63, 65-66,74,77-78, 81,88) 6 WS (1955,59,63,65,81,88)	• Brooklyn (1890-1957) Los Angeles (1958–)
Milwaukee Brewers	1969	1 AL (1982)	• Seattle (1969) Milwaukee (1970–)
Montreal Expos	1969	None	• Montreal (1969–)
New York Mets	1962	4 NL (1969,73,86,00) 2 WS (1969,86)	• New York (1962–)
Philadelphia Phillies	1883	5 NL (1915,50,80,83,93) 1 WS (1980)	• Philadelphia (1883–)
Pittsburgh Pirates	1887	7 NL (1903,09,25,27,60,71,79) 5 WS (1909,25,60,71,79)	• Pittsburgh (1887–)
St. Louis Cardinals	1892	15 NL (1926,28,30-31,34,42-44,46,64, 67-68,82,85,87) 9 WS (1926,31,34,42,44,46,64,67,82)	• St. Louis (1892–)
San Diego Padres	1969	2 NL (1984,98)	• San Diego (1969–)
San Francisco Giants	1883	16 NL (1905,11-13,17,21-24,33,36-37,51, 54,62,89) 5 WS (1905,21-22,33,54)	• New York (1883–1957) San Francisco (1958–)

American League

	1st Year	Pennants & World Series	Franchise Stops
Anaheim Angels	1961	None	• Los Angeles (1961–65) Anaheim, CA (1966–)

Baltimore Orioles	1901	7 AL (1944,66,69-71,79,83)
		3 WS (1966,70,83)
			• Milwaukee (1901)
			  St. Louis (1902–53)
			  Baltimore (1954–)

Boston Red Sox	1901	9 AL (1903,12,15-16,18,46,67,75,86) 5 WS (1903,12,15-16,18)	• Boston (1901–)
Chicago White Sox	1901	4 AL (1906,17,19,59) 2 WS (1906,17)	• Chicago (1901–)
Cleveland Indians	1901	5 AL (1920,48,54,95,97) 2 WS (1920,48)	• Cleveland (1901–)
Detroit Tigers	1901	9 AL (1907-09,34-35,40,45,68,84) 4 WS (1935,45,68,84)	• Detroit (1901–)
Kansas City Royals	1969	2 AL (1980,85) 1 WS (1985)	• Kansas City (1969–)

Minnesota Twins	1901	6 AL (1924-25,33,65,87,91)
		3 WS (1924,87,91)
			• Washington, DC (1901–60)
			  Bloomington, MN (1961–81)
			  Minneapolis (1982–)

New York Yankees	1901	38 AL (1921-23,26-28,32,36-39,41-43,47, 49-53,55-58,60-64,76-78,81,96,98-01) 26 WS (1923,27-28,32,36-39,41,43,47, 49-53,56,58,61-62,77-78,96,98-00)	• Baltimore (1901–02) New York (1903–)

Oakland Athletics	1901	14 AL (1905,10-11,13-14,29-31,72-74;
		88-90)
		9 WS (1910-11,13,29-30,72-74,89)
			• Philadelphia (1901-54)
			  Kansas City (1955–67)
			  Oakland (1968–)

Seattle Mariners	1977	None	• Seattle (1977–)
Tampa Bay Devil Rays	1998	None	• Tampa Bay (1998–)
Texas Rangers	1961	None	• Washington, DC (1961–71) Arlington, TX (1972–)
Toronto Blue Jays	1977	2 AL (1992-93) 2 WS (1992-93)	• Toronto (1977–)

The Growth of Major League Baseball

The National League (founded in 1876) and the American League (founded in 1901) were both eight-team circuits at the turn of the century and remained that way until expansion finally came to Major League Baseball in the 1960s. The AL added two teams in 1961 and the NL did the same a year later. Both leagues went to 12 teams and split into two divisions in 1969. The AL then grew by two more teams in 1977, but the NL didn't follow suit until adding its 13th and 14th clubs in 1993. The NL added two teams in 1998 when the expansion Arizona Diamondbacks entered the league and the Milwaukee Brewers moved over from the AL.

Expansion Timetable (Since 1901)

1961—Los Angeles Angels (now Anaheim) and Washington Senators (now Texas Rangers) join AL; **1962**—Houston Colt .45s (now Astros) and New York Mets join NL; **1969**—Kansas City Royals and Seattle Pilots (now Milwaukee Brewers) join AL, while Montreal Expos and San Diego Padres join NL; **1977**—Seattle Mariners and Toronto Blue Jays join AL; **1993**—Colorado Rockies and Florida Marlins join NL; **1998**—Arizona Diamondbacks join NL and Tampa Bay Devil Rays join AL.

City and Nickname Changes
National League

1953—Boston Braves move to Milwaukee; **1958**—Brooklyn Dodgers move to Los Angeles and New York Giants move to San Francisco; **1965**—Houston Colt .45s renamed Astros; **1966**—Milwaukee Braves move to Atlanta.

Other nicknames: Boston (Beaneaters and Doves through 1908, and Bees from 1936-40); **Brooklyn** (Superbas through 1926, then Robins from 1927-31; then Dodgers from 1932-57); **Cincinnati** (Red Legs from 1944-45, then Redlegs from 1954-60, then Reds since 1961); **Philadelphia** (Blue Jays from 1943-44).

American League

1902—Milwaukee Brewers move to St. Louis and become Browns; **1903**—Baltimore Orioles move to New York and become Highlanders; **1913**—NY Highlanders renamed Yankees; **1954**—St. Louis Browns move to Baltimore and become Orioles; **1955**—Philadelphia Athletics move to Kansas City; **1961**—Washington Senators move to Bloomington, Minn., and become Minnesota Twins; **1965**—LA Angels renamed California Angels; **1966**—California Angels move to Anaheim; **1968**—KC Athletics move to Oakland and become A's; **1970**—Seattle Pilots move to Milwaukee and become Brewers; **1972**—Washington Senators move to Arlington, Texas, and become Rangers; **1982**—Minnesota Twins move to Minneapolis; **1987**—Oakland A's renamed Athletics; **1997**—California Angels renamed Anaheim Angels.

Other nicknames: Boston (Pilgrims, Puritans, Plymouth Rocks and Somersets through 1906); **Cleveland** (Broncos, Blues, Naps and Molly McGuires through 1914); **Washington** (Senators through 1904, then Nationals from 1905-44, then Senators again from 1945-60).

National League Pennant Winners from 1876-99

Founded in 1876, the National League played 24 seasons before the turn of the century and its eventual rivalry with the younger American League.

Multiple winners: Boston (8); Chicago (6); Baltimore (3); Brooklyn, New York and Providence (2).

Year		Year		Year		Year	
1876	Chicago	1882	Chicago	1888	New York	1894	Baltimore
1877	Boston	1883	Boston	1889	New York	1895	Baltimore
1878	Boston	1884	Providence	1890	Brooklyn	1896	Baltimore
1879	Providence	1885	Chicago	1891	Boston	1897	Boston
1880	Chicago	1886	Chicago	1892	Boston	1898	Boston
1881	Chicago	1887	Detroit	1893	Boston	1899	Brooklyn

Champions of Leagues That No Longer Exist

A Special Baseball Records Committee appointed by the commissioner found in 1968 that four extinct leagues qualified for major league status—the American Association (1882-91), the Union Association (1884), the Players' League (1890) and the Federal League (1914-15). The first years of the American League (1900) and Federal League (1913) were not recognized.

American Association

Year	Champion	Manager	Year	Champion	Manager	Year	Champion	Manager
1882	Cincinnati	Pop Snyder	1886	St. Louis	Charlie Comiskey	1890	Louisville	Jack Chapman
1883	Philadelphia	Lew Simmons	1887	St. Louis	Charlie Comiskey	1891	Boston	Arthur Irwin
1884	New York	Jim Mutrie	1888	St. Louis	Charlie Comiskey			
1885	St. Louis	Charlie Comiskey	1889	Brooklyn	Bill McGunnigle			

Union Association

Year	Champion	Manager
1884	St. Louis	Henry Lucas

Players' League

Year	Champion	Manager
1890	Boston	King Kelly

Federal League

Year	Champion	Manager
1914	Indianapolis	Bill Phillips
1915	Chicago	Joe Tinker

Annual Batting Leaders (since 1900)
Batting Average
National League

Multiple winners: Tony Gwynn and Honus Wagner (8); Rogers Hornsby and Stan Musial (7); Roberto Clemente and Bill Madlock (4); Pete Rose, Larry Walker and Paul Waner (3); Hank Aaron, Richie Ashburn, Jake Daubert, Tommy Davis, Ernie Lombardi, Willie McGee, Lefty O'Doul, Dave Parker and Edd Roush (2).

Year		Avg	Year		Avg	Year		Avg
1900	Honus Wagner, Pit	.381	1934	Paul Waner, Pit	.362	1968	Pete Rose, Cin	.335
1901	Jesse Burkett, St.L	.382	1935	Arky Vaughan, Pit	.385	1969	Pete Rose, Cin	.348
1902	Ginger Beaumont, Pit	.357	1936	Paul Waner, Pit	.373			
1903	Honus Wagner, Pit	.355	1937	Joe Medwick, St.L	.374	1970	Rico Carty, Atl	.366
1904	Honus Wagner, Pit	.349	1938	Ernie Lombardi, Cin	.342	1971	Joe Torre, St.L	.363
1905	Cy Seymour, Cin	.377	1939	Johnny Mize, St.L	.349	1972	Billy Williams, Chi	.333
1906	Honus Wagner, Pit	.339				1973	Pete Rose, Cin	.338
1907	Honus Wagner, Pit	.350	1940	Debs Garms, Pit	.355	1974	Ralph Garr, Atl	.353
1908	Honus Wagner, Pit	.354	1941	Pete Reiser, Bklyn	.343	1975	Bill Madlock, Chi	.354
1909	Honus Wagner, Pit	.339	1942	Ernie Lombardi, Bos	.330	1976	Bill Madlock, Chi	.339
			1943	Stan Musial, St.L	.357	1977	Dave Parker, Pit	.338
1910	Sherry Magee, Phi	.331	1944	Dixie Walker, Bklyn	.357	1978	Dave Parker, Pit	.334
1911	Honus Wagner, Pit	.334	1945	Phil Cavarretta, Chi	.355	1979	Keith Hernandez, St.L	.344
1912	Heinie Zimmerman, Chi	.372	1946	Stan Musial, St.L	.365			
1913	Jake Daubert, Bklyn	.350	1947	Harry Walker, St.L-Phi	.363	1980	Bill Buckner, Chi	.324
1914	Jake Daubert, Bklyn	.329	1948	Stan Musial, St.L	.376	1981	Bill Madlock, Pit	.341
1915	Larry Doyle, NY	.320	1949	Jackie Robinson, Bklyn	.342	1982	Al Oliver, Mon	.331
1916	Hal Chase, Cin	.339				1983	Bill Madlock, Pit	.323
1917	Edd Roush, Cin	.341	1950	Stan Musial, St.L	.346	1984	Tony Gwynn, SD	.351
1918	Zack Wheat, Bklyn	.335	1951	Stan Musial, St.L	.355	1985	Willie McGee, St.L	.353
1919	Edd Roush, Cin	.321	1952	Stan Musial, St.L	.336	1986	Tim Raines, Mon	.334
			1953	Carl Furillo, Bklyn	.344	1987	Tony Gwynn, SD	.370
1920	Rogers Hornsby, St.L	.370	1954	Willie Mays, NY	.345	1988	Tony Gwynn, SD	.313
1921	Rogers Hornsby, St.L	.397	1955	Richie Ashburn, Phi	.338	1989	Tony Gwynn, SD	.336
1922	Rogers Hornsby, St.L	.401	1956	Hank Aaron, Mil	.328			
1923	Rogers Hornsby, St.L	.384	1957	Stan Musial, St.L	.351	1990	Willie McGee, St.L	.335
1924	Rogers Hornsby, St.L	.424	1958	Richie Ashburn, Phi	.350	1991	Terry Pendleton, Atl	.319
1925	Rogers Hornsby, St.L	.403	1959	Hank Aaron, Mil	.355	1992	Gary Sheffield, SD	.330
1926	Bubbles Hargrave, Cin	.353				1993	Andres Galarraga, Col	.370
1927	Paul Waner, Pit	.380	1960	Dick Groat, Pit	.325	1994	Tony Gwynn, SD	.394
1928	Rogers Hornsby, Bos	.387	1961	Roberto Clemente, Pit	.351	1995	Tony Gwynn, SD	.368
1929	Lefty O'Doul, Phi	.398	1962	Tommy Davis, LA	.346	1996	Tony Gwynn, SD	.353
			1963	Tommy Davis, LA	.326	1997	Tony Gwynn, SD	.372
1930	Bill Terry, NY	.401	1964	Roberto Clemente, Pit	.339	1998	Larry Walker, Col.	.363
1931	Chick Hafey, St.L	.349	1965	Roberto Clemente, Pit	.329	1999	Larry Walker, Col.	.379
1932	Lefty O'Doul, Bklyn	.368	1966	Matty Alou, Pit	.342			
1933	Chuck Klein, Phi	.368	1967	Roberto Clemente, Pit	.357	2000	Todd Helton, Col	.372
						2001	Larry Walker, Col.	.350

American League

Multiple winners: Ty Cobb (12); Rod Carew (7); Ted Williams (6); Wade Boggs (5); Harry Heilmann (4); George Brett, Nap Lajoie, Tony Oliva and Carl Yastrzemski (3); Luke Appling, Joe DiMaggio, Ferris Fain, Jimmie Foxx, Nomar Garciaparra, Edgar Martinez, Pete Runnels, Al Simmons, George Sisler and Mickey Vernon (2).

Year		Avg	Year		Avg	Year		Avg
1901	Nap Lajoie, Phi	.422	1925	Harry Heilmann, Det	.393	1949	George Kell, Det.	.343
1902	Ed Delahanty, Wash.	.376	1926	Heinie Manush, Det	.378	1950	Billy Goodman, Bos	.354
1903	Nap Lajoie, Cle	.355	1927	Harry Heilmann, Det	.398	1951	Ferris Fain, Phi	.344
1904	Nap Lajoie, Cle	.381	1928	Goose Goslin, Wash	.379	1952	Ferris Fain, Phi	.327
1905	Elmer Flick, Cle	.306	1929	Lew Fonseca, Cle	.369	1953	Mickey Vernon, Wash	.337
1906	George Stone, St.L	.358				1954	Bobby Avila, Clev	.341
1907	Ty Cobb, Det	.350	1930	Al Simmons, Phi	.381	1955	Al Kaline, Det	.340
1908	Ty Cobb, Det	.324	1931	Al Simmons, Phi	.390	1956	Mickey Mantle, NY	.353
1909	Ty Cobb, Det	.377	1932	Dale Alexander, Det-Bos	.367	1957	Ted Williams, Bos	.388
			1933	Jimmie Foxx, Phi	.356	1958	Ted Williams, Bos	.328
1910	Ty Cobb, Det	.385	1934	Lou Gehrig, NY	.363	1959	Harvey Kuenn, Det	.353
1911	Ty Cobb, Det	.420	1935	Buddy Myer, Wash	.349			
1912	Ty Cobb, Det	.410	1936	Luke Appling, Chi	.388	1960	Pete Runnels, Bos	.320
1913	Ty Cobb, Det	.390	1937	Charlie Gehringer, Det	.371	1961	Norm Cash, Det	.361*
1914	Ty Cobb, Det	.368	1938	Jimmie Foxx, Bos.	.349	1962	Pete Runnels, Bos	.326
1915	Ty Cobb, Det	.369	1939	Joe DiMaggio, NY	.381	1963	Carl Yastrzemski, Bos.	.321
1916	Tris Speaker, Cle.	.386	1940	Joe DiMaggio, NY	.352	1964	Tony Oliva, Min	.323
1917	Ty Cobb, Det	.383	1941	Ted Williams, Bos	.406	1965	Tony Oliva, Min	.321
1918	Ty Cobb, Det	.382	1942	Ted Williams, Bos	.356	1966	Frank Robinson, Bal	.316
1919	Ty Cobb, Det	.384	1943	Luke Appling, Chi	.328	1967	Carl Yastrzemski, Bos.	.326
			1944	Lou Boudreau, Clev	.327	1968	Carl Yastrzemski, Bos.	.301
1920	George Sisler, St.L	.407	1945	Snuffy Stirnweiss, NY.	.309	1969	Rod Carew, Min	.332
1921	Harry Heilmann, Det	.394	1946	Mickey Vernon, Wash	.353			
1922	George Sisler, St.L	.420	1947	Ted Williams, Bos	.343	1970	Alex Johnson, Cal	.329
1923	Harry Heilmann, Det	.403	1948	Ted Williams, Bos	.369	1971	Tony Oliva, Min	.337
1924	Babe Ruth, NY	.378						

Year	Avg	Year	Avg	Year	Avg
1972 Rod Carew, Min	.318	1984 Don Mattingly, NY	.343	1996 Alex Rodriguez, Sea	.358
1973 Rod Carew, Min	.350	1985 Wade Boggs, Bos	.368	1997 Frank Thomas, Chi	.347
1974 Rod Carew, Min	.364	1986 Wade Boggs, Bos	.357	1998 Bernie Williams, NY	.339
1975 Rod Carew, Min	.359	1987 Wade Boggs, Bos	.363	1999 Nomar Garciaparra, Bos	.357
1976 George Brett, KC	.333	1988 Wade Boggs, Bos	.366		
1977 Rod Carew, Min	.388	1989 Kirby Puckett, Min	.339	2000 Nomar Garciaparra, Bos	.372
1978 Rod Carew, Min	.333			2001 Ichiro Suzuki, Sea	.350
1979 Fred Lynn, Bos	.333	1990 George Brett, KC	.329		
		1991 Julio Franco, Tex	.341	*Norm Cash later admitted to using a	
1980 George Brett, KC	.390	1992 Edgar Martinez, Sea	.343	corked bat the entire season. He	
1981 Carney Lansford, Bos	.336	1993 John Olerud, Tor	.363	played 16 other seasons and never hit	
1982 Willie Wilson, KC	.332	1994 Paul O'Neill, NY	.359	better than .286.	
1983 Wade Boggs, Bos	.361	1995 Edgar Martinez, Sea	.356		

Home Runs
National League

Multiple winners: Mike Schmidt (8); Ralph Kiner (7); Gavvy Cravath and Mel Ott (6); Hank Aaron, Chuck Klein, Willie Mays, Johnny Mize, Cy Williams and Hack Wilson (4); Willie McCovey (3); Ernie Banks, Johnny Bench, Barry Bonds, George Foster, Rogers Hornsby, Tim Jordan, Dave Kingman, Eddie Mathews, Mark McGwire, Dale Murphy, Bill Nicholson, Dave Robertson, Wildfire Schulte and Willie Stargell (2).

Year	HR	Year	HR	Year	HR
1900 Herman Long, Bos	12	1934 Rip Collins, St.L	35	1968 Willie McCovey, SF	36
1901 Sam Crawford, Cin	16	& Mel Ott, NY	35	1969 Willie McCovey, SF	45
1902 Tommy Leach, Pit	6	1935 Wally Berger, Bos	34		
1903 Jimmy Sheckard, Bklyn	9	1936 Mel Ott, NY	33	1970 Johnny Bench, Cin	45
1904 Harry Lumley, Bklyn	9	1937 Joe Medwick, St.L	31	1971 Willie Stargell, Pit	48
1905 Fred Odwell, Cin	9	& Mel Ott, NY	31	1972 Johnny Bench, Cin	40
1906 Tim Jordan, Bklyn	12	1938 Mel Ott, NY	36	1973 Willie Stargell, Pit	44
1907 Dave Brain, Bos	10	1939 Johnny Mize, St.L	28	1974 Mike Schmidt, Phi	36
1908 Tim Jordan, Bklyn	12			1975 Mike Schmidt, Phi	38
1909 Red Murray, NY	7	1940 Johnny Mize, St.L	43	1976 Mike Schmidt, Phi	38
		1941 Dolph Camilli, Bklyn	34	1977 George Foster, Cin	52
1910 Fred Beck, Bos	10	1942 Mel Ott, NY	30	1978 George Foster, Cin	40
& Wildfire Schulte, Chi	10	1943 Bill Nicholson, Chi	29	1979 Dave Kingman, Chi	48
1911 Wildfire Schulte, Chi	21	1944 Bill Nicholson, Chi	33		
1912 Heinie Zimmerman, Chi	14	1945 Tommy Holmes, Bos	28	1980 Mike Schmidt, Phi	48
1913 Gavvy Cravath, Phi	19	1946 Ralph Kiner, Pit	23	1981 Mike Schmidt, Phi	31
1914 Gavvy Cravath, Phi	19	1947 Ralph Kiner, Pit	51	1982 Dave Kingman, NY	37
1915 Gavvy Cravath, Phi	24	& Johnny Mize, NY	51	1983 Mike Schmidt, Phi	40
1916 Cy Williams, Chi	12	1948 Ralph Kiner, Pit	40	1984 Dale Murphy, Atl	36
& Dave Robertson, NY	12	& Johnny Mize, NY	40	& Mike Schmidt, Phi	36
1917 Gavvy Cravath, Phi	12	1949 Ralph Kiner, Pit	54	1985 Dale Murphy, Atl	37
& Dave Robertson, NY	12			1986 Mike Schmidt, Phi	37
1918 Gavvy Cravath, Phi	8	1950 Ralph Kiner, Pit	47	1987 Andre Dawson, Chi	49
1919 Gavvy Cravath, Phi	12	1951 Ralph Kiner, Pit	42	1988 Darryl Strawberry, NY	39
		1952 Ralph Kiner, Pit	37	1989 Kevin Mitchell, SF	47
1920 Cy Williams, Phi	15	& Hank Sauer, Chi	37		
1921 George Kelly, NY	23	1953 Eddie Mathews, Mil	47	1990 Ryne Sandberg, Chi	40
1922 Rogers Hornsby, St.L	42	1954 Ted Kluszewski, Cin	49	1991 Howard Johnson, NY	38
1923 Cy Williams, Phi	41	1955 Willie Mays, NY	51	1992 Fred McGriff, SD	35
1924 Jack Fournier, Bklyn	27	1956 Duke Snider, Bklyn	43	1993 Barry Bonds, SF	46
1925 Rogers Hornsby, St.L	39	1957 Hank Aaron, Mil	44	1994 Matt Williams, SF	43
1926 Hack Wilson, Chi	21	1958 Ernie Banks, Chi	47	1995 Dante Bichette, Col	40
1927 Cy Williams, Phi	30	1959 Eddie Mathews, Mil	46	1996 Andres Galarraga, Col	47
& Hack Wilson, Chi	30			1997 Larry Walker, Col	49
1928 Jim Bottomley, St.L	31	1960 Ernie Banks, Chi	41	1998 Mark McGwire, St.L	70
& Hack Wilson, Chi	31	1961 Orlando Cepeda, SF	46	1999 Mark McGwire, St.L	65
· 1929 Chuck Klein, Phi	43	1962 Willie Mays, SF	49		
		1963 Hank Aaron, Mil	44	2000 Sammy Sosa, Chi	50
1930 Hack Wilson, Chi	56	& Willie McCovey, SF	44	2001 Barry Bonds, SF	73
1931 Chuck Klein, Phi	31	1964 Willie Mays, SF	47	**Note:** In 1997 Mark McGwire hit 58	
1932 Chuck Klein, Phi	38	1965 Willie Mays, SF	52	home runs but hit 34 of them in the AL	
& Mel Ott, NY	38	1966 Hank Aaron, Atl	44	with Oakland before getting traded to	
1933 Chuck Klein, Phi	28	1967 Hank Aaron, Atl	39	St. Louis.	

American League

Multiple winners: Babe Ruth (12); Harmon Killebrew (6); Home Run Baker, Harry Davis, Jimmie Foxx, Hank Greenberg, Ken Griffey Jr., Reggie Jackson, Mickey Mantle and Ted Williams (4); Lou Gehrig and Jim Rice (3); Dick Allen, Tony Armas, Jose Canseco, Joe DiMaggio, Larry Doby, Cecil Fielder, Juan Gonzalez, Mark McGwire, Wally Pipp, Al Rosen and Gorman Thomas (2).

Year	HR	Year	HR	Year	HR
1901 Nap Lajoie, Phi	14	1906 Harry Davis, Phi	12	1910 Jake Stahl, Bos	10
1902 Socks Seybold, Phi	16	1907 Harry Davis, Phi	8	1911 Home Run Baker, Phi	11
1903 Buck Freeman, Bos	13	1908 Sam Crawford, Det	7	1912 Home Run Baker, Phi	10
1904 Harry Davis, Phi	10	1909 Ty Cobb, Det	9	& Tris Speaker, Bos	10
1905 Harry Davis, Phi	8			1913 Home Run Baker, Phi	12

Year		HR
1914	Home Run Baker, Phi	.9
1915	Braggo Roth, Chi-Cle	.7
1916	Wally Pipp, NY	.12
1917	Wally Pipp, NY	.9
1918	Babe Ruth, Bos	.11
	& Tilly Walker, Phi	.11
1919	Babe Ruth, Bos	.29
1920	Babe Ruth, NY	.54
1921	Babe Ruth, NY	.59
1922	Ken Williams, St.L.	.39
1923	Babe Ruth, NY	.41
1924	Babe Ruth, NY	.46
1925	Bob Meusel, NY	.33
1926	Babe Ruth, NY	.47
1927	Babe Ruth, NY	.60
1928	Babe Ruth, NY	.54
1929	Babe Ruth, NY	.46
1930	Babe Ruth, NY	.49
1931	Lou Gehrig, NY	.46
	& Babe Ruth, NY	.46
1932	Jimmie Foxx, Phi	.58
1933	Jimmie Foxx, Phi	.48
1934	Lou Gehrig, NY	.49
1935	Jimmie Foxx, Phi	.36
	& Hank Greenberg, Det.	.36
1936	Lou Gehrig, NY	.49
1937	Joe DiMaggio, NY	.46
1938	Hank Greenberg, Det.	.58
1939	Jimmie Foxx, Bos.	.35
1940	Hank Greenberg, Det.	.41
1941	Ted Williams, Bos.	.37
1942	Ted Williams, Bos.	.36
1943	Rudy York, Det.	.34
1944	Nick Etten, NY	.22
1945	Vern Stephens, St.L	.24

Year		HR
1946	Hank Greenberg, Det.	.44
1947	Ted Williams, Bos	.32
1948	Joe DiMaggio, NY	.39
1949	Ted Williams, Bos	.43
1950	Al Rosen, Cle.	.37
1951	Gus Zernial, Chi-Phi	.33
1952	Larry Doby, Cle.	.32
1953	Al Rosen, Cle.	.43
1954	Larry Doby, Cle.	.32
1955	Mickey Mantle, NY	.37
1956	Mickey Mantle, NY	.52
1957	Roy Sievers, Wash	.42
1958	Mickey Mantle, NY	.42
1959	Rocky Colavito, Cle	.42
	& Harmon Killebrew, Wash	.42
1960	Mickey Mantle, NY	.40
1961	Roger Maris, NY.	.61
1962	Harmon Killebrew, Min	.48
1963	Harmon Killebrew, Min	.45
1964	Harmon Killebrew, Min	.49
1965	Tony Conigliaro, Bos	.32
1966	Frank Robinson, Bal	.49
1967	Harmon Killebrew, Min	.44
	& Carl Yastrzemski, Bos.	.44
1968	Frank Howard, Wash.	.44
1969	Harmon Killebrew, Min	.49
1970	Frank Howard, Wash.	.44
1971	Bill Melton, Chi	.33
1972	Dick Allen, Chi	.37
1973	Reggie Jackson, Oak	.32
1974	Dick Allen, Chi	.32
1975	Reggie Jackson, Oak	.36
	& George Scott, Mil	.36
1976	Graig Nettles, NY	.32
1977	Jim Rice, Bos	.39

Year		HR
1978	Jim Rice, Bos	.46
1979	Gorman Thomas, Mil	.45
1980	Reggie Jackson, NY	.41
	& Ben Oglivie, Mil	.41
1981	Tony Armas, Oak	.22
	Dwight Evans, Bos	.22
	Bobby Grich, Cal	.22
	& Eddie Murray, Bal.	.22
1982	Reggie Jackson, Cal	.39
	& Gorman Thomas, Mil	.39
1983	Jim Rice, Bos	.39
1984	Tony Armas, Bos	.43
1985	Darrell Evans, Det	.40
1986	Jesse Barfield, Tor	.40
1987	Mark McGwire, Oak	.49
1988	Jose Canseco, Oak	.42
1989	Fred McGriff, Tor	.36
1990	Cecil Fielder, Det	.51
1991	Jose Canseco, Oak	.44
	& Cecil Fielder, Det	.44
1992	Juan Gonzalez, Tex	.43
1993	Juan Gonzalez, Tex	.46
1994	Ken Griffey Jr., Sea	.40
1995	Albert Belle, Cle	.50
1996	Mark McGwire, Oak	.52
1997	Ken Griffey Jr., Sea	.56
1998	Ken Griffey Jr., Sea	.56
1999	Ken Griffey Jr., Sea	.48
2000	Troy Glaus, Ana	.47
2001	Alex Rodriguez, Tex	.52

Note: In 1997 Mark McGwire hit 58 home runs but hit 24 of them in the NL with St. Louis after getting traded from Oakland.

Runs Batted In
National League

Multiple winners: Hank Aaron, Rogers Hornsby, Sherry Magee, Mike Schmidt and Honus Wagner (4); Johnny Bench, George Foster, Joe Medwick, Johnny Mize and Heinie Zimmerman (3); Ernie Banks, Jim Bottomley, Orlando Cepeda, Gavvy Cravath, Andres Galarraga, George Kelly, Chuck Klein, Willie McCovey, Dale Murphy, Stan Musial, Bill Nicholson, Sammy Sosa and Hack Wilson (2).

Year		RBI
1900	Elmer Flick, Phi	.110
1901	Honus Wagner, Pit	.126
1902	Honus Wagner, Pit	.91
1903	Sam Mertes, NY	.104
1904	Bill Dahlen, NY	.80
1905	Cy Seymour, Cin	.121
1906	Jim Nealon, Pit	.83
	& Harry Steinfeldt, Chi.	.83
1907	Sherry Magee, Phi	.85
1908	Honus Wagner, Pit	.109
1909	Honus Wagner, Pit	.100
1910	Sherry Magee, Phi	.123
1911	Wildfire Schulte, Chi	.121
1912	Heinie Zimmerman, Chi	.103
1913	Gavvy Cravath, Phi	.128
1914	Sherry Magee, Phi	.103
1915	Gavvy Cravath, Phi	.115
1916	Heinie Zimmerman, Chi-NY	.83
1917	Heinie Zimmerman, NY.	.102
1918	Sherry Magee, Cin.	.76
1919	Hy Myers, Bklyn	.73
1920	Rogers Hornsby, St.L.	.94
	& George Kelly, NY	.94
1921	Rogers Hornsby, St.L	.126
1922	Rogers Hornsby, St.L	.152
1923	Irish Meusel, NY.	.125
1924	George Kelly, NY	.136

Year		RBI
1925	Rogers Hornsby, St.L	.143
1926	Jim Bottomley, St.L	.120
1927	Paul Waner, Pit	.131
1928	Jim Bottomley, St.L	.136
1929	Hack Wilson, Chi.	.159
1930	Hack Wilson, Chi.	.191
1931	Chuck Klein, Phi	.121
1932	Don Hurst, Phi	.143
1933	Chuck Klein, Phi.	.120
1934	Mel Ott, NY	.135
1935	Wally Berger, Bos	.130
1936	Joe Medwick, St.L.	.138
1937	Joe Medwick, St.L.	.154
1938	Joe Medwick, St.L.	.122
1939	Frank McCormick, Cin	.128
1940	Johnny Mize, St.L.	.137
1941	Dolph Camilli, Bklyn	.120
1942	Johnny Mize, NY	.110
1943	Bill Nicholson, Chi	.128
1944	Bill Nicholson, Chi	.122
1945	Dixie Walker, Bklyn	.124
1946	Enos Slaughter, St.L.	.130
1947	Johnny Mize, NY	.138
1948	Stan Musial, St.L.	.131
1949	Ralph Kiner, Pit	.127
1950	Del Ennis, Phi	.126

Year		RBI
1951	Monte Irvin, NY	.121
1952	Hank Sauer, Chi	.121
1953	Roy Campanella, Bklyn	.142
1954	Ted Kluszewski, Cin	.141
1955	Duke Snider, Bklyn	.136
1956	Stan Musial, St.L.	.109
1957	Hank Aaron, Mil	.132
1958	Ernie Banks, Chi	.129
1959	Ernie Banks, Chi	.143
1960	Hank Aaron, Mil	.126
1961	Orlando Cepeda, SF	.142
1962	Tommy Davis, LA	.153
1963	Hank Aaron, Mil	.130
1964	Ken Boyer, St.L	.119
1965	Deron Johnson, Cin	.130
1966	Hank Aaron, Atl	.127
1967	Orlando Cepeda, St.L.	.111
1968	Willie McCovey, SF	.105
1969	Willie McCovey, SF	.126
1970	Johnny Bench, Cin	.148
1971	Joe Torre, St.L	.137
1972	Johnny Bench, Cin	.125
1973	Willie Stargell, Pit.	.119
1974	Johnny Bench, Cin	.129
1975	Greg Luzinski, Phi	.120
1976	George Foster, Cin.	.121
1977	George Foster, Cin.	.149

Year	RBI	Year	RBI	Year	RBI
1978 George Foster, Cin	120	1986 Mike Schmidt, Phi	119	1996 Andres Galarraga, Col	150
1979 Dave Winfield, SD	118	1987 Andre Dawson, Chi	137	1997 Andres Galarraga, Col	140
1980 Mike Schmidt, Phi	121	1988 Will Clark, SF	109	1998 Sammy Sosa, Chi	158
1981 Mike Schmidt, Phi	91	1989 Kevin Mitchell, SF	125	1999 Mark McGwire, St.L	147
1982 Dale Murphy, Atl	109			2000 Todd Helton, Col	147
& Al Oliver, Mon	109	1990 Matt Williams, SF	122	2001 Sammy Sosa, Chi	160
1983 Dale Murphy, Atl	121	1991 Howard Johnson, NY	117		
1984 Gary Carter, Mon	106	1992 Darren Daulton, Phi	109		
& Mike Schmidt, Phi	106	1993 Barry Bonds, SF	123		
1985 Dave Parker, Cin	125	1994 Jeff Bagwell, Hou	116		
		1995 Dante Bichette, Col	128		

American League

Multiple winners: Babe Ruth (6); Lou Gehrig (5); Ty Cobb, Hank Greenberg and Ted Williams (4); Albert Belle, Sam Crawford, Cecil Fielder, Jimmie Foxx, Jackie Jensen, Harmon Killebrew, Vern Stephens and Bobby Veach (3); Home Run Baker, Cecil Cooper, Harry Davis, Joe DiMaggio, Buck Freeman, Nap Lajoie, Roger Maris, Al Rosen, and Bobby Veach (2).

Year	RBI	Year	RBI	Year	RBI
1901 Nap Lajoie, Phi	125	1935 Hank Greenberg, Det	170	1968 Ken Harrelson, Bos	109
1902 Buck Freeman, Bos	121	1936 Hal Trosky, Cle	162	1969 Harmon Killebrew, Min	140
1903 Buck Freeman, Bos	104	1937 Hank Greenberg, Det	183		
1904 Nap Lajoie, Cle	102	1938 Jimmie Foxx, Bos	175	1970 Frank Howard, Wash	126
1905 Harry Davis, Phi	83	1939 Ted Williams, Bos	145	1971 Harmon Killebrew, Min	119
1906 Harry Davis, Phi	96			1972 Dick Allen, Chi	113
1907 Ty Cobb, Det	116	1940 Hank Greenberg, Det	150	1973 Reggie Jackson, Oak	117
1908 Ty Cobb, Det	108	1941 Joe DiMaggio, NY	125	1974 Jeff Burroughs, Tex	118
1909 Ty Cobb, Det	107	1942 Ted Williams, Bos	137	1975 George Scott, Mil	109
1910 Sam Crawford, Det	120	1943 Rudy York, Det	118	1976 Lee May, Bal	109
1911 Ty Cobb, Det	144	1944 Vern Stephens, St.L	109	1977 Larry Hisle, Min	119
1912 Home Run Baker, Phi	133	1945 Nick Etten, NY	111	1978 Jim Rice, Bos	139
1913 Home Run Baker, Phi	126	1946 Hank Greenberg, Det	127	1979 Don Baylor, Cal	139
1914 Sam Crawford, Det	104	1947 Ted Williams, Bos	114		
1915 Sam Crawford, Det	112	1948 Joe DiMaggio, NY	155	1980 Cecil Cooper, Mil	122
& Bobby Veach, Det	112	1949 Ted Williams, Bos	159	1981 Eddie Murray, Bal	78
1916 Del Pratt, St.L	103	& Vern Stephens, Bos	159	1982 Hal McRae, KC	133
1917 Bobby Veach, Det	103			1983 Cecil Cooper, Mil	126
1918 Bobby Veach, Det	78	1950 Walt Dropo, Bos	144	& Jim Rice, Bos	126
1919 Babe Ruth, Bos	114	& Vern Stephens, Bos	144	1984 Tony Armas, Bos	123
1920 Babe Ruth, NY	137	1951 Gus Zernial, Chi-Phi	129	1985 Don Mattingly, NY	145
1921 Babe Ruth, NY	171	1952 Al Rosen, Cle	105	1986 Joe Carter, Cle	121
1922 Ken Williams, St.L	155	1953 Al Rosen, Cle	145	1987 George Bell, Tor	134
1923 Babe Ruth, NY	131	1954 Larry Doby, Cle	126	1988 Jose Canseco, Oak	124
1924 Goose Goslin, Wash	129	1955 Ray Boone, Det	116	1989 Ruben Sierra, Tex	119
1925 Bob Meusel, NY	138	& Jackie Jensen, Bos	116		
1926 Babe Ruth, NY	145	1956 Mickey Mantle, NY	130	1990 Cecil Fielder, Det	132
1927 Lou Gehrig, NY	175	1957 Roy Sievers, Wash	114	1991 Cecil Fielder, Det	133
1928 Lou Gehrig, NY	142	1958 Jackie Jensen, Bos	122	1992 Cecil Fielder, Det	124
& Babe Ruth, NY	142	1959 Jackie Jensen, Bos	112	1993 Albert Belle, Cle	129
1929 Al Simmons, Phi	157			1994 Kirby Puckett, Min	112
1930 Lou Gehrig, NY	174	1960 Roger Maris, NY	112	1995 Albert Belle, Cle	126
1931 Lou Gehrig, NY	184	1961 Roger Maris, NY	142	& Mo Vaughn, Bos	126
1932 Jimmie Foxx, Phi	169	1962 Harmon Killebrew, Min	126	1996 Albert Belle, Cle	148
1933 Jimmie Foxx, Phi	163	1963 Dick Stuart, Bos	118	1997 Ken Griffey Jr., Sea	147
1934 Lou Gehrig, NY	165	1964 Brooks Robinson, Bal	118	1998 Juan Gonzalez, Tex	157
		1965 Rocky Colavito, Cle	108	1999 Manny Ramirez, Cle	165
		1966 Frank Robinson, Bal	122		
		1967 Carl Yastrzemski, Bos	121	2000 Edgar Martinez, Sea	145
				2001 Bret Boone, Sea	141

Batting Triple Crown Winners

Players who led either league in Batting Average, Home Runs and Runs Batted In over a single season.

National League

	Year	Avg	HR	RBI
Paul Hines, Providence	1878	.358	4	50
Hugh Duffy, Boston	1894	.438	18	145
Heinie Zimmerman, Chicago	1912	.372	14	103
Rogers Hornsby, St. Louis	1922	.401	42	152
Rogers Hornsby, St. Louis	1925	.403	39	143
Chuck Klein, Philadelphia	1933	.368	28	120
Joe Medwick, St. Louis	1937	.374	31*	154

*Tied for league lead in HRs with Mel Ott, NY.

American League

	Year	Avg	HR	RBI
Nap Lajoie, Philadelphia	1901	.422	14	125
Ty Cobb, Detroit	1909	.377	9	115
Jimmie Foxx, Philadelphia	1933	.356	48	163
Lou Gehrig, New York	1934	.363	49	165
Ted Williams, Boston	1942	.356	36	137
Ted Williams, Boston	1947	.343	32	114
Mickey Mantle, New York	1956	.353	52	130
Frank Robinson, Baltimore	1966	.316	49	122
Carl Yastrzemski, Boston	1967	.326	44*	121

*Tied for league lead in HRs with Harmon Killebrew, Min.

Stolen Bases
National League

Multiple winners: Max Carey (10); Lou Brock (8); Vince Coleman and Maury Wills (6); Honus Wagner (5); Bob Bescher, Kiki Cuyler, Willie Mays and Tim Raines (4); Bill Bruton, Frankie Frisch, Pepper Martin and Tony Womack (3); George Burns, Frank Chance, Augie Galan, Marquis Grissom, Stan Hack, Sam Jethroe, Davey Lopes, Omar Moreno, Pete Reiser and Jackie Robinson (2).

Year		SB	Year		SB	Year		SB
1900	Patsy Donovan, St.L	.45	1933	Pepper Martin, St.L	.26	1968	Lou Brock, St.L	.62
	& George Van Haltren, NY	.45	1934	Pepper Martin, St.L	.23	1969	Lou Brock, St.L	.53
1901	Honus Wagner, Pit	.49	1935	Augie Galan, Chi	.22	1970	Bobby Tolan, Cin	.57
1902	Honus Wagner, Pit	.42	1936	Pepper Martin, St.L	.23	1971	Lou Brock, St.L	.64
1903	Frank Chance, Chi	.67	1937	Augie Galan, Chi	.23	1972	Lou Brock, St.L	.63
	& Jimmy Sheckard, Bklyn	.67	1938	Stan Hack, Chi	.16	1973	Lou Brock, St.L	.70
1904	Honus Wagner, Pit	.53	1939	Stan Hack, Chi	.17	1974	Lou Brock, St.L	.118
1905	Art Devlin, NY	.59		& Lee Handley, Pit	.17	1975	Davey Lopes, LA	.77
	& Billy Maloney, Chi	.59	1940	Lonny Frey, Cin	.22	1976	Davey Lopes, LA	.63
1906	Frank Chance, Chi	.57	1941	Danny Murtaugh, Phi	.18	1977	Frank Taveras, Pit	.70
1907	Honus Wagner, Pit	.61	1942	Pete Reiser, Bklyn	.20	1978	Omar Moreno, Pit.	.71
1908	Honus Wagner, Pit	.53	1943	Arky Vaughan, Bklyn	.20	1979	Omar Moreno, Pit.	.77
1909	Bob Bescher, Cin	.54	1944	Johnny Barrett, Pit	.28	1980	Ron LeFlore, Mon	.97
1910	Bob Bescher, Cin	.70	1945	Red Schoendienst, St.L	.26	1981	Tim Raines, Mon	.71
1911	Bob Bescher, Cin	.81	1946	Pete Reiser, Bklyn	.34	1982	Tim Raines, Mon	.78
1912	Bob Bescher, Cin	.67	1947	Jackie Robinson, Bklyn	.29	1983	Tim Raines, Mon	.90
1913	Max Carey, Pit	.61	1948	Richie Ashburn, Phi.	.32	1984	Tim Raines, Mon	.75
1914	George Burns, NY	.62	1949	Jackie Robinson, Bklyn	.37	1985	Vince Coleman, St.L	.110
1915	Max Carey, Pit	.36	1950	Sam Jethroe, Bos	.35	1986	Vince Coleman, St.L	.107
1916	Max Carey, Pit	.63	1951	Sam Jethroe, Bos	.35	1987	Vince Coleman, St.L	.109
1917	Max Carey, Pit	.46	1952	Pee Wee Reese, Bklyn	.30	1988	Vince Coleman, St.L	.81
1918	Max Carey, Pit	.58	1953	Bill Bruton, Mil.	.26	1989	Vince Coleman, St.L	.65
1919	George Burns, NY	.40	1954	Bill Bruton, Mil.	.34	1990	Vince Coleman, St.L	.77
1920	Max Carey, Pit	.52	1955	Bill Bruton, Mil.	.25	1991	Marquis Grissom, Mon	.76
1921	Frankie Frisch, NY	.49	1956	Willie Mays, NY	.40	1992	Marquis Grissom, Mon	.78
1922	Max Carey, Pit	.51	1957	Willie Mays, NY	.38	1993	Chuck Carr, Fla	.58
1923	Max Carey, Pit	.51	1958	Willie Mays, SF	.31	1994	Craig Biggio, Hou	.39
1924	Max Carey, Pit	.49	1959	Willie Mays, SF	.27	1995	Quilvio Veras, Fla	.56
1925	Max Carey, Pit	.46	1960	Maury Wills, LA	.50	1996	Eric Young, Col	.53
1926	Kiki Cuyler, Pit.	.35	1961	Maury Wills, LA	.35	1997	Tony Womack, Pit.	.60
1927	Frankie Frisch, St.L	.48	1962	Maury Wills, LA	.104	1998	Tony Womack, Pit.	.58
1928	Kiki Cuyler, Chi	.37	1963	Maury Wills, LA	.40	1999	Tony Womack, Ari	.72
1929	Kiki Cuyler, Chi	.43	1964	Maury Wills, LA	.53	2000	Luis Castillo, Fla	.62
1930	Kiki Cuyler, Chi	.37	1965	Maury Wills, LA	.94	2001	Juan Pierre, Col	.46
1931	Frankie Frisch, St.L	.28	1966	Lou Brock, St.L	.74		& Jimmy Rollins, Phi	.46
1932	Chuck Klein, Phi	.20	1967	Lou Brock, St.L	.52			

30 Homers & 30 Stolen Bases in One Season

National League

	Year	Gm	HR	SB
Willie Mays, NY Giants	1956	152	36	40
Willie Mays, NY Giants	1957	152	35	38
Hank Aaron, Milwaukee	1963	161	44	31
Bobby Bonds, San Francisco	1969	158	32	45
Bobby Bonds, San Francisco	1973	160	39	43
Dale Murphy, Atlanta	1983	162	36	30
Eric Davis, Cincinnati	1987	129	37	50
Howard Johnson, NY Mets	1987	157	36	32
Darryl Strawberry, NY Mets	1987	154	39	36
Howard Johnson, NY Mets	1989	153	36	41
Ron Gant, Atlanta	1990	152	32	33
Barry Bonds, Pittsburgh	1990	151	33	52
Ron Gant, Atlanta	1991	154	32	34
Howard Johnson, NY Mets	1991	156	38	30
Barry Bonds, Pittsburgh	1992	140	34	39
Sammy Sosa, Chicago	1993	159	33	36
Barry Bonds, San Francisco	1995	144	33	31
Sammy Sosa, Chicago	1995	144	36	34
Barry Bonds, San Francisco	1996	158	42	40
Ellis Burks, Colorado	1996	156	40	32
Dante Bichette, Colorado	1996	159	31	31
Barry Larkin, Cincinnati	1996	152	33	36
Larry Walker, Colorado	1997	153	49	33
Barry Bonds, San Francisco	1997	159	40	37
Raul Mondesi, Los Angeles	1997	159	30	32
Jeff Bagwell, Houston	1997	162	43	31
Jeff Bagwell, Houston	1999	162	42	30
Raul Mondesi, Los Angeles	1999	159	33	36
Preston Wilson, Florida	2000	161	31	36
Vladimir Guerrero, Montreal	2001	159	34	37
Bobby Abreu, Philadelphia	2001	162	31	36

American League

	Year	Gm	HR	SB
Kenny Williams, St. Louis	1922	153	39	37
Tommy Harper, Milwaukee	1970	154	31	38
Bobby Bonds, New York	1975	145	32	30
Bobby Bonds, California	1977	158	37	41
Bobby Bonds, Chicago-Texas	1978	156	31	43
Joe Carter, Cleveland	1987	149	32	31
Jose Canseco, Oakland	1988	158	42	40
Alex Rodriguez, Seattle	1998	161	42	46
Shawn Green, Toronto	1998	158	35	35
Jose Cruz Jr., Toronto	2001	146	34	32

American League

Multiple winners: Rickey Henderson (12); Luis Aparicio (9); Bert Campaneris, George Case and Ty Cobb (6); Kenny Lofton (5); Ben Chapman, Eddie Collins and George Sisler (4); Bob Dillinger, Minnie Minoso and Bill Werber (3); Elmer Flick, Tommy Harper, Brian Hunter, Clyde Milan, Johnny Mostil, Bill North and Snuffy Stirnweiss (2).

Year		SB	Year		SB	Year		SB
1901	Frank Isbell, Chi	52	1935	Bill Werber, Bos	29	1969	Tommy Harper, Sea	73
1902	Topsy Hartsel, Phi	47	1936	Lyn Lary, St.L	37	1970	Bert Campaneris, Oak	42
1903	Harry Bay, Cle	45	1937	Ben Chapman, Wash-Bos	35	1971	Amos Otis, KC	52
1904	Elmer Flick, Cle	42		& Bill Werber, Phi	35	1972	Bert Campaneris, Oak	52
1905	Danny Hoffman, Phi	46	1938	Frank Crosetti, NY	27	1973	Tommy Harper, Bos	54
1906	John Anderson, Wash	39	1939	George Case, Wash	51	1974	Bill North, Oak	54
	& Elmer Flick, Cle	39	1940	George Case, Wash	35	1975	Mickey Rivers, CA	70
1907	Ty Cobb, Det	49	1941	George Case, Wash	33	1976	Bill North, Oak	75
1908	Patsy Dougherty, Chi	47	1942	George Case, Wash	44	1977	Freddie Patek, KC	53
1909	Ty Cobb, Det	76	1943	George Case, Wash	61	1978	Ron LeFlore, Det	68
1910	Eddie Collins, Phi	81	1944	Snuffy Stirnweiss, NY	55	1979	Willie Wilson, KC	83
1911	Ty Cobb, Det	83	1945	Snuffy Stirnweiss, NY	33	1980	Rickey Henderson, Oak	100
1912	Clyde Milan, Wash	88	1946	George Case, Cle	28	1981	Rickey Henderson, Oak	56
1913	Clyde Milan, Wash	75	1947	Bob Dillinger, St.L	34	1982	Rickey Henderson, Oak	130
1914	Fritz Maisel, NY	74	1948	Bob Dillinger, St.L	28	1983	Rickey Henderson, Oak	108
1915	Ty Cobb, Det	96	1949	Bob Dillinger, St.L	20	1984	Rickey Henderson, Oak	66
1916	Ty Cobb, Det	68	1950	Dom DiMaggio, Bos	15	1985	Rickey Henderson, NY	80
1917	Ty Cobb, Det	55	1951	Minnie Minoso, Cle-Chi	31	1986	Rickey Henderson, NY	87
1918	George Sisler, St.L	45	1952	Minnie Minoso, Chi	22	1987	Harold Reynolds, Sea	60
1919	Eddie Collins, Chi	33	1953	Minnie Minoso, Chi	25	1988	Rickey Henderson, NY	93
1920	Sam Rice, Wash	63	1954	Jackie Jensen, Bos	22	1989	R. Henderson, NY-Oak	77
1921	George Sisler, St.L	35	1955	Jim Rivera, Chi	25	1990	Rickey Henderson, Oak	65
1922	George Sisler, St.L	51	1956	Luis Aparicio, Chi	21	1991	Rickey Henderson, Oak	58
1923	Eddie Collins, Chi	47	1957	Luis Aparicio, Chi	28	1992	Kenny Lofton, Cle	66
1924	Eddie Collins, Chi	42	1958	Luis Aparicio, Chi	29	1993	Kenny Lofton, Cle	70
1925	Johnny Mostil, Chi	43	1959	Luis Aparicio, Chi	56	1994	Kenny Lofton, Cle	60
1926	Johnny Mostil, Chi	35	1960	Luis Aparicio, Chi	51	1995	Kenny Lofton, Cle	54
1927	George Sisler, St.L	27	1961	Luis Aparicio, Chi	53	1996	Kenny Lofton, Cle	75
1928	Buddy Myer, Bos	30	1962	Luis Aparicio, Chi	31	1997	Brian Hunter, Det	74
1929	Charlie Gehringer, Det	28	1963	Luis Aparicio, Bal	40	1998	Rickey Henderson, Oak	66
1930	Marty McManus, Det	23	1964	Luis Aparicio, Bal	57	1999	Brian Hunter, Det-Sea	44
1931	Ben Chapman, NY	61	1965	Bert Campaneris, KC	51	2000	Johnny Damon, KC	46
1932	Ben Chapman, NY	38	1966	Bert Campaneris, KC	52	2001	Ichiro Suzuki, Sea	56
1933	Ben Chapman, NY	27	1967	Bert Campaneris, KC	55			
1934	Bill Werber, Bos	40	1968	Bert Campaneris, Oak	62			

Consecutive Game Streaks
Regular season games through 2001.

Games Played

Gm		Dates of Streak
2632	Cal Ripken Jr., Bal	5/30/82 to 9/19/98
2130	Lou Gehrig, NY	6/1/25 to 4/30/39
1307	Everett Scott, Bos-NY	6/20/16 to 5/5/25
1207	Steve Garvey, LA-SD	9/3/75 to 7/29/83
1117	Billy Williams, Cubs	9/22/63 to 9/2/70
1103	Joe Sewell, Cle	9/13/22 to 4/30/30
895	Stan Musial, St.L	4/15/52 to 8/23/57
829	Eddie Yost, Wash	4/30/49 to 5/11/55
822	Gus Suhr, Pit	9/11/31 to 6/4/37
798	Nellie Fox, Chisox	8/8/55 to 9/3/60
745	Pete Rose, Cin-Phi	9/2/78 to 8/23/83
740	Dale Murphy, Atl	9/26/81 to 7/8/86
730	Richie Ashburn, Phi	6/7/50 to 4/13/55
717	Ernie Banks, Cubs	8/28/56 to 6/22/61
678	Pete Rose, Cin	9/28/73 to 5/7/78

Others

Gm		Gm	
673	Earl Averill	565	Aaron Ward
652	Frank McCormick	540	Candy LaChance
648	Sandy Alomar Sr.	535	Buck Freeman
618	Eddie Brown	533	Fred Luderus
585	Roy McMillan	511	Clyde Milan
577	George Pinckney	511	Charlie Gehringer
574	Steve Brodie	508	Vada Pinson

Hitting

	Gm	Year
Joe DiMaggio, New York (AL)	56	1941
Willie Keeler, Baltimore (NL)	44	1897
Pete Rose, Cincinnati (NL)	44	1978
Bill Dahlen, Chicago (NL)	42	1894
George Sisler, St. Louis (AL)	41	1922
Ty Cobb, Detroit (AL)	40	1911
Paul Molitor, Milwaukee (AL)	39	1987
Tommy Holmes, Boston (NL)	37	1945
Billy Hamilton, Philadelphia (NL)	36	1894
Fred Clarke, Louisville (NL)	35	1895
Ty Cobb, Detroit (AL)	35	1917
Ty Cobb, Detroit (AL)	34	1912
George Sisler, St. Louis (AL)	34	1925
George McQuinn, St. Louis (AL)	34	1938
Dom DiMaggio, Boston (AL)	34	1949
Benito Santiago, San Diego (NL)	34	1987
George Davis, New York (NL)	33	1893
Hal Chase, New York (AL)	33	1907
Rogers Hornsby, St. Louis (NL)	33	1922
Heinie Manush, Washington (AL)	33	1933
Ed Delahanty, Philadelphia (NL)	31	1899
Nap Lajoie, Cleveland (AL)	31	1906
Sam Rice, Washington, (AL)	31	1924
Willie Davis, Los Angeles (NL)	31	1969
Rico Carty, Atlanta (NL)	31	1970
Ken Landreaux, Minnesota (AL)	31	1980
Vladimir Guerrero, Montreal (NL)	31	1999

Annual Pitching Leaders (since 1900)
Winning Percentage
At least 15 wins, except in strike years of 1981 and 1994 (when the minimum was 10).

National League
Multiple winners: Ed Reulbach and Tom Seaver (3); Larry Benton, Harry Brecheen, Jack Chesbro, Paul Derringer, Freddie Fitzsimmons, Don Gullett, Claude Hendrix, Carl Hubbell, Sandy Koufax, Bill Lee, Greg Maddux, Christy Mathewson, Don Newcombe, Preacher Roe and John Smoltz (2).

Year		W-L	Pct	Year		W-L	Pct
1900	Jesse Tannehill, Pittsburgh	20-6	.769	1952	Hoyt Wilhelm, New York	15-3	.833
1901	Jack Chesbro, Pittsburgh	21-10	.677	1953	Carl Erskine, Brooklyn	20-6	.769
1902	Jack Chesbro, Pittsburgh	28-6	.824	1954	Johnny Antonelli, New York	21-7	.750
1903	Sam Leever, Pittsburgh	25-7	.781	1955	Don Newcombe, Brooklyn	20-5	.800
1904	Joe McGinnity, New York	35-8	.814	1956	Don Newcombe, Brooklyn	27-7	.794
1905	Christy Mathewson, New York	31-8	.795	1957	Bob Buhl, Milwaukee	18-7	.720
1906	Ed Reulbach, Chicago	19-4	.826	1958	Warren Spahn, Milwaukee	22-11	.667
1907	Ed Reulbach, Chicago	17-4	.810		& Lew Burdette, Milwaukee	20-10	.667
1908	Ed Reulbach, Chicago	24-7	.774	1959	Roy Face, Pittsburgh	18-1	.947
1909	Howie Camnitz, Pittsburgh	25-6	.806	1960	Ernie Broglio, St. Louis	21-9	.700
	& Christy Mathewson, New York	25-6	.806	1961	Johnny Podres, Los Angeles	18-5	.783
1910	King Cole, Chicago	20-4	.833	1962	Bob Purkey, Cincinnati	23-5	.821
1911	Rube Marquard, New York	24-7	.774	1963	Ron Perranoski, Los Angeles	16-3	.842
1912	Claude Hendrix, Pittsburgh	24-9	.727	1964	Sandy Koufax, Los Angeles	19-5	.792
1913	Bert Humphries, Chicago	16-4	.800	1965	Sandy Koufax, Los Angeles	26-8	.765
1914	Bill James, Boston	26-7	.788	1966	Juan Marichal, San Francisco	25-6	.806
1915	Grover Alexander, Phila.	31-10	.756	1967	Dick Hughes, St. Louis	16-6	.727
1916	Tom Hughes, Boston	16-3	.842	1968	Steve Blass, Pittsburgh	18-6	.750
1917	Ferdie Schupp, New York	21-7	.750	1969	Tom Seaver, New York	25-7	.781
1918	Claude Hendrix, Chicago	19-7	.731	1970	Bob Gibson, St. Louis	23-7	.767
1919	Dutch Ruether, Cincinnati	19-6	.760	1971	Don Gullett, Cincinnati	16-6	.727
1920	Burleigh Grimes, Brooklyn	23-11	.676	1972	Gary Nolan, Cincinnati	15-5	.750
1921	Bill Doak, St. Louis	15-6	.714	1973	Tommy John, Los Angeles	16-7	.696
1922	Pete Donohue, Cincinnati	18-9	.667	1974	Andy Messersmith, Los Angeles	20-6	.769
1923	Dolf Luque, Cincinnati	27-8	.771	1975	Don Gullett, Cincinnati	15-4	.789
1924	Emil Yde, Pittsburgh	16-3	.842	1976	Steve Carlton, Philadelphia	20-7	.741
1925	Bill Sherdel, St. Louis	15-6	.714	1977	John Candelaria, Pittsburgh	20-5	.800
1926	Ray Kremer, Pittsburgh	20-6	.769	1978	Gaylord Perry, San Diego	21-6	.778
1927	Larry Benton, Boston-NY	17-7	.708	1979	Tom Seaver, Cincinnati	16-6	.727
1928	Larry Benton, New York	25-9	.735	1980	Jim Bibby, Pittsburgh	19-6	.760
1929	Charlie Root, Chicago	19-6	.760	1981	Tom Seaver, Cincinnati	14-2	.875
1930	Freddie Fitzsimmons, NY	19-7	.731	1982	Phil Niekro, Atlanta	17-4	.810
1931	Paul Derringer, St. Louis	18-8	.692	1983	John Denny, Philadelphia	19-6	.760
1932	Lon Warneke, Chicago	22-6	.786	1984	Rick Sutcliffe, Chicago	16-1	.941
1933	Ben Cantwell, Boston	20-10	.667	1985	Orel Hershiser, Los Angeles	19-3	.864
1934	Dizzy Dean, St. Louis	30-7	.811	1986	Bob Ojeda, New York	18-5	.783
1935	Bill Lee, Chicago	20-6	.769	1987	Dwight Gooden, New York	15-7	.682
1936	Carl Hubbell, New York	26-6	.813	1988	David Cone, New York	20-3	.870
1937	Carl Hubbell, New York	22-8	.733	1989	Mike Bielecki, Chicago	18-7	.720
1938	Bill Lee, Chicago	22-9	.710	1990	Doug Drabek, Pittsburgh	22-6	.786
1939	Paul Derringer, Cincinnati	25-7	.781	1991	John Smiley, Pittsburgh	20-8	.714
1940	Freddie Fitzsimmons, Bklyn	16-2	.889		& Jose Rijo, Cincinnati	15-6	.714
1941	Elmer Riddle, Cincinnati	19-4	.826	1992	Bob Tewksbury, St. Louis	16-5	.762
1942	Larry French, Brooklyn	15-4	.789	1993	Mark Portugal, Houston	18-4	.818
1943	Mort Cooper, St. Louis	21-8	.724	1994	Marvin Freeman, Colorado	10-2	.833
1944	Ted Wilks, St. Louis	17-4	.810	1995	Greg Maddux, Atlanta	19-2	.905
1945	Harry Brecheen, St. Louis	14-4	.778	1996	John Smoltz, Atlanta	24-8	.750
1946	Murray Dickson, St. Louis	15-6	.714	1997	Greg Maddux, Atlanta	19-4	.826
1947	Larry Jansen, New York	21-5	.808	1998	John Smoltz, Atlanta	17-3	.850
1948	Harry Brecheen, St. Louis	20-7	.741	1999	Mike Hampton, Houston	22-4	.846
1949	Preacher Roe, Brooklyn	15-6	.714	2000	Randy Johnson, Arizona	19-7	.731
1950	Sal Maglie, New York	18-4	.818	2001	Curt Schilling, Arizona	22-6	.786
1951	Preacher Roe, Brooklyn	22-3	.880				

Note: In 1984, Sutcliffe was also 4-5 with Cleveland for a combined AL-NL record of 20-6 (.769).

American League
Multiple winners: Lefty Grove (5); Chief Bender, Roger Clemens and Whitey Ford (3); Johnny Allen, Eddie Cicotte, Mike Cuellar, Lefty Gomez, Ron Guidry, Catfish Hunter, Randy Johnson, Walter Johnson, Jim Palmer, Pete Vuckovich and Smokey Joe Wood (2).

Year		W-L	Pct	Year		W-L	Pct
1901	Clark Griffith, Chicago	24-7	.774	1904	Jack Chesbro, New York	41-12	.774
1902	Bill Bernhard, Phila-Cleve	18-5	.783	1905	Andy Coakley, Philadelphia	20-7	.741
1903	Cy Young, Boston	28-9	.757	1906	Eddie Plank, Philadelphia	19-6	.760

Year		W-L	Pct	Year		W-L	Pct
1907	Wild Bill Donovan, Detroit	25-4	.862	1956	Whitey Ford, New York	19-6	.760
1908	Ed Walsh, Chicago	40-15	.727	1957	Dick Donovan, Chicago	16-6	.727
1909	George Mullin, Detroit	29-8	.784		& Tom Sturdivant, New York	16-6	.727
1910	Chief Bender, Philadelphia	23-5	.821	1958	Bob Turley, New York	21-7	.750
1911	Chief Bender, Philadelphia	17-5	.773	1959	Bob Shaw, Chicago	18-6	.750
1912	Smokey Joe Wood, Boston	34-5	.872	1960	Jim Perry, Cleveland	18-10	.643
1913	Walter Johnson, Washington	36-7	.837	1961	Whitey Ford, New York	25-4	.862
1914	Chief Bender, Philadelphia	17-3	.850	1962	Ray Herbert, Chicago	20-9	.690
1915	Smokey Joe Wood, Boston	15-5	.750	1963	Whitey Ford, New York	24-7	.774
1916	Eddie Cicotte, Chicago	15-7	.682	1964	Wally Bunker, Baltimore	19-5	.792
1917	Reb Russell, Chicago	15-5	.750	1965	Mudcat Grant, Minnesota	21-7	.750
1918	Sad Sam Jones, Boston	16-5	.762	1966	Sonny Siebert, Cleveland	16-8	.667
1919	Eddie Cicotte, Chicago	29-7	.806	1967	Joe Horlen, Chicago	19-7	.731
1920	Jim Bagby, Cleveland	31-12	.721	1968	Denny McLain, Detroit	31-6	.838
1921	Carl Mays, New York	27-9	.750	1969	Jim Palmer, Baltimore	16-4	.800
1922	Joe Bush, New York	26-7	.788	1970	Mike Cuellar, Baltimore	24-8	.750
1923	Herb Pennock, New York	19-6	.760	1971	Dave McNally, Baltimore	21-5	.808
1924	Walter Johnson, Washington	23-7	.767	1972	Catfish Hunter, Oakland	21-7	.750
1925	Stan Coveleski, Washington	20-5	.800	1973	Catfish Hunter, Oakland	21-5	.808
1926	George Uhle, Cleveland	27-11	.711	1974	Mike Cuellar, Baltimore	22-10	.688
1927	Waite Hoyt, New York	22-7	.759	1975	Mike Torrez, Baltimore	20-9	.690
1928	General Crowder, St. Louis	21-5	.808	1976	Bill Campbell, Minnesota	17-5	.773
1929	Lefty Grove, Philadelphia	20-6	.769	1977	Paul Splittorff, Kansas City	16-6	.727
1930	Lefty Grove, Philadelphia	28-5	.848	1978	Ron Guidry, New York	25-3	.893
1931	Lefty Grove, Philadelphia	31-4	.886	1979	Mike Caldwell, Milwaukee	16-6	.727
1932	Johnny Allen, New York	17-4	.810	1980	Steve Stone, Baltimore	25-7	.781
1933	Lefty Grove, Philadelphia	24-8	.750	1981	Pete Vuckovich, Milwaukee	14-4	.778
1934	Lefty Gomez, New York	26-5	.839	1982	Pete Vuckovich, Milwaukee	18-6	.750
1935	Eldon Auker, Detroit	18-7	.720		& Jim Palmer, Baltimore	15-5	.750
1936	Monte Pearson, New York	19-7	.731	1983	Rich Dotson, Chicago	22-7	.759
1937	Johnny Allen, Cleveland	15-1	.938	1984	Doyle Alexander, Toronto	17-6	.739
1938	Red Ruffing, New York	21-7	.750	1985	Ron Guidry, New York	22-6	.786
1939	Lefty Grove, Boston	15-4	.789	1986	Roger Clemens, Boston	24-4	.857
1940	Schoolboy Rowe, Detroit	16-3	.842	1987	Roger Clemens, Boston	20-9	.690
1941	Lefty Gomez, New York	15-5	.750	1988	Frank Viola, Minnesota	24-7	.774
1942	Ernie Bonham, New York	21-5	.808	1989	Bret Saberhagen, Kansas City	23-6	.793
1943	Spud Chandler, New York	20-4	.833	1990	Bob Welch, Oakland	27-6	.818
1944	Tex Hughson, Boston	18-5	.783	1991	Scott Erickson, Minnesota	20-8	.714
1945	Hal Newhouser, Detroit	25-9	.735	1992	Mike Mussina, Baltimore	18-5	.783
1946	Boo Ferriss, Boston	25-6	.806	1993	Jimmy Key, New York	18-6	.750
1947	Allie Reynolds, New York	19-8	.704	1994	Jason Bere, Chicago	12-2	.857
1948	Jack Kramer, Boston	18-5	.783	1995	Randy Johnson, Seattle	18-2	.900
1949	Ellis Kinder, Boston	23-6	.793	1996	Charles Nagy, Cleveland	17-5	.773
1950	Vic Raschi, New York	21-8	.724	1997	Randy Johnson, Seattle	20-4	.833
1951	Bob Feller, Cleveland	22-8	.733	1998	David Wells, New York	18-4	.818
1952	Bobby Shantz, Philadelphia	24-7	.774	1999	Pedro Martinez, Boston	23-4	.852
1953	Ed Lopat, New York	16-4	.800	2000	Tim Hudson, Oakland	20-6	.769
1954	Sandy Consuegra, Chicago	16-3	.842	2001	Roger Clemens, New York	20-3	.870
1955	Tommy Byrne, New York	16-5	.762				

Earned Run Average

Earned Run Averages were based on at least 10 complete games pitched (1900-49), at least 154 innings pitched (1950-60), and at least 162 innings pitched since 1961 in the AL and 1962 in the NL. In the strike years of 1981, '94 and '95, qualifiers had to pitch at least as many innings as the total number of games their team played that season.

National League

Multiple winners: Grover Alexander, Sandy Koufax and Christy Mathewson (5); Greg Maddux (4); Carl Hubbell, Tom Seaver, Warren Spahn and Dazzy Vance (3); Kevin Brown, Bill Doak, Randy Johnson, Ray Kremer, Dolf Luque, Howie Pollet, Nolan Ryan, Bill Walker and Bucky Walters (2).

Year		ERA	Year		ERA	Year		ERA
1900	Rube Waddell, Pit	2.37	1909	Christy Mathewson, NY	1.14	1918	Hippo Vaughn, Chi	1.74
1901	Jesse Tannehill, Pit	2.18	1910	George McQuillan, Phi	1.60	1919	Grover Alexander, Chi	1.72
1902	Jack Taylor, Chi	1.33	1911	Christy Mathewson, NY	1.99	1920	Grover Alexander, Chi	1.91
1903	Sam Leever, Pit	2.06	1912	Jeff Tesreau, NY	1.96	1921	Bill Doak, St.L	2.59
1904	Joe McGinnity, NY	1.61	1913	Christy Mathewson, NY	2.06	1922	Rosy Ryan, NY	3.01
1905	Christy Mathewson, NY	1.27	1914	Bill Doak, St.L	1.72	1923	Dolf Luque, Cin	1.93
1906	Three Finger Brown, Chi	1.04	1915	Grover Alexander, Phi	1.22	1924	Dazzy Vance, Bklyn	2.16
1907	Jack Pfiester, Chi	1.15	1916	Grover Alexander, Phi	1.55	1925	Dolf Luque, Cin	2.63
1908	Christy Mathewson, NY	1.43	1917	Grover Alexander, Phi	1.86	1926	Ray Kremer, Pit	2.61

Year		ERA	Year		ERA	Year		ERA
1927	Ray Kremer, Pit	2.47	1953	Warren Spahn, Mil	2.10	1979	J.R. Richard, Hou	2.71
1928	Dazzy Vance, Bklyn	2.09	1954	Johnny Antonelli, NY	2.30	1980	Don Sutton, LA	2.21
1929	Bill Walker, NY	3.09	1955	Bob Friend, Pit	2.83	1981	Nolan Ryan, Hou	1.69
1930	Dazzy Vance, Bklyn	2.61	1956	Lew Burdette, Mil	2.70	1982	Steve Rogers, Mon	2.40
1931	Bill Walker, NY	2.26	1957	Johnny Podres, Bklyn	2.66	1983	Atlee Hammaker, SF	2.25
1932	Lon Warneke, Chi	2.37	1958	Stu Miller, SF	2.47	1984	Alejandro Peña, LA	2.48
1933	Carl Hubbell, NY	1.66	1959	Sam Jones, SF	2.83	1985	Dwight Gooden, NY	1.53
1934	Carl Hubbell, NY	2.30	1960	Mike McCormick, SF	2.70	1986	Mike Scott, Hou	2.22
1935	Cy Blanton, Pit	2.58	1961	Warren Spahn, Mil	3.02	1987	Nolan Ryan, Hou	2.76
1936	Carl Hubbell, NY	2.31	1962	Sandy Koufax, LA	2.54	1988	Joe Magrane, St.L	2.18
1937	Jim Turner, Bos	2.38	1963	Sandy Koufax, LA	1.88	1989	Scott Garrelts, SF	2.28
1938	Bill Lee, Chi	2.66	1964	Sandy Koufax, LA	1.74	1990	Danny Darwin, Hou	2.21
1939	Bucky Walters, Cin	2.29	1965	Sandy Koufax, LA	2.04	1991	Dennis Martinez, Mon	2.39
1940	Bucky Walters, Cin	2.48	1966	Sandy Koufax, LA	1.73	1992	Bill Swift, SF	2.08
1941	Elmer Riddle, Cin	2.24	1967	Phil Niekro, Atl	1.87	1993	Greg Maddux, Atl	2.36
1942	Mort Cooper, St.L	1.78	1968	Bob Gibson, St.L	1.12	1994	Greg Maddux, Atl	1.56
1943	Howie Pollet, St.L	1.75	1969	Juan Marichal, SF	2.10	1995	Greg Maddux, Atl	1.63
1944	Ed Heusser, Cin	2.38	1970	Tom Seaver, NY	2.81	1996	Kevin Brown, Fla	1.89
1945	Hank Borowy, Chi	2.13	1971	Tom Seaver, NY	1.76	1997	Pedro Martinez, Mon	1.90
1946	Howie Pollet, St.L	2.10	1972	Steve Carlton, Phi	1.97	1998	Greg Maddux, Atl	2.22
1947	Warren Spahn, Bos	2.33	1973	Tom Seaver, NY	2.08	1999	Randy Johnson, Ari	2.48
1948	Harry Brecheen, St.L	2.24	1974	Buzz Capra, Atl	2.28	2000	Kevin Brown, LA	2.58
1949	Dave Koslo, NY	2.50	1975	Randy Jones, SD	2.24	2001	Randy Johnson, Ari	2.49
1950	Jim Hearn, St.L-NY	2.49	1976	John Denny, St.L	2.52			
1951	Chet Nichols, Bos	2.88	1977	John Candelaria, Pit	2.34			
1952	Hoyt Wilhelm, NY	2.43	1978	Craig Swan, NY	2.43			

Note: In 1945, Borowy had a 3.13 ERA in 18 games with New York (AL) for a combined ERA of 2.65.

American League

Multiple winners: Lefty Grove (9); Roger Clemens (6); Walter Johnson (5); Spud Chandler, Stan Coveleski, Red Faber, Whitey Ford, Lefty Gomez, Ron Guidry, Addie Joss, Pedro Martinez, Hal Newhouser, Jim Palmer, Gary Peters, Luis Tiant and Ed Walsh (2).

Year		ERA	Year		ERA	Year		ERA
1901	Cy Young, Bos	1.62	1935	Lefty Grove, Bos	2.70	1969	Dick Bosman, Wash	2.19
1902	Ed Siever, Det	1.91	1936	Lefty Grove, Bos	2.81	1970	Diego Segui, Oak	2.56
1903	Earl Moore, Cle	1.77	1937	Lefty Gomez, NY	2.33	1971	Vida Blue, Oak	1.82
1904	Addie Joss, Cle	1.59	1938	Lefty Grove, Bos	3.08	1972	Luis Tiant, Bos	1.91
1905	Rube Waddell, Phi	1.48	1939	Lefty Grove, Bos	2.54	1973	Jim Palmer, Bal	2.40
1906	Doc White, Chi	1.52	1940	Ernie Bonham, NY	1.90	1974	Catfish Hunter, Oak	2.49
1907	Ed Walsh, Chi	1.60	1941	Thornton Lee, Chi	2.37	1975	Jim Palmer, Bal	2.09
1908	Addie Joss, Cle	1.16	1942	Ted Lyons, Chi	2.10	1976	Mark Fidrych, Det	2.34
1909	Harry Krause, Phi	1.39	1943	Spud Chandler, NY	1.64	1977	Frank Tanana, Cal	2.54
1910	Ed Walsh, Chi	1.27	1944	Dizzy Trout, Det	2.12	1978	Ron Guidry, NY	1.74
1911	Vean Gregg, Cle	1.81	1945	Hal Newhouser, Det	1.81	1979	Ron Guidry, NY	2.78
1912	Walter Johnson, Wash	1.39	1946	Hal Newhouser, Det	1.94	1980	Rudy May, NY	2.47
1913	Walter Johnson, Wash	1.09	1947	Spud Chandler, NY	2.46	1981	Steve McCatty, Oak	2.32
1914	Dutch Leonard, Bos	1.01	1948	Gene Bearden, Cle	2.43	1982	Rick Sutcliffe, Cle	2.96
1915	Smokey Joe Wood, Bos	1.49	1949	Mel Parnell, Bos	2.77	1983	Rick Honeycutt, Tex	2.42
1916	Babe Ruth, Bos	1.75	1950	Early Wynn, Cle	3.20	1984	Mike Boddicker, Bal	2.79
1917	Eddie Cicotte, Chi	1.53	1951	Saul Rogovin, Det-Chi	2.78	1985	Dave Stieb, Tor	2.48
1918	Walter Johnson, Wash	1.27	1952	Allie Reynolds, NY	2.06	1986	Roger Clemens, Bos	2.48
1919	Walter Johnson, Wash	1.49	1953	Ed Lopat, NY	2.42	1987	Jimmy Key, Tor	2.76
1920	Bob Shawkey, NY	2.45	1954	Mike Garcia, Cle	2.64	1988	Allan Anderson, Min	2.45
1921	Red Faber, Chi	2.48	1955	Billy Pierce, Chi	1.97	1989	Bret Saberhagen, KC	2.16
1922	Red Faber, Chi	2.80	1956	Whitey Ford, NY	2.47	1990	Roger Clemens, Bos	1.93
1923	Stan Coveleski, Cle	2.76	1957	Bobby Shantz, NY	2.45	1991	Roger Clemens, Bos	2.62
1924	Walter Johnson, Wash	2.72	1958	Whitey Ford, NY	2.01	1992	Roger Clemens, Bos	2.41
1925	Stan Coveleski, Wash	2.84	1959	Hoyt Wilhelm, Bal	2.19	1993	Kevin Appier, KC	2.56
1926	Lefty Grove, Phi	2.51	1960	Frank Baumann, Chi	2.67	1994	Steve Ontiveros, Oak	2.65
1927	Wilcy Moore, NY	2.28	1961	Dick Donovan, Wash	2.40	1995	Randy Johnson, Sea	2.48
1928	Garland Braxton, Wash	2.51	1962	Hank Aguirre, Det	2.21	1996	Juan Guzman, Tor	2.93
1929	Lefty Grove, Phi	2.81	1963	Gary Peters, Chi	2.33	1997	Roger Clemens, Tor	2.05
1930	Lefty Grove, Phi	2.54	1964	Dean Chance, LA	1.65	1998	Roger Clemens, Tor	2.65
1931	Lefty Grove, Phi	2.06	1965	Sam McDowell, Cle	2.18	1999	Pedro Martinez, Bos	2.07
1932	Lefty Grove, Phi	2.84	1966	Gary Peters, Chi	1.98	2000	Pedro Martinez, Bos	1.74
1933	Monte Pearson, Cle	2.33	1967	Joe Horlen, Chi	2.06	2001	Freddy Garcia, Sea	3.05
1934	Lefty Gomez, NY	2.33	1968	Luis Tiant, Cle	1.60			

Strikeouts
National League

Multiple winners: Dazzy Vance (7); Grover Alexander (6); Steve Carlton, Christy Mathewson and Tom Seaver (5); Dizzy Dean, Sandy Koufax and Warren Spahn (4); Don Drysdale, Randy Johnson, Sam Jones and Johnny Vander Meer (3); David Cone, Dwight Gooden, Bill Hallahan, J.R. Richard, Robin Roberts, Nolan Ryan, Curt Schilling, John Smoltz and Hippo Vaughn (2).

Year	SO	Year	SO	Year	SO
1900 Rube Waddell, Pit	.130	1935 Dizzy Dean, St.L	.190	1968 Bob Gibson, St.L	.268
1901 Noodles Hahn, Cin	.239	1936 Van Lingle Mungo, Bklyn	.238	1969 Ferguson Jenkins, Chi	.273
1902 Vic Willis, Bos	.225	1937 Carl Hubbell, NY	.159	1970 Tom Seaver, NY	.283
1903 Christy Mathewson, NY	.267	1938 Clay Bryant, Chi	.135	1971 Tom Seaver, NY	.289
1904 Christy Mathewson, NY	.212	1939 Claude Passeau, Phi-Chi	.137	1972 Steve Carlton, Phi	.310
1905 Christy Mathewson, NY	.206	& Bucky Walters, Cin	.137	1973 Tom Seaver, NY	.251
1906 Fred Beebe, Chi-St.L	.171			1974 Steve Carlton, Phi	.240
1907 Christy Mathewson, NY	.178	1940 Kirby Higbe, Phi	.137	1975 Tom Seaver, NY	.243
1908 Christy Mathewson, NY	.259	1941 John Vander Meer, Cin	.202	1976 Tom Seaver, NY	.235
1909 Orval Overall, Chi	.205	1942 John Vander Meer, Cin	.186	1977 Phil Niekro, Atl	.262
		1943 John Vander Meer, Cin	.174	1978 J.R. Richard, Hou	.303
1910 Earl Moore, Phi	.185	1944 Bill Voiselle, NY	.161	1979 J.R. Richard, Hou	.313
1911 Rube Marquard, NY	.237	1945 Preacher Roe, Pit	.148		
1912 Grover Alexander, Phi	.195	1946 Johnny Schmitz, Chi	.135	1980 Steve Carlton, Phi	.286
1913 Tom Seaton, Phi	.168	1947 Ewell Blackwell, Cin	.193	1981 F. Valenzuela, LA	.180
1914 Grover Alexander, Phi	.214	1948 Harry Brecheen, St.L	.149	1982 Steve Carlton, Phi	.286
1915 Grover Alexander, Phi	.241	1949 Warren Spahn, Bos	.151	1983 Steve Carlton, Phi	.275
1916 Grover Alexander, Phi	.167			1984 Dwight Gooden, NY	.276
1917 Grover Alexander, Phi	.201	1950 Warren Spahn, Bos	.191	1985 Dwight Gooden, NY	.268
1918 Hippo Vaughn, Chi	.148	1951 Don Newcombe, Bklyn	.164	1986 Mike Scott, Hou	.306
1919 Hippo Vaughn, Chi	.141	& Warren Spahn, Bos	.164	1987 Nolan Ryan, Hou	.270
		1952 Warren Spahn, Bos	.183	1988 Nolan Ryan, Hou	.228
1920 Grover Alexander, Chi	.173	1953 Robin Roberts, Phi	.198	1989 Jose DeLeon, St.L	.201
1921 Burleigh Grimes, Bklyn	.136	1954 Robin Roberts, Phi	.185		
1922 Dazzy Vance, Bklyn	.134	1955 Sam Jones, Chi	.198	1990 David Cone, NY	.233
1923 Dazzy Vance, Bklyn	.197	1956 Sam Jones, Chi	.176	1991 David Cone, NY	.241
1924 Dazzy Vance, Bklyn	.262	1957 Jack Sanford, Phi	.188	1992 John Smoltz, Atl	.215
1925 Dazzy Vance, Bklyn	.221	1958 Sam Jones, St.L	.225	1993 Jose Rijo, Cin	.227
1926 Dazzy Vance, Bklyn	.140	1959 Don Drysdale, LA	.242	1994 Andy Benes, SD	.189
1927 Dazzy Vance, Bklyn	.184			1995 Hideo Nomo, LA	.236
1928 Dazzy Vance, Bklyn	.200	1960 Don Drysdale, LA	.246	1996 John Smoltz, Atl	.276
1929 Pat Malone, Chi	.166	1961 Sandy Koufax, LA	.269	1997 Curt Schilling, Phi	.319
		1962 Don Drysdale, LA	.232	1998 Curt Schilling, Phi	.300
1930 Bill Hallahan, St.L	.177	1963 Sandy Koufax, LA	.306	1999 Randy Johnson, Ari	.364
1931 Bill Hallahan, St.L	.159	1964 Bob Veale, Pit	.250		
1932 Dizzy Dean, St.L	.191	1965 Sandy Koufax, LA	.382	2000 Randy Johnson, Ari	.347
1933 Dizzy Dean, St.L	.199	1966 Sandy Koufax, LA	.317	2001 Randy Johnson, Ari	.372
1934 Dizzy Dean, St.L	.195	1967 Jim Bunning, Phi	.253		

Pitching Triple Crown Winners

Pitchers who led either league in Earned Run Average, Wins and Strikeouts over a single season.

National League

	Year	ERA	W-L	SO
Tommy Bond, Bos	1877	2.11	40-17	170
Hoss Radbourne, Prov	1884	1.38	60-12	441
Tim Keefe, NY	1888	1.74	35-12	333
John Clarkson, Bos	1889	2.73	49-19	284
Amos Rusie, NY	1894	2.78	36-13	195
Christy Mathewson, NY	1905	1.27	31-8	206
Christy Mathewson, NY	1908	1.43	37-11	259
Grover Alexander, Phi	1915	1.22	31-10	241
Grover Alexander, Phi	1916	1.55	33-12	167
Grover Alexander, Phi	1917	1.86	30-13	201
Hippo Vaughn, Chi	1918	1.74	22-10	148
Grover Alexander, Chi	1920	1.91	27-14	173
Dazzy Vance, Bklyn	1924	2.16	28-6	262
Bucky Walters, Cin	1939	2.29	27-11	137
Sandy Koufax, LA	1963	1.88	25-5	306
Sandy Koufax, LA	1965	2.04	26-8	382
Sandy Koufax, LA	1966	1.73	27-9	317
Steve Carlton, Phi	1972	1.97	27-10	310
Dwight Gooden, NY	1985	1.53	24-4	268

Ties: In 1894, Rusie tied for league lead in wins with Jouett Meekin, NY (36-10); in 1939, Walters tied for league lead in strikeouts with Claude Passeau, Phi-Chi; in 1963, Koufax tied for the league lead in wins with Juan Marichal, SF.

American League

	Year	ERA	W-L	SO
Cy Young, Bos	1901	1.62	33-10	158
Rube Waddell, Phi	1905	1.48	26-11	287
Walter Johnson, Wash	1913	1.09	36-7	243
Walter Johnson, Wash	1918	1.27	23-13	162
Walter Johnson, Wash	1924	2.72	23-7	158
Lefty Grove, Phi	1930	2.54	28-5	209
Lefty Grove, Phi	1931	2.06	31-4	175
Lefty Gomez, NY	1934	2.33	26-5	158
Lefty Gomez, NY	1937	2.33	21-11	194
Hal Newhouser, Det	1945	1.81	25-9	212
Roger Clemens, Tor	1997	2.05	21-7	292
Roger Clemens, Tor	1998	2.65	20-6	271
Pedro Martinez, Bos	1999	2.07	23-4	313

Ties: In 1998, Clemens tied for league lead in wins with David Cone, NY (20-7) and Rick Helling, Tex (20-7).

American League

Multiple winners: Walter Johnson (12); Nolan Ryan (9); Bob Feller and Lefty Grove (7); Rube Waddell (6); Roger Clemens and Sam McDowell (5); Randy Johnson (4); Lefty Gomez, Mark Langston and Camilo Pascual (3); Len Barker, Tommy Bridges, Jim Bunning, Pedro Martinez, Hal Newhouser, Allie Reynolds, Herb Score, Ed Walsh and Early Wynn (2).

Year	SO	Year	SO	Year	SO
1901 Cy Young, Bos	158	1935 Tommy Bridges, Det	163	1968 Sam McDowell, Cle	283
1902 Rube Waddell, Phi	210	1936 Tommy Bridges, Det	175	1969 Sam McDowell, Cle	279
1903 Rube Waddell, Phi	302	1937 Lefty Gomez, NY	194	1970 Sam McDowell, Cle	304
1904 Rube Waddell, Phi	349	1938 Bob Feller, Cle	240	1971 Mickey Lolich, Det	308
1905 Rube Waddell, Phi	287	1939 Bob Feller, Cle	246	1972 Nolan Ryan, Cal	329
1906 Rube Waddell, Phi	196			1973 Nolan Ryan, Cal	383
1907 Rube Waddell, Phi	232	1940 Bob Feller, Cle	261	1974 Nolan Ryan, Cal	367
1908 Ed Walsh, Chi	269	1941 Bob Feller, Cle	260	1975 Frank Tanana, Cal	269
1909 Frank Smith, Chi	177	1942 Tex Hughson, Bos	113	1976 Nolan Ryan, Cal	327
		& Bobo Newsom, Wash	113	1977 Nolan Ryan, Cal	341
1910 Walter Johnson, Wash	313	1943 Allie Reynolds, Cle	151	1978 Nolan Ryan, Cal	260
1911 Ed Walsh, Chi	255	1944 Hal Newhouser, Det	187	1979 Nolan Ryan, Cal	223
1912 Walter Johnson, Wash	303	1945 Hal Newhouser, Det	212		
1913 Walter Johnson, Wash	243	1946 Bob Feller, Cle	348	1980 Len Barker, Cle	187
1914 Walter Johnson, Wash	225	1947 Bob Feller, Cle	196	1981 Len Barker, Cle	127
1915 Walter Johnson, Wash	203	1948 Bob Feller, Cle	164	1982 Floyd Bannister, Sea	209
1916 Walter Johnson, Wash	228	1949 Virgil Trucks, Det	153	1983 Jack Morris, Det	232
1917 Walter Johnson, Wash	188			1984 Mark Langston, Sea	204
1918 Walter Johnson, Wash	162	1950 Bob Lemon, Cle	170	1985 Bert Blyleven, Cle-Min	206
1919 Walter Johnson, Wash	147	1951 Vic Raschi, NY	164	1986 Mark Langston, Sea	245
		1952 Allie Reynolds, NY	160	1987 Mark Langston, Sea	262
1920 Stan Coveleski, Cle	133	1953 Billy Pierce, Chi	186	1988 Roger Clemens, Bos	291
1921 Walter Johnson, Wash	143	1954 Bob Turley, Bal	185	1989 Nolan Ryan, Tex	301
1922 Urban Shocker, St.L	149	1955 Herb Score, Cle	245		
1923 Walter Johnson, Wash	130	1956 Herb Score, Cle	263	1990 Nolan Ryan, Tex	232
1924 Walter Johnson, Wash	158	1957 Early Wynn, Cle	184	1991 Roger Clemens, Bos	241
1925 Lefty Grove, Phi	116	1958 Early Wynn, Chi	179	1992 Randy Johnson, Sea	241
1926 Lefty Grove, Phi	194	1959 Jim Bunning, Det	201	1993 Randy Johnson, Sea	308
1927 Lefty Grove, Phi	174			1994 Randy Johnson, Sea	204
1928 Lefty Grove, Phi	183	1960 Jim Bunning, Det	201	1995 Randy Johnson, Sea	294
1929 Lefty Grove, Phi	170	1961 Camilo Pascual, Min	221	1996 Roger Clemens, Bos	257
		1962 Camilo Pascual, Min	206	1997 Roger Clemens, Tor	292
1930 Lefty Grove, Phi	209	1963 Camilo Pascual, Min	202	1998 Roger Clemens, Tor	271
1931 Lefty Grove, Phi	175	1964 Al Downing, NY	217	1999 Pedro Martinez, Bos	313
1932 Red Ruffing, NY	190	1965 Sam McDowell, Cle	325		
1933 Lefty Gomez, NY	163	1966 Sam McDowell, Cle	225	2000 Pedro Martinez, Bos	284
1934 Lefty Gomez, NY	158	1967 Jim Lonborg, Bos	246	2001 Hideo Nomo, Bos	220

Perfect Games

Seventeen pitchers have thrown perfect games (27 up, 27 down) in major league history. However, the game pitched by Ernie Shore is not considered to be official.

National League

	Game	Date	Score
Lee Richmond	Wor. vs Cle.	6/12/1880	1-0
Monte Ward	Prov. vs Bos.	6/17/1880	5-0
Jim Bunning	Phi. at NY	6/21/1964	6-0
Sandy Koufax	LA vs Chi.	9/9/1965	1-0
Tom Browning	Cin. vs LA	9/16/1988	1-0
Dennis Martinez	Mon. at LA	7/28/1991	2-0

Note: Pittsburgh's Harvey Haddix pitched 12 perfect innings against the Milwaukee Braves on May 26, 1959 before losing, 1-0, in the 13th. Braves' lead-off batter Felix Mantilla reached on a throwing error by Pirates 3B Don Hoak, Eddie Mathews sacrificed Mantilla to 2nd, Hank Aaron was walked intentionally, and Joe Adcock hit a 3-run HR. Adcock, however, passed Aaron on the bases and was only credited with a 1-run double.

Note: Montreal's Pedro Martinez pitched nine perfect innings against the San Diego Padres on June 3, 1995 before surrendering a leadoff double to Bip Roberts in the 10th. He was then relieved by Mel Rojas, who finished the game, which Montreal won, 1-0.

American League

	Game	Date	Score
Cy Young	Bos. vs Phi.	5/5/1904	3-0
Addie Joss	Cle. vs Chi.	10/2/1908	1-0
Ernie Shore	Bos. vs Wash.	6/23/1917	4-0*
Charlie Robertson	Chi. at Det.	4/30/1922	2-0
Catfish Hunter	Oak. vs Min.	5/8/1968	4-0
Len Barker	Cle. vs Tor.	5/15/1981	3-0
Mike Witt	Cal. at Tex.	9/30/1984	1-0
Kenny Rogers	Tex. vs Cal.	7/28/1994	4-0
David Wells	NY vs Min.	5/17/1998	4-0
David Cone	NY vs Mon.	7/18/1999	6-0

*Babe Ruth started for Boston, walking Senators' lead-off batter Ray Morgan, then was thrown out of game by umpire Brick Owens for arguing the call. Shore came on in relief. Morgan was caught stealing and Shore retired the next 26 batters in a row. While technically not a perfect game—since he didn't start—Shore gets credit anyway.

World Series

Pitcher	Game	Date	Score
Don Larsen	NY vs Bklyn	10/8/1956	2-0

No-Hit Games

Nine innings or more, including perfect games, since 1876. Losing pitchers in **bold** type. **Multiple no-hitters:** Nolan Ryan (7); Sandy Koufax (4); Larry Cocoran, Bob Feller and Cy Young (3); Jim Bunning, Steve Busby, Carl Erskine, Bob Forsch, Pud Galvin, Ken Holtzman, Addie Joss, Hub Leonard, Jim Maloney, Christy Mathewson, Hideo Nomo, Allie Reynolds, Warren Spahn, Bill Stoneham, Virgil Trucks, Johnny Vander Meer and Don Wilson (2).

National League

Year	Date	Pitcher	Result
1876	7/15	George Bradley	St.L vs Har, 2-0
1880	6/12	Lee Richmond	Wor vs Cle, 1-0
			(perfect game)
	6/17	Monte Ward	Prov vs Buf, 5-0
			(perfect game)
	8/19	Larry Corcoran	Chi vs Bos, 6-0
	8/20	Pud Galvin	Buf at Wor, 1-0
1882	9/20	Larry Corcoran	Chi vs Wor, 1-0
1883	7/25	Old Hoss Radbourne	Prov at Cle, 8-0
	9/13	Hugh Daily	Cle at Phi, 1-0
1884	6/27	Larry Corcoran	Chi vs Prov, 6-0
	8/4	Pud Galvin	Buf at Det, 18-0
1885	7/27	John Clarkson	Chi vs Prov, 6-0
	8/29	Charlie Ferguson	Phi vs Prov, 1-0
1891	6/22	Tom Lovett	Bklyn vs NY, 4-0
	7/31	Amos Rusie	NY vs Bklyn, 11-0
1892	8/6	John Stivetts	Bos vs Wash, 4-0
	8/22	Ben Sanders	Lou vs Bal, 6-2
	10/22	Bumpus Jones	Cin vs Pit, 7-1
			(1st major league game)
1893	8/16	Bill Hawke	Bal vs Wash, 5-0
1897	9/18	Cy Young	Cle vs Cin, 6-0
1898	4/22	Ted Breitenstein	Cin vs Pit, 11-0
	4/22	Jim Hughes	Bal vs Bos, 8-0
	7/8	Frank Donahue	Phi vs Bos, 5-0
	8/21	Walter Thornton	Chi vs Bklyn, 2-0
1899	5/25	Deacon Phillippe	Lou vs NY, 7-0
1900	7/12	Noodles Hahn	Cin vs Phi, 4-0
1901	7/15	Christy Mathewson	NY vs St.L, 5-0
1903	9/18	Chick Fraser	Phi at Chi, 10-0
1905	6/13	Christy Mathewson	NY at Chi, 1-0
1906	5/1	John Lush	Phi at Bklyn, 1-0
	7/20	Mal Eason	Bklyn at St.L, 2-0
1907	5/8	Frank Pfeffer	Bos vs Cin, 6-0
	9/20	Nick Maddox	Pit vs Bkn, 2-1
1908	7/4	Hooks Wiltse	NY vs Phi, 1-0 (10)
	9/5	Nap Rucker	Bklyn vs Bos, 6-0
1912	9/6	Jeff Tesreau	NY at Phi, 3-0
1914	9/9	George Davis	Bos vs Phi, 7-0
1915	4/15	Rube Marquard	NY vs Bklyn, 2-0
	8/31	Jimmy Lavender	Chi at N.Y, 2-0
1916	6/16	Tom Hughes	Bos vs. Pit, 2-0
1917	5/2	Fred Toney	Cin at Chi, 1-0 (10)
1919	5/11	Hod Eller	Cin at St.L, 6-0
1922	5/7	Jesse Barnes	NY vs Phi, 6-0
1924	7/17	Jesse Haines	St.L vs Bos, 5-0
1925	9/17	Dazzy Vance	Bklyn vs Phi, 10-1
1929	5/8	Carl Hubbell	NY vs Pit, 2-0
1934	9/21	Paul Dean	St.L vs Bklyn, 3-0
1938	6/11	Johnny Vander Meer	Cin vs Bos, 3-0
	6/15	Johnny Vander Meer	Cin at Bklyn, 6-0
			(consecutive starts)
1940	4/30	Tex Carleton	Bklyn at Cin, 3-0
1941	8/30	Lon Warneke	St.L at Cin, 2-0
1944	4/27	Jim Tobin	Bos vs Bklyn, 2-0
	5/15	Clyde Shoun	Cin vs Bos, 1-0
1946	4/23	Ed Head	Bklyn at NY, 2-0
1947	6/18	Ewell Blackwell	Cin vs Bos, 6-0
1948	9/9	Rex Barney	Bklyn at NY, 2-0
1950	8/11	Vern Bickford	Bos vs Bklyn, 7-0
1951	5/6	Cliff Chambers	Pit at Bos, 3-0
1952	6/19	Carl Erskine	Bklyn vs Chi, 5-0
1954	6/12	Jim Wilson	Mil vs Phi, 2-0
1955	5/12	Sam Jones	Chi vs Pit, 4-0
1956	5/12	Carl Erskine	Bklyn vs NY, 3-0
	9/25	Sal Maglie	Bklyn vs Phi, 5-0
1960	5/15	Don Cardwell	Chi vs St.L, 4-0
	8/18	Lew Burdette	Mil vs Phi, 1-0
	9/16	Warren Spahn	Mil vs Phi, 4-0
1961	4/28	Warren Spahn	Mil vs SF, 1-0
1962	6/30	Sandy Koufax	LA vs NY, 5-0
1963	5/11	Sandy Koufax	LA vs SF, 1-0
	5/17	Don Nottebart	Hou vs Phi, 4-1
	6/15	Juan Marichal	SF vs Hou, 1-0
1964	4/23	**Ken Johnson**	Hou vs Cin, 0-1
	6/4	Sandy Koufax	LA at Phi, 3-0
	6/21	Jim Bunning	Phi at NY, 6-0
			(perfect game)
1965	8/19	Jim Maloney	Cin at Chi, 1-0 (10)
	9/9	Sandy Koufax	LA vs Chi, 1-0
			(perfect game)
1967	6/18	Don Wilson	Hou vs Atl, 2-0
1968	7/29	George Culver	Cin at Phi, 6-1
	9/17	Gaylord Perry	SF vs St.L, 1-0
	9/18	Ray Washburn	St.L at SF, 2-0
			(next day, same park)
1969	4/17	Bill Stoneman	Mon at Phi, 7-0
	4/30	Jim Maloney	Cin vs Hou, 10-0
	5/1	Don Wilson	Hou at Cin, 4-0
	8/19	Ken Holtzman	Chi vs Atl, 3-0
	9/20	Bob Moose	Pit at NY, 4-0
1970	6/12	Dock Ellis	Pit at SD, 2-0
	7/20	Bill Singer	LA vs Phi, 5-0
1971	6/3	Ken Holtzman	Chi at Cin, 1-0
	6/23	Rick Wise	Phi at Cin, 4-0
	8/14	Bob Gibson	St.L at Pit, 11-0
1972	4/16	Burt Hooton	Chi vs Phi, 4-0
	9/2	Milt Pappas	Chi vs SD, 8-0
	10/2	Bill Stoneman	Mon vs NY, 7-0
1973	8/5	Phil Niekro	Atl vs SD, 9-0
1975	8/24	Ed Halicki	SF vs NY, 6-0
1976	7/9	Larry Dierker	Hou vs Mon, 6-0
	8/9	John Candelaria	Pit vs LA, 2-0
	9/29	John Montefusco	SF vs Atl, 9-0
1978	4/16	Bob Forsch	St.L vs Phi, 5-0
	6/16	Tom Seaver	Cin vs St.L, 4-0
1979	4/7	Ken Forsch	Hou vs Atl, 6-0
1980	6/27	Jerry Reuss	LA at SF, 4-0
1981	5/10	Charlie Lea	Mon vs SF, 4-0
	9/26	Nolan Ryan	Hou vs LA, 5-0
1983	9/26	Bob Forsch	St.L vs Mon, 3-0
1986	9/25	Mike Scott	Hou vs SF, 2-0
1988	9/16	Tom Browning	Cin vs LA, 1-0
			(perfect game)
1990	6/29	Fernando Valenzuela	LA vs St.L, 6-0
	8/15	Terry Mulholland	Phi vs SF, 6-0
1991	5/23	Tommy Greene	Phi at Mon, 2-0
	7/28	Dennis Martinez	Mon at LA, 2-0
			(perfect game)
	9/11	Kent Mercker (6), Mark Wohlers (2) & Alejandro Peña (1)	Atl vs SD, 1-0 (combined no-hitter)
1992	8/17	Kevin Gross	LA vs SF, 2-0
1993	9/8	Darryl Kile	Hou vs NY, 7-1
1994	4/8	Kent Mercker	Atl at LA, 6-0
1995	7/14	Ramon Martinez	LA vs Fla, 7-0
1996	5/11	Al Leiter	Fla vs Col, 11-0
	9/17	Hideo Nomo	LA at Col, 9-0
1997	6/10	Kevin Brown	Fla at SF, 9-0
	7/12	Francisco Cordova (9) Ricardo Rincon (1)	Pit vs. Hou, 3-0 (10 inn.) (combined no-hitter)
1999	6/25	Jose Jimenez	St.L vs Ari, 1-0
2001	5/12	A.J. Burnett	Fla vs SD, 3-0
	9/3	Bud Smith	St.L at SD, 4-0

No-Hit Games (Cont.)
American League

Year	Date	Pitcher	Result
1902	9/20	Jimmy Callahan	Chi vs Det, 3-0
1904	5/5	Cy Young	Bos vs Phi, 3-0 (perfect game)
	8/17	Jesse Tannehill	Bos vs Chi, 6-0
1905	7/22	Weldon Henley	Phi at St. L, 6-0
	9/6	Frank Smith	Chi at Det, 15-0
	9/27	Bill Dinneen	Bos vs Chi, 2-0
1908	6/30	Cy Young	Bos at NY, 8-0
	9/18	Dusty Rhoades	Cle vs Bos, 2-0
	9/20	Frank Smith	Chi vs Phi, 1-0
	10/2	Addie Joss	Cle vs Chi, 1-0 (perfect game)
1910	4/20	Addie Joss	Cle at Chi, 1-0
	5/12	Chief Bender	Phi vs Cle, 4-0
1911	7/19	Smokey Joe Wood	Bos vs St. L, 5-0
	8/27	Ed Walsh	Chi vs Bos, 5-0
1912	7/4	George Mullin	Det vs St. L, 7-0
	8/30	Earl Hamilton	St. L at Det, 5-1
1914	5/31	Joe Benz	Chi vs Cle, 6-1
1916	6/16	Rube Foster	Bos vs NY, 2-0
	8/26	Joe Bush	Phi vs Cle, 5-0
	8/30	Hub Leonard	Bos vs St. L, 4-0
1917	4/14	Ed Cicotte	Chi at St. L, 11-0
	4/24	George Mogridge	NY at Bos, 2-1
	5/5	Ernie Koob	St. L vs Chi, 1-0
	5/6	Bob Groom	St. L vs Chi, 3-0
	6/23	Babe Ruth (0) & Ernie Shore (9)	Bos vs Wash, 4-0 (combined no-hitter)
1918	6/3	Hub Leonard	Bos at Det, 5-0
1919	9/10	Ray Caldwell	Cle at NY, 3-0
1920	7/1	Walter Johnson	Wash at Bos, 1-0
1922	4/30	Charlie Robertson	Chi at Det, 2-0 (perfect game)
1923	9/4	Sam Jones	NY at Phi, 2-0
	9/7	Howard Ehmke	Bos at Phi, 4-0
1926	8/21	Ted Lyons	Chi at Bos, 6-0
1931	4/29	Wes Ferrell	Cle vs St. L, 9-0
	8/8	Bob Burke	Wash vs Bos, 5-0
1935	8/31	Vern Kennedy	Chi vs Cle, 5-0
1937	6/1	Bill Dietrich	Chi vs St. L, 8-0
1938	8/27	Monte Pearson	NY vs Cle, 13-0
1940	4/16	Bob Feller	Cle at Chi, 1-0 (Opening Day)
1945	9/9	Dick Fowler	Phi vs St. L, 1-0
1946	4/30	Bob Feller	Cle vs NY, 1-0
1947	7/10	Don Black	Cle vs Phi, 3-0
	9/3	Bill McCahan	Phi vs Wash, 3-0
1948	6/30	Bob Lemon	Cle at Det, 2-0
1951	7/1	Bob Feller	Cle vs Det, 2-1
	7/12	Allie Reynolds	NY vs Cle, 1-0
	9/28	Allie Reynolds	NY vs Bos, 8-0
1952	5/15	Virgil Trucks	Det vs Wash, 1-0
	8/25	Virgil Trucks	Det at NY, 1-0
1953	5/6	Bobo Holloman	St. L vs Phi, 6-0 (first major league start)
1956	7/14	Mel Parnell	Bos vs Chi, 4-0
	10/8	Don Larsen	NY vs Bklyn, 2-0 (perfect W. Series game)
1957	8/20	Bob Keegan	Chi vs Wash, 6-0
1958	7/20	Jim Bunning	Det at Bos, 3-0
	9/2	Hoyt Wilhelm	Bal at NY, 1-0
1962	5/5	Bo Belinsky	LA vs Bal, 2-0
	6/26	Earl Wilson	Bos vs LA, 2-0
	8/1	Bill Monbouquette	Bos at Chi, 1-0
	8/26	Jack Kralick	Min vs KC, 1-0

Year	Date	Pitcher	Result
1965	9/16	Dave Morehead	Bos vs Cle, 2-0
1966	6/10	Sonny Siebert	Cle vs Wash, 2-0
1967	4/30	**Steve Barber** (8⅔) & **Stu Miller** (⅓)	Bal vs Det, 1-2 (combined no-hitter)
	8/25	Dean Chance	Min at Cle, 2-1
	9/10	Joel Horlen	Chi vs Det, 6-0
1968	4/27	Tom Phoebus	Bal vs Bos, 6-0
	5/8	Catfish Hunter	Oak vs Min, 4-0 (perfect game)
1969	8/13	Jim Palmer	Bal vs Oak, 8-0
1970	7/3	Clyde Wright	Cal vs Oak, 4-0
	9/21	Vida Blue	Oak vs Min, 6-0
1973	4/27	Steve Busby	KC at Det, 3-0
	5/15	Nolan Ryan	Cal at KC, 3-0
	7/15	Nolan Ryan	Cal at Det, 6-0
	7/30	Jim Bibby	Tex at Oak, 6-0
1974	6/19	Steve Busby	KC at Mil, 2-0
	7/19	Dick Bosman	Cle at Oak, 4-0
	9/28	Nolan Ryan	Cal at Min, 4-0
1975	6/1	Nolan Ryan	Cal vs Bal, 1-0
	9/28	Vida Blue (5), Glenn Abbott (1), Paul Lindblad (1), & Rollie Fingers (2)	Oak vs Cal, 5-0 (combined no-hitter)
1976	7/28	John Odom (5) & Francisco Barrios (4)	Chi at Oak, 2-1 (combined no-hitter)
1977	5/14	Jim Colborn	KC vs Tex, 6-0
	5/30	Dennis Eckersley	Cle vs Cal, 1-0
	9/22	Bert Blyleven	Tex at Cal, 6-0
1981	5/15	Len Barker	Cle vs Tor, 3-0 (perfect game)
1983	7/4	Dave Righetti	NY vs Bos, 4-0
	9/29	Mike Warren	Oak vs Chi, 3-0
1984	4/7	Jack Morris	Det at Chi, 4-0
	9/30	Mike Witt	Cal at Tex, 1-0 (perfect game)
1986	9/19	Joe Cowley	Chi at Cal, 7-1
1987	4/15	Juan Nieves	Mil at Bal, 7-0
1990	4/11	Mark Langston (7) & Mike Witt (2)	Cal vs Sea, 1-0 (combined no-hitter)
	6/2	Randy Johnson	Sea vs Det, 2-0
	6/11	Nolan Ryan	Tex at Oak, 5-0
	6/29	Dave Stewart	Oak at Tor, 5-0
	9/2	Dave Stieb	Tor at Cle, 3-0
1991	5/1	Nolan Ryan	Tex vs Tor, 3-0
	7/13	Bob Milacki (6), Mike Flanagan (1), Mark Williamson (1) & Gregg Olson (1)	Bal at Oak, 2-0 (combined no-hitter)
	8/11	Wilson Alvarez	Chi at Bal, 7-0
	8/26	Bret Saberhagen	KC vs Chi, 7-0
1993	4/22	Chris Bosio	Sea vs Bos, 7-0
	9/4	Jim Abbott	NY vs Cle, 4-0
1994	4/27	Scott Erickson	Min vs Mil, 6-0
	7/28	Kenny Rogers	Tex vs Cal, 4-0 (perfect game)
1996	5/14	Dwight Gooden	NY vs Sea, 2-0
1998	5/17	David Wells	NY vs Min, 4-0 (perfect game)
1999	7/18	David Cone	NY vs Mon, 6-0 (perfect game)
	9/11	Eric Milton	Min vs Ana, 7-0
2001	4/4	Hideo Nomo	Bos at Bal, 3-0

All-Time Major League Leaders
Based on statistics compiled by *The Baseball Encyclopedia* (9th ed.); through 2001 regular season.

CAREER
Players active in 2001 in **bold** type.

Batting
Note that (*) indicates left-handed hitter and (†) indicates switch-hitter.

Batting Average
(Minimum 3,000 AB)

		Yrs	AB	H	Avg
1	Ty Cobb*	24	11,429	4191	.367
2	Rogers Hornsby	23	8,173	2930	.358
3	Joe Jackson*	13	4,981	1774	.356
4	Ed Delahanty	16	7,509	2597	.346
5	Tris Speaker*	22	10,197	3514	.345
6	Ted Williams*	19	7,706	2654	.344
7	Billy Hamilton*	14	6,284	2163	.344
8	Willie Keeler*	19	8,585	2947	.343
9	Dan Brouthers*	19	6,711	2296	.342
10	Babe Ruth*	22	8,399	2873	.342
11	Harry Heilmann	17	7,787	2660	.342
12	Pete Browning	13	4,820	1646	.341
13	Bill Terry*	14	6,428	2193	.341
14	George Sisler*	15	8,267	2812	.340
15	Lou Gehrig*	17	8,001	2721	.340
16	Jesse Burkett*	16	8,413	2853	.339
17	Nap Lajoie	21	9,592	3244	.338
18	**Tony Gwynn***	20	9,288	3141	.338
19	Riggs Stephenson	14	4,508	1515	.336
20	Al Simmons	20	8,761	2927	.334
21	Paul Waner*	20	9,459	3152	.333
22	Eddie Collins*	25	9,951	3313	.333
23	Stan Musial*	22	10,972	3630	.331
24	Sam Thompson*	14	6,005	1986	.331
25	Heinie Manush*	17	17,654	2524	.330

Hits

		Yrs	AB	H	Avg
1	Pete Rose†	24	14,053	**4256**	.303
2	Ty Cobb*	24	11,429	**4191**	.367
3	Hank Aaron	23	12,364	**3771**	.305
4	Stan Musial*	22	10,972	**3630**	.331
5	Tris Speaker*	22	10,197	**3514**	.345
6	Carl Yastrzemski*	23	11,988	**3419**	.285
7	Honus Wagner	21	10,443	**3418**	.327
8	Paul Molitor	21	10,835	**3319**	.306
9	Eddie Collins*	25	9,951	**3313**	.333
10	Willie Mays	22	10,881	**3283**	.302
11	Eddie Murray†	21	11,336	**3255**	.287
12	Nap Lajoie	21	9,592	**3244**	.338
13	**Cal Ripken Jr.**	21	11,551	**3184**	.276
14	George Brett*	21	10,349	**3154**	.305
15	Paul Waner*	20	9,459	**3152**	.333
16	Robin Yount	20	11,008	**3142**	.285
17	**Tony Gwynn***	20	9,288	**3141**	.338
18	Dave Winfield	22	11,003	**3110**	.283
19	Rod Carew*	19	9,315	**3053**	.328
20	Lou Brock*	19	10,332	**3023**	.293
21	Wade Boggs*	18	9,180	**3010**	.328
22	Al Kaline	22	10,116	**3007**	.297
23	Cap Anson	22	9,108	**3000**	.329
	Roberto Clemente	18	9,454	**3000**	.317
	Rickey Henderson	23	10,710	**3000**	.280

Players Active in 2001

		Yrs	AB	H	Avg
1	Tony Gwynn*	20	9,288	3141	.338
2	Mike Piazza	10	4,638	1507	.325
3	Derek Jeter	7	3,744	1199	.320
4	Frank Thomas	12	5,542	1770	.319
5	Edgar Martinez	15	5,902	1882	.319
6	Larry Walker*	13	5,403	1702	.315
7	Manny Ramirez	9	3,999	1248	.312
8	Jeff Cirillo	8	3,937	1224	.311
9	Alex Rodriguez	8	3,758	1167	.311
10	Jason Giambi*	7	3,398	1048	.308
11	Mark Grace*	14	7,632	2343	.307
12	Chipper Jones†	8	4,041	1240	.307
13	Roberto Alomar†	14	7,796	2389	.306

Players Active in 2001

		Yrs	AB	H	Avg
1	Cal Ripken Jr.	21	11,551	**3184**	.276
2	Tony Gwynn*	20	9,288	**3141**	.338
3	Rickey Henderson	23	10,710	**3000**	.280
4	Harold Baines*	22	9,908	**2866**	.289
5	Tim Raines†	22	8,783	**2588**	.295
6	Rafael Palmeiro*	16	8,446	**2485**	.294
7	Roberto Alomar†	14	7,796	**2389**	.306
8	Mark Grace*	14	7,632	**2343**	.307
9	Barry Bonds*	16	7,932	**2313**	.292
10	Tony Fernandez†	17	7,911	**2276**	.288
11	Fred McGriff*	16	7,865	**2260**	.287
12	Julio Franco	17	7,334	**2204**	.301
13	Andres Galarraga	16	7,522	**2172**	.289

Games Played

1	Pete Rose	3562
2	Carl Yastrzemski	3308
3	Hank Aaron	3298
4	Ty Cobb	3034
5	Stan Musial	3026
	Eddie Murray	3026
7	**Cal Ripken Jr.**	3001
8	Willie Mays	2992
9	**Rickey Henderson**	2979
10	Dave Winfield	2973
11	Rusty Staub	2951
12	Brooks Robinson	2896
13	Robin Yount	2856
14	Al Kaline	2834
15	**Harold Baines**	2830
16	Eddie Collins	2826
17	Reggie Jackson	2820
18	Frank Robinson	2808
19	Tris Speaker	2789
	Honus Wagner	2789

At Bats

1	Pete Rose	14,053
2	Hank Aaron	12,364
3	Carl Yastrzemski	11,988
4	**Cal Ripken Jr.**	11,551
5	Ty Cobb	11,429
6	Eddie Murray	11,336
7	Robin Yount	11,008
8	Dave Winfield	11,003
9	Stan Musial	10,972
10	Willie Mays	10,881
11	Paul Molitor	10,835
12	**Rickey Henderson**	10,710
13	Brooks Robinson	10,654
14	Honus Wagner	10,441
15	George Brett	10,349
16	Lou Brock	10,332
17	Luis Aparicio	10,230
18	Tris Speaker	10,197
19	Al Kaline	10,116
20	Rabbit Maranville	10,078

Total Bases

1	Hank Aaron	6856
2	Stan Musial	6134
3	Willie Mays	6066
4	Ty Cobb	5863
5	Babe Ruth	5793
6	Pete Rose	5752
7	Carl Yastrzemski	5539
8	Eddie Murray	5397
9	Frank Robinson	5373
10	Dave Winfield	5221
11	**Cal Ripken Jr.**	5168
12	Tris Speaker	5103
13	Lou Gehrig	5059
14	George Brett	5044
15	Mel Ott	5041
16	Jimmie Foxx	4956
17	Ted Williams	4884
18	Honus Wagner	4868
19	Paul Molitor	4854
20	Al Kaline	4852

Home Runs

		Yrs	AB	HR	AB/HR
1	Hank Aaron	23	12,364	755	16.4
2	Babe Ruth*	22	8,399	714	11.8
3	Willie Mays	22	10,881	660	16.5
4	Frank Robinson	21	10,006	586	17.1
5	**Mark McGwire**	16	6,187	583	10.6
6	Harmon Killebrew	22	8,147	573	14.2
7	**Barry Bonds***	16	7,932	567	14.0
8	Reggie Jackson*	21	9,864	563	17.5
9	Mike Schmidt	18	8,352	548	15.2
10	Mickey Mantle†	18	8,102	536	15.1
11	Jimmie Foxx	20	8,134	534	15.2
12	Ted Williams*	19	7,706	521	14.8
	Willie McCovey*	22	8,197	521	15.7
14	Eddie Mathews*	17	8,537	512	16.7
	Ernie Banks	19	9,421	512	18.4
16	Mel Ott*	22	9,456	511	18.5
17	Eddie Murray†	21	11,336	504	22.5
18	Lou Gehrig*	17	8,001	493	16.2
19	Willie Stargell*	21	7,927	475	16.7
	Stan Musial*	22	10,972	475	23.1
21	Dave Winfield	22	11,003	465	23.7
22	**Jose Canseco**	17	7,057	462	15.3
23	**Ken Griffey Jr.***	13	6,716	460	14.6
24	Carl Yastrzemski*	23	11,988	452	26.5
25	**Sammy Sosa**	13	6,470	450	14.4

Runs Batted In

		Yrs	Gm	RBI	P/G
1	Hank Aaron	23	3298	2297	.70
2	Babe Ruth*	22	2503	2211	.88
3	Lou Gehrig*	17	2164	1990	.92
4	Ty Cobb*	24	3034	1961	.65
5	Stan Musial*	22	3026	1951	.64
6	Jimmie Foxx	20	2317	1921	.83
7	Eddie Murray†	21	2980	1917	.64
8	Willie Mays	22	2992	1903	.64
9	Mel Ott*	22	2732	1861	.68
10	Carl Yastrzemski*	23	3308	1844	.56
11	Ted Williams*	19	2292	1839	.80
12	Dave Winfield	22	2973	1833	.62
13	Al Simmons	20	2215	1827	.82
14	Frank Robinson	21	2808	1812	.65
15	Honus Wagner	21	2786	1732	.62
16	Cap Anson	22	2276	1715	.75
17	Reggie Jackson*	21	2820	1702	.60
18	**Cal Ripken Jr.**	21	3001	1695	.56
19	Tony Perez	23	2777	1652	.59
20	Ernie Banks	19	2528	1636	.65
21	**Harold Baines***	22	2830	1628	.58
22	Goose Goslin*	18	2287	1609	.70
23	Nap Lajoie	21	2475	1599	.65
24	Mike Schmidt	18	2404	1595	.66
	George Brett*	21	2707	1595	.59

Players Active in 2001

		Yrs	AB	HR	AB/HR
1	Mark McGwire	16	6,187	583	10.6
2	Barry Bonds*	16	7,932	567	14.0
3	Jose Canseco	17	7,057	462	15.3
4	Ken Griffey Jr.*	13	6,716	460	14.6
5	Sammy Sosa	13	6,470	450	14.4
6	Fred McGriff*	16	7,865	448	17.6
7	Rafael Palmeiro*	16	8,446	447	18.9
8	Cal Ripken Jr.	21	11,551	431	26.8
9	Juan Gonzalez	13	5,824	397	14.7
10	Harold Baines*	22	9,908	384	25.8
11	Andres Galarraga	16	7,522	377	20.0
12	Matt Williams	15	6,651	362	18.4
13	Jeff Bagwell	11	5,949	349	17.0
14	Frank Thomas	12	5,542	348	15.9
15	Greg Vaughn	13	5,815	344	16.9

Players Active in 2001

		Yrs	Gm	RBI	P/G
1	Cal Ripken Jr.	21	3001	1695	.56
2	Harold Baines*	22	2830	1628	.58
3	Barry Bonds*	16	2296	1542	.67
4	Rafael Palmeiro*	16	2258	1470	.65
5	Mark McGwire	16	1874	1414	.75
6	Jose Canseco	17	1887	1407	.75
7	Fred McGriff*	16	2201	1400	.64
8	Andres Galarraga	16	2036	1341	.66
9	Ken Griffey Jr.*	13	1791	1335	.75
10	Juan Gonzalez	13	1503	1282	.85
11	Paul O'Neill*	17	2053	1269	.62
12	Sammy Sosa	13	1725	1239	.72
13	Jeff Bagwell	11	1637	1223	.75
14	Frank Thomas	12	1550	1193	.77
15	Bobby Bonilla†	16	2113	1173	.56

Runs

1	**Rickey Henderson**	2248
2	Ty Cobb	2245
3	Babe Ruth	2174
	Hank Aaron	2174
5	Pete Rose	2165
6	Willie Mays	2062
7	Stan Musial	1949
8	Lou Gehrig	1888
9	Tris Speaker	1881
10	Mel Ott	1859
11	Frank Robinson	1829
12	Eddie Collins	1820
13	Carl Yastrzemski	1816
14	Ted Williams	1798
15	Paul Molitor	1782
16	Charlie Gehringer	1774
17	Jimmie Foxx	1751
18	Honus Wagner	1735
19	Willie Keeler	1727
20	Cap Anson	1719

Extra Base Hits

1	Hank Aaron	1477
2	Stan Musial	1377
3	Babe Ruth	1356
4	Willie Mays	1323
5	Lou Gehrig	1190
6	Frank Robinson	1186
7	Carl Yastrzemski	1157
8	Ty Cobb	1139
9	Tris Speaker	1132
10	**Barry Bonds**	1121
11	George Brett	1119
12	Ted Williams	1117
	Jimmie Foxx	1117
14	Eddie Murray	1099
15	Dave Winfield	1093
16	**Cal Ripken Jr.**	1078
17	Reggie Jackson	1075
18	Mel Ott	1071
19	Pete Rose	1041
20	Andre Dawson	1039

Slugging Percentage
(Minimum 3,000 AB)

1	Babe Ruth	.690
2	Ted Williams	.634
3	Lou Gehrig	.632
4	Jimmie Foxx	.609
5	Hank Greenberg	.605
6	**Manny Ramirez**	.594
7	**Mark McGwire**	.588
8	**Barry Bonds**	.585
9	**Mike Piazza**	.579
10	Joe DiMaggio	.579
11	**Frank Thomas**	.577
12	Rogers Hornsby	.577
13	**Larry Walker**	.572
14	**Alex Rodriguez**	.571
15	**Juan Gonzalez**	.568
16	**Ken Griffey Jr.**	.566
17	Albert Belle	.564
18	Johnny Mize	.562
19	Stan Musial	.559
20	Willie Mays	.557

Stolen Bases

1	**Rickey Henderson**	1395
2	Lou Brock	938
3	Billy Hamilton	937
4	Ty Cobb	892
5	**Tim Raines**	808
6	Vince Coleman	752
7	Eddie Collins	743
8	Max Carey	738
9	Honus Wagner	720
10	Joe Morgan	689
11	Arlie Latham	679
12	Willie Wilson	668
13	Bert Campaneris	649
14	Tom Brown	627
15	Otis Nixon	620
16	George Davis	615
17	Dummy Hoy	597
18	Maury Wills	586
19	Hugh Duffy	583
	George Van Haltren	583

Walks

1	**Rickey Henderson**	2141
2	Babe Ruth	2062
3	Ted Williams	2019
4	Joe Morgan	1865
5	Carl Yastrzemski	1845
6	Mickey Mantle	1734
7	**Barry Bonds**	1724
8	Mel Ott	1708
9	Eddie Yost	1614
10	Darrell Evans	1605
11	Stan Musial	1599
12	Pete Rose	1566
13	Harmon Killebrew	1559
14	Lou Gehrig	1508
15	Mike Schmidt	1507
16	Eddie Collins	1503
17	Willie Mays	1463
18	Jimmie Foxx	1452
19	Eddie Mathews	1444
20	Frank Robinson	1420

Strikeouts

1	Reggie Jackson	2597
2	**Jose Canseco**	1942
3	Willie Stargell	1936
4	Mike Schmidt	1883
5	Tony Perez	1867
6	**Andres Galarraga**	1858
7	Dave Kingman	1816
8	Bobby Bonds	1757
9	Dale Murphy	1748
10	Lou Brock	1730
11	Mickey Mantle	1710
12	Harmon Killebrew	1699
13	Chili Davis	1698
	Fred McGriff	1698
15	Dwight Evans	1697
16	**Sammy Sosa**	1690
17	Dave Winfield	1686
18	**Rickey Henderson**	1631
19	Gary Gaetti	1602
20	**Mark McGwire**	1596

Pitching

Note that (*) indicates left-handed pitcher. Active pitching leaders are listed for wins and strikeouts.

Wins

		Yrs	GS	W	L	Pct
1	Cy Young	22	815	**511**	316	.618
2	Walter Johnson	21	666	**417**	279	.599
3	Christy Mathewson	17	551	**373**	188	.665
	Grover Alexander	20	598	**373**	208	.642
5	Warren Spahn*	21	665	**363**	245	.597
6	Kid Nichols	15	561	**361**	208	.634
	Pud Galvin	14	682	**361**	308	.540
8	Tim Keefe	14	594	**342**	225	.603
9	Steve Carlton*	24	709	**329**	244	.574
10	Eddie Plank*	17	527	**327**	193	.629
11	John Clarkson	12	518	**326**	177	.648
12	Don Sutton	23	756	**324**	256	.559
13	Nolan Ryan	27	773	**324**	292	.526
14	Phil Niekro	24	716	**318**	274	.537
15	Gaylord Perry	22	690	**314**	265	.542
16	Old Hoss Radbourne	12	503	**311**	194	.616
	Tom Seaver	20	647	**311**	205	.603
18	Mickey Welch	13	549	**308**	209	.596
19	Lefty Grove*	17	456	**300**	141	.680
	Early Wynn	23	612	**300**	244	.551
21	Tommy John*	26	700	**288**	231	.555
22	Bert Blyleven	22	685	**287**	250	.534
23	Robin Roberts	19	609	**286**	245	.539
24	Tony Mullane	13	505	**285**	220	.564
25	Ferguson Jenkins	19	594	**284**	226	.557
26	Jim Kaat*	25	625	**283**	237	.544
27	**Roger Clemens**	18	544	**280**	145	.659
28	Red Ruffing	22	536	**273**	225	.548
29	Burleigh Grimes	19	495	**270**	212	.560
30	Jim Palmer	19	521	**268**	152	.638

Strikeouts

		Yrs	IP	SO	P/9
1	Nolan Ryan	27	5386.0	**5714**	9.55
2	Steve Carlton*	24	5217.1	**4136**	7.13
3	**Roger Clemens**	18	3887.0	**3717**	8.61
4	Bert Blyleven	22	4970.0	**3701**	6.70
5	Tom Seaver	20	4782.2	**3640**	6.85
6	Don Sutton	23	5282.1	**3574**	6.09
7	Gaylord Perry	22	5350.1	**3534**	5.94
8	Walter Johnson	21	5923.2	**3508**	5.33
9	**Randy Johnson***	14	2748.1	**3412**	11.17
10	Phil Niekro	24	5404.1	**3342**	5.57
11	Ferguson Jenkins	19	4500.2	**3192**	6.38
12	Bob Gibson	17	3884.1	**3117**	7.22
13	Jim Bunning	17	3760.1	**2855**	6.83
14	Mickey Lolich*	16	3638.1	**2832**	7.01
15	Cy Young	22	7356.0	**2796**	3.42
16	Frank Tanana*	21	4186.2	**2773**	5.96
17	**David Cone**	16	2880.2	**2655**	8.29
18	Warren Spahn*	21	5243.2	**2583**	4.43
19	Bob Feller	18	3827.0	**2581**	6.07
20	Jerry Koosman*	19	3839.1	**2556**	5.99
21	Tim Keefe	14	5061.1	**2527**	4.50
22	**Greg Maddux**	16	3551.0	**2523**	6.39
23	Christy Mathewson	17	4781.0	**2502**	4.71
24	Don Drysdale	14	3432.0	**2486**	6.52
25	Jack Morris	18	3824.2	**2478**	5.83
26	Mark Langston*	16	2962.2	**2464**	7.49
27	Jim Kaat*	25	4530.1	**2461**	4.89
28	Sam McDowell*	15	2492.1	**2453**	8.86
29	**Chuck Finley***	16	3006.2	**2436**	7.29
30	Luis Tiant	19	3486.1	**2416**	6.24

Pitchers Active in 2001

		Yrs	GS	W	L	Pct
1	Roger Clemens	18	544	**280**	145	.659
2	Greg Maddux	16	501	**257**	146	.638
3	Tom Glavine*	15	469	**224**	132	.629
4	Randy Johnson*	14	391	**200**	101	.664
5	David Cone	16	415	**193**	123	.611
6	Chuck Finley*	16	435	**189**	158	.545
7	Kevin Brown	15	399	**180**	118	.604
8	Bret Saberhagen	17	371	**167**	117	.588
9	David Wells	15	325	**166**	114	.593
10	Mike Mussina	11	322	**164**	92	.641

Pitchers Active in 2001

		Yrs	IP	SO	P/9
1	Roger Clemens	18	3887.0	**3717**	8.61
2	Randy Johnson*	14	2748.1	**3412**	11.17
3	David Cone	16	2880.2	**2655**	8.29
4	Greg Maddux	16	3551.0	**2523**	6.39
5	Chuck Finley*	16	3006.2	**2436**	7.29
6	John Smoltz	14	2473.1	**2155**	7.84
7	Curt Schilling	14	2158.2	**2032**	8.47
8	Kevin Brown	15	2776.1	**2021**	6.55
9	Pedro Martinez	10	1693.0	**1981**	10.53
10	Bobby Witt	15	2465.0	**1955**	7.14

Winning Pct.
(Minimum 100 wins)

		Yrs	W-L	Pct
1	Bob Caruthers	9	218-97	.692
2	**Pedro Martinez**	10	132-59	.691
3	Dave Foutz	11	147-66	.690
4	Whitey Ford*	16	236-106	.690
5	Don Gullett*	9	109-50	.686
6	Lefty Grove*	17	300-141	.680
7	Vic Raschi	10	132-66	.667
8	Christy Mathewson	17	373-188	.665
9	**Randy Johnson***	14	200-101	.664
10	Larry Corcoran	8	177-90	.663
11	**Roger Clemens**	18	280-145	.659
12	Sam Leever	13	194-101	.658
13	Sal Maglie	10	119-62	.657
14	Sandy Koufax*	12	165-87	.655
15	Johnny Allen	13	142-75	.654

Losses

		Yrs	GS	W	L	Pct
1	Cy Young	22	815	511	**316**	.618
2	Pud Galvin	14	682	361	**308**	.540
3	Nolan Ryan	27	773	324	**292**	.526
4	Walter Johnson	21	666	417	**279**	.599
5	Phil Niekro	24	716	318	**274**	.537
6	Gaylord Perry	22	690	314	**265**	.542
7	Jack Powell	16	517	245	**256**	.489
	Don Sutton	23	756	324	**256**	.559
9	Eppa Rixey*	21	552	266	**251**	.515
10	Bert Blyleven	22	685	287	**250**	.534
11	Robin Roberts	19	609	286	**245**	.539
	Warren Spahn*	21	665	363	**245**	.597
13	Early Wynn	23	612	300	**244**	.551
	Steve Carlton*	24	709	329	**244**	.574
15	Jim Kaat*	25	625	283	**237**	.544

Appearances

1	**Jesse Orosco**	1131
2	Dennis Eckersley	1071
3	Hoyt Wilhelm	1070
4	Kent Tekulve	1050
5	Lee Smith	1022
6	Rich Gossage	1002
7	**John Franco**	998
8	Lindy McDaniel	987
9	**Dan Plesac**	946
10	Rollie Fingers	944
11	Gene Garber	931
12	Cy Young	906
13	**Mike Jackson**	902
14	Sparky Lyle	899
15	Jim Kaat	898

Innings Pitched

1	Cy Young	7356.0
2	Pud Galvin	5941.1
3	Walter Johnson	5923.2
4	Phil Niekro	5404.1
5	Nolan Ryan	5386.0
6	Gaylord Perry	5350.1
7	Don Sutton	5282.1
8	Warren Spahn	5243.2
9	Steve Carlton	5217.1
10	Grover Alexander	5189.2
11	Kid Nichols	5084.0
12	Tim Keefe	5061.1
13	Bert Blyleven	4970.0
14	Mickey Welch	4802.0
15	Tom Seaver	4782.2

Earned Run Avg.
(Minimum 1500 IP)

1	Ed Walsh	1.82
2	Addie Joss	1.88
3	Three Finger Brown	2.06
4	Monte Ward	2.10
5	Christy Mathewson	2.13
6	Rube Waddell	2.16
7	Walter Johnson	2.17
8	Orval Overall	2.24
9	Tommy Bond	2.25
10	Will White	2.28
11	Ed Reulbach	2.28
12	Jim Scott	2.32
13	Eddie Plank	2.34
14	Larry Corcoran	2.36
15	Eddie Cicotte	2.37

Shutouts

1	Walter Johnson	110
2	Grover Alexander	90
3	Christy Mathewson	80
4	Cy Young	76
5	Eddie Plank	69
6	Warren Spahn	63
7	Nolan Ryan	61
	Tom Seaver	61
9	Bert Blyleven	60
10	Don Sutton	58
11	Three Finger Brown	57
	Pud Galvin	57
	Ed Walsh	57
14	Bob Gibson	56
15	Steve Carlton	55

Walks Allowed

1	Nolan Ryan	2795
2	Steve Carlton	1833
3	Phil Niekro	1809
4	Early Wynn	1775
5	Bob Feller	1764
6	Bobo Newsom	1732
7	Amos Rusie	1704
8	Charlie Hough	1665
9	Gus Weyhing	1566
10	Red Ruffing	1541
11	Bump Hadley	1442
12	Warren Spahn	1434
13	Earl Whitehill	1431
14	Tony Mullane	1409
15	Sad Sam Jones	1396

HRs Allowed

1	Robin Roberts	505
2	Ferguson Jenkins	484
3	Phil Niekro	482
4	Don Sutton	472
5	Frank Tanana	448
6	Warren Spahn	434
7	Bert Blyleven	430
8	Steve Carlton	414
9	Gaylord Perry	399
10	Jim Kaat	395
11	Jack Morris	389
12	Charlie Hough	383
13	Tom Seaver	380
14	Catfish Hunter	374
15	Jim Bunning	372
	Dennis Martinez	372

Saves

1	Lee Smith	478
2	**John Franco**	422
3	Dennis Eckersley	390
4	Jeff Reardon	367
5	Randy Myers	347
6	Rollie Fingers	341
7	John Wetteland	330
8	Rick Aguilera	318
9	**Trevor Hoffman**	314
10	Tom Henke	311
11	Rich Gossage	310
12	Jeff Montgomery	304
13	Doug Jones	303
14	Bruce Sutter	300
15	**Roberto Hernandez**	294
16	**Robb Nen**	271
17	**Rod Beck**	266
18	Todd Worrell	256
19	Dave Righetti	252
20	Dan Quisenberry	244
21	Sparky Lyle	238
22	Hoyt Wilhelm	227
23	Gene Garber	218
24	**Gregg Olson**	217
25	Dave Smith	216
26	**Mariano Rivera**	215
27	**Troy Percival**	210
28	**Jeff Shaw**	203
29	Bobby Thigpen	201
30	Roy Face	193
	Mike Henneman	193

SINGLE SEASON

Through 2001 regular season.

Batting

Home Runs

	Name	Year	Gm	AB	HR
1	**Barry Bonds**, SF	2001	153	476	73
2	Mark McGwire, St.L	1998	155	509	70
3	Sammy Sosa, Chi-NL	1998	159	643	66
4	Mark McGwire, St.L	1999	153	521	65
5	**Sammy Sosa**, Chi-NL	2001	160	577	64
6	Sammy Sosa, Chi-NL	1999	162	625	63
7	Roger Maris, NY-AL	1961	162	590	61
8	Babe Ruth, NY-AL	1927	151	540	60
9	Babe Ruth, NY-AL	1921	152	540	59
10	Mark McGwire, Oak-St.L	1997	156	540	58
	Hank Greenberg, Det	1938	155	556	58
	Jimmie Foxx, Phi-AL	1932	154	585	58
13	**Luis Gonzalez**, Ari	2001	162	609	57
14	Hack Wilson, Chi-NL	1930	155	585	56
	Ken Griffey Jr., Sea	1997	157	608	56
	Ken Griffey Jr., Sea	1998	161	633	56
17	Babe Ruth, NY-AL	1920	142	458	54
	Mickey Mantle, NY-AL	1961	153	514	54
	Babe Ruth, NY-AL	1928	154	536	54
	Ralph Kiner, Pit	1949	152	549	54

Hits

	Name	Year	AB	H	Avg
1	George Sisler, StL-AL	1920	631	**257**	.407
2	Bill Terry, NY-NL	1930	633	**254**	.401
	Lefty O'Doul, Phi-NL	1929	638	**254**	.398
4	Al Simmons, Phi-AL	1925	658	**253**	.384
5	Rogers Hornsby, StL-NL	1922	623	**250**	.401
	Chuck Klein, Phi-NL	1930	648	**250**	.386
7	Ty Cobb, Det	1911	591	**248**	.420
8	George Sisler, StL-AL	1922	586	**246**	.420
9	**Ichiro Suzuki**, Sea	2001	692	**242**	.350
10	Babe Herman, Bklyn	1930	614	**241**	.393
	Heinie Manush, StL-AL	1928	638	**241**	.378
12	Wade Boggs, Bos	1985	653	**240**	.368
	Darin Erstad, Ana	2000	676	**240**	.355
14	Rod Carew, Min	1977	616	**239**	.388
15	Don Mattingly, NY-AL	1986	677	**238**	.352
16	Harry Heilmann, Det	1921	602	**237**	.394
	Paul Waner, Pit	1927	623	**237**	.380
	Joe Medwick, StL-NL	1937	633	**237**	.374
19	Jack Tobin, StL-AL	1921	671	**236**	.352
20	Rogers Hornsby, StL-NL	1921	592	**235**	.397

Batting Average

From 1900-49

	Name	Year	AB	H	Avg
1	Rogers Hornsby, StL-NL	1924	536	227	.424
2	Nap Lajoie, Phi-AL	1901	543	229	.422
3	George Sisler, StL-AL	1922	586	246	.420
4	Ty Cobb, Det	1911	591	248	.420
5	Ty Cobb, Det	1912	533	227	.410
6	Joe Jackson, Cle	1911	571	233	.408
7	George Sisler, StL-AL	1920	631	257	.407
8	Ted Williams, Bos-AL	1941	456	185	.406
9	Rogers Hornsby, StL-NL	1925	504	203	.403
10	Harry Heilmann, Det	1923	524	211	.403

Since 1950

	Name	Year	AB	H	Avg
1	Tony Gwynn, SD	1994	419	175	.394
2	George Brett, KC	1980	449	175	.390
3	Ted Williams, Bos	1957	420	163	.388
4	Rod Carew, Min	1977	616	239	.388
5	Larry Walker, Col	1999	438	166	.379
6	Todd Helton, Col	2000	580	216	.372
7	Nomar Garciaparra, Bos	2000	529	197	.372
8	Tony Gwynn, SD	1997	592	220	.372
9	Andres Galarraga, Col	1993	470	174	.370
10	Tony Gwynn, SD	1987	589	218	.370

Total Bases

From 1900-49

	Name	Year	TB
1	Babe Ruth, New York-AL	1921	457
2	Rogers Hornsby, St. Louis-NL	1922	450
3	Lou Gehrig, New York-AL	1927	447
4	Chuck Klein, Philadelphia-NL	1930	445
5	Jimmie Foxx, Philadelphia-AL	1932	438
6	Stan Musial, St. Louis-NL	1948	429
7	Hack Wilson, Chicago-NL	1930	423
8	Chuck Klein, Philadelphia-NL	1932	420
9	Lou Gehrig, New York-AL	1930	419
10	Joe DiMaggio, New York-AL	1937	418

Since 1950

	Name	Year	TB
1	**Sammy Sosa**, Chicago-NL	2001	425
2	**Luis Gonzalez**, Arizona	2001	419
3	Sammy Sosa, Chicago-NL	1998	416
4	**Barry Bonds**, San Francisco	2001	411
5	Larry Walker, Colorado	1997	409
6	Jim Rice, Boston	1978	406
7	Todd Helton, Colorado	2000	405
8	**Todd Helton**, Colorado	2001	402
9	Hank Aaron, Milwaukee	1959	400
10	Albert Belle, Chicago-AL	1998	399

Runs Batted In

From 1900-49

	Name	Year	Avg	HR	RBI
1	Hack Wilson, Chi-NL	1930	.356	56	191
2	Lou Gehrig, NY-AL	1931	.341	46	184
3	Hank Greenberg, Det	1937	.337	40	183
4	Lou Gehrig, NY-AL	1927	.373	47	175
	Jimmie Foxx, Bos-AL	1938	.349	50	175
6	Lou Gehrig, NY-AL	1930	.379	41	174
7	Babe Ruth, NY-AL	1921	.378	59	171
8	Chuck Klein, Phi-NL	1930	.386	40	170
	Hank Greenberg, Det	1935	.328	36	170
10	Jimmie Foxx, Phi-AL	1932	.364	58	169

Since 1950

	Name	Year	Avg	HR	RBI
1	Manny Ramirez, Cle	1999	.333	44	165
2	**Sammy Sosa**, Chi-NL	2001	.328	64	160
3	Sammy Sosa, Chi-NL	1998	.308	66	158
4	Juan Gonzalez, Tex	1998	.318	45	157
5	Tommy Davis, LA-NL	1962	.346	27	153
6	Albert Belle, Chi-AL	1998	.328	49	152
7	Andres Galarraga, Col	1996	.304	47	150
8	George Foster, Cin	1977	.320	52	149
9	Rafael Palmeiro, Tex	1999	.324	47	148
	Johnny Bench, Cin	1970	.293	45	148
	Albert Belle, Cle	1996	.311	48	148

Runs

		Year	Runs
1	Babe Ruth, New York-AL	1921	177
2	Lou Gehrig, New York-AL	1936	167
3	Babe Ruth, New York-AL	1928	163
	Lou Gehrig, New York-AL	1931	163
5	Babe Ruth, New York-AL	1920	158
	Babe Ruth, New York-AL	1927	158
	Chuck Klein, Philadelphia-NL	1930	158
8	Rogers Hornsby, Chicago-NL	1929	156
9	Kiki Cuyler, Chicago-NL	1930	155
10	Lefty O'Doul, Philadelphia-NL	1929	152
	Woody English, Chicago-NL	1930	152
	Al Simmons, Philadelphia-AL	1930	152
	Chuck Klein, Philadelphia-NL	1932	152
	Jeff Bagwell, Houston	2000	152
15	Babe Ruth, New York-AL	1923	151
	Jimmie Foxx, Philadelphia-AL	1932	151
	Joe DiMaggio, New York-AL	1937	151
18	Babe Ruth, New York-AL	1930	150
	Ted Williams, Boston-AL	1940	150
20	Lou Gehrig, New York-AL	1927	149
	Babe Ruth, New York-AL	1931	149

Walks

		Year	BB
1	**Barry Bonds**, San Francisco	2001	177
2	Babe Ruth, New York-AL	1923	170
3	Ted Williams, Boston-AL	1947	162
	Ted Williams, Boston-AL	1949	162
	Mark McGwire, St. Louis	1998	162
6	Ted Williams, Boston-AL	1946	156
7	Barry Bonds, San Francisco	1996	151
	Eddie Yost, Washington	1956	151
9	Jeff Bagwell, Houston	1999	149
	Eddie Joost, Philadelphia-AL	1949	149

Extra Base Hits

		Year	EBH
1	Babe Ruth, New York-AL	1921	119
2	Lou Gehrig, New York-AL	1927	117
3	Chuck Klein, Philadelphia-NL	1930	107
	Barry Bonds, San Francisco	2001	107
5	**Todd Helton**, Colorado	2001	105
6	Chuck Klein, Philadelphia-NL	1932	103
	Hank Greenberg, Detroit	1937	103
	Stan Musial, St. Louis-NL	1948	103
	Albert Belle, Cleveland	1995	103
	Todd Helton, Colorado	2000	103
	Sammy Sosa, Chicago-NL	2001	103

Slugging Percentage

From 1900-49

		Year	Pct
1	Babe Ruth, New York-AL	1920	.847
2	Babe Ruth, New York-AL	1921	.846
3	Babe Ruth, New York-AL	1927	.772
4	Lou Gehrig, New York-AL	1927	.765
5	Babe Ruth, New York-AL	1923	.764
6	Rogers Hornsby, St. Louis-NL	1925	.756
7	Jimmie Foxx, Philadelphia-AL	1932	.749
8	Babe Ruth, New York-AL	1924	.739
9	Babe Ruth, New York-AL	1926	.737
10	Ted Williams, Boston-AL	1941	.735

Since 1950

		Year	Pct
1	**Barry Bonds**, San Francisco	2001	.863
2	Mark McGwire, St. Louis	1998	.752
3	Jeff Bagwell, Houston	1994	.750
4	**Sammy Sosa**, Chicago-NL	2001	.737
5	Ted Williams, Boston	1957	.731
6	Mark McGwire, Oakland	1996	.730
7	Frank Thomas, Chicago-AL	1994	.729
8	Larry Walker, Colorado	1997	.720

Doubles

		Year	2B
1	Earl Webb, Boston-AL	1931	67
2	George Burns, Cleveland	1926	64
	Joe Medwick, St. Louis-NL	1936	64
4	Hank Greenberg, Detroit	1934	63
5	Paul Waner, Pittsburgh	1932	62
6	Charlie Gehringer, Detroit	1936	60
7	Tris Speaker, Cleveland	1923	59
	Chuck Klein, Philadelphia-NL	1930	59
	Todd Helton, Colorado	2000	59
10	Three tied with 57 each.		

Triples

From 1900-49

		Year	3B
1	Chief Wilson, Pittsburgh	1912	36
2	Joe Jackson, Cleveland	1912	26
3	Sam Crawford, Detroit	1914	26
4	Kiki Cuyler, Pittsburgh	1925	26
5	Three tied with 25 each.		

Since 1950

		Year	3B
1	Willie Wilson, Kansas City	1985	21
	Lance Johnson, New York-NL	1996	21
3	Willie Mays, New York-NL	1957	20
	George Brett, Kansas City	1979	20
	Cristian Guzman, Minnesota	2000	20

Stolen Bases

		Year	SB
1	Rickey Henderson, Oakland	1982	130
2	Lou Brock, St. Louis	1974	118
3	Vince Coleman, St. Louis	1985	110
4	Vince Coleman, St. Louis	1987	109
5	Rickey Henderson, Oakland	1983	108
6	Vince Coleman, St. Louis	1986	107
7	Maury Wills, Los Angeles-NL	1962	104
8	Rickey Henderson, Oakland	1980	100
9	Ron LeFlore, Montreal	1980	97
10	Ty Cobb, Detroit	1915	96
	Omar Moreno, Pittsburgh	1980	96
12	Maury Wills, Los Angeles	1965	94
13	Rickey Henderson, New York-AL	1988	93
14	Tim Raines, Montreal	1983	90
15	Clyde Milan, Washington	1912	88

Strikeouts

		Year	SO
1	Bobby Bonds, San Francisco	1970	189
2	Bobby Bonds, San Francisco	1969	187
	Preston Wilson, Florida	2000	187
4	Rob Deer, Milwaukee	1987	186
5	Pete Incaviglia, Texas	1986	185
	Jose Hernandez, Milwaukee	2001	185
	Jim Thome, Cleveland	2001	185
8	Cecil Fielder, Detroit	1990	182
9	Mo Vaughn, Anaheim	2000	181
10	Mike Schmidt, Philadelphia	1975	180

Pinch Hits

Career pinch hits in parentheses.

		Year	PH	
1	John Vander Wal, Colorado	1995	28	(116)
2	Lenny Harris, Col-Ari	1999	26	(151)
3	Jose Morales, Montreal	1976	25	(123)
4	Dave Philley, Baltimore	1961	24	(93)
	Vic Davalillo, St. Louis	1970	24	(95)
	Rusty Staub, New York-NL	1983	24	(100)
	Gerald Perry, St. Louis	1993	24	(95)

Note: Harris (151) is the career leader.

Pitching
Wins

From 1900-49

		Year	W	L	Pct
1	Jack Chesbro, NY-AL	1904	**41**	12	.774
2	Ed Walsh, Chi-AL	1908	**40**	15	.727
3	Christy Mathewson, NY-NL	1908	**37**	11	.771
4	Walter Johnson, Wash	1913	**36**	7	.837
5	Joe McGinnity, NY-NL	1904	**35**	8	.814
6	Smokey Joe Wood, Bos-AL	1912	**34**	5	.872
7	Cy Young, Bos-AL	1901	**33**	10	.767
	Grover Alexander, Phi-NL	1916	**33**	12	.733
	Christy Mathewson, NY-NL	1904	**33**	12	.733
10	Cy Young, Bos-AL	1902	**32**	11	.744

Since 1950

		Year	W	L	Pct
1	Denny McLain, Det.	1968	**31**	6	.838
2	Robin Roberts, Phi-NL	1952	**28**	7	.800
3	Bob Welch, Oak	1990	**27**	6	.818
	Don Newcombe, Bklyn	1956	**27**	7	.794
	Sandy Koufax, LA	1966	**27**	9	.750
	Steve Carlton, Phi.	1972	**27**	10	.730
7	Sandy Koufax, LA	1965	**26**	8	.765
	Juan Marichal, SF	1968	**26**	9	.743

Note: 11 pitchers tied with 25 wins, including Marichal twice.

Earned Run Average

From 1900-49

		Year	ShO	ERA
1	Dutch Leonard, Bos-AL	1914	7	1.01
2	Three Finger Brown, Chi-NL	1906	10	1.04
3	Walter Johnson, Wash	1913	11	1.09
4	Christy Mathewson, NY-NL	1909	8	1.14
5	Jack Pfiester, Chi-NL	1907	3	1.15
6	Addie Joss, Cle.	1908	9	1.16
7	Carl Lundgren, Chi-NL	1907	7	1.17
8	Grover Alexander, Phi-NL	1915	12	1.22
9	Cy Young, Bos-AL	1908	3	1.26
10	Three pitchers tied at 1.27			

Since 1950

		Year	ShO	ERA
1	Bob Gibson, St.L	1968	13	1.12
2	Dwight Gooden, NY-NL	1985	8	1.53
3	Greg Maddux, Atl.	1994	3	1.56
4	Luis Tiant, Cle	1968	9	1.60
5	Greg Maddux, Atl	1995	3	1.63
6	Dean Chance, LA-AL	1964	11	1.65
7	Nolan Ryan, Cal	1981	3	1.69
8	Sandy Koufax, LA	1966	5	1.73
9	Sandy Koufax, LA	1964	7	1.74
10	Pedro Martinez, Bos	2000	4	1.74

Note: Koufax's ERA in 1964 was 1.735. Martinez' ERA in 2000 was 1.742. The Yankees' Ron Guidry narrowly missed the top 10 list with an ERA of 1.743 in 1978.

Winning Pct.

		Year	W-L	Pct
1	Roy Face, Pit	1959	18-1	.947
2	Rick Sutcliffe, Chi-NL*	1984	16-1	.941
3	Johnny Allen, Cle	1937	15-1	.938
4	Greg Maddux, Atl	1995	19-2	.904
5	Randy Johnson, Sea.	1995	18-2	.900
6	Ron Guidry, NY-AL	1978	25-3	.893
7	Freddie Fitzsimmons, Bklyn	1940	16-2	.889
8	Lefty Grove, Phi-AL	1931	31-4	.886
9	Bob Stanley, Bos.	1978	15-2	.882
10	Preacher Roe, Bklyn	1951	22-3	.880

*Sutcliffe began 1984 with Cleveland and was 4-5 before being traded to the Cubs; his overall winning pct. was .769 (20-6).

Strikeouts

		Year	SO	P/9
1	Nolan Ryan, Cal	1973	**383**	10.57
2	Sandy Koufax, LA	1965	**382**	10.24
3	**Randy Johnson**, Ari	2001	**372**	13.41
4	Nolan Ryan, Cal	1974	**367**	9.93
5	Randy Johnson, Ari	1999	**364**	12.06
6	Rube Waddell, Phi-AL	1904	**349**	8.20
7	Bob Feller, Cle	1946	**348**	8.43
8	Randy Johnson, Ari	2000	**347**	12.56
9	Nolan Ryan, Cal	1977	**341**	10.26
10	Nolan Ryan, Cal	1972	**329**	10.43
	Randy Johnson, Sea-Hou	1998	**329**	12.12

Appearances

		Year	App	Sv
1	Mike Marshall, LA	1974	**106**	21
2	Kent Tekulve, Pit	1979	**94**	31
3	Mike Marshall, LA	1973	**92**	31
4	Kent Tekulve, Pit	1978	**91**	31
5	Wayne Granger, Cin.	1969	**90**	27
	Mike Marshall, Min	1979	**90**	32
	Kent Tekulve, Phi.	1987	**90**	3

Saves

		Year	App	Sv
1	Bobby Thigpen, Chi-AL	1990	77	57
2	Randy Myers, Chi-NL	1993	73	53
	Trevor Hoffman, SD	1998	66	53
4	Dennis Eckersley, Oak.	1992	69	51
	Rod Beck, Chi-NL	1998	81	51
6	**Mariano Rivera**, NY-AL	2001	71	50
7	Dennis Eckersley, Oak.	1990	63	48
	Rod Beck, SF.	1993	76	48
	Jeff Shaw, Cin-LA	1998	73	48
10	Lee Smith, St.L.	1991	67	47

Innings Pitched (since 1920)

		Year	IP	W-L
1	Wilbur Wood, Chi-AL	1972	**376.2**	24-17
2	Mickey Lolich, Det	1971	**376.0**	25-14
3	Bob Feller, Cle	1946	**371.1**	26-15
4	Grover Alexander, Chi-NL	1920	**363.1**	27-14
5	Wilbur Wood, Chi-AL	1973	**359.1**	24-20

Shutouts

		Year	ShO	ERA
1	Grover Alexander, Phi-NL	1916	**16**	1.55
2	Jack Coombs, Phi-AL	1910	**13**	1.30
	Bob Gibson, St.L	1968	**13**	1.12
4	Christy Mathewson, NY-NL	1908	**12**	1.43
	Grover Alexander, Phi-NL	1915	**12**	1.22

Walks Allowed (since 1920)

		Year	BB	SO
1	Bob Feller, Cle	1938	**208**	240
2	Nolan Ryan, Cal	1977	**204**	341
3	Nolan Ryan, Cal	1974	**202**	367
4	Bob Feller, Cle	1941	**194**	260
5	Bobo Newsom, St.L-AL	1938	**192**	226

Home Runs Allowed

		Year	HRs
1	Bert Blyleven, Minnesota	1986	50
2	Jose Lima, Houston	2000	48
3	Robin Roberts, Philadelphia	1956	46
	Bert Blyleven, Minnesota	1987	46
5	Pedro Ramos, Washington	1957	43

SINGLE GAME

Through 2001 regular season.

Batting

Home Runs

No		Date	Inn
4	Bobby Lowe, Boston-NL	5/30/1894	9
	Ed Delahanty, Philadelphia-NL	7/13/1896	9
	Lou Gehrig, New York-AL	6/3/1932	9
	Chuck Klein, Philadelphia-NL	7/10/1936	10
	Pat Seerey, Chicago-AL	7/18/1948	11
	Gil Hodges, Brooklyn	8/31/1950	9
	Joe Adcock, Milwaukee	7/31/1954	9
	Rocky Colavito, Cleveland	6/10/1959	9
	Willie Mays, San Francisco	4/30/1961	9
	Mike Schmidt, Philadelphia	4/17/1976	10
	Bob Horner, Atlanta	7/6/1986	9
	Mark Whiten, St. Louis	9/7/1993	9

Hits

No		Date	Inn
9	Johnny Burnett, Cleveland (9-for-11)	7/10/1932	18
7	Wilbert Robinson, Baltimore (7-for-7)	6/10/1892	9
	Rennie Stennett, Pittsburgh (7-for-7)	9/16/1975	9
	Cesar Gutierrez, Detroit (7-for-7)	6/21/1970	12
	Rocky Colavito, Detroit (7-for-10)	6/24/1962	22

Runs

No		Date	Inn
7	Guy Hecker, Louisville	8/15/1886	9

Runs Batted In

No		Date	Inn
12	Jim Bottomley, St. Louis-NL	9/16/1924	9
	Mark Whiten, St. Louis	9/7/1993	9

Pitching

Strikeouts

No		Date	Inn
21	Tom Cheney, Washington	9/12/1962	16
20	Roger Clemens, Boston	4/29/1986	9
	Roger Clemens, Boston	9/18/1996	9
	Kerry Wood, Chicago-NL	5/6/1998	9
	Randy Johnson, Arizona	5/8/2001	9*

Innings Pitched

No		Date
26	Leon Cadore, Brooklyn (tie, 1-1)	5/1/1920
	Joe Oeschger, Boston-NL (tie, 1-1)	5/1/1920

*Johnson struck out 20 in nine innings and was removed with the game tied, 1-1. Arizona beat Cincinnati, 4-3, in 11 innings.

Unassisted Triple Plays

One of the rarest feats in baseball, the unassisted triple play has been accomplished only 12 times in major league history. Ironically, in what can only be described as a statistic anomaly, the trick was turned twice in two days in May of 1927.

Player, Position, Team	Date	Opponent
Paul Hines, OF, Providence	May 8, 1878	Boston-NL
Neal Ball, SS, Cleveland	July 19, 1909	Boston-AL
Bill Wambganss, 2B, Cleveland*	Oct. 10, 1920	Brooklyn
George Burns, 1B, Boston-AL	Sept. 14, 1923	Cleveland
Ernie Padgett, SS, Boston-NL	Oct. 6, 1923	Philadelphia
Glenn Wright, SS, Pittsburgh	May 7, 1925	St.Louis-NL
Jimmy Cooney, SS, Chicago-NL	May 30, 1927	Pittsburgh
Johnny Neun, 1B, Detroit	May 31, 1927	Cleveland
Ron Hansen, SS, Washington	July 30, 1968	Cleveland
Mickey Morandini, 2B, Philadelphia	Sept. 20, 1992	Pittsburgh
John Valentin, SS, Boston	July 8, 1994	Seattle
Randy Velarde, 2B, Oakland	May 29, 2000	NY Yankees

*World Series game

Most Gold Gloves (by position)

Gold Gloves have been awarded since the 1957 season by Rawlings Sporting Goods to superior major league fielders at each position in both leagues. Voting has been conducted by a panel of sportswriters appointed by *The Sporting News* publisher J.G. Taylor Spink (1957), major league players (1958-1964) and managers and coaches (1965-present). Top 5 in each position are listed, through the 2000 season.

Pitchers	No
1 Jim Kaat	16
2 Greg Maddux	11
3 Bob Gibson	9
4 Bobby Shantz	8
5 Mark Langston	7

Catchers	No
1 Johnny Bench	10
2 Ivan Rodriguez	9
3 Bob Boone	7
4 Jim Sundberg	6
5 Bill Freehan	5

First Basemen	No
1 Keith Hernandez	11
2 Don Mattingly	9
3 George Scott	8
4 Vic Power	7
Bill White	7

Second Basemen	No
1 Roberto Alomar	9
Ryne Sandberg	9
3 Bill Mazeroski	8
Frank White	8
5 Two tied with 5 each.	

Third Basemen	No
1 Brooks Robinson	16
2 Mike Schmidt	10
3 Buddy Bell	6
4 Robin Ventura	6
5 Three tied with 5 each.	

Shortstops	No
1 Ozzie Smith	13
2 Luis Aparicio	9
3 Mark Belanger	8
Omar Vizquel	8
5 Dave Concepcion	5

Outfielders	No
1 Roberto Clemente	12
Willie Mays	12
3 Ken Griffey Jr.	10
Al Kaline	10
5 Five tied with 8 each.	

All-Time Winningest Managers

Top 20 Major League career victories through the 2001 season. Career, regular season and postseason (playoffs and World Series) records are noted along with AL and NL pennants and World Series titles won. Managers active during 2001 season in **bold** type.

		Career			Regular Season			Postseason			
		Yrs	W	L	Pct	W	L	Pct	W	L	Pct	Titles
1	Connie Mack	53	**3755**	3967	.486	3731	3948	.486	24	19	.558	9 AL, 5 WS
2	John McGraw	33	**2866**	2012	.588	2840	1984	.589	26	28	.482	10 NL, 3 WS
3	Sparky Anderson	26	**2228**	1855	.547	2194	1834	.545	34	21	.618	4 NL, 1 AL, 3 WS
4	Bucky Harris	29	**2168**	2228	.493	2157	2218	.493	11	10	.524	3 AL, 2 WS
5	Joe McCarthy	24	**2155**	1346	.616	2125	1333	.615	30	13	.698	1 NL, 8 AL, 7 WS
6	Walter Alston	23	**2063**	1634	.558	2040	1613	.558	23	21	.523	7 NL, 4 WS
7	Leo Durocher	24	**2015**	1717	.540	2008	1709	.540	7	8	.467	3 NL, 1 WS
8	Casey Stengel	25	**1942**	1868	.510	1905	1842	.508	37	26	.587	10 AL, 7 WS
9	Gene Mauch	26	**1907**	2044	.483	1902	2037	.483	5	7	.417	—None—
10	Bill McKechnie	25	**1904**	1737	.523	1896	1723	.524	8	14	.364	4 NL, 2 WS
11	**Tony La Russa**	23	**1859**	1674	.526	1827	1647	.526	32	27	.542	3 AL, 1 WS
12	**Bobby Cox**	20	**1763**	1398	.558	1704	1345	.559	59	53	.527	5 NL, 1 WS
13	Tommy Lasorda	21	**1630**	1469	.526	1599	1439	.526	31	30	.508	4 NL, 2 WS
14	Ralph Houk	20	**1627**	1539	.514	1619	1531	.514	8	8	.500	3 AL, 2 WS
15	Fred Clarke	19	**1609**	1189	.575	1602	1181	.576	7	8	.467	4 NL, 1 WS
16	Dick Williams	21	**1592**	1474	.519	1571	1451	.520	21	23	.477	3 AL, 1 NL, 2 WS
17	**Joe Torre**	20	**1532**	1415	.520	1476	1390	.515	56	25	.691	5 AL, 4 WS
18	Earl Weaver	17	**1506**	1080	.582	1480	1060	.583	26	20	.565	4 AL, 1 WS
19	Clark Griffith	20	**1491**	1367	.522	1491	1367	.522	0	0	.000	1 AL (1901)
20	Miller Huggins	17	**1431**	1149	.555	1413	1134	.555	18	15	.545	6 AL, 3 WS

Notes: John McGraw's postseason record also includes two World Series tie games (1912,'22); Miller Huggins postseason record also includes one World Series tie game (1922).

Where They Managed

Alston—Brooklyn/Los Angeles NL (1954-76); **Anderson**—Cincinnati NL (1970-78), Detroit AL (1979-95); **Clarke**—Louisville NL (1897-99), Pittsburgh NL (1900-15); **Cox**—Atlanta (1978-81, 1990-), Toronto (1982-85); **Durocher**—Brooklyn NL (1939-46,48), New York NL (1948-55), Chicago NL (1966-72), Houston NL (1972-73); **Griffith**—Chicago AL (1901-02), New York AL (1903-08), Cincinnati NL (1909-11), Washington AL (1912-20); **Harris**—Washington AL (1924-28,35-42,50-54), Detroit AL (1929-33,55-56), Boston AL (1934), Philadelphia NL (1943), New York AL (1947-48); **Houk**—New York AL (1961-63,66-73), Detroit AL (1974-78), Boston AL (1981-84); **Huggins**—St. Louis NL (1913-17), New York AL (1918-29); **La Russa**—Chicago AL (1979-86), Oakland (1986-95); St. Louis (1996-); **Lasorda**—Los Angeles NL (1976-96); **Mack**—Pittsburgh NL (1894-96), Philadelphia AL (1901-50).

Mauch—Philadelphia NL (1960-68), Montreal NL (1969-75), Minnesota AL (1976-80), California AL (1981-82,85-87); **McCarthy**—Chicago NL (1926-30), New York AL (1931-46), Boston AL (1948-50); **McGraw**—Baltimore NL (1899), Baltimore AL (1901-02), New York NL (1902-32); **McKechnie**—Newark FL (1915), Pittsburgh NL (1922-26), St. Louis NL (1928-29), Boston NL (1930-37), Cincinnati NL (1938-46); **Stengel**—Brooklyn NL (1934-36), Boston NL (1938-43), New York AL (1949-60), New York NL (1962-65); **Torre**—New York NL (1977-81), Atlanta (1982-84), St. Louis (1990-95), New York AL (1996-); **Weaver**—Baltimore AL (1968-82,85-86); **Williams**—Boston AL (1967-69), Oakland AL (1971-73), California AL (1974-76), Montreal NL (1977-81), San Diego NL (1982-85), Seattle AL (1986-88).

Regular Season Winning Pct.

Minimum of 750 victories.

		Yrs	W	L	Pct	Pen
1	Joe McCarthy	24	2125	1333	**.615**	9
2	Charlie Comiskey	12	838	541	**.608**	4
3	Frank Selee	16	1284	862	**.598**	5
4	Billy Southworth	13	1044	704	**.597**	4
5	Frank Chance	11	946	648	**.593**	4
6	John McGraw	33	2840	1984	**.589**	10
7	Al Lopez	17	1410	1004	**.584**	2
8	Earl Weaver	17	1480	1060	**.583**	4
9	Cap Anson	20	1296	947	**.578**	5
10	Fred Clarke	19	1602	1181	**.576**	4
11	Davey Johnson	14	1148	888	**.564**	1
12	**Bobby Cox**	20	1704	1345	**.559**	5
13	Steve O'Neill	14	1040	821	**.559**	1
14	Walter Alston	23	2040	1613	**.558**	7
15	Bill Terry	10	823	661	**.555**	3
16	Miller Huggins	17	1413	1134	**.555**	6
17	Billy Martin	16	1253	1013	**.553**	2
18	Harry Wright	18	1000	825	**.548**	3
19	Charlie Grimm	19	1287	1067	**.547**	3
20	Sparky Anderson	26	2194	1834	**.545**	5

World Series Victories

		App	W	L	T	Pct	WS
1	Casey Stengel	10	**37**	26	0	.587	7
2	Joe McCarthy	9	**30**	13	0	.698	7
3	John McGraw	9	**26**	28	2	.482	3
4	Connie Mack	8	**24**	19	0	.558	5
5	Walter Alston	7	**20**	20	0	.500	4
6	**Joe Torre**	5	**19**	7	0	.731	4
7	Miller Huggins	6	**18**	15	1	.544	3
8	Sparky Anderson	5	**16**	12	0	.571	3
9	Tommy Lasorda	4	**12**	11	0	.522	2
	Dick Williams	4	**12**	14	0	.462	2
11	Frank Chance	4	**11**	9	1	.548	2
	Bucky Harris	3	**11**	10	0	.524	2
	Billy Southworth	4	**11**	11	0	.500	2
	Earl Weaver	4	**11**	13	0	.458	1
	Bobby Cox	5	**11**	18	0	.379	1
16	Whitey Herzog	3	**10**	11	0	.476	1
17	Bill Carrigan	2	**8**	2	0	.800	2
	Danny Murtaugh	2	**8**	6	0	.571	2
	Cito Gaston	2	**8**	6	0	.571	2
	Tom Kelly	2	**8**	6	0	.571	2
	Ralph Houk	2	**8**	8	0	.500	2
	Bill McKechnie	4	**8**	14	0	.364	2

Active Managers' Records

Regular season games only; through 2001 (updated as of Nov. 1).

National League

		Yrs	W	L	Pct
1	Tony La Russa, St.L	23	**1827**	1647	.526
2	Bobby Cox, Atl	20	**1704**	1345	.559
3	Bobby Valentine, NY	14	**1042**	986	.514
4	Dusty Baker, SF	9	**745**	649	.534
5	Jimy Williams, Hou.	9	**695**	593	.540
6	Don Baylor, Chi.	8	**593**	640	.481
7	Bruce Bochy, SD	7	**564**	552	.505
8	Jeff Torborg, Mon.	9	**539**	613	.468
9	Buddy Bell, Col	5	**339**	446	.432
10	Bob Boone, Cin	4	**247**	302	.450
11	Larry Bowa, Phi	3	**167**	203	.451
12	Davey Lopes, Mil	2	**141**	183	.435
13	Bob Brenly, Arizona	1	**92**	70	.568
14	Jim Tracy, LA.	1	**86**	76	.531
15	Lloyd McClendon, Pit.	1	**62**	100	.383
	Florida				

American League

		Yrs	W	L	Pct
1	Joe Torre, NY	20	**1476**	1390	.515
2	Lou Piniella, Sea.	15	**1226**	1066	.535
3	Art Howe, Oak.	11	**889**	892	.499
4	Mike Hargrove, Bal	11	**858**	777	.525
5	Phil Garner, Det.	10	**708**	796	.471
6	Hal McRae, TB	5	**344**	367	.484
7	Jerry Manuel, Chi.	4	**333**	314	.515
8	Tony Muser, KC	5	**309**	416	.426
9	Charlie Manuel, Cle	2	**181**	143	.559
10	Mike Scioscia, Ana.	2	**157**	167	.485
11	Buck Martinez, Tor	1	**80**	82	.494
12	Jerry Narron, Tex.	1	**62**	72	.463
13	Joe Kerrigan, Bos	1	**17**	26	.395
	Minnesota				

Annual Awards

MOST VALUABLE PLAYER

There have been three different Most Valuable Player awards in baseball since 1911—the Chalmers Award (1911-14), presented by the Detroit-based automobile company; the League Award (1922-29), presented by the National and American Leagues; and the Baseball Writers' Award (since 1931), presented by the Baseball Writers' Association of America. Statistics for winning players are provided below. Stats for winning pitchers before advent of Cy Young Award are in MVP Pitchers' Statistics table.

Multiple winners: NL—Barry Bonds, Roy Campanella, Stan Musial and Mike Schmidt (3); Ernie Banks, Johnny Bench, Rogers Hornsby, Carl Hubbell, Willie Mays, Joe Morgan and Dale Murphy (2). **AL**—Yogi Berra, Joe DiMaggio, Jimmie Foxx and Mickey Mantle (3); Mickey Cochrane, Lou Gehrig, Juan Gonzalez, Hank Greenberg, Walter Johnson, Roger Maris, Hal Newhouser, Cal Ripken Jr., Frank Thomas, Ted Williams and Robin Yount (2). **NL & AL**—Frank Robinson (2, one in each).

Chalmers Award

National League

Year		Pos	HR	RBI	Avg
1911	Wildfire Schulte, Chi	OF	21	121	.300
1912	Larry Doyle, NY	2B	10	90	.330
1913	Jake Daubert, Bklyn	1B	2	52	.350
1914	Johnny Evers, Bos	2B	1	40	.279

American League

Year		Pos	HR	RBI	Avg
1911	Ty Cobb, Det	OF	8	144	.420
1912	Tris Speaker, Bos	OF	10	98	.383
1913	Walter Johnson, Wash	P	—	—	—
1914	Eddie Collins, Phi	2B	2	85	.344

League Award

National League

Year		Pos	HR	RBI	Avg
1922	No selection				
1923	No selection				
1924	Dazzy Vance, Bklyn	P	—	—	—
1925	Rogers Hornsby, St.L	2B-Mgr	39	143	.403
1926	Bob O'Farrell, St.L	C	7	68	.293
1927	Paul Waner, Pit	OF	9	131	.380
1928	Jim Bottomley, St.L	1B	31	136	.325
1929	Rogers Hornsby, Chi	2B	39	149	.380

American League

Year		Pos	HR	RBI	Avg
1922	George Sisler, St.L	1B	8	105	.420
1923	Babe Ruth, NY	OF	41	131	.393
1924	Walter Johnson, Wash	P	—	—	—
1925	Roger Peckinpaugh, Wash.	SS	4	64	.294
1926	George Burns, Cle	1B	4	114	.358
1927	Lou Gehrig, NY	1B	47	175	.373
1928	Mickey Cochrane, Phi	C	10	57	.293
1929	No selection				

Most Valuable Player
National League

Year		Pos	HR	RBI	Avg	Year		Pos	HR	RBI	Avg
1931	Frankie Frisch, St.L	2B	4	82	.311	1949	Jackie Robinson, Bklyn	2B	16	124	.342
1932	Chuck Klein, Phi	OF	38	137	.348	1950	Jim Konstanty, Phi	P	—	—	—
1933	Carl Hubbell, NY	P	—	—	—	1951	Roy Campanella, Bklyn	C	33	108	.325
1934	Dizzy Dean, St.L	P	—	—	—	1952	Hank Sauer, Chi	OF	37	121	.270
1935	Gabby Hartnett, Chi.	C	13	91	.344	1953	Roy Campanella, Bklyn	C	41	142	.312
1936	Carl Hubbell, NY	P	—	—	—	1954	Willie Mays, NY	OF	41	110	.345
1937	Joe Medwick, St.L	OF	31	154	.374	1955	Roy Campanella, Bklyn	C	32	107	.318
1938	Ernie Lombardi, Cin	C	19	95	.342	1956	Don Newcombe, Bklyn	P	—	—	—
1939	Bucky Walters, Cin	P	—	—	—	1957	Hank Aaron, Mil	OF	44	132	.322
1940	Frank McCormick, Cin	1B	19	127	.309	1958	Ernie Banks, Chi	SS	47	129	.313
1941	Dolf Camilli, Bklyn	1B	34	120	.285	1959	Ernie Banks, Chi	SS	45	143	.304
1942	Mort Cooper, St.L	P	—	—	—	1960	Dick Groat, Pit	SS	2	50	.325
1943	Stan Musial, St.L	OF	13	81	.357	1961	Frank Robinson, Cin	OF	37	124	.323
1944	Marty Marion, St.L	SS	6	63	.267	1962	Maury Wills, LA	SS	6	48	.299
1945	Phil Cavarretta, Chi	1B	6	97	.355	1963	Sandy Koufax, LA	P	—	—	—
1946	Stan Musial, St.L	1B-OF	16	103	.365	1964	Ken Boyer, St.L	3B	24	119	.295
1947	Bob Elliott, Bos	3B	22	113	.317	1965	Willie Mays, SF	OF	52	112	.317
1948	Stan Musial, St.L	OF	39	131	.376						

Year		Pos	HR	RBI	Avg
1966	Roberto Clemente, Pit	OF	29	119	.317
1967	Orlando Cepeda, St.L	1B	25	111	.325
1968	Bob Gibson, St.L	P	—	—	—
1969	Willie McCovey, SF	1B	45	126	.320
1970	Johnny Bench, Cin	C	45	148	.293
1971	Joe Torre, St.L	3B	24	137	.363
1972	Johnny Bench, Cin	C	40	125	.270
1973	Pete Rose, Cin	OF	5	64	.338
1974	Steve Garvey, LA	1B	21	111	.312
1975	Joe Morgan, Cin	2B	17	94	.327
1976	Joe Morgan, Cin	2B	27	111	.320
1977	George Foster, Cin	OF	52	149	.320
1978	Dave Parker, Pit	OF	30	117	.334
1979	Keith Hernandez, St.L	1B	11	105	.344
	Willie Stargell, Pit	1B	32	82	.281
1980	Mike Schmidt, Phi	3B	48	121	.286
1981	Mike Schmidt, Phi	3B	31	91	.316
1982	Dale Murphy, Atl	OF	36	109	.281
1983	Dale Murphy, Atl	OF	36	121	.302
1984	Ryne Sandberg, Chi	2B	19	84	.314
1985	Willie McGee, St.L	OF	10	82	.353
1986	Mike Schmidt, Phi	3B	37	119	.290
1987	Andre Dawson, Chi	OF	49	137	.287
1988	Kirk Gibson, LA	OF	25	76	.290
1989	Kevin Mitchell, SF	OF	47	125	.291
1990	Barry Bonds, Pit	OF	33	114	.301
1991	Terry Pendleton, Atl	3B	22	86	.319
1992	Barry Bonds, Pit	OF	34	103	.311
1993	Barry Bonds, SF	OF	46	123	.336
1994	Jeff Bagwell, Hou	1B	39	116	.368
1995	Barry Larkin, Cin	SS	15	66	.319
1996	Ken Caminiti, SD	3B	40	130	.326
1997	Larry Walker, Col	OF	49	130	.366
1998	Sammy Sosa, Chi	OF	66	158	.308
1999	Chipper Jones, Atl	3B	45	110	.319
2000	Jeff Kent, SF	2B	33	125	.334

American League

Year		Pos	HR	RBI	Avg
1931	Lefty Grove, Phi	P	—	—	—
1932	Jimmie Foxx, Phi	1B	58	169	.364
1933	Jimmie Foxx, Phi	1B	48	163	.356
1934	Mickey Cochrane, Det	C-Mgr	2	76	.320
1935	Hank Greenberg, Det	1B	36	170	.328
1936	Lou Gehrig, NY	1B	49	152	.354
1937	Charlie Gehringer, Det	2B	14	96	.371
1938	Jimmie Foxx, Bos	1B	50	175	.349
1939	Joe DiMaggio, NY	OF	30	126	.381
1940	Hank Greenberg, Det	OF	41	150	.340
1941	Joe DiMaggio, NY	OF	30	125	.357
1942	Joe Gordon, NY	2B	18	103	.322
1943	Spud Chandler, NY	P	—	—	—
1944	Hal Hewhouser, Det	P	—	—	—
1945	Hal Newhouser, Det	P	—	—	—
1946	Ted Williams, Bos	OF	38	123	.342

Year		Pos	HR	RBI	Avg
1947	Joe DiMaggio, NY	OF	20	97	.315
1948	Lou Boudreau, Cle	SS-Mgr	18	106	.355
1949	Ted Williams, Bos	OF	43	159	.343
1950	Phil Rizzuto, NY	SS	7	66	.324
1951	Yogi Berra, NY	C	27	88	.294
1952	Bobby Shantz, Phi	P	—	—	—
1953	Al Rosen, Cle	3B	43	145	.336
1954	Yogi Berra, NY	C	22	125	.307
1955	Yogi Berra, NY	C	27	108	.272
1956	Mickey Mantle, NY	OF	52	130	.353
1957	Mickey Mantle, NY	OF	34	94	.365
1958	Jackie Jensen, Bos	OF	35	122	.286
1959	Nellie Fox, Chi	2B	2	70	.306
1960	Roger Maris, NY	OF	39	112	.283
1961	Roger Maris, NY	OF	61	142	.269
1962	Mickey Mantle, NY	OF	30	89	.321
1963	Elston Howard, NY	C	28	85	.287
1964	Brooks Robinson, Bal	3B	28	118	.317
1965	Zoilo Versalles, Min	SS	19	77	.273
1966	Frank Robinson, Bal	OF	49	122	.316
1967	Carl Yastrzemski, Bos	OF	44	121	.326
1968	Denny McLain, Det	P	—	—	—
1969	Harmon Killebrew, Min	3B-1B	49	140	.276
1970	Boog Powell, Bal	1B	35	114	.297
1971	Vida Blue, Oak	P	—	—	—
1972	Dick Allen, Chi	1B	37	113	.308
1973	Reggie Jackson, Oak	OF	32	117	.293
1974	Jeff Burroughs, Tex	OF	25	118	.301
1975	Fred Lynn, Bos	OF	21	105	.331
1976	Thurman Munson, NY	C	17	105	.302
1977	Rod Carew, Min	1B	14	100	.388
1978	Jim Rice, Bos	OF-DH	46	139	.315
1979	Don Baylor, Cal	OF-DH	36	139	.296
1980	George Brett, KC	3B	24	118	.390
1981	Rollie Fingers, Mil	P	—	—	—
1982	Robin Yount, Mil	SS	29	114	.331
1983	Cal Ripken Jr., Bal	SS	27	102	.318
1984	Willie Hernandez, Det	P	—	—	—
1985	Don Mattingly, NY	1B	35	145	.324
1986	Roger Clemens, Bos	P	—	—	—
1987	George Bell, Tor	OF	47	134	.308
1988	Jose Canseco, Oak	OF	42	124	.307
1989	Robin Yount, Mil	OF	21	103	.318
1990	Rickey Henderson, Oak	OF	28	61	.325
1991	Cal Ripken Jr., Bal	SS	34	114	.323
1992	Dennis Eckersley, Oak	P	—	—	—
1993	Frank Thomas, Chi	1B	41	128	.317
1994	Frank Thomas, Chi	1B	38	101	.353
1995	Mo Vaughn, Bos	1B	39	126	.300
1996	Juan Gonzalez, Tex	OF-DH	47	144	.314
1997	Ken Griffey Jr., Sea	OF	56	147	.304
1998	Juan Gonzalez, Tex	OF	45	157	.318
1999	Ivan Rodriguez, Tex	C	35	113	.332
2000	Jason Giambi, Oak	1B	43	137	.333

MVP Pitchers' Statistics

Pitchers have been named Most Valuable Player on 23 occasions, 10 times in the NL and 13 in the AL. Four have been relief pitchers—Jim Konstanty, Rollie Fingers, Willie Hernandez and Dennis Eckersley. For statistics of MVP pitchers since 1956, see Cy Young Award tables on following page.

National League

Year		Gm	W-L	SV	ERA
1924	Dazzy Vance, Bklyn	35	28-6	0	2.16
1933	Carl Hubbell, NY	45	23-12	5	1.66
1934	Dizzy Dean, St.L	50	30-7	7	2.66
1936	Carl Hubbell, NY	42	26-6	3	2.31
1939	Bucky Walters, Cin	39	27-11	0	2.29
1942	Mort Cooper, St.L	37	22-7	0	1.78
1950	Jim Konstanty, Phi	74	16-7	22	2.66

American League

Year		Gm	W-L	SV	ERA
1913	Walter Johnson, Wash	47	36-7	2	1.09
1924	Walter Johnson, Wash	38	23-7	0	2.72
1931	Lefty Grove, Phi	41	31-4	5	2.06
1943	Spud Chandler, NY	30	20-4	0	1.64
1944	Hal Newhouser, Det	47	29-9	2	2.22
1945	Hal Newhouser, Det	40	25-9	2	1.81
1952	Bobby Shantz, Phi	33	24-7	0	2.48

CY YOUNG AWARD

Voted on by the Baseball Writers Association of America. One award was presented from 1956-66, two since 1967. Pitchers who won the MVP and Cy Young awards in the same season are in **bold** type.

Multiple winners: NL—Steve Carlton and Greg Maddux (4); Sandy Koufax and Tom Seaver (3); Bob Gibson and Tom Glavine (2). **AL**—Roger Clemens (5); Jim Palmer (3); Denny McLain (2). **NL & AL**— Pedro Martinez (3, two in AL, one in NL), Randy Johnson (3, two in NL, one in AL) and Gaylord Perry (2, one in each).

NL and AL Combined

Year	National League	Gm	W-L	SV	ERA	Year	American League	Gm	W-L	SV	ERA
1956	**Don Newcombe**, Bklyn	38	27-7	0	3.06	1958	Bob Turley, NY	33	21-7	1	2.97
1957	Warren Spahn, Mil	39	21-11	3	2.69	1959	Early Wynn, Chi	37	22-10	0	3.17
1960	Vernon Law, Pit	35	20-9	0	3.08	1961	Whitey Ford, NY	39	25-4	0	3.21
1962	Don Drysdale, LA	43	25-9	1	2.83	1964	Dean Chance, LA	46	20-9	4	1.65
1963	**Sandy Koufax**, LA	40	25-5	0	1.88						
1965	Sandy Koufax, LA	43	26-8	2	2.04						
1966	Sandy Koufax, LA	41	27-9	0	1.73						

Separate League Awards

	National League						American League				
Year		Gm	W-L	SV	ERA	Year		Gm	W-L	SV	ERA
1967	Mike McCormick, SF	40	22-10	0	2.85	1967	Jim Lonborg, Bos	39	22-9	0	3.16
1968	**Bob Gibson**, St.L	34	22-9	0	1.12	1968	**Denny McLain**, Det	41	31-6	0	1.96
1969	Tom Seaver, NY	36	25-7	0	2.21	1969	Denny McLain, Det	42	24-9	0	2.80
1970	Bob Gibson, St.L	34	23-7	0	3.12		Mike Cuellar, Bal	39	23-11	0	2.38
1971	Ferguson Jenkins, Chi	39	24-13	0	2.77	1970	Jim Perry, Min	40	24-12	0	3.03
1972	Steve Carlton, Phi	41	27-10	0	1.97	1971	**Vida Blue**, Oak	39	24-8	0	1.82
1973	Tom Seaver, NY	36	19-10	0	2.08	1972	Gaylord Perry, Cle	41	24-16	1	1.92
1974	Mike Marshall, LA	106	15-12	21	2.42	1973	Jim Palmer, Bal	38	22-9	1	2.40
1975	Tom Seaver, NY	36	22-9	0	2.38	1974	Catfish Hunter, Oak	41	25-12	0	2.49
1976	Randy Jones, SD	40	22-14	0	2.74	1975	Jim Palmer, Bal	39	23-11	1	2.09
1977	Steve Carlton, Phi	36	23-10	0	2.64	1976	Jim Palmer, Bal	40	22-13	0	2.51
1978	Gaylord Perry, SD	37	21-6	0	2.72	1977	Sparky Lyle, NY	72	13-5	26	2.17
1979	Bruce Sutter, Chi	62	6-6	37	2.23	1978	Ron Guidry, NY	35	25-3	0	1.74
1980	Steve Carlton, Phi	38	24-9	0	2.34	1979	Mike Flanagan, Bal	39	23-9	0	3.08
1981	Fernando Valenzuela, LA	25	13-7	0	2.48	1980	Steve Stone, Bal	37	25-7	0	3.23
1982	Steve Carlton, Phi	38	23-11	0	3.10	1981	**Rollie Fingers**, Mil	47	6-3	28	1.04
1983	John Denny, Phi	36	19-6	0	2.37	1982	Pete Vuckovich, Mil	30	18-6	0	3.34
1984	Rick Sutcliffe, Chi	20*	16-1	0	2.69	1983	LaMarr Hoyt, Chi	36	24-10	0	3.66
1985	Dwight Gooden, NY	35	24-4	0	1.53	1984	**Willie Hernandez**, Det	80	9-3	32	1.92
1986	Mike Scott, Hou	37	18-10	0	2.22	1985	Bret Saberhagen, KC	32	20-6	0	2.87
1987	Steve Bedrosian, Phi	65	5-3	40	2.83	1986	**Roger Clemens**, Bos	33	24-4	0	2.48
1988	Orel Hershiser, LA	35	23-8	1	2.26	1987	Roger Clemens, Bos	36	20-9	0	2.97
1989	Mark Davis, SD	70	4-3	44	1.85	1988	Frank Viola, Min	35	24-7	0	2.64
1990	Doug Drabek, Pit	33	22-6	0	2.76	1989	Bret Saberhagen, KC	36	23-6	0	2.16
1991	Tom Glavine, Atl	34	20-11	0	2.55	1990	Bob Welch, Oak	35	27-6	0	2.95
1992	Greg Maddux, Chi	35	20-11	0	2.18	1991	Roger Clemens, Bos	35	18-10	0	2.62
1993	Greg Maddux, Atl	36	20-10	0	2.36	1992	**Dennis Eckersley**, Oak	69	7-1	51	1.91
1994	Greg Maddux, Atl	25	16-6	0	1.56	1993	Jack McDowell, Chi	34	22-10	0	3.37
1995	Greg Maddux, Atl	28	19-2	0	1.63	1994	David Cone, KC	23	16-5	0	2.94
1996	John Smoltz, Atl	35	24-8	0	2.94	1995	Randy Johnson, Sea	30	18-2	0	2.48
1997	Pedro Martinez, Mon	31	17-8	0	1.90	1996	Pat Hentgen, Tor	35	20-10	0	3.22
1998	Tom Glavine, Atl	33	20-6	0	2.47	1997	Roger Clemens, Tor	34	21-7	0	2.05
1999	Randy Johnson, Ari	35	17-9	0	2.48	1998	Roger Clemens, Tor	33	20-6	0	2.65
2000	Randy Johnson, Ari	35	19-7	0	2.64	1999	Pedro Martinez, Bos	31	23-4	0	2.07
						2000	Pedro Martinez, Bos	29	18-6	0	1.74

*NL games only, Sutcliffe pitched 15 games with Cleveland before being traded to the Cubs.

ROOKIE OF THE YEAR

Voted on by the Baseball Writers Assn. of America. One award was presented from 1947-48. Two awards (one for each league) have been presented since 1949. Winner who was also named MVP is in **bold** type.

NL and AL Combined

Year		Pos	Year		Pos
1947	Jackie Robinson, Brooklyn	1B	1948	Alvin Dark, Boston-NL	SS

National League

Year		Pos	Year		Pos	Year		Pos
1949	Don Newcombe, Bklyn	P	1955	Bill Virdon, St.L	OF	1961	Billy Williams, Chi	OF
1950	Sam Jethroe, Bos	OF	1956	Frank Robinson, Cin	OF	1962	Ken Hubbs, Chi	2B
1951	Willie Mays, NY	OF	1957	Jack Sanford, Phi	P	1963	Pete Rose, Cin	2B
1952	Joe Black, Bklyn	P	1958	Orlando Cepeda, SF	1B	1964	Richie Allen, Phi	3B
1953	Jim Gilliam, Bklyn	2B	1959	Willie McCovey, SF	1B	1965	Jim Lefebvre, LA	2B
1954	Wally Moon, St.L	OF	1960	Frank Howard, LA	OF	1966	Tommy Helms, Cin	3B

Year		Pos
1967	Tom Seaver, NY	P
1968	Johnny Bench, Cin	C
1969	Ted Sizemore, LA	2B
1970	Carl Morton, Mon	P
1971	Earl Williams, Atl	C
1972	Jon Matlack, NY	P
1973	Gary Matthews, SF	OF
1974	Bake McBride, St.L	P
1975	John Montefusco, SF	P
1976	Butch Metzger, SD	P
	& Pat Zachry, Cin	P
1977	Andre Dawson, Mon	OF

Year		Pos
1978	Bob Horner, Atl	3B
1979	Rick Sutcliffe, LA	P
1980	Steve Howe, LA	P
1981	Fernando Valenzuela, LA	P
1982	Steve Sax, LA	2B
1983	Darryl Strawberry, NY	OF
1984	Dwight Gooden, NY	P
1985	Vince Coleman, St.L	OF
1986	Todd Worrell, St.L	P
1987	Benito Santiago, SD	C
1988	Chris Sabo, Cin	3B
1989	Jerome Walton, Chi	OF

Year		Pos
1990	David Justice, Atl	OF
1991	Jeff Bagwell, Hou	1B
1992	Eric Karros, LA	1B
1993	Mike Piazza, LA	C
1994	Raul Mondesi, LA	OF
1995	Hideo Nomo, LA	P
1996	Todd Hollandsworth, LA	OF
1997	Scott Rolen, Phi	3B
1998	Kerry Wood, Chi	P
1999	Scott Williamson, Cin	P
2000	Rafael Furcal, Atl	SS

American League

Year		Pos
1949	Roy Sievers, St.L	OF
1950	Walt Dropo, Bos	1B
1951	Gil McDougald, NY	3B
1952	Harry Byrd, Phi	P
1953	Harvey Kuenn, Det	SS
1954	Bob Grim, NY	P
1955	Herb Score, Cle	P
1956	Luis Aparicio, Chi	SS
1957	Tony Kubek, NY	INF-OF
1958	Albie Pearson, Wash	OF
1959	Bob Allison, Wash	OF
1960	Ron Hansen, Bal	SS
1961	Don Schwall, Bos	P
1962	Tom Tresh, NY	SS-OF
1963	Gary Peters, Chi	P
1964	Tony Oliva, Min	OF
1965	Curt Blefary, Bal	OF
1966	Tommie Agee, Chi	OF

Year		Pos
1967	Rod Carew, Min	2B
1968	Stan Bahnsen, NY	P
1969	Lou Piniella, KC	OF
1970	Thurman Munson, NY	C
1971	Chris Chambliss, Cle	1B
1972	Carlton Fisk, Bos	C
1973	Al Bumbry, Bal	OF
1974	Mike Hargrove, Tex	1B
1975	**Fred Lynn**, Bos	OF
1976	Mark Fidrych, Det	P
1977	Eddie Murray, Bal	DH-1B
1978	Lou Whitaker, Det	2B
1979	John Castino, Min	3B
	& Alfredo Griffin, Tor	SS
1980	Joe Charboneau, Cle	OF-DH
1981	Dave Righetti, NY	P
1982	Cal Ripken Jr., Bal	SS-3B
1983	Ron Kittle, Chi	OF

Year		Pos
1984	Alvin Davis, Sea	1B
1985	Ozzie Guillen, Chi	SS
1986	Jose Canseco, Oak	OF
1987	Mark McGwire, Oak	1B
1988	Walt Weiss, Oak	SS
1989	Gregg Olson, Bal	P
1990	Sandy Alomar Jr., Cle	C
1991	Chuck Knoblauch, Min	2B
1992	Pat Listach, Mil	SS
1993	Tim Salmon, Cal	OF
1994	Bob Hamelin, KC	DH
1995	Marty Cordova, Min	OF
1996	Derek Jeter, NY	SS
1997	Nomar Garciaparra, Bos	SS
1998	Ben Grieve, Oak	OF
1999	Carlos Beltran, KC	OF
2000	Kazuhiro Sasaki, Sea	P

MANAGER OF THE YEAR

Voted on by the Baseball Writers Association of America. Two awards (one for each league) presented since 1983. Note that (*) indicates manager's team won division championship and (†) indicates unofficial division won in 1994.

Multiple winners: Dusty Baker and Tony La Russa (3), Sparky Anderson, Bobby Cox, Tommy Lasorda, Jim Leyland and Joe Torre (2).

National League

Year		Improvement		
1983	Tommy Lasorda, LA	88-74	to	91-71*
1984	Jim Frey, Chi	71-91	to	96-75*
1985	Whitey Herzog, St. L	84-78	to	101-61*
1986	Hal Lanier, Hou	83-79	to	96-66*
1987	Buck Rodgers, Mon	78-83	to	91-71
1988	Tommy Lasorda, LA	73-89	to	94-67*
1989	Don Zimmer, Chi	77-85	to	93-69*
1990	Jim Leyland, Pit	74-88	to	95-67*
1991	Bobby Cox, Atl	65-97	to	94-68*
1992	Jim Leyland, Pit	98-64*	to	96-66*
1993	Dusty Baker, SF	72-90	to	103-59
1994	Felipe Alou, Mon	94-68	to	74-40†
1995	Don Baylor, Col	53-64	to	77-67
1996	Bruce Bochy, SD	70-74	to	91-71
1997	Dusty Baker, SF	68-94	to	90-72
1998	Larry Dierker, Hou	84-78	to	102-60*
1999	Jack McKeon, Cin	77-85	to	96-67
2000	Dusty Baker, SF	86-76	to	97-65*

American League

Year		Improvement		
1983	Tony La Russa, Chi	87-75	to	99-63*
1984	Sparky Anderson, Det	92-70	to	104-58*
1985	Bobby Cox, Tor	89-73	to	99-62*
1986	John McNamara, Bos	81-81	to	95-66*
1987	Sparky Anderson, Det	87-75	to	98-64*
1988	Tony La Russa, Oak	81-81	to	104-58*
1989	Frank Robinson, Bal	54-107	to	87-75
1990	Jeff Torborg, Chi	69-92	to	94-68
1991	Tom Kelly, Min	74-88	to	95-67*
1992	Tony La Russa, Oak	84-78	to	96-66*
1993	Gene Lamont, Chi	86-76	to	94-68*
1994	Buck Showalter, NY	88-74	to	70-43†
1995	Lou Piniella, Sea	49-63	to	79-66*
1996	Joe Torre, NY	79-65	to	92-70
	& Johnny Oates, Tex	74-70	to	90-72
1997	Davey Johnson, Bal	88-74	to	98-64
1998	Joe Torre, NY	96-66	to	114-48*
1999	Jimy Williams, Bos	92-70	to	94-68
2000	Jerry Manuel, Chi	75-86	to	95-67*

HANK AARON AWARD

The inaugural award was presented in 1999 to the best "complete" hitter in both the American and National leagues. In 1999, hitters received one point for every hit, home run and RBI. Beginning in 2000, winners were selected by a panel of broadcasters.

National League

Year		H	HR	RBI	Avg
1999	Sammy Sosa, Chi	180	63	141	.288
2000	Todd Helton, Col	216	42	147	.372

American League

Year		H	HR	RBI	Avg
1999	Manny Ramirez, Cle	174	44	165	.333
2000	Carlos Delgado, Tor	196	41	137	.344

COLLEGE BASEBALL

College World Series

The NCAA Division I College World Series has been held in Kalamazoo, Mich. (1947-48), Wichita, Kan. (1949) and Omaha, Neb. (since 1950).

Multiple winners: USC (12); Arizona St. and LSU (5); Miami-FL and Texas (4); Arizona, CS-Fullerton and Minnesota (3); California, Michigan, Oklahoma and Stanford (2).

Year	Winner	Coach	Score	Runner-up	Year	Winner	Coach	Score	Runner-up
1947	California	Clint Evans	8-7	Yale	1975	Texas	Cliff Gustafson	5-1	S. Carolina
1948	USC	Sam Barry	9-2	Yale	1976	Arizona	Jerry Kindall	7-1	E. Michigan
1949	Texas	Bibb Falk	10-3	W. Forest	1977	Arizona St.	Jim Brock	2-1	S. Carolina
1950	Texas	Bibb Falk	3-0	Wash. St.	1978	USC	Rod Dedeaux	10-3	Ariz. St.
1951	Oklahoma	Jack Baer	3-2	Tennessee	1979	CS-Fullerton	Augie Garrido	2-1	Arkansas
1952	Holy Cross	Jack Barry	8-4	Missouri	1980	Arizona	Jerry Kindall	5-3	Hawaii
1953	Michigan	Ray Fisher	7-5	Texas	1981	Arizona St.	Jim Brock	7-4	Okla. St.
1954	Missouri	Hi Simmons	4-1	Rollins	1982	Miami-FL	Ron Fraser	9-3	Wichita St.
1955	Wake Forest	Taylor Sanford	7-6	W. Mich.	1983	Texas	Cliff Gustafson	4-3	Alabama
1956	Minnesota	Dick Siebert	12-1	Arizona	1984	CS-Fullerton	Augie Garrido	3-1	Texas
1957	California	Geo. Wolfman	1-0	Penn St.	1985	Miami-FL	Ron Fraser	10-6	Texas
1958	USC	Rod Dedeaux	8-7	Missouri	1986	Arizona	Jerry Kindall	10-2	Fla. St.
1959	Oklahoma St.	Toby Greene	5-3	Arizona	1987	Stanford	M. Marquess	9-5	Okla. St.
					1988	Stanford	M. Marquess	9-4	Ariz. St.
1960	Minnesota	Dick Siebert	2-1	USC	1989	Wichita St.	G.Stephenson	5-3	Texas
1961	USC	Rod Dedeaux	1-0	Okla. St.					
1962	Michigan	Don Lund	5-4	S. Clara	1990	Georgia	Steve Webber	2-1	Okla. St.
1963	USC	Rod Dedeaux	5-2	Arizona	1991	LSU	Skip Bertman	6-3	Wichita St.
1964	Minnesota	Dick Siebert	5-1	Missouri	1992	Pepperdine	Andy Lopez	3-2	CS-Fullerton
1965	Arizona St.	Bobby Winkles	2-1	Ohio St.	1993	LSU	Skip Bertman	8-0	Wichita St.
1966	Ohio St.	Marty Karow	8-2	Okla. St.	1994	Oklahoma	Larry Cochell	13-5	Ga. Tech
1967	Arizona St.	Bobby Winkles	11-2	Houston	1995	CS-Fullerton	Augie Garrido	11-5	USC
1968	USC	Rod Dedeaux	4-3	So. Ill.	1996	LSU	Skip Bertman	9-8	Miami-FL
1969	Arizona St.	Bobby Winkles	10-1	Tulsa	1997	LSU	Skip Bertman	13-6	Alabama
					1998	USC	Mike Gillespie	21-14	Arizona St.
1970	USC	Rod Dedeaux	2-1	Fla. St.	1999	Miami-FL	Jim Morris	6-5	Fla. St.
1971	USC	Rod Dedeaux	7-2	So. Ill.					
1972	USC	Rod Dedeaux	1-0	Ariz. St.	2000	LSU	Skip Bertman	6-5	Stanford
1973	USC	Rod Dedeaux	4-3	Ariz. St.	2001	Miami-FL	Jim Morris	12-1	Stanford
1974	USC	Rod Dedeaux	7-3	Miami-FL					

Most Outstanding Player

The Most Outstanding Player has been selected every year of the College World Series since 1949. Winners who did not play for the CWS champion are listed in **bold** type. No player has won the award more than once.

Year		Year		Year	
1949	**Charles Teague,** W. Forest, 2B	1967	Ron Davini, Ariz. St., C	1985	Greg Ellena, Miami-FL, LF
1950	**Ray VanCleef,** Rutgers, CF	1968	Bill Seinsoth, USC, 1B	1986	Mike Senne, Arizona, DH
1951	**Sidney Hatfield,** Tenn., P-1B	1969	John Dolinsek, Ariz. St., LF	1987	Paul Carey, Stanford, RF
1952	James O'Neill, Holy Cross, P	1970	**Gene Ammann,** Fla. St., P	1988	Lee Plemel, Stanford, P
1953	**J.L. Smith,** Texas, P	1971	**Jerry Tabb,** Tulsa, 1B	1989	Greg Brummett, Wich. St., P
1954	**Tom Yewcic,** Mich. St., C	1972	Russ McQueen, USC, P	1990	Mike Rebhan, Georgia, P
1955	**Tom Borland,** Okla. St., P	1973	**Dave Winfield,** Minn., P-OF	1991	Gary Hymel, LSU, C
1956	Jerry Thomas, Minn., P	1974	George Milke, USC, P	1992	**Phil Nevin,** CS-Fullerton, 3B
1957	**Cal Emery,** Penn St., P-1B	1975	Mickey Reichenbach, Texas, 1B	1993	Todd Walker, LSU, 2B
1958	Bill Thom, USC, P	1976	Steve Powers, Arizona, P-DH	1994	Chip Glass, Oklahoma, OF
1959	Jim Dobson, Okla. St., 3B	1977	Bob Horner, Ariz. St., 3B	1995	Mark Kotsay, CS-Fullerton, OF
1960	John Erickson, Minn., 2B	1978	Rod Boxberger, USC, P	1996	**Pat Burrell,** Miami-FL, 3B
1961	**Littleton Fowler,** Okla. St., P	1979	Tony Hudson, CS-Fullerton, P	1997	Brandon Larson, LSU, SS
1962	**Bob Garibaldi,** Santa Clara, P	1980	Terry Francona, Arizona, LF	1998	Wes Rachels, USC, 2B
1963	Bud Hollowell, USC, C	1981	Stan Holmes, Ariz. St., LF	1999	**Marshall McDougall,** Fla. St., 2B
1964	**Joe Ferris,** Maine, P	1982	Dan Smith, Miami-FL, P	2000	Trey Hodges, LSU, P
1965	Sal Bando, Ariz. St., 3B	1983	Calvin Schiraldi, Texas, P	2001	Charlton Jimerson, Miami-FL, CF
1966	Steve Arlin, Ohio St., P	1984	John Fishel, CS-Fullerton, P		

Annual Awards
Golden Spikes Award

First presented in 1978 by USA Baseball, honoring the nation's best amateur player. Alex Fernandez, the 1990 winner, has been the only junior college player chosen.

Year		Year		Year	
1978	Bob Horner, Ariz. St, 2B	1986	Mike Loynd, Fla. St., P	1994	Jason Varitek, Ga. Tech, C
1979	Tim Wallach, CS-Fullerton, 1B	1987	Jim Abbott, Michigan, P	1995	Mark Kotsay, CS-Fullerton, OF
1980	Terry Francona, Arizona, OF	1988	Robin Ventura, Okla. St., 3B	1996	Travis Lee, San Diego St., 1B
1981	Mike Fuentes, Fla. St., OF	1989	Ben McDonald, LSU, P	1997	J.D. Drew, Florida St., OF
1982	Augie Schmidt, N. Orleans, SS	1990	Alex Fernandez, Miami-Dade, P	1998	Pat Burrell, Miami-FL, 3B
1983	Dave Magadan, Alabama, 1B	1991	Mike Kelly, Ariz. St., OF	1999	Jason Jennings, Baylor, DH/P
1984	Oddibe McDowell, Ariz. St., OF	1992	Phil Nevin, CS-Fullerton, 3B	2000	Kip Bouknight, South Carolina, P
1985	Will Clark, Miss. St., 1B	1993	Darren Dreifort, Wichita St., P		

Baseball America Player of the Year
Presented to the College Player of the Year since 1981 by *Baseball America.*

Year	Year	Year
1981 Mike Sodders, Ariz. St., 3B	1988 John Olerud, Wash. St., 1B/P	1995 Todd Helton, Tenn., 1B/P
1982 Jeff Ledbetter, Fla. St., OF/P	1989 Ben McDonald, LSU, P	1996 Kris Benson, Clemson, P
1983 Dave Magadan, Alabama, 1B	1990 Mike Kelly, Ariz. St., OF	1997 J.D. Drew, Florida St., OF
1984 Oddibe McDowell, Ariz. St., OF	1991 David McCarty, Stanford, 1B	1998 Jeff Austin, Stanford, P
1985 Pete Incaviglia, Okla. St., OF	1992 Phil Nevin, CS-Fullerton, 3B	1999 Jason Jennings, Baylor, DH/P
1986 Casey Close, Michigan, OF	1993 Brooks Kieschnick, Texas, DH/P	2000 Mark Teixeira, Ga. Tech, 3B
1987 Robin Ventura, Okla. St., 3B	1994 Jason Varitek, Ga. Tech, C	2001 Mark Prior, USC, P

Dick Howser Trophy
Presented to the College Player of the Year since 1987, by the American Baseball Coaches Association (ABCA) from 1987-98 and the National Collegiate Baseball Writers Association (NCBWA) beginning in 1999. Named after the late two-time All-America shortstop and college coach at Florida State. Howser was also a major league manager with Kansas City and the New York Yankees.
Multiple winner: Brooks Kieschnick (2).

Year	Year	Year
1987 Mike Fiore, Miami-FL, OF	1992 Brooks Kieschnick, Texas, DH/P	1997 J.D. Drew, Florida St., OF
1988 Robin Ventura, Okla. St., 3B	1993 Brooks Kieschnick, Texas, DH/P	1998 Eddie Furniss, LSU, 1B
1989 Scott Bryant, Texas, DH	1994 Jason Varitek, Ga. Tech, C	1999 Jason Jennings, Baylor, DH/P
1990 Paul Ellis, UCLA, C	1995 Todd Helton, Tenn., 1B/P	2000 Mark Teixeira, Ga. Tech, 3B
1991 Bobby Jones, Fresno St., P	1996 Kris Benson, Clemson, P	2001 Mark Prior, USC, P

Baseball America Coach of the Year
Presented to the College Coach of the Year since 1981 by *Baseball America.*
Multiple winners: Skip Bertman, Dave Snow and Gene Stephenson (2).

Year	Year	Year
1981 Ron Fraser, Miami-FL	1988 Jim Brock, Arizona St.	1996 Skip Bertman, LSU
1982 Gene Stephenson, Wichita St.	1989 Dave Snow, Long Beach St.	1997 Jim Wells, Alabama
1983 Barry Shollenberger, Alabama	1990 Steve Webber, Georgia	1998 Pat Murphy, Arizona St.
1984 Augie Garrido, CS-Fullerton	1991 Jim Hendry, Creighton	1999 Wayne Graham, Rice
1985 Ron Polk, Mississippi St.	1992 Andy Lopez, Pepperdine	2000 Ray Tanner, S. Carolina
1986 Skip Bertman, LSU	1993 Gene Stephenson, Wichita St.	2001 Dave Van Horn, Nebraska
& Dave Snow, Loyola-CA	1994 Jim Morris, Miami-FL	
1987 Mark Marquess, Stanford	1995 Rod Delmonico, Tennessee	

All-Time Winningest Coaches
Coaches active in 2001 are in **bold** type. Records given are for four-year colleges only. For winning percentage, a minimum 10 years in Division I is required.

Top 25 Winning Percentage

		Yrs	W	L	T	Pct
1	John Barry	40	619	147	6	.806
2	W.J. Disch	29	465	115	0	.802
3	Cliff Gustafson	29	1427	373	2	.792
4	Harry Carlson	17	143	41	0	.777
5	**Gene Stephenson**	24	1310	405	3	.763
6	George Jacobs	11	76	25	0	.752
7	Bobby Winkles	13	524	173	0	.752
8	**Gary Ward**	20	985	336	1	.745
9	**Mike Martin**	22	1179	402	3	.745
10	Frank Sancet	23	831	283	8	.744
11	Ron Fraser	30	1271	438	9	.742
12	Bob Wren	23	464	160	4	.742
13	Bibb Falk	25	435	152	0	.741
14	**Skip Bertman**	18	870	330	3	.724
15	Bud Middaugh	22	821	319	1	.720
16	J.F. "Pop" McKale	30	302	118	7	.715
17	Jim Brock	28	1100	440	0	.714
18	**Jim Morris**	20	897	363	2	.712
19	Toby Green	21	318	132	0	.707
20	Joe Arnold	18	750	313	2	.705
21	**Rick Jones**	13	520	220	1	.702
22	Joe Bedenk	32	380	159	3	.701
23	Rod Dedeaux	45	1332	571	11	.699
24	Enos Semore	22	851	370	1	.697
25	**Ray Tanner**	14	612	268	3	.695

Top 25 Victories

		Yrs	W	L	T	Pct
1	Cliff Gustafson	29	**1427**	373	2	.792
2	Rod Dedeaux	45	**1332**	571	11	.699
3	**Augie Garrido**	33	**1323**	651	8	.670
4	**Gene Stephenson**	24	**1310**	405	3	.763
5	**Chuck Hartman**	42	**1305**	679	8	.657
6	**Larry Hays**	31	**1278**	686	2	.651
7	Ron Fraser	30	**1271**	438	9	.742
8	**Bob Bennett**	33	**1268**	730	8	.634
9	Jack Stallings	39	**1258**	796	5	.612
10	Al Ogletree	41	**1217**	713	1	.631
11	**Larry Cochell**	35	**1211**	712	3	.630
12	**Jim Dietz**	30	**1188**	727	18	.619
13	**Mike Martin**	22	**1179**	402	3	.745
14	Chuck Brayton	33	**1162**	523	8	.689
15	Bill Wilhelm	36	**1161**	536	10	.683
16	**Richard Jones**	35	**1128**	651	5	.634
17	**Norm DeBriyn**	32	**1126**	622	6	.644
18	**Ron Polk**	28	**1123**	534	0	.678
19	Jim Brock	23	**1100**	440	0	.714
20	**Gary Adams**	32	**1083**	797	12	.576
21	Les Murakami	30	**1077**	570	4	.654
22	Bob Hannah	36	**1053**	464	6	.693
23	**Mark Marquess**	25	**1046**	515	5	.670
24	**Gary Ward**	20	**985**	336	1	.745
25	**Jay Bergman**	25	**972**	540	3	.643

Other NCAA Champions
Division II

Multiple winners: Florida Southern (8); Cal Poly Pomona and Tampa (3); CS-Chico, CS-Northridge, Jacksonville St., Troy St., UC-Irvine and UC-Riverside (2).

Year		Year		Year		Year	
1968	Chapman, CA	1977	UC-Riverside	1986	Troy St., AL	1995	Florida Southern
1969	Illinois St.	1978	Florida Southern	1987	Troy St., AL	1996	Kennesaw St., GA
1970	CS-Northridge	1979	Valdosta St., GA	1988	Florida Southern	1997	CS-Chico
1971	Florida Southern	1980	Cal Poly Pomona	1989	Cal Poly SLO	1998	Tampa
1972	Florida Southern	1981	Florida Southern	1990	Jacksonville St., AL	1999	CS-Chico
1973	UC-Irvine	1982	UC-Riverside	1991	Jacksonville St., AL	2000	Southeastern Okla.
1974	UC-Irvine	1983	Cal Poly Pomona	1992	Tampa	2001	St. Mary's, TX
1975	Florida Southern	1984	CS-Northridge	1993	Tampa		
1976	Cal Poly Pomona	1985	Florida Southern	1994	Central Missouri St.		

Division III

Multiple winners: Eastern Conn. St., Marietta, and Montclair St. (3); CS-Stanislaus, Glassboro St., Ithaca, NC-Wesleyan, Southern Maine and Wm. Paterson, NJ (2).

Year		Year		Year		Year	
1976	CS-Stanislaus	1983	Marietta, OH	1990	Eastern Conn. St.	1997	Southern Maine
1977	CS-Stanislaus	1984	Ramapo, NJ	1991	Southern Maine	1998	Eastern Conn. St.
1978	Glassboro St., NJ	1985	Wisconsin-Oshkosh	1992	Wm. Paterson, NJ	1999	NC-Wesleyan
1979	Glassboro St., NJ	1986	Marietta, OH	1993	Montclair St., NJ	2000	Montclair St., NJ
1980	Ithaca, NY	1987	Monclair St., NJ	1994	Wisconsin-Oshkosh	2001	St. Thomas, MN
1981	Marietta, OH	1988	Ithaca, NY	1995	La Verne, CA		
1982	Eastern Conn. St.	1989	NC-Wesleyan	1996	Wm. Paterson, NJ		

Major League Number One Draft Picks

The Major League First-Year Player Draft has been held every year since 1965. Clubs select in reverse order of their won-loss records from the previous regular season with National League and American League teams alternating. AL teams select first in odd-numbered years while NL teams go first in even-numbered years. The pool of draftees consists of graduated high school players, junior or senior college players, Junior college players and anyone over the age of 21. Listed are the top selections from each draft.

Year		Pos	Team	Year		Pos	Team
1965	Rick Monday	OF	Kansas City Athletics	1984	Shawn Abner	OF	New York Mets
1966	Steve Chilcott	C	New York Mets	1985	B.J. Surhoff	C	Milwaukee Brewers
1967	Rom Blomberg	1B	New York Yankees	1986	Jeff King	IF	Pittsburgh Pirates
1968	Tim Foli	IF	New York Mets	1987	Ken Griffey Jr.	OF	Seattle Mariners
1969	Jeff Burroughs	OF	Washington Senators	1988	Andy Benes	P	San Diego Padres
1970	Mike Ivie	C	San Diego Padres	1989	Ben McDonald	P	Baltimore Orioles
1971	Danny Goodwin	C	Chicago White Sox	1990	Chipper Jones	SS	Atlanta Braves
1972	Dave Roberts	IF	San Diego Padres	1991	Brien Taylor	P	New York Yankees
1973	David Clyde	P	Texas Rangers	1992	Phil Nevin	3B	Houston Astros
1974	Bill Almon	IF	San Diego Padres	1993	Alex Rodriguez	SS	Seattle Mariners
1975	Danny Goodwin	C	California Angels	1994	Paul Wilson	P	New York Mets
1976	Floyd Bannister	P	Houston Astros	1995	Darin Erstad	OF/P	California Angels
1977	Harold Baines	OF	Chicago White Sox	1996	Kris Benson	P	Pittsburgh Pirates
1978	Bob Horner	3B	Atlanta Braves	1997	Matt Anderson	P	Detroit Tigers
1979	Al Chambers	OF	Seattle Mariners	1998	Pat Burrell	3B	Philadelphia Phillies
1980	Darryl Strawberry	OF	New York Mets	1999	Josh Hamilton	OF	T.B. Devil Rays
1981	Mike Moore	P	Seattle Mariners	2000	Adrian Gonzalez	1B	Florida Marlins
1982	Shawon Dunston	SS	Chicago Cubs	2001	Joe Mauer	C	Minnesota Twins
1983	Tim Belcher	P	Minnesota Twins				

Straight to the Majors

Since Major League baseball began its First-Year Player Draft in 1965, 19 selections have advanced directly to the major leagues without first playing in the minors.

Draft		Pos	Team	Draft		Pos	Team
1967	Mike Adamson, USC	P	Baltimore	1978	Tim Conroy, Gateway HS (Pa.)	P	Oakland
1969	Steve Dunning, Stanford	P	Cleveland		Bob Horner, Arizona St.	3B	Atlanta
1971	Pete Broberg, Dartmouth	P	Washington		Brian Milner, Southwest HS (Tex.)	C	Toronto
	Rob Ellis, Michigan St.	OF	Milwaukee		Mike Morgan, Valley HS (Nev.)	P	Oakland
	Burt Hooton, Texas	P	Chicago-NL	1985	Pete Incaviglia, Oklahoma St.	OF	Montreal
1972	Dave Roberts, Oregon	3B	San Diego	1988	Jim Abbott, Michigan	P	California
1973	Dick Ruthven, Fresno St.	P	Philadelphia	1989	John Olerud, Washington St.	1B	Toronto
	David Clyde, Westchester HS (Tex.)	P	Texas	1995	Ariel Prieto, Fajardo U (Cuba)	P	Oakland
	Dave Winfield, Minnesota	OF	San Diego	2000	Xavier Nady, California	3B	San Diego
	Eddie Bane, Arizona St.	P	Minnesota				

College Football

Sooners coach **Bob Stoops** raises the Sears Trophy following his team's Orange Bowl win.

Oklahoma Stoops to Another Level

Oklahoma's defense locks down Florida State's high-powered offense for a national title.

Chris Fowler
is the host of ESPN's College GameDay

The college football season was over, but the Oklahoma Sooners were still swarming.

In the postgame emptiness of Miami's Pro Player Stadium, the new champions had invaded our College GameDay set on the far corner of the field. About 50 of them surrounded us. Would our suddenly flimsy-feeling platform hold up under a couple of unexpected extra tons of human bulk? Our crew looked legitimately concerned.

Headsets were slapped on Sooner stars Josh Heupel and Torrance Marshall and they shouted answers over their jubilant teammates. The segments were fun and lively, and fortunately, our set survived the Sooner assault.

The same could not be said for Florida State's offense. Seminole quarterback Chris Weinke and company had just been strangled, suffocated by the most dominant defensive effort in any championship game, ever. The Sooners controlled the evening like they controlled the stage,

claiming a 13–2 Orange Bowl victory for their first national championship in 15 years.

Abandoned by academic casualty Snoop Minnis, his top receiver, and robbed of a running game by the Sooners' impressive lateral speed, Weinke, the Heisman winner, had never looked so helpless. An offensive attack that routinely amassed 500 yards and 40 points a game and, even in defeat, cut to ribbons an exhausted University of Miami defense, was reduced to repeated three-and-outs. Only an Oklahoma punt snap wilder than a Rick Ankiel fastball, which led to a safety, spoiled the potential shutout.

We were honored that the Sooners had come to our corner of the field for their postgame pep rally. It was role-reversal. We had been shadowing their unlikely championship journey for the last three months.

It was an amazing season to witness. Teams coming off a loss in the Independence Bowl, with a preseason

AP/Wide World Photos

The Oklahoma Sooners *celebrate their national title on stage following their Orange Bowl win.*

ranking of 19, are just not supposed to reel off 13 straight victories and cart home the Sears Trophy as national champs. A true Cinderella is rarer in today's college football than a well-dressed bowl rep.

Many images of the Sooners' 2000 uprising remain. On the fringe of the postgame glee following Oklahoma's breakthrough triumph at Kansas State in October two of Bob Stoops' Sooner assistants shared wide smiles and a heartfelt hug.

Mark Mangino and Brent Venables had returned to Manhattan, Kan., and beaten former boss and Wildcat head coach Bill Snyder. They still respected the man but relished besting Snyder, the

taskmaster they had toiled under (and in Venables' case played for) until switching sides to follow Mike Stoops to big brother Bob's OU staff.

Since then, old friendships had soured. For Mangino, Venables and the Stoops brothers, it made the victory much sweeter. The nine-point underdog Sooners had whipped the second-ranked Wildcats and they were on their way back to the top of the national-title picture.

The march appeared halted just a couple of weeks later. Old enemy Nebraska had rumbled to a quick and easy two-touchdown lead, silencing a Sooner home crowd that, beneath a veneer of bravado, had deep-down doubts about the team's mettle.

AP/Wide World Photos

*FSU quarterback and Heisman winner **Chris Weinke** had Sooners in his face all night at the Orange Bowl.*

After all, weren't these mostly the same players who had stumbled and bumbled under John Blake's tutelage?

Well, yes. One of the exceptions was Heupel, the quarterback who had somehow found his way to Oklahoma from South Dakota, via a junior college in Utah, thanks to an assistant coach who came from Kentucky and has since moved on to west Texas. Heupel's circuitous journey to stardom was as unorthodox as his southpaw delivery.

He would zip short sidearm darts under the outstretched arms of oncoming rushers to one of several criss-crossing targets. Or he might loop wobbly arcs down the sideline, like the one

Andre Woolfolk acrobatically snatched while flat on his back, and tangled up with a Nebraska defender.

It was the catch of the year and a few moments later OU was in the end zone, its skeptical crowd in delirium. Confidence and momentum had been seized. The Cornhuskers were buried in an avalanche of 31 straight points. Oklahoma went to #1 the next day.

From then onward, nothing came easily. Fueled by the unmatched spirit of their fans, the Aggies of Texas A&M had OU in deep trouble, until linebacker Marshall positioned himself in the path

continued on page 134 ▶

Lee Corso's Ten Biggest Stories of the Year in College Football

10 Lee Corso's rental car is struck by lightning just before the Black Coaches Association Classic in Blacksburg, Va. between Virginia Tech and Georgia Tech. Coaches around the country were overheard saying, "Too bad Corso wasn't in it at the time."

9 Michael Vick opts to take his considerable talent to the NFL after two seasons as Virginia Tech's quarterback.

8 Oregon State and South Carolina join college football's elite with big seasons. Oregon State enjoys back-to-back winning seasons for the first time since 1969 and whips Notre Dame, 41–9, in the Fiesta Bowl. Meanwhile South Carolina rebounds from an 0–11 record in 1999 and caps an 8–4 season by defeating the Ohio State Buckeyes, 24–7, in the Outback Bowl.

7 Veteran coaches LaVell Edwards (BYU), Don Nehlen (West Virginia), George Welsh (Virginia) and Dick Tomey (Arizona) announce their retirement.

6 Florida loses to Florida State and Miami by a combined score of 67–27 and is only #3 in the state of Florida.

5 Ohio State fires coach John Cooper after season-ending losses to arch-rival Michigan and then South Carolina in the Outback Bowl. Despite an 8–4 record and a 111–43–4 career mark, Cooper was only 2–10–1 against Michigan and 3–8 in bowls while at Ohio State.

4 Not only does Joe Paterno fail to get seven wins to break Bear Bryant's major-college record of 323 victories, but Penn State (5-7) records only the second losing season in his 35 years with the Nittany Lions.

3 Alabama, one of college football's premier programs, stumbles to a 3–8 record. Its 'Bama's worst season since 1957 and results in the firing of Mike DuBose and the hiring of Dennis Franchione from TCU.

2 The furor surrounding the Bush/Gore election mess in Florida pales in comparison to the uproar when the Bowl Championship Series rankings pick Florida State, #3 in the polls, over #2 Miami to face Oklahoma in the Orange Bowl.

1 Oklahoma returns to national prominence by winning its seventh national championship, and first in 15 years, with a convincing 13–2 upset victory over Florida State in the 2001 Orange Bowl.

of a short pass and rambled the other way for a turnaround touchdown.

Late defensive heroics were also required at Oklahoma State, which had frustrated Heupel all game with gimmicky wrinkles. Surviving a grudge match with K-State in the Big 12 Championship on a frigid night in Arrowhead was the final tension- packed test before Oklahoma completed its mission at the Orange Bowl.

The rapid rebirth of OU football had surprised everybody except perhaps Stoops. The Sooner boss was born of coaching bloodlines with an almost absurd confidence, the kind that fills those around him with belief. He's very smart and he knows it. And, a head coach for just two years, he has yet to feel the humbling sting of professional embarrassment that follows a sound whipping.

He will. Eventually, they all do. But in 2000, the Sooners' perfect campaign justified Stoops' supreme self-assurance. So, when the football season's final order was issued, you better believe OU stepped to it.

It was time to take the championship team photo, and when the coaches whistled, the players came running, jumping off our stage and crossing through camera shots in the midst of that live postgame segment.

The point had been made. The University of Oklahoma is back on college football's main stage. And it is likely to stay there, at least as long as Stoops does.

inside
···inside the numbers

Top-ranked Losers

In two years as Oklahoma's head coach Bob Stoops is 6–0 against Top 10 teams. Here is a look at how the Sooners have fared against top-ranked competition in the Stoops era.

2000	#2 Florida State	W, 13–2
2000	#7 Kansas State	W, 27–24
2000	#1 Nebraska	W, 31–14
2000	#3 Kansas State	W, 41–31
2000	#10 Texas	W, 63–14
1999	#10 Texas A&M	W, 51–6

Note: Above rankings reflect the ESPN/*USA Today* Coaches' Poll.

Saviors

Before the 1999 season, three great college coaches returned to the sidelines in seemingly hopeless situations. Look at 1998, the year before Dennis Erickson, Lou Holtz and John Robinson arrived. Now all three have taken their teams to bowl wins within two years. Below is a table with the win totals for each school over the past three seasons.

	'98	'99	'00
D. Erickson, Ore. St.	5	7	11
L. Holtz, S. Carolina	1	0	8
J. Robinson, UNLV	0	3	8

2000-2001 Season in Review

information please® SPORTS ALMANAC

Final AP Top 25 Poll

Voted on by panel of 71 sportswriters & broadcasters and released on Jan. 4, 2001, following the Orange Bowl: winning team receives the Bear Bryant Trophy, given since 1983; first place votes in parentheses, records, total points (based on 25 for 1st, 24 for 2nd, etc.) bowl game result, head coach and career record, preseason rank (released Aug. 6, 2000) and final regular season rank (released Dec. 4, 2000).

		Final Record	Points	Bowl Game	Head Coach	Aug. 6 Rank	Dec. 4 Rank
1	Oklahoma (71)	13-0	1775	won Orange	Bob Stoops (2 yrs: 20-5)	19	1
2	Miami-FL	11-1	1690	won Sugar	Butch Davis (6 yrs: 51-20)	5	2
3	Washington	11-1	1634	won Rose	Rick Neuheisel (5 yrs: 44-15)	13	4
4	Oregon St.	11-1	1539	won Fiesta	Dennis Erickson (15 yrs: 131-46-1)	NR	5
5	Florida St.	11-2	1488	lost Orange	Bobby Bowden (35 yrs: 315-87-4)	2	3
6	Virginia Tech	11-1	1432	won Gator	Frank Beamer (20 yrs: 141-84-4)	11	6
7	Oregon	10-2	1299	won Holiday	Mike Bellotti (11 yrs: 70-47-2)	NR	8
8	Nebraska	10-2	1282	won Alamo	Frank Solich (3 yrs: 31-7)	1	9
9	Kansas St.	11-3	1258	won Cotton	Bill Snyder (12 yrs: 99-43-1)	8	11
10	Florida	10-3	1128	lost Rose	Steve Spurrier (14 yrs: 132-38-2)	9	7
11	Michigan	9-3	1061	won Citrus	Lloyd Carr (6 yrs: 58-16)	6	17
12	Texas	9-3	894	lost Holiday	Mack Brown (17 yrs: 113-85-1)	7	12
13	Purdue	8-4	765	lost Rose	Joe Tiller (10 yrs: 72-46-1)	14	14
14	Colorado St.	10-2	640	won Liberty	Sonny Lubick (12 yrs: 88-48)	NR	23
15	Notre Dame	9-3	611	lost Fiesta	Bob Davie (4 yrs: 30-19)	NR	10
16	Clemson	9-3	563	lost Gator	Tommy Bowden (4 yrs: 33-13)	17	16
17	Georgia Tech	9-3	545	lost Peach	George O'Leary (7 yrs: 45-28-0)	NR	15
18	Auburn	9-4	498	lost Citrus	Tommy Tuberville (6 yrs: 39-30)	NR	20
19	South Carolina	8-4	486	won Outback	Lou Holtz (29 yrs: 224-110-7)	NR	NR
20	Georgia	8-4	430	won Oahu	Jim Donnan (11 yrs: 104-40-0)	10	24
21	TCU	10-2	406	lost Mobile	Dennis Franchione (18 yrs: 138-65-2) & Gary Patterson (1 yr: 0-1-0)	20	13
22	LSU	8-4	340	won Peach	Nick Saban (7 yrs: 51-30-1)	NR	NR
23	Wisconsin	9-4	208	won Sun	Barry Alvarez (11 yrs: 79-48-4)	4	NR
24	Mississippi St.	8-4	197	won Independence	Jackie Sherrill (23 yrs: 172-93-4)	NR	NR
25	Iowa St.	9-3	188	won Insight.com	Dan McCarney (6 yrs: 22-45-0)	NR	NR

Other teams receiving votes: 26. **Tennessee** (8-4, 187 points, lost Cotton); 27. **Toledo** (10-1, 173 pts, no bowl); 28. **Northwestern** (8-4, 103 pts, lost Alamo); 29. **Ohio State** (8-4, 62 pts, lost Outback); 30. **Louisville** (9-3, 53 pts, lost Liberty); 31. **Southern Mississippi** (8-4, 47 pts, won Mobile); 32. **Air Force** (9-3, 40 pts, won Silicon Valley); 33. **Boise State** (10-2, 24 pts, won Humanitarian); 34. **N.C. State** (8-4, 13 pts, won MicronPC.com); 35. **East Carolina** (8-4, 8 pts, won GalleryFurniture.com); 36. **Boston College** (7-5, 4 pts, won Aloha); 37. **Texas A&M** (7-5, 2 pts, lost Independence); 38. **UNLV** (8-5, 1 pt, won Las Vegas) and **West Virginia** (7-5, 1 pt, won Music City).

AP Preseason and Final Regular Season Polls

First place votes in parentheses.

Top 25
(Aug. 6, 2000)

		Pts
1	Nebraska (36)	1732
2	Florida St. (29)	1720
3	Alabama (3)	1570
4	Wisconsin (1)	1408
5	Miami-FL	1392
6	Michigan	1380
7	Texas (2)	1297
8	Kansas St.	1276
9	Florida	1255
10	Georgia	1226
11	Virginia Tech	1044
12	Tennessee	940
13	Washington	816
14	Purdue	751
15	USC	723
16	Ohio St.	601
17	Clemson	599
18	Mississippi	541
19	Oklahoma	455
20	TCU	404
21	Illinois	361
22	Penn St.	359
23	So. Miss.	224
24	Colorado	166
25	Michigan St.	145

Top 25
(Dec. 4, 2000)

		Pts
1	Oklahoma (67)	1768
2	Miami-FL (3)	1693
3	Florida St. (1)	1640
4	Washington	1571
5	Oregon St.	1473
6	Virginia Tech	1396
7	Florida	1349
8	Oregon	1207
9	Nebraska	1160
10	Notre Dame	1086
11	Kansas St.	1084
12	Texas	941
13	TCU	867
14	Purdue	810
15	Georgia Tech	803
16	Clemson	776
17	Michigan	754
18	Northwestern	553
19	Ohio State	481
20	Auburn	450
21	Tennessee	366
22	Louisville	232
23	Colorado St.	198
24	Georgia	110
25	Toledo	84

2000-2001 Bowl Games

Listed by bowls matching highest-ranked teams as of final regular season AP poll (released Dec. 4, 2000). Attendance figures indicate tickets sold.

Bowl		Winner	Regular Season		Loser	Regular Season	Score	Date	Attendance
Orange	#1	Oklahoma	12-0	#3	Florida St.	11-1	13-2	Jan. 3	76,835
Sugar	#2	Miami-FL	10-1	#7	Florida	10-2	37-20	Jan. 2	64,407
Rose	#4	Washington	10-1	#14	Purdue	8-3	34-24	Jan. 1	94,392
Fiesta	#5	Oregon St.	10-1	#10	Notre Dame	9-2	41-9	Jan. 1	75,428
Gator	#6	Virginia Tech	10-1	#16	Clemson	9-2	41-20	Jan. 1	68,741
Holiday	#8	Oregon	9-2	#12	Texas	9-2	35-30	Dec. 29	63,278
Alamo	#9	Nebraska	9-2	#18	Northwestern	8-3	66-17	Dec. 30	60,028
Cotton	#11	Kansas St.	10-3	#21	Tennessee	8-3	35-21	Jan. 1	63,465
Mobile		So. Miss.	7-4	#13	TCU	10-1	28-21	Dec. 20	40,300
Peach		LSU	7-4	#15	Georgia Tech	9-2	28-14	Dec. 29	73,614
Citrus	#17	Michigan	8-3	#20	Auburn	9-3	31-28	Jan. 1	66,928
Outback		South Carolina	7-4	#19	Ohio St.	8-3	24-7	Jan. 1	65,229
Liberty	#23	Colorado St.	9-2	#22	Louisville	9-2	22-17	Dec. 29	58,302
Oahu	#24	Georgia	7-4		Virginia	6-5	37-14	Dec. 24	24,187
Motor City		Marshall	7-5		Cincinnati	7-4	25-14	Dec. 27	52,911
Sun		Wisconsin	8-4		UCLA	6-5	21-20	Dec. 29	49,093
Insight.com		Iowa St.	8-3		Pittsburgh	7-4	37-29	Dec. 28	41,813
Aloha		Boston College	6-5		Arizona St.	6-5	31-17	Dec. 25	24,397
MicronPC.com		N.C. State	7-4		Minnesota	6-5	38-30	Dec. 28	28,359
Independence		Mississippi St.	7-4		Texas A&M	7-5	43-41	Dec. 31	36,974
Humanitarian		Boise St.	9-2		UTEP	7-4	38-23	Dec. 28	26,203
Music City		West Virginia	6-5		Mississippi	7-4	49-38	Dec. 28	47,119
Las Vegas		UNLV	7-5		Arkansas	6-5	31-14	Dec. 21	29,113
Silicon Valley		Air Force	8-3		Fresno St.	7-4	37-34	Dec. 31	26,542
GalleryFurniture.com		East Carolina	7-4		Texas Tech	7-5	40-27	Dec. 27	33,899

FAVORITES:

Orange (Florida St. by 11); **Sugar** (Miami-FL by 6); **Rose** (Purdue by 1); **Fiesta** (Oregon St. by 3½); **Gator** (Virginia Tech by 6); **Holiday** (Texas by 7); **Alamo** (Nebraska by 14½); **Cotton** (Kansas St. by 3½); **Mobile** (TCU by 7); **Peach** (Georgia Tech by 8½); **Citrus** (Michigan by 7½); **Outback** (Ohio St. by 1½); **Liberty** (Colorado St. by 1½); **Oahu** (Georgia by 9½); **Motor City** (Cincinnati by 3); **Sun** (Wisconsin by 5); **Insight.com** (Pittsburgh by 1½); **Aloha** (Arizona St. by 3); **MicronPC.com** (Minnesota by 3½); **Independence** (Texas A&M by 1½); **Humanitarian** (Boise St. by 7); **Music City** (Mississippi by 3½); **Las Vegas** (UNLV by 1); **Silicon Valley** (Fresno St. by 1); **GalleryFurniture.com** (Texas Tech by 1).

PER TEAM PAYOUTS:

Nokia Sugar, Tostitos Fiesta, FedEx Orange and **Rose** ($13 million); **Capital One Florida Citrus** ($4 million); **Southwestern Bell Cotton** ($2.5 million); **Outback** ($2 million); **Culligan Holiday** ($1.9 million); **Chick-fil-A Peach** ($1.7 million); **Toyota Gator** ($1.4 million); **AXA Liberty** ($1.25 million); **Sylvania Alamo** ($1.2 million); **Sanford Independence** ($1.1 million); **Wells Fargo Sun** ($1 million); **Silicon Valley** ($975,000); **Jeep Aloha, Jeep Oahu, Las Vegas,** ($800,000); **Insight.com, GMAC Mobile, MicronPC.com, Ford Motor City, GalleryFurniture.com, Music City** and **Crucial.com Humanitarian** ($750,000).

Final BCS Rankings

The Bowl Championship Series rankings were used for the first time during the 1998 season to determine BCS bowl match-ups and revised slightly for the 1999 season. The final rankings were released Dec. 3, 2000. Note that S-rank refers to schedule rank and L refers to games lost.

		Polls		Computer Rankings										
		AP	ESPN	Bill.	D.I.	K.M.	NYT	D.R.	Sag.	S.H.	S.T.	Sched.	S-rank	L	Total
1	Oklahoma	1	1	3	2	3	1	3	2	1	11	0.44	0	3.30
2	Florida St.	3	3	2	1	1	2	1	1	3	2	0.08	1	5.37
3	Miami-FL	2	2	3	2	3	3	2	3	4	3	0.12	1	5.69
4	Washington	4	4	10	11	5	5	4	8	4	2	6	0.24	1	10.67
5	Va. Tech	5	6	5	5	4	4	7	5	7	6	14	0.56	1	12.20
6	Oregon St.	6	5	7	9	8	8	5	7	5	5	42	1.68	1	14.68
7	Florida	7	7	4	4	9	6	9	6	6	7	1	0.04	2	14.75
8	Nebraska	8	9	6	13	6	10	6	4	8	9	18	0.72	2	18.22
9	Kansas St.	9	11	8	12	11	12	8	9	11	12	29	1.16	3	24.30
10	Oregon	11	8	12	17	14	15	11	14	9	8	24	0.96	2	24.32
11	Notre Dame	10	10	14	15	15	8	12	16	10	10	25	1.00	1	25.07
12	Texas	12	12	11	6	9	11	10	10	12	15	84	3.36	2	27.22
13	Ga. Tech	17	15	9	8	10	7	14	11	13	11	44	1.76	2	29.62
14	TCU	16	13	16	7	12	20	15	12	14	20	95	3.80	1	33.01
15	Clemson	13	16	13	21	13	19	13	15	15	13	56	2.24	2	33.17

Explanation Key

Schedule Rank—Rank of schedule strength compared to other Division I-A teams divided by 25. This component is calculated by determining the cumulative wins/loss records of the team's opponents (66.6 percent) and the cumulative won/loss record of the team's opponents' opponents (33.3 percent).

Losses—One point for each loss during the season.

National Championship Game

Oklahoma and Florida State were ranked first and second, respectively, in the final Bowl Championship Series rankings (released Dec. 3, 2000) and according to the BCS plan met in the so-called National Championship Game at the Orange Bowl on Jan. 3. Opponents' records and AP rank listed below are day of game.

Oklahoma Sooners (12-0)

Date	AP Rank	Opponent	Result
Sept. 2	#19	UTEP (0-0)	55-14
Sept. 9	#20	Arkansas State (0-1)	45-7
Sept. 23	#17	Rice (1-2)	42-14
Sept. 30	#14	Kansas (2-1)	34-16
Oct. 7	#10	at #11 Texas (3-1)	63-14
Oct. 14	#8	at #2 Kansas State (6-0)	41-31
Oct. 28	#3	#1 Nebraska (7-0)	31-14
Nov. 4	#1	at Baylor (2-6)	56-7
Nov. 11	#1	at #24 Texas A&M (7-2)	35-31
Nov. 18	#1	Texas Tech (7-4)	27-13
Nov. 25	#1	at Oklahoma St. (3-7)	12-7
Dec. 2	#1	#8 Kansas St. (10-2)	27-24

Florida State Seminoles (11-1)

Date	AP Rank	Opponent	Result
Aug. 26	#2	BYU (0-0)	29-3
Sept. 9	#2	at Georgia Tech (1-0)	26-21
Sept. 16	#2	North Carolina (2-0)	63-14
Sept. 23	#2	Louisville (2-0)	31-0
Sept. 28	#2	at Maryland (2-1)	59-7
Oct. 7	#1	at #7 Miami-FL (3-1)	24-27
Oct. 14	#7	Duke (0-5)	63-14
Oct. 21	#6	Virginia (4-2)	37-3
Oct. 28	#6	at #21 N.C. State (5-1)	58-14
Nov. 4	#6	#10 Clemson (8-1)	54-7
Nov. 11	#3	at Wake Forest (1-7)	35-6
Nov. 18	#3	#4 Florida (9-1)	30-7

Final Statistics — Oklahoma

Passing (5 Att)

	Att	Cmp	Pct.	Yds	TD	Rate
Josh Heupel	472	305	64.6	3606	20	136.42
Nate Hybl	16	9	56.3	144	2	148.10

Interceptions: Heupel 15, Hybl 2.

Top Receivers

	No	Yds	Avg	Long	TD
Quentin Griffin	51	429	8.4	36	0
Antwone Savage	50	621	12.4	74	3
Andre Woolfolk	42	614	14.6	57	5
Curtis Fagan	41	606	14.8	51	7
Josh Norman	34	518	15.2	55	1
Trent Smith	31	323	10.4	50	3
Damian Mackey	30	298	9.9	42	1

Top Rushers

	Car	Yds	Avg	Long	TD
Quentin Griffin	200	823	4.1	49	17
Renaldo Works	89	393	4.4	75	5
Josh Heupel	83	167	2.0	21	7
Antwone Savage	12	160	13.3	40	1
Seth Littrell	24	78	3.3	11	1
Josh Norman	6	30	5.0	11	1
Jay Hunt	1	13	13.0	13	0
Andre Woolfolk	1	11	11.0	11	0

Most Touchdowns

	TD	Run	Rec	Ret	Pts
Quentin Griffin	17	17	0	0	102
Curtis Fagan	8	1	7	0	48
Josh Heupel	7	7	0	0	42
Renaldo Works	6	5	1	0	36
Andre Woolfolk	5	0	5	0	30
Antwone Savage	4	1	3	0	24
Trent Smith	3	0	3	0	18
J.T. Thatcher	3	0	0	3	18

Kicking

	FG/Att	Lg	PAT/Att	Pts
Tim Duncan	15/24	46	60/61	105

Punting

	No	Yds	Long	Blk	Avg
Jeff Ferguson	56	2437	66	3	43.5

Most Interceptions

J.T. Thatcher	8
Ontei Jones	5
Torrance Marshall	3

Most Sacks

Torrance Marshall	5
Corey Callens	5

Final Statistics — Florida State

Passing (5 Att)

	Att	Cmp	Pct.	Yds	TD	Rate
Chris Weinke	431	266	61.7	4167	33	163.09
Marcus Outzen	35	24	68.6	441	3	185.55

Interceptions: Weinke 11, Outzen 3.

Top Receivers

	No	Yds	Avg	Long	TD
Marvin Minnis	63	1340	21.3	98	11
Travis Minor	42	333	7.9	23	0
Anquan Boldin	41	664	16.2	60	6
Atrews Bell	37	675	18.2	48	10
Javon Walker	20	313	15.6	63	3
Robert Morgan	19	366	19.3	71	3

Top Rushers

	Car	Yds	Avg	Long	TD
Travis Minor	181	923	5.1	67	5
Jeff Chaney	71	346	4.9	29	3
Greg Jones	41	266	6.5	34	2
Davy Ford	38	239	6.3	82	3
William McCray	45	131	2.9	8	11
Nick Maddox	7	70	10.0	41	0
Randy Golightly	16	49	3.1	10	4
Marcus Outzen	15	27	1.8	13	0
Talman Gardner	2	24	12.0	29	0

Most Touchdowns

	TD	Run	Rec	Ret	Pts
Atrews Bell	11	1	10	0	66
Marvin Minnis	11	0	11	0	66
William McCray	8	8	0	0	48
Anquan Boldin	6	0	6	0	36
Travis Minor	5	5	0	0	30
Randy Golightly	4	4	0	0	24
Jeff Chaney	4	3	1	0	24

Kicking

	FG/Att	Lg	PAT/Att	Pts
Matt Munyon	3/8	44	18/22	27
Chance Gwaltney	5/7	39	18/20	33
Brett Cimorelli	6/9	38	23/24	41

Punting

	No	Yds	Long	Blk	Avg
Keith Cottrell	48	1983	60	0	41.3
Chance Gwaltney	1	39	39	0	39.0

Most Interceptions

Tay Cody	6

Most Sacks

Jamal Reynolds	12
Darnell Dockett	7

Orange Bowl

Tuesday, Jan. 3, 2001 at Pro Player Stadium, in Miami, Florida.

#3 **Florida St.** (ACC) 0   0   0   2   **—2**
#1 **Oklahoma** (Big 12) 3   0   3   7   **—13**

1st; 7:16; **Oklahoma**— Tim Duncan 27-yard field goal.
3rd; 04:24; **Oklahoma**— Duncan 42-yd field goal.
4th; 07:46; **Oklahoma**— Quentin Griffin 10-yd run (Duncan kick).
4th; 00:55; **Florida St.**— Safety, Jeff Ferguson was tackled in end zone.

Favorite: Florida St. by 11   **Attendance:** 76,835
Field: Grass   **Weather:** Mostly cloudy
Time: 3:37   **TV Rating:** 17.8/28 (ABC)
MVP: Torrance Marshall, Oklahoma LB

Team Statistics

	FSU	OU
Touchdowns	0	1
Rushing	0	1
Passing	0	0
Kick/Punt returns	0	0
Interception returns	0	0
Safeties	1	0
Time of possession	23:27	36:33
First downs	14	12
Rushing	1	2
Passing	12	10
Penalty	1	0
Total Plays	69	75
Carries/yards (includ. sacks)	17/27	36/56
Passing yards	274	214
Completions/attempts	25/52	25/39
Return yardage	21	48
Fumbles/lost	3/1	2/1
Penalties/yards	6/38	7/45
Punts/average	10/45.0	8/41.0
3rd down conversions	1/15	7/19
4th down conversions	0/2	0/1

INDIVIDUAL STATISTICS
Florida State Seminoles

Passing (5 Att)

	Att	Cmp	Pct.	Yds	TD	Int
Chris Weinke	51	25	49.0	274	0	2
Team	1	0	0.0	0	0	0
TOTAL	52	25	48.1	274	0	2

Rushing

	Car	Yds	Avg	Long	TD
Travis Minor	13	20	1.5	4	0
Chris Weinke	4	7	1.8	5	0
TOTAL	17	27	1.6	5	0

Receiving

	No	Yds	Avg	Long	TD
Atrews Bell	7	137	19.6	43	0
Travis Minor	5	9	1.8	5	0
Anquan Boldin	3	31	10.3	19	0
Robert Morgan	3	21	7.0	16	0
Randy Golightly	3	15	5.0	8	0
Javon Walker	1	25	25.0	25	0
Talman Gardner	1	16	16.0	16	0
Ryan Sprague	1	14	14.0	14	0
Nick Franklin	1	6	6.0	6	0
TOTAL	25	274	11.0	43	0

Field Goals

	20-29	30-39	40-49	50-59	Total
Brett Cimorelli	0-0	0-1	0-0	0-0	0-1

Punting

	No	Yds	Long	Blk	Avg
Keith Cottrell	10	447	58	0	44.7

Punt Returns

	No	Yds	Long	Avg	TD
Clevan Thomas	3	5	3	1.7	0
Nick Maddox	1	-3	0	-3.0	0
TOTAL	4	2	3	0.5	0

Kickoff Returns

	No	Yds	Long	Avg	TD
Slade Douglas	1	2	2	2.0	0
TOTAL	1	2	2	2.0	0

Sacks
Jamal Reynolds 1
David Warren 1
Darnell Dockett 1

Interceptions
Tay Cody 1

Oklahoma Sooners

Passing (5 Att)

	Att	Cmp	Pct.	Yds	TD	Int
Josh Heupel	39	25	64.1	214	0	1

Rushing

	Car	Yds	Avg	Long	TD
Quentin Griffin	11	40	3.6	10	1
Josh Heupel	13	23	1.8	7	0
Renaldo Works	6	16	2.7	7	0
Seth Littrell	2	8	4.0	5	0
Damian Mackey	2	5	2.5	5	0
Team	2	-36	-18.0	0	0
TOTAL	36	56	1.6	10	1

Receiving

	No	Yds	Avg	Long	TD
Quentin Griffin	6	23	3.8	12	0
Damian Mackey	4	23	5.8	11	0
Renaldo Works	4	3	0.8	4	0
Josh Norman	3	49	16.3	36	0
Andre Woolfolk	3	41	13.7	22	0
Antwone Savage	2	23	11.5	14	0
Trent Smith	2	13	6.5	8	0
Curtis Fagan	1	39	39.0	39	0
TOTAL	25	214	8.6	39	0

Field Goals

	20-29	30-39	40-49	50-59	Total
Tim Duncan	1-1	0-1	1-1	0-0	2-3

Punting

	No	Yds	Long	Blk	Avg
Jeff Ferguson	8	329	52	0	41.1

Punt Returns

	No	Yds	Long	Avg	TD
J.T. Thatcher	5	35	16	7.0	0

Kickoff Returns

	No	Yds	Long	Avg	TD
Antwone Savage	1	36	36	36.0	0

Sacks
Kory Klein 1

Interceptions
Torrance Marshall 1
Ontei Jones 1

Other Final Division I-A Polls

FWAA Poll

Voted on by a five-person panel comprised of Tony Barnhart of the *Atlanta Journal-Constitution*, Chris Dufresne of the *Los Angeles Times*, Blair Kerkhoff of the *Kansas City Star*, Dick Weiss of the *New York Daily News*, and Kelly Whiteside of *USA Today*. Each selector voted for one team. Winning team receives the Grantland Rice Award, given since 1954.

Oklahoma (5)

NFF's MacArthur Bowl

In the past the MacArthur Bowl was awarded following a vote by a panel of members of the National Football Foundation and College Football Hall of Fame but since the advent of the Bowl Championship Series it has been awarded to the BCS champion; winning team receives the NFF's MacArthur Bowl, given since 1959; The MacArthur Bowl was the gift of an anonymous donor in the name of General Douglas MacArthur who served for several years as chairman of the Foundation's National Advisory Board. Almost 400 ounces of silver went into the bowl which represents a huge stadium with rows of seats carved in relief.

Oklahoma

AP Weekly Ratings

The Associated Press Top 25 college football polls on a weekly basis are listed below. The table starts with the preseason and progresses through the season.

	Aug		Sep				Oct					Nov				Dec	Jan
	Pre	28	4	11	18	25	2	9	16	23	30	6	13	20	27	4	4
Nebraska	1	1	1	1	1	1	2	1	1	1	5	4	10	9	10	9	8
Florida St.	2	2	2	2	2	2	1	7	6	6	4	3	3	3	3	3	5
Alabama	3	3	13	15	NR	NR	NR	NR	NR	NR	NR	NR	NR	NR	NR	NR	NR
Wisconsin	4	4	5	4	7	17	24	NR	NR	NR	NR	NR	NR	NR	NR	2	23
Miami-FL	5	5	4	12	12	10	7	4	4	4	3	2	2	2	2	2	2
Michigan	6	6	3	3	10	9	6	18	16	15	12	20	19	16	16	17	11
Texas	7	7	6	5	15	13	11	25	NR	22	20	19	14	12	12	12	12
Kansas St.	8	8	7	7	4	5	4	2	10	10	19	16	9	8	8	11	9
Florida	9	9	8	6	3	3	12	10	8	8	6	5	4	7	7	7	10
Georgia	10	10	9	23	24	25	19	14	12	13	17	14	22	19	24	24	20
Virginia Tech	11	11	10	8	5	4	3	3	2	2	2	8	7	6	6	6	6
Tennessee	12	13	12	11	13	11	21	NR	NR	NR	NR	NR	NR	25	21	21	NR
Washington	13	14	15	9	8	6	13	11	9	9	8	7	6	4	4	4	3
Purdue	14	15	14	13	21	22	NR	21	17	16	11	9	17	14	14	14	13
USC	15	12	11	10	9	8	18	NR	NR	NR	NR	NR	NR	NR	NR	NR	NR
Ohio St.	16	16	18	17	14	12	8	6	14	12	16	13	12	21	20	19	NR
Clemson	17	17	17	16	11	7	5	5	5	5	10	17	16	15	15	16	16
Mississippi	18	18	19	NR	NR	NR	NR	NR	NR	NR	NR	NR	NR	NR	NR	NR	NR
Oklahoma	19	19	20	18	17	14	10	8	3	3	1	1	1	1	1	1	1
TCU	20	20	22	20	18	16	14	12	11	11	9	18	15	13	13	13	21
Illinois	21	21	21	19	19	24	NR	NR	NR	NR	NR	NR	NR	NR	NR	NR	NR
Penn St.	22	NR	NR	NR	NR	NR	NR	NR	NR	NR	NR	NR	NR	NR	NR	NR	NR
So. Mississippi	23	22	25	25	22	21	17	16	15	14	13	25	24	NR	NR	NR	NR
Colorado	24	23	NR	NR	NR	NR	NR	NR	NR	NR	NR	NR	NR	NR	NR	NR	NR
Michigan St.	25	24	24	22	23	18	NR	NR	NR	NR	NR	NR	NR	NR	NR	NR	NR
Texas A&M	NR	25	NR	NR	NR	NR	NR	NR	NR	24	23	21	22	NR	NR	NR	NR
UCLA	NR	NR	16	14	6	15	16	13	23	NR	NR	NR	NR	NR	NR	NR	NR
Notre Dame	NR	NR	23	21	16	20	25	20	20	19	15	11	11	11	11	10	15
Auburn	NR	NR	NR	24	20	19	15	19	NR	25	23	22	18	17	18	20	18
Mississippi St.	NR	NR	NR	NR	25	NR	20	15	13	20	18	15	13	23	NR	NR	24
Oregon	NR	NR	NR	NR	NR	20	9	9	7	7	7	6	5	10	9	8	7
South Carolina	NR	NR	NR	NR	NR	23	NR	24	18	17	22	21	25	NR	NR	NR	19
Northwestern	NR	NR	NR	NR	NR	NR	22	17	25	23	21	12	23	20	19	18	NR
Oregon St.	NR	NR	NR	NR	NR	NR	23	23	19	18	14	10	8	5	5	5	4
Arizona	NR	NR	NR	NR	NR	NR	NR	22	21	24	NR	NR	NR	NR	NR	NR	NR
Minnesota	NR	NR	NR	NR	NR	NR	NR	22	NR	NR	NR	NR	NR	NR	NR	NR	NR
N.C. State	NR	NR	NR	NR	NR	NR	NR	24	21	NR	NR	NR	NR	NR	NR	NR	NR
Georgia Tech	NR	NR	NR	NR	NR	NR	NR	NR	NR	25	24	20	18	17	17	15	17
LSU	NR	NR	NR	NR	NR	NR	NR	NR	NR	NR	NR	NR	24	NR	NR	NR	22
Louisville	NR	NR	NR	NR	NR	NR	NR	NR	NR	NR	NR	NR	NR	NR	22	22	NR
Colorado St.	NR	NR	NR	NR	NR	NR	NR	NR	NR	NR	NR	NR	NR	NR	23	23	14
Toledo	NR	NR	NR	NR	NR	NR	NR	NR	NR	NR	NR	NR	NR	NR	25	25	NR
Iowa St.	NR	NR	NR	NR	NR	NR	NR	NR	NR	NR	NR	NR	NR	NR	NR	NR	25

NCAA Division I-A Final Standings

Standings based on conference games only; overall records include postseason games.

Atlantic Coast Conference

	Conference				Overall			
	W	L	PF	PA	W	L	PF	PA
*Florida St.	8	0	395	86	11	2	511	136
*Clemson	6	2	280	189	9	3	416	253
*Georgia Tech	6	2	284	164	9	3	386	237
*Virginia	5	3	138	169	6	6	242	292
*N.C. State	4	4	221	239	8	4	379	338
North Carolina	3	5	199	243	6	5	269	284
Maryland	3	5	168	217	5	6	247	284
Wake Forest	1	7	106	299	2	9	181	362
Duke	0	8	143	328	0	11	155	430

Bowls (1-4): Florida St. (lost Orange); Clemson (lost Gator); Georgia Tech (lost Peach); Virginia (lost Oahu); N.C. State (won MicronPC.com).

Big East Conference

	Conference				Overall			
	W	L	PF	PA	W	L	PF	PA
*Miami-FL	7	0	310	67	11	1	506	190
*Virginia Tech	6	1	260	156	11	1	484	269
*Pittsburgh	4	3	174	167	7	5	196	247
Syracuse	4	3	162	145	6	5	294	212
*Boston College	3	4	173	205	7	5	378	277
*West Virginia	3	4	179	226	7	5	356	363
Temple	1	6	117	192	4	7	224	269
Rutgers	0	7	95	312	3	8	233	399

Bowls (4-1): Miami-FL (won Sugar); Virginia Tech (won Gator); Pittsburgh (lost Insight.com); Boston College (won Aloha); West Virginia (won Music City).

Big Ten Conference

	Conference				Overall			
	W	L	PF	PA	W	L	PF	PA
*Michigan	6	2	273	164	9	3	404	229
*Northwestern	6	2	337	271	8	4	441	400
*Purdue	6	2	243	199	8	4	381	266
*Ohio St.	5	3	227	155	8	4	331	222
*Wisconsin	4	4	199	172	9	4	328	265
*Minnesota	4	4	247	238	6	6	375	318
Penn St.	4	4	186	221	5	7	264	293
Iowa	3	5	148	210	3	9	203	330
Illinois	2	6	193	252	5	6	294	286
Michigan St.	2	6	123	178	5	6	197	233
Indiana	2	6	223	339	3	8	337	427

Bowls (2-4): Michigan (won Citrus); Northwestern (lost Alamo); Purdue (lost Rose); Ohio St. (lost Outback); Wisconsin (won Sun); Minnesota (lost MicronPC.com).

Conference Bowling Results

Postseason records for 2000 season.

	W-L	Pct
Mountain West	3-0	1.000
Big West	1-0	1.000
Mid-American	1-0	1.000
Big East	4-1	.800
Pac-10	3-2	.600
Big 12	4-3	.571
Conference USA	2-2	.500
SEC	4-5	.444
Big Ten	2-4	.333
ACC	1-4	.200
WAC	0-3	.000

Big 12 Conference

North	Conference				Overall			
	W	L	PF	PA	W	L	PF	PA
*Nebraska	6	2	338	163	10	2	522	230
*Kansas St.	6	3	302	213	11	3	549	261
*Iowa St.	5	3	220	242	9	3	343	322
Colorado	3	5	200	222	3	8	252	284
Kansas	2	6	179	308	4	7	261	359
Missouri	2	6	186	253	3	8	255	348

South	Conference				Overall			
	W	L	PF	PA	W	L	PF	PA
*Oklahoma	9	0	326	157	13	0	481	194
*Texas	7	1	301	160	9	3	455	232
*Texas A&M	5	3	201	152	7	5	348	239
*Texas Tech	3	5	202	212	7	6	330	278
Oklahoma St.	1	7	137	249	3	8	202	303
Baylor	0	8	82	343	2	9	139	397

Big 12 championship game: Oklahoma 27, Kansas St. 24 (Dec. 2).

Bowls (4-3): Oklahoma (won Orange); Nebraska (won Alamo); Kansas St. (won Cotton); Iowa St. (won Insight.com); Texas (lost Holiday); Texas A&M (lost Independence); Texas Tech (lost GalleryFurniture.com).

Big West Conference

	Conference				Overall			
	W	L	PF	PA	W	L	PF	PA
*Boise St.	5	0	267	107	10	2	532	274
Utah St.	4	1	174	160	5	6	292	356
Idaho	3	2	140	177	5	6	321	377
New Mexico St.	1	4	167	181	3	8	295	357
North Texas	1	4	84	168	3	8	162	300
Arkansas St.	1	4	152	191	1	10	247	410

Bowl (1-0): Boise St. (won Humanitarian).

Conference USA

	Conference				Overall			
	W	L	PF	PA	W	L	PF	PA
*Louisville	6	1	255	159	9	3	405	268
*East Carolina	5	2	206	125	8	4	370	256
*Cincinnati	5	2	187	165	7	5	289	285
*Southern Miss.	4	3	180	150	8	4	314	203
UAB	3	4	144	156	7	4	238	192
Tulane	3	4	192	205	6	5	329	346
Memphis	2	5	109	146	4	7	176	199
Houston	2	5	154	249	3	8	211	370
Army	1	6	129	204	1	10	224	372

Bowls (2-2): Louisville (lost Liberty); East Carolina (won GalleryFurniture.com); Cincinnati (lost Motor City); Southern Miss. (won Mobile).

Mid-American Conference

Eastern	Conference				Overall			
	W	L	PF	PA	W	L	PF	PA
*Marshall	5	1	211	136	8	5	367	297
Akron	5	1	198	112	6	5	333	295
Ohio	4	2	191	126	7	4	343	208
Miami-OH	4	2	164	152	6	5	272	286
Buffalo	2	4	104	189	2	9	177	452
Bowling Green	1	5	100	125	2	9	174	289
Kent St.	0	6	67	195	1	10	128	359

Western	Conference				Overall			
	W	L	PF	PA	W	L	PF	PA
Toledo	4	1	166	62	10	1	400	125
Western Michigan	4	1	160	60	9	3	359	139
Northern Illinois	2	3	161	149	6	5	409	280
Ball St.	2	3	91	164	5	6	212	349
Eastern Michigan	2	3	98	150	3	8	209	350
Central Michigan	1	4	76	167	2	9	137	376

MAC championship game: Marshall 19, Western Michigan 14.

Bowl (1-0): Marshall (won Motor City).

Mountain West Conference

	Conference				Overall		
	W	L	PF	PA	W	L	PF	PA
*Colorado State 6	1	217	150	10	2	363	225
*Air Force.........5	2	230	198	9	3	421	312
*UNLV...........4	3	167	142	8	5	370	275
BYU............4	3	159	146	6	6	280	310
New Mexico 3	4	141	125	5	7	229	249
Utah 3	4	154	114	4	7	234	207
San Diego St......3	4	144	162	3	8	170	273
Wyoming.........0	7	87	262	1	10	170	393

Bowls (3-0): Colorado St. (won Liberty), Air Force (won Silicon Valley); UNLV (won Las Vegas).

Pacific 10 Conference

	Conference				Overall		
	W	L	PF	PA	W	L	PF	PA
*Oregon St........7	1	275	161	11	1	400	212
*Washington 7	1	258	183	11	1	387	270
*Oregon..........7	2	215	172	10	2	351	249
Stanford 4	4	193	210	5	6	261	294
*Arizona St.........3	5	229	235	6	6	313	303
*UCLA...........3	5	251	282	6	6	353	368
Arizona.........3	5	203	204	6	6	254	237
USC............2	6	280	256	5	7	309	337
Washington St....2	6	167	260	4	7	281	354
California........2	6	204	240	3	8	246	295

Bowls (3-2): Oregon St. (won Fiesta); Washington (won Rose); Oregon (won Holiday); Arizona St. (lost Aloha); UCLA (lost Sun).

Southeastern Conference

	Conference				Overall		
Eastern	W	L	PF	PA	W	L	PF	PA
*Florida 8	1	346	187	10	3	468	273
*Georgia 5	3	213	164	8	4	331	212
*South Carolina 5	3	173	152	8	4	283	181
*Tennessee 5	3	251	176	8	4	380	247
Vanderbilt........1	7	120	223	3	8	193	273
Kentucky........0	8	152	300	2	9	254	383

Western

	Conference				Overall		
Western	W	L	PF	PA	W	L	PF	PA
*Auburn 6	3	184	172	9	4	316	266
*LSU 5	3	196	195	8	4	320	235
*Mississippi St. 4	4	225	199	8	4	390	306
*Mississippi 4	4	187	210	7	5	352	329
*Arkansas.........3	5	136	221	6	6	278	289
Alabama 3	5	166	150	3	8	228	246

SEC championship game: Florida beat Auburn, 28-6 (Dec. 2).

Bowls (4-5): Florida (lost Sugar); Auburn (lost Citrus); Georgia (won Oahu); South Carolina (won Outback); Tennessee (lost Cotton); LSU (won Peach); Mississippi St. (won Independence); Arkansas (lost Las Vegas); Mississippi (lost Music City).

Western Athletic Conference

	Conference				Overall		
	W	L	PF	PA	W	L	PF	PA
*TCU..............7	1	293	89	10	2	431	134
*UTEP............7	1	283	167	8	4	378	336
*Fresno St.........6	2	235	144	7	5	317	251
San Jose St. 5	3	250	240	7	5	374	357
Tulsa 4	4	155	165	5	7	240	283
Rice.............2	6	186	215	3	8	237	322
Hawaii 2	6	197	276	3	9	294	399
SMU 2	6	118	248	3	9	181	352
Nevada 1	7	144	317	2	10	207	464

Bowls (0-3): TCU (lost Mobile); UTEP (lost Humanitarian); Fresno St. (lost Silicon Valley).

I-A Independents

	W	L	PF	PA
*Notre Dame...................9	3	353	267
Central Florida..................7	4	333	221
Middle Tennessee 6	5	350	316
Connecticut 3	8	210	368
Louisiana Tech 3	9	317	396
Navy..........................1	10	182	391
UL-Monroe 1	10	96	415
UL-Lafayette 1	10	171	355

Bowls (0-1): Notre Dame (lost Fiesta).

NCAA Division I-A Individual Leaders

REGULAR SEASON

Total Offense

		Rushing				Passing		Total Offense			
	Cl	Car	Gain	Loss	Net	Att	Yds	Plays	Yds	YdsPP	YdsPG
Drew Brees, Purdue...............	Sr.	91	601	55	546	473	3393	564	3939	6.98	358.1
Jared Lorenzen, Kentucky..........	Fr.	76	321	181	140	559	3687	635	3827	6.03	347.9
Chris Weinke, Florida St............	Sr.	30	50	147	-97	431	4167	461	4070	8.83	339.2
Bart Hendricks, Boise St............	Sr.	85	415	146	269	347	3364	432	3633	8.41	330.3
Timmy Chang, Hawaii	Fr.	23	25	74	-49	469	3041	492	2992	6.08	299.2
Josh Heupel, Oklahoma	Sr.	70	270	126	144	433	3392	503	3536	7.03	294.7
John Welsh, Idaho................	Jr.	80	237	209	28	399	3171	479	3199	6.68	290.8
Patrick Ramsey, Tulane	Jr.	39	120	67	53	389	2833	428	2886	6.74	288.6
Byron Leftwich, Marshall..........	So.	82	287	204	83	457	3358	539	3441	6.38	286.8
Kliff Kingsbury, Texas Tech	So.	78	248	229	19	584	3412	662	3431	5.18	285.9

All-Purpose Yards

	Cl	Gm	Rush	Rec	PR	KOR	Total Yds	YdsPG
Emmett White, Utah St..........................	Jr.	11	1322	592	183	531	2628	238.91
LaDainian Tomlinson, TCU	Sr.	11	2158	40	0	0	2198	199.82
Robert Kilow, Arkansas St.......................	Sr.	10	42	1002	133	724	1901	190.10
Damien Anderson, Northwestern	Sr.	11	1914	120	0	0	2034	184.91
Justin McCareins, N. Illinois	Sr.	11	73	1168	362	411	2014	183.09
Brock Forsey, Boise St.	So.	10	914	399	0	517	1830	183.00
Deonce Whitaker, San Jose St.	Sr.	10	1577	37	0	151	1765	176.50
Hodges Mitchell, Texas.........................	Sr.	11	1118	386	427	0	1931	175.55
Michael Bennett, Wisconsin.....................	Jr.	10	1598	23	0	94	1715	171.50
Koren Robinson, N.C. State	So.	11	95	1061	218	506	1880	170.91

Utah State
Emmett White
All-Purpose Yards

Virginia Tech
Lee Suggs
Scoring

Louisiana Tech
James Jordan
Receptions

Purdue
Drew Brees
Total Offense

Passing Efficiency
(Minimum 15 attempts per game)

	Cl	Gm	Att	Cmp	Cmp Pct	Int	Int Pct	Yds	Yds/ Att	TD	TD Pct	Rating Points
Bart Hendricks, Boise St.	Sr.	11	347	210	60.52	8	2.31	3364	9.69	35	10.09	170.6
Chris Weinke, Florida St.	Sr.	12	431	266	61.72	11	2.55	4167	9.67	33	7.66	163.1
Rex Grossman, Florida	Fr.	11	212	131	61.79	7	3.30	1866	8.80	21	9.91	161.8
Casey Printers, TCU	So.	11	176	102	57.95	6	3.41	1584	9.00	16	9.09	156.7
Ken Dorsey, Miami-FL	So.	11	322	188	58.39	5	1.55	2737	8.50	25	7.76	152.3
George Godsey, Ga. Tech	Jr.	11	349	222	63.61	6	1.72	2906	8.33	23	6.59	151.9
John Turman, Pittsburgh	Sr.	11	233	128	54.94	7	3.00	2135	9.16	18	7.73	151.4
Rocky Perez, UTEP	Sr.	11	338	200	59.17	6	1.78	2661	7.87	26	7.69	147.1
Mike Thiessen, Air Force	Sr.	11	195	112	57.44	5	2.56	1687	8.65	13	6.67	147.0
Ryan Schneider, C. Florida	Fr.	9	286	177	61.89	11	3.85	2334	8.16	21	7.34	147.0
Casey Clausen, Tennessee	Fr.	9	194	121	62.37	6	3.09	1473	7.59	15	7.73	145.5
Dave Ragone, Louisville	So.	11	354	216	61.02	11	3.11	2621	7.40	27	7.63	142.2

Rushing

	Cl	Car	Yds	TD	YdsPG
LaDainian Tomlinson, TCU	Sr.	369	2158	22	196.18
Damien Anderson, Northwestern	Sr.	293	1914	22	174.00
Michael Bennett, Wisconsin	Jr.	294	1598	10	159.80
Deonce Whitaker, San Jose St.	Sr.	224	1577	15	157.70
Anthony Thomas, Michigan	Sr.	287	1551	16	141.00
Ken Simonton, Oregon St.	Jr.	266	1474	18	134.00
Chester Taylor, Toledo	Sr.	250	1470	18	133.64
Robert Sanford, W. Mich.	Sr.	293	1571	18	130.92
Rudi Johnson, Auburn	Jr.	324	1567	13	130.58
Ennis Haywood, Iowa St.	Jr.	230	1237	8	123.70
T.J. Duckett, Michigan St.	So.	240	1353	7	123.00
Thomas Hammock, N. Illinois	So.	215	1083	16	120.33

Games: All played 11, except Bennett, Whitaker and Haywood (10) and Sanford and Johnson (12) and Hammock (9).

Receptions

	Cl	No	Yds	TD	P/Gm
James Jordan, La. Tech	Sr.	109	1003	4	9.08
Tyson Hinshaw, C. Fla.	Sr.	89	1089	13	8.09
Kenny Christian, E. Michigan	Jr.	78	808	3	7.80
Robert Kilow, Arkansas St.	Sr.	72	1002	3	7.20
Brian Robinson, Houston	So.	79	892	6	7.18
DeRonnie Pitts, Stanford	Sr.	77	882	8	7.00
Kevin Kasper, Iowa	Sr.	82	1010	7	6.83
Antonio Bryant, Pittsburgh	So.	68	1302	11	6.80
Adrian Burnette, Tulane	Sr.	74	1075	14	6.73
Kendall Newson, Md. Tenn. St.	Jr.	74	945	5	6.73
Don Shoals, Tulsa	Jr.	80	1195	5	6.67
Vinny Sutherland, Purdue	Sr.	65	926	11	6.50

Games: All played 11, except Jordan, Kasper and Shoals (12), Christian, Kilow, Bryant and Sutherland (10).

Field Goals

	Cl	FG/Att	Pct	Lg
Jonathan Ruffin, Cincinnati	So.	26/29	89.7	42
Dan Nystrom, Minnesota	So.	22/34	64.7	52
Kris Stockton, Texas	Sr.	22/26	84.6	47
Dave Stultz, Ohio St.	Sr.	19/23	82.6	49
Rhett Gallego, UAB	So.	19/24	79.2	47
Dave Adams, Air Force	Sr.	19/24	79.2	54
Owen Pochman, BYU	Sr.	19/24	79.2	56

Games: All played 11, except Pochman (12).
Longest FG of season: 56 yards by Owen Pochman, BYU vs. New Mexico (Nov. 18).

Interceptions

	Cl	No	Yds	TD	Lg
Dwight Smith, Akron	Sr.	10	208	2	68
Anthony Floyd, Louisville	So.	10	152	1	51
Ed Reed, Miami-FL	Jr.	8	92	2	44
J.T. Thatcher, Oklahoma	Sr.	8	162	1	85
Dan Dawson, Rice	Jr.	7	206	1	68
Nate Jackson, Hawaii	Jr.	7	57	0	32

Games: All played 11 except Thatcher and Jackson (12)

Scoring

Non-Kickers

	Cl	TD	Pts	P/Gm
Lee Suggs, Va. Tech	So.	28	168	15.27
LaDainian Tomlinson, TCU	Sr.	22	132	12.00
Damien Anderson, Northwestern	Sr.	22	132	12.00
Dwone Hicks, Mid. Tenn St.	So.	21	126	11.45
Eric Crouch, Nebraska	Jr.	20	120	10.91
Thomas Hammock, N. Illinois	So.	16	96	10.67
Chester Taylor, Toledo	Sr.	19	114	10.36
Ken Simonton, Oregon St.	Jr.	18	110	10.00
Deonce Whitaker, San Jose St.	Sr.	16	98	9.80
Brock Forsey, Boise St.	So.	16	96	9.60

Games: All played 11, except Hammock (9), Whitaker and Forsey (10).

Kickers

	FG/Att	PAT/Att	Pts	P/Gm
Kris Stockton, Texas	22/26	41/44	107	9.73
Nick Calaycay, Boise St.	15/16	59/61	104	9.45
Jonathan Ruffin, Cincinnati	26/29	26/27	104	9.45
Chris Kaylakie, TCU	16/18	50/51	98	8.91
Steve Azar, N. Illinois	14/15	38/40	80	8.89
Dan Nystrom, Minnesota	22/34	31/33	97	8.82
Todd France, Toledo	15/19	49/49	94	8.55
Dave Adams, Air Force	19/24	37/39	94	8.55
Alex Walls, Tennessee	18/20	39/39	93	8.45
Jaime Rheem, Kansas St.	17/20	49/50	100	8.33

Games: All played 11, except Azar (9) and Rheem (12).

Punting

(Minimum of 3.6 per game)

	Cl	No	Yds	Avg
Preston Gruening, Minnesota	So.	46	2080	45.22
Brian Morton, Duke	Sr.	77	3478	45.17
Kevin Stemke, Wisconsin	Sr.	65	2915	44.85
Brooks Barnard, Maryland	So.	49	2191	44.71
Dave Zastudil, Ohio	Jr.	47	2084	44.34
Casey Roussel, Tulane	Jr.	59	2609	44.22
Jeff Ferguson, Oklahoma	Jr.	48	2108	43.92

Punt Returns

(Minimum of 1.2 per game)

	Cl	No	Yds	TD	Avg
Aaron Lockett, Kansas St.	Jr.	22	501	3	22.77
Andre Davis, Va. Tech	Jr.	18	396	3	22.00
Justin McCareins, N. Illinois	Sr.	19	362	1	19.05
Santana Moss, Miami-FL	Sr.	36	655	4	18.19
Jemeel Powell, California	So.	12	218	1	18.17
Pete Rebstock, Colorado St.	Jr.	28	469	1	16.75
Troy Mason, UNLV	So.	23	378	1	16.43
Joey Getherall, Notre Dame	Sr.	24	392	2	16.33
J.T. Thatcher, Oklahoma	Sr.	38	599	2	15.76
Don Shoals, Tulsa	Jr.	17	266	2	15.65

Kickoff Returns

(Minimum of 1.2 per game)

	Cl	No	Yds	TD	Avg
LaTarence Dunbar, TCU	So.	15	506	2	33.73
Zek Parker, Louisville	Sr.	26	752	0	28.92
David Mikell, Boise St.	Fr.	16	459	1	28.69
Julius Jones, Notre Dame	So.	15	427	1	28.47
Ken-Yon Rambo, Ohio St.	Sr.	17	478	0	28.12
Kahlil Hill, Iowa	Jr.	25	680	1	27.20
Robert Kilow, Arkansas St.	Sr.	27	724	0	26.81
Shawn Terry, West Virginia	Jr.	27	720	2	26.67
Kyle Moore, Duke	Jr.	13	335	0	25.77
James Hickenbocham, Arkansas St.	So.	17	435	1	25.59

NCAA Division I-A Team Leaders

REGULAR SEASON

Scoring Offense

	Gm	Record	Pts	Avg
Boise St.	11	9-2	494	44.91
Miami-FL	11	10-1	469	42.64
Florida St.	12	11-1	509	42.42
Nebraska	11	9-2	456	41.45
Virginia Tech	11	10-1	443	40.27
Kansas St.	13	10-3	514	39.54
Oklahoma	12	12-0	468	39.00
Texas	11	9-2	425	38.64
Northwestern	11	8-3	424	38.55
Florida	12	10-2	448	37.33

Scoring Defense

	Gm	Record	Pts	Avg
TCU	11	10-1	106	9.6
Florida St.	12	11-1	123	10.3
Toledo	11	10-1	125	11.4
W. Michigan	12	9-3	139	11.6
Miami-FL	11	10-1	170	15.5
South Carolina	11	7-4	174	15.8
Oklahoma	12	12-0	192	16.0
Southern Miss.	11	7-4	182	16.5
UAB	11	7-4	192	17.5
Texas A&M	11	7-4	196	17.8

Total Offense

	Gm	Plays	Yds	Avg	TD	YdsPG
Florida St.	12	924	6588	7.13	67	549.00
Boise St.	11	812	5459	6.72	64	496.27
Northwestern	11	911	5232	5.74	56	475.64
Purdue	11	904	5183	5.73	47	471.18
Miami-FL	11	774	5069	6.55	63	460.82
Nebraska	11	808	5059	6.26	63	459.91
Tulane	11	897	4989	5.56	40	453.55
Idaho	11	846	4985	5.89	42	453.18
Air Force	11	852	4971	5.83	47	451.91
Clemson	11	853	4911	5.76	53	446.45

Note: Touchdowns scored by rushing and passing only.

Total Defense

	Gm	Plays	Yds	Avg	TD	YdsPG
TCU	11	718	2695	3.75	13	245.00
Southern Miss.	11	784	2950	3.76	21	268.18
Toledo	11	703	2959	4.21	16	269.00
Kansas St.	13	872	3517	4.03	29	270.54
Memphis	11	755	3028	4.01	20	275.27
Florida St.	12	834	3324	3.99	15	277.00
Texas	11	766	3061	4.00	26	278.27
Oklahoma	12	809	3347	4.14	25	278.92
W. Michigan	12	803	3399	4.23	16	283.25
Utah	11	735	3171	4.31	24	288.27

Note: Opponents' TDs scored by rushing and passing only.

Single Game Highs
INDIVIDUAL

Rushing Yards

Yds
322   Emmett White, Utah St. vs. New Mexico St.
       (Nov. 4, 2000)

Receiving Yards

Yds
297   Aaron Jones, Utah St. vs. Boise St.
       (Nov. 11, 2000)

Total Offense

Yds
527   Chris Weinke, Florida St. vs. Duke
       (Oct. 14, 2000)

Passing Yards

Yds
536   Chris Weinke, Florida St. vs. Duke
       (Oct. 14, 2000)

Receptions

Att
20   Kenny Christian, E. Michigan vs. Temple
       (Sept. 23, 2000)

Passes Completed

No
47   Luke McCown, La. Tech vs. Auburn
       (Oct. 21, 2000)

TEAM

Total Offense Yards Gained

Yds
771   Florida St. vs. Clemson
       (Nov. 4, 2000)

Total Defense Yards Allowed

Yds
51   Kansas St. vs. Ball St.
       (Sept. 16, 2000)

Annual Awards

Player of the Year

Chris Weinke, FSU ....Heisman
Josh Heupel, Oklahoma......................AP, Camp
Drew Brees, Purdue ....Maxwell

Position Players of the Year

O'Brien Award (Quarterback)............Chris Weinke, FSU
Walker Award (Running Back) .....LaDainian Tomlinson, TCU
Biletnikoff Award (Receiver) ....Antonio Bryant, Pittsburgh
Groza Award (Kicker) ....Jonathan Ruffin, Cincinnati
Outland Trophy (Interior Lineman) . John Henderson, Tennessee
Lombardi Award (Lineman)............ Jamal Reynolds, FSU
Butkus Award (Linebacker) ....Dan Morgan, Miami-FL
Thorpe Award (Defensive Back).... Jamar Fletcher, Wisconsin
Nagurski Award (Defensive Player) ....Dan Morgan, Miami-FL
Payton Award (IAA Player of the Year) ....Louis Ivory, Furman
Hill Trophy (Div. II Player of the Year).Dusty Bonner, Valdosta St.
Melberger Award (Div. III Player of the Year) ......R.J. Bowers,
                                              Grove City (PA)

Coach of the Year

Bob Stoops, Oklahoma....AFCA, AP, Camp, Dodd, FWAA

Heisman Trophy Vote

Presented since 1935 by the Downtown Athletic Club of New York City and named after former college coach and DAC athletic director John W. Heisman. Voting done by national media and former Heisman winners. Each ballot allows for three names (points based on 3 for 1st, 2 for 2nd and 1 for 3rd).

Top 10 Vote-Getters

	Pos	1st	2nd	3rd	Pts
Chris Weinke, Florida St. ...QB		369	216	89	1628
Josh Heupel, Oklahoma ...QB		286	290	114	1552
Drew Brees, Purdue .....QB		69	107	198	619
LaDainian Tomlinson, TCU...RB		47	110	205	566
Damien Anderson, Northwestern ....RB		6	20	43	101
Michael Vick, Va. Tech .....QB		7	14	34	83
Santana Moss, Miami-FL ...WR		3	9	28	55
Marques Tuiasosopo, Washington................QB		5	8	10	41
Ken Simonton, Oregon St....RB		1	5	12	25
Rudi Johnson, Auburn ....RB		3	1	9	20

Consensus All-America Team

NCAA Division I-A players cited most frequently by the following selectors: AFCA, AP, and Walter Camp Foundation. (*) indicates unanimous selection.

Offense

	Player	Class	Ht	Wt
WR	Santana Moss*, Miami-FL ....Sr.		5-10	180
WR	Marvin Minnis*, FSU ....Sr.		6-1	185
TE	Brian Natkin*, UTEP ....Sr.		6-4	245
OL	Chris Brown, Ga. Tech ....Sr.		6-6	315
OL	Leonard Davis, Texas ....Sr.		6-6	365
OL	Steve Hutchinson*, Michigan ....Sr.		6-5	299
OL	Ben Hamilton, Minnesota............Sr.		6-5	285
C	Dominic Raiola*, Nebraska ....Jr.		6-2	300
QB	Josh Heupel, Oklahoma..............Sr.		6-2	214
RB	LaDainian Tomlinson*, TCU..........Sr.		5-11	220
RB	Damien Anderson, Northwestern.....Jr.		5-11	208
K	Jonathan Ruffin, Cincinnati ....So.		5-10	184

Defense

	Player	Class	Ht	Wt
DL	Jamal Reynolds*, FSU................Sr.		6-4	254
DL	Andre Carter*, California ....Sr.		6-5	260
DL	Casey Hampton*, Texas..............Sr.		6-1	310
DL	Richard Seymour, Georgia ....Sr.		6-6	300
LB	Dan Morgan*, Miami-FL ....Sr.		6-3	245
LB	Carlos Polk, Nebraska ....Sr.		6-2	260
LB	Rocky Calmus*, Oklahoma ....Jr.		6-3	240
LB	Keith Adams, Clemson ....Jr.		5-11	220
DB	Jamar Fletcher*, Wisconsin ....Jr.		5-10	175
DB	Dwight Smith*, Akron................Sr.		5-11	205
DB	Fred Smoot, Mississippi St............Sr.		6-1	179
P	Nick Harris*, California..............Sr.		6-3	225

Underclassmen who declared for the 2001 draft

Thirty-six players forfeited the remainder of their college eligibility and declared for the NFL draft in 2001. NFL teams drafted 28 underclassmen. Players listed in alphabetical order; first round selections in **bold** type.

	Pos	Drafted by	Overall pick		Pos	Drafted by	Overall pick
Keith Adams, Clemson	LB	Tennessee	232	Delvin Jones, Minnesota	DB	Not drafted	—
Hakim Akbar, Washington	S	New England	163	George Layne, TCU	RB	Kansas City	108
Alex Ardley, Clemson	DB	Not drafted	—	**Willie Middlebrooks**,			
Idrees Bashir, Memphis	DB	Indianapolis	37	Minnesota	CB	Denver	24
Michael Bennett, Wisconsin	RB	Minnesota	27	**Freddie Mitchell**, UCLA	CB	Philadelphia	25
Josh Booty, LSU	QB	Seattle	172	Jonathan Ordway, Boston Coll.	DB	Not drafted	—
Jerametrius Butler, Kansas St.	DB	St. Louis	145	**Ryan Pickett**, Ohio St.	DT	St. Louis	29
John Capel, Florida	WR	Chicago	208	Dominic Raiola, Nebraska	C	Detroit	50
Quincy Carter, Georgia	QB	Dallas	53	**Koren Robinson**, N.C. State	WR	Seattle	9
Nate Clements, Ohio St.	CB	Buffalo	21	**Justin Smith**, Missouri	DE	Cincinnati	4
Jameel Cook, Illinois	RB	Tampa Bay	174	**David Terrell**, Michigan	WR	Chicago	8
Ronney Daniels, Auburn	WR	Not drafted	—	Ja'Mar Toombs, Texas A&M	FB	Not drafted	—
Heath Evans, Auburn	FB	Seattle	82	**Michael Vick**, Va. Tech	QB	Atlanta	1
Robert Ferguson, Texas A&M	WR	Green Bay	41	**Kenyatta Walker**, Florida	OL	Tampa Bay	14
Jamar Fletcher, Wisconsin	CB	Miami	26	**Gerard Warren**, Florida	DL	Cleveland	3
Lloyd Garden, Cincinnati	RB	Not drafted	—	Reggie White, Oklahoma St.	RB	Not drafted	—
Derin Graham, Indiana	WR	Not drafted	—	Adrian Wilson, N.C. State	S	Arizona	64
Todd Heap, Arizona St.	TE	Baltimore	31	Jamie Winborn, Vanderbilt	LB	San Fran.	47
Rudi Johnson, Auburn	RB	Cincinnati	100				

NCAA Division I-AA Final Standings

Standings based on conference games only; overall records include postseason games.

Atlantic 10 Conference

	Conference				Overall			
	W	L	PF	PA	W	L	PF	PA
*Delaware	7	1	290	161	12	2	570	238
*Richmond	7	1	179	112	10	3	255	217
Massachusetts	5	3	216	166	7	4	312	246
James Madison	4	4	183	152	6	5	300	185
New Hampshire	4	4	181	238	6	5	289	314
Wm. & Mary	4	4	196	213	6	6	268	314
Maine	3	5	206	184	5	6	319	256
Villanova	3	5	211	313	5	6	385	361
Rhode Island	2	6	118	177	3	8	175	257
Northeastern	1	7	133	257	4	7	279	305

*Playoffs (3-2): Delaware (2-1), Richmond (1-1).

Big Sky Conference

	Conference				Overall			
	W	L	PF	PA	W	L	PF	PA
*Montana	8	0	245	161	13	2	475	288
*Portland St.	5	3	270	201	8	4	406	325
Sacramento St.	5	3	258	227	7	4	329	279
Weber St.	5	3	187	145	7	4	272	219
Eastern Wash.	5	3	218	175	6	5	288	243
Idaho St.	4	4	220	255	6	5	329	351
CS-Northridge	2	6	238	296	4	7	308	391
Northern Arizona	2	6	162	189	3	8	245	275
Montana St.	0	8	96	245	0	11	131	359

*Playoffs (3-2): Montana (3-1), Portland St. (0-1).

Gateway Athletic Conference

	Conference				Overall			
	W	L	PF	PA	W	L	PF	PA
*Western Ill.	5	1	191	110	9	3	390	231
*Youngstown St.	4	2	133	101	9	3	296	189
Illinois St.	4	2	153	90	7	4	361	221
Northern Iowa	3	3	193	164	7	4	397	305
SW Missouri St.	2	4	94	120	5	6	237	200
Southern Ill.	2	4	120	153	3	8	208	316
Indiana St.	1	5	61	207	1	10	122	408

*Playoffs (0-2): Youngstown St. (0-1), Western Ill. (0-1).

Ivy League

	Conference				Overall			
	W	L	PF	PA	W	L	PF	PA
Pennsylvania	6	1	277	178	7	3	349	257
Cornell	5	2	217	238	5	5	264	334
Brown	4	3	266	245	7	3	375	301
Yale	4	3	177	133	7	3	276	183
Harvard	4	3	247	164	5	5	327	255
Princeton	3	4	207	208	3	7	248	286
Columbia	1	6	156	246	3	7	256	306
Dartmouth	1	6	155	290	2	8	231	388

Playoffs: League does not play postseason games.

Metro Atlantic Athletic Conference

	Conference				Overall			
	W	L	PF	PA	W	L	PF	PA
Duquesne	7	0	286	89	10	1	424	189
Fairfield	6	1	304	90	8	2	387	154
Marist	5	2	155	121	6	4	221	236
La Salle	4	3	127	159	4	7	217	211
Iona	3	4	189	197	4	7	259	333
St. Peter's	2	5	60	145	4	7	145	201
Siena	1	6	128	220	1	9	167	313
Canisius	0	7	53	281	0	10	100	373

Playoffs: No teams invited.

Best Conference Playoff Records

Postseason records for 2000 season.

	W-L	Pct
Southern	6-2	.750
Atlantic 10	3-2	.600
Big Sky	3-2	.600
Patriot	1-1	.500
Ohio Valley	1-2	.333
Mid-Eastern Athletic	0-1	.000
Gateway Athletic	0-2	.000
Southland	0-2	.000

NCAA Division I-AA Final Standings (Cont.)

Mid-Eastern Athletic Conference

	Conference				Overall			
	W	L	PF	PA	W	L	PF	PA
*Florida A&M	7	1	348	151	9	3	439	245
†Bethune-Cookman	6	2	265	138	9	2	330	168
N. Carolina A&T	6	2	267	140	8	3	323	174
Delaware St.	5	3	287	298	7	4	380	378
Hampton	5	3	281	240	7	4	380	311
Howard	3	5	147	245	3	8	190	355
Norfolk St.	2	6	110	209	3	8	153	292
South Carolina St.	2	6	222	350	3	8	308	460
Morgan St.	0	8	137	293	1	10	173	403

*Playoffs (0-1): Florida A&M (0-1).

†Heritage Bowl: Southern defeated Bethune-Cookman (28-2).

Northeast Conference

	Conference				Overall			
	W	L	PF	PA	W	L	PF	PA
Robert Morris	8	0	318	107	10	0	365	140
Sacred Heart	6	1	167	98	10	1	314	147
Wagner	6	2	232	122	6	5	306	215
Albany	5	3	297	169	5	6	342	318
Monmouth (N.J.)	4	4	161	114	5	6	200	174
Central Conn.	3	5	130	240	4	6	174	285
St. John's	0	5	39	147	5	6	169	216
Stony Brook	0	6	76	210	2	8	182	262
St. Francis (Pa.)	0	6	43	256	0	11	71	436

Playoffs: No teams invited.

Ohio Valley Conference

	Conference				Overall			
	W	L	PF	PA	W	L	PF	PA
*Western Ky.	7	0	266	95	11	2	404	145
*Eastern Ill.	6	1	249	98	8	4	443	242
Tennessee Tech	5	2	208	103	8	3	317	217
Murray St.	4	3	238	225	6	5	366	332
Eastern Ky.	3	4	137	112	6	5	267	156
Tennessee St.	2	5	180	270	3	8	278	372
SE Missouri St.	1	6	148	258	3	8	224	403
Tenn.-Martin	0	7	36	301	2	9	122	453

*Playoffs (1-2): Western Ky. (1-1), Eastern Ill. (0-1).

Patriot League

	Conference				Overall			
	W	L	PF	PA	W	L	PF	PA
*Lehigh	6	0	186	89	12	1	396	214
Colgate	4	2	109	120	7	4	235	240
Holy Cross	4	2	105	95	7	4	245	223
Towson	3	3	155	135	7	4	299	216
Bucknell	2	4	126	113	6	5	242	172
Fordham	1	5	100	190	3	8	211	318
Lafayette	1	5	137	176	2	9	244	350

*Playoffs (1-1): Lehigh (1-1).

Pioneer League

	Conference				Overall			
	W	L	PF	PA	W	L	PF	PA
Dayton	3	1	126	69	8	3	376	192
Drake	3	1	181	101	7	4	410	267
Valparaiso	3	1	88	86	7	4	275	239
San Diego	1	3	74	148	4	6	242	313
Butler	0	4	111	176	2	8	356	378

Playoffs: No teams invited.

Southern Conference

	Conference				Overall			
	W	L	PF	PA	W	L	PF	PA
*Ga. Southern	6	1	235	134	13	2	506	274
*Furman	6	2	261	155	9	3	379	209
*Appalachian St.	6	2	293	152	10	4	441	278
Wofford	5	3	243	226	7	4	305	276
E. Tenn St.	4	4	183	199	6	5	282	267
Tenn.-Chatt.	3	4	212	205	5	6	332	279
W. Carolina	3	5	228	266	4	7	316	371
The Citadel	1	7	99	243	2	9	144	335
VMI	1	7	141	315	2	9	227	434

*Playoffs (6-2): Georgia Southern (4-0), Appalachian St. (2-1), Furman (0-1).

Southland Conference

	Conference				Overall			
	W	L	PF	PA	W	L	PF	PA
*Troy St.	6	1	166	80	9	3	330	193
*McNeese St.	5	2	176	90	8	4	315	224
SW Texas St.	5	2	146	121	7	4	220	183
Sam Houston St.	4	3	187	176	7	4	290	228
Northwestern St.	3	4	138	165	6	5	256	236
Stephen F. Austin	3	4	139	177	6	5	289	297
Jacksonville St.	2	5	106	164	4	6	170	234
Nicholls St.	0	7	84	169	1	10	170	312

*Playoffs (0-2): Troy St. (0-1), McNeese St. (0-1).

Southwestern Athletic Conference

Eastern	Conference				Overall			
	W	L	PF	PA	W	L	PF	PA
Alabama St.	5	2	231	188	6	5	327	351
Alabama A&M	5	3	210	134	7	5	312	227
Jackson St.	4	3	221	174	7	4	365	299
Miss. Valley St.	1	6	116	256	2	9	199	433
Alcorn St.	0	7	114	175	0	11	159	297

Western	Conference				Overall			
	W	L	PF	PA	W	L	PF	PA
Grambling	7	1	226	109	10	2	300	207
Texas Southern	5	2	174	145	8	3	280	201
Ark.-Pine Bluff	4	3	185	151	6	5	325	250
†Southern	4	3	230	158	6	5	368	282
Prairie View	1	6	82	299	1	10	103	497

†Heritage Bowl: Southern defeated Bethune-Cookman (28-2).

NCAA I-AA Independents

	W	L	PF	PA
Davidson	10	0	271	135
*Hofstra	9	4	445	384
Morehead St.	6	3	374	291
Elon College	7	4	278	223
Southern Utah	7	4	386	306
South Florida	7	4	278	201
St. Mary's (Ca.)	6	5	349	359
Charleston Southern	5	6	246	244
Georgetown	5	6	282	326
Samford	4	7	183	290
Cal Poly-SLO	3	8	301	395
Liberty	3	8	195	320
Jacksonville	3	8	183	297
Austin Peay	2	8	180	390

*Playoffs (1-1): Hofstra (1-1)

Morehead State
David Dinkins
Total Offense

Southern-BR
Terrence Levy
Passing Efficiency

Hampton University
Montrell Coley
Scoring

Furman University
Louis Ivory
Rushing

NCAA Division I-AA Regular Season Leaders
INDIVIDUAL

Passing Efficiency
Minimum 15 attempts per game

	Cl	Gm	Att	Cmp	Cmp Pct	Int	Int Pct	Yds	Yds/ Att	TD	TD Pct	Rating Points
Terrence Levy, Southern	Jr.	11	233	139	59.66	6	2.58	2249	9.65	23	9.87	168.2
Tony Romo, E. Illinois	So.	11	278	164	58.99	12	4.32	2583	9.29	27	9.71	160.5
Gavin Hoffman, Pennsylvania	Jr.	10	386	272	70.47	14	3.63	3214	8.33	24	6.22	153.7
Brett Gordon, Villanova	So.	11	281	184	65.48	9	3.20	2293	8.16	22	7.83	153.5
Matt Nagy, Delaware	Sr.	11	288	151	52.43	12	4.17	2718	9.44	25	8.68	152.0
Seth Burford, Cal Poly	Jr.	11	304	174	57.24	7	2.30	2655	8.73	23	7.57	151.0
Tony Zimmerman, Duquesne	Sr.	11	309	166	53.72	9	2.91	2670	8.64	28	9.06	150.4
Ira Vandever, Drake	So.	11	195	104	53.33	2	1.03	1669	8.56	15	7.69	148.6
Ryan Helming, N. Iowa	Sr.	11	380	219	57.63	9	2.37	3145	8.28	30	7.89	148.5
DeWayne Ewing, Butler	Jr.	10	388	246	63.40	8	2.06	3182	8.20	22	5.67	146.9

Total Offense

	Cl	Rush	Pass	Yds	YdsPG
David Dinkins, Morehead St.	Sr.	1405	1704	3109	345.4
Chris Sanders, Chattanooga	Sr.	65	3691	3756	341.5
Darnell Kennedy, Alabama St.	Jr.	-13	3488	3475	315.9
Gavin Hoffman, Pennsylvania	Jr.	-65	3214	3149	314.9
Eric Webber, Brown	Sr.	-40	3175	3135	313.5
DeWayne Ewing, Butler	Jr.	-103	3182	3079	307.9
Ricky Rahne, Cornell	Jr.	92	2944	3036	303.6
Ryan Helming, N. Iowa	Sr.	112	3145	3257	296.1
Neil Rose, Harvard	Jr.	206	2655	2861	286.1
Quinn Gray, Florida A&M	Jr.	328	2787	3115	283.2

Rushing

	Cl	Car	Yds	TD	YdsPG
Louis Ivory, Furman	Jr.	286	2079	16	189.00
Charles Dunn, Portland St.	Sr.	302	1792	21	162.91
David Dinkins, Morehead St.	Sr.	190	1405	21	156.11
Adrian Peterson, Ga. Southern	Jr.	230	1361	13	151.22
Charles Roberts, CS-Sacramento	Sr.	296	1624	14	147.64
Matt Cannon, Southern Utah	Sr.	218	1602	22	145.61
Montrell Coley, Hampton	Sr.	307	1582	27	143.82
Charles Tharp, Western Ill.	Sr.	238	1523	17	138.45
Ralph Saldiveri, Iona	Sr.	277	1520	10	138.18
Rashad Bartholomew, Yale	Sr.	216	1233	11	137.00

Games: All played 11, except Dinkins, Peterson and Bartholomew (9).

Receptions

	Cl	No	Yds	TD	P/Gm
Steve Campbell, Brown	Sr.	120	1332	11	12.00
Eric Johnson, Yale	Sr.	87	1017	14	8.70
Jacquay Nunnally, Florida A&M	Jr.	95	1082	9	8.64
Richmond Flowers, Chattanooga	Sr.	86	1035	2	7.82
Rob Milanese, Pennsylvania	Jr.	76	936	6	7.60
Kassim Osgood, Cal Poly	So.	83	1377	14	7.55
Cos DeMatteo, Chattanooga	Jr.	75	971	11	7.50
Michael Hayes, Southern	Jr.	80	1328	15	7.27
Phil Yarborough, Lafayette	Sr.	77	1139	7	7.00
Eddie Berlin, N. Iowa	Sr.	74	1195	16	6.73

Games: All played 11, except Campbell, Johnson, Milanese and DeMatteo (10).

Interceptions

	Cl	No	Yds	TD	Int/Gm
Steve Dogmanits, Fairfield	Sr.	11	113	2	1.10
Rashean Mathis, Bethune-Cookman	So.	11	157	0	1.00
Don Milligan, Fairfield	Jr.	9	165	1	.90
Bobby Sippio, Western Ky.	So.	9	236	2	.90
Leigh Bodden, Duquesne	So.	9	175	2	.82
Eric Martinson, La Salle	Sr.	8	23	0	.82

Games: All played 11, except Dogmanits, Milligan and Sippio (10).

NCAA Division I-AA Regular Season Leaders (Cont.)

Scoring
Non-Kickers

	Cl	TD	XPt	Pts	P/Gm
Montrell Coley, Hampton	Sr.	28	0	172	15.64
David Dinkins, Morehead St.	Sr.	21	0	128	14.22
Brian Westbrook, Villanova	Jr.	22	0	136	12.36
Matt Cannon, Southern Utah	Sr.	22	0	132	12.00
Charles Dunn, Portland St.	Sr.	21	0	126	11.45

Games: All played 11, except Dinkins (9).

Kickers

	Cl	FG/Att	PAT/Att	Pts
Billy Cundiff, Drake	Jr.	20/27	40/44	100
Matt Vick, Chattanooga	Sr.	22/26	31/31	97
Jason Feinberg, Pennsylvania	Sr.	15/21	38/40	83
Peter Martinez, Western Ky.	So.	15/20	44/45	89
Juan Vasques, Florida A&M	Fr.	14/21	44/49	86

Games: All played 11, except Feinberg (10).

Field Goals

	Cl	FG/Att	Pct	LG
Matt Vick, Chattanooga	Sr.	22/26	.846	51
Billy Cundiff, Drake	Jr.	20/27	.741	62
Brett Sterba, Wm. & Mary	Sr.	17/19	.895	53

Four tied with 16 each.

Games: All played 11.

Longest FG of season: 63 yards by Bill Gramatica, So. Florida vs. Austin Peay (Nov. 18).

Punt/Kickoff Leaders

Punting	Cl	No	Yds	Avg
David Beckford, Alabama St.	So.	48	2121	44.19

Punt Returns	Cl	No	Yds	TD	Avg
Terrence McGee, N'western St.	So.	18	427	3	23.72

Kickoff Returns	Cl	No	Yds	TD	Avg
Richard Holland, VMI	Sr.	19	628	1	33.05

TEAM
REGULAR SEASON
Scoring Offense

	Gm	Record	Pts	Avg
Morehead St.	9	6-3	374	41.56
Delaware	11	10-1	456	41.45
Florida A&M	11	9-2	436	39.64
Eastern Ill.	11	8-3	430	39.09
Fairfield	10	8-2	387	38.70
Duquesne	11	10-1	424	38.55
Brown	10	7-3	375	37.50
Drake	11	7-4	410	37.27
Robert Morris	10	10-0	365	36.50
Northern Iowa	11	7-4	397	36.09
Hofstra	11	8-3	394	35.82
Portland St.	11	8-3	392	35.64
Butler	10	10-0	356	35.60
Southern Utah	11	7-4	386	35.09
Villanova	11	5-6	385	35.00
Pennsylvania	10	7-3	349	34.90

Scoring Defense

	Gm	Record	Pts	Avg
Western Ky.	11	10-1	128	11.6
Sacred Heart	11	10-1	147	13.4
Davidson	10	10-0	135	13.5
Robert Morris	10	10-0	140	14.0
Eastern Ky.	11	6-5	156	14.2
Lehigh	11	11-0	160	14.5
Troy St.	11	9-2	160	14.5
Bethune-Cookman	11	9-2	168	15.3
Fairfield	10	8-2	154	15.4
Bucknell	11	6-5	172	15.6
Monmouth	11	5-6	174	15.8
N.C. A&T	11	8-3	174	15.8
Delaware	11	10-1	175	15.9
Furman	11	9-2	178	16.2
Youngstown St.	11	9-2	179	16.3
Richmond	11	9-2	180	16.4

Total Offense

	Record	Plays	Yds	Avg
Morehead St.	6-3	698	4715	523.89
Brown	7-3	788	4832	483.20
Southern Utah	7-4	815	5291	481.00
Pennsylvania	7-3	769	4746	474.60
Harvard	5-5	782	4679	467.90
Southern	6-5	838	5130	466.36
Illinois St.	7-4	846	5036	457.82
Chattanooga	5-6	802	4989	453.55
Butler	2-8	744	4530	453.00
Eastern Ill.	8-3	746	4979	452.64
Murray St.	6-5	801	4975	452.27
Appalachian St.	8-3	827	4962	451.09
Ga. Southern	9-2	768	4931	448.27
W. Carolina	4-7	810	4929	448.09
Delaware	10-1	790	4905	445.91
Montana	10-1	827	4905	445.91

Total Defense

	Record	Plays	Yds	Avg
Monmouth	5-6	678	2553	232.09
St. John's-NY	5-6	731	2687	244.27
Wagner	6-5	682	2705	245.91
Eastern Ky.	6-5	713	2855	259.55
N.C. A&T	8-3	739	2873	261.18
McNeese St.	8-3	680	2874	261.27
St. Peter's	8-3	658	2893	263.00
Montana	10-1	722	2915	265.00
Fairfield	8-2	677	2677	267.70
Alabama A&M	7-5	823	3309	275.75
Towson	7-4	787	3042	276.55
Western Ill.	9-2	749	3058	278.00
Texas Southern	8-3	777	3073	279.36
Sacred Heart	10-1	725	3085	280.45
Southern Ill.	4-7	682	3088	280.73

NCAA Playoffs

Division I-AA

First Round (Nov. 25)

at Montana 45 ....Eastern Ill. 13
at Richmond 13 ....Youngstown St. 3
at Western Ky. 27 ....Florida A&M 0
Appalachian St. 33 ....at Troy St. 30
at Georgia Southern 42 ....McNeese St. 17
Hofstra 31 ....at Furman 24
Lehigh 37 ....at Western Ill. 7
at Delaware 49 ....Portland St. 14

Quarterfinals (Dec. 2)

at Montana 34 ....Richmond 20
Appalachian St. 17 ....at Western Ky. 14
at Georgia Southern 48.....................Hofstra 20
at Delaware 47..............................Lehigh 22

Semifinals (Dec. 9)

at Georgia Southern 27.................Delaware 18
at Montana 19.....................Appalachian St. 16

Championship Game
Dec. 16 at Chattanooga, Tenn. (Att: 17,156)

Georgia Southern 27 ....Montana 25
(13-2)   (13-2)

Division II

First Round (Nov. 18)

North Dakota St. 31 ....at Northwest Mo. St. 17
at Nebraska-Omaha 14...................Pittsburg St. 3
at Catawba 28 ....West Ga. 24
at Delta St. 49 ....Valdosta St. 12
at Northwood 28........................Indiana-PA 0
at Bloomsburg 46.................Saginaw Valley 32
at UC Davis 48 ....Chadron St. 10
Mesa St. 40................at Northeastern St. 21

Quarterfinals (Nov. 25)

North Dakota St. 43 ....at Nebraska-Omaha 21
Delta St. 20 ....at Catawba 14
at Bloomsburg 38 ....Northwood 14
at UC Davis 62.............................Mesa St. 18

Semifinals (Dec. 2)

at Delta St. 34 ....North Dakota St. 16
Bloomsburg 58 ....at UC Davis 48

Championship Game
Dec. 9 at Florence, Ala. (Att: 7,123)

Delta St. 63 ....Bloomsburg 34
(14-1)   (13-2)

Division III

First Round (Nov. 18)

at Ohio Northern 47 ....Millikin 21
Hanover 20.................................at Hope 3
at Wittenberg 31...........................Aurora 20
at Springfield 31 ....Montclair St. 29
Widener 33...............................at Union 26
at Hobart 25 ....Bridgewater St. 0
at Central-IA 29 ....St. Norbert 14
Pacific Lutheran 41........................at Bethel 13
St. John's-MN 26 ....at WI-Stout 19
W. Maryland 38 ....at Emory and Henry 14
at Trinity-TX 21 ....Wesley 3
Bridgewater-VA 59 ....at Wash. & Jeff. 42

Second Round (Nov. 25)

at Mt. Union 59 ....Ohio Northern 28
at Wittenberg 32 ....Hanover 21
Springfield 13 ....at Brockport St. 6
at Widener 40..............................Hobart 14
Central 20 ....OT ....at Linfield 17
St. John's 28 ....OT ...at Pacific Lutheran 21
at Hardin-Simmons 32 ....Western Maryland 14
at Trinity 47 ....OT.............Bridgewater 41

Quarterfinals (Dec. 2)

at Mt. Union 32 ....Wittenberg 15
Widener 61 ....at Springfield 27
St. John's 21 ....at Central 18
at Hardin-Simmons 33 ....at Trinity 30

Semifinals (Dec. 9)

at Mt. Union 70 ....Widener 30
at St. John's 38 ....at Hardin-Simmons 14

Amos Alonzo Stagg Bowl
Dec. 16 at Salem, Va. (Att: 4,643)

Mt. Union 10 ....St. John's 7
(14-0)   (12-2)

NAIA Playoffs
Division I

First Round (Nov. 18)

at NW Oklahoma St. 40 ....Nebraska Wesleyan 13
at Georgetown (Ky.) 55 ....Olivet Nazarene (Ill.) 6
Northwestern (Ia.) 27 ....at Benedictine (Ks.) 26
at St. Francis (Ind.) 48 ....Lambuth (Tenn.) 33
at MidAm. Nazarene (Ks.) 27 ......Azusa Pacific (Ca.) 21
Carroll 24 ....at Valley City St. (N.D.) 21
at St. Ambrose (Ia.) 27 ....Mary (N.D.) 7
at Huron (S.D.) 47.....................Ottawa (Ks.) 17

Quarterfinals (Nov. 25)

at Georgetown 37......................St. Francis 19
at NW Oklahoma St. 31...........MidAm. Nazarene 27
Northwestern 21 ....at St. Ambrose 14
Carroll 31 ....at Huron 17

Semifinals (Dec. 2)

at NW Oklahoma St. 42.................Northwestern 7
at Georgetown 28....................Carroll 21

Championship
Dec. 16 at Savannah, Tenn. (Att: 6,650)

Georgetown 20...................NW Oklahoma St. 0
(14-0)   (13-1)

1869-2001 Through the Years

ESPN information please® SPORTS ALMANAC

National Champions

Over the last 132 years, there have been 25 major selectors of national champions by way of polls (11), mathematical rating systems (10) and historical research (4). The best-known and most widely circulated of these surveys, the Associated Press poll of sportswriters and broadcasters, first appeared during the 1936 season. Champions prior to 1936 have been determined by retro polls, ratings and historical research.

The Early Years (1869-1935)

National champions based on the Dickinson mathematical system (DS) and three historical retro polls taken by the College Football Researchers Association (CFRA), the National Championship Foundation (NCF) and the Helms Athletic Foundation (HF). The CFRA and NCF polls start in 1869, college football's inaugural year, while the Helms poll begins in 1883, the first season the game adopted a point system for scoring. Frank Dickinson, an economics professor at Illinois, introduced his system in 1926 and retro-picked winners in 1924 and '25. Bowl game results were counted in the Helms selections, but not in the other three.

Multiple champions: Yale (18); Princeton (17); Harvard (9); Michigan (7); Notre Dame and Penn (4); Alabama, California, Cornell, Illinois, Pittsburgh and USC (3); Georgia Tech, Minnesota and Penn St. (2).

Year		Record	Year		Record	Year		Record
1869	**Princeton**	1-1-0	1880	**Yale** (CFRA)	4-0-1	1891	**Yale**	13-0-0
1870	**Princeton**	1-0-0		& **Princeton** (NCF)	4-0-1	1892	**Yale**	13-0-0
1871	No games played		1881	**Yale**	5-0-1	1893	**Princeton**	11-0-0
1872	**Princeton**	1-0-0	1882	**Yale**	8-0-0	1894	**Yale**	16-0-0
1873	**Princeton**	1-0-0	1883	**Yale**	8-0-0	1895	**Penn**	14-0-0
1874	**Yale**	3-0-0	1884	**Yale**	8-0-1	1896	**Princeton** (CFRA)	10-0-1
1875	**Princeton** (CFRA)	2-0-0	1885	**Princeton**	9-0-0		& **Lafayette** (NCF)	11-0-1
	& **Harvard** (NCF)	4-0-0	1886	**Yale**	9-0-1	1897	**Penn**	15-0-0
1876	**Yale**	3-0-0	1887	**Yale**	9-0-0	1898	**Harvard**	11-0-0
1877	**Yale**	3-0-1	1888	**Yale**	13-0-0	1899	**Princeton** (CFRA)	12-1-0
1878	**Princeton**	6-0-0	1889	**Princeton**	10-0-0		& **Harvard** (NCF, HF)	10-0-1
1879	**Princeton**	4-0-1	1890	**Harvard**	11-0-0			

Year		Record	Bowl Game	Head Coach	Outstanding Player
1900	**Yale**	12-0-0	No bowl	Malcolm McBride	Perry Hale, HB
1901	**Harvard** (CFRA)	12-0-0	No bowl	Bill Reid	Bob Kernan, HB
	& **Michigan** (NCF, HF)	11-0-0	Won Rose	Hurry Up Yost	Neil Snow, E
1902	**Michigan**	11-0-0	No bowl	Hurry Up Yost	Boss Weeks, QB
1903	**Princeton**	11-0-0	No bowl	Art Hillebrand	John DeWitt, G
1904	**Penn** (CFRA, HF)	12-0-0	No bowl	Carl Williams	Andy Smith, FB
	& **Michigan** (NCF)	10-0-0	No bowl	Hurry Up Yost	Willie Heston, HB
1905	**Chicago**	10-0-0	No bowl	Amos Alonzo Stagg	Walter Eckersall, QB
1906	**Princeton**	9-0-1	No bowl	Bill Roper	Cap Wister, E
1907	**Yale**	9-0-1	No bowl	Bill Knox	Tad Jones, HB
1908	**Penn** (CFRA, HF)	11-0-1	No bowl	Sol Metzger	Hunter Scarlett, E
	& **LSU** (NCF)	10-0-0	No bowl	Edgar Wingard	Doc Fenton, QB
1909	**Yale**	12-1-0	No bowl	Howard Jones	Ted Coy, FB
1910	**Harvard** (CFRA, HF)	8-0-1	No bowl	Percy Haughton	Percy Wendell, HB
	& **Pittsburgh** (NCF)	9-0-0	No bowl	Joe Thompson	Ralph Galvin, C
1911	**Princeton** (CFRA, HF)	8-0-2	No bowl	Bill Roper	Sam White, E
	& **Penn St.** (NCF)	8-0-1	No bowl	Bill Hollenback	Dexter Very, E
1912	**Harvard** (CFRA, HF)	9-0-0	No bowl	Percy Haughton	Charley Brickley, HB
	& **Penn St.** (NCF)	8-0-0	No bowl	Bill Hollenback	Dexter Very, E
1913	**Harvard**	9-0-0	No bowl	Percy Haughton	Eddie Mahan, FB
1914	**Army**	9-0-0	No bowl	Charley Daly	John McEwan, C
1915	**Cornell**	9-0-0	No bowl	Al Sharpe	Charley Barrett, QB
1916	**Pittsburgh**	8-0-0	No bowl	Pop Warner	Bob Peck, C
1917	**Georgia Tech**	9-0-0	No bowl	John Heisman	Ev Strupper, HB
1918	**Pittsburgh** (CFRA, HF)	4-1-0	No bowl	Pop Warner	Tom Davies, HB
	& **Michigan** (NCF)	5-0-0	No bowl	Hurry Up Yost	Frank Steketee, FB
1919	**Harvard** (CFRA-tie, HF)	9-0-1	Won Rose	Bob Fisher	Eddie Casey, HB
	Illinois (CFRA-tie)	6-1-0	No bowl	Bob Zuppke	Chuck Carney, E
	& **Notre Dame** (NCF)	9-0-0	No bowl	Knute Rockne	George Gipp, HB
1920	**California**	9-0-0	Won Rose	Andy Smith	Dan McMillan, T
1921	**California** (CFRA)	9-0-1	Tied Rose	Andy Smith	Brick Muller, E
	& **Cornell** (NCF, HF)	8-0-0	No bowl	Gil Dobie	Eddie Kaw, HB
1922	**Princeton** (CFRA)	8-0-0	No bowl	Bill Roper	Herb Treat, T
	California (NCF)	9-0-0	No bowl	Andy Smith	Brick Muller, E
	& **Cornell** (HF)	8-0-0	No bowl	Gil Dobie	Eddie Kaw, HB

Year		Record	Bowl Game	Head Coach	Outstanding Player
1923	**Illinois** (CFRA, HF)	8-0-0	No bowl	Bob Zuppke	Red Grange, HB
	& Michigan (NCF)	8-0-0	No bowl	Hurry Up Yost	Jack Blott, C
1924	**Notre Dame**	10-0-0	Won Rose	Knute Rockne	"The Four Horsemen"*
1925	**Alabama** (CFRA, HF)	10-0-0	Won Rose	Wallace Wade	Johnny Mack Brown, HB
	& Dartmouth (DS)	8-0-0	No bowl	Jesse Hawley	Swede Oberlander, HB
1926	**Alabama** (CFRA, HF)	9-0-1	Tied Rose	Wallace Wade	Hoyt Winslett, E
	& Stanford (DS)	10-0-1	Tied Rose	Pop Warner	Ted Shipkey, E
1927	**Yale** (CFRA)	7-1-0	No bowl	Tad Jones	Bill Webster, G
	& Illinois (NCF, HF, DS)	7-0-1	No bowl	Bob Zuppke	Bob Reitsch, C
1928	**Georgia Tech** (CFRA, NCF, HF)	10-0-0	Won Rose	Bill Alexander	Pete Pund, C
	& USC (DS)	9-0-1	No bowl	Howard Jones	Jesse Hibbs, T
1929	**Notre Dame**	9-0-0	No bowl	Knute Rockne	Frank Carideo, QB
1930	**Alabama** (CFRA)	10-0-0	Won Rose	Wallace Wade	Fred Sington, T
	& Notre Dame (NCF, HF, DS)	10-0-0	No bowl	Knute Rockne	Marchy Schwartz, HB
1931	**USC**	10-1-0	Won Rose	Howard Jones	John Baker, G
1932	**USC** (CFRA, NCF, HF)	10-0-0	Won Rose	Howard Jones	Ernie Smith, T
	& Michigan (DS)	8-0-0	No bowl	Harry Kipke	Harry Newman, QB
1933	**Michigan**	8-0-0	No bowl	Harry Kipke	Chuck Bernard, C
1934	**Minnesota**	8-0-0	No bowl	Bernie Bierman	Pug Lund, HB
1935	**Minnesota** (CFRA, NCF, HF)	8-0-0	No bowl	Bernie Bierman	Dick Smith, T
	& SMU (DS)	12-1-0	Lost Rose	Matty Bell	Bobby Wilson, HB

*Notre Dame's Four Horsemen were Harry Stuhldreher (QB), Jim Crowley (HB), Don Miller (HB-P) and Elmer Layden (FB).

The Media Poll Years (since 1936)

National champions according to seven media and coaches' polls: Associated Press (since 1936), United Press (1950-57), International News Service (1952-57), United Press International (1958-92), Football Writers Association of America (since 1954), National Football Foundation and Hall of Fame (since 1959) and USA Today/CNN (since 1991). In 1991, the American Football Coaches Association switched outlets for its poll from UPI to USA Today/CNN and then to USA Today/ESPN in 1997.

After 29 years of releasing its final Top 20 poll in early December, AP named its 1965 national champion following that season's bowl games. AP returned to a pre-bowls final vote in 1966 and '67, but has polled its writers and broadcasters after the bowl games since the 1968 season. The FWAA has selected its champion after the bowl games since the 1955 season, the NFF-Hall of Fame since 1971, UPI after 1974, USA Today/CNN 1991-96, and USA Today/ESPN since 1997.

The Associated Press changed the name of its national championship award from the AP trophy to the Bear Bryant Trophy after the legendary Alabama coach's death in 1983. The Football Writers' trophy is called the Grantland Rice Award (after the celebrated sportswriter) and the NFF-Hall of Fame trophy is called the MacArthur Bowl (in honor of Gen. Douglas MacArthur).

Multiple champions: Notre Dame (9); Alabama and Oklahoma (7); Ohio St. (6); USC and Nebraska (5); Miami-FL and Minnesota (4); Michigan St. and Texas (3); Army, Florida St., Georgia Tech, Michigan, Penn St., Pittsburgh and Tennessee (2).

Year		Record	Bowl Game	Head Coach	Outstanding Player
1936	**Minnesota**	7-1-0	No bowl	Bernie Bierman	Ed Widseth, T
1937	**Pittsburgh**	9-0-1	No bowl	Jock Sutherland	Marshall Goldberg, HB
1938	**TCU**	11-0-0	Won Sugar	Dutch Meyer	Davey O'Brien, QB
1939	**Texas A&M**	11-0-0	Won Sugar	Homer Norton	John Kimbrough, FB
1940	**Minnesota**	8-0-0	No Bowl	Bernie Bierman	George Franck, HB
1941	**Minnesota**	8-0-0	No bowl	Bernie Bierman	Bruce Smith, HB
1942	**Ohio St.**	9-1-0	No bowl	Paul Brown	Gene Fekete, FB
1943	**Notre Dame**	9-1-0	No bowl	Frank Leahy	Angelo Bertelli, QB
1944	**Army**	9-0-0	No bowl	Red Blaik	Glenn Davis, HB
1945	**Army**	9-0-0	No bowl	Red Blaik	Doc Blanchard, FB
1946	**Notre Dame**	8-0-1	No bowl	Frank Leahy	Johnny Lujack, QB
1947	**Notre Dame**	9-0-0	No bowl	Frank Leahy	Johnny Lujack, QB
1948	**Michigan**	9-0-0	No bowl	Bennie Oosterbaan	Dick Rifenburg, E
1949	**Notre Dame**	10-0-0	No bowl	Frank Leahy	Leon Hart, E
1950	**Oklahoma**	10-1-0	Lost Sugar	Bud Wilkinson	Leon Heath, FB
1951	**Tennessee**	10-0-0	Lost Sugar	Bob Neyland	Hank Lauricella, TB
1952	**Michigan St.** (AP, UP)	9-0-0	No bowl	Biggie Munn	Don McAuliffe, HB
	& Georgia Tech (INS)	12-0-0	Won Sugar	Bobby Dodd	Hal Miller, T
1953	**Maryland**	10-1-0	Lost Orange	Jim Tatum	Bernie Faloney, QB
1954	**Ohio St.** (AP, INS)	10-0-0	Won Rose	Woody Hayes	Howard Cassady, HB
	& UCLA (UP, FW)	9-0-0	No bowl	Red Sanders	Jack Ellena, T
1955	**Oklahoma**	11-0-0	Won Orange	Bud Wilkinson	Jerry Tubbs, C
1956	**Oklahoma**	10-0-0	No bowl	Bud Wilkinson	Tommy McDonald, HB
1957	**Auburn** (AP)	10-0-0	No bowl	Shug Jordan	Jimmy Phillips, E
	& Ohio St. (UP, FW, INS)	9-1-0	Won Rose	Woody Hayes	Bob White, FB
1958	**LSU** (AP, UPI)	11-0-0	Won Sugar	Paul Dietzel	Billy Cannon, HB
	& Iowa (FW)	8-1-1	Won Rose	Forest Evashevski	Randy Duncan, QB
1959	**Syracuse**	11-0-0	Won Cotton	Ben Schwartzwalder	Ernie Davis, HB
1960	**Minnesota** (AP, UPI, NFF)	8-2-0	Lost Rose	Murray Warmath	Tom Brown, G
	& Mississippi (FW)	10-0-1	Won Sugar	Johnny Vaught	Jake Gibbs, QB

National Champions (Cont.)

Year		Record	Bowl Game	Head Coach	Outstanding Player
1961	**Alabama** (AP, UPI, NFF)	11-0-0	Won Sugar	Bear Bryant	Billy Neighbors, T
	& **Ohio St.** (FW)	8-0-1	No bowl	Woody Hayes	Bob Ferguson, HB
1962	**USC**	11-0-0	Won Rose	John McKay	Hal Bedsole, E
1963	**Texas**	11-0-0	Won Cotton	Darrell Royal	Scott Appleton, T
1964	**Alabama** (AP, UPI)	10-1-0	Lost Orange	Bear Bryant	Joe Namath, QB
	Arkansas (FW)	11-0-0	Won Cotton	Frank Broyles	Ronnie Caveness, LB
	& **Notre Dame** (NFF)	9-1-0	No bowl	Ara Parseghian	John Huarte, QB
1965	**Alabama** (AP, FW-tie)	9-1-1	Won Orange	Bear Bryant	Paul Crane, C
	& **Michigan St.** (UPI, NFF, FW-tie)	10-1-0	Lost Rose	Duffy Daugherty	George Webster, LB
1966	**Notre Dame** (AP, UPI, FW, NFF-tie)	9-0-1	No bowl	Ara Parseghian	Jim Lynch, LB
	& **Michigan St.** (NFF-tie)	9-0-1	No bowl	Duffy Daugherty	Bubba Smith, DE
1967	**USC**	10-1-0	Won Rose	John McKay	O.J. Simpson, HB
1968	**Ohio St.**	10-0-0	Won Rose	Woody Hayes	Rex Kern, QB
1969	**Texas**	11-0-0	Won Cotton	Darrell Royal	James Street, QB
1970	**Nebraska** (AP, FW)	11-0-1	Won Orange	Bob Devaney	Jerry Tagge, QB
	Texas (UPI, NFF-tie)	10-1-0	Lost Cotton	Darrell Royal	Steve Worster, RB
	& **Ohio St.** (NFF-tie)	9-1-0	Lost Rose	Woody Hayes	Jim Stillwagon, MG
1971	**Nebraska**	13-0-0	Won Orange	Bob Devaney	Johnny Rodgers, WR
1972	**USC**	12-0-0	Won Rose	John McKay	Charles Young, TE
1973	**Notre Dame** (AP, FW, NFF)	11-0-0	Won Sugar	Ara Parseghian	Mike Townsend, DB
	& **Alabama** (UPI)	11-1-0	Lost Sugar	Bear Bryant	Buddy Brown, OT
1974	**Oklahoma** (AP)	11-0-0	No bowl	Barry Switzer	Joe Washington, RB
	& **USC** (UPI, FW, NFF)	10-1-1	Won Rose	John McKay	Anthony Davis, RB
1975	**Oklahoma**	11-1-0	Won Orange	Barry Switzer	Lee Roy Selmon, DT
1976	**Pittsburgh**	12-0-0	Won Sugar	Johnny Majors	Tony Dorsett, RB
1977	**Notre Dame**	11-1-0	Won Cotton	Dan Devine	Ross Browner, DE
1978	**Alabama** (AP, FW, NFF)	11-1-0	Won Sugar	Bear Bryant	Marty Lyons, DT
	& **USC** (UPI)	12-1-0	Won Rose	John Robinson	Charles White, RB
1979	**Alabama**	12-0-0	Won Sugar	Bear Bryant	Jim Bunch, OT
1980	**Georgia**	12-0-0	Won Sugar	Vince Dooley	Herschel Walker, RB
1981	**Clemson**	12-0-0	Won Orange	Danny Ford	Jeff Davis, LB
1982	**Penn St.**	11-1-0	Won Sugar	Joe Paterno	Todd Blackledge, QB
1983	**Miami-FL**	11-1-0	Won Orange	H. Schnellenberger	Bernie Kosar, QB
1984	**BYU**	13-0-0	Won Holiday	LaVell Edwards	Robbie Bosco, QB
1985	**Oklahoma**	11-1-0	Won Orange	Barry Switzer	Brian Bosworth, LB
1986	**Penn St.**	12-0-0	Won Fiesta	Joe Paterno	D.J. Dozier, RB
1987	**Miami-FL**	12-0-0	Won Orange	Jimmy Johnson	Steve Walsh, QB
1988	**Notre Dame**	12-0-0	Won Fiesta	Lou Holtz	Tony Rice, QB
1989	**Miami-FL**	11-1-0	Won Sugar	Dennis Erickson	Craig Erickson, QB
1990	**Colorado** (AP, FW, NFF)	11-1-1	Won Orange	Bill McCartney	Eric Bieniemy, RB
	& **Georgia Tech** (UPI)	11-0-1	Won Citrus	Bobby Ross	Shawn Jones, QB
1991	**Miami-FL** (AP)	12-0-0	Won Orange	Dennis Erickson	Gino Torretta, QB
	& **Washington** (USA, FW, NFF)	12-0-0	Won Rose	Don James	Steve Emtman, DT
1992	**Alabama**	13-0-0	Won Sugar	Gene Stallings	Eric Curry, DE
1993	**Florida St.**	12-1-0	Won Orange	Bobby Bowden	Charlie Ward, QB
1994	**Nebraska**	13-0-0	Won Orange	Tom Osborne	Zach Wiegert, OT
1995	**Nebraska**	12-0-0	Won Fiesta	Tom Osborne	Tommie Frazier, QB
1996	**Florida**	12-1*	Won Sugar	Steve Spurrier	Danny Wuerffel, QB
1997	**Michigan** (AP, FW, NFF)	12-0	Won Rose	Lloyd Carr	Charles Woodson, DB
	& **Nebraska** (ESPN/USA)	13-0	Won Orange	Tom Osborne	Ahman Green, RB
1998	**Tennessee**	13-0	Won Fiesta	Phillip Fulmer	Peerless Price, WR
1999	**Florida St.**	12-0	Won Sugar	Bobby Bowden	Peter Warrick, WR
2000	**Oklahoma**	13-0	Won Orange	Bob Stoops	Josh Heupel, QB

*The NCAA instituted overtime for regular season games in 1996.

Number 1 vs. Number 2

Since the Associated Press writers poll started keeping track of such things in 1936, the No. 1 and No. 2 ranked teams in the country have met 33 times; 20 during the regular season and 13 in bowl games. Since the first showdown in 1943, the No. 1 team has beaten the No. 2 team 21 times, lost 10 and there have been two ties. Each showdown is listed below with the date, the match-up, each team's record going into the game, the final score, the stadium and site.

Date	Match-up		Stadium	Date	Match-up		Stadium
Oct. 9 1943	#1 Notre Dame (2-0)	35	Michigan	Nov. 10 1945	#1 Army (6-0)	48	Yankee
	#2 Michigan (3-0)	12	(Ann Arbor)		#2 Notre Dame (5-0-1)	0	(New York)
Nov. 20 1943	#1 Notre Dame (8-0)	14	Notre Dame	Dec. 1 1945	#1 Army (8-0)	32	Municipal
	#2 Iowa Pre-Flight (8-0)	13	(South Bend)		#2 Navy (7-0-1)	13	(Philadelphia)
Dec. 2 1944	#1 Army (8-0)	23	Municipal	Nov. 9 1946	#1 Army (7-0)	0	Yankee
	#2 Navy (6-2)	7	(Baltimore)		#2 Notre Dame (5-0)	0	(New York)

Date	Match-up		Stadium
Jan. 1 1963	#1 USC (10-0)	42	ROSE BOWL
	#2 Wisconsin (8-1)	37	(Pasadena)
Oct. 12 1963	#2 Texas (3-0)	28	Cotton Bowl
	#1 Oklahoma (2-0)	7	(Dallas)
Jan. 1 1964	#1 Texas (10-0)	28	COTTON BOWL
	#2 Navy (9-1)	6	(Dallas)
Nov. 19 1966	#1 Notre Dame (8-0)	10	Spartan
	#2 Michigan St. (9-0)	10	(East Lansing)
Sept. 28 1968	#1 Purdue (1-0)	37	Notre Dame
	#2 Notre Dame (1-0)	22	(South Bend)
Jan. 1 1969	#1 Ohio St. (9-0)	27	ROSE BOWL
	#2 USC (9-0-1)	16	(Pasadena)
Dec. 6 1969	#1 Texas (9-0)	15	Razorback
	#2 Arkansas (9-0)	14	(Fayetteville)
Nov. 25 1971	#1 Nebraska (10-0)	35	Owen Field
	#2 Oklahoma (9-0)	31	(Norman)
Jan. 1 1972	#1 Nebraska (12-0)	38	ORANGE BOWL
	#2 Alabama (11-0)	6	(Miami)
Jan. 1 1979	#2 Alabama (10-1)	14	SUGAR BOWL
	#1 Penn St. (11-0)	7	(New Orleans)
Sept. 26 1981	#1 USC (2-0)	28	Coliseum
	#2 Oklahoma (1-0)	24	(Los Angeles)
Jan. 1 1983	#2 Penn St. (10-1)	27	SUGAR BOWL
	#1 Georgia (11-0)	23	(New Orleans)
Oct. 19 1985	#1 Iowa (5-0)	12	Kinnick
	#2 Michigan (5-0)	10	(Iowa City)
Sept. 27 1986	#2 Miami-FL (3-0)	28	Orange Bowl
	#1 Oklahoma (2-0)	16	(Miami)
Jan. 2 1987	#2 Penn St. (11-0)	14	FIESTA BOWL
	#1 Miami-FL (11-0)	10	(Tempe)
Nov. 21 1987	#2 Oklahoma (10-0)	17	Memorial
	#1 Nebraska (11-0)	7	(Lincoln)
Jan. 1 1988	#2 Miami-FL (11-0)	20	ORANGE BOWL
	#1 Oklahoma (11-0)	14	(Miami)
Nov. 26 1988	#1 Notre Dame (10-0)	27	Coliseum
	#2 USC (10-0)	10	(Los Angeles)
Sept. 16 1989	#1 Notre Dame (1-0)	24	Michigan
	#2 Michigan (0-0)	19	(Ann Arbor)
Nov. 16 1991	#2 Miami-FL (8-0)	17	Doak Campbell
	#1 Florida St. (10-0)	16	(Tallahassee)
Jan. 1 1993	#2 Alabama (12-0)	34	SUGAR BOWL
	#1 Miami-FL (11-0)	13	(New Orleans)
Nov. 13 1993	#2 Notre Dame (9-0)	31	Notre Dame
	#1 Florida St. (9-0)	24	(South Bend)
Jan. 1 1994	#1 Florida St. (11-1)	18	ORANGE BOWL
	#2 Nebraska (11-0)	16	(Miami)
Jan. 2 1996	#1 Nebraska (11-0)	62	FIESTA BOWL
	#2 Florida (12-0)	24	(Tempe)
Nov. 30 1996	#2 Florida St. (10-0)	24	Doak Campbell
	#1 Florida (10-1)	21	(Tallahassee)
Jan. 4 1999	#1 Tennessee (12-0)	23	FIESTA BOWL
	#2 Florida St. (11-1)	16	(Tempe)
Jan. 4 2000	#1 Florida St. (11-0)	46	SUGAR BOWL
	#2 Virginia Tech (11-0)	29	(New Orleans)

Note: Bowl games are listed in CAPITAL letters.

Top 50 Rivalries

Top Division I-A and I-AA series records, including games through the 2000 season. All rivalries listed below are renewed annually with the following exceptions. **LSU-Tulane** stopped playing in 1996 but will renew the rivalry in 2001. **Nebraska-Oklahoma** now play only when matched up as part of the rotating Big 12 schedule.

RECENTLY DISCONTINUED SERIES: **Baylor vs TCU** in 1995 after 102 games (Baylor ahead 48-47-7); **Florida vs Miami-FL** in 1991 after 49 games (Florida ahead, 25-24); **Miami-FL vs Notre Dame** in 1990 after 23 games (ND ahead, 15-7-1). Note that Miami beat Florida in the 2000 Sugar Bowl.

	Gm	Series Leader		Gm	Series Leader
Air Force-Army	35	Air Force (22-12-1)	**Michigan-Notre Dame**	29	Michigan (17-11-1)
Air Force-Navy	33	Air Force (23-10-0)	**Michigan-Ohio St.**	97	Michigan (56-35-6)
Alabama-Auburn	65	Alabama (37-27-1)	**Minnesota-Wisconsin**	110	Minnesota (57-45-8)
Alabama-Tennessee	83	Alabama (42-34-7)	**Mississippi-Miss. St.**	97	Ole Miss (55-36-6)
Arizona-Arizona St.	74	Arizona (42-31-1)	**Missouri-Kansas**	109	Tied (53-53-9)
Army-Navy	101	Army (48-46-7)	**Nebraska-Oklahoma**	79	Oklahoma (40-36-3)
Auburn-Georgia	104	Auburn (50-46-8)	**N. Mexico-N. Mexico St.**	90	New Mexico (58-27-5)
California-Stanford	103	Stanford (53-39-11)	**N. Carolina-N.C. State**	90	N. Carolina (59-25-6)
The Citadel-VMI	60	Tied (29-29-2)	**Notre Dame-Purdue**	72	Notre Dame (47-23-2)
Clemson-S. Carolina	98	Clemson (59-35-4)	**Notre Dame-USC**	72	Notre Dame (41-26-5)
Colorado-Nebraska	59	Nebraska (43-14-2)	**Oklahoma-Okla. St.**	95	Oklahoma (74-14-7)
Colo. St.-Wyoming	90	Colorado St. (47-38-5)	**Oregon-Oregon St.**	104	Oregon (54-42-10)
Duke-N. Carolina	86	N. Carolina (47-36-4)*	**Penn-Cornell**	107	Penn (61-41-5)
Florida-Florida St.	45	Florida (26-17-2)	**Penn St.-Pittsburgh**	96	Penn St. (50-42-4)
Florida-Georgia	79	Georgia (46-31-2)	**Pittsburgh-West Va**	93	Pitt (57-33-3)
Florida St.-Miami,FL	45	Miami (24-20-0)	**Princeton-Yale**	123	Yale (66-47-10)
Georgia-Georgia Tech	95	Georgia (52-38-5)*	**Purdue-Indiana**	103	Purdue (63-34-6)
Grambling-Southern	49	Southern (26-23-0)	**Richmond-Wm. & Mary**	110	Wm. & Mary (56-49-5)
Harvard-Yale	117	Yale (64-45-8)	**Tennessee-Vanderbilt**	94	Tennessee (63-26-5)
Kansas-Kansas St.	98	Kansas (61-32-5)	**Texas-Oklahoma**	95	Texas (55-35-5)
Kentucky-Tennessee	96	Tennessee (64-23-9)	**Texas-Texas A&M**	107	Texas (68-34-5)
Lafayette-Lehigh	136	Lafayette (71-60-5)	**UCLA-USC**	70	USC (36-27-7)
LSU-Tulane	93	LSU (64-22-7)*	**Utah-BYU**	76	Utah (45-27-4)*
Miami,OH-Cincinnati	105	Miami (55-43-7)	**Utah-Utah St.**	98	Utah (65-29-4)
Michigan-Michigan St.	93	Michigan (61-27-5)	**Washington-Wash. St.**	93	Washington (61-26-6)

*Disputed series records: UNC claims lead of 48-35-4; Georgia claims lead of 52-36-5; Tulane claims LSU leads 61-23-7; Utah claims lead of 48-30-4

Associated Press Final Polls

The Associated Press introduced its weekly college football poll of sportswriters (later, sportswriters and broadcasters) in 1936. The final AP poll was released at the end of the regular season until 1965, when bowl results were included for one year. After a two-year return to regular season games only, the final poll has come out after the bowls since 1968. Starting in 1989, the AP Poll has ranked 25 teams.

1936

Final poll released Nov. 30. Top 20 regular season results after that: **Dec. 5**—#8 Notre Dame tied USC, 13-13; #17 Tennessee tied Ole Miss, 0-0; #18 Arkansas over Texas, 6-0. **Dec. 12**—#16 TCU over #6 Santa Clara, 9-0.

		As of Nov. 30	Head Coach	After Bowls
1	Minnesota	7-1-0	Bernie Bierman	same
2	LSU	9-0-1	Bernie Moore	9-1-1
3	Pittsburgh	7-1-1	Jock Sutherland	8-1-1
4	Alabama	8-0-1	Frank Thomas	same
5	Washington	7-1-1	Jimmy Phelan	7-2-1
6	Santa Clara	7-0-0	Buck Shaw	8-1-0
7	Northwestern	7-1-0	Pappy Waldorf	same
8	Notre Dame	6-2-0	Elmer Layden	6-2-1
9	Nebraska	7-2-0	Dana X. Bible	same
10	Penn	7-1-0	Harvey Harman	same
11	Duke	9-1-0	Wallace Wade	same
12	Yale	7-1-0	Ducky Pond	same
13	Dartmouth	7-1-1	Red Blaik	same
14	Duquesne	7-2-0	John Smith	8-2-0
15	Fordham	5-1-2	Jim Crowley	same
16	TCU	7-2-2	Dutch Meyer	9-2-2
17	Tennessee	6-2-1	Bob Neyland	6-2-2
18	Arkansas	6-3-0	Fred Thomsen	7-3-0
	Navy	6-3-0	Tom Hamilton	same
20	Marquette	7-1-0	Frank Murray	7-2-0

Key Bowl Games

Sugar—#6 Santa Clara over #2 LSU, 21-14; **Rose**—#3 Pitt over #5 Washington, 21-0; **Orange**—#14 Duquesne over Mississippi St., 13-12; **Cotton**—#16 TCU over #20 Marquette, 16-6.

1937

Final poll released Nov. 29. Top 20 regular season results after that: **Dec. 4**—#18 Rice over SMU, 15-7.

		As of Nov. 29	Head Coach	After Bowls
1	Pittsburgh	9-0-1	Jock Sutherland	same
2	California	9-0-1	Stub Allison	10-0-1
3	Fordham	7-0-1	Jim Crowley	same
4	Alabama	9-0-0	Frank Thomas	9-1-0
5	Minnesota	6-2-0	Bernie Bierman	same
6	Villanova	8-0-1	Clipper Smith	same
7	Dartmouth	7-0-2	Red Blaik	same
8	LSU	9-1-0	Bernie Moore	9-2-0
9	Notre Dame	6-2-1	Elmer Layden	same
	Santa Clara	8-0-0	Buck Shaw	9-0-0
11	Nebraska	6-1-2	Biff Jones	same
12	Yale	6-1-1	Ducky Pond	same
13	Ohio St.	6-2-0	Francis Schmidt	same
14	Holy Cross	8-0-2	Eddie Anderson	same
	Arkansas	6-2-2	Fred Thomsen	same
16	TCU	4-2-2	Dutch Meyer	same
17	Colorado	8-0-0	Bunnie Oakes	8-1-0
18	Rice	4-3-2	Jimmy Kitts	6-3-2
19	North Carolina	7-1-1	Ray Wolf	same
20	Duke	7-2-1	Wallace Wade	same

Key Bowl Games

Rose—#2 Cal over #4 Alabama, 13-0; **Sugar**—#9 Santa Clara over #8 LSU, 6-0; **Cotton**—#18 Rice over #17 Colorado, 28-14; **Orange**—Auburn over Michigan St., 6-0.

1938

Final poll released Dec. 5. Top 20 regular season results after that: **Dec. 26**—#14 Cal over Georgia Tech, 13-7.

		As of Dec. 5	Head Coach	After Bowls
1	TCU	10-0-0	Dutch Meyer	11-0-0
2	Tennessee	10-0-0	Bob Neyland	11-0-0
3	Duke	9-0-0	Wallace Wade	9-1-0
4	Oklahoma	10-0-0	Tom Stidham	10-1-0
5	Notre Dame	8-1-0	Elmer Layden	same
6	Carnegie Tech	7-1-0	Bill Kern	7-2-0
7	USC	8-2-0	Howard Jones	9-2-0
8	Pittsburgh	8-2-0	Jock Sutherland	same
9	Holy Cross	8-1-0	Eddie Anderson	same
10	Minnesota	6-2-0	Bernie Bierman	same
11	Texas Tech	10-0-0	Pete Cawthon	10-1-0
12	Cornell	5-1-1	Carl Snavely	same
13	Alabama	7-1-1	Frank Thomas	same
14	California	9-1-0	Stub Allison	10-1-0
15	Fordham	6-1-2	Jim Crowley	same
16	Michigan	6-1-1	Fritz Crisler	same
17	Northwestern	4-2-2	Pappy Waldorf	same
18	Villanova	8-0-1	Clipper Smith	same
19	Tulane	7-2-1	Red Dawson	same
20	Dartmouth	7-2-0	Red Blaik	same

Key Bowl Games

Sugar—#1 TCU over #6 Carnegie Tech, 15-7; **Orange**—#2 Tennessee over #4 Oklahoma, 17-0; **Rose**—#7 USC over #3 Duke, 7-3; **Cotton**—St. Mary's over #11 Texas Tech 20-13.

1939

Final poll released Dec. 11. Top 20 regular season results after that: None.

		As of Dec. 11	Head Coach	After Bowls
1	Texas A&M	10-0-0	Homer Norton	11-0-0
2	Tennessee	10-0-0	Bob Neyland	10-1-0
3	USC	7-0-2	Howard Jones	8-0-2
4	Cornell	8-0-0	Carl Snavely	same
5	Tulane	8-0-1	Red Dawson	8-1-1
6	Missouri	8-1-0	Don Faurot	8-2-0
7	UCLA	6-0-4	Babe Horrell	same
8	Duke	8-1-0	Wallace Wade	same
9	Iowa	6-1-1	Eddie Anderson	same
10	Duquesne	8-0-1	Buff Donelli	same
11	Boston College	9-1-0	Frank Leahy	9-2-0
12	Clemson	8-1-0	Jess Neely	9-1-0
13	Notre Dame	7-2-0	Elmer Layden	same
14	Santa Clara	5-1-3	Buck Shaw	same
15	Ohio St.	6-2-0	Francis Schmidt	same
16	Georgia Tech	7-2-0	Bill Alexander	8-2-0
17	Fordham	6-2-0	Jim Crowley	same
18	Nebraska	7-1-1	Biff Jones	same
19	Oklahoma	6-2-1	Tom Stidham	same
20	Michigan	6-2-0	Fritz Crisler	same

Key Bowl Games

Sugar—#1 Texas A&M over #5 Tulane, 14-13; **Rose**—#3 USC over #2 Tennessee, 14-0; **Orange**—#16 Georgia Tech over #6 Missouri, 21-7; **Cotton**—#12 Clemson over #11 Boston College, 6-3.

1940

Final poll released Dec. 2. Top 20 regular season results after that: **Dec. 7**–#16 SMU over Rice, 7-6.

		As of Dec. 2	Head Coach	After Bowls
1	Minnesota	8-0-0	Bernie Bierman	same
2	Stanford	9-0-0	Clark Shaughnessy	10-0-0
3	Michigan	7-1-0	Fritz Crisler	same
4	Tennessee	10-0-0	Bob Neyland	10-1-0
5	Boston College	10-0-0	Frank Leahy	11-0-0
6	Texas A&M	8-1-0	Homer Norton	9-1-0
7	Nebraska	8-1-0	Biff Jones	8-2-0
8	Northwestern	6-2-0	Pappy Waldorf	same
9	Mississippi St.	9-0-1	Allyn McKeen	10-0-1
10	Washington	7-2-0	Jimmy Phelan	same
11	Santa Clara	6-1-1	Buck Shaw	same
12	Fordham	7-1-0	Jim Crowley	7-2-0
13	Georgetown	8-1-0	Jack Hagerty	8-2-0
14	Penn	6-1-1	George Munger	same
15	Cornell	6-2-0	Carl Snavely	same
16	SMU	7-1-1	Matty Bell	8-1-1
17	Hardin-Simmons	9-0-0	Warren Woodson	same
18	Duke	7-2-0	Wallace Wade	same
19	Lafayette	9-0-0	Hooks Mylin	same
20	–			

Note: Only 19 teams ranked.

Key Bowl Games

Rose–#2 Stanford over #7 Nebraska, 21-13; **Sugar**– #5 Boston College over #4 Tennessee, 19-13; **Cotton**–#6 Texas A&M over #12 Fordham, 13-12; **Orange**–#9 Mississippi St. over #13 Georgetown, 14-7.

1941

Final poll released Dec. 1. Top 20 regular season results after that: **Dec. 6**–#4 Texas over Oregon, 71-7; #9 Texas A&M over #19 Washington St., 7-0; #16 Mississippi St. over San Francisco, 26-13.

		As of Dec. 1	Head Coach	After Bowls
1	Minnesota	8-0-0	Bernie Bierman	same
2	Duke	9-0-0	Wallace Wade	9-1-0
3	Notre Dame	8-0-1	Frank Leahy	same
4	Texas	7-1-1	Dana X. Bible	8-1-1
5	Michigan	6-1-1	Fritz Crisler	same
6	Fordham	7-1-0	Jim Crowley	8-1-0
7	Missouri	8-1-0	Don Faurot	8-2-0
8	Duquesne	8-0-0	Buff Donelli	same
9	Texas A&M	8-1-0	Homer Norton	9-2-0
10	Navy	7-1-1	Swede Larson	same
11	Northwestern	5-3-0	Pappy Waldorf	same
12	Oregon St.	7-2-0	Lon Stiner	8-2-0
13	Ohio St.	6-1-1	Paul Brown	same
14	Georgia	8-1-1	Wally Butts	9-1-1
15	Penn	7-1-1	George Munger	same
16	Mississippi St.	7-1-1	Allyn McKeen	8-1-1
17	Mississippi	6-2-1	Harry Mehre	same
18	Tennessee	8-2-0	John Barnhill	same
19	Washington St.	6-3-0	Babe Hollingbery	6-4-0
20	Alabama	8-2-0	Frank Thomas	9-2-0

Note: 1942 Rose Bowl moved to Durham, N.C., for one year after outbreak of World War II.

Key Bowl Games

Rose–#12 Oregon St. over #2 Duke, 20-16; **Sugar**– #6 Fordham over #7 Missouri, 2-0; **Cotton**–#20 Alabama over #9 Texas A&M, 29-21; **Orange**–#14 Georgia over TCU, 40-26.

1942

Final poll released Nov. 30. Top 20 regular season results after that: **Dec. 5**–#6 Notre Dame tied Great Lakes Naval Station, 13-13; #13 UCLA over Idaho, 40-13; #14 William & Mary over Oklahoma, 14-7; #17 Washington St. lost to Texas A&M, 21-0; #18 Mississippi St. over San Francisco, 19-7. **Dec. 12**–#13 UCLA over USC, 14-7.

		As of Nov. 30	Head Coach	After Bowls
1	Ohio St.	9-1-0	Paul Brown	same
2	Georgia	10-1-0	Wally Butts	11-1-0
3	Wisconsin	8-1-1	Harry Stuhldreher	same
4	Tulsa	10-0-0	Henry Frnka	10-1-0
5	Georgia Tech	9-1-0	Bill Alexander	9-2-0
6	Notre Dame	7-2-1	Frank Leahy	7-2-2
7	Tennessee	8-1-1	John Barnhill	9-1-1
8	Boston College	8-1-0	Denny Myers	8-2-0
9	Michigan	7-3-0	Fritz Crisler	same
10	Alabama	7-3-0	Frank Thomas	8-3-0
11	Texas	8-2-0	Dana X. Bible	9-2-0
12	Stanford	6-4-0	Marchy Schwartz	same
13	UCLA	5-3-0	Babe Horrell	7-4-0
14	William & Mary	8-1-1	Carl Voyles	9-1-1
15	Santa Clara	7-2-0	Buck Shaw	same
16	Auburn	6-4-1	Jack Meagher	same
17	Washington St.	6-1-2	Babe Hollingbery	6-2-2
18	Mississippi St.	7-2-0	Allyn McKeen	8-2-0
19	Minnesota	5-4-0	George Hauser	same
	Holy Cross	5-4-1	Ank Scanlon	same
	Penn St.	6-1-1	Bob Higgins	same

Key Bowl Games

Rose–#2 Georgia over #13 UCLA, 9-0; **Sugar**–#7 Tennessee over #4 Tulsa, 14-7; **Cotton**–#11 Texas over #5 Georgia Tech, 14-7; **Orange**–#10 Alabama over #8 Boston College, 37-21.

1943

Final poll released Nov. 29. Top 20 regular season results after that: **Dec. 11**–#10 March Field over #19 Pacific, 19-0.

		As of Nov. 29	Head Coach	After Bowls
1	Notre Dame	9-1-0	Frank Leahy	same
2	Iowa Pre-Flight	9-1-0	Don Faurot	same
3	Michigan	8-1-0	Fritz Crisler	same
4	Navy	8-1-0	Billick Whelchel	same
5	Purdue	9-0-0	Elmer Burnham	same
6	Great Lakes Naval Station	10-2-0	Tony Hinkle	same
7	Duke	8-1-0	Eddie Cameron	same
8	DelMonte Pre-Flight	7-1-0	Bill Kern	same
9	Northwestern	6-2-0	Pappy Waldorf	same
10	March Field	8-1-0	Paul Schissler	9-1-0
11	Army	7-2-1	Red Blaik	same
12	Washington	4-0-0	Ralph Welch	4-1-0
13	Georgia Tech	7-3-0	Bill Alexander	8-3-0
14	Texas	7-1-0	Dana X. Bible	7-1-1
15	Tulsa	6-0-1	Henry Frnka	6-1-1
16	Dartmouth	6-1-0	Earl Brown	same
17	Bainbridge Navy Training School	7-0-0	Joe Maniaci	same
18	Colorado College	7-0-0	Hal White	same
19	Pacific	7-1-0	Amos A. Stagg	7-2-0
20	Penn	6-2-1	George Munger	same

Key Bowl Games

Rose–USC over #12 Washington, 29-0; **Sugar**–#13 Georgia Tech over #15 Tulsa, 20-18; **Cotton**–#14 Texas tied Randolph Field, 7-7; **Orange**–LSU over Texas A&M, 19-14.

Associated Press Final Polls (Cont.)

1944

Final poll released Dec. 4. Top 20 regular season results after that: **Dec. 10**–#3 Randolph Field over #10 March Field, 20-7; #18 Fort Pierce over Kessler Field, 34-7; Morris Field over #20 Second Air Force, 14-7.

	As of Dec. 4	Head Coach	After Bowls
1	Army.............9-0-0	Red Blaik	same
2	Ohio St. 9-0-0	Carroll Widdoes	same
3	Randolph Field 10-0-0	Frank Tritico	12-0-0
4	Navy.............6-3-0	Oscar Hagberg	same
5	Bainbridge Navy		
	Training School.....10-0-0	Joe Maniaci	same
6	Iowa Pre-Flight 10-1-0	Jack Meagher	same
7	USC ..../...7-0-2	Jeff Cravath	8-0-2
8	Michigan 8-2-0	Fritz Crisler	same
9	Notre Dame 8-2-0	Ed McKeever	same
10	March Field 7-0-2	Paul Schissler	7-1-2
11	Duke 5-4-0	Eddie Cameron	6-4-0
12	Tennessee 7-0-1	John Barnhill	7-1-1
13	Georgia Tech.......8-2-0	Bill Alexander	8-3-0
14	Norman Pre-Flight...6-0-0	John Gregg	same
15	Illinois 5-4-1	Ray Eliot	same
16	El Toro Marines......8-1-0	Dick Hanley	same
17	Great Lakes		
	Naval Station 9-2-1	Paul Brown	same
18	Fort Pierce 8-0-0	Hamp Pool	9-0-0
19	St. Mary's Pre-Flight .4-4-0	Jules Sikes	same
20	Second Air Force ...10-2-1	Bill Reese	10-4-1

Key Bowl Games
Treasury–#3 Randolph Field over #20 Second Air Force, 13-6; **Rose**–#7 USC over #12 Tennessee, 25-0; **Sugar**–#11 Duke over Alabama, 29-26; **Orange**–Tulsa over #13 Georgia Tech, 26-12; **Cotton**–Oklahoma A&M over TCU, 34-0.

1945

Final poll released Dec. 3. Top 20 regular season results after that: None.

	As of Dec. 3	Head Coach	After Bowls
1	Army.............9-0-0	Red Blaik	same
2	Alabama 9-0-0	Frank Thomas	10-0-0
3	Navy.............7-1-1	Oscar Hagberg	same
4	Indiana...........9-0-1	Bo McMillan	same
5	Oklahoma A&M ...8-0-0	Jim Lookabaugh	9-0-0
6	Michigan 7-3-0	Fritz Crisler	same
7	St. Mary's-CA 7-1-0	Jimmy Phelan	7-2-0
8	Penn 6-2-0	George Munger	same
9	Notre Dame 7-2-1	Hugh Devore	same
10	Texas 9-1-0	Dana X. Bible	10-1-0
11	USC 7-3-0	Jeff Cravath	7-4-0
12	Ohio St. 7-2-0	Carroll Widdoes	same
13	Duke 6-2-0	Eddie Cameron	same
14	Tennessee.........8-1-0	John Barnhill	same
15	LSU 7-2-0	Bernie Moore	same
16	Holy Cross 8-1-0	John DeGrosa	8-2-0
17	Tulsa 8-2-0	Henry Frnka	8-3-0
18	Georgia 8-2-0	Wally Butts	9-2-0
19	Wake Forest.......4-3-1	Peahead Walker	5-3-1
20	Columbia 8-1-0	Lou Little	same

Key Bowl Games
Rose–#2 Alabama over #11 USC, 34-14; **Sugar**– #5 Oklahoma A&M over #7 St. Mary's, 33-13; **Cotton**–#10 Texas over Missouri, 40-27; **Orange**–Miami-FL over #16 Holy Cross, 13-6.

1946

Final poll released Dec. 2. Top 20 regular season results after that: None.

	As of Dec. 2	Head Coach	After Bowls
1	Notre Dame......8-0-1	Frank Leahy	same
2	Army.............9-0-1	Red Blaik	same
3	Georgia 10-0-0	Wally Butts	11-0-0
4	UCLA 10-0-0	Bert LaBrucherie	10-1-0
5	Illinois 7-2-0	Ray Eliot	8-2-0
6	Michigan 6-2-1	Fritz Crisler	same
7	Tennessee 9-1-0	Bob Neyland	9-2-0
8	LSU 9-1-0	Bernie Moore	9-1-1
9	North Carolina 8-1-1	Carl Snavely	8-2-1
10	Rice 8-2-0	Jess Neely	9-2-0
11	Georgia Tech......8-2-0	Bobby Dodd	9-2-0
12	Yale 7-1-1	Howard Odell	same
13	Penn 6-2-0	George Munger	same
14	Oklahoma 7-3-0	Jim Tatum	8-3-0
15	Texas 8-2-0	Dana X. Bible	same
16	Arkansas 6-3-1	John Barnhill	6-3-2
17	Tulsa 9-1-0	J.O. Brothers	same
18	N.C. State 8-2-0	Beattie Feathers	8-3-0
19	Delaware 9-0-0	Bill Murray	10-0-0
20	Indiana...........6-3-0	Bo McMillan	same

Key Bowl Games
Sugar–#3 Georgia over #9 N. Carolina, 20-10; **Rose**–#5 Illinois over #4 UCLA, 45-14; **Orange**–#10 Rice over #7 Tennessee, 8-0; **Cotton**–#8 LSU tied #16 Arkansas, 0-0.

1947

Final poll released Dec. 8. Top 20 regular season results after that: None.

	As of Dec. 8	Head Coach	After Bowls
1	Notre Dame......9-0-0	Frank Leahy	same
2	Michigan 9-0-0	Fritz Crisler	10-0-0
3	SMU 9-0-1	Matty Bell	9-0-2
4	Penn St. 9-0-0	Bob Higgins	9-0-1
5	Texas 9-1-0	Blair Cherry	10-1-0
6	Alabama 8-2-0	Red Drew	8-3-0
7	Penn 7-0-1	George Munger	same
8	USC 7-1-1	Jeff Cravath	7-2-1
9	North Carolina 8-2-0	Carl Snavely	same
10	Georgia Tech......9-1-0	Bobby Dodd	10-1-0
11	Army 5-2-2	Red Blaik	same
12	Kansas 8-0-2	George Sauer	8-1-2
13	Mississippi 8-2-0	Johnny Vaught	9-2-0
14	William & Mary ...9-1-0	Rube McCray	9-2-0
15	California 9-1-0	Pappy Waldorf	same
16	Oklahoma 7-2-1	Bud Wilkinson	same
17	N.C. State 5-3-1	Beattie Feathers	same
18	Rice 6-3-1	Jess Neely	same
19	Duke 4-3-2	Wallace Wade	same
20	Columbia 7-2-0	Lou Little	same

Key Bowl Games
Rose–#2 Michigan over #8 USC, 49-0; **Cotton**–#3 SMU tied #4 Penn St., 13-13; **Sugar**–#5 Texas over #6 Alabama, 27-7; **Orange**–#10 Georgia Tech over #12 Kansas, 20-14.

Note: An unprecedented "Who's No. 1?" poll was conducted by AP after the Rose Bowl game, pitting Notre Dame against Michigan. The Wolverines won the vote, 226-119, but AP ruled that the Irish would be the No. 1 team of record. For more information see the box on page 167.

1948

Final poll released Nov. 29. Top 20 regular season results after that: **Dec. 3**–#12 Vanderbilt over Miami-FL, 33-6. **Dec. 4**–#2 Notre Dame tied USC, 14-14; #11 Clemson over The Citadel, 20-0.

		As of Nov. 29	Head Coach	After Bowls
1	Michigan	9-0-0	Bennie Oosterbaan	same
2	Notre Dame	9-0-0	Frank Leahy	9-0-1
3	North Carolina	9-0-1	Carl Snavely	9-1-1
4	California	10-0-0	Pappy Waldorf	10-1-0
5	Oklahoma	9-1-0	Bud Wilkinson	10-1-0
6	Army	8-0-1	Red Blaik	same
7	Northwestern	7-2-0	Bob Voigts	8-2-0
8	Georgia	9-1-0	Wally Butts	9-2-0
9	Oregon	9-1-0	Jim Aiken	9-2-0
10	SMU	8-1-1	Matty Bell	9-1-1
11	Clemson	9-0-0	Frank Howard	11-0-0
12	Vanderbilt	7-2-1	Red Sanders	8-2-1
13	Tulane	9-1-0	Henry Frnka	same
14	Michigan St.	6-2-2	Biggie Munn	same
15	Mississippi	8-1-0	Johnny Vaught	same
16	Minnesota	7-2-0	Bernie Bierman	same
17	William & Mary	6-2-2	Rube McCray	7-2-2
18	Penn St.	7-1-1	Bob Higgins	same
19	Cornell	8-1-0	Lefty James	same
20	Wake Forest	6-3-0	Peahead Walker	6-4-0

Note: Big Nine "no-repeat" rule kept Michigan from Rose Bowl.

Key Bowl Games

Sugar–#5 Oklahoma over #3 North Carolina, 14-6; **Rose**–#7 Northwestern over #4 Cal, 20-14; **Orange**–Texas over #8 Georgia, 41-28; **Cotton**–#10 SMU over #9 Oregon, 21-13.

1949

Final poll released Nov. 28. Top 20 regular season results after that: **Dec. 2**–#14 Maryland over Miami-FL, 13-0. **Dec. 3**–#1 Notre Dame over SMU, 27-20; #10 Pacific over Hawaii, 75-0.

		As of Nov. 28	Head Coach	After Bowls
1	Notre Dame	9-0-0	Frank Leahy	10-0-0
2	Oklahoma	10-0-0	Bud Wilkinson	11-0-0
3	California	10-0-0	Pappy Waldorf	10-1-0
4	Army	9-0-0	Red Blaik	same
5	Rice	9-1-0	Jess Neely	10-1-0
6	Ohio St.	6-1-2	Wes Fesler	7-1-2
7	Michigan	6-2-1	Bennie Oosterbaan	same
8	Minnesota	7-2-0	Bernie Bierman	same
9	LSU	8-2-0	Gaynell Tinsley	8-3-0
10	Pacific	10-0-0	Larry Siemering	11-0-0
11	Kentucky	9-2-0	Bear Bryant	9-3-0
12	Cornell	8-1-0	Lefty James	same
13	Villanova	8-1-0	Jim Leonard	same
14	Maryland	7-1-0	Jim Tatum	9-1-0
15	Santa Clara	7-2-1	Len Casanova	8-2-1
16	North Carolina	7-3-0	Carl Snavely	7-4-0
17	Tennessee	7-2-1	Bob Neyland	same
18	Princeton	6-3-0	Charlie Caldwell	same
19	Michigan St.	6-3-0	Biggie Munn	same
20	Missouri	7-3-0	Don Faurot	7-4-0
	Baylor	8-2-0	Bob Woodruff	same

Key Bowl Games

Sugar–#2 Oklahoma over #9 LSU, 35-0; **Rose**–#6 Ohio St. over #3 Cal, 17-14; **Cotton**–#5 Rice over #16 North Carolina, 27-13; **Orange**–#15 Santa Clara over #11 Kentucky, 21-13.

1950

Final poll released Nov. 27. Top 20 regular season results after that: **Nov. 30**–#3 Texas over Texas A&M, 17-0. **Dec. 1**–#15 Miami-FL over Missouri, 27-9. **Dec. 2**–#1 Oklahoma over Okla. A&M, 41-14; Navy over #2 Army, 14-2; #4 Tennessee over Vanderbilt, 43-0; #16 Alabama over Auburn, 34-0; #19 Tulsa over Houston, 28-21; #20 Tulane tied LSU, 14-14. **Dec. 9**–#3 Texas over LSU, 21-6.

		As of Nov. 27	Head Coach	After Bowls
1	Oklahoma	9-0-0	Bud Wilkinson	10-1-0
2	Army	8-0-0	Red Blaik	8-1-0
3	Texas	7-1-0	Blair Cherry	9-2-0
4	Tennessee	9-1-0	Bob Neyland	11-1-0
5	California	9-0-1	Pappy Waldorf	9-1-1
6	Princeton	9-0-0	Charlie Caldwell	same
7	Kentucky	10-1-0	Bear Bryant	11-1-0
8	Michigan St.	8-1-0	Biggie Munn	same
9	Michigan	5-3-1	Bennie Oosterbaan	6-3-1
10	Clemson	8-0-1	Frank Howard	9-0-1
11	Washington	8-2-0	Howard Odell	same
12	Wyoming	9-0-0	Bowden Wyatt	10-0-0
13	Illinois	7-2-0	Ray Eliot	same
14	Ohio St.	6-3-0	Wes Fesler	same
15	Miami-FL	8-0-1	Andy Gustafson	9-1-1
16	Alabama	8-2-0	Red Drew	9-2-0
17	Nebraska	6-2-1	Bill Glassford	same
18	Wash. & Lee	8-2-0	George Barclay	8-3-0
19	Tulsa	8-1-1	J.O. Brothers	9-1-1
20	Tulane	6-2-0	Henry Frnka	6-2-1

Key Bowl Games

Sugar–#7 Kentucky over #1 Oklahoma, 13-7; **Cotton**–#4 Tennessee over #3 Texas, 20-14; **Rose**–#9 Michigan over #5 Cal, 14-6; **Orange**–#10 Clemson over #15 Miami-FL, 15-14.

1951

Final poll released Dec. 3. Top 20 regular season results after that: None.

		As of Dec. 3	Head Coach	After Bowls
1	Tennessee	10-0-0	Bob Neyland	10-1-0
2	Michigan St.	9-0-0	Biggie Munn	same
3	Maryland	9-0-0	Jim Tatum	10-0-0
4	Illinois	8-0-1	Ray Eliot	9-0-1
5	Georgia Tech	10-0-1	Bobby Dodd	11-0-1
6	Princeton	9-0-0	Charlie Caldwell	same
7	Stanford	9-1-0	Chuck Taylor	9-2-0
8	Wisconsin	7-1-1	Ivy Williamson	same
9	Baylor	8-1-1	George Sauer	8-2-1
10	Oklahoma	8-2-0	Bud Wilkinson	same
11	TCU	6-4-0	Dutch Meyer	6-5-0
12	California	8-2-0	Pappy Waldorf	same
13	Virginia	8-1-0	Art Guepe	same
14	San Francisco	9-0-0	Joe Kuharich	same
15	Kentucky	7-4-0	Bear Bryant	8-4-0
16	Boston Univ.	6-4-0	Buff Donelli	same
17	UCLA	5-3-1	Red Sanders	same
18	Washington St.	7-3-0	Forest Evashevski	same
19	Holy Cross	8-2-0	Eddie Anderson	same
20	Clemson	7-2-0	Frank Howard	7-3-0

Key Bowl Games

Sugar–#3 Maryland over #1 Tennessee, 28-13; **Rose**–#4 Illinois over #7 Stanford, 40-7; **Orange**–#5 Georgia Tech over #9 Baylor, 17-14; **Cotton**–#15 Kentucky over #11 TCU, 20-7.

Associated Press Final Polls (Cont.)

1952

Final poll released Dec. 1. Top 20 regular season results after that: **Dec. 6**–#15 Florida over #20 Kentucky, 27-20.

			As of Dec. 1	Head Coach	After Bowls
1	Michigan St.		9-0-0	Biggie Munn	same
2	Georgia Tech		11-0-0	Bobby Dodd	12-0-0
3	Notre Dame		7-2-1	Frank Leahy	same
4	Oklahoma		8-1-1	Bud Wilkinson	same
5	USC		9-1-0	Jess Hill	10-1-0
6	UCLA		8-1-0	Red Sanders	same
7	Mississippi		8-0-2	Johnny Vaught	8-1-2
8	Tennessee		8-1-1	Bob Neyland	8-2-1
9	Alabama		9-2-0	Red Drew	10-2-0
10	Texas		8-2-0	Ed Price	9-2-0
11	Wisconsin		6-2-1	Ivy Williamson	6-3-1
12	Tulsa		8-1-1	J.O. Brothers	8-2-1
13	Maryland		7-2-0	Jim Tatum	same
14	Syracuse		7-2-0	Ben Schwartzwalder	7-3-0
15	Florida		6-3-0	Bob Woodruff	8-3-0
16	Duke		8-2-0	Bill Murray	same
17	Ohio St.		6-3-0	Woody Hayes	same
18	Purdue		4-3-2	Stu Holcomb	same
19	Princeton		8-1-0	Charlie Caldwell	same
20	Kentucky		5-3-2	Bear Bryant	5-4-2

Note: Michigan St. would officially join Big Ten in 1953.

Key Bowl Games

Sugar–#2 Georgia Tech over #7 Ole Miss, 24-7; **Rose**–#5 USC over #11 Wisconsin, 7-0; **Cotton**–#10 Texas over #8 Tennessee, 16-0; **Orange**–#9 Alabama over #14 Syracuse, 61-6.

1953

Final poll released Nov. 30. Top 20 regular season results after that: **Dec. 5**–#2 Notre Dame over SMU, 40-14.

			As of Nov. 30	Head Coach	After Bowls
1	Maryland		10-0-0	Jim Tatum	10-1-0
2	Notre Dame		8-0-1	Frank Leahy	9-0-1
3	Michigan St.		8-1-0	Biggie Munn	9-1-0
4	Oklahoma		8-1-1	Bud Wilkinson	9-1-1
5	UCLA		8-1-0	Red Sanders	8-2-0
6	Rice		8-2-0	Jess Neely	9-2-0
7	Illinois		7-1-1	Ray Eliot	same
8	Georgia Tech		8-2-1	Bobby Dodd	9-2-1
9	Iowa		5-3-1	Forest Evashevski	same
10	West Virginia		8-1-0	Art Lewis	8-2-0
11	Texas		7-3-0	Ed Price	same
12	Texas Tech		10-1-0	DeWitt Weaver	11-1-0
13	Alabama		6-2-3	Red Drew	6-3-3
14	Army		7-1-1	Red Blaik	same
15	Wisconsin		6-2-1	Ivy Williamson	same
16	Kentucky		7-2-1	Bear Bryant	same
17	Auburn		7-2-1	Shug Jordan	7-3-1
18	Duke		7-2-1	Bill Murray	same
19	Stanford		6-3-1	Chuck Taylor	same
20	Michigan		6-3-0	Bennie Oosterbaan	same

Key Bowl Games

Orange–#4 Oklahoma over #1 Maryland, 7-0; **Rose**–#3 Michigan St. over #5 UCLA, 28-20; **Cotton**–#6 Rice over #13 Alabama, 28-6; **Sugar**–#8 Georgia Tech over #10 West Virginia, 42-19.

1954

Final poll released Nov. 29. Top 20 regular season results after that: **Dec. 4**–#4 Notre Dame over SMU, 26-14.

			As of Nov. 29	Head Coach	After Bowls
1	Ohio St.		9-0-0	Woody Hayes	10-0-0
2	UCLA		9-0-0	Red Sanders	same
3	Oklahoma		10-0-0	Bud Wilkinson	same
4	Notre Dame		8-1-0	Terry Brennan	9-1-0
5	Navy		7-2-0	Eddie Erdelatz	8-2-0
6	Mississippi		9-1-0	Johnny Vaught	9-2-0
7	Army		7-2-0	Red Blaik	same
8	Maryland		7-2-1	Jim Tatum	same
9	Wisconsin		7-2-0	Ivy Williamson	same
10	Arkansas		8-2-0	Bowden Wyatt	8-3-0
11	Miami-FL		8-1-0	Andy Gustafson	same
12	West Virginia		8-1-0	Art Lewis	same
13	Auburn		7-3-0	Shug Jordan	8-3-0
14	Duke		7-2-1	Bill Murray	8-2-1
15	Michigan		6-3-0	Bennie Oosterbaan	same
16	Virginia Tech		8-0-1	Frank Moseley	same
17	USC		8-3-0	Jess Hill	8-4-0
18	Baylor		7-3-0	George Sauer	7-4-0
19	Rice		7-3-0	Jess Neely	same
20	Penn St.		7-2-0	Rip Engle	same

Note: PCC and Big Seven "no-repeat" rules kept UCLA and Oklahoma from Rose and Orange bowls, respectively.

Key Bowl Games

Rose–#1 Ohio St. over #17 USC, 20-7; **Sugar**–#5 Navy over #6 Ole Miss, 21-0; **Cotton**–Georgia Tech over #10 Arkansas, 14-6; **Orange**–#14 Duke over Nebraska, 34-7.

1955

Final poll released Nov. 28. Top 20 regular season results after that: None.

			As of Nov. 28	Head Coach	After Bowls
1	Oklahoma		10-0-0	Bud Wilkinson	11-0-0
2	Michigan St.		8-1-0	Duffy Daugherty	9-1-0
3	Maryland		10-0-0	Jim Tatum	10-1-0
4	UCLA		9-1-0	Red Sanders	9-2-0
5	Ohio St.		7-2-0	Woody Hayes	same
6	TCU		9-1-0	Abe Martin	9-2-0
7	Georgia Tech		8-1-1	Bobby Dodd	9-1-1
8	Auburn		8-1-1	Shug Jordan	8-2-1
9	Notre Dame		8-2-0	Terry Brennan	same
10	Mississippi		9-1-0	Johnny Vaught	10-1-0
11	Pittsburgh		7-3-0	John Michelosen	7-4-0
12	Michigan		7-2-0	Bennie Oosterbaan	same
13	USC		6-4-0	Jess Hill	same
14	Miami-FL		6-3-0	Andy Gustafson	same
15	Miami-OH		9-0-0	Ara Parseghian	same
16	Stanford		6-3-1	Chuck Taylor	same
17	Texas A&M		7-2-1	Bear Bryant	same
18	Navy		6-2-1	Eddie Erdelatz	same
19	West Virginia		8-2-0	Art Lewis	same
20	Army		6-3-0	Red Blaik	same

Note: Big Ten "no-repeat" rule kept Ohio St. from Rose Bowl.

Key Bowl Games

Orange–#1 Oklahoma over #3 Maryland, 20-6; **Rose**–#2 Michigan St. over #4 UCLA, 17-14; **Cotton**–#10 Ole Miss over #6 TCU, 14-13; **Sugar**–#7 Georgia Tech over #11 Pitt, 7-0; **Gator**–Vanderbilt over #8 Auburn, 25-13.

1956

Final poll released Dec. 3. Top 20 regular season results after that: **Dec. 8**–#13 Pitt over #6 Miami-FL, 14-7.

		As of Dec. 3	Head Coach	After Bowls
1	Oklahoma	10-0-0	Bud Wilkinson	same
2	Tennessee	10-0-0	Bowden Wyatt	10-1-0
3	Iowa	8-1-0	Forest Evashevski	9-1-0
4	Georgia Tech	9-1-0	Bobby Dodd	10-1-0
5	Texas A&M	9-0-1	Bear Bryant	same
6	Miami-FL	8-0-1	Andy Gustafson	8-1-1
7	Michigan	7-2-0	Bennie Oosterbaan	same
8	Syracuse	7-1-0	Ben Schwartzwalder	7-2-0
9	Michigan St.	7-2-0	Duffy Daugherty	same
10	Oregon St.	7-2-1	Tommy Prothro	7-3-1
11	Baylor	8-2-0	Sam Boyd	9-2-0
12	Minnesota	6-1-2	Murray Warmath	same
13	Pittsburgh	6-2-1	John Michelosen	7-3-1
14	TCU	7-3-0	Abe Martin	8-3-0
15	Ohio St.	6-3-0	Woody Hayes	same
16	Navy	6-1-2	Eddie Erdelatz	same
17	G. Washington	7-1-1	Gene Sherman	8-1-1
18	USC	8-2-0	Jess Hill	same
19	Clemson	7-1-2	Frank Howard	7-2-2
20	Colorado	7-2-1	Dallas Ward	8-2-1

Note: Big Seven "no-repeat" rule kept Oklahoma from Orange Bowl and Texas A&M was on probation.

Key Bowl Games

Sugar–#11 Baylor over #2 Tennessee, 13-7; **Rose**– #3 Iowa over #10 Oregon St., 35-19; **Gator**–#4 Georgia Tech over #13 Pitt, 21-14; **Cotton**–#14 TCU over #8 Syracuse, 28-27; **Orange**–#20 Colorado over #19 Clemson, 27-21.

1957

Final poll released Dec. 2. Top 20 regular season results after that: **Dec. 7**–#10 Notre Dame over SMU, 54-21.

		As of Dec. 2	Head Coach	After Bowls
1	Auburn	10-0-0	Shug Jordan	same
2	Ohio St.	8-1-0	Woody Hayes	9-1-0
3	Michigan St.	8-1-0	Duffy Daugherty	same
4	Oklahoma	9-1-0	Bud Wilkinson	10-1-0
5	Navy	8-1-1	Eddie Erdelatz	9-1-1
6	Iowa	7-1-1	Forest Evashevski	same
7	Mississippi	8-1-1	Johnny Vaught	9-1-1
8	Rice	7-3-0	Jess Neely	7-4-0
9	Texas A&M	8-2-0	Bear Bryant	8-3-0
10	Notre Dame	6-3-0	Terry Brennan	7-3-0
11	Texas	6-3-1	Darrell Royal	6-4-1
12	Arizona St.	10-0-0	Dan Devine	same
13	Tennessee	7-3-0	Bowden Wyatt	8-3-0
14	Mississippi St.	6-2-1	Wade Walker	same
15	N.C. State	7-1-2	Earle Edwards	same
16	Duke	6-2-2	Bill Murray	6-3-2
17	Florida	6-2-1	Bob Woodruff	same
18	Army	7-2-0	Red Blaik	same
19	Wisconsin	6-3-0	Milt Bruhn	same
20	VMI	9-0-1	John McKenna	same

Note: Auburn on probation, ineligible for bowl game.

Key Bowl Games

Rose–#2 Ohio St. over Oregon, 10-7; **Orange**–#4 Oklahoma over #16 Duke, 48-21; **Cotton**–#5 Navy over #8 Rice, 20-7; **Sugar**–#7 Ole Miss over #11 Texas, 39-7; **Gator**–#13 Tennessee over #9 Texas A&M, 3-0.

1958

Final poll released Dec. 1. Top 20 regular season results after that: None.

		As of Dec. 1	Head Coach	After Bowls
1	LSU	10-0-0	Paul Dietzel	11-0-0
2	Iowa	7-1-1	Forest Evashevski	8-1-1
3	Army	8-0-1	Red Blaik	same
4	Auburn	9-0-1	Shug Jordan	same
5	Oklahoma	9-1-0	Bud Wilkinson	10-1-0
6	Air Force	9-0-1	Ben Martin	9-0-2
7	Wisconsin	7-1-1	Milt Bruhn	same
8	Ohio St.	6-1-2	Woody Hayes	same
9	Syracuse	8-1-0	Ben Schwartzwalder	8-2-0
10	TCU	8-2-0	Abe Martin	8-2-1
11	Mississippi	8-2-0	Johnny Vaught	9-2-0
12	Clemson	8-2-0	Frank Howard	8-3-0
13	Purdue	6-1-2	Jack Mollenkopf	same
14	Florida	6-3-1	Bob Woodruff	6-4-1
15	South Carolina	7-3-0	Warren Giese	same
16	California	7-3-0	Pete Elliott	7-4-0
17	Notre Dame	6-4-0	Terry Brennan	same
18	SMU	6-4-0	Bill Meek	same
19	Oklahoma St.	7-3-0	Cliff Speegle	8-3-0
20	Rutgers	8-1-0	John Stiegman	same

Key Bowl Games

Sugar–#1 LSU over #12 Clemson, 7-0; **Rose**–#2 Iowa over #16 Cal, 38-12; **Orange**–#5 Oklahoma over #9 Syracuse, 21-6; **Cotton**–#6 Air Force tied #10 TCU, 0-0.

1959

Final poll released Dec. 7. Top 20 regular season results after that: None.

		As of Dec. 7	Head Coach	After Bowls
1	Syracuse	10-0-0	Ben Schwartzwalder	11-0-0
2	Mississippi	9-1-0	Johnny Vaught	10-1-0
3	LSU	9-1-0	Paul Dietzel	9-2-0
4	Texas	9-1-0	Darrell Royal	9-2-0
5	Georgia	9-1-0	Wally Butts	10-1-0
6	Wisconsin	7-2-0	Milt Bruhn	7-3-0
7	TCU	8-2-0	Abe Martin	8-3-0
8	Washington	9-1-0	Jim Owens	10-1-0
9	Arkansas	8-2-0	Frank Broyles	9-2-0
10	Alabama	7-1-2	Bear Bryant	7-2-2
11	Clemson	8-2-0	Frank Howard	9-2-0
12	Penn St.	8-2-0	Rip Engle	9-2-0
13	Illinois	5-3-1	Ray Eliot	same
14	USC	8-2-0	Don Clark	same
15	Oklahoma	7-3-0	Bud Wilkinson	same
16	Wyoming	9-1-0	Bob Devaney	same
17	Notre Dame	5-5-0	Joe Kuharich	same
18	Missouri	6-4-0	Dan Devine	6-5-0
19	Florida	5-4-1	Bob Woodruff	same
20	Pittsburgh	6-4-0	John Michelosen	same

Note: Big Seven "no-repeat" rule kept Oklahoma from Orange Bowl.

Key Bowl Games

Cotton–#1 Syracuse over #4 Texas, 23-14; **Sugar**– #2 Ole Miss over #3 LSU, 21-0; **Orange**–#5 Georgia over #18 Missouri, 14-0; **Rose**–#8 Washington over #6 Wisconsin, 44-8; **Bluebonnet**–#11 Clemson over #7 TCU, 23-7; **Gator**–#9 Arkansas over Georgia Tech, 14-7; **Liberty**–#12 Penn St. over #10 Alabama, 7-0.

Associated Press Final Polls (Cont.)

1960

Final poll released Nov. 28. Top 20 regular season results after that: **Dec. 3**–UCLA over #10 Duke, 27-6.

			As of Nov. 28	Head Coach	After Bowls
1	Minnesota		8-1-0	Murray Warmath	8-2-0
2	Mississippi		9-0-1	Johnny Vaught	10-0-1
3	Iowa		8-1-0	Forest Evashevski	same
4	Navy		9-1-0	Wayne Hardin	9-2-0
5	Missouri		9-1-0	Dan Devine	10-1-0
6	Washington		9-1-0	Jim Owens	10-1-0
7	Arkansas		8-2-0	Frank Broyles	8-3-0
8	Ohio St.		7-2-0	Woody Hayes	same
9	Alabama		8-1-1	Bear Bryant	8-1-2
10	Duke		7-2-0	Bill Murray	8-3-0
11	Kansas		7-2-1	Jack Mitchell	same
12	Baylor		8-2-0	John Bridgers	8-3-0
13	Auburn		8-2-0	Shug Jordan	same
14	Yale		9-0-0	Jordan Olivar	same
15	Michigan St.		6-2-1	Duffy Daugherty	same
16	Penn St.		6-3-0	Rip Engle	7-3-0
17	New Mexico St.		10-0-0	Warren Woodson	11-0-0
18	Florida		8-2-0	Ray Graves	9-2-0
19	Syracuse		7-2-0	Ben Schwartzwalder	same
	Purdue		4-4-1	Jack Mollenkopf	same

Key Bowl Games

Rose–#6 Washington over #1 Minnesota, 17-7; **Sugar**–#2 Ole Miss over Rice, 14-6; **Orange**–#5 Missouri over #4 Navy, 21-14; **Cotton**–#10 Duke over #7 Arkansas, 7-6; **Bluebonnet**–#9 Alabama tied Texas, 3-3.

1961

Final poll released Dec. 4. Top 20 regular season results after that: None.

			As of Dec. 4	Head Coach	After Bowls
1	Alabama		10-0-0	Bear Bryant	11-0-0
2	Ohio St.		8-0-1	Woody Hayes	same
3	Texas		9-1-0	Darrell Royal	10-1-0
4	LSU		9-1-0	Paul Dietzel	10-1-0
5	Mississippi		9-1-0	Johnny Vaught	9-2-0
6	Minnesota		7-2-0	Murray Warmath	8-2-0
7	Colorado		9-1-0	Sonny Grandelius	9-2-0
8	Michigan St.		7-2-0	Duffy Daugherty	same
9	Arkansas		8-2-0	Frank Broyles	8-3-0
10	Utah St.		9-0-1	John Ralston	9-1-1
11	Missouri		7-2-1	Dan Devine	same
12	Purdue		6-3-0	Jack Mollenkopf	same
13	Georgia Tech		7-3-0	Bobby Dodd	7-4-0
14	Syracuse		7-3-0	Ben Schwartzwalder	8-3-0
15	Rutgers		9-0-0	John Bateman	same
16	UCLA		7-3-0	Bill Barnes	7-4-0
17	Rice		7-3-0	Jess Neely	7-4-0
	Penn St.		7-3-0	Rip Engle	8-3-0
	Arizona		8-1-1	Jim LaRue	same
20	Duke		7-3-0	Bill Murray	same

Note: Ohio St. faculty council turned down Rose Bowl invitation citing concern with OSU's overemphasis on sports.

Key Bowl Games

Sugar–#1 Alabama over #9 Arkansas, 10-3; **Cotton**–#3 Texas over #5 Ole Miss, 12-7; **Orange**–#4 LSU over #7 Colorado, 25-7; **Rose**–#6 Minnesota over #16 UCLA, 21-3; **Gotham**–Baylor over #10 Utah St., 24-9.

1962

Final poll released Dec. 3. Top 10 regular season results after that: None.

			As of Dec. 3	Head Coach	After Bowls
1	USC		10-0-0	John McKay	11-0-0
2	Wisconsin		8-1-0	Milt Bruhn	8-2-0
3	Mississippi		9-0-0	Johnny Vaught	10-0-0
4	Texas		9-0-1	Darrell Royal	9-1-1
5	Alabama		9-1-0	Bear Bryant	10-1-0
6	Arkansas		9-1-0	Frank Broyles	9-2-0
7	LSU		8-1-1	Charlie McClendon	9-1-1
8	Oklahoma		8-2-0	Bud Wilkinson	8-3-0
9	Penn St.		9-1-0	Rip Engle	9-2-0
10	Minnesota		6-2-1	Murray Warmath	same

Key Bowl Games

Rose–#1 USC over #2 Wisconsin, 42-37; **Sugar**–#3 Ole Miss over #6 Arkansas, 17-13; **Cotton**–#7 LSU over #4 Texas, 13-0; **Orange**–#5 Alabama over #8 Oklahoma, 17-0; **Gator**–Florida over #9 Penn St.,17-7.

1963

Final poll released Dec. 9. Top 10 regular season results after that: **Dec.14**–#8 Alabama over Miami-FL, 17-12.

			As of Dec. 9	Head Coach	After Bowls
1	Texas		10-0-0	Darrell Royal	11-0-0
2	Navy		9-1-0	Wayne Hardin	9-2-0
3	Illinois		7-1-1	Pete Elliott	8-1-1
4	Pittsburgh		9-1-0	John Michelosen	same
5	Auburn		9-1-0	Shug Jordan	9-2-0
6	Nebraska		9-1-0	Bob Devaney	10-1-0
7	Mississippi		7-0-2	Johnny Vaught	7-1-2
8	Alabama		7-2-0	Bear Bryant	9-2-0
9	Michigan St.		6-2-1	Duffy Daugherty	same
10	Oklahoma		8-2-0	Bud Wilkinson	same

Key Bowl Games

Cotton–#1 Texas over #2 Navy, 28-6; **Rose**–#3 Illinois over Washington, 17-7; **Orange**–#6 Nebraska over #5 Auburn, 13-7; **Sugar**–#8 Alabama over #7 Ole Miss, 12-7.

1964

Final poll released Nov. 30. Top 10 regular season results after that: **Dec. 5**–Florida over #7 LSU, 20-6.

			As of Nov. 30	Head Coach	After Bowls
1	Alabama		10-0-0	Bear Bryant	10-1-0
2	Arkansas		10-0-0	Frank Broyles	11-0-0
3	Notre Dame		9-1-0	Ara Parseghian	same
4	Michigan		8-1-0	Bump Elliott	9-1-0
5	Texas		9-1-0	Darrell Royal	10-1-0
6	Nebraska		9-1-0	Bob Devaney	9-2-0
7	LSU		7-1-1	Charlie McClendon	8-2-1
8	Oregon St.		8-2-0	Tommy Prothro	8-3-0
9	Ohio St.		7-2-0	Woody Hayes	same
10	USC		7-3-0	John McKay	same

Key Bowl Games

Orange–#5 Texas over #1 Alabama, 21-17; **Cotton**–#2 Arkansas over #6 Nebraska, 10-7; **Rose**– #4 Michigan over #8 Oregon St., 34-7; **Sugar**–#7 LSU over Syracuse, 13-10.

1965

Final poll taken after bowl games for the first time.

	After Bowls	Head Coach	Regular Season
1 Alabama	9-1-1	Bear Bryant	8-1-1
2 Michigan St.	10-1-0	Duffy Daugherty	10-0-0
3 Arkansas	10-1-0	Frank Broyles	10-0-0
4 UCLA	8-2-1	Tommy Prothro	7-1-1
5 Nebraska	10-1-0	Bob Devaney	10-0-0
6 Missouri	8-2-1	Dan Devine	7-2-1
7 Tennessee	8-1-2	Doug Dickey	6-1-2
8 LSU	8-3-0	Charlie McClendon	7-3-0
9 Notre Dame	7-2-1	Ara Parseghian	same
10 USC	7-2-1	John McKay	same

Key Bowl Games

Rankings below reflect final regular season poll, released Nov. 29. No bowls for then #8 USC or #9 Notre Dame. **Rose**–#5 UCLA over #1 Michigan St., 14-12; **Cotton**–LSU over #2 Arkansas, 14-7; **Orange**–#4 Alabama over #3 Nebraska, 39-28; **Sugar**–#6 Missouri over Florida, 20-18; **Bluebonnet**–#7 Tennessee over Tulsa, 27-6; **Gator**–Georgia Tech over #10 Texas Tech, 31-21.

1966

Final poll released Dec. 5, returning to pre-bowl status. Top 10 regular season results after that: None.

	As of Dec. 5	Head Coach	After Bowls
1 Notre Dame	9-0-1	Ara Parseghian	same
2 Michigan St.	9-0-1	Duffy Daugherty	same
3 Alabama	10-0-0	Bear Bryant	11-0-0
4 Georgia	9-1-0	Vince Dooley	10-1-0
5 UCLA	9-1-0	Tommy Prothro	same
6 Nebraska	9-1-0	Bob Devaney	9-2-0
7 Purdue	8-2-0	Jack Mollenkopf	9-2-0
8 Georgia Tech	9-1-0	Bobby Dodd	9-2-0
9 Miami-FL	7-2-1	Charlie Tate	8-2-1
10 SMU	8-2-0	Hayden Fry	8-3-0

Key Bowl Games

Sugar–#3 Alabama over #6 Nebraska, 34-7; **Cotton**–#4 Georgia over #10 SMU, 24-9; **Rose**–#7 Purdue over USC, 14-13; **Orange**–Florida over #8 Georgia Tech, 27-12; **Liberty**–#9 Miami-FL over Virginia Tech, 14-7.

1967

Final poll released Nov. 27. Top 10 regular season results after that: **Dec. 2**–#2 Tennessee over Vanderbilt, 41-14; #3 Oklahoma over Oklahoma St., 38-14; #8 Alabama over Auburn, 7-3.

	As of Nov. 27	Head Coach	After Bowls
1 USC	9-1-0	John McKay	10-1-0
2 Tennessee	8-1-0	Doug Dickey	9-2-0
3 Oklahoma	8-1-0	Chuck Fairbanks	10-1-0
4 Indiana	9-1-0	John Pont	9-2-0
5 Notre Dame	8-2-0	Ara Parseghian	same
6 Wyoming	10-0-0	Lloyd Eaton	10-1-0
7 Oregon St.	7-2-1	Dee Andros	same
8 Alabama	7-1-1	Bear Bryant	8-2-1
9 Purdue	8-2-0	Jack Mollenkopf	same
10 Penn St.	8-2-0	Joe Paterno	8-2-1

Key Bowl Games

Rose–#1 USC over #4 Indiana, 14-3; **Orange**–#3 Oklahoma over #2 Tennessee, 26-24; **Sugar**–LSU over #6 Wyoming, 20-13; **Cotton**–Texas A&M over #8 Alabama, 20-16; **Gator**–#10 Penn St. tied Florida St. 17-17.

1968

Final poll taken after bowl games for first time since close of 1965 season.

	After Bowls	Head Coach	Regular Season
1 Ohio St.	10-0-0	Woody Hayes	9-0-0
2 Penn St.	11-0-0	Joe Paterno	10-0-0
3 Texas	9-1-1	Darrell Royal	8-1-1
4 USC	9-1-1	John McKay	9-0-1
5 Notre Dame	7-2-1	Ara Parseghian	same
6 Arkansas	10-1-0	Frank Broyles	9-1-0
7 Kansas	9-2-0	Pepper Rodgers	9-1-0
8 Georgia	8-1-2	Vince Dooley	8-0-2
9 Missouri	8-3-0	Dan Devine	7-3-0
10 Purdue	8-2-0	Jack Mollenkopf	same
11 Oklahoma	7-4-0	Chuck Fairbanks	7-3-0
12 Michigan	8-2-0	Bump Elliott	same
13 Tennessee	8-2-1	Doug Dickey	8-1-1
14 SMU	8-3-0	Hayden Fry	7-3-0
15 Oregon St.	7-3-0	Dee Andros	same
16 Auburn	7-4-0	Shug Jordan	6-4-0
17 Alabama	8-3-0	Bear Bryant	8-2-0
18 Houston	6-2-2	Bill Yeoman	same
19 LSU	8-3-0	Charlie McClendon	7-3-0
20 Ohio Univ.	10-1-0	Bill Hess	10-0-0

Key Bowl Games

Rankings below reflect final regular season poll, released Dec. 2. No bowls for then #7 Notre Dame and #11 Purdue. **Rose**–#1 Ohio St. over #2 USC, 27-16; **Orange**–#3 Penn St. over #6 Kansas, 15-14; **Sugar**–#9 Arkansas over #4 Georgia, 16-2; **Cotton**–#5 Texas over #8 Tennessee, 36-13; **Bluebonnet**–#20 SMU over #10 Oklahoma, 28-27; **Gator**–#16 Missouri over #12 Alabama, 35-10.

1969

Final poll taken after bowl games.

	After Bowls	Head Coach	Regular Season
1 Texas	11-0-0	Darrell Royal	10-0-0
2 Penn St.	11-0-0	Joe Paterno	10-0-0
3 USC	10-0-1	John McKay	9-0-1
4 Ohio St.	8-1-0	Woody Hayes	same
5 Notre Dame	8-2-1	Ara Parseghian	8-1-1
6 Missouri	9-2-0	Dan Devine	9-1-0
7 Arkansas	9-2-0	Frank Broyles	9-1-0
8 Mississippi	8-3-0	Johnny Vaught	7-3-0
9 Michigan	8-3-0	Bo Schembechler	8-2-0
10 LSU	9-1-0	Charlie McClendon	same
11 Nebraska	9-2-0	Bob Devaney	8-2-0
12 Houston	9-2-0	Bill Yeoman	8-2-0
13 UCLA	8-1-1	Tommy Prothro	same
14 Florida	9-1-1	Ray Graves	8-1-1
15 Tennessee	9-2-0	Doug Dickey	9-1-0
16 Colorado	8-3-0	Eddie Crowder	7-3-0
17 West Virginia	10-1-0	Jim Carlen	9-1-0
18 Purdue	8-2-0	Jack Mollenkopf	same
19 Stanford	7-2-1	John Ralston	same
20 Auburn	8-3-0	Shug Jordan	8-2-0

Key Bowl Games

Rankings below reflect final regular season poll, released Dec. 8. No bowls for then #4 Ohio St., #8 LSU and #10 UCLA.

Cotton–#1 Texas over #9 Notre Dame, 21-17; **Orange**–#2 Penn St. over #6 Missouri, 10-3; **Sugar**–#13 Ole Miss over #3 Arkansas, 27-22; **Rose**–#5 USC over #7 Michigan, 10-3.

Associated Press Final Polls (Cont.)

1970

		After Bowls	Head Coach	Regular Season
1	Nebraska	11-0-1	Bob Devaney	10-0-1
2	Notre Dame	10-1-0	Ara Parseghian	9-0-1
3	Texas	10-1-0	Darrell Royal	10-0-0
4	Tennessee	11-1-0	Bill Battle	10-1-0
5	Ohio St.	9-1-0	Woody Hayes	9-0-0
6	Arizona St.	11-0-0	Frank Kush	10-0-0
7	LSU	9-3-0	Charlie McClendon	9-2-0
8	Stanford	9-3-0	John Ralston	8-3-0
9	Michigan	9-1-0	Bo Schembechler	same
10	Auburn	9-2-0	Shug Jordan	8-2-0
11	Arkansas	9-2-0	Frank Broyles	same
12	Toledo	12-0-0	Frank Lauterbur	11-0-0
13	Georgia Tech	9-3-0	Bud Carson	8-3-0
14	Dartmouth	9-0-0	Bob Blackman	same
15	USC	6-4-1	John McKay	same
16	Air Force	9-3-0	Ben Martin	9-2-0
17	Tulane	8-4-0	Jim Pittman	7-4-0
18	Penn St.	7-3-0	Joe Paterno	same
19	Houston	8-3-0	Bill Yeoman	same
20	Oklahoma	7-4-1	Chuck Fairbanks	7-4-0
	Mississippi	7-4-0	Johnny Vaught	7-3-0

Key Bowl Games

Rankings below reflect final regular season poll, released Dec. 7. No bowls for then #4 Arkansas and #7 Michigan.

Cotton–#6 Notre Dame over #1 Texas, 24-11; **Rose**– #12 Stanford over #2 Ohio St., 27-17; **Orange**–#3 Nebraska over #8 LSU, 17-12; **Sugar**– #5 Tennessee over #11 Air Force, 34-13; **Peach**–#9 Ariz. St. over N. Carolina, 48-26.

1972

		After Bowls	Head Coach	Regular Season
1	USC	12-0-0	John McKay	11-0-0
2	Oklahoma	11-1-0	Chuck Fairbanks	10-1-0
3	Texas	10-1-0	Darrell Royal	9-1-0
4	Nebraska	9-2-1	Bob Devaney	8-2-1
5	Auburn	10-1-0	Shug Jordan	9-1-0
6	Michigan	10-1-0	Bo Schembechler	same
7	Alabama	10-2-0	Bear Bryant	10-1-0
8	Tennessee	10-2-0	Bill Battle	9-2-0
9	Ohio St.	9-2-0	Woody Hayes	9-1-0
10	Penn St.	10-2-0	Joe Paterno	10-1-0
11	LSU	9-2-1	Charlie McClendon	9-1-1
12	North Carolina	11-1-0	Bill Dooley	10-1-0
13	Arizona St.	10-2-0	Frank Kush	9-2-0
14	Notre Dame	8-3-0	Ara Parseghian	8-2-0
15	UCLA	8-3-0	Pepper Rodgers	same
16	Colorado	8-4-0	Eddie Crowder	8-3-0
17	N.C. State	8-3-1	Lou Holtz	7-3-1
18	Louisville	9-1-0	Lee Corso	same
19	Washington St.	7-4-0	Jim Sweeney	same
20	Georgia Tech	7-4-1	Bill Fulcher	6-4-1

Key Bowl Games

Rankings below reflect final regular season poll, released Dec. 4. No bowl for then #8 Michigan.

Rose–#1 USC over #3 Ohio St., 42-17; **Sugar**–#2 Oklahoma over #5 Penn St., 14-0; **Cotton**–#7 Texas over #4 Alabama, 17-13; **Orange**–#9 Nebraska over #12 Notre Dame, 40-6; **Gator**–#6 Auburn over #13 Colorado, 24-3; **Bluebonnet**–#11 Tennessee over #10 LSU, 24-17.

1971

		After Bowls	Head Coach	Regular Season
1	Nebraska	13-0-0	Bob Devaney	12-0-0
2	Oklahoma	11-1-0	Chuck Fairbanks	10-1-0
3	Colorado	10-2-0	Eddie Crowder	9-2-0
4	Alabama	11-1-0	Bear Bryant	11-0-0
5	Penn St.	11-1-0	Joe Paterno	10-1-0
6	Michigan	11-1-0	Bo Schembechler	11-0-0
7	Georgia	11-1-0	Vince Dooley	10-1-0
8	Arizona St.	11-1-0	Frank Kush	10-1-0
9	Tennessee	10-2-0	Bill Battle	9-2-0
10	Stanford	9-3-0	John Ralston	8-3-0
11	LSU	9-3-0	Charlie McClendon	8-3-0
12	Auburn	9-2-0	Shug Jordan	9-1-0
13	Notre Dame	8-2-0	Ara Parseghian	same
14	Toledo	12-0-0	John Murphy	11-0-0
15	Mississippi	10-2-0	Billy Kinard	9-2-0
16	Arkansas	8-3-1	Frank Broyles	8-2-1
17	Houston	9-3-0	Bill Yeoman	9-2-0
18	Texas	8-3-0	Darrell Royal	8-2-0
19	Washington	8-3-0	Jim Owens	same
20	USC	6-4-1	John McKay	same

Key Bowl Games

Rankings below reflect final regular season poll, released Dec. 6.

Orange–#1 Nebraska over #2 Alabama, 38-6; **Sugar**–#3 Oklahoma over #5 Auburn, 40-22; **Rose**–#16 Stanford over #4 Michigan, 13-12; **Gator**–#6 Georgia over N. Carolina, 7-3; **Bluebonnet**–#7 Colorado over #15 Houston, 29-17; **Fiesta**–#8 Ariz. St. over Florida St., 45-38; **Cotton**–#10 Penn St. over #12 Texas, 30-6.

1973

		After Bowls	Head Coach	Regular Season
1	Notre Dame	11-0-0	Ara Parseghian	10-0-0
2	Ohio St.	10-0-1	Woody Hayes	9-0-1
3	Oklahoma	10-0-1	Barry Switzer	same
4	Alabama	11-1-0	Bear Bryant	11-0-0
5	Penn St.	12-0-0	Joe Paterno	11-0-0
6	Michigan	10-0-1	Bo Schembechler	same
7	Nebraska	9-2-1	Tom Osborne	8-2-1
8	USC	9-2-1	John McKay	9-1-1
9	Arizona St.	11-1-0	Frank Kush	10-1-0
	Houston	11-1-0	Bill Yeoman	10-1-0
11	Texas Tech	11-1-0	Jim Carlen	10-1-0
12	UCLA	9-2-0	Pepper Rodgers	same
13	LSU	9-3-0	Charlie McClendon	9-2-0
14	Texas	8-3-0	Darrell Royal	8-2-0
15	Miami-OH	11-1-0	Bill Mallory	10-0-0
16	N.C. State	9-3-0	Lou Holtz	8-3-0
17	Missouri	8-4-0	Al Onofrio	7-4-0
18	Kansas	7-4-1	Don Fambrough	7-3-1
19	Tennessee	8-4-0	Bill Battle	8-3-0
20	Maryland	8-4-0	Jerry Claiborne	8-3-0
	Tulane	9-3-0	Bennie Ellender	9-2-0

Key Bowl Games

Rankings below reflect final regular season poll, released Dec. 3. No bowls for then #2 Oklahoma (probation), #5 Michigan and #9 UCLA.

Sugar–#3 Notre Dame over #1 Alabama, 24-23; **Rose**–#4 Ohio St. over #7 USC, 42-21; **Orange**–#6 Penn St. over #13 LSU, 16-9; **Cotton**–#12 Nebraska over #8 Texas, 19-3; **Fiesta**–#10 Ariz. St. over Pitt, 28-7; **Bluebonnet**–#14 Houston over #17 Tulane, 47-7.

1974

		After Bowls	Head Coach	Regular Season
1	Oklahoma	11-0-0	Barry Switzer	same
2	USC	10-1-1	John McKay	9-1-1
3	Michigan	10-1-0	Bo Schembechler	same
4	Ohio St.	10-2-0	Woody Hayes	10-1-0
5	Alabama	11-1-0	Bear Bryant	11-0-0
6	Notre Dame	10-2-0	Ara Parseghian	9-2-0
7	Penn St.	10-2-0	Joe Paterno	9-2-0
8	Auburn	10-2-0	Shug Jordan	9-2-0
9	Nebraska	9-3-0	Tom Osborne	8-3-0
10	Miami-OH	10-0-1	Dick Crum	9-0-1
11	N.C. State	9-2-1	Lou Holtz	9-2-0
12	Michigan St.	7-3-1	Denny Stolz	same
13	Maryland	8-4-0	Jerry Claiborne	8-3-0
14	Baylor	8-4-0	Grant Teaff	8-3-0
15	Florida	8-4-0	Doug Dickey	8-3-0
16	Texas A&M	8-3-0	Emory Ballard	same
17	Mississippi St.	9-3-0	Bob Tyler	8-3-0
	Texas	8-4-0	Darrell Royal	8-3-0
19	Houston	8-3-1	Bill Yeoman	8-3-0
20	Tennessee	7-3-2	Bill Battle	6-3-2

Key Bowl Games

Rankings below reflect final regular season poll, released Dec. 2. No bowls for #1 Oklahoma (probation) and then #4 Michigan.

Orange–#9 Notre Dame over #2 Alabama, 13-11; **Rose**–#5 USC over #3 Ohio St., 18-17; **Gator**–#6 Auburn over #11 Texas, 27-3; **Cotton**–#7 Penn St. over #12 Baylor, 41-20; **Sugar**–#8 Nebraska over #18 Florida, 13-10; **Liberty**–Tennessee over #10 Maryland, 7-3.

1975

		After Bowls	Head Coach	Regular Season
1	Oklahoma	11-1-0	Barry Switzer	10-1-0
2	Arizona St.	12-0-0	Frank Kush	11-0-0
3	Alabama	11-1-0	Bear Bryant	10-1-0
4	Ohio St.	11-1-0	Woody Hayes	11-0-0
5	UCLA	9-2-1	Dick Vermeil	8-2-1
6	Texas	10-2-0	Darrell Royal	9-2-0
7	Arkansas	10-2-0	Frank Broyles	9-2-0
8	Michigan	8-2-2	Bo Schembechler	8-1-2
9	Nebraska	10-2-0	Tom Osborne	10-1-0
10	Penn St.	9-3-0	Joe Paterno	9-2-0
11	Texas A&M	10-2-0	Emory Bellard	10-1-0
12	Miami-OH	11-1-0	Dick Crum	10-1-0
13	Maryland	9-2-1	Jerry Claiborne	8-2-1
14	California	8-3-0	Mike White	same
15	Pittsburgh	8-4-0	Johnny Majors	7-4-0
16	Colorado	9-3-0	Bill Mallory	9-2-0
17	USC	8-4-0	John McKay	7-4-0
18	Arizona	9-2-0	Jim Young	same
19	Georgia	9-3-0	Vince Dooley	9-2-0
20	West Virginia	9-3-0	Bobby Bowden	8-3-0

Key Bowl Games

Rankings below reflect final regular season poll, released Dec. 1. Texas A&M was unbeaten and ranked 2nd in that poll, but lost to #18 Arkansas, 31-6, in its final regular season game on Dec. 6.

Rose–#11 UCLA over #1 Ohio St., 23-10; **Liberty**–#17 USC over #2 Texas A&M, 20-0; **Orange**–#3 Oklahoma over #5 Michigan, 14-6; **Sugar**–#4 Alabama over #8 Penn St., 13-6; **Fiesta**–#7 Ariz. St. over #6 Nebraska, 17-14; **Bluebonnet**–#9 Texas over #10 Colorado, 38-21; **Cotton**–#18 Arkansas over #12 Georgia, 31-10.

1976

		After Bowls	Head Coach	Regular Season
1	Pittsburgh	12-0-0	Johnny Majors	11-0-0
2	USC	11-1-0	John Robinson	10-1-0
3	Michigan	10-2-0	Bo Schembechler	10-1-0
4	Houston	10-2-0	Bill Yeoman	9-2-0
5	Oklahoma	9-2-1	Barry Switzer	8-2-1
6	Ohio St.	9-2-1	Woody Hayes	8-2-1
7	Texas A&M	10-2-0	Emory Bellard	9-2-0
8	Maryland	11-1-0	Jerry Claiborne	11-0-0
9	Nebraska	9-3-1	Tom Osborne	8-3-1
10	Georgia	10-2-0	Vince Dooley	10-1-0
11	Alabama	9-3-0	Bear Bryant	8-3-0
12	Notre Dame	9-3-0	Dan Devine	8-3-0
13	Texas Tech	10-2-0	Steve Sloan	10-1-0
14	Oklahoma St.	9-3-0	Jim Stanley	8-3-0
15	UCLA	9-2-1	Terry Donahue	9-1-1
16	Colorado	8-4-0	Bill Mallory	8-3-0
17	Rutgers	11-0-0	Frank Burns	same
18	Kentucky	8-4-0	Fran Curci	7-4-0
19	Iowa St.	8-3-0	Earle Bruce	same
20	Mississippi St.	9-2-0	Bob Tyler	same

Key Bowl Games

Rankings below reflect final regular season poll, released Nov. 29. No bowl for then #20 Miss. St. (probation).

Sugar–#1 Pitt over #5 Georgia, 27-3; **Rose**–#3 USC over #2 Michigan, 14-6; **Cotton**–#6 Houston over #4 Maryland, 30-21; **Liberty**–#16 Alabama over #7 UCLA, 36-6; **Fiesta**–#8 Oklahoma over Wyoming, 41-7; **Bluebonnet**–#13 Nebraska over #9 Texas Tech, 27-24; **Sun**–#10 Texas A&M over Florida, 37-14; **Orange**–#11 Ohio St. over #12 Colorado, 27-10.

1977

		After Bowls	Head Coach	Regular Season
1	Notre Dame	11-1-0	Dan Devine	10-1-0
2	Alabama	11-1-0	Bear Bryant	10-1-0
3	Arkansas	11-1-0	Lou Holtz	10-1-0
4	Texas	11-1-0	Fred Akers	11-0-0
5	Penn St.	11-1-0	Joe Paterno	10-1-0
6	Kentucky	10-1-0	Fran Curci	same
7	Oklahoma	10-2-0	Barry Switzer	10-1-0
8	Pittsburgh	9-2-1	Jackie Sherrill	8-2-1
9	Michigan	10-2-0	Bo Schembechler	10-1-0
10	Washington	8-4-0	Don James	7-4-0
11	Ohio St.	9-3-0	Woody Hayes	9-2-0
12	Nebraska	9-3-0	Tom Osborne	8-3-0
13	USC	8-4-0	John Robinson	7-4-0
14	Florida St.	10-2-0	Bobby Bowden	9-2-0
15	Stanford	9-3-0	Bill Walsh	8-3-0
16	San Diego St.	10-1-0	Claude Gilbert	same
17	North Carolina	8-3-1	Bill Dooley	8-2-1
18	Arizona St.	9-3-0	Frank Kush	9-2-0
19	Clemson	8-3-1	Charley Pell	8-2-1
20	BYU	9-2-0	LaVell Edwards	same

Key Bowl Games

Rankings below reflect final regular season poll, released Nov. 28. No bowl for then #7 Kentucky (probation).

Cotton–#5 Notre Dame over #1 Texas, 38-10; **Orange**–#6 Arkansas over #2 Oklahoma, 31-6; **Sugar**–#3 Alabama over #9 Ohio St., 35-6; **Rose**–#13 Washington over #4 Michigan, 27-20; **Fiesta**–#8 Penn St. over #15 Ariz. St., 42-30; **Gator**–#10 Pitt over #11 Clemson, 34-3.

Associated Press Final Polls (Cont.)

1978

	After Bowls	Head Coach	Regular Season
1	Alabama 11-1-0	Bear Bryant	10-1-0
2	USC 12-1-0	John Robinson	11-1-0
3	Oklahoma 11-1-0	Barry Switzer	10-1-0
4	Penn St. 11-1-0	Joe Paterno	11-0-0
5	Michigan 10-2-0	Bo Schembechler	10-1-0
6	Clemson 11-1-0	Charley Pell	10-1-0
7	Notre Dame 9-3-0	Dan Devine	8-3-0
8	Nebraska 9-3-0	Tom Osborne	9-2-0
9	Texas 9-3-0	Fred Akers	8-3-0
10	Houston 9-3-0	Bill Yeoman	9-2-0
11	Arkansas 9-2-1	Lou Holtz	9-2-0
12	Michigan St. 8-3-0	Darryl Rogers	same
13	Purdue 9-2-1	Jim Young	8-2-1
14	UCLA 8-3-1	Terry Donahue	8-3-0
15	Missouri 8-4-0	Warren Powers	7-4-0
16	Georgia 9-2-1	Vince Dooley	9-1-1
17	Stanford 8-4-0	Bill Walsh	7-4-0
18	N.C. State 9-3-0	Bo Rein	8-3-0
19	Texas A&M 8-4-0	Emory Bellard (4-2) & Tom Wilson (4-2)	7-4-0
20	Maryland 9-3-0	Jerry Claiborne	9-2-0

Key Bowl Games

Rankings below reflect final regular season poll, released Dec. 4. No bowl for then #12 Michigan St. (probation).
Sugar–#2 Alabama over #1 Penn St., 14-7; **Rose**–#3 USC over #5 Michigan, 17-10; **Orange**–#4 Oklahoma over #6 Nebraska, 31-24; **Gator**–#7 Clemson over #20 Ohio St., 17-15; **Fiesta**–#8 Arkansas tied #15 UCLA, 10-10; **Cotton**–#10 Notre Dame over #9 Houston, 35-34.

1980

	After Bowls	Head Coach	Regular Season
1	Georgia 12-0-0	Vince Dooley	11-0-0
2	Pittsburgh 11-1-0	Jackie Sherrill	10-1-0
3	Oklahoma 10-2-0	Barry Switzer	9-2-0
4	Michigan 10-2-0	Bo Schembechler	9-2-0
5	Florida St. 10-2-0	Bobby Bowden	10-1-0
6	Alabama 10-2-0	Bear Bryant	9-2-0
7	Nebraska 10-2-0	Tom Osborne	9-2-0
8	Penn St. 10-2-0	Joe Paterno	9-2-0
9	Notre Dame 9-2-1	Dan Devine	9-1-1
10	North Carolina . . 11-1-0	Dick Crum	10-1-0
11	USC 8-2-1	John Robinson	same
12	BYU 12-1-0	LaVell Edwards	11-1-0
13	UCLA 9-2-0	Terry Donahue	same
14	Baylor 10-2-0	Grant Teaff	10-1-0
15	Ohio St. 9-3-0	Earle Bruce	9-2-0
16	Washington 9-3-0	Don James	9-2-0
17	Purdue 9-3-0	Jim Young	8-3-0
18	Miami-FL 9-3-0	H. Schnellenberger	8-3-0
19	Mississippi St. 9-3-0	Emory Bellard	9-2-0
20	SMU 8-4-0	Ron Meyer	8-3-0

Key Bowl Games

Rankings below reflect final regular season poll, released Dec. 8.
Sugar–#1 Georgia over #7 Notre Dame, 17-10; **Orange**–#4 Oklahoma over #2 Florida St., 18-17; **Gator**–#3 Pitt over #18 S. Carolina, 37-9; **Rose**–#5 Michigan over #16 Washington, 23-6; **Cotton**–#9 Alabama over #6 Baylor, 30-2; **Sun**–#8 Nebraska over #17 Miss. St., 31-17; **Fiesta**–#10 Penn St. over #11 Ohio St., 31-19; **Bluebonnet**–#13 N. Carolina over Texas, 16-7.

1979

	After Bowls	Head Coach	Regular Season
1	Alabama 12-0-0	Bear Bryant	11-0-0
2	USC 11-0-1	John Robinson	10-0-1
3	Oklahoma 11-1-0	Barry Switzer	10-1-0
4	Ohio St. 11-1-0	Earle Bruce	11-0-0
5	Houston 11-1-0	Bill Yeoman	10-1-0
6	Florida St. 11-1-0	Bobby Bowden	11-0-0
7	Pittsburgh 11-1-0	Jackie Sherrill	10-1-0
8	Arkansas 10-2-0	Lou Holtz	10-1-0
9	Nebraska 10-2-0	Tom Osborne	10-1-0
10	Purdue 10-2-0	Jim Young	9-2-0
11	Washington 9-3-0	Don James	8-3-0
12	Texas 9-3-0	Fred Akers	9-2-0
13	BYU 11-1-0	LaVell Edwards	11-0-0
14	Baylor 8-4-0	Grant Teaff	7-4-0
15	North Carolina 8-3-1	Dick Crum	7-3-1
16	Auburn 8-3-0	Doug Barfield	same
17	Temple 10-2-0	Wayne Hardin	9-2-0
18	Michigan 8-4-0	Bo Schembechler	8-3-0
19	Indiana 8-4-0	Lee Corso	7-4-0
20	Penn St. 8-4-0	Joe Paterno	7-4-0

Key Bowl Games

Rankings below reflect final regular season poll, released Dec. 3. No bowl for then #17 Auburn (probation).
Sugar–#2 Alabama over #6 Arkansas, 24-9; **Rose**–#3 USC over #1 Ohio St., 17-16; **Orange**–#5 Oklahoma over #4 Florida St., 24-7; **Sun**–#13 Washington over #11 Texas, 14-7; **Cotton**–#8 Houston over #7 Nebraska, 17-14; **Fiesta**–#10 Pitt over Arizona, 16-10.

1981

	After Bowls	Head Coach	Regular Season
1	Clemson 12-0-0	Danny Ford	11-0-0
2	Texas 10-1-1	Fred Akers	9-1-1
3	Penn St. 10-2-0	Joe Paterno	9-2-0
4	Pittsburgh 11-1-0	Jackie Sherrill	10-1-0
5	SMU 10-1-0	Ron Meyer	same
6	Georgia 10-2-0	Vince Dooley	10-1-0
7	Alabama 9-2-1	Bear Bryant	9-1-1
8	Miami-FL 9-2-0	H. Schnellenberger	same
9	North Carolina 10-2-0	Dick Crum	9-2-0
10	Washington 10-2-0	Don James	9-2-0
11	Nebraska 9-3-0	Tom Osborne	9-2-0
12	Michigan 9-3-0	Bo Schembechler	8-3-0
13	BYU 11-2-0	LaVell Edwards	10-2-0
14	USC 9-3-0	John Robinson	9-2-0
15	Ohio St. 9-3-0	Earle Bruce	8-3-0
16	Arizona St. 9-2-0	Darryl Rogers	same
17	West Virginia 9-3-0	Don Nehlen	8-3-0
18	Iowa 8-4-0	Hayden Fry	8-3-0
19	Missouri 8-4-0	Warren Powers	7-4-0
20	Oklahoma 7-4-1	Barry Switzer	6-4-1

Key Bowl Games

Rankings below reflect final regular season poll, released Nov. 30. No bowl for then #5 SMU (probation), #9 Miami-FL (probation), and #17 Ariz. St. (probation).
Orange–#1 Clemson over #4 Nebraska, 22-15; **Sugar**–#10 Pitt over #2 Georgia, 24-20; **Cotton**–#6 Texas over #3 Alabama, 14-12; **Fiesta**–#7 Penn St. over #8 USC, 26-10; **Gator**–#11 N. Carolina over Arkansas, 31-27; **Rose**–#12 Washington over #13 Iowa, 28-0.

1982

		After Bowls	Head Coach	Regular Season
1	Penn St.	11-1-0	Joe Paterno	10-1-0
2	SMU	11-0-1	Bobby Collins	10-0-1
3	Nebraska	12-1-0	Tom Osborne	11-1-0
4	Georgia	11-1-0	Vince Dooley	11-0-0
5	UCLA	10-1-1	Terry Donahue	9-1-1
6	Arizona St.	10-2-0	Darryl Rogers	9-2-0
7	Washington	10-2-0	Don James	9-2-0
8	Clemson	9-1-1	Danny Ford	same
9	Arkansas	9-2-1	Lou Holtz	8-2-1
10	Pittsburgh	9-3-0	Foge Fazio	9-2-0
11	LSU	8-3-1	Jerry Stovall	8-2-1
12	Ohio St.	9-3-0	Earle Bruce	8-3-0
13	Florida St.	9-3-0	Bobby Bowden	8-3-0
14	Auburn	9-3-0	Pat Dye	8-3-0
15	USC	8-3-0	John Robinson	same
16	Oklahoma	8-4-0	Barry Switzer	8-3-0
17	Texas	9-3-0	Fred Akers	9-2-0
18	North Carolina	8-4-0	Dick Crum	7-4-0
19	West Virginia	9-3-0	Don Nehlen	9-2-0
20	Maryland	8-4-0	Bobby Ross	8-3-0

Key Bowl Games

Rankings below reflect final regular season poll, released Dec. 6. No bowl for then #7 Clemson (probation) and #15 USC (probation).

Sugar–#2 Penn St. over #1 Georgia, 27-23; **Orange**–#3 Nebraska over #13 LSU, 21-20; **Cotton**–#4 SMU over #6 Pitt, 7-3; **Rose**–#5 UCLA over #19 Michigan, 24-14; **Aloha**–#9 Washington over #16 Maryland, 21-20; **Fiesta**–#11 Ariz. St. over #12 Oklahoma, 32-21; **Bluebonnet**–#14 Arkansas over Florida, 28-24.

1983

		After Bowls	Head Coach	Regular Season
1	Miami-FL	11-1-0	H. Schnellenberger	10-1-0
2	Nebraska	12-1-0	Tom Osborne	12-0-0
3	Auburn	11-1-0	Pat Dye	10-1-0
4	Georgia	10-1-1	Vince Dooley	9-1-1
5	Texas	11-1-0	Fred Akers	11-0-0
6	Florida	9-2-1	Charley Pell	8-2-1
7	BYU	11-1-0	LaVell Edwards	10-1-0
8	Michigan	9-3-0	Bo Schembechler	9-2-0
9	Ohio St.	9-3-0	Earle Bruce	8-3-0
10	Illinois	10-2-0	Mike White	10-1-0
11	Clemson	9-1-1	Danny Ford	same
12	SMU	10-2-0	Bobby Collins	10-1-0
13	Air Force	10-2-0	Ken Hatfield	9-2-0
14	Iowa	9-3-0	Hayden Fry	9-2-0
15	Alabama	8-4-0	Ray Perkins	7-4-0
16	West Virginia	9-3-0	Don Nehlen	8-3-0
17	UCLA	7-4-1	Terry Donahue	6-4-1
18	Pittsburgh	8-3-1	Foge Fazio	8-2-1
19	Boston College	9-3-0	Jack Bicknell	9-2-0
20	East Carolina	8-3-0	Ed Emory	same

Key Bowl Games

Rankings below reflect final regular season poll, released Dec. 5. No bowl for then #12 Clemson (probation).

Orange–#5 Miami-FL over #1 Nebraska, 31-30; **Cotton**–#7 Georgia over #2 Texas, 10-9; **Sugar**– #3 Auburn over #8 Michigan, 9-7; **Rose**–UCLA over #4 Illinois, 45-9; **Holiday**–#9 BYU over Missouri, 21-17; **Gator**–#11 Florida over #10 Iowa, 14-6; **Fiesta**–#14 Ohio St. over #15 Pitt, 28-23.

1984

		After Bowls	Head Coach	Regular Season
1	BYU	13-0-0	LaVell Edwards	12-0-0
2	Washington	11-1-0	Don James	10-1-0
3	Florida	9-1-1	Charley Pell (0-1-1) & Galen Hall (9-0)	same
4	Nebraska	10-2-0	Tom Osborne	9-2-0
5	Boston College	10-2-0	Jack Bicknell	9-2-0
6	Oklahoma	9-2-1	Barry Switzer	9-1-1
7	Oklahoma St.	10-2-0	Pat Jones	9-2-0
8	SMU	10-2-0	Bobby Collins	9-2-0
9	UCLA	9-3-0	Terry Donahue	8-3-0
10	USC	9-3-0	Ted Tollner	8-3-0
11	South Carolina	10-2-0	Joe Morrison	10-1-0
12	Maryland	9-3-0	Bobby Ross	8-3-0
13	Ohio St.	9-3-0	Earle Bruce	9-2-0
14	Auburn	9-4-0	Pat Dye	8-4-0
15	LSU	8-3-1	Bill Arnsparger	8-2-1
16	Iowa	8-4-1	Hayden Fry	7-4-1
17	Florida St.	7-3-2	Bobby Bowden	7-3-1
18	Miami-FL	8-5-0	Jimmy Johnson	8-4-0
19	Kentucky	9-3-0	Jerry Claiborne	8-3-0
20	Virginia	8-2-2	George Welsh	7-2-2

Key Bowl Games

Rankings below reflect final regular season poll, released Dec. 3. No bowl for then #3 Florida (probation).

Holiday–#1 BYU over Michigan, 24-17.

Orange–#4 Washington over #2 Oklahoma, 28-17; **Sugar**–#11 Nebraska over #5 LSU, 28-10; **Rose**–#18 USC over #6 Ohio St., 20-17; **Gator**–#9 Okla. St. over #7 S. Carolina, 21-14; **Cotton**–#8 BC over Houston, 45-28; **Aloha**–#10 SMU over #17 Notre Dame, 27-20.

1985

		After Bowls	Head Coach	Regular Season
1	Oklahoma	11-1-0	Barry Switzer	10-1-0
2	Michigan	10-1-1	Bo Schembechler	9-1-1
3	Penn St.	11-1-0	Joe Paterno	11-0-0
4	Tennessee	9-1-2	Johnny Majors	8-1-2
5	Florida	9-1-1	Galen Hall	same
6	Texas A&M	10-2-0	Jackie Sherrill	9-2-0
7	UCLA	9-2-1	Terry Donahue	8-2-1
8	Air Force	12-1-0	Fisher DeBerry	11-1-0
9	Miami-FL	10-2-0	Jimmy Johnson	10-1-0
10	Iowa	10-2-0	Hayden Fry	10-1-0
11	Nebraska	9-3-0	Tom Osborne	9-2-0
12	Arkansas	10-2-0	Ken Hatfield	9-2-0
13	Alabama	9-2-1	Ray Perkins	8-2-1
14	Ohio St.	9-3-0	Earle Bruce	8-3-0
15	Florida St.	9-3-0	Bobby Bowden	8-3-0
16	BYU	11-3-0	LaVell Edwards	11-2-0
17	Baylor	9-3-0	Grant Teaff	8-3-0
18	Maryland	9-3-0	Bobby Ross	8-3-0
19	Georgia Tech	9-2-1	Bill Curry	8-2-1
20	LSU	9-2-1	Bill Arnsparger	9-1-1

Key Bowl Games

Rankings below reflect final regular season poll, released Dec. 9. No bowl for then #6 Florida (probation).

Orange–#3 Oklahoma over #1 Penn St., 25-10; **Sugar**–#8 Tennessee over #2 Miami-FL, 35-7; **Rose**–#13 UCLA over #4 Iowa, 45-28; **Fiesta**–#5 Michigan over #7 Nebraska, 27-23; **Bluebonnet**–#10 Air Force over Texas, 24-16; **Cotton**–#11 Texas A&M over #16 Auburn, 36-16.

Associated Press Final Polls (Cont.)

1986

		After Bowls	Head Coach	Regular Season
1	Penn St.	12-0-0	Joe Paterno	11-0-0
2	Miami-FL	11-1-0	Jimmy Johnson	11-0-0
3	Oklahoma	11-1-0	Barry Switzer	10-1-0
4	Arizona St.	10-1-1	John Cooper	9-1-1
5	Nebraska	10-2-0	Tom Osborne	9-2-0
6	Auburn	10-2-0	Pat Dye	9-2-0
7	Ohio St.	10-3-0	Earle Bruce	9-3-0
8	Michigan	11-2-0	Bo Schembechler	11-1-0
9	Alabama	10-3-0	Ray Perkins	9-3-0
10	LSU	9-3-0	Bill Arnsparger	9-2-0
11	Arizona	9-3-0	Larry Smith	8-3-0
12	Baylor	9-3-0	Grant Teaff	8-3-0
13	Texas A&M	9-3-0	Jackie Sherrill	9-2-0
14	UCLA	8-3-1	Terry Donahue	7-3-1
15	Arkansas	9-3-0	Ken Hatfield	9-2-0
16	Iowa	9-3-0	Hayden Fry	8-3-0
17	Clemson	8-2-2	Danny Ford	7-2-2
18	Washington	8-3-1	Don James	8-2-1
19	Boston College	9-3-0	Jack Bicknell	8-3-0
20	Virginia Tech	9-2-1	Bill Dooley	8-2-1

Key Bowl Games

Rankings below reflect final regular season poll, released Dec. 1.

Fiesta—#2 Penn St. over #1 Miami-FL, 14-10; **Orange**—#3 Oklahoma over #9 Arkansas, 42-8; **Rose**— #7 Ariz. St. over #4 Michigan, 22-15; **Sugar**—#6 Nebraska over #5 LSU, 30-15; **Cotton**—#11 Ohio St. over #8 Texas A&M, 28-12; **Citrus**—#10 Auburn over USC, 16-7; **Sun** over #12 Washington, 28-6.

1988

		After Bowls	Head Coach	Regular Season
1	Notre Dame	12-0-0	Lou Holtz	11-0-0
2	Miami-FL	11-1-0	Jimmy Johnson	10-1-0
3	Florida St.	11-1-0	Bobby Bowden	10-1-0
4	Michigan	9-2-1	Bo Schembechler	8-2-1
5	West Virginia	11-1-0	Don Nehlen	11-0-0
6	UCLA	10-2-0	Terry Donahue	9-2-0
7	USC	10-2-0	Larry Smith	10-1-0
8	Auburn	10-2-0	Pat Dye	10-1-0
9	Clemson	10-2-0	Danny Ford	9-2-0
10	Nebraska	11-2-0	Tom Osborne	11-1-0
11	Oklahoma St.	10-2-0	Pat Jones	9-2-0
12	Arkansas	10-2-0	Ken Hatfield	10-1-0
13	Syracuse	10-2-0	Dick MacPherson	9-2-0
14	Oklahoma	9-3-0	Barry Switzer	9-2-0
15	Georgia	9-3-0	Vince Dooley	8-3-0
16	Washington St.	9-3-0	Dennis Erickson	8-3-0
17	Alabama	9-3-0	Bill Curry	8-3-0
18	Houston	9-3-0	Jack Pardee	9-2-0
19	LSU	8-4-0	Mike Archer	8-3-0
20	Indiana	8-3-1	Bill Mallory	7-3-1

Key Bowl Games

Rankings below reflect final regular season poll, released Dec. 5.

Fiesta—#1 Notre Dame over #3 West Va., 34-21; **Orange**—#2 Miami-FL over #6 Nebraska, 23-3; **Sugar**—#4 Florida St. over #7 Auburn, 13-7; **Rose**—#11 Michigan over #5 USC, 22-14; **Cotton**—#9 UCLA over #8 Arkansas, 17-3; **Citrus**—#13 Clemson over #10 Oklahoma, 13-6.

1987

		After Bowls	Head Coach	Regular Season
1	Miami-FL	12-0-0	Jimmy Johnson	11-0-0
2	Florida St.	11-1-0	Bobby Bowden	10-1-0
3	Oklahoma	11-1-0	Barry Switzer	11-0-0
4	Syracuse	11-0-1	Dick MacPherson	11-0-0
5	LSU	10-1-1	Mike Archer	9-1-1
6	Nebraska	10-2-0	Tom Osborne	10-1-0
7	Auburn	9-1-2	Pat Dye	9-1-1
8	Michigan St.	9-2-1	George Perles	8-2-1
9	UCLA	10-2-0	Terry Donahue	9-2-0
10	Texas A&M	10-2-0	Jackie Sherrill	9-2-0
11	Oklahoma St.	10-2-0	Pat Jones	9-2-0
12	Clemson	10-2-0	Danny Ford	9-2-0
13	Georgia	9-3-0	Vince Dooley	8-3-0
14	Tennessee	10-2-1	Johnny Majors	9-2-1
15	South Carolina	8-4-0	Joe Morrison	8-3-0
16	Iowa	10-3-0	Hayden Fry	9-3-0
17	Notre Dame	8-4-0	Lou Holtz	8-3-0
18	USC	8-4-0	Larry Smith	8-3-0
19	Michigan	8-4-0	Bo Schembechler	7-4-0
20	Arizona St.	7-4-1	John Cooper	6-4-1

Key Bowl Games

Rankings below reflect final regular season poll, released Dec. 7.

Orange—#2 Miami-FL over #1 Oklahoma, 20-14; **Fiesta**—#3 Florida St. over #5 Nebraska, 31-28; **Sugar**—#4 Syracuse tied #6 Auburn, 16-16; **Gator**—#7 LSU over #9 S. Carolina, 30-13; **Rose**—#8 Mich. St. over #16 USC, 20-17; **Aloha**—#10 UCLA over Florida, 20-16; **Cotton**—#13 Texas A&M over #12 Notre Dame, 35-10.

1989

		After Bowls	Head Coach	Regular Season
1	Miami-FL	11-1-0	Dennis Erickson	10-1-0
2	Notre Dame	12-1-0	Lou Holtz	11-1-0
3	Florida St.	10-2-0	Bobby Bowden	9-2-0
4	Colorado	11-1-0	Bill McCartney	11-0-0
5	Tennessee	11-1-0	Johnny Majors	10-1-0
6	Auburn	10-2-0	Pat Dye	9-2-0
7	Michigan	10-2-0	Bo Schembechler	10-1-0
8	USC	9-2-1	Larry Smith	8-2-1
9	Alabama	10-2-0	Bill Curry	10-1-0
10	Illinois	10-2-0	John Mackovic	9-2-0
11	Nebraska	10-2-0	Tom Osborne	10-1-0
12	Clemson	10-2-0	Danny Ford	9-2-0
13	Arkansas	10-2-0	Ken Hatfield	10-1-0
14	Houston	9-2-0	Jack Pardee	same
15	Penn St.	8-3-1	Joe Paterno	7-3-1
16	Michigan St.	8-4-0	George Perles	7-4-0
17	Pittsburgh	8-3-1	Mike Gottfried (7-3-1) & Paul Hackett (1-0)	7-3-1
18	Virginia	10-3-0	George Welsh	10-2-0
19	Texas Tech	9-3-0	Spike Dykes	8-3-0
20	Texas A&M	8-4-0	R.C. Slocum	8-3-0
21	West Virginia	8-3-1	Don Nehlen	8-2-1
22	BYU	10-3-0	LaVell Edwards	10-2-0
23	Washington	8-4-0	Don James	7-4-0
24	Ohio St.	8-4-0	John Cooper	8-3-0
25	Arizona	8-4-0	Dick Tomey	7-4-0

Key Bowl Games

Rankings below reflect final regular season poll, released Dec. 11. No bowl for then #13 Houston (probation).

Orange—#4 Notre Dame over #1 Colorado, 21-6; **Sugar**—#2 Miami-FL over #7 Alabama, 33-25; **Rose**— #12 USC over #3 Michigan, 17-10; **Fiesta**—#5 Florida St. over #6 Nebraska, 41-17; **Cotton**—#8 Tennessee over #10 Arkansas, 31-27; **Hall of Fame**—#9 Auburn over #21 Ohio St., 31-14; **Citrus**—#11 Illinois over #15 Virginia, 31-21.

1990

		After Bowls	Head Coach	Regular Season
1	Colorado	11-1-1	Bill McCartney	10-1-1
2	Georgia Tech	11-0-1	Bobby Ross	10-0-1
3	Miami-FL	10-2-0	Dennis Erickson	9-2-0
4	Florida St.	10-2-0	Bobby Bowden	9-2-0
5	Washington	10-2-0	Don James	9-2-0
6	Notre Dame	9-3-0	Lou Holtz	9-2-0
7	Michigan	9-3-0	Gary Moeller	8-3-0
8	Tennessee	9-2-2	Johnny Majors	8-2-2
9	Clemson	10-2-0	Ken Hatfield	9-2-0
10	Houston	10-1-0	John Jenkins	same
11	Penn St.	9-3-0	Joe Paterno	9-2-0
12	Texas	10-2-0	David McWilliams	10-1-0
13	Florida	9-2-0	Steve Spurrier	same
14	Louisville	10-1-1	H. Schnellenberger	9-1-1
15	Texas A&M	9-3-1	R.C. Slocum	8-3-1
16	Michigan St.	8-3-1	George Perles	7-3-1
17	Oklahoma	8-3-0	Gary Gibbs	same
18	Iowa	8-4-0	Hayden Fry	8-3-0
19	Auburn	8-3-1	Pat Dye	7-3-1
20	USC	8-4-1	Larry Smith	8-3-1
21	Mississippi	9-3-0	Billy Brewer	9-2-0
22	BYU	10-3-0	LaVell Edwards	10-2-0
23	Virginia	8-4-0	George Welsh	8-3-0
24	Nebraska	9-3-0	Tom Osborne	9-2-0
25	Illinois	8-4-0	John Mackovic	8-3-0

Key Bowl Games

Rankings below reflect final regular season poll, released Dec. 3. No bowl for then #9 Houston (probation), #11 Florida (probation) and #20 Oklahoma (probation).

Orange—#1 Colorado over #5 Notre Dame, 10-9; **Citrus**—#2 Ga. Tech over #19 Nebraska, 45-21; **Cotton**—#4 Miami-FL over #3 Texas, 46-3; **Blockbuster**—#6 Florida St. over #7 Penn St., 24-17; **Rose**—#8 Washington over #17 Iowa, 46-34; **Sugar**—#10 Tennessee over Virginia, 23-22; **Gator**—#12 Michigan over #15 Ole Miss, 35-3.

1991

		After Bowls	Head Coach	Regular Season
1	Miami-FL	12-0-0	Dennis Erickson	11-0-0
2	Washington	12-0-0	Don James	11-0-0
3	Penn St.	11-2-0	Joe Paterno	10-2-0
4	Florida St.	11-2-0	Bobby Bowden	10-2-0
5	Alabama	11-1-0	Gene Stallings	10-1-0
6	Michigan	10-2-0	Gary Moeller	10-1-0
7	Florida	10-2-0	Steve Spurrier	10-1-0
8	California	10-2-0	Bruce Snyder	9-2-0
9	East Carolina	11-1-0	Bill Lewis	10-1-0
10	Iowa	10-1-1	Hayden Fry	10-1-0
11	Syracuse	10-2-0	Paul Pasqualoni	9-2-0
12	Texas A&M	10-2-0	R.C. Slocum	10-1-0
13	Notre Dame	10-3-0	Lou Holtz	9-3-0
14	Tennessee	9-3-0	Johnny Majors	9-2-0
15	Nebraska	9-2-1	Tom Osborne	9-1-1
16	Oklahoma	9-3-0	Gary Gibbs	8-3-0
17	Georgia	9-3-0	Ray Goff	8-3-0
18	Clemson	9-2-1	Ken Hatfield	9-1-1
19	UCLA	9-3-0	Terry Donahue	8-3-0
20	Colorado	8-3-1	Bill McCartney	8-2-1
21	Tulsa	10-2-0	David Rader	9-2-0
22	Stanford	8-4-0	Dennis Green	8-3-0
23	BYU	8-3-2	LaVell Edwards	8-3-1
24	N.C. State	9-3-0	Dick Sheridan	9-2-0
25	Air Force	9-3-0	Fisher DeBerry	9-3-0

Key Bowl Games

Rankings below reflect final regular season poll, taken Dec. 2.

Orange—#1 Miami-FL over #11 Nebraska, 22-0; **Rose**—#2 Washington over #4 Michigan, 34-14; **Sugar**—#18 Notre Dame over #3 Florida, 39-28; **Cotton**—#5 Florida St. over #9 Texas A&M, 10-2; **Fiesta**—#6 Penn St. over #10 Tennessee, 42-17; **Holiday**—#7 Iowa tied BYU, 13-13; **Blockbuster**—#8 Alabama over #15 Colorado, 30-25; **Citrus**—#14 California over #13 Clemson, 37-13; **Peach**—#12 East Carolina over #21 N.C. State, 37-34.

1992

		After Bowls	Head Coach	Regular Season
1	Alabama	13-0-0	Gene Stallings	12-0-0
2	Florida St.	11-1-0	Bobby Bowden	10-1-0
3	Miami-FL	11-1-0	Dennis Erickson	11-0-0
4	Notre Dame	10-1-1	Lou Holtz	9-1-1
5	Michigan	9-0-3	Gary Moeller	8-0-3
6	Syracuse	10-2-0	Paul Pasqualoni	9-2-0
7	Texas A&M	12-1-0	R.C. Slocum	12-0-0
8	Georgia	10-2-0	Ray Goff	9-2-0
9	Stanford	10-3-0	Bill Walsh	9-3-0
10	Florida	9-4-0	Steve Spurrier	8-4-0
11	Washington	9-3-0	Don James	9-2-0
12	Tennessee	9-3-0	Johnny Majors (5-3) & Phillip Fulmer (4-0)	8-3-0
13	Colorado	9-2-1	Bill McCartney	9-1-1
14	Nebraska	9-3-0	Tom Osborne	9-2-0
15	Washington St.	9-3-0	Mike Price	8-3-0
16	Mississippi	9-3-0	Billy Brewer	8-3-0
17	N.C. State	9-3-1	Dick Sheridan	9-2-1
18	Ohio St.	8-3-1	John Cooper	8-2-1
19	North Carolina	9-3-0	Mack Brown	8-3-0
20	Hawaii	11-2-0	Bob Wagner	10-2-0
21	Boston College	8-3-1	Tom Coughlin	8-2-1
22	Kansas	8-4-0	Glen Mason	7-4-0
23	Mississippi St.	7-5-0	Jackie Sherrill	7-4-0
24	Fresno St.	9-4-0	Jim Sweeney	9-3-0
25	Wake Forest	8-4-0	Bill Dooley	7-4-0

Key Bowl Games

Rankings below reflect final regular season poll, taken Dec. 5.

Sugar—#2 Alabama over #1 Miami-FL, 34-13; **Orange**—#3 Florida St. over #11 Nebraska, 27-14; **Cotton**—#5 Notre Dame over #4 Texas A&M, 28-3; **Fiesta**—#6 Syracuse over #10 Colorado, 26-22; **Rose**—#7 Michigan over #9 Washington, 38-31; **Citrus**—#8 Georgia over #15 Ohio St., 21-14.

The Special Election That Didn't Count

There was one No. 1 vs No. 2 confrontation not noted in the Number 1 vs. Number 2 table on pages 152-53. It came in a special election or re-vote of AP selectors following the 1948 Rose Bowl. Here's what happened: Unbeaten Notre Dame was declared 1947 national champion by AP on Dec. 8, two days after closing out an undefeated season with a 38-7 rout of then third-ranked USC in Los Angeles. Twenty-four days later, however, unbeaten Michigan, AP's final No. 2 team, clobbered now 8th-ranked USC, 49-0, in the Rose Bowl. An immediate cry went up for an unprecedented two-team, "Who's No. 1" ballot and AP gave in. Michigan won the election, 226-119, with 12 voters calling it even. However, AP ruled that the Dec. 8 final poll won by Notre Dame would be the vote of record.

Associated Press Final Polls (Cont.)

1993

	After Bowls	Head Coach	Regular Season
1	Florida St 12-1-0	Bobby Bowden	11-1-0
2	Notre Dame 11-1-0	Lou Holtz	10-1-0
3	Nebraska........11-1-0	Tom Osborne	11-0-0
4	Auburn 11-0-0	Terry Bowden	11-0-0
5	Florida 11-2-0	Steve Spurrier	10-2-0
6	Wisconsin 10-1-1	Barry Alvarez	9-1-1
7	West Virginia 11-1-0	Don Nehlen	11-0-0
8	Penn St..........10-2-0	Joe Paterno	9-2-0
9	Texas A&M 10-2-0	R.C. Slocum	10-1-0
10	Arizona 10-2-0	Dick Tomey	9-2-0
11	Ohio St 10-1-1	John Cooper	9-1-1
12	Tennessee........9-2-1	Phillip Fulmer	9-1-1
13	Boston College 9-3-0	Tom Coughlin	8-3-0
14	Alabama 9-3-1	Gene Stallings	8-3-1
15	Miami-FL 9-3-0	Dennis Erickson	9-2-0
16	Colorado 8-3-1	Bill McCartney	7-3-1
17	Oklahoma 9-3-0	Gary Gibbs	8-3-0
18	UCLA 8-4-0	Terry Donahue	8-3-0
19	North Carolina ...10-3-0	Mack Brown	10-2-0
20	Kansas St........9-2-1	Bill Snyder	8-2-1
21	Michigan 8-4-0	Gary Moeller	7-4-0
22	Va. Tech 9-3-0	Frank Beamer	9-2-0
23	Clemson 9-3-0	Ken Hatfield (8-3)	8-3-0
		& Tommy West (1-0)	
24	Louisville 9-3-0	H. Schnellenberger	8-3-0
25	California........9-4-0	Keith Gilbertson	8-4-0

Key Bowl Games

Rankings below reflect final regular season poll, taken Dec. 5. No bowl for then #5 Auburn (probation).

Orange–#1 Florida St. over #2 Nebraska, 18-16; **Sugar**–#8 Florida over #3 West Virginia, 41-7; **Cotton**–#4 Notre Dame over #7 Texas A&M, 24-21; **Citrus**–#13 Penn St. over #6 Tennessee, 31-13; **Rose**–#9 Wisconsin over #14 UCLA, 21-16; **Fiesta**–#16 Arizona over #10 Miami-FL, 29-0; **Holiday**–#11 Ohio St. over BYU, 28-21; **Gator**–#18 Alabama over #12 North Carolina, 24-10; **Carquest**–#15 Boston College over Virginia, 31-13.

1994

	After Bowls	Head Coach	Regular Season
1	Nebraska........13-0-0	Tom Osborne	12-0-0
2	Penn St........12-0-0	Joe Paterno	11-0-0
3	Colorado 11-1-0	Bill McCartney	10-1-0
4	Florida St........10-1-1	Bobby Bowden	9-1-1
5	Alabama 12-1-0	Gene Stallings	11-1-0
6	Miami-FL 10-2-0	Dennis Erickson	10-1-0
7	Florida 10-2-1	Steve Spurrier	10-1-1
8	Texas A&M 10-0-1	R.C. Slocum	same
9	Auburn 9-1-1	Terry Bowden	same
10	Utah 10-2-0	Ron McBride	9-2-0
11	Oregon 9-4-0	Rich Brooks	9-3-0
12	Michigan 8-4-0	Gary Moeller	7-4-0
13	USC 8-3-1	John Robinson	7-3-1
14	Ohio St..........9-4-0	John Cooper	9-3-0
15	Virginia 9-3-0	George Welsh	8-3-0
16	Colorado St......10-2-0	Sonny Lubick	10-1-0
17	N.C. State 9-3-0	Mike O'Cain	8-3-0
18	BYU 10-3-0	LaVell Edwards	9-3-0
19	Kansas St........9-3-0	Bill Snyder	9-2-0
20	Arizona 8-4-0	Dick Tomey	8-3-0
21	Washington St.....8-4-0	Mike Price	7-4-0
22	Tennessee........8-4-0	Phillip Fulmer	7-4-0
23	Boston College 7-4-1	Dan Henning	6-4-1
24	Mississippi St......8-4-0	Jackie Sherrill	8-3-0
25	Texas...........8-4-0	John Mackovic	7-4-0

Key Bowl Games

Rankings below reflect final regular season poll, taken Dec. 4. No bowls for then #8 Texas A&M (probation) and #9 Auburn (probation).

Orange–#1 Nebraska over #3 Miami-FL, 24-17; **Rose**–#2 Penn St. over #12 Oregon, 38-20; **Fiesta**–#4 Colorado over Notre Dame, 41-24; **Sugar**–#7 Florida St. over #5 Florida, 23-17; **Citrus**–#6 Alabama over #13 Ohio St., 24-17; **Freedom**–#14 Utah over #15 Arizona, 16-13.

1995

	After Bowls	Head Coach	Regular Season
1	Nebraska........12-0-0	Tom Osborne	11-0-0
2	Florida 12-1-0	Steve Spurrier	12-0-0
3	Tennessee........11-1-0	Phillip Fulmer	10-1-0
4	Florida St........10-2-0	Bobby Bowden	9-2-0
5	Colorado 10-2-0	Rick Neuheisel	9-2-0
6	Ohio St..........11-2-0	John Cooper	11-1-0
7	Kansas St........10-2-0	Bill Snyder	9-2-0
8	Northwestern 10-2-0	Gary Barnett	10-1-0
9	Kansas 10-2-0	Glen Mason	9-2-0
10	Va. Tech 10-2-0	Frank Beamer	9-2-0
11	Notre Dame.......9-3-0	Lou Holtz	9-2-0
12	USC 9-2-1	John Robinson	8-2-1
13	Penn St..........9-3-0	Joe Paterno	8-3-0
14	Texas 10-2-1	John Mackovic	10-1-1
15	Texas A&M 9-3-0	R.C. Slocum	8-3-0
16	Virginia 9-4-0	George Welsh	8-4-0
17	Michigan 9-4-0	Lloyd Carr	9-3-0
18	Oregon 9-3-0	Mike Bellotti	9-2-0
19	Syracuse 9-3-0	Paul Pasqualoni	8-3-0
20	Miami-FL..........8-3-0	Butch Davis	same
21	Alabama 8-3-0	Gene Stallings	same
22	Auburn 8-4-0	Terry Bowden	8-3-0
23	Texas Tech 9-3-0	Spike Dykes	8-3-0
24	Toledo 11-0-1	Gary Pinkel	10-0-1
25	Iowa 8-4-0	Hayden Fry	7-4-0

Key Bowl Games

Rankings below reflect final regular season poll, taken Dec. 3. No bowl for then #21 Alabama (probation) and #22 Miami-FL (probation).

Fiesta–#1 Nebraska over #2 Florida, 62-24; **Rose**–#17 USC over #3 Northwestern, 41-32; **Citrus**–#4 (tie) Tennessee over #4 (tie) Ohio St., 20-14; **Orange**–#8 Florida St. over #6 Notre Dame, 31-26; **Cotton**–#7 Colorado over #12 Oregon, 38-6; **Sugar**–#13 Va. Tech over #9 Texas, 28-10; **Aloha**–#11 Kansas over UCLA, 51-30; **Alamo**–#19 Texas A&M over #14 Michigan, 22-20; **Outback**–#15 Penn St. over #16 Auburn, 43-14; **Peach**–#18 Virginia over Georgia, 34-27; **Gator**–Syracuse over #23 Clemson, 41-0.

1996

	After Bowls	Head Coach	Regular Season
1 Florida	12-1	Steve Spurrier	11-1
2 Ohio St.	11-1	John Cooper	10-1
3 Florida St	11-1	Bobby Bowden	11-0
4 Arizona St.	11-1	Bruce Snyder	11-0
5 BYU	14-1	LaVell Edwards	13-1
6 Nebraska	11-2	Tom Osborne	10-2
7 Penn St.	11-2	Joe Paterno	10-2
8 Colorado	10-2	Rick Neuheisel	9-2
9 Tennessee	10-2	Phillip Fulmer	9-2
10 North Carolina	10-2	Mack Brown	9-2
11 Alabama	10-3	Gene Stallings	9-3
12 LSU	10-2	Gerry DiNardo	9-2
13 Virginia Tech	10-2	Frank Beamer	10-1
14 Miami-FL	9-3	Butch Davis	8-3
15 Northwestern	9-3	Gary Barnett	9-2
16 Washington	9-3	Jim Lambright	9-2
17 Kansas St.	9-3	Bill Snyder	9-2
18 Iowa	9-3	Hayden Fry	8-3
19 Notre Dame	8-3	Lou Holtz	same
20 Michigan	8-4	Lloyd Carr	8-3
21 Syracuse	9-3	Paul Pasqualoni	8-3
22 Wyoming	10-2	Joe Tiller	same
23 Texas	8-5	John Mackovic	8-4
24 Auburn	8-4	Terry Bowden	7-4
25 Army	10-1	Bob Sutton	10-1

Key Bowl Games

Rankings below reflect final regular season poll, taken Dec. 8. No bowl for then #18 Notre Dame and #22 Wyoming. **Sugar**– #3 Florida over #1 Florida St., 52-20; **Rose**– #4 Ohio St. over #2 Arizona St., 20-17; **Fiesta**– #7 Penn St. over #20 Texas, 38-15; **Cotton**– #5 BYU over #14 Kansas St., 19-15; **Citrus**– #9 Tennessee over #11 Northwestern, 48-28; **Orange**– #6 Nebraska over #10 Virginia Tech, 41-21; **Gator**– #12 North Carolina over #25 West Virginia, 20-13; **Outback**– #16 Alabama over #15 Michigan, 17-14. **Carquest**– #19 Miami over Virginia, 31-21.

1997

	After Bowls	Head Coach	Regular Season
1 Michigan	12-0	Lloyd Carr	11-0
2 Nebraska	13-0	Tom Osborne	12-0
3 Florida St	11-1	Bobby Bowden	10-1
4 Florida	10-2	Steve Spurrier	9-2
5 UCLA	10-2	Bob Toledo	9-2
6 North Carolina	11-1	Mack Brown (10-1) & Carl Torbush (1-0)	10-1
7 Tennessee	11-2	Phillip Fulmer	11-1
8 Kansas St.	11-1	Bill Snyder	10-1
9 Washington St.	10-2	Mike Price	10-1
10 Georgia	10-2	Jim Donnan	9-2
11 Auburn	10-3	Terry Bowden	9-3
12 Ohio St.	10-3	John Cooper	10-2
13 LSU	9-3	Gerry DiNardo	8-3
14 Arizona St.	8-3	Bruce Snyder	7-3
15 Purdue	9-3	Joe Tiller	8-3
16 Penn St.	9-3	Joe Paterno	9-2
17 Colorado St.	11-2	Sonny Lubick	10-2
18 Washington	8-4	Jim Lambright	7-4
19 So. Mississippi	9-3	Jeff Bower	8-3
20 Texas A&M	9-4	R.C. Slocum	9-3
21 Syracuse	9-4	Paul Pasqualoni	9-3
22 Mississippi	8-4	Tommy Tuberville	7-4
23 Missouri	7-5	Larry Smith	6-5
24 Oklahoma St.	8-4	Bobby Simmons	8-3
25 Georgia Tech	7-5	George O'Leary	6-5

Key Bowl Games

Rankings below reflect final regular season poll, taken Dec. 7. **Rose**– #1 Michigan over #7 Washington St., 21-16; **Orange**– #2 Nebraska over #3 Tennessee, 42-17; **Sugar**– #4 Florida St. over #10 Ohio St., 31-14; **Gator**– #5 North Carolina over Virginia Tech, 42-3; **Cotton**– #6 UCLA over #19 Texas A&M, 29-23; **Citrus**– #8 Florida over #12 Penn St., 21-6; **Fiesta**– #9 Kansas St. over #14 Syracuse, 35-18; **Outback**– #11 Georgia over Wisconsin, 33-6; **Peach**– #13 Auburn over Clemson, 21-17; **Independence**– #15 LSU over Notre Dame, 27-9; **Alamo**– #16 Purdue over #24 Oklahoma St., 33-20; **Holiday**– #17 Colorado St. over #20 Missouri, 35-24.

1998

	After Bowls	Head Coach	Regular Season
1 Tennessee	13-0	Phillip Fulmer	12-0
2 Ohio St.	11-1	John Cooper	10-1
3 Florida St.	11-2	Bobby Bowden	11-1
4 Arizona	12-1	Dick Tomey	11-1
5 Florida	10-2	Steve Spurrier	9-2
6 Wisconsin	11-1	Barry Alvarez	10-1
7 Tulane	12-0	Tommy Bowden	11-0
8 UCLA	10-2	Bob Toledo	10-1
9 Georgia Tech	10-2	George O'Leary	9-2
10 Kansas St.	11-2	Bill Snyder	11-1
11 Texas A&M	11-3	R.C. Slocum	11-2
12 Michigan	10-3	Lloyd Carr	9-3
13 Air Force	12-1	Fisher DeBerry	11-1
14 Georgia	9-3	Jim Donnan	8-3
15 Texas	9-3	Mack Brown	8-3
16 Arkansas	9-3	Houston Nutt	9-2
17 Penn St.	9-3	Joe Paterno	8-3
18 Virginia	9-3	George Welsh	9-2
19 Nebraska	9-4	Frank Solich	9-3
20 Miami-FL	9-3	Butch Davis	8-3
21 Missouri	8-4	Larry Smith	7-4
22 Notre Dame	9-3	Bob Davie	9-2
23 Va. Tech	9-3	Frank Beamer	8-3
24 Purdue	9-4	Joe Tiller	8-4
25 Syracuse	8-4	Paul Pasqualoni	8-3

Key Bowl Games

Rankings below reflect final regular season poll, taken Dec. 6. **Fiesta**– #1 Tennessee over #2 Florida St., 23-16; **Sugar**– #3 Ohio St. over #8 Texas A&M, 24-14; **Orange**– #7 Florida over #18 Syracuse, 31-10; **Rose**– #9 Wisconsin over #6 UCLA, 38-31; **Holiday**– #5 Arizona over #14 Nebraska, 23-20; **Citrus**– #15 Michigan over #11 Arkansas, 45-31; **Gator**– #12 Georgia Tech over #17 Notre Dame, 35-28; **Cotton**– #20 Texas over #25 Mississippi St., 38-11; **Peach**– #19 Georgia over #13 Virginia, 35-33; **Alamo**– Purdue over #4 Kansas St., 37-34; **Outback**– #22 Penn St. over Kentucky, 26-14.

Associated Press Final Polls (Cont.)

1999

		After Bowls	Head Coach	Regular Season
1	Florida St.	12-0	Bobby Bowden	11-0
2	Va. Tech.	11-1	Frank Beamer	11-0
3	Nebraska	12-1	Frank Solich	11-1
4	Wisconsin	10-2	Barry Alvarez	9-2
5	Michigan	10-2	Lloyd Carr	9-2
6	Kansas St.	11-1	Bill Snyder	10-1
7	Michigan St.	10-2	Nick Saban (9-2) & B. Williams (1-0)	9-2
8	Alabama	10-3	Mike DuBose	10-2
9	Tennessee	9-3	Phillip Fulmer	8-3
10	Marshall	13-0	Bob Pruett	12-0
11	Penn St.	10-3	Joe Paterno	9-3
12	Florida	9-4	Steve Spurrier	9-3
13	Mississippi St.	10-2	Jackie Sherrill	9-2
14	Southern Miss.	9-3	Jeff Bower	8-3
15	Miami-FL	9-4	Butch Davis	8-4
16	Georgia	8-4	Jim Donnan	7-4
17	Arkansas	8-4	Houston Nutt	7-4
18	Minnesota	8-4	Glen Mason	8-3
19	Oregon	9-3	Mike Bellotti	8-3
20	Georgia Tech	8-4	George O'Leary	8-3
21	Texas	9-5	Mack Brown	9-4
22	Mississippi	8-4	David Cutcliffe	7-4
23	Texas A&M	8-4	R.C. Slocum	7-4
24	Illinois	8-4	Ron Turner	7-4
25	Purdue	7-5	Joe Tiller	7-4

Key Bowl Games

Rankings below reflect final regular season poll, taken Dec. 5.

Sugar– #1 Florida St. over #2 Va. Tech, 46-29; **Fiesta**– #3 Nebraska over #6 Tennessee, 31-21; **Rose**– #4 Wisconsin over #22 Stanford, 17-9; **Orange**– #8 Michigan over #5 Alabama, 35-34; **Holiday**– #7 Kansas St. over Washington, 24-20; **Citrus**– #9 Michigan St. over #10 Florida, 37-34; **Motor City**– #11 Marshall over BYU, 21-3; **Sun**– Oregon over #12 Minnesota, 24-20; **Alamo**– #13 Penn St. over #18 Texas A&M, 24-0; **Cotton**– #24 Arkansas over #14 Texas, 27-6; **Peach**– #15 Mississippi St. over Clemson, 17-7; **Liberty**– #16 Southern Miss. over Colorado St., 23-17; **Gator**– #23 Miami-FL over #17 Georgia Tech, 28-13; **Outback**– #21 Georgia over #19 Purdue, 28-25.

2000

		After Bowls	Head Coach	Regular Season
1	Oklahoma	13-0	Bob Stoops	12-0
2	Miami-FL	11-1	Butch Davis	10-1
3	Washington	11-1	Rick Neuheisel	10-1
4	Oregon St.	11-1	Dennis Erickson	10-1
5	Florida St.	11-2	Bobby Bowden	11-1
6	Va. Tech.	11-1	Frank Beamer	10-1
7	Oregon	10-2	Mike Bellotti	9-2
8	Nebraska	10-2	Frank Solich	9-2
9	Kansas St.	11-3	Bill Snyder	10-3
10	Florida	10-3	Steve Spurrier	10-2
11	Michigan	9-3	Lloyd Carr	8-3
12	Texas	9-3	Mack Brown	9-2
13	Purdue	8-4	Joe Tiller	8-3
14	Colorado St.	10-2	Sonny Lubick	9-2
15	Notre Dame	9-3	Bob Davie	9-2
16	Clemson	9-3	Tommy Bowden	9-2
17	Georgia Tech	9-3	George O'Leary	9-2
18	Auburn	9-4	Tommy Tuberville	9-3
19	South Carolina	8-4	Lou Holtz	7-4
20	Georgia	8-4	Jim Donnan	7-4
21	TCU	10-2	D. Franchione (10-1) & G. Patterson (0-1)	10-1
22	LSU	8-4	Nick Saban	7-4
23	Wisconsin	9-4	Barry Alvarez	8-4
24	Mississippi St.	8-4	Jackie Sherrill	7-4
25	Iowa St.	9-3	Dan McCarney	8-3

Key Bowl Games

Rankings below reflect final regular season poll, taken Dec. 4.

Orange– #1 Oklahoma over #3 Florida St., 13-2; **Sugar**– #2 Miami-FL over #7 Florida, 37-20; **Rose**– #4 Washington over #14 Purdue, 34-24; **Fiesta**– #5 Oregon St. over #10 Notre Dame, 41-9; **Gator**– #6 Virginia Tech over #16 Clemson, 41-20; **Holiday**– #8 Oregon over #12 Texas, 35-30; **Alamo**– #9 Nebraska over #18 Northwestern, 66-17; **Cotton**– #11 Kansas St. over #21 Tennessee, 35-21; **Mobile**– Southern Miss. over #13 TCU, 28-21; **Peach**– LSU over #15 Georgia Tech, 28-14; **Citrus**– #17 Michigan over #20 Auburn, 31-28; **Outback**– South Carolina over #19 Ohio St., 24-7; **Liberty**– #23 Colorado St. over #22 Louisville, 22-17; **Oahu**– #24 Georgia over Virginia, 37-14.

All-Time AP Top 20

The composite AP Top 20 from the 1936 season through the 2000 season, based on the final rankings of each year. The final AP poll has been taken after the bowl games in 1965 and since 1968. Team point totals are based on 20 points for all 1st place finishes, 19 for each 2nd, etc. Also listed are the number of times each team has been named national champion by AP and times ranked in the final Top 10 and Top 20.

		Pts	No.1	Top 10	Top 20			Pts	No.1	Top 10	Top 20
1	Notre Dame	632	8	34	45	11	UCLA	322	0	16	29
2	Michigan	611	2	34	48	12	Florida St.	308	2	16	20
3	Oklahoma	578	7	30	42	13	Miami-FL	290	4	14	24
4	Alabama	564	6	31	42	14	Auburn	284	1	14	27
5	Nebraska	533	4	29	40	15	LSU	277	1	14	25
6	Ohio St.	518	3	24	41	16	Arkansas	267	0	13	25
7	Tennessee	433	2	21	36	17	Georgia	262	1	14	24
8	Texas	415	2	19	33	18	Michigan St.	252	1	13	20
9	USC	414	3	20	36	19	Florida	239	1	12	21
10	Penn St.	403	2	21	35	20	Washington	220	0	11	20

Bowl Games

From Jan. 1, 1902 through Jan. 3, 2001. Corporate title sponsors and automatic berths updated through Jan. 3, 2001. Please note that the Bowl selection process is now dominated by the recently inaugurated Bowl Championship Series (which includes the Fiesta, Orange, Rose and Sugar bowls) and the following non-BCS bowls' so called "automatic berths" are contingent upon several factors, including the leftovers from the BCS, Notre Dame's record and the record of their designated choices.

Rose Bowl

City: Pasadena, Calif. **Stadium:** Rose Bowl. **Capacity:** 102,083. **Playing surface:** Grass. **First game:** Jan. 1, 1902. **Playing sites:** Tournament Park (1902, 1916-22), Rose Bowl (1923-41 and since 1943) and Duke Stadium in Durham, N.C. (1942, due to wartime restrictions following Japan's attack on Pearl Harbor on Dec. 7, 1941). **Corporate sponsor:** AT&T (since 1998).

Automatic berths: Pacific Coast Conference champion vs. opponent selected by PCC (1924-45 seasons); Big Ten champion vs. Pac-10 champion (1946-97); Bowl Championship Series: Big Ten champion vs. Pac-10 champion, if available (1998-2000 seasons) and #1 vs. #2 on Jan. 3, 2002.

Multiple wins: USC (20); Michigan (8); Washington (7); Ohio St. (6); Stanford and UCLA (5); Alabama (4); Illinois, Michigan St. and Wisconsin (3); California and Iowa (2).

Year		Year		Year	
1902*	Michigan 49, Stanford 0	1945	USC 25, Tennessee 0	1975	USC 18, Ohio St. 17
1916	Washington St. 14, Brown 0	1946	Alabama 34, USC 14	1976	UCLA 23, Ohio St. 10
1917	Oregon 14, Penn 0	1947	Illinois 45, UCLA 14	1977	USC 14, Michigan 6
1918	Mare Island 19, Camp Lewis 7	1948	Michigan 49, USC 0	1978	Washington 27, Michigan 20
1919	Great Lakes 17, Mare Island 0	1949	Northwestern 20, California 14	1979	USC 17, Michigan 10
1920	Harvard 7, Oregon 6	1950	Ohio St. 17, California 14	1980	USC 17, Ohio St. 16
1921	California 28, Ohio St. 0	1951	Michigan 14, California 6	1981	Michigan 23, Washington 6
1922	0-0, California vs Wash. & Jeff.	1952	Illinois 40, Stanford 7	1982	Washington 28, Iowa 0
1923	USC 14, Penn St. 0	1953	USC 7, Wisconsin 0	1983	UCLA 24, Michigan 14
1924	14-14, Navy vs Washington	1954	Michigan St. 28, UCLA 20	1984	UCLA 45, Illinois 9
1925	Notre Dame 27, Stanford 10	1955	Ohio St. 20, USC 7	1985	USC 20, Ohio St. 17
1926	Alabama 20, Washington 19	1956	Michigan St. 17, UCLA 14	1986	UCLA 45, Iowa 28
1927	7-7, Alabama vs Stanford	1957	Iowa 35, Oregon St. 19	1987	Arizona St. 22, Michigan 15
1928	Stanford 7, Pittsburgh 6	1958	Ohio St. 10, Oregon 7	1988	Michigan St. 20, USC 17
1929	Georgia Tech 8, California 7	1959	Iowa 38, California 12	1989	Michigan 22, USC 14
1930	USC 47, Pittsburgh 14	1960	Washington 44, Wisconsin 8	1990	USC 17, Michigan 10
1931	Alabama 24, Washington St. 0	1961	Washington 17, Minnesota 7	1991	Washington 46, Iowa 34
1932	USC 21, Tulane 12	1962	Minnesota 21, UCLA 3	1992	Washington 34, Michigan 14
1933	USC 35, Pittsburgh 0	1963	USC 42, Wisconsin 37	1993	Michigan 38, Washington 31
1934	Columbia 7, Stanford 0	1964	Illinois 17, Washington 7	1994	Wisconsin 21, UCLA 16
1935	Alabama 29, Stanford 13	1965	Michigan 34, Oregon St. 7	1995	Penn St. 38, Oregon 20
1936	Stanford 7, SMU 0	1966	UCLA 14, Michigan St. 12	1996	USC 41, Northwestern 32
1937	Pittsburgh 21, Washington 0	1967	Purdue 14, USC 13	1997	Ohio St. 20, Arizona St. 17
1938	California 13, Alabama 0	1968	USC 14, Indiana 3	1998	Michigan 21, Washington St. 16
1939	USC 7, Duke 3	1969	Ohio St. 27, USC 16	1999	Wisconsin 38, UCLA 31
1940	USC 14, Tennessee 0	1970	USC 10, Michigan 3	2000	Wisconsin 17, Stanford 9
1941	Stanford 21, Nebraska 13	1971	Stanford 27, Ohio St. 17	2001	Washington 34, Purdue 24
1942	Oregon St. 20, Duke 16	1972	Stanford 13, Michigan 12		
1943	Georgia 9, UCLA 0	1973	USC 42, Ohio St. 17	*January game since 1902.	
1944	USC 29, Washington 0	1974	Ohio St. 42, USC 21		

Fiesta Bowl

City: Tempe, Ariz. **Stadium:** Sun Devil. **Capacity:** 73,656. **Playing surface:** Grass. **First game:** Dec. 27, 1971. **Playing site:** Sun Devil Stadium (since 1971). **Corporate title sponsors:** Sunkist Citrus Growers (1986-91), IBM OS/2 (1993-95) and Frito-Lay Tostitos chips (since 1996).

Automatic berths: Western Athletic Conference champion vs. at-large opponent (1971-79 seasons); Two of first five picks from 8-team Bowl Coalition pool (1992-94). Bowl Alliance (#1 vs. #2 on Jan. 2, 1996; #3 vs. #5 on Jan. 1, 1997; and #4 vs. #6 on Dec. 31, 1997); Big 12 champion vs. next best team in pool (New Bowl Alliance 1995-1997 seasons); Bowl Championship Series: #1 vs. #2 on Jan. 4, 1999 and Big 12 champion, if available, vs. at-large (1999-2001 seasons).

Multiple wins: Penn St. (6); Arizona St. (5); Florida St. and Nebraska (2).

Year		Year		Year	
1971†	Arizona St. 45, Florida St. 38	1983	Arizona St. 32, Oklahoma 21	1994	Arizona 29, Miami-FL 0
1972	Arizona St. 49, Missouri 35	1984	Ohio St. 28, Pittsburgh 23	1995	Colorado 41, Notre Dame 24
1973	Arizona St. 28, Pittsburgh 7	1985	UCLA 39, Miami-FL 37	1996	Nebraska 62, Florida 24
1974	Oklahoma 16, BYU 6	1986	Michigan 27, Nebraska 23	1997	Penn St. 38, Texas 15
1975	Arizona St. 17, Nebraska 14	1987	Penn St. 14, Miami-FL 10	1997†	Kansas St. 35, Syracuse 18
1976	Oklahoma 41, Wyoming 7	1988	Florida St. 31, Nebraska 28	1999	Tennessee 23, Florida St. 16
1977	Penn St. 42, Arizona St. 30	1989	Notre Dame 34, West Va. 21	2000	Nebraska 31, Tennessee 21
1978	10-10, Arkansas vs UCLA	1990	Florida St. 41, Nebraska 17	2001	Oregon St. 41, Notre Dame 9
1979	Pittsburgh 16, Arizona 10	1991	Louisville 34, Alabama 7		
1980	Penn St. 31, Ohio St. 19	1992	Penn St. 42, Tennessee 17	†December game from 1971-80 and in '97.	
1982*	Penn St. 26, USC 10	1993	Syracuse 26, Colorado 22	* January game since 1982.	

Bowl Games (Cont.)

Sugar Bowl

City: New Orleans, La. **Stadium:** Louisiana Superdome. **Capacity:** 77,446. **Playing surface:** AstroTurf. **First game:** Jan. 1, 1935. **Playing sites:** Tulane Stadium (1935-74) and Superdome (since 1975). **Corporate title sponsors:** USF&G Financial Services (1987-95) and Nokia cellular telephones of Finland (starting in 1995).

Automatic berths: SEC champion vs. at-large opponent (1976-91 seasons); SEC champion vs. one of first five picks from 8-team Bowl Coalition pool (1992-94 seasons); #4 vs. #6 on Dec. 31, 1995; #1 vs. #2 on Jan. 2, 1997; and #3 vs. #5 on Jan. 1, 1998; Bowl Championship Series: SEC champion, if available, vs. at-large (1998-99, 2000 seasons) and #1 vs. #2 on Jan. 4, 2000.

Multiple wins: Alabama (8); Mississippi (5); Florida St., Georgia Tech, Oklahoma and Tennessee (4); LSU and Nebraska (3); Florida, Georgia, Miami-FL, Notre Dame, Pittsburgh, Santa Clara and TCU (2).

Year		Year		Year	
1935*	Tulane 20, Temple 14	1959	LSU 7, Clemson 0	1983	Penn St. 27, Georgia 23
1936	TCU 3, LSU 2			1984	Auburn 9, Michigan 7
1937	Santa Clara 21, LSU 14	1960	Mississippi 21, LSU 0	1985	Nebraska 28, LSU 10
1938	Santa Clara 6, LSU 0	1961	Mississippi 14, Rice 6	1986	Tennessee 35, Miami-FL 7
1939	TCU 15, Carnegie Tech 7	1962	Alabama 10, Arkansas 3	1987	Nebraska 30, LSU 15
		1963	Mississippi 17, Arkansas 13	1988	16-16, Syracuse vs Auburn
1940	Texas A&M 14, Tulane 13	1964	Alabama 12, Mississippi 7	1989	Florida St. 13, Auburn 7
1941	Boston College 19, Tennessee 13	1965	LSU 13, Syracuse 10		
1942	Fordham 2, Missouri 0	1966	Missouri 20, Florida 18	1990	Miami-FL 33, Alabama 25
1943	Tennessee 14, Tulsa 7	1967	Alabama 34, Nebraska 7	1991	Tennessee 23, Virginia 22
1944	Georgia Tech 20, Tulsa 18	1968	LSU 20, Wyoming 13	1992	Notre Dame 39, Florida 28
1945	Duke 29, Alabama 26	1969	Arkansas 16, Georgia 2	1993	Alabama 34, Miami-FL 13
1946	Okla. A&M 33, St.Mary's 13			1994	Florida 41, West Va. 7
1947	Georgia 20, N. Carolina 10	1970	Mississippi 27, Arkansas 22	1995	Florida St. 23, Florida 17
1948	Texas 27, Alabama 7	1971	Tennessee 34, Air Force 13	1995†	Va. Tech 28, Texas 10
1949	Oklahoma 14, N. Carolina 6	1972	Oklahoma 40, Auburn 22	1997	Florida 52, Florida St. 20
		1972†	Oklahoma 14, Penn St. 0	1998	Florida St. 31, Ohio St. 14
1950	Oklahoma 35, LSU 0	1973	Notre Dame 24, Alabama 23	1999	Ohio St. 24, Texas A&M 14
1951	Kentucky 13, Oklahoma 7	1974	Nebraska 13, Florida 10		
1952	Maryland 28, Tennessee 13	1975	Alabama 13, Penn St. 6	2000	Florida St. 46, Va. Tech 29
1953	Georgia Tech 24, Mississippi 7	1977*	Pittsburgh 27, Georgia 3	2001	Miami-FL 37, Florida 20
1954	Georgia Tech 42, West Va. 19	1978	Alabama 35, Ohio St. 6	*January game from 1935-72 and
1955	Navy 21, Mississippi 0	1979	Alabama 14, Penn St. 7	since 1977 (except in 1995).
1956	Georgia Tech 7, Pittsburgh 0			†Game played on Dec. 31 from
1957	Baylor 13, Tennessee 7	1980	Alabama 24, Arkansas 9	1972-75 and in 1995.
1958	Mississippi 39, Texas 7	1981	Georgia 17, Notre Dame 10	
		1982	Pittsburgh 24, Georgia 20	

Orange Bowl

City: Miami, Fla. **Stadium:** Pro Player. **Capacity:** 74,916. **Playing surface:** Grass. **First game:** Jan. 1, 1935. **Playing sites:** Orange Bowl (1935-95); Pro Player Stadium (since 1996). **Corporate title sponsor:** Federal Express (since 1989).

Automatic berths: Big 8 champion vs. Atlantic Coast Conference champion (1953-57 seasons); Big 8 champion vs. at-large opponent (1958-63 seasons and 1975-91 seasons); Big 8 champion vs. one of first five picks from 8-team Bowl Coalition pool (1992-94 seasons); #3 vs. #5 on Jan. 1, 1996; #4 vs. #6 on Dec. 31, 1996; and #1 vs. #2 on Jan. 2, 1998 (New Bowl Alliance 1995-97 seasons); Bowl Championship Series: Big East or ACC champion, if available, vs. at-large (1998-99, 2001 seasons) and #1 vs. #2 Jan. 3, 2001.

Multiple wins: Oklahoma (12); Nebraska (8); Miami-FL (5); Alabama (4); Florida State, Georgia Tech and Penn St. (3); Clemson, Colorado, Florida, Georgia, LSU, Notre Dame and Texas (2).

Year		Year		Year	
1935*	Bucknell 26, Miami-FL 0	1955	Duke 34, Nebraska 7	1975	Notre Dame 13, Alabama 11
1936	Catholic U. 20, Mississippi 19	1956	Oklahoma 20, Maryland 6	1976	Oklahoma 14, Michigan 6
1937	Duquesne 13, Mississippi St. 12	1957	Colorado 27, Clemson 21	1977	Ohio St. 27, Colorado 10
1938	Auburn 6, Michigan St. 0	1958	Oklahoma 48, Duke 21	1978	Arkansas 31, Oklahoma 6
1939	Tennessee 17, Oklahoma 0	1959	Oklahoma 21, Syracuse 6	1979	Oklahoma 31, Nebraska 24
1940	Georgia Tech 21, Missouri 7	1960	Georgia 14, Missouri 0	1980	Oklahoma 24, Florida St. 7
1941	Mississippi St. 14, Georgetown 7	1961	Missouri 21, Navy 14	1981	Oklahoma 18, Florida St. 17
1942	Georgia 40, TCU 26	1962	LSU 25, Colorado 7	1982	Clemson 22, Nebraska 15
1943	Alabama 37, Boston College 21	1963	Alabama 17, Oklahoma 0	1983	Nebraska 21, LSU 20
1944	LSU 19, Texas A&M 14	1964	Nebraska 13, Auburn 7	1984	Miami-FL 31, Nebraska 30
1945	Tulsa 26, Georgia Tech 12	1965†	Texas 21, Alabama 17	1985	Washington 28, Oklahoma 17
1946	Miami-FL 13, Holy Cross 6	1966	Alabama 39, Nebraska 28	1986	Oklahoma 25, Penn St. 10
1947	Rice 8, Tennessee 0	1967	Florida 27, Georgia Tech 12	1987	Oklahoma 42, Arkansas 8
1948	Georgia Tech 20, Kansas 14	1968	Oklahoma 26, Tennessee 24	1988	Miami-FL 20, Oklahoma 14
1949	Texas 41, Georgia 28	1969	Penn St. 15, Kansas 14	1989	Miami-FL 23, Nebraska 3
1950	Santa Clara 21, Kentucky 13	1970	Penn St. 10, Missouri 3	1990	Notre Dame, 21, Colorado 6
1951	Clemson 15, Miami-FL 6	1971	Nebraska 17, LSU 12	1991	Colorado 10, Notre Dame 9
1952	Georgia Tech 17, Baylor 14	1972	Nebraska 38, Alabama 6	1992	Miami-FL 22, Nebraska 0
1953	Alabama 61, Syracuse 6	1973	Nebraska 40, Notre Dame 6	1993	Florida St. 27, Nebraska 14
1954	Oklahoma 7, Maryland 0	1974	Penn St. 16, LSU 9	1994	Florida St. 18, Nebraska 16

Year		
1995	Nebraska 24, Miami-FL 17	
1996	Florida St. 31, Notre Dame 26	
1996**	Nebraska 41, Virginia Tech 21	
1998*	Nebraska 42, Tennessee 17	

Year		
1999	Florida 31, Syracuse 10	
2000	Michigan 35, Alabama 34	
2001	Oklahoma 13, Florida St. 2	

*January game 1935-1996 and since '98.

**December game in 1996

†Night game since 1965.

Cotton Bowl

City: Dallas, Tex. **Stadium:** Cotton Bowl. **Capacity:** 68,252. **Playing surface:** Grass. **First game:** Jan 1, 1937. **Playing sites:** Fair Park Stadium (1937) and Cotton Bowl (since 1938). **Corporate title sponsor:** Mobil Corporation (1988-95), SBC Communications Inc., previously Southwestern Bell, (since 1997).

Automatic berths: SWC champion vs. at-large opponent (1941-91 seasons); SWC champion vs. one of first five picks from 8-team Bowl Coalition pool (1992-1994 seasons); second pick from Big 12 vs. first choice of WAC champion or second pick from Pac-10 (1995-97 seasons); Big 12 vs. SEC (since 1998).

Multiple wins: Texas (10); Notre Dame (5); Texas A&M (4); Arkansas and Rice (3); Alabama, Georgia, Houston, LSU, Penn St., SMU, Tennessee, TCU and UCLA (2).

Year		
1937*	TCU 16, Marquette 6	
1938	Rice 28, Colorado 14	
1939	St. Mary's 20, Texas Tech 13	
1940	Clemson 6, Boston College 3	
1941	Texas A&M 13, Fordham 12	
1942	Alabama 29, Texas A&M 21	
1943	Texas 14, Georgia Tech 7	
1944	7-7, Texas vs Randolph Field	
1945	Oklahoma A&M 34, TCU 0	
1946	Texas 40, Missouri 27	
1947	0-0, Arkansas vs LSU	
1948	13-13, SMU vs Penn St.	
1949	SMU 21, Oregon 13	
1950	Rice 27, N. Carolina 13	
1951	Tennessee 20, Texas 14	
1952	Kentucky 20, TCU 7	
1953	Texas 16, Tennessee 0	
1954	Rice 28, Alabama 6	
1955	Georgia Tech 14, Arkansas 6	
1956	Mississippi 14, TCU 13	
1957	TCU 28, Syracuse 27	
1958	Navy 20, Rice 7	
1959	0-0, TCU vs Air Force	

Year		
1960	Syracuse 23, Texas 14	
1961	Duke 7, Arkansas 6	
1962	Texas 12, Mississippi 7	
1963	LSU 13, Texas 0	
1964	Texas 28, Navy 6	
1965	Arkansas 10, Nebraska 7	
1966	LSU 14, Arkansas 7	
1966†	Georgia 24, SMU 9	
1968*	Texas A&M 20, Alabama 16	
1969	Texas 36, Tennessee 13	
1970	Texas 21, Notre Dame 17	
1971	Notre Dame 24, Texas 11	
1972	Penn St. 30, Texas 6	
1973	Texas 17, Alabama 13	
1974	Nebraska 19, Texas 3	
1975	Penn St. 41, Baylor 20	
1976	Arkansas 31, Georgia 10	
1977	Houston 30, Maryland 21	
1978	Notre Dame 38, Texas 10	
1979	Notre Dame 35, Houston 34	
1980	Houston 17, Nebraska 14	
1981	Alabama 30, Baylor 2	
1982	Texas 14, Alabama 12	

Year		
1983	SMU 7, Pittsburgh 3	
1984	Georgia 10, Texas 9	
1985	Boston College 45, Houston 28	
1986	Texas A&M 36, Auburn 16	
1987	Ohio St. 28, Texas A&M 12	
1988	Texas A&M 35, Notre Dame 10	
1989	UCLA 17, Arkansas 3	
1990	Tennessee 31, Arkansas 27	
1991	Miami-FL 46, Texas 3	
1992	Florida St. 10, Texas A&M 2	
1993	Notre Dame 28, Texas A&M 3	
1994	Notre Dame 24, Texas A&M 21	
1995	USC 55, Texas Tech 14	
1996	Colorado 38, Oregon 6	
1997	BYU 19, Kansas St. 15	
1998	UCLA 29, Texas A&M 23	
1999	Texas 38, Mississippi St. 11	
2000	Arkansas 27, Texas 6	
2001	Kansas St. 35, Tennessee 21	

*January game from 1937-66 and since 1968.

†Game played on Dec. 31, 1966.

Florida Citrus Bowl

City: Orlando, Fla. **Stadium:** Florida Citrus Bowl. **Capacity:** 70,188. **Playing surface:** Grass. **First game:** Jan. 1, 1947. **Name change:** Tangerine Bowl (1947-82) and Florida Citrus Bowl (since 1983). **Playing sites:** Tangerine Bowl (1947-72, 1974-82), Florida Field in Gainesville (1973), Orlando Stadium (1983-85) and Florida Citrus Bowl (since 1986). The Tangerine Bowl, Orlando Stadium and Florida Citrus Bowl are all the same stadium. **Corporate title sponsors:** Florida Department of Citrus (since 1983), CompUSA (1992-99) and Ourhouse.com (since 2000).

Automatic berths: Championship game of Atlantic Coast Regional Conference (1964-67 seasons); Mid-American Conference champion vs. Southern Conference champion (1968-71 seasons); ACC champion vs. at-large opponent (1988-91 seasons); second pick from SEC, if available, vs. second pick from Big 10, if available (since 1992 season).

Multiple wins: East Texas St., Miami-OH, Tennessee and Toledo (3); Auburn, Catawba, Clemson, East Carolina, Florida and Michigan (2).

Year		
1947*	Catawba 31, Maryville 6	
1948	Catawba 7, Marshall 0	
1949	21-21, Murray St. vs Sul Ross St.	
1950	St. Vincent 7, Emory & Henry 6	
1951	M. Harvey 35, Emory & Henry 14	
1952	Stetson 35, Arkansas St. 20	
1953	E. Texas St. 33, Tenn. Tech 0	
1954	7-7, E. Texas St. vs Arkansas St.	
1955	Neb.-Omaha 7, Eastern Ky. 6	
1956	6-6, Juniata vs Missouri Valley	
1957	W. Texas St. 20, So. Miss. 13	
1958	E. Texas St. 10, So. Miss. 9	
1958†	E. Texas St. 26, Mo. Valley 7	
1960*	Mid. Tenn. 21, Presbyterian 12	
1960†	Citadel 27, Tenn. Tech 0	
1961	Lamar 21, Middle Tenn. 14	
1962	Houston 49, Miami-OH 21	
1963	Western Ky. 27, Coast Guard 0	
1964	E. Carolina 14, Massachusetts 13	
1965	E. Carolina 31, Maine 0	

Year		
1966	Morgan St. 14, West Chester 6	
1967	Tenn-Martin 25, West Chester 8	
1968	Richmond 49, Ohio U. 42	
1969	Toledo 56, Davidson 33	
1970	Toledo 40, Wm. & Mary 12	
1971	Toledo 28, Richmond 3	
1972	Tampa 21, Kent St. 18	
1973	Miami-OH 16, Florida 7	
1974	Miami-OH 21, Georgia 10	
1975	Miami-OH 20, S. Carolina 7	
1976	Oklahoma 49, BYU 21	
1977	Florida St. 40, Texas Tech 17	
1978	N.C. State 30, Pittsburgh 17	
1979	LSU 34, Wake Forest 10	
1980	Florida 35, Maryland 20	
1981	Missouri 19, Southern Miss. 17	
1982	Auburn 33, Boston College 26	
1983	Tennessee 30, Maryland 23	
1984	17-17, Florida St. vs Georgia	
1985	Ohio St. 10, BYU 7	

Year		
1987*	Auburn 16, USC 7	
1988	Clemson 35, Penn St. 10	
1989	Clemson 13, Oklahoma 6	
1990	Illinois 31, Virginia 21	
1991	Georgia Tech 45, Nebraska 21	
1992	California 37, Clemson 13	
1993	Georgia 21, Ohio St. 14	
1994	Penn St. 31, Tennessee 13	
1995	Alabama 24, Ohio St. 17	
1996	Tennessee 20, Ohio St. 14	
1997	Tennessee 48, Northwestern 28	
1998	Florida 21, Penn St. 6	
1999	Michigan 45, Arkansas 31	
2000	Michigan St. 37, Florida 34	
2001	Michigan 31, Auburn 28	

*January game from 1947-58, in 1960 and since 1987.

†December game in 1958 and 1960-85.

Bowl Games (Cont.)
Gator Bowl

City: Jacksonville, Fla. **Stadium:** ALLTEL Stadium. **Capacity:** 73,000. **Playing surface:** Grass. **First game:** Jan. 1, 1946. **Playing sites:** Gator Bowl (1946-93), Florida Field in Gainesville (1994) and New Gator Bowl (since 1995). Name was changed to ALLTEL Stadium in 1997. **Corporate title sponsors:** Mazda Motors of America, Inc. (1986-91), Outback Steakhouse, Inc. (1992-94) and Toyota Motor Co. (since 1995).

Automatic berths: Third pick from SEC vs. sixth pick from 8-team Bowl Coalition pool (1992-94 seasons); second pick from ACC, if available, vs. second pick from Big East or Notre Dame, if available (since 1995 season).

Multiple wins: Florida (6); North Carolina (5); Auburn and Clemson (4); Florida St., Georgia Tech and Tennessee (3); Georgia, Maryland, Miami-FL, Oklahoma, Pittsburgh, and Texas Tech (2).

Year		Year		Year	
1946*	Wake Forest 26, S. Carolina 14	1966	Tennessee 18, Syracuse 12	1987	LSU 30, S. Carolina 13
1947	Oklahoma 34, N.C. State 13	1967	17-17, Florida St. vs Penn St.	1989*	Georgia 34, Michigan St. 27
1948	20-20, Maryland vs Georgia	1968	Missouri 35, Alabama 10	1989†	Clemson 27, West Va. 7
1949	Clemson 24, Missouri 23	1969	Florida 14, Tennessee 13	1991*	Michigan 35, Mississippi 3
1950	Maryland 20, Missouri 7	1971*	Auburn 35, Mississippi 28	1991†	Oklahoma 48, Virginia 14
1951	Wyoming 20, Wash. & Lee 7	1971†	Georgia 7, N. Carolina 3	1992	Florida 27, N.C. State 10
1952	Miami-FL 14, Clemson 0	1972	Auburn 24, Colorado 3	1993	Alabama 24, N. Carolina 10
1953	Florida 14, Tulsa 13	1973	Texas Tech 28, Tennessee 19	1994	Tennessee 45, Va. Tech 23
1954	Texas Tech 35, Auburn 13	1974	Auburn 27, Texas 3	1996*	Syracuse 41, Clemson 0
1954†	Auburn 33, Baylor 13	1975	Maryland 13, Florida 0	1997	N. Carolina 20, West Va. 13
1955	Vanderbilt 25, Auburn 13	1976	Notre Dame 20, Penn St. 9	1998	N. Carolina 42, Va. Tech 3
1956	Georgia Tech 21, Pittsburgh 14	1977	Pittsburgh 34, Clemson 3	1999	Ga. Tech 35, Notre Dame 28
1957	Tennessee 3, Texas A&M 0	1978	Clemson 17, Ohio St. 15	2000	Miami-FL 28, Ga. Tech 13
1958	Mississippi 7, Florida 3	1979	N. Carolina 17, Michigan 15	2001	Va. Tech 41, Clemson 20
1960*	Arkansas 14, Georgia Tech 7	1980	Pittsburgh 37, S. Carolina 9	*January game from 1946-54, 1960,
1960†	Florida 13, Baylor 12	1981	N. Carolina 31, Arkansas 27	1965, 1971, 1989, 1991 and since
1961	Penn St. 30, Georgia Tech 15	1982	Florida St. 31, West Va. 12	1996.
1962	Florida 17, Penn St. 7	1983	Florida 14, Iowa 6	
1963	N. Carolina 35, Air Force 0	1984	Oklahoma St. 21, S. Carolina 14	†December game from 1954-58,
1965*	Florida St. 36, Oklahoma 19	1985	Florida St. 34, Oklahoma St. 23	1960-63, 1965-69, 1971-87, 1989
1965†	Georgia Tech 31, Texas Tech 21	1986	Clemson 27, Stanford 21	and 1991-94.

Bowl Championship Series

Division I-A football remains the only NCAA sport on any level that does not have a sanctioned national champion. To that end, the Bowl Coalition was formed in 1992 and was updated and renamed the Bowl Alliance in 1995 in an attempt to keep the bowl system intact while forcing an annual championship game between the regular season's two top-ranked teams.

The Bowl Championship Series is the organizers' latest attempt to finally guarantee that the teams ranked #1 and #2 will play each other in a "national title game" come January. The key difference from the 1992-97 Bowl Coalition/Bowl Alliance is that the Bowl Championship Series includes the Big 10 and Pac-10 champions. These teams, which were originally locked into playing in the Rose Bowl, are allowed under the new system to move to another bowl game in order to create a match-up featuring the #1 and #2 teams.

The bowls (the Fiesta, Orange, and Sugar) which made up the old Bowl Alliance kept their spots when the Rose Bowl joined this new four-bowl alliance. The Fiesta Bowl held the first national championship (#1 vs. #2) game under the Bowl Championship Series contract (Jan. 4, 1999), it was followed by the Sugar (Jan. 4, 2000) and the Orange (Jan. 3, 2001) and will continue at the Rose Bowl (Jan. 3, 2002). The BCS has successfully matched the top two teams in the country (according to the AP Poll) in two of the last three years.

Oklahoma played Florida St. in the BCS title game on Jan. 3, 2001 despite the fact that Miami-FL was #2 in the AP poll. FSU was the second-ranked team in the BCS rankings and therefore met Oklahoma, the top-ranked team, even though the Seminoles lost to Miami during the regular season. Controversy was averted when Oklahoma beat FSU 13-2 in the Orange Bowl.

Originally, ABC paid the BCS members $525 million over seven years in rights fees for the four "title" games, with a three year option clause. The option was exercised in January 2000 and ABC and the BCS agreed on an additional eighth year as well. The future schedule for the BCS championship game: Fiesta (2003), Sugar (2004), Orange (2005) and Rose (2006).

The 1992 Coalition, which lasted three seasons, consolidated the resources of four major bowl games (the Cotton, Fiesta, Orange and Sugar), the champions of five major conferences (the ACC, Big East, Big Eight, Southeastern and Southwest) and the national following of independent Notre Dame. It worked two out of three years with #1 vs. #2 showdowns in the 1993 Sugar Bowl (#2 Alabama over #1 Miami-FL) and 1994 Orange Bowl (#1 Florida St. over #2 Nebraska). The 1995 Orange Bowl had to settle for #1 Nebraska beating #3 Miami-FL because #2 Penn St., the Big Ten champion, was obligated to play in the Rose Bowl.

The Bowl Alliance, which ended a three-year run after the 1997 season, was an updated version of the Coalition.

Holiday Bowl

City: San Diego, Calif. **Stadium:** Qualcomm. **Capacity:** 71,000. **Playing surface:** Grass. **First game:** Dec. 22, 1978. **Playing site:** San Diego/Jack Murphy Stadium (since 1978). Name changed to Qualcomm Stadium in 1997. **Corporate title sponsors:** Sea World (1986-90), Thrifty Car Rental (1991-94), Chrysler-Plymouth Division of Chrysler Corp. (1995-97) and U.S. Filter/Culligan Water Tech. (since 1998).

Automatic berths: WAC champion vs. at-large opponent (1978-84, 1986-90 seasons); WAC champ vs. second pick from Big 10 (1991 season); WAC.champ vs. third pick from Big 10 (1992-94 seasons); choice of WAC champion, if available, or second pick from Pac-10, if available vs. third pick from Big 12, if available (1995-99); second pick from Pac-10 vs. third pick from Big 12 (2000 season).

Multiple wins: BYU (4); Iowa, Kansas St. and Ohio St. (2).

Year		Year		Year	
1978†	Navy 23, BYU 16	1986	Iowa 39, San Diego St. 38	1994	Michigan 24, Colo. St. 14
1979	Indiana 38, BYU 37	1987	Iowa 20, Wyoming 19	1995	Kansas St. 54, Colorado St. 21
		1988	Oklahoma St. 62, Wyoming 14	1996	Colorado 33, Washington 21
1980	BYU 46, SMU 45	1989	Penn St. 50, BYU 39	1997	Colorado St. 35, Missouri 24
1981	BYU 38, Washington St. 36			1998	Arizona 23, Nebraska 20
1982	Ohio St. 47, BYU 17	1990	Texas A&M 65, BYU 14	1999	Kansas St. 24, Washington 20
1983	BYU 21, Missouri 17	1991	13-13, Iowa vs BYU		
1984	BYU 24, Michigan 17	1992	Hawaii 27, Illinois 17	2000	Oregon 35, Texas 30
1985	Arkansas 18, Arizona St. 17	1993	Ohio St. 28, BYU 21	†December game since 1978.	

Outback Bowl

City: Tampa, Fla. **Stadium:** Raymond James. **Capacity:** 66,005. **Playing surface:** Grass. **First game:** Dec. 23, 1986. **Name change:** Hall of Fame Bowl (1986-95) and Outback Bowl (since 1995). **Playing sites:** Tampa/Houlihan's Stadium (1986-98) and Raymond James Stadium (since 1999). **Corporate title sponsor:** Outback Steakhouse, Inc. (since 1995).

Automatic berths: Fourth pick from ACC vs. fourth pick from Big 10 (1993-94 seasons); third pick from Big 10, if available, vs. third pick from SEC, if available (1995-99); fourth pick from Big 10 vs. third pick from SEC (2000 season).

Multiple wins: Georgia, Michigan, Penn St. and Syracuse (2).

Year		Year		Year	
1986†	Boston College 27, Georgia 24	1993	Tennessee 38, Boston Col. 23	1999	Penn St. 26, Kentucky 14
1988*	Michigan 28, Alabama 24	1994	Michigan 42, N.C. State 7	2000	Georgia 28, Purdue 25
1989	Syracuse 23, LSU 10	1995	Wisconsin 34, Duke 20	2001	S. Carolina 24, Ohio St. 7
		1996	Penn St. 43, Auburn 14		
1990	Auburn 31, Ohio St. 14	1997	Alabama 17, Michigan 14	†December game in 1986.	
1991	Clemson 30, Illinois 0	1998	Georgia 33, Wisconsin 6	*January game since 1988.	
1992	Syracuse 24, Ohio St. 17				

Peach Bowl

City: Atlanta, Ga. **Stadium:** Georgia Dome. **Capacity:** 71,228. **Playing surface:** AstroTurf. **First game:** Dec. 30, 1968. **Playing sites:** Grant Field (1968-70), Atlanta-Fulton County Stadium (1971-92) and Georgia Dome (since 1993). **Corporate title sponsor:** Chick-fil-A.

Automatic berths: Third pick from ACC vs. at-large opponent (1992 season); third pick from ACC vs. fourth pick from SEC (1993-94 seasons); third pick from ACC, if available, vs. fourth pick from SEC, if available (since 1995 season).

Multiple wins: N.C. State (4); LSU and West Virginia (3); Auburn, Georgia and Virginia (2).

Year		Year		Year	
1968†	LSU 31, Florida St. 27	1981†	West Va. 26, Florida 6	1995*	N.C. State 24, Miss. St. 24
1969	West Va. 14, S. Carolina 3	1982	Iowa 28, Tennessee 22	1995†	Virginia 34, Georgia 27
		1983	Florida St. 28, N. Carolina 3	1996	LSU 10, Clemson 7
1970	Arizona St. 48, N. Carolina 26	1984	Virginia 27, Purdue 24	1998*	Auburn 21, Clemson 17
1971	Mississippi 41, Georgia Tech 18	1985	Army 31, Illinois 29	1998†	Georgia 35, Virginia 33
1972	N.C. State 49, West Va. 13	1986	Va. Tech 25, N.C. State 24	1999	Mississippi St. 17, Clemson 7
1973	Georgia 17, Maryland 16	1988*	Tennessee 27, Indiana 22		
1974	6-6, Vanderbilt vs Texas Tech	1988†	N.C. State 28, Iowa 23	2000	LSU 28, Ga. Tech 14
1975	West Va. 13, N.C. State 10	1989	Syracuse 19, Georgia 18	†December game from 1968-79,
1976	Kentucky 21, N. Carolina 0			1981-86, 1988-90, 1993, 1995,
1977	N.C. State 24, Iowa St. 14	1990	Auburn 27, Indiana 23	1996, 1998 and since 1999.
1978	Purdue 41, Georgia Tech 21	1992*	E. Carolina 37, N.C. State 34	*January game in 1981, 1988, 1992-
1979	Baylor 24, Clemson 18	1993	N. Carolina 21, Miss. St. 17	93, 1995 and 1998.
		1993†	Clemson 14, Kentucky 13		
1981*	Miami-FL 20, Va. Tech 10				

Alamo Bowl

City: San Antonio, Tex. **Stadium:** Alamodome. **Capacity:** 65,000. **Playing surface:** AstroTurf. **First game:** Dec. 31, 1993. **Playing site:** Alamodome (since 1993). **Corporate title sponsor:** Builders Square (1993-98) and Sylvania (since 1999).

Automatic berths: third pick from SWC vs. fourth pick from Pac-10 (1993-94 seasons); fourth pick from Big 10, if available vs. fourth pick from Big 12, if available (1995-99 seasons); fourth pick from Big 12 vs. third pick from Big 10 (2000 season).

Multiple wins: Purdue (2).

Year		Year		Year	
1993†	California 37, Iowa 3	1996	Iowa 27, Texas Tech 0	1999	Penn St. 24, Texas A&M 0
1994	Washington St. 10, Baylor 3	1997	Purdue 33, Oklahoma St. 20	2000	Nebraska 66, Northwestern 17
1995	Texas A&M 22, Michigan 20	1998	Purdue 37, Kansas St. 34	†December game since 1993.	

Bowl Games (Cont.)
Sun Bowl

City: El Paso, Tex. **Stadium:** Sun Bowl. **Capacity:** 52,000. **Playing surface:** AstroTurf. **First game:** Jan. 1, 1936. **Name changes:** Sun Bowl (1936-85), John Hancock Sun Bowl (1986-88), John Hancock Bowl (1989-93) and Sun Bowl (since 1994). **Playing sites:** Kidd Field (1936-62) and Sun Bowl (since 1963). **Corporate title sponsors:** John Hancock Financial Services (1986-93), Norwest Bank (1996-98), Wells Fargo (since 1999).

Automatic berths: Eighth pick from 8-team Bowl Coalition pool vs. at-large opponent (1992); Seventh and eighth picks from 8-team Bowl Coalition pool (1993-94 seasons); third pick from Pac-10, if available, vs. fifth pick from Big 10, if available (since 1995 season).

Multiple wins: Texas Western/UTEP (5); Alabama and Wyoming (3); Nebraska, New Mexico St., North Carolina, Oklahoma, Oregon, Pittsburgh, Southwestern, Stanford, Texas, West Texas St. and West Virginia (2).

Year		Year		Year	
1936*	14-14, Hardin-Simmons vs New Mexico St.	1958*	Louisville 34, Drake 20	1981	Oklahoma 40, Houston 14
1937	Hardin-Simmons 34, Texas Mines 6	1958†	Wyoming 14, Hardin-Simmons 6	1982	N. Carolina 26, Texas 10
1938	West Va. 7, Texas Tech 6	1959	New Mexico St. 28, N. Texas 8	1983	Alabama 28, SMU 7
1939	Utah 26, New Mexico 0	1960	New Mexico St. 20, Utah St. 13	1984	Maryland 28, Tennessee 27
		1961	Villanova 17, Wichita 9	1985	13-13, Georgia vs Arizona
1940	0-0, Catholic U. vs Arizona St.	1962	West Texas 15, Ohio U. 14	1986	Alabama 28, Washington 6
1941	W. Reserve 26, Arizona St. 13	1963	Oregon 21, SMU 14	1987	Oklahoma St. 35, West Va. 33
1942	Tulsa 6, Texas Tech 0	1964	Georgia 7, Texas Tech 0	1988	Alabama 29, Army 28
1943	Second Air Force 13, Hardin-Simmons 7	1965	Texas Western 13, TCU 12	1989	Pittsburgh 31, Texas A&M 28
		1966	Wyoming 28, Florida St. 20		
1944	Southwestern 7, New Mexico 0	1967	UTEP 14, Mississippi 7	1990	Michigan St. 17, USC 16
1945	Southwestern 35, U. of Mexico 0	1968	Auburn 34, Arizona 10	1991	UCLA 6, Illinois 3
1946	New Mexico 34, Denver 24	1969	Nebraska 45, Georgia 6	1992	Baylor 20, Arizona 15
1947	Cincinnati 18, Va. Tech 6	1970	Georgia Tech 17, Texas Tech 9	1993	Oklahoma 41, Texas Tech 10
1948	Miami-OH 13, Texas Tech 12	1971	LSU 33, Iowa St. 15	1994	Texas 35, N. Carolina 31
1949	West Va. 21, Texas Mines 12	1972	N. Carolina 32, Texas Tech 28	1995	Iowa 38, Washington 18
		1973	Missouri 34, Auburn 17	1996	Stanford 38, Michigan St. 0
1950	Tex. Western 33, Georgetown 20	1974	Miss. St. 26, N. Carolina 24	1997	Arizona St. 17, Iowa 7
1951	West Texas 14, Cincinnati 13	1975	Pittsburgh 33, Kansas 19	1998	TCU 28, USC 19
1952	Texas Tech 25, Pacific 14	1977*	Texas A&M 37, Florida 14	1999	Oregon 24, Minnesota 20
1953	Pacific 26, Southern Miss. 7	1977†	Stanford 24, LSU 14	2000	Wisconsin 21, UCLA 20
1954	Tex. Western 37, So. Miss. 14	1978	Texas 42, Maryland 0		
1955	Tex. Western 47, Florida St. 20	1979	Washington 14, Texas 7	*January game from 1936-58 and in 1977.
1956	Wyoming 21, Texas Tech 14	1980	Nebraska 31, Miss. St. 17	†December game from 1958-75 and since 1977.
1957	Geo. Wash. 13, Tex. Western 0				

Insight.com Bowl

City: Tucson, Ariz. **Stadium:** Arizona. **Capacity:** 57,803. **Playing surface:** Grass. **First game:** Dec. 31, 1989. **Name change:** Copper Bowl (1989-1996), Insight.com Bowl (since 1997). **Playing site:** Arizona Stadium (since 1989). **Corporate title sponsors:** Domino's Pizza (1990-91), Weiser Lock (1992-1996) and Insight Enterprises (since 1997).

Automatic berths: Third pick from WAC vs. at-large opponent (1992 season); third pick from WAC vs. fourth pick from Big Eight (1993-94 seasons); second pick from WAC vs. sixth pick from Big 12 (1995-97); third pick from Big East or Notre Dame, if available vs. fifth pick from Big 12, if available (since 1998 season).

Multiple wins: Arizona (2).

Year		Year		Year	
1989†	Arizona 17, N.C. State 10	1994	BYU 31, Oklahoma 6	1999	Colorado 62, Boston College 28
1990	California 17, Wyoming 15	1995	Texas Tech 55, Air Force 41	2000	Iowa St. 37, Pittsburgh 29
1991	Indiana 24, Baylor 0	1996	Wisconsin 38, Utah 10		
1992	Washington St. 31, Utah 28	1997	Arizona 20, New Mexico 14	†December game since 1989.
1993	Kansas St. 52, Wyoming 17	1998	Missouri 34, W. Virginia 31		

Liberty Bowl

City: Memphis, Tenn. **Stadium:** Liberty Bowl Memorial. **Capacity:** 62,380. **Playing surface:** Grass. **First game:** Dec. 19, 1959. **Playing sites:** Municipal Stadium in Philadelphia (1959-63), Convention Hall in Atlantic City, N.J. (1964), Memphis Memorial Stadium (1965-75) and Liberty Bowl Memorial Stadium (since 1976). Memphis Memorial Stadium renamed Liberty Bowl Memorial in 1976. **Corporate title sponsors:** St. Jude's Hospital (since 1993), AXA/Equitable (since 1997).

Automatic berths: Commander-in-Chief's Trophy winner (Army, Navy or Air Force) vs. at-large opponent (1989-92 seasons); none (1993 season); first pick from independent group of Cincinnati, East Carolina, Memphis, Southern Miss. and Tulane vs. at-large opponent (for 1994 and '95 seasons); Conference USA champion vs. at-large opponent (for 1994 and '95 seasons); Conference USA champion vs. fourth pick from the Big East (1996-97 seasons); Conference USA champion, if available, vs. fifth, sixth or seventh pick or at-large from SEC (1998-99 seasons); Mountain West champion vs. Conference USA champion, if available (2000 season).

Multiple wins: Mississippi (4); Penn St. and Tennessee (3); Air Force, Alabama, N.C. State, Southern Miss., Syracuse and Tulane (2).

Year		Year		Year	
1959†	Penn St. 7, Alabama 0	1966	Miami-FL 14, Virginia Tech 7	1973	N.C. State 31, Kansas 18
1960	Penn St. 41, Oregon 12	1967	N.C. State 14, Georgia 7	1974	Tennessee 7, Maryland 3
1961	Syracuse 15, Miami-FL 14	1968	Mississippi 34, Virginia Tech 17	1975	USC 20, Texas A&M 0
1962	Oregon St. 6, Villanova 0	1969	Colorado 47, Alabama 33	1976	Alabama 36, UCLA 6
1963	Mississippi St. 16, N.C. State 12	1970	Tulane 17, Colorado 3	1977	Nebraska 21, N. Carolina 17
1964	Utah 32, West Virginia 6	1971	Tennessee 14, Arkansas 13	1978	Missouri 20, LSU 15
1965	Mississippi 13, Auburn 7	1972	Georgia Tech 31, Iowa St. 30	1979	Penn St. 9, Tulane 6

Year		Year		Year	
1980	Purdue 28, Missouri 25	1988	Indiana 34, S. Carolina 10	1996	Syracuse 30, Houston 17
1981	Ohio St. 31, Navy 28	1989	Mississippi 42, Air Force 29	1997	Southern Miss. 41, Pittsburgh 7
1982	Alabama 21, Illinois 15	1990	Air Force 23, Ohio St. 11	1998	Tulane 41, BYU 27
1983	Notre Dame 19, Boston Col. 18	1991	Air Force 38, Mississippi St. 15	1999	Southern Miss. 23, Colorado St. 17
1984	Auburn 21, Arkansas 15	1992	Mississippi 13, Air Force 0	2000	Colorado St. 22, Louisville 17
1985	Baylor 21, LSU 7	1993	Louisville 18, Michigan St. 7	†December game since 1959.
1986	Tennessee 21, Minnesota 14	1994	Illinois 30, E. Carolina 0		
1987	Georgia 20, Arkansas 17	1995	E. Carolina 19, Stanford 13		

MicronPC.com Bowl

City: Miami, Fla. **Stadium:** Pro Player. **Capacity:** 74,915. **Playing surface:** Grass. **First game:** Dec. 28, 1990. **Name change:** Blockbuster Bowl (1990-93), Carquest Bowl (1994-97), Micron PC Bowl (1998) and MicronPC.com Bowl (since 1999). The game was called the Sunshine Football Classic for a short time in the offseason after Carquest Auto Parts dropped its sponsorship and before Micron signed on. **Playing site:** Joe Robbie Stadium (since 1990). Name changed to Pro Player Stadium in 1996. **Corporate title sponsors:** Blockbuster Video (1990-93), Carquest Auto Parts (1993-97) and Micron Electronics (since 1998).

Automatic berths: Penn St. vs. seventh pick from 8-team Bowl Coalition pool (1992 season); third pick from Big East vs. fifth pick from SEC (1993-94 seasons); third pick from Big East vs. fifth pick from SEC (1995 season); third pick from Big East vs. fourth pick from ACC (1996-97 season); sixth pick from Big Ten, if available, vs. fourth pick from ACC, if available (since 1998 season).

Multiple wins: Miami-FL (2).

Year		Year		Year	
1990†	Florida St. 24, Penn St. 17	1995†	N. Carolina 20, Arkansas 10	2000	N.C. State 38, Minnesota 30
1991	Alabama 30, Colorado 25	1996	Miami-FL 31, Virginia 21	†December game from 1990-91 and
1993*	Stanford 24, Penn St. 3	1997	Ga. Tech 35, W. Virginia 30	since 1995.
1994	Boston College 31, Virginia 13	1998	Miami-FL 46, N.C. State 23	*January game 1993-95.
1995	S. Carolina 24, West Va. 21	1999	Illinois 63, Virginia 21		

San Francisco Bowl

City: San Francisco, Calif. **Stadium:** Pacific Bell Park. **Capacity:** 40,800 (for baseball). **Playing surface:** Grass. **First game:** Dec. 25, 1982. **Name change:** Aloha Bowl (1982-2000), San Francisco Bowl (since 2001). **Playing sites:** Aloha Stadium (1982-2000); Pacific Bell Park (2001–). **Corporate title sponsor:** Jeep Eagle Division of Chrysler (since 1987).

Automatic berths: Second or third pick from Big Eight (1992-93 seasons); third pick from Big Eight vs. at-large (1994 season); fifth pick from Big 12 vs. fourth pick from Pac-10 (1995-97 season); fourth pick from Pac-10, if available vs. at-large (1998-99); fourth or fifth pick from Pac-10 vs. fourth or fifth pick from Big East or fourth pick from ACC (2000 season).

Multiple wins: Boston College, Colorado, Kansas and Washington (2).

Year		Year		Year	
1982†	Washington 21, Maryland 20	1989	Michigan St. 33, Hawaii 13	1996	Navy 42, California 38
1983	Penn St. 13, Washington 10	1990	Syracuse 28, Arizona 0	1997	Washington 51, Michigan St. 23
1984	SMU 27, Notre Dame 20	1991	Georgia Tech 18, Stanford 17	1998	Colorado 51, Oregon 43
1985	Alabama 24, USC 3	1992	Kansas 23, BYU 20	1999	Wake Forest 23, Arizona St. 3
1986	Arizona 30, N. Carolina 21	1993	Colorado 41, Fresno St. 30	2000	Boston Col. 31, Arizona St. 17
1987	UCLA 20, Florida 16	1994	Boston Col. 12, Kansas St. 7	†December game since 1982.
1988	Washington St. 24, Houston 22	1995	Kansas 51, UCLA 30		

Seattle Bowl

City: Seattle, Wash. **Stadium:** Safeco Field. **Capacity:** 47,116 (for baseball). **Playing surface:** Grass. **First game:** Dec. 25, 1998. **Name change:** Oahu Bowl (1998-2000); Seattle Bowl (since 2001). **Playing sites:** Aloha Stadium (1998-2000), Safeco Field (2001), new Seahawks stadium (2002–). **Corporate title sponsor:** Jeep Eagle Division of Chrysler (since 1998).

Automatic berths: second or third pick from WAC, if available, vs. fifth pick from Pac-10, if available (1998-99 seasons); fourth or fifth pick from Pac-10 vs. fourth or fifth pick from Big East or fourth pick from ACC (2000 season).

Year		Year			
1998†	Air Force 45, Washington 25	2000	Georgia 37, Virginia 14	†December game since 1998.	
1999	Hawaii 23, Oregon St. 17				

Humanitarian Bowl

City: Boise, Idaho. **Stadium:** Bronco. **Capacity:** 30,000. **Playing surface:** AstroTurf. **First game:** Dec. 29, 1997. **Playing sites:** Bronco Stadium (since 1997). **Corporate title sponsor:** World Sports Humanitarian Hall of Fame (since 1997) and Crucial.com (since 1999).

Automatic berths: Big West champion, if available, vs. at-large (since 1997 season).

Multiple wins: Boise St. (2).

Year		Year			
1997†	Cincinnati 35, Utah St. 19	1999	Boise St. 34, Louisville 31	†December game since 1997.	
1998	Idaho 42, Southern Miss. 35	2000	Boise St. 38, UTEP 23		

Las Vegas Bowl

City: Las Vegas, Nev. **Stadium:** Sam Boyd. **Capacity:** 40,000. **Playing surface:** AstroTurf. **First game:** Dec. 18, 1992. **Playing site:** Sam Boyd Stadium (since 1992). **Corporate title sponsor:** EA Sports (since 1999).

Automatic berths: Mid-American champion vs. Big West champion (1992-96 season); none (1997 season); second or third pick from WAC, if available vs. at-large (since 1998 season).

Multiple wins: Fresno St. (4); UNLV (3); Bowling Green, San Jose St. and Toledo (2).

Bowl Games (Cont.)

Year		Year		Year	
1981†	Toledo 27, San Jose St. 25	1989	Fresno St. 27, Ball St. 6	1997	Oregon 41, Air Force 13
1982	Fresno St. 29, Bowling Green 28	1990	San Jose St. 48, C. Michigan 24	1998	N. Carolina 20, San Diego St. 13
1983	Northern Ill. 20, CS-Fullerton 13	1991	Bowling Green 28, Fresno St. 21	1999	Utah 17, Fresno St. 16
1984*	UNLV 30, Toledo 13	1992	Bowling Green 35, Nevada 34	2000	UNLV 31, Arkansas 14
1985	Fresno St. 51, Bowling Green 7	1993	Utah St. 42, Ball St. 33		
1986	San Jose St. 37, Miami-OH 7	1994	UNLV 52, C. Michigan 24		†December game since 1981.
• 1987	E. Michigan 30, San Jose St. 27	1995	Toledo 40, Nevada 37 (OT)		* Toledo later ruled winner of 1984
1988	Fresno St. 35, W. Michigan 30	1996	Nevada 18, Ball St. 15		game by forfeit because UNLV used ineligible players.

Note: The MAC and Big West champs met in a bowl game from 1981 to 1996, originally in Fresno at the California Bowl (1981-88, 1992) and California Raisin Bowl (1989-91). The results from 1981-91 are included below.

Independence Bowl

City: Shreveport, La. **Stadium:** Independence. **Capacity:** 50,832. **Playing surface:** Grass. **First game:** Dec. 13, 1976. **Playing site:** Independence Stadium (since 1976). **Corporate title sponsors:** Poulan/Weed Eater (1990-97) and Sanford (since 1998). **Automatic berths:** Southland Conference champion vs. at-large opponent (1976-81 seasons); none (1982-95 seasons); fifth pick from SEC, if available, vs. at-large (1995-97 season); fifth, sixth or seventh pick from SEC, if available, vs. at-large (1998-99 season); sixth pick from Big 12 vs. SEC (2000 season).
Multiple wins: Mississippi (3); Air Force, LSU and Southern Miss (2).

Year		Year		Year	
1976†	McNeese St. 20, Tulsa 16	1985	Minnesota 20, Clemson 13	1994	Virginia 20, TCU 10
1977	La. Tech 24, Louisville 14	1986	Mississippi 20, Texas Tech 17	1995	LSU 45, Michigan St. 26
1978	E. Carolina 35, La. Tech 13	1987	Washington 24, Tulane 12	1996	Auburn 32, Army 29
1979	Syracuse 31, McNeese St. 7	1988	Southern Miss 38, UTEP 18	1997	LSU 27, Notre Dame 9
1980	Southern Miss 16, McNeese St. 14	1989	Oregon 27, Tulsa 24	1998	Mississippi 35, Texas Tech 18
1981	Texas A&M 33, Oklahoma St. 16			1999	Mississippi 27, Oklahoma 25
1982	Wisconsin 14, Kansas St. 3	1990	34-34, La. Tech vs Maryland		
1983	Air Force 9, Mississippi 3	1991	Georgia 24, Arkansas 15	2000	Mississippi St. 43, Texas A&M 41
1984	Air Force 23, Va. Tech 7	1992	Wake Forest 39, Oregon 35		†December game since 1976.
		1993	Va. Tech 45, Indiana 20		

Motor City Bowl

City: Pontiac, Mich. **Stadium:** Pontiac Silverdome. **Capacity:** 80,368. **Playing surface:** Turf. **First game:** Dec. 26, 1997. **Playing site:** Pontiac Silverdome (since 1997). **Corporate title sponsor:** Ford Division of Ford Motor Company (since 1997). **Automatic berths:** Mid-American champions vs at-large (1997-99 season); Mid-American champions vs. fourth pick from Conference USA (2000 season).
Multiple wins: Marshall (3).

Year		Year			
1997†	Mississippi 34, Marshall 31	1999	Marshall 21, BYU 3	†December game since 1997.	
1998	Marshall 48, Louisville 29	2000	Marshall 25, Cincinnati 14		

Music City Bowl

City: Nashville, Tenn. **Stadium:** Adelphia Coliseum. **Capacity:** 67,000. **Playing surface:** Grass. **First game:** Dec. 29, 1998. **Playing sites:** Vanderbilt Stadium (1998) and Adelphia Coliseum (since 1999). **Corporate title sponsors:** American General (1998) and HomePoint.com (since 1999). **Automatic berths:** sixth choice from the SEC, if available, vs. at-large (1998-99 season); fourth pick from Big East, if available vs. SEC (2000 season).

Year		Year		Year	
1998†	Va. Tech 38, Alabama 7	1999	Syracuse 20, Kentucky 13	2000	West Va. 49, Mississippi 38
		†December game since 1998.			

Mobile Bowl

City: Mobile, Ala. **Stadium:** Ladd-Peebles. **Capacity:** 40,646. **Playing surface:** Grass. **First game:** Dec. 22, 1999. **Playing sites:** Ladd-Peebles Stadium (since 1999). **Automatic berths:** WAC champions (if team is from the east) or second pick from WAC vs. second pick from Conference USA, if available (2000 season).

Year		Year			
1999†	TCU 28, E. Carolina 14	2000	So. Miss 28, TCU 21	†December game since 1999.	

GalleryFurniture.com Bowl

City: Houston, Tex. **Stadium:** Astrodome. **Capacity:** 59,969. **Playing surface:** Turf. **First game:** Dec. 27, 2000. **Playing sites:** Astrodome (since 2000). **Corporate title sponsors:** GalleryFurniture.com (since 2000). **Automatic berths:** Big 12 vs. Conference USA.

Year			
2000†	E. Carolina 40, Tex. Tech 27	†December game since 2000.	

Silicon Valley Classic Bowl

City: San Jose, Calif.. **Stadium:** Spartan. **Capacity:** 30,578. **Playing surface:** Grass. **First game:** Dec. 31, 2000. **Playing sites:** Spartan Stadium (since 2000). **Corporate title sponsors:** none. **Automatic berths:** WAC vs. at-large

Year			
2000†	Air Force 37, Fresno St. 34	†December game since 2000.	

All-Time Winningest Division I-A Teams

Schools classified as Division I-A for at least 10 years; through 2000 season (including bowl games).

Top 25 Winning Percentage

		Yrs	Gm	W	L	T	Pct	Bowls App	Bowls Record	2000 Season Bowl	2000 Season Record
1	Notre Dame	112	1059	776	241	42	.753	24	13-11-0	Lost Fiesta	9-3
2	Michigan	121	1103	805	262	36	.746	32	17-15-0	Won Citrus	9-3
3	Alabama*	106	1056	737	276	43	.718	50	28-19-3	None	3-8
4	Nebraska	111	1092	753	299	40	.708	39	20-19-0	Won Alamo	10-2
5	Ohio St.	111	1064	724	287	53	.705	32	14-18-0	Lost Outback	8-4
6	Oklahoma	106	1033	702	278	53	.705	34	21-12-1	Won Orange	13-0
7	Texas	108	1079	744	302	33	.705	40	18-20-2	Lost Holiday	9-3
8	Tennessee*	104	1051	707	292	52	.697	41	22-19-0	Lost Cotton	8-4
9	Penn St.	114	1092	739	312	41	.696	36	23-11-2	None	5-7
10	USC	108	1020	678	288	54	.691	39	25-14-0	None	5-7
11	Florida St.*	54	594	392	185	17	.674	29	17-10-2	Won Rose	11-2
12	Washington*	111	1004	617	337	50	.639	27	14-12-1	Won Rose	11-1
13	Miami-OH*	112	973	597	332	44	.636	7	5-2-0	None	6-5
14	Georgia	107	1057	641	362	54	.632	36	19-14-3	Won Oahu	8-4
15	LSU*	107	1025	618	360	47	.626	32	15-16-1	Won Peach	8-4
16	Arizona St.	88	804	490	290	24	.624	19	10-8-1	Lost Aloha	6-6
17	Central Michigan	100	849	512	301	36	.624	2	0-2-0	None	2-9
18	Miami-FL	74	773	472	282	19	.623	25	14-11-0	Won Sugar	11-1
19	Auburn*	108	1022	610	365	47	.620	27	14-11-2	Lost Citrus	9-4
20	Army	111	1043	618	374	51	.617	4	2-2-0	None	1-10
21	Colorado*	111	1023	611	376	36	.615	23	11-12-0	None	3-8
22	Florida	94	951	564	347	40	.614	28	13-15-0	Lost Sugar	10-3
23	Texas A&M	106	1043	609	386	48	.607	26	12-14-0	Lost Independence	7-5
24	UCLA	82	835	484	314	37	.605	23	11-11-1	Lost Sun	6-6
25	Syracuse	111	1098	638	411	49	.603	20	11-8-1	None	6-5

*Includes games forfeited following rulings by the NCAA Executive Council and/or the Committee on Infractions.

Top 50 Victories

		Wins			Wins			Wins
1	Michigan	805	18	Texas A&M	609	35	Missouri	540
2	Notre Dame	776	19	West Virginia	603	36	Boston College	536
3	Nebraska	753	20	Georgia Tech	601		Wisconsin	536
4	Texas	744	21	North Carolina	600	38	Maryland	535
5	Penn St.	739	22	Miami-OH	597	39	Illinois	526
6	Alabama	737	23	Pittsburgh	596	40	Vanderbilt	525
7	Ohio St.	724	24	Arkansas	594	41	Utah	524
8	Tennessee	707	25	Minnesota	587	42	Kentucky	519
9	Oklahoma	702	26	Navy	579	43	Stanford	518
10	USC	678		Virginia Tech	579	44	Purdue	516
11	Georgia	641	28	Clemson	571	45	Kansas	515
12	Syracuse	638	29	Florida	564	46	Central Michigan	512
13	Army	618	30	Michigan St.	561	47	Arizona	508
	LSU	618	31	Mississippi	559	48	Iowa	501
15	Washington	617	32	California	558	49	Tulsa	498
16	Colorado	611	33	Virginia	555	50	Louisiana Tech	494
17	Auburn	610	34	Rutgers	550			

Top 30 Bowl Appearances

		App	Record			App	Record			App	Record
1	Alabama	50	28-19-3	12	Arkansas	31	10-18-3	21	Texas Tech	24	5-18-1
2	Tennessee	41	22-19-0	13	Georgia Tech	29	19-10-0		Notre Dame	24	13-11-0
3	Texas	40	18-20-2		Florida St	29	17-10-2		Clemson	24	12-12-0
4	USC	39	25-14-0		Mississippi	29	17-12-0	24	North Carolina	23	11-12-0
	Nebraska	39	20-19-0	16	Florida	28	13-15-0		Colorado	23	11-12-0
6	Penn St	36	23-11-2	17	Auburn	27	14-11-2		UCLA	23	11-11-1
	Georgia	36	19-14-3		Washington	27	14-12-1	27	BYU	22	7-14-1
8	Oklahoma	34	21-12-1	19	Texas A&M	26	12-14-0	28	Missouri	21	9-12-0
9	LSU	32	15-16-1	20	Miami-FL	25	14-11-0		West Virginia	21	9-12-0
	Ohio St	32	14-18-0					30	Syracuse	20	11-8-1
	Michigan	32	17-15-0						Pittsburgh	20	8-12-0

Note: Alabama, Georgia, Georgia Tech, Notre Dame, Ohio State and Penn State are the only schools that have won all four of the traditional major bowl games—the Rose, Orange, Sugar and Cotton. Ohio State, Penn State and Notre Dame are the only schools to have won those four and the recently prestigious Fiesta bowl.

Major Conference Champions
Atlantic Coast Conference

Founded in 1953 when charter members all left Southern Conference to form ACC. **Charter members** (7): Clemson, Duke, Maryland, North Carolina, N.C. State, South Carolina and Wake Forest. **Admitted later** (3): Virginia in 1953 (began play in '54), Georgia Tech in 1979 (began play in '83), Florida St. in 1990 (began play in '92). **Withdrew later** (1): South Carolina in 1971 (became an independent after '70 season).

2001 playing membership (9): Clemson, Duke, Florida St., Georgia Tech, Maryland, North Carolina, N.C. State, Virginia and Wake Forest.

Multiple titles: Clemson (13); Florida St. (9); Maryland (8); Duke and N.C. State (7); North Carolina (5); Georgia Tech & Virginia (2).

Year		Year		Year		Year	
1953	Duke (4-0) & Maryland (3-0)	1965	Clemson (5-2) & N.C. State (5-2)	1979	N.C. State (5-1)	1991	Clemson (6-0-1)
1954	Duke (4-0)	1966	Clemson (6-1)	1980	North Carolina (6-0)	1992	Florida St. (8-0)
1955	Maryland (4-0) & Duke (4-0)	1967	Clemson (6-0)	1981	Clemson (6-0)	1993	Florida St. (8-0)
1956	Clemson (4-0-1)	1968	N.C. State (6-1)	1982	Clemson (6-0)	1994	Florida St. (8-0)
1957	N.C. State (5-0-1)	1969	South Carolina (6-0)	1983	Clemson (7-0) † & Maryland (5-0)	1995	Virginia (7-1) & Florida St. (7-1)
1958	Clemson (5-1)	1970	Wake Forest (5-1)	1984	Maryland (5-0)	1996	Florida St. (8-0)
1959	Clemson (6-1)	1971	North Carolina (6-0)	1985	Maryland (6-0)	1997	Florida St. (8-0)
1960	Duke (5-1)	1972	North Carolina (6-0)	1986	Clemson (5-1-1)	1998	Florida St. (7-1) & Georgia Tech (7-1)
1961	Duke (5-1)	1973	N.C. State (6-0)	1987	Clemson (6-1)	1999	Florida St. (8-0)
1962	Duke (6-0)	1974	Maryland (6-0)	1988	Clemson (6-1)	2000	Florida St. (8-0)
1963	North Carolina (6-1) & N.C. State (6-1)	1975	Maryland (5-0)	1989	Virginia (6-1) & Duke (6-1)	†On probation, ineligible for championship.	
1964	N.C. State (5-2)	1976	Maryland (5-0)	1990	Georgia Tech (6-0-1)		
		1977	North Carolina (5-0-1)				
		1978	Clemson (5-1)				

Big East Conference

Founded in 1991 when charter members gave up independent football status to form Big East. **Charter members** (8): Boston College, Miami-FL, Pittsburgh, Rutgers, Syracuse, Temple, Virginia Tech and West Virginia. **Note:** Temple and Virginia Tech are Big East members in football only.

2001 playing membership (8): Boston College, Miami-FL, Pittsburgh, Rutgers, Syracuse, Temple, Virginia Tech and West Virginia.

Conference champion: Member schools needed two years to adjust their regular season schedules in order to begin round-robin conference play in 1993. In the meantime, the 1991 and '92 Big East titles went to the highest-ranked member in the final regular season *USA Today*/CNN coaches' poll.

Multiple titles: Miami-FL (6); Syracuse (4); Virginia Tech (3).

Year		Year		Year		Year	
1991	Miami-FL (2-0, #1) & Syracuse (5-0, #16)	1994	Miami-FL (7-0)	1996	Virginia Tech (6-1), Miami-FL (6-1) & Syracuse (6-1)	1997	Syracuse (6-1)
1992	Miami-FL (4-0, #1)	1995	Virginia Tech (6-1) & Miami-FL (6-1)			1998	Syracuse (6-1)
1993	West Virginia (7-0)					1999	Virginia Tech (7-0)
						2000	Miami-FL (7-0)

Big Ten Conference

Originally founded in 1895 as the Intercollegiate Conference of Faculty Representatives, better known as the Western Conference. **Charter members** (7): Chicago, Illinois, Michigan, Minnesota, Northwestern, Purdue and Wisconsin. **Admitted later** (5): Indiana and Iowa in 1899; Ohio St. in 1912; Michigan St. in 1950 (began play in '53); Penn St. in 1990 (began play in '93). **Withdrew later** (2): Michigan in 1917 (rejoined in '17); Chicago in 1940 (dropped football after '39 season). **Note:** Iowa belonged to both the Western and Missouri Valley conferences from 1907-10.

Unofficially called the **Big Ten** from 1912 until Chicago's withdrawal in 1939, then the **Big Nine** from 1940 until Michigan St. began conference play in 1953. Formally named the **Big Ten** in 1984 and has kept the name even after adding Penn St. as its 11th member in 1990.

2001 playing membership (11): Illinois, Indiana, Iowa, Michigan, Michigan St., Minnesota, Northwestern, Ohio St., Penn St., Purdue and Wisconsin.

Multiple titles: Michigan (40); Ohio St. (28); Minnesota (18); Illinois (14); Wisconsin (11); Iowa (9); Purdue and Northwestern (8); Chicago and Michigan St. (6); Indiana (2).

Year		Year		Year		Year	
1896	Wisconsin (2-0-1)	1906	Wisconsin (3-0), Minnesota (2-0) & Michigan (1-0)	1917	Ohio St. (4-0)	1927	Illinois (5-0)
1897	Wisconsin (3-0)			1918	Illinois (4-0), Michigan (2-0) & Purdue (1-0)		& Minnesota (3-0-1)
1898	Michigan (3-0)	1907	Chicago (4-0)			1928	Illinois (4-1)
1899	Chicago (4-0)	1908	Chicago (5-0)	1919	Illinois (6-1)	1929	Purdue (5-0)
1900	Iowa (3-0-1) & Minnesota (3-0-1)	1909	Minnesota (3-0)	1920	Ohio St. (5-0)	1930	Michigan (5-0) & Northwestern (5-0)
1901	Michigan (4-0) & Wisconsin (2-0)	1910	Illinois (4-0) & Minnesota (2-0)	1921	Iowa (5-0)	1931	Purdue (5-1), Michigan (5-1) & Northwestern (5-1)
				1922	Iowa (5-0) & Michigan (4-0)		
1902	Michigan (5-0)	1911	Minnesota (3-0-1)	1923	Illinois (5-0) & Michigan (4-0)	1932	Michigan (6-0) & Purdue (5-0-1)
1903	Michigan (3-0-1), Minnesota (3-0-1) & Northwestern (1-0-2)	1912	Wisconsin (6-0)			1933	Michigan (5-0-1) & Minnesota (2-0-4)
		1913	Chicago (7-0)	1924	Chicago (3-0-3)		
		1914	Illinois (6-0)	1925	Michigan (5-1)	1934	Minnesota (5-0)
1904	Minnesota (3-0) & Michigan (2-0)	1915	Minnesota (3-0-1) & Illinois (3-0-2)	1926	Michigan (5-0) & Northwestern (5-0)	1935	Minnesota (5-0) & Ohio St. (5-0)
1905	Chicago (7-0)	1916	Ohio St. (4-0)				

Year		Year		Year		Year	
1936	Northwestern (6-0)	1955	Ohio St. (6-0)	1973	Ohio St. (7-0-1)	1989	Michigan (8-0)
1937	Minnesota (5-0)	1956	Iowa (5-1)		& Michigan (7-0-1)	1990	Iowa (6-2),
1938	Minnesota (4-1)	1957	Ohio St. (7-0)	1974	Ohio St. (7-1)		Michigan (6-2),
1939	Ohio St. (5-1)	1958	Iowa (5-1)		& Michigan (7-1)		Michigan St. (6-2)
1940	Minnesota (6-0)	1959	Wisconsin (5-2)	1975	Ohio St. (8-0)		& Illinois (6-2)
1941	Minnesota (5-0)	1960	Minnesota (5-1)	1976	Michigan (7-1)	1991	Michigan (8-0)
1942	Ohio St. (5-1)		& Iowa (5-1)		& Ohio St. (7-1)	1992	Michigan (6-0-2)
1943	Purdue (6-0)	1961	Ohio St. (6-0)	1977	Michigan (7-1)	1993	Wisconsin (6-1-1)
	& Michigan (6-0)	1962	Wisconsin (6-1)		& Ohio St. (7-1)		& Ohio St. (6-1-1)
1944	Ohio St. (6-0)	1963	Illinois (5-1-1)	1978	Michigan (7-1)	1994	Penn St. (8-0)
1945	Indiana (5-0-1)	1964	Michigan (6-1)		& Michigan St. (7-1)	1995	Northwestern (8-0)
1946	Illinois (6-1)	1965	Michigan St. (7-0)	1979	Ohio St. (8-0)	1996	Ohio St. (7-1)
1947	Michigan (6-0)	1966	Michigan St. (7-0)	1980	Michigan (8-0)		& Northwestern (7-1)
1948	Michigan (6-0)	1967	Indiana (6-1),	1981	Iowa (6-2)	1997	Michigan (8-0)
1949	Ohio St. (4-1-1)		Purdue (6-1)		& Ohio St. (6-2)	1998	Ohio St. (7-1),
	& Michigan (4-1-1)		& Minnesota (6-1)	1982	Michigan (8-1)		Wisconsin (7-1)
1950	Michigan (4-1-1)	1968	Ohio St. (7-0)	1983	Illinois (9-0)		& Michigan (7-1)
1951	Illinois (5-0-1)	1969	Ohio St. (6-1)	1984	Ohio St. (7-2)	1999	Wisconsin (7-1)
1952	Wisconsin (4-1-1)		& Michigan (6-1)	1985	Iowa (7-1)	2000	Purdue (6-2),
	& Purdue (4-1-1)	1970	Ohio St. (7-0)	1986	Michigan (7-1)		Michigan (6-2)
1953	Michigan St. (5-1)	1971	Michigan (8-0)		& Ohio St. (7-1)		& Northwestern (6-2)
	& Illinois (5-1)	1972	Ohio St. (7-1)	1987	Michigan St. (7-0-1)		
1954	Ohio St. (7-0)		& Michigan (7-1)	1988	Michigan (7-0-1)		

Big Eight Conference (1907-1996)

Originally founded in 1907 as the Missouri Valley Intercollegiate Athletic Assn. **Charter members** (5): Iowa, Kansas, Missouri, Nebraska and Washington University of St. Louis. **Admitted later** (11): Drake and Iowa St. (then Ames College) in 1908; Kansas St. (then Kansas College of Applied Science and Agriculture) in 1913; Grinnell (Iowa) College in 1919; Oklahoma in 1920; Oklahoma A&M (now Oklahoma St.) in 1925; Colorado in 1947 (began play in '48).

Withdrew later (9): Iowa in 1911 (left for Big Ten after 1910 season), Colorado, Iowa St., Kansas, Kansas St. Missouri, Nebraska, Oklahoma and Oklahoma St. in 1996 (left for Big 12 after 1995 season); **Excluded later** (4): Drake, Grinnell, Oklahoma A&M and Washington-MO (left out when MVIAA cut membership to six teams in 1928).

Streamlined MVIAA unofficially called **Big Six** from 1928-47 with surviving members Iowa St., Kansas, Kansas St., Missouri, Nebraska and Oklahoma. Became the **Big Seven** after 1947 season when Colorado came over from the Skyline Conference, and then the **Big Eight** with the return of Oklahoma A&M in 1957. A&M, which resumed conference play in '60, became Oklahoma St. on July 10, 1957. The MVIAA was officially renamed the Big Eight in 1964. The league folded in 1996 when the existing members formed the newly created Big 12 along with four schools from the Southwest Conference.

Multiple titles: Nebraska (43), Oklahoma (34), Missouri (12), Colorado and Kansas (5), Iowa St. and Oklahoma St. (2).

Year		Year		Year		Year	
1907	Iowa (1-0)	1928	Nebraska (4-0)	1952	Oklahoma (5-0-1)	1976	Colorado (5-2),
	& Nebraska (1-0)	1929	Nebraska (3-0-2)	1953	Oklahoma (6-0)		Oklahoma (5-2)
1908	Kansas (4-0)	1930	Kansas (4-1)	1954	Oklahoma (6-0)		& Oklahoma St.
1909	Missouri (4-0-1)	1931	Nebraska (5-0)	1955	Oklahoma (6-0)		(5-2)
1910	Nebraska (2-0)	1932	Nebraska (5-0)	1956	Oklahoma (6-0)	1977	Oklahoma (7-0)
1911	Iowa St. (2-0-1)	1933	Nebraska (5-0)	1957	Oklahoma (6-0)	1978	Nebraska (6-1)
	& Nebraska (2-0-1)	1934	Kansas St. (5-0)	1958	Oklahoma (6-0)		& Oklahoma (6-1)
1912	Iowa St. (2-0)	1935	Nebraska (4-0-1)	1959	Oklahoma (5-1)	1979	Oklahoma (7-0)
	& Nebraska (2-0)	1936	Nebraska (5-0)	1960	Missouri (7-0)	1980	Oklahoma (7-0)
1913	Missouri (4-0)	1937	Nebraska (3-0-2)	1961	Colorado (7-0)	1981	Nebraska (7-0)
	& Nebraska (3-0)	1938	Oklahoma (5-0)	1962	Oklahoma (7-0)	1982	Nebraska (7-0)
1914	Nebraska (3-0)	1939	Missouri (5-0)	1963	Nebraska (7-0)	1983	Nebraska (7-0)
1915	Nebraska (4-0)	1940	Nebraska (5-0)	1964	Nebraska (6-1)	1984	Oklahoma (6-1)
1916	Nebraska (3-1)	1941	Missouri (5-0)	1965	Nebraska (7-0)		& Nebraska (6-1)
1917	Nebraska (2-0)	1942	Missouri (4-0-1)	1966	Nebraska (6-1)	1985	Oklahoma (7-0)
1918	Vacant (WW I)	1943	Oklahoma (4-0-1)	1967	Oklahoma (7-0)	1986	Oklahoma (7-0)
1919	Missouri (4-0-1)	1944	Oklahoma (4-0-1)	1968	Kansas (6-1)	1987	Oklahoma (7-0)
1920	Oklahoma (4-0-1)	1945	Missouri (5-0)		& Oklahoma (6-1)	1988	Nebraska (7-0)
1921	Nebraska (3-0)	1946	Oklahoma (4-1)	1969	Missouri (6-1)	1989	Colorado (7-0)
1922	Nebraska (5-0)		& Kansas (4-1)		& Nebraska (6-1)	1990	Colorado (7-0)
1923	Nebraska (3-0-2)	1947	Kansas (4-0)	1970	Nebraska (7-0)	1991	Nebraska (6-1)
	& Kansas (3-0-3)		& Oklahoma (4-0-1)	1971	Nebraska (7-0)		& Colorado (6-0-1)
1924	Missouri (5-1)	1948	Oklahoma (5-0)	1972	Nebraska (5-1-1)*	1992	Nebraska (6-1)
1925	Missouri (5-1)	1949	Oklahoma (5-0)	1973	Oklahoma (7-0)	1993	Nebraska (7-0)
1926	Okla. A&M (3-0-1)	1950	Oklahoma (6-0)	1974	Oklahoma (7-0)	1994	Nebraska (7-0)
1927	Missouri (5-1)	1951	Oklahoma (6-0)	1975	Nebraska (6-1)	1995	Nebraska (7-0)
					& Oklahoma (6-1)		

*Oklahoma (6-1) forfeited title in 1972 after a player was ruled ineligible.

Major Conference Champions (Cont.)
Big 12 Conference

Originally founded in 1996 by the former teams of the Big Eight and four schools from the Southwest Conference. The league stages a conference championship game between the two division winners on the first Saturday in December. The game has been played at the Trans World Dome in St. Louis (1996, 1998), the Alamodome in San Antonio (1997, 1999) and Arrowhead Stadium in Kansas City, Mo. (2000).

2001 playing membership: NORTH— Colorado, Iowa St., Kansas, Kansas St., Missouri and Nebraska; SOUTH— Baylor, Oklahoma, Oklahoma St., Texas, Texas A&M and Texas Tech.

Multiple titles: Nebraska (2).

Year	Year	Year
1996 Texas 37, Nebraska 27	1998 Texas A&M 36, Kansas St. 33	2000 Oklahoma 27, Kansas St. 24
1997 Nebraska 54, Texas A&M 15	1999 Nebraska 22, Texas 6	

Big West Conference

Originally founded in 1969 as Pacific Coast Athletic Assn. **Charter members** (7): CS-Los Angeles, Fresno St., Long Beach St., Pacific, San Diego St., San Jose St. and UC-Santa Barbara. **Admitted later** (12): CS-Fullerton in 1974; Utah St. in 1977 (began play in '78); UNLV in 1982; New Mexico St. in 1983 (began play in '84); Nevada in 1991 (began play in '92); Arkansas St., Louisiana Tech, Northern Illinois and SW Louisiana in 1992 (all four began play in football only in '93); Boise St., Idaho and North Texas in 1994 (all three began play in '96); Arkansas St. rejoined in 1999 (in football only). **Withdrew later** (14): CS-Los Angeles and UC-Santa Barbara in 1972 (both dropped football after '71 season); San Diego St. in 1975 (became an independent after '75 season); Fresno St. in 1991 (left for WAC after '91 season); Long Beach St. in 1991 (dropped football after '91 season); CS-Fullerton in 1992 (dropped football after '92 season); San Jose St. and UNLV in 1994 (left for WAC after '95 season); Pacific in 1995 (dropped football after '95 season); Arkansas St., Louisiana Tech, Northern Illinois and SW Louisiana in 1995 (all four returned to independent football status after '95 season); Nevada in 2000 (left for WAC after '99 season). **Conference renamed** Big West in 1988.

2001 playing membership (0): Big West dropped football following the 2000 season.

Multiple titles: San Jose St. (8); Fresno St. (6); Nevada, San Diego St. and Utah St. (5); Long Beach St. (3); Boise St., CS-Fullerton and SW Louisiana (2).

Year		Year		Year	
1969	San Diego St. (6-0)	1981	San Jose St. (5-0)	1993	Utah St. (5-1)
1970	Long Beach St. (5-1)	1982	Fresno St. (6-0)		& SW Louisiana (5-1)
	& San Diego St. (5-1)	1983	CS-Fullerton (5-1)	1994	UNLV (5-1),
1971	Long Beach St. (5-1)	1984	CS-Fullerton (6-1)†		Nevada (5-1),
1972	San Diego St. (4-0)	1985	Fresno St. (7-0)		& SW Louisiana (5-1)
1973	San Diego St. (3-0-1)	1986	San Jose St. (7-0)	1995	Nevada (6-0)
1974	San Diego St. (4-0)	1987	San Jose St. (7-0)	1996	Nevada (4-1)
1975	San Jose St. (5-0)	1988	Fresno St. (7-0)		& Utah St. (4-1)
1976	San Jose St. (4-0)	1989	Fresno St. (7-0)	1997	Utah St. (4-1)
1977	Fresno St. (4-0)	1990	San Jose St. (7-0)		& Nevada (4-1)
1978	San Diego St. (4-1)	1991	Fresno St. (6-1)	1998	Idaho (4-1)
	& Utah St. (4-1)		& San Jose St. (6-1)	1999	Boise St. (5-1)
1979	Utah St. (4-0-1)*	1992	Nevada (5-1)	2000	Boise St. (5-0)
1980	Long Beach St. (5-0)				

*San Jose St. (4-0-1) forfeited share of title in 1979 for use of an ineligible player.
†UNLV (7-0) forfeited title in 1984 for use of ineligible players.

Conference USA

Founded in 1994 by six independent football schools which began play as a conference in 1996. **Charter members** (6): Cincinnati, Houston, Louisville, Memphis, Southern Mississippi and Tulane. **Admitted later** (4): East Carolina in 1997, Army in 1998, Univ. of Alabama-Birmingham in 1999, Texas Christian Univ. in 2001; **2001 playing members** (10): Alabama-Birmingham, Army, Cincinnati, East Carolina, Houston, Louisville, Memphis, Southern Mississippi, TCU and Tulane.

Multiple titles: Southern Mississippi (3).

Year	Year	Year
1996 Southern Mississippi (4-1)	1997 Southern Mississippi (6-0)	1999 Southern Mississippi (6-0)
& Houston (4-1)	1998 Tulane (6-0)	2000 Louisville (6-1)

Mid-American Conference

Founded in 1946. **Charter members** (6): Butler, Cincinnati, Miami-OH, Ohio University, Western Michigan and Western Reserve (Miami and WMU began play in '48). **Admitted later** (12): Kent St. (now Kent) and Toledo in 1951 (Toledo began play in '52); Bowling Green in 1952; Marshall in 1954; Central Michigan and Eastern Michigan in 1972 (CMU began play in '75 and EMU in '76); Ball St. and Northern Illinois in 1973 (both began play in '75); Akron in 1991 (began play in '92); Marshall and Northern Illinois in 1995 (both resumed play in '97); Buffalo in 1995 (resumed play in '99). **Withdrew later** (5): Butler in 1950 (left for the Indiana Collegiate Conference); Cincinnati in 1953 (went independent); Western Reserve (now Case Western) in 1955 (left for President's Athletic Conference); Marshall in 1969 (went independent); and Northern Illinois in 1986 (went independent).

2001 playing membership (13): EAST—Akron, Bowling Green, Buffalo, Kent St., Marshall, Miami-OH, Ohio University; WEST—Ball St., Central Michigan, Eastern Michigan, Northern Illinois, Toledo and Western Michigan.

Multiple titles: Miami-OH (13); Bowling Green (10); Toledo (8); Ball St. and Ohio University (5); Central Michigan, Cincinnati and Marshall (4); Western Michigan (2).

Year
1947 Cincinnati (3-1)
1948 Miami-OH (4-0)
1949 Cincinnati (4-0)
1950 Miami-OH (4-0)
1951 Cincinnati (3-0)
1952 Cincinnati (3-0)
1953 Ohio Univ. (5-0-1) & Miami-OH (3-0-1)
1954 Miami-OH (4-0)
1955 Miami-OH (5-0)
1956 Bowling Green (5-0-1) & Miami-OH (4-0-1)
1957 Miami-OH (5-0)
1958 Miami-OH (5-0)

Year
1959 Bowling Green (6-0)
1960 Ohio Univ. (6-0)
1961 Bowling Green (5-1)
1962 Bowling Green (5-0-1)
1963 Ohio Univ. (5-1)
1964 Bowling Green (5-1)
1965 Bowling Green (5-1) & Miami-OH (5-1)
1966 Miami-OH (5-1) & Western Mich. (5-1)
1967 Toledo (5-1) & Ohio Univ. (5-1)
1968 Ohio Univ. (6-0)
1969 Toledo (5-0)

Year
1970 Toledo (5-0)
1971 Toledo (5-0)
1972 Kent St. (4-1)
1973 Miami-OH (5-0)
1974 Miami-OH (5-0)
1975 Miami-OH (6-0)
1976 Ball St. (4-1)
1977 Miami-OH (5-0)
1978 Ball St. (8-0)
1979 Central Mich. (8-0-1)
1980 Central Mich. (7-2)
1981 Toledo (8-1)
1982 Bowling Green (7-2)
1983 Northern Ill. (8-1)

Year
1984 Toledo (7-1-1)
1985 Bowling Green (9-0)
1986 Miami-OH (6-2)
1987 Eastern Mich. (7-1)
1988 Western Mich. (7-1)
1989 Ball St. (6-1-1)
1990 Central Mich. (7-1) & Toledo (7-1)
1991 Bowling Green (8-0)
1992 Bowling Green (8-0)
1993 Ball St. (7-0-1)
1994 Central Mich. (8-1)
1995 Toledo (7-0-1)
1996 Ball St. (7-1)

MAC Championship Game

After expanding to 12 teams (and then 13 in 1999 with the addition of Buffalo) and splitting into two divisions in 1997, the MAC now stages a conference championship game between the two division winners on the first Saturday in December. The game has been played each year at Marshall Stadium in Huntington, West Virginia.

Year
1997 Marshall 34, Toledo 13
1998 Marshall 23, Toledo 17

Year
1999 Marshall 34, W. Michigan 30

Year
2000 Marshall 19, W. Michigan 14

Mountain West Conference

Founded in 1999. **Charter members** (8): Air Force, Brigham Young, Colorado St., New Mexico, Nevada-Las Vegas, San Diego St., Utah and Wyoming.
　2001 playing membership (8): Air Force, Brigham Young, Colorado St., New Mexico, Nevada-Las Vegas, San Diego St., Utah and Wyoming.
　Multiple titles: Colorado St. (2).

Year
1999 BYU (5-2), Colorado St. (5-2) & Utah (5-2)

Year
2000 Colorado St. (6-1)

Pacific-10 Conference

Originally founded in 1915 as Pacific Coast Conference. **Charter members** (4): California, Oregon, Oregon St. and Washington. **Admitted later** (6): Washington St. in 1917; Stanford in 1918; Idaho and USC (Southern Cal) in 1922; Montana in 1924; and UCLA in 1928. **Withdrew later** (1): Montana in 1950 (left for the Mountain States Conf.).
　The **PCC** dissolved in 1959 and the **AAWU** (Athletic Assn. of Western Universities) was founded. **Charter members** (5): California, Stanford, UCLA, USC and Washington. **Admitted later** (5): Washington St. in 1962; Oregon and Oregon St. in 1964; Arizona and Arizona St. in 1978. **Conference renamed** Pacific-10 in 1968 and Pacific-10 in 1978.
　2001 playing membership (10): Arizona, Arizona St., California, Oregon, Oregon St., Stanford, UCLA, USC, Washington and Washington St.
　Multiple titles: USC (31); UCLA (17); Washington (15); California (13); Stanford (12); Oregon (6); Oregon St. (5); Washington St. (3); Arizona St. (2).

Year
1916 Washington (3-0-1)
1917 Washington St. (3-0)
1918 California (3-0)
1919 Oregon (2-1) & Washington (2-1)
1920 California (3-0)
1921 California (5-0)
1922 California (3-0)
1923 California (5-0)
1924 Stanford (3-0-1)
1925 Washington (5-0)
1926 Stanford (4-0)
1927 USC (4-0-1) & Stanford (4-0-1)
1928 USC (4-0-1)
1929 USC (6-1)
1930 Washington St. (6-0)
1931 USC (7-0)
1932 USC (6-0)
1933 Oregon (4-1) & Stanford (4-1)
1934 Stanford (5-0)
1935 California (4-1), Stanford (4-1) & UCLA (4-1)
1936 Washington (6-0-1)

Year
1937 California (6-0-1)
1938 USC (6-1) & California (6-1)
1939 USC (5-0-2) & UCLA (5-0-3)
1940 Stanford (7-0)
1941 Oregon St. (7-2)
1942 UCLA (6-1)
1943 USC (4-0)
1944 USC (3-0-2)
1945 USC (5-1)
1946 UCLA (7-0)
1947 USC (6-0)
1948 California (6-0) & Oregon (6-0)
1949 California (7-0)
1950 California (5-0-1)
1951 Stanford (6-1)
1952 USC (6-0)
1953 UCLA (6-1)
1954 UCLA (6-0)
1955 UCLA (6-0)
1956 Oregon St. (6-1-1)
1957 Oregon (6-2) & Oregon St. (6-2)
1958 California (6-1)

Year
1959 Washington (3-1), USC (3-1) & UCLA (3-1)
1960 Washington (4-0)
1961 UCLA (3-1)
1962 USC (4-0)
1963 Washington (4-1)
1964 Oregon St. (3-1) & USC (3-1)
1965 UCLA (4-0)
1966 USC (4-1)
1967 USC (6-1)
1968 USC (6-0)
1969 USC (6-0)
1970 Stanford (6-1)
1971 Stanford (6-1)
1972 USC (7-0)
1973 USC (7-0)
1974 USC (6-0-1)
1975 UCLA (6-1) & California (6-1)
1976 USC (7-0)
1977 Washington (6-1)
1978 USC (6-1)
1979 USC (6-0-1)
1980 Washington (6-1)
1981 Washington (6-2)

Year
1982 UCLA (5-1-1)
1983 UCLA (6-1-1)
1984 USC (7-1)
1985 UCLA (6-2)
1986 Arizona St. (5-1-1)
1987 USC (7-1) & UCLA (7-1)
1988 USC (8-0)
1989 USC (6-0-1)
1990 Washington (7-1)
1991 Washington (8-0)
1992 Washington (6-2) & Stanford (6-2)
1993 UCLA (6-2), Arizona (6-2) & USC (6-2)
1994 Oregon (7-1)
1995 USC (6-1-1) & Washington (6-1-1)
1996 Arizona St. (8-0)
1997 Washington St. (7-1) & UCLA (7-1)
1998 UCLA (8-0)
1999 Stanford (7-1)
2000 Washington (7-1), Oregon St. (7-1) & Oregon (7-1)

Major Conference Champions (Cont.)

Southeastern Conference

Founded in 1933 when charter members all left Southern Conference to form SEC. **Charter members** (13): Alabama, Auburn, Florida, Georgia, Georgia Tech, Kentucky, LSU (Louisiana St.), Mississippi, Mississippi St., Sewanee, Tennessee, Tulane and Vanderbilt. **Admitted later** (2): Arkansas and South Carolina in 1990 (both began play in '92). **Withdrew later** (3): Sewanee in 1940; Georgia Tech in 1964; and Tulane in 1966.

2001 playing membership (12): Alabama, Arkansas, Auburn, Florida, Georgia, Kentucky, LSU, Mississippi, Mississippi St., South Carolina, Tennessee and Vanderbilt. **Note:** Conference title decided by championship game between Western and Eastern division winners since 1992.

Multiple titles: Alabama (21); Tennessee (13); Georgia (10); Florida (9); LSU (7); Mississippi (6); Auburn and Georgia Tech (5); Kentucky and Tulane (3).

Year		Year		Year		Year	
1933	Alabama (5-0-1)	1948	Georgia (6-0)	1965	Alabama (6-1-1)	1981	Georgia (6-0)
1934	Tulane (8-0)	1949	Tulane (5-1)	1966	Alabama (6-0)		& Alabama (6-0)
	& Alabama (7-0)	1950	Kentucky (5-1)		& Georgia (6-0)	1982	Georgia (6-0)
1935	LSU (5-0)	1951	Georgia Tech (7-0)	1967	Tennessee (6-0)	1983	Auburn (6-0)
1936	LSU (6-0)		& Tennessee (5-0)	1968	Georgia (5-0-1)	1984	Florida (5-0-1)*
1937	Alabama (6-0)	1952	Georgia Tech (6-0)	1969	Tennessee (5-1)	1985	Florida (5-1)†
1938	Tennessee (7-0)	1953	Alabama (4-0-3)	1970	LSU (5-0)		& Tennessee (5-1)
1939	Tennessee (6-0),	1954	Mississippi (5-1)	1971	Alabama (7-0)	1986	LSU (5-1)
	Georgia Tech (6-0)	1955	Mississippi (5-1)	1972	Alabama (7-1)	1987	Auburn (5-0-1)
	& Tulane (5-0)	1956	Tennessee (6-0)	1973	Alabama (8-0)	1988	Auburn (6-1)
1940	Tennessee (5-0)	1957	Auburn (7-0)	1974	Alabama (6-0)		& LSU (6-1)
1941	Mississippi St. (4-0-1)	1958	LSU (6-0)	1975	Alabama (6-0)	1989	Alabama (6-1),
1942	Georgia (6-1)	1959	Georgia (7-0)	1976	Georgia (5-1)		Tennessee (6-1)
1943	Georgia Tech (3-0)	1960	Mississippi (5-0-1)		& Kentucky (5-1)		& Auburn (6-1)
1944	Georgia Tech (4-0)	1961	Alabama (7-0)	1977	Alabama (7-0)	1990	Florida (6-1)†
1945	Alabama (6-0)		& LSU (6-0)		& Kentucky (6-0)		& Tennessee (5-1-1)
1946	Georgia (5-0)	1962	Mississippi (6-0)	1978	Alabama (6-0)	1991	Florida (7-0)
	& Tennessee (5-0)	1963	Mississippi (5-0-1)	1979	Alabama (6-0)	*Title vacated.
1947	Mississippi (6-1)	1964	Alabama (8-0)	1980	Georgia (6-0)	†On probation, ineligible for championship.

Southwest Conference (1914-95)

Founded in 1914 as Southwest Intercollegiate Athletic Conference. **Charter members** (8): Arkansas, Baylor, Oklahoma, Oklahoma A&M (now Oklahoma St.), Rice, Southwestern, Texas and Texas A&M. **Admitted later** (5): SMU (Southern Methodist) in 1918; Phillips University in 1920; TCU (Texas Christian) in 1923; Texas Tech in 1956 (began play in '60); Houston in 1971 (began play in '76). **Withdrew later** (5): Southwestern in 1917 (went independent); Oklahoma in 1920 (left for Missouri Valley after '19 season); Phillips in 1921; Oklahoma A&M (now Oklahoma St.) in 1925 (left for Big Six); Arkansas in 1990 (left for SEC after '91 season); Baylor, Texas, Texas A&M and Texas Tech in 1994 (all four left for Big 12 after '95 season); Rice, SMU and TCU in 1994 (all three left for WAC after '95 season); Houston in 1994 (left for Conference USA after '95 season). Conference folded on June 30, 1996.

Multiple titles: Texas (25); Texas A&M (17); Arkansas (13); SMU (9); TCU (9); Rice (7); Baylor (5); Houston (4); Texas Tech (2).

Year		Year		Year		Year	
1914	No champion	1940	Texas A&M (5-1)	1961	Texas (6-1)	1981	SMU (7-1)
1915	Oklahoma (3-0)	1941	Texas A&M (5-1)		& Arkansas (6-1)	1982	SMU (7-0-1)
1916	No champion	1942	Texas (5-1)	1962	Texas (6-0-1)	1983	Texas (8-0)
1917	Texas A&M (2-0)	1943	Texas (5-0)	1963	Texas (7-0)	1984	SMU (6-2)
1918	No champion	1944	TCU (3-1-1)	1964	Arkansas (7-0)		& Houston (6-2)
1919	Texas A&M (4-0)	1945	Texas (5-1)	1965	Arkansas (7-0)	1985	Texas A&M (7-1)
1920	Texas (5-0)	1946	Rice (5-1)	1966	SMU (6-1)	1986	Texas A&M (7-1)
1921	Texas A&M (3-0-2)		& Arkansas (5-1)	1967	Texas A&M (6-1)	1987	Texas A&M (6-1)
1922	Baylor (5-0)	1947	SMU (5-0-1)	1968	Arkansas (6-1)	1988	Arkansas (7-0)
1923	SMU (5-0)	1948	SMU (5-0-1)		& Texas (6-1)	1989	Arkansas (7-1)
1924	Baylor (4-0-1)	1949	Rice (6-0)	1969	Texas (7-0)	1990	Texas (8-0)
1925	Texas A&M (4-1)	1950	Texas (6-0)	1970	Texas (7-0)	1991	Texas A&M (8-0)
1926	SMU (5-0)	1951	TCU (5-1)	1971	Texas (6-1)	1992	Texas A&M (7-0)
1927	Texas A&M (4-0-1)	1952	Texas (6-0)	1972	Texas (7-0)	1993	Texas A&M (7-0)
1928	Texas (5-1)	1953	Rice (5-1)	1973	Texas (7-0)	1994	Baylor, Rice, TCU,
1929	TCU (4-0-1)		& Texas (5-1)	1974	Baylor (6-1)		Texas and Texas Tech†
1930	Texas (4-1)	1954	Arkansas (5-1)	1975	Arkansas (6-1),		(4-3)
1931	SMU (5-0-1)	1955	TCU (5-1)		Texas (6-1)	1995	Texas (7-0)
1932	TCU (6-0)	1956	Texas A&M (6-0)		& Texas A&M (6-1)	*Arkansas (4-1) forced to
1933	Arkansas (4-1)*	1957	Rice (5-1)	1976	Houston (7-1)	vacate 1933 title for use of
1934	Rice (5-1)	1958	TCU (5-1)		& Texas Tech (7-1)	ineligible player.
1935	SMU (6-0)	1959	Texas (5-1),	1977	Texas (8-0)	†Texas A&M had the best
1936	Arkansas (5-1)		TCU (5-1)	1978	Houston (7-1)	record (6-0-1) in 1994 but
1937	Rice (4-1-1)		& Arkansas (5-1)	1979	Houston (7-1)	was on probation and there-
1938	TCU (6-0)	1960	Arkansas (6-1)		& Arkansas (7-1)	fore ineligible for the South-
1939	Texas A&M (6-0)			1980	Baylor (8-0)	west championship.

SEC Championship Game

Since expanding to 12 teams and splitting into two divisions in 1992, the SEC has staged a conference championship game between the two division winners on the first Saturday in December. The game has been played at Legion Field in Birmingham, Ala., (1992-93) and the Georgia Dome in Atlanta (since 1994). The divisions: EAST— Florida, Georgia, Kentucky, South Carolina, Tennessee and Vanderbilt; WEST— Alabama, Arkansas, Auburn, LSU, Mississippi and Mississippi St.

Year	Result
1992	Alabama 28, Florida 21
1993	Florida 28, Alabama 23
1994	Florida 24, Alabama 23
1995	Florida 34, Arkansas 3
1996	Florida 45, Alabama 30
1997	Tennessee 30, Auburn 29
1998	Tennessee 24, Miss. St. 14
1999	Alabama 34, Florida 7
2000	Florida 28, Auburn 6

Western Athletic Conference

Founded in 1962 when charter members left the Skyline and Border conferences to form the WAC. **Charter members** (6): Arizona and Arizona St. from Border; BYU (Brigham Young), New Mexico, Utah and Wyoming from Skyline. **Admitted later** (15): Colorado St. and UTEP (Texas-El Paso) in 1967 (both began play in '68); San Diego St. in 1978; Hawaii in 1979; Air Force in 1980; Fresno St. in 1991 (began play in '92); Rice, San Jose St., SMU (Southern Methodist), TCU (Texas Christian), Tulsa and UNLV (Nevada-Las Vegas) in 1994 (all began play in '96); Nevada in 2000; Boise St. and Louisiana Tech in 2001. **Withdrew later** (11): Arizona and Arizona St. in 1978 (left for Pac-10 after '77 season); Air Force, BYU, Colorado St., New Mexico, San Diego St., UNLV, Utah and Wyoming (left to form Mountain West conference in '99); TCU in 2000 (left for Conference USA after 2000 season).

2001 playing membership (10): Boise St., Fresno St., Hawaii, Louisiana Tech, Nevada, Rice, San Jose St., SMU, Tulsa and UTEP.

Multiple titles: BYU (19); Arizona St. and Wyoming (7); Air Force, Fresno St., New Mexico and Colorado St. (3); Arizona, Hawaii, TCU and Utah (2).

Year	Champion
1962	New Mexico (2-1-1)
1963	New Mexico (3-1)
1964	Utah (3-1), New Mexico (3-1) & Arizona (3-1)
1965	BYU (4-1)
1966	Wyoming (5-0)
1967	Wyoming (5-0)
1968	Wyoming (6-1)
1969	Arizona St. (6-1)
1970	Arizona St. (7-0)
1971	Arizona St. (7-0)
1972	Arizona St. (5-1)
1973	Arizona St. (6-1) & Arizona (6-1)
1974	BYU (6-0-1)
1975	Arizona St. (7-0)
1976	BYU (6-1) & Wyoming (6-1)
1977	Arizona St. (6-1) & BYU (6-1)
1978	BYU (5-1)
1979	BYU (7-0)
1980	BYU (6-1)
1981	BYU (7-1)
1982	BYU (7-1)
1983	BYU (7-0)
1984	BYU (8-0)
1985	Air Force (7-1) & BYU (7-1)
1986	San Diego St. (7-1)
1987	Wyoming (8-0)
1988	Wyoming (8-0)
1989	BYU (7-1)
1990	BYU (7-1)
1991	BYU (7-0-1)
1992	Hawaii (6-2), BYU (6-2) & Fresno St. (6-2)
1993	BYU (6-2), Fresno St. (6-2) & Wyoming (6-2)
1994	Colorado St. (7-1)
1995	Colorado St. (6-2), Air Force (6-2), BYU (6-2) & Utah (6-2)
1999	Fresno St. (5-2), Hawaii (7-2) & TCU (7-2)
2000	TCU (7-1) & UTEP (7-1)

Longest Division I Streaks

Winning Streaks

(Including bowl games)

No		Seasons	Spoiler	Score
47	Oklahoma	1953-57	Notre Dame	7-0
39	Washington	1908-14	Oregon St.	0-0
37	Yale	1890-93	Princeton	6-0
37	Yale	1887-89	Princeton	10-0
35	Toledo	1969-71	Tampa	21-0
34	Penn	1894-96	Lafayette	6-4
31	Oklahoma	1948-50	Kentucky	13-7*
31	Pittsburgh	1914-18	Cleve. Naval	10-9
31	Penn	1896-98	Harvard	10-0
30	Texas	1968-70	Notre Dame	24-11*
29	Miami-FL	1990-93	Alabama	34-13
29	Michigan	1901-03	Minnesota	6-6
28	Alabama†	1991-93	Tennessee	17-17
28	Alabama	1978-80	Mississippi St.	6-3
28	Oklahoma	1973-75	Kansas	23-3
28	Michigan St.	1950-53	Purdue	6-0
27	Nebraska	1901-04	Colorado	6-0
26	Nebraska	1994-96	Arizona St.	19-0
26	Cornell	1921-24	Williams	14-7
26	Michigan	1903-05	Chicago	2-0
25	BYU	1983-85	UCLA	27-24
25	San Diego St.	1965-67	Utah St.	31-25
25	Michigan	1946-49	Army	21-7
25	Army	1944-46	Notre Dame	0-0
25	USC	1931-33	Oregon St.	0-0

*Kentucky beat Oklahoma in 1951 Sugar Bowl and Notre Dame beat Texas in 1971 Cotton Bowl.

†Alabama was forced to forfeit eight victories and one tie in 1993 by the NCAA Committee on Infractions.

Unbeaten Streaks

(Including bowl games)

No	W-T		Seasons	Spoiler	Score
63	59-4	Washington	1907-17	California	27-0
56	55-1	Michigan	1901-05	Chicago	2-0
50	46-4	California	1920-25	Olympic Club	15-0
48	47-1	Oklahoma	1953-57	N. Dame	7-0
48	47-1	Yale	1885-89	Princeton	10-0
47	42-5	Yale	1879-85	Princeton	6-5
44	42-2	Yale	1894-96	Princeton	24-6
42	39-3	Yale	1904-08	Harvard	4-0
39	37-2	N. Dame	1946-50	Purdue	28-14
37	36-1	Oklahoma	1972-75	Kansas	23-3
37	37-0	Yale	1890-93	Princeton	6-0
35	35-0	Toledo	1967-71	Tampa	21-0
35	34-1	Minnesota	1903-05	Wisconsin	16-12

Losing Streaks

No		Seasons	Victim	Score
80	Prairie View	1989-98	Langston	14-12
44	Columbia	1983-88	Princeton	16-14
34	Northwestern	1979-82	No. Illinois	31-6
28	Virginia	1958-60	Wm. & Mary	21-6
28	Kansas St.	1944-48	Arkansas St.	37-6
27	Eastern Mich.	1980-82	Kent St.	9-7
27	New Mexico St.	1988-90	CS-Fullerton	43-9

Note: Virginia ended its losing streak in the opening game of the 1961 season.

Major Conference Champions (Cont.)
WAC Championship Game

In addition to expanding to 16 teams and splitting into two divisions in 1996, the WAC staged a conference championship game between the two division winners on the first Saturday in December at Sam Boyd Stadium in Las Vegas until eight teams split off and formed the Mountain West Conference in 1999. The divisions: PACIFIC—BYU, Fresno St., Hawaii, New Mexico, San Diego St., San Jose St., UTEP, Utah; MOUNTAIN—Air Force, Colorado St., Rice, SMU, TCU, Tulsa, UNLV, Wyoming.

Year	Year	Year
1996 BYU 28, Wyoming 25 (OT)	1997 Colorado St. 41, New Mexico 13	1998 Air Force 20, BYU 13

Annual NCAA Division I-A Leaders

Note that Oklahoma A&M is now Oklahoma St. and Texas Mines is now UTEP.

Rushing

Individual championship decided on Rushing Yards (1937-69), and on Yards Per Game (since 1970).

Multiple winners: Troy Davis, Marshall Faulk, Art Luppino, Ed Marinaro, Rudy Mobley, Jim Pilot, O.J. Simpson, LaDainian Tomlinson and Ricky Williams (2).

Year		Car	Yards
1937	Byron (Whizzer) White, Colorado	181	1121
1938	Len Eshmont, Fordham	132	831
1939	John Polanski, Wake Forest	137	882
1940	Al Ghesquiere, Detroit	146	957
1941	Frank Sinkwich, Georgia	209	1103
1942	Rudy Mobley, Hardin-Simmons	187	1281
1943	Creighton Miller, Notre Dame	151	911
1944	Red Williams, Minnesota	136	911
1945	Bob Fenimore, Oklahoma A&M	142	1048
1946	Rudy Mobley, Hardin-Simmons	227	1262
1947	Wilton Davis, Hardin-Simmons	193	1173
1948	Fred Wendt, Texas Mines	184	1570
1949	John Dottley, Ole Miss	208	1312
1950	Wilford White, Arizona St	199	1502
1951	Ollie Matson, San Francisco	245	1566
1952	Howie Waugh, Tulsa	164	1372
1953	J.C. Caroline, Illinois	194	1256
1954	Art Luppino, Arizona	179	1359
1955	Art Luppino, Arizona	209	1313
1956	Jim Crawford, Wyoming	200	1104
1957	Leon Burton, Arizona St	117	1126
1958	Dick Bass, Pacific	205	1361
1959	Pervis Atkins, New Mexico St	130	971
1960	Bob Gaiters, New Mexico St	197	1338
1961	Jim Pilot, New Mexico St.	191	1278
1962	Jim Pilot, New Mexico St.	208	1247
1963	Dave Casinelli, Memphis St	219	1016
1964	Brian Piccolo, Wake Forest	252	1044
1965	Mike Garrett, USC	267	1440
1966	Ray McDonald, Idaho	259	1329
1967	O.J. Simpson, USC	266	1415
1968	O.J. Simpson, USC	355	1709

Year		Car	Yards	
1969	Steve Owens, Oklahoma	358	1523	

Year		Car	Yards	P/Gm
1970	Ed Marinaro, Cornell	285	1425	158.3
1971	Ed Marinaro, Cornell	356	1881	209.0
1972	Pete VanValkenburg, BYU	232	1386	138.6
1973	Mark Kellar, Northern Ill	291	1719	156.3
1974	Louie Giammona, Utah St.	329	1534	153.4
1975	Ricky Bell, USC	357	1875	170.5
1976	Tony Dorsett, Pittsburgh	338	1948	177.1
1977	Earl Campbell, Texas	267	1744	158.5
1978	Billy Sims, Oklahoma	231	1762	160.2
1979	Charles White, USC.	293	1803	180.3
1980	George Rogers, S. Carolina	297	1781	161.9
1981	Marcus Allen, USC	403	2342	212.9
1982	Ernest Anderson, Okla. St.	353	1877	170.6
1983	Mike Rozier, Nebraska	275	2148	179.0
1984	Keith Byars, Ohio St.	313	1655	150.5
1985	Lorenzo White, Mich. St.	386	1908	173.5
1986	Paul Palmer, Temple	346	1866	169.6
1987	Ickey Woods, UNLV	259	1658	150.7
1988	Barry Sanders, Okla. St.	344	2628	238.9
1989	Anthony Thompson, Ind.	358	1793	163.0
1990	Gerald Hudson, Okla. St.	279	1642	149.3
1991	Marshall Faulk, S. Diego St.	201	1429	158.8
1992	Marshall Faulk, S. Diego St.	265	1630	163.0
1993	LeShon Johnson, No. Ill.	327	1976	179.6
1994	Rashaan Salaam, Colorado	298	2055	186.8
1995	Troy Davis, Iowa St.	345	2010	182.7
1996	Troy Davis, Iowa St.	402	2185	198.6
1997	Ricky Williams, Texas	279	1893	172.1
1998	Ricky Williams, Texas	361	2124	193.1
1999	LaDainian Tomlinson, TCU	268	1850	168.2
2000	LaDainian Tomlinson, TCU	369	2158	196.2

All-Purpose Yardage

Multiple winners: Marcus Allen, Pervis Atkins, Ryan Benjamin, Troy Davis, Troy Edwards, Louie Giammona, Tom Harmon, Art Luppino, Napolean McCallum, O.J. Simpson, Charles White and Gary Wood (2).

Year		Yards	P/Gm
1937	Byron (Whizzer) White, Colorado	1970	246.3
1938	Parker Hall, Ole Miss	1420	129.1
1939	Tom Harmon, Michigan	1208	151.0
1940	Tom Harmon, Michigan	1312	164.0
1941	Bill Dudley, Virginia	1674	186.0
1942	Complete records not available		
1943	Stan Koslowski, Holy Cross	1411	176.4
1944	Red Williams, Minnesota	1467	163.0
1945	Bob Fenimore, Oklahoma A&M	1577	197.1
1946	Rudy Mobley, Hardin-Simmons	1765	176.5
1947	Wilton Davis, Hardin-Simmons	1798	179.8
1948	Lou Kusserow, Columbia	1737	193.0
1949	Johnny Papit, Virginia	1611	179.0
1950	Wilford White, Arizona St.	2065	206.5
1951	Ollie Matson, San Francisco	2037	226.3
1952	Billy Vessels, Oklahoma	1512	151.2
1953	J.C. Caroline, Illinois	1470	163.3

Year		Yards	P/Gm
1954	Art Luppino, Arizona	2193	219.3
1955	Jim Swink, TCU	1702	170.2
	& Art Luppino, Arizona	1702	170.2
1956	Jack Hill, Utah St.	1691	169.1
1957	Overton Curtis, Utah St	1608	160.8
1958	Dick Bass, Pacific	1878	187.8
1959	Pervis Atkins, New Mexico St	1800	180.0
1960	Pervis Atkins, New Mexico St	1613	161.3
1961	Jim Pilot, New Mexico St	1606	160.6
1962	Gary Wood, Cornell	1395	155.0
1963	Gary Wood, Cornell	1508	167.6
1964	Donny Anderson, Texas Tech	1710	171.0
1965	Floyd Little, Syracuse	1990	199.0
1966	Frank Quayle, Virginia	1616	161.6
1967	O.J. Simpson, USC	1700	188.9
1968	O.J. Simpson, USC	1966	196.6
1969	Lynn Moore, Army	1795	179.5

Year		Yards	P/Gm
1970	Don McCauley, North Carolina	2021	183.7
1971	Ed Marinaro, Cornell	1932	214.7
1972	Howard Stevens, Louisville	2132	213.2
1973	Willard Harrell, Pacific	1777	177.7
1974	Louie Giammona, Utah St	1984	198.4
1975	Louie Giammona, Utah St	2045	185.9
1976	Tony Dorsett, Pittsburgh	2021	183.7
1977	Earl Campbell, Texas	1855	168.6
1978	Charles White, USC	2096	174.7
1979	Charles White, USC	1941	194.1
1980	Marcus Allen, USC	1794	179.4
1981	Marcus Allen, USC	2559	232.6
1982	Carl Monroe, Utah	2036	185.1
1983	Napoleon McCallum, Navy	2385	216.8
1984	Keith Byars, Ohio St	2284	207.6
1985	Napoleon McCallum, Navy	2330	211.8

Year		Yards	P/Gm
1986	Paul Palmer, Temple	2633	239.4
1987	Eric Wilkerson, Kent St.	2074	188.6
1988	Barry Sanders, Oklahoma St.	3250	295.5
1989	Mike Pringle, CS-Fullerton	2690	244.6
1990	Glyn Milburn, Stanford	2222	202.0
1991	Ryan Benjamin, Pacific	2995	249.6
1992	Ryan Benjamin, Pacific	2597	236.1
1993	LeShon Johnson, Northern Ill.	2082	189.3
1994	Rashaan Salaam, Colorado	2349	213.5
1995	Troy Davis, Iowa St.	2466	224.2
1996	Troy Davis, Iowa St.	2364	214.9
1997	Troy Edwards, La. Tech	2144	194.9
1998	Troy Edwards, La. Tech	2784	232.0
1999	Trevor Insley, Nevada	2176	197.8
2000	Emmett White, Utah St.	2628	238.9

Total Offense

Individual championship decided on Total Yards (1937-69) and on Yards Per Game (since 1970).

Multiple winners: Tim Rattay (3); Johnny Bright, Bob Fenimore, Mike Maxwell and Jim McMahon (2).

Year		Plays	Yards
1937	Byron (Whizzer) White, Colorado	224	1596
1938	Davey O'Brien, TCU	291	1847
1939	Kenny Washington, UCLA	259	1370
1940	Johnny Knolla, Creighton	298	1420
1941	Bud Schwenk, Washington-MO	354	1928
1942	Frank Sinkwich, Georgia	341	2187
1943	Bob Hoernschemeyer, Indiana	355	1648
1944	Bob Fenimore, Oklahoma A&M	241	1758
1945	Bob Fenimore, Oklahoma A&M	203	1641
1946	Travis Bidwell, Auburn	339	1715
1947	Fred Enke, Arizona	329	1941
1948	Stan Heath, Nevada-Reno	233	1992
1949	Johnny Bright, Drake	275	1950
1950	Johnny Bright, Drake	320	2400
1951	Dick Kazmaier, Princeton	272	1827
1952	Ted Marchibroda, Detroit	305	1813
1953	Paul Larson, California	262	1572
1954	George Shaw, Oregon	276	1536
1955	George Welsh, Navy	203	1348
1956	John Brodie, Stanford	295	1642
1957	Bob Newman, Washington St	263	1444
1958	Dick Bass, Pacific	218	1440
1959	Dick Norman, Stanford	319	2018
1960	Billy Kilmer, UCLA	292	1889
1961	Dave Hoppmann, Iowa St	320	1638
1962	Terry Baker, Oregon St	318	2276
1963	George Mira, Miami-FL	394	2318
1964	Jerry Rhome, Tulsa	470	3128
1965	Bill Anderson, Tulsa	580	3343
1966	Virgil Carter, BYU	388	2545
1967	Sal Olivas, New Mexico St.	368	2184
1968	Greg Cook Cincinnati	507	3210
1969	Dennis Shaw, San Diego St	388	3197

Year		Plays	Yards	P/Gm
1970	Pat Sullivan, Auburn	333	2856	285.6
1971	Gary Huff, Florida St	386	2653	241.2
1972	Don Strock, Va. Tech	480	3170	288.2
1973	Jesse Freitas, San Diego St.	410	2901	263.7
1974	Steve Joachim, Temple	331	2227	222.7
1975	Gene Swick, Toledo	490	2706	246.0
1976	Tommy Kramer, Rice	562	3272	297.5
1977	Doug Williams, Gambling	377	3229	293.5
1978	Mike Ford, SMU	459	2957	268.8
1979	Marc Wilson, BYU	488	3580	325.5
1980	Jim McMahon, BYU	540	4627	385.6
1981	Jim McMahon, BYU	487	3458	345.8
1982	Todd Dillon, Long Beach St	585	3587	326.1
1983	Steve Young, BYU	531	4346	395.1
1984	Robbie Bosco, BYU	543	3932	327.7
1985	Jim Everett, Purdue	518	3589	326.3
1986	Mike Perez, San Jose St.	425	2969	329.9
1987	Todd Santos, San Diego St.	562	3668	307.3
1988	Scott Mitchell, Utah	589	4299	390.8
1989	Andre Ware, Houston	628	4661	423.7
1990	David Klingler, Houston	704	5221	474.6
1991	Ty Detmer, BYU	478	4001	333.4
1992	Jimmy Klingler, Houston	544	3768	342.6
1993	Chris Vargas, Nevada	535	4332	393.8
1994	Mike Maxwell, Nevada	477	3498	318.0
1995	Mike Maxwell, Nevada	443	3623	402.6
1996	Josh Wallwork, Wyoming	525	4209	350.8
1997	Tim Rattay, La. Tech	541	3968	360.7
1998	Tim Rattay, La. Tech	602	4840	403.3
1999	Tim Rattay, La. Tech	562	3810	381.0
2000	Drew Brees, Purdue	564	3939	358.1

Passing

Individual championship decided on Completions (1937-69), on Completions Per Game (1970-78) and on Passing Efficiency rating points (since 1979).

Multiple winners: Elvis Grbac, Don Heinrich, Jim McMahon, Davey O'Brien and Don Trull (2).

Year		Cmp	Pct	TD	Yds
1937	Davey O'Brien, TCU	94	.402	–	969
1938	Davey O'Brien, TCU	93	.557	–	1457
1939	Kay Eakin, Arkansas	78	.404	–	962
1940	Billy Sewell, Wash. St.	86	.494	–	1023
1941	Bud Schwenk, Wash.-MO	114	.487	–	1457
1942	Ray Evans, Kansas	101	.505	–	1117
1943	Johnny Cook, Georgia	73	.465	–	1007
1944	Paul Rickards, Pittsburgh	84	.472	–	997
1945	Al Dekdebrun, Cornell	90	.464	–	1227
1946	Travis Tidwell, Auburn	79	.500	5	943
1947	Charlie Conerly, Ole Miss	133	.571	18	1367

Year		Cmp	Pct	TD	Yds
1948	Stan Heath, Nev-Reno	126	.568	22	2005
1949	Adrian Burk, Baylor	110	.576	14	1428
1950	Don Heinrich, Washington	134	.606	14	1846
1951	Don Klosterman, Loyola-CA	159	.505	9	1843
1952	Don Heinrich, Washington	137	.507	13	1647
1953	Bob Garrett, Stanford	118	.576	17	1637
1954	Paul Larson, California	125	.641	10	1537
1955	George Welsh, Navy	94	.627	8	1319
1956	John Brodie, Stanford	139	.579	12	1633
1957	Ken Ford, H-Simmons	115	.561	14	1254
1958	Buddy Humphrey, Baylor	112	.574	7	1316

Annual NCAA Division I-A Leaders (Cont.)

Year		Cmp	Pct	TD	Yds	Year		Cmp	TD	Yds	Rating
1959	Dick Norman, Stanford	152	.578	11	1963	1979	Turk Schonert, Stanford	148	19	1922	163.0
1960	Harold Stephens, H-Simm.	145	.566	3	1254	1980	Jim McMahon, BYU	284	47	4571	176.9
1961	Chon Gallegos, S. Jose St.	117	.594	14	1480	1981	Jim McMahon, BYU	272	30	3555	155.0
1962	Don Trull, Baylor	125	.546	11	1627	1982	Tom Ramsey, UCLA	191	21	2824	153.5
1963	Don Trull, Baylor	174	.565	12	2157	1983	Steve Young, BYU	306	33	3902	168.5
1964	Jerry Rhome, Tulsa	224	.687	32	2870	1984	Doug Flutie, BC	233	27	3454	152.9
1965	Bill Anderson, Tulsa	296	.582	30	3464	1985	Jim Harbaugh, Michigan	139	18	1913	163.7
1966	John Eckman, Wichita St.	195	.426	7	2339	1986	Vinny Testaverde, Miami-FL	175	26	2557	165.8
1967	Terry Stone, N. Mexico	160	.476	9	1946	1987	Don McPherson, Syracuse	129	22	2341	164.3
1968	Chuck Hixson, SMU	265	.566	21	3103	1988	Timm Rosenbach, Wash. St.	199	23	2791	162.0
1969	John Reaves, Florida	222	.561	24	2896	1989	Ty Detmer, BYU	265	32	4560	175.6
						1990	Shawn Moore, Virginia	144	21	2262	160.7

Year		Cmp	P/Gm	TD	Yds						
1970	Sonny Sixkiller, Wash	186	18.6	15	2303	1991	Elvis Grbac, Michigan	152	24	1955	169.0
1971	Brian Sipe, S. Diego St.	196	17.8	17	2532	1992	Elvis Grbac, Michigan	112	15	1465	154.2
1972	Don Strock, Va. Tech	228	20.7	16	3243	1993	Trent Dilfer, Fresno St.	217	28	3276	173.1
1973	Jesse Freitas, S. Diego St.	227	20.6	21	2993	1994	Kerry Collins, Penn St.	176	21	2679	172.9
1974	Steve Bartkowski, Cal	182	16.5	12	2580	1995	Danny Wuerffel, Florida	210	35	3266	178.4
1975	Craig Penrose, S. Diego St.	198	18.0	15	2660	1996	Steve Sarkisian, BYU	278	33	4027	173.6
1976	Tommy Kramer, Rice	269	24.5	21	3317	1997	Cade McNown, UCLA	173	22	2877	168.6
1977	Guy Benjamin, Stanford	208	20.8	19	2521	1998	Shaun King, Tulane	223	36	3232	183.3
1978	Steve Dils, Stanford	247	22.5	22	2943	1999	Michael Vick, Va. Tech	90	12	1840	180.4
						2000	Bart Hendricks, Boise St.	210	35	3364	170.6

Receptions

Championship decided on Passes Caught (1937-69) and on Catches Per Game (since 1970). Touchdown totals unavailable in 1939 and 1941-45.

Multiple winners: Neil Armstrong, Hugh Campell, Manny Hazard, Reid Moseley, Jason Phillips, Howard Twilley and Alex Van Dyke (2).

Year		No	TD	Yds	Year		No	P/Gm	TD	Yds
1937	Jim Benton, Arkansas	47	7	754	1970	Mike Mikolayunas, Davidson	87	8.7	8	1128
1938	Sam Boyd, Baylor	32	5	537	1971	Tom Reynolds, San Diego St	67	6.7	7	1070
1939	Ken Kavanaugh, LSU	30	–	467	1972	Tom Forzani, Utah St	85	7.7	8	1169
1940	Eddie Bryant, Virginia	30	2	222	1973	Jay Miller, BYU	100	9.1	8	1181
1941	Hank Stanton, Arizona	50	–	820	1974	D. McDonald, San Diego St	86	7.8	7	1157
1942	Bill Rogers, Texas A&M	39	–	432	1975	Bob Farnham, Brown	56	6.2	2	701
1943	Neil Armstrong, Okla. A&M	39	–	317	1976	Billy Ryckman, La. Tech	77	7.0	10	1382
1944	Reid Moseley, Georgia	32	–	506	1977	W. Tolleson, W. Carolina	73	6.6	7	1101
1945	Reid Moseley, Georgia	31	–	662	1978	Dave Petzke, Northern Ill	91	8.3	11	1217
1946	Neil Armstrong, Okla. A&M	32	1	479	1979	Rick Beasley, Appalach. St	74	6.7	12	1205
1947	Barney Poole, Ole Miss	52	8	513	1980	Dave Young, Purdue	67	6.1	8	917
1948	Red O'Quinn, Wake Forest	39	7	605	1981	Pete Harvey, N. Texas St	57	6.3	3	743
1949	Art Weiner, N. Carolina	52	7	762	1982	Vincent White, Stanford	68	6.8	8	677
1950	Gordon Cooper, Denver	46	8	569	1983	Keith Edwards, Vanderbilt	97	8.8	8	909
1951	Dewey McConnell, Wyoming	47	9	725	1984	David Williams, Illinois	101	9.2	8	1278
1952	Ed Brown, Fordham	57	6	774	1985	Rodney Carter, Purdue	98	8.9	4	1099
1953	John Carson, Georgia	45	4	663	1986	Mark Templeton, L. Beach St	99	9.0	2	688
1954	Jim Hanifan, California	44	7	569	1987	Jason Phillips, Houston	99	9.0	3	875
1955	Hank Burnine, Missouri	44	2	594	1988	Jason Phillips, Houston	108	9.8	15	1444
1956	Art Powell, San Jose St.	40	5	583	1989	Manny Hazard, Houston	142	12.9	22	1689
1957	Stuart Vaughan, Utah	53	5	756	1990	Manny Hazard, Houston	78	7.8	9	946
1958	Dave Hibbert, Arizona	61	4	606	1991	Fred Gilbert, Houston	106	9.6	7	957
1959	Chris Burford, Stanford	61	6	756	1992	Sherman Smith, Houston	103	9.4	6	923
1960	Hugh Campbell, Wash. St.	66	10	881	1993	Chris Penn, Tulsa	105	9.6	12	1578
1961	Hugh Campbell, Wash. St.	53	5	723	1994	Alex Van Dyke, Nevada	98	8.9	10	1246
1962	Vern Burke, Oregon St	69	10	1007	1995	Alex Van Dyke, Nevada	129	11.7	16	1854
1963	Lawrence Elkins, Baylor	70	8	873	1996	Damond Wilkins, Nevada	114	10.4	4	1121
1964	Howard Twilley, Tulsa	95	13	1178	1997	Eugene Baker, Kent	103	9.4	18	1549
1965	Howard Twilley, Tulsa	134	16	1779	1998	Troy Edwards, La. Tech	140	11.7	27	1996
1966	Glenn Meltzer, Wichita St	91	4	1115	1999	Trevor Insley, Nevada	134	12.2	13	2060
1967	Bob Goodridge, Vanderbilt	79	6	1114	2000	James Jordan, La. Tech	109	9.1	4	1003
1968	Ron Sellers, Florida St.	86	12	1496						
1969	Jerry Hendren, Idaho	95	12	1452						

Scoring

Championship decided on Total Points (1937-69) and on Points Per Game (since 1970).

Multiple winners: Tom Harmon and Billy Sims (2).

Year		TD	XP	FG	Pts	Year		TD	XP	FG	Pts
1937	Byron (Whizzer) White, Colo.	16	23	1	122	1941	Bill Dudley, Virginia	18	23	1	134
1938	Parker Hall, Ole Miss	11	7	0	73	1942	Bob Steuber, Missouri	18	13	0	121
1939	Tom Harmon, Michigan	14	15	1	102	1943	Steve Van Buren, LSU	14	14	0	98
1940	Tom Harmon, Michigan	16	18	1	117	1944	Glenn Davis, Army	20	0	0	120

Year		TD	XP	FG	Pts
1945	Doc Blanchard, Army	19	1	0	115
1946	Gene Roberts, Tenn-Chatt	18	9	0	117
1947	Lou Gambino, Maryland	16	0	0	96
1948	Fred Wendt, Texas Mines	20	32	0	152
1949	George Thomas, Oklahoma	19	3	0	117
1950	Bobby Reynolds, Nebraska	22	25	0	157
1951	Ollie Matson, San Francisco	21	0	0	126
1952	Jackie Parker, Miss. St.	16	24	0	120
1953	Earl Lindley, Utah St.	13	3	0	81
1954	Art Luppino, Arizona	24	22	0	166
1955	Jim Swink, TCU	20	5	0	125
1956	Clendon Thomas, Oklahoma	18	0	0	108
1957	Leon Burton, Ariz. St.	16	0	0	96
1958	Dick Bass, Pacific	18	8	0	116
1959	Pervis Atkins, N. Mexico St.	17	5	0	107
1960	Bob Gaiters, N. Mexico St.	23	7	0	145
1961	Jim Pilot, N. Mexico St.	21	12	0	138
1962	Jerry Logan, W. Texas St.	13	32	0	110
1963	Cosmo Iacavazzi, Princeton	14	0	0	84
	& Dave Casinelli, Memphis St.	14	0	0	84
1964	Brian Piccolo, Wake Forest	17	9	0	111
1965	Howard Twilley, Tulsa	16	31	0	127
1966	Ken Hebert, Houston	11	41	2	113
1967	Leroy Keyes, Purdue	19	0	0	114
1968	Jim O'Brien, Cincinnati	12	31	13	142
1969	Steve Owens, Oklahoma	23	0	0	138

Year		TD	XP	FG	Pts	P/Gm
1970	Brian Bream, Air Force	20	0	0	120	12.0
	& Gary Kosins, Dayton	18	0	0	108	12.0

Year		TD	XP	FG	Pts	P/Gm
1971	Ed Marinaro, Cornell	24	4	0	148	16.4
1972	Harold Henson, Ohio St.	20	0	0	120	12.0
1973	Jim Jennings, Rutgers	21	2	0	128	11.6
1974	Bill Marek, Wisconsin	19	0	0	114	12.7
1975	Pete Johnson, Ohio St.	25	0	0	150	13.6
1976	Tony Dorsett, Pitt	22	2	0	134	12.2
1977	Earl Campbell, Texas	19	0	0	114	10.4
1978	Billy Sims, Oklahoma	20	0	0	120	10.9
1979	Billy Sims, Oklahoma	22	0	0	132	12.0
1980	Sammy Winder, So. Miss.	20	0	0	120	10.9
1981	Marcus Allen, USC	23	0	0	138	12.5
1982	Greg Allen, Fla. St.	21	0	0	126	11.5
1983	Mike Rozier, Nebraska	29	0	0	174	14.5
1984	Keith Byars, Ohio St.	24	0	0	144	13.1
1985	Bernard White, B. Green	19	0	0	114	10.4
1986	Steve Bartalo, Colo. St.	19	0	0	114	10.4
1987	Paul Hewitt, S. Diego St.	24	0	0	144	12.0
1988	Barry Sanders, Okla.St.	39	0	0	234	21.3
1989	Anthony Thompson, Ind	25	4	0	154	14.0
1990	Stacey Robinson, No. Ill.	19	6	0	120	10.9
1991	Marshall Faulk, S.D. St.	23	2	0	140	15.6
1992	Garrison Hearst, Georgia	21	0	0	126	11.5
1993	Bam Morris, Texas Tech	22	2	0	134	12.2
1994	Rashaan Salaam, Colo.	24	0	0	144	13.1
1995	Eddie George, Ohio St.	24	0	0	144	12.0
1996	Corey Dillon, Washington	23	0	0	138	12.6
1997	Ricky Williams, Texas	25	2	0	152	13.8
1998	Troy Edwards, La. Tech	31	2	0	188	15.7
1999	Shaun Alexander, Alabama	24	0	0	144	13.1
2000	Lee Suggs, Va. Tech	28	0	0	168	15.3

All-Time NCAA Division I-A Leaders

Through the 2000 regular season. The NCAA does not recognize active players among career Per Game leaders.

CAREER

Passing

(Minimum 500 Completions)

	Passing Efficiency	Years	Rating
1	Danny Wuerffel, Florida	1993-96	163.6
2	Ty Detmer, BYU	1988-91	162.7
3	Steve Sarkisian, BYU	1995-96	162.0
4	Billy Blanton, San Diego St.	1993-96	157.1
5	Jim McMahon, BYU	1977-78, 80-81	156.9

	Yards Gained	Years	Yards
1	Ty Detmer, BYU	1988-91	15,031
2	Tim Rattay, La. Tech	1997-99	12,746
3	Chris Redman, Louisville	1996-99	12,541
4	Todd Santos, San Diego St	1984-87	11,425
5	Tim Lester, W. Michigan	1996-99	11,299

	Completions	Years	No
1	Chris Redman, Louisville	1996-99	1031
2	Tim Rattay, La. Tech	1997-99	1015
3	Ty Detmer, BYU	1988-91	958
4	Drew Brees, Purdue	1997-00	942
5	Todd Santos, San Diego St	1984-87	910

Rushing

	Yards Gained	Years	Yards
1	Ron Dayne, Wisconsin	1996-99	6397
2	Ricky Williams, Texas	1995-98	6279
3	Tony Dorsett, Pittsburgh	1973-76	6082
4	Charles White, USC	1976-79	5598
5	Travis Prentice, Miami-OH	1996-99	5596

	Yards Per Game	Years	Yards	P/Gm
1	Ed Marinaro, Cornell	1969-71	4715	174.6
2	O.J. Simpson, USC	1967-68	3124	164.4
3	Herschel Walker, Georgia	1980-82	5259	159.4
4	LeShon Johnson, No. Ill.	1992-93	3314	150.6
5	Ron Dayne, Wisconsin	1996-99	6397	148.8

Receptions

	Catches	Years	No
1	Arnold Jackson, Louisville	1997-00	300
2	Trevor Insley, Nevada	1996-99	298
3	Geoff Noisy, Nevada	1995-98	295
4	Troy Edwards, La. Tech	1996-98	280
5	Aaron Turner, Pacific	1989-92	266

	Catches Per Game	Years	No	P/Gm
1	Manny Hazard, Houston	1989-90	220	10.5
2	Alex Van Dyke, Nevada	1994-95	227	10.3
3	Howard Twilley, Tulsa	1963-65	261	10.0
4	Jason Phillips, Houston	1987-88	207	9.4
5	Troy Edwards, La. Tech	1996-98	280	8.2

	Yards Gained	Years	No	Yards
1	Trevor Insley, Nevada	1996-99	298	5005
2	Marcus Harris, Wyoming	1993-96	259	4518
3	Ryan Yarborough, Wyoming	1990-93	229	4357
4	Troy Edwards, La. Tech	1996-98	280	4352
5	Aaron Turner, Pacific	1989-92	266	4345

Total Offense

	Yards Gained	Years	Yards
1	Ty Detmer, BYU	1988-91	14,665
2	Tim Rattay, La. Tech	1997-99	12,689
3	Chris Redman, Louisville	1996-99	12,129
4	Drew Brees, Purdue	1997-00	11,815
5	Doug Flutie, Boston College	1981-84	11,317

	Yards Per Game	Years	Yards	P/Gm
1	Tim Rattay, La. Tech	1997-99	12,689	382.4
2	Chris Vargas, Nevada	1992-93	6,417	320.9
3	Ty Detmer, BYU	1988-91	14,665	318.8
4	Daunte Culpepper*, C. Fla.	1996-98	10,344	313.5
5	Mike Perez, San Jose St	1986-87	6,182	309.1

*Culpepper played I-AA with Central Florida in 1995.

All-Time NCAA Division I-A Leaders (Cont.)
All-Purpose Yardage

	Yards Gained	Years	Yards
1	Ricky Williams, Texas	1995-98	7206
2	Napoleon McCallum, Navy	1981-85	7172
3	Darrin Nelson, Stanford	1977-78, 80-81	6885
4	Kevin Faulk, LSU	1995-98	6833
5	Ron Dayne, Wisconsin	1996-99	6701

	Yards Per Game	Years	Yards	P/Gm
1	Ryan Benjamin, Pacific	1990-92	5706	237.8
2	Sheldon Canley, S. Jose St.	1988-90	5146	205.8
3	Howard Stevens, Louisville	1971-72	3873	193.7
4	O.J. Simpson, USC	1967-68	3666	192.9
5	Alex Van Dyke, Nevada	1994-95	4146	188.5

Miscellaneous

	Interceptions	Years	No
1	Al Brosky, Illinois	1950-52	29
2	John Provost, Holy Cross	1972-74	27
	Martin Bayless, Bowling Green	1980-83	27
4	Tom Curtis, Michigan	1967-69	25
	Tony Thurman, Boston College	1981-84	25
	Tracy Saul, Texas Tech.	1989-92	25

	Punt Return Average*	Years	Avg
1	Jack Mitchell, Oklahoma	1946-48	23.6
2	Gene Gibson, Cincinnati	1949-50	20.5
3	Eddie Macon, Pacific	1949-51	18.9
4	Jackie Robinson, UCLA	1939-40	18.8
5	Two tied at 17.7 each.		

*Minimum 1.2 punt returns per game and 30 career returns.

	Punting Average*	Years	Avg
1	Todd Sauerbrun, West Va.	1991-94	46.3
2	Reggie Roby, Iowa	1979-82	45.6
3	Greg Montgomery, Mich. St.	1985-87	45.4
4	Tom Tupa, Ohio St.	1984-87	45.2
5	Barry Helton, Colorado	1984-87	44.9

*At least 150 punts.

	Kickoff Return Average*	Years	Avg
1	Anthony Davis, USC	1972-74	35.1
2	Eric Booth, So. Miss.	1994-97	32.4
3	Overton Curtis, Utah St	1957-58	31.0
4	Fred Montgomery, New Mexico St.	1991-92	30.5
5	Allie Taylor, Utah St.	1966-68	29.3

*Minimum 1.2 kickoff returns per game and 30 career returns.

Scoring
Non-kickers

	Points	Years	TD	Xpt	FG	Pts
1	Travis Prentice, Miami-OH	1996-99	78	0	0	468
2	Ricky Williams, Texas	1995-98	75	2	0	452
3	Anthony Thompson, Ind.	1986-89	65	4	0	394
4	Ron Dayne, Wisconsin	1996-99	63	0	0	378
5	Marshall Faulk, S.D. St.	1991-93	62	4	0	376

	Touchdown Catches	Years	No
1	Troy Edwards, La. Tech	1996-98	50
2	Aaron Turner, Pacific	1989-92	43
3	Ryan Yarborough, Wyoming	1990-93	42
4	Clarkston Hines, Duke	1986-89	38
	Marcus Harris, Wyoming	1993-96	38

	Points Per Game	Years	Pts	P/Gm
1	Marshall Faulk, S. Diego St.	1991-93	376	12.1
2	Ed Marinaro, Cornell	1969-71	318	11.8
3	Bill Burnett, Arkansas	1968-70	294	11.3
4	Steve Owens, Oklahoma	1967-69	336	11.2
5	Eddie Talboom, Wyoming	1948-50	303	10.8

Kickers

	Points	Years	FG	XP	Pts
1	Roman Anderson, Hou	1988-91	70	213	423
2	Carlos Huerta, Mia-FL	1988-91	73	178	397
3	Jason Elam, Hawaii	1988-89, 91-92	79	158	395
4	Derek Schmidt, Fla. St	1984-87	73	174	393
5	Kris Brown, Nebraska	1995-98	57	217	388

	Field Goals	Years	No
1	Jeff Jaeger, Washington	1983-86	80
2	John Lee, UCLA	1982-85	79
	Jason Elam, Hawaii	1988-89, 91-92	79
4	Philip Doyle, Alabama	1987-90	78
	Luis Zendejas, Arizona St	1981-84	78

	Touchdowns Rushing	Years	No
1	Travis Prentice, Miami-OH	1996-99	73
2	Ricky Williams, Texas	1995-98	72
3	Anthony Thompson, Indiana	1986-89	64
4	Ron Dayne, Wisconsin	1996-99	63
5	Marshall Faulk, S. Diego St.	1991-93	57

	Touchdowns Passing	Years	No
1	Ty Detmer, BYU	1988-91	121
2	Tim Rattay, La. Tech	1997-99	115
3	Danny Wuerffel, Florida	1993-96	114
4	Chad Pennington, Marshall	1997-99	100
5	David Klingler, Houston	1988-91	91

SINGLE SEASON

Rushing

Yards Gained	Year	Gm	Car	Yards
Barry Sanders, Okla. St	1988	11	344	2628
Marcus Allen, USC	1981	11	403	2342
Troy Davis, Iowa St.	1996	11	402	2185
LaDainian Tomlinson, TCU	2000	11	369	2158
Mike Rozier, Nebraska	1983	12	275	2148

Yards Per Game	Year	Gm	Yards	P/Gm
Barry Sanders, Okla. St	1988	11	2628	238.9
Marcus Allen, USC	1981	11	2342	212.9
Ed Marinaro, Cornell	1971	9	1881	209.0
Troy Davis, Iowa St.	1996	11	2185	198.6
LaDainian Tomlinson, TCU	2000	11	2158	196.2

Passing
(Minimum 15 Attempts Per Game)

Passing Efficiency	Year	Rating
Shaun King, Tulane	1998	183.3
Michael Vick, Va. Tech	1999	180.4
Danny Wuerffel, Florida	1995	178.4
Jim McMahon, BYU	1980	176.9
Ty Detmer, BYU	1989	175.6

Yards Gained	Year	Yards
Ty Detmer, BYU	1990	5188
David Klingler, Houston	1990	5140
Tim Rattay, La. Tech	1998	4943
Andre Ware, Houston	1989	4699
Jim McMahon, BYU	1980	4571

Completions

Player	Year	Att	No
Tim Rattay, La. Tech	1998	559	380
David Klingler, Houston	1990	643	374
Andre Ware, Houston	1989	578	365
Tim Couch, Kentucky	1997	547	363
Ty Detmer, BYU	1990	562	361

Total Offense

Yards Gained

Player	Year	Gm	Plays	Yards
David Klingler, Houston	1990	11	704	5221
Ty Detmer, BYU	1990	12	635	5022
Tim Rattay, La. Tech	1998	12	602	4840
Andre Ware, Houston	1989	11	628	4661
Jim McMahon, BYU	1980	12	540	4627

Yards Per Game

Player	Year	Gm	Yards	P/Gm
David Klingler, Houston	1990	11	5221	474.6
Andre Ware, Houston	1989	11	4661	423.7
Ty Detmer, BYU	1990	12	5022	418.5
Tim Rattay, La. Tech	1998	12	4840	403.3
Mike Maxwell, Nevada	1995	9	3623	402.6

Receptions

Catches

Player	Year	Gm	No
Manny Hazard, Houston	1989	11	142
Troy Edwards, La. Tech	1998	12	140
Howard Twilley, Tulsa	1965	10	134
Trevor Insley, Nevada	1999	11	134
Alex Van Dyke, Nevada	1995	11	129

Catches Per Game

Player	Year	No	P/Gm
Howard Twilley, Tulsa	1965	134	13.4
Manny Hazard, Houston	1989	142	12.9
Trevor Insley, Nevada	1999	134	12.2
Alex Van Dyke, Nevada	1995	129	11.7
Troy Edwards, La. Tech	1998	140	11.7
Damond Wilkins, Nevada	1996	114	10.4

Yards Gained

Player	Year	No	Yards
Trevor Insley, Nevada	1999	134	2060
Troy Edwards, La. Tech	1998	140	1996
Alex Van Dyke, Nevada	1995	129	1854
Howard Twilley, Tulsa	1965	134	1779
Troy Edwards, La. Tech	1997	102	1707

All-Purpose Yardage

Yards Gained

Player	Year	Yards
Barry Sanders, Okla. St	1988	3250
Ryan Benjamin, Pacific	1991	2995
Troy Edwards, La. Tech	1998	2784
Mike Pringle, CS-Fullerton	1989	2690
Paul Palmer, Temple	1986	2633

Yards Per Game

Player	Year	Yards	P/Gm
Barry Sanders, Okla. St	1988	3250	295.5
Ryan Benjamin, Pacific	1991	2995	249.6
Byron (Whizzer) White, Colo	1937	1970	246.3
Mike Pringle, CS-Fullerton	1989	2690	244.6
Paul Palmer, Temple	1986	2633	239.4

Scoring

Points

Player	Year	TD	Xpt	FG	Pts
Barry Sanders, Okla. St	1988	39	0	0	234
Troy Edwards, La. Tech	1998	31	2	0	188
Mike Rozier, Nebraska	1983	29	0	0	174
Lydell Mitchell, Penn St	1971	29	0	0	174
Lee Suggs, Va. Tech	2000	28	0	0	168

Points Per Game

Player	Year	Pts	P/Gm
Barry Sanders, Okla. St	1988	234	21.0
Bobby Reynolds, Nebraska	1950	157	17.4
Art Luppino, Arizona	1954	166	16.6
Ed Marinaro, Cornell	1971	148	16.4
Lydell Mitchell, Penn St	1971	174	15.8

Touchdowns Rushing

Player	Year	No
Barry Sanders, Okla. St	1988	37
Mike Rozier, Nebraska	1983	29
Ricky Williams, Texas	1998	27
Lee Suggs, Va. Tech	2000	27
Ricky Williams, Texas	1997	25
Travis Prentice, Miami-OH	1997	25

Touchdowns Passing

Player	Year	No
David Klingler, Houston	1990	54
Jim McMahon, BYU	1980	47
Andre Ware, Houston	1989	46
Tim Rattay, La. Tech	1998	46
Ty Detmer, BYU	1990	41

Touchdown Catches

Player	Year	No
Troy Edwards, La. Tech	1998	27
Randy Moss, Marshall	1997	25
Manny Hazard, Houston	1989	22
Desmond Howard, Michigan	1991	19
Five tied with 18 each.		

Field Goals

Player	Year	No
John Lee, UCLA	1984	29
Paul Woodside, West Virginia	1982	28
Luis Zendejas, Arizona St	1983	28
Fuad Reveiz, Tennessee	1982	27
Sebastian Janikowski, FSU	1998	27

Miscellaneous

Interceptions

Player	Year	No
Al Worley, Washington	1968	14
George Shaw, Oregon	1951	13
Eight tied with 12 each.		

Punting Average*

Player	Year	Avg
Chad Kessler, LSU	1997	50.3
Reggie Roby, Iowa	1981	49.8
Kirk Wilson, UCLA	1956	49.3
Todd Sauerbrun, West Virginia	1994	48.4
Zack Jordan, Colorado	1950	48.2

*Qualifiers for championship.

Punt Return Average*

Player	Year	Avg
Bill Blackstock, Tennessee	1951	25.9
George Sims, Baylor	1948	25.0
Gene Derricotte, Michigan	1947	24.8

*At least 1.2 returns per game.

Kickoff Return Average*

Player	Year	Avg
Paul Allen, BYU	1961	40.1
Tremain Mack, Miami-FL	1996	39.5
Leeland McElroy, Texas A&M	1993	39.3
Forrest Hall, San Francisco	1946	38.2
Tony Ball, Tenn-Chattanooga	1977	36.4

*At least 1.2 kickoff returns per game.

All-Time NCAA Division I-A Leaders (Cont.)
SINGLE GAME

Rushing

Yards Gained	Opponent	Year	Yds
LaDainian Tomlinson, TCU	UTEP	1999	406
Tony Sands, Kansas	Missouri	1991	396
Marshall Faulk, San Diego St	Pacific	1991	386
Troy Davis, Iowa St.	Missouri	1996	378
Anthony Thompson, Indiana	Wisconsin	1989	377

Total Offense

Yards Gained	Opponent	Year	Yds
David Klingler, Houston	Arizona St.	1990	732
Matt Vogler, TCU	Houston	1990	696
David Klingler, Houston	TCU	1990	625
Scott Mitchell, Utah	Air Force	1988	625
Jimmy Klingler, Houston	Rice	1992	612

Passing

Yards Gained	Opponent	Year	Yds
David Klingler, Houston	Arizona St.	1990	716
Matt Vogler, TCU	Houston	1990	690
Scott Mitchell, Utah	Air Force	1988	631
Jeremy Leach, New Mexico	Utah	1989	622
Dave Wilson, Illinois	Ohio St.	1980	621

Receiving

Catches	Opponent	Year	No
Randy Gatewood, UNLV	Idaho	1994	23
Jay Miller, BYU	New Mexico	1973	22
Troy Edwards, La. Tech	Nebraska	1998	21
Chris Daniels, Purdue	Mich. St.	1999	21
Two tied with 20 each.			

Completions	Opponent	Year	No
Drew Brees, Purdue	Wisconsin	1998	55
Rusty LaRue, Wake Forest	Duke	1995	55
Rusty LaRue, Wake Forest	N.C. St.	1995	50
David Klingler, Houston	SMU	1990	48
Two tied with 47 each.			

Yards Gained	Opponent	Year	Yds
Troy Edwards, La. Tech	Nebraska	1998	405
Randy Gatewood, UNLV	Idaho	1994	363
Chuck Hughes, UTEP*	N. Texas St.	1965	349
Rick Eber, Tulsa	Idaho St.	1967	322
Harry Wood, Tulsa	Idaho St.	1967	318

*UTEP was Texas Western in 1965.

Scoring

Points

Points	Opponent	Year	Pts
Howard Griffith, Illinois	So. Ill.	1990	48
Marshall Faulk, S. Diego St.	Pacific	1991	44
Jim Brown, Syracuse	Colgate	1956	43
Showboat Boykin, Ole Miss	Miss. St.	1951	42
Fred Wendt, UTEP*	N. Mex. St.	1948	42

*UTEP was Texas Mines in 1948.

Touchdown Catches	Opponent	Year	No
Tim Delaney, S. Diego St	N. Mex. St.	1969	6

Note: Delaney's TD catches (2-22-34-31-30-9).

Field Goals	Opponent	Year	No
Dale Klein, Nebraska	Missouri	1985	7
Mike Prindle, W. Mich.	Marshall	1984	7

Note: Klein's FGs (32-22-43-44-29-43-43); Prindle's FGs (32-44-42-23-48-41-27).

Touchdowns Rushing	Opponent	Year	No
Howard Griffith, Illinois	So. Ill	1990	8
Showboat Boykin, Ole Miss	Miss. St.	1951	7

Note: Griffith's TD runs (5-51-7-41-5-18-5-3).

Extra Points (Kick)	Opponent	Year	No
Terry Leiweke, Houston	Tulsa	1968	13
Derek Mahoney, Fresno St	New Mexico	1991	13

Touchdowns Passing	Opponent	Year	No
David Klingler, Houston	E. Wash.	1990	11
Dennis Shaw, San Diego St	N. Mex. St.	1969	9

Note: Klingler's TD passes (5-48-29-7-3-7-40-8-7-8-51).

Longest Plays (since 1941)

Rushing

Rushing	Opponent	Year	Yds
Gale Sayers, Kansas	Nebraska	1963	99
Max Anderson, Ariz. St.	Wyoming	1967	99
Ralph Thompson, W. Texas St	Wich. St.	1970	99
Kelsey Finch, Tennessee	Florida	1977	99
Eric Vann, Kansas	Oklahoma	1997	99
Eleven tied at 98 each.			

Passing

Passing	Opponent	Year	Yds
Scott Ankrom to James Maness, TCU	Rice	1984	99
Gino Torretta to Horace Copeland, Miami-FL	Ark.	1991	99
John Paci to Thomas Lewis, Indiana	Penn St.	1993	99
Drew Brees to Vinny Sutherland, Purdue	Northwestern	1999	99

Passing	Opponent	Year	Yds
Fred Owens to Jack Ford, Portland	St. Mary's	1947	99
Bo Burris to Warren McVea, Houston	Wash. St.	1966	99
Colin Clapton to Eddie Jenkins, Holy Cross	Boston U.	1970	99
Terry Peel to Robert Ford, Houston	Syracuse	1970	99
Terry Peel to Robert Ford, Houston	S. Diego St.	1972	99
Cris Collinsworth to Derrick Gaffney, Florida	Rice	1977	99

Field Goals	Opponent	Year	Yds
Steve Little, Arkansas	Texas	1977	67
Russell Erxleben, Texas	Rice	1977	67
Joe Williams, Wichita St	So. Ill.	1978	67
Tony Franklin, Tex. A&M	Baylor	1976	65
Martin Gramatica, Kan. St.	No. Ill.	1998	65

Annual Awards
Heisman Trophy

Originally presented in 1935 as the DAC Trophy by the Downtown Athletic Club of New York City to the best college football player east of the Mississippi. In 1936, players across the country were eligible and the award was renamed the Heisman Trophy following the death of former college coach and DAC athletic director John W. Heisman.

Multiple winner: Archie Griffin (2).

Winners in junior year (13): Doc Blanchard (1945), Ty Detmer (1990); Archie Griffin (1974), Desmond Howard (1991), Vic Janowicz (1950), Rashaan Salaam (1994), Barry Sanders (1988), Billy Sims (1978), Roger Staubach (1963), Doak Walker (1948), Herschel Walker (1982), Andre Ware (1989) and Charles Woodson (1997).

Winners on AP national champions (10): Angelo Bertelli (Notre Dame, 1943); Doc Blanchard (Army, 1945); Tony Dorsett (Pittsburgh, 1976); Leon Hart (Notre Dame, 1949); Johnny Lujack (Notre Dame, 1947); Davey O'Brien (TCU, 1938); Bruce Smith (Minnesota, 1941); Charlie Ward (Florida St., 1993); Danny Wuerffel (Florida, 1996); and Charles Woodson (Michigan, 1997).

Year	Points
1935 **Jay Berwanger,** Chicago, HB	.84
2nd–Monk Meyer, Army, HB	.29
3rd–Bill Shakespeare, Notre Dame, HB	.23
4th–Pepper Constable, Princeton, FB	.20
1936 **Larry Kelley,** Yale, E.	.219
2nd–Sam Francis, Nebraska, FB	.47
3rd–Ray Buivid, Marquette, HB	.43
4th–Sammy Baugh, TCU, HB	.39
1937 **Clint Frank,** Yale, HB	.524
2nd–Byron (Whizzer) White, Colo., HB	.264
3rd–Marshall Goldberg, Pitt, HB	.211
4th–Alex Wojciechowicz, Fordham, C	.85
1938 **Davey O'Brien,** TCU, QB	.519
2nd–Marshall Goldberg, Pitt, HB	.294
3rd–Sid Luckman, Columbia, QB	.154
4th–Bob MacLeod, Dartmouth, HB	.78
1939 **Nile Kinnick,** Iowa, HB	.651
2nd–Tom Harmon, Michigan, HB	.405
3rd–Paul Christman, Missouri, QB	.391
4th–George Cafego, Tennessee, QB	.296
1940 **Tom Harmon,** Michigan, HB	.1303
2nd–John Kimbrough, Texas A&M, FB	.841
3rd–George Franck, Minnesota, HB	.102
4th–Frankie Albert, Stanford, QB	.90
1941 **Bruce Smith,** Minnesota, HB	.554
2nd–Angelo Bertelli, Notre Dame, QB	.345
3rd–Frankie Albert, Stanford, QB	.336
4th–Frank Sinkwich, Georgia, HB	.249
1942 **Frank Sinkwich,** Georgia, HB	.1059
2nd–Paul Governali, Columbia, QB	.218
3rd–Clint Castleberry, Ga. Tech, HB	.99
4th–Mike Holovak, Boston College, FB	.95
1943 **Angelo Bertelli,** Notre Dame, QB	.648
2nd–Bob Odell, Penn, HB	.177
3rd–Otto Graham, Northwestern, QB	.140
4th–Creighton Miller, Notre Dame, HB	.134
1944 **Les Horvath,** Ohio St., TB-QB	.412
2nd–Glenn Davis, Army, HB	.287
3rd–Doc Blanchard, Army, FB	.237
4th–Don Whitmire, Navy, T	.115
1945 **Doc Blanchard,** Army, FB	.860
2nd–Glenn Davis, Army, HB	.638
3rd–Bob Fenimore, Oklahoma A&M, HB	.187
4th–Herman Wedemeyer, St. Mary's, HB	.152
1946 **Glenn Davis,** Army, HB	.792
2nd–Charlie Trippi, Georgia, HB	.435
3rd–Johnny Lujack, Notre Dame, QB	.379
4th–Doc Blanchard, Army, FB	.267
1947 **Johnny Lujack,** Notre Dame, QB	.742
2nd–Bob Chappuis, Michigan, HB	.555
3rd–Doak Walker, SMU, HB	.196
4th–Charlie Conerly, Mississippi, QB	.186
1948 **Doak Walker,** SMU, HB	.778
2nd–Charlie Justice, N. Carolina, HB	.443
3rd–Chuck Bednarik, Penn, C	.336
4th–Jackie Jensen, California, HB	.143
1949 **Leon Hart,** Notre Dame, E	.995
2nd–Charlie Justice, N. Carolina, HB	.272
3rd–Doak Walker, SMU, HB	.229
4th–Arnold Galiffa, Army QB	.196
1950 **Vic Janowicz,** Ohio St., HB	.633
2nd–Kyle Rote, SMU, HB	.280
3rd–Reds Bagnell, Penn, HB	.231
4th–Babe Parilli, Kentucky, QB	.214
1951 **Dick Kazmaier,** Princeton, TB	.1777
2nd–Hank Lauricella, Tennessee, HB	.424
3rd–Babe Parilli, Kentucky, QB	.344
4th–Bill McColl, Stanford, E	.313
1952 **Billy Vessels,** Oklahoma, HB	.525
2nd–Jack Scarbath, Maryland, QB	.367
3rd–Paul Giel, Minnesota, HB	.329
4th–Donn Moomaw, UCLA, C	.257

Year	Points
1953 **Johnny Lattner,** Notre Dame, HB	.1850
2nd–Paul Giel, Minnesota, HB	.1794
3rd–Paul Cameron, UCLA, HB	.444
4th–Bernie Faloney, Maryland, QB	.258
1954 **Alan Ameche,** Wisconsin, FB	.1068
2nd–Kurt Burris, Oklahoma, C	.838
3rd–Howard Cassady, Ohio St., HB	.810
4th–Ralph Guglielmi, Notre Dame, QB	.691
1955 **Howard Cassady,** Ohio St., HB	.2219
2nd–Jim Swink, TCU, HB	.742
3rd–George Welsh, Navy, QB	.383
4th–Earl Morrall, Michigan St., QB	.323
1956 **Paul Hornung,** Notre Dame, QB	.1066
2nd–Johnny Majors, Tennessee, HB	.994
3rd–Tommy McDonald, Oklahoma, HB	.973
4th–Jerry Tubbs, Oklahoma, C	.724
1957 **John David Crow,** Texas A&M, HB	.1183
2nd–Alex Karras, Iowa, T	.693
3rd–Walt Kowalczyk, Mich. St., HB	.630
4th–Lou Michaels, Kentucky, T	.330
1958 **Pete Dawkins,** Army, HB	.1394
2nd–Randy Duncan, Iowa, QB	.1021
3rd–Billy Cannon, LSU, HB	.975
4th–Bob White, Ohio St., FB	.365
1959 **Billy Cannon,** LSU, HB	.1929
2nd–Richie Lucas, Penn St., QB	.613
3rd–Don Meredith, SMU, QB	.286
4th–Bill Burrell, Illinois, G	.196
1960 **Joe Bellino,** Navy, HB	.1793
2nd–Tom Brown, Minnesota, G	.731
3rd–Jake Gibbs, Mississippi, QB	.453
4th–Ed Dyas, Auburn, HB	.319
1961 **Ernie Davis,** Syracuse, HB	.824
2nd–Bob Ferguson, Ohio St., HB	.771
3rd–Jimmy Saxton, Texas, HB	.551
4th–Sandy Stephens, Minnesota, QB	.543
1962 **Terry Baker,** Oregon St., QB	.707
2nd–Jerry Stovall, LSU, HB	.618
3rd–Bobby Bell, Minnesota, T	.429
4th–Lee Roy Jordan, Alabama, C	.321
1963 **Roger Staubach,** Navy, QB	.1860
2nd–Billy Lothridge, Ga. Tech, QB	.504
3rd–Sherman Lewis, Mich. St., HB	.369
4th–Don Trull, Baylor, QB	.253
1964 **John Huarte,** Notre Dame, QB	.1026
2nd–Jerry Rhome, Tulsa, QB	.952
3rd–Dick Butkus, Illinois, C	.505
4th–Bob Timberlake, Michigan, QB	.361
1965 **Mike Garrett,** USC, HB	.926
2nd–Howard Twilley, Tulsa, E	.528
3rd–Jim Grabowski, Illinois, FB	.481
4th–Donny Anderson, Texas Tech, HB	.408
1966 **Steve Spurrier,** Florida, QB	.1679
2nd–Bob Griese, Purdue, QB	.816
3rd–Nick Eddy, Notre Dame, HB	.456
4th–Gary Beban, UCLA, QB	.318
1967 **Gary Beban,** UCLA, QB	.1968
2nd–O.J. Simpson, USC, HB	.1722
3rd–Leroy Keyes, Purdue, HB	.1366
4th–Larry Csonka, Syracuse, FB	.136
1968 **O.J. Simpson,** USC, HB	.2853
2nd–Leroy Keyes, Purdue, HB	.1103
3rd–Terry Hanratty, Notre Dame, QB	.387
4th–Ted Kwalick, Penn St., TE	.254
1969 **Steve Owens,** Oklahoma, HB	.1488
2nd–Mike Phipps, Purdue, QB	.1344
3rd–Rex Kern, Ohio St., QB	.856
4th–Archie Manning, Mississippi, QB	.582
1970 **Jim Plunkett,** Stanford, QB	.2229
2nd–Joe Theismann, Notre Dame, QB	.1410
3rd–Archie Manning, Mississippi, QB	.849
4th–Steve Worster, Texas, RB	.398

Annual Awards (Cont.)

Year		Points
1971	**Pat Sullivan,** Auburn, QB	1597
	2nd–Ed Marinaro, Cornell, RB	1445
	3rd–Greg Pruitt, Oklahoma, RB	586
	4th–John Musso, Alabama, RB	365
1972	**Johnny Rodgers,** Nebraska, FL	1310
	2nd–Greg Pruitt, Oklahoma, RB	966
	3rd–Rich Glover, Nebraska, MG	652
	4th–Bert Jones, LSU, QB	351
1973	**John Cappelletti,** Penn St., RB	1057
	2nd–John Hicks, Ohio St., OT	524
	3rd–Roosevelt Leaks, Texas, RB	482
	4th–David Jaynes, Kansas, QB	394
1974	**Archie Griffin,** Ohio St., RB	1920
	2nd–Anthony Davis, USC, RB	819
	3rd–Joe Washington, Oklahoma, RB	661
	4th–Tom Clements, Notre Dame, QB	244
1975	**Archie Griffin,** Ohio St., RB	1800
	2nd–Chuck Muncie, California, RB	730
	3rd–Ricky Bell, USC, RB	708
	4th–Tony Dorsett, Pitt, RB	616
1976	**Tony Dorsett,** Pittsburgh, RB	2357
	2nd–Ricky Bell, USC, RB	1346
	3rd–Rob Lytle, Michigan, RB	413
	4th–Terry Miller, Oklahoma St., RB	197
1977	**Earl Campbell,** Texas, RB	1547
	2nd–Terry Miller, Oklahoma St., RB	812
	3rd–Ken MacAfee, Notre Dame, TE	343
	4th–Doug Williams, Grambling, QB	266
1978	**Billy Sims,** Oklahoma, RB	827
	2nd–Chuck Fusina, Penn St., QB	750
	3rd–Rick Leach, Michigan, QB	435
	4th–Charles White, USC, RB	354
1979	**Charles White,** USC, RB	1695
	2nd–Billy Sims, Oklahoma, RB	773
	3rd–Marc Wilson, BYU, QB	589
	4th–Art Schlichter, Ohio St., QB	251
1980	**George Rogers,** South Carolina, RB	1128
	2nd–Hugh Green, Pittsburgh, DE	861
	3rd–Herschel Walker, Georgia, RB	683
	4th–Mark Herrmann, Purdue, QB	405
1981	**Marcus Allen,** USC, RB	1797
	2nd–Herschel Walker, Georgia, RB	1199
	3rd–Jim McMahon, BYU, QB	706
	4th–Dan Marino, Pitt, QB	256
1982	**Herschel Walker,** Georgia, RB	1926
	2nd–John Elway, Stanford, QB	1231
	3rd–Eric Dickerson, SMU, RB	465
	4th–Anthony Carter, Michigan, WR	142
1983	**Mike Rozier,** Nebraska, RB	1801
	2nd–Steve Young, BYU, QB	1172
	3rd–Doug Flutie, Boston College, QB	253
	4th–Turner Gill, Nebraska, QB	190
1984	**Doug Flutie,** Boston College, QB	2240
	2nd–Keith Byars, Ohio St., RB	1251
	3rd–Robbie Bosco, BYU, QB	443
	4th–Bernie Kosar, Miami-FL, QB	320
1985	**Bo Jackson,** Auburn, RB	1509
	2nd–Chuck Long, Iowa, QB	1464
	3rd–Robbie Bosco, BYU, QB	459
	4th–Lorenzo White, Michigan St., RB	391

Year		Points
1986	**Vinny Testaverde,** Miami-FL, QB	2213
	2nd–Paul Palmer, Temple, RB	672
	3rd–Jim Harbaugh, Michigan, QB	458
	4th–Brian Bosworth, Oklahoma, LB	395
1987	**Tim Brown,** Notre Dame, WR	1442
	2nd–Don McPherson, Syracuse, QB	831
	3rd–Gordie Lockbaum, Holy Cross, WR-DB	657
	4th–Lorenzo White, Michigan St., RB	632
1988	**Barry Sanders,** Oklahoma St., RB	1878
	2nd–Rodney Peete, USC, QB	912
	3rd–Troy Aikman, UCLA, QB	582
	4th–Steve Walsh, Miami-FL, QB	341
1989	**Andre Ware,** Houston, QB	1073
	2nd–Anthony Thompson, Ind., RB	1003
	3rd–Major Harris, West Va., QB	709
	4th–Tony Rice, Notre Dame, QB	523
1990	**Ty Detmer,** BYU, QB	1482
	2nd–Rocket Ismail, Notre Dame, FL	1177
	3rd–Eric Bieniemy, Colorado, RB	798
	4th–Shawn Moore, Virginia, QB	465
1991	**Desmond Howard,** Michigan, WR	2077
	2nd–Casey Weldon, Florida St., QB	503
	3rd–Ty Detmer, BYU, QB	445
	4th–Steve Emtman, Washington, DT	357
1992	**Gino Torretta,** Miami-FL, QB	1400
	2nd–Marshall Faulk, San Diego St., RB	1080
	3rd–Garrison Hearst, Georgia, RB	982
	4th–Marvin Jones, Florida St., LB	392
1993	**Charlie Ward,** Florida St., QB	2310
	2nd–Heath Shuler, Tennessee, QB	688
	3rd–David Palmer, Alabama, RB	292
	4th–Marshall Faulk, S. Diego St., RB	250
1994	**Rashaan Salaam,** Colorado, RB	1743
	2nd–Ki-Jana Carter, Penn St., RB	901
	3rd–Steve McNair, Alcorn St., QB	655
	4th–Kerry Collins, Penn St., QB	639
1995	**Eddie George,** Ohio St., RB	1460
	2nd–Tommie Frazier, Nebraska, QB	1196
	3rd–Danny Wuerffel, Florida, QB	987
	4th–Darnell Autry, Northwestern, RB	535
1996	**Danny Wuerffel,** Florida, QB	1363
	2nd–Troy Davis, Iowa St., RB	1174
	3rd–Jake Plummer, Arizona St., QB	685
	4th–Orlando Pace, Ohio St., OT	599
1997	**Charles Woodson,** Michigan, DB-WR	1815
	2nd–Peyton Manning, Tennessee, QB	1543
	3rd–Ryan Leaf, Washington St., QB	861
	4th–Randy Moss, Marshall, WR	253
1998	**Ricky Williams,** Texas, RB	2355
	2nd–Michael Bishop, Kansas St., QB	792
	3rd–Cade McNown, UCLA, QB	696
	4th–Tim Couch, Kentucky, QB	527
1999	**Ron Dayne,** Wisconsin, RB	2042
	2nd–Joe Hamilton, Ga. Tech, QB	994
	3rd–Michael Vick, Va. Tech, QB	319
	4th–Drew Brees, Purdue, QB	308
2000	**Chris Weinke,** Florida St., QB	1628
	2nd–Josh Heupel, Oklahoma, QB	1552
	3rd–Drew Brees, Purdue, QB	619
	4th–LaDainian Tomlinson, TCU, RB	566

Maxwell Award

First presented in 1937 by the Maxwell Memorial Football Club of Philadelphia, the award is named after Robert (Tiny) Maxwell, a Philadelphia native who was a standout lineman at the University of Chicago at the turn of the century. Like the Heisman, the Maxwell is given to the outstanding college player in the nation. Both awards have gone to the same player in the same season 34 times. Those players are preceded by (#). Glenn Davis of Army and Doak Walker of SMU won both but in different years.

Multiple winner: Johnny Lattner (2).

Year		
1937 #Clint Frank, Yale, HB	1959 Rich Lucas, Penn St., QB	1980 Hugh Green, Pitt, DE
1938 #Davey O'Brien, TCU, QB	1960 #Joe Bellino, Navy, HB	1981 #Marcus Allen, USC, RB
1939 #Nile Kinnick, Iowa, HB	1961 Bob Ferguson, Ohio St., HB	1982 #Herschel Walker, Georgia, RB
1940 #Tom Harmon, Michigan, HB	1962 #Terry Baker, Oregon St., QB	1983 #Mike Rozier, Nebraska, RB
1941 Bill Dudley, Virginia, HB	1963 #Roger Staubach, Navy, QB	1984 #Doug Flutie, Boston Col., QB
1942 Paul Governali, Columbia, QB	1964 Glenn Ressler, Penn St., G	1985 Chuck Long, Iowa, QB
1943 Bob Odell, Penn, HB	1965 Tommy Nobis, Texas, LB	1986 #V. Testaverde, Miami-FL, QB
1944 Glenn Davis, Army, HB	1966 Jim Lynch, Notre Dame, LB	1987 Don McPherson, Syracuse, QB
1945 #Doc Blanchard, Army, FB	1967 #Gary Beban, UCLA, QB	1988 #Barry Sanders, Okla. St., RB
1946 Charley Trippi, Georgia, HB	1968 #O.J. Simpson, USC, HB	1989 Anthony Thompson, Indiana, RB
1947 Doak Walker, SMU, HB	1969 Mike Reid, Penn St., DT	
1948 Chuck Bednarik, Penn, C		1990 #Ty Detmer, BYU, QB
1949 #Leon Hart, Notre Dame, E	1970 #Jim Plunkett, Stanford, QB	1991 #Desmond Howard, Mich., WR
	1971 Ed Marinaro, Cornell, RB	1992 #Gino Torretta, Miami-FL, QB
1950 Reds Bagnell, Penn, HB	1972 Brad Van Pelt, Michigan St., DB	1993 #Charlie Ward, Florida St., QB
1951 #Dick Kazmaier, Princeton, TB	1973 #John Cappelletti, Penn St., RB	1994 Kerry Collins, Penn St., QB
1952 Johnny Lattner, Notre Dame, HB	1974 Steve Joachim, Temple, QB	1995 #Eddie George, Ohio St., RB
1953 #Johnny Lattner, N. Dame, HB	1975 #Archie Griffin, Ohio St., RB	1996 #Danny Wuerffel, Florida, QB
1954 Ron Beagle, Navy, E	1976 #Tony Dorsett, Pitt, RB	1997 Peyton Manning, Tennessee, QB
1955 #Howard Cassady, Ohio St., HB	1977 Ross Browner, Notre Dame, DE	1998 #Ricky Williams, Texas, RB
1956 Tommy McDonald, Okla., HB	1978 Chuck Fusina, Penn St., QB	1999 #Ron Dayne, Wisconsin, RB
1957 Bob Reifsnyder, Navy, T	1979 #Charles White, USC, RB	
1958 #Pete Dawkins, Army, HB		2000 Drew Brees, Purdue, QB

Outland Trophy

First presented in 1946 by the Football Writers Association of America, honoring the nation's outstanding interior lineman. The award is named after its benefactor, Dr. John H. Outland (Kansas, Class of 1898). Players listed in **bold** type helped lead their team to a national championship (according to AP).

Multiple winner: Dave Rimington (2). **Winners in junior year:** Ross Browner (1976), Steve Emtman (1991), Orlando Pace (1996) and Rimington (1981).

Year		
1946 **George Connor**, N. Dame, T	1965 Tommy Nobis, Texas, G	1984 Bruce Smith, Virginia Tech, DT
1947 Joe Steffy, Army, G	1966 Loyd Phillips, Arkansas, T	1985 Mike Ruth, Boston College, NG
1948 Bill Fischer, Notre Dame, G	1967 **Ron Yary**, USC, T	1986 Jason Buck, BYU, DT
1949 Ed Bagdon, Michigan St., G	1968 Bill Stanfill, Georgia, T	1987 Chad Hennings, Air Force, DT
	1969 Mike Reid, Penn St., DT	1988 Tracy Rocker, Auburn, DT
1950 Bob Gain, Kentucky, T		1989 Mohammed Elewonibi, BYU, G
1951 Jim Weatherall, Oklahoma, T	1970 Jim Stillwagon, Ohio St., MG	
1952 Dick Modzelewski, Maryland, T	1971 **Larry Jacobson**, Neb., DT	1990 Russell Maryland, Miami-FL, NT
1953 J.D. Roberts, Oklahoma, G	1972 Rich Glover, Nebraska, MG	1991 Steve Emtman, Washington, DT
1954 Bill Brooks, Arkansas, G	1973 John Hicks, Ohio St., OT	1992 Will Shields, Nebraska, G
1955 Calvin Jones, Iowa, G	1974 Randy White, Maryland, DT	1993 Rob Waldrop, Arizona, NG
1956 Jim Parker, Ohio St., G	1975 **Lee Roy Selmon**, Okla., DT	1994 **Zach Wiegert**, Nebraska, OT
1957 Alex Karras, Iowa, T	1976 Ross Browner, Notre Dame, DE	1995 Jonathan Ogden, UCLA, OT
1958 Zeke Smith, Auburn, G	1977 Brad Shearer, Texas, DT	1996 Orlando Pace, Ohio St., OT
1959 Mike McGee, Duke, T	1978 Greg Roberts, Oklahoma, G	1997 Aaron Taylor, Nebraska, G
	1979 Jim Richter, N.C. State, C	1998 Kris Farris, UCLA, OT
1960 **Tom Brown**, Minnesota, G		1999 Chris Samuels, Alabama, OT
1961 Merlin Olsen, Utah St., T	1980 Mark May, Pittsburgh, OT	
1962 Bobby Bell, Minnesota, T	1981 Dave Rimington, Nebraska, C	2000 John Henderson, Tennessee, DT
1963 **Scott Appleton**, Texas, T	1982 Dave Rimington, Nebraska, C	
1964 Steve DeLong, Tennessee, T	1983 Dean Steinkuhler, Nebraska, G	

Butkus Award

First presented in 1985 by the Downtown Athletic Club of Orlando, Fla., to honor the nation's outstanding linebacker. The award is named after Dick Butkus, two-time consensus All-America at Illinois and six-time All-Pro with the Chicago Bears.

Multiple winner: Brian Bosworth (2).

Year	Year	Year
1985 Brian Bosworth, Oklahoma	1991 Erick Anderson, Michigan	1997 Andy Katzenmoyer, Ohio St.
1986 Brian Bosworth, Oklahoma	1992 Marvin Jones, Florida St.	1998 Chris Claiborne, USC
1987 Paul McGowan, Florida St.	1993 Trev Alberts, Nebraska	1999 LaVar Arrington, Penn St.
1988 Derrick Thomas, Alabama	1994 Dana Howard, Illinois	2000 Dan Morgan, Miami-FL
1989 Percy Snow, Michigan St.	1995 Kevin Hardy, Illinois	
1990 Alfred Williams, Colorado	1996 Matt Russell, Colorado	

Lombardi Award

First presented in 1970 by the Rotary Club of Houston, honoring the nation's best lineman. The award is named after pro football coach Vince Lombardi, who, as a guard, was a member of the famous "Seven Blocks of Granite" at Fordham in the 1930s. The Lombardi and Outland awards have gone to the same player in the same year ten times. Those players are preceded by (#). Ross Browner of Notre Dame won both, but in different years.

Multiple winner: Orlando Pace (2).

Year	Year	Year
1970 #Jim Stillwagon, Ohio St., MG	1972 #Rich Glover, Nebraska, MG	1974 #Randy White, Maryland, DT
1971 Walt Patulski, Notre Dame, DE	1973 #John Hicks, Ohio St., OT	1975 #Lee Roy Selmon, Okla., DT

Annual Awards (Cont.)

Year		Year		Year	
1976	Wilson Whitley, Houston, DT	1985	Tony Casillas, Oklahoma, NG	1994	Warren Sapp, Miami-FL, DT
1977	Ross Browner, Notre Dame, DE	1986	Cornelius Bennett, Alabama, LB	1995	Orlando Pace, Ohio St., OT
1978	Bruce Clark, Penn St., DT	1987	Chris Spielman, Ohio St., LB	1996	#Orlando Pace, Ohio St., OT
1979	Brad Budde, USC, G	1988	#Tracy Rocker, Auburn, DT	1997	Grant Wistrom, Nebraska, DE
1980	Hugh Green, Pitt, DE	1989	Percy Snow, Michigan St., LB	1998	Dat Nguyen, Tex. A&M, LB
1981	Kenneth Sims, Texas, DT	1990	Chris Zorich, Notre Dame, NT	1999	Corey Moore, Va. Tech, DE
1982	#Dave Rimington, Neb., C	1991	#Steve Emtman, Wash., DT	2000	Jamal Reynolds, Florida St., DE
1983	#Dean Steinkuhler, Neb., G	1992	Marvin Jones, Florida St., LB		
1984	Tony Degrate, Texas, DT	1993	Aaron Taylor, Notre Dame, OT		

O'Brien Quarterback Award

First presented in 1977 as the O'Brien Memorial Trophy, the award went to the outstanding player in the Southwest. In 1981, however, the Davey O'Brien Educational and Charitable Trust of Ft. Worth renamed the prize the O'Brien National Quarterback Award and now honors the nation's best quarterback. The award is named after 1938 Heisman Trophy-winning QB Davey O'Brien of Texas Christian.

Multiple winners: Ty Detmer, Mike Singletary and Danny Wuerffel (2).

Memorial Trophy

Year		Year	
1977	Earl Campbell, Texas, RB	1979	Mike Singletary, Baylor, LB
1978	Billy Sims, Oklahoma, RB	1980	Mike Singletary, Baylor, LB

National QB Award

Year		Year		Year	
1981	Jim McMahon, BYU	1988	Troy Aikman, UCLA	1995	Danny Wuerffel, Florida
1982	Todd Blackledge, Penn St.	1989	Andre Ware, Houston	1996	Danny Wuerffel, Florida
1983	Steve Young, BYU	1990	Ty Detmer, BYU	1997	Peyton Manning, Tennessee
1984	Doug Flutie, Boston College	1991	Ty Detmer, BYU	1998	Michael Bishop, Kansas St.
1985	Chuck Long, Iowa	1992	Gino Torretta, Miami-FL	1999	Joe Hamilton, Ga. Tech
1986	Vinny Testaverde, Miami, FL	1993	Charlie Ward, Florida St.	2000	Chris Weinke, Florida St.
1987	Don McPherson, Syracuse	1994	Kerry Collins, Penn St.		

Thorpe Award

First presented in 1986 by the Jim Thorpe Athletic Club of Oklahoma City to honor the nation's outstanding defensive back. The award is named after Jim Thorpe—Olympic champion and two-time consensus All-America halfback at Carlisle.

Year		Year		Year	
1986	Thomas Everett, Baylor	1991	Terrell Buckley, Florida St.	1997	Charles Woodson, Michigan
1987	Bennie Blades, Miami-FL & Rickey Dixon, Oklahoma	1992	Deon Figures, Colorado	1998	Antoine Winfield, Ohio St.
		1993	Antonio Langham, Alabama	1999	Tyrone Carter, Minnesota
1988	Deion Sanders, Florida St.	1994	Chris Hudson, Colorado	2000	Jamar Fletcher, Wisconsin
1989	Mike Carrier, USC	1995	Greg Myers, Colorado St.		
1990	Darryl Lewis, Arizona	1996	Lawrence Wright, Florida		

Payton Award

First presented in 1987 by the Sports Network and Division I-AA sports information directors to honor the nation's outstanding Division I-AA player. The award is named after Walter Payton, the NFL's all-time leading rusher who was an All-America running back at Jackson St.

Year		Year		Year	
1987	Kenny Gamble, Colgate, RB	1992	Michael Payton, Marshall, QB	1997	Brian Finneran, Villanova, WR
1988	Dave Meggett, Towson St., RB	1993	Doug Nussmeier, Idaho, QB	1998	Jerry Azumah, N. Hampshire, RB
1989	John Friesz, Idaho, QB	1994	Steve McNair, Alcorn St., QB	1999	Adrian Peterson, Ga. Southern, RB
1990	Walter Dean, Grambling, RB	1995	Dave Dickenson, Montana, QB	2000	Louis Ivory, Furman, RB
1991	Jamie Martin, Weber St., QB	1996	Archie Amerson, N. Arizona, RB		

Hill Trophy

First presented in 1986 by the Harlon Hill Awards Committee in Florence, Ala., to honor the nation's outstanding Division II player. The award is named after three-time NFL All-Pro Harlon Hill, who played college ball at North Alabama.

Multiple winner: Johnny Bailey (3).

Year		Year		Year	
1986	Jeff Bentrim, N. Dakota St., QB	1991	Ronnie West, Pittsburg St., WR	1996	Jarrett Anderson, Truman St., RB
1987	Johnny Bailey, Texas A&I, RB	1992	Ronald Moore, Pittsburg St., RB	1997	Irv Sigler, Bloomsburg, RB
1988	Johnny Bailey, Texas A&I, RB	1993	Roger Graham, New Haven, RB	1998	Brian Shay, Emporia St., RB
1989	Johnny Bailey, Texas A&I, RB	1994	Chris Hatcher, Valdosta St., QB	1999	Corte McGuffet, N. Colo., RB
1990	Chris Simdorn, N. Dakota St., QB	1995	Ronald McKinnon, N. Alabama, LB	2000	Dusty Bonner, Valdosta St., QB

All-Time Winningest Division I-A Coaches

Minimum of 10 years in Division I-A through 2000 season. Regular season and bowl games included. Coaches active in 2000 in **bold** type.

Top 25 Winning Percentage

		Yrs	W	L	T	Pct
1	Knute Rockne	13	105	12	5	.881
2	Frank Leahy	13	107	13	9	.864
3	George Woodruff	12	142	25	2	.846
4	Barry Switzer	16	157	29	4	.837
5	Tom Osborne	25	255	49	3	.836
6	Percy Haughton	13	96	17	6	.832
7	Bob Neyland	21	173	31	12	.829
8	Hurry Up Yost	29	196	36	12	.828
9	Bud Wilkinson	17	145	29	4	.826
10	Jock Sutherland	20	144	28	14	.812
11	Bob Devaney	16	136	30	7	.806
12	Frank Thomas	19	141	33	9	.795
13	Henry Williams	23	141	34	12	.786
14	Gil Dobie	33	180	45	15	.781
15	**Bobby Bowden**	35	315	87	4	.781
16	Bear Bryant	38	323	85	17	.780
17	**Joe Paterno**	35	322	90	3	.780
18	Fred Folsom	19	106	28	6	.779
19	Bo Schembechler	27	234	65	8	.775
20	**Steve Spurrier**	14	132	38	2	.773
21	Fritz Crisler	18	116	32	9	.768
22	Charley Moran	18	122	33	12	.766
23	Wallace Wade	24	171	49	10	.765
24	Frank Kush	22	176	54	1	.764
25	Dan McGugin	30	197	55	19	.762

Top 25 Victories

		Yrs	W	L	T	Pct
1	Bear Bryant	38	323	85	17	.780
2	**Joe Paterno**	35	322	90	3	.780
3	Pop Warner	44	319	106	32	.733
4	**Bobby Bowden**	35	315	87	4	.781
5	Amos Alonzo Stagg	57	314	199	35	.605
6	**LaVell Edwards**	29	257	101	3	.722
7	Tom Osborne	25	255	49	3	.836
8	Woody Hayes	33	238	72	10	.759
9	Bo Schembechler	27	234	65	8	.775
10	Hayden Fry	37	232	178	10	.564
11	**Lou Holtz**	29	224	110	7	.667
12	Jess Neely	40	207	176	19	.539
13	Warren Woodson	31	203	95	14	.673
14	**Don Nehlen**	30	202	128	8	.609
15	Vince Dooley	25	201	77	10	.715
	Eddie Anderson	39	201	128	15	.606
17	Jim Sweeney	32	200	154	4	.564
18	Dana X. Bible	33	198	72	23	.715
19	Dan McGugin	30	197	55	19	.762
20	Hurry Up Yost	29	196	36	12	.828
21	Howard Jones	29	194	64	21	.733
22	**John Cooper**	24	192	84	6	.691
23	Johnny Vaught	25	190	61	12	.745
24	**George Welsh**	28	189	132	4	.588
25	John Heisman	36	185	70	17	.711
	Johnny Majors	29	185	137	10	.572

Note: Eddie Robinson of Division I-AA Grambling St. (1941-42, 1945-97) is the all-time NCAA leader in coaching wins with a 408-165-15 record and .708 winning pct. over 55 seasons.

Where They Coached

Anderson–Loras (1922-24), DePaul (1925-31), Holy Cross (1933-38), Iowa (1939-42), Holy Cross (1950-64); **Bible**–Mississippi College (1913-15), LSU (1916), Texas A&M (1917, 1919-28), Nebraska (1929-36), Texas (1937-46); **Bowden**–Samford (1959-62), West Virginia (1970-75), Florida St. (1976–); **Bryant**–Maryland (1945), Kentucky (1946-53), Texas A&M (1954-57), Alabama (1958-82); **Cooper**–Tulsa (1977-84), Arizona St. (1985-87), Ohio St. (1988-2000); **Crisler**–Minnesota (1930-31), Princeton (1932-37), Michigan (1938-47); **Devaney**–Wyoming (1957-61), Nebraska (1962-72); **Dobie**–North Dakota St. (1906-07), Washington (1908-16), Navy (1917-19), Cornell (1920-35), Boston College (1936-38); **V. Dooley**–Georgia (1964-88); **Edwards**–BYU (1972-2000); **Folsom**–Colorado (1895-99, 1901-02), Dartmouth (1903-06), Colorado (1908-15).

Fry–SMU (1962-72), North Texas (1973-78), Iowa (1979-98); **Haughton**–Cornell (1899-1900), Harvard (1908-16), Columbia (1923-24); **Hayes**–Denison (1946-48), Miami-OH (1949-50), Ohio St. (1951-78); **Heisman**–Oberlin (1892), Akron (1893), Oberlin (1894), Auburn (1895-99), Clemson (1900-03), Georgia Tech (1904-19), Penn (1920-22), Washington & Jefferson (1923), Rice (1924-27); **Holtz**–William & Mary (1969-71), N.C. State (1972-75), Arkansas (1977-83), Minnesota (1984-85), Notre Dame (1986-96), South Carolina (1999–); **Jones**–Syracuse (1908), Yale (1909), Ohio St. (1910), Yale (1913), Iowa (1916-23), Duke (1924), USC (1925-40); **Kush**–Arizona St. (1958-79); **Leahy**–Boston College (1939-40), Notre Dame (1941-43, 1946-53); **Majors**–Iowa St. (1968-72), Pittsburgh (1973-76, 93-96), Tennessee (1977-92); **McGugin**–Michigan (1904), Vanderbilt (1904-17, 1919-34); **Moran**–Texas A&M (1909-14), Centre (1919-23), Bucknell (1924-26), Catawba (1930-33).

Neely–Rhodes (1924-27), Clemson (1931-39), Rice (1940-66); **Nehlen**–Bowling Green (1968-76), West Virginia (1980-2000); **Neyland**–Tennessee (1926-34, 1936-40, 1946-52); **Osborne**–Nebraska (1973-97); **Paterno**–Penn St. (1966–); **Rockne**–Notre Dame (1918-30); **Schembechler**–Miami-OH (1963-68), Michigan (1969-89); **Spurrier**–Duke (1987-89), Florida (1990–); **Stagg**–Springfield College (1890-91), Chicago (1892-1932), Pacific (1933-46); **Sutherland**–Lafayette (1919-23), Pittsburgh (1924-38); **Sweeney**–Montana St. (1963-67), Washington St. (1968-75), Fresno St. (1976-96); **Switzer**–Oklahoma (1973-88).

Thomas–Chattanooga (1925-28), Alabama (1931-42, 1944-46); **Vaught**–Mississippi (1947-70); **Wade**–Alabama (1923-30), Duke (1931-41, -1946-50); **Warner**–Georgia (1895-96), Cornell (1897-98), Carlisle (1899-1903), Cornell (1904-06), Carlisle (1907-13), Pittsburgh (1915-23), Stanford (1924-32), Temple (1933-38); **Welsh**–Navy (1973-81), Virginia (1982-2000); **Wilkinson**–Oklahoma (1947-63); **Williams**–Army (1891), Minnesota (1900-21); **Woodruff**–Penn (1892-1901), Illinois (1903), Carlisle (1905); **Woodson**–Central Arkansas (1935-39), Hardin-Simmons (1941-42, 1946-51), Arizona (1952-56), New Mexico St. (1958-67), Trinity-TX (1972-73); **Yost**–Ohio Wesleyan (1897), Nebraska (1898), Kansas (1899), Stanford (1900), Michigan (1901-23, 1925-26).

All-Time Winningest Division I-A Coaches (Cont.)

All-Time Bowl Appearances

Coaches active in 2000 in **bold** type.

Active Coaches' Victories

(Minimum 5 years in Division I-A.)

		Overall		
		App	W	L	T
1	**Joe Paterno**	.30	20	9	1
2	Bear Bryant	.29	15	12	2
3	Tom Osborne	.25	12	13	0
4	**Bobby Bowden**	.24	17	6	1
5	**LaVell Edwards**	.22	7	14	1
6	**Lou Holtz**	.20	10	8	2
	Vince Dooley	.20	8	10	2
8	Johnny Vaught	.18	10	8	0
9	Hayden Fry	.17	7	9	1
	Bo Schembechler	.17	5	12	0
11	Johnny Majors	.16	9	7	0
	Darrell Royal	.16	8	7	1
13	Don James	.15	10	5	0
	George Welsh	.15	5	10	0
15	**John Cooper**	.14	5	9	0
16	Bobby Dodd	.13	9	4	0
	Terry Donahue	.13	8	4	1
	Barry Switzer	.13	8	5	0
	Charlie McClendon	.13	7	6	0
	Jackie Sherrill	.13	7	6	0

		Yrs	W	L	T	Pct
1	Joe Paterno, Penn St.	.35	**322**	90	3	.780
2	Bobby Bowden, Fla. St.	.35	**315**	87	4	.781
3	Lou Holtz, South Carolina	.29	**224**	110	7	.667
4	Jackie Sherrill, Miss. St.	.22	**172**	93	4	.647
5	Ken Hatfield, Rice	.21	**147**	104	4	.584
6	Frank Beamer, Va. Tech	.20	**141**	84	4	.624
7	Dennis Franchione, Alabama	.17	**138**	66	2	.675
8	Fisher DeBerry, Air Force	.17	**135**	72	1	.651
9	Steve Spurrier, Florida	.14	**132**	38	2	.773
10	Dennis Erickson, Oregon St.	.15	**131**	46	1	.739
11	Paul Pasqualoni, Syracuse	.15	**115**	53	1	.683
	John Robinson, UNLV	.14	**115**	48	4	.701
13	Mack Brown, Texas	.17	**113**	85	1	.570
14	Mike Price, Wash. St.	.20	**109**	117	0	.482
	R.C. Slocum, Texas A&M	.12	**109**	37	2	.743
16	Bill Snyder, Kansas St.	.12	**99**	43	1	.696
17	Sonny Lubick, Colorado St.	.12	**88**	48	0	.647
18	Phillip Fulmer, Tennessee	.9	**84**	18	0	.824
19	Glen Mason, Minnesota	.15	**81**	89	1	.477
20	Barry Alvarez, Wisconsin	.11	**79**	48	4	.618

Note: Only four coaches — **Bill Alexander** of Georgia Tech (1920-44); **Bob Neyland** of Tennessee (1926-34, 36-40, 46-52); **Frank Thomas** of Alabama (1931-42, 44-46) and **Joe Paterno** of Penn State (1966–) — have taken teams to the Rose, Orange, Sugar and Cotton Bowls. Paterno has won all four, while Alexander and Thomas won three and Neyland two.

AFCA Coach of the Year

First presented in 1935 by the American Football Coaches Association.

Multiple winners: Joe Paterno (4), Bear Bryant (3), John McKay and Darrell Royal (2).

Years

1935 Pappy Waldorf, Northwestern
1936 Dick Harlow, Harvard
1937 Hooks Mylin, Lafayette
1938 Bill Kern, Carnegie Tech
1939 Eddie Anderson, Iowa
1940 Clark Shaughnessy, Stanford
1941 Frank Leahy, Notre Dame
1942 Bill Alexander, Georgia Tech
1943 Amos Alonzo Stagg, Pacific
1944 Carroll Widdoes, Ohio St.
1945 Bo McMillin, Indiana
1946 Red Blaik, Army
1947 Fritz Crisler, Michigan
1948 Bennie Oosterbaan, Michigan
1949 Bud Wilkinson, Oklahoma
1950 Charlie Caldwell, Princeton
1951 Chuck Taylor, Stanford
1952 Biggie Munn, Michigan St.
1953 Jim Tatum, Maryland
1954 Red Sanders, UCLA
1955 Duffy Daugherty, Michigan St.
1956 Bowden Wyatt, Tennessee
1957 Woody Hayes, Ohio St.

Years

1958 Paul Dietzel, LSU
1959 Ben Schwartzwalder, Syracuse
1960 Murray Warmath, Minnesota
1961 Bear Bryant, Alabama
1962 John McKay, USC
1963 Darrell Royal, Texas
1964 Frank Broyles, Arkansas
      & Ara Parseghian, Notre Dame
1965 Tommy Prothro, UCLA
1966 Tom Cahill, Army
1967 John Pont, Indiana
1968 Joe Paterno, Penn St.
1969 Bo Schembechler, Michigan
1970 Charlie McClendon, LSU
      & Darrell Royal, Texas
1971 Bear Bryant, Alabama
1972 John McKay, USC
1973 Bear Bryant, Alabama
1974 Grant Teaff, Baylor
1975 Frank Kush, Arizona St.
1976 Johnny Majors, Pittsburgh
1977 Don James, Washington
1978 Joe Paterno, Penn St.

Years

1979 Earle Bruce, Ohio St.
1980 Vince Dooley, Georgia
1981 Danny Ford, Clemson
1982 Joe Paterno, Penn St.
1983 Ken Hatfield, Air Force
1984 LaVell Edwards, BYU
1985 Fisher DeBerry, Air Force
1986 Joe Paterno, Penn St.
1987 Dick MacPherson, Syracuse
1988 Don Nehlen, West Virginia
1989 Bill McCartney, Colorado
1990 Bobby Ross, Georgia Tech
1991 Bill Lewis, East Carolina
1992 Gene Stallings, Alabama
1993 Barry Alvarez, Wisconsin
1994 Tom Osborne, Nebraska
1995 Gary Barnett, Northwestern
1996 Bruce Snyder, Arizona St.
1997 Lloyd Carr, Michigan
1998 Phillip Fulmer, Tennessee
1999 Frank Beamer, Va. Tech
2000 Bob Stoops, Oklahoma

FWAA Coach of the Year

First presented in 1957 by the Football Writers Association of America. The FWAA and AFCA awards have both gone to the same coach in the same season 30 times. Those double winners are preceded by (#).

Multiple winners: Woody Hayes and Joe Paterno (3); Lou Holtz, Johnny Majors and John McKay (2).

Year

1957 #Woody Hayes, Ohio St.
1958 #Paul Dietzel, LSU
1959 #Ben Schwartzwalder, Syracuse
1960 #Murray Warmath, Minnesota
1961 Darrell Royal, Texas
1962 #John McKay, USC
1963 #Darrell Royal, Texas
1964 #Ara Parseghian, Notre Dame

Year

1965 #Duffy Daugherty, Michigan St.
1966 #Tom Cahill, Army
1967 #John Pont, Indiana
1968 Woody Hayes, Ohio St.
1969 #Bo Schembechler, Michigan
1970 Alex Agase, Northwestern
1971 Bob Devaney, Nebraska
1972 #John McKay, USC

Year

1973 Johnny Majors, Pitt
1974 #Grant Teaff, Baylor
1975 Woody Hayes, Ohio St.
1976 Johnny Majors, Pitt
1977 Lou Holtz, Arkansas
1978 #Joe Paterno, Penn St.
1979 #Earle Bruce, Ohio St.
1980 #Vince Dooley, Georgia

Year		Year		Year	
1981	#Danny Ford, Clemson	1988	Lou Holtz, Notre Dame	1995	#Gary Barnett, Northwestern
1982	#Joe Paterno, Penn St.	1989	#Bill McCartney, Colorado	1996	#Bruce Snyder, Arizona St.
1983	Howard Schnellenberger, Miami-FL	1990	#Bobby Ross, Georgia Tech	1997	Mike Price, Washington St.
1984	#LaVell Edwards, BYU	1991	Don James, Washington	1998	#Phillip Fulmer, Tennessee
1985	#Fisher DeBerry, Air Force	1992	#Gene Stallings, Alabama	1999	#Frank Beamer, Va. Tech
1986	#Joe Paterno, Penn St.	1993	Terry Bowden, Auburn	2000	#Bob Stoops, Oklahoma
1987	#Dick MacPherson, Syracuse	1994	Rich Brooks, Oregon		

All-Time NCAA Division I-AA Leaders
CAREER

Total Offense

Yards Gained

		Years	Yards
1	Steve McNair, Alcorn St.	1991-94	16,823
2	Willie Totten, Miss. Valley	1982-85	13,007
3	Jamie Martin, Weber St.	1989-92	12,287
4	Doug Nussmeier, Idaho	1990-93	12,054
5	Neil Lomax, Portland St.	1978-80	11,647

Yards per Game

		Years	Yards	P/Gm
1	Steve McNair, Alcorn St.	1991-94	16,823	400.5
2	Neil Lomax, Portland St.	1978-80	11,647	352.9
3	Aaron Flowers, CS-N'ridge	1996-97	6,754	337.7
4	Chris Sanders, Chatt.	1999-00	7,247	329.4
5	Dave Dickenson, Montana	1992-95	11,523	329.2

Passing
(Minimum 500 Completions)

Passing Efficiency

		Years	Rating
1	Shawn Knight, William & Mary	1991-94	170.8
2	Dave Dickenson, Montana	1992-95	166.3
3	Drew Miller, Montana	1999-00	160.5
4	Doug Nussmeier, Idaho	1990-93	154.4
5	Mark Washington, Jackson St.	1996-99	153.5

Yards Gained

		Years	Yards
1	Steve McNair, Alcorn St.	1991-94	14,496
2	Willie Totten, Miss. Valley	1982-85	12,711
3	Jamie Martin, Weber St.	1989-92	12,037
4	Neil Lomax, Portland St.	1978-80	11,550
5	Travis Brown, N. Arizona	1996-99	11,400

Receiving

Catches

		Years	No
1	Jacquay Nunnally, Fla. A&M	1997-00	317
2	Stephen Campbell, Brown	1997-00	305
3	Jerry Rice, Miss. Valley	1981-84	301
4	Kasey Dunn, Idaho	1988-91	268
5	Sean Morey, Brown	1995-98	251

Yards Gained

		Years	No	Yards
1	Jerry Rice, Miss. Valley	1981-84	301	4693
2	Jacquay Nunnally, Fla. A&M	1997-00	317	4239
3	Cedric Ward, N. Iowa	1993-96	176	3876
4	Sean Morey, Brown	1995-98	251	3850
5	Kasey Dunn, Idaho	1988-91	268	3847

Rushing

Yards Gained

		Years	Yards
1	Charles Roberts, CS-Sac.	1997-00	6553
2	Jerry Azumah, N. Hampshire	1995-98	6193
3	Matt Cannon, S. Utah	1997-00	5489
4	Reggie Green, Siena	1994-97	5415
5	Marcell Shipp, UMass	1997-00	5383

Yards per Game

		Years	Yards	P/Gm
1	Arnold Mickens, Butler	1994-95	3813	190.7
2	Aaron Stecker, W. Ill.	1997-98	3081	151.1
3	Tim Hall, Robert Morris	1994-95	2908	153.1
4	Jerry Azumah, N. Hampshire	1995-98	6193	151.0
5	Reggie Green, Siena	1994-97	5415	150.4

Miscellaneous

Interceptions

		Years	No
1	Dave Murphy, Holy Cross	1986-89	28
2	Cedric Walker, S.F. Austin	1990-93	25
3	Issiac Holt, Alcorn St.	1981-84	24
	Bill McGovern, Holy Cross	1981-84	24
	Darren Sharper, Wm. & Mary	1993-96	24

Punting Average

		Years	Avg
1	Pumpy Tudors, Tenn.-Chatt.	1989-91	44.4
2	Case de Brujin, Idaho St.	1978-81	43.7
3	Terry Belden, Northern Ariz.	1990-93	43.4
4	Chad Stanley, SF Austin	1996-98	43.3
5	George Cimadevilla, East Tenn. St.	1983-86	43.0

Punt Return Average*

		Years	Avg
1	Willie Ware, Miss. Valley	1982-85	16.4
2	Buck Phillips, Western Ill.	1994-95	16.4
3	Tim Egerton, Delaware St.	1986-89	16.1
4	Mark Orlando, Towson St.	1991-94	15.7
5	John Armstrong, Richmond	1984-85	14.5

Kickoff Return Average*

		Years	Avg
1	Lamont Brightful, E. Wash.	1998-00	33.3
2	Troy Brown, Marshall	1991-92	29.7
3	Charles Swann, Indiana St.	1989-91	29.3
4	Craig Richardson, Eastern Wash.	1983-86	28.5
5	Ramondo North, N.C. A&T	1998-00	28.3

*(Minimum 1.2 returns per game)

Scoring
NON-KICKERS

Points

		Years	TD	XP	Pts
1	Matt Cannon, S. Utah	1997-00	69	3	420
2	Jerry Azumah, N. Hampshire	1995-98	69	2	418
3	Adrian Peterson, Ga. Southern	1998–	69	0	414
4	Sherriden May, Idaho	1991-94	61	0	366
5	David Dinkins, Morehead St.	1997-00	63	3	384

Touchdowns Passing

		Years	No
1	Willie Totten, Miss. Valley	1982-85	139
2	Steve McNair, Alcorn St.	1991-94	119
3	Dave Dickenson, Montana	1992-95	96
4	Chris Boden, Villanova	1996-99	93
5	Ted White, Howard	1995-98	92

Touchdowns Rushing

		Years	No
1	Matt Cannon, S. Utah	1997-00	69
2	Adrian Peterson, Ga. Southern	1998–	66
3	David Dinkins, Morehead St.	1997-00	63
4	Jerry Azumah, N. Hampshire	1995-98	60
5	Charles Roberts, CS-Sacramento	1997-00	56

Touchdown Catches

		Years	No
1	Jerry Rice, Miss. Valley	1981-84	50
2	Rennie Benn, Lehigh	1982-85	44
3	Dedric Ward, N. Iowa	1993-96	41
4	Sean Morey, Brown	1995-98	39
5	Gharun Hester, Georgetown	1997-00	39

All-Time NCAA Division I-AA Leaders (Cont.)

KICKERS

	Points	Years	FG	XP	Pts
1	Marty Zendejas, Nevada	1984-87	72	169	385
2	Dave Ettinger, Hofstra	1994-97	62	140	326
3	B. Mitchell, Marshall/				
	N. Iowa	1987, 89-91	64	130	322
	Scott Shields, Weber St.	1995-98	67	109	322
5	Thayne Doyle, Idaho	1988-91	49	160	307

	Field Goals	Years	No
1	Marty Zendejas, Nevada	1984-87	72
2	Kirk Roach, Western Carolina	1984-87	71
3	Tony Zendejas, Nevada	1981-83	70
4	Scott Shields, Weber St.	1995-98	67
5	B. Mitchell, Marshall/N. Iowa	1987,89-91	64

All-Time Winningest Division I-AA Teams

Includes record at a senior college only, minimum of 20 seasons of competition. Bowl and·playoff games are included.

Top 20 Winning Percentage

		Yrs	Gm	W	L	T	Pct.	Playoffs W-L-T
1	Yale	128	1161	806	300	55	.718	0-0-0
2	Florida A&M	68	692	483	191	18	.711	5-7-0
3	Grambling St.	58	622	430	177	15	.703	9-7-0
4	Tennessee St.	73	683	461	192	30	.697	8-4-1
5	Princeton	131	1114	740	324	50	.687	0-0-0
6	Harvard	126	1143	734	359	50	.664	1-0-0
7	Jackson St.	55	566	362	191	13	.651	1-11-1
8	Georgia Southern	32	363	232	124	7	.649	34-6-0
9	Southern	79	770	475	270	25	.633	6-1-0
10	Eastern Kentucky	77	767	470	270	27	.630	17-17-0
11	Dartmouth	119	1030	626	358	46	.630	6-1-0
12	Fordham	102	1137	689	395	53	.629	2-3-0
13	Pennsylvania	124	1216	742	432	42	.628	0-1-0
14	Hofstra	60	579	356	212	11	.624	4-11-0
15	Dayton	93	881	533	322	26	.620	16-11-0
16	Appalachian St.	71	748	448	271	29	.618	8-14-0
17	McNeese St.	50	541	326	201	14	.616	11-11-0
18	S. Carolina St.	73	677	401	249	27	.612	6-5-0
19	Delaware	109	982	571	368	43	.603	24-14-0
20	Youngstown St.	60	613	361	235	17	.603	26-9-0

Top 50 Victories

		Wins			Wins			Wins
1	Yale	806	18	Drake	496	35	VMI	430
2	Pennsylvania	742	19	Villanova	488		Grambling St.	430
3	Princeton	740	20	Florida A&M	483	37	Western Ill.	429
4	Harvard	734	21	Furman	482	38	Richmond	428
5	Fordham	689	22	Southern	475	39	Maine	427
6	Dartmouth	626		Massachusetts	475	40	SW Texas St.	425
7	Lafayette	590	24	William & Mary	474	41	Montana	424
8	Cornell	586	25	E. Kentucky	470	42	Citadel	416
9	Delaware	571	26	Tennessee St.	461	43	Idaho St.	408
10	Lehigh	565	27	Hampton	454	44	Murray St.	405
11	Holy Cross	544	28	W. Kentucky	451	45	Eastern Ill.	404
12	Dayton	533	29	Tenn-Chat	448	46	S. Carolina St.	401
13	Bucknell	523		Appalachian St.	448	47	SW Missouri St.	396
14	Brown	521	31	Northwestern St.	441		Wofford	396
	Colgate	521		New Hampshire	441	49	E. Washington	395
16	N. Iowa	520	33	Georgetown	438	50	N.C. A&T	393
17	Butler	502	34	Howard	431			

Top 10 Playoff Game Appearances

Ranked by NCAA playoff games played from 1978-2000. CH refers to championships won.

		Years	Games	Record	CH			Years	Games	Record	CH
1	Georgia Southern	12	40	34-6	6	6	Delaware	11	22	11-11	0
2	Eastern Ky.	17	31	16-15	2	7	Furman	10	20	11-9	1
3	Marshall*	8	29	23-6	2	8	Northern Iowa	9	18	9-9	0
	Youngstown St.	10	29	23-6	4	9	Appalachian St.	10	17	7-10	0
5	Montana	11	23	14-10	1		Idaho*	11	17	6-11	0

*Marshall (1997), Idaho (1996) and Nevada (1992) have all moved up to I-A.

Active Division I-AA Coaches

Minimum of 5 years as a Division I-A and/or Division I-AA through 2000 season.

Top 10 Winning Percentage

		Yrs	W	L	T	Pct
1	Mike Kelly, Dayton	.20	185	39	1	.824
2	Al Bagnoli, Pennsylvania	.19	150	44	0	.773
3	Pete Richardson, Southern	.13	113	37	1	.752
4	Larry Blakeney, Troy St.	.10	91	30	1	.750
5	Greg Gattuso, Duquesne	.8	63	22	0	.741
6	Joe Gardi, Hofstra	.11	90	33	3	.726
7	Tubby Raymond, Delaware	.35	296	113	3	.722
8	Roy Kidd, Eastern Ky.	.37	299	117	8	.715
9	Billy Joe, Florida A&M	.27	214	85	4	.713
10	Joe Taylor, Hampton	.18	139	55	4	.712

Top 10 Victories

		Yrs	W	L	T	Pct
1	Roy Kidd, Eastern Ky.	.37	299	117	8	.715
2	Tubby Raymond, Delaware	.35	296	113	3	.722
3	Billy Joe, Florida A&M	.27	214	85	4	.713
4	Ron Randleman, Sam Houston St.	.32	191	145	6	.567
5	Mike Kelly, Dayton	.20	185	39	1	.824
6	Bill Hayes, N. Carolina A&T	.25	183	93	2	.662
7	Willie Jeffries, S. Carolina St.	.28	173	127	6	.575
8	Al Bagnoli, Pennsylvania	.19	150	44	0	.773
9	Walt Hameline, Wagner	.20	147	61	2	.705
10	Bob Ricca, St. John's	.23	145	91	1	.614

Note: Eddie Robinson of Grambling St. (1941-42, 1945-97) retired following the 1997 season as the all-time NCAA leader in coaching wins with a 408-165-15 record and a .707 winning pct. over 55 seasons.

Division I-AA Coach of the Year

First presented in 1983 by the American Football Coaches Association.

Multiple winners: Mark Duffner, Paul Johnson and Erk Russell (2).

Year		Year		Year	
1983	Rey Dempsey, Southern Ill.	1989	Erk Russell, Ga. Southern	1995	Don Read, Montana
1984	Dave Arnold, Montana St.	1990	Tim Stowers, Ga. Southern	1996	Ray Tellier, Columbia
1985	Dick Sheridan, Furman	1991	Mark Duffner, Holy Cross	1997	Andy Talley, Villanova
1986	Erk Russell, Ga. Southern	1992	Charlie Taafe, Citadel	1998	Mark Whipple, Massachusetts
1987	Mark Duffner, Holy Cross	1993	Dan Allen, Boston Univ.	1999	Paul Johnson, Ga. Southern
1988	Jimmy Satterfield, Furman	1994	Jim Tressel, Youngstown St.	2000	Paul Johnson, Ga. Southern

NCAA Playoffs

Division I-AA

Established in 1978 as a four-team playoff. Tournament field increased to eight teams in 1981, 12 teams in 1982 and 16 teams in 1986. Automatic berths are awarded to champions of the Big Sky, Gateway, Mid-Eastern Athletic, Ohio Valley, Patriot, Southern, Southland and Atlantic 10 (formerly Yankee) conferences.

Multiple winners: Georgia Southern (6); Youngstown St. (4); Eastern Kentucky and Marshall (2).

Year	Winner	Score	Loser	Year	Winner	Score	Loser
1978	Florida A&M	35-28	Massachusetts	1990	Georgia Southern	36-13	Nevada-Reno
1979	Eastern Kentucky	30-7	Lehigh, PA	1991	Youngstown St., OH	25-17	Marshall
1980	Boise St., ID	31-29	Eastern Kentucky	1992	Marshall	31-28	Youngstown St.
1981	Idaho St.	34-23	Eastern Kentucky	1993	Youngstown St.	17-5	Marshall
1982	Eastern Kentucky	17-14	Delaware	1994	Youngstown St.	28-14	Boise St.
1983	Southern Illinois	43-7	Western Carolina	1995	Montana	22-20	Marshall
1984	Montana St.	19-6	Louisiana Tech	1996	Marshall	49-29	Montana
1985	Georgia Southern	44-42	Furman, SC	1997	Youngstown St.	10-9	McNeese St.
1986	Georgia Southern	48-21	Arkansas St.	1998	Massachusetts	55-43	Georgia Southern
1987	NE Louisiana	43-42	Marshall, WV	1999	Georgia Southern	59-24	Youngstown St.
1988	Furman, SC	17-12	Georgia Southern	2000	Georgia Southern	27-25	Montana
1989	Georgia Southern	37-34	S.F. Austin St.				

Division II

Established in 1973 as an eight-team playoff. Tournament field increased to 16 teams in 1988. From 1964-72, eight qualifying NCAA College Division member institutions competed in four regional bowl games, but there was no tournament and no national championship until 1973.

Multiple winners: North Dakota St. (5); North Alabama (3); Northern Colorado, Northwest Missouri St., Southwest Texas St. and Troy St. (2).

Year	Winner	Score	Loser	Year	Winner	Score	Loser
1973	Louisiana Tech	34-0	Western Kentucky	1987	Troy St., AL	31-17	Portland St., OR
1974	Central Michigan	54-14	Delaware	1988	North Dakota St.	35-21	Portland St., OR
1975	Northern Michigan	16-14	Western Kentucky	1989	Mississippi Col.	3-0	Jacksonville St., AL
1976	Montana St.	24-13	Akron, OH	1990	North Dakota St.	51-11	Indiana, PA
1977	Lehigh, PA	33-0	Jacksonville St., AL	1991	Pittsburg St., KS	23-6	Jacksonville St., AL
1978	Eastern Illinois	10-9	Delaware	1992	Jacksonville St., AL	17-13	Pittsburg St., KS
1979	Delaware	38-21	Youngstown St., OH	1993	North Alabama	41-34	Indiana, PA
1980	Cal Poly-SLO	21-13	Eastern Illinois	1994	North Alabama	16-10	Tex. A&M (Kings.)
1981	SW Texas St.	42-13	North Dakota St.	1995	North Alabama	27-7	Pittsburg St., KS
1982	SW Texas St.	34-9	UC-Davis	1996	Northern Colorado	23-14	Carson-Newman
1983	North Dakota St.	41-21	Central St., OH	1997	Northern Colorado	51-0	New Haven
1984	Troy St., AL	18-17	North Dakota St.	1998	NW Missouri St.	24-6	Carson-Newman
1985	North Dakota St.	35-7	North Alabama	1999	NW Missouri St.	58-52*	Carson-Newman
1986	North Dakota St.	27-7	South Dakota	2000	Delta St., MS	63-34	Bloomsburg, PA

*Four overtimes

Division III

Established in 1973 as a four-team playoff. Tournament field increased to eight teams in 1975, 16 teams in 1985 and 28 teams in 1999. From 1969-72, four qualifying NCAA College Division member institutions competed in two regional bowl games, but there was no tournament and no national championship until 1973. (*) denotes overtime.

Multiple winners: Mt. Union (5); Augustana (4); Ithaca (3); Dayton, Widener, WI-La Crosse and Wittenberg (2).

Year	Winner	Score	Loser	Year	Winner	Score	Loser
1973	Wittenberg, OH	41-0	Juniata, PA	1987	Wagner, NY	19-3	Dayton
1974	Central, IA	10-8	Ithaca, NY	1988	Ithaca	39-24	Central, IA
1975	Wittenberg	28-0	Ithaca	1989	Dayton	17-7	Union
1976	St. John's, MN	31-28	Towson St., MD	1990	Allegheny, PA	21-14*	Lycoming, PA
1977	Widener, PA	39-36	Wabash, IN	1991	Ithaca	34-20	Dayton
1978	Baldwin-Wallace	24-10	Wittenberg	1992	WI-La Crosse	16-12	Wash. & Jeff., PA
1979	Ithaca, NY	14-10	Wittenberg	1993	Mt. Union, OH	34-24	Rowan, NJ
1980	Dayton, OH	63-0	Ithaca	1994	Albion, MI	38-15	Wash. & Jeff.
1981	Widener, PA	17-10	Dayton, OH	1995	WI-La Crosse	36-7	Rowan
1982	West Georgia	14-0	Augustana, IL	1996	Mt. Union	56-24	Rowan
1983	Augustana	21-17	Union, NY	1997	Mt. Union	61-12	Lycoming
1984	Augustana	21-12	Central, IA	1998	Mt. Union	44-24	Rowan
1985	Augustana	20-7	Ithaca	1999	Pacific Lutheran	42-13	Rowan
1986	Augustana	31-3	Salisbury St., MD	2000	Mt. Union	10-7	St. John's, MN

NAIA Playoffs

Division I

Established in 1956 as two-team playoff. Tournament field increased to four teams in 1958, eight teams in 1978 and 16 teams in 1987 before cutting back to eight teams in 1989. NAIA went back to a single division 16-team playoff in 1997. The title game has ended in a tie four times (1956, '64, '84 and '85).

Multiple winners: Texas A&I (7); Carson-Newman (5); Central Arkansas and Central St., OH (3); Abilene Christian, Central St-OK, Elon, Pittsburg St. and St. John's-MN (2).

Year	Winner	Score	Loser	Year	Winner	Score	Loser
1956	Montana St.	0-0	St. Joseph's, IN	1979	Texas A&I	20-14	Central St., OK
1957	Pittsburg St., KS	27-26	Hillsdale, MI	1980	Elon, NC	17-10	NE Oklahoma
1958	NE Oklahoma	19-13	Northern Arizona	1981	Elon, NC	3-0	Pittsburg St., KS
1959	Texas A&I	20-7	Lenoir-Rhyne, NC	1982	Central St., OK	14-11	Mesa, CO
1960	Lenoir-Rhyne, NC	15-14	Humboldt St., CA	1983	Car-Newman, TN	36-28	Mesa, CO
1961	Pittsburg St., KS	12-7	Linfield, OR	1984	Car-Newman, TN	19-19	Central Arkansas
1962	Central St., OK	28-13	Lenoir-Rhyne, NC	1985	Hillsdale, MI	10-10	Central Arkansas
1963	St. John's, MN	33-27	Prairie View, TX	1986	Car-Newman, TN	17-0	Cameron, OK
1964	Concordia, MN	7-7	Sam Houston, TX	1987	Cameron, OK	30-2	Car-Newman, TN
1965	St. John's, MN	33-0	Linfield, OR	1988	Car-Newman, TN	56-21	Adams St., CO
1966	Waynesburg, PA	42-21	WI-Whitewater	1989	Car-Newman, TN	34-20	Emporia St., KS
1967	Fairmont St., WV	28-21	Eastern Wash.	1990	Central St., OH	38-16	Mesa, CO
1968	Troy St., AL	43-35	Texas A&I	1991	Central Arkansas	19-16	Central St., OH
1969	Texas A&I	32-7	Concordia, MN	1992	Central St., OH	19-16	Gardner-Webb, NC
1970	Texas A&I	48-7	Wofford, SC	1993	E. Central, OK	49-35	Glenville St., WV
1971	Livingston, AL	14-12	Arkansas Tech	1994	N'eastern St., OK	13-12	Ark-Pine Bluff
1972	East Texas St.	21-18	Car-Newman, TN	1995	Central St., OH	37-7	N'eastern St., OK
1973	Abilene Christian	42-14	Elon, NC	1996	SW Oklahoma St.	33-31	Montana Tech
1974	Texas A&I	34-23	Henderson St., AR	1997	Findlay, OH	14-7	Willamette, ORE
1975	Texas A&I	37-0	Salem, WV	1998	Azusa Pacific, CA	17-14	Olivet Nazarene, IL
1976	Texas A&I	26-0	Central Arkansas	1999	NW Oklahoma St.	34-26	Georgetown, KY
1977	Abilene Christian	24-7	SW Oklahoma	2000	Georgetown, KY	20-0	NW Oklahoma St.
1978	Angelo St., TX	34-14	Elon, NC				

Division II

Established in 1970 as four-team playoff. Tournament field increased to eight teams in 1978 and 16 teams in 1987. NAIA went back to a single division playoff in 1997. The title game has ended in a tie twice (1981 and '87).

Multiple winners: Westminster (6); Findlay, Linfield and Pacific Lutheran (3); Concordia-MN, Northwestern-IA and Texas Lutheran (2).

Year	Winner	Score	Loser	Year	Winner	Score	Loser
1970	Westminster, PA	21-16	Anderson, IN	1984	Linfield, OR	33-22	Northwestern, IA
1971	Calif. Lutheran	20-14	Westminster, PA	1985	WI-La Crosse	24-7	Pacific Lutheran
1972	Missouri Southern	21-14	Northwestern, IA	1986	Linfield, OR	17-0	Baker, KS
1973	Northwestern, IA	10-3	Glenville St., WV	1987	Pacific Lutheran	16-16	WI-Stevens Pt.*
1974	Texas Lutheran	42-0	Missouri Valley	1988	Westminster, PA	21-14	WI-La Crosse
1975	Texas Lutheran	34-8	Calif. Lutheran	1989	Westminster, PA	51-30	WI-La Crosse
1976	Westminster, PA	20-13	Redlands, CA	1990	Peru St., NE	17-7	Westminster, PA
1977	Westminster, PA	17-9	Calif. Lutheran	1991	Georgetown, KY	28-20	Pacific Lutheran
1978	Concordia, MN	7-0	Findlay, OH	1992	Findlay, OH	26-13	Linfield, OR
1979	Findlay, OH	51-6	Northwestern, IA	1993	Pacific Lutheran	50-20	Westminster, PA
1980	Pacific Lutheran	38-10	Wilmington, OH	1994	Westminster, PA	27-7	Pacific Lutheran
1981	Austin College, TX	24-24	Concordia, MN	1995	Findlay, OH	21-21	Central Wash.
1982	Linfield, OR	33-15	Wm. Jewell, MO	1996	Sioux Falls, S.D.	47-25	W. Washington
1983	Northwestern, IA	25-21	Pacific Lutheran				

*Wisconsin-Stevens Point forfeited its entire 1987 schedule due to its use of an ineligible player.

Pro Football

Stifling defensive play, led by MVP **Ray Lewis,** carried
the Ravens to a giant win in Super Bowl XXXV.

Up for Grabs

*With no clear favorite,
the Ravens swooped in and
grabbed their first title.*

Chris Berman
is the host of ESPN's NFL Prime Time.

Even The Swami has a hard time figuring out the National Football League these days.

One year after the high-flying Rams stunned the football world with their explosive attack that led to a thrilling win in Super Bowl XXXIV, the upstart Baltimore Ravens pounded the opposition into submission with one of the best defensive performances in league history. They eventually rolled over the equally surprising New York Football Giants, 34-7, in Super Bowl XXXV.

Think about it. The Rams entered the 1999 season with the worst record in the 90's and walked (flew) away with a championship. The Ravens switched their quarterback at midseason (Tony Banks to Trent Dilfer) and failed to win their division, but became the second wild card team in four years to claim the Vince Lombardi Trophy.

Noted offensive mind Brian Billick must have bit his tongue a while as his club struggled to score points for most of the season. During one stretch, the Ravens went 21 consecutive quarters without reaching the end zone, and following a three-game losing streak sat at just 5-4. But Dilfer seemed to be the right medicine as Baltimore won its final 11 games (including playoffs) with the much-maligned former Buccaneer, and irony of ironies saw Dilfer and company win the Super Bowl in Tampa.

The postseason included a win over the Broncos, as well as road victories at Tennessee (24-10) and Oakland (16-3)—the latter in the AFC title game—as Baltimore allowed just 23 points and one offensive touchdown in four post-season victories.

The Ravens' unexpected title run epitomized what has been a recent trend in the NFL. Unpredictability. Over the last four seasons, 21 different teams have won division titles, and all but five of the 31 clubs have made it to the playoffs. Teams like the Saints (1992) and Raiders (1993) ended long postseason droughts, while Andy Reid's Eagles

AP/Wide World Photos

*Giants QB **Kerry Collins** couldn't escape the immense pressure from the Ravens defense in Super Bowl XXXV. He was sacked four times and threw four interceptions.*

more than doubled their five wins in '99 (11-5) and grabbed a wild card invitation. Even the Giants' Super Bowl appearance was a surprise considering the team was just 7-4 after 11 games. But head coach Jim Fassel assured us all that his club would be in the playoffs, and the G-Men reeled off seven straight wins, including a mind-numbing 41-0 rout of the favored Vikings in the NFC Championship Game, before running into those Ravens.

What about the defending NFC champions? There was talk of the Rams going undefeated following an explosive 6-0 start, but injuries to quarterback Kurt Warner and running back Marshall Faulk, combined with one of the worst defenses in the league, eventually did in Mike Martz's club.

The New Orleans Saints dethroned the Rams in the NFC West, becoming the fifth different team to win that division in the last five years. The Rams were relegated to wild card status and were eliminated from the playoffs by those same Saints.

As for Tennessee, Jeff Fisher's defending AFC champs finished with the NFL's best record (13-3) on the strength of the legs of Eddie George and the arm of Steve McNair but ran into that Baltimore buzzsaw in the playoffs. In just two seasons the Titans have turned Adelphia Coliseum into one of the league's best home-field advantages (16-2, including

*Rams running back **Marshall Faulk** breaks free and crosses the goal line against the Saints on Dec. 24. It was a familiar sight in 2000 as Faulk scored an NFL-record 26 touchdowns.*

playoffs), with their only two losses coming courtesy of Baltimore.

There were also tremendous individual performances to note. Despite missing two games, Faulk set a new NFL record by scoring 26 touchdowns and captured league MVP honors. And one of the league's most coveted records fell as Cincinnati's Corey Dillon ran through the Denver Broncos for 278 yards, eclipsing the mark (275) set by Hall of Famer Walter Payton in 1977. Unheralded Broncos back Mike Anderson set a rookie record by rushing for 251 yards against the Saints, breaking Dillon's mark (246) set in 1996. San Francisco wide receiver Terrell Owens set a new standard for receptions in a game, grabbing 20 against the Bears in December to break Tom Fears' mark of 18 set in 1950. Also, Vikings placekicker Gary Anderson became the NFL's all-time leader in scoring, ending the season with 2,059 points, joining George Blanda (2,002) as the only players in history to top the 2,000-point plateau.

The Rams won it all with offense in 1999. The Ravens got it done with defense in 2000. Different formulas, but identical results. Perhaps it will be a kicking game that leads a team to victory in Super Bowl XXXVI.

John Clayton's Ten Biggest Stories of the Year in Pro Football

10 ▪ What an opening! With Dennis Miller making his regular season Monday Night debut in Week 1, Kurt Warner and the Rams pick up where they left off with a 41-36 shootout win over the Broncos.

9 ▪ Cincinnati halfback Corey Dillon has the greatest rushing day in NFL history, gashing the Broncos for 278 yards on 22 carries in a 31-21 Bengals victory. Dillon tops Walter Payton's single-game mark of 275 yards set in 1977.

8 ▪ With the state of Indiana lamenting Bobby Knight's departure in early September, the Raiders catch the Colts napping before a distracted crowd at the RCA Dome. Rich Gannon runs for three TDs and rallies the Raiders from a 21-0 deficit to a 38-31 win.

7 ▪ In Week 2, Baltimore tight end Shannon Sharpe urges quarterback Tony Banks to get him the ball with the Ravens trailing Jacksonville 36-32 late in the fourth quarter. Banks obliges, tossing a 29-yard TD strike with 41 seconds remaining for a 39-36 Ravens win. Banks finishes with five TD passes (four in the second half) while Jags wideout Jimmy Smith gains 291 receiving yards.

6 ▪ Mike Anderson, a former Marine whose last venture into the Superdome was as a member of his high school band, runs for an NFL rookie record 251 yards against a great Saints defense to power the Broncos to a 38-23 victory in Week 14. Anderson is later named offensive rookie of the year, while filling in for injured running backs Terrell Davis and Olandis Gary.

5 ▪ Jets wide receiver Wayne Chrebet, who absorbed an offseason of criticism from his former teammate (now Buccaneer) Keyshawn Johnson, gets his revenge in Week 4. With 52 seconds remaining, Chrebet stuns Tampa Bay by catching an 18-yard halfback option pass from Curtis Martin to give the Jets a 21-17 come-from-behind victory.

4 ▪ Dolphins running back Lamar Smith becomes part of playoff history, rushing for 209 yards on a record 40 carries in a 23-17 overtime victory over the rival Colts. The Dolphins come back from a 14-0 deficit to tie the game behind sensational defense, Smith's running, and the clutch play of quarterback Jay Fiedler. They finally win on Smith's 17-yard TD run in overtime.

3 ■ Brian Griese stages one of the most courageous acts of leadership by fighting off the pain of a third degree right shoulder separation to lead the Broncos to a 27-24 victory over the Raiders in Week 11. Griese drives the team 44 yards in 66 seconds to set up the game-winning field goal. It is his last drive of the regular season.

2 ■ The longest game in Monday Night Football history turns into one of the best. The Jets, trailing the Dolphins 30-7 at the end of three quarters in the Meadowlands, score 30 fourth-quarter points. The capper comes when Vinny Testaverde tosses a touchdown pass to tackle Jumbo Elliott to send the game into overtime. The Jets eventually win 40-37 on a John Hall 40-yard field goal to complete the four-hour, 10-minute marathon.

1 ■ Certainly not known for his speed, Ravens tight end Shannon Sharpe hauls in a Trent Dilfer pass on 3rd-and-18, eludes Raiders strong safety Marquez Pope, and scampers 96 yards for a touchdown to break a scoreless tie in the AFC Championship Game. The Ravens knock out quarterback Rich Gannon and win 16-3 to advance to the Super Bowl, which they win going away.

The Defense Rests

The 2000 Ravens allowed fewer points than any other team in NFL history over a 16-game schedule (since 1978).

Year	Team	Points
2000	Baltimore Ravens*	165
1986	Chicago Bears	187
2000	Tennessee Titans	191
1978	Pittsburgh Steelers*	195
1985	Chicago Bears*	198
1978	Denver Broncos	198

* won Super Bowl

Troy's Story

Dallas quarterback Troy Aikman hung up his cleats after the 2000 season. Listed below are just some of the marks he left behind.

		Rank
Wins in a Decade	90	1st
Super Bowl Wins*	3	3rd
Completion Pct.	61.5	4th
Passing Yards	32,942	19th

* among starting quarterbacks

Running Mates

Just how important is a strong running attack? Listed are the most successful running back duos from 2000. Note that two of the top three teams met in Super Bowl XXXV.

	Team	Yards
J. Lewis/P. Holmes	Bal.	1,952
M. Anderson/T. Davis	Den.	1,782
T. Barber/R. Dayne	NYG	1,776
C. Dillon/B. Bennett	Cin.	1,759
E. James/L. Gordon	Ind.	1,722

2000-2001 Season in Review

 **information please® SPORTS ALMANAC**

Final NFL Standings

Division champions (*) and wild card playoff qualifiers (†) are noted; division champions with two best records received first round byes. Number of seasons listed after each head coach refers to latest tenure with club through 2000 season.

American Football Conference
Eastern Division

	W	L	T	PF	PA	vs Div	vs AFC
*Miami	11	5	0	323	226	5-3	9-3
†Indianapolis	10	6	0	429	326	5-3	8-4
NY Jets	9	7	0	321	321	6-2	6-6
Buffalo	8	8	0	315	350	2-6	6-6
New England	5	11	0	276	338	2-6	5-7

2000 Head Coaches: Mia—Dave Wannstedt (1st season); **Ind**—Jim Mora (3rd); **NY**—Al Groh (1st); **Buf**—Wade Phillips (3rd); **NE**—Bill Belichick (1st).
1999 Standings: 1. Indianapolis (13-3); 2. Buffalo (11-5); 3. Miami (9-7); 4. NY Jets (8-8); 5. New England (8-8).

Central Division

	W	L	T	PF	PA	vs Div	vs AFC
*Tennessee	13	3	0	346	191	8-2	9-3
†Baltimore	12	4	0	333	165	8-2	10-3
Pittsburgh	9	7	0	321	255	5-5	8-5
Jacksonville	7	9	0	367	327	5-5	5-7
Cincinnati	4	12	0	185	359	2-8	3-10
Cleveland	3	13	0	161	419	2-8	3-10

2000 Head Coaches: Ten—Jeff Fisher (7th season); **Bal**—Brian Billick (2nd); **Pit**—Bill Cowher (9th); **Jax**—Tom Coughlin (6th); **Cin**—Bruce Coslet (5th, 0-3) quit on Sept. 25, 2000 and was replaced by defensive coordinator Dick LeBeau (4-9); **Cle**—Chris Palmer (2nd).
1999 Standings: 1. Jacksonville (14-2); 2. Tennessee (13-3); 3. Baltimore (8-8); 4. Pittsburgh (6-10); 5. Cincinnati (4-12); 6. Cleveland (2-14).

Western Division

	W	L	T	PF	PA	vs Div	vs AFC
*Oakland	12	4	0	479	299	5-3	8-4
†Denver	11	5	0	485	369	6-2	8-4
Kansas City	7	9	0	355	354	5-3	5-7
Seattle	6	10	0	320	405	3-5	4-8
San Diego	1	15	0	269	440	1-7	1-11

2000 Head Coaches: Oak—Jon Gruden (3rd season); **Den**—Mike Shanahan (6th); **KC**—Gunther Cunningham (2nd); **Sea**—Mike Holmgren (2nd); **SD**—Mike Riley (2nd).
1999 Standings: 1. Seattle (9-7); 2. Kansas City (9-7); 3. San Diego (8-8); 4. Oakland (8-8); 5. Denver (6-10).

National Football Conference
Eastern Division

	W	L	T	PF	PA	vs Div	vs NFC
*NY Giants	12	4	0	328	246	7-1	9-3
†Philadelphia	11	5	0	351	245	5-3	8-4
Washington	8	8	0	281	269	3-5	6-6
Dallas	5	11	0	294	361	3-5	4-8
Arizona	3	13	0	210	443	2-6	2-10

2000 Head Coaches: NY—Jim Fassel (4th season); **Phi**—Andy Reid (2nd); **Wash**—Norv Turner (7th, 7-6) was fired on Dec. 4, 2000 and replaced by passing game coordinator Terry Robiskie (1-2); **Dal**—Dave Campo (1st); **Ariz**—Vince Tobin (5th, 2-5) was fired on Oct. 23, 2000 and replaced by defensive coordinator Dave McGinnis (1-8).
1999 Standings: 1. Washington (10-6); 2. Dallas (8-8); 3. NY Giants (7-9); Arizona (6-10); Philadelphia (5-11).

Central Division

	W	L	T	PF	PA	vs Div	vs NFC
*Minnesota	11	5	0	397	371	5-3	8-4
†Tampa Bay	10	6	0	388	269	4-4	7-5
Green Bay	9	7	0	353	323	5-3	8-4
Detroit	9	7	0	307	307	3-5	7-5
Chicago	5	11	0	216	355	3-5	3-9

2000 Head Coaches: Min—Dennis Green (9th season); **TB**—Tony Dungy (5th); **GB**—Mike Sherman (1st); **Det**—Bobby Ross (5-4) resigned on Nov. 6, 2000 and was replaced by assistant head coach Gary Moeller (4-3); **Chi**—Dick Jauron (2nd).
1999 Standings: 1. Tampa Bay (11-5); 2. Minnesota (10-6); 3. Detroit (8-8); 4. Green Bay (8-8); 5. Chicago (6-10).

Western Division

	W	L	T	PF	PA	vs Div	vs NFC
*New Orleans	10	6	0	354	305	7-1	9-3
†St. Louis	10	6	0	540	471	5-3	7-5
Carolina	7	9	0	310	310	4-4	5-7
San Francisco	6	10	0	388	422	1-7	4-8
Atlanta	4	12	0	252	413	3-5	3-9

2000 Head Coaches: NO—Jim Haslett (1st season); **St.L**—Mike Martz (1st); **Car**—George Seifert (2nd); **SF**—Steve Mariucci (4th); **Atl**—Dan Reeves (4th).
1999 Standings: 1. St. Louis (13-3); 2. Carolina (8-8); 3. Atlanta (5-11); 4. San Fran. (4-12); 5. N. Orleans (3-13).

2002 NFL Realignment

With the addition of the Houston Texans to the NFL beginning in the 2002 season, the NFL's 32 teams will be realigned into eight divisions of four teams each.

AFC
East: Buffalo, Miami, New England, NY Jets
South: Houston, Indianapolis, Jacksonville, Tennessee
North: Baltimore, Cincinnati, Cleveland, Pittsburgh
West: Denver, Kansas City, Oakland, San Diego

NFC
East: Dallas, NY Giants, Philadelphia, Washington
South: Atlanta, Carolina, New Orleans, Tampa Bay
North: Chicago, Detroit, Green Bay, Minnesota
West: Arizona, St. Louis, San Francisco, Seattle

NFL Regular Season Individual Leaders

(* indicates rookies)

Passing Efficiency

(Minimum of 224 attempts)

AFC	Att	Cmp	Cmp Pct	Yds	Yds/ Att	TD	Long	Int	Sack/Lost	Rating Points
Brian Griese, Den.	336	216	64.3	2688	8.00	19	61	4	17/139	102.9
Peyton Manning, Ind.	571	357	62.5	4413	7.73	33	78-td	15	20/131	94.7
Rich Gannon, Oak.	473	284	60.0	3430	7.25	28	84-td	11	28/124	92.4
Elvis Grbac, KC	547	326	59.6	4169	7.62	28	81-td	14	29/213	89.9
Doug Flutie, Buf.	231	132	57.1	1700	7.36	8	52	3	10/68	86.5
Mark Brunell, Jax	512	311	60.7	3640	7.11	20	67-td	14	54/289	84.0
Steve McNair, Ten.	396	248	62.6	2847	7.19	15	56-td	13	24/141	83.2
Rob Johnson, Buf.	306	175	57.2	2125	6.94	12	74-td	7	49/292	82.2
Gus Frerotte, Den.	232	138	59.5	1776	7.66	9	44	8	12/77	82.1
Drew Bledsoe, NE	531	312	58.8	3291	6.20	17	59	13	45/264	77.3
Trent Dilfer, Bal.	226	134	59.3	1502	6.65	12	59-td	11	23/135	76.6
Jon Kitna, Sea.	418	259	62.0	2658	6.36	18	71	19	33/166	75.6
Jay Fiedler, Mia.	357	204	57.1	2402	6.73	14	61	14	23/129	74.5
Kordell Stewart, Pit.	289	151	52.2	1860	6.44	11	45-td	8	30/150	73.6
Tony Banks, Bal.	274	150	54.7	1578	5.76	8	53-td	8	20/152	69.3

NFC	Att	Cmp	Cmp Pct	Yds	Yds/ Att	TD	Long	Int	Sack/Lost	Rating Points
Trent Green, St.L	240	145	60.4	2063	8.60	16	64	5	24/145	101.8
Kurt Warner, St.L	347	235	67.7	3429	9.88	21	85-td	18	20/115	98.3
Daunte Culpepper, Min.	474	297	62.7	3937	8.31	33	78-td	16	34/181	98.0
Jeff Garcia, SF	561	355	63.3	4278	7.63	31	69-td	10	24/155	97.6
Kerry Collins, NYG	529	311	58.8	3610	6.82	22	59	13	28/243	83.1
Jeff Blake, NO	302	184	60.9	2025	6.71	13	49-td	9	24/150	82.7
Steve Beuerlein, Car.	533	324	60.8	3730	7.00	19	54	18	62/331	79.7
Brett Favre, GB	580	338	58.3	3812	6.57	20	67-td	16	33/236	78.0
Donovan McNabb, Phi.	569	330	58.0	3365	5.91	21	70-td	13	45/262	77.8
Shaun King, TB	428	233	54.4	2769	6.47	18	75	13	37/240	75.8
Brad Johnson, Wash.	364	227	62.4	2505	6.88	11	77-td	15	20/150	75.6
Chris Chandler, Atl.	331	192	58.0	2236	6.76	10	55	12	40/251	73.5
Cade McNown, Chi.	280	154	55.0	1646	5.88	8	68-td	9	27/169	68.5
Charlie Batch, Det.	412	221	53.6	2489	6.04	13	59	15	41/242	67.3
Jake Plummer, Ari.	475	270	56.8	2946	6.20	13	70-td	21	22/151	66.0

Receptions

AFC	No	Yds	Avg	Long	TD
Marvin Harrison, Ind.	102	1413	13.9	78-td	14
Ed McCaffrey, Den.	101	1317	13.0	61	9
Rod Smith, Den.	100	1602	16.0	49	8
Eric Moulds, Buf.	94	1326	14.1	52	5
Keenan McCardell, Jax	94	1207	12.8	67-td	5
Tony Gonzalez, KC	93	1203	12.9	39	9
Jimmy Smith, Jax	91	1213	13.3	65-td	8
Richie Anderson, NYJ	88	853	9.7	41	2
Troy Brown, NE	83	944	11.4	44-td	4
Terry Glenn, NE	79	963	12.2	39-td	6
Derrick Alexander, KC	78	1391	17.8	81-td	10
Tim Brown, Oak.	76	1128	14.8	45	11
Freddie Jones, SD	71	766	10.8	44	5
Frank Wycheck, Ten.	70	636	9.1	26	4
Curtis Martin, NYJ	70	508	7.3	31	2

NFC	No	Yds	Avg	Long	TD
Mushin Muhammad, Car.	102	1183	11.6	36	6
Terrell Owens, SF	97	1451	15.0	69-td	13
Cris Carter, Min.	96	1274	13.3	53	9
Joe Horn, NO	94	1340	14.3	52	8
Isaac Bruce, St.L	87	1471	16.9	78-td	9
Torry Holt, St.L	82	1635	19.9	85-td	6
Marshall Faulk, St.L	81	830	10.2	72-td	8
Larry Centers, Wash.	80	600	7.5	26	3
Amani Toomer, NYG	78	1094	14.0	54-td	7
Randy Moss. Min.	77	1437	18.7	78-td	15
Jerry Rice, SF	75	805	10.7	68-td	7
Michael Pittman, Ari.	73	579	7.9	36-td	2
Ahman Green, GB	73	559	7.7	31	3
David Boston, Ari.	71	1156	16.3	70-td	7
Keyshawn Johnson, TB	71	874	12.3	38	8

Rushing

AFC	Att	Yds	Avg	Long	TD
Edgerrin James, Ind.	387	1709	4.4	30	13
Eddie George, Ten.	403	1509	3.7	35-td	14
Mike Anderson*, Den.	297	1500	5.1	80-td	15
Corey Dillon, Cin.	315	1435	4.6	80-td	7
Fred Taylor, Jax.	292	1399	4.8	71	12
Jamal Lewis*, Bal.	309	1364	4.4	45	6
Jerome Bettis, Pit.	355	1341	3.8	30	8
Ricky Watters, Sea.	278	1242	4.5	55	7
Curtis Martin, NYJ	316	1204	3.8	55	9
Lamar Smith, Mia.	309	1139	3.7	68-td	14
Tyrone Wheatley, Oak.	232	1046	4.5	80-td	9
Tony Richardson, KC	147	697	4.7	33	3
Shawn Bryson*, Buf.	161	591	3.7	24	0
Priest Holmes, Bal.	137	588	4.3	21	2
Kevin Faulk, NE	164	570	3.5	18	4

NFC	Att	Yds	Avg	Long	TD
Robert Smith, Min.	295	1521	5.2	72-td	7
Marshall Faulk, St.L	253	1359	5.4	36	18
Stephen Davis, Wash.	332	1318	4.0	50-td	11
Emmitt Smith, Dal.	294	1203	4.1	52	9
James Stewart, Det.	339	1184	3.5	34	10
Ahman Green, GB	263	1175	4.5	39-td	10
Charlie Garner, SF	258	1142	4.4	42	7
Warrick Dunn, TB	248	1133	4.6	70-td	8
James Allen, Chi.	290	1120	3.9	29	2
Jamal Anderson, Atl.	282	1024	3.6	42	6
Tiki Barber, NYG	213	1006	4.7	78-td	8
Ricky Williams, NO	248	1000	4.0	26-td	8
Ron Dayne*, NYG	228	770	3.4	50	5
Michael Pittman, Ari.	184	719	3.9	29	4
Donovan McNabb, Phi.	86	629	7.3	54	6

Denver Broncos
Brian Griese
Passing Efficiency

St. Louis Rams
Marshall Faulk
Scoring

Indianapolis Colts
Edgerrin James
Rushing

Green Bay Packers
Darren Sharper
Interceptions

All-Purpose Yardage

AFC	Rush	Rec	Ret	Total	NFC	Rush	Rec	Ret	Total
Derrick Mason, Ten. 1		895	1794	2690	MarTay Jenkins, Ari............-4		219	2187	2402
Edgerrin James, Ind. 1709		594	0	2303	Marshall Faulk, St.L 1359		830	18	2207
Charlie Rogers, Sea............0		0	1992	1992	Tiki Barber, NYG 1006		719	360	2085
Eddie George, Ten. 1509		453	0	1962	Desmond Howard, Det. 0		14	1858	1872
Kevin Faulk, NE 570		465	874	1909	Robert Smith, Min............1521		348	0	1869
Ricky Watters, Sea.........1242		613	0	1855	James Thrash, Wash........82		653	1106	1841
Curtis Martin, NYJ 1204		508	0	1712	Charlie Garner, SF.........1142		647	0	1789
Rod Smith, Den. 99		1602	0	1701	Glyn Milburn, Chi. 6		8	1768	1782
Mike Anderson*, Den. 1500		169	0	1669	Brian Mitchell, Phi. 187		89	1459	1735
Jamal Lewis*, Bal. 1364		296	0	1660	Ahman Green, GB.........1175		559	0	1734
Fred Taylor, Jax............1399		240	0	1639	Chad Morton*, NO.........136		213	1307	1656
Corey Dillon, Cin. 1435		158	0	1593	Torry Holt, St.L 7		1635	0	1642
Ronney Jenkins*, SD..........6		-1	1531	1538	Stephen Davis, Wash......1318		313	0	1631
Troy Brown, NE..............46		944	519	1509	Warrick Dunn, TB.........1133		422	0	1555
Deltha O'Neal*, Den..........0		0	1456	1456	Allen Rossum, GB 0		0	1536	1536

Ret column indicates all kickoff, punt, fumble and interception returns.

Scoring

Touchdowns

AFC	TD	Rush	Rec	Ret	Pts
Edgerrin James, Ind........18		13	5	0	110†
Eddie George, Ten..........16		14	2	0	96
Lamar Smith, Mia..........16		14	2	0	96
Mike Anderson*, Den......15		15	0	0	92†
Marvin Harrison, Ind.......14		0	14	0	84
Fred Taylor, Jax 14		12	2	0	84
Tim Brown, Oak............11		0	11	0	66
Curtis Martin, NYJ 11		9	2	0	66
Derrick Alexander, KC 10		0	10	0	60
Tyrone Wheatley, Oak......10		9	1	0	60
Ed McCaffrey, Den..........9		0	9	0	56†
Tony Gonzalez, KC..........9		0	9	0	54
Rod Smith, Den...........9		1	8	0	54
Ricky Watters, Sea..........9		7	2	0	54

NFC	TD	Rush	Rec	Ret	Pts
Marshall Faulk, St.L........26		18	8	0	160&
Randy Moss, Min...........15		0	15	0	92†
Terrell Owens, SF 13		0	13	0	80†
Ahman Green, GB 13		10	3	0	78
James Stewart, Det..........11		10	1	0	72@
Stephen Davis, Wash. 11		11	0	0	66
Charlie Garner, SF 10		7	3	0	60
Robert Smith, Min..........10		7	3	0	60

Seven tied with 9 TDs each for 54 pts.

† Includes one 2-point conversion.

& Includes two 2-point conversions.

@ Includes three 2-point conversions.

Kickers

AFC	PAT	FG	Long	Pts
Matt Stover, Bal. 30/30	35/39	51	135
Mike Vanderjagt, Ind.......46/46	25/27	48	121
Al Del Greco, Ten..........37/38	27/33	50	118
Olindo Mare, Mia. 33/34	28/31	49	117
Sebastian Janikowski*, Oak..46/46	22/32	54	112
Steve Christie, Buf...........31/31	26/35	48	109
Kris Brown, Pit............32/33	25/30	52	107
Adam Vinatieri, NE 25/25	27/33	53	106
Mike Hollis, Jax 33/33	24/26	51	105
Jason Elam, Den...........49/49	18/24	51	103
John Hall, NYJ 30/30	21/32	51	93
John Carney, SD 27/27	18/25	54	81

Two tied with 70 pts each.

NFC	PAT	FG	Long	Pts
Ryan Longwell, GB 32/32	33/38	52	131
Martin Gramatica, TB 42/42	28/34	55	126
Joe Nedney, Den.-Car.......24/24	34/38	52	126
David Akers, Phi...........34/36	29/33	51	121
Gary Anderson, Min. 45/45	22/23	49	111
Tim Seder*, Dal...........27/27	25/33	48	108
Doug Brien, NO 37/37	23/29	48	106
Jason Hanson, Det. 29/29	24/30	54	101
Morten Andersen, Atl........23/23	25/31	51	98
Jeff Wilkins, St.L...........38/38	17/17	51	89
Wade Richey, SF 43/45	15/22	47	88
Brad Daluiso, NYG 34/34	17/23	46	85
Paul Edinger*, Chi..........21/21	21/27	54	84

NFL Regular Season Individual Leaders (Cont.)

Interceptions

AFC	No	Yds	Long	TD
Samari Rolle, Ten.	7	140	81-td	1
Brian Walker, Mia.	7	80	31	0
Eric Allen, Oak.	6	145	50-td	3
Victor Green, NYJ	6	144	43	1
Duane Starks, Bal.	6	125	64	0
Terrell Buckley, Den.	6	110	33	1
Rodney Harrison, SD	6	97	63-td	1
William Thomas, Oak.	6	68	46-td	1

NFC	No	Yds	Long	TD
Darren Sharper, GB	9	109	47	0
Dexter McCleon, St.L	8	28	23	0
Donnie Abraham, TB	7	82	23	0
Kurt Schulz, Det.	7	53	19	0

Four tied with 4 Ints. each.

Sacks

AFC	No
Trace Armstrong, Mia.	16.5
Jason Taylor, Mia.	14.5
Eric Hicks, KC	14.0
Jason Gildon, Pit.	13.5
Trevor Pryce, Den.	12.0
Jevon Kearse, Ten.	11.5

NFC	No
La'Roi Glover, NO	17.0
Warren Sapp, TB	16.5
Hugh Douglas, Phi.	15.0
Marcus Jones, TB	13.0
Marco Coleman, Wash.	12.0
Joe Johnson, NO	12.0

Punting

AFC	No	Yds	Lg	Avg	In20
Darren Bennett, SD	92	4248	66	46.2	23
Shane Lechler*, Oak.	65	2984	69	45.9	24
Chris Gardocki, Cle.	108	4919	67	45.5	25
Tom Tupa, NYJ.	83	3714	70	44.7	18
Hunter Smith, Ind.	65	2906	65	44.7	20

NFC	No	Yds	Lg	Avg	In20
Mitch Berger, Min.	62	2773	60	44.7	16
Scott Player, Ari.	65	2871	55	44.2	17
John Jett, Det.	93	4044	59	43.5	33
Micah Knorr*, Dal.	58	2485	60	42.8	12
Sean Landeta, Phi.	86	3635	60	42.3	23

Punt Returns

(Minimum of 20 returns)

AFC	No	Yds	Avg	Long	TD
Jermaine Lewis, Bal.	36	578	16.1	89-td	2
Charlie Rogers, Sea.	26	363	14.0	43	0
Derrick Mason, Ten.	51	662	13.0	69-td	1
Hank Poteat*, Pit.	36	467	13.0	54	1
Troy Brown, NE.	39	504	12.9	66-td	1

NFC	No	Yds	Avg	Long	TD
Az-Zahir Hakim, St.L.	32	489	15.3	86-td	1
Desmond Howard, Det.	31	457	14.7	95-td	1
Wane McGarity, Dal.	30	353	11.8	64-td	2
Brian Mitchell, Phi.	32	335	10.5	72-td	1
Tim Dwight, Atl.	33	309	9.4	70-td	1

Kickoff Returns

(Minimum of 20 returns)

AFC	No	Yds	Avg	Long	TD
Derrick Mason, Ten.	42	1132	27.0	66	0
Kevin Williams, NYJ-Mia.	24	615	25.6	97-td	1
Autry Denson, Mia.	20	495	24.8	56	0
Charlie Rogers, Sea.	66	1629	24.7	81-td	1
David Dunn, Oak.	44	1073	24.4	88-td	1

NFC	No	Yds	Avg	Long	TD
Darrick Vaughn*, Atl.	39	1082	27.7	100-td	3
MarTay Jenkins, Ari.	82	2186	26.7	98-td	1
Allen Rossum, GB	50	1288	25.8	92-td	1
Desmond Howard, Det.	57	1401	24.6	70	0
Tony Horne, St.L	57	1379	24.2	103-td	1

Single Game Highs

Passing

AFC	Cmp/Att	Yds	TD
Elvis Grbac, KC vs. Oak. (11/5)	39/53	504	2
Vinny Testaverde, NYJ vs. Bal. (12/24)	36/69	481	2
Gus Frerotte, Den. vs. SD (11/19)	36/58	462	5
Peyton Manning, Ind. vs. Jax (9/25)	23/36	440	4
Mark Brunell, Jax vs. Bal. (9/10)	28/50	386	1

NFC	Cmp/Att	Yds	TD
Kurt Warner, St.L vs. Den. (9/4)	25/35	441	3
Aaron Brooks, NO vs. Den. (12/3)	30/48	441	2
Trent Green, St.L vs. Car. (11/5)	29/42	431	2
Jeff Garcia, SF vs. Chi. (12/17)	36/44	402	2
Kurt Warner, St.L vs. SF (9/17)	23/34	394	2

Rushing

AFC	Car	Yds	TD
Corey Dillon, Cin. vs. Den. (10/22)	22	278	2
Mike Anderson*, Den. vs. NO (12/3)	37	251	4
Fred Taylor, Jax vs. Pit. (11/19)	30	234	3
Edgerrin James, Ind. vs. Sea. (10/15)	38	219	3
Corey Dillon, Cin. vs. Ari. (12/3)	35	216	1

NFC	Car	Yds	TD
Marshall Faulk, St.L vs. NO (12/24)	32	220	2
Warrick Dunn, TB vs. Dal. (12/3)	22	210	2
Marshall Faulk, St.L vs. Atl. (10/15)	25	208	1
Charlie Garner, SF vs. Dal. (9/24)	36	201	1
Duce Staley, Phi. vs. Dal. (9/3)	26	201	1

Receiving Yards

AFC	Ct	Yds	TD
Jimmy Smith, Jax vs. Bal. (9/10)	15	291	3
Rod Smith, Den. vs. SD (11/19)	11	187	1
Tim Brown, Oak. vs. SF (10/8)	7	172	2
Eric Moulds, Buf. vs. SD (10/15)	11	170	0
Rod Smith, Den. vs. NE (10/1)	13	160	0

NFC	Ct	Yds	TD
Terrell Owens, SF vs. Chi. (12/17)	20	283	1
Albert Connell, Wash. vs. Jax (10/22)	7	211	3
Amani Toomer, NYG vs. Jax (12/23)	8	193	1
Torry Holt, St.L vs. Atl. (9/24)	3	189	2
Isaac Bruce, St.L vs. SF (9/17)	8	188	1

NFL Bests

Longest Field Goal
55 yds. . . . . Martin Gramatica, TB vs. Det. (10/19)

Longest Run from Scrimmage
85 yds. . . . . Brian Mitchell, Phi. vs. Atl. (10/1) TD

Longest Pass Play
85 yds . . . Kurt Warner to Torry Holt, St.L vs. Atl. (9/24) TD

Longest Interception Return
101 yds . . . . Bryant Westbrook, Det. vs. NE (11/23) TD

Longest Punt Return
95 yds . . . . Desmond Howard, Det. vs. NO (9/3) TD

Longest Kickoff Return
103 yds . . . . Tony Horne, St.L vs. Atl. (10/15) TD

NFL Regular Season Team Leaders

Offense

AFC	Points For	Avg	Yardage Rush	Pass	Total	Avg
Denver	485	30.3	2324	4243	6567	410.4
Indianapolis	429	26.8	1859	4282	6141	383.8
Oakland	479	29.9	2470	3306	5776	361.0
Jacksonville	367	22.9	2032	3658	5690	355.6
Kansas City	355	22.2	1465	4149	5614	350.9
Buffalo	315	19.7	1922	3576	5498	343.6
NY Jets	321	20.1	1471	3924	5395	337.2
Tennessee	346	21.6	2085	3265	5350	334.4
Baltimore	333	20.8	2199	2815	5014	313.4
Pittsburgh	321	20.1	2248	2518	4766	297.9
Seattle	320	20.0	1720	2960	4680	292.5
New England	276	17.3	1390	3181	4571	285.7
Miami	323	20.2	1894	2567	4461	278.8
San Diego	269	16.8	1062	3238	4300	268.8
Cincinnati	185	11.6	2314	1946	4260	266.3
Cleveland	161	10.1	1085	2445	3530	220.6

NFC	Points For	Avg	Yardage Rush	Pass	Total	Avg
St. Louis	540	33.8	1843	5232	7075	442.2
San Francisco	388	24.3	1801	4239	6040	377.5
Minnesota	397	24.8	2129	3832	5961	372.6
New Orleans	354	22.1	2068	3329	5397	337.3
Washington	281	17.6	1748	3648	5396	337.3
NY Giants	328	20.5	2009	3367	5376	336.0
Green Bay	353	22.1	1643	3678	5321	332.6
Philadelphia	351	21.9	1882	3124	5006	312.9
Carolina	310	19.4	1186	3468	4654	290.9
Tampa Bay	388	24.3	2066	2583	4649	290.6
Chicago	216	13.5	1736	2805	4541	283.8
Arizona	210	13.1	1278	3250	4528	283.0
Dallas	294	18.4	1953	2523	4476	279.8
Detroit	307	19.2	1747	2675	4422	276.4
Atlanta	252	15.8	1214	2780	3994	249.6

Defense

AFC	Points Opp	Avg	Yardage Rush	Pass	Total	Avg
Tennessee	191	11.9	1390	2424	3814	238.4
Baltimore	165	10.3	970	2997	3967	247.9
Buffalo	350	21.9	1559	2867	4426	276.6
Miami	226	14.1	1736	2900	4636	289.8
Pittsburgh	255	15.9	1693	3020	4713	294.6
NY Jets	321	20.1	1888	2932	4820	301.3
Jacksonville	327	20.4	1685	3160	4845	302.8
San Diego	440	27.5	1422	3537	4959	309.9
Oakland	299	18.7	1551	3698	5249	328.1
Kansas City	354	22.1	1822	3471	5293	330.8
New England	338	21.1	1831	3522	5353	334.6
Indianapolis	326	20.4	1935	3422	5357	334.8
Cincinnati	359	22.4	1925	3562	5487	342.9
Denver	369	23.1	1598	3946	5544	346.5
Cleveland	419	26.2	2505	3138	5643	352.7
Seattle	405	25.3	2454	3937	6391	399.4

NFC	Points Opp	Avg	Yardage Rush	Pass	Total	Avg
Washington	269	16.8	1853	2621	4474	279.6
NY Giants	246	15.4	1156	3390	4546	284.1
New Orleans	305	19.1	1672	3071	4743	296.4
Tampa Bay	269	16.8	1648	3152	4800	300.0
Philadelphia	245	15.3	1830	2990	4820	301.3
Detroit	307	19.2	1823	3210	5033	314.6
Green Bay	323	20.2	1618	3451	5069	316.8
Chicago	355	22.2	1827	3407	5234	327.1
Dallas	361	22.3	2637	2692	5329	333.1
St. Louis	471	29.4	1697	3797	5494	343.4
Atlanta	413	25.8	1983	3624	5607	350.4
Carolina	310	19.4	1944	3712	5656	353.5
Minnesota	371	23.2	1788	3913	5701	356.3
San Francisco	422	26.4	1794	3915	5709	356.8
Arizona	443	27.7	2609	3128	5737	358.6

Offensive Downs

AFC	Tot	First Downs Rush	Pass	Pen	3rd Downs Made	All	Pct	4th Downs Made	All	Pct
Denver	383	124	223	36	97	218	44.5	9	17	52.9
Indianapolis	357	111	213	33	94	201	46.8	9	10	90.0
Oakland	337	128	177	32	89	206	43.2	3	8	37.5
Kansas City	321	84	207	30	75	204	36.8	4	13	30.8
Jacksonville	318	109	193	16	100	235	42.6	5	14	35.7
Buffalo	309	111	174	24	92	247	37.2	9	12	75.0
NY Jets	308	84	192	32	89	233	38.2	11	17	64.7
Tennessee	299	107	167	25	97	228	42.5	4	11	36.4
Baltimore	288	116	156	16	95	236	40.3	1	6	16.7
New England	283	80	172	31	82	234	35.0	13	26	50.0
Pittsburgh	283	124	128	31	86	229	37.6	5	10	50.0
Seattle	281	98	168	15	83	205	40.5	7	14	50.0
Cincinnati	254	119	109	26	77	227	33.9	10	25	40.0
Miami	251	104	122	25	75	214	35.0	4	6	66.7
San Diego	251	63	156	32	72	219	32.9	3	14	21.4
Cleveland	176	53	110	13	58	210	27.6	6	19	31.6

NFC	Tot	First Downs Rush	Pass	Pen	3rd Downs Made	Att	Pct	4th Downs Made	Att	Pct
St. Louis	380	112	247	21	86	181	47.5	8	13	61.5
San Francisco	334	98	211	25	84	202	41.6	10	20	50.0
Minnesota	319	107	193	19	86	188	45.7	8	13	61.5
Green Bay	315	88	197	30	85	218	39.0	7	12	58.3
New Orleans	312	117	169	26	97	227	42.7	10	17	58.8
NY Giants	310	100	195	15	92	229	40.2	7	15	46.7
Washington	308	98	185	25	84	213	39.4	4	10	40.0
Carolina	304	63	201	40	78	198	39.4	8	14	57.1
Philadelphia	295	88	182	25	90	224	40.2	7	11	63.6
Dallas	376	116	128	32	70	195	35.9	10	18	55.6
Tampa Bay	275	111	144	20	66	198	33.3	5	12	41.7
Detroit	264	101	143	20	72	224	32.1	6	13	46.2
Atlanta	256	65	156	35	57	197	28.9	6	13	46.2
Arizona	253	71	156	26	75	199	37.7	8	27	29.6
Chicago	239	89	143	7	67	222	30.2	11	25	44.0

AFC Team by Team Results
(*) indicates overtime game

Baltimore Ravens (12-4)

at Pittsburgh	W, 16-0
Jacksonville	W, 39-36
at Miami	L, 6-19
Cincinnati	W, 37-0
at Cleveland	W, 12-0
at Jacksonville	W, 15-10
at Washington	L, 3-10
Tennessee	L, 6-14
Pittsburgh	L, 6-9
at Cincinnati	W, 27-7
at Tennessee	W, 24-23
Dallas	W, 27-0
Cleveland	W, 44-7
OPEN	—
San Diego	W, 24-3
at Arizona	W, 13-7
NY Jets	W, 34-20

Buffalo Bills (8-8)

Tennessee	W, 16-13
Green Bay	W, 27-18
at NY Jets	L, 14-27
OPEN	—
Indianapolis	L, 16-18
at Miami	L, 13-22
San Diego	W, 27-24*
at Minnesota	L, 27-31
NY Jets	W, 23-20
at N. England	W, 16-13*
Chicago	W, 20-3
at Kansas City	W, 21-17
at Tampa Bay	L, 17-31
Miami	L, 6-33
at Indianapolis	L, 20-44
N. England	L, 10-13*
at Seattle	W, 42-23

Cincinnati Bengals (4-12)

OPEN	—
Cleveland	L, 7-24
at Jacksonville	L, 0-13
at Baltimore	L, 0-37
Miami	L, 16-31
Tennessee	L, 14-23
at Pittsburgh	L, 0-15
Denver	W, 31-21
at Cleveland	W, 12-3
Baltimore	L, 7-27
at Dallas	L, 6-23
at N. England	L, 13-16
Pittsburgh	L, 28-48
Arizona	W, 24-13
at Tennessee	L, 3-35
Jacksonville	W, 17-14
at Philadelphia	L, 7-16

Cleveland Browns (3-13)

Jacksonville	L, 7-27
at Cincinnati	W, 24-7
Pittsburgh	W, 23-20
at Oakland	L, 10-36
Baltimore	L, 0-12
at Arizona	L, 21-29
at Denver	L, 10-44
at Pittsburgh	L, 0-22
Cincinnati	L, 3-12
NY Giants	L, 3-24
N. England	W, 19-11
at Tennessee	L, 10-24
at Baltimore	L, 7-44
at Jacksonville	L, 0-48
Philadelphia	L, 24-35
Tennessee	L, 0-24
OPEN	—

Denver Broncos (11-5)

at St. Louis	L, 36-41
Atlanta	W, 42-14
at Oakland	W, 33-24
Kansas City	L, 22-23
N. England	L, 19-28
at San Diego	W, 21-7
Cleveland	W, 44-10
at Cincinnati	L, 21-31
OPEN	—
at NY Jets	W, 30-23
Oakland	W, 27-24
San Diego	W, 38-37
at Seattle	W, 38-31
at New Orleans	W, 38-23
Seattle	W, 31-24
at Kansas City	L, 7-20
San Francisco	W, 38-9

Indianapolis Colts (10-6)

at Kansas City	W, 27-14
Oakland	L, 31-38
OPEN	—
Jacksonville	W, 43-14
at Buffalo	W, 18-16
at N. England	L, 16-24
at Seattle	W, 37-24
N. England	W, 30-23
Detroit	W, 30-18
at Chicago	L, 24-27
NY Jets	W, 23-15
at Green Bay	L, 24-26
Miami	L, 14-17
at NY Jets	L, 17-27
Buffalo	W, 44-20
at Miami	W, 20-13
Minnesota	W, 31-10

Jacksonville Jaguars (7-9)

at Cleveland	W, 27-7
at Baltimore	L, 36-39
Cincinnati	W, 13-0
at Indianapolis	L, 14-43
Pittsburgh	L, 13-24
Baltimore	L, 10-15
at Tennessee	L, 13-27
Washington	L, 16-35
at Dallas	W, 23-17*
OPEN	—
Seattle	L, 21-28
at Pittsburgh	W, 34-24
Tennessee	W, 16-13
Cleveland	W, 48-0
Arizona	W, 44-10
at Cincinnati	L, 14-17
at NY Giants	L, 25-28

Kansas City Chiefs (7-9)

Indianapolis	L, 14-27
at Tennessee	L, 14-17*
San Diego	W, 42-10
at Denver	W, 23-22
Seattle	W, 24-17
OPEN	—
Oakland	L, 17-20
St. Louis	W, 54-34
at Seattle	W, 24-19
at Oakland	L, 31-49
at San Fran.	L, 7-21
Buffalo	L, 17-21
at San Diego	L, 16-17
at N. England	L, 24-30
Carolina	W, 15-14
Denver	W, 20-7
at Atlanta	L, 13-29

Miami Dolphins (11-5)

Seattle	W, 23-0
at Minnesota	L, 7-13
Baltimore	W, 19-6
N. England	W, 10-3
at Cincinnati	W, 31-16
Buffalo	W, 22-13
OPEN	—
at NY Jets	L, 37-40*
Green Bay	W, 28-20
at Detroit	W, 23-8
at San Diego	W, 17-7
NY Jets	L, 3-20
at Indianapolis	W, 17-14
at Buffalo	W, 33-6
Tampa Bay	L, 13-16
Indianapolis	L, 13-20
at N. England	W, 27-24

New England Patriots (5-11)

Tampa Bay	L, 16-21
at NY Jets	L, 19-20
Minnesota	L, 13-21
at Miami	L, 3-10
at Denver	W, 28-19
Indianapolis	W, 24-16
NY Jets	L, 17-34
at Indianapolis	L, 23-30
OPEN	—
Buffalo	L, 13-16*
at Cleveland	L, 11-19
Cincinnati	W, 16-13
at Detroit	L, 9-34
Kansas City	W, 30-24
at Chicago	L, 17-24
at Buffalo	W, 13-10*
Miami	L, 24-27

New York Jets (9-7)

at Green Bay	W, 20-16
N. England	W, 20-19
Buffalo	W, 27-14
at Tampa Bay	W, 21-17
OPEN	—
Pittsburgh	L, 3-20
at N. England	W, 34-17
Miami	W, 40-37*
at Buffalo	L, 20-23
Denver	L, 23-30
at Indianapolis	L, 15-23
at Miami	W, 20-3
Chicago	W, 17-10
Indianapolis	W, 27-17
at Oakland	L, 7-31
Detroit	L, 7-10
at Baltimore	L, 20-34

Oakland Raiders (12-4)

San Diego	W, 9-6
at Indianapolis	W, 38-31
Denver	L, 24-33
Cleveland	W, 36-10
OPEN	—
at San Fran.	W, 34-28*
at Kansas City	W, 20-17
Seattle	W, 31-3
at San Diego	W, 15-13
Kansas City	W, 49-31
at Denver	L, 24-27
at New Orleans	W, 31-22
Atlanta	W, 41-14
at Pittsburgh	L, 20-21
NY Jets	W, 31-7
at Seattle	L, 24-27
Carolina	W, 52-9

Pittsburgh Steelers (9-7)

Baltimore	L, 0-16
OPEN	—
at Cleveland	L, 20-23
Tennessee	L, 20-23
at Jacksonville	W, 24-13
at NY Jets	W, 20-3
Cincinnati	W, 15-0
Cleveland	W, 22-0
at Baltimore	W, 9-6
at Tennessee	L, 7-9
Philadelphia	L, 23-26*
Jacksonville	L, 24-34
at Cincinnati	W, 48-28
Oakland	W, 21-20
at NY Giants	L, 10-30
Washington	W, 24-3
at San Diego	W, 34-21

San Diego Chargers (1-15)

at Oakland	L, 6-9
New Orleans	L, 27-28
at Kansas City	L, 10-42
Seattle	L, 12-20
at St. Louis	L, 31-57
Denver	L, 7-21
at Buffalo	L, 24-27*
OPEN	—
Oakland	L, 13-15
at Seattle	L, 15-17
Miami	L, 7-17
at Denver	L, 37-38
Kansas City	W, 17-16
San Fran.	L, 17-45
at Baltimore	L, 3-24
at Carolina	L, 22-30
Pittsburgh	L, 21-34

Seattle Seahawks (6-10)

at Miami	L, 0-23
St. Louis	L, 34-37
New Orleans	W, 20-10
at San Diego	W, 20-12
at Kansas City	L, 17-24
at Carolina	L, 3-26
Indianapolis	L, 24-37
at Oakland	L, 3-31
Kansas City	L, 19-24
San Diego	W, 17-15
at Jacksonville	W, 28-21
OPEN	—
Denver	L, 31-38
at Atlanta	W, 30-10
at Denver	L, 24-31
Oakland	W, 27-24
Buffalo	L, 23-42

Tennessee Titans (13-3)

at Buffalo	L, 13-16
Kansas City	W, 17-14*
OPEN	—
at Pittsburgh	W, 23-20
NY Giants	W, 28-14
at Cincinnati	W, 23-14
Jacksonville	W, 27-13
at Baltimore	W, 14-6
at Washington	W, 27-21
Pittsburgh	W, 9-7
Baltimore	L, 23-24
Cleveland	W, 24-10
at Jacksonville	L, 13-16
at Philadelphia	W, 15-13
Cincinnati	W, 35-3
at Cleveland	W, 24-0
Dallas	W, 31-0

NFC Team by Team Results

(*) indicates overtime game

Arizona Cardinals (3-13)

at NY Giants	L, 16-21
Dallas	W, 32-31
OPEN	—
Green Bay	L, 3-29
at San Fran.	L, 20-27
Cleveland	W, 29-21
Philadelphia	L, 14-33
at Dallas	L, 7-48
New Orleans	L, 10-21
Washington	W, 16-15
at Minnesota	L, 14-31
at Philadelphia	L, 9-34
NY Giants	L, 7-31
at Cincinnati	L, 13-24
at Jacksonville	L, 10-44
Baltimore	L, 7-13
at Washington	L, 3-20

Atlanta Falcons (4-12)

San Fran.	W, 36-28
at Denver	L, 14-42
at Carolina	W, 15-10
St. Louis	L, 20-41
at Philadelphia	L, 10-38
NY Giants	L, 6-13
at St. Louis	L, 29-45
New Orleans	L, 19-21
Carolina	W, 13-12
Tampa Bay	L, 14-27
at Detroit	L, 10-13
at San Fran.	L, 6-16
at Oakland	L, 14-41
Seattle	L, 10-30
OPEN	—
at New Orleans	L, 7-23
Kansas City	W, 29-13

Carolina Panthers (7-9)

at Washington	L, 17-20
at San Fran.	W, 38-22
Atlanta	L, 10-15
OPEN	—
Dallas	L, 13-16*
Seattle	W, 26-3
at New Orleans	L, 6-24
San Fran.	W, 34-16
at Atlanta	L, 12-13
at St. Louis	W, 27-24
New Orleans	L, 10-20
at Minnesota	L, 17-31
Green Bay	W, 31-14
St. Louis	W, 16-3
at Kansas City	L, 14-15
San Diego	W, 30-22
at Oakland	L, 9-52

Chicago Bears (5-11)

at Minnesota	L, 27-30
at Tampa Bay	L, 0-41
NY Giants	L, 7-14
Detroit	L, 14-21
at Green Bay	W, 27-24
New Orleans	L, 10-31
Minnesota	L, 16-28
at Philadelphia	L, 9-13
OPEN	—
Indianapolis	W, 27-24
at Buffalo	L, 3-20
Tampa Bay	W, 13-10
at NY Jets	L, 10-17
Green Bay	L, 6-28
N. England	W, 24-17
at San Fran.	L, 0-17
at Detroit	W, 23-20

Dallas Cowboys (5-11)

Philadelphia	L, 14-41
at Arizona	L, 31-32
at Washington	W, 27-21
San Fran.	L, 24-41
at Carolina	W, 16-13*
OPEN	—
at NY Giants	L, 14-19
Arizona	W, 48-7
Jacksonville	L, 17-23*
at Philadelphia	L, 13-16*
Cincinnati	W, 23-6
at Baltimore	L, 0-27
Minnesota	L, 15-27
at Tampa Bay	L, 7-27
Washington	W, 32-13
NY Giants	L, 13-17
at Tennessee	L, 0-31

Detroit Lions (9-7)

at New Orleans	W, 14-10
Washington	W, 15-10
Tampa Bay	L, 10-31
at Chicago	W, 21-14
Minnesota	L, 24-31
Green Bay	W, 31-24
OPEN	—
at Tampa Bay	W, 28-14
at Indianapolis	L, 18-30
Miami	L, 8-23
Atlanta	W, 13-10
at NY Giants	W, 31-21
N. England	W, 34-9
at Minnesota	L, 17-24
at Green Bay	L, 13-26
at NY Jets	W, 10-7
Chicago	L, 20-23

Green Bay Packers (9-7)

NY Jets	L, 16-20
at Buffalo	L, 18-27
Philadelphia	W, 6-3
at Arizona	W, 29-3
Chicago	L, 24-27
at Detroit	L, 24-31
San Fran.	W, 31-28
OPEN	—
at Miami	L, 20-28
Minnesota	W, 26-20*
at Tampa Bay	L, 15-20
Indianapolis	W, 26-24
at Carolina	L, 14-31
at Chicago	W, 28-6
Detroit	W, 26-13
at Minnesota	W, 33-28
Tampa Bay	W, 17-14*

Minnesota Vikings (11-5)

Chicago	W, 30-27
Miami	W, 13-7
at N. England	W, 21-13
OPEN	—
at Detroit	W, 31-24
Tampa Bay	W, 30-23
at Chicago	W, 28-16
Buffalo	W, 31-27
at Tampa Bay	L, 13-41
at Green Bay	L, 20-26*
Arizona	W, 31-14
Carolina	W, 31-17
at Dallas	W, 27-15
Detroit	W, 24-17
at St. Louis	L, 29-40
Green Bay	L, 28-33
at Indianapolis	L, 10-31

NFC Team by Team Results (Cont.)

New Orleans Saints (10-6)

Detroit	L, 10-14
at San Diego	W, 28-27
at Seattle	L, 10-20
Philadelphia	L, 7-21
OPEN	—
at Chicago	W, 31-10
Carolina	W, 24-6
at Atlanta	W, 21-19
at Arizona	W, 21-10
San Fran.	W, 31-15
at Carolina	W, 20-10
Oakland	L, 22-31
at St. Louis	W, 31-24
Denver	L, 23-38
at San Fran.	W, 31-27
Atlanta	W, 23-7
St. Louis	L, 21-26

New York Giants (12-4)

Arizona	W, 21-16
at Philadelphia	W, 33-18
at Chicago	W, 14-7
Washington	L, 6-16
at Tennessee	L, 14-28
at Atlanta	W, 13-6
Dallas	W, 19-14
OPEN	—
Philadelphia	W, 24-7
at Cleveland	W, 24-3
St. Louis	L, 24-38
Detroit	L, 21-31
at Arizona	W, 31-7
at Washington	W, 9-7
Pittsburgh	W, 30-10
at Dallas	W, 17-13
Jacksonville	W, 28-25

Philadelphia Eagles (11-5)

at Dallas	W, 41-14
NY Giants	L, 18-33
at Green Bay	L, 3-6
at New Orleans	W, 21-7
Atlanta	W, 38-10
Washington	L, 14-17
at Arizona	W, 33-14
Chicago	W, 13-9
at NY Giants	L, 7-24
Dallas	W, 16-13*
at Pittsburgh	W, 26-23*
Arizona	W, 34-9
at Washington	W, 23-20
Tennessee	L, 13-15
at Cleveland	W, 35-24
OPEN	—
Cincinnati	W, 16-7

St. Louis Rams (10-6)

Denver	W, 41-36
at Seattle	W, 37-34
San Fran.	W, 41-24
at Atlanta	W, 41-20
San Diego	W, 57-31
OPEN	—
Atlanta	W, 45-29
at Kansas City	L, 34-54
at San Fran.	W, 34-24
Carolina	L, 24-27
at NY Giants	W, 38-24
Washington	L, 20-33
New Orleans	L, 24-31
at Carolina	L, 3-16
Minnesota	W, 40-29
at Tampa Bay	L, 35-38
at New Orleans	W, 26-21

San Francisco 49ers (6-10)

at Atlanta	L, 28-36
Carolina	L, 22-38
at St. Louis	L, 24-41
at Dallas	W, 41-24
Arizona	W, 27-20
Oakland	L, 28-34*
at Green Bay	L, 28-31
at Carolina	L, 16-34
St. Louis	L, 24-34
at New Orleans	L, 15-31
Kansas City	W, 21-7
Atlanta	W, 16-6
OPEN	—
at San Diego	W, 45-17
New Orleans	L, 27-31
Chicago	W, 17-0
at Denver	L, 9-38

Tampa Bay Buccaneers (10-6)

at N. England	W, 21-16
Chicago	W, 41-0
at Detroit	W, 31-10
NY Jets	L, 17-21
at Washington	L, 17-20*
at Minnesota	L, 23-30
OPEN	—
Detroit	L, 14-28
Minnesota	W, 41-13
at Atlanta	W, 27-14
Green Bay	W, 20-15
at Chicago	L, 10-13
Buffalo	W, 31-17
Dallas	W, 27-7
at Miami	W, 16-13
St. Louis	W, 38-35
at Green Bay	L, 14-17*

Washington Redskins (8-8)

Carolina	W, 20-17
at Detroit	L, 10-15
Dallas	L, 21-27
at NY Giants	W, 16-6
Tampa Bay	W, 20-17*
at Philadelphia	W, 17-14
Baltimore	W, 10-3
at Jacksonville	W, 35-16
Tennessee	L, 21-27
at Arizona	L, 15-16
OPEN	—
at St. Louis	W, 33-20
Philadelphia	L, 20-23
NY Giants	L, 7-9
at Dallas	L, 13-32
at Pittsburgh	L, 3-24
Arizona	W, 20-3

Takeaways/Giveaways

AFC	Takeaways Int	Fum	Total	Giveaways Int	Fum	Total	Net Diff	NFC	Takeaways Int	Fum	Total	Giveaways Int	Fum	Total	Net Diff
Baltimore	23	26	49	19	7	26	+23	Tampa Bay	25	16	41	13	11	24	+17
Denver	27	17	44	12	13	25	+19	Detroit	25	17	42	19	12	31	+11
Oakland	21	16	37	11	9	20	+17	New Orleans	20	15	35	15	11	26	+9
Miami	28	13	41	17	9	26	+15	NY Giants	20	11	31	13	11	24	+7
Pittsburgh	17	18	35	10	11	21	+14	Carolina	17	21	38	19	16	35	+3
Buffalo	16	13	29	10	13	23	+6	Philadelphia	19	12	31	15	14	29	+2
Kansas City	15	14	29	15	11	26	+3	San Francisco	13	8	21	10	9	19	+2
Jacksonville	12	18	30	15	14	29	+1	Washington	17	16	33	21	12	33	0
Tennessee	17	13	30	16	14	30	0	Green Bay	21	7	28	16	17	33	-5
New England	10	13	23	15	10	25	-2	Atlanta	15	10	25	20	14	34	-9
Cleveland	12	13	25	19	9	28	-3	Chicago	11	9	20	16	13	29	-9
NY Jets	21	14	35	29	11	40	-5	Minnesota	8	10	18	18	10	28	-10
Indianapolis	14	8	22	15	14	29	-7	St. Louis	19	6	25	23	12	35	-10
Seattle	17	12	29	21	17	38	-9	Dallas	16	9	25	21	18	39	-14
Cincinnati	9	12	21	14	21	35	-14	Arizona	10	10	20	24	20	44	-24
San Diego	16	6	22	30	20	50	-28	TOTALS	256	177	433	263	200	463	-30
TOTALS	275	226	501	268	203	471	+30								

AFC Team by Team Statistics

Players with more than one team during the regular season are listed with club they ended season with; (*) indicates rookies.

Baltimore Ravens

Passing (5 Att)	Att	Cmp	Pct	Yds	TD	Rate
Tony Banks	.274	150	54.7	1578	8	69.3
Trent Dilfer	.226	134	59.3	1502	12	76.6

Interceptions: Dilfer 11, Banks 8.

Top Receivers	No	Yds	Avg	Long	TD
Shannon Sharpe	.67	810	12.1	59-td	5
Qadry Ismail	.49	655	13.4	53-td	5
Priest Holmes	.32	221	6.9	27	0
Travis Taylor*	.28	276	9.9	40	3
Jamal Lewis*	.27	296	11.0	45	0
Obafemi Ayanbadejo	.23	168	7.3	26	1

Top Rushers	Car	Yds	Avg	Long	TD
Jamal Lewis*	.309	1364	4.4	45	6
Priest Holmes	.137	588	4.3	21	2
Trent Dilfer	.20	75	3.8	19	0
Tony Banks	.19	57	3.0	10	0

Most Touchdowns	TD	Run	Rec	Ret	Pts
Jamal Lewis*	.6	6	0	0	38
Qadry Ismail	.5	0	5	0	30
Shannon Sharpe	.5	0	5	0	30
Jermaine Lewis	.3	0	1	2	18
Travis Taylor*	.3	0	3	0	18

2-Pt. Conversions: (2-2) Lewis, Ben Coates.

Kicking	PAT/Att	FG/Att	Lg	Pts
Matt Stover	.30/30	35/39	51	135

Punts (10 or more)	No	Yds	Long	Avg	In20
Kyle Richardson	.86	3457	55	40.2	35

Most Interceptions		Most Sacks	
Duane Starks	.6	Rob Burnett	.10.5

Buffalo Bills

Passing (5 Att)	Att	Cmp	Pct	Yds	TD	Rate
Rob Johnson	.306	175	57.2	2125	12	82.2
Doug Flutie	.231	132	57.1	1700	8	86.5

Interceptions: Johnson 7, Flutie 3.

Top Receivers	No	Yds	Avg	Long	TD
Eric Moulds	.94	1326	14.1	52	5
Peerless Price	.52	762	14.7	42	3
Jeremy McDaniel*	.43	697	16.2	74-td	4
Sammy Morris*	.37	268	7.2	24	1
Shawn Bryson*	.32	271	8.5	32	2
Jay Riemersma	.31	372	12.0	35	5
Bobby Collins	.6	72	12.0	23	0

Top Rushers	Car	Yds	Avg	Long	TD
Shawn Bryson*	.161	591	3.7	24	0
Antowain Smith	.101	354	3.5	59	4
Sammy Morris*	.93	341	3.7	32-td	5
Rob Johnson	.42	307	7.3	23	1

Most Touchdowns	TD	Run	Rec	Ret	Pts
Sammy Morris*	.6	5	1	0	36
Eric Moulds	.5	0	5	0	30
Jay Riemersma	.5	0	5	0	30
Antowain Smith	.4	4	0	0	24
Peerless Price	.3	0	3	0	18

2-Pt. Conversions: (1-3) Bryson.

Kicking	PAT/Att	FG/Att	Lg	Pts
Steve Christie	.31/31	26/35	48	109

Punts (10 or more)	No	Yds	Long	Avg	In20
Chris Mohr	.95	3661	57	38.5	19

Most Interceptions		Most Sacks	
Keion Carpenter	.5	Marcellus Wiley	.10.5

Cincinnati Bengals

Passing (5 Att)	Att	Cmp	Pct	Yds	TD	Rate
Akili Smith	.267	118	44.2	1253	3	52.8
Scott Mitchell	.187	89	47.6	966	3	50.8

Interceptions: Mitchell 8, Smith 6.

Top Receivers	No	Yds	Avg	Long	TD
Peter Warrick*	.51	592	11.6	46	4
Tony McGee	.26	309	11.9	39	1
Craig Yeast	.24	301	12.5	27	0
Danny Farmer*	.19	268	14.1	38	0
Brandon Bennett	.19	168	8.8	25	0
Corey Dillon	.18	158	8.8	31	0

Top Rushers	Car	Yds	Avg	Long	TD
Corey Dillon	.315	1435	4.6	80-td	7
Brandon Bennett	.90	324	3.6	37-td	3
Akili Smith	.41	232	5.7	21	0
Peter Warrick*	.16	148	9.3	77-td	2

Most Touchdowns	TD	Run	Rec	Ret	Pts
Corey Dillon	.7	7	0	0	42
Peter Warrick*	.7	2	4	1	42
Brandon Bennett	.3	3	0	0	18
Four tied with 1 each for 6 pts.					

2-Pt. Conversions: (0-0).

Kicking	PAT/Att	FG/Att	Lg	Pts
Neil Rackers*	.21/21	12/21	45	57

Punts (10 or more)	No	Yds	Long	Avg	In20
Daniel Pope	.94	3775	57	40.2	18

Most Interceptions		Most Sacks	
Tom Carter	.2	Steve Foley	.4
Takeo Spikes	.2	Oliver Gibson	.4
		Cory Hall	.4

Cleveland Browns

Passing (5 Att)	Att	Cmp	Pct	Yds	TD	Rate
Tim Couch	.215	137	63.7	1483	7	77.3
Doug Pederson	.210	117	55.7	1047	2	56.6
Spergon Wynn*	.54	22	40.7	167	0	41.2

Interceptions: Couch 9, Pederson 8, Wynn and Kevin Johnson 1.

Top Receivers	No	Yds	Avg	Long	TD
Kevin Johnson	.57	669	11.7	79	0
Dennis Northcutt*	.39	422	10.8	37	0
David Patten	.38	546	14.4	65	1
Travis Prentice*	.37	191	5.2	13	1
Aaron Shea*	.30	302	10.1	37	2
Marc Edwards	.16	128	8.0	21-td	2

Top Rushers	Car	Yds	Avg	Long	TD
Travis Prentice	.173	512	3.0	17	7
Errict Rhett	.71	258	3.6	42	0
Jamel White*	.47	145	3.1	14	0
Doug Pederson	.18	68	3.8	15	0

Most Touchdowns	TD	Run	Rec	Ret	Pts
Travis Prentice*	.8	7	1	0	48
Marc Edwards	.2	0	2	0	12
Aaron Shea*	.2	0	2	0	12
Five tied with 1 each for 6 pts.					

2-Pt. Conversions: (0-0).

Kicking	PAT/Att	FG/Att	Lg	Pts
Phil Dawson	.17/17	14/17	45	59

Punts (10 or more)	No	Yds	Long	Avg	In20
Chris Gardocki	.108	4919	67	45.5	25

Most Interceptions		Most Sacks	
Corey Fuller	.3	Keith McKenzie	.8

Denver Broncos

Passing (5 Att)	Att	Cmp	Pct	Yds	TD	Rate
Brian Griese	336	216	64.3	2688	19	102.9
Gus Frerotte	232	138	59.5	1776	9	82.1

Interceptions: Frerotte 8, Griese 4.

Top Receivers	No	Yds	Avg	Long	TD
Ed McCaffrey	101	1317	13.0	61	9
Rod Smith	100	1602	16.0	49	8
Dwayne Carswell	49	495	10.1	43-td	3
Desmond Clark	27	339	12.6	44	3
Mike Anderson*	23	169	7.3	18	0
Byron Chamberlain	22	283	12.9	38	1

Top Rushers	Car	Yds	Avg	Long	TD
Mike Anderson*	297	1487	5.0	80-td	15
Terrell Davis	78	282	3.6	24	2
KaRon Coleman*	54	183	3.4	24-td	1
Brian Griese	29	102	3.5	18	1
Rod Smith	6	99	16.5	50-td	1

Most Touchdowns	TD	Run	Rec	Ret	Pts
Mike Anderson*	15	15	0	0	92
Ed McCaffrey	9	0	9	0	56
Rod Smith	9	1	8	0	54
Dwayne Carswell	3	0	3	0	18
Desmond Clark	3	0	3	0	18

2-Pt. Conversions: (2-5) Anderson, McCaffrey.

Kicking	PAT/Att	FG/Att	Lg	Pts
Jason Elam	49/49	18/24	51	103

Signed: Joe Nedney on Sept. 12. **Released:** Nedney on Oct. 2 (see Carolina).

Punts (10 or more)	No	Yds	Long	Avg	In20
Tom Rouen	61	2455	62	40.2	18

Most Interceptions		Most Sacks	
Terrell Buckley	6	Trevor Pryce	12

Indianapolis Colts

Passing (5 Att)	Att	Cmp	Pct	Yds	TD	Rate
Peyton Manning	571	357	62.5	4413	33	94.7

Interceptions: Manning 14.

Top Receivers	No	Yds	Avg	Long	TD
Marvin Harrison	102	1413	13.9	78-td	14
Edgerrin James	63	594	9.4	60	5
Jerome Pathon	50	646	12.9	38	3
Ken Dilger	47	538	11.4	32	3
Terrence Wilkins	43	569	13.2	43-td	3
Marcus Pollard	30	439	14.6	50-td	3
E.G. Green	18	201	11.2	34-td	1

Top Rushers	Car	Yds	Avg	Long	TD
Edgerrin James	387	1709	4.4	30	13
Peyton Manning	37	116	3.1	14	1
Lennox Gordon	4	13	3.3	6	0

Most Touchdowns	TD	Run	Rec	Ret	Pts
Edgerrin James	18	13	5	0	110
Marvin Harrison	14	0	14	0	84
Marcus Pollard	3	0	3	0	20
Ken Dilger	3	0	3	0	18
Jerome Pathon	3	0	3	0	18
Terrence Wilkins	3	0	3	0	18

2-Pt. Conversions: (2-4) James, Pollard.

Kicking	PAT/Att	FG/Att	Lg	Pts
Mike Vanderjagt	46/46	25/27	48	121

Punts (10 or more)	No	Yds	Long	Avg	In20
Hunter Smith	65	2906	65	44.7	20

Most Interceptions		Most Sacks	
Jeff Burris	4	Chad Bratzke	7.5

Jacksonville Jaguars

Passing (5 Att)	Att	Cmp	Pct	Yds	TD	Rate
Mark Brunell	512	311	60.7	3640	20	84.0
Jamie Martin	33	22	66.7	307	2	104.0

Interceptions: Brunell 14, Martin 1.

Top Receivers	No	Yds	Avg	Long	TD
Keenan McCardell	94	1207	12.8	67-td	5
Jimmy Smith	91	1213	13.3	65-td	8
Kyle Brady	64	729	11.4	36	3
Fred Taylor	36	240	6.7	19	2
R. Jay Soward*	14	154	11.0	45	1
Alvis Whitted	13	137	10.5	37-td	3

Top Rushers	Car	Yds	Avg	Long	TD
Fred Taylor	292	1399	4.8	71	12
Mark Brunell	48	236	4.9	16	2
Stacey Mack	54	145	2.7	14	1
Anthony Johnson	28	112	4.0	19	1

Most Touchdowns	TD	Run	Rec	Ret	Pts
Fred Taylor	14	12	2	0	84
Jimmy Smith	8	0	8	0	48
Keenan McCardell	5	0	5	0	30
Kyle Brady	3	0	3	0	20
Alvis Whitted	3	0	3	0	18

2-Pt. Conversions: (1-1) Brady.

Kicking	PAT/Att	FG/Att	Lg	Pts
Mike Hollis	33/33	24/26	51	105
Steve Lindsey	5/5	5/7	49	20

Released: Lindsey on Nov. 15.

Punts (10 or more)	No	Yds	Long	Avg	In20
Bryan Barker	76	3194	65	42.0	29

Most Interceptions		Most Sacks	
Rayna Stewart	2	Tony Brackens	7.5
Donovin Darius	2		
Mike Logan	2		

Kansas City Chiefs

Passing (5 Att)	Att	Cmp	Pct	Yds	TD	Rate
Elvis Grbac	547	326	59.6	4169	28	89.9
Warren Moon	34	15	44.1	208	1	61.9

Interceptions: Grbac 14, Moon 1.

Top Receivers	No	Yds	Avg	Long	TD
Tony Gonzalez	93	1203	12.9	39	9
Derrick Alexander	78	1391	17.8	81-td	10
Tony Richardson	58	468	8.1	24	3
Sylvester Morris*	48	678	14.1	47	3
Kevin Lockett	33	422	12.8	34-td	2

Top Rushers	Car	Yds	Avg	Long	TD
Tony Richardson	147	697	4.7	33	3
Kimble Anders	76	331	4.4	69	2
Frank Moreau*	67	179	2.7	22	4
Elvis Grbac	30	110	3.7	22	1

Most Touchdowns	TD	Run	Rec	Ret	Pts
Derrick Alexander	10	0	10	0	60
Tony Gonzalez	9	0	9	0	54
Tony Richardson	6	3	3	0	36
Frank Moreau*	4	4	0	0	24

2-Pt. Conversions: (0-4)

Kicking	PAT/Att	FG/Att	Lg	Pts
Todd Peterson	25/25	15/20	42	70

Signed: Peterson on Oct. 11. **Released:** Pete Stoyanovich on Oct. 11 (see St. Louis).

Punts (10 or more)	No	Yds	Long	Avg	In20
Todd Sauerbrun	82	3656	68	44.6	28

Most Interceptions		Most Sacks	
James Hasty	4	Eric Hicks	14

Miami Dolphins

Passing (5 Att)	Att	Cmp	Pct	Yds	TD	Rate
Jay Fiedler	.357	204	57.1	2402	14	74.5
Damon Huard	.63	39	61.9	318	1	60.2

Interceptions: Fiedler 14, Huard 3.

Top Receivers	No	Yds	Avg	Long	TD
Oronde Gadsden	.56	786	14.0	61	6
Leslie Shepherd	.35	446	12.7	46-td	4
Lamar Smith	.31	201	6.5	28	2
Tony Martin	.26	393	15.1	44	0
Thurman Thomas	.16	117	7.3	15	1
O.J. McDuffie	.14	143	10.2	24	0
Autry Denson	.14	105	7.5	28	0
Rob Konrad	.14	83	5.9	18	0

Top Rushers	Car	Yds	Avg	Long	TD
Lamar Smith	.309	1139	3.7	68-td	14
Jay Fiedler	.54	267	4.9	30	1
J.J. Johnson	.50	168	3.4	16	1
Thurman Thomas	.28	136	4.9	25	0

Most Touchdowns	TD	Run	Rec	Ret	Pts
Lamar Smith	.16	14	2	0	96
Oronde Gadsden	.6	0	6	0	36
Leslie Shepherd	.4	0	4	0	24

2-Pt. Conversions: (0-0).

Kicking	PAT/Att	FG/Att	Lg	Pts
Olindo Mare	.33/34	28/31	49	117

Punts (10 or more)	No	Yds	Long	Avg	In20
Matt Turk	.92	3870	70	42.1	25

Most Interceptions		Most Sacks	
Brian Walker	.7	Trace Armstrong	.16.5

New England Patriots

Passing (5 Att)	Att	Cmp	Pct	Yds	TD	Rate
Drew Bledsoe	.531	312	58.8	3291	17	77.3
John Friesz	.21	11	52.4	66	0	39.0
Michael Bishop	.9	3	33.3	80	1	64.4

Interceptions: Bledsoe 13, Bishop and Friesz 1.

Top Receivers	No	Yds	Avg	Long	TD
Troy Brown	.83	944	11.4	44-td	4
Terry Glenn	.79	963	12.2	39-td	6
Kevin Faulk	.51	465	9.1	52-td	1
Eric Bjornson	.20	152	7.6	19	2
J.R. Redmond*	.20	126	6.3	20	2
Jermaine Wiggins	.18	207	11.5	59	2
NYJ	.2	4	2.0	3	1
NE	.16	203	12.7	59	1

Claimed: Wiggins off waivers from NY Jets (Nov. 28).
Released: Bjornson on Nov. 15.

Top Rushers	Car	Yds	Avg	Long	TD
Kevin Faulk	.164	570	3.5	18	4
J.R. Redmond*	.125	406	3.2	20	1
Drew Bledsoe	.47	158	3.4	16	2
Tony Carter	.37	90	2.4	9	2

Most Touchdowns	TD	Run	Rec	Ret	Pts
Terry Glenn	.6	0	6	0	36
Kevin Faulk	.5	4	1	0	32
Troy Brown	.5	0	4	1	30
J.R. Redmond*	.3	1	2	0	18

2-Pt. Conversions: (1-3) Faulk.

Kicking	PAT/Att	FG/Att	Lg	Pts
Adam Vinatieri	.25/25	27/33	53	106

Punts (10 or more)	No	Yds	Long	Avg	In20
Lee Johnson	.89	3798	62	42.7	31

Most Interceptions		Most Sacks	
Lawyer Milloy	.2	Willie McGinest	.6
Ty Law	.2	Greg Spires	.6
Tebucky Jones	.2		

New York Jets

Passing (5 Att)	Att	Cmp	Pct	Yds	TD	Rate
Vinny Testaverde	.590	328	55.6	3732	21	69.0
Ray Lucas	.41	21	51.2	206	0	26.1
Chad Pennington*	.5	2	40.0	67	1	127.1

Interceptions: Testaverde 25, Lucas 4.

Top Receivers	No	Yds	Avg	Long	TD
Richie Anderson	.88	853	9.7	41	2
Curtis Martin	.70	508	7.3	31	2
Wayne Chrebet	.69	937	13.6	50	8
Dedric Ward	.54	801	14.8	61	3
Laveranues Coles*	.22	370	16.8	63	1

Top Rushers	No	Yds	Avg	Long	TD
Curtis Martin	.316	1204	3.8	55	9
Bernie Parmalee	.27	87	3.2	18-td	2
Richie Anderson	.27	63	2.3	9	0

Most Touchdowns	TD	Run	Rec	Ret	Pts
Curtis Martin	.11	9	2	0	66
Wayne Chrebet	.8	0	8	0	48
Dedric Ward	.3	0	3	0	18

2-Pt. Conversions: (2-4) Coles, Marcus Coleman.

Kicking	PAT/Att	FG/Att	Lg	Pts
John Hall	.30/30	21/32	51	93
Brett Conway	.8/8	6/6	40	26
WASH	.3/3	3/3	26	12
OAK	.3/3	1/1	19	6
NYJ	.2/2	2/2	40	8

Signed: Conway off waivers from Oakland (Dec. 18).

Punts (10 or more)	No	Yds	Long	Avg	In20
Tom Tupa	83	3714	70	44.7	18

Most Interceptions		Most Sacks	
Victor Green	.6	Mo Lewis	.10

Oakland Raiders

Passing (5 Att)	Att	Cmp	Pct	Yds	TD	Rate
Rich Gannon	.473	284	60.0	3430	28	92.4

Interceptions: Gannon 11.

Top Receivers	No	Yds	Avg	Long	TD
Tim Brown	.76	1128	14.8	45	11
Andre Rison	.41	606	14.8	49	6
Rickey Dudley	.29	350	12.1	30	4
Randy Jordan	.27	299	11.1	55	1
Jon Ritchie	.26	173	6.7	17	0
James Jett	.20	356	17.8	84-td	2
Tyrone Wheatley	.20	156	7.8	17	1

Top Rushers	Car	Yds	Avg	Long	TD
Tyrone Wheatley	.232	1046	4.5	80-td	9
Rich Gannon	.89	529	5.9	23	4
Napoleon Kaufman	.93	499	5.4	60	0
Randy Jordan	.46	213	4.6	43-td	3

Most Touchdowns	TD	Run	Rec	Ret	Pts
Tim Brown	.11	0	11	0	66
Tyrone Wheatley	.10	9	1	0	60
Zack Crockett	.7	7	0	0	42
Andre Rison	.6	0	6	0	36

2-Pt. Conversions: (1-1) Gannon.

Kicking	PAT/Att	FG/Att	Lg	Pts
Sebastian Janikowski*	.46/46	22/32	54	112
Shane Lechler*	.7/7	0/1	—	7

Signed: Brett Conway off waivers from Washington (Sept. 18). **Waived:** Conway on Nov. 22 (see NY Jets).

Punts (10 or more)	No	Yds	Long	Avg	In20
Shane Lechler*	.65	2984	69	45.9	24

Most Interceptions		Most Sacks	
Eric Allen	.6	Grady Jackson	.8
William Thomas	.6		

Pittsburgh Steelers

Passing (5 Att)	Att	Cmp	Pct	Yds	TD	Rate
Kordell Stewart	289	151	52.2	1860	11	73.6
Kent Graham	148	66	44.6	878	1	63.4

Interceptions: Stewart 8, Graham 1.

Top Receivers	No	Yds	Avg	Long	TD
Hines Ward	48	672	14.0	77-td	4
Bobby Shaw	40	672	16.8	45-td	4
Plaxico Burress*	22	273	12.4	39	0
Courtney Hawkins	19	238	12.5	33	1
Troy Edwards	18	215	11.9	27	0
Mark Bruener	17	192	11.3	30-td	3

Top Rushers	Car	Yds	Avg	Long	TD
Jerome Bettis	355	1341	3.8	30	8
Kordell Stewart	78	436	5.6	45-td	2
Richard Huntley	46	215	4.7	30-td	3
Chris Fuamatu-Ma'afala	21	149	7.1	23	1

Most Touchdowns	TD	Run	Rec	Ret	Pts
Jerome Bettis	8	8	0	0	48
Kordell Stewart	7	7	0	0	42
Bobby Shaw	4	0	4	0	24
Hines Ward	4	0	4	0	24
Richard Huntley	3	3	0	0	20
Mark Bruener	3	0	3	0	18

2-Pt. Conversions: (1-2) Huntley.

Kicking	PAT/Att	FG/Att	Lg	Pts
Kris Brown	32/33	25/30	52	107

Punts (10 or more)	No	Yds	Long	Avg	In20
Josh Miller	90	3944	67	43.8	34

Most Interceptions		Most Sacks	
Chad Scott	5	Jason Gildon	13.5
Dewayne Washington	5		

San Diego Chargers

Passing (5 Att)	Att	Cmp	Pct	Yds	TD	Rate
Ryan Leaf	322	161	50.0	1883	11	56.2
Jim Harbaugh	202	123	60.9	1416	8	74.6
Moses Moreno	53	27	50.9	241	0	47.8

Interceptions: Leaf 18, Harbaugh 10, Moreno 2.

Top Receivers	No	Yds	Avg	Long	TD
Freddie Jones	71	766	10.8	44	5
Jeff Graham	55	907	16.5	83-td	4
Curtis Conway	53	712	13.4	68-td	5
Terrell Fletcher	48	355	7.4	26	1
Reggie Jones	22	253	11.5	34	0
Fred McCrary	18	141	7.8	19	2

Top Rushers	No	Yds	Avg	Long	TD
Terrell Fletcher	116	384	3.3	21	3
Jermaine Fazande	119	368	3.1	26	2
Robert Chancey	42	141	3.4	14	2
Ryan Leaf	28	54	1.9	14	0

Most Touchdowns	TD	Run	Rec	Ret	Pts
Curtis Conway	5	0	5	0	30
Freddie Jones	5	0	5	0	30
Terrell Fletcher	4	3	1	0	24
Jeff Graham	4	0	4	0	24

Three tied with 2 each for 12 pts.

2-Pt. Conversions: (0-4).

Kicking	PAT/Att	FG/Att	Lg	Pts
John Carney	27/27	18/25	54	81

Punts (10 or more)	No	Yds	Long	Avg	In20
Darren Bennett	92	4248	66	46.2	23

Most Interceptions		Most Sacks	
Rodney Harrison	6	John Parrella	7

Seattle Seahawks

Passing (5 Att)	Att	Cmp	Pct	Yds	TD	Rate
Jon Kitna	418	259	62.0	2658	18	75.6
Brock Huard	87	49	56.3	540	3	76.8

Interceptions: Kitna 19, Huard 2.

Top Receivers	No	Yds	Avg	Long	TD
Sean Dawkins	63	731	11.6	40	5
Ricky Watters	63	613	9.7	59	2
Darrell Jackson*	53	713	13.5	71	6
Derrick Mayes	29	264	9.1	40	1
Itula Mili	28	288	10.3	34	3
Christian Fauria	28	237	8.5	16	2
Mack Strong	23	141	6.1	24	1

Top Rushers	Car	Yds	Avg	Long	TD
Ricky Watters	278	1242	4.5	55	7
Shaun Alexander*	64	313	4.9	50	2
Jon Kitna	48	127	2.6	13	1
Brock Huard	5	29	5.8	10	0

Most Touchdowns	TD	Run	Rec	Ret	Pts
Ricky Watters	9	7	2	0	54
Darrell Jackson*	6	0	6	0	36
Sean Dawkins	5	0	5	0	30
Itula Mili	3	0	3	0	18

2-Pt. Conversions: (0-4).

Kicking	PAT/Att	FG/Att	Lg	Pts
Rian Lindell*	25/25	15/17	52	70

Signed: Lindell on Sept. 26. **Waived:** Kris Heppner on Sept. 26 (see Washington).

Punts (10 or more)	No	Yds	Lg	Avg	In20
Jeff Feagles	74	2960	57	40.0	24

Most Interceptions		Most Sacks	
Jay Bellamy	4	Chad Brown	6
Willie Williams	4	Lamar King	6

Tennessee Titans

Passing (5 Att)	Att	Cmp	Pct	Yds	TD	Rate
Steve McNair	396	248	62.6	2847	15	83.2
Neil O'Donnell	64	36	56.3	530	2	74.3

Interceptions: McNair 13, O'Donnell 3.

Top Receivers	No	Yds	Avg	Long	TD
Frank Wycheck	70	636	9.1	26	4
Derrick Mason	63	895	14.2	34	5
Eddie George	50	453	9.1	24	2
Chris Sanders	33	536	16.2	54	0
Erron Kinney*	19	197	10.4	19	1
Yancey Thigpen	15	289	19.3	56-td	2
Carl Pickens	10	242	24.2	67	0

Top Rushers	Car	Yds	Avg	Long	TD
Eddie George	403	1509	3.7	35-td	14
Steve McNair	72	403	5.6	25	0
Rodney Thomas	61	175	2.9	20	0

Most Touchdowns	TD	Run	Rec	Ret	Pts
Eddie George	16	14	2	0	96
Derrick Mason	6	0	5	1	36
Frank Wycheck	4	0	4	0	24
Lorenzo Neal	2	0	2	0	12
Yancey Thigpen	2	0	2	0	12

2-Pt. Conversions: (0-0).

Kicking	PAT/Att	FG/Att	Lg	Pts
Al Del Greco	37/38	27/33	50	118
Craig Hentrich	0/0	0/1	—	0

Punts (10 or more)	No	Yds	Long	Avg	In20
Craig Hentrich	76	3101	67	40.8	33

Most Interceptions		Most Sacks	
Samari Rolle	7	Jevon Kearse	11.5

NFC Team by Team Statistics

Players with more than one team during the regular season are listed with club they ended season with; (*) indicates rookies.

Arizona Cardinals

Passing (5 Att)	Att	Cmp	Pct	Yds	TD	Rate
Jake Plummer	475	270	56.8	2946	13	66.0
Dave Brown	69	40	58.0	467	2	70.1
Chris Greisen	10	6	60.0	65	1	112.5

Interceptions: Plummer 21, Brown 3.

Top Receivers	No	Yds	Avg	Long	TD
Michael Pittman	73	579	7.9	36-td	2
David Boston	71	1156	16.3	70-td	7
Frank Sanders	54	749	13.9	53-td	6
Thomas Jones*	32	208	6.5	20	0
Terry Hardy	27	160	5.9	13	1
MarTay Jenkins	17	219	12.9	34	0
Mac Cody	17	212	12.5	24	0

Top Rushers	Car	Yds	Avg	Long	TD
Michael Pittman	184	719	3.9	29	4
Thomas Jones*	112	373	3.3	29	2
Jake Plummer	37	183	4.9	24	0

Most Touchdowns	TD	Run	Rec	Ret	Pts
David Boston	7	0	7	0	42
Michael Pittman	6	4	2	0	36
Frank Sanders	6	0	6	0	36
Thomas Jones*	2	2	0	0	12

2-Pt. Conversions: (0-5).

Kicking	PAT/Att	FG/Att	Lg	Pts
Cary Blanchard	18/19	16/23	54	66

Punts (10 or more)	No	Yds	Long	Avg	In20
Scott Player	65	2871	55	44.2	17

Most Interceptions		Most Sacks	
Aeneas Williams	5	Simeon Rice	7.5

Atlanta Falcons

Passing (5 Att)	Att	Cmp	Pct	Yds	TD	Rate
Chris Chandler	331	192	58.0	2236	10	73.5
Danny Kanell	116	57	49.1	524	2	49.6
Doug Johnson*	67	36	53.7	406	2	63.4

Interceptions: Chandler 12, Kanell 5, Johnson 3.

Top Receivers	No	Yds	Avg	Long	TD
Shawn Jefferson	60	822	13.7	49	2
Terance Mathis	57	679	11.9	44-td	5
Bob Christian	44	315	7.2	19	0
Jamal Anderson	42	382	9.1	55	0
Reggie Kelly	31	340	11.0	37-td	2
Tim Dwight	26	406	15.6	52-td	3
Brian Kozlowski	15	151	10.1	30	2

Top Rushers	Car	Yds	Avg	Long	TD
Jamal Anderson	282	1024	3.6	42	6
Maurice Smith*	19	69	3.6	16	0
Chris Chandler	21	60	2.9	16	0
Ron Rivers	8	27	3.4	10	0

Most Touchdowns	TD	Run	Rec	Ret	Pts
Jamal Anderson	6	6	0	0	38
Terance Mathis	5	0	5	0	30
Tim Dwight	4	0	3	1	24
Darrick Vaughn*	3	0	0	3	18

2-Pt. Conversions: (1-2) Anderson.

Kicking	PAT/Att	FG/Att	Lg	Pts
Morten Anderson	23/23	25/31	51	98

Punts (10 or more)	No	Yds	Long	Avg	In20
Dan Stryzinski	84	3447	60	41.0	27

Most Interceptions		Most Sacks	
Ray Buchanan	6	Travis Hall	4.5
		Brady Smith	4.5

Carolina Panthers

Passing (5 Att)	Att	Cmp	Pct	Yds	TD	Rate
Steve Beuerlein	533	324	60.8	3730	19	79.7
Jeff Lewis	32	16	50.0	120	0	46.4

Interceptions: Beuerlein 18, Lewis 1.

Top Receivers	No	Yds	Avg	Long	TD
Mushin Muhammad	102	1183	11.6	36	6
Donald Hayes	66	926	14.0	43-td	3
Tim Biakabutuka	34	341	10.0	25	2
Wesley Walls	31	422	13.6	54	2

Top Rushers	Car	Yds	Avg	Long	TD
Tim Biakabutuka	173	627	3.6	43	2
Brad Hoover*	89	290	3.3	35	1
Steve Beuerlein	44	106	2.4	15	1

Most Touchdowns	TD	Run	Rec	Ret	Pts
Mushin Muhammad	6	0	6	0	36
Tim Biakabutuka	4	2	2	0	24
Donald Hayes	3	0	3	0	18
Chris Hetherington	3	2	1	0	18

2-Pt. Conversions: (1-2) Beuerlein.

Kicking	PAT/Att	FG/Att	Lg	Pts
Joe Nedney	24/24	34/38	52	126
DEN	4/4	8/10	43	28
CAR	20/20	26/28	52	98
Richie Cunningham	9/9	5/7	39	24

Released: Cunningham (Oct. 4). **Signed:** Nedney off waivers from Denver (Oct. 4)

Punts (10 or more)	No	Yds	Long	Avg	In20
Ken Walter	64	2459	66	38.4	19

Most Interceptions		Most Sacks	
Eric Davis	5	Jay Williams	6

Chicago Bears

Passing (5 Att)	Att	Cmp	Pct	Yds	TD	Rate
Cade McNown	280	154	55.0	1646	8	68.5
Shane Matthews	178	102	57.3	964	3	64.0
Jim Miller	82	47	57.3	382	1	68.2

Interceptions: McNown 9, Matthews 6, Miller 1.

Top Receivers	No	Yds	Avg	Long	TD
Marcus Robinson	55	738	13.4	68-td	5
Eddie Kennison	55	549	10.0	26	2
Marty Booker	47	490	10.4	41	2
James Allen	39	291	7.5	26	1

Top Rushers	Car	Yds	Avg	Long	TD
James Allen	290	1120	3.9	29	2
Cade McNown	50	326	6.5	30	3
Curtis Enis	36	84	2.3	11-td	1
Marlon Barnes*	15	81	5.4	20	0

Most Touchdowns	TD	Run	Rec	Ret	Pts
Marcus Robinson	5	0	5	0	30
James Allen	3	2	1	0	18
Cade McNown	3	3	0	0	18

Two tied with 2 each for 12 pts.

2-Pt. Conversions: (0-1).

Kicking	PAT/Att	FG/Att	Lg	Pts
Paul Edinger*	21/21	21/27	54	84

Punts (10 or more)	No	Yds	Lg	Avg	In20
Louie Aguiar	52	2017	56	38.8	8
Brent Bartholomew	44	1607	52	36.5	12

Signed: Aguiar (Oct. 18).

Most Interceptions		Most Sacks	
Tony Parrish	3	Brian Urlacher*	8

Dallas Cowboys

Passing (10 Att)	Att	Cmp	Pct	Yds	TD	Rate
Troy Aikman	262	156	59.5	1632	7	64.3
R. Cunningham	125	74	59.2	849	6	82.4
Anthony Wright	53	22	41.5	237	0	31.7

Interceptions: Aikman 14, Cunningham 4, Wright 3.

Top Receivers	No	Yds	Avg	Long	TD
James McKnight	52	926	17.8	48	2
Jackie Harris	39	306	7.8	21	5
Raghib Ismail	25	350	14.0	44	1
Wane McGarity	25	250	10.0	25	0
Robert Thomas	23	117	5.1	14	2

Top Rushers	Car	Yds	Avg	Long	TD
Emmitt Smith	294	1203	4.1	52	9
Randall Cunningham	23	89	3.9	19	1
Michael Wiley*	24	88	3.7	11	0
Raghib Ismail	8	73	9.1	37	0

Most Touchdowns	TD	Run	Rec	Ret	Pts
Emmitt Smith	9	9	0	0	54
Jackie Harris	5	0	5	0	32
Wane McGarity	3	1	0	2	18
James McKnight	2	0	2	0	12
Robert Thomas	2	0	2	0	12

2-Pt. Conversions: (2-4) Harris, Ismail.

Kicking	PAT/Att	FG/Att	Lg	Pts
Tim Seder*	27/27	25/33	48	108

Punts (10 or more)	No	Yds	Long	Avg	In20
Micah Knorr*	58	2485	60	42.8	12
Barry Cantrell*	10	367	40	36.7	3

Signed: Cantrell (Nov. 15).

Most Interceptions		Most Sacks	
Phillippi Sparks	5	Ebenezer Ekuban	6.5

Detroit Lions

Passing (5 Att)	Att	Cmp	Pct	Yds	TD	Rate
Charlie Batch	412	221	53.6	2489	13	67.3
Stoney Case	91	56	61.5	503	1	61.7

Interceptions: Batch 15, Case 4.

Top Receivers	No	Yds	Avg	Long	TD
Johnnie Morton	61	788	12.9	42-td	3
Herman Moore	40	434	10.9	30-td	3
Germane Crowell	34	430	12.6	50-td	3
David Sloan	32	379	11.8	59	2
James Stewart	32	287	9.0	32	1
Larry Foster*	17	175	10.3	40-td	1
Mario Bates	15	109	7.3	17	0

Top Rushers	Car	Yds	Avg	Long	TD
James Stewart	339	1184	3.5	34	10
Charlie Batch	44	199	4.5	19	2
Mario Bates	31	127	4.1	23	2
Stoney Case	16	117	7.3	27	1

Most Touchdowns	TD	Run	Rec	Ret	Pts
James Stewart	11	10	1	0	72
Johnnie Morton	3	0	3	0	20
Germane Crowell	3	0	3	0	18
Herman Moore	3	0	3	0	18

Three tied with 2 each for 12 pts.

2-Pt. Conversions: (4-4) Stewart 3, Morton 1.

Kicking	PAT/Att	FG/Att	Lg	Pts
Jason Hanson	29/29	24/30	54	101

Punts (10 or more)	No	Yds	Long	Avg	In20
John Jett	93	4044	59	43.5	33

Most Interceptions		Most Sacks	
Kurt Schulz	7	Robert Porcher	8

Green Bay Packers

Passing (5 Att)	Att	Cmp	Pct	Yds	TD	Rate
Brett Favre	580	338	58.3	3812	20	78.0
Matt Hasselbeck	19	10	52.6	104	1	86.3

Interceptions: Favre 16.

Top Receivers	No	Yds	Avg	Long	TD
Ahman Green	73	559	7.7	35	3
Bill Schroeder	65	999	15.4	55-td	4
Antonio Freeman	62	912	14.7	67-td	9
William Henderson*	35	234	6.7	25	1
Bubba Franks*	34	363	10.7	27-td	1
Donald Driver	21	322	15.3	49	1
Tyrone Davis	19	177	9.3	41	2

Top Rushers	Car	Yds	Avg	Long	TD
Ahman Green	263	1175	4.5	39-td	10
Dorsey Levens	77	224	2.9	17	3
Brett Favre	27	108	4.0	18	0
De'Mond Parker	18	85	4.7	24	0

Most Touchdowns	TD	Run	Rec	Ret	Pts
Ahman Green	13	10	3	0	78
Antonio Freeman	9	0	9	0	54
Bill Schroeder	4	0	4	0	24
Dorsey Levens	3	3	0	0	18
Tyrone Davis	2	0	2	0	14

2-Pt. Conversions: (2-3) Davis, Driver.

Kicking	PAT/Att	FG/Att	Lg	Pts
Ryan Longwell	32/32	33/38	52	131

Punts (10 or more)	No	Yds	Long	Avg	In20
Josh Bidwell	78	3003	53	38.5	22

Most Interceptions		Most Sacks	
Darren Sharper	9	John Thierry	6.5

Minnesota Vikings

Passing (5 Att)	Att	Cmp	Pct	Yds	TD	Rate
Daunte Culpepper	474	297	62.7	3937	33	98.0
Bubby Brister	20	10	50.0	82	0	40.0

Interceptions: Culpepper 16, Brister 1.

Top Receivers	No	Yds	Avg	Long	TD
Cris Carter	96	1274	13.3	53	9
Randy Moss	77	1437	18.7	78-td	15
Robert Smith	36	348	9.7	53-td	3
Johnny McWilliams	22	180	8.2	26	3
Chris Walsh	18	191	10.6	21	0
John Davis	17	202	11.9	37	1

Top Rushers	Car	Yds	Avg	Long	TD
Robert Smith	295	1521	5.2	72-td	7
Daunte Culpepper	89	470	5.3	27-td	7
Moe Williams	23	67	2.9	10	0
Jimmy Kleinsasser	12	43	3.6	7	0

Most Touchdowns	TD	Run	Rec	Ret	Pts
Randy Moss	15	0	15	0	92
Robert Smith	10	7	3	0	60
Cris Carter	9	0	9	0	54
Daunte Culpepper	7	7	0	0	42
Johnny McWilliams	3	0	3	0	18
Matt Hatchette	2	0	2	0	12

2-Pt. Conversions: (2-2) Moss, Williams.

Kicking	PAT/Att	FG/Att	Lg	Pts
Gary Anderson	45/45	22/23	49	111

Punts (10 or more)	No	Yds	Long	Avg	In20
Mitch Berger	62	2773	60	44.7	16

Most Interceptions		Most Sacks	
Kailee Wong	2	John Randle	8
Robert Tate	2		

New Orleans Saints

Passing (5 Att)	Att	Cmp	Pct	Yds	TD	Rate
Jeff Blake	302	184	60.9	2025	13	82.7
Aaron Brooks	194	113	58.2	1514	9	85.7

Interceptions: Blake 9, Brooks 6.

Top Receivers	No	Yds	Avg	Long	TD
Joe Horn	94	1340	14.3	52	8
Ricky Williams	44	409	9.3	24	1
Willie Jackson	37	523	14.1	53-td	6
Chad Morton*	30	213	7.1	35	0
Keith Poole	21	293	14.0	49-td	1
Andrew Glover	21	281	13.4	39	4
Jake Reed	16	206	12.9	22	0

Top Rushers	Car	Yds	Avg	Long	TD
Ricky Williams	248	1000	4.0	26-td	8
Jeff Blake	57	243	4.3	20	1
Terry Allen	46	179	3.9	18	2
Aaron Brooks	41	170	4.1	29	2
Jerald Moore	37	156	4.2	40	1

Signed: Allen (Nov. 14).

Most Touchdowns	TD	Run	Rec	Ret	Pts
Ricky Williams	9	8	1	0	54
Joe Horn	8	0	8	0	48
Willie Jackson	6	0	6	0	36
Andrew Glover	4	0	4	0	24

2-Pt. Conversions: (1-4) Allen.

Kicking	PAT/Att	FG/Att	Lg	Pts
Doug Brien	37/37	23/29	48	106

Punts (10 or more)	No	Yds	Long	Avg	In20
Toby Gowin	74	3043	58	41.1	22

Most Interceptions | | **Most Sacks** |
---|---|---|---
Sammy Knight | 5 | La'Roi Glover | 17

New York Giants

Passing (5 Att)	Att	Cmp	Pct	Yds	TD	Rate
Kerry Collins	529	311	58.8	3610	22	83.1

Interceptions: Collins 13.

Top Receivers	No	Yds	Avg	Long	TD
Amani Toomer	78	1094	14.0	54-td	7
Tiki Barber	70	719	10.3	36	1
Ike Hilliard	55	787	14.3	59	8
Greg Comella	36	274	7.6	25	0
Pete Mitchell	25	245	9.8	22	1
Joe Jurevicius	24	272	11.3	43	1

Top Rushers	Car	Yds	Avg	Long	TD
Tiki Barber	213	1006	4.7	78-td	8
Ron Dayne*	228	770	3.4	50	5
Amani Toomer	5	91	18.2	28	1
Kerry Collins	41	65	1.6	15	-1
Greg Comella	10	45	4.5	16	0

Most Touchdowns	TD	Run	Rec	Ret	Pts
Tiki Barber	9	8	1	0	54
Ike Hilliard	8	0	8	0	48
Amani Toomer	8	1	7	0	48
Ron Dayne*	5	5	0	0	30
Dan Campbell	3	0	3	0	18

2-Pt. Conversions: (0-2).

Kicking	PAT/Att	FG/Att	Lg	Pts
Brad Daluiso	34/34	17/23	46	85
Jaret Holmes	3/3	2/2	34	9

Signed: Holmes (Oct. 1).

Punts (10 or more)	No	Yds	Long	Avg	In20
Brad Maynard	79	3210	64	40.6	26

Most Interceptions | | **Most Sacks** |
---|---|---|---
Emmanuel McDaniel | 6 | Keith Hamilton | 10

Philadelphia Eagles

Passing (5 Att)	Att	Cmp	Pct	Yds	TD	Rate
Donovan McNabb	569	330	58.0	3365	21	77.8

Interceptions: McNabb 13.

Top Receivers	No	Yds	Avg	Long	TD
Chad Lewis	69	735	10.7	52	3
Charles Johnson	56	642	11.5	59	7
Torrance Small	40	569	14.2	70-td	3
Chris Warren	32	303	9.5	76-td	1
DAL	31	302	9.7	76-td	1
PHI	1	1	1.0	1	0

Signed: Warren off waivers from Dallas (Dec. 7).

Top Rushers	Car	Yds	Avg	Long	TD
Donovan McNabb	86	629	7.3	54	6
Duce Staley	79	344	4.4	60	1
Darnell Autry	112	334	3.0	15	3
Chris Warren	74	296	4.0	32-td	2
DAL	59	254	4.3	32-td	2
PHI	15	42	2.8	11	0

Most Touchdowns	TD	Run	Rec	Ret	Pts
Charles Johnson	7	0	7	0	42
Donovan McNabb	6	6	0	0	36
Brian Mitchell	5	2	1	2	30
Jeff Thomason	5	0	5	0	30

2-Pt. Conversions: (1-2) Small.

Kicking	PAT/Att	FG/Att	Lg	Pts
David Akers	34/36	29/33	51	121

Punts (10 or more)	No	Yds	Long	Avg	In20
Sean Landeta	86	3635	60	42.3	23

Most Interceptions | | **Most Sacks** |
---|---|---|---
Troy Vincent | 5 | Hugh Douglas | 15

St. Louis Rams

Passing (5 Att)	Att	Cmp	Pct	Yds	TD	Rate
Kurt Warner	347	235	67.7	3429	21	98.3
Trent Green	240	145	60.4	2063	16	101.8

Interceptions: Warner 18, Green 5.

Top Receivers	No	Yds	Avg	Long	TD
Isaac Bruce	87	1471	16.9	78-td	9
Torry Holt	82	1635	19.9	85-td	6
Marshall Faulk	81	830	10.2	72-td	8
Az-Zahir Hakim	53	734	13.8	80-td	4

Top Rushers	Car	Yds	Avg	Long	TD
Marshall Faulk	253	1359	5.4	36	18
Justin Watson	54	249	4.6	49	4
Robert Holcombe	21	70	3.3	11	3

Most Touchdowns	TD	Run	Rec	Ret	PTS
Marshall Faulk	26	18	8	0	160
Isaac Bruce	9	0	9	0	54
Torry Holt	6	0	6	0	36
Az-Zahir Hakim	5	0	4	1	30

2-Pt. Conversions: (4-9) Faulk 2, Roland Williams and London Fletcher 1.

Top Kickers	PAT/Att	FG/Att	Lg	Pts
Jeff Wilkins	38/38	17/17	51	89
Pete Stoyanovich	26/26	5/9	48	41
KC	15/15	2/4	42	21
ST.L	11/11	3/5	48	20

Signed: Stoyanovich off waivers from Kansas City (Oct. 18).
Released: Stoyanovich (Nov. 6).

Punts (10 or more)	No	Yds	Long	Avg	In20
John Baker*	43	1736	59	40.4	13

Most Interceptions | | **Most Sacks** |
---|---|---|---
Dexter McCleon | 8 | Grant Wistrom | 11

San Francisco 49ers

Passing (5 Att)	Att	Cmp	Pct	Yds	TD	Rate
Jeff Garcia	561	355	63.3	4278	31	97.6
Rick Mirer	20	10	50.0	126	1	86.7

Interceptions: Garcia 10.

Top Receivers	No	Yds	Avg	Long	TD
Terrell Owens	97	1451	15.0	69-td	13
Jerry Rice	75	805	10.7	68-td	7
Charlie Garner	68	647	9.5	62	3
Greg Clark	38	342	9.0	34	2
Fred Beasley	31	233	7.5	34	1
J.J. Stokes	30	524	17.5	53	3

Top Rushers	Car	Yds	Avg	Long	TD
Charlie Garner	258	1142	4.4	42	7
Jeff Garcia	72	414	5.8	33	4
Fred Beasley	50	147	2.9	9	3
Paul Smith*	18	72	4.0	14	0

Most Touchdowns	TD	Run	Rec	Ret	Pts
Terrell Owens	13	0	13	0	80
Charlie Garner	10	7	3	0	60
Jerry Rice	7	0	7	0	42
Fred Beasley	6	3	3	0	36
Jeff Garcia	4	4	0	0	24

2-Pt. Conversions: (3-4) Owens, Stokes, Terry Jackson.

Kicking	PAT/Att	FG/Att	Lg	Pts
Wade Richey	43/45	15/22	47	88

Punts (10 or more)	No	Yds	Long	Avg	In20
Chad Stanley	69	2727	56	39.5	15

Most Interceptions		Most Sacks	
Zack Bronson	3	Bryant Young	9.5
Monty Montgomery	3		

Tampa Bay Buccaneers

Passing (5 Att)	Att	Cmp	Pct	Yds	TD	Rate
Shaun King	428	233	54.4	2769	18	75.8

Interceptions: King 13.

Top Receivers	No	Yds	Avg	Long	TD
Keyshawn Johnson	71	874	12.3	38	8
Jacquez Green	51	773	15.2	75	1
Warrick Dunn	44	422	9.6	45	1
Dave Moore	29	288	9.9	28	3
Reidel Anthony	15	232	15.5	46-td	4
Mike Alstott	13	93	7.2	21	0
Patrick Hape	6	39	6.5	13	0

Top Rushers	Car	Yds	Avg	Long	TD
Warrick Dunn	248	1133	4.6	70-td	8
Mike Alstott	131	465	3.5	20-td	5
Shaun King	73	353	4.8	19	5
Rabih Abdullah	16	70	4.4	19	0

Most Touchdowns	TD	Run	Rec	Ret	Pts
Warrick Dunn	9	8	1	0	54
Keyshawn Johnson	8	0	8	0	48
Shaun King	5	5	0	0	32
Mike Alstott	5	5	0	0	30
Reidel Anthony	4	0	4	0	24
Dave Moore	3	0	3	0	18

2-Pt. Conversions: (1-1) King.

Kicking	PAT/Att	FG/Att	Lg	Pts
Martin Gramatica	42/42	28/34	55	126

Punts (10 or more)	No	Yds	Long	Avg	In20
Mark Royals	85	3551	63	41.8	17

Most Interceptions		Most Sacks	
Donnie Abraham	7	Warren Sapp	16.5

Washington Redskins

Passing (5 Att)	Att	Cmp	Pct	Yds	TD	Rate
Brad Johnson	365	228	62.5	2505	11	75.7
Jeff George	194	113	58.2	1389	7	79.6

Interceptions: Johnson 15, George 6.

Top Receivers	No	Yds	Avg	Long	TD
Larry Centers	81	600	7.4	26	3
James Thrash	50	653	13.1	50	2
Stephen Alexander	47	510	10.9	30	2
Irving Fryar	41	548	13.4	34-td	5

Top Rushers	Car	Yds	Avg	Long	TD
Stephen Davis	332	1318	4.0	50-td	11
Larry Centers	19	103	5.4	14	0
James Thrash	10	82	8.2	34	0

Most Touchdowns	TD	Run	Rec	Ret	Pts
Stephen Davis	11	11	0	0	66
Irving Fryar	5	0	5	0	30
Larry Centers	3	0	3	0	18
Albert Connell	3	0	3	0	18

2-Pt. Conversions: (0-3).

Top Kickers	PAT/Att	FG/Att	Lg	Pts
Kris Heppner	17/17	10/15	45	47
SEA	8/8	6/9	45	26
WASH	9/9	4/6	37	21
Eddie Murray	7/8	8/12	47	31

Signed: Heppner off waivers from Seattle (Oct. 10); Murray (Nov. 9). **Released:** Heppner (Nov. 6).

Punts (10 or more)	No	Yds	Long	Avg	In20
Tommy Barnhardt	79	3160	53	40.0	23

Most Interceptions		Most Sacks	
Champ Bailey	5	Marco Coleman	12

Overall Club Rankings

Combined AFC and NFC rankings by yards gained on offense and yards given up on defense. Teams are ranked by offense with AFC teams in *italics*.

	Offense			Defense		
	Rush	Pass	Rank	Rush	Pass	Rank
St. Louis	17	1	**1**	13	27	23
Denver	2	3	**2**	7	31	24
Indianapolis	16	2	**3**	25	18	21
San Francisco	18	4	**4**	16	29	29
Minnesota	6	7	**5**	15	28	28
Oakland	1	5	**6**	5	25	17
Jacksonville	10	9	**7**	11	14	12
Kansas City	25	5	**8**	17	20	18
Buffalo	13	11	**9**	6	4	3
New Orleans	8	14	**10**	10	10	8
Washington	19	10	**11**	22	2	4
NY Jets	24	6	**12**	23	6	10t
NY Giants	11	13	**13**	2	16	5
Tennessee	7	16	**14**	3	1	1
Green Bay	23	8	**15**	8	19	15
Baltimore	5	22	**16**	1	8	2
Philadelphia	15	20	**17**	20	7	10t
Pittsburgh	4	29	**18**	12	9	7
Seattle	22	19	**19**	28	30	31
Carolina	29	12	**20**	26	26	27
Tampa Bay	9	26	**21**	9	13	9
New England	26	19	**22**	21	21	20
Chicago	21	23	**23**	19	17	16
Arizona	27	17	**24**	30	11	30
Dallas	12	28	**25**	31	3	19
Miami	14	27	**26**	14	5	6
Detroit	20	25	**27**	18	15	14
San Diego	31	18	**28**	4	22	13
Cincinnati	3	31	**29**	24	23	22
Atlanta	28	24	**30**	27	24	25
Cleveland	30	30	**31**	29	12	26

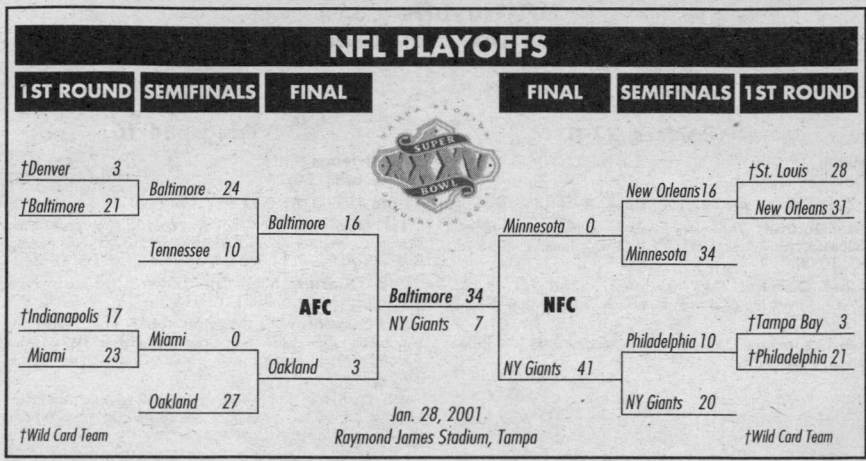

NFL PLAYOFFS

| 1ST ROUND | SEMIFINALS | FINAL | | FINAL | SEMIFINALS | 1ST ROUND |

†Denver   3
†Baltimore   21
　　　　　Baltimore   24
Baltimore   16
Tennessee   10

New Orleans 16
　　　　　　　　†St. Louis   28
New Orleans 31

†Indianapolis 17
Miami   23
　　　　　Miami   0
Oakland   3
Oakland   27

AFC

Baltimore   34
NY Giants   7

NFC

NY Giants   41

Minnesota   0
Minnesota   34

Philadelphia 10
　　　　　　　　†Tampa Bay   3
　　　　　　　　†Philadelphia 21

NY Giants   20

†Wild Card Team

Jan. 28, 2001
Raymond James Stadium, Tampa

†Wild Card Team

Playoff Game Summaries
Team records listed in parentheses indicate records before game.
WILD CARD ROUND

AFC

Dolphins, 23-17 (OT)

Indianapolis (10-6)	3	11	0	3 0—	**17**
Miami (11-5)	0	0	7	10 6—	**23**

Date—Dec. 30. **Att**—73,193. **Time**—3:09.

1st Quarter: IND—Mike Vanderjagt 32-yd FG, 7:11.

2nd Quarter: IND—Vanderjagt 26-yd FG, 5:27; IND—Jerome Pathon 17-yd pass from Peyton Manning (Ken Dilger pass from Manning), 7:13.

3rd Quarter: MIA—Lamar Smith 2-yd run (Olindo Mare kick), 6:51.

4th Quarter: MIA—Mare 38-yd FG, 4:37; IND—Vanderjagt 50-yd FG, 10:05; MIA—Jed Weaver 9-yd pass from Jay Fiedler (Mare kick), 14:26.

Overtime: MIA—Smith 17-yd run, 11:26.

Ravens, 21-3

Denver (11-5)	0	3	0	0—	**3**
Baltimore (12-4)	0	14	7	0—	**21**

Date—Dec. 31. **Att**—69,638. **Time**—2:54.

2nd Quarter: BAL—Jamal Lewis 1-yd run (Matt Stover kick), 3:17; DEN—Jason Elam 31-yd FG, 10:29; BAL—Shannon Sharpe 58-yd pass from Trent Dilfer (Stover kick), 10:54.

3rd Quarter: BAL—Lewis 27-yd run (Stover kick), 11:41.

NFC

Saints, 31-28

St. Louis (10-6)	7	0	0	21—	**28**
New Orleans (10-6)	0	10	7	14—	**31**

Date—Dec. 30. **Att**—64,900. **Time**—3:16.

1st Quarter: ST.L—Isaac Bruce 17-yd pass from Kurt Warner (Jeff Wilkins kick), 9:02.

2nd Quarter: NO—Robert Wilson 12-yd pass from Aaron Brooks (Doug Brien kick), 0:04; NO—Brien 33-yd FG, 13:30.

3rd Quarter: NO—Willie Jackson 10-yd pass from Brooks (Brien kick), 6:20.

4th Quarter: NO—Jackson 49-yd pass from Brooks (Brien kick), 1:38; NO—Jackson 16-yd pass from Brooks (Brien kick), 3:03; ST.L—Ricky Proehl 17-yd pass from Warner (2-pt attempt failed), 5:24; ST.L—Marshall Faulk 25-yd pass from Warner (Wilkins kick), 11:08; ST.L—Warner 5-yd run (Faulk pass from Warner), 12:24.

Eagles, 21-3

Tampa Bay (10-6)	0	3	0	0—	**3**
Philadelphia (11-5)	0	14	0	7—	**21**

Date—Dec. 31. **Att**—65,813. **Time**—2:55.

2nd Quarter: TB—Martin Gramatica 29-yd FG, 4:44; PHI—Donovan McNabb 5-yd run (David Akers kick), 11:39; PHI—Na Brown 5-yd pass from McNabb (Akers kick), 14:48.

4th Quarter: PHI—Jeff Thomason 2-yd pass from McNabb (Akers kick), 0:47.

NFL Playoffs (Cont.)
DIVISIONAL SEMIFINALS

AFC

🏈 Raiders, 27-0

Miami (12-5)	0	0	0	0—	**0**
Oakland (12-4)	10	10	7	0—	**27**

Date—Jan. 6. **Att**—61,998. **Time**—3:04.

1st Quarter: OAK—Tory James 90-yd interception return (Sebastian Janikowski kick), 3:24; OAK— Janikowski 36-yd FG, 10:08.

2nd Quarter: OAK—Janikowski 33-yd FG, 6:24; OAK— James Jett 6-yd pass from Rich Gannon (Janikowski kick), 13:07.

3rd Quarter: OAK—Tyrone Wheatley 2-yd run (Janikowski kick), 9:04.

🏈 Ravens, 24-10

Baltimore (13-4)	0	7	3	14—	**24**
Tennessee (13-3)	7	0	3	0—	**10**

Date—Jan. 7. **Att**—68,527. **Time**—3:01.

1st Quarter: TEN—Eddie George 2-yd run (Al Del Greco kick), 7:17.

2nd Quarter: BAL—Jamal Lewis 1-yd run (Matt Stover kick), 5:14.

3rd Quarter: TEN—Del Greco 21-yd FG, 6:40; BAL—Stover 38-yd FG, 11:55.

4th Quarter: BAL—Anthony Mitchell 90-yd return of a blocked FG (Stover kick), 2:48; BAL—Ray Lewis 50-yd interception return (Stover kick), 8:19.

NFC

🏈 Vikings, 34-16

New Orleans (11-6)	3	0	7	6—	**16**
Minnesota (11-5)	10	7	10	7—	**34**

Date—Jan. 6. **Att**—63,881. **Time**—3:15.

1st Quarter: MIN—Randy Moss 53-yd pass from Daunte Culpepper (Gary Anderson kick), 3:03; NO—Doug Brien 33-yd FG, 7:14; MIN—Anderson 24-yd FG, 13:24.

2nd Quarter: MIN—Cris Carter 17-yd pass from Culpepper (Anderson kick), 13:31.

3rd Quarter: MIN—Moss 68-yd pass from Culpepper (Anderson kick), 1:27; NO—Dave Stachelski 2-yd pass from Aaron Brooks (Brien kick), 5:27; MIN—Anderson 44-yd FG, 10:29.

4th Quarter: MIN—Robert Smith 2-yd run (Anderson kick), 4:14; NO—Willie Jackson 48-yd pass from Brooks (2-pt attempt failed), 12:41.

🏈 Giants, 20-10

Philadelphia (12-5)	0	3	0	7—	**10**
NY Giants (12-4)	7	10	0	3—	**20**

Date—Jan. 7. **Att**—78,765. **Time**—3:15.

1st Quarter: NYG—Ron Dixon 97-yd kickoff return (Brad Daluiso kick), 0:17.

2nd Quarter: NYG—Daluiso 37-yd FG, 0:05; NYG—Jason Sehorn 32-yd interception return (Daluiso kick), 13:20; PHI—David Akers 28-yd FG, 14:34.

4th Quarter: NYG—Daluiso 25-yd FG, 6:19; PHI—Torrance Small 10-yd pass from Donovan McNabb (Akers kick), 13:04.

CONFERENCE CHAMPIONSHIPS

AFC

🏈 Ravens, 16-3

Baltimore (14-4)	0	10	3	3—	**16**
Oakland (13-4)	0	0	3	0—	**3**

Date—Jan. 14. **Att**—62,784. **Time**—3:08.

2nd Quarter: BAL—Shannon Sharpe 96-yd pass from Trent Dilfer (Matt Stover kick), 3:52; BAL—Stover 31-yd FG, 6:41.

3rd Quarter: OAK—Sebastian Janikowski 24-yd FG, 4:53; BAL—Stover 28-yd FG, 9:52.

4th Quarter: BAL—Stover 21-yd FG, 7:32.

NFC

🏈 Giants, 41-0

Minnesota (12-5)	0	0	0	0—	**0**
NY Giants (13-4)	14	20	7	0—	**41**

Date—Jan. 14. **Att**—79,310. **Time**—3:04.

1st Quarter: NYG—Ike Hilliard 46-yd pass from Kerry Collins (Brad Daluiso kick), 1:57; NYG—Greg Comella 18-yd pass from Collins (Daluiso kick), 2:13.

2nd Quarter: NYG—Daluiso 21-yd FG, 0:04; NYG—Joe Jurevicius 8-yd pass from Collins (Daluiso kick), 4:36; NYG—Daluiso 22-yd FG, 9:38; NYG—Hilliard 7-yd pass from Collins (Daluiso kick), 14:48.

3rd Quarter: NYG—Amani Toomer 7-yd pass from Collins (Daluiso kick), 2:54.

Super Bowl XXXV

Sunday, Jan. 28, 2001 at Raymond James Stadium, Tampa, Fla.

Baltimore (15-4)	7	3	14	10—	**34**
NY Giants (14-4)	0	0	7	0—	**7**

1st: BAL—Brandon Stokley 38-yd pass from Trent Dilfer (Matt Stover kick), 8:10. Drive: 41 yards in 2 plays. Key play: Jermaine Lewis 43-yd punt return to NYG 22.

2nd: BAL—Stover 47-yd FG, 13:19. Drive: 59 yards in 7 plays. Key play: Qadry Ismail 44-yd pass from Dilfer to NYG 36.

3rd: BAL—Duane Starks 49-yd interception return (Stover kick), 11:11. **NYG**—Ron Dixon 97-yd kickoff return (Brad Daluiso kick), 11:29. **BAL**—Je. Lewis 84-yd kickoff return (Stover kick), 11:47.

4th: BAL—Jamal Lewis 3-yd run (Stover kick), 6:15. Drive: 38 yards in 6 plays. Key play: Ben Coates 17-yd pass from Dilfer to NYG 21. **BAL**—Stover 34-yd FG, 9:33. Drive: 18 yards in 5 plays. Key play: Robert Bailey recovery of Dixon fumble during kickoff return at NYG 34.

Favorite: Ravens by 3 **Attendance:** 71,921
Field: Grass **Time:** 3:23
Start time: 6:28 EST **TV Rating:** 40.3/60 share (CBS)

MVP—Ray Lewis, Baltimore LB (5 tackles, 4 passes defended)

Officials: Gerard Austin (referee); Chad Brown (umpire); Walt Anderson (LJ); Doug Toole (SJ); Tony Veteri (HL); Bill Schmitz (BJ); Bill Lovett (FJ).

Team Statistics

	Ravens	Giants
First downs	13	11
Rushing	6	2
Passing	6	6
Penalty	1	3
3rd down efficiency	3/16	2/14
4th down efficiency	0/0	1/1
Total offense (net yards)	244	152
Plays	62	59
Average gain	3.9	2.6
Rushes/yards	33/111	16/66
Yards per rush	3.4	4.1
Passing yards (net)	133	86
Times sacked/yards lost	3/20	4/26
Passing yards (gross)	153	112
Completions/attempts	12/26	15/39
Yards per pass	4.6	2.0
Times intercepted	0	4
Return yardage	204	217
Punt returns/yards	3/34	5/46
Kickoff returns/yards	2/111	7/171
Interceptions/yards	4/59	0/0
Fumbles/lost	2/0	2/1
Penalties/yards	9/70	6/27
Punts/average	10/43.0	11/38.4
Field Goals made/attempted	2/3	0/0
Time of possession	34:06	25:54

Individual Statistics

Baltimore Ravens

Passing	Att	Cmp	Pct.	Yds	TD	Int
Trent Dilfer	25	12	48.0	153	1	0
Tony Banks	1	0	0.0	0	0	0
TOTAL	26	12	46.2	153	1	0

Receiving	No	Yds	Avg	Long	TD
Brandon Stokley	3	52	17.3	38-td	1
Ben Coates	3	30	10.0	17	0
Qadry Ismail	1	44	44.0	44	0
Patrick Johnson	1	8	8.0	8	0
Jermaine Lewis	1	6	6.0	6	0
Shannon Sharpe	1	5	5.0	5	0
Jamal Lewis	1	4	4.0	4	0
Priest Holmes	1	4	4.0	4	0
TOTAL	12	153	12.8	44	1

Rushing	Car	Yds	Avg	Long	TD
Jamal Lewis	27	102	3.8	19	1
Priest Holmes	4	8	2.0	6	0
Jermaine Lewis	1	1	1.0	1	0
Trent Dilfer	1	0	0.0	0	0
TOTAL	33	111	3.4	19	1

Field Goals	20-29	30-39	40-49	50-59	Total
Matt Stover	0-0	1-1	1-2	0-0	2-3

Punting	No	Yds	Avg	Long	In 20	TB
Kyle Richardson	10	430	43.0	53	4	0

Punt Returns	Ret	Yds	Long	Avg	FC	TD
Jermaine Lewis	3	34	34	11.3	4	0

Kickoff Returns	Ret	Yds	Long	Avg	FC	TD
Jermaine Lewis	2	111	84-td	55.5	0	1

Interceptions	No	Yds	Long	Avg	TD
Duane Starks	1	49	49-td	49.0	1
Chris McAlister	1	4	4	4.0	0
Jamie Sharper	1	4	4	4.0	0
Kim Herring	1	2	2	2.0	0
TOTAL	4	59	49-td	14.8	1

Sacks		Most Tackles (solo)	
Michael McCrary	2	Rod Woodson	5
Rob Burnett	1	Duane Starks	5
Keith Washington	1		

New York Giants

Passing	Att	Cmp	Pct.	Yds	TD	Int
Kerry Collins	39	15	38.5	112	0	4

Receiving	No	Yds	Avg	Long	TD
Tiki Barber	6	26	4.3	7	0
Ike Hilliard	3	30	10.0	13	0
Amani Toomer	2	24	12.0	19	0
Ron Dixon	1	16	16.0	16	0
Howard Cross	1	7	7.0	7	0
Pete Mitchell	1	7	7.0	7	0
Greg Comella	1	2	2.0	2	0
TOTAL	15	112	7.5	19	0

Rushing	Car	Yds	Avg	Long	TD
Tiki Barber	11	49	4.5	27	0
Kerry Collins	3	12	4.0	5	0
Joe Montgomery	2	5	2.5	4	0
TOTAL	16	66	4.1	27	0

Field Goals	20-29	30-39	40-49	50-59	Total
none					

Punting	No	Yds	Avg	Long	In 20	TB
Brad Maynard	11	422	38.4	46	3	0

Punt Returns	Ret	Yds	Long	Avg	FC	TD
Ike Hilliard	3	33	19	11.0	1	0
Tiki Barber	2	13	9	6.5	2	0
TOTAL	5	46	19	9.2	3	0

Kickoff Returns	Ret	Yds	Long	Avg	FC	TD
Ron Dixon	6	154	97-td	25.7	0	1
Damon Washington	1	17	17	17.0	0	0
TOTAL	7	171	97-td	24.4	0	1

Interceptions	No	Yds	Long	Avg	TD
none					

Sacks		Most Tackles (solo)	
Michael Strahan	1.5	Michael Barrow	6
Cornelius Griffin	1.5	Jason Sehorn	6

Super Bowl Finalists' Playoff Statistics

Baltimore Ravens (4-0)

Passing	Att	Cmp	Pct.	Yds	TD	Rating
Trent Dilfer	73	35	47.9	590	3	83.7
Tony Banks	3	0	0.0	0	0	39.6

Interceptions: Dilfer 1.

Top Receivers	No	Yds	Avg	Long	TD
Qadry Ismail	9	150	16.7	44	0
Brandon Stokley	7	91	13.0	38-td	1
Shannon Sharpe	6	230	38.3	96-td	2
Jamal Lewis	5	40	8.0	15	0
Ben Coates	4	54	13.5	24	0

Top Rushers	Car	Yds	Avg	Long	TD
Jamal Lewis	103	338	3.3	27-td	4
Priest Holmes	18	45	2.5	11	0
Jermaine Lewis	3	7	2.3	5	0
Trent Dilfer	13	7	0.5	6	0

Touchdowns	TD	Run	Rec	Ret	Pts
Jamal Lewis	4	4	0	0	24
Shannon Sharpe	2	0	2	0	12
Five tied with 1 each for 6 pts.					

Kicking	PAT/Att	FG/Att	Lg	Pts
Matt Stover	11/11	6/8	47	29

Punts	No	Yds	Avg	Long	In20
Kyle Richardson	33	1318	39.9	66	14

Most Interceptions
Duane Starks 3
Ray Lewis 2
Jamie Sharper 2

Most Sacks
Michael McCrary 6
Three tied with 2 each.

NY Giants (2-1)

Passing	Att	Cmp	Pct.	Yds	TD	Rate
Kerry Collins	97	55	56.7	618	5	67.3
Jason Garrett	1	1	100.0	4	0	83.3

Interceptions: Collins 6.

Top Receivers	No	Yds	Avg	Long	TD
Ike Hilliard	16	220	13.8	46-td	2
Tiki Barber	13	60	4.6	12	0
Amani Toomer	10	135	13.5	24	1
Greg Comella	6	41	6.8	18-td	1
Two tied with 3 each.					

Top Rushers	Car	Yds	Avg	Long	TD
Tiki Barber	38	153	4.0	27	0
Ron Dayne	27	82	3.0	18	0
Joe Montgomery	18	48	2.7	8	0
Kerry Collins	11	29	2.6	9	0

Touchdowns	TD	Run	Rec	Ret	Pts
Ike Hilliard	2	0	2	0	12
Ron Dixon	2	0	0	2	12
Four tied with 1 each for 6 pts.					

Kicking	PAT/Att	FG/Att	Lg	Pts
Brad Daluiso	8/8	4/5	37	20

Punts	No	Yds	Avg	Long	In20
Brad Maynard	18	684	38.0	52	4

Most Interceptions
Jason Sehorn 2
Sam Garnes 1
Emmanuel McDaniel 1

Most Sacks
Michael Strahan 4.5
Cornelius Griffin 3
Jessie Armstead 1.5

NFL Playoff Leaders

Passing Efficiency
(Minimum of 25 attempts)

	Gm	Att	Cmp	Cmp%	Yards	Avg Gain	TD	TD%	Int	Int%	Rating
Aaron Brooks, NO	2	77	46	59.7	561	7.29	6	7.8	3	3.9	92.0
Kurt Warner, St.L	1	40	24	60.0	365	9.13	3	7.5	3	7.5	83.9
Trent Dilfer, Bal.	4	73	35	47.9	590	8.08	3	4.1	1	1.4	83.7
Peyton Manning, Ind.	1	32	17	53.1	194	6.06	1	3.1	0	0.0	82.0
Donovan McNabb, Phi.	2	74	44	59.5	342	4.62	3	4.1	2	2.7	73.1

Receptions

	No	Yds	Avg	Long	TD
Ike Hilliard, NYG	16	220	13.8	46-td	2
Willie Jackson, NO	15	267	17.8	50	4
Chad Morton, NO	15	140	9.3	23	0
Tiki Barber, NYG	13	60	4.6	12	0
Cris Carter, Min.	11	144	13.1	34	1

Rushing

	No	Yds	Avg	Long	TD
Jamal Lewis, Bal.	103	338	3.3	27-td	4
Lamar Smith, Mia.	48	214	4.5	24	2
Tiki Barber, NYG	38	153	4.0	27	0
Robert Smith, Min.	32	118	3.7	25	1
Edgerrin James, Ind.	21	107	5.1	34	0

Touchdowns

	TD	Rush	Rec	Ret	Pts
Willie Jackson, NO	4	0	4	0	24
Jamal Lewis, Bal.	4	4	0	0	24
Ike Hilliard, NYG	2	0	2	0	12
Randy Moss, Min.	2	0	2	0	12
Shannon Sharpe, Bal.	2	0	2	0	12
Lamar Smith, Mia.	2	2	0	0	12
Ron Dixon, NYG	2	0	0	2	12

Kicking

	PAT	FG	Long	Pts
Matt Stover, Bal.	11/11	6/8	47	29
Brad Daluiso, NYG	8/8	4/5	37	20
Sebastian Janikowski, Oak.	3/3	3/4	36	12
Doug Brien, NO	5/5	2/2	33	11
Gary Anderson, Min.	4/4	2/2	44	10

Interceptions

	No	Yds	Long	TD
Duane Starks, Bal.	3	93	49-td	1
Seven tied with 2 each.				

Sacks

	No
Michael McCrary, Bal.	6
Michael Strahan, NYG	4.5
Cornelius Griffin, NYG	3
Peter Boulware, Bal.	2
Jamie Sharper, Bal.	2
Rob Burnett, Bal.	2
Hugh Douglas, Phi.	2

NFL Pro Bowl

51st NFL Pro Bowl Game and 31st AFC-NFC contest (NFC leads series, 16-15). **Date:** Feb. 4, 2001 at Aloha Stadium in Honolulu. **Coaches:** Dennis Green, Min. (NFC) and Jon Gruden, Oak. (AFC). **Most Valuable Player:** QB Rich Gannon, Oak. (12 for 14, 160 yds, 2 TD).

NFC	 0	3	14	0—	**17**
AFC	 14	10	7	7—	**38**

1st: AFC—Tony Gonzalez 8-yd pass from Rich Gannon (Matt Stover kick), 5:22; AFC—Marvin Harrison 16-yd pass from Gannon (Stover kick), 10:52.

2nd: AFC—Stover 29-yd FG, 1:19; NFC—Martin Gramatica 48-yd FG, 5:43; AFC—Jimmy Smith 2-yd pass from Peyton Manning (Stover kick), 14:06.

3rd: NFC—Terrell Owens 17-yd pass from Donovan McNabb (Gramatica kick), 1:21; AFC—Harrison 24-yd pass from Manning (Stover kick), 3:50; NFC—Torry Holt 20-yd pass from Daunte Culpepper (Gramatica kick), 11:38.

4th: AFC—Edgerrin James 20-yd run (Stover kick), 3:41. **Attendance**— 50,128. **TV Rating**— 4.7/9 share (ABC). **Time**— 3:01.

STARTING LINEUPS

As voted on by NFL players, coaches, and fans. (*) denotes injured and unable to play.

American Conference

Pos	Offense	Pos	Defense
WR	Marvin Harrison, Ind.	E	Jason Taylor, Mia.
WR	Eric Moulds, Buf.	E	Trace Armstrong, Mia.
TE	Tony Gonzalez, KC	T	Trevor Pryce, Den.
T	Tony Boselli*, Jax.	T	Sam Adams, Bal.
T	Jonathan Ogden, Bal.	LB	Junior Seau, SD
G	Ruben Brown, Buf.	LB	Mo Lewis, NYJ
G	Bruce Matthews*, Ten.	LB	Ray Lewis, Bal.
C	Kevin Mawae, NYJ	CB	Sam Madison, Mia.
QB	Rich Gannon, Oak.	CB	Samari Rolle, Ten.
RB	Edgerrin James, Ind.	SS	Blaine Bishop, Ten.
FB	Richie Anderson, NYJ	FS	Rod Woodson, Bal.
K	Matt Stover, Bal.	P	Darren Bennett, SD
KR	Derrick Mason, Ten.	ST	Larry Izzo, Mia.

Reserves

Offense: WR—Rod Smith. Den. and Jimmy Smith, Jax; **TE**—Frank Wycheck, Ten.; **T**—Brad Hopkins, Ten.; **G**—Steve Wisniewski, Oak.; **C**—Tom Nalen*, Den.; **QB**—Peyton Manning, Ind. and Brian Griese*, Den.; **RB**—Corey Dillon, Cin. and Eddie George, Ten.

Defense: E—Jevon Kearse, Ten.; **T**—Ted Washington, Buf.; **LB**—Jason Gildon, Pit. and Sam Cowart, Buf.; **CB**—Charles Woodson, Oak.; **FS**—Brock Marion, Mia.

Replacements: OFFENSE—T Lincoln Kennedy, Oak. for Boselli; T Will Shields, KC for Matthews; C Tim Ruddy, Mia. for Nalen; QB—Elvis Grbac, KC for Griese. NEED PLAYER—LB Zach Thomas, Mia.

National Conference

Pos	Offense	Pos	Defense
WR	Isaac Bruce*, St.L	E	Hugh Douglas, Phi.
WR	Randy Moss*, Min.	E	Joe Johnson, NO
TE	Chad Lewis, Phi.	T	La'Roi Glover, NO
T	Orlando Pace, St.L	T	Warren Sapp, TB
G	William Roaf, NO	LB	Jessie Armstead, NYG
G	Larry Allen, Dal.	LB	Derrick Brooks, TB
G	Randall McDaniel, TB	LB	Stephen Boyd*, Det.
C	Jeff Christy, TB	CB	Champ Bailey, Wash.
QB	Daunte Culpepper, Min.	CB	Troy Vincent, Phi.
RB	Marshall Faulk*, St.L	SS	John Lynch, TB
FB	Mike Alstott, TB	FS	Darren Sharper, GB
K	Martin Gramatica, TB	P	Scott Player, Ari.
KR	Desmond Howard, Det.	ST	Michael Bates, Car.

Reserves

Offense: WR—Cris Carter, Min. and Terrell Owens, SF; **TE**—Stephen Alexander, Wash.; **T**— Korey Stringer, Min.; **G**—Ron Stone, NYG; **C**—Matt Birk, Min.; **QB**—Jeff Garcia, SF and Kurt Warner*, St.L; **RB**—Robert Smith*, Min. and Charlie Garner, SF.

Defense: E—Marco Coleman, Wash.; **T**—Luther Elliss, Det.; **LB**—Keith Mitchell, NO and Jeremiah Trotter, Phi.; **CB**—Donnie Abraham, TB; **S**—Robert Griffith, Min.

Replacements: OFFENSE—WR Joe Horn, NO and Torry Holt, St.L for Moss and Bruce; QB Donovan McNabb, Phi. for Warner; RB Stephen Davis, Wash. and Warrick Dunn, TB for Faulk and Smith. DEFENSE—LB Brian Urlacher, Chi. for Boyd. NEED PLAYER—LB Mark Fields, NO.

Annual Awards

The NFL does not sanction any of the major postseason awards for players and coaches, but many are given out. Among the presenters for the 2000 regular season were AP, The Maxwell Football Club of Philadelphia (Bert Bell Award for player; Greasy Neale Award for coach), *The Sporting News* and the Pro Football Writers of America/*Pro Football Weekly*.

Most Valuable Player

Marshall Faulk, St. Louis, RB .... AP, *TSN*, PFWA
Rich Gannon, Oakland, QB .... Bell

Offensive Players of the Year

Marshall Faulk, St. Louis, RB .... AP, PFWA

Defensive Player of the Year

Ray Lewis, Baltimore, LB .... AP, PFWA

Rookies of the Year

NFL	Brian Urlacher, Chicago, LB .... *TSN*	
Offense	Mike Anderson, Denver, RB .... AP, PFWA	
Defense	Brian Urlacher, Chicago, LB .... AP, PFWA	

Coach of the Year

Jim Haslett, New Orleans .... AP, PFWA
Andy Reid, Philadelphia..................... Neale, *TSN*

2000 All-NFL Team

The 2000 All-NFL team combining the All-Pro selections of the Associated Press, *The Sporting News* (TSN) and the Pro Football Writers of America/*Pro Football Weekly* (PFWA). Holdovers from the 1999 All-NFL Team in **bold** type.

Offense

Pos		Selectors
WR—	Randy Moss, Minnesota	AP, PFWA, *TSN*
WR—	Terrell Owens, San Francisco	AP
WR—	**Marvin Harrison**, Indianapolis	PFWA, *TSN*
TE—	**Tony Gonzalez**, Kansas City	AP, PFWA, *TSN*
T—	Jonathan Ogden, Baltimore	AP, PFWA, *TSN*
T—	Kyle Turley, New Orleans	AP
T—	William Roaf, New Orleans	PFWA
T—	Orlando Pace, St. Louis	*TSN*
G—	**Bruce Matthews**, Tennessee	AP, PFWA, *TSN*
G—	**Larry Allen**, Dallas	AP, PFWA, *TSN*
C—	**Tom Nalen**, Denver	AP, *TSN*
C—	**Kevin Mawae**, NY Jets	PFWA
QB—	Rich Gannon, Oakland	AP, PFWA, *TSN*
RB—	**Marshall Faulk**, St. Louis	AP, PFWA, *TSN*
RB—	Eddie George, Tennessee	AP, PFWA
RB—	**Edgerrin James**, Indianapolis	*TSN*

Defense

Pos		Selectors
DE—	Hugh Douglas, Philadelphia	AP, PFWA, *TSN*
DE—	Jason Taylor, Miami	AP, PFWA, *TSN*
DT—	**Warren Sapp**, Tampa Bay	AP, PFWA, *TSN*
DT—	La'Roi Glover, New Orleans	AP, PFWA, *TSN*
LB—	**Derrick Brooks**, Tampa Bay	AP, PFWA, *TSN*
LB—	**Ray Lewis**, Baltimore	AP, PFWA, *TSN*
LB—	Junior Seau, San Diego	AP, PFWA, *TSN*
LB—	Jeremiah Trotter, Philadelphia	AP
CB—	Samari Rolle, Tennessee	AP, PFWA, *TSN*
CB—	**Sam Madison**, Miami	AP, PFWA, *TSN*
S—	**John Lynch**, Tampa Bay	AP, PFWA, *TSN*
S—	Darren Sharper, Green Bay	AP, PFWA, *TSN*

Specialists

Pos		Selectors
PK—	Matt Stover, Baltimore	AP, PFWA, *TSN*
P—	Shane Lechler, Oakland	AP, *TSN*
P—	Darren Bennett, San Diego	PFWA

Pos		Selectors
KR—	Derrick Mason, Tennessee	AP, PFWA, *TSN*
PR—	Az-Zahir Hakim, St. Louis	PFWA, *TSN*
ST—	**Michael Bates**, Carolina	PFWA

2001 College Draft

First and second round selections at the 66th annual NFL College Draft held April 21-22, 2001, in New York City. Eighteen underclassmen were among the first 62 players chosen and are listed in capital LETTERS.

First Round

No	Team		Pos
1	Atlanta	MICHAEL VICK, Virginia Tech	QB
2	Arizona	Leonard Davis, Texas	OT
3	Cleveland	GERARD WARREN, Florida	DT
4	Cincinnati	JUSTIN SMITH, Missouri	DE
5	San Diego	LaDainian Tomlinson, TCU	RB
6	New England	Richard Seymour, Georgia	DT
7	San Francisco	Andre Carter, California	DE
8	Chicago	DAVID TERRELL, Michigan	WR
9	Seattle	KOREN ROBINSON, N.C. State	WR
10	Green Bay	Jamal Reynolds, Florida St.	DE
11	Carolina	Dan Morgan, Miami-FL	LB
12	St. Louis	Damione Lewis, Miami-FL	DT
13	Jacksonville	Marcus Stroud, Georgia	DT
14	Tampa Bay	KENYATTA WALKER, Florida	OT
15	Washington	Rod Gardner, Clemson	WR
16	NY Jets	Santana Moss, Miami-FL	WR
17	Seattle	Steve Hutchinson, Michigan	G
18	Detroit	Jeff Backus, Michigan	OT
19	Pittsburgh	Casey Hampton, Texas	DT
20	St. Louis	Adam Archuleta, Arizona St.	S
21	Buffalo	NATE CLEMENTS, Ohio St.	CB
22	NY Giants	Will Allen, Syracuse	CB
23	New Orleans	Deuce McAllister, Mississippi	RB
24	Denver	WILLIE MIDDLEBROOKS, Minnesota	CB
25	Philadelphia	FREDDIE MITCHELL, UCLA	WR
26	Miami	JAMAR FLETCHER, Wisconsin	CB
27	Minnesota	MICHAEL BENNETT, Wisconsin	RB
28	Oakland	Derrick Gibson, Florida St.	S
29	St. Louis	RYAN PICKETT, Ohio St.	DT
30	Indianapolis	Reggie Wayne, Miami-FL	WR
31	Baltimore	TODD HEAP, Arizona St.	TE

Second Round

No	Team		Pos
32	San Diego	Drew Brees, Purdue	QB
33	Cleveland	Quincy Morgan, Kansas St.	WR
34	Arizona	Kyle Vanden Bosch, Nebraska	DE
35	Atlanta	Alge Crumpler, North Carolina	TE
36	Cincinnati	Chad Johnson, Oregon St.	WR
37	Indianapolis	IDREES BASHIR, Memphis	S
38	Chicago	Anthony Thomas, Michigan	RB
39	Pittsburgh	Kendrell Bell, Georgia	LB
40	Seattle	Ken Lucas, Mississippi	CB
41	Green Bay	ROBERT FERGUSON, Texas A&M	WR
42	St. Louis	Tommy Polley, Florida St.	LB
43	Jacksonville	Maurice Williams, Michigan	OT
44	Carolina	Kris Jenkins, Maryland	DT
45	Washington	Fred Smoot, Mississippi St.	CB
46	Buffalo	Aaron Schobel, TCU	DE
47	San Francisco	JAMIE WINBORN, Vanderbilt	LB
48	New England	Matt Light, Purdue	OT
49	NY Jets	Lamont Jordan, Maryland	RB
50	Detroit	DOMINIC RAIOLA, Nebraska	C
51	Denver	Paul Toviessi, Marshall	DE
52	Miami	Chris Chambers, Wisconsin	WR
53	Dallas	QUINCY CARTER, Georgia	QB
54	Arizona	Michael Stone, Memphis	CB
55	Philadelphia	Quinton Caver, Arkansas	LB
56	Dallas	Tony Dixon, Alabama	S
57	Minnesota	Willie Howard, Stanford	DT
58	Buffalo	Travis Henry, Tennessee	RB
59	Oakland	Marques Tuiasosopo, Washington	QB
60	Tennessee	Andre Dyson, Utah	CB
61	Detroit	Shaun Rogers, Texas	DT
62	Baltimore	Gary Baxter, Baylor	CB

NFL Europe

Final 2001 Standings

	W	L	T	Pct.	PF	PA
*Barcelona	8	2	0	.800	252	191
*Berlin	6	4	0	.600	270	239
Rhein	5	5	0	.500	174	179
Scotland	4	6	0	.400	168	188
Amsterdam	4	6	0	.400	194	226
Frankfurt	3	7	0	.300	199	234

*World Bowl participants

Note: The teams with the top two records after the regular season advance directly to the World Bowl.

World Bowl IX

June 30, 2001 at the Amsterdam ArenA, the Netherlands

(Att: 32,116)

Berlin (6-4)	4	6	0	14 —	24
Barcelona (8-2)	3	6	8	0 —	17

MVP: Jonathan Quinn, Berlin, QB (25-38 for 308 yards and 3 TDs)

Regular Season Individual Leaders

Passing Efficiency
(Min. 140 pass attempts)

	Att	Cmp	Cmp Pct	Yds	Yds/ Att	TD	TD Pct	Long	Int	Int Pct	Rating
Jonathan Quinn, Ber	296	167	56.4	2257	7.63	24	8.1	82-td	9	3.0	95.3
Jarious Jackson, Bar	223	125	56.1	1544	6.92	13	5.8	74-td	6	2.7	85.9
Michael Bishop, Fra	153	76	49.7	1090	7.12	11	7.2	80-td	7	4.6	78.1
Spergon Wynn, Ams	337	193	57.3	2041	6.06	14	4.2	45-td	9	2.7	77.8
Clint Stoerner, Sco	307	171	55.7	1966	6.08	10	3.3	79-td	8	2.6	73.8

Scoring

Touchdowns

	TD	Rus	Rec	Ret	Pts
Chris Coleman, Ams	8	0	8	0	48
Mike Green, Bar	8	8	0	0	48
Tony Simmons, Bar	7	0	7	0	42
Bryan Gilmore, Bar	6	1	5	0	36
Ahmad Merritt, Ber	6	0	6	0	36

Kicking

	PAT	FG/FGA	Lg	Pts
Jesus Angoy, Bar	30/30	12/16	43	66
Rob Hart, Sco	16/16	16/19	39	64
Axel Kruse, Ber	33/33	4/5	29	45
Silvio Diliberto, Ams	22/23	5/5	31	37
Ola Kimrin, Fra	7/7	10/13	47	37

Rushing

	Car	Yards	Avg	Long	TD
Mike Green, Bar	183	1057	5.8	55	8
Pepe Pearson, Rhe	166	597	3.6	19	3
Denvis Manns, Fra	143	513	3.6	30	1
Anthony Gray, Sco	111	445	4.0	53	2
Madre Hill, Ber	69	388	5.6	60-td	2

Punting

	No	Yards	Avg	Long	In20
Brian Moorman, Ber	38	1645	43.3	77	7
Brad Costello, Sco	45	1887	41.9	64	16
Jason Malecki, Ams	55	2239	40.7	59	18
Rodney Williams, Rhe	50	2014	40.3	74	12
Bill LaFleur, Bar	44	1702	38.7	54	17

Receptions

	No	Yards	Avg	Long	TD
James Whalen, Sco	66	691	10.5	47	3
Trevor Insley, Bar	61	659	10.8	54	2
Chris Coleman, Ams	51	710	13.9	45-td	8
Andy McCullough, Fra	41	460	11.2	38	3
Ahmad Merritt, Ber	39	582	14.9	62	6

Sacks

	No
Roshaun Matthews, Ams	9.5
Gary Stills, Fra	9.5
Winfield Garnett, Ams	8.0
Chris Ward, Sco	7.5
Tim Englehardt, Bar	6.5

All-NFL Europe League Team

The All-NFL Europe League Team as selected by members of the NFL Europe media and by fan vote.

Offense

QB	Jonathan Quinn, Ber
WR	Trevor Insley, Bar
WR	Chris Coleman, Ams
WR	Tony Simmons, Bar
RB	Mike Green, Bar
TE	James Whalen, Sco
T	Josh Rawlings, Fra
G	Donnie Young, Bar
C	Michael Early, Rhe
G	Steve Herndon, Bar
T	John Feugill, Bar

Special Teams

K	Rob Hart, Sco
P	Brian Moorman, Ber
Spec.	Jordan Younger, Rhe

Defense

DE	Roshaun Matthews, Ams
DT	Tim Englehardt, Bar
DT	Winfield Garnett, Ams
DE	Chris Ward, Sco
LB	Scott Zimmerman, Rhe
LB	Dwan Epps, Ams
LB	Gary Stills, Fra
CB	Anthony Malbrough, Bar
S	Deke Cooper, Rhe
S	Clarence LeBlanc, Rhe
CB	Todd McMillon, Fra

Interceptions

	No	Yds	Long	TD
Deke Cooper, Rhe	6	30	18	0
Clarence LeBlanc, Rhe	4	153	73-td	3
Anthony Malbrough, Bar	4	140	75-td	2
Billy Gustin, Ber	4	44	21	0
Samyr Hamoudi, Bar	4	35	18	0

Annual Awards

Offensive MVP	Mike Green, Barcelona, RB
Defensive MVP	Roshaun Matthews, Amsterdam, DE
Coach of the Year	Jack Bicknell, Barcelona

Canadian Football League
Final 2000 Standings

Division champions (*) and playoff qualifiers (†) are noted. Ties and overtime losses (OTL) are each worth one point in the standings.

East Division

	W	L	T	OTL	Pts	PF	PA
*Montreal	12	6	0	0	24	594	379
†Hamilton	9	9	0	2	20	470	446
†Winnipeg	7	10	1	1	16	539	596
Toronto	7	10	1	0	15	390	562

West Division

	W	L	T	OTL	Pts	PF	PA
*Calgary	12	5	1	0	25	604	495
†Edmonton	10	7	0	1	21	527	520
†Brit. Columbia	8	10	0	1	17	513	529
Saskatchewan	5	12	1	0	11	516	626

Playoffs
Division Semifinals (Nov. 12)
East: Winnipeg 22 ....at Hamilton 20
West: B.C. 34 ....at Edmonton 32

Division Finals (Nov. 19)
East: at Montreal 35 ....Winnipeg 24
West: B.C. 37 ....at Calgary 23

88th Grey Cup Championship
November 26, 2000 at McMahon Stadium in Calgary, Alberta

(Att: 43,822)

Montreal	3	0	7	16 —	**26**
British Columbia	8	4	0	16 —	**28**

MVP: Robert Drummond, British Columbia, RB (10 carries for 122 yds, 1 TD; 3 catches for 41 yds)

Regular Season Individual Leaders
Passing Efficiency

	Att	Cmp	Cmp Pct	Yds	Yds/ Att	TD	TD Pct	Int	Int Pct	Rating
Dave Dickenson, Calg.	493	317	64.3	4636	9.4	36	7.3	6	1.2	114.1
Anthony Calvillo, Mon.	435	272	62.5	4277	9.8	27	6.2	5	1.1	111.1
Damon Allen, B.C.	525	324	61.7	4840	9.2	24	4.6	11	2.1	98.4
Nealon Greene, Edm.	397	247	62.2	3059	7.7	22	5.5	6	1.5	98.2
Kerwin Bell, Win.-Tor.	429	254	59.2	3085	7.2	17	4.0	14	3.3	81.0

Scoring

Touchdowns

	TD	Rus	Rec	Ret	Pts
Mike Pringle, Mon.	19	19	0	0	114
Derrell Mitchell, Tor.	16	1	14	1	96
Milt Stegall, Win.	15	0	15	0	90
Travis Moore, Calg.	15	0	15	0	90
Kez McCorvey, Edm.	15	0	15	0	90
Ronald Williams, Ham.	15	13	2	0	90

Kicking

	PAT	FG	S*	Pts
Terry Baker, Mon.	60/60	46/60	22	220
Mark McLoughlin, Calg.	63/63	43/55	7	199
Troy Westwood, Win.	52/52	45/58	8	195
Sean Fleming, Edm.	53/53	37/55	21	185
Paul Osbaldiston, Ham.	42/42	43/53	7	178

*Singles (or Rouges)

Rushing

	Car	Yards	Avg	TD
Mike Pringle, Mon.	326	1778	5.5	19
Ronald Williams, Ham.	267	1264	4.7	13
Kelvin Anderson, Calg.	203	1048	5.2	6
Darren Davis, Sask.	161	1024	6.4	4
Sean Millington, B.C.	156	1010	6.5	6

Receptions

	No	Yards	Avg	TD
Curtis Marsh, Sask.	102	1560	15.3	10
Derrell Mitchell, Tor.	100	1398	14.0	14
Terry Vaughn, Edm.	94	1216	12.9	6
Robert Gordon, Win.	89	1395	15.7	7
Darren Flutie, Ham.	79	1120	14.2	4

All-CFL Team

Offense
WR Curtis Marsh, Sask.
WR Travis Moore, Calg.
T   Bruce Beaton, Edm.
T   Christopher Perez, B.C.
G   Andrew Greene, Sask.
G   Pierre Vercheval, Mon.
C   Bryan Chiu, Mon.
QB Dave Dickenson, Calg.
RB Sean Millington, B.C.
RB Mike Pringle, Mon.
SB Derrell Mitchell, Tor.
SB Milt Stegall, Win.

Specialists
K—Lui Passaglia, B.C.
P—Noel Prefontaine, Tor.
Special Teams—Albert Johnson III, Win.

Defense
E   Shont'e Peoples, Calg.
E   Joe Montford, Ham.
T   Joe Fleming, Calg.
T   Demetrious Maxie, Sask.
LB Alondra Johnson, Calg.
LB Terry Ray, Edm.
LB George White, Sask.
DB Marvin Coleman, Calg.
DB Davis Sanchez, Mon.
DB Eddie Davis, Calg.
DB Barron Miles, Mon.
S   Greg Frers, Calg.

Most Outstanding Awards

Player ....Dave Dickenson, Calgary, QB	Rookie...........Albert Johnson III, Winnipeg, WR/ST
Canadian.........Sean Millington, British Columbia, RB	Tom Pate Award (Sportsmanship) ....Mike Morreale,
Offensive Lineman ....Pierre Vercheval, Montreal, G	Hamilton, SB
Defensive Player...........Joe Montford, Hamilton, DE	Coach ....Charlie Taaffe, Montreal

Arena Football
Final 2001 Standings

Division champions (*) and playoff qualifiers (†) are noted; top twelve teams advance to the playoffs, with top four receiving first-round byes.

American Conference
Central Division

	W	L	T	Pct.	PF	PA
*Grand Rapids	11	3	0	.786	801	776
†Indiana	9	5	0	.643	814	717
†Chicago	7	7	0	.500	684	699
†Detroit	7	7	0	.500	639	666
Milwaukee	3	11	0	.214	598	768

Western Division

	W	L	T	Pct.	PF	PA
*San Jose	10	4	0	.714	831	673
†Arizona	8	6	0	.571	750	640
Los Angeles	5	9	0	.357	564	716
Oklahoma	5	9	0	.357	630	759
Houston	3	11	0	.214	683	803

National Conference
Eastern Division

	W	L	T	Pct.	PF	PA
*New York	8	6	0	.571	898	828
†Toronto	8	6	0	.571	694	706
†Carolina	7	7	0	.500	786	685
Buffalo	6	8	0	.429	649	739
New Jersey	2	12	0	.143	543	693

Southern Division

	W	L	T	Pct.	PF	PA
*Nashville	10	4	0	.714	724	550
†Tampa Bay	10	4	0	.714	756	615
†Orlando	8	6	0	.571	675	627
Florida	6	8	0	.429	658	717

Annual Awards

Tinactin Ironman of the Year . . . . . . Dameon Porter, Chicago
Offensive Player of the Year . . . . Aaron Garcia, New York
Defensive Player of the Year . . . . . Kenny McEntyre, Orlando
Rookie of the Year . . . . R-Kal Truluck, Detroit
Coach of the Year . . . . Michael Trigg, G. Rapids

---

ArenaBowl XV

August 19, 2001 at Van Andel Arena in Grand Rapids, Mich.

(Att: 11,217)

Nashville	14	7	14	7 —	**42**
Grand Rapids	14	23	14	13 —	**64**

MVP: Terrill Shaw, Grand Rapids, offensive specialist (12 catches for 172 yards and 5 TDs.)

XFL
Final 2001 Standings

Division champions (*) and playoff qualifiers (†) are noted.

East Division

	W	L	T	Pct.	PF	PA
*Orlando	8	2	0	.800	213	185
†Chicago	5	5	0	.500	186	184
NY/NJ	4	6	0	.400	132	145
Birmingham	2	8	0	.200	131	239

West Division

	W	L	T	Pct.	PF	PA
*Los Angeles	7	3	0	.700	235	166
†San Francisco	5	5	0	.500	156	161
Memphis	5	5	0	.500	167	166
Las Vegas	4	6	0	.400	169	143

Playoffs

Semifinals (April 14-15)

San Francisco 26 . . . . at Orlando 25
at Los Angeles 33 . . . . Chicago 16

The Million Dollar Game

April 21, 2001 at the Los Angeles Coliseum
(Att: 24,153)

San Francisco	0	0	0	6 —	**6**
Los Angeles	3	18	10	7 —	**38**

Regular Season Individual Leaders

Passing Yards 2186   Tommy Maddox, LA
Receptions 67   Jeremaine Copeland, LA
Receiving Yards 828   Stepfret Williams, Bir.
Rushing Yards 800   John Avery, Chi.
Touchdowns 8   Darnell McDonald, LA

Points (Kicking) 60   Jose Cortez, LA
Sacks 7   Antonio Edwards, LV
       & Kelvin Kinney, LV
Interceptions 5   Corey Ivy, Chi.

Annual Awards

Player of the Year . . . . . . Tommy Maddox, Los Angeles, QB
Offensive Player of the Year . . . . . John Avery, Chicago, RB

Defensive Player of the Year . James Willis, Birmingham, LB
Coach of the Year . . . . Galen Hall, Orlando

Professional Football

1920-2001 Through the Years

ESPN information please®
SPORTS ALMANAC

PAGE
234

The Super Bowl

The first AFL-NFL World Championship Game, as it was originally called, was played seven months after the two leagues agreed to merge in June of 1966. It became the Super Bowl (complete with roman numerals) by the third game in 1969. The Super Bowl winner has been presented the Vince Lombardi Trophy since 1971. Lombardi, whose Green Bay teams won the first two title games, died in 19700. NFL champions (1966-69) and NFC champions (since 1970) are listed in CAPITAL letters.

Multiple winners: Dallas and San Francisco (5); Pittsburgh (4); Green Bay, Oakland-LA Raiders and Washington (3); Denver, Miami and NY Giants (2).

Bowl	Date	Winner	Head Coach	Score	Loser	Head Coach	Site
I	1/15/67	GREEN BAY	Vince Lombardi	35-10	Kansas City	Hank Stram	Los Angeles
II	1/14/68	GREEN BAY	Vince Lombardi	33-14	Oakland	John Rauch	Miami
III	1/12/69	NY Jets	Weeb Ewbank	16-7	BALT. COLTS	Don Shula	Miami
IV	1/11/70	Kansas City	Hank Stram	23-7	MINNESOTA	Bud Grant	New Orleans
V	1/17/71	Balt. Colts	Don McCafferty	16-13	DALLAS	Tom Landry	Miami
VI	1/16/72	DALLAS	Tom Landry	24-3	Miami	Don Shula	New Orleans
VII	1/14/73	Miami	Don Shula	14-7	WASHINGTON	George Allen	Los Angeles
VIII	1/13/74	Miami	Don Shula	24-7	MINNESOTA	Bud Grant	Houston
IX	1/12/75	Pittsburgh	Chuck Noll	16-6	MINNESOTA	Bud Grant	New Orleans
X	1/18/76	Pittsburgh	Chuck Noll	21-17	DALLAS	Tom Landry	Miami
XI	1/9/77	Oakland	John Madden	32-14	MINNESOTA	Bud Grant	Pasadena
XII	1/15/78	DALLAS	Tom Landry	27-10	Denver	Red Miller	New Orleans
XIII	1/21/79	Pittsburgh	Chuck Noll	35-31	DALLAS	Tom Landry	Miami
XIV	1/20/80	Pittsburgh	Chuck Noll	31-19	LA RAMS	Ray Malavasi	Pasadena
XV	1/25/81	Oakland	Tom Flores	27-10	PHILADELPHIA	Dick Vermeil	New Orleans
XVI	1/24/82	SAN FRANCISCO	Bill Walsh	26-21	Cincinnati	Forrest Gregg	Pontiac, MI
XVII	1/30/83	WASHINGTON	Joe Gibbs	27-17	Miami	Don Shula	Pasadena
XVIII	1/22/84	LA Raiders	Tom Flores	38-9	WASHINGTON	Joe Gibbs	Tampa
XIX	1/20/85	SAN FRANCISCO	Bill Walsh	38-16	Miami	Don Shula	Stanford
XX	1/26/86	CHICAGO	Mike Ditka	46-10	New England	Raymond Berry	New Orleans
XXI	1/25/87	NY GIANTS	Bill Parcells	39-20	Denver	Dan Reeves	Pasadena
XXII	1/31/88	WASHINGTON	Joe Gibbs	42-10	Denver	Dan Reeves	San Diego
XXIII	1/22/89	SAN FRANCISCO	Bill Walsh	20-16	Cincinnati	Sam Wyche	Miami
XXIV	1/28/90	SAN FRANCISCO	George Seifert	55-10	Denver	Dan Reeves	New Orleans
XXV	1/27/91	NY GIANTS	Bill Parcells	20-19	Buffalo	Marv Levy	Tampa
XXVI	1/26/92	WASHINGTON	Joe Gibbs	37-24	Buffalo	Marv Levy	Minneapolis
XXVII	1/31/93	DALLAS	Jimmy Johnson	52-17	Buffalo	Marv Levy	Pasadena
XXVIII	1/30/94	DALLAS	Jimmy Johnson	30-13	Buffalo	Marv Levy	Atlanta
XXIX	1/29/95	SAN FRANCISCO	George Seifert	49-26	San Diego	Bobby Ross	Miami
XXX	1/28/96	DALLAS	Barry Switzer	27-17	Pittsburgh	Bill Cowher	Tempe, AZ
XXXI	1/26/97	GREEN BAY	Mike Holmgren	35-21	New England	Bill Parcells	New Orleans
XXXII	1/25/98	Denver	Mike Shanahan	31-24	GREEN BAY	Mike Holmgren	San Diego
XXXIII	1/31/99	Denver	Mike Shanahan	34-19	ATLANTA	Dan Reeves	Miami
XXXIV	1/30/00	ST. LOUIS	Dick Vermeil	23-16	Tennessee	Jeff Fisher	Atlanta
XXXV	1/28/01	Balt. Ravens	Brian Billick	34-7	NY GIANTS	Jim Fassel	Tampa

Super Bowl Appearances

App		W	L	Pct	PF	PA	App		W	L	Pct	PF	PA
8	Dallas	5	3	.625	221	132	2	Kansas City	1	1	.500	33	42
6	Denver	2	4	.333	115	206	2	LA/St.L Rams	1	1	.500	42	47
5	San Francisco	5	0	1.000	188	89	2	Cincinnati	0	2	.000	37	46
5	Pittsburgh	4	1	.800	120	100	2	New England	0	2	.000	31	81
5	Washington	3	2	.600	122	103	1	Baltimore Ravens	1	0	1.000	34	7
5	Miami	2	3	.400	74	103	1	Chicago	1	0	1.000	46	10
4	Green Bay	3	1	.750	127	76	1	NY Jets	1	0	1.000	16	7
4	Oak/LA Raiders	3	1	.750	111	66	1	Atlanta	0	1	.000	19	34
4	Buffalo	0	4	.000	73	139	1	Philadelphia	0	1	.000	10	27
4	Minnesota	0	4	.000	34	95	1	San Diego	0	1	.000	26	49
3	NY Giants	2	1	.667	66	73	1	Tennessee	0	1	.000	16	23
2	Baltimore Colts	1	1	.500	23	29							

Pete Rozelle Award (MVP)

The Most Valuable Player in the Super Bowl. Currently selected by a 15-member panel made up of national pro football writers and broadcasters chosen by the NFL (80 percent) and fans voting via the internet (20 percent). Presented by *Sport* magazine from 1967-89 and by the NFL since 1990. Named after former NFL commissioner Pete Rozelle in 1990. Winner who did not play for Super Bowl champion is in **bold** type.

Multiple winners: Joe Montana (3); Terry Bradshaw and Bart Starr (2).

Bowl		Bowl		Bowl	
I	Bart Starr, Green Bay, QB	XIII	Terry Bradshaw, Pittsburgh, QB	XXVI	Mark Rypien, Washington, QB
II	Bart Starr, Green Bay, QB	XIV	Terry Bradshaw, Pittsburgh, QB	XXVII	Troy Aikman, Dallas, QB
III	Joe Namath, NY Jets, QB	XV	Jim Plunkett, Oakland, QB	XXVIII	Emmitt Smith, Dallas, RB
IV	Len Dawson, Kansas City, QB	XVI	Joe Montana, San Francisco, QB	XXIX	Steve Young, San Francisco, QB
V	**Chuck Howley**, Dallas, LB	XVII	John Riggins, Washington, RB	XXX	Larry Brown, Dallas, CB
VI	Roger Staubach, Dallas, QB	XVIII	Marcus Allen, LA Raiders, RB	XXXI	Desmond Howard, Green Bay, KR
VII	Jake Scott, Miami, S	XIX	Joe Montana, San Francisco, QB	XXXII	Terrell Davis, Denver, RB
VIII	Larry Csonka, Miami, RB	XX	Richard Dent, Chicago, DE	XXXIII	John Elway, Denver, QB
IX	Franco Harris, Pittsburgh, RB	XXI	Phil Simms, NY Giants, QB	XXXIV	Kurt Warner, St. Louis, QB
X	Lynn Swann, Pittsburgh, WR	XXII	Doug Williams, Washington, QB	XXXV	Ray Lewis, Baltimore, LB
XI	Fred Biletnikoff, Oakland, WR	XXIII	Jerry Rice, San Francisco, WR		
XII	Harvey Martin, Dallas, DE	XXIV	Joe Montana, San Francisco, QB		
	& Randy White, Dallas, DT	XXV	Ottis Anderson, NY Giants, RB		

All-Time Super Bowl Leaders

Through 2001; participants in Super Bowl XXXV in **bold** type.

CAREER

Passing Efficiency

		Gm	Att	Cmp	Cmp%	Yards	Avg Gain	TD	TD%	Int	Int%	Rating
1	Phil Simms, NYG	1	25	22	88.0	268	10.72	3	12.0	0	0.0	150.9
2	Steve Young, SF	2	39	26	66.7	345	8.85	6	15.4	0	0.0	134.8
3	Doug Williams, Wash	1	29	18	62.1	340	11.72	4	13.8	1	3.4	128.1
4	Joe Montana, SF	4	122	83	68.0	1142	9.36	11	9.0	0	0.0	127.8
5	Jim Plunkett, Raiders	2	46	29	63.0	433	9.41	4	8.7	0	0.0	122.8
6	Terry Bradshaw, Pit	4	84	49	58.3	932	11.10	9	10.7	4	4.8	112.8
7	Troy Aikman, Dal	3	80	56	70.0	689	8.61	5	6.3	1	1.3	111.9
8	Bart Starr, GB	2	47	29	61.7	452	9.62	3	6.4	1	2.1	106.0
9	Kurt Warner, St.L	1	45	24	53.3	414	9.20	2	4.4	0	0.0	99.7
10	Brett Favre, GB	2	69	39	56.5	502	7.28	5	7.2	1	1.4	97.6

Ratings based on performance standards established for completion percentage, average gain, touchdown percentage and interception percentage. Quarterbacks are allocated points according to how their statistics measure up to those standards. Minimum 25 passing attempts.

Passing Yards

		Gm	Att	Cmp	Pct	Yds
1	Joe Montana, SF	4	122	83	68.0	1142
2	John Elway, Den	5	152	76	50.0	1128
3	Terry Bradshaw, Pit	4	84	49	58.3	932
4	Jim Kelly, Buf	4	145	81	55.9	829
5	Roger Staubach, Dal	4	98	61	62.2	734
6	Troy Aikman, Dal	3	80	56	70.0	689
7	Brett Favre, GB	2	69	39	56.5	502
8	Fran Tarkenton, Min	3	89	46	51.7	489
9	Bart Starr, GB	2	47	29	61.7	452
10	Jim Plunkett, Raiders	2	46	29	63.0	433
11	Kurt Warner, St.L	1	45	24	53.3	414
12	Joe Theismann, Wash	2	58	31	53.4	386
13	Len Dawson, KC	2	44	28	63.6	353
14	Steve Young, SF	2	26	39	66.7	345
15	Doug Williams, Wash	1	29	18	62.1	340

Receptions

		Gm	No	Yds	Avg	TD
1	Jerry Rice, SF	3	28	512	18.3	7
2	Andre Reed, Buf	4	27	323	12.0	0
3	Roger Craig, SF	3	20	212	10.6	3
	Thurman Thomas, Buf	4	20	144	7.2	0
5	Jay Novacek, Dal	3	17	148	8.7	2
6	Lynn Swann, Pit	4	16	364	22.8	3
7	Michael Irvin, Dal	3	16	256	16.0	2
8	Chuck Foreman, Min	3	15	139	9.3	0
9	Cliff Branch, Raiders	3	14	181	12.9	3
10	Don Beebe, Buf	3	12	171	14.3	2
	Preston Pearson, Bal-Pit-Dal	5	12	105	8.8	0
	Kenneth Davis, Buf	4	12	72	6.0	0
	Antonio Freeman, GB	2	12	231	19.3	3
14	John Stallworth, Pit	4	11	268	24.4	3
	Dan Ross, Cin	1	11	104	9.5	2

Rushing

		Gm	Car	Yds	Avg	TD
1	Franco Harris, Pit	4	101	354	3.5	4
2	Larry Csonka, Mia	3	57	297	5.2	2
3	Emmitt Smith, Dal	3	70	289	4.1	5
4	Terrell Davis, Den	2	55	259	4.7	3
5	John Riggins, Wash	2	64	230	3.6	2
6	Timmy Smith, Wash	1	22	204	9.3	2
	Thurman Thomas, Buf	4	52	204	3.9	4
8	Roger Craig, SF	3	52	201	3.9	2
9	Marcus Allen, Raiders	1	20	191	9.5	2
10	Tony Dorsett, Dal	2	31	162	5.2	1

All-Purpose Yards

		Gm	Rush	Rec	Ret	Total
1	Jerry Rice, SF	3	15	512	0	527
2	Franco Harris, Pit	4	354	114	0	468
3	Roger Craig, SF	3	201	212	0	413
4	Lynn Swann, Pit	4	-7	364	34	391
5	Thurman Thomas, Buf	4	204	144	0	348
6	Emmitt Smith, Dal	3	289	56	0	345
7	Antonio Freeman, GB	2	0	231	104	335
8	Andre Reed, Buf	4	0	323	0	323
9	Terrell Davis, Den	2	259	58	0	317
10	Larry Csonka, Mia	3	297	17	0	314

All-Time Super Bowl Leaders (Cont.)
Scoring

Points

		Gm	TD	FG	PAT	Pts
1	Jerry Rice, SF	3	7	0	0	42
2	Emmitt Smith, Dal.	3	5	0	0	30
3	Roger Craig, SF	3	4	0	0	24
	Franco Harris, Pit.	4	4	0	0	24
	Thurman Thomas, Buf	4	4	0	0	24
	John Elway, Den	5	4	0	0	24
7	Ray Wersching, SF	2	0	5	7	22
8	Don Chandler, GB	2	0	4	8	20
9	Cliff Branch, Raiders	3	3	0	0	18
	John Stallworth, Pit	3	3	0	0	18
	Lynn Swann, Pit	4	3	0	0	18
	Ricky Watters, SF	1	3	0	0	18
	Terrell Davis, Den.	2	3	0	0	18
	Antonio Freeman, GB	2	3	0	0	18
15	Chris Bahr, Raiders	2	0	3	8	17
	Jason Elam, Den	2	0	3	8	17

Punting
(Minimum 10 Punts)

		Gm	No	Yds	Avg.
1	Jerrel Wilson, KC	2	11	511	46.5
2	**Kyle Richardson**, Bal	1	10	430	43.0
3	Ray Guy, Raiders	3	14	587	41.9
4	Larry Seiple, Mia	3	15	620	41.3
5	Mike Eischeid, Raiders-Min	3	17	698	41.1

Punt Returns
(Minimum 4 returns)

		Gm	No	Yds	Avg.	TD
1	John Taylor, SF	3	6	94	15.7	0
2	Desmond Howard, GB	1	6	90	15.0	0
3	Neal Colzie, Raiders	1	4	43	10.8	0
4	Dana McLemore, SF	1	5	51	10.2	0
5	Mike Fuller, Cin	1	4	35	8.8	0

Kickoff Returns
(Minimum 4 returns)

		Gm	No	Yds	Avg.	TD
1	Tim Dwight, Atl	1	5	210	42.0	1
2	Desmond Howard, GB	1	4	154	38.5	1
3	Fulton Walker, Mia	2	8	283	35.4	1
4	Andre Coleman, SD	1	8	242	30.3	1
5	Larry Anderson, Pit	2	8	207	25.9	0

Touchdowns

		Gm	Rush	Rec	Ret	TD
1	Jerry Rice, SF	3	0	7	0	7
2	Emmitt Smith, Dal.	3	5	0	0	5
3	Roger Craig, SF	3	2	2	0	4
	Franco Harris, Pit.	4	4	0	0	4
	John Elway, Den	5	4	0	0	4
	Thurman Thomas, Buf	4	4	0	0	4
7	Cliff Branch, Raiders	3	0	3	0	3
	John Stallworth, Pit	4	0	3	0	3
	Lynn Swann, Pit	4	0	3	0	3
	Ricky Watters, SF	1	1	2	0	3
	Terrell Davis, Den.	2	3	0	0	3
	Antonio Freeman, GB	2	0	3	0	3
13	Twenty-four tied with 2 TDs each:					

Marcus Allen, Raiders; Ottis Anderson, NYG; Pete Banaszak, Raiders; Don Beebe, Buf.; Gary Clark, Wash.; Larry Csonka, Mia.; Eddie George, Ten.; Howard Griffith, Den.; Michael Irvin, Dal.; Butch Johnson, Dal.; Jim Kiick, Mia.; Max McGee, GB; Jim McMahon, Chi.; Bill Miller, Raiders; Joe Montana, SF; Elijah Pitts, GB; Tom Rathman, SF; John Riggins, Wash.; Gerald Riggs, Wash.; Dan Ross, Cin.; Ricky Sanders, Wash.; Timmy Smith, Wash.; John Taylor, SF and Duane Thomas, Dal.

Interceptions

		Gm	No	Yds	TD
1	Larry Brown, Dal	2	3	77	0
	Chuck Howley, Dal	2	3	63	0
	Rod Martin, Raiders	2	3	44	0
4	Randy Beverly, NYJ	1	2	0	0
	Mel Blount, Pit	4	2	23	0
	Brad Edwards, Wash	1	2	56	0
	Thomas Everett, Dal.	2	2	22	0
	Darrien Gordon, Den.	3	2	108	0
	Jake Scott, Mia	2	2	63	0
	Mike Wagner, Pit.	3	2	45	0
	James Washington, Dal	2	2	25	0
	Barry Wilburn, Wash	1	2	11	0
	Eric Wright, SF	4	2	25	0

Sacks

		Gm	No
1	Charles Haley, SF-Dal	5	4.5
2	Reggie White, GB	2	3
	Leonard Marshall, NYG	2	3
	Danny Stubbs, SF	2	3
	Jeff Wright, Buf	4	3

Four or More Super Bowl Wins
Dallas Cowboys (5)

Year	Bowl	Head Coach	Quarterback	MVP	Opponent	Score	Site
1972	VI	Tom Landry	Roger Staubach	Staubach	Miami	24-3	New Orleans
1978	XII	Tom Landry	Roger Staubach	Harvey Martin & Randy White	Denver	27-10	New Orleans
1993	XXVII	Jimmy Johnson	Troy Aikman	Aikman	Buffalo	52-17	Pasadena
1994	XXVIII	Jimmy Johnson	Troy Aikman	Emmitt Smith	Buffalo	30-13	Atlanta
1996	XXX	Barry Switzer	Troy Aikman	Larry Brown	Pittsburgh	27-17	Tempe

San Francisco 49ers (5)

Year	Bowl	Head Coach	Quarterback	MVP	Opponent	Score	Site
1982	XVI	Bill Walsh	Joe Montana	Montana	Cincinnati	26-21	Pontiac
1985	XIX	Bill Walsh	Joe Montana	Montana	Miami	38-16	Stanford
1989	XXIII	Bill Walsh	Joe Montana	Jerry Rice	Cincinnati	20-16	Miami
1990	XXIV	George Seifert	Joe Montana	Montana	Denver	55-10	New Orleans
1995	XXIX	George Seifert	Steve Young	Young	San Diego	49-26	Miami

Pittsburgh Steelers (4)

Year	Bowl	Head Coach	Quarterback	MVP	Opponent	Score	Site
1975	IX	Chuck Noll	Terry Bradshaw	Franco Harris	Minnesota	16-6	New Orleans
1976	X	Chuck Noll	Terry Bradshaw	Lynn Swann	Dallas	21-17	Miami
1979	XIII	Chuck Noll	Terry Bradshaw	Bradshaw	Dallas	35-31	Miami
1980	XIV	Chuck Noll	Terry Bradshaw	Bradshaw	LA Rams	31-19	Pasadena

SINGLE GAME

Passing

Yards Gained	Year	Att/Cmp	Yds
1 Kurt Warner, St.L vs Ten	2000	45/24	414
2 Joe Montana, SF vs Cin	1989	36/23	357
3 Doug Williams, Wash vs Den	1988	29/18	340
4 John Elway, Den vs Atl	1999	29/18	336
5 Joe Montana, SF vs Mia	1985	35/24	331
6 Steve Young, SF vs SD	1995	36/24	325
7 Terry Bradshaw, Pit vs Dal	1979	30/17	318
Dan Marino, Mia vs SF	1985	50/29	318
9 Terry Bradshaw, Pit vs Rams	1980	21/14	309
10 John Elway, Den vs NYG	1987	37/22	304

Touchdown Passes	Year	TD	Int
1 Steve Young, SF vs SD	1995	6	0
2 Joe Montana, SF vs Den	1990	5	0
3 Terry Bradshaw, Pit vs Dal	1979	4	1
Doug Williams, Wash vs Den	1988	4	1
Troy Aikman, Dal vs Buf	1993	4	0
6 Roger Staubach, Dal vs Pit	1979	3	1
Jim Plunkett, Raiders vs Phi	1981	3	0
Joe Montana, SF vs Mia	1985	3	0
Phil Simms, NYG vs Den	1987	3	0
Brett Favre, GB vs Den	1998	3	1

Receiving

Catches	Year	No	Yds	TD
1 Dan Ross, Cin vs SF	1982	11	104	2
Jerry Rice, SF vs Cin	1989	11	215	1
3 Tony Nathan, Mia vs SF	1985	10	83	0
Jerry Rice, SF vs SD	1995	10	149	3
Andre Hastings, Pit vs Dal	1996	10	98	0
6 Ricky Sanders, Wash vs Den	1988	9	193	1
Antonio Freeman, GB vs Den	1998	9	126	2

Five tied with 8 each, including twice by Andre Reed.

Yards Gained	Year	No	Yds	TD
1 Jerry Rice, SF vs Cin	1989	11	215	1
2 Ricky Sanders, Wash vs Den	1988	9	193	2
3 Isaac Bruce, St.L vs Ten	2000	6	162	1
4 Lynn Swann, Pit vs Dal	1976	4	161	1
5 Andre Reed, Buf vs Dal	1993	8	152	0
Rod Smith, Den vs Atl	1999	5	152	1
7 Jerry Rice, SF vs SD	1995	10	149	3
8 Jerry Rice, SF vs Den	1990	7	148	3
9 Max McGee, GB vs KC	1967	7	138	2
10 George Sauer, NYJ vs Bal	1969	8	133	0

Rushing

Yards Gained	Year	Car	Yds	TD
1 Timmy Smith, Wash vs Den	1988	22	204	2
2 Marcus Allen, Raiders vs Wash	1984	20	191	2
3 John Riggins, Wash vs Mia	1983	38	166	1
4 Franco Harris, Pit vs Min	1975	34	158	1
5 Terrell Davis, Den vs GB	1998	30	157	3
6 Larry Csonka, Mia vs Min	1974	33	145	2
7 Clarence Davis, Raiders vs Min	1977	16	137	0
8 Thurman Thomas, Buf vs NYG	1991	15	135	1
9 Emmitt Smith, Dal vs Buf	1994	30	132	2
10 Matt Snell, NYJ vs Bal	1969	30	121	1
11 Tom Matte, Bal vs NYJ	1969	11	116	0
12 Larry Csonka, Mia vs Wash	1973	15	112	1
13 Emmitt Smith, Dal vs Buf	1993	22	108	1
14 Ottis Anderson, NYG vs Buf	1991	21	102	1
Terrell Davis, Den vs Atl	1999	25	102	0
Jamal Lewis, Bal vs NYG	2001	27	102	1

Scoring

Points	Year	TD	FG	PAT	Pts
1 Roger Craig, SF vs Mia	1985	3	0	0	18
Jerry Rice, SF vs Den	1990	3	0	0	18
Jerry Rice, SF vs SD	1995	3	0	0	18
Ricky Watters, SF vs SD	1995	3	0	0	18
Terrell Davis, Den vs GB	1998	3	0	0	18
6 Don Chandler, GB vs Raiders	1968	0	4	3	15

Touchdowns	Year	TD	Rush	Rec
1 Roger Craig, SF vs Mia	1985	3	1	2
Jerry Rice, SF vs Den	1990	3	0	3
Jerry Rice, SF vs SD	1995	3	0	3
Ricky Watters, SF vs SD	1995	3	1	2
Terrell Davis, Den vs GB	1998	3	3	0

Punt Returns

(Minimum 3 returns)

	Year	No	Yds	Avg
1 John Taylor, SF vs Cin	1989	3	56	18.7
2 Desmond Howard, GB vs NE	1997	6	90	15.0
3 John Taylor, SF vs Den	1990	3	38	12.7
4 Kelvin Martin, Dal vs Buf	1993	3	35	11.7

All-Purpose Yards

Yards Gained	Year	Run	Rec	Tot
1 Desmond Howard, GB vs NE	1997	0	0	244
2 Andre Coleman, SD vs SF	1995	0	0	242
3 Ricky Sanders, Wash vs Den	1988	193	-4	235
4 Antonio Freeman, GB vs Den	1998	0	126	230
5 Jerry Rice, SF vs Cin	1989	215	5	220
6 Tim Dwight, Atl vs Den	1999	5	0	215
7 Timmy Smith, Wash vs Den	1988	204	9	213
8 Marcus Allen, Raiders vs Wash	1984	191	18	209
9 Stephen Starring, NE vs Chi	1986	0	39	192
10 Fulton Walker, Mia vs Wash	1983	0	0	190
Thurman Thomas, Buf vs NYG	1991	135	55	190

Return Yardage: Howard 244, Coleman 242, Sanders 46, Freeman 104, Dwight 210, Starring 153, Walker 190.

Interceptions

	Year	No	Yds	TD
1 Rod Martin, Raiders vs Phi	1981	3	44	0

Eight tied with 2 each.

Punting

(Minimum 4 punts)

	Year	No	Yds	Avg
1 Bryan Wagner, SD vs SF	1995	4	195	48.8
2 Jerrel Wilson, KC vs Min	1970	4	194	48.5
3 Jim Miller, SF vs Cin	1982	4	185	46.3

Kickoff Returns

(Minimum 3 returns)

	Year	No	Yds	Avg
1 Fulton Walker, Mia vs Wash	1983	4	190	47.5
2 Tim Dwight, Atl vs Den	1999	5	210	42.0
3 Desmond Howard, GB vs NE	1997	4	154	38.5
4 Larry Anderson, Pit vs Rams	1980	5	162	32.4
5 Rick Upchurch, Den vs Dal	1978	3	94	31.3

Super Bowl Playoffs

The Super Bowl forced the NFL to set up pro football's first guaranteed multiple-game playoff format. Over the years, the NFL-AFL merger, the creation of two conferences comprised of three divisions each and the proliferation of wild card entries has seen the postseason field grow from four teams (1966), to six (1967-68), to eight (1969-77), to 10 (1978-81, 1983-89), to the present 12 (since 1990).

In 1966, there was a special playoff between Oakland and Kansas City which were both 12-2 and tied for first in the AFL's Western Division. In 1982, when a 57-day players' strike shortened the regular season to just nine games, playoff berths were extended to 16 teams (eight from each conference) and a 15-game tournament was played.

Note that in the following year-by-year summary, records of finalists include all games leading up to the Super Bowl; (*) indicates non-division winners or wild card teams.

1966 Season

AFL Playoffs

Championship . . . . .Kansas City 31, at Buffalo 7

NFL Playoffs

Championship . . . . :Green Bay 34, at Dallas 27

Super Bowl I
Jan. 15, 1967
Memorial Coliseum, Los Angeles
Favorite: Packers by 14   Attendance: 61,946

Kansas City (12-2-1) 0   10   0   0 **—10**
Green Bay (13-2) 7   7 14   7 **—35**
MVP: Green Bay QB Bart Starr (16 for 23, 250 yds, 2 TD, 1 Int)

1967 Season

AFL Playoffs

Championship . . . . .at Oakland 40, Houston 7

NFL Playoffs

Eastern Conference . . . . .at Dallas 52, Cleveland 14
Western Conference . . . . .at Green Bay 28, LA Rams 7
Championship . . . . .at Green Bay 21, Dallas 17

Super Bowl II
Jan. 14, 1968
Orange Bowl, Miami
Favorite: Packers by 13½   Attendance: 75,546

Green Bay (11-4-1) 3   13 10   7 **—33**
Oakland (14-1) 0   7   0   7 **—14**
MVP: Green Bay QB Bart Starr (13 for 24, 202 yds, 1 TD)

1968 Season

AFL Playoffs

Western Div. Playoff . . . . .at Oakland 41, Kansas City 6
AFL Championship . . . . .at NY Jets 27, Oakland 23

NFL Playoffs

Eastern Conference . . . . .at Cleveland 31, Dallas 20
Western Conference . . . . . .at Baltimore 24, Minnesota 14
NFL Championship . . . . .Baltimore 34, at Cleveland 0

Super Bowl III
Jan. 12, 1969
Orange Bowl, Miami
Favorite: Colts by 18   Attendance: 75,389

NY Jets (12-3) 0   7   6   3 **—16**
Baltimore (15-1) 0   0   0   7   **—7**
MVP: NY Jets QB Joe Namath (17 for 28, 206 yds)

1969 Season

AFL Playoffs

Inter-Division . . . .*Kansas City 13, at NY Jets 6
                                            at Oakland 56, *Houston 7
AFL Championship . . . . .Kansas City 17, at Oakland 7

NFL Playoffs

Eastern Conference . . . . .Cleveland 38, at Dallas 14
Western Conference . . . . . . .at Minnesota 23, LA Rams 20
NFL Championship . . . . .at Minnesota 27, Cleveland 7

Super Bowl IV
Jan. 11, 1970
Tulane Stadium, New Orleans
Favorite: Vikings by 12   Attendance: 80,562

Minnesota (14-2) 0   0   7   0   **—7**
Kansas City (13-3) 3   13   7   0 **—23**
MVP: KC QB Len Dawson (12 for 17, 142 yds, 1 TD, 1 Int)

1970 Season

AFC Playoffs

First Round . . . . .at Baltimore 17, Cincinnati 0
                                            at Oakland 21,*Miami 14
Championship . . . . .at Baltimore 27, Oakland 17

NFC Playoffs

First Round. . . . . .at Dallas 5, *Detroit 0
                                            San Francisco 17, at Minnesota 14
Championship . . . . .Dallas 17, at San Francisco 10

Super Bowl V
Jan. 17, 1971
Orange Bowl, Miami
Favorite: Cowboys by 2½   Attendance: 79,204

Baltimore (13-2-1) 0   6   0 10 **—16**
Dallas (12-4) 3   10   0   0 **—13**
MVP: Dallas LB Chuck Howley (2 interceptions for 22 yds)

1971 Season

AFC Playoffs

First Round . . . . : . .Miami 27, at Kansas City 24 (OT)
                                            *Baltimore 20, at Cleveland 3
Championship . . . . .at Miami 21, Baltimore 0

NFC Playoffs

First Round . . . . .Dallas 20, at Minnesota 12
                                            at San Francisco 24,*Washington 20
Championship . . . . .at Dallas 14, San Francisco 3

Super Bowl VI
Jan. 16, 1972
Tulane Stadium, New Orleans
Favorite: Cowboys by 6   Attendance: 81,023

Dallas (13-3) 3   7   7   7 **—24**
Miami (12-3-1) 0   3   0   0   **—3**
MVP: Dallas QB Roger Staubach (12 for 19, 119 yds, 2 TD)

1972 Season

AFC Playoffs

First Round . . . . .at Pittsburgh 13, Oakland 7
at Miami 20, *Cleveland 14
Championship . . . . .Miami 21, at Pittsburgh 17

NFC Playoffs

First Round . . . .*Dallas 30, at San Francisco 28
at Washington 16, Green Bay 3
Championship . . . . .at Washington 26, Dallas 3

Super Bowl VII
Jan. 14, 1973
Memorial Coliseum, Los Angeles
Favorite: Redskins by 1½   Attendance: 90,182

Miami (16-0)	7	7	0	0	**—14**
Washington (13-3)	0	0	0	7	**—7**

MVP: Miami safety Jake Scott (2 Interceptions for 63 yds)

1973 Season

AFC Playoffs

First Round . . . . .at Oakland 33, *Pittsburgh 14
at Miami 34, Cincinnati 16
Championship . . . . .at Miami 27, Oakland 10

NFC Playoffs

First Round . . . . .at Minnesota 27, *Washington 20
at Dallas 27, LA Rams 16
Championship . . . . .Minnesota 27, at Dallas 10

Super Bowl VIII
Jan. 13, 1974
Rice Stadium, Houston
Favorite: Dolphins by 6½   Attendance: 71,882

Minnesota (14-2)	0	0	0	7	**—7**
Miami (12-4)	14	3	7	0	**—24**

MVP: Miami FB Larry Csonka (33 carries, 145 yds, 2 TD)

1974 Season

AFC Playoffs

First Round . . . . .at Oakland 28, Miami 26
at Pittsburgh 32, *Buffalo 14
Championship . . . . .Pittsburgh 24, at Oakland 13

NFC Playoffs

First Round . . . . .at Minnesota 30, St. Louis 14
at LA Rams 19, *Washington 10
Championship . . . . .at Minnesota 14, LA Rams 10

Super Bowl IX
Jan. 12, 1975
Tulane Stadium, New Orleans
Favorite: Steelers by 3   Attendance: 80,997

Pittsburgh (12-3-1)	0	2	7	7	**—16**
Minnesota (12-4)	0	0	0	6	**—6**

MVP: Pittsburgh RB Franco Harris (34 carries, 158 yds, 1 TD)

1975 Season

AFC Playoffs

First Round . . . . .at Pittsburgh 28, Baltimore 10
at Oakland 31, *Cincinnati 28
Championship . . . . .at Pittsburgh 16, Oakland 10

NFC Playoffs

First Round . . . . .at LA Rams 35, St. Louis 23
*Dallas 17, at Minnesota 14
Championship . . . . .Dallas 37, at LA Rams 7

Super Bowl X
Jan. 18, 1976
Orange Bowl, Miami
Favorite: Steelers by 6½   Attendance: 80,187

Dallas (12-4)	7	3	0	7	**—17**
Pittsburgh (14-2)	7	0	0	14	**—21**

MVP: Pittsburgh WR Lynn Swann (4 catches, 161 yds, 1 TD)

1976 Season

AFC Playoffs

First Round . . . . .at Oakland 24, *New England 21
Pittsburgh 40, at New England 14
Championship . . .*. . . . . .at Oakland 24, Pittsburgh 7

NFC Playoffs

First Round . . . . .at Minnesota 35, *Washington 20
LA Rams 14, at Dallas 12
Championship . . . . .at Minnesota 24, LA Rams 13

Super Bowl XI
Jan. 9, 1977
Rose Bowl, Pasadena
Favorite: Raiders by 4½   Attendance: 103,438

Oakland (15-1)	0	16	3	13	**—32**
Minnesota (13-2-1)	0	0	7	7	**—14**

MVP: Oakland WR Fred Biletnikoff (4 catches, 79 yds)

1977 Season

AFC Playoffs

First Round . . . . .at Denver 34, Pittsburgh 21
*Oakland 37, at Baltimore 31 (OT)
Championship . . . . .at Denver 20, Oakland 17

NFC Playoffs

First Round . . . . .at Dallas 37, *Chicago 7
Minnesota 14, at LA Rams 7
Championship . . . . .at Dallas 23, Minnesota 6

Super Bowl XII
Jan. 15, 1978
Louisiana Superdome, New Orleans
Favorite: Cowboys by 6   Attendance: 75,583

Dallas (14-2)	10	3	7	7	**—27**
Denver (14-2)	0	0	10	0	**—10**

MVPs: Dallas DE Harvey Martin and DT Randy White (Cowboys' defense forced 8 turnovers)

1978 Season

AFC Playoffs

First Round . . . .*Houston 17, at *Miami 9
Second Round . . . . .Houston 31, at New England 14
at Pittsburgh 33, Denver 10
Championship . . . . .at Pittsburgh 34, Houston 5

NFC Playoffs

First Round . . . . .at *Atlanta 14, *Philadelphia 13
Second Round . . . . .at Dallas 27, Atlanta 20
at LA Rams 34, Minnesota 10
Championship . . . . .Dallas 28, at LA Rams 0

Super Bowl XIII
Jan. 21, 1979
Orange Bowl, Miami
Favorite: Steelers by 4   Attendance: 79,484

Pittsburgh (16-2)	7	14	0	14	**—35**
Dallas (14-4)	7	7	3	14	**—31**

MVP: Pittsburgh QB Terry Bradshaw (17 for 30, 318 yds, 4 TD, 1 Int)

Super Bowl Playoffs (Cont.)

1979 Season

AFC Playoffs

First Round...................at *Houston 13, *Denver 7
Second Round.............Houston 17, at San Diego 14
at Pittsburgh 34, Miami 14
Championship ....at Pittsburgh 27, Houston 13

NFC Playoffs

First Round ....at *Philadelphia 27, *Chicago 17
Second Round ....at Tampa Bay 24, Philadelphia 17
LA Rams 21, at Dallas 19
Championship ....LA Rams 9, at Tampa Bay 0

Super Bowl XIV
Jan. 20, 1980
Rose Bowl, Pasadena
Favorite: Steelers by 10½ Attendance: 103,985

LA Rams (11-7)	.7	6	6	0	**—19**
Pittsburgh (14-4)	.3	7	7	14	**—31**

MVP: Pittsburgh QB Terry Bradshaw (14 for 21, 309 yds, 2 TD, 3 Int)

1980 Season

AFC Playoffs

First Round ....at *Oakland 27, *Houston 7
Second Round...............at San Diego 20, Buffalo 14
Oakland 14, at Cleveland 12
Championship ....Oakland 34, at San Diego 27

NFC Playoffs

First Round ....at *Dallas 34, *LA Rams 13
Second Round ....at Philadelphia 31, Minnesota 16
Dallas 30, at Atlanta 27
Championship ....at Philadelphia 20, Dallas 7

Super Bowl XV
Jan. 25, 1981
Louisiana Superdome, New Orleans
Favorite: Eagles by 3 Attendance: 76,135

Oakland (14-5)	.14	0	10	3	**—27**
Philadelphia (14-4)	.0	3	0	7	**—10**

MVP: Oakland QB Jim Plunkett (13 for 21, 261 yds, 3 TD)

1981 Season

AFC Playoffs

First Round ....*Buffalo 31, at *NY Jets 27
Second Round..........San Diego 41, at Miami 38 (OT)
at Cincinnati 28, Buffalo 21
Championship ....at Cincinnati 27, San Diego 7

NFC Playoffs

First Round..........*NY Giants 27, at *Philadelphia 21
Second Round...............at Dallas 38, Tampa Bay 0
at San Francisco 38, NY Giants 24
Championship ....at San Francisco 28, Dallas 27

Super Bowl XVI
Jan. 24, 1982
Pontiac Silverdome, Pontiac, Mich.
Favorite: Pick'em Attendance: 81,270

San Francisco (15-3)	.7	13	0	6	**—26**
Cincinnati (14-4)	.0	0	7	14	**—21**

MVP: San Francisco QB Joe Montana (14 for 22, 157 yds, 1 TD; 6 carries, 18 yds, 1 TD)

1982 Season

A 57-day players' strike shortened the regular season from 16 games to nine. The playoff format was changed to a 16-team tournament open to the top eight teams in each conference.

AFC Playoffs

First Round..............at LA Raiders 27, Cleveland 10
at Miami 28, New England 3
NY Jets 44, at Cincinnati 17
San Diego 31, at Pittsburgh 28
Second Round ....NY Jets 17, at LA Raiders 14
at Miami 34, San Diego 13
Championship ....at Miami 14, NY Jets 0

NFC Playoffs

First Round.................at Washington 31, Detroit 7
at Dallas 30, Tampa Bay 17
at Green Bay 41, St. Louis 16
at Minnesota 30, Atlanta 24
Second Round..........at Washington 21, Minnesota 7
at Dallas 37, Green Bay 26
Championship ....at Washington 31, Dallas 17

Super Bowl XVII
Jan. 30, 1983
Rose Bowl, Pasadena
Favorite: Dolphins by 3 Attendance: 103,667

Miami (10-2)	.7	10	0	0	**—17**
Washington (11-1)	.0	10	3	14	**—27**

MVP: Washington RB John Riggins (38 carries, 166 yds, 1 TD; 1 catch, 15 yds)

1983 Season

AFC Playoffs

First Round...................at *Seattle 31, *Denver 7
Second Round ....Seattle 27, at Miami 20
at LA Raiders 38, Pittsburgh 10
Championship...............at LA Raiders 30, Seattle 14

NFC Playoffs

First Round..............*LA Rams 24, at *Dallas 17
Second Round...........at San Francisco 24, Detroit 23
at Washington 51, LA Rams 7
Championship ....at Washington 24, San Francisco 21

Super Bowl XVIII
Jan. 22, 1984
Tampa Stadium, Tampa
Favorite: Redskins by 3 Attendance: 72,920

Washington (16-2)	.0	3	6	0	**—9**
LA Raiders (14-4)	.7	14	14	3	**—38**

MVP: LA Raiders RB Marcus Allen (20 carries, 191 yds, 2 TD; 2 catches, 18 yds)

Most Popular Playing Sites
Stadiums hosting more than one Super Bowl.

No		Years
5	Orange Bowl (Miami)	1968-69, 71, 76, 79
5	Rose Bowl (Pasadena)	1977, 80, 83, 87, 93
5	Superdome (N. Orleans)	1978, 81, 86, 90, 97
3	Tulane Stadium (N. Orleans)	1970, 72, 75
3	Joe Robbie/Pro Player Stadium (Miami)	1989, 95, 99
2	LA Memorial Coliseum	1967, 73
2	Tampa Stadium	1984, 91
2	Jack Murphy/Qualcomm Stadium (San Diego)	1988, 98
2	Georgia Dome (Atlanta)	1994, 2000

1984 Season

AFC Playoffs

First Round . . . . .at *Seattle 13, *LA Raiders 7
Second Round . . . . .at Miami 31, Seattle 10
Pittsburgh 24, at Denver 17
Championship . . . . .at Miami 45, Pittsburgh 28

NFC Playoffs

First Round . . . . *NY Giants 16, at *LA Rams 13
Second Round . . . . .at San Francisco 21, NY Giants 10
Chicago 23, at Washington 19
Championship . . . . .at San Francisco 23, Chicago 0

Super Bowl XIX
Jan. 20, 1985
Stanford Stadium, Stanford, Calif.
Favorite: 49ers by 3   Attendance: 84,059

Miami (16-2) 10   6   0   0 **—16**
San Francisco (17-1) 7   21 10   0 **—38**
MVP: San Francisco QB Joe Montana (24 for 35, 331 yds, 2 TD; 5 carries, 59 yards, 1 TD)

1985 Season

AFC Playoffs

First Round . . . . *New England 26, at *NY Jets 14
Second Round . . . . .at Miami 24, Cleveland 21
New England 27, at LA Raiders 20
Championship . . . . .New England 31, at Miami 14

NFC Playoffs

First Round . . . . .at *NY Giants 17, *San Francisco 3
Second Round . . . . .at LA Rams 20, Dallas 0
at Chicago 21, NY Giants 0
Championship . . . . .at Chicago 24, LA Rams 0

Super Bowl XX
Jan. 26, 1986
Louisiana Superdome, New Orleans
Favorite: Bears by 10   Attendance: 73,818

Chicago Bears (17-1) . . . . .13 10 21   2 **—46**
New England (14-5) 3   0   0   7 **—10**
MVP: Chicago DE Richard Dent (Bears defense: 7 sacks, 6 turnovers, 1 safety and gave up just 123 total yards)

1986 Season

AFC Playoffs

First Round . . . . .at *NY Jets 35, *Kansas City 15
Second Round . . . . .at Cleveland 23, NY Jets 20 (OT)
at Denver 22, New England 17
Championship . . . . .Denver 23, at Cleveland 20 (OT)

NFC Playoffs

First Round . . . . .at *Washington 19, *LA Rams 7
Second Round . . . . .Washington 27, at Chicago 13
at NY Giants 49, San Francisco 3
Championship . . . . .at NY Giants 17, Washington 0

Super Bowl XXI
Jan. 25, 1987
Rose Bowl, Pasadena
Favorite: Giants by 9½   Attendance: 101,063

Denver (13-5) 10   0   0 10 **—20**
NY Giants (16-2) 7   2 17 13 **—39**
MVP: NY Giants QB Phil Simms (22 for 25, 268 yds, 3 TD; 3 carries, 25 yds)

1987 Season

A 24-day players' strike shortened the regular season to 15 games with replacement teams playing for three weeks.

AFC Playoffs

First Round . . . . .at *Houston 23, *Seattle 20 (OT)
Second Round . . . . .at Cleveland 38, Indianapolis 21
at Denver 34, Houston 10
Championship . . . . .at Denver 38, Cleveland 33

NFC Playoffs

First Round . . . .*Minnesota 44, at *New Orleans 10
Second Round . . . . .Minnesota 36, at San Francisco 24
Washington 21, at Chicago 17
Championship . . . . .at Washington 17, Minnesota 10

Super Bowl XXII
Jan. 31, 1988
San Diego/Jack Murphy Stadium
Favorite: Broncos by 3½   Attendance: 73,302

Washington (13-4) . . . . .0 35   0   7 **—42**
Denver (12-4-1) 10   0   0   0 **—10**
MVP: Washington QB Doug Williams (18 for 29, 340 yds, 4 TD, 1 Int)

1988 Season

AFC Playoffs

First Round . . . .*Houston 24, at *Cleveland 23
Second Round . . . . .at Buffalo 17, Houston 10
at Cincinnati 21, Seattle 13
Championship . . . . .at Cincinnati 21, Buffalo 10

NFC Playoffs

First Round . . . . .at *Minnesota 28, *LA Rams 17
Second Round . . . . .at San Francisco 34, Minnesota 9
at Chicago 20, Philadelphia 12
Championship . . . . .San Francisco 28, at Chicago 3

Super Bowl XXIII
Jan. 22, 1989
Joe Robbie Stadium, Miami
Favorite: 49ers by 7   Attendance: 75,129

Cincinnati (14-4) 0   3 10   3 **—16**
San Francisco (12-6) 3   0   3 14 **—20**
MVP: San Francisco WR Jerry Rice (11 catches, 215 yds, 1 TD; 1 carry, 5 yds)

1989 Season

AFC Playoffs

First Round . . . .*Pittsburgh 26, at *Houston 23
Second Round . . . . .at Cleveland 34, Buffalo 30
at Denver 24, Pittsburgh 23
Championship . . . . .at Denver 37, Cleveland 21

NFC Playoffs

First Round . . . .*LA Rams 21, at *Philadelphia 7
Second Round . . . . .LA Rams 19, NY Giants 13 (OT)
at San Francisco 41, Minnesota 13
Championship . . . . .at San Francisco 30, LA Rams 3

Super Bowl XXIV
Jan. 28, 1990
Louisiana Superdome, New Orleans
Favorite: 49ers by 12½   Attendance: 72,919

San Francisco (17-2) . . . . .13 14 14 14 **—55**
Denver (13-6) 3   0   7   0 **—10**
MVP: San Francisco QB Joe Montana (22 for 29, 297 yds, 5 TD)

Super Bowl Playoffs (Cont.)

1990 Season

AFC Playoffs
First Round..............at *Miami 17, *Kansas City 16
at Cincinnati 41, *Houston 14
Second Round..................at Buffalo 44, Miami 34
at LA Raiders 20, Cincinnati 10
Championship................at Buffalo 51, LA Raiders 3

NFC Playoffs
First Round..........*Washington 20, at *Philadelphia 6
at Chicago 16, *New Orleans 6
Second Round.......at San Francisco 28, Washington 10
at NY Giants 31, Chicago 3
Championship........NY Giants 15, at San Francisco 13

Super Bowl XXV
Jan. 27, 1991
Tampa Stadium, Tampa
Favorite: Bills by 7   Attendance: 73,813

Buffalo (15-4)	3	9	0	7	—19
NY Giants (16-3)	3	7	7	3	—20

MVP: NY Giants RB Ottis Anderson (21 carries, 102 yds, 1 TD; 1 catch, 7 yds)

1991 Season

AFC Playoffs
First Round............at *Kansas City 10, *LA Raiders 6
at Houston 17, *NY Jets 10
Second Round................at Denver 26, Houston 24
at Buffalo 37, Kansas City 14
Championship..................at Buffalo 10, Denver 7

NFC Playoffs
First Round.............*Atlanta 27, at New Orleans 20
+*Dallas 17, at *Chicago 13
Second Round...........at Washington 24, Atlanta 7
at Detroit 38, Dallas 6
Championship............at Washington 41, Detroit 10

Super Bowl XXVI
Jan. 26, 1992
Hubert Humphrey Metrodome, Minneapolis
Favorite: Redskins by 7   Attendance: 63,130

Washington (16-2)	0	17	14	6	—37
Buffalo (15-3)	0	0	10	14	—24

MVP: Washington QB Mark Rypien (18 for 33, 292 yds, 2 TD, 1 Int)

1992 Season

AFC Playoffs
First Round.............at *Buffalo 41, *Houston 38 (OT)
at San Diego 17, *Kansas City 0
Second Round.................Buffalo 24, at Pittsburgh 3
at Miami 31, San Diego 0
Championship.................Buffalo 29, at Miami 10

NFC Playoffs
First Round.............*Washington 24, at Minnesota 7
*Philadelphia 36, at *New Orleans 20
Second Round.......at San Francisco 20, Washington 13
at Dallas 34, Philadelphia 10
Championship.........Dallas 30, at San Francisco 20

Super Bowl XXVII
Jan. 31, 1993
Rose Bowl, Pasadena
Favorite: Cowboys by 7   Attendance: 98,374

Buffalo (14-5)	7	3	7	0	—17
Dallas (15-3)	14	14	3	21	—52

MVP: Dallas QB Troy Aikman (22 for 30, 273 yds, 4 TD)

1993 Season

AFC Playoffs
First Round........at Kansas City 27, *Pittsburgh 24 (OT)
at *LA Raiders 42, *Denver 24
Second Round..............at Buffalo 29, LA Raiders 23
Kansas City 28, at Houston 20
Championship.............at Buffalo 30, Kansas City 13

NFC Playoffs
First Round................*Green Bay 28, at Detroit 24
at *NY Giants 17, *Minnesota 10
Second Round..........at San Francisco 44, NY Giants 3
at Dallas 27, Green Bay 17
Championship.............at Dallas 38, San Francisco 21

Super Bowl XXVIII
Jan. 30, 1994
Georgia Dome, Atlanta
Favorite: Cowboys by 10½   Attendance: 72,817

Dallas (15-4)	6	0	14	10	—30
Buffalo (14-5)	3	10	0	0	—13

MVP: Dallas RB Emmitt Smith (30 carries, 132 yds, 2 TDs; 4 catches, 26 yds)

1994 Season

AFC Playoffs
First Round................at Miami 27, *Kansas City 17
at *Cleveland 20, *New England 13
Second Round..............at Pittsburgh 29, Cleveland 9
at San Diego 22, Miami 21
Championship.........San Diego 17, at Pittsburgh 13

NFC Playoffs
First Round.............at *Green Bay 16, *Detroit 12
*Chicago 25, at Minnesota 18
Second Round..........at San Francisco 44, Chicago 15
at Dallas 35, Green Bay 9
Championship............at San Francisco 38, Dallas 28

Super Bowl XXIX
Jan. 29, 1995
Joe Robbie Stadium, Miami
Favorite: 49ers by 18   Attendance: 74,107

San Diego (13-5)	7	3	8	8	—26
San Francisco (15-3)	14	14	14	7	—49

MVP: San Francisco QB Steve Young (24 for 36, 325 yds, 6 TD)

1995 Season

AFC Playoffs
First Round....................at Buffalo 37, *Miami 22
*Indianapolis 35, at *San Diego 20
Second Round..............at Pittsburgh 40, Buffalo 21
Indianapolis 10, at Kansas City 7
Championship...........at Pittsburgh 20, Indianapolis 16

NFC Playoffs
First Round.............at *Philadelphia 58, *Detroit 37
at Green Bay 37, *Atlanta 20
Second Round........Green Bay 27, at San Francisco 17
at Dallas 30, Philadelphia 11
Championship........at Dallas 38, Green Bay 27

Super Bowl XXX
Jan. 28, 1996
Sun Devil Stadium, Tempe, Ariz.
Favorite: Cowboys by 13½   Attendance: 76,347

Dallas (14-4)	10	3	7	7	—27
Pittsburgh (13-5)	0	7	0	10	—17

MVP: Dallas CB Larry Brown (2 interceptions for 77 yds)

1996 Season

AFC Playoffs

First Round . . . .*Jacksonville 30, at *Buffalo 27
at Pittsburgh 42, *Indianapolis 14
Second Round. . . . . Jacksonville 30, at Denver 27
at New England 28, Pittsburgh 3
Championship . . . . .at New England 20, Jacksonville 6

NFC Playoffs

First Round. . . . . at Dallas 40, *Minnesota 15
at *San Francisco 14, *Philadelphia 0
Second Round. . . . . . . at Green Bay 35, San Francisco 14
at Carolina 26, Dallas 17
Championship . . . . at Green Bay 30, Carolina.13

Super Bowl XXXI

Jan. 26, 1997
Louisiana Superdome, New Orleans
Favorite: Packers by 14 Attendance: 72,301
New England (13-5). 14   0   7   0 **—21**
Green Bay (15-3) 10   17   8   0 **—35**
MVP: Green Bay KR Desmond Howard (4 kickoff returns for 154 yds and 1 TD, also 6 punt returns for 90 yds)

1997 Season

AFC Playoffs

First Round . . . . .at *Denver 42, *Jacksonville 17
at New England 17, *Miami 3
Second Round . . . . .at Pittsburgh 7, New England 6
Denver 14, at Kansas City 10
Championship. . . . . Denver 24, at Pittsburgh 21

NFC Playoffs

First Round . . . .*Minnesota 23, at NY Giants 22
at *Tampa Bay 20, *Detroit 10
Second Round. . . . . . . .at San Francisco 38, Minnesota 22
at Green Bay 21, Tampa Bay 7
Championship . . . . .Green Bay 23, at San Francisco 10

Super Bowl XXXII

Jan. 25, 1998
Qualcomm Stadium, San Diego
Favorite: Packers by 11½ Attendance: 68,912
Green Bay (15-3). 7   7   3   7 **—24**
Denver (15-4). 7   10   7   7 **—31**
MVP: Denver RB Terrell Davis (30 carries, 157 yds, 3 TDs; 2 catches, 8 yds)

1998 Season

AFC Playoffs

First Round . . . . .at *Miami 24, *Buffalo 17
at Jacksonville 25, *New England 10
Second Round . . . . .at NY Jets 34, Jacksonville 24
at Denver 38, Miami 3
Championship. . . . . at Denver 23, NY Jets 10

NFC Playoffs

First Round . . . . .at *San Francisco 30, *Green Bay 27
*Arizona 20, at Dallas 7
Second Round . . . . .at Atlanta 20, San Francisco 18
at Minnesota 41, Arizona 21
Championship . . . . .Atlanta 30, at Minnesota 27 (OT)

Super Bowl XXXIII

Jan. 31, 1999
Pro Player Stadium, Miami
Favorite: Broncos by 7½ Attendance: 74,803
Denver (16-2) 7   10   0 17 **—34**
Atlanta (16-2). 3   3   0 13 **—19**
MVP: Denver QB John Elway (18 for 29, 336 yds, 1 TD, 1 Int and 1 rushing TD)

1999 Season

AFC Playoffs

First Round. . . . . .at *Tennessee 22, *Buffalo 16
*Miami 20, at Seattle 17
Second Round . . . . .at Jacksonville 62, Miami 7
Tennessee 19, at Indianapolis 16
Championship . . . . Tennessee 33, at Jacksonville 14

NFC Playoffs

First Round . . . . .at Washington 27, *Detroit 13
at *Minnesota 27, *Dallas 10
Second Round. . . . . .at Tampa Bay 14, Washington 13
at St. Louis 49, Minnesota 37
Championship . . . . .at St. Louis 11, Tampa Bay 6

Super Bowl XXXIV

Jan. 30, 2000
Georgia Dome, Atlanta
Favorite: Rams by 7 Attendance: 72,625
St. Louis (15-3) 3   6   7   7 **—23**
Tennessee (16-3). 0   0   6 10 **—16**
MVP: St. Louis QB Kurt Warner (24 for 45, 414 yds, 2 TD)

2000 Season

AFC Playoffs

First Round . . . . .at Miami 23, *Indianapolis 17 (OT)
at *Baltimore 21, *Denver 3
Second Round. . . . . .at Oakland 27, Miami 0
Baltimore 24, at Tennessee 10
Championship. . . . . Baltimore 16, at Oakland 3

NFC Playoffs

First Round . . . . .at New Orleans 31, *St. Louis 28
at *Philadelphia 21, *Tampa Bay 3
Second Round . . . . .at Minnesota 34, New Orleans 16
at NY Giants 20, Philadelphia 10
Championship . . . . .at NY Giants 41, Minnesota 0

Super Bowl XXXV

Jan. 28, 2001
Raymond James Stadium, Tampa
Favorite: Ravens by 3 Attendance: 71,921
Baltimore (15-4). 7   3 14 10 **—34**
NY Giants (14-4). 0   0   7   0 **—7**
MVP: Baltimore LB Ray Lewis (5 tackles, 4 passes defended)

A Year Later . . .

Super Bowl champions who did not qualify for the playoffs the following season.

Season		Record	Finish	Season		Record	Finish
1968	Green Bay	6-7-1	3rd in NFL Central	1987	NY Giants	6-9-0*	5th in NFC East
1970	Kansas City	7-5-2	2nd in AFC West	1988	Washington	7-9-0	3rd in NFC East
1980	Pittsburgh	9-7-0	3rd in AFC Central	1991	NY Giants	8-8-0	4th in NFC East
1981	Oakland	7-9-0	4th in AFC West	1999	Denver	6-10-0	5th in AFC West
1982	San Francisco	3-6-0*	11th in overall NFC				

* Seasons when player strikes interrupted schedule.

Before the Super Bowl

The first NFL champion was the Akron Pros in 1920, when the league was called the American Professional Football Association (APFA) and the title went to the team with the best regular season record. The APFA changed its name to the National Football League in 1922.

The first playoff game with the championship at stake came in 1932, when the Chicago Bears (6-1-6) and Portsmouth (Ohio) Spartans (6-1-4) ended the regular season tied for first place. The Bears won the subsequent playoff, 9-0. Due to a snowstorm and cold weather, the game was moved from Wrigley Field to an improvised 80-yard dirt field at Chicago Stadium, making it the first indoor title game as well.

The NFL Championship Game decided the league title until the NFL merged with the AFL and the first Super Bowl was played following the 1966 season.

NFL Champions, 1920-32

Winning player-coaches noted by position.

Multiple winners: Canton-Cleveland Bulldogs and Green Bay (3); Chicago Staleys/Bears (2).

Year	Champion	Head Coach	Year	Champion	Head Coach
1920	Akron Pros	Fritz Pollard, HB & Elgie Tobin, QB	1927	New York Giants	Earl Potteiger, QB
			1928	Providence Steam Roller	Jimmy Conzelman, HB
1921	Chicago Staleys	George Halas, E	1929	Green Bay Packers	Curly Lambeau, QB
1922	Canton Bulldogs	Guy Chamberlin, E	1930	Green Bay Packers	Curly Lambeau
1923	Canton Bulldogs	Guy Chamberlin, E	1931	Green Bay Packers	Curly Lambeau
1924	Cleveland Bulldogs	Guy Chamberlin, E	1932	Chicago Bears	Ralph Jones
1925	Chicago Cardinals	Norm Barry	(Bears beat Portsmouth-OH in playoff, 9-0)		
1926	Frankford Yellow Jackets	Guy Chamberlin, E			

NFL-NFC Championship Game

NFL Championship games from 1933-69 and NFC Championship games since the completion of the NFL-AFL merger following the 1969 season.

Multiple winners: Green Bay (10); Dallas (8); Chicago Bears and Washington (7); NY Giants (6); San Francisco (5); Cleveland Browns, Detroit, Minnesota, and Philadelphia (4); Baltimore Colts and Cle-LA-St.L Rams (3).

Season	Winner	Head Coach	Score	Loser	Head Coach	Site
1933	Chicago Bears	George Halas	23-21	New York	Steve Owen	Chicago
1934	New York	Steve Owen	30-13	Chicago Bears	George Halas	New York
1935	Detroit	Potsy Clark	26- 7	New York	Steve Owen	Detroit
1936	Green Bay	Curly Lambeau	21- 6	Boston Redskins	Ray Flaherty	New York
1937	Washington Redskins	Ray Flaherty	28-21	Chicago Bears	George Halas	Chicago
1938	New York	Steve Owen	23-17	Green Bay	Curly Lambeau	New York
1939	Green Bay	Curly Lambeau	27- 0	New York	Steve Owen	Milwaukee
1940	Chicago Bears	George Halas	73- 0	Washington	Ray Flaherty	Washington
1941	Chicago Bears	George Halas	37- 9	New York	Steve Owen	Chicago
1942	Washington	Ray Flaherty	14- 6	Chicago Bears	Hunk Anderson & Luke Johnsos	Washington
1943	Chicago Bears	Hunk Anderson & Luke Johnsos	41-21	Washington	Arthur Bergman	Chicago
1944	Green Bay	Curly Lambeau	14- 7	New York	Steve Owen	New York
1945	Cleveland Rams	Adam Walsh	15-14	Washington	Dudley DeGroot	Cleveland
1946	Chicago Bears	George Halas	24-14	New York	Steve Owen	New York
1947	Chicago Cardinals	Jimmy Conzelman	28-21	Philadelphia	Greasy Neale	Chicago
1948	Philadelphia	Greasy Neale	7- 0	Chicago Cardinals	Jimmy Conzelman	Philadelphia
1949	Philadelphia	Greasy Neale	14- 0	Los Angeles Rams	Clark Shaughnessy	Los Angeles
1950	Cleveland Browns	Paul Brown	30-28	Los Angeles	Joe Stydahar	Cleveland
1951	Los Angeles	Joe Stydahar	24-17	Cleveland	Paul Brown	Los Angeles
1952	Detroit	Buddy Parker	17- 7	Cleveland·	Paul Brown	Cleveland
1953	Detroit	Buddy Parker	17-16	Cleveland	Paul Brown	Detroit
1954	Cleveland	Paul Brown	56-10	Detroit	Buddy Parker	Cleveland
1955	Cleveland	Paul Brown	38-14	Los Angeles	Sid Gillman	Los Angeles
1956	New York	Jim Lee Howell	47- 7	Chicago Bears	Paddy Driscoll	New York
1957	Detroit	George Wilson	59-14	Cleveland	Paul Brown	Detroit
1958	Balt. Colts	Weeb Ewbank	23-17*	New York	Jim Lee Howell	New York
1959	Balt. Colts	Weeb Ewbank	31-16	New York	Jim Lee Howell	Baltimore
1960	Philadelphia	Buck Shaw	17-13	Green Bay	Vince Lombardi	Philadelphia
1961	Green Bay	Vince Lombardi	37- 0	New York	Allie Sherman	Green Bay
1962	Green Bay	Vince Lombardi	16- 7	New York	Allie Sherman	New York
1963	Chicago	George Halas	14-10	New York	Allie Sherman	Chicago
1964	Cleveland	Blanton Collier	27- 0	Balt. Colts	Don Shula	Cleveland
1965	Green Bay	Vince Lombardi	23-12	Cleveland	Blanton Collier	Green Bay
1966	Green Bay	Vince Lombardi	34-27	Dallas	Tom Landry	Dallas
1967	Green Bay	Vince Lombardi	21-17	Dallas	Tom Landry	Green Bay
1968	Balt. Colts	Don Shula	34- 0	Cleveland	Blanton Collier	Cleveland
1969	Minnesota	Bud Grant	27- 7	Cleveland	Blanton Collier	Minnesota
1970	Dallas	Tom Landry	17-10	San Francisco	Dick Nolan	San Francisco
1971	Dallas	Tom Landry	14- 3	San Francisco	Dick Nolan	Dallas
1972	Washington	George Allen	26- 3	Dallas	Tom Landry	Washington

Season	Winner	Head Coach	Score	Loser	Head Coach	Site
1973	Minnesota	Bud Grant	27-10	Dallas	Tom Landry	Dallas
1974	Minnesota	Bud Grant	14-10	Los Angeles	Chuck Knox	Minnesota
1975	Dallas	Tom Landry	37- 7	Los Angeles	Chuck Knox	Los Angeles
1976	Minnesota	Bud Grant	24-13	Los Angeles	Chuck Knox	Minnesota
1977	Dallas	Tom Landry	23- 6	Minnesota	Bud Grant	Dallas
1978	Dallas	Tom Landry	28- 0	Los Angeles	Ray Malavasi	Los Angeles
1979	Los Angeles	Ray Malavasi	9- 0	Tampa Bay	John McKay	Tampa Bay
1980	Philadelphia	Dick Vermeil	20- 7	Dallas	Tom Landry	Philadelphia
1981	San Francisco	Bill Walsh	28-27	Dallas	Tom Landry	San Francisco
1982	Washington	Joe Gibbs	31-17	Dallas	Tom Landry	Washington
1983	Washington	Joe Gibbs	24-21	San Francisco	Bill Walsh	Washington
1984	San Francisco	Bill Walsh	23- 0	Chicago	Mike Ditka	San Francisco
1985	Chicago	Mike Ditka	24- 0	Los Angeles	John Robinson	Chicago
1986	New York	Bill Parcells	17- 0	Washington	Joe Gibbs	New York
1987	Washington	Joe Gibbs	17-10	Minnesota	Jerry Burns	Washington
1988	San Francisco	Bill Walsh	28- 3	Chicago	Mike Ditka	Chicago
1989	San Francisco	George Seifert	30- 3	Los Angeles	John Robinson	San Francisco
1990	New York	Bill Parcells	15-13	San Francisco	George Seifert	San Francisco
1991	Washington	Joe Gibbs	41-10	Detroit	Wayne Fontes	Washington
1992	Dallas	Jimmy Johnson	30-20	San Francisco	George Seifert	San Francisco
1993	Dallas	Jimmy Johnson	38-21	San Francisco	George Seifert	Dallas
1994	San Francisco	George Seifert	38-28	Dallas	Barry Switzer	San Francisco
1995	Dallas	Barry Switzer	38-27	Green Bay	Mike Holmgren	Dallas
1996	Green Bay	Mike Holmgren	30-13	Carolina	Dom Capers	Green Bay
1997	Green Bay	Mike Holmgren	23-10	San Francisco	Steve Mariucci	San Francisco
1998	Atlanta	Dan Reeves	30-27*	Minnesota	Dennis Green	Minnesota
1999	St. Louis	Dick Vermeil	11-6	Tampa Bay	Tony Dungy	St. Louis
2000	New York	Jim Fassel	41-0	Minnesota	Dennis Green	New York

*Sudden death overtime

NFL-NFC Championship Game Appearances

App		W	L	Pct	PF	PA	App		W	L	Pct	PF	PA
17	NY Giants	6	11	.353	281	322	8	Minnesota	4	4	.500	135	151
16	Dallas Cowboys	8	8	.500	361	319	6	Detroit	4	2	.667	139	141
13	Green Bay Packers	10	3	.769	303	177	5	Philadelphia	4	1	.800	79	48
13	Chicago Bears	7	6	.538	286	245	4	Baltimore Colts	3	1	.750	88	60
13	Cle-LA-St.L Rams	4	9	.308	134	276	2	Chicago Cardinals	1	1	.500	28	28
12	Boston-Wash. Redskins	7	5	.583	222	255	2	Tampa Bay	0	2	.000	6	20
12	San Francisco	5	7	.417	245	222	1	Atlanta	1	0	1.000	30	27
11	Cleveland Browns	4	7	.364	224	253	1	Carolina	0	1	.000	13	30

AFL-AFC Championship Game

AFL Championship games from 1960-69 and AFC Championship games since the completion of the NFL-AFL merger following the 1969 season.

Multiple winners: Buffalo and Denver (6); Miami and Pittsburgh (5); Oakland-LA Raiders (4); Dallas Texans-KC Chiefs and Houston Oilers-Tennessee Titans (3); Cincinnati, Jacksonville, New England and San Diego (2).

Season	Winner	Head Coach	Score	Loser	Head Coach	Site
1960	Houston	Lou Rymkus	24-16	LA Chargers	Sid Gillman	Houston
1961	Houston	Wally Lemm	10- 3	SD Chargers	Sid Gillman	San Diego
1962	Dallas	Hank Stram	20-17*	Houston	Pop Ivy	Houston
1963	San Diego	Sid Gillman	51-10	Boston Patriots	Mike Holovak	San Diego
1964	Buffalo	Lou Saban	20- 7	San Diego	Sid Gillman	Buffalo
1965	Buffalo	Lou Saban	23- 0	San Diego	Sid Gillman	San Diego
1966	Kansas City	Hank Stram	31- 7	Buffalo	Joel Collier	Buffalo
1967	Oakland	John Rauch	40- 7	Houston	Wally Lemm	Oakland
1968	NY Jets	Weeb Ewbank	27-23	Oakland	John Rauch	New York
1969	Kansas City	Hank Stram	17- 7	Oakland	John Madden	Oakland
1970	Balt. Colts	Don McCafferty	27-17	Oakland	John Madden	Baltimore
1971	Miami	Don Shula	21- 0	Balt. Colts	Don McCafferty	Miami
1972	Miami	Don Shula	21-17	Pittsburgh	Chuck Noll	Pittsburgh
1973	Miami	Don Shula	27-10	Oakland	John Madden	Miami
1974	Pittsburgh	Chuck Noll	24-13	Oakland	John Madden	Oakland
1975	Pittsburgh	Chuck Noll	16-10	Oakland	John Madden	Pittsburgh
1976	Oakland	John Madden	24- 7	Pittsburgh	Chuck Noll	Oakland
1977	Denver	Red Miller	20-17	Oakland	John Madden	Denver
1978	Pittsburgh	Chuck Noll	34- 5	Houston	Bum Phillips	Pittsburgh
1979	Pittsburgh	Chuck Noll	27-13	Houston	Bum Phillips	Pittsburgh
1980	Oakland	Tom Flores	34-27	San Diego	Don Coryell	San Diego
1981	Cincinnati	Forrest Gregg	27- 7	San Diego	Don Coryell	Cincinnati
1982	Miami	Don Shula	14- 0	NY Jets	Walt Michaels	Miami
1983	LA Raiders	Tom Flores	30-14	Seattle	Chuck Knox	Los Angeles
1984	Miami	Don Shula	45-28	Pittsburgh	Chuck Noll	Miami
1985	New England	Raymond Berry	31-14	Miami	Don Shula	Miami

AFL-AFC Championship Game (Cont.)

Season	Winner	Head Coach	Score	Loser	Head Coach	Site
1986	Denver	Dan Reeves	23-20*	Cleveland	Marty Schottenheimer	Cleveland
1987	Denver	Dan Reeves	38-33	Cleveland	Marty Schottenheimer	Denver
1988	Cincinnati	Sam Wyche	21-10	Buffalo	Marv Levy	Cincinnati
1989	Denver	Dan Reeves	37-21	Cleveland	Bud Carson	Denver
1990	Buffalo	Marv Levy	51-3	LA Raiders	Art Shell	Buffalo
1991	Buffalo	Marv Levy	10-7	Denver	Dan Reeves	Buffalo
1992	Buffalo	Marv Levy	29-10	Miami	Don Shula	Miami
1993	Buffalo	Marv Levy	30-13	Kansas City	Marty Schottenheimer	Buffalo
1994	San Diego	Bobby Ross	17-13	Pittsburgh	Bill Cowher	Pittsburgh
1995	Pittsburgh	Bill Cowher	20-16	Indianapolis	Ted Marchibroda	Pittsburgh
1996	New England	Bill Parcells	20-6	Jacksonville	Tom Coughlin	New England
1997	Denver	Mike Shanahan	24-21	Pittsburgh	Bill Cowher	Pittsburgh
1998	Denver	Mike Shanahan	23-10	NY Jets	Bill Parcells	Denver
1999	Tennessee	Jeff Fisher	33-14	Jacksonville	Tom Coughlin	Jacksonville
2000	Balt. Ravens	Brian Billick	16-3	Oakland	Jon Gruden	Oakland

*Sudden death overtime

AFL-AFC Championship Game Appearances

App		W	L	Pct	PF	PA	App		W	L	Pct	PF	PA
13	Oakland-LA Raiders	4	9	.308	231	280	3	Boston-NE Patriots	2	1	.667	61	71
10	Pittsburgh	5	5	.500	207	188	3	Baltimore-Indy Colts	1	2	.333	43	58
8	Buffalo	6	2	.750	180	92	3	NY Jets	1	2	.333	37	60
8	LA-San Diego Chargers	2	6	.250	128	161	3	Cleveland	0	3	.000	74	98
7	Denver	6	1	.857	172	132	2	Cincinnati	2	0	1.000	48	17
7	Miami	5	2	.714	152	115	2	Jacksonville	0	2	.000	20	53
7	Houston Oilers/Ten. Titans	3	4	.429	109	154	1	Baltimore Ravens	1	0	1.000	16	3
4	Dallas Texans/KC Chiefs	3	1	.750	81	61	1	Seattle	0	1	.000	14	30

NFL Divisional Champions

The NFL adopted divisional play for the first time in 1967, splitting both conferences into two four-team divisions—the Capitol and Century divisions in the East and the Central and Coastal divisions in the West. A merger with the AFL in 1970 increased NFL membership to 26 teams and made it necessary for realignment. Two 13-team conferences—the AFC and NFC—were formed by moving established NFL clubs in Baltimore, Cleveland and Pittsburgh to the AFC and rearranging both conferences into Eastern, Central and Western divisions. Expansion has since increased the league to 31 teams with 16 teams in the AFC and 15 in the NFC. The AFC Central currently has six teams and all others have five.

Division champions are listed below; teams that went on to win the Super Bowl are in **bold** type. Note that in the 1980 season, Oakland won the Super Bowl as a wild card team, as did Denver in 1997 and Baltimore in 2000; and in 1982, the players' strike shortened the regular season to nine games and eliminated divisional play for one season.

Multiple champions (since 1970): AFC—Pittsburgh (14); Miami (12); Oakland-LA Raiders (10); Denver (9); Buffalo (7); Baltimore-Indianapolis Colts and Cleveland (6); Cincinnati and San Diego (5); Kansas City and New England (4); Houston Oilers-Tennessee Titans (3); Jacksonville and Seattle (2). NFC—San Francisco (16); Dallas (15); Minnesota (14); LA-St. Louis Rams (9); Chicago and Washington (6); NY Giants (5); Green Bay (4); Detroit and Tampa Bay (3); Atlanta, New Orleans, Philadelphia and St. Louis Cardinals (2).

American Football League / National Football League

Season	East	West	Season	East		Central	West
1966	Buffalo	Kansas City	1966	Dallas			**Green Bay**

Season	East	West	Season	Capitol	Century	Central	Coastal
1967	Houston	Oakland	1967	Dallas	Cleveland	**Green Bay**	LA Rams
1968	**NY Jets**	Oakland	1968	Dallas	Cleveland	Minnesota	Baltimore
1969	NY Jets	Oakland	1969	Dallas	Cleveland	Minnesota	LA Rams

Note: Kansas City, an AFL second-place team, won the Super Bowl in the 1969 season.

American Football Conference / National Football Conference

Season	East	Central	West	Season	East	Central	West
1970	**Balt. Colts**	Cincinnati	Oakland	1970	Dallas	Minnesota	San Francisco
1971	Miami	Cleveland	Kansas City	1971	**Dallas**	Minnesota	San Francisco
1972	**Miami**	Pittsburgh	Oakland	1972	Washington	Green Bay	San Francisco
1973	**Miami**	Cincinnati	Oakland	1973	Dallas	Minnesota	LA Rams
1974	Miami	**Pittsburgh**	Oakland	1974	St. Louis	Minnesota	LA Rams
1975	Balt. Colts	**Pittsburgh**	Oakland	1975	St. Louis	Minnesota	LA Rams
1976	Balt. Colts	Pittsburgh	**Oakland**	1976	Dallas	Minnesota	LA Rams
1977	Balt. Colts	Pittsburgh	Denver	1977	**Dallas**	Minnesota	LA Rams
1978	New England	**Pittsburgh**	Denver	1978	Dallas	Minnesota	LA Rams
1979	Miami	**Pittsburgh**	San Diego	1979	Dallas	Tampa Bay	LA Rams
1980	Buffalo	Cleveland	San Diego	1980	Philadelphia	Minnesota	Atlanta
1981	Miami	Cincinnati	San Diego	1981	Dallas	Tampa Bay	**San Francisco**
1982	—	—	—	1982	—	—	San Francisco
1983	Miami	Pittsburgh	**LA Raiders**	1983	Washington	Detroit	San Francisco
1984	Miami	Pittsburgh	Denver	1984	Washington	Chicago	**San Francisco**
1985	Miami	Cleveland	LA Raiders	1985	Dallas	**Chicago**	LA Rams
1986	New England	Cleveland	Denver	1986	**NY Giants**	Chicago	San Francisco
1987	Indianapolis	Cleveland	Denver	1987	**Washington**	Chicago	San Francisco
1988	Buffalo	Cincinnati	Seattle	1988	Philadelphia	Chicago	**San Francisco**
1989	Buffalo	Cleveland	Denver	1989	NY Giants	Minnesota	**San Francisco**

	American Football Conference				National Football Conference		
Season	**East**	**Central**	**West**	**Season**	**East**	**Central**	**West**
1990	Buffalo	Cincinnati	LA Raiders	1990	**NY Giants**	Chicago	San Francisco
1991	Buffalo	Houston	Denver	1991	**Washington**	Detroit	New Orleans
1992	Miami	Pittsburgh	San Diego	1992	**Dallas**	Minnesota	San Francisco
1993	Buffalo	Houston	Kansas City	1993	**Dallas**	Detroit	San Francisco
1994	Miami	Pittsburgh	San Diego	1994	Dallas	Minnesota	**San Francisco**
1995	Buffalo	Pittsburgh	Kansas City	1995	**Dallas**	Green Bay	San Francisco
1996	New England	Pittsburgh	Denver	1996	Dallas	**Green Bay**	Carolina
1997	New England	Pittsburgh	Kansas City	1997	NY Giants	Green Bay	San Francisco
1998	NY Jets	Jacksonville	**Denver**	1998	Dallas	Minnesota	Atlanta
1999	Indianapolis	Jacksonville	Seattle	1999	Washington	Tampa Bay	**St. Louis**
2000	Miami	Tennessee	Oakland	2000	NY Giants	Minnesota	New Orleans

Overall Postseason Games

The postseason records of all NFL teams, ranked by number of playoff games participated in from 1933–2000.

Gm		W	L	Pct	PF	PA	Gm		W	L	Pct	PF	PA
53	Dallas Cowboys	32	21	.604	1274	979	22	Philadelphia Eagles	10	12	.455	387	392
40	Minnesota Vikings	17	23	.425	779	913	19	Dallas Texans/KC Chiefs	8	11	.421	301	384
39	San Francisco 49ers	24	15	.615	984	759	18	LA-San Diego Chargers	7	11	.389	332	428
38	Oakland-LA Raiders	22	16	.579	885	675	17	Boston-NE Patriots	7	10	.412	310	357
38	Miami Dolphins	20	18	.526	777	828	17	Detroit Lions	7	10	.412	365	404
37	Boston-Wash. Redskins	22	15	.595	778	652	13	New York Jets	6	7	.462	260	247
37	Cle-LA-St.L Rams	16	21	.432	612	787	12	Cincinnati Bengals	5	7	.417	246	257
36	Pittsburgh Steelers	21	15	.583	801	707	10	Atlanta Falcons	4	6	.400	208	260
36	New York Giants	16	20	.444	619	660	9	Tampa Bay Buccaneers	3	6	.333	91	170
32	Green Bay Packers	22	10	.688	772	558	8	Jacksonville Jaguars	4	4	.500	208	204
30	Cleveland Browns	11	19	.367	596	702	8	Seattle Seahawks	3	5	.375	145	159
29	Buffalo Bills	14	15	.483	681	658	7	Chi-St.L.-Ari. Cardinals	2	5	.286	122	182
28	Denver Broncos	16	12	.571	616	657	6	New Orleans Saints	1	5	.167	103	185
28	Chicago Bears	14	14	.500	579	552	4	Baltimore Ravens	4	0	1.000	95	23
27	Houston Oilers/Ten. Titans	12	15	.444	471	626	2	Carolina Panthers	1	1	.500	39	47
22	Balt-Indianapolis Colts	10	12	.455	393	431							

All-Time Postseason Leaders

Through Super Bowl XXXV in 2001; participants in 2000 season playoffs in **bold** type.

CAREER

Passing Efficiency

Ratings based on performance standards established for completion percentage, average gain, touchdown percentage and interception percentage. Minimum 150 passing attempts.

		Gm	Cmp%	Yds	TD	Int	Rtg
1	Bart Starr	10	61.0	1753	15	3	104.8
2	**Kurt Warner**	4	62.7	1428	11	7	96.0
3	Joe Montana	23	62.7	5772	45	21	95.6
4	Kenny Anderson	6	66.3	1321	9	6	93.5
5	Joe Theismann	10	60.7	1782	11	7	91.4

Passing

Completions

		Gm	Cmp
1	Joe Montana, SF-KC	23	460
2	Dan Marino, Miami	18	385
3	John Elway, Denver	22	355

Yards Gained

		Gm	Yds
1	Joe Montana, SF-KC	23	5772
2	John Elway, Denver	22	4964
3	Dan Marino, Miami	18	4510

Games

Played

		Gm
1	D.D. Lewis, Dallas	27
2	Larry Cole, Dallas	26
3	Charlie Waters, Dallas	25

Coached

		Gm
1	Tom Landry, Dallas	36
	Don Shula, Balt. Colts-Miami	36
3	Chuck Noll, Pittsburgh	24

Rushing

		Gm	Car	Yds	Avg
1	Emmitt Smith, Dallas	17	349	1586	4.54
2	Franco Harris, Pittsburgh	19	400	1556	3.89
3	Thurman Thomas, Buffalo	21	339	1442	4.25

Receiving

Catches

		Gm	No	Yds	Avg
1	Jerry Rice, San Francisco	23	124	1811	14.6
2	Michael Irvin, Dallas	16	87	1315	15.1
3	Andre Reed, Buffalo	21	85	1229	14.5

Yards Gained

		Gm	Yds
1	Jerry Rice, San Francisco	23	1811
2	Michael Irvin, Dallas	16	1315
3	Cliff Branch, Oakland-LA	22	1289

Scoring

Points

		Gm	TD	FG	PAT	Pts
1	Gary Anderson, Pit-Phi-SF-Min	21	0	30	53	143
2	Thurman Thomas, Buffalo	21	21	0	0	126
	Emmitt Smith, Dallas	17	21	0	0	126

Touchdowns

		Gm	Run	Rec	Ret	No
1	Thurman Thomas, Buffalo	21	16	5	0	21
	Emmitt Smith, Dallas	17	19	2	0	21
3	Jerry Rice, San Francisco	23	0	19	0	19

Field Goals

		Gm	Att	FG	Pct
1	Gary Anderson, Pit-Phi-SF-Min	21	37	30	.811
2	George Blanda, Chi-Hou-Oak	19	39	22	.564
	Steve Christie, Buffalo	12	25	22	.880

Champions of Leagues That No Longer Exist

No professional league in American sports has had to contend with more pretenders to the throne than the NFL. Eight times in nine decades, a rival league has risen up to challenge the NFL and seven of them (including the XFL) went under in less than five seasons. Only the fourth American Football League (1960-69) succeeded, forcing the older league to sue for peace and a full partnership in 1966.

Of the seven leagues that didn't make it, only the All-America Football Conference (1946-49) lives on—the Cleveland Browns and San Francisco 49ers joined the NFL after the AAFC folded in 1949. The champions of leagues past are listed below.

American Football League I

Year		Head Coach
1926	Philadelphia Quakers (8-2)	Bob Folwell

Note: Philadelphia was challenged to a postseason game by the 7th place New York Giants (8-4-1) of the NFL. The Giants won, 31-0, in a snowstorm.

American Football League II

Year		Head Coach
1936	Boston Shamrocks (8-3)	George Kennealy
1937	Los Angeles Bulldogs (9-0)	Gus Henderson

Note: Boston was scheduled to play 2nd place Cleveland (5-2-2) in the '36 championship game, but the Shamrock players refused to participate because they were owed pay for past games.

American Football League III

Year		Head Coach
1940	Columbus Bullies (8-1-1)	Phil Bucklew
1941	Columbus Bullies (5-1-2)	Phil Bucklew

All-America Football Conference

Year	Winner	Head Coach	Score	Loser	Head Coach	Site
1946	Cleveland Browns	Paul Brown	14-9	NY Yankees	Ray Flaherty	Cleveland
1947	Cleveland Browns	Paul Brown	14-3	NY Yankees	Ray Flaherty	New York
1948	Cleveland Browns	Paul Brown	49-7	Buffalo Bills	Red Dawson	Cleveland
1949	Cleveland Browns	Paul Brown	21-7	S.F. 49ers	Buck Shaw	Cleveland

World Football League

Year	Winner	Head Coach	Score	Loser	Head Coach	Site
1974	Birmingham Americans	Jack Gotta	22-21	Florida Blazers	Jack Pardee	Birmingham

United States Football League

Year	Winner	Head Coach	Score	Loser	Head Coach	Site
1983	Michigan Panthers	Jim Stanley	24-22	Philadelphia Stars	Jim Mora	Denver
1984	Philadelphia Stars	Jim Mora	23-3	Arizona Wranglers	George Allen	Tampa
1985	Baltimore Stars	Jim Mora	28-24	Oakland Invaders	Charlie Sumner	E. Rutherford

XFL

Year	Winner	Head Coach	Score	Loser	Head Coach	Site
2001	Los Angeles Xtreme	Al Luginbill	38-6	San Fran. Demons	Jim Skipper	Los Angeles

Defunct Leagues

AFL I (1926): Boston Bulldogs, Brooklyn Horseman, Chicago Bulls, Cleveland Panthers, Los Angeles Wildcats, New York Yankees, Newark Bears, Philadelphia Quakers, Rock Island Independents.

AFL II (1936-37): Boston Shamrocks (1936-37); Brooklyn Tigers (1936); Cincinnati Bengals (1937); Cleveland Rams (1936); Los Angeles Bulldogs (1937); New York Yankees (1936-37); Pittsburgh Americans (1936-37); Rochester Tigers (1936-37).

AFL III (1940-41): Boston Bears (1940); Buffalo Indians (1940-41); Cincinnati Bengals (1940-41); Columbus Bullies (1940-41); Milwaukee Chiefs (1940-41); New York Yankees (1940) renamed Americans (1941).

AAFC (1946-49): Brooklyn Dodgers (1946-48) merged to become Brooklyn-New York Yankees (1949); Buffalo Bisons (1946) renamed Bills (1947-49); Chicago Rockets (1946-48) renamed Hornets (1949); Cleveland Browns (1946-49); Los Angeles Dons (1946-49); Miami Seahawks (1946) became Baltimore Colts (1947-49); New York Yankees (1946-48) merged to become Brooklyn-New York Yankees (1949); San Francisco 49ers (1946-49).

WFL (1974-75): Birmingham Americans (1974) renamed Vulcans (1975); Chicago Fire (1974) renamed Winds (1975); Detroit Wheels (1974); Florida Blazers (1974) became San Antonio Wings (1975); The Hawaiians (1974-75); Houston Texans (1974) became Shreveport (La.) Steamer (1974-75); Jacksonville Sharks (1974) renamed Express (1975); Memphis Southmen (1974) also known as Grizzlies (1975); New York Stars (1974) became Charlotte Hornets (1974-75); Philadelphia Bell (1974-75); Portland Storm (1974) renamed Thunder (1975); Southern California Sun (1974-75).

USFL (1983-85): Arizona Wranglers (1983-84) merged with Oklahoma to become Arizona Outlaws (1985); Birmingham Stallions (1983-85); Boston Breakers (1983) became New Orleans Breakers (1984) and then Portland Breakers (1985); Chicago Blitz (1983-84); Denver Gold (1983-85); Houston Gamblers (1984-85); Jacksonville Bulls (1984-85); Los Angeles Express (1983-85); Memphis Showboats (1984-85).

Michigan Panthers (1983-84) merged with Oakland (1985); New Jersey Generals (1983-85); Oakland Invaders (1983-85); Oklahoma Outlaws (1984) merged with Arizona to become Arizona Outlaws (1985); Philadelphia Stars (1983-84) became Baltimore Stars (1985); Pittsburgh Maulers (1984); San Antonio Gunslingers (1984-85); Tampa Bay Bandits (1983-85); Washington Federals (1983-84) became Orlando Renegades (1985).

XFL (2001): Birmingham Thunderbolts, Chicago Enforcers, Las Vegas Outlaws, Los Angeles Xtreme, Memphis Maniax, New York/New Jersey Hitmen, Orlando Rage, San Francisco Demons.

NFL Pro Bowl

A postseason All-Star game between the new league champion and a team of professional all-stars was added to the NFL schedule in 1939. In the first game at Wrigley Field in Los Angeles, the NY Giants beat a team made up of players from NFL teams and two independent clubs in Los Angeles (the LA Bulldogs and Hollywood Stars). An all-NFL All-Star team provided the opposition over the next four seasons, but the game was cancelled in 1943.

The Pro Bowl was revived in 1951 as a contest between conference all-star teams: American vs National (1951-53), Eastern vs Western (1954-70), and AFC vs NFC (since 1971). The NFC leads the current series with the AFC, 16-15.

The MVP trophy was named the Dan McGuire Award in 1984 after the late SF 49ers publicist and Honolulu Advertiser sports columnist.

Year	Winner	Score	Loser
1939	NY Giants	13-10	All-Stars
1940	Green Bay	16-7	All-Stars
1940	Chicago Bears	28-14	All-Stars
1942	Chicago Bears	35-24	All-Stars
1942	All-Stars	17-14	Washington
1943-50		No game	

Year	Winner	MVP
1951	American, 28-27	Otto Graham, Cle., QB
1952	National, 30-13	Dan Towler, LA Rams, HB
1953	National, 27-7	Don Doll, Det., DB
1954	East, 20-9	Chuck Bednarik, Phi., LB
1955	West, 26-19	Billy Wilson, SF, E
1956	East, 31-30	Ollie Matson, Cards, HB
1957	West, 19-10	Back–Bert Rechichar, Bal.
		Line–Ernie Stautner, Pit.
1958	West, 26-7	Back–Hugh McElhenny, SF
		Line–Gene Brito, Wash.
1959	East, 28-21	Back–Frank Gifford, NY
		Line–Doug Atkins, Chi.
1960	West, 38-21	Back–Johnny Unitas, Bal.
		Line–Big Daddy Lipscomb, Pit.
1961	West, 35-31	Back–Johnny Unitas, Bal.
		Line–Sam Huff, NY
1962	West, 31-30	Back–Jim Brown, Cle.
		Line–Henry Jordan, GB
1963	East, 30-20	Back–Jim Brown, Cle.
		Line–Big Daddy Lipscomb, Pit.
1964	West, 31-17	Back–Johnny Unitas, Bal.
		Line–Gino Marchetti, Bal.
1965	West, 34-14	Back–Fran Tarkenton, Min.
		Line–Terry Barr, Det.
1966	East, 36-7	Back–Jim Brown, Cle.
		Line–Dale Meinhart, St. L.
1967	East, 20-10	Back–Gale Sayers, Chi.
		Line–Floyd Peters, Phi.
1968	West, 38-20	Back–Gale Sayers, Chi.
		Line–Dave Robinson, GB
1969	West, 10-7	Back–Roman Gabriel, LA Rams
		Line–Merlin Olsen, LA Rams

Year	Winner	MVP
1970	West, 16-13	Back–Gale Sayers, Chi.
		Line–George Andrie, Dal.
1971	NFC, 27-6	Back–Mel Renfro, Dal.
		Line–Fred Carr, GB
1972	AFC, 26-13	Off–Jan Stenerud, KC
		Def–Willie Lanier, KC
1973	AFC, 33-28	O.J. Simpson, Buf., RB
1974	AFC, 15-13	Garo Yepremian, Mia., PK
1975	NFC, 17-10	James Harris, LA Rams, QB
1976	NFC, 23-20	Billy Johnson, Hou., KR
1977	AFC, 24-14	Mel Blount, Pit., CB
1978	NFC, 14-13	Walter Payton, Chi., RB
1979	NFC, 13-7	Ahmad Rashad, Min., WR
1980	NFC, 37-27	Chuck Muncie, NO, RB
1981	NFC, 21-7	Eddie Murray, Det., PK
1982	AFC, 16-13	Kellen Winslow, SD, WR
		& Lee Roy Selmon, TB, DE
1983	NFC, 20-19	Dan Fouts, SD, QB
		& John Jefferson, GB, WR
1984	NFC, 45-3	Joe Theismann, Wash., QB
1985	AFC, 22-14	Mark Gastineau, NYJ, DE
1986	NFC, 28-24	Phil Simms, NYG, QB
1987	AFC, 10-6	Reggie White, Phi., DE
1988	AFC, 15-6	Bruce Smith, Buf., DE
1989	NFC, 34-3	Randall Cunningham, Phi., QB
1990	NFC, 27-21	Jerry Gray, LA Rams, CB
1991	AFC, 23-21	Jim Kelly, Buf., QB
1992	NFC, 21-15	Michael Irvin, Dal., WR
1993	AFC, 23-20 (OT)	Steve Tasker, Buf., Sp. Teams
1994	NFC, 17-3	Andre Rison, Atl., WR
1995	AFC, 41-13	Marshall Faulk, Ind., RB
1996	NFC, 20-13	Jerry Rice, SF, WR
1997	AFC, 26-23 (OT)	Mark Brunell, Jax, QB
1998	AFC, 29-24	Warren Moon, Sea., QB
1999	AFC, 23-10	Ty Law, NE, CB
		& Keyshawn Johnson, NYJ, WR
2000	NFC, 51-31	Randy Moss, Min., WR
2001	AFC, 38-17	Rich Gannon, Oak., QB

Playing sites: Wrigley Field in Los Angeles (1939); Gilmore Stadium in Los Angeles (1940–both games); Polo Grounds in New York (Jan., 1942); Shibe Park in Philadelphia (Dec., 1942); Memorial Coliseum in Los Angeles (1951-72 and 1979); Texas Stadium in Irving, TX (1973); Arrowhead Stadium in Kansas City (1974); Orange Bowl in Miami (1975); Superdome in New Orleans (1976); Kingdome in Seattle (1977); Tampa Stadium in Tampa (1978) and Aloha Stadium in Honolulu (since 1980).

AFL All-Star Game

The AFL did not play an All-Star game after its first season in 1960 but did stage All-Star games from 1962-70. All-Star teams from the Eastern and Western divisions played each other every year except 1966 with the West winning the series, 6-2. In 1966, the league champion Buffalo Bills met an elite squad made up of the best players from the league's other eight clubs and lost, 30-19.

Year	Winner	MVP
1962	West, 47-27	Cotton Davidson, Oak., QB
1963	West, 21-14	Off–Curtis McClinton, Dal.
		Def–Earl Faison, SD
1964	West, 27-24	Off–Keith Lincoln, SD
		Def–Archie Matsos, Oak.
1965	West, 38-14	Off–Keith Lincoln, SD
		Def–Willie Brown, Den.
1966	All-Stars 30	Off–Joe Namath, NY
	Buffalo 19	Def–Frank Buncom, SD

Year	Winner	MVP
1967	East, 30-23	Off–Babe Parilli, Bos.
		Def–Verlon Biggs, NY
1968	East, 25-24	Off–Joe Namath, NY
		& Don Maynard, NY
		Def–Speedy Duncan, SD
1969	West, 38-25	Off–Len Dawson, KC
		Def–George Webster, Hou.
1970	West, 26-3	John Hadl, SD, QB

Playing sites: Balboa Stadium in San Diego (1962-64); Jeppesen Stadium in Houston (1965); Rice Stadium in Houston (1966); Oakland Coliseum (1967); Gator Bowl in Jacksonville (1968-69) and Astrodome in Houston (1970).

NFL Franchise Origins

Here is what the current 31 teams in the National Football League have to show for the years they have put in as members of the American Professional Football Association (APFA), the NFL, the All-America Football Conference (AAFC) and the American Football League (AFL). Years given for league titles indicate seasons championships were won.

American Football Conference

	First Season	League Titles	Franchise Stops
Baltimore Ravens	1996 (NFL)	1 Super Bowl (2000)	• Baltimore (1996—)
Buffalo Bills	1960 (AFL)	2 AFL (1964-65)	• Buffalo (1960-72) Orchard Park, NY (1973—)
Cincinnati Bengals	1968 (AFL)	None	• Cincinnati (1968—)
Cleveland Browns	1946 (AAFC)	4 AAFC (1946-49) 4 NFL (1950,54-55,64)	• Cleveland (1946-95, 99—)
Denver Broncos	1960 (AFL)	2 Super Bowls (1997-98)	• Denver (1960—)
Indianapolis Colts	1953 (NFL)	3 NFL (1958-59,68) 1 Super Bowl (1970)	• Baltimore (1953-83) Indianapolis (1984—)
Jacksonville Jaguars	1995 (NFL)	None	• Jacksonville, FL (1995—)
Kansas City Chiefs	1960 (AFL)	3 AFL (1962,66,69) 1 Super Bowl (1969)	• Dallas (1960-62) Kansas City (1963—)
Miami Dolphins	1966 (AFL)	2 Super Bowls (1972-73)	• Miami (1966—)
New England Patriots	1960 (AFL)	None	• Boston (1960-70) Foxboro, MA (1971—)
New York Jets	1960 (AFL)	1 AFL (1968) 1 Super Bowl (1968)	• New York (1960-83) E. Rutherford, NJ (1984—)
Oakland Raiders	1960 (AFL)	1 AFL (1967) 3 Super Bowls (1976,80,83)	• Oakland (1960-81, 1995—) Los Angeles (1982-94)
Pittsburgh Steelers	1933 (NFL)	4 Super Bowls (1974-75,78-79)	• Pittsburgh (1933—)
San Diego Chargers	1960 (AFL)	1 AFL (1963)	• Los Angeles (1960) San Diego (1961—)
Seattle Seahawks	1976 (NFL)	None	• Seattle (1976—)
Tennessee Titans	1960 (AFL)	2 AFL (1960-61)	• Houston (1960-96) Memphis (1997) Nashville (1998—)

National Football Conference

	First Season	League Titles	Franchise Stops
Arizona Cardinals	1920 (APFA)	2 NFL (1925,47)	• Chicago (1920-59) St. Louis (1960-87) Tempe, AZ (1988—)
Atlanta Falcons	1966 (NFL)	None	• Atlanta (1966—)
Carolina Panthers	1995 (NFL)	None	• Clemson, SC (1995) Charlotte, NC (1996—)
Chicago Bears	1920 (APFA)	8 NFL (1921, 32-33,40-41,43,46,63) 1 Super Bowl (1985)	• Decatur, IL (1920) Chicago (1921—)
Dallas Cowboys	1960 (NFL)	5 Super Bowls (1971,77,92-93,95)	• Dallas (1960-70) Irving, TX (1971—)
Detroit Lions	1930 (NFL)	4 NFL (1935,52-53,57)	• Portsmouth, OH (1930-33) Detroit (1934-74) Pontiac, MI (1975—)
Green Bay Packers	1921 (APFA)	11 NFL (1929-31,36,39,44,61-62,65-67) 3 Super Bowls (1966-67,96)	• Green Bay (1921—)
Minnesota Vikings	1961 (NFL)	1 NFL (1969)	• Bloomington, MN (1961-81) Minneapolis, MN (1982—)
New Orleans Saints	1967 (NFL)	None	• New Orleans (1967—)
New York Giants	1925 (NFL)	4 NFL (1927,34,38,56) 2 Super Bowls (1986,90)	• New York (1925-73,75) New Haven, CT (1973-74) E. Rutherford, NJ (1976—)
Philadelphia Eagles	1933 (NFL)	3 NFL (1948-49,60)	• Philadelphia (1933—)
St. Louis Rams	1937 (NFL)	2 NFL (1945,51) 1 Super Bowl (1999)	• Cleveland (1937-45) Los Angeles (1946-79) Anaheim (1980-94) St. Louis (1995—)
San Francisco 49ers	1946 (AAFC)	5 Super Bowls (1981,84,88-89,94)	• San Francisco (1946—)
Tampa Bay Buccaneers	1976 (NFL)	None	• Tampa, FL (1976—)
Washington Redskins	1932 (NFL)	2 NFL (1937,42) 3 Super Bowls (1982,87,91)	• Boston (1932-36) Washington, DC (1937-96) Raljon, MD (1997—)

The Growth of the NFL

Of the 14 franchises that comprised the American Professional Football Association in 1920, only two remain—the Arizona Cardinals (then the Chicago Cardinals) and the Chicago Bears (originally the Decatur-IL Staleys). Green Bay joined the APFC in 1921 and the league changed its name to the NFL in 1922. Since then, 54 NFL clubs have come and gone, six rival leagues have expired and two other leagues have been swallowed up.

The NFL merged with the **All-America Football Conference** (1946-49) following the 1949 season and adopted three of its seven clubs—the Baltimore Colts, Cleveland Browns and San Francisco 49ers. The four remaining AAFC teams—the Brooklyn/NY Yankees, Buffalo Bills, Chicago Hornets and Los Angeles Dons—did not survive. After the 1950 season, the financially troubled Colts were sold back to the NFL. The league folded the team and added its players to the 1951 college draft pool. A new Baltimore franchise, also named the Colts, joined the NFL in 1953.

The formation of the **American Football League** (1960-69) was announced in 1959 with ownership lined up in eight cities—Boston, Buffalo, Dallas, Denver, Houston, Los Angeles, Minneapolis and New York. Set to begin play in the autumn of 1960, the AFL was stunned early that year when Minneapolis withdrew to accept an offer to join the NFL as an expansion team in 1961. The new league responded by choosing Oakland to replace Minneapolis and inherit the departed team's draft picks. Since no AFL team actually played in Minneapolis, it is not considered the original home of the Oakland Raiders.

In 1966, the NFL and AFL agreed to a merger that resulted in the first Super Bowl (originally called the AFL-NFL World Championship Game) following the '66 league playoffs. In 1970, the now 10-member AFL officially joined the NFL, forming a 26-team league made up of two conferences of three divisions each.

Expansion/Merger Timetable

For teams currently in NFL.

1921—Green Bay Packers; **1925**—New York Giants; **1930**—Portsmouth-OH Spartans (now Detroit Lions); **1932**—Boston Braves (now Washington Redskins); **1933**—Philadelphia Eagles and Pittsburgh Pirates (now Steelers); **1937**—Cleveland Rams (now St. Louis); **1950**—added AAFC's Cleveland Browns and San Francisco 49ers; **1953**—Baltimore Colts (now Indianapolis). **1960**—Dallas Cowboys; **1961**—Minnesota Vikings; **1966**—Atlanta Falcons; **1967**—New Orleans Saints; **1970**—added AFL's Boston Patriots (now New England), Buffalo Bills, Cincinnati Bengals (1968 expansion team), Denver Broncos, Houston Oilers (now Tennessee Titans), Kansas City Chiefs, Miami Dolphins (1966 expansion team), New York Jets, Oakland Raiders and San Diego Chargers (the AFL-NFL merger divided the league into two 13-team conferences with old-line NFL clubs Baltimore, Cleveland and Pittsburgh moving to the AFC); **1976**—Seattle Seahawks and Tampa Bay Buccaneers (Seattle was originally in the NFC West and Tampa Bay in the AFC West, but were switched to their current divisions in 1977); **1995**—Carolina Panthers and Jacksonville Jaguars; **1996**—Cleveland Browns move to Baltimore and become Ravens. City of Cleveland retains rights to team name, colors and all memorabilia; **1999**—Cleveland Browns return to the NFL.

Looking forward: 2002—Houston Texans.

City and Nickname Changes

1921—Decatur Staleys move to Chicago; **1922**—Chicago Staleys renamed Bears; **1933**—Boston Braves renamed Redskins; **1937**—Boston Redskins move to Washington; **1934**—Portsmouth (Ohio) Spartans move to Detroit and become Lions; **1941**—Pittsburgh Pirates renamed Steelers; **1943**—Philadelphia and Pittsburgh merge for one season and become Phil-Pitt, or the "Steagles"; **1944**—Chicago Cardinals and Pittsburgh merge for one season and become Card-Pitt; **1946**—Cleveland Rams move to Los Angeles.

1960—Chicago Cardinals move to St. Louis; **1961**—Los Angeles Chargers (AFL) move to San Diego; **1963**—New York Titans (AFL) renamed Jets and Dallas Texans (AFL) move to Kansas City and become Chiefs; **1971**—Boston Patriots become New England Patriots; **1982**—Oakland Raiders move to Los Angeles; **1984**—Baltimore Colts move to Indianapolis; **1988**—St. Louis Cardinals move to Phoenix; **1994**—Phoenix Cardinals become Arizona Cardinals; **1995**—L.A. Rams move to St. Louis and L.A. Raiders move back to Oakland; **1996**—Cleveland Browns move to Baltimore and become Ravens. City of Cleveland retains rights to team name, colors and all memorabilia; **1997**—Houston Oilers move to Memphis and become Tennessee Oilers; **1998**—Tennessee Oilers move to Nashville; **1999**—Tennessee Oilers renamed Titans.

Defunct NFL Teams

Teams that once played in the APFA and NFL, but no longer exist.

Akron-OH—Pros (1920-25) and Indians (1926); **Baltimore**—Colts (1950); **Boston**—Bulldogs (1926) and Yanks (1944-48); **Brooklyn**—Lions (1926), Dodgers (1930-43) and Tigers (1944); **Buffalo**—All-Americans (1920-23), Bisons (1924-25), Rangers (1926), Bisons (1927,1929); **Canton-OH**—Bulldogs (1920-23,1925-26); **Chicago**—Tigers (1920); **Cincinnati**—Celts (1921) and Reds (1933-34); **Cleveland**—Tigers (1920), Indians (1921), Indians (1923), Bulldogs (1924-25,1927) and Indians (1931); **Columbus-OH**—Panhandles (1920-22) and Tigers (1923-26); **Dallas**—Texans (1952); **Dayton-OH**—Triangles (1920-29).

Detroit—Heralds (1920-21), Panthers (1925-26) and Wolverines (1928); **Duluth-MN**—Kelleys (1923-25) and Eskimos (1926-27); **Evansville-IN**—Crimson Giants (1921-22); **Frankford-PA**—Yellow Jackets (1924-31); **Hammond-IN**—Pros (1920-26); **Hartford**—Blues (1926); **Kansas City**—Blues (1924) and Cowboys (1925-26); **Kenosha-WI**—Maroons (1924); **Los Angeles**—Buccaneers (1926); **Louisville**—Brecks (1921-23) and Colonels (1926); **Marion-OH**—Oorang Indians (1922-23); **Milwaukee**—Badgers (1922-26); **Minneapolis**—Marines (1922-24) and Red Jackets (1929-30); **Muncie-IN**—Flyers (1920-21).

New York—Giants (1921), Yankees (1927-28), Bulldogs (1949) and Yanks (1950-51); **Newark-NJ**—Tornadoes (1930); **Orange-NJ**—Tornadoes (1929); **Pottsville-PA**—Maroons (1925-28); **Providence-RI**—Steam Roller (1925-31); **Racine-WI**—Legion (1922-24) and Tornadoes (1926); **Rochester-NY**—Jeffersons (1920-25); **Rock Island-IL**—Independents (1920-26); **Staten Island-NY**—Stapletons (1929-32); **St. Louis**—All-Stars (1923) and Gunners (1934); **Toledo-OH**—Maroons (1922-23); **Tonawanda-NY**—Kardex (1921), also called Lumbermen; **Washington**—Senators (1921).

Annual NFL Leaders

Individual leaders in NFL (1932-69), NFC (since 1970), AFL (1960-69) and AFC (since 1970).

Passing

Since 1932, the NFL has used several formulas to determine passing leadership, from Total Yards alone (1932-37), to the current rating system—adopted in 1973—that takes Completions, Completion Percentage, Yards Gained, TD Passes, Interceptions, Interception Percentage and other factors into account. The quarterbacks listed below all led the league according to the system in use at the time.

Multiple winners: Sammy Baugh and Steve Young (6); Joe Montana and Roger Staubach (5); Arnie Herber, Sonny Jurgensen, Bart Starr and Norm Van Brocklin (3); Ed Danowski, Otto Graham, Cecil Isbell, Milt Plum and Bob Waterfield (2).

NFL-NFC

Year		Att	Cmp	Yds	TD	Year		Att	Cmp	Yds	TD
1932	Arnie Herber, GB	101	37	639	9	1966	Bart Starr, GB	251	156	2257	14
1933	Harry Newman, NY	136	53	973	11	1967	Sonny Jurgensen, Wash	508	288	3747	31
1934	Arnie Herber, GB	115	42	799	8	1968	Earl Morrall, Bal	317	182	2909	26
1935	Ed Danowski, NY	113	57	794	10	1969	Sonny Jurgensen, Wash	442	274	3102	22
1936	Arnie Herber, GB	173	77	1239	11	1970	John Brodie, SF	378	223	2941	24
1937	Sammy Baugh, Wash	171	81	1127	8	1971	Roger Staubach, Dal	211	126	1882	15
1938	Ed Danowski, NY	129	70	848	7	1972	Norm Snead, NY	325	196	2307	17
1939	Parker Hall, Cle. Rams	208	106	1227	9	1973	Roger Staubach, Dal	286	179	2428	23
1940	Sammy Baugh, Wash	177	111	1367	12	1974	Sonny Jurgensen, Wash	167	107	1185	11
1941	Cecil Isbell, GB	206	117	1479	15	1975	Fran Tarkenton, Min	425	273	2994	25
1942	Cecil Isbell, GB	268	146	2021	24	1976	James Harris, LA	158	91	1460	8
1943	Sammy Baugh, Wash	239	133	1754	23	1977	Roger Staubach, Dal	361	210	2620	18
1944	Frank Filchock, Wash	147	84	1139	13	1978	Roger Staubach, Dal	413	231	3190	25
1945	Sammy Baugh, Wash	182	128	1669	11	1979	Roger Staubach, Dal	461	267	3586	27
	& Sid Luckman, Chi. Bears	217	117	1725	14	1980	Ron Jaworski, Phi	451	257	3529	27
1946	Bob Waterfield, LA	251	127	1747	18	1981	Joe Montana, SF	488	311	3565	19
1947	Sammy Baugh, Wash	354	210	2938	25	1982	Joe Theismann, Wash	252	161	2033	13
1948	Tommy Thompson, Phi	246	141	1965	25	1983	Steve Bartkowski, Atl	432	274	3167	22
1949	Sammy Baugh, Wash	255	145	1903	18	1984	Joe Montana, SF	432	279	3630	28
1950	Norm Van Brocklin, LA	233	127	2061	18	1985	Joe Montana, SF	494	303	3653	27
1951	Bob Waterfield, LA	176	88	1566	13	1986	Tommy Kramer, Min	372	208	3000	24
1952	Norm Van Brocklin, LA	205	113	1736	14	1987	Joe Montana, SF	398	266	3054	31
1953	Otto Graham, Cle	258	167	2722	11	1988	Wade Wilson, Min	332	204	2746	15
1954	Norm Van Brocklin, LA	260	139	2637	13	1989	Don Majkowski, GB	599	353	4318	27
1955	Otto Graham, Cle	185	98	1721	15	1990	Joe Montana, SF	520	321	3944	26
1956	Ed Brown, Chi. Bears	168	96	1667	11	1991	Steve Young, SF	279	180	2517	17
1957	Tommy O'Connell, Cle	110	63	1229	9	1992	Steve Young, SF	402	268	3465	25
1958	Eddie LeBaron, Wash	145	79	1365	11	1993	Steve Young, SF	462	314	4023	29
1959	Charlie Conerly, NY	194	113	1706	14	1994	Steve Young, SF	461	324	3969	35
1960	Milt Plum, Cle	250	151	2297	21	1995	Brett Favre, GB	570	359	4413	38
1961	Milt Plum, Cle	302	177	2416	16	1996	Steve Young, SF	316	214	2410	14
1962	Bart Starr, GB	285	178	2438	12	1997	Steve Young, SF	356	241	3029	19
1963	Y.A. Tittle, NY	367	221	3145	36	1998	Randall Cunningham, Min	425	259	3704	34
1964	Bart Starr, GB	272	163	2144	15	1999	Kurt Warner, St.L	499	325	4353	41
1965	Rudy Bukich, Chi	312	176	2641	20	2000	Trent Green, St.L	240	145	2063	16

Note: In 1945, Sammy Baugh and Sid Luckman tied with 8 points on an inverse rating system.

AFL-AFC

Multiple winners: Dan Marino (5); Ken Anderson and Len Dawson (4); Bob Griese, Daryle Lamonica, Warren Moon and Ken Stabler (2).

Year		Att	Cmp	Yds	TD	Year		Att	Cmp	Yds	TD
1960	Jack Kemp, LA	406	211	3018	20	1981	Ken Anderson, Cin	479	300	3753	29
1961	George Blanda, Hou	362	187	3330	36	1982	Ken Anderson, Cin	309	218	2495	12
1962	Len Dawson, Dal	310	189	2759	29	1983	Dan Marino, Mia	296	173	2210	20
1963	Tobin Rote, SD	286	170	2510	20	1984	Dan Marino, Mia	564	362	5084	48
1964	Len Dawson, KC	354	199	2879	30	1985	Ken O'Brien, NY	488	297	3888	25
1965	John Hadl, SD	348	174	2798	20	1986	Dan Marino, Mia	623	378	4746	44
1966	Len Dawson, KC	284	159	2527	26	1987	Bernie Kosar, Cle	389	241	3033	22
1967	Daryle Lamonica, Oak	425	220	3228	30	1988	Boomer Esiason, Cin	388	223	3572	28
1968	Len Dawson, KC	224	131	2109	17	1989	Dan Marino, Mia	550	308	3997	24
1969	Greg Cook, Cin	197	106	1854	15	1990	Warren Moon, Hou	584	362	4689	33
1970	Daryle Lamonica, Oak	356	179	2516	22	1991	Jim Kelly, Buf	474	304	3844	33
1971	Bob Griese, Mia	263	145	2089	19	1992	Warren Moon, Hou	346	224	2521	18
1972	Earl Morrall, Mia	150	83	1360	11	1993	John Elway, Den	551	348	4030	25
1973	Ken Stabler, Oak	260	163	1997	14	1994	Dan Marino, Mia	615	385	4453	30
1974	Ken Anderson, Cin	328	213	2667	18	1995	Jim Harbaugh, Ind	314	200	2575	17
1975	Ken Anderson, Cin	377	228	3169	21	1996	John Elway, Den	466	287	3328	26
1976	Ken Stabler, Oak	291	194	2737	27	1997	Mark Brunell, Jax	435	264	3281	18
1977	Bob Griese, Mia	307	180	2252	22	1998	Vinny Testaverde, NYJ	421	259	3256	29
1978	Terry Bradshaw, Pit	368	207	2915	28	1999	Peyton Manning, Ind	533	331	4135	26
1979	Dan Fouts, SD	530	332	4082	24	2000	Brian Griese, Den	336	216	2688	19
1980	Brian Sipe, Cle	554	337	4132	30						

Receptions
NFL-NFC

Multiple winners: Don Hutson (8); Raymond Berry, Tom Fears, Pete Pihos, Jerry Rice, Sterling Sharpe and Billy Wilson (3); Dwight Clark, Herman Moore, Mushin Muhammad, Ahmad Rashad and Charley Taylor (2).

Year		No	Yds	Avg	TD	Year		No	Yds	Avg	TD
1932	Ray Flaherty, NY	21	350	16.7	3	1966	Charley Taylor, Wash	72	1119	15.5	12
1933	Shipwreck Kelly, Bklyn	22	246	11.2	3	1967	Charley Taylor, Wash	70	990	14.1	9
1934	Joe Carter, Phi	16	238	14.9	4	1968	Clifton McNeil, SF	71	994	14.0	7
	& Red Badgro, NY	16	206	12.9	1	1969	Dan Abramowicz, NO	73	1015	13.9	7
1935	Tod Goodwin, NY	26	432	16.6	4	1970	Dick Gordon, Chi	71	1026	14.5	13
1936	Don Hutson, GB	34	536	15.8	8	1971	Bob Tucker, NY	59	791	13.4	4
1937	Don Hutson, GB	41	552	13.5	7	1972	Harold Jackson, Phi	62	1048	16.9	4
1938	Gaynell Tinsley, Chi. Cards	41	516	12.6	1	1973	Harold Carmichael, Phi	67	1116	16.7	9
1939	Don Hutson, GB	34	846	24.9	6	1974	Charles Young, Phi	63	696	11.0	3
1940	Don Looney, Phi	58	707	12.2	4	1975	Chuck Foreman, Min	73	691	9.5	9
1941	Don Hutson, GB	58	739	12.7	10	1976	Drew Pearson, Dal	58	806	13.9	6
1942	Don Hutson, GB	74	1211	16.4	17	1977	Ahmad Rashad, Min	51	681	13.4	2
1943	Don Hutson, GB	47	776	16.5	11	1978	Rickey Young, Min	88	704	8.0	5
1944	Don Hutson, GB	58	866	14.9	9	1979	Ahmad Rashad, Min	80	1156	14.5	9
1945	Don Hutson, GB	47	834	17.7	9	1980	Earl Cooper, SF	83	567	6.8	4
1946	Jim Benton, LA	63	981	15.6	6	1981	Dwight Clark, SF	85	1105	13.0	4
1947	Jim Keane, Chi. Bears	64	910	14.2	10	1982	Dwight Clark, SF	60	913	12.2	5
1948	Tom Fears, LA	51	698	13.7	4	1983	Roy Green, St. L	78	1227	15.7	14
1949	Tom Fears, LA	77	1013	13.2	9		Charlie Brown, Wash	78	1225	15.7	8
1950	Tom Fears, LA	84	1116	13.3	7		& Earnest Gray, NY	78	1139	14.6	5
1951	Elroy Hirsch, LA	66	1495	22.7	17	1984	Art Monk, Wash	106	1372	12.9	7
1952	Mac Speedie, Cle	62	911	14.7	5	1985	Roger Craig, SF	92	1016	11.0	6
1953	Pete Pihos, Phi	63	1049	16.7	10	1986	Jerry Rice, SF	86	1570	18.3	15
1954	Pete Pihos, Phi	60	872	14.5	10	1987	J.T. Smith, St. L	91	1117	12.3	8
	& Billy Wilson, SF	60	830	13.8	5	1988	Henry Ellard, LA	86	1414	16.4	10
1955	Pete Pihos, Phi	62	864	13.9	7	1989	Sterling Sharpe, GB	90	1423	15.8	12
1956	Billy Wilson, SF	60	889	14.8	5	1990	Jerry Rice, SF	100	1502	15.0	13
1957	Billy Wilson, SF	52	757	14.6	6	1991	Michael Irvin, Dal	93	1523	16.4	8
1958	Raymond Berry, Bal	56	794	14.2	9	1992	Sterling Sharpe, GB	108	1461	13.5	13
	& Pete Retzlaff, Phi	56	766	13.7	2	1993	Sterling Sharpe, GB	112	1274	11.4	11
1959	Raymond Berry, Bal	66	959	14.5	14	1994	Cris Carter, Min	122	1256	10.3	7
1960	Raymond Berry, Bal	74	1298	17.5	10	1995	Herman Moore, Det	123	1686	13.7	14
1961	Red Phillips, LA	78	1092	14.0	5	1996	Jerry Rice, SF	108	1254	11.6	8
1962	Bobby Mitchell, Wash	72	1384	19.2	11	1997	Herman Moore, Det	104	1293	12.4	8
1963	Bobby Joe Conrad, St. L	73	967	13.2	10	1998	Frank Sanders, Ari	89	1145	12.9	3
1964	Johnny Morris, Chi. Bears	93	1200	12.9	10	1999	Mushin Muhammad, Car	96	1253	13.1	6
1965	Dave Parks, SF	80	1344	16.8	12	2000	Mushin Muhammad, Car	102	1183	11.6	6

AFL-AFC

Multiple winners: Lionel Taylor (5); Lance Alworth, Haywood Jeffires, Lydell Mitchell and Kellen Winslow (3); Fred Biletnikoff, Todd Christensen, Carl Pickens and Al Toon (2).

Year		No	Yds	Avg	TD	Year		No	Yds	Avg	TD
1960	Lionel Taylor, Den	92	1235	13.4	12	1981	Kellen Winslow, SD	88	1075	12.2	10
1961	Lionel Taylor, Den	100	1176	11.8	4	1982	Kellen Winslow, SD	54	721	13.4	6
1962	Lionel Taylor, Den	77	908	11.8	4	1983	Todd Christensen, LA	92	1247	13.6	12
1963	Lionel Taylor, Den	78	1101	14.1	10	1984	Ozzie Newsome, Cle	89	1001	11.2	5
1964	Charley Hennigan, Hou	101	1546	15:3	8	1985	Lionel James, SD	86	1027	11.9	6
1965	Lionel Taylor, Den	85	1131	13.3	6	1986	Todd Christensen, LA	95	1153	12.1	8
1966	Lance Alworth, SD	73	1383	18.9	13	1987	Al Toon, NY	68	976	14.4	5
1967	George Sauer, NY	75	1189	15.9	6	1988	Al Toon, NY	93	1067	11.5	5
1968	Lance Alworth, SD	68	1312	19.3	10	1989	Andre Reed, Buf	88	1312	14.9	9
1969	Lance Alworth, SD	64	1003	15.7	4	1990	Haywood Jeffires, Hou	74	1048	14.2	8
1970	Marlin Briscoe, Buf	57	1036	18.2	8		& Drew Hill, Hou	74	1019	13.8	5
1971	Fred Biletnikoff, Oak	61	929	15.2	9	1991	Haywood Jeffires, Hou	100	1181	11.8	7
1972	Fred Biletnikoff, Oak	58	802	13.8	7	1992	Haywood Jeffires, Hou	90	913	10.1	9
1973	Fred Willis, Hou	57	371	6.5	1	1993	Reggie Langhorne, Ind	85	1038	12.2	3
1974	Lydell Mitchell, Bal	72	544	7.6	2	1994	Ben Coates, NE	96	1174	12.2	7
1975	Reggie Rucker, Cle	60	770	12.8	3	1995	Carl Pickens, Cin	99	1234	12.5	17
	& Lydell Mitchell, Bal	60	544	9.1	4	1996	Carl Pickens, Cin	100	1180	11.8	12
1976	MacArthur Lane, KC	66	686	10.4	1	1997	Tim Brown, Oak	104	1408	13.5	5
1977	Lydell Mitchell, Bal	71	620	8.7	4	1998	O.J. McDuffie, Mia	90	1050	11.7	7
1978	Steve Largent, Sea	71	1168	16.5	8	1999	Jimmy Smith, Jax	116	1636	14.1	6
1979	Joe Washington, Bal	82	750	9.1	3	2000	Marvin Harrison, Ind	102	1413	13.9	14
1980	Kellen Winslow, SD	89	1290	14.5	9						

Annual NFL Leaders (Cont.)
Rushing

NFL-NFC

Multiple winners: Jim Brown (8); Walter Payton and Barry Sanders (5); Emmitt Smith and Steve Van Buren (4); Eric Dickerson (3); Cliff Battles, John Brockington, Larry Brown, Bill Dudley, Leroy Kelly, Bill Paschal, Joe Perry, Gale Sayers and Whizzer White (2).

Year		Car	Yds	Avg	TD	Year		Car	Yds	Avg	TD
1932	Cliff Battles, Bos	148	576	3.9	3	1967	Leroy Kelly, Cle	235	1205	5.1	11
1933	Jim Musick, Bos.	173	809	4.7	5	1968	Leroy Kelly, Cle	248	1239	5.0	16
1934	Beattie Feathers, Chi. Bears	119	1004	8.4	8	1969	Gale Sayers, Chi	236	1032	4.4	8
1935	Doug Russell, Chi. Cards.	140	499	3.6	0	1970	Larry Brown, Wash	237	1125	4.7	5
1936	Tuffy Leemans, NY	206	830	4.0	2	1971	John Brockington, GB	216	1105	5.1	4
1937	Cliff Battles, Wash	216	874	4.0	5	1972	Larry Brown, Wash	285	1216	4.3	8
1938	Whizzer White, Pit.	152	567	3.7	4	1973	John Brockington, GB	265	1144	4.3	3
1939	Bill Osmanski, Chi. Bears	121	699	5.8	7	1974	Lawrence McCutcheon, LA	236	1109	4.7	3
1940	Whizzer White, Det.	146	514	3.5	5	1975	Jim Otis, St.L.	269	1076	4.0	5
1941	Pug Manders, Bklyn	111	486	4.4	5	1976	Walter Payton, Chi	311	1390	4.5	13
1942	Bill Dudley, Pit	162	696	4.3	5	1977	Walter Payton, Chi	339	1852	5.5	14
1943	Bill Paschal, NY	147	572	3.9	10	1978	Walter Payton, Chi	333	1395	4.2	11
1944	Bill Paschal, NY	196	737	3.8	9	1979	Walter Payton, Chi	369	1610	4.4	14
1945	Steve Van Buren, Phi	143	832	5.8	15	1980	Walter Payton, Chi	317	1460	4.6	6
1946	Bill Dudley, Pit	146	604	4.1	3	1981	George Rogers, NO	378	1674	4.4	13
1947	Steve Van Buren, Phi	217	1008	4.6	13	1982	Tony Dorsett, Dal	177	745	4.2	5
1948	Steve Van Buren, Phi	201	945	4.7	10	1983	Eric Dickerson, LA	390	1808	4.6	18
1949	Steve Van Buren, Phi	263	1146	4.4	11	1984	Eric Dickerson, LA	379	2105	5.6	14
1950	Marion Motley, Cle	140	810	5.8	3	1985	Gerald Riggs, Atl	397	1719	4.3	10
1951	Eddie Price, NY Giants	271	971	3.6	7	1986	Eric Dickerson, LA	404	1821	4.5	11
1952	Dan Towler, LA	156	894	5.7	10	1987	Charles White, LA	324	1374	4.2	11
1953	Joe Perry, SF	192	1018	5.3	10	1988	Herschel Walker, Dal	361	1514	4.2	5
1954	Joe Perry, SF	173	1049	6.1	8	1989	Barry Sanders, Det	280	1470	5.3	14
1955	Alan Ameche, Bal.	213	961	4.5	9	1990	Barry Sanders, Det	255	1304	5.1	13
1956	Rick Casares, Chi. Bears	234	1126	4.8	12	1991	Emmitt Smith, Dal.	365	1563	4.3	12
1957	Jim Brown, Cle	202	942	4.7	9	1992	Emmitt Smith, Dal.	373	1713	4.6	18
1958	Jim Brown, Cle	257	1527	5.9	17	1993	Emmitt Smith, Dal.	283	1486	5.3	9
1959	Jim Brown, Cle	290	1329	4.6	14	1994	Barry Sanders, Det	331	1883	5.7	7
1960	Jim Brown, Cle	215	1257	5.8	9	1995	Emmitt Smith, Dal.	377	1773	4.7	25
1961	Jim Brown, Cle	305	1408	4.6	8	1996	Barry Sanders, Det	307	1553	5.1	11
1962	Jim Taylor, GB	272	1474	5.4	19	1997	Barry Sanders, Det	335	2053	6.1	11
1963	Jim Brown, Cle	291	1863	6.4	12	1998	Jamal Anderson, Atl	410	1846	4.5	14
1964	Jim Brown, Cle	280	1446	5.2	7	1999	Stephen Davis, Wash	290	1405	4.8	17
1965	Jim Brown, Cle	289	1544	5.3	17	2000	Robert Smith, Min	295	1521	5.2	7
1966	Gale Sayers, Chi	229	1231	5.4	8						

Note: Jim Brown led the NFL in rushing eight of his nine years in the league. The one season he didn't win (1962) he finished fourth (996 yds) behind Jim Taylor, John Henry Johnson of Pittsburgh (1,141 yds) and Dick Bass of the LA Rams (1,033 yds).

AFL-AFC

Multiple winners: Earl Campbell and O.J. Simpson (4); Terrell Davis and Thurman Thomas (3); Eric Dickerson, Cookie Gilchrist, Edgerrin James, Floyd Little, Jim Nance and Curt Warner (2).

Year		Car	Yds	Avg	TD	Year		Car	Yds	Avg	TD
1960	Abner Haynes, Dal.	157	875	5.6	9	1981	Earl Campbell, Hou	361	1376	3.8	10
1961	Billy Cannon, Hou	200	948	4.7	6	1982	Freeman McNeil, NY	151	786	5.2	6
1962	Cookie Gilchrist, Buf	214	1096	5.1	13	1983	Curt Warner, Sea.	335	1449	4.3	13
1963	Clem Daniels, Oak	215	1099	5.1	3	1984	Earnest Jackson, SD	296	1179	4.0	8
1964	Cookie Gilchrist, Buf	230	981	4.3	6	1985	Marcus Allen, LA	380	1759	4.6	11
1965	Paul Lowe, SD	222	1121	5.0	7	1986	Curt Warner, Sea.	319	1481	4.6	13
1966	Jim Nance, Bos.	299	1458	4.9	11	1987	Eric Dickerson, Ind.	223	1011	4.5	5
1967	Jim Nance, Bos.	269	1216	4.5	7	1988	Eric Dickerson, Ind.	388	1659	4.3	14
1968	Paul Robinson, Cin	238	1023	4.3	8	1989	Christian Okoye, KC	370	1480	4.0	12
1969	Dickie Post, SD	182	873	4.8	6	1990	Thurman Thomas, Buf	271	1297	4.8	11
1970	Floyd Little, Den	209	901	4.3	3	1991	Thurman Thomas, Buf	288	1407	4.9	7
1971	Floyd Little, Den	284	1133	4.0	6	1992	Barry Foster, Pit	390	1690	4.3	11
1972	O.J. Simpson, Buf.	292	1251	4.3	6	1993	Thurman Thomas, Buf	355	1315	3.7	6
1973	O.J. Simpson, Buf.	332	2003	6.0	12	1994	Chris Warren, Sea.	333	1545	4.6	9
1974	Otis Armstrong, Den	263	1407	5.3	9	1995	Curtis Martin, NE.	368	1487	4.0	14
1975	O.J. Simpson, Buf.	329	1817	5.5	16	1996	Terrell Davis, Den.	345	1538	4.5	13
1976	O.J. Simpson, Buf.	290	1503	5.2	8	1997	Terrell Davis, Den.	369	1750	4.7	15
1977	Mark van Eeghen, Oak	324	1273	3.9	7	1998	Terrell Davis, Den.	392	2008	5.1	21
1978	Earl Campbell, Hou	302	1450	4.8	13	1999	Edgerrin James, Ind.	369	1553	4.2	13
1979	Earl Campbell, Hou	368	1697	4.6	19	2000	Edgerrin James, Ind.	387	1709	4.4	13
1980	Earl Campbell, Hou	373	1934	5.2	13						

Note: Eric Dickerson was traded to Indianapolis from the NFC's LA Rams during the 1987 season. In three games with the Rams, he carried the ball 60 times for 277 yds, a 4.6 avg and 1 TD. His official AFC statistics above came in nine games with the Colts.

Scoring
NFL-NFC

Multiple winners: Don Hutson (5); Dutch Clark, Pat Harder, Paul Hornung, Chip Lohmiller and Mark Moseley (3); Kevin Butler, Mike Cofer, Fred Cox, Jack Manders, Chester Marcol, Eddie Murray, Emmitt Smith, Gordy Soltau and Doak Walker (2).

Year		TD	FG	PAT	Pts	Year		TD	FG	PAT	Pts
1932	Dutch Clark, Portsmouth	6	3	10	55	1967	Jim Bakken, St.L	0	27	36	117
1933	Glenn Presnell, Portsmouth	6	6	10	64	1968	Leroy Kelly, Cle	20	0	0	120
	& Ken Strong, NY	6	5	13	64	1969	Fred Cox, Min	0	26	43	121
1934	Jack Manders, Chi. Bears	3	10	31	79	1970	Fred Cox, Min	0	30	35	125
1935	Dutch Clark, Det	6	1	16	55	1971	Curt Knight, Wash.	0	29	27	114
1936	Dutch Clark, Det	7	4	19	73	1972	Chester Marcol, GB	0	33	29	128
1937	Jack Manders, Chi. Bears	5	8	15	69	1973	David Ray, LA	0	30	40	130
1938	Clarke Hinkle, GB	7	3	7	58	1974	Chester Marcol, GB	0	25	19	94
1939	Andy Farkas, Wash	11	0	2	68	1975	Chuck Foreman, Min	22	0	0	132
1940	Don Hutson, GB	7	0	15	57	1976	Mark Moseley, Wash	0	22	31	97
1941	Don Hutson, GB	12	1	20	95	1977	Walter Payton, Chi	16	0	0	96
1942	Don Hutson, GB	17	1	33	138	1978	Frank Corral, LA	0	29	31	118
1943	Don Hutson, GB	12	3	26	117	1979	Mark Moseley, Wash	0	25	39	114
1944	Don Hutson, GB	9	0	31	85	1980	Eddie Murray, Det	0	27	35	116
1945	Steve Van Buren, Phi	18	0	2	110	1981	Rafael Septien, Dal	0	27	40	121
1946	Ted Fritsch, GB	10	9	13	100		& Eddie Murray, Det	0	25	46	121
1947	Pat Harder, Chi. Cards	7	7	39	102	1982	Wendell Tyler, LA	13	0	0	78
1948	Pat Harder, Chi. Cards	6	7	53	110	1983	Mark Moseley, Wash	0	33	62	161
1949	Gene Roberts, NY Giants	17	0	0	102	1984	Ray Wersching, SF	0	25	56	131
	& Pat Harder, Chi. Cards	8	3	45	102	1985	Kevin Butler, Chi	0	31	51	144
1950	Doak Walker, Det	11	8	38	128	1986	Kevin Butler, Chi	0	28	36	120
1951	Elroy Hirsch, LA	17	0	0	102	1987	Jerry Rice, SF	23	0	0	138
1952	Gordy Soltau, SF	7	6	34	94	1988	Mike Cofer, SF	0	27	40	121
1953	Gordy Soltau, SF	6	10	48	114	1989	Mike Cofer, SF	0	29	49	136
1954	Bobby Walston, Phi	11	4	36	114	1990	Chip Lohmiller, Wash	0	30	41	131
1955	Doak Walker, Det	7	9	27	96	1991	Chip Lohmiller, Wash	0	31	56	149
1956	Bobby Layne, Det	5	12	33	99	1992	Chip Lohmiller, Wash	0	30	30	120
1957	Sam Baker, Wash	1	14	29	77		& Morten Andersen, NO	0	29	33	120
	& Lou Groza, Cle	0	15	32	77	1993	Jason Hanson, Det	0	34	28	130
1958	Jim Brown, Cle	18	0	0	108	1994	Emmitt Smith, Dal	22	0	0	132
1959	Paul Hornung, GB	7	7	31	94		& Fuad Reveiz, Min	0	34	30	132
1960	Paul Hornung, GB	15	15	41	176	1995	Emmitt Smith, Dal	25	0	0	150
1961	Paul Hornung, GB	10	15	41	146	1996	John Kasay, Car.	0	37	34	145
1962	Jim Taylor, GB	19	0	0	114	1997	Richie Cunningham, Dal.	0	34	24	126
1963	Don Chandler, NY	0	18	52	106	1998	Gary Anderson, Min.	0	35	59	164
1964	Lenny Moore, Bal	20	0	0	120	1999	Jeff Wilkins, St.L.	0	20	64	124
1965	Gale Sayers, Chi.	22	0	0	132	2000	Ryan Longwell, GB	0	33	32	131
1966	Bruce Gossett, LA	0	28	29	113						

AFL-AFC

Multiple winners: Gino Cappelletti (5); Gary Anderson (3); Jim Breech, Roy Gerela, Gene Mingo, Nick Lowery, John Smith, Pete Stoyanovich and Jim Turner (2).

Year		TD	FG	PAT	Pts	Year		TD	FG	PAT	Pts
1960	Gene Mingo, Den	6	18	33	123	1981	Nick Lowery, KC	0	26	37	115
1961	Gino Cappelletti, Bos	8	17	48	147		& Jim Breech, Cin	0	22	49	115
1962	Gene Mingo, Den	4	27	32	137	1982	Marcus Allen, LA.	14	0	0	84
1963	Gino Cappelletti, Bos	2	22	35	113	1983	Gary Anderson, Pit	0	27	38	119
1964	Gino Cappelletti, Bos	7	25	36	155	1984	Gary Anderson, Pit	0	24	45	117
1965	Gino Cappelletti, Bos	9	17	27	132	1985	Gary Anderson, Pit	0	33	40	139
1966	Gino Cappelletti, Bos	6	16	35	119	1986	Tony Franklin, NE	0	32	44	140
1967	George Blanda, Oak	0	20	56	116	1987	Jim Breech, Cin	0	24	25	97
1968	Jim Turner, NY	0	34	43	145	1988	Scott Norwood, Buf	0	32	33	129
1969	Jim Turner, NY	0	32	33	129	1989	David Treadwell, Den	0	27	39	120
1970	Jan Stenerud, KC	0	30	26	116	1990	Nick Lowery, KC	0	34	37	139
1971	Garo Yepremian, Mia	0	28	33	117	1991	Pete Stoyanovich, Mia	0	31	28	121
1972	Bobby Howfield, NY	0	27	40	121	1992	Pete Stoyanovich, Mia	0	30	34	124
1973	Roy Gerela, Pit	0	29	36	123	1993	Jeff Jaeger, LA	0	35	27	132
1974	Roy Gerela, Pit	0	20	33	93	1994	John Carney, SD	0	34	33	135
1975	O.J. Simpson, Buf	23	0	0	138	1995	Norm Johnson, Pit	0	34	39	141
1976	Toni Linhart, Bal	0	20	49	109	1996	Cary Blanchard, Ind	0	36	27	135
1977	Errol Mann, Oak	0	20	39	99	1997	Mike Hollis, Jax	0	31	41	134
1978	Pat Leahy, NY	0	22	41	107	1998	Steve Christie, Buf	0	33	41	140
1979	John Smith, NE	0	23	46	115	1999	Mike Vanderjagt, Ind	0	34	43	145
1980	John Smith, NE	0	26	51	129	2000	Matt Stover, Bal	0	35	30	135

All-Time NFL Leaders
Through 2000 regular season.
CAREER
Players active in 2000 in **bold** type.
Passing Efficiency
Ratings based on performance standards established for completion percentage, average gain, touchdown percentage and interception percentage. Quarterbacks are allocated points according to how their statistics measure up to those standards. Minimum 1500 passing attempts.

		Yrs	Att	Cmp	Cmp%	Yards	Avg Gain	TD	TD%	Int	Int%	Rating
1	Steve Young	15	4149	2667	64.4	33,124	7.98	232	5.6	107	2.6	96.8
2	Joe Montana	15	5391	3409	63.2	40,551	7.52	273	5.1	139	2.6	92.3
3	Dan Marino	17	8358	4967	59.4	61,361	7.34	420	5.0	252	3.0	86.4
4	**Brett Favre**	10	4932	2997	60.8	34,706	7.04	255	5.2	157	3.2	86.0
5	**Peyton Manning**	3	1679	1014	60.4	12,287	7.32	85	5.1	58	3.5	85.4
6	**Mark Brunell**	7	2672	1608	60.2	19,212	7.19	106	4.0	66	2.5	85.1
7	**Brad Johnson**	9	1821	1126	61.8	12,973	7.12	79	4.3	57	3.1	84.7
8	Jim Kelly	11	4779	2874	60.1	35,467	7.42	237	5.0	175	3.7	84.4
9	Roger Staubach	11	2958	1685	57.0	22,700	7.67	153	5.2	109	3.7	83.4
10	Neil Lomax	8	3153	1817	57.6	22,771	7.22	136	4.3	90	2.9	82.7
11	Sonny Jurgensen	18	4262	2433	57.1	32,224	7.56	255	6.0	189	4.4	82.625
12	Len Dawson	19	3741	2136	57.1	28,711	7.67	239	6.4	183	4.9	82.555
13	**Neil O'Donnell**	11	3121	1802	57.7	20,938	6.71	116	3.7	65	2.1	81.863
14	Ken Anderson	16	4475	2654	59.3	32,838	7.34	197	4.4	160	3.6	81.858
15	Bernie Kosar	12	3365	1994	59.3	23,301	6.92	124	3.7	87	2.6	81.8
16	Danny White	13	2950	1761	59.7	21,959	7.44	155	5.3	132	4.5	81.715
17	**Elvis Grbac**	8	1978	1181	59.7	13,741	6.95	84	4.2	63	3.2	81.669
18	**Troy Aikman**	12	4715	2898	61.5	32,942	6.99	165	3.5	141	3.0	81.6
19	Dave Krieg	19	5311	3105	58.5	38,147	7.18	261	4.9	199	3.7	81.499
20	**Randall Cunningham**	15	4200	2375	56.6	29,406	7.00	204	4.9	132	3.1	81.474
21	Boomer Esiason	14	5205	2969	57.0	37,920	7.29	247	4.7	184	3.5	81.1
22	**Jeff George**	11	3925	2275	58.0	27,434	6.99	154	3.9	110	2.8	80.909
23	**Warren Moon**	17	6823	3988	58.5	49,325	7.23	291	4.3	233	3.4	80.901
24	**Steve Beuerlein**	12	3148	1793	57.0	22,732	7.22	139	4.4	102	3.2	80.853
25	**Rich Gannon**	13	2746	1588	57.8	18,428	6.71	118	4.3	79	2.9	80.573

Note: The NFL does not recognize records from the All-American Football Conference (1946-49). If it did, **Otto Graham** would rank 3rd (after Montana) with the following stats: 10 Yrs; 2,626 Att; 1,464 Comp; 55.8 Comp Pct; 23,584 Yards; 8.98 Avg Gain; 174 TD; 6.6 TD Pct; 135 Int; 5.1 Int Pct; and 86.6 Rating Pts.

Touchdown Passes

		No			No			No
1	Dan Marino	420	16	Steve Young	232	31	Ken Stabler	194
2	Fran Tarkenton	342	17	**Vinny Testaverde**	226	32	Bob Griese	192
3	John Elway	300	18	John Brodie	214	33	Sammy Baugh	187
4	**Warren Moon**	291	19	Terry Bradshaw	212	34	Craig Morton	183
5	Johnny Unitas	290		Y.A. Tittle	212	35	Steve Grogan	182
6	Joe Montana	273	21	Jim Hart	209	36	Ron Jaworski	179
7	Dave Krieg	261	22	**Randall Cunningham**	204	37	Babe Parilli	178
8	**Brett Favre**	255	23	Jim Everett	203	38	Charlie Conerly	173
	Sonny Jurgensen	255	24	Roman Gabriel	201		Joe Namath	173
10	Dan Fouts	254	25	Phil Simms	199		Norm Van Brocklin	173
11	Boomer Esiason	247	26	Ken Anderson	197	41	Charley Johnson	170
12	John Hadl	244	27	Joe Ferguson	196	42	**Troy Aikman**	165
13	Len Dawson	239		Bobby Layne	196	43	**Drew Bledsoe**	164
14	Jim Kelly	237		Steve DeBerg	196		Daryle Lamonica	164
15	George Blanda	236		Norm Snead	196		Jim Plunkett	164

Note: The NFL does not recognize records from the All-American Football Conference (1946-49). If it did, **Y.A. Tittle** would move up from 19th to 13th (after Hadl) with 242 TDs and **Otto Graham** would rank 38th (after Parilli) with 174 TDs.

Passes Intercepted

		No			No			No
1	George Blanda	277	10	**Warren Moon**	233	19	Joe Ferguson	209
2	John Hadl	268	11	John Elway	226	20	Steve Grogan	208
3	Fran Tarkenton	266	12	John Brodie	224	21	Steve DeBerg	204
4	Norm Snead	257	13	Ken Stabler	222	22	Sammy Baugh	203
5	Johnny Unitas	253	14	Y.A. Tittle	221	23	Dave Krieg	199
6	Dan Marino	252	15	Joe Namath	220	24	Jim Plunkett	198
7	Jim Hart	247		Babe Parilli	220	25	Tobin Rote	191
8	Bobby Layne	245	17	**Vinny Testaverde**	216			
9	Dan Fouts	242	18	Terry Bradshaw	210			

Passing Yards

		Yrs	Att	Comp	Pct	Yards
1	Dan Marino	17	8358	4967	59.4	61,361
2	John Elway	16	7250	4123	56.9	51,475
3	Warren Moon	17	6823	3988	58.5	49,325
4	Fran Tarkenton	18	6467	3686	57.0	47,003
5	Dan Fouts	15	5604	3297	58.8	43,040
6	Joe Montana	15	5391	3409	63.2	40,551
7	Johnny Unitas	18	5186	2830	54.6	40,239
8	Dave Krieg	19	5311	3105	58.5	38,147
9	Boomer Esiason	14	5205	2969	57.0	37,920
10	Vinny Testaverde	14	5203	2897	55.7	36,307
11	Jim Kelly	11	4779	2874	60.1	35,467
12	Jim Everett	12	4923	2841	57.7	34,837
13	Brett Favre	10	4932	2997	60.8	34,706
14	Jim Hart	19	5076	2593	51.1	34,665
15	Steve DeBerg	17	5024	2874	57.2	34,241
16	John Hadl	16	4687	2363	50.4	33,503
17	Phil Simms	14	4647	2576	55.4	33,462
18	Steve Young	15	4149	2667	64.3	33,124
19	Troy Aikman	12	4715	2898	61.5	32,942
20	Ken Anderson	16	4475	2654	59.3	32,838
21	Sonny Jurgensen	18	4262	2433	57.1	32,224
22	John Brodie	17	4491	2469	55.0	31,548
23	Norm Snead	15	4353	2276	52.3	30,797
24	Joe Ferguson	18	4519	2369	52.4	29,817
25	Roman Gabriel	16	4498	2366	52.6	29,444

Note: The NFL does not recognize records from the All-American Football Conference (1946-49). If it did, **Y.A. Tittle** would rank 19th (after Young) with the following stats: 17 Yrs; 4,395 Att; 2,427 Comp; 55.2 Pct; and 33,070 Yards.

Receptions

		Yrs	No	Yards	Avg	TD
1	Jerry Rice	16	1281	19,247	15.0	176
2	Cris Carter	14	1020	12,962	12.7	123
3	Andre Reed	16	951	13,198	13.9	87
4	Art Monk	16	940	12,721	13.5	68
5	Irving Fryar	17	851	12,785	15.0	84
6	Tim Brown	13	846	12,072	14.3	86
7	Steve Largent	14	819	13,089	16.0	100
8	Henry Ellard	16	814	13,777	16.9	65
9	James Lofton	16	764	14,004	18.3	75
10	Charlie Joiner	18	750	12,146	16.2	65
	Michael Irvin	12	750	11,904	15.9	65
12	Andre Rison	12	743	10,205	13.7	84
13	Gary Clark	11	699	10,856	15.5	65
14	Larry Centers	11	685	5,683	8.3	25
15	Herman Moore	10	666	9,098	13.7	62
16	Ozzie Newsome	13	662	7,980	12.1	47
17	Charley Taylor	13	649	9,110	14.0	79
18	Drew Hill	15	634	9,831	15.5	60
19	Don Maynard	15	633	11,834	18.7	88
20	Raymond Berry	13	631	9,275	14.7	68
21	Rob Moore	10	628	9,368	14.9	49
22	Shannon Sharpe	11	619	7,793	12.6	49
23	Terance Mathis	13	615	8,027	13.1	59
24	Keith Byars	13	610	5,661	9.3	31
25	Sterling Sharpe	7	595	8,134	13.7	65
	Anthony Miller	10	595	9,148	15.4	63

Rushing

		Yrs	Car	Yards	Avg	TD
1	Walter Payton	13	3838	16,726	4.4	110
2	Barry Sanders	10	3062	15,269	5.0	99
3	Emmitt Smith	11	3537	15,166	4.3	145
4	Eric Dickerson	11	2996	13,259	4.4	90
5	Tony Dorsett	12	2936	12,739	4.3	77
6	Jim Brown	9	2359	12,312	5.2	106
7	Marcus Allen	16	3022	12,243	4.1	123
8	Franco Harris	13	2949	12,120	4.1	91
9	Thurman Thomas	13	2877	12,074	4.2	65
10	John Riggins	14	2916	11,352	3.9	104
11	O.J. Simpson	11	2404	11,236	4.7	61
12	Ricky Watters	9	2550	10,325	4.1	77
13	Ottis Anderson	14	2562	10,273	4.0	81
14	Jerome Bettis	8	2461	9,804	4.0	49
15	Earl Campbell	8	2187	9,407	4.3	74
16	Jim Taylor	10	1941	8,597	4.4	83
17	Joe Perry	14	1737	8,378	4.8	53
18	Ernest Byner	14	2095	8,261	3.9	56
19	Herschel Walker	12	1954	8,225	4.2	61
20	Roger Craig	11	1991	8,189	4.1	56
21	Gerald Riggs	10	1989	8,188	4.1	69
22	Larry Csonka	11	1891	8,081	4.3	64
23	Freeman McNeil	12	1798	8,074	4.5	38
24	Marshall Faulk	7	1895	8,060	4.3	67
25	James Brooks	12	1685	7,962	4.7	49

Note: The NFL does not recognize records from the All-American Football Conference (1946-49). If it did, **Joe Perry** would move up from 17th to 15th (after Bettis) with the following stats: 16 Yrs; 1,929 Att; 9,723 Yards; 5.0 Avg; and 71 TD.

All-Purpose Yards

		Rush	Rec	Ret	Total
1	Walter Payton	16,726	4,538	539	21,803
2	Jerry Rice	625	19,247	6	19,878
3	Brian Mitchell	1,938	2,176	14,526	18,640
4	Barry Sanders	15,269	2,921	118	18,308
5	Herschel Walker	8,225	4,859	5,084	18,168
6	Emmitt Smith	15,166	2,807	0	17,973
7	Marcus Allen	12,243	5,411	-6	17,648
8	Eric Metcalf	2,385	5,553	8,789	16,727
9	Tim Brown	132	12,072	4,344	16,548
10	Thurman Thomas	12,074	4,458	0	16,532
11	Tony Dorsett	12,739	3,554	33	16,326
12	Henry Ellard	50	13,777	1,891	15,718
13	Irving Fryar	242	12,785	2,567	15,594
14	Jim Brown	12,312	2,499	648	15,459
15	Eric Dickerson	13,259	2,137	15	15,411
16	James Brooks	7,962	3,621	3,327	14,910
17	Franco Harris	12,120	2,287	215	14,622
18	Glyn Milburn	814	1,313	12,448	14,575
19	Ricky Watters	10,325	4,141	0	14,466
20	O.J. Simpson	11,236	2,142	990	14,368
21	James Lofton	246	14,004	27	14,277
22	Bobby Mitchell	2,735	7,954	3,389	14,078
23	Dave Meggett	1,684	3,038	9,274	13,996
24	Andre Reed	500	13,198	14	13,712
25	Earnest Byner	8,261	4,605	631	13,497

Years played: Allen (16), Brooks (12), J. Brown (9), T. Brown (14), Byner (14), Dickerson (11), Dorsett (12), Ellard (16), Fryar (17), Harris (13), Lofton (16), Meggett (10), Metcalf (11), Milburn (8), Bri. Mitchell (11), Bo. Mitchell (11), Payton (13), Reed (16), Rice (16), Sanders (10), Simpson (11), Smith (11), Thomas (13), Walker (12) and Watters (10).

All-Time NFL Leaders (Cont.)
Scoring

	Points	Yrs	TD	FG	PAT	Total
1	**Gary Anderson**	19	0	461	676	2059
2	George Blanda	26	9	335	943	2002
3	**Morten Andersen**	19	0	441	615	1938
4	Norm Johnson	18	0	366	638	1736
5	Nick Lowery	18	0	383	562	1711
6	Jan Stenerud	19	0	373	580	1699
7	**Eddie Murray**	19	0	352	538	1594
8	**Al Del Greco**	17	0	347	543	1584
9	Pat Leahy	18	0	304	558	1470
10	Jim Turner	16	1	304	521	1439
11	Matt Bahr	17	0	300	522	1422
12	Mark Moseley	16	0	300	482	1382
13	Jim Bakken	17	0	282	534	1380
14	Fred Cox	15	0	282	519	1365
15	Lou Groza	17	1	234	641	1349
16	Jim Breech	14	0	243	517	1246
17	**Pete Stoyanovich**	12	0	272	420	1236
18	Chris Bahr	14	0	241	490	1213
19	Kevin Butler	13	0	265	413	1208
20	**Steve Christie**	11	0	272	358	1174
21	Gino Cappelletti	11	42	176	350	1130†
	Jerry Rice	16	187	0	0	1130†
23	Ray Wersching	15	0	222	456	1122
24	**John Carney**	13	0	263	299	1088
25	Don Cockroft	13	0	216	432	1080

† Cappelletti's total and Rice's total both include four 2-point conversions.

Note: The NFL does not recognize records from the All-American Football Conference (1946-49). If it did, **Lou Groza** would move up from 15th to 7th (after Stenerud) with the following stats: 21 Yrs; 1 TD; 264 FG, 810 PAT; 1,608 Pts.

Touchdowns

		Yrs	Rush	Rec	Ret	Total
1	Jerry Rice	16	10	176	1	187
2	Emmitt Smith	11	145	11	0	156
3	Marcus Allen	16	123	21	1	145
4	Jim Brown	9	106	20	0	126
5	Walter Payton	13	110	15	0	125
6	Cris Carter	14	0	123	1	124
7	John Riggins	14	104	12	0	116
8	Lenny Moore	12	63	48	2	113
9	Barry Sanders	10	99	10	0	109
10	Don Hutson	11	3	99	3	105
11	Steve Largent	14	1	100	0	101
12	Franco Harris	13	91	9	0	100
13	Eric Dickerson	11	90	6	0	96
14	Jim Taylor	10	83	10	0	93
15	Tony Dorsett	12	77	13	1	91
	Bobby Mitchell	11	18	65	8	91
17	Tim Brown	13	1	86	3	90
	Leroy Kelly	10	74	13	3	90
	Charley Taylor	13	11	79	0	90
	Ricky Watters	10	77	13	0	90
21	**Marshall Faulk**	7	67	22	0	89
22	**Irving Fryar**	17	1	84	3	88
	Don Maynard	15	0	88	0	88
	Andre Reed	16	1	87	0	88
	Thurman Thomas	13	65	23	0	88

Interceptions

		Yrs	No	Yards	TD
1	Paul Krause	16	81	1185	3
2	Emlen Tunnell	14	79	1282	4
3	Dick (Night Train) Lane	14	68	1207	5
4	Ken Riley	15	65	596	5
5	Ronnie Lott	14	63	730	5

Sacks

		Yrs	No
1	**Reggie White**	15	198
2	**Bruce Smith**	16	181
3	Kevin Greene	15	160
4	**Chris Doleman**	15	151
5	Richard Dent	15	137.5

Note: The NFL did not begin officially compiling sacks until 1982. Deacon Jones, who played with the Rams, Chargers and Redskins from 1961-74, is often credited with 173½ sacks.

Safeties

		Yrs	No
1	Ted Hendricks	15	4
	Doug English	10	4
3	Seventeen players tied with 3 each.		

Kickoff Returns
Minimum 75 returns.

		Yrs	No	Yards	Avg	TD
1	Gale Sayers	7	91	2781	30.6	6
2	Lynn Chandnois	7	92	2720	29.6	3
3	Abe Woodson	9	193	5538	28.7	5
4	Buddy Young	6	90	2514	27.9	2
5	Travis Williams	5	102	2801	27.5	6

Punting
Minimum 300 punts.

		Yrs	No	Yards	Avg
1	Sammy Baugh	16	338	15,245	45.1
2	**Darren Bennett**	6	524	23,492	44.8
3	Tommy Davis	11	511	22,833	44.7
4	Yale Lary	11	503	22,279	44.3
5	**Tom Tupa**	12	530	23,297	44.0

Punt Returns
Minimum 75 returns.

		Yrs	No	Yards	Avg	TD
1	George McAfee	8	112	1431	12.8	2
2	Jack Christiansen	8	85	1084	12.8	8
3	Claude Gibson	5	110	1381	12.6	3
4	**Az-Zahir Hakim**	3	76	951	12.5	2
5	**Desmond Howard**	9	213	2646	12.4	8

Long-Playing Records

Seasons

		No
1	George Blanda, QB-K	26
2	Earl Morrall, QB	21
3	Jim Marshall, DE	20
	Jackie Slater, OL	20

Games

		No
1	George Blanda, QB-K	340
2	**Gary Anderson**, K	293
3	**Morten Andersen**, K	292

Consecutive Games

		No
1	Jim Marshall, DE	282
2	Mick Tingelhoff, C	240
3	Jim Bakken, K	234

SINGLE SEASON

Passing

Yards Gained	Year	Att	Cmp	Pct	Yds
Dan Marino, Mia.	1984	564	362	64.2	5084
Dan Fouts, SD.	1981	609	360	59.1	4802
Dan Marino, Mia.	1986	623	378	60.7	4746
Dan Fouts, SD.	1980	589	348	59.1	4715
Warren Moon, Hou	1991	655	404	61.7	4690
Warren Moon, Hou	1990	584	362	62.0	4689
Neil Lomax, St.L	1984	560	345	61.6	4614
Drew Bledsoe, NE	1994	691	400	57.9	4555
Lynn Dickey, GB	1983	484	286	59.7	4458
Steve Beuerlein, Car	1999	571	343	60.1	4436

Efficiency	Year	Att/Cmp	TD	Rtg
Steve Young, SF	1994	461/324	35	112.8
Joe Montana, SF	1989	386/271	26	112.4
Milt Plum, Cle	1960	250/151	21	110.4
Sammy Baugh, Wash	1945	182/128	11	109.9
Kurt Warner, St.L	1999	499/325	41	109.2
Dan Marino, Mia.	1984	564/362	48	108.9
Sid Luckman, Bears	1943	202/110	28	107.5
Steve Young, SF	1992	402/268	25	107.0
Randall Cunningham, Min	1998	425/259	34	106.0
Bart Starr, GB	1966	251/156	14	105.0

Receptions

Catches	Year	No	Yds
Herman Moore, Det.	1995	123	1686
Jerry Rice, SF	1995	122	1848
Cris Carter, Min	1995	122	1371
Cris Carter, Min	1994	122	1256
Isaac Bruce, St.L	1995	119	1781
Jimmy Smith, Jax	1999	116	1636
Marvin Harrison, Ind	1999	115	1663
Jerry Rice, SF	1994	112	1499
Sterling Sharpe, GB	1993	112	1274
Michael Irvin, Dal	1995	111	1603
Terance Mathis, Atl	1994	111	1342
Brett Perriman, Det	1995	108	1488
Sterling Sharpe, GB	1992	108	1461

Rushing

Yards Gained	Year	Car	Yds	Avg
Eric Dickerson, LA Rams	1984	379	2105	5.6
Barry Sanders, Det.	1997	335	2053	6.1
Terrell Davis, Den	1998	392	2008	5.1
O.J. Simpson, Buf.	1973	332	2003	6.0
Earl Campbell, Hou	1980	373	1934	5.2
Barry Sanders, Det.	1994	331	1883	5.7
Jim Brown, Cle	1963	291	1863	6.4
Walter Payton, Chi	1977	339	1852	5.5
Jamal Anderson, Atl.	1998	410	1846	4.5
Eric Dickerson, LA Rams	1986	404	1821	4.5
O.J. Simpson, Buf.	1975	329	1817	5.5
Eric Dickerson, LA Rams	1983	390	1808	4.6

Scoring

Points

	Year	TD	PAT	FG	Pts
Paul Hornung, GB	1960	15	41	15	176
Gary Anderson, Min	1998	0	59	35	164
Mark Moseley, Wash	1983	0	62	33	161
Marshall Faulk, St.L	2000	26	4	0	160
Gino Cappelletti, Bos	1964	7	38	25	155
Emmitt Smith, Dal	1995	25	0	0	150
Chip Lohmiller, Wash	1991	0	56	31	149
Gino Cappelletti, Bos	1961	8	48	17	147
Paul Hornung, GB	1961	10	41	15	146
Jim Turner, Jets	1968	0	43	34	145
John Kasay, Car.	1996	0	34	37	145
Mike Vanderjagt, Ind.	1999	0	43	34	145
John Riggins, Wash	1983	24	0	0	144
Kevin Butler, Chi	1985	0	51	31	144
Olindo Mare, Mia	1999	0	27	39	144

Touchdowns

	Year	Rush	Rec	Ret	Total
Marshall Faulk, St.L	2000	18	8	0	26
Emmitt Smith, Dal	1995	25	0	0	25
John Riggins, Wash	1983	24	0	0	24
Terrell Davis, Den	1998	21	2	0	23
O.J. Simpson, Buf.	1975	16	7	0	23
Jerry Rice, SF	1987	1	22	0	23
Gale Sayers, Chi	1966	14	6	2	22
Chuck Foreman, Min	1975	13	9	0	22
Emmitt Smith, Dal	1994	21	1	0	22
Jim Brown, Cle	1965	17	4	0	21
Joe Morris, NY Giants	1985	21	0	0	21
Terry Allen, Wash	1996	21	0	0	21
Lenny Moore, Bal	1964	16	3	1	20
Leroy Kelly, Cle.	1968	16	4	0	20
Eric Dickerson, LA Rams	1983	18	2	0	20

Note: The NFL regular season schedule grew from 12 games (1947-60) to 14 (1961-77) to 16 (1978-present). The AFL regular season schedule was always 14 games (1960-69).

Touchdowns Passing

	Year	No
Dan Marino, Miami	1984	48
Dan Marino, Miami	1986	44
Kurt Warner, St. Louis	1999	41
Brett Favre, Green Bay	1996	39
Brett Favre, Green Bay	1995	38
George Blanda, Houston	1961	36
Y.A. Tittle, NY Giants	1963	36
Steve Young, San Francisco	1998	36
Steve Beuerlein, Carolina	1999	36
Brett Favre, Green Bay	1997	35
Steve Young, San Francisco	1994	35
Randall Cunningham, Minnesota	1998	34
Y.A. Tittle, NY Giants	1962	33
Dan Fouts, San Diego	1981	33
Warren Moon, Houston	1990	33
Jim Kelly, Buffalo	1991	33
Brett Favre, Green Bay	1994	33
Warren Moon, Minnesota	1995	33
Vinny Testaverde, Baltimore	1996	33
Daunte Culpepper, Minnesota	2000	33
Peyton Manning, Indianapolis	2000	33

Touchdowns Receiving

	Year	No
Jerry Rice, San Francisco	1987	22
Mark Clayton, Miami	1984	18
Sterling Sharpe, Green Bay	1994	18
Don Hutson, Green Bay	1942	17
Elroy (Crazylegs) Hirsch, LA Rams	1951	17
Bill Groman, Houston	1961	17
Jerry Rice, San Francisco	1989	17
Cris Carter, Minnesota	1995	17
Carl Pickens, Cincinnati	1995	17
Randy Moss, Minnesota	1998	17
Art Powell, Oakland	1963	16
Cloyce Box, Detroit	1952	15
Sonny Randle, St. Louis	1960	15
Jerry Rice, San Francisco	1986	15
Jerry Rice, San Francisco	1993	15
Andre Rison, Atlanta	1993	15
Jerry Rice, San Francisco	1995	15
Randy Moss, Minnesota	2000	15

All-Time NFL Leaders (Cont.)

Touchdowns Rushing

	Year	No
Emmitt Smith, Dallas	1995	25
John Riggins, Washington	1983	24
Joe Morris, NY Giants	1985	21
Emmitt Smith, Dallas	1994	21
Terry Allen, Washington	1996	21
Terrell Davis, Denver	1998	21
Jim Taylor, Green Bay	1962	19
Earl Campbell, Houston	1979	19
Chuck Muncie, San Diego	1981	19
Eric Dickerson, LA Rams	1983	18
George Rogers, Washington	1986	18
Emmitt Smith, Dallas	1992	18
Marshall Faulk, St. Louis	2000	18
Jim Brown, Cleveland	1958	17
Jim Brown, Cleveland	1965	17
Stephen Davis, Washington	1999	17

Field Goals

	Year	Att	No
Olindo Mare, Miami	1999	46	39
John Kasay, Carolina	1996	45	37
Cary Blanchard, Indianapolis	1996	40	36
Al Del Greco, Tennessee	1998	39	36
Ali Haji-Sheikh, NY Giants	1983	42	35
Jeff Jaeger, LA Raiders	1993	44	35
Gary Anderson, Minnesota	1998	35	35
Matt Stover, Baltimore	2000	39	35
Jim Turner, NY Jets	1968	46	34
Nick Lowery, Kansas City	1990	37	34
Jason Hanson, Detroit	1993	43	34
John Carney, San Diego	1994	38	34
Fuad Reveiz, Minnesota	1994	39	34
Norm Johnson, Pittsburgh	1995	41	34
Richie Cunningham, Dallas	1997	37	34
Mike Vanderjagt, Indianapolis	1999	38	34
Todd Peterson, Seattle	1999	40	34
Joe Nedney, Den.-Car.	2000	38	34

Interceptions

	Year	No
Dick (Night Train) Lane, Detroit	1952	14
Dan Sandifer, Washington	1948	13
Spec Sanders, NY Yanks	1950	13
Lester Hayes, Oakland	1980	13

Punting

Qualifiers	Year	Avg
Sammy Baugh, Washington	1940	51.4
Yale Lary, Detroit	1963	48.9
Sammy Baugh, Washington	1941	48.7
Yale Lary, Detroit	1961	48.4

Kickoff Returns

	Year	Avg
Travis Williams, Green Bay	1967	41.1
Gale Sayers, Chicago Bears	1967	37.7
Ollie Matson, Chicago Cards	1958	35.5

Punt Returns

	Year	Avg
Herb Rich, Baltimore	1950	23.0
Jack Christiansen, Detroit	1952	21.5
Dick Christy, NY Titans	1961	21.3
Bob Hayes, Dallas	1968	20.8

Sacks

	Year	No		Year	No
Mark Gastineau, NY Jets	1984	22	Chris Doleman, Minnesota	1989	21
Reggie White, Philadelphia	1987	21	Lawrence Taylor, NY Giants	1986	20.5

Note: The NFL did not begin officially compiling sacks until 1982. Cincinnati's Coy Bacon is widely, although not officially, credited with 26 sacks during the 1976 season.

SINGLE GAME

Passing

Yards Gained	Date	Yds
Norm Van Brocklin, LA vs NY Yanks	9/28/51	554
Warren Moon, Hou vs KC	12/16/90	527
Boomer Esiason, Ariz vs Wash.	11/10/96	522
Dan Marino, Mia vs NYJ	10/23/88	521
Phil Simms, NYG vs Cin	10/13/85	513

Completions	Date	No
Drew Bledsoe, NE vs Min	11/13/94	45
Richard Todd, NYJ vs SF	9/21/80	42
Vinny Testaverde, NYJ vs Sea	12/6/98	42
Warren Moon, Hou vs Dal	11/10/91	41
Ken Anderson, Cin vs SD	12/20/82	40
Phil Simms, NYG vs Cin	10/13/85	40

Receiving

Catches	Date	No
Terrell Owens, SF vs Chi	12/17/00	20
Tom Fears, LA vs GB	12/3/50	18
Clark Gaines, NYJ vs SF	9/21/80	17
Sonny Randle, St.L vs NYG	11/4/62	16
Keenan McCardell, Jax vs St.L	10/20/96	16
Jerry Rice, SF vs LA Rams	11/20/94	16

Yards Gained	Date	Yds
Flipper Anderson, LA Rams vs NO	11/26/89	336
Stephone Paige, KC vs SD	12/22/85	309
Jim Benton, Cle vs Det	11/22/45	303
Cloyce Box, Det vs Bal	12/3/50	302
Jimmy Smith, Jax vs Bal	9/10/00	291
Jerry Rice, SF vs Det	9/25/95	289

Rushing

Yards Gained	Date	Yds
Corey Dillon, Cin vs Den	10/22/00	278
Walter Payton, Chi vs Min	11/20/77	275
O.J. Simpson, Buf vs Det	11/25/76	273
Mike Anderson, Den vs NO	12/3/00	251
O.J. Simpson, Buf vs NE	9/16/73	250
Willie Ellison, LA Rams vs NO	12/5/71	247
Corey Dillon, Cin vs Ten	12/4/97	246

All-Purpose Yards

	Date	Yds
Glyn Milburn, Den vs Sea	12/10/95	404
Billy Cannon, Hou vs NY Titans	12/10/61	373
Tyrone Hughes, NO vs LA Rams	10/23/94	347
Lionel James, SD vs Raiders	11/10/85	345
Timmy Brown, Phi vs St.L	12/16/62	341
Gale Sayers, Chi vs Min	12/18/66	339
Gale Sayers, Chi vs SF	12/12/65	336
Flipper Anderson, LA Rams vs NO	11/26/89	336

Scoring

Points

	Date	Pts
Ernie Nevers, Chi. Cards vs Chi. Bears	..11/28/29	40
Dub Jones, Cle vs Chi. Bears	...........11/25/51	36
Gale Sayers, Chi vs SF	................12/12/65	36
Paul Hornung, GB vs Bal	...............10/8/61	33
Bob Shaw, Chi. Cards vs Bal	............10/2/50	30
Jim Brown, Cle vs Bal	..................11/1/59	30
Abner Haynes, Dal. Texans vs Oak	.....11/26/61	30
Billy Cannon, Hou vs NY Titans	.........12/10/61	30
Cookie Gilchrist, Buf vs NY Jets	.........12/8/63	30
Kellen Winslow, SD vs Oak	............11/22/81	30
Jerry Rice, SF vs Atl	....................10/14/90	30
James Stewart, Jax vs Phi	..............10/12/97	30

Note: Nevers celebrated Thanksgiving, 1929, by scoring all of the Chicago Cardinals' points on six rushing TDs and four PATs. The Cards beat Red Grange and the Chicago Bears, 40-6.

Touchdowns Passing

	Date	No
Sid Luckman, Chi. Bears vs NYG	........11/14/43	7
Adrian Burk, Phi vs Wash	..............10/17/54	7
George Blanda, Hou vs NY Titans	.......11/19/61	7
Y.A. Tittle, NYG vs Wash	..............10/28/62	7
Joe Kapp, Min vs Bal	...................9/28/69	7

Touchdowns Receiving

	Date	No
Bob Shaw, Chi. Cards vs Bal	............10/2/50	5
Kellen Winslow, SD vs Oak	.............11/22/81	5
Jerry Rice, SF vs Atl	....................10/14/90	5

Touchdowns Rushing

	Date	No
Ernie Nevers, Chi. Cards vs Chi. Bears	..11/28/29	6
Jim Brown, Cle vs Bal	..................11/ 1/59	5
Cookie Gilchrist, Buf vs NY Jets	.........12/ 8/63	5
James Stewart, Jax vs Phi	..............10/12/97	5

Field Goals

	Date	No
Jim Bakken, St.L vs Pit	..................9/24/67	7
Chris Boniol, Dal vs GB	.................11/18/96	7
Rich Karlis, Min vs LA Rams	..............11/5/89	7
Fourteen players tied with 6 FGs.		

Note: Bakken was 7-for-9, Boniol and Karlis 7-for-7.

Extra Point Kicks

	Date	No
Pat Harder, Cards vs NYG	..............10/17/48	9
Bob Waterfield, LA Rams vs Bal	........10/22/50	9
Charlie Gogolak, Wash vs NYG	........11/27/66	9

Interceptions

	No
By 17 players	4

Sacks

	Date	No
Derrick Thomas, KC vs Sea	.............11/11/90	7
Fred Dean, SF vs NO	...................11/13/83	6
Derrick Thomas, KC vs Oak	.............9/6/98	6
William Gay, Det vs TB	..................9/4/83	5.5

Longest Plays

Passing (all for TDs)

	Date	Yds
Frank Filchock to Andy Farkas, Wash vs Pit	....10/15/39	99
George Izo to Bobby Mitchell, Wash vs Cle	...........9/15/63	99
Karl Sweetan to Pat Studstill, Det vs Bal	...........10/16/66	99
Sonny Jurgensen to Gerry Allen, Wash vs Chi	...........9/15/68	99
Jim Plunkett to Cliff Branch, LA Raiders vs Wash	..........10/2/83	99
Ron Jaworski to Mike Quick, Phi vs Atl	.....11/10/85	99
Stan Humphries to Tony Martin, SD vs Sea	..........9/18/94	99
Brett Favre to Robert Brooks, GB vs Chi	...........9/11/95	99

Runs from Scrimmage (all for TDs)

	Date	Yds
Tony Dorsett, Dal vs Min	...................1/3/83	99
Andy Uram, GB vs Chi. Cards	...........10/8/39	97
Bob Gage, Pit vs Bears	...............12/4/49	97
Jim Spavital, Balt. Colts vs GB	...........11/5/50	96
Bob Hoernschemeyer, Det vs NY Yanks	..11/23/50	96
Garrison Hearst, SF vs NYJ	...............9/6/98	96

Punts

	Date	Yds
Steve O'Neal, NYJ vs Den	..............9/21/69	98
Joe Lintzenich, Chi. Bears vs NYG	.......11/15/31	94
Shawn McCarthy, NE vs Buf	............11/3/91	93

Field Goals

	Date	Yds
Tom Dempsey, NO vs Det	..............11/8/70	63
Jason Elam, Den vs Jax	................10/25/98	63
Steve Cox, Cle vs Cin	..................10/21/84	60
Morten Andersen, NO vs Chi	............10/27/91	60
Tony Franklin, Phi vs Dal	...............11/12/79	59
Pete Stoyanovich, Mia vs NYJ	..........11/12/89	59
Steve Christie, Buf vs Mia	...............9/26/93	59
Morten Andersen, Atl vs SF	............12/24/95	59

Punt Returns (all for TDs)

	Date	Yds
Robert Bailey, Rams vs NO	............10/23/94	103
Gil LeFebvre, Cin vs Bklyn	..............12/3/33	98
Charlie West, Min vs Wash	..............11/3/68	98
Dennis Morgan, Dal vs St.L	............10/13/74	98
Terance Mathis, NYJ vs Dal	............11/4/90	98
Greg Pruitt, LA Raiders vs Wash	.........10/2/83	97

Kickoff Returns (all for TDs)

	Date	Yds
Al Carmichael, GB vs Chi. Bears	.........10/7/56	106
Noland Smith, KC vs Den	..............12/17/67	106
Roy Green, St.L vs Dal	.................10/21/79	106

Interception Returns (all for TDs)

	Date	Yds
James Willis (14 yds) lateral to Troy Vincent (90 yds), Phi vs Dal	.......11/3/96	104
Vencie Glenn, SD vs Den	..............11/29/87	103
Louis Oliver, Mia vs Buf	................10/4/92	103
Six players tied with 102-yd returns.		

Chicago College All-Star Game

On Aug. 31, 1934, a year after sponsoring Major League Baseball's first All-Star Game, *Chicago Tribune* sports editor Arch Ward presented the first Chicago College All-Star Game at Soldier Field. A crowd of 79,432 turned out to see an all-star team of graduated college seniors battle the 1933 NFL champion Chicago Bears to a scoreless tie. The preseason game was played at Soldier Field and pitted the College All-Stars against the defending NFL champions (1933-1966) or Super Bowl champions (1967-75) every year except 1935 until it was cancelled in 1977. The NFL champs won the series, 31-9-1.

Year		Year		Year	
1934	Chi. Bears 0, All-Stars 0	1949	Philadelphia 38, All-Stars 0	1964	Chi. Bears 28, All-Stars 17
1935	Chi. Bears 5, All-Stars 0			1965	Cleveland 24, All-Stars 16
1936	Detroit 7, All-Stars 0	1950	All-Stars 17, Philadelphia 7	1966	Green Bay 38, All-Stars 0
1937	All-Stars 6, Green Bay 0	1951	Cleveland 33, All-Stars 0	1967	Green Bay 27, All-Stars 0
1938	All-Stars 28, Washington 16	1952	LA Rams 10, All-Stars 7	1968	Green Bay 34, All-Stars 17
1939	NY Giants 9, All-Stars 0	1953	Detroit 24, All-Stars 10	1969	NY Jets 26, All-Stars 24
		1954	Detroit 31, All-Stars 6		
1940	Green Bay 45, All-Stars 28	1955	All-Stars 30, Cleveland 27	1970	Kansas City 24, All-Stars 3
1941	Chi. Bears 37, All-Stars 13	1956	Cleveland 26, All-Stars 0	1971	Baltimore 24, All-Stars 17
1942	Chi. Bears 21, All-Stars 0	1957	NY Giants 22, All-Stars 12	1972	Dallas 20, All-Stars 7
1943	All-Stars 27, Washington 7	1958	All-Stars 35, Detroit 19	1973	Miami 14, All-Stars 3
1944	Chi. Bears 24, All-Stars 21	1959	Baltimore 29, All-Stars 0	1974	No Game (NFLPA Strike)
1945	Green Bay 19, All-Stars 7			1975	Pittsburgh 21, All-Stars 14
1946	All-Stars 16, LA Rams 0	1960	Baltimore 32, All-Stars 7	1976	Pittsburgh 24, All-Stars 0*
1947	All-Stars 16, Chi. Bears 0	1961	Philadelphia 28, All-Stars 14		
1948	Chi. Cards 28, All-Stars 0	1962	Green Bay 42, All-Stars 20	*Downpour flooded field, game called
		1963	All-Stars 20, Green Bay 17	with 1:22 left in 3rd quarter.

Number One Draft Choices

In an effort to blunt the dominance of the Chicago Bears and New York Giants in the 1930s and distribute talent more evenly throughout the league, the NFL established the college draft in 1936. The first player chosen in the first draft was Jay Berwanger, who was also college football's first Heisman Trophy winner. In all, 16 Heisman winners have also been the NFL's No. 1 draft choice. They are noted in **bold** type. The American Football League (formed in 1960) held its own draft for six years before agreeing to merge with the NFL and select players in a common draft starting in 1967.

Year	Team		Year	Team	
1936	Philadelphia	**Jay Berwanger**, HB, Chicago	1967	Baltimore	Bubba Smith, DT, Michigan St.
1937	Philadelphia	Sam Francis, FB, Nebraska	1968	Minnesota	Ron Yary, T, USC
1938	Cleveland Rams	Corbett Davis, FB, Indiana	1969	Buffalo	**O.J. Simpson**, RB, USC
1939	Chicago Cards	Ki Aldrich, C, TCU	1970	Pittsburgh	Terry Bradshaw, QB, La.Tech
1940	Chicago Cards	George Cafego, HB, Tennessee	1971	New England	**Jim Plunkett**, QB, Stanford
1941	Chicago Bears	**Tom Harmon**, HB, Michigan	1972	Buffalo	Walt Patulski, DE, Notre Dame
1942	Pittsburgh	Bill Dudley, HB, Virginia	1973	Houston	John Matuszak, DE, Tampa
1943	Detroit	**Frank Sinkwich**, HB, Georgia	1974	Dallas	Ed (Too Tall) Jones, DE, Tenn. St.
1944	Boston Yanks	**Angelo Bertelli**, QB, N. Dame	1975	Atlanta	Steve Bartkowski, QB, Calif.
1945	Chicago Cards	Charley Trippi, HB, Georgia	1976	Tampa Bay	Lee Roy Selmon, DE, Oklahoma
1946	Boston Yanks	Frank Dancewicz, QB, N. Dame	1977	Tampa Bay	Ricky Bell, RB, USC
1947	Chicago Bears	Bob Fenimore, HB, Okla. A&M	1978	Houston	**Earl Campbell**, RB, Texas
1948	Washington	Harry Gilmer, QB, Alabama	1979	Buffalo	Tom Cousineau, LB, Ohio St.
1949	Philadelphia	Chuck Bednarik, C, Penn	1980	Detroit	**Billy Sims**, RB, Oklahoma
1950	Detroit	**Leon Hart**, E, Notre Dame	1981	New Orleans	**George Rogers**, RB, S. Carolina
1951	NY Giants	Kyle Rote, HB, SMU	1982	New England	Kenneth Sims, DT, Texas
1952	LA Rams	Bill Wade, QB, Vanderbilt	1983	Baltimore	John Elway, QB, Stanford
1953	San Francisco	Harry Babcock, E, Georgia	1984	New England	Irving Fryar, WR, Nebraska
1954	Cleveland	Bobby Garrett, QB, Stanford	1985	Buffalo	Bruce Smith, DE, Va. Tech
1955	Baltimore	George Shaw, QB, Oregon	1986	Tampa Bay	**Bo Jackson**, RB, Auburn
1956	Pittsburgh	Gary Glick, DB, Colo. A&M	1987	Tampa Bay	**V. Testaverde**, QB, Miami-FL
1957	Green Bay	**Paul Hornung**, QB, N. Dame	1988	Atlanta	Aundray Bruce, LB, Auburn
1958	Chicago Cards	King Hill, QB, Rice	1989	Dallas	Troy Aikman, QB, UCLA
1959	Green Bay	Randy Duncan, QB, Iowa	1990	Indianapolis	Jeff George, QB, Illinois
1960	NFL–LA Rams	**Billy Cannon**, HB, LSU	1991	Dallas	Russell Maryland, DT, Miami-FL
	AFL–No choice		1992	Indianapolis	Steve Emtman, DT, Washington
1961	NFL–Minnesota	Tommy Mason, HB, Tulane	1993	New England	Drew Bledsoe, QB, Washington St.
	AFL–Buffalo	Ken Rice, G, Auburn	1994	Cincinnati	Dan Wilkinson, DT, Ohio St.
1962	NFL–Washington	**Ernie Davis**, HB, Syracuse	1995	Cincinnati	Ki-Jana Carter, RB, Penn St.
	AFL–Oakland	Roman Gabriel, QB, N.C. State	1996	NY Jets	Keyshawn Johnson, WR, USC
1963	NFL–LA Rams	**Terry Baker**, QB, Oregon St.	1997	St. Louis	Orlando Pace, OT, Ohio St.
	AFL–Kan.City	Buck Buchanan, DT, Grambling	1998	Indianapolis	Peyton Manning, QB, Tennessee
1964	NFL–San Fran	Dave Parks, E, Texas Tech	1999	Cleveland	Tim Couch, QB, Kentucky
	AFL–Boston	Jack Concannon, QB, Boston Col.	2000	Cleveland	Courtney Brown, DE, Penn St.
1965	NFL–NY Giants	Tucker Frederickson, FB, Auburn	2001	Atlanta	Michael Vick, QB, Va. Tech
	AFL–Houston	Lawrence Elkins, E, Baylor			
1966	NFL–Atlanta	Tommy Nobis, LB, Texas			
	AFL–Miami	Jim Grabowski, FB, Illinois			

AP/Wide World Photos
Don Shula

AP/Wide World Photos
Bill Parcells

Indianapolis Colts
Jim Mora

AP/Wide World Photos
Vince Lombardi

All-Time Winningest NFL Coaches

NFL career victories through the 2000 season. Career, regular season and playoff records are noted along with NFL, AFL and Super Bowl titles won. Coaches active during 2000 season are noted in **bold** type.

		Yrs	Career W	L	T	Pct	Regular Season W	L	T	Pct	Playoffs W	L	Pct.	League Titles
1	Don Shula	33	**347**	173	6	.665	328	156	6	.676	19	17	.528	2 Super Bowls and 1 NFL
2	George Halas	40	**324**	151	31	.671	318	148	31	.671	6	3	.667	5 NFL
3	Tom Landry	29	**270**	178	6	.601	250	162	6	.605	20	16	.556	2 Super Bowls
4	Curly Lambeau	33	**229**	134	22	.623	226	132	22	.624	3	2	.600	6 NFL
5	Chuck Noll	23	**209**	156	1	.572	193	148	1	.566	16	8	.667	4 Super Bowls
6	Chuck Knox	22	**193**	158	1	.550	186	147	1	.558	7	11	.389	—None—
7	**Dan Reeves**	20	**181**	148	1	.550	171	140	1	.550	10	8	.556	—None—
8	Paul Brown	21	**170**	108	6	.609	166	100	6	.621	4	8	.333	3 NFL
9	Bud Grant	18	**168**	108	5	.607	158	96	5	.620	10	12	.455	1 NFL
10	Marv Levy	17	**154**	120	0	.562	143	112	0	.561	11	8	.579	—None—
11	Steve Owen	23	**153**	108	17	.581	151	100	17	.595	2	8	.200	2 NFL
12	Marty Schottenheimer	15	**150**	96	1	.609	145	85	1	.630	5	11	.313	—None—
13	Bill Parcells	15	**149**	106	1	.584	138	100	1	.579	11	6	.647	2 Super Bowls
14	Joe Gibbs	12	**140**	65	0	.683	124	60	0	.674	16	5	.762	3 Super Bowls
15	Hank Stram	17	**136**	100	10	.573	131	97	10	.571	5	3	.625	1 Super Bowl and 3 AFL
16	Weeb Ewbank	20	**134**	130	7	.507	130	129	7	.502	4	1	.800	1 Super Bowl, 2 NFL, and 1 AFL
17	Mike Ditka	14	**127**	101	0	.557	121	95	0	.560	6	6	.500	1 Super Bowl
18	**George Seifert**	10	**123**	52	0	.703	113	47	0	.706	10	5	.667	2 Super Bowls
	Sid Gillman	18	**123**	104	7	.541	122	99	7	.550	1	5	.167	1 AFL
20	**Jim Mora**	14	**119**	102	0	.538	119	96	0	.553	0	6	.000	—None—
21	George Allen	12	**118**	54	5	.681	116	47	5	.705	2	7	.222	—None—
22	Don Coryell	14	**114**	89	1	.561	111	83	1	.572	3	6	.333	—None—
23	John Madden	10	**112**	39	7	.731	103	32	7	.750	9	7	.563	1 Super Bowl
24	Buddy Parker	15	**107**	76	9	.581	104	75	9	.577	3	1	.750	2 NFL
25	Vince Lombardi	10	**105**	35	6	.740	96	34	6	.728	9	1	.900	2 Super Bowls and 5 NFL
	Tom Flores	12	**105**	90	0	.538	97	87	0	.527	8	3	.727	2 Super Bowls

Notes: The NFL does not recognize records from the All-American Football Conference (1946-49). If it did, **Paul Brown** (52-4-3 in four AAFC seasons) would move up from 8th to 5th on the all-time list with the following career stats— 25 Yrs; 222 Wins; 112 Losses; 9 Ties; .660 Pct; 9-8 playoff record; and 4 AAFC titles.

The NFL also considers the Playoff Bowl or "Runner-up Bowl" (officially: the Bert Bell Benefit Bowl) as a postseason exhibition game. The Playoff Bowl was contested every year from 1960-69 in Miami between Eastern and Western Conference second place teams. While the games did not count, six of the coaches above went to the Playoff Bowl at least once and came away with the following records— Allen (2-0), Brown (0-1), Grant (0-1), Landry (1-2), Lombardi (1-1) and Shula (2-0).

Where They Coached

Allen—LA Rams (1966-70), Washington (1971-77); **Brown**—Cleveland (1950-62), Cincinnati (1968-75); **Coryell**—St. Louis (1973-77), San Diego (1978-86); **Ditka**—Chicago (1982-92), New Orleans (1997-99); **Ewbank**— Baltimore (1954-62), NY Jets (1963-73); **Flores**—Oakland-LA Raiders (1979-87), Seattle (1992-94); **Gibbs**—Washington (1981-92); **Gillman**—LA Rams (1955-59), LA-San Diego Chargers (1960-69), Houston (1973-74).

Grant—Minnesota (1967-83,1985); **Halas**—Chicago Bears (1920-29,33-42,46-55,58-67); **Knox**— LA Rams (1973-77, 1992-94); Buffalo (1978-82), Seattle (1983-91); **Lambeau**— Green Bay (1921-49), Chicago Cards (1950-51), Washington (1952-53); **Landry**—Dallas (1960-88); **Levy**— Kansas City (1978-82), Buffalo (1986-97); **Lombardi**— Green Bay (1959-67), Washington (1969); **Madden**—Oakland (1969-78); **Mora**—New Orleans (1986-1995), Indianapolis (1998—).

Noll—Pittsburgh (1969-91); **Owen**—NY Giants (1931-53); **Parcells**— NY Giants (1983-90), New England (1993-97), NY Jets (1997-99); **Parker**—Chicago Cards (1949), Detroit (1951-56), Pittsburgh (1957-64); **Reeves**— Denver (1981-92), NY Giants (1993-96), Atlanta (1997—); **Schottenheimer**—Cleveland (1984-88), Kansas City (1989-98), Washington (2001—); **Seifert**—San Francisco (1989-96), Carolina (1999—); **Shula**—Baltimore (1963-69), Miami (1970-95); **Stram**—Dallas-Kansas City (1960-74), New Orleans (1976-77).

Top Winning Percentages

Minimum of 85 NFL victories, including playoffs.

		Yrs	W	L	T	Pct
1	Vince Lombardi	10	105	35	6	.740
2	John Madden	10	112	39	7	.731
3	**George Seifert**	10	123	52	0	.703
4	Joe Gibbs	12	140	65	0	.683
5	George Allen	12	118	54	5	.681
6	George Halas	40	324	151	31	.671
7	Don Shula	33	347	173	6	.665
8	Curly Lambeau	33	229	134	22	.623
9	**Mike Holmgren**	9	99	60	0	.623
10	Bill Walsh	10	102	63	1	.617
11	**Dennis Green**	9	96	60	0	.615
12	Marty Schottenheimer	15	150	96	1	.609
13	Paul Brown	21	170	108	6	.609
14	Bud Grant	18	168	108	5	.607
15	Tom Landry	29	270	178	6	.601
16	**Bill Cowher**	9	91	64	0	.587
17	Bill Parcells	15	149	106	1	.584
18	Steve Owen	23	153	108	17	.581
19	Buddy Parker	15	107	76	9	.581
20	Hank Stram	17	136	100	10	.573
21	Chuck Noll	23	209	156	1	.572
22	Jimmy Johnson	9	89	68	0	.567
23	Marv Levy	17	154	120	0	.562
24	Don Coryell	14	114	89	1	.561
25	Jimmy Conzelman	15	89	68	17	.560

Note: If AAFC records are included, **Paul Brown** moves from 13th to 8th with a percentage of .660 (25 yrs, 222-112-9) and Buck Shaw would be 11th at .619 (8 yrs, 91-55-5).

Active Coaches' Victories

Through 2000 season, including playoffs.

		Yrs	W	L	T	Pct
1	Dan Reeves, Atlanta	20	181	148	1	.550
2	Marty Schottenheimer, Wash.	15	150	96	1	.609
3	George Seifert, Carolina	10	123	52	0	.703
4	Jim Mora, Indianapolis	14	119	102	0	.538
5	Mike Holmgren, Seattle	9	99	60	0	.623
6	Dennis Green, Minnesota	9	96	60	0	.615
7	Bill Cowher, Pittsburgh	9	91	64	0	.587
8	Dick Vermeil, KC	10	82	77	0	.516
9	Mike Shanahan, Denver	8	79	46	0	.632
10	Jeff Fisher, Tennessee	7	61	46	0	.570
11	Tom Coughlin, Jacksonville	6	60	44	0	.577
12	Dave Wannstedt, Miami	7	53	63	0	.457
13	Tony Dungy, Tampa Bay	5	47	38	0	.553
14	Bill Belichick, New England	6	42	56	0	.429
15	Jim Fassel, NY Giants	4	39	28	1	.581
16	Steve Mariucci, San Fran	4	37	31	0	.544
17	Jon Gruden, Oakland	3	29	21	0	.580
18	Brian Billick, Baltimore	2	24	12	0	.667
19	Andy Reid, Philadelphia	2	17	17	0	.500
20	Jim Haslett, New Orleans	1	11	7	0	.611
	Dick Jauron, Chicago	2	11	21	0	.344
22	Mike Martz, St. Louis	1	10	7	0	.588
23	Mike Sherman, Green Bay	1	9	7	0	.563
	Mike Riley, San Diego	2	9	23	0	.281
25	Dave Campo, Dallas	1	5	11	0	.313
26	Dick LeBeau, Cincinnati	1	4	9	0	.308
27	Dave McGinnis, Arizona	1	1	8	0	.111
28	Butch Davis, Cleveland	0	0	0	0	.000
	Herman Edwards, NY Jets	0	0	0	0	.000
	Marty Mornhinweg, Detroit	0	0	0	0	.000
	Gregg Williams, Buffalo	0	0	0	0	.000

Annual Awards
Most Valuable Player

Currently, the NFL does not sanction an official MVP award. It awarded the Joe F. Carr Trophy (Carr was NFL president from 1921-39) to the league MVP from 1938 to 1946. Since then, four principal MVP awards have been given out throughout the years and are noted below: UPI (1953-69), AP (since 1957), the Maxwell Club of Philadelphia's Bert Bell Trophy (since 1959) and the Pro Football Writers Assn. (since 1976). UPI switched to AFC and NFC Player of the Year awards in 1970 and then discontinued its awards in 1997.

Multiple winners (more than one season): Jim Brown (4); Randall Cunningham, Brett Favre, Johnny Unitas and Y.A. Tittle (3); Earl Campbell, Otto Graham, Don Hutson, Joe Montana, Walter Payton, Barry Sanders, Ken Stabler, Joe Theismann and Steve Young (2).

Year		Awards
1938	Mel Hein, NY Giants, C	Carr
1939	Parker Hall, Cleveland Rams, HB	Carr
1940	Ace Parker, Brooklyn, HB	Carr
1941	Don Hutson, Green Bay, E	Carr
1942	Don Hutson, Green Bay, E	Carr
1943	Sid Luckman, Chicago Bears, QB	Carr
1944	Frank Sinkwich, Detroit, HB	Carr
1945	Bob Waterfield, Cleveland Rams, QB	Carr
1946	Bill Dudley, Pittsburgh, HB	Carr
1947-52	No award	
1953	Otto Graham, Cleveland Browns, QB	UPI
1954	Joe Perry, San Francisco, FB	UPI
1955	Otto Graham, Cleveland, QB	UPI
1956	Frank Gifford, NY Giants, HB	UPI
1957	Y.A. Tittle, San Francisco, QB	UPI
	& Jim Brown, Cleveland, FB	AP
1958	Jim Brown, Cleveland, FB	UPI
	& Gino Marchetti, Baltimore, DE	AP
1959	Johnny Unitas, Baltimore, QB	UPI, Bell
	& Charley Conerly, NY Giants, QB	AP
1960	Norm Van Brocklin, Phi., QB	UPI, AP (tie), Bell
	& Joe Schmidt, Detroit, LB	AP (tie)
1961	Paul Hornung, Green Bay, HB	UPI, AP, Bell
1962	Y.A. Tittle, NY Giants, QB	UPI
	Jim Taylor, Green Bay, FB	AP
	& Andy Robustelli, NY Giants, DE	Bell
1963	Jim Brown, Cleveland, FB	UPI, Bell
	& Y.A. Tittle, NY Giants, QB	AP
1964	Johnny Unitas, Baltimore, QB	UPI, AP, Bell
1965	Jim Brown, Cleveland, FB	UPI, AP
	& Pete Retzlaff, Philadelphia, TE	Bell
1966	Bart Starr, Green Bay, QB	UPI, AP
	& Don Meredith, Dallas, QB	Bell
1967	Johnny Unitas, Baltimore, QB	UPI, AP, Bell
1968	Earl Morrall, Baltimore, QB	UPI, AP
	& Leroy Kelly, Cleveland, RB	Bell
1969	Roman Gabriel, LA Rams, QB	UPI, AP, Bell
1970	John Brodie, San Francisco, QB	AP
	& George Blanda, Oakland, QB-PK	Bell
1971	Alan Page, Minnesota, DT	AP
	& Roger Staubach, Dallas, QB	Bell
1972	Larry Brown, Washington, RB	AP, Bell
1973	O.J. Simpson, Buffalo, RB	AP, Bell
1974	Ken Stabler, Oakland, QB	AP
	& Merlin Olsen, LA Rams, DT	Bell
1975	Fran Tarkenton, Minnesota, QB	AP, Bell
1976	Bert Jones, Baltimore, QB	AP, PFWA
	& Ken Stabler, Oakland, QB	Bell
1977	Walter Payton, Chicago, RB	AP, PFWA
	& Bob Griese, Miami, QB	Bell
1978	Terry Bradshaw, Pittsburgh, QB	AP, Bell
	& Earl Campbell, Houston, RB	PFWA
1979	Earl Campbell, Houston, RB	AP, Bell, PFWA
1980	Brian Sipe, Cleveland, QB	AP, PFWA
	& Ron Jaworski, Philadelphia, QB	Bell
1981	Ken Anderson, Cincinnati, QB	AP, Bell, PFWA

Year		Awards
1982	Mark Moseley, Washington, PK	AP
	Joe Theismann, Washington, QB	Bell
	& Dan Fouts, San Diego, QB	PFWA
1983	Joe Theismann, Washington, QB	AP, PFWA
	& John Riggins, Washington, RB	Bell
1984	Dan Marino, Miami, QB	AP, Bell, PFWA
1985	Marcus Allen, LA Raiders, RB	AP, PFWA
	& Walter Payton, Chicago, RB	Bell
1986	Lawrence Taylor, NY Giants, LB	AP, Bell, PFWA
1987	Jerry Rice, San Francisco, WR	Bell, PFWA
	& John Elway, Denver, QB	AP
1988	Boomer Esiason, Cincinnati, QB	AP, PFWA
	& Randall Cunningham, Phila., QB	Bell
1989	Joe Montana, San Francisco, QB	AP, Bell, PFWA
1990	Randall Cunningham, Phila., QB	Bell, PFWA
	& Joe Montana, San Francisco, QB	AP

Year		Awards
1991	Thurman Thomas, Buffalo, RB	AP, PFWA
	& Barry Sanders, Detroit, RB	Bell
1992	Steve Young, San Francisco, QB	AP, Bell, PFWA
1993	Emmitt Smith, Dallas, RB	AP, Bell, PFWA
1994	Steve Young, San Francisco, QB	AP, Bell, PFWA
1995	Brett Favre, Green Bay, QB	AP, Bell, PFWA
1996	Brett Favre, Green Bay, QB	AP, Bell, PFWA
1997	Barry Sanders, Detroit, RB	AP*, Bell, PFWA
	& Brett Favre, Green Bay, QB	AP*
1998	Terrell Davis, Denver, RB	AP, PFWA
	& Randall Cunningham, Minnesota, QB	Bell
1999	Kurt Warner, St. Louis, QB	AP, Bell, PFWA
2000	Marshall Faulk, St. Louis, RB	AP, PFWA
	& Edgerrin James, Indianapolis, RB	Bell

*In 1997 for the first time in history, two players tied for the AP MVP award.

AP Offensive Player of the Year

Selected by The Associated Press in balloting by a nationwide media panel. Given out since 1972. Rookie winners are in **bold** type.

Multiple winners: Earl Campbell (3); Terrell Davis, Marshall Faulk, Jerry Rice and Barry Sanders (2).

Year		Pos	Year		Pos	Year		Pos
1972	Larry Brown, Was	RB	1982	Dan Fouts, SD	QB	1992	Steve Young, SF	QB
1973	O.J. Simpson, Buf	RB	1983	Joe Theismann, Was	QB	1993	Jerry Rice, SF	WR
1974	Ken Stabler, Oak	QB	1984	Dan Marino, Mia	QB	1994	Barry Sanders, Det	RB
1975	Fran Tarkenton, Min	QB	1985	Marcus Allen, Raiders	RB	1995	Brett Favre, GB	QB
1976	Bert Jones, Bal	QB	1986	Eric Dickerson, Rams	RB	1996	Terrell Davis, Den.	RB
1977	Walter Payton, Chi	RB	1987	Jerry Rice, SF	WR	1997	Barry Sanders, Det	RB
1978	**Earl Campbell**, Hou	RB	1988	Roger Craig, SF	RB	1998	Terrell Davis, Den.	RB
1979	Earl Campbell, Hou	RB	1989	Joe Montana, SF	QB	1999	Marshall Faulk, St.L.	RB
1980	Earl Campbell, Hou	RB	1990	Warren Moon, Hou	QB	2000	Marshall Faulk, St.L.	RB
1981	Ken Anderson, Cin.	QB	1991	Thurman Thomas, Buf	RB			

AP Defensive Player of the Year

Selected by The Associated Press in balloting by a nationwide media panel. Given out since 1971. Rookie winners are in **bold** type.

Multiple winners: Lawrence Taylor (3); Joe Greene, Mike Singletary, Bruce Smith and Reggie White (2).

Year		Pos	Year		Pos	Year		Pos
1971	Alan Page, Min	DT	1981	**Lawrence Taylor**, NYG	LB	1991	Pat Swilling, NO	LB
1972	Joe Greene, Pit	DT	1982	Lawrence Taylor, NYG	LB	1992	Cortez Kennedy, Sea	DT
1973	Dick Anderson, Mia	S	1983	Doug Betters, Mia	DE	1993	Rod Woodson, Pit	CB
1974	Joe Greene, Pit	DT	1984	Kenny Easley, Sea	S	1994	Deion Sanders, SF	CB
1975	Mel Blount, Pit	CB	1985	Mike Singletary, Chi	LB	1995	Bryce Paup, Buf	LB
1976	Jack Lambert, Pit	LB	1986	Lawrence Taylor, NYG	LB	1996	Bruce Smith, Buf	DE
1977	Harvey Martin, Dal	DE	1987	Reggie White, Phi	DE	1997	Dana Stubblefield, SF	DT
1978	Randy Gradishar, Den.	LB	1988	Mike Singletary, Chi	LB	1998	Reggie White, GB	DE
1979	Lee Roy Selmon, TB	DE	1989	Keith Millard, Min	DT	1999	Warren Sapp, TB	DT
1980	Lester Hayes, Oak	CB	1990	Bruce Smith, Buf	DE	2000	Ray Lewis, Bal.	LB

UPI NFC Player of the Year

Given out by UPI from 1970-96. Offensive and defensive players honored since 1983. Rookie winners are in **bold** type.

Multiple winners: Eric Dickerson, Reggie White and Mike Singletary (3); Brett Favre, Charles Haley, Walter Payton, Lawrence Taylor and Steve Young (2).

Year		Pos	Year		Pos	Year		Pos
1970	John Brodie, SF	QB	1984	Off—Eric Dickerson, Rams	RB	1991	Off—Mark Rypien, Was	QB
1971	Alan Page, Min	DT		Def—Mike Singletary, Chi	LB		Def—Reggie White, Phi	DE
1972	Larry Brown, Was	RB	1985	Off—Walter Payton, Chi	RB	1992	Off—Steve Young, SF	QB
1973	John Hadl, Rams	QB		Def—Mike Singletary, Chi	LB		Def—Chris Doleman, Min	DE
1974	Jim Hart, St.L.	QB	1986	Off—Eric Dickerson, Rams	RB	1993	Off—Emmitt Smith, Dal	RB
1975	Fran Tarkenton, Min	QB		Def—Lawrence Taylor, NYG	LB		Def—Eric Allen, Phi	CB
1976	Chuck Foreman, Min	RB	1987	Off—Jerry Rice, SF	WR	1994	Off—Steve Young, SF	QB
1977	Walter Payton, Chi	RB		Def—Reggie White, Phi	DE		Def—Charles Haley, Dal	DE
1978	Archie Manning, NO	QB	1988	Off—Roger Craig, SF	RB	1995	Off—Brett Favre, GB	QB
1979	Ottis Anderson, St.L.	RB		Def—Mike Singletary, Chi	LB		Def—Reggie White, GB	DE
1980	Ron Jaworski, Phi	QB	1989	Off—Joe Montana, SF	QB	1996	Off—Brett Favre, GB	QB
1981	Tony Dorsett, Dal	RB		Def—Keith Millard, Min	DT		Def—Kevin Greene, Car	LB
1982	Mark Moseley, Was	PK	1990	Off—Randall Cunningham, Phi.	QB	1997	Award discontinued.	
1983	Off—Eric Dickerson, Rams	RB		Def—Charles Haley, SF	LB			
	Def—Lawrence Taylor, NYG	LB						

Annual Awards (Cont.)
UPI AFL-AFC Player of the Year

Presented by UPI to the top player in the AFL (1960-69) and AFC (1970-96). Offensive and defensive players have been honored since 1983. Rookie winners are in **bold** type.

Multiple winners: Bruce Smith (4); O.J. Simpson (3); Cornelius Bennett, George Blanda, John Elway, Dan Fouts, Daryle Lamonica, Dan Marino and Curt Warner (2).

Year		Pos	Year		Pos	Year		Pos
1960	**Abner Haynes**, Dal	HB	1978	**Earl Campbell**, Hou	RB	1989	Off—Christian Okoye, KC	RB
1961	George Blanda, Hou	QB	1979	Dan Fouts, SD	QB		Def—Michael Dean Perry, Cle	NT
1962	Cookie Gilchrist, Buf	FB	1980	Brian Sipe, Cle	QB	1990	Off—Warren Moon, Hou	QB
1963	Lance Alworth, SD	FL	1981	Ken Anderson, Cin	QB		Def—Bruce Smith, Buf	DE
1964	Gino Cappelletti, Bos	FL-PK	1982	Dan Fouts, SD	QB	1991	Off—Thurman Thomas, Buf	RB
1965	Paul Lowe, SD	HB	1983	Off—**Curt Warner**, Sea	RB		Def—Cornelius Bennett, Buf	LB
1966	Jim Nance, Bos	FB		Def—Rod Martin, Raiders	LB	1992	Off—Barry Foster, Pit	RB
1967	Daryle Lamonica, Raiders	QB	1984	Off—Dan Marino, Mia	QB		Def—Junior Seau, SD	LB
1968	Joe Namath, NYJ	QB		Def—Mark Gastineau, NYJ	DE	1993	Off—John Elway, Den	QB
1969	Daryle Lamonica, Raiders	QB	1985	Off—Marcus Allen, Raiders	RB		Def—Rod Woodson, Pit	CB
1970	George Blanda, Raiders	QB-PK		Def—Andre Tippett, NE	LB	1994	Off—Dan Marino, Mia	QB
1971	Otis Taylor, KC	WR	1986	Off—Curt Warner, Sea	RB		Def—Greg Lloyd, Pit	LB
1972	O.J. Simpson, Buf	RB		Def—Rulon Jones, Den	DE	1995	Off—Jim Harbaugh, Ind	QB
1973	O.J. Simpson, Buf	RB	1987	Off—John Elway, Den	QB		Def—Bryce Paup, Buf	LB
1974	Ken Stabler, Raiders	QB		Def—Bruce Smith, Buf	DE	1996	Off—Terrell Davis, Den	RB
1975	O.J. Simpson, Buf	RB	1988	Off—Boomer Esiason, Cin	QB		Def—Bruce Smith, Buf	DE
1976	Bert Jones, Bal	QB		Def—Bruce Smith, Buf	DE	1997	Award discontinued.	
1977	Craig Morton, Den	QB		& Cornelius Bennett, Buf	LB			

UPI NFL-NFC Rookie of the Year

Presented by UPI to the top rookie in the NFL (1955-69) and NFC (1970-96). Players who were the overall first pick in the NFL draft are in **bold** type.

Year		Pos	Year		Pos	Year		Pos
1955	Alan Ameche, Bal	FB	1970	Bruce Taylor, SF	DB	1985	Jerry Rice, SF	WR
1956	Lenny Moore, Bal	HB	1971	John Brockington, GB	RB	1986	Reuben Mayes, NO	RB
1957	Jim Brown, Cle	FB	1972	Chester Marcol, GB	PK	1987	Robert Awalt, St.L	TE
1958	Jimmy Orr, Pit	FL	1973	Charle Young, Phi	TE	1988	Keith Jackson, Phi	TE
1959	Boyd Dowler, GB	FL	1974	John Hicks, NY	G	1989	Barry Sanders, Det	RB
1960	Gail Cogdill, Det	FL	1975	Mike Thomas, Wash	RB	1990	Mark Carrier, Chi	S
1961	Mike Ditka, Chi	TE	1976	Sammy White, Min	WR	1991	Lawrence Dawsey, TB	WR
1962	Ronnie Bull, Chi	RB	1977	Tony Dorsett, Dal	RB	1992	Robert Jones, Dal	LB
1963	Paul Flatley, Min	FL	1978	Bubba Baker, Det	DE	1993	Jerome Bettis, LA	RB
1964	Charley Taylor, Wash	HB	1979	Ottis Anderson, St.L	RB	1994	Bryant Young, SF	DT
1965	Gale Sayers, Chi	HB	1980	**Billy Sims**, Det	RB	1995	Rashaan Salaam, Chi	RB
1966	Johnny Roland, St.L	HB	1981	**George Rogers**, NO	RB	1996	Simeon Rice, Ari	DE
1967	Mel Farr, Det	RB	1982	Jim McMahon, Chi	QB	1997	Award discontinued.	
1968	Earl McCullough, Det	FL	1983	Eric Dickerson, LA	RB			
1969	Calvin Hill, Dal	RB	1984	Paul McFadden, Phi	PK			

UPI AFL-AFC Rookie of the Year

Presented by UPI to the top rookie in the AFL (1960-69) and AFC (1970-96). Players who were the overall first pick in the AFL or NFL draft are in **bold** type.

Year		Pos	Year		Pos	Year		Pos
1960	Abner Haynes, Dal	HB	1973	Bobbie Clark, Cin	RB	1986	Leslie O'Neal, SD	DE
1961	Earl Faison, SD	DE	1974	Don Woods, SD	RB	1987	Shane Conlan, Buf	LB
1962	Curtis McClinton, Dal	FB	1975	Robert Brazile, Hou	LB	1988	John Stephens, NE	RB
1963	Billy Joe, Den	FB	1976	Mike Haynes, NE	DB	1989	Derrick Thomas, KC	LB
1964	Matt Snell, NY	FB	1977	A.J. Duhe, Mia	DE	1990	Richmond Webb, Mia	OT
1965	Joe Namath, NY	QB	1978	**Earl Campbell**, Hou	RB	1991	Mike Croel, Den	LB
1966	Bobby Burnett, Buf	RB	1979	Jerry Butler, Buf	WR	1992	Dale Carter, KC	CB
1967	George Webster, Hou	LB	1980	Joe Cribbs, Buf	RB	1993	Rick Mirer, Sea	QB
1968	Paul Robinson, Cin	RB	1981	Joe Delaney, KC	RB	1994	Marshall Faulk, Ind	RB
1969	Greg Cook, Cin	QB	1982	Marcus Allen, LA	RB	1995	Curtis Martin, NE	RB
1970	Dennis Shaw, Buf	QB	1983	Curt Warner, Sea	RB	1996	Terry Glenn, NE	WR
1971	**Jim Plunkett**, NE	QB	1984	Louis Lipps, Pit	WR	1997	Award discontinued.	
1972	Franco Harris, Pit	RB	1985	Kevin Mack, Cle	RB			

AP Offensive Rookie of the Year

Selected by The Associated Press in balloting by a nationwide media panel. Given out since 1967.

Year		Pos	Year		Pos	Year		Pos
1967	Mel Farr, Det	RB	1979	Ottis Anderson, St.L.	RB	1990	Emmitt Smith, Dal.	RB
1968	Earl McCullouch, Det	OE	1980	Billy Sims, Det	RB	1991	Leonard Russell, NE	RB
1969	Calvin Hill, Dal	RB	1981	George Rogers, NO	RB	1992	Carl Pickens, Cin	WR
1970	Dennis Shaw, Buf	QB	1982	Marcus Allen, Raiders:	RB	1993	Jerome Bettis, Rams	RB
1971	John Brockington, GB	RB	1983	Eric Dickerson, Rams	RB	1994	Marshall Faulk, Ind	RB
1972	Franco Harris, Pit	RB	1984	Louis Lipps, Pit	WR	1995	Curtis Martin, NE	RB
1973	Chuck Foreman, Min	RB	1985	Eddie Brown, Cin	WR	1996	Eddie George, Hou	RB
1974	Don Woods, SD	RB	1986	Reuben Mayes, NO	RB	1997	Warrick Dunn, TB	RB
1975	Mike Thomas, Was	RB	1987	Troy Stradford, Mia	RB	1998	Randy Moss, Min	WR
1976	Sammy White, Min	WR	1988	John Stephens, NE	RB	1999	Edgerrin James, Ind.	RB
1977	Tony Dorsett, Dal	RB	1989	Barry Sanders, Det	RB	2000	Mike Anderson, Den	RB
1978	Earl Campbell, Hou	RB						

AP Defensive Rookie of the Year

Selected by The Associated Press in balloting by a nationwide media panel. Given out since 1967.

Year		Pos	Year		Pos	Year		Pos
1967	Lem Barney, Det	CB	1979	Jim Haslett, Buf	LB	1990	Mark Carrier, Chi	S
1968	Claude Humphrey, Atl	DE	1980	Buddy Curry, Atl.	LB	1991	Mike Croel, Den	LB
1969	Joe Greene, Pit	DT		& Al Richardson, Atl	LB	1992	Dale Carter, KC	CB
1970	Bruce Taylor, SF.	CB	1981	Lawrence Taylor, NYG	LB	1993	Dana Stubblefield, SF	DT
1971	Isiah Robertson, Rams	LB	1982	Chip Banks, Cle	LB	1994	Tim Bowens, Mia.	DT
1972	Willie Buchanon, GB	CB	1983	Vernon Maxwell, Bal	LB	1995	Hugh Douglas, NYJ	DE
1973	Wally Chambers, Chi	DT	1984	Bill Maas, KC	DT	1996	Simeon Rice, Ari	DE
1974	Jack Lambert, Pit	LB	1985	Duane Bickett, Ind	LB	1997	Peter Boulware, Bal	LB
1975	Robert Brazile, Hou	LB	1986	Leslie O'Neal, SD	DE	1998	Charles Woodson, Raiders	CB
1976	Mike Haynes, NE	CB	1987	Shane Conlan, Buf	LB	1999	Jevon Kearse, Ten	DE
1977	A.J. Duhe, Mia	DE	1988	Erik McMillan, NYJ	S	2000	Brian Urlacher, Chi	LB
1978	Al Baker, Det	DE	1989	Derrick Thomas, KC	LB			

Coach of the Year

Presented by UPI to the top coach in the AFL-NFL (1955-69) and AFC-NFC (1970-96). In 1997, the UPI awards were discontinued. Awards beginning in 1997 are the consensus selections from presenters such as AP, The Maxwell Football Club of Philadelphia, *The Sporting News* and the Pro Football Writers Association. Records indicate the team's change in record from the previous season.

Multiple winners: Dan Reeves (4); Paul Brown, Chuck Knox and Don Shula (3); George Allen, Leeman Bennett, Mike Ditka, George Halas, Tom Landry, Marv Levy, Bill Parcells, Jack Pardee, Sam Rutigliano, Lou Saban, Allie Sherman, Marty Schottenheimer, Dick Vermeil and Bill Walsh (2).

Year		Improvement	Year		Improvement
1955	NFL–Joe Kuharich, Washington	3-9 to 8-4	1973	NFC–Chuck Knox, Los Angeles	6-7-1 to 12-2
1956	NFL–Buddy Parker, Detroit	3-9 to 9-3		AFC–John Ralston, Denver	5-9 to 7-5-2
1957	NFL–Paul Brown, Cleveland	5-7 to 9-2-1	1974	NFC–Don Coryell, St. Louis	4-9-1 to 10-4
1958	NFL–Weeb Ewbank, Baltimore	7-5 to 9-3		AFC–Sid Gillman, Houston	1-13 to 7-7
1959	NFL–Vince Lombardi, Green Bay	1-10-1 to 7-5	1975	NFC–Tom Landry, Dallas	8-6 to 10-4
1960	NFL–Buck Shaw, Philadelphia	7-5 to 10-2		AFC–Ted Marchibroda, Baltimore	2-12 to 10-4
	AFL–Lou Rymkus, Houston	10-4	1976	NFC–Jack Pardee, Chicago	4-10 to 7-7
1961	NFL–Allie Sherman, New York	6-4-2 to 10-3-1		AFC–Chuck Fairbanks, New England	3-11 to 11-3
	AFL–Wally Lemm, Houston	10-4 to 10-3-1	1977	NFC–Leeman Bennett, Atlanta	4-10 to 7-7
1962	NFL–Allie Sherman, New York	10-3-1 to 12-2		AFC–Red Miller, Denver	9-5 to 12-2
	AFL–Jack Faulkner, Denver	3-11 to 7-7	1978	NFC–Dick Vermeil, Philadelphia	5-9 to 9-7
1963	NFL–George Halas, Chicago	9-5 to 11-1-2		AFC–Walt Michaels, New York	3-11 to 8-8
	AFL–Al Davis, Oakland	1-13 to 10-4	1979	NFC–Jack Pardee, Washington	8-8 to 10-6
1964	NFL–Don Shula, Baltimore	8-6 to 12-2		AFC–Sam Rutigliano, Cleveland	8-8 to 9-7
	AFL–Lou Saban, Buffalo	7-6-1 to 12-2	1980	NFC–Leeman Bennett, Atlanta	6-10 to 12-4
1965	NFL–George Halas, Chicago	5-9 to 9-5		AFC–Sam Rutigliano, Cleveland	9-7 to 11-5
	AFL–Lou Saban, Buffalo	12-2 to 10-3-1	1981	NFC–Bill Walsh, San Francisco	6-10 to 13-3
1966	NFL–Tom Landry, Dallas	7-7 to 10-3-1		AFC–Forrest Gregg, Cincinnati	6-10 to 12-4
	AFL–Mike Holovak, Boston	4-8-2 to 8-4-2	1982	NFC–Joe Gibbs, Washington	8-8 to 8-1
1967	NFL–George Allen, Los Angeles	8-6 to 11-1-2		AFC–Tom Flores, Los Angeles	7-9 to 8-1
	AFL–John Rauch, Oakland	8-5-1 to 13-1	1983	NFC–John Robinson, Los Angeles	2-7 to 9-7
1968	NFL–Don Shula, Baltimore	11-1-2 to 13-1		AFC–Chuck Knox, Seattle	4-6 to 9-7
	AFL–Hank Stram, Kansas City	9-5 to 12-2	1984	NFC–Bill Walsh, San Francisco	10-6 to 15-1
1969	NFL–Bud Grant, Minnesota	8-6 to 12-2		AFC–Chuck Knox, Seattle	9-7 to 12-4
	AFL–Paul Brown, Cincinnati	3-11 to 4-9-1	1985	NFC–Mike Ditka, Chicago	10-6 to 15-1
1970	NFC–Alex Webster, New York	6-8 to 9-5		AFC–Raymond Berry, New England	9-7 to 11-5
	AFC–Paul Brown, Cincinnati	4-9-1 to 8-6	1986	NFC–Bill Parcells, New York	10-6 to 14-2
1971	NFC–George Allen, Washington	6-8 to 9-4-1		AFC–Marty Schottenheimer, Cleveland	8-8 to 12-4
	AFC–Don Shula, Miami	10-4 to 10-3-1	1987	NFC–Jim Mora, New Orleans	7-9 to 12-3
1972	NFC–Dan Devine, Green Bay	4-8-2 to 10-4		AFC–Ron Meyer, Indianapolis	3-13 to 9-6
	AFC–Chuck Noll, Pittsburgh	6-8 to 11-3	1988	NFC–Mike Ditka, Chicago	11-4 to 12-4
				AFC–Marv Levy, Buffalo	7-8 to 12-4

Annual Awards (Cont.)

Year		Improvement	Year		Improvement
1989	NFC–Lindy Infante, Green Bay	4-12 to 10-6	1994	NFC–Dave Wannstedt, Chicago	7-9 to 9-7
	AFC–Dan Reeves, Denver	8-8 to 11-5		AFC–Bill Parcells, New England	5-11 to 10-6
1990	NFC–Jimmy Johnson, Dallas	1-15 to 7-9	1995	NFC–Ray Rhodes, Philadelphia	7-9 to 10-6
	AFC–Art Shell, Los Angeles	8-8 to 12-4		AFC–Marty Schottenheimer, Kansas City	9-7 to 13-3
1991	NFC–Wayne Fontes, Detroit	6-10 to 12-4	1996	NFC–Dom Capers, Carolina	7-9 to 12-4
	AFC–Dan Reeves, Denver	5-11 to 12-4		AFC–Tom Coughlin, Jacksonville	4-12 to 9-7
1992	NFC–Dennis Green, Minnesota	8-8 to 11-5	1997	NFL–Jim Fassel, NY Giants	6-10 to 10-5-1
	AFC–Bobby Ross, San Diego	4-12 to 11-5	1998	NFL–Dan Reeves, Atlanta	7-9 to 14-2
1993	NFC–Dan Reeves, New York	6-10 to 11-5	1999	NFL–Dick Vermeil, St. Louis	4-12 to 13-3
	AFC–Marv Levy, Buffalo	11-5 to 12-4	2000	NFL–Jim Haslett, New Orleans	3-13 to 10-6

CANADIAN FOOTBALL

The Grey Cup

Earl Grey, the Governor-General of Canada (1904-11), donated a trophy in 1909 for the Rugby Football Championship of Canada. The trophy, which later became known as the Grey Cup, was originally open to competition for teams registered with the Canada Rugby Union. Since 1954, the Cup has gone to the champion of the Canadian Football League (CFL).

Overall multiple winners: Toronto Argonauts (14); Edmonton Eskimos (11); Winnipeg Blue Bombers (9); Hamilton Tiger-Cats (8); Ottawa Rough Riders (7); Hamilton Tigers (5); B.C. Lions, Calgary Stampeders, Montreal Alouettes and University of Toronto (4); Queen's University (3); Ottawa Senators, Sarnia Imperials, Saskatchewan Roughriders and Toronto Balmy Beach (2).

CFL multiple winners (since 1954): Edmonton (11); Hamilton and Winnipeg (7); Ottawa (5); B.C. Lions and Toronto (4); Calgary and Montreal (3); Saskatchewan (2).

Year	Cup Final	Year	Cup Final
1909	Univ. of Toronto 26, Toronto Parkdale 6	1934	Sarnia Imperials 20, Regina Roughriders 12
1910	Univ. of Toronto 16, Hamilton Tigers 7	1935	Winnipeg 'Pegs 18, Hamilton Tigers 12
1911	Univ. of Toronto 14, Toronto Argonauts 7	1936	Sarnia Imperials 26, Ottawa Rough Riders 20
1912	Hamilton Alerts 11, Toronto Argonauts 4	1937	Toronto Argonauts 4, Winnipeg Blue Bombers 3
1913	Hamilton Tigers 44, Toronto Parkdale 2	1938	Toronto Argonauts 30, Winnipeg Blue Bombers 7
1914	Toronto Argonauts 14, Univ. of Toronto 2	1939	Winnipeg Blue Bombers 8, Ottawa Rough Riders 7
1915	Hamilton Tigers 13, Toronto Rowing 7	1940	Gm 1: Ottawa Rough Riders 8, Toronto B-Beach 2
1916-19	Not held (WWI)		Gm 2: Ottawa Rough Riders 12, Toronto B-Beach 5
1920	Univ. of Toronto 16, Toronto Argonauts 3	1941	Winnipeg Blue Bombers 18, Ottawa Rough Riders 16
1921	Toronto Argonauts 23, Edmonton Eskimos 0	1942	Toronto RACF 8, Winnipeg RACF 5
1922	Queens Univ. 13, Edmonton Elks 1	1943	Hamilton Wildcats 23, Winnipeg RACF 14
1923	Queens Univ. 54, Regina Roughriders 0	1944	Montreal HMCS 7, Hamilton Wildcats 6
1924	Queens Univ. 11, Toronto Balmy Beach 3	1945	Toronto Argonauts 35, Winnipeg Blue Bombers 0
1925	Ottawa Senators 24, Winnipeg Tigers 1	1946	Toronto Argonauts 28, Winnipeg Blue Bombers 6
1926	Ottawa Senators 10, Univ. of Toronto 7	1947	Toronto Argonauts 10, Winnipeg Blue Bombers 9
1927	Toronto Balmy Beach 9, Hamilton Tigers 6	1948	Calgary Stampeders 12, Ottawa Rough Riders 7
1928	Hamilton Tigers 30, Regina Roughriders 0	1949	Montreal Alouettes 28, Calgary Stampeders 15
1929	Hamilton Tigers 14, Regina Roughriders 3	1950	Toronto Argonauts 13, Winnipeg Blue Bombers 0
1930	Toronto Balmy Beach 11, Regina Roughriders 6	1951	Ottawa Rough Riders 21, Saskatch. Roughriders 14
1931	Montreal AAA 22, Regina Roughriders 0	1952	Toronto Argonauts 21, Edmonton Eskimos 11
1932	Hamilton Tigers 25, Regina Roughriders 6	1953	Hamilton Tiger-Cats 12, Winnipeg Blue Bombers 6
1933	Toronto Argonauts 4, Sarnia Imperials 3		

Year	Winner	Head Coach	Score	Loser	Head Coach	Site
1954	Edmonton	Frank (Pop) Ivy	26-25	Montreal	Doug Walker	Toronto
1955	Edmonton	Frank (Pop) Ivy	34-19	Montreal	Doug Walker	Vancouver
1956	Edmonton	Frank (Pop) Ivy	50-27	Montreal	Doug Walker	Toronto
1957	Hamilton	Jim Trimble	32-7	Winnipeg	Bud Grant	Toronto
1958	Winnipeg	Bud Grant	35-28	Hamilton	Jim Trimble	Vancouver
1959	Winnipeg	Bud Grant	21-7	Hamilton	Jim Trimble	Toronto
1960	Ottawa	Frank Clair	16-6	Edmonton	Eagle Keys	Vancouver
1961	Winnipeg	Bud Grant	21-14(OT)	Hamilton	Jim Trimble	Toronto
1962	Winnipeg	Bud Grant	28-27*	Hamilton	Jim Trimble	Toronto
1963	Hamilton	Ralph Sazio	21-10	B.C. Lions	Dave Skrien	Vancouver
1964	B.C. Lions	Dave Skrien	34-24	Hamilton	Ralph Sazio	Toronto
1965	Hamilton	Ralph Sazio	22-16	Winnipeg	Bud Grant	Toronto
1966	Saskatchewan	Eagle Keys	29-14	Ottawa	Frank Clair	Vancouver
1967	Hamilton	Ralph Sazio	24-1	Saskatchewan	Eagle Keys	Ottawa
1968	Ottawa	Frank Clair	24-21	Calgary	Jerry Williams	Toronto
1969	Ottawa	Frank Clair	29-11	Saskatchewan	Eagle Keys	Montreal
1970	Montreal	Sam Etcheverry	23-10	Calgary	Jim Duncan	Toronto
1971	Calgary	Jim Duncan	14-11	Toronto	Leo Cahill	Vancouver
1972	Hamilton	Jerry Williams	13-10	Saskatchewan	Dave Skrien	Hamilton
1973	Ottawa	Jack Gotta	22-18	Edmonton	Ray Jauch	Toronto

Year	Winner	Head Coach	Score	Loser	Head Coach	Site
1974	Montreal	Marv Levy	20-7	Edmonton	Ray Jauch	Vancouver
1975	Edmonton	Ray Jauch	9-8	Montreal	Marv Levy	Calgary
1976	Ottawa	George Brancato	23-20	Saskatchewan	John Payne	Toronto
1977	Montreal	Marv Levy	41-6	Edmonton	Hugh Campbell	Montreal
1978	Edmonton	Hugh Campbell	20-13	Montreal	Joe Scannella	Toronto
1979	Edmonton	Hugh Campbell	17-9	Montreal	Joe Scannella	Montreal
1980	Edmonton	Hugh Campbell	48-10	Hamilton	John Payne	Toronto
1981	Edmonton	Hugh Campbell	26-23	Ottawa	George Brancato	Montreal
1982	Edmonton	Hugh Campbell	32-16	Toronto	Bob O'Billovich	Toronto
1983	Toronto	Bob O'Billovich	18-17	B.C. Lions	Don Matthews	Vancouver
1984	Winnipeg	Cal Murphy	47-17	Hamilton	Al Bruno	Edmonton
1985	B.C. Lions	Don Matthews	37-24	Hamilton	Al Bruno	Montreal
1986	Hamilton	Al Bruno	39-15	Edmonton	Jack Parker	Vancouver
1987	Edmonton	Joe Faragalli	38-36	Toronto	Bob O'Billovich	Vancouver
1988	Winnipeg	Mike Riley	22-21	B.C. Lions	Larry Donovan	Ottawa
1989	Saskatchewan	John Gregory	43-40	Hamilton	Al Bruno	Toronto
1990	Winnipeg	Mike Riley	50-11	Edmonton	Joe Faragalli	Vancouver
1991	Toronto	Adam Rita	36-21	Calgary	Wally Buono	Winnipeg
1992	Calgary	Wally Buono	24-10	Winnipeg	Urban Bowman	Toronto
1993	Edmonton	Ron Lancaster	33-23	Winnipeg	Cal Murphy	Calgary
1994	B.C. Lions	Dave Ritchie	26-23	Baltimore	Don Matthews	Vancouver
1995	Baltimore	Don Matthews	37-20	Calgary	Wally Buono	Regina
1996	Toronto	Don Matthews	43-37	Edmonton	Ron Lancaster	Hamilton
1997	Toronto	Don Matthews	47-23	Saskatchewan	Jim Daley	Edmonton
1998	Calgary	Wally Buono	26-24	Hamilton	Ron Lancaster	Winnipeg
1999	Hamilton	Ron Lancaster	32-21	Calgary	Wally Buono	Vancouver
2000	B.C. Lions	Steve Buratto	28-26	Montreal	Charlie Taaffe	Calgary

*Halted by fog in 4th quarter, final 9:29 played the following day.

CFL Most Outstanding Player

Regular season Player of the Year as selected by The Football Reporters of Canada since 1953.
Multiple winners: Doug Flutie (6); Russ Jackson and Jackie Parker (3); Dieter Brock, Ron Lancaster and Mike Pringle (2).

Year	Year	Year
1953 Billy Vessels, Edmonton, RB	1969 Russ Jackson, Ottawa, QB	1985 Merv Fernandez, B.C. Lions, WR
1954 Sam Etcheverry, Montreal, QB	1970 Ron Lancaster, Saskatch., QB	1986 James Murphy, Winnipeg, WR
1955 Pat Abbruzzi, Montreal, RB	1971 Don Jonas, Winnipeg, QB	1987 Tom Clements, Winnipeg, QB
1956 Hal Patterson, Montreal, E-DB	1972 Garney Henley, Hamilton, WR	1988 David Williams, B.C. Lions, WR
1957 Jackie Parker, Edmonton, RB	1973 Geo. McGowan, Edmonton, WR	1989 Tracy Ham, Edmonton, QB
1958 Jackie Parker, Edmonton, QB	1974 Tom Wilkinson, Edmonton, QB	1990 Mike Clemons, Toronto, RB
1959 Johnny Bright, Edmonton, RB	1975 Willie Burden, Calgary, RB	1991 Doug Flutie, B.C. Lions, QB
1960 Jackie Parker, Edmonton, QB	1976 Ron Lancaster, Saskatch., QB	1992 Doug Flutie, Calgary, QB
1961 Bernie Faloney, Hamilton, QB	1977 Jimmy Edwards, Hamilton, RB	1993 Doug Flutie, Calgary, QB
1962 George Dixon, Montreal, RB	1978 Tony Gabriel, Ottawa, TE	1994 Doug Flutie, Calgary, QB
1963 Russ Jackson, Ottawa, QB	1979 David Green, Montreal, RB	1995 Mike Pringle, Baltimore, RB
1964 Lovell Coleman, Calgary, RB	1980 Dieter Brock, Winnipeg, QB	1996 Doug Flutie, Toronto, QB
1965 George Reed, Saskatchewan, RB	1981 Dieter Brock, Winnipeg, QB	1997 Doug Flutie, Toronto, QB
1966 Russ Jackson, Ottawa, QB	1982 Condredge Holloway, Tor., QB	1998 Mike Pringle, Montreal, RB
1967 Peter Liske, Calgary, QB	1983 Warren Moon, Edmonton, QB	1999 Danny McManus, Hamilton, QB
1968 Bill Symons, Toronto, RB	1984 Willard Reaves, Winnipeg, RB	2000 Dave Dickenson, Calgary, QB

All-Time CFL Leaders

Through the 2000 season. Players active in 2000 are in **bold** type.

Passing Yards

		Yrs	Att	Cmp	Yards	Cmp Pct	Avg Gain	TD	Int	Rating
1	**Damon Allen**	16	6480	3588	50,789	55.4	14.2	277	214	81.4
2	Ron Lancaster	19	6233	3384	50,535	54.3	14.9	333	396	72.4
3	Matt Dunigan	14	5476	3057	43,857	55.8	14.3	306	211	84.5
4	Doug Flutie	8	4854	2975	41,355	61.3	13.9	270	155	93.9
5	Tracy Ham	12	4945	2670	40,534	53.9	15.2	284	164	86.4

Rushing Yards

		Yrs	Car	Yards	Avg	TD
1	George Reed	13	3243	16,116	5.0	134
2	**Mike Pringle**	9	2129	12,357	5.8	88
3	Johnny Bright	13	1969	10,909	5.5	69
4	**Damon Allen**	16	1380	9,463	6.9	76
5	Normie Kwong	13	1745	9,022	5.2	78

Receiving Yards

		Yrs	Ct	Yards	Avg	TD
1	Allen Pitts	11	966	14,891	15.4	117
2	Ray Elgaard	14	830	13,198	15.9	78
3	Don Narcisse	13	919	12,366	13.5	75
4	**Darren Flutie**	10	828	12,224	14.8	56
5	Brian Kelly	9	575	11,169	19.4	97

NFL EUROPE

The World League of American Football was formed in 1991 with hopes of expanding the popularity of the NFL to overseas markets. Funded by the NFL, the inaugural league in 1991 consisted of three European teams (London, Barcelona and Frankfurt), and seven North American teams (New York/New Jersey, Orlando, Montreal, Raleigh-Durham, Birmingham, Sacramento and San Antonio). The second season used the same format with Columbus, Ohio, replacing Raleigh-Durham.

In the fall of 1992, the NFL and WLAF Board of Directors voted to restructure the league to include more European teams. Play was subsequently suspended. In 1993, NFL clubs approved a six-team European-only league to resume play in 1995 with teams in Amsterdam, Barcelona, Frankfurt, London, Rhein and Scotland. In January 1998, the name of the league was changed to NFL Europe. Berlin was added for the 1999 season and London was disbanded.

The World Bowl

The first World Bowl was held in 1991 in front of 61,108 fans at London's Wembley Stadium. In 1991 and 1992, when the league consisted of three divisions, the top team from each division and one wild-card team advanced to the playoffs, with the winners of each game advancing to the World Bowl. There was no game played in 1993 or 1994. Since 1995, the top two regular season teams advance directly to the World Bowl.

Year	Winner	Head Coach	Score	Loser	Head Coach	Site
1991	London	Larry Kennan	21-0	Barcelona	Jack Bicknell	London
1992	Sacramento	Kay Stephenson	21-17	Orlando	Galen Hall	Montreal
1995	Frankfurt	Ernie Stautner	26-22	Amsterdam	Al Luginbill	Amsterdam
1996	Scotland	Jim Criner	32-27	Frankfurt	Ernie Stautner	Edinburgh, Scot.
1997	Barcelona	Jack Bicknell	38-24	Rhein	Galen Hall	Barcelona
1998	Rhein	Galen Hall	34-10	Frankfurt	Dick Curl	Frankfurt
1999	Frankfurt	Dick Curl	38-24	Barcelona	Jack Bicknell	Dusseldorf
2000	Rhein	Galen Hall	13-10	Scotland	Jim Criner	Frankfurt
2001	Berlin	Peter Vaas	24-17	Barcelona	Jack Bicknell	Amsterdam

World Bowl MVP

Year		Year		Year	
1991	Dan Crossman, London, S	1996	Yo Murphy, Scotland, WR	1999	Andy McCullough, Frankfurt, WR
1992	Davis Archer, Sacramento, QB	1997	Jon Kitna, Barcelona, QB	2000	Aaron Stecker, Scotland, RB
1995	Paul Justin, Frankfurt, QB	1998	Jim Arellanes, Rhein, QB	2001	Jonathan Quinn, Berlin, QB

Most Valuable Player

Regular season Offensive and Defensive Most Valuable Players as selected by league head coaches since 1991.

Year		Year		Year	
1991	Off—Stan Gelbaugh, Lon., QB	1996	Off—Sean LaChapelle, Sco., WR	1999	Off—Lawrence Phillips, Bar., RB
	Def—Anthony Parker, NY/NJ, CB		Def—Ty Parten, Sco., DL		Def—Mike Maslowski, Bar., LB
	& Danny Lockett, Lon., LB	1997	Off—T.J. Rubley, Rhe., QB	2000	Off—Aaron Stecker, Sco., RB
1992	Off—David Archer, Sac., QB		Def—Jason Simmons, Sco., DE		Def—Jonathan Brown, Ber., DE
	Def—Adrian Jones, Bar., CB	1998	Off—Marcus Robinson, Rhe., WR		& Duane Hawthorne, Sco., CB
1995	Off—Paul Justin, Fra., QB		Def—Josh Taves, Bar., DE	2001	Off—Mike Green, Bar., RB
	Def—Malcolm Showell, Ams., DE				Def—Roshaun Matthews, Ams., DE

ARENA FOOTBALL

The Arena Football League debuted in June of 1987 with four teams in Chicago, Denver, Pittsburgh and Washington D.C. Currently there are 19 teams in the league, divided into two conferences and four divisions.

ArenaBowl

Bowl	Year	Winner	Head Coach	Score	Loser	Head Coach	Site
I	1987	Denver	Tim Marcum	45-16	Pittsburgh	Joe Haering	Pittsburgh
II	1988	Detroit	Tim Marcum	24-13	Chicago	Perry Moss	Chicago
III	1989	Detroit	Tim Marcum	39-26	Pittsburgh	Joe Haering	Detroit
IV	1990	Detroit	Perry Moss	51-27	Dallas	Ernie Stautner	Detroit
V	1991	Tampa Bay	Fran Curci	48-42	Detroit	Tim Marcum	Detroit
VI	1992	Detroit	Tim Marcum	56-38	Orlando	Perry Moss	Orlando
VII	1993	Tampa Bay	Lary Kuharich	51-31	Detroit	Tim Marcum	Detroit
VIII	1994	Arizona	Danny White	36-31	Orlando	Perry Moss	Orlando
IX	1995	Tampa Bay	Tim Marcum	48-35	Orlando	Perry Moss	St. Petersburg
X	1996	Tampa Bay	Tim Marcum	42-38	Iowa	John Gregory	Des Moines
XI	1997	Arizona	Danny White	55-33	Iowa	John Gregory	Phoenix
XII	1998	Orlando	Jay Gruden	62-31	Tampa Bay	Tim Marcum	Tampa
XIII	1999	Albany	Mike Dailey	59-48	Orlando	Jay Gruden	Albany
XIV	2000	Orlando	Jay Gruden	41-38	Nashville	Pat Sperduto	Orlando
XV	2001	Grand Rapids	Michael Trigg	64-42	Nashville	Pat Sperduto	Grand Rapids

ArenaBowl MVP

Year		Year		Year	
1987	Gary Mullen, Denver, WR	1992	George LaFrance, Detroit, OS	1997	Donnie Davis, Arizona, QB
1988	Steve Griffin, Detroit, WR/DB	1993	Jay Gruden, Tampa Bay, QB	1998	Rick Hamilton, Orlando, FB/LB
1989	George LaFrance, Detroit, WR/DB	1994	Sherdrick Bonner, Arizona, QB	1999	Eddie Brown, Albany, OS
1990	Art Schlichter, Detroit, QB	1995	George LaFrance, Tampa Bay, OS	2000	Connell Maynor, Orlando, QB
1991	Jay Gruden, Tampa Bay, QB	1996	Stevie Thomas, Tampa Bay, WR/LB	2001	Terrill Shaw, Grand Rapids, OS

College Basketball

Longtime Louisville head coach **Denny Crum** retired in 2001 after 30 seasons, 675 wins, six Final Fours and two NCAA titles.

Mission Accomplished

All-American Shane Battier finally gets his title after Duke marches through the NCAA tourney.

Chris Fowler
is the host of ESPN's College GameDay

College basketball has no Ray Bourques; legends who sustain individual excellence for decades, in pursuit of the single goal that matters to them most: a championship. Here, it is the coaches who endure, while too many of their stars' careers are only brief pit stops on the path to NBA riches.

College basketball players rarely bother to hang around long enough to create compelling public melodramas surrounding their personal quests for a national title. And it's even rarer that they make such an impact on the court and exhibit such unqualified class away from the game that otherwise neutral folks take a special interest in seeing the fitting completion of their legacy.

But then, Shane Battier was, indeed, very rare. If there could ever be a Bourque in college hoops—a guy who deserved nothing more than the sweet taste of his first title as his final minutes in uniform passed into history—it was Battier.

The most complete player and complete person to grace the game in years was finally completed on the first Monday in April, when Duke dispatched an Arizona bunch that believed destiny was riding in its bus to the Metrodome that night. Perhaps only the ardent anti-Dukies (and there were plenty around) could argue with the ending.

Battier arrived at Duke as a super-recruit, and made himself a superb college player, perfecting the game's details as an underclassman, while patiently deferring to flashier guys. He became the rarest of stars. Not only did he defend, block shots, take charges, rebound and pass, he actually relished doing the Blue Devils' blue-collar stuff. Oh yeah, he also hit big shots from all spots on the court.

And all his skills couldn't begin to measure the value of his toughness and leadership. Battier embodies such ideals that the question wasn't: Will he win Player of the Year? But what year will he win the Presidency? Then again, maybe Shane is too smart to be prez these days. Or too well behaved.

AP/Wide World Photos

The Blue Devils were led to the NCAA title by the threesome of **Jason Williams, Shane Battier** *and coach* **Mike Krzyzewski**.

Imagine having your jersey hoisted to the rafters at Cameron alongside those of former Duke greats Danny Ferry, Christian Laettner, Bobby Hurley, and Grant Hill, among others. Now imagine having to play the most important games of your life after receiving that honor, knowing that a single loss would leave a huge hollow spot in you forever.

A year earlier, Battier had nearly promised a championship to Mike Krzyzewski. The coach had been in agony, laid up from back surgery and still smarting from Duke's early dismissal from the 2000 tournament by Florida. The team's mission for 2000–01 had already been undermined by the early

defections of Will Avery and Corey Maggette to the pros the previous spring. Battier's commitment to return for his senior season and bust his butt for a national title was a milestone moment.

Not only did Battier return, he returned with a vengeance, as did sophomore point guard Jason Williams. The two of them set the pace all season, forcing turnovers on the defensive end and hitting big three-pointers on offense.

How fitting to find Maryland waiting in Minneapolis. The Terrapins had brought out the best in Duke all season, but had also bested the Devils, spoiling Battier's final Cameron performance. Months earlier, Duke's impossible rally

AP/Wide World Photos

Bob Knight had both guns blazing when he returned to college basketball with Texas Tech.

from 10 points down in the final minute at Maryland symbolized the find-a-way heroics that the Blue Devils believe their legacy is built upon. Remember the stunner over Tark's unbeatable UNLV gang in the 1991 Final Four? Not to mention the Laettner buzzer-beater against Kentucky?

So when a Maryland barrage built a 39–17 lead in the first half of the national semis, no Blue Devil panicked, least of all Battier. This time, Duke's comeback was slow and grinding, spawned from mental strength, not expert marksmanship. The Blue Devils remained sound and steady and in the end their stronger wills won out.

Bourque would have approved. Sure, Battier was still in Pampers when Bourque was turning pro. True, he played only four years, not 22.

But in college basketball, Battier accomplished all the things one can accomplish, carried himself immaculately and stayed the course.

Number 77, meet number 31.

And as it turned out, their 2000–01 seasons ended the only way they should have for both of them, with hugs, tears and trophies.

Dick Vitale's Ten Biggest Stories of the Year in College Basketball

10 Tennessee's Collapse—After opening the season 16–1, the Volunteers just fall apart down the stretch and it costs head coach Jerry Green his job.

9 Georgia on Our Minds and in Our Brackets—Coaches Lefty Driesell (Georgia State) and Jim Harrick (Univ. of Georgia) take their fourth schools to the NCAA tourney, tying Eddie Sutton's Record. Georgia State finished 29–5, losing the second round of the NCAA tourney.

8 In the Iz-zone—Michigan State and coach Tom Izzo lose their two stars, Mateen Cleaves and Morris Peterson, from their 2000 national champion squad yet still get back to the Final Four in 2001.

7 Stanford's Super Season—The Cardinal were #1 for a good part of the regular season, with a 28–2 record heading into the NCAA tournament. Their 28 wins include one over eventual national champion Duke, but Mike Montgomery's team later loses to Maryland in the Elite Eight.

6 The Surprise Teams—Boston College soars with the play of star guard Troy Bell and the coaching of Al Skinner. St. Joseph's wins with Phil Martelli and stand out Marvin O'Connor leading the charge, and Mississippi succeeds with coach Rod Barnes getting the job done.

5 Maryland Breaks Through—Gary Williams finally gets to a Final Four. Juan Dixon, Lonny Baxter, Terence Morris and company were 15–9 before coming on strong to make it to Minneapolis but squander a 22-point lead in the national semi-final against Duke.

4 Denny Crum's Farewell—It was a disappointing season at Louisville, leading to the return to college basketball for former Kentucky coach Rick Pitino.

3 Mike Davis for Bob Knight in Indiana—Talk about pressure, the Hoosiers make it to the Big Dance before being upset by Kent State. But Davis still goes from interim to full-time head coach.

2 For Bobbi—Arizona gets off to a slow start, going 8–5. The Wildcats overcome adversity with the passing of Lute Olson's wife, Bobbi, plus early suspensions to Loren Woods and Richard Jefferson. They win 20 of their last 23 games, but lose in the National Championship Game against Duke.

1 Duke wins it all—Shane Battier ends his collegiate career in style by cutting down the nets in Minneapolis. Jason Williams steps up in the tourney and Mike Dunleavy hits the key 3's in the title game. Coach K gets his third national title as Duke dominates the ACC again.

King Duke

This season Duke won its third NCAA title since 1991, continuing its recent domination in the tourney. Here's a look at the best all-time winning percentages in NCAA tournament history (minimum 30 games played).

School	W–L	Pct.
Duke	73–22	.768
UCLA	78–28	.736
Michigan St.	33–14	.702
Kentucky	87–37	.702

Note: The NCAA officially voided the tournament appearances of UCLA (5–1 in 1980 and 0–1 in 1999) and Kentucky (2–1 in 1988) and those totals are not included above.

Upsetting First Round

After a tame 2000, with only three numerical upsets in round one of the NCAA Tournament, it was a completely different story in 2001. In fact, the 2001 first round set a tournament record for most upsets. Here's a look at the most first-round upsets by seeding.

Tournament	Upsets
2001	13
1999	12
1989	12
1996	10

Finally Four

The Maryland Terrapins finally ended their long streak of NCAA tournament trips without making a Final Four appearance. Here's a look at the longest stretches of NCAA bids without making it all the way to the Final Four (entering the 2001 tournament).

School	Years
Missouri	18
Brigham Young	18
Maryland	17
Miami-Ohio	16
Utah State	13

Winningest Era

Duke not only capped its 2000–01 season with a third national championship, but the Blue Devils also set the Division I record for most wins in a four-year stretch, previously held by the University of Kentucky teams of the 1990's.

School (Years)	Wins
Duke (1998–2001)	133
Kentucky (1995–98)	132
Kentucky (1996–99)	132
Kentucky (1946–49)	130
Kentucky (1947–50)	127
UNLV (1984–87)	127

2000-2001 Season in Review

information please®
SPORTS ALMANAC

Final Regular Season AP Men's Top 25 Poll
Taken **before** start of NCAA tournament.

The sportswriters & broadcasters poll: first place votes in parentheses; records through Monday, March 12, 2001; total points (based on 25 for 1st, 24 for 2nd, etc.); record in NCAA tourney and team lost to; head coach (career years and record including 2001 postseason), and preseason ranking. Teams in **bold** type went on to reach NCAA Final Four.

		Mar. 12 Record	Points	NCAA Recap	Head Coach	Preseason Rank
1	**Duke** (45)	29-4	1701	6-0	Mike Krzyzewski (26 yrs: 606-223)	2
2	Stanford (23)	28-2	1674	3-1 (Maryland)	Mike Montgomery (23 yrs: 473-223)	4
3	**Michigan St.**	24-4	1537	4-1 (Arizona)	Tom Izzo (6 yrs: 148-53)	3
4	Illinois	24-7	1450	3-1 (Arizona)	Bill Self (8 yrs: 157-88)	8
5	**Arizona** (1)	23-7	1439	5-1 (Duke)	Lute Olson (28 yrs: 639-225)	1
6	North Carolina	25-6	1357	1-1 (Penn St.)	Matt Doherty (2 yrs: 48-22)	6
7	Boston College	26-4	1264	1-1 (USC)	Al Skinner (13 yrs: 197-187)	NR
8	Florida	23-6	1236	1-1 (Temple)	Billy Donovan (7 yrs: 137-76)	11
9	Kentucky	22-9	1133	2-1 (USC)	Tubby Smith (10 yrs: 234-95)	12
10	Iowa St.	25-5	1113	0-1 (Hampton)	Larry Eustachy (11 yrs: 231-111)	25
11	**Maryland**	21-10	1065	4-1 (Duke)	Gary Williams (23 yrs: 449-267)	5
12	Kansas	24-6	903	2-1 (Illinois)	Roy Williams (13 yrs: 355-89)	7
13	Oklahoma	26-6	885	0-1 (Indiana St.)	Kelvin Sampson (18 yrs: 332-217)	22
14	Mississippi	25-7	853	2-1 (Arizona)	Rod Barnes (3 yrs: 66-35)	NR
15	UCLA	21-8	753	2-1 (Duke)	Steve Lavin (5 yrs: 111-47)	17
16	Virginia	20-8	706	0-1 (Gonzaga)	Pete Gillen (15 yrs: 327-165)	24
17	Syracuse	24-8	605	1-1 (Kansas)	Jim Boeheim (25 yrs: 591-208)	NR
18	Texas	25-8	547	0-1 (Temple)	Rick Barnes (14 yrs: 270-165)	NR
19	Notre Dame	19-9	305	1-1 (Mississippi)	Mike Brey (6 yrs: 119-62)	15
20	Indiana	21-12	282	0-1 (Kent St.)	Mike Davis (1 yr: 21-13)	NR
21	Georgetown	23-7	263	2-1 (Maryland)	Craig Esherick (3 yrs: 52-33)	NR
22	St. Joseph's	25-6	206	1-1 (Stanford)	Phil Martelli (6 yrs: 119-78)	NR
23	Wake Forest	19-10	178	0-1 (Butler)	Dave Odom (15 yrs: 270-174)	20
24	Iowa	22-11	163	1-1 (Kentucky)	Steve Alford (10 yrs: 193-105)	NR
25	Wisconsin	18-10	145	0-1 (Georgia St.)	Dick Bennett (25 yrs: 455-266) & Brad Soderberg (1 yr: 16-10)	19

Others receiving votes: 26. **Ohio State** (20-10) 116 pts; 27. **Cincinnati** (23-9) 62; 28. **Arkansas** (20-10) 61; 29. **Gonzaga** (24-6) 59; 30. **Fresno St.** (25-6) 51; 31. **Tennessee** (22-10) 44; 32. **Georgia State** (28-4) and **Providence** (21-9) 43; 34. **Alabama** (22-10) 37, 35. **USC** (21-9) 21; 36. **Creighton** (24-7) 18; 37. **Charlotte** (21-10) 16; 38. **Hofstra** (26-4) 15; 39. **Georgia Tech** (17-12) 12; 40. **Temple** (21-12) 11; 41. **Penn State** (19-11) and **Western Kentucky** (24-6) 8; 43. **BYU** (24-8), **Oklahoma** (26-6), **Utah St.** (19-11) and **Southern Utah** (25-5) 6; 47. **Butler** (23-7), **Seton Hall** (16-14)and **Xavier** (21-7) 3; 50. **California** (20-10) 2; 51. **Hawaii** (17-13), **Holy Cross** (22-7), **Kent State** (23-9), **Richmond** (21-6) and **Southern Mississippi** (22-8) 1.

NCAA Men's Division I Tournament Seeds

	WEST		MIDWEST		SOUTH		EAST
1	Stanford (28-2)	1	Illinois (24-7)	1	Michigan St. (24-4)	1	Duke (29-4)
2	Iowa St. (25-5)	2	Arizona (23-7)	2	North Carolina (25-6)	2	Kentucky (22-9)
3	Maryland (21-10)	3	Mississippi (25-7)	3	Florida (23-6)	3	Boston College (26-4)
4	Indiana (21-12)	4	Kansas (24-6)	4	Oklahoma (26-6)	4	UCLA (21-8)
5	Cincinnati (23-9)	5	Syracuse (24-8)	5	Virginia (20-8)	5	Ohio St. (20-10)
6	Wisconsin (18-10)	6	Notre Dame (19-9)	6	Texas (25-8)	6	USC (21-9)
7	Arkansas (20-10)	7	Wake Forest (19-10)	7	Penn St. (19-11)	7	Iowa (22-11)
8	Georgia Tech (17-12)	8	Tennessee (22-10)	8	California (20-10)	8	Georgia (16-14)
9	St. Joseph's (25-6)	9	Charlotte (21-10)	9	Fresno St. (25-6)	9	Missouri (19-12)
10	Georgetown (23-7)	10	Butler (23-7)	10	Providence (21-9)	10	Creighton (24-7)
11	Georgia St. (28-4)	11	Xavier (21-7)	11	Temple (21-12)	11	Oklahoma St. (20-9)
12	BYU (24-8)	12	Hawaii (17-13)	12	Gonzaga (24-6)	12	Utah St. (27-5)
13	Kent St. (24-8)	13	CS-Northridge (22-9)	13	Indiana St. (21-11)	13	Hofstra (26-4)
14	George Mason (18-11)	14	Iona (22-10)	14	Western Ky. (24-6)	14	Southern Utah (25-5)
15	Hampton (24-6)	15	Eastern Ill. (24-9)	15	Princeton (16-10)	15	Holy Cross (22-7)
16	NC-Greensboro (19-11)	16	Northwestern St.* (18-12)	16	Alabama St. (22-8)	16	Monmouth (21-9)

*Northwestern St. defeated Winthrop, 71-67, in the NCAA Tournament play-in game for a berth in the field of 64.

2001 NCAA BASKETBALL MEN'S DIVISION I

EAST

1st ROUND March 15	2nd ROUND March 1	SWEET 16 March 22	ELITE EIGHT March 24
(1) Duke 95			
(16) Monmouth NJ 52	(1) Duke 94		
(8) Georgia 68			
(9) Missouri 70	(9) Missouri 81	(1) Duke 76	
(5) Ohio St 68			
(12) Utah St 77	(12) Utah St 50		(1) Duke 79
(4) UCLA 61		(4) UCLA 63	
(13) Hofstra 48	(4) UCLA 75		
(6) USC 69			
(11) Oklahoma St 54	(6) USC 74	(6) USC 80	
(3) Boston College 68			(6) USC 69
(14) Southern Utah 65	(6) Boston College 71		
(7) Iowa 56		(2) Kentucky 76	
(10) Creighton 72	(7) Iowa 79		
(2) Kentucky 72			
(15) Holy Cross 68	(2) Kentucky 92		

WEST

1st ROUND March 15	2nd ROUND March 1	SWEET 16 March 22	ELITE EIGHT March 24
(1) Stanford 89			
(16) N.C.Greensboro 60	(1) Stanford 90		
(8) Georgia Tech 62			
(9) St Joseph's 66	(9) St Joseph's 83	(1) Stanford 78	
(5) Cincinnati 84			
(12) BYU 59	(5) Cincinnati 66		(1) Stanford 73
(4) Indiana 73		(5) Cincinnati 65	
(13) Kent State 77	(13) Kent State 43		
(6) Wisconsin 49			
(11) Georgia St 50	(11) Georgia St 60	(3) Maryland 76	
(3) Maryland 83			(3) Maryland 87
(14) George Mason 80	(3) Maryland 79		
(7) Arkansas 61		(15) Hampton 66	
(10) Georgetown 63	(10) Georgetown 76		
(2) Iowa St 57			
(15) Hampton 58	(15) Hampton 57		

SOUTH

1st ROUND March 16	2nd ROUND March 18	SWEET 16 March 23	ELITE EIGHT March 25
(1) Michigan St 69			
(16) Alabama St 35	(1) Michigan St 81		
(8) California 70			
(9) Fresno St 82	(9) Fresno St 65	(1) Michigan St 77	
(5) Virginia 85			
(12) Gonzaga 86	(12) Gonzaga 85		(1) Michigan St 69
(4) Oklahoma 68		(12) Gonzaga 62	
(13) Indiana St 70	(13) Indiana St 68		
(6) Texas 65			
(11) Temple 79	(11) Temple 75	(11) Temple 84	
(3) Florida 69			(11) Temple 62
(14) Western KY 56	(3) Florida 54		
(7) Penn St 69		(2) Penn St 72	
(10) Providence 59	(7) Penn St 82		
(2) North Carolina 70			
(15) Princeton 48	(2) North Carolina 74		

Play-in Game to Midwest (16) seed

Northwestern St 71
Winthrop 67

MIDWEST

1st ROUND March 16	2nd ROUND March 18	SWEET 16 March 23	ELITE EIGHT March 25
(1) Illinois 96			
(16) Northwestern St 54	(1) Illinois 79		
(8) Tennessee 63			
(9) Charlotte 61	(9) Charlotte 61	(1) Illinois 80	
(5) Syracuse 79			
(12) Hawaii 69	(5) Syracuse 58		(1) Illinois 81
(4) Kansas 99		(4) Kansas 64	
(13) CS Northridge 75	(4) Kansas 87		
(6) Notre Dame 83			
(11) Xavier 71	(6) Notre Dame 56	(3) Mississippi 56	
(3) Mississippi 72			(2) Arizona 87
(14) Iona 70	(3) Mississippi 59		
(7) Wake Forest 83		(2) Arizona 66	
(10) Butler 79	(10) Butler 52		
(2) Arizona 101			
(15) Eastern Ill 76	(2) Arizona 73		

FINAL FOUR March 3

(1) Duke 95

(3) Maryland 84

(1) Michigan St 61

(2) Arizona 80

NATIONAL CHAMPIONSHIP

(1) Duke **82**

(2) Arizona 72

Hubert H. Humphrey Metrodome
Minneapolis, Minnesota
Monday, April 2, 2001

NCAA Men's Championship Game

63rd NCAA Division I Championship Game. **Date:** Monday, April 2, at the HHH Metrodome in Minneapolis. **Coaches:** Mike Krzyzewski of Duke and Lute Olson of Arizona. **Favorite:** Duke by 3½.
Attendance: 45,994; **Officials:** Scott Thornley, Frankie Bordeaux, Ed Corbett; **TV Rating:** 15.6/24 share (CBS).

Arizona 72

	Min	FG M-A	FT M-A	Pts	Reb O-T	A	PF
Michael Wright	28	5-9	0-1	10	4-11	0	4
Richard Jefferson	35	7-13	1-3	19	2-8	3	2
Loren Woods	37	8-15	6-8	22	4-11	1	4
Gilbert Arenas	34	4-17	2-3	10	2-4	4	1
Jason Gardner	40	2-11	3-4	7	1-3	2	2
Justin Wessel	2	0-0	0-0	0	0-0	0	0
Eugene Edgerson	8	0-0	0-0	0	0-1	0	4
Luke Walton	16	2-6	0-0	4	2-3	4	3
TOTALS	200	28-71	12-19	72	15-41	14	20

Three-point FG: 4-22 (Jefferson 4-8, Woods 0-1, Arenas 0-4, Gardner 0-8, Walton 0-1); **Team Rebounds:** 4; **Blocked Shots:** 7 (Woods 4, Wright 2, Jefferson); **Turnovers:** 9 (Jefferson 5, Arenas, Walton, Woods, Wright); **Steals:** 5 (Arenas, Gardner, Jefferson, Woods, Wright); **Percentages:** 2-Pt FG (.490), 3-Pt FG (.182), Total FG (.394), Free Throws (.632).

Duke 82

	Min	FG M-A	FT M-A	Pts	Reb O-T	A	PF
Shane Battier	40	7-14	3-6	18	4-11	6	1
Mike Dunleavy	32	8-17	0-1	32	2-3	0	3
Casey Sanders	10	0-1	0-0	0	0-2	1	1
Chris Duhon	39	3-5	2-3	9	1-4	6	2
Jason Williams	29	5-15	4-6	16	0-3	4	4
Carlos Boozer	30	5-9	2-3	12	1-12	1	3
Nate James	20	2-3	2-3	6	1-3	0	3
TOTALS	200	30-64	13-22	82	9-38	18	17

Three-point FG: 9-27 (Battier 1-5, Dunleavy 5-9, Duhon 1-1, Williams 2-11, James 0-1); **Team Rebounds:** 4; **Blocked Shots:** 5 (Battier 2, Boozer 2, James); **Turnovers:** 11 (Williams 6, Boozer 2, James 2, Duhon); **Steals:** 5 (Williams 3, James, Sanders); **Percentages:** 2-Pt FG (.568), 3-Pt FG (.333), Total FG (.469), Free Throws (.591).

Arizona (Pac-10)	33	39 —	**72**
Duke (ACC)	35	47 —	**82**

Final ESPN/USA Today Coaches' Poll

Taken **after** NCAA Tournament.

Voted on by a panel of 31 Division I head coaches following the NCAA tournament: first place votes in parentheses with total points (based on 25 for 1st, 24 for 2nd, etc.). Schools on major probation are ineligible to be ranked.

		W-L	Pts	Before NCAAs W-L	Rank
1	Duke (31)	35-4	775	29-4	1
2	Arizona	28-8	744	23-7	4
3	Michigan St.	28-5	697	24-4	3
4	Maryland	25-11	688	21-10	11
5	Stanford	31-3	642	28-2	2
6	Illinois	27-8	635	24-7	6
7	Kansas	26-7	483	24-6	12
8	Kentucky	24-10	461	22-9	10
9	Mississippi	27-8	455	25-7	13
10	North Carolina	26-7	427	25-6	5
11	Boston College	27-5	414	26-4	7
12	UCLA	23-9	386	21-8	18
13	Florida	24-7	380	23-6	8
14	USC	24-10	379	21-9	NR
15	Iowa St.	25-6	321	25-5	9
16	Temple	24-13	308	21-12	NR
17	Georgetown	25-8	256	23-7	20
18	Syracuse	25-9	216	24-8	16
19	Oklahoma	26-7	183	26-6	14
20	Gonzaga	26-7	179	24-6	NR
21	Virginia	20-9	171	20-8	15
22	Cincinnati	25-10	160	23-9	NR
23	Notre Dame	20-10	138	19-9	19
24	St. Joseph's	26-7	137	25-6	23
25	Penn St.	21-12	110	19-11	NR

Others receiving votes: 26. **Texas** (25-9, 71 pts); 27. **Indiana** (21-13, 39); 28. **Tulsa** (26-11, 38); 29. **Iowa** (23-12, 34); 30. **Wake Forest** (19-11, 31); 31. **Fresno State** (26-7, 30); 32. **Tennessee** (22-11, 15); 33. **Alabama** (25-11) and **Butler** (24-8, 12); 35. **Georgia State** (29-5), **Utah State** (28-6) and **Xavier** (21-8, 8); 38. **Missouri** (20-13) and **Ohio State** (20-11, 6); 40. **Charlotte** (22-11) and **Georgia Tech** (17-13, 3); 42. **Indiana State** (21-12, 2) and **Wisconsin** (18-11, 2); 44. **Kent State** (23-10) and **Richmond** (22-7, 1).

THE FINAL FOUR

HHH Metrodome in Minneapolis.
(Mar. 31-April 2).

Semifinal—Game One

Midwest Regional champ Arizona vs. South Regional champ Michigan State; Saturday, Mar. 31 (5:31 p.m. tipoff). **Coaches:** Lute Olson, Arizona and Tom Izzo, Michigan State. **Favorite:** Arizona by 1.

Arizona (Pac-10)	32	48—	**80**
Michigan State (Big Ten)	30	31—	**61**

High scorers— Jason Gardner, Arizona (21) and Andre Hutson, Michigan State (20). **Att**—45,406; **TV rating**—9.1/20 share (CBS).

Semifinal—Game Two

West Regional champion Maryland vs. East Regional champ Duke; Saturday, Mar. 31 (8:12 p.m. tipoff). **Coaches:** Gary Williams, Maryland and Mike Krzyzewski, Duke. **Favorite:** Duke by 4½.

Maryland (ACC)	49	35—	**84**
Duke (ACC)	38	57—	**95**

High scorers— Juan Dixon, Maryland (19) and Shane Battier, Duke (25); **Att**—45,406; **TV rating**—11.6/21 share (CBS).

Most Outstanding Player

Shane Battier, senior forward, Duke. SEMIFINAL—40 minutes, 25 points, 8 rebounds, 4 blocks, 2 steals; FINAL—40 minutes, 18 points, 11 rebounds, 6 assists, 2 blocks.

All-Final Four Team

Battier, guard/forward Mike Dunleavy and guard Jason Williams of Duke; center Loren Woods and forward Richard Jefferson of Arizona.

NCAA Finalists' Tournament and Season Statistics

At least 10 games played during the overall season.

Arizona (28-8)

| | NCAA Tournament | | | | | Overall Season | | | | | |
| | | | —Per Game— | | | | | | —Per Game— | | |
	Gm	FG%	TPts	Pts	Reb	Ast	Gm	FG%	TPts	Pts	Reb	Ast
Loren Woods............	6	52.4	96	16.0	7.7	1.7	29	50.4	384	13.2	6.5	2.1
Gilbert Arenas..........	6	45.2	87	14.5	4.3	3.0	36	47.9	582	16.2	3.6	2.3
Richard Jefferson........	6	50.0	81	13.5	6.3	2.0	35	47.9	397	11.3	5.4	2.7
Jason Gardner..........	6	37.0	75	12.5	2.7	2.5	36	38.1	393	10.9	3.0	4.1
Michael Wright.........	6	61.4	68	11.3	6.0	0.2	36	59.4	561	15.6	7.8	0.3
Eugene Edgerson........	6	71.4	31	5.2	4.8	0.2	34	57.6	157	4.6	4.0	0.2
Luke Walton............	6	36.0	27	4.5	3.8	2.5	36	42.0	198	5.5	3.9	3.2
Lamont Frazier.........	4	57.1	9	2.2	0.5	0.2	32	37.7	77	2.4	1.3	0.9
Travis Hanour..........	2	50.0	3	1.5	1.0	0.0	20	33.9	61	3.1	1.4	0.5
Justin Wessel...........	5	16.7	2	0.4	0.6	0.2	35	46.7	92	2.6	1.6	0.5
ARIZONA...............	6	48.3	479	79.8	40.3	12.5	36	47.6	2926	81.3	39.8	16.3
OPPONENTS............	6	39.7	408	68.0	33.8	13.5	36	39.7	2386	66.3	33.2	13.1

Three-pointers: NCAA TOURNAMENT—Gardner (8-34), Jefferson (8-20), Arenas (5-19), Hanour (1-2), Walton (1-4), Team (23-80 for .288 pct.); OVERALL—Gardner (76-207), Arenas (69-166), Jefferson (31-90), Walton (9-41), Hanour (5-27), Woods (1-3), Wessel (1-3), Schwertley (1-1), Ash (0-1), Ranne (0-2), Wright (0-3), Team (193-544 for .355 pct.).

Duke (35-4)

| | NCAA Tournament | | | | | Overall Season | | | | | |
| | | | —Per Game— | | | | | | —Per Game— | | |
	Gm	FG%	TPts	Pts	Reb	Ast	Gm	FG%	TPts	Pts	Reb	Ast
Jason Williams.........	6	46.0	154	25.7	3.3	5.2	39	47.3	841	21.6	3.3	6.1
Shane Battier..........	6	47.7	135	22.5	10.2	2.3	39	47.1	778	19.9	7.3	1.8
Mike Dunleavy..........	6	46.7	72	12.0	4.3	1.7	39	47.4	493	12.6	5.7	2.6
Carlos Boozer..........	4	61.9	34	8.5	6.5	0.5	32	60.4	425	13.3	6.5	2.8
Chris Duhon...........	6	40.0	49	8.2	3.5	4.8	39	42.4	280	7.2	3.2	4.5
Nate James...........	6	55.9	44	7.3	5.3	1.0	39	49.4	480	12.3	5.2	1.1
Matt Christensen.......	1	75.0	6	6.0	7.0	0.0	30	58.6	48	1.6	2.3	0.1
Casey Sanders........	6	60.0	16	2.7	2.5	0.2	35	46.7	87	2.5	1.8	0.2
J.D. Simpson..........	2	40.0	5	2.5	0.0	0.0	22	33.3	20	0.9	0.5	0.2
Reggie Love...........	3	100.0	6	2.0	1.3	0.0	21	52.9	28	1.3	1.6	0.1
Ryan Caldbeck.........	1	0.0	0	0.0	1.0	2.0	13	0.0	1	0.1	0.5	0.2
DUKE.................	6	47.9	521	86.8	39.2	16.2	39	48.1	3538	90.7	38.6	18.0
OPPONENTS............	6	39.9	421	70.2	38.3	12.2	39	41.6	2750	70.5	37.5	13.3

Three-pointers: NCAA TOURNAMENT— Williams (23-66), Battier (15-42), Dunleavy (11-28), Duhon (7-18), James (3-13), Simpson (1-3), Caldbeck (0-2), Borman (0-2), Buckner (0-1), Team (60-175 for .343 pct.); OVERALL— Williams (132-309), Battier (124-296), Dunleavy (57-153), Duhon (44-122), James (43-137), Simpson (3-10), Love (0-1), Buckner (0-3), Caldbeck (0-6), Team (407-1057 for .385 pct.).

Arizona's Schedule

Reg. Season

(23-7)

W	Chaminade 97-57
W	Dayton 76-59
W	Illinois 79-76
L	Purdue..........69-72
W	Gonzaga 101-87
W	St. Mary's-CA ...101-41
L	at UConn 69-71
L	Illinois 73-81
W	Louisiana St...... .88-75
W	Butler...........72-60
L	Mississippi St...74-75
W	California 78-75
L	Stanford 76-85
W	Washington St. ...84-51
W	at Washington ...89-64
W	USC...........71-58
W	UCLA...........88-63
W	Arizona St......86-75
W	Texas..........80-52

L	at Oregon........67-79
W	at Oregon St......68-41
W	Washington 82-62
W	Washington St...86-51
L	at UCLA (OT).....77-79
W	at USC 105-61
W	at Arizona St......88-58
W	Oregon St......65-54
W	Oregon.........104-65
W	at Stanford 76-75
W	at California......78-76

NCAA Tourney

(5-1)

W	E. Illinois.........101-76
W	Butler..........73-52
W	Mississippi 66-56
W	Illinois 87-81
W	Michigan St......80-61
L	Duke 72-82

Duke's Schedule

Reg. Season

(26-4)

W	Princeton.........87-50
W	Villanova 98-85
W	Texas 95-69
W	Temple..........63-61
W	Army 91-48
W	Illinois 78-77
W	Temple..........93-68
W	Davidson 102-60
W	Michigan 104-61
W	Portland 97-64
L	Stanford 83-84
W	North Carolina	
	A&T...........108-73
W	at Florida St......99-72
W	Clemson........115-74
W	at N.C. State 84-78
W	Virginia 103-61
W	Boston College....97-75
W	at Georgia Tech...98-77
W	Wake Forest.....85-62
W	at Maryland (OT) .98-96
L	North Carolina ...83-85

W	Florida St......100-58
W	at Clemson......81-64
W	N.C. State 101-75
L	at Virginia 89-91
W	at St. John's 91-59
W	Georgia Tech.....98-54
W	at Wake Forest ...82-80
L	Maryland........80-91
W	at North Carolina .95-81

ACC Tourney

(3-0)

W	N.C. State 76-61
W	Maryland........84-82
W	North Carolina ...79-53

NCAA Tourney

(6-0)

W	Monmouth 95-52
W	Missouri 94-81
W	UCLA...........76-63
W	USC............79-69
W	Maryland........95-84
W	Arizona.........82-72

Final NCAA Men's Division I Standings

Conference records include regular season games only. Overall records include all postseason tournament games.

America East Conference

Team	Conference			Overall		
	W	L	Pct	W	L	Pct
*Hofstra	16	2	.889	26	5	.839
Delaware	14	4	.778	20	10	.667
Drexel	12	6	.667	15	12	.556
Maine	10	8	.556	18	11	.621
Boston University	9	9	.500	14	14	.500
Northeastern	8	10	.444	10	19	.345
Vermont	7	11	.389	12	17	.414
Towson	7	11	.389	12	17	.414
New Hampshire	6	12	.333	7	21	.250
Hartford	1	17	.056	4	24	.143

Conf. Tourney Final: Hofstra 68, Delaware 54.
*NCAA Tourney (0-1): Hofstra (0-1).

Atlantic Coast Conference

Team	Conference			Overall		
	W	L	Pct	W	L	Pct
*Duke	13	3	.813	35	4	.897
*North Carolina	13	3	.813	26	7	.788
*Maryland	10	6	.625	25	11	.694
*Virginia	9	7	.563	20	9	.690
*Wake Forest	8	8	.500	19	11	.633
*Georgia Tech	8	8	.500	17	13	.567
N.C. State	5	11	.313	13	16	.448
Florida St	4	12	.250	9	21	.300
Clemson	2	14	.125	12	19	.387

Conf. Tourney Final: Duke 79, North Carolina 53.
*NCAA Tourney (11-5): North Carolina (1-1), Duke (6-0), Maryland (4-1), Virginia (0-1), Wake Forest (0-1), Georgia Tech (0-1).

Atlantic 10 Conference

Team	Conference			Overall		
	W	L	Pct	W	L	Pct
*St. Joseph's	14	2	.975	26	7	.788
*Xavier-OH	12	4	.750	21	8	.724
*Temple	12	4	.750	24	13	.649
Massachusetts	11	5	.688	15	15	.500
†St. Bonaventure	9	7	.563	18	12	.600
†Dayton	9	7	.563	21	13	.618
Geo. Washington	6	10	.375	14	18	.438
La Salle	5	11	.313	12	17	.414
Fordham	4	12	.250	12	17	.414
Duquesne	3	13	.188	9	21	.300
Rhode Island	3	13	.188	7	23	.233

Note: There are 11 teams in the Atlantic 10.
Conf. Tourney Final: Temple 76, UMass 65.
*NCAA Tourney (4-3): Temple (3-1), St. Joseph's (1-1), Xavier (0-1).
†NIT (2-2): Dayton (2-1), St. Bonaventure (0-1).

Big East Conference

East	Conference			Overall		
	W	L	Pct	W	L	Pct
*Boston College	13	3	.813	27	5	.844
*Providence	11	5	.688	21	10	.677
St. John's	8	8	.500	14	15	.483
†Miami-FL	8	8	.500	16	13	.552
†Villanova	8	8	.500	18	13	.581
†Connecticut	8	8	.500	20	12	.625
Virginia Tech	2	14	.125	8	19	.296
West	**W**	**L**	**Pct**	**W**	**L**	**Pct**
*Notre Dame	11	5	.688	20	10	.667
*Georgetown	10	6	.625	25	8	.758
*Syracuse	10	6	.625	25	9	.735
†West Virginia	8	8	.500	17	12	.586
†Pittsburgh	7	9	.438	19	14	.576
†Seton Hall	5	11	.313	16	15	.516
Rutgers	3	13	.188	11	16	.407

Conf. Tourney Final: Boston College 79, Pittsburgh 57.
*NCAA Tourney (5-5): Georgetown (2-1), Boston College (1-1), Syracuse (1-1), Notre Dame (1-1), Providence (0-1).
†NIT (2-6): UConn (1-1), Pittsburgh (1-1), Miami-FL (0-1), Seton Hall (0-1), West Virginia (0-1), Villanova (0-1).

Big Sky Conference

Team	Conference			Overall		
	W	L	Pct	W	L	Pct
*Cal St. Northridge	13	3	.812	20	9	.690
Eastern Washington	11	5	.688	16	10	.615
Idaho St	10	6	.625	14	13	.519
Montana St	8	8	.500	16	13	.552
Weber St	8	8	.500	14	13	.519
Northern Arizona	8	8	.500	14	13	.519
Montana	6	10	.375	11	16	.407
Portland St.	6	10	.375	9	18	.333
Sacramento St.	2	14	.125	5	22	.185

Conf. Tourney Final: Cal St. Northridge 73, Eastern Washington 58.
*NCAA Tourney (0-1): Cal St. Northridge (0-1).

Big South Conference

Team	Conference			Overall		
	W	L	Pct	W	L	Pct
Radford	12	2	.857	19	10	.655
*Winthrop	11	3	.786	18	12	.600
NC-Asheville	9	5	.643	15	13	.536
Charleston Southern	6	8	.429	10	19	.345
Coastal Carolina	6	8	.429	8	20	.286
Liberty	5	9	.357	13	15	.464
Elon	4	10	.286	9	20	.310
High Point	3	11	.214	8	20	.286

Conf. Tourney Final: Winthrop 67, Radford 65.
*NCAA Tourney (0-1): Winthrop (0-1).

Best in Show

Conferences with at least two wins in the 2001 NCAA's; number of tournament teams in parentheses.

	W-L	Pct		W-L	Pct
Pac-10 (5)	13-5	.722	Atlantic 10 (3)	4-3	.571
ACC (6)	11-5	.688	Big East (5)	5-5	.500
West Coast (1)	2-1	.667	SEC (6)	5-6	.455
CUSA (2)	3-2	.600	Big 12 (6)	3-6	.333
Big Ten (7)	10-7	.588			

Final NCAA Men's Division I Standings (Cont.)

Big Ten Conference

Team	Conference			Overall		
	W	L	Pct	W	L	Pct
*Michigan St	13	3	.813	28	5	.848
*Illinois	13	3	.813	27	8	.771
*Ohio St	11	5	.688	20	11	.645
*Indiana	10	6	.625	21	13	.618
*Wisconsin	9	7	.563	18	11	.621
*Iowa	7	9	.438	23	12	.657
*Penn St	7	9	.438	21	12	.636
†Purdue	6	10	.375	17	15	.531
†Minnesota	5	11	.313	18	14	.562
Michigan	4	12	.250	10	18	.357
Northwestern	3	13	.188	11	19	.367

Note: There are 11 teams in the Big Ten.
Conf. Tourney Final: Iowa 63, Indiana 61.
*NCAA Tourney (10-7): Michigan St. (4-1), Illinois (3-1), Penn St. (2-1), Iowa (1-1), Ohio St. (0-1), Wisconsin (0-1), Indiana (0-1).
†NIT (3-2): Purdue (2-1), Minnesota (1-1).

Big 12 Conference

Team	Conference			Overall		
	W	L	Pct	W	L	Pct
*Iowa St	13	3	.813	25	6	.806
*Kansas	12	4	.750	26	7	.788
*Oklahoma	12	4	.750	26	7	.788
*Texas	12	4	.750	25	9	.735
*Oklahoma St	10	6	.625	20	10	.667
*Missouri	9	7	.563	20	13	.606
Nebraska	7	9	.438	14	16	.467
†Baylor	6	10	.375	19	12	.613
Colorado	5	11	.313	15	15	.500
Kansas St	4	12	.250	11	18	.379
Texas A&M	3	13	.188	10	20	.333
Texas Tech	3	13	.188	9	19	.321

Conf. Tourney Final: Oklahoma 54, Texas 45.
*NCAA Tourney (3-6): Kansas (2-1), Missouri (1-1), Iowa St. (0-1), Oklahoma St. (0-1), Texas (0-1), Oklahoma (0-1).
†NIT (0-1): Baylor (0-1).

Big West Conference

Team	Conference			Overall		
	W	L	Pct	W	L	Pct
†UC-Irvine	15	1	.938	25	5	.833
*Utah St	13	3	.813	28	6	.824
Long Beach St	10	6	.625	18	13	.581
UC-Santa Barbara	9	7	.563	13	15	.464
Pacific	8	8	.500	18	12	.600
Boise St	8	8	.500	17	14	.548
Cal St.-Fullerton	3	13	.188	5	23	.179
Cal Poly-SLO	3	13	.188	9	19	.321
Idaho	3	13	.188	6	21	.222

Conf. Tourney Final: Utah State 50, Pacific 38.
*NCAA Tourney (1-1): Utah State (1-1).
†NIT (0-1): UC-Irvine (0-1).

Colonial Athletic Association

Team	Conference			Overall		
	W	L	Pct	W	L	Pct
†Richmond	12	4	.750	22	7	.759
†NC-Wilmington	11	5	.688	19	11	.633
*George Mason	11	5	.688	18	12	.600
Va. Commonwealth	9	7	.562	16	14	.533
William & Mary	7	9	.438	17	13	.393
Old Dominion	7	9	.438	13	18	.419
James Madison	6	10	.375	12	17	.414
East Carolina	6	10	.375	14	14	.500
American	3	13	.188	7	20	.259

Conf. Tourney Final: George Mason 35, NC-Wilmington 33.
*NCAA Tourney (0-1): George Mason (0-1).
†NIT (1-2): NC-Wilmington (0-1), Richmond (1-1).

Conference USA

American Division	Conference			Overall		
	W	L	Pct	W	L	Pct
*Cincinnati	11	5	.688	25	10	.714
*Charlotte	10	6	.625	22	11	.667
Marquette	9	7	.563	15	14	.517
Saint Louis	8	8	.500	17	14	.548
Louisville	8	8	.500	12	19	.387
DePaul	4	12	.250	12	18	.400

National Division	Conference			Overall		
	W	L	Pct	W	L	Pct
†So. Mississippi	11	5	.688	22	9	.710
†Memphis	10	6	.625	19	14	.576
So. Florida	9	7	.563	18	13	.581
Ala-Birmingham	8	8	.500	17	14	.548
Houston	6	10	.375	9	20	.310
Tulane	2	14	.125	9	21	.300

Conf. Tourney Final: Charlotte 80, Cincinnati 72.
*NCAA Tourney (3-2): Cincinnati (2-1), Charlotte (1-1).
†NIT (3-2): Memphis (3-1), So. Mississippi (0-1).

Ivy League

Team	Conference			Overall		
	W	L	Pct	W	L	Pct
*Princeton	11	3	.786	16	11	.593
Brown	9	5	.643	15	12	.556
Pennsylvania	9	5	.643	12	17	.414
Harvard	7	7	.500	14	12	.538
Columbia	7	7	.500	12	15	.444
Yale	7	7	.500	10	17	.370
Dartmouth	3	11	.214	8	19	.296
Cornell	3	11	.214	7	20	.259

Conf. Tourney Final: Ivy League has no tournament.
*NCAA Tourney (0-1): Princeton (0-1).

Metro Atlantic Athletic Conference

Team	Conference			Overall		
	W	L	Pct	W	L	Pct
*Iona	12	6	.667	22	11	.667
Siena	12	6	.667	20	11	.645
Marist	11	7	.611	17	13	.567
Rider	11	7	.611	16	12	.571
Niagara	12	6	.667	15	13	.536
Manhattan	11	7	.611	14	15	.483
Canisius	9	9	.500	20	11	.645
Fairfield	8	10	.444	12	16	.414
Loyola	2	16	.111	6	23	.207
St. Peter's	2	16	.111	4	24	.143

Conf. Tourney Final: Iona 74, Canisius 67.
*NCAA Tourney (0-1): Iona (0-1).

Mid-American Conference

East	Conference			Overall		
	W	L	Pct	W	L	Pct
*Kent St.	13	5	.722	24	10	.706
Marshall	12	6	.667	18	9	.667
Ohio	12	6	.667	19	11	.633
Bowling Green	10	8	.556	15	14	.517
Miami-OH	10	8	.556	17	16	.515
Akron	9	9	.500	12	16	.429
Buffalo	2	16	.111	4	24	.143

West	Conference			Overall		
	W	L	Pct	W	L	Pct
Central Mich	14	4	.778	20	8	.714
†Toledo	12	6	.667	22	11	.667
Ball St.	11	7	.611	18	12	.600
Western Mich	7	11	.389	7	21	.250
N. Illinois	4	14	.222	5	23	.179
Eastern Mich	1	17	.056	3	25	.107

Conf. Tourney Final: Kent State 67, Miami-OH 61.
*NCAA Tourney (1-1): Kent State (1-1).
†NIT (1-1): Toledo (1-1).

Mid-Continent Conference

Team	Conference			Overall		
	W	L	Pct	W	L	Pct
Southern Utah	13	3	.813	25	6	.806
*Valparaiso	13	3	.813	24	8	.750
Youngstown St.	11	5	.688	19	11	.633
Missouri-KC	9	7	.563	14	16	.467
Oakland	8	8	.500	12	16	.429
Indiana-Purdue	6	10	.375	11	18	.379
Oral Roberts	5	11	.313	10	19	.345
Western Illinois	5	11	.313	5	23	.179
Chicago St.	2	14	.125	5	23	.179

Conf. Tourney Final: Southern Utah 62, Valparaiso 59.
*NCAA Tourney (0-1): Southern Utah (0-1).
Note: Oakland was a provisional member of the Mid-Continent Conference in 2000-01 and not eligible for the conference championship.

Mid-Eastern Athletic Conference

Team	Conference			Overall		
	W	L	Pct	W	L	Pct
*Hampton	14	4	.778	24	6	.800
S.C. State	14	4	.778	19	13	.594
Delaware St.	11	7	.611	13	15	.464
Norfolk St.	11	7	.611	12	17	.414
Coppin St.	11	8	.579	13	15	.464
MD-Eastern Shore	10	8	.556	12	16	.429
N. Carolina A&T	8	10	.444	12	16	.429
Howard	8	10	.444	10	18	.357
Bethune-Cookman	5	13	.278	10	19	.345
Florida A&M	4	14	.222	6	22	.214
Morgan St.	4	15	.211	6	23	.207

Conf. Tourney Final: Hampton 70, S.C. State 58.
*NCAA Tourney (1-1): Hampton (1-1).

Midwestern Collegiate Conference

Team	Conference			Overall		
	W	L	Pct	W	L	Pct
*Butler	11	3	.786	24	8	.750
†Detroit	10	4	.714	25	12	.676
Cleveland St.	9	5	.643	19	13	.594
Wright St.	8	6	.571	18	11	.621
WI-Milwaukee	7	7	.500	15	13	.536
Illinois-Chicago	5	9	.357	11	17	.393
WI-Green Bay	4	10	.286	11	17	.393
Loyola-IL	2	12	.143	7	21	.250

Conf. Tourney Final: Butler 53, Detroit 38.
*NCAA Tourney (1-1): Butler (1-1).
†NIT Tourney (3-1): Detroit (3-1).

Missouri Valley Conference

Team	Conference			Overall		
	W	L	Pct	W	L	Pct
*Creighton	14	4	.778	24	8	.750
†Illinois St.	12	6	.667	21	9	.700
†Bradley	12	6	.667	19	12	.613
*Indiana St.	10	8	.556	22	12	.647
Southern Illinois	10	8	.556	16	14	.533
Evansville	9	9	.500	14	16	.467
SW Missouri St.	8	10	.444	13	16	.448
Drake	8	10	.444	12	16	.429
Wichita St.	4	14	.222	9	19	.321
Northern Iowa	3	15	.167	7	24	.226

Conf. Tourney Final: Indiana St. 69, Bradley 63.
*NCAA Tourney (1-2): Indiana St. (1-1), Creighton (0-1).
†NIT (0-2): Bradley (0-1), Illinois St. (0-1).

Mountain West Conference

Team	Conference			Overall		
	W	L	Pct	W	L	Pct
*Brigham Young	10	4	.714	24	9	.727
†Wyoming	10	4	.714	20	10	.667
†Utah	10	4	.714	19	12	.613
UNLV	7	7	.500	16	13	.552
†New Mexico	6	8	.429	21	13	.618
Colorado St.	6	8	.429	15	13	.536
San Diego St.	4	10	.286	14	14	.500
Air Force	3	11	.214	8	21	.276

Conf. Tourney Final: Brigham Young 69, New Mexico 65.
*NCAA Tourney (0-1): Brigham Young (0-1).
†NIT (2-3): New Mexico (2-1), Wyoming (0-1), Utah (0-1).

Northeast Conference

Team	Conference			Overall		
	W	L	Pct	W	L	Pct
St. Francis-NY	16	4	.800	18	11	.621
*Monmouth	15	5	.750	21	10	.677
MD-Baltimore County	13	7	.650	18	11	.621
LIU Brooklyn	12	8	.600	12	16	.429
Wagner	11	9	.550	16	13	.552
Central Connecticut St.	11	9	.550	14	14	.500
Fairleigh Dickinson	10	10	.500	13	15	.464
St. Francis-PA	9	11	.450	9	18	.333
Mt. St. Mary's	7	13	.350	7	21	.250
Robert Morris	7	19	.350	7	22	.241
Sacred Heart	6	14	.300	7	21	.250
Quinnipiac	3	17	.150	6	21	.222

Conf. Tourney Final: Monmouth 67, St. Francis-NY 64.
*NCAA Tourney (0-1): Monmouth (0-1).

Ohio Valley Conference

Team	Conference			Overall		
	W	L	Pct	W	L	Pct
Tennessee Tech	13	3	.813	20	9	.690
*Eastern Illinois	11	5	.688	21	10	.677
Murray St.	11	5	.688	17	12	.586
Austin Peay	10	6	.625	22	10	.688
SE Missouri St	8	8	.500	18	12	.600
Tennessee St.	7	9	.438	10	19	.345
Morehead St	6	10	.375	12	16	.429
Tennessee-Martin	5	11	.313	10	18	.357
Eastern Kentucky	1	15	.063	7	19	.269

Conf. Tourney Final: Eastern Illinois 84, Austin Peay 83.
*NCAA Tourney (0-1): Eastern Illinois (0-1).

Final NCAA Men's Division I Standings (Cont.)

Pacific-10 Conference

Team	Conference W	L	Pct	Overall W	L	Pct
*Stanford	16	2	.889	31	3	.912
*Arizona	15	3	.833	28	8	.778
*UCLA	14	4	.778	23	9	.719
*California	11	7	.611	20	11	.645
*USC	11	7	.611	24	10	.706
Arizona St	5	13	.278	13	16	.448
Washington St	5	13	.278	12	16	.429
Oregon	5	13	.278	14	14	.500
Oregon St	4	14	.222	10	20	.333
Washington	4	14	.222	10	20	.333

Conf. Tourney Final: Pac-10 has no tournament.

***NCAA Tourney (13-5):** Arizona (5-1), Stanford (3-1), USC (3-1), UCLA (2-1), California (0-1).

Patriot League

Team	Conference W	L	Pct	Overall W	L	Pct
*Holy Cross	10	2	.833	22	8	.733
Navy	9	3	.750	19	12	.613
Colgate	6	6	.500	13	15	.464
Lehigh	6	6	.500	13	16	.448
Lafayette	4	8	.333	12	16	.429
Bucknell	4	8	.333	14	15	.483
Army	3	9	.250	9	19	.321

Conf. Tourney Final: Holy Cross 68, Navy 64 (OT).

***NCAA Tourney (0-1):** Holy Cross (0-1).

Southeastern Conference

Eastern Div.	Conference W	L	Pct	Overall W	L	Pct
*Kentucky	12	4	.750	24	10	.706
*Florida	12	4	.750	24	7	.774
*Georgia	9	7	.563	16	15	.516
*Tennessee	8	8	.500	22	11	.667
†South Carolina	6	10	.375	15	15	.500
Vanderbilt	4	12	.250	15	15	.500

Western Div.	Conference W	L	Pct	Overall W	L	Pct
*Mississippi	11	5	.688	27	8	.771
*Arkansas	10	6	.625	20	11	.645
†Alabama	8	8	.500	25	11	.694
†Mississippi St	7	9	.438	18	13	.581
†Auburn	7	9	.438	18	14	.563
LSU	2	14	.125	13	16	.448

Conf. Tourney Final: Kentucky 77, Mississippi 55.

***NCAA Tourney (5-6):** Kentucky (2-1), Mississippi (2-1), Florida (1-1), Arkansas (0-1), Georgia (0-1), Tennessee (0-1).

†**NIT (7-4):** Alabama (4-1), Mississippi St. (2-1), Auburn (1-1), South Carolina (0-1).

Southern Conference

North Div.	Conference W	L	Pct	Overall W	L	Pct
East Tennessee St	13	3	.812	18	10	.643
*NC-Greensboro	10	6	.625	19	11	.633
Davidson	7	9	.438	15	17	.469
Appalachian St	7	9	.438	11	20	.355
Virginia Military	5	11	.312	9	19	.321
W. Carolina	3	13	.188	6	25	.194

South Div.	Conference W	L	Pct	Overall W	L	Pct
College of Charleston	12	4	.750	22	7	.759
The Citadel	9	7	.562	16	12	.571
Chattanooga	9	7	.562	17	13	.567
Georgia Southern	9	7	.562	15	15	.500
Wofford	7	9	.438	12	16	.429
Furman	5	11	.312	10	16	.385

Conf. Tourney Final: NC-Greensboro 67, Chattanooga 66.

***NCAA Tourney (0-1):** NC-Greensboro (0-1).

Southland Conference

Team	Conference W	L	Pct	Overall W	L	Pct
†McNeese St	17	3	.850	22	9	.710
Nicholls St	12	8	.600	14	14	.500
Texas-San Antonio	12	8	.600	14	15	.483
*Northwestern St	11	9	.550	19	13	.594
Sam Houston St	11	9	.550	16	13	.552
Texas-Arlington	11	9	.550	13	15	.464
SW Texas St	10	10	.500	13	15	.464
Louisiana-Monroe	8	12	.400	11	17	.393
Lamar	7	13	.350	9	18	.333
Stephen F. Austin	6	14	.300	9	17	.346
SE Louisiana	5	15	.250	8	21	.276

Conf. Tourney Final: Northwestern St. 72, McNeese St. 71.

***NCAA Tourney (1-1):** Northwestern St. (1-1).

†**NIT (0-1):** McNeese St. (0-1).

Southwestern Athletic Conference

Team	Conference W	L	Pct	Overall W	L	Pct
*Alabama St	15	3	.833	22	9	.710
Miss. Valley St	14	4	.778	18	9	.667
Alabama A&M	13	5	.722	17	11	.607
Alcorn St	13	5	.722	15	15	.500
Southern	8	10	.444	11	16	.407
Grambling	8	10	.444	8	18	.308
Jackson St	7	11	.389	7	23	.233
Texas Southern	5	13	.278	7	22	.241
Prairie View A&M	5	13	.278	6	22	.214
Ark-Pine Bluff	2	16	.111	2	25	.074

Conf. Tourney Final: Alabama St. 64, Alcorn St. 52.

***NCAA Tourney (0-1):** Alabama St. (0-1).

Sun Belt Conference

East	Conference W	L	Pct	Overall W	L	Pct
*Western Kentucky	14	2	.875	24	7	.774
Arkansas St	10	6	.625	17	13	.567
Louisiana Tech	10	6	.625	17	12	.586
Ark-Little Rock	9	7	.563	18	11	.621
Florida International	5	11	.313	8	21	.276
Middle Tennessee	1	15	.063	5	22	.185

West	Conference W	L	Pct	Overall W	L	Pct
†South Alabama	11	5	.688	22	11	.667
Louisiana-Lafayette	10	6	.625	16	13	.552
New Mexico St	10	6	.625	14	14	.500
New Orleans	10	6	.625	17	12	.586
Denver	5	11	.313	10	18	.357
North Texas	1	15	.063	4	24	.143

Conf. Tourney Final: Western Kentucky 64, South Alabama 54.

***NCAA Tourney (0-1):** Western Kentucky (0-1).

†**NIT (0-1):** South Alabama (0-1).

Trans America Athletic Conference

Team	Conference			Overall		
	W	L	Pct	W	L	Pct
*Georgia St.	16	2	.889	29	5	.853
Troy St.	12	6	.667	19	12	.613
Stetson	11	7	.611	17	12	.586
Jacksonville	11	7	.611	18	10	.543
Samford	11	7	.611	15	14	.517
Mercer	10	8	.556	13	15	.464
Jacksonville St.	6	12	.333	9	19	.321
Campbell	5	13	.278	7	21	.250
Florida Atlantic	5	13	.278	7	24	.226
Central Florida	3	15	.167	8	23	.258

Conf. Tourney Final: Georgia St. 79, Troy St. 55.
***NCAA Tourney (1-1):** Georgia St. (1-1).

West Coast Conference

Team	Conference			Overall		
	W	L	Pct	W	L	Pct
*Gonzaga	13	1	.929	26	7	.788
†Pepperdine	12	2	.857	22	9	.710
Santa Clara	10	4	.714	20	12	.625
San Diego	7	7	.500	15	13	.536
San Francisco	5	9	.357	12	18	.400
Loyola Marymount	5	9	.357	9	19	.321
Portland	4	10	.286	11	17	.393
St. Mary's-CA	0	14	.000	2	27	.069

Conf. Tourney Final: Gonzaga 80, Santa Clara 77.
***NCAA Tourney (2-1):** Gonzaga (2-1).
†NIT Tourney (1-1): Pepperdine (1-1).

Western Athletic Conference

Team	Conference			Overall		
	W	L	Pct	W	L	Pct
*Fresno St.	14	4	.778	26	7	.788
†Tulsa	12	7	.632	25	11	.694
†UTEP	11	7	.611	23	9	.719
*Hawaii	11	8	.579	17	14	.548
TCU	9	8	.529	20	11	.645
SMU	8	9	.471	18	12	.600
San Jose St.	6	11	.353	14	14	.500
Rice	6	12	.333	14	16	.467
Nevada	3	14	.176	10	18	.357

Conf. Tourney Final: Hawaii 78, Tulsa 72 (OT).
***NCAA Tourney (1-2):** Fresno St. (1-1), Hawaii (0-1).
†NIT (6-1): Tulsa (5-0), UTEP (1-1).

Division I Independents

Team	W	L	Pct
Stony Brook	17	11	.607
Belmont	13	15	.464
Texas A&M-Corpus Christi	12	14	.462
Texas-Pan American	12	17	.414
Centenary	8	19	.296
Albany	6	22	.214

Annual Awards

Player of the Year

Shane Battier, Duke . . . . AP, USBWA, Naismith, Wooden
Jason Williams, Duke . . . . NABC

Wooden Award Voting

Presented since 1977 by the Los Angeles Athletic Club and named after the former Purdue All-America and UCLA coach John Wooden. Voting done by 1,047-member panel of national media; candidates must have a cumulative college grade point average of 2.0 (out of 4.0) and be making progress toward graduation.

		Cl	Pos	Pts
1	Shane Battier, Duke	Sr.	F	4892
2	Jason Williams, Duke	So.	G	3764
3	Joseph Forte, North Carolina	So.	G	2899
4	Casey Jacobsen, Stanford	So.	G/F	2831
5	Troy Murphy, Notre Dame	Jr.	F	2768
6	Tayshaun Prince, Kentucky	Jr.	G/F	1398
7	Charlie Bell, Michigan St.	Sr.	G	1386
8	Frank Williams, Illinois	So.	G	1147
9	Casey Calvary, Gonzaga	Sr.	F	977
10	Jarron Collins, Stanford	Sr.	F	939

Div. II and III Annual Awards

Awarded by the National Association of Basketball Coaches.

Players of the Year
Div. II . . . . Colin Ducharme, Longwood, F/C
Div. III . . . . Horace Jenkins, William Paterson, G
Coaches of the Year
Div. II . . . . Ray Harper, Ky. Wesleyan
Div. III . . . . Mike Lonergan, Catholic
NAIA . . . . Don Lane, Transylvania
JuCo . . . . Jay Spoonhour, Wabash Valley

Coaches of the Year

Matt Doherty, North Carolina . . . . AP
Al Skinner, Boston College . . . . USBWA
Tom Izzo, Michigan St. . . . . NABC
Rod Barnes, Mississippi . . . . Naismith

Consensus All-America Team

The NCAA Division I players cited most frequently by the following All-America selectors: AP, U.S. Basketball Writers, National Assn. of Basketball Coaches and Wooden Award Committee. (*) indicates unanimous first team selection. Holdover from 1999-2000 first team in **bold** type.

First Team

	Class	Hgt	Pos
Shane Battier*, Duke	Sr.	6-8	F
Troy Murphy*, Notre Dame	Jr.	6-11	F
Casey Jacobsen, Stanford	So.	6-6	F
Jason Williams*, Duke	So.	6-2	G
Joseph Forte, N. Carolina	So.	6-4	G

Second Team

	Class	Hgt	Pos
Michael Bradley, Villanova	Jr.	6-10	F
Jason Richardson, Michigan St.	So.	6-6	F
Jamaal Tinsley, Iowa St.	Sr.	6-3	G
Troy Bell, Boston College	So.	6-1	G
Tayshaun Prince, Kentucky	Jr.	6-9	G

Third Team

	Class	Hgt	Pos
Kirk Haston, Indiana	Jr.	6-10	F
Udonis Haslem, Florida	Jr.	6-8	C
Charlie Bell, Michigan St.	Sr.	6-3	G
Frank Williams, Illinois	So.	6-3	G
Juan Dixon, Maryland	Jr.	6-3	G

NCAA Men's Division I Leaders

Includes games through NCAA and NIT tourneys.

INDIVIDUAL

Scoring

	Cl	Gm	FG%	3FG/Att	FT%	Reb	Ast	Stl	Blk	Pts	Avg	Hi
Ronnie McCollum, Centenary	Sr.	27	41.2	85/232	90.7	101	32	27	1	787	29.1	44
Kyle Hill, Eastern Ill.	Sr.	31	47.3	86/199	83.9	151	125	46	23	737	23.8	40
DeWayne Jefferson, Miss. Valley St.	Sr.	27	43.2	107/285	81.0	173	78	38	6	637	23.6	41
Tarise Bryson, Illinois St.	Sr.	30	46.5	62/174	82.1	118	72	56	13	685	22.8	41
Henry Domercant, Eastern Ill.	So.	31	49.3	79/179	81.6	211	66	35	20	706	22.8	35
Rashad Phillips, Detroit	Sr.	35	43.4	136/328	91.6	88	145	35	0	785	22.4	41
Brandon Wolfram, UTEP	Sr.	32	59.1	6/18	82.4	242	29	17	13	714	22.3	36
Rasual Butler, La Salle	Jr.	29	40.2	97/272	84.5	187	57	34	20	641	22.1	39
Brandon Armstrong, Pepperdine	Jr.	31	44.7	76/198	82.6	101	46	46	6	684	22.1	41
Marvin O'Connor, St. Joseph's	Jr.	31	46.3	99/265	67.6	119	82	26	1	706	22.1	37
Tarvis Williams, Hampton	Sr.	32	53.5	0/0	72.7	220	32	16	147	702	21.9	37
Troy Murphy, Notre Dame	Jr.	30	47.1	30/86	76.6	277	62	27	50	653	21.8	37
Trenton Hassell, Austin Peay	Sr.	32	48.5	32/136	79.6	249	144	39	15	693	21.7	33
Isaac Spencer, Murray St.	Sr.	29	48.8	6/36	70.5	206	112	35	20	626	21.6	42
Jason Williams, Duke	So.	39	47.3	132/309	65.9	128	237	78	5	841	21.6	34
Demond Mallet, McNeese St.	Sr.	31	43.1	107/275	79.6	103	67	66	5	660	21.3	40
Carlos Arroyo, Florida Int'l.	Sr.	29	43.1	52/176	74.3	100	117	51	6	616	21.2	39
Kareem Rush, Missouri	So.	26	44.2	69/154	80.0	174	51	34	21	549	21.1	32
Joseph Forte, N. Carolina	So.	33	45.0	55/146	85.3	201	116	67	12	690	20.9	38
Michael Bradley, Villanova	Jr.	31	69.2	12/34	59.0	303	81	28	56	645	20.8	29

Rebounding

	Cl	Gm	No	Avg
Chris Marcus, Western Ky.	Jr.	31	374	12.1
Reggie Evans, Iowa	Jr.	35	416	11.9
J.R. VanHoose, Marshall	Jr.	27	299	11.1
David West, Xavier	So.	29	316	10.9
Eddie Griffin, Seton Hall	Fr.	30	323	10.8
Jeremy Jefferson, Ark-Pine Bluff	Jr.	23	246	10.7
Brian Carroll, Loyola-MD	Sr.	27	286	10.6
Eric Mann, VMI	Sr.	28	294	10.5
Joe Breakenridge, N. Iowa	Sr.	28	294	10.5
Alvin Jones, Georgia Tech	Sr.	30	312	10.4
Kelly Wise, Memphis	Jr.	36	363	10.1
Erwin Dudley, Alabama	So.	36	361	10.0
Andy Savtchenko, Radford	Sr.	29	290	10.0
Chris Miller, Texas Southern	So.	26	259	10.0
Bruce Jenkins, N.C. A&T	Jr.	27	266	9.9

Assists

	Cl	Gm	No	Avg
Markus Carr, CS-Northridge	Jr.	32	286	8.9
Omar Cook, St. John's	Fr.	29	252	8.7
Sean Kennedy, Marist	Jr.	27	219	8.1
Tito Maddox, Fresno St.	So.	25	200	8.0
Ashley Robinson, Miss. Valley St.	Jr.	27	201	7.4
Brandon Pardon, Bowling Green	Jr.	29	204	7.0
Jeremy Stanton, Evansville	Sr.	26	181	7.0
Kirk Hinrich, Kansas	So.	33	229	6.9
Steve Blake, Maryland	So.	36	248	6.9
Allen Griffin, Syracuse	Sr.	34	220	6.5
Jose Winston, Colorado	Jr.	30	194	6.5
Jameer Nelson, St. Joseph's	Fr.	33	213	6.5
Martin Ingelsby, Notre Dame	Sr.	30	193	6.4
Elliott Prasse-Freeman, Harvard	So.	26	164	6.3
Jamal Brown, Texas Tech	Jr.	28	175	6.3

Field Goal Percentage

Minimum 5 Field Goals made per game.

	Cl	Gm	FG	FGA	Pct
Michael Bradley, Villanova	Jr.	31	254	367	69.2
Nakiea Miller, Iona	Sr.	27	163	244	66.8
Kimani Ffriend, Nebraska	Sr.	28	144	231	62.3
Andre Hutson, Michigan St.	Sr.	32	173	278	62.2
George Evans, George Mason	Sr.	30	233	380	61.3
Carlos Boozer, Duke	So.	32	160	265	60.4
Steffon Bradford, Nebraska	Sr.	30	155	257	60.3
Terry Black, Baylor	Sr.	31	191	317	60.3
Joe Linderman, Drexel	Sr.	24	146	244	59.8
Nick Collison, Kansas	So.	33	187	313	59.7
Udonis Haslem, Florida	Jr.	31	188	315	59.7
Michael Wright, Arizona	Jr.	36	202	340	59.4
Brandon Wolfram, UTEP	Sr.	32	251	425	59.1
Jermaine Hall, Wagner	So.	29	211	359	58.8
Melvin Ely, Fresno St.	Sr.	33	208	357	58.3

Free Throw Percentage

Minimum 2.5 Free Throws made per game.

	Cl	Gm	FT	FTA	Pct
Gary Buchanan, Villanova	So.	31	97	103	94.2
Brent Jolly, Tennessee Tech	So.	29	95	102	93.1
Ryan Mendez, Stanford	Sr.	34	94	101	93.1
Rashad Phillips, Detroit	Sr.	35	185	202	91.6
Ronnie McCollum, Centenary	Sr.	27	214	236	90.7
Titus Ivory, Penn St.	Sr.	33	125	139	89.9
Chris Spatola, Army	Jr.	28	149	166	89.8
Albert Mouring, Connecticut	Sr.	32	104	117	88.9
Scott Knapp, Siena	Sr.	31	80	90	88.9
Dominic Smith, Houston	Jr.	29	142	160	88.8
Roger Mason, Virginia	So.	29	122	138	88.4
Chad Pleiness, C. Michigan	So.	28	76	86	88.4
Mark Linebaugh, Colgate	Fr.	28	90	102	88.2
Adam Lopez, N. Arizona	Jr.	29	89	101	88.1
Steve Logan, Cincinnati	Jr.	34	132	150	88.0

Cal. St. Northridge	Univ. of Iowa	Villanova	Stanford
Markus Carr	**Reggie Evans**	**Michael Bradley**	**Ryan Mendez**
Assists	Rebounding	Field Goal Pct.	Free Throw Pct.

3-Pt Field Goal Percentage

Minimum 1.5 Three-Point FGs made per game.

	Cl	Gm	FG	FGA	Pct
Amory Sanders, SE Missouri	Sr.	24	53	95	55.8
David Falknor, Akron	Jr.	22	47	87	54.0
Cary Cochran, Nebraska	Jr.	30	78	165	47.3
Casey Jacobsen, Stanford	So.	34	84	178	47.2
Tim Erickson, Idaho St.	Sr.	28	82	177	46.3
Justin Brown, Montana St.	Jr.	30	60	130	46.2
Luke McDonald, Drake	Fr.	28	86	187	46.0
Sean Jackson, UC-Irvine	Sr.	30	62	135	45.9
Brian Chase, Virginia Tech	So.	23	60	131	45.8
Jason Kapono, UCLA	So.	32	84	184	45.7

3-Pt Field Goals Per Game

	Cl	Gm	No	Avg
DeWayne Jefferson, Miss. Valley	Sr.	27	107	4.0
Rashad Phillips, Detroit	Sr.	35	136	3.9
Brian Merriweather, TX Pan Am	Sr.	29	108	3.7
Cory Schwab, N. Arizona	Sr.	29	105	3.6
Demond Mallet, McNeese St.	Sr.	31	107	3.5
Tony Orciari, Vermont	Sr.	27	92	3.4
Jason Williams, Duke	So.	39	132	3.4
Rasual Butler, La Salle	Jr.	29	97	3.3
Darius Lane, Seton Hall	Jr.	31	103	3.3
Wes Burtner, Belmont	Jr.	28	93	3.3
E.J. Hallup, Albany	Fr.	28	93	3.3

Blocked Shots

	Cl	Gm	No	Avg
Tarvis Williams, Hampton	Sr.	32	147	4.6
Eddie Griffin, Seton Hall	Fr.	30	133	4.4
Wojciech Myrda, La.-Monroe	Jr.	28	123	4.4
Kris Hunter, Jacksonville	Sr.	28	114	4.1
Ken Johnson, Ohio St.	Sr.	31	125	4.0
Hondre Brewer, San Francisco	Jr.	30	114	3.8
Brendan Haywood, N. Carolina	Sr.	33	120	3.6
Jason Jennings, Arkansas St.	Jr.	29	102	3.5
Patrick Flomo, Ohio	Jr.	30	105	3.5
Alvin Jones, Georgia Tech	Sr.	30	101	3.4
Chris Marcus, Western Ky.	Jr.	31	97	3.1
Nakiea Miller, Iona	Sr.	27	84	3.1

Steals

	Cl	Gm	No	Avg
Greedy Daniels, TCU	Jr.	25	108	4.3
Desmond Cambridge, Ala. A&M	Jr.	28	107	3.8
Senecca Wall, Sam Houston St.	Sr.	29	103	3.6
John Linehan, Providence	Jr.	26	81	3.1
Fred House, Southern Utah	Sr.	31	93	3.0
Andy Woodley, Northern Iowa	Jr.	27	80	3.0
Kevin Braswell, Georgetown	Jr.	33	94	2.8
Andrew Gellert, Harvard	Jr.	26	72	2.8
Cookie Belcher, Nebraska	Sr.	30	82	2.7
Mire Chatman, TX-Pan Am.	Jr.	29	78	2.7

Single Game Highs

Points

No		Opponent	Date
50	Oliver Morton, Chattanooga	Pikeville	Jan. 24
49	Trevor Diggs, UNLV	Wyoming	Mar. 3

Rebounds

No		Opponent	Date
23	Clifton Jones, Old Dominion	NC-Wilmington	Feb. 26

Assists

No		Opponent	Date
17	Omar Cook, St. John's	Stony Brook	Nov. 18
	Tito Maddox, Fresno St.	TCU	Jan. 10

Blocks

No		Opponent	Date
13	D'or Fischer, Northwestern St.	SW Texas St.	Jan. 22

Steals

No		Opponent	Date
12	Greedy Daniels, TCU	Ark-Pine Bluff	Dec. 30

3-point FGs

No		Opponent	Date
11	Cory Schwab, N. Arizona	Cal Poly	Dec. 2
	Ron Williamson, Howard	Georgetown	Dec. 16

NCAA Men's Division I Leaders (Cont.)
TEAM

Scoring Offense

	Gm	W-L	Pts	Avg
TCU	31	20-11	2902	93.6
Duke	39	35-4	3538	90.7
Maryland	36	25-11	3067	85.2
Virginia	29	20-9	2464	85.0
McNeese St.	31	22-9	2580	83.2
Stanford	34	31-3	2829	83.2
CS-Northridge	32	22-10	2650	82.8
Eastern Illinois	31	21-10	2564	82.7
Wagner	29	16-13	2393	82.5
Gonzaga	33	26-7	2720	82.4
Kansas	33	26-7	2707	82.0
Fresno St.	33	26-7	2689	81.5
Arizona	36	28-8	2926	81.3
Florida	31	24-7	2509	80.9
Tennessee	33	22-11	2668	80.8

Won-Lost Percentage

	W	L	Pct
Stanford	31	3	.912
Duke	35	4	.897
Georgia St.	29	5	.853
Michigan St.	28	5	.848
Boston College	27	5	.844
Hofstra	26	5	.839
UC-Irvine	25	5	.833
Utah St.	28	6	.824
Iowa St.	25	6	.806
Southern Utah	25	6	.806
Fresno St.	26	7	.788
Gonzaga	26	7	.788
Kansas	26	7	.788
North Carolina	26	7	.788
Oklahoma	26	7	.788
St. Joseph's	26	7	.788

Scoring Defense

	Gm	W-L	Pts	Avg
Wisconsin	29	18-11	1641	56.6
Utah St.	34	28-6	1959	57.6
Princeton	27	16-11	1569	58.1
NC-Wilmington	30	19-11	1751	58.4
Miami-OH	33	17-16	1928	58.4
Columbia	27	12-15	1591	58.9
College of Charleston	29	22-7	1739	60.0
UMKC	30	14-16	1815	60.5
Richmond	29	22-7	1763	60.8
Butler	32	24-8	1946	60.8
Western Ky.	31	24-7	1889	60.9
Stephen F. Austin	26	9-17	1595	61.3
Michigan St.	33	28-5	2039	61.8
Winthrop	31	18-13	1917	61.8
Hofstra	31	26-5	1929	62.2

Field Goal Percentage

	FG	FGA	Pct
Stanford	953	1865	51.1
Gonzaga	915	1793	51.0
Austin Peay	935	1845	50.7
Kansas	1002	1996	50.2
Villanova	845	1708	49.5
CS-Northridge	910	1842	49.4
UTEP	878	1786	49.2
Michigan St.	957	1957	48.9
Southern Utah	783	1602	48.9
Central Michigan	669	1370	48.8
Nebraska	775	1591	48.7
Montana St.	771	1588	48.6
Utah St.	852	1755	48.5
Bowling Green	761	1571	48.4
Maryland	1120	2313	48.4
Evansville	733	1515	48.4

Scoring Margin

	Off	Def	Mar
Duke	90.7	70.5	20.2
Stanford	83.2	65.5	17.7
Michigan St.	77.4	61.8	15.6
Arizona	81.3	66.3	15.0
Florida	80.9	67.1	13.8
Gonzaga	82.4	68.8	13.6
Western Ky.	74.3	60.9	13.4
Utah St.	70.7	57.6	13.1
Boston College	79.6	66.5	13.1
Maryland	85.2	72.4	12.8
Kansas	82.0	69.3	12.8
Illinois	77.9	65.9	11.9
TCU	93.6	82.3	11.4
Arkansas	79.9	68.8	11.1
Iowa St.	79.1	68.2	10.8

Field Goal Percentage Defense

	FG	FGA	Pct
Kansas	782	2069	37.8
Holy Cross	628	1642	38.2
Illinois	748	1936	38.6
Georgetown	745	1922	38.8
Texas	734	1889	38.9
Alabama St.	728	1869	39.0
Columbia	525	1344	39.1
North Carolina	859	2196	39.1
Indiana	761	1930	39.4
Utah St.	708	1795	39.4
Gonzaga	794	2009	39.5
Bradley	668	1686	39.6
Arizona	862	2174	39.7
St. Louis	667	1682	39.7
NC-Asheville	662	1667	39.7

Rebound Margin

	Off	Def	Mar
Michigan St.	42.5	27.1	15.4
Western Ky.	40.0	30.4	9.6
Georgetown	44.9	35.6	9.2
Iowa St.	39.6	30.8	8.8
Mississippi St.	41.2	33.3	7.9
Holy Cross	38.5	30.8	7.7
Kansas	42.6	35.0	7.6
Stanford	36.6	29.2	7.4
Valparaiso	37.5	30.3	7.3
Alabama	42.2	35.0	7.2
Illinois	40.0	33.0	7.0
Central Conn. St.	38.9	32.2	6.8
Iowa	38.6	31.9	6.7
Arizona	39.8	33.2	6.6
Utah	36.8	30.5	6.4

Free Throw Percentage

	FT	FTA	Pct
BYU	651	835	78.0
Eastern Ill.	504	650	77.5
NC-Greensboro	552	718	76.9
Bowling Green	546	712	76.7
Penn St.	587	768	76.4
Kent St.	564	739	76.3
Manhattan	471	739	76.3
Drake	428	562	76.2
UMKC	315	414	76.1
Col. of Charleston	467	615	75.9
Long Island	354	467	75.8
Centenary	483	641	75.4
Idaho St.	421	559	75.3
UTEP	633	841	75.3
Army	567	756	75.0

3-point FG Percentage

	3PT	3PTA	Pct
Akron	189	436	43.3
Stanford	252	587	42.9
New Orleans	106	444	41.9
Iowa St.	182	436	41.7
Montana St.	226	544	41.5
N. Arizona	237	571	41.5
Butler	251	617	40.7
Ark.-Little Rock	200	492	40.7
Ball St.	193	477	40.5
Gonzaga	245	606	40.4
Colorado St.	183	454	40.3
Providence	249	622	40.0
Southern Utah	197	493	40.0
SE Missouri St.	209	525	39.8
Oral Roberts	188	473	39.7

3-point FG Made Per Game

	Gm	No	Avg
Duke	39	407	10.4
Belmont	28	288	10.3
Samford	29	284	9.8
Miss. Valley St.	27	250	9.3
Charlotte	33	305	9.2
Tennessee St.	29	260	9.0
Arkansas	31	273	8.8
WI-Milwaukee	28	244	8.7
Georgia Tech	30	260	8.7
TCU	31	268	8.6
Siena	31	266	8.6
Missouri	33	279	8.5
Troy St.	31	262	8.5
Air Force	29	245	8.4
Penn St.	33	278	8.4

Underclassmen in NBA Draft

Thirty-three division I players (17 juniors, 10 sophomores and 6 freshmen), 8 junior college players, and 6 high school seniors forfeited the remainder of their college eligibility and declared for the 2001 NBA Draft which took place at Madison Square Garden in New York City on June 27.

Players are listed in alphabetical order; first round selections in **bold** type, high school players in *italics*.

	Cl	Drafted by	Overall Pick
Gilbert Arenas, Arizona	So.	Golden State	31
B. Armstrong, Pepperdine	Jr.	New Jersey	23
Malcolm Battles, New Mexico	Jr.	not drafted	—
Tavorris Bell, Rhode Island	Jr.	not drafted	—
Preston Bennett, Grayson CC	Fr.	not drafted	—
Michael Bradley, Villanova	Jr.	Toronto	17
Jamison Brewer, Auburn	So.	Indiana	41
K. Brown, Okaloosa-Walton CC	So.	Boston	11
Kwame Brown, Glynn Acad.	HS	Washington	1
SirValiant Brown, George Wash.	So.	not drafted	—
Nick Burwell, Orange CC	So.	not drafted	—
Tyson Chandler, Dominguez	HS	L.A. Clippers	2
Ousmane Cisse, St. Jude Cath.	HS	Denver	47
Jason Collins, Stanford	So.	Houston	18
Omar Cook, St. John's	Fr.	Denver	32
Eddy Curry, Thorwood HS (Ill.)	HS	Chicago	4
Samuel Dalembert, Seton Hall	So.	Philadelphia	26
Greedy Daniels, TCU	Fr.	not drafted	—
DeSagana Diop, Oak Hill Acad.	HS	Cleveland	8
Maurice Evans, Texas	Jr.	not drafted	—
Benjamin Eze, Col.of S. Idaho	Fr.	not drafted	—
Alton Ford, Houston	Fr.	Phoenix	51
Joseph Forte, North Carolina	So.	Boston	21
Jerry Green, UC-Irvine	Jr.	not drafted	—
Eddie Griffin, Seton Hall	Fr.	New Jersey	7
Rob Griffin, Iowa	Jr.	not drafted	—
Rashid Hardwick, E. Okla. St.	Jr.	not drafted	—
Trenton Hassell, Austin Peay	Jr.	Chicago	30
Kirk Haston, Indiana	Jr.	Charlotte	16
Draper Housley, Lee College	So.	not drafted	—
Steven Hunter, DePaul	So.	Orlando	15
Richard Jefferson, Arizona	Jr.	Houston	13
Joe Johnson, Arkansas	So.	Boston	10
Tony Key, Centennial HS (Calif.)	HS	not drafted	—
D.A. Layne, Georgia	Jr.	not drafted	—
Zach Marbury, Rhode Island	Jr.	not drafted	—
Jamario Moon, Meridian CC	So.	not drafted	—
Troy Murphy, Notre Dame	Jr.	Golden State	14
Zach Randolph, Michigan St.	Fr.	Portland	19
Jason Richardson, Mich. St.	So.	Golden State	5
Kenny Satterfield, Cincinnati	So.	Dallas	54
Bobby Simmons, DePaul	Jr.	Seattle	42
Will Solomon, Clemson	Jr.	Vancouver	33
Clifton Terry, Kennedy-King Col.	So.	not drafted	—
Gerald Wallace, Alabama	Fr.	Sacramento	25
Rodney White, Charlotte	Fr.	Detroit	9
Michael Wright, Arizona	Jr.	New York	39

Note: Twenty-one players who initially declared themselves eligible for the 2001 NBA Draft withdrew their names before the June 20 deadline. The list of players who pulled their names back included Keith Bogans and Tayshaun Price of Kentucky, Sam Clancy of USC and Tito Maddox of Fresno State.

Other 2001 Men's Tournaments

NIT Tournament

The 64th annual National Invitation Tournament had a 32-team field. First three rounds played on home courts of higher seeded teams. Semifinal, Third Place and Championship games played March 27-29 at Madison Square Garden in New York City.

1st Round

at Connecticut 72 . . . . South Carolina 65
Detroit 68 . . . . at Bradley 49
at Richmond 79 . . . . West Virginia 56
at Dayton 68 . . . . NC-Wilmington 59
at Alabama 85. . . . . Seton Hall 79
at Toledo 76 . . . . OT . . . . South Alabama 67
at Purdue 90 . . . . Illinois St. 79
at Auburn 60 . . . . Miami-FL 58
at Minnesota 87 . . . . Villanova 78
at Tulsa 75 . . . . UC-Irvine 71
at Pittsburgh 84. . . . . St. Bonaventure 75
at Mississippi St. 75. . . . . Southern Mississippi 68
Pepperdine 72 . . . . at Wyoming 69
at New Mexico 83. . . . . Baylor 73
at UTEP 84 . . . . McNeese St. 74
Memphis 71. . . . . at Utah 62

2nd Round

Detroit 67. . . . . at Connecticut 61
at Dayton 71. . . . . Richmond 56
at Alabama 79 . . . . Toledo 69
at Purdue 79 . . . . Auburn 61
Tulsa 76 . . . . at Minnesota 73
Mississippi St. 66 . . . . at Pittsburgh 61
at New Mexico 81 . . . . Pepperdine 75
at Memphis 90 . . . . UTEP 65

Quarterfinals

Detroit 59. . . . . at Dayton 42
Alabama 85. . . . . 2 OT . . . . at Purdue 77
Tulsa 77 . . . . at Mississippi St. 75
at Memphis 81 . . . . New Mexico 63

Semifinals

Tulsa 72. . . . . Memphis 64
Alabama 74. . . . . Detroit 63

Third Place

Memphis 86 . . . . Detroit 71

Championship

Tulsa 79 . . . . Alabama 60

Most Valuable Players

NIT
Marcus Hill, Tulsa guard

NCAA Division II
Lorico Duncan, Ky. Wesleyan guard

NCAA Division III
Pat Maloney, Catholic guard

NAIA Division I
Paul Little, Faulkner (Ala.) center

NAIA Division II
Brandon Woudstra, Northwestern (Iowa) guard

NCAA Division II

The eight regional winners of the 48-team field: NORTHEAST—Adelphi (31-0); EAST—Queens-NC (26-5); SOUTH ATLANTIC—Johnson C. Smith (27-4); SOUTH—Tampa (24-6); SOUTH CENTRAL—Washburn (27-4); GREAT LAKES—Kentucky Wesleyan (28-3); NORTH CENTRAL—Southwest St. (28-6); WEST—Western Wash. (26-3).

The Elite Eight was played March 21-24, at Bakersfield, Calif. There was no Third Place game.

Quarterfinals

Ky. Wesleyan 85 . . . . Southwest St. 66
Tampa 82 . . . . Adelphi 68
Washburn 70 . . . . Johnson C. Smith 64
Western Wash. 89. . . . . Queens (N.C.) 85

Semifinals

Ky. Wesleyan 85 . . . . OT . . . . Tampa 84
Washburn 96 . . . . Western Wash. 90

Championship

Ky. Wesleyan 72 . . . . Washburn 63

NCAA Division III

Sixty-four teams played into the 32-team Division III field. The four sectional winners: MIDDLE ATLANTIC—William Paterson-NJ (24-4); EAST/NORTHEAST—Catholic (25-5); NORTH—Ohio Northern (26-2); MIDWEST—Illinois Wesleyan (22-6).

The Final Four was played March 16-17, at Salem Civic Center in Salem, Va.

Semifinals

Catholic 82. . . . . Ohio Northern 77
Wm. Paterson 67 . . . . Ill. Wesleyan 52

Third Place

Ill. Wesleyan 76. Ohio Northern 73

Championship

Catholic 76 . . . . Wm. Paterson 62

NAIA Division I

The quarterfinalists, in alphabetical order, after two rounds of the 32-team NAIA tournament: Azusa Pacific, Calif. (35-3); Christian Heritage, Calif. (29-7); Faulkner, Ala. (32-5); Lubbock Christian, Tex. (21-10); Oklahoma Baptist (25-9); Pikeville, Ky (27-11); Science and Arts, Okla. (28-2); Spring Hill, Ala. (29-8).

All tournament games played, March 14-20, at the Convention Center of Tulsa, Okla. There was no Third Place game.

Quarterfinals: Christian Heritage def. Lubbock Christian, 75-61; Science and Arts def. Spring Hill, 63-57; Pikeville def. Oklahoma Baptist, 88-83; Faulkner def. Azusa Pacific, 79-75.

Semifinals: Science and Arts def. Christian Heritage, 99-88; Faulkner def. Pikeville, 87-78.

Championship: Faulkner def. Science and Arts, 63-59.

NAIA Division II

The semifinalists, in alphabetical order, after three rounds of the 32-team NAIA tournament: Cornerstone, Mich. (30-8); MidAmerica Nazarene (29-8); Northwestern, Iowa (27-6); Rio Grande, Ohio (29-8).

All tournament games played, March 7-13, at Point Lookout, Missouri. There was no Third Place game.

Semifinals: MidAmerica Nazarene def. Cornerstone, 81-61; Northwestern def. Rio Grande, 110-91.

Championship: Northwestern def. MidAmerica Nazarene, 82-78.

Irish March to the Arch

by Nancy Lieberman

It was supposed to be another year of the same old, same old. UConn and Tennessee were going to fight for the crown again. Both teams had player of the year candidates in UConn's Svetlana Abrosimova and Tennessee's Tamika Catchings. But devastating injuries to UConn's All-Americans Abrosimova and Shea Ralph proved too much for the Huskies to overcome in the end. Tennessee also saw their chances dim when 2000 National Player of the Year Catchings tore her ACL in January.

So the door to a national title was left open, and many pretenders became viable contenders in the March to the Arch in St. Louis. It was Muffet McGraw's Notre Dame team that was most ready for the challenges. It was a season of firsts for the Irish; their first sellout at home, first win versus UConn, and first national championship.

The inside-out balance of the Irish was a thing of beauty. Led by Player of the Year Ruth Riley, Notre Dame was hitting on all cylinders. The senior All-

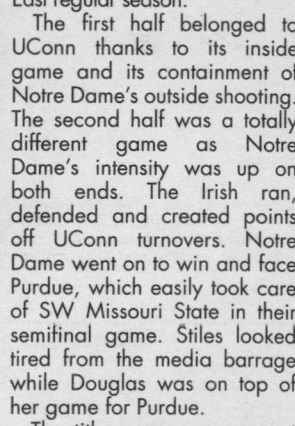

Ruth Riley

American improved on her incredible offensive game, passing out of constant double teams and denying opponents' shots. But it wasn't just Riley. Team chemistry proved to be a major factor. Niele Ivey ran the team with excellent poise and decision-making. Alicia Ratay shot three's with the best, Kelley Siemon was the unsung hero with her intensity, garbage buckets, and layups off of Riley double-teams.

Although many others thought the door was open for a title shot, the Big East made sure our attention was squarely on the newest and biggest rivalry in the country. Although Notre Dame thought they could beat UConn, a rivalry isn't a rivalry until you win at least one, and this year the Irish finally won—twice.

The top seeds in the NCAA tournament were Tennessee, Connecticut, Notre Dame and Duke. Xavier, which bumped Tennessee

out of the regionals, and SW Missouri State, led by the NCAA's all-time scoring leader Jackie Stiles, both were pleasant surprises. They gave hope to the little guy that anything can happen if you have a little talent, chemistry, and a willingness to believe.

It was the best and most enjoyable Final Four in recent years. UConn, the defending champs, were going for a repeat. Purdue, the 1999 national champs, were back in the Final Four with All-American Katie Douglas. Notre Dame was making its second Final Four and the newcomer, SW Missouri State, had Stiles, the local favorite.

It was Notre Dame and UConn in the semis in a dream match up. Like Ali-Frazier III, they had split their two previous meetings and were co-champs of the Big East regular season.

The first half belonged to UConn thanks to its inside game and its containment of Notre Dame's outside shooting. The second half was a totally different game as Notre Dame's intensity was up on both ends. The Irish ran, defended and created points off UConn turnovers. Notre Dame went on to win and face Purdue, which easily took care of SW Missouri State in their semifinal game. Stiles looked tired from the media barrage while Douglas was on top of her game for Purdue.

The title game was a great match-up on paper and even better on the court. Purdue started quickly and again Notre Dame had to come from behind to make a game of it. In the end both teams relied on their stars—Notre Dame's Riley played sensational along with teammate Ivey. Purdue's Douglas and Kelly Komara wouldn't give in.

Riley made a great catch in the post and was fouled with seconds remaining on the clock and the score tied 66-66. She hit both free throws for a 68-66 lead. The luck of the Irish held, as Douglas missed an elbow jumper at the buzzer and Notre Dame had its first NCAA basketball title ever. It was quite a year for the Irish. ∎

Nancy Lieberman is ESPN's women's college basketball analyst.
Photo source: AP/Wide World Photos

Final Regular Season AP Women's Top 25 Poll

Taken **before** start of NCAA tournament.

The sportswriters & broadcasters poll: first place votes in parentheses; records through Sunday, March 11, 2001; total points (based on 25 for 1st, 24 for 2nd, etc.); record in NCAA tourney and team lost to; head coach (career years and career record including 2001 postseason), and preseason ranking. Teams in **bold** type went on to reach the NCAA Final Four.

		Mar. 11 Record	Points	NCAA Recap	Head Coach	Preseason Rank
1	**Connecticut** (32)	28-2	990	4-1 (Notre Dame)	Geno Auriemma (16 yrs: 425-98)	1
2	**Notre Dame** (5)	28-2	951	6-0	Muffet McGraw (19 yrs: 410-158)	6
3	Tennessee (3)	29-2	934	2-1 (Xavier)	Pat Summitt (27 yrs: 759-153)	2
4	Georgia	26-5	860	1-1 (Missouri)	Andy Landers (26 yrs: 627-179)	3
5	Duke	28-3	851	2-1 (SW Mo. St.)	Gail Goestenkors (9 yrs: 206-78)	5
6	Louisiana Tech	28-4	778	3-1 (UConn)	Leon Barmore (18 yrs: 551-82)	9
7	Oklahoma	26-5	722	2-1 (Washington)	Sherri Coale (5 yrs: 81-69)	14
8	Iowa St.	25-5	715	2-1 (Vanderbilt)	Bill Fennelly (13 yrs: 304-103)	10
9	**Purdue**	26-6	642	5-1 (Notre Dame)	Kristy Curry (2 yrs: 54-15)	4
10	Vanderbilt	21-9	618	3-1 (Notre Dame)	Jim Foster (23 yrs: 474-218)	20
11	Rutgers	22-7	598	1-1 (SW Mo. St.)	C. Vivian Stringer (29 yrs: 644-199)	8
12	Xavier	28-2	566	3-1 (Purdue)	Melanie Balcomb (8 yrs: 151-85)	NR
13	Texas Tech	23-6	522	2-1 (Purdue)	Marsha Sharp (19 yrs: 459-141)	16
14	Florida	23-5	492	1-1 (Washington)	Carol Ross (11 yrs: 229-110)	NR
15	**SW Missouri St.**	25-5	399	4-1 (Purdue)	Cheryl Burnett (14 yrs: 303-123)	21
16	Iowa	20-9	374	1-1 (Utah)	Lisa Bluder (17 yrs: 377-152)	NR
17	Utah	26-3	371	2-1 (Notre Dame)	Elaine Elliott (18 yrs: 374-152)	NR
18	LSU	19-10	303	1-1 (Purdue)	Sue Gunter (31 yrs: 633-284)	7
19	N.C. State	20-10	287	2-1 (UConn)	Kay Yow (30 yrs: 611-253)	NR
20	Colorado	21-8	236	1-1 (Vanderbilt)	Ceal Barry (22 yrs: 431-239)	NR
21	Penn St.	19-9	161	0-1 (TCU)	Rene Portland (25 yrs: 572-195)	13
22	Clemson	20-9	120	1-1 (Xavier)	Jim Davis (15 yrs: 318-146)	NR
23	Baylor	21-8	85	0-1 (Arkansas)	Kim Mulkey-Robinson (1 yr: 21-9)	NR
24	Wisconsin	18-9	82	0-1 (Missouri)	Jane Albright (18 yrs: 323-184)	18
25	Arizona St.	20-10	35	0-1 (LSU)	Charli Turner Thorne (8 yrs: 105-117)	NR
	Virginia Tech	21-8	35	1-1 (Texas Tech)	Bonnie Henrickson (4 yrs: 92-33)	NR

Others receiving votes: 27. **Drake** (30 pts); 28. **Stanford** and **Villanova** (29); 30. **Colorado St.** (27); 31. **Toledo** (24); 32. **Washington** (23); 33. **Michigan** (15); 34. **Idaho St.**, **St. Mary's-CA** and **Texas** (14); 37. **TCU** (11); 38. **Missouri** (10); 39. **Arkansas** (8); 40. **George Washington** (7); 41. **UC-Santa Barbara** (5); 42. **Florida St.** and **Tulane** (4); 44. **Arizona** (3); 45. **Virginia** (2).

NCAA Women's Division I Tournament Seeds

	WEST		MIDWEST		MIDEAST		EAST
1	Duke (28-3)	1	Notre Dame (28-2)	1	Tennessee (29-2)	1	Connecticut (28-2)
2	Oklahoma (26-5)	2	Iowa St. (25-5)	2	Texas Tech (23-6)	2	Georgia (26-5)
3	Florida (23-5)	3	Vanderbilt (21-9)	3	Purdue (26-6)	3	La. Tech (28-4)
4	Rutgers (22-7)	4	Iowa (20-9)	4	Xavier (28-2)	4	N.C. State (20-10)
5	SW Missouri St. (25-5)	5	Utah (26-3)	5	Clemson (20-9)	5	Villanova (21-8)
6	Washington (19-9)	6	Colorado (21-8)	6	LSU (19-10)	6	Penn St. (19-9)
7	Geo. Washington (22-9)	7	Florida St. (18-11)	7	Va. Tech (21-8)	7	Wisconsin (18-9)
8	Baylor (21-8)	8	Michigan (18-11)	8	Texas (20-12)	8	Maryland (17-11)
9	Arkansas (19-12)	9	Virginia (18-13)	9	St. Mary's-CA (25-5)	9	Colorado St. (24-6)
10	Stanford (18-10)	10	Tulane (22-9)	10	Denver (24-6)	10	Missouri (20-9)
11	Old Dominion (21-8)	11	Siena (24-5)	11	Arizona St. (20-10)	11	TCU (24-7)
12	Toledo (25-5)	12	Fairfield (25-5)	12	Chattanooga (24-6)	12	Drake (23-6)
13	Stephen F. Austin (26-6)	13	Oregon (17-11)	13	Louisville (19-9)	13	Delaware (26-4)
14	Holy Cross (21-8)	14	Idaho St. (25-4)	14	UC-Santa Barbara (22-8)	14	Georgia St. (24-6)
15	Oral Roberts (20-10)	15	Howard (21-9)	15	Pennsylvania (22-5)	15	Liberty (18-11)
16	WI-Milwaukee (19-10)	16	Alcorn St. (21-10)	16	Austin Peay (17-13)	16	Long Island (16-14)

2001 NCAA BASKETBALL WOMEN'S DIVISION I

MIDWEST

1st ROUND March 16-17
- (1) Notre Dame 98
- (16) Alcorn St 49
- (8) Michigan 81
- (9) Virginia 71
- (5) Utah 79
- (12) Fairfield 57
- (4) Iowa 89
- (13) Oregon 82
- (6) Colorado 98
- (11) Siena 78
- (3) Vanderbilt 83
- (14) Idaho St 57
- (7) Florida St 72
- (10) Tulane 70
- (2) Iowa St 100
- (15) Howard 61

2nd ROUND March 18-19
- (1) Notre Dame 88
- (8) Michigan 54
- (5) Utah 78
- (4) Iowa 69
- (6) Colorado 59
- (3) Vanderbilt 65
- (7) Florida St 70
- (2) Iowa St 85

SWEET 16 March 24
- (1) Notre Dame 69
- (5) Utah 54
- (3) Vanderbilt 84
- (2) Iowa St 65

ELITE EIGHT March 26
- (1) Notre Dame 72
- (3) Vanderbilt 64

FINAL FOUR March 30
- (1) Notre Dame 90

EAST

1st ROUND March 16-17
- (1) Connecticut 101
- (16) Long Island 29
- (8) Maryland 69
- (9) Colorado St 83
- (5) Villanova 66
- (12) Drake 58
- (4) N Carolina St 76
- (13) Delaware 57
- (6) Penn St 75
- (11) TCU 77
- (3) Louisiana Tech 84
- (14) Georgia St 48
- (7) Wisconsin 68
- (10) Missouri 71
- (2) Georgia 77
- (15) Liberty 48

2nd ROUND March 18-19
- (1) Connecticut 89
- (9) Colorado St 44
- (5) Villanova 64
- (4) N Carolina St 68
- (11) TCU 59
- (3) Louisiana Tech 80
- (10) Missouri 78
- (2) Georgia 65

SWEET 16 March 24
- (1) Connecticut 72
- (4) N Carolina St 58
- (3) Louisiana Tech 78
- (10) Missouri 67

ELITE EIGHT March 26
- (1) Connecticut 67
- (3) Louisiana Tech 48

FINAL FOUR March 30
- (1) Connecticut 75

NATIONAL CHAMPIONSHIP

- (1) Notre Dame 68
- (3) Purdue 66

Savvis Center
St. Louis, Missouri
Sunday, April 1, 2001

MIDEAST

FINAL FOUR March 30
- (3) Purdue 81

ELITE EIGHT March 26
- (4) Xavier 78
- (3) Purdue 88

SWEET 16 March 24
- (1) Tennessee 65
- (4) Xavier 80
- (3) Purdue 74
- (2) Texas Tech 72

2nd ROUND March 18-19
- (1) Tennessee 92
- (9) St Mary's (CA) 75
- (5) Clemson 62
- (4) Xavier 77
- (13) LSU 70
- (3) Purdue 73
- (7) Virginia Tech 52
- (2) Texas Tech 73

1st ROUND March 16-17
- (1) Tennessee 80
- (16) Austin Peay 38
- (8) Texas 64
- (9) St Mary's (CA) 68
- (5) Clemson 51
- (12) Chattanooga 49
- (4) Xavier 80
- (13) Louisville 52
- (6) LSU 83
- (11) Arizona St 66
- (3) Purdue 75
- (14) Santa Barbara 62
- (7) Virginia Tech 77
- (10) Denver 57
- (2) Texas Tech 100
- (15) Pennsylvania 57

WEST

FINAL FOUR March 30
- (9) SW Missouri St 64

ELITE EIGHT March 26
- (9) SW Missouri St 104
- (6) Washington 87

SWEET 16 March 24
- (1) Duke 71
- (9) SW Missouri St 81
- (6) Washington 84
- (2) Oklahoma 67

2nd ROUND March 18-19
- (1) Duke 75
- (8) Arkansas 54
- (5) SW Missouri St 60
- (4) Rutgers 53
- (6) Washington 86
- (3) Florida 75
- (10) Stanford 50
- (2) Oklahoma 67

1st ROUND March 16-17
- (1) Duke 96
- (16) WI Milwaukee 63
- (8) Baylor 59
- (9) Arkansas 68
- (5) SW Missouri St 89
- (12) Toledo 71
- (4) Rutgers 80
- (13) SFA 43
- (6) Washington 67
- (11) Old Dominion 65
- (3) Florida 84
- (14) Holy Cross 52
- (10) Geo Washington 51
- (10) Stanford 76
- (2) Oklahoma 70
- (15) Oral Roberts 64

NCAA Championship Game

Purdue 66

	Min	FG M-A	FT M-A	Pts	Reb O-T	A	PF
Shalicia Hurns	39	7-13	3-5	17	4-7	0	0
Shereka Wright	34	6-15	3-5	17	2-4	0	2
Camille Cooper	23	3-9	0-0	6	1-6	2	4
Katie Douglas	40	6-15	3-3	18	1-7	5	2
Kelly Komara	37	3-9	0-0	8	0-2	2	1
Lindsey Hicks	1	0-0	0-0	0	0-0	0	0
Shinika Parks	12	0-3	0-0	0	1-2	1	1
Candi Crawford	11	0-2	0-2	0	3-4	2	4
Mary Jo Noon	3	0-1	0-0	0	0-0	0	2
TOTALS	200	25-67	9-15	66	12-32	12	16

Three-point FG: 7-17 (Wright 2-4, Douglas 3-6, Komara 2-5, Parks 0-2); **Team Rebounds:** 9; **Blocked Shots:** 4 (Cooper 2, Wright, Hurns); **Turnovers:** 15 (Douglas 6, Cooper 2, Hurns 2, Wright 2, Crawford, Komara, Parks); **Steals:** 10 (Douglas 5, Cooper, Crawford, Hurns, Komara, Wright); **Percentages:** 2-Pt FG (.360); 3-Pt FG (.412); Total FG (.373); Free Throws (.600).

Notre Dame 68

	Min	FG M-A	FT M-A	Pts	Reb O-T	A	PF
Ericka Haney	35	6-11	1-2	13	1-5	2	3
Kelley Siemon	40	5-11	0-0	10	2-9	6	3
Ruth Riley	35	9-13	10-14	28	6-13	1	3
Alicia Ratay	25	1-6	0-0	3	0-4	2	4
Niele Ivey	40	5-13	2-3	12	1-5	4	0
Jeneka Joyce	20	0-2	2-2	2	0-0	1	1
Amanda Barksdale	5	0-0	0-0	0	1-2	0	0
TOTALS	200	26-56	15-21	68	11-38	16	14

Three-point FG: 1-10 (Ratay 1-4, Ivey 0-4, Joyce 0-2); **Team Rebounds:** 0; **Blocked Shots:** 11 (Riley 7, Barksdale 2, Haney, Ivey); **Turnovers:** 15 (Siemon 7, Ivey 4, Riley 3, Ratay); **Steals:** 8 (Ivey 6, Haney, Ratay); **Percentages:** 2-Pt FG (.543); 3-Pt FG (.100); Total FG (.464); Free Throws (.714).

Purdue (Big Ten) .... 32 34— **66**
Notre Dame (Big East) .... 26 42— **68**

Technical Fouls: None. **Officials:** Sally Bell, Scott Yarbrough, Lisa Mattingly. **Attendance:** 20,551. **TV Rating:** 2.7/5 share (ESPN).

Final ESPN/USA Today Coaches' Poll

Taken **after** NCAA tournament.

Voted on by panel of 10 women's coaches and media following the NCAA tournament: first place votes in parentheses.

		Pts			Pts
1	Notre Dame (10)	1,000	14	Washington	439
2	Purdue	948	15	Utah	414
3	Connecticut	925	16	N.C. State	382
4	SW Missouri St.	817	17	Rutgers	367
5	Tennessee	758	18	Florida	301
6	Louisiana Tech	748	19	Missouri	270
7	Vanderbilt	736	20	LSU	265
8	Duke	719	21	Iowa	198
9	Xavier	712	22	Clemson	161
10	Oklahoma	590	23	Colorado	154
11	Texas Tech	544	24	Villanova	70
12	Iowa St.	542	25	Florida St.	64
13	Georgia	534			

WOMEN'S FINAL FOUR

at St. Louis, Missouri (March 30-April 1).

Semifinals

Purdue 81 .... SW Missouri St. 64
Notre Dame 90 .... Connecticut 75

Championship

Notre Dame 68 .... Purdue 66

Final Records: Notre Dame (34-2), Purdue (31-7), Connecticut (32-3), SW Missouri St. (29-6).

Most Outstanding Player: Ruth Riley, Notre Dame center. SEMIFINAL— 32 minutes, 18 points, 7 rebounds, 5 blocks; FINAL— 35 minutes, 28 points, 13 rebounds, 7 blocks.

All-Tournament Team: Riley, guard Niele Ivey from Notre Dame, and guard/forward Katie Douglas and forwards Shalicia Hurns and Shereka Wright from Purdue.

Annual Awards

Player of the Year

Ruth Riley, Notre Dame ..... AP, Naismith, USBWA, WBCA
Jackie Stiles, SW Missouri St. .... Broderick, Wade

Coach of the Year

Muffet McGraw, Notre Dame .... AP, Naismith, WBCA, USBWA

Consensus All-America Team

The NCAA Division I players cited most frequently by the Associated Press, US Basketball Writers Assn., the Women's Basketball Coaches Assn. and the Women's Basketball News Service. Holdover from 1999-2000 All-America first team in **bold** type; (*) indicates unanimous first team selection.

First Team

	Class	Hgt	Pos
Katie Douglas, Purdue*	Sr.	6-1	F/G
Stacey Dales, Oklahoma*	Jr.	6-0	G
Kelly Miller, Georgia*	Sr.	5-10	G
Ruth Riley, Notre Dame*	Sr.	6-5	C
Jackie Stiles, SW Missouri St.*	Sr.	5-8	G

Second Team

	Class	Hgt	Pos
Svetlana Abrosimova, Connecticut	Sr.	6-2	F
Tamika Catchings, Tennessee	Sr.	6-1	F
LaToya Thomas, Mississippi St.	So.	6-2	C
Chantelle Anderson, Vanderbilt	So.	6-6	C
Marie Ferdinand, LSU	Sr.	5-9	G

Other Women's Tournaments

WNIT (Mar. 28 at Albuquerque, N.M.): Final— Ohio St. def. New Mexico, 62-61.
NCAA Division II (Mar. 24 at Rochester, Minn.): Final— Cal Poly-Pomona def. North Dakota, 87-80.
NCAA Division III (Mar. 17 at Danbury, Conn.): Final— Washington (Mo.) def. Messiah College, 67-45.
NAIA Division I (Mar. 20 at Jackson, Tenn.): Final— Oklahoma City def. Auburn Montgomery (Ala.), 69-52.
NAIA Division II (Mar. 13 at Sioux City, Iowa): Final— Northwestern College (Iowa) def. Albertson (Idaho), 77-50.

NCAA Women's Division I Leaders
Includes games through NCAA and NIT tourneys.

INDIVIDUAL

Scoring

	Cl	Gm	Pts	Avg
Jackie Stiles, SW Missouri St.	Sr.	35	1062	30.3
Deanna Jackson, UAB	Jr.	31	777	25.1
Janet Holt, Tennessee Tech	Jr.	30	738	24.6
LaToya Thomas, Mississippi	So.	31	752	24.3
Susan Moran, St. Joseph's	Jr.	28	633	22.6
Natalie Powers, Western Ky.	Jr.	33	736	22.3
Brooke Armistead, Austin Peay	So.	31	685	22.1
Sheila Lambert, Baylor	Jr.	30	662	22.1
Jaynetta Saunders, Texas A&M	Sr.	28	611	21.8
Diana Caramanico, Pennsylvania	Sr.	28	607	21.7
Michelle Maslowski, Drexel	Jr.	29	625	21.6
Jamie Thomatis, Md. Tenn. St.	Jr.	30	639	21.3
Chantelle Anderson, Vanderbilt	So.	34	722	21.2
Danielle Crockrom, Baylor	Jr.	30	637	21.2
Marie Ferdinand, LSU	Sr.	31	654	21.1
Kiesha Brooks, Coppin St.	Sr.	27	565	20.9
Michelle Greco, UCLA	Jr.	27	537	19.9
Angela Hassell, Tennessee St.	Sr.	27	537	19.9
Leslie McElrath, Georgia St.	Jr.	30	596	19.9
Gergana Slavtcheva, Florida	Jr.	30	593	19.8

Rebounding

	Cl	Gm	No	Avg
Andrea Gardner, Howard	Jr.	31	439	14.2
Angela Buckner, Wichita St.	Fr.	27	341	12.6
Malveata Johnson, N.C. A&T	Sr.	29	356	12.3
Schuye LaRue, Virginia	So.	32	379	11.8
Danielle Crockrom, Baylor	Jr.	30	347	11.6
Deanna Jackson, UAB	Jr.	31	358	11.5
LaQuanda Barksdale, N. Carolina	Sr.	29	334	11.5
Anne Tierney, Lehigh	So.	30	335	11.2
Brenda Abakwue, Sam Houston St.	Sr.	27	297	11.0
Sheena Johnson, TX-Arlington	Fr.	27	292	10.8
Janell Burse, Tulane	Sr.	32	342	10.7
Kieshu Burse, Tulane	Sr.	27	288	10.7
Christina Rible, Delaware	Jr.	31	324	10.5
Lani Lawrence, Northeastern	Jr.	29	302	10.4
Jermisha Dosty, St. Mary's-CA	Jr.	32	333	10.4

Assists

	Cl	Gm	No	Avg
Natasha Pointer, Rutgers	Sr.	31	257	8.3
Reetta Piipari, Xavier	So.	34	281	8.3
Angela Zampella, St. Joseph's	Sr.	27	220	8.1
Jamie Lewis, Ohio St.	Sr.	33	257	7.8
Sara Nord, Louisville	Fr.	29	222	7.7
Reshea Bristol, Arizona	Sr.	32	242	7.6
Michele Koclanes, Richmond	Jr.	28	208	7.4
Stacey Dales, Oklahoma	Jr.	34	248	7.3
Toccara Williams, Texas A&M	Fr.	28	196	7.0
Misty Garrett, Tennessee Tech.	Jr.	30	209	7.0
Niele Ivey, Notre Dame	Sr.	36	247	6.9
Ivelina Vrancheva, Fla. Int'l.	So.	30	205	6.8
Coretta Brown, N. Carolina	So.	29	193	6.7
Joana Fogaca, E. Carolina	Sr.	28	180	6.4
Shala Crook, Ball St.	Jr.	28	179	6.4
Marica Maddox, Georgia St.	Jr.	31	197	6.4
Cara Consuegra, Iowa	Sr.	31	191	6.2
Ashley McElhiney, Vanderbilt	So.	31	191	6.2
Sheila Lambert, Baylor	Jr.	30	182	6.1
Amy Wright, Arkansas	Jr.	33	198	6.0
Jessie Brown, UMBC	So.	28	168	6.0

Blocked Shots

	Cl	Gm	No	Avg
Malveata Johnson, N.C. A&T	Sr.	29	95	3.3
Ruth Riley, Notre Dame	Sr.	36	113	3.1
Tawana McDonald, Georgia	Jr.	33	103	3.1
Ruta Griniute, Fla. Atlantic	Sr.	28	86	3.1
Jordan Adams, New Mexico	So.	35	105	3.0

Steals

	Cl	Gm	No	Avg
Rochelle Luckett, VCU	Jr.	28	119	4.3
Shrieka Evans, Grambling	So.	29	116	4.0
LaNeishea Caufield, Oklahoma	Jr.	34	135	4.0
Shakira Smith, Morgan St.	Sr.	27	107	4.0
Toccara Williams, Texas A&M	Fr.	28	107	3.8

TEAM

Scoring Offense

	Gm	W-L	Pts	Avg
Eastern Ky.	28	22-6	2474	88.4
Connecticut	35	32-3	3035	86.7
SW Missouri St.	35	29-6	2898	82.8
Tennessee	34	31-3	2812	82.7
Ball St.	28	19-9	2312	82.6
Howard	31	21-10	2554	82.4
Oklahoma	34	28-6	2783	81.9
Tennessee Tech	30	24-6	2437	81.2
Georgia	33	27-6	2626	79.6

Scoring Defense

	Gm	W-L	Pts	Avg
Utah	32	28-4	1635	51.1
TX-San Antonio	29	16-13	1582	54.6
Connecticut	35	32-3	1921	54.9
Stephen F. Austin	33	26-7	1820	55.2
Notre Dame	36	34-2	2008	55.8
Rutgers	31	23-8	1750	56.5
Idaho St.	30	25-5	1710	57.0
Weber St.	29	14-15	1662	57.3
Louisiana Tech	36	31-5	2072	57.6
Villanova	31	22-9	1792	57.8

Scoring Margin

	Off	Def	Mar
Connecticut	86.7	54.9	31.8
Notre Dame	77.2	55.8	21.4
Tennessee	82.7	61.9	20.9
Louisiana Tech	75.4	57.6	17.9
Georgia	79.6	62.1	17.5
SW Missouri St.	82.8	66.5	16.3
Utah	66.8	51.1	15.8
Iowa St.	79.5	63.9	15.5
Florida	78.4	63.4	15.1

High-Point Games

Individual

No		Opponent	Date
49	Jackie Stiles, SW Mo. St.	Northern Iowa	1/20
48	LaToya Thomas, Mississippi St.	Memphis	11/21
47	Jackie Stiles, SW Mo. St.	Drake	3/10
43	Brianne Kenneally, Youngstown St.	Ga. St.	11/24
43	Jackie Stiles, SW Mo. St.	Southern Ill.	2/9

1901-2001 Through the Years

National Champions and NCAA Final Four

The Helms Foundation of Los Angeles, under the direction of founder Bill Schroeder, selected national college basketball champions from 1942-82 and researched retroactive picks from 1901-41. The first NIT tournament and then the NCAA tournament have settled the national championship since 1938, but there are four years (1939, '40, '44 and '54) where the Helms selections differ. In 1939, Helms picked undefeated LIU-Brooklyn (24-0), winners of the NIT. In 1940, Helms picked USC (20-3) although they were beaten by Kansas in the West Regionals of the NCAA tourney. In 1944, Helms picked unbeaten Army (15-0). Army did not lift its policy barring postseason play until the 1961 NIT. In 1954, Helms chose unbeaten Kentucky (25-0), even though Kentucky refused its NCAA bid after seniors Cliff Hagan, Frank Ramsey and Lou Tsioropoulos were declared ineligible.

Multiple champions (1901-37): Chicago, Columbia and Wisconsin (3); Kansas, Minnesota, Notre Dame, Penn, Pittsburgh, Syracuse and Yale (2). **Multiple champions (since 1938):** UCLA (11); Kentucky (7); Indiana (5); Duke and North Carolina (3); Cincinnati, Kansas, Louisville, Michigan St., N.C. State, Oklahoma A&M (now Oklahoma St.) and San Francisco (2).

Year		Record	Head Coach	Outstanding Player
1901	Yale	10-4	No coach	G.M. Clark, F
1902	Minnesota	11-0	Louis Cooke	W.C. Deering, F
1903	Yale	15-1	W.H. Murphy	R.B. Hyatt, F
1904	Columbia	17-1	No coach	Harry Fisher, F
1905	Columbia	19-1	No coach	Harry Fisher, F
1906	Dartmouth	16-2	No coach	George Grebenstein, F
1907	Chicago	22-2	Joseph Raycroft	John Schommer, C
1908	Chicago	21-2	Joseph Raycroft	John Schommer, C
1909	Chicago	12-0	Joseph Raycroft	John Schommer, C
1910	Columbia	11-1	Harry Fisher	Ted Kiendl, F
1911	St. John's-NY	14-0	Claude Allen	John Keenan, F/C
1912	Wisconsin	15-0	Doc Meanwell	Otto Stangel, F
1913	Navy	9-0	Louis Wenzell	Laurence Wild, F
1914	Wisconsin	15-0	Doc Meanwell	Gene Van Gent, C
1915	Illinois	16-0	Ralph Jones	Ray Woods, G
1916	Wisconsin	20-1	Doc Meanwell	George Levis, G
1917	Washington St.	25-1	Doc Bohler	Roy Bohler, G
1918	Syracuse	16-1	Edmund Dollard	Joe Schwarzer, G
1919	Minnesota	13-0	Louis Cooke	Arnold Oss, F
1920	Penn	22-1	Lon Jourdet	George Sweeney, F
1921	Penn	21-2	Edward McNichol	Danny McNichol, G
1922	Kansas	16-2	Phog Allen	Paul Endacott, G
1923	Kansas	17-1	Phog Allen	Paul Endacott, G
1924	North Carolina	25-0	Bo Shepard	Jack Cobb, F
1925	Princeton	21-2	Al Wittmer	Art Loeb, G
1926	Syracuse	19-1	Lew Andreas	Vic Hanson, F
1927	Notre Dame	19-1	George Keogan	John Nyikos, C
1928	Pittsburgh	21-0	Doc Carlson	Chuck Hyatt, F
1929	Montana St.	36-2	Schubert Dyche	John (Cat) Thompson, F
1930	Pittsburgh	23-2	Doc Carlson	Chuck Hyatt, F
1931	Northwestern	16-1	Dutch Lonborg	Joe Reiff, C
1932	Purdue	17-1	Piggy Lambert	John Wooden, G
1933	Kentucky	20-3	Adolph Rupp	Forest Sale, F
1934	Wyoming	26-3	Willard Witte	Les Witte, G
1935	NYU	19-1	Howard Cann	Sid Gross, F
1936	Notre Dame	22-2-1	George Keogan	John Moir, F
1937	Stanford	25-2	John Bunn	Hank Luisetti, F

Year		Record	Winner	Head Coach	Outstanding Player
1938	Temple	23-2	NIT	James Usilton	Meyer Bloom, G

Year	Champion	Runner-up	Score	Final Two		Third Place
1939	Oregon	Ohio St.	46-33	@ Evanston, IL	Oklahoma	Villanova
1940	Indiana	Kansas	60-42	@ Kansas City	Duquesne	USC
1941	Wisconsin	Washington St.	39-34	@ Kansas City	Arkansas	Pittsburgh
1942	Stanford	Dartmouth	53-38	@ Kansas City	Colorado	Kentucky
1943	Wyoming	Georgetown	46-34	@ New York	DePaul	Texas
1944	Utah	Dartmouth	42-40 (OT)	@ New York	Iowa St.	Ohio St.
1945	Oklahoma A&M	NYU	49-45	@ New York	Arkansas	Ohio St.

Year	Champion	Runner-up	Score	Final Two	Third Place	Fourth Place
1946	Oklahoma A&M	North Carolina	43-40	@ New York	Ohio St.	California
1947	Holy Cross	Oklahoma	58-47	@ New York	Texas	CCNY
1948	Kentucky	Baylor	58-42	@ New York	Holy Cross	Kansas St.
1949	Kentucky	Oklahoma A&M	46-36	@ Seattle	Illinois	Oregon St.
1950	CCNY	Bradley	71-68	@ New York	N.C. State	Baylor
1951	Kentucky	Kansas St.	68-58	@ Minneapolis	Illinois	Oklahoma A&M

Year	Champion	Runner-up	Score	Third Place	Fourth Place	Final Four
1952	Kansas	St. John's	80-63	Illinois	Santa Clara	@ Seattle
1953	Indiana	Kansas	69-68	Washington	LSU	@ Kansas City
1954	La Salle	Bradley	92-76	Penn St.	USC	@ Kansas City
1955	San Francisco	La Salle	77-63	Colorado	Iowa	@ Kansas City
1956	San Francisco	Iowa	83-71	Temple	SMU	@ Evanston, IL
1957	North Carolina	Kansas	54-53 (3OT)	San Francisco	Michigan St.	@ Kansas City
1958	Kentucky	Seattle	84-72	Temple	Kansas St.	@ Louisville
1959	California	West Virginia	71-70	Cincinnati	Louisville	@ Louisville
1960	Ohio St.	California	75-55	Cincinnati	NYU	@ San Francisco
1961	Cincinnati	Ohio St.	70-65 (OT)	St. Joseph's-PA	Utah	@ Kansas City
1962	Cincinnati	Ohio St.	71-59	Wake Forest	UCLA	@ Louisville
1963	Loyola-IL	Cincinnati	60-58 (OT)	Duke	Oregon St.	@ Louisville
1964	UCLA	Duke	98-83	Michigan	Kansas St.	@ Kansas City
1965	UCLA	Michigan	91-80	Princeton	Wichita St.	@ Portland, OR
1966	Texas Western	Kentucky	72-65	Duke	Utah	@ College Park, MD
1967	UCLA	Dayton	79-64	Houston	North Carolina	@ Louisville
1968	UCLA	North Carolina	78-55	Ohio St.	Houston	@ Los Angeles
1969	UCLA	Purdue	92-72	Drake	North Carolina	@ Louisville
1970	UCLA	Jacksonville	80-69	New Mexico St.	St. Bonaventure	@ College Park, MD
1971	UCLA	Villanova	68-62	Western Ky.	Kansas	@ Houston
1972	UCLA	Florida St.	81-76	North Carolina	Louisville	@ Los Angeles
1973	UCLA	Memphis St.	87-66	Indiana	Providence	@ St. Louis
1974	N.C. State	Marquette	76-64	UCLA	Kansas	@ Greensboro, NC
1975	UCLA	Kentucky	92-85	Louisville	Syracuse	@ San Diego
1976	Indiana	Michigan	86-68	UCLA	Rutgers	@ Philadelphia
1977	Marquette	North Carolina	67-59	UNLV	NC-Charlotte	@ Atlanta
1978	Kentucky	Duke	94-88	Arkansas	Notre Dame	@ St. Louis
1979	Michigan St.	Indiana St.	75-64	DePaul	Penn	@ Salt Lake City
1980	Louisville	UCLA	59-54	Purdue	Iowa	@ Indianapolis
1981	Indiana	North Carolina	63-50	Virginia	LSU	@ Philadelphia

Year	Champion	Runner-up	Score	Third Place		Final Four
1982	North Carolina	Georgetown	63-62	Houston	Louisville	@ New Orleans
1983	N.C. State	Houston	54-52	Georgia	Louisville	@ Albuquerque
1984	Georgetown	Houston	84-75	Kentucky	Virginia	@ Seattle
1985	Villanova	Georgetown	66-64	Memphis St.	St. John's	@ Lexington
1986	Louisville	Duke	72-69	Kansas	LSU	@ Dallas
1987	Indiana	Syracuse	74-73	Providence	UNLV	@ New Orleans
1988	Kansas	Oklahoma	83-79	Arizona	Duke	@ Kansas City
1989	Michigan	Seton Hall	80-79 (OT)	Duke	Illinois	@ Seattle
1990	UNLV	Duke	103-73	Arkansas	Georgia Tech	@ Denver
1991	Duke	Kansas	72-65	North Carolina	UNLV	@ Indianapolis
1992	Duke	Michigan	71-51	Cincinnati	Indiana	@ Minneapolis
1993	North Carolina	Michigan	77-71	Kansas	Kentucky	@ New Orleans
1994	Arkansas	Duke	76-72	Arizona	Florida	@ Charlotte
1995	UCLA	Arkansas	89-78	North Carolina	Oklahoma St.	@ Seattle
1996	Kentucky	Syracuse	76-67	UMass	Mississippi St.	@ E. Rutherford, NJ
1997	Arizona	Kentucky	84-79 (OT)	Minnesota	North Carolina	@ Indianapolis
1998	Kentucky	Utah	78-69	Stanford	North Carolina	@ San Antonio
1999	Connecticut	Duke	77-74	Michigan St.	Ohio St.	@ St. Petersburg, FL
2000	Michigan St.	Florida	89-76	Wisconsin	North Carolina	@ Indianapolis
2001	Duke	Arizona	82-72	Michigan St.	Maryland	@ Minneapolis

Note: Six teams have had their standing in the Final Four vacated for using ineligible players: 1961–St. Joseph's-PA (3rd place); 1971–Villanova (Runner-up) and Western Kentucky (3rd); 1980–UCLA (Runner-up); 1985–Memphis St. (3rd); 1996–UMass (3rd).

The Red Cross Benefit Games, 1943-45

For three seasons during World War II, the NCAA and NIT champions met in a benefit game at Madison Square Garden in New York to raise money for the Red Cross. The NCAA champs won all three games.

Year	Winner	Score	Loser
1943	Wyoming (NCAA)	52-47	St. John's (NIT)
1944	Utah (NCAA)	43-36	St. John's (NIT)
1945	Oklahoma A&M (NCAA)	52-44	DePaul (NIT)

Most Outstanding Player

A Most Outstanding Player has been selected every year of the NCAA tournament. Winners who did not play for the tournament champion are listed in **bold** type. The 1939 and 1951 winners are unofficial and not recognized by the NCAA. Statistics listed are for Final Four games only.

Multiple winners: Lew Alcindor (3); Alex Groza, Bob Kurland, Jerry Lucas and Bill Walton (2).

Year		Gm	FGM	Pct	3PTM	3PTA	FTM	Pct	Reb	Ast	Blk	Stl	PPG
1939	**Jimmy Hull**, Ohio St.	2	15	—	—	—	10	.833	—	—	—	—	20.0
1940	Marv Huffman, Indiana	2	7	—	—	—	4	—	—	—	—	—	9.0
1941	John Kotz, Wisconsin	2	8	—	—	—	6	—	—	—	—	—	11.0
1942	Howie Dallmar, Stanford	2	8	—	—	—	4	.667	—	—	—	—	10.0
1943	Kenny Sailors, Wyoming	2	10	—	—	—	8	.727	—	—	—	—	14.0
1944	Arnie Ferrin, Utah	2	11	—	—	—	6	—	—	—	—	—	14.0
1945	Bob Kurland, Okla. A&M	2	16	—	—	—	5	—	—	—	—	—	18.5
1946	Bob Kurland, Okla. A&M	2	21	—	—	—	10	.667	—	—	—	—	26.0
1947	George Kaftan, Holy Cross	2	18	—	—	—	12	.706	—	—	—	—	24.0
1948	Alex Groza, Kentucky	2	16	—	—	—	5	—	—	—	—	—	18.5
1949	Alex Groza, Kentucky	2	19	—	—	—	14	—	—	—	—	—	26.0
1950	Irwin Dambrot, CCNY	2	12	.429	—	—	4	.500	—	—	—	—	14.0
1951	Bill Spivey, Kentucky	2	20	.400	—	—	10	.625	37	—	—	—	25.0
1952	Clyde Lovellette, Kansas	2	24	—	—	—	18	—	—	—	—	—	33.0
1953	**B.H. Born**, Kansas	2	17	—	—	—	17	—	—	—	—	—	25.5
1954	Tom Gola, La Salle	2	12	—	—	—	14	—	—	—	—	—	19.0
1955	Bill Russell, San Francisco	2	19	—	—	—	9	—	—	—	—	—	23.5
1956	**Hal Lear**, Temple	2	32	—	—	—	16	—	—	—	—	—	40.0
1957	**Wilt Chamberlain**, Kansas	2	18	.514	—	—	19	.704	25	—	—	—	32.5
1958	**Elgin Baylor**, Seattle	2	18	.340	—	—	12	.750	41	—	—	—	24.0
1959	Jerry West, West Virginia	2	22	.667	—	—	22	.688	25	—	—	—	33.0
1960	Jerry Lucas, Ohio St.	2	16	.667	—	—	3	1.000	23	—	—	—	17.5
1961	**Jerry Lucas**, Ohio St.	2	20	.714	—	—	16	.941	25	—	—	—	28.0
1962	Paul Hogue, Cincinnati	2	23	.639	—	—	12	.632	38	—	—	—	29.0
1963	**Art Heyman**, Duke	2	18	.409	—	—	15	.682	19	—	—	—	25.5
1964	Walt Hazzard, UCLA	2	11	.550	—	—	8	.667	10	—	—	—	15.0
1965	**Bill Bradley**, Princeton	2	34	.630	—	—	19	.950	24	—	—	—	43.5
1966	Jerry Chambers, Utah	2	25	.532	—	—	20	.833	35	—	—	—	35.0
1967	Lew Alcindor, UCLA	2	14	.609	—	—	11	.458	38	—	—	—	19.5
1968	Lew Alcindor, UCLA	2	22	.629	—	—	9	.900	34	—	—	—	26.5
1969	Lew Alcindor, UCLA	2	23	.676	—	—	16	.640	41	—	—	—	31.0
1970	Sidney Wicks, UCLA	2	15	.714	—	—	9	.600	34	—	—	—	19.5
1971	**Howard Porter**, Villanova	2	20	.488	—	—	7	.778	24	—	—	—	23.5
1972	Bill Walton, UCLA	2	20	.690	—	—	17	.739	41	—	—	—	28.5
1973	Bill Walton, UCLA	2	28	.824	—	—	2	.400	30	—	—	—	29.0
1974	David Thompson, N.C. State	2	19	.514	—	—	11	.786	17	—	—	—	24.5
1975	Richard Washington, UCLA	2	23	.548	—	—	8	.727	20	—	—	—	27.0
1976	Kent Benson, Indiana	2	17	.500	—	—	7	.636	18	—	—	—	20.5
1977	Butch Lee, Marquette	2	11	.344	—	—	8	1.000	6	2	1	1	15.0
1978	Jack Givens, Kentucky	2	28	.651	—	—	8	.667	17	4	1	3	32.0
1979	Magic Johnson, Michigan St.	2	17	.680	—	—	19	.864	17	3	0	2	26.5
1980	Darrell Griffith, Louisville	2	23	.622	—	—	11	.688	7	15	0	2	28.5
1981	Isiah Thomas, Indiana	2	14	.560	—	—	9	.818	4	9	3	4	18.5
1982	James Worthy, N. Carolina	2	20	.741	—	—	2	.286	8	9	0	4	21.0
1983	**Akeem Olajuwon**, Houston	2	16	.552	—	—	9	.643	40	3	2	5	20.5
1984	Patrick Ewing, Georgetown	2	8	.571	—	—	2	1.000	18	1	15	1	9.0
1985	Ed Pinckney, Villanova	2	8	.571	—	—	12	.750	15	6	3	0	14.0
1986	Pervis Ellison, Louisville	2	15	.600	—	—	6	.750	24	2	3	1	18.0
1987	Keith Smart, Indiana	2	14	.636	0	1	7	.778	7	7	0	2	17.5
1988	Danny Manning, Kansas	2	25	.556	0	1	6	.667	17	4	8	9	28.0
1989	Glen Rice, Michigan	2	24	.490	7	16	4	1.000	16	1	0	3	29.5
1990	Anderson Hunt, UNLV	2	19	.613	9	16	2	.500	4	9	1	1	24.5
1991	Christian Laettner, Duke	2	12	.545	1	1	21	.913	17	2	1	2	23.0
1992	Bobby Hurley, Duke	2	10	.417	7	12	8	.800	3	11	0	3	17.5
1993	Donald Williams, N. Carolina	2	15	.652	10	14	10	1.000	4	1	0	2	25.0
1994	Corliss Williamson, Arkansas	2	21	.500	0	0	10	.714	21	8	3	4	26.0
1995	Ed O'Bannon, UCLA	2	16	.457	3	8	10	.769	25	3	1	7	22.5
1996	Tony Delk, Kentucky	2	15	.417	8	16	6	.546	9	2	3	2	22.0
1997	Miles Simon, Arizona	2	17	.459	3	10	17	.773	8	6	0	1	27.0
1998	Jeff Sheppard, Kentucky	2	16	.552	4	10	7	.778	10	7	0	4	21.5
1999	Richard Hamilton, Connecticut	2	20	.513	3	7	8	.727	12	4	1	2	25.5
2000	Mateen Cleaves, Michigan St.	2	8	.444	3	4	10	.833	6	5	0	2	14.5
2001	Shane Battier, Duke	2	13	.464	5	12	12	.706	19	8	6	2	21.5

Final Four All-Decade Teams

To celebrate the 50th anniversary of the NCAA tournament in 1989, five All-Decade teams were selected by a blue ribbon panel of coaches and administrators. An All-Time Final Four team was also chosen. Selections were actually made prior to the 1988 tournament.

Selection panel: Vic Bubas, Denny Crum, Wayne Duke, Dave Gavitt, Joe B. Hall, Jud Heathcote, Hank Iba, Pete Newell, Dean Smith, John Thompson and John Wooden.

All-1950s

	Years
Elgin Baylor, Seattle	1958
Wilt Chamberlain, Kansas	1957
Tom Gola, La Salle	1954
K.C. Jones, San Francisco	1955
Clyde Lovellette, Kansas	1952
Oscar Robertson, Cinn.	1959-60
Guy Rodgers, Temple	1958
Lennie Rosenbluth, N. Carolina	1957
Bill Russell, San Francisco	1955-56
Jerry West, West Virginia	1959

All-1970s

	Years
Kent Benson, Indiana	1976
Larry Bird, Indiana St	1979
Jack Givens, Kentucky	1978
Magic Johnson, Mich. St.	1979
Marques Johnson, UCLA	1975-76
Scott May, Indiana	1976
David Thompson, N.C. State	1974
Bill Walton, UCLA	1972-74
Sidney Wicks, UCLA	1969-71
Keith Wilkes, UCLA	1972-74

All-Time Team

	Years
Lew Alcindor, UCLA	1967-69
Larry Bird, Indiana St.	1979
Wilt Chamberlain, Kansas	1957
Magic Johnson, Mich. St	1979
Michael Jordan, N. Carolina	1982

All-1940s

	Years
Ralph Beard, Kentucky	1948-49
Howie Dallmar, Stanford	1942
Dwight Eddleman, Illinois	1949
Arnie Ferrin, Utah	1944
Alex Groza, Kentucky	1948-49
George Kaftan, Holy Cross	1947
Bob Kurland, Okla. A&M	1945-46
Jim Pollard, Stanford	1942
Kenny Sailors, Wyoming	1943
Gerry Tucker, Oklahoma	1947

All-1960s

	Years
Lew Alcindor, UCLA	1967-69
Bill Bradley, Princeton	1965
Gail Goodrich, UCLA	1964-65
John Havlicek, Ohio St.	1961-62
Elvin Hayes, Houston	1967
Walt Hazzard, UCLA	1964
Jerry Lucas, Ohio St	1960-61
Jeff Mullins, Duke	1964
Cazzie Russell, Michigan	1965
Charlie Scott, N. Carolina	1968-69

All-1980s

	Years
Steve Alford, Indiana	1987
Johnny Dawkins, Duke	1986
Patrick Ewing, Georgetown	1982-84
Darrell Griffith, Louisville	1980
Michael Jordan, N. Carolina	1982
Rodney McCray, Louisville	1980
Akeem Olajuwon, Houston	1983-84
Ed Pinckney, Villanova	1985
Isiah Thomas, Indiana	1981
James Worthy, N. Carolina	1982

Note: Lew Alcindor later changed his name to Kareem Abdul-Jabbar; Keith Wilkes later changed his first name to Jamaal; and Akeem Olajuwon later changed the spelling of his first name to Hakeem.

Seeds at the Final Four

Year	Seeds (Total)	Teams
1979	1,2,2,9 (14)	Indiana St., **Michigan St.**, DePaul, Pennsylvania
1980	2,5,6,8 (21)	**Louisville**, Iowa, Purdue, UCLA
1981	1,1,2,3 (7)	Virginia, LSU, N. Carolina, **Indiana**
1982	1,1,3,6 (11)	**N. Carolina**, Georgetown, Louisville, Houston
1983	1,1,4,6 (12)	Houston, Louisville, Georgia, **N.C. State**
1984	1,1,2,7 (11)	Kentucky, **Georgetown**, Houston, Virginia
1985	1,1,2,8 (12)	St. John's, Georgetown, Memphis, **Villanova**
1986	1,1,2,11 (15)	Duke, Kansas, **Louisville**, LSU
1987	1,1,2,6 (10)	UNLV, **Indiana**, Syracuse, Providence
1988	1,1,2,6 (10)	Arizona, Oklahoma, Duke, **Kansas**
1989	1,2,3,3 (9)	Illinois, Duke, Seton Hall, **Michigan**
1990	1,3,4,4 (12)	**UNLV**, Duke, Ga. Tech, Arkansas
1991	1,1,2,3 (7)	UNLV, N. Carolina, **Duke**, Kansas
1992	1,2,4,6 (13)	**Duke**, Indiana, Cincinnati, Michigan
1993	1,1,1,2 (5)	**N. Carolina**, Kentucky, Michigan, Kansas
1994	1,2,2,3 (8)	**Arkansas**, Arizona, Duke, Florida
1995	1,2,2,4 (9)	**UCLA**, Arkansas, N. Carolina, Okla. St.
1996	1,1,4,5 (11)	**Kentucky**, UMass, Syracuse, Miss. St.
1997	1,1,1,4 (7)	Kentucky, N. Carolina, Minnesota, **Arizona**
1998	1,2,3,3 (9)	N. Carolina, **Kentucky**, Stanford, Utah
1999	1,1,1,4 (7)	**Connecticut**, Duke, Michigan St., Ohio St.
2000	1,5,8,8 (22)	**Michigan St.**, Florida, Wisconsin, N. Carolina
2001	1,1,2,3 (7)	**Duke,** Michigan St., Arizona, Maryland

All-Time Seeds Records

All-time records of NCAA tournament seeds since tourney began seeding teams in 1979. Records are through the 2001 NCAA Tournament. Note that 1st refers to championships. 2nd refers to runners-up and FF refers to Final Four appearances not including 1st and 2nd place finishes.

Seed	W	L	Pct.	1st	2nd	FF
1	280	81	.776	12	9	18
2	200	87	.697	5	6	8
3	138	90	.605	2	4	4
4	128	91	.584	1	1	6
5	104	93	.528	0	1	2
6	127	90	.585	2	1	3
7	74	92	.446	0	0	1
8	70	91	.435	1	1	2
9	55	93	.372	0	0	1
10	62	92	.403	0	0	0
11	40	88	.313	0	0	1
12	34	88	.279	0	0	0
13	17	68	.200	0	0	0
14	15	68	.181	0	0	0
15	4	68	.056	0	0	0
16	0	68	.000	0	0	0

Collegiate Commissioners Association Tournament

The Collegiate Commissioners Association staged an eight-team tournament for teams that didn't make the NCAA tournament in 1974 and '75.

Most Valuable Players: 1974–Kent Benson, Indiana: 1975–Bob Elliot, Arizona.

Year	Winner	Score	Loser	Site
1974	Indiana	85-60	USC	St. Louis
1975	Drake	83-76	Arizona	Louisville

NCAA Tournament Appearances

App		W-L	F4	Championships	App		W-L	F4	Championships
43	Kentucky	89-38	13	7 (1948-49,51,58,78,96,98)	21	DePaul	20-24	2	None
37	UCLA	83-30	15	11 (1964-65,67-73,75,95)	21	Ohio St.	36-20	9	1 (1960)
35	N. Carolina	81-35	15	3 (1957,82,93)	21	Illinois	27-22	4	None
30	Indiana	52-25	7	5 (1940,53,76,81,87)	20	Michigan	41-19	6	1 (1989)
30	Kansas	61-30	10	2 (1952,88)	20	Arizona	32-19	3	1 (1997)
29	Louisville	48-31	7	2 (1980,86)	20	Cincinnati	37-19	6	2 (1961-62)
27	Syracuse	40-28	3	None	20	Iowa	27-22	3	None
26	St. John's	27-28	2	None	20	Oklahoma	23-20	3	None
26	Arkansas	39-26	6	1 (1994)	19	Purdue	26-19	2	None
25	Duke	73-22	13	3 (1991-92, 2001)	19	Texas	17-22	2	None
25	Villanova	37-25	3	1 (1985)	19	Missouri	14-19	0	None
25	Notre Dame	26-29	1	None	19	BYU	11-22	0	None
25	Temple	31-25	2	None	18	Houston	26-23	5	None
22	Connecticut	27-22	1	1 (1999)	18	Oklahoma St.	30-17	5	2 (1945-46)
22	Kansas St.	27-26	4	None	18	Maryland	26-18	1	None
22	Utah	32-25	4	1 (1944)	18	West Virginia	13-18	1	None
22	Georgetown	38-21	4	1 (1984)	18	Pennsylvania	13-20	1	None
22	Princeton	13-26	1	None	17	N.C. State	27-16	3	2 (1974,83)
21	Marquette	28-22	2	1 (1977)	17	Western Ky.	15-18	1	None

Note: Although all NCAA tournament appearances are included above, the NCAA has officially voided the records of Villanova (4-1) and Western Ky. (4-1) in 1971; UCLA (5-1) in 1980 and again (0-1) in 1999; Oregon St. (2-3) from 1980-82; Memphis (9-5) from 1982-86; DePaul (6-4) from 1986-89; N.C. State (0-2) from 1987-88; Kentucky (2-1) and Maryland (1-1) in 1988; Missouri (3-1) in 1994; Connecticut (2-1) and Purdue (1-1) in 1996; Arizona (0-1) in 1999.

All-Time NCAA Division I Tournament Leaders

Through 2001; minimum of six games; **Last** column indicates final year played.

CAREER

Scoring

	Points	Yrs	Last	Gm	Pts
1	Christian Laettner, Duke	4	1992	23	407
2	Elvin Hayes, Houston	3	1968	13	358
3	Danny Manning, Kansas	4	1988	16	328
4	Oscar Robertson, Cincinnati	3	1960	10	324
5	Glen Rice, Michigan	4	1989	13	308
6	Lew Alcindor, UCLA	3	1969	12	304
7	Bill Bradley, Princeton	3	1965	9	303
	Corliss Williamson, Arkansas	3	1995	15	303
9	Austin Carr, Notre Dame	3	1971	7	289
10	Juwan Howard, Michigan	3	1994	16	280

	Average	Yrs	Last	Pts	Avg
1	Austin Carr, Notre Dame	3	1971	289	41.3
2	Bill Bradley, Princeton	3	1965	303	33.7
3	Oscar Robertson, Cincinnati	3	1960	324	32.4
4	Jerry West, West Virginia	3	1960	275	30.6
5	Bob Pettit, LSU	2	1954	183	30.5
6	Dan Issel, Kentucky	3	1970	176	29.3
	Jim McDaniels, Western Ky	2	1971	176	29.3
8	Dwight Lamar, SW Louisiana	2	1973	175	29.2
9	Bo Kimble, Loyola-CA	3	1990	204	29.1
10	David Robinson, Navy	3	1987	200	28.6

Rebounds

	Total	Yrs	Last	Gm	No
1	Elvin Hayes, Houston	3	1968	13	222
2	Lew Alcindor, UCLA	3	1969	12	201
3	Jerry Lucas, Ohio St.	3	1962	12	197
4	Bill Walton, UCLA	3	1974	12	176
5	Christian Laettner, Duke	4	1992	23	169
6	Tim Duncan, Wake Forest	4	1997	11	165
7	Paul Hogue, Cincinnati	3	1962	12	160
8	Sam Lacey, New Mexico St.	3	1970	11	157
9	Derrick Coleman, Syracuse	4	1990	14	155
10	Akeem Olajuwon, Houston	3	1984	15	153

	Average	Yrs	Last	Reb	Avg
1	Johnny Green, Michigan St.	2	1959	118	19.7
2	Artis Gilmore, Jacksonville	2	1971	115	19.2
3	Paul Silas, Creighton	3	1964	111	18.5
4	Len Chappell, Wake Forest	2	1962	137	17.1
5	Elvin Hayes, Houston	3	1968	222	17.1
6	Lew Alcindor, UCLA	3	1969	201	16.8
7	Jerry Lucas, Ohio St.	3	1962	197	16.4
8	Tim Duncan, Wake Forest	4	1997	165	15.0
9	Bill Walton, UCLA	3	1974	176	14.7
10	Sam Lacey, New Mexico St.	3	1970	157	14.3

3-Pt Field Goals

	Total	Yrs	Last	Gm	No
1	Bobby Hurley, Duke	4	1993	20	42
2	Tony Delk, Kentucky	4	1996	17	40
3	Jeff Fryer, Loyola-CA	3	1990	7	38
	Donald Williams, North Carolina	4	1995	15	38
5	Scotty Thurman, Arkansas	3	1995	15	36

Assists

	Total	Yrs	Last	Gm	No
1	Bobby Hurley, Duke	4	1993	20	145
2	Sherman Douglas, Syracuse	4	1989	14	106
3	Greg Anthony, UNLV	3	1991	15	100
4	Mark Wade, UNLV	2	1987	8	93
	Rumeal Robinson, Michigan	3	1990	11	93
	Jacque Vaughn, Kansas	4	1997	13	93
	Anthony Epps, Kentucky	4	1997	18	93

SINGLE TOURNAMENT

Scoring

	Points	Year	Gm	Pts
1	Glen Rice, Michigan	1989	6	184
2	Bill Bradley, Princeton	1965	5	177
3	Elvin Hayes, Houston	1968	5	167
4	Danny Manning, Kansas	1988	6	163
5	Hal Lear, Temple	1956	5	160
	Jerry West, West Virginia	1959	5	160

	Average	Year	Gm	Pts	Avg
1	Austin Carr, Notre Dame	1970	3	158	52.7
2	Austin Carr, Notre Dame	1971	3	125	41.7
3	Jerry Chambers, Utah	1966	4	143	35.8
	Bo Kimble, Loyola-CA	1990	4	143	35.8
5	Bill Bradley, Princeton	1965	5	177	35.4
6	Clyde Lovellette, Kansas	1952	4	141	35.3

Rebounds

Total	Year	Gm	No	Avg
1 Elvin Hayes, Houston...........1968		5	97	19.4
2 Artis Gilmore, Jacksonville 1970		5	93	18.6
3 Elgin Baylor, Seattle............1958		5	91	18.2
4 Sam Lacey, New Mexico St. 1970		5	90	18.0
5 Clarence Glover, Western Ky....1971		5	89	17.8

Assists

Total	Year	Gm	No	Avg
1 Mark Wade, UNLV 1987		5	61	12.2
2 Rumeal Robinson, Michigan.....1989		6	56	9.3
3 Sherman Douglas, Syracuse.....1987		6	49	8.2
4 Bobby Hurley, Duke............1992		6	47	7.8
5 Lazarus Sims, Syracuse.........1996		6	46	7.7

SINGLE GAME

Scoring

Points	Year	Pts
1 Austin Carr, Notre Dame vs Ohio Univ 1970		61
2 Bill Bradley, Princeton vs Wichita St.........1965		58
3 Oscar Robertson, Cincinnati vs Arkansas....1958		56
4 Austin Carr, Notre Dame vs Kentucky.......1970		52
Austin Carr, Notre Dame vs TCU...........1971		52
6 David Robinson, Navy vs Michigan 1987		50
7 Elvin Hayes, Houston vs Loyola-IL 1968		49
8 Hal Lear, Temple vs SMU 1956		48
9 Austin Carr, Notre Dame vs Houston 1971		47
10 Dave Corzine, DePaul vs Louisville.........1978		46
11 Bob Houbregs, Washington vs Seattle 1953		45
Austin Carr, Notre Dame vs Iowa 1970		45
Bo Kimble, Loyola-CA vs New Mexico St....1990		45
14 Seven players tied with 44 each.		

Rebounds

Total	Year	No
1 Fred Cohen, Temple vs UConn.............1956		34
2 Nate Thurmond, Bowl. Green vs Miss. St....1963		31
3 Jerry Lucas, Ohio St. vs Kentucky.........1961		30
4 Toby Kimball, UConn vs St. Joseph's-PA 1965		29
5 Elvin Hayes, Houston vs Pacific 1966		28

Assists

Total	Year	No
1 Mark Wade, UNLV vs Indiana............1987		18
2 Sam Crawford, N. Mexico St. vs Nebraska .1993		16
3 Kenny Patterson, DePaul vs Syracuse 1985		15
Keith Smart, Indiana vs Auburn..........1987		15
5 Six players tied with 14 each.		

SINGLE FINAL FOUR GAME

Letters in the **Year** column indicate the following: C for Consolation Game, F for Final and S for Semifinal.

Scoring

Points	Year	Pts
1 Bill Bradley, Princeton vs Wichita St 1965-C		58
2 Hal Lear, Temple vs SMU................1956-C		48
3 Bill Walton, UCLA vs Memphis St.........1973-F		44
4 Bob Houbregs, Washington vs LSU 1953-C		42
Jack Egan, St. Joseph's-PA vs Utah 1961-C		42*
Gail Goodrich, UCLA vs Michigan 1965-C		42
7 Jack Givens, Kentucky vs Duke 1978-F		41
8 Oscar Robertson, Cincinnati vs L'ville 1959-C		39
Al Wood, N. Carolina vs Virginia 1981-S		39
10 Jerry West, West Va. vs Louisville.........1959-S		38
Jerry Chambers, Utah vs Texas Western ...1966-S		38
Freddie Banks, UNLV vs Indiana..........1987-S		38

*Four overtimes.

Rebounds

Total	Year	No
1 Bill Russell, San Francisco vs Iowa 1956-F		27
2 Elvin Hayes, Houston vs UCLA 1967-S		24
3 Bill Russell, San Francisco vs SMU 1956-S		23
4 Four players tied with 22 each.		

Assists

Total	Year	No
1 Mark Wade, UNLV vs Indiana 1987-S		18
2 Rumeal Robinson, Michigan vs Illinois....1989-S		12
Edgar Padilla, UMass vs. Ky...........1996-S		12
4 Michael Jackson, G'town vs St. John's....1985-S		11
Milt Wagner, Louisville vs LSU............1986-S		11
Rumeal Robinson, Mich. vs Seton Hall.....1989-F		11*

*Overtime.

Teams in Both NCAA and NIT

Fourteen teams played in both the NCAA and NIT tournaments from 1940-52. Colorado (1940), Utah (1944), Kentucky (1949) and BYU (1951) won one of the titles, while CCNY won two in 1950, beating Bradley in both championship games.

Year	NIT	NCAA
1940 Colorado ....**Won Final**		Lost 1st Rd
Duquesne ....Lost Final		Lost 2nd Rd
1944 Utah ....Lost 1st Rd		**Won Final**
1949 Kentucky ....Lost 2nd Rd		**Won Final**
1950 CCNY ....**Won Final**		**Won Final**
Bradley ....Lost Final		Lost Final
1951 BYU ....**Won Final**		Lost 2nd Rd
St. John's ....Lost 3rd Rd		Lost 2nd Rd
N.C. State .....Lost 2nd Rd		Lost 2nd Rd
Arizona ......Lost 2nd Rd		Lost 1st Rd
1952 St. John's ....Lost 2nd Rd		Lost Final
Dayton ....Lost Final		Lost 1st Rd
Duquesne ......Lost 3rd Rd		Lost 2nd Rd
Saint Louis ......Lost 2nd Rd		Lost 2nd Rd

Most Popular Final Four Sites

The NCAA has staged its Men's Division I championship--the Final Two (1939-51) and Final Four (since 1952)--at 31 different arenas and indoor stadiums in 27 different cities. The following facilities have all hosted the event more than once.

No	Arena	Years
9	Municipal Auditorium (KC)	1940-42, 53-55, 57, 61, 64
7	Madison Sq. Garden (NYC)	1943-48, 50
6	Freedom Hall (Louisville)	1958-59, 62-63, 67, 69
3	Kingdome (Seattle)	1984, 89, 95
	RCA Dome (Indianapolis)	1991, 97, 2000
	Superdome (New Orleans)	1982, 87, 93
2	Cole Field House (College Park, Md.)	1966, 70
	Edmundson Pavilion (Seattle)	1949, 52
	HHH Metrodome (Minneapolis)	1992, 2001
	LA Sports Arena	1968, 72
	St. Louis Arena	1973, 78
	Spectrum (Philadelphia)	1976, 81

NIT Championship

The National Invitation Tournament began under the sponsorship of the Metropolitan New York Basketball Writers Association in 1938. The NIT is now administered by the Metropolitan Intercollegiate Basketball Association. All championship games have been played at Madison Square Garden.

Multiple winners: St. John's (5); Bradley (4); BYU, Dayton, Kentucky, LIU-Brooklyn, Michigan, Minnesota, Providence, Temple, Tulsa, Virginia and Virginia Tech (2).

Year	Winner	Score	Loser	Year	Winner	Score	Loser
1938	Temple	60-36	Colorado	1970	Marquette	65-53	St. John's
1939	LIU-Brooklyn	44-32	Loyola-IL	1971	North Carolina	84-66	Georgia Tech
1940	Colorado	51-40	Duquesne	1972	Maryland	100-69	Niagara
1941	LIU-Brooklyn	56-42	Ohio Univ.	1973	Virginia Tech	92-91 (OT)	Notre Dame
1942	West Virginia	47-45	Western Ky.	1974	Purdue	97-81	Utah
1943	St. John's	48-27	Toledo	1975	Princeton	80-69	Providence
1944	St. John's	47-39	DePaul	1976	Kentucky	71-67	NC-Charlotte
1945	DePaul	71-54	Bowling Green	1977	St. Bonaventure	94-91	Houston
1946	Kentucky	46-45	Rhode Island	1978	Texas	101-93	N.C. State
1947	Utah	49-45	Kentucky	1979	Indiana	53-52	Purdue
1948	Saint Louis	65-52	NYU	1980	Virginia	58-55	Minnesota
1949	San Francisco	48-47	Loyola-IL	1981	Tulsa	86-84 (OT)	Syracuse
1950	CCNY	69-61	Bradley	1982	Bradley	67-58	Purdue
1951	BYU	62-43	Dayton	1983	Fresno St.	69-60	DePaul
1952	La Salle	75-64	Dayton	1984	Michigan	83-63	Notre Dame
1953	Seton Hall	58-46	St. John's	1985	UCLA	65-62	Indiana
1954	Holy Cross	71-62	Duquesne	1986	Ohio St.	73-63	Wyoming
1955	Duquesne	70-58	Dayton	1987	Southern Miss.	84-80	La Salle
1956	Louisville	93-80	Dayton	1988	Connecticut	72-67	Ohio St.
1957	Bradley	84-83	Memphis St.	1989	St. John's	73-65	Saint Louis
1958	Xavier-OH	78-74 (OT)	Dayton	1990	Vanderbilt	74-72	Saint Louis
1959	St. John's	76-71 (OT)	Bradley	1991	Stanford	78-72	Oklahoma
1960	Bradley	88-72	Providence	1992	Virginia	81-76 (OT)	Notre Dame
1961	Providence	62-59	Saint Louis	1993	Minnesota	62-61	Georgetown
1962	Dayton	73-67	St. John's	1994	Villanova	80-73	Vanderbilt
1963	Providence	81-66	Canisius	1995	Virginia Tech	65-64 (OT)	Marquette
1964	Bradley	86-54	New Mexico	1996	Nebraska	60-56	St. Joseph's
1965	St. John's	55-51	Villanova	1997	Michigan	82-72	Florida St.
1966	BYU	97-84	NYU	1998	Minnesota	79-72	Penn St.
1967	Southern Illinois	71-56	Marquette	1999	California	61-60	Clemson
1968	Dayton	61-48	Kansas	2000	Wake Forest	71-61	Notre Dame
1969	Temple	89-76	Boston Coll.	2001	Tulsa	79-60	Alabama

Most Valuable Player

A Most Valuable Player has been selected every year of the NIT tournament. Winners who did not play for the tournament champion are listed in **bold** type.

Multiple winners: None. However, Tom Gola of La Salle is the only player to be named MVP in the NIT (1952) and Most Outstanding Player of the NCAA tournament (1954).

Year		Year		Year	
1938	Don Shields, Temple	1964	Lavern Tart, Bradley	1989	Jayson Williams, St. John's
1939	**Bill Lloyd**, St. John's	1965	Ken McIntyre, St. John's	1990	Scott Draud, Vanderbilt
1940	Bob Doll, Colorado	1966	**Bill Melchionni**, Villanova	1991	Adam Keefe, Stanford
1941	**Frank Baumholtz**, Ohio U.	1967	Walt Frazier, So. Illinois	1992	Bryant Stith, Virginia
1942	Rudy Baric, West Virginia	1968	Don May, Dayton	1993	Voshon Lenard, Minnesota
1943	Harry Boykoff, St. John's	1969	**Terry Driscoll,** Boston College	1994	**Doremus Bennerman**, Siena
1944	Bill Kotsores, St. John's	1970	Dean Meminger, Marquette	1995	Shawn Smith, Va. Tech
1945	George Mikan, DePaul	1971	Bill Chamberlain, N. Carolina	1996	Erick Strickland, Nebraska
1946	**Ernie Calverley**, Rhode Island	1972	Tom McMillen, Maryland	1997	Robert Traylor, Michigan
1947	Vern Gardner, Utah	1973	**John Shumate**, Notre Dame	1998	Kevin Clark, Minnesota
1948	Ed Macauley, Saint Louis	1974	**Mike Sojourner**, Utah	1999	Sean Lampley, California
1949	Don Lofgran, San Francisco	1975	**Ron Lee**, Oregon	2000	Robert O'Kelley, Wake Forest
1950	Ed Warner, CCNY	1976	**Cedric Maxwell**, NC-Charlotte	2001	Marcus Hill, Tulsa
1951	Roland Minson, BYU	1977	Greg Sanders, St. Bonaventure		
1952	Tom Gola, La Salle & Norm Grekin, La Salle	1978	Ron Baxter, Texas & Jim Krivacs, Texas		
1953	Walter Dukes, Seton Hall	1979	Clarence Carter, Indiana & Ray Tolbert, Indiana		
1954	Togo Palazzi, Holy Cross	1980	Ralph Sampson, Virginia		
1955	**Maurice Stokes**, St. Francis-PA	1981	Greg Stewart, Tulsa		
1956	Charlie Tyra, Louisville	1982	Mitchell Anderson, Bradley		
1957	**Win Wilfong**, Memphis St.	1983	Ron Anderson, Fresno St.		
1958	Hank Stein, Xavier-OH	1984	Tim McCormick, Michigan		
1959	Tony Jackson, St. John's	1985	Reggie Miller, UCLA		
1960	**Lenny Wilkens**, Providence	1986	Brad Sellers, Ohio St.		
1961	Vinny Ernst, Providence	1987	Randolph Keys, So. Miss.		
1962	Bill Chmielewski, Dayton	1988	Phil Gamble, Connecticut		
1963	Ray Flynn, Providence				

All-Time NIT Team

As selected by a media panel (Mar. 15, 1997).

Walt Frazier, S. Illinois
George Mikan, DePaul
Tom Gola, La Salle
Maurice Stokes, St. Francis-PA
Ralph Beard, Kentucky

All-Time Winningest Division I Teams
Top 25 Winning Percentage

Division I schools with best winning percentages through 2000-01 season (including tournament games). Years in Division I only; minimum 20 years. NCAA tournament columns indicate years in tournament, record and number of championships.

		First Year	Yrs	Games	Won	Lost	Tied	Pct	NCAA Tourney Yrs	W-L	Titles
1	Kentucky	1903	98	2354	1795	558	1	.763	43	89-38	7
2	North Carolina	1911	91	2411	1781	630	0	.739	35	81-35	3
3	UNLV	1959	43	1224	883	341	0	.721	14	30-13	1
4	Kansas	1899	103	2479	1738	741	0	.701	30	61-30	2
5	UCLA	1920	82	2132	1489	643	0	.698	37	83-30	11
6	St. John's	1908	94	2359	1621	738	0	.687	26	27-28	0
7	Syracuse	1901	100	2268	1549	719	0	.683	27	40-28	0
8	Duke	1906	96	2413	1649	764	0	.683	25	73-22	3
9	Western Kentucky	1915	82	2121	1411	710	0	.665	17	15-18	0
10	Arkansas	1924	78	2062	1354	708	0	.657	26	39-26	1
11	Utah	1909	93	2204	1446	758	0	.656	22	32-25	1
12	Indiana	1901	101	2294	1494	800	0	.651	30	52-25	5
13	Temple	1895	105	2414	1571	843	0	.651	25	31-25	0
14	Louisville	1912	87	2415	1387	758	0	.647	29	48-31	2
15	Notre Dame	1898	96	2301	1483	817	1	.645	25	26-29	0
16	DePaul	1924	78	1915	1231	684	0	.643	21	20-24	0
17	Illinois	1906	96	2189	1407	782	0	.643	21	27-22	0
18	Weber St.	1963	39	1107	711	396	0	.642	12	6-13	0
19	Arizona	1905	96	2160	1386	774	0	.642	20	32-19	1
20	Purdue	1897	103	2231	1421	820	0	.637	19	26-19	0
21	Pennsylvania	1897	101	2373	1508	863	2	.636	18	13-20	0
22	Villanova	1921	81	2086	1327	759	0	.636	25	37-25	1
23	Murray St.	1926	76	1956	1237	719	0	.632	10	1-10	0
24	Cincinnati	1902	100	2211	1392	819	0	.630	20	37-19	2
25	New Orleans	1970	32	911	571	340	0	.627	4	1-4	0

Top 35 All-Time Victories

Division I schools with most victories through 2000-01 (including postseason tournaments). Minimum 20 years in Division I.

		Wins			Wins			Wins			Wins
1	Kentucky	1795	10	Oregon St.	1491	19	Cincinnati	1392	28	Washington St.	1339
2	North Carolina	1781	11	UCLA	1489	20	West Virginia	1390	29	Ohio St	1334
3	Kansas	1738	12	Notre Dame	1483	21	Louisville	1387	30	Montana St.	1328
4	Duke	1649	13	Utah	1446		Bradley	1387	31	Villanova	1327
5	St. John's	1621	14	Princeton	1442	23	Arizona	1386	32	Iowa	1322
6	Temple	1571	15	Washington	1422	24	N.C. State	1378	33	Alabama	1321
7	Syracuse	1549	16	Purdue	1421	25	Texas	1364	34	USC	1313
8	Penn	1508	17	Western Ky.	1411	26	Fordham	1357	35	St. Joseph's-PA	1311
9	Indiana	1494	18	Illinois	1407	27	Arkansas	1354			

Top 29 Single-Season Victories

Division I schools with most victories in a season through 2000-01 (including postseason tournaments). NCAA champions in **bold** type.

		Year	Record		Year	Record		Year	Record
1	UNLV	1987	37-2	Kansas	1997	34-2	Connecticut*	1996	32-3
	Duke	1999	37-2	Kentucky	1947	34-3	Duke	1998	32-4
	Duke	1986	37-3	**Georgetown**	1984	34-3	Louisville	1983	32-4
4	**Kentucky**	1948	36-3	Arkansas	1991	34-4	Kentucky	1986	32-4
5	Massachusetts*	1996	35-2	**N. Carolina**	1993	34-4	N. Carolina	1987	32-4
	Georgetown	1985	35-3	N. Carolina	1998	34-4	Temple	1987	32-4
	Arizona	1988	35-3	25 Indiana St	1979	33-1	Bradley	1950	32-5
	Duke	2001	35-4	**Louisville**	1980	33-3	Connecticut	1998	32-5
	Kansas	1986	35-4	Michigan St.	1999	33-5	Tulsa	2000	32-5
	Kansas	1998	35-4	UNLV	1986	33-5	Iowa St.	2000	32-5
	Kentucky	1998	35-4	29 **N. Carolina**	1957	32-0	Marshall	1947	32-5
	Oklahoma	1988	35-4	**Indiana**	1976	32-0	Houston	1984	32-5
	UNLV	1990	35-5	**Kentucky**	1949	32-2	Bradley	1951	32-6
	Kentucky	1997	35-5	**Kentucky**	1951	32-2	**Louisville**	1986	32-7
15	UNLV	1991	34-1	**N. Carolina**	1982	32-2	**Duke**	1991	32-7
	Connecticut	1999	34-2	Temple	1988	32-2	Arkansas	1995	32-7
	Duke	1992	34-2	Arkansas	1978	32-3	**Michigan St.**	2000	32-7
	Kentucky	1996	34-2	Bradley	1986	32-3			

*NCAA later stripped UMass of its four 1996 tournament victories after learning that center Marcus Camby accepted gifts from an agent. UConn was stripped of its two 1996 tournament victories because two players illegally accepted plane tickets.

Associated Press Final Polls

Taken before NCAA, NIT and Collegiate Commissioner's Association (1974-75) tournaments.

The Associated Press introduced its weekly college basketball poll of sportswriters (later, sportswriters and broadcasters) during the 1948-49 season.

Since the NCAA Division I tournament has determined the national champion since 1939, the final AP poll ranks the nation's best teams through the regular season and conference tournaments.

Except for four seasons (see AP Post-Tournament Final Polls), the final AP poll has been released prior to the NCAA and NIT tournaments and has gone from a Top 10 (1949 and 1963-67) to a Top 20 (1950-62 and 1968-89) to a Top 25 (since 1990).

Tournament champions are in **bold** type.

1949

		Before Tourns	Head Coach	Final Record
1	**Kentucky**	29-1	Adolph Rupp	32-2
2	Oklahoma A&M	21-4	Hank Iba	23-5
3	Saint Louis	22-3	Eddie Hickey	22-4
4	Illinois	19-3	Harry Combes	21-4
5	Western Ky.	25-3	Ed Diddle	25-4
6	Minnesota	18-3	Ozzie Cowles	same
7	Bradley	25-6	Forddy Anderson	27-8
8	**San Francisco**	21-5	Pete Newell	25-5
9	Tulane	24-4	Cliff Wells	same
10	Bowling Green	21-6	Harold Anderson	24-7

NCAA Final Four (at Edmundson Pavilion, Seattle): **Third Place**—Illinois 57, Oregon St. 53. **Championship**—Kentucky 46, Oklahoma A&M 36.

NIT Final Four (at Madison Square Garden): **Semifinals**—San Francisco 49, Bowling Green 39; Loyola-IL 55, Bradley 50. **Third Place**—Bowling Green 82, Bradley 77. **Championship**—San Francisco 48, Loyola-IL 47.

1950

		Before Tourns	Head Coach	Final Record
1	Bradley	28-3	Forddy Anderson	32-5
2	Ohio St.	21-3	Tippy Dye	22-4
3	Kentucky	25-4	Adolph Rupp	25-5
4	Holy Cross	27-2	Buster Sheary	27-4
5	N.C. State	25-5	Everett Case	27-6
6	Duquesne	22-5	Dudey Moore	23-6
7	UCLA	24-5	John Wooden	24-7
8	Western Ky.	24-5	Ed Diddle	25-6
9	St. John's	23-4	Frank McGuire	24-5
10	La Salle	20-3	Ken Loeffler	21-4
11	Villanova	25-4	Al Severance	same
12	San Francisco	19-6	Pete Newell	19-7
13	LIU-Brooklyn	20-4	Clair Bee	20-5
14	Kansas St.	17-7	Jack Gardner	same
15	Arizona	26-4	Fred Enke	26-5
16	Wisconsin	17-5	Bud Foster	same
17	San Jose St.	21-7	Walter McPherson	same
18	Washington St.	19-13	Jack Friel	same
19	Kansas	14-11	Phog Allen	same
20	Indiana	17-5	Branch McCracken	same

Note: Unranked **CCNY**, coached by Nat Holman, won both the NCAAs and NIT. The Beavers entered the postseason at 17-5 and had a final record of 24-5.

NCAA Final Four (at Madison Square Garden): **Third Place**—N. Carolina St. 53, Baylor 41. **Championship**—CCNY 71, Bradley 68.

NIT Final Four (at Madison Square Garden): **Semifinals**—Bradley 83, St. John's 72; CCNY 62, Duquesne 52. **Third Place**—St. John's 69, Duquesne 67 (OT). **Championship**—CCNY 69, Bradley 61.

1951

		Before Tourns	Head Coach	Final Record
1	**Kentucky**	28-2	Adolph Rupp	32-2
2	Oklahoma A&M	27-4	Hank Iba	29-6
3	Columbia	22-0	Lou Rossini	22-1
4	Kansas St.	22-3	Jack Gardner	25-4
5	Illinois	19-4	Harry Combes	22-5
6	Bradley	32-6	Forddy Anderson	same
7	Indiana	19-3	Branch McCracken	same
8	N.C. State	29-4	Everett Case	30-7
9	St. John's	22-3	Frank McGuire	26-5
10	Saint Louis	21-7	Eddie Hickey	22-8
11	**BYU**	22-8	Stan Watts	26-10
12	Arizona	24-4	Fred Enke	24-6
13	Dayton	24-4	Tom Blackburn	27-5
14	Toledo	23-8	Jerry Bush	same
15	Washington	22-5	Tippy Dye	24-6
16	Murray St.	21-6	Harlan Hodges	same
17	Cincinnati	18-3	John Wiethe	18-4
18	Siena	19-8	Dan Cunha	same
19	USC	21-6	Forrest Twogood	same
20	Villanova	25-6	Al Severance	25-7

NCAA Final Four (at Williams Arena, Minneapolis): **Third Place**—Illinois 61, Oklahoma St. 46. **Championship**—Kentucky 68, Kansas St. 58.

NIT Final Four (at Madison Sq. Garden): **Semifinals**—Dayton 69, St. John's 62 (OT); BYU 69, Seton Hall 59. **Third Place**—St. John's 70, Seton Hall 68 (2 OT). **Championship**—BYU 62, Dayton 43.

1952

		Before Tourns	Head Coach	Final Record
1	Kentucky	28-2	Adolph Rupp	29-3
2	Illinois	19-3	Harry Combes	22-4
3	Kansas St.	19-5	Jack Gardner	same
4	Duquesne	21-1	Dudey Moore	23-4
5	Saint Louis	22-6	Eddie Hickey	23-8
6	Washington	25-6	Tippy Dye	same
7	Iowa	19-3	Bucky O'Connor	same
8	**Kansas**	24-3	Phog Allen	28-3
9	West Virginia	23-4	Red Brown	same
10	St. John's	22-3	Frank McGuire	25-5
11	Dayton	24-3	Tom Blackburn	28-5
12	Duke	24-6	Harold Bradley	same
13	Holy Cross	23-3	Buster Sheary	24-4
14	Seton Hall	25-2	Honey Russell	25-3
15	St. Bonaventure	19-5	Ed Melvin	21-6
16	Wyoming	27-6	Everett Shelton	28-7
17	Louisville	20-5	Peck Hickman	20-6
18	Seattle	29-7	Al Brightman	29-8
19	UCLA	19-10	John Wooden	19-12
20	SW Texas St.	30-1	Milton Jowers	same

Note: Unranked La Salle, coached by Ken Loeffler, won the NIT. The Explorers entered the postseason at 21-7 and had a final record of 25-7.

NCAA Final Four (at Edmundson Pavillion, Seattle): **Semifinals**—St. John's 61, Illinois 59; Kansas 74, Santa Clara 59. **Third Place**—Illinois 67, Santa Clara 64. **Championship**—Kansas 80, St. John's 63.

NIT Final Four (at Madison Sq. Garden): **Semifinals**—La Salle 59, Duquesne 46; Dayton 69, St. Bonaventure 62. **Third Place**—St. Bonaventure 48, Duquesne 34. **Championship**—La Salle 75, Dayton 64.

1953

	Before Tourns	Head Coach	Final Record
1	Indiana 18-3	Branch McCracken	23-3
2	La Salle 25-2	Ken Loeffler	25-3
3	Seton Hall 28-2	Honey Russell	31-2
4	Washington 27-2	Tippy Dye	30-3
5	LSU.............22-1	Harry Rabenhorst	24-3
6	Kansas..........16-5	Phog Allen	19-6
7	Oklahoma A&M .22-6	Hank Iba	23-7
	Kansas St........17-4	Jack Gardner	same
9	Western Ky. 25-5	Ed Diddle	25-6
10	Illinois 18-4	Harry Combes	same
11	Oklahoma City...18-4	Doyle Parrick	18-6
12	N.C. State.......26-6	Everett Case	same
13	Notre Dame 17-4	John Jordan	19-5
14	Louisville 21-5	Peck Hickman	22-6
	Seattle 27-3	Al Brightman	29-4
16	Miami-OH.......17-5	Bill Rohr	17-6
17	Eastern Ky. 16-8	Paul McBrayer	16-9
18	Duquesne 18-7	Dudey Moore	21-8
	Navy 16-4	Ben Carnevale	16-5
20	Holy Cross 18-5	Buster Sheary	20-6

NCAA Final Four (at Municipal Auditorium, Kansas City): **Semifinals**—Indiana 80, LSU 67; Kansas 79, Washington 53. **Third Place**—Washington 88, LSU 69. **Championship**—Indiana 69, Kansas 68.

NIT Final Four (at Madison Sq. Garden): **Semifinals**—Seton Hall 74, Manhattan 56; St. John's 64, Duquesne 55. **Third Place**—Duquesne 81, Manhattan 67. **Championship**—Seton Hall 58, St. John's 46.

1954

	Before Tourns	Head Coach	Final Record
1	Kentucky 25-0	Adolph Rupp	same*
2	Indiana 19-3	Branch McCracken	20-4
3	Duquesne 24-2	Dudey Moore	26-3
4	Western Ky. 28-1	Ed Diddle	29-3
5	Oklahoma A&M .23-4	Hank Iba	24-5
6	Notre Dame 20-2	John Jordan	22-3
7	Kansas..........16-5	Phog Allen	same
8	Holy Cross 23-2	Buster Sheary	26-2
9	LSU.............21-3	Harry Rabenhorst	21-5
10	La Salle 21-4	Ken Loeffler	26-4
11	Iowa............17-5	Bucky O'Connor	same
12	Duke 22-6	Harold Bradley	same
13	Colorado A&M ..22-5	Bill Strannigan	22-7
14	Illinois 17-5	Harry Combes	same
15	Wichita 27-3	Ralph Miller	27-4
16	Seattle 26-1	Al Brightman	26-2
17	N.C. State.......26-6	Everett Case	28-7
18	Dayton..........24-6	Tom Blackburn	25-7
	Minnesota.......17-5	Ozzie Cowles	same
20	Oregon St......19-10	Slats Gill	same
	UCLA...........18-7	John Wooden	same
	USC............17-12	Forrest Twogood	19-14

*Kentucky turned down invitation to NCAA tournament after NCAA declared seniors Cliff Hagan, Frank Ramsey and Lou Tsioropoulos ineligible for postseason play.

NCAA Final Four (at Municipal Auditorium, Kansas City): **Semifinals**—La Salle 69, Penn St. 54; Bradley 74, USC 72. **Third Place**—Penn St. 70, USC 61. **Championship**—La Salle 92, Bradley 76.

NIT Final Four (at Madison Square Garden): **Semifinals**—Duquesne 51, Niagara 51; Holy Cross 75, Western Ky. 69. **Third Place**—Niagara 71, Western Ky. 65. **Championship**—Holy Cross 71, Duquesne 62.

1955

	Before Tourns	Head Coach	Final Record
1	San Francisco ..23-1	Phil Woolpert	28-1
2	Kentucky 22-2	Adolph Rupp	23-3
3	La Salle 22-4	Ken Loeffler	26-5
4	N.C. State.......28-4	Everett Case	same
5	Iowa............17-5	Bucky O'Connor	19-7
6	Duquesne 19-4	Dudey Moore	22-4
7	Utah............23-3	Jack Gardner	24-4
8	Marquette 22-2	Jack Nagle	24-3
9	Dayton..........23-3	Tom Blackburn	25-4
10	Oregon St........21-7	Slats Gill	22-8
11	Minnesota.......15-7	Ozzie Cowles	same
12	Alabama.........19-5	Johnny Dee	same
13	UCLA...........21-5	John Wooden	same
14	G. Washington ..24-6	Bill Reinhart	same
15	Colorado........16-5	Bebe Lee	19-6
16	Tulsa............20-6	Clarence Iba	21-7
17	Vanderbilt 16-6	Bob Polk	same
18	Illinois 17-5	Harry Combes	same
19	West Virginia ...19-10	Fred Schaus	19-11
20	Saint Louis.......19-7	Eddie Hickey	20-8

NCAA Final Four (at Municipal Auditorium, Kansas City): **Semifinals**—La Salle 76, Iowa 73; San Francisco 62, Colorado 50. **Third Place**—Colorado 75, Iowa 74. **Championship**—San Francisco 77, La Salle 63.

NIT Final Four (at Madison Square Garden): **Semifinals**—Dayton 79, St. Francis-PA 73 (OT); Duquesne 65, Cincinnati 51. **Third Place**—Cincinnati 96, St. Francis-PA 91 (OT). **Championship**—Duquesne 70, Dayton 58.

1956

	Before Tourns	Head Coach	Final Record
1	San Francisco ..25-0	Phil Woolpert	29-0
2	N.C. State.......24-3	Everett Case	24-4
3	Dayton..........23-3	Tom Blackburn	25-4
4	Iowa............17-5	Bucky O'Connor	20-6
5	Alabama.........21-3	Johnny Dee	same
6	Louisville 23-3	Peck Hickman	26-3
7	SMU 22-2	Doc Hayes	25-4
8	UCLA...........21-5	John Wooden	22-6
9	Kentucky 19-5	Adolph Rupp	20-6
10	Illinois 18-4	Harry Combes	same
11	Oklahoma City...18-6	Abe Lemons	20-7
12	Vanderbilt 19-4	Bob Polk	same
13	North Carolina ..18-5	Frank McGuire	same
14	Holy Cross 22-4	Roy Leenig	22-5
15	Temple 23-3	Harry Litwack	27-4
16	Wake Forest 19-9	Murray Greason	same
17	Duke 19-7	Harold Bradley	same
18	Utah............21-5	Jack Gardner	22-6
19	Oklahoma A&M .18-8	Hank Iba	18-9
20	West Virginia ...21-8	Fred Schaus	21-9

NCAA Final Four (at McGaw Hall, Evanston, IL): **Semifinals**—Iowa 83, Temple 76; San Francisco 86, SMU 68. **Third Place**—Temple 90, SMU 81. **Championship**—San Francisco 83, Iowa 71.

NIT Final Four (at Madison Square Garden): **Semifinals**—Dayton 89, St. Francis-NY 58; Louisville 89, St. Joseph's-PA 79. **Third Place**—St. Joseph's-PA 93, St. Francis-NY 82. **Championship**—Louisville 93, Dayton 80.

Associated Press Final Polls (Cont.)

1957

		Before Tourns	Head Coach	Final Record
1	N. Carolina	27-0	Frank McGuire	32-0
2	Kansas	21-2	Dick Harp	24-3
3	Kentucky	22-4	Adolph Rupp	23-5
4	SMU	21-3	Doc Hayes	22-4
5	Seattle	24-2	John Castellani	24-3
6	Louisville	21-5	Peck Hickman	same
7	West Va.	25-4	Fred Schaus	25-5
8	Vanderbilt	17-5	Bob Polk	same
9	Oklahoma City	17-8	Abe Lemons	19-9
10	Saint Louis	19-7	Eddie Hickey	19-9
11	Michigan St.	14-8	Forddy Anderson	16-10
12	Memphis St.	21-5	Bob Vanatta	24-6
13	California	20-4	Pete Newell	21-5
14	UCLA	22-4	John Wooden	same
15	Mississippi St.	17-8	Babe McCarthy	same
16	Idaho St.	24-2	John Grayson	25-4
17	Notre Dame	18-7	John Jordan	20-8
18	Wake Forest	19-9	Murray Greason	same
19	Canisius	20-5	Joe Curran	22-6
20	Oklahoma A&M	17-9	Hank Iba	same

Note: Unranked **Bradley**, coached by Chuck Orsborn, won the NIT. The Braves entered the tourney at 19-7 and had a final record of 22-7.
NCAA Final Four (at Municipal Auditorium, Kansas City): **Semifinals**–North Carolina 74, Michigan St. 70 (3 OT); Kansas 80, San Francisco 56. **Third Place**–San Francisco 67, Michigan St. 60. **Championship**–North Carolina 54, Kansas 53 (3 OT).
NIT Final Four (at Madison Square Garden): **Semifinals**–Memphis St. 80, St. Bonaventure 78; Bradley 78, Temple 66. **Third Place**–Temple 67, St. Bonaventure 50. **Championship**–Bradley 84, Memphis St. 83.

1958

		Before Tourns	Head Coach	Final Record
1	West Virginia	26-1	Fred Schaus	26-2
2	Cincinnati	24-2	George Smith	25-3
3	Kansas St.	20-3	Tex Winter	22-5
4	San Francisco	24-1	Phil Woolpert	25-2
5	Temple	24-2	Harry Litwack	27-3
6	Maryland	20-6	Bud Millikan	22-7
7	Kansas	18-5	Dick Harp	same
8	Notre Dame	22-4	John Jordan	24-5
9	Kentucky	19-6	Adolph Rupp	23-6
10	Duke	18-7	Harold Bradley	same
11	Dayton	23-3	Tom Blackburn	25-4
12	Indiana	12-10	Branch McCracken	13-11
13	North Carolina	19-7	Frank McGuire	same
14	Bradley	20-6	Chuck Orsborn	20-7
15	Mississippi St.	20-5	Babe McCarthy	same
16	Auburn	16-6	Joel Eaves	same
17	Michigan St.	16-6	Forddy Anderson	same
18	Seattle	20-6	John Castellani	24-7
19	Oklahoma St.	19-7	Hank Iba	21-8
20	N.C. State	18-6	Everett Case	same

Note: Unranked **Xavier-OH**, coached by Jim McCafferty, won the NIT. The Musketeers entered the tourney at 15-11 and had a final record of 19-11.
NCAA Final Four (at Freedom Hall, Louisville): **Semifinals**–Kentucky 61, Temple 60; Seattle 73, Kansas St. 51. **Third Place**–Temple 67, Kansas St. 57. **Championship**–Kentucky 84, Seattle 72.
NIT Final Four (at Madison Square Garden): **Semifinals**–Dayton 80, St. John's 56; Xavier-OH 72, St. Bonaventure 53. **Third Place**–St. Bonaventure 84, St. John's 69. **Championship**–Xavier-OH 78, Dayton 74 (OT).

1959

		Before Tourns	Head Coach	Final Record
1	Kansas St.	24-1	Tex Winter	25-2
2	Kentucky	23-2	Adolph Rupp	24-3
3	Mississippi St.	24-1	Babe McCarthy	same*
4	Bradley	23-3	Chuck Orsborn	25-4
5	Cincinnati	23-3	George Smith	26-4
6	N.C. State	22-4	Everett Case	same
7	Michigan St.	18-3	Forddy Anderson	19-4
8	Auburn	20-2	Joel Eaves	same
9	North Carolina	20-4	Frank McGuire	20-5
10	West Virginia	25-4	Fred Schaus	29-5
11	California	21-4	Pete Newell	25-4
12	Saint Louis	20-5	John Benington	20-6
13	Seattle	23-6	Vince Cazzetta	same
14	St. Joseph's-PA	22-3	Jack Ramsay	22-5
15	St. Mary's-CA	18-5	Jim Weaver	19-6
16	TCU	19-5	Buster Brannon	20-6
17	Oklahoma City	20-6	Abe Lemons	20-7
18	Utah	21-5	Jack Gardner	21-7
19	St. Bonaventure	20-2	Eddie Donovan	20-3
20	Marquette	22-4	Eddie Hickey	23-6

*Mississippi St. turned down invitation to NCAA tournament because it was an integrated event.
Note: Unranked **St. John's**, coached by Joe Lapchick, won the NIT. The Redmen entered the tourney at 16-6 and had a final record of 20-6.
NCAA Final Four (at Freedom Hall, Louisville): **Semifinals**–West Virginia 94, Louisville 79; California 64, Cincinnati 58. **Third Place**–Cincinnati 98, Louisville 85. **Championship**–California 71, West Virginia 70.
NIT Final Four (at Madison Square Garden): **Semifinals**–Bradley 59, NYU 57; St. John's 76, Providence 55. **Third Place**–NYU 71, Providence 57. **Championship**–St. John's 76, Bradley 71 (OT).

1960

		Before Tourns	Head Coach	Final Record
1	Cincinnati	25-1	George Smith	28-2
2	California	24-1	Pete Newell	28-2
3	Ohio St.	21-3	Fred Taylor	25-3
4	Bradley	24-2	Chuck Orsborn	27-2
5	West Virginia	24-4	Fred Schaus	26-5
6	Utah	24-2	Jack Gardner	26-3
7	Indiana	20-4	Branch McCracken	same
8	Utah St.	22-4	Cecil Baker	24-5
9	St. Bonaventure	19-3	Eddie Donovan	21-5
10	Miami-FL	23-3	Bruce Hale	23-4
11	Auburn	19-3	Joel Eaves	same
12	NYU	19-4	Lou Rossini	22-5
13	Georgia Tech	21-5	Whack Hyder	22-6
14	Providence	21-4	Joe Mullaney	24-5
15	Saint Louis	19-7	John Benington	19-8
16	Holy Cross	20-5	Roy Leenig	20-6
17	Villanova	19-5	Al Severance	20-6
18	Duke	15-10	Vic Bubas	17-11
19	Wake Forest	21-7	Bones McKinney	same
20	St. John's	17-7	Joe Lapchick	17-8

NCAA Final Four (at the Cow Palace, San Fran.): **Semifinals**–Ohio St. 76, NYU 54; California 77, Cincinnati 69. **Third Place**–Cincinnati 95, NYU 71. **Championship**–Ohio St. 75, California 55.
NIT Final Four (at Madison Square Garden): **Semifinals**–Bradley 82, St. Bonaventure 71; Providence 68, Utah St. 62. **Third Place**–Utah St. 99, St. Bonaventure 93. **Championship**–Bradley 88, Providence 72.

1961

		Before Tourns	Head Coach	Final Record
1	Ohio St.	..24-0	Fred Taylor	27-1
2	**Cincinnati**	..23-3	Ed Jucker	27-3
3	St. Bonaventure	..22-3	Eddie Donovan	24-4
4	Kansas St.	..22-3	Tex Winter	23-4
5	North Carolina	..19-4	Frank McGuire	same
6	Bradley	..21-5	Chuck Orsborn	same
7	USC	..20-6	Forrest Twogood	21-8
8	Iowa	..18-6	S. Scheuerman	same
9	West Virginia	..23-4	George King	same
10	Duke	..22-6	Vic Bubas	same
11	Utah	..21-6	Jack Gardner	23-8
12	Texas Tech	..14-9	Polk Robison	15-10
13	Niagara	..16-4	Taps Gallagher	16-5
14	Memphis St.	..20-2	Bob Vanatta	20-3
15	Wake Forest	..17-10	Bones McKinney	19-11
16	St. John's	..20-4	Joe Lapchick	20-5
17	St. Joseph's-PA	..22-4	Jack Ramsay	25-5
18	Drake	..19-7	Maury John	same
19	Holy Cross	..19-4	Roy Leenig	22-5
20	Kentucky	..18-8	Adolph Rupp	19-9

Note: Unranked **Providence**, coached by Joe Mullaney, won the NIT. The Friars entered the tourney at 20-5 and had a final record of 24-5.

NCAA Final Four (at Municipal Auditorium, Kansas City): **Semifinals**–Ohio St. 95, St. Joseph's-PA 69; Cincinnati 82, Utah 67. **Third Place**–St. Joseph's-PA 127, Utah 120 (4 OT). **Championship**–Cincinnati 70, Ohio St. 65 (OT).

NIT Final Four (at Madison Square Garden) **Semifinals**– St. Louis 67, Dayton 60; Providence 90, Holy Cross 83 (OT). **Third Place**–Holy Cross 85, Dayton 67. **Championship**– Providence 62, St. Louis 59.

1962

		Before Tourns	Head Coach	Final Record
1	Ohio St.	..23-1	Fred Taylor	26-2
2	**Cincinnati**	..25-2	Ed Jucker	29-2
3	Kentucky	..22-2	Adolph Rupp	23-3
4	Mississippi St.	..19-6	Babe McCarthy	same
5	Bradley	..21-6	Chuck Orsborn	21-7
6	Kansas St.	..22-3	Tex Winter	same
7	Utah	..23-3	Jack Gardner	same
8	Bowling Green	..21-3	Harold Anderson	same
9	Colorado	..18-6	Sox Walseth	19-7
10	Duke	..20-5	Vic Bubas	same
11	Loyola-IL	..21-3	George Ireland	23-4
12	St. John's	..19-4	Joe Lapchick	21-5
13	Wake Forest	..18-8	Bones McKinney	22-9
14	Oregon St.	..22-4	Slats Gill	24-5
15	West Virginia	..24-5	George King	24-6
16	Arizona St.	..23-3	Ned Wulk	23-4
17	Duquesne	..20-5	Red Manning	22-7
18	Utah St.	..21-5	Ladell Andersen	22-7
19	UCLA	..16-9	John Wooden	18-11
20	Villanova	..19-6	Jack Kraft	21-7

Note: Unranked **Dayton**, coached by Tom Blackburn, won the NIT. The Flyers entered the tourney at 20-6 and had a final record of 24-6.

NCAA Final Four (at Freedom Hall, Louisville): **Semifinals**–Ohio St. 84, Wake Forest 68; Cincinnati 72, UCLA 70. **Third Place**–Wake Forest 82, UCLA 80. **Championship**–Cincinnati 71, Ohio St. 59.

NIT Final Four (at Madison Square Garden): **Semifinals**–Dayton 98, Loyola-IL 82; St. John's 76, Duquesne 65. **Third Place**–Loyola-IL 95, Duquesne 84. **Championship**–Dayton 73, St. John's 67.

1963

AP ranked only 10 teams from the 1962-63 season through 1967-68.

		Before Tourns	Head Coach	Final Record
1	Cincinnati	..23-1	Ed Jucker	26-2
2	Duke	..24-2	Vic Bubas	27-3
3	**Loyola-IL**	..24-2	George Ireland	29-2
4	Arizona St.	..24-2	Ned Wulk	26-3
5	Wichita	..19-7	Ralph Miller	19-8
6	Mississippi St.	..21-5	Babe McCarthy	22-6
7	Ohio St.	..20-4	Fred Taylor	same
8	Illinois	..19-5	Harry Combes	20-6
9	NYU	..17-3	Lou Rossini	18-5
10	Colorado	..18-6	Sox Walseth	19-7

Note: Unranked **Providence**, coached by Joe Mullaney, won the NIT. The Friars entered the tourney at 21-4 and had a final record of 24-4.

NCAA Final Four (at Freedom Hall, Louisville): **Semifinals**–Loyola-IL 94, Duke 75; Cincinnati 80, Oregon St. 46. **Third Place**–Duke 85, Oregon St. 63. **Championship**–Loyola-IL 60, Cincinnati 58 (OT).

NIT Final Four (at Madison Square Garden): **Semifinals**–Providence 70, Marquette 64; Canisius 61, Villanova 46. **Third Place**–Marquette 64, Villanova 53. **Championship**–Providence 81, Canisius 66.

1964

AP ranked only 10 teams from the 1962-63 season through 1967-68.

		Before Tourns	Head Coach	Final Record
1	**UCLA**	..26-0	John Wooden	30-0
2	Michigan	..20-4	Dave Strack	23-5
3	Duke	..23-4	Vic Bubas	26-5
4	Kentucky	..21-4	Adolph Rupp	21-6
5	Wichita St.	..22-5	Ralph Miller	23-6
6	Oregon St.	..25-3	Slats Gill	25-4
7	Villanova	..22-3	Jack Kraft	24-4
8	Loyola-IL	..20-5	George Ireland	22-6
9	DePaul	..21-3	Ray Meyer	21-4
10	Davidson	..22-4	Lefty Driesell	same

Note: Unranked **Bradley**, coached by Chuck Orsborn, won the NIT. The Braves entered the tourney at 20-6 and finished with a record of 23-6.

NCAA Final Four (at Municipal Auditorium, Kansas City): **Semifinals**–Duke 91, Michigan 80; UCLA 90, Kansas St. 84. **Third Place**–Michigan 100, Kansas St. 90. **Championship**–UCLA 98, Duke 83.

NIT Final Four (at Madison Square Garden): **Semifinals**–New Mexico 72, NYU 65; Bradley 67, Army 52. **Third Place**–Army 60, NYU 59. **Championship**–Bradley 86, New Mexico 54.

Undefeated National Champions

Seven NCAA seasons have ended with an undefeated national champion. UCLA has accomplished the feat four times.

Year		W-L
1956	San Francisco	..29-0
1957	North Carolina	..32-0
1964	UCLA	..30-0
1967	UCLA	..30-0
1972	UCLA	..30-0
1973	UCLA	..30-0
1976	Indiana	..32-0

Associated Press Final Polls (Cont.)

1965

AP ranked only 10 teams from the 1962-63 season through 1967-68.

		Before Tourns	Head Coach	Final Record
1	Michigan	21-3	Dave Strack	24-4
2	UCLA	24-2	John Wooden	28-2
3	St. Joseph's-PA	25-1	Jack Ramsay	26-3
4	Providence	22-1	Joe Mullaney	24-2
5	Vanderbilt	23-3	Roy Skinner	24-4
6	Davidson	24-2	Lefty Driesell	same
7	Minnesota	19-5	John Kundla	same
8	Villanova	21-4	Jack Kraft	23-5
9	BYU	21-5	Stan Watts	21-7
10	Duke	20-5	Vic Bubas	same

Note: Unranked **St. John's,** coached by Joe Lapchick, won the NIT. The Redmen entered the tourney at 17-8 and finished with a record of 21-8.
NCAA Final Four (at Memorial Coliseum, Portland, OR): **Semifinals**–Michigan 93, Princeton 76; UCLA 108, Wichita St. 89. **Third Place**–Princeton 118, Wichita St. 82. **Championship**–UCLA 91, Michigan 80.
NIT Final Four (at Madison Square Garden): **Semifinals**–Villanova 91, NYU 69; St. John's 67, Army 60. **Third Place**–Army 75, NYU 74. **Championship**– St. John's 55, Villanova 51.

1966

AP ranked only 10 teams from the 1962-63 season through 1967-68.

		Before Tourns	Head Coach	Final Record
1	Kentucky	24-1	Adolph Rupp	27-2
2	Duke	23-3	Vic Bubas	26-4
3	**Texas Western**	23-1	Don Haskins	28-1
4	Kansas	22-3	Ted Owens	23-4
5	St. Joseph's-PA	22-4	Jack Ramsay	24-5
6	Loyola-IL	22-2	George Ireland	22-3
7	Cincinnati	21-5	Tay Baker	21-7
8	Vanderbilt	22-4	Roy Skinner	same
9	Michigan	17-7	Dave Strack	18-8
10	Western Ky.	23-2	Johnny Oldham	25-3

Note: Unranked **BYU** coached by Stan Watts, won the NIT. The Cougars entered the tourney at 17-5 and had a final record of 20-5.
NCAA Final Four (at Cole Fieldhouse, College Park, MD): **Semifinals**–Kentucky 83, Duke 79; Texas Western 85, Utah 78. **Third Place**–Duke 79, Utah 77. **Championship**–Texas Western 72, Kentucky 65.
NIT Final Four (at Madison Square Garden): **Semifinals**–BYU 66, Army 60; NYU 69, Villanova 63. **Third Place**–Villanova 76, Army 65. **Championship**–BYU 97, NYU 84.

1967

AP ranked only 10 teams from the 1962-63 season through 1967-68.

		Before Tourns	Head Coach	Final Record
1	UCLA	26-0	John Wooden	30-0
2	Louisville	23-3	Peck Hickman	23-5
3	Kansas	22-3	Ted Owens	23-4
4	North Carolina	24-4	Dean Smith	26-6
5	Princeton	23-2	B. van Breda Kolff	25-3
6	Western Ky.	23-2	Johnny Oldham	23-3
7	Houston	23-3	Guy Lewis	27-4
8	Tennessee	21-5	Ray Mears	21-7
9	Boston College	19-2	Bob Cousy	21-3
10	Texas Western	20-5	Don Haskins	22-6

Note: Unranked **Southern Illinois,** coached by Jack Hartman, won the NIT. The Salukis entered the tourney at 20-2 and had a final record of 24-2.
NCAA Final Four (at Freedom Hall, Louisville): **Semifinals**–Dayton 76, N. Carolina 62; UCLA 73, Houston 58. **Third Place**–Houston 84, N. Carolina 62. **Championship**–UCLA 79, Dayton 64.
NIT Final Four (at Madison Square Garden): **Semifinals**–Marquette 83, Marshall 78; Southern Ill. 79, Rutgers 70. **Third Place**–Rutgers 93, Marshall 76. **Championship**–Southern Ill. 71, Marquette 56.

1968

AP ranked only 10 teams from the 1962-63 season through 1967-68.

		Before Tourns	Head Coach	Final Record
1	Houston	28-0	Guy Lewis	31-2
2	UCLA	25-1	John Wooden	29-1
3	St. Bonaventure	22-0	Larry Weise	23-2
4	North Carolina	25-3	Dean Smith	28-4
5	Kentucky	21-4	Adolph Rupp	22-5
6	New Mexico	23-3	Bob King	23-5
7	Columbia	21-4	Jack Rohan	23-5
8	Davidson	22-4	Lefty Driesell	24-5
9	Louisville	20-6	John Dromo	21-7
10	Duke	21-5	Vic Bubas	22-6

Note: Unranked **Dayton,** coached by Don Donoher, won the NIT. The Flyers entered the tourney at 17-9 and had a final record of 21-9.
NCAA Final Four (at the Sports Arena, Los Angeles): **Semifinals**–N. Carolina 80, Ohio St. 66; UCLA 101, Houston 69. **Third Place**–Ohio St. 89, Houston 85. **Championship**–UCLA 78, N. Carolina 55.
NIT Final Four (at Madison Square Garden): **Semifinals**–Dayton 76, Notre Dame 74 (OT); Kansas 58, St. Peter's 46. **Third Place**–Notre Dame 81, St.Peter's 78. **Championship**–Dayton 61, Kansas 48.

All-Time AP Top 20

The composite AP Top 20 from the 1948-49 season through 2000-01, based on the final regular season rankings of each year. The final AP poll has been taken before the NCAA and NIT tournaments each season since 1949 except in 1953 and '54 and again in 1974 and '75 when the final poll came out after the postseason. Team point totals are based on 20 points for all 1st place finishes, 19 for each 2nd, etc. Also listed are the number of times ranked No.1 by AP going into the tournaments, and times ranked in the pre-tournament Top 10 and Top 20.

		Pts	No.1	Top 10	Top 20			Pts	No.1	Top 10	Top 20
1	Kentucky	614	7	35	41	11	Notre Dame	190	0	12	18
2	North Carolina	510	5	28	36	12	Illinois	181	0	9	19
3	UCLA	449	7	22	35	13	N.C. State	176	1	9	16
4	Duke	395	5	22	31	14	UNLV	173	2	8	13
5	Kansas	321	1	17	25	15	Ohio St.	169	2	10	12
6	Indiana	293	4	16	24	16	Marquette	166	0	11	15
7	Cincinnati	233	2	12	17		Arkansas	166	0	9	15
	Louisville	233	0	11	22	18	Syracuse	160	0	9	17
9	Michigan	200	2	10	15	19	Utah	152	0	7	16
	Arizona	200	1	9	17	20	Michigan St.	151	0	7	12

1969

		Before Tourns	Head Coach	Final Record
1	UCLA	25-1	John Wooden	29-1
2	La Salle	23-1	Tom Gola	same*
3	Santa Clara	26-1	Dick Garibaldi	27-2
4	North Carolina	25-3	Dean Smith	27-5
5	Davidson	24-2	Lefty Driesell	26-3
6	Purdue	20-4	George King	23-5
7	Kentucky	22-4	Adolph Rupp	23-5
8	St. John's	22-4	Lou Carnesecca	23-6
9	Duquesne	19-4	Red Manning	21-5
10	Villanova	21-4	Jack Kraft	21-5
11	Drake	23-4	Maury John	26-5
12	New Mexico St.	23-3	Lou Henson	24-5
13	South Carolina	20-6	Frank McGuire	21-7
14	Marquette	22-4	Al McGuire	24-5
15	Louisville	20-5	John Dromo	21-6
16	Boston College	21-3	Bob Cousy	24-4
17	Notre Dame	20-6	Johnny Dee	20-7
18	Colorado	20-6	Sox Walseth	21-7
19	Kansas	20-6	Ted Owens	20-7
20	Illinois	19-5	Harvey Schmidt	same

*On probation

Note: Unranked **Temple,** coached by Harry Litwack, won the NIT. The Owls entered the tourney at 18-8 and finished with a record of 22-8.

NCAA Final Four (at Freedom Hall, Louisville): **Semifinals**—Purdue 92, N. Carolina 65; UCLA 85, Drake 82. **Third Place**—Drake 104, N. Carolina 84. **Championship**—UCLA 92, Purdue 72.

NIT Final Four (at Madison Square Garden): **Semifinals**—Temple 63, Tennessee 58; Boston College 73, Army 61. **Third Place**—Tennessee 64, Army 52. **Championship**—Temple 89, Boston College 76.

1970

		Before Tourns	Head Coach	Final Record
1	Kentucky	25-1	Adolph Rupp	26-2
2	UCLA	24-2	John Wooden	28-2
3	St. Bonaventure	22-1	Larry Weise	25-3
4	Jacksonville	23-1	Joe Williams	27-2
5	New Mexico St.	23-2	Lou Henson	27-3
6	South Carolina	25-3	Frank McGuire	25-3
7	Iowa	19-4	Ralph Miller	20-5
8	Marquette	22-3	Al McGuire	26-3
9	Notre Dame	20-6	Johnny Dee	21-8
10	N.C. State	22-6	Norm Sloan	23-7
11	Florida St.	23-3	Hugh Durham	23-3
12	Houston	24-3	Guy Lewis	25-5
13	Penn	25-1	Dick Harter	25-2
14	Drake	21-6	Maury John	22-7
15	Davidson	22-4	Terry Holland	22-5
16	Utah St.	20-6	Ladell Andersen	22-7
17	Niagara	21-5	Frank Layden	22-7
18	Western Ky.	22-2	John Oldham	22-3
19	Long Beach St.	23-3	Jerry Tarkanian	24-5
20	USC	18-8	Bob Boyd	18-8

NCAA Final Four (at Cole Fieldhouse, College Park, MD): **Semifinals**—Jacksonville 91, St. Bonaventure 83; UCLA 93, New Mexico St. 77. **Third Place**—N. Mexico St. 79, St. Bonaventure 73. **Championship**—UCLA 80, Jacksonville 69.

NIT Final Four (at Madison Square Garden): **Semifinals**—St. John's 60, Army 59; Marquette 101, LSU 79. **Third Place**—Army 75, LSU 68. **Championship**—Marquette 65, St. John's 53.

1971

		Before Tourns	Head Coach	Final Record
1	UCLA	25-1	John Wooden	29-1
2	Marquette	26-0	Al McGuire	28-1
3	Penn	26-0	Dick Harter	28-1
4	Kansas	25-1	Ted Owens	27-3
5	USC	24-2	Bob Boyd	24-2
6	South Carolina	23-4	Frank McGuire	23-6
7	Western Ky.	20-5	John Oldham	24-6
8	Kentucky	22-4	Adolph Rupp	22-6
9	Fordham	25-1	Digger Phelps	26-3
10	Ohio St.	19-5	Fred Taylor	20-6
11	Jacksonville	22-3	Tom Wasdin	22-4
12	Notre Dame	19-7	Johnny Dee	20-9
13	N. Carolina	22-6	Dean Smith	26-6
14	Houston	20-6	Guy Lewis	22-7
15	Duquesne	21-3	Red Manning	21-4
16	Long Beach St.	21-4	Jerry Tarkanian	23-5
17	Tennessee	20-6	Ray Mears	21-7
18	Villanova	19-5	Jack Kraft	23-6
19	Drake	20-7	Maury John	21-8
20	BYU	18-9	Stan Watts	18-11

NCAA Final Four (at the Astrodome, Houston): **Semifinals**—Villanova 92, Western Ky. 89 (2 OT); UCLA 68, Kansas 60. **Third Place**—Western Ky. 77, Kansas 75. **Championship**—UCLA 68, Villanova 62.

NIT Final Four (at Madison Square Garden): **Semifinals**—N. Carolina 73, Duke 69; Ga.Tech 76, St. Bonaventure 71 (2 OT). **Third Place**—St. Bonaventure 92, Duke 88 (OT). **Championship**—N. Carolina 84, Ga.Tech 66.

1972

		Before Tourns	Head Coach	Final Record
1	UCLA	26-0	John Wooden	30-0
2	North Carolina	23-4	Dean Smith	26-5
3	Penn	23-2	Chuck Daly	25-3
4	Louisville	23-4	Denny Crum	26-5
5	Long Beach St.	23-3	Jerry Tarkanian	25-4
6	South Carolina	22-4	Frank McGuire	24-5
7	Marquette	24-2	Al McGuire	25-4
8	SW Louisiana	23-3	Beryl Shipley	25-4
9	BYU	21-4	Stan Watts	21-5
10	Florida St.	23-5	Hugh Durham	27-6
11	Minnesota	17-6	Bill Musselman	18-7
12	Marshall	23-3	Carl Tacy	23-4
13	Memphis St.	21-6	Gene Bartow	21-7
14	Maryland	23-5	Lefty Driesell	27-5
15	Villanova	19-6	Jack Kraft	20-8
16	Oral Roberts	25-1	Ken Trickey	26-2
17	Indiana	17-7	Bob Knight	17-8
18	Kentucky	20-6	Adolph Rupp	21-7
19	Ohio St.	18-6	Fred Taylor	same
20	Virginia	21-6	Bill Gibson	21-7

NCAA Final Four (at the Sports Arena, Los Angeles): **Semifinals**—Florida St. 79, N. Carolina 75; UCLA 96, Louisville 77. **Third Place**—N. Carolina 105, Louisville 91. **Championship**—UCLA 81, Florida St. 76.

NIT Final Four (at Madison Square Garden): **Semifinals**—Maryland 91, Jacksonville 77; Niagara 69, St. John's 67. **Third Place**—Jacksonville 83, St. John's 80. **Championship**—Maryland 100, Niagara 69.

Associated Press Final Polls (Cont.)

1973

		Head Coach	Before Tourns	Final Record
1	UCLA	John Wooden	26-0	30-0
2	N.C. State	Norm Sloan	27-0	same*
3	Long Beach St.	Jerry Tarkanian	24-2	26-3
4	Providence	Dave Gavitt	24-2	27-4
5	Marquette	Al McGuire	23-3	25-4
6	Indiana	Bob Knight	19-5	22-6
7	SW Louisiana	Beryl Shipley	23-2	24-5
8	Maryland	Lefty Driesell	22-6	23-7
9	Kansas St.	Jack Hartman	22-4	23-5
10	Minnesota	Bill Musselman	20-4	21-5
11	North Carolina	Dean Smith	22-7	25-8
12	Memphis St.	Gene Bartow	21-5	24-6
13	Houston	Guy Lewis	23-3	23-4
14	Syracuse	Roy Danforth	22-4	24-5
15	Missouri	Norm Stewart	21-5	21-6
16	Arizona St.	Ned Wulk	18-7	19-9
17	Kentucky	Joe B. Hall	19-7	20-8
18	Penn	Chuck Daly	20-5	21-7
19	Austin Peay	Lake Kelly	21-5	22-7
20	San Francisco	Bob Gaillard	22-4	23-5

*N.C. State was ineligible for NCAA tournament for using improper methods to recruit David Thompson.
Note: Unranked **Virginia Tech**, coached by Don DeVoe, won the NIT. The Hokies entered the tourney at 18-5 and finished with a record of 22-5.
NCAA Final Four (at The Arena, St. Louis): **Semifinals**—Memphis St. 98, Providence 85; UCLA 70, Indiana 59. **Third Place**—Indiana 97, Providence 79. **Championship**—UCLA 87, Memphis St. 66.
NIT Final Four (at Madison Square Garden): **Semifinals**—Va. Tech 74, Alabama 73; Notre Dame 78, N. Carolina 71. **Third Place**—N. Carolina 88, Alabama 69. **Championship**—Va. Tech 92, Notre Dame 91 (OT).

1974

		Head Coach	Before Tourns	Final Record
1	N.C. State	Norm Sloan	26-1	30-1
2	UCLA	John Wooden	23-3	26-4
3	Notre Dame	Digger Phelps	24-2	26-3
4	Maryland	Lefty Driesell	23-5	same
5	Providence	Dave Gavitt	26-3	28-4
6	Vanderbilt	Roy Skinner	23-3	23-5
7	Marquette	Al McGuire	22-4	26-5
8	North Carolina	Dean Smith	22-5	22-6
9	Long Beach St.	Lute Olson	24-2	same
10	Indiana	Bob Knight	20-5	23-5
11	Alabama	C.M. Newton	22-4	same
12	Michigan	Johnny Orr	21-4	22-5
13	Pittsburgh	Buzz Ridl	23-3	25-4
14	Kansas	Ted Owens	21-5	23-7
15	USC	Bob Boyd	22-4	24-5
16	Louisville	Denny Crum	21-6	21-7
17	New Mexico	Norm Ellenberger	21-6	22-7
18	South Carolina	Frank McGuire	22-4	22-5
19	Creighton	Eddie Sutton	22-6	23-7
20	Dayton	Don Donoher	19-7	20-9

NCAA Final Four (at Greensboro, NC, Coliseum): **Semifinals**—N.C. State 80, UCLA 77 (2 OT); Marquette 64, Kansas 51. **Third Place**—UCLA 78, Kansas 61. **Championship**—N.C. State 76, Marquette 64.
NIT Final Four (at Madison Square Garden): **Semifinals**—Purdue 78, Jacksonville 63; Utah 117, Boston Col. 93. **Third Place**—Boston Col. 87, Jacksonville 77. **Championship**—Purdue 87, Utah 81.
CCA Final Four (at The Arena, St. Louis): **Semifinals**—Indiana 73, Toledo 72; USC 74, Bradley 73. **Championship**—Indiana 85, USC 60.

1975

		Head Coach	Before Tourns	Final Record
1	Indiana	Bob Knight	29-0	31-1
2	UCLA	John Wooden	23-3	28-3
3	Louisville	Denny Crum	24-2	28-3
4	Maryland	Lefty Driesell	22-4	24-5
5	Kentucky	Joe B. Hall	22-4	26-5
6	North Carolina	Dean Smith	21-7	23-8
7	Arizona St.	Ned Wulk	23-3	25-4
8	N.C.State	Norm Sloan	22-6	22-6
9	Notre Dame	Digger Phelps	18-8	19-10
10	Marquette	Al McGuire	23-3	23-4
11	Alabama	C.M. Newton	22-4	22-5
12	Cincinnati	Gale Catlett	23-4	23-6
13	Oregon St.	Ralph Miller	18-10	19-12
14	Drake	Bob Ortegel	16-10	19-10
15	Penn	Chuck Daly	23-4	23-5
16	UNLV	Jerry Tarkanian	22-4	24-5
17	Kansas St.	Jack Hartman	18-8	20-9
18	USC	Bob Boyd	18-7	18-8
19	Centenary	Larry Little	25-4	same
20	Syracuse	Roy Danforth	20-7	23-9

NCAA Final Four (at San Diego Sports Arena): **Semifinals**—Kentucky 95, Syracuse 79; UCLA 75, Louisville 74 (OT). **Third Place**—Louisville 96, Syracuse 88 (OT). **Championship**—UCLA 92, Kentucky 85.
NIT Championship (at Madison Sq. Garden): Princeton 80, Providence 69. No Top 20 teams played in NIT.
CCA Championship (at Freedom Hall, Louisville): Drake 83, Arizona 76. No.14 Drake and No.18 USC were only Top 20 teams in CCA.

1976

		Head Coach	Before Tourns	Final Record
1	Indiana	Bob Knight	27-0	32-0
2	Marquette	Al McGuire	25-1	27-2
3	UNLV	Jerry Tarkanian	28-1	29-2
4	Rutgers	Tom Young	28-0	31-2
5	UCLA	Gene Bartow	24-3	28-4
6	Alabama	C.M. Newton	22-4	23-5
7	Notre Dame	Digger Phelps	22-5	23-6
8	North Carolina	Dean Smith	25-3	25-4
9	Michigan	Johnny Orr	21-6	25-7
10	Western Mich.	Eldon Miller	24-2	25-3
11	Maryland	Lefty Driesell	22-6	same
12	Cincinnati	Gale Catlett	25-5	25-6
13	Tennessee	Ray Mears	21-5	21-6
14	Missouri	Norm Stewart	24-4	26-5
15	Arizona	Fred Snowden	22-8	24-9
16	Texas Tech	Gerald Myers	24-5	25-6
17	DePaul	Ray Meyer	19-8	20-9
18	Virginia	Terry Holland	18-11	18-12
19	Centenary	Larry Little	22-5	same
20	Pepperdine	Gary Colson	21-5	22-6

NCAA Final Four (at the Spectrum, Phila.); **Semifinals**—Michigan 86, Rutgers 70; Indiana 65, UCLA 51. **Third Place**—UCLA 106, Rutgers 92. **Championship**—Indiana 86, Michigan 68.
NIT Championship (at Madison Square Garden): Kentucky 71, NC-Charlotte 67. No Top 20 teams played in NIT.

1977

		Before Tours	Head Coach	Final Record
1	Michigan	24-3	Johnny Orr	26-4
2	UCLA	24-3	Gene Bartow	25-4
3	Kentucky	24-3	Joe B. Hall	26-4
4	UNLV	25-2	Jerry Tarkanian	29-3
5	North Carolina	24-4	Dean Smith	28-5
6	Syracuse	25-3	Jim Boeheim	26-4
7	**Marquette**	20-7	Al McGuire	25-7
8	San Francisco	29-1	Bob Gaillard	29-2
9	Wake Forest	20-7	Carl Tacy	22-8
10	Notre Dame	21-6	Digger Phelps	22-7
11	Alabama	23-4	C.M. Newton	25-6
12	Detroit	24-3	Dick Vitale	25-4
13	Minnesota	24-3	Jim Dutcher	same*
14	Utah	22-6	Jerry Pimm	23-7
15	Tennessee	22-5	Ray Mears	22-6
16	Kansas St.	23-6	Jack Hartman	24-7
17	NC-Charlotte	25-3	Lee Rose	28-5
18	Arkansas	26-1	Eddie Sutton	26-2
19	Louisville	21-6	Denny Crum	21-7
20	VMI	25-3	Charlie Schmaus	26-4

*On probation

NCAA Final Four (at the Omni, Atlanta): **Semifinals**–Marquette 51, NC-Charlotte, 49; N. Carolina 84, UNLV 83. **Third Place**–UNLV 106, NC-Charlotte 94. **Championship**–Marquette 67, N. Carolina 59.

NIT Championship (at Madison Square Garden): St. Bonaventure 94, Houston 91. No.11 Alabama was only Top 20 team in NIT.

1979

		Before Tours	Head Coach	Final Record
1	Indiana St.	29-0	Bill Hodges	33-1
2	UCLA	23-4	Gary Cunningham	25-5
3	**Michigan St.**	21-6	Jud Heathcote	26-6
4	Notre Dame	22-5	Digger Phelps	24-6
5	Arkansas	23-4	Eddie Sutton	25-5
6	DePaul	22-5	Ray Meyer	26-6
7	LSU	22-5	Dale Brown	23-6
8	Syracuse	25-3	Jim Boeheim	26-4
9	North Carolina	23-5	Dean Smith	23-6
10	Marquette	21-6	Hank Raymonds	22-7
11	Duke	22-7	Bill Foster	22-8
12	San Francisco	21-6	Dan Belluomini	22-7
13	Louisville	23-7	Denny Crum	24-8
14	Penn	21-5	Bob Weinhauer	25-7
15	Purdue	23-7	Lee Rose	27-8
16	Oklahoma	20-9	Dave Bliss	21-10
17	St. John's	18-10	Lou Carnesecca	21-11
18	Rutgers	21-8	Tom Young	22-9
19	Toledo	21-6	Bob Nichols	22-7
20	Iowa	20-7	Lute Olson	20-8

NCAA Final Four (at Special Events Center, Salt Lake City): **Semifinals**–Michigan St. 101, Penn 67; Indiana St. 76, DePaul 74; **Third Place**–DePaul 96, Penn 93; **Championship**–Michigan St. 75, Indiana St. 64.

NIT Championship (at Madison Square Garden): Indiana 53, Purdue 52. No. 15 Purdue was the only Top 20 team in NIT.

1978

		Before Tours	Head Coach	Final Record
1	**Kentucky**	25-2	Joe B. Hall	30-2
2	UCLA	24-2	Gary Cunningham	25-3
3	DePaul	25-2	Ray Meyer	27-3
4	Michigan St.	23-4	Jud Heathcote	25-5
5	Arkansas	28-3	Eddie Sutton	32-3
6	Notre Dame	20-6	Digger Phelps	23-8
7	Duke	23-6	Bill Foster	27-7
8	Marquette	24-3	Hank Raymonds	24-4
9	Louisville	22-6	Denny Crum	23-7
10	Kansas	24-4	Ted Owens	24-5
11	San Francisco	22-5	Bob Gaillard	23-6
12	New Mexico	24-3	Norm Ellenberger	24-4
13	Indiana	20-7	Bob Knight	21-8
14	Utah	22-5	Jerry Pimm	23-6
15	Florida St.	23-5	Hugh Durham	23-6
16	North Carolina	23-7	Dean Smith	23-8
17	**Texas**	22-5	Abe Lemons	26-5
18	Detroit	24-3	Dave Gaines	25-4
19	Miami-OH	18-8	Darrell Hedric	19-9
20	Penn	19-7	Bob Weinhauer	20-8

NCAA Final Four (at the Checkerdome, St. Louis): **Semifinals**–Kentucky 64, Arkansas 59; Duke 90, Notre Dame 86. **Third Place**–Arkansas 71, Notre Dame 69. **Championship**–Kentucky 94, Duke 88.

NIT Championship (at Madison Square Garden): Texas 101, N.C. State 93. No. 17 Texas and No. 18 Detroit were only Top 20 teams in NIT.

1980

		Before Tours	Head Coach	Final Record
1	DePaul	26-1	Ray Meyer	26-2
2	**Louisville**	28-3	Denny Crum	33-3
3	LSU	24-5	Dale Brown	26-6
4	Kentucky	28-3	Joe B. Hall	29-6
5	Oregon St.	26-3	Ralph Miller	26-4
6	Syracuse	25-3	Jim Boeheim	26-4
7	Indiana	20-7	Bob Knight	21-8
8	Maryland	23-6	Lefty Driesell	24-7
9	Notre Dame	20-7	Digger Phelps	20-8
10	Ohio St.	24-5	Eldon Miller	21-8
11	Georgetown	24-5	John Thompson	26-6
12	BYU	24-4	Frank Arnold	24-5
13	St. John's	24-4	Lou Carnesecca	24-5
14	Duke	22-8	Bill Foster	24-9
15	North Carolina	21-7	Dean Smith	21-8
16	Missouri	23-5	Norm Stewart	25-6
17	Weber St.	26-2	Neil McCarthy	26-3
18	Arizona St.	21-6	Ned Wulk	22-7
19	Iona	28-4	Jim Valvano	29-5
20	Purdue	19-9	Lee Rose	23-10

NCAA Final Four (at Market Square Arena, Indianapolis): **Semifinals**–Louisville 80, Iowa 72; UCLA 67, Purdue 62; **Championship**–Louisville 59, UCLA 54.

NIT Championship (at Madison Square Garden): Virginia 58, Minnesota 55. No Top 20 teams played in NIT.

Associated Press Final Polls (Cont.)

1981

		Before Tourns	Head Coach	Final Record
1	DePaul	27-1	Ray Meyer	27-2
2	Oregon St.	26-1	Ralph Miller	26-2
3	Arizona St.	24-3	Ned Wulk	24-4
4	LSU	28-3	Dale Brown	31-5
5	Virginia	25-3	Terry Holland	29-4
6	North Carolina	25-7	Dean Smith	29-8
7	Notre Dame	22-5	Digger Phelps	23-6
8	Kentucky	22-5	Joe B. Hall	22-6
9	**Indiana**	21-9	Bob Knight	26-9
10	UCLA	20-6	Larry Brown	20-7
11	Wake Forest	22-6	Carl Tacy	22-7
12	Louisville	21-8	Denny Crum	21-9
13	Iowa	21-6	Lute Olson	21-7
14	Utah	24-4	Jerry Pimm	25-5
15	Tennessee	20-7	Don DeVoe	21-8
16	BYU	22-6	Frank Arnold	25-7
17	Wyoming	23-5	Jim Brandenburg	24-6
18	Maryland	20-9	Lefty Driesell	21-10
19	Illinois	20-7	Lou Henson	21-8
20	Arkansas	22-7	Eddie Sutton	24-8

NCAA Final Four (at the Spectrum, Phila.): **Semifinals**–N. Carolina 78, Virginia 65; Indiana 67, LSU 49. **Third Place**–Virginia 78, LSU 74. **Championship**–Indiana 63, N. Carolina 50.

NIT Championship (at Madison Square Garden): Tulsa 86, Syracuse 84. No Top 20 teams played in NIT.

1982

		Before Tourns	Head Coach	Final Record
1	**N. Carolina**	27-2	Dean Smith	32-2
2	DePaul	26-1	Ray Meyer	26-2
3	Virginia	29-3	Terry Holland	30-4
4	Oregon St.	23-4	Ralph Miller	25-5
5	Missouri	26-3	Norm Stewart	27-4
6	Georgetown	26-6	John Thompson	30-7
7	Minnesota	22-5	Jim Dutcher	23-6
8	Idaho	26-2	Don Monson	27-3
9	Memphis St.	23-4	Dana Kirk	24-5
10	Tulsa	24-5	Nolan Richardson	24-6
11	Fresno St.	26-2	Boyd Grant	27-3
12	Arkansas	23-5	Eddie Sutton	23-6
13	Alabama	23-6	Wimp Sanderson	24-7
14	West Virginia	26-3	Gale Catlett	27-4
15	Kentucky	22-7	Joe B. Hall	22-8
16	Iowa	20-7	Lute Olson	21-8
17	Ala-Birmingham	23-5	Gene Bartow	25-6
18	Wake Forest	20-8	Carl Tacy	21-9
19	UCLA	21-6	Larry Farmer	21-6
20	Louisville	20-9	Denny Crum	23-10

NCAA Final Four (at the Superdome, New Orleans): **Semifinals**–N. Carolina 68, Houston 63; Georgetown 50, Louisville 46. **Championship**–N. Carolina 63, Georgetown 62.

NIT Championship (at Madison Square Garden): Bradley 67, Purdue 58. No Top 20 teams played in NIT.

1983

		Before Tourns	Head Coach	Final Record
1	Houston	27-2	Guy Lewis	31-3
2	Louisville	29-3	Denny Crum	32-4
3	St. John's	27-4	Lou Carnesecca	28-5
4	Virginia	27-4	Terry Holland	29-5
5	Indiana	23-5	Bob Knight	24-6
6	UNLV	28-2	Jerry Tarkanian	28-3
7	UCLA	23-5	Larry Farmer	23-6
8	North Carolina	26-7	Dean Smith	28-8
9	Arkansas	25-3	Eddie Sutton	26-4
10	Missouri	26-7	Norm Stewart	26-8
11	Boston College	24-6	Gary Williams	25-7
12	Kentucky	22-7	Joe B. Hall	23-8
13	Villanova	22-7	Rollie Massimino	24-8
14	Wichita St.	25-3	Gene Smithson	same*
15	Tenn-Chatt.	26-3	Murray Arnold	26-4
16	**N.C. State**	20-10	Jim Valvano	26-10
17	Memphis St.	22-7	Dana Kirk	23-8
18	Georgia	21-9	Hugh Durham	24-10
19	Oklahoma St.	24-6	Paul Hansen	24-7
20	Georgetown	21-9	John Thompson	22-10

*On probation

NCAA Final Four (at The Pit, Albuquerque, NM): **Semifinals**–N.C. State 67, Georgia 60; Houston 94, Louisville 81. **Championship**–N.C. State 54, Houston 52.

NIT Championship (at Madison Square Garden): Fresno St. 69, DePaul 60. No Top 20 teams played in NIT.

1984

		Before Tourns	Head Coach	Final Record
1	North Carolina	27-2	Dean Smith	28-3
2	**Georgetown**	29-3	John Thompson	34-3
3	Kentucky	26-4	Joe B. Hall	29-5
4	DePaul	26-2	Ray Meyer	27-3
5	Houston	28-4	Guy Lewis	32-5
6	Illinois	24-4	Lou Henson	26-5
7	Oklahoma	29-4	Billy Tubbs	29-5
8	Arkansas	25-6	Eddie Sutton	25-7
9	UTEP	27-3	Don Haskins	27-4
10	Purdue	22-6	Gene Keady	22-7
11	Maryland	23-7	Lefty Driesell	24-8
12	Tulsa	27-3	Nolan Richardson	27-4
13	UNLV	27-5	Jerry Tarkanian	29-6
14	Duke	24-9	Mike Krzyzewski	24-10
15	Washington	22-6	Marv Harshman	24-7
16	Memphis St.	24-6	Dana Kirk	26-7
17	Oregon St.	22-6	Ralph Miller	22-7
18	Syracuse	22-8	Jim Boeheim	23-9
19	Wake Forest	21-8	Carl Tacy	23-9
20	Temple	25-4	John Chaney	26-5

NCAA Final Four (at the Kingdome, Seattle): **Semifinals**–Houston 49, Virginia 47 (OT); Georgetown 53, Kentucky 40. **Championship**–Georgetown 84, Houston 75.

NIT Championship (at Madison Square Garden): Michigan 83, Notre Dame 63. No Top 20 teams played in NIT.

Highest-Rated College Games on TV

The dozen highest-rated college basketball games seen on U.S. television have been NCAA tournament championship games, led by the 1979 Michigan State-Indiana State final that featured Magic Johnson and Larry Bird.

Listed below are the finalists (winning team first), date of game, TV network, and TV rating and audience share (according to Nielson Media Research).

		Date	Net	Rtg/Sh
1	Michigan St.-Indiana St.	3/26/79	NBC	24.1/38
2	Villanova-Georgetown	4/1/85	CBS	23.3/33
3	Duke-Michigan	4/6/92	CBS	22.7/35
4	N.C. State-Houston	4/4/83	CBS	22.3/32
5	N. Carolina-Michigan	4/5/93	CBS	22.2/34
6	Arkansas-Duke	4/4/94	CBS	21.6/33

		Date	Net	Rtg/Sh
7	N. Carolina-Georgetown	3/29/82	CBS	21.6/31
8	UCLA-Kentucky	3/31/75	NBC	21.3/33
9	Michigan-Seton Hall	4/3/89	CBS	21.3/33
10	Louisville-Duke	3/31/86	CBS	20.7/31
11	Indiana-N. Carolina	3/30/81	NBC	20.7/29
12	UCLA-Memphis St.	3/26/73	NBC	20.5/32

1985

		Before Tourns	Head Coach	Final Record
1	Georgetown	30-2	John Thompson	35-3
2	Michigan	25-3	Bill Frieder	26-4
3	St. John's	27-3	Lou Carnesecca	31-4
4	Oklahoma	28-5	Billy Tubbs	31-6
5	Memphis St.	27-3	Dana Kirk	31-4
6	Georgia Tech	24-7	Bobby Cremins	27-8
7	North Carolina	24-8	Dean Smith	27-9
8	Louisiana Tech	27-2	Andy Russo	29-3
9	UNLV	27-3	Jerry Tarkanian	28-4
10	Duke	22-7	Mike Krzyzewski	23-8
11	VCU	25-5	J.D. Barnett	26-6
12	Illinois	24-8	Lou Henson	26-9
13	Kansas	25-7	Larry Brown	26-8
14	Loyola-IL	25-5	Gene Sullivan	27-6
15	Syracuse	21-8	Jim Boeheim	22-9
16	N.C. State	20-9	Jim Valvano	23-10
17	Texas Tech	23-7	Gerald Myers	23-8
18	Tulsa	23-7	Nolan Richardson	23-8
19	Georgia	21-8	Hugh Durham	22-9
20	LSU	19-9	Dale Brown	19-10

Note: Unranked **Villanova**, coached by Rollie Massimino, won the NCAAs. The Wildcats entered the tourney at 19-10 and had a final record of 25-10.

NCAA Final Four (at Rupp Arena, Lexington, KY): **Semifinals**—Georgetown 77, St. John's 59; Villanova 52, Memphis St. 45. **Championship**—Villanova 66, Georgetown 64.

NIT Championship (at Madison Square Garden): UCLA 65, Indiana 62. No Top 20 teams played in NIT.

1986

		Before Tourns	Head Coach	Final Record
1	Duke	32-2	Mike Krzyzewski	37-3
2	Kansas	31-3	Larry Brown	35-4
3	Kentucky	29-3	Eddie Sutton	32-4
4	St. John's	30-4	Lou Carnesecca	31-5
5	Michigan	27-4	Bill Frieder	28-5
6	Georgia Tech	25-6	Bobby Cremins	27-7
7	**Louisville**	26-7	Denny Crum	32-7
8	North Carolina	26-5	Dean Smith	28-6
9	Syracuse	25-5	Jim Boeheim	26-6
10	Notre Dame	23-5	Digger Phelps	23-6
11	UNLV	31-4	Jerry Tarkanian	33-5
12	Memphis St.	27-5	Dana Kirk	28-6
13	Georgetown	23-7	John Thompson	24-8
14	Bradley	31-2	Dick Versace	32-3
15	Oklahoma	25-8	Billy Tubbs	26-9
16	Indiana	21-7	Bob Knight	21-8
17	Navy	27-4	Paul Evans	30-5
18	Michigan St.	21-7	Jud Heathcote	23-8
19	Illinois	21-9	Lou Henson	22-10
20	UTEP	27-5	Don Haskins	27-6

NCAA Final Four (at Reunion Arena, Dallas): **Semifinals**—Duke 71, Kansas 67; Louisville 88, LSU 77. **Championship**—Louisville 72, Duke 69.

NIT Championship (at Madison Square Garden): Ohio St. 73, Wyoming 63. No Top 20 teams played in NIT.

1987

		Before Tourns	Head Coach	Final Record
1	UNLV	33-1	Jerry Tarkanian	37-2
2	North Carolina	29-3	Dean Smith	32-4
3	**Indiana**	24-4	Bob Knight	30-4
4	Georgetown	26-4	John Thompson	29-5
5	DePaul	26-2	Joey Meyer	28-3
6	Iowa	27-4	Tom Davis	30-5
7	Purdue	24-4	Gene Keady	25-5
8	Temple	31-3	John Chaney	32-4
9	Alabama	26-4	Wimp Sanderson	28-5
10	Syracuse	26-6	Jim Boeheim	31-7
11	Illinois	23-7	Lou Henson	23-8
12	Pittsburgh	24-7	Paul Evans	25-8
13	Clemson	25-5	Cliff Ellis	25-6
14	Missouri	24-9	Norm Stewart	24-10
15	UCLA	24-6	Walt Hazzard	25-7
16	New Orleans	25-3	Benny Dees	26-4
17	Duke	22-8	Mike Krzyzewski	24-9
18	Notre Dame	22-7	Digger Phelps	24-8
19	TCU	23-6	Jim Killingsworth	24-7
20	Kansas	23-10	Larry Brown	25-11

NCAA Final Four (at the Superdome, New Orleans): **Semifinals**—Syracuse 77, Providence 63; Indiana 97, UNLV 93. **Championship**—Indiana 74, Syracuse 73.

NIT Championship (at Madison Square Garden): Southern Miss. 84, La Salle 80. No Top 20 teams played in NIT.

1988

		Before Tourns	Head Coach	Final Record
1	Temple	29-1	John Chaney	32-2
2	Arizona	31-2	Lute Olson	35-3
3	Purdue	27-3	Gene Keady	29-4
4	Oklahoma	30-3	Billy Tubbs	35-4
5	Duke	24-6	Mike Krzyzewski	28-7
6	Kentucky	25-5	Eddie Sutton	27-6
7	North Carolina	24-6	Dean Smith	27-7
8	Pittsburgh	23-6	Paul Evans	24-7
9	Syracuse	25-8	Jim Boeheim	26-9
10	Michigan	24-7	Bill Frieder	26-8
11	Bradley	26-4	Stan Albeck	26-5
12	UNLV	27-5	Jerry Tarkanian	28-6
13	Wyoming	26-5	Benny Dees	26-6
14	N.C. State	24-7	Jim Valvano	24-8
15	Loyola-CA	27-3	Paul Westhead	28-4
16	Illinois	22-9	Lou Henson	23-10
17	Iowa	22-9	Tom Davis	24-10
18	Xavier-OH	26-3	Pete Gillen	26-4
19	BYU	25-5	Ladell Andersen	26-6
20	Kansas St.	22-8	Lon Kruger	25-9

Note: Unranked **Kansas**, coached by Larry Brown, won the NCAAs. The Jayhawks entered the tourney at 21-11 and had a final record of 27-11.

NCAA Final Four (at Kemper Arena, Kansas City): **Semifinals**—Kansas 66, Duke 59; Oklahoma 86, Arizona 78. **Championship**—Kansas 83, Oklahoma 79.

NIT Championship (at Madison Square Garden): Connecticut 72, Ohio St. 67. No Top 20 teams played in NIT.

Associated Press Final Polls (Cont.)

1989

		Before Tourns	Head Coach	Final Record
1	Arizona	27-3	Lute Olson	29-4
2	Georgetown	26-4	John Thompson	29-5
3	Illinois	27-4	Lou Henson	31-5
4	Oklahoma	28-5	Billy Tubbs	30-6
5	North Carolina	27-7	Dean Smith	29-8
6	Missouri	27-7	Norm Stewart & Rich Daly*	29-8
7	Syracuse	27-7	Jim Boeheim	30-8
8	Indiana	25-7	Bob Knight	27-8
9	Duke	24-7	Mike Krzyzewski	28-8
10	**Michigan**	24-7	Bill Frieder (24-7) & Steve Fisher (6-0)	30-7
11	Seton Hall	26-6	P.J. Carlesimo	31-7
12	Louisville	22-8	Denny Crum	24-9
13	Stanford	26-6	Mike Montgomery	26-7
14	Iowa	22-9	Tom Davis	23-10
15	UNLV	26-7	Jerry Tarkanian	29-8
16	Florida St.	22-7	Pat Kennedy	22-8
17	West Virginia	25-4	Gale Catlett	26-5
18	Ball State	28-2	Rick Majerus	29-3
19	N.C. State	20-8	Jim Valvano	22-9
20	Alabama	23-7	Wimp Sanderson	23-8

NCAA Final Four (at The Kingdome, Seattle): **Semifinals**–Seton Hall 95, Duke 78; Michigan 83, Illinois 81. **Championship**–Michigan 80, Seton Hall 79 (OT).

NIT Championship (at Madison Square Garden): St. John's 73, St. Louis 65. No Top 20 teams played in NIT.

*Norm Stewart's assistant Rich Daly temporarily took over for his ailing boss (Daly coached the final 14 games of the season) but returned to his role as an assistant when Stewart recovered before the start of the following season.

1991

		Before Tourns	Head Coach	Final Record
1	UNLV	30-0	Jerry Tarkanian	34-1
2	Arkansas	31-3	Nolan Richardson	34-4
3	Indiana	27-4	Bob Knight	29-5
4	North Carolina	25-5	Dean Smith	29-6
5	Ohio St.	25-3	Randy Ayers	27-4
6	Duke	26-7	Mike Krzyzewski	32-7
7	Syracuse	26-5	Jim Boeheim	26-6
8	Arizona	26-6	Lute Olson	28-7
9	Kentucky	22-6	Rick Pitino	same*
10	Utah	28-3	Rick Majerus	30-4
11	Nebraska	26-7	Danny Nee	26-8
12	Kansas	22-7	Roy Williams	27-8
13	Seton Hall	22-8	P.J. Carlesimo	25-9
14	Oklahoma St.	22-7	Eddie Sutton	24-8
15	New Mexico St.	23-5	Neil McCarthy	23-6
16	UCLA	23-8	Jim Harrick	23-9
17	E.Tennessee St.	28-4	Alan LaForce	28-5
18	Princeton	24-2	Pete Carril	24-3
19	Alabama	21-9	Wimp Sanderson	23-10
20	St. John's	20-8	Lou Carnesecca	23-9
21	Mississippi St.	20-8	Richard Williams	20-9
22	LSU	20-9	Dale Brown	20-10
23	Texas	22-8	Tom Penders	23-9
24	DePaul	20-8	Joey Meyer	20-9
25	Southern Miss.	21-7	M.K. Turk	21-8

*On probation

NCAA Final Four (at the Hoosier Dome, Indianapolis): **Semifinals**–Kansas 79, North Carolina 73; Duke 79, UNLV 77. **Championship**–Duke 72, Kansas 65.

NIT Championship (at Madison Square Garden): Stanford 78, Oklahoma 72. No Top 25 teams played in NIT.

1990

		Before Tourns	Head Coach	Final Record
1	Oklahoma	26-4	Billy Tubbs	27-5
2	**UNLV**	29-5	Jerry Tarkanian	35-5
3	Connecticut	28-5	Jim Calhoun	31-6
4	Michigan St.	26-5	Jud Heathcote	28-6
5	Kansas	29-4	Roy Williams	30-5
6	Syracuse	24-6	Jim Boeheim	26-7
7	Arkansas	26-4	Nolan Richardson	30-5
8	Georgetown	23-6	John Thompson	24-7
9	Georgia Tech	24-6	Bobby Cremins	28-7
10	Purdue	21-7	Gene Keady	22-8
11	Missouri	26-5	Norm Stewart	26-6
12	La Salle	29-1	Speedy Morris	30-2
13	Michigan	22-7	Steve Fisher	23-8
14	Arizona	24-6	Lute Olson	25-7
15	Duke	24-8	Mike Krzyzewski	29-9
16	Louisville	26-7	Denny Crum	27-8
17	Clemson	24-8	Cliff Ellis	26-9
18	Illinois	21-7	Lou Henson	21-8
19	LSU	23-8	Dale Brown	23-9
20	Minnesota	20-8	Clem Haskins	23-9
21	Loyola-CA	23-5	Paul Westhead	26-6
22	Oregon St.	22-6	Jim Anderson	22-7
23	Alabama	24-8	Wimp Sanderson	26-9
24	New Mexico St.	26-4	Neil McCarthy	26-5
25	Xavier-OH	26-4	Pete Gillen	28-5

NCAA Final Four (at McNichols Sports Arena, Denver): **Semifinals**–Duke 97, Arkansas 83; UNLV 90, Georgia Tech 81. **Championship**–UNLV 103, Duke 73.

NIT Championship (at Madison Square Garden): Vanderbilt 74, St.Louis 72. No Top 25 teams played in NIT.

1992

		Before Tourns	Head Coach	Final Record
1	**Duke**	28-2	Mike Krzyzewski	34-2
2	Kansas	26-4	Roy Williams	27-5
3	Ohio St.	23-5	Randy Ayers	26-6
4	UCLA	25-4	Jim Harrick	28-5
5	Indiana	23-6	Bob Knight	27-7
6	Kentucky	26-6	Rick Pitino	29-7
7	UNLV	26-2	Jerry Tarkanian	same*
8	USC	23-5	George Raveling	24-6
9	Arkansas	25-7	Nolan Richardson	26-8
10	Arizona	24-6	Lute Olson	24-7
11	Oklahoma St.	26-7	Eddie Sutton	28-8
12	Cincinnati	25-4	Bob Huggins	29-5
13	Alabama	25-8	Wimp Sanderson	26-9
14	Michigan St.	21-7	Jud Heathcote	22-8
15	Michigan	20-8	Steve Fisher	25-9
16	Missouri	20-8	Norm Stewart	21-9
17	Massachusetts	28-4	John Calipari	30-5
18	North Carolina	21-9	Dean Smith	23-10
19	Seton Hall	21-8	P.J. Carlesimo	23-9
20	Florida St.	20-9	Pat Kennedy	22-10
21	Syracuse	21-9	Jim Boeheim	22-10
22	Georgetown	21-9	John Thompson	22-10
23	Oklahoma	21-8	Billy Tubbs	21-9
24	DePaul	20-8	Joey Meyer	20-9
25	LSU	20-9	Dale Brown	21-10

*On probation

NCAA Final Four (at the Metrodome, Minneapolis): **Semifinals**–Michigan 76, Cincinnati 72; Duke 81, Indiana 78. **Championship**–Duke 71, Michigan 51.

NIT Championship (at Madison Square Garden): Virginia 81, Notre Dame 76 (OT). No Top 25 teams played in NIT.

1993

		Before Tourns	Head Coach	Final Record
1	Indiana	28-3	Bob Knight	31-4
2	Kentucky	26-3	Rick Pitino	30-4
3	Michigan	26-4	Steve Fisher	31-5
4	**N. Carolina**	28-4	Dean Smith	34-4
5	Arizona	24-3	Lute Olson	24-4
6	Seton Hall	27-6	P.J. Carlesimo	28-7
7	Cincinnati	24-4	Bob Huggins	27-5
8	Vanderbilt	26-5	Eddie Fogler	28-6
9	Kansas	25-6	Roy Williams	29-7
10	Duke	23-7	Mike Krzyzewski	24-8
11	Florida St.	22-9	Pat Kennedy	25-10
12	Arkansas	20-8	Nolan Richardson	22-9
13	Iowa	22-8	Tom Davis	23-9
14	Massachusetts	23-6	John Calipari	24-7
15	Louisville	20-8	Denny Crum	22-9
16	Wake Forest	19-8	Dave Odom	21-9
17	New Orleans	26-3	Tim Floyd	26-4
18	Georgia Tech	19-10	Bobby Cremins	19-11
19	Utah	23-6	Rick Majerus	24-7
20	Western Ky.	24-5	Ralph Willard	26-6
21	New Mexico	24-6	Dave Bliss	24-7
22	Purdue	18-9	Gene Keady	18-10
23	Oklahoma St.	19-8	Eddie Sutton	20-9
24	New Mexico St.	25-7	Neil McCarthy	26-8
25	UNLV	21-7	Rollie Massimino	21-8

NCAA Final Four (at the Superdome, New Orleans): **Semifinals**—North Carolina 78, Kansas 68; Michigan 81, Kentucky 78 (OT). **Championship**—North Carolina 77, Michigan 71.

NIT Championship (at Madison Square Garden): Minnesota 62, Georgetown 61. No. 25 UNLV was the only Top 25 team that played in the NIT.

1994

		Before Tourns	Head Coach	Final Record
1	North Carolina	27-6	Dean Smith	28-7
2	**Arkansas**	25-3	Nolan Richardson	31-3
3	Purdue	26-4	Gene Keady	29-5
4	Connecticut	27-4	Jim Calhoun	29-5
5	Missouri	25-3	Norm Stewart	28-4
6	Duke	23-5	Mike Krzyzewski	28-6
7	Kentucky	26-6	Rick Pitino	27-7
8	Massachusetts	27-6	John Calipari	28-7
9	Arizona	25-5	Lute Olson	29-6
10	Louisville	26-5	Denny Crum	28-6
11	Michigan	21-7	Steve Fisher	24-8
12	Temple	22-7	John Chaney	23-8
13	Kansas	25-7	Roy Williams	27-8
14	Florida	25-7	Lon Kruger	29-8
15	Syracuse	21-6	Jim Boeheim	23-7
16	California	22-7	Todd Bozeman	22-8
17	UCLA	21-6	Jim Harrick	21-7
18	Indiana	19-8	Bob Knight	21-9
19	Oklahoma St.	23-9	Eddie Sutton	24-10
20	Texas	25-7	Tom Penders	26-8
21	Marquette	22-8	Kevin O'Neill	24-9
22	Nebraska	20-9	Danny Nee	20-10
23	Minnesota	20-11	Clem Haskins	21-12
24	Saint Louis	23-5	Charlie Spoonhour	23-6
25	Cincinnati	22-9	Bob Huggins	22-9

NCAA Final Four (at the Charlotte Coliseum): **Semifinals**— Arkansas 91, Arizona 82; Duke 70, Florida 65. **Championship**— Arkansas 76, Duke 72.

NIT Championship (at Madison Square Garden): Villanova 80, Vanderbilt 73. No top 25 teams played in NIT.

1995

		Before Tourns	Head Coach	Final Record
1	UCLA	25-2	Jim Harrick	31-2
2	Kentucky	25-4	Rick Pitino	28-5
3	Wake Forest	24-5	Dave Odom	26-6
4	North Carolina	24-5	Dean Smith	28-6
5	Kansas	23-5	Roy Williams	25-6
6	Arkansas	27-6	Nolan Richardson	32-7
7	Massachusetts	26-4	John Calipari	26-5
8	Connecticut	25-4	Jim Calhoun	28-5
9	Villanova	25-7	Steve Lappas	25-8
10	Maryland	24-7	Gary Williams	26-8
11	Michigan St.	22-5	Jud Heathcote	22-6
12	Purdue	24-6	Gene Keady	25-7
13	Virginia	22-8	Jeff Jones	25-9
14	Oklahoma St.	23-9	Eddie Sutton	27-10
15	Arizona	23-7	Lute Olson	23-8
16	Arizona St.	22-8	Bill Frieder	24-9
17	Oklahoma	23-8	Kelvin Sampson	23-9
18	Mississippi St.	20-7	Richard Williams	22-8
19	Utah	27-5	Rick Majerus	28-6
20	Alabama	22-9	David Hobbs	23-10
21	Western Ky.	26-3	Matt Kilcullen	27-4
22	Georgetown	19-9	John Thompson	21-10
23	Missouri	19-8	Norm Stewart	20-9
24	Iowa St.	22-10	Tim Floyd	23-11
25	Syracuse	19-9	Jim Boeheim	20-10

NCAA Final Four (at the Kingdome, Seattle): **Semifinals**— UCLA 74, Oklahoma St. 61; Arkansas 75, North Carolina 68. **Championship**— UCLA 89, Arkansas 78.

NIT Championship (at Madison Square Garden): Virginia Tech 65, Marquette 64 (OT). No top 25 teams played in NIT.

1996

		Before Tourns	Head Coach	Final Record
1	Massachusetts	31-1	John Calipari	35-2
2	**Kentucky**	28-2	Rick Pitino	34-2
3	Connecticut	30-2	Jim Calhoun	32-3
4	Georgetown	26-7	John Thompson	29-8
5	Kansas	26-4	Roy Williams	29-5
6	Purdue	25-5	Gene Keady	26-6
7	Cincinnati	25-4	Bob Huggins	28-5
8	Texas Tech	28-1	James Dickey	30-2
9	Wake Forest	23-5	Dave Odom	26-6
10	Villanova	25-6	Steve Lappas	26-7
11	Arizona	24-6	Lute Olson	26-7
12	Utah	25-6	Rick Majerus	27-7
13	Georgia Tech	22-11	Bobby Cremins	24-12
14	UCLA	23-7	Jim Harrick	23-8
15	Syracuse	24-8	Jim Boeheim	29-9
16	Memphis	22-7	Larry Finch	22-8
17	Iowa St.	23-8	Tim Floyd	24-9
18	Penn St.	21-6	Jerry Dunn	21-7
19	Mississippi St.	22-7	Richard Williams	26-8
20	Marquette	22-7	Mike Deane	23-8
21	Iowa	22-8	Tom Davis	23-9
22	Virginia Tech	22-5	Bill Foster	23-6
23	New Mexico	27-4	Dave Bliss	28-5
24	Louisville	20-11	Denny Crum	22-12
25	North Carolina	20-10	Dean Smith	21-11

NCAA Final Four (at the Meadowlands, E. Rutherford, N.J.): **Semifinals**— Kentucky 81, Massachusetts 74; Syracuse 77, Mississippi St. 69. **Championship**— Kentucky 76, Syracuse 67.

NIT Championship (at Madison Square Garden): Nebraska 60, St. Joseph's 56. No top 25 teams played in NIT.

Associated Press Final Polls (Cont.)

	1997				1998		
		Before Tourns	**Head Coach**	**Final Record**		**Before Tourns**	**Head Coach**	**Final Record**

	1997					1998		
		Before Tourns	Head Coach	Final Record		Before Tourns	Head Coach	Final Record
1	Kansas	32-1	Roy Williams	34-2	North Carolina	30-3	Bill Guthridge	34-4
2	Utah	26-3	Rick Majerus	29-4	Kansas	34-3	Roy Williams	35-4
3	Minnesota	27-3	Clem Haskins	31-4	Duke	29-3	Mike Krzyzewski	32-4
4	North Carolina	24-6	Dean Smith	28-7	Arizona	27-4	Lute Olson	30-5
5	Kentucky	30-4	Rick Pitino	35-5	Kentucky	29-4	Tubby Smith	35-4
6	South Carolina	24-7	Eddie Fogler	24-8	Connecticut	29-4	Jim Calhoun	32-5
7	UCLA	21-7	Steve Lavin	24-8	Utah	25-3	Rick Majerus	30-4
8	Duke	23-8	Mike Krzyzewski	24-9	Princeton	26-1	Bill Carmody	27-2
9	Wake Forest	23-6	Dave Odom	24-7	Cincinnati	26-5	Bob Huggins	27-6
10	Cincinnati	25-7	Bob Huggins	26-8	Stanford	26-4	Mike Montgomery	30-5
11	New Mexico	24-7	Dave Bliss	25-8	Purdue	26-7	Gene Keady	28-8
12	St. Joseph's	24-6	Phil Martelli	26-7	Michigan	24-8	Brian Ellerbe	25-9
13	Xavier	22-5	Skip Prosser	23-6	Mississippi	22-6	Rob Evans	22-7
14	Clemson	21-9	Rick Barnes	23-10	South Carolina	23-7	Eddie Fogler	23-8
15	**Arizona**	19-9	Lute Olson	25-9	TCU	27-5	Billy Tubbs	27-6
16	Charleston	28-2	John Kresse	29-3	Michigan St.	20-7	Tom Izzo	22-8
17	Georgia	24-8	Tubby Smith	24-9	Arkansas	23-8	Nolan Richardson	24-9
18	Iowa St.	20-8	Tim Floyd	22-9	New Mexico	23-7	Dave Bliss	24-8
19	Illinois	21-9	Lon Kruger	22-10	UCLA	22-8	Steve Lavin	24-9
20	Villanova	23-9	Steve Lappas	24-10	Maryland	19-10	Gary Williams	21-11
21	Stanford	20-7	Mike Montgomery	22-8	Syracuse	24-8	Jim Boeheim	26-9
22	Maryland	21-10	Gary Williams	21-11	Illinois	22-9	Lon Kruger	23-10
23	Boston College	21-8	Jim O'Brien	22-9	Xavier	22-7	Skip Prosser	22-8
24	Colorado	21-9	Ricardo Patton	22-10	Temple	21-8	John Chaney	21-9
25	Louisville	23-8	Denny Crum	26-9	Murray St.	29-3	Mark Gottfried	29-4

NCAA Final Four (at the RCA Dome, Indianapolis):
Semifinals– Kentucky 78, Minnesota 69; Arizona 66, North Carolina 58. **Championship–** Arizona 84, Kentucky 79 (OT).

NIT Championship (at Madison Square Garden): Michigan 82, Florida St. 72. No top 25 teams played in NIT.

NCAA Final Four (at the Alamodome, San Antonio):
Semifinals– Kentucky 86, Stanford 85 (OT); Utah 65, North Carolina 59. **Championship–** Kentucky 78, Utah 69.

NIT Championship (at Madison Square Garden): Minnesota 79, Penn St. 72. No top 25 teams played in NIT.

AP Post-Tournament Final Polls

The final AP Top 20 poll has been released after the NCAA tournament and NIT four times– in 1953 and '54 and again in 1974 and '75. Those four polls are listed below; teams that were not included in the last regular season polls are in *CAPITAL* italic letters.

	1953	Final Record		1954	Final Record		1974	Final Record		1975	Final Record
1	Indiana	23-3	1	Kentucky	25-0	1	N.C. State	30-1	1	UCLA	28-3
2	Seton Hall	31-2	2	La Salle	26-4	2	UCLA	26-4	2	Kentucky	26-5
3	Kansas	19-6	3	Holy Cross	26-2	3	Marquette	26-5	3	Indiana	31-1
4	Washington	30-3	4	Indiana	20-4	4	Maryland	23-5	4	Louisville	28-3
5	LSU	24-3	5	Duquesne	26-3	5	Notre Dame	26-3	5	Maryland	24-5
6	La Salle	25-3	6	Notre Dame	22-3	6	Michigan	22-5	6	Syracuse	23-9
7	*ST. JOHN'S*	17-6	7	*BRADLEY*	19-13	7	Kansas	23-7	7	N.C. State	22-6
8	Okla. A&M	23-7	8	Western Ky.	29-3	8	Providence	28-4	8	Arizona St.	25-4
9	Duquesne	21-8	9	*PENN ST.*	18-6	9	Indiana	23-5	9	North Carolina	23-8
10	Notre Dame	19-5	10	Okla. A&M	24-5	10	Long Beach St.	24-2	10	Alabama	22-5
11	Illinois	18-4	11	USC	19-14	11	*PURDUE*	22-8	11	Marquette	23-4
12	Kansas St.	17-4	12	*GEO. WASH.*	23-3	12	North Carolina	22-6	12	*PRINCETON*	22-8
13	Holy Cross	20-6	13	Iowa	17-5	13	Vanderbilt	23-5	13	Cincinnati	23-6
14	Seattle	29-4	14	LSU	21-5	14	Alabama	22-4	14	Notre Dame	19-10
15	*WAKE FOREST*	22-7	15	Duke	22-6	15	*UTAH*	22-8	15	Kansas St.	20-9
16	*SANTA CLARA*	20-7	16	*NIAGARA*	24-6	16	Pittsburgh	25-4	16	Drake	19-10
17	Western Ky.	25-6	17	Seattle	26-2	17	USC	24-5	17	UNLV	24-5
18	N.C. State	26-6	18	Kansas	16-5	18	*ORAL ROBERTS*	23-6	18	Oregon St.	19-12
19	*DEPAUL*	19-9	19	Illinois	17-5	19	South Carolina	22-5	19	*MICHIGAN*	19-8
20	*SW MISSOURI*	24-4	20	*MARYLAND*	23-7	20	Dayton	20-9	20	Penn	23-5

Pre-Tournament Records

1953– St. John's (Al DeStefano, 14-5); Wake Forest (Murray Greason, 21-6); Santa Clara (Bob Feerick, 18-6); DePaul (Ray Meyer, 18-7); SW Missouri St. (Bob Vanatta, 19-4 before NAIA tourney). **1954–** Bradley (Forddy Anderson, 15-12); Penn St. (Elmer Gross, 14-5); George Washington (Bill Reinhart, 23-2); Niagara (Taps Gallagher, 22-5); Maryland (Bud Millikan, 23-7). **1974–** Purdue (Fred Schaus, 18-8); Utah (Bill Foster, 19-7); Oral Roberts (Ken Trickey, 21-5). **1975–** Princeton (Pete Carril, 18-8); Michigan (Johnny Orr, 19-7).

1999

		Before Tourns	Head Coach	Final Record
1	Duke	32-1	Mike Krzyzewski	37-2
2	Michigan St.	29-4	Tom Izzo	33-5
3	**Connecticut**	28-2	Jim Calhoun	34-2
4	Auburn	27-3	Cliff Ellis	29-4
5	Maryland	26-5	Gary Williams	28-6
6	Utah	27-4	Rick Majerus	28-5
7	Stanford	25-6	Mike Montgomery	26-7
8	Kentucky	25-8	Tubby Smith	28-9
9	St. John's	25-8	Mike Jarvis	28-9
10	Miami-FL	22-6	Leonard Hamilton	23-7
11	Cincinnati	26-5	Bob Huggins	27-6
12	Arizona	22-6	Lute Olson	22-7
13	North Carolina	24-9	Bill Guthridge	24-10
14	Ohio St.	23-8	Jim O'Brien	27-9
15	UCLA	22-8	Steve Lavin	22-9
16	College of Charleston	28-2	John Kresse	28-3
17	Arkansas	22-10	Nolan Richardson	23-11
18	Wisconsin	22-9	Dick Bennett	22-10
19	Indiana	22-10	Bobby Knight	23-11
20	Tennessee	20-8	Jerry Green	21-9
21	Iowa	18-9	Tom Davis	20-10
22	Kansas	22-9	Roy Williams	23-10
23	Florida	20-8	Billy Donovan	22-9
24	NC-Charlotte	22-10	Bob Lutz	23-11
25	New Mexico	24-8	Dave Bliss	25-9

NCAA Final Four (at the Tropicana Field, St. Petersburg): **Semifinals**– Duke 68, Michigan St. 62; Connecticut 64, Ohio St. 58. **Championship**– Connecticut 77, Duke 74.
NIT Championship (at Madison Square Garden): California 61, Clemson 60. No top 25 teams played in NIT.

2000

		Before Tourns	Head Coach	Final Record
1	Duke	27-4	Mike Krzyzewski	29-5
2	**Michigan St.**	26-7	Tom Izzo	32-7
3	Stanford	26-3	Mike Montgomery	27-4
4	Arizona	26-6	Lute Olson	27-7
5	Temple	26-5	John Chaney	27-6
6	Iowa St.	29-4	Larry Eustachy	32-5
7	Cincinnati	28-3	Bob Huggins	29-4
8	Ohio St.	22-6	Jim O'Brien	23-7
9	St. John's	24-7	Mike Jarvis	25-8
10	LSU	26-5	John Brady	28-6
11	Tennessee	24-6	Jerry Green	26-7
12	Oklahoma	26-6	Kelvin Sampson	27-7
13	Florida	24-7	Billy Donovan	29-8
14	Oklahoma St.	24-6	Eddie Sutton	27-7
15	Texas	23-8	Rick Barnes	24-9
16	Syracuse	26-6	Jim Boeheim	26-6
17	Maryland	24-9	Gary Williams	25-10
18	Tulsa	29-4	Bill Self	32-5
19	Kentucky	22-9	Tubby Smith	23-10
20	Connecticut	24-9	Jim Calhoun	25-10
21	Illinois	21-9	Lon Kruger	22-10
22	Indiana	20-8	Bobby Knight	20-9
23	Miami-FL	21-10	Leonard Hamilton	23-11
24	Auburn	23-9	Cliff Ellis	24-10
25	Purdue	21-9	Gene Keady	24-10

NCAA Final Four (at the RCA Dome, Indianapolis): **Semifinals**– Michigan St. 53, Wisconsin 41; Florida 71, North Carolina 59. **Championship**– Michigan St. 89, Florida 76.
NIT Championship (at Madison Square Garden): Wake Forest 71, Notre Dame 61. No top 25 teams played in NIT.

2001

		Before Tourns	Head Coach	Final Record
1	**Duke**	29-4	Mike Krzyzewski	35-4
2	Stanford	28-2	Mike Montgomery	31-3
3	Michigan St.	24-4	Tom Izzo	28-5
4	Illinois	24-7	Bill Self	27-8
5	Arizona	23-7	Lute Olson	28-8
6	North Carolina	25-6	Matt Doherty	26-7
7	Boston College	26-4	Al Skinner	27-5
8	Florida	23-6	Billy Donovan	24-7
9	Kentucky	22-9	Tubby Smith	24-10
10	Iowa St.	25-5	Larry Eustachy	25-6
11	Maryland	21-10	Gary Williams	25-11
12	Kansas	24-6	Roy Williams	26-7
13	Oklahoma	26-6	Kelvin Sampson	26-7
14	Mississippi	25-7	Rod Barnes	27-8
15	UCLA	21-8	Steve Lavin	23-9
16	Virginia	20-8	Pete Gillen	20-9
17	Syracuse	24-8	Jim Boeheim	25-9
18	Texas	25-8	Rick Barnes	25-9
19	Notre Dame	19-9	Mike Brey	20-10
20	Indiana	21-12	Mike Davis	21-13
21	Georgetown	23-7	Craig Esherick	25-0
22	St. Joseph's	25-6	Phil Martelli	26-7
23	Wake Forest	19-10	Dave Odom	19-11
24	Iowa	22-11	Steve Alford	23-12
25	Wisconsin	18-10	Dick Bennett (2-1) & Brad Soderberg (16-10)	18-11

NCAA Final Four (at the HHH Metrodome, Minneapolis): **Semifinals**– Duke 95, Maryland 84; Arizona 80, Michigan St. 61. **Championship**– Duke 82, Arizona 72.
NIT Championship (at Madison Square Garden): Tulsa 79, Alabama 60. No top 25 teams played in NIT.

Division I Winning Streaks

Full Season
(Including tournaments)

No		Seasons	Broken by	Score
88	UCLA	1971-74	Notre Dame	71-70
60	San Francisco	1955-57	Illinois	62-33
47	UCLA	1966-68	Houston	71-69
45	UNLV	1990-91	Duke	79-77
44	Texas	1913-17	Rice	24-18
43	Seton Hall	1939-41	LIU-Bklyn	49-26
43	LIU-Brooklyn	1935-37	Stanford	45-31
41	UCLA	1968-69	USC	46-44
39	Marquette	1970-71	Ohio St.	60-59
37	Cincinnati	1962-63	Wichita St.	65-64
37	North Carolina	1957-58	West Virginia	75-64
36	N.C. State	1974-75	Wake Forest	83-78
35	Arkansas	1927-29	Texas	26-25

Regular Season
(Not including tournaments)

No		Seasons	Broken by	Score
76	UCLA	1971-74	Notre Dame	71-70
57	Indiana	1975-77	Toledo	59-57
56	Marquette	1970-72	Detroit	70-49
54	Kentucky	1952-55	Georgia Tech	59-58
51	San Francisco	1955-57	Illinois	62-33
48	Penn	1970-72	Temple	57-52
47	Ohio St	1960-62	Wisconsin	86-67
44	Texas	1913-17	Rice	24-18
43	UCLA	1966-68	Houston	71-69
43	LIU-Brooklyn	1935-37	Stanford	45-31
42	Seton Hall	1939-41	LIU-Bklyn	49-26

Home Court

No		Seasons	Broken By	Score	No		Seasons	Broken By	Score
129	Kentucky	1943-55	Georgia Tech	59-58	81	Marquette	1967-73	Notre Dame	71-69
99	St. Bonaventure	1948-61	Detroit	77-70	80	Lamar	1978-84	Louisiana Tech	68-65
98	UCLA	1970-76	Oregon	65-45	75	Long Beach St.	1968-74	San Francisco	94-84
86	Cincinnati	1957-64	Kansas	51-47	72	UNLV	1974-78	New Mexico	102-98
81	Arizona	1945-51	Kansas St.	76-57	71	Arizona	1987-92	UCLA	89-87

Annual NCAA Division I Leaders
Scoring

The NCAA did not begin keeping individual scoring records until the 1947-48 season. All averages include postseason games where applicable.

Multiple winners: Pete Maravich and Oscar Robertson (3); Darrell Floyd, Charles Jones, Harry Kelly, Frank Selvy and Freeman Williams (2).

Year		Gm	Pts	Avg	Year		Gm	Pts	Avg
1948	Murray Wier, Iowa	19	399	21.0	1975	Bob McCurdy, Richmond	26	855	32.9
1949	Tony Lavelli, Yale	30	671	22.4	1976	Marshall Rodgers, Texas-Pan Am	25	919	36.8
1950	Paul Arizin, Villanova	29	735	25.3	1977	Freeman Williams, Portland St.	26	1010	38.8
1951	Bill Mlkvy, Temple	25	731	29.2	1978	Freeman Williams, Portland St.	27	969	35.9
1952	Clyde Lovellette, Kansas	28	795	28.4	1979	Lawrence Butler, Idaho St.	27	812	30.1
1953	Frank Selvy, Furman	25	738	29.5	1980	Tony Murphy, Southern-BR	29	932	32.1
1954	Frank Selvy, Furman	29	1209	41.7	1981	Zam Fredrick, S. Carolina	27	781	28.9
1955	Darrell Floyd, Furman	25	897	35.9	1982	Harry Kelly, Texas Southern	29	862	29.7
1956	Darrell Floyd, Furman	28	946	33.8	1983	Harry Kelly, Texas Southern	29	835	28.8
1957	Grady Wallace, S. Carolina	29	906	31.2	1984	Joe Jakubick, Akron	27	814	30.1
1958	Oscar Robertson, Cincinnati	28	984	35.1	1985	Xavier McDaniel, Wichita St	31	844	27.2
1959	Oscar Robertson, Cincinnati	30	978	32.6	1986	Terrance Bailey, Wagner	29	854	29.4
1960	Oscar Robertson, Cincinnati	30	1011	33.7	1987	Kevin Houston, Army	29	953	32.9
1961	Frank Burgess, Gonzaga	26	842	32.4	1988	Hersey Hawkins, Bradley	31	1125	36.3
1962	Billy McGill, Utah	26	1009	38.8	1989	Hank Gathers, Loyola-CA	31	1015	32.7
1963	Nick Werkman, Seton Hall	22	650	29.5	1990	Bo Kimble, Loyola-CA	32	1131	35.3
1964	Howie Komives, Bowling Green	23	844	36.7	1991	Kevin Bradshaw, US Int'l	28	1054	37.6
1965	Rick Barry, Miami-FL	26	973	37.4	1992	Brett Roberts, Morehead St	29	815	28.1
1966	Dave Schellhase, Purdue	24	781	32.5	1993	Greg Guy, Texas-Pan Am	19	556	29.3
1967	Jimmy Walker, Providence	28	851	30.4	1994	Glenn Robinson, Purdue	34	1030	30.3
1968	Pete Maravich, LSU	26	1138	43.8	1995	Kurt Thomas, TCU	27	781	28.9
1969	Pete Maravich, LSU	26	1148	44.2	1996	Kevin Granger, Texas Southern	24	648	27.0
1970	Pete Maravich, LSU	31	1381	44.5	1997	Charles Jones, LIU-Brooklyn	30	903	30.1
1971	Johnny Neumann, Ole Miss	23	923	40.1	1998	Charles Jones, LIU-Brooklyn	30	869	29.0
1972	Dwight Lamar, SW La.	29	1054	36.3	1999	Alvin Young, Niagara	29	728	25.1
1973	Bird Averitt, Pepperdine	25	848	33.9	2000	Courtney Alexander, Fresno St.	27	669	24.8
1974	Larry Fogle, Canisius	25	835	33.4	2001	Ronnie McCollum, Centenary	27	787	29.1

Note: Seventeen underclassmen have won the title. **Sophomores** (4)–Robertson (1958), Maravich (1968), Neumann (1971) and Fogle (1974); **Juniors** (13)–Selvy (1953), Floyd (1955), Robertson (1959), Werkman (1963), Maravich (1969), Lamar (1972), Williams (1977), Kelly (1982), Bailey (1986), Gathers (1989), Guy (1993), Robinson (1994) and Jones (1997).

Rebounds

The NCAA did not begin keeping individual rebounding records until the 1950-51 season. From 1956-62, the championship was decided on highest percentage of recoveries out of all rebounds made by both teams in all games. All averages include postseason games where applicable.

Multiple winners: Artis Gilmore, Jerry Lucas, Xavier McDaniel, Kermit Washington and Leroy Wright (2).

Year		Gm	No	Avg	Year		Gm	No	Avg
1951	Ernie Beck, Penn	27	556	20.6	1972	Kermit Washington, American	23	455	19.8
1952	Bill Hannon, Army	17	355	20.9	1973	Kermit Washington, American	22	439	20.0
1953	Ed Conlin, Fordham	26	612	23.5	1974	Marvin Barnes, Providence	32	597	18.7
1954	Art Quimby, Connecticut	26	588	22.6	1975	John Irving, Hofstra	21	323	15.4
1955	Charlie Slack, Marshall	21	538	25.6	1976	Sam Pellom, Buffalo	26	420	16.2
1956	Joe Holup, G. Washington	26	604	25.6	1977	Glenn Mosley, Seton Hall	29	473	16.3
1957	Elgin Baylor, Seattle	25	508	23.5	1978	Ken Williams, N. Texas	28	411	14.7
1958	Alex Ellis, Niagara	25	536	26.2	1979	Monti Davis, Tennessee St.	26	421	16.2
1959	Leroy Wright, Pacific	26	652	23.8	1980	Larry Smith, Alcorn State	26	392	15.1
1960	Leroy Wright, Pacific	17	380	23.4	1981	Darryl Watson, Miss. Valley St.	27	379	14.0
1961	Jerry Lucas, Ohio St.	27	470	19.8	1982	LaSalle Thompson, Texas	27	365	13.5
1962	Jerry Lucas, Ohio St.	28	499	21.1	1983	Xavier McDaniel, Wichita St.	28	403	14.4
1963	Paul Silas, Creighton	27	557	20.6	1984	Akeem Olajuwon, Houston	37	500	13.5
1964	Bob Pelkington, Xavier-OH	26	567	21.8	1985	Xavier McDaniel, Wichita St.	31	460	14.8
1965	Toby Kimball, Connecticut	23	483	21.0	1986	David Robinson, Navy	35	455	13.0
1966	Jim Ware, Oklahoma City	29	607	20.9	1987	Jerome Lane, Pittsburgh	33	444	13.5
1967	Dick Cunningham, Murray St.	22	479	21.8	1988	Kenny Miller, Loyola-CA	29	395	13.6
1968	Neal Walk, Florida	25	494	19.8	1989	Hank Gathers, Loyola-CA	31	426	13.7
1969	Spencer Haywood, Detroit	22	472	21.5	1990	Anthony Bonner, St. Louis	33	456	13.8
1970	Artis Gilmore, Jacksonville	28	621	22.2	1991	Shaquille O'Neal, LSU	28	411	14.7
1971	Artis Gilmore, Jacksonville	26	603	23.2	1992	Popeye Jones, Murray St.	30	431	14.4

Year		Gm	No	Avg
1993	Warren Kidd, Mid. Tenn. St.	26	386	14.8
1994	Jerome Lambert, Baylor	24	355	14.8
1995	Kurt Thomas, TCU	27	393	14.6
1996	Marcus Mann, Miss. Valley St.	29	394	13.6
1997	Tim Duncan, Wake Forest	31	457	14.7

Year		Gm	No	Avg
1998	Ryan Perryman, Dayton	33	412	12.5
1999	Ian McGinnis, Dartmouth	26	317	12.2
2000	Darren Phillip, Fairfield	29	405	14.0
2001	Chris Marcus, Western Ky.	31	374	12.1

Note: Only three players have ever led the NCAA in scoring and rebounding in the same season: Xavier McDaniel of Wichita St. (1985), Hank Gathers of Loyola-Marymount (1989) and Kurt Thomas of TCU (1995).

Assists

The NCAA did not begin keeping individual assist records until the 1983-84 season. All averages include postseason games where applicable.

Multiple winner: Avery Johnson (2).

Year		Gm	No	Avg
1984	Craig Lathen, IL-Chicago	29	274	9.45
1985	Rob Weingard, Hofstra	24	228	9.50
1986	Mark Jackson, St. John's	36	328	9.11
1987	Avery Johnson, Southern-BR	31	333	10.74
1988	Avery Johnson, Southern-BR	30	399	13.30
1989	Glenn Williams, Holy Cross	28	278	9.93
1990	Todd Lehmann, Drexel	28	260	9.29
1991	Chris Corchiani, N.C. State	31	299	9.65
1992	Van Usher, Tennessee Tech	29	254	8.76
1993	Sam Crawford, N. Mexico St	34	310	9.12
1994	Jason Kidd, California	30	272	9.06
1995	Nelson Haggerty, Baylor	28	284	10.14
1996	Raimonds Miglinieks, UC-Irvine	27	230	8.52
1997	Kenny Mitchell, Dartmouth	26	203	7.81
1998	Ahlon Lewis, Arizona St.	32	294	9.19
1999	Doug Gottlieb, Oklahoma St.	34	299	8.79
2000	Mark Dickel, UNLV	31	280	9.03
2001	Markus Carr, CS-Northridge	32	286	8.94

Blocked Shots

The NCAA did not begin keeping individual blocked shots records until the 1985-86 season. All averages include postseason games where applicable.

Multiple winners: Keith Closs, David Robinson and Tarvis Williams (2).

Year		Gm	No	Avg
1986	David Robinson, Navy	35	207	5.91
1987	David Robinson, Navy	32	144	4.50
1988	Rodney Blake, St. Joe's-PA	29	116	4.00
1989	Alonzo Mourning, G'town	34	169	4.97
1990	Kenny Green, Rhode Island	26	124	4.77
1991	Shawn Bradley, BYU	34	177	5.21
1992	Shaquille O'Neal, LSU	30	157	5.23
1993	Theo Ratliff, Wyoming	28	124	4.43
1994	Grady Livingston, Howard	26	115	4.42
1995	Keith Closs, Cen. Conn. St.	26	139	5.35
1996	Keith Closs, Cen. Conn. St.	28	178	6.36
1997	Adonal Foyle, Colgate	28	180	6.43
1998	Jerome James, Florida A&M	27	125	4.63
1999	Tarvis Williams, Hampton	27	135	5.00
2000	Ken Johnson, Ohio St.	30	161	5.37
2001	Tarvis Williams, Hampton	32	147	4.59

All-Time NCAA Division I Individual Leaders

Through 2000-01; includes regular season and tournament games; **Last** column indicates final year played.

CAREER

Scoring

	Points	Yrs	Last	Gm	Pts
1	Pete Maravich, LSU	3	1970	83	3667
2	Freeman Williams, Port. St.	4	1978	106	3249
3	Lionel Simmons, La Salle	4	1990	131	3217
4	Alphonso Ford, Miss. Val. St.	4	1993	109	3165
5	Harry Kelly, Texas Southern	4	1983	110	3066
6	Hersey Hawkins, Bradley	4	1988	125	3008
7	Oscar Robertson, Cincinnati	3	1960	88	2973
8	Danny Manning, Kansas	4	1988	147	2951
9	Alfredrick Hughes, Loyola-IL	4	1985	120	2914
10	Elvin Hayes, Houston	3	1968	93	2884
11	Larry Bird, Indiana St.	3	1979	94	2850
12	Otis Birdsong, Houston	4	1977	116	2832
13	Kevin Bradshaw, Beth-Cook/US Int'l	4	1991	111	2804
14	Allan Houston, Tennessee	4	1993	128	2801
15	Hank Gathers, USC/Loyola-CA	4	1990	117	2723
16	Reggie Lewis, Northeastern	4	1987	122	2708
17	Daren Queenan, Lehigh	4	1988	118	2703
18	Byron Larkin, Xavier-OH	4	1988	121	2696
19	David Robinson, Navy	4	1987	127	2669
20	Wayman Tisdale, Oklahoma	3	1985	104	2661

	Average	Yrs	Last	Pts	Avg
1	Pete Maravich, LSU	3	1970	3667	44.2
2	Austin Carr, Notre Dame	3	1971	2560	34.6
3	Oscar Robertson, Cinn	3	1960	2973	33.8
4	Calvin Murphy, Niagara	3	1970	2548	33.1
5	Dwight Lamar, SW La	2	1973	1862	32.7
6	Frank Selvy, Furman	3	1954	2538	32.5
7	Rick Mount, Purdue	3	1970	2323	32.3
8	Darrell Floyd, Furman	3	1956	2281	32.1
9	Nick Werkman, Seton Hall	3	1964	2273	32.0
10	Willie Humes, Idaho St.	2	1971	1510	31.5
11	William Averitt, Pepperdine	2	1973	1541	31.4
12	Elgin Baylor, Idaho/Seattle	3	1958	2500	31.3
13	Elvin Hayes, Houston	3	1968	2884	31.0
14	Freeman Williams, Port. St.	4	1978	3249	30.7
15	Larry Bird, Indiana St.	3	1979	2850	30.3
16	Bill Bradley, Princeton	3	1965	2503	30.2
17	Rich Fuqua, Oral Roberts	2	1973	1617	29.9
18	Wilt Chamberlain, Kansas	2	1958	1433	29.9
19	Rick Barry, Miami-FL	3	1965	2298	29.8
20	Doug Collins, Illinois St.	3	1973	2240	29.1

	Field Goal Pct.	Yrs	Last	FG	FGA	Pct
1	Steve Johnson, Ore. St.	4	1981	828	1222	.678
2	Michael Bradley, Ky./Villanova	3	2001	441	651	.677
3	Murray Brown, Fla. St.	4	1980	566	847	.668
4	Lee Campbell, M.Tenn St./SW Mo.St.	3	1990	411	618	.665
5	Warren Kidd, M.Tenn.St.	3	1993	496	747	.664
6	Todd MacCulloch, Wash.	4	1999	702	1058	.664
7	Joe Senser, West Chester	4	1979	476	719	.662
8	Kevin McGee, UC-Irvine	2	1982	552	841	.656
9	O. Phillips, Pepperdine	2	1983	404	618	.654
10	Bill Walton, UCLA	3	1974	747	1147	.651

Note: minimum 400 FGs made and an average of four per game.

	Free Throw Pct.	Yrs	Last	FT	FTA	Pct
1	Greg Starrick, Ky/So.Ill	4	1972	341	375	.909
2	Jack Moore, Nebraska	4	1982	446	495	.901
3	Steve Henson, Kansas St.	4	1990	361	401	.900
4	Steve Alford, Indiana	4	1987	535	596	.898
5	Bob Lloyd, Rutgers	3	1967	543	605	.898
6	Jim Barton, Dartmouth	4	1989	394	440	.895
7	Tommy Boyer, Arkansas	3	1963	315	353	.892
8	Rob Robbins, N. Mexico	4	1991	309	348	.888
9	Marcus Wilson, Evansville	4	1999	455	513	.887
10	Sean Miller, Pitt	4	1992	317	358	.885

Note: minimum 300 FTs made and an average of two per game.

All-Time NCAA Division I Individual Leaders (Cont.)

3-Pt Field Goals

		Yrs	Last	Gm	3FG
1	Curtis Staples, Virginia	4	1998	122	413
2	Keith Veney, Lamar/Marshall	4	1997	111	409
3	Doug Day, Radford	4	1993	117	401
4	Ronnie Schmitz, Missouri-KC	4	1993	112	378
5	Mark Alberts, Akron	4	1993	107	375

3-Pt Field Goal Pct.

		Yrs	Last	3FG	Att	Pct
1	Tony Bennett, Wisc-GB	4	1992	290	584	.497
2	Keith Jennings, E.Tenn.St.	4	1991	223	452	.493
3	Kirk Manns, Michigan St.	4	1990	212	446	.475
4	Tim Locum, Wisconsin	4	1991	227	481	.472
5	David Olson, Eastern Ill.	4	1992	262	562	.466

Note: minimum 200 3FGs made.

All-Time Highest Scoring Teams
SINGLE SEASON
Scoring Offense

Team	Season	Gm	Pts	Avg
Loyola-CA	1990	32	3918	122.4
Loyola-CA	1989	31	3486	112.5
UNLV	1976	31	3426	110.5
Loyola-CA	1988	32	3528	110.3
UNLV	1977	32	3426	107.1
Oral Roberts	1972	28	2943	105.1
Southern-BR	1991	28	2924	104.4
Loyola-CA	1991	31	3211	103.6
Oklahoma	1988	39	4012	102.9
Oklahoma	1989	36	3680	102.2

Rebounds

Total (before 1973)

		Yrs	Last	Gm	No
1	Tom Gola, La Salle	4	1955	118	2201
2	Joe Holup, G. Washington	4	1956	104	2030
3	Charlie Slack, Marshall	4	1956	88	1916
4	Ed Conlin, Fordham	4	1955	102	1884
5	Dickie Hemric, Wake Forest	4	1955	104	1802
6	Paul Silas, Creighton	3	1964	81	1751
7	Art Quimby, Connecticut	4	1955	80	1716
8	Jerry Harper, Alabama	4	1956	93	1688
9	Jeff Cohen, Wm. & Mary	4	1961	103	1679
10	Steve Hamilton, Morehead St.	4	1958	102	1675

Average (before 1973)

		Yrs	Last	No	Avg
1	Artis Gilmore, Jacksonville	2	1971	1224	22.7
2	Charlie Slack, Marshall	4	1956	1916	21.8
3	Paul Silas, Creighton	3	1964	1751	21.6
4	Leroy Wright, Pacific	3	1960	1442	21.5
5	Art Quimby, Connecticut	4	1955	1716	21.5

Note: minimum 800 rebounds.

Total (since 1973)

		Yrs	Last	Gm	No
1	Tim Duncan, Wake Forest	4	1997	128	1570
2	Derrick Coleman, Syracuse	4	1990	143	1537
3	Malik Rose, Drexel	4	1996	120	1514
4	Ralph Sampson, Virginia	4	1983	132	1511
5	Pete Padgett, Nevada-Reno	4	1976	104	1464
6	Lionel Simmons, La Salle	4	1990	131	1429
7	Anthony Bonner, St. Louis	4	1990	133	1424
8	Tyrone Hill, Xavier-OH	4	1990	126	1380
9	Popeye Jones, Murray St.	4	1992	123	1374
10	Michael Brooks, La Salle	4	1980	114	1372

Average (since 1973)

		Yrs	Last	No	Avg
1	Glenn Mosley, Seton Hall	4	1977	1263	15.2
2	Bill Campion, Manhattan	3	1975	1070	14.2
3	Pete Padgett, Nevada-Reno	4	1976	1464	14.1
4	Bob Warner, Maine	4	1976	1304	13.6
5	Shaquille O'Neal, LSU	3	1992	1217	13.5

Note: minimum 650 rebounds.

Assists

Total

		Yrs	Last	Gm	No
1	Bobby Hurley, Duke	4	1993	140	1076
2	Chris Corchiani, N.C. State	4	1991	124	1038
3	Ed Cota, N. Carolina	4	2000	138	1030
4	Keith Jennings, E. Tenn. St.	4	1991	127	983
5	Sherman Douglas, Syracuse	4	1989	138	960
6	Tony Miller, Marquette	4	1995	123	956
7	Greg Anthony, Portland/UNLV	4	1991	138	950
8	Doug Gottlieb, ND/Okla St.	4	2000	124	947
9	Gary Payton, Oregon St.	4	1990	120	938
10	Orlando Smart, San Fran.	4	1994	116	902
11	Andre LaFleur, Northeastern	4	1987	128	894

Average

		Yrs	Last	No	Avg
1	A. Johnson, Cameron/Southern	3	1988	838	8.91
2	Sam Crawford, N. Mexico St.	2	1993	592	8.84
3	Mark Wade, Okla/UNLV	3	1987	693	8.77
4	Chris Corchiani, N.C. State	4	1991	1038	8.37
5	Taurence Chisholm, Delaware	4	1988	877	7.97
6	Van Usher, Tennessee Tech	3	1992	676	7.95
7	Anthony Manuel, Bradley	3	1989	855	7.92
8	Chico Fletcher, Ark. St.	4	2000	893	7.83
9	Gary Payton, Oregon St.	4	1990	938	7.82
10	Orlando Smart, San Fran.	4	1994	902	7.78

Note: minimum 550 assists.

Blocked Shots

Average

		Yrs	Last	No	Avg
1	Keith Closs, Cen. Conn. St.	2	1996	317	5.87
2	Adonal Foyle, Colgate	3	1997	492	5.66
3	David Robinson, Navy	2	1987	351	5.24
4	Shaquille O'Neal, LSU	3	1992	412	4.58
5	Troy Murphy, Notre Dame	3	2001	425	4.52

Note: minimum 225 blocked shots.

Steals

Average

		Yrs	Last	No	Avg
1	Mookie Blaylock, Oklahoma	2	1989	281	3.80
2	Ronn McMahon, Eastern Wash.	3	1990	225	3.52
3	Eric Murdock, Providence	4	1991	376	3.21
4	Van Usher, Tennessee Tech	3	1992	270	3.18
5	Pepe Sanchez, Temple	4	2000	365	3.15

Note: minimum 225 steals.

2000 Points/1000 Rebounds
For a combined total of 4000 or more.

		Gm	Pts	Reb	Total			Gm	Pts	Reb	Total
1	Tom Gola, La Salle	118	2462	2201	4663	7	Harry Kelly, TX-Southern	110	3066	1085	4151
2	Lionel Simmons, La Salle	131	3217	1429	4646	8	Danny Manning, Kansas	147	2951	1187	4138
3	Elvin Hayes, Houston	93	2884	1602	4486	9	Larry Bird, Indiana St.	94	2850	1247	4097
4	Dickie Hemric, W. Forest	104	2587	1802	4389	10	Elgin Baylor, Col. Idaho/				
5	Oscar Robertson, Cinn.	88	2973	1338	4311		Seattle	80	2500	1559	4059
6	Joe Holup, G. Wash	104	2226	2030	4256	11	Michael Brooks, La Salle	114	2628	1372	4000

Years Played—Baylor (1956-58); **Bird** (1977-79); **Brooks** (1977-80); **Gola** (1952-55); **Hayes** (1966-68); **Hemric** (1952-55); **Holup** (1953-56); **Kelly** (1980-83); **Manning** (1985-88); **Robertson** (1958-60); **Simmons** (1987-90).

SINGLE SEASON

Scoring

Points

		Year	Gm	Pts
1	Pete Maravich, LSU	1970	31	1381
2	Elvin Hayes, Houston	1968	33	1214
3	Frank Selvy, Furman	1954	29	1209
4	Pete Maravich, LSU	1969	26	1148
5	Pete Maravich, LSU	1968	26	1138
6	Bo Kimble, Loyola-CA	1990	32	1131
7	Hersey Hawkins, Bradley	1988	31	1125
8	Austin Carr, Notre Dame	1970	29	1106
9	Austin Carr, Notre Dame	1971	29	1101
10	Otis Birdsong, Houston	1977	36	1090

Average

		Year	Gm	Pts	Avg
1	Pete Maravich, LSU	1970	31	1381	44.5
2	Pete Maravich, LSU	1969	26	1148	44.2
3	Pete Maravich, LSU	1968	26	1138	43.8
4	Frank Selvy, Furman	1954	29	1209	41.7
5	Johnny Neumann, Ole Miss	1971	23	923	40.1
6	Freeman Williams, Port. St.	1977	26	1010	38.8
7	Billy McGill, Utah	1962	26	1009	38.8
8	Calvin Murphy, Niagara	1968	24	916	38.2
9	Austin Carr, Notre Dame	1970	29	1106	38.1
10	Austin Carr, Notre Dame	1971	29	1101	38.0

Field Goal Pct.

		Year	FG	FGA	Pct
1	Steve Johnson, Oregon St.	1981	235	315	.746
2	Dwayne Davis, Florida	1989	179	248	.722
3	Keith Walker, Utica	1985	154	216	.713
4	Steve Johnson, Oregon St.	1980	211	297	.710
5	Oliver Miller, Arkansas	1991	254	361	.704

Free Throw Pct.

		Year	FT	FTA	Pct
1	Craig Collins, Penn St.	1985	94	98	.959
2	Rod Foster, UCLA	1982	95	100	.950
3	Clay McKnight, Pacific	2000	74	78	.949
4	Carlos Gibson, Marshall	1978	84	89	.944
5	Danny Basile, Marist	1994	84	89	.944

3-Pt Field Goal Pct.

		Year	3FG	Att	Pct
1	Glenn Tropf, Holy Cross	1988	52	82	.634
2	Sean Wightman, W. Mich	1992	48	76	.632
3	Keith Jennings, E. Tenn. St.	1991	84	142	.592
4	Dave Calloway, Monmouth	1989	48	82	.585
5	Steve Kerr, Arizona	1988	114	199	.573

Assists

Average

		Year	Gm	No	Avg
1	Avery Johnson, Southern-BR	1988	30	399	13.3
2	Anthony Manuel, Bradley	1988	31	373	12.0
3	Avery Johnson, Southern-BR	1987	31	333	10.7
4	Mark Wade, UNLV	1987	38	406	10.7
5	Glenn Williams, Holy Cross	1989	28	278	9.9

Rebounds

Average (before 1973)

		Year	Gm	No	Avg
1	Charlie Slack, Marshall	1955	21	538	25.6
2	Leroy Wright, Pacific	1959	26	652	25.1
3	Art Quimby, Connecticut	1955	25	611	24.4
4	Charlie Slack, Marshall	1956	22	520	23.6
5	Ed Conlin, Fordham	1953	26	612	23.5

Average (since 1973)

		Year	Gm	No	Avg
1	Kermit Washington, American	1973	25	511	20.4
2	Marvin Barnes, Providence	1973	30	571	19.0
3	Marvin Barnes, Providence	1974	32	597	18.7
4	Pete Padgett, Nevada	1973	26	462	17.8
5	Jim Bradley, Northern Ill	1973	24	426	17.8

Blocked Shots

Average

		Year	Gm	No	Avg
1	Adonal Foyle, Colgate	1997	28	180	6.42
2	Keith Closs, Cen. Conn. St.	1996	28	178	6.36
3	David Robinson, Navy	1986	35	207	5.91
4	Ken Johnson, Ohio St.	2000	30	161	5.37
5	Keith Closs, Cen. Conn. St.	1995	26	139	5.35

Steals

Average

		Year	Gm	No	Avg
1	Darron Brittman, Chicago St.	1986	28	139	4.96
2	Aldwin Ware, Florida A&M	1988	29	142	4.90
3	Ronn McMahon, East Wash.	1990	29	130	4.48
4	Pointer Williams, McNeese St.	1996	27	118	4.37
5	Greedy Daniels, TCU	2001	25	108	4.32

SINGLE GAME
Scoring

Points vs Div. I Team

		Year	Pts
1	Kevin Bradshaw, US Int'l vs Loyola-CA	1991	72
2	Pete Maravich, LSU vs Alabama	1970	69
3	Calvin Murphy, Niagara vs Syracuse	1969	68
4	Jay Handlan, Wash. & Lee vs Furman	1951	66
	Pete Maravich, LSU vs Tulane	1969	66
	Anthony Roberts, Oral Rbts vs N.C. A&T	1977	66
7	Anthony Roberts, Oral Rbts vs Ore	1977	65
	Scott Haffner, Evansville vs Dayton	1989	65
9	Pete Maravich, LSU vs Kentucky	1970	64
10	Johnny Neumann, Ole Miss vs LSU	1971	63
	Hersey Hawkins, Bradley vs Detroit	1988	63

Points vs Non-Div. I Team

		Year	Pts
1	Frank Selvy, Furman vs Newberry	1954	100
2	Paul Arizin, Villanova vs Phi. NAMC	1949	85
3	Freeman Williams, Port. St. vs Rocky Mt	1978	81
4	Bill Mlkvy, Temple vs Wilkes	1951	73
5	Freeman Williams, Port. St. vs So. Ore	1977	71

Note: Bevo Francis of Division II Rio Grande (Ohio) scored an overall collegiate record 113 points against Hillsdale in 1954. He also scored 84 against Alliance and 82 against Bluffton that same season.

All-Time NCAA Division I Individual Leaders (Cont.)

Assists

		Year	No
1	Tony Fairley, Baptist vs Armstrong St.	1987	22
	Avery Johnson, Southern-BR vs TX-South	1988	22
	Sherman Douglas, Syracuse vs Providence	1989	22
4	Mark Wade, UNLV vs Navy	1986	21
	Kelvin Scarborough, N. Mexico vs Hawaii	1987	21
	Anthony Manuel, Bradley vs UC-Irvine	1987	21
	Avery Johnson, Southern-BR vs Ala. St.	1988	21

Rebounds

Total (before 1973)

		Year	No
1	Bill Chambers, Wm. & Mary vs Virginia	1953	51
2	Charlie Slack, Marshall vs M. Harvey	1954	43
3	Tom Heinsohn, Holy Cross vs BC	1955	42
4	Art Quimby, UConn vs BU	1955	40
5	Three players tied with 39 each.		

Total (since 1973)

		Year	No
1	Larry Abney, Fresno St. vs SMU	2000	35
2	David Vaughn, Oral Roberts vs Brandeis	1973	34
3	Robert Parish, Centenary vs So. Miss	1973	33
4	Durand Macklin, LSU vs Tulane	1976	32
	Jervaughn Scales, South-BR vs Grambling	1994	32

3-Pt Field Goals

		Year	No
1	Keith Veney, Marshall vs Morehead St.	1996	15
2	Dave Jamerson, Ohio U. vs Charleston	1989	14
	Askia Jones, Kansas St. vs Fresno St.	1994	14
4	Gary Bosserd, Niagara vs Siena	1987	12
	Darrin Fitzgerald, Butler vs Detroit	1987	12
	Al Dillard, Arkansas vs Delaware St.	1993	12
	Mitch Taylor, South-BR vs La. Christian	1995	12
	David McMahan, Winthrop vs C. Carolina	1996	12

Blocked Shots

		Year	No
1	David Robinson, Navy vs NC-Wilmington	1986	14
	Shawn Bradley, BYU vs Eastern Ky	1990	14
	Roy Rogers, Alabama vs Georgia	1996	14
	Loren Woods, Arizona vs Oregon	2000	14
5	Kevin Roberson, Vermont vs UNH	1992	13
	Jim McIlvaine, Marquette vs No. III	1993	13
	Keith Closs, C. Conn. St. vs St. Fran-PA.	1994	13
	D'or Fischer, N'Western St. vs SW Tex. St.	2001	13

Steals

		Year	No
1	Mookie Blaylock, Oklahoma vs Centenary	1987	13
	Mookie Blaylock, Oklahoma vs Loyola-CA	1988	13
3	Kenny Robertson, Cleve. St. vs Wagner	1988	12
	Terry Evans, Oklahoma vs Florida A&M	1993	12
	Richard Duncan, Mid. Tenn St. vs E. Ky.	1999	12
	Greedy Daniels, TCU vs Ark-Pine Bluff	2001	12

Players of the Year and Top Draft Picks

Consensus College Players of the Year and first overall selections in NBA draft since the abolition of the NBA's territorial draft in 1966. Top draft picks who became Rookie of the Year are in **bold** type; (*) indicates top draft pick chosen as junior, (**) indicates top draft pick chosen as sophomore, (†) indicates top draft pick chosen as a high school senior.

Year	Player of the Year	Top Draft Pick
1966	Cazzie Russell, Mich.	Cazzie Russell, NY
1967	Lew Alcindor, UCLA	Jimmy Walker, Det.
1968	Elvin Hayes, Houston	Elvin Hayes, SD
1969	Lew Alcindor, UCLA	**Lew Alcindor**, Mil.
1970	Pete Maravich, LSU	Bob Lanier, Det.
1971	Sidney Wicks, UCLA	Austin Carr, Cle.
1972	Bill Walton, UCLA	LaRue Martin, Por.
1973	Bill Walton, UCLA	Doug Collins, Phi.
1974	Bill Walton, UCLA	**Bill Walton**, Por.
1975	David Thompson, N.C. St.	David Thompson, Atl.
1976	Scott May, Indiana	John Lucas, Hou.
1977	Marques Johnson, UCLA	Kent Benson, Ind.
1978	Butch Lee, Marquette & Phil Ford, N. Caro.	Mychal Thompson, Por.
1979	Larry Bird, Indiana St.	**Magic Johnson**, LAL**
1980	Mark Aguirre, DePaul	Joe Barry Carroll, G. St.
1981	Ralph Sampson, Va. & Danny Ainge, BYU	Mark Aguirre, Dal.
1982	Ralph Sampson, Va.	James Worthy, LAL*
1983	Ralph Sampson, Va.	**Ralph Sampson**, Hou.
1984	Michael Jordan, N. Caro.	Akeem Olajuwon, Hou.
1985	Patrick Ewing, G'town & Chris Mullin, St. John's	**Patrick Ewing**, NY

Year	Player of the Year	Top Draft Pick
1986	Walter Berry, St. John's	Brad Daugherty, Cle.
1987	David Robinson, Navy	**David Robinson**, SA
1988	Hersey Hawkins, Bradley & Danny Manning, Kan.	Danny Manning, LAC
1989	Sean Elliott, Arizona & Danny Ferry, Duke	Pervis Ellison, Sac.
1990	Lionel Simmons, La Salle	**Derrick Coleman**, NJ
1991	Larry Johnson, UNLV & Shaquille O'Neal, LSU	**Larry Johnson**, Cha.
1992	Christian Laettner, Duke	**Shaquille O'Neal**, Orl.*
1993	Calbert Cheaney, Ind.	**Chris Webber**, Orl.**
1994	Glenn Robinson, Purdue	Glenn Robinson, Mil.*
1995	Ed O'Bannon, UCLA & Joe Smith, Maryland	Joe Smith, G. St.**
1996	Marcus Camby, UMass	**Allen Iverson**, Phi.**
1997	Tim Duncan, Wake Forest	**Tim Duncan**, SA
1998	Antawn Jamison, N. Caro.	M. Olowokandi, LAC
1999	Elton Brand, Duke	**Elton Brand**, Chi.**
2000	Kenyon Martin, Cincinnati	Kenyon Martin, NJ
2001	Shane Battier, Duke & Jason Williams, Duke	Kwame Brown, Wash.†

Annual Awards

UPI picked the first national Division I Player of the Year in 1955. Since then, the U.S. Basketball Writers Assn. (1959), the Commonwealth Athletic Club of Kentucky's Adolph Rupp Trophy (1961), the Atlanta Tip-Off Club (1969), the National Assn. of Basketball Coaches (1975), and the LA Athletic Club's John Wooden Award (1977) have joined in. UPI discontinued its award in 1997.

Since 1977, the first year all the following awards were given out, the same player has won all of them in the same season 13 times: Marques Johnson in 1977, Larry Bird in 1979, Ralph Sampson in both 1982 and '83, Michael Jordan in 1984, David Robinson in 1987, Lionel Simmons in 1990, Calbert Cheaney in 1993, Glenn Robinson in 1994, Tim Duncan in 1997, Antawn Jamison in 1998, Elton Brand in 1999 and Kenyon Martin in 2000.

United Press International

Voted on by a panel of UPI college basketball writers and first presented in 1955.

Multiple winners: Oscar Robertson, Ralph Sampson and Bill Walton (3); Lew Alcindor and Jerry Lucas (2).

Year	Year	Year
1955 Tom Gola, La Salle	1957 Chet Forte, Columbia	1959 Oscar Robertson, Cincinnati
1956 Bill Russell, San Francisco	1958 Oscar Robertson, Cincinnati	1960 Oscar Robertson, Cincinnati

Year		Year		Year	
1961	Jerry Lucas, Ohio St.	1974	Bill Walton, UCLA	1987	David Robinson, Navy
1962	Jerry Lucas, Ohio St.	1975	David Thompson, N.C. State	1988	Hersey Hawkins, Bradley
1963	Art Heyman, Duke	1976	Scott May, Indiana	1989	Danny Ferry, Duke
1964	Gary Bradds, Ohio St.	1977	Marques Johnson, UCLA	1990	Lionel Simmons, La Salle
1965	Bill Bradley, Princeton	1978	Butch Lee, Marquette	1991	Shaquille O'Neal, LSU
1966	Cazzie Russell, Michigan	1979	Larry Bird, Indiana St.	1992	Jim Jackson, Ohio St.
1967	Lew Alcindor, UCLA	1980	Mark Aguirre, DePaul	1993	Calbert Cheaney, Indiana
1968	Elvin Hayes, Houston	1981	Ralph Sampson, Virginia	1994	Glenn Robinson, Purdue
1969	Lew Alcindor, UCLA	1982	Ralph Sampson, Virginia	1995	Joe Smith, Maryland
1970	Pete Maravich, LSU	1983	Ralph Sampson, Virginia	1996	Ray Allen, UConn
1971	Austin Carr, Notre Dame	1984	Michael Jordan, N. Carolina	1997	award discontinued
1972	Bill Walton, UCLA	1985	Chris Mullin, St. John's		
1973	Bill Walton, UCLA	1986	Walter Berry, St. John's		

U.S. Basketball Writers Association

Voted on by the USBWA and first presented in 1959.

Multiple winners: Ralph Sampson and Bill Walton (3); Lew Alcindor, Jerry Lucas and Oscar Robertson (2).

Year		Year		Year	
1959	Oscar Robertson, Cincinnati	1974	Bill Walton, UCLA	1989	Danny Ferry, Duke
1960	Oscar Robertson, Cincinnati	1975	David Thompson, N.C. State	1990	Lionel Simmons, La Salle
1961	Jerry Lucas, Ohio St.	1976	Adrian Dantley, Notre Dame	1991	Larry Johnson, UNLV
1962	Jerry Lucas, Ohio St.	1977	Marques Johnson, UCLA	1992	Christian Laettner, Duke
1963	Art Heyman, Duke	1978	Phil Ford, North Carolina	1993	Calbert Cheaney, Indiana
1964	Walt Hazzard, UCLA	1979	Larry Bird, Indiana St.	1994	Glenn Robinson, Purdue
1965	Bill Bradley, Princeton	1980	Mark Aguirre, DePaul	1995	Ed O'Bannon, UCLA
1966	Cazzie Russell, Michigan	1981	Ralph Sampson, Virginia	1996	Marcus Camby, UMass
1967	Lew Alcindor, UCLA	1982	Ralph Sampson, Virginia	1997	Tim Duncan, Wake Forest
1968	Elvin Hayes, Houston	1983	Ralph Sampson, Virginia	1998	Antawn Jamison, N. Carolina
1969	Lew Alcindor, UCLA	1984	Michael Jordan, N. Carolina	1999	Elton Brand, Duke
1970	Pete Maravich, LSU	1985	Chris Mullin, St. John's	2000	Kenyon Martin, Cincinnati
1971	Sidney Wicks, UCLA	1986	Walter Berry, St. John's	2001	Shane Battier, Duke
1972	Bill Walton, UCLA	1987	David Robinson, Navy		
1973	Bill Walton, UCLA	1988	Hersey Hawkins, Bradley		

Rupp Trophy

Voted on by AP sportswriters and broadcasters and first presented in 1961 by the Commonwealth Athletic Club of Kentucky in the name of former University of Kentucky coach Adolph Rupp.

Multiple winners: Ralph Sampson (3); Lew Alcindor, Jerry Lucas, David Thompson and Bill Walton (2).

Year		Year		Year	
1961	Jerry Lucas, Ohio St.	1975	David Thompson, N.C. State	1989	Sean Elliott, Arizona
1962	Jerry Lucas, Ohio St.	1976	Scott May, Indiana	1990	Lionel Simmons, La Salle
1963	Art Heyman, Duke	1977	Marques Johnson, UCLA	1991	Shaquille O'Neal, LSU
1964	Gary Bradds, Ohio St.	1978	Butch Lee, Marquette	1992	Christian Laettner, Duke
1965	Bill Bradley, Princeton	1979	Larry Bird, Indiana St.	1993	Calbert Cheaney, Indiana
1966	Cazzie Russell, Michigan	1980	Mark Aguirre, DePaul	1994	Glenn Robinson, Purdue
1967	Lew Alcindor, UCLA	1981	Ralph Sampson, Virginia	1995	Joe Smith, Maryland
1968	Elvin Hayes, Houston	1982	Ralph Sampson, Virginia	1996	Marcus Camby, UMass
1969	Lew Alcindor, UCLA	1983	Ralph Sampson, Virginia	1997	Tim Duncan, Wake Forest
1970	Pete Maravich, LSU	1984	Michael Jordan, N. Carolina	1998	Antawn Jamison, N. Carolina
1971	Austin Carr, Notre Dame	1985	Patrick Ewing, Georgetown	1999	Elton Brand, Duke
1972	Bill Walton, UCLA	1986	Walter Berry, St. John's	2000	Kenyon Martin, Cincinnati
1973	Bill Walton, UCLA	1987	David Robinson, Navy	2001	Shane Battier, Duke
1974	David Thompson, N.C. State	1988	Hersey Hawkins, Bradley		

Naismith Award

Voted on by a panel of coaches, sportswriters and broadcasters and first presented in 1969 by the Atlanta Tip-Off Club in 1969 in the name of the inventor of basketball, Dr. James Naismith.

Multiple winners: Ralph Sampson and Bill Walton (3).

Year		Year		Year	
1969	Lew Alcindor, UCLA	1980	Mark Aguirre, DePaul	1991	Larry Johnson, UNLV
1970	Pete Maravich, LSU	1981	Ralph Sampson, Virginia	1992	Christian Laettner, Duke
1971	Austin Carr, Notre Dame	1982	Ralph Sampson, Virginia	1993	Calbert Cheaney, Indiana
1972	Bill Walton, UCLA	1983	Ralph Sampson, Virginia	1994	Glenn Robinson, Purdue
1973	Bill Walton, UCLA	1984	Michael Jordan, N. Carolina	1995	Joe Smith, Maryland
1974	Bill Walton, UCLA	1985	Patrick Ewing, Georgetown	1996	Marcus Camby, UMass
1975	David Thompson, N.C. State	1986	Johnny Dawkins, Duke	1997	Tim Duncan, Wake Forest
1976	Scott May, Indiana	1987	David Robinson, Navy	1998	Antawn Jamison, N. Carolina
1977	Marques Johnson, UCLA	1988	Danny Manning, Kansas	1999	Elton Brand, Duke
1978	Butch Lee, Marquette	1989	Danny Ferry, Duke	2000	Kenyon Martin, Cincinnati
1979	Larry Bird, Indiana St.	1990	Lionel Simmons, La Salle	2001	Shane Battier, Duke

National Association of Basketball Coaches

Voted on by the National Assn. of Basketball Coaches and presented by the Eastman Kodak Co. from 1975-94.

Multiple winner: Ralph Sampson (2).

Year	Year	Year
1975 David Thompson, N.C. State	1984 Michael Jordan, N. Carolina	1993 Calbert Cheaney, Indiana
1976 Scott May, Indiana	1985 Patrick Ewing, Georgetown	1994 Glenn Robinson, Purdue
1977 Marques Johnson, UCLA	1986 Walter Berry, St. John's	1995 Shawn Respert, Mich. St.
1978 Phil Ford, North Carolina	1987 David Robinson, Navy	1996 Marcus Camby, UMass
1979 Larry Bird, Indiana St.	1988 Danny Manning, Kansas	1997 Tim Duncan, Wake Forest
1980 Michael Brooks, La Salle	1989 Sean Elliott, Arizona	1998 Antawn Jamison, N. Carolina
1981 Danny Ainge, BYU	1990 Lionel Simmons, La Salle	1999 Elton Brand, Duke
1982 Ralph Sampson, Virginia	1991 Larry Johnson, UNLV	2000 Kenyon Martin, Cincinnati
1983 Ralph Sampson, Virginia	1992 Christian Laettner, Duke	2001 Jason Williams, Duke

Wooden Award

Voted on by a panel of coaches, sportswriters and broadcasters and first presented in 1977 by the Los Angeles Athletic Club in the name of former Purdue All-American and UCLA coach John Wooden. Unlike the other five player of the year awards, candidates for the Wooden must have a minimum grade point average of 2.00 (out of 4.00).

Multiple winner: Ralph Sampson (2).

Year	Year	Year
1977 Marques Johnson, UCLA	1986 Walter Berry St. John's	1995 Ed O'Bannon, UCLA
1978 Phil Ford, North Carolina	1987 David Robinson, Navy	1996 Marcus Camby, UMass
1979 Larry Bird, Indiana St.	1988 Danny Manning, Kansas	1997 Tim Duncan, Wake Forest
1980 Darrell Griffith, Louisville	1989 Sean Elliott, Arizona	1998 Antawn Jamison, N. Carolina
1981 Danny Ainge, BYU	1990 Lionel Simmons, La Salle	1999 Elton Brand, Duke
1982 Ralph Sampson, Virginia	1991 Larry Johnson, UNLV	2000 Kenyon Martin, Cincinnati
1983 Ralph Sampson, Virginia	1992 Christian Laettner, Duke	2001 Shane Battier, Duke
1984 Michael Jordan, N. Carolina	1993 Calbert Cheaney, Indiana	
1985 Chris Mullin, St. John's	1994 Glenn Robinson, Purdue	

All-Time Winningest Division I Coaches

Minimum of 10 seasons as Division I head coach; regular season and tournament games included; coaches active during 2000-01 in **bold** type.

Top 30 Winning Percentage

		Yrs	W	L	Pct
1	Clair Bee	21	412	87	**.826**
2	Adolph Rupp	41	876	190	**.822**
3	John Wooden	29	664	162	**.804**
4	**Jerry Tarkanian**	30	759	187	**.802**
5	**John Kresse**	22	538	134	**.801**
6	**Roy Williams**	13	353	89	**.799**
7	Dean Smith	36	879	254	**.776**
8	Harry Fisher	13	147	44	**.770**
9	Frank Keaney	27	387	117	**.768**
10	George Keogan	24	385	117	**.767**
11	Jack Ramsay	11	231	71	**.765**
12	Vic Bubas	10	213	67	**.761**
13	Chick Davies	21	314	106	**.748**
14	Ray Mears	21	399	135	**.747**
15	**Jim Boeheim**	25	600	208	**.743**
16	Rick Pitino	15	352	124	**.739**
17	Al McGuire	20	405	143	**.739**
18	Everett Case	18	376	133	**.739**
19	Phog Allen	48	746	264	**.739**
20	**Lute Olson**	28	640	228	**.737**
21	**Bob Huggins**	20	469	168	**.736**
22	Walter Meanwell	22	280	101	**.735**
23	**John Chaney**	29	656	238	**.734**
24	**Rick Majerus**	17	376	137	**.733**
25	Bill Musselman	12	232	85	**.732**
26	**Mike Krzyzewski**	26	606	222	**.731**
27	Lew Andreas	25	355	134	**.726**
28	Bob Knight	35	763	290	**.725**
29	Lou Carnesecca	24	526	200	**.725**
30	Fred Schaus	12	251	96	**.723**

Top 30 Victories

		Yrs	W	L	Pct
1	Dean Smith	36	**879**	254	.776
2	Adolph Rupp	41	**876**	190	.822
3	Jim Phelan	47	**816**	484	.628
4	Hank Iba	41	**767**	338	.694
5	Bob Knight	35	**763**	290	.725
6	**Lefty Driesell**	39	**761**	377	.669
7	Ed Diddle	42	**759**	302	.715
	Jerry Tarkanian	30	**759**	187	.802
9	Phog Allen	48	**746**	264	.739
10	**Lou Henson**	38	**739**	377	.662
11	Norm Stewart	38	**731**	375	.661
12	Ray Meyer	42	**724**	354	.672
13	Don Haskins	38	**719**	353	.671
14	**Eddie Sutton**	31	**678**	269	.716
15	**Denny Crum**	30	**675**	295	.696
16	John Wooden	29	**664**	162	.804
17	Ralph Miller	38	**657**	382	.632
18	**John Chaney**	29	**656**	238	.734
19	Marv Harshman	40	**654**	449	.593
20	Gene Bartow	34	**647**	353	.647
21	**Lute Olson**	28	**640**	228	.737
22	Cam Henderson	35	**630**	243	.722
23	Norm Sloan	37	**624**	393	.614
24	**Mike Krzyzewski**	26	**606**	222	.731
25	**Jim Boeheim**	25	**600**	208	.743
26	Slats Gill	36	**599**	392	.604
27	Abe Lemons	34	**597**	344	.634
28	John Thompson	27	**596**	239	.714
	Jim Calhoun	29	**596**	279	.681
30	Guy Lewis	30	**592**	279	.680

Note: Clarence (Bighouse) Gaines of Division II Winston-Salem St. (1947-93) retired after the 1992-93 season to finish his 47-year career ranked No. 3 on the all-time NCAA list of all coaches regardless of division. His record is 828-446 with a .650 winning percentage.

Where They Coached

Allen–Baker (1906-08), Kansas (1908-09), Haskell (1909), Central Mo. St. (1913-19), Kansas (1920-56); **Andreas**–Syracuse (1925-43; 45-50); **Bartow**–Central Mo. St. (1962-64), Valparaiso (1965-70), Memphis St. (1971-74), Illinois (1975), UCLA (1976-77), UAB (1979-96); **Bee**–Rider (1929-31), LIU-Brooklyn (1932-45, 46-51); **Boeheim**–Syracuse (1977–); **Bubas**–Duke (1960-69); **Calhoun**–Northeastern (1973-86), Connecticut (1987–); **Carnesecca**–St. John's (1966-70, 74-92); **Case**–N.C. State (1947-64); **Chaney**–Cheyney St. (1973-82), Temple (1983–); **Crum**–Louisville (1972-01); **Davies**–Duquesne (1925-43, 47-48); **Diddle**–Western Ky. (1923-64); **Driesell**–Davidson (1961-69), Maryland (1970-86), J. Madison (1989-97), Georgia St. (1997–); **Fisher**–Columbia (1907-16), Army (1922-23, 25).

Gill–Oregon St. (1929-64); **Harshman**–Pacific Lutheran (1946-58), Wash. St. (1959-71), Washington (1972-85); **Haskins**–UTEP (1962-99); **Henderson**–Muskingum (1920-22), Davis & Elkins (1923-35), Marshall (1936-55); **Henson**–Hardin-Simmons (1963-66), N. Mexico St. (1967-75), Illinois (1976-96), N. Mexico St. (1997–); **Huggins**–Walsh (1981-83), Akron (1985-89), Cincinnati (1990–); **Iba**–NW Missouri St. (1930-33), Colorado (1934), Oklahoma St. (1935-70); **Keaney**–Rhode Island (1921-48); **Keogan**–St. Louis (1916), Allegheny (1919), Valparaiso (1920-21), Notre Dame (1924-43); **Knight**–Army (1966-71), Indiana (1972-00), Texas Tech (2001–); **Kresse**–Charleston (1979–); **Krzyzewski**–Army (1976-80), Duke (1981–).

Lemons–Okla. City (1956-73), Pan American (1974-76), Texas (1977-82), Okla. City (1984-90); **Lewis**– Houston (1957-86); **Majerus**–Marquette (1984-86), Ball St. (1988-89), Utah (1991–); **A. McGuire**–Belmont Abbey (1958-64), Marquette (1965-77); **Meanwell**–Wisconsin (1912-17, 21-34), Missouri (1918-20); **Mears**–Wittenberg (1957-62), Tennessee (1963-77); **Meyer**–DePaul (1943-84); **E. Miller**–Western Mich. (1970-75), Ohio St. (1976-85), Northern Iowa (1986-98); **R. Miller**–Wichita St. (1952-64), Iowa (1965-70), Oregon St. (1971-89); **Musselman**–Ashland (1966-71), Minnesota (1972-75), S. Alabama (1996-97); **Olson**–Long Beach St. (1974), Iowa (1975-83), Arizona (1984–); **Phelan**–Mount St. Mary's (1955–); **Pitino**–Boston Univ. (1979-83), Providence (1986-87), Kentucky (1989-97).

Ramsay–St. Joseph's-PA (1956-66); **Rupp**–Kentucky (1931-72); **Schaus**–West Va. (1955-60), Purdue (1973-78); **Sloan**–Presbyterian (1952-55), Citadel (1957-60), Florida (1961-66), N.C. State (1967-80), Florida (1981-89); **Smith**–North Carolina (1962-97); **Stewart**–No. Iowa (1962-67), Missouri (1968-99); **Sutton**–Creighton (1970-74), Arkansas (1975-85), Kentucky (1986-89), Oklahoma St. (1991–); **Tarkanian**–Long Beach St. (1969-73), UNLV (1974-92), Fresno St. (1995–); **Thompson**–Georgetown (1973-99); **Williams**– Kansas (1989–); **Wooden**–Indiana St. (1947-48), UCLA (1949-75).

Most NCAA Tournaments

Through 2001; listed are number of appearances, overall tournament record, times reaching Final Four, and number of NCAA championships. (*) denotes that actual records are different from official NCAA records.

App		W-L	F4	Championships
27	Dean Smith	65-27	11	2 (1982, 93)
24	Bob Knight	42-21	5	3 (1976, 81, 87)
23	Denny Crum	42-23	6	2 (1980, 86)
22	**Lute Olson***	37-22	5	1 (1997)
22	**Eddie Sutton***	32-22	2	None
21	**Jim Boeheim**	32-21	2	None
20	Adolph Rupp	30-18	6	4 (1948-49, 51, 50)
20	John Thompson	34-19	3	1 (1984)
19	**Lou Henson**	19-20	2	None
18	Lou Carnesecca	17-20	1	None
18	Jerry Tarkanian	38-18	4	1 (1990)
17	**Mike Krzyzewski**	56-14	9	3 (1991-92, 2001)
17	John Chaney	23-17	0	None
17	Gene Keady*	18-17	0	None
16	John Wooden	47-10	12	10 (1964-65, 67-73, 75)
16	Norm Stewart*	12-16	0	None
16	**Nolan Richardson**	26-15	3	1 (1994)
15	Digger Phelps	17-17	1	None
15	**Jim Harrick**	17-14	1	1 (1995)
14	Don Haskins	14-13	1	1 (1966)
14	Guy Lewis	26-18	5	None
14	**Jim Calhoun***	26-13	1	1 (1999)
13	Dale Brown	15-14	2	None
13	Ray Meyer	14-16	2	None
13	**Lefty Driesell**	16-14	0	None

Active Coaches' Victories

Minimum five seasons in Division I.

		Yrs	W	L	Pct
1	Jim Phelan, Mt. St. Mary's	47	**816**	484	.628
2	Bob Knight, Texas Tech	35	**763**	290	.725
3	Lefty Driesell, Georgia St.	39	**761**	377	.669
4	Jerry Tarkanian, Fresno St.	30	**759**	187	.802
5	Lou Henson, N. Mexico St.	38	**739**	377	.662
6	Eddie Sutton, Okla. St.	31	**678**	269	.716
7	John Chaney, Temple	29	**656**	238	.734
8	Lute Olson, Arizona	28	**640**	228	.737
9	Mike Krzyzewski, Duke	26	**622**	231	.729
10	Jim Boeheim, Syracuse	25	**600**	208	.743
11	Jim Calhoun, UConn	29	**596**	279	.681
12	Billy Tubbs, TCU	27	**575**	283	.670
13	Hugh Durham, Jacksonville	33	**570**	372	.605
14	Gale Catlett, West Va.	29	**557**	304	.647
15	John Kresse, C. of Charleston	22	**538**	134	.801
16	Davey Whitney, Alcorn St.	30	**528**	327	.618
17	Dave Bliss, Baylor	26	**496**	298	.625
18	Rollie Massimino, Cleveland St.	27	**495**	353	.584
	Nolan Richardson, Arkansas	21	**495**	192	.721
20	Gene Keady, Purdue	23	**494**	225	.687
21	Don DeVoe, Navy	27	**487**	326	.599
22	Cliff Ellis, Auburn	26	**486**	295	.622
23	Homer Drew, Valparaiso	25	**477**	299	.615
24	Mike Montgomery, Stanford	23	**472**	223	.679
25	Bob Huggins, Cincinnati	20	**469**	168	.736

Annual Awards

UPI picked the first national Division I Coach of the Year in 1955. Since then, the U.S. Basketball Writers Assn. (1959), AP (1967), the National Assn. of Basketball Coaches (1969), and the Atlanta Tip-Off Club (1987) have joined in. Since 1987, the first year all five awards were given out, no coach has won all of them in the same season.

United Press International

Voted on by a panel of UPI college basketball writers and first presented in 1955.

Multiple winners: John Wooden (6); Bob Knight, Ray Meyer, Adolph Rupp, Norm Stewart, Fred Taylor and Phil Woolpert (2).

Year		Year		Year	
1955	Phil Woolpert, San Francisco	1958	Tex Winter, Kansas St.	1961	Fred Taylor, Ohio St.
1956	Phil Woolpert, San Francisco	1959	Adolph Rupp, Kentucky	1962	Fred Taylor, Ohio St.
1957	Frank McGuire, North Carolina	1960	Pete Newell, California	1963	Ed Jucker, Cincinnati

Annual Awards (Cont.)

Year
1964 John Wooden, UCLA
1965 Dave Strack, Michigan
1966 Adolph Rupp, Kentucky
1967 John Wooden, UCLA
1968 Guy Lewis, Houston
1969 John Wooden, UCLA
1970 John Wooden, UCLA
1971 Al McGuire, Marquette
1972 John Wooden, UCLA
1973 John Wooden, UCLA
1974 Digger Phelps, Notre Dame

Year
1975 Bob Knight, Indiana
1976 Tom Young, Rutgers
1977 Bob Gaillard, San Francisco
1978 Eddie Sutton, Arkansas
1979 Bill Hodges, Indiana St.
1980 Ray Meyer, DePaul
1981 Ralph Miller, Oregon St.
1982 Norm Stewart, Missouri
1983 Jerry Tarkanian, UNLV
1984 Ray Meyer, DePaul
1985 Lou Carnesecca, St. John's

Year
1986 Mike Krzyzewski, Duke
1987 John Thompson, Georgetown
1988 John Chaney, Temple
1989 Bob Knight, Indiana
1990 Jim Calhoun, Connecticut
1991 Rick Majerus, Utah
1992 Perry Clark, Tulane
1993 Eddie Fogler, Vanderbilt
1994 Norm Stewart, Missouri
1995 Leonard Hamilton, Miami-FL
1996 Gene Keady, Purdue
1997 award discontinued

U.S. Basketball Writers Association

Voted on by the USBWA and first presented in 1959.
Multiple winners: John Wooden (5); Bob Knight (3); Lou Carnesecca, John Chaney, Ray Meyer and Fred Taylor (2).

Year
1959 Eddie Hickey, Marquette
1960 Pete Newell, California
1961 Fred Taylor, Ohio St.
1962 Fred Taylor, Ohio St.
1963 Ed Jucker, Cincinnati
1964 John Wooden, UCLA
1965 Butch van Breda Kolff, Princeton
1966 Adolph Rupp, Kentucky
1967 John Wooden, UCLA
1968 Guy Lewis, Houston
1969 Maury John, Drake
1970 John Wooden, UCLA
1971 Al McGuire, Marquette
1972 John Wooden, UCLA
1973 John Wooden, UCLA

Year
1974 Norm Sloan, N.C. State
1975 Bob Knight, Indiana
1976 Bob Knight, Indiana
1977 Eddie Sutton, Arkansas
1978 Ray Meyer, DePaul
1979 Dean Smith, North Carolina
1980 Ray Meyer, DePaul
1981 Ralph Miller, Oregon St.
1982 John Thompson, Georgetown
1983 Lou Carnesecca, St. John's
1984 Gene Keady, Purdue
1985 Lou Carnesecca, St. John's
1986 Dick Versace, Bradley
1987 John Chaney, Temple
1988 John Chaney, Temple

Year
1989 Bob Knight, Indiana
1990 Roy Williams, Kansas
1991 Randy Ayers, Ohio St.
1992 Perry Clark, Tulane
1993 Eddie Fogler, Vanderbilt
1994 Charlie Spoonhour, St. Louis
1995 Kelvin Sampson, Oklahoma
1996 Gene Keady, Purdue
1997 Clem Haskins, Minnesota
1998 Tom Izzo, Michigan St.
1999 Cliff Ellis, Auburn
2000 Larry Eustachy, Iowa St.
2001 Al Skinner, Boston College

Associated Press

Voted on by AP sportswriters and broadcasters and first presented in 1967.
Multiple winners: John Wooden (5); Bob Knight (3); Guy Lewis, Ray Meyer, Ralph Miller and Eddie Sutton (2).

Year
1967 John Wooden, UCLA
1968 Guy Lewis, Houston
1969 John Wooden, UCLA
1970 John Wooden, UCLA
1971 Al McGuire, Marquette
1972 John Wooden, UCLA
1973 John Wooden, UCLA
1974 Norm Sloan, N.C. State
1975 Bob Knight, Indiana
1976 Bob Knight, Indiana
1977 Bob Gaillard, San Francisco
1978 Eddie Sutton, Arkansas

Year
1979 Bill Hodges, Indiana St.
1980 Ray Meyer, DePaul
1981 Ralph Miller, Oregon St.
1982 Ralph Miller, Oregon St.
1983 Guy Lewis, Houston
1984 Ray Meyer, DePaul
1985 Bill Frieder, Michigan
1986 Eddie Sutton, Kentucky
1987 Tom Davis, Iowa
1988 John Chaney, Temple
1989 Bob Knight, Indiana
1990 Jim Calhoun, Connecticut

Year
1991 Randy Ayers, Ohio St.
1992 Roy Williams, Kansas
1993 Eddie Fogler, Vanderbilt
1994 Norm Stewart, Missouri
1995 Kelvin Sampson, Oklahoma
1996 Gene Keady, Purdue
1997 Clem Haskins, Minnesota
1998 Tom Izzo, Michigan St.
1999 Cliff Ellis, Auburn
2000 Larry Eustachy, Iowa St.
2001 Matt Doherty, North Carolina

National Association of Basketball Coaches

Voted on by NABC membership and first presented in 1969.
Multiple winners: John Wooden (3); Gene Keady and Mike Krzyzewski (2).

Year
1969 John Wooden, UCLA
1970 John Wooden, UCLA
1971 Jack Kraft, Villanova
1972 John Wooden, UCLA
1973 Gene Bartow, Memphis St.
1974 Al McGuire, Marquette
1975 Bob Knight, Indiana
1976 Johnny Orr, Michigan
1977 Dean Smith, North Carolina
1978 Bill Foster, Duke
    & Abe Lemons, Texas
1979 Ray Meyer, DePaul
1980 Lute Olson, Iowa

Year
1981 Ralph Miller, Oregon St.
    & Jack Hartman, Kansas St.
1982 Don Monson, Idaho
1983 Lou Carnesecca, St. John's
1984 Marv Harshman, Washington
1985 John Thompson, Georgetown
1986 Eddie Sutton, Kentucky
1987 Rick Pitino, Providence
1988 John Chaney, Temple
1989 P.J. Carlesimo, Seton Hall
1990 Jud Heathcote, Michigan St.
1991 Mike Krzyzewski, Duke
1992 George Raveling, USC

Year
1993 Eddie Fogler, Vanderbilt
1994 Nolan Richardson, Arkansas
    & Gene Keady, Purdue
1995 Jim Harrick, UCLA
1996 John Calipari, UMass
1997 Clem Haskins, Minnesota
1998 Bill Guthridge, N. Carolina
1999 Mike Krzyzewski, Duke
    & Jim O'Brien, Ohio St.
2000 Gene Keady, Purdue
2001 Tom Izzo, Michigan St.

Naismith Award

Voted on by a panel of coaches, sportswriters and broadcasters and first presented by the Atlanta Tip-Off Club in 1987 in the name of the inventor of basketball, Dr. James Naismith.

Multiple winner: Mike Krzyzewski (3).

Year		Year		Year	
1987	Bob Knight, Indiana	1992	Mike Krzyzewski, Duke	1997	Roy Williams, Kansas
1988	Larry Brown, Kansas	1993	Dean Smith, North Carolina	1998	Bill Guthridge, N. Carolina
1989	Mike Krzyzewski, Duke	1994	Nolan Richardson, Arkansas	1999	Mike Krzyzewski, Duke
1990	Bobby Cremins, Georgia Tech	1995	Jim Harrick, UCLA	2000	Mike Montgomery, Stanford
1991	Randy Ayers, Ohio St.	1996	John Calipari, UMass	2001	Rod Barnes, Mississippi

Player of the Year and NBA MVP

College Players of the Year who have gone on to win the NBA's Most Valuable Player award:

Bill Russell COLLEGE–San Francisco (1956); PROS–Boston Celtics (1958, 1961, 1962, 1963 and 1965).

Oscar Robertson COLLEGE–Cincinnati (1958, 1959 and 1960); PROS–Cincinnati Royals (1964).

Kareem Abdul-Jabbar COLLEGE–UCLA (1967 and 1969); PROS–Milwaukee Bucks (1971, 1972 and 1974) and LA Lakers (1976, 1977 and 1980).

Bill Walton COLLEGE–UCLA (1972, 1973 and 1974); PROS–Portland Trail Blazers (1978).

Larry Bird COLLEGE–Indiana St. (1979); PROS–Boston Celtics (1984, 1985, and 1986).

Michael Jordan COLLEGE–North Carolina (1984); PROS–Chicago Bulls (1988, 1991, 1992, 1996 and 1998).

David Robinson COLLEGE–Navy (1987); PROS–San Antonio Spurs (1995).

Shaquille O'Neal COLLEGE–LSU (1991); PROS–LA Lakers (2000).

Other Men's Champions

The NCAA has sanctioned national championship tournaments for Division II since 1957 and Division III since 1975. The NAIA sanctioned a single tournament from 1937-91, then split into two divisions in 1992.

NCAA Div. II Finals

Multiple winners: Kentucky Wesleyan (8); Evansville (5); CS-Bakersfield (3); North Alabama and Virginia Union (2).

Year	Winner	Score	Loser	Year	Winner	Score	Loser
1957	Wheaton, IL	89-65	Ky. Wesleyan	1981	Florida Southern	73-68	Mt. St. Mary's, MD
1958	South Dakota	75-53	St. Michael's, VT	1982	Dist. of Columbia	73-63	Florida Southern
1959	Evansville, IN	83-67	SW Missouri St.	1983	Wright St., OH	92-73	Dist. of Columbia
1960	Evansville	90-69	Chapman, CA	1984	Central Mo. St.	81-77	St. Augustine's, NC
1961	Wittenberg, OH	42-38	SE Missouri St.	1985	Jacksonville St.	74-73	South Dakota St.
1962	Mt. St. Mary's, MD	58-57*	CS-Sacramento	1986	Sacred Heart, CT	93-87	SE Missouri St.
1963	South Dakota St.	42-40	Wittenberg, OH	1987	Ky. Wesleyan	92-74	Gannon, PA
1964	Evansville	72-59	Akron, OH	1988	Lowell, MA	75-72	AK-Anchorage
1965	Evansville	85-82*	Southern Illinois	1989	N.C. Central	73-46	SE Missouri St.
1966	Ky. Wesleyan	54-51	Southern Illinois	1990	Ky. Wesleyan	93-79	CS-Bakersfield
1967	Winston-Salem, NC	77-74	SW Missouri St.	1991	North Alabama	79-72	Bridgeport, CT
1968	Ky. Wesleyan	63-52	Indiana St.	1992	Virginia Union	100-75	Bridgeport
1969	Ky. Wesleyan	75-71	SW Missouri St.	1993	CS-Bakersfield	85-72	Troy St., AL
1970	Phila. Textile	76-65	Tennessee St.	1994	CS-Bakersfield	92-86	Southern Ind.
1971	Evansville	97-82	Old Dominion, VA	1995	Southern Indiana	71-63	UC-Riverside
1972	Roanoke, VA	84-72	Akron, OH	1996	Fort Hays St.	70-63	N. Kentucky
1973	Ky. Wesleyan	78-76*	Tennessee St.	1997	CS-Bakersfield	57-56	N. Kentucky
1974	Morgan St., MD	67-52	SW Missouri St.	1998	UC-Davis	83-77	Ky. Wesleyan
1975	Old Dominion	76-74	New Orleans	1999	Ky. Wesleyan	75-60	Metropolitan St.
1976	Puget Sound, WA	83-74	Tennessee-Chatt.	2000	Metropolitan St.	97-79	Ky. Wesleyan
1977	Tennessee-Chatt.	71-62	Randolph-Macon	2001	Ky. Wesleyan	72-63	Washburn, KS
1978	Cheyney, PA	47-40	WI-Green Bay	*Overtime			
1979	North Alabama	64-50	WI-Green Bay				
1980	Virginia Union	80-74	New York Tech				

NCAA Div. III Finals

Multiple winners: North Park (5); WI-Platteville (4); Calvin, Potsdam St., Scranton and WI-Whitewater (2).

Year	Winner	Score	Loser	Year	Winner	Score	Loser
1975	LeMoyne-Owen, TN	57-54	Glassboro St., NJ	1986	Potsdam St., NY	76-73	LeMoyne-Owen, TN
1976	Scranton, PA	60-57	Wittenberg, OH				
1977	Wittenberg, OH	79-66	Oneonta St., NY	1987	North Park, IL	106-100	Clark, MA
1978	North Park, IL	69-57	Widener, PA	1988	Ohio Wesleyan	92-70	Scranton, PA
1979	North Park, IL	66-62	Potsdam St., NY	1989	WI-Whitewater	94-86	Trenton St., NJ
1980	North Park, IL	83-76	Upsala, NJ	1990	Rochester, NY	43-42	DePauw, IN
1981	Potsdam St., NY	67-65*	Augustana, IL	1991	WI-Platteville	81-74	Franklin Marshall
1982	Wabash, IN	83-62	Potsdam St., NY	1992	Calvin, MI	62-49	Rochester, NY
1983	Scranton, PA	64-63	Wittenberg, OH	1993	Ohio Northern	71-68	Augustana, IL
1984	WI-Whitewater	103-86	Clark, MA	1994	Lebanon Valley, PA	66-59*	NYU
1985	North Park, IL	72-71	Potsdam St., NY				

Year	Winner	Score	Loser
1995	WI-Platteville	69-55	Manchester, IN
1996	Rowan, NJ	100-93	Hope, MI
1997	Illinois Wesleyan	89-86	Neb-Wesleyan
1998	WI-Platteville	69-56	Hope, MI
1999	WI-Platteville	76-75**	Hampden-Sydney

Year	Winner	Score	Loser
2000	Calvin, MI	79-74	WI-Eau Claire
2001	Catholic, DC	76-62	Wm. Paterson

*Overtime
**Double overtime

NAIA Finals, 1937-91

Multiple winners: Grand Canyon, Hamline, Kentucky St. and Tennessee St. (3); Central Missouri, Central St., Fort Hays St. and SW Missouri St. (2).

Year	Winner	Score	Loser
1937	Central Missouri	35-24	Morningside, IA
1938	Central Missouri	45-30	Roanoke, VA
1939	Southwestern, KS	32-31	San Diego St.
1940	Tarkio, MO	52-31	San Diego St.
1941	San Diego St.	36-32	Murray St., KY
1942	Hamline, MN	33-31	SE Oklahoma
1943	SE Missouri St.	34-32	NW Missouri St.
1944	Not held		
1945	Loyola-LA	49-36	Pepperdine, CA
1946	Southern Illinois	49-40	Indiana St.
1947	Marshall, WV	73-59	Mankato St., MN
1948	Louisville, KY	82-70	Indiana St.
1949	Hamline, MN	57-46	Regis, CO
1950	Indiana St.	61-47	East Central, OK
1951	Hamline, MN	69-61	Millikin, IL
1952	SW Missouri St.	73-64	Murray St., KY
1953	SW Missouri St.	79-71	Hamline, MN
1954	St.Benedict's, KS	62-56	Western Illinois
1955	East Texas St.	71-54	SE Oklahoma
1956	McNeese St., LA	60-55	Texas Southern
1957	Tennessee St.	92-73	SE Oklahoma
1958	Tennessee St.	85-73	Western Illinois
1959	Tennessee St.	97-87	Pacific-Luth., WA
1960	SW Texas St.	66-44	Westminster, PA
1961	Grambling, LA	95-75	Georgetown, KY
1962	Prairie View, TX	62-53	Westminster, PA
1963	Pan American, TX	73-62	Western Carolina
1964	Rockhurst, MO	66-56	Pan American, TX
1965	Central St., OH	85-51	Oklahoma Baptist
1966	Oklahoma Baptist	88-59	Georgia Southern
1967	St.Benedict's, KS	71-65	Oklahoma Baptist
1968	Central St., OH	51-48	Fairmont St., WV
1969	Eastern N. Mex	99-76	MD-Eastern Shore
1970	Kentucky St.	79-71	Central Wash.
1971	Kentucky St.	102-82	Eastern Michigan
1972	Kentucky St.	71-62	WI-Eau Claire

Year	Winner	Score	Loser
1973	Guilford, NC	99-96	MD-Eastern Shore
1974	West Georgia	97-79	Alcorn St., MS
1975	Grand Canyon, AZ	65-54	M'western St., TX
1976	Coppin St., MD	96-91	Henderson St., AR
1977	Texas Southern	71-44	Campbell, NC
1978	Grand Canyon	79-75	Kearney St., NE
1979	Drury, MO	60-54	Henderson St., AR
1980	Cameron, OK	84-77	Alabama St.
1981	Beth. Nazarene, OK	86-85*	AL-Huntsville
1982	SC-Spartanburg	51-38	Biola, CA
1983	Charleston, SC	57-53	WV-Wesleyan
1984	Fort Hays St., KS	48-46*	WI-Stevens Pt.
1985	Fort Hays St.	82-80*	Wayland Bapt., TX
1986	David Lipscomb, TN	67-54	AR-Monticello
1987	Washburn, KS	79-77	West Virginia St.
1988	Grand Canyon	88-86*	Auburn-Montg, AL
1989	St.Mary's, TX	61-58	East Central, OK
1990	Birm-Southern, AL	88-80	WI-Eau Claire
1991	Oklahoma City	77-74	Central Arkansas

*Overtime

NAIA Div. I Finals

NAIA split tournament into two divisions in 1992.

Multiple winners: Life, GA and Oklahoma City (3).

Year	Winner	Score	Loser
1992	Oklahoma City	82-73*	Central Arkansas
1993	Hawaii Pacific	88-83	Okla. Baptist
1994	Oklahoma City	99-81	Life, GA
1995	Birm-Southern	92-76	Pfeiffer, NC
1996	Oklahoma City	86-80	Georgetown, KY
1997	Life, GA	73-64	Okla. Baptist
1998	Georgetown, KY	83-69	So. Nazarene
1999	Life, GA	63-60	Mobile, AL
2000	Life, GA	61-59	Georgetown, KY
2001	Faulkner, AL	63-59	Science & Arts, OK

*Overtime

NAIA Div. II Finals

NAIA split tournament into two divisions in 1992.

Multiple winner: Bethel, IN (3).

Year	Winner	Score	Loser
1992	Grace, IN	85-79*	Northwestern-IA
1993	Williamette, OR	63-56	Northern St., SD
1994	Eureka, IL	98-95*	Northern St.
1995	Bethel, IN	103-95*	NW Nazarene, ID
1996	Albertson, ID	81-72*	Whitworth, WA
1997	Bethel	95-94	Siena Heights, MI

Year	Winner	Score	Loser
1998	Bethel	89-87	Oregon Tech
1999	Cornerstone, MI	113-109	Bethel
2000	Embry-Riddle, FL	75-63	Ozarks, MO
2001	Northwestern, IA	82-78	Mid. Am. Nazarene, KS

*Overtime

WOMEN

NCAA Final Four

Replaced the Association of Intercollegiate Athletics for Women (AIAW) tournament in 1982 as the official playoff for the national championship.

Multiple winners: Tennessee (6); Connecticut, Louisiana Tech, Stanford and USC (2).

Year	Champion	Head Coach	Score	Runner-up	——Third Place——	
1982	Louisiana Tech	Sonya Hogg	76-62	Cheyney	Maryland	Tennessee
1983	USC	Linda Sharp	69-67	Louisiana Tech	Georgia	Old Dominion
1984	USC	Linda Sharp	72-61	Tennessee	Cheyney	Louisiana Tech
1985	Old Dominion	Marianne Stanley	70-65	Georgia	NE Louisiana	Western Ky.
1986	Texas	Jody Conradt	97-81	USC	Tennessee	Western Ky.
1987	Tennessee	Pat Summitt	67-44	Louisiana Tech	Long Beach St.	Texas

Year	Champion	Head Coach	Score	Runner-up	——Third Place——	
1988	Louisiana Tech	Leon Barmore	56-54	Auburn	Long Beach St.	Tennessee
1989	Tennessee	Pat Summitt	76-60	Auburn	Louisiana Tech	Maryland
1990	Stanford	Tara VanDerveer	88-81	Auburn	Louisiana Tech	Virginia
1991	Tennessee	Pat Summitt	70-67(OT)	Virginia	Connecticut	Stanford
1992	Stanford	Tara VanDerveer	78-62	Western Kentucky	SW Missouri St.	Virginia
1993	Texas Tech	Marsha Sharp	84-82	Ohio St.	Iowa	Vanderbilt
1994	N. Carolina	Sylvia Hatchell	60-59	Louisiana Tech	Alabama	Purdue
1995	Connecticut	Geno Auriemma	70-64	Tennessee	Georgia	Stanford
1996	Tennessee	Pat Summitt	83-65	Georgia	Connecticut	Stanford
1997	Tennessee	Pat Summitt	68-59	Old Dominion	Stanford	Notre Dame
1998	Tennessee	Pat Summitt	93-75	Louisiana Tech	Arkansas	N.C. State
1999	Purdue	Carolyn Peck	62-45	Duke	Louisiana Tech	Georgia
2000	Connecticut	Geno Auriemma	71-52	Tennessee	Penn St.	Rutgers
2001	Notre Dame	Muffet McGraw	68-66	Purdue	Connecticut	SW Missouri St.

Final Four sites: 1982 (Norfolk, Va.), **1983** (Norfolk, Va.), **1984** (Los Angeles), **1985** (Austin), **1986** (Lexington), **1987** (Austin), **1988** (Tacoma), **1989** (Tacoma), **1990** (Knoxville), **1991** (New Orleans), **1992** (Los Angeles), **1993** (Atlanta), **1994** (Richmond), **1995** (Minneapolis), **1996** (Charlotte), **1997** (Cincinnati), **1998** (Kansas City), **1999** (San Jose), **2000** (Philadelphia), **2001** (St. Louis).

Most Outstanding Player

A Most Outstanding Player has been selected every year of the NCAA tournament. Winner who did not play for the tournament champion is listed in **bold,** type.

Multiple winners: Chamique Holdsclaw and Cheryl Miller (2).

Year		Year		Year	
1982	Janice Lawrence, La. Tech	1989	Bridgette Gordon, Tennessee	1996	Michelle Marciniak, Tennessee
1983	Cheryl Miller, USC	1990	Jennifer Azzi, Stanford	1997	Chamique Holdsclaw, Tenn.
1984	Cheryl Miller, USC	1991	**Dawn Staley**, Virginia	1998	Chamique Holdsclaw, Tenn.
1985	Tracy Claxton, Old Dominion	1992	Molly Goodenbour, Stanford	1999	Ukari Figgs, Purdue
1986	Clarissa Davis, Texas	1993	Sheryl Swoopes, Texas Tech	2000	Shea Ralph, Connecticut
1987	Tonya Edwards, Tennessee	1994	Charlotte Smith, N. Carolina	2001	Ruth Riley, Notre Dame
1988	Erica Westbrooks, La. Tech	1995	Rebecca Lobo, Connecticut		

All-Time NCAA Division I Tournament Leaders

Through 2000-01; minimum of six games; **Last** column indicates final year played.

CAREER

Scoring

	Total Points	Yrs	Last	Pts	Avg
1	Chamique Holdsclaw, Tenn	4	1999	**479**	21.8
2	Bridgette Gordon, Tenn	4	1989	**388**	21.6
3	Cheryl Miller, USC	4	1986	**333**	20.8
4	Janice Lawrence, La. Tech	3	1984	**312**	22.3
5	Penny Toler, Long Beach St.	4	1989	**291**	22.4
6	Dawn Staley, Virginia	4	1992	**274**	18.3
7	Cindy Brown, Long Beach St	4	1987	**263**	21.9
	Venus Lacy, La. Tech	3	1990	**263**	18.8
9	Clarissa Davis, Texas	3	1989	**261**	21.8
10	Janet Harris, Georgia	4	1985	**254**	19.5

Rebounds

	Total Rebounds	Yrs	Last	No	Avg
1	Chamique Holdsclaw, Tenn	4	1999	**188**	8.5
2	Cheryl Miller, USC	4	1986	**170**	10.6
3	Sheila Frost, Tennessee	4	1989	**162**	9.0
4	Val Whiting, Stanford	4	1993	**161**	10.1
5	Venus Lacy, La. Tech	3	1990	**148**	10.6
6	Bridgette Gordon, Tenn	4	1989	**142**	7.9
7	Kirsten Cummings, Long Beach St.	4	1985	**136**	10.5
8	Nora Lewis, La. Tech	3	1989	**130**	9.3
9	Pam McGee, USC	3	1984	**127**	9.8
10	Daedra Charles, Tenn	3	1991	**125**	9.6
	Paula McGee, USC	3	1984	**125**	9.6

SINGLE GAME

Scoring

		Year	Pts
1	Lorri Bauman, Drake vs Maryland	1982	50
2	Sheryl Swoopes, Texas Tech vs Ohio St	1993	47
3	Barbara Kennedy, Clemson vs Penn St	1982	43
4	Jackie Stiles, SW Mo. St. vs. Duke	2001	41
5	LaTaunya Pollard, L. Beach St. vs Howard	1982	40
	Cindy Brown, L. Beach St. vs Ohio St.	1987	40
	Tamika Whitmore, Memphis vs. YSU	1998	40
	Tara Mitchem, SW Mo. St. vs. Toledo	2001	40

Rebounds

		Year	No
1	Cheryl Taylor, Tenn. Tech vs Georgia	1985	23
	Charlotte Smith, N. Car. vs La. Tech	1994	23
3	Daedra Charles, Tenn. vs SW Missouri	1991	22
4	Cherie Nelson, USC vs Western Ky	1987	21
5	Alison Lang, Oregon vs Missouri	1982	20
	Shelda Arceneaux, S.D. St. vs L. Beach St.	1984	20
	Tracy Claxton, ODU vs Georgia	1985	20
	Brigette Combs, West. Ky. vs West Va	1989	20
	Tandreia Green, West. Ky. vs West Va	1989	20

Associated Press Final Top 10 Polls

The Associated Press weekly women's college basketball poll was begun by Mel Greenberg of *The Philadelphia Inquirer* during the 1976-77 season. Although the poll was started as a Top 20 in 1977 and was expanded to a Top 25 in 1990, only the Top 10 from each poll are listed below due to space constraints. The Association of Intercollegiate Athletics for Women (AIAW) Tournament determined the Division I national champion from 1972-81. The NCAA began its women's Division I tournament in 1982. The final AP Polls were taken before the NCAA tournament. Eventual national champions are in **bold** type.

1977
1 **Delta St.**
2 Immaculata
3 St. Joseph's-PA
4 CS-Fullerton
5 Tennessee
6 Tennessee Tech
7 Wayland Baptist
8 Montclair St.
9 S.F. Austin St.
10 N.C. State

1978
1 Tennessee
2 Wayland Baptist
3 N.C. State
4 Montclair St.
5 **UCLA**
6 Maryland
7 Queens-NY
8 Valdosta St.
9 Delta St.
10 LSU

1979
1 **Old Dominion**
2 Louisiana Tech
3 Tennessee
4 Texas
5 S.F. Austin St.
6 UCLA
7 Rutgers
8 Maryland
9 Cheyney
10 Wayland Baptist

1980
1 **Old Dominion**
2 Tennessee
3 Louisiana Tech
4 South Carolina
5 S.F. Austin St.
6 Maryland
7 Texas
8 Rutgers
9 Long Beach St.
10 N.C. State

1981
1 **Louisiana Tech**
2 Tennessee
3 Old Dominion
4 USC
5 Cheyney
6 Long Beach St.
7 UCLA
8 Maryland
9 Rutgers
10 Kansas

1982
1 **Louisiana Tech**
2 Cheyney
3 Maryland
4 Tennessee
5 Texas
6 USC
7 Old Dominion
8 Rutgers
9 Long Beach St.
10 Penn St.

1983
1 **USC**
2 Louisiana Tech
3 Texas
4 Old Dominion
5 Cheyney
6 Long Beach St.
7 Maryland
8 Penn St.
9 Georgia
10 Tennessee

1984
1 Texas
2 Louisiana Tech
3 Georgia
4 Old Dominion
5 **USC**
6 Long Beach St.
7 Kansas St.
8 LSU
9 Cheyney
10 Mississippi

1985
1 Texas
2 NE Louisiana
3 Long Beach St.
4 Louisiana Tech
5 **Old Dominion**
6 Mississippi
7 Ohio St.
8 Georgia
9 Penn St.
10 Auburn

1986
1 **Texas**
2 Georgia
3 USC
4 Louisiana Tech
5 Western Ky.
6 Virginia
7 Auburn
8 Long Beach St.
9 LSU
10 Rutgers

1987
1 Texas
2 Auburn
3 Louisiana Tech
4 Long Beach St.
5 Rutgers
6 Georgia
7 **Tennessee**
8 Mississippi
9 Iowa
10 Ohio St.

1988
1 Tennessee
2 Iowa
3 Auburn
4 Texas
5 **Louisiana Tech**
6 Ohio St.
7 Long Beach St.
8 Rutgers
9 Maryland
10 Virginia

1989
1 **Tennessee**
2 Auburn
3 Louisiana Tech
4 Stanford
5 Maryland
6 Texas
7 Long Beach St.
8 Iowa
9 Colorado
10 Georgia

1990
1 Louisiana Tech
2 **Stanford**
3 Washington
4 Tennessee
5 UNLV
6 S.F. Austin St.
7 Georgia
8 Texas
9 Auburn
10 Iowa

1991
1 Penn St.
2 Virginia
3 Georgia
4 **Tennessee**
5 Purdue
6 Auburn
7 N.C. State
8 LSU
9 Arkansas
10 Western Ky.

1992
1 Virginia
2 Tennessee
3 **Stanford**
4 S.F. Austin St.
5 Mississippi
6 Miami-FL
7 Iowa
8 Maryland
9 Penn St.
10 SW Missouri St.

1993
1 Vanderbilt
2 Tennessee
3 Ohio St.
4 Iowa
5 **Texas Tech**
6 Stanford
7 Auburn
8 Penn St.
9 Virginia
10 Colorado

1994
1 Tennessee
2 Penn St.
3 Connecticut
4 **North Carolina**
5 Colorado
6 Louisiana Tech
7 USC
8 Purdue
9 Texas Tech
10 Virginia

1995
1 **Connecticut**
2 Colorado
3 Tennessee
4 Stanford
5 Texas Tech
6 Vanderbilt
7 Penn St.
8 Louisiana Tech
9 Western Ky.
10 Virginia

1996
1 Louisiana Tech
2 Connecticut
3 Stanford
4 **Tennessee**
5 Georgia
6 Old Dominion
7 Iowa
8 Penn St.
9 Texas Tech
10 Alabama

1997
1 Connecticut
2 Old Dominion
3 Stanford
4 North Carolina
5 Louisiana Tech
6 Georgia
7 Florida
8 Alabama
9 LSU
10 **Tennessee**

1998
1 **Tennessee**
2 Old Dominion
3 Connecticut
4 Louisiana Tech
5 Stanford
6 Texas Tech
7 North Carolina
8 Duke
9 Arizona
10 N.C. State

1999
1 **Purdue**
2 Tennessee
3 Louisiana Tech
4 Colorado St.
5 Old Dominion
6 Connecticut
7 Rutgers
8 Notre Dame
9 Texas Tech
10 Duke

2000
1 **Connecticut**
2 Tennessee
3 Louisiana Tech
4 Georgia
5 Notre Dame
6 Penn St.
7 Iowa St.
8 Rutgers
9 UC-Santa Barbara
10 Duke

2001
1 Connecticut
2 **Notre Dame**
3 Tennessee
4 Georgia
5 Duke
6 Louisiana Tech
7 Oklahoma
8 Iowa St.
9 Purdue
10 Vanderbilt

All-Time AP Top 10

The composite AP Top 10 from the 1976-77 season through 2000-01, based on the final regular season rankings of each year. Team points are based on 10 points for all 1st place finishes, 9 for each 2nd, etc. Also listed are the number of times ranked No. 1 by AP going into the tournaments, and times ranked in the pre-tournament Top 10.

		Pts	No. 1	Top 10				Pts	No. 1	Top 10
1	Tennessee	177	5	23	6	Connecticut		70	4	8
2	Louisiana Tech	161	4	21	7	Stanford		58	0	8
3	Old Dominion	81	2	11	8	Penn St.		46	1	10
4	Texas	80	4	17	9	Long Beach St.		45	0	10
5	Georgia	72	0	13	10	Auburn		42	0	8

All-Time Winningest Division I Teams

Division I schools with best winning percentages and most victories through 2000-01 (including postseason tournaments). Although official NCAA women's basketball records didn't begin until the 1981-82 season, results from previous seasons are included below.

Top 10 Winning Percentage

		Yrs	W	L	Pct
1	Louisiana Tech	27	768	128	.857
2	Tennessee	56	852	210	.802
3	Montana	23	535	148	.783
4	Texas	27	687	205	.770
5	Old Dominion	32	707	226	.758
6	S. F. Austin St.	29	690	222	.757
7	Mount St. Mary's*	27	534	196	.732
8	Utah	27	559	215	.722
9	Virginia	28	590	228	.721
10	Penn St.	37	616	242	.718

*Includes records prior to Division I.

Top 10 Victories

		Yrs	W	L	Pct
1	Tennessee	56	852	210	.802
2	Louisiana Tech	27	768	128	.857
3	Old Dominion	32	707	226	.758
4	S.F. Austin St.	29	690	222	.757
5	James Madison	79	688	386	.641
6	Texas	27	687	205	.770
7	Long Beach St.	39	677	285	.704
8	Tennessee Tech	31	674	276	.709
9	Richmond	81	629	431	.593
10	Penn St.	37	616	242	.718

Annual NCAA Division I Leaders

All averages include postseason games

Scoring

Multiple winners: Cindy Blodgett, Andrea Congreaves and Jackie Stiles (2).

Year		Gm	Pts	Avg
1982	Barbara Kennedy, Clemson	31	908	29.3
1983	LaTaunya Pollard, L. Beach St	31	907	29.3
1984	Deborah Temple, Delta St	28	873	31.2
1985	Anucha Browne, Northwestern	28	855	30.5
1986	Wanda Ford, Drake	30	919	30.6
1987	Tresa Spaulding, BYU	28	810	28.9
1988	LeChandra LeDay, Grambling	28	850	30.4
1989	Patricia Hoskins, Miss. Valley	27	908	33.6
1990	Kim Perrot, SW Louisiana	28	839	30.0
1991	Jan Jensen, Drake	30	888	29.6
1992	Andrea Congreaves, Mercer	28	925	33.0
1993	Andrea Congreaves, Mercer	26	805	31.0
1994	Kristy Ryan, CS-Sacramento	26	727	28.0
1995	Koko Lahanas, CS-Fullerton	29	778	26.8
1996	Cindy Blodgett, Maine	32	889	27.8
1997	Cindy Blodgett, Maine	30	810	27.0
1998	Allison Feaster, Harvard	28	797	28.5
1999	Tamika Whitmore, Memphis	32	843	26.3
2000	Jackie Stiles, SW Missouri St.	32	890	27.8
2001	Jackie Stiles, SW Missouri St.	35	1062	30.3

Rebounds

Multiple winner: Patricia Hoskins (2).

Year		Gm	No	Avg
1982	Anne Donovan, Old Dominion	28	412	14.7
1983	Deborah Mitchell, Miss. Col	28	447	16.0
1984	Joy Kellog, Oklahoma City	23	373	16.2
1985	Rosina Pearson, Beth-Cookman	26	480	18.5
1986	Wanda Ford, Drake	30	506	16.9
1987	Patricia Hoskins, Miss. Valley St.	28	476	17.0
1988	Katie Beck, East Tenn. St.	25	441	17.6
1989	Patricia Hoskins, Miss. Valley St.	27	440	16.3
1990	Pam Hudson, Northwestern St	29	438	15.1
1991	Tarcha Hollis, Grambling	29	443	15.3
1992	Christy Greis, Evansville	28	383	13.7
1993	Ann Barry, Nevada	25	355	14.2
1994	DeShawne Blocker, E. Tenn. St.	26	450	17.3
1995	Tera Sheriff, Jackson St.	29	401	13.8
1996	Dana Wynne, Seton Hall	29	372	12.8
1997	Etolia Mitchell, Georgia St.	25	330	13.2
1998	Alisha Hill, Howard	30	397	13.2
1999	Monica Logan, UMBC	27	364	13.5
2000	Malveata Johnson, N.C. A&T	27	363	13.4
2001	Andrea Gardner, Howard	31	439	14.2

Note: Wanda Ford (1986) and Patricia Hoskins (1989) each led the country in scoring and rebounds in the same year.

All-Time NCAA Division I Individual Leaders

Through 2000-01; includes regular season and tournament games; Official NCAA women's basketball records began with 1981-82 season. Players who competed earlier than that are not included below; **Last** column indicates final year played.

CAREER

Scoring

Average

		Yrs	Last	Pts	Avg
1	Patricia Hoskins, Miss. Valley St.	4	1989	3122	28.4
2	Sandra Hodge, New Orleans	4	1984	2860	26.7
3	Jackie Stiles, SW Mo. St.	4	2001	3206	26.1
4	Lorri Bauman, Drake	4	1984	3115	26.0
5	Andrea Congreaves, Mercer	4	1993	2796	25.9
6	Cindy Blodgett, Maine	4	1998	3005	25.5
7	Valorie Whiteside, Aplach St.	4	1988	2944	25.4
8	Joyce Walker, LSU	4	1984	2906	24.8
9	Tarcha Hollis, Grambling	4	1991	2058	24.2
10	Korie Hlede, Duquesne	4	1998	2631	24.1

Rebounds

		Yrs	Last	Reb	Avg
1	Wanda Ford, Drake	4	1986	1887	16.1
2	Patricia Hoskins, Miss. Valley St.	4	1989	1662	15.1
3	Tarcha Hollis, Grambling	4	1991	1185	13.9
4	Katie Beck, East Tenn. St.	4	1988	1404	13.4
5	Marilyn Stephens, Temple	4	1984	1519	13.0
6	Natalie Williams, UCLA	4	1994	1137	12.8
7	Cheryl Taylor, Tenn. Tech	4	1987	1532	12.8
8	DeShawne Blocker, E. Tenn. St.	4	1995	1361	12.7
9	Olivia Bradley, West Virginia	4	1985	1484	12.7
10	Judy Mosley, Hawaii	4	1990	1441	12.6

SINGLE SEASON

Scoring

Average

		Year	Gm	Pts	Avg
1	Patricia Hoskins, Miss.Valley St.	1989	27	908	33.6
2	Andrea Congreaves, Mercer	1992	28	925	33.0
3	Deborah Temple, Delta St.	1984	28	873	31.2
4	Andrea Congreaves, Mercer	1993	26	805	31.0
5	Wanda Ford, Drake	1986	30	919	30.6
6	Anucha Browne, Northwestern	1985	28	855	30.5
7	LeChandra LeDay, Grambling	1988	28	850	30.4
8	Jackie Stiles, SW Mo. St.	2001	35	1062	30.3
9	Kim Perrot, SW Louisiana	1990	28	841	30.0
10	Tina Hutchinson, San Diego St.	1984	30	898	29.9

SINGLE GAME

Scoring

		Year	Pts
1	Cindy Brown, Long Beach St. vs San Jose St.	1987	60
2	Lorri Bauman, Drake vs SW Missouri St.	1984	58
	Kim Perrot, SW La. vs SE La.	1990	58
4	Jackie Stiles, SW Mo. St. vs Evansville	2000	56
5	Patricia Hoskins, Miss.Valley St. vs South-BR	1989	55
	Patricia Hoskins, Miss.Valley St. vs Ala. St.	1989	55
7	Wanda Ford, Drake vs SW Missouri St.	1986	54
	Anjinea Hopson, Grambling vs Jackson St.	1994	54
	Mary Lowry, Baylor vs Texas	1994	54
10	Chris Starr, Nevada vs CS-Sacramento	1983	53
	Felisha Edwards, NE La. vs Southern Miss.	1991	53
	Sheryl Swoopes, Texas Tech vs Texas	1993	53

Winningest Active Division I Coaches

Minimum of five seasons as Division I head coach; regular season and tournament games included.

Top 10 Winning Percentage

		Yrs	W	L	Pct
1	Leon Barmore, La. Tech	19	551	82	**.870**
2	Pat Summitt, Tennessee	27	759	152	**.833**
3	Geno Auriemma, Connecticut	16	425	98	**.813**
4	Robin Selvig, Montana	23	536	148	**.784**
5	Andy Landers, Georgia	22	545	158	**.775**
6	Tara VanDerveer, Stanford	22	516	153	**.771**
7	Marsha Sharp, Texas Tech	19	458	141	**.765**
8	Vivian Stringer, Rutgers	29	644	199	**.764**
9	Jody Conradt, Texas	32	766	248	**.755**
10	Joe Ciampi, Auburn	24	546	180	**.752**

Top 10 Victories

		Yrs	W	L	Pct
1	Jody Conradt, Texas	32	**766**	248	.755
2	Pat Summitt, Tennessee	27	**759**	152	.833
3	Vivian Stringer, Rutgers	29	**644**	199	.764
4	Sue Gunter, LSU	31	**633**	284	.690
5	Kay Yow, N.C. State	30	**609**	252	.707
6	Theresa Grentz, Illinois	27	**577**	227	.718
7	Sylvia Hatchell, N. Carolina	26	**576**	240	.706
8	Rene Portland, Penn St.	25	**572**	195	.746
9	Mike Granelli, St. Peter's	29	**553**	214	.721
10	Leon Barmore, La. Tech	19	**551**	82	.870

Annual Awards

The Broderick Award was first given out to the Women's Division I or Large School Player of the Year in 1977. Since then, the National Assn. for Girls and Women in Sports (1978), the Women's Basketball Coaches Assn. (1983), the Atlanta Tip-Off Club (1983) and the Associated Press (1995) have joined in.

Since 1983, the first year as many as four awards were given out, the same player has won all of them in the same season twice: Cheryl Miller of USC in 1985 and Rebecca Lobo of Connecticut in 1995.

Associated Press

Voted on by AP sportswriters and broadcasters and first presented in 1995.

Multiple winner: Chamique Holdsclaw (2).

Year		Year		Year	
1995	Rebecca Lobo, Connecticut	1998	Chamique Holdsclaw, Tennessee	2001	Ruth Riley, Notre Dame
1996	Jennifer Rizzotti, Connecticut	1999	Chamique Holdsclaw, Tennessee		
1997	Kara Wolters, Connecticut	2000	Tamika Catchings, Tennessee		

Broderick Award

Voted on by a national panel of women's collegiate athletic directors and first presented by the late Thomas Broderick, an athletic outfitter, in 1977. Honda has presented the award since 1987. Basketball Player of the Year is one of 10 nominated for Collegiate Woman Athlete of the Year; (*) indicates player also won Athlete of the Year.

Multiple winners: Chamique Holdsclaw, Nancy Lieberman, Cheryl Miller and Dawn Staley (2).

Year		Year		Year	
1977	Lucy Harris, Delta St.*	1979	Nancy Lieberman, Old Dominion*	1981	Lynette Woodard, Kansas
1978	Ann Meyers, UCLA*	1980	Nancy Lieberman, Old Dominion*	1982	Pam Kelly, La. Tech

Year	Year	Year
1983 Anne Donovan, Old Dominion	1989 Bridgette Gordon, Tennessee	1995 Rebecca Lobo, Connecticut
1984 Cheryl Miller, USC*	1990 Jennifer Azzi, Stanford	1996 Jennifer Rizzotti, Connecticut
1985 Cheryl Miller, USC	1991 Dawn Staley, Virginia	1997 Chamique Holdsclaw, Tennessee
1986 Kamie Ethridge, Texas*	1992 Dawn Staley, Virginia	1998 Chamique Holdsclaw, Tennessee*
1987 Katrina McClain, Georgia	1993 Sheryl Swoopes, Texas Tech	1999 Stephanie White-McCarty, Purdue
1988 Teresa Weatherspoon, La. Tech*	1994 Lisa Leslie, USC	2000 Jackie Stiles, SW Missouri St.

Wade Trophy

Voted on by the National Assn. for Girls and Women in Sports (NAGWS) and awarded for academics and community service as well as player performance. First presented in 1978 in the name of former Delta St. coach Margaret Wade.

Multiple winner: Nancy Lieberman (2).

Year	Year	Year
1978 Carol Blazejowski, Montclair St.	1986 Kamie Ethridge, Texas	1994 Carol Ann Shudlick, Minnesota
1979 Nancy Lieberman, Old Dominion	1987 Shelly Pennefather, Villanova	1995 Rebecca Lobo, Connecticut
1980 Nancy Lieberman, Old Dominion	1988 Teresa Weatherspoon, La. Tech	1996 Jennifer Rizzotti, Connecticut
1981 Lynette Woodard, Kansas	1989 Clarissa Davis, Texas	1997 DeLisha Milton, Florida
1982 Pam Kelly, La. Tech	1990 Jennifer Azzi, Stanford	1998 Ticha Penicheiro, Old Dominion
1983 LaTaunya Pollard, L. Beach St.	1991 Daedra Charles, Tennessee	1999 Stephanie White-McCarty, Purdue
1984 Janice Lawrence, La. Tech	1992 Susan Robinson, Penn St.	2000 Edwina Brown, Texas
1985 Cheryl Miller, USC	1993 Karen Jennings, Nebraska	2001 Jackie Stiles, SW Missouri St.

Naismith Trophy

Voted on by a panel of coaches, sportswriters and broadcasters and first presented in 1983 by the Atlanta Tip-Off Club in the name of the inventor of basketball, Dr. James Naismith.

Multiple winners: Cheryl Miller (3); Clarissa Davis, Chamique Holdsclaw and Dawn Staley (2).

Year	Year	Year
1983 Anne Donovan, Old Dominion	1990 Jennifer Azzi, Stanford	1997 Kate Starbird, Stanford
1984 Cheryl Miller, USC	1991 Dawn Staley, Virgina	1998 Chamique Holdsclaw, Tennessee
1985 Cheryl Miller, USC	1992 Dawn Staley, Virginia	1999 Chamique Holdsclaw, Tennessee
1986 Cheryl Miller, USC	1993 Sheryl Swoopes, Texas Tech	2000 Tamika Catchings, Tennessee
1987 Clarissa Davis, Texas	1994 Lisa Leslie, USC	2001 Ruth Riley, Notre Dame
1988 Sue Wicks, Rutgers	1995 Rebecca Lobo, Connecticut	
1989 Clarissa Davis, Texas	1996 Saudia Roundtree, Georgia	

Women's Basketball Coaches Association

Voted on by the WBCA and first presented by Champion athletic outfitters in 1983.

Multiple winners: Chamique Holdsclaw, Cheryl Miller and Dawn Staley (2).

Year	Year	Year
1983 Anne Donovan, Old Dominion	1990 Venus Lacy, La. Tech	1997 Kate Starbird, Stanford
1984 Janice Lawrence, La. Tech	1991 Dawn Staley, Virgina	1998 Chamique Holdsclaw, Tennessee
1985 Cheryl Miller, USC	1992 Dawn Staley, Virginia	1999 Chamique Holdsclaw, Tennessee
1986 Cheryl Miller, USC	1993 Sheryl Swoopes, Texas Tech	2000 Tamika Catchings, Tennessee
1987 Katrina McClain, Georgia	1994 Lisa Leslie, USC	2001 Ruth Riley, Notre Dame
1988 Michelle Edwards, Iowa	1995 Rebecca Lobo, Connecticut	
1989 Clarissa Davis, Texas	1996 Saudia Roundtree, Georgia	

Coach of the Year Award

Voted on by the Women's Basketball Coaches Assn. and first presented by Converse athletic outfitters in 1983.

Multiple winners: Pat Summitt (3), Geno Auriemma, Jody Conradt and Vivian Stringer (2).

Year	Year	Year
1983 Pat Summitt, Tennessee	1990 Kay Yow, N.C. State	1997 Geno Auriemma, Connecticut
1984 Jody Conradt, Texas	1991 Rene Portland, Penn St.	1998 Pat Summitt, Tennessee
1985 Jim Foster, St. Joseph's-PA	1992 Ferne Labati, Miami-FL	1999 Carolyn Peck, Purdue
1986 Jody Conradt, Texas	1993 Vivian Stringer, Iowa	2000 Geno Auriemma, Connecticut
1987 Theresa Grentz, Rutgers	1994 Marsha Sharp, Texas Tech	2001 Muffet McGraw, Notre Dame
1988 Vivian Stringer, Iowa	1995 Pat Summitt, Tennessee	
1989 Tara VanDerveer, Stanford	1996 Leon Barmore, La. Tech	

Other Women's Champions

The NCAA has sanctioned national championship tournaments for Division II and Division III since 1982. The NAIA sanctioned a single tournament from 1981-91, then split to two divisions in 1992.

NCAA Div. II Finals

Multiple winners: North Dakota St. (5); Cal Poly Pomona (4); Delta St. and North Dakota (3).

Year	Winner	Score	Loser
1982	Cal Poly Pomona	93-74	Tuskegee, AL
1983	Virginia Union	73-60	Cal Poly Pomona
1984	Central Mo.St.	80-73	Virginia Union
1985	Cal Poly Pomona	80-69	Central Mo.St.
1986	Cal Poly Pomona	70-63	North Dakota St.
1987	New Haven, CT	77-75	Cal Poly Pomona
1988	Hampton, VA	65-48	West Texas St.
1989	Delta St., MS	88-58	Cal Poly Pomona
1990	Delta St., MS	77-43	Bentley, MA
1991	North Dakota St.	81-74	SE Missouri St.
1992	Delta St., MS	65-63	North Dakota St.
1993	North Dakota St.	95-63	Delta St.
1994	North Dakota St.	89-56	CS-San Bernadino
1995	North Dakota St.	98-85	Portland St.
1996	North Dakota St.	104-78	Shippensburg, PA
1997	North Dakota	94-78	S. Indiana
1998	North Dakota	92-76	Emporia St.
1999	North Dakota	80-63	Arkansas Tech
2000	Northern Kentucky	71-62	North Dakota St.
2001	Cal Poly Pomona	87-80*	North Dakota

*Overtime

NCAA Div. III Finals

Multiple winners: Washington (4); Capital and Elizabethtown.

Year	Winner	Score	Loser
1982	Elizabethtown, PA	67-66*	NC-Greensboro
1983	North Central, IL	83-71	Elizabethtown, PA
1984	Rust College, MS	51-49	Elizabethtown, PA
1985	Scranton, PA	68-59	New Rochelle, NY
1986	Salem St., MA	89-85	Bishop, TX
1987	WI-Stevens Pt.	81-74	Concordia, MN
1988	Concordia, MN	65-57	St. John Fisher, NY
1989	Elizabethtown, PA	66-65	CS-Stanislaus
1990	Hope, MI	65-63	St. John Fisher
1991	St. Thomas, MN	73-55	Muskingum, OH
1992	Alma, MI	79-75	Moravian, PA
1993	Central Iowa	71-63	Capital, OH
1994	Capital, OH	82-63	Washington, MO
1995	Capital, OH	59-55	WI-Oshkosh
1996	WI-Oshkosh	66-50	Mt. Union, OH
1997	NYU	72-70	WI-Eau Claire
1998	Washington, MO	77-69	So. Maine
1999	Washington, MO	74-65	College of St. Benedict, MN
2000	Washington, MO	79-33	So. Maine
2001	Washington, MO	67-45	Messiah, PA

*Overtime

NAIA Finals

Multiple winners: One tournament–SW Oklahoma (4); Div. I tourney–Southern Nazarene and Oklahoma City (4); Arkansas Tech (2); Div. II tourney–Northern St. and Western Oregon (2).

Year	Winner	Score	Loser
1981	Kentucky St.	73-67	Texas Southern
1982	SW Oklahoma	80-45	Mo. Southern
1983	SW Oklahoma	80-68	AL-Huntsville
1984	NC-Asheville	72-70*	Portland, OR
1985	SW Oklahoma	55-54	Saginaw Val., MI
1986	Francis Marion, SC	75-65	Wayland Baptist, TX
1987	SW Oklahoma	60-58	North Georgia
1988	Oklahoma City	113-95	Claflin, SC
1989	So. Nazarene, OK	98-96	Claflin, SC
1990	SW Oklahoma	82-75	AR-Monticello
1991	Ft. Hays St., KS	57-53	SW Oklahoma
1992	I– Arkansas Tech	84-68	Wayland Baptist, TX
	II– Northern St., SD	73-56	Tarleton St., TX
1993	I– Arkansas Tech	76-75	Union, TN
	II– No. Montana	71-68	Northern St., SD
1994	I– So. Nazarene	97-74	David Lipscomb, TN
	II– Northern St., SD	48-45	Western Oregon
1995	I– So. Nazarene	78-77	SE Oklahoma
	II– Western Oregon	75-67	NW Nazarene, ID
1996	I– So. Nazarene	80-79	SE Oklahoma
	II– Western Oregon	80-77	Huron, SD
1997	I– So. Nazarene	78-73	Union, TN
	II– NW Nazarene	64-46	Black Hills St., SD
1998	I– Union, TN	73-70	So. Nazarene
	II– Walsh, OH	73-66	Mary Hardin-Baylor
1999	I– Oklahoma City	72-55	Simon Fraser, B.C.
	II– Shawnee St., OH	80-65	St. Francis, IN
2000	I– Oklahoma City	64-55	Simon Fraser, B.C.
	II– Mary, N.D.	59-49	Northwestern, IA
2001	I– Oklahoma City	69-52	Auburn Montgomery, AL
	II– Northwestern, IA	77-50	Albertson, ID

*Overtime

AIAW Finals

The Association of Intercollegiate Athletics for Women Large College tournament determined the women's national champion for 10 years until supplanted by the NCAA.

In 1982, most Division I teams entered the first NCAA tournament rather than the last one staged by the AIAW.

Year	Winner	Score	Loser
1972	Immaculata, PA	52-48	West Chester, PA
1973	Immaculata, PA	59-52	Queens College, NY
1974	Immaculata, PA	68-53	Mississippi College
1975	Delta St., MS	90-81	Immaculata, PA
1976	Delta St., MS	69-64	Immaculata, PA
1977	Delta St., MS	68-55	LSU
1978	UCLA	90-74	Maryland
1979	Old Dominion	75-65	Louisiana Tech
1980	Old Dominion	68-53	Tennessee
1981	Louisiana Tech	79-59	Tennessee
1982	Rutgers	83-77	Texas

Pro Basketball

The 76ers' **Allen Iverson** blew past the rest of the league on his way to the NBA MVP award.

Ooh L.A., L.A. Lakers Repeat

Shaq, Kobe and Co. nearly run the table, going 15-1 in an impressive playoff run.

Ric Bucher
is an NBA analyst for ESPN.

In keeping with the recent retro fashion groove—big 'fros, long socks and classic Air Jordans, along with their namesake showing signs of a comeback—the power of peace, love and harmony asserted itself by season's end.

Larry Brown and Allen Iverson kissed and made up (sort of), then led the 76ers to an Eastern Conference title and respective Coach of the Year and league MVP awards.

Kobe Bryant and Shaquille O'Neal settled their differences, then looked nearly invincible leading the Lakers to a second straight NBA title. Antonio Davis embraced the Frozen North and signed a big contract with the Toronto Raptors (a match made in salary-cap heaven). Suddenly it was a group hug, with Vince Carter included, saving basketball in Canada in the process.

"We," said longtime NBA commissioner David Stern, "are a resilient league."

Nothing demonstrated that better than the mixed reaction to Michael Jordan indicating he might like to un-retire again. A year earlier the clamor would've been deafening, what with the league desperately needing a shot of something to reverse the steady decline in TV ratings, attendance and general satisfaction with NBA-style basketball.

Even midway through the season, Stern was concerned enough that he allowed Phoenix Suns owner and ally Jerry Colangelo to form a special group to devise rule changes intended to enliven the game, most notably abolishing illegal-defense rules instituted in 1947.

Other rule changes will allow incidental contact on defense, reduce the time allowed to bring the ball out of the backcourt from 10 seconds to eight and institute a defensive three-second rule.

But those changes suddenly looked premature as the playoffs produced some elements missing since His Airness

AP/Wide World Photos

*It seems that the sky's the limit for two-time defending NBA champions **Shaquille O'Neal** and **Kobe Bryant**.*

went ether in 1998: a bona-fide top dog for the rest of the league to target (the Lakers) and a one-man show carrying his team to unthinkable heights (Iverson).

The postseason also saw an infusion of new O(as in offense)-positive blood as the Miami Heat, New York Knicks and Utah Jazz all fell to young, up-tempo teams.

The Milwaukee Bucks rode three jump-shooters (Ray Allen, Sam Cassell and Glenn Robinson) nearly to the Finals. A similar trio (Dirk Nowitzki, Steve Nash and Michael Finley) ended the Dallas Mavericks' 10-year playoff hiatus with a somewhat surprising second-round appearance.

The Charlotte Hornets did their part by sweeping away the Heat and coach Pat Riley's clock-milking, 70-point-producing, three-quarters trap by an average of 22 points a game. Iverson and Carter conjured visions of Bird and 'Nique going at it with alternating top-this-no-top-this, 50-plus-point performances.

All of this resulted in an excitement about the playoffs that hadn't been felt since before Jordan left and the league's lockout-shortened 1998–99 season.

AP/Wide World Photos

The successful return to the NHL of golfing buddy **Mario Lemeiux** had **Michael Jordan** pondering a comeback of his own in 2001.

The increase in TV ratings reflected it. In fact, they were the highest since Jordan's dramatic come-from-behind victory to earn himself, and the Bulls, a sixth ring while denying veterans Karl Malone, John Stockton and the rest of the Utah Jazz in what seemed to be their best (and perhaps their last) shot at their first.

All the talk about asterisked championships (the San Antonio Spurs in 1999) and champions by default (the Lakers in 2000) gave way to the debates over exactly where the Lakers' dominating 15-1 playoff run placed them historically among the league's all-time greatest teams.

Your grandfather might say it doesn't quite put them among the great Celtics, Lakers, Knicks and 76ers teams of the past.

No problem.

At least you and your grandfather will finally have something to talk about again.

Ric Bucher's Ten Biggest Stories of the Year in Pro Basketball

10 ▪ Mavs Make Their Mark— A basketball wasteland spawns a playoff team and a convention-challenging billionaire owner, Mark Cuban, who in his first year draws a series of five-figure fines much to the delight of the media and consternation of the league.

9 ▪ Blazers' Meltdown—No team entered the season with a greater assemblage of talent. No team, comparatively, did less with what it had. Shawn Kemp goes into rehab, coach Mike Dunleavy is fired and Rasheed Wallace continues to get teed off and T'd up at a record pace.

8 ▪ Grant Hill Motors—The five-time all-star bolts Detroit but the five screws in his surgically repaired ankle signifcantly cloud his visions of leading the Orlando Magic back to glory. Tracy McGrady emerges while Hill misses all but four games, and doubts linger if he'll ever be the same player.

7 ▪ New Rules—The rule tweaking that took place two years back, intended to enhance ball and player movement, achieved the exact opposite effect. So the NBA

takes more drastic measures without the precaution of testing any of them first.

6 ▪ Oh, Canada!—The NBA's foray across the border appeared to be on the brink of failure with the Vancouver Grizzlies moving to Memphis and indications that Raptors superstar Vince Carter was ready to leave Toronto. But veteran Antonio Davis leads a wave of three free-agent re-signings, prompting Carter to re-up for another six years as well.

5 ▪ Zo's Kidneys—The Heat, title contenders with the offseason additions of Brian Grant and Eddie Jones, are eliminated in training camp when Alonzo Mourning is diagnosed with the same kidney ailment that threatened Sean Elliott's career. Zo returns, briefly, but Miami is bounced in the first round and Zo's long-term future remains cloudy.

4 ▪ Philly Feud—Coach Larry Brown, fed up with Allen Iverson's poor punctuality and practice habits, entertains trade offers for his young star. AI straightens up and the Sixers fly right into the NBA Finals.

3 • Joe Must Go—NBA commissioner David Stern finds documented proof of an under-the-table deal between Joe Smith and the Minnesota Timberwolves and drops the hammer—one-year suspensions for VP Kevin McHale and owner Glen Taylor, forfeiture of four future first-round picks and temporary exclusion from re-signing Smith.*

2 • Kobe–Shaq Feud—The Lakers' two stars battle over whom the offense should revolve around, nearly tearing the team apart and foreclosing their bid to repeat as league champions. Injuries to both opened the way to mutual appreciation, a discord-toughened solidarity and, ultimately, a second title with the promise of more to come.

1 • Sir Charles Talks of a Jordan Comeback—Barkley becomes an instant hit as a TNT analyst thanks to his candid appraisals, including weekly updates on pal Jordan potentially returning with him to play in the NBA. Barkley soon scratched his own comeback plans but MJ's preparations to play after a two-year absence became a soap opera that added drama to everything the otherwise moribund Wizards did.

Most Finals Meetings

The Los Angeles Lakers and Philadelphia 76ers faced each other for the sixth time in NBA Finals history in 2001. The only franchises to square off more often with a title at stake are the Lakers and Boston Celtics.

	Times Met
Celtics vs. Lakers	10
Lakers vs. 76ers	6
Lakers vs. Knicks	5
Celtics vs. Hawks	4

Note: The Celtics lead the Lakers, 8-2, in the all-time Finals series. The Lakers lead the 76ers, 5-1. The Lakers lead the Knicks, 3-2. The Celtics lead the Hawks, 3-1.

Final Scorers

With back-to-back Finals MVP performances, Shaquille O'Neal now has the highest Finals scoring average in NBA history (with a minimum of 12 games played). He is at the top of a pretty good list. Here's a look at the top five Finals scorers:

	PPG
Shaquille O'Neal	33.7
Michael Jordan	33.6
Jerry West	30.5
Bob Pettit	28.4
Hakeem Olajuwon	27.5

2000-2001 Season in Review

information please® SPORTS ALMANAC

Final NBA Standings

Division champions (*) and playoff qualifiers (†) are noted. Number of seasons listed after each head coach refers to current tenure with club.

Western Conference

Midwest Division

	W	L	Pct	GB	Per Game For	Opp
*San Antonio	58	24	.707	—	96.2	88.4
†Utah	53	29	.646	5	97.1	92.4
†Dallas	53	29	.646	5	100.5	96.2
†Minnesota	47	35	.573	11	97.3	96.0
Houston	45	37	.549	13	97.2	94.9
Denver	40	42	.488	18	96.6	99.0
Vancouver	23	59	.280	35	91.7	97.5

Head Coaches: SA—Gregg Popovich (5th season); **Utah**—Jerry Sloan (13th); **Dal**—Don Nelson (4th); **Min**—Phil Saunders (6th); **Hou**—Rudy Tomjanovich (10th); **Den**—Dan Issel (2nd); **Van**—Sidney Lowe (1st).

1999-00 Standings: 1. Utah (55-27); 2. San Antonio (53-29); 3. Minnesota (50-32); 4. Dallas (40-42); 5. Denver (35-47); 6. Houston (34-48); 7. Vancouver (22-60).

Pacific Division

	W	L	Pct	GB	Per Game For	Opp
*LA Lakers	56	26	.683	—	100.6	97.2
†Sacramento	55	27	.671	1	101.7	95.9
†Phoenix	51	31	.622	5	94.0	91.8
†Portland	50	32	.610	6	95.4	91.2
Seattle	44	38	.537	12	97.3	97.3
LA Clippers	31	51	.378	25	92.5	95.3
Golden St.	17	65	.207	39	92.5	101.5

Head Coaches: LAL—Phil Jackson (2nd season); **Sac**—Rick Adelman (3rd); **Pho**—Scott Skiles (2nd); **Port**—Mike Dunleavy (4th); **Sea**—Paul Westphal fired Nov. 27, 2000 (6-9) and replaced by Nate McMillan (38-29); **LAC**—Alvin Gentry (1st); **G. St.**—Dave Cowens (1st).

1999-2000 Standings: 1. LA Lakers (67-15); 2. Portland (59-23); 3. Phoenix (53-29); 4. Seattle (45-37); 5. Sacramento (44-38); 6. Golden St. (19-63); 7. LA Clippers (15-67).

Eastern Conference

Atlantic Division

	W	L	Pct	GB	Per Game For	Opp
*Philadelphia	56	26	.683	—	94.7	90.4
†Miami	50	32	.610	6	88.9	86.6
†New York	48	34	.585	8	88.7	86.1
†Orlando	43	39	.524	13	97.5	96.5
Boston	36	46	.439	20	94.6	96.8
New Jersey	26	56	.317	30	92.1	97.1
Washington	19	63	.232	37	93.2	99.9

Head Coaches: Phi—Larry Brown (4th season); **Mia**—Pat Riley (6th); **NY**—Jeff Van Gundy (6th); **Orl**—Doc Rivers (2nd); **Bos**—Rick Pitino (12-22) resigned Jan. 8, 2001 and was replaced by assistant Jim O'Brien (24-24); **NJ**—Don Casey (3rd); **Wash**—Leonard Hamilton (1st).

1999-2000 Standings: 1. Miami (52-30); 2. New York (50-32); 3. Philadelphia (49-33); 4. Orlando (41-41); 5. Boston (35-47); 6. New Jersey (31-51); 7. Washington (29-53).

Central Division

	W	L	Pct	GB	Per Game For	Opp
*Milwaukee	52	30	.634	—	100.7	96.9
†Toronto	47	35	.573	5	97.6	95.4
†Charlotte	46	36	.561	6	91.9	89.8
†Indiana	41	41	.500	11	92.6	92.8
Detroit	32	50	.390	20	95.6	97.3
Cleveland	30	52	.366	22	92.2	96.5
Atlanta	25	57	.305	27	91.0	96.2
Chicago	15	67	.183	37	87.6	96.7

Head Coaches: Mil—George Karl (3rd season); **Tor**—Lenny Wilkens (1st); **Char**—Paul Silas (3rd); **Ind**—Isiah Thomas (1st); **Det**—George Irvine (2nd); **Cle**—Randy Wittman (2nd); **Atl**—Lon Kruger (1st); **Chi**—Tim Floyd (3rd).

1999-2000 Standings: 1. Indiana (56-26); 2. Charlotte (49-33); 3. Toronto (45-37); 4. Detroit (42-40); 5. Milwaukee (42-40); 6. Cleveland (32-50); 7. Atlanta (28-54); 8. Chicago (17-65).

Overall Conference Standings

Sixteen teams—eight from each conference—qualify for the NBA Playoffs; (*) indicates division champions.

Western Conference

		W	L	Home	Away	Div	Conf
1	San Antonio*	58	24	33-8	25-16	19-5	39-13
2	LA Lakers*	56	26	31-10	25-16	14-10	34-18
3	Sacramento	55	27	33-8	22-19	16-8	35-19
4	Utah	53	29	28-13	25-16	14-10	31-21
5	Dallas	53	29	28-13	25-16	14-10	30-22
6	Phoenix	51	31	31-10	20-21	12-12	30-22
7	Portland	50	32	28-13	22-19	12-12	26-26
8	Minnesota	47	35	30-11	17-24	11-13	27-25
	Houston	45	37	24-17	21-20	11-13	20-32
	Seattle	44	38	26-15	18-23	17-7	27-25
	Denver	40	42	29-12	11-30	13-11	27-25
	LA Clippers	31	51	22-19	9-32	9-15	18-34
	Vancouver	23	59	15-26	8-33	2-22	11-41
	Golden St.	17	65	11-30	6-35	4-20	9-43

Eastern Conference

		W	L	Home	Away	Div	Conf
1	Philadelphia*	56	26	29-12	27-14	18-6	40-14
2	Milwaukee*	52	30	31-10	21-20	19-9	38-16
3	Miami	50	32	29-12	21-20	15-10	34-20
4	New York	48	34	30-11	18-23	16-9	32-22
5	Toronto	47	35	27-14	20-21	18-10	36-18
6	Charlotte	46	36	28-13	18-23	20-8	37-17
7	Orlando	43	39	26-15	17-24	14-10	30-24
8	Indiana	41	41	26-15	15-26	15-13	29-25
	Boston	36	46	20-21	16-25	11-13	24-30
	Detroit	32	50	18-23	14-27	16-12	25-29
	Cleveland	30	52	20-21	10-31	11-17	22-32
	New Jersey	26	56	18-23	8-33	8-16	16-38
	Atlanta	25	57	18-23	7-34	9-19	16-38
	Washington	19	63	12-29	7-34	3-21	13-41
	Chicago	15	67	10-31	5-36	4-24	13-41

2001 NBA All-Star Game
East, 111-110

50th NBA All-Star Game. **Date:** Feb. 11, at The MCI Center in Washington, D.C.; **Coaches:** Larry Brown, Philadelphia (East) and Rick Adelman, Sacramento (West); **MVP:** Allen Iverson, Philadelphia (25 points, 5 assists, 4 steals); Starters chosen by fan vote, (Toronto's Vince Carter was the leading vote-getter, receiving 1,717,687); bench chosen by conference coaches' vote.

Western Conference

Pos	Starters	Min	FG M-A	Pts	Reb	A
F	Tim Duncan, SA	28	5-11	14	14	1
F	Chris Webber, Sac	29	6-14	14	9	3
C	Kevin Garnett, Min.	27	7-12	14	4	4
G	Kobe Bryant, LAL	30	9-17	19	4	7
G	Jason Kidd, Pho	30	4-6	11	4	2
	Bench					
F	Michael Finley, Dal	19	5-15	12	3	5
G	Gary Payton, Sea	18	0-5	0	4	5
F	Rasheed Wallace, Por . .	21	1-7	2	4	2
C	David Robinson, SA . . .	10	3-5	8.	4	0
G	Antonio McDyess, Den . .	15	4-9	8	8	2
C	Vlade Divac, Sac	9	4-6	8	3	1
F	Karl Malone, Utah	4	0-2	0	1	0
	TOTALS	240	48-109	110	62	32

Three-Point FG: 4-11 (Kidd 3-4, Bryant 1-2, Webber 0-1, Wallace 0-1, Divac 0-1, Finley 0-2); **Free Throws:** 10-14 (Duncan 4-4, Finley 2-2, Webber 2-4, Robinson 2-4); **Percentages:** FG (.440), Three-Pt. FG (.364), Free Throws (.714); **Turnovers:** 19 (Kidd 5, Bryant 3, Duncan 2, Garnett 2, Wallace 2, Webber, Finley, Payton, Robinson, Divac); **Steals:** 16 (Kidd 5, Duncan 2, Payton 2, Divac 2, Webber, Garnett, Bryant, Wallace, McDyess); **Blocked Shots:** 4 (Garnett 3, Duncan); **Fouls:** 16 (Bryant 3, Kidd 3, Robinson 3, Webber 2, Payton 2, McDyess 2, Duncan); **Team Rebounds:** 6.

	1	2	3	4	F
West	30	31	28	21	—110
East	17	33	20	41	—111

Eastern Conference

Pos	Starters	Min	FG M-A	Pts	Reb	A
F	Vince Carter, Tor	24	7-18	16	3	4
F	Anthony Mason, Cha . .	20	0-3	0	4	1
C	Antonio Davis, Ind	20	4-11	8	9	0
G	Allen Iverson, Phi	27	9-21	25	2	5
G	Tracy McGrady, Orl . . .	21	1-4	2	1	0
	Bench					
G	Stephon Marbury, NJ . .	18	5-9	12	0	4
G	Ray Allen, Mil	19	7-15	15	3	2
F	Glenn Robinson, Mil . . .	18	4-7	8	4	1
G	Allan Houston, NY	15	2-5	5	3	3
G	Jerry Stackhouse, Det . .	15	3-8	7	2	2
F	Latrell Sprewell, NY	15	3-6	7	2	2
C	Dikembe Mutombo, Atl .	28	2-2	6	22	0
	TOTALS	240	47-109	111	54	26

Three-Point FG: 7-20 (Marbury 2-3, Iverson 1-1, Stackhouse 1-1, Houston 1-2, Carter 1-4, Allen 1-7, McGrady 0-1, Sprewell 0-1); **Free Throws:** 10-16 (Iverson 6-6, Mutombo 2-2, Carter 1-1, Sprewell 1-3, Marbury 0-2, Stackhouse 0-2); **Percentages:** FG (.431), Three-Pt. FG (.350), Free Throws (.625); **Turnovers:** 21 (Iverson 4, McGrady 4, Carter 3, Marbury 3, Mason 2, Mutombo 2, Allen, Houston, Sprewell); **Steals:** 13 (Iverson 4, McGrady 2, Mutombo 2, Carter, Mason, Davis, Allen, Robinson); **Blocked Shots:** 8 (Mutombo 3, Carter, Davis, McGrady, Allen, Robinson); **Fouls:** 12 (Mutombo 5, Mason 2, Marbury 2, Carter, Stackhouse, Sprewell); **Team Rebounds:** 11.

Halftime— West, 61-50; **Third Quarter—** West, 89-70; **Technical Fouls—** none; **Officials—** Dan Crawford, Don Vaden, Ed F. Rush; **Attendance—** 20,374; **Time—** 2:15; **TV Rating—** 5.1/8 share (NBC).

NBA 3-point Shootout

Eight players are invited to compete in the annual three-point shooting contest held during All-Star Weekend, since 1986. Each shooter has 60 seconds to shoot the 25 balls in five racks outside the three-point line. Each ball is worth one point, except the last ball in each rack, which is worth two. Highest scores advance. First prize: $25,000.

First Round	Pts
Ray Allen, Mil	20
Dirk Nowitzki, Dal	19
Predrag Stojakovic, Sac.	17

Failed to advance	Pts
Pat Garrity, Orl	15
Steve Nash, Dal	14
Rashard Lewis, Sea	12
Allan Houston, NY	11
Bryon Russell, Utah	10

Finals	Pts
Ray Allen	19
Predrag Stojakovic	17
Dirk Nowitzki	10

Slam Dunk Contest

Six players are invited to compete in the slam dunk contest based on "the creativity and artistry they have displayed in dunking" over the course of the season. In the first round, everyone attempts three dunks, one of which must involve a teammate. The dunks are judged by five judges on a scale from six to ten. The top three advance to the final round and attempt two dunks. The combined score of the two dunks determines the winner. First prize: $25,000.

First Round	Pts
DeShawn Stevenson, Utah.	95
Baron Davis, Cha	94
Desmond Mason, Sea	91
Jonathan Bender, Ind	90
Stromile Swift, Van	90
Corey Maggette, LAC	88

Finals	Pts
Desmond Mason	89
DeShawn Stevenson	85
Baron Davis	77

NBA/WNBA All-Star 2Ball

In 2Ball one NBA and one WNBA player, who compete on teams from the same city, are paired up in a competition in which they alternate taking shots from seven designated spots on the half court, accumulating points for every made basket. Each team has one minute to perform, and the point amounts differ according to each spot's distance away from the basket. First prize: $25,000. **Teams: Charlotte—**Dawn Staley and David Wesley; **Cleveland—**Eva Nemcova and Trajan Langdon; **Houston—**Sheryl Swoopes and Cuttino Mobley; **Orlando—**Nykesha Sales and Tracy McGrady; **Phoenix—** Brandy Reed and Jason Kidd; **Sacramento—**Ruthie Bolton-Holifield and Predrag Stojakovic; **Utah—**Natalie Williams and Byron Russell; **Washington—**Nikki McCray and Richard Hamilton. **Finals:** Sacramento def. Cleveland, 62-57.

Philadelphia 76ers
Allen Iverson
Scoring

Phoenix Suns
Jason Kidd
Assists & Triple Doubles

Philadelphia 76ers
Dikembe Mutombo
Rebounds

Atlanta Hawks
Theo Ratliff
Blocked Shots

NBA Regular Season Individual Leaders
Scoring
(*indicates rookie)

	Gm	Min	FG	FG%	3pt/Att	FT	FT%	Reb	Ast	Stl	Blk	Pts	Avg	Hi
Allen Iverson, Phi.	71	42.0	762	.420	98/306	585	.814	273	325	178	20	2207	**31.1**	54
Jerry Stackhouse, Det	80	40.2	774	.402	166/473	666	.822	315	410	97	54	2380	**29.8**	57
Shaquille O'Neal, LAL	74	39.5	813	.572	0/2	499	.513	940	277	47	204	2125	**28.7**	41
Kobe Bryant, LAL	68	31.0	701	.454	61/200	475	.853	399	338	114	43	1938	**28.5**	51
Vince Carter, Tor	75	38.0	862	.460	162/397	384	.765	416	291	114	82	2070	**27.6**	48
Chris Webber, Sac	70	40.5	786	.481	2/28	324	.703	777	294	93	118	1898	**27.1**	51
Tracy McGrady, Orl	77	40.1	788	.457	59/166	430	.733	580	352	116	118	2065	**26.8**	49
Paul Pierce, Bos	82	38.0	687	.454	147/384	550	.745	522	253	138	69	2071	**25.3**	44
Antawn Jamison, G. St.	82	41.4	800	.442	62/205	382	.715	715	164	114	28	2044	**24.9**	51
Stephon Marbury, NJ	67	38.2	563	.420	110/335	362	.790	205	506	79	5	1598	**23.9**	50
Antoine Walker, Bos	81	41.9	711	.413	221/603	249	.716	719	445	138	49	1892	**23.4**	47
Karl Malone, Utah	81	35.7	670	.498	2/5	536	.793	669	361	93	62	1878	**23.2**	41
Gary Payton, Sea	79	41.1	725	.456	102/272	271	.766	361	642	127	26	1824	**23.1**	44
Tim Duncan, SA.	82	38.7	702	.499	7/27	409	.618	997	245	70	192	1820	**22.2**	42
Glenn Robinson, Mil	76	37.0	684	.468	55/184	227	.820	526	252	86	62	1674	**22.0**	45
Kevin Garnett, Min	81	39.5	704	.477	19/66	357	.764	921	401	111	145	1784	**22.0**	40
Ray Allen, Mil	82	38.2	628	.480	202/467	348	.888	428	374	124	20	1806	**22.0**	43
Dirk Nowitzki, Dal	82	38.1	591	.474	151/390	451	.838	754	173	79	101	1784	**21.8**	38
Michael Finley, Dal	82	42.0	711	.458	91/263	252	.775	425	360	118	32	1765	**21.5**	38
Antonio McDyess, Den	70	36.5	577	.495	0/0	304	.700	845	146	43	102	1458	**20.8**	40
Shareef Abdur-Rahim, Van.	81	40.0	604	.472	12/64	443	.834	734	250	90	77	1663	**20.5**	38
Jalen Rose, Ind.	72	40.9	567	.457	59/174	285	.828	359	435	65	43	1478	**20.5**	42
Predrag Stojakovic, Sac.	75	38.7	559	.470	144/360	267	.853	434	164	91	13	1529	**20.4**	39
Elton Brand, Chi	74	39.3	578	.476	0/2	334	.708	746	240	71	118	1490	**20.1**	31
Jamal Mashburn, Cha	76	39.3	573	.413	103/289	279	.766	576	411	85	13	1528	**20.1**	33

Rebounds

	Gm	Off	Def	Tot	Avg
Dikembe Mutombo, Atl-Phi	75	4.1	9.4	1015	13.5
Ben Wallace, Det	80	3.8	9.4	1052	13.2
Shaquille O'Neal, LAL	74	3.9	8.8	940	12.7
Tim Duncan, SA.	82	3.2	9.0	997	12.2
Antonio McDyess, Den	70	3.4	8.6	845	12.1
Kevin Garnett, Min	81	2.7	8.7	921	11.4
Chris Webber, Sac	70	2.6	8.5	777	11.1
Shawn Marion, Pho	79	2.8	7.9	848	10.7
Antonio Davis, Tor.	78	3.5	6.6	787	10.1
Elton Brand, Chi	74	3.9	6.2	746	10.1
Jermaine O'Neal, Ind.	81	3.1	6.7	794	9.8
C. Weatherspoon, Cle	82	2.7	7.0	796	9.7
Anthony Mason, Mia	80	2.1	7.5	770	9.6
Charles Oakley, Tor	78	1.8	7.7	741	9.5
P.J. Brown, Cha	80	3.2	6.1	742	9.3

Assists

	Gm	Ast	Avg
Jason Kidd, Pho.	77	753	9.8
John Stockton, Utah	82	713	8.7
Nick Van Exel, Den.	71	600	8.5
Mike Bibby, Van.	82	685	8.4
Gary Payton, Sea	79	642	8.1
Andre Miller, Cle.	82	657	8.0
Mark Jackson, Tor-NY.	83	661	8.0
Sam Cassell, Mil	76	580	7.6
Stephon Marbury, NJ	67	506	7.6
Terrell Brandon, Min	78	583	7.5
Baron Davis, Cha	82	598	7.3
Steve Nash, Dal	70	509	7.3
Darrell Armstrong, Orl	74	524	7.0
Mookie Blaylock, G. St.	69	462	6.7
Steve Francis, Hou	80	517	6.5

Field Goal Pct.

	Gm	FG	Att	Pct
Shaquille O'Neal, LAL	.74	813	1422	.572
Bonzi Wells, Por	.75	387	726	.533
Marcus Camby, NY	.63	304	580	.524
Kurt Thomas, NY	.77	314	614	.511
Wally Szczerbiak, Min.	.82	469	920	.510
Darius Miles*, LAC	.81	318	630	.505
John Stockton, Utah	.82	328	651	.504
Donyell Marshall, Utah	.81	427	849	.503
Corliss Williamson, Tor-Det	.79	325	647	.502
Clarence Weatherspoon, Cle	.82	347	692	.501
Rasheed Wallace, Por	.77	590	1178	.501
Tim Duncan, SA	.82	702	1406	.499

Free Throw Pct.

	Gm	FT	Att	Pct
Reggie Miller, Ind	.81	323	348	.928
Allan Houston, NY	.78	279	307	.909
Doug Christie, Sac	.81	280	312	.897
Steve Nash, Dal	.70	231	258	.895
Mitch Richmond, Wash	.37	143	160	.894
Steve Smith, Por	.81	309	347	.890
Ray Allen, Mil	.82	348	392	.888
Darrell Armstrong, Orl	.75	220	249	.884
Eric Piatkowski, LAC	.81	158	181	.873
Terrell Brandon, Cle	.78	195	224	.871
Wally Szczerbiak, Min.	.72	181	208	.870
Richard Hamilton, Wash	.78	277	319	.868

3-Point Field Goal Pct.

	Gm	3FG	Att	Pct
Brent Barry, Sea	.67	109	229	.476
John Stockton, Utah	.82	61	132	.462
Shammond Williams, Sea	.69	61	133	.459
Hubert Davis, Dal-Wash.	.66	78	171	.456
Danny Ferry, SA	.80	70	156	.449
Toni Kukoc, Phi-Atl.	.65	70	157	.446
Pat Garrity, Orl	.76	97	224	.433
Rashard Lewis, Sea.	.78	123	285	.432
Dell Curry, Tor	.71	62	145	.428

High-Point Games

	Opp	Date	FG-FT—Pts
Jerry Stackhouse, Det	@ Chi	Apr. 3, 2001	21-11-57
Allen Iverson, Phi	@ Cle	Jan. 6, 2001	20-10-54
Tony Delk, Pho	@ Sac	Jan. 2, 2001	20-13-53
Allen Iverson, Phi	vs. Tor	Jan 21, 2001	20-7-51
Chris Webber, Sac	vs. Ind	Jan. 5, 2001	24-3-51
Kobe Bryant, LAL	@ G. St	Dec. 6, 2000	18-13-51
Antawn Jamison, G. St	@ Sea	Dec. 3, 2000	23-3-51
Antawn Jamison, G. St	vs. LAL	Dec. 6, 2000	21-7-51
Stephon Marbury, NJ	vs. LAL	Feb. 13, 2001	17-12-50
Allen Iverson, Phi	@ Mil	Feb. 13, 2001	17-12-49

Blocked Shots

	Gm	Blk	Avg
Theo Ratliff, Phi-Atl	.50	187	3.74
Jermaine O'Neal, Ind.	.81	228	2.81
Shawn Bradley, Dal	.82	228	2.78
Shaquille O'Neal, LAL	.74	204	2.76
Dikembe Mutombo, Atl-Phi	.75	203	2.71
Adonal Foyle, G. St	.58	156	2.69
Raef LaFrentz, Den	.78	206	2.64
David Robinson, SA	.80	197	2.46
Tim Duncan, SA.	.82	192	2.34
Ben Wallace, Det	.80	186	2.33

Steals

	Gm	Stl	Avg
Allen Iverson, Phi.	.71	178	2.51
Mookie Blaylock, G. St.	.69	163	2.36
Doug Christie, Sac	.81	183	2.26
Jason Kidd, Pho.	.77	166	2.16
Baron Davis, Cha	.82	170	2.07
Terrell Brandon, Min.	.78	161	2.06
Ron Artest, Chi	.76	152	2.00
Darrell Armstrong, Orl	.75	135	1.80
Steve Francis, Hou	.80	141	1.76
Antoine Walker, Bos.	.81	138	1.70

Rookie Leaders

Scoring

	Gm	FG	FT	Pts	Avg
Marc Jackson, G. St.	.48	237	154	633	13.2
Kenyon Martin, NJ	.68	346	121	814	12.0
Mike Miller, Orl.	.82	368	91	975	11.9
Courtney Alexander, Wash.	.65	239	123	618	9.5
Marcus Fizer, Chi	.72	278	117	683	9.5

Field Goal Pct.

	Gm	FG	Att	Pct
Darius Miles, LAC	.81	318	630	.505
Marc Jackson, G. St.	.48	237	508	.467
Stromile Swift, Van	.80	153	339	.451
Kenyon Martin, NJ	.68	346	777	.445
Chris Mihm, Cle	.59	173	391	.442

Rebounds

	Gm	Off	Def	Tot	Avg
Marc Jackson, G. St.	.48	119	242	361	7.5
Kenyon Martin, NJ	.68	137	365	502	7.4
Darius Miles, LAC	.81	127	350	477	5.9
Chris Mihm, Cle	.59	106	174	280	4.7
Marcus Fizer, Chi	.72	76	237	313	4.3

Assists

	Gm	No	Avg
Mateen Cleaves, Det	.78	207	2.7
Keyon Dooling, LAC	.76	177	2.3
Jamal Crawford, Chi	.61	141	2.3
Kenyon Martin, NJ	.68	131	1.9
Stephen Jackson, NJ	.77	140	1.8

Personal Fouls

Aaron Williams, NJ	.319
Brian Grant, Mia	.293
Juwan Howard, Dal	.292
Raef LaFrentz, Den	.290
LaPhonso Ellis, Min	.290
Kurt Thomas, NY	.287

Triple Doubles

Jason Kidd, Pho	.7
Antoine Walker, Bos	.5
Lamar Odom, LAC	.4
Seven tied with 2 each.	

Disqualifications

Rasheed Wallace, Por	.7
Jermaine O'Neal, Ind	.3
Bonzi Wells, Por	.3
Chris Gatling, Cle	.3
Nick Van Exel, Den	.3
Bimbo Coles, Cle	.3

Minutes Played

Michael Finley, Dal.	.3443
Antoine Walker, Bos.	.3396
Antawn Jamison, G. St.	.3394
Anthony Mason, Mia	.3254
Gary Payton, Sea	.3244

Turnovers

Jerry Stackhouse, Det	.326
Antoine Walker, Bos	.301
Jason Kidd, Pho	.286
Steve Francis, Hou	.265
Andre Miller, Cle	.265

Technical Fouls

Rasheed Wallace, Por	.40
Steve Francis, Hou	.23
Karl Malone, Utah	.21
Chris Gatling, Cle	.19
Allen Iverson, Phi	.18
Shawn Bradley, Dal	.18

Team by Team Statistics

Players who competed for more than one team during the regular season are listed with their final club; (*) indicates rookies.

Atlanta Hawks

	Gm	FG%	Tpts	PPG	RPG	APG
Jason Terry	82	.436	1619	19.7	3.3	4.9
Theo Ratliff	50	.499	621	12.4	8.3	1.2
Toni Kukoc	65	.473	721	11.1	4.0	3.1
Alan Henderson	73	.444	769	10.5	5.6	0.7
Nazr Mohammed	58	.477	441	7.6	5.3	0.3
Chris Crawford	47	.452	318	6.8	2.3	0.8
Matt Maloney	55	.420	369	6.7	2.1	2.8
Brevin Knight	53	.375	333	6.3	3.2	5.9
Dion Glover	57	.420	338	5.9	2.3	1.2
Larry Robinson	34	.364	199	5.9	2.6	1.1
DerMarr Johnson*	78	.374	397	5.1	2.3	0.8
Hanno Mottola*	73	.444	319	4.4	2.4	0.3
Cal Bowdler	44	.465	140	3.2	1.8	0.1
Tony Smith	6	.348	17	2.8	0.5	1.7
Ira Bowman	3	.000	0	0.0	0.7	2.3
Andy Panko*	1	.000	0	0.0	0.0	0.0

Triple Doubles: Kukoc (2). **3-pt FG leader:** Terry (124).
Steals leader: Terry (104). **Blocks leader:** Lorenzen Wright (63).
Signed: G Smith (Jan. 25), F Panko (Jan. 5), G Bowman (Feb. 16), G Robinson (Feb. 15).
Traded: G Jim Jackson, G Larry Robinson, G Anthony Johnson to Cleveland for G Knight (Jan. 2); C Dikembe Mutombo and F Roshown McLeod to Philadelphia for C Ratliff, F Kukoc, C Mohammed and G Pepe Sanchez (Feb. 22).

Boston Celtics

	Gm	FG%	Tpts	PPG	RPG	APG
Paul Pierce	82	.454	2071	25.3	6.4	3.1
Antoine Walker	81	.413	1892	23.4	8.9	5.5
Bryant Stith	78	.401	756	9.7	3.6	2.2
Kenny Anderson	33	.388	246	7.5	2.2	4.1
Vitaly Potapenko	82	.476	611	7.5	6.0	0.8
Eric Williams	81	.362	535	6.6	2.6	1.4
Tony Battie	40	.537	260	6.5	5.8	0.4
Milt Palacio	58	.472	342	3.9	1.8	2.6
Chris Carr	35	.473	169	4.8	1.3	0.3
Randy Brown	54	.422	223	4.1	1.8	2.9
Mark Blount*	64	.505	248	3.9	3.6	0.5
Chris Herren	25	.302	83	3.3	0.8	2.2
Walter McCarty	60	.357	131	2.2	1.4	0.6
Adrian Griffin	44	.340	93	2.1	2.0	0.6
Jerome Moiso*	24	.400	35	1.5	1.8	0.1

Triple Doubles: Walker (5). **3-pt FG leader:** Walker (221).
Steals leaders: Pierce & Walker (138). **Blocks leader:** Blount (76).
Signed G Palacio (Dec. 6).

Charlotte Hornets

	Gm	FG%	Tpts	PPG	RPG	APG
Jamal Mashburn	76	.413	1528	20.1	7.6	5.4
David Wesley	82	.422	1414	17.2	2.7	4.4
Baron Davis	82	.427	1131	13.8	5.0	7.3
Elden Campbell	78	.440	1022	13.1	7.8	1.3
P.J. Brown	80	.444	676	8.5	9.3	1.6
Derrick Coleman	34	.380	277	8.1	5.4	1.1
Eddie Robinson	67	.532	498	7.4	3.0	0.9
Jamaal Magloire*	74	.450	339	4.6	4.0	0.4
Scott Burrell	4	.467	17	4.3	0.8	0.2
Lee Nailon*	42	.485	164	3.9	2.2	0.6
Hersey Hawkins	59	.409	183	3.1	1.4	1.2
Otis Thorpe	49	.450	138	2.8	3.0	0.6
Eldridge Recasner	43	.333	103	2.4	1.2	0.9
Tim James	30	.308	45	1.5	1.2	0.3
Terrance Roberson	3	.000	0	0.0	0.3	0.3

Triple Doubles: Davis (2). **3-pt FG leader:** Mashburn (103).
Steals leader: Davis (170). **Blocks leader:** Campbell (140).
Signed: G-F Burrell (Apr. 10).

Chicago Bulls

	Gm	FG%	Tpts	PPG	RPG	APG
Elton Brand	74	.476	1490	20.1	10.1	3.2
Ron Mercer	61	.446	1202	19.7	3.9	3.3
Ron Artest	76	.401	907	11.9	3.9	3.0
Marcus Fizer*	72	.430	683	9.5	4.3	1.1
Fred Hoiberg	74	.438	673	9.1	4.2	3.6
Brad Miller	57	.435	505	8.9	7.4	1.9
Bryce Drew	48	.379	302	6.3	1.4	3.9
Khalid El-Amin	50	.370	314	6.3	1.6	2.9
A.J. Guyton*	33	.406	198	6.0	1.1	1.9
Corey Benjamin	65	.381	307	4.7	1.5	1.1
Jamal Crawford*	61	.352	282	4.6	1.5	2.3
Michael Ruffin	45	.444	119	2.6	5.8	0.9
Dragan Tarlac	43	.394	103	2.4	2.8	0.7
Jake Voskuhl*	16	.440	30	1.9	2.1	0.3
Steve Goodrich	12	.389	19	1.6	1.8	0.5
Dalibor Bagaric*	35	.262	47	1.3	1.6	0.3

Triple Doubles: None. **3-pt FG leader:** Hoiberg (103).
Steals leader: Artest (152). **Blocks leader:** Brand (118).
Signed: F Goodrich (Mar. 28).

Cleveland Cavaliers

	Gm	FG%	Tpts	PPG	RPG	APG
Andre Miller	82	.452	1296	15.8	4.4	8.0
Lamond Murray	78	.423	998	12.8	4.4	1.6
Zydrunas Ilgauskas	24	.487	281	11.7	6.7	0.8
Jim Jackson	56	.378	643	11.5	4.0	2.9
Chris Gatling	74	.449	842	11.4	5.3	0.8
Clarence Weatherspoon	82	.501	924	11.3	9.7	1.3
Matt Harpring	56	.454	623	11.1	4.3	1.8
Chris Mihm*	59	.442	446	7.6	4.7	0.3
Wesley Person	44	.438	314	7.1	3.0	1.5
Irajan Langdon	65	.431	389	6.0	1.4	1.2
Robert Traylor	70	.497	402	5.7	4.3	0.9
Bimbo Coles	47	.381	232	4.9	1.0	2.9
Cedric Henderson	55	.389	235	4.3	1.6	1.4
Chucky Brown	26	.421	102	3.9	2.1	0.4
Anthony Johnson	53	.349	130	2.5	0.8	1.5
J.R. Reid	6	.400	10	1.7	1.3	0.2
Etdrick Bohannon	6	.500	8	1.3	1.2	0.0
Michael Hawkins	10	.333	8	0.8	0.5	1.3

Triple Doubles: None. **3-pt FG leader:** Murray (61).
Steals leader: Miller (119). **Blocks leader:** Weatherspoon (105).
Signed: F Brown (Jan. 29), F Bohannon (Jan. 18).
Traded: G Brevin Knight to Atlanta for G Jackson, G Johnson and G Larry Robinson (Jan. 2).

Individual Single Game Highs
Most Field Goals Made

24 . . . . Chris Webber, Sac. vs Ind. (1/5)

Most Field Goals Attempted

47 . . . . Chris Webber, Sac. vs Ind. (1/5)

Most Assists	Most Rebounds
22 . . . . George McCloud, Den. at Chi. (3/26)	29 . . Dikembe Mutombo, Atl. vs. Tor. (1/31)

Dallas Mavericks

	Gm	FG%	Tpts	PPG	RPG	APG
Dirk Nowitzki	82	.474	1784	21.8	9.2	2.1
Michael Finley	82	.458	1765	21.5	5.2	4.4
Juwan Howard	81	.479	1462	18.0	7.1	2.8
Steve Nash	70	.487	1092	15.6	3.2	7.3
Howard Eisley	82	.393	741	9.0	2.4	3.6
Calvin Booth	55	.476	293	5.3	4.5	0.8
Shawn Bradley	82	.490	579	7.1	7.4	0.5
Greg Buckner	37	.438	229	6.2	4.2	1.3
Zhizhi Wang*	5	.421	24	4.8	1.4	0.0
Vernon Maxwell	43	.327	201	4.7	1.5	1.1
Gary Trent	33	.438	133	4.0	2.8	0.3
Eduardo Najera*	40	.523	131	3.3	2.4	0.7
Obinna Ekezie	33	.395	101	3.1	2.4	0.3
Donnell Harvey*	18	.571	22	1.2	1.1	0.1
Mark Bryant	18	.400	19	1.1	1.2	0.2

Triple Doubles: Finley (1). **3-pt FG leader:** Nowitzki (151).
Steals leader: Finley (118). **Blocks leader:** Bradley (228).
Signed: F Bryant (Nov. 28), G Maxwell (Feb. 28), C Zhizhi (Apr. 4).
Traded: F Christian Laettner, F Loy Vaught, F Etan Thomas, G Hubert Davis, G Courtney Alexander and cash to Washington for F Howard, C Booth, and C Ekezie (Feb. 22).

Denver Nuggets

	Gm	FG%	Tpts	PPG	RPG	APG
Antonio McDyess	70	.495	1458	20.8	12.1	2.1
Nick Van Exel	71	.414	1259	17.7	3.4	8.5
Raef LaFrentz	78	.477	1008	12.9	7.8	1.4
Voshon Leonard	80	.397	972	12.2	2.9	2.4
Kevin Willis	78	.441	722	9.3	6.8	0.6
George McCloud	76	.382	729	9.6	2.9	3.7
James Posey	82	.412	666	8.1	5.3	2.0
Robert Pack	74	.425	479	6.5	1.9	4.0
Anthony Goldwire	20	.375	82	4.1	0.6	1.7
Tariq Abdul-Wahad	29	.387	111	3.8	2.0	0.8
Ryan Bowen	57	.556	191	3.4	2.0	0.5
Dan McClintock*	6	.500	18	3.0	2.8	0.2
Calbert Chaney	9	.333	21	2.3	2.2	1.0
Terry Davis	19	.480	33	1.7	2.8	0.4
Garth Joseph	4	.200	2	0.5	0.5	0.2

Triple Doubles: Pack (1). **3-pt FG leader:** Leonard (147).
Steals leader: Posey (93). **Blocks leader:** LaFrentz (206).
Signed: G Goldwire (Feb. 19), C McClintock (Apr. 4).
Traded: F-C Keon Clark, F Tracy Murray and C Mamadou N'diaye to Toronto for F-C Willis, C Aleksandar Radojevic, C Joseph and a 2nd rd. draft choice in 2001 or 2002 (Jan. 12).

Detroit Pistons

	Gm	FG%	Tpts	PPG	RPG	APG
Jerry Stackhouse	80	.402	2380	29.8	3.9	5.1
Corliss Williamson	69	.502	801	11.6	4.7	0.9
Joe Smith	69	.403	847	12.3	7.1	1.1
Chucky Atkins	81	.399	971	12.0	2.1	4.1
Dana Barros	60	.444	478	8.0	1.6	1.8
Ben Wallace	80	.490	511	6.4	13.1	1.5
Mateen Cleaves*	78	.400	422	5.4	1.7	2.7
Michael Curry	68	.455	356	5.2	1.8	1.9
Mikki Moore	81	.493	359	4.4	3.9	0.4
Billy Owens	45	.383	198	4.4	4.6	1.2
Jud Buechler	57	.463	193	3.4	1.6	0.7
Kornel David	27	.490	62	2.3	1.9	0.3
Brian Cardinal*	15	.323	31	2.1	1.5	0.2

Triple Doubles: Stackhouse (1). **3-pt FG leader:** Stackhouse (166).
Steals leader: Wallace (107). **Blocks leader:** Wallace (186).
Signed: F Smith (Nov. 20). **Traded:** F Jerome Williams and C Eric Montross to Toronto for F Williamson, F Tyrone Corbin and F David (Feb. 22).

Golden St. Warriors

	Gm	FG%	Tpts	PPG	RPG	APG
Antawn Jamison	82	.442	2044	24.9	8.7	2.0
Danny Fortson	6	.580	100	16.7	16.3	0.8
Larry Hughes	50	.383	823	16.5	5.5	4.5
Marc Jackson	48	.467	633	13.2	7.5	1.2
Chris Mills	15	.372	180	12.0	6.2	1.2
Bob Sura	53	.390	586	11.1	4.3	4.6
Mookie Blaylock	69	.396	760	11.0	3.9	6.7
Chris Porter*	51	.389	440	8.6	3.7	1.2
Erick Dampier	43	.401	319	7.4	5.8	1.4
Vonteego Cummings	66	.344	483	7.3	2.1	3.4
Adonal Foyle	58	.416	342	5.9	7.0	0.8
Chris Mullin	20	.340	115	5.8	2.0	0.9
Paul McPherson*	55	.505	262	4.8	1.4	0.7
Corie Blount	68	.442	313	4.6	5.9	0.9
Bill Curley	20	.532	63	3.2	1.9	0.2
Adam Keefe	67	.403	168	2.5	3.1	0.5
Chris Garner	8	.189	19	2.4	1.5	2.2
Ruben Garces	13	.318	16	1.2	2.2	0.4
John Coker	6	.125	2	0.3	0.8	0.3
Randy Livingston	2	.000	0	0.0	0.5	0.5

Triple Doubles: Blaylock (1). **3-pt FG leader:** Jamison (62).
Steals leader: Blaylock (163). **Blocks leader:** Foyle (156).
Signed: G Livingston (Nov. 15), F Curley (Dec. 1), C Coker (Jan. 8), G Garner (Apr. 16).
Traded: G Vinny Del Negro to Phoenix for F Blount, F Garces, and G McPherson (Jan. 26).

Houston Rockets

	Gm	FG%	Tpts	PPG	RPG	APG
Steve Francis	80	.451	1591	19.9	6.9	6.5
Cuttino Mobley	79	.434	1538	19.5	5.0	2.5
Maurice Taylor	69	.489	899	13.0	5.5	1.5
Hakeem Olajuwon	58	.498	689	11.9	7.4	1.2
Shandon Anderson	82	.446	710	8.7	4.1	2.3
Walt Williams	72	.394	599	8.3	3.4	1.3
Kenny Thomas	74	.443	528	7.1	5.6	1.0
Moochie Norris	82	.446	544	6.6	2.4	3.5
Matt Bullard	61	.423	354	5.8	2.1	0.7
Kelvin Cato	35	.577	165	4.7	4.0	0.3
Carlos Rogers	39	.682	179	4.6	3.6	0.2
Jason Collier	23	.380	71	3.1	1.6	0.3
Dan Langhi*	33	.374	90	2.7	1.2	0.1
Sean Colson*	13	.250	15	1.2	0.5	0.8

Triple Doubles: Francis (2). **3-pt FG leader:** Francis (133).
Steals leader: Francis (141). **Blocks leader:** Olajuwon (88).
Signed: F-C Anthony Miller (Dec. 8), G Colson (Feb. 28).

Indiana Pacers

	Gm	FG%	Tpts	PPG	RPG	APG
Jalen Rose	72	.457	1478	20.5	5.0	6.0
Reggie Miller	81	.440	1527	18.9	3.5	3.2
Jermaine O'Neal	81	.465	1041	12.9	9.8	1.2
Travis Best	77	.440	918	11.9	2.9	6.1
Austin Croshere	81	.394	822	10.1	4.8	1.1
Al Harrington	78	.444	586	7.5	4.9	1.7
Tyus Edney	24	.385	106	4.4	4.1	2.2
Zan Tabak	55	.527	216	3.9	3.9	0.6
Bruno Sundov	11	.488	43	3.9	2.1	0.2
Sam Perkins	64	.381	242	3.8	2.6	0.6
Jeff Foster	71	.469	249	3.5	5.5	0.5
Jonathan Bender	59	.355	193	3.3	1.3	0.5
Derrick McKey	66	.441	145	2.2	2.7	1.1
Terry Mills	14	.324	25	1.8	1.5	0.4
Lari Ketner	3	.000	0	0.0	0.0	0.0

Triple Doubles: None. **3-pt FG leader:** Miller (170).
Steals leader: Best (110). **Blocks leader:** O'Neal (228).

Los Angeles Clippers

	Gm	FG%	Tpts	PPG	RPG	APG
Lamar Odom 76		.460	1304	17.2	7.8	5.2
Jeff McInnis 81		.463	1046	12.9	2.7	5.5
Eric Piatkowski......81		.433	860	10.6	3.0	1.2
Corey Maggette 69		.462	690	10.0	4.2	1.2
Darius Miles* 81		.505	761	9.4	5.9	1.2
Michael Olowokandi .82		.435	701	8.5	6.4	0.6
Quentin Richardson* .76		.442	613	8.1	3.4	0.8
Earl Boykins 10		.397	65	6.5	1.1	3.2
Keyon Dooling* 76		.409	449	5.9	1.2	2.3
Sean Rooks 82		.428	446	5.4	3.7	0.9
Cherokee Parks......65		.489	299	4.6	3.5	0.7
Derek Strong 28		.385	118	4.2	3.9	0.2
Brian Skinner 39		.398	160	4.1	4.3	0.5
Zendon Hamilton*....3		.222	9	3.0	2.7	0.0

Triple Doubles: Odom (4), McInnis (1). **3-pt FG leader:** Piatkowski (120).
Steals leader: McInnis (75). **Blocks leader:** Miles (125).
Traded: F Tyrone Nesby to Washington for F-C Parks and F Obinna Ekezie (Nov. 28).

Los Angeles Lakers

	Gm	FG%	Tpts	PPG	RPG	APG
Shaquille O'Neal 74		.572	2125	28.7	12.7	3.7
Kobe Bryant.........68		.464	1938	28.5	5.9	5.0
Derek Fisher 20		.412	229	11.5	3.0	4.3
Rick Fox 82		.444	787	9.6	4.0	3.2
Horace Grant 77		.462	657	8.5	7.1	1.6
Isaiah Rider 67		.426	507	7.6	2.3	1.7
Ron Harper 47		.469	307	6.5	3.5	2.4
Brian Shaw 80		.399	421	5.3	3.8	3.2
Robert Horry 79		.387	407	5.2	3.7	1.6
Mike Penberthy 53		.414	267	5.0	1.2	1.3
Stanislav Medvedenko .7		.480	32	4.6	1.3	0.3
Tyronn Lue 38		.427	130	3.4	0.8	1.2
Devean George 59		.309	182	3.1	1.9	0.3
Mark Madsen* 70		.487	137	2.0	2.2	0.3
Greg Foster 62		.421	125	2.0	1.8	0.5

Triple Doubles: Bryant (2). **3-pt FG leader:** Fox (118).
Steals leader: Bryant (114). **Blocks leader:** O'Neal (204).

Miami Heat

	Gm	FG%	Tpts	PPG	RPG	APG
Eddie Jones 63		.445	1094	17.4	4.6	2.7
Anthony Mason 80		.482	1290	16.1	9.6	3.1
Brian Grant 82		.479	1250	15.2	8.8	1.2
Tim Hardaway.......77		.392	1150	14.9	2.6	6.3
Alonzo Mourning 13		.518	147	13.6	7.8	0.9
Bruce Bowen 82		.363	623	7.6	3.0	1.6
Cedric Ceballos 40		.441	261	6.5	2.7	0.5
Anthony Carter 72		.406	461	6.4	2.5	3.7
Dan Majerle 53		.336	267	5.0	3.1	1.7
Eddie House* 50		.421	251	5.0	0.8	1.0
Ricky Davis..........7		.414	32	4.6	1.0	1.6
A.C. Green 82		.444	367	4.5	3.8	0.5
Don MacLean 8		.500	31	3.9	2.2	0.5
Todd Fuller 10		.286	28	2.8	1.8	0.1
Duane Causwell 31		.376	76	2.5	2.7	0.2
Jamal Robinson 6		.136	6	1.0	1.8	0.3

Triple Doubles: None. **3-pt FG leader:** Hardaway (189).
Steals leader: Jones (110). **Blocks leader:** Grant (71).

Milwaukee Bucks

	Gm	FG%	Tpts	PPG	RPG	APG
Ray Allen 82		.480	1806	22.0	5.2	4.6
Glenn Robinson 76		.468	1674	22.0	6.9	3.3
Sam Cassell 76		.474	1381	18.2	3.8	7.6
Tim Thomas 76		.430	954	12.6	4.1	1.8
Lindsey Hunter 82		.381	825	10.1	2.1	2.7
Jason Caffey 70		.488	500	7.1	5.0	0.8
Scott Williams 66		.474	403	6.1	5.5	0.5
Darvin Ham 29		.488	109	3.8	4.2	0.9
Jerome Kersey 22		.464	72	3.3	2.0	0.7
Ervin Johnson 82		.545	266	3.2	7.5	0.5
Mark Pope 63		.437	151	2.4	2.3	0.6
Michael Redd* 6		.263	13	2.2	.07	0.2
Rafer Alston 31		.357	77	2.1	.08	1.8
Jason Hart* 1		1.000	2	2.0	0.0	1.0
Joel Przybilla* 33		.343	27	0.8	2.2	0.1

Triple Doubles: Allen (1). **3-pt FG leader:** Allen (202).
Steals leader: Allen (124). **Blocks leader:** Johnson (97).

Minnesota Timberwolves

	Gm	FG%	Tpts	PPG	RPG	APG
Kevin Garnett........81		.477	1784	22.0	11.4	5.0
Terrell Brandon 78		.451	1250	16.0	3.8	7.5
Wally Szczerbiak 82		.510	1145	14.0	5.5	3.2
Anthony Peeler 75		.421	791	10.5	2.6	2.6
LaPhonso Ellis 82		.464	772	9.4	6.0	1.1
Chauncey Billups 77		.422	713	9.3	2.1	3.4
Felipe Lopez.........70		.441	550	7.9	3.3	1.5
Reggie Slater 55		.514	254	4.6	3.4	0.5
Radoslav Nesterovic .73		.461	328	4.5	3.9	0.6
Todd Day 31		.373	132	4.3	1.2	0.9
Sam Mitchell 82		.408	285	3.5	1.5	0.7
William Avery 55		.382	154	2.8	0.5	1.4
Dean Garrett 70		.481	177	2.5	3.1	0.3
Sam Jacobson 14		.500	20	1.4	0.4	0.3
Tom Hammonds.......7		.300	7	1.0	0.6	0.1

Triple Doubles: Brandon & Garnett (1). **3-pt FG leader:** Peeler (100).
Steals leader: Brandon (161). **Blocks leader:** Garnett (145).
Signed: G Lopez (Feb. 28).

New Jersey Nets

	Gm	FG%	Tpts	PPG	RPG	APG
Stephon Marbury 67		.441	1598	23.9	3.1	7.6
Keith Van Horn 49		.435	831	17.0	7.1	1.7
Kenyon Martin* 68		.445	814	12.0	7.4	1.9
Johnny Newman 82		.419	895	10.9	2.1	1.4
Aaron Williams 82		.457	838	10.2	7.2	1.1
Lucious Harris 73		.425	683	9.4	3.9	1.8
Kendall Gill 31		.331	283	9.1	4.2	2.8
Stephen Jackson*....77		.425	635	8.2	2.7	1.8
Doug Overton 21		.374	125	6.0	1.9	3.4
Mark Strickland 55		.431	252	4.6	2.9	0.4
Sherman Douglas ...59		.403	338	5.7	1.3	2.4
Eddie Gill* 8		.390	39	4.9	1.1	3.0
Jamie Feick...........6		.348	22	3.7	9.3	0.8
Evan Eschmeyer 74		.460	251	3.4	4.9	0.5
Vladimir Stepania ...29		.318	82	2.8	3.8	0.6
Jamel Thomas.........5		.316	13	2.6	1.8	0.0
Jim McIlvaine 18		.357	28	1.6	1.9	0.2
Soumaila Samake*...34		.375	46	1.4	1.6	0.0

Triple Doubles: Marbury & Martin (1). **3-pt FG leader:** Marbury (110).
Steals leader: Marbury (79). **Blocks leaders:** Martin & Williams (113).
Signed: C Stepania (Dec. 15), G Overton (Mar. 22), F Strickland (Mar. 28), G Gill (Mar. 29), F Thomas (Apr. 6).

New York Knicks

	Gm	FG%	Tpts	PPG	RPG	APG
Allan Houston	78	.449	1459	18.7	3.6	2.2
Latrell Sprewell	77	.430	1364	17.7	4.5	3.5
Marcus Camby	63	.524	759	12.0	11.5	0.8
Glen Rice	75	.440	899	12.0	4.1	1.2
Kurt Thomas	77	.511	800	10.4	6.7	0.8
Larry Johnson	65	.411	645	9.9	5.6	2.0
Charlie Ward	61	.416	433	7.1	2.6	4.5
Othella Harrington	74	.487	665	9.0	5.2	0.8
Mark Jackson	83	.419	631	7.6	3.7	8.0
Lavor Postell*	26	.315	59	2.3	1.0	0.2
Felton Spencer	18	.600	39	2.2	1.9	0.1
Luc Longley	25	.333	49	2.0	2.6	0.3
Rick Brunson	22	.333	21	0.9	1.0	1.4
Travis Knight	45	.189	29	0.6	1.2	0.1
Muggsy Bogues	3	.000	0	0.0	1.0	1.7

Triple Doubles: Jackson (1). **3-pt FG leader:** Houston (96).
Steals leader: Sprewell (106). **Blocks leader:** Camby (136).
Claimed: G Brunson off waivers (Nov. 27). **Traded:** G Erick Strickland, the 2001 1st rd. draft pick acquired from LAL and NY's 2001 2nd rd. draft pick to Vancouver for F Harrington (Jan. 30); G Chris Childs and 2001 1st rd. draft pick to Toronto for G Jackson and G Bogues (Feb. 22).

Orlando Magic

	Gm	FG%	Tpts	PPG	RPG	APG
Tracy McGrady	77	.457	2065	26.8	7.5	4.6
Darrell Armstrong	75	.412	1189	15.9	4.6	7.0
Grant Hill	4	.442	55	13.8	6.2	6.2
Mike Miller*	82	.436	975	11.9	4.0	1.7
Pat Garrity	76	.387	628	8.3	2.8	0.7
John Amaechi	82	.400	650	7.9	3.3	0.9
Bo Outlaw	80	.614	582	7.3	7.7	2.8
Dee Brown	7	.364	48	6.9	1.6	1.7
Michael Doleac	77	.417	490	6.4	3.5	0.8
Monty Williams	82	.445	410	5.0	3.0	1.0
Troy Hudson	75	.336	357	4.8	1.4	2.2
Andrew DeClercq	67	.554	261	3.9	3.5	0.5
Don Reid	64	.566	210	3.3	3.8	0.3
Cory Alexander	26	.321	52	2.0	1.0	1.4
James Robinson	6	.364	10	1.7	1.3	0.0

Triple Doubles: None. **3-pt FG leader:** Miller (148).
Steals leader: Armstrong (135). **Blocks leader:** Outlaw (137).
Signed: G Alexander (Jan. 29), G Robinson (Jan. 18).

Philadelphia 76ers

	Gm	FG%	Tpts	PPG	RPG	APG
Allen Iverson	71	.420	2207	31.1	3.8	4.6
Aaron McKie	76	.473	878	11.6	4.1	5.0
Dikembe Mutombo	75	.494	749	10.0	13.5	1.4
Eric Snow	50	.418	491	9.8	3.3	7.4
Roshown McLeod	35	.437	337	9.6	3.4	1.7
Tyrone Hill	76	.474	728	9.6	9.0	0.6
George Lynch	82	.445	686	8.4	7.2	1.7
Matt Geiger	35	.393	213	6.1	4.0	0.4
Rodney Buford	47	.432	248	5.3	1.6	0.4
Jumaine Jones	65	.444	304	4.7	2.9	0.5
Todd MacCulloch	63	.589	260	4.1	2.7	0.2
Kevin Ollie	70	.396	216	3.1	1.4	2.1
Raja Bell*	5	.286	5	1.0	0.2	0.0
Pepe Sanchez	29	.321	20	0.7	0.5	1.4
Anthony Miller	4	.500	2	0.5	0.0	0.0

Triple Doubles: McKie (2). **3-pt FG leader:** Iverson (98).
Steals leader: Iverson (178). **Blocks leader:** Mutombo (203).
Signed: G-F Buford (Dec. 23), G Ollie (Dec. 22), G Bell (Apr. 6), F Miller (Mar. 15), G Sanchez (Mar. 15). **Traded:** C Theo Ratliff, F Toni Kukoc, C Nazr Mohammed and G Pepe Sanchez to Atlanta for C Mutombo and F McLeod (Feb. 22).

Phoenix Suns

	Gm	FG%	Tpts	PPG	RPG	APG
Shawn Marion	79	.480	1369	17.3	10.7	2.0
Jason Kidd	77	.411	1299	16.9	6.4	9.8
Cliff Robinson	82	.422	1345	16.4	4.1	2.9
Tony Delk	82	.415	1005	12.3	3.2	2.0
Rodney Rogers	82	.430	998	12.2	4.4	2.2
Anfernee Hardaway	4	.417	39	9.8	4.5	3.8
Tom Gugliotta	57	.392	362	6.4	4.5	1.0
Iakovos Tsakalidis*	57	.470	256	4.5	4.2	0.3
Mario Elie	68	.423	299	4.4	2.3	1.9
Vinny Del Negro	65	.453	254	3.9	1.3	1.9
Daniel Santiago*	54	.478	170	3.1	1.9	0.2
Elliot Perry	49	.464	147	3.0	0.9	1.6
Chris Dudley	53	.397	72	1.4	3.5	0.3

Triple Doubles: Kidd (7), Hardaway (1). **3-pt FG leader:** Robinson (90).
Steals leader: Kidd (166). **Blocks leader:** Marion (108).
Signed: G Perry (Dec. 8). **Traded:** F Corie Blount, F Ruben Garces and G Paul McPherson to Golden State for G Del Negro (Jan. 26).

Portland Trailblazers

	Gm	FG%	Tpts	PPG	RPG	APG
Rasheed Wallace	77	.501	1477	19.2	7.8	2.8
Steve Smith	81	.456	1105	13.6	3.4	2.6
Damon Stoudamire	82	.434	1066	13.0	3.7	5.7
Bonzi Wells	75	.533	950	12.7	4.9	2.8
Scottie Pippen	64	.451	721	11.3	5.2	4.6
Arvydas Sabonis	61	.479	616	10.1	5.4	1.4
Rod Strickland	54	.424	498	9.2	2.6	5.6
Dale Davis	81	.498	580	7.2	7.5	1.3
Shawn Kemp	68	.407	441	6.5	3.8	1.0
Greg Anthony	58	.383	284	4.9	1.1	1.4
Stacey Augmon	66	.477	311	4.7	2.4	1.5
Detlef Schrempf	26	.411	104	4.0	3.0	1.7
Antonio Harvey	12	.464	31	2.6	1.2	0.3
Gary Grant	4	.714	10	2.5	0.0	0.2
Erick Barkley*	8	.364	19	2.4	0.4	0.8
Will Perdue	13	.667	14	1.1	1.4	0.2

Triple Doubles: Stoudamire (1). **3-pt FG leader:** Stoudamire (82).
Steals leader: Stoudamire (106). **Blocks leader:** Wallace (135). **Signed:** G Strickland (Mar. 5).

Sacramento Kings

	Gm	FG%	Tpts	PPG	RPG	APG
Chris Webber	70	.481	1898	27.1	11.1	4.2
Predrag Stjakovic	75	.470	1529	20.4	5.8	2.2
Doug Christie	81	.395	996	12.3	4.4	3.6
Vlade Divac	81	.482	974	12.0	8.3	2.9
Jason Williams	77	.407	720	9.4	2.4	5.4
Bobby Jackson	79	.439	566	7.2	3.1	2.0
Scot Pollard	77	.468	498	6.5	6.0	0.6
Hidayet Turkoglu*	74	.412	391	5.3	2.8	0.9
Jon Barry	62	.404	316	5.1	1.5	2.1
Lawrence Funderburke	59	.496	288	4.9	3.3	0.3
Darrick Martin	31	.382	103	3.3	0.5	0.5
Jabari Smith	9	.500	26	2.9	0.9	0.7
Nick Anderson	21	.246	38	1.8	1.2	0.6
Art Long*	9	.000	0	0.0	0.9	0.1

Triple Doubles: Webber (1). **3-pt FG leader:** Stojakovic (144).
Steals leader: Christie (183). **Blocks leader:** Webber (118).
Signed: F. Long (Feb. 27).

San Antonio Spurs

	Gm	FG%	Tpts	PPG	RPG	APG
Tim Duncan	82	.499	1820	22.2	12.2	3.0
Derek Anderson	82	.416	1269	15.5	4.4	3.7
David Robinson	80	.486	1151	14.4	8.6	1.5
Antonio Daniels	79	.468	745	9.4	2.1	3.8
Sean Elliott	52	.434	409	7.9	3.3	1.6
Malik Rose	57	.435	437	7.7	5.4	0.8
Terry Porter	80	.448	573	7.2	2.5	3.1
Avery Johnson	55	.447	310	5.6	1.5	4.3
Danny Ferry	80	.475	448	5.6	2.8	0.9
Samaki Walker	61	.480	321	5.3	4.0	0.5
Steve Kerr	55	.421	181	3.3	0.6	1.0
Derrick Dial	33	.434	86	2.6	1.2	0.6
Jaren Jackson	16	.400	39	2.4	0.8	0.4
Ira Newble*	27	.382	54	2.0	1.3	0.2
Shawnelle Scott	27	.415	43	1.6	1.9	0.1

Triple Doubles: Duncan (1). **3-pt FG leader:** Anderson (101). **Steals leader:** Anderson (120). **Blocks leader:** Robinson (197).

Seattle Supersonics

	Gm	FG%	Tpts	PPG	RPG	APG
Gary Payton	79	.456	1823	23.1	4.6	8.1
Rashard Lewis	78	.480	1151	14.8	6.9	1.6
Ruben Patterson	76	.494	988	13.0	5.0	2.1
Vin Baker	76	.422	927	12.2	5.7	1.2
Patrick Ewing	79	.430	760	9.6	7.4	1.2
Brent Barry	67	.494	589	8.8	3.1	3.4
Shammond Williams	69	.438	467	6.8	1.9	2.8
David Wingate	1	1.000	6	6.0	0.0	2.0
Desmond Mason*	78	.431	463	5.9	3.2	0.8
Emanuel Davis	62	.418	361	5.8	2.5	2.2
Jelani McCoy	70	.523	317	4.5	3.6	0.8
Ruben Wolkowyski*	34	.316	75	2.2	1.4	0.1
Olumide Oyedeji*	30	.486	45	1.5	2.2	0.1
Pervis Ellison	9	.286	6	0.7	1.3	0.3

Triple Doubles: Payton (2). **3-pt FG leader:** Lewis (123). **Steals leader:** Payton (127). **Blocks leader:** Ewing (91).

Toronto Raptors

	Gm	FG%	Tpts	PPG	RPG	APG
Vince Carter	75	.460	2070	27.6	5.5	3.9
Antonio Davis	78	.433	1069	13.7	10.1	1.4
Alvin Williams	82	.430	802	9.8	2.6	5.0
Charles Oakley	78	.388	748	9.6	9.5	3.4
Morris Peterson*	80	.431	747	9.3	3.2	1.3
Keon Clark	81	.480	640	7.9	5.4	0.9
Dell Curry	71	.424	429	6.0	1.2	1.1
Tracy Murray	51	.379	257	5.0	1.6	0.5
Jerome Williams	59	.463	372	6.3	6.5	0.8
Chris Childs	77	.403	362	4.7	2.6	4.6
Eric Montross	54	.406	120	2.2	3.2	0.4
Michael Stewart	26	.324	33	1.3	1.1	0.1
Tyrone Corbin	15	.237	20	1.3	0.9	0.3
Mamadou N'diaye*	3	.250	4	1.3	0.7	0.0

Triple Doubles: Oakley & A. Williams (1). **3-pt FG leader:** Carter (162). **Steals leader:** A. Williams (123). **Blocks leader:** Davis (151).
Traded: F-C Kevin Willis, C Aleksandar Radojevic, C Garth Joseph and a 2nd. rd. draft pick in 2001 or 2002 to Denver for F-C Clark, F Murray and C N'diaye (Jan. 12); F Corliss Williamson, F Tyrone Corbin, and F Kornel David to Detroit for F Williams and C Montross (Feb. 22); G Mark Jackson and G Muggsy Bogues to NY for G Childs and a 2001 1st-rd. draft pick (Feb. 22).

Utah Jazz

	Gm	FG%	Tpts	PPG	RPG	APG
Karl Malone	81	.498	1878	23.2	8.3	4.5
Donyell Marshall	81	.503	1100	13.6	7.0	1.6
Bryon Russell	78	.440	933	12.0	4.2	2.1
John Stockton	82	.504	944	11.5	2.8	8.7
John Starks	75	.398	699	9.3	2.1	2.4
Danny Manning	82	.494	603	7.4	2.6	1.1
Jacque Vaughn	82	.433	498	6.1	1.8	3.9
Olden Polynice	81	.496	429	5.3	4.7	0.4
Greg Ostertag	81	.495	363	4.5	5.1	0.3
David Benoit	49	.483	178	3.6	1.7	0.4
Quincy Lewis	35	.407	124	3.5	1.3	0.5
DeShawn Stevenson*	40	.341	89	2.2	0.7	0.4
John Crotty	31	.338	65	2.1	0.9	1.1
Scott Padgett	27	.419	56	2.1	1.4	0.2

Triple Doubles: None. **3-pt FG leader:** Russell (95). **Steals leader:** Stockton (132). **Blocks leader:** Ostertag (142).

Vancouver Grizzlies

	Gm	FG%	Tpts	PPG	RPG	APG
Shareef Abdur-Rahim	81	.472	1663	20.5	9.1	3.1
Michael Dickerson	70	.417	1142	16.3	3.3	3.3
Mike Bibby	82	.454	1301	15.9	3.7	8.4
Bryant Reeves	75	.460	622	8.3	6.0	1.1
Damon Jones	71	.409	461	6.5	1.7	3.2
Mahmoud Abdul-Rauf	41	.488	266	6.5	0.6	1.9
Grant Long	66	.439	396	6.0	4.2	1.3
Erick Strickland	50	.303	260	5.2	2.6	1.9
Stromile Swift*	80	.451	391	4.9	3.5	0.3
Tony Massenberg	52	.462	233	4.5	4.0	0.2
Isaac Austin	52	.356	226	4.3	4.3	1.1
Kevin Edwards	46	.329	160	3.5	1.8	1.1
Brent Price	6	.273	13	2.2	0.7	0.8
Doug West	15	.289	28	1.9	1.0	0.9

Triple Doubles: None. **3-pt FG leader:** Bibby (108). **Steals leader:** Bibby (107). **Blocks leader:** Swift (82).
Traded: F Othella Harrington to New York for G Strickland, the 2001 1st rd. pick acquired from LAL and NY's 2001 2nd rd. pick (Jan. 30).

Washington Wizards

	Gm	FG%	Tpts	PPG	RPG	APG
Richard Hamilton	78	.438	1411	18.1	3.1	2.9
Mitch Richmond	37	.407	598	16.2	2.9	3.0
Christian Laettner	78	.503	728	9.3	4.7	1.6
Courtney Alexander*	65	.417	618	9.5	2.2	1.0
Chris Whitney	59	.387	558	9.5	1.8	4.2
Jahidi White	68	.498	583	8.6	7.6	0.3
Tyrone Nesby	62	.357	512	8.3	2.8	1.2
Hubert Davis	66	.453	524	7.9	2.1	1.7
David Vanterpool*	22	.418	122	5.5	1.7	3.0
Gerald King	45	.511	216	4.8	2.9	0.7
Laron Profit	35	.394	152	4.3	1.8	2.5
Loy Vaught	51	.473	168	3.3	3.4	0.5
Michael Smith	79	.486	301	3.8	7.1	1.3
Popeye Jones	45	.392	162	3.6	4.9	0.7
Mike Smith*	17	.322	51	3.0	1.3	0.6

Triple Doubles: None. **3-pt FG leader:** Whitney (93). **Steals leader:** Hamilton (75). **Blocks leader:** White (111). **Signed:** G Vanterpool (Mar. 5). **Claimed:** F Obinna Ekezie (Dec. 1).
Traded: F Juwan Howard, C Calvin Booth and C Obinna Ekezie to Dallas for F Laettner, F Vaught, F Etan Thomas, G Davis, G Alexander and cash (Feb. 22).

NBA Regular Season Team Leaders
Offense

WEST	Pts	Reb	Ast	FGM-FGA	FG%	3PM-3PA	3Pt%	FTM-FTA	FT%	OFF-DEF	TRB	TO	BLKS
Sacramento	101.7	45.0	22.6	3132-6969	.449	479-1353	.354	1600-2075	.771	987-2705	3734	1178	432
LA Lakers	100.6	44.7	23.0	3109-6685	.465	439-1275	.344	1594-2333	.683	1085-2583	3668	1137	490
Dallas	100.5	41.5	21.2	3085-6716	.459	517-1357	.381	1552-1954	.794	831-2571	3402	1094	492
Minnesota	97.3	42.3	25.4	3148-6871	.458	322-901	.357	1364-1737	.785	1002-2470	3472	1105	456
Seattle	97.3	41.7	21.9	3029-6649	.456	466-1169	.399	1454-1986	.732	999-2422	3421	1201	409
Houston	97.2	42.0	19.7	2943-6494	.453	504-1412	.357	1582-2086	.758	919-2524	3443	1136	358
Utah	97.1	40.6	25.7	2960-6289	.471	325-825	.381	1714-2280	.752	943-2383	3326	1251	463
Denver	96.6	44.2	24.0	2979-6877	.433	512-1444	.355	1448-1964	.737	1004-2583	3627	1136	538
San Antonio	96.2	44.1	21.7	2884-6262	.461	445-1094	.407	1673-2340	.715	902-2712	3614	1145	576
Portland	95.4	42.0	23.9	3004-6416	.468	369-1057	.349	1447-1899	.762	959-2481	3440	1257	419
Phoenix	94.0	42.7	23.2	2944-6757	.436	332-1054	.315	1490-1973	.755	970-2529	3499	1250	429
Golden State	92.5	45.5	21.8	2937-7175	.409	282-964	.293	1428-2024	.706	1345-2385	3730	1253	410
LA Clippers	92.5	42.9	19.3	2896-6467	.448	360-1063	.339	1429-2061	.693	962-2559	3521	1212	513
Vancouver	91.7	40.5	23.2	2870-6539	.439	325-947	.343	1457-1892	.770	894-2431	3325	1237	359

EAST	Pts	Reb	Ast	FGM-FGA	FG%	3PM-3PA	3Pt%	FTM-FTA	FT%	ORB-DRB	TRB	TO	BLKS
Milwaukee	100.7	42.4	22.5	3112-6798	.449	562-1481	.354	1474-1874	.771	975-2500	3475	1082	386
Toronto	97.6	44.5	24.4	3048-6972	.437	429-1164	.369	1482-1984	.747	1118-2529	3647	1043	519
Orlando	97.5	42.9	22.0	3013-6873	.438	490-1346	.364	1476-2068	.714	1069-2450	3519	1216	481
Detroit	95.6	45.5	19.9	2919-6880	.424	389-1112	.350	1610-2233	.721	1108-2626	3734	1265	447
Philadelphia	94.7	44.8	20.6	2902-6487	.447	262-803	.326	1697-2277	.745	1075-2600	3675	1231	408
Boston	94.6	39.8	20.8	2773-6485	.428	592-1633	.363	1621-2190	.740	897-2367	3264	1238	336
Washington	93.2	41.3	20.1	2833-6453	.439	275-848	.324	1704-2245	.759	1016-2370	3386	1321	383
Indiana	92.6	42.9	21.5	2828-6431	.440	396-1159	.342	1539-2009	.766	921-2595	3516	1173	487
Cleveland	92.2	42.1	20.8	2890-6532	.442	220-659	.334	1561-2040	.765	1015-2440	3455	1297	436
New Jersey	92.1	39.6	19.5	2781-6550	.425	361-1084	.333	1629-2146	.759	909-2337	3246	1139	407
Charlotte	91.9	44.4	23.2	2800-6501	.431	340-984	.346	1599-2146	.745	1033-2608	3641	1124	455
Atlanta	91.0	42.9	19.0	2876-6668	.431	333-933	.357	1374-1811	.759	1029-2489	3518	1292	387
Miami	88.9	39.6	19.9	2694-6258	.430	478-1384	.345	1423-1874	.759	813-2435	3248	1076	304
New York	88.7	40.2	18.5	2755-6198	.444	391-1115	.351	1374-1727	.796	773-2524	3297	1132	346
Chicago	87.6	38.9	22.1	2721-6411	.424	329-950	.346	1410-1909	.739	926-2260	3186	1197	379

Defense

WEST	Pts	Reb	Ast	FGM-FGA	FG%	3PM-3PA	3Pt%	FTM-FTA	FT%	OFF-DEF	TRB	TO	BLKS
San Antonio	88.1	41.5	19.7	2837-6770	.419	343-1043	.329	1233-1664	.741	967-2432	3399	1060	426
Portland	91.2	38.8	21.3	2819-6436	.438	406-1103	.368	1436-1930	.744	946-2238	3184	1169	324
Phoenix	91.8	42.6	20.2	2792-6422	.435	327-937	.349	1618-2127	.761	902-2588	3490	1383	416
Utah	92.4	37.3	19.1	2667-6076	.439	410-1194	.343	1830-2391	.765	875-2182	3057	1269	453
Houston	94.9	41.6	21.2	3020-6733	.449	359-1015	.354	1385-1862	.744	988-2420	3408	1055	400
LA Clippers	95.3	42.4	21.8	2995-6800	.441	354-1075	.329	1474-1983	.743	1041-2439	3480	996	412
Sacramento	95.9	45.9	22.1	3087-7139	.432	401-1131	.355	1291-1724	.749	1121-2643	3764	1277	476
Minnesota	96.0	42.3	22.4	2977-6588	.452	350-996	.351	1567-2164	.724	967-2505	3472	1181	357
Dallas	96.2	45.0	21.7	2938-6693	.439	381-1140	.334	1631-2231	.731	1068-2623	3691	1211	379
Vancouver	97.5	43.7	23.6	3143-6791	.463	389-1075	.362	1317-1798	.732	1052-2534	3586	1190	476
LA Lakers	97.2	41.3	20.2	2983-6815	.438	413-1168	.354	1595-2114	.754	981-2407	3388	1021	324
Seattle	97.3	42.4	23.9	3076-6783	.453	471-1351	.349	1353-1824	.742	1046-2431	3477	1171	510
Denver	99.0	44.6	24.9	3081-6914	.446	416-1168	.356	1542-2049	.753	1012-2642	3654	1040	497
Golden State	101.5	45.5	24.9	3179-6740	.472	439-1159	.379	1529-2011	.760	1039-2693	3732	1303	493

EAST	Pts	Reb	Ast	FGM-FGA	FG%	3PM-3PA	3Pt%	FTM-FTA	FT%	OFF-DEF	TRB	TO	BLKS
New York	86.1	40.1	19.2	2568-6159	.417	445-1266	.352	1478-2015	.733	872-2418	3290	1147	338
Miami	86.6	42.0	17.3	2701-6261	.431	360-1087	.331	1339-1818	.737	914-2528	3442	1208	424
Charlotte	89.8	40.6	21.3	2767-6501	.426	389-1081	.360	1444-1910	.756	892-2436	3328	1145	375
Philadelphia	90.4	40.9	21.6	2871-6699	.429	427-1248	.342	1243-1660	.749	985-2366	3351	1216	458
Indiana	92.8	43.1	20.7	2829-6683	.423	377-1121	.336	1572-2074	.758	1042-2495	3537	1071	387
Toronto	95.4	41.9	20.7	3009-6725	.447	379-1045	.363	1425-1890	.754	926-2511	3437	1095	439
Atlanta	96.2	43.5	21.2	2922-6609	.442	396-1080	.367	1646-2153	.765	1029-2534	3563	1159	513
Cleveland	96.5	41.3	22.9	2927-6582	.445	422-1155	.365	1633-2125	.768	990-2400	3390	1174	542
Orlando	96.5	44.8	21.9	2830-6499	.435	366-1059	.346	1885-2566	.735	1061-2609	3670	1325	440
Chicago	96.7	42.8	23.6	2987-6330	.472	346-973	.356	1607-2202	.730	957-2551	3508	1176	426
Boston	96.8	43.1	23.0	2935-6392	.459	430-1170	.368	1634-2178	.750	888-2650	3538	1325	440
Milwaukee	96.9	42.7	23.0	2912-6626	.439	439-1246	.352	1679-2186	.768	1014-2490	3504	1216	350
New Jersey	97.1	44.2	22.4	2937-6452	.455	428-1189	.360	1664-2231	.746	1001-2622	3623	1258	522
Detroit	97.3	44.0	22.7	2976-6850	.434	428-1229	.348	1596-2169	.736	1012-2671	3683	1219	397
Washington	99.9	40.7	23.2	3100-6596	.470	433-1093	.396	1559-2088	.747	931-2410	3341	1181	511

2001 NBA PLAYOFFS

| 1ST ROUND | SEMIFINALS | FINAL | | FINAL | SEMIFINALS | 1ST ROUND |

(1) Philadelphia 3
(8) Indiana 1 — *(1) Philadelphia 4*
(4) New York 2 — *(1) Philadelphia 4*
(5) Toronto 3 — *(5) Toronto 3*

EASTERN CONFERENCE
(2) LA Lakers 4
(1) Philadelphia 1

(3) Miami 0
(6) Charlotte 3 — *(6) Charlotte 3*
(2) Milwaukee 3 — *(2) Milwaukee 3*
(7) Orlando 1 — *(2) Milwaukee 4*

(1) San Antonio 0

WESTERN CONFERENCE
(2) LA Lakers 4

(1) San Antonio 3
(8) Minnesota 1 — *(1) San Antonio 4*
(4) Utah 2 — *(5) Dallas 1*
(5) Dallas 3 — *(5) Dallas 3*

(3) Sacramento 0
(3) Sacramento 3
(6) Phoenix 1 — *(3) Sacramento 3*
(2) LA Lakers 4
(2) LA Lakers 3
(7) Portland 0 — *(2) LA Lakers 4*

Series Summaries

WESTERN CONFERENCE

FIRST ROUND (Best of 5)

	W-L	Avg.	Leading Scorer
Portland	0-3	89.0	Stoudamire (17.7)
LA Lakers	3-0	103.7	O'Neal (27.0)

Date	Winner	Home Court
Apr. 22	Lakers, 106-93	at Los Angeles
Apr. 26	Lakers, 106-88	at Los Angeles
Apr. 29	Lakers, 99-86	at Portland

	W-L	Avg.	Leading Scorer
Dallas	3-2	93.8	Finley & Nowitzki (23.8)
Utah	2-3	89.6	Malone (27.6)

Date	Winner	Home Court
Apr. 21	Jazz, 88-86	at Utah
Apr. 24	Jazz, 109-98	at Utah
Apr. 28	Mavericks, 94-91	at Dallas
May 1	Mavericks, 107-77	at Dallas
May 3	Mavericks, 84-83	at Utah

	W-L	Avg.	Leading Scorer
Minnesota	1-3	82.0	Garnett (21.0)
San Antonio	3-1	88.5	Duncan (22.5)

Date	Winner	Home Court
Apr. 21	Spurs, 87-82	at San Antonio
Apr. 23	Spurs, 86-69	at San Antonio
Apr. 28	Timberwolves, 93-84	at Timberwolves
Apr. 30	Spurs, 97-84	at San Antonio

	W-L	Avg.	Leading Scorer
Phoenix	1-3	88.5	Robinson (15.0)
Sacramento	3-1	98.0	Stojakovic (23.3)

Date	Winner	Home Court
Apr. 22	Suns, 86-83	at Sacramento
Apr. 25	Kings, 116-90	at Sacramento
Apr. 29	Kings, 102-96	at Phoenix
May 2	Kings, 89-82	at Phoenix

SEMIFINALS (Best of 7)

	W-L	Avg.	Leading Scorer
Sacramento	0-4	97.3	Webber (26.3)
LA Lakers	4-0	106.5	Bryant (35.0)

Date	Winner	Home Court
May 6	Lakers, 108-105	at Los Angeles
May 8	Lakers, 96-90	at Los Angeles
May 11	Lakers, 103-81	at Sacramento
May 13	Lakers, 119-113	at Sacramento

	W-L	Avg.	Leading Scorer
Dallas	1-4	90.6	Nowitzki (23.0)
San Antonio	4-1	102.2	Duncan (27.0)

Date	Winner	Home Court
May 5	Spurs, 94-78	at San Antonio
May 7	Spurs, 100-86	at San Antonio
May 9	Spurs, 104-90	at Dallas
May 12	Mavericks, 112-108	at Dallas
May 14	Spurs, 105-87	at San Antonio

CHAMPIONSHIP (Best of 7)

	W-L	Avg.	Leading Scorer
San Antonio	0-4	81.3	Duncan (23.0)
LA Lakers	4-0	103.5	Bryant (33.3)

Date	Winner	Home Court
May 19	Lakers, 104-90	at Los Angeles
May 21	Lakers, 88-81	at Los Angeles
May 25	Lakers, 111-72	at San Antonio
May 27	Lakers, 111-82	at San Antonio

EASTERN CONFERENCE

FIRST ROUND (Best of 5)

	W-L	Avg.	Leading Scorer
Indiana	1-3	87.3	Miller (31.3)
Philadelphia	3-1	93.5	Iverson (31.5)

Date	Winner	Home Court
Apr. 21	Pacers, 79-78	at Philadelphia
Apr. 24	76ers, 116-98	at Philadelphia
Apr. 28	76ers, 92-87	at Indiana
May 2	76ers, 88-85	at Indiana

	W-L	Avg.	Leading Scorer
Orlando	1-3	102.8	McGrady (33.8)
Milwaukee	3-1	108.5	Allen (24.5)

Date	Winner	Home Court
Apr. 22	Bucks, 103-90	at Milwaukee
Apr. 25	Bucks, 103-96	at Milwaukee
Apr. 28	Magic, 121-116 (OT)	at Orlando
May 1	Bucks, 112-104	at Orlando

	W-L	Avg.	Leading Scorer
Charlotte	3-0	100.7	Mashburn (23.7)
Miami	0-3	78.3	Jones (19.0)

Date	Winner	Home Court
Apr. 21	Hornets, 106-80	at Miami
Apr. 23	Hornets, 102-76	at Miami
Apr. 27	Hornets, 94-79	at Charlotte

	W-L	Avg.	Leading Scorer
Toronto	3-2	92.2	Carter (22.8)
New York	2-3	89.0	Houston (20.8)

Date	Winner	Home Court
Apr. 22	Knicks, 92-85	at New York
Apr. 26	Raptors, 94-74	at New York
Apr. 29	Knicks, 97-89	at Toronto
May 2	Raptors, 100-93	at Toronto
May 4	Raptors, 93-89	at New York

SEMIFINALS (Best of 7)

	W-L	Avg.	Leading Scorer
Toronto	3-4	92.1	Carter (30.4)
Philadelphia	4-3	92.9	Iverson (33.7)

Date	Winner	Home Court
May 6	Raptors, 96-93	at Philadelphia
May 9	76ers, 97-92	at Philadelphia
May 11	Raptors, 102-78	at Toronto
May 13	76ers, 84-79	at Toronto
May 16	76ers, 121-88	at Philadelphia
May 18	Raptors, 101-89	at Toronto
May 20	76ers, 88-87	at Philadelphia

	W-L	Avg.	Leading Scorer
Charlotte	3-4	93.6	Mashburn (25.4)
Milwaukee	4-3	94.1	Allen (23.4)

Date	Winner	Home Court
May 6	Bucks, 104-94	at Milwaukee
May 8	Bucks, 91-90	at Milwaukee
May 10	Hornets, 102-92	at Charlotte
May 13	Hornets, 85-78	at Charlotte
May 15	Hornets, 94-86	at Milwaukee
May 17	Bucks, 104-97	at Charlotte
May 20	Bucks, 104-95	at Milwaukee

CHAMPIONSHIP (Best of 7)

	W-L	Avg.	Leading Scorer
Milwaukee	3-4	89.9	Allen (27.1)
Philadelphia	4-3	90.1	Iverson (30.5)

Date	Winner	Home Court
May 22	76ers, 93-85	at Philadelphia
May 24	Bucks, 92-78	at Philadelphia
May 26	Bucks, 80-74	at Milwaukee
May 28	76ers, 89-83	at Milwaukee
May 30	76ers, 89-88	at Philadelphia
June 1	Bucks, 110-100	at Milwaukee
June 3	76ers, 108-91	at Philadelphia

NBA FINALS (Best of 7)

	W-L	Avg.	Leading Scorer
Philadelphia	1-4	93.8	Iverson (35.6)
LA Lakers	4-1	100.6	O'Neal (33.0)

Date	Winner	Home Court
June 6	76ers, 107-101 (OT)	at Los Angeles
June 8	Lakers, 98-89	at Los Angeles
June 10	Lakers, 96-91	at Philadelphia
June 13	Lakers, 100-86	at Philadelphia
June 15	Lakers, 108-96	at Philadelphia

Most Valuable Player
Shaquille O'Neal, Lakers, C
33.0 points, 15.8 rebounds, 3.4 blocks

Final Playoff Standings
(Ranked by victories)

	Gm	W	L	Pct	Per Game For	Opp
LA Lakers	16	15	1	.938	103.4	90.6
Philadelphia	23	12	11	.522	92.3	92.4
Milwaukee	18	10	8	.555	95.7	94.3
San Antonio	13	7	6	.538	91.5	91.9
Charlotte	10	6	4	.600	95.7	89.4
Toronto	12	6	6	.500	92.2	91.3
Dallas	10	4	6	.400	92.2	95.9
Sacramento	8	3	5	.375	97.6	97.5
New York	5	2	3	.400	89.0	92.2
Utah	5	2	3	.400	89.6	93.8
Indiana	4	1	3	.250	87.3	93.5
Orlando	4	1	3	.250	102.8	108.5
Minnesota	4	1	3	.250	82.0	88.5
Phoenix	4	1	3	.250	88.5	98.0
Portland	3	0	3	.000	89.0	103.7
Miami	3	0	3	.000	78.3	100.7

Off-Season Coaching Changes in 2001

Team	Old Coach	Why left?	New Coach	Old Job
Cleveland	Randy Wittman	Fired	John Lucas	Asst., Denver
Detroit	George Irvine	Fired	Rick Carlisle	Asst., Pacers
Portland	Mike Dunleavy	Fired	Maurice Cheeks	Asst., 76ers
Washington	Leonard Hamilton	Resigned	Doug Collins	TV analyst

NBA Finals Box Scores

Game 1

Date: June 6, 2001; **Attendance:** 18,997; **Time:** 3:00;
Officials: Dick Bavetta, Ron Garretson, Joe Crawford.

	1	2	3	4	OT	F
Philadelphia	22	34	23	15	13	—107
LA Lakers	23	27	27	17	7	—101

		FG	FT		Reb		
Philadelphia	Min	M-A	M-A	Pts	O-T	A	PF
Tyrone Hill	40	1-6	2-2	4	1-6	0	3
Jumaine Jones	11	2-3	0-0	4	0-0	0	1
Dikembe Mutombo	44	4-7	5-7	13	5-16	0	5
Allen Iverson	52	18-41	9-9	48	2-5	6	0
Aaron McKie	51	3-7	2-2	9	2-7	9	1
Eric Snow	31	5-10	3-3	13	0-4	5	2
Raja Bell	19	2-2	2-2	6	1-4	1	2
Kevin Ollie	1	0-0	0-0	0	0-0	0	0
Matt Geiger	14	5-7	0-0	10	0-0	0	5
Todd MacCulloch	2	0-0	0-0	0	0-0	0	1
TOTALS	265	40-83	23-25	107	11-42	21	21

Three-point FG: 4–11 (Jones 0–1, Iverson. 3–8, McKie 1–1, Snow 0–1); **Team Rebounds:** 7; **Blocked Shots:** 8 (Mutombo 5, Hill, McKie, Jones); **Turnovers:** 18 (McKie 5, Snow 5, Iverson 3, Hill 3, Geiger, Bell); **Steals:** 10 (Iverson 5, McKie 2, Bell 2, Geiger); **Percentages:** Total FG (.482), 3-Pt FG (.364), Free Throws (.920) **Technicals:** 2 (Snow, Head Coach Larry Brown).

		FG	FT		Reb		
LA Lakers	Min	M-A	M-A	Pts	O-T	A	PF
Rick Fox	44	7-12	2-2	19	1-7	5	3
Horace Grant	27	3-11	2-2	8	4-5	0	1
Shaquille O'Neal	52	17-28	10-22	44	6-20	5	3
Kobe Bryant	52	7-22	1-1	15	0-3	5	4
Derek Fisher	23	0-4	0-0	0	0-0	1	3
Brian Shaw	18	3-5	0-0	7	2-4	3	1
Robert Horry	27	1-5	0-0	3	3-4	1	5
Tyronn Lue	22	2-3	0-0	5	0-1	3	2
TOTALS	265	40-90	15-27	101	16-44	23	22

Three-point FG: 6–13 (Fox 3–6, Fisher 0–1, Shaw 1–2, Horry 1–3, Lue 1–1); **Team Rebounds:** 14; **Blocked Shots:** 9 (Bryant 3, Horry 2, Grant 2, Fox, Lue) **Turnovers:** 19 (Bryant 6, Fox 4, O'Neal 4, Grant 2, Shaw, Horry, Lue); **Steals:** 14 (Lue 5, Fox 2, Horry 2, Grant, O'Neal, Bryant, Fisher, Shaw); **Percentages:** Total FG (.444), 3-Pt FG (.462), Free Throws (.556); **Technicals:** 2 (Fox, Head Coach Phil Jackson).

Game 2

Date: June 8, 2001; **Attendance:** 18,997; **Time:** 2:39;
Officials: Bernie Fryer, Ronnie Nunn, Steve Javie.

	1	2	3	4	F
Philadelphia	24	23	20	22	—89
LA Lakers	25	24	28	21	—98

		FG	FT		Reb		
Philadelphia	Min	M-A	M-A	Pts	O-T	A	PF
Tyrone Hill	22	1-3	0-0	2	1-5	0	5
Jumaine Jones	15	1-2	0-0	3	0-3	0	1
Dikembe Mutombo	36	5-12	6-6	16	4-13	1	3
Allen Iverson	47	10-29	0-4	23	0-4	3	3
Aaron McKie	40	6-17	0-2	14	4-6	6	3
Eric Snow	28	4-9	4-4	12	1-2	4	1
Matt Geiger	13	2-4	0-0	4	1-2	0	1
Todd MacCulloch	16	5-9	3-4	13	3-5	0	3
Raja Bell	18	0-1	2-6	2	0-2	1	3
Rodney Buford	1	0-0	0-0	0	0-0	0	0
Kevin Ollie	4	0-1	0-0	0	0-0	1	0
TOTALS	240	34-87	15-26	89	14-42	16	28

Three-point FG: 6–15 (Jones 1–1, Iverson 3–10, McKie 2–4); **Team Rebounds:** 11; **Blocked Shots:** 5 (Hill 3, Mutombo, Jones); **Turnovers:** 11 (Iverson 3, Snow 3, McKie 2, Mutombo, MacCulloch, Bell); **Steals:** 8 (Iverson 3, Snow 2, Mutombo, Iverson); **Percentages:** Total FG (.391), 3-Pt FG (.400), Free Throws (.557); **Technical:** 1 (Iverson).

		FG	FT		Reb		
LA Lakers	Min	M-A	M-A	Pts	O-T	A	PF
Rick Fox	28	0-4	0-0	0	1-6	2	4
Horace Grant	18	2-7	2-2	6	2-5	2	0
Shaquille O'Neal	45	12-19	4-10	28	8-20	9	5
Kobe Bryant	47	11-23	8-8	31	1-8	6	4
Derek Fisher	34	5-11	2-2	14	0-0	3	4
Brian Shaw	25	1-7	1-2	4	0-5	5	3
Robert Horry	26	4-6	0-0	8	3-7	1	3
Tyronn Lue	10	1-1	0-0	2	0-0	1	0
Ron Harper	7	2-3	1-2	5	0-1	1	0
TOTALS	240	38-81	18-26	98	15-52	29	24

Three-point FG: 4–16 (Fox 0–2, Bryant 1–2, Fisher 2–5, Shaw 1–5, Horry 0–1, Harper 0–1); **Team Rebounds:** 11; **Blocked Shots:** 8 (Horry 4, O'Neal 3, Bryant); **Turnovers:** 16 (Fox 5, O'Neal 5, Bryant 2, Shaw 2, Fisher, Lue); **Steals:** 7 (Bryant 2, Fisher 2, Horry, O'Neal, Shaw); **Percentages:** Total FG (.469), 3-Pt FG (.250), Free Throws (.692); **Technical:** 1 (O'Neal).

Game 3

Date: June 10, 2001; **Attendance:** 20,900; **Time:** 2:53; **Officials:** Bennett Salvatore, Bob Delaney, Dan Crawford.

	1	2	3	4	F
LA Lakers	25	30	18	23	—96
Philadelphia	25	20	21	25	—91

		FG	FT		Reb		
LA Lakers	Min	M-A	M-A	Pts	O-T	A	PF
Rick Fox	22	1-3	1-2	3	0-3	2	2
Horace Grant	29	2-5	0-0	4	3-7	1	3
Shaquille O'Neal	41	11-20	8-9	30	3-12	3	6
Kobe Bryant	48	13-30	6-6	32	0-6	3	2
Derek Fisher	31	2-5	3-4	7	1-2	6	4
Brian Shaw	28	0-3	0-0	0	1-5	3	3
Robert Horry	24	4-5	4-4	15	1-4	3	2
Tyronn Lue	17	2-4	0-0	5	1-1	1	2
TOTALS	240	35-75	22-25	96	10-40	18	26

Three-point FG: 4–10 (Fox 0–1, Bryant 0–2, Fisher 0–1, Shaw 0–1, Horry 3–3, Lue 1–2); **Team Rebounds:** 7; **Blocked Shots:** 6 (O'Neal 4, Horry 2); **Turnovers:** 13 (O'Neal 3, Bryant 3, Fox 2, Shaw 2, Fisher, Horry, Lue); **Percentages:** Total FG (.467), 3-Pt FG (.400), Free Throws (.880) **Technicals:** 2 (Lue, Grant).

		FG	FT		Reb		
Philadelphia	Min	M-A	M-A	Pts	O-T	A	PF
Tyrone Hill	26	1-7	0-0	2	0-2	0	4
Jumaine Jones	18	1-2	0-0	3	0-1	0	1
Dikembe Mutombo	42	9-14	5-8	23	5-12	0	4
Allen Iverson	47	12-30	10-13	35	2-12	4	1
Aaron McKie	42	2-8	1-1	5	1-6	8	1
Eric Snow	34	4-11	6-7	14	4-6	5	4
Matt Geiger	5	2-2	0-0	4	0-0	0	3
Raja Bell	17	1-5	0-0	2	0-2	0	3
Todd MacCulloch	8	0-0	0-0	0	0-0	0	0
Kevin Ollie	1	1-1	1-1	3	1-1	0	1
TOTALS	240	33-80	23-30	91	13-42	17	22

Three-point FG: 2–12 (Jones 1–2, Iverson 1–6, McKie 0–1, Snow 0–1, Bell 0–2); **Team Rebounds:** 8; **Blocked Shots:** 6 (McKie 2, Mutombo 2, Iverson, Hill); **Turnovers:** 14 (McKie 3, Snow 3, Mutombo 2, Geiger 2, Hill, Jones, Iverson, Bell); **Steals:** 5 (Bell 3, Mutombo, Snow); **Percentages:** Total FG (.413), 3-Pt FG (.167), Free Throws (.767); **Technical:** 1 (Iverson).

Game 4

Date: June 13, 2001; **Attendance:** 20,896; **Time:** 2:35;
Officials: Hugh Evans, Ed F. Rush, Jack Nies.

	1	2	3	4	F
LA Lakers	22	29	26	23	—100
Philadelphia	14	23	22	27	—86

		FG	FT		Reb		
LA Lakers	Min	M-A	M-A	Pts	O-T	A	PF
Rick Fox	30	2-7	2-2	7	0-1	4	3
Horace Grant	25	1-4	0-0	2	0-5	0	2
Shaquille O'Neal	42	13-25	8-16	34	8-14	5	4
Kobe Bryant	43	6-13	7-12	19	2-10	9	2
Derek Fisher	34	4-7	0-0	10	0-1	1	3
Brian Shaw	10	2-3	0-1	5	0-2	1	3
Robert Horry	24	3-4	0-0	9	1-4	0	3
Tyronn Lue	14	2-3	0-0	6	0-1	2	0
Ron Harper	16	3-5	1-1	8	0-4	2	2
Mark Madsen	2	0-1	0-0	0	1-1	0	0
TOTALS	240	36-72	18-32	100	12-43	24	24

Three-point FG: 10-19 (Fox 1-3, Bryant 0-2, Fisher 2-4, Shaw 1-2, Horry 3-3, Lue 2-3, Harper 1-2); **Team Rebounds:** 13; **Blocked Shots:** 6 (Grant 2, Harper, Bryant, Horry, Madsen); **Turnovers:** 14 (Bryant 4, O'Neal 3, Fisher 3, Shaw 2, Fox, Lue); **Steals:** 6 (Fisher 3, Bryant, Lue, Harper); **Percentages:** Total FG (.500), 3-Pt FG (.526), Free Throws (.563); **Technical:** 1 (Assistant Coach Cleamons).

		FG	FT		Reb		
Philadelphia	Min	M-A	M-A	Pts	O-T	A	PF
Tyrone Hill	21	3-4	1-1	7	2-7	1	5
Jumaine Jones	11	0-3	0-0	0	1-3	1	1
Dikembe Mutombo	44	9-11	1-3	19	3-9	0	5
Allen Iverson	46	12-30	10-14	35	1-4	4	3
Aaron McKie	40	1-9	3-4	5	0-3	2	1
Eric Snow	29	5-10	1-4	11	0-4	4	4
George Lynch	8	0-0	0-0	0	0-2	1	2
Raja Bell	20	0-2	1-2	1	0-0	1	2
Matt Geiger	11	2-4	2-2	6	0-2	1	4
Rodney Buford	5	1-3	0-0	2	1-3	0	0
Kevin Ollie	3	0-1	0-0	0	0-0	0	0
Todd MacCulloch	2	0-0	0-0	0	0-0	0	0
TOTALS	240	33-77	19-30	86	8-37	15	27

Three-point FG: 1-6 (Iverson 1-6, McKie 0-2); **Team Rebounds:** 12; **Blocked Shots:** 1 (Mutombo); **Turnovers:** 9 (Iverson 3, Hill, Jones, Mutombo, McKie, Snow, Bell, MacCulloch); **Steals:** 9 (Snow 3, Lynch 2, Bell 2, Jones, Iverson); **Percentages:** Total FG (.429), 3-Pt FG (.167), Free Throws (.633); **Technical:** 1 (Iverson).

Game 5

Date: June 15, 2001; **Attendance:** 20,890; **Time:** 2:47;
Officials: Dick Bavetta, Bernie Fryer, Joe Crawford.

	1	2	3	4	F
LA Lakers	24	28	31	25	—108
Philadelphia	27	21	20	28	—96

		FG	FT		Reb		
LA Lakers	Min	M-A	M-A	Pts	O-T	A	PF
Rick Fox	40	5-8	7-7	20	1-6	6	2
Horace Grant	24	2-7	2-4	6	3-6	0	3
Shaquille O'Neal	45	10-18	9-19	29	6-13	2	2
Kobe Bryant	44	7-18	10-11	26.	2-12	6	3
Derek Fisher	36	6-12	0-0	18	0-3	3	4
Robert Horry	26	2-5	2-2	7	2-6	1	4
Brian Shaw	12	0-2	2-2	2	0-0	2	2
Tyronn Lue	10	0-1	0-0	0	0-1	1	2
Mark Madsen	1	0-0	0-0	0	0-0	0	0
Ron Harper	2	0-0	0-0	0	0-0	0	0
TOTALS	240	32-71	32-45	108	14-47	21	22

Three-point FG: 12-17 (Fox 3-3, Bryant 2-3, Fisher 6-8, Horry 1-3); **Team Rebounds:** 8; **Blocked Shots:** 10 (O'Neal 5, Horry 2, Bryant, Fisher, Grant); **Turnovers:** 12 (O'Neal 5, Bryant 3, Fox 2, Fisher, Lue); **Steals:** 6 (Fisher 2, Fox, Grant, Bryant, Shaw); **Percentages:** Total FG (.451), 3-Pt FG (.706), Free Throws (.711); **Technical:** 1 (O'Neal).

		FG	FT		Reb		
Philadelphia	Min	M-A	M-A	Pts	O-T	A	PF
Tyrone Hill	32	7-13	4-6	18	3-13	1	4
Aaron McKie	34	3-7	0-0	7	0-5	5	4
Dikembe Mutombo	42	6-11	1-2	13	3-11	1	6
Allen Iverson	45	14-32	6-8	37	0-3	2	5
Eric Snow	42	4-14	5-8	13	6-6	12	3
George Lynch	6	1-3	0-0	2	2-3	0	1
Raja Bell	5	1-3	0-0	2	1-1	1	0
Kevin Ollie	6	0-0	2-2	2	0-0	0	0
Jumaine Jones	7	0-0	0-0	0	1-3	0	1
Rodney Buford	7	0-3	0-0	0	1-3	0	2
Matt Geiger	11	1-1	0-0	2	1-1	1	6
Todd MacCulloch	3	0-0	0-0	0	2-2	0	0
TOTALS	240	37-90	18-26	96	20-51	23	32

Three-point FG: 4-15 (McKie 1-1, Iverson 3-11, Snow 0-1, Bell 0-1, Buford 0-1); **Team Rebounds:** 7; **Blocked Shots:** 4 (Mutombo 2, Snow, Hill); **Turnovers:** 10 (McKie 3, Iverson 3, Snow 2, Mutombo, Buford); **Steals:** 6 (McKie 2, Iverson 2, Snow 2); **Percentages:** Total FG (.411), 3-Pt FG (.267), Free Throws (.692); **Technicals:** 2 (Iverson, Geiger).

NBA Playoff Leaders

Scoring

	Gm	FG	FT	Pts	Avg
Tracy McGrady, Orlando	4	51	31	135	33.8
Allen Iverson, Philadelphia	22	257	161	723	32.9
Reggie Miller, Indiana	4	28	125	31.3
Shaquille O'Neal, LA Lakers	16	191	105	487	30.4
Kobe Bryant, LA Lakers	16	168	124	471	29.4
Karl Malone, Utah	5	49	39	138	27.6
Vince Carter, Toronto	12	122	58	327	27.3
Ray Allen, Milwaukee	18	158	79	452	25.1
Jamal Mashburn, Charlotte	10	84	74	249	24.9
Tim Duncan, San Antonio	13	120	76	317	24.4
Chris Webber, Sacramento	8	76	34	186	23.3
Predrag Stojakovic, Sacramento	8	52	60	173	21.6
Kevin Garnett, Minnesota	4	27	30	84	21.0
Allan Houston, New York	5	38	22	104	20.8
Michael Finley, Dallas	10	72	36	197	19.7
Glenn Robinson, Milwaukee	18	138	50	350	19.4
Eddie Jones, Miami	3	22	6	57	19.0
Latrell Sprewell, New York	5	35	19	92	18.4
Jalen Rose, Indiana	4	30	7	67	18.0

High Point Games

	Date	FG-FT—Pts
Allen Iverson, Phi vs. Tor	May 9	21-9—54
Allen Iverson, Phi vs. Tor	May 16	21-2—52
Vince Carter, Tor vs. Phi	May 11	19-3—50
Kobe Bryant, LAL vs. Sac	May 13	15-17—48
Allen Iverson, Phi at LAL	June 6	18-9—48

Rebounds

	Gm	Off	Def	Tot	Avg
Shaquille O'Neal, LAL	16	91	156	247	15.4
Tim Duncan, SA	13	54	134	188	14.5
Dikembe Mutombo, Phi	23	113	203	316	13.7
Jermaine O'Neal, Ind	4	12	38	50	12.5
Kevin Garnett, Minnesota	4	10	38	48	12.0

Assists

	Gm	No	Avg
Jason Kidd, Pho	4	53	13.3
John Stockton, Utah	5	57	11.4
Travis Best, Ind	4	37	9.3
Tracy McGrady, Orl	4	33	8.3
Sam Cassell, Mil	18	120	6.7

NBA Finalists' Composite Box Scores
Philadelphia 76ers (12-11)

| | | Overall Playoffs | | | | | | | Finals vs. Los Angeles | | | | |
| | | | —Per Game— | | | | | | | —Per Game— | | | |
	Gm	FG%	TPts	Pts	Reb	Ast	Gm	FG%	TPts	Pts	Reb	Ast
Allen Iverson	22	.389	723	32.9	4.7	6.1	5	.407	178	35.6	5.6	3.8
Aaron McKie	23	.415	336	14.6	5.2	5.3	5	.312	40	8.0	5.4	6.0
Dikembe Mutombo	23	.490	319	13.9	13.7	0.7	5	.600	84	16.8	12.2	0.4
Eric Snow	23	.414	214	9.3	3.7	4.5	5	.407	63	12.6	4.4	6.0
Tyrone Hill	23	.409	166	7.2	7.3	0.4	5	.394	33	6.6	5.2	0.4
George Lynch	10	.480	127	5.7	5.1	1.2	2	.333	2	1.0	2.5	0.5
Jumaine Jones	23	.416	57	5.5	3.7	0.7	5	.400	10	2.0	2.0	0.2
Matt Geiger	12	.586	56	3.2	1.5	0.6	5	.667	26	5.2	1.0	0.4
Todd MacCulloch	18	.632	38	3.1	1.6	0.2	5	.417	13	2.6	1.4	0.0
Raja Bell	15	.444	34	2.3	0.9	0.5	5	.308	13	2.6	1.8	0.8
Kevin Ollie	23	.370	33	1.4	0.4	1.0	5	.333	5	1.0	0.2	0.2
Rodney Buford	15	.333	21	1.4	0.8	0.2	3	.167	2	0.7	2.0	0.0
76ERS	23	.421	2124	92.3	43.9	20.0	5	.424	469	93.8	42.8	18.4
OPPONENTS	23	.440	523	93.2	41.9	22.2	5	.465	503	100.6	45.2	23.0

Three-pointers: PLAYOFFS—Iverson (48-for-142), McKie (27-64), Jones (8-32), Buford (3-6), Bell (2-8), Lynch (0-10), Snow (0-7), Hill (0-1), Mutombo (0-1), Team (88-262, .336); FINALS— Iverson (11-for-39), McKie (4-9), Bell (0-3), Snow (0-3), Jones (0-2), Buford (0-1), Team (17-59, .288).

Los Angeles Lakers (15-1)

| | | Overall Playoffs | | | | | | | Finals vs. Philadelphia | | | | |
| | | | —Per Game— | | | | | | | —Per Game— | | | |
	Gm	FG%	TPts	Pts	Reb	Ast	Gm	FG%	TPts	Pts	Reb	Ast
Shaquille O'Neal	16	.555	487	30.4	15.4	3.2	5	.573	165	33.0	15.8	4.8
Kobe Bryant	16	.469	471	29.4	7.2	6.1	5	.415	123	24.6	7.8	5.8
Derek Fisher	16	.484	215	13.4	3.8	3.0	5	.436	49	9.8	1.2	2.0
Rick Fox	16	.450	160	10.0	4.9	3.6	5	.441	49	9.8	4.6	3.8
Horace Grant	16	.385	96	6.0	6.0	1.2	5	.294	26	5.2	5.6	0.6
Robert Horry	16	.368	94	5.9	5.2	1.9	5	.560	42	8.4	5.0	1.2
Brian Shaw	16	.375	70	4.4	3.4	2.7	5	.300	18	3.6	3.2	2.8
Ron Harper	6	.500	13	2.2	1.3	0.7	3	.625	13	4.3	1.7	1.0
Devean George	7	.500	14	2.0	0.7	0.1	0	.000	0	0.0	0.0	0.0
Tyronn Lue	16	.345	29	1.9	0.7	0.8	5	.583	18	3.6	0.8	1.4
Mark Madsen	13	.077	5	0.4	0.8	0.3	2	.000	0	0.0	0.0	0.0
Greg Foster	1	.000	0	0.0	0.0	0.0	0	.000	0	0.0	0.0	0.0
LAKERS	16	.460	1654	103.4	40.2	22.0	5	.465	503	100.6	45.2	23.0
OPPONENTS	16	.407	1484	89.9	40.8	16.8	5	.424	469	93.8	42.8	18.4

Three-pointers: PLAYOFFS— Fisher (35-for-68), Fox (18-57), Horry (17-47), Bryant (11-34), Shaw (10-29), Lue (5-13), George (1-2), Harper (1-4), Team (98-254, .386); FINALS— Fisher (10-for-19), Horry (8-13), Fox (7-15), Lue (4-6), Bryant (3-9), Shaw (3-10), Harper (1-3), Team (36-75, .480).

Annual Awards

Most Valuable Player

The Maurice Podoloff Trophy; voting by 124-member panel of local and national pro basketball writers and broadcasters. Each ballot has five entries; points awarded on 10-7-5-3-1 basis.

	1st	2nd	3rd	4th	5th	Pts
Allen Iverson, Philadelphia	93	20	9	2	0	1121
Tim Duncan, San Antonio	18	41	34	21	6	706
Shaquille O'Neal, LA Lakers	7	26	45	29	14	578
Chris Webber, Sacramento	5	29	27	39	16	521
Kevin Garnett, Minnesota	1	5	4	17	35	151
Tracy McGrady, Orlando	0	2	3	6	17	64
Karl Malone, Utah	0	0	0	4	9	21
Jason Kidd, Phoenix	0	0	0	3	9	18
Kobe Bryant, LA Lakers	0	0	1	0	6	11
Glenn Robinson, Milwaukee	0	1	0	0	1	8
Ray Allen, Milwaukee	0	0	0	2	1	7
Vince Carter, Toronto	0	0	0	1	4	7
Paul Pierce, Boston	0	0	1	0	0	5
Jerry Stackhouse, Detroit	0	0	0	0	3	3
Michael Finley, Dallas	0	0	0	0	1	1
Anthony Mason, Miami	0	0	0	0	1	1
John Stockton, Utah	0	0	0	0	1	1

All-NBA Teams

Voting by a 124-member panel of local and national pro basketball writers and broadcasters. Each ballot has entries for three teams; points awarded on 5-3-1 basis. First Team repeaters from 1999-2000 are in **bold** type.

Pos	First Team	1st	Pts
F	Chris Webber, Sacramento	109	596
F	**Tim Duncan**, San Antonio	115	608
C	**Shaquille O'Neal**, LA Lakers	115	581
G	Allen Iverson, Philadelphia	120	612
G	**Jason Kidd**, Phoenix	54	423

Pos	Second Team	1st	Pts
F	Kevin Garnett, Minnesota	25	424
F	Vince Carter, Toronto	11	287
C	Dikembe Mutombo, Philadelphia	0	238
G	Kobe Bryant, LA Lakers	36	411
G	Tracy McGrady, Orlando	21	318

Pos	Third Team	1st	Pts
F	Karl Malone, Utah	0	197
F	Dirk Nowitzki, Dallas	0	56
C	David Robinson, San Antonio	0	165
G	Gary Payton, Seattle	1	117
G	Ray Allen, Milwaukee	3	105

Annual Awards (Cont.)

All-Defensive Teams

Voting by NBA head coaches. Each ballot has entries for two teams; two points given for 1st team, one for 2nd. Coaches cannot vote for own players. First Team repeaters from 1999-2000 are in **bold** type.

Pos	First Team	1st	Pts
F	**Tim Duncan**, San Antonio	19	40
F	**Kevin Garnett**, Minnesota	9	24
C	Dikembe Mutombo, Philadelphia	19	43
G	**Gary Payton**, Seattle	17	38
G	Jason Kidd, Phoenix	14	39

Pos	Second Team	1st	Pts
F	Bruce Bowen, Miami	7	18
F	P.J. Brown, Miami	4	13
C	Shaquille O'Neal, LA Lakers	5	17
G	Kobe Bryant, LA Lakers	9	26
G	Doug Christie, Sacramento	6	20

Coach of the Year

The Red Auerbach Trophy; voting by 124-member panel of local and national pro basketball writers and broadcasters. Each ballot has one entry.

	Votes	Improvement
Larry Brown, Philadelphia	43	49-33 to 56-26
Rick Adelman, Sacramento	11	44-38 to 55-27
Don Nelson, Dallas	8	40-42 to 53-29
Pat Riley, Miami	5	52-30 to 50-32
Alvin Gentry, LA Clippers	4	15-67 to 31-51
Gregg Popovich, San Antonio	3	53-29 to 58-24
Flip Saunders, Minnesota	3	50-32 to 47-35
Jerry Sloan, Utah	1	55-27 to 53-29

Rookie of the Year

The Eddie Gottlieb Trophy; voting by 124-member panel of local and national pro basketball writers and broadcasters. Each ballot has one entry.

	Pos	Votes
Mike Miller, Orlando	G/F	75
Kenyon Martin, New Jersey	F	36
Marc Jackson, Golden St.	C	7
Morris Peterson, Toronto	F	3
Darius Miles, LA Clippers	F	3

All-Rookie Team

Voting by NBA's 29 head coaches, who cannot vote for players on their team. Each ballot has entries for two five-man teams, regardless of position; two points given for 1st team, one for 2nd. First team votes in parentheses.

First Team	College	Pts
Mike Miller, Orlando (28)	Florida	56
Kenyon Martin, New Jersey (27)	Cincinnati	54
Marc Jackson, Golden State (24)	Temple	51
Morris Peterson, Toronto (22)	Mich. St.	50
Darius Miles, LA Clippers (21)	HS	48

Second Team	College	Pts
Hidayet Turkoglu, Sacramento (9)	None	34
Desmond Mason, Seattle (5)	Oklahoma St.	28
Courtney Alexander, Washington (2)	Fresno St.	16
Marcus Fizer, Chicago (1)	Iowa St.	16
Chris Mihm, Cleveland (1)	Texas	13

IBM Award

Created prior to the 1983-84 season to honor the player who contributes most to his team's overall success and utilizes a computer evaluation of key offensive and defensive statistics to determine an overall leader. The formula is as follows: (Player points-FGA+REB+AST+STL+BLK-PF-TO+(team wins x 10) x 250)/(team points-FGA+REB+AST+STL+BLK-PF-TO).

	Pos	Pts
Shaquille O'Neal, LA Lakers	C	110.21
Kevin Garnett, Minnesota	F	100.83
Anthony Mason, Miami	F	96.86
Jason Kidd, Phoenix	G	95.04
Ben Wallace, Detroit	C	94.09
Dirk Nowitzki, Dallas	F	93.77
Karl Malone, Utah	F	92.60
Tracy McGrady, Orlando	F	92.23
Tim Duncan, San Antonio	C	91.92
Marcus Camby, New York	C	91.62

Sixth-Man Award

Voted on by a 124-member panel of local and national pro basketball writers and broadcasters.

	Pos	Votes
Aaron McKie, Philadelphia	G	57
Tim Thomas, Milwaukee	F	27
LaPhonso Ellis, Minnesota	F	10
Bobby Jackson, Sacramento	G	9
Travis Best, Indiana	G	5
Ruben Patterson, Seattle	F/G	4
Rodney Rogers, Phoenix	F	4
Steve Smith, Portland	G/F	4
Donyell Marshall, Utah	F	2
Austin Croshere, Indiana	F	1
Tony Delk, Phoenix	G	1

Most Improved Player Award

Voted on by a 124-member panel of local and national pro basketball writers and broadcasters.

	Pos	Votes
Tracy McGrady, Orlando	F	74
Peja Stojakovic, Sacramento	G	14
Steve Nash, Dallas	G	12
Shawn Marion, Phoenix	F	6
Baron Davis, Charlotte	G	4
Dirk Nowitzki, Dallas	F	4
Travis Best, Indiana	G	2
Jason Terry, Atlanta	G	2
Ben Wallace, Detroit	C/F	1
Bonzi Wells, Portland	G/F	1
Donyell Marshall, Utah	F	1
Richard Hamilton, Washington	G/F	1
Alvin Williams, Toronto	G	1
Jeff McInnis, LA Clippers	G	1

Defensive Player of the Year Award

Voted on by a 124-member panel of local and national pro basketball writers and broadcasters.

	Pos	Votes
Dikembe Mutombo, Philadelphia	C	48
Kevin Garnett, Minnesota	F	26
Tim Duncan, San Antonio	F/C	14
Doug Christie, Sacramento	G	9
Ben Wallace, Detroit	C/F	6
David Robinson, San Antonio	C	6
Theo Ratliff, Atlanta	C/F	4
Bruce Bowen, Miami	F/G	2
Anthony Mason, Miami	F	2
Shaquille O'Neal, LA Lakers	C	2
Kobe Bryant, LA Lakers	G	1
Allen Iverson, Philadelphia	G	1
Jason Kidd, Phoenix	G	1
Shawn Marion, Phoenix	F	1

2001 College Draft

First and second round picks at the 55th annual NBA College Draft held June 27, 2001 held in New York City at the Theatre at Madison Square Garden. The order of the first 13 positions were determined by a Draft Lottery held May 20, in Secaucus, N.J. Positions 14 through 28 reflect regular season records in reverse order. Minnesota was stripped of their first round pick due to an illegal contract agreement with Joe Smith. Underclassmen selected are noted in CAPITAL letters.

First Round

	Team	Pos
1	Washington . .KWAME BROWN, Glynn Academy	PF
2	**ab-** Chicago .TYSON CHANDLER; Dominguez HS	PF
3	Atlanta.....................Pau Gasol, Spain	SF
4	Chicago...........EDDY CURRY, Thornwood HS	C
5	Golden State... JASON RICHARDSON, Mich. St.	SF
6	Vancouver.................Shane Battier, Duke	SF
7	**c-** Houston...........EDDIE GRIFFIN, Seton Hall	PF
8	Cleveland. .DeSAGANA DIOP, Oak Hill Acad. HS	C
9	Detroit..............RODNEY WHITE, Charlotte	PF
10	Boston..............JOE JOHNSON, Arkansas	SF
11	**d-** Boston .KEDRICK BROWN, Okaloosa-Walton CC	SF
12	Seattle.........Vladimir Radmanovic, Yugoslavia	PF
13	**e-** New Jersey....RICHARD JEFFERSON, Arizona	SF
14	**f-** Golden State .....TROY MURPHY, Notre Dame	PF
15	Orlando.............STEVEN HUNTER, Depaul	C
16	Charlotte...............KIRK HASTON, Indiana	PF
17	Toronto...........MICHAEL BRADLEY, Villanova	PF
18	**g-** New Jersey.........JASON COLLINS, Stanford	C
19	Portland........ZACH RANDOLPH, Michigan State	PF
20	**h-** Orlando . .Brendan Haywood, North Carolina	C
21	**i-** Boston.......JOSEPH FORTE, North Carolina	SG
22	**j-** Orlando..................Jeryl Sasser, SMU	PG
23	**k-** New Jersey...B. ARMSTRONG, Pepperdine	SG
24	Utah.......................Raul Lopez, Spain	PG
25	Sacramento......:.GERALD WALLACE, Alabama	SF
26	Philadelphia.....SAMUEL DALEMBERT, Seton Hall	C
27	**lmn-** Vancouver......Jamaal Tinsley, Iowa State	PG
28	San Antonio...............Tony Parker, France	PG

Second Round

	Team	Pos
30	Chicago...........Trenton Hassell, Austin Peay	SG
31	Golden State.........GILBERT ARENAS, Arizona	SG
32	**o-** Denver.........OMAR COOK, St. John's	PG
33	Vancouver...........WILL SOLOMON, Clemson	PG
34	**p-** Houston...........Terence Morris, Maryland	SF
35	New Jersey.............Brian Scalabrine, USC	PF
36	Cleveland.................Jeff Trepagnier, USC	SG
37	**q-** Philadelphia........Damone Brown, Syracuse	SF
38	Detroit............:....Mehmet Okur, Turkey	PF
39	**r-** New York.......MICHAEL WRIGHT, Arizona	PF
40	**s-** Seattle..................Earl Watson, UCLA	PG
41	Indiana.........JAMISON BREWER, Auburn	PG
42	**tu-** Washington......BOBBY SIMMONS, Depaul	SG
43	**v-** New York............Eric Chenowith, Kansas	C
44	**w-** Dallas.............Kyle Hill, Eastern Illinois	SG
45	**x-** Chicago.............Sean Lampley, California	SF
46	Minnesota...............Loren Woods, Arizona	C
47	**y-** Denver.....OUSMANE CISSE, St. Jude HS	PF
48	Vancouver.................Antonis Fotsis, Greece	SF
49	Miami...............Ken Johnson, Ohio State	C
50	Portland....Ruben Boumtje Boumtje, Georgetown	C
51	Phoenix.............ALTON FORD, Houston	PF
52	Milwaukee........Andre Hutson, Michigan State	PF
53	Utah..................Jarron Collins, Stanford	C
54	Dallas.......KENNY SATTERFIELD, Cincinnati	PG
55	Sacramento........Maurice Jeffers, St. Louis	SG
56	**z-** San Antonio......Robertas Javtokas, Lithuania	PF
57	Philadelphia..........Alvin Jones, Georgia Tech	C
58	San Antonio.............Bryan Bracey, Oregon	SF

Acquired Picks

FIRST ROUND: **a-**from LA Clippers; **b-**Chicago traded F Elton Brand to the LA Clippers for F Brian Skinner and the rights to F-C Tyson Chandler; **c-**from New Jersey for the rights to F Richard Jefferson, C Jason Collins and G Brandon Armstrong; **d-**from Denver; **e-**from Houston; **f-**from Indiana; **g-**from Houston; **h-**from Cleveland for C Michael Doleac; **i-**from Phoenix via Denver; **j-**from Milwaukee via Houston; **k-**from Houston; **l-**from LA Lakers via New York; **m-** Vancouver trades F Shareef Abdur-Rahim and the rights to G Jamaal Tinsley for F-C Lorenzen Wright, G Brevin Knight and the rights to F Pau Gasol; **n-** Atlanta traded a future first-round pick to Atlanta for the rights to G Jamaal Tinsley. SECOND ROUND: **o-**from Orlando for a future first round pick; **p-**from Atlanta for a future first-round pick; **q-**from LA Clippers for an undisclosed amount of cash; **r-**from Boston via Seattle; **s-**from Denver via Boston; **t-**from Seattle; **u-** Seattle traded the rights to G Bobby Simmons for the rights to F Predrag Drobnjak; **v-**from Seattle; **w-**from Houston; **x-**from Charlotte; **w-**from Toronto; **z-**from LA Lakers.

2001 FIBA SuproLeague Championships

FIBA, the international basketball federation sponsors the newly-dubbed SuproLeague, featuring 20 European clubs and formerly called the European Championships of Men's Clubs. The expanded league debuted in September of 2000 and climaxed May 11-13, 2001 with the "FIBA SuproLeague Final Four" in Paris.

Round of 16

Games played Mar. 27-Apr. 5, 2001. Series were best-of-three.

Panathinaikos BSA (Greece) 2 . .KK Krka Telekom (Slovenia) 0
CSKA (Russia) 2.................Oostende (Belgium) 0
Croatia Osiguranje 2.........EB PAU Orthez (France) 0
Scavolini Basket (Italy) 2...........Ülker SC (Turkey) 1
ALBA (Germany) 2...........Iraklis BC SA (Greece) 1
ASVEL (France) 2......Partizan ICN (Yugoslavia) 1
Efes Pilsen (Turkey) 2.....BC Lietuvos Rytas (Lithuania) 1
Maccabi Elite (Israel) 2 .Zepter Slask Wroclaw (Poland) 0

Quarterfinals

Games played Apr. 17-26, 2001.

Panathinaikos BSA 2........................ALBA 0
CSKA 2..............................ASVEL 0
Efes Pilsen 2....................Croatia Osiguranje 1
Maccabi Elite 2................Scavolini Basket 0

Semifinals

Maccabi Elite 86......................CSKA 80
Panathinaikos BSA 74..............Efes Pilsen 66

Third Place Game

Efes Pilsen 91..........................CSKA 85

Championship

Held May 13, 2001 at Bercy Arena in Paris. Attendance: 13,200

	1	2	F
Panathinaikos BSA	23	44	— 67
Maccabi Elite	37	44	— 81

Women's National Basketball Association
Final WNBA Standings

Conference champions (*) and playoff qualifiers (†) are noted. GB refers to Games Behind leader. Number of seasons listed after each head coach refers to current tenure with club.

Eastern Conference

	W	L	Pct	GB	Home	Road
*Cleveland	22	10	.688	—	14-2	8-8
†New York	21	11	.656	1	13-3	8-8
†Miami	20	12	.625	2	10-6	10-6
†Charlotte	18	14	.563	4	11-5	7-9
Orlando	13	19	.406	9	10-6	3-13
Indiana	10	22	.313	12	7-9	3-13
Detroit	10	22	.313	12	6-10	4-12
Washington	10	22	.313	12	8-8	2-14

Head Coaches: Cle–Dan Hughes (2nd season); **NY**–Richie Adubato (3rd); **Mia**–Ron Rothstein (2nd); **Cha**–Anne Donovan (1st); **Orl**–Carolyn Peck (3rd); **Ind**–Nell Fortner (1st); **Det**–Greg Williams (1st); **Wash**–Tom Maher (1st).

2000 Standings: 1. New York (20-12); 2. Cleveland (17-15); 3. Orlando (16-16); 4. Washington (14-18); 5. Detroit (14-18); 6. Miami (13-19); 7. Indiana (9-23); 8. Charlotte (8-24).

Western Conference

	W	L	Pct	GB	Home	Road
*Los Angeles	28	4	.875	—	16-0	12-4
†Sacramento	20	12	.625	8	12-4	8-8
†Utah	19	13	.594	9	9-7	10-6
†Houston	19	13	.594	9	11-5	8-8
Phoenix	13	19	.406	15	10-6	3-13
Minnesota	12	20	.375	16	6-10	6-10
Portland	11	21	.344	17	6-10	5-11
Seattle	10	22	.313	18	5-11	5-11

Head Coaches: LA–Michael Cooper (2nd season); **Sac**–Maura McHugh (1st); **Utah**–Candi Harvey (1st); **Hou**–Van Chancellor (5th); **Pho**–Cynthia Cooper (1st); **Min**–Brian Agler (3rd); **Port**–Linda Hargrove (2nd); **Sea**–Lin Dunn (2nd).

2000 Standings: 1. Los Angeles (28-4); 2. Houston (27-5); 3. Sacramento (21-11); 4. Phoenix (20-12); 5. Utah (18-14); 6. Minnesota (15-17); 7. Portland (10-22); 8. Seattle (6-26).

WNBA Regular Season Individual Leaders

Scoring

	Gm	Pts	Avg
Katie Smith, Minnesota	32	739	23.1
Lisa Leslie, Los Angeles	31	606	19.5
Tina Thompson, Houston	30	579	19.3
Janeth Arcain, Houston	32	591	18.5
Chamique Holdsclaw, Washington	29	486	16.8
Yolanda Griffith, Sacramento	32	518	16.2
Tari Phillips, New York	32	489	15.3
Lauren Jackson, Seattle	29	442	15.2
Jackie Stiles, Portland	32	478	14.9
Natalie Williams, Utah	31	439	14.2

Rebounding

	Gm	Reb	Avg
Yolanda Griffith, Sacramento	32	357	11.2
Natalie Williams, Utah	31	308	9.9
Lisa Leslie, Los Angeles	31	298	9.6
Chamique Holdsclaw, Washington	29	256	8.8
Tari Phillips, New York	32	257	8.0
Tina Thompson, Houston	30	233	7.8
Kristin Folkl, Portland	32	245	7.7
Margo Dydek, Utah	32	243	7.6
Taj McWilliams-Franklin, Orlando	32	243	7.6
Vicky Bullett, Washington	32	231	7.2

Field Goal Pct.

	Gm	FGM	FGA	Pct
Latasha Byears, Los Angeles	32	133	221	.602
Ann Wauters, Cleveland	24	87	153	.569
Yolanda Griffith, Sacramento	32	192	368	.522
Rushia Brown, Cleveland	30	101	195	.518
Tari Phillips, New York	32	208	410	.507
Maria Stepanova, Phoenix	32	143	282	.507
Marie Ferdinand, Utah	32	143	290	.493
Trisha Fallon, Phoenix	31	127	259	.490
Natalie Williams, Utah	31	171	349	.490
Andrea Stinson, Charlotte	32	179	370	.484

Free Throw Pct.

	Gm	FTM	FTA	Pct
Elena Baranova, Miami	32	66	71	.930
Allison Feaster, Charlotte	32	58	63	.921
Jennifer Azzi, Utah	32	88	96	.917
Janeth Arcain, Houston	32	135	150	.900
Katie Smith, Minnesota	32	246	275	.895
Dawn Staley, Charlotte	32	51	57	.895
Elena Tornikidou, Detroit	32	63	71	.887
Nadine Malcolm, Indiana	31	54	62	.871
Lisa Harrison, Phoenix	32	51	59	.864
Kamila Vodichkova, Seattle	29	38	44	.864

WNBA Annual Awards

Most Valuable Player Lisa Leslie, LA	**Def. Player of the Year** Debbie Black, Mia
Rookie of the Year Jackie Stiles, Por	**Coach of the Year** Dan Hughes, Cle
Most Improved Janeth Arcain, Hou	**Sportsmanship Award** Sue Wicks, NY

AP/Wide World Photos

The **Los Angeles Sparks** celebrate their first WNBA title following their series-clinching Game 2 win over the Charlotte Sting. Los Angeles center Lisa Leslie, right, was named Most Valuable Player of the 2001 WNBA Championship Series.

3-Point Field Goal Pct.

	Gm	FGM	FGA	Pct
Jennifer Azzi, Utah	32	38	74	.514
Ukari Figgs, Los Angeles	32	54	117	.462
Edna Campbell, Sacramento	32	43	94	.457
Elena Tornikidou, Detroit	32	22	49	.449
Andrea Stinson, Charlotte	32	29	65	.446
Jackie Stiles, Portland	32	50	116	.431
Crystal Robinson, New York	32	70	168	.417
Nadine Malcolm, Indiana	31	23	56	.411
Stephanie McCarty, Indiana	30	23	57	.404
Sandy Brondello, Miami	29	26	66	.394

Blocks

	Gm	Blk	Avg
Margo Dydek, Utah	32	113	3.53
Lisa Leslie, Los Angeles	31	71	2.29
Lauren Jackson, Seattle	29	64	2.21
Maria Stepanova, Phoenix	32	64	2.00
Vicky Bullett, Washington	32	58	1.81
Elena Baranova, Miami	32	57	1.78
Tangela Smith, Sacramento	32	55	1.72
Taj McWilliams-Franklin, Orlando	32	50	1.56
Ruth Riley, Miami	32	46	1.44
Tammy Sutton-Brown, Charlotte	29	39	1.34

Assists

	Gm	Ast	Avg
Ticha Penicheiro, Sacramento	23	172	7.5
Teresa Weatherspoon, New York	32	203	6.3
Dawn Staley, Charlotte	32	179	5.6
Jennifer Azzi, Utah	32	171	5.3
Kristen Veal, Phoenix	29	125	4.3
Michele Timms, Phoenix	21	87	4.1
Tamecka Dixon, Los Angeles	29	114	3.9
Ukari Figgs, Los Angeles	32	126	3.9
Debbie Black, Miami	32	123	3.8
Coquese Washington, Houston	32	122	3.8

Steals

	Gm	Stl	Avg
Debbie Black, Miami	32	82	2.56
Rita Williams, Indiana	32	72	2.25
Nykesha Sales, Orlando	32	70	2.19
Coquese Washington, Houston	32	69	2.16
Yolanda Griffith, Sacramento	32	63	1.97
Tully Bevilaqua, Portland	31	59	1.90
Janeth Arcain, Houston	32	60	1.88
Lauren Jackson, Seattle	29	54	1.86
Kendra Hollard-Corn, Sacramento	32	56	1.75
Ticha Penicheiro, Sacramento	23	40	1.74

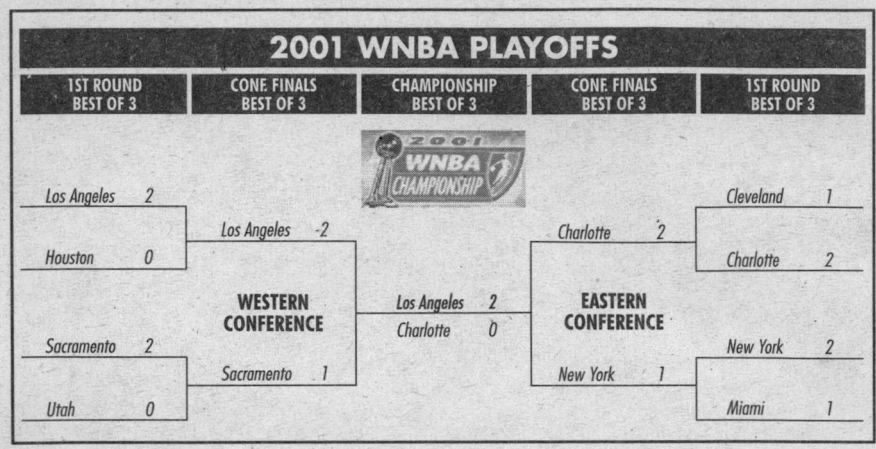

WNBA Playoffs

First Round (Best of 3)

East

Aug. 16 Charlotte 53 . . . . Cleveland 46
Aug. 18 Cleveland 69 . . . . Charlotte 51
Aug. 20 Charlotte 72 . . . . Cleveland 64
Charlotte Sting wins series, 2-1

Aug. 17 New York 62 . . . . Miami 46
Aug. 19 Miami 53 . . . . New York 50
Aug. 21 New York 72 . . . . Miami 61
New York Liberty wins series, 2-1

West

Aug. 18 Los Angeles 64 . . . . Houston 59
Aug. 20 Los Angeles 70 . . . . Houston 58
Los Angeles Sparks win series, 2-0

Aug. 17 Sacramento 89 . . . . Utah 65
Aug. 19 Sacramento 71 . . . . Utah 66
Sacramento Monarchs wins series, 2-0

Conference Finals (Best of 3)

East

Aug. 24 New York 61 . . . . Charlotte 57
Aug. 26 Charlotte 62 . . . . New York 53
Aug. 27 Charlotte 48 . . . . New York 44
Charlotte Sting win series, 2-1

West

Aug. 24 Los Angeles 74 . . . . Sacramento 73
Aug. 26 Sacramento 80 . . . . Los Angeles 60
Aug. 27 Los Angeles 93 . . . . Sacramento 62
Los Angeles Sparks win series, 2-1

Championship Series (Best of 3)

Los Angeles wins series, 2 games to 0

	W-L	Avg	Leading Scorer
Charlotte	0-2	60.0	Stinson (12.0 ppg)
Los Angeles	2-0	78.5	Leslie (24.0 ppg)

Date	Winner	Home Court
Aug. 30	Sparks, 75-66	at Charlotte
Sept. 1	Sparks, 82-54	at Los Angeles

Finals MVP: Lisa Leslie, LA Sparks center, (24.0 ppg, 10.5 rpg, 5.0 apg)

WNBA 2001 Attendance

Attendance figures below are for the regular season and teams are listed in alphabetical order.

Team	Home Games	Total Attendance	Average Attendance
Charlotte Sting	16	105,525	6,595
Cleveland Rockers	16	147,373	9,211
Detroit Shock	16	109,348	6,834
Houston Comets	16	181,115	11,320
Indiana Fever	16	138,922	8,683
Los Angeles Sparks	16	148,446	9,278
Miami Sol	16	141,517	8,845
Minnesota Lynx	16	120,607	7,538
New York Liberty	16	250,565	15,660
Orlando Miracle	16	118,874	7,430
Phoenix Mercury	16	136,982	8,561
Portland Fire	16	137,656	8,604
Sacramento Monarchs	16	133,601	8,350
Seattle Storm	16	95,257	5,954
Utah Starzz	16	110,507	6,907
Washington Mystics	16	246,667	15,417
WNBA TOTALS	256	2,322,962	9,074

1938-2001 Through the Years

information please® SPORTS ALMANAC

The NBA Finals

Although the National Basketball Association traces its first championship back to the 1946-47 season, the league was then called the Basketball Association of America (BAA). It did not become the NBA until after the 1948-49 season when the BAA and the National Basketball League (NBL) agreed to merge.

In the chart below, the Eastern finalists (representing the NBA Eastern Division from 1947-70, and the NBA Eastern Conference since 1971) are listed in CAPITAL letters. Also, each NBA champion's wins and losses are noted in parentheses after the series score.

Multiple winners: Boston (16); Minneapolis-LA Lakers (13); Chicago Bulls (6); Phi-SF-Golden St. Warriors and Syracuse Nationals-Phi. 76ers (3); Detroit, Houston and New York (2).

Year	Winner	Head Coach	Series	Loser	Head Coach
1947	PHILADELPHIA WARRIORS	Eddie Gottlieb	4-1 (WWWLW)	Chicago Stags	Harold Olsen
1948	Baltimore Bullets	Buddy Jeannette	4-2 (LWWWLW)	PHILA. WARRIORS	Eddie Gottlieb
1949	Minneapolis Lakers	John Kundla	4-2 (WWWLLW)	WASH. CAPITOLS	Red Auerbach
1950	Minneapolis Lakers	John Kundla	4-2 (WLWWLW)	SYRACUSE	Al Cervi
1951	Rochester	Les Harrison	4-3 (WWWLLLW)	NEW YORK	Joe Lapchick
1952	Minneapolis Lakers	John Kundla	4-3 (WLWLWLW)	NEW YORK	Joe Lapchick
1953	Minneapolis Lakers	John Kundla	4-1 (LWWWW)	NEW YORK	Joe Lapchick
1954	Minneapolis Lakers	John Kundla	4-3 (WLWLWLW)	SYRACUSE	Al Cervi
1955	SYRACUSE	Al Cervi	4-3 (WWLLLWW)	Ft. Wayne Pistons	Charley Eckman
1956	PHILADELPHIA WARRIORS	George Senesky	4-1 (WWWLW)	Ft. Wayne Pistons	Charley Eckman
1957	BOSTON	Red Auerbach	4-3 (LWLWWLW)	St. Louis Hawks	Alex Hannum
1958	St. Louis Hawks	Alex Hannum	4-2 (WLWLWW)	BOSTON	Red Auerbach
1959	BOSTON	Red Auerbach	4-0	Mpls. Lakers	John Kundla
1960	BOSTON	Red Auerbach	4-3 (WLWLWLW)	St. Louis Hawks	Ed Macauley
1961	BOSTON	Red Auerbach	4-1 (WWLWW)	St. Louis Hawks	Paul Seymour
1962	BOSTON	Red Auerbach	4-3 (WLLWLWW)	LA Lakers	Fred Schaus
1963	BOSTON	Red Auerbach	4-2 (WWLWLW)	LA Lakers	Fred Schaus
1964	BOSTON	Red Auerbach	4-1 (WWIWW)	SF Warriors	Alex Hannum
1965	BOSTON	Red Auerbach	4-1 (WLWWW)	LA Lakers	Fred Schaus
1966	BOSTON	Red Auerbach	4-3 (LWWLWLW)	LA Lakers	Fred Schaus
1967	PHILADELPHIA 76ERS	Alex Hannum	4-2 (WWLWLW)	SF Warriors	Bill Sharman
1968	BOSTON	Bill Russell	4-2 (WLWLWW)	LA Lakers	B.van Breda Kolff
1969	BOSTON	Bill Russell	4-3 (LLWWLWW)	LA Lakers	B.van Breda Kolff
1970	NEW YORK	Red Holzman	4-3 (WLWLWLW)	LA Lakers	Joe Mullaney
1971	Milwaukee	Larry Costello	4-0	BALT. BULLETS	Gene Shue
1972	LA Lakers	Bill Sharman	4-1 (LWWWW)	NEW YORK	Red Holzman
1973	NEW YORK	Red Holzman	4-1 (LWWWW)	LA Lakers	Bill Sharman
1974	BOSTON	Tommy Heinsohn	4-3 (WLWLWLW)	Milwaukee	Larry Costello
1975	Golden St. Warriors	Al Attles	4-0	WASH. BULLETS	K.C. Jones
1976	BOSTON	Tommy Heinsohn	4-2 (WWLLWW)	Phoenix	John MacLeod
1977	Portland	Jack Ramsay	4-2 (LLWWWW)	PHILA. 76ERS	Gene Shue
1978	WASHINGTON BULLETS	Dick Motta	4-3 (LWWLWLW)	Seattle	Lenny Wilkens
1979	Seattle	Lenny Wilkens	4-1 (LWWWW)	WASH. BULLETS	Dick Motta
1980	LA Lakers	Paul Westhead	4-2 (WLWLWW)	PHILA. 76ERS	Billy Cunningham
1981	BOSTON	Bill Fitch	4-2 (WLWLWW)	Houston	Del Harris
1982	LA Lakers	Pat Riley	4-2 (WLWLWW)	PHILA. 76ERS	Billy Cunningham
1983	PHILADELPHIA 76ERS	Billy Cunningham	4-0	LA Lakers	Pat Riley
1984	BOSTON	K.C. Jones	4-3 (LWWLWLW)	LA Lakers	Pat Riley
1985	LA Lakers	Pat Riley	4-2 (LWLWWW)	BOSTON	K.C. Jones
1986	BOSTON	K.C. Jones	4-2 (WWLWLW)	Houston	Bill Fitch
1987	LA Lakers	Pat Riley	4-2 (WWLWLW)	BOSTON	K.C. Jones
1988	LA Lakers	Pat Riley	4-3 (LWWLLWW)	DETROIT PISTONS	Chuck Daly
1989	DETROIT PISTONS	Chuck Daly	4-0	LA Lakers	Pat Riley
1990	DETROIT	Chuck Daly	4-1 (WLWWW)	Portland	Rick Adelman
1991	CHICAGO	Phil Jackson	4-1 (LWWWW)	LA Lakers	Mike Dunleavy
1992	CHICAGO	Phil Jackson	4-2 (WWLWLW)	Portland	Rick Adelman
1993	CHICAGO	Phil Jackson	4-2 (WWLWLW)	Phoenix	Paul Westphal
1994	Houston	Rudy Tomjanovich	4-3 (WLWLLWW)	NEW YORK	Pat Riley
1995	Houston	Rudy Tomjanovich	4-0	ORLANDO	Brian Hill

Year	Winner	Head Coach	Series	Loser	Head Coach
1996	CHICAGO	Phil Jackson	4-2 (WWWLLW)	Seattle	George Karl
1997	CHICAGO	Phil Jackson	4-2 (WWLLWW)	Utah	Jerry Sloan
1998	CHICAGO	Phil Jackson	4-2 (LWWWLW)	Utah	Jerry Sloan
1999	San Antonio	Gregg Popovich	4-1 (WWLWW)	NEW YORK	Jeff Van Gundy
2000	LA Lakers	Phil Jackson	4-2 (WWLWLW)	INDIANA	Larry Bird
2001	LA Lakers	Phil Jackson	4-1 (LWWWW)	PHILA. 76ERS	Larry Brown

Note: Four finalists were led by player-coaches: **1948**—Buddy Jeannette (guard) of Baltimore; **1950**—Al Cervi (guard) of Syracuse; **1968**—Bill Russell (center) of Boston; **1969**—Bill Russell (center) of Boston.

Most Valuable Player

Selected by an 11-member media panel. Winner who did not play for the NBA champion is in **bold** type.

Multiple winners: Michael Jordan (6); Magic Johnson (3); Kareem Abdul-Jabbar, Larry Bird, Hakeem Olajuwon, Shaquille O'Neal and Willis Reed (2).

Year		Year		Year	
1969	**Jerry West**, LA Lakers, G	1980	Magic Johnson, LA Lakers, G/C	1991	Michael Jordan, Chicago, G
1970	Willis Reed, New York, C	1981	Cedric Maxwell, Boston, F	1992	Michael Jordan, Chicago, G
1971	Lew Alcindor, Milwaukee, C	1982	Magic Johnson, LA Lakers, G	1993	Michael Jordan, Chicago, G
1972	Wilt Chamberlain, LA Lakers, C	1983	Moses Malone, Philadelphia, C	1994	Hakeem Olajuwon, Houston, C
1973	Willis Reed, New York, C	1984	Larry Bird, Boston, F	1995	Hakeem Olajuwon, Houston, C
1974	John Havlicek, Boston, F	1985	K. Abdul-Jabbar, LA Lakers, C	1996	Michael Jordan, Chicago, G
1975	Rick Barry, Golden State, F	1986	Larry Bird, Boston, F	1997	Michael Jordan, Chicago, G
1976	Jo Jo White, Boston, G	1987	Magic Johnson, LA Lakers, G	1998	Michael Jordan, Chicago, G
1977	Bill Walton, Portland, C	1988	James Worthy, LA Lakers, F	1999	Tim Duncan, San Antonio, F/C
1978	Wes Unseld, Washington, C	1989	Joe Dumars, Detroit, G	2000	Shaquille O'Neal, LA Lakers, C
1979	Dennis Johnson, Seattle, G	1990	Isiah Thomas, Detroit, G	2001	Shaquille O'Neal, LA Lakers, C

Note: Lew Alcindor changed his name to Kareem Abdul-Jabbar after the 1970-71 season.

All-Time NBA Playoff Leaders

Through the 2001 playoffs.

CAREER

Years listed indicate number of playoff appearances. Players active in 2001 in **bold** type. DNP indicates player that was active in 2001 but did not participate in playoffs.

Points

		Yrs	Gm	Pts	Avg
1	Michael Jordan	13	179	5987	33.4
2	Kareem Abdul-Jabbar	18	237	5762	24.3
3	Jerry West	13	153	4457	29.1
4	**Karl Malone**	16	163	4341	26.6
5	Larry Bird	12	164	3897	23.8
6	John Havlicek	13	172	3776	22.0
7	**Hakeem Olajuwon** (DNP)	14	140	3727	26.6
8	Magic Johnson	13	190	3701	19.5
9	Elgin Baylor	12	134	3623	27.0
10	Wilt Chamberlain	13	160	3607	22.5
11	**Scottie Pippen**	14	201	3570	17.8
12	Kevin McHale	13	169	3182	18.8
13	Dennis Johnson	13	180	3116	17.3
14	Julius Erving	11	141	3088	21.9
15	James Worthy	9	143	3022	21.1
16	Clyde Drexler	15	145	2963	20.4
17	**Shaquille O'Neal**	8	105	2956	28.2
18	Sam Jones	12	154	2909	18.9
19	Charles Barkley	13	123	2833	23.0
20	Robert Parish	16	184	2820	15.3

Scoring Average

Minimum of 25 games or 700 points.

		Yrs	Gm	Pts	Avg
1	Michael Jordan	13	179	5987	33.4
2	**Allen Iverson**	3	40	1213	30.3
3	Jerry West	13	153	4457	29.1
4	**Shaquille O'Neal**	8	105	2956	28.2
5	Elgin Baylor	12	134	3623	27.0
6	George Gervin	9	59	1592	27.0
7	**Hakeem Olajuwon** (DNP)	14	140	3727	26.6
8	**Karl Malone**	16	163	4341	26.6
9	Dominique Wilkins	9	55	1421	25.8
10	Bob Pettit	9	88	2240	25.5
11	Rick Barry	7	74	1833	24.8
12	Bernard King	5	28	687	24.5
13	Alex English	10	68	1661	24.4
14	Kareem Abdul-Jabbar	18	237	5762	24.3
15	Paul Arizin	8	49	1186	24.2
16	Larry Bird	12	164	3897	23.8
17	George Mikan	9	91	2141	23.5
18	**Reggie Miller**	11	104	2445	23.5
19	Charles Barkley	13	123	2833	23.0
20	**Tim Duncan**	3	39	898	23.0

Field Goals

		Yrs	FG	Att	Pct
1	Kareem Abdul-Jabbar	18	2356	4422	.533
2	Michael Jordan	13	2188	4497	.487
3	Jerry West	13	1622	3460	.469
4	**Karl Malone**	16	1581	3393	.466
5	**Hakeem Olajuwon** (DNP)	14	1492	2825	.528
6	Larry Bird	12	1458	3090	.472
7	John Havlicek	13	1451	3329	.436
8	Wilt Chamberlain	13	1425	2728	.522
9	Elgin Baylor	12	1388	3161	.439
10	**Scottie Pippen**	14	1308	2948	.444

Free Throws

		Yrs	FT	Att	Pct
1	Michael Jordan	13	1463	1766	.828
2	Jerry West	13	1213	1507	.805
3	**Karl Malone**	16	1173	1583	.741
4	Kareem Abdul-Jabbar	18	1050	1419	.740
5	Magic Johnson	12	1040	1241	.838
6	Larry Bird	12	901	1012	.891
7	John Havlicek	13	874	1046	.836
8	Elgin Baylor	12	847	1101	.769
9	Kevin McHale	13	766	972	.788
10	**Scottie Pippen**	14	763	1057	.722

Assists

		Yrs	Gm	No	Avg
1	Magic Johnson	13	190	2346	12.3
2	John Stockton	17	173	1773	10.2
3	Larry Bird	12	164	1062	6.5
4	Michael Jordan	13	179	1022	5.7
5	Scottie Pippen	14	201	1018	5.1

Rebounds

		Yrs	Gm	No	Avg
1	Bill Russell	13	165	4104	24.9
2	Wilt Chamberlain	13	160	3913	24.5
3	Kareem Abdul-Jabbar	18	237	2481	10.5
4	Wes Unseld	12	119	1777	14.9
5	Karl Malone	16	163	1813	11.1

Appearances

	No
Kareem Abdul-Jabbar	18
John Stockton	17
Robert Parish	16
Karl Malone	16
Jerome Kersey (DNP)	15
Dolph Schayes	15
Paul Silas	14
Hakeem Olajuwon (DNP)	14

Games Played

	No		No
K. Abdul-Jabbar	237	John Stockton	173
Scottie Pippen	201	John Havlicek	170
Danny Ainge	193	Kevin McHale	169
Magic Johnson	190	Michael Cooper	168
Robert Parish	184	Bill Russell	165
Byron Scott	183	Larry Bird	164
Dennis Johnson	180	Paul Silas	163
Michael Jordan	179	Karl Malone	163

SINGLE GAME

Points

	Date	FG-FT-Pts
Michael Jordan, Chi at Bos*	4/20/86	22-19-63
Elgin Baylor, LA at Bos	4/14/62	22-17-61
Wilt Chamberlain, Phi vs Syr	3/22/62	22-12-56
Michael Jordan, Chi at Mia.	4/29/92	20-16-56
Charles Barkley, Pho vs G.St.	5/4/94	23-7-56
Rick Barry, SF vs Phi	4/18/67	22-11-55
Michael Jordan, Chi vs Cle	5/1/88	24-7-55
Michael Jordan, Chi vs Pho	4/16/93	21-13-55
Michael Jordan, Chi vs. Wash	4/27/97	22-10-55

*Double overtime.

Field Goals

	Date	FG	Att
Wilt Chamberlain, Phi vs Syr	3/14/60	24	42
John Havlicek, Bos vs Atl	4/1/73	24	36
Michael Jordan, Chi vs Cle	5/1/88	24	45

Eight tied with 22 each.

Miscellaneous

3-Pt Field Goals

	Date	No
Rex Chapman, Pho at Sea	4/25/97	9
Dan Majerle, Pho vs Sea	6/1/93	8
Allen Iverson, Phi vs Tor	5/16/01	8

Eight tied with 7 each.

Assists

	Date	No
Magic Johnson, LA vs Pho	5/15/84	24
John Stockton, Utah at LA Lakers	5/17/88	24
Magic Johnson, LA Lakers at Port	5/3/85	23
John Stockton, Utah vs Port	4/25/96	23
Doc Rivers, Atl vs Bos	5/16/88	22

Four tied with 21 each.

Rebounds

	Date	No
Wilt Chamberlain, Phi vs Bos	4/5/67	41
Bill Russell, Bos vs Phi	3/23/58	40
Bill Russell, Bos vs St.L	3/29/60	40
Bill Russell, Bos vs LA*	4/18/62	40

Three tied with 39 each.

*Overtime.

Appearances in NBA Finals

Standings of all NBA teams that have reached the NBA Finals since 1947.

App		Titles	Last Won
26	Minneapolis-LA Lakers	13	2001
19	Boston Celtics	16	1986
9	Syracuse Nats-Phila. 76ers	3	1983
8	New York Knicks	2	1973
6	Chicago Bulls	6	1998
6	Phila-SF-Golden St. Warriors	3	1975
5	Ft. Wayne-Detroit Pistons	2	1990
4	Houston Rockets	2	1995
4	St. Louis Hawks	1	1958
4	Baltimore-Washington Bullets	1	1978
3	Portland Trail Blazers	1	1977
3	Seattle SuperSonics	1	1979
2	Milwaukee Bucks	1	1971
2	Phoenix Suns	0	—
2	Utah Jazz	0	—
1	Baltimore Bullets	1	1948
1	Rochester Royals	1	1951
1	San Antonio Spurs	1	1999
1	Chicago Stags	0	—
1	Orlando Magic	0	—
1	Washington Capitols	0	—
1	Indiana Pacers	0	—

Change of address: The St. Louis Hawks now play in Atlanta and the Rochester Royals are now the Sacramento Kings.

Teams now defunct: Baltimore Bullets (1947-55), Chicago Stags (1946-50) and Washington Capitols (1946-51).

NBA FINALS

Points

Series		Year	Pts
4-Gm	Hakeem Olajuwon, Hou vs Orl	1995	131
5-Gm	Allen Iverson, Phi vs LAL	2001	178
6-Gm	Michael Jordan, Chi vs Pho	1993	246
7-Gm	Elgin Baylor, LA vs Bos	1962	284

Field Goals

Series		Year	No
4-Gm	Hakeem Olajuwon, Hou vs Orl	1995	56
5-Gm	Allen Iverson, Phi vs LAL	2001	66
6-Gm	Michael Jordan, Chi vs Pho	1993	101
7-Gm	Elgin Baylor, LA vs Bos	1962	101

Assists

Series		Year	No
4-Gm	Bob Cousy, Bos vs Mpls	1959	51
5-Gm	Magic Johnson, LAL vs Chi	1991	62
6-Gm	Magic Johnson, LAL vs Bos	1985	84
7-Gm	Magic Johnson, LA vs Bos	1984	95

Rebounds

Series		Year	No
4-Gm	Bill Russell, Bos vs Mpls	1959	118
5-Gm	Bill Russell, Bos vs St.L	1961	144
6-Gm	Wilt Chamberlain, Phi vs SF	1967	171
7-Gm	Bill Russell, Bos vs LA	1962	189

The National Basketball League

The NBL started with 13 previously independent teams in 1937-38 and although GE, Firestone and Goodyear were gone by late 1942, ran 12 years before merging with the three-year-old Basketball Association of America in 1949 to form the NBA.

Multiple champions: Akron Firestone Non-Skids, Fort Wayne Zollner Pistons, Oshkosh All-Stars (2).

Year	Winner	Series	Loser	Year	Winner	Series	Loser
1938	Goodyear Wingfoots	2-1	Oshkosh All-Stars	1944	Ft. Wayne Pistons	3-0	Sheboygan Redskins
1939	Firestone Non-Skids	3-2	Oshkosh All-Stars	1945	Ft. Wayne Pistons	3-2	Sheboygan Redskins
1940	Firestone Non-Skids	3-2	Oshkosh All-Stars	1946	Rochester Royals	3-0	Sheboygan Redskins
1941	Oshkosh All-Stars	3-0	Sheboygan Redskins	1947	Chicago Gears	3-2	Rochester Royals
1942	Oshkosh All-Stars	2-1	Ft. Wayne Pistons	1948	Minneapolis Lakers	3-1	Rochester Royals
1943	Sheboygan Redskins	2-1	Ft. Wayne Pistons	1949	Anderson Packers	3-0	Oshkosh All-Stars

NBA All-Star Game

The NBA staged its first All-Star Game before 10,094 at Boston Garden on March 2, 1951. From that year on, the game has matched the best players in the East against the best in the West. Winning coaches are listed first. East leads series, 32-18.

Multiple MVP winners: Bob Pettit (4); Michael Jordan and Oscar Robertson (3); Bob Cousy, Julius Erving, Magic Johnson, Karl Malone and Isiah Thomas (2).

Year		Host	Coaches	Most Valuable Player
1951	East 111, West 94	Boston	Joe Lapchick, John Kundla	Ed Macauley, Boston
1952	East 108, West 91	Boston	Al Cervi, John Kundla	Paul Arizin, Philadelphia
1953	West 79, East 75	Ft. Wayne	John Kundla, Joe Lapchick	George Mikan, Minneapolis
1954	East 98, West 93 (OT)	New York	Joe Lapchick, John Kundla	Bob Cousy, Boston
1955	East 100, West 91	New York	Al Cervi, Charley Eckman	Bill Sharman, Boston
1956	West 108, East 94	Rochester	Charley Eckman, George Senesky	Bob Pettit, St. Louis
1957	East 109, West 97	Boston	Red Auerbach, Bobby Wanzer	Bob Cousy, Boston
1958	East 130, West 118	St. Louis	Red Auerbach, Alex Hannum	Bob Pettit, St. Louis
1959	West 124, East 108	Detroit	Ed Macauley, Red Auerbach	Bob Pettit, St. Louis
				& Elgin Baylor, Minneapolis
1960	East 125, West 115	Philadelphia	Red Auerbach, Ed Macauley	Wilt Chamberlain, Philadelphia
1961	West 153, East 131	Syracuse	Paul Seymour, Red Auerbach	Oscar Robertson, Cincinnati
1962	West 150, East 130	St. Louis	Fred Schaus, Red Auerbach	Bob Pettit, St. Louis
1963	East 115, West 108	Los Angeles	Red Auerbach, Fred Schaus	Bill Russell, Boston
1964	East 111, West 107	Boston	Red Auerbach, Fred Schaus	Oscar Robertson, Cincinnati
1965	East 124, West 123	St. Louis	Red Auerbach, Alex Hannum	Jerry Lucas, Cincinnati
1966	East 137, West 94	Cincinnati	Red Auerbach, Fred Schaus	Adrian Smith, Cincinnati
1967	West 135, East 120	San Francisco	Fred Schaus, Red Auerbach	Rick Barry, San Francisco
1968	East 144, West 124	New York	Alex Hannum, Bill Sharman	Hal Greer, Philadelphia
1969	East 123, West 112	Baltimore	Gene Shue, Richie Guerin	Oscar Robertson, Cincinnati
1970	East 142, West 135	Philadelphia	Red Holzman, Richie Guerin	Willis Reed, New York
1971	West 108, East 107	San Diego	Larry Costello, Red Holzman	Lenny Wilkens, Seattle
1972	West 112, East 110	Los Angeles	Bill Sharman, Tom Heinsohn	Jerry West, Los Angeles
1973	East 104, West 84	Chicago	Tom Heinsohn, Bill Sharman	Dave Cowens, Boston
1974	West 134, East 123	Seattle	Larry Costello, Tom Heinsohn	Bob Lanier, Detroit
1975	East 108, West 102	Phoenix	K.C. Jones, Al Attles	Walt Frazier, New York
1976	East 123, West 109	Philadelphia	Tom Heinsohn, Al Attles	Dave Bing, Washington
1977	West 125, East 124	Milwaukee	Larry Brown, Gene Shue	Julius Erving, Philadelphia
1978	East 133, West 125	Atlanta	Billy Cunningham, Jack Ramsay	Randy Smith, Buffalo
1979	West 134, East 129	Detroit	Lenny Wilkens, Dick Motta	David Thompson, Denver
1980	East 144, West 136 (OT)	Washington	Billy Cunningham, Lenny Wilkens	George Gervin, San Antonio
1981	East 123, West 120	Cleveland	Billy Cunningham, John MacLeod	Nate Archibald, Boston
1982	East 120, West 118	New Jersey	Bill Fitch, Pat Riley	Larry Bird, Boston
1983	East 132, West 123	Los Angeles	Billy Cunningham, Pat Riley	Julius Erving, Philadelphia
1984	East 154, West 145 (OT)	Denver	K.C. Jones, Frank Layden	Isiah Thomas, Detroit
1985	West 140, East 129	Indiana	Pat Riley, K.C. Jones	Ralph Sampson, Houston
1986	East 139, West 132	Dallas	K.C. Jones, Pat Riley	Isiah Thomas, Detroit
1987	West 154, East 149 (OT)	Seattle	Pat Riley, K.C. Jones	Tom Chambers, Seattle
1988	East 138, West 133	Chicago	Mike Fratello, Pat Riley	Michael Jordan, Chicago
1989	West 143, East 134	Houston	Pat Riley, Lenny Wilkens	Karl Malone, Utah
1990	East 130, West 113	Miami	Chuck Daly, Pat Riley	Magic Johnson, LA Lakers
1991	East 116, West 114	Charlotte	Chris Ford, Rick Adelman	Charles Barkley, Philadelphia
1992	West 153, East 113	Orlando	Don Nelson, Phil Jackson	Magic Johnson, LA Lakers
1993	West 135, East 132 (OT)	Salt Lake City	Paul Westphal, Pat Riley	Karl Malone, Utah
				& John Stockton, Utah
1994	East 127, West 118	Minneapolis	Lenny Wilkens, George Karl	Scottie Pippen, Chicago
1995	West 139, East 112	Phoenix	Paul Westphal, Brian Hill	Mitch Richmond, Sacramento
1996	East 129, West 118	San Antonio	Phil Jackson, George Karl	Michael Jordan, Chicago
1997	East 132, West 120	Cleveland	Doug Collins, Rudy Tomjanovich	Glen Rice, Charlotte
1998	East 135, West 114	New York	Larry Bird, George Karl	Michael Jordan, Chicago
1999	Not held—due to lockout			
2000	West 137, East 126	Oakland	Jeff Van Gundy, Phil Jackson	Tim Duncan, San Antonio
				& Shaquille O'Neal, LA Lakers
2001	East 111, West 110	Washington	Larry Brown, Rick Adelman	Allen Iverson, Philadelphia

NBA Franchise Origins

Here is what the current 29 teams in the National Basketball Association have to show for the years they have put in as members of the National Basketball League (NBL), Basketball Association of America (BAA), the NBA, and the American Basketball Association (ABA). League titles are noted by year won.

Western Conference

	First Season	League Titles	Franchise Stops
Dallas Mavericks	1980-81 (NBA)	None	•Dallas (1980–)
Denver Nuggets	1967-68 (ABA)	None	•Denver (1967–)
Golden St. Warriors	1946-47 (BAA)	1 BAA (1947) 2 NBA (1956,75)	•Philadelphia (1946-62) San Francisco (1962-71) Oakland (1971–)
Houston Rockets	1967-68 (NBA)	2 NBA (1994-95)	•San Diego (1967-71) Houston (1971–)
Los Angeles Clippers	1970-71 (NBA)	None	•Buffalo (1970-78) San Diego (1978-84) Los Angeles (1984–)
Los Angeles Lakers	1947-48 (NBL)	1 NBL (1948) 1 BAA (1949) 12 NBA (1950,52-54,72, 80,82,85,87-88,00-01)	•Minneapolis (1947-60) Los Angeles (1960-67) Inglewood, CA (1967-99) Los Angeles (1999–)
Memphis Grizzlies	1995-96 (NBA)	None	•Vancouver (1995-01) Memphis, TN (2001–)
Minnesota Timberwolves	1989-90 (NBA)	None	•Minneapolis (1989–)
Phoenix Suns	1968-69 (NBA)	None	•Phoenix (1968–)
Portland Trail Blazers	1970-71 (NBA)	1 NBA (1977)	•Portland (1970–)
Sacramento Kings	1945-46 (NBL)	1 NBL (1946) 1 NBA (1951)	•Rochester, NY (1945-58) Cincinnati (1958-72) KC-Omaha (1972-75) Kansas City (1975-85) Sacramento (1985–)
San Antonio Spurs	1967-68 (ABA)	1 NBA (1999)	•Dallas (1967-73) San Antonio (1973–)
Seattle SuperSonics	1967-68 (NBA)	1 NBA (1979)	•Seattle (1967–)
Utah Jazz	1974-75 (NBA)	None	•New Orleans (1974-79) Salt Lake City (1979–)

Eastern Conference

	First Season	League Titles	Franchise Stops
Atlanta Hawks	1946-47 (NBL)	1 NBA (1958)	•Tri-Cities (1946-51) Milwaukee (1951-55) St. Louis (1955-68) Atlanta (1968–)
Boston Celtics	1946-47 (BAA)	16 NBA (1957,59-66,68-69 74,76,81,84,86)	•Boston (1946–)
Charlotte Hornets	1988-89 (NBA)	None	•Charlotte (1988–)
Chicago Bulls	1966-67 (NBA)	6 NBA (1991-93,96-98)	•Chicago (1966–)
Cleveland Cavaliers	1970-71 (NBA)	None	•Cleveland (1970-74) Richfield, OH (1974-94) Cleveland (1994–)
Detroit Pistons	1941-42 (NBL)	2 NBL (1944-45) 2 NBA (1989-90)	•Ft. Wayne, IN (1941-57) Detroit (1957-78) Pontiac, MI (1978-88) Auburn Hills, MI (1988–)
Indiana Pacers	1967-68 (ABA)	3 ABA (1970,72-73)	•Indianapolis (1967–)
Miami Heat	1988-89 (NBA)	None	•Miami (1988–)
Milwaukee Bucks	1968-69 (NBA)	1 NBA (1971)	•Milwaukee (1968–)
New Jersey Nets	1967-68 (ABA)	2 ABA (1974,76)	•Teaneck, NJ (1967-68) Commack, NY (1968-69) W. Hempstead, NY (1969-71) Uniondale, NY (1971-77) Piscataway, NJ (1977-81) E. Rutherford, NJ (1981–)
New York Knicks	1946-47 (BAA)	2 NBA (1970,73)	•New York (1946–)
Orlando Magic	1989-90 (NBA)	None	•Orlando, FL (1989–)
Philadelphia 76ers	1949-50 (NBA)	3 NBA (1955,67,83)	•Syracuse, NY (1949-63) Philadelphia (1963–)
Toronto Raptors	1995-96 (NBA)	None	•Toronto (1995–)
Washington Wizards	1961-62 (NBA)	1 NBA (1978)	•Chicago (1961-63) Baltimore (1963-73) Landover, MD (1973–)

Note: The Tri-Cities Blackhawks represented Moline and Rock Island, Ill., and Davenport, Iowa.

The Growth of the NBA

Of the 11 franchises that comprised the Basketball Association of America (BAA) at the start of the 1946-47 season, only three remain—the Boston Celtics, New York Knickerbockers and Golden State Warriors (originally Philadelphia Warriors).

Just before the start of the 1948-49 season, four teams from the more established **National Basketball League** (NBL)—the Ft. Wayne Pistons (now Detroit), Indianapolis Jets, Minneapolis Lakers (now Los Angeles) and Rochester Royals (now Sacramento Kings)—joined the BAA.

A year later, the six remaining NBL franchises—Anderson (Ind.), Denver, Sheboygan (Wisc.), the Syracuse Nationals (now Philadelphia 76ers), Tri-Cities Blackhawks (now Atlanta Hawks) and Waterloo (Iowa)—joined along with the new Indianapolis Olympians and the BAA became the 17-team **National Basketball Association**.

The NBA was down to 10 teams by the 1950-51 season and slipped to eight by 1954-55 with Boston, New York, Philadelphia and Syracuse in the Eastern Division, and Ft. Wayne, Milwaukee (formerly Tri-Cities), Minneapolis and Rochester in the West.

By 1960, five of those surviving eight teams had moved to other cities but by the end of the decade the NBA was a 14-team league. It also had a rival, the **American Basketball Association**, which began play in 1967 with a red, white and blue ball, a three-point line and 11 teams. After a nine-year run, the ABA merged four clubs—the Denver Nuggets, Indiana Pacers, New York Nets and San Antonio Spurs—with the NBA following the 1975-76 season. The NBA adopted the three-point shot in 1979-80.

Expansion/Merger Timetable

For teams currently in NBA.

1948—Added NBL's Ft. Wayne Pistons (now Detroit), Minneapolis Lakers (now Los Angeles) and Rochester Royals (now Sacramento Kings); **1949**—Syracuse Nationals (now Philadelphia 76ers) and Tri-Cities Blackhawks (now Atlanta Hawks).

1961—Chicago Packers (now Washington Wizards); **1966**—Chicago Bulls; **1967**—San Diego Rockets (now Houston) and Seattle SuperSonics; **1968**—Milwaukee Bucks and Phoenix Suns.

1970—Buffalo Braves (now Los Angeles Clippers), Cleveland Cavaliers and Portland Trail Blazers; **1974**—New Orleans Jazz (now Utah); **1976**—added ABA's Denver Nuggets, Indiana Pacers, New York Nets (now New Jersey) and San Antonio Spurs.

1980—Dallas Mavericks; **1988**—Charlotte Hornets and Miami Heat; **1989**—Minnesota Timberwolves and Orlando Magic.

1995—Toronto Raptors and Vancouver Grizzlies (Now Memphis).

City and Nickname Changes

1951—Tri-Cities Blackhawks, who divided home games between Moline and Rock Island, Ill., and Davenport, Iowa, move to Milwaukee and become the Hawks; **1955**—Milwaukee Hawks move to St. Louis; **.1957**—Ft. Wayne Pistons move to Detroit, while Rochester Royals move to Cincinnati.

1960—Minneapolis Lakers move to Los Angeles; **1962**—Chicago Packers renamed Zephyrs, while Philadelphia Warriors move to San Francisco; **1963**—Chicago Zephyrs move to Baltimore and become Bullets, while Syracuse Nationals move to Philadelphia and become 76ers; **1968**—St. Louis Hawks move to Atlanta.

1971—San Diego Rockets move to Houston, while San Francisco Warriors move to Oakland and become Golden State Warriors; **1972**—Cincinnati Royals move to Midwest, divide home games between Kansas City, Mo., and Omaha, Neb., and become Kings; **1973**—Baltimore Bullets move to Landover, Md., outside Washington and become Capital Bullets; **1974**—Capital Bullets renamed Washington Bullets; **1975**—KC-Omaha Kings settle in Kansas City; **1977**—New York Nets move from Uniondale, N.Y., to Piscataway, N.J. (later East Rutherford) and become New Jersey Nets; **1978**—Buffalo Braves move to San Diego and become Clippers; **1979**—New Orleans Jazz move to Salt Lake City and become Utah Jazz.

1984—San Diego Clippers move to Los Angeles; **1985**—Kansas City Kings move to Sacramento.

1997—Washington Bullets become Washington Wizards.

2001—Vancouver Grizzlies move to Memphis, Tenn.

Defunct NBA Teams

Teams that once played in the BAA and NBA, but no longer exist.

Anderson (Ind.)—Packers (1949-50); **Baltimore**—Bullets (1947-55); **Chicago**—Stags (1946-50); **Cleveland**—Rebels (1946-47); **Denver**—Nuggets (1949-50); **Detroit**—Falcons (1946-47); **Indianapolis**—Jets (1948-49) and Olympians (1949-53); **Pittsburgh**—Ironmen (1946-47); **Providence**—Steamrollers (1946-49); **St. Louis**—Bombers (1946-50); **Sheboygan (Wisc.)**—Redskins (1949-50); **Toronto**—Huskies (1946-47); **Washington**—Capitols (1946-51); **Waterloo (Iowa)**—Hawks (1949-50).

ABA Teams (1967-76)

Anaheim—Amigos (1967-68, moved to LA); **Baltimore**—Claws (1975, never played); **Carolina**—Cougars (1969-74, moved to St. Louis); **Dallas**—Chaparrals (1967-73, called Texas Chaparrals in 1970-71, moved to San Antonio); **Denver**—Rockets (1967-76, renamed Nuggets in 1974-76); **Miami**—Floridians (1968-72, called simply Floridians from 1970-72).

Houston—Mavericks (1967-69, moved to North Carolina); **Indiana**—Pacers (1967-76); **Kentucky**—Colonels (1967-76); **Los Angeles**—Stars (1968-70, moved to Utah); **Memphis**—Pros (1970-75, renamed Tams in 1972 and Sounds in 1974, moved to Baltimore); **Minnesota**—Muskies (1967-68, moved to Miami) and Pipers (1968-69, moved back to Pittsburgh); **New Jersey**—Americans (1967-68, moved to New York).

New Orleans—Buccaneers (1967-70, moved to Memphis); **New York**—Nets (1968-76); **Oakland**—Oaks (1967-69, moved to Washington); **Pittsburgh**—Pipers (1967-68, moved to Minnesota), Pipers (1969-72, renamed Condors in 1970); **St. Louis**—Spirits of St. Louis (1974-76); **San Antonio**—Spurs (1973-76); **San Diego**—Conquistadors (1972-75, renamed Sails in 1975); **Utah**—Stars (1970-75); **Virginia**—Squires (1970-76); **Washington**—Caps (1969-70, moved to Virginia).

Annual NBA Leaders
Scoring

Decided by total points from 1947-69, and per game average since 1970. A lockout in 1999 shortened the regular season to 50 games.

Multiple winners: Michael Jordan (10); Wilt Chamberlain (7); George Gervin (4); Neil Johnston, Bob McAdoo and George Mikan (3); Kareem Abdul-Jabbar, Paul Arizin, Adrian Dantley, Allen Iverson, Shaquille O'Neal and Bob Pettit (2).

Year		Gm	Pts	Avg	Year		Gm	Pts	Avg
1947	Joe Fulks, Phi	60	1389	23.2	1975	Bob McAdoo, Buf	82	2831	34.5
1948	Max Zaslofsky, Chi	48	1007	21.0	1976	Bob McAdoo, Buf	78	2427	31.1
1949	George Mikan, Mpls	60	1698	28.3	1977	Pete Maravich, NO	73	2273	31.1
					1978	George Gervin, SA	82	2232	27.2
1950	George Mikan, Mpls	68	1865	27.4	1979	George Gervin, SA	80	2365	29.6
1951	George Mikan, Mpls	68	1932	28.4					
1952	Paul Arizin, Phi	66	1674	25.4	1980	George Gervin, SA	78	2585	33.1
1953	Neil Johnston, Phi	70	1564	22.3	1981	Adrian Dantley, Utah	80	2452	30.7
1954	Neil Johnston, Phi	72	1759	24.4	1982	George Gervin, SA	79	2551	32.3
1955	Neil Johnston, Phi	72	1631	22.7	1983	Alex English, Den	82	2326	28.4
1956	Bob Pettit, St.L	72	1849	25.7	1984	Adrian Dantley, Utah	79	2418	30.6
1957	Paul Arizin, Phi	71	1817	25.6	1985	Bernard King, NY	55	1809	32.9
1958	George Yardley, Det	72	2001	27.8	1986	Dominique Wilkins, Atl	78	2366	30.3
1959	Bob Pettit, St.L	72	2105	29.2	1987	Michael Jordan, Chi	82	3041	37.1
					1988	Michael Jordan, Chi	82	2868	35.0
1960	Wilt Chamberlain, Phi	72	2707	37.6	1989	Michael Jordan, Chi	81	2633	32.5
1961	Wilt Chamberlain, Phi	79	3033	38.4					
1962	Wilt Chamberlain, Phi	80	4029	50.4	1990	Michael Jordan, Chi	82	2753	33.6
1963	Wilt Chamberlain, SF	80	3586	44.8	1991	Michael Jordan, Chi	82	2580	31.5
1964	Wilt Chamberlain, SF	80	2948	36.9	1992	Michael Jordan, Chi	80	2404	30.1
1965	Wilt Chamberlain, SF-Phi	73	2534	34.7	1993	Michael Jordan, Chi	78	2541	32.6
1966	Wilt Chamberlain, Phi	79	2649	33.5	1994	David Robinson, SA	80	2383	29.8
1967	Rick Barry, SF	78	2775	35.6	1995	Shaquille O'Neal, Orl	79	2315	29.3
1968	Dave Bing, Det	79	2142	27.1	1996	Michael Jordan, Chi	82	2491	30.4
1969	Elvin Hayes, SD	82	2327	28.4	1997	Michael Jordan, Chi	82	2431	29.7
					1998	Michael Jordan, Chi	82	2357	28.7
1970	Jerry West, LA	74	2309	31.2	1999	Allen Iverson, Phi	48	1284	26.8
1971	Lew Alcindor, Mil	82	2596	31.7					
1972	Kareem Abdul-Jabbar, Mil	81	2822	34.8	2000	Shaquille O'Neal, LAL	79	2344	29.7
1973	Nate Archibald, KC-Omaha	80	2719	34.0	2001	Allen Iverson, Phi	71	2207	31.1
1974	Bob McAdoo, Buf	74	2261	30.6					

Note: Lew Alcindor changed his name to Kareem Abdul-Jabbar after the 1970-71 season.

Rebounds

Decided by total rebounds from 1951-69 and per game average since 1970.

Multiple winners: Wilt Chamberlain (11); Dennis Rodman (7); Moses Malone (6); Bill Russell (4); Elvin Hayes, Dikembe Mutombo and Hakeem Olajuwon (2).

Year		Gm	No	Avg	Year		Gm	No	Avg
1951	Dolph Schayes, Syr	66	1080	16.4	1977	Bill Walton, Port	65	934	14.4
1952	Larry Foust, Ft. Wayne	66	880	13.3	1978	Len Robinson, NO	82	1288	15.7
	& Mel Hutchins, Mil	66	880	13.3	1979	Moses Malone, Hou	82	1444	17.6
1953	George Mikan, Mpls	70	1007	14.4					
1954	Harry Gallatin, NY	72	1098	15.3	1980	Swen Nater, SD	81	1216	15.0
1955	Neil Johnston, Phi	72	1085	15.1	1981	Moses Malone, Hou	80	1180	14.8
1956	Bob Pettit, St.L	72	1164	16.2	1982	Moses Malone, Hou	81	1188	14.7
1957	Maurice Stokes, Roch	72	1256	17.4	1983	Moses Malone, Phi	78	1194	15.3
1958	Bill Russell, Bos	69	1564	22.7	1984	Moses Malone, Phi	71	950	13.4
1959	Bill Russell, Bos	70	1612	23.0	1985	Moses Malone, Phi	79	1031	13.1
					1986	Bill Laimbeer, Det	82	1075	13.1
1960	Wilt Chamberlain, Phi	72	1941	27.0	1987	Charles Barkley, Phi	68	994	14.6
1961	Wilt Chamberlain, Phi	79	2149	27.2	1988	Michael Cage, LAC	72	938	13.0
1962	Wilt Chamberlain, Phi	80	2052	25.7	1989	Hakeem Olajuwon, Hou	82	1105	13.5
1963	Wilt Chamberlain, SF	80	1946	24.3					
1964	Bill Russell, Bos	78	1930	24.7	1990	Hakeem Olajuwon, Hou	82	1149	14.0
1965	Bill Russell, Bos	78	1878	24.1	1991	David Robinson, SA	82	1063	13.0
1966	Wilt Chamberlain, Phi	79	1943	24.6	1992	Dennis Rodman, Det	82	1530	18.7
1967	Wilt Chamberlain, Phi	81	1957	24.2	1993	Dennis Rodman, Det	62	1232	18.3
1968	Wilt Chamberlain, Phi	82	1952	23.8	1994	Dennis Rodman, SA	79	1132	17.3
1969	Wilt Chamberlain, LA	81	1712	21.1	1995	Dennis Rodman, SA	49	823	16.8
					1996	Dennis Rodman, Chi	64	952	14.9
1970	Elvin Hayes, SD	82	1386	16.9	1997	Dennis Rodman, Chi	55	883	16.1
1971	Wilt Chamberlain, LA	82	1493	18.2	1998	Dennis Rodman, Chi	80	1201	15.0
1972	Wilt Chamberlain, LA	82	1572	19.2	1999	Chris Webber, Sac	42	545	13.0
1973	Wilt Chamberlain, LA	82	1526	18.6					
1974	Elvin Hayes, Cap*	81	1463	18.1	2000	Dikembe Mutombo, Atl	82	1157	14.1
1975	Wes Unseld, Wash	73	1077	14.8	2001	Dikembe Mutombo, Atl-Phi	75	1015	13.5
1976	Kareem Abdul-Jabbar, LA	82	1383	16.9					

*The Baltimore Bullets moved to Landover, Md. in 1973-74 and became first the Capital Bullets, then the Washington Bullets in 1974-75.

Annual NBA Leaders (Cont.)
Assists

Decided by total assists from 1952-69 and per game average since 1970.

Multiple winners: John Stockton (9); Bob Cousy (8); Oscar Robertson (6); Magic Johnson and Kevin Porter (4); Jason Kidd (3); Andy Phillip and Guy Rodgers (2).

Year		No	Year		No	Year		No
1947	Ernie Calverly, Prov	.202	1966	Oscar Robertson, Cin	.847	1985	Isiah Thomas, Det	13.9
1948	Howie Dallmar, Phi	.120	1967	Guy Rodgers, Chi	.908	1986	Magic Johnson, LAL	12.6
1949	Bob Davies, Roch	.321	1968	Wilt Chamberlain, Phi	.702	1987	Magic Johnson, LAL	12.2
1950	Dick McGuire, NY	.386	1969	Oscar Robertson, Cin	.772	1988	John Stockton, Utah	13.8
1951	Andy Phillip, Phi	.414	1970	Lenny Wilkens, Sea	9.1	1989	John Stockton, Utah	13.6
1952	Andy Phillip, Phi	.539	1971	Norm Van Lier, Chi	10.1	1990	John Stockton, Utah	14.5
1953	Bob Cousy, Bos	.547	1972	Jerry West, LA	9.7	1991	John Stockton, Utah	14.2
1954	Bob Cousy, Bos	.518	1973	Nate Archibald, KC-O	11.4	1992	John Stockton, Utah	13.7
1955	Bob Cousy, Bos	.557	1974	Ernie DiGregorio, Buf	8.2	1993	John Stockton, Utah	12.0
1956	Bob Cousy, Bos	.642	1975	Kevin Porter, Wash	8.0	1994	John Stockton, Utah	12.6
1957	Bob Cousy, Bos	.478	1976	Slick Watts, Sea	8.1	1995	John Stockton, Utah	12.3
1958	Bob Cousy, Bos	.463	1977	Don Buse, Ind	8.5	1996	John Stockton, Utah	11.2
1959	Bob Cousy, Bos	.557	1978	Kevin Porter, Det-NJ	10.2	1997	Mark Jackson, Den-Ind	11.4
1960	Bob Cousy, Bos	.715	1979	Kevin Porter, Det	13.4	1998	Rod Strickland, Wash	10.5
1961	Oscar Robertson, Cin	.690	1980	M.R. Richardson, NY	10.1	1999	Jason Kidd, Pho	10.8
1962	Oscar Robertson, Cin	.899	1981	Kevin Porter, Wash	9.1	2000	Jason Kidd, Pho	10.1
1963	Guy Rodgers, SF	.825	1982	Johnny Moore, SA	9.6	2001	Jason Kidd, Pho	9.8
1964	Oscar Robertson, Cin	.868	1983	Magic Johnson, LA	10.5			
1965	Oscar Robertson, Cin	.861	1984	Magic Johnson, LA	13.1			

Field Goal Percentage

Multiple winners: Wilt Chamberlain (9); Shaquille O'Neal (5); Artis Gilmore (4); Neil Johnston (3); Bob Feerick, Johnny Green, Alex Groza, Cedric Maxwell, Kevin McHale, Gheorghe Muresan, Kenny Sears and Buck Williams (2).

Year		Pct	Year		Pct	Year		Pct
1947	Bob Feerick, Wash	.401	1966	Wilt Chamberlain, Phi	.540	1985	James Donaldson, LAC	.637
1948	Bob Feerick, Wash	.340	1967	Wilt Chamberlain, Phi	.683	1986	Steve Johnson, SA	.632
1949	Arnie Risen, Roch	.423	1968	Wilt Chamberlain, Phi	.595	1987	Kevin McHale, Bos	.604
1950	Alex Groza, Indpls	.478	1969	Wilt Chamberlain, LA	.583	1988	Kevin McHale, Bos	.604
1951	Alex Groza, Indpls	.470	1970	Johnny Green, Cin	.559	1989	Dennis Rodman, Det.	.595
1952	Paul Arizin, Phi	.448	1971	Johnny Green, Cin	.587	1990	Mark West, Pho.	.625
1953	Neil Johnston, Phi	.452	1972	Wilt Chamberlain, LA	.649	1991	Buck Williams, Port	.602
1954	Ed Macauley, Bos	.486	1973	Wilt Chamberlain, LA	.727	1992	Buck Williams, Port	.604
1955	Larry Foust, Ft.W	.487	1974	Bob McAdoo, Buf	.547	1993	Cedric Ceballos, Pho	.576
1956	Neil Johnston, Phi.	.457	1975	Don Nelson, Bos	.539	1994	Shaquille O'Neal, Orl	.599
1957	Neil Johnston, Phi.	.447	1976	Wes Unseld, Wash	.561	1995	Chris Gatling, G.St	.633
1958	Jack Twyman, Cin	.452	1977	K. Abdul-Jabbar, LA	.579	1996	Gheorghe Muresan, Wash.	.584
1959	Kenny Sears, NY	.490	1978	Bobby Jones, Den	.578	1997	Gheorghe Muresan, Wash.	.604
1960	Kenny Sears, NY	.477	1979	Cedric Maxwell, Bos	.584	1998	Shaquille O'Neal, LAL	.584
1961	Wilt Chamberlain, Phi	.509	1980	Cedric Maxwell, Bos	.609	1999	Shaquille O'Neal, LAL	.576
1962	Walt Bellamy, Chi	.519	1981	Artis Gilmore, Chi	.670	2000	Shaquille O'Neal, LAL	.574
1963	Wilt Chamberlain, SF	.528	1982	Artis Gilmore, Chi	.652	2001	Shaquille O'Neal, LAL	.572
1964	Jerry Lucas, Cin	.527	1983	Artis Gilmore, SA	.626			
1965	W. Chamberlain, SF-Phi	.510	1984	Artis Gilmore, SA	.631			

Free Throw Percentage

Multiple winners: Bill Sharman (7); Rick Barry (6); Larry Bird (4); Reggie Miller, Mark Price and Dolph Schayes (3); Mahmoud Abdul-Rauf, Larry Costello, Ernie DiGregorio, Bob Feerick, Kyle Macy, Calvin Murphy, Oscar Robertson and Larry Siegfried (2).

Year		Pct	Year		Pct	Year		Pct
1947	Fred Scolari, Wash	.811	1966	Larry Siegfried, Bos	.881	1985	Kyle Macy, Pho	.907
1948	Bob Feerick, Wash	.788	1967	Adrian Smith, Cin	.903	1986	Larry Bird, Bos	.896
1949	Bob Feerick, Wash	.859	1968	Oscar Robertson, Cin	.873	1987	Larry Bird, Bos	.910
1950	Max Zaslofsky, Chi	.843	1969	Larry Siegfried, NY	.864	1988	Jack Sikma, Mil	.922
1951	Joe Fulks, Phi	.855	1970	Flynn Robinson, Mil	.898	1989	Magic Johnson, LAL	.911
1952	Bob Wanzer, Roch	.904	1971	Chet Walker, Chi	.859	1990	Larry Bird, Bos	.930
1953	Bill Sharman, Bos	.850	1972	Jack Marin, Bal	.894	1991	Reggie Miller, Ind	.918
1954	Bill Sharman, Bos	.844	1973	Rick Barry, G.St.	.902	1992	Mark Price, Cle	.947
1955	Bill Sharman, Bos	.897	1974	Ernie DiGregorio, Buf	.902	1993	Mark Price, Cle	.948
1956	Bill Sharman, Bos	.867	1975	Rick Barry, G.St.	.904	1994	M. Abdul-Rauf, Den	.956
1957	Bill Sharman, Bos	.905	1976	Rick Barry, G.St.	.923	1995	Spud Webb, Sac	.934
1958	Dolph Schayes, Syr	.904	1977	Ernie DiGregorio, Buf	.945	1996	M. Abdul-Rauf, Den	.930
1959	Bill Sharman, Bos	.932	1978	Rick Barry, G.St.	.924	1997	Mark Price, G.St.	.906
1960	Dolph Schayes, Syr	.892	1979	Rick Barry, Hou	.947	1998	Chris Mullin, Ind.	.939
1961	Bill Sharman, Bos	.921	1980	Rick Barry, Hou	.935	1999	Reggie Miller, Ind	.915
1962	Dolph Schayes, Syr	.896	1981	Calvin Murphy, Hou	.958	2000	Jeff Hornacek, Utah	.950
1963	Larry Costello, Syr	.881	1982	Kyle Macy, Pho	.899	2001	Reggie Miller, Ind	.928
1964	Oscar Robertson, Cin	.853	1983	Calvin Murphy, Hou	.920			
1965	Larry Costello, Phi	.877	1984	Larry Bird, Bos	.888			

Blocked Shots

Decided by per game average since 1973-74 season.

Multiple winners: Kareem Abdul-Jabbar and Mark Eaton (4); George Johnson, Dikembe Mutombo and Hakeem Olajuwon (3); Manute Bol and Alonzo Mourning (2).

Year		Gm	No	Avg
1974	Elmore Smith, LA	.81	393	4.85
1975	Kareem Abdul-Jabbar, Mil	.65	212	3.26
1976	Kareem Abdul-Jabbar, LA	.82	338	4.12
1977	Bill Walton, Port	.65	211	3.25
1978	George Johnson, NJ	.81	274	3.38
1979	Kareem Abdul-Jabbar, LA	.80	316	3.95
1980	Kareem Abdul-Jabbar, LA	.82	280	3.41
1981	George Johnson, SA	.82	278	3.39
1982	George Johnson, SA	.75	234	3.12
1983	Tree Rollins, Atl	.80	343	4.29
1984	Mark Eaton, Utah	.82	351	4.28
1985	Mark Eaton, Utah	.82	456	5.56
1986	Manute Bol, Wash	.80	397	4.96
1987	Mark Eaton, Utah	.79	321	4.06
1988	Mark Eaton, Utah	.82	304	3.71
1989	Manute Bol, G.St.	.80	345	4.31
1990	Akeem Olajuwon, Hou	.82	376	4.59
1991	Hakeem Olajuwon, Hou	.56	221	3.95
1992	David Robinson, SA	.68	305	4.49
1993	Hakeem Olajuwon, Hou	.82	342	4.17
1994	Dikembe Mutombo, Den	.82	336	4.10
1995	Dikembe Mutombo, Den	.82	321	3.91
1996	Dikembe Mutombo, Den	.74	332	4.49
1997	Shawn Bradley, Dal-NJ	.73	248	3.40
1998	Marcus Camby, Tor	.63	230	3.65
1999	Alonzo Mourning, Mia	.46	180	3.91
2000	Alonzo Mourning, Mia	.79	294	3.72
2001	Theo Ratliff, Phi-Atl	.50	187	3.74

Note: Akeem Olajuwon changed the spelling of his first name to Hakeem during the 1990-91 season.

Steals

Decided by per game average since 1973-74 season.

Multiple winners: Michael Jordan, Micheal Ray Richardson and Alvin Robertson (3); Mookie Blaylock, Magic Johnson and John Stockton (2).

Year		Gm	No	Avg
1974	Larry Steele, Port	.81	217	2.68
1975	Rick Barry, G.St.	.80	228	2.85
1976	Slick Watts, Sea	.82	261	3.18
1977	Don Buse, Ind	.81	281	3.47
1978	Ron Lee, Pho	.82	225	2.74
1979	M.L. Carr, Det	.80	197	2.46
1980	Micheal Ray Richardson, NY	.82	265	3.23
1981	Magic Johnson, LA	.37	127	3.43
1982	Magic Johnson, LA	.78	208	2.67
1983	Micheal Ray Richardson, G. ST-NJ	.64	182	2.84
1984	Rickey Green, Utah	.81	215	2.65
1985	Micheal Ray Richardson, NJ	.82	243	2.96
1986	Alvin Robertson, SA	.82	301	3.67
1987	Alvin Robertson, SA	.81	260	3.21
1988	Michael Jordan, Chi	.82	259	3.16
1989	John Stockton, Utah	.82	263	3.21
1990	Michael Jordan, Chi	.82	227	2.77
1991	Alvin Robertson, SA	.81	246	3.04
1992	John Stockton, Utah	.82	244	2.98
1993	Michael Jordan, Chi	.78	221	2.83
1994	Nate McMillan, Sea	.73	216	2.96
1995	Scottie Pippen, Chi	.79	232	2.94
1996	Gary Payton, Sea	.81	231	2.85
1997	Mookie Blaylock, Atl	.78	212	2.72
1998	Mookie Blaylock, Atl	.70	183	2.61
1999	Kendall Gill, NJ	.50	134	2.68
2000	Eddie Jones, Cha	.72	192	2.67
2001	Allen Iverson, Phi	.71	178	2.51

All-Time NBA Regular Season Leaders

Through the 2000-01 regular season.

CAREER

Players active in 2000-01 in **bold** type.

Points

		Yrs	Gm	Pts	Avg
1	Kareem Abdul-Jabbar	20	1560	38,387	24.6
2	**Karl Malone**	16	1273	32,919	25.9
3	Wilt Chamberlain	14	1045	31,419	30.1
4	Michael Jordan	13	930	29,277	31.5
5	Moses Malone	19	1329	27,409	20.6
6	Elvin Hayes	16	1303	27,313	21.0
7	Oscar Robertson	14	1040	26,710	25.7
8	Dominique Wilkins	15	1074	26,668	24.8
9	**Hakeem Olajuwon**	17	1177	26,511	22.5
10	John Havlicek	16	1270	26,395	20.8
11	Alex English	15	1193	25,613	21.5
12	Jerry West	14	932	25,192	27.0
13	**Patrick Ewing**	16	1118	24,425	21.8
14	Charles Barkley	16	1073	23,757	22.1
15	Robert Parish	21	1611	23,334	14.5
16	Adrian Dantley	15	955	23,177	24.3
17	Elgin Baylor	14	846	23,149	27.4
18	Clyde Drexler	15	1086	22,195	20.4
19	Larry Bird	13	897	21,791	24.3
20	Hal Greer	15	1122	21,586	19.2
21	**Reggie Miller**	14	1094	21,319	19.5
22	Walt Bellamy	14	1043	20,941	20.1
23	Bob Pettit	11	792	20,880	26.4
24	George Gervin	10	791	20,708	26.2
25	**Mitch Richmond**	13	912	20,237	22.2
26	Tom Chambers	16	1107	20,049	18.1
27	Bernard King	14	874	19,655	22.5
28	Walter Davis	15	1033	19,521	18.9
29	Terry Cummings	18	1183	19,460	16.4
30	**David Robinson**	12	845	19,293	22.8

Scoring Average

Minimum of 400 games or 10,000 points.

		Yrs	Gm	Pts	Avg
1	Michael Jordan	13	930	29,277	31.5
2	Wilt Chamberlain	14	1045	31,419	30.1
3	**Shaquille O'Neal**	9	608	16,812	27.7
4	Elgin Baylor	14	846	23,149	27.4
5	Jerry West	14	932	25,192	27.0
6	Bob Pettit	11	792	20,880	26.4
7	George Gervin	10	791	20,708	26.2
8	**Karl Malone**	16	1273	32,919	25.9
9	Oscar Robertson	14	1040	26,710	25.7
10	Dominique Wilkins	15	1074	26,668	24.8
11	Kareem Abdul-Jabbar	20	1560	38,387	24.6
12	Larry Bird	13	897	21,791	24.3
13	Adrian Dantley	15	955	23,177	24.3
14	Pete Maravich	10	658	15,948	24.2
15	Rick Barry	10	794	18,395	23.2
16	**David Robinson**	12	845	19,293	22.8
17	Paul Arizin	10	713	16,266	22.8
18	George Mikan	9	520	11,764	22.6
19	**Hakeem Olajuwon**	17	1177	26,511	22.5
20	Bernard King	14	874	19,655	22.5
21	**Mitch Richmond**	13	912	20,237	22.2
22	David Thompson	8	509	11,264	22.1
23	Charles Barkley	16	1073	23,757	22.1
24	Bob McAdoo	14	852	18,787	22.1
25	Julius Erving	11	836	18,364	22.0
26	**Patrick Ewing**	16	1118	24,425	21.8
27	**Chris Webber**	8	475	10,345	21.8
28	Alex English	15	1193	25,613	21.5
29	**Jerry Stackhouse**	7	436	9,238	21.2
30	Elvin Hayes	16	1303	27,313	21.0

All-Time NBA Regular Season Leaders (Cont.)

NBA-ABA Top 20

Points

All-Time combined regular season scoring leaders, including ABA service (1968-76). NBA players with ABA experience are listed in CAPITAL letters. Players active during 1999-2000 are in **bold** type.

		Yrs	Pts	Avg
1	Kareem Abdul-Jabbar	20	38,387	24.6
2	**Karl Malone**	16	32,919	25.9
3	Wilt Chamberlain	14	31,419	30.1
4	JULIUS ERVING	16	30,026	24.2
5	MOSES MALONE	21	29,580	20.3
5	Michael Jordan	13	29,277	31.5
7	DAN ISSEL	15	27,482	22.6
8	Elvin Hayes	16	27,313	21.0
9	Oscar Robertson	14	26,710	25.7
10	Dominique Wilkins	15	26,668	24.8
11	GEORGE GERVIN	14	26,595	25.1
12	**Hakeem Olajuwon**	17	26,511	22.5
13	John Havlicek	16	26,395	20.8
14	Alex English	15	25,613	21.5
15	RICK BARRY	14	25,279	24.8
16	Jerry West	14	25,192	27.0
17	ARTIS GILMORE	17	24,941	18.8
18	**Patrick Ewing**	16	24,425	21.8
19	Charles Barkley	16	23,757	22.1
20	Robert Parish	21	23,334	14.5

ABA Totals: BARRY (4 yrs, 226 gm, 6884 pts, 30.5 avg); ERVING (5 yrs, 407 gm, 11,662 pts, 28.7 avg); GERVIN (4 yrs, 269 gm, 5887 pts, 21.9 avg); GILMORE (5 yrs, 420 gm, 9362 pts, 22.3 avg); ISSEL (6 yrs, 500 gm, 12,823 pts, 25.6 avg); MALONE (2 yrs, 126 gm, 2171 pts, 17.2 avg).

Field Goals

		Yrs	FG	Att	Pct
1	Kareem Abdul-Jabbar	20	15,837	28,307	.559
2	Wilt Chamberlain	14	12,681	23,497	.540
3	**Karl Malone**	16	12,102	23,122	.523
4	Elvin Hayes	16	10,976	24,272	.452
5	Michael Jordan	13	10,958	21,686	.505
6	Alex English	15	10,659	21,036	.507
7	John Havlicek	16	10,513	23,930	.439
8	**Hakeem Olajuwon**	17	10,555	20,573	.513
9	Dominique Wilkins	15	9,963	21,589	.461
10	Robert Parish	21	9,614	17,914	.537

Note: If field goals made in the ABA are included, consider these NBA-ABA totals: Julius Erving (11,818), Dan Issel (10,431), George Gervin (10,368), Moses Malone (10,277) and Rick Barry (9,695).

Free Throws

		Yrs	FT	Att	Pct
1	**Karl Malone**	16	8636	11,703	.738
2	Moses Malone	19	8531	11,090	.769
3	Oscar Robertson	14	7694	9,185	.838
4	Jerry West	14	7160	8,801	.814
5	Dolph Schayes	16	6979	8,273	.844
6	Adrian Dantley	15	6832	8,351	.818
7	Michael Jordan	13	6798	8,115	.838
8	Kareem Abdul-Jabbar	20	6712	9,304	.721
9	Charles Barkley	16	6349	8,643	.734
10	Bob Pettit	11	6182	8,119	.761

Note: If free throws made in the ABA are included, consider these totals: Moses Malone (9,018), Dan Issel (6,591), and Julius Erving (6,256).

Assists

		Yrs	Gm	No	Avg
1	**John Stockton**	17	1340	14,503	10.8
2	Magic Johnson	13	906	10,141	11.2
3	Oscar Robertson	14	1040	9,887	9.5
4	**Mark Jackson**	14	1090	9,235	8.5
5	Isiah Thomas	13	979	9,061	9.3
6	Maurice Cheeks	15	1101	7,392	6.7
7	Lenny Wilkens	15	1077	7,211	6.7
8	**Rod Strickland**	13	894	7,027	7.9
9	Bob Cousy	14	924	6,955	7.5
10	Guy Rodgers	12	892	6,917	7.8

Rebounds

		Yrs	Gm	No	Avg
1	Wilt Chamberlain	14	1045	23,924	22.9
2	Bill Russell	13	963	21,620	22.5
3	Kareem Abdul-Jabbar	20	1560	17,440	11.2
4	Elvin Hayes	16	1303	16,279	12.5
5	Moses Malone	19	1329	16,212	12.2
6	Robert Parish	21	1611	14,715	9.1
7	Nate Thurmond	14	964	14,464	15.0
8	Walt Bellamy	14	1043	14,241	13.7
9	Wes Unseld	13	984	13,769	14.0
10	**Hakeem Olajuwon**	17	1177	13,381	11.4

Note: If rebounds accumulated in the ABA are included, consider the following totals: Moses Malone (17,834) and Artis Gilmore (16,330).

Steals

		Yrs	Gm	No
1	**John Stockton**	17	1340	2976
2	Maurice Cheeks	15	1101	2310
3	Michael Jordan	13	930	2306
4	Clyde Drexler	15	1086	2207
5	Alvin Robertson	10	779	2112

Note: Steals have only been an official stat since the 1973-74 season.

Blocked Shots

		Yrs	Gm	No
1	**Hakeem Olajuwon**	17	1177	3740
2	Kareem Abdul-Jabbar	20	1560	3189
3	Mark Eaton	11	875	3064
4	**Patrick Ewing**	16	1118	2849
5	**David Robinson**	12	845	2703

Note: Blocked shots have only been an official stat since the 1973-74 season. Also, note that if ABA records are included, consider the following block totals: Artis Gilmore (3,178).

Games Played

		Yrs	Career	Gm
1	Robert Parish	21	1976-97	1611
2	Kareem Abdul-Jabbar	20	1970-89	1560
3	**John Stockton**	17	1984–	1340
4	Moses Malone	19	1976-95	1329
5	Buck Williams	17	1982-98	1307

Note: If ABA records are included, consider the following game totals: Moses Malone (1,455) and Artis Gilmore (1,329).

Personal Fouls

		Yrs	Gm	Fouls	DQ
1	Kareem Abdul-Jabbar	20	1560	4657	48
2	Robert Parish	21	1611	4443	86
3	Buck Williams	17	1307	4267	58
4	**Hakeem Olajuwon**	17	1177	4236	80
5	Elvin Hayes	16	1303	4193	53

Note: If ABA records are included, consider the following personal foul totals: Artis Gilmore (4,529) and Caldwell Jones (4,436).

SINGLE SEASON

Scoring Average

		Season	Avg
1	Wilt Chamberlain, Phi	1961-62	50.4
2	Wilt Chamberlain, SF	1962-63	44.8
3	Wilt Chamberlain, Phi	1960-61	38.4
4	Elgin Baylor, LA	1961-62	38.3
5	Wilt Chamberlain, Phi	1959-60	37.6
6	Michael Jordan, Chi	1986-87	37.1
7	Wilt Chamberlain, SF	1963-64	36.9
8	Rick Barry, SF	1966-67	35.6
9	Michael Jordan, Chi	1987-88	35.0
10	Elgin Baylor, LA	1960-61	34.8
	Kareem Abdul-Jabbar, Mil	1971-72	34.8

Assists

		Season	Avg
1	John Stockton, Utah	1989-90	14.5
2	John Stockton, Utah	1990-91	14.2
3	Isiah Thomas, Det	1984-85	13.9
4	John Stockton, Utah	1987-88	13.8
5	John Stockton, Utah	1991-92	13.7
6	John Stockton, Utah	1988-89	13.6
7	Kevin Porter, Det	1978-79	13.4
8	Magic Johnson, LAL	1983-84	13.1
9	Magic Johnson, LAL	1988-89	12.8
10	Magic Johnson, LAL	1984-85	12.6
	John Stockton, Utah	1993-94	12.6

Field Goal Pct.

		Season	Pct
1	Wilt Chamberlain, LA	1972-73	.727
2	Wilt Chamberlain, SF	1966-67	.683
3	Artis Gilmore, Chi	1980-81	.670
4	Artis Gilmore, Chi	1981-82	.652
5	Wilt Chamberlain, LA	1971-72	.649

Rebounds

		Season	Avg
1	Wilt Chamberlain, Phi	1960-61	27.2
2	Wilt Chamberlain, Phi	1959-60	27.0
3	Wilt Chamberlain, Phi	1961-62	25.7
4	Bill Russell, Bos	1963-64	24.7
5	Wilt Chamberlain, Phi	1965-66	24.6

Free Throw Pct.

		Season	Pct
1	Calvin Murphy, Hou	1980-81	.958
2	Mahmoud Abdul-Rauf, Den	1993-94	.956
3	Mark Price, Cle	1992-93	.948
4	Mark Price, Cle	1991-92	.947
	Rick Barry, Hou	1978-79	.947

Blocked Shots

		Season	Avg
1	Mark Eaton, Utah	1984-85	5.56
2	Manute Bol, Wash	1985-86	4.96
3	Elmore Smith, LA	1973-74	4.85
4	Mark Eaton, Utah	1985-86	4.61
5	Hakeem Olajuwon, Hou	1989-90	4.59

3-Pt Field Goal Pct.

		Season	Pct
1.	Steve Kerr, Chi	1994-95	.524
2	Jon Sundvold, Mia	1988-89	.522
3	Tim Legler, Wash	1995-96	.522
4	Steve Kerr, Chi	1995-96	.515
5	Detlef Schrempf, Sea	1994-95	.514

Steals

		Season	Avg
1	Alvin Robertson, SA	1985-86	3.67
2	Don Buse, Ind	1976-77	3.47
3	Magic Johnson, LAL	1980-81	3.43
4	Micheal Ray Richardson, NY	1979-80	3.23
5	Alvin Robertson, SA	1986-87	3.21

SINGLE GAME

Points

	Date	FG-FT	Pts
Wilt Chamberlain, Phi vs NY	3/2/62	36-28-	100
Wilt Chamberlain, Phi vs LA***	12/8/61	31-16-	78
Wilt Chamberlain, Phi vs Chi	1/13/62	29-15-	73
Wilt Chamberlain, SF at NY	11/16/62	29-15-	73
David Thompson, Den at Det	4/9/78	28-17-	73
Wilt Chamberlain, SF at LA	11/3/62	29-14-	72
Elgin Baylor, LA at NY	11/15/60	28-15-	71
David Robinson, SA at LAC	4/24/94	26-18-	71
Wilt Chamberlain, SF at Syr	3/10/63	27-16-	70
Michael Jordan, Chi at Cle*	3/28/90	23-21-	69
Wilt Chamberlain, Phi at Chi	12/16/67	30-8-	68
Pete Maravich, NO vs NYK	2/25/77	26-16-	68
Wilt Chamberlain, Phi vs NY	3/9/61	27-13-	67
Wilt Chamberlain, Phi at St. L	2/17/62	26-15-	67
Wilt Chamberlain, Phi vs NY	2/25/62	25-17-	67
Wilt Chamberlain, SF vs LA	1/11/63	28-11-	67
Wilt Chamberlain, LA vs Pho	2/9/69	29-8-	66
Wilt Chamberlain, Phi at Cin	2/13/62	24-17-	65
Wilt Chamberlain, Phi at St. L	2/27/62	25-15-	65
Wilt Chamberlain, Phi vs LA	2/7/66	28-9-	65
Elgin Baylor, Mpls vs Bos	11/8/59	25-14-	64
Rick Barry, G.St. vs Port	3/26/74	30-4-	64
Michael Jordan, Chi vs Orl	1/16/93	27-9-	64

*Overtime
***Triple overtime.

Note: Wilt Chamberlain's 100-point game vs New York was played at Hershey, Penn.

Field Goals

	Date	FG	Att
Wilt Chamberlain, Phi vs NY	3/2/62	36	63
Wilt Chamberlain, Phi vs LA***	12/8/61	31	62
Wilt Chamberlain, Phi at Chi	12/16/67	30	40
Rick Barry, G.St. vs Port	2/26/74	30	45
Wilt Chamberlain made 29 four times.			

***Triple overtime.

Free Throws

	Date	FT	Att
Wilt Chamberlain, Phi vs NY	3/2/62	28	32
Adrian Dantley, Utah vs Hou	1/4/84	28	29
Adrian Dantley, Utah vs Den	11/25/83	27	31
Adrian Dantley, Utah vs Dal	10/31/80	26	29
Michael Jordan, Chi vs NJ	2/26/87	26	27

3-Pt Field Goals

	Date	No
Dennis Scott, Orl vs Atl	4/18/96	11
Brian Shaw, Mia at Mil	4/8/93	10
Joe Dumars, Det vs Min	11/8/94	10
George McCloud, Dal vs Pho	12/16/95	10*
Many tied with 9 each		

* Overtime

All-Time NBA Regular Season Leaders (Cont.)

Assists

	Date	No
Scott Skiles, Orl vs Den	12/30/90	30
Kevin Porter, NJ vs Hou	2/24/78	29
Bob Cousy, Bos vs Mpls	2/27/59	28
Guy Rodgers, SF vs St.L	3/14/63	28
John Stockton, Utah vs SA	1/15/91	28

Rebounds

	Date	No
Wilt Chamberlain, Phi vs Bos	11/24/60	55
Bill Russell, Bos vs Syr	2/5/60	51
Bill Russell, Bos vs Phi	11/16/57	49
Bill Russell, Bos vs Det	3/11/65	49
Wilt Chamberlain, Phi vs Syr	2/6/60	45
Wilt Chamberlain, Phi vs LA	1/21/61	45

Blocked Shots

	Date	No
Elmore Smith, LA vs Port	10/28/73	17
Manute Bol, Wash vs Atl	1/25/86	15
Manute Bol, Wash vs Ind	2/26/87	15
Shaquille O'Neal, Orl at NJ	11/20/93	15

Steals

	Date	No
Larry Kenon, San Antonio at KC	12/26/76	11
Kendall Gill, NJ vs Mia	4/3/99	11
14 different players tied with 10 each, including Alvin Robertson, who had 10 steals in a game four times.		

All-Time Winningest NBA Coaches

Top 25 NBA career victories through the 2000-01 season. Career, regular season and playoff records are noted along with NBA titles won. Coaches active during 2000-01 season in **bold** type.

		Yrs	Career W	L	Pct	Regular Season W	L	Pct	Playoffs W	L	Pct	NBA Titles
1	**Lenny Wilkens**	28	**1304**	1107	.541	1226	1016	.547	78	91	.462	1 (1979)
2	**Pat Riley**	19	**1204**	566	.680	1049	466	.692	155	100	.608	4 (1982,85,87-88)
3	Red Auerbach	20	**1037**	548	.654	938	479	.662	99	69	.589	9 (1957, 59-66)
4	**Don Nelson**	23	**1034**	848	.550	979	781	.556	55	67	.451	None
5	Bill Fitch	25	**999**	1157	.463	944	1106	.460	55	54	.505	1 (1981)
6	Dick Motta	25	**991**	1087	.477	935	1017	.479	56	70	.444	1 (1978)
7	Jack Ramsay	21	**908**	841	.519	864	783	.525	44	58	.431	1 (1977)
8	Cotton Fitzsimmons	21	**867**	824	.513	832	775	.518	35	49	.417	None
9	**Jerry Sloan**	16	**860**	521	.623	784	448	.636	76	73	.510	None
10	**Larry Brown**	18	**849**	675	.557	788	612	.563	61	63	.492	None
11	Gene Shue	22	**814**	908	.473	784	861	.477	30	47	.390	None
12	**Phil Jackson**	11	**809**	284	.740	668	234	.741	141	50	.738	8 (1991-93,96-98,00,01)
13	Red Holzman	18	**754**	652	.536	696	604	.535	58	48	.547	2 (1970, 73)
	John MacLeod	18	**754**	711	.515	707	657	.518	47	54	.465	None
15	Chuck Daly	14	**713**	488	.594	638	437	.593	75	51	.595	2 (1989-90)
16	**George Karl**	14	**682**	481	.586	625	418	.599	57	63	.475	None
17	Doug Moe	15	**661**	579	.533	628	529	.543	33	50	.398	None
18	K.C. Jones	10	**603**	309	.661	522	252	.674	81	57	.587	2 (1984,86)
19	Del Harris	14	**594**	507	.540	556	457	.549	38	50	.432	None
20	Mike Fratello	14	**592**	499	.543	572	465	.552	20	34	.370	None
21	Al Attles	14	**588**	548	.518	557	518	.518	31	30	.508	1 (1975)
22	**Rick Adelman**	11	**526**	384	.578	483	340	.587	43	44	.494	None
23	Billy Cunningham	8	**520**	235	.689	454	196	.698	66	39	.629	1 (1983)
24	Alex Hannum	12	**518**	446	.537	471	412	.533	47	34	.580	2 (1958, 67)
25	John Kundla	11	**485**	338	.589	423	302	.583	62	36	.633	5 (1949-50, 52-54)

Note: The NBA does not recognize records from the National Basketball League (1937-49), the American Basketball League (1961-62) or the American Basketball Assn. (1968-76), so the following NBL, ABL and ABA overall coaching records are not included above: NBL—**John Kundla** (51-19 and a title in 1 year); ABA—**Larry Brown** (249-129 in 4 yrs), **Alex Hannum** (194-164 and one title in 4 yrs), **K.C. Jones** (30-58 in 1 yr); **Kevin Loughery** (189-95 and one title in 3 yrs).

Where They Coached

Adelman—Portland (1988-94), Golden State (1995-97), Sacramento (1998–); **Attles**—Golden St. (1970-80,80-83); **Auerbach**—Washington (1946-49), Tri-Cities (1949-50), Boston (1950-66); **Brown**—Denver (1976-79), New Jersey (1981-83), San Antonio (1988-92), LA Clippers (1992-93), Indiana (1993-97), Philadelphia (1997–); **Cunningham**—Philadelphia (1977-85); **Daly**—Cleveland (1981-82), Detroit (1983-92), New Jersey (1992-94), Orlando (1997-99); **Fitch**—Cleveland (1970-79), Boston (1979-83), Houston (1983-88), New Jersey (1989-92), LA Clippers (1994-98); **Fitzsimmons**—Phoenix (1970-72), Atlanta (1972-76), Buffalo (1977-78), Kansas City (1978-84), San Antonio (1984-86), Phoenix (1988-92, 95-96); **Fratello**—Atlanta (1980-90), Cleveland (1993-99).

Hannum—St. Louis (1957-58), Syracuse (1960-63), San Francisco (1963-66), Phila. 76ers (1966-68), Houston (1970-71); **Harris**—Houston (1979-83), Milwaukee (1987-92), LA Lakers (1994-99); **Holzman**—Milwaukee-St. Louis Hawks (1954-57), NY Knicks (1968-77,78-82); **Jackson**—Chicago (1989-98), LA Lakers (1999–); **Jones**—Washington (1973-76), Boston (1983-88), Seattle (1990-92); **Karl**—Cleveland (1984-86); Golden St. (1986-88), Seattle (1991-98), Milwaukee (1999–); **Kundla**—Minneapolis (1948-57,58-59); **MacLeod**—Phoenix (1973-87), Dallas (1987-89), NY Knicks (1990-91); **Moe**—San Antonio (1976-80), Denver (1981-90), Philadelphia (1992-93).

Motta—Chicago (1968-76), Washington (1976-80), Dallas (1980-87), Sacramento (1990-91), Dallas (1994-96), Denver (1997); **Nelson**—Milwaukee (1976-87), Golden St. (1988-95), New York (1995-96), Dallas (1997–); **Ramsay**—Philadelphia (1968-72), Buffalo (1972-76), Portland (1976-86), Indiana (1986-89); **Riley**—LA Lakers (1981-90), New York (1991-95), Miami (1995–); **Shue**—Baltimore (1967-73), Philadelphia (1973-77), San Diego Clippers (1978-80), Washington (1980-86), LA Clippers (1987-89); **Sloan**—Chicago (1979-82), Utah (1988–); **Wilkens**—Seattle (1969-72), Portland (1974-76), Seattle (1977-85), Cleveland (1986-93), Atlanta (1993-00), Toronto (2000–).

Top Winning Percentages

Minimum of 350 victories, including playoffs; coaches active during 2000-01 season in **bold** type.

		Yrs	W	L	Pct
1	**Phil Jackson**	11	809	284	**.740**
2	Billy Cunningham	8	520	235	**.689**
3	**Pat Riley**	19	1204	566	**.680**
4	K.C. Jones	10	603	309	**.661**
5	Red Auerbach	20	1037	548	**.654**
6	**Jerry Sloan**	16	860	521	**.623**
7	Tommy Heinsohn	9	474	296	**.616**
8	Chuck Daly	14	713	488	**.594**
9	Larry Costello	10	467	323	**.591**
10	John Kundla	11	485	338	**.589**
11	**George Karl**	14	682	481	**.586**
12	**Rudy Tomjanovich**	10	483	343	**.585**
13	Bill Sharman	7	368	267	**.580**
14	**Rick Adelman**	11	526	384	**.578**
15	Al Cervi	9	359	267	**.573**
16	Joe Lapchick	9	356	277	**.562**
17	**Larry Brown**	18	849	675	**.557**
18	**Don Nelson**	23	1034	848	**.550**
19	Mike Fratello	14	592	499	**.543**
20	Bill Russell	8	375	317	**.542**
21	**Lenny Wilkens**	28	1304	1107	**.541**
22	Del Harris	14	594	507	**.540**
23	Alex Hannum	12	518	446	**.537**
24	Red Holzman	18	754	652	**.536**
25	Doug Moe	15	661	579	**.533**

Active Coaches' Victories

Through 2000-01 season, including playoffs.

		Yrs	W	L	Pct
1	Lenny Wilkens, Toronto	28	1304	1107	.541
2	Pat Riley, Miami	19	1204	566	.680
3	Don Nelson, Dallas	23	1034	848	.550
4	Jerry Sloan, Utah	16	860	521	.623
5	Larry Brown, Philadelphia	18	849	675	.557
6	Phil Jackson, LA Lakers	11	809	284	.740
7	George Karl, Milwaukee	14	682	481	.586
8	Rick Adelman, Sacramento	11	526	384	.578
9	Rudy Tomjanovich, Houston	10	483	343	.585
10	Jeff Van Gundy, New York	6	275	195	.585
11	Doug Collins, Washington	6	273	220	.554
12	Gregg Popovich, San Antonio	5	248	155	.615
13	Phil Saunders, Minnesota	6	232	228	.504
14	Paul Silas, Charlotte	6	202	257	.440
15	Dan Issel, Denver	5	177	197	.473
16	Dave Cowens, Golden St.	6	157	184	.460
17	John Lucas, Cleveland	4	142	179	.442
18	Alvin Gentry, LA Clippers	5	121	147	.451
19	Scott Skiles, Phoenix	2	96	61	.611
20	Doc Rivers, Orlando	2	85	83	.506
21	Sidney Lowe, Memphis	3	56	161	.258
22	Tim Floyd, Chicago	3	45	169	.210
23	Isiah Thomas, Indiana	1	41	41	.500
24	Nate McMillan, Seattle	1	38	29	.567
25	Byron Scott, New Jersey	1	26	56	.317
26	Lon Kruger, Atlanta	1	25	57	.305
27	Jim O'Brien, Boston	1	24	24	.500
28	Maurice Cheeks, Portland	0	0	0	—
29	Rick Carlisle, Detroit	0	0	0	—

Annual Awards

Most Valuable Player

The Maurice Podoloff Trophy for regular season MVP. Named after the first commissioner (then president) of the NBA. Winners first selected by the NBA players (1956-80) then a national panel of pro basketball writers and broadcasters (since 1981). Winners' scoring averages are provided; (^) indicates led league.

Multiple winners: Kareem Abdul-Jabbar (6); Michael Jordan and Bill Russell (5); Wilt Chamberlain (4); Larry Bird, Magic Johnson and Moses Malone (3); Karl Malone and Bob Pettit (2).

Year		Avg
1956	Bob Pettit, St. Louis, F	25.7*
1957	Bob Cousy, Boston, G	20.6
1958	Bill Russell, Boston, C	16.6
1959	Bob Pettit, St. Louis, F	29.2*
1960	Wilt Chamberlain, Philadelphia, C	37.6*
1961	Bill Russell, Boston, C	16.9
1962	Bill Russell, Boston, C	18.9
1963	Bill Russell, Boston, C	16.8
1964	Oscar Robertson, Cincinnati, G	31.4
1965	Bill Russell, Boston, C	14.1
1966	Wilt Chamberlain, Philadelphia, C	33.5*
1967	Wilt Chamberlain, Philadelphia, C	24.1
1968	Wilt Chamberlain, Philadelphia, C	24.3
1969	Wes Unseld, Baltimore, C	13.8
1970	Willis Reed, New York, C	21.7
1971	Lew Alcindor, Milwaukee, C	31.7*
1972	Kareem Abdul-Jabbar, Milwaukee, C	34.8*
1973	Dave Cowens, Boston, C	20.5
1974	Kareem Abdul-Jabbar, Milwaukee, C	27.0
1975	Bob McAdoo, Buffalo, F	34.5*
1976	Kareem Abdul-Jabbar, LA, C	27.7
1977	Kareem Abdul-Jabbar, LA, C	26.2
1978	Bill Walton, Portland, C	18.9
1979	Moses Malone, Houston, C	24.8

Year		Avg
1980	Kareem Abdul-Jabbar, LA, C	24.8
1981	Julius Erving, Philadelphia, F	24.6
1982	Moses Malone, Houston, C	31.1
1983	Moses Malone, Philadelphia, C	24.5
1984	Larry Bird, Boston, F	24.2
1985	Larry Bird, Boston, F	28.7
1986	Larry Bird, Boston, F	25.8
1987	Magic Johnson, LAL, G	23.9
1988	Michael Jordan, Chicago, G	35.0*
1989	Magic Johnson, LAL, G	22.5
1990	Magic Johnson, LAL, G	22.3
1991	Michael Jordan, Chicago, G	31.5*
1992	Michael Jordan, Chicago, G	30.1*
1993	Charles Barkley, Phoenix, F	25.6
1994	Hakeem Olajuwon, Houston, C	27.3
1995	David Robinson, San Antonio, C	27.6
1996	Michael Jordan, Chicago, G	30.4*
1997	Karl Malone, Utah, F	27.4
1998	Michael Jordan, Chicago, G	28.7*
1999	Karl Malone, Utah, F	23.8
2000	Shaquille O'Neal, LAL, C	29.7*
2001	Allen Iverson, Philadelphia, G	31.1*

Note: Lew Alcindor changed his name to Kareem Abdul-Jabbar after the 1970-71 season.

Annual Awards (Cont.)
Rookie of the Year

The Eddie Gottlieb Trophy for outstanding rookie of the regular season. Named after the pro basketball pioneer and owner-coach of the first NBA champion Philadelphia Warriors. Winners selected by a national panel of pro basketball writers and broadcasters. Winners' scoring averages provided; (*) indicates led league; winners who were also named MVP are in **bold** type.

Year		Avg	Year		Avg
1953	Don Meineke, Ft. Wayne, F	10.8	1978	Walter Davis, Phoenix, G	24.2
1954	Ray Felix, Baltimore, C	17.6	1979	Phil Ford, Kansas City, G	15.9
1955	Bob Pettit, Milwaukee Hawks, F.	20.4	1980	Larry Bird, Boston, F	21.3
1956	Maurice Stokes, Rochester, F/C	16.8	1981	Darrell Griffith, Utah, G	20.6
1957	Tommy Heinsohn, Boston, F	16.2	1982	Buck Williams, New Jersey, F	15.5
1958	Woody Sauldsberry, Philadelphia, F/C	12.8	1983	Terry Cummings, San Diego, F	23.7
1959	Elgin Baylor, Minneapolis, F	24.9	1984	Ralph Sampson, Houston, C	21.0
1960	**Wilt Chamberlain**, Philadelphia, C	37.6*	1985	Michael Jordan, Chicago, G	28.2
1961	Oscar Robertson, Cincinnati, G	30.5	1986	Patrick Ewing, New York, C	20.0
1962	Walt Bellamy, Chicago Packers, C	31.6	1987	Chuck Person, Indiana, F	18.8
1963	Terry Dischinger, Chicago Zephyrs, F	25.5	1988	Mark Jackson, New York, G	13.6
1964	Jerry Lucas, Cincinnati, F/C	17.7	1989	Mitch Richmond, Golden St., G	22.0
1965	Willis Reed, New York, C	19.5	1990	David Robinson, San Antonio, C	24.3
1966	Rick Barry, San Francisco, F	25.7	1991	Derrick Coleman, New Jersey, F	18.4
1967	Dave Bing, Detroit, G	20.0	1992	Larry Johnson, Charlotte, F	19.2
1968	Earl Monroe, Baltimore, G	24.3	1993	Shaquille O'Neal, Orlando, C	23.4
1969	**Wes Unseld**, Baltimore, C	13.8	1994	Chris Webber, Golden St., F	17.5
1970	Lew Alcindor, Milwaukee Bucks, C	28.8	1995	Grant Hill, Detroit, F	19.9
1971	Dave Cowens, Boston, C	17.0		& Jason Kidd, Dallas, G	11.7
	& Geoff Petrie, Portland, G	24.8	1996	Damon Stoudamire, Toronto, G	19.0
1972	Sidney Wicks, Portland, F	24.5	1997	Allen Iverson, Philadelphia, G	23.5
1973	Bob McAdoo, Buffalo, C/F	18.0	1998	Tim Duncan, San Antonio, F/C	21.6
1974	Ernie DiGregorio, Buffalo, G	15.2	1999	Vince Carter, Toronto, F	18.3
1975	Keith Wilkes, Golden St., F	14.2	2000	Elton Brand, Chicago, F	20.1
1976	Alvan Adams, Phoenix, C	19.0		& Steve Francis, Houston, G	18.0
1977	Adrian Dantley, Buffalo, F	20.3	2001	Mike Miller, Orlando, G/F	11.9

Note: The Chicago Packers changed their name to the Zephyrs after 1961-62 season. Also, Lew Alcindor changed his name to Kareem Abdul-Jabbar after the 1970-71 season.

Sixth Man Award

Awarded to the Best Player Off the Bench for the regular season. Winners selected by a national panel of pro basketball writers and broadcasters.

Multiple winners: Kevin McHale, Ricky Pierce and Detlef Schrempf (2).

Year		Year		Year	
1983	Bobby Jones, Phi., F	1990	Ricky Pierce, Mil., G/F	1997	John Starks, NY, G
1984	Kevin McHale, Bos., F	1991	Detlef Schrempf, Ind., F	1998	Danny Manning, Pho., F
1985	Kevin McHale, Bos., F	1992	Detlef Schrempf, Ind., F	1999	Darrell Armstrong, Orl., G
1986	Bill Walton, Bos., F/C	1993	Cliff Robinson, Port., F	2000	Rodney Rogers, Pho., F
1987	Ricky Pierce, Mil., G/F	1994	Dell Curry, Char., G	2001	Aaron McKie, Phi., G
1988	Roy Tarpley, Dal., F	1995	Anthony Mason, NY, F		
1989	Eddie Johnson, Pho., F	1996	Toni Kukoc, Chi., F		

Number One Draft Choices

Overall first choices in the NBA draft since the abolition of the territorial draft in 1966. Players who became Rookie of the Year are in **bold** type. The draft lottery began in 1985.

Year		Overall 1st Pick	Year		Overall 1st Pick
1966	New York	Cazzie Russell, Michigan	1984	Houston	Akeem Olajuwon, Houston
1967	Detroit	Jimmy Walker, Providence	1985	New York	**Patrick Ewing**, Georgetown
1968	San Diego	Elvin Hayes, Houston	1986	Cleveland	Brad Daugherty, N. Carolina
1969	Milwaukee	**Lew Alcindor**, UCLA	1987	San Antonio	**David Robinson**, Navy
1970	Detroit	Bob Lanier, St. Bonaventure	1988	LA Clippers	Danny Manning, Kansas
1971	Cleveland	Austin Carr, Notre Dame	1989	Sacramento	Pervis Ellison, Louisville
1972	Portland	LaRue Martin, Loyola-Chicago	1990	New Jersey	**Derrick Coleman**, Syracuse
1973	Philadelphia	Doug Collins, Illinois St.	1991	Charlotte	**Larry Johnson**, UNLV
1974	Portland	Bill Walton, UCLA	1992	Orlando	**Shaquille O'Neal**, LSU
1975	Atlanta	David Thompson, N.C. State	1993	Orlando	**Chris Webber**, Michigan
1976	Houston	John Lucas, Maryland	1994	Milwaukee	Glenn Robinson, Purdue
1977	Milwaukee	Kent Benson, Indiana	1995	Golden St.	Joe Smith, Maryland
1978	Portland	Mychal Thompson, Minnesota	1996	Philadelphia	**Allen Iverson**, Georgetown
1979	LA Lakers	Magic Johnson, Michigan St.	1997	San Antonio	**Tim Duncan**, Wake Forest
1980	Golden St	Joe Barry Carroll, Purdue	1998	LA Clippers	Michael Olowokandi, Pacific
1981	Dallas	Mark Aguirre, DePaul	1999	Chicago	**Elton Brand**, Duke
1982	LA Lakers	James Worthy, N. Carolina	2000	New Jersey	Kenyon Martin, Cincinnati
1983	Houston	**Ralph Sampson**, Virginia	2001	Washington	Kwame Brown, Glynn Acad.

Note: Lew Alcindor changed his name to Kareem Abdul-Jabbar after the 1970-71 season; Akeem Olajuwon changed his first name to Hakeem in 1991; in 1975 David Thompson signed with Denver of the ABA and did not play for Atlanta; David Robinson joined NBA for 1989-90 season after fulfilling military obligation.

Defensive Player of the Year

Awarded to the Best Defensive Player for the regular season. Winners selected by a national panel of pro basketball writers and broadcasters.

Multiple winners: Dikembe Mutombo (4); Mark Eaton, Sidney Moncrief, Alonzo Mourning, Hakeem Olajuwon and Dennis Rodman (2).

Year		Year		Year	
1983	Sidney Moncrief, Mil., G	1990	Dennis Rodman, Det., F	1996	Gary Payton, Sea., G
1984	Sidney Moncrief, Mil., G	1991	Dennis Rodman, Det., F	1997	Dikembe Mutombo, Atl., C
1985	Mark Eaton, Utah, C	1992	David Robinson, SA, C	1998	Dikembe Mutombo, Atl., C
1986	Alvin Robertson, SA, G	1993	Hakeem Olajuwon, Hou., C	1999	Alonzo Mourning, Mia., C
1987	Michael Cooper, LAL, F	1994	Hakeem Olajuwon, Hou., C	2000	Alonzo Mourning, Mia., C
1988	Michael Jordan, Chi., G	1995	Dikembe Mutombo, Den., C	2001	Dikembe Mutombo, Atl.-Phi., C
1989	Mark Eaton, Utah, C				

Most Improved Player

Awarded to the Most Improved Player for the regular season. Winners selected by a national panel of pro basketball writers and broadcasters.

Year		Year		Year	
1986	Alvin Robertson, SA, G	1992	Pervis Ellison, Wash., C	1997	Isaac Austin, Miami, C
1987	Dale Ellis, Sea., G	1993	Mahmoud Abdul-Rauf, Den., G	1998	Alan Henderson, Atl., F
1988	Kevin Duckworth, Port., C	1994	Don MacLean, Wash., F	1999	Darrell Armstrong, Orl., G
1989	Kevin Johnson, Pho., G	1995	Dana Barros, Phi., G	2000	Jalen Rose, Ind., G
1990	Rony Seikaly, Mia., C	1996	Gheorghe Muresan, Wash., C	2001	Tracy McGrady, Orl., F
1991	Scott Skiles, Orl., G				

Coach of the Year

The Red Auerbach Trophy for outstanding coach of the year. Renamed in 1967 for the former Boston coach who led the Celtics to nine NBA titles. Winners selected by a national panel of pro basketball writers and broadcasters. Previous season and winning season records are provided; (*) indicates division title.

Multiple winners: Don Nelson and Pat Riley (3); Bill Fitch, Cotton Fitzsimmons and Gene Shue (2).

Year			Improvement		Year			Improvement	
1963	Harry Gallatin, St. L	29-51	to	48-32	1983	Don Nelson, Mil	55-27*	to	51-31*
1964	Alex Hannum, SF	31-49	to	48-32*	1984	Frank Layden, Utah	30-52	to	45-37*
1965	Red Auerbach, Bos	59-21*	to	61-18*	1985	Don Nelson, Mil	50-32*	to	59-23*
1966	Dolph Schayes, Phi	40-40	to	55-25*	1986	Mike Fratello, Atl	34-48	to	50-32
1967	Johnny Kerr, Chi.	Expan.	to	33-48	1987	Mike Schuler, Port	40-42	to	49-33
1968	Richie Guerin, St. L	39-42	to	56-26*	1988	Doug Moe, Den	37-45	to	54-28*
1969	Gene Shue, Balt	36-46	to	57-25*	1989	Cotton Fitzsimmons, Pho	28-54	to	55-27
1970	Red Holzman, NY	54-28	to	60-22*	1990	Pat Riley, LA Lakers	57-25*	to	63-19*
1971	Dick Motta, Chi	39-43	to	51-31	1991	Don Chaney, Hou	41-41	to	52-30
1972	Bill Sharman, LA	48-34*	to	69-13*	1992	Don Nelson, GS	44-38	to	55-27
1973	Tommy Heinsohn, Bos	56-26*	to	68-14*	1993	Pat Riley, NY	51-31	to	60-22
1974	Ray Scott, Det	40-42	to	52-30	1994	Lenny Wilkens, Atl	43-39	to	57-25*
1975	Phil Johnson, KC-Omaha	33-49	to	44-38	1995	Del Harris, LA Lakers	33-49	to	48-34
1976	Bill Fitch, Cle	40-42	to	49-33*	1996	Phil Jackson, Chi	47-35	to	72-10*
1977	Tom Nissalke, Hou	40-42	to	49-33*	1997	Pat Riley, Mia	42-40	to	61-21
1978	Hubie Brown, Atl	31-51	to	41-41	1998	Larry Bird, Ind	39-43	to	58-24
1979	Cotton Fitzsimmons, KC	31-51	to	48-34*	1999	Mike Dunleavy, Port	46-36	to	35-15*
1980	Bill Fitch, Bos	29-53	to	61-21*	2000	Doc Rivers, Orlando	33-17	to	41-41
1981	Jack McKinney, Ind	37-45	to	44-38	2001	Larry Brown, Phila.	49-33	to	56-26*
1982	Gene Shue, Wash	39-43	to	43-39					

World Championships

The World Basketball Championships for men and women have been played regularly at four-year intervals (give or take a year) since 1970. The men's tournament began in 1950 and the women's in 1953. The Federation Internationale de Basketball Amateur (FIBA), which governs the World and Olympic tournaments, was founded in 1932. FIBA first allowed professional players from the NBA to participate in 1994. A team of collegians represented the USA in 1998.

Men

Multiple wins: Yugoslavia (4); Soviet Union and USA (3); Brazil (2).

Year	
1950	**Argentina**, United States, Chile
1954	**United States**, Brazil, Philippines
1959	**Brazil**, United States, Chile
1963	**Brazil**, Yugoslavia, Soviet Union
1967	**Soviet Union**, Yugoslavia, Brazil
1970	**Yugoslavia**, Brazil, Soviet Union
1974	**Soviet Union**, Yugoslavia, United States
1978	**Yugoslavia**, Soviet Union, Brazil
1982	**Soviet Union**, United States, Yugoslavia
1986	**United States**, Soviet Union, Yugoslavia
1990	**Yugoslavia**, Soviet Union, United States
1994	**United States**, Russia, Croatia
1998	**Yugoslavia**, Russia, United States
2002	at Indianapolis (August)

Women

Multiple wins: Soviet Union and USA (6).

Year	
1953	**United States**, Chile, France
1957	**United States**, Soviet Union, Czechoslovakia
1959	**Soviet Union**, Bulgaria, Czechoslovakia
1964	**Soviet Union**, Czechoslovakia, Bulgaria
1967	**Soviet Union**, South Korea, Czechoslovakia
1971	**Soviet Union**, Czechoslovakia, Brazil
1975	**Soviet Union**, Japan, Czechoslovakia
1979	**United States**, South Korea, Canada
1983	**Soviet Union**, United States, China
1986	**United States**, Soviet Union, Canada
1990	**United States**, Yugoslavia, Cuba
1994	**Brazil**, China, United States
1998	**United States**, Russia, Australia
2002	at China (May)

NBA Photos

NBA's 50 Greatest Players

In October 1996, as part of its 50th anniversary celebration, the NBA named the 50 greatest players in league history. The voting was done by a league-approved panel of media, former players and coaches, current and former general managers and team executives. The players are listed alphabetically along with the dates of their professional careers and positions. Active players are in **bold** type.

Player	Pos	Player	Pos	Player	Pos
Kareem Abdul-Jabbar, 1969-89	C	George Gervin, 1972-86	G	Bob Pettit, 1954-65	F/C
Nate Archibald, 1970-84	G	Hal Greer, 1958-73	G	**Scottie Pippen**, 1987—	F
Paul Arizin, 1950-61	F/G	John Havlicek, 1962-78	F/G	Willis Reed, 1964-74	C
Charles Barkley, 1984-00	F	Elvin Hayes, 1968-84	F/C	Oscar Robertson, 1960-74	G
Rick Barry, 1965-80	F	Magic Johnson, 1979-91, 96	G	**David Robinson**, 1989—	C
Elgin Baylor, 1958-72	F	Sam Jones, 1957-69	G	Bill Russell, 1956-69	C
Dave Bing, 1966-78	G	Michael Jordan, 1984-93, 95-98	G	Dolph Schayes, 1948-64	F/C
Larry Bird, 1979-92	F	Jerry Lucas, 1963-74	F/C	Bill Sharman, 1950-61	G
Wilt Chamberlain, 1959-73	C	**Karl Malone**, 1985—	F	**John Stockton**, 1984—	G
Bob Cousy, 1950-63, 69-70	G	Moses Malone, 1974-95	C	Isiah Thomas, 1981-94	G
Dave Cowens, 1970-80, 1982-83	C	Pete Maravich, 1970-80	G	Nate Thurmond, 1963-77	C/F
Billy Cunningham, 1965-76	G	Kevin McHale, 1980-93	F	Wes Unseld, 1968-81	C/F
Dave DeBusschere, 1962-74	F	George Mikan, 1946-54, 55-56	C	Bill Walton, 1974-88	C
Clyde Drexler, 1983-98	G	Earl Monroe, 1967-80	G	Jerry West, 1960-74	G
Julius Erving, 1971-87	F	**Hakeem Olajuwon**, 1984—	C	Lenny Wilkens, 1960-75	G
Patrick Ewing, 1985—	C	**Shaquille O'Neal**, 1992—	C	James Worthy, 1982-94	F
Walt Frazier, 1967-80	G	Robert Parish, 1976-97	C		

Note: Rick Barry, Billy Cunningham, Julius Erving, George Gervin and Moses Malone all played part of their pro careers in the ABA.

NBA's 10 Greatest Coaches

In December 1996, as part of its 50th anniversary celebration, the NBA named the 10 greatest coaches in league history. The voting was done by a league-approved panel of media. The coaches are listed alphabetically along with the dates of their professional coaching careers and overall records, including playoff games, and number of NBA titles won. Active coaches are in **bold** type.

Coach	W	L	Pct.	Titles	Coach	W	L	Pct.	Titles
Red Auerbach, 1946-66	1037	548	.654	9	**Don Nelson**, 1976-96, 97—	1034	848	.549	0
Chuck Daly, 1981-94, 97-99	713	488	.594	2	Jack Ramsay, 1968-89	908	841	.519	1
Bill Fitch, 1970-98	999	1157	.463	1	**Pat Riley**, 1981—	1204	566	.680	4
Red Holzman, 1953-82	754	652	.536	2	**Lenny Wilkens**, 1969—	1304	1107	.541	1
Phil Jackson, 1989-98, 99—	.810	284	.740	8	TOTALS	9248	6829	.575	33
John Kundla, 1947-59	.485	338	.589	5					

American Basketball Association
ABA Finals

The American Basketball Assn. began play in 1967-68 as a 10-team rival of the 21-year-old NBA. The ABA, which introduced the three-point basket, a multi-colored ball and the All-Star Game Slam Dunk Contest, lasted nine seasons before folding following the 1975-76 season. Four ABA teams—Denver, Indiana, New York and San Antonio—survived to enter the NBA in 1976-77. The NBA also adopted the three-point basket (in 1979-80) and the All-Star Game Slam Dunk Contest. The older league, however, refused to take in the ABA ball.

Multiple winners: Indiana (3); New York (2).

Year	Winner	Head Coach	Series	Loser	Head Coach
1968	Pittsburgh Pipers	Vince Cazzetta	4-3 (WLLWLWW)	New Orleans Bucs	Babe McCarthy
1969	Oakland Oaks	Alex Hannum	4-1 (WLWWW)	Indiana Pacers	Bob Leonard
1970	Indiana Pacers	Bob Leonard	4-2 (WWLWLW)	Los Angeles Stars	Bill Sharman
1971	Utah Stars	Bill Sharman	4-3 (WWLLWLW)	Kentucky Colonels	Frank Ramsey
1972	Indiana Pacers	Bob Leonard	4-2 (WLWLWW)	New York Nets	Lou Carnesecca
1973	Indiana Pacers	Bob Leonard	4-3 (WLLWWLW)	Kentucky Colonels	Joe Mullaney
1974	New York Nets	Kevin Loughery	4-1 (WWWLW)	Utah Stars	Joe Mullaney
1975	Kentucky Colonels	Hubie Brown	4-1 (WWWLW)	Indiana Pacers	Bob Leonard
1976	New York Nets	Kevin Loughery	4-2 (WLWWLW)	Denver Nuggets	Larry Brown

Most Valuable Player

Winners' scoring averages provided; (*) indicates led league.

Multiple winners: Julius Erving (3); Mel Daniels (2).

Year		Avg
1968	Connie Hawkins, Pittsburgh, C	26.8*
1969	Mel Daniels, Indiana, C	24.0
1970	Spencer Haywood, Denver, C	30.0*
1971	Mel Daniels, Indiana, C	21.0
1972	Artis Gilmore, Kentucky, C	23.8
1973	Billy Cunningham, Carolina, F	24.1
1974	Julius Erving, New York, F	27.4*
1975	George McGinnis, Indiana, F	29.8*
	& Julius Erving, New York, F	27.9
1976	Julius Erving, New York, F	29.3*

Rookie of the Year

Winners' scoring averages provided; (*) indicates led league. Rookies who were also named Most Valuable Player are in **bold** type.

Year		Avg
1968	Mel Daniels, Minnesota, C	22.2
1969	Warren Armstrong, Oakland, G	21.5
1970	**Spencer Haywood**, Denver, C	30.0*
1971	Dan Issel, Kentucky, C	29.8*
	& Charlie Scott, Virginia, G	27.1
1972	**Artis Gilmore**, Kentucky, C	23.8
1973	Brian Taylor, New York, G	15.3
1974	Swen Nater, Virginia-SA, C	14.1
1975	Marvin Barnes, St. Louis, C	24.0
1976	David Thompson, Denver, F	26.0

Note: Warren Armstrong changed his name to Warren Jabali after the 1970-71 season.

Coach of the Year

Previous season and winning season records are provided; (*) indicates division title.

Multiple winner: Larry Brown (3).

Year		Improvement
1968	Vince Cazzetta, Pittsburgh	54-24*
1969	Alex Hannum, Oakland	22-56 to 60-18*
1970	Joe Belmont, Denver	44-34 to 51-33*
	& Bill Sharman, LA Stars	33-45 to 43-41
1971	Al Bianchi, Virginia	44-40 to 55-29*
1972	Tom Nissalke, Dallas	30-54 to 42-42
1973	Larry Brown, Carolina	35-49 to 57-27*
1974	Babe McCarthy, Kentucky	56-28 to 53-31
	& Joe Mullaney, Utah	55-29* to 51-33*
1975	Larry Brown, Denver	37-47 to 65-19*
1976	Larry Brown, Denver	65-19* to 60-24*

Scoring Leaders

Scoring championship decided by per game point average every season.

Multiple winner: Julius Erving (3).

Year		Gm	Avg	Pts
1968	Connie Hawkins, Pittsburgh	70	1875	26.8
1969	Rick Barry, Oakland	35	1190	34.0
1970	Spencer Haywood, Denver	84	2519	30.0
1971	Dan Issel, Kentucky	83	2480	29.8
1972	Charlie Scott, Virginia	73	2524	34.6
1973	Julius Erving, Virginia	71	2268	31.9
1974	Julius Erving, New York	84	2299	27.4
1975	George McGinnis, Indiana	79	2353	29.8
1976	Julius Erving, New York	84	2462	29.3

ABA All-Star Game

The ABA All-Star Game was an Eastern Division vs. Western Division contest from 1968-75. League membership had dropped to seven teams by 1976, the ABA's last season, so the team in first place at the break (Denver) played an All-Star team made up from the other six clubs.

Series: East won 5, West 3 and Denver 1.

Year	Result	Host	Coaches	Most Valuable Player
1968	East 126, West 120	Indiana	Jim Pollard, Babe McCarthy	Larry Brown, New Orleans
1969	West 133, East 127	Louisville	Alex Hannum, Gene Rhodes	John Beasley, Dallas
1970	West 128, East 98	Indiana	Babe McCarthy, Bob Leonard	Spencer Haywood, Denver
1971	East 126, West 122	Carolina	Al Bianchi, Bill Sharman	Mel Daniels, Indiana
1972	East 142, West 115	Louisville	Joe Mullaney, Ladell Andersen	Dan Issel, Kentucky
1973	West 123, East 111	Utah	Ladell Andersen, Larry Brown	Warren Jabali, Denver
1974	East 128, West 112	Virginia	Babe McCarthy, Joe Mullaney	Artis Gilmore, Kentucky
1975	East 151, West 124	San Antonio	Kevin Loughery, Larry Brown	Freddie Lewis, St. Louis
1976	Denver 144, ABA 138	Denver	Larry Brown, Kevin Loughery	David Thompson, Denver

Continental Basketball Association

Originally named the Eastern Pennsylvania Basketball League when it formed on April 23, 1946, the league changed names several times before becoming known as the Eastern Basketball Association. In 1978, the EBA was redubbed the CBA. The CBA suspended operations following the 2000 season.

Multiple champions: Allentown and Wilkes-Barre (8); Scranton, Tampa Bay and Williamsport (3); Albany, La Crosse, Pottsville, Rochester, Wilmington and Yakima (2).

Year		Year		Year		Year	
1947	Wilkes-Barre Barons	1963	Allentown Jets	1977	Scranton Apollos	1992	La Crosse Catbirds
1948	Reading Keys	1964	Camden Bullets	1978	Wilkes-Barre Barons	1993	Omaha Racers
1949	Pottsville Packers	1965	Allentown Jets	1979	Rochester Zeniths	1994	Quad City Thunder
1950	Williamsport Billies	1966	Wilmington Blue	1980	Anchorage Northern	1995	Yakima Sun Kings
1951	Sunbury Mercuries		Bombers		Knights	1996	Sioux Falls Skyforce
1952	Pottsville Packers	1967	Wilmington Blue	1981	Rochester Zeniths	1997	Oklahoma City
1953	Williamsport Billies		Bombers	1982	Lancaster Lightning		Calvary
1954	Williamsport Billies	1968	Allentown Jets	1983	Detroit Spirits	1998	Quad City Thunder
1955	Wilkes-Barre Barons	1969	Wilkes-Barre Barons	1984	Albany Patroons	1999	Connecticut Pride
1956	Wilkes-Barre Barons	1970	Allentown Jets	1985	Tampa Bay Thrillers	2000	Yakima Sun Kings
1957	Scranton Miners	1971	Scranton Apollos	1986	Tampa Bay Thrillers		
1958	Wilkes-Barre Barons	1972	Allentown Jets	1987	Rapid City Thrillers*	*The Tampa Bay Thrillers	
1959	Wilkes-Barre Barons	1973	Wilkes-Barre Barons	1988	Albany Patroons	moved to Rapid City, S.D.	
1960	Easton Madisons	1974	Hartford Capitols	1989	Tulsa Fast Breakers	at the end of the 1987 regu-	
1961	Baltimore Bullets	1975	Allentown Jets	1990	La Crosse Catbirds	lar season.	
1962	Allentown Jets	1976	Allentown Jets	1991	Wichita Falls Texans		

WOMEN

American Basketball League (1997–98)
League Champions

The American Basketball League began play in 1996 as an eight-team league. Before the 1997-98 season the league added an expansion franchise in Long Beach, Calif. while the Richmond Rage was relocated to Philadelphia. In the spring of 1998, the league announced plans to dissolve an original franchise, the Atlanta Glory, and expand to Chicago and Nashville before the 1998-99 season, increasing the league's size to 10 teams. The ABL finals was a best of five series. Each ABL champion's wins and losses are noted in parentheses after the series score. The ABL folded before the 1999 season.

Multiple winner: Columbus (2).

Year	Champions	Head Coach	Series	Runners-up	Head Coach
1997	Columbus Quest	Brian Agler	3-2 (WLLLWW)	Richmond Rage	Lisa Boyer
1998	Columbus Quest	Brian Agler	3-2 (LLWWW)	Long Beach StingRays	Maura McHugh
1999	league folded				

Most Valuable Player

Winner's scoring averages provided; (*) indicates led league.

Year		Avg
1997	Nikki McCray, Columbus	19.9
1998	Natalie Williams, Portland	21.9*

Coach of the Year

Previous season and winning season's record are provided; (*) indicates division title.

Year		Improvement
1997	Brian Agler, Columbus	31-9*
1998	Lin Dunn, Portland	14-26 to 27-17

Women's National Basketball Association
League Champions

The WNBA, owned and operated by the NBA, began play in 1997 as an eight-team summer league. The league added two teams prior to its second season (1998) and again expanded by two teams before its third season in 1999. Four more teams were added before the 2000 season, bringing the total number of teams to 16. The WNBA champion was determined by a single-game playoff between the winners of the semifinals in the league's 1997 inaugural season, before going to a best-of-three championship series in 1998.

Multiple winner: Houston (4).

Year	Champions	Head Coach	Score	Runners-up	Head Coach
1997	Houston Comets	Van Chancellor	65-51	New York Liberty	Nancy Darsch
1998	Houston Comets	Van Chancellor	2-1 (LWW)	Phoenix Mercury	Cheryl Miller
1999	Houston Comets	Van Chancellor	2-1 (WLW)	New York Liberty	Richie Adubato
2000	Houston Comets	Van Chancellor	2-0	New York Liberty	Richie Adubato
2001	Los Angeles Sparks	Michael Cooper	2-0	Charlotte Sting	Anne Donovan

Most Valuable Player

Winner's scoring averages provided; (*) indicates led league.
Multiple winner: Cynthia Cooper (2).

Year		Avg
1997	Cynthia Cooper, Houston	22.2*
1998	Cynthia Cooper, Houston	22.7*
1999	Yolanda Griffith, Sacramento	18.8
2000	Sheryl Swoopes, Houston	20.7*
2001	Lisa Leslie, Los Angeles	19.5

Coach of the Year

Previous season and winning season's record are provided; (*) indicates division title.
Multiple winner: Van Chancellor (3).

Year		Improvement
1997	Van Chancellor, Houston	18-10*
1998	Van Chancellor, Houston	18-10 to 27-3*
1999	Van Chancellor, Houston	27-3 to 26-6*
2000	Michael Cooper, Los Angeles	20-12 to 28-4*
2001	Dan Hughes, Cleveland	17-15 to 22-10*

Hockey

After 22 years of service, **Ray Bourque** finally had his chance to raise the Stanley Cup.

Rocky Mountain High, Colorado

Sakic, Roy and Co. see to it that Ray Bourque gets what he came for.

Steve Levy *is a hockey play-by-play announcer and host of ESPN's National Hockey Night.*

It's 2:25 a.m. at Denver's ChopHouse & Brewery, a restaurant frequented by the Colorado Avalanche, and I'm minding my own business as usual. About five hours earlier, the Avalanche skated around the Pepsi Center with sports' greatest trophy after winning Game 7 of the Stanley Cup Finals.

There before me is none other than Raymond Bourque. He and I shake hands, I wish him congratulations, and he proceeds to apologize for his second period interview on ABC in which he told me, "What's said in the room, stays in the room." He now says "I wish I could've said more."

That's the kind of individual Ray Bourque is—with everything going on in his life, on the greatest night of his stellar professional career, he remembers a 45-second interview we did between the second and third periods. It's something I'll never forget.

It's now 2:30 a.m. when I'm hit with what has become my lasting image of the 2000–01 NHL campaign.

As I walk out of the restaurant, I bump into Av's forward Shjon Podein. Let me start at the top...of his head, where he's sporting a brand new Avalanche championship hat. As I glance farther down, I notice that he's still wearing his game-worn, sweaty Av's sweater. He even has his shoulder pads on underneath it. From there I look down farther...elbow pads—ON; hockey pants—ON; shin guards—ON; socks—ON. The only pieces of equipment he isn't still wearing are his helmet and gloves.

Think I've forgotten something? No way! Skates—ON!

The man is walking outside on the sidewalk with his skates still on five hours after the game ended. I'm told later that ESPN analyst Barry Melrose told Podein that he once knew an AHL player who

AP/Wide World Photos

*From left, **Ray Bourque**, coach **Bob Hartley**, Conn Smythe winner **Patrick Roy** and captain **Joe Sakic** celebrate their come-from-behind Stanley Cup win over New Jersey.*

won the championship and left all of his equipment on for a full 24 hours.

Sure enough, the next night Podein called Melrose to tell him he was 10 minutes away from the 25-hour mark...and that his feet were really hurting.

I'd be hard-pressed to think up a better ending to the season— Bourque winning the cup in Game 7 against the defending champion New Jersey Devils.

When you get right down to it, while it's tough to complain about a Stanley Cup Finals that goes to seven games, this one still wouldn't be considered a classic. In every game it seemed like one team played well while the other floundered. Not once did both goaltenders, Patrick Roy and Martin Brodeur, play at their best in the same game. Truth be told, when the Avalanche won their first cup in a sweep over Florida in 1996, three of the four games (culminating with Game 4's triple-overtime thriller) were better than any of the seven Colorado played against the Devils. But who's complaining?

The NHL season was made truly memorable by the triumphant return of No. 66. I just couldn't get enough of Mario this year and judging by the ratings on ESPN, few could. One thing we all got too much of, however, was the

AP/Wide-World Photos

*After a three-plus year hiatus, Pittsburgh owner **Mario Lemieux** returned to the ice in December and revitalized the league, his city and his star Jaromir Jagr.*

Eric Lindros saga. It played on far too long and wasn't fair to Lindros or the Flyers. Their relationship couldn't end soon enough.

Player movement took center stage towards the end of the season as superstars changed addresses like never before. Rob Blake (Los Angeles to Colorado), Keith Tkachuk (Phoenix to St. Louis) and Teemu Selanne (Anaheim to San Jose) were just three of the league's big names to finish the season with different teams.

In the offseason, the league's best player Jaromir Jagr was the hottest property up for bid. Is all of this movement good for the league? Time will tell, but sometimes a change of scenery works for all involved. I think Penguins fans had enough of Jagr but I also think Capitals fans won't be able to get enough of him. Either way, having a live franchise in our nation's capital will energize the entire league.

The best playoff team not to make the Stanley Cup Finals this year was the Los Angeles Kings. They didn't just lose the first two games to Detroit in the first round, they looked like they didn't belong in the same league. For them to win the next four games and advance to the second round (only to take Colorado to seven games before succumbing) was

continued on page 384 ▶

Steve Levy's Ten Biggest Stories of the Year in Hockey

10 ▪ The soft Senators are swept in the first round of the playoffs. They finish the regular season second-best in the East and fourth-best overall, but it proves to be meaningless come playoff time…again.

9 ▪ Goaltender Roman Turek lets the Blues down in the Western Conference finals against the Avalanche, seemingly allowing the worst goals at the worst times. It's so bad that Blues coach Joel Quenneville opts to start rookie Brent Johnson in the final game of the series.

8 ▪ Four of the league's Original Six—the Bruins, Rangers, Canadiens and Blackhawks—miss out on the postseason fun again, turning hockey cities into baseball cities way too early in the year.

7 ▪ Despite losing top scorer and captain Markus Naslund down the stretch, the Vancouver Canucks still find a way to fight their way into the playoffs.

6 ▪ Rookie goaltender Johan Hedberg gives Penguins fans something to cheer for besides Mario and Jaromir. The ex-Manitoba Moose star comes from the minors and provides the Pens with much-needed stability. And 17,000 sets of antlers inside the Igloo are truly something to see.

5 ▪ The playoffs are fit for the Kings. The Staples Center is electric as seventh-seeded Los Angeles shocks the heavily favored Red Wings in the first round and nearly does the same thing to the Avalanche in round two.

4 ▪ Colorado scores a hat trick in the offseason. GM Pierre Lacroix and Avalanche ownership take care of business, re-signing stars Joe Sakic, Patrick Roy and Rob Blake. Lacroix has a lot of resources to work with, but he and New Jersey's Lou Lamoriello are the best in the game.

3 ▪ Jaromir Jagr knew it was coming…and it came. The biggest surprise was that he was traded to the Capitals instead of the Rangers, but one thing's for sure—the Capitals will no longer be boring to watch.

2 ▪ The Penguins and the league are given an immeasurable boost as No. 66 Mario Lemieux returns to the ice. He looks like his old self, recording 76 points in 43 games.

1 ▪ Ray Bourque finally hoists Lord Stanley. I'm a sucker for happy endings and I'll admit it—even though it's a no-no in the press room, I couldn't help but stand up and cheer when it was all over. I just hope the NHL doesn't confiscate my press pass.

one of the great shockers in recent NHL history. The Big Four (Avalanche, Red Wings, Blues, and Stars) might have to make some more room for the California Kids because the Kings showed they're ready to step up in the highly skilled Western Conference in 2000–01.

Super Mario vs The Great One

At the conclusion of the 2000-01 season, Mario Lemieux had scored 648 goals in 788 games, more than even Wayne Gretzky had at that point in his career.

(through 788 games)

	Wayne Gretzky	Mario Lemieux
Goals	646	648
Assists	1217	922
Points	1863	1570
+/−.	+563	+158
PP Goals	139	217

Comeback Kids

The 2000–01 Avalanche became only the fifth team in NHL history to trail 3-2 in the Stanley Cup Finals and come back to win it all.

2001	Colorado Avalanche
1971	Montreal Canadiens
1964	Toronto Maple Leafs
1950	Detroit Red Wings
1942	Toronto Maple Leafs

Cup Combos

Colorado captain Joe Sakic is just the sixth player since expansion (in 1967) to win the Stanley Cup and the Hart Trophy (as league MVP) in the same season.

Joe Sakic, Col	2001
Mark Messier, Edm	1990
W. Gretzky, Edm	1984, 85, 87
Guy Lafleur, Mon	1977, 78
Bob Clarke, Phi	1975
Bobby Orr, Bos	1970, 72

Happy Endings

Penguins wing Jaromir Jagr led the league in scoring in 2000–01 and was dealt to the Washington Capitals in the offseason. Below are the most points scored by a player who began the following season with a new team.

	Pts.	New Team
W. Gretzky, Edm, '88	149	LA
J. Jagr, Pit, '01	121	Wash
M. Dionne, Det, '75	121	LA
J. Carson, LA, '88	107	Edm
M. Rogers, Hart, '81	105	NYR

2000-2001 Season in Review

information please®
SPORTS ALMANAC

Final NHL Standings

Division champions (*) and playoff qualifiers (†) are noted. OL signifies any game that was tied after regulation play but lost in overtime. Number of seasons listed after each head coach refers to current tenure with club through 2000-01 season.

Western Conference

Central Division

	W	L	T	OL	Pts	GF	GA
*Detroit	49	20	9	4	111	253	202
†St. Louis	43	22	12	5	103	249	195
Nashville	34	36	9	3	80	186	200
Chicago	29	40	8	5	71	210	246
Columbus	28	39	9	6	71	190	233

Head Coaches: Det—Scotty Bowman (8th season); **St.L**—Joel Quenneville (5th); **Nash**—Barry Trotz (3rd); **Chi**—Alpo Suhonen (1st; 29-35-7-4) was replaced on an interim basis by asst. Denis Savard (0-5-1-1) on Mar. 27; **Clb**—Dave King (1st).

Northwest Division

	W	L	T	OL	Pts	GF	GA
*Colorado	52	16	10	4	118	270	192
†Edmonton	39	28	12	3	93	243	222
†Vancouver	36	28	11	7	90	239	238
Calgary	27	36	15	4	73	197	236
Minnesota	25	39	13	5	68	168	210

Head Coaches: Col— Bob Hartley (3rd season); **Edm**—Craig MacTavish (1st); **Van**—Marc Crawford (3rd); **Calg**—Don Hay (1st; 23-28-13-4) was replaced by asst. Greg Gilbert (4-8-2-0) on March 14; **Min**—Jacques Lemaire (1st).

Pacific Division

	W	L	T	OL	Pts	GF	GA
*Dallas	48	24	8	2	106	241	187
†San Jose	40	27	12	3	95	217	192
†Los Angeles	38	28	13	3	92	252	228
Phoenix	35	27	17	3	90	214	212
Anaheim	25	41	11	5	66	188	245

Head Coaches: Dal— Ken Hitchcock (6th season); **SJ**—Darryl Sutter (4th); **LA**—Andy Murray (2nd); **Pho**—Bob Francis (2nd); **Ana**—Craig Hartsburg (3rd; 11-15-4-3) was replaced on an interim basis by asst. Guy Charron (14-26-7-2) on Dec. 14.

Eastern Conference

Northeast Division

	W	L	T	OL	Pts	GF	GA
*Ottawa	48	21	9	4	109	274	205
†Buffalo	46	30	5	1	98	218	184
†Toronto	37	29	11	5	90	232	207
Boston	36	30	8	8	88	227	249
Montreal	28	40	8	6	70	206	232

Head Coaches: Ott—Jacques Martin (6th season); **Buf**—Lindy Ruff (4th); **Tor**—Pat Quinn (3rd); **Bos**—Pat Burns (4th; 3-4-1-0) was replaced by Mike Keenan (33-26-7-8) on Oct. 25; **Mon**—Alain Vigneault (4th; 5-13-2-0) was replaced by Michel Therrien (23-27-6-6) on Nov. 20.

Atlantic Division

	W	L	T	OL	Pts	GF	GA
*New Jersey	48	19	12	3	111	295	195
†Philadelphia	43	25	11	3	100	240	207
†Pittsburgh	42	28	9	3	96	281	256
NY Rangers	33	43	5	1	72	250	290
NY Islanders	21	51	7	3	52	185	268

Head Coaches: NJ—Larry Robinson (2nd season); **Phi**—Craig Ramsey (2nd; 12-12-4-0) was replaced by asst. Bill Barber (31-13-7-3) on Dec. 10; **Pit**— Ivan Hlinka (1st); **NYR**—Ron Low (1st); **NYI**—Butch Goring (2nd; 17-40-5-3) was replaced on an interim basis by asst. Lorne Henning (4-11-2-0) on March 4.

Southeast Division

	W	L	T	OL	Pts	GF	GA
*Washington	41	27	10	4	96	233	211
†Carolina	38	32	9	3	88	212	225
Florida	22	38	13	9	66	200	246
Atlanta	23	45	12	2	60	211	289
Tampa Bay	24	47	6	5	59	201	280

Head Coaches: Wash—Ron Wilson (4th season); **Car**—Paul Maurice (6th); **Fla**—Terry Murray (3rd; 6-18-7-5) was replaced by Duane Sutter (16-20-6-4) on Dec. 28; **Atl**—Curt Fraser (2nd); **TB**—Steve Ludzik (2nd; 12-20-5-2) was replaced by asst. John Tortorella (12-27-1-3) on Jan. 6.

Home & Away, Division, Conference Records

Sixteen teams—eight from each conference—qualify for the Stanley Cup Playoffs; (*) indicates division champions.

Western Conference

		Pts	Home	Away	Div
1	Colorado*	118	28-6-5-2	24-10-5-2	14-5-1-0
2	Detroit*	111	27-9-3-2	22-11-6-2	11-3-3-3
3	Dallas*	106	26-10-5-0	22-14-3-2	11-6-3-0
4	St. Louis	103	28-5-5-3	15-17-7-2	9-7-4-0
5	San Jose	95	22-15-4-1	18-13-8-2	11-5-2-2
6	Edmonton	93	23-9-7-2	16-19-5-1	11-5-3-1
7	Los Angeles	92	20-12-8-1	18-17-5-2	8-7-4-1
8	Vancouver	90	21-12-5-3	15-16-6-4	10-6-1-3
	Phoenix	90	21-11-7-2	14-16-10-1	7-7-5-1
	Nashville	80	16-8-7-0	18-18-2-3	8-11-1-0
	Calgary	73	12-18-9-2	15-18-6-2	5-10-3-2
	Chicago	71	16-14-6-2	15-19-4-2	11-7-0-2
	Columbus	71	19-15-4-3	9-24-5-3	6-10-2-2
	Minnesota	68	14-13-10-4	11-26-3-1	4-10-4-2
	Anaheim	66	15-20-4-2	10-21-7-3	5-9-2-3

Eastern Conference

		Pts	Home	Away	Div
1	New Jersey*	111	24-11-6-0	24-8-6-3	7-5-7-1
2	Ottawa*	109	26-7-5-3	22-14-4-1	13-5-1-1
3	Washington*	96	24-9-6-2	17-18-4-2	12-4-3-1
4	Philadelphia	100	26-11-4-0	17-14-7-3	11-5-2-2
5	Buffalo	98	26-12-3-0	20-18-2-1	11-7-2-0
6	Pittsburgh	96	24-15-2-0	18-14-7-3	12-5-2-1
7	Toronto	90	19-11-7-4	18-18-4-1	7-10-2-1
8	Carolina	88	23-15-3-0	15-17-6-3	11-5-4-0
	Boston	88	21-12-5-3	15-18-3-5	11-6-1-2
	NY Rangers	72	17-20-3-1	16-23-2-0	5-12-3-0
	Montreal	70	15-20-4-2	13-20-4-4	5-13-0-2
	Florida	66	12-18-7-4	10-20-6-5	5-10-3-2
	Atlanta	60	10-23-6-2	13-22-6-0	6-10-4-0
	Tampa Bay	59	17-19-3-2	7-28-3-3	9-8-0-3
	NY Islanders	52	12-27-1-1	9-24-6-2	7-10-2-1

2001 NHL All-Star Game
North America 14, World 12

51st NHL All-Star Game. **Date:** Feb. 4 at the Pepsi Center in Denver; **Coaches:** Joel Quenneville, St. Louis (North America) and Jacques Martin, Ottawa (World); **MVP:** Bill Guerin, Boston right wing (North America)—three goals, two assists.

Starters were chosen by fan vote while reserves were selected by the NHL's Hockey Operations Department, after consultation with NHL general managers. Head coaches whose teams had the best winning percentage in the Eastern Conference (World) and Western Conference (North America) on Jan. 7 were named all-star head coaches.

Defenseman Ed Jovanovski, defenseman Scott Niedermayer, and left wing Simon Gagne were added to the **North American** team as injury replacements for Chris Pronger, Al MacInnis, and Vincent Damphousse, respectively. Defenseman Rob Blake assumed Pronger's spot in the starting lineup.

Right wing Milan Hejduk and right wing Sergei Samsonov were added to the **World** team as injury replacements for Alexander Mogilny and Jaromir Jagr, respectively. Hejduk assumed Jagr's spot in the starting lineup.

North America

	Starters	G	A	Pts	PM
W	Theoren Fleury, NY Rangers	2	1	3	0
W	Paul Kariya, Anaheim	0	3	3	0
D	Rob Blake, Los Angeles	0	1	1	0
C	Joe Sakic, Colorado	1	0	1	0
D	Ray Bourque, Colorado	0	0	0	0
	Reserves				
W	Bill Guerin, Boston	3	2	5	0
W	Tony Amonte, Chicago	2	2	4	0
C	Doug Weight, Edmonton	1	3	4	0
C	Simon Gagne, Philadelphia	2	0	2	0
C	Mario Lemieux, Pittsburgh	1	1	2	0
W	Luc Robitaille, Los Angeles	2	0	2	0
D	Scott Stevens, New Jersey	0	2	2	0
C	Jason Allison, Boston	0	1	1	0
W	Donald Audette, Atlanta	0	1	1	0
W	Brett Hull, Dallas	0	1	1	0
D	Ed Jovanovski, Vancouver	0	1	1	0
D	Brian Leetch, NY Rangers	0	1	1	0
D	Scott Niedermayer, New Jersey	0	0	0	0
	TOTALS	14	20	34	0

Goaltenders	Mins	Shots	Saves	GA
Patrick Roy, Col.	20:00	11	8	3
Sean Burke, Pho	20:00	11	7	4
Martin Brodeur, NJ (W)	20:00	23	18	5
TOTALS	60:00	45	33	12

World

	Starters	G	A	Pts	PM
C	Peter Forsberg, Colorado	1	2	3	0
D	Nicklas Lidstrom, Detroit	1	2	3	0
W	Pavel Bure, Florida	0	2	2	0
W	Milan Hejduk, Colorado	1	0	1	0
D	Sandis Ozolinsh, Carolina	0	1	1	0
	Reserves				
W	Fredrik Modin, Tampa Bay	0	4	4	0
C	Mats Sundin, Toronto	2	2	4	0
C	Sergei Fedorov, Detroit	2	0	2	0
D	Sergei Gonchar, Washington	0	2	2	0
W	Marian Hossa, Colorado	0	2	2	0
W	Alexei Kovalev, Pittsburgh	1	1	2	0
W	Markus Naslund, Vancouver	1	1	2	0
D	Teppo Numminen, Phoenix	0	2	2	0
W	Zigmund Palffy, Los Angeles	1	1	2	0
W	Sergei Samsonov, Boston	1	1	2	0
C	Radek Bonk, Ottawa	1	0	1	0
D	Janne Niinimaa, Edmonton	0	0	0	0
D	Marcus Ragnarsson, San Jose	0	0	0	0
	TOTALS	12	23	35	0

Goaltenders	Mins	Shots	Saves	GA
Dominik Hasek, Buf	20:00	17	14	3
Roman Cechmanek, Phi	20:00	20	14	6
Evgeni Nabokov, SJ	20:00	16	11	5
TOTALS	60:00	53	39	14

Score by Periods

	1	2	3	Final
North America	3	6	5	— 14
World	3	4	5	— 12

Power plays: North America—0/0; World—0/0. **Officials:** Michael McGeough and Richard Trottier (referees), Randy Mitton and Mark Wheler (linesmen). **Attendance:** 18,646. **TV Rating:** 2.4/5 share (ABC).

2001 NHL Skills Competition
North America, 15-13

Puck Control Relay
Team: North America (Sakic, Jovanovski, Gagne)
Individual: Paul Kariya (North America)
Fastest Skater
Team: North America (Avg.13.896 sec.: Amonte, Guerin, Gagne)
Individual: Bill Guerin, North America (13.690 sec.)
Hardest Shot
Team: World (Avg. 97.9 mph: Modin, Fedorov, Bonk, Lidstrom)
Individual: Fredrik Modin, World (102.1 mph)

Shooting Accuracy (targets/shots)
Team: World (14/30: Naslund, Hossa, Hejduk, Forsberg)
Individual: Ray Bourque, North America (4/6)
Pass and Score
Team: North America wins, 5-3
Breakaway Relay
Team: World wins, 7-5
Goaltender Competition
(combined Pass and Score + Breakaway Relay)
Individual: Sean Burke, North America

Pittsburgh Penguins
Jaromir Jagr
Scoring, Assists

Florida Panthers
Pavel Bure
Goals, Shots

New York Rangers
Brian Leetch
Defensemen Points

New Jersey Devils
Martin Brodeur
Wins

NHL Regular Season Individual Leaders

(*) indicates rookie eligible for Calder Trophy.

Scoring

	Pos	Gm	G	A	Pts	+/-	PM	PP	SH	GW	GT	Shots	Pct
Jaromir Jagr, Pittsburgh	R	81	52	69	**121**	19	42	14	1	10	1	317	16.4
Joe Sakic, Colorado	C	82	54	64	**118**	45	30	19	3	12	2	332	16.3
Patrik Elias, New Jersey	L	82	40	56	**96**	45	51	8	3	6	1	220	18.2
Alexei Kovalev, Pittsburgh	R	79	44	51	**95**	12	96	12	2	9	1	307	14.3
Jason Allison, Boston	C	82	36	59	**95**	-8	85	11	3	6	0	185	19.5
Martin Straka, Pittsburgh	L	82	27	68	**95**	19	38	7	1	4	1	185	14.6
Pavel Bure, Florida	R	82	59	33	**92**	-2	58	19	5	8	3	384	15.4
Doug Weight, Edmonton	C	82	25	65	**90**	12	91	8	0	3	2	188	13.3
Zigmund Palffy, Los Angeles	R	73	38	51	**89**	22	20	12	4	8	0	217	17.5
Peter Forsberg, Colorado	C	73	27	62	**89**	23	54	12	2	5	0	178	15.2
Alexei Yashin, Ottawa	C	82	40	48	**88**	10	30	13	2	10	1	263	15.2
Luc Robitaille, Los Angeles	L	82	37	51	**88**	10	66	16	1	4	1	235	15.7
Bill Guerin, Edm.-Bos.	R	85	40	45	**85**	7	140	11	1	5	0	289	13.8
Mike Modano, Dallas	C	81	33	51	**84**	26	52	8	3	7	1	208	15.9
Alexander Mogilny, New Jersey	R	75	43	40	**83**	10	43	12	0	7	0	240	17.9
Pierre Turgeon, St. Louis	C	79	30	52	**82**	14	37	11	0	6	1	171	17.5
Adam Oates, Washington	C	81	13	69	**82**	-9	28	5	0	4	0	72	18.1
Peter Bondra, Washington	L	82	45	36	**81**	8	60	22	4	8	0	305	14.8
Petr Sykora, New Jersey	R	73	35	46	**81**	36	32	9	2	3	0	249	14.1
Robert Lang, Pittsburgh	C	82	32	48	**80**	20	28	10	0	2	0	177	18.1

Goals

Bure, Fla.	59
Sakic, Col.	54
Jagr, Pit.	52
Bondra, Wash.	45
Kovalev, Pit.	44
Mogilny, NJ	43
Naslund, Van.	41
Hejduk, Col.	41
O'Neill, Car.	41
Young, St.L	40
Elias, NJ	40
Yashin, Ott.	40
Guerin, Edm.-Bos.	40

Assists

Jagr, Pit.	69
Oates, Wash.	69
Straka, Pit.	68
Weight, Edm.	65
Sakic, Col.	64
Forsberg, Col.	62
Allison, Bos.	59
Leetch, NYR	58
Elias, NJ	56
Lidstrom, Det.	56
Turgeon, St.L	52
Bourque, Col.	52

Defensemen Points

Leetch, NYR	79
Lidstrom, Det.	71
Blake, LA-Col.	59
Bourque, Col.	59
Gonchar, Wash.	57
MacInnis, St.L	54
Tverdovsky, Ana.	53
Rafalski, NJ	52
Schneider, LA	51
Zubov, Dal.	51

Rookie Points

Richards, TB	62
Willis, Car.	44
Havlat, Ott.	42
Visnovsky, LA	39
Reinprecht, LA-Col.	36
Gaborik, Min.	36
Fedotenko, Phi.	36
D. Sedin, Van.	34
Rachunek, Ott.	33
Vyborny, Clb.	32

Plus/Minus

Elias, NJ	45
Sakic, Col.	45
Stevens, NJ	40
Sykora, NJ	36
Rafalski, NJ	36
Tanguay, Col.	35
Hejduk, Col.	32
White*, NJ	32
Lukowich, Dal.	28
Demitra, St.L	27
Bonk, Ott.	27

Penalty Minutes

Barnaby, Pit.-TB	265
Worrell, Fla.	248
Grimson, LA	235
Nazarov, Ana.-Bos.	229
Odgers, Atl.	226
Lambert, Atl.	215
Domi, Tor.	214
Ray, Buf.	210
Marchment, SJ	204
Corson, Tor.	189

Power Play Goals

Bondra, Wash.	22
Thornton, Bos.	19
Bure, Fla.	19
Sakic, Col.	19
Naslund, Van.	18
Kariya, Ana.	18
Tkachuk, Pho.-St.L	17
O'Neill, Car.	17
Lemieux, Pit.	16
Bure, Calg.	16
Robitaille, LA	16

Short-Handed Goals

Sullivan, Chi.	8
Walz, Min.	7
Fleury, NYR	7
Bure, Fla.	5
Bondra, Wash.	4
Conroy, St.L-Calg.	4
Palffy, LA	4
Schaefer, Van.	4
Marchant, Edm.	4

Shots

Bure, Fla.	.384
Sakic, Col.	.332
Young, St.L.	.321
Jagr, Pit.	.317
Kovalev, Pit.	.307
Bondra, Wash.	.305
Guerin, Edm.-Bos.	.289
Czerkawski, NYI	.287
Rolston, Bos.	.286
Shanahan, Det.	.278

Shooting Pct.
(Min. 70 shots)

Holmstrom, Det.	.21.6
Arvedson, Ott.	.21.5
Roberts, Tor.	.21.0
Primeau, Phi.	.20.6
Lemieux, Pit.	.20.5
Thornton, Bos.	.20.4
Tanguay, Col.	.20.0
Allison, Bos.	.19.5
Handzus, St.L-Pho.	.19.4
Hejduk, Col.	.19.2

Hits

Chara, NYI	.373
Svehla, Fla.	.354
Kasparaitis, Pit.	.351
McGillis, Phi.	.292
Vishnevski, Ana.	.286
O'Neill, Car.	.263
Lapointe, Det.	.259
Smith, Edm.	.254
Gauthier, Calg.	.252
Hatcher, Dal.	.250

Minutes/Game
(Min. 50 Games)

Leetch, NYR	.29:21
Lidstrom, Det.	.28:26
Bure, Fla.	.26:52
Zubov, Dal.	.26:36
Desjardins, Phi.	.26:26
Bourque, Col.	.26:05
Blake, LA-Col.	.26:02
Hatcher, Dal.	.25:52
Weinrich, Mon.-Bos.	.25:51
Svehla, Fla.	.25:34

Goaltending
(Minimum 26 games)

	Gm	Min	GAA	GA	Shots	Sv%	EN	ShO	Record	G	A	Pts	PM
Marty Turco*, Dallas	26	1266	**1.90**	40	532	.925	1	3	13-6-1	0	0	0	12
Roman Cechmanek, Philadelphia	59	3431	**2.01**	115	1464	.921	2	10	35-15-6	0	1	1	4
Manny Legace, Detroit	39	2136	**2.05**	73	909	.920	1	2	24-5-5	0	2	2	4
Dominik Hasek, Buffalo	67	3904	**2.11**	137	1726	.921	2	11	37-24-4	0	3	3	22
Brent Johnson*, St. Louis	31	1744	**2.17**	63	676	.907	2	4	19-9-2	0	0	0	2
Evgeni Nabokov*, San Jose	66	3700	**2.19**	135	1582	.915	3	6	32-21-7	0	2	2	8
Patrick Roy, Colorado	62	3585	**2.21**	132	1513	.913	5	4	40-13-7	0	5	5	10
David Aebischer*, Colorado	26	1393	**2.24**	52	538	.903	3	3	12-7-3	0	1	1	0
Manny Fernandez, Minnesota	42	2461	**2.24**	92	1147	.920	1	4	19-17-4	0	0	0	6
Sean Burke, Phoenix	62	3644	**2.27**	138	1766	.922	5	4	25-22-13	0	1	1	16
Roman Turek, St. Louis	54	3232	**2.28**	123	1248	.901	7	6	24-18-10	0	1	1	6
Mike Dunham, Nashville	48	2810	**2.28**	107	1381	.923	2	4	21-21-4	0	0	0	2
Martin Brodeur, New Jersey	72	4297	**2.32**	166	1762	.906	2	9	42-17-11	0	1	1	14
Fred Brathwaite, Calgary	49	2742	**2.32**	106	1181	.910	6	5	15-17-10	0	1	1	2
Ed Belfour, Dallas	63	3687	**2.34**	144	1508	.905	2	8	35-20-7	0	1	1	4

Wins

Brodeur, NJ	.42
Roy, Col.	.40
Hasek, Buf.	.37
Irbe, Car.	.37
Kolzig, Wash.	.37
Salo, Edm.	.36
Lalime, Ott.	.36
Belfour, Dal.	.35
Cechmanek, Phi.	.35
Joseph, Tor.	.33
Nabokov*, SJ	.32

Shutouts

Hasek, Buf.	.11
Cechmanek, Phi.	.10
Brodeur, NJ	.9
Belfour, Dal.	.8
Salo, Edm.	.8
Lalime, Ott.	.7
Irbe, Car.	.6
Thibault, Chi.	.6
Potvin, Van.-LA	.6
Nabokov*, SJ	.6
Turek, St.L	.6
Joseph, Tor.	.6

Save Pct.

Turco*, Dal.	.925
Dunham, Nash.	.923
Burke, Pho.	.922
Cechmanek, Phi.	.921
Hasek, Buf.	.921
Fernandez, Min.	.920
Luongo*, Fla.	.920
Legace, Det.	.920
Tugnutt, Clb.	.917
Nabokov*, SJ	.915
Joseph, Tor.	.915

Losses

Weekes, TB	.33
Thibault, Chi.	.32
Hebert, Ana.-NYR	.30
Irbe, Car.	.29
Theodore, Mon.	.29
Joseph, Tor.	.27
Kolzig, Wash.	.26
Tugnutt, Clb.	.25
Salo, Edm.	.25
Vanbiesbrouck, NYI-NJ	.25
Hasek, Buf.	.24
Luongo*, Fla.	.24

Team Goaltending

WESTERN	GAA	Mins	GA	Shots	Sv%	EN	SO	EASTERN	GAA	Mins	GA	Shots	Sv%	EN	SO
Dallas	**2.26**	4970	187	2043	.908	3	11	Buffalo	**2.23**	4956	184	2195	.916	3	13
San Jose	**2.30**	5008	192	2169	.911	5	9	New Jersey	**2.34**	5001	195	2024	.904	2	10
Colorado	**2.31**	4993	192	2059	.907	8	7	Ottawa	**2.47**	4977	205	2235	.908	7	9
St. Louis	**2.34**	5001	195	1933	.899	9	10	Philadelphia	**2.48**	5001	207	2144	.903	9	11
Nashville	**2.41**	4984	200	2347	.915	6	6	Toronto	**2.49**	4990	207	2244	.908	6	6
Detroit	**2.43**	4994	202	2221	.909	2	3	Washington	**2.54**	4986	211	2273	.907	7	5
Minnesota	**2.52**	5005	210	2307	.909	4	6	Carolina	**2.71**	4986	225	2206	.898	8	6
Phoenix	**2.54**	5010	212	2429	.913	6	6	Montreal	**2.80**	4978	232	2297	.899	9	4
Edmonton	**2.67**	4997	222	2139	.896	7	8	Florida	**2.95**	5006	246	2559	.904	9	6
Los Angeles	**2.74**	4995	228	2160	.894	9	10	Boston	**2.99**	4991	249	2191	.886	8	2
Columbus	**2.80**	4988	233	2475	.906	7	4	Pittsburgh	**3.09**	4978	256	2397	.893	7	3
Calgary	**2.83**	5009	236	2224	.894	9	8	NY Islanders	**3.24**	4968	268	2378	.887	11	2
Vancouver	**2.85**	5006	238	2122	.888	6	2	Tampa Bay	**3.38**	4968	280	2557	.890	12	5
Anaheim	**2.94**	4995	245	2417	.899	5	6	Atlanta	**3.48**	4983	289	2655	.891	9	2
Chicago	**2.96**	4981	246	2190	.888	8	6	NY Rangers	**3.50**	4966	290	2575	.887	7	0

Power Play/Penalty Killing

Power play and penalty killing conversions. Power play: No—number of opportunities; GF—goals for; Pct—percentage. Penalty killing: No—number of times shorthanded; GA—goals against; Pct—percentage of penalties killed; SH—shorthanded goals for.

WESTERN	—Power Play—			—Penalty Killing—				EASTERN	—Power Play—			—Penalty Killing—		
	No	GF	Pct	No	GA	Pct	SH		No	GF	Pct	No	GA	Pct	SH
Detroit	384	85	22.1	385	55	85.7	10	New Jersey	310	71	22.9	320	49	84.7	9
Colorado	363	80	22.0	342	59	82.7	11	Washington	353	75	21.2	391	62	84.1	6
Dallas	367	72	19.6	355	49	86.2	7	Pittsburgh	375	76	20.3	405	78	80.7	7
Los Angeles	367	71	19.3	382	72	81.2	14	Carolina	382	72	18.8	351	45	87.2	6
St. Louis	385	72	18.7	389	57	85.3	15	Ottawa	381	71	18.6	361	49	86.4	10
Anaheim	373	66	17.7	390	71	81.8	6	NY Rangers	363	65	17.9	400	86	78.5	16
Vancouver	416	71	17.1	387	74	80.9	12	Boston	390	64	16.4	377	65	82.8	8
Phoenix	343	57	16.6	432	64	85.2	9	Montreal	421	68	16.2	337	60	82.2	5
Calgary	435	65	14.9	378	76	79.9	3	Buffalo	373	60	16.1	334	40	88.0	6
Edmonton	398	59	14.8	382	62	83.8	13	Toronto	355	57	16.1	366	55	85.0	2
Columbus	381	56	14.7	363	70	80.7	3	Philadelphia	350	55	15.7	314	55	82.5	11
Nashville	361	51	14.1	331	49	85.2	7	Atlanta	395	54	13.7	408	90	77.9	9
San Jose	406	57	14.0	441	61	86.2	8	NY Islanders	386	51	13.2	445	79	82.2	9
Chicago	318	41	12.9	323	52	83.9	15	Florida	353	46	13.0	398	64	83.9	8
Minnesota	374	36	9.6	373	57	84.7	13	Tampa Bay	424	53	12.5	422	72	82.9	9

Single Game Highs
INDIVIDUAL

Goals		Opponent	Date
4	Jaromir Jagr, Pittsburgh	NY Rangers	Oct. 14
4	John Madden, New Jersey	Pittsburgh	Oct. 28
4	Randy McKay, New Jersey	Pittsburgh	Oct. 28
4	Peter Bondra, Washington	Ottawa	Dec. 27
4	Pavel Bure, Florida	Atlanta	Feb. 10
4	Brendan Shanahan, Detroit	Calgary	Mar. 15
4	Brett Hull, Dallas	Anaheim	Mar. 21
4	Radek Dvorak, NY Rangers	NY Islanders	Mar. 29

Assists		Opponent	Date
5	Marian Hossa, Ottawa	Tampa Bay	Jan. 4
5	Keith Tkachuk, Phoenix	Buffalo	Feb. 23
5	Espen Knutsen, Columbus	Calgary	Mar. 24

Points		Opponent	Date
6	Radek Bonk, Ottawa	Tampa Bay	Jan. 4

Saves		Opponent	Date
49	Jeff Hackett, Montreal	Pittsburgh	Dec. 16

Team by Team Statistics

High scorers and goaltenders with at least ten games played. Players who competed for more than one team during the regular season are listed with their final club; (*) indicates rookies eligible for Calder Trophy.

Mighty Ducks of Anaheim

Top Scorers	Gm	G	A	Pts	+/-	PM	PP
Paul Kariya	66	33	34	67	-9	20	18
Oleg Tverdovsky	82	14	39	53	-11	32	8
Jeff Friesen	79	14	34	48	5	66	4
SJ	64	12	24	36	7	56	2
ANA	15	2	10	12	-2	10	2
Marty McInnis	75	20	22	42	-21	40	10
Matt Cullen	82	10	30	40	23	38	4
Tony Hrkac	80	13	25	38	0	29	0
Mike LeClerc	54	15	20	35	-1	26	3
German Titov	71	9	11	20	-21	61	1
Petr Tenkrat*	46	5	9	14	-11	16	0
Niclas Havelid	47	4	10	14	-6	34	2
Jim Cummins	79	5	6	11	-11	167	0
Mike Crowley	39	1	10	11	-16	20	0
Vitaly Vishnevski	76	1	10	11	-1	99	0
Pascal Trepanier	57	6	4	10	-12	73	3
Dan Bylsma	82	1	9	10	-12	22	0
Samuel Pahlsson*	76	4	5	9	-14	20	1
BOS	17	1	1	2	-5	6	0
ANA	59	3	4	7	-9	14	1
Steve Rucchin	16	3	5	8	-5	0	2
Pavel Trnka	59	1	7	8	-12	42	0

Acquired: C Pahlsson from Bos. for D Patrick Traverse and LW Andrei Nazarov (Nov. 18); LW Friesen, G Shields, and a conditional pick from SJ for RW Teemu Selanne (Mar. 5).

Goalies (10 Gm)	Gm	Min	GAA	Record	SV%
Steve Shields	21	1135	2.48	6-8-5	.911
SJ	21	1135	2.48	6-8-5	.911
J.S. Giguere	34	2031	2.57	11-17-5	.911
ANAHEIM	82	4995	2.94	25-46-11	.899

Shutouts: Giguere (4); Shields (2 with SJ). **Assists:** Giguere (2). **PM:** Giguere (8), Shields (2 with SJ).

Atlanta Thrashers

Top Scorers	Gm	G	A	Pts	+/-	PM	PP
Ray Ferraro	81	29	47	76	-11	91	11
Andrew Brunette	77	15	44	59	-5	26	6
Jiri Slegr	75	8	26	34	-10	96	2
PIT	42	5	10	15	-9	60	0
ATL	33	3	16	19	-1	36	2
Patrik Stefan	66	10	21	31	-3	22	0
Stephen Guolla	63	12	16	28	-6	23	2
Hnat Domenichelli	63	15	12	27	-9	18	4
Tomi Kallio*	56	14	13	27	-3	22	2
Shean Donovan	63	12	11	23	-14	47	1
Steve Staios	70	9	13	22	-23	137	4
Per Svartvadet	69	10	11	21	-6	20	0
Chris Tamer	82	4	13	17	-1	128	0
Andreas Karlsson	60	5	11	16	-2	16	0
Frantisek Kaberle	51	4	11	15	11	18	1
Ladislav Kohn	77	7	7	14	-27	86	0
ANA	51	4	3	7	-15	42	0
ATL	26	3	4	7	-12	44	0
Gord Murphy	27	3	11	14	-11	12	2
Jeff Odgers	82	6	7	13	-8	226	0
Yannick Tremblay	46	4	8	12	-6	30	1
Dean Sylvester	43	5	6	11	-16	8	1

Acquired: D Slegr from Pit. for a '01 3rd-round pick (Jan. 14); RW Kohn from Ana. for D Sergei Vyshedkevich and G Scott Langkow (Feb. 9).

Goalies (10 Gm)	Gm	Min	GAA	Record	SV%
Milan Hnilicka	36	1879	3.35	12-19-2	.890
Damian Rhodes	38	2072	3.36	7-19-7	.897
Norm Maracle	13	753	3.43	2-8-3	.894
ATLANTA	82	4983	3.48	23-47-12	.891

Shutouts: Hnilicka (2). **Assists:** none. **PM:** Rhodes (16), Hnilicka (4).

Boston Bruins

Top Scorers	Gm	G	A	Pts	+/-	PM	PP
Jason Allison	82	36	59	95	-8	85	11
Bill Guerin	85	40	45	85	7	140	11
EDM	21	12	10	22	11	18	4
BOS	64	28	35	63	-4	122	7
Sergei Samsonov	82	29	46	75	6	18	3
Joe Thornton	72	37	34	71	-4	107	19
Brian Rolston	77	19	39	58	6	28	5
Andrei Kovalenko	76	16	21	37	-14	27	7
Eric Weinrich	82	7	24	31	-9	44	3
MON	60	6	19	25	-1	34	2
BOS	22	1	5	6	-8	10	1
Mikko Eloranta	62	12	11	23	2	38	1
P.J. Axelsson	81	8	15	23	-12	27	0
Mike Knuble	82	7	13	20	0	37	0
Dixon Ward	63	5	13	18	-1	65	0
Kyle McLaren	58	5	12	17	-5	53	2
Jonathan Girard	31	3	13	16	2	14	2
Darren Van Impe	31	3	10	13	-9	41	2
Don Sweeney	72	2	10	12	-1	26	1
Hall Gill	80	1	10	11	-2	71	0
Jarno Kultanen	62	2	8	10	-3	26	0

Acquired: RW Guerin from Edm. for LW Anson Carter, a '02 2nd-round pick and an optional swap of 1st-round picks in '01 or '02 (Nov. 15); D Weinrich from Mon. for D Patrick Traverse (Feb. 21). **Signed:** free agent C Ward (Nov. 3). **Claimed:** G Skudra off waivers from Buf. (Nov. 14).

Goalies (10 Gm)	Gm	Min	GAA	Record	SV%
Byron Dafoe	45	2536	2.39	22-14-7	.906
Andrew Raycroft*	15	649	2.96	4-6-0	.890
Peter Skudra	26	1116	3.33	6-12-1	.879
John Grahame	10	471	3.57	3-4-0	.867
BOSTON	82	4991	2.99	36-38-8	.886

Shutouts: Dafoe (2). **Assists:** Dafoe (2). **PM:** Dafoe (6), Grahame (2).

Buffalo Sabres

Top Scorers	Gm	G	A	Pts	+/-	PM	PP
Donald Audette	76	34	45	79	-2	76	14
ATL	64	32	39	71	-3	64	13
BUF	12	2	6	8	1	12	1
Miroslav Satan	82	29	33	62	5	36	8
Steve Heinze	79	27	27	54	-13	46	15
CLB	65	22	20	42	-19	38	14
BUF	14	5	7	12	6	8	1
J.P. Dumont	79	23	28	51	1	54	9
Stu Barnes	75	19	24	43	-2	26	3
Chris Gratton	82	19	21	40	0	102	5
Doug Gilmour	71	7	31	38	3	70	4
Alexei Zhitnik	78	8	29	37	-3	75	5
Maxim Afinogenov	78	14	22	36	1	40	3
Dave Andreychuk	74	20	13	33	0	32	8
Curtis Brown	70	10	22	32	15	34	2
Erik Rasmussen	82	12	19	31	0	51	1
Vaclav Varada	75	10	21	31	-2	81	2
Jason Woolley	67	5	18	23	0	46	4
Dmitri Kalinin*	79	4	18	22	-2	38	2
Rhett Warrener	77	3	16	19	10	78	0
Richard Smehlik	56	3	12	15	6	4	0
Vladimir Tsyplakov	36	7	7	14	2	10	0
James Patrick	54	4	9	13	9	12	1
Denis Hamel*	41	8	3	11	-2	22	1
Jay McKee	74	1	10	11	9	76	0

Acquired: RW Audette from Atl. for C Kamil Piros and a '01 4th-round pick (Mar. 13); RW Heinze from Clb. for a '01 3rd-round pick (Mar. 13).

Goalies (10 Gm)	Gm	Min	GAA	Record	Sv%
Dominik Hasek	67	3904	2.11	37-24-4	.921
Martin Biron	18	918	2.55	7-7-1	.909
BUFFALO	82	4956	2.23	46-31-5	.916

Shutouts: Hasek (11), Biron (2). **Assists:** Hasek (3). **PM:** Hasek (22).

Calgary Flames

Top Scorers	Gm	G	A	Pts	+/-	PM	PP
Jarome Iginla	77	31	40	71	-2	62	10
Marc Savard	77	23	42	65	-12	46	10
Valeri Bure	78	22	28	55	-21	26	16
Dave Lowry	79	18	17	35	-2	47	5
Phil Housley	69	4	30	34	-15	24	0
Craig Conroy	83	14	18	32	2	60	0
ST.L	69	11	14	25	2	46	0
CALG	14	3	4	7	0	14	0
Derek Morris	51	5	23	28	-15	56	3
Oleg Saprykin*	59	9	14	23	4	43	2
Jeff Shantz	73	5	15	20	-7	58	0
Tommy Albelin	77	1	19	20	2	22	1
Toni Lydman*	62	3	16	19	-7	30	1
Jason Wiemer	65	10	5	15	-15	177	3
Clarke Wilm	81	7	8	15	-11	69	2
Igor Kravchuk	52	1	13	14	-8	18	0
OTT	15	1	5	6	4	14	0
CALG	37	0	8	8	-12	4	0
Jeff Cowan*	51	9	4	13	-8	74	2
Daniel Tkaczuk*	19	4	7	11	1	14	1
Ronald Petrovicky*	30	4	5	9	0	54	1
Denis Gauthier	62	2	6	8	3	78	0
Chris Clark*	29	5	1	6	0	38	1
Brad Werenka	33	1	4	5	-3	16	0

Acquired: C Conroy and a '01 7th-round pick from St.L for C Cory Stillman (Mar. 13). **Claimed:** D Kravchuk off waivers from Ott. (Nov. 10).

Goalies (10 Gm)	Gm	Min	GAA	Record	SV%
Fred Brathwaite	49	2742	2.32	15-17-10	.910
Mike Vernon	41	2246	3.23	12-23-5	.883
CALGARY	82	5009	2.83	27-40-15	.894

Shutouts: Brathwaite (5), Vernon (3). **Assists:** Brathwaite and Vernon (1). **PM:** Vernon (16), Brathwaite (2).

Carolina Hurricanes

Top Scorers	Gm	G	A	Pts	+/-	PM	PP
Jeff O'Neill	82	41	26	67	-18	106	17
Ron Francis	82	15	50	65	-15	32	7
Sami Kapanen	82	20	37	57	-12	24	7
Rod Brind'Amour	79	20	36	56	-7	47	5
Martin Gelinas	79	23	29	52	-4	59	6
Shane Willis*	73	20	24	44	-6	45	9
Sandis Ozolinsh	72	12	32	44	-25	71	4
Scott Pellerin	77	11	33	44	2	51	2
MIN	58	11	28	39	6	45	2
CAR	19	0	5	5	-4	6	0
David Tanabe	74	7	22	29	-9	42	5
Bates Battaglia	80	12	15	27	-14	76	2
Rob DiMaio	74	6	18	24	-14	54	0
Josef Vasicek*	76	8	13	21	-8	53	1
Glen Wesley	71	5	16	21	-2	42	3
Marek Malik	61	6	14	20	-4	34	1
Kevin Hatcher	57	4	14	18	2	38	3
David Karpa	80	4	6	10	-19	159	2
Tommy Westlund	79	5	3	8	-9	23	0
Niclas Wallin*	37	2	3	5	-11	21	0
Jeff Daniels	67	1	1	2	-3	14	0
Darren Langdon	54	0	2	2	-4	94	0
Craig Adams*	44	1	0	1	-7	20	0
Steve Halko	48	0	1	1	-10	6	0

Acquired: LW Pellerin from Min. for LW Ashkat Rakhmatullin, a '01 3rd-round pick, and future considerations (Mar. 1).

Goalies (10 Gm)	Gm	Min	GAA	Record	Sv%
Arturs Irbe	77	4406	2.45	37-29-9	.908
Tyler Moss	12	557	3.99	1-6-0	.853
CAROLINA	82	4986	2.71	38-35-9	.898

Shutouts: Irbe (6). **Assists:** Irbe (2). **PM:** Irbe (6).

Chicago Blackhawks

Top Scorers

Top Scorers	Gm	G	A	Pts	+/-	PM	PP
Steve Sullivan..........81	81	34	41	75	3	54	6
Tony Amonte..........82	82	35	29	64	-22	54	9
Michael Nylander......82	82	25	39	64	7	32	4
Eric Daze............79	79	33	24	57	1	16	9
Alexei Zhamnov 63	63	13	36	49	-12	40	3
Jaroslav Spacek.......62	62	7	19	26	3	28	3
FLA 12	12	2	1	3	-4	8	1
CHI 50	50	5	18	23	7	20	2
Chris Herperger 61	61	10	15	25	0	20	0
Boris Mironov 66	66	5	17	22	-14	42	3
Bob Probert 79	79	7	12	19	-13	103	1
Stephane Quintal 72	72	1	18	19	-9	60	0
Kyle Calder* 43	43	5	10	15	-4	14	0
Alexander Karpovtsev .53	53	2	13	15	-4	39	1
Kevin Dean 69	69	0	11	11	-16	30	0
Steve Dubinsky 60	60	6	4	10	-4	33	0
Jean-Yves Leroux 59	59	4	4	8	-9	22	1
Valeri Zelepukin 36	36	3	4	7	-14	18	0
Ryan VandenBussche ...64	64	2	5	7	-8	146	0
Chris McAlpine 50	50	0	6	6	5	32	0
Steve Poapst 36	36	2	3	5	3	12	0
Steve McCarthy* 44	44	0	5	5	-7	8	0
Reto Von Arx* 19	19	3	1	4	-4	4	0
Jamie Allison 44	44	1	3	4	7	53	0

Acquired: D Spacek from Fla. for D Anders Eriksson (Nov. 6); G Passmore from LA for a '01 8th-round pick (Feb. 28).

Goalies (10 Gm)

Goalies (10 Gm)	Gm	Min	GAA	Record	SV%
Jocelyn Thibault........66	66	3844	2.81	27-32-7	.895
Steve Passmore 20	20	1058	2.89	3-12-2	.888
LA 14	14	718	3.09	3-8-1	.881
CHI 6	6	340	2.47	0-4-1	.905
Rob Tallas 12	12	627	3.35	2-7-0	.868
CHICAGO 82	82	4981	2.96	29-45-8	.888

Shutouts: Thibault (6), Passmore (1 with LA). **Assists:** Thibault (3). **PM:** Passmore (4), Thibault (2).

Colorado Avalanche

Top Scorers

Top Scorers	Gm	G	A	Pts	+/-	PM	PP
Joe Sakic 82	82	54	64	118	45	30	19
Peter Forsberg 73	73	27	62	89	23	54	12
Milan Hejduk 80	80	41	38	79	32	36	12
Alex Tanguay 82	82	27	50	77	35	37	7
Chris Drury 71	71	24	41	65	6	47	11
Rob Blake 67	67	19	40	59	3	77	10
LA 54	54	17	32	49	-8	69	9
COL...........13	13	2	8	10	11	8	1
Ray Bourque 80	80	7	52	59	25	48	2
Steve Reinprecht 80	80	15	21	36	10	14	3
LA 59	59	12	17	29	11	12	3
COL...........21	21	3	4	7	-1	2	0
Shjon Podein 82	82	15	17	32	7	68	0
Martin Skoula 82	82	8	17	25	8	38	3
Ville Nieminen*........50	50	14	8	22	8	38	2
Greg de Vries 79	79	5	12	17	23	51	0
Dan Hinote 76	76	5	10	15	1	51	1
Jon Klemm 78	78	4	11	15	2	54	2
Adam Foote 35	35	3	12	15	6	42	1
Stephane Yelle 50	50	4	10	14	-3	20	0
Eric Messier 64	64	5	7	12	-3	26	0
Dave Reid 73	73	1	9	10	1	21	0
Scott Parker 69	69	2	3	5	-2	155	0

Acquired: D Blake and C Reinprecht from LA for RW Adam Deadmarsh, D Aaron Miller, a '01 1st-round pick, and future considerations (Feb. 22).

Goalies (10 Gm)

Goalies (10 Gm)	Gm	Min	GAA	Record	SV%
Patrick Roy 62	62	3585	2.21	40-13-7	.913
David Aebischer* 26	26	1393	2.24	12-7-3	.903
COLORADO 82	82	4993	2.31	52-20-10	.907

Shutouts: Roy (4), Aebischer (3). **Assists:** Roy (5), Aebischer (1). **PM:** Roy (10).

Columbus Blue Jackets

Top Scorers

Top Scorers	Gm	G	A	Pts	+/-	PM	PP
Geoff Sanderson.......68	68	30	26	56	4	46	9
Espen Knutsen 66	66	11	42	53	-3	30	2
Ray Whitney 46	46	10	24	34	-17	30	5
FLA 43	43	10	21	31	-16	28	5
CLB 3	3	0	3	3	-1	2	0
Tyler Wright 76	76	16	16	32	-9	140	4
David Vyborny* 79	79	13	19	32	-9	22	5
Serge Aubin* 81	81	13	17	30	-20	107	0
Jamie Heward 69	69	11	16	27	3	33	9
Deron Quint 57	57	7	16	23	-19	16	3
Bruce Gardiner 73	73	7	15	22	-1	78	0
Robert Kron 59	59	8	11	19	4	10	0
Alexander Selivanov....59	59	8	11	19	-11	38	5
Lyle Odelein 81	81	3	14	17	-16	118	1
Petteri Nummelin 61	61	4	12	16	-11	10	2
Kevin Dineen 66	66	8	7	15	2	126	0
Jamie Pushor 75	75	3	10	13	7	94	0
Mattias Timander 76	76	2	9	11	-8	24	0
Chris Nielsen*........29	29	4	5	9	4	4	0
Mike Maneluk 39	39	5	1	6	-11	33	2
Blake Sloan 47	47	3	2	5	-4	17	0
DAL...........33	33	2	2	4	-2	4	0
CLB 14	14	1	0	1	-2	13	0
Jean-Luc Grand-Pierre..64	64	1	4	5	-6	73	0

Acquired: LW Whitney from Fla. for C Kevyn Adams and a conditional pick (Mar. 13). **Claims:** RW Sloan off waivers from Dal. (Mar. 13).

Goalies (10 Gm)

Goalies (10 Gm)	Gm	Min	GAA	Record	SV%
Ron Tugnutt..........53	53	3129	2.44	22-25-5	.917
Marc Denis 32	32	1830	3.25	6-20-4	.895
COLUMBUS..........82	82	4988	2.80	28-45-9	.906

Shutouts: Tugnutt (4). **Assists:** Tugnutt (1). **PM:** Tugnutt and Denis (2).

Dallas Stars

Top Scorers

Top Scorers	Gm	G	A	Pts	+/-	PM	PP
Mike Modano 81	81	33	51	84	26	52	8
Brett Hull............79	79	39	40	79	10	18	11
Joe Nieuwendyk 69	69	29	23	52	5	30	12
Sergei Zubov 79	79	10	41	51	22	24	6
Darryl Sydor 81	81	10	37	47	-5	34	3
Jere Lehtinen 74	74	20	25	45	14	24	7
Brenden Morrow 82	82	20	24	44	18	128	7
Grant Marshall 75	75	13	24	37	1	64	4
Jamie Langenbrunner ..53	53	12	18	30	4	57	3
Ted Donato 65	65	8	17	25	6	26	1
Mike Keane 67	67	10	14	24	4	35	1
Shaun Van Allen 59	59	7	16	23	5	16	0
Derian Hatcher 80	80	2	21	23	5	77	1
Richard Matvichuk 78	78	4	16	20	5	62	2
Brad Lukowich 80	80	4	10	14	28	76	0
Benoit Hogue 34	34	3	7	10	-1	26	0
Kirk Muller 55	55	1	9	10	-4	26	0
Roman Lyashenko 60	60	6	3	9	-1	45	0
Tyler Bouck* 48	48	2	5	7	-3	29	0
John MacLean 30	30	4	2	6	-2	17	1
NYR...........2	2	0	0	0	-2	0	0
DAL...........28	28	4	2	6	0	17	1
Grant Ledyard 22	22	2	3	5	-2	16	0
TB 14	14	2	2	4	1	4	0
DAL...........8	8	0	1	1	-3	4	0

Acquired: RW MacLean from NYR for future considerations (Feb. 1); D Ledyard from TB for a '01 7th-round pick (Mar. 13). **Signed:** free agent LW Hogue (Jan. 5).

Goalies (10 Gm)

Goalies (10 Gm)	Gm	Min	GAA	Record	SV%
Marty Turco* 26	26	1266	1.90	13-6-1	.925
Ed Belfour 63	63	3687	2.34	35-20-7	.905
DALLAS.............82	82	4970	2.26	48-26-8	.908

Shutouts: Belfour (8), Turco (3). **Assists:** Belfour (1). **PM:** Turco (12), Belfour (4).

Detroit Red Wings

Top Scorers	Gm	G	A	Pts	+/-	PM	PP
Brendan Shanahan	81	31	45	76	9	81	15
Nicklas Lidstrom	82	15	56	71	9	18	8
Sergei Fedorov	75	32	37	69	12	40	14
Martin Lapointe	82	27	30	57	3	127	13
Steve Yzerman	54	18	34	52	4	18	5
Tomas Holmstrom	73	16	24	40	-12	40	9
Igor Larionov	65	9	31	40	-5	38	4
FLA	26	5	6	11	-11	10	2
DET	39	4	25	29	6	28	2
Vyacheslav Kozlov	72	20	18	38	9	30	4
Pat Verbeek	67	15	15	30	0	73	7
Mathieu Dandenault	73	10	15	25	11	38	2
Kris Draper	75	8	17	25	17	38	0
Steve Duchesne	54	6	19	25	9	48	2
Darren McCarty	72	12	10	22	-5	123	1
Doug Brown	60	9	13	22	0	14	2
Larry Murphy	57	2	19	21	-6	12	0
Kirk Maltby	79	12	7	19	16	22	1
Boyd Devereaux	55	5	6	11	1	14	0
Todd Gill	68	3	8	11	17	53	0
Aaron Ward	73	4	5	9	-4	57	0
Jiri Fischer	55	1	8	9	3	59	0
Brent Gilchrist	60	1	8	9	-8	41	0
Maxim Kuznetsov*	25	1	2	3	-1	23	0
Jason Williams*	5	0	3	3	1	2	0
Chris Chelios	24	0	3	3	4	45	0

Acquired: C Larionov from Fla. for D Yan Golubovsky (Dec. 28).

Goalies (10 Gm)	Gm	Min	GAA	Record	Sv%
Manny Legace	39	2136	2.05	24-5-5	.920
Chris Osgood	52	2834	2.69	25-19-4	.903
DETROIT	82	4994	2.43	49-24-9	.909

Shutouts: Legace (2), Osgood (1). **Assists:** Legace (2). **PM:** Osgood (8), Legace (4).

Florida Panthers

Top Scorers	Gm	G	A	Pts	+/-	PM	PP
Pavel Bure	82	59	33	92	-2	58	19
Viktor Kozlov	51	14	23	37	-4	10	6
Marcus Nilson	78	12	24	36	-3	74	0
Rob Niedermayer	67	12	20	32	-12	50	3
Kevyn Adams	78	11	18	29	3	54	0
CLB	66	8	12	20	-4	52	0
FLA	12	3	6	9	7	2	0
Vaclav Prospal	74	5	24	29	-1	22	1
OTT	40	1	12	13	1	12	0
FLA	34	4	12	16	-2	10	1
Robert Svehla	82	6	22	28	-8	76	0
Anders Eriksson	73	2	24	26	-2	30	1
CHI	13	2	3	5	-4	2	1
FLA	60	0	21	21	2	28	0
Greg Adams	60	11	12	23	-3	10	2
Len Barrie	60	5	18	23	4	135	0
Dan Boyle	69	4	18	22	-14	28	1
Bret Hedican	70	5	15	20	-7	72	4
Denis Shvidki*	43	6	10	16	6	16	0
Ollie Jokinen	78	6	10	16	-22	106	0
Peter Worrell	71	3	7	10	-10	248	0
Ivan Novoseltsev*	38	3	6	9	-4	16	0

Acquired: D Eriksson from Chi. for D Jaroslav Spacek (Nov. 6); C Prospal from Ott. for a '01 4th-round pick or a '02 3rd-round pick (Jan. 21); C K. Adams and a conditional pick from Clb. for LW Ray Whitney (Mar. 13). **Signed:** free agent LW G. Adams (Nov. 6).

Goalies (10 Gm)	Gm	Min	GAA	Record	Sv%
Roberto Luongo*	47	2628	2.44	12-24-7	.920
Trevor Kidd	42	2354	3.31	10-23-6	.893
FLORIDA	82	5006	2.95	22-47-13	.904

Shutouts: Luongo (5), Kidd (1). **Assists:** Kidd (1). **PM:** Kidd (6), Luongo (2).

Edmonton Oilers

Top Scorers	Gm	G	A	Pts	+/-	PM	PP
Doug Weight	82	25	65	90	12	91	8
Ryan Smyth	82	31	39	70	10	58	11
Janne Niinimaa	82	12	34	46	6	90	8
Anson Carter	61	16	26	42	1	23	7
Todd Marchant	71	13	26	39	1	51	0
Mike Grier	74	20	16	36	11	20	2
Rem Murray	82	15	21	36	5	24	1
Dan Cleary	81	14	21	35	5	37	2
Tom Poti	81	12	20	32	-4	60	6
Sergei Zholtok	69	5	26	31	-7	30	1
MON	32	1	10	11	-15	8	0
EDM	37	4	16	20	8	22	1
Georges Laraque	82	13	16	29	5	148	1
Igor Ulanov	67	3	20	23	15	90	1
Mike Comrie*	41	8	14	22	6	14	3
Eric Brewer	77	7	14	21	15	53	2
Jason Smith	82	5	15	20	14	120	1
Ethan Moreau	68	9	10	19	-6	90	0
Shawn Horcoff*	49	9	7	16	8	10	0
Domenic Pittis*	47	4	5	9	-5	49	0
Sean Brown	62	2	3	5	2	110	0

Acquired: LW Carter, a '02 2nd-round pick and an optional swap of 1st-round picks in '01 or '02 from Bos. for RW Bill Guerin (Nov. 15); C Zholtok from Mon. for C Chad Kilger (Dec. 18). **Claimed:** G Roussel off waivers from Ana. (Jan. 10).

Goalies (10 Gm)	Gm	Min	GAA	Record	Sv%
Tommy Salo	73	4364	2.46	36-25-12	.904
Dominic Roussel	21	1001	3.12	3-9-2	.883
ANA	13	653	2.85	2-5-2	.895
EDM	8	348	3.62	1-4-0	.861
EDMONTON	82	4997	2.67	39-31-12	.896

Shutouts: Salo (8). **Assists:** Salo (1). **PM:** Salo (4), Roussel (2).

Los Angeles Kings

Top Scorers	Gm	G	A	Pts	+/-	PM	PP
Zigmund Palffy	73	38	51	89	22	20	12
Luc Robitaille	82	37	51	88	10	66	16
Bryan Smolinski	78	27	32	59	10	40	5
Jozef Stumpel	63	16	39	55	20	14	9
Mathieu Schneider	73	16	35	51	0	56	7
Glen Murray	64	18	21	39	9	32	3
Lubomir Visnovsky*	81	7	32	39	16	36	3
Adam Deadmarsh	57	17	15	32	1	63	7
COL	39	13	13	26	-2	59	7
LA	18	4	2	6	3	4	0
Nelson Emerson	78	11	11	22	-13	54	0
Eric Belanger*	62	9	12	21	14	16	1
Kelly Buchberger	82	6	14	20	-10	75	0
Jaroslav Modry	63	4	15	19	16	48	0
Ian Laperriere	79	8	10	18	5	141	0
Aaron Miller	69	4	14	18	22	43	0
COL	56	4	9	13	19	29	0
LA	13	0	5	5	3	14	0
Mattias Norstrom	82	0	18	18	10	60	0
Craig Johnson	26	4	5	9	0	16	0
Jere Karalahti	56	2	7	9	8	38	0
Philippe Boucher	22	2	4	6	8	20	0

Acquired: G Potvin from Van. for future considerations (Feb. 15); RW Deadmarsh, D Miller, a '01 1st-round pick, and future considerations from Col. for D Rob Blake and C Steve Reinprecht (Feb. 22).

Goalies (10 Gm)	Gm	Min	GAA	Record	Sv%
Felix Potvin	58	3416	2.62	27-22-8	.900
VAN	35	2006	3.08	14-17-3	.887
LA	23	1410	1.96	13-5-5	.919
Jamie Storr	45	2498	2.74	19-18-6	.894
LOS ANGELES	82	4995	2.74	38-31-13	.894

Shutouts: Potvin (6 incl. 1 with Van.), Storr (4). **Assists:** Potvin (5 incl. 2 with Van.). **PM:** Potvin (4 incl. 2 with Van.), Storr (4).

Minnesota Wild

Top Scorers	Gm	G	A	Pts	+/-	PM	PP
Marian Gaborik*	71	18	18	36	-6	32	6
Lubomir Sekeras	80	11	23	34	-8	52	4
Wes Walz	82	18	12	30	-8	37	0
Filip Kuba*	75	9	21	30	-6	28	4
Darby Hendrickson	72	18	11	29	1	36	3
Jim Dowd	68	7	22	29	-6	80	0
Antti Laaksonen	82	12	16	28	-7	24	0
Stacy Roest	76	7	20	27	3	20	1
Aaron Gavey	75	10	14	24	-8	52	1
Sergei Krivokrasov	54	7	15	22	-1	20	2
Roman Simicek	57	5	10	15	-9	51	3
PIT	29	3	6	9	-5	30	1
MIN	28	2	4	6	-4	21	2
Brad Bombardir	70	0	15	15	-6	42	0
Cam Stewart	54	4	9	13	-3	18	0
Maxim Sushinsky	30	7	4	11	-7	29	3
Jeff Nielsen	59	3	8	11	-16	4	1
Willie Mitchell*	33	1	9	10	4	40	0
NJ	16	0	2	2	0	29	0
MIN	17	1	7	8	4	11	0
Andy Sutton	69	3	4	7	-11	131	2
Ladislav Benysek*	71	2	5	7	-11	38	1
Peter Bartos	13	4	2	6	2	6	1
Sylvain Blouin	41	3	2	5	-5	117	0

Acquired: C Simicek from Pit for LW Steve McKenna (Jan. 13); D Mitchell and future considerations from NJ for D Sean O'Donnell (Mar. 4).

Goalies (10 Gm)	Gm	Min	GAA	Record	Sv%
Manny Fernandez	42	2461	2.24	19-17-4	.920
Jamie McLennan	38	2230	2.64	5-23-9	.905
MINNESOTA	82	5005	2.52	25-44-13	.909

Shutouts: Fernandez (4), McLennan (2). **Assists:** McLennan (1). **PM:** Fernandez (6), McLennan (4).

Montreal Canadiens

Top Scorers	Gm	G	A	Pts	+/-	PM	PP
Saku Koivu	54	17	30	47	2	40	7
Oleg Petrov	81	17	30	47	-11	24	4
Brian Savage	62	21	24	45	-13	26	12
Richard Zednik	74	19	25	44	-4	71	5
WASH	62	16	19	35	-2	61	4
MON	12	3	6	9	-2	10	1
Martin Rucinsky	57	16	22	38	-5	66	5
Patrice Brisebois	77	15	21	36	-31	28	11
Chad Kilger	77	14	18	32	-8	51	2
EDM	34	5	2	7	-7	17	1
MON	43	9	16	25	-1	34	1
Craig Darby	78	12	16	28	-17	16	0
Andrei Markov*	63	6	17	23	-6	18	2
Jan Bulis	51	5	18	23	-1	26	1
WASH	39	5	13	18	0	26	1
MON	12	0	5	5	-1	0	0
Patrick Poulin	52	9	11	20	1	13	0
Jim Campbell	57	9	11	20	-3	53	6
Karl Dykhuis	67	8	9	17	9	44	2
Patrick Traverse	71	5	9	14	-10	30	1
ANA	15	1	0	1	-6	6	0
BOS	37	2	6	8	4	14	1
MON	19	2	3	5	-8	10	0
Benoit Brunet	35	3	11	14	-4	12	0
Stephane Robidas*	65	6	6	12	0	14	1

Acquired: C Kilger from Edm. for C Sergei Zholtok (Dec. 18); D Traverse from Bos. for D Eric Weinrich (Feb. 21); RW Zednik, C Bulis, and a '01 1st-round pick from Wash. for C Trevor Linden, RW Dainius Zubrus and a '01 2nd-round pick (Mar. 13).

Goalies (10 Gm)	Gm	Min	GAA	Record	Sv%
Mathieu Garon*	11	589	2.44	4-5-1	.897
Jose Theodore	59	3298	2.57	20-29-5	.909
Jeff Hackett	19	998	3.25	4-10-2	.887
MONTREAL	82	4978	2.80	28-46-8	.899

Shutouts: Garon and Theodore (2). **Assists:** Hackett (1). **PM:** Theodore (6).

Nashville Predators

Top Scorers	Gm	G	A	Pts	+/-	PM	PP
Cliff Ronning	80	19	43	62	4	28	6
Scott Walker	74	25	29	54	-2	66	9
Patric Kjellberg	81	14	31	45	-2	12	5
David Legwand	81	13	28	41	1	38	3
Vitali Yachmenev	78	15	19	34	-5	10	4
Greg Johnson	82	15	17	32	-6	46	1
Marian Cisar*	60	12	15	27	-7	45	5
Randy Robitaille	62	9	17	26	-11	12	5
Kimmo Timonen	82	12	13	25	-6	50	6
Tom Fitzgerald	82	9	9	18	-5	70	0
Bill Houlder	81	4	12	16	-7	40	0
Scott Harnell*	75	2	14	16	-8	48	0
Rob Valicevic	60	8	6	14	-2	26	1
Denis Arkhipov*	40	6	7	13	0	4	0
Karlis Skrastins	82	1	11	12	-12	30	0
Mark Eaton	34	3	8	11	7	14	1
Richard Lintner	50	3	5	8	2	22	1
Cale Hulse	82	1	7	8	-5	128	0
Greg Classen*	27	2	4	6	-4	14	1
Ville Peltonen	23	3	1	4	-7	2	0

Goalies (10 Gm)	Gm	Min	GAA	Record	Sv%
Mike Dunham	48	2810	2.28	21-21-4	.923
Tomas Vokoun	37	2088	2.44	13-17-5	.910
NASHVILLE	82	4984	2.41	34-39-9	.915

Shutouts: Dunham (4), Vokoun (2). **Assists:** none. **PM:** Dunham and Vokoun (6).

New Jersey Devils

Top Scorers	Gm	G	A	Pts	+/-	PM	PP
Patrik Elias	82	40	56	96	45	51	8
Alexander Mogilny	75	43	40	83	10	43	12
Petr Sykora	73	35	46	81	36	32	9
Scott Gomez	76	14	49	63	-1	46	2
Jason Arnott	54	21	34	55	23	75	8
Sergei Brylin	75	23	29	52	25	24	3
Brian Rafalski	78	9	43	52	36	26	6
Bobby Holik	80	15	35	50	19	97	3
Randy McKay	77	23	20	43	3	50	12
John Madden	80	23	15	38	24	12	0
Scott Niedermayer	57	6	29	35	14	22	1
Scott Stevens	81	9	22	31	40	71	3
Sergei Nemchinov	65	8	22	30	11	16	1
Turner Stevenson	69	8	18	26	11	97	2
Colin White*	82	1	19	20	32	155	0
Sean O'Donnell	80	4	13	17	0	161	1
MIN	63	4	12	16	-2	128	1
NJ	17	0	1	1	2	33	0
Jay Pandolfo	63	4	12	16	3	16	0
Bob Corkum	75	7	7	14	-8	22	1
LA	58	4	6	10	-12	18	1
NJ	17	3	1	4	4	4	0
Ken Sutton	53	1	7	8	9	37	0
Pierre Dagenais*	9	3	2	5	1	6	1
Mike Commodore*	20	1	4	5	5	14	0
Jim McKenzie	53	2	2	4	0	119	0
Ken Daneyko	77	0	4	4	8	87	0

Acquired: C Corkum from LA for future considerations (Feb. 23); D O'Donnell from Min. for D Willie Mitchell and future considerations (Mar. 4); G Vanbiesbrouck from NYI for G Chris Terreri and a '01 9th-round pick (Mar. 12).

Goalies (10 Gm)	Gm	Min	GAA	Record	Sv%
Martin Brodeur	72	4297	2.32	42-17-11	.906
John Vanbiesbrouck	48	2630	2.87	14-25-5	.901
NYI	44	2390	3.01	10-25-5	.898
NJ	4	240	1.50	4-0-0	.935
NEW JERSEY	82	5001	2.34	48-22-12	.904

Shutouts: Brodeur (9), Vanbiesbrouck (2, incl. 1 with NYI). **Assists:** Brodeur (1). **PM:** Brodeur (14), Vanbiesbrouck (8 with NYI).

New York Islanders

Top Scorers

Top Scorers	Gm	G	A	Pts	+/-	PM	PP
Mariusz Czerkawski	82	30	32	62	-25	48	10
Roman Hamrlik	76	16	30	46	-20	92	5
Dave Scatchard	81	21	24	45	-9	114	4
Tim Connolly	82	10	31	41	-14	42	5
Brad Isbister	51	18	14	32	-19	59	7
Claude Lapointe	80	9	23	32	-2	56	1
Mark Parrish	70	17	13	30	-27	28	6
Kenny Jonsson	65	8	21	29	-22	30	5
Bill Muckalt	60	11	15	26	-3	33	1
Oleg Kvasha	62	11	9	20	-15	46	0
Garry Galley	56	6	14	20	-4	59	4
Taylor Pyatt*	78	4	14	18	-17	39	1
Jason Blake	47	5	11	16	-20	34	1
LA	17	1	3	4	-8	10	0
NYI	30	4	8	12	-12	24	1
Zdeno Chara	82	2	7	9	-27	157	0
Aris Brimanis	56	0	8	8	-12	26	0
Juraj Kolnik*	29	4	3	7	-8	12	0
Mats Lindgren	20	3	4	7	4	10	0
Mark Lawrence	36	3	4	7	-9	32	1

Acquired: C Blake from LA for a '02 conditional pick (Jan. 3); G Terreri and a '01 9th-round pick from NJ for G John Vanbiesbrouck (Mar. 12).

Goalies (10 Gm)	Gm	Min	GAA	Record	Sv%
Chris Terreri	18	895	2.61	4-9-2	.895
NJ	10	453	2.78	2-5-1	.874
NYI	8	442	2.44	2-4-1	.912
Rick DiPietro*	20	1083	3.49	3-15-1	.878
NY ISLANDERS	82	4968	3.24	21-54-7	.887

Shutouts: none. **Assists:** DiPietro (2). **PM:** Terreri and DiPietro (2).

Ottawa Senators

Top Scorers

Top Scorers	Gm	G	A	Pts	+/-	PM	PP
Alexei Yashin	82	40	48	88	10	30	13
Marian Hossa	81	32	43	75	19	44	11
Shawn McEachern	82	32	40	72	10	62	9
Daniel Alfredsson	68	24	46	70	11	30	10
Radek Bonk	74	23	36	59	27	52	5
Wade Redden	78	10	37	47	22	49	4
Martin Havlat*	73	19	23	42	8	20	7
Mike Sillinger	68	16	25	41	-11	48	1
FLA	55	13	21	34	-12	44	1
OTT	13	3	4	7	1	4	0
Rob Zamuner	79	19	18	37	7	52	1
Magnus Arvedson	51	17	16	33	23	24	1
Karel Rachunek*	71	3	30	33	17	60	3
Andreas Dackell	81	13	18	31	7	24	1
Jason York	74	6	16	22	7	72	3
Mike Fisher	60	7	12	19	-1	46	0
Sami Salo	31	2	16	18	9	10	1
Chris Phillips	73	2	12	14	8	31	2
Curtis Leschyshyn	65	2	7	9	5	-19	1
MIN	54	2	3	5	-2	19	1
OTT	11	0	4	4	7	0	0
Ricard Persson	33	1	8	9	8	35	0
Andre Roy	64	3	5	8	1	169	0

Acquired: C Sillinger from Fla. for past considerations (Mar. 13); D Leschyshyn from Min. for a '01 3rd-round pick (Mar. 13).

Goalies (10 Gm)	Gm	Min	GAA	Record	Sv%
Patrick Lalime	60	3607	2.35	36-19-5	.914
Jani Hurme*	22	1296	2.50	12-5-4	.904
OTTAWA	82	4977	2.47	48-25-9	.908

Shutouts: Lalime (7), Hurme (2). **Assists:** Lalime (1). **PM:** Lalime (2).

New York Rangers

Top Scorers

Top Scorers	Gm	G	A	Pts	+/-	PM	PP
Brian Leetch	82	21	58	79	-18	34	10
Petr Nedved	79	32	46	78	10	54	9
Theo Fleury	62	30	44	74	0	122	8
Radek Dvorak	82	31	36	67	9	20	5
Mark Messier	82	24	43	67	-25	89	12
Jan Hlavac	79	28	36	64	3	20	5
Valeri Kamensky	65	14	20	34	-18	36	6
Mike York	79	14	17	31	1	20	3
Adam Graves	82	10	16	26	-16	77	1
Kim Johnsson	75	5	21	26	-3	40	4
Sandy McCarthy	81	11	10	21	3	171	0
Michal Grosek	65	9	11	20	-10	61	2
Sylvain Lefebvre	71	2	13	15	3	55	0
Manny Malhotra	50	4	8	12	-10	31	0
Rich Pilon	69	2	9	11	-2	175	0
Jeff Toms	54	3	5	8	-10	10	0
NYI	39	2	4	6	-7	10	0
NYR	15	1	1	2	-3	0	0
Tim Taylor	38	2	5	7	-6	16	0
Colin Forbes	58	1	5	6	4	46	0
OTT	39	0	1	1	-3	31	0
NYR	19	1	4	5	-3	15	0

Acquired: LW Forbes from Ott. for LW Eric Lacroix (Mar. 1). **Claimed:** LW Toms off waivers from NYI (Jan. 13); G Hebert off waivers from Ana. (Mar. 7).

Goalies (10 Gm)	Gm	Min	GAA	Record	Sv%
Guy Hebert	54	2950	3.19	17-30-5	.897
ANA	41	2215	3.12	12-23-4	.897
NYR	13	735	3.43	5-7-1	.897
Mike Richter	45	2635	3.28	20-21-3	.893
Kirk McLean	23	1220	3.49	8-10-1	.889
NY RANGERS	82	4966	3.50	33-44-5	.887

Shutouts: Hebert (2 with Ana.). **Assists:** none. **PM:** none.

Philadelphia Flyers

Top Scorers

Top Scorers	Gm	G	A	Pts	+/-	PM	PP
Mark Recchi	69	27	50	77	15	33	7
Keith Primeau	71	34	39	73	17	76	11
Simon Gagne	69	27	32	59	-24	18	6
Daymond Langkow	71	13	41	54	12	50	3
Dan McGillis	82	14	35	49	13	86	4
Eric Desjardins	79	15	33	48	-3	50	6
Ruslan Fedotenko*	74	16	20	36	8	72	3
Rick Tocchet	60	14	22	36	10	83	5
Dean McAmmond	71	11	17	28	3	43	2
CHI	61	10	16	26	4	43	1
PHI	10	1	1	2	-1	0	1
Justin Williams*	63	12	13	25	6	22	0
Peter White	77	9	16	25	1	16	1
Paul Ranheim	80	10	7	17	2	14	0
Michal Sykora	49	5	11	16	9	26	1
Jody Hull	71	7	8	15	-1	10	0
Kent Manderville	82	5	10	15	-2	47	0
Andy Delmore	66	5	9	14	2	16	2
Chris Therien	73	2	12	14	22	48	1
John LeClair	16	7	5	12	2	0	3
Todd Fedoruk*	53	5	5	10	0	109	0
Luke Richardson	82	2	6	8	23	131	0
P.J. Stock	51	2	5	7	-3	110	1
MON	20	1	2	3	-1	32	0
PHI	31	1	3	4	-2	78	0

Acquired: C Stock and a '01 6th-round pick from Mon. for LW Gino Odjick (Dec. 7); LW McAmmond from Chi. for a '01 3rd-round pick (Mar. 13).

Goalies (10 Gm)	Gm	Min	GAA	Record	Sv%
Roman Cechmanek	59	3431	2.01	35-15-6	.921
Brian Boucher	27	1470	3.27	8-12-5	.876
PHILADELPHIA	82	5001	2.48	43-28-11	.903

Shutouts: Cechmanek (10), Boucher (1). **Assists:** Cechmanek (1). **PM:** Cechmanek (4), Boucher (2).

Phoenix Coyotes

Top Scorers	Gm	G	A	Pts	+/-	PM	PP
Jeremy Roenick	80	30	46	76	-1	114	13
Shane Doan	76	26	37	63	0	89	6
Mike Johnson	76	13	30	43	-10	42	4
TB	64	11	27	38	-10	38	3
PHO	12	2	3	5	0	4	1
Joe Juneau	69	10	23	33	-2	28	5
Michal Handzus	46	14	18	32	16	33	3
ST.L	36	10	14	24	11	12	3
PHO	10	4	4	8	5	21	0
Landon Wilson	70	18	13	31	3	92	2
Teppo Numminen	72	5	26	31	9	36	1
Travis Green	69	13	15	28	-11	63	3
Claude Lemieux	46	10	16	26	1	58	2
Brad May	62	11	14	25	10	107	0
Jyrki Lumme	58	4	21	25	3	44	0
Juha Ylonen	69	4	14	23	10	38	0
Trevor Letowski	77	7	15	22	-2	32	0
Paul Mara	62	6	14	20	-16	54	2
TB	46	6	40	16	-17	40	2
PHO	16	0	4	4	1	14	0
Mika Alatalo	70	7	12	19	1	22	0
Ladislav Nagy*	46	8	9	17	-2	22	2
ST.L	40	8	8	16	-2	20	2
PHO	6	0	1	1	0	2	0
Ossi Vaananen*	81	4	12	16	9	90	0
Keith Carney	82	2	14	16	15	86	0

Acquired: RW Johnson, D Mara, RW Ruslan Zainullin, and a '01 2nd-round pick from TB for D Stan Neckar and G Nikolai Khabibulin (Mar. 5); C Nagy, C Handzus, C Jeff Taffe, and a '01 1st-round pick from St.L for LW Keith Tkachuk (Mar. 13). **Signed:** free agent RW Lemieux (Dec. 2).

Goalies (10 Gm)	Gm	Min	GAA	Record	Sv%
Sean Burke	62	3644	2.27	25-22-13	.922
Robert Esche*	25	1350	3.02	10-8-4	.896
PHOENIX	82	5010	2.54	35-30-17	.913

Shutouts: Burke (4), Esche (2). **Assists:** Esche (3), Burke (1). **PM:** Burke (16), Esche (2).

Pittsburgh Penguins

Top Scorers	Gm	G	A	Pts	+/-	PM	PP
Jaromir Jagr	81	52	69	121	19	42	14
Alexei Kovalev	79	44	51	95	12	96	12
Martin Straka	82	27	68	95	19	38	7
Robert Lang	82	32	48	80	20	28	10
Mario Lemieux	43	35	41	76	15	18	16
Jan Hrdina	78	15	28	43	19	48	3
Kevin Stevens	55	10	22	32	-6	73	2
PHI	23	2	7	9	-2	18	0
PIT	32	8	15	23	-4	55	2
Josef Beranek	70	9	14	23	-7	43	2
Hans Jonsson	58	4	18	22	11	22	2
Wayne Primeau	75	3	19	22	-17	131	0
TB	47	2	13	15	-17	77	0
PIT	28	1	6	7	0	54	0
Janne Laukkanen	50	3	17	20	9	34	0
Aleksey Morozov	66	5	14	19	-8	6	0
Darius Kasparaitis	77	3	16	19	11	111	1
Rene Corbet	43	8	9	17	-3	57	2
Andrew Ference	36	4	11	15	6	28	1
Milan Kraft	42	7	7	14	-6	8	1
Kip Miller	33	3	8	11	0	6	1
Frantisek Kucera	55	2	7	9	-7	12	0
CLB	48	2	5	7	-5	12	0
PIT	7	0	2	2	-2	0	0

Acquired: LW Stevens from Phi. for D John Slaney (Jan. 14); C Primeau from TB for RW Matthew Barnaby (Feb. 1); D Kucera from Clb. for a '01 6th-round pick (Mar. 13).

Goalies (10 Gm)	Gm	Min	GAA	Record	Sv%
Garth Snow	35	2032	2.98	14-15-4	.900
J-S Aubin	36	2050	3.13	20-14-1	.890
PITTSBURGH	82	4978	3.09	42-31-9	.893

Shutouts: Snow (3). **Assists:** Aubin (1). **PM:** Snow (8), Aubin (4).

St. Louis Blues

Top Scorers	Gm	G	A	Pts	+/-	PM	PP
Pierre Turgeon	79	30	52	82	14	37	11
Keith Tkachuk	76	35	44	79	3	122	17
PHO	64	29	42	71	6	108	15
ST.L	12	6	2	8	-3	14	2
Scott Young	81	40	33	73	15	30	14
Al MacInnis	59	12	42	54	23	52	6
Cory Stillman	78	24	28	52	-8	51	10
CALG	66	21	24	45	-6	45	7
ST.L	12	3	4	7	-2	6	3
Chris Pronger	51	8	39	47	21	75	4
Pavol Demitra	44	20	25	45	27	16	5
Jochen Hecht	72	19	25	44	11	48	8
Dallas Drake	82	12	29	41	18	71	2
Alexander Khavanov	74	7	16	23	16	52	2
Mike Eastwood	77	6	17	23	4	28	0
Scott Mellanby	63	11	10	21	-13	71	3
FLA	40	4	9	13	-13	46	1
ST.L	23	7	1	8	0	25	2
Jamal Mayers	77	8	13	21	-3	117	0
Tyson Nash	57	8	7	15	8	110	0
Daniel Corso*	28	10	3	13	0	14	5
Lubos Bartecko	50	5	8	13	-1	12	0
Marty Reasoner	41	4	9	13	-5	14	0
Sean Hill	48	1	10	11	5	51	0
Jeff Finley	72	2	8	10	7	38	0
Bryce Salvador*	75	2	8	10	-4	69	0

Acquired: RW Mellanby from Fla. for RW Dave Morisset and a '02 conditional pick (Feb. 9); LW Tkachuk from Pho. for C Ladislav Nagy, C Michal Handzus, C Jeff Taffe, and a '01 1st-round pick (Mar. 13); C Stillman from Calg. for C Craig Conroy and a '01 7th-round pick (Mar. 13).

Goalies (10 Gm)	Gm	Min	GAA	Record	Sv%
Brent Johnson*	31	1744	2.17	19-9-2	.907
Roman Turek	54	3232	2.28	24-18-10	.901
ST. LOUIS	82	5001	2.34	43-27-12	.899

Shutouts: Turek (6), Johnson (4). **Assists:** Turek (1). **PM:** Turek (6), Johnson (2).

San Jose Sharks

Top Scorers	Gm	G	A	Pts	+/-	PM	PP
Teemu Selanne	73	33	39	72	-7	36	12
ANA	61	26	33	59	-8	36	10
SJ	12	7	6	13	1	0	2
Patrick Marleau	81	25	27	52	7	22	5
Owen Nolan	57	24	25	49	0	75	10
Niklas Sundstrom	82	10	39	49	10	28	4
Vincent Damphousse	45	9	37	46	17	62	4
Mike Ricci	81	22	22	44	3	65	9
Scott Thornton	73	19	17	36	4	114	4
Gary Suter	68	10	24	34	8	84	4
Marco Sturm	81	14	18	32	9	28	2
Stephane Matteau	80	13	19	32	5	32	1
Alex Korolyuk	70	12	13	25	2	41	3
Brad Stuart	77	5	18	23	10	56	1
Todd Harvey	69	10	11	21	6	72	1
Bryan Marchment	75	7	11	18	15	204	1
Scott Hannan	75	3	14	17	10	51	0
Marcus Ragnarsson	68	3	12	15	2	44	1
Bill Lindsay	68	1	13	14	-6	126	0
CALG	52	1	9	10	-8	97	0
SJ	16	0	4	4	2	29	0
Jeff Norton	42	2	11	13	12	28	1
PIT	32	2	10	12	8	20	1
SJ	10	0	1	1	4	8	0

Acquired: RW Selanne from Ana. for LW Jeff Friesen, G Steve Shields, and a conditional pick (Mar. 5); LW Lindsay from Calg. for a '01 8th-round pick (Mar. 6); D Norton from Pit. for D Bobby Dollas and G Johan Hedberg (Mar. 12).

Goalies (10 Gm)	Gm	Min	GAA	Record	Sv%
Evgeni Nabokov*	66	3700	2.19	32-21-7	.915
SAN JOSE	82	5008	2.30	40-30-12	.911

Shutouts: Nabokov (6). **Assists:** Nabokov (2). **PM:** Nabokov (8).

Tampa Bay Lightning

Top Scorers	Gm	G	A	Pts	+/-	PM	PP
Brad Richards*	82	21	41	62	-10	14	7
Fredrik Modin	76	32	24	56	-1	48	8
Vincent Lecavalier	68	23	28	51	-26	66	7
Martin St. Louis	78	18	22	40	-4	12	3
Brian Holzinger	70	11	25	36	-9	64	3
Pavel Kubina	70	11	19	30	-13	103	6
Adrian Aucoin	73	4	24	28	5	45	2
VAN	47	3	13	16	13	20	1
TB	26	1	11	12	-8	25	1
Alexander Kharitonov*	66	7	15	22	-9	8	0
Todd Warriner	64	10	11	21	-13	46	3
Ryan Johnson	80	7	14	21	-20	44	1
Nils Ekman	43	9	11	20	-15	40	2
Andrei Zyuzin	64	4	16	20	-8	76	2
Matthew Barnaby	76	5	8	13	-10	265	1
PIT	47	1	4	5	-7	168	0
TB	29	4	4	8	-3	97	1
Cory Sarich	73	1	8	9	-26	106	0
Jassen Cullimore	74	1	6	7	-6	80	0
Ben Clymer	23	5	1	6	-7	21	3
Stan Drulia	34	2	4	6	-11	18	1
Stan Neckar	69	2	4	6	-3	71	0
PHO	53	2	2	4	-2	63	0
TB	16	0	2	2	1	8	0

Acquired: RW Barnaby from Pit. for C Wayne Primeau (Feb. 1); D Aucoin for a '01 2nd-round pick from Van. for G Dan Cloutier (Feb. 7); G Flaherty from NYI for a conditional pick (Feb. 16); D Neckar and G Nikolai Khabibulin from Pho. for RW Mike Johnson, D Paul Mara, RW Ruslan Zainullin, and a '01 2nd-round pick (Mar. 5).

Goalies (10 Gm)	Gm	Min	GAA	Record	Sv%
Kevin Weekes	61	3378	3.14	20-33-3	.898
Wade Flaherty	22	1135	3.38	6-12-0	.878
NYI	20	1017	3.30	6-10-0	.881
TB	2	118	4.07	0-2-0	.855
Dieter Kochan*	10	314	3.44	0-3-0	.870
TAMPA BAY	82	4968	3.38	24-52-6	.890

Shutouts: Weekes (4), Flaherty (1 with NYI). **Assists:** Weekes (1). **PM:** Weekes (4), Flaherty (2 with NYI).

Toronto Maple Leafs

Top Scorers	Gm	G	A	Pts	+/-	PM	PP
Mats Sundin	82	28	46	74	15	76	9
Gary Roberts	82	29	24	53	16	109	8
Yanic Perreault	76	24	28	52	0	52	5
Sergei Berezin	79	22	28	50	2	8	10
Jonas Hoglund	82	23	26	49	1	14	5
Tomas Kaberle	82	6	39	45	10	24	0
Darcy Tucker	82	16	21	37	6	141	2
Steve Thomas	57	8	26	34	0	46	1
Igor Korolev	73	10	19	29	3	28	2
Bryan McCabe	82	5	24	29	16	123	3
Garry Valk	74	8	18	26	4	46	1
Shayne Corson	77	8	18	26	1	189	0
Dimitri Yushkevich	81	5	19	24	-2	52	1
Tie Domi	82	13	7	20	2	214	1
Nikolai Antropov	52	6	11	17	5	30	0
Danny Markov	59	3	13	16	6	34	1
Dave Manson	74	4	7	11	14	93	0
Nathan Dempsey	25	1	9	10	13	4	1
Cory Cross	41	3	5	8	7	50	1
Aki Berg	59	3	4	7	-3	45	3
LA	47	0	4	4	3	43	0
TOR	12	3	0	3	-6	2	3

Acquired: D Berg from LA for C Adam Mair and a '01 2nd-round pick (Mar. 13).

Goalies (10 Gm)	Gm	Min	GAA	Record	Sv%
Curtis Joseph	68	4100	2.39	33-27-8	.915
Glenn Healy	15	871	2.62	4-7-3	.885
TORONTO	82	4990	2.49	37-34-11	.908

Shutouts: Joseph (6). **Assists:** Joseph (1). **PM:** Joseph (8).

Vancouver Canucks

Top Scorers	Gm	G	A	Pts	+/-	PM	PP
Markus Naslund	72	41	34	75	-2	58	18
Andrew Cassels	66	12	44	56	1	10	2
Todd Bertuzzi	79	25	30	55	-18	93	14
Brendan Morrison	82	16	38	54	2	42	3
Ed Jovanovski	79	12	35	47	-1	102	4
Peter Schaefer	82	16	20	36	4	22	3
Daniel Sedin*	75	20	14	34	-3	24	10
Trent Klatt	77	13	20	33	8	31	3
Harold Druken	55	15	15	30	2	14	6
Henrik Sedin*	82	9	20	29	-2	38	2
Donald Brashear	79	9	19	28	0	145	0
Mattias Ohlund	65	8	20	28	-16	46	1
Matt Cooke	81	14	13	27	5	94	0
Drake Berehowsky	80	7	19	26	-9	121	4
NASH	66	6	18	24	-9	100	3
VAN	14	1	1	2	0	21	1
Brent Sopel*	52	4	10	14	4	10	0
Scott Lachance	76	3	11	14	5	46	0
Denis Pederson	61	4	8	12	0	65	0
Murray Baron	82	3	8	11	-13	63	0
Mike Stapleton	52	2	6	8	-11	10	1
NYI	34	1	4	5	-2	0	0
VAN	18	1	2	3	-6	4	0

Acquired: C Stapleton from NYI for a '01 9th-round pick (Dec. 28); G Cloutier from TB for D Adrian Aucoin and a '01 2nd-round pick (Feb. 7); D Berehowsky from Nash. for a '01 2nd-round pick (Mar. 9).

Goalies (10 Gm)	Gm	Min	GAA	Record	Sv%
Bob Essensa	39	2059	2.68	18-12-3	.892
Dan Cloutier	40	1920	3.00	7-19-8	.892
TB	24	1005	3.52	3-13-3	.891
VAN	16	914	2.43	4-6-5	.894
VANCOUVER	82	5006	2.85	36-35-11	.888

Shutouts: Essensa (1), Cloutier (1 with TB). **Assists:** none. **PM:** Essensa (4), Cloutier (4 with TB).

Washington Capitals

Top Scorers	Gm	G	A	Pts	+/-	PM	PP
Adam Oates	81	13	69	82	-9	28	5
Peter Bondra	82	45	36	81	8	60	22
Sergei Gonchar	76	19	38	57	12	70	8
Ulf Dahlen	73	15	33	48	11	6	6
Steve Konowalchuk	82	24	23	47	8	87	6
Jeff Halpern	80	21	21	42	13	60	2
Dmitri Khristich	70	13	25	38	0	16	6
TOR	27	3	6	9	8	2	0
WASH	43	10	19	29	-8	8	4
Andrei Nikolishin	81	13	25	38	9	34	4
Trevor Linden	69	15	22	37	0	60	6
MON	57	12	21	33	-2	52	6
WASH	12	3	1	4	2	8	0
Calle Johansson	76	7	29	36	11	26	5
Dainius Zubrus	61	13	13	26	-11	37	4
MON	49	12	12	24	-7	30	3
WASH	12	1	1	2	-4	7	1
Chris Simon	60	10	10	20	-12	109	4
Sylvain Cote	68	7	11	18	-3	18	1
Joe Sacco	69	7	7	14	4	48	0
Joe Reekie	74	2	9	11	14	77	0
Dmitri Mironov	36	3	5	8	-7	6	1
Jason Marshall	55	3	4	7	-13	122	2
ANA	50	3	4	7	-12	105	2
WASH	5	0	0	0	1	17	0

Acquired: RW Khristich from Tor. for a '01 3rd-round pick (Dec. 11); C Linden; RW Zubrus and a '01 2nd-round pick from Mon. for RW Richard Zednik, C Jan Bulis, and a '01 1st-round pick (Mar. 13); D Marshall from Ana. for D Alexei Tezikov and a '01 4th-round pick (Mar. 13).

Goalies (10 Gm)	Gm	Min	GAA	Record	Sv%
Craig Billington	12	660	2.45	3-5-2	.915
Olaf Kolzig	72	4279	2.48	37-26-8	.909
WASHINGTON	82	4986	2.54	41-31-10	.907

Shutouts: Kolzig (5). **Assists:** Kolzig (2), Billington (1). **PM:** Kolzig (14).

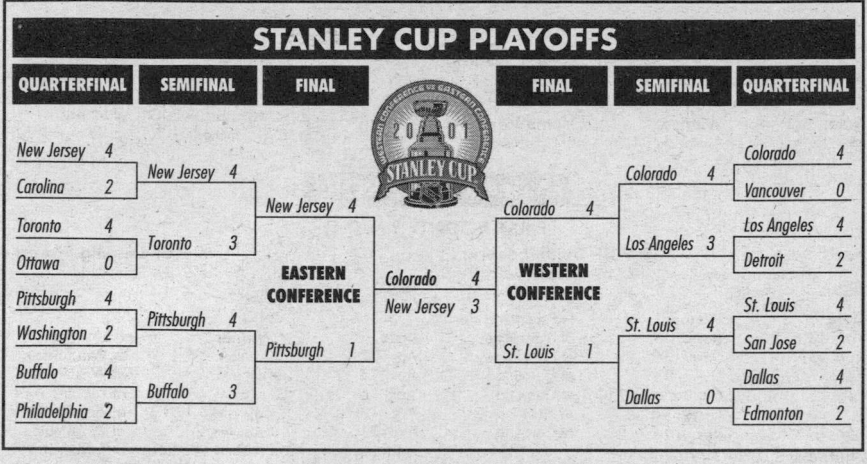

STANLEY CUP PLAYOFFS

| QUARTERFINAL | SEMIFINAL | FINAL | | FINAL | SEMIFINAL | QUARTERFINAL |

EASTERN CONFERENCE | **WESTERN CONFERENCE**

- New Jersey 4 / Carolina 2
- New Jersey 4
- Toronto 4 / Ottawa 0
- Toronto 3
- New Jersey 4
- Pittsburgh 4 / Washington 2
- Pittsburgh 4
- Pittsburgh 1
- Buffalo 4 / Philadelphia 2
- Buffalo 3

- Colorado 4 / New Jersey 3

- Colorado 4
- St. Louis 1

- Colorado 4 / Los Angeles 3
- St. Louis 4 / Dallas 0

- Colorado 4 / Vancouver 0
- Los Angeles 4 / Detroit 2
- St. Louis 4 / San Jose 2
- Dallas 4 / Edmonton 2

Stanley Cup Playoffs
Series Summaries

WESTERN CONFERENCE

FIRST ROUND (Best of 7)

	W-L	GF	Leading Scorers
Colorado	4-0	16	Sakic (4-3–7)
Vancouver	0-4	9	Three tied with 4 each.

Date	Winner	Home Ice
April 12	Avalanche, 5-4	at Colorado
April 14	Avalanche, 2-1	at Colorado
April 16	Avalanche, 4-3 (OT)	at Vancouver
April 18	Avalanche, 5-1	at Vancouver

	W-L	GF	Leading Scorers
St. Louis	4-2	16	Matteau (1-3–4)
San Jose	2-4	11	Turgeon (2-7–9)

Date	Winner	Home Ice
April 12	Blues, 3-1	at St. Louis
April 14	Sharks, 1-0	at St. Louis
April 16	Blues, 6-3	at San Jose
April 17	Sharks, 3-2	at San Jose
April 19	Blues, 3-2 (OT)	at St. Louis
April 21	Blues, 2-1	at San Jose

Shutout: Nabokov, San Jose.

	W-L	GF	Leading Scorers
Los Angeles	4-2	15	Stumpel (3-4–7)
Detroit	2-4	17	Lidstrom (1-7–8)

Date	Winner	Home Ice
April 11	Red Wings, 5-3	at Detroit
April 14	Red Wings, 4-0	at Detroit
April 15	Kings, 2-1	at Los Angeles
April 18	Kings, 4-3 (OT)	at Los Angeles
April 21	Kings, 3-2	at Detroit
April 23	Kings, 3-2 (OT)	at Los Angeles

Shutout: Osgood, Detroit.

	W-L	GF	Leading Scorers
Dallas	4-2	16	Three tied with 4 each.
Edmonton	2-4	13	Smyth (3-4–7)

Date	Winner	Home Ice
April 11	Stars, 2-1 (OT)	at Dallas
April 14	Oilers, 4-3	at Dallas
April 15	Stars, 3-2 (OT)	at Edmonton
April 17	Oilers, 2-1 (OT)	at Edmonton
April 19	Stars, 4-3 (OT)	at Dallas
April 21	Stars, 3-1	at Edmonton

SEMIFINALS (Best of 7)

	W-L	GF	Leading Scorers
Colorado	4-3	17	Hejduk (3-5–8) & Forsberg (2-6–8)
Los Angeles	3-4	10	Murray (4-1–5) & Schneider (0-5-5)

Date	Winner	Home Ice
April 26	Kings, 4-3 (OT)	at Colorado
April 28	Avalanche, 2-0	at Colorado
April 30	Avalanche, 4-3	at Los Angeles
May 2	Avalanche, 3-0	at Los Angeles
May 4	Kings, 1-0	at Colorado
May 6	Kings, 1-0 (2OT)	at Los Angeles
May 9	Avalanche, 5-1	at Colorado

Shutouts: Roy, Colorado (2); Potvin, Los Angeles (2).

	W-L	GF	Leading Scorers
St. Louis	4-0	13	Three tied with 4 each.
Dallas	0-4	6	Three tied with 2 each.

Date	Winner	Home Ice
April 27	Blues, 4-2	at Dallas
April 29	Blues, 2-1	at Dallas
May 1	Blues, 3-2 (OT)	at St. Louis
May 3	Blues, 4-1	at St. Louis

CHAMPIONSHIP (Best of 7)

	W-L	GF	Leading Scorers
Colorado	4-1	17	Sakic (4-4–8)
St. Louis	1-4	11	MacInnis (1-3–4)

Date	Winner	Home Ice
May 12	Avalanche, 4-1	at Colorado
May 14	Avalanche, 4-2	at Colorado
May 16	Blues, 4-3 (2OT)	at St. Louis
May 18	Avalanche, 4-3 (OT)	at St. Louis
May 21	Avalanche, 2-1 (OT)	at Colorado

EASTERN CONFERENCE

FIRST ROUND (Best of 7)

	W-L	GF	Leading Scorers
New Jersey	4-2	20	Holik (4-4–8)
Carolina	2-4	8	Kapanen (2-3–5)

Date	Winner	Home Ice
April 12	Devils, 5-1	at New Jersey
April 15	Devils, 2-0	at New Jersey
April 17	Devils, 4-0	at Carolina
April 18	Hurricanes, 3-2 (OT)	at Carolina
April 20	Hurricanes, 3-2	at New Jersey
April 22	Devils, 5-1	at Carolina

Shutouts: Brodeur, New Jersey (2).

	W-L	GF	Leading Scorers
Toronto	4-0	10	Sundin (2-2–5)
			& Berezin (1-3–4)
Ottawa	0-4	3	Hossa (1-1–2)
			& McEachern (0-2–2)

Date	Winner	Home Ice
April 13	Maple Leafs, 1-0 (OT)	at Ottawa
April 14	Maple Leafs, 3-0	at Ottawa
April 16	Maple Leafs, 3-2 (OT)	at Toronto
April 18	Maple Leafs, 3-1	at Toronto

Shutouts: Joseph, Toronto (2).

	W-L	GF	Leading Scorers
Pittsburgh	4-2	14	Lemieux (4-3-7)
Washington	2-4	10	Konowalchuk (2-3-5)
			& Halpern (2-3-5)

Date	Winner	Home Ice
April 12	Capitals, 1-0	at Washington
April 14	Penguins, 2-1	at Washington
April 16	Penguins, 3-0	at Pittsburgh
April 18	Capitals, 4-3 (OT)	at Pittsburgh
April 21	Penguins, 2-1	at Washington
April 23	Penguins, 4-3 (OT)	at Pittsburgh

Shutouts: Kolzig, Washington (1); Hedberg, Pittsburgh (1).

	W-L	GF	Leading Scorers
Buffalo	4-2	21	Satan (2-7–9)
Philadelphia	2-4	13	Langkow (2-4–6)

Date	Winner	Home Ice
April 11	Sabres, 2-1	at Philadelphia
April 14	Sabres, 4-3 (OT)	at Philadelphia
April 16	Flyers, 3-2	at Buffalo
April 17	Sabres, 4-3 (OT)	at Buffalo
April 19	Flyers, 3-1	at Philadelphia
April 21	Sabres, 8-0	at Buffalo

Shutout: Hasek, Buffalo (1).

SEMIFINALS (Best of 7)

	W-L	GF	Leading Scorers
New Jersey	4-3	21	Mogilny (2-5–7)
			& Sykora (2-5-7)
Toronto	3-4	18	Sundin (4-5–9)

Date	Winner	Home Ice
April 26	Maple Leafs, 2-0	at New Jersey
April 28	Devils, 6-5 (OT)	at New Jersey
May 1	Devils, 3-2 (OT)	at Toronto
May 3	Maple Leafs, 3-1	at Toronto
May 5	Maple Leafs, 3-2	at Toronto
May 7	Devils, 4-2	at Toronto*
May 9	Devils, 5-1	at New Jersey

Shutout: Joseph, Toronto (1).

	W-L	GF	Leading Scorers
Pittsburgh	4-3	17	Straka (2-6–8)
Buffalo	3-4	17	Barnes (4-2–6)
			& Audette (1-5–6)

Date	Winner	Home Ice
April 26	Penguins, 3-0	at Buffalo
April 28	Penguins, 3-1	at Buffalo
April 30	Sabres, 4-1	at Pittsburgh
May 2	Sabres, 5-2	at Pittsburgh
May 5	Sabres, 3-2 (OT)	at Buffalo
May 8	Penguins, 3-2 (OT)	at Pittsburgh
May 10	Penguins, 3-2 (OT)	at Buffalo

Shutout: Hedberg, Pittsburgh.

CHAMPIONSHIP (Best of 7)

	W-L	GF	Leading Scorers
New Jersey	4-1	17	Rafalski (3-5–8)
Pittsburgh	1-4	7	Straka (2-1–3)
			& Lemieux (0-3–3)

Date	Winner	Home Ice
May 12	Devils, 3-1	at New Jersey
May 15	Penguins, 4-2	at New Jersey
May 17	Devils, 3-0	at Pittsburgh
May 19	Devils, 5-0	at Pittsburgh
May 22	Devils, 4-2	at New Jersey

Shutouts: Brodeur, New Jersey (2).

STANLEY CUP FINAL (Best of 7)

	W-L	GF	Leading Scorers
Colorado	4-3	19	Sakic (4-5–9)
New Jersey	3-4	11	Elias (2-3–5)

Date	Winner	Home Ice
May 26	Avalanche, 5-0	at Colorado
May 29	Devils, 2-1	at Colorado
May 31	Avalanche, 3-1	at New Jersey
June 2	Devils, 3-2	at New Jersey
June 4	Devils, 4-1	at Colorado
June 7	Avalanche, 4-0	at New Jersey
June 9	Avalanche, 3-1	at Colorado

Shutout: Roy, Colorado (2).

Conn Smythe Trophy (Playoff MVP)
Patrick Roy, Colorado, G
16-7, 1.70 GAA, .934 save pct., 4 ShO

Stanley Cup Final Box Scores

Game 1

Saturday, May 26, at Colorado

```
New Jersey ........................0  0  0 — 0
Colorado .........................1  2  2 — 5
```

1st Period: COL—Sakic 10 (Hejduk, Blake), 11:07.
2nd Period: COL—Drury 9 (Hinote, Nieminen), 9:35; COL—Sakic 11 (Blake, Skoula), 15:06.
3rd Period: COL—Blake 5 (Tanguay, Sakic), 5:36 (pp); COL—Reinprecht 2 (Dingman, Reid), 17:36.
Shots on Goal: New Jersey— 7-11-7-25; Colorado—14-7-9-30. **Power plays:** New Jersey 0-6; Colorado 1-5. **Goalies:** New Jersey, Brodeur (30 shots, 25 saves); Colorado, Roy (25 shots, 25 saves). **Attendance:** 18,007.

Game 2

Tuesday, May 29, at Colorado

```
New Jersey ........................2  0  0 — 2
Colorado .........................1  0  0 — 1
```

1st Period: COL—Sakic 12 (Hejduk, Blake), 5:58 (pp); NJ—Corkum 1 (Rafalski), 14:29; NJ—Stevenson 1 (Niedermayer, Mogilny), 17:20.
Shots on Goal: New Jersey—12-6-2-20; Colorado—8-4-8-20. **Power plays:** New Jersey 0-3; Colorado 1-6. **Goalies:** New Jersey, Brodeur (20 shots, 19 saves); Colorado, Roy (20 shots, 18 saves). **Attendance:** 18,007.

Game 3

Thursday, May 31, at New Jersey

```
Colorado .........................1  0  2 — 3
New Jersey ........................1  0  0 — 1
```

1st Period: NJ—Arnott 8 (Holik, Elias) 3:16 (pp); COL—Skoula 1 (Podein, Messier) 10:38.
3rd Period: COL—Bourque 4 (Sakic) 0:31 (pp); COL—Hinote 2 (Nieminen, Drury) 6:28.
Shots on Goal: Colorado—5-11-5-21; New Jersey—8-3-11-22. **Power plays:** Colorado 1-4; New Jersey 1-6. **Goalies:** Colorado, Roy (22 shots, 21 saves); New Jersey, Brodeur (21 shots, 18 saves). **Attendance:** 19,040.

Game 4

Saturday, June 2, at New Jersey

```
Colorado .........................1  1  0 — 2
New Jersey ........................0  1  2 — 3
```

1st Period: COL— Blake 6 (Tanguay) 3:58.
2nd Period: NJ—Elias 8 (Sykora) 3:42 (sh); COL—Drury 10 (Dingman, Hinote) 13:54.
3rd Period: NJ—Gomez 5 (Pandolfo, Corkum) 8:09; NJ—Sykora 9 (Elias, Holik) 17:23.

Game 5

Monday, June 4, at Colorado

```
New Jersey ........................2  1  1 — 4
Colorado .........................1  0  0 — 1
```

1st period: NJ—Elias 9 (Sykora, Rafalski) 3:09; COL—Tanguay 3 (Sakic, Bourque) 10:09 (pp); NJ—Mogilny 5 (Gomez, Rafalski) 18:47.
2nd period: NJ—Brylin 3 (Mogilny, Niedermayer) 4:39 (pp).
3rd period: NJ—Madden 4 (Stevenson, Brylin) 18:05.
Shots on Goal: New Jersey—6-10-10-26; Colorado—6-9-8-23. **Power plays:** New Jersey 1-1; Colorado 1-4. **Goalies:** New Jersey, Brodeur (23 shots, 22 saves); Colorado, Roy (26 shots, 22 saves). **Attendance:** 18,007.

Game 6

Thursday, June 7, at New Jersey

```
Colorado .........................1  2  1 — 4
New Jersey ........................0  0  0 — 0
```

1st Period: COL—Foote 3 (unassisted) 18:02.
2nd Period: COL—Nieminen 4 (Skoula, Foote) 2:26 (pp); COL—Drury 11 (Reinprecht, Foote) 18:27.
3rd Period: COL—Tanguay 4 (Reid, Sakic) 13:46.
Shots on Goal: Colorado—5-7-6-18; New Jersey—12-7-5-24. **Power plays:** Colorado 1-7; New Jersey 0-6. **Goalies:** Colorado, Roy (24 shots, 24 saves); New Jersey, Brodeur (18 shots, 14 saves). **Attendance:** 19,040.

Game 7

Saturday, June 9, at Colorado

```
New Jersey ........................0  1  0 — 1
Colorado .........................1  2  0 — 3
```

1st Period: COL—Tanguay 5 (Hinote) 7:58.
2nd Period: COL—Tanguay 6 (Sakic, Foote) 4:57; COL—Sakic 13 (Hejduk, Tanguay) 6:16 (pp); NJ—Sykora 10 (Elias, Arnott) 9:33 (pp).
Shots on Goal: New Jersey—9-12-5-26; Colorado—10-7-5-22. **Power plays:** New Jersey 1-3; Colorado 1-5. **Goalies:** New Jersey, Brodeur (22 shots, 19 saves); Colorado, Roy (26 shots, 25 saves). **Attendance:** 18,007.

Stanley Cup Leaders

Scoring

	Gm	G	A	Pts	+/-	PM	PP
Joe Sakic, Col	21	13	13	**26**	6	6	5
Patrik Elias, NJ	25	9	14	**23**	11	10	3
Milan Hejduk, Col	23	7	16	**23**	8	6	4
Petr Sykora, NJ	25	10	12	**22**	15	12	2
Alex Tanguay, Col	23	6	15	**21**	13	8	1
Rob Blake, Col	23	6	13	**19**	6	16	3
Brian Rafalski, NJ	25	7	11	**18**	10	7	1
Mario Lemieux, Pit	18	6	11	**17**	4	4	1

Goals

Sakic, Col	13
Drury, Col	11
Sykora, NJ	10
Elias, NJ	9
Arnott, NJ	8
Hejduk, Col	7
Rafalski, NJ	7

Assists

Hejduk, Col	16
Tanguay, Col	15
Elias, NJ	14
Sakic, Col	13
Blake, Col	13
Sykora, NJ	12

Goaltending

(Minimum 420 minutes)

	Gm	Min	W-L	ShO	GAA
Patrick Roy, Col	23	1451	16-7	4	1.70
Roman Turek, St.L	14	908	9-5	0	2.05
Martin Brodeur, NJ	25	1505	15-10	4	2.07
Dominik Hasek, Buf	13	833	7-6	1	2.09
Curtis Joseph, Tor	11	685	7-4	3	2.10
Ed Belfour, Dal	10	671	4-6	0	2.24
Johan Hedberg, Pit	18	1123	9-9	2	2.30
Felix Potvin, LA	13	812	7-6	2	2.44

Wins

Roy, Col	16-7
Brodeur, NJ	15-10
Turek, St.L	9-5
Hedberg, Pit	9-9
Three tied with 7 each.	

Save Pct.

Roy, Col	.934
Joseph, Tor	.927
Turek, St.L	.919
Hasek, Buf	.916
Hedberg, Pit	.911

Finalists' Composite Box Scores
Colorado Avalanche (16-7)

Top Scorers	Pos	Overall Playoffs								Finals vs New Jersey							
		Gm	G	A	Pts	+/-	PM	PP	S	Gm	G	A	Pts	+/-	PM	PP	S
Joe Sakic	C	21	13	13	26	6	6	5	79	7	4	5	9	2	2	2	23
Milan Hejduk	R	23	7	16	23	8	6	4	51	7	0	3	3	0	0	0	8
Alex Tanguay	L	23	6	15	21	13	8	1	37	7	4	3	7	4	4	1	15
Rob Blake	D	23	6	13	19	6	16	3	83	7	2	3	5	0	4	1	23
Chris Drury	L	23	11	5	16	5	4	2	62	7	3	1	4	3	0	0	13
Peter Forsberg	C	11	4	10	14	5	6	1	23	0	0	0	0	0	0	0	0
Ray Bourque	D	21	4	6	10	9	12	3	49	7	1	1	2	3	2	1	8
Ville Nieminen*	L	23	4	6	10	-1	69	3	39	7	1	2	3	1	6	1	8
Adam Foote	D	23	3	4	7	5	47	1	28	7	1	3	4	2	14	0	7
Dan Hinote	C	23	2	4	6	4	21	0	16	7	1	3	4	3	11	0	5
Steve Reinprecht	C	22	2	3	5	0	2	0	14	7	1	1	2	0	0	0	4
Shjon Podein	R	23	2	3	5	3	14	0	16	7	0	1	1	1	6	0	3
Martin Skoula	D	23	1	4	5	1	8	0	14	7	1	2	3	3	6	0	4
Eric Messier	L	23	2	2	4	0	14	0	20	7	0	1	1	-2	6	0	4
Chris Dingman	L	16	0	4	4	3	14	0	8	7	0	2	2	2	10	0	2
Dave Reid	R	18	0	4	4	2	6	0	8	7	0	2	2	1	2	0	4
Jon Klemm	D	22	1	2	3	7	16	0	14	7	0	0	0	0	0	0	1
Stephane Yelle	C	23	1	2	3	2	8	0	23	7	0	0	0	0	4	0	8
Greg de Vries	D	23	0	1	1	5	20	0	20	7	0	0	0	1	6	0	6
Bryan Muir	D	3	0	0	0	0	0	0	0	0	0	0	0	0	0	0	0
Scott Parker	R	4	0	0	0	2	0	0	0	0	0	0	0	0	0	0	0

Overtime goals—OVERALL (Sakic, Forsberg, Yelle); FINALS (none). **Shorthanded goals**—OVERALL (none); FINALS (none). **Power Play conversions**—OVERALL (23 for 116, 19.8%); FINALS (6 for 36, 16.7%).

Goaltending	Gm	Min	GAA	GA	SA	Sv%	W-L	Gm	Min	GAA	GA	SA	Sv%	W-L
David Aebischer	1	1	0.00	0	0	.000	0-0	0	0	0.00	0	0	.000	0-0
Patrick Roy	23	1451	1.70	41	622	.934	16-7	7	418	1.58	11	178	.938	4-3
TOTAL	23	1455	1.69	41	622	.934	16-7	7	420	1.57	11	178	.938	4-3

Empty Net Goals—OVERALL (none), FINALS (none). **Shutouts**—OVERALL (Roy 4), FINALS (Roy 2). **Assists**—OVERALL (Roy 1), FINALS (none). **Penalty Minutes**—OVERALL (none), FINALS (none).

New Jersey Devils (15-10)

Top Scorers	Pos	Overall Playoffs								Finals vs Colorado							
		Gm	G	A	Pts	+/-	PM	PP	S	Gm	G	A	Pts	+/-	PM	PP	S
Patrik Elias	L	25	9	14	23	11	10	3	58	7	2	3	5	2	2	0	21
Petr Sykora	R	25	10	12	22	15	12	2	71	7	2	2	4	2	4	1	19
Brian Rafalski	D	25	7	11	18	10	7	1	47	7	0	3	3	0	0	0	6
Bobby Holik	C	25	6	10	16	1	37	1	66	7	0	2	2	-6	6	0	17
Alexander Mogilny	R	25	5	11	16	3	8	1	76	7	1	2	3	-5	4	0	18
Jason Arnott	C	23	8	7	15	8	16	5	42	6	1	1	2	-1	4	1	9
Scott Gomez	C	25	5	9	14	7	24	0	70	7	1	1	2	1	4	0	15
Randy McKay	R	19	6	3	9	3	8	2	31	1	0	0	0	0	0	0	0
Scott Stevens	D	25	1	7	8	3	37	0	34	7	0	0	0	-3	6	0	0
John Madden	L	25	4	3	7	2	6	0	62	7	1	0	1	-2	2	0	13
Sergei Brylin	L	20	3	4	7	1	6	1	23	7	1	1	2	-2	6	1	6
Scott Niedermayer	D	21	0	6	6	7	14	0	29	7	0	2	2	-1	8	0	10
Jay Pandolfo	L	25	1	4	5	-1	4	0	19	7	0	1	1	0	0	0	8
Turner Stevenson	R	23	1	3	4	2	20	0	14	7	1	1	2	1	6	0	3
Sergei Nemchinov	C	25	1	3	4	0	16	0	14	7	0	0	0	-5	0	0	7
Bob Corkum	C	12	1	2	3	-2	0	0	11	6	1	1	2	-1	0	0	10
Sean O'Donnell	D	23	1	2	3	5	41	0	9	5	0	0	0	-1	25	0	1
Ken Daneyko	D	25	0	3	3	4	21	0	13	7	0	0	0	1	13	0	3
Colin White	D	25	0	3	3	7	42	0	25	7	0	0	0	-4	14	0	6
Jim McKenzie	L	3	0	0	0	1	2	0	1	1	0	0	0	1	2	0	0
Ken Sutton	D	6	0	0	0	1	13	0	7	2	0	0	0	-2	9	0	0

Overtime goals—OVERALL (Rafalski, McKay); FINALS (none). **Shorthanded goals**—OVERALL (Sykora 2, Elias); FINALS (Elias). **Power Play conversions**—OVERALL (16 for 101, 15.8%); FINALS (3 for 27, 11.1%).

Goaltending	Gm	Min	GAA	GA	SA	Sv%	W-L	Gm	Min	GAA	GA	SA	Sv%	W-L
Martin Brodeur	25	1505	2.07	52	507	.897	15-10	7	416	2.74	19	146	.870	3-4
TOTAL	25	1513	2.06	52	507	.897	15-10	7	420	2.71	19	146	.870	3-4

Empty Net Goals—OVERALL (none); FINALS (none). **Shutouts**—OVERALL (Brodeur 4); FINALS (none). **Assists**—OVERALL (Brodeur); FINALS (none). **Penalty Minutes**—OVERALL (none), FINALS (none).

Annual Awards

Voting for the Hart, Calder, Norris, Lady Byng, Selke, and Masterton Trophies is conducted after the regular season by the Professional Hockey Writers' Association. The Vezina Trophy is selected by the NHL general managers, while the Jack Adams Award is selected by NHL broadcasters. Points are awarded on 10–7–5–3–1 basis except for the Vezina Trophy and the Adams Award which are awarded 5–3–1.

Hart Trophy
For Most Valuable Player

	Pos	1st	2nd	3rd	4th	5th	Pts
Joe Sakic, Col	C	53	6	2	1	0—	585
Mario Lemieux, Pit	C	8	17	10	6	5—	272
Jaromir Jagr, Pit	R	0	20	10	5	5—	210
Roman Cechmanek, Phi.	G	0	2	8	10	5—	89
Martin Brodeur, NJ	G	0	4	4	4	4—	64

Calder Trophy
For Rookie of the Year

	Pos	1st	2nd	3rd	4th	5th	Pts
Evgeni Nabokov, SJ	G	50	7	2	2	0—	565
Brad Richards, TB	C	9	38	10	3	1—	416
Martin Havlat, Ott	R	2	5	26	17	4—	240
Lubomir Visnovsky, LA	D	0	5	9	12	8—	124
Shane Willis, Car	R	1	2	3	13	13—	91

Norris Trophy
For Best Defenseman

	1st	2nd	3rd	4th	5th	Pts
Nicklas Lidstrom, Det	56	5	1	0	0—	600
Ray Bourque, Col	4	16	12	10	9—	251
Scott Stevens, NJ	1	15	14	4	6—	203
Rob Blake, LA-Col	1	11	8	14	7—	176
Brian Leetch, NYR	0	9	7	5	13—	126

Vezina Trophy
For Outstanding Goaltender

	1st	2nd	3rd	Pts
Dominik Hasek, Buf	9	12	4—	85
Roman Cechmanek, Phi	7	9	3—	65
Martin Brodeur, NJ	7	2	1—	42
Evgeni Nabokov, SJ	3	3	5—	29
Patrick Roy, Col	2	1	6—	19

Lady Byng Trophy
For Sportsmanship and Gentlemanly Play

	Pos	1st	2nd	3rd	4th	5th	Pts
Joe Sakic, Col	C	15	18	5	3	2—	312
Nicklas Lidstrom, Det	D	21	7	7	4	2—	308
Adam Oates, Wash	C	7	7	13	3	2—	195
Brett Hull, Dal	R	2	3	9	6	6—	110
Zigmund Palffy, LA	R	2	4	4	8	3—	95

Selke Trophy
For Best Defensive Forward

	Pos	1st	2nd	3rd	4th	5th	Pts
John Madden, NJ	L	14	10	10	2	3—	269
Joe Sakic, Col	C	15	9	3	6	3—	249
Mike Modano, Dal	C	8	8	7	8	4—	199
Mike Ricci, SJ	C	6	2	6	6	3—	125
Steve Yzerman, Det	C	3	7	3	3	5—	108

Adams Award
For Coach of the Year

	1st	2nd	3rd	Pts
Bill Barber, Phi	17	11	7—	125
Scotty Bowman, Det	14	6	7—	95
Jacques Martin, Ott	10	13	3—	92
Larry Robinson, NJ	11	7	7—	83
Bob Hartley, Col	5	10	4—	59

AP/Wide World Photos
Joe Sakic's stellar season resulted in the Hart (r) and Lady Byng Trophies, but he's holding the one he really wanted.

Other Awards

Lester B. Pearson Award (NHL Players Assn. MVP)—Joe Sakic, Colorado; **Jennings Trophy** (goaltenders with a minimum of 25 games played for team with fewest goals against)—Dominik Hasek, Buffalo; **Maurice "Rocket" Richard Trophy** (regular season goal-scoring leader)—Pavel Bure, Florida; **Art Ross Trophy** (regular season points leader)—Jaromir Jagr, Pittsburgh; **Masterton Trophy** (perseverance, sportsmanship, and dedication to hockey)—Adam Graves, NY Rangers; **King Clancy Trophy** (leadership and humanitarian contributions to community)—Shjon Podein, Colorado; **Lester Patrick Trophy** (outstanding service to hockey in the U.S.)—NHL commissioner Gary Bettman, Detroit Red Wings coach Scotty Bowman, and Nashville Predators GM David Poile.

All-NHL Team

Voting by Pro Hockey Writers' Association (PHWA). Holdovers from 1999-2000 All-NHL first team in **bold** type.

	First Team		Second Team
G	Dominik Hasek, Buf	G	Roman Cechmanek, Phi
D	Ray Bourque, Col	D	Rob Blake, LA-Col
D	**Nicklas Lidstrom**, Det	D	Scott Stevens, NJ
C	Joe Sakic, Col	C	Mario Lemieux, Pit
R	**Jaromir Jagr**, Pit	R	Pavel Bure, Fla
L	Patrik Elias, NJ	L	Luc Robitaille, LA

All-Rookie Team

Voting by PHWA. Vote totals not released.

Pos		Pos	
G	Evgeni Nabokov, SJ	F	Martin Havlat, Ott
D	Lubomir Visnovsky, LA	F	Brad Richards, TB
D	Colin White, NJ	F	Shane Willis, Car

2001 NHL Draft

The top 50 selections at the 39th annual NHL Entry Draft held June 23-24, 2001, in Sunrise, Fla. The order of the first 14 positions were determined by a draft lottery of non-playoff teams held April 10 in New York. Positions 15 through 30 reflect regular season records in reverse order. The top 30 picks are first round selections and the remaining 20 are from the second round. (*) denotes compensatory pick.

Top 50 Picks

	Team	Player, Last Team	Pos			Team	Player, Last Team	Pos
1	Atlanta	Ilya Kovalchuk, Spartak (Rus)	R		26	Dallas	Jason Bacashihua, Chicago (NAHL)	G
2	a-Ottawa	Jason Spezza, Windsor (OHL)	C		27	i-Philadelphia	Jeff Woywitka, Red Deer (WHL)	D
3	Tampa Bay	Alexander Svitov, Omsk (Rus)	C		28	New Jersey	Adrian Foster, Saskatoon (WHL)	L
4	Florida	Stephen Weiss, Plymouth (OHL)	C		29	j-Chicago	Adam Munro, Erie (OHL)	G
5	Anaheim	Stanislav Chistov, Omsk (Rus)	C		30	k-Los Angeles	David Steckel, Ohio St. (CCHA)	C
6	Minnesota	Mikko Koivu, TPS Turku (Fin)	C		31	l-Phoenix	Matthew Spiller, Seattle (WHL)	D
7	Montreal	Mike Komisarek, Michigan (CCHA)	D		32	m-Buffalo	Derek Roy, Kitchener (OHL)	C
8	Columbus	Pascal Leclaire, Halifax (QMJHL)	G		33	n-Nashville	Timofei Shishkanov, Spartak (Rus)	L
9	Chicago	Tuomo Ruutu, Jokerit (Fin)	C		34	Florida	Greg Watson, Prince Albert (WHL)	C
10	NY Rangers	Dan Blackburn, Kootenay (WHL)	G		35	Anaheim	Mark Popovic, St. Michael's (OHL)	D
11	b-Phoenix	Fredrik Sjostrom, Frolunda (Swe)	R		36	Minnesota	Kyle Wanvig, Red Deer (WHL)	R
12	Nashville	Dan Hamhuis, Prince George (WHL)	D		37	Montreal	Duncan Milroy, Swift Current (WHL)	R
13	c-Edmonton	Ales Hemsky, Hull (QMJHL)	R		38	Columbus	Tim Jackman, MSU-Mankato (WCHA)	R
14	d-Calgary	Chuck Kobasew, Boston Coll. (HE)	R		39	o-Toronto	Karel Pilar, Litvinov (Cze)	D
15	Carolina	Igor Knyazev, Spartak (Rus)	D		40	NY Rangers	Fedor Tjutin, St. Petersburg (Rus)	D
16	Vancouver	R.J. Umberger, Ohio St. (CCHA)	C		41	Calgary	Andrei Taratukhin, Omsk (Rus)	C
17	Toronto	Carlo Colaiacovo, Erie (OHL)	D		42	Nashville	Tomas Slovak, Kosice (Svk)	D
18	Los Angeles	Jens Karlsson, Frolunda (Swe)	R		43	c-Edmonton	Doug Lynch, Red Deer (WHL)	D
19	e-Boston	Shaone Morrisonn, Kamloops (WHL)	D		44	d-New Jersey	Igor Pohanka, Prince Albert (WHL)	C
20	San Jose	Marcel Goc, Schwenningen (Ger)	C		45	Phoenix*	Martin Podlesak, Lethbridge (WHL)	C
21	Pittsburgh	Colby Armstrong, Red Deer (WHL)	R		46	Carolina	Michael Zigomanis, Kingston (OHL)	C
22	Buffalo	Jiri Novotny, Budejovice Jr. (Cze)	C		47	p-Tampa Bay	Alexander Polushin, Tver (Rus)	L
23	f-Ottawa	Tim Gleason, Windsor (OHL)	D		48	p-New Jersey*	Thomas Pihlman, Jyvaskyla (Fin)	L
24	g-Florida	Lukas Krajicek, Peterborough (OHL)	D		49	q-Los Angeles	Mike Cammalleri, Michigan (CCHA)	C
25	h-Montreal	Alexander Perejougin, Omsk (Rus)	C		50	Buffalo	Chris Thorburn, North Bay (OHL)	C

Acquired picks: a—from NY Islanders; **b**—from Calgary; **c**—from Boston; **d**—from Phoenix; **e**—from Edmonton; **f**—from Philadelphia; **g**—from St. Louis via New Jersey; **h**—from Washington; **i**—from Ottawa; **j**—from Detroit; **k**—from Colorado; **l**—from NY Islanders via Tampa Bay; **m**—from Tampa Bay; **n**—from Atlanta via Vancouver; **o**—from Chicago; **p**—from Vancouver; **q**—from Toronto.

U.S. Division I College Hockey

Final regular season standings; overall records, including all postseason tournament games, in parentheses.

Central Collegiate Hockey Assn.

	W	L	T	Pts	GF	GA
*Michigan St. (33-5-4)	21	4	3	45	86	37
Miami-OH (20-16-2)	17	10	1	35	95	71
*Michigan (27-13-5)	16	9	3	35	102	60
Nebraska-Omaha (24-15-3)	15	10	3	33	86	80
N. Michigan (18-13-7)	12	10	6	30	76	71
W. Michigan (20-13-6)	12	10	6	30	97	96
Ohio St. (17-18-2)	13	13	2	28	81	89
Ferris St. (13-20-5)	9	15	4	22	64	81
Bowling Green (16-19-5)	8	15	5	21	72	82
Alaska-Fairbanks (9-19-8)	7	14	7	21	67	91
Notre Dame (10-22-7)	7	15	6	20	72	98
Lake Superior St. (13-23-0)	8	20	0	16	53	95

Conf. Tourney Final: Michigan St. 2, Michigan 0.

*NCAA Tourney (3-2): Michigan (2-1), Michigan St. (1-1).

College Hockey America

	W	L	T	Pts	GF	GA
Alab.-Huntsville (21-12-1)	15	4	1	31	78	49
Niagara (14-19-5)	10	7	3	23	59	52
Wayne State (18-14-3)	8	9	3	19	59	68
Findlay (10-15-2)	8	10	2	18	57	63
Air Force (16-17-4)	6	9	4	18	51	61
Bemidji State (4-26-4)	4	12	3	11	51	62

Conf. Tourney Final: Wayne State 4, Alab.-Huntsville 1.

*NCAA Tourney: No teams invited.

Note: On Dec. 3, Air Force and Bemidji State played a game worth four points in the standings, as opposed to the usual two. Air Force won 3-0.

Eastern Collegiate Athletic Conf.

	W	L	T	Pts	GF	GA
Clarkson (21-11-3)	15	5	2	32	81	45
*St. Lawrence (20-13-4)	13	6	3	29	83	70
Harvard (16-15-2)	12	8	2	26	68	60
Cornell (16-12-5)	11	8	3	25	44	44
Dartmouth (16-14-4)	10	8	4	24	67	62
Rensselaer (17-15-2)	11	9	2	24	62	54
Princeton (10-16-5)	9	9	4	22	70	66
Yale (14-16-1)	10	11	1	21	72	80
Union (12-18-4)	8	12	2	18	54	75
Vermont (14-18-2)	8	12	2	18	68	69
Colgate (10-20-4)	8	13	1	17	60	67
Brown (4-21-4)	2	16	4	8	43	80

Conf. Tourney Final: St. Lawrence 3, Cornell 1.

*NCAA Tourney (0-1): St. Lawrence (0-1).

Hockey East Association

	W	L	T	Pts	GF	GA
*Boston College (33-8-2)	17	5	2	36	103	57
*Maine (20-12-7)	12	7	5	29	70	62
*Providence (22-13-5)	13	8	3	29	76	71
New Hampshire (21-12-6)	11	8	5	27	61	47
UMass-Lowell (19-16-3)	10	11	3	23	67	66
Boston University (14-20-3)	9	12	3	21	66	71
Northeastern (13-19-4)	7	13	4	18	58	73
Merrimack (14-20-4)	7	13	3	17	60	86
UMass-Amherst (8-22-4)	7	15	2	16	53	81

Conf. Tourney Final: Boston College 5, Providence 3.

*NCAA Tourney (4-2): Boston College (3-0), Maine (1-1), Providence (0-1).

Metro Atlantic Athletic Conf.

	W	L	T	Pts	GF	GA
*Mercyhurst (22-12-2)	19	6	1	39	110	52
Quinnipiac (22-11-4)	17	7	2	36	106	67
Iona (18-13-4)	16	6	4	36	122	84
Canisius (17-12-4)	13	9	4	30	95	90
Connecticut (12-19-4)	12	11	3	27	94	86
Sacred Heart (14-12-5)	11	10	5	27	81	76
Army (12-20-0)	11	15	0	22	84	101
Fairfield (11-19-2)	10	14	2	22	82	104
American Int'l (10-20-1)	10	15	1	21	75	96
Holy Cross (8-22-2)	8	16	2	18	81	99
Bentley (4-23-2)	3	21	2	8	67	142

Conf. Tourney Final: Mercyhurst 6, Quinnipiac 5.
NCAA Tourney (0-1): Mercyhurst (0-1).

Western Collegiate Hockey Assn.

	W	L	T	Pts	GF	GA
*North Dakota (29-8-9)	18	4	6	42	115	80
*St. Cloud St. (31-9-1)	20	8	0	40	111	69
*Minnesota (27-13-2)	18	8	2	38	107	70
*Colorado College (27-13-1)	17	11	0	34	106	81
*Wisconsin (22-15-4)	14	10	4	32	81	86
Denver (19-15-4)	14	11	3	31	84	78
MSU-Mankato (19-18-1)	13	14	1	27	91	99
Michigan Tech (8-24-4)	6	19	3	15	69	105
Alaska-Anchorage (7-24-5)	4	20	4	12	61	104
Minnesota-Duluth (7-28-4)	3	22	3	9	68	121

Conf. Tourney Final: St. Cloud St. 6, North Dakota 5 (OT).

*NCAA Tourney (4-5): North Dakota (2-1), Colorado College (1-1), Wisconsin (1-1), Minnesota (0-1), St. Cloud St. (0-1).

USA Today/American Hockey Magazine Coaches Poll

Taken April 7, 2001 after the NCAA Tournament. First place votes are in parentheses.

	League	W	L	T	Pts
1 Boston College (18)	HE	33	8	2	270
2 North Dakota	WCHA	29	8	9	252
3 Michigan St.	CCHA	33	5	4	234
4 Michigan	CCHA	27	13	5	216
5 St. Cloud St.	WCHA	31	9	1	193
6 Colorado College	WCHA	27	13	1	175
7 Maine	HE	20	12	7	172
8 Wisconsin	WCHA	22	15	4	143
9 Minnesota	WCHA	27	13	2	127
10 St. Lawrence	ECAC	20	13	4	108

Scoring Leaders

Including postseason games; minimum 20 games.

	Cl	Gm	G	A	Pts	Avg
Mike Bishai, Western Mich.	Jr	37	23	45	68	**1.84**
Jeff Hamilton, Yale	Sr	31	23	32	55	**1.77**
Jeff Panzer, N. Dakota	Sr	46	26	55	81	**1.76**
Mark Cullen, Colorado Coll.	Jr	31	20	33	53	**1.71**
Erik Anderson, St. Lawrence	Sr	32	17	34	51	**1.59**

Goaltending Leaders

Including postseason games; minimum 15 games.

	Cl	Record	Sv%	GAA
Ryan Miller, Michigan St.	So	31-5-4	.950	1.32
Mike Walsh, Clarkson	So	15-4-1	.922	1.86
Matt Underhill, Cornell	Jr	13-8-3	.928	1.88
Ty Conklin, UNH	Sr	17-12-5	.920	2.05
Scott Clemmensen, BC	Sr	30-7-2	.914	2.12

Hobey Baker Award

For College Hockey Player of the Year. Voting is done by a 24-member panel of national media, college coaches, pro scouts, and officials.

		Cl	Pos
Winner: Ryan Miller, Michigan St.		So	G

NCAA Division I Tournament

Regional Seeds

Frozen Four teams in **bold**.

	West		East
1	**Michigan St.** (32-4-4)	1	**Boston College** (30-8-2)
2	St. Cloud St. (31-8-1)	2	**North Dakota** (27-7-9)
3	**Michigan** (25-12-5)	3	Colorado Coll. (26-12-1)
4	Wisconsin (21-14-4)	4	Minnesota (27-12-2)
5	Providence (22-12-5)	5	Maine (19-11-7)
6	Mercyhurst (22-11-2)	6	St. Lawrence (20-12-4)

West Regional

Held at Van Andel Arena in Grand Rapids, Mich., March 24-25. Single elimination, two second round winners advance to Frozen Four.

First Round

Wisconsin 4	Providence 1
Michigan 4	Mercyhurst 3

(Byes: Michigan St. and St. Cloud St.)

Second Round

Michigan St. 5	Wisconsin 1
Michigan 4	St. Cloud St. 3

East Regional

Held at the Worcester (Mass.) Centrum, March 23-24. Single elimination, two second round winners advance to Frozen Four.

First Round

Colorado College 3	2OT	St. Lawrence 2
Maine 5	OT	Minnesota 4

(Byes: Boston College and North Dakota)

Second Round

North Dakota 4	Colorado College 1
Boston College 3	Maine 1

THE FROZEN FOUR

Held at Pepsi Arena in Albany, N.Y., April 5 and April 7. Single elimination; no consolation game.

Semifinals

North Dakota 2	Michigan St. 0
Boston College 4	Michigan 2

Championship Game

Boston College, 3-2 (OT)

North Dakota (WCHA)	0	0	2	0	**2**
Boston College (HE)	0	2	0	1	**3**

2nd Period: BC—Chuck Kobasew 27 (Jeff Giuliano) 5:26 (pp); BC—Mike Lephart 15 (J.D. Forrest, Bobby Allen) 8:50.
3rd Period: ND—Tim Skarperud 10 (Travis Roche, Bryan Lundbohm) 16:18 (pp); ND—Wes Dorey 17 (Aaron Schneekloth, Lundbohm) 19:24.
Overtime: BC—Krys Kolanos 25 (Tony Voce, Kobasew) 4:43.
Goalies: ND—Karl Goehring (31 shots, 28 saves); BC—Scott Clemmensen (37 shots, 35 saves). **Attendance:** 13,667.
Final records: Boston College (33-8-2); North Dakota (29-8-9); Michigan St. (33-5-4); Michigan (27-13-5).
Most Outstanding Player: Chuck Kobasew, freshman forward; 2 goals in semifinal game; 1 goal, 1 assist in final game.
All-Tournament Team: Kobasew, forward Krys Kolanos, defenseman Rob Scuderi, and goalie Scott Clemmensen of Boston College; forward Bryan Lundbohm and defenseman Travis Roche of North Dakota.

Division III
Frozen Four
March 16-17 in Rochester, N.Y.

Semifinals

Rochester Inst. (N.Y.) 5 . . . . .Wisc.-River Falls 2
Plattsburgh St. (N.Y.) 5 . . . . .Wisc.-Superior 3

Third Place: Wisc.-Superior 3 . . . . .Wisc.-River Falls 1
Championship: Plattsburgh St. 6 . . . . . .Rochester Inst. 2
Final records: Plattsburgh St. (29-5-0); Rochester Inst. (27-1-1); Wisc.-Superior (30-4-1); Wisc.-River Falls (23-10-2).

Women's College Hockey

In 2000-01, women's college hockey was sanctioned as an official NCAA sport for the first time in history. Division III championships, however, are sponsored by the American Women's College Hockey Alliance (AWCHA).

NCAA Frozen Four
Held March 23 and 25 at Mariucci Arena in Minneapolis, Minn.

Semifinals

St. Lawrence 3 . . . . .Dartmouth 1
Minnesota-Duluth 6 . . . . .Harvard 3

Third Place: Harvard 3 . . . . .Dartmouth 2
Championship: Minnesota-Duluth 4 . . . . . .St. Lawrence 2
Final records: Minnesota-Duluth (28-5-4); St. Lawrence (24-8-3); Harvard (24-10-0); Dartmouth (26-5-1).

Division III Championship
Held March 9-10 at ESL Sports Centre in Rochester, N.Y.

Semifinals

Middlebury (Vt.) 3 . . . . .St. Mary's (Minn.) 1
Gustavus Adolphus (Minn.) 2 . . . . .Williams (Mass.) 1

Third Place: St. Mary's 2 . . . . .Williams 1
Championship: Middlebury 6 . . . . .G. Adolphus 0
Final records: Middlebury (23-1-1); Gustavus Adolphus (23-6-1); St. Mary's (22-7-1); Williams (20-6-1).

Patty Kazmaier Award

For Women's College Hockey Player of the Year. Voting is done by an 11-member panel of national media, college coaches, and one USA Hockey member.

		Cl	Pos
Winner: Jennifer Botterill, Harvard	. . . .	Jr	F

MINOR LEAGUE HOCKEY

American Hockey League

Division champions (*) and playoff qualifiers (†) are noted. T denotes any game that was tied after regulation play and a five-minute overtime period. OL signifies any game that was tied after regulation play but lost in overtime. They are each worth one point in the standings.

Eastern Conference
Canadian Division

Team (Affiliate)	W	L	T	OL	Pts	GF	GA
*Saint John (Calg.)	44	24	7	5	100	269	210
†Quebec (Mon.)	41	32	3	4	89	264	252
†St. John's (Tor.)	35	35	8	2	80	247	244
Hamilton (Edm.)	28	41	6	5	67	227	281

New England Division

Team (Affiliate)	W	L	T	OL	Pts	GF	GA
*Worcester (St.L)	48	20	9	3	108	264	205
†Hartford (NYR)	40	26	8	6	94	263	247
†Providence (Bos.)	35	31	10	4	84	245	242
†Lowell (LA & NYI)	35	35	5	5	80	225	244
Portland (Wash.)	34	40	4	2	74	250	280
Springfield (Pho.)	29	37	8	6	72	253	280

Western Conference
Southern Division

Team (Affiliate)	W	L	T	OL	Pts	GF	GA
*Kentucky (SJ)	42	25	12	1	97	273	212
†Cincinnati (Ana. & Det.)	41	26	9	4	95	254	240
†Norfolk (Chicago)	36	26	13	5	90	241	208
Louisville (Florida)	21	51	5	3	50	200	285

Mid-Atlantic Division

Team (Affiliate)	W	L	T	OL	Pts	GF	GA
*Rochester (Buf.)	46	22	9	3	104	224	192
†Wilkes-Barre (Pit.)	36	33	9	2	83	252	248
†Syracuse (Clb.)	33	30	12	5	83	235	254
†Philadelphia (Phi.)	36	34	5	5	82	246	244
Hershey (Col.)	34	39	4	3	75	216	234
Albany (NJ)	30	40	6	4	70	216	262

Scoring Leaders

	Gm	G	A	Pts	PM
Derek Armstrong, Har.	75	32	69	101	73
Jean-Guy Trudel, Spr.	80	34	65	99	89
Ryan Kraft, Ken.	77	38	50	88	36
Mark Greig, Phi.	74	31	57	88	98
Brad Smyth, Har.	77	50	29	79	110

Goaltending Leaders

(At least 1590 minutes)	GP	GAA	Sv%	Record
Dwayne Roloson, Wor.	52	2.17	.929	32-15-5
Mika Noronen, Roch.	47	2.18	.913	26-15-5
Miikka Kiprusoff, Ken.	36	2.24	.926	19-9-6

Calder Cup Finals

	W-L	GF	Leading Scorers
Saint John	4-2	20	Tkaczuk (6-4—10)
Wilkes-Barre	2-4	17	Kelleher (3-4—7)

Date	Winner	Home Ice
May 17	Wilkes-Barre, 4-3	at Saint John
May 19	Saint John, 4-3	at Saint John
May 21	Saint John, 4-1	at Wilkes-Barre
May 23	Wilkes-Barre, 6-4	at Wilkes-Barre
May 25	Saint John, 4-3	at Wilkes-Barre
May 28	Saint John, 1-0	at Saint John

International Hockey League

Division champions (*) and playoff qualifiers (†) are noted. GF and GA refer to goals for and against. SOL refers to shootout losses and are worth one point in the standings.

Eastern Conference

Team (Affiliate)	W	L	SOL	Pts	GF	GA
*Grand Rapids (Ott.)	53	22	7	113	279	196
†Orlando (Atl.)	47	28	7	101	241	193
†Cincinnati (Car.)	44	29	9	97	267	259
†Cleveland (Min.)	43	32	7	93	270	258
†Milwaukee (Nash.)	42	33	7	91	244	217
Detroit (TB)	23	53	6	52	184	311

Scoring Leaders

	Gm	G	A	Pts	PM
Derek King, GR	72	32	49	81	19
Steve Larouche, Chi.	72	31	50	81	78
Brett Harkins, Hou.	81	16	63	79	51
Rob Brown, Chi.	72	24	53	77	97
Kai Nurminen, Cle.	72	28	43	71	32

Goaltending Leaders

(At least 1500 minutes)	GP	GAA	Sv%	Record
Richard Shulmistra, Chi.	28	1.82	.940	20-7-0
Norm Maracle, Orl.	49	2.01	.925	31-13-3
Mike Fountain, GR	50	2.08	.924	33-9-6

Western Conference

Team (Affiliate)	W	L	SOL	Pts	GF	GA
*Chicago (NYI)	43	32	7	93	267	249
†Houston (Indep.)	42	32	8	92	229	245
†Manitoba (Det.)	39	31	12	90	222	230
†Utah (Dal.)	38	36	8	84	208	220
Kansas City (Van.)	37	42	3	77	240	273

Turner Cup Finals

	W-L	GF	Leading Scorers
Orlando	4-1	20	Beaufait (1-5-6)
			& Mason (1-5-6)
Chicago	1-4	8	Maltais (2-2-4)

Date	Winner	Home Ice
May 19	Orlando, 7-2	at Orlando
May 20	Orlando, 5-1	at Orlando
May 23	Chicago, 3-1	at Chicago
May 25	Orlando, 2-1 (OT)	at Chicago
May 26	Orlando, 5-1	at Orlando

Note: The IHL ceased its operations after the 2000-01 season. Six teams—Chicago, Grand Rapids, Houston, Manitoba, Milwaukee, and Utah—will join the AHL beginning in 2001-02.

East Coast Hockey League

Division champions (*) and playoff qualifiers (†) are noted. GF and GA refer to goals for and against. SOL refers to shootout losses and are worth one point in the standings.

Northern Conference

Northeast Division

Team (Affiliate)	W	L	T	Pts	GF	GA
*Trenton (Phi./NYI)	50	18	4	104	236	164
†Roanoke (Indep.)	38	30	4	80	231	195
†Charlotte (NYR)	34	26	12	80	247	252
†Richmond (SJ/Wash.)	35	31	6	76	223	228
Greensboro (Indep.)	26	39	7	59	215	277

Northwest Division

Team (Affiliate)	W	L	T	Pts	GF	GA
*Peoria (St.L)	45	17	10	100	238	182
†Dayton (Clb.)	45	21	6	96	247	194
†Toledo (Det.)	37	27	8	82	262	259
†Johnstown (Calg. & TB)	28	36	8	64	207	238
Wheeling (Pit.)	24	40	8	56	192	277

Scoring Leaders

	Gm	G	A	Pts	PM
Scott King, Cha.	72	40	61	101	34
Jeff Bes, Pens.-Jac.	68	35	65	100	103
Andrew Williamson, Tol.	66	52	45	97	53
James Patterson, Tol.	65	40	56	96	59
Jamie Ling, Day.	72	26	67	93	40

Goaltending Leaders

(At least 1440 minutes)	GP	GAA	Sv%	Record
Curtis Sanford, Peo.	27	1.91	.925	15-7-4
Scott Stirling, Tre.	48	2.14	.922	32-10-3
Alex Westlund, Day.	29	2.22	.930	19-5-4

Southern Conference

Southeast Division

Team (Affiliate)	W	L	T	Pts	GF	GA
*South Carolina (Buf.)	42	23	7	91	240	210
†Florida (Car.)	38	26	8	84	236	242
Tallahassee (Edm. & Mon.)	38	27	7	83	248	219
†Pee Dee (Ott.)	38	28	6	82	242	231
†Augusta (Indep.)	36	29	7	79	259	253
Greenville (Bos. & Atl.)	34	33	5	73	219	239

Note: At the conclusion of the regular season, Tallahassee was penalized 15 points in the standings (from 83 to 68) due to salary cap violations.

Southwest Division

Team (Affiliate)	W	L	T	Pts	GF	GA
*Louisiana (Indep.)	42	24	6	90	237	209
†Jackson (Min.)	39	24	9	87	206	209
†Mobile (Ott.)	38	28	6	82	240	233
†New Orleans (SJ & Nash.)	35	25	12	82	247	239
†Arkansas (Indep.)	34	24	14	82	237	232
†Baton Rouge (Indep.)	35	26	11	81	216	225
Mississippi (LA & Pho.)	34	33	5	73	221	218
Birmingham (Indep.)	28	40	4	60	224	296
Pensacola (Indep.)	27	40	5	59	201	250

Kelly Cup Finals

	W-L	GF	Leading Scorers
South Carolina	4-1	20	Seitz (4-4-8)
Trenton	1-4	16	Bertoli (2-5-7)

Date	Winner	Home Ice
May 18	South Carolina, 3-2 (OT)	at Trenton
May 20	South Carolina, 5-3	at Trenton
May 22	Trenton, 4-3 (2OT)	at South Carolina
May 24	South Carolina, 6-5	at South Carolina
May 27	South Carolina, 3-2	at South Carolina

World Hockey Championships

MEN

The World Hockey Championships, held in Hanover, Cologne, and Nuremberg, Germany from April 28-May 13, 2001. Top three teams (*) in each group after preliminary round-robin advance to the second round. Fourth-place teams play in a consolation round. Top four teams from each group of the second round advance to the quarterfinals.

Final Round Robin Standings

GROUP A	W-L-T	Pts	GF	GA
*Czech Republic	.2-0-1	5	10	4
*Germany	.1-1-1	3	5	5
*Switzerland	.1-2-0	2	7	8
Belarus	.1-2-0	2	5	10

GROUP B	W-L-T	Pts	GF	GA
*Finland	.3-0-0	6	18	3
*Slovakia	.2-1-0	4	15	9
*Austria	.1-2-0	2	4	12
Japan	.0-3-0	0	6	19

GROUP C	W-L-T	Pts	GF	GA
*Sweden	.2-0-1	5	12	4
*United States	.1-1-1	3	8	7
*Ukraine	.1-2-0	2	7	13
Latvia	.1-2-0	2	6	9

GROUP D	W-L-T	Pts	GF	GA
*Canada	.3-0-0	6	13	2
*Russia	.2-1-0	4	12	5
*Italy	.0-2-1	1	5	14
Norway	.0-2-1	1	4	13

Second Round

GROUP E	W-L-T	Pts	GF	GA
*Czech Republic	.4-0-1	9	24	8
*Canada	.3-1-1	7	19	11
*Russia	.3-2-0	6	16	11
*Germany	.1-2-2	4	10	12
Switzerland	.1-4-0	2	13	15
Italy	.1-4-0	2	5	30

GROUP F	W-L-T	Pts	GF	GA
*Finland	.4-1-0	8	23	12
*Sweden	.3-1-1	7	25	8
*United States	.3-1-1	7	15	10
*Slovakia	.2-3-0	4	12	12
Ukraine	.1-4-0	2	7	21
Austria	.1-4-0	2	4	23

Quarterfinals

Czech Republic 2 . . . . .Slovakia 0
Finland 4 . . . . .Germany 1
United States 4 . . . . .OT . . . . .Canada 3
Sweden 4 . . . . .OT . . . . .Russia 3

Semifinals

Czech Republic 3 . . . . .OT* . . . . .Sweden 2
Finland 3 . . . . .United States 1
* After a scoreless overtime, Czech Republic won the penalty shootout.

Bronze Medal: Sweden 3 . . . . .United States 2
Gold Medal: Czech Rep. 3 . .OT . . . . .Finland 2

Scoring Leaders

	Gm	G	A	Pts	PM
Juha Ylonen, Finland	9	5	9	**14**	2
Petteri Nummelin, Finland	9	1	12	**13**	0
Robert Reichel, Czech Republic	9	5	7	**12**	4
Sami Kapanen, Finland	8	7	4	**11**	8
Sami Salo, Finland	9	3	6	**9**	6
P.J. Axelsson, Sweden	9	3	6	**9**	12

Goaltending Leaders

(At least 200 minutes)	Gm	Min	Sv%	GAA
Milan Hnilicka, Czech Rep.	9	541	.952	**1.44**
Maxim Sokolov, Russia	7	322	.928	**1.68**
Pasi Nurminen, Finland	7	411	.938	**1.75**
Tommy Salo, Sweden	8	494	.920	**1.94**
Pavol Rybar, Slovakia	4	239	.911	**2.01**

WOMEN

The seventh sanctioned Women's World Hockey Championship, held in Minneapolis, Minn. and surrounding areas, April 2-8, 2001. Top two teams (*) in each group after preliminary round-robin advance to the medal round.

Pool A Final Standings

GROUP A	W-L-T	Pts	GF	GA
*Canada	.3-0-0	6	29	1
*Russia	.2-1-0	4	12	7
Sweden	.1-2-0	2	3	17
Kazakstan	.0-3-0	0	3	22

GROUP B	W-L-T	Pts	GF	GA
*United States	.3-0-0	6	35	0
*Finland	.2-1-0	4	12	17
China	.0-2-1	1	6	20
Germany	.0-2-1	1	2	18

Medal Round

Canada 8 . . . . .Finland 0
United States 6 . . . . .Russia 1

Bronze Medal: Russia 2 . . . . .Finland 1
Gold Medal: Canada 3 . . . . .United States 2

Scoring Leaders

	Gm	G	A	Pts	PM
Cammi Granato, USA	5	7	6	**13**	0
Krissy Wendell, USA	5	3	9	**12**	4
Nancy Drolet, Canada	5	4	7	**11**	4
Jennifer Botterill, Canada	5	8	2	**10**	4
Ekaterina Pashkevich, Russia	5	6	4	**10**	2
Jenny Schmidgall, USA	5	3	7	**10**	4
Kelly Bechard, Canada	5	1	9	**10**	8

Goaltending Leaders

(At least 120 minutes)	Gm	Min	Sv%	GAA
Sara DeCosta, USA	2	120	.975	**0.50**
Sami Jo Small, Canada	2	120	.952	**0.50**
Kim St-Pierre, Canada	3	180	.969	**0.67**
Sarah Tueting, USA	3	179	.933	**1.01**
Irina Gachennikova, Russia	5	286	.913	**2.73**

1893-2001 Through the Years

information please®
SPORTS ALMANAC

The Stanley Cup

The Stanley Cup was originally donated to the Canadian Amateur Hockey Association by Sir Frederick Arthur Stanley, Lord Stanley of Preston and 16th Earl of Derby, who had become interested in the sport while Governor General of Canada from 1888 to 1893. Stanley wanted the trophy to be a challenge cup, contested for each year by the best amateur hockey teams in Canada.

In 1893, the Cup was presented without a challenge to the AHA champion Montreal Amateur Athletic Association team. Every year since, however, there has been a playoff. In 1914, Cup trustees limited the field challenging for the trophy to the champion of the eastern professional National Hockey Association (NHA, organized in 1910) and the western professional Pacific Coast Hockey Association (PCHA, organized in 1912).

The NHA disbanded in 1917 and the National Hockey League (NHL) was formed. From 1918 to 1926, the NHL and PCHA champions played for the Cup with the Western Canada Hockey League (WCHL) champion joining in a three-way challenge in 1923 and '24. The PCHA disbanded in 1924, while the WCHL became the Western Hockey League (WHL) for the 1925-26 season and folded the following year. The NHL playoffs have decided the winner of the Stanley Cup ever since.

Champions, 1893-1917

Multiple winners: Montreal Victorias and Montreal Wanderers (4); Montreal Amateur Athletic Association and Ottawa Silver Seven (3); Montreal Shamrocks, Ottawa Senators, Quebec Bulldogs and Winnipeg Victorias (2).

Year		Year		Year	
1893	Montreal AAA	1901	Winnipeg Victorias	1909	Ottawa Senators
1894	Montreal AAA	1902	Montreal AAA	1910	Montreal Wanderers
1895	Montreal Victorias	1903	Ottawa Silver Seven	1911	Ottawa Senators
1896	(Feb.) Winnipeg Victorias	1904	Ottawa Silver Seven	1912	Quebec Bulldogs
	(Dec.) Montreal Victorias	1905	Ottawa Silver Seven	1913	Quebec Bulldogs
1897	Montreal Victorias	1906	Montreal Wanderers	1914	Toronto Blueshirts (NHA)
1898	Montreal Victorias	1907	(Jan.) Kenora Thistles	1915	Vancouver Millionaires (PCHA)
1899	Montreal Shamrocks		(Mar.) Montreal Wanderers	1916	Montreal Canadiens (NHA)
1900	Montreal Shamrocks	1908	Montreal Wanderers	1917	Seattle Metropolitans (PCHA)

Champions Since 1918

Multiple winners: Montreal Canadiens (23); Toronto Arenas-St. Pats-Maple Leafs (13); Detroit Red Wings (9); Boston Bruins and Edmonton Oilers (5); NY Islanders, NY Rangers and Ottawa Senators (4); Chicago Blackhawks (3); Colorado Avalanche, Montreal Maroons, New Jersey Devils, Philadelphia Flyers and Pittsburgh Penguins (2).

Year	Winner	Head Coach	Series	Loser	Head Coach
1918	Toronto Arenas	Dick Carroll	3-2 (WLWLW)	Vancouver (PCHA)	Frank Patrick
1919	No Decision*				
1920	Ottawa	Pete Green	3-2 (WWLLW)	Seattle (PCHA)	Pete Muldoon
1921	Ottawa	Pete Green	3-2 (LWWLW)	Vancouver (PCHA)	Frank Patrick
1922	Toronto St. Pats	Eddie Powers	3-2 (LWLWW)	Vancouver (PCHA)	Frank Patrick
1923	Ottawa	Pete Green	3-1 (WLWW)	Vancouver (PCHA)	Frank Patrick
			2-0	Edmonton (WCHL)	K.C. McKenzie
1924	Montreal	Leo Dandurand	2-0	Vancouver (PCHA)	Frank Patrick
			2-0	Calgary (WCHL)	Eddie Oatman
1925	Victoria (WCHL)	Lester Patrick	3-1 (WWLW)	Montreal	Leo Dandurand
1926	Montreal Maroons	Eddie Gerard	3-1 (WWLW)	Victoria (WHL)	Lester Patrick
1927	Ottawa	Dave Gill	2-0-2 (TWTW)	Boston	Art Ross
1928	NY Rangers	Lester Patrick	3-2 (LWLWW)	Montreal Maroons	Eddie Gerard
1929	Boston	Cy Denneny	2-0	NY Rangers	Lester Patrick
1930	Montreal	Cecil Hart	2-0	Boston	Art Ross
1931	Montreal	Cecil Hart	3-2 (WLLWW)	Chicago	Art Duncan
1932	Toronto	Dick Irvin	3-0	NY Rangers	Lester Patrick
1933	NY Rangers	Lester Patrick	3-1 (WWLW)	Toronto	Dick Irvin
1934	Chicago	Tommy Gorman	3-1 (WWLW)	Detroit	Jack Adams
1935	Montreal Maroons	Tommy Gorman	3-0	Toronto	Dick Irvin
1936	Detroit	Jack Adams	3-1 (WWLW)	Toronto	Dick Irvin
1937	Detroit	Jack Adams	3-2 (LWLWW)	NY Rangers	Lester Patrick
1938	Chicago	Bill Stewart	3-1 (WLWW)	Toronto	Dick Irvin
1939	Boston	Art Ross	4-1 (WLWWW)	Toronto	Dick Irvin

* The 1919 finals were cancelled after five games due to an influenza epidemic with Montreal and Seattle (PCHA) tied at 2-2-1.

The Stanley Cup (Cont.)

Year	Winner	Head Coach	Series	Loser	Head Coach
1940	NY Rangers	Frank Boucher	4-2 (WWLLWW)	Toronto	Dick Irvin
1941	Boston	Cooney Weiland	4-0	Detroit	Jack Adams
1942	Toronto	Hap Day	4-3 (LLLWWWW)	Detroit	Jack Adams
1943	Detroit	Ebbie Goodfellow	4-0	Boston	Art Ross
1944	Montreal	Dick Irvin	4-0	Chicago	Paul Thompson
1945	Toronto	Hap Day	4-3 (WWWLLLW)	Detroit	Jack Adams
1946	Montreal	Dick Irvin	4-1 (WWWLW)	Boston	Dit Clapper
1947	Toronto	Hap Day	4-2 (LWWWLW)	Montreal	Dick Irvin
1948	Toronto	Hap Day	4-0	Detroit	Tommy Ivan
1949	Toronto	Hap Day	4-0	Detroit	Tommy Ivan
1950	Detroit	Tommy Ivan	4-3 (WLWLLWW)	NY Rangers	Lynn Patrick
1951	Toronto	Joe Primeau	4-1 (WLWWW)	Montreal	Dick Irvin
1952	Detroit	Tommy Ivan	4-0	Montreal	Dick Irvin
1953	Montreal	Dick Irvin	4-1 (WLWWW)	Boston	Lynn Patrick
1954	Detroit	Tommy Ivan	4-3 (WLWWLLW)	Montreal	Dick Irvin
1955	Detroit	Jimmy Skinner	4-3 (WWLLWLW)	Montreal	Dick Irvin
1956	Montreal	Toe Blake	4-1 (WWLWW)	Detroit	Jimmy Skinner
1957	Montreal	Toe Blake	4-1 (WWWLW)	Boston	Milt Schmidt
1958	Montreal	Toe Blake	4-2 (WWLWW)	Boston	Milt Schmidt
1959	Montreal	Toe Blake	4-1 (WWLWW)	Toronto	Punch Imlach
1960	Montreal	Toe Blake	4-0	Toronto	Punch Imlach
1961	Chicago	Rudy Pilous	4-2 (WLWLWW)	Detroit	Sid Abel
1962	Toronto	Punch Imlach	4-2 (WWLLWW)	Chicago	Rudy Pilous
1963	Toronto	Punch Imlach	4-1 (WWLWW)	Detroit	Sid Abel
1964	Toronto	Punch Imlach	4-3 (WLLWLWW)	Detroit	Sid Abel
1965	Montreal	Toe Blake	4-3 (WWLLWLW)	Chicago	Billy Reay
1966	Montreal	Toe Blake	4-2 (LLWWWW)	Detroit	Sid Abel
1967	Toronto	Punch Imlach	4-2 (LWWLWW)	Montreal	Toe Blake
1968	Montreal	Toe Blake	4-0	St. Louis	Scotty Bowman
1969	Montreal	Claude Ruel	4-0	St. Louis	Scotty Bowman
1970	Boston	Harry Sinden	4-0	St. Louis	Scotty Bowman
1971	Montreal	Al MacNeil	4-3 (LLWWLWW)	Chicago	Billy Reay
1972	Boston	Tom Johnson	4-2 (WWWLWW)	NY Rangers	Emile Francis
1973	Montreal	Scotty Bowman	4-2 (WWWLWW)	Chicago	Billy Reay
1974	Philadelphia	Fred Shero	4-2 (LWWWLW)	Boston	Bep Guidolin
1975	Philadelphia	Fred Shero	4-2 (WWLLWW)	Buffalo	Floyd Smith
1976	Montreal	Scotty Bowman	4-0	Philadelphia	Fred Shero
1977	Montreal	Scotty Bowman	4-0	Boston	Don Cherry
1978	Montreal	Scotty Bowman	4-2 (WWLLWW)	Boston	Don Cherry
1979	Montreal	Scotty Bowman	4-1 (LWWWW)	NY Rangers	Fred Shero
1980	NY Islanders	Al Arbour	4-2 (WLWWLW)	Philadelphia	Pat Quinn
1981	NY Islanders	Al Arbour	4-1 (WWWLW)	Minnesota	Glen Sonmor
1982	NY Islanders	Al Arbour	4-0	Vancouver	Roger Neilson
1983	NY Islanders	Al Arbour	4-0	Edmonton	Glen Sather
1984	Edmonton	Glen Sather	4-1 (WLWWW)	NY Islanders	Al Arbour
1985	Edmonton	Glen Sather	4-1 (LWWWW)	Philadelphia	Mike Keenan
1986	Montreal	Jean Perron	4-1 (LWWWW)	Calgary	Bob Johnson
1987	Edmonton	Glen Sather	4-3 (WWLWLLW)	Philadelphia	Mike Keenan
1988	Edmonton	Glen Sather	4-0	Boston	Terry O'Reilly
1989	Calgary	Terry Crisp	4-2 (WLLWWW)	Montreal	Pat Burns
1990	Edmonton	John Muckler	4-1 (WWLWW)	Boston	Mike Milbury
1991	Pittsburgh	Bob Johnson	4-2 (LWLWWW)	Minnesota	Bob Gainey
1992	Pittsburgh	Scotty Bowman	4-0	Chicago	Mike Keenan
1993	Montreal	Jacques Demers	4-1 (LWWWW)	Los Angeles	Barry Melrose
1994	NY Rangers	Mike Keenan	4-3 (LWWWLLW)	Vancouver	Pat Quinn
1995	New Jersey	Jacques Lemaire	4-0	Detroit	Scotty Bowman
1996	Colorado	Marc Crawford	4-0	Florida	Doug MacLean
1997	Detroit	Scotty Bowman	4-0	Philadelphia	Terry Murray
1998	Detroit	Scotty Bowman	4-0	Washington	Ron Wilson
1999	Dallas	Ken Hitchcock	4-2 (LWWLWW)	Buffalo	Lindy Ruff
2000	New Jersey	Larry Robinson	4-2 (WLWWLW)	Dallas	Ken Hitchcock
2001	Colorado	Bob Hartley	4-3 (WLWLLWW)	New Jersey	Larry Robinson

M.J. O'Brien Trophy

Donated by Canadian mining magnate M.J. O'Brien, whose son Ambrose founded the National Hockey Association in 1910. Originally presented to the NHA champion until the league's demise in 1917, the trophy then passed to the NHL champion through 1927. It was awarded to the NHL's Canadian Division winner from 1927-38 and the Stanley Cup runner-up from 1939-50 before being retired in 1950.

NHA winners included the Montreal Wanderers (1910), original Ottawa Senators (1911 and '15), Quebec Bulldogs (1912 and '13), Toronto Blueshirts (1914) and Montreal Canadiens (1916 and '17).

Conn Smythe Trophy

The Most Valuable Player of the Stanley Cup Playoffs, as selected by the Pro Hockey Writers Association. Presented since 1965 by Maple Leaf Gardens Limited in the name of the former Toronto coach, GM and owner, Conn Smythe. Winners who did not play for the Cup champion are in **bold** type.

Multiple winners: Patrick Roy (3); Wayne Gretzky, Mario Lemieux, Bobby Orr and Bernie Parent (2).

Year		Year		Year	
1965	Jean Beliveau, Mon., C	1978	Larry Robinson, Mon., D	1991	Mario Lemieux, Pit., C
1966	**Roger Crozier**, Det., G	1979	Bob Gainey, Mon., LW	1992	Mario Lemieux, Pit., C
1967	Dave Keon, Tor., C	1980	Bryan Trottier, NYI, C	1993	Patrick Roy, Mon., G
1968	**Glenn Hall**, St.L., G	1981	Butch Goring, NYI, C	1994	Brian Leetch, NYR, D
1969	Serge Savard, Mon., D	1982	Mike Bossy, NYI, RW	1995	Claude Lemieux, NJ, RW
1970	Bobby Orr, Bos., D	1983	Billy Smith, NYI, G	1996	Joe Sakic, Col., C
1971	Ken Dryden, Mon., G	1984	Mark Messier, Edm., LW	1997	Mike Vernon, Det., G
1972	Bobby Orr, Bos., D	1985	Wayne Gretzky, Edm., C	1998	Steve Yzerman, Det., C
1973	Yvan Cournoyer, Mon., RW	1986	Patrick Roy, Mon., G	1999	Joe Nieuwendyk, Dal., C
1974	Bernie Parent, Phi., G	1987	**Ron Hextall**, Phi., G	2000	Scott Stevens, NJ, D
1975	Bernie Parent, Phi., G	1988	Wayne Gretzky, Edm., C	2001	Patrick Roy, Col., G
1976	**Reggie Leach**, Phi., RW	1989	Al MacInnis, Calg., D		
1977	Guy Lafleur, Mon., RW	1990	Bill Ranford, Edm., G		

Note: Ken Dryden (1971) and Patrick Roy (1986) are the only players to win as rookies.

All-Time Stanley Cup Playoff Leaders
CAREER

Stanley Cup Playoff leaders through 2001. Years listed indicate number of playoff appearances. Players active in 2001 are in **bold** type; (DNP) indicates player that was active in 2001 but did not participate in playoffs.

Scoring

Points

		Yrs	Gm	G	A	Pts
1	Wayne Gretzky	16	208	122	260	382
2	**Mark Messier** (DNP)	17	236	109	186	295
3	Jari Kurri	14	200	106	127	233
4	Glenn Anderson	15	225	93	121	214
5	**Paul Coffey** (DNP)	16	194	59	137	196
6	Bryan Trottier	17	221	71	113	184
7	**Ray Bourque**	21	214	41	139	180
8	**Doug Gilmour**	16	170	56	122	178
9	Jean Beliveau	17	162	79	97	176
10	Denis Savard	16	169	66	109	175
11	**Mario Lemieux**	8	107	76	96	172
12	**Brett Hull**	16	163	90	76	166
13	Denis Potvin	14	185	56	108	164
14	Mike Bossy	10	129	85	75	160
	Gordie Howe	20	157	68	92	160
	Bobby Smith	13	184	64	96	160
17	**Claude Lemieux** (DNP)	15	221	80	77	157
18	**Steve Yzerman**	16	154	61	91	152
	Al MacInnis	17	164	39	113	152
	Larry Murphy	20	215	37	115	152
21	Stan Mikita	18	155	59	91	150
22	Brian Propp	13	160	64	84	148
23	**Jaromir Jagr**	11	140	65	82	147
24	Larry Robinson	20	227	28	116	144
25	**Sergei Fedorov**	11	135	44	97	141
	Adam Oates	13	137	38	103	141

Goals

		Yrs	Gm	G
1	Wayne Gretzky	16	208	122
2	**Mark Messier** (DNP)	17	236	109
3	Jari Kurri	15	200	106
4	Glenn Anderson	15	225	93
5	**Brett Hull**	16	163	90
6	Mike Bossy	10	129	85
7	Maurice Richard	15	133	82
8	**Claude Lemieux** (DNP)	15	221	80
9	Jean Beliveau	17	162	79
10	**Mario Lemieux**	8	107	76

Assists

		Yrs	Gm	A
1	Wayne Gretzky	16	208	260
2	**Mark Messier** (DNP)	17	236	186
3	**Ray Bourque**	21	214	139
4	**Paul Coffey** (DNP)	16	194	137
5	Jari Kurri	15	200	127
6	**Doug Gilmour**	16	170	122
7	Glenn Anderson	15	225	121
8	Larry Robinson	20	227	116
9	**Larry Murphy**	20	215	115
10	**Al MacInnis**	17	164	113
	Bryan Trottier	17	221	113

The Stanley Cup (Cont.)

Goaltending

Wins

		Gm	W-L	Pct	GAA
1	**Patrick Roy**	219	137-80	.631	2.29
2	Grant Fuhr	150	92-50	.648	2.92
3	Billy Smith	132	88-36	.710	2.73
4	Ken Dryden	112	80-32	.714	2.40
5	**Ed Belfour**	141	79-57	.581	2.14
6	**Mike Vernon** (DNP)	138	77-56	.579	2.68
7	Jacques Plante	112	71-37	.657	2.17
8	Andy Moog	132	68-57	.544	3.04
9	**Martin Brodeur**	109	65-44	.596	1.91
10	Tom Barrasso	119	61-54	.530	3.01

Shutouts

		Gm	GAA	No
1	**Patrick Roy**	219	2.29	19
2	Clint Benedict	48	1.80	15
	Jacques Plante	112	2.17	15
4	Turk Broda	102	1.98	13
5	Three tied with 12 each.			

Appearances in Cup Finals

Standings of all teams that have reached the Stanley Cup championship round, since 1918.

App		Cups	Last Won
32	Montreal Canadiens	23*	1993
21	Toronto Maple Leafs	13†	1967
21	Detroit Red Wings	9	1998
17	Boston Bruins	5	1972
10	New York Rangers	4	1994
10	Chicago Blackhawks	3	1961
7	Philadelphia Flyers	2	1975
6	Edmonton Oilers	5	1990
5	New York Islanders	4	1983
5	Vancouver Millionaires (PCHA)	0	—
4	(original) Ottawa Senators	4	1927
4	Minnesota/Dallas (North) Stars	1	1999
3	New Jersey Devils	2	2000
3	Montreal Maroons	2	1935
3	St. Louis Blues	0	—
2	Colorado Avalanche	2	2001
2	Pittsburgh Penguins	2	1992
2	Calgary Flames	1	1989
2	Victoria Cougars (WCHL-WHL)	1	1925
2	Buffalo Sabres	0	—
2	Seattle Metropolitans (PCHA)	0	—
2	Vancouver Canucks	0	—
1	Calgary Tigers (WCHL)	0	—
1	Edmonton Eskimos (WCHL)	0	—
1	Florida Panthers	0	—
1	Los Angeles Kings	0	—
1	Washington Capitals	0	—

*Les Canadiens also won the Cup in 1916 for a total of 24. Also, their final with Seattle in 1919 was cancelled due to an influenza epidemic that claimed the life of the Habs' Joe Hall.

†Toronto has won the Cup under three nicknames—Arenas (1918), St. Pats (1922) and Maple Leafs (1932,42,45,47-49,51,62-64,67).

Teams now defunct (7): Calgary Tigers, Edmonton Eskimos, Montreal Maroons, (original) Ottawa Senators, Seattle, Vancouver Millionaires and Victoria. Edmonton (1923) and Calgary (1924) represented the WCHL and later the WHL, while Vancouver (1918,1921-24) and Seattle (1919-20) played out of the PCHA.

Goals Against Average

Minimum of 50 games played

		Gm	Min	GA	GAA
1	**Martin Brodeur**	109	6830	217	1.91
2	George Hainsworth	52	3486	112	1.93
3	Turk Broda	101	6389	211	1.98
4	**Dominik Hasek**	74	4517	157	2.09
5	**Ed Belfour**	141	8639	308	2.14
6	Jacques Plante	112	6652	240	2.16
7	**Chris Osgood**	68	3989	144	2.17
8	**Patrick Roy**	219	13545	516	2.29
9	Ken Dryden	112	6846	274	2.40
10	Bernie Parent	71	4302	174	2.43

Note: Clint Benedict had an average of 1.80 but played in only 48 games.

Games Played

		Yrs	Gm
1	**Patrick Roy**, Mon-Col	15	219
2	Grant Fuhr, Edm-Buf-St.L	14	150
3	**Ed Belfour**, Chi-Dal	11	141
4	**Mike Vernon**, Calg-Det-SJ-Fla (DNP)	14	138
5	Billy Smith, NY Islanders	13	132
	Andy Moog, Edm-Bos-Dal-Mon	16	132

Miscellaneous

Championships

		Yrs	Cups
1	Henri Richard, Montreal	18	11
2	Yvan Cournoyer, Montreal	15	10
	Jean Beliveau, Montreal	17	10
4	Claude Provost, Montreal	14	9
5	Jacques Lemaire, Montreal	11	8
	Maurice Richard, Montreal	15	8
	Red Kelly, Detroit-Toronto	19	8

Years in Playoffs

		Yrs	Gm
1	**Ray Bourque**, Boston-Colorado	21	214
2	Gordie Howe, Detroit-Hartford	20	157
	Larry Robinson, Montreal-Los Angeles	20	227
	Larry Murphy, LA-Wash-Min-Pit-Tor-Det	20	215
5	Red Kelly, Detroit-Toronto	19	164

Games Played

		Yrs	Gm
1	**Mark Messier**, Edm-NYR-Van (DNP)	17	236
2	Guy Carbonneau, Mon-St.L-Dal	17	231
3	Larry Robinson, Montreal-Los Angeles	20	227
4	Glenn Anderson, Edm-Tor-NYR-St.L	15	225
5	Bryan Trottier, NY Isles-Pittsburgh	17	221
	Claude Lemieux, Mon-NJ-Col-NJ (DNP)	15	221

Penalty Minutes

		Yrs	Gm	Min
1	Dale Hunter, Que-Wash-Col	18	186	729
2	Chris Nilan, Mon-NYR-Bos-Mon	12	111	541
3	**Claude Lemieux**, Mon-NJ-Col-NJ (DNP)	15	221	517
4	**Rick Tocchet**, Phi-Pit-Bos-Pho-Phi	13	145	471
5	Willi Plett, Atl-Calg-Min-Bos	10	83	466

SINGLE SEASON
Scoring
Points

		Year	Gm	G	A	Pts
1	Wayne Gretzky, Edm	1985	18	17	30	47
2	Mario Lemieux, Pit	1991	23	16	28	44
3	Wayne Gretzky, Edm	1988	19	12	31	43
4	Wayne Gretzky, LA	1993	24	15	25	40
5	Wayne Gretzky, Edm	1983	16	12	26	38
6	Paul Coffey, Edm	1985	18	12	25	37
7	Mike Bossy, NYI	1981	18	17	18	35
	Wayne Gretzky, Edm	1984	19	13	22	35
	Doug Gilmour, Tor	1993	21	10	25	35
10	Six tied with 34 each.					

Goals

		Year	Gm	No
1	Reggie Leach, Philadelphia	1976	16	19
	Jari Kurri, Edmonton	1985	18	19
3	Joe Sakic, Colorado	1996	22	18
4	Seven tied with 17 each, including three times by Mike Bossy.			

Assists

		Year	Gm	No
1	Wayne Gretzky, Edmonton	1988	19	31
2	Wayne Gretzky, Edmonton	1985	18	30
3	Wayne Gretzky, Edmonton	1987	21	29
4	Mario Lemieux, Pittsburgh	1991	23	28
5	Wayne Gretzky, Edmonton	1983	16	26

Goaltending
Wins

1	13 tied with 16 each.

Shutouts

1	13 tied with 4 each.

Goals Against Average

	Min. 8 games played	Year	Gm	Min	GA	GAA
1	Terry Sawchuk, Det	1952	8	480	5	0.63
2	Clint Benedict, Mon-M	1928	9	555	8	0.89
3	Turk Broda, Tor	1951	9	509	9	1.06
4	Dave Kerr, NYR	1937	9	553	10	1.11
5	Jacques Plante, Mon	1960	8	489	11	1.35

Note: Average determined by games played through 1942-43 season and by minutes played since then.

SINGLE SERIES
Points

	Year	Rd	G-A—Pts
Rick Middleton, Bos vs Buf	1983	DF	5-14—19
Wayne Gretzky, Edm vs Chi	1985	CF	4-14—18
Mario Lemieux, Pit vs Wash	1992	DSF	7-10—17
Barry Pederson, Bos vs Buf	1983	DF	7-9—16
Doug Gilmour, Tor vs SJ	1994	CSF	3-13—16

Goals

	Year	Rd	No
Jari Kurri, Edm vs Chi	1985	CF	12
Newsy Lalonde, Mon vs Ott	1919	SF*	11
Tim Kerr, Phi vs Pit	1989	DF	10
Five tied with 9 each.			

*NHL final prior to Stanley Cup series with Seattle (PCHA).

Assists

	Year	Rd	No
Rick Middleton, Bos vs Buf	1983	DF	14
Wayne Gretzky, Edm vs Chi	1985	CF	14
Wayne Gretzky, Edm vs LA	1987	DSF	13
Doug Gilmour, Tor vs SJ	1994	CSF	13
Four tied with 11 each.			

SINGLE GAME
Points

	Date	G	A	Pts
Patrik Sundstrom, NJ vs Wash	4/22/88	3	5	8
Mario Lemieux, Pit vs Phi	4/25/89	5	3	8
Wayne Gretzky, Edm at Calg	4/17/83	4	3	7
Wayne Gretzky, Edm at Win	4/25/85	3	4	7
Wayne Gretzky, Edm vs LA	4/9/87	1	6	7

Goals

	Date	No
Newsy Lalonde, Mon vs Ott	3/1/19	5
Maurice Richard, Mon vs Tor	3/23/44	5
Darryl Sittler, Tor vs Phi	4/22/76	5
Reggie Leach, Phi vs Bos	5/6/76	5
Mario Lemieux, Pit vs Phi	4/25/89	5

Assists

	Date	No
Mikko Leinonen, NYR vs Phi	4/8/82	6
Wayne Gretzky, Edm vs LA	4/9/87	6
10 tied with 5 each.		

Five Longest Playoff Overtime Games

The 5 longest overtime games in Stanley Cup history. Note the following Series initials: SF (semifinals), CQF (conference quarterfinal), CSF (conference semifinal), DSF (division semifinal), QF (quarterfinal) and Final (Cup final). Series winners are in **bold** type; (*) indicates deciding game of series.

		OTs	Elapsed Time	Goal Scorer	Date	Series	Location
1	**Detroit** 1, Montreal Maroons 0	6	176:30	Mud Bruneteau	3/24/36	SF, Gm 1	Montreal
2	**Toronto** 1, Boston 0	6	164:46	Ken Doraty	4/3/33	SF, Gm 5	Toronto
3	**Philadelphia** 2, Pittsburgh 1	5	152:01	Keith Primeau	5/4/00	CSF, Gm 4	Pittsburgh
4	**Pittsburgh** 3 Washington 2	4	139:15	Petr Nedved	4/24/96	CQF, Gm 4	Washington
5	Toronto 3, **Detroit** 2	4	130:18	Jack McLean	3/23/43	SF, Gm 2	Detroit

NHL All-Star Game

Three benefit NHL All-Star Games were staged in the 1930s for forward Ace Bailey and the families of Howie Morenz and Babe Siebert. Bailey, of Toronto, suffered a fractured skull on a career-ending check by Boston's Eddie Shore. Morenz, the Montreal Canadiens' legend, died of a heart attack at 35 after a severely broken leg ended his career. Siebert, who played with both Montreal teams, drowned at age 35.

The All-Star Game was revived at the start of the 1947-48 season as an annual exhibition match between the defending Stanley Cup champion and all-stars from the league's other five teams. The format has changed several times since then. The game was moved to midseason in 1966-67 and became an East vs. West contest in 1968-69. The Eastern (East, 1968-1974; Wales, 1975-93) Conference leads the series 18-7-1. In 1998, the East-West format was abandoned for one pitting North American all-stars against all-stars from the rest of the world. North America leads that series 3-1.

NHL All-Star Game (Cont.)
Benefit Games

Date	Occasion		Host	Coaches
2/14/34	Ace Bailey Benefit	Toronto 7, All-Stars 3	Toronto	Dick Irvin, Lester Patrick
11/3/37	Howie Morenz Memorial	All-Stars 6, Montreals* 5	Montreal	Jack Adams, Ceil Hart
10/29/39	Babe Seibert Memorial	All-Stars 5, Canadiens 3	Montreal	Art Ross, Pit Lepine

*Combined squad of Montreal Canadiens and Montreal Maroons.

All-Star Games

Multiple MVP winners: Wayne Gretzky and Mario Lemieux (3); Bobby Hull and Frank Mahovlich (2).

Year		Host	Coaches	Most Valuable Player
1947	All-Stars 4, Toronto 3	Toronto	Dick Irvin, Hap Day	No award
1948	All-Stars 3, Toronto 1	Chicago	Tommy Ivan, Hap Day	No award
1949	All-Stars 3, Toronto 1	Toronto	Tommy Ivan, Hap Day	No award
1950	Detroit 7, All-Stars 1	Detroit	Tommy Ivan, Lynn Patrick	No award
1951	1st Team 2, 2nd Team 2	Toronto	Joe Primeau, Hap Day	No award
1952	1st Team 1, 2nd Team 1	Detroit	Tommy Ivan, Dick Irvin	No award
1953	All-Stars 3, Montreal 1	Montreal	Lynn Patrick, Dick Irvin	No award
1954	All-Stars 2, Detroit 2	Detroit	King Clancy, Jim Skinner	No award
1955	Detroit 3, All-Stars 1	Detroit	Jim Skinner, Dick Irvin	No award
1956	All-Stars 1, Montreal 1	Montreal	Jim Skinner, Toe Blake	No award
1957	All-Stars 5, Montreal 3	Montreal	Milt Schmidt, Toe Blake	No award
1958	Montreal 6, All-Stars 3	Montreal	Toe Blake, Milt Schmidt	No award
1959	Montreal 6, All-Stars 1	Montreal	Toe Blake, Punch Imlach	No award
1960	All-Stars 2, Montreal 1	Montreal	Punch Imlach, Toe Blake	No award
1961	All-Stars 3, Chicago 1	Chicago	Sid Abel, Rudy Pilous	No award
1962	Toronto 4, All-Stars 1	Toronto	Punch Imlach, Rudy Pilous	Eddie Shack, Tor., RW
1963	All-Stars 3, Toronto 3	Toronto	Sid Abel, Punch Imlach	Frank Mahovlich, Tor., LW
1964	All-Stars 3, Toronto 2	Toronto	Sid Abel, Punch Imlach	Jean Beliveau, Mon., C
1965	All-Stars 5, Montreal 2	Montreal	Billy Reay, Toe Blake	Gordie Howe, Det., RW
1966	No game (see below)			
1967	Montreal 3, All-Stars 0	Montreal	Toe Blake, Sid Abel	Henri Richard, Mon., C
1968	Toronto 4, All-Stars 3	Toronto	Punch Imlach, Toe Blake	Bruce Gamble, Tor., G
1969	West 3, East 3	Montreal	Scotty Bowman, Toe Blake	Frank Mahovlich, Det., LW
1970	East 4, West 1	St. Louis	Claude Ruel, Scotty Bowman	Bobby Hull, Chi., LW
1971	West 2, East 1	Boston	Scotty Bowman, Harry Sinden	Bobby Hull, Chi., LW
1972	East 3, West 2	Minnesota	Al MacNeil, Billy Reay	Bobby Orr, Bos., D
1973	East 5, West 4	NY Rangers	Tom Johnson, Billy Reay	Greg Polis, Pit., LW
1974	West 6, East 4	Chicago	Billy Reay, Scotty Bowman	Garry Unger, St.L., C
1975	Wales 7, Campbell 1	Montreal	Bep Guidolin, Fred Shero	Syl Apps Jr., Pit., C
1976	Wales 7, Campbell 5	Philadelphia	Floyd Smith, Fred Shero	Peter Mahovlich, Mon., C
1977	Wales 4, Campbell 3	Vancouver	Scotty Bowman, Fred Shero	Rick Martin, Buf., LW
1978	Wales 3, Campbell 2 (OT)	Buffalo	Scotty Bowman, Fred Shero	Billy Smith, NYI, G
1979	No game (see below)			
1980	Wales 6, Campbell 3	Detroit	Scotty Bowman, Al Arbour	Reggie Leach, Phi., RW
1981	Campbell 4, Wales 1	Los Angeles	Pat Quinn, Scotty Bowman	Mike Liut, St.L., G
1982	Wales 4, Campbell 2	Washington	Al Arbour, Glen Sonmor	Mike Bossy, NYI, RW
1983	Campbell 9, Wales 3	NY Islanders	Roger Neilson, Al Arbour	Wayne Gretzky, Edm., C
1984	Wales 7, Campbell 6	New Jersey	Al Arbour, Glen Sather	Don Maloney, NYR, LW
1985	Wales 6, Campbell 4	Calgary	Al Arbour, Glen Sather	Mario Lemieux, Pit., C
1986	Wales 4, Campbell 3 (OT)	Hartford	Mike Keenan, Glen Sather	Grant Fuhr, Edm., G
1987	No game (see below)			
1988	Wales 6, Campbell 5 (OT)	St. Louis	Mike Keenan, Glen Sather	Mario Lemieux, Pit., C
1989	Campbell 9, Wales 5	Edmonton	Glen Sather, Terry O'Reilly	Wayne Gretzky, LA, C
1990	Wales 12, Campbell 7	Pittsburgh	Pat Burns, Terry Crisp	Mario Lemieux, Pit., C
1991	Campbell 11, Wales 5	Chicago	John Muckler, Mike Milbury	Vincent Damphousse, Tor., LW
1992	Campbell 10, Wales 6	Philadelphia	Bob Gainey, Scotty Bowman	Brett Hull, St.L., RW
1993	Wales 16, Campbell 6	Montreal	Scotty Bowman, Mike Keenan	Mike Gartner, NYR, RW
1994	East 9, West 8	NY Rangers	Jacques Demers, Barry Melrose	Mike Richter, NYR, G
1995	No game (see below)			
1996	East 5, West 4	Boston	Doug MacLean, Scotty Bowman	Ray Bourque, Bos., D
1997	East 11, West 7	San Jose	Doug MacLean, Ken Hitchcock	Mark Recchi, Mon., RW
1998	North America 8, World 7	Vancouver	Jacques Lemaire, Ken Hitchcock	Teemu Selanne, Ana., RW
1999	North America 8, World 6	Tampa	Ken Hitchcock, Lindy Ruff	Wayne Gretzky, NYR, C
2000	World 9, North America 4	Toronto	Scotty Bowman, Pat Quinn	Pavel Bure, Fla., RW
2001	North America 14, World 12	Denver	Joel Quenneville, Jacques Martin	Bill Guerin, Bos., RW

No All-Star Game: in 1966 (moved from start of season to mid-season); in 1979 (replaced by Challenge Cup series with USSR); in 1987 (replaced by Rendez-Vous '87 series with USSR); and in 1995 (cancelled when NHL lockout shortened season to 48 games).

NHL Franchise Origins

Here is what the current 30 teams in the National Hockey League have to show for the years they have put in as members of the NHL, the early National Hockey Association (NHA) and the more recent World Hockey Association (WHA). League titles and Stanley Cup championships are noted by year won. The Stanley Cup has automatically gone to the NHL champion since the 1926-27 season. Following the 1992-93 season, the NHL renamed the Clarence Campbell Conference the Western Conference, while the Prince of Wales Conference became the Eastern Conference.

Western Conference

	First Season	League Titles	Franchise Stops
Anaheim, Mighty Ducks of	1993-94 (NHL)	None	•Anaheim, CA (1993—)
Calgary Flames	1972-73 (NHL)	1 Cup (1989)	•Atlanta (1972-80)
			Calgary (1980—)
Chicago Blackhawks	1926-27 (NHL)	3 Cups (1934,38,61)	•Chicago (1926—)
Colorado Avalanche	1972-73 (WHA)	1 WHA (1977)	•Quebec City (1972-95)
		2 Cups (1996, 2001)	Denver (1995—)
Columbus Blue Jackets	2000-01 (NHL)	None	•Columbus, OH (2000—)
Dallas Stars	1967-68 (NHL)	1 Cup (1999)	•Bloomington, MN (1967-93)
			Dallas (1993—)
Detroit Red Wings	1926-27 (NHL)	9 Cups (1936-37,43,50,52,54-55,97,98)	•Detroit (1926—)
Edmonton Oilers	1973-74 (WHA)	5 Cups (1984-85,87-88,90)	•Edmonton (1972—)
Los Angeles Kings	1967-68 (NHL)	None	•Inglewood, CA (1967-99)
			Los Angeles (1999—)
Minnesota Wild	2000-01 (NHL)	None	•St. Paul, MN (2000—)
Nashville Predators	1998-99 (NHL)	None	•Nashville, TN (1998—)
Phoenix Coyotes	1972-73 (WHA)	3 WHA (1976, 78-79)	•Winnipeg (1972-96)
			Phoenix (1996—)
St. Louis Blues	1967-68 (NHL)	None	•St. Louis (1967—)
San Jose Sharks	1991-92 (NHL)	None	•San Francisco (1991-93)
			San Jose (1993—)
Vancouver Canucks	1970-71 (NHL)	None	•Vancouver (1970—)

Eastern Conference

	First Season	League Titles	Franchise Stops
Atlanta Thrashers	1999-00 (NHL)	None	•Atlanta (1999—)
Boston Bruins	1924-25 (NHL)	5 Cups (1929,39,41,70,72)	•Boston (1924—)
Buffalo Sabres	1970-71 (NHL)	None	•Buffalo (1970—)
Carolina Hurricanes	1972-73 (WHA)	1 WHA (1973)	•Boston (1972-74)
			W. Springfield, MA (1974-75)
			Hartford, CT (1975-78)
			Springfield, MA (1978-80)
			Hartford (1980-97)
			Greensboro (1997-99)
			Raleigh (1999—)
Florida Panthers	1993-94 (NHL)	None	•Miami (1993-98)
			Sunrise, FL (1998—)
Montreal Canadiens	1909-10 (NHA)	2 NHA (1916-17)	•Montreal (1909—)
		2 NHL (1924-25)	
		24 Cups (1916,24,30-31,44,46,53,56-60,65-66,68-69,71,73,76-79,86,93)	
New Jersey Devils	1974-75 (NHL)	2 Cups (1995, 2000)	•Kansas City (1974-76)
			Denver (1976-82)
			E. Rutherford, NJ (1982—)
New York Islanders	1972-73 (NHL)	4 Cups (1980-83)	•Uniondale, NY (1972—)
New York Rangers	1926-27 (NHL)	4 Cups (1928,33,40,94)	•New York (1926—)
Ottawa Senators	1992-93 (NHL)	None	•Ottawa (1992-1996)
			Kanata, Ont. (1996—)
Philadelphia Flyers	1967-68 (NHL)	2 Cups (1974-75)	•Philadelphia (1967—)
Pittsburgh Penguins	1967-68 (NHL)	2 Cups (1991-92)	•Pittsburgh (1967—)
Tampa Bay Lightning	1992-93 (NHL)	None	•Tampa, FL (1992-93)
			St. Petersburg, FL (1993-96)
			Tampa, FL (1996—)
Toronto Maple Leafs	1916-17 (NHA)	2 NHL (1918,22)	•Toronto (1916—)
		13 Cups (1918,22,32,42,45,47-49,51,62-64,67)	
Washington Capitals	1974-75 (NHL)	None	•Landover, MD (1974-97)
			Washington, D.C. (1997—)

Note: The Hartford Civic Center roof collapsed after a snowstorm in January 1978, forcing the Whalers to move their home games to Springfield, Mass., for two years.

The Growth of the NHL

Of the four franchises that comprised the National Hockey League (NHL) at the start of the 1917-18 season, only two remain—the Montreal Canadiens and the Toronto Maple Leafs (originally the Toronto Arenas). From 1919-26, eight new teams joined the league, but only four—the Boston Bruins, Chicago Blackhawks (originally Black Hawks), Detroit Red Wings (originally Cougars) and New York Rangers—survived.

It was 41 years before the NHL expanded again, doubling in size for the 1967-68 season with new teams in Los Angeles, Minnesota, Oakland, Philadelphia, Pittsburgh and St. Louis. The league had 16 clubs by the start of the 1972-73 season, but it also had a rival in the **World Hockey Association**, which debuted that year with 12 teams.

The NHL added two more teams in 1974 and merged the struggling Cleveland Barons (originally the Oakland Seals) and Minnesota North Stars in 1978, before absorbing four WHA clubs—the Edmonton Oilers, Hartford Whalers, Quebec Nordiques and Winnipeg Jets—in time for the 1979-80 season. Seven expansion teams joined the league in the 1990s, with two more being added in 2000 to make it an even 30.

Expansion/Merger Timetable
For teams currently in NHL.

1919—Quebec Bulldogs finally take the ice after sitting out NHL's first two seasons; **1924**—Boston Bruins and Montreal Maroons; **1925**—New York Americans and Pittsburgh Pirates; **1926**—Chicago Black Hawks (now Blackhawks), Detroit Cougars (now Red Wings) and New York Rangers; **1932**—Ottawa Senators return after sitting out 1931-32 season.

1967—California Seals (later Cleveland Barons), Los Angeles Kings, Minnesota North Stars, Philadelphia Flyers, Pittsburgh Penguins and St. Louis Blues.

1970—Buffalo Sabres and Vancouver Canucks; **1972**—Atlanta Flames (now Calgary) and New York Islanders; **1974**—Kansas City Scouts (now New Jersey Devils) and Washington Capitals; **1978**—Cleveland Barons merge with Minnesota North Stars (now Dallas Stars) and team remains in Minnesota; **1979**—added WHA's Edmonton Oilers, Hartford Whalers, Quebec Nordiques (now Colorado Avalanche) and Winnipeg Jets (now Phoenix Coyotes).

1991—San Jose Sharks; **1992**—Ottawa Senators and Tampa Bay Lightning; **1993**—Mighty Ducks of Anaheim and Florida Panthers; **1998**—Nashville Predators; **1999**—Atlanta Thrashers.

2000—Columbus Blue Jackets and Minnesota Wild.

City and Nickname Changes

1919—Toronto Arenas renamed St. Pats; **1920**—Quebec moves to Hamilton and becomes Tigers (will fold in 1925); **1926**—Toronto St. Pats renamed Maple Leafs; **1929**—Detroit Cougars renamed Falcons.

1930—Pittsburgh Pirates move to Philadelphia and become Quakers (will fold in 1931); **1932**—Detroit Falcons renamed Red Wings; **1934**—Ottawa Senators move to St. Louis and become Eagles (will fold in 1935); **1941**—New York Americans renamed Brooklyn Americans (will fold in 1942).

1967—California Seals renamed Oakland Seals three months into first season; **1970**—Oakland Seals renamed California Golden Seals; **1975**—California Golden Seals renamed Seals; **1976**—California Seals move to Cleveland and become Barons, while Kansas City Scouts move to Denver and become Colorado Rockies; **1978**—Cleveland Barons merge with Minnesota North Stars and become Minnesota North Stars.

1980—Atlanta Flames move to Calgary; **1982**—Colorado Rockies move to East Rutherford, N.J., and become New Jersey Devils; **1986**—Chicago Black Hawks renamed Blackhawks; **1993**—Minnesota North Stars move to Dallas and become Stars. **1995**—Quebec Nordiques move to Denver and become Colorado Avalanche; **1996**—Winnipeg Jets move to Phoenix and become Coyotes; **1997**—Hartford Whalers move to Greensboro and become Carolina Hurricanes; **1999**—Carolina Hurricanes move to Raleigh.

Defunct NHL Teams
Teams that once played in the NHL, but no longer exist.

Brooklyn—Americans (1941-42, formerly NY Americans from 1925-41); **Cleveland**—Barons (1976-78, originally California-Oakland Seals from 1967-76); **Hamilton (Ont.)**—Tigers (1920-25, originally Quebec Bulldogs from 1919-20); **Montreal**—Maroons (1924-38) and Wanderers (1917-18); **New York**—Americans (1925-41, later Brooklyn Americans for 1941-42); **Oakland**—Seals (1967-76, also known as California Seals and Golden Seals and later Cleveland Barons from 1976-78); **Ottawa**—Senators (1917-31 and 1932-34, later St. Louis Eagles for 1934-35); **Philadelphia**—Quakers (1930-31, originally Pittsburgh Pirates from 1925-30); **Pittsburgh**—Pirates (1925-30, later Philadelphia Quakers for 1930-31); **Quebec**—Bulldogs (1919-20, later Hamilton Tigers from 1920-25); **St. Louis**—Eagles (1934-35), originally Ottawa Senators (1917-31 and 1932-34).

WHA Teams (1972-79)

Baltimore—Blades (1975); **Birmingham**—Bulls (1976-78); **Calgary**—Cowboys (1975-77); **Chicago**—Cougars (1972-75); **Cincinnati**—Stingers (1975-79); **Cleveland**—Crusaders (1972-76, moved to Minnesota); **Denver**—Spurs (1975-76, moved to Ottawa); **Edmonton**—Oilers (1972-79, originally called Alberta Oilers in 1972-73); **Houston**—Aeros (1972-78); **Indianapolis**—Racers (1974-78).

Los Angeles—Sharks (1972-74, moved to Michigan); **Michigan**—Stags (1974-75, moved to Baltimore); **Minnesota**—Fighting Saints (1972-76) and New Fighting Saints (1976-77); **New England**—Whalers (1972-79, played in Boston from 1972-74, West Springfield, MA from 1974-75, Hartford from 1975-78 and Springfield, MA in 1979); **New Jersey**—Knights (1973-74, moved to San Diego); **New York**—Raiders (1972-73, renamed Golden Blades in 1973, moved to New Jersey).

Ottawa—Nationals (1972-73, moved to Toronto) and Civics (1976); **Philadelphia**—Blazers (1972-73, moved to Vancouver); **Phoenix**—Roadrunners (1974-77); **Quebec**—Nordiques (1972-79); **San Diego**—Mariners (1974-77); **Toronto**—Toros (1973-76, moved to Birmingham, AL); **Vancouver**—Blazers (1973-75, moved to Calgary); **Winnipeg**—Jets (1972-79).

Annual NHL Leaders
Art Ross Trophy (Scoring)

Given to the player who leads the league in points scored and named after the former Boston Bruins general manager-coach. First presented in 1948, names of prior leading scorers have been added retroactively. A tie for the scoring championship is broken three ways: 1. total goals; 2. fewest games played; 3. first goal scored.

Multiple Winners: Wayne Gretzky (10); Gordie Howe and Mario Lemieux (6); Phil Esposito and Jaromir Jagr (5); Stan Mikita (4); Bobby Hull and Guy Lafleur (3); Max Bentley, Charlie Conacher, Bill Cook, Babe Dye, Bernie Geoffrion, Elmer Lach, Newsy Lalonde, Joe Malone, Dickie Moore, Howie Morenz, Bobby Orr and Sweeney Schriner (2).

Year		Gm	G	A	Pts	Year		Gm	G	A	Pts
1918	Joe Malone, Mon	20	44	0	44	1960	Bobby Hull, Chi	70	39	42	81
1919	Newsy Lalonde, Mon	17	23	9	32	1961	Bernie Geoffrion, Mon	64	50	45	95
						1962	Bobby Hull, Chi	70	50	34	84
1920	Joe Malone, Que	24	39	6	45	1963	Gordie Howe, Det	70	38	48	86
1921	Newsy Lalonde, Mon	24	33	8	41	1964	Stan Mikita, Chi	70	39	50	89
1922	Punch Broadbent, Ott	24	32	14	46	1965	Stan Mikita, Chi	70	28	59	87
1923	Babe Dye, Tor	22	26	11	37	1966	Bobby Hull, Chi	65	54	43	97
1924	Cy Denneny, Ott	21	22	1	23	1967	Stan Mikita, Chi	70	35	62	97
1925	Babe Dye, Tor	29	38	6	44	1968	Stan Mikita, Chi	72	40	47	87
1926	Nels Stewart, Maroons	36	34	8	42	1969	Phil Esposito, Bos	74	49	77	126
1927	Bill Cook, NYR	44	33	4	37						
1928	Howie Morenz, Mon	43	33	18	51	1970	Bobby Orr, Bos	76	33	87	120
1929	Ace Bailey, Tor	44	22	10	32	1971	Phil Esposito, Bos	78	76	76	152
						1972	Phil Esposito, Bos	76	66	67	133
1930	Cooney Weiland, Bos	44	43	30	73	1973	Phil Esposito, Bos	78	55	75	130
1931	Howie Morenz, Mon	39	28	23	51	1974	Phil Esposito, Bos	78	68	77	145
1932	Busher Jackson, Tor	48	28	25	53	1975	Bobby Orr, Bos	80	46	89	135
1933	Bill Cook, NYR	48	28	22	50	1976	Guy Lafleur, Mon	80	56	69	125
1934	Charlie Conacher, Tor	42	32	20	52	1977	Guy Lafleur, Mon	80	56	80	136
1935	Charlie Conacher, Tor	47	36	21	57	1978	Guy Lafleur, Mon	79	60	72	132
1936	Sweeney Schriner, NYA	48	19	26	45	1979	Bryan Trottier, NYI	76	47	87	134
1937	Sweeney Schriner, NYA	48	21	25	46						
1938	Gordie Drillon, Tor	48	26	26	52	1980	Marcel Dionne, LA	80	53	84	137
1939	Toe Blake, Mon	48	24	23	47	1981	Wayne Gretzky, Edm	80	55	109	164
						1982	Wayne Gretzky, Edm	80	92	120	212
1940	Milt Schmidt, Bos	48	22	30	52	1983	Wayne Gretzky, Edm	80	71	125	196
1941	Bill Cowley, Bos	46	17	45	62	1984	Wayne Gretzky, Edm	74	87	118	205
1942	Bryan Hextall, NYR	48	24	32	56	1985	Wayne Gretzky, Edm	80	73	135	208
1943	Doug Bentley, Chi	50	33	40	73	1986	Wayne Gretzky, Edm	80	52	163	215
1944	Herbie Cain, Bos	48	36	46	82	1987	Wayne Gretzky, Edm	79	62	121	183
1945	Elmer Lach, Mon	50	26	54	80	1988	Mario Lemieux, Pit	77	70	98	168
1946	Max Bentley, Chi	47	31	30	61	1989	Mario Lemieux, Pit	76	85	114	199
1947	Max Bentley, Chi	60	29	43	72						
1948	Elmer Lach, Mon	60	30	31	61	1990	Wayne Gretzky, LA	73	40	102	142
1949	Roy Conacher, Chi	60	26	42	68	1991	Wayne Gretzky, LA	78	41	122	163
						1992	Mario Lemieux, Pit	64	44	87	131
1950	Ted Lindsay, Det	69	23	55	78	1993	Mario Lemieux, Pit	60	69	91	160
1951	Gordie Howe, Det	70	43	43	86	1994	Wayne Gretzky, LA	81	38	92	130
1952	Gordie Howe, Det	70	47	39	86	1995	Jaromir Jagr, Pit	48	32	38	70
1953	Gordie Howe, Det	70	49	46	95	1996	Mario Lemieux, Pit	70	69	92	161
1954	Gordie Howe, Det	70	33	48	81	1997	Mario Lemieux, Pit	76	50	72	122
1955	Bernie Geoffrion, Mon	70	38	37	75	1998	Jaromir Jagr, Pit	77	35	67	102
1956	Jean Beliveau, Mon	70	47	41	88	1999	Jaromir Jagr, Pit	81	44	83	127
1957	Gordie Howe, Det	70	44	45	89						
1958	Dickie Moore, Mon	70	36	48	84	2000	Jaromir Jagr, Pit	63	42	54	96
1959	Dickie Moore, Mon	70	41	55	96	2001	Jaromir Jagr, Pit	81	52	69	121

Note: The three times players have tied for total points in one season the player with more goals has won the trophy. In 1961-62, Hull outscored Andy Bathgate of NY Rangers, 50 goals to 28. In 1979-80, Dionne outscored Wayne Gretzky of Edmonton, 53-51. In 1995, Jagr outscored Eric Lindros of Philadelphia, 32-29.

Goals

Multiple Winners: Bobby Hull (7); Phil Esposito (6); Charlie Conacher, Wayne Gretzky, Gordie Howe and Maurice Richard (5); Bill Cooke, Babe Dye, Brett Hull, Mario Lemieux, Pavel Bure and Teemu Selanne (3); Jean Beliveau, Doug Bentley, Peter Bondra, Mike Bossy, Bernie Geoffrion, Bryan Hextall, Joe Malone and Nels Stewart (2).

Year		No	Year		No	Year		No
1918	Joe Malone, Mon	44	1928	Howie Morenz, Mon	33	1937	Larry Aurie, Det	23
1919	Odie Cleghorn, Mon	23	1929	Ace Bailey, Tor	22		& Nels Stewart, Bos-NYA	23
	& Newsy Lalonde, Mon	23				1938	Gordie Drillon, Tor	26
			1930	Cooney Weiland, Bos	43	1939	Roy Conacher, Bos	26
1920	Joe Malone, Que	39	1931	Charlie Conacher, Tor	31			
1921	Babe Dye, Ham-Tor	35	1932	Charlie Conacher, Tor	34	1940	Bryan Hextall, NYR	24
1922	Punch Broadbent, Ott	32		& Bill Cook, NYR	34	1941	Bryan Hextall, NYR	26
1923	Babe Dye, Tor	26	1933	Bill Cook, NYR	28	1942	Lynn Patrick, NYR	32
1924	Cy Denneny, Ott	22	1934	Charlie Conacher, Tor	32	1943	Doug Bentley, Chi	33
1925	Babe Dye, Tor	38	1935	Charlie Conacher, Tor	36	1944	Doug Bentley, Chi	38
1926	Nels Stewart, Maroons	34	1936	Charlie Conacher, Tor	23	1945	Maurice Richard, Mon	50
1927	Bill Cook, NYR	33		& Bill Thoms, Tor	23	1946	Gaye Stewart, Tor	37

Annual NHL Leaders (Cont.)

Year	No	Year	No	Year	No
1947 Maurice Richard, Mon	.45	1966 Bobby Hull, Chi	.54	1985 Wayne Gretzky, Edm	.73
1948 Ted Lindsay, Det	.33	1967 Bobby Hull, Chi	.52	1986 Jari Kurri, Edm	.68
1949 Sid Abel, Det	.28	1968 Bobby Hull, Chi	.44	1987 Wayne Gretzky, Edm	.62
1950 Maurice Richard, Mon	.43	1969 Bobby Hull, Chi	.58	1988 Mario Lemieux, Pit	.70
1951 Gordie Howe, Det	.43	1970 Phil Esposito, Bos	.43	1989 Mario Lemieux, Pit	.85
1952 Gordie Howe, Det	.47	1971 Phil Esposito, Bos	.76		
1953 Gordie Howe, Det	.49	1972 Phil Esposito, Bos	.66	1990 Brett Hull, St.L	.72
1954 Maurice Richard, Mon	.37	1973 Phil Esposito, Bos	.55	1991 Brett Hull, St.L	.86
1955 Bernie Geoffrion, Mon	.38	1974 Phil Esposito, Bos	.68	1992 Brett Hull, St.L	.70
& Maurice Richard, Mon	.38	1975 Phil Esposito, Bos	.61	1993 Alexander Mogilny, Buf	.76
1956 Jean Beliveau, Mon	.47	1976 Reggie Leach, Phi	.61	& Teemu Selanne, Win	.76
1957 Gordie Howe, Det	.44	1977 Steve Shutt, Mon	.60	1994 Pavel Bure, Van	.60
1958 Dickie Moore, Mon	.36	1978 Guy Lafleur, Mon	.60	1995 Peter Bondra, Wash	.34
1959 Jean Beliveau, Mon	.45	1979 Mike Bossy, NYI	.69	1996 Mario Lemieux, Pit	.69
1960 Bronco Horvath, Bos	.39	1980 Danny Gare, Buf	.56	1997 Keith Tkachuk, Pho	.52
& Bobby Hull, Chi	.39	Charlie Simmer, LA	.56	1998 Teemu Selanne, Ana	.52
1961 Bernie Geoffrion, Mon	.50	& Blaine Stoughton, Hart	.56	& Peter Bondra, Wash	.52
1962 Bobby Hull, Chi	.50	1981 Mike Bossy, NYI	.68	1999 Teemu Selanne, Ana	.47
1963 Gordie Howe, Det	.38	1982 Wayne Gretzky, Edm	.92		
1964 Bobby Hull, Chi	.43	1983 Wayne Gretzky, Edm	.71	2000 Pavel Bure, Fla	.58
1965 Norm Ullman, Tor	.42	1984 Wayne Gretzky, Edm	.87	2001 Pavel Bure, Fla	.59

Assists

Multiple Winners: Wayne Gretzky (16); Bobby Orr (5); Frank Boucher, Bill Cowley, Phil Esposito, Gordie Howe, Jaromir Jagr, Elmer Lach, Mario Lemieux, Stan Mikita and Joe Primeau (3); Syl Apps, Andy Bathgate, Jean Beliveau, Doug Bentley, Art Chapman, Bobby Clarke, Ron Francis, Ted Lindsay, Adam Oates, Bert Olmstead, Henri Richard and Bryan Trottier (2).

Year	No	Year	No	Year	No
1918 No official records kept.		1948 Doug Bentley, Chi	.37	1977 Guy Lafleur, Mon	.80
1919 Newsy Lalonde, Mon	.9	1949 Doug Bentley, Chi	.43	1978 Bryan Trottier, NYI	.77
1920 Corbett Denneny, Tor	.12	1950 Ted Lindsay, Det	.55	1979 Bryan Trottier, NYI	.87
1921 Louis Berlinquette, Mon	.9	1951 Gordie Howe, Det	.43	1980 Wayne Gretzky, Edm	.86
Harry Cameron, Tor	.9	& Teeder Kennedy, Tor	.43	1981 Wayne Gretzky, Edm	.109
& Joe Matte, Ham	.9	1952 Elmer Lach, Mon	.50	1982 Wayne Gretzky, Edm	.120
1922 Punch Broadbent, Ott	.14	1953 Gordie Howe, Det	.46	1983 Wayne Gretzky, Edm	.125
& Leo Reise, Ham	.14	1954 Gordie Howe, Det	.48	1984 Wayne Gretzky, Edm	.118
1923 Ed Bouchard, Ham	.12	1955 Bert Olmstead, Mon	.48	1985 Wayne Gretzky, Edm	.135
1924 King Clancy, Ott	.8	1956 Bert Olmstead, Mon	.56	1986 Wayne Gretzky, Edm	.163
1925 Cy Denneny, Ott	.15	1957 Ted Lindsay, Det	.55	1987 Wayne Gretzky, Edm	.121
1926 Frank Nighbor, Ott	.13	1958 Henri Richard, Mon	.52	1988 Wayne Gretzky, Edm	.109
1927 Dick Irvin, Chi	.18	1959 Dickie Moore, Mon	.55	1989 Wayne Gretzky, LA	.114
1928 Howie Morenz, Mon	.18	1960 Don McKenney, Bos	.49	& Mario Lemieux, Pit	.114
1929 Frank Boucher, NYR	.16	1961 Jean Beliveau, Mon	.58	1990 Wayne Gretzky, LA	.102
1930 Frank Boucher, NYR	.36	1962 Andy Bathgate, NYR	.56	1991 Wayne Gretzky, LA	.122
1931 Joe Primeau, Tor	.32	1963 Henri Richard, Mon	.50	1992 Wayne Gretzky, LA	.90
1932 Joe Primeau, Tor	.37	1964 Andy Bathgate, NYR-Tor	.58	1993 Adam Oates, Bos	.97
1933 Frank Boucher, NYR	.28	1965 Stan Mikita, Chi	.59	1994 Wayne Gretzky, LA	.92
1934 Joe Primeau, Tor	.32	1966 Jean Beliveau, Mon	.48	1995 Ron Francis, Pit	.48
1935 Art Chapman, NYA	.34	Stan Mikita, Chi	.48	1996 Ron Francis, Pit	.92
1936 Art Chapman, NYA	.28	& Bobby Rousseau, Mon	.48	& Mario Lemieux, Pit	.92
1937 Syl Apps, Tor	.29	1967 Stan Mikita, Chi	.62	1997 Mario Lemieux, Pit	.72
1938 Syl Apps, Tor	.29	1968 Phil Esposito, Bos	.49	& Wayne Gretzky, NYR	.72
1939 Bill Cowley, Bos	.34	1969 Phil Esposito, Bos	.77	1998 Jaromir Jagr, Pit	.67
1940 Milt Schmidt, Bos	.30	1970 Bobby Orr, Bos	.87	& Wayne Gretzky, NYR	.67
1941 Bill Cowley, Bos	.45	1971 Bobby Orr, Bos	.102	1999 Jaromir Jagr, Pit	.83
1942 Phil Watson, NYR	.37	1972 Bobby Orr, Bos	.80	2000 Mark Recchi, Phi	.63
1943 Bill Cowley, Bos	.45	1973 Phil Esposito, Bos	.75	2001 Jaromir Jagr, Pit	.69
1944 Clint Smith, Chi	.49	1974 Bobby Orr, Bos	.90	& Adam Oates, Wash	.69
1945 Elmer Lach, Mon	.54	1975 Bobby Clarke, Phi	.89		
1946 Elmer Lach, Mon	.34	& Bobby Orr, Bos	.89		
1947 Billy Taylor, Det	.46	1976 Bobby Clarke, Phi	.89		

Goals Against Average

Average determined by games played through 1942-43 season and by minutes played since then. Minimum of 15 games from 1917-18 season through 1925-26; minimum of 25 games since 1926-27 season. Not to be confused with the Vezina Trophy. Goaltenders who posted the season's lowest goals against average, but did not win the Vezina are in **bold** type.

Multiple Winners: Jacques Plante (9); Clint Benedict and Bill Durnan (6); Johnny Bower, Ken Dryden and Tiny Thompson (4); Patrick Roy and Georges Vezina (3); Ed Belfour, Frankie Brimsek, Turk Broda, George Hainsworth, Dominik Hasek, Harry Lumley, Bernie Parent, Pete Peeters and Terry Sawchuk (2).

Year	Player	GAA	Year	Player	GAA	Year	Player	GAA
1918	Georges Vezina, Mon	3.82	1947	Bill Durnan, Mon	2.30	1975	Bernie Parent, Phi	2.03
1919	Clint Benedict, Ott	2.94	1948	Turk Broda, Tor	2.38	1976	Ken Dryden, Mon	2.03
1920	Clint Benedict, Ott	2.67	1949	Bill Durnan, Mon	2.10	1977	Bunny Larocque, Mon	2.09
1921	Clint Benedict, Ott	3.13	1950	Bill Durnan, Mon	2.20	1978	Ken Dryden, Mon	2.05
1922	Clint Benedict, Ott	3.50				1979	Ken Dryden, Mon	2.30
1923	Clint Benedict, Ott	2.25	1951	Al Rollins, Tor	1.77			
1924	Georges Vezina, Mon	2.00	1952	Terry Sawchuk, Det	1.90	1980	Bob Sauve, Buf	2.36
1925	Georges Vezina, Mon	1.87	1953	Terry Sawchuk, Det	1.90	1981	Richard Sevigny, Mon	2.40
1926	Alex Connell, Ott	1.17	1954	Harry Lumley, Tor	1.86	1982	**Denis Herron**, Mon	2.64
1927	**Clint Benedict,** Mon-M	1.51	1955	**Harry Lumley,** Tor	1.94	1983	Pete Peeters, Bos	2.36
1928	Geo. Hainsworth, Mon	1.09	1956	Jacques Plante, Mon	1.86	1984	**Pat Riggin,** Wash	2.66
1929	Geo. Hainsworth, Mon	0.98	1957	Jacques Plante, Mon	2.02	1985	**Tom Barrasso,** Buf	2.66
1930	Tiny Thompson, Bos	2.23	1958	Jacques Plante, Mon	2.11	1986	**Bob Froese,** Phi	2.55
1931	Roy Worters, NYA	1.68	1959	Jacques Plante, Mon	2.16	1987	**Brian Hayward,** Mon	2.81
1932	Chuck Gardiner, Chi	1.92	1960	Jacques Plante, Mon	2.54	1988	**Pete Peeters,** Wash	2.78
1933	Tiny Thompson, Bos	1.83	1961	Johnny Bower, Tor	2.50	1989	Patrick Roy, Mon	2.47
1934	**Wilf Cude,** Det-Mon	1.57	1962	Jacques Plante, Mon	2.37	1990	**Mike Liut,** Hart-Wash	2.53
1935	Lorne Chabot, Chi	1.83	1963	**Jacques Plante,** Mon	2.49	1991	Ed Belfour, Chi	2.47
1936	Tiny Thompson, Bos	1.71	1964	**Johnny Bower,** Tor	2.11	1992	Patrick Roy, Mon	2.36
1937	Norm Smith, Det	2.13	1965	Johnny Bower, Tor	2.38	1993	**Felix Potvin,** Tor	2.50
1938	Tiny Thompson, Bos	1.85	1966	**Johnny Bower,** Tor	2.25	1994	Dominik Hasek, Buf	1.95
1939	Frankie Brimsek, Bos	1.58	1967	Glenn Hall, Chi	2.38	1995	Dominik Hasek, Buf	2.11
1940	Dave Kerr, NYR	1.60	1968	Gump Worsley, Mon	1.98	1996	**Ron Hextall,** Phi	2.17
1941	Turk Broda, Tor	2.06	1969	**Jacques Plante,** St.L	1.96	1997	**Martin Brodeur,** NJ	1.88
1942	Frankie Brimsek, Mon	2.45	1970	**Ernie Wakely,** St.L	2.11	1998	**Ed Belfour,** Dal	1.88
1943	John Mowers, Det	2.47	1971	**Jacques Plante,** Tor	1.88	1999	**Ron Tugnutt,** Ott	1.79
1944	Bill Durnan, Mon	2.18	1972	Tony Esposito, Chi	1.77			
1945	Bill Durnan, Mon	2.42	1973	Ken Dryden, Mon	2.26	2000	**Brian Boucher**, Phi	1.91
1946	Bill Durnan, Mon	2.60	1974	Bernie Parent, Phi	1.89	2001	**Marty Turco**, Dal	1.90

Penalty Minutes

Multiple Winners: Red Horner (8); Gus Mortson and Dave Schultz (4); Bert Corbeau, Lou Fontinato and Tiger Williams (3); Matthew Barnaby, Billy Boucher, Carl Brewer, Red Dutton, Pat Egan, Bill Ezinicki, Joe Hall, Tim Hunter, Keith Magnuson, Chris Nilan, Jimmy Orlando and Rob Ray (2).

Year	Player	Min	Year	Player	Min	Year	Player	Min
1918	Joe Hall, Mon	60	1946	Jack Stewart, Det	73	1974	Dave Schultz, Phi	348
1919	Joe Hall, Mon	85	1947	Gus Mortson, Tor	133	1975	Dave Schultz, Phi	472
1920	Cully Wilson, Tor	79	1948	Bill Barilko, Tor	147	1976	Steve Durbano, Pit-KC	370
1921	Bert Corbeau, Mon	86	1949	Bill Ezinicki, Tor	145	1977	Tiger Williams, Tor	338
1922	Sprague Cleghorn, Mon	63	1950	Bill Ezinicki, Tor	144	1978	Dave Schultz, LA-Pit	405
1923	Billy Boucher, Mon	52	1951	Gus Mortson, Tor	142	1979	Tiger Williams, Tor	298
1924	Bert Corbeau, Tor	55	1952	Gus Kyle, Bos	127	1980	Jimmy Mann, Win	287
1925	Billy Boucher, Mon	92	1953	Maurice Richard, Mon	112	1981	Tiger Williams, Van	343
1926	Bert Corbeau, Tor	121	1954	Gus Mortson, Chi	132	1982	Paul Baxter, Pit	409
1927	Nels Stewart, Mon-M	133	1955	Fern Flaman, Bos	150	1983	Randy Holt, Wash	275
1928	Eddie Shore, Bos	165	1956	Lou Fontinato, NYR	202	1984	Chris Nilan, Mon	338
1929	Red Dutton, Mon-M	139	1957	Gus Mortson, Chi	147	1985	Chris Nilan, Mon	358
1930	Joe Lamb, Ott	119	1958	Lou Fontinato, NYR	152	1986	Joey Kocur, Det	377
1931	Harvey Rockburn, Det	118	1959	Ted Lindsay, Chi	184	1987	Tim Hunter, Calg	361
1932	Red Dutton, NYA	107	1960	Carl Brewer, Tor	150	1988	Bob Probert, Det	398
1933	Red Horner, Tor	144	1961	Pierre Pilote, Chi	165	1989	Tim Hunter, Calg	375
1934	Red Horner, Tor	146	1962	Lou Fontinato, Mon	167	1990	Basil McRae, Min	351
1935	Red Horner, Tor	125	1963	Howie Young, Det	273	1991	Rob Ray, Buf	350
1936	Red Horner, Tor	167	1964	Vic Hadfield, NYR	151	1992	Mike Peluso, Chi	408
1937	Red Horner, Tor	124	1965	Carl Brewer, Tor	177	1993	Mike McSorley, LA	399
1938	Red Horner, Tor	82	1966	Reg Fleming, Bos-NYR	166	1994	Tie Domi, Win	347
1939	Red Horner, Tor	85	1967	John Ferguson, Mon	177	1995	Enrico Ciccone, TB	225
1940	Red Horner, Tor	87	1968	Barclay Plager, St.L	153	1996	Matthew Barnaby, Buf	335
1941	Jimmy Orlando, Det	99	1969	Forbes Kennedy, Phi-Tor	219	1997	Gino Odjick, Van	371
1942	Pat Egan, NYA	124	1970	Keith Magnuson, Chi	213	1998	Donald Brashear, Van	372
1943	Jimmy Orlando, Det	99	1971	Keith Magnuson, Chi	291	1999	Rob Ray, Buf	261
1944	Mike McMahon, Mon	98	1972	Bryan Watson, Pit	212	2000	Denny Lambert, Atl	219
1945	Pat Egan, Bos	86	1973	Dave Schultz, Phi	259	2001	Matthew Barnaby, Pit-TB	265

All-Time NHL Regular Season Leaders

Through 2001 regular season.

CAREER

Players active during 2001 season in **bold** type.

Points

		Yrs	Gm	G	A	Pts
1	Wayne Gretzky	.20	1487	894	1963	2857
2	Gordie Howe	.26	1767	801	1049	1850
3	**Mark Messier**	.22	1561	651	1130	1781
4	Marcel Dionne	.18	1348	731	1040	1771
5	**Ron Francis**	.20	1489	487	1137	1624
6	**Steve Yzerman**	.18	1310	645	969	1614
7	Phil Esposito	.18	1282	717	873	1590
8	**Ray Bourque**	.22	1612	410	1169	1579
9	**Mario Lemieux**	.13	788	648	922	1570
10	**Paul Coffey**	.21	1409	396	1135	1531
11	Stan Mikita	.22	1394	541	926	1467
12	Bryan Trottier	.18	1279	524	901	1425
13	Dale Hawerchuk	.16	1188	518	891	1409
14	Jari Kurri	.17	1251	601	797	1398
15	John Bucyk	.23	1540	556	813	1369
16	Guy Lafleur	.17	1126	560	793	1353
17	**Doug Gilmour**	.18	1342	429	914	1343
18	Denis Savard	.17	1196	473	865	1338
19	Mike Gartner	.19	1432	708	627	1335
20	Gilbert Perreault	.17	1191	512	814	1326
21	Alex Delvecchio	.24	1549	456	825	1281
22	**Adam Oates**	.16	1130	316	963	1279
23	Jean Ratelle	.21	1281	491	776	1267
24	Peter Stastny	.15	977	450	789	1239
25	**Luc Robitaille**	.15	1124	590	648	1238
26	Norm Ullman	.20	1410	490	739	1229
27	Jean Beliveau	.20	1125	507	712	1219
28	**Larry Murphy**	.21	1615	287	929	1216
29	Bobby Clarke	.15	1144	358	852	1210
30	**Dave Andreychuk**	.19	1361	572	637	1209
	Bernie Nicholls	.18	1127	475	734	1209

Goals

		Yrs	Gm	No
1	Wayne Gretzky	.20	1487	894
2	Gordie Howe	.26	1767	801
3	Marcel Dionne	.18	1348	731
4	Phil Esposito	.18	1282	717
5	Mike Gartner	.19	1432	708
6	**Mark Messier**	.22	1561	651
7	**Brett Hull**	.16	1019	649
8	**Mario Lemieux**	.13	788	648
9	**Steve Yzerman**	.18	1310	645
10	Bobby Hull	.16	1063	610
11	Dino Ciccarelli	.19	1232	608
12	Jari Kurri	.17	1251	601
13	**Luc Robitaille**	.15	1124	590
14	Mike Bossy	.10	752	573
15	**Dave Andreychuk**	.19	1361	572
16	Guy Lafleur	.17	1126	560
17	John Bucyk	.23	1540	556
18	Michel Goulet	.15	1089	548
19	Maurice Richard	.18	978	544
20	Stan Mikita	.22	1394	541
21	Frank Mahovlich	.18	1181	533
22	Bryan Trottier	.18	1279	524
23	Dale Hawerchuk	.16	1188	518
24	**Pat Verbeek**	.19	1360	515
25	Gilbert Perreault	.17	1191	512
26	Jean Beliveau	.20	1125	507
27	Joe Mullen	.17	1062	502
28	Lanny McDonald	.16	1111	500
29	Glenn Anderson	.16	1128	498
30	Jean Ratelle	.21	1281	491

Assists

		Yrs	Gm	No
1	Wayne Gretzky	.20	1487	1963
2	**Ray Bourque**	.22	1612	1169
3	**Ron Francis**	.20	1489	1137
4	**Paul Coffey**	.21	1409	1135
5	**Mark Messier**	.22	1561	1130
6	Gordie Howe	.26	1767	1049
7	Marcel Dionne	.18	1348	1040
8	**Steve Yzerman**	.18	1310	969
9	**Adam Oates**	.16	1130	963
10	**Larry Murphy**	.21	1615	929
11	Stan Mikita	.22	1394	926
12	**Mario Lemieux**	.13	788	922
13	**Doug Gilmour**	.18	1342	914
14	Bryan Trottier	.18	1279	901
15	Dale Hawerchuk	.16	1188	891
16	Phil Esposito	.18	1281	873
17	Denis Savard	.17	1196	865
18	Bobby Clarke	.15	1144	852
19	**Phil Housley**	.19	1357	847
20	**Al MacInnis**	.20	1262	845

Penalty Minutes

		Yrs	Gm	Min
1	Tiger Williams	.14	962	3966
2	Dale Hunter	.19	1407	3565
3	Marty McSorley	.17	961	3381
4	Tim Hunter	.16	815	3146
5	**Bob Probert**	.15	874	3124
6	Chris Nilan	.13	688	3043
7	**Rick Tocchet**	.17	1130	2946
8	**Rob Ray**	.12	777	2897
9	**Craig Berube**	.15	933	2885
10	**Tie Domi**	.12	710	2870
11	**Pat Verbeek**	.19	1360	2833
12	Dave Manson	.15	1056	2759
13	**Scott Stevens**	.19	1434	2678
14	Willi Plett	.12	834	2572
15	Joey Kocur	.15	820	2519

NHL-WHA Top 15

All-time regular season scoring leaders, including games played in World Hockey Association (1972-79). NHL players with WHA experience are listed in CAPITAL letters. Players active during 2001 are in **bold** type.

Points

		Yrs	G	A	Pts
1	WAYNE GRETZKY	.21	940	2027	2967
2	GORDIE HOWE	.32	975	1383	2358
3	BOBBY HULL	.23	913	895	1808
4	**MARK MESSIER**	.23	652	1140	1792
5	Marcel Dionne	.18	731	1040	1771
6	**Ron Francis**	.20	487	1137	1624
7	**Steve Yzerman**	.18	645	969	1614
8	Phil Esposito	.18	717	873	1590
9	**Ray Bourque**	.22	410	1169	1579
10	**Mario Lemieux**	.13	648	922	1570
11	**Paul Coffey**	.21	396	1135	1531
12	Stan Mikita	.22	541	926	1467
13	Bryan Trottier	.18	524	901	1425
14	Dale Hawerchuk	.16	512	891	1409
15	Jari Kurri	.17	601	797	1398

WHA Totals: GRETZKY (1 yr, 80 gm, 46-64—110); HOWE (6 yrs, 419 gm, 174-334—508); HULL (7 yrs, 411 gm, 303-335—638); MESSIER (1 yr, 52 gm, 1-10—11).

Years Played

		Yrs	Career	Gm
1	Gordie Howe	26	1946-71, 79-80	1767
2	Alex Delvecchio	24	1950-74	1549
	Tim Horton	24	1949-50, 51-74	1446
4	John Bucyk	23	1955-78	1540
5	**Ray Bourque**	22	1979-2001	1612
	Mark Messier	22	1979-	1561
	Stan Mikita	22	1958-80	1394
	Doug Mohns	22	1953-75	1390
	Dean Prentice	22	1952-74	1378
10	**Larry Murphy**	21	1980-	1615
	Harry Howell	21	1952-73	1411
	Paul Coffey	21	1980-	1409
	Ron Stewart	21	1952-73	1353
	Jean Ratelle	21	1960-81	1281
	Allan Stanley	21	1948-69	1244
	Eric Nesterenko	21	1951-72	1219
	Marcel Pronovost	21	1950-70	1206
	George Armstrong	21	1949-50, 51-71	1187
	Terry Sawchuk	21	1949-70	971
	Gump Worsley	21	1952-53, 54-74	862

Note: Combined NHL-WHA years played: Howe (32); Howell (24); Bobby Hull and Messier (23); Norm Ullman, Nesterenko, Frank Mahovlich and Dave Keon (22); Wayne Gretzky (21).

Games Played

		Yrs	Career	Gm
1	Gordie Howe	26	1946-71, 79-80	1767
2	**Larry Murphy**	21	1980-	1615
3	**Ray Bourque**	22	1979-2001	1612
4	**Mark Messier**	22	1979-	1561
5	Alex Delvecchio	24	1950-74	1549
6	John Bucyk	23	1955-78	1540
7	**Ron Francis**	20	1981-	1489
8	Wayne Gretzky	20	1979-99	1487
9	Tim Horton	24	1949-50, 51-74	1446
10	**Scott Stevens**	19	1982-	1434
11	Mike Gartner	19	1979-98	1432
12	Harry Howell	21	1952-73	1411
13	Norm Ullman	20	1955-75	1410
14	**Paul Coffey**	21	1980-	1409
15	Dale Hunter	19	1980-99	1407

Note: Combined NHL-WHA games played: Howe (2,186), Messier (1,613), Dave Keon (1,597), Howell (1,581), Gretzky (1,567), Ullman (1,554), Gartner (1,510), Bobby Hull (1,474) and Frank Mahovlich (1,418).

Goaltending

Wins

		Yrs	Gm	W	L	T	Pct
1	**Patrick Roy**	17	903	484	277	110	.619
2	Terry Sawchuk	21	971	447	330	172	.562
3	Jacques Plante	18	837	434	247	146	.614
4	Tony Esposito	16	886	423	306	152	.566
5	Glenn Hall	18	906	407	326	163	.545
6	Grant Fuhr	19	868	403	295	114	.567
7	**Mike Vernon**	18	763	383	264	91	.581
8	Andy Moog	18	713	372	209	88	.622
	J. Vanbiesbrouck	19	877	372	343	119	.517
10	Rogie Vachon	16	795	355	291	127	.541
11	Tom Barrasso	17	733	353	259	81	.568
12	**Ed Belfour**	13	675	343	215	89	.599
13	Gump Worsley	21	861	335	352	150	.490
14	Harry Lumley	16	804	330	329	143	.501
15	**Curtis Joseph**	12	655	317	243	76	.558
16	Billy Smith	18	680	305	233	105	.556
17	Turk Broda	12	629	302	224	101	.562
18	Ron Hextall	13	608	296	214	69	.571
19	Mike Liut	13	663	294	271	74	.518
20	Ed Giacomin	13	610	289	208	97	.568

Shutouts

		Yrs	Games	No
1	Terry Sawchuk	21	971	103
2	George Hainsworth	11	465	94
3	Glenn Hall	18	906	84
4	Jacques Plante	18	837	82
5	Alex Connell	12	417	81
	Tiny Thompson	12	553	81
7	Tony Esposito	16	886	76
8	Lorne Chabot	11	411	73
9	Harry Lumley	16	804	71
10	Roy Worters	12	484	66
11	Turk Broda	14	629	62
12	John Roach	14	491	58
13	Clint Benedict	13	362	57
	Ed Belfour	13	675	57
15	**Dominik Hasek**	11	516	56

Losses

		Yrs	Gm	W	L	T	Pct
1	Gump Worsley	21	861	335	352	150	.490
2	Gilles Meloche	18	788	270	351	131	.446
3	**J. Vanbiesbrouck**	19	877	372	343	119	.517
4	Terry Sawchuk	21	971	447	330	172	.562
5	Harry Lumley	16	804	330	329	143	.501

Goals Against Average
Minimum of 300 games played.

Before 1950

		Gm	Min	GA	GAA
1	George Hainsworth	465	29,415	937	1.91
2	Alex Connell	417	26,050	830	1.91
3	Chuck Gardiner	316	19,687	664	2.02
4	Lorne Chabot	411	25,307	860	2.04
5	Tiny Thompson	553	34,175	1183	2.08

Since 1950

		Gm	Min	GA	GAA
1	**Martin Brodeur**	519	30,235	1116	2.21
2	Ken Dryden	397	23,352	870	2.24
3	**Dominik Hasek**	516	29,873	1114	2.24
4	Jacques Plante	837	49,533	1965	2.38
5	**Chris Osgood**	389	22,475	900	2.40

NHL-WHA Top 15

All-Time regular season wins leaders, including games played in World Hockey Association (1972-79). NHL goaltenders with WHA experience are listed in CAPITAL letters. Players active during 2001 are in **bold** type.

Wins

		Yrs	W	L	T	Pct
1	**Patrick Roy**	17	484	277	110	.619
2	JACQUES PLANTE	19	449	261	147	.610
3	Terry Sawchuk	21	447	330	172	.562
4	Tony Esposito	16	423	306	152	.566
5	Glenn Hall	18	407	326	163	.545
6	Grant Fuhr	19	403	295	114	.567
7	**Mike Vernon**	18	383	264	91	.581
8	Andy Moog	18	372	209	88	.622
	J. Vanbiesbrouck	19	372	343	119	.517
10	Rogie Vachon	16	355	291	127	.541
11	Tom Barrasso	17	353	259	81	.568
12	**Ed Belfour**	13	343	215	89	.599
13	Gump Worsley	21	335	352	150	.490
14	Harry Lumley	16	330	329	143	.501
15	GERRY CHEEVERS	17	329	180	83	.626

WHA Totals: PLANTE (1 yr, 31 gm, 15-14-1); CHEEVERS (4 yrs, 191 gm, 99-78-9).

All-Time NHL Regular Season Leaders (Cont.)
SINGLE SEASON

Scoring
Points

		Season	G	A	Pts
1	Wayne Gretzky, Edm	1985-86	52	163	215
2	Wayne Gretzky, Edm	1981-82	92	120	212
3	Wayne Gretzky, Edm	1984-85	73	135	208
4	Wayne Gretzky, Edm	1983-84	87	118	205
5	Mario Lemieux, Pit	1988-89	85	114	199
6	Wayne Gretzky, Edm	1982-83	71	125	196
7	Wayne Gretzky, Edm	1986-87	62	121	183
8	Mario Lemieux, Pit	1987-88	70	98	168
9	Wayne Gretzky, LA	1988-89	54	114	168
10	Wayne Gretzky, Edm	1980-81	55	109	164
11	Wayne Gretzky, LA	1990-91	41	122	163
12	Mario Lemieux, Pit	1995-96	69	92	161
13	Mario Lemieux, Pit	1992-93	69	91	160
14	Steve Yzerman, Det	1988-89	65	90	155
15	Phil Esposito, Bos	1970-71	76	76	152
16	Bernie Nicholls, LA	1988-89	70	80	150
17	Jaromir Jagr, Pit	1995-96	62	87	149
	Wayne Gretzky, Edm	1987-88	40	109	149
19	Pat LaFontaine, Buf	1992-93	53	95	148
20	Mike Bossy, NYI	1981-82	64	83	147

WHA 150 points or more: 154—Marc Tardif, Que. (1977-78).

Goals

		Season	Gm	No
1	Wayne Gretzky, Edm	1981-82	80	92
2	Wayne Gretzky, Edm	1983-84	74	87
3	Brett Hull, St.L	1990-91	78	86
4	Mario Lemieux, Pit	1988-89	76	85
5	Alexander Mogilny, Buf	1992-93	77	76
	Phil Esposito, Bos	1970-71	78	76
	Teemu Selanne, Win	1992-93	84	76
8	Wayne Gretzky, Edm	1984-85	80	73
9	Brett Hull, St.L	1989-90	80	72
10	Jari Kurri, Edm	1984-85	73	71
	Wayne Gretzky, Edm	1982-83	80	71
12	Brett Hull, St.L	1991-92	73	70
	Mario Lemieux, Pit	1987-88	77	70
	Bernie Nicholls, LA	1988-89	79	70
15	Mario Lemieux, Pit	1992-93	60	69
	Mario Lemieux, Pit	1995-96	70	69
	Mike Bossy, NYI	1978-79	80	69
18	Phil Esposito, Bos	1973-74	78	68
	Jari Kurri, Edm	1985-86	78	68
	Mike Bossy, NYI	1980-81	79	68

WHA 70 goals or more: 77—Bobby Hull, Win. (1974-75); 75—Real Cloutier, Que. (1978-79); 71—Marc Tardif, Que. (1975-76); 70—Anders Hedberg, Win. (1976-77).

Assists

		Season	Gm	No
1	Wayne Gretzky, Edm	1985-86	80	163
2	Wayne Gretzky, Edm	1984-85	80	135
3	Wayne Gretzky, Edm	1982-83	80	125
4	Wayne Gretzky, LA	1990-91	78	122
5	Wayne Gretzky, Edm	1986-87	79	121
6	Wayne Gretzky, Edm	1981-82	80	120
7	Wayne Gretzky, Edm	1983-84	74	118
8	Mario Lemieux, Pit	1988-89	76	114
	Wayne Gretzky, LA	1988-89	78	114
10	Wayne Gretzky, Edm	1987-88	64	109
	Wayne Gretzky, Edm	1980-81	80	109
12	Wayne Gretzky, LA	1989-90	73	102
	Bobby Orr, Bos	1970-71	78	102
14	Mario Lemieux, Pit	1987-88	77	98
15	Adam Oates, Bos	1992-93	84	97

WHA 95 assists or more: 106—Andre Lacroix, San Diego (1974-75).

Goaltending
Wins

		Season	Record
1	Bernie Parent, Phi	1973-74	47-13-12
2	Bernie Parent, Phi	1974-75	44-14- 9
	Terry Sawchuk, Det	1950-51	44-13-13
	Terry Sawchuk, Det	1951-52	44-14-12
5	Martin Brodeur, NJ	1999-00	43-20- 8
	Martin Brodeur, NJ	1997-98	43-17- 8
	Tom Barrasso, Pit	1992-93	43-14- 5
	Ed Belfour, Chi	1990-91	43-19- 7
9	Jacques Plante, Mon	1955-56	42-12-10
	Jacques Plante, Mon	1961-62	42-14-14
	Ken Dryden, Mon	1975-76	42-10- 8
	Mike Richter, NYR	1993-94	42-12- 6
	Roman Turek, St.L	1999-00	42-15- 9
	Martin Brodeur, NJ	2000-01	42-17-11

Most WHA wins in one season: 44—Richard Brodeur, Que. (1975-76).

Losses

		Season	Record
1	Gary Smith, Cal	1970-71	19-48- 4
2	Al Rollins, Chi	1953-54	12-47- 7
3	Peter Sidorkiewicz, Ott	1992-93	8-46- 3
4	Harry Lumley, Chi	1951-52	17-44- 9
5	Harry Lumley, Chi	1950-51	12-41-10
	Craig Billington, Ott	1993-94	11-41- 4

Most WHA losses in one season: 36—Don McLeod, Van. (1974-75) and Andy Brown, Ind. (1974-75).

Shutouts

		Season	Gm	No
1	George Hainsworth, Mon	1928-29	44	22
2	Alex Connell, Ottawa	1925-26	36	15
	Alex Connell, Ottawa	1927-28	44	15
	Hal Winkler, Bos	1927-28	44	15
	Tony Esposito, Chi	1969-70	63	15

Most WHA shutouts in one season: 5—Gerry Cheevers, Cle. (1972-73) and Joe Daly, Win. (1975-76).

Goals Against Average

Before 1950

		Season	Gm	GAA
1	George Hainsworth, Mon	1928-29	44	0.98
2	George Hainsworth, Mon	1927-28	44	1.09
3	Alex Connell, Ottawa	1925-26	36	1.17
4	Tiny Thompson, Bos	1928-29	44	1.18
5	Roy Worters, NY Americans	1928-29	38	1.21

Since 1950

		Season	Gm	GAA
1	Tony Esposito, Chi	1971-72	48	1.77
2	Al Rollins, Tor	1950-51	40	1.77
3	Ron Tugnutt, Ott	1998-99	43	1.79
4	Harry Lumley, Tor	1953-54	69	1.86
5	Jacques Plante, Mon	1955-56	64	1.86

Penalty Minutes

		Season	PM
1	Dave Schultz, Phi	1974-75	472
2	Paul Baxter, Pit	1981-82	409
3	Mike Peluso, Chi	1991-92	408
4	Dave Schultz, LA-Pit	1977-78	405
5	Marty McSorley, LA	1992-93	399
6	Bob Probert, Det	1987-88	398
7	Basil McRae, Min	1987-88	382
8	Joey Kocur, Det	1985-86	377
9	Tim Hunter, Calg.	1988-89	375
10	Donald Brashear, Van	1997-98	372

WHA 355 minutes or more: 365—Curt Brackenbury, Min-Que. (1975-76).

SINGLE GAME
Scoring

Points

	Date	G-A—Pts
Darryl Sittler, Tor vs Bos	2/7/76	6-4—10
Maurice Richard, Mon vs Det	12/28/44	5-3— 8
Bert Olmstead, Mon vs Chi	1/9/54	4-4— 8
Tom Bladon, Phi vs Cle	12/11/77	4-4— 8
Bryan Trottier, NYI vs NYR	12/23/78	5-3— 8
Peter Stastny, Que at Wash	2/22/81	4-4— 8
Anton Stastny, Que at Wash	2/22/81	3-5— 8
Wayne Gretzky, Edm vs NJ	11/19/83	3-5— 8
Wayne Gretzky, Edm vs Min	1/4/84	4-4— 8
Paul Coffey, Edm vs Det	3/14/86	2-6— 8
Mario Lemieux, Pit vs St.L	10/15/88	2-6— 8
Bernie Nicholls, LA vs Tor	12/1/88	2-6— 8
Mario Lemieux, Pit vs NJ	12/31/88	5-3— 8

Goals

	Date	No
Joe Malone, Que vs Tor	1/31/20	7
Newsy Lalonde, Mon vs Tor	1/10/20	6
Joe Malone, Que vs Ott	3/10/20	6
Corb Denneny, Tor vs Ham	1/26/21	6
Cy Denneny, Ott vs Ham	3/7/21	6
Syd Howe, Det vs NYR	2/3/44	6
Red Berenson, St.L at Phi	11/7/68	6
Darryl Sittler, Tor vs Bos	2/7/76	6

Assists

	Date	No
Billy Taylor, Det at Chi	3/16/47	7
Wayne Gretzky, Edm vs Wash	2/15/80	7
Wayne Gretzky, Edm at Chi	12/11/85	7
Wayne Gretzky, Edm vs Que	2/14/86	7
24 players tied with 6 each.		

Penalty Minutes

	Date	Min
Randy Holt, LA at Phi	3/11/79	67
Frank Bathe, Phi vs LA	3/11/79	55
Russ Anderson, Pit vs Edm	1/19/80	51

Penalties

	Date	No
Chris Nilan, Bos vs Har	3/31/91	10*
Eight tied with 9 each.		

* Nilan accumulated six minors, two majors, one 10-minute misconduct and one game misconduct.

All-Time Winningest NHL Coaches

Top 20 NHL career victories through the 2001 season. Career, regular season and playoff records are noted along with NHL titles won. Coaches active during 2001 season in **bold** type. **Note:** In the following tables, overtime losses are considered losses.

		Career				Regular Season				Playoffs				
	Yrs	W	L	T	Pct	W	L	T	Pct	W	L	T	Pct	Stanley Cups
1 Scotty Bowman	29	1400	685	304	.650	1193	562	304	.653	207	123	0	.627	8 (1973, 76-79, 92, 97-98)
2 Al Arbour	22	904	663	248	.566	781	577	248	.564	123	86	0	.589	4 (1980-83)
3 Dick Irvin	26	790	609	228	.556	690	521	226	.559	100	88	2	.532	4 (1932,44,46,53)
4 Mike Keenan	15	630	475	124	.563	539	406	124	.562	91	69	0	.569	1 (1994)
5 Billy Reay	16	599	445	175	.563	542	385	175	.571	57	60	0	.487	None
6 Toe Blake	13	582	292	159	.640	500	255	159	.634	82	37	0	.689	8 (1956-60,65-66,68)
7 Pat Quinn	15	559	447	127	.549	484	379	127	.553	75	68	0	.524	None
8 Glen Sather	11	553	305	110	.628	464	268	110	.616	89	37	0	.706	4 (1984-85,87-88)
9 Bryan Murray	13	518	412	123	.550	484	368	123	.559	34	44	0	.436	None
10 Roger Neilson	15	510	435	159	.534	459	380	159	.541	51	55	0	.481	None
11 Jack Adams	21	475	449	163	.512	423	397	162	.513	52	52	1	.500	3 (1936-37, 43)
12 Pat Burns	12	473	373	129	.551	412	314	129	.557	61	59	0	.508	None
13 Jacques Demers	14	464	510	130	.479	409	467	130	.471	55	43	0	.561	1 (1993)
14 Fred Shero	10	451	272	119	.606	390	225	119	.612	61	47	0	.565	2 (1974-75)
15 Punch Imlach	15	439	384	148	.528	395	336	148	.534	44	48	0	.478	4 (1962-64,67)
16 Emile Francis	13	433	326	112	.561	393	273	112	.577	40	53	0	.430	None
17 Sid Abel	16	414	470	155	.473	382	426	155	.477	32	44	0	.421	None
18 Terry Murray	11	406	331	89	.545	360	288	89	.549	46	43	0	.517	None
19 Bob Berry	11	395	377	121	.510	384	355	121	.517	11	22	0	.333	None
20 Art Ross	18	393	310	95	.552	361	277	90	.558	32	33	5	.493	1 (1939)

Where They Coached

Abel—Chicago (1952-54), Detroit (1957-68,69-70), St. Louis (1971-72), Kansas City (1975-76); **Adams**—Toronto (1922-23), Detroit (1927-47); **Arbour**—St. Louis (1970-73), NY Islanders (1973-86,88-94); **Berry**—Los Angeles (1978-81), Montreal (1981-84), Pittsburgh (1984-87), St. Louis (1992-94); **Blake**—Montreal (1955-68); **Bowman**—St. Louis (1967-71), Montreal (1971-79), Buffalo (1979-87), Pittsburgh (1991-93), Detroit (1993—); **Burns**—Montreal (1988-92), Toronto (1992-96), Boston (1997-2000).

Demers—Quebec (1979-80), St. Louis (1983-86), Detroit (1986-90), Montreal (1992-95), Tampa Bay (1997-99); **Francis**—NY Rangers (1965-75), St. Louis (1976-77,81-83); **Imlach**—Toronto (1958-69), Buffalo (1970-72), Toronto (1979-81); **Irvin**—Chicago (1930-31,55-56), Toronto (1931-40), Montreal (1940-55); **Keenan**—Philadelphia (1984-88), Chicago (1988-92), NY Rangers (1993-94), St. Louis (1994-96), Vancouver (1997-99), Boston (2000-01); **B. Murray**—Washington (1982-90), Detroit (1990-93), Florida (1997-98), Anaheim (2001—); **T. Murray**— Washington (1990-94), Philadelphia (1994-97), Florida (1998-2000).

Neilson—Toronto (1977-79), Buffalo (1979-81), Vancouver (1982-83), Los Angeles (1984), NY Rangers (1989-93), Florida (1993-95), Philadelphia (1998-00), Toronto (1980—); **Quinn**—Philadelphia (1978-82), Los Angeles (1984-87), Vancouver (1990-94, 96), Toronto (1998—); **Reay**—Toronto (1957-59), Chicago (1963-77); **Ross**—Montreal Wanderers (1917-18), Hamilton (1922-23), Boston (1924-28,29-34,36-39,41-45); **Sather**—Edmonton (1979-89, 93-94); **Shero**—Philadelphia (1971-78), NY Rangers (1978-81).

Top Winning Percentages

Minimum of 275 victories, including playoffs.

		Yrs	W	L	T	Pct.
1	**Scotty Bowman**	29	1400	685	304	**.650**
2	Toe Blake	13	582	292	159	**.640**
3	Glen Sather	11	553	305	110	**.628**
4	**Ken Hitchcock**	6	301	178	54	**.615**
5	Fred Shero	10	451	272	119	**.606**
6	Don Cherry	6	281	177	77	**.597**
7	Tommy Ivan	9	324	205	111	**.593**
8	Al Arbour	22	904	663	248	**.566**
9	**Jacques Lemaire**	8	321	237	82	**.566**
10	Billy Reay	16	599	445	175	**.563**
11	**Mike Keenan**	15	630	475	124	**.563**
12	Emile Francis	13	433	326	112	**.561**
13	Hap Day	10	308	237	81	**.557**
14	Dick Irvin	26	790	609	228	**.556**
15	Lester Patrick	13	312	242	115	**.552**
16	Art Ross	18	393	310	95	**.552**
17	**Pat Burns**	12	473	373	129	**.551**
18	Bryan Murray	13	518	412	123	**.550**
19	**Pat Quinn**	15	559	447	127	**.549**
20	Bob Johnson	6	275	223	58	**.547**
21	**Terry Murray**	11	406	331	89	**.545**
22	Roger Neilson	15	510	435	159	**.534**
23	Punch Imlach	15	439	384	148	**.528**
24	Brian Sutter	10	387	355	103	**.519**
25	Terry Crisp	9	310	286	78	**.518**

Active Coaches' Victories

Through 2001 season, including playoffs.

		Yrs	W	L	T	Pct.
1	Scotty Bowman, Det.	29	1400	685	304	.650
2	Pat Quinn, Tor.	15	559	447	127	.549
3	Bryan Murray, Ana.	13	518	412	123	.550
4	Brian Sutter, Chi.	10	387	355	103	.519
5	Jacques Lemaire, Min.	8	321	237	82	.566
6	Ken Hitchcock, Dal.	6	301	178	54	.615
7	Ron Wilson, Wash.	8	295	301	71	.496
8	Jacques Martin, Ott.	8	291	273	92	.514
9	Darryl Sutter, SJ	7	272	252	76	.517
10	Marc Crawford, Van.	7	270	208	73	.556
11	Joel Quenneville, St.L	5	220	148	51	.586
12	Paul Maurice, Car.	6	207	221	64	.486
13	Larry Robinson, NJ	6	205	208	57	.497
14	Lindy Ruff, Buf	4	186	146	50	.552
15	Ron Low, NYR	6	182	224	45	.453
16	Bob Hartley, Col.	3	176	98	31	.628
17	Robbie Ftorek, Bos.	4	161	120	30	.566
18	Dave King, Clb.	4	145	133	40	.519
19	Barry Trotz, Nash.	3	90	133	23	.413
20	Andy Murray, LA	2	84	72	25	.533
21	Bob Francis, Pho	2	75	69	25	.518
22	Ivan Hlinka, Pit	1	51	40	9	.555
23	Craig MacTavish, Edm.	1	41	35	12	.534
24	Curt Fraser, Atl.	2	37	108	19	.284
25	Bill Barber, Phi	1	33	20	7	.608
26	Michel Therrien, Mon.	1	23	33	6	.419
27	Duane Sutter, Fla.	1	16	24	6	.413
28	John Tortorella, TB	2	12	33	2	.277
29	Greg Gilbert, Calg.	1	4	8	2	.357
30	Peter Laviolette, NYI	0	0	0	0	.000

Annual Awards

Hart Memorial Trophy

Awarded to the player "adjudged to be the most valuable to his team" and named after Cecil Hart, the former manager-coach of the Montreal Canadiens. Winners selected by Pro Hockey Writers Assn. (PHWA). Winners' scoring statistics or goaltender W-L records and goals against average are provided; (*) indicates led or tied for league lead.

Multiple Winners: Wayne Gretzky (9); Gordie Howe (6); Eddie Shore (4); Bobby Clarke, Mario Lemieux, Howie Morenz and Bobby Orr (3); Jean Beliveau, Bill Cowley, Phil Esposito, Dominik Hasek, Bobby Hull, Guy Lafleur, Mark Messier, Stan Mikita and Nels Stewart (2).

Year		G	A	Pts	Year		G	A	Pts
1924	Frank Nighbor, Ottawa, C	10	3	13	1950	Chuck Rayner, NYR, G	28-30-11;		2.62
1925	Billy Burch, Hamilton, C	20	4	24	1951	Milt Schmidt, Bos., C	22	39	61
1926	Nels Stewart, Maroons, C	34	8	42*	1952	Gordie Howe, Det., RW	47	39	86*
1927	Herb Gardiner, Mon., D	6	6	12	1953	Gordie Howe, Det., RW	49	46	95*
1928	Howie Morenz, Mon., C	33	18	51	1954	Al Rollins, Chi., G	12-47-7;		3.23
1929	Roy Worters, NYA, G	16-13-9;		1.21	1955	Ted Kennedy, Tor., C	10	42	52
					1956	Jean Beliveau, Mon., C	47	41	88
1930	Nels Stewart, Maroons, C	39	16	55	1957	Gordie Howe, Det., RW	44	45	89*
1931	Howie Morenz, Mon., C	28	23	51*	1958	Gordie Howe, Det., RW	33	44	77
1932	Howie Morenz, Mon., C	24	25	49	1959	Andy Bathgate, NYR, RW	40	48	88
1933	Eddie Shore, Bos., D	8	27	35					
1934	Aurel Joliat, Mon., LW	22	15	37	1960	Gordie Howe., Det., RW	28	45	73
1935	Eddie Shore, Bos., D	7	26	33	1961	Bernie Geoffrion, Mon., RW	50	45	95*
1936	Eddie Shore, Bos., D	3	16	19	1962	Jacques Plante, Mon., G	42-14-14;		2.37*
1937	Babe Siebert, Mon., D	8	20	28	1963	Gordie Howe, Det., RW	38	48	86*
1938	Eddie Shore, Bos., D	3	14	17	1964	Jean Beliveau, Mon., C	28	50	78
1939	Toe Blake, Mon., LW	24	23	47*	1965	Bobby Hull, Chi., LW	39	32	71
					1966	Bobby Hull, Chi., LW	54	43	97*
1940	Ebbie Goodfellow, Det., D	11	17	28	1967	Stan Mikita, Chi., C	35	62	97*
1941	Bill Cowley, Bos., C	17	45	62*	1968	Stan Mikita, Chi., C	40	47	87*
1942	Tommy Anderson, NYA, D	12	29	41	1969	Phil Esposito, Bos., C	49	77	126*
1943	Bill Cowley, Bos., C	27	45	72					
1944	Babe Pratt, Tor., D	17	40	57	1970	Bobby Orr, Bos., D	33	87	120*
1945	Elmer Lach, Mon., C	26	54	80*	1971	Bobby Orr, Bos., D	37	102	139
1946	Max Bentley, Chi., C	31	30	61*	1972	Bobby Orr, Bos., D	37	80	117
1947	Maurice Richard, Mon., RW	45	26	71	1973	Bobby Clarke, Phi., C	37	67	104
1948	Buddy O'Connor, NYR, C	24	36	60	1974	Phil Esposito, Bos., C	68	77	145*
1949	Sid Abel, Det., C	28	26	54	1975	Bobby Clarke, Phi., C	27	89	116
					1976	Bobby Clarke, Phi., C	30	89	119

Year		G	A	Pts	Year		G	A	Pts
1977	Guy Lafleur, Mon., RW	56	80	136*	1990	Mark Messier, Edm., C	45	84	129
1978	Guy Lafleur, Mon., RW	60	72	132*	1991	Brett Hull, St. L., RW	86	45	131
1979	Bryan Trottier, NYI., C	47	87	134*	1992	Mark Messier, NYR, C	35	72	107
					1993	Mario Lemieux, Pit., C	69	91	160*
1980	Wayne Gretzky, Edm., C	51	86	137*	1994	Sergei Fedorov, Det., C	56	64	120
1981	Wayne Gretzky, Edm., C	55	109	164*	1995	Eric Lindros, Phi., C	29	41	70*
1982	Wayne Gretzky, Edm., C	92	120	212*	1996	Mario Lemieux, Pit., C	69	92	161*
1983	Wayne Gretzky, Edm., C	71	125	196*	1997	Dominik Hasek, Buf., G	37-20-10;		2.27
1984	Wayne Gretzky, Edm., C	87	118	205*	1998	Dominik Hasek, NYR, G	33-23-13,		2.09
1985	Wayne Gretzky, Edm., C	73	135	208*	1999	Jaromir Jagr, Pit., RW	44	83	127*
1986	Wayne Gretzky, Edm., C	52	163	215*					
1987	Wayne Gretzky, Edm., C	62	121	183*	2000	Chris Pronger, St.L, D	14	48	62
1988	Mario Lemieux, Pit., C	70	98	168*	2001	Joe Sakic, Col., C	54	64	118
1989	Wayne Gretzky, LA, C	54	114	168					

Calder Memorial Trophy

Awarded to the most outstanding rookie of the year and named after Frank Calder, the late NHL president (1917-43). Since the 1990-91 season, all eligible candidates must not have attained their 26th birthday by Sept. 15 of their rookie year. Winners selected by PHWA. Winners' scoring statistics or goaltender W-L record & goals against average are provided.

Year		G	A	Pts	Year		G	A	Pts
1933	Carl Voss, NYR-Det., C	8	15	23	1968	Derek Sanderson, Bos., C	24	25	49
1934	Russ Blinco, Maroons, C	14	9	23	1969	Danny Grant, Min., LW	34	31	65
1935	Sweeney Schriner, NYA, LW	18	22	40					
1936	Mike Karakas, Chi., G	21-19-8;		1.92	1970	Tony Esposito, Chi., G	38-17-8;		2.17
1937	Syl Apps, Tor., C	16	29	45	1971	Gilbert Perreault, Buf., C	38	34	72
1938	Cully Dahlstrom, Chi., C	10	9	19	1972	Ken Dryden, Mon., G	39-8-15;		2.24
1939	Frankie Brimsek, Bos., G	33-9-1;		1.58	1973	Steve Vickers, NYR, LW	30	23	53
					1974	Denis Potvin, NYI, D	17	37	54
1940	Kilby MacDonald, NYR, LW	15	13	28	1975	Eric Vail, Atl., LW	39	21	60
1941	John Quilty, Mon., C	18	16	34	1976	Bryan Trottier, NYI, C	32	63	95
1942	Knobby Warwick, NYR, RW	16	17	33	1977	Willi Plett, Atl., RW	33	23	56
1943	Gaye Stewart, Tor., LW	24	23	47	1978	Mike Bossy, NYI, RW	53	38	91
1944	Gus Bodnar, Tor., C	22	40	62	1979	Bobby Smith, Min., C	30	44	74
1945	Frank McCool, Tor., G	24-22-4;		3.22					
1946	Edgar Laprade, NYR, C	15	19	34	1980	Ray Bourque, Bos., D	17	48	65
1947	Howie Meeker, Tor., RW	27	18	45	1981	Peter Stastny, Que., C	39	70	109
1948	Jim McFadden, Det., C	24	24	48	1982	Dale Hawerchuk, Win., C	45	58	103
1949	Penny Lund, NYR, RW	14	16	30	1983	Steve Larmer, Chi., RW	43	47	90
					1984	Tom Barrasso, Buf., G	26-12-3;		2.84
1950	Jack Gelineau, Bos., G	22-30-15;		3.28	1985	Mario Lemieux, Pit., C	43	57	100
1951	Terry Sawchuk, Det., G	44-13-13;		1.99	1986	Gary Suter, Calg., D	18	50	68
1952	Bernie Geoffrion, Mon., RW	30	24	54	1987	Luc Robitaille, LA, LW	45	39	84
1953	Gump Worsley, NYR, G	13-29-8;		3.06	1988	Joe Nieuwendyk, Calg., C	51	41	92
1954	Camille Henry, NYR, LW	24	15	39	1989	Brian Leetch, NYR, D	23	48	71
1955	Ed Litzenberger, Mon-Chi., RW	23	28	51					
1956	Glenn Hall, Det., G	30-24-16;		2.11	1990	Sergei Makarov, Calg., RW	24	62	86
1957	Larry Regan, Bos., RW	14	19	33	1991	Ed Belfour, Chi., G	43-19-7;		2.47
1958	Frank Mahovlich, Tor., LW	20	16	36	1992	Pavel Bure, Van., RW	34	26	60
1959	Ralph Backstrom, Mon., C	18	22	40	1993	Teemu Selanne, Win., RW	76	56	132
					1994	Martin Brodeur, NJ, G	27-11-8;		2.40
1960	Billy Hay, Chi., C	18	37	55	1995	Peter Forsberg, Que., C	15	35	50
1961	Dave Keon, Tor., C	20	25	45	1996	Daniel Alfredsson, Ott., RW	26	35	61
1962	Bobby Rousseau, Mon., RW	21	24	45	1997	Bryan Berard, NYI, D	8	40	48
1963	Kent Douglas, Tor., D	7	15	22	1998	Sergei Samsonov, Bos., LW	22	25	47
1964	Jacques Laperriere, Mon., D	2	28	30	1999	Chris Drury, Col., C	20	24	44
1965	Roger Crozier, Det., G	40-23-7;		2.42					
1966	Brit Selby, Tor., LW	14	13	27	2000	Scott Gomez, NJ, C	19	51	70
1967	Bobby Orr, Bos., D	13	28	41	2001	Evgeni Nabokov, SJ, G	32-21-7;		2.19

Vezina Trophy

From 1927-80, given to the principal goaltender(s) on the team allowing the fewest goals during the regular season. Trophy named after 1920's goalie Georges Vezina of the Montreal Canadiens, who died of tuberculosis in 1926. Since the 1980-81 season, the trophy has been awarded to the most outstanding goaltender of the year as selected by the league's general managers.

Multiple Winners: Jacques Plante (7, one of them shared); Bill Durnan and Dominik Hasek (6); Ken Dryden (5, three shared); Bunny Larocque (4, all shared); Terry Sawchuk (4, one shared); Tiny Thompson (3, one shared); Tony Esposito (3, one shared); George Hainsworth (3); Glenn Hall (3, two shared); Patrick Roy (3); Ed Belfour (2); Johnny Bower (2, one shared); Frankie Brimsek (2); Turk Broda (2); Chuck Gardiner (2); Charlie Hodge (2, one shared); Bernie Parent (2, one shared); Gump Worsley (2, both shared).

Year		Record	GAA	Year		Record	GAA
1927	George Hainsworth, Mon.	28-14-2	1.52	1931	Roy Worters, NYA	18-16-10	1.68
1928	George Hainsworth, Mon.	26-11-7	1.09	1932	Chuck Gardiner, Chi	18-19-11	1.92
1929	George Hainsworth, Mon.	22-7-15	0.98	1933	Tiny Thompson, Bos	25-15-8	1.83
				1934	Chuck Gardiner, Chi	20-17-11	1.73
1930	Tiny Thompson, Bos	38-5-1	2.23	1935	Lorne Chabot, Chi	26-17-5	1.83

Annual Awards (Cont.)

Year		Record	GAA
1936	Tiny Thompson, Bos	22-20-6	1.71
1937	Norm Smith, Det	25-14-9	2.13
1938	Tiny Thompson, Bos	30-11-7	1.85
1939	Frankie Brimsek, Bos	33-9-1	1.58
1940	Dave Kerr, NYR	27-11-10	1.60
1941	Turk Broda, Tor	28-14-6	2.06
1942	Frankie Brimsek, Bos	24-17-6	2.45
1943	John Mowers, Det	25-14-11	2.47
1944	Bill Durnan, Mon	38-5-7	2.18
1945	Bill Durnan, Mon	38-8-4	2.42
1946	Bill Durnan, Mon	24-11-5	2.60
1947	Bill Durnan, Mon	34-16-10	2.30
1948	Turk Broda, Tor	32-15-13	2.38
1949	Bill Durnan, Mon	28-23-9	2.10
1950	Bill Durnan, Mon	26-21-17	2.20
1951	Al Rollins, Tor	27-5-8	1.77
1952	Terry Sawchuk, Det	44-14-12	1.90
1953	Terry Sawchuk, Det	32-15-16	1.90
1954	Harry Lumley, Tor	32-24-13	1.86
1955	Terry Sawchuk, Det	40-17-11	1.96
1956	Jacques Plante, Mon	42-12-10	1.86
1957	Jacques Plante, Mon	31-18-12	2.02
1958	Jacques Plante, Mon	34-14-8	2.11
1959	Jacques Plante, Mon	38-16-13	2.16
1960	Jacques Plante, Mon	40-17-12	2.54
1961	Johnny Bower, Tor	33-15-10	2.50
1962	Jacques Plante, Mon	42-14-14	2.37
1963	Glenn Hall, Chi	30-20-16	2.55
1964	Charlie Hodge, Mon	33-18-11	2.26
1965	Johnny Bower, Tor	13-13-8	2.38
	& Terry Sawchuk, Tor	17-13-6	2.56
1966	Gump Worsley, Mon	29-14-6	2.36
	& Charlie Hodge, Mon	12-7-2	2.58
1967	Glenn Hall, Chi	19-5-5	2.38
	& Denis Dejordy, Chi	22-12-7	2.46
1968	Gump Worsley, Mon	19-9-8	1.98
	& Rogie Vachon, Mon	23-13-2	2.48
1969	Jacques Plante, St.L	18-12-6	1.96
	& Glenn Hall, St.L	19-12-8	2.17
1970	Tony Esposito, Chi	38-17-8	2.17

Year		Record	GAA
1971	Ed Giacomin, NYR	27-10-7	2.16
	& Gilles Villemure, NYR	22-8-4	2.30
1972	Tony Esposito, Chi	31-10-6	1.77
	& Gary Smith, Chi	14-5-6	2.42
1973	Ken Dryden, Mon	33-7-13	2.26
1974	(Tie) Bernie Parent, Phi	47-13-12	1.89
	Tony Esposito, Chi	34-14-21	2.04
1975	Bernie Parent, Phi	44-14-10	2.03
1976	Ken Dryden, Mon	42-10-8	2.03
1977	Ken Dryden, Mon	41-6-8	2.14
	& Bunny Larocque, Mon	19-2-4	2.09
1978	Ken Dryden, Mon	37-7-7	2.05
	& Bunny Larocque, Mon	22-3-4	2.67
1979	Ken Dryden, Mon	30-10-7	2.30
	& Bunny Larocque, Mon	22-7-4	2.84
1980	Bob Sauve, Buf	20-8-4	2.36
	& Don Edwards, Buf	27-9-12	2.57
1981	Richard Sevigny, Mon	20-4-3	2.40
	Denis Herron, Mon	6-9-6	3.50
	& Bunny Larocque, Mon	16-9-3	3.03
1982	Billy Smith, NYI	32-9-4	2.97
1983	Pete Peeters, Bos	40-11-9	2.36
1984	Tom Barrasso, Buf	26-12-3	2.84
1985	Pelle Lindbergh, Phi	40-17-7	3.02
1986	John Vanbiesbrouck, NYR	31-21-5	3.32
1987	Ron Hextall, Phi	37-21-6	3.00
1988	Grant Fuhr, Edm	40-24-9	3.43
1989	Patrick Roy, Mon	33-5-6	2.47
1990	Patrick Roy, Mon	31-16-5	2.53
1991	Ed Belfour, Chi	43-19-7	2.47
1992	Patrick Roy, Mon	36-22-8	2.36
1993	Ed Belfour, Chi	41-18-11	2.59
1994	Dominik Hasek, Buf	30-20-6	1.95
1995	Dominik Hasek, Buf	19-14-7	2.11
1996	Jim Carey, Wash	35-24-9	2.26
1997	Dominik Hasek, Buf	37-20-10	2.27
1998	Dominik Hasek, Buf	33-23-13	2.09
1999	Dominik Hasek, Buf	30-18-14	1.87
2000	Olaf Kolzig, Wash	41-20-11	2.24
2001	Dominik Hasek, Buf	37-24-4	2.11

Lady Byng Memorial Trophy

Awarded to the player "adjudged to have exhibited the best type of sportsmanship and gentlemanly conduct combined with a high standard of playing ability" and named after Lady Evelyn Byng, the wife of former Canadian Governor General (1921-26) Baron Byng of Vimy. Winners selected by PHWA.

Multiple winners: Frank Boucher (7); Wayne Gretzky (5); Red Kelly (4); Bobby Bauer, Mike Bossy and Alex Delvecchio (3); Johnny Bucyk, Marcel Dionne, Ron Francis, Paul Kariya, Dave Keon, Stan Mikita, Joey Mullen, Frank Nighbor, Jean Ratelle, Clint Smith and Sid Smith (2).

Year		Year		Year	
1925	Frank Nighbor, Ott., C	1944	Clint Smith, Chi., C	1963	Dave Keon, Tor., C
1926	Frank Nighbor, Ott., C	1945	Bill Mosienko, Chi., RW	1964	Ken Wharram, Chi., RW
1927	Billy Burch, NYA, C	1946	Toe Blake, Mon., LW	1965	Bobby Hull, Chi., LW
1928	Frank Boucher, NYR, C	1947	Bobby Bauer, Bos., RW	1966	Alex Delvecchio, Det., LW
1929	Frank Boucher, NYR, C	1948	Buddy O'Connor, NYR, C	1967	Stan Mikita, Chi., C
1930	Frank Boucher, NYR, C	1949	Bill Quackenbush, Det., D	1968	Stan Mikita, Chi., C
1931	Frank Boucher, NYR, C	1950	Edgar Laprade, NYR, C	1969	Alex Delvecchio, Det., LW
1932	Joe Primeau, Tor., C	1951	Red Kelly, Det., D	1970	Phil Goyette, St.L., C
1933	Frank Boucher, NYR, C	1952	Sid Smith, Tor., LW	1971	Johnny Bucyk, Bos., LW
1934	Frank Boucher, NYR, C	1953	Red Kelly, Det., D	1972	Jean Ratelle, NYR, C
1935	Frank Boucher, NYR, C	1954	Red Kelly, Det., D	1973	Gilbert Perreault, Buf., C
1936	Doc Romnes, Chi., F	1955	Sid Smith, Tor., LW	1974	Johnny Bucyk, Bos., LW
1937	Marty Barry, Det., C	1956	Earl Reibel, Det., C	1975	Marcel Dionne, Det., C
1938	Gordie Drillon, Tor., RW	1957	Andy Hebenton, NYR, RW	1976	Jean Ratelle, NY-Bos., C
1939	Clint Smith, NYR, C	1958	Camille Henry, NYR, LW	1977	Marcel Dionne, LA, C
1940	Bobby Bauer, Bos., RW	1959	Alex Delvecchio, Det., LW	1978	Butch Goring, LA, C
1941	Bobby Bauer, Bos., RW	1960	Don McKenney, Bos., C	1979	Bob MacMillan, Atl., RW
1942	Syl Apps, Tor., C	1961	Red Kelly, Tor., D	1980	Wayne Gretzky, Edm., C
1943	Max Bentley, Chi., C	1962	Dave Keon, Tor., C	1981	Rick Kehoe, Pit., RW

Year	Year	Year
1982 Rick Middleton, Bos., RW	1989 Joey Mullen, Calg., RW	1996 Paul Kariya, Ana., LW
1983 Mike Bossy, NYI, RW		1997 Paul Kariya, Ana., LW
1984 Mike Bossy, NYI, RW	1990 Brett Hull, St.L., RW	1998 Ron Francis, Pit., C
1985 Jari Kurri, Edm., RW	1991 Wayne Gretzky, LA, C	1999 Wayne Gretzky, NYR, C
1986 Mike Bossy, NYI, RW	1992 Wayne Gretzky, LA, C	
1987 Joey Mullen, Calg., RW	1993 Pierre Turgeon, NYI, C	2000 Pavol Demitra, St.L, RW
1988 Mats Naslund, Mon., LW	1994 Wayne Gretzky, LA, C	2001 Joe Sakic, Col., C
	1995 Ron Francis, Pit., C	

Note: Bill Quackenbush and Red Kelly are the only defensemen to win the Lady Byng.

James Norris Memorial Trophy

Awarded to the most outstanding defenseman of the year and named after James Norris, the late Detroit Red Wings owner-president. Winners selected by PHWA.

Multiple winners: Bobby Orr (8); Doug Harvey (7); Ray Bourque (5); Chris Chelios, Paul Coffey, Pierre Pilote and Denis Potvin (3); Rod Langway, Brian Leetch and Larry Robinson (2).

Year	Year	Year
1954 Red Kelly, Detroit	1970 Bobby Orr, Boston	1986 Paul Coffey, Edmonton
1955 Doug Harvey, Montreal	1971 Bobby Orr, Boston	1987 Ray Bourque, Boston
1956 Doug Harvey, Montreal	1972 Bobby Orr, Boston	1988 Ray Bourque, Boston
1957 Doug Harvey, Montreal	1973 Bobby Orr, Boston	1989 Chris Chelios, Montreal
1958 Doug Harvey, Montreal	1974 Bobby Orr, Boston	
1959 Tom Johnson, Montreal	1975 Bobby Orr, Boston	1990 Ray Bourque, Boston
	1976 Denis Potvin, NY Islanders	1991 Ray Bourque, Boston
1960 Doug Harvey, Montreal	1977 Larry Robinson, Montreal	1992 Brian Leetch, NY Rangers
1961 Doug Harvey, Montreal	1978 Denis Potvin, NY Islanders	1993 Chris Chelios, Chicago
1962 Doug Harvey, NY Rangers	1979 Denis Potvin, NY Islanders	1994 Ray Bourque, Boston
1963 Pierre Pilote, Chicago		1995 Paul Coffey, Detroit
1964 Pierre Pilote, Chicago	1980 Larry Robinson, Montreal	1996 Chris Chelios, Chicago
1965 Pierre Pilote, Chicago	1981 Randy Carlyle, Pittsburgh	1997 Brian Leetch, NY Rangers
1966 Jacques Laperriere, Montreal	1982 Doug Wilson, Chicago	1998 Rob Blake, Los Angeles
1967 Harry Howell, NY Rangers	1983 Rod Langway, Washington	1999 Al MacInnis, St. Louis
1968 Bobby Orr, Boston	1984 Rod Langway, Washington	
1969 Bobby Orr, Boston	1985 Paul Coffey, Edmonton	2000 Chris Pronger, St. Louis
		2001 Nicklas Lidstrom, Detroit

Frank Selke Trophy

Awarded to the outstanding defensive forward of the year and named after the late Montreal Canadiens general manager. Winners selected by the PHWA.

Multiple winners: Bob Gainey (4); Guy Carbonneau (3); Sergei Fedorov and Jere Lehtinen (2).

Year	Year	Year
1978 Bob Gainey, Mon., LW	1986 Troy Murray, Chi., C	1994 Sergei Fedorov, Det., C
1979 Bob Gainey, Mon., LW	1987 Dave Poulin, Phi., C	1995 Ron Francis, Pit., C
1980 Bob Gainey, Mon., LW	1988 Guy Carbonneau, Mon., C	1996 Sergei Fedorov, Det., C
1981 Bob Gainey, Mon., LW	1989 Guy Carbonneau, Mon., C	1997 Michael Peca, Buf., C
1982 Steve Kasper, Bos., C	1990 Rick Meagher, St.L., C	1998 Jere Lehtinen, Dal., RW
1983 Bobby Clarke, Phi., C	1991 Dirk Graham, Chi., RW	1999 Jere Lehtinen, Dal., RW
1984 Doug Jarvis, Wash., C	1992 Guy Carbonneau, Mon., C	2000 Steve Yzerman, Det., C
1985 Craig Ramsay, Buf., LW	1993 Doug Gilmour, Tor., C	2001 John Madden, NJ, LW

Jack Adams Award

Awarded to the coach "adjudged to have contributed the most to his team's success" and named after the late Detroit Red Wings coach and general manager. Winners selected by NHL Broadcasters' Assn.; (*) indicates division champion.

Multiple winners: Pat Burns (3); Scotty Bowman, Jacques Demers and Pat Quinn (2).

Year		Improvement	Year		Improvement
1974 Fred Shero, Phi	37-30-11	to 50-16-12*	1988 Jacques Demers, Det	34-36-10	to 41-28-11*
1975 Bob Pulford, LA	41-14-23	to 37-35-8	1989 Pat Burns, Mon	45-22-13	to 53-18- 9*
1976 Don Cherry, Bos	40-26-14	to 48-15-17*	1990 Bob Murdoch, Win	26-42-12	to 37-32-11
1977 Scotty Bowman, Mon	58-11-11*	to 60- 8-12*	1991 Brian Sutter, St.L	37-34-9	to 47-22-11
1978 Bobby Kromm, Det	6-55-9	to 32-34-14	1992 Pat Quinn, Van	28-43-9	to 42-26-12*
1979 Al Arbour, NYI	48-17-15*	to 51-15-14*	1993 Pat Burns, Tor	30-43-7	to 44-29-11
1980 Pat Quinn, Phi	40-25-15	to 48-12-20*	1994 Jacques Lemaire, NJ	40-37-7	to 47-25-12
1981 Red Berenson, St.L	34-34-12	to 45-18-17*	1995 Marc Crawford, Que	34-42-8	to 30-13-5*
1982 Tom Watt, Win	9-57-14	to 33-33-14	1996 Scotty Bowman, Det	33-11-4*	to 62-13-7*
1983 Orval Tessier, Chi	30-38-12	to 47-23-10	1997 Ted Nolan, Buf	33-42-7	to 40-30-12*
1984 Bryan Murray, Wash	39-25-16	to 48-27-5	1998 Pat Burns, Bos	26-47-9	to 39-30-13
1985 Mike Keenan, Phi	44-26-10	to 53-20-7*	1999 Jacques Martin, Ott	34-33-15	to 44-23-15*
1986 Glen Sather, Edm	49-20-11*	to 56-17-7*	2000 Joel Quenneville, St.L	37-32-13	to 51-20-11*
1987 Jacques Demers, Det	17-57-6	to 34-36-10	2001 Bill Barber, Phi	45-25-12	to 43-25-14

Annual Awards (Cont.)

Lester B. Pearson Award

Awarded to the season's most outstanding player and named after the former diplomat, Nobel Peace Prize winner and Canadian prime minister. Winners selected by the NHL Players Assn.

Multiple winners: Wayne Gretzky (5); Mario Lemieux (4); Guy Lafleur (3); Marcel Dionne, Phil Esposito, Dominik Hasek, Jaromir Jagr and Mark Messier (2).

Year	Year	Year
1971 Phil Esposito, Bos., C	1982 Wayne Gretzky, Edm., C	1993 Mario Lemieux, Pit., C
1972 Jean Ratelle, NYR, C	1983 Wayne Gretzky, Edm., C	1994 Sergei Fedorov, Det., C
1973 Bobby Clarke, Phi., C	1984 Wayne Gretzky, Edm., C	1995 Eric Lindros, Phi., C
1974 Phil Esposito, Bos., C	1985 Wayne Gretzky, Edm., C	1996 Mario Lemieux, Pit., C
1975 Bobby Orr, Bos., D	1986 Mario Lemieux, Pit., C	1997 Dominik Hasek, Buf., G
1976 Guy Lafleur, Mon., RW	1987 Wayne Gretzky, Edm., C	1998 Dominik Hasek, Buf., G
1977 Guy Lafleur, Mon., RW	1988 Mario Lemieux, Pit., C	1999 Jaromir Jagr, Pit., RW
1978 Guy Lafleur, Mon., RW	1989 Steve Yzerman, Det., C	2000 Jaromir Jagr, Pit., RW
1979 Marcel Dionne, LA, C	1990 Mark Messier, Edm., C	2001 Joe Sakic, Col., C
1980 Marcel Dionne, LA, C	1991 Brett Hull, St.L., RW	
1981 Mike Liut, St.L., G	1992 Mark Messier, NYR, C	

King Clancy Memorial Trophy

Awarded to the player who "best exemplifies leadership on and off the ice and who has made a noteworthy humanitarian contribution to his community" and named after former player, coach, official and executive Frank "King" Clancy. Presented by the NHL's Board of Governors.

Year	Year	Year
1988 Lanny McDonald, Calg., RW	1993 Dave Poulin, Bos., C	1998 Kelly Chase, St.L, RW
1989 Bryan Trottier, NYI, C	1994 Adam Graves, NYR, LW	1999 Rob Ray, Buf., RW
1990 Kevin Lowe, Edm., D	1995 Joe Nieuwendyk, Calg., C	2000 Curtis Joseph, Tor., G
1991 Dave Taylor, LA, RW	1996 Kris King, Win., LW	2001 Shjon Podein, Col., LW
1992 Ray Bourque, Bos., D	1997 Trevor Linden, Van., C	

Bill Masterton Trophy

Awarded to the player who "best exemplifies the qualities of perseverance, sportsmanship and dedication to hockey" and named after the 29-year-old rookie center of the Minnesota North Stars who died of a head injury sustained in a 1968 NHL game. Presented by the PHWA.

Year	Year	Year
1968 Claude Provost, Mon., RW	1980 Al MacAdam, Min., RW	1992 Mark Fitzpatrick, NYI, G
1969 Ted Hampson, Oak., C	1981 Blake Dunlop, St.L., C	1993 Mario Lemieux, Pit., C
1970 Pit Martin, Chi., C	1982 Chico Resch, Colo., G	1994 Cam Neely, Bos., RW
1971 Jean Ratelle, NYR, C	1983 Lanny McDonald, Calg., RW	1995 Pat LaFontaine, Buf., C
1972 Bobby Clarke, Phi., C	1984 Brad Park, Det., D	1996 Gary Roberts, Calg., LW
1973 Lowell MacDonald, Pit., RW	1985 Anders Hedberg, NYR, RW	1997 Tony Granato, SJ, LW
1974 Henri Richard, Mon., C	1986 Charlie Simmer, Bos., LW	1998 Jamie McLennan, St.L, C
1975 Don Luce, Buf., C	1987 Doug Jarvis, Hart., C	1999 John Cullen, TB, C
1976 Rod Gilbert, NYR, RW	1988 Bob Bourne, LA, C	2000 Ken Daneyko, NJ, D
1977 Ed Westfall, NYI, RW	1989 Tim Kerr, Phi., C	2001 Adam Graves, NYR, LW
1978 Butch Goring, LA, C	1990 Gord Kluzak, Bos., D	
1979 Serge Savard, Mon., D	1991 Dave Taylor, LA, RW	

Number One Draft Choices

Overall first choices in the NHL draft since the league staged its first universal amateur draft in 1969. Players are listed with team that selected them; those who became Rookie of the Year are in **bold** type.

Year	Year	Year
1969 Rejean Houle, Mon., LW	1980 Doug Wickenheiser, Mon., C	1991 Eric Lindros, Que., C
1970 **Gilbert Perreault,** Buf., C	1981 **Dale Hawerchuk,** Win., C	1992 Roman Hamrlik, TB, D
1971 Guy Lafleur, Mon., RW	1982 Gord Kluzak, Bos., D	1993 Alexandre Daigle, Ott., C
1972 Billy Harris, NYI, RW	1983 Brian Lawton, Min., C	1994 Ed Jovanovski, Fla., D
1973 **Denis Potvin,** NYI, D	1984 **Mario Lemieux,** Pit., C	1995 **Bryan Berard,** Ott., D
1974 Greg Joly, Wash., D	1985 Wendel Clark, Tor., LW/D	1996 Chris Phillips, Ott., D
1975 Mel Bridgman, Phi., C	1986 Joe Murphy, Det., C	1997 Joe Thornton, Bos., C
1976 Rick Green, Wash., D	1987 Pierre Turgeon, Buf., C	1998 Vincent Lecavalier, TB, C
1977 Dale McCourt, Det., C	1988 Mike Modano, Min., C	1999 Patrik Stefan, Atl., C
1978 **Bobby Smith,** Min., C	1989 Mats Sundin, Que., RW	2000 Rick DiPietro, NYI, G
1979 Rob Ramage, Colo., D	1990 Owen Nolan, Que., RW	2001 Ilya Kovalchuk, Atl., RW

World Hockey Association
WHA Finals

The World Hockey Association began play in 1972-73 as a 12-team rival of the 56-year-old NHL. The WHA played for the AVCO World Trophy in its seven playoff finals (Avco Financial Services underwrote the playoffs).

Multiple winners: Winnipeg (3); Houston (2).

Year	Winner	Head Coach	Series	Loser	Head Coach
1973	New England Whalers	Jack Kelley	4-1 (WWLWW)	Winnipeg Jets	Bobby Hull
1974	Houston Aeros	Bill Dineen	4-0	Chicago Cougars	Pat Stapleton
1975	Houston Aeros	Bill Dineen	4-0	Quebec Nordiques	Jean-Guy Gendron
1976	Winnipeg Jets	Bobby Kromm	4-0	Houston Aeros	Bill Dineen
1977	Quebec Nordiques	Marc Boileau	4-3 (LWLWWLW)	Winnipeg Jets	Bobby Kromm
1978	Winnipeg Jets	Larry Hillman	4-0	NE Whalers	Harry Neale
1979	Winnipeg Jets	Larry Hillman	4-2 (WWLWLW)	Edmonton Oilers	Glen Sather

Playoff MVPs—1973—No award; **1974**—No award; **1975**—Ron Grahame, Houston, G; **1976**—Ulf Nilsson, Winnipeg, C; **1977**—Serg Bernier, Quebec, C; **1978**—Bobby Guindon, Winnipeg, C; **1979**—Rich Preston, Winnipeg, RW.

Most Valuable Player
(Gordie Howe Trophy, 1976-79)

Year		G	A	Pts
1973	Bobby Hull, Win., LW	51	52	103
1974	Gordie Howe, Hou., RW	31	69	100
1975	Bobby Hull, Win., LW	77	65	142
1976	Marc Tardif, Que., LW	71	77	148
1977	Robbie Ftorek, Pho., C	46	71	117
1978	Marc Tardif, Que., LW	65	89	154
1979	Dave Dryden, Edm., G	41-17-2; 2.89		

Scoring Leaders

Year		Gm	G	A	Pts
1973	Andre Lacroix, Phi.	78	50	74	124
1974	Mike Walton, Min.	78	57	60	117
1975	Andre Lacroix, S. Diego	78	41	106	147
1976	Marc Tardif, Que	81	71	77	148
1977	Real Cloutier, Que	76	66	75	141
1978	Marc Tardif, Que	78	65	89	154
1979	Real Cloutier, Que	77	75	54	129

Note: In 1979, 18 year-old Rookie of the Year Wayne Gretzky finished third in scoring (46-64—110).

Rookie of the Year

Year		G	A	Pts
1973	Terry Caffery, N. Eng., C	39	61	100
1974	Mark Howe, Hou., LW	38	41	79
1975	Anders Hedberg, Win., RW	53	47	100
1976	Mark Napier, Tor., RW	43	50	93
1977	George Lyle, N. Eng., LW	39	33	72
1978	Kent Nilsson, Win., C	42	65	107
1979	Wayne Gretzky, Ind.-Edm., C	46	64	110

Best Goaltender

Year		Record	GAA
1973	Gerry Cheevers, Cleveland	32-20-0	2.84
1974	Don McLeod, Houston	33-13-3	2.56
1975	Ron Grahame, Houston	33-10-0	3.03
1976	Michel Dion, Indianapolis	14-15-1	2.74
1977	Ron Grahame, Houston	27-10-2	2.74
1978	Al Smith, New England	30-20-3	3.22
1979	Dave Dryden, Edmonton	41-17-2	2.89

Best Defenseman

Year	
1973	J.C. Tremblay, Quebec
1974	Pat Stapleton, Chicago
1975	J.C. Tremblay, Quebec
1976	Paul Shmyr, Cleveland
1977	Ron Plumb, Cincinnati
1978	Lars-Erik Sjoberg, Winnipeg
1979	Rick Ley, New England

Coach of the Year

Year		Improvement	
1973	Jack Kelley, N. Eng		46-30-2*
1974	Billy Harris, Tor	35-39-4	to 41-33-4
1975	Sandy Hucul, Pho	Expan.	to 39-31-8
1976	Bobby Kromm, Win	38-35-5	to 52-27-2*
1977	Bill Dineen, Hou	53-27-0*	to 50-24-6*
1978	Bill Dineen, Hou	50-24-6*	to 42-34-4
1979	John Brophy, Birm	36-41-3	to 32-42-6

*Won Division.

WHA All-Star Game

The WHA All-Star Game was an Eastern Division vs Western Division contest from 1973-75. In 1976, the league's five Canadian-based teams played the nine teams in the US. Over the final three seasons–East played West in 1977; AVCO Cup champion Quebec played a WHA All-Star team in 1978; and in 1979, a full WHA All-Star team played a three-game series with Moscow Dynamo of the Soviet Union.

Year	Result	Host	Coaches	Most Valuable Player
1973	East 6, West 2	Quebec	Jack Kelley, Bobby Hull	Wayne Carleton, Ottawa
1974	East 8, West 4	St. Paul, MN	Jack Kelley, Bobby Hull	Mike Walton, Minnesota
1975	West 6, East 4	Edmonton	Bill Dineen, Ron Ryan	Rejean Houle, Quebec
1976	Canada 6, USA 1	Cleveland	Jean-Guy Gendron, Bill Dineen	Can—Real Cloutier, Que. USA—Paul Shmyr, Cleve.
1977	East 4, West 2	Hartford	Jacques Demers, Bobby Kromm	East—L. Levasseur, Min. West—W. Lindstrom, Win.
1978	Quebec 5, WHA 4	Quebec	Marc Boileau, Bill Dineen	Quebec—Marc Tardif WHA—Mark Howe, NE
1979	WHA def. Moscow Dynamo 3 games to none (4-2, 4-2, 4-3)	Edmonton	Larry Hillman, P. Iburtovich	No awards

World Championship
Men

The World Hockey Championship tournament has been played regularly since 1930. The International Ice Hockey Federation (IIHF), which governs both the World and Winter Olympic tournaments, considers the Olympic champions from 1920-68 to also be the World champions. However the IIHF has not recognized an Olympic champion as World champion since 1968. The IIHF has sanctioned separate World Championships in Olympic years three times—in 1972, 1976 and again in 1992. The world championship is officially vacant for the three Olympic years from 1980-88.

Multiple winners: Soviet Union/Russia (23); Canada (21); Sweden (7); Czechoslovakia (6) Czech Republic (4), USA (2).

Year		Year		Year		Year	
1920	Canada	1951	Canada	1969	Soviet Union	1987	Sweden
1924	Canada	1952	Canada	1970	Soviet Union	1988	Not held
1928	Canada	1953	Sweden	1971	Soviet Union	1989	Soviet Union
1930	Canada	1954	Soviet Union	1972	Czechoslovakia	1990	Soviet Union
1931	Canada	1955	Canada	1973	Soviet Union	1991	Sweden
1932	Canada	1956	Soviet Union	1974	Soviet Union	1992	Sweden
1933	United States	1957	Sweden	1975	Soviet Union	1993	Russia
1934	Canada	1958	Canada	1976	Czechoslovakia	1994	Canada
1935	Canada	1959	Canada	1977	Czechoslovakia	1995	Finland
1936	Great Britain	1960	United States	1978	Soviet Union	1996	Czech Republic
1937	Canada	1961	Canada	1979	Soviet Union	1997	Canada
1938	Canada	1962	Sweden	1980	Not held	1998	Sweden
1939	Canada	1963	Soviet Union	1981	Soviet Union	1999	Czech Republic
1940-46	Not held	1964	Soviet Union	1982	Soviet Union	2000	Czech Republic
1947	Czechoslovakia	1965	Soviet Union	1983	Soviet Union	2001	Czech Republic
1948	Canada	1966	Soviet Union	1984	Not held		
1949	Czechoslovakia	1967	Soviet Union	1985	Czechoslovakia		
1950	Canada	1968	Soviet Union	1986	Soviet Union		

Women

The women's World Hockey Championship tournament is governed by the International Ice Hockey Federation (IIHF).

Multiple winners: Canada (7).

Year		Year		Year		Year	
1990	Canada	1994	Canada	1999	Canada	2001	Canada
1992	Canada	1997	Canada	2000	Canada		

Canada vs. USSR Summits

The first competition between the Soviet National Team and the NHL took place Sept. 2-28, 1972. A team of NHL All-Stars emerged as the winner of the heralded 8-game series, but just barely—winning with a record of 4-3-1 after trailing 1-3-1.

Two years later a WHA All-Star team played the Soviet Nationals and could win only one game and tie three others in eight contests. Two other Canada vs USSR series took place during NHL All-Star breaks: the three-game Challenge Cup at New York in 1979, and the two-game Rendez-Vous '87 in Quebec City in 1987.

The NHL All-Stars played the USSR in a three-game Challenge Cup series in 1979.

1972 Team Canada vs. USSR

NHL All-Stars vs Soviet National Team.

Date	City	Result	Goaltenders
9/2	Montreal	USSR, 7-3	Tretiak/Dryden
9/4	Toronto	Canada, 4-1	Esposito/Tretiak
9/6	Winnipeg	Tie, 4-4	Tretiak/Esposito
9/8	Vancouver	USSR, 5-3	Tretiak/Dryden
9/22	Moscow	USSR, 5-4	Tretiak/Esposito
9/24	Moscow	Canada, 3-2	Dryden/Tretiak
9/26	Moscow	Canada, 4-3	Esposito/Tretiak
9/28	Moscow	Canada, 6-5	Dryden/Tretiak

Standings

	W	L	T	Pts	GF	GA
Team Canada (NHL)	4	3	1	9	32	32
Soviet Union	3	4	1	7	32	32

Leading Scorers

1. Phil Esposito, Canada, (7-6—13); **2.** Aleksandr Yakushev, USSR (7-4—11); **3.** Paul Henderson, Canada (7-2—9); **4.** Boris Shadrin (3-5—8); **5.** Valeri Kharlamov, USSR (3-4—7) and Vladimir Petrov, USSR (3-4—7).

1974 Team Canada vs. USSR

WHA All-Stars vs Soviet National Team.

Date	City	Result	Goaltenders
9/17	Quebec City	Tie, 3-3	Tretiak/Cheevers
9/19	Toronto	Canada, 4-1	Cheevers/Tretiak
9/21	Winnipeg	Tie, 8-8	Tretiak/McLeod
9/23	Vancouver	Tie, 5-5	Tretiak/Cheevers
10/1	Moscow	USSR, 3-2	Tretiak/Cheevers
10/3	Moscow	USSR, 5-2	Tretiak/Cheevers
10/5	Moscow	Tie, 4-4	Cheevers/Tretiak
10/6	Moscow	USSR, 3-2	Sidelinkov/Cheevers

Standings

	W	L	T	Pts	GF	GA
Soviet Union	4	1	3	11	32	27
Team Canada (WHA)	1	4	3	5	27	32

Leading Scorers

1. Bobby Hull, Canada (7-2—9); **2.** Aleksandr Yakushev, USSR (6-2—8), Ralph Backstrom, Canada (4-4—8) and Valeri Kharlamov, USSR (2-6—8); **5.** Gordie Howe, Canada (3-4—7), Andre Lacroix, Canada (1-6—7) and Vladimir Petrov, USSR (1-6—7).

1979 Challenge Cup Series

NHL All-Stars vs Soviet National Team

Date	City	Result	Goaltenders
2/8	New York	NHL, 4-2	K. Dryden/Tretiak
2/10	New York	USSR, 5-4	Tretiak/K. Dryden
2/11	New York	USSR, 6-0	Myshkin/Cheevers

Rendez-Vous '87

NHL All-Stars vs Soviet National Team

Date	City	Result	Goaltenders
2/11	Quebec	NHL, 4-3	Fuhr/Belosheykhin
2/13	Quebec	USSR, 5-3	Belosheykhin/Fuhr

The Canada Cup

After organizing the historic 8-game Team Canada-Soviet Union series of 1972, NHL Players Association executive director Alan Eagleson and the NHL created the Canada Cup in 1976. For the first time, the best players from the world's six major hockey powers—Canada, Czechoslovakia, Finland, Russia, Sweden and the USA—competed together in one tournament.

1976
Round Robin Standings

	W	L	T	Pts	GF	GA
Canada	4	1	0	8	22	6
Czechoslovakia	3	1	1	7	19	9
Soviet Union	2	2	1	5	23	14
Sweden	2	2	1	5	16	18
United States	1	3	1	3	14	21
Finland	1	4	0	2	16	42

Finals (Best of 3)

Date	City	Score
9/13	Toronto	Canada 6, Czechoslovakia 0
9/15	Montreal	Canada 5, Czechoslovakia 4 (OT)

Note: Darryl Sittler scored the winning goal for Canada at 11:33 in overtime to clinch the Cup, 2 games to none.

Leading Scorers

1. Victor Hluktov, USSR (5-4—9), Bobby Orr, Canada (2-7—9) and Denis Potvin, Canada (1-8—9); **4.** Bobby Hull, Canada (5-3—8) and Milan Novy, Czechoslovakia (5-3—8).

Team MVPs

Canada—Rogie Vachon
Czech.—Milan Novy
USSR—Alexandr Maltsev
Sweden—Borje Salming
USA—Robbie Ftorek
Finland—Matti Hagman
Tournament MVP—Bobby Orr, Canada

1981
Round Robin Standings

	W	L	T	Pts	GF	GA
Canada	4	0	1	9	32	13
Soviet Union	3	1	1	7	20	13
Czechoslovakia	2	1	2	6	21	13
United States	2	2	1	5	17	19
Sweden	1	4	0	2	13	20
Finland	0	4	1	1	6	31

Semifinals

Date	City	Score
9/11	Ottawa	USSR 4, Czechoslovakia 1
9/11	Montreal	Canada 4, United States 1

Finals

Date	City	Score
9/13	Montreal	USSR 8, Canada 1

Leading Scorers

1. Wayne Gretzky, Canada (5-7—12); **2.** Mike Bossy, Canada (8-3—11), Bryan Trottier, Canada (3-8—11), Guy Lafleur, Canada (2-9—11), Alexei Kasatonov, USSR (1-10—11).

All-Star Team

Goal—Vladislav Tretiak, USSR; **Defense**—Arnold Kadlec, Czech. and Alexei Kasatonov, USSR; **Forwards**—Mike Bossy, Canada, Gil Perreault, Canada, and Sergei Shepelev, USSR. **Tournament MVP**—Tretiak.

1984
Round Robin Standings

	W	L	T	Pts	GF	GA
Soviet Union	5	0	0	10	22	7
United States	3	1	1	7	21	13
Sweden	3	2	0	6	15	16
Canada	2	2	1	5	23	18
West Germany	0	4	1	1	13	29
Czechoslovakia	0	4	1	1	10	21

Semifinals

Date	City	Score
9/12	Edmonton	Sweden 9, United States 2
9/15	Montreal	Canada 3, USSR 2 (OT)

Note: Mike Bossy scored the winning goal for Canada at 12:29 in overtime.

Finals (Best of 3)

Date	City	Score
9/16	Calgary	Canada 5, Sweden 2
9/18	Edmonton	Canada 6, Sweden 5

Leading Scorers

1. Wayne Gretzky, Canada (5-7—12); **2.** Michel Goulet, Canada (5-6—11), Kent Nilsson, Sweden (3-8—11), Paul Coffey, Canada (3-8—11); **5.** Hakan Loob, Sweden (6-4—10).

All-Star Team

Goal—Vladimir Myshkin, USSR; **Defense**—Paul Coffey, Canada and Rod Langway, USA; **Forwards**—Wayne Gretzky, Canada, John Tonelli, Canada, and Sergei Makarov, USSR. **Tournament MVP**—Tonelli.

1987
Round Robin Standings

	W	L	T	Pts	GF	GA
Canada	3	0	2	8	19	13
Soviet Union	3	1	1	7	22	13
Sweden	3	2	0	6	17	14
Czechoslovakia	2	2	1	5	12	15
United States	2	3	0	4	13	14
Finland	0	5	0	0	9	23

Semifinals

Date	City	Score
9/8	Hamilton	USSR 4, Sweden 2
9/9	Montreal	Canada 5, Czechoslovakia 3

Finals (Best of 3)

Date	City	Score
9/11	Montreal	USSR 6, Canada 5 (OT)
9/13	Hamilton	Canada 6, USSR 5 (2 OT)
9/15	Hamilton	Canada 6, USSR 5

Note: In Game 1, Alexander Semak of USSR scored at 5:33 in overtime. In Game 2, Mario Lemieux of Canada scored at 10:01 in the second overtime period. Lemieux also won Game 3 on a goal with 1:26 left in regulation time.

Leading Scorers

1. Wayne Gretzky, Canada (3-18—21); **2.** Mario Lemieux, Canada (11-7—18); **3.** Sergei Makarov, USSR (7-8—15); **4.** Vladimir Krutov, USSR (7-7—14); **5.** Viacheslav Bykov, USSR (2-7—9); **6.** Ray Bourque, Canada (2-6—8).

All-Star Team

Goal—Grant Fuhr, Canada; **Defense**—Ray Bourque, Canada and Viacheslav Fetisov, USSR; **Forwards**—Wayne Gretzky, Canada, Mario Lemieux, Canada, and Vladimir Krutov, USSR. **Tournament MVP**—Gretzky.

1991

Round Robin Standings

	W	L	T	Pts	GF	GA
Canada	3	0	2	8	21	11
United States	4	1	0	8	19	15
Finland	2	2	1	5	10	13
Sweden	2	3	0	4	13	17
Soviet Union	1	3	1	3	14	14
Czechoslovakia	1	4	0	2	11	18

Semifinals

Date	City	Score
9/11	Hamilton	United States 7, Finland 3
9/12	Toronto	Canada 4, Sweden 0

Finals (Best of 3)

Date	City	Score
9/14	Montreal	Canada 4, United States 1
9/16	Hamilton	Canada 4, United States 2

Leading Scorers

1. Wayne Gretzky, Canada (4-8—12); **2.** Steve Larmer, Canada (6-5—11); **3.** Brett Hull, USA (2-7—9); **4.** Mike Modano, USA (2-7—9); **5.** Mark Messier, Canada (2-6—8).

All-Star Team

Goal—Bill Ranford, Canada; **Defense**—Al MacInnis, Canada and Chris Chelios, USA; **Forwards**—Wayne Gretzky, Canada, Jeremy Roenick, USA and Mats Sundin, Sweden. **Tournament MVP**—Bill Ranford.

The World Cup

Formed jointly by the NHL and the NHL Players Association in cooperation with the International Ice Hockey Federation. The inaugural World Cup held games in nine different cities throughout North America and Europe, the most ever by a single international hockey tournament.

1996

Round Robin Standings

European Pool	W	L	T	Pts	GF	GA
Sweden	3	0	0	6	14	3
Finland	2	1	0	4	17	11
Germany	1	2	0	2	11	15
Czech Republic	0	3	0	0	4	17

North American Pool	W	L	T	Pts	GF	GA
United States	3	0	0	6	19	8
Canada	2	1	0	4	11	10
Russia	1	2	0	2	12	14
Slovakia	0	3	0	0	10	18

Semifinals

Date	City	Score
9/7	Philadelphia	Canada 3, Sweden 2 (OT)
9/8	Ottawa	United States 5, Russia 2

Finals (Best of 3)

Date	City	Score
9/10	Philadelphia	Canada 4, United States 3 (OT)
9/12	Montreal	United States 5, Canada 2
9/14	Montreal	United States 5, Canada 2

Leading Scorers

1. Brett Hull, USA (7-4—11); **2.** John LeClair, USA (6-4—10); **3.** Mats Sundin, Sweden (4-3—7); Wayne Gretzky, Canada (3-4—7); Doug Weight, USA (3-4—7); Paul Coffey, Canada (0-7—7); Brian Leetch, USA (0-7—7).

All-Tournament Team

Goal—Mike Richter, USA; **Defense**—Calle Johansson, Sweden and Chris Chelios, USA; **Forwards**—Brett Hull, USA; John LeClair, USA and Mats Sundin, Sweden. **Tournament MVP**—Mike Richter, USA.

U.S. DIVISION I COLLEGE HOCKEY

NCAA Frozen Four

The NCAA Division I hockey tournament began in 1948 and was played at the Broadmoor Ice Palace in Colorado Springs from 1948-57. Since 1958, the tournament has moved around the country, stopping for consecutive years only at Boston Garden from 1972-74. Consolation games to determine third place were played from 1949-89 and discontinued in 1990.

Multiple Winners: Michigan (9); North Dakota (7); Denver and Wisconsin (5); Boston University (4); Lake Superior St., Michigan Tech and Minnesota (3); Boston College, Colorado College, Cornell, Maine, Michigan St. and RPI (2).

Year	Champion	Head Coach	Score	Runner-up	Third Place		
1948	Michigan	Vic Heyliger	8-4	Dartmouth	Colorado College and Boston College		

Year	Champion	Head Coach	Score	Runner-up	Third Place	Score	Fourth Place
1949	Boston College	Snooks Kelley	4-3	Dartmouth	Michigan	10-4	Colorado Col.
1950	Colorado College	Cheddy Thompson	13-4	Boston Univ.	Michigan	10-6	Boston College
1951	Michigan	Vic Heyliger	7-1	Brown	Boston Univ.	7-4	Colorado College
1952	Michigan	Vic Heyliger	4-1	Colorado Col.	Yale	4-1	St. Lawrence
1953	Michigan	Vic Heyliger	7-3	Minnesota	RPI	6-3	Boston Univ.
1954	RPI	Ned Harkness	5-4*	Minnesota	Michigan	7-2	Boston College
1955	Michigan	Vic Heyliger	5-3	Colorado Col.	Harvard	6-3	St. Lawrence
1956	Michigan	Vic Heyliger	7-5	Michigan Tech	St. Lawrence	6-2	Boston College
1957	Colorado College	Tom Bedecki	13-6	Michigan	Clarkson	2-1†	Harvard
1958	Denver	Murray Armstrong	6-2	North Dakota	Clarkson	5-1	Harvard
1959	North Dakota	Bob May	4-3*	Michigan St.	Boston College	7-6†	St. Lawrence
1960	Denver	Murray Armstrong	5-3	Michigan Tech	Boston Univ.	7-6	St. Lawrence
1961	Denver	Murray Armstrong	12-2	St. Lawrence	Minnesota	4-3	RPI
1962	Michigan Tech	John MacInnes	7-1	Clarkson	Michigan	5-1	St. Lawrence
1963	North Dakota	Barry Thorndycraft	6-5	Denver	Clarkson	5-3	Boston College
1964	Michigan	Allen Renfrew	6-3	Denver	RPI	2-1	Providence
1965	Michigan Tech	John MacInnes	8-2	Boston College	North Dakota	9-5	Brown
1966	Michigan St.	Amo Bessone	6-1	Clarkson	Denver	4-3	Boston Univ.
1967	Cornell	Ned Harkness	4-1	Boston Univ.	Michigan St.	6-1	North Dakota
1968	Denver	Murray Armstrong	4-0	North Dakota	Cornell	6-1	Boston College
1969	Denver	Murray Armstrong	4-3	Cornell	Harvard	6-5†	Michigan Tech

Year	Champion	Head Coach	Score	Runner-up	Third Place	Score	Fourth Place
1970	Cornell	Ned Harkness	6-4	Clarkson	Wisconsin	6-5	Michigan Tech
1971	Boston Univ.	Jack Kelley	4-2	Minnesota	Denver	1-0	Harvard
1972	Boston Univ.	Jack Kelley	4-0	Cornell	Wisconsin	5-2	Denver
1973	Wisconsin	Bob Johnson	4-2	Denver	Boston College	3-1	Cornell
1974	Minnesota	Herb Brooks	4-2	Michigan Tech	Boston Univ.	7-5	Harvard
1975	Michigan Tech	John MacInnes	6-1	Minnesota	Boston Univ.	10-5	Harvard
1976	Minnesota	Herb Brooks	6-4	Michigan Tech	Brown	8-7	Boston Univ.
1977	Wisconsin	Bob Johnson	6-5*	Michigan	Boston Univ.	6-5	N. Hampshire
1978	Boston Univ.	Jack Parker	5-3	Boston College	Bowl. Green	4-3	Wisconsin
1979	Minnesota	Herb Brooks	4-3	North Dakota	Dartmouth	7-3	N. Hampshire
1980	North Dakota	Gino Gasparini	5-2	N. Michigan	Dartmouth	8-4	Cornell
1981	Wisconsin	Bob Johnson	6-3	Minnesota	Mich. Tech	5-2	N. Michigan
1982	North Dakota	Gino Gasparini	5-2	Wisconsin	Northeastern	10-4	N. Hampshire
1983	Wisconsin	Jeff Sauer	6-2	Harvard	Providence	4-3	Minnesota
1984	Bowling Green	Jerry York	5-4*	Minn-Duluth	North Dakota	6-5†	Michigan St.
1985	RPI	Mike Addesa	2-1	Providence	Minn-Duluth	7-6†	Boston College
1986	Michigan St.	Ron Mason	6-5	Harvard	Minnesota	6-4	Denver
1987	North Dakota	Gino Gasparini	5-3	Michigan St.	Minnesota	6-3	Harvard
1988	Lake Superior St.	Frank Anzalone	4-3*	St. Lawrence	Maine	5-2	Minnesota
1989	Harvard	Billy Cleary	4-3*	Minnesota	Michigan St.	7-4	Maine

Year	Champion	Head Coach	Score	Runner-up	Third Place
1990	Wisconsin	Jeff Sauer	7-3	Colgate	Boston College and Boston Univ.
1991	Northern Michigan	Rick Comley	8-7*	Boston Univ.	Maine and Clarkson
1992	Lake Superior St.	Jeff Jackson	5-3	Wisconsin	Michigan and Michigan St.
1993	Maine	Shawn Walsh	5-4	Lake Superior St.	Boston Univ. and Michigan
1994	Lake Superior St.	Jeff Jackson	9-1	Boston Univ.	Harvard and Minnesota
1995	Boston Univ.	Jack Parker	6-2	Maine	Michigan and Minnesota
1996	Michigan	Red Berenson	3-2*	Colorado Col.	Vermont and Boston Univ.
1997	North Dakota	Dean Blais	6-4	Boston Univ.	Colorado College and Michigan
1998	Michigan	Red Berenson	3-2*	Boston College	New Hampshire and Ohio St.
1999	Maine	Shawn Walsh	3-2*	New Hampshire	Boston College and Michigan St.
2000	North Dakota	Dean Blais	4-2	Boston College	St. Lawrence and Maine
2001	Boston College	Jerry York	3-2*	North Dakota	Michigan and Michigan St.

*Championship game overtime goals: **1954**—1:54; **1959**—4:22; **1977**—0: 23; **1984**—7:11 in 4th OT; **1988**—4:46; **1989**—4:16; **1991**—1:57 in 3rd OT; **1996**—3:35; **1998**—17:51; **1999**—10:50; **2001**—4:43.

†Consolation game overtimes ended in 1st OT except in 1957, '59, and '69, which all ended in 2nd OT.

Note: Runners-up Denver (1973) and Wisconsin (1992) had participation voided by the NCAA for using ineligible players.

Most Outstanding Player

The Most Outstanding Players of each NCAA Div. I tournament since 1948. Winners of the award who did not play for the tournament champion are in **bold** type. In 1960, three players, none on the winning team, shared the award.

Multiple Winners: Lou Angotti and Marc Behrend (2).

Year
- 1948 **Joe Riley,** Dartmouth, F
- 1949 **Dick Desmond,** Dart., G
- 1950 **Ralph Bevins,** Boston U., G
- 1951 **Ed Whiston,** Brown, G
- 1952 **Ken Kinsley,** Colo. Col., G
- 1953 John Matchefts, Mich., F
- 1954 Abbie Moore, RPI, F
- 1955 **Phil Hilton,** Colo. Col., D
- 1956 Lorne Howes, Mich., G
- 1957 Bob McCusker, Colo. Col., F
- 1958 Murray Massier, Denver, F
- 1959 Reg Morelli, N. Dakota, F
- 1960 **Lou Angotti,** Mich. Tech, F;
  Bob Marquis, Boston U., F;
  & Barry Urbanski, BU, G
- 1961 Bill Masterton, Denver, F
- 1962 Lou Angotti, Mich. Tech, F
- 1963 Al McLean, N. Dakota, F
- 1964 Bob Gray, Michigan, G

Year
- 1965 Gary Milroy, Mich. Tech, F
- 1966 Gaye Cooley, Mich. St., G
- 1967 Walt Stanowski, Cornell, D
- 1968 Gerry Powers, Denver, G
- 1969 Keith Magnuson, Denver, D
- 1970 Dan Lodboa, Cornell, D
- 1971 Dan Brady, Boston U., G
- 1972 Tim Regan, Boston, U., G
- 1973 Dean Talafous, Wisc., F
- 1974 Brad Shelstad, Minn., G
- 1975 Jim Warden, Mich. Tech, G
- 1976 Tom Vanelli, Minn., F
- 1977 Julian Baretta, Wisc., G
- 1978 Jack O'Callahan, Boston U., D
- 1979 Steve Janaszak, Minn., G
- 1980 Doug Smail, N. Dakota, F
- 1981 Marc Behrend, Wisc., G
- 1982 Phil Sykes, N. Dakota, F
- 1983 Marc Behrend, Wisc., G

Year
- 1984 Gary Kruzich, Bowl. Green, G
- 1985 **Chris Terreri,** Prov., G
- 1986 Mike Donnelly, Mich. St., F
- 1987 Tony Hrkac, N. Dakota, F
- 1988 Bruce Hoffort, Lk. Superior, G
- 1989 Ted Donato, Harvard, F
- 1990 Chris Tancill, Wisconsin, F
- 1991 Scott Beattie, No. Mich., F
- 1992 Paul Constantin, Lk. Superior, F
- 1993 Jim Montgomery, Maine, F
- 1994 Sean Tallaire, Lk. Superior, F
- 1995 Chris O'Sullivan, Boston U., F
- 1996 Brendan Morrison, Michigan, F
- 1997 Matt Henderson, N. Dakota, F
- 1998 Marty Turco, Michigan, G
- 1999 Alfie Michaud, Maine, G
- 2000 Lee Goren, N. Dakota, F
- 2001 Chuck Kobasew, Boston College, F

U.S. Division I College Hockey (Cont.)
Hobey Baker Award

College hockey's Player of the Year award; voted on by a national panel of sportswriters, broadcasters, college coaches and pro scouts. First presented in 1981 by the Decathlon Athletic Club of Bloomington, Minn., in the name of the Princeton collegiate hockey and football star who was killed in a plane crash.

Year	Year	Year
1981 Neal Broten, Minnesota, F	1988 Robb Stauber, Minnesota, G	1995 Brian Holzinger, Bowl. Green, F
1982 George McPhee, Bowl. Green, F	1989 Lane MacDonald, Harvard, F	1996 Brian Bonin, Minnesota, F
1983 Mark Fusco, Harvard, D	1990 Kip Miller, Michigan St., F	1997 Brendan Morrison, Michigan, F
1984 Tom Kurvers, Minn-Duluth, D	1991 Dave Emma, Boston College, F	1998 Chris Drury, Boston U., F
1985 Bill Watson, Minn-Duluth, F	1992 Scott Pellerin, Maine, F	1999 Jason Krog, UNH, F
1986 Scott Fusco, Harvard, F	1993 Paul Kariya, Maine, F	2000 Mike Mottau, Boston College, D
1987 Tony Hrkac, North Dakota, F	1994 Chris Marinucci, Minn-Duluth, F	2001 Ryan Miller, Michigan St., G

Coach of the Year

The Penrose Memorial Trophy, voted on by the American Hockey Coaches Association and first presented in 1951 in the name of Colorado gold and copper magnate Spencer T. Penrose. Penrose built the Broadmoor hotel and athletic complex in Colorado Springs that originally hosted the NCAA hockey championship from 1948-57.

Multiple winners: Len Ceglarski and Charlie Holt (3); Dean Blais, Rick Comley, Eddie Jeremiah, Snooks Kelly, John MacInnes, Joe Marsh, Jack Parker, Jack Riley and Cooney Weiland (2).

Year	Year	Year
1951 Eddie Jeremiah, Dartmouth	1969 Charlie Holt, New Hampshire	1988 Frank Anzalone, Lk. Superior
1952 Cheddy Thompson, Colo. Col.	1970 John MacInnes, Michigan Tech	1989 Joe Marsh, St. Lawrence
1953 John Mariucci, Minnesota	1971 Cooney Weiland, Harvard	
1954 Vic Heyliger, Michigan	1972 Snooks Kelly, BC	1990 Terry Slater, Colgate
1955 Cooney Weiland, Harvard	1973 Len Ceglarski, BC	1991 Rick Comley, No. Michigan
1956 Bill Harrison, Clarkson	1974 Charlie Holt, New Hampshire	1992 Ron Mason, Michigan St.
1957 Jack Riley, Army	1975 Jack Parker, BU	1993 George Gwozdecky, Miami-OH
1958 Harry Cleverly, BU	1976 John MacInnes, Michigan Tech	1994 Don Lucia, Colorado Col.
1959 Snooks Kelly, BC	1977 Jerry York, Clarkson	1995 Shawn Walsh, Maine
	1978 Jack Parker, BU	1996 Bruce Crowder, UMass-Lowell
1960 Jack Riley, Army	1979 Charlie Holt, New Hampshire	1997 Dean Blais, N. Dakota
1961 Murray Armstrong, Denver		1998 Tim Taylor, Yale
1962 Jack Kelley, Colby	1980 Rick Comley, No. Michigan	1999 Dick Umile, UNH
1963 Tony Frasca, Colorado Col.	1981 Bill O'Flarety, Clarkson	
1964 Tom Eccleston, Providence	1982 Fern Flaman, Northeastern	2000 Joe Marsh, St. Lawrence
1965 Jim Fullerton, Brown	1983 Bill Cleary, Harvard	2001 Dean Blais, N. Dakota
1966 Amo Bessone, Michigan St.	1984 Mike Sertich, Minn-Duluth	**Note:** 1960 winner Jack Riley won
& Len Ceglarski, Clarkson	1985 Len Ceglarski, BC	the award for coaching the USA to its
1967 Eddie Jeremiah, Dartmouth	1986 Ralph Backstrom, Denver	first hockey gold medal in the Winter
1968 Ned Harkness, Cornell	1987 Gino Gasparini, N. Dakota	Olympics at Squaw Valley.

All-Time Tournament Appearances

	App	Record		App	Record
Minnesota	25	39-28-0	RPI	8	7-8-1
Boston Univ.	25	32-27-0	N. Michigan	7	10-9-0
Michigan	24	38-17-0	Minn.-Duluth	4	6-6-0
Boston College	22	23-32-0	Dartmouth	4	4-4-0
Michigan St.	21	24-24-1	Brown	4	2-5-0
Wisconsin	18	28-16-2	Northeastern	3	3-3-1
Clarkson	18	12-21-1	Colgate	3	3-4-0
North Dakota	17	30-12-0	UMass-Lowell	3	2-3-1
Harvard	16	14-24-1	Ala-Anchorage	3	2-5-0
St. Lawrence	15	5-24-0	Vermont	3	1-4-0
Denver	14	17-12-0	St. Cloud St.	3	0-4-0
Colorado Coll.	14	13-14-0	W. Michigan	3	0-4-0
Cornell	12	11-13-0	Ohio St.	2	2-2-0
Maine	11	20-13-0	Yale	2	1-2-0
New Hampshire	11	7-15-0	Miami-OH.	2	0-2-0
Lake Superior St.	10	20-11-1	Merrimack	1	2-2-0
Michigan Tech	10	13-9-0	Niagara	1	1-1-0
Providence	9	9-15-0	Mercyhurst	1	0-1-0
Bowling Green	9	7-13-1	Princeton	1	0-1-0

Note: The NCAA voided tournament participation of Denver in 1973 and Wisconsin in 1992 for using ineligible players.

College Sports

Women's water polo and women's ice hockey each
made their NCAA debut in 2000-01.

AP/Wide World Photos

Twenty-Three Days in January

*Tragedy sways Oklahoma
from a state of euphoria
to a state of sorrow.*

Steve Cyphers *is a reporter for ESPN's
SportsCenter and College GameDay.*

There, on a field in South Florida, thousands roared in celebration. Millions watched from home while cameras captured the excitement and the giddy chaos. And just like that, the Sooners were champions.

There, on a field in eastern Colorado, the frozen silence was deafening. Dreaded rumors followed by solemn confirmations trickled back home. And just like that, 10 Cowboys were gone.

Twenty-three days separated the glory and the grief in the state of Oklahoma in January. Just 23 days.

With a perfect record (12-0) Oklahoma entered the Orange Bowl against Florida State as a decided underdog (11 points). It was only ranked #19 in the preseason AP poll, but a high-scoring offense led by Heisman Trophy runner-up Josh Heupel had thrust Bob Stoops' Sooners to the top of the polls by November. In the end, however, it was

Oklahoma's defense that secured the title. No one knew that more than Chris Weinke, the 28-year-old Florida State quarterback who edged Heupel in the Heisman voting.

Only once in 15 third-down situations did Bobby Bowden's Seminoles convert. They could muster just 27 yards on the ground, forcing Weinke to throw, which he did 51 times. It was utter domination. Linebacker Torrance Marshall, a Miami native, spearheaded the Sooners' defensive attack with six tackles, an interception, and a pass broken up. For that he was named the game's most valuable player, but seeing the speedy Sooners swarm around any unfortunate Seminole ball carrier, it was clear that this was a team effort.

The 13-2 final wasn't the kind of score that appeals to the offense-first, more-points-the-better generation of football fans. Yet because of the stakes, the tension, the strategy, the subtle nuances of a field-position game, and because of

AP/Wide World Photos

*A tale of triumph and tragedy: Oklahoma football coach **Bob Stoops** (left) celebrates after the Orange Bowl, and Oklahoma State basketball coach **Eddie Sutton** (right) mourns weeks later.*

Oklahoma's near-flawless execution, I considered myself privileged to be standing on the field.

I never stood on the field in eastern Colorado. Only on TV did I see the wreckage of the small plane that was carrying 10 men associated with the Oklahoma State basketball team, including players Daniel Lawson and Nate Fleming, home from their game against Colorado.

I watched from Stillwater, Okla. where wet, dreary skies enveloped the somber mood of a school, a city and a state, once again forced to grieve together as they had after the April 1995 bombing of the Alfred P. Murrah Federal Building and the May 1999 tornado that killed 41 and injured hundreds more.

Eddie Sutton, as fierce a coach and as strong a man as he is, shelved the importance of basketball. Games were postponed. Scheduled practices and meetings were cancelled. Instead, players gathered on their own in the basketball office or sought solace on the court.

Support came from every corner of the Big 12 and from every corner of the nation, but no matter where they went in Stillwater, everything they saw or heard

AP/Wide World Photos

*Wrestling legend **Dan Gable** (left) congratulates Iowa State's **Cael Sanderson** (right) after Sanderson tied his NCAA Division I record of 100 consecutive wins on Jan. 14.*

was about the fallen Cowboys. From the flowers, signs and makeshift memorials scattered about campus to the wet, gray skies overhead, sorrow hung in the Oklahoma air.

But on Wednesday, four days after the crash, the sun came out again. It was fitting on a day when the 10 men would be memorialized inside Gallagher-Iba Arena, the very same building where they had worked and played.

Individual services would begin the following day but on that afternoon thousands came to remember them all. Some students lined up in front of the arena over three hours before the service began. Upon entering the lobby of the arena there were portraits of the 10 men to the left. To the right was a temporary wall where classmates, friends, relatives and other mourners could write notes to the victims.

These notes were personal and compelling. They were stories. They were memories. They were tributes. They were words that left any of us who'd met any of the 10 men, feeling privileged.

Twenty-three days separated the glory and the grief in the state of Oklahoma in January. Just 23 days.

Steve Cyphers' Ten Biggest Stories of the Year in College Sports

10 ■ The Knight Commission provides grist for sportstalk radio when it recommends, among other things, that Division I-A football and basketball programs that do not graduate at least 50 percent of their players be ineligible for postseason play. Unfortunately the following day the topic was met with a yawn.

9 ■ Led by sophomore Matt Emmons, Alaska-Fairbanks rallies to win both the smallbore and air rifle team events en route to its third consecutive NCAA rifle championship and fourth in the last eight years.

8 ■ Coaches Bobby Knight and Rick Pitino each hold press conferences *during* their job interviews at Texas Tech and Louisville, respectively, leading most astute basketball observers to believe that they were the leading candidates for those jobs.

7 ■ After the death of Lute Olson's wife Bobbi, an inspired Arizona basketball squad makes its way to the NCAA Championship Game. Then all five of its starters (four of them underclassmen) declare their eligibility for the NBA draft. Eventually guard Jason Gardner withdraws his name from consideration, but the other four are taken in the draft.

6 ■ Hawaii football coach June Jones is nearly killed in a single-car accident after driving his car into a concrete pillar in Honolulu in February. In April he miraculously returns to work, and by August he is back on the field for his third season at the helm of the Rainbows.

5 ■ Division II experiences a power surge as the Bentley baseball team and Mesa State softball team set NCAA records for home runs (per game) by a team in a single season. Bentley wallops 2.39 per game (98 overall) while Mesa State hits 1.81 per game (also 98 overall).

4 ■ For the first time in school history, Nebraska, under head coach Dave Van Horn, qualifies for the College World Series held annually just 60 miles away in Omaha. Two games and two losses later, the Huskers make the long drive home.

3 ■ Following the plane crash that took the lives of 10 men associated with its basketball team, including two players, Oklahoma State plays through the loss and qualifies for the NCAA tournament. OSU finishes the regular season at 20-9 before eventually bowing out to USC in the first round of the tourney.

2 ■ The effects of Title IX shine through as women's ice hockey and women's water polo stage their first officially sanctioned NCAA championships. Minnesota-Duluth captures the first hockey crown with a 4-2 win over St. Lawrence in front of over 3,000 fans, while UCLA takes the inaugural water polo title over rival powerhouse Stanford.

1 ■ Iowa State wrestler Cael Sanderson breaks Dan Gable's record for consecutive wins in Division I and ends his junior season with a career mark of 119-0. He has three national titles under his belt and is approaching Pitt-Johnstown's Carlton Haselrig's all-division mark of 122 matches without a defeat.

inside the numbers

Major Hurricane

Since 1980, no school has won more Division I men's national titles in the four major sports (baseball, basketball, football, hockey) than Miami-FL. The Hurricanes have four national football titles and just won their fourth College World Series in 2001.

School	Titles	Sports
Miami-FL	8	4 FB, 4 Baseball
Louisiana St.	5	5 Baseball
North Dakota	5	5 Hockey
Michigan	4	2 Hockey, 1 FB, 1 Basketball

Note: Six schools are tied with three titles each: Arizona, Duke, Lake Superior State, Nebraska, Oklahoma, Wisconsin.

Clockwork Orange

Lacrosse has long been recognized as an East Coast sport. For over a decade two teams, Princeton and Syracuse, have emerged as the cream of the crop. The closeness of the two programs was never more evident than in 2001 when they battled into overtime of the championship game with Princeton finally notching the 10-9 win.

School	Titles (since 1988)
Princeton	6
Syracuse	6
North Carolina	1
Virginia	1

Note: Syracuse's title in 1990 was later revoked by the NCAA for rules infractions. It is included here.

NCAA Schools & Champs

ESP*n* information please®
SPORTS ALMANAC

NCAA Division I-A Football Schools
2001 Season
Conferences and coaches as of Sept. 10, 2001.

Joining Conference USA in 2001: TCU from WAC.
Joining WAC in 2001: BOISE ST. from Big West; LOUISIANA TECH from Independent.
New Conference in 2001: Sun Belt (7 teams)— ARKANSAS ST., IDAHO, MIDDLE TENN. ST., NEW MEXICO ST., NORTH TEXAS from Big West; LA-LAFAYETTE, LA-MONROE from Independent.
To I-A Independent in 2001: SOUTH FLORIDA, TROY STATE from Division I-AA; UTAH ST. from Big West.
Joining Conference USA in 2003: SOUTH FLORIDA from Independent.

	Nickname	Conference	Head Coach	Location	Colors
Air Force	Falcons	Mountain West	Fisher DeBerry	Colo. Springs, CO	Blue/Silver
Akron	Zips	Mid-American	Lee Owens	Akron, OH	Blue/Gold
Alabama	Crimson Tide	SEC-West	Dennis Franchione	Tuscaloosa, AL	Crimson/White
Arizona	Wildcats	Pac-10	John Mackovic	Tucson, AZ	Cardinal/Navy
Arizona St.	Sun Devils	Pac-10	Dirk Koetter	Tempe, AZ	Maroon/Gold
Arkansas	Razorbacks	SEC-West	Houston Nutt	Fayetteville, AR	Cardinal/White
Arkansas St.	Indians	Sun Belt	Joe Hollis	State Univ., AR	Scarlet/Black
Army	Cadets, Black Knights	USA	Todd Berry	West Point, NY	Black/Gold/Gray
Auburn	Tigers	SEC-West	Tommy Tuberville	Auburn, AL	Orange/Blue
Ball St.	Cardinals	Mid-American	Bill Lynch	Muncie, IN	Cardinal/White
Baylor	Bears	Big 12	Kevin Steele	Waco, TX	Green/Gold
Boise St.	Broncos	WAC	Dan Hawkins	Boise, ID	Orange/Blue
Boston College	Eagles	Big East	Tom O'Brien	Chestnut Hill, MA	Maroon/Gold
Bowling Green	Falcons	Mid-American	Urban Meyer	Bowling Green, OH	Orange/Brown
Brigham Young	Cougars	Mountain West	Gary Crowton	Provo, UT	Royal Blue/White
Buffalo	Bulls	Mid-American	Jim Hofher	Buffalo, NY	Royal Blue/White
California	Golden Bears	Pac-10	Tom Holmoe	Berkeley, CA	Blue/Gold
Central Florida	Golden Knights	Independent	Mike Kruczek	Orlando, FL	Black/Gold
Central Michigan	Chippewas	Mid-American	Mike DeBord	Mt. Pleasant, MI	Maroon/Gold
Cincinnati	Bearcats	USA	Rick Minter	Cincinnati, OH	Red/Black
Clemson	Tigers	ACC	Tommy Bowden	Clemson, SC	Purple/Orange
Colorado	Buffaloes	Big 12	Gary Barnett	Boulder, CO	Silver/Gold/Black
Colorado St.	Rams	Mountain West	Sonny Lubick	Ft. Collins, CO	Green/Gold
Connecticut	Huskies	Independent	Randy Edsall	Storrs, CT	Blue/White
Duke	Blue Devils	ACC	Carl Franks	Durham, NC	Royal Blue/White
East Carolina	Pirates	USA	Steve Logan	Greenville, NC	Purple/Gold
Eastern Michigan	Eagles	Mid-American	Jeff Woodruff	Ypsilanti, MI	Green/White
Florida	Gators	SEC-East	Steve Spurrier	Gainesville, FL	Orange/Blue
Florida St.	Seminoles	ACC	Bobby Bowden	Tallahassee, FL	Garnet/Gold
Fresno St.	Bulldogs	WAC	Pat Hill	Fresno, CA	Cardinal/Blue
Georgia	Bulldogs	SEC-East	Mark Richt	Athens, GA	Red/Black
Georgia Tech	Yellow Jackets	ACC	George O'Leary	Atlanta, GA	Old Gold/White
Hawaii	Warriors	WAC	June Jones	Honolulu, HI	Green/White
Houston	Cougars	USA	Dana Dimel	Houston, TX	Scarlet/White
Idaho	Vandals	Sun Belt	Tom Cable	Moscow, ID	Silver/Gold
Illinois	Fighting Illini	Big Ten	Ron Turner	Champaign, IL	Orange/Blue
Indiana	Hoosiers	Big Ten	Cam Cameron	Bloomington, IN	Cream/Crimson
Iowa	Hawkeyes	Big Ten	Kirk Ferentz	Iowa City, IA	Old Gold/Black
Iowa St.	Cyclones	Big 12	Dan McCarney	Ames, IA	Cardinal/Gold
Kansas	Jayhawks	Big 12	Terry Allen	Lawrence, KS	Crimson/Blue
Kansas St.	Wildcats	Big 12	Bill Snyder	Manhattan, KS	Purple/White
Kent St.	Golden Flashes	Mid-American	Dean Pees	Kent, OH	Navy Blue/Gold
Kentucky	Wildcats	SEC-East	Guy Morriss	Lexington, KY	Blue/White
LSU	Fighting Tigers	SEC-West	Nick Saban	Baton Rouge, LA	Purple/Gold
LA-Lafayette	Ragin' Cajuns	Sun Belt	Jerry Baldwin	Lafayette, LA	Vermilion/White
LA-Monroe	Indians	Sun Belt	Bobby Keasler	Monroe, LA	Maroon/Gold
Louisiana Tech	Bulldogs	WAC	Jack Bicknell III	Ruston, LA	Red/Blue
Louisville	Cardinals	USA	John L. Smith	Louisville, KY	Red/Black/White

	Nickname	Conference	Head Coach	Location	Colors
Marshall	Thundering Herd	Mid-American	Bob Pruett	Huntington, WV	Green/White
Maryland	Terrapins, Terps	ACC	Ralph Friedgen	College Park, MD	Red/White/Black/Gold
Memphis	Tigers	USA	Tommy West	Memphis, TN	Blue/Gray
Miami-FL	Hurricanes	Big East	Larry Coker	Coral Gables, FL	Orange/Grn./Wt.
Miami-OH	RedHawks	Mid-American	Terry Hoeppner	Oxford, OH	Red/White
Michigan	Wolverines	Big Ten	Lloyd Carr	Ann Arbor, MI	Maize/Blue
Michigan St.	Spartans	Big Ten	Bobby Williams	E. Lansing, MI	Green/White
Middle Tenn. St.	Blue Raiders	Sun Belt	Andy McCollum	Murfreesboro, TN	Blue/White
Minnesota	Golden Gophers	Big Ten	Glen Mason	Minneapolis, MN	Maroon/Gold
Mississippi	Ole Miss, Rebels	SEC-West	David Cutcliffe	Oxford, MS	Cardinal/Navy Bl.
Mississippi St.	Bulldogs	SEC-West	Jackie Sherrill	Starkville, MS	Maroon/White
Missouri	Tigers	Big 12	Gary Pinkel	Columbia, MO	Old Gold/Black
Navy	Midshipmen	Independent	Charlie Weatherbie	Annapolis, MD	Navy Blue/Gold
Nebraska	Cornhuskers	Big 12	Frank Solich	Lincoln, NE	Scarlet/Cream
Nevada	Wolf Pack	WAC	Chris Tormey	Reno, NV	Silver/Blue
New Mexico	Lobos	Mountain West	Rocky Long	Albuquerque, NM	Cherry/Silver
New Mexico St.	Aggies	Sun Belt	Tony Samuel	Las Cruces, NM	Crimson/White
North Carolina	Tar Heels	ACC	John Bunting	Chapel Hill, NC	Carolina Blue/Wt.
North Carolina St.	Wolfpack	ACC	Chuck Amato	Raleigh, NC	Red/White
North Texas	Mean Green	Sun Belt	Darrell Dickey	Denton, TX	Green/White
Northern Illinois	Huskies	Mid-American	Joe Novak	De Kalb, IL	Cardinal/Black
Northwestern	Wildcats	Big Ten	Randy Walker	Evanston, IL	Purple/White
Notre Dame	Fighting Irish	Independent	Bob Davie	Notre Dame, IN	Gold/Blue
Ohio University	Bobcats	Mid-American	Brian Knorr	Athens, OH	Ohio Grn./Wt.
Ohio St.	Buckeyes	Big Ten	Jim Tressel	Columbus, OH	Scarlet/Gray
Oklahoma	Sooners	Big 12	Bob Stoops	Norman, OK	Crimson/Cream
Oklahoma St.	Cowboys	Big 12	Les Miles	Stillwater, OK	Orange/Black
Oregon	Ducks	Pac-10	Mike Bellotti	Eugene, OR	Green/Yellow
Oregon St.	Beavers	Pac-10	Dennis Erickson	Corvallis, OR	Orange/Black
Penn St.	Nittany Lions	Big Ten	Joe Paterno	University Park, PA	Blue/White
Pittsburgh	Panthers	Big East	Walt Harris	Pittsburgh, PA	Blue/Gold
Purdue	Boilermakers	Big Ten	Joe Tiller	W. Lafayette, IN	Old Gold/Black
Rice	Owls	WAC	Ken Hatfield	Houston, TX	Blue/Gray
Rutgers	Scarlet Knights	Big East	Greg Schiano	New Brunswick, NJ	Scarlet
San Diego St.	Aztecs	Mountain West	Ted Tollner	San Diego, CA	Scarlet/Black
San Jose St.	Spartans	WAC	Fitz Hill	San Jose, CA	Gold/White/Blue
South Carolina	Gamecocks	SEC-East	Lou Holtz	Columbia, SC	Garnet/Black
South Florida	Bulls	Independent	Jim Leavitt	Tampa, FL	Green/Gold
SMU	Mustangs	WAC	Mike Cavan	Dallas, TX	Red/Blue
Southern Miss.	Golden Eagles	USA	Jeff Bower	Hattiesburg, MS	Black/Gold
Stanford	Cardinal	Pac-10	Tyrone Willingham	Stanford, CA	Cardinal/White
Syracuse	Orangemen	Big East	Paul Pasqualoni	Syracuse, NY	Orange
Temple	Owls	Big East	Bobby Wallace	Philadelphia, PA	Cherry/White
Tennessee	Volunteers	SEC-East	Phillip Fulmer	Knoxville, TN	Orange/White
Texas	Longhorns	Big 12	Mack Brown	Austin, TX	Burnt Orange/Wt.
Texas A&M	Aggies	Big 12	R.C. Slocum	College Station, TX	Maroon/White
TCU	Horned Frogs	USA	Gary Patterson	Ft. Worth, TX	Purple/White
Texas Tech	Red Raiders	Big 12	Mike Leach	Lubbock, TX	Scarlet/Black
Toledo	Rockets	Mid-American	Tom Amstutz	Toledo, OH	Blue/Gold
Troy State	Trojans	Independent	Larry Blakeney	Troy, AL	Cardinal/Slvr./Blk.
Tulane	Green Wave	USA	Chris Scelfo	New Orleans, LA	Olive Grn./Sky Bl.
Tulsa	Golden Hurricane	WAC	Keith Burns	Tulsa, OK	Blue/Gold
UAB	Blazers	USA	Watson Brown	Birmingham, AL	Green/Gold
UCLA	Bruins	Pac-10	Bob Toledo	Los Angeles, CA	Blue/Gold
UNLV	Rebels	Mountain West	John Robinson	Las Vegas, NV	Scarlet/Gray
USC	Trojans	Pac-10	Pete Carroll	Los Angeles, CA	Cardinal/Gold
Utah	Utes	Mountain West	Ron McBride	Salt Lake City, UT	Crimson/White
Utah St.	Aggies	Independent	Mick Dennehy	Logan, UT	Navy Blue/White
UTEP	Miners	WAC	Gary Nord	El Paso, TX	Orange/Blue/Wt.
Vanderbilt	Commodores	SEC-East	Woody Widenhofer	Nashville, TN	Black/Gold
Virginia	Cavaliers	ACC	Al Groh	Charlottesville, VA	Orange/Blue
Virginia Tech	Hokies, Gobblers	Big East	Frank Beamer	Blacksburg, VA	Orange/Maroon
Wake Forest	Demon Deacons	ACC	Jim Grobe	Winston-Salem, NC	Old Gold/Black
Washington	Huskies	Pac-10	Rick Neuheisel	Seattle, WA	Purple/Gold
Washington St.	Cougars	Pac-10	Mike Price	Pullman, WA	Crimson/Gray
West Virginia	Mountaineers	Big East	Rich Rodriguez	Morgantown, WV	Old Gold/Blue
Western Michigan	Broncos	Mid-American	Gary Darnell	Kalamazoo, MI	Brown/Gold
Wisconsin	Badgers	Big Ten	Barry Alvarez	Madison, WI	Cardinal/White
Wyoming	Cowboys	Mountain West	Vic Koenning	Laramie, WY	Brown/Yellow

NCAA Division I-AA Football Schools

2001 Season

Conferences and coaches as of Sept. 10, 2001.

Joining Atlantic 10 in 2001: HOFSTRA from Independent.
Joining Gateway in 2001: WESTERN KENTUCKY from Ohio Valley.
Joining Patriot in 2001: GEORGETOWN from Independent.
Joining Pioneer in 2001: AUSTIN PEAY ST., DAVIDSON, JACKSONVILLE, MOREHEAD ST. from Independent.
To I-AA Independent in 2001: CAL STATE NORTHRIDGE from Big Sky; MORRIS BROWN, SAVANNAH ST. from Division II; FLORIDA ATLANTIC (new program).
New Conference in 2002: Big South (5 teams) — CHARLESTON SOUTHERN, ELON, LIBERTY, GARDNER-WEBB (in 2002); COASTAL CAROLINA (in 2003).
Joining Ohio Valley in 2003: SAMFORD from Independent.
To I-AA Independent in 2003: SOUTHEASTERN LOUISIANA (program reinstated).

	Nickname	Conference	Head Coach	Location	Colors
Alabama A&M	Bulldogs	SWAC	Ron Cooper	Huntsville, AL	Maroon/White
Alabama St.	Hornets	SWAC	L.C. Cole	Montgomery, AL	Black/Gold
Albany	Great Danes	Northeast	Bob Ford	Albany, NY	Purple/Gold
Alcorn St.	Braves	SWAC	Johnny Thomas	Lorman, MS	Purple/Gold
Appalachian St.	Mountaineers	Southern	Jerry Moore	Boone, NC	Black/Gold
Ark.-Pine Bluff	Golden Lions	SWAC	Lee Hardman	Pine Bluff, AR	Black/Gold
Austin Peay St.	Governors	Pioneer	Bill Schmitz	Clarksville, TN	Red/White
Bethune-Cookman	Wildcats	Mid-Eastern	Alvin Wyatt	Daytona Beach, FL	Maroon/Gold
Brown	Bears	Ivy	Phil Estes	Providence, RI	Brown/Red/White
Bucknell	Bison	Patriot	Tom Gadd	Lewisburg, PA	Orange/Blue
Butler	Bulldogs	Pioneer	Ken LaRose	Indianapolis, IN	Blue/White
Cal Poly	Mustangs	Independent	Rich Ellerson	San Luis Obispo, CA	Green/Gold
CS-Northridge	Matadors	Independent	Jeff Kearin	Northridge, CA	Red/White/Black
CS-Sacramento	Hornets	Big Sky	John Volek	Sacramento, CA	Green/Gold
Canisius	Golden Griffins	Metro Atlantic	Edward Argast	Buffalo, NY	Blue/Gold
Central Conn. St.	Blue Devils	Northeast	Paul Schudel	New Britain, CT	Blue/White
Charleston So.	Buccaneers	Independent	David Dowd	Charleston, SC	Blue/Gold
The Citadel	Bulldogs	Southern	Ellis Johnson	Charleston, SC	Blue/White
Colgate	Raiders	Patriot	Dick Biddle	Hamilton, NY	Maroon/White/Gray
Columbia	Lions	Ivy	Ray Tellier	New York, NY	Lt. Blue/White
Cornell	Big Red	Ivy	Tim Pendergast	Ithaca, NY	Carnelian/White
Dartmouth	Big Green	Ivy	John Lyons	Hanover, NH	Green/White
Davidson	Wildcats	Pioneer	Mike Toop	Davidson, NC	Red/Black
Dayton	Flyers	Pioneer	Mike Kelly	Dayton, OH	Red/Blue
Delaware	Blue Hens	Atlantic 10	Tubby Raymond	Newark, DE	Blue/Gold
Delaware St.	Hornets	Mid-Eastern	Ben Blacknall	Dover, DE	Red/Blue
Drake	Bulldogs	Pioneer	Rob Ash	Des Moines, IA	Blue/White
Duquesne	Dukes	Metro Atlantic	Greg Gattuso	Pittsburgh, PA	Red/Blue
East Tenn. St.	Buccaneers	Southern	Paul Hamilton	Johnson City, TN	Blue/Gold
Eastern Illinois	Panthers	Ohio Valley	Bob Spoo	Charleston, IL	Blue/Gray
Eastern Kentucky	Colonels	Ohio Valley	Roy Kidd	Richmond, KY	Maroon/White
Eastern Washington	Eagles	Big Sky	Paul Wulff	Cheney, WA	Red/White
Elon	Phoenix	Independent	Al Seagraves	Elon, NC	Maroon/Gold
Fairfield	Stags	Metro Atlantic	Joe Bernard	Fairfield, CT	Cardinal Red
Florida A&M	Rattlers	Mid-Eastern	Billy Joe	Tallahassee, FL	Orange/Green
Florida Atlantic	Owls	Independent	H. Schnellenberger	Boca Raton, FL	Blue/Red
Fordham	Rams	Patriot	Dave Clawson	Bronx, NY	Maroon/White
Furman	Paladins	Southern	Bobby Johnson	Greenville, SC	Purple/White
Gardner-Webb	Bulldogs	Independent	Steve Patton	Boiling Springs, NC	Scarlet/Black
Georgetown	Hoyas	Patriot	Bob Benson	Washington, DC	Blue/Gray
Georgia Southern	Eagles	Southern	Paul Johnson	Statesboro, GA	Blue/White
Grambling St.	Tigers	SWAC	Doug Williams	Grambling, LA	Black/Gold
Hampton	Pirates	Mid-Eastern	Joe Taylor	Hampton, VA	Royal Blue/White
Harvard	Crimson	Ivy	Tim Murphy	Cambridge, MA	Crimson/Black/White
Hofstra	Flying Dutchmen	Atlantic 10	Joe Gardi	Hempstead, NY	Gray/White/Gold
Holy Cross	Crusaders	Patriot	Dan Allen	Worcester, MA	Royal Purple
Howard	Bison	Mid-Eastern	Steve Wilson	Washington, DC	Blue/Wt./Red
Idaho St.	Bengals	Big Sky	Larry Lewis	Pocatello, ID	Orange/Black
Illinois St.	Redbirds	Gateway	Denver Johnson	Normal, IL	Red/White
Indiana St.	Sycamores	Gateway	Tim McGuire	Terre Haute, IN	Royal Blue/White
Iona	Gaels	Metro Atlantic	Fred Mariani	New Rochelle, NY	Maroon/Gold
Jackson St.	Tigers	SWAC	Robert Hughes	Jackson, MS	Blue/White
Jacksonville	Dolphins	Pioneer	Steve Gilbert	Jacksonville, FL	Green/White
Jacksonville St.	Gamecocks	Southland	Jack Crowe	Jacksonville, AL	Red/White
James Madison	Dukes	Atlantic 10	Mickey Matthews	Harrisonburg, VA	Purple/Gold

	Nickname	Conference	Head Coach	Location	Colors
Lafayette	Leopards	Patriot	Frank Tavani	Easton, PA	Maroon/White
La Salle	Explorers	Metro Atlantic	Bill Manlove	Philadelphia, PA	Blue/Gold
Lehigh	Engineers	Patriot	Pete Lembo	Bethlehem, PA	Brown/White
Liberty	Flames	Independent	Ken Karcher	Lynchburg, VA	Red/White/Blue
Maine	Black Bears	Atlantic 10	Jack Cosgrove	Orono, ME	Blue/White
Marist	Red Foxes	Metro Atlantic	Jim Parady	Poughkeepsie, NY	Red/White
Massachusetts	Minutemen	Atlantic 10	Mark Whipple	Amherst, MA	Maroon/White
McNeese St.	Cowboys	Southland	Tommy Tate	Lake Charles, LA	Blue/Gold
Miss. Valley St.	Delta Devils	SWAC	LaTraia Jones	Itta Bena, MS	Green/White
Monmouth	Hawks	Northeast	Kevin Callahan	W. Long Branch, NJ	Royal Blue/White
Montana	Grizzlies	Big Sky	Joe Glenn	Missoula, MT	Maroon/Gray
Montana St.	Bobcats	Big Sky	Mike Kramer	Bozeman, MT	Blue/Gold
Morehead St.	Eagles	Pioneer	Matt Ballard	Morehead, KY	Blue/Gold
Morgan St.	Bears	Mid-Eastern	Stanley Mitchell	Baltimore, MD	Blue/Orange
Morris Brown	Wolverines	Independent	Solomon Brannan	Atlanta, GA	Purple/Black
Murray St.	Racers	Ohio Valley	Joe Pannunzio	Murray, KY	Blue/Gold
New Hampshire	Wildcats	Atlantic 10	Sean McDonnell	Durham, NH	Blue/White
Nicholls St.	Colonels	Southland	Daryl Daye	Thibodaux, LA	Red/Gray
Norfolk State	Spartans	Mid-Eastern	Maurice Forte	Norfolk, VA	Green/Gold
North Carolina A&T	Aggies	Mid-Eastern	Bill Hayes	Greensboro, NC	Blue/Gold
Northeastern	Huskies	Atlantic 10	Don Brown	Boston, MA	Red/Black
Northern Arizona	Lumberjacks	Big Sky	Jerome Souers	Flagstaff, AZ	Blue/Gold
Northern Iowa	Panthers	Gateway	Mark Farley	Cedar Falls, IA	Purple/Old Gold
Northwestern St.	Demons	Southland	Steve Roberts	Natchitoches, LA	Purple/White
Pennsylvania	Quakers	Ivy	Al Bagnoli	Philadelphia, PA	Red/Blue
Portland St.	Vikings	Big Sky	Tim Walsh	Portland, OR	Green/Gray
Prairie View A&M	Panthers	SWAC	Larry Dorsey	Prairie View, TX	Purple/Gold
Princeton	Tigers	Ivy	Roger Hughes	Princeton, NJ	Orange/Black
Rhode Island	Rams	Atlantic 10	Tim Stowers	Kingston, RI	Light Blue/Navy/Wt.
Richmond	Spiders	Atlantic 10	Jim Reid	Richmond, VA	Red/Blue
Robert Morris	Colonials	Northeast	Joe Walton	Moon Township, PA	Blue/White
Sacred Heart	Pioneers	Northeast	Jim Fleming	Fairfield, CT	Scarlet/White
St. Francis-PA	Red Flash	Northeast	David Jaumotte	Loretto, PA	Red/White
St. John's-NY	Red Storm	Northeast	Bob Ricca	Jamaica, NY	Red/White
St. Mary's-CA	Gaels	Independent	Tim Landis	Moraga, CA	Red/Blue
St. Peter's	Peacocks	Metro Atlantic	Rob Stern	Jersey City, NJ	Blue/White
Sam Houston St.	Bearkats	Southland	Ron Randleman	Huntsville, TX	Orange/White
Samford	Bulldogs	Independent	Pete Hurt	Birmingham, AL	Crimson/Blue
San Diego	Toreros	Pioneer	Kevin McGarry	San Diego, CA	Lt. Blue/Navy
Savannah St.	Tigers	Independent	Bill Davis	Savannah, GA	Orange/Blue
Siena	Saints	Metro Atlantic	Jay Bateman	Loudonville, NY	Green/Gold
South Carolina St.	Bulldogs	Mid-Eastern	Willie Jeffries	Orangeburg, SC	Garnet/Blue
SE Missouri St.	Indians	Ohio Valley	Tim Billings	Cape Girardeau, MO	Red/Black
Southern-BR	Jaguars	SWAC	Pete Richardson	Baton Rouge, LA	Blue/Gold
Southern Illinois	Salukis	Gateway	Jerry Kill	Cardondale, IL	Maroon/White
Southern Utah	Thunderbirds	Independent	C. Ray Gregory	Cedar City, UT	Scarlet/White
SW Missouri St.	Bears	Gateway	Randy Ball	Springfield, MO	Maroon/White
SW Texas St.	Bobcats	Southland	Bob DeBesse	San Marcos, TX	Maroon/Gold
S.F. Austin St.	Lumberjacks	Southland	Mike Santiago	Nacogdoches, TX	Purple/White
Stony Brook	Seawolves	Northeast	Sam Kornhauser	Stony Brook, NY	Scarlet/Gray
Tenn-Chattanooga	Mocs	Southern	Donnie Kirkpatrick	Chattanooga, TN	Navy Blue/Old Gold
Tennessee-Martin	Skyhawks	Ohio Valley	Sam McCorkle	Martin, TN	Orange/White/Blue
Tennessee St.	Tigers	Ohio Valley	James Reese	Nashville, TN	Blue/White
Tennessee Tech	Golden Eagles	Ohio Valley	Mike Hennigan	Cookeville, TN	Purple/Gold
Texas Southern	Tigers	SWAC	Bill Thomas	Houston, TX	Maroon/Gray
Towson	Tigers	Patriot	Gordy Combs	Towson, MD	Gold/White
Valparaiso	Crusaders	Pioneer	Tom Horne	Valparaiso, IN	Brown/Gold
Villanova	Wildcats	Atlantic 10	Andy Talley	Villanova, PA	Blue/White
VMI	Keydets	Southern	Cal McCombs	Lexington, VA	Red/White/Yellow
Wagner	Seahawks	Northeast	Walt Hameline	Staten Island, NY	Green/White
Weber St.	Wildcats	Big Sky	Jerry Graybeal	Ogden, UT	Royal Purple/White
Western Carolina	Catamounts	Southern	Bill Bleil	Cullowhee, NC	Purple/Gold
Western Illinois	Leathernecks	Gateway	Don Patterson	Macomb, IL	Purple/Gold
Western Kentucky	Hilltoppers	Gateway	Jack Harbaugh	Bowling Green, KY	Red/White
William & Mary	Tribe	Atlantic 10	Jimmye Laycock	Williamsburg, VA	Green/Gold/Silver
Wofford	Terriers	Southern	Mike Ayers	Spartanburg, SC	Old Gold/Black
Yale	Bulldogs, Elis	Ivy	Jack Siedlecki	New Haven, CT	Yale Blue/White
Youngstown St.	Penguins	Gateway	Jon Heacock	Youngstown, OH	Red/White

NCAA Division I Basketball Schools
2001-2002 Season
Conferences and coaches as of Sept. 10, 2001.

Joining America East in 2001-2002: ALBANY, STONY BROOK from Independent; BINGHAMTON from Division II.
Joining Atlantic 10 in 2001-2002: RICHMOND from Colonial.
Joining Atlantic Sun (formerly Trans America) in 2001-2002: BELMONT from Independent.
Joining Big South in 2001-2002: BIRMINGHAM SOUTHERN from Independent.
Joining Big West in 2001-2002: CAL STATE NORTHRIDGE from Big Sky; UC-RIVERSIDE from Division II.
Joining Colonial 2001-2002: DELAWARE, DREXEL, HOFSTRA, TOWSON from America East.
Joining Conference USA in 2001-2002: EAST CAROLINA from Colonial; TCU from WAC.
Joining Horizon League (formerly Midwestern) in 2001-2002: YOUNGSTOWN ST. from Mid-Continent.
Joining Patriot in 2001-2002: AMERICAN from Colonial.
Joining WAC in 2001-2002: BOISE ST. from Big West; LOUISIANA TECH from Sun Belt.
Joining Atlantic Sun (formerly Trans America) in 2002-2003: GARDNER-WEBB from Independent.
Joining Ohio Valley in 2003-2004: JACKSONVILLE ST., SAMFORD from Atlantic Sun.

	Nickname	Conference	Head Coach	Location	Colors
Air Force	Falcons	Mountain West	Joe Scott	Colo. Springs, CO	Blue/Silver
Akron	Zips	Mid-American	Dan Hipsher	Akron, OH	Blue/Gold
Alabama	Crimson Tide	SEC-West	Mark Gottfried	Tuscaloosa, AL	Crimson/White
Alabama A&M	Bulldogs	SWAC	Vann Pettaway	Huntsville, AL	Maroon/White
Alabama St.	Hornets	SWAC	Rob Spivery	Montgomery, AL	Black/Gold
Albany	Great Danes	America East	Scott Beeten	Albany, NY	Purple/Gold
Alcorn St.	Braves	SWAC	Davey Whitney	Lorman, MS	Purple/Gold
American	Eagles	Patriot	Jeff Jones	Washington, DC	Red/Blue
Appalachian St.	Mountaineers	Southern	Houston Fancher	Boone, NC	Black/Gold
Arizona	Wildcats	Pac-10	Lute Olson	Tucson, AZ	Cardinal/Navy
Arizona St.	Sun Devils	Pac-10	Rob Evans	Tempe, AZ	Maroon/Gold
Arkansas	Razorbacks	SEC-West	Nolan Richardson	Fayetteville, AR	Cardinal/White
Ark.-Little Rock	Trojans	Sun Belt	Porter Moser	Little Rock, AR	Maroon/White
Ark.-Pine Bluff	Golden Lions	SWAC	Harold Blevins	Pine Bluff, AR	Black/Gold
Arkansas St.	Indians	Sun Belt	Dickey Nutt	State Univ., AR	Scarlet/Black
Army	Black Knights	Patriot	Pat Harris	West Point, NY	Black/Gold/Gray
Auburn	Tigers	SEC-West	Cliff Ellis	Auburn, AL	Orange/Blue
Austin Peay St.	Governors	Ohio Valley	Dave Loos	Clarksville, TN	Red/White
Ball St.	Cardinals	Mid-American	Tim Buckley	Muncie, IN	Cardinal/White
Baylor	Bears	Big 12	Dave Bliss	Waco, TX	Green/Gold
Belmont	Bruins	Atlantic Sun	Rick Byrd	Nashville, TN	Navy Blue/Red
Bethune-Cookman	Wildcats	Mid-Eastern	Horace Broadnax	Daytona Beach, FL	Maroon/Gold
Binghamton	Bearcats	America East	Al Walker	Binghamton, NY	Green/Black/White
Birmingham Southern	Panthers	Big South	Duane Reboul	Birmingham, AL	Black/Gold
Boise St.	Broncos	WAC	Rod Jensen	Boise, ID	Orange/Blue
Boston College	Eagles	Big East	Al Skinner	Chestnut Hill, MA	Maroon/Gold
Boston University	Terriers	America East	Dennis Wolff	Boston, MA	Scarlet/White
Bowling Green	Falcons	Mid-American	Dan Dakich	Bowling Green, OH	Orange/Brown
Bradley	Braves	Mo. Valley	Jim Molinari	Peoria, IL	Red/White
Brigham Young	Cougars	Mountain West	Steve Cleveland	Provo, UT	Royal Blue/White
Brown	Bears	Ivy	Glen Miller	Providence, RI	Brown/Cardinal/White
Bucknell	Bison	Patriot	Pat Flannery	Lewisburg, PA	Orange/Blue
Buffalo	Bulls	Mid-American	R. Witherspoon	Buffalo, NY	Royal Blue/White
Butler	Bulldogs	Horizon	Todd Lickliter	Indianapolis, IN	Blue/White
California	Golden Bears	Pac-10	Ben Braun	Berkeley, CA	Blue/Gold
Cal Poly	Mustangs	Big West	Kevin Bromley	San Luis Obispo, CA	Green/Gold
CS-Fullerton	Titans	Big West	Donny Daniels	Fullerton, CA	Blue/Orange/White
CS-Northridge	Matadors	Big West	Bobby Braswell	Northridge, CA	Red/White/Black
CS-Sacramento	Hornets	Big Sky	Jerome Jenkins	Sacramento, CA	Green/Gold
Campbell	Fighting Camels	Atlantic Sun	Billy Lee	Buies Creek, NC	Orange/Black
Canisius	Golden Griffins	Metro Atlantic	Mike MacDonald	Buffalo, NY	Blue/Gold
Centenary	Gentlemen	Independent	Kevin Johnson	Shreveport, LA	Maroon/White
Central Conn. St.	Blue Devils	Northeast	Howie Dickenman	New Britain, CT	Blue/White
Central Florida	Golden Knights	Atlantic Sun	Kirk Speraw	Orlando, FL	Black/Gold
Central Michigan	Chippewas	Mid-American	Jay Smith	Mt. Pleasant, MI	Maroon/Gold
Charleston So.	Buccaneers	Big South	Jim Platt	Charleston, SC	Blue/Gold
Chicago St.	Cougars	Mid-Continent	Bo Ellis	Chicago, IL	Green/White
Cincinnati	Bearcats	USA	Bob Huggins	Cincinnati, OH	Red/Black
The Citadel	Bulldogs	Southern	Pat Dennis	Charleston, SC	Blue/White
Clemson	Tigers	ACC	Larry Shyatt	Clemson, SC	Purple/Orange
Cleveland St.	Vikings	Horizon	Rollie Massimino	Cleveland, OH	Forest Green/White
Coastal Carolina	Chanticleers	Big South	Pete Strickland	Conway, SC	Green/Bronze/Black
Colgate	Raiders	Patriot	Emmett Davis	Hamilton, NY	Maroon/Gray/White
College of Charleston	Cougars	Southern	John Kresse	Charleston, SC	Maroon/White

NCAA Division I Basketball Schools (Cont.)

	Nickname	Conference	Head Coach	Location	Colors
Colorado	Buffaloes	Big 12	Ricardo Patton	Boulder, CO	Silver/Gold/Black
Colorado St.	Rams	Mountain West	Dale Layer	Ft. Collins, CO	Green/Gold
Columbia	Lions	Ivy	Armond Hill	New York, NY	Lt. Blue/White
Connecticut	Huskies	Big East	Jim Calhoun	Storrs, CT	Blue/White
Coppin St.	Eagles	Mid-Eastern	Ron Mitchell	Baltimore, MD	Royal Blue/Gold
Cornell	Big Red	Ivy	Steve Donahue	Ithaca, NY	Carnelian/White
Creighton	Bluejays	Mo. Valley	Dana Altman	Omaha, NE	Blue/White
Dartmouth	Big Green	Ivy	Dave Faucher	Hanover, NH	Green/White
Davidson	Wildcats	Southern	Bob McKillop	Davidson, NC	Red/Black
Dayton	Flyers	Atlantic 10	Oliver Purnell	Dayton, OH	Red/Blue
Delaware	Fightin' Blue Hens	Colonial	David Henderson	Newark, DE	Blue/Gold
Delaware St.	Hornets	Mid-Eastern	Greg Jackson	Dover, DE	Red/Columbia Blue
Denver	Pioneers	Sun Belt	Terry Carroll	Denver, CO	Crimson/Gold
DePaul	Blue Demons	USA	Pat Kennedy	Chicago, IL	Scarlet/Blue
Detroit Mercy	Titans	Horizon	Perry Watson	Detroit, MI	Red/White/Blue
Drake	Bulldogs	Mo. Valley	Kurt Kanaskie	Des Moines, IA	Blue/White
Drexel	Dragons	Colonial	Bruiser Flint	Philadelphia, PA	Navy Blue/Gold
Duke	Blue Devils	ACC	Mike Krzyzewski	Durham, NC	Royal Blue/White
Duquesne	Dukes	Atlantic 10	Danny Nee	Pittsburgh, PA	Red/Blue
East Carolina	Pirates	USA	Bill Herrion	Greenville, NC	Purple/Gold
East Tenn. St.	Buccaneers	Southern	Ed DeChellis	Johnson City, TN	Blue/Gold
Eastern Illinois	Panthers	Ohio Valley	Rick Samuels	Charleston, IL	Blue/Gray
Eastern Kentucky	Colonels	Ohio Valley	Travis Ford	Richmond, KY	Maroon/White
Eastern Michigan	Eagles	Mid-American	Jim Boone	Ypsilanti, MI	Green/White
Eastern Washington	Eagles	Big Sky	Ray Giacoletti	Cheney, WA	Red/White
Elon	Phoenix	Big South	Mark Simons	Elon, NC	Maroon/Gold
Evansville	Aces	Mo. Valley	Jim Crews	Evansville, IN	Purple/White
Fairfield	Stags	Metro Atlantic	Tim O'Toole	Fairfield, CT	Cardinal Red
Fairleigh Dickinson	Knights	Northeast	Tom Green	Teaneck, NJ	Blue/Black
Florida	Gators	SEC-East	Billy Donovan	Gainesville, FL	Orange/Blue
Florida A&M	Rattlers	Mid-Eastern	Mike Gillespie	Tallahassee, FL	Orange/Green
Florida Atlantic	Owls	Atlantic Sun	Sidney Green	Boca Raton, FL	Blue/Red
Florida Int'l	Golden Panthers	Sun Belt	Donnie Marsh	Miami, FL	Blue/Gold
Florida St.	Seminoles	ACC	Steve Robinson	Tallahassee, FL	Garnet/Gold
Fordham	Rams	Atlantic 10	Bob Hill	Bronx, NY	Maroon/White
Fresno St.	Bulldogs	WAC	Jerry Tarkanian	Fresno, CA	Cardinal/Blue
Furman	Paladins	Southern	Larry Davis	Greenville, SC	Purple/White
Gardner-Webb	Bulldogs	Independent	Rick Scruggs	Boiling Springs, NC	Scarlet/Black
George Mason	Patriots	Colonial	Jim Larranaga	Fairfax, VA	Green/Gold
George Washington	Colonials	Atlantic 10	Karl Hobbs	Washington, DC	Buff/Blue
Georgetown	Hoyas	Big East	Craig Esherick	Washington, DC	Blue/Gray
Georgia	Bulldogs, 'Dawgs	SEC-East	Jim Harrick	Athens, GA	Red/Black
Georgia Southern	Eagles	Southern	Jeff Price	Statesboro, GA	Blue/White
Georgia St.	Panthers	Atlantic Sun	Lefty Driesell	Atlanta, GA	Roy. Blue/White
Georgia Tech	Yellow Jackets	ACC	Paul Hewitt	Atlanta, GA	Old Gold/White
Gonzaga	Bulldogs, Zags	West Coast	Mark Few	Spokane, WA	Blue/White/Red
Grambling St.	Tigers	SWAC	Larry Wright	Grambling, LA	Black/Gold
Hampton	Pirates	Mid-Eastern	Steve Merfeld	Hampton, VA	Royal Blue/White
Hartford	Hawks	America East	Larry Harrison	W. Hartford, CT	Scarlet/White
Harvard	Crimson	Ivy	Frank Sullivan	Cambridge, MA	Crimson/Black/White
Hawaii	Rainbows	WAC	Riley Wallace	Honolulu, HI	Green/White
High Point	Panthers	Big South	Jerry Steele	High Point, NC	Purple/White
Hofstra	Flying Dutchmen	Colonial	Tom Pecora	Hempstead, NY	Blue/White/Gold
Holy Cross	Crusaders	Patriot	Ralph Willard	Worcester, MA	Royal Purple
Houston	Cougars	USA	Ray McCallum	Houston, TX	Scarlet/White
Howard	Bison	Mid-Eastern	Frankie Allen	Washington, DC	Blue/White/Red
Idaho	Vandals	Big West	Leonard Perry	Moscow, ID	Silver/Gold
Idaho St.	Bengals	Big Sky	Doug Oliver	Pocatello, ID	Orange/Black
Illinois	Fighting Illini	Big Ten	Bill Self	Champaign, IL	Orange/Blue
Illinois-Chicago	Flames	Horizon	Jim Collins	Chicago, IL	Navy Blue/Red
Illinois St.	Redbirds	Mo. Valley	Tom Richardson	Normal, IL	Red/White
Indiana	Hoosiers	Big Ten	Mike Davis	Bloomington, IN	Cream/Crimson
IU/PU-Indianapolis	Jaguars	Mid-Continent	Ron Hunter	Indianapolis, IN	Red/Gold
Indiana St.	Sycamores	Mo. Valley	Royce Waltman	Terre Haute, IN	Blue/White
Iona	Gaels	Metro Atlantic	Jeff Ruland	New Rochelle, NY	Maroon/Gold
Iowa	Hawkeyes	Big Ten	Steve Alford	Iowa City, IA	Old Gold/Black
Iowa St.	Cyclones	Big 12	Larry Eustachy	Ames, IA	Cardinal/Gold

	Nickname	Conference	Head Coach	Location	Colors
Jackson St.	Tigers	SWAC	Andy Stoglin	Jackson, MS	Blue/White
Jacksonville	Dolphins	Atlantic Sun	Hugh Durham	Jacksonville, FL	Green/White
Jacksonville St.	Gamecocks	Atlantic Sun	Mike LaPlante	Jacksonville, FL	Red/White
James Madison	Dukes	Colonial	Sherman Dillard	Harrisonburg, VA	Purple/Gold
Kansas	Jayhawks	Big 12	Roy Williams	Lawrence, KS	Crimson/Blue
Kansas St.	Wildcats	Big 12	Jim Wooldridge	Manhattan, KS	Purple/White
Kent St.	Golden Flashes	Mid-American	Stan Heath	Kent, OH	Navy Blue/Gold
Kentucky	Wildcats	SEC-East	Tubby Smith	Lexington, KY	Blue/White
La Salle	Explorers	Atlantic 10	Bill Hahn	Philadelphia, PA	Blue/Gold
Lafayette	Leopards	Patriot	Fran O'Hanlon	Easton, PA	Maroon/White
Lamar	Cardinals	Southland	Mike Deane	Beaumont, TX	Red/White
Lehigh	Mountain Hawks, Engineers	Patriot	Sal Mentesana	Bethlehem, PA	Brown/White
Liberty	Flames	Big South	Mel Hankinson	Lynchburg, VA	Red/White/Blue
Lipscomb	Bisons	Independent	Scott Sanderson	Nashville, TN	Purple/Gold
Long Beach St.	49ers	Big West	Wayne Morgan	Long Beach, CA	Black/Gold
LIU-Brooklyn	Blackbirds	Northeast	Ray Martin	Brooklyn, NY	Blue/White
LSU	Fighting Tigers	SEC-West	John Brady	Baton Rouge, LA	Purple/Gold
LA-Lafayette	Ragin' Cajuns	Sun Belt	Jessie Evans	Lafayette, LA	Vermilion/White
LA-Monroe	Indians	Southland	Mike Vining	Monroe, LA	Maroon/Gold
Louisiana Tech	Bulldogs	WAC	Keith Richard	Ruston, LA	Red/Blue
Louisville	Cardinals	USA	Rick Pitino	Louisville, KY	Red/Black/White
Loyola Marymount	Lions	West Coast	Steve Aggers	Los Angeles, CA	Crimson/Blue
Loyola-IL	Ramblers	Horizon	Larry Farmer	Chicago, IL	Maroon/Gold
Loyola-MD	Greyhounds	Metro Atlantic	Scott Hicks	Baltimore, MD	Green/Gray
Maine	Black Bears	America East	John Giannini	Orono, ME	Blue/White
Manhattan	Jaspers	Metro Atlantic	Bobby Gonzalez	Riverdale, NY	Kelly Green/White
Marist	Red Foxes	Metro Atlantic	Dave Magarity	Poughkeepsie, NY	Red/White
Marquette	Golden Eagles	USA	Tom Crean	Milwaukee, WI	Blue/Gold
Marshall	Thundering Herd	Mid-American	Greg Whim	Huntington, WV	Green/White
Maryland	Terrapins, Terps	ACC	Gary Williams	College Park, MD	Red/Wt./Black/Gold
MD-Balt. County	Retrievers	Northeast	Tom Sullivan	Baltimore, MD	Black/Gold/Red
MD-Eastern Shore	Hawks	Mid-Eastern	Thomas Trotter	Princess Anne, MD	Maroon/Gray
Massachusetts	Minutemen	Atlantic 10	Steve Lappas	Amherst, MA	Maroon/White
McNeese St.	Cowboys	Southland	Tic Price	Lake Charles, LA	Blue/Gold
Memphis	Tigers	USA	John Calipari	Memphis, TN	Blue/Gray
Mercer	Bears	Atlantic Sun	Mark Slonaker	Macon, GA	Orange/Black
Miami-FL	Hurricanes	Big East	Perry Clark	Coral Gables, FL	Orange/Grn./White
Miami-OH	RedHawks	Mid-American	Charlie Coles	Oxford, OH	Red/White
Michigan	Wolverines	Big Ten	Tommy Amaker	Ann Arbor, MI	Maize/Blue
Michigan St.	Spartans	Big Ten	Tom Izzo	East Lansing, MI	Green/White
Middle Tenn. St.	Blue Raiders	Sun Belt	Randy Wiel	Murfreesboro, TN	Blue/White
Minnesota	Golden Gophers	Big Ten	Dan Monson	Minneapolis, MN	Maroon/Gold
Mississippi	Ole Miss, Rebels	SEC-West	Rod Barnes	Oxford, MS	Red/Blue
Mississippi St.	Bulldogs	SEC-West	Rick Stansbury	Starkville, MS	Maroon/White
Miss. Valley St.	Delta Devils	SWAC	Lafayette Stribling	Itta Bena, MS	Green/White
Missouri	Tigers	Big 12	Quin Snyder	Columbia, MO	Old Gold/Black
Missouri-KC	Kangaroos	Mid-Continent	Rich Zvosec	Kansas City, MO	Blue/Gold
Monmouth	Hawks	Northeast	Dave Calloway	W. Long Branch, NJ	Royal Blue/White
Montana	Grizzlies	Big Sky	Don Holst	Missoula, MT	Copper/Silver/Gold
Montana St.	Bobcats	Big Sky	Mick Durham	Bozeman, MT	Blue/Gold
Morehead St.	Eagles	Ohio Valley	Kyle Macy	Morehead, KY	Blue/Gold
Morgan St.	Bears	Mid-Eastern	Butch Beard	Baltimore, MD	Blue/Orange
Morris Brown	Wolverines	Independent	Dereck Thompson	Atlanta, GA	Purple/Black
Mt. St. Mary's	Mountaineers	Northeast	Jim Phelan	Emmitsburg, MD	Blue/White
Murray St.	Racers	Ohio Valley	Tevester Anderson	Murray, KY	Blue/Gold
Navy	Midshipmen	Patriot	Don DeVoe	Annapolis, MD	Navy Blue/Gold
Nebraska	Cornhuskers	Big 12	Barry Collier	Lincoln, NE	Scarlet/Cream
Nevada	Wolf Pack	WAC	Trent Johnson	Reno, NV	Silver/Blue
New Hampshire	Wildcats	America East	Phil Rowe	Durham, NH	Blue/White
New Mexico	Lobos	Mountain West	Fran Fraschilla	Albuquerque, NM	Cherry/Silver
New Mexico St.	Aggies	Sun Belt	Lou Henson	Las Cruces, NM	Crimson/White
New Orleans	Privateers	Sun Belt	Monte Towe	New Orleans, LA	Royal Blue/Silver
Niagara	Purple Eagles	Metro Atlantic	Joe Mihalich	Lewiston, NY	Purple/White/Gold
Nicholls St.	Colonels	Southland	Rickey Broussard	Thibodaux, LA	Red/Gray
Norfolk State	Spartans	Mid-Eastern	Mel Coleman	Norfolk, VA	Green/Gold
North Carolina	Tar Heels	ACC	Matt Doherty	Chapel Hill, NC	Carolina Blue/Wht.
North Carolina A&T	Aggies	Mid-Eastern	Curtis Hunter	Greensboro, NC	Blue/Gold
North Carolina St.	Wolfpack	ACC	Herb Sendek	Raleigh, NC	Red/White
NC-Asheville	Bulldogs	Big South	Eddie Biedenbach	Asheville, NC	Royal Blue/White
NC-Charlotte	49ers	USA	Bobby Lutz	Charlotte, NC	Green/White

NCAA Division I Basketball Schools (Cont.)

	Nickname	Conference	Head Coach	Location	Colors
NC-Greensboro	Spartans	Southern	Fran McCaffrey	Greensboro, NC	Gold/White/Navy
NC-Wilmington	Seahawks	Colonial	Jerry Wainwright	Wilmington, NC	Green/Gold/Navy
North Texas	Mean Green	Sun Belt	Johnny Jones	Denton, TX	Green/White
Northeastern	Huskies	America East	Ron Everhart	Boston, MA	Red/Black
Northern Arizona	Lumberjacks	Big Sky	Mike Adras	Flagstaff, AZ	Blue/Gold
Northern Illinois	Huskies	Mid-American	Rob Judson	De Kalb, IL	Cardinal/Black
Northern Iowa	Panthers	Mo. Valley	Greg McDermott	Cedar Falls, IA	Purple/Old Gold
Northwestern	Wildcats	Big Ten	Bill Carmody	Evanston, IL	Purple/White
Northwestern St.	Demons	Southland	Mike McConathy	Natchitoches, LA	Purple/Orange/Wt.
Notre Dame	Fighting Irish	Big East	Mike Brey	Notre Dame, IN	Gold/Blue
Oakland-MI	Pioneers	Mid-Continent	Greg Kampe	Rochester, MI	Black/Gold
Ohio	Bobcats	Mid-American	Tim O'Shea	Athens, OH	Hunter Green/White
Ohio St.	Buckeyes	Big Ten	Jim O'Brien	Columbus, OH	Scarlet/Gray
Oklahoma	Sooners	Big 12	Kelvin Sampson	Norman, OK	Crimson/Cream
Oklahoma St.	Cowboys	Big 12	Eddie Sutton	Stillwater, OK	Orange/Black
Old Dominion	Monarchs	Colonial	Blaine Taylor	Norfolk, VA	Slate Blue/Silver
Oral Roberts	Golden Eagles	Mid-Continent	Scott Sutton	Tulsa, OK	Navy Blue/White
Oregon	Ducks	Pac-10	Ernie Kent	Eugene, OR	Green/Yellow
Oregon St.	Beavers	Pac-10	Ritchie McKay	Corvallis, OR	Orange/Black
Pacific	Tigers	Big West	Bob Thomason	Stockton, CA	Orange/Black
Pennsylvania	Quakers	Ivy	Fran Dunphy	Philadelphia, PA	Red/Blue
Penn St.	Nittany Lions	Big Ten	Jerry Dunn	University Park, PA	Blue/White
Pepperdine	Waves	West Coast	Paul Westphal	Malibu, CA	Blue/Orange
Pittsburgh	Panthers	Big East	Ben Howland	Pittsburgh, PA	Gold/Blue
Portland	Pilots	West Coast	Mike Holton	Portland, OR	Purple/White
Portland St.	Vikings	Big Sky	Joel Sobotka	Portland, OR	Green/White
Prairie View A&M	Panthers	SWAC	Elwood Plummer	Prairie View, TX	Purple/Gold
Princeton	Tigers	Ivy	J. Thompson III	Princeton, NJ	Orange/Black
Providence	Friars	Big East	Tim Welsh	Providence, RI	Black/White
Purdue	Boilermakers	Big Ten	Gene Keady	W. Lafayette, IN	Old Gold/Black
Quinnipiac	Braves	Northeast	Joe DeSantis	Hamden, CT	Blue/Gold
Radford	Highlanders	Big South	Ron Bradley	Radford, VA	Blue/Red/Green/Wt.
Rhode Island	Rams	Atlantic 10	Jim Baron	Kingston, RI	Lt. Blue/White/Navy
Rice	Owls	WAC	Willis Wilson	Houston, TX	Blue/Gray
Richmond	Spiders	Atlantic 10	John Beilein	Richmond, VA	Red/Blue
Rider	Broncs	Metro Atlantic	Don Harnum	Lawrenceville, NJ	Cranberry/White
Robert Morris	Colonials	Northeast	Mark Schmidt	Moon Township, PA	Blue/White
Rutgers	Scarlet Knights	Big East	Gary Waters	New Brunswick, NJ	Scarlet
Sacred Heart	Pioneers	Northeast	Dave Bike	Fairfield, CT	Scarlet/White
St. Bonaventure	Bonnies	Atlantic 10	J. Van Breda Kolff	St. Bonaventure, NY	Brown/White
St. Francis-NY	Terriers	Northeast	Ron Ganulin	Brooklyn, NY	Red/Blue
St. Francis-PA	Red Flash	Northeast	Bobby Jones	Loretto, PA	Red/White
St. John's	Red Storm	Big East	Mike Jarvis	Jamaica, NY	Red/White
St. Joseph's-PA	Hawks	Atlantic 10	Phil Martelli	Philadelphia, PA	Crimson/Gray
Saint Louis	Billikens	USA	Lorenzo Romar	St. Louis, MO	Blue/White
St. Mary's-CA	Gaels	West Coast	Randy Bennett	Moraga, CA	Red/Blue
St. Peter's	Peacocks	Metro Atlantic	Bob Leckie	Jersey City, NJ	Blue/White
Sam Houston St.	Bearkats	Southland	Bob Marlin	Huntsville, TX	Orange/White
Samford	Bulldogs	Atlantic Sun	Jimmy Tillette	Birmingham, AL	Red/Blue
San Diego	Toreros	West Coast	Brad Holland	San Diego, CA	Lt. Blue/Navy
San Diego St.	Aztecs	Mountain West	Steve Fisher	San Diego, CA	Scarlet/Black
San Francisco	Dons	West Coast	Phil Mathews	San Francisco, CA	Green/Gold
San Jose St.	Spartans	WAC	Steve Barnes	San Jose, CA	Gold/White/Blue
Santa Clara	Broncos	West Coast	Dick Davey	Santa Clara, CA	Bronco Red/White
Savannah St.	Tigers	Independent	Jack Grant	Savannah, GA	Orange/Blue
Seton Hall	Pirates	Big East	Louis Orr	South Orange, NJ	Blue/White
Siena	Saints	Metro Atlantic	Rob Lanier	Loudonville, NY	Green/Gold
South Alabama	Jaguars	Sun Belt	Bob Weltlich	Mobile, AL	Red/White/Blue
South Carolina	Gamecocks	SEC-East	Dave Odom	Columbia, SC	Garnet/Black
South Carolina St.	Bulldogs	Mid-Eastern	Cy Alexander	Orangeburg, SC	Garnet/Blue
South Florida	Bulls	USA	Seth Greenberg	Tampa, FL	Green/Gold
SE Missouri St.	Indians	Ohio Valley	Gary Garner	Cape Girardeau, MO	Red/Black
SE Louisiana	Lions	Southland	Billy Kennedy	Hammond, LA	Green/Gold
Southern Illinois	Salukis	Mo. Valley	Bruce Weber	Carbondale, IL	Maroon/White
SMU	Mustangs	WAC	Mike Dement	Dallas, TX	Red/Blue
Southern Miss	Golden Eagles	USA	James Green	Hattiesburg, MS	Black/Gold
Southern Utah	Thunderbirds	Mid-Continent	Bill Evans	Cedar City, UT	Scarlet/White
Southern-BR	Jaguars	SWAC	Ben Jobe	Baton Rouge, LA	Blue/Gold

	Nickname	Conference	Head Coach	Location	Colors
SW Missouri St.	Bears	Mo. Valley	Barry Hinson	Springfield, MO	Maroon/White
SW Texas St.	Bobcats	Southland	Dennis Nutt	San Marcos, TX	Maroon/Gold
Stanford	Cardinal	Pac-10	Mike Montgomery	Stanford, CA	Cardinal/White
S.F. Austin St.	Lumberjacks	Southland	Danny Kaspar	Nacogdoches, TX	Purple/White
Stetson	Hatters	Atlantic Sun	Derek Waugh	DeLand, FL	Green/White
Stony Brook	Seawolves	America East	Nick Macarchuk	Stony Brook, NY	Scarlet/Gray
Syracuse	Orangemen	Big East	Jim Boeheim	Syracuse, NY	Orange
Temple	Owls	Atlantic 10	John Chaney	Philadelphia, PA	Cherry/White
Tennessee	Volunteers	SEC-East	Buzz Peterson	Knoxville, TN	Orange/White
Tenn-Chattanooga	Mocs	Southern	Henry Dickerson	Chattanooga, TN	Navy Blue/Old Gold
Tenn-Martin	Skyhawks	Ohio Valley	Bret Campbell	Martin, TN	Orange/Wt./Royal Blue
Tennessee St.	Tigers	Ohio Valley	N. Richardson III	Nashville, TN	Blue/White
Tennessee Tech	Golden Eagles	Ohio Valley	Jeff Lebo	Cookeville, TN	Purple/Gold
Texas	Longhorns	Big 12	Rick Barnes	Austin, TX	Burnt Orange/White
Texas A&M	Aggies	Big 12	Melvin Watkins	College Station, TX	Maroon/White
TX A&M Corpus-Christi	Islanders	Independent	Ronnie Arrow	Corpus Christi, TX	Blue/Green/Silver
TCU	Horned Frogs	USA	Billy Tubbs	Ft. Worth, TX	Purple/White
Texas Southern	Tigers	SWAC	Ronnie Courtney	Houston, TX	Maroon/Gray
Texas Tech	Red Raiders	Big 12	Bob Knight	Lubbock, TX	Scarlet/Black
TX-Arlington	Mavericks	Southland	Eddie McCarter	Arlington, TX	Royal Blue/White
TX-Pan American	Broncs	Independent	Bob Hoffman	Edinburg, TX	Green/White
TX-San Antonio	Roadrunners	Independent	Tim Carter	San Antonio, TX	Orange/Navy/White
Toledo	Rockets	Mid-American	Stan Joplin	Toledo, OH	Blue/Gold
Towson	Tigers	Colonial	Michael Hunt	Towson, MD	Gold/White/Black
Troy St.	Trojans	Atlantic Sun	Don Maestri	Troy, AL	Cardinal/Silver/Black
Tulane	Green Wave	USA	Shawn Finney	New Orleans, LA	Olive Grn./Sky Blue
Tulsa	Golden Hurricane	WAC	John Phillips	Tulsa, OK	Blue/Red/Gold
UAB	Blazers	USA	Murray Bartow	Birmingham, AL	Green/Gold
UC-Irvine	Anteaters	Big West	Pat Douglass	Irvine, CA	Blue/Gold
UCLA	Bruins	Pac-10	Steve Lavin	Los Angeles, CA	Blue/Gold
UC-Riverside	Highlanders	Big West	John Masi	Riverside, CA	Blue/Gold
UC-Santa Barbara	Gauchos	Big West	Bob Williams	Santa Barbara, CA	Blue/Gold
UNLV	Runnin' Rebels	Mountain West	Charlie Spoonhour	Las Vegas, NV	Scarlet/Gray
USC	Trojans	Pac-10	Henry Bibby	Los Angeles, CA	Cardinal/Gold
Utah	Utes	Mountain West	Rick Majerus	Salt Lake City, UT	Crimson/White
Utah St.	Aggies	Big West	Stew Morrill	Logan, UT	Navy Blue/White
UTEP	Miners	WAC	Jason Rabedeaux	El Paso, TX	Orange/Blue/Wt.
Valparaiso	Crusaders	Mid-Continent	Homer Drew	Valparaiso, IN	Brown/Gold
Vanderbilt	Commodores	SEC-East	Kevin Stallings	Nashville, TN	Black/Gold
Vermont	Catamounts	America East	Tom Brennan	Burlington, VT	Green/Gold
Villanova	Wildcats	Big East	Jay Wright	Villanova, PA	Blue/White
Virginia	Cavaliers	ACC	Pete Gillen	Charlottesville, VA	Orange/Blue
VCU	Rams	Colonial	Mack McCarthy	Richmond, VA	Black/Gold
VMI	Keydets	Southern	Bart Bellairs	Lexington, VA	Red/White/Yellow
Virginia Tech	Hokies, Gobblers	Big East	Ricky Stokes	Blacksburg, VA	Orange/Maroon
Wagner	Seahawks	Northeast	D. Whittenburg	Staten Island, NY	Green/White
Wake Forest	Demon Deacons	ACC	Skip Prosser	Winston-Salem, NC	Old Gold/Black
Washington	Huskies	Pac-10	Bob Bender	Seattle, WA	Purple/Gold
Washington St.	Cougars	Pac-10	Paul Graham	Pullman, WA	Crimson/Gray
Weber St.	Wildcats	Big Sky	Joe Cravens	Ogden, UT	Purple/White
West Virginia	Mountaineers	Big East	Gale Catlett	Morgantown, WV	Old Gold/Blue
Western Carolina	Catamounts	Southern	Steve Shurina	Cullowhee, NC	Purple/Gold
Western Illinois	Leathernecks	Mid-Continent	Jim Kerwin	Macomb, IL	Purple/Gold
Western Kentucky	Hilltoppers	Sun Belt	Dennis Felton	Bowling Green, KY	Red/White
Western Michigan	Broncos	Mid-American	Robert McCullum	Kalamazoo, MI	Brown/Gold
Wichita St.	Shockers	Mo. Valley	Mark Turgeon	Wichita, KS	Yellow/Black
William & Mary	Tribe	Colonial	Rick Boyages	Williamsburg, VA	Green/Gold/Silver
Winthrop	Eagles	Big South	Gregg Marshall	Rock Hill, SC	Garnet/Gold
Wisconsin	Badgers	Big Ten	Bo Ryan	Madison, WI	Cardinal/White
WI-Green Bay	Phoenix	Horizon	Mike Heideman	Green Bay, WI	Green/White/Red
WI-Milwaukee	Panthers	Horizon	Bruce Pearl	Milwaukee, WI	Black/Gold
Wofford	Terriers	Southern	Richard Johnson	Spartanburg, SC	Old Gold/Black
Wright St.	Raiders	Horizon	Ed Schilling	Dayton, OH	Green/Gold
Wyoming	Cowboys	Mountain West	Steve McClain	Laramie, WY	Brown/Yellow
Xavier	Musketeers	Atlantic 10	Thad Matta	Cincinnati, OH	Blue/White
Yale	Bulldogs, Elis	Ivy	James Jones	New Haven, CT	Yale Blue/White
Youngstown St.	Penguins	Horizon	John Robic	Youngstown, OH	Red/White

Ohio St.   USC   Drexel   Seton Hall

Jim Tressel   **Pete Carroll**   **Bruiser Flint**   **Louis Orr**
Youngstown to Ohio St.   USC   UMass to Drexel   Siena to Seton Hall

Coaching Changes

New head coaches were named at 25 Division 1-A and 11 Division 1-AA football schools while 47 Division 1 basketball schools changed head coaches after the 2000-01 season. Coaching changes listed below are as of September 1, 2001.

Division I-A Football

	Old Coach	Record	Why Left?	New Coach	Old Job
Alabama	Mike DuBose	3-8	resigned	Dennis Franchione	Coach, TCU
Arizona	Dick Tomey	5-6	resigned	John Mackovic	Former coach, Texas
Arizona State	Bruce Snyder	6-6	fired	Dirk Koetter	Coach, Boise State
Boise State	Dirk Koetter	10-2	to Arizona State*	Dan Hawkins	Asst., Boise State
Bowling Green	Gary Blackney	2-9	resigned	Urban Meyer	Asst., Notre Dame
Buffalo	Craig Cirbus	2-9	fired	Jim Hofher	Asst., Syracuse
BYU	LaVell Edwards	6-6	retired	Gary Crowton	Off. Coor., NFL Chicago
Georgia	Jim Donnan	8-4	fired	Mark Richt	Off. Coor., Florida St.
Kentucky	Hal Mumme	2-9	resigned	Guy Morriss	Asst., Kentucky
Maryland	Ron Vanderlinden	5-6	fired	Ralph Friedgen	Off. Coor., Georgia Tech
Memphis	Rip Scherer	4-7	fired	Tommy West	Def. Coor., Memphis
Miami-FL.	Butch Davis	11-1	to NFL Cleveland*	Larry Coker	Off. Coor., Miami
Missouri	Larry Smith	3-8	fired	Gary Pinkel	Coach, Toledo
North Carolina	Carl Torbush	6-5	fired	John Bunting	Asst., NFL New Orleans
Ohio	Jim Grobe	7-4	to Wake Forest*	Brian Knorr	Def. Coor., Ohio
Ohio State	John Cooper	8-4	fired	Jim Tressel	Coach, Youngstown St.
Oklahoma State	Bob Simmons	3-8	resigned	Les Miles	Asst., NFL Dallas
Rutgers	Terry Shea	3-8	resigned	Greg Schiano	Def. Coor., Miami-FL
San Jose State	Dave Baldwin	7-5	resigned	Fitz Hill	Asst., Arkansas
Toledo	Gary Pinkel	10-1	to Missouri*	Tom Amstutz	Asst., Toledo
TCU	Dennis Franchione	10-2	to Alabama*	Gary Patterson	Def. Coor., TCU
USC	Paul Hackett	5-7	fired	Pete Carroll	Former coach, NFL New Englc
Virginia	George Welsh	6-6	retired	Al Groh	Coach, NFL NY Jets
Wake Forest	Jim Caldwell	2-9	fired	Jim Grobe	Coach, Ohio
West Virginia	Don Nehlen	7-5	retired	Rich Rodriguez	Off. Coor., Clemson

* as head coach

Division I-AA Football

	Old Coach	Record	Why Left?	New Coach	Old Job
Cal Poly	Larry Welsh	3-8	fired	Rich Ellerson	Def. Coor., Arizona
Central Conn. St.	Sal Cintorino	4-6	resigned	Paul Schudel	Asst., Virginia
The Citadel	Don Powers	2-9	resigned	Ellis Johnson	Def. Coor., Alabama
Cornell	Pete Mangurian	5-5	to NFL Atlanta**	Tim Pendergast	Coach, Hamilton
Davidson	Joe Susan	10-0	to Rutgers**	Mike Toop	Def. Coor., Connecticut
Fairfield	Kevin Kiesel	8-2	to Millersville*	Joe Bernard	Def. Coor., Fairfield
Lehigh	Kevin Higgins	12-1	to NFL Detroit**	Pete Lembo	Asst., Lehigh
Morris Brown	Joe Crosby	4-6	resigned	Solomon Brannan	Asst., Morris Brown
Northern Iowa	Mike Dunbar	7-4	to Northwestern**	Mark Farley	Asst., Kansas
Southern Illinois	Jan Quarless	3-8	fired	Jerry Kill	Coach, Emporia St.
Youngstown State	Jim Tressel	9-3	to Ohio State*	Jon Heacock	Def. Coor., Youngstown State

* as head coach
** as assistant coach

Division I Basketball

	Old Coach	Record	Why Left?	New Coach	Old Job
Butler	Thad Matta	24-8	to Xavier*	Todd Lickliter	Asst., Xavier
Cal Poly	Jeff Schneider	9-19&	interim	Kevin Bromley	Assoc., Cal Poly
Denver	Martin Fletcher	10-18	fired	Terry Carroll	Asst., Iowa State
Drexel	Steve Seymour	15-12	fired	Bruiser Flint	Coach, UMass
Duquesne	Darelle Porter	9-21	resigned	Danny Nee	Coach, Robert Morris
Florida A&M	Mickey Clayton	6-23	fired	Mike Gillespie	Coach, Tallahassee CC
George Washington	Tom Penders	14-18	retired	Karl Hobbs	Asst., UConn
Hofstra	Jay Wright	26-5	to Villanova*	Tom Pecora	Asst., Hofstra
Idaho	David Farrar	6-21	fired	Leonard Perry	Asst., Iowa State
Kent State	Gary Waters	24-10	to Rutgers*	Stan Heath	Asst., Michigan St.
La Salle	Speedy Morris	12-17	fired	Billy Hahn	Asst., Maryland
Louisville	Denny Crum	12-19	retired	Rick Pitino	Coach, NBA Boston
Massachusetts	Bruiser Flint	15-15	resigned	Steve Lappas	Coach, Villanova
McNeese St.	Ron Everhart	22-9	to Northeastern*	Tic Price	Assoc., McNeese St.
Michigan	Brian Ellerbe	10-18	fired	Tommy Amaker	Coach, Seton Hall
Missouri-Kansas City	Dean Demopoulos	14-16	to NBA Seattle**	Rich Zvosec	Asst., Missouri-KC
Morgan State	Chris Fuller	6-23	fired	Butch Beard	Asst., NBA Washington
New Orleans	Joey Stiebling	17-12	fired	Monte Towe	Coach, Santa Fe CC (FL)
North Texas	Vic Trilli	4-24	fired	Johnny Jones	Asst., Alabama
Northeastern	Rudy Keeling	10-19	resigned	Ron Everhart	Coach, McNeese St.
Northern Illinois	Andy Greer	4-17#	interim	Rob Judson	Asst., Illinois
Northern Iowa	Sam Weaver	7-24	fired	Greg McDermott	Coach, N. Dakota St.
Ohio	Larry Hunter	19-11	fired	Tim O'Shea	Asst., Boston College
Old Dominion	Jeff Capel	13-18	resigned	Blaine Taylor	Asst., Stanford
Pepperdine	Jan van Breda Kolff	22-9	to St. Bona.*	Paul Westphal	Coach, NBA Seattle
Portland	Rob Chavez	11-17	fired	Michael Holton	Asst., UCLA
Rhode Island	Jerry DeGregorio	7-23	resigned	Jim Baron	Coach, St. Bonaventure
Robert Morris	Danny Nee	7-22	fired	Mark Schmidt	Asst., Xavier
Rutgers	Kevin Bannon	11-16	fired	Gary Waters	Coach, Kent State
St. Bonaventure	Jim Baron	18-12	to Rhode Island*	Jan van Breda Kolff	Coach, Pepperdine
St. Mary's-CA	David Bollwinkel	2-27	fired	Randy Bennett	Asst., St. Louis
Seton Hall	Tommy Amaker	16-15	to Michigan*	Louis Orr	Coach, Siena
Siena	Louis Orr	20-11	to Seton Hall*	Rob Lanier	Asst., Texas
South Carolina	Eddie Fogler	15-15	resigned	Dave Odom	Coach, Wake Forest
Southern-BR	Tommy Green	11-16	fired	Ben Jobe	Former coach, Tuskegee
Stetson	Murray Arnold	17-12†	retired	Derek Waugh	Asst., Stetson
Tennessee	Jerry Green	22-11	fired	Buzz Peterson	Coach, Tulsa
Texas Southern	Robert Moreland	7-22	fired	Ronnie Courtney	Coach, Willowridge HS
Texas Tech	James Dickey	9-19	fired	Bob Knight	Former coach, Indiana
Towson	Mike Jaskulski	12-17	fired	Michael Hunt	Asst., Tennessee
Tulsa	Buzz Peterson	26-11	to Tennessee*	John Phillips	Asst., Tulsa
UNLV	Max Good	16-13@	interim	Charlie Spoonhour	Former coach, St. Louis
Villanova	Steve Lappas	18-13	to Massachusetts*	Jay Wright	Coach, Hofstra
Wake Forest	Dave Odom	19-11	to South Carolina*	Skip Prosser	Coach, Xavier
Wisconsin	Brad Soderberg	18-11%	interim	Bo Ryan	Coach, WI-Milwaukee
WI-Milwaukee	Bo Ryan	15-13	to Wisconsin*	Bruce Pearl	Coach, Southern Indiana
Xavier	Skip Prosser	21-8	to Wake Forest*	Thad Matta	Coach, Butler

* as head coach
** as assistant coach
& Schneider (5-7) resigned on Jan. 10 and was replaced by Bromley for the remainder of the season.
# Brian Hammel (1-6) resigned on Dec. 6, 2000 and was replaced by Greer for the remainder of the season.
† Arnold (4-4) retired for health reasons on Dec. 27, 2000 and was replaced by Waugh for the remainder of the season.
@ Bill Bayno (3-4) was fired on Dec. 12, 2000 and replaced by Good for the remainder of the season.
% Dick Bennett (2-1) resigned on Nov. 30, 2000 and was replaced by Soderberg for the remainder of the season.

Housecleaning

There are five Division I member institutions with new football and men's basketball head coaches for the 2001-02 season.

	Football		Basketball	
School	**Old Coach**	**New Coach**	**Old Coach**	**New Coach**
Cal Poly	Larry Welsh	Rich Ellerson	Jeff Schneider	Kevin Bromley
Northern Iowa	Mike Dunbar	Mark Farley	Sam Weaver	Greg McDermott
Ohio	Jim Grobe	Brian Knorr	Larry Hunter	Tim O'Shea
Rutgers	Terry Shea	Greg Schiano	Kevin Bannon	Gary Waters
Wake Forest	Jim Caldwell	Jim Grobe	Dave Odom	Skip Prosser

2000-01 Directors' Cup

Officially, the Sears Directors' Cup and sponsored by the National Association of Collegiate Directors of Athletics. Introduced in 1993-94 to honor the nation's best overall NCAA Division I athletic department (combining men's and women's sports), winners in NCAA Division II and III and NAIA were named for the first time following the 1995-96 season.

Standings are computed by NACDA with points awarded for each Div. I school's finish in 20 sports (top 10 scoring sports for both men and women). Div. II schools are awarded points in 14 sports (top 7 scoring sports for both men and women). Div III schools are awarded points in 18 sports (top 9 scoring sports for both men and women). NAIA schools are awarded points in 12 sports (top 6 scoring sports for both men and women). National champions in each sport earn 100 points, while 2nd through 64th-place finishers earn decreasing points depending on the size of the tournament field. Division I-A football points are based on the final ESPN/*USA Today* Coaches' Top 25 poll. Listed below are team conferences (for Div. I only), combined Final Four finishes (1st through 4th place) for men's and women's programs, overall points in **bold** type, and the previous year's ranking (for Div. I only).

Multiple winners: Stanford (7); Simon Fraser, BC and Williams, MA (5); UC-Davis (4)

Division I

		Conf	1-2-3-4	Pts	99-00 Rank			Conf	1-2-3-4	Pts	99-00 Rank
1	Stanford	Pac-10	1-4-2-3	**1359**	1	14	Washington	Pac-10	1-0-1-0	**748**	30
2	UCLA	Pac-10	4-4-0-0	**1138**	2	15	N. Carolina	ACC	1-1-0-0	**729.5**	5
3	Georgia	SEC	3-1-1-0	**890.5**	12	16	Duke	ACC	1-1-0-0	**722**	24
4	Michigan	Big Ten	0-1-2-1	**864.5**	3	17	BYU	Mountain West	1-1-0-0	**708**	18
5	Arizona	Pac-10	1-1-3-0	**863**	8	18	Oklahoma	Big 12	1-1-0-1	**698.5**	25
6	Ohio St.	Big Ten	1-0-1-1	**862**	14	19	Texas	Big 12	1-0-2-0	**672**	9
7	Florida	SEC	1-0-1-0	**847**	7	20	Wisconsin	Big Ten	0-1-0-0	**671.5**	17
8	Southern Cal.	Pac-10	1-0-2-1	**817.5**	16	21	Tennessee	SEC	1-1-2-0	**661.5**	20
9	Arizona St.	Pac-10	0-0-0-0	**801**	11	22	LSU	SEC	1-0-1-0	**653.5**	10
10	Penn St.	Big Ten	0-1-1-0	**775.5**	4	23	Minnesota	Big Ten	1-0-0-0	**639**	19
11	Notre Dame	Big East	1-0-3-0	**764.5**	21	24	Princeton	Ivy	1-0-1-0	**569.5**	33
12	California	Pac-10	0-0-1-0	**761**	15	25	S. Carolina	SEC	0-1-0-1	**539**	32
13	Nebraska	Big 12	1-0-0-0	**753**	6						

Division II

		1-2-3-4	Pts			1-2-3-4	Pts
1	UC-Davis	0-0-3-2	**703**	14	North Dakota St.	1-0-2-0	**383**
2	North Dakota	0-3-1-1	**539**	15	Northern Colorado	0-0-0-0	**383**
3	CS-Bakersfield	1-0-0-0	**536**	16	Ashland, OH	0-0-0-0	**376**
4	UC-San Diego	1-1-1-0	**524**	17	South Dakota St.	0-1-0-0	**373.5**
5	Western St., CO	2-1-1-0	**500**	18	Rollins, FL	1-1-0-1	**360**
6	Abilene Christian, TX	0-3-1-1	**461.5**	19	Barry, FL	0-1-2-0	**355**
7	Central Missouri St.	0-1-0-1	**447.5**	20	Nebraska-Omaha	1-0-1-0	**352**
8	Indianapolis, IN	0-0-0-0	**438**	21	North Florida	0-0-1-0	**347**
9	Truman St., MO	1-0-0-0	**422**	22	Tampa, FL	0-0-1-0	**345**
10	Lewis, IL	0-1-2-1	**396**	23	St. Cloud St., MN	0-0-0-0	**337.5**
11	Delta St., MS	1-0-1-0	**395**	24	Drury, MO	0-2-1-0	**334**
12	Adams St., CO	0-0-1-0	**394.5**	25	Central Washington	0-0-0-0	**326.5**
13	Bloomsburg, PA	0-1-0-1	**391**				

Division III

		1-2-3-4	Pts			1-2-3-4	Pts
1	Williams, MA	2-1-2-0	**897.5**	14	Amherst, MA	0-1-0-1	**451**
2	Middlebury, VT	3-0-0-0	**728.5**	15	Salisbury St., MD	0-0-1-1	**435**
3	College of New Jersey	1-0-1-0	**713.5**	16	Washington, MO	1-0-1-0	**430.5**
4	Emory, GA	0-1-1-1	**633**	17	Wisconsin-La Crosse	2-2-0-0	**426**
5	Ithaca, NY	0-0-0-0	**584**	18	Gustavus Adolphus, MN	0-1-0-1	**407.5**
6	Wisconsin-Stevens Pt.	0-0-2-2	**538**	19	Denison, OH	1-0-1-0	**404**
7	Wisconsin-Oshkosh	0-1-2-1	**529**	20	Nebraska Wesleyan	0-0-0-0	**402**
8	Wisconsin-Eau Claire	1-0-0-0	**476.5**	21	Wisconsin-Whitewater	0-0-1-0	**384.5**
9	Calvin, MI	1-1-0-0	**474**	22	Ohio Wesleyan	0-0-1-0	**368**
10	Wartburg, IA	0-0-0-0	**473**	23	Wheaton, MA	2-0-1-0	**356.5**
11	Trinity, TX	0-1-1-0	**463**	24	Tufts, MA	0-1-0-0	**354.5**
12	Central, IA	1-1-0-0	**459**	25	St. Thomas, MN	1-0-0-0	**353.5**
13	Cortland St., NY	0-0-0-0	**453.5**				

NAIA

		1-2-3-4	Pts			1-2-3-4	Pts
1	Simon Fraser, BC	3-1-0-2	**820**	14	Briar Cliff, IA	0-0-1-0	**340**
2	Oklahoma City	4-1-1-0	**715**	15	CS-San Marcos	0-0-0-0	**334.5**
3	Azusa Pacific, CA	1-1-1-2	**630**	16	McKendree, IL	2-0-1-0	**334**
4	Lindenwood, MO	0-1-1-2	**586.5**	17	Oklahoma Christian	0-1-0-0	**332.5**
5	Cumberland, KY	0-0-0-1	**473**	18	Southern Nazarene, OK	0-0-1-1	**332**
6	California Baptist	0-2-0-1	**460**	19	Oklahoma Baptist	0-0-0-0	**330.5**
7	Pt. Loma Nazarene, CA	0-0-1-0	**450.5**	20	Biola, CA	0-0-0-0	**328.5**
8	Northwestern, IA	2-0-1-0	**438**	21	Embry-Riddle, FL	0-0-0-0	**315**
9	Life, GA	2-2-0-0	**422**	22	Georgetown, KY	1-0-0-0	**300**
10	Auburn-Montgomery, AL	1-2-1-0	**405**	23	Mary, ND	0-0-1-0	**294.5**
11	Mobile, AL	0-0-2-1	**386.5**	24	Birmingham Southern, AL	1-0-0-0	**293**
12	Malone, OH	0-0-1-0	**379**	25	Brevard, NC	0-0-0-1	**292**
13	Aquinas, MI	0-0-0-0	**347.5**				

NCAA Division I Schools on Probation

As of September 1, 2001, there were 22 Division I member institutions serving NCAA probations.

School	Sport	Yrs	Penalty To End	School	Sport	Yrs	Penalty To End
Arkansas-LR	M & W Basketball	2	9/24/01	SMU	Football	2	12/13/02
LSU	M Basketball	3	9/26/01	Baylor	M Tennis	2	12/21/02
Michigan St.	Wrestling	2	12/2/01	Tennessee St.	Football	3	1/4/03
	& W Track and XC	2	12/2/01		M Tennis	3	1/4/03
Notre Dame	Football	2	12/16/01		& M Golf	3	1/4/03
Prairie View	Football	1	4/17/02	Miss. Valley St.	No specific sport	2	1/23/03
Texas Tech	M & W Basketball	4	4/23/02	Bucknell	M Wrestling	4	2/6/03
	Football	4	4/23/02	Buffalo	M Basketball	2	3/21/03
	Baseball	4	4/23/02	Dayton	M Basketball	3	4/18/03
	Golf	4	4/23/02	CS-Northridge	Football	3	6/1/03
	M Track	4	4/23/02	USC	Football	2	8/22/03
	W Soccer	4	4/23/02		& W Swimming	2	8/22/03
	W Volleyball	4	4/23/02	Northern Arizona	Football	3	4/17/04
	& M Tennis	4	4/23/02	Minnesota	M Basketball	4	10/23/04
UTEP	M & W Basketball	5	4/30/02	UNLV	M Basketball	4	12/11/04
	Football	5	4/30/02	Jackson St.	M Track and XC	5	5/16/05
	& W Rifle	5	4/30/02	New Mexico St.	M Basketball	4	6/19/05
Gonzaga	M Basketball	4	6/4/02	Jacksonville	M Soccer	5	8/30/06
CS-Fullerton	M Basketball	4	11/13/02				

Remaining postseason and TV sanctions
2001-2002 postseason ban: Jackson St. mens track and XC.
2001-2002 television ban: None.

NCAA Graduation Rates

The following table compares graduation rates of NCAA Division I student athletes with the entire student body in those schools. Years given denote the year in which students entered college. Rates are based on students who enrolled as freshmen, received an athletics scholarship and graduated in six years or less. All figures are percentages.
Source: NCAA Graduation-Rate Report, 2000.

	1988	**1989**	**1990**	**1991**	**1992**	**1993**
All Student Athletes	58	58	58	57	58	58
Entire Student Body	57	57	56	56	56	56
Male Student Athletes	53	53	53	51	52	51
Male Student Body	55	55	54	53	54	54
Female Student Athletes	69	67	68	67	68	68
Female Student Body	58	59	58	58	59	59
Div. I-A Football Players	56	56	52	50	51	48
Male Basketball Players	42	44	45	41	41	42
Female Basketball Players	65	65	67	66	62	63

2000-01 NCAA Team Champions

Eight schools won two or more national championships during the 2000-01 academic year, led by Division I UCLA and Div. II St. Augustine's, NC with four each.

Multiple winners: Four— UCLA (National Div. men's and women's water polo, National Div. women's gymnastics, Div. I women's indoor track); ST. AUGUSTINE'S, NC (Div. II men's and women's indoor track, Div II men's and women's outdoor track). **Three**— GEORGIA (Div. I men's tennis, Div. I women's golf, Div. 1 women's swimming and diving); MIDDLEBURY, VT (Div. III men's and women's lacrosse, Div. III women's cross country).

Two— WESTERN ST., CO (Div. II men's and women's cross country); WHEATON, MA (Div. III women's indoor and outdoor track); WILLIAMS, MA (Div. III men's and women's tennis); WISC.-LA CROSSE (Div. III men's indoor and outdoor track).

Overall titles in parentheses; (*) indicates defending champions.

FALL

Cross Country

Men

Div.	Winner		Runner-Up	Score
I	Arkansas*	(11)	Colorado	83-94
II	Western St., CO*	(3)	Abilene Christian	29-62
III	Calvin, MI	(1)	Keene St., NH	65-87

Women

Div.	Winner		Runner-Up	Score
I	Colorado	(1)	Brigham Young*	117-167
II	Western St., CO	(1)	North Dakota	38-131
III	Middlebury, VT	(1)	Williams, MA	103-123

Field Hockey

Div.	Winner		Runner-Up	Score
I	Old Dominion	(9)	North Carolina	3-1
II	Lock Haven, PA	(5)	Bentley, MA	2-0
III	William Smith, NY	(3)	Springfield, MA	1-0

Football

Div.	Winner		Runner-Up	Score
I-A	Oklahoma	(7)	Florida St.*	13-2
I-AA	Georgia Southern*	(6)	Montana	27-25
II	Delta St., MS	(1)	Bloomsburg, PA	63-34
III	Mt. Union, OH	(5)	St. John's, MN	10-7

Note: There is no official Div. I-A playoff. Oklahoma defeated Florida St. in the BCS Championship Game (Orange Bowl).

Soccer

Men

Div.	Winner		Runner-Up	Score
I	Connecticut	(2)	Creighton	2-0
II	CS-Dominguez Hills	(1)	Barry, FL	2-1 (4OT)
III	Messiah, PA	(1)	Rowan, NJ	2-0

Women

Div.	Winner		Runner-Up	Score
I	North Carolina*	(16)	UCLA	2-1
II	UC San Diego	(1)	Northern Kentucky	2-1
III	College of NJ	(3)	Tufts, MA	2-1

Volleyball

Women

Div.	Winner		Runner-Up	Score
I	Nebraska	(2)	Wisconsin	5 games
II	Hawaii Pacific	(2)	Augustana, SD	3 games
III	Central, IA*	(3)	Wisc.-Whitewater	3 games

Water Polo

Men

Div.	Winner		Runner-Up	Score
National	UCLA*	(7)	UC San Diego	11-2

WINTER

Basketball

Men

Div.	Winner		Runner-Up	Score
I	Duke	(3)	Arizona	82-72
II	Kentucky Wesleyan	(8)	Washburn, KS	72-63
III	Catholic, DC	(1)	William Paterson, NJ	76-62

Women

Div.	Winner		Runner-Up	Score
I	Notre Dame	(1)	Purdue	68-66
II	Cal Poly Pomona	(4)	North Dakota	87-80 (OT)
III	Washington, MO*	(4)	Messiah, PA	67-45

Fencing

Div.	Winner		Runner-Up	Score
Combined	St. John's, NY	(1)	Penn St.*	180-172

Gymnastics

Div.	Winner		Runner-Up	Margin
Men	Ohio St.	(3)	Oklahoma	by .350
Women	UCLA*	(3)	Georgia	by .175

Ice Hockey

Men

Div.	Winner		Runner-Up	Score
I	Boston College	(2)	North Dakota*	3-2 (OT)
III	Plattsburgh St., NY	(2)	Rochester Inst., NY	6-2

Women

Div.	Winner		Runner-Up	Score
National	Minn.-Duluth	(1)	St. Lawrence, NY	4-2

Note: The 2001 National Collegiate Women's Ice Hockey Championship was the first to be sponsored by the NCAA. National championships had been sponsored by the American Women's College Hockey Alliance (AWCHA) since 1998.

Rifle

Div.	Winner		Runner-Up	Score
Combined	AK-Fairbanks*	(4)	Kentucky	6283-6175

Skiing

Div.	Winner		Runner-Up	Score
Combined	Denver*	(16)	Vermont	649-605

Swimming & Diving

Men

Div.	Winner		Runner-Up	Score
I	Texas*	(8)	Stanford	597½-457½
II	CS-Bakersfield*	(11)	Drury, MO	621-562½
III	Kenyon, OH*	(22)	Emory, GA	669-289½

Women

Div.	Winner		Runner-Up	Score
I	Georgia*	(3)	Stanford	389-387½
II	Truman, MO	(1)	Drury, MO*	656-610½
III	Denison, OH	(1)	Kenyon, OH*	588-572

Indoor Track

Men

Div.	Winner		Runner-Up	Score
I	LSU	(1)	Texas Christian	34-33
II	St. Augustine's, NC	(8)	New York Tech	74-48
III	Wisc.-La Crosse	(8)	Wisc.-Oshkosh	58-44

Women

Div.	Winner		Runner-Up	Score
I	UCLA*	(2)	South Carolina	53½-40
II	St. Augustine's, NC	(3)	Abilene Christian*	63-48
III	Wheaton, MA*	(3)	Wisc.-La Crosse	63-35

Wrestling

Div.	Winner		Runner-Up	Score
I	Minnesota	(1)	Iowa*	138½-125½
II	North Dakota St.*	(4)	South Dakota St.	98½-91
III	Augsburg, MN	(7)	Wisc.-La Crosse	119½-72

SPRING

Baseball

Div.	Winner		Runner-Up	Score
I	Miami-FL	(4)	Stanford	12-1
II	St. Mary's, TX	(1)	Central Mo. St.	11-3
III	St. Thomas, MN	(1)	Marietta, OH	8-4

Golf

Men

Div.	Winner		Runner-Up	Score
I	Florida	(4)	Clemson	1126-1144
II	West Florida	(1)	Florida Southern*	1148-1163
III	Wisc.-Eau Claire	(1)	Guilford, NC	1162-1163

Women

Div.	Winner		Runner-Up	Score
I	Georgia	(1)	Duke	1176-1179
II	Fla. Southern^	(2)	Rollins, FL	1250-1266
III	Methodist, NC*	(5)	Concordia, MN	1214-1264

Lacrosse

Men

Div.	Winner		Runner-Up	Score
I	Princeton	(6)	Syracuse*	10-9 (OT)
II	Adelphi, NY	(7)	Limestone, SC*	14-10
III	Middlebury, VT*	(2)	Gettysburg, PA	15-10

Women

Div.	Winner		Runner-Up	Score
I	Maryland*	(9)	Georgetown	14-13 (OT)
II	C.W. Post, NY	(1)	West Chester, PA	13-9
III	Middlebury, VT	(3)	Amherst, MA	11-10 (OT)

Note: A Division II women's lacrosse championship was held for the first time in 2001.

Rowing

Women

Div.	Winner		Runner-Up	Score
National	Washington	(3)	Michigan	58-53

Note: The 1997 National Collegiate Women's Rowing Championship was the first to be sponsored by the NCAA. National championships had been held without NCAA sponsorship since 1979.

Softball

Div.	Winner		Runner-Up	Score
I	Arizona	(6)	UCLA	1-0
II	Neb.-Omaha	(1)	Lewis, IL	4-0
III	Muskingum, OH	(1)	Central, IA	4-1

Tennis

Note that both Div. II tournaments were team-only.

Men

Div.	Winner		Runner-Up	Score
I	Georgia	(4)	Tennessee	4-1
II	Rollins, FL	(4)	Hawaii Pacific	5-0
III	Williams, MA	(2)	UC Santa Cruz	4-1

Women

Div.	Winner		Runner-Up	Score
I	Stanford	(11)	Vanderbilt	4-0
II	Lynn, FL	(3)	BYU-Hawaii*	5-3
III	Williams, MA	(1)	Trinity, TX*	6-3

Outdoor Track

Men

Div.	Winner		Runner-Up	Score
I	Tennessee	(3)	Texas Christian	50-49
II	St. Augustine's, NC	(9)	Abilene Christian*	80-59
III	Wisc.-La Crosse	(6)	Lincoln, PA*	80-60

Women

Div.	Winner		Runner-Up	Score
I	USC	(1)	UCLA	64-55
II	St. Augustine's, NC*	(3)	Western St., CO	80-59
III	Wheaton, MA	(1)	Calvin, MI	83½-49

Volleyball

Men

Div.	Winner		Runner-Up	Score
National	BYU	(2)	UCLA*	3 games

Water Polo

Women

Div.	Winner		Runner-Up	Score
National	UCLA	(1)	Stanford	5-4

Note: The 2001 National Collegiate Women's Water Polo Championship was the first to be sponsored by the NCAA. National championships had been held without NCAA sponsorship since 1995.

Real Gender Equity

Schools whose men's and women's teams won NCAA championships in the same sport, or its equivalent during the 2000-01 season.

School	Div.	Sports
Middlebury, VT	III	Men's Lacrosse
		Women's Lacrosse
St. Augustine's, NC	II	Men's Indoor Track
		Women's Indoor Track
		Men's Outdoor Track
		Women's Outdoor Track

School	Div.	Sports
UCLA	Nat.	Men's Water Polo
		Women's Water Polo
Western St., CO	II	Men's Cross Country
		Women's Cross Country
Williams, MA	III	Men's Tennis
		Women's Tennis

St. John's
Emese Takács
Fencing

AK-Fairbanks
Matthew Emmons
Rifle

South Carolina
Demetria Washington
Track and Field

Texas
Nate Dusing
Swimming

2000-01 Division I Individual Champions
Repeat champions in **bold** type.

FALL

Cross Country

Men (10,000 meters)	Time
1 Keith Kelly, Providence	30:14.5
2 Stephen Ondieki, Fairleigh Dickinson	30:16.3
3 Jorge Torres, Colorado	30:21.4

Women (6,000 meters)	Time
1 Kara Grgas-Wheeler, Colorado	20:30.5
2 Sabrina Monro, Montana	20:37.8
3 Erica Palmer, Wisconsin	20:39.9

WINTER

Fencing
Men

Event		Score
Foil	William Jed Dupree, Columbia	14-10
Epee	Soren Thompson, Princeton	15-12
Sabre	Ivan Lee, St. John's, NY	15-13

Women

Event		Score
Foil	Iris Zimmerman, Stanford	15-3
Epee	Emese Takács, St. John's, NY	15-13
Sabre	Sada Jacobson, Yale	15-6

Gymnastics
Men

Event		Points
All-Around	**Jamie Natalie**, Ohio St.	55.700
Floor Exercise	Clay Strother, Minnesota	9.525
Pommel Horse	Clay Strother, Minnesota	9.662
Rings	Chris Lakeman, Penn St.	9.550
Vault	Daren Lynch, Ohio St.	9.500
Parallel Bars	Raj Bhavsar, Ohio St.	9.412
Horizontal Bar	**Michael Ashe**, California	9.512

Women

Event		Points
All-Around	Onnie Willis, UCLA	39.525
	& Elise Ray, Michigan	39.525
Vault	Cory Fritzinger, Georgia	9.881
Uneven Bars	Yvonne Tousek, UCLA	9.9375
Balance Beam	Theresa Kulikowski, Utah	9.9375
Floor Exercise	Mohini Bhardwaj, UCLA	9.963

Rifle
Combined
Smallbore

	Points
1 Matthew Emmons, AK-Fairbanks	1178
2 Per Sandberg, AK-Fairbanks	1177
3 Karl Olsson, AK-Fairbanks	1174

Air Rifle

	Points
1 Matthew Emmons, AK-Fairbanks	392
2 Amanda Trujillo, Nebraska	392
3 Maxim Shub, Tennessee	391
& Thrine Kane, Xavier	391

Note: Emmons won the event over Trujillo with more inner tens (30-27).

Skiing
Men

Event		Time
Slalom	Jernej Bukovec, Utah	1:24.50
Giant Slalom	John Minahan, Vermont	1:59.52
10-k Classic	Wolf Wallendorf, Denver	28:37.5
20-k Freestyle	**Pietro Broggini**, Denver	50:44.8

Women

Event		Time
Slalom	Petra Svet, Utah	1:28.76
Giant Slalom	Erica MacConnell, Vermont	2:06.32
5-k Classic	**Katerina Hanusova**, Nevada	15:59.4
15-k Freestyle	Katerina Hanusova, Nevada	44:23.2

Wrestling

Wgt	Champion	Runner-Up
125	Stephen Abas, Fresno St.	J. Strittmatter, Iowa
133	**Eric Juergens**, Iowa	J. Thompson, Okla. St.
141	Michael Lightner, Oklahoma	D. Schwab, Iowa
149	Adam Tirapelle, Illinois	D. Esposito, Lehigh
157	T.J. Williams, Iowa	B. Snyder, Nebraska
165	**Don Pritzlaff**, Wisconsin	J. Heskett, Iowa St.
174	Josh Koscheck, Edinboro	M. Worthy, Army
184	**Cael Sanderson**, Iowa St.	D. Cormier, Okla. St.
197	Mark Munoz, Okla. St.	P. Quirk, Illinois
Hvy	John Lockhart, Illinois	T. Rowlands, Ohio St.

Florida
Nick Gilliam
Golf

Stanford
Laura Granville
Tennis

Tennessee
Justin Gatlin
Track & Field

USC
Angela Williams
Track and Field

Swimming & Diving
(*) indicates meet record. (†) indicates tied meet record.

Men

Event (yards)	Time
50 free ....Anthony Robinson, Stanford	19.15
100 free........**Anthony Ervin**, California	41.80†
200 free................Klete Keller, USC	1:34.43
500 free.................Klete Keller, USC	4:14.67
1650 free.......Chris Thompson, Michigan	14:26.62*
100 back........Michael Gilliam, Tennessee	45.97
200 back..............Nate Dusing, Texas	1:41.52
100 breast.........Brendan Hansen, Texas	52.35
200 breast.........Brendan Hansen, Texas	1:53.11*
100 butterfly.............Ian Crocker, Texas	45.96
200 butterfly....**Adam Messner**, Stanford	1:43.12
200 IM ....Nate Dusing, Texas	1:42.85*
400 IM ....**Tim Siciliano**, Michigan	3:40.77
200 free relay ....Stanford	1:16.83
400 free relay ....**Texas**	2:49.80*
800 free relay ....**Texas**	6:18.00*
200 medley relay ....**Texas**	1:24.47*
400 medley relay ....**Texas**	3:05.37*

Diving	Points
1-meter...............**Troy Dumais**, Texas	397.60
3-meter...............**Troy Dumais**, Texas	664.70
Platform ....Kyle Prandi, Miami-FL	591.75

Women

Event (yards)	Time
50 free ....Colleen Lanne, Texas	21.99
100 free ....Colleen Lanne, Texas	48.29
200 free ....Sarah Tolar, Stanford	1:45.21
500 free ....Jessica Foschi, Stanford	4:37.81
1650 free.............**Cara Lane**, Virginia	15:53.86
100 back........Natalie Coughlin, California	51.23*
200 back........Natalie Coughlin, California	1:51.02*
100 breast ....Tara Kirk, Stanford	59.18
200 breast ....Amanda Beard, Arizona	2:09.09
100 butterfly ...Natalie Coughlin, California	51.18*
200 butterfly ....Misty Hyman, Stanford	1:53.63
200 IM ....Maggie Bowen, Auburn	1:55.49*
400 IM ....Maggie Bowen, Auburn	4:07.26
200 free relay......................Texas	1:28.89*
400 free relay ....Texas	3:14.52*
800 free relay ....Georgia	7:06.48
200 medley relay ....Stanford	1:38.43
400 medley relay ....Stanford	3:32.43*

Diving	Points
1-meter............Yulia Pakhalina, Houston	329.60
3-meter............Yulia Pakhalina, Houston	573.20
Platform ....Erin Sones, Stanford	463.05

Indoor Track
(*) indicates meet record

Men

Event	Time
60 meters................Kim Collins, TCU	6.58
200 meters ....Kim Collins, TCU	20.55
400 meters ....Rickey Harris, Florida	45.78
800 meters.....Patrick Nduwimana, Arizona	1:45.33*
Mile ....Bryan Berryhill, Colorado St.	3:56.84
3000 meters ....**David Kimani**, Alabama	8:03.29
5000 meters ......**David Kimani**, Alabama	13:42.32
60-m hurdles.....Aubrey Herring, Indiana St.	7.61
4x400-m relay ....LSU	3:04.44
Distance medley relay...........**Stanford**	9:30.01

Event	Hgt/Dist
High Jump ....Charles Clinger, Weber St.	7-5
Pole Vault ....Jacob Pauli, Northern Iowa	18-7½
Long Jump...Savante Stringfellow, Mississippi	26-6¼
Triple Jump...............Walter Davis, LSU	55-5
Shot Put..............**Janus Robberts**, SMU	70-1*
35-lb Throw ....Andras Haklits, Georgia	80-2#

The implement thrown by Haklits did not meet specifications for record purposes. However, second-place finisher Libor Charfreitag from SMU threw 78-9¾ and was given credit for setting a new meet record.

Women

Event	Time
60 meters.......Monique Tubbs, Jacksonville	7.29
200 meters ....Cydonie Mothersill, Clemson	22.89
400 meters .Demetria Washington, S. Carolina	52.37
800 meters .....Svetlana Badrankova, UTEP	2:06.58
Mile ....Tracy Robertson, Arkansas	4:39.10
3000 meters ..Shannon Smith, Boston College	9:11.25
5000 meters ....Jodie Hughes, Colorado	16:08.61
60-m hurdles .....Donica Merriman, Ohio St.	7.95
4x400-m relay ....South Carolina	3:30.08*
Distance medley relay.............Missouri	11:06.77

Event	Hgt/Dist
High Jump ....Kart Siilats, Harvard	6-0¾
Pole Vault ....Thorey Elisdottir, Georgia	14-9½*
Long Jump ....Jenny Adams, Houston	21-11
Triple Jump ....Gi-Gi Miller, Arkansas	44-4
Shot Put ....Christina Tolson, UCLA	55-9¾
20-lb Throw ....**Florence Ezeh**, SMU	69-10¼

SPRING
Golf
Men

		Total
1 Nick Gilliam, Florida...........69-70-66-71—276		
2 Camilo Benedetti, Florida.......74-71-69-65—279		
& Jamie Elson, Augusta St.......73-65-70-71—279		

Women

		Total
1	Candy Hannemann, Duke	75-72-69-69—285*
2	Lorena Ochoa, Arizona	73-71-72-69—285
3	Candie Kung, USC	72-74-71-70—287
	& Katy Harris, LSU	72-70-70-75—287

* Hannemann won on the first sudden death playoff hole.

Tennis

Men

Singles— Matias Boeker (Georgia) def. Brian Vahaly (Virginia), 6-2, 6-4.

Doubles— Boeker & Travis Parrott (Georgia) def. Johan Brunstrom & Jon Wallmark (SMU), 6-4, 7-5.

Women

Singles— Laura Granville (Stanford) def. Lauren Kalvaria (Stanford), 6-3, 7-6.

Doubles— Whitney Laiho & Jessica Lehnhoff (Florida) def. Granville & Gabriela Lastra (Stanford), 4-6, 6-1, 6-3.

Outdoor Track

(*) indicates meet record

Men

Event		Time
100 meters	Justin Gatlin, Tennessee	10.08
200 meters	Justin Gatlin, Tennessee	20.11
400 meters	**Avard Moncur**, Auburn	44.84
800 meters	Otukile Lekote, S. Carolina	1:46.68
1500 meters	Bryan Berryhill, Colorado St.	3:37.05
5000 meters	Jonathon Riley, Stanford	13:42.51
10,000 meters	Ryan Shay, Notre Dame	29:05.44
110-m hurdles	Ron Bramlett, Alabama	13.54
400-m hurdles	Bayano Kamani, Baylor	48.99
3000-m steeple	Daniel Lincoln, Arkansas	8:42.31
4x100-m relay	TCU	38.58
4x400-m relay	**Baylor**	3:03.89

Event		Hgt/Dist
High Jump	Charles Clinger, Weber St.	7-6½
Pole Vault	Dennis Kholev, USC	18-6½
Long Jump	**Savante Stringfellow**, Mississippi	27-1¾
Triple Jump	Walter Davis, LSU	54-4
Shot Put	Janus Robberts, SMU	72-1
Discus	Tolga Koseoglu, Texas A&M	204-10
Javelin	John Stiegeler, Oregon	252-10
Hammer	Andras Haklits, Georgia	247-8
Decathlon	Santiago Lorenzo, Oregon	7889 pts

Women

Event		Time
100 meters	**Angela Williams**, USC	11.05
200 meters	Brianna Glenn, Arizona	22.92
400 meters	Allison Beckford, Rice	52.33
800 meters	Brigita Langerholc, USC	2:01.61
1500 meters	Mary Jayne Harrelson, App. St.	4:14.30
3000 meters	Elizabeth Jackson, BYU	9:49.73
5000 meters	Lauren Fleshman, Stanford	15:52.21
10,000 meters	Amy Yoder-Begley, Arkansas	33:59.96
100-m hurdles	Donica Merriman, Ohio St.	12.73
400-m hurdles	Brenda Taylor, Harvard	55.88
4x100-m relay	LSU	43.54
4x400-m relay	Clemson	3:29.97

Event		Hgt/Dist
High Jump	Dora Gyorffy, Harvard	6-2¾
Pole Vault	Andrea Dutoit, Arizona	13-9¼
Long Jump	Brianna Glenn, Arizona	21-6¼
Triple Jump	Shelly-Ann Gallimore, Auburn	43-7¼
Shot Put	Christina Tolson, UCLA	57-0¾
Discus	Katja Schreiber, Idaho	197-11
Javelin	Inga Stasiulionyte, USC	172-4
Hammer	**Florence Ezeh**, SMU	219-4*
Heptathlon	Austra Skujyte, Kansas St.	5857 pts*

Championships
Most Outstanding Players
Men

Baseball	Charlton Jimerson, Miami-FL
Basketball	Shane Battier, Duke
Cross Country	Keith Kelly, Providence*
Golf	Nick Gilliam, Florida*
Gymnastics	Jamie Natalie, Ohio St.*
Ice Hockey	Chuck Kobasew, Boston Coll.
Lacrosse	B.J. Prager, Princeton
Soccer: Offense	Darin Lewis, UConn
Soccer: Defense	Chris Gbandi, UConn
Swimming & Diving	Nate Dusing, Texas
Tennis	Matias Boeker, Georgia*
Track: Indoor	Kim Collins, TCU*
	& David Kimani, S. Alabama*
Track: Outdoor	Justin Gatlin, Tennessee*
Volleyball	Mike Wall, BYU
Water Polo	Sean Kern, UCLA
Wrestling	Cael Sanderson, Iowa St.

Women

Basketball	Ruth Riley, Notre Dame
Cross Country	Kara Grgas-Wheeler, Colorado*
Golf	Candy Hannemann, Duke*
Gymnastics	Onnie Willis, UCLA*
	& Elise Ray, Michigan*
Ice Hockey	Maria Rooth, Minn.-Duluth
Lacrosse	Courtney Martinez, Maryland
Soccer: Offense	Meredith Florance, N. Carolina
Soccer: Defense	Catherine Reddick, N. Carolina
Softball	Jennie Finch, Arizona
Swimming & Diving	Natalie Coughlin, California
Tennis	Laura Granville, Stanford*
Track: Indoor	Demetria Washington, S. Carolina*
	& Christina Tolson, UCLA*
Track: Outdoor	Brianna Glenn, Arizona*
Volleyball	Greichaly Cepero, Nebraska
Water Polo	Coralie Simmons, UCLA

(*) indicates won individual or all-around NCAA championship; There were no official Outstanding Players in fencing, field hockey, I-AA football, riflery, rowing and skiing. Outstanding players in indoor and outdoor track are the individuals earning the most points in the NCAA Championships.

2000-01 NAIA Team Champions

Total NAIA titles in parentheses.

FALL

Cross Country: MEN'S–Life, GA (3); WOMEN'S– Concordia, CA (1). **Football:** MEN'S– Georgetown, KY (2). **Soccer:** MEN'S– Lindsey Wilson, KY (5); WOMEN'S– Simon Fraser, BC (2). **Volleyball:** WOMEN'S– Dickinson St., ND (1).

WINTER

Basketball: MEN'S– Division I: Faulkner, AL (1) and Division II: Northwestern, IA (1); WOMEN'S– Division I: Oklahoma City (4) and Division II: Northwestern, IA (1). **Swimming & Diving:** MEN'S– Simon Fraser, BC (4); WOMEN'S– Simon Fraser, BC (8). **Indoor Track:** MEN'S– McKendree, IL (1); WOMEN'S– McKendree, IL (3). **Wrestling:** MEN'S– Southern Oregon (4).

SPRING

Baseball: MEN'S– Birmingham-Southern, AL (1). **Golf:** MEN'S– Oklahoma City (1); WOMEN'S– British Columbia (1). **Softball:** WOMEN'S– Oklahoma City (6). **Tennis:** MEN'S– Oklahoma City (4); WOMEN'S– Auburn-Montgomery, AL (4). **Outdoor Track:** MEN'S– Azusa Pacific, CA (12); WOMEN'S– (tie) Life, GA (2) and Doane, NE (1).

Annual NCAA Division I Team Champions

Men's and women's NCAA Division I team champions from Cross Country to Wrestling. Also see team champions for base-ball, basketball, football, golf, ice hockey, soccer and tennis in the appropriate chapters throughout the almanac. See pages 454-456 for list of 2000-01 individual champions.

CROSS COUNTRY

Men

Despite no top-10 finishers, Arkansas won its third consecutive men's cross country title and 11th overall in the freezing cold temperatures and whipping winds of Iowa. Balance was the key as four of the meet's top 24 finishers wore Arkansas colors. Led by senior James Karanu (11th place), Arkansas registered 83 points to top runner-up Colorado (94) and third-place Providence (121). Keith Kelly of Providence was the meet's individual winner, completing the 10,000-meter course in 30:14.5, while Fairleigh Dickinson's Stephen Ondieki followed in second at 30:16.3. (Ames, IA; Nov. 20, 2000.)

Multiple winners: Arkansas (11); Michigan St. (8); UTEP (7); Oregon and Villanova (4); Drake, Indiana, Penn St. and Wisconsin (3); Iowa St., San Jose St., Stanford and Western Michigan (2).

Year		Year		Year		Year		Year	
1938	Indiana	1950	Penn St.	1963	San Jose St.	1976	UTEP	1989	Iowa St.
1939	Michigan St.	1951	Syracuse	1964	Western Mich.	1977	Oregon	1990	Arkansas
1940	Indiana	1952	Michigan St.	1965	Western Mich.	1978	UTEP	1991	Arkansas
1941	Rhode Island	1953	Kansas	1966	Villanova	1979	UTEP	1992	Arkansas
1942	Indiana	1954	Oklahoma St.	1967	Villanova	1980	UTEP	1993	Arkansas
	& Penn St.	1955	Michigan St.	1968	Villanova	1981	UTEP	1994	Iowa St.
1943	Not held	1956	Michigan St.	1969	UTEP	1982	Wisconsin	1995	Arkansas
1944	Drake	1957	Notre Dame	1970	Villanova	1983	Vacated	1996	Stanford
1945	Drake	1958	Michigan St.	1971	Oregon	1984	Arkansas	1997	Stanford
1946	Drake	1959	Michigan St.	1972	Tennessee	1985	Wisconsin	1998	Arkansas
1947	Penn St.	1960	Houston	1973	Oregon	1986	Arkansas	1999	Arkansas
1948	Michigan St.	1961	Oregon St.	1974	Oregon	1987	Arkansas	2000	Arkansas
1949	Michigan St.	1962	San Jose St.	1975	UTEP	1988	Wisconsin		

Women

Colorado literally ran away with its first Division I Women's Cross Country Championship by an impressive 50 points over defend-ing champion Brigham Young. Kara Grgas-Wheeler was the star for the Buffaloes, winning the meet with a time of 20:30.5 over the 6,000-meter course. Colorado's cause was also bolstered by the eighth-place finish of freshman Sara Gorton (20:51.3). They tallied 117 points, while Brigham Young and Stanford followed with 167 and 198, respectively. Sabrina Monro of Montana was the meet's runner-up (20:37.8) and last year's champ Erica Palmer of Wisconsin placed third. (Ames, IA; Nov. 20, 2000.)

Multiple winners: Villanova (7); Brigham Young, Oregon, Virginia and Wisconsin (2).

Year		Year		Year		Year		Year	
1981	Virginia	1985	Wisconsin	1989	Villanova	1993	Villanova	1997	Brigham Young
1982	Virginia	1986	Texas	1990	Villanova	1994	Villanova	1998	Villanova
1983	Oregon	1987	Oregon	1991	Villanova	1995	Providence	1999	Brigham Young
1984	Wisconsin	1988	Kentucky	1992	Villanova	1996	Stanford	2000	Colorado

FENCING

Men & Women

After finishing runner-up to Penn St. last year, St. John's finally broke through to win their first NCAA fencing championship, ending the Nittany Lions' six-year streak. The Red Storm accumulated 180 points overall on the strength of 1-2 finishes in two disciplines. Ivan Lee won the men's sabre, besting teammate Keeth Smart, while Emese Takács defeated Arlene Stevens in the women's epee. Penn St. followed in second place with 172 points and Notre Dame was third with 153. (Kenosha, WI; Mar. 22-25, 2001.)

Multiple winners: Penn St. (8); Columbia/Barnard (2). **Note:** Prior to 1990, men and women held separate champion-ships. Men's multiple winners included: NYU (12); Columbia (11); Wayne St. (7); Navy, Notre Dame and Penn (3); Illinois (2). Women's multiple winners included: Wayne St. (3); Yale (2).

Year		Year		Year		Year	
1990	Penn St.	1993	Columbia/Barnard	1996	Penn St.	1999	Penn St.
1991	Penn St.	1994	Notre Dame	1997	Penn St.	2000	Penn St.
1992	Columbia/Barnard	1995	Penn St.	1998	Penn St.	2001	St. John's

FIELD HOCKEY

Women

All-time NCAA points leader Marina DiGiacomo scored the opening goal of the game and top-seeded Old Dominion added two second-half goals to beat North Carolina 3-1 in the Division I Field Hockey Championship Game. It was the fifth time the two field hockey powerhouses faced each other in the finals. The title is the Lady Monarchs' ninth overall and the victory put them at 25-1 for the season. Julie Miracle and Laura Steadman added the other two goals for ODU, and goaltender Marybeth Freeman turned away six shots. (Norfolk, VA; Nov. 19, 2000.)

Multiple winners: Old Dominion (9); North Carolina (4); Maryland (3); Connecticut (2).

Year		Year		Year		Year		Year	
1981	Connecticut	1985	Connecticut	1989	North Carolina	1993	Maryland	1997	North Carolina
1982	Old Dominion	1986	Iowa	1990	Old Dominion	1994	J. Madison	1998	Old Dominion
1983	Old Dominion	1987	Maryland	1991	Old Dominion	1995	North Carolina	1999	Maryland
1984	Old Dominion	1988	Old Dominion	1992	Old Dominion	1996	North Carolina	2000	Old Dominion

Annual NCAA Division I Team Champions (Cont.)

GYMNASTICS

Men

In front of its home crowd, Ohio St. won its third men's gymnastics title and first since 1996. The Buckeyes amassed 218.125 points to edge runner-up Oklahoma (217.775) and California (216.775). Jamie Natalie took home the individual all-around championship for the second consecutive year for Ohio St., teammate Daren Lynch won the vault competition and Raj Bhavsar was first in the parallel bars. Minnesota's Clay Strother was the only double victor with individual wins in the floor exercise and pommel horse. *(Columbus, OH; Apr. 5-7, 2001.)*

Multiple winners: Penn St. (10); Illinois (9); Nebraska (8); California and So. Illinois (4); Iowa St., Michigan, Ohio St., Oklahoma and Stanford (3); Florida St and UCLA (2).

Year		Year		Year		Year		Year	
1938	Chicago	1956	Illinois	1969	Iowa	1980	Nebraska	1994	Nebraska
1939	Illinois	1957	Penn St.		& Michigan (T)	1981	Nebraska	1995	Stanford
1940	Illinois	1958	Michigan St.	1970	Michigan	1982	Nebraska	1996	Ohio St.
1941	Illinois		& Illinois		& Michigan (T)	1983	Nebraska	1997	California
1942	Illinois	1959	Penn St.	1971	Iowa St.	1984	UCLA	1998	California
1943-47	Not held	1960	Penn St.	1972	So. Illinois	1985	Ohio St.	1999	Michigan
1948	Penn St.	1961	Penn St.	1973	Iowa St.	1986	Arizona St.	2000	Penn St.
1949	Temple	1962	USC	1974	Iowa St.	1987	UCLA	2001	Ohio St.
1950	Illinois	1963	Michigan	1975	California	1988	Nebraska		
1951	Florida St.	1964	So. Illinois	1976	Penn St.	1989	Illinois	(T) indicates won	
1952	Florida St.	1965	Penn St.	1977	Indiana St.	1990	Nebraska	trampoline competi-	
1953	Penn St.	1966	So. Illinois		& Oklahoma	1991	Oklahoma	tion (1969-70).	
1954	Penn St.	1967	So. Illinois	1978	Oklahoma	1992	Stanford		
1955	Illinois	1968	California	1979	Nebraska	1993	Stanford		

Women

UCLA overcame two late falls to win its second consecutive women's gymnastics title and third in the last five. Despite falls in the floor exercise and the balance beam, the Bruins rallied to score 197.575 points to finish ahead of host Georgia (197.400) and Michigan (197.275). UCLA's Onnie Willis tied for the individual all-around title with Sydney Olympian Elise Ray of Michigan. Also winning individual titles for the Bruins were Yvonne Toucek in the uneven bars and Mohini Bhardwaj in the floor exercise. *(Athens, GA; Apr. 19-21, 2001.)*

Multiple winners: Utah (9); Georgia (5); Alabama and UCLA (3).

Year		Year		Year		Year		Year	
1982	Utah	1986	Utah	1990	Utah	1994	Utah	1998	Georgia
1983	Utah	1987	Georgia	1991	Alabama	1995	Utah	1999	Georgia
1984	Utah	1988	Alabama	1992	Utah	1996	Alabama	2000	UCLA
1985	Utah	1989	Georgia	1993	Georgia	1997	UCLA	2001	UCLA

LACROSSE

Men

The 2001 men's lacrosse title matchup was a repeat of last year's, only this time it was Princeton getting the better of Syracuse in a 10-9 overtime thriller. It was the sixth lacrosse championship for Princeton and fourth in the last six years. Syracuse trailed 8-4 entering the fourth period but fought back to tie it on Michael Powell's goal with 16 seconds remaining. In overtime, B.J. Prager scored the game-winner with 41 seconds left on a feed from Ryan Boyle. *(New Brunswick, N.J.; May 26-28, 2001.)*

Multiple winners: Johns Hopkins (7); Princeton and Syracuse (6); North Carolina (4); Cornell (3); Maryland and Virginia (2).

Year		Year		Year		Year		Year	
1971	Cornell	1977	Cornell	1983	Syracuse	1989	Syracuse	1995	Syracuse
1972	Virginia	1978	Johns Hopkins	1984	Johns Hopkins	1990	Syracuse*	1996	Princeton
1973	Maryland	1979	Johns Hopkins	1985	Johns Hopkins	1991	North Carolina	1997	Princeton
1974	Johns Hopkins	1980	Johns Hopkins	1986	North Carolina	1992	Princeton	1998	Princeton
1975	Maryland	1981	North Carolina	1987	Johns Hopkins	1993	Syracuse	1999	Virginia
1976	Cornell	1982	North Carolina	1988	Syracuse	1994	Princeton	2000	Syracuse
								2001	Princeton

*Title was later vacated due to action by the NCAA Committee on Infractions.

Women

It was anything but easy, but Maryland won its seventh consecutive women's lacrosse title and ninth overall with a 14-13 sudden-death overtime victory over Georgetown. The hero for the Terps was senior Allison Comito, who netted the game-winner with eight seconds left in overtime. Maryland held an early 8-1 lead but Georgetown wouldn't quit, tying the game at 12-12 with just under six minutes left. Erin Elbe scored six goals for the Hoyas. *(Baltimore, MD; May 18-20, 2001.)*

Multiple winners: Maryland (9); Penn St., Temple and Virginia (2).

Year		Year		Year		Year		Year	
1982	Massachusetts	1986	Maryland	1990	Harvard	1994	Princeton	1998	Maryland
1983	Delaware	1987	Penn St.	1991	Virginia	1995	Maryland	1999	Maryland
1984	Temple	1988	Temple	1992	Maryland	1996	Maryland	2000	Maryland
1985	New Hampshire	1989	Penn St.	1993	Virginia	1997	Maryland	2001	Maryland

RIFLE

Men & Women

Matthew Emmons won both the individual smallbore and air rifle disciplines and Alaska-Fairbanks came away with its third consecutive NCAA rifle championship. The Nanooks squad of Emmons, Melissa Mulloy, Per Sandberg and Karl Olsson recorded an aggregate score of 6,283 points (4,710 in smallbore and 1,573 in air rifle) to better runner-up Kentucky (6,175) and West Virginia (6,174). It was the fourth overall rifle title for Alaska-Fairbanks. (*Columbus, OH; Mar. 8-10, 2001.*)

Multiple winners: West Virginia (13); Alaska-Fairbanks (4); Tennessee Tech (3); Murray St. (2).

Year	Year	Year	Year	Year
1980 Tenn. Tech	1985 Murray St.	1990 West Virginia	1995 West Virginia	2000 AK-Fairbanks
1981 Tenn. Tech	1986 West Virginia	1991 West Virginia	1996 West Virginia	2001 AK-Fairbanks
1982 Tenn. Tech	1987 Murray St.	1992 West Virginia	1997 West Virginia	
1983 West Virginia	1988 West Virginia	1993 West Virginia	1998 West Virginia	
1984 West Virginia	1989 West Virginia	1994 AK-Fairbanks	1999 AK-Fairbanks	

ROWING

NCAA Championships

Women

The Washington Huskies returned to Lake Lanier, the site of their last NCAA championship, and once again came away with a hard-fought victory for their third overall title. Washington trailed Michigan heading into the all-important Varsity I Eights but was spurred to victory by coxswain Mary Whipple in a time of 7:04.03 over the 2,000-meter course. Brown finished a close second in 7:05.34 while Michigan placed third in 7:08.45. In the overall standings, Washington amassed 58 points, followed by Michigan (53) and Brown (49). Washington also won the Fours race and placed second to Michigan in the II Eights event. (*Gainesville, GA; May 24-26, 2001*).

Multiple winners: Washington (3); Brown (2).

Year	Overall winner	Varsity Eights	Year	Overall winner	Varsity Eights
1997	Washington	Washington	2000	Brown	Brown
1998	Washington	Washington	2001	Washington	Washington
1999	Brown	Brown			

Intercollegiate Rowing Association Regatta

VARSITY EIGHTS

Men

California grabbed an early lead and powered through to the finish to win the Varsity Eights title at the 99th IRA Championships Regatta. It was the third consecutive win and 13th overall for the Bears. By 400 meters, Cal (5:34.62) had a half-length lead and came in over three seconds ahead of runner-up Princeton (5:37.76). Washington took third in 5:39.46. (*Cooper River, Camden NJ; June 1-3, 2000.*)

The IRA was formed in 1895 by several Northeastern colleges after Harvard and Yale quit the Rowing Association (established in 1871) to stage an annual race of their own. Since then the IRA Regatta has been contested over courses of varying lengths in Poughkeepsie, N.Y., Marietta, Ohio, Syracuse, N.Y. and Camden, N.J.

Distances: 4 miles (1895-97,1899-1916,1925-41); 3 miles (1898,1921-24,1947-49,1952-63,1965-67); 2 miles (1920,1950-51); 2000 meters (1964, since 1968).

Multiple winners: Cornell (24); California and Navy (13); Washington (11); Penn (9); Brown and Wisconsin (7); Syracuse (6); Columbia (4); Princeton (3); Northeastern (2).

Year	Year	Year	Year	Year
1895 Columbia	1916 Syracuse	1939 California	1964 California	1985 Princeton
1896 Cornell	1917-19 Not held	1940 Washington	1965 Navy	1986 Brown
1897 Cornell	1920 Syracuse	1941 Washington	1966 Wisconsin	1987 Brown
1898 Penn	1921 Navy	1942-46 Not held	1967 Penn	1988 Northeastern
1899 Penn	1922 Navy	1947 Navy	1968 Penn	1989 Penn
1900 Penn	1923 Washington	1948 Washington	1969 Penn	1990 Wisconsin
1901 Cornell	1924 Washington	1949 California	1970 Washington	1991 Northeastern
1902 Cornell	1925 Navy	1950 Washington	1971 Cornell	1992 Dartmouth,
1903 Cornell	1926 Washington	1951 Wisconsin	1972 Penn	Navy & Penn†
1904 Syracuse	1927 Columbia	1952 Navy	1973 Wisconsin	1993 Brown
1905 Cornell	1928 California	1953 Navy	1974 Wisconsin	1994 Brown
1906 Cornell	1929 Columbia	1954 Navy*	1975 Wisconsin	1995 Brown
1907 Cornell	1930 Cornell	1955 Cornell	1976 California	1996 Princeton
1908 Syracuse	1931 Navy	1956 Cornell	1977 Cornell	1997 Washington
1909 Cornell	1932 California	1957 Cornell	1978 Syracuse	1998 Princeton
1910 Cornell	1933 Not held	1958 Cornell	1979 Brown	1999 California
1911 Cornell	1934 California	1959 Wisconsin	1980 Navy	2000 California
1912 Cornell	1935 California	1960 California	1981 Cornell	2001 California
1913 Syracuse	1936 Washington	1961 California	1982 Cornell	
1914 Columbia	1937 Washington	1962 Cornell	1983 Brown	
1915 Cornell	1938 Navy	1963 Cornell	1984 Navy	

*In 1954, Navy was disqualified because of an ineligible coxswain; no trophies were given.
†First dead heat in history of IRA Regatta.

Annual NCAA Division I Team Champions (Cont.)

National Rowing Championship
VARSITY EIGHTS
Men

National championship raced annually from 1982-96 in Bantam, Ohio over a 2,000-meter course on Lake Harsha. Winner received the Herschede Cup. Regatta discontinued in 1997.

Multiple winners: Harvard (6); Brown (3); Wisconsin (2).

Year	Champion	Time	Runner-up	Time	Year	Champion	Time	Runner-up	Time
1982	Yale	5:50.8	Cornell	5:54.15	1990	Wisconsin	5:52.5	Harvard	5:56.84
1983	Harvard	5:59.6	Washington	6:00.0	1991	Penn	5:58.21	Northeastern	5:58.48
1984	Washington	5:51.1	Yale	5:55.6	1992	Harvard	5:33.97	Dartmouth	5:34.28
1985	Harvard	5:44.4	Princeton	5:44.87	1993	Brown	5:54.15	Penn	5:56.98
1986	Wisconsin	5:57.8	Brown	5:59.9	1994	Brown	5:24.52	Harvard	5:25.83
1987	Harvard	5:35.17	Brown	5:35.63	1995	Brown	5:23.40	Princeton	5:25.83
1988	Harvard	5:35.98	Northeastern	5:37.07	1996	Princeton	5:57.47	Penn	6:03.28
1989	Harvard	5:36.6	Washington	5:38.93	1997	discontinued			

Women

National championship held over various distances at 10 different venues from 1979-96. Distances– 1000 meters (1979-81); 1500 meters (1982-83); 1000 meters (1984); 1750 meters (1985); 2000 meters (1986-88, since 1991); 1852 meters (1989-90). Winner received the Ferguson Bowl. Regatta discontinued in 1997.

Multiple winners: Washington (7); Princeton (4); Boston University (2).

Year	Champion	Time	Runner-up	Time	Year	Champion	Time	Runner-up	Time
1979	Yale	3:06	California	3:08.6	1988	Washington	6:41.0	Yale	6:42.37
1980	California	3:05.4	Oregon St.	3:05.8	1989	Cornell	5:34.9	Wisconsin	5:37.5
1981	Washington	3:20.6	Yale	3:22.9	1991	Boston Univ.	7:03.2	Cornell	7:06.21
1982	Washington	4:56.4	Wisconsin	4:59.83	1992	Boston Univ.	6:28.79	Cornell	6:32.79
1983	Washington	4:57.5	Dartmouth	5:03.02	1993	Princeton	6:40.75	Washington	6:43.86
1984	Washington	3:29.48	Radcliffe	3:31.08	1994	Princeton	6:11.38	Yale	6:14.46
1985	Washington	5:28.4	Wisconsin	5:32.0	1995	Princeton	6:11.98	Washington	6:12.69
1986	Wisconsin	6:53.28	Radcliffe	6:53.34	1996	Brown	6:45.7	Princeton	6:49.3
1987	Washington	6:33.8	Yale	6:37.4	1997	discontinued			

The Harvard-Yale Regatta

Harvard made it two in a row and 15 of the last 17 by cruising to a sweep over Yale at the 136th running of the Harvard/Yale Regatta on June 3, 2001. Harvard's Varsity Eights squad was simply dominant, completing the four-mile course on the Thames River in New London, Conn. in 18:55.6, more than 11 lengths and 37 seconds ahead of the Bulldogs (19:32.7). Harvard's second varsity and freshman teams also won with relative ease. The Harvard/Yale Regatta is the nation's oldest intercollegiate sporting event. Harvard holds an 83-53 series edge.

SKIING

Men & Women

Denver had won 14 of the first 18 NCAA skiing championships from 1954 through 1971 and then took a 28-year championship hiatus until its title in 2000. The dynasty is officially back as the Pioneers captured their second consecutive and 16th overall national skiing championship in 2001. Denver amassed 649 points to beat runner-up Vermont (605) and third-place Colorado (595.5). Wolf Wallendorf and Pietro Broggini each won individual titles to pace the Pioneers, Wallendorf in the men's 10-k classic and Broggini in the 20-k freestyle. Nevada's Katerina Hanusova was the competition's only double winner, taking both the women's 5-k classic and the women's 15-k freestyle. (Middlebury, VT; March 7-10, 2000.)

Multiple winners: Denver (16); Colorado (15); Utah (9); Vermont (5); Dartmouth and Wyoming (2).

Year		Year		Year		Year		Year	
1954	Denver	1964	Denver	1974	Colorado	1983	Utah	1993	Utah
1955	Denver	1965	Denver	1975	Colorado	1984	Utah	1994	Vermont
1956	Denver	1966	Denver	1976	Colorado	1985	Wyoming	1995	Colorado
1957	Denver	1967	Denver		& Dartmouth	1986	Utah	1996	Utah
1958	Dartmouth	1968	Wyoming	1977	Colorado	1987	Utah	1997	Utah
1959	Colorado	1969	Denver	1978	Colorado	1988	Utah	1998	Colorado
1960	Colorado	1970	Denver	1979	Colorado	1989	Vermont	1999	Colorado
1961	Denver	1971	Denver	1980	Vermont	1990	Vermont	2000	Denver
1962	Denver	1972	Colorado	1981	Utah	1991	Colorado	2001	Denver
1963	Denver	1973	Colorado	1982	Colorado	1992	Vermont		

SOFTBALL

Women

Arizona flamethrower Jennie Finch threw seven shutout innings, giving up four hits while fanning seven, to lead the Wildcats to a 1-0 nailbiter over UCLA in the NCAA Women's Softball Championship Game. It was the sixth title overall for Arizona, second only to UCLA with eight. The two rivals were locked in a scoreless tie until the top of the fourth inning when senior catcher Lindsey Collins launched an Amanda Freed offering over the fence in right-center field. It was Freed's only mistake as she gave up just three hits in seven innings. Finch was named most outstanding player of the tournament and ended her season with a perfect 32-0 mark. (*Oklahoma City, OK; May 24-28, 2001.*)

Multiple winners: UCLA (8); Arizona (6); Texas A&M (2).

Year		Year		Year		Year		Year	
1982	UCLA	1986	CS-Fullerton	1990	UCLA	1994	Arizona	1998	Fresno St.
1983	Texas A&M	1987	Texas A&M	1991	Arizona	1995	UCLA*	1999	UCLA
1984	UCLA	1988	UCLA	1992	UCLA	1996	Arizona	2000	Oklahoma
1985	UCLA	1989	UCLA	1993	Arizona	1997	Arizona	2001	Arizona

*Title was later vacated due to action by the NCAA Committee on Infractions.

SWIMMING & DIVING

Men

Texas left no doubt this year, steamrolling to its second consecutive and eighth overall title at the NCAA Division I Men's Swimming and Diving Championships. The Longhorns registered a total of 597½ points, well ahead of runner-up Stanford (457½) and third-place Tennessee (330½). In all, eight NCAA records were set or tied at the meet, six of them by the Longhorns. Nate Dusing took home Swimmer of the Meet honors, recording 57 points for Texas. He won the 200-yard backstroke and 200-yard individual medley and was a member on each of Texas' four relay victories. Dusing also finished second to teammate Ian Crocker in the 100-yard butterfly.

Brendan Hansen (100- and 200-yard breaststrokes) and Troy Dumais (one- and three-meter diving) were the other double winners for Texas. Olympian Klete Keller was a double winner for USC, capturing both the 200- and 500-yard freestyle events, and Michigan's Chris Thompson wowed the Texas A&M crowd by breaking Olympian Tom Dolan's NCAA and American mark in the 1,650-freestyle. (*College Station, TX; Mar. 22-24, 2001.*)

Multiple winners: Michigan and Ohio St. (11); USC (9); Stanford and Texas (8); Indiana (6); Yale (4); Auburn, California and Florida (2).

Year		Year		Year		Year		Year	
1937	Michigan	1950	Ohio St.	1963	USC	1976	USC	1989	Texas
1938	Michigan	1951	Yale	1964	USC	1977	USC	1990	Texas
1939	Michigan	1952	Ohio St.	1965	USC	1978	Tennessee	1991	Texas
1940	Michigan	1953	Yale	1966	USC	1979	California	1992	Stanford
1941	Michigan	1954	Ohio St.	1967	Stanford	1980	California	1993	Stanford
1942	Yale	1955	Ohio St.	1968	Indiana	1981	Texas	1994	Stanford
1943	Ohio St.	1956	Ohio St.	1969	Indiana	1982	UCLA	1995	Michigan
1944	Yale	1957	Michigan	1970	Indiana	1983	Florida	1996	Texas
1945	Ohio St.	1958	Michigan	1971	Indiana	1984	Florida	1997	Auburn
1946	Ohio St.	1959	Michigan	1972	Indiana	1985	Stanford	1998	Stanford
1947	Ohio St.	1960	USC	1973	Indiana	1986	Stanford	1999	Auburn
1948	Michigan	1961	Michigan	1974	USC	1987	Stanford	2000	Texas
1949	Ohio St.	1962	Ohio St.	1975	USC	1988	Texas	2001	Texas

Women

The graduation of Olympians Kristy Kowal and Courtney Shealy was supposed to knock Georgia from contention in 2001. But the Lady Bulldogs wouldn't hear of it, storming to their third consecutive win at the NCAA Division I Women's Swimming and Diving Championships. Georgia, whose only event win came at the NCAA Division I Women's Swimming and Diving Championships, finished with 389 points to barely edge out eight-time champ Stanford (387½). Texas finished in third with 350½ points.

Swimmer of the Meet honors went to Natalie Coughlin of California, who not only won the 100-yard butterfly and the 100- and 200-yard backstrokes, she set meet records in each. Texas' Colleen Lanne was a double winner in the 50- and 100-yard freestyle, as was Auburn's Maggie Bowen (200- and 400-yard individual medley) and diver Yulia Pakhalina of Houston. (*East Meadow, N.Y.; Mar. 15-17, 2001.*)

Multiple winners: Stanford (8); Texas (7); Georgia (3).

Year		Year		Year		Year		Year	
1982	Florida	1986	Texas	1990	Texas	1994	Stanford	1998	Stanford
1983	Stanford	1987	Texas	1991	Texas	1995	Stanford	1999	Georgia
1984	Texas	1988	Texas	1992	Stanford	1996	Stanford	2000	Georgia
1985	Texas	1989	Stanford	1993	Stanford	1997	USC	2001	Georgia

Annual NCAA Division I Team Champions (Cont.)

INDOOR TRACK

Men

It would have been almost impossible for the NCAA Division I Men's Indoor Track and Field Championships to end any more dramatically. But when the smoke had cleared it was LSU which had secured its first-ever title, ending the four-year streak of host Arkansas. Entering the final race of the day, the 1,600-meter relay, LSU trailed TCU by nine points. To win the title, the Tigers needed to win the race and have TCU finish out of the top eight. When Alleyne Francique of LSU crossed the line first and the TCU squad dropped its baton, LSU's dream became reality.

All told, LSU accumulated 34 points and was followed by TCU (33), Arkansas (32) and Alabama (31). Walter Davis was instrumental in leading LSU, winning the triple jump and taking second in the long jump. TCU's Kim Collins and Alabama's David Kimani were the meet's double winners, Collins taking the 60- and 200-meter dashes, and Kimani winning the 3,000- and 5,000-meter runs. (*Fayetteville, AR; March 9-10, 2001.*)

Multiple winners: Arkansas (16); UTEP (7); Kansas and Villanova (3); USC (2).

Year		Year		Year		Year		Year	
1965	Missouri	1973	Manhattan	1981	UTEP	1989	Arkansas	1997	Arkansas
1966	Kansas	1974	UTEP	1982	UTEP	1990	Arkansas	1998	Arkansas
1967	USC	1975	UTEP	1983	SMU	1991	Arkansas	1999	Arkansas
1968	Villanova	1976	UTEP	1984	Arkansas	1992	Arkansas	2000	Arkansas
1969	Kansas	1977	Washington St.	1985	Arkansas	1993	Arkansas	2001	LSU
1970	Kansas	1978	UTEP	1986	Arkansas	1994	Arkansas		
1971	Villanova	1979	Villanova	1987	Arkansas	1995	Arkansas		
1972	USC	1980	UTEP	1988	Arkansas	1996	George Mason		

Women

UCLA won its second consecutive Division I women's track and field title behind an impressive showing by Christina Tolson in the throwing events. Tolson won the shot put and placed second in the 20-lb weight throw behind defending champ Florence Ezeh from SMU. The Bruins tallied 53½ points to outpace last year's runner-up South Carolina (40). Arizona and Clemson tied for third with 30 points each.

Tolson was UCLA's only individual event winner, while Tracey O'Hara (pole vault) and Deana Simmons (triple jump) grabbed seconds. Meet records were set by Georgia's Thorey Elisdottir in the pole vault (14-9½) and by South Carolina's 4x400-meter relay team (3:30.08). (*Fayetteville, AR; March 9-10, 2001.*)

Multiple winners: LSU (8); Texas (5); Nebraska and UCLA (2).

Year		Year		Year		Year		Year	
1983	Nebraska	1987	LSU	1991	LSU	1995	LSU	1999	Texas
1984	Nebraska	1988	Texas	1992	Florida	1996	LSU	2000	UCLA
1985	Florida St.	1989	LSU	1993	LSU	1997	LSU	2001	UCLA
1986	Texas	1990	Texas	1994	LSU	1998	Texas		

OUTDOOR TRACK

Men

Entering the meet's final event, the 4x400-meter relay, Tennessee needed just one point to break its tie with TCU and win its third outdoor track and field title, and first since 1991. Caution was even more important than speed as the squad carefully passed the baton and finished the race in eighth, giving them one point and the championship. The Vols amassed a total of 50 points to edge runner-up TCU (49). Baylor finished third with 36½ points. Justin Gatlin was a double winner for Tennessee, claiming victories in the 100- and 200-meter dashes. The freshman also ran a leg on Tennessee's second place 4x100-meter relay team.

Only two athletes successfully defended titles won in 2000 — Auburn's Avard Moncur in the 400-meter run and Mississippi's Savante Stringfellow in the long jump. (*Eugene, OR; May 30-June 2, 2001.*)

Multiple winners: USC (26); Arkansas (9); UCLA (8); UTEP (6); Illinois and Oregon (5); Stanford (4); Kansas, LSU and Tennessee (3); SMU (2).

Year		Year		Year		Year		Year	
1921	Illinois	1938	USC	1955	USC	1971	UCLA	1988	UCLA
1922	California	1939	USC	1956	UCLA	1972	UCLA	1989	LSU
1923	Michigan	1940	USC	1957	Villanova	1973	UCLA	1990	LSU
1924	Not held	1941	USC	1958	USC	1974	Tennessee	1991	Tennessee
1925	Stanford*	1942	USC	1959	Kansas	1975	UTEP	1992	Arkansas
1926	USC*	1943	USC			1976	USC	1993	Arkansas
1927	Illinois*	1944	Illinois	1960	Kansas	1977	Arizona St.	1994	Arkansas
1928	Stanford	1945	Navy	1961	USC	1978	UCLA & UTEP	1995	Arkansas
1929	Ohio St.	1946	Illinois	1962	Oregon	1979	UTEP	1996	Arkansas
1930	USC	1947	Illinois	1963	USC	1980	UTEP	1997	Arkansas
1931	USC	1948	Minnesota	1964	Oregon	1981	UTEP	1998	Arkansas
1932	Indiana	1949	USC	1965	Oregon & USC	1982	UTEP	1999	Arkansas
1933	LSU	1950	USC	1966	UCLA	1983	SMU		
1934	Stanford	1951	USC	1967	USC	1984	Oregon	2000	Stanford
1935	USC	1952	USC	1968	USC	1985	Arkansas	2001	Tennessee
1936	USC	1953	USC	1969	San Jose St.	1986	SMU		
1937	USC	1954	USC	1970	BYU, Kansas & Oregon	1987	UCLA		

(*) indicates unofficial championship.

AP/Wide World Photos

Arizona's **Jennie Finch** *was virtually untouchable in 2001, going 32-0 and capping off her season with a shutout win over UCLA in the championship game. The junior broke the NCAA all-time mark for wins in a season without a loss.*

Women

Sprinter Angela Williams won the 100-meter dash for the third consecutive year to lead her USC Trojans to their first NCAA outdoor track and field championship. It was an all Pac-10 top three as the Trojans finished with 64 points to outpace runner-up UCLA (55) and Arizona (44). Williams became the first athlete to win the 100 three years in row in the meet's 20-year history. Brigita Langerholc and Inga Stasiulionyte also registered wins for USC in the 800-meter run and javelin throw, respectively.

The meet's only double winner was Arizona's Brianna Glenn who captured her first titles in the 200-meter dash and the long jump. SMU's Florence Ezeh won the hammer throw for the third consecutive year and Appalachian St.'s Mary Jayne Harrelson won the 1,500-meter run, an event she also won in 1999. (*Eugene, OR; May 30-June 2, 2001.*)

Multiple winners: LSU (12); Texas (3); UCLA (2).

Year		Year		Year		Year		Year	
1982	UCLA	1986	Texas	1990	LSU	1994	LSU	1998	Texas
1983	UCLA	1987	LSU	1991	LSU	1995	LSU	1999	Texas
1984	Florida St.	1988	LSU	1992	LSU	1996	LSU	2000	LSU
1985	Oregon	1989	LSU	1993	LSU	1997	LSU	2001	USC

VOLLEYBALL

Men

Brigham Young upset favorite UCLA for its second men's volleyball title in the last three years. With the new rally-scoring format in place for the first time, the Cougars put away the Bruins in three games — 30-26, 30-26, 32-30. Mike Wall recorded 16 kills for Brigham Young to win the award for the tournament's most outstanding player. Hector Lebron dished out 43 assists but it was the Cougars' defense at the net that solidified the win. Adam Naeve led UCLA with 16 kills and just one error. In the semifinals, Brigham Young bested Penn St. in four games while UCLA took care of Ohio St. (*Long Beach, CA; May 5, 2001.*)

Multiple winners: UCLA (18); Pepperdine and USC (4); Brigham Young (2).

Year		Year		Year		Year		Year	
1970	UCLA	1977	USC	1984	UCLA	1991	Long Beach St.	1998	UCLA
1971	UCLA	1978	Pepperdine	1985	Pepperdine	1992	Pepperdine	1999	Brigham Young
1972	UCLA	1979	UCLA	1986	Pepperdine	1993	UCLA	2000	UCLA
1973	San Diego St.	1980	USC	1987	UCLA	1994	Penn St.	2001	Brigham Young
1974	UCLA	1981	UCLA	1988	USC	1995	UCLA		
1975	UCLA	1982	UCLA	1989	UCLA	1996	UCLA		
1976	UCLA	1983	UCLA	1990	USC	1997	Stanford		

Annual NCAA Division I Team Champions (Cont.)

Women

Nebraska capped off a perfect season by winning its second overall NCAA Women's Volleyball Championship over Wisconsin. It was a hard-fought match as the Cornhuskers escaped with a 15-9, 9-15, 7-15, 15-2, 15-9 victory to run their record to 34-0, only the second time in history a championship team finished with a perfect record.

Outside hitter Laura Pilakowski and Amber Holmquist led the Huskers offensively with 23 and 16 kills, respectively. National player of the year Greichaly Cepero dished out 52 assists and was named the tournament's most outstanding player. Sherisa Livingston recorded 19 kills for Wisconsin in a losing effort. (*Richmond, VA; Dec. 16, 2000.*)

Multiple winners: Stanford (4); Hawaii, Long Beach St. and UCLA (3); Nebraska and Pacific (2).

Year		Year		Year		Year		Year	
1981	USC	1985	Pacific	1989	Long Beach St.	1993	Long Beach St.	1997	Stanford
1982	Hawaii	1986	Pacific	1990	UCLA	1994	Stanford	1998	Long Beach St.
1983	Hawaii	1987	Hawaii	1991	UCLA	1995	Nebraska	1999	Penn St.
1984	UCLA	1988	Texas	1992	Stanford	1996	Stanford	2000	Nebraska

WATER POLO

Men

UCLA scored eight unanswered goals en route to an 11-2 thrashing of UC-San Diego in the National Collegiate Men's Water Polo Championship. The win was the Bruins' second consecutive and fourth in the last six years. Last year's tournament most outstanding player Sean Kern scored twice in the semifinal match against Navy and twice in the finals to earn the honors once again. Brian Brown contributed three goals for the Bruins in the finals and was named to the all-tournament team. Bruins goalie Brandon Brooks stopped 11 UC-San Diego shots. (*Malibu, CA; Dec. 3, 2000.*)

Multiple winners: California (11); Stanford (8); UCLA (7); UC-Irvine (3).

Year		Year		Year		Year		Year	
1969	UCLA	1976	Stanford	1983	California	1990	California	1997	Pepperdine
1970	UC-Irvine	1977	California	1984	California	1991	California	1998	USC
1971	UCLA	1978	Stanford	1985	Stanford	1992	California	1999	UCLA
1972	UCLA	1979	UC-S. Barbara	1986	Stanford	1993	Stanford	2000	UCLA
1973	California	1980	Stanford	1987	California	1994	Stanford		
1974	California	1981	Stanford	1988	California	1995	UCLA		
1975	California	1982	UC-Irvine	1989	UC-Irvine	1996	UCLA		

Women

With just 1:28 remaining on the clock, UCLA playmaker Coralie Simmons scored to give the Bruins a 5-4 victory over Stanford in the inaugural National Collegiate Women's Water Polo Championship. UCLA (19-4) acted out the ultimate revenge on Stanford, which dealt the Bruins all four of their losses during the season. The Cardinal finished the season at 27-1. UCLA pounded Loyola Marymount, 11-1 while Stanford blanked Brown, 12-0 in the semifinals to set up the anticipated final battle. It was UCLA's fifth national title in the last six years, although this was the first championship officially sanctioned by the NCAA. (*Stanford, CA; May 13, 2001.*)

Year	
2001	UCLA

WRESTLING

Men

Despite having no individual class winners, Minnesota ended the six-year reign of Iowa and won its first Division I wrestling championship. The Golden Gophers accumulated 138½ points and were followed by Iowa (125½) and Oklahoma St. (115½). Garrett Lowney took third in the heavyweight division to lead Minnesota, but ultimately it was the team's depth that proved to be the difference as they became the first school in history to have 10 wrestlers finish in eighth place or higher.

Individually, Iowa State's Cael Sanderson ran his college record to 119-0. The junior defeated Oklahoma State's Daniel Cormier at 184 pounds to win the class for the third consecutive year and once again was selected as the competition's most outstanding wrestler. (*Iowa City, IA; Mar. 15-17, 2001.*)

Multiple winners: Oklahoma St. (30); Iowa (20); Iowa St. (8); Oklahoma (7).

Year		Year		Year		Year		Year	
1928	Okla. A&M*	1942	Okla. A&M	1959	Okla. St.	1974	Oklahoma	1989	Okla. St.
1929	Okla. A&M	1943-45	Not held	1960	Oklahoma	1975	Iowa	1990	Okla. St.
1930	Okla. A&M	1946	Okla. A&M	1961	Okla. St.	1976	Iowa	1991	Iowa
1931	Okla. A&M*	1947	Cornell Col.	1962	Okla. St.	1977	Iowa St.	1992	Iowa
1932	Indiana*	1948	Okla. A&M	1963	Oklahoma	1978	Iowa	1993	Iowa
1933	Okla. A&M*	1949	Okla. A&M	1964	Okla. St.	1979	Iowa	1994	Okla. St.
	& Iowa St.*	1950	Northern Iowa	1965	Iowa St.	1980	Iowa	1995	Iowa
1934	Okla. A&M	1951	Oklahoma	1966	Okla. St.	1981	Iowa	1996	Iowa
1935	Okla. A&M	1952	Oklahoma	1967	Michigan St.	1982	Iowa	1997	Iowa
1936	Oklahoma	1953	Penn St.	1968	Okla. St.	1983	Iowa	1998	Iowa
1937	Okla. A&M	1954	Okla. A&M	1969	Iowa St.	1984	Iowa	1999	Iowa
1938	Okla. A&M	1955	Okla. A&M	1970	Iowa St.	1985	Iowa	2000	Iowa
1939	Okla. A&M	1956	Okla. A&M	1971	Okla. St.	1986	Iowa	2001	Minnesota
1940	Okla. A&M	1957	Oklahoma	1972	Iowa St.	1987	Iowa St.		
1941	Okla. A&M	1958	Okla. St.	1973	Iowa St.	1988	Arizona St.		

(*) indicates unofficial champions. **Note:** Oklahoma A&M became Oklahoma St. in 1958.

Halls of Fame & Awards

Newly enshrined Pro Football Hall of Famer
Nick Buoniconti with his presenter, and son, Marc.

BASEBALL

National Baseball Hall of Fame & Museum

Established in 1935 by Major League Baseball to celebrate the game's 100th anniversary. **Address:** P.O. Box 590, Cooperstown, NY 13326. **Telephone:** (607) 547-7200.

Eligibility: In August 2001, the Hall of Fame announced changes in the way players are elected via the Veterans Committee. The voting done by Baseball Writers' Association of America remains unchanged. Nominated players must have played at least parts of 10 seasons in the major leagues and be retired for at least five. Certain nominated players not elected by the writers can become eligible via the Veterans Committee. The new Veterans Committee will be comprised of all living Hall of Famers (currently 60 people) as well as all living winners of the Ford Frick (13) and J.G. Taylor Spink (13) Awards and three members of the old 15-member Veterans Committee with unexpired terms. There will be no Veterans Committee vote in 2002. Beginning in 2003 the new Veterans Committee will vote every two years on former players and every four years on managers, umpires and executives. Previously, the committee voted annually.

Also, the eligibility of all players that had been dropped from the ballots for not receiving five percent of the vote was restored and those players can now be immediately considered by the new Veterans Committee. The players on baseball's ineligible list are still excluded from consideration. Pete Rose is the only living ex-player on that list.

Class of 2001 (4): BBWAA vote—center fielder **Kirby Puckett**, Minnesota (1984-95); right fielder **Dave Winfield**, San Diego (1973-80), NY Yankees (1980-89), California (1990-91), Toronto (1992), Minnesota (1993-94), Cleveland (1995); VETERANS COMMITTEE vote—second baseman **Bill Mazeroski**, Pittsburgh (1954-74); pitcher **Hilton Smith**, several clubs (1931-35), Kansas City Monarchs (1936-48).

2001 Top 10 vote-getters (515 BBWAA ballots cast, 387 needed to elect): 1. **Dave Winfield** (435), 2. **Kirby Puckett** (423), 3. **Gary Carter** (334), 4. **Jim Rice** (298), 5. **Rich Gossage** (228), 7. **Steve Garvey** (176), 8. **Tommy John** (146), 9. **Don Mattingly** (145), 10. **Jim Kaat** (139).

Elected first year on ballot (36): Hank Aaron, Ernie Banks, Johnny Bench, George Brett, Lou Brock, Rod Carew, Steve Carlton, Ty Cobb, Bob Feller, Bob Gibson, Reggie Jackson, Walter Johnson, Al Kaline, Sandy Koufax, Mickey Mantle, Christy Mathewson, Willie Mays, Willie McCovey, Joe Morgan, Stan Musial, Jim Palmer, Kirby Puckett, Brooks Robinson, Frank Robinson, Jackie Robinson, Babe Ruth, Nolan Ryan, Mike Schmidt, Tom Seaver, Warren Spahn, Willie Stargell, Honus Wagner, Ted Williams, Dave Winfield, Carl Yastrzemski and Robin Yount.

Members are listed with years of induction; (+) indicates deceased members.

Catchers

Bench, Johnny 1989	+ Cochrane, Mickey. 1947	Fisk, Carlton 2000
Berra, Yogi 1972	+ Dickey, Bill 1954	+ Hartnett, Gabby 1955
+ Bresnahan, Roger 1945	+ Ewing, Buck 1939	+ Lombardi, Ernie 1986
+ Campanella, Roy 1969	+ Ferrell, Rick. 1984	+ Schalk, Ray 1955

1st Basemen

+ Anson, Cap 1939	+ Connor, Roger 1976	McCovey, Willie 1986
+ Beckley, Jake 1971	+ Foxx, Jimmie. 1951	+ Mize, Johnny 1981
+ Bottomley, Jim. 1974	+ Gehrig, Lou 1939	Perez, Tony. 2000
+ Brouthers, Dan 1945	+ Greenberg, Hank 1956	+ Sisler, George 1939
Cepeda, Orlando 1999	+ Kelly, George 1973	+ Terry, Bill 1954
+ Chance, Frank 1946	Killebrew, Harmon 1984	

2nd Basemen

Carew, Rod 1991	+ Gehringer, Charlie 1949	+ McPhee, Bid 2000
+ Collins, Eddie 1939	+ Herman, Billy 1975	Morgan, Joe 1990
Doerr, Bobby 1986	+ Hornsby, Rogers 1942	+ Robinson, Jackie 1962
+ Evers, Johnny 1946	+ Lajoie, Nap 1937	Schoendienst, Red. 1989
+ Fox, Nellie 1997	+ Lazzeri, Tony 1991	
+ Frisch, Frankie 1947	Mazeroski, Bill. 2001	

Shortstops

Aparicio, Luis. 1984	+ Jackson, Travis 1982	+ Vaughan, Arky 1985
+ Appling, Luke. 1964	+ Jennings, Hugh 1945	+ Wagner, Honus 1936
+ Bancroft, Dave 1971	+ Maranville, Rabbit. 1954	+ Wallace, Bobby 1953
Banks, Ernie 1977	+ Reese, Pee Wee 1984	+ Ward, Monte 1964
+ Boudreau, Lou 1970	Rizzuto, Phil 1994	Yount, Robin 1999
+ Cronin, Joe 1956	+ Sewell, Joe 1977	
+ Davis, George 1998	+ Tinker, Joe. 1946	

3rd Basemen

+ Baker, Frank. 1955	Kell, George. 1983	Robinson, Brooks. 1983
Brett, George 1999	+ Lindstrom, Fred 1976	Schmidt, Mike 1995
+ Collins, Jimmy 1945	+ Mathews, Eddie 1978	+ Traynor, Pie 1948

Center Fielders

+ Ashburn, Richie 1995	Doby, Larry. 1998	+ Roush, Edd 1962
+ Averill, Earl. 1975	+ Duffy, Hugh 1945	Snider, Duke. 1980
+ Carey, Max 1961	+ Hamilton, Billy 1961	+ Speaker, Tris. 1937
+ Cobb, Ty 1936	+ Mantle, Mickey 1974	+ Waner, Lloyd 1967
+ Combs, Earle 1970	Mays, Willie. 1979	+ Wilson, Hack 1979
+ DiMaggio, Joe. 1955	Puckett, Kirby 2001	

Left Fielders

Brock, Lou...............1985	+ Kelley, Joe................1971	+ Simmons, Al.............1953
+ Burkett, Jesse.............1946	Kiner, Ralph...............1975	+ Stargell, Willie............1988
+ Clarke, Fred.............1945	+ Manush, Heinie...........1964	+ Wheat, Zack.............1959
+ Delahanty, Ed............1945	+ Medwick, Joe.............1968	Williams, Billy............1987
+ Goslin, Goose............1968	Musial, Stan...............1969	+ Williams, Ted.............1966
+ Hafey, Chick.............1971	+ O'Rourke, Jim............1945	Yastrzemski, Carl........1989

Right Fielders

Aaron, Hank.............1982	Kaline, Al.................1980	+ Ruth, Babe..............1936
+ Clemente, Roberto.........1973	+ Keeler, Willie.............1939	Slaughter, Enos...........1985
+ Crawford, Sam............1957	+ Kelly, King...............1945	+ Thompson, Sam...........1974
+ Cuyler, Kiki..............1968	+ Klein, Chuck.............1980	+ Waner, Paul.............1952
+ Flick, Elmer...............1963	+ McCarthy, Tommy.........1946	Winfield, Dave...........2001
+ Heilmann, Harry..........1952	+ Ott, Mel.................1951	+ Youngs, Ross.............1972
+ Hooper, Harry...........1971	+ Rice, Sam...............1963	
Jackson, Reggie...........1993	Robinson, Frank..........1982	

Pitchers

+ Alexander, Grover.........1938	+ Coveleski, Stan............1969	+ Galvin, Pud...............1965
+ Bender, Chief.............1953	+ Dean, Dizzy.............1953	Gibson, Bob.............1981
+ Brown, Mordecai..........1949	+ Drysdale, Don.............1984	+ Gomez, Lefty.............1972
Bunning, Jim..............1996	+ Faber, Red...............1964	+ Grimes, Burleigh........1964
Carlton, Steve.............1994	Feller, Bob................1962	+ Grove, Lefty.............1947
+ Chesbro, Jack.............1946	Fingers, Rollie.............1992	+ Haines, Jess.............1970
+ Clarkson, John...........1963	Ford, Whitey..............1974	+ Hoyt, Waite.............1969

Major League Baseball's All-Time Team—Then and Now

The Baseball Writers' Association of America originally selected an all-time team as part of major league baseball's 100th anniversary, announcing the outcome of its vote on July 21, 1969. Vote totals were not released. Recently, another vote was released when a panel of 36 BWAA members picked an all-time team for the Classic Sports Network just before the 1997 All-Star Game. This time vote totals were given, the single outfield category was divided into three (left, center and right) and two recently popularized positions—the designated hitter and relief pitcher—were added. In the most recent vote two points were awarded for first-place votes and one point for second place. Point totals follow the names with the number of first-place votes in parentheses. All-time team members are listed in **bold** type

1969 Vote

C	**Mickey Cochrane**, Bill Dickey, Roy Campanella	OF	**Babe Ruth, Ty Cobb, Joe DiMaggio**, Ted Williams, Tris Speaker, Willie Mays
1B	**Lou Gehrig**, George Sisler, Stan Musial		
2B	**Rogers Hornsby**, Charlie Gehringer, Eddie Collins	RHP	**Walter Johnson**, Christy Mathewson, Cy Young
SS	**Honus Wagner**, Joe Cronin, Ernie Banks	LHP	**Lefty Grove**, Sandy Koufax, Carl Hubbell
3B	**Pie Traynor**, Brooks Robinson, Jackie Robinson	Mgr.	**John McGraw**, Casey Stengel, Joe McCarthy

1969 Vote All-Time Outstanding Player: **Ruth**, Cobb, Wagner, DiMaggio

1997 Vote

C **Johnny Bench** (24) 52; Yogi Berra (4) 22; Roy Campanella (4) 17; Mickey Cochrane (1) 5; Bill Dickey (1) 4; Gabby Hartnett (1) 3; Carlton Fisk 2.

1B **Lou Gehrig** (31) 66½; Jimmie Foxx (3) 19; George Sisler (2) 8; Willie McCovey 6; Hank Greenberg 2½; Stan Musial, Eddie Murray, Mark McGwire and Frank Thomas 1.

2B **Rogers Hornsby** (17) 44; Joe Morgan (6) 23; Jackie Robinson (6) 15; Charley Gehringer (4) and Napolean Lajoie (3) 11; Eddie Collins (1) 3; Rod Carew 2; Ryne Sandberg 1.

SS **Honus Wagner** (23) 55; Cal Ripken Jr. (6) 24; Ozzie Smith (5) 16; Ernie Banks (1) 8; Lou Boudreau and Luke Appling 1.

3B **Mike Schmidt** (21) 50; Brooks Robinson (13) 37; Eddie Mathews 5; George Brett (1) 8; Pie Traynor 3; Pete Rose (1) 2; Frank Baker, Al Rosen and Wade Boggs 1.

LF **Ted Williams** (32) 68; Stan Musial (4) 36; Pete Rose, Ralph Kiner, Rickey Henderson and Barry Bonds 1.

CF **Willie Mays** (25) 57; Ty Cobb (7) 22; Joe DiMaggio (3) 17; Mickey Mantle (1) 10; Tris Speaker 2.

RF **Babe Ruth** (31) 67; Hank Aaron (5) 36; Frank Robinson 2; Al Kaline, Roberto Clemente and Tony Gwynn 1.

DH **Paul Molitor** (22) 48; Harold Baines (3) 12; Don Baylor (1) 10; Edgar Martinez (2) 9; Ty Cobb (2) 6; Hal McRae (1) 5; Mickey Mantle (1) and Dave Parker (1) 3; Joe DiMaggio (1) 2; Lee May, Frank Robinson and Tony Oliva 1.

RHP **Walter Johnson** (9) 30, Cy Young (12) 25; Christy Mathewson (5) 18; Bob Feller (4) 10; Bob Gibson (2) 9; Nolan Ryan (2) 7; Tom Seaver (1) 3; Greg Maddux (1), Grover Cleveland Alexander and Juan Marichal 2.

LHP **Sandy Koufax** (11) 32; Warren Spahn (11) 28; Lefty Grove (8) 25; Steve Carlton (4) 12; Carl Hubbell (1) 3; Whitey Ford (1) 3; Eddie Plank (1) 2.

RP **Dennis Eckersley** (16) 40; Rollie Fingers (9) 29; Lee Smith (4) 13; Hoyt Wilhelm (3) 10; Rich Gossage (3) 9; Bruce Sutter (1) 6, Dan Quisenberry 1.

Mgr. **Casey Stengel** (6) 22, Joe McCarthy (6) 18; Connie Mack (7) 17; John McGraw (6) 14; Sparky Anderson (3) 11; Leo Durocher (2) 6; Dick Williams (1) 4; Billy Martin (1) 3; Al Lopez (1), Ned Hanlon (1), Whitey Herzog (1), Earl Weaver and Bobby Cox 2; Tony La Russa 1.

Baseball (Cont.)

+ Hubbell, Carl 1947	Niekro, Phil 1997	Seaver, Tom 1992
+ Hunter, Catfish 1987	+ Newhouser, Hal. 1992	Spahn, Warren 1973
Jenkins, Ferguson. 1991	+ Nichols, Kid 1949	Sutton, Don. 1998
+ Johnson, Walter. 1936	Palmer, Jim 1990	+ Vance, Dazzy. 1955
+ Joss, Addie 1978	+ Pennock, Herb 1948	+ Waddell, Rube. 1946
+ Keefe, Tim. 1964	Perry, Gaylord 1991	+ Walsh, Ed. 1946
Koufax, Sandy 1972	+ Plank, Eddie 1946	+ Welch, Mickey 1973
+ Lemon, Bob 1976	+ Radbourne, Old Hoss 1939	Wilhelm, Hoyt 1985
+ Lyons, Ted 1955	+ Rixey, Eppa 1963	+ Willis, Vic. 1995
Marichal, Juan 1983	Roberts, Robin 1976	+ Wynn, Early. 1972
+ Marquard, Rube 1971	+ Ruffing, Red 1967	+ Young, Cy. 1937
+ Mathewson, Christy 1936	+ Rusie, Amos 1977	
+ McGinnity, Joe 1946	Ryan, Nolan. 1999	

Managers

+ Alston, Walter 1983	Lasorda, Tommy. 1997	+ Robinson, Wilbert 1945
Anderson, Sparky 2000	Lopez, Al 1977	+ Selee, Frank. 1999
+ Durocher, Leo 1994	+ Mack, Connie 1937	+ Stengel, Casey. 1966
+ Hanlon, Ned 1996	+ McCarthy, Joe 1957	Weaver, Earl 1996
+ Harris, Bucky 1975	+ McGraw, John 1937	
+ Huggins, Miller 1964	+ McKechnie, Bill 1962	

Umpires

+ Barlick, Al. 1989	+ Connolly, Tom 1953	+ Hubbard, Cal. 1976
+ Chylak, Nestor. 1999	+ Evans, Billy 1973	+ Klem, Bill. 1953
+ Conlan, Jocko 1974		+ McGowan, Bill. 1992

From Negro Leagues

+ Bell, Cool Papa (OF) 1974	+ Foster, Willie (P) 1996	+ Paige, Satchel (P) 1971
+ Charleston, Oscar (1B-OF) . . .1976	+ Gibson, Josh (C) 1972	+ Rogan, Wilber (P) 1998
+ Dandridge, Ray (3B) 1987	Irvin, Monte (OF) 1973	+ Smith, Hilton. 2001
+ Day, Leon (P-OF-2B) 1995	+ Johnson, Judy (3B). 1975	+ Stearns, Turkey (OF) 2000
+ Dihigo, Martin (P-OF) 1977	+ Leonard, Buck (1B) 1972	+ Wells, Willie (SS). 1997
+ Foster, Rube (P-Mgr) 1981	+ Lloyd, Pop (SS) 1977	+ Williams, Joe (P) 1999

Pioneers and Executives

+ Barrow, Ed 1953	+ Giles, Warren 1979	+ Rickey, Branch 1967
+ Bulkeley, Morgan. 1937	+ Griffith, Clark. 1946	+ Spalding, Al 1939
+ Cartwright, Alexander 1938	+ Harridge, Will 1972	+ Veeck, Bill. 1991
+ Chadwick, Henry 1938	+ Hulbert, William 1995	+ Weiss, George. 1971
+ Chandler, Happy. 1982	+ Johnson, Ban 1937	+ Wright, George. 1937
+ Comiskey, Charles. 1939	+ Landis, Kenesaw 1944	+ Wright, Harry 1953
+ Cummings, Candy. 1939	+ MacPhail, Larry 1978	+ Yawkey, Tom. 1980
+ Frick, Ford 1970	MacPhail, Lee 1998	

Ford Frick Award

First presented in 1978 by the Hall of Fame for meritorious contributions by baseball broadcasters. Named in honor of the late newspaper reporter, broadcaster, National League president and commissioner, the Frick Award does not constitute induction into the Hall of Fame.

Year		Year		Year	
1978	Mel Allen & Red Barber	1986	Bob Prince	1994	Bob Murphy
1979	Bob Elson	1987	Jack Buck	1995	Bob Wolff
1980	Russ Hodges	1988	Lindsey Nelson	1996	Herb Carneal
1981	Ernie Harwell	1989	Harry Caray	1997	Jimmy Dudley
1982	Vin Scully	1990	Byrum Saam	1998	Jaime Jarrin
1983	Jack Brickhouse	1991	Joe Garagiola	1999	Arch McDonald
1984	Curt Gowdy	1992	Milo Hamilton	2000	Marty Brennaman
1985	Buck Canel	1993	Chuck Thompson	2001	Felo Ramirez

J.G. Taylor Spink Award

First presented in 1962 by the Baseball Writers' Association of America for meritorious contributions by members of the BBWAA. Named in honor of the late publisher of *The Sporting News*, the Spink Award does not constitute induction into the Hall of Fame. Winners are honored in the year following their selection.

Year		Year		Year	
1962	J.G. Taylor Spink		& J. Roy Stockton	1980	Joe Reichler & Milt Richman
1963	Ring Lardner	1973	Warren Brown, John Drebinger	1981	Bob Addie & Allen Lewis
1964	Hugh Fullerton		& John F. Kieran	1982	Si Burick
1965	Charley Dryden	1974	John Carmichael	1983	Ken Smith
1966	Grantland Rice		& James Isaminger	1984	Joe McGuff
1967	Damon Runyon	1975	Tom Meany & Shirley Povich	1985	Earl Lawson
1968	H.G. Salsinger	1976	Harold Kaese & Red Smith	1986	Jack Lang
1969	Sid Mercer	1977	Gordon Cobbledick	1987	Jim Murray
1970	Heywood C. Broun		& Edgar Munzel	1988	Bob Hunter & Ray Kelly
1971	Frank Graham	1978	Tim Murnane & Dick Young	1989	Jerome Holtzman
1972	Dan Daniel, Fred Lieb	1979	Bob Broeg & Tommy Holmes	1990	Phil Collier

Year		Year		Year	
1991	Ritter Collett	1994	No award	1998	Bob Stevens
1992	Leonard Koppett	1995	Joseph Durso	1999	Hal Lebovitz
	& Buzz Saidt	1996	Charley Feeney	2000	Ross Newhan
1993	John Wendell Smith	1997	Sam Lacy		

BASKETBALL

Naismith Memorial Basketball Hall of Fame

Established in 1949 by the National Association of Basketball Coaches in memory of the sport's inventor, Dr. James Naismith. Original Hall opened in 1968 and current Hall in 1985. Construction of a new home for the Hall began in August 2000. Completion is expected by early summer 2002. **Address:** 1150 West Columbus Avenue, Springfield, MA 01105. **Telephone:** (413) 781-6500.

Eligibility: Nominated players and referees must be retired for five years, coaches must have coached 25 years or be retired for five, and contributors must have already completed their noteworthy service to the game. Voting done by 24-member honors committee made up of media representatives, Hall of Fame members and trustees. Any nominee not elected after five years becomes eligible for consideration by the Veterans' Committee after a five-year wait.

Class of 2001 (3): PLAYERS— center **Moses Malone**, Utah-ABA (1974-75), St. Louis-ABA (1975-76), Buffalo (1976), Houston (1977-82), Philadelphia (1982-86, 1993-94), Washington (1986-88), Atlanta (1988-91), Milwaukee (1991-93), San Antonio (1994-95); COACHES— **Mike Krzyzewski**, Army (1976-80), Duke (1981-); **John Chaney**, Cheyney St. (1973-82), Temple (1983-).

2001 finalists (nominated but not elected): PLAYERS—Adrian Dantley, Bobby Jones and James Worthy. COACHES— Larry Brown, Lute Olson and Jerry Tarkanian. CONTRIBUTORS—Junius Kellogg and Tex Winter. INTERNATIONAL—Drazen Petrovic and Dino Meneghin. VETS—Earl Lloyd and Grady Lewis. WOMEN'S—Cathy Rush and Kay Yow.

Note: John Wooden and Lenny Wilkens, who was rehonored by the Hall in 1998, are the only members to be inducted as both a player and a coach.

Members are listed with years of induction; (+) indicates deceased members.

Men

Abdul-Jabbar, Kareem	1995	Goodrich, Gail	1996	Mikan, George	1959
Archibald, Nate	1991	Greer, Hal	1981	Mikkelsen, Vern	1995
Arizin, Paul	1977	+ Gruenig, Robert	1963	Monroe, Earl	1990
+ Barlow, Thomas (Babe)	1980	Hagan, Cliff	1977	Murphy, Calvin	1993
Barry, Rick	1987	+ Hanson, Victor	1960	+ Murphy, Charles (Stretch)	1960
Baylor, Elgin	1976	Havlicek, John	1983	+ Page, Harlan (Pat)	1962
+ Beckman, John	1972	Hawkins, Connie	1992	Pettit, Bob	1970
Bellamy, Walt	1993	Hayes, Elvin	1990	+ Phillip, Andy	1961
Belov, Sergei	1992	Haynes, Marques	1998	+ Pollard, Jim	1977
Bing, Dave	1990	Heinsohn, Tom	1986	Ramsey, Frank	1981
Bird, Larry	1998	+ Holman, Nat	1964	Reed, Willis	1981
+ Borgmann, Benny	1961	Houbregs, Bob	1987	Risen, Arnie	1998
Bradley, Bill	1982	Howell, Bailey	1997	Robertson, Oscar	1979
+ Brennan, Joe	1974	+ Hyatt, Chuck	1959	+ Roosma, John	1961
Cervi, Al	1984	Issel, Dan	1993	Russell, Bill	1974
+ Chamberlain, Wilt	1978	+ Jeannette, Buddy	1994	+ Russell, John (Honey)	1964
+ Cooper, Charles (Tarzan)	1976	+ Johnson, Bill (Skinny)	1976	Schayes, Dolph	1972
+ Cosic, Kresimir	1996	+ Johnston, Neil	1990	+ Schmidt, Ernest J	1973
Cousy, Bob	1970	Jones, K. C.	1989	+ Schommer, John	1959
Cowens, Dave	1991	Jones, Sam	1983	+ Sedran, Barney	1962
Cunningham, Billy	1986	+ Krause, Edward (Moose)	1975	Sharman, Bill	1975
+ Davies, Bob	1969	Kurland, Bob	1961	+ Steinmetz, Christian	1961
+ DeBernardi, Forrest	1961	Lanier, Bob	1992	Thomas, Isiah	2000
DeBusschere, Dave	1982	+ Lapchick, Joe	1966	Thompson, David	1996
+ Dehnert, Dutch	1968	Lovellette, Clyde	1988	+ Thompson, John (Cat)	1962
+ Endacott, Paul	1971	Lucas, Jerry	1979	Thurmond, Nate	1984
English, Alex	1997	Luisetti, Hank	1959	Twyman, Jack	1982
Erving, Julius (Dr. J)	1993	Macauley, Ed	1960	Unseld, Wes	1988
+ Foster, Bud	1964	Malone, Moses	2001	+ Vandivier, Robert (Fuzzy)	1974
Frazier, Walt	1987	+ Maravich, Pete	1987	+ Wachter, Ed	1961
+ Friedman, Marty	1971	Martin, Slater	1981	Walton, Bill	1993
Fulks, Joe	1977	McAdoo, Bob	2000	Wanzer, Bobby	1987
Gale, Laddie	1976	+ McCracken, Branch	1960	West, Jerry	1979
Gallatin, Harry	1991	+ McCracken, Jack	1962	Wilkens, Lenny	1989
+ Gates, William (Pop)	1989	+ McDermott, Bobby	1988	Wooden, John	1960
Gervin, George	1996	McGuire, Dick	1993	Yardley, George	1996
Gola, Tom	1975	McHale, Kevin	1999		

Women

Blazejowski, Carol	1994	Harris-Stewart, Lucia	1992	Semenova, Juliana	1993
Crawford, Joan	1997	Lieberman, Nancy	1996	White, Nera	1992
Curry, Denise	1997	Meyers, Ann	1993		
Donovan, Anne	1995	Miller, Cheryl	1995		

Teams

Buffalo Germans	1961	New York Renaissance	1963	Original Celtics	1959
First Team	1959				

Basketball (Cont.)
Referees

+ Enright, Jim 1978
+ Hepbron, George 1960
+ Hoyt, George 1961
+ Kennedy, Pat 1959

+ Leith, Lloyd 1982
+ Mihalik, Red 1986
+ Nucatola, John. 1977
+ Quigley, Ernest (Quig) 1961

+ Shirley, J. Dallas 1979
+ Strom, Earl 1995
+ Tobey, Dave 1961
+ Walsh, David. 1961

Coaches

+ Allen, Forrest (Phog) 1959
+ Anderson, Harold (Andy) 1984
  Auerbach, Red. 1968
· Barry, Sam 1978
+ Blood, Ernest (Prof) 1960
+ Cann, Howard. 1967
+ Carlson, Henry (Doc) 1959
  Carnesecca, Lou 1992
  Carnevale, Ben 1969
  Carril, Pete 1997
+ Case, Everett 1981
  Chaney, John 2001
  Conradt, Judy. 1998
  Crum, Denny 1994
  Daly, Chuck 1994
+ Dean, Everett 1966
  Diaz-Miguel, Antonio 1997
+ Diddle, Ed 1971
+ Drake, Bruce 1972
  Gaines, Clarence (Bighouse) .1981
+ Gardner, Jack 1983
+ Gill, Amory (Slats) 1967

  Gomelsky, Aleksandr 1995
  Hannum, Alex 1998
  Harshman, Marv. 1984
  Haskins, Don 1997
+ Hickey, Eddie 1978
+ Hobson, Howard (Hobby) . . .1965
+ Holzman, Red 1986
+ Iba, Hank 1968
+ Julian, Alvin (Doggie) 1967
+ Keaney, Frank 1960
+ Keogan, George 1961
  Knight, Bob 1991
  Krzyzewski, Mike 2001
  Kundla, John 1995
+ Lambert, Ward (Piggy) 1960
+ Litwack, Harry 1975
+ Loeffler, Ken 1964
+ Lonborg, Dutch 1972
+ McCutchan, Arad 1980
+ McGuire, Al 1992
+ McGuire, Frank 1976
+ McLendon, John. 1978

+ Meanwell, Walter (Doc) 1959
  Meyer, Ray 1978
+ Miller, Ralph. 1988
  Moore, Billie. 1999
  Newell, Pete. 1978
+ Nikolic, Aleksandar 1998
  Ramsay, Jack 1992
  Rubini, Cesare 1994
+ Rupp, Adolph. 1968
+ Sachs, Leonard 1961
+ Shelton, Everett 1979
  Smith, Dean 1982
  Summitt, Pat 2000
  Taylor, Fred. 1985
  Thompson, John. 1999
+ Wade, Margaret 1984
  Watts, Stan. 1985
  Wilkens, Lenny. 1998
  Wooden, John 1972
+ Woolpert, Phil 1992
  Wooten, Morgan. 2000

Contributors

+ Abbott, Senda Berenson 1984
+ Bee, Clair 1967
+ Biasone, Danny 2000
+ Brown, Walter A 1965
+ Bunn, John 1964
  Douglas, Bob 1971
+ Duer, Al. 1981
  Embry, Wayne 1999
+ Fagen, Clifford B 1983
+ Fisher, Harry 1973
+ Fleisher, Larry 1991
+ Gottlieb, Eddie. 1971
+ Gulick, Luther 1959
+ Harrison, Les 1979
+ Hepp, Ferenc 1980
+ Hickox, Ed 1959

+ Hinkle, Tony 1965
+ Irish, Ned 1964
+ Jones, R. William 1964
+ Kennedy, Walter 1980
+ Liston, Emil (Liz) 1974
+ Mokray, Bill 1965
+ Morgan, Ralph. 1959
+ Morgenweck, Frank (Pop) . . .1962
+ Naismith, James. 1959
  Newton, Charles M. 2000
+ O'Brien, John J. (Jack) 1961
+ O'Brien, Larry 1991
+ Olsen, Harold G 1959
+ Podoloff, Maurice 1973
+ Porter, Henry (H.V.) 1960
+ Reid, William A 1963

+ Ripley, Elmer. 1972
+ St. John, Lynn W 1962
+ Saperstein, Abe. 1970
+ Schabinger, Arthur 1961
+ Stagg, Amos Alonzo. 1959
  Stankovic, Boris 1991
+ Steitz, Ed. 1983
+ Taylor, Chuck 1968
+ Teague, Bertha. 1984
+ Tower, Oswald. 1959
+ Trester, Arthur (A.L.) 1961
+ Wells, Cliff 1971
+ Wilke, Lou 1982
+ Zollner, Fred 1999

Curt Gowdy Award

First presented in 1990 by the Hall of Fame Board of Trustees for meritorious contributions by the media. Named in honor of the former NBC sportscaster, the Gowdy Award does not constitute induction into the Hall of Fame.

Year
1990 Curt Gowdy & Dick Herbert
1991 Dave Dorr & Marty Glickman
1992 Sam Goldaper & Chick Hearn
1993 Leonard Lewin & Johnny Most
1994 Leonard Koppett
    & Cawood Ledford

Year
1995 Dick Enberg & Bob Hammel
1996 Billy Packer & Bob Hentzen
1997 Marv Albert & Bob Ryan
1998 Dick Vitale, Larry Donald
    & Dick Weiss
1999 Smith Barrier & Bob Costas

Year
2000 Dave Kindred & Hubie Brown
2001 Dick Stockton
    & Curry Kirkpatrick

BOWLING

International Bowling Hall of Fame & Museum

The National Bowling Hall is one museum with separate wings for honorees of the American Bowling Congress (ABC), Professional Bowlers' Association (PBA) and Women's International Bowling Congress (WIBC). The museum does not include the Pro Women Bowlers Hall of Fame, which is located in Las Vegas. **Address:** 111 Stadium Plaza, St. Louis, MO 63102. **Telephone:** (314) 231-6340.

Professional Bowlers Association

Established in 1975. **Eligibility:** Nominees must be PBA members and at least 35 years old. Voting done by 50-member panel that includes writers who have covered bowling for at least 12 years.

Note: The PBA will wait until 2002 to induct their next class.

Members are listed with years of induction; (+) indicates deceased members.

Performance

+ Allen, Bill 1983	+ Fazio, Buzz 1976	Roth, Mark 1987
+ Anthony, Earl 1986	Ferraro, Dave. 1997	Salvino, Carmen 1975
Aulby, Mike 1996	+ Godman, Jim 1987	Semiz, Teata. 1998
Berardi, Joe 1990	Hardwick, Billy 1977	Smith, Harry. 1975
Bluth, Ray 1975	Holman, Marshall 1990	Soutar, Dave 1979
Bohn, Parker III. 2000	Hudson, Tommy 1989	Stefanich, Jim 1980
Buckley, Roy 1992	Husted, Dave 1996	Voss, Brian 1994
Burton, Nelson Jr 1979	Johnson, Don 1977	Webb, Wayne. 1993
Carter, Don 1975	Laub, Larry 1985	Weber, Dick 1975
Colwell, Paul 1991	Monacelli, Amleto 1997	Weber, Pete 1998
Cook, Steve 1993	Ozio, David 1995	+ Welu, Billy. 1975
Davis, Dave 1978	Pappas, George 1986	Williams, Mark 1999
Dickinson, Gary. 1988	Petraglia, John 1982	Williams, Walter Ray Jr. 1995
Durbin, Mike 1984	Ritger, Dick. 1978	Zahn, Wayne. 1981

Veterans

Allison, Glenn . . . . : . . .1984	+ Joseph, Joe 1985	Schlegel, Ernie. 1997
Asher, Barry 1988	Limongello, Mike 1994	+ St. John, Jim 1989
Baker, Tom 1999	Marzich, Andy. 1990	Strampe, Bob 1987
Foremsky, Skee 1992	McCune, Don. 1991	
Guenther, Johnny. 1986	McGrath, Mike 1988	

Meritorious Service

+ Antenora, Joe. 1993	+ Fitzgerald, Jim 2000	Nakano, Keijiro 1999
Archibald, John 1989	+ Frantz, Lou 1978	Pezzano, Chuck. 1975
Clemens, Chuck. 1994	Golden, Harry 1983	Reichert, Jack 1992
+ Elias, Eddie 1976	Hoffman, Ted Jr 1985	+ Richards, Joe 1976
Esposito, Frank. 1975	Jowdy, John 1988	Schenkel, Chris 1976
Evans, Dick. 1986	Kelley, Joe. 1989	Stitzlein, Lorraine. 1980
Firestone, Raymond. 1987	Lichstein, Larry 1996	Thompson, Al 1991
Fisher, E.A. (Bud) . . . . : . . .1984	+ Nagy, Steve 1977	Zeller, Roger. 1995

American Bowling Congress

Established in 1941 and open to professional and amateur bowlers. **Eligibility:** Nominated bowlers must have competed in at least 20 years of ABC tournaments. Voting done by 170-member panel made up of ABC officials, Hall of Fame members and media representatives.

Class of 2001 (4): PERFORMANCE—**Mike Aulby** and **Gary Bower**; MERITORIOUS SERVICE— **John Jowdy** and **Bill Spigner**.

Members are listed with years of induction; (+) indicates deceased members.

Performance

Allison, Glenn 1979	Davis, Dave 1990	+ Klares, John 1982
+ Anthony, Earl 1986	+ Daw, Charlie 1941	+ Knox, Billy 1954
Asher, Barry 1998	+ Day, Ned 1952	+ Koster, John 1941
+ Asplund, Harold 1978	Dickinson, Gary. 1992	+ Krems, Eddie 1973
Aulby, Mike 2001	+ Easter, Sarge 1963	Kristof, Joe 1968
Baer, Gordy 1987	Ellis, Don. 1981	+ Krumske, Paul. 1968
Beach, Bill 1991	+ Falcaro, Joe 1968	+ Lange, Herb 1941
+ Benkovic, Frank. 1958	+ Faragalli, Lindy 1968	+ Lauman, Hank . . : 1976
Berlin, Mike 1994	+ Fazio, Buzz 1963	Lillard, Bill. 1972
+ Billick, George 1982	Fehr, Steve 1993	Lindemann, Tony 1979
+ Blouin, Jimmy 1953	+ Gersonde, Russ 1968	+ Lindsey, Mort 1941
Bluth, Ray 1973	+ Gibson, Therm 1965	+ Lippe, Harry 1989
+ Bodis, Joe 1941	Godman, Jim 1987	Lubanski, Ed 1971
+ Bomar, Buddy 1966	Goike, Robert. 1996	Lucci, Vince Sr 1978
Bower, Gary 2001	+ Golembiewski, Billy. 1979	+ Marino, Hank. 1941
+ Brandt, Allie 1960	Griffo, Greg 1995	+ Martino, John 1969
+ Brosius, Eddie 1976	Guenther, Johnny. 1988	Marzich, Andy. 1993
+ Bujack, Fred. 1967	Hardwick, Billy 1985	McGrath, Mike 1993
Bunetta, Bill 1968	Hart, Bob 1994	+ McMahon, Junie 1967
Burton, Nelson Jr 1981	+ Hennessey, Tom 1976	+ Meisel, Darold 1998
+ Burton, Nelson Sr 1964	Hoover, Dick 1974	+ Mercurio, Skang 1967
+ Campi, Lou. 1968	Horn, Bud. 1992	+ Meyers, Norm 1984
+ Carlson, Adolph 1941	Howard, George. 1986	+ Nagy, Steve 1963
Carter, Don 1970	Jackson, Eddie 1988	+ Norris, Joe 1954
+ Caruana, Frank 1977	Johnson, Don 1982	O'Donnell, Chuck 1968
+ Cassio, Marty 1972	Johnson, Earl 1987	Pappas, George 1989
+ Castellano, Graz. 1976	+ Joseph, Joe 1969	+ Patterson, Pat 1974
+ Clause, Frank. 1980	+ Jouglard, Lee 1979	Ritger, Dick. 1984
Cohn, Alfred 1985	+ Kartheiser, Frank 1967	+ Rogoznica, Andy. 1993
Colwell, Paul 1999	+ Kawolics, Ed 1968	Salvino, Carmen 1979
+ Crimmins, Johnny 1962	+ Kissoff, Joe 1976	Schissler, Les. 1991

Bowling (Cont.)

Schlegel, Ernie............1997
Schroeder, Jim 1990
+ Schwoegler, Connie 1968
Scudder, Don 1999
Semiz, Teata.............1991
+ Sielaff, Lou 1968
+ Sinke, Joe 1977
+ Sixty, Billy 1961
Smith, Harry.............1978
+ Smith, Jimmy 1941
Soutar, Dave 1985
+ Sparando, Tony 1968

+ Spinella, Barney 1968
+ Steers, Harry 1941
Stefanich, Jim 1983
+ Stein, Otto Jr 1971
Stoudt, Bud.............1991
Strampe, Bob............1977
+ Thoma, Sykes 1971
Toft, Rod 1991
Tountas, Pete 1989
+ Totsky, Mike 1996
Tucker, Bill.............1988
Tuttle, Tommy 1995

+ Varipapa, Andy...........1957
+ Ward, Walter............1959
Weber, Dick 1970
+ Welu, Billy 1975
+ Wilman, Joe.............1951
+ Wolf, Phil 1961
Wonders, Rich 1990
+ Young, George 1959
Zahn, Wayne.............1980
Zikes, Les 1983
+ Zunker, Gil 1941

Pioneers

+ Allen, Lafayette Jr. 1994
+ Briell, Frank 1996
+ Carow, Rev. Charles 1995
+ Celestine, Sydney 1993
+ Curtis, Thomas 1993
+ de Freitas, Eric...........1994
Hall, William Sr. 1994

Hirashima, Hirohito........1995
+ Karpf, Samuel 1993
+ Moore, Henry 1996
+ Pasdeloup, Frank 1993
+ Rhodman, Bill...........1997
+ Satow, Masao 1994
+ Schutte, Louis 1993

Shimada, Fuzzy...........1997
+ Stein, Louis 1997
+ Thompson, William V........1993
+ Timm, Dr. Henry...........1993
Wilcox, John 1999

Meritorious Service

+ Allen, Harold 1966
Archibald, John 1996
+ Baker, Frank 1975
+ Baumgarten, Elmer 1963
+ Bellisimo, Lou 1986
+ Bensinger, Bob 1969
+ Chase, LeRoy 1972
+ Coker, John 1980
+ Collier, Chuck 1963
+ Cruchon, Steve 1983
+ Ditzen, Walt.............1973
+ Dobs, Darold 1999
+ Doehrman, Bill 1968
+ Elias, Eddie 1985
Esposito, Frank...........1997
Evans, Dick 1992
Franklin, Bill 1992

+ Hagerty, Jack 1963
+ Hattstrom, H.A. (Doc).......1980
+ Hermann, Cornelius 1968
+ Howley, Pete 1941
Jowdy, John 2001
+ Kennedy, Bob............1981
+ Langtry, Abe 1963
+ Levine, Sam 1971
+ Luby, David.............1969
Luby, Mort Jr.............1988
+ Luby, Mort Sr.............1974
Matzelle, Al 1995
+ McCullough, Howard 1971
+ Patterson, Morehead 1985
+ Petersen, Louie 1963
Pezzano, Chuck...........1982
Picchietti, Remo 1993

Pluckhahn, Bruce 1989
+ Powell, John 2000
+ Raymer, Milt 1972
+ Reed, Elmer 1978
Reichert, Jack 1998
Rudo, Milt.............1984
Schenkel, Chris 1988
Spigner, Bill 2001
+ Sweeney, Dennis 1974
Tessman, Roger 1994
+ Thum, Joe 1980
Weinstein, Sam 1970
+ Whitney, Eli 1975
+ Wolf, Fred 1976

Women's International Bowling Congress

Established in 1953. **Eligibility:** Performance nominees must have won at least one WIBC Championship Tournament title, a WIBC Queens tournament title or an international competition title and have bowled in at least 15 national WIBC Championship Tournaments (unless injury or illness cut career short).

Class of 2001 (3): PERFORMANCE—**Louise Fulton**; MERITORIOUS SERVICE—**Clara Morton** and **Carol Norman**. Members are listed with years of induction; (+) indicates deceased members.

Performance

Abel, Joy.................1984
Adamek, Donna 1996
Ann, Patty.............1995
Bolt, Mae 1978
Bouvia, Gloria 1987
Boxberger, Loa...........1984
Buckner, Pam Rutherford....1990
+ Burling, Catherine 1958
+ Burns, Nina 1977
Cantaline, Anita 1979
Carter, LaVerne 1977
Carter, Paula Sperba 1994
Coburn, Cindy C...........1998
Coburn, Doris 1976
Costello, Pat.............1986
Costello, Patty 1989
Dryer, Pat.............1978
Duval, Helen 1970
Fellmeth, Catherine 1970
Fothergill, Dotty 1980
+ Fulton, Louise 2001
+ Fritz, Deane 1966
Garms, Shirley 1971
Gianulias, Nikki 1997

Giovinco-Sandelin, Lucy 1999
+ Gloor, Olga 1976
Gonzalez, Ashie 1998
Graham, Linda 1992
Graham, Mary Lou 1989
+ Greenwald, Goldie 1953
Grinfelds, Vesma 1991
+ Harman, Janet 1985
+ Hartrick, Stella 1972
+ Hatch, Grayce 1953
Havlish, Jean 1987
+ Hoffman, Martha 1979
Holm, Joan 1974
+ Humphreys, Birdie 1979
Ignizio, Mildred...........1975
Jacobson, D.D............1981
+ Jaeger, Emma 1953
Kelly, Annese 1985
+ Knechtges, Doris 1983
Kuczynski, Betty...........1981
Ladewig, Marion 1964
Martin, Sylvia Wene 1966
Martorella, Millie 1975
+ Matthews, Merle 1974

+ McCutcheon, Floretta 1956
Merrick, Marge 1980
+ Mikiel, Val 1979
Miller-Mackey, Dana........2000
Miller, Carol.............1997
+ Miller, Dorothy 1954
Mivelaz, Betty 1991
Mohacsi, Mary 1994
Morris, Betty 1983
Naccarato, Jeanne 1999
Nichols, Lorrie Koch 1989
Norman, Edie Jo 1993
Norton, Virginia 1988
Notaro, Phyllis 1979
Ortner, Bev.............1972
+ Powers, Connie 1973
Reichley, Susie 2000
Rickard, Robbie 1994
+ Robinson, Leona 1969
Romeo, Robin 1995
+ Rump, Anita 1962
Ruschmeyer, Addie 1961
+ Ryan, Esther 1963
+ Sablatnik, Ethel 1979

+ Schulte, Myrtle 1965	+ Smith, Grace 1968	Wagner, Lisa 2000
+ Shablis, Helen 1977	Soutar, Judy 1976	+ Warmbier, Marie. 1953
Sill, Aleta 1996	+ Stockdale, Louise. 1953	Wilkinson, Dorothy 1990
+ Simon, Violet (Billy) 1960	Toepfer, Elvira 1976	+ Winandy, Cecelia 1975
+ Small, Tess 1971	+ Twyford, Sally 1964	Zimmerman, Donna 1982

Meritorious Service

Baetz, Helen. 1977	+ Higley, Margaret 1969	+ Phaler, Emma 1965
+ Baker, Helen. 1989	+ Hochstadter, Bee 1967	+ Porter, Cora 1986
+ Banker, Gladys 1994	+ Kay, Nora. 1964	+ Quin, Zoe. 1979
+ Bayley, Clover 1992	Keller, Pearl 1999	+ Rishling, Gertrude 1972
+ Berger, Winifred 1976	+ Kelly, Ellen 1979	Robinson, Jeanette. 2000
+ Bohlen, Philena 1955	Kelone, Theresa 1978	Simone, Anne 1991
Borschuk, Lo 1988	+ Knepprath, Jeannette 1963	Sloan, Catherine 1985
+ Botkin, Freda 1986	+ Lasher, Iolia 1967	+ Speck, Berdie. 1966
+ Chapman, Emily 1957	Marrs, Mabel. 1979	Spitalnick, Mildred 1994
+ Crowe, Alberta 1982	+ McBride, Bertha. 1968	+ Spring, Alma 1979
+ Dornblaser, Gertrude 1979	McCleary, Hazel 2000	+ Switzer, Pearl 1973
Duffy, Agnes. 1987	+ Menne, Catherine 1979	Todd, Trudy. 1993
Finke, Gertrude 1990	Mitchell, Flora 1996	+ Veatch, Georgia 1974
+ Fisk, Rae. 1983	Morton, Clara 2001	+ White, Mildred 1975
+ Haas, Dorothy 1977	+ Mraz, Jo 1959	+ Wood, Ann. 1970
Hagin, Elaine. 2000	Norman, Carol 2001	
Herold, Mitzi 1998	O'Connor, Billie. 1992	

Professional Women Bowlers Hall of Fame

Established in 1995 by the Ladies Pro Bowlers Tour. The LPBT has since been renamed the Professional Women Bowlers Association. **Address:** Sam's Town Hotel, Gambling Hall and Bowling Center, 5111 Boulder Highway, Las Vegas, NV 89122. **Telephone:** (815) 332-5756.

Eligibility: Nominees in performance category must have at least five titles from organizations including All-Star, World Invitational, LPBT, WPBA, PWBA, TPA and LPBA. Voting done by 10-member committee of bowling writers appointed by PWBA president John Falzone.

Note: The PWB Hall of Fame has not inducted any bowlers since 1998, but is considering an upcoming class.

Members are listed with year of induction; (+) indicates deceased member.

Performance

Adamek, Donna 1995	Gianulias, Nikki 1996	Morris, Betty. 1995
Colburn-Carroll, Cindy 1997	Grinfelds, Vesma 1997	Nichols, Lorrie 1996
Costello, Pat. 1997	Johnson, Tish 1998	Romeo, Robin. 1996
Costello, Patty 1995	Ladewig, Marion 1995	Sill, Aleta 1998
Fothergill, Dotty 1995	Martorella, Millie. 1995	Wagner, Lisa 1996

Pioneers

Able, Joy. 1998	Coburn, Doris 1996	Ortner, Bev. 1998
Boxberger, Loa. 1997	Duval, Helen 1995	Soutar, Judy 1997
Carter, LaVerne 1995	Garms, Shirley. 1995	Zimmerman, Donna 1996

Builders

Buhler, Janet. 1996	Robinson, Jeanette. 1996	+ Veatch, Georgia 1995
Keller, Pearl 1997	Sommer Jr., John 1997	

BOXING

International Boxing Hall of Fame

Established in 1989 and opened in 1990. **Address:** 1 Hall of Fame Drive, Canastota, NY 13032. **Tel.:** (315) 697-7095.

Eligibility: All nominees must be retired for five years. Voting done by 142-member panel made up of Boxing Writers' Association members and world-wide boxing historians.

Class of 2001 (16): MODERN ERA—**Ismael Laguna, Laszlo Papp, Willie Pastrano, Ultiminio "Sugar" Ramos** and **Randy Turpin.** OLD TIMERS—**Paul Berlenbach, Jim Braddock, Billy Papke** and **Midget Wolgast.** PIONEER—**Barney Aaron.** NON-PARTICIPANTS—**George Benton, Don Chargin** and **Sam Ichinose.** OBSERVERS—**Lester Bromberg, Ralph Citro** and **Bill Gallo.**

Members are listed with year of induction; (+) indicates deceased member.

Modern Era

Ali, Muhammad. 1990	Bivins, Jimmy 1999	Chandler, Jeff. 2000
+ Angott, Sammy 1998	+ Brown, Joe 1996	+ Charles, Ezzard. 1990
Arguello, Alexis. 1992	Buchanan, Ken 2000	+ Conn, Billy 1990
+ Armstrong, Henry 1990	+ Burley, Charley 1992	+ Elorde, Gabriel (Flash) 1993
Basilio, Carmen. 1990	Canto, Miguel 1998	Foster, Bob 1990
Benitez, Wilfredo 1996	+ Carter, Jimmy 2000	Frazier, Joe. 1990
Benvenuti, Nino. 1992	+ Cerdan, Marcel. 1991	Fullmer, Gene. 1991
+ Berg, Jackie (Kid) 1994	Cervantes, Antonio 1998	Galaxy, Khaosai 1999

Boxing (Cont.)

Gavilan, Kid..............1990
Giardello, Joey...........1993
Gomez, Wilfredo.........1995
+ Graham, Billy............1992
+ Graziano, Rocky..........1991
Griffith, Emile............1990
Hagler, Marvelous Marvin..1993
Harada, Masahiko (Fighting).1995
Jack, Beau................1991
+ Jenkins, Lew..............1999
Jofre, Eder...............1992
Johnson, Harold...........1993
Laguna, Ismael...........2001
LaMotta, Jake............1990
Leonard, Sugar Ray........1997
+ Liston, Sonny.............1991
+ Louis, Joe................1990
+ Marciano, Rocky...........1990

+ Maxim, Joey..............1994
+ Montgomery, Bob.........1995
+ Monzon, Carlos...........1990
+ Moore, Archie............1990
Muhammad, Matthew Saad.1998
Napoles, Jose.............1990
Norton, Ken...............1992
Olivares, Ruben...........1991
Olson, Carl...............2000
Ortiz, Carlos.............1991
+ Ortiz, Manuel.............1996
Papp, Laszlo..............2001
+ Pastrano, Willie...........2001
Patterson, Floyd..........1991
Pedroza, Eusebio.........1999
Pep, Willie...............1990
+ Perez, Pascual............1995
Pryor, Aaron..............1996

Ramos, Ultiminio..........2001
+ Robinson, Sugar Ray.......1990
+ Rodriguez, Luis...........1997
+ Saddler, Sandy............1990
+ Saldivar, Vicente..........1999
+ Sanchez, Salvador.........1991
Schmeling, Max...........1992
Spinks, Michael...........1994
+ Tiger, Dick...............1991
Torres, Jose..............1997
+ Turpin, Randy.............2001
+ Walcott, Jersey Joe........1990
+ Williams, Ike.............1990
+ Wright, Chalky............1997
+ Zale, Tony...............1991
Zarate, Carlos............1994
+ Zivic, Fritzie.............1993

Old-Timers

Ambers, Lou..............1992
+ Attell, Abe...............1990
+ Baer, Max................1995
+ Barry, Jimmy..............2000
+ Berlenbach, Paul..........2001
+ Braddock, Jim.............2001
+ Britton, Jack.............1990
+ Brown, Panama Al.........1992
+ Burns, Tommy.............1996
+ Canzoneri, Tony...........1990
+ Carpentier, Georges.......1991
+ Chocolate, Kid............1991
+ Choynski, Joe.............1998
+ Corbett, James J...........1990
+ Coulon, Johnny............1999
+ Darcy, Les................1993
+ Delaney, Jack.............1996
+ Dempsey, Jack.............1990
+ Dempsey, Jack (Nonpareil)..1992
+ Dillon, Jack..............1995
+ Dixon, George.............1990
+ Driscoll, Jim.............1990
+ Dundee, Johnny...........1991
+ Fitzsimmons, Bob..........1990
+ Flowers, Theodore (Tiger)...1993
+ Gans, Joe................1990

+ Genaro, Frankie...........1998
+ Gibbons, Mike............1992
+ Gibbons, Tommy..........1993
+ Greb, Harry..............1990
+ Griffo, Young.............1991
+ Herman, Pete.............1997
+ Jackson, Peter............1990
+ Jeanette, Joe.............1997
+ Jeffries, James J...........1990
+ Johnson, Jack.............1990
+ Ketchel, Stanley..........1990
+ Kilbane, Johnny...........1995
+ LaBarba, Fidel............1996
+ Langford, Sam............1990
+ Lavigne, George (Kid).....1998
+ Leonard, Benny...........1990
+ Levinsky, Battling.........2000
+ Lewis, John Henry.........1994
+ Lewis, Ted (Kid)..........1992
+ Loughran, Tommy.........1991
+ Lynch, Benny.............1998
+ Mandell, Sammy..........1998
+ McAuliffe, Jack...........1995
+ McCoy, Charles (Kid).....1991
+ McFarland, Packey.........1992
+ McGovern, Terry..........1990

McLarnin, Jimmy..........1991
+ McVey, Sam..............1999
+ Miller, Freddie...........1997
+ Nelson, Battling..........1992
+ O'Brien, Philadelphia Jack..1994
+ Papke, Billy..............2001
+ Petrolle, Billy............2000
+ Rosenbloom, Maxie........1993
+ Ross, Barney.............1990
+ Ryan, Tommy.............1991
+ Sharkey, Jack............1994
+ Steele, Freddie...........1999
+ Stribling, Young..........1996
+ Tendler, Lew.............1999
+ Tunney, Gene.............1990
+ Villa, Pancho.............1994
+ Walcott, Joe (Barbados)....1991
+ Walker, Mickey...........1990
+ Welsh, Freddie...........1997
+ Wilde, Jimmy.............1990
+ Williams, Kid.............1996
+ Wills, Harry..............1992
+ Wolgast, Ad..............2000
+ Wolgast, Midget..........2001

Pioneers

+ Aaron, Barney............2001
+ Belcher, Jem.............1992
+ Brain, Ben...............1994
+ Broughton, Jack..........1990
+ Burke, James (Deaf)......1992
+ Chambers, Arthur.........2000
+ Cribb, Tom...............1991
+ Donovan, Prof. Mike.......1998
+ Duffy, Paddy.............1994

+ Figg, James..............1992
+ Jackson, Gentleman John...1992
+ Johnson, Tom.............1995
+ King, Tom...............1992
+ Langham, Nat............1992
+ Mace, Jem...............1990
+ Mendoza, Daniel..........1990
+ Molineaux, Tom...........1997
+ Morrissey, John..........1996

+ Pearce, Henry............1993
+ Richmond, Bill...........1999
+ Sam, Dutch..............1997
+ Sayers, Tom..............1990
Spring, Tom..............1992
+ Sullivan, John L..........1990
+ Thompson, William........1991
+ Ward, Jem...............1995

Non-Participants

+ Andrews, Thomas S........1992
+ Arcel, Ray...............1991
Arum, Bob...............1999
+ Ballarati, Giuseppe........1999
Benton, George...........2001
+ Blackburn, Jack...........1992
+ Brady, William A..........1998
Brenner, Teddy...........1993
+ Chambers, John Graham...1990
Chargin, Don.............2001
Clancy, Gil...............1993
+ Coffroth, James W..........1991
+ D'Amato, Cus.............1995
Dickson, Jeff.............2000

+ Donovan, Arthur..........1993
Duff, Mickey.............1999
Dundee, Angelo..........1992
+ Dundee, Chris............1994
+ Dunphy, Don.............1993
Duva, Lou...............1998
+ Egan, Pierce.............1991
+ Fleischer, Nat............1990
+ Fox, Richard K............1997
+ Futch, Eddie.............1994
+ Goldman, Charley.........1992
+ Goldstein, Ruby..........1994
Goodman, Murray.........1999
+ Humphreys, Joe..........1997

+ Ichinose, Sam............2001
+ Jacobs, Jimmy............1993
+ Jacobs, Mike.............1990
+ Johnston, Jimmy..........1999
+ Kearns, Jack (Doc).........1990
King, Don...............1997
Lectoure, Tito............2000
+ Liebling, A.J.............1992
+ Lonsdale, Lord............1990
+ Markson, Harry...........1992
Mercante, Arthur.........1995
+ Morgan, Dan.............2000
+ Muldoon, William.........1996
Odd, Gilbert.............1995

+ O'Rourke, Tom 1999
+ Parker, Dan 1996
+ Parnassus, George 1991
+ Queensberry, Marquis of 1990

+ Rickard, Tex 1990
+ Rudd, Irving 1999
+ Siler, George 1995
+ Solomons, Jack 1995

Steward, Emanuel 1996
+ Taub, Sam. 1994
+ Taylor, Herman 1998
+ Walker, James J. (Jimmy) 1992

Observers

+ Bromberg, Lester 2001

Citro, Ralph 2001

Gallo, Bill 2001

Old *Ring* Hall Members Not in Int'l. Boxing Hall

Nat Fleischer, the late founder and editor-in-chief of *The Ring*, established his magazine's Boxing Hall of Fame in 1954, but it was abandoned after the 1987 inductions. One hundred and twenty members of the old *Ring* Hall have been elected to the International Hall since 1989. The 34 boxers and one sportswriter who have yet to be elected to the International Hall are listed below with their year of induction into the *Ring* Hall.

Modern Group

+ Apostoli, Fred. 1978
+ Escobar, Sixto 1975

+ Garcia, Ceferino 1977
+ Lesnevich, Gus. 1973

+ Shirai, Yoshio 1977

Old-Timers

+ Britt, Jimmy 1976
+ Chaney, George (K.O.) 1974
+ Corbett, Young II 1965
+ Fields, Jackie 1977
+ Houck, Leo 1969
+ Jeffra, Harry 1982

+ Kid, The Dixie 1975
+ Klaus, Frank 1974
+ Maher, Peter. 1978
+ Mitchell, Charley 1957
+ Ritchie, Willie 1962
+ Root, Jack 1961

+ Sharkey, Tom 1959
+ Smith, Jeff. 1969
+ Taylor, Bud 1986
+ Willard, Jess. 1977

Pioneers

+ Chandler, Tom 1972
+ Clark, Nobby 1971
+ Collyer, Sam 1964
+ Donnelly, Dan 1960
+ Goss, Joe 1969

+ Gully, John 1959
+ Heenan, John C 1954
+ Hyer, Jacob 1968
+ Hyer, Tom 1954
+ Jackling, Thomas 1985

+ Kilrain, Jack 1965
+ Price, Ned 1962
+ Ryan, Paddy 1973

Non-Participant

+ Daniel, Dan (sportswriter). . . .1977

FOOTBALL

College Football Hall of Fame

Established in 1955 by the National Football Foundation. **Address:** 111 South St. Joseph St., South Bend, IN 46601. **Telephone:** (219) 235-9999.

Eligibility: Nominated players must be out of college 10 years and a first team All-America pick by a major selector during their careers; coaches must be retired three years. Voting done by 12-member panel of athletic directors, conference and bowl officials and media representatives. The first year representatives from NCAA Div. I-AA, II, and III, and the NAIA were eligible for induction was 1996.

Class of 2001 (18): LARGE COLLEGE—RB/DB **Jon Arnett**, USC (1954-56); K **Kevin Butler**, Georgia (1981-84); WR **Anthony Carter**, Michigan (1979-82); DE **Dick Duden**, Navy (1943-45); DT **Tim Green**, Syracuse (1982-85); QB **Ralph Guglielmi**, Notre Dame (1951-54); T **John Hicks**, Ohio State (1970, 72-73); TE **Keith Jackson**, Oklahoma (1984-87); DB **Terry Kinard**, Clemson (1979-82); LB **D.D. Lewis**, Mississippi State (1965-68); RB **Donald McCauley**, North Carolina (1968-70); T **John Outland**, Kansas/Penn. (1895, 97-99); C/G **Glenn Ressler**, Penn. St. (1962-64); DB **Brad Van Pelt**, Michigan St. (1970-72); QB **Steve Young**, BYU (1981-83); COACHES—**Barry Switzer**, Oklahoma (1973-88); **Grant Teaff**, McMurry (1960-65), Angelo St. (1969-71), Baylor (1972-92); **Bill Yeoman**, Houston (1962-86).

Note: Bobby Dodd and **Amos Alonzo Stagg** are the only members to be honored as both players and coaches.

Players are listed with final year they played in college and coaches are listed with year of induction; (+) indicates deceased members.

Players

+ Abell, Earl-Colgate 1915
Agase, Alex-Purdue/Ill 1946
+ Agganis, Harry-Boston U 1952
Albert, Frank-Stanford. 1941
+ Aldrich, Ki-TCU 1938
+ Aldrich, Malcolm-Yale. 1921
+ Alexander, Joe-Syracuse. 1920
Allen, Marcus-USC 1981
Alworth, Lance-Arkansas 1961
+ Ameche, Alan-Wisconsin 1954
+ Ames, Knowlton-Princeton . . .1889
Amling, Warren-Ohio St.. 1946
Anderson, Dick-Colorado. 1967
Anderson, Donny-Tex.Tech . . .1966
+ Anderson, Hunk-N.Dame 1921
Arnett, Jon-USC 1956
Atkins, Doug-Tennessee. 1952
Babich, Bob-Miami-OH 1968
+ Bacon, Everett-Wesleyan 1912
+ Bagnell, Reds-Penn 1950

+ Baker, Hobey-Princeton. 1913
+ Baker, John-USC 1931
+ Baker, Moon-N'western 1926
Baker, Terry-Oregon St 1962
+ Ballin, Harold-Princeton 1914
+ Banker, Bill-Tulane 1929
Banonis, Vince-Detroit. 1941
+ Barnes, Stan-California. 1921
+ Barrett, Charles-Cornell. 1915
+ Baston, Bert-Minnesota 1916
+ Battles, Cliff-WV Wesleyan . . .1931
Baugh, Sammy-TCU 1936
Baughan, Maxie-Ga.Tech. 1959
+ Bausch, James-Kansas. 1930
Beagle, Ron-Navy 1955
Beban, Gary-UCLA 1967
Bechtol, Hub-Texas 1946
Beck, Ray-Ga. Tech 1951
+ Beckett, John-Oregon 1916
Bednarik, Chuck-Penn. 1948

Behm, Forrest-Nebraska 1940
Bell, Bobby-Minnesota 1962
Bellino, Joe-Navy. 1960
Below, Marty-Wisconsin. 1923
+ Benbrook, Al-Michigan. 1910
+ Berry, Charlie-Lafayette. 1924
+ Bertelli, Angelo-N.Dame. 1943
Berwanger, Jay-Chicago 1935
+ Bettencourt, L.-St.Mary's 1927
Biletnikoff, Fred-Fla.St. 1964
Blanchard, Doc-Army 1946
+ Blozis, Al-Georgetown 1942
Bock, Ed-Iowa St 1938
Bomar, Lynn-Vanderbilt 1924
+ Bomeisler, Bo-Yale 1913
+ Booth, Albie-Yale. 1931
. + Borries, Fred-Navy 1934
+ Bosley, Bruce-West Va. 1955
Bosseler, Don-Miami,FL. 1956
Bottari, Vic-California 1938

College Football Hall of Fame (Cont.)

+ Boynton, Ben-Williams 1920
+ Brewer, Charles-Harvard 1895
+ Bright, Johnny-Drake 1951
  Brodie, John-Stanford 1956
+ Brooke, George-Penn 1895
  Brosky, Al-Illinois 1952
  Brown, Bob-Nebraska 1963
  Brown, Geo-Navy/S.Diego St.1947
+ Brown, Gordon-Yale 1900
  Brown, Jim-Syracuse 1956
+ Brown, John, Jr.-Navy 1913
+ Brown, Johnny Mack-Ala 1925
+ Brown, Tay-USC 1932
  Browner, Ross-Notre Dame ...1977
  Buddie, Brad-USC 1979
+ Bunker, Paul-Army 1902
  Burford, Chris-Stanford 1959
+ Burris, Kurt-Oklahoma.......1954
  Burton, Ron-N'western 1959
+ Butkus, Dick-Illinois 1964
  Butler, Kevin-Georgia 1984
+ Butler, Robert-Wisconsin 1912
+ Cafego, George-Tenn 1939
+ Cagle, Red-SWLa/Army......1929
+ Cain, John-Alabama 1932
  Cameron, Ed-Wash.& Lee ...1924
+ Campbell, David-Harvard ...1901
  Campbell, Earl-Texas.......1977
+ Cannon, Jack-N.Dame 1929
  Cappelletti, John-Penn St 1973
+ Carideo, Frank-N.Dame......1930
+ Carney, Charles-Illinois 1921
+ Caroline, J.C.-Illinois 1954
  Carpenter, Bill-Army 1959
+ Carpenter, Hunter-Va.Tech ...1905
  Carroll, Chas.-Washington....1928
  Carter, Anthony-Michigan ...1982
  Casanova, Tommy-LSU 1971
+ Casey, Edward-Harvard 1919
  Cassady, Howard-Ohio St 1955
+ Chamberlin, Guy-Neb.......1915
  Chapman, Sam-California 1938
  Chappuis, Bob-Michigan 1947
+ Christman, Paul-Missouri 1940
+ Clark, Dutch-Colo. Col. 1929
  Cleary, Paul-USC 1947
+ Clevenger, Zora-Indiana......1903
  Cloud, Jack-Wm. & Mary ...1948
+ Cochran, Gary-Princeton 1897
+ Cody, Josh-Vanderbilt 1919
  Coleman, Don-Mich.St 1951
+ Conerly, Charlie-Miss 1947
+ Connor, George-HC/ND 1947
+ Corbin, William-Yale........1888
  Corbus, William-Stanford....1933
+ Cowan, Hector-Princeton 1889
+ Coy, Edward (Tad)-Yale 1909
+ Crawford, Fred-Duke........1933
  Crow, John David-Tex.A&M...1957
+ Crowley, Jim-Notre Dame ...1924
  Csonka, Larry-Syracuse 1967
  Cutter, Slade-Navy 1934
+ Czarobski, Ziggie-N.Dame ...1947
  Dale, Carroll-Va.Tech 1959
+ Dalrymple, Gerald-Tulane ...1931
+ Dalton, John-Navy..........1911
+ Daly, Chas.-Harvard/Army ...1902
  Daniell, Averell-Pitt........1936
+ Daniell, James-Ohio St 1941
+ Davies, Tom-Pittsburgh 1921
  Davis, Ernie-Syracuse 1961
  Davis, Glenn-Army 1946
  Davis, Robert-Ga.Tech 1947

  Dawkins, Pete-Army 1958
  DeLong, Steve-Tennessee 1964
+ DeRogatis, Al-Duke.........1948
+ DesJardien, Paul-Chicago....1914
+ Devine, Aubrey-Iowa 1921
+ DeWitt, John-Princeton 1903
  Dial, Buddy-Rice 1958
  Dicus, Chuck-Arkansas......1970
  Dierdorf, Dan-Michigan 1970
  Ditka, Mike-Pittsburgh......1960
  Dobbs, Glenn-Tulsa 1942
+ Dodd, Bobby-Tennessee 1930
  Donan, Holland-Princeton....1950
+ Donchess, Joseph-Pitt.......1929
  Dorsett, Tony-Pitt...........1976
+ Dougherty, Nathan-Tenn.....1909
  Dove, Bob-Notre Dame 1942
  Drahos, Nick-Cornell........1940
+ Driscoll, Paddy-N'western ...1917
  Drury, Morley-USC 1927
  Duden, Dick-Navy 1945
  Dudley, Bill-Virginia 1941
  Duncan, Randy-Iowa 1958
  Easley, Kenny-UCLA 1980
+ Eckersall, Walter-Chicago ...1906
+ Edwards, Turk-Wash.St......1931
+ Edwards, Wm.-Princeton 1899
+ Eichenlaub, Ray-N.Dame 1914
  Eisenhauer, Steve-Navy 1953
  Elkins, Larry-Baylor 1964
  Elliott, Bump-Mich/Purdue ..1947
  Elliott, Pete-Michigan 1948
  Elmendorf, Dave-Tex. A&M ..1970
  Elway, John-Stanford 1982
+ Evans, Ray-Kansas..........1947
+ Exendine, Albert-Carlisle 1907
  Falaschi, Nello-S.Clara......1936
  Fears, Tom-S.Clara/UCLA ...1947
+ Feathers, Beattie-Tenn 1933
  Fenimore, Bob-Okla.St......1946
+ Fenton, Doc-LSU 1909
  Ferguson, Bob-Ohio St. 1961
+ Ferraro, John-USC 1944
  Fesler, Wes-Ohio St. 1930
+ Fincher, Bill-Ga.Tech 1920
  Fischer, Bill-Notre Dame 1948
+ Fish, Hamilton-Harvard 1909
+ Fisher, Robert-Harvard 1911
+ Flowers, Allen-Ga.Tech 1920
  Flowers, Charlie-Ole Miss....1959
+ Fortmann, Danny-Colgate ...1935
  Fralic, Bill-Pittsburgh 1984
  Francis, Sam-Nebraska 1936
  Franco, Ed-Fordham 1937
+ Frank, Clint-Yale...........1937
  Franz, Rodney-California 1949
  Frederickson, Tucker-Auburn .1964
+ Friedman, Benny-Michigan ..1926
  Gabriel, Roman-N.C. State ..1961
  Gain, Bob-Kentucky 1950
+ Galiffa, Arnold-Army 1949
+ Gallarneau, Hugh-Stanford ..1940
+ Garbisch, Edgar-W.& J./Army.1924
  Garrett, Mike-USC..........1965
+ Gelbert, Charles-Penn.......1896
+ Geyer, Forest-Oklahoma.....1915
  Gibbs, Jake-Miss 1960
  Giel, Paul-Minnesota 1953
  Gifford, Frank-USC 1951
  Gilbert, Chris-Texas.........1968
+ Gilbert, Walter-Auburn 1936
  Gilmer, Harry-Alabama 1947
+ Gipp, George-N.Dame 1920

+ Gladchuk, Chet-Boston Col ..1940
  Glass, Bill-Baylor 1956
  Glover, Rich-Nebraska 1972
  Goldberg, Marshall-Pitt......1938
  Goodreault, Gene-BC 1940
+ Gordon, Walter-Calif........1918
+ Governali, Paul-Columbia ...1942
  Grabowski, Jim-Illinois 1965
  Gradishar, Randy-Ohio St....1973
  Graham, Otto-N'western 1943
+ Grange, Red-Illinois 1925
+ Grayson, Bobby-Stanford....1935
  Green, Hugh-Pitt 1980
+ Green, Jack-Tulane/Army.....1945
  Green, Tim-Syracuse 1985
  Greene, Joe-N.Texas St 1968
  Griese, Bob-Purdue 1966
  Griffin, Archie-Ohio St 1975
  Groom, Jerry-Notre Dame ...1950
+ Gulick, Merle-Toledo/Hobart.1929
  Guglielmi, Ralph-N.Dame ...1954
+ Guyon, Joe-Ga.Tech 1918
  Hadl, John-Kansas..........1961
+ Hale, Edwin-Miss.College ...1921
  Hall, Parker-Miss 1938
  Ham, Jack-Penn St 1970
+ Hamilton, Bob-Stanford.....1935
+ Hamilton, Tom-Navy 1926
  Hannah, John-Alabama 1972
  Hanson, Vic-Syracuse 1926
+ Harder, Pat-Wisconsin 1942
+ Hardwick, Tack-Harvard 1914
+ Hare, T.Truxton-Penn 1900
+ Harley, Chick-Ohio St. 1919
+ Harmon, Tom-Michigan 1940
+ Harpster, Howard-Carnegie..1928
+ Hart, Edward-Princeton 1911
  Hart, Leon-Notre Dame......1949
  Hartman, Bill-Georgia 1937
  Haynes, Michael-Arizona St .1975
+ Hazel, Homer-Rutgers 1924
+ Hazeltine, Matt-Calif........1954
+ Healey, Ed.-Dartmouth 1916
+ Heffelfinger, Pudge-Yale 1891
+ Hein, Mel-Washington St 1930
+ Heinrich, Don-Washington...1952
  Hendricks, Ted-Miami,FL.....1968
+ Henry, Pete-Wash&Jeff 1919
+ Herschberger, C.-Chicago ...1898
+ Herwig, Robert-Calif.........1937
+ Heston, Willie-Michigan 1904
+ Hickman, Herman-Tenn......1931
+ Hickok, William-Yale........1894
  Hicks, John-Ohio State 1973
  Hill, Dan-Duke 1938
+ Hillebrand, Art-Princeton 1899
+ Hinkey, Frank-Yale..........1894
+ Hinkle, Carl-Vanderbilt 1937
  Hinkle, Clarke-Bucknell......1931
  Hirsch, Elroy-Wisc./Mich.....1943
+ Hitchcock, James-Auburn 1932
  Hoage, Terry-Georgia........1983
  Hoffmann, Frank-N.Dame ...1931
+ Hogan, James J.-Yale 1904
+ Holland, Brud-Cornell 1938
+ Holleder, Don-Army.........1955
+ Hollenback, Bill-Penn.......1908
+ Holovak, Mike-Boston Col ...1942
+ Holub, E.J.-Texas Tech 1960
  Hornung, Paul-N.Dame 1956
+ Horrell, Edwin-California 1924
+ Horvath, Les-Ohio St.........1944
+ Howe, Arthur-Yale..........1911

+ Howell, Dixie-Alabama......1934
+ Hubbard, Cal-Centenary....1926
+ Hubbard, John-Amherst....1906
+ Hubert, Pooley-Ala.........1925
  Huff, Sam-West Virginia....1955
  Humble, Weldon-Rice.......1946
  Hunley, Ricky-Arizona.......1983
+ Hunt, Joe-Texas A&M.......1927
  Huntington, Ellery-Colgate...1914
+ Hutson, Don-Alabama.......1934
+ Ingram, Jonas-Navy........1906
+ Isbell, Cecil-Purdue........1937
+ Jablonsky, J.-Army/Wash...1933
  Jackson, Bo-Auburn.........1985
  Jackson, Keith-Oklahoma.'...1987
+ Janowicz, Vic-Ohio St.......1951
+ Jenkins, Darold-Missouri....1941
+ Jensen, Jackie-California....1948
+ Joesting, Herbert-Minn.....1927
  Johnson, Bob-Tennessee....1967
+ Johnson, Jimmie-Carlisle/
    Northwestern...............1903
  Johnson, Ron-Michigan......1968
+ Jones, Calvin-Iowa..........1955
+ Jones, Gomer-Ohio St.......1935
  Jones, Stan-Maryland.......1953
  Jordan, Lee Roy-Alabama....1962
+ Juhan, Frank-U.of South....1910
  Justice, Charlie-N.Car.......1949
+ Kaer, Mort-USC.............1926
  Karras, Alex-Iowa...........1957
  Kavanaugh, Ken-LSU.........1939
+ Kaw, Edgar-Cornell.........1922
  Kazmaier, Dick-Princeton...1951
+ Keck, James-Princeton......1921
+ Kelley, Larry-Yale...........1936
+ Kelly, Wild Bill-Montana.....1926
  Kenna, Doug-Army..........1944
+ Kerr, George-Boston Col.....1941
  Ketcham, Henry-Yale........1913
  Keyes, Leroy-Purdue........1968
+ Killinger, Glenn-Penn St......1921
  Kilmer, Billy-UCLA...........1960
+ Kilpatrick, John-Yale........1910
  Kimbrough, John-Tex A&M...1940
+ Kinard, Frank-Mississippi....1937
  Kinard, Terry-Clemson.......1982
  Kiner, Steve-Tennessee......1969
+ King, Phillip-Princeton.......1893
+ Kinnick, Nile-Iowa...........1939
+ Kipke, Harry-Michigan.......1923
+ Kitzmiller, John-Oregon......1930
+ Koch, Barton-Baylor........1931
+ Koppisch, Walt-Columbia....1924
  Kramer, Ron-Michigan.......1956
  Kroll, Alex-Rutgers..........1961
  Krueger, Charlie-Tex. A&M..1957
  Kutner, Malcolm-Texas......1941
  Kwalick, Ted-Penn St........1968
+ Lach, Steve-Duke...........1941
+ Lane, Myles-Dartmouth.....1927
  Lattner, Johnny-N.Dame....1953
  Lauricella, Hank-Tenn.......1952
+ Lautenschlaeger, Les-Tulane...1925
+ Layden, Elmer-N.Dame......1924
  Layne, Bobby-Texas.........1947
+ Lea, Langdon-Princeton.....1895
  LeBaron, Eddie-Pacific......1949
+ Leech, James-VMI...........1920
+ Lester, Darrell-TCU.........1935
  Lewis, D.D.-Mississippi State.1968
  Lilly, Bob-TCU..............1960
  Little, Floyd-Syracuse.......1966
+ Lio, Augie-Georgetown......1940
+ Locke, Gordon-Iowa........1922

  Long, Chuck-Iowa.........:...1985
  Long, Mel-Toledo...........1971
+ Loria, Frank-Virginia Tech....1967
+ Lourie, Don-Princeton.......1921
  Lucas, Richie-Penn St........1959
+ Luckman, Sid-Columbia....1938
  Lujack, Johnny-N.Dame.....1947
+ Lund, Pug-Minnesota.......1934
  Lynch, Jim-Notre Dame.....1966
+ Macomber, Bart-Illinois......1915
  MacLeod, Robert-Dart......1938
  Maegle, Dick-Rice..........1954
+ Mahan, Eddie-Harvard......1915
  Majors, John-Tennessee.....1956
+ Mallory, William-Yale.......1923
  Mancha, Vaughn-Ala.......1947
+ Mann, Gerald-SMU.........1927
  Manning, Archie-Miss.......1970
  Manske, Edgar-N'western...1933
  Marinaro, Ed-Cornell.......1971
+ Markov, Vic-Washington....1937
+ Marshall, Bobby-Minn.....1906
  Martin, Jim-Notre Dame....1949
  Matson, Ollie-San Fran......1952
  Matthews, Ray-TCU........1927
+ Maulbetsch, John-Mich.....1914
+ Mauthe, Pete-Penn St.......1912
+ Maxwell, Robert-Chicago/
    Swarthmore...............1906
  McAfee, George-Duke......1939
  McAfee, Ken-Notre Dame...1977
  McCauley, Donald-N. Carolina.1970
+ McClung, Thomas-Yale......1891
  McColl, Bill-Stanford........1951
+ McCormick, Jim-Princeton...1907
  McDonald, Tommy-Okla....1956
+ McDowall, Jack-N.C.State...1927
  McElhenny, Hugh-Wash....1951
+ McEver, Gene-Tennessee...1931
+ McEwan, John-Army........1916
  McFadden, Banks-Clemson...1939
  McFadin, Bud-Texas........1950
  McGee, Mike-Duke.........1959
+ McGinley, Edward-Penn....1924
+ McGovern, John-Minn......1910
  McGraw, Thurman-Colo.St...1949
+ McKeever, Mike-USC........1960
+ McLaren, George-Pitt.......1918
  McMahon, Jim-BYU.........1981
+ McMillan, Dan-USC/Calif...1922
+ McMillin, Bo-Centre........1921
+ McWhorter, Bob-Georgia...1913
+ Mercer, LeRoy-Penn........1912
  Meredith, Don-SMU.........1959
  Merritt, Frank-Army.........1943
+ Metzger, Bert-N.Dame......1930
+ Meylan, Wayne-Nebraska....1967
  Michaels, Lou-Kentucky.....1957
  Michels, John-Tennessee.....1952
  Mickal, Abe-LSU............1935
  Miller, Creighton-N.Dame....1943
+ Miller, Don-Notre Dame.....1924
+ Miller, Eugene-Penn St.......1913
+ Miller, Fred-Notre Dame.....1928
  Miller, Rip-Notre Dame......1924
  Millner, Wayne-N.Dame.....1935
+ Milstead, C.A.-Wabash/Yale...1923
+ Minds, John-Penn..........1897
  Minisi, Skip-Penn/Navy......1947
  Modzelewski, Dick-Md......1952
+ Moffat, Alex-Princeton.......1883
+ Molinski, Ed-Tenn..........1940
  Montgomery, Cliff-Columbia.1933
  Moomaw, Donn-UCLA......1952
+ Morley, William-Columbia...1902

  Morris, George-Ga.Tech.....1952
  Morris, Larry-Ga.Tech.......1954
+ Morton, Bill-Dartmouth.....1931
  Morton, Craig-California.....1964
+ Moscrip, Monk-Stanford.....1935
+ Muller, Brick-California.....1922
  Musso, Johnny-Alabama.....1971
+ Nagurski, Bronko-Minn......1929
+ Nevers, Ernie-Stanford.......1925
+ Newell, Marshall-Harvard....1893
+ Newman, Harry-Michigan...1932
  Newsome, Ozzie-Alabama...1977
  Nielson, Gifford-BYU........1977
  Nobis, Tommy-Texas........1965
  Nomellini, Leo-Minnesota...1949
+ Oberlander, Andrew-Dart...1925
+ O'Brien, Davey-TCU........1938
+ O'Dea, Pat-Wisconsin.......1899
  Odell, Bob-Penn...........1943
+ O'Hearn, Jack-Cornell.......1915
  Olds, Robin-Army..........1942
+ Oliphant, Elmer-Army/Pur...1917
  Olsen, Merlin-Utah St.......1961
  Onkotz, Dennis-Penn St......1969
+ Oosterbaan, Bennie-Mich...1927
  O'Rourke, Charles-BC.......1940
+ Orsi, John-Colgate..........1931
+ Osgood, Win-Cornell/Penn..1892
  Osmanski, Bill-Holy Cross...1938
+ Outland, John-Penn........1899
+ Owen, George-Harvard.....1922
  Owens, Jim-Oklahoma......1949
  Owens, Steve-Oklahoma....1969
  Page, Alan-Notre Dame.....1966
  Palumbo, Joe-Virginia.......1951
  Pardee, Jack-Texas A&M....1956
  Parilli, Babe-Kentucky.......1951
  Parker, Ace-Duke..........1936
  Parker, Jackie-Miss.St.......1953
  Parker, Jim-Ohio St.........1956
+ Pazzetti, Vince-Lehigh.......1912
+ Peabody, Chub-Harvard.....1941
+ Peck, Robert-Pittsburgh.....1916
  Pellegrini, Bob-Maryland....1955
+ Pennock, Stan-Harvard......1914
  Pfann, George-Cornell......1923
+ Phillips, H.D.-Sewanee......1904
  Phillips, Loyd-Arkansas......1966
  Pihos, Pete-Indiana.........1946
  Pingel, John-Michigan St....1938
+ Pinckert, Erny-USC.........1931
  Plunkett, Jim-Stanford......1970
+ Poe, Arthur-Princeton.......1899
+ Pollard, Fritz-Brown........1916
  Poole, B.-Miss/NC/Army....1947
  Powell, Marvin-USC........1976
  Pregulman, Merv-Michigan..1943
+ Price, Eddie-Tulane.........1949
  Pruitt, Greg-Oklahoma......1972
+ Pund, Peter-Georgia Tech....1928
  Ramsey, G.-Wm&Mary.....1942
  Redman, Rick-Wash........1964
+ Reeds, Claude-Oklahoma...1913
  Reid, Mike-Penn St..........1969
  Reid, Steve-Northwestern....1936
+ Reid, William-Harvard......1899
  Reifsnyder, Bob-Navy.......1958
  Renfro, Mel-Oregon........1963
+ Rentner, Pug-N'western.....1932
  Ressler, Glenn-Penn St......1964
+ Reynolds, Bob-Stanford.....1935
+ Reynolds, Bobby-Nebraska...1952
  Rhome, Jerry-SMU/Tulsa...1964
  Richter, Les-California.......1951
  Richter, Pat-Wisconsin.......1962

College Football Hall of Fame (Cont.)

+ Riley, Jack-Northwestern 1931
  Rimington, Dave-Nebraska . .1982
+ Rinehart, Chas.-Lafayette 1897
  Ritcher, Jim-NC St. 1979
  Roberts, J. D.-Oklahoma 1953
+ Robeson, Paul-Rutgers 1918
  Robinson, Dave-Penn St. 1962
  Robinson, Jerry-UCLA 1978
+ Rodgers, Ira-West Va. 1919
  Rodgers, Johnny-Nebraska . .2000
+ Rogers, Ed-Carlisle/Minn 1903
  Rogers, George-S. Carolina. .1980
  Roland, Johnny-Missouri 1965
+ Romig, Joe-Colorado. 1961
+ Rosenberg, Aaron-USC. 1933
  Rote, Kyle-SMU 1950
+ Routt, Joe-Texas A&M 1937
+ Salmon, Red-Notre Dame. . . .1903
  Sarkisian, Alex. 1948
+ Sauer, George-Nebraska 1933
  Savitsky, George-Penn 1947
  Saxton, Jimmy-Texas 1961
  Sayers, Gale-Kansas 1964
  Scarbath, Jack-Maryland 1952
+ Scarlett, Hunter-Penn 1908
  Schloredt, Bob-Wash 1960
  Schmidt, Joe-Pittsburgh 1952
+ Schoonover, Wear-Ark. 1929
+ Schreiner, Dave-Wisconsin. . .1942
+ Schultz, Germany-Mich 1908
+ Schwab, Dutch-Lafayette. 1922
+ Schwartz, Marchy-N.Dame . . .1931
+ Schwegler, Paul-Wash 1931
  Scott, Clyde-Navy/Arkansas .1948
  Scott, Richard-Navy 1947
  Scott, Tom-Virginia. 1953
+ Seibels, Henry-Sewanee 1899
  Sellers, Ron-Florida St 1968
  Selmon, Lee Roy-Okla 1975
  Sewell, Harley-Texas 1952
+ Shakespeare, Bill-N.Dame 1935
  Shell, Donnie-S.Carolina St. .1998
+ Shelton, Murray-Cornell 1915
+ Shevlin, Tom-Yale 1905
+ Shively, Bernie-Illinois 1926
+ Simons, Monk-Tulane 1934
  Simpson, O.J.-USC 1968
  Sims, Billy-Oklahoma 1979
  Singletary, Mike-Baylor. 1980
  Sington, Fred-Alabama 1930
+ Sinkwich, Frank-Georgia 1942
+ Sitko, Emil-Notre Dame. 1949
+ Skladany, Joe-Pittsburgh 1933
+ Slater, Duke-Iowa. 1921
  Smith, Billy Ray-Arkansas 1982
+ Smith, Bruce-Minnesota 1941
  Smith, Bubba-Michigan St . . .1966
+ Smith, Clipper-N.Dame. 1927
+ Smith, Ernie-USC 1932
  Smith, Harry-USC 1939

  Smith, Jim Ray-Baylor 1954
  Smith, Riley-Alabama 1935
+ Smith, Vernon-Georgia 1931
+ Snow, Neil-Michigan 1901
  Sparlis, Al-UCLA 1945
+ Spears, Clarence-Dart. 1915
  Spears, W.D.-Vanderbilt 1927
+ Sprackling, Wm.-Brown 1911
+ Sprague, Bud-Army/Texas . . .1928
  Spurrier, Steve-Florida 1966
+ Stafford, Harrison-Texas 1932
+ Stagg, Amos Alonzo-Yale. . . .1889
  Stanfill, Bill-Georgia 1968
+ Starcevich, Max-Wash 1936
  Staubach, Roger-Navy 1964
+ Steffen, Walter-Chicago 1908
+ Steffy, Joe-Tenn/Army 1947
+ Stein, Herbert-Pitt 1921
  Steuber, Bob-Missouri 1943
+ Stevens, Mal-Yale. 1923
  Stillwagon, Jim-Ohio St. 1970
+ Stinchcomb, Pete-Ohio St. . . .1920
+ Stevenson, Vincent-Penn 1905
  Strom, Brock-Air Force 1959
+ Strong, Ken-NYU 1928
+ Strupper, Ev-Ga.Tech. 1917
+ Stuhldreher, Harry-N.Dame. . .1924
+ Sturhan, Herb-Yale. 1926
+ Stydahar, Joe-West Va 1935
+ Suffridge, Bob-Tennessee 1940
+ Suhey, Steve-Penn St 1947
  Sullivan, Pat-Auburn 1971
+ Sundstrom, Frank-Cornell 1923
  Swann, Lynn-USC 1973
+ Swanson, Clarence-Neb. 1921
+ Swiacki, Bill-Columbia/HC . . .1947
  Swink, Jim-TCU 1956
+ Talboom, Eddie-Wyoming 1950
  Taliafarro, Geo.-Indiana 1948
+ Tarkenton, Fran-Georgia. 1960
+ Tavener, John-Indiana 1944
+ Taylor, Chuck-Stanford 1942
  Thomas, Aurelius-Ohio St. . . .1957
+ Thompson, Joe-Pittsburgh 1907
+ Thorne, Samuel-Yale 1895
+ Thorpe, Jim-Carlisle 1912
+ Ticknor, Ben-Harvard 1930
+ Tigert, John-Vanderbilt. 1904
  Tinsley, Gaynell-LSU 1936
+ Tipton, Eric-Duke 1938
+ Tonnemaker, Clayton-Minn. . .1949
+ Torrey, Bob-Pennsylvania 1905
+ Travis, Brick-Missouri. 1920
  Trippi, Charley-Georgia 1946
+ Tryon, Edward-Colgate. 1925
  Tubbs, Jerry-Oklahoma 1956
  Turner, Bulldog-H.Simmons: . .1949
  Twilley, Howard-Tulsa 1965
+ Utay, Joe-Texas A&M 1907
+ Van Brocklin, Norm-Ore 1948
+ Van Pelt, Brad-Michigan St. . .1972
+ Van Sickel, Dale-Florida 1929

+ Van Surdam, H.-Wesleyan . . .1905
+ Very, Dexter-Penn St 1912
  Vessels, Billy-Oklahoma 1952
+ Vick, Ernie-Michigan 1921-
+ Wagner, Hube-Pittsburgh 1913
+ Walker, Doak-SMU 1949
  Walker, Herschel-Georgia 1982
+ Wallace, Bill-Rice. 1935
+ Walsh, Adam-N.Dame 1924
+ Warburton, Cotton, USC 1934
  Ward, Bob-Maryland 1951
+ Warner, William-Cornell 1904
+ Washington, Kenny-UCLA . . .1939
+ Weatherall, Jim-Okla. 1951
  Webster, George-Mich. St 1966
+ Wedemeyer, H.-St. Mary's . . .1947
+ Weekes, Harold-Columbia . . .1902
  Weiner, Art-N. Carolina. 1949
+ Weir, Ed-Nebraska 1925
+ Welch, Gus-Carlisle. 1914
+ Weller, John-Princeton 1935
+ Wendell, Percy-Harvard 1912
+ West, Belford-Colgate 1919
+ Westfall, Bob-Michigan 1941
+ Weyand, Babe-Army. 1915
+ Wharton, Buck-Penn 1896
+ Wheeler, Arthur-Princeton 1894
  White, Byron-Colorado 1938
  White, Charles-USC 1979
  White, Danny-Ariz. St. 1973
  White, Ed-Cal.Berkeley. 1968
  White, Randy-Maryland. 1974
  Whitmire, Don-Navy/Ala. 1944
+ Wickhorst, Frank-Navy. 1926
  Widseth, Ed-Minnesota 1936
+ Wildung, Dick-Minnesota 1942
  Williams, Bob-N. Dame 1950
  Williams, Froggie-Rice 1949
  Willis, Bill-Ohio St 1944
+ Wilson, Bobby-SMU 1935
+ Wilson, George-Lafayette. 1928
+ Wilson, George-Wash 1925
+ Wilson, Harry-Army/Penn St.1926
  Wilson, Marc-BYU 1979
  Wilson, Mike-Lafayette 1928-
  Wistert, Albert-Michigan 1942
  Wistert, Alvin-Michigan 1949
+ Wistert, Whitey-Michigan 1933
+ Wojciechowicz, Alex-Fordham.1937
+ Wood, Barry-Harvard 1931
+ Wyant, Andy-Chicago 1894
+ Wyatt, Bowden-Tenn. 1938
+ Wyckoff, Clint-Cornell. 1895
+ Yarr, Tommy-N.Dame 1931
  Yary, Ron-USC 1967
+ Yoder, Lloyd-Carnegie. 1926
+ Young, Claude-Illinois 1946
+ Young, Harry-Wash.& Lee . . .1916
  Young, Steve-Brigham Young .1983
+ Young, Waddy-Okla 1938
  Youngblood, Jack-Florida 1970
  Zarnas, Gustave-Ohio St. 1937

Coaches

+ Aillet, Joe 1989
+ Alexander, Bill 1951
+ Anderson, Ed 1971
+ Armstrong, Ike 1957
+ Bachman, Charlie 1978
+ Banks, Earl 1992
+ Baujan, Harry 1990
+ Bell, Matty 1955
+ Bezdek, Hugo 1954
+ Bible, Dana X. 1951

+ Bierman, Bernie. 1955
  Blackman, Bob. 1987
+ Blaik, Earl (Red) 1965
+ Broyles, Frank 1983
+ Bryant, Paul (Bear) 1986
+ Butts, Wally 1997
+ Caldwell, Charlie 1961
+ Camp, Walter 1951
  Casanova, Len. 1977
+ Cavanaugh, Frank. 1954

+ Claiborne, Jerry. 1999
+ Colman, Dick. 1990
  Coryell, Don. 1999
+ Crisler, Fritz 1954
+ Daugherty, Duffy 1984
+ Devaney, Bob. 1981
  Devine, Dan 1985
+ Dobie, Gil. 1951
+ Dodd, Bobby 1993
  Donahue, Tom 2000

+ Donohue, Michael.........1951	+ Little, Lou 1960	+ Romney, Dick 1954
Dooley, Vince.............1994	+ Madigan, Slip 1974	+ Roper, Bill 1951
+ Dorais, Gus 1954	Maurer, Dave..............1991	Royal,Darrell 1983
+ Edwards, Bill 1986	McClendon, Charley.......1986	+ Sanders, Henry (Red) 1996
+ Engle, Rip 1973	+ McCracken, Herb 1973	+ Sanford, George 1971
Evashevski, Forest 2000	+ McGugin, Dan............1951	Schembechler, Bo 1993
Faurot, Don 1961	+ McKay, John..............1988	+ Schmidt, Francis 1971
+ Gaither, Jake 1973	+ McKeen, Allyn 1991	+ Schwartzwalder, Ben 1982
Gillman, Sid 1989	+ McLaughry, Tuss 1962	+ Shaughnessy, Clark 1968
+ Godfrey, Ernest 1972	+ Merritt, John 1994	+ Shaw, Buck...............1972
Graves, Ray 1990	+ Meyer, Dutch 1956	+ Smith, Andy 1951
+ Gustafson, Andy 1985	+ Mollenkopf, Jack 1988	+ Snavely, Carl 1965
+ Hall, Edward 1951	+ Moore, Bernie 1954	+ Stagg, Amos Alonzo 1951
+ Harding, Jack............1980	+ Moore, Scrappy 1980	+ Sutherland, Jock..........1951
+ Harlow, Richard...........1954	+ Morrison, Ray 1954	Switzer, Barry 2001
+ Harman, Harvey 1981	+ Munger, George 1976	+ Tatum, Jim 1984
+ Harper, Jesse 1971	+ Munn, Clarence (Biggie) ...1959	Teaff, Grant 2001
+ Haughton, Percy 1951	+ Murray, Bill..............1974	+ Thomas, Frank 1951
+ Hayes, Woody.............1983	+ Murray, Frank 1983	+ Vann, Thad 1987
+ Heisman, John W 1954	+ Mylin, Ed (Hooks) 1974	Vaught, Johnny...........1979
+ Higgins, Robert 1954	+ Neale, Earle (Greasy).......1967	+ Wade, Wallace 1955
+ Hollingberry, Babe 1979	+ Neely, Jess 1971	+ Waldorf, Lynn (Pappy) 1966
+ Howard, Frank............1989	+ Nelson, David 1987	+ Warner, Glenn (Pop).......1951
+ Ingram, Bill 1973	+ Neyland, Robert 1956	+ Wieman, E.E. (Tad)........1956
James, Don 1997	+ Norton, Homer 1971	+ Wilce, John 1954
+ Jennings, Morley 1973	+ O'Neill, Frank (Buck) 1951	+ Wilkinson, Bud 1969
+ Jones, Biff 1954	+ Osborne, Tom 1998	+ Williams, Henry...........1951
+ Jones, Howard 1951	+ Owen, Bennie 1951	+ Woodruff, George.........1963
+ Jones, Tad 1958	Parseghian, Ara 1980	+ Woodson, Warren 1989
+ Jordan, Lloyd 1978	+ Perry, Doyt 1988	+ Wyatt, Bowden 1997
+ Jordan, Ralph (Shug).......1982	+ Phelan, Jimmy 1973	Yeoman, Bill 2001
+ Kerr, Andy 1951	+ Prothro, Tommy 1991	Young, Jim 1999
Kush, Frank...............1995	Ralston, John 1992	+ Yost, Fielding (Hurry Up) ..1951
+ Leahy, Frank 1970	+ Robinson, E.N.............1955	+ Zuppke, Bob..............1951
+ Little, George 1955	+ Rockne, Knute 1951	

Pro Football Hall of Fame

Established in 1963 by National Football League to commemorate the sport's professional origins. **Address:** 2121 George Halas Drive NW, Canton, OH 44708. **Telephone:** (330) 456-8207.

Eligibility: Nominated players must be retired five years, coaches must be retired, and contributors can still be active. Voting done by 38-member panel made up of media representatives from all 30 NFL cities (two from New York), one PFWA representative and six selectors-at-large.

Class of 2001 (7): PLAYERS—LB **Nick Buoniconti**, Boston Patriots (1962-68), Miami Dolphins (1969-74, 76); G **Mike Munchak**, Houston Oilers (1982-93); T **Jackie Slater**, LA/St.Louis Rams (1976-95); WR **Lynn Swann**, Pittsburgh Steelers (1974-82); T **Ron Yary**, Minnesota Vikings (1968-81), LA Rams (1982); DE **Jack Youngblood**, LA Rams (1971-84); COACH—**Marv Levy**, Kansas City Chiefs (1978-82), Buffalo Bills (1986-97).

Quarterbacks

Baugh, Sammy.............1963	Graham, Otto 1965	Parker, Clarence (Ace) 1972
Blanda, George (also PK) ...1981	Griese, Bob 1990	Starr, Bart................1977
Bradshaw, Terry...........1989	+ Herber, Arnie 1966	Staubach, Roger 1985
+ Clark, Dutch 1963	Jurgensen, Sonny.........1983	Tarkenton, Fran 1986
+ Conzelman, Jimmy 1964	+ Layne, Bobby............1967	Tittle, Y.A................1971
Dawson, Len..............1987	+ Luckman, Sid 1965	Unitas, Johnny 1979
+ Driscoll, Paddy...........1965	Montana, Joe.............2000	+ Van Brocklin, Norm........1971
Fouts, Dan 1993	Namath, Joe..............1985	+ Waterfield, Bob 1965

Running Backs

+ Battles, Cliff 1968	+ Hinkle, Clarke 1964	+ Nevers, Ernie 1963
Brown, Jim 1971	Hornung, Paul 1986	+ Payton, Walter 1993
Campbell, Earl............1991	Johnson, John Henry.......1987	Perry, Joe 1969
Canadeo, Tony 1974	Kelly, Leroy 1994	Riggins, John 1992
Csonka, Larry............1987	+ Leemans, Tuffy 1978	Sayers, Gale 1977
Dickerson, Eric 1999	Matson, Ollie 1972	Simpson, O.J. 1985
Dorsett, Tony.............1994	McAfee, George 1966	+ Strong, Ken 1967
Dudley, Bill...............1966	McElhenny, Hugh 1970	Taylor, Jim 1976
Gifford, Frank 1977	+ McNally, Johnny (Blood) ...1963	+ Thorpe, Jim 1963
+ Grange, Red 1963	Moore, Lenny 1975	Trippi, Charley...........1968
+ Guyon, Joe 1966	+ Motley, Marion 1968	Van Buren, Steve 1965
Harris, Franco 1990	+ Nagurski, Bronko 1963	+ Walker, Doak 1986

Ends & Wide Receivers

Alworth, Lance 1978	Ditka, Mike 1988	Joiner, Charlie 1996
+ Badgro, Red 1981	+ Fears, Tom 1970	Largent, Steve 1995
Berry, Raymond 1973	+ Hewitt, Bill 1971	Lavelli, Dante 1975
Biletnikoff, Fred 1988	Hirsch, Elroy (Crazylegs) ...1968	Mackey, John 1992
+ Chamberlin, Guy..........1965	+ Hutson, Don 1963	Maynard, Don 1987

Pro Football (Cont.)

McDonald, Tommy 1998	Pihos, Pete 1970	Warfield, Paul 1983
+ Millner, Wayne 1968	Smith, Jackie 1994	Winslow, Kellen.........1995
Mitchell, Bobby 1983	Swann, Lynn...........2001	
Newsome, Ozzie 1999	Taylor, Charley.........1984	

Linemen (pre-World War II)

+ Edwards, Turk (T).........1969	+ Hubbard, Cal (T).........1963	+ Musso, George (T-G).......1982
+ Fortmann, Dan (G) 1985	+ Kiesling, Walt (G) 1966	+ Stydahar, Joe (T) 1967
+ Healey, Ed (T)............1964	+ Kinard, Bruiser (T) 1971	+ Trafton, George (C).........1964
+ Hein, Mel (C) 1963	+ Lyman, Link (T)...........1964	+ Turner, Bulldog (C).........1966
+ Henry, Pete (T) 1963	+ Michalske, Mike (G) 1964	+ Wojciechowicz, Alex (C) 1968

Offensive Linemen

Bednarik, Chuck (C-LB) 1967	Little, Larry (G) 1993	Ringo, Jim (C)............1981
Brown, Roosevelt (T) 1975	Mack, Tom (G) 1999	St. Clair, Bob (T) 1990
Dierdorf, Dan (T) 1996	McCormack, Mike (T).......1984	Shaw, Billy (G) 1999
Gatski, Frank (C) 1985	Mix, Ron (T-G) 1979	Shell, Art (T) 1989
Gregg, Forrest (T-G) 1977	Munchak, Mike (G).........2001	Slater, Jackie (T)..........2001
+ Groza, Lou (T-PK)..........1974	Munoz, Anthony (T) 1998	Stephenson, Dwight (C) 1998
Hannah, John (G) 1991	+ Musso, George (T-G).......1982	Upshaw, Gene (G) 1987
Jones, Stan (T-G-DT)........1991	Otto, Jim (C) 1980	Yary, Ron (T) 2001
Langer, Jim (C)............1987	Parker, Jim (G) 1973	Webster, Mike (C).........1997

Defensive Linemen

Atkins, Doug.............1982	+ Jordan, Henry 1995	Selmon, Lee Roy 1995
+ Buchanan, Buck 1990	Lilly, Bob 1980	Stautner, Ernie 1969
Creekmur, Lou 1996	Long, Howie.............2000	+ Weinmeister, Arnie 1984
Davis, Willie.............1981	Marchetti, Gino 1972	White, Randy.............1994
Donovan, Art 1968	+ Nomellini, Leo 1969	Willis, Bill 1977
+ Ford, Len...............1976	Olsen, Merlin 1982	Youngblood, Jack 2001
Greene, Joe 1987	Page, Alan 1988	
Jones, Deacon 1980	Robustelli, Andy...........1971	

Linebackers

Bell, Bobby 1983	Ham, Jack 1988	+ Nitschke, Ray 1978
Buoniconti, Nick 2001	Hendricks, Ted 1990	Schmidt, Joe 1973
Butkus, Dick 1979	Huff, Sam 1982	Singletary, Mike...........1998
Connor, George (DT-OT) 1975	Lambert, Jack 1990	Taylor, Lawrence 1999
+ George, Bill 1974	Lanier, Willie 1986	Wilcox, Dave.............2000

Defensive Backs

Adderley, Herb 1980	Johnson, Jimmy 1994	Wilson, Larry 1978
Barney, Lem 1992	Krause, Paul 1998	Wood, Willie 1989
Blount, Mel.............1989	Lane, Dick (Night Train) 1974	
Brown, Mel 1984	Lary, Yale 1979	
+ Christiansen, Jack 1970	Lott, Ronnie.............2000	**Placekicker**
Haynes, Michael 1997	Renfro, Mel 1996	Stenerud, Jan 1991
Houston, Ken 1986	+ Tunnell, Emlen 1967	

Coaches

+ Brown, Paul 1967	+ Halas, George 1963	Noll, Chuck 1993
+ Ewbank, Weeb 1978	+ Lambeau, Curly 1963	+ Owen, Steve 1966
+ Flaherty, Ray 1976	+ Landry, Tom 1990	Shula, Don 1997
Gibbs, Joe 1996	Levy, Marv 2001	Walsh, Bill 1993
Gillman, Sid.............1983	+ Lombardi, Vince...........1971	
Grant, Bud 1994	+ Neale, Earle (Greasy).......1969	

NFL's All-Time Team

Selected by the Pro Football Hall of Fame voters and released Aug. 1, 2000 as part of the NFL Century celebration.

Offense

Wide Receivers: Don Hutson and Jerry Rice
Tight End: John Mackey
Tackles: Roosevelt Brown and Anthony Munoz
Guards: John Hannah and Jim Parker
Center: Mike Webster
Quarterback: Johnny Unitas
Running Backs: Jim Brown and Walter Payton

Defense

Ends: Deacon Jones and Reggie White
Tackles: Joe Greene and Bob Lilly
Linebackers: Dick Butkus, Jack Ham and Lawrence Taylor
Cornerbacks: Mel Blount and Dick (Night Train) Lane
Safeties: Ronnie Lott and Larry Wilson

Specialists

Placekicker: Jan Stenerud
Punter: Ray Guy
Kick Returner: Gale Sayers

Punt Returner: Deion Sanders
Special Teams: Steve Tasker

Contributors

+ Bell, Bert 1963
+ Bidwill, Charles 1967
+ Carr, Joe 1963
  Davis, Al 1992
+ Finks, Jim 1995
+ Halas, George 1963

  Hunt, Lamar 1972
+ Mara, Tim 1963
  Mara, Wellington 1997
+ Marshall, George 1963
+ Ray, Hugh (Shorty) 1966
+ Reeves, Dan 1967

+ Rooney, Art 1964
  Rooney, Dan 2000
+ Rozelle, Pete 1985
  Schramm, Tex 1991

Dick McCann Award

First presented in 1969 by the Pro Football Writers of America for long and distinguished reporting on pro football. Named in honor of the first director of the Hall, the McCann Award does not constitute induction into the Hall of Fame.

Year	Year	Year	Year
1969 George Strickler	1978 Murray Olderman	1987 Jerry Magee	1996 Paul Zimmerman
1970 Arthur Daley	1979 Pat Livingston	1988 Gordon Forbes	1997 Bob Roesler
1971 Joe King	1980 Chuck Heaton	1989 Vito Stellino	1998 Dave Anderson
1972 Lewis Atchison	1981 Norm Miller	1990 Will McDonough	1999 Art Spander
1973 Dave Brady	1982 Cameron Snyder	1991 Dick Connor	2000 Tom McEwen
1974 Bob Oates	1983 Hugh Brown	1992 Frank Luska	2001 Leonard Shapiro
1975 John Steadman	1984 Larry Felser	1993 Ira Miller	
1976 Jack Hand	1985 Cooper Rollow	1994 Don Pierson	
1977 Art Daley	1986 Bill Wallace	1995 Ray Didinger	

Pete Rozelle Award

First presented in 1989 by the Hall of Fame for exceptional longtime contributions to radio and TV in pro football. Named in honor of the former NFL commissioner, who was also a publicist and GM for the LA Rams, the Rozelle Award does not constitute induction into the Hall of Fame.

Year	Year	Year	Year
1989 Bill McPhail	1993 Curt Gowdy	1997 Charlie Jones	2001 Roone Arledge
1990 Lindsey Nelson	1994 Pat Summerall	1998 Val Pinchbeck Jr.	
1991 Ed Sabol	1995 Frank Gifford	1999 Dick Enberg	
1992 Chris Schenkel	1996 Jack Buck	2000 Ray Scott	

Canadian Football Hall of Fame

Established in 1963. Current Hall opened in 1972. **Address:** 58 Jackson Street West, Hamilton, Ontario, L8P 1L4. **Telephone:** (905) 528-7566.

Eligibility: Nominated players must be retired three years, but coaches and builders can still be active. Voting done by 15-member panel of Canadian pro and amateur football officials.

Class of 2001 (5): PLAYERS—LB **Willie Burden**, Calgary (1974-81); **Bill Frank**, BC (1962-65), Toronto (1965-69), Winnipeg (1969-77); QB **Warren Moon**, Edmonton (1978-83); DE **James Parker**, Edmonton (1980-83), BC (1984-89), Toronto (1990-91); BUILDER—**Sidney Forster**.

Members are listed with year of induction; (+) indicates deceased members.

Players

  Ah You, Junior 1997
  Atchison, Ron 1978
+ Bailey, Byron 1975
  Baker, Bill 1994
  Barrow, John 1976
  Bass, Danny 2000
+ Batstone, Harry 1963
+ Beach, Ormond 1963
  Benecick, Al 1996
+ Box, Ab. 1965
+ Breen, Joe 1963
+ Bright, Johnny 1970
  Brown, Tom 1984
  Brock, Dieter 1995
  Burden, Willie 2001
  Campbell, Jerry (Soupy) 1996
  Casey, Tom 1964
  Charlton, Ken 1992
+ Clarke, Bill 1996
  Clements, Tom 1994
  Coffey, Tommy Joe 1977
+ Conacher, Lionel 1963
  Copeland, Royal 1988
  Corrigall, Jim 1990
  Covington, Grover 2000
+ Cox, Ernest 1963
+ Craig, Ross 1964
+ Cronin, Carl 1967
+ Cutler, Dave 1998
+ Cutler, Wes. 1968
  Dalla Riva, Peter 1993
  DiPietro, Rocky. 1997

+ Dixon, George. 1974
+ Eliowitz, Abe 1969
+ Emerson, Eddie 1963
  Etcheverry, Sam 1969
  Evanshen, Terry 1984
+ Faloney, Bernie 1974
+ Fear, A.H. (Cap) 1967
  Fennell, Dave 1990
+ Ferraro, John 1966
  Fieldgate, Norm 1979
  Fleming, Willie. 1982
  Frank, Bill 2001
  Gabriel, Tony 1985
  Gaines, Gene 1994
+ Gall, Hugh 1963
  Golab, Tony 1964
  Grant, Tom 1995
  Gray, Herbert. 1983
+ Griffing, Dean 1965
  Halloway, Condredge 1999
  Hanson, Fritz 1963
  Harris, Dickie 1999
  Harris, Wayne 1976
  Harrison, Herm 1993
  Helton, John 1986
  Henley, Garney 1979
  Hinton, Tom 1991
+ Huffman, Dick 1987
+ Isbister, Bob Sr 1965
  Jackson, Russ 1973
+ Jacobs, Jack 1963
+ James, Eddie (Dynamite) 1963

  James, Gerry 1981
+ Kabat, Greg. 1966
  Kapp, Joe 1984
  Keeling, Jerry 1989
  Kelly, Brian 1991
  Kelly, Ellison 1992
  Kepley, Dan 1996
  Krol, Joe 1963
  Kwong, Normie. 1969
  Lancaster, Ron 1982
+ Lawson, Smirle. 1963
+ Leadlay, Frank (Pep) 1963
+ Lear, Les 1974
  Lewis, Leo 1973
  Lunsford, Earl 1983
  Luster, Marv 1990
  Luzzi, Don 1986
+ McCance, Ches. 1976
+ McGill, Frank 1965
  McQuarters, Ed 1988
  Miles, Rollie 1980
+ Molson, Percy 1963
  Moon, Warren 2001
  Morris, Frank 1983
+ Morris, Ted 1964
  Mosca, Angelo 1987
  Murphy, James. 2000
+ Nelson, Roger 1986
  Neumann, Peter. 1979
  O'Quinn, John (Red) 1981
  Pajaczkowski, Tony 1988
  Parker, Jackie 1971

Canadian Football (Cont.)

Parker, James 2001	Ruby, Martin 1974	Tinsley, Bud 1982
Patterson, Hal. 1971	+ Russel, Jeff 1963	+ Tommy, Andy 1989
Poplawski, Joe 1998	Scott, Tom 1998	+ Trawick, Herb 1975
Perry, Gordon 1970	+ Scott, Vince 1982	+ Tubman, Joe 1968
+ Perry, Norm 1963	Shatto, Dick 1975	Tucker, Whit 1993
Ploen, Ken 1975	+ Simpson, Ben 1963	Urness, Ted 1989
+ Quilty, S.P. (Silver) 1966	Simpson, Bob 1976	Vaughan, Kaye 1978
Raimey, Dave. 2000	+ Sprague, David 1963	Wagner, Virgil 1980
+ Rebholz, Russ. 1963	+ Stevenson, Art 1969	+ Welch, Hawley (Huck) 1964
Reed, George . . . . .1979 ·	Stewart, Ron 1977	Wilkinson, Tom 1987
+ Reeve, Ted 1963	+ Stirling, Hugh (Bummer) 1966	Wilson, Al 1997
Rigney, Frank 1985	Sutherin, Don 1992	Wylie, Harvey 1980
Robinson, Larry 1998	Symons, Bill 1997	Young, Jim 1991
+ Rodden, Mike 1964	Thelen, Dave 1989	+ Zock, Bill. 1985
+ Rowe, Paul 1964	+ Timmis, Brian 1963	

Builders

+ Back, Leonard 1971	+ Forster, Sidney 2001	+ McPherson, Don 1983
+ Bailey, Harold 1965	+ Foulds, Willliam 1963	+ Metras, Johnny. 1980
+ Ballard, Harold 1987	Fulton, Greg 1995	+ Montgomery, Ken 1970
Barker, Donald. 1999	Gaudaur, J.G. (Jake) 1984	+ Newton, Jack 1964
+ Berger, Sam 1993	Gibson, Frank 1996	+ Preston, Ken 1990
+ Brook, Tom 1975	Grant, Bud 1983	+ Ritchie, Alvin 1963
+ Brown, D. Wes 1963	+ Grey, Lord Earl. 1963	+ Ryan, Joe B. 1968
Cambell, Hugh. 2000	+ Griffith, Dr. Harry 1963	Sazio, Ralph 1988
+ Chipman, Arthur 1969	+ Halter, Sydney 1966	+ Shaughnessy, Frank (Shag) . .1963
Clair, Frank. 1981	+ Hannibal, Frank 1963	+ Shouldice, W.T. (Hap). 1977
+ Cooper, Ralph 1992	+ Hayman, Lew 1975	+ Simpson, Jimmie 1986
+ Coulter, Bruce 1997	+ Hughes, W.P. (Billy) 1974	+ Slocomb, Karl 1989
+ Crighton, Hec 1986	Keys, Eagle 1990	+ Spring, Harry 1976
+ Currie, Andrew 1974	Kimball, Norman 1991	Stukus, Annis 1974
Custis, Bernard 1998	+ Kramer, R.A. (Bob) 1987	+ Taylor, N.J. (Piffles) 1963
+ Davies, Dr. Andrew. 1969	+ Lieberman, M.I. (Moe) 1973	+ Tindall, Frank 1985
+ DeGruchy, John 1963	+ McBrien, Harry 1978	+ Warner, Clair. 1965
Dojack, Paul 1978	+ McCaffrey, Jimmy 1967	+ Warwick, Bert 1964
+ Duggan, Eck. 1981	+ McCann, Dave 1966	+ Wilson, Seymour 1984
+ DuMoulin, Seppi 1963	McNaughton, Don 1994	

GOLF

World Golf Hall of Fame

A new World Golf Hall of Fame opened its doors in 1998 at the World Golf Village outside of Jacksonville, Fla. **Address:** 21 World Golf Place, St. Augustine, FL 32092. **Telephone:** (904) 940-4000.

Eligibility: Professionals have three avenues into the WGHF. A PGA Tour player qualifies for the ballot if he has at least 10 victories in approved tournaments, or at least two victories among The Players Championship, Masters, U.S. Open, British Open and PGA Championship, is at least 40 years old and has been a member of the Tour for 10 years. A senior PGA Tour player qualifies if he has been a Senior Tour member for five years and has 20 wins between the PGA Tour and Senior Tour or five wins among the PGA majors, the Players Championship and the senior majors (U.S. Senior Open, Tradition, PGA Seniors' Championship and Senior Players Championship).

Any player qualifying for the LPGA Hall automatically qualifies for the WGHF. Until 1999, nominees must have had played 10 years on the LPGA tour and won 30 official events, including two major championships; 35 official events and one major; or 40 official events and no majors. The eligibility requirements were loosened somewhat in 1999. The new guidelines are based on a system which awards two points for winning a major and one point for winning other tournaments, the Vare trophy (for lowest scoring average) and the player of the year award. Players must win at least one major, Vare trophy, or player of the year award and accumulate a total of 27 points to be inducted. For players not eligible for either the PGA Tour or the LPGA Hall of Fame, a body of over 300 international golf writers and historians will vote each year.

Members are listed with year of induction; (+) indicates deceased members.

Class of 2001 (6): MEN—**Greg Norman, Allan Robertson** and **Payne Stewart**; WOMEN—**Donna Caponi**; CONTRIBUTORS—**Judy Bell** and **Karsten Solheim**.

Note: Annika Sorenstam (2003) and Karrie Webb (2005) already have enough points for entrance into the Hall but will be inducted after their 10th LPGA season.

Men

+ Anderson, Willie 1975	Cooper, Lighthorse Harry 1992	Jacobs, John 2000
+ Armour, Tommy 1976	+ Cotton, Thomas 1980	+ Jones, Bobby 1974
+ Ball, John, Jr. 1977	+ Demaret, Jimmy 1983	+ Little, Lawson 1980
Ballesteros, Seve 1999	De Vicenzo, Roberto 1989	Littler, Gene 1990
+ Barnes, Jim 1989	+ Evans, Chick 1975	+ Locke, Bobby 1977
Beman, Deane 2000	Faldo, Nick 1998	+ Mangrum, Lloyd 1999
Bonallack, Sir Michael 2000	Floyd, Ray 1989	+ Middlecoff, Cary 1986
+ Boros, Julius 1982	+ Guldahl, Ralph 1981	Miller, Johnny 1998
+ Braid, James. 1976	+ Hagen, Walter 1974	+ Morris, Tom Jr. 1975
Burke, Jack Jr.. 2000	+ Hilton, Harold 1978	+ Morris, Tom Sr 1976
Casper, Billy 1978	+ Hogan, Ben 1974	Nelson, Byron 1974
Coles, Neil 2000	Irwin, Hale 1992	Nicklaus, Jack 1974

Norman, Greg............2001	+ Sarazen, Gene 1974	+ Travers, Jerry 1976
+ Ouimet, Francis..........1974	+ Smith, Horton............1990	+ Travis, Walter 1979
Palmer, Arnold...........1974	Snead, Sam 1974	Trevino, Lee 1981
Player, Gary.............1974	+ Stewart, Payne...........2001	+ Vardon, Harry 1974
Robertson, Allan 2001	+ Taylor, John H 1975	Watson, Tom 1988
Runyan, Paul 1990	Thomson, Peter...........1988	

Women

Alcott, Amy..............1999	Inkster, Julie 2000	Suggs, Louise.............1979
Berg, Patty 1974	Jameson, Betty 1951	+ Vare, Glenna Collett.......1975
Bradley, Pat 1991	King, Betsy 1995	+ Wethered, Joyce 1975
Carner, JoAnne 1985	Lopez, Nancy 1989	Whitworth, Kathy 1982
Caponi, Donna 2001	Mann, Carol...............1977	Wright, Mickey 1976
Daniel, Beth 2000	Rankin, Judy..............2000	+ Zaharias, Babe Didrikson ...1974
Haynie, Sandra...........1977	Rawls, Betsy 1987	
+ Howe, Dorothy C.H 1978	Sheehan, Patty............1993	

Contributors

Bell, Judy................2001	+ Graffis, Herb 1977	Rodriguez, Chi Chi 1992
Campbell, William 1990	+ Harlow, Robert...........1988	+ Ross, Donald 1977
+ Corcoran, Fred 1975	Hope, Bob 1983	+ Solheim, Karsten 2001
+ Crosby, Bing.............1978	+ Jones, Robert Trent 1987	+ Shore, Dinah 1994
+ Dey, Joe 1975	+ Roberts, Clifford 1978	+ Tufts, Richard 1992

Old PGA Hall Members Not in PGA/World Hall

The original PGA Hall of Fame was established in 1940 by the PGA of America, but abandoned after the 1982 inductions in favor of the PGA/World Hall of Fame. Twenty-nine members of the old PGA Hall have been elected to the PGA/World Hall since then. Players yet to make the cut are listed below with year of induction into old PGA Hall.

+ Brady, Mike 1960	Ford, Doug................1975	+ McLeod, Fred............1960
+ Burke, Jim 1966	+ Ghezzi, Vic 1965	+ Picard, Henry............1961
+ Cruickshank, Bobby 1967	+ Harbert, Chick 1968	+ Revolta, Johnny 1963
+ Diegel, Leo 1955	Harper, Chandler 1969	+ Shute, Denny 1957
+ Dudley, Ed 1964	+ Harrison, Dutch 1962	+ Smith, Alex 1940
+ Dutra, Olin 1962	+ Hutchison, Jock Sr 1959	+ Smith, Macdonald.........1954
+ Farroll, Johnny 1961	+ McDermott, John 1940	+ Wood, Craig 1956

HOCKEY

Hockey Hall of Fame

Established in 1945 by the National Hockey League and opened in 1961. **Address:** BCE Place, 30 Yonge Street, Toronto, Ontario, M5E 1X8. **Telephone:** (416) 360-7735.

Eligibility: Nominated players and referees must be retired three years. However that waiting period has now been waived 10 times. Players that have had the waiting period waived are indicated with an asterisk. Voting done by 18-member panel made up of pro and amateur hockey personalities and media representatives. A 15-member Veterans Committee that selected older players was eliminated in 2000.

Class of 2001 (5): PLAYERS— defense **Viacheslav Fetisov**, USSR National Team and CSKA Moscow (1973-89), New Jersey (1989-95), Detroit (1995-98); forward **Mike Gartner**, Washington (1982-88), Minnesota North Stars (1988-89), NY Rangers (1989-93), Toronto (1993-96), Phoenix (1996-1998); forward **Dale Hawerchuk**, Winnipeg Jets (1981-90), Buffalo (1990-95), St. Louis (1995-96), Philadelphia (1995-97); forward **Jari Kurri**, Edmonton (1980-90), Los Angeles (1991-96), NY Rangers (1995-96), Anaheim (1996-97), Colorado (1997-98). BUILDER— **Craig Patrick**, contributions to USA Hockey.

Members are listed with year of induction; (+) indicates deceased members.

Forwards

+ Abel, Sid................1969	+ Conacher, Charlie..........1961	+ Gardner, Jimmy 1962
+ Adams, Jack.............1959	Conacher, Roy.............1998	Gartner, Mike 2001
+ Apps, Syl 1961	+ Cook, Bill 1952	Geoffrion, Bernie..........1972
Armstrong, George 1975	+ Cook, Bun...............1995	+ Gerard, Eddie 1945
+ Bailey, Ace..............1975	Cournoyer, Yvan 1982	Gilbert, Rod 1982
+ Bain, Dan...............1945	+ Cowley, Bill 1968	+ Gilmour, Billy 1962
+ Baker, Hobey............1945	+ Crawford, Rusty 1962	Goulet, Michel 1998
Barber, Bill 1990	+ Darragh, Jack............1962	Gretzky, Wayne* 1999
+ Barry, Marty.............1965	+ Davidson, Scotty 1950	+ Griffis, Si...............1950
Bathgate, Andy 1978	+ Day, Hap 1961	Hawerchuk, Dale 2001
+ Bauer, Bobby 1996	Delvecchio, Alex 1977	+ Hay, George 1958
Beliveau, Jean* 1972	+ Denneny, Cy.............1959	+ Hextall, Bryan 1969
+ Bentley, Doug............1964	Dionne, Marcel 1992	+ Hooper, Tom............1962
+ Bentley, Max 1966	+ Drillon, Gordie 1975	Howe, Gordie* 1972
+ Blake, Toe..............1966	+ Drinkwater, Graham 1950	+ Howe, Syd 1965
Bossy, Mike 1991	Dumart, Woody 1992	Hull, Bobby 1983
+ Boucher, Frank 1958	+ Dunderdale, Tommy 1974	+ Hyland, Harry 1962
+ Bowie, Dubbie 1945	+ Dye, Babe...............1970	+ Irvin, Dick 1958
+ Broadbent, Punch 1962	Esposito, Phil 1984	+ Jackson, Busher 1971
Bucyk, John (Chief) 1981	+ Farrell, Arthur...........1965	+ Joliat, Aurel 1947
+ Burch, Billy 1974	+ Foyston, Frank 1958	+ Keats, Duke 1958
Clarke, Bobby 1987	+ Frederickson, Frank 1958	Kennedy, Ted (Teeder).......1966
+ Colville, Neil 1967	Gainey, Bob 1992	Keon, Dave 1986

Hockey (Cont.)

Kurri, Jari 2001
Lach, Elmer. 1966
Lafleur, Guy 1988
+ Lalonde, Newsy. 1950
Laprade, Edgar 1993
Lemaire, Jacques 1984
Lemieux, Mario* 1997
+ Lewis, Herbie 1989
Lindsay, Ted* 1966
+ MacKay, Mickey. 1952
Mahovlich, Frank. 1981
+ Malone, Joe 1950
+ Marshall, Jack 1965
+ Maxwell, Fred 1962
McDonald, Lanny 1992
+ McGee, Frank 1945
+ McGimsie, Billy 1962
Mikita, Stan 1983
Moore, Dickie 1974
+ Morenz, Howie 1945
+ Mosienko, Bill 1965
Mullen, Joe. 2000
+ Nighbor, Frank 1947

+ Benedict, Clint 1965
Bower, Johnny 1976
+ Brimsek, Frankie 1966
+ Broda, Turk. 1967
Cheevers, Gerry 1985
+ Connell, Alex 1958
Dryden, Ken. 1983
+ Durnan, Bill. 1964
Esposito, Tony 1988
+ Gardiner, Chuck 1945

Boivin, Leo 1986
+ Boon, Dickie 1952
Bouchard, Butch 1966
+ Boucher, George 1960
+ Cameron, Harry 1962
+ Clancy, King. 1958
+ Clapper, Dit* 1947
+ Cleghorn, Sprague 1958
+ Conacher, Lionel 1994
Coulter, Art. 1974
+ Dutton, Red. 1958
Fetisov, Viacheslav 2001
Flaman, Fernie 1990
Gadsby, Bill 1970
+ Gardiner, Herb 1958
+ Goheen, F.X. (Moose) 1952
+ Goodfellow, Ebbie 1963
+ Grant, Mike 1950
+ Green, Wilf (Shorty) 1962

Armstrong, Neil. 1991
Ashley, John 1981
Chadwick, Bill 1964
D'Amico, John 1993
+ Elliott, Chaucer 1961

+ Adams, Charles 1960
+ Adams, Weston W. Sr 1972
+ Ahearn, Frank 1962
+ Ahearne, J:F. (Bunny) 1977
+ Allan, Sir Montagu 1945
Allen, Keith. 1992
Arbour, Al. 1996
+ Ballard, Harold 1977
+ Bauer, Fr. David. 1989
+ Bickell, J.P.. 1978
Bowman, Scotty 1991
+ Brown, George 1961

+ Noble, Reg. 1962
+ O'Connor, Buddy 1988
+ Oliver, Harry 1967
Olmstead, Bert. 1985
+ Patrick, Lynn 1980
Perreault, Gilbert 1990
Phillips, Tom 1945
+ Primeau, Joe. 1963
Pulford, Bob 1991
+ Rankin, Frank 1961
Ratelle, Jean 1985
Richard, Henri 1979
+ Richard, Maurice (Rocket)* . .1961
+ Richardson, George 1950
Roberts, Gordie 1971
+ Russel, Blair 1965
+ Russell, Ernie 1965
+ Ruttan, Jack 1962
Savard, Denis 2000
+ Scanlan, Fred. 1965
Schmidt, Milt 1961
+ Schriner, Sweeney. 1962
+ Seibert, Oliver 1961

Goaltenders

Giacomin, Eddie 1987
+ Hainsworth, George 1961
Hall, Glenn 1975
+ Hern, Riley 1962
+ Holmes, Hap 1972
+ Hutton, J.B. (Bouse) 1962
+ Lehman, Hughie 1958
+ LeSueur, Percy 1961
+ Lumley, Harry 1980
+ Moran, Paddy 1958

Defensemen

+ Hall, Joe 1961
+ Harvey, Doug. 1973
Horner, Red 1965
+ Horton, Tim. 1977
Howell, Harry 1979
+ Johnson, Ching 1958
+ Johnson, Ernie 1952
Johnson, Tom 1970
Kelly, Red* 1969
Laperriere, Jacques 1987
Lapointe, Guy 1993
+ Laviolette, Jack 1962
+ Mantha, Sylvio 1960
+ McNamara, George. 1958
Orr, Bobby* 1979
Park, Brad. 1988
+ Patrick, Lester 1947
Pilote, Pierre 1975
+ Pitre, Didier 1962

Referees & Linesmen

+ Hayes, George 1988
+ Hewitson, Bobby. 1963
+ Ion, Mickey. 1961
Pavelich, Matt 1987
+ Rodden, Mike 1962

Builders

+ Brown, Walter 1962
+ Buckland, Frank. 1975
Bush, Walter. 2000
Butterfield, Jack 1980
+ Calder, Frank. 1945
+ Campbell, Angus. 1964
+ Campbell, Clarence 1966
+ Cattarinich, Joseph 1977
+ Dandurand, Leo. 1963
Dilio, Frank. 1964
+ Dudley, George. 1958
+ Dunn, James. 1968

Shutt, Steve. 1993
+ Siebert, Babe. 1964
Sittler, Darryl 1989
+ Smith, Alf 1962
Smith, Clint. 1991
+ Smith, Hooley. 1972
+ Smith, Tommy. 1973
+ Stanley, Barney 1962
Stastny, Peter 1998
+ Stewart, Nels 1962
+ Stuart, Bruce. 1961
+ Taylor, Fred (Cyclone) 1947
+ Trihey, Harry 1950
Trottier, Bryan. 1997
Ullman, Norm 1982
+ Walker, Jack. 1960
+ Walsh, Marty. 1962
Watson, Harry. 1994
+ Watson, Harry (Moose) 1962
+ Weiland, Cooney 1971
+ Westwick, Harry (Rat). 1962
+ Whitcroft, Fred. 1962

Parent, Bernie. 1984
+ Plante, Jacques 1978
Rayner, Chuck 1973
+ Sawchuk, Terry* 1971
Smith, Billy 1993
+ Thompson, Tiny 1959
Tretiak, Vladislav 1989
+ Vezina, Georges 1945
Worsley, Gump 1980
+ Worters, Roy 1969

Potvin, Denis 1991
+ Pratt, Babe 1966
Pronovost, Marcel 1978
+ Pulford, Harvey 1945
Quackenbush, Bill 1976
Reardon, Kenny 1966
Robinson, Larry 1995
+ Ross, Art 1945
Salming, Borje 1996
Savard, Serge 1986
Seibert, Earl. 1963
+ Shore, Eddie 1947
+ Simpson, Joe 1962
Stanley, Allan 1981
+ Stewart, Jack 1964
+ Stuart, Hod. 1945
+ Wilson, Gordon (Phat) 1962

+ Smeaton, J. Cooper 1961
Storey, Red. 1967
Udvari, Frank. 1973
van Hellemond, Andy. 1999

Francis, Emile. 1982
+ Gibson, Jack 1976
+ Gorman, Tommy 1963
+ Griffiths, Frank A. 1993
+ Hanley, Bill 1986
+ Hay, Charles 1984
+ Hendy, Jim 1968
+ Hewitt, Foster 1965
+ Hewitt, W.A. 1945
+ Hume, Fred. 1962
+ Imlach, Punch 1984
+ Ivan, Tommy 1964

+ Jennings, Bill. 1975
+ Johnson, Bob 1992
+ Juckes, Gordon 1979
+ Kilpatrick, John 1960
+ Knox, Seymour III 1993
+ Leader, Al 1969
  LeBel, Bob. 1970
+ Lockhart, Tom 1965
+ Loicq, Paul 1961
+ Mariucci, John 1985
  Mathers, Frank. 1992
+ McLaughlin, Frederic 1963
+ Milford, Jake 1984
  Molson, Hartland 1973
  Morrison, Ian (Scotty) 1999
+ Murray, Athol (Pere) 1998
+ Nelson, Francis 1945
+ Norris, Bruce 1969
+ Norris, James D 1962

+ Norris, James Sr 1958
+ Northey, William 1945
+ O'Brien, J.A 1962
  O'Neill, Brian 1994
  Page, Fred 1993
  Patrick, Craig. 2001
+ Patrick, Frank. 1958
+ Pickard, Allan 1958
+ Pilous, Rudy 1985
  Poile, Bud 1990
  Pollock, Sam. 1978
+ Raymond, Donat 1958
+ Robertson, John Ross. 1945
+ Robinson, Claude 1945
+ Ross, Philip 1976
  Sather, Glen 1997
  Sebetzki, Gunther 1995
+ Selke, Frank 1960
  Sinden, Harry 1983

+ Smith, Frank 1962
+ Smythe, Conn. 1958
  Snider, Ed 1988
+ Stanley, Lord of Preston 1945
+ Sutherland, James 1945
+ Tarasov, Anatoli 1974
  Torrey, Bill. 1995
+ Turner, Lloyd 1958
+ Tutt, William Thayer 1978
  Voss, Carl 1974
+ Waghorne, Fred 1961
+ Wirtz, Arthur 1971
  Wirtz, Bill. 1976
  Ziegler, John 1987

Note: Alan Eagleson was inducted into the Hockey Hall of Fame in 1989 but resigned in 1998 after being found guilty of fraud.

Elmer Ferguson Award

First presented in 1984 by the Professional Hockey Writers' Association for meritorious contributions by members of the PHWA. Named in honor of the late Montreal newspaper reporter, the Ferguson Award does not constitute induction into the Hall of Fame and is not necessarily an annual presentation.

Year		
1984 Jacques Beauchamp, Jim Burchard, Red Burnett, Dink Carroll, Jim Coleman, Ted Damata, Marcel Desjardins, Jack Dulmage, Milt Dunnell, Elmer Ferguson, Tom Fitzgerald, Trent Frayne, Al Laney, Joe Nichols, Basil O'Meara, Jim Vipond & Lewis Walter	1986 Dick Johnston, Leo Monahan & Tim Moriarty	1995 Jake Gatecliff
	1987 Bill Brennan, Rex MacLeod, Ben Olan & Fran Rosa	1996 No award
	1988 Jim Proudfoot & Scott Young	1997 Ken McKenzie
	1989 Claude Larochelle & Frank Orr	1998 Yvon Pedneault
	1990 Bertrand Raymond	1999 Russ Conway
	1991 Hugh Delano	2000 Jim Matheson
1985 Charlie Barton, Red Fisher, George Gross, Zotique L'Esperance, Charles Mayer & Andy O'Brien	1992 No award	2001 Eric Duhatschek
	1993 Al Strachan	
	1994 No award	

Foster Hewitt Award

First presented in 1984 by the NHL Broadcasters' Association for meritorious contributions by members of the NHLBA. Named in honor of Canada's legendary "Voice of Hockey," the Hewitt Award does not constitute induction into the Hall of Fame and is not necessarily an annual presentation.

Year	Year	Year	Year	Year
1984 Fred Cusick, Foster Hewitt, Danny Gallivan & Rene Lecavelier	1986 Wes McKnight & Lloyd Pettit	1990 Jiggs McDonald	1995 Brian McFarlane	2000 Bob Miller
	1987 Bob Wilson	1991 Bruce Martyn	1996 Bob Cole	2001 Mike Lange
	1988 Dick Irvin	1992 Jim Robson	1997 Gene Hart	
	1989 Dan Kelly	1993 Al Shaver	1998 Howie Meeker	
1985 Budd Lynch & Doug Smith		1994 Ted Darling	1999 Richard Garneau	

U.S. Hockey Hall of Fame

Established in 1968 by the Eveleth (Minn.) Civic Association Project H Committee and opened in 1973. **Address:** 801 Hat Trick Ave., P.O. Box 657, Eveleth, MN 55734. **Telephone:** (218) 744-5167.

Eligibility: Nominated players and referees must be American-born and retired five years; coaches must be American-born and must have coached predominantly American teams. Voting done by 12-member panel made up of Hall of Fame members and U.S. hockey officials.

Class of 2001 (3): PLAYERS—**Dave Christian**, **Paul Johnson** and **Mike Ramsey**.

Members are listed with year of induction; (+) indicates deceased members.

Players

+ Abel, Clarence (Taffy). 1973
+ Baker, Hobey 1973
  Bartholome, Earl 1977
+ Bessone, Peter 1978
  Blake, Bob 1985
  Boucha, Henry 1995
+ Brimsek, Frankie 1973
  Broten, Neal. 2000
  Cavanaugh, Joe 1994
+ Chaisson, Ray 1974
  Chase, John 1973
  Christian, Bill 1984
  Christian, Dave 2001
  Christian, Roger. 1989
  Cleary, Bill 1976
  Cleary, Bob 1981
+ Conroy, Tony 1975

  Curran, Mike 1998
+ Dahlstrom, Carl (Cully) 1973
+ DesJardins, Vic. 1974
+ Desmond, Richard. 1988
+ Dill, Bob 1979
+ Everett, Doug 1974
  Ftorek, Robbie 1991
+ Garrison, John 1974
  Garrity, Jack. 1986
+ Goheen, Frank (Moose) 1973
  Grant, Wally 1994
+ Harding, Austie 1975
  Iglehart, Stewart 1975
  Ikola, Willard. 1990
  Johnson, Paul. 2001
  Johnson, Virgil 1974
+ Karakas, Mike 1973

  Kirrane, Jack 1987
+ Lane, Myles 1973
  Langevin, Dave 1993
  Langway, Rod 1999
  Larson, Reed. 1996
+ Linder, Joe. 1975
+ LoPresti, Sam 1973
+ Mariucci, John 1973
  Matchefts, John 1991
+ Mather, Bruce. 1998
  Mayasich, John 1976
  McCartan, Jack 1983
  Moe, Bill 1974
  Morrow, Ken 1995
+ Moseley, Fred. 1975
  Mullen, Joe 1998
+ Murray, Hugh (Muzz) Sr.. 1987

Hockey (Cont.)

+ Nelson, Hub 1978	+ Purpur, Clifford (Fido) 1974	Watson, Gordie 1999
+ Nyrop, William D. 1997	Ramsey, Mike 2001	+ Williams, Tom 1981
Olson, Eddie 1977	Riley, Bill 1977	+ Winters, Frank (Coddy) 1973
+ Owen, George 1973	+ Romnes, Elwin (Doc) 1973	+ Yackel, Ken 1986
+ Palmer, Winthrop 1973	+ Rondeau, Dick 1985	
Paradise, Bob 1989	Sheehey, Timothy 1997	

Coaches

+ Almquist, Oscar 1983	+ Holt Jr., Charles E. 1997	Ramsay, Mike 2001
Bessone, Amo 1992	Ikola, Willard 1990	Riley, Jack 1979
Brooks, Herb 1990	+ Jeremiah, Eddie 1973	+ Ross, Larry 1988
Ceglarski, Len 1992	+ Johnson, Bob 1991	+ Thompson, Cliff 1973
+ Fullerton, James 1992	Johnson, Paul 2001	+ Stewart, Bill 1982
Gambucci, Sergio 1996	Kelley, Jack 1993	Watson, Sid 1999
+ Gordon, Malcolm 1973	+ Kelly, John (Snooks) 1974	+ Winsor, Ralph 1973
Harkness, Ned. 1994	Nanne, Lou 1998	
Heyliger, Vic. 1974	Pleban, Connie 1990	

Referee

Chadwick, Bill 1974

Contributor

+ Schulz, Charles M. 1993

Administrators

+ Brown, George 1973	+ Jennings, Bill. 1981	Pleau, Larry 2000
+ Brown, Walter 1973	+ Kahler, Nick 1980	Ridder, Bob 1976
Bush, Walter 1980	+ Lockhart, Tom 1973	Trumble, Hal 1970
+ Clark, Don 1978	Marvin, Cal 1982	+ Tutt, Thayer 1973
Claypool, Jim 1995	Palazzari, Doug. 2000	Wirtz, Bill 1967
+ Gibson, J.L. (Doc) 1973	Patrick, Craig. 1996	+ Wright, Lyle 1973

Members of Both Hockey and U.S. Hockey Halls of Fame

Players	**Coach**	**Builders**	
Hobey Baker	Bob Johnson	George Brown	Tom Lockhart
Frankie Brimsek		Walter Brown	Craig Patrick
Frank (Moose) Goheen	**Referee**	Walter Bush	Thayer Tutt
John Mariucci	Bill Chadwick	Doc Gibson	Bill Wirtz
Joe Mullen		Bill Jennings	

HORSE RACING

National Museum of Racing and Hall of Fame

Established in 1950 by the Saratoga Springs Racing Association and opened in 1955. **Address:** National Museum of Racing and Hall of Fame, 191 Union Ave., Saratoga Springs, NY 12866. **Telephone:** (518) 584-0400.

Eligibility: Nominated horses must be retired five years; jockeys must be active at least 15 years; trainers must be active at least 25 years. Voting done by 100-member panel of horse racing media.

Class of 2001 (6): JOCKEY—**Earlie Fires**. TRAINER—**Richard Mandella** and **Tom Smith**. HORSES—**Holy Bull**, **Maskette** and **Paseana**.

Members are listed with year of induction; (+) indicates deceased members.

Jockeys

+ Adams, Frank (Dooley)* 1970	Delahoussaye, Eddie 1993	+ McKinney, Rigan 1968
+ Adams, John 1965	+ Ensor, Lavelle (Buddy). 1962	+ McLaughlin, James 1955
+ Aitcheson, Joe Jr.* 1978	+ Fator, Laverne 1955	+ Miller, Walter 1955
+ Arcaro, Eddie 1958	Fires, Earlie. 2001	+ Murphy, Isaac 1955
Atkinson, Ted 1957	Fishback, Jerry* 1992	+ Neves, Ralph 1960
Baeza, Braulio 1976	+ Garner, Andrew (Mack) 1969	+ Notter, Joe 1963
Bailey, Jerry 1995	+ Garrison, Snapper 1955	+ O'Connor, Winnie 1956
+ Barbee, George. 1996	+ Gomez, Avelino 1982	+ Odom, George 1955
+ Bassett, Carroll* 1972	+ Griffin, Henry 1956	+ O'Neill, Frank 1956
Baze, Russell 1999	+ Guerin, Eric 1972	+ Parke, Ivan 1978
+ Blum, Walter 1987	Hartack, Bill 1959	+ Patrick, Gil 1970
+ Bostwick, George H.* 1968	Hawley, Sandy 1992	Pincay, Laffit Jr. 1975
+ Boulmetis, Sam 1973	+ Johnson, Albert 1971	+ Purdy, Sam 1970
+ Brooks, Steve 1963	+ Knapp, Willie 1969	+ Reiff, John 1956
Brumfield, Don 1996	Krone, Julie 2000	+ Robertson, Alfred. 1971
+ Burns, Tommy. 1983	+ Kummer, Clarence 1972	Rotz, John L. 1983
+ Butwell, Jimmy 1984	+ Kurtsinger, Charley 1967	+ Sande, Earl. 1955
+ Byers, J.D. (Dolly) 1967	+ Loftus, Johnny 1959	+ Schilling, Carroll 1970
Cauthen, Steve. 1994	Longden, Johnny 1958	Shoemaker, Bill 1958
+ Coltiletti, Frank. 1970	Maher, Danny 1955	+ Simms, Willie 1977
Cordero, Angel Jr. 1988	+ McAtee, Linus. 1956	+ Sloan, Todhunter 1955
+ Crawford, Robert (Specs)*. . .1973	McCarron, Chris 1989	+ Smithwick, A. Patrick* 1973
Day, Pat 1991	+ McCreary, Conn 1975	Stevens, Gary 1997

+ Stout, James	1968	+ Turner, Nash	1955	+ Woolfe, George	1955

+ Stout, James 1968
+ Taral, Fred 1955
+ Tuckman, Bayard Jr.* 1973
Turcotte, Ron. 1979

+ Turner, Nash. 1955
Ussery, Robert 1980
Vasquez, Jacinto 1998
Velasquez, Jorge 1990

+ Woolfe, George 1955
+ Workman, Raymond 1956
Ycaza, Manuel 1977
*Steeplechase jockey

Trainers

+ Barrera, Laz 1979
+ Bedwell, H. Guy 1971
+ Brown, Edward D. 1984
Burch, Elliot 1980
+ Burch, Preston M. 1963
+ Burch, W.P. 1955
+ Burlew, Fred 1973
+ Childs, Frank E. 1968
+ Clark, Henry 1982
+ Cocks, W. Burling 1985
Conway, James P. 1996
Croll, Jimmy 1994
Drysdale, Neil 2000
+ Duke, William 1956
+ Feustel, Louis 1964
+ Fitzsimmons, J. (Sunny Jim) . .1958
Frankel, Bobby. 1995
+ Gaver, John M. 1966
+ Healey, Thomas 1955
+ Hildreth, Samuel 1955
+ Hirsch, Max 1959
+ Hirsch, W.J. (Buddy) 1982
+ Hitchcock, Thomas Sr. 1973
+ Hughes, Hollie 1973
+ Hyland, John 1956

+ Jacobs, Hirsch 1958
+ Jerkens, H. Allen 1975
Johnson, Philip 1997
+ Johnson, William R. 1986
+ Jolley, LeRoy 1987
+ Jones, Ben A. 1958
+ Jones, H.A. (Jimmy) 1959
+ Joyner, Andrew 1955
Kelly, Tom 1993
+ Laurin, Lucien 1977
+ Lewis, J. Howard 1969
Lukas, D. Wayne 1999
+ Luro, Horatio 1980
Mandella, Richard. 2001
+ Madden, John 1983
+ Maloney, Jim 1989
Martin, Frank (Pancho) 1981
McAnally, Ron 1990
+ McDaniel, Henry 1956
+ Miller, MacKenzie 1987
+ Molter, William, Jr. 1960
Mott, Bill 1998
+ Mulholland, Winbert. 1967
+ Neloy, Eddie 1983
Nerud, John 1972

+ Parke, Burley 1986
+ Penna, Angel Sr. 1988
+ Pincus, Jacob 1988
+ Rogers, John. 1955
+ Rowe, James Sr. 1955
Schulhofer, Scotty 1992
Sheppard, Jonathan 1990
+ Smith, Robert A. 1976
Smith, Tom 2001
+ Smithwick, Mike 1976
+ Stephens, Woody 1976
Tenny, Mesh 1991
+ Thompson, H.J. 1969
+ Trotsek, Harry 1984
Van Berg, Jack. 1985
+ Van Berg, Marion 1970
+ Veitch, Sylvester 1977
+ Walden, Robert 1970
Walsh, Michael 1997
+ Ward, Sherrill 1978
Whiteley, Frank Jr. 1978
+ Whittingham, Charlie 1974
+ Williamson, Ansel 1998
Winfrey, W.C. (Bill) 1971

Horses
Year foaled in parentheses.

A.P. Indy (1989) 2000
+ Ack Ack (1966) 1986
Affectionately (1960) 1989
Affirmed (1975) 1980
All-Along (1979) 1990
+ Alsab (1939) 1976
+ Alydar (1975) 1989
Alysheba (1984) 1993
+ American Eclipse (1814) 1970
+ Armed (1941) 1963
Artful (1902) 1956
+ Arts and Letters (1966) 1994
+ Assault (1943) 1964
+ Battleship (1927) 1969

+ Bayakoa (1984) 1998
+ Bed O'Roses (1947) 1976
Beldame (1901) 1956
+ Ben Brush (1893) 1955
Bewitch (1945) 1977
Bimelech (1937) 1990
Black Gold (1919) 1989
i Black Helen (1932) 1991
+ Blue Larkspur (1926) 1957
+ Bold 'n Determined (1977) . . .1997
+ Bold Ruler (1954) 1973
+ Bon Nouvel (1960) 1976
+ Boston (1833) 1955
+ Broomstick (1901) 1956

+ Buckpasser (1963) 1970
+ Busher (1942) 1964
+ Bushranger (1930) 1967
+ Cafe Prince (1970) 1985
+ Carry Back (1958) 1975
+ Cavalcade (1931) 1993
+ Challendon (1936) 1977
+ Chris Evert (1971) 1988
+ Cicada (1959) 1967
+ Citation (1945) 1959
+ Coaltown (1945) 1983
+ Colin (1905) 1956
+ Commando (1898) 1956
+ Count Fleet (1940) 1961

Harness Racing Museum and Hall of Fame

Established by the U.S. Harness Writers Association (USHWA) in 1958. **Address:** Trotting Horse Museum, 240 Main Street, P.O. Box 590, Goshen, NY 10924; **Telephone:** (845) 294-6330.

Eligibility: Open to all harness racing drivers, trainers and executives. Voting done by USHWA membership. There are 76 members of the Living Hall of Fame, but only the 41 drivers and trainer-drivers are listed below.

Class of 2001 (3): DRIVER—**Catello Manzi**; TRAINER/DRIVER—**Jim Dennis** and **Harry Harvey**.

Members are listed with years of induction; (+) indicates deceased members.

Trainer-Drivers

Abbatiello, Carmine 1986
Abbatiello, Tony 1995
Ackerman, Doug 1995
+ Avery, Earle 1975
+ Baldwin, Ralph 1972
Beissinger, Howard 1975
Bostwick, Dunbar 1989
+ Cameron, Del 1975
Campbell, John 1991
+ Chapman, John 1980
Cruise, Jimmy 1987
Dancer, Stanley 1970
Dennis, Jim 2001
+ Ervin, Frank. 1969

Farrington, Bob 1980
Filion, Herve 1976
+ Garnsey, Glen 1983
Galbraith, Clint. 1990
Gilmour, Buddy 1990
Harner, Levi 1986
Harvey, Harry 2001
+ Haughton, Billy 1969
Hodgins, Clint. 1973
Insko, Del 1981
Kopas, Jack. 1996
Lachance, Mike 1996
Miller, Del 1969
+ O'Brien, Joe 1971

O'Donnell, Bill 1991
Patterson, John Sr. 1994
+ Pownall, Harry 1971
Remmem, Ray 1998
Riegle, Gene. 1992
+ Russell, Sanders 1971
+ Shively, Bion 1968
Sholty, George 1985
Simpson, John Sr 1972
+ Smart, Curly 1970
Sylvester, Charles. 1998
Waples, Keith 1987
Waples, Ron 1994

Horse Racing (Cont.)

+ Crusader (1923) 1995	Holy Bull (1991) 2001	+ Roamer (1911) 1981
+ Dahlia (1971) 1981	+ Imp (1894) 1965	+ Roseben (1901) 1956
+ Damascus (1964) 1974	+ Jay Trump (1957) 1971	+ Round Table (1954) 1972
+ Dark Mirage (1965) 1974	John Henry (1975) 1990	+ Ruffian (1972) 1976
+ Davona Dale (1976) 1985	+ Johnstown (1936) 1992	+ Ruthless (1864) 1975
+ Desert Vixen (1970) 1979	+ Jolly Roger (1922) 1965	+ Salvator (1886) 1955
+ Devil Diver (1939) 1980	+ Kingston (1884) 1955	+ Sarazen (1921) 1957
+ Discovery (1931) 1969	+ Kelso (1957) 1967	+ Seabiscuit (1933) 1958
+ Domino (1891) 1955	+ Kentucky (1861) 1983	+ Searching (1952) 1978
+ Dr. Fager (1964) 1971	Lady's Secret (1982) 1992	Seattle Slew (1974) 1981
Easy Goer (1986) 1997	+ La Prevoyante (1970) 1995	+ Secretariat (1970) 1974
+ Eight 30 (1936) 1994	+ L'Escargot (1963) 1977	+ Shuvee (1966) 1975
+ Elkridge (1938) 1966	+ Lexington (1850) 1955	+ Silver Spoon (1956) 1978
+ Emperor of Norfolk (1885) . . .1988	+ Longfellow (1867) 1971	+ Sir Archy (1805) 1955
+ Equipoise (1928) 1957	+ Luke Blackburn (1877) 1956	+ Sir Barton (1916) 1957
+ Exceller (1973) 1999	+ Majestic Prince (1966) 1988	Slew o'Gold (1980) 1992
+ Exterminator (1915) 1957	+ Man o' War (1917) 1957	+ Sun Beau (1925) 1996
+ Fairmount (1921) 1985	Maskette (1906) 2001	Sunday Silence (1986) 1996
+ Fair Play (1905) 1956	Miesque (1984) 1999	+ Stymie (1941) 1975
+ Firenze (1885) 1981	+ Miss Woodford (1880) 1967	+ Susan's Girl (1969) 1976
Flatterer (1994) 1994	+ Myrtlewood (1933) 1979	+ Swaps (1952) 1966
+ Foolish Pleasure (1972) 1995	+ Nashua (1952) 1965	+ Sword Dancer (1956) 1977
+ Forego (1971) 1979	+ Native Dancer (1950) 1963	+ Sysonby (1902) 1956
+ Fort Marcy (1964) 1998	+ Native Diver (1959) 1978	+ Ta Wee (1966) 1994
+ Gallant Bloom (1966) 1977	+ Needles (1953) 2000	+ Tim Tam (1955) 1985
+ Gallant Fox (1927) 1957	+ Northern Dancer (1961) 1976	+ Tom Fool (1949) 1960
+ Gallant Man (1954) 1987	+ Neji (1950) 1966	+ Top Flight (1929) 1966
+ Gallorette (1942) 1962	+ Oedipus (1941) 1978	+ Tosmah (1961) 1984
+ Gamely (1964) 1980	+ Old Rosebud (1911) 1968	+ Twenty Grand (1928) 1957
Genuine Risk (1977) 1986	+ Omaha (1932) 1965	+ Twilight Tear (1941) 1963
+ Good and Plenty (1900) 1956	+ Pan Zareta (1910) 1972	+ War Admiral (1934) 1958
+ Go For Wand (1987) 1996	+ Parole (1873) 1984	+ Whirlaway (1938) 1959
+ Granville (1933) 1997	Personal Ensign (1984) 1993	+ Whisk Broom II (1907) 1979
+ Grey Lag (1918) 1957	Paseana (1987) 2001	Winning Colors (1985) 2000
+ Gun Bow (1960) 1999	+ Peter Pan (1904) 1956	Zaccio (1976) 1990
+ Hamburg (1895) 1986	Princess Rooney (1980) 1991	+ Zev (1920) 1983
+ Hanover (1884) 1955	+ Real Delight (1949) 1987	
+ Henry of Navarre (1891) . . .1985	+ Regret (1912) 1957	
+ Hill Prince (1947) 1991	+ Reigh Count (1925) 1978	
+ Hindoo (1878) 1955	Riva Ridge (1969) 1998	

Exemplars of Racing

+ Hanes, John W 1982	+ Mellon, Paul 1989	Widener, George D 1971
+ Jeffords, Walter M 1973		

MEDIA

National Sportscasters and Sportswriters Hall of Fame

Established in 1959 by the National Sportscasters and Sportswriters Association. A permanent museum for the NSSA Hall of Fame opened on May 1, 2000. **Address:** 322 East Innes St., Salisbury, NC 28144. **Telephone:** (704) 633-4275.

Eligibility: Nominees must be active for at least 25 years. Voting done by NSSA membership and other media representatives. **Class of 2001** (3): **W.C. Heinz**, **George Vecsey** and **Jack Whitaker**.

Members are listed with year of induction; (+) indicates deceased members.

Sportscasters

+ Allen, Mel 1972	Gowdy, Curt 1981	Miller, Jon 1999
+ Barber, Walter (Red) 1973	Harwell, Ernie 1989	+ Nelson, Lindsey 1979
+ Brickhouse, Jack 1983	Hearn, Chick 1997	+ Prince, Bob 1986
Buck, Jack 1990	+ Hodges, Russ 1975	Schenkel, Chris 1981
+ Caray, Harry 1989	+ Hoyt, Waite 1987	+ Scott, Ray 1982
+ Cosell, Howard 1993	+ Husing, Ted 1963	Scully, Vin 1991
+ Dean, Dizzy 1976	Jackson, Keith 1995	Simpson, Jim 2000
+ Dunphy, Don 1986	+ McCarthy, Clem 1970	+ Stern, Bill 1974
+ Elson, Bob 1995	McKay, Jim 1987	Summerall, Pat 1994
Enberg, Dick 1996	+ McNamee, Graham 1964	Whitaker, Jack 2001
+ Glickman, Marty 1992	Michaels, Al 1998	

Sportswriters

	+ Cannon, Jimmy 1986	+ Daley, Arthur 1976
Anderson, Dave 1990	+ Carmichael, John P. 1994	Deford, Frank 1998
Bisher, Furman 1989	+ Connor, Dick 1992	Durslag, Mel 1995
Broeg, Bob 1997	+ Considine, Bob 1980	+ Gould, Alan 1990
Burick, Si 1985		

+ Graham, Frank Sr..........1995	+ Murray, Jim................1978
+ Grimsley, Will 1987	Olderman, Murray 1993
Heinz, W.C................2001	+ Parker, Dan 1975
Izenberg, Jerry............2000	Pope, Edwin 1994
Jenkins, Dan 1996	+ Povich, Shirley 1984
+ Kieran, John 1971	+ Rice, Grantland 1962
+ Lardner, Ring 1967	+ Runyon, Damon 1964
+ Murphy, Jack 1988	Russell, Fred 1988

Sherrod, Blackie 1991
+ Smith, Walter (Red)........1977
+ Spink, J.G. Taylor 1969
+ Stedman, John 1999
Vecsey, George 2001
+ Ward, Arch 1973
+ Woodward, Stanley 1974

MOTORSPORTS

Motorsports Hall of Fame of America

Established in 1989. **Mailing Address:** P.O. Box 194, Novi, MI 48376. **Telephone:** (248) 349-7223.

Eligibility: Nominees must be retired at least three years or engaged in their area of motorsports for at least 20 years. Areas include: open wheel, stock car, dragster, sports car, motorcycle, off road, power boat, air racing, land speed records, historic and at-large.

Class of 2001 (9): DRIVERS—**Earl Cooper** (historic), **Emerson Fittipaldi** (open wheel racing), **Fred Lorenzen** (stock car), **Tom McEwen** (drag racing), **Ken Miles** (sports car), **Freddie Spencer** (motorcycle) and **Mira Slovak** (powerboat). PILOT—**Tony LeVier**. CONTRIBUTOR—**Andy Granatelli**.

Members are listed with year of induction; (+) indicates deceased members.

Drivers

Allison, Bobby 1992	Gurney, Dan..............1991	+ Musson, Ron...........1993
Andretti, Mario 1990	Hanauer, Chip............1995	Nordskog, Bob 1997
Arfons, Art 1991	Hannah, Bob 2000	+ Oldfield, Barney 1989
+ Baker, Cannonball 1989	+ Hanks, Sam 2000	Ongais, Danny...........2000
Bettenhausen, Tony 1997	+ Harroun, Ray 2000	Parks, Wally.............1993
Brabham, Jack 1998	Hart, C.J.................1999	Pearson, David 1993
Breedlove, Craig..........1993	Hill, Phil 1989	+ Petrali, Joe 1992
Bryan, Jimmy 1999	+ Holbert, Al 1993	+ Petty, Lee...............1996
+ Campbell, Sir Malcolm.....1994	+ Horn, Ted 1993	Petty, Richard 1989
Cantrell, Bill 1992	Jarrett, Ned 1997	Prudhomme, Don 1991
+ Chenoweth, Dean 1991	Jenkins, Bill (Grumpy) 1996	+ Revson, Peter 1996
Chrisman, Art.............1997	Johnson, Junior............1991	+ Roberts, Fireball.........1995
+ Clark, Jim 1990	Jones, Parnelli 1992	Roberts, Kenny 1990
+ Cook, Betty..............1996	Kalitta, Connie 1992	Rutherford, Johnny........1996
Cooper, Earl..............2001	Kurtis, Frank 1999	Seebold, Bill..............1999
Cunningham, Briggs........1997	Leonard, Joe..............1991	+ Shaw, Wilbur 1991
+ Davis, Jim 1997	Lockhart, Frank 1999	Slock, Tim................1999
D'Eath, Tom 2000	Lorenzen, Fred 2001	Slovak, Mira..............2001
DeCoster, Roger...........1994	+ McLaren, Bruce 1995	Smith, Malcolm 1996
+ DePalma, Ralph 1992	Mann, Dick...............1993	Spencer, Freddie 2001
+ DePaolo, Peter 1995	Markle, Bart 1999	+ Thompson, Mickey 1990
+ Donahue, Mark 1990	+ Mays, Rex...............1995	Unser, Al.................1991
Fittipaldi, Emerson..........2001	McEwen, Tom.............2001	Unser, Bobby 1994
Follmer, George 1999	Mears, Rick 1998	+ Vukovich, Bill Sr.........1992
Foyt, A.J 1989	+ Meyer, Louis 1993	Ward, Rodger 1995
Garlits, Don 1989	+ Miles, Ken 2001	+ Wood, Gar...............1990
Glidden, Bob 1994	Muldowney, Shirley........1990	Yarborough, Cale 1994
+ Gregg, Peter 2000	+ Muncy, Bill 1989	

Pilots

Cleland, Cook 2000	+ Earhart, Amelia 1992	Shelton, Lyle 1999
+ Cochran, Jacqueline 1993	+ Falck, Bill 1994	+ Turner, Roscoe 1991
+ Curtiss, Glenn 1990	Greenmayer, Darryl 1997	
+ Doolittle, Jimmy 1989	LeVier, Tony 2001	

Contributors

+ Agajanian, J.C............1992	+ France, Bill Sr. 1990	+ Rose, Mauri 1996
Bignotti, George 1993	Granatelli, Andy 2001	Shelby, Carroll 1992
+ Black, Keith 1995	Hall, Jim 1994	Watson, A.J...............1996
Chapman, Colin 1997	+ Hulman, Tony.............1991	Wood, Glen...............2000
+ Chevrolet, Louis 1995	Little, Bernie 1994	Wood, Leonard 2000
Duesenberg, Fred 1997	Miller, Harry 1999	+ Yunick, Smokey 2000
Economaki, Chris 1994	Penske, Roger 1995	
+ Ford, Henry 1996	+ Rickenbacker, Eddie 1994	

International Motorsports Hall of Fame

Established in 1990 by the International Motorsports Hall of Fame Commission. **Mailing Address:** P.O. Box 1018, Talladega, AL 35160. **Telephone:** (256) 362-5002.

Eligibility: Nominees must be retired from their specialty in motorsports for five years. Voting done by 150-member panel made up of the world-wide auto racing media.

Class of 2001 (4): DRIVERS—**Neil Bonnett**, **Jimmy Bryan** and **Mike Hailwood**. CONTRIBUTOR—**Fred Offenhauser**.

Members are listed with year of induction; (+) indicates deceased members.

Motorsports (Cont.)
Drivers

Allison, Bobby 1993	+ Haley, Donald 1996	Piquet, Nelson 2000
Andretti, Mario 2000	+ Hill, Graham 1990	Prodhomme, Don. 2000
+ Ascari, Alberto. 1992	Hill, Phil 1991	Prost, Alain 1999
+ Ascari, Alberto. 1992	+ Holbert, Al 1993	+ Roberts, Fireball. 1990
Baker, Buck. 1990	+ Isaac, Bobby 1996	Roberts, Kenny 1992
Bonnett, Neil 2001	Jarrett, Ned 1991	Rose, Mauri 1994
+ Bettenhausen, Tony 1991	Johncock, Gordon 1999	Rutherford, Johnny. 1996
Brabham, Jack 1990	Johnson, Junior. 1990	Scott, Wendell 1999
Bryan, Jimmy 2001	Jones, Parnelli 1990	+ Senna, Ayrton 2000
+ Campbell, Sir Malcolm. 1990	Lauda, Niki. 1993	+ Shaw, Wilbur 1991
+ Caracciola, Rudolph 1998	Lorenzen, Fred 1991	Smith, Louise 1999
+ Clark, Jim 1990	+ Lund, Tiny 1994	Stewart, Jackie. 1990
+ DePalma, Ralph 1991	+ Mays, Rex. 1993	Surtees, John 1996
+ Donahue, Mark 1990	+ McLaren, Bruce 1991	+ Thomas, Herb. 1994
+ Evans, Richie 1996	+ Meyer, Louis 1992	+ Turner, Curtis 1992
+ Fangio, Juan Manuel 1990	Moss, Stirling 1990	Unser, Al Sr.. 1998
+ Flock, Tim 1991	+ Nuvolari, Tazio 1998	Unser, Bobby 1990
Foyt, A.J.. 2000	+ Oldfield, Barney 1990	+ Vukovich, Bill 1991
+ Gregg, Peter . . . . :. .1992	Parsons, Benny. 1994	Ward Rodger 1992
Gurney, Dan. 1990	Pearson, David 1993	+ Weatherly, Joe 1994
Hailwood, Mike. 2001	+ Petty, Lee. 1990	Yarborough, Cale 1993
Bignotti, George 1993	### Contributors	
Breedlove, Craig 2000	+ Hulman, Tony 1990	Penske, Roger 1998
+ Chapman, Colin 1994	Hyde, Harry 1999	+ Porsche, Ferdinand 1996
+ Chevrolet, Louis 1992	Marcum, John 1994	+ Rickenbacker, Eddie 1992
+ Ferrari, Enzo 1994	+ Matthews, Banjo 1998	Shelby, Carroll 1991
+ Ford, Henry 1993	Moody, Ralph 1994	+ Thompson, Mickey 1990
+ France, Bill Sr.. 1990	Offenhauser, Fred 2001	+ Yunick, Smokey 1990
Granatelli, Andy 1992	Parks, Wally 1992	

OLYMPICS

U.S. Olympic Hall of Fame

Established in 1983 by the United States Olympic Committee. **Mailing Address:** U.S. Olympic Committee, 1750 East Boulder Street, Colorado Springs, CO 80909. Plans for a permanent museum site have been suspended due to lack of funding. **Telephone:** (719) 578-4529.

Eligibility: Nominated athletes must be five years removed from active competition. Voting done by National Sportscasters and Sportswriters Association, Hall of Fame members and the USOC board members of directors.

Voting for membership in the Hall was suspended in 1993.

Members are listed with year of induction; (+) indicates deceased members.

Teams

1956 Basketball Dick Boushka, Carl Cain, Chuck Darling, Bill Evans, Gib Ford, Burdy Haldorson, Bill Hougland, Bob Jeangerard, K.C. Jones, Bill Russell, Ron Tomsic, +Jim Walsh and coach +Gerald Tucker.

1960 Basketball Jay Arnette, Walt Bellamy, Bob Boozer, Terry Dischinger, Burdy Haldorson, Darrall Imhoff, Allen Kelley, +Lester Lane, Jerry Lucas, Oscar Robertson, Adrian Smith, Jerry West and coach Pete Newell.

1964 Basketball Jim Barnes, Bill Bradley, Larry Brown, Joe Caldwell, Mel Counts, Richard Davies, Walt Hazzard, Luke Jackson, John McCaffrey, Jeff Mullins, Jerry Shipp, George Wilson and coach +Hank Iba.

1960 Ice Hockey Billy Christian, Roger Christian, Billy Cleary, Bob Cleary, Gene Grazia, Paul Johnson, Jack Kirrane, John Mayasich, Jack McCartan, Bob McKay, Dick Meredith, Weldon Olson, Ed Owen, Rod Paavola, Larry Palmer, Dick Rodenheiser, +Tom Williams and coach Jack Riley.

1980 Ice Hockey Bill Baker, Neal Broten, Dave Christian, Steve Christoff, Jim Craig, Mike Eruzione, John Harrington, Steve Janaszak, Mark Johnson, Ken Morrow, Rob McClanahan, Jack O'Callahan, Mark Pavelich, Mike Ramsey, Buzz Schneider, Dave Silk, Eric Strobel, Bob Suter, Phil Verchota, Mark Wells and coach Herb Brooks.

Alpine Skiing
Mahre, Phil. 1992

Bobsled
+ Eagan, Eddie (see Boxing). . .1983

Boxing
Clay, Cassius* 1983
+ Eagan, Eddie (see Bobsled). .1983
Foreman, George 1990
Frazier, Joe. 1989
Leonard, Sugar Ray 1985
Patterson, Floyd 1987
*Clay changed name to Muhammad Ali in 1964.

Cycling
Carpenter-Phinney, Connie. . .1992

Diving
King, Miki. 1992
Lee, Sammy 1990
Louganis, Greg 1985
McCormick, Pat 1985

Figure Skating
Albright, Tenley 1988
Button, Dick 1983
Fleming, Peggy 1983
Hamill, Dorothy 1991
Hamilton, Scott 1990

Gymnastics
Conner, Bart. 1991
Retton, Mary Lou 1985
Vidmar, Peter 1991

Rowing
+ Kelly, Jack Sr.. 1990

Speed Skating
Heiden, Eric 1983

Swimming
Babashoff, Shirley 1987
Caulkins, Tracy 1990
+ Daniels, Charles 1988
de Varona, Donna. 1987
+ Kahanamoku, Duke. 1984
+ Madison, Helene. 1992
Meyer, Debbie. 1986
Naber, John 1984
Schollander, Don 1983
Spitz, Mark. 1983
+ Weissmuller, Johnny 1983

Track & Field

Beamon, Bob	1983
Boston, Ralph	1985
+ Calhoun, Lee	1991
Campbell, Milt.	1992
Davenport, Willie	1991
Davis, Glenn	1986
+ Didrikson, Babe	1983
Dillard, Harrison	1983
Evans, Lee	1989
+ Ewry, Ray	1983
Fosbury, Dick	1992
Jenner, Bruce	1986
Johnson, Rafer	1983
+ Kraenzlein, Alvin	1985
Lewis, Carl	1985
Mathias, Bob	1983
Mills, Billy	1984

Morrow, Bobby	1989
Moses, Edwin	1985
O'Brien, Parry	1984
Oerter, Al	1983
+ Owens, Jesse	1983
+ Paddock, Charley	1991
Richards, Bob	1983
+ Rudolph, Wilma	1983
+ Sheppard, Mel	1989
Shorter, Frank	1984
+ Thorpe, Jim	1983
Toomey, Bill	1984
Tyus, Wyomia	1985
Whitfield, Mal	1988
+ Wykoff, Frank	1984

Weight Lifting

+ Davis, John	1989
Kono, Tommy	1990

Wrestling

Gable, Dan	1985

Contributors

Arledge, Roone	1989
+ Brundage, Avery	1983
+ Bushnell, Asa	1990
Hull, Col. Don	1992
+ Iba, Hank	1985
+ Kane, Robert	1986
+ Kelly, Jack Jr.	1992
McKay, Jim	1988
Miller, Don	1984
+ Simon, William	1991
Walker, LeRoy	1987

The Olympic Order

Established in 1974 by the International Olympic Committee (IOC) to honor athletes, officials and media members who have made remarkable contributions to the Olympic movement. The IOC's Council of the Olympic Order is presided over by the IOC president and active IOC members are not eligible for consideration. Through 1998, only three American officials have received the Order's highest commendation—the gold medal:

Avery Brundage, president of USOC (1928-53) and IOC (1952-72), was given the award posthumously in 1975.

Peter Ueberroth, president of Los Angeles Olympic Organizing Committee, was given the award in 1984.

Billy Payne, president of the Atlanta Committee for the Olympic Games, was given the award in 1996.

SOCCER

International Soccer Hall of Champions

Established in 1998 by FIFA, soccer's international governing body. Located at Disneyland Paris.

Eligibility: Nominated players and coaches must be retired at least five years. Nominations made by a committee composed of FIFA members, the Hall of Champions management and three ad hoc members then submit a list to a panel of 32 soccer journalists from around the world who also have the chance to add nominees of their own as well as voting for a specific number of candidates in each category.

Class of 2000 (6): PLAYERS—**George Best** (N. Ireland); **Didi** (Brazil); **Marko Van Basten** (Holland); **Zico** (Brazil); CLUB TEAM—**FC Barcelona**; NATIONAL TEAMS—**Italy**.

Players

Beckenbauer, Franz (W. Ger)	1998
Best, George (N. Ire)	2000
Charlton, Sir Bobby (ENG)	1998
Cruyff, Johan (NED)	1998
+ Didi (BRA)	2000
Distefano, Alfredo (ARG/SPA)	1998
Eusebio (POR)	1998

Fontaine, Just (FRA)	1999
+ Garrincha (BRA)	1999
+ Matthews, Sir Stanley (ENG)	1998
+ Moore, Bobby (ENG)	1999
Müller, Gerd (W. Ger)	1999
Pele (BRA)	1998
Plantini, Michel (FRA)	1998

Puskas, Ferenc (HUN/SPA)	1998
Van Basten, Marko (HOL)	2000
+ Yashin, Lev (RUS)	1998
Zico (BRA)	2000
Zoff, Dino (ITA)	1999

Managers

+ Busby, Sir Matt (SCO)	1998
Michels, Rinus (NED)	1998
+ Shankly, Bill (SCO)	1999

Referees

Taylor, Jack (ENG)	1999
Vautrot, Michel (FRA)	1998

Pioneers

Havelange, Joao (BRA)	1999
+ Rimet, Jules (FRA)	1998

Club Teams

Ajax Amsterdam (NED)	1999
FC Barcelona (SPA)	2000
Real Madrid (SPA)	1998

National Teams

Brazil	1998
Germany	1999
Italy	2000

Media

Ferran, Jacques (FRA)	1999
Goddett, Jacques (FRA)	1998

For the Good of the Game

+ Dassler, Horst (GER)	1998
+ Sastre, Fernard (FRA)	1999

National Soccer Hall of Fame

Established in 1950 by the Philadelphia Oldtimers Association. First exhibit unveiled in Oneonta, NY in 1982. Moved into new Hall of Fame building in the summer of 1999. **Address:** 18 Stadium Circle, Oneonta, NY 13820. **Telephone:** (607) 432-3351.

Eligibility: Nominated players must have represented the U.S. in international competition and be retired five years; other categories include Meritorious Service and Special Commendation.

Nominations made by state organizations and a veterans' committee. Voting done by nine-member committee made up of Hall of Famers, U.S. Soccer officials and members of the national media.

Class of 2001 (3): **Rick Davis, Robert Hermann** and **Bill Looby**.

Members are listed with home state and year of induction; (+) indicates deceased members.

Members

Abronzino, Umberto (CA) ...1971
Aimi, Milton (TX) 1991
+ Alonso, Julie (NY) 1972
+ Andersen, William (NY) 1956
+ Ardizzone, John (CA) 1971
+ Armstrong, James (NY) 1952
+ Auld, Andrew (RI) 1986
Bahr, Walter (PA) 1976
Barr, George (NY) 1983
+ Barriskill, Joe (NY) 1953
+ Beardsworth, Fred (MA) 1965
Beckenbauer, Franz (Ger) ...1998
Berling, Clay (CA) 1995
Bernabei, Ray (PA) 1978
Best, John O. (CA) 1982
+ Bookie, Michael (PA) 1986
+ Booth, Joseph (CT) 1952
Borghi, Frank (MO) 1976
Boulos, Frenchy (NY) 1980
+ Boxer, Matt (CA) 1961
Bradley, Gordon (Eng) 1996
+ Briggs, Lawrence E. (MA) ...1978
+ Brittan, Harold (PA) 1951
+ Brock, John (MA) 1950
+ Brown, Andrew M. (OH) 1950
+ Brown, David (NJ) 1951
Brown, George (NJ) 1995
Brown, James (NY) 1986
+ Cahill, Thomas W (NY) 1950
+ Carenza, Joe (MO) 1982
+ Caraffi, Ralph (OH) 1959
Chacurian, Chico (CT) 1992
+ Chesney, Stan (NY) 1966
Chinaglia, Giorgio (Italy) 2000
Chyzowych, Walter (PA) 1997
+ Coll, John (NY) 1986
+ Collins, George M. (MA) 1951
Collins, Peter (NY) 1998
+ Colombo, Charlie (MO) 1976
+ Commander, Colin (OH) 1967
+ Cordery, Ted (CA) 1975
+ Craddock, Robert (PA) 1959
+ Craggs, Edmund (WA) 1969
Craggs, George (WA) 1981
+ Cummings, Wilfred R. (IL) ..1953
Davis, Rick (CA) 2001
+ Delach, Joseph (PA) 1973
DeLuca, Enzo (NY) 1979
+ Dick, Walter (CA) 1989
Diorio, Nick (PA) 1974
+ Donaghy, Edward J. (NY) ...1951
+ Donelli, Buff (PA) 1954
+ Donnelly, George (NY) 1989
+ Douglas, Jimmy (NJ) 1954
+ Dresmich, John W. (PA) 1968
+ Duff, Duncan (CA) 1972
+ Dugan, Thomas (NJ) 1951
+ Dunn, James (MO) 1974
Edwards, Gene (WI) 1985
Ely, Alexander (PA) 1997
+ Epperleim, Rudy (NJ) 1951
+ Fairfield, Harry (PA) 1951
Feibusch, Ernst (CA) 1984
+ Ferguson, John (PA) 1950
+ Fernley, John A. (MA) 1951
+ Ferro, Charles (NY) 1958
+ Fishwick, George E. (IL) 1974
+ Flamhaft, Jack (NY) 1964
+ Fleming, Harry G. (PA) 1967
+ Florie, Thomas (NJ) 1986
+ Foulds, Pal (MA) 1953
+ Foulds, Sam (MA) 1969
+ Fowler, Dan (NY) 1970
+ Fowler, Peg (NY) 1979

+ Fricker, Werner (PA) 1992
+ Fryer, William J. (NJ) 1951
Gabarra, Carin (CA) 2000
+ Gaetjens, Joe (NY) 1976
+ Gallagher, James (NY) 1986
+ Garcia, Pete (MO) 1964
+ Gentle, James (PA) 1986
Getzinger, Rudy (IL) 1991
+ Giesler, Walter (MO) 1962
Glover, Teddy (NY) 1965
+ Gonsalves, Billy (MA) 1950
Gormley, Bob (PA) 1989
+ Gould, David L. (PA) 1953
+ Govier, Sheldon (IL) 1950
Greer, Don (CA) 1985
Gryzik, Joe (IL) 1973
+ Guelker, Bob (MO) 1980
Guennel, Joe (CO) 1980
Harker, Al (PA) 1979
+ Healy, George (MI) 1951
Heilpern, Herb (NY) 1988
Heinrichs, April (CO) 1998
+ Hemmings, William (IL) 1961
Hermann, Robert (MO) 2001
+ Hudson, Maurice (CA) 1966
Hunt, Lamar (TX) 1982
Hynes, John (NY) 1977
+ Iglehart, Alfredda (MD) 1951
+ Japp, John (PA) 1953
+ Jeffrey, William (PA) 1951
Jewell, Frank (FA) 1996
+ Johnson, Jack (IL) 1952
Kabanica, Mike (WI) 1987
Kehoe, Bob (MO) 1990
Kelly, Frank (NJ) 1994
+ Kempton, George (WA) 1950
Keough, Harry (MO) 1976
+ Klein, Paul (NJ) 1953
Kleinaitis, Al (IN) 1995
+ Koszma, Oscar (CA) 1964
Kracher, Frank (IL) 1983
Kraft, Granny (MD) 1984
+ Kraus, Harry (NY) 1963
Kropfelder, Nicholas 1996
+ Kunter, Rudy (NY) 1963
+ Lamm, Kurt (NY) 1979
Lang, Millard (MD) 1950
Larson, Bert (CT) 1988
Leonard, Abbot (Eng) 1996
+ Lewis, H. Edgar (PA) 1950
Lombardo, Joe (NY) 1984
Long, Denny (NY) 1993
Looby, Bill (MO) 2001
+ MacEwan, John J. (MI) 1953
+ Maca, Joe (NY) 1976
+ Magnozzi, Enzo (NY) 1978
+ Maher, Jack (IL) 1970
+ Manning, Dr. Randolf (NY) ..1950
+ Marre, John (MO) 1953
McBride, Pat (MO) 1994
+ McClay, Allan (MA) 1971
+ McGhee, Bart (NY) 1986
+ McGrath, Frank (MA) 1978
+ McGuire, Jimmy (NY) 1951
+ McGuire, John (NY) 1951
+ McIlveney, Eddie (PA) 1976
McLaughlin, Bennie (PA) 1977
+ McSkimming, Dent (MO) 1951
Merovich, Pete (PA) 1971
+ Mieth, Werner (NJ) 1974
+ Millar, Robert (NY) 1950
Miller, Al (OH) 1995
+ Miller, Milton (NY) 1971
+ Mills, Jimmy (NY) 1954

Monson, Lloyd (NY) 1994
Moore, James F. (MO) 1971
Moore, Johnny (CA) 1997
+ Moorehouse, George (NY) ..1986
+ Morrison, Robert (PA) 1951
+ Morrissette, Bill (MA) 1967
Nanoski, Jukey (PA) 1993
+ Netto, Fred (IL) 1958
Newman, Ron (CA) 1992
+ Niotis, D.J. (IL) 1963
+ O'Brien, Shamus (NY) 1990
Olaff, Gene (NJ) 1971
+ Oliver, Arnie (MA) 1968
Oliver, Len (PA) 1996
+ Palmer, William (PA) 1952
Pariani, Gino (MO) 1976
+ Patenaude, Bert (MA) 1971
+ Pearson, Eddie (GA) 1990
+ Peel, Peter (IL) 1951
Pelé (Brazil) 1993
Peters, Wally (NJ) 1967
Phillipson, Don (CO) 1987
+ Piscopo, Giorgio (NY) 1978
+ Pomeroy, Edgar (CA) 1955
+ Ramsden, Arnold (TX) 1957
+ Ratican, Harry (MO) 1950
Reese, Doc (MD) 1957
+ Renzulli, Pete (NY)..........1951
Ringsdorf, Gene (MD) 1979
Roe, James (MO) 1997
Roth, Werner (NY) 1989
+ Rottenberg, Jack (NJ) 1971
Roy, Willy (IL) 1989
+ Ryan, Hun (PA) 1958
+ Sager, Tom (PA) 1968
Saunders, Harry (NY) 1981
Schaller, Willy (IL) 1995
Schellscheidt, Mannie (NJ)...1990
Schillinger, Emil (PA) 1960
+ Schroeder, Elmer (PA) 1951
+ Scwarcz, Erno (NY) 1951
+ Shields, Fred (PA) 1968
+ Single, Erwin (NY)...........1981
+ Slone, Philip (NY) 1986
+ Smith, Alfred (PA) 1951
Smith, Patrick (OH) 1998
+ Souza, Ed (MA) 1976
Souza, Clarkie (MA) 1976
+ Spalding, Dick (PA) 1951
+ Stark, Archie (NJ) 1950
+ Steelink, Nicolaas (CA) 1971
+ Steur, August (NY) 1969
+ Stewart, Douglas (PA) 1950
+ Stone, Robert T. (CO) 1971
+ Swords, Thomas (MA) 1976
+ Tintle, Joseph (NJ) 1952
+ Tracey, Ralph (MO) 1986
+ Triner, Joseph (IL) 1951
+ Vaughan, Frank (MO) 1986
+ Walder, Jimmy (NY) 1971
+ Wallace, Frank (MO) 1976
+ Washauer, Adolph (CA) 1977
+ Webb, Tom (WA) 1987
+ Weir, Alex (NY) 1975
+ Weston, Victor (WA) 1956
+ Wilson, Peter (NJ) 1950
+ Wood, Alex (MI) 1986
+ Woods, John W. (IL) 1952
Woosnam, Phil (GA) 1997
Yeagley, Jerry (IN) 1989
+ Young, John (CA) 1958
+ Zampini, Dan (PA) 1963
Zerhusen, Al (CA) 1978

SWIMMING

International Swimming Hall of Fame

Established in 1965 by the U.S. College Coaches' Swim Forum. **Address:** One Hall of Fame Drive, Ft. Lauderdale, FL 33316. **Telephone:** (954) 462-6536.

Categories for induction are: swimming, diving, water polo, synchronized swimming, coaching, pioneers and contributors. Contributors are not included in the following list. Only U.S. men, women and coaches listed below.

Class of 2001 (5): U.S. WOMEN—**Janet Evans, Patty Robinson Fulton** and **Wendy Wyland**; U.S. MEN—**Tom Jager** and **Jeff Rouse** .

Members are listed with year of induction; (+) indicates deceased members.

U.S. Men

+ Anderson, Miller	1967
Barrowman, Mike	1997
Biondi, Matt	1997
+ Boggs, Phil	1985
Brack, Walter	1997
Breen, George	1975
+ Browning, Skippy	1975
Bruner, Mike	1988
Burton, Mike	1977
+ Cann, Tedford	1967
Carey, Rick	1993
Clark, Earl	1972
Clark, Steve	1966
Cleveland, Dick	1991
Clotworthy, Robert	1980
+ Crabbe, Buster	1965
+ Daniels, Charlie	1965
Degener, Dick	1971
DeMont, Rick	1990
Dempsey, Frank	1996
+ Desjardins, Pete	1966
Edgar, David	1996
+ Faricy, John	1990
+ Farrell, Jeff	1968
+ Fick, Peter	1978
+ Flanagan, Ralph	1978
Ford, Alan	1966
Furniss, Bruce	1987
Gaines, Rowdy	1995
Garton, Tim	1997
Glancy, Harrison	1990
+ Goodwin, Budd	1971
Graef, Jed	1988
Haines, George	1977
Hall, Gary	1981
+ Harlan, Bruce	1973
+ Hebner, Harry	1968
Hencken, John	1988
Hickcox, Charles	1976

Higgins, John	1971
+ Holiday, Harry	1991
Irwin, Juno Stover	1980
Jager, Tom	2001
Jastremski, Chet	1977
+ Kahanamoku, Duke	1965
+ Kealoha, Warren	1968
Kiefer, Adolph	1965
Kinsella, John	1986
+ Kojac, George	1968
Konno, Ford	1972
+ Kruger, Stubby	1986
+ Kuehn, Louis	1988
+ Langer, G. Harold Gus	1995
+ Langer, Ludy	1988
Larson, Lance	1980
Lee, Dr. Sammy	1968
Lemmons, Kelley	1999
+ LeMoyne, Harry	1988
Louganis, Greg	1993
Lundquist, Steve	1990
Mann, Thompson	1984
+ Martin, G. Harold	1999
McCormick, Pat	1965
+ McDermott, Turk	1969
+ McGillivray, Perry	1981
McKenzie, Don	1989
McKinney, Frank	1975
McLane, Jimmy	1970
+ Medica, Jack	1966
Montgomery, Jim	1986
Mullikan, Bill	1984
Naber, John	1982
Nakama, Keo	1975
+ O'Connor, Wally	1966
Oyakawa, Yoshi	1979
+ Patnik, Al	1969
Phillips, William Berge	1997
+ Riley, Mickey	1977

+ Ris, Wally	1966
Robie, Carl	1976
Roper, Gail	1997
Ross, Clarence	1988
+ Ross, Norman	1967
Roth, Dick	1987
Rouse, Jeff	2001
+ Ruddy, Joe	1986
Russell, Doug	1985
Saari, Roy	1976
+ Schaeffer, E. Carroll	1968
Scholes, Clarke	1980
Schollander, Don	1965
Shaw, Tim	1989
+ Sheldon, George	1989
+ Skelton, Robert	1988
Smith, Bill	1966
+ Smith, Dutch	1979
+ Smith, Jimmy	1992
Smith, R. Jackson	1983
Spitz, Mark	1977
+ Stack, Allen	1979
Stickles, Ted	1995
Stock, Tom	1989
+ Swendsen, Clyde	1991
Tobian, Gary	1978
Troy, Mike	1971
Vande Weghe, Albert	1990
Vassallo, Jesse	1997
+ Verdeur, Joe	1966
Vogel, Matt	1996
+ Vollmer, Hal	1990
+ Wayne, Marshall	1981
Webster, Bob	1970
+ Weissmuller, Johnny	1965
+ White, Al	1965
Wrightson, Bernie	1984
Yorzyk, Bill	1971

U.S. Women

Anderson, Terry	1986
Atwood, Sue	1992
Babashoff, Shirley	1982
Babb-Sprigue, Kristen	1999
Ball, Catie	1976
+ Bauer, Sybil	1967
Bean, Dawn Pawson	1996
Belote, Melissa	1983
Bleibtrey, Ethelda	1967
+ Boyle, Charlotte	1988
Burke, Lynne	1978
Bush, Lesley	1986
Callen, Gloria	1984
Caretto, Patty	1987
Carr, Cathy	1988
Caulkins, Tracy	1990
+ Chadwick, Florence	1970
Chandler, Jennifer	1987
Cohen, Tiffany	1996
+ Coleman, Georgia	1966
Cone, Carin	1984
Costie, Candy	1995
Cox, Lynne	2000

Crlenkovich, Helen	1981
Curtis, Ann	1966
Daniel, Ellie	1997
de Varona, Donna	1969
Dean, Penny	1996
+ Dorfner, Olga	1970
Draves, Vickie	1969
Duenkel, Ginny	1985
Dunbar, Barbara	2000
Ederle, Gertrude	1965
Ellis, Kathy	1991
Evans, Janet	2001
Ferguson, Cathy	1978
Finneran, Sharon	1985
+ Fulton, Patty Robinson	2001
+ Galligan, Claire	1970
+ Garatti-Seville, Eleanor	1992
Gestring, Marjorie	1976
Gossick, Sue	1988
+ Guest, Irene	1990
Hall, Kaye	1979
Henne, Jan	1979
Holm, Eleanor	1966

Hunt-Newman, Virginia	1993
Johnson, Gail	1983
Josephson, Karen	1997
Josephson, Sarah	1997
Kane, Marion	1981
+ Kaufman, Beth	1967
+ Kight, Lenore	1981
King, Micki	1978
Kolb, Claudia	1975
+ Lackie, Ethel	1969
+ Landon, Alice-Lord	1993
Linehan, Kim	1997
+ Madison, Helene	1966
Mann, Shelly	1966
McCormick, Kelly	1999
McGrath, Margo	1989
McKim, Josephine	1991
Meagher, Mary T.	1993
+ Meany, Helen	1971
Merlino, Maxine	1999
Meyer, Debbie	1977
Mitchell, Michele	1995
Moe, Karen	1992

Morris, Pam 1965
Neilson, Sandra 1986
Neyer, Megan 1997
+ Norelius, Martha 1967
Olsen, Zoe-Ann 1989
O'Rourke, Heidi 1980
+ Osipowich, Albina 1986
Pedersen, Susan 1995
Pinkston, Betty Becker 1967
Pope, Paula Jean Meyers 1979
Potter, Cynthia 1987
+ Poynton, Dorothy 1968
Rawls, Katherine 1965

+ Armbruster, Dave. 1966
+ Bachrach, Bill. 1966
Billingsley, Hobie. 1983
+ Brandsten, Ernst. 1966
+ Brauninger, Stan 1972
Bussard, Ray 1999
+ Cady, Fred 1969
+ Center, George (Dad). 1991
Chavoor, Sherman 1977
+ Cody, Jack 1970
Counsilman, Dr. James. 1976
+ Curtis, Katherine 1979
Daland, Peter. 1977
+ Daughters, Ray 1971
Emery, Gail 2000

Redmond, Carol 1989
Riggin, Aileen 1967
Ross, Anne 1984
Rothammer, Keena 1991
Ruiz-Conforto, Tracie. 1993
Ruuska, Sylvia 1976
Schuler, Carolyn 1989
Seller, Peg. 1988
+ Smith, Caroline 1988
Steinseifer, Carrie 1999
Stouder, Sharon. 1972
+ Toner, Vee. 1995
+ Vilen, Kay. 1978

U.S. Coaches

Gambril, Don. 1983
Gambril, Don. 1983
Haines, George. 1977
Handley, L. de B. 1967
Hannula, Dick 1987
Kimball, Dick 1985
+ Kiphuth, Bob 1965
Mann, Matt II 1965
+ McCormick, Glen 1995
Moriarty, Phil 1980
Mowerson, Robert. 1986
Muir, Bob 1989
+ Neuschaufer, Al. 1967
Nitzkowski, Monte 1991
O'Brien, Ron 1988

Von Saltza, Chris. 1966
Oho Wahle 1996
+ Wainwright, Helen 1972
+ Watson, Lillian (Pokey) 1984
Wayte, Mary 2000
Wehselau, Mariechen. 1989
Welshons, Kim 1988
Wichman, Sharon 1991
Williams, Esther. 1966
+ Woodbridge, Margaret 1989
Wyland, Wendy 2001

+ Papenguth, Richard. 1986
+ Peppe, Mike. 1966
+ Pinkston, Clarence. 1966
Quick, Richard. 2000
+ Robinson, Tom 1965
Sakamoto, Soichi 1966
+ Sava, Charlie. 1970
+ Schlueter, Walt. 1978
Schubert, Mark 1997
Smith, Dick 1979
Stager, Gus 1982
Thornton, Nort 1995
Tinkham, Stan 1989

TENNIS

International Tennis Hall of Fame

Originally the National Tennis Hall of Fame. Established in 1953 by James Van Alen and sanctioned by the U.S. Tennis Association in 1954. Renamed the International Tennis Hall of Fame in 1976. **Address:** 194 Bellevue Ave., Newport, RI 02840. **Telephone:** (401) 849-3990.

Eligibility: Nominated players must be five years removed from being a "significant factor" in competitive tennis. Voting done by members of the international tennis media.

Class of 2001 (2): PLAYERS— **Ivan Lendl** and **Mervyn Rose**.

Members are listed with year of induction; (+) indicates deceased members.

Men

+ Adee, George 1964
+ Alexander, Fred. 1961
+ Allison, Wilmer 1963
+ Alonso, Manuel 1977
Anderson, Malcolm. 2000
+ Ashe, Arthur. 1985
+ Austin, Bunny 1997
+ Behr, Karl 1969
Borg, Bjorn 1987
+ Borotra, Jean 1976
Bromwich, John 1984
+ Brookes, Norman 1977
+ Brugnon, Jacques 1976
+ Budge, Don 1964
+ Campbell, Oliver. 1955
+ Chace, Malcolm 1961
+ Clark, Clarence 1983
+ Clark, Joseph 1955
+ Clothier, William 1956
+ Cochet, Henri. 1976
Connors, Jimmy 1998
Cooper, Ashley 1991
+ Crawford, Jack 1979
David, Herman 1998
+ Doeg, John 1962
+ Doherty, Lawrence. 1980
+ Doherty, Reginald 1980
+ Drobny, Jaroslav 1983
+ Dwight, James 1955
Emerson, Roy 1982
+ Etchebaster, Pierre. 1978
Falkenburg, Bob 1974
Fraser, Neale 1984
+ Garland, Chuck. 1969

+ Gonzales, Pancho. 1968
+ Grant, Bryan (Bitsy). 1972
+ Griffin, Clarence 1970
+ Hackett, Harold 1961
Hewitt, Bob 1992
+ Hoad, Lew 1980
+ Hovey, Fred 1974
+ Hunt, Joe. 1966
+ Hunter, Frank 1961
+ Johnston, Bill. 1958
+ Jones, Perry 1970
Kelleher, Robert 2000
Kodes, Jan 1990
Kramer, Jack. 1968
+ Lacoste, Rene 1976
+ Larned, William 1956
Larsen, Art 1969
Laver, Rod 1981
Lendl, Ivan 2001
+ Lott, George 1964
Mako, Gene. 1973
McEnroe, John 1999
McGregor, Ken 1999
+ McKinley, Chuck 1986
+ McLoughlin, Maurice 1957
McMillan, Frew 1992
+ McNeill, Don 1965
Mulloy, Gardnar 1972
+ Murray, Lindley 1958
+ Myrick, Julian 1963
Nastase, Ilie. 1991
Newcombe, John. 1986
+ Nielsen, Arthur 1971
Olmedo, Alex 1987

+ Osuna, Rafael 1979
Parker, Frank 1966
+ Patterson, Gerald 1989
Patty, Budge 1977
+ Perry, Fred 1975
+ Pettitt, Tom. 1982
Pietrangeli, Nicola 1986
+ Quist, Adrian 1984
Ralston, Dennis 1987
+ Renshaw, Ernest. 1983
+ Renshaw, William 1983
+ Richards, Vincent. 1961
+ Riggs, Bobby 1967
Roche, Tony 1986
Rose, Mervyn 2001
Rosewall, Ken 1980
Santana, Manuel. 1984
Savitt, Dick 1976
Schroeder, Ted 1966
+ Sears, Richard 1955
Sedgman, Frank 1979
Segura, Pancho 1984
Seixas, Vic 1971
+ Shields, Frank 1964
+ Slocum, Henry 1955
Smith, Stan 1987
Stolle, Fred 1985
+ Talbert, Bill 1967
+ Tilden, Bill 1959
Trabert, Tony 1970
Van Ryn, John. 1963
Vilas, Guillermo 1991
+ Vines, Ellsworth 1962
+ von Cramm, Gottfried. 1977

+ Ward, Holcombe 1956
+ Washburn, Watson 1965
+ Whitman, Malcolm 1955

+ Wilding, Anthony 1978
+ Williams, Richard 2nd 1957
   Wood, Sidney 1964

+ Wrenn, Robert 1955
+ Wright, Beals 1956

Women

+ Atkinson, Juliette 1974
   Austin, Tracy 1992
+ Barger-Wallach, Maud 1958
   Betz Addie, Pauline. 1965
+ Bjurstedt Mallory, Molla 1958
   Bowrey, Lesley Turner 1997
   Brough Clapp, Louise 1967
+ Browne, Mary 1957
   Bueno, Maria 1978
+ Cahill, Mabel. 1976
   Casals, Rosie 1996
+ Connolly Brinker, Maureen . .1968
+ Dod, Charlotte (Lottie) 1983
+ Douglass Chambers, Dorothy. .1981
   Evert, Chris 1995
   Fry Irvin, Shirley 1970

   Gibson, Althea 1971
   Goolagong Cawley, Evonne . .1988
+ Hansell, Dorea 1965
   Hard, Darlene 1973
   Hart, Doris 1969
   Haydon Jones, Ann 1985
   Heldman, Gladys 1979
+ Hotchkiss Wightman, Hazel . . .1957
+ Jacobs, Helen Hull 1962
   King, Billie Jean 1987
+ Lenglen, Suzanne 1978
   Mandlikova, Hana 1994
+ Marble, Alice 1964
+ McKane Godfree, Kitty 1978
+ Moore, Elisabeth 1971
   Mortimer Barrett, Angela 1993

   Navratilova, Martina 2000
+ Nuthall Shoemaker, Betty 1977
   Osborne duPont, Margaret. . . .1967
+ Palfrey Danzig, Sarah 1963
+ Roosevelt, Ellen 1975
+ Round Little, Dorothy 1986
+ Ryan, Elizabeth 1972
+ Sears, Eleanora 1968
   Smith Court, Margaret 1979
+ Sutton Bundy, May 1956
+ Townsend Toulmin, Bertha 1974
   Wade, Virginia 1989
+ Wagner, Marie 1969
+ Wills Moody Roark, Helen 1959

Contributors

+ Baker, Lawrence Sr 1975
+ Chatrier, Philippe. 1992
   Collins, Bud 1994
   Cullman, Joseph F. 3rd 1990
+ Danzig, Allison 1968
+ Davis, Dwight. 1956
+ Gray, David 1985

+ Gustaf, V (King of Sweden) . .1980
+ Hester, W.E. (Slew) 1981
.+ Hopman, Harry 1978
   Hunt, Lamar 1993
+ Laney, Al 1979
   Martin, Alastair 1973
   Martin, William M. 1982

   Maskell, Dan 1996
+ Outerbridge, Mary 1981
+ Pell, Theodore 1966
+ Tingay, Lance 1982
+ Tinling, Ted 1986
+ Van Alen, James 1965
+ Wingfield, Walter Clopton. . .1997

TRACK & FIELD

National Track & Field Hall of Fame

Established in 1974 by the The Athletics Congress (now USA Track & Field). Originally located in Charleston, WV, the Hall moved to Indianapolis in 1983 and reopened at the Hoosier Dome (now RCA Dome) in 1986. **Address:** One RCA Dome, Indianapolis, IN 46225. **Telephone:** (317) 261-0500.

   Eligibility: Nominated athletes must be retired three years and coaches must have coached at least 20 years if retired or 35 years if still coaching. Voting done by 800-member panel made up of Hall of Fame and USA Track & Field officials, Hall of Fame members, current U.S. champions and members of the Track & Field Writers of America.

   Class of 2000 (4): MEN—**Arnie Robinson** (long jump); WOMEN—**Chandra Cheeseborough** (sprints) and **Maren Seidler** (shot put); COACH—**Bill Dellinger**.

   Members are listed with year of induction; (+) indicates deceased members.

Men

+ Albritton, Dave 1980
   Ashenfelter, Horace 1975
   Banks, Willie 2000
+ Bausch, James 1979
   Beamon, Bob 1977
   Beatty, Jim. 1990
   Bell, Greg 1988
+ Boeckmann, Dee 1976
   Boston, Ralph 1974
   Bragg, Don 1996
+ Calhoun, Lee 1974
   Campbell, Milt. 1989
   Carr, Henry 1997
+ Clark, Ellery 1991
   Connolly, Harold 1984
   Courtney, Tom 1978
+ Cunningham, Glenn 1974
+ Curtis, William. 1979
   Davenport, Willie 1982
   Davis, Glenn 1974
   Davis, Harold 1974
   Dillard, Harrison 1974
   Dumas, Charley 1990
+ Ellis, Larry 2000
   Evans, Lee. 1983
+ Ewell, Barney 1986
+ Ewry, Ray 1974
+ Flanagan, John 1975
   Fosbury, Dick 1981
   Foster, Greg 1998
+ Gordien, Fortune 1979
   Greene, Charlie. 1992

+ Hahn, Archie 1983
+ Hardin, Glenn 1978
   Hayes, Bob 1976
   Held, Bud 1987
   Hines, Jim 1979
+ Houser, Bud 1979
+ Hubbard, DeHart 1979
   Jenkins, Charlie 1992
   Jenner, Bruce 1980
+ Johnson, Cornelius 1994
   Johnson, Rafer 1974
   Jones, Hayes 1976
   Kelley, John 1980
   Kiviat, Abel. 1985
+ Kraenzlein, Alvin 1974
   Laird, Ron 1986
+ Lash, Don 1995
+ Laskau, Henry 1997
   Liquori, Marty. 1995
   Long, Dr. Dallas 1996
   Mathias, Bob 1974
   Matson, Randy. 1984
   McCluskey, Joe 1996
+ Meadows, Earle 1996
+ Meredith, Ted 1982
+ Metcalfe, Ralph 1975
+ Milburn, Rod 1993
   Mills, Billy 1976
   Moore, Charles 2000
   Moore, Tom 1988
   Morrow, Bobby 1975
+ Mortensen, Jess 1992

   Moses, Edwin 1994
+ Myers, Lawrence 1974
   Nehemiah, Renaldo 1997
   O'Brien, Parry 1974
   Oerter, Al 1974
+ Osborn, Harold 1974
+ Owens, Jesse 1974
+ Paddock, Charley 1976
   Patton, Mel 1985
+ Peacock, Eulace 1987
+ Prefontaine, Steve 1976
+ Ray, Joie 1976
+ Rice, Greg 1977
   Richards, Bob. 1975
   Rodgers, Bill 2000
   Robinson, Arnie 2001
+ Rose, Ralph 1976
   Ryun, Jim. 1980
+ Scholz, Jackson 1977
   Schul, Bob 1991
   Seagren, Bob 1986
+ Sheppard, Mel 1976
+ Sheridan, Martin 1988
   Shorter, Frank. 1989
   Silvester, Jay 1998
   Sime, Dave. 1981
+ Simpson, Robert. 1974
   Smith, Tommie 1978
+ Stanfield, Andy 1977
   Steers, Les 1974
   Stones, Dwight. 1998
+ Tewksbury, Dr. Walter 1996

Thomas, John 1985	+ Towns, Forrest (Spec) 1976	Wohlhuter, Rick 1990
+ Thomson, Earl 1977	Warmerdam, Cornelius 1974	Woodruff, John 1978
+ Thorpe, Jim 1975	Whitfield, Mal 1974	Wottle, Dave 1982
+ Tolan, Eddie 1982	Wilkins, Mac 1993	+ Wykoff, Frank 1977
Toomey, Bill 1975	+ Williams, Archie 1992	Young, George 1981

Women

Ashford, Evelyn 1997	+ Hall Adams, Evelyne 1988	+ Rudolph, Wilma 1974
Brisco, Valerie 1995	Heritage, Doris Brown 1990	+ Schmidt, Kate 1994
Cheeseborough, Chandra . . .2001	+ Jackson, Nell 1989	Seidler, Maren 2001
Coachman, Alice 1975	Larrieu Smith, Francie 1998	+ Shiley Newhouse, Jean 1993
+ Copeland, Lillian 1994	Manning, Madeline 1984	+ Stephens, Helen 1975
Didrikson, Babe 1974	McDaniel, Mildred 1983	Tyus, Wyomia 1980
+ Faggs, Mae 1976	McGuire, Edith 1979	+ Walsh, Stella 1975
Ferrell, Barbara 1988	Ritter, Louise 1995	Watson, Martha 1987
+ Griffith Joyner, Florence 1995	+ Robinson, Betty 1977	White, Willye 1981

Coaches

+ Abbott, Cleve 1996	+ Giegengack, Bob 1978	+ Moakley, Jack 1988
+ Baskin, Weems 1982	+ Hamilton, Brutus 1974	+ Murphy, Michael 1974
+ Beard, Percy 1981	+ Haydon, Ted 1975	Rosen, Mel 1995
Bell, Sam 1992	+ Hayes, Billy 1976	+ Snyder, Larry 1978
+ Botts, Tom 1983	+ Haylett, Ward 1979	Temple, Ed 1989
+ Bowerman, Bill 1981	+ Higgins, Ralph 1982	+ Templeton, Dink 1976
Bush, Jim 1987	+ Hillman, Harry 1976	Walker, LeRoy 1983
+ Cromwell, Dean 1974	+ Hurt, Edward 1975	+ Wilt, Fred 1981
Dellinger, Bill 2001	+ Hutsell, Wilbur 1977	+ Winter, Bud 1985
+ Doherty, Ken 1976	+ Jones, Thomas 1977	+ Wolfe, Vern 1996
+ Easton, Bill 1975	Jordan, Payton 1982	Wright, Stan. 1993
+ Elliott, Jumbo 1981	+ Littlefield, Clyde 1981	+ Yancy, Joseph 1984

Contributors

+ Abramson, Jesse 1981	+ Ferris, Dan 1974	Nelson, Cordner 1988
Andersen, Roxanne 1991	+ Griffith, John 1979	+ Sullivan, James 1977
+ Bakjian, Andy 1986	+ Lebow, Fred 1994	
+ Brundage, Avery 1974	+ Nelson, Bert 1991	

WOMEN

International Women's Sports Hall of Fame

Established in 1980 by the Women's Sports Foundation. **Address:** Women's Sports Foundation, Eisenhower Park, East Meadow, NY 11554. **Telephone:** (516) 542-4700.

Eligibility: Nominees' achievements and commitment to the development of women's sports must be internationally recognized. Athletes are elected in two categories—Pioneer (before 1960) and Contemporary (since 1960). Members are divided below by sport for the sake of easy reference; (*) indicates member inducted in Pioneer category. Coaching nominees must have coached at least 10 years.

Class of 2001 (3): CONTEMPORARY—**Tracie Ruiz-Conforto** (swimming); PIONEER—**Marjorie Jackson Nelson** (track & field); COACH—**Chris Carver**.

Note: Charlotte Dod is inducted for tennis, as well as archery and golf; **Marie Marvingt** is inducted for aviation, as well as mountaineering; **Eleanora Sears** is inducted for golf, as well as polo and squash.

Members are listed with year of induction; (+) indicates deceased members.

Alpine Skiing
Cranz, Christl* 1991	
+ Golden Brosnihan, Diana 1997	
Lawrence, Andrea Mead* . . .1983	
Moser-Pröll, Annemarie 1982	

Auto Racing
Guthrie, Janet 1980

Aviation
+ Coleman, Bessie* 1992	
+ Earhart, Amelia* 1980	
+ Marvingt, Marie* 1987	

Badminton
Hashman, Judy Devlin* 1995

Baseball
Stone, Toni* 1993

Basketball
Meyers, Ann 1985	
Miller, Cheryl 1991	

Bowling
Ladewig, Marion* 1984

Cycling
Carpenter Phinney, Connie . .1990

Diving
King, Micki 1983	
McCormick, Pat* 1984	
Riggin, Aileen* 1988	

Equestrian
Hartel, Lis 1994

Fencing
Schacherer-Elek, Ilona* 1989

Figure Skating
Albright, Tenley* 1983	
+ Blanchard, Theresa Weld* . .1989	
Fleming, Peggy 1981	
Heiss Jenkins, Carol* 1992	
+ Henie, Sonja* 1982	
Protopopov, Ludmila 1992	
Rodnina, Irena 1988	
Scott-King, Barbara Ann* . . .1997	

Golf
Berg, Patty* 1980	
Carner, JoAnne 1987	
Haynie, Sandra 1999	
Hicks, Betty* 1995	
Jameson, Betty* 1999	
Mann, Carol 1982	
Rawls, Betsy* 1986	
+ Sears, Eleanora 1984	
Suggs, Louise* 1987	
+ Vare, Glenna Collett* 1981	
Whitworth, Kathy 1984	
Wright, Mickey 1981	

Golf/Track & Field
+ Zaharias, Babe Didrikson* . .1980

Gymnastics
Caslavska, Vera 1991	
Comaneci, Nadia 1990	
Korbut, Olga 1982	
Latynina, Larysa* 1985	
Retton, Mary Lou 1993	
Tourischeva, Lyudmila 1987	

Orienteering
Kringstad, Annichen 1995

Shooting
Murdock, Margaret 1988

Softball
Joyce, Joan 1989

de Varona, Donna.........1983
Ederle, Gertrude*.........1980
Fraser, Dawn.............1985
Holm, Eleanor*...........1980
Meagher, Mary T..........1993
Meyer-Reyes, Debbie......1987
Ruiz-Confronto, Tracie......2001

Tennis

+ Connolly, Maureen*......1987
+ Dod, Charlotte (Lottie)*......1986
  Evert, Chris.............1981
  Gibson, Althea*.........1980
  Goolagong Cawley, Evonne .1989
+ Hotchkiss Wightman, Hazel* .1986
  King, Billie Jean.........1980
+ Lenglen, Suzanne*........1984
  Navratilova, Martina.......1984
  Osbourne du Pont, Margaret*.1998
+ Sears, Eleanora*..........1984
  Smith Court, Margaret......1986

Track & Field

Ashford, Evelyn...........1997
Blankers-Koen, Fanny*.....1982
Cheng, Chi...............1994
Coachman Davis, Alice*....1991
+ Faggs Star, Aeriwentha Mae*.1996
+ Griffith Joyner, Florence ...1998
  Manning Mims, Madeline ...1987
  Nelson, Marjorie Jackson* .2001
+ Rudolph, Wilma...........1980
  Samuelson, Joan Benoit 1999
+ Stephens, Helen*.........1983
  Strickland de la Hunty, Shirley* .1998
  Szewinska, Irena...........1992
  Tyus, Wyomia.............1981
  Waitz, Grete.............1995
  White, Willye.............1988

Volleyball

+ Hyman, Flo...............1986

Water Skiing

McGuire, Willa Worthington*...1990

Coaches

+ Applebee, Constance.......1991
  Backus, Sharron...........1993
  Carver, Chris.............2001
  Conradt, Judy.............1995
  Emery, Gail..............1997
  Green, Tina Sloan.........1999
  Grossfeld, Muriel..........1991
  Holum, Diana............1996
  Jacket, Barbara..........1995
+ Jackson, Nell.............1990
  Kanakogi, Rusty..........1994
  Summitt, Pat Head........1990
  Van Derveer, Tara.........1998
+ Wade, Margaret..........1992

RETIRED NUMBERS

Major League Baseball

The New York Yankees have retired the most uniform numbers (14) in the major leagues; followed by the Brooklyn/Los Angeles Dodgers (10), the St. Louis Cardinals (9), the Chicago White Sox and the Pittsburgh Pirates (8) and the New York/San Francisco Giants (7). **Jackie Robinson** had his #42 retired by Major League Baseball in 1997. Players who were already wearing the number were allowed to continue to do so. Los Angeles had already retired Robinson's number so he's only listed with the Dodgers below. **Nolan Ryan** has had his number retired by three teams—#34 by Texas and Houston and #30 by California (now Anaheim). Five players and a manager have had their numbers retired by two teams: **Hank Aaron**—#44 by the Boston/Milwaukee/Atlanta Braves and the Milwaukee Brewers; **Rod Carew**—#29 by Minnesota and California (now Anaheim); **Rollie Fingers**—#34 by Milwaukee and Oakland; **Carlton Fisk**—#27 by Boston and #72 by the Chicago White Sox; **Frank Robinson**—#20 by Cincinnati and Baltimore; **Casey Stengel**—#37 by the New York Yankees and New York Mets.

Numbers retired in 2001 (3): CLEVELAND—#455 for the number of **consecutive sellouts** that the Indians had from June 12, 1995 to Apr. 2, 2001; PHILADELPHIA—#14 worn by pitcher **Jim Bunning** (1964-67, 1970-71 with Phillies); SAN DIEGO—#31 worn by right fielder **Dave Winfield** (1973-80 with Padres).

American League

Two AL teams—the Seattle Mariners and the Toronto Blue Jays—have not retired any numbers. The Blue Jays have a "level of excellence" which includes Dave Steib (#11), George Bell (#37), and Cito Gaston (#43). All numbers have been used in recent years, however.

Anaheim Angels

11 Jim Fregosi
26 Gene Autry
29 Rod Carew
30 Nolan Ryan
50 Jimmie Reese

Baltimore Orioles

4 Earl Weaver
5 Brooks Robinson
20 Frank Robinson
22 Jim Palmer
33 Eddie Murray

Boston Red Sox

1 Bobby Doerr
4 Joe Cronin
8 Carl Yastrzemski
9 Ted Williams
27 Carlton Fisk

Chicago White Sox

2 Nellie Fox
3 Harold Baines
4 Luke Appling
9 Minnie Minoso
11 Luis Aparicio
16 Ted Lyons
19 Billy Pierce
72 Carlton Fisk

Cleveland Indians

3 Earl Averill
5 Lou Boudreau
14 Larry Doby
18 Mel Harder
19 Bob Feller
21 Bob Lemon
455 Fans (# of consecutive sellouts)

Detroit Tigers

2 Charlie Gehringer
5 Hank Greenberg
6 Al Kaline
16 Hal Newhouser
23 Willie Horton

Kansas City Royals

5 George Brett
10 Dick Howser
20 Frank White

Minnesota Twins

3 Harmon Killebrew
6 Tony Oliva
14 Kent Hrbek
29 Rod Carew
34 Kirby Puckett

Oakland Athletics

27 Catfish Hunter
34 Rollie Fingers

New York Yankees

1 Billy Martin
3 Babe Ruth
4 Lou Gehrig
5 Joe DiMaggio
7 Mickey Mantle
8 Yogi Berra & Bill Dickey
9 Roger Maris
10 Phil Rizzuto
15 Thurman Munson
16 Whitey Ford
23 Don Mattingly
32 Elston Howard
37 Casey Stengel
44 Reggie Jackson

Tampa Bay Devil Rays

12 Wade Boggs

Texas Rangers

34 Nolan Ryan

Retired Numbers (Cont.)
National League

Two NL teams—the Arizona Diamondbacks and Colorado Rockies—have not retired any numbers. San Francisco has honored former NY Giants Christy Mathewson and John McGraw even though they played before numbers were worn. As did the Philadelphia Phillies for Grover Cleveland Alexander and Chuck Klein.

Atlanta Braves
3 Dale Murphy
21 Warren Spahn
35 Phil Niekro
41 Eddie Mathews
44 Hank Aaron

Chicago Cubs
14 Ernie Banks
26 Billy Williams

Cincinnati Reds
1 Fred Hutchinson
5 Johnny Bench
8 Joe Morgan
18 Ted Kluszewski
20 Frank Robinson
24 Tony Perez

Florida Marlins
5 Carl Barger

Houston Astros
25 Jose Cruz
32 Jim Umbricht
33 Mike Scott
34 Nolan Ryan
40 Don Wilson

Los Angeles Dodgers
1 Pee Wee Reese
2 Tommy Lasorda
4 Duke Snider
19 Jim Gilliam
20 Don Sutton
24 Walter Alston
32 Sandy Koufax
39 Roy Campanella
42 Jackie Robinson
53 Don Drysdale

Milwaukee Brewers
4 Paul Molitor
19 Robin Yount
34 Rollie Fingers
44 Hank Aaron

Montreal Expos
8 Gary Carter
10 Rusty Staub
& Andre Dawson

New York Mets
14 Gil Hodges
37 Casey Stengel
41 Tom Seaver

Philadelphia Phillies
1 Richie Ashburn
14 Jim Bunning
20 Mike Schmidt
32 Steve Carlton
36 Robin Roberts

Pittsburgh Pirates
1 Billy Meyer
4 Ralph Kiner
8 Willie Stargell
9 Bill Mazeroski
20 Pie Traynor
21 Roberto Clemente
33 Honus Wagner
40 Danny Murtaugh

St. Louis Cardinals
1 Ozzie Smith
2 Red Schoendienst
6 Stan Musial
9 Enos Slaughter
14 Ken Boyer
17 Dizzy Dean
20 Lou Brock
45 Bob Gibson
85 August (Gussie) Busch

San Diego Padres
6 Steve Garvey
31 Dave Winfield
35 Randy Jones

San Francisco Giants
3 Bill Terry
4 Mel Ott
11 Carl Hubbell
24 Willie Mays
27 Juan Marichal
30 Orlando Cepeda
44 Willie McCovey

National Basketball Association

Boston has retired the most numbers (20) in the NBA, followed by Portland (9); Detroit, Los Angeles Lakers, Milwaukee, New York Knicks, Syracuse Nats/Philadelphia 76ers, Phoenix Suns and the KC/Sacramento Kings have (7); Cleveland, New Jersey, the Rochester/Cincinnati Royals and have (6). **Wilt Chamberlain** is the only player to have his number retired by three teams: #13 by the LA Lakers, Golden State and Philadelphia; Six players have had their numbers retired by two teams: **Kareem Abdul-Jabbar**—#33 by LA Lakers and Milwaukee; **Clyde Drexler**—#22 by Houston and Portland; **Julius Erving**—#6 by Philadelphia and #32 by New Jersey; **Bob Lanier**—#16 by Detroit and Milwaukee; **Oscar Robertson**—#1 by Milwaukee and #14 by Sacramento; **Nate Thurmond**—#42 by Cleveland and Golden State.

Numbers retired in 2000-01 (7): ATLANTA—#21 worn by forward **Dominique Wilkins** (1982-93 with Hawks); INDIANA—#529 won as coach **Bob "Slick" Leonard** (1968-80 with Pacers); ORLANDO—#6 for **the fans**, or the "Sixth Man"; PHILADELPHIA—#34 worn by forward **Charles Barkley** (1984-92 with 76ers); PHOENIX—#7 worn by guard **Kevin Johnson** (1987-2000 with Suns) and #24 worn by forward **Tom Chambers** (1988-92 with Suns); PORTLAND—#22 worn by guard **Clyde Drexler** (1983-95 with Trail Blazers).

Eastern Conference

Two Eastern teams—the Miami Heat and Toronto Raptors—have not retired any numbers.

Boston Celtics
1 Walter A. Brown
2 Red Auerbach
3 Dennis Johnson
6 Bill Russell
10 Jo Jo White
14 Bob Cousy
15 Tom Heinsohn
16 Tom (Satch) Sanders
17 John Havlicek
18 Dave Cowens
19 Don Nelson
21 Bill Sharman
22 Ed Macauley
23 Frank Ramsey
24 Sam Jones
25 K.C. Jones
32 Kevin McHale
33 Larry Bird
35 Reggie Lewis
00 Robert Parish
Loscy Jim Loscutoff
Radio mic Johnny Most

Atlanta Hawks
9 Bob Pettit
21 Dominique Wilkins
23 Lou Hudson

Charlotte Hornets
13 Bobby Phills

Chicago Bulls
4 Jerry Sloan
10 Bob Love
23 Michael Jordan

Cleveland Cavaliers
7 Bingo Smith
22 Larry Nance
25 Mark Price
34 Austin Carr
42 Nate Thurmond
43 Brad Daugherty

Detroit Pistons
2 Chuck Daly
4 Joe Dumars
11 Isiah Thomas
15 Vinnie Johnson
16 Bob Lanier
21 Dave Bing
40 Bill Laimbeer

Indiana Pacers
30 George McGinnis
34 Mel Daniels
35 Roger Brown
529 Bob "Slick" Leonard

Milwaukee Bucks
1 Oscar Robertson
2 Junior Bridgeman
14 Sidney Moncrief
14 Jon McGlocklin
16 Bob Lanier
32 Brian Winters
33 Kareem Abdul-Jabbar

New York Knicks
10 Walt Frazier
12 Dick Barnett
15 Dick McGuire
& Earl Monroe
19 Willis Reed
22 Dave DeBusschere
24 Bill Bradley
613 Red Holzman

New Jersey Nets
3 Drazen Petrovic
4 Wendell Ladner
23 John Williamson
25 Bill Melchionni
32 Julius Erving
52 Buck Williams

Orlando Magic
6 Fans ("Sixth Man")

Philadelphia 76ers
6 Julius Erving
10 Maurice Cheeks
13 Wilt Chamberlain
15 Hal Greer
24 Bobby Jones
32 Billy Cunningham
34 Charles Barkley
P.A. mic Dave Zinkoff

Washington Wizards
11 Elvin Hayes
25 Gus Johnson
41 Wes Unseld

Western Conference

Three Western teams—the Los Angeles Clippers, Memphis Grizzlies and Minnesota Timberwolves—have not retired any numbers.

Dallas Mavericks
15 Brad Davis
22 Rolando Blackman

Denver Nuggets
2 Alex English
33 David Thompson
40 Byron Beck
44 Dan Issel

Golden St. Warriors
13 Wilt Chamberlain
14 Tom Meschery
16 Al Attles
24 Rick Barry
42 Nate Thurmond

Houston Rockets
22 Clyde Drexler
23 Calvin Murphy
24 Moses Malone
45 Rudy Tomjanovich

Los Angeles Lakers
13 Wilt Chamberlain
22 Elgin Baylor
25 Gail Goodrich
32 Magic Johnson
33 Kareem Abdul-Jabbar
42 James Worthy
44 Jerry West

Phoenix Suns
5 Dick Van Arsdale
6 Walter Davis
7 Kevin Johnson
24 Tom Chambers
33 Alvan Adams
42 Connie Hawkins
44 Paul Westphal

Portland Trail Blazers
1 Larry Weinberg
13 Dave Twardzik
15 Larry Steele
20 Maurice Lucas
22 Clyde Drexler
32 Bill Walton
36 Lloyd Neal
45 Geoff Petrie
77 Jack Ramsay

Sacramento Kings
1 Nate Archibald
6 Fans ("Sixth Man")
11 Bob Davies
12 Maurice Stokes
14 Oscar Robertson
27 Jack Twyman
44 Sam Lacey

San Antonio Spurs
13 James Silas
44 George Gervin
00 Johnny Moore

Seattle SuperSonics
10 Nate McMillan
19 Lenny Wilkens
32 Fred Brown
43 Jack Sikma
Radio mic Bob Blackburn

Utah Jazz
1 Frank Layden
7 Pete Maravich
35 Darrell Griffith
53 Mark Eaton

National Football League

The Chicago Bears have retired the most uniform numbers (13) in the NFL; followed by the New York Giants (11); the Dallas Texans/Kansas City Chiefs and San Francisco (8); the Baltimore-Indianapolis Colts (7); Detroit, Boston-New England Patriots and Philadelphia (6); Cleveland (5). No player has ever had his number retired by more than one NFL team. The NFL has recently discouraged (though not eliminated) the practice of retiring numbers. As a result, the Green Bay Packers retired the jersey (but not the #92) of defensive end Reggie White in 1999. Nonetheless, Packers GM Ron Wolf announced that there are no plans to reissue the number.

Numbers retired in 2000-01 (8): ATLANTA—#31 worn by running back **William Andrews** (1979-83, 86 with Falcons), #57 worn by center **Jeff Van Note** (1969-86 with Falcons) and #60 worn by linebacker **Tommy Nobis** (1966-76 with Falcons); MINNESOTA—#53 worn by center **Mick Tingelhoff** (1962-78 with Vikings) and #77 worn by offensive tackle **Korey Stringer** (1995-2000 with Vikings); NY GIANTS—#16 worn by half back/wide receiver **Frank Gifford** (1952-64 with Giants); PITTSBURGH—#70 worn by guard **Ernie Stautner** (1950-63 with Steelers); ST. LOUIS—#85 worn by defensive end **Jack Youngblood** (1971-84 with Rams).

AFC

Four AFC teams—the Baltimore Ravens, Buffalo Bills, Oakland Raiders and Jacksonville Jaguars—have not retired any numbers.

Cincinnati Bengals
54 Bob Johnson

Cleveland Browns
14 Otto Graham
32 Jim Brown
45 Ernie Davis
46 Don Fleming
76 Lou Groza

Denver Broncos
7 John Elway
18 Frank Tripucka
44 Floyd Little

Indianapolis Colts
19 Johnny Unitas
22 Buddy Young
24 Lenny Moore
70 Art Donovan
77 Jim Parker
82 Raymond Berry
89 Gino Marchetti

Kansas City Chiefs
3 Jan Stenerud
16 Len Dawson
28 Abner Haynes
33 Stone Johnson
36 Mack Lee Hill
63 Willie Lanier
78 Bobby Bell
86 Buck Buchanan

Miami Dolphins
12 Bob Griese
13 Dan Marino

New England Patriots
20 Gino Cappelletti
40 Mike Haynes
56 Andre Tippett
57 Steve Nelson
73 John Hannah
79 Jim Hunt
89 Bob Dee

New York Jets
12 Joe Namath
13 Don Maynard

Pittsburgh Steelers
70 Ernie Stautner

San Diego Chargers
14 Dan Fouts

Seattle Seahawks
12 Fans ("12th Man")
80 Steve Largent

Tennessee Titans
34 Earl Campbell
43 Jim Norton
63 Mike Munchak
65 Elvin Bethea

Retired Numbers (Cont.)

NFC

Dallas and the Carolina Panthers are the only NFC teams that haven't officially retired any numbers. The Falcons haven't issued uniform #10 (Steve Bartowski) and #78 (Mike Kenn) since those players retired. The Cowboys have a "Ring of Honor" at Texas Stadium that includes 10 players and one coach—Tony Dorsett, Bob Hayes, Chuck Howley, Lee Roy Jordan, Tom Landry, Bob Lilly, Don Meredith, Don Perkins, Mel Renfro, Roger Staubach and Randy White.

Arizona Cardinals
- 8 Larry Wilson
- 77 Stan Mauldin
- 88 J.V. Cain
- 99 Marshall Goldberg

Atlanta Falcons
- 31 William Andrews
- 57 Jeff Van Note
- 60 Tommy Nobis

Chicago Bears
- 3 Bronko Nagurski
- 5 George McAfee
- 7 George Halas
- 28 Willie Galimore
- 34 Walter Payton
- 40 Gale Sayers
- 41 Brian Piccolo
- 42 Sid Luckman
- 51 Dick Butkus
- 56 Bill Hewitt
- 61 Bill George
- 66 Bulldog Turner
- 77 Red Grange

Detroit Lions
- 7 Dutch Clark
- 22 Bobby Layne
- 37 Doak Walker
- 56 Joe Schmidt
- 85 Chuck Hughes
- 88 Charlie Sanders

Green Bay Packers
- 3 Tony Canadeo
- 14 Don Hutson
- 15 Bart Starr
- 66 Ray Nitschke

Minnesota Vikings
- 10 Fran Tarkenton
- 53 Mick Tingelhoff
- 70 Jim Marshall
- 77 Korey Stringer
- 88 Alan Page

New Orleans Saints
- 31 Jim Taylor
- 81 Doug Atkins

New York Giants
- 1 Ray Flaherty
- 4 Tuffy Leemans
- 7 Mel Hein
- 11 Phil Simms
- 14 Y.A. Tittle
- 16 Frank Gifford
- 32 Al Blozis
- 40 Joe Morrison
- 42 Charlie Conerly
- 50 Ken Strong
- 56 Lawrence Taylor

Philadelphia Eagles
- 15 Steve Van Buren
- 40 Tom Brookshier
- 44 Pete Retzlaff
- 60 Chuck Bednarik
- 70 Al Wistert
- 99 Jerome Brown

St. Louis Rams
- 7 Bob Waterfield
- 29 Eric Dickerson
- 74 Merlin Olsen
- 78 Jackie Slater
- 85 Jack Youngblood

San Francisco 49ers
- 12 John Brodie
- 16 Joe Montana
- 34 Joe Perry
- 37 Jimmy Johnson
- 39 Hugh McElhenny
- 70 Charlie Krueger
- 73 Leo Nomellini
- 87 Dwight Clark

Tampa Bay Bucs
- 63 Lee Roy Selmon

Wash. Redskins
- 33 Sammy Baugh

National Hockey League

The Boston Bruins have retired the most uniform numbers (8) in the NHL; followed by Montreal (7); Detroit and N.Y. Islanders (6); Chicago (5); Buffalo, St. Louis and Philadelphia (4). Following his retirement in 1999, the NHL announced that the league would retire **Wayne Gretzky**'s #99. Three players have had their numbers retired by two teams: **Gordie Howe**—#9 by Detroit and Hartford; **Bobby Hull**—#9 by Chicago and Winnipeg (now Phoenix); and **Ray Bourque**—#77 by Boston and Colorado.

Numbers retired in 2001 (4): BOSTON—#77 worn by **Ray Bourque** (1979-2000 with Bruins); COLORADO—#77 worn by **Ray Bourque** (2000-01 with Avalanche); EDMONTON—#17 worn by **Jari Kurri** (1980-90 with Oilers); N.Y. ISLANDERS—#19 worn by **Bryan Trottier** (1975-90 with Islanders).

Eastern Conference

Five Eastern teams—the Atlanta Thrashers, Carolina Hurricanes, Florida Panthers, New Jersey Devils and Tampa Bay Lightning—have not retired any numbers. The Hartford Whalers had retired three numbers: #2 Rick Ley, #9 Gordie Howe and #19 John McKenzie.

Boston Bruins
- 2 Eddie Shore
- 3 Lionel Hitchman
- 4 Bobby Orr
- 5 Dit Clapper
- 7 Phil Esposito
- 9 John Bucyk
- 15 Milt Schmidt
- 77 Ray Bourque

Buffalo Sabres
- 2 Tim Horton
- 7 Rick Martin
- 11 Gilbert Perreault
- 14 Rene Robert

Montreal Canadiens
- 1 Jacques Plante
- 2 Doug Harvey
- 4 Jean Beliveau
- 7 Howie Morenz
- 9 Maurice Richard
- 10 Guy Lafleur
- 16 Henri Richard

New York Islanders
- 5 Denis Potvin
- 9 Clark Gilles
- 19 Bryan Trottier
- 22 Mike Bossy
- 23 Bob Nystrom
- 31 Billy Smith

New York Rangers
- 1 Eddie Giacomin
- 7 Rod Gilbert

Ottawa Senators
- 8 Frank Finnigan

Philadelphia Flyers
- 1 Bernie Parent
- 4 Barry Ashbee
- 7 Bill Barber
- 16 Bobby Clarke

Pittsburgh Penguins
- 21 Michel Briere
- 66 Mario Lemieux

Toronto Maple Leafs
- 5 Bill Barilko
- 6 Ace Bailey

Washington Capitals
- 5 Rod Langway
- 7 Yvon Labre
- 32 Dale Hunter

Western Conference

Five western teams—the Columbus Blue Jackets, Mighty Ducks of Anaheim, Minnesota Wild, Nashville Predators and San Jose Sharks —have not retired any numbers. Note, the Quebec Nordiques retired the numbers of J.C. Tremblay (3), Marc Tardiff (8) and Michel Goulet (16) but these numbers have been worn since the team moved to Colorado.

Calgary Flames
9 Lanny McDonald

Chicago Blackhawks
1 Glenn Hall
9 Bobby Hull
18 Denis Savard
21 Stan Mikita
35 Tony Esposito

Colorado Avalanche
77 Ray Bourque

Dallas Stars
7 Neal Broten
8 Bill Goldsworthy
19 Bill Masterton

Detroit Red Wings
1 Terry Sawchuk
7 Ted Lindsay
9 Gordie Howe
10 Alex Delvecchio
12 Sid Abel

Edmonton Oilers
3 Al Hamilton
17 Jari Kurri

Los Angeles Kings
16 Marcel Dionne
18 Dave Taylor
30 Rogie Vachon

Phoenix Coyotes
9 Bobby Hull
25 Thomas Steen

St. Louis Blues
3 Bob Gassoff
8 Barclay Plager
11 Brian Sutter
24 Bernie Federko

Vancouver Canucks
12 Stan Smyl

AWARDS

Associated Press Athletes of the Year

Selected annually by AP newspaper sports editors since 1931.

Male

Tiger Woods won his third AP Athlete of the Year Award in 2000. His stellar season included eleven victories, nine on the PGA tour, and featured three straight major titles. Tiger led the U.S. team to the World Cup title while earning $9,188,321 on the PGA Tour ($11,034,530 worldwide), breaking his own record of $6,616,585, which he set in 1999. Woods also completed the career Grand Slam (and actually held all four Major titles simultaneously for a time), winning his first British Open.

The Top 10 vote-getters (first place votes in parentheses): 1. **Tiger Woods**, golf (47), 160 pts; 2. **Lance Armstrong**, cycling (8), 72 pts; 3. **Kurt Warner**, football (3), 34 pts; 4. **Pedro Martinez**, baseball (3), 31 pts; 5. **Shaquille O'Neal**, basketball (1), 22 pts; 6. **Rulon Gardner**, wrestling (3), 18 pts; 7. **Jason Giambi**, baseball (2), 13 pts; 8. **Derek Jeter**, baseball, 8 pts; 9. **Marshall Faulk**, football, 7 pts. and Josh Heupel, college football (2), 7 pts.

Multiple winners: Michael Jordan and Tiger Woods (3); Don Budge, Sandy Koufax, Carl Lewis, Joe Montana and Byron Nelson (2).

Year		
1931 **Pepper Martin**, baseball	1953 **Ben Hogan**, golf	1977 **Steve Cauthen**, horse racing
1932 **Gene Sarazen**, golf	1954 **Willie Mays**, baseball	1978 **Ron Guidry**, baseball
1933 **Carl Hubbell**, baseball	1955 **Hopalong Cassady**, col. football	1979 **Willie Stargell**, baseball
1934 **Dizzy Dean**, baseball		1980 **U.S. Olympic hockey team**
1935 **Joe Louis**, boxing	1956 **Mickey Mantle**, baseball	1981 **John McEnroe**, tennis
1936 **Jesse Owens**, track	1957 **Ted Williams**, baseball	1982 **Wayne Gretzky**, hockey
1937 **Don Budge**, tennis	1958 **Herb Elliott**, track	1983 **Carl Lewis**, track
1938 **Don Budge**, tennis	1959 **Ingemar Johansson**, boxing	1984 **Carl Lewis**, track
1939 **Nile Kinnick**, college football	1960 **Rafer Johnson**, track	1985 **Dwight Gooden**, baseball
1940 **Tom Harmon**, college football	1961 **Roger Maris**, baseball	1986 **Larry Bird**, pro basketball
1941 **Joe DiMaggio**, baseball	1962 **Maury Wills**, baseball	1987 **Ben Johnson**, track
1942 **Frank Sinkwich**, college football	1963 **Sandy Koufax**, baseball	1988 **Orel Hershiser**, baseball
1943 **Gunder Haegg**, track	1964 **Don Schollander**, swimming	1989 **Joe Montana**, pro football
1944 **Byron Nelson**, golf	1965 **Sandy Koufax**, baseball	1990 **Joe Montana**, pro football
1945 **Byron Nelson**, golf	1966 **Frank Robinson**, baseball	1991 **Michael Jordan**, pro basketball
1946 **Glenn Davis**, college football	1967 **Carl Yastrzemski**, baseball	1992 **Michael Jordan**, pro basketball
1947 **Johnny Lujack**, college football	1968 **Denny McLain**, baseball	1993 **Michael Jordan**, pro basketball
1948 **Lou Boudreau**, baseball	1969 **Tom Seaver**, baseball	1994 **George Foreman**, boxing
1949 **Leon Hart**, college football	1970 **George Blanda**, pro football	1995 **Cal Ripken Jr.**, baseball
1950 **Jim Konstanty**, baseball	1971 **Lee Trevino**, golf	1996 **Michael Johnson**, track
1951 **Dick Kazmaier**, college football	1972 **Mark Spitz**, swimming	1997 **Tiger Woods**, golf
1952 **Bob Mathias**, track	1973 **O.J. Simpson**, pro football	1998 **Mark McGwire**, baseball
	1974 **Muhammad Ali**, boxing	1999 **Tiger Woods**, golf
	1975 **Fred Lynn**, baseball	2000 **Tiger Woods**, golf
	1976 **Bruce Jenner**, track	

Female

Marion Jones ran away with five medals at the 2000 Summer Games in Sydney, Australia becoming the first female track athlete to do so. Jones took home the gold in the 100m, 200m and 4x400m relay and bronze in the 4x200m relay and long jump.

The Top 3 vote-getters (first place votes in parentheses): 1. **Marion Jones**, track (27), 112 pts; 2. **Venus Williams**, tennis (16.5), 104.5 pts; 3. **Karrie Webb**, golf, 30 pts.

Multiple winners: Babe Didrikson Zaharias (6); Chris Evert (4); Patty Berg and Maureen Connolly (3); Tracy Austin, Althea Gibson, Billie Jean King, Nancy Lopez, Alice Marble, Martina Navratilova, Wilma Rudolph, Monica Seles, Kathy Whitworth and Mickey Wright (2).

Year		
1931 **Helene Madison**, swimming	1934 **Virginia Van Wie**, golf	1937 **Katherine Rawls**, swimming
1932 **Babe Didrikson**, track	1935 **Helen Wills Moody**, tennis	1938 **Patty Berg**, golf
1933 **Helen Jacobs**, tennis	1936 **Helen Stephens**, track	1939 **Alice Marble**, tennis

Awards (Cont.)

Year		Year		Year	
1940	**Alice Marble**, tennis	1961	**Wilma Rudolph**, track	1982	**Mary Decker Tabb**, track
1941	**Betty Hicks Newell**, golf	1962	**Dawn Fraser**, swimming	1983	**Martina Navratilova**, tennis
1942	**Gloria Callen**, swimming	1963	**Mickey Wright**, golf	1984	**Mary Lou Retton**, gymnastics
1943	**Patty Berg**, golf	1964	**Mickey Wright**, golf	1985	**Nancy Lopez**, golf
1944	**Ann Curtis**, swimming	1965	**Kathy Whitworth**, golf	1986	**Martina Navratilova**, tennis
1945	**Babe Didrikson Zaharias**, golf	1966	**Kathy Whitworth**, golf	1987	**Jackie Joyner-Kersee**, track
1946	**Babe Didrikson Zaharias**, golf	1967	**Billie Jean King**, tennis	1988	**Florence Griffith Joyner**, track
1947	**Babe Didrikson Zaharias**, golf	1968	**Peggy Fleming**, skating	1989	**Steffi Graf**, tennis
1948	**Fanny Blankers-Koen**, track	1969	**Debbie Meyer**, swimming	1990	**Beth Daniel**, golf
1949	**Marlene Bauer**, golf	1970	**Chi Cheng**, track	1991	**Monica Seles**, tennis
1950	**Babe Didrikson Zaharias**, golf	1971	**Evonne Goolagong**, tennis	1992	**Monica Seles**, tennis
1951	**Maureen Connolly**, tennis	1972	**Olga Korbut**, gymnastics	1993	**Sheryl Swoopes**, basketball
1952	**Maureen Connolly**, tennis	1973	**Billie Jean King**, tennis	1994	**Bonnie Blair**, speed skating
1953	**Maureen Connolly**, tennis	1974	**Chris Evert**, tennis	1995	**Rebecca Lobo**, col. basketball
1954	**Babe Didrikson Zaharias**, golf	1975	**Chris Evert**, tennis	1996	**Amy Van Dyken**, swimming
1955	**Patty Berg**, golf	1976	**Nadia Comaneci**, gymnastics	1997	**Martina Hingis**, tennis
1956	**Pat McCormick**, diving	1977	**Chris Evert**, tennis	1998	**Se Ri Pak**, golf
1957	**Althea Gibson**, tennis	1978	**Nancy Lopez**, golf	1999	**U.S. Soccer Team**
1958	**Althea Gibson**, tennis	1979	**Tracy Austin**, tennis	2000	**Marion Jones**, track
1959	**Maria Bueno**, tennis	1980	**Chris Evert Lloyd**, tennis		
1960	**Wilma Rudolph**, track	1981	**Tracy Austin**, tennis		

USOC Sportsman & Sportswoman of the Year

To the outstanding overall male and female athletes from within the U.S. Olympic Committee member organizations. Winners are chosen from nominees of the national governing bodies for Olympic and Pan American Games and affiliated organizations. Voting is done by members of the national media, USOC board of directors and Athletes' Advisory Council.

Sportsman

Multiple winners: Eric Heiden and Michael Johnson (3); Matt Biondi and Greg Louganis (2).

Year		Year		Year	
1974	**Jim Bolding**, track	1983	**Rick McKinney**, archery	1992	**Pablo Morales**, swimming
1975	**Clint Jackson**, boxing	1984	**Edwin Moses**, track	1993	**Michael Johnson**, track
1976	**John Naber**, swimming	1985	**Willie Banks**, track	1994	**Dan Jansen**, speed skating
1977	**Eric Heiden**, speed skating	1986	**Matt Biondi**, swimming	1995	**Michael Johnson**, track
1978	**Bruce Davidson**, equestrian	1987	**Greg Louganis**, diving	1996	**Michael Johnson**, track
1979	**Eric Heiden**, speed skating	1988	**Matt Biondi**, swimming	1997	**Pete Sampras**, tennis
1980	**Eric Heiden**, speed skating	1989	**Roger Kingdom**, track	1998	**Jonny Moseley**, skiing
1981	**Scott Hamilton**, fig. skating	1990	**John Smith**, wrestling	1999	**Lance Armstrong**, cycling
1982	**Greg Louganis**, diving	1991	**Carl Lewis**, track	2000	**Rulon Gardner**, wrestling

Sportswoman

Multiple winners: Bonnie Blair, Tracy Caulkins, Jackie Joyner-Kersee, Picabo Street and Sheila Young Ochowicz (2).

Year		Year		Year	
1974	**Shirley Babashoff**, swimming	1983	**Tamara McKinney**, skiing	1993	**Gail Devers**; track
1975	**Kathy Heddy**, swimming	1984	**Tracy Caulkins**, swimming	1994	**Bonnie Blair**, speed skating
1976	**Sheila Young**, speedskating	1985	**Mary Decker Slaney**, track	1995	**Picabo Street**, skiing
1977	**Linda Fratianne**, fig. skating	1986	**Jackie Joyner-Kersee**, track	1996	**Amy Van Dyken**, swimming
1978	**Tracy Caulkins**, swimming	1987	**Jackie Joyner-Kersee**, track	1997	**Tara Lipinski**, figure skating
1979	**Sippy Woodhead**, swimming	1988	**Florence Griffith Joyner**, track	1998	**Picabo Street**, skiing
1980	**Beth Heiden**, speed skating	1989	**Janet Evans**, swimming	1999	**Jenny Thompson**, swimming
1981	**Sheila Ochowicz**, speed skating & cycling	1990	**Lynn Jennings**, track	2000	**Marion Jones**, track
1982	**Melanie Smith**, equestrian	1991	**Kim Zmeskal**, gymnastics		
		1992	**Bonnie Blair**, speed skating		

UPI International Athletes of the Year

Selected annually by United Press International's European newspaper sports editors from 1974-95.

Male

Multiple winners: Sebastian Coe, Alberto Juantorena and Carl Lewis (2).

Year		Year		Year	
1974	**Muhammad Ali**, boxing	1982	**Daley Thompson**, track	1990	**Stefan Edberg**, tennis
1975	**Joao Oliveira**, track	1983	**Carl Lewis**, track	1991	**Sergei Bubka**, track
1976	**Alberto Juantorena**, track	1984	**Carl Lewis**, track	1992	**Kevin Young**, track
1977	**Alberto Juantorena**, track	1985	**Steve Cram**, track	1993	**Miguel Indurain**, cycling
1978	**Henry Rono**, track	1986	**Diego Maradona**, soccer	1994	**Johan Olav Koss**, speed skating
1979	**Sebastian Coe**, track	1987	**Ben Johnson**, track	1995	**Jonathan Edwards**, track
1980	**Eric Heiden**, speed skating	1988	**Matt Biondi**, swimming	1996	discontinued
1981	**Sebastian Coe**, track	1989	**Boris Becker**, tennis		

Female

Multiple winners: Nadia Comaneci, Steffi Graf, Marita Koch and Monica Seles (2).

Year		Year		Year	
1974	**Irena Szewinska**, track	1983	**Jarmila Kratochvilova**, track	1992	**Monica Seles**, tennis
1975	**Nadia Comaneci**, gymnastics	1984	**Martina Navratilova**, tennis	1993	**Wang Junxia**, track
1976	**Nadia Comaneci**, gymnastics	1985	**Mary Decker Slaney**, track	1994	**Le Jingyi**, swimming
1977	**Rosie Ackermann**, track	1986	**Heike Drechsler**, track	1995	**Gwen Torrence**, track
1978	**Tracy Caulkins**, swimming	1987	**Steffi Graf**, tennis	1996	discontinued
1979	**Marita Koch**, track	1988	**Florence Griffith Joyner**, track		
1980	**Hanni Wenzel**, alpine skiing	1989	**Steffi Graf**, tennis		
1981	**Chris Evert Lloyd**, tennis	1990	**Merlene Ottey**, track		
1982	**Marita Koch**, track	1991	**Monica Seles**, tennis		

Jesse Owens International Trophy

Presented annually by the International Amateur Athletic Association since 1981 and selected by a worldwide panel of electors. The Jesse Owens International Trophy is named after the late American Olympic champion, who won four gold medals at the 1936 Summer Games in Berlin.

Multiple winners: Michael Johnson and Marion Jones (2).

Year		Year		Year	
1981	**Eric Heiden**, speed skating	1990	**Roger Kingdom**, track	1997	**Michael Johnson**, track
1982	**Sebastian Coe**, track	1991	**Greg LeMond**, cycling	1998	**Haile Gebrselassie**, track
1983	**Mary Decker**, track	1992	**Mike Powell**, track	1999	**Marion Jones**, track
1984	**Edwin Moses**, track	1993	**Vitaly Scherbo**, gymnastics	2000	**Lance Armstrong**, cycling
1985	**Carl Lewis**, track	1994	**Wang Junxia**, track	2001	**Marion Jones**, track
1986	**Said Aouita**, track	1995	**Johan Olva Koss**, speed		
1987	**Greg Louganis**, diving		skating		
1988	**Ben Johnson**, track	1996	**Michael Johnson**, track		

Honda Broderick Cup

To the outstanding collegiate woman athlete of the year in NCAA competition. Winner is chosen from nominees in each of the NCAA's 10 competitive sports. Final voting is done by member athletic directors. Award is named after founder and sportswear manufacturer Thomas Broderick.

Multiple winner: Tracy Caulkins (2).

Year		Year	
1977	**Lucy Harris**, Delta St ....basketball	1989	**Vicki Huber**, Villanova ....track
1978	**Ann Meyers**, UCLA ....basketball	1990	**Suzy Favor**, Wisconsin....................track
1979	**Nancy Lieberman**, Old Dominion .....basketball	1991	**Dawn Staley**, Virginia......,..........basketball
1980	**Julie Shea**, N.C. State ....track & field	1992	**Missy Marlowe**, Utah ....gymnastics
1981	**Jill Sterkel**, Texas ....swimming	1993	**Lisa Fernandez**, UCLA ....softball
1982	**Tracy Caulkins**, Florida..............swimming	1994	**Mia Hamm**, North Carolina ....soccer
1983	**Deitre Collins**, Hawaii ....volleyball	1995	**Rebecca Lobo**, UConn...............basketball
1984	**Tracy Caulkins**, Florida..............swimming	1996	**Jennifer Rizzotti**, UConn ....basketball
	& **Cheryl Miller**, USC................basketball	1997	**Cindy Daws**, Notre Dame ....soccer
1985	**Jackie Joyner**, UCLA.................track & field	1998	**Chamique Holdsclaw**, Tennessee ......basketball
1986	**Kamie Ethridge**, Texas ....basketball	1999	**Misty May**, Long Beach St.............volleyball
1987	**Mary T. Meagher**, California..........swimming	2000	**Cristina Teuscher**, Columbia ....swimming
1988	**Teresa Weatherspoon**, La. Tech ....basketball	2001	**Jackie Stiles**, SW Missouri St. ....basketball

Flo Hyman Award

Presented annually since 1987 by the Women's Sports Foundation for "exemplifying dignity, spirit and commitment to excellence" and named in honor of the late captain of the 1984 U.S. Women's Volleyball team. Voting by WSF members.

Year		Year		Year	
1987	**Martina Navratilova**, tennis	1992	**Nancy Lopez**, golf	1997	**Billie Jean King**, tennis
1988	**Jackie Joyner-Kersee**, track	1993	**Lynette Woodward**, basketball	1998	**Nadia Comaneci**, gymnastics
1989	**Evelyn Ashford**, track	1994	**Patty Sheehan**, golf	1999	**Bonnie Blair**, speed skating
1990	**Chris Evert**, tennis	1995	**Mary Lou Retton**, gymnastics	2000	**Monica Seles**, tennis
1991	**Diana Golden**, skiing	1996	**Donna de Varona**, swimming	2001	**Lisa Leslie**, basketball

Awards (Cont.)

AP/Wide World Photos

*Olympic wrestler **Rulon Gardner** won the 2000 Sullivan Award, as the nation's best amateur athlete, for his stunning gold-medal performance at the Summer Games in Sydney.*

James E. Sullivan Memorial Award

Presented annually by the Amateur Athletic Union since 1930. The Sullivan Award is named after the former AAU president and given to the athlete who, "by his or her performance, example and influence as an amateur, has done the most during the year to advance the cause of sportsmanship." An athlete cannot win the award more than once.

Olympic Greco-Roman wrestler **Rulon Gardner** won the 2000 Sullivan Award. Gardner bested Russian Alexandre Kareline in the 2000 Olympic super heavyweight championship match by a score of 1-0. It marked the first time in 10 years that an opposing grappler had scored a single point against Kareline and it broke the Russian's incredible 13-year winning streak. The four additional finalists are listed alphabetically: **Lisa Fernandez**, softball; **Josh Heupel**, football; **Lenny Krayzelburg**, swimming; **Laura Wilkinson**, diving. Vote totals were not released.

Year		Year		Year	
1930	**Bobby Jones**, golf	1955	**Harrison Dillard**, track	1979	**Kurt Thomas**, gymnastics
1931	**Barney Berlinger**, track	1956	**Pat McCormick**, diving	1980	**Eric Heiden**, speed skating
1932	**Jim Bausch**, track	1957	**Bobby Morrow**, track	1981	**Carl Lewis**, track
1933	**Glenn Cunningham**, track	1958	**Glenn Davis**, track	1982	**Mary Decker**, track
1934	**Bill Bonthron**, track	1959	**Parry O'Brien**, track	1983	**Edwin Moses**, track
1935	**Lawson Little**, golf	1960	**Rafer Johnson**, track	1984	**Greg Louganis**, diving
1936	**Glenn Morris**, track	1961	**Wilma Rudolph**, track	1985	**Joan B. Samuelson**, track
1937	**Don Budge**, tennis	1962	**Jim Beatty**, track	1986	**Jackie Joyner-Kersee**, track
1938	**Don Lash**, track	1963	**John Pennel**, track	1987	**Jim Abbott**, baseball
1939	**Joe Burk**, rowing	1964	**Don Schollander**, swimming	1988	**Florence Griffith Joyner**, track
1940	**Greg Rice**, track	1965	**Bill Bradley**, basketball	1989	**Janet Evans**, swimming
1941	**Leslie MacMitchell**, track	1966	**Jim Ryun**, track	1990	**John Smith**, wrestling
1942	**Cornelius Warmerdam**, track	1967	**Randy Matson**, track	1991	**Mike Powell**, track
1943	**Gilbert Dodds**, track	1968	**Debbie Meyer**, swimming	1992	**Bonnie Blair**, speed skating
1944	**Ann Curtis**, swimming	1969	**Bill Toomey**, track	1993	**Charlie Ward**, football
1945	**Doc Blanchard**, football	1970	**John Kinsella**, swimming	1994	**Dan Jansen**, speed skating
1946	**Arnold Tucker**, football	1971	**Mark Spitz**, swimming	1995	**Bruce Baumgartner**, wrestling
1947	**John B. Kelly, Jr.**, rowing	1972	**Frank Shorter**, track	1996	**Michael Johnson**, track
1948	**Bob Mathias**, track	1973	**Bill Walton**, basketball	1997	**Peyton Manning**, football
1949	**Dick Button**, skating	1974	**Rich Wohlhuter**, track	1998	**Chamique Holdsclaw**,
1950	**Fred Wilt**, track	1975	**Tim Shaw**, swimming		basketball
1951	**Bob Richards**, track	1976	**Bruce Jenner**, track	1999	**Coco and Kelly Miller**,
1952	**Horace Ashenfelter**, track	1977	**John Naber**, swimming		basketball
1953	**Sammy Lee**, diving	1978	**Tracy Caulkins**, swimming	2000	**Rulon Gardner**, wrestling
1954	**Mal Whitfield**, track				

ESPY Awards

The ESPY Awards, which represent the convergence of the sports and entertainment communities, were created by ESPN in 1993 and are given for Excellence in Sports Performance in more than 30 categories. ESPYs are awarded by a panel of sports executives, journalists and retired athletes whose decisions are based on the performances of the nominees during the year preceding the awards ceremony. Note that not all categories are listed below.

Breakthrough Athlete of the Year

1993 Gary Sheffield, San Diego Padres
1994 Mike Piazza, Los Angeles Dodgers
1995 Jeff Bagwell, Houston Astros
1996 Hideo Nomo, Los Angeles Dodgers
1997 Tiger Woods, golf
1998 Nomar Garciaparra, Boston Red Sox
1999 Randy Moss, Minnesota Vikings
2000 Kurt Warner, St. Louis Rams
2001 Daunte Culpepper, Minnesota Vikings

Coach/Manager of the Year

1993 Jimmy Johnson, Dallas Cowboys
1994 Jimmy Johnson, Dallas Cowboys
1995 George Siefert, San Francisco 49ers
1996 Gary Barnett, Northwestern
1997 Joe Torre, New York Yankees
1998 Jim Leyland, Florida Marlins
1999 Joe Torre, New York Yankees
2000 Joe Torre, New York Yankees
2001 Joe Torre, New York Yankees

Comeback Athlete of the Year

1993 Dave Winfield, Toronto Blue Jays
1994 Mario Lemieux, Pittsburgh Penguins
1995 Dan Marino, Miami Dolphins
1996 Michael Jordan, Chicago Bulls
1997 Evander Holyfield, boxer
1998 Roger Clemens, Toronto Blue Jays
1999 Eric Davis, Baltimore Orioles
2000 Lance Armstrong, cycling
2001 Andres Galarraga, baseball

Outstanding Female Athlete of the Year

1993 Monica Seles, tennis
1994 Julie Krone, jockey
1995 Bonnie Blair, speed skater
1996 Rebecca Lobo, basketball
1997 Amy Van Dyken, swimming
1998 Mia Hamm, soccer
1999 Chamique Holdsclaw, college basketball
2000 Mia Hamm, soccer
2001 Marion Jones, track

Outstanding Male Athlete of the Year

1993 Michael Jordan, Chicago Bulls
1994 Barry Bonds, San Francisco Giants
1995 Steve Young, San Francisco 49ers
1996 Cal Ripken, Baltimore Orioles
1997 Michael Johnson, Olympic sprinter
1998 Tiger Woods, golf
1999 Mark McGwire, St. Louis Cardinals
2000 Tiger Woods, golf
2001 Tiger Woods, golf

Outstanding Performance Under Pressure

1993 Christian Laettner, Duke
1994 Joe Carter, Toronto Blue Jays
1995 Mark Messier, New York Rangers
1996 Martin Broduer, New Jersey Devils
1997 Kerri Strug, Olympic gymnast
1998 Terrell Davis, Denver Broncos
1999 Mark O'Meara, golf
2000 discontinued

Outstanding Team

1993 Dallas Cowboys
1994 Toronto Blue Jays
1995 New York Rangers
1996 UConn women's hoops
1997 New York Yankees
1998 Denver Broncos
1999 New York Yankees
2000 U.S. Women's World Cup Soccer Team
2001 New York Yankees

Outstanding Baseball Performer of the Year

1993 Dennis Eckersley, Oakland A's
1994 Barry Bonds, San Francisco Giants
1995 Jeff Bagwell, Houston Astros
1996 Greg Maddux, Atlanta Braves
1997 Ken Caminiti, San Diego Padres
1998 Larry Walker, Colorado Rockies
1999 Mark McGwire, St. Louis Cardinals
2000 Pedro Martinez, Boston Red Sox
2001 Pedro Martinez, Boston Red Sox

Outstanding Pro Football Performer of the Year

1993 Emmitt Smith, Dallas Cowboys
1994 Emmitt Smith, Dallas Cowboys
1995 Barry Sanders, Detroit Lions
1996 Brett Favre, Green Bay Packers
1997 Brett Favre, Green Bay Packers
1998 Barry Sanders, Detroit Lions
1999 Terrell Davis, Denver Broncos
2000 Kurt Warner, St. Louis Rams
2001 Marshall Faulk, St. Louis Rams

Outstanding Pro Basketball Performer of the Year

1993 Michael Jordan, Chicago Bulls
1994 Charles Barkley, Phoenix Suns
1995 Hakeem Olajuwon, Houston Rockets
1996 Hakeem Olajuwon, Houston Rockets
1997 Michael Jordan, Chicago Bulls
1998 Michael Jordan, Chicago Bulls
1999 Michael Jordan, Chicago Bulls
2000 Tim Duncan, San Antonio Spurs
2001 Shaquille O'Neal, Los Angeles Lakers

Outstanding Women's Pro Basketball Performer of the Year

1998 Cynthia Cooper, Houston Comets
1999 Cynthia Cooper, Houston Comets
2000 Cynthia Cooper, Houston Comets
2001 Sheryl Swoopes, Houston Comets

Outstanding Pro Hockey Performer of the Year

1993 Mario Lemieux, Pittsburgh Penguins
1994 Mario Lemieux, Pittsburgh Penguins
1995 Mark Messier, New York Rangers
1996 Eric Lindros, Philadelphia Flyers
1997 Joe Sakic, Colorado Avalanche
1998 Mario Lemieux, Pittsburgh Penguins
1999 Dominik Hasek, Buffalo Sabres
2000 Dominik Hasek, Buffalo Sabres
2001 Chris Pronger, St. Louis Blues

Awards (Cont.)

Outstanding College Football Performer of the Year

1993   Garrison Hearst, Georgia
1994   Charlie Ward, Florida State
1995   Rashaan Salaam, Colorado
1996   Eddie George, Ohio State
1997   Danny Wuerffel, Florida
1998   Peyton Manning, Tennessee
1999   Ricky Williams, Texas
2000   Michael Vick, Virginia Tech
2001   Chris Weinke, Florida State

Outstanding College Basketball Performer of the Year

1993   Christian Laettner, Duke
1994   Bobby Hurley, Duke
1995   Grant Hill, Duke
1996   Ed O'Bannon, UCLA
1997   Tim Duncan, Wake Forest
1998   Keith Van Horn, Utah
1999   Antawn Jamison, North Carolina
2000   Flton Brand, Duke
2001   Kenyon Martin, Cincinnati

Outstanding Women's College Hoops Performer of the Year

1993   Dawn Staley, Virginia
1994   Sheryl Swoopes, Texas Tech
1995   Charlotte Smith, North Carolina
1996   Rebecca Lobo, Connecticut
1997   Saudia Roundtree, Georgia
1998   Chamique Holdsclaw, Tennessee
1999   Chamique Holdsclaw, Tennessee
2000   Chamique Holdsclaw, Tennessee
2001   Tamika Catchings, Tennessee

Outstanding Men's Tennis Performer of the Year

1993   Jim Courier
1994   Pete Sampras
1995   Pete Sampras
1996   Pete Sampras
1997   Pete Sampras
1998   Pete Sampras
1999   Pete Sampras
2000   Andre Agassi
2001   Pete Sampras

Outstanding Women's Tennis Performer of the Year

1993   Monica Seles
1994   Steffi Graf
1995   Aranxta Sanchez Vicario
1996   Steffi Graf
1997   Steffi Graf
1998   Martina Hingis
1999   Lindsay Davenport
2000   Lindsay Davenport
2001   Venus Williams

Outstanding Men's Golf Performer of the Year

1993   Fred Couples
1994   Nick Price
1995   Nick Price
1996   Corey Pavin
1997   Tom Lehman
1998   Tiger Woods
1999   Mark O'Meara
2000   Tiger Woods
2001   Tiger Woods

Outstanding Women's Golf Performer of the Year

1993   Dottie Mochrie
1994   Betsy King
1995   Laura Davies
1996   Annika Sorenstam
1997   Karrie Webb
1998   Annika Sorenstam
1999   Annika Sorenstam
2000   Julie Inkster
2001   Karrie Webb

Outstanding Jockey of the Year

1994   Mike Smith
1995   Chris McCarron
1996   Jerry Bailey
1997   Jerry Bailey
1998   Gary Stevens
1999   Kent Desormeaux
2000   Chris Antley
2001   Kent Desormeaux

Outstanding Bowling Performer of the Year

1995   Norm Duke
1996   Mike Aulby
1997   Bob Learn Jr.
1998   Walter Ray Williams Jr.
1999   Walter Ray Williams Jr.
2000   Parker Bohn III
2001   Walter Ray Williams Jr.

Outstanding Auto Racing Performer of the Year

1993   Nigel Mansell
1994   Nigel Mansell
1995   Al Unser Jr.
1996   Jeff Gordon
1997   Jimmy Vasser
1998   Jeff Gordon
1999   Jeff Gordon
2000   Dale Jarrett
2001   Bobby Labonte

Outstanding Men's Track Performer of the Year

1993   Kevin Young
1994   Michael Johnson
1995   Dennis Mitchell
1996   Michael Johnson
1997   Michael Johnson
1998   Wilson Kipketer
1999   Maurice Greene
2000   Michael Johnson
2001   Maurice Greene

Outstanding Women's Track Performer of the Year

1993 Evelyn Ashford
1994 Gail Devers
1995 Gwen Torrence
1996 Kim Batten
1997 Marie-Jose Perec
1998 Marion Jones
1999 Marion Jones
2000 Marion Jones
2001 Marion Jones

Outstanding Boxing Performer of the Year

1993 Riddick Bowe
1994 Evander Holyfield
1995 George Foreman
1996 Roy Jones Jr.
1997 Evander Holyfield
1998 Evander Holyfield
1999 Oscar De La Hoya
2000 Roy Jones Jr.
2001 Felix Trinidad

Game of the Year

1996 AFC championship between Colts and Steelers
1997 Ohio State edges Arizona State in the Rose Bowl
1998 Super Bowl XXXII, Broncos over Packers
1999 discontinued

Arthur Ashe Award for Courage

Presented since 1993 on the annual ESPN "ESPYs" telecast. Given to a member of the sports community who has exemplified the same courage, spirit and determination to help others despite personal hardship that characterized Arthur Ashe, the late tennis champion and humanitarian. Voting done by select 26-member committee of media and sports personalities.

Year		Year		Year	
1993	**Jim Valvano**, basketball	1997	**Muhammad Ali**, boxing	2001	**Cathy Freeman**, track
1994	**Steve Palermo**, baseball	1998	**Dean Smith**, college basketball		
1995	**Howard Cosell**, TV & radio	1999	**Billie Jean King**, tennis		
1996	**Loretta Clairborne**, special olympics	2000	**Dave Sanders**, Columbine H.S. coach		

The Hickok Belt

Officially known as the S. Rae Hickok Professional Athlete of the Year Award and presented by the Kickik Manufacturing Co. of Arlington, Texas, from 1950-76. The trophy was a large belt of gold, diamonds and other jewels, reportedly worth $30,000 in 1976, the last year it was handed out. Voting was done by 270 newspaper sports editors from around the country.
Multiple winner: Sandy Koufax (2).

Year		Year		Year	
1950	**Phil Rizzuto**, baseball	1960	**Arnold Palmer**, golf	1970	**Brooks Robinson**, baseball
1951	**Allie Reynolds**, baseball	1961	**Roger Maris**, baseball	1971	**Lee Trevino**, golf
1952	**Rocky Marciano**, boxing	1962	**Maury Wills**, baseball	1972	**Steve Carlton**, baseball
1953	**Ben Hogan**, golf	1963	**Sandy Koufax**, baseball	1973	**O.J. Simpson**, football
1954	**Willie Mays**, baseball	1964	**Jim Brown**, football	1974	**Muhammad Ali**, boxing
1955	**Otto Graham**, football	1965	**Sandy Koufax**, baseball	1975	**Pete Rose**, baseball
1956	**Mickey Mantle**, baseball	1966	**Frank Robinson**, baseball	1976	**Ken Stabler**, football
1957	**Carmen Basilio**, boxing	1967	**Carl Yastrzemski**, baseball	1977	Discontinued
1958	**Bob Turley**, baseball	1968	**Joe Namath**, football		
1959	**Ingemar Johansson**, boxing	1969	**Tom Seaver**, baseball *		

Presidential Medal of Freedom

Since President John F. Kennedy established the Medal of Freedom as America's highest civilian honor in 1963, only nine sports figures have won the award. Note that (*) indicates the presentation was made posthumously.

Year		President	Year		President
1963	**Bob Kiphuth**, swimming	Kennedy	1986	**Earl (Red) Blaik**, football	Reagan
1976	**Jesse Owens**, track & field	Ford	1991	**Ted Williams**, baseball	Bush
1977	**Joe DiMaggio**, baseball	Ford	1992	**Richard Petty**, auto racing	Bush
1983	**Paul (Bear) Bryant***, football	Reagan	1993	**Arthur Ashe***, tennis	Clinton
1984	**Jackie Robinson***, baseball	Reagan			

Awards (Cont.)
ABC's "Wide World of Sports" Athlete of the Year
Selected annually by the producers of ABC Sports since 1962.

Multiple winners: Greg LeMond and Tiger Woods (2).

Year		Year		Year	
1962	**Jim Beatty**, track	1977	**Steve Cauthen**, horse racing	1992	**Bonnie Blair**, speed skating
1963	**Valery Brumel**, track	1978	**Ron Guidry**, baseball	1993	**Evander Holyfield**, boxing
1964	**Don Schollander**, swimming	1979	**Willie Stargell**, baseball	1994	**Al Unser Jr.**, auto racing
1965	**Jim Clark**, auto racing	1980	**U.S. Olympic hockey team**	1995	**Miguel Induráin**, cycling
1966	**Jim Ryun**, track	1981	**Sugar Ray Leonard**, boxing	1996	**Michael Johnson**, track
1967	**Peggy Fleming**, figure skating	1982	**Wayne Gretzky**, hockey	1997	**Tiger Woods**, golf
1968	**Bill Toomey**, track	1983	**Australia II**, yachting	1998	**Mark McGwire**, baseball
1969	**Mario Andretti**, auto racing	1984	**Edwin Moses**, track	1999	**Lance Armstrong**, cycling
1970	**Willis Reed**, basketball	1985	**Pete Rose**, baseball	2000	**Tiger Woods**, golf
1971	**Lee Trevino**, golf	1986	**Debi Thomas**, figure skating		
1972	**Olga Korbut**, gymnastics	1987	**Dennis Conner**, yachting		
1973	**O.J. Simpson**, football	1988	**Greg Louganis**, diving		
	& **Jackie Stewart**, auto racing	1989	**Greg LeMond**, cycling		
1974	**Muhammad Ali**, boxing	1990	**Greg LeMond**, cycling		
1975	**Jack Nicklaus**, golf	1991	**Carl Lewis**, track		
1976	**Nadia Comaneci**, gymnastics		& **Kim Zmeskal**, gymnastics		

The *Sporting News* Sportsman of the Year
Selected annually by the editors of *The Sporting News* since 1968. 'Man of the Year' changed to 'Sportsman' of the Year in 1993.

Multiple Winner: Mark McGwire (2).

Year		Year		Year	
1968	**Denny McLain**, baseball	1982	**Whitey Herzog**, baseball	1995	**Cal Ripken Jr.**, baseball
1969	**Tom Seaver**, baseball	1983	**Bowie Kuhn**, baseball	1996	**Joe Torre**, baseball
1970	**John Wooden**, basketball	1984	**Peter Ueberroth**, LA Olympics	1997	**Mark McGwire**, baseball
1971	**Lee Trevino**, golf	1985	**Pete Rose**, baseball	1998	**Mark McGwire**
1972	**Charles O. Finley**, baseball	1986	**Larry Bird**, pro basketball		& **Sammy Sosa**, baseball
1973	**O.J. Simpson**, pro football	1987	No award	1999	**New York Yankees**, base-
1974	**Lou Brock**, baseball	1988	**Jackie Joyner-Kersee**, track		ball
1975	**Archie Griffin**, football	1989	**Joe Montana**, football	2000	**Kurt Warner**
1976	**Larry O'Brien**, basketball	1990	**Nolan Ryan**, baseball		& **Marshall Faulk**, football
1977	**Steve Cauthen**, horse racing	1991	**Michael Jordan**, basketball		
1978	**Ron Guidry**, baseball	1992	**Mike Krzyzewski**, col. bask.		
1979	**Willie Stargell**, baseball	1993	**Cito Gaston**		
1980	**George Brett**, baseball		& **Pat Gillick**, baseball		
1981	**Wayne Gretzky**, hockey	1994	**Emmitt Smith**, pro football		

Time Person of the Year
Since Charles Lindbergh was named *Time* magazine's first Man of the Year for 1927, two individuals with significant sports credentials have won the honor.

Year	
1984	**Peter Ueberroth**, president of the Los Angeles Olympic Organizing Committee.
1991	**Ted Turner**, owner-president of Turner Broadcasting System, founder of CNN cable news network, owner of the Atlanta Braves (NL) and Atlanta Hawks (NBA), and former winning America's Cup skipper.

TROPHY CASE

From the first organized track meet at Olympia in 776 B.C., to the Sydney Summer Olympics over 2,700 years later, championships have been officially recognized with prizes that are symbolically rich and eagerly pursued. Here are 15 of the most coveted trophies in America.

(Illustrations by Lynn Mercer Michaud)

America's Cup

First presented by England's Royal Yacht Squadron to the winner of an invitational race around the Isle of Wight on Aug. 22, 1851. . . originally called the Hundred Guinea Cup. . . renamed after the U.S. boat America, winner of the first race. . . made of sterling silver and designed by London jewelers R. & G. Garrard. . . measures 2 feet, 3 inches high and weighs 16 lbs. . . originally cost 100 guineas ($500), now valued at $250,000 . . . bell-shaped base added in 1958. . . challenged for every three to four years. . . trophy held by yacht club sponsoring winning boat...Cup was badly damaged when a Maori protester repeatedly smashed it with a sledgehammer on March 14, 1997. It was sent back to the original maker and fully restored.

Vince Lombardi Trophy

First presented at the AFL-NFL World Championship Game (now Super Bowl) on Jan. 15, 1967. . . originally called the World Championship Game Trophy . . . renamed in 1971 in honor of former Green Bay Packers GM-coach and two-time Super Bowl winner Vince Lombardi, who died in 1970 as coach of Washington . . . made of sterling silver and designed by Tiffany & Co. of New York . . . measures 21 inches high and weighs 7 lbs (football depicted is regulation size). . . valued at $12,500. . . competed for annually-. . . winning team keeps trophy.

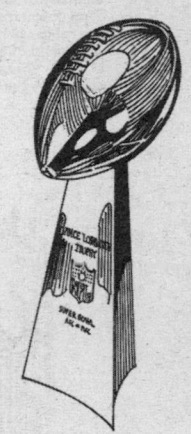

Olympic Gold Medal

First presented by International Olympic Committee in 1908 (until then winners received silver medals). . . second and third place finishers also got medals of silver and bronze for first time in 1908. . . each medal must be at least 2.4 inches in diameter and 0.12 inches thick. . . the gold medal is actually made of silver, but must be gilded with at least 6 grams (0.21 ounces) of pure gold. . . the medals for the 1996 Atlanta Games were designed by Malcolm Grear Designers and produced by Reed & Barton of Taunton, Mass...604 gold, 604 silver and 630 bronze medals were made. . . competed for every two years as Winter and Summer Games alternate. . . winners keep medals.

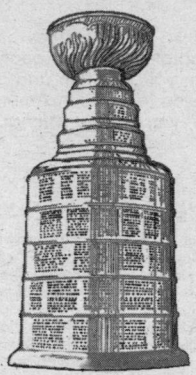

Stanley Cup

Donated by Lord Stanley of Preston, the Governor General of Canada and first presented in 1893. . . original cup was made of sterling silver by an unknown London silversmith and measured 7 inches high with an 11½-inch diameter. . . in order to accommodate all the rosters of winning teams, the cup now measures 35½ inches high with a base 54 inches around and weighs 32 lbs. . . in order to add new names each year, bands on the trophy are often retired and displayed at the Hall of Fame. . . originally bought for 10 guineas ($48.67), it is now insured for $75,000. . . actual cup retired to Hall of Fame and replaced in 1970. . . presented to NHL playoff champion since 1918. . . trophy loaned to winning team for one year.

World Cup

First presented by the Federation Internationale de Football Association (FIFA). . . originally called the World Cup Trophy. . . renamed the Jules Rimet Cup (after the then FIFA president) in 1946, but retired by Brazil after that country's third title in 1970. . . new World Cup trophy created in 1974. . . designed by Italian sculptor Silvio Gazzaniga and made of solid 18 carat gold with two malachite rings inlaid at the base. . . measures 14.2 inches high and weighs 11 lbs. . . insured for $200,000 (U.S.). . . competed for every four years. . . winning team gets gold-plated replica.

Commissioner's Trophy

First presented by the Commissioner of baseball to the winner of the 1967 World Series. . . also known as the World Championship Trophy. . . made of brass and gold plate with an ebony base and a baseball in the center made of pewter with a silver finish. . . designed by Balfour & Co. of Attleboro, Mass. . . 30 pennants represent 14 AL and 16 NL teams . . . measures 30 inches high and 36 inches around at the base and weighs 30 lbs. . . valued at $15,000. . . competed for annually. . . winning team keeps trophy.

Larry O'Brien Trophy

First presented in 1978 to winner of NBA Finals. . . originally called the Walter A. Brown Trophy after the league pioneer and Boston Celtics owner (an earlier NBA championship bowl was also named after Brown). . . renamed in 1984 in honor of outgoing commissioner O'Brien, who served from 1975-84 . . . made of sterling silver with 24 carat gold overlay and designed by Tiffany & Co. of New York. . . measures 2 feet high and weighs 14½ lbs (basketball depicted is regulation size). . . valued at $13,500. . . competed for annually. . . winning team keeps trophy.

Heisman Trophy

First presented in 1935 to the best college football player east of the Mississippi by the Downtown Athletic Club of New York. . . players across the entire country eligible since 1936. . . originally called the DAC Trophy. . . renamed in 1936 following the death of DAC athletic director and former college coach John W. Heisman. . . made of bronze and designed by New York sculptor Frank Eliscu, it measures 13½ in. high, 6½ in. wide and 14 in. long at the base and weighs 25 lbs. . . valued at $2,000 . . . voting done by national media and former Heisman winners. . . trophy sponsor American Suzuki announced plans for limited fan voting starting in 1999. . . awarded annually. . . winner keeps trophy.

James E. Sullivan Memorial Award

First presented by the Amateur Athletic Union (AAU) in 1930 as a gold medal and given to the nation's outstanding amateur athlete. . . trophy given since 1933. . . named after the amateur sports movement pioneer, who was a founder and past president of AAU and the director of the 1904 Olympic Games in St. Louis. . . made of bronze with a marble base, it measures 17½ in. high and 11 in. wide at the base and weighs 13½ lbs. . . valued at $2,500. . . voting done by AAU and USOC officials, former winners and selected media. . . awarded annually. . . winner keeps trophy.

Ryder Cup

Donated in 1927 by English seed merchant Samuel Ryder, who offered the gold cup for a biennial match between teams of golfing pros from Great Britain and the United States. . . the format changed in 1977 to include the best players on the European PGA Tour . . . made of 14 carat gold on a wood base and designed by Mappin and Webb of London. . . the golfer depicted on the top of the trophy is Ryder's friend and teaching pro Abe Mitchell. . . . the cup measures 16 in. high and weighs 4 lbs. . . insured for $50,000 . . . competed for every two years at alternating European and U.S. sites . . . the cup is held by the PGA headquarters of the winning side.

Davis Cup

Donated by American college student and U.S. doubles champion Dwight F. Davis in 1900 and presented by the International Tennis Federation (ITF) to the winner of the annual 16-team men's competition. . . officially called the International Lawn Tennis Challenge Trophy. . . made of sterling silver and designed by Shreve, Crump and Low of Boston, the cup has a matching tray (added in 1921) and a very heavy two-tiered base containing rosters of past winning teams. . . it stands 34½ in. high and 108 in. around at the base and weighs 400 lbs. . . insured for $150,000. . . competed for annually. . . trophy loaned to winning country for one year.

Borg-Warner Trophy

First presented by the Borg-Warner Automotive Co. of Chicago in 1936 to the winner of the Indianapolis 500. . . replaced the Wheeler-Schebler Trophy which went to the 400-mile leader from 1911-32. . . made of sterling silver with bas-relief sculptured heads of each winning driver and a gold bas-relief head of Tony Hulman, the owner of the Indy Speedway from 1945-77 . . . designed by Robert J. Hill and made by Gorham, Inc. of Rhode Island . . . measures 51½ in. high and weighs over 80 lbs. . . new base added in 1988 and the entire trophy restored in 1991. . . competed for annually. . . insured for $1 million. . . trophy stays at Speedway Hall of Fame. . . winner gets a 14-in. high replica valued at $30,000.

NCAA Championship Trophy

First presented in 1952 by the NCAA to all 1st, 2nd and 3rd place teams in sports with sanctioned tournaments. . . 1st place teams receive gold-plated awards, 2nd place award is silver-plated and 3rd is bronze. . . replaced silver cup given to championship teams from 1939-1951. . . made of walnut, the trophy stands 24¾ in. high, 14⅛ in. wide and 4½ in. deep at the base and weighs 15 lbs . . . designed by Medallic Art Co. of Danbury, Conn. and made by House of Usher of Kansas City since 1990. . . valued at $500. . . competed for annually. . . winning teams keep trophies.

World Championship Belt

First presented in 1921 by the World Boxing Association, one of the three organizations (the World Boxing Council and International Boxing Federation are the others) generally accepted as sanctioning legitimate world championship fights. . . belt weighs 8 lbs. and is made of hand tanned leather. . . the outsized buckle measures 10½ in. high and 8 in. wide, is made of pewter with 24 carat gold plate and contains crystal and semi-precious stones . . . side panels of polished brass are for engraving title bout results . . . currently made by Champbelts by Ronn Scala in Pittsburgh . . . champions keep belts even if they lose their title.

World Championship Ring

Rings decorated with gems and engraving date back to ancient Egypt where the wealthy wore heavy gold and silver rings to indicate social status. . . championship rings in sports serve much the same purpose, indicating the wearer is a champion. . . As an example, the Dallas Cowboys' ring for winning Superbowl XXX on Jan. 28, 1996 was designed by Diamond Cutters International of Houston. . . each ring is made of 14-carat yellow gold, weighs 48-51 penny weights and features five trimmed marquis diamonds interlocking in the shape of the Cowboys' star logo as well as five more marquis diamonds (for the team's five Super Bowl wins) on a bed of 51 smaller diamonds. . . rings were appraised at over $30,000 each.

Who's Who

Jim Thorpe and ***Babe Didrikson Zaharias***
were named AP Athletes of the half century in 1950.

Sports Personalities

Eight hundred sixty five entries dating back to the turn of the century. Entries updated through September 21, 2001.

Hank Aaron (b. Feb. 5, 1934): Baseball OF; led NL in HRs and RBI 4 times each and batting twice with Milwaukee and Atlanta Braves; MVP in 1957; played in 24 All-Star Games, all-time leader in HRs (755) and RBI (2,297), 3rd in hits (3,771); executive with Braves and TBS, Inc.

Kareem Abdul-Jabbar (b. Lew Alcindor, Apr. 16, 1947): Basketball C; led UCLA to 3 NCAA titles (1967-69); Final 4 MOP 3 times; Player of Year twice; led Milwaukee (1) and LA Lakers (5) to 6 NBA titles; playoff MVP twice (1971,85), regular season MVP 6 times (1971-72,74,76-77,80); retired in 1989 after 20 seasons as all-time leader in over 20 categories.

Andre Agassi (b. Apr. 29, 1970): Tennis; 49 career tournament wins including the career grand slam; Wimbledon (1992), U.S. Open (1994,99), Australian Open (1995,2000,01), French Open (1999); helped U.S. win 2 Davis Cup finals (1990,92); regained the world No. 1 ranking in 1999 for the first time since 1996.

Troy Aikman (b. Nov. 21, 1966): Football QB; consensus All-America at UCLA (1988); 1st overall pick in 1989 NFL Draft (by Dallas); led Cowboys to 3 Super Bowl titles (1992,93,95 seasons); MVP in Super Bowl XXVII.

Marv Albert (b. June 12, 1941): Radio-TV; NBC announcer and radio broadcaster for the New York Knicks, Rangers and Giants who pled guilty to a misdemeanor assault charge amid embarrassing allegations of his sex life. Rehired to MSG and Turner networks in 1998 and NBC in '99.

Tenley Albright (b. July 18, 1935): Figure skater; 2-time world champion (1953,55); won Olympic silver (1952) and gold (1956) medals; became a surgeon.

Amy Alcott (b. Feb. 22, 1956): Golfer; 29 career wins, including five majors; inducted into World Golf Hall of Fame in 1999.

Grover Cleveland (Pete) Alexander (b. Feb. 26, 1887, d. Nov. 4, 1950): Baseball RHP; won 20 or more games 9 times; 373 career wins and 90 shutouts.

Muhammad Ali (b. Cassius Clay, Jan. 17, 1942): Boxer; 1960 Olympic light heavyweight champion; 3-time world heavyweight champ (1964-67, 1974-78,1978-79); defeated Sonny Liston (1964), George Foreman (1974) and Leon Spinks (1978) for title; fought Joe Frazier in 3 memorable bouts (1971-75), winning twice; adopted Black Muslim faith in 1964 and changed name; stripped of title in 1967 after conviction for refusing induction into U.S. Army; verdict reversed by Supreme Court in 1971; career record of 56-5 with 37 KOs and 19 successful title defenses; lit the flaming cauldron to signal the beginning of the 1996 Summer Olympics in Atlanta.

Forrest (Phog) Allen (b. Nov. 18, 1885, d. Sept. 16, 1974): Basketball; college coach 48 years; directed Kansas to NCAA title (1952); 746 wins.

Bobby Allison (b. Dec. 3, 1937): Auto racer; 3-time winner of Daytona 500 (1978,82,88); NASCAR national champion in 1983; father of Davey.

Davey Allison (b. Feb. 25, 1961, d. July 13, 1993): Auto racer; stock car Rookie of Year (1987); winner of 19 NASCAR races, including 1992 Daytona 500; killed at age 32 in helicopter accident at Talladega Superspeedway; son of Bobby.

Roberto Alomar (b. Feb. 5, 1968): Baseball; perennial Gold Glove second baseman and All-Star; MVP of 1992 ALCS; became known well beyond baseball for spitting in the face of umpire John Hirschbeck during final weekend of 1996 season; named MVP of 1998 All-Star Game.

Walter Alston (b. Dec. 1, 1911, d. Oct. 1, 1984): Baseball; managed Brooklyn-LA Dodgers 23 years, won 7 pennants and 4 World Series (1955,59,63,65); retired after 1976 season with 2,063 wins (2,040 regular season and 23 postseason).

Sparky Anderson (b. Feb. 22, 1934): Baseball; only manager to win World Series in each league—Cincinnati in NL (1975-76) and Detroit in AL (1984); 3rd-ranked skipper on all-time career list with 2,228 wins (2,194 regular season and 34 postseason); inducted into the Baseball Hall of Fame in 2000.

Mario Andretti (b. Feb. 28, 1940): Auto racer; 4-time USAC-CART national champion (1965-66,69,84); only driver to win Daytona 500 (1967), Indy 500 (1969) and Formula One world title (1978); Indy 500 Rookie of Year (1965); retired after 1994 racing season ranked 1st in poles (67) and starts (407) and 2nd in wins (52) on all-time CART list; father of Michael and Jeff, uncle of John.

Michael Andretti (b. Oct. 5, 1962): Auto racer; 1991 CART national champion with single-season record 8 wins; Indy 500 Rookie of Year (1984); left IndyCar circuit for ill-fated Formula One try in 1993; returned to IndyCar (now CART) in '94; son of Mario.

Earl Anthony (b. Apr. 27, 1938, d. Aug. 14, 2001): Bowler; 6-time PBA Bowler of Year; 41 career titles; first to earn $100,000 in 1 season (1975); first to earn $1 million in career; came out of retirement in '96; ranked 11th on list of PBA career money leaders through 2000.

Said Aouita (b. Nov. 2, 1959): Moroccan runner; won gold (5000m) and bronze (800m) in 1984 Olympics; won 5000m at 1987 World Championships; formerly held 2 world records recognized by IAAF—2000m and 5000m.

Luis Aparicio (b. Apr. 29, 1934): Baseball SS; retired as all-time leader in most games, assists and double plays by shortstop; led AL in stolen bases 9 times (1956-64); 506 career steals.

Al Arbour (b. Nov. 1, 1932): Hockey; coached NY Islanders to 4 straight Stanley Cup titles (1980-83); retired after 1993-94 season; 2nd on all-time career list with 904 wins (781 regular season and 123 postseason); elected to Hockey Hall of Fame in 1996.

Eddie Arcaro (b. Feb. 19, 1916, d. Nov. 14, 1997): Jockey; 2-time Triple Crown winner (Whirlaway in 1941, Citation in '48); he won Kentucky Derby 5 times, Preakness and Belmont 6 times each.

Henry Armstrong (b. Dec. 12, 1912, d. Oct. 22, 1988): Boxer; held feather-, light- and welterweight titles simultaneously in 1938; pro record 152-21-8 with 100 KOs.

Lance Armstrong (b. Sept. 18, 1971): Cyclist; 3-time winner of the Tour de France (1999-2001); returned from treatment for testicular cancer to become improbable winner of '99 Tour de France; only the second American winner in the race's history.

Arthur Ashe (b. July 10, 1943, d. Feb. 6, 1993): Tennis; first black man to win U.S. Championship (1968) and Wimbledon (1975); 1st U.S. player to earn $100,000 in 1 year (1970); won Davis Cup as player (1968-70) and captain (1981-82); wrote black sports history, *Hard Road to Glory*; announced in 1992 that he was infected with AIDS virus from a blood transfusion during 1983 heart surgery; in 1997, the new home for the U.S. Open was named Arthur Ashe Stadium.

Evelyn Ashford (b. Apr. 15, 1957): Track & Field; winner of 4 Olympic gold medals—100m in 1984, and 4x100m in 1984, '88 and '92; also won silver medal in 100m in '88; member of 5 U.S. Olympic teams (1976-92); inducted into Track and Field and Women's Sports Halls of Fame in 1997.

Red Auerbach (b. Sept. 20, 1917): Basketball; 3rd winningest coach (regular season and playoffs) in NBA history; won 1,037 times in 20 years; as coach-GM, led Boston to 9 NBA titles, including 8 in a row (1959-66); also coached defunct Washington Capitols (1946-49); NBA Coach of the Year award named after him; retired as Celtics coach in 1966 and as GM in '84; club president from 1970 to 1997.

Tracy Austin (b. Dec. 12, 1962): Tennis; youngest player to win U.S. Open (age 16 in 1979); won 2nd U.S. Open in '81; named AP Female Athlete of Year twice before she was 20; recurring neck and back injuries shortened career after 1983; youngest player ever inducted into Tennis Hall of Fame (age 29 in 1992).

Donovan Bailey (b. Dec. 16, 1967): Track; Jamaican-born Canadian sprinter who set world record in the 100m (9.84) in gold medal-winning performance at 1996 Olympics which stood until '99; set indoor record in 50m (5.56) in 1996; member of Canadian 4x100 relay that won gold in 1996 Olympics.

Oksana Baiul (b. Feb. 26, 1977): Ukrainian figure skater; 1993 world champion at age 15; edged Nancy Kerrigan by a 5-4 judges' vote for 1994 Olympic gold medal.

Hobey Baker (b. Jan. 15, 1892, d. Dec. 21, 1918): Football and hockey star at Princeton (1911-14); member of college football and pro hockey Halls of Fame; college hockey Player of Year award named after him; killed in plane crash.

Bob Baffert (b. Jan. 13, 1953): Horse racing; 3-time Eclipse Award winner as outstanding trainer; trained 2 Kentucky Derby winners (1997,98) and 3 Preakness winners (1997,98,01); leading annual money leader for trainers in 1998 and '99.

Seve Ballesteros (b. Apr. 9, 1957): Spanish golfer; has won British Open 3 times (1979,84,88) and Masters twice (1980,83); 3-time European Golfer of Year (1986,88,91); has led Europe to 5 Ryder Cup titles (1985,87,89,95,97); 72 world-wide victories.

Ernie Banks (b. Jan. 31, 1931): Baseball SS-1B; led NL in home runs and RBI twice each; 2-time MVP (1958-59) with Chicago Cubs; 512 career HRs.

Roger Bannister (b. Mar. 23, 1929): British runner; first to run mile in less than 4 minutes (3:59.4 on May 6, 1954).

Walter (Red) Barber (b. Feb. 17, 1908, d. Oct. 22, 1992): Radio-TV; renowned baseball play-by-play broadcaster for Cincinnati, Brooklyn and N.Y. Yankees from 1934-66; won Peabody Award for radio commentary in 1991.

Charles Barkley (b. Feb. 20, 1963): Basketball F; 5-time All-NBA 1st team with Philadelphia and Phoenix; traded to Suns for 3 players (June 17, 1992); U.S. Olympic Dream Team member in '92; NBA regular season MVP in 1993.

Rick Barry (b. Mar. 28, 1944): Basketball F; only player to lead both NBA and ABA in scoring; 5-time All-NBA 1st team; Finals MVP with Golden St. in 1975.

Sammy Baugh (b. Mar. 17, 1914): Football QB-DB-P; led Washington to NFL titles in 1937 (his rookie year) and '42; led league in passing 6 times, punting 4 times and interceptions once.

Elgin Baylor (b. Sept. 16, 1934): Basketball F; MOP of Final 4 in 1958; led Minneapolis-LA Lakers to 8 NBA Finals; 10-time All-NBA 1st team (1959-65,67-69); LA Clippers' vice president of basketball operations.

Bob Beamon (b. Aug. 29, 1946): Track & Field; won 1968 Olympic gold medal in long jump with world record (29-ft, 2½in.) that shattered old mark by nearly 2 feet; record finally broken by 2 inches in 1991 by Mike Powell.

Franz Beckenbauer (b. Sept. 11, 1945): Soccer; captain of West German World Cup champions in 1974 then coached West German to World Cup title in 1990; invented sweeper position; played in U.S. for NY Cosmos (1977-80,83); Member of International Soccer Hall of Champions.

Boris Becker (b. Nov. 22, 1967): German tennis player; 3-time Wimbledon champ (1985-86,89); youngest male (17) to win Wimbledon; led country to 1st Davis Cup win in 1988; has also won U.S. (1989) and Australian (1991,96) Opens.

Chuck Bednarik (b. May 1, 1925): Football C-LB; 2-time All-America at Penn and 7-time All-Pro with NFL Eagles as both center (1950) and linebacker (1951-56); missed only 3 games in 14 seasons; led Eagles to 1960 NFL title as a 35-year-old two-way player.

Clair Bee (b. Mar. 2, 1896, d. May 20, 1983): Basketball coach who led LIU to 2 undefeated seasons (1936,39) and 2 NIT titles (1939,41); his teams won 95 percent of their games between 1931-51, including 43 in a row from 1935-37; coached NBA Baltimore Bullets from 1952-54, but was only 34-116; contributions to game include 1-3-1 zone defense, 3-second rule and NBA 24-second clock.

Jean Beliveau (b. Aug. 31, 1931): Hockey C; led Montreal to 10 Stanley Cups in 17 playoffs; playoff MVP (1965); 2-time regular season MVP (1956,64).

Bert Bell (b. Feb. 25, 1895, d. Oct. 11, 1959): Football; team owner and 2nd NFL commissioner (1946-59); proposed college draft in 1935 and instituted TV blackout rule.

James (Cool Papa) Bell (b. May 17, 1903, d. Mar. 8, 1991): Baseball; member of the Negro Leagues; widely considered the fastest player ever to play baseball; tremendous hitter and base runner; also coached for the Kansas City Monarchs, teaching such players as Jackie Robinson; member of the National Baseball Hall of Fame.

Deane Beman (b. Apr. 22, 1938): Golf; 1st commissioner of PGA Tour (1974-94); introduced "stadium golf"; as player, won U.S. Amateur twice and British Amateur once; inducted into the World Golf Hall of Fame in 2000.

Johnny Bench (b. Dec. 7, 1947): Baseball C; led NL in HRs twice and RBI 3 times; 2-time regular season MVP (1970,72) with Cincinnati, World Series MVP in 1976; 389 career HRs.

Patty Berg (b. Feb. 13, 1918): Golfer; 57 career pro wins, including 15 majors; 3-time AP Female Athlete of Year (1938,43,55).

Yogi Berra (b. May 12, 1925): Baseball C; played on 10 World Series winners with NY Yankees; holds WS records for games played (75), at bats (259) and hits (71); 3-time AL MVP (1951,54-55); managed both Yankees (1964) and NY Mets (1973) to pennants.

Jay Berwanger (b. Mar. 19, 1914): Football HB; Univ. of Chicago star; won 1st Heisman Trophy in 1935.

Gary Bettman (b. June 2, 1952): Hockey; former NBA executive, who was named first commissioner of NHL on Dec. 11, 1992; took office on Feb. 1, 1993.

Abebe Bikila (b. Aug. 7, 1932, d. Oct. 25, 1973): Ethiopian runner; 1st to win consecutive Olympic marathons (1960,64).

Matt Biondi (b. Oct. 8, 1965): Swimmer; won 7 medals in 1988 Olympics, including 5 gold (2 individual, 3 relay); has won a total of 11 medals (8 gold, 2 silver and a bronze) in 3 Olympics (1984,88,92).

Larry Bird (b. Dec. 7, 1956): Basketball F; college Player of Year (1979) at Indiana St.; 1980 NBA Rookie of Year; 9-time All-NBA 1st team; 3-time regular season MVP (1984-86); led Boston to 3 NBA titles (1981,84, 86); 2-time Finals MVP (1984,86); U.S. Olympic Dream Team member in '92; inducted into Hall of Fame in 1998; in 1997, named coach of Indiana Pacers and won Coach of the Year honors in first season; led the Pacers to the NBA finals in 2000 but lost in 6 games to the Lakers; retired from coaching in 2000.

The Black Sox: Eight Chicago White Sox players who were banned from baseball for life in 1921 for allegedly throwing the 1919 World Series— RHP Eddie Cicotte (1884-1969), OF Happy Felsch (1891-1964), 1B Chick Gandil (1887-1970), OF Shoeless Joe Jackson (1889-1951), INF Fred McMullin (1891-1952), SS Swede Risberg (1894-1975), 3B-SS Buck Weaver (1890-1956), and LHP Lefty Williams (1893-1959).

Earl (Red) Blaik (b. Feb. 15, 1897, d. May 6, 1989): Football; coached Army to consecutive national titles in 1944-45; 166 career wins and 3 Heisman winners (Blanchard, Davis, Dawkins).

Bonnie Blair (b. Mar. 18, 1964): Speedskater; only American woman to win 5 Olympic gold medals in Winter Games; won 500-meters in 1988, then 500m and 1,000m in both 1992 and '94; added 1,000m bronze in 1988; Sullivan Award winner (1992); retired on 31st birthday as reigning world sprint champ.

Hector (Toe) Blake (b. Aug. 21, 1912, d. May 17, 1995): Hockey LW; led Montreal to 2 Stanley Cups as a player and 8 more as coach; regular season MVP in 1939.

Felix (Doc) Blanchard (b. Dec. 11, 1924): Football FB; 3-time All-America; led Army to national titles in 1944-45; Glenn Davis' running mate; won Heisman Trophy and Sullivan Award in 1945.

George Blanda (b. Sept. 17, 1927): Football QB-PK; was pro football's all-time leading scorer (2,002 points) until 2000 when he was finally passed by kicker Gary Anderson; led Houston to 2 AFL titles (1960-61); played 26 pro seasons; retired at 48.

Fanny Blankers-Koen (b. Apr. 26, 1918): Dutch sprinter; 30-year-old mother of two, who won 4 gold medals (100m, 200m, 800m hurdles and 4x100m relay) at 1948 Olympics.

Wade Boggs (b. June 15, 1958): Baseball 3B; 5 AL batting titles (1983,85-88) with Boston Red Sox; 11-time All-Star; two Gold Gloves; later played with NY Yankees and Tampa Bay; got 3000th career hit with a home run Aug. 7, 1999 against Cleveland.

Barry Bonds (b. July 24, 1964): Baseball OF; 3-time NL MVP, twice with Pitt (1990,92) and once with San Fran (1993); NL's HR and RBI leader in 1993; one of only 3 players with 40 HRs and 40 SBs in same season (1996); made a run at single season HR record in 2001; son of Bobby.

Bjorn Borg (b. June 6, 1956): Swedish tennis player; 2-time Player of Year (1979-80); won 6 French Opens and 5 straight Wimbledons (1976-80); led Sweden to 1st Davis Cup win in 1975; retired in 1983 at age 26; attempted unsuccessful comeback in 1991.

Mike Bossy (b. Jan. 22, 1957): Hockey RW; led NY Isles to 4 Stanley Cups; playoff MVP in 1982; 50 goals or more 9 straight years; 573 career goals.

Ralph Boston (b. May 9, 1939): Track & Field; medaled in 3 consecutive Olympic long jumps— gold (1960), silver (1964), bronze (1968).

Ray Bourque (b. Dec. 28, 1960): Hockey D; 12-time All-NHL 1st team; won Norris Trophy 5 times (1987-88,1990-91,94) with Boston; '96 All-Star Game MVP; all-time leader for points and assists by a defenseman; traded to Colorado Avalanche in 2000 and won his only Stanley Cup in 2001; retired after 2000-01 season ranked 8th in career scoring (1,579 points) and 3rd in games played (1,612).

Bobby Bowden (b. Nov. 8, 1929): Football; coached Florida St. to a national title in 1993 and again in 1999; 2001 season with 315 wins including a 17-6-1 bowl record in 35 years as coach at Samford, West Va. and FSU; father of Clemson head coach Tommy and former Auburn coach Terry.

Scotty Bowman (b. Sept. 18, 1933): Hockey coach; all-time winningest NHL coach in both regular season (1,147) and playoffs (202) over 28 seasons entering 2001-02; coached a record-tying eight Stanley Cup winners with Montreal (1973,76-79), Pittsburgh (1992) and Detroit (1997,98).

Jack Brabham (b. Apr. 2, 1926): Australian auto racer; 3-time Formula One champion (1959-60,66); 14 career wins; member of the Hall of Fame.

Bill Bradley (b. July 28, 1943): Basketball F; 2-time All-America at Princeton; Player of the Year and Final 4 MOP in 1965; captain of gold medal-winning 1964 U.S. Olympic team; Sullivan Award winner (1965); led NY Knicks to 2 NBA titles (1970,73); U.S. Senator (D, N.J.) 1979-95; ran for President in 2000.

Pat Bradley (b. Mar. 24, 1951): Golfer; 2-time LPGA Player of Year (1986,91); has won all four majors on LPGA tour, including 3 du Maurier Classics; inducted into the LPGA Hall of Fame on Jan. 18, 1992; among all-time LPGA money leaders and tournament winners (31); captained the 2000 U.S. Solheim Cup team.

Terry Bradshaw (b. Sept. 2, 1948): Football QB; led Pittsburgh to 4 Super Bowl titles (1975-76,79-80); 2-time Super Bowl MVP (1979-80) and regular season MVP in 1978; Fox TV studio analyst.

George Brett (b. May 15, 1953): Baseball 3B-1B; AL batting champion in 3 different decades (1976,80,90); MVP in 1980; led KC to World Series title in 1985; retired after 1993 season with 3,154 hits and .305 career average; inducted into Hall of Fame in '99.

Valerie Brisco-Hooks (b. July 6, 1960): Track & Field; won three gold medals at the 1984 Olympics (200 meters, 400 meters and 4x100 relay); first athlete to ever win the 200 and 400 in the same Olympics.

Lou Brock (b. June 18, 1939): Baseball OF; former all-time stolen base leader (938); led NL in steals 8 times; led St. Louis to 2 World Series titles (1964,67); had 3,023 career hits.

Herb Brooks (b. Aug. 5, 1937): Hockey; former U.S. Olympic player (1964,68) who coached 1980 team to gold medal; coached Minnesota to 3 NCAA titles (1974,76,78); also coached NY Rangers, Minnesota, New Jersey and Pittsburgh in NHL.

Jim Brown (b. Feb. 17, 1936): Football FB; All-America at Syracuse (1956) and NFL Rookie of Year (1957); led NFL in rushing 8 times; 8-time All-Pro (1957-61,63-65); 3-time MVP (1958,63,65) with Cleveland; ran for 12,312 yards and scored 126 touchdowns in just 9 seasons.

Larry Brown (b. Sept. 14, 1940): Basketball; played in ACC, AAU, 1964 Olympics and ABA; 3-time assist leader (1968-70) and 3-time Coach of Year (1973,75-76) in ABA; coached ABA's Carolina and Denver and NBA's Denver, N. J., San Antonio, LA Clippers, Indiana and Phila.; also coached UCLA to NCAA Final (1980) and Kansas to NCAA title (1988).

Mordecai (Three-Finger) Brown (b. Oct. 18, 1876, d. Feb. 14, 1948): Baseball; nickname derived from injury in a childhood accident that left him with three digits on right hand; injury gave him a particularly nasty curve ball; won the decisive game of the the 1907 World Series as a Chicago Cub; in 1908, first pitcher to record 4 consecutive shutouts and finished at 29-9; career record of 239-130 with lifetime ERA of 2.06; member of Hall of Fame.

Paul Brown (b. Sept. 7, 1908, d. Aug. 5, 1991): Football innovator; coached Ohio St. to national title in 1942; in pros, directed Cleveland Browns to 4 straight AAFC titles (1946-49) and 3 NFL titles (1950,54-55); formed Cincinnati Bengals as head coach and part-owner in 1968 (reached playoffs in '70).

Valery Brumel (b. Apr. 14, 1942): Soviet high jumper; dominated event from 1961-64; broke world record 5 times; won silver medal in 1960 Olympics and gold in 1964; highest jump was 7-5 ¾.

Avery Brundage (b. Sept. 28, 1887, d. May 5, 1975): Amateur sports czar for over 40 years as president of AAU (1928-35), U.S. Olympic Committee (1929-53) and Int'l Olympic Committee (1952-72).

Kobe Bryant (b. Aug. 23, 1978): Basketball; guard/forward for the LA Lakers; graduated from Lower Merion (Penn.) HS and made the jump directly to the NBA; youngest player (18 yrs., 2 mos., 11 days) ever to appear in an NBA game; became the youngest all-star in NBA history in 1998 and scored a team-high 18 points; won titles with the Lakers in 2000 and 2001.

Paul (Bear) Bryant (b. Sept. 11, 1913, d. Jan. 26, 1983): Football; coached at 4 colleges over 38 years; directed Alabama to 5 national titles (1961,64-65,78-79); retired as the winningest coach of all time (323-85-17 record); 15 bowl wins, including 8 Sugar Bowls.

Sergey Bubka (b. Dec. 4, 1963): Ukrainian pole vaulter; 1st man to clear 20 feet both indoors and out (1991); holder of indoor (20-2) and outdoor (20-1¾) world records as of Sept. 21, 2001; 6-time world champion (1983,87,91,93,95,97); won Olympic gold medal in 1988, but failed to clear any height in 1992 Games.

Buck Buchanan (b. Sept. 10, 1940, d. July 16, 1992): Football; played both ways in college at Grambling; first player chosen in the first AFL draft by the Dallas Texans who later became the KC Chiefs; missed one game in a 13-year pro career; played in six AFL All-Star games and two Pro Bowls at def. tackle; defensive star of the Chiefs team that won Super Bowl IV; later coached for the New Orleans Saints and Cleveland Browns; member of Pro Football Hall of Fame.

Don Budge (b. June 13, 1915, d. Jan. 26, 2000): Tennis; in 1938 became 1st player to win the Grand Slam— the French, Wimbledon, U.S. and Australian titles in 1 year; led U.S. to 2 Davis Cups (1937-38); turned pro in late '38.

Maria Bueno (b. Oct. 11, 1939): Brazilian tennis player; won 4 U.S. Championships (1959,63-64,66) and 3 Wimbledons (1959-60,64).

Leroy Burrell (b. Feb. 21, 1967): Track & Field; set former world record of 9.85 in 100 meters, July 6, 1994; previously held record (9.90) in 1991; member of 4 world record-breaking 4x100m relay teams.

Susan Butcher (b. Dec. 26, 1956): Sled Dog racer; 4-time winner of Iditarod Trail race (1986-88,90).

Dick Butkus (b. Dec. 9, 1942): Football LB; 2-time All-America at Illinois (1963-64); All-Pro 7 of 9 NFL seasons with Chicago Bears; worked with XFL in 2001.

Dick Button (b. July 18, 1929): Figure skater; 5-time world champion (1948-52); 2-time Olympic champ (1948,52); Sullivan Award winner (1949); won Emmy Award as Best Analyst for 1980-81 TV season.

Walter Byers (b. Mar. 13, 1922): College athletics; 1st exec. director of NCAA, serving from 1951-88.

Frank Calder (b. Nov. 17, 1877, d. Feb. 4, 1943): Hockey, 1st NHL president (1917-43); guided league through its formative years; NHL's Rookie of the Year award named after him.

Lee Calhoun (b. Feb. 23, 1933, d. June 22, 1989): Track & Field; won consecutive Olympic gold medals in the 110m hurdles (1956,60).

Walter Camp (b. Apr. 7, 1859, d. Mar. 14, 1925): Football coach and innovator; established scrimmage line, center snap, downs, 11 players per side; elected 1st All-America team (1889).

Roy Campanella (b. Nov. 19, 1921, d. June 26, 1993): Baseball C; 3-time NL MVP (1951,53,55); led Brooklyn to 5 pennants and 1st World Series title (1955); career cut short when 1958 car accident left him paralyzed.

Clarence Campbell (b. July 9, 1905, d. June 24, 1984): Hockey; 3rd NHL president (1946-77), league tripled in size from 6 to 18 teams during his tenure.

Earl Campbell (b. Mar. 29, 1955): Football RB; won Heisman Trophy in 1977; led NFL in rushing 3 times; 3-time All-Pro; 2-time MVP (1978-79) at Houston.

John Campbell (b. Apr. 8, 1955): Harness racing; 5-time winner of Hambletonian (1987,88,90,95,98); 3-time Driver of Year; first driver to go over $100 million in career winnings.

Milt Campbell (b. Dec. 9, 1933): Track & Field; won silver medal in 1952 Olympic decathlon and gold medal in '56.

Jimmy Cannon (b. 1910, d. Dec. 5, 1973): Tough, opinionated New York sportswriter and essayist who viewed sports as an extension of show business; protégé of Damon Runyon; covered World War II for Stars & Stripes.

Jose Canseco (b. July 2, 1964): Baseball OF/DH; AL Rookie of the Year in 1986 and Most Valuable Player in 1988 with the Oakland A's; in 1988 he became the first player in history with 40 HRs and 40 steals in a season; led AL in HRs in 1988 and tied for lead in 1991.

Tony Canzoneri (b. Nov. 6, 1908, d. Dec. 9, 1959): Boxer; 2-time world lightweight champion (1930-33,35-36); pro record 141-24-10 with 44 KOs.

Jennifer Capriati (b. Mar. 29, 1976): Tennis; youngest Grand Slam semifinalist ever (age 14 in 1990 French Open); surprise gold medal winner at 1992 Olympics; left tour from 1994 to '96 due to personal problems including an arrest for marijuana possession; comeback complete with 2001 Australian and French Open titles.

Harry Caray (b. Mar. 1, 1917, d. Feb. 18, 1998): Radio-TV; baseball play-by-play broadcaster for St. Louis Cardinals, Oakland, Chicago White Sox and Cubs 1945-98; father of sportscaster Skip and grandfather of sportscaster Chip.

Rod Carew (b. Oct. 1, 1945): Baseball 2B-1B; led AL in batting 7 times (1969,72-75,77-78) with Minnesota; MVP in 1977; had 3,053 career hits.

Steve Carlton (b. Dec. 22, 1944): Baseball LHP; won 20 or more games 6 times; 4-time Cy Young winner (1972,77,80,82) with Philadelphia; 329-244 career record.

JoAnne Carner (b. Apr. 4, 1939): Golfer; 5-time U.S. Amateur champion; 2-time U.S. Open champ; 3-time LPGA Player of Year (1974,81-82); 7th in career wins (42).

Cris Carter (b. Nov. 25, 1965): Football; WR for the Minnesota Vikings; twice caught 122 passes in a season (1994, '95), the first time establishing an NFL record for catches in a season that was beaten a year later; 2nd player to reach 1000 career catches.

Don Carter (b. July 29, 1926): Bowler; 6-time Bowler of Year (1953-54,57-58,60-61); voted Greatest of All-Time in 1970.

Alexander Cartwright (b. Apr. 17, 1820, d. July 12, 1892): Baseball; engineer and draftsman who spread gospel of baseball from New York City to California gold fields; widely regarded as the father of modern game; his guidelines included setting 3 strikes for an out and 3 outs for each half inning.

Billy Casper (b. June 24, 1931): Golfer; 2-time PGA Player of Year (1966,70); has won U.S. Open (1959,66), Masters (1970), U.S. Senior Open (1983); compiled 51 PGA Tour wins and 9 on Senior Tour.

Tracy Caulkins (b. Jan. 11, 1963): Swimmer; won 3 gold medals (2 individual) at 1984 Olympics; set 5 world records and won 48 U.S. national titles from 1978-84; Sullivan Award winner (1978); 2-time Honda Broderick Cup winner (1982,84).

Steve Cauthen (b. May 1, 1960): Jockey; became youngest jockey (18) to win the Triple Crown with Affirmed in 1978; won a record $6.1 million in 1977, winning the Eclipse Award as the nation's top rider and the award for AP male athlete of the year.

Evonne Goolagong Cawley (b. July 31, 1951): Australian tennis player; won Australian Open 4 times, Wimbledon twice (1971,80), French once (1971).

Florence Chadwick (b. Nov. 9, 1917, d. Mar. 15, 1995): Dominant distance swimmer of 1950s; set English Channel records from France to England (1950) and England to France (1951 and '55).

Wilt Chamberlain (b. Aug. 21, 1936, d. Oct. 12, 1999): Basketball C; consensus All-America in 1957 and '58 at Kansas; Final Four MOP in 1957; led NBA in scoring 7 times and rebounding 11 times; 7-time All-NBA first team; 4-time MVP (1960,66-68) in Philadelphia; scored 100 points vs. NY Knicks in Hershey, Pa., Mar. 2, 1962; led 76ers (1967) and LA Lakers (1972) to NBA titles; Finals MVP in 1972.

A.B. (Happy) Chandler (b. July 14, 1898, d. June 15, 1991): Baseball; former Kentucky governor and U.S. Senator who succeeded Judge Landis as commissioner in 1945; backed Branch Rickey's move in 1947 to make Jackie Robinson 1st black player in major leagues; deemed too pro-player and ousted by owners in 1951.

Michael Chang (b. Feb. 22, 1972): Tennis; won the 1989 French Open , becoming the youngest men's champion of a grand slam event (17 years, 3 months.); went 11 consecutive years (1988-98) with at least one title; finished in top 10 in the ATP year-end rankings from 1992-97 (career high no. 2 in 1996).

Julio Cesar Chavez (b. July 12, 1962): Mexican boxer; world jr. welterweight champ (1989-94); also held titles as jr. lightweight (1984-87) and lightweight (1987-89); career record of 101-2-2 record with 84 KOs; 90-bout unbeaten streak ended Jan. 29, 1994 when Frankie Randall won title on split decision; Chavez won title back four months later.

Linford Christie (b. Apr. 2, 1960): British sprinter; won 100-meter gold medals at both 1992 Olympics (9.96) and '93 World Championships (9.87).

Jim Clark (b. Mar. 14, 1936, d. Apr. 7, 1968): Scottish auto racer; 2-time Formula One world champion (1963,65); won Indy 500 in 1965; killed in car crash.

Bobby Clarke (b. Aug. 13, 1949): Hockey C; led Philadelphia Flyers to consecutive Stanley Cups in 1974-75; 3-time regular season MVP (1973,75-76); currently Flyers President/GM.

Ron Clarke (b. Feb. 21, 1937): Australian runner; from 1963-70 set 17 world records in races from 2 miles to 20,000m; never won Olympic gold medal.

Roger Clemens (b. Aug. 4, 1962): Baseball RHP; twice fanned MLB record 20 batters in 9-inning game (April 29, 1986 and Sept. 18, 1996); 5 Cy Young Awards with Boston (1986-87,91) and Toronto (1997,98); AL MVP in 1986; won pitching Triple Crown in 1997 and 98; traded from Toronto to the NY Yankees and won World Series rings in 1999 and 2000.

Roberto Clemente (b. Aug. 18, 1934, d. Dec. 31, 1972): Baseball OF; hit over .300 13 times with Pittsburgh; led NL in batting 4 times; World Series MVP in 1971; regular season MVP in 1966; had 3,000 career hits; killed in plane crash.

Alice Coachman (b. Nov. 9, 1923): Track & Field; became the first black woman to win an Olympic gold medal with her win in the high jump in 1948 (London); broke the high school and college high jump records despite not wearing any shoes; member of the National Track & Field Hall of Fame.

Ty Cobb (b. Dec. 18, 1886, d. July 17, 1961): Baseball OF; all-time highest career batting average (.367); hit over .400 3 times; led AL in batting 12 times and stolen bases 6 times with Detroit; MVP in 1911; had 4,191 career hits and 892 steals.

Mickey Cochrane (b. Apr. 6, 1903, d. June 28, 1962): Baseball C; led Philadelphia A's (1929-30) and Detroit (1935) to 3 World Series titles; 2-time AL MVP (1928,34).

Sebastian Coe (b. Sept. 29, 1956): British runner; won gold medal in 1500m and silver medal in 800m at both 1980 and '84 Olympics; long-time world record holder in 800m and 1000m; elected to Parliament as Conservative in 1992.

Paul Coffey (b. June 1, 1961): Hockey D; 3-time Norris Trophy winner; member of four Stanley Cup championship teams at Edmonton (1984-85,87) and Pittsburgh (1991).

Rocky Colavito (b. August 10, 1933): Baseball OF; six-time all-star who hit 374 HRs over his 14-year career; hugely popular in Cleveland where he played from 1955-59 and then 1965-67; led the league in HRs in 1959 with 42 and RBI in 1965 with 108; hit four consecutive HRs in one game.

Eddie Collins (b. May 2, 1887, d. Mar. 25, 1951): Baseball 2B; led Phila. A's (1910-11) and Chicago White Sox (1917) to 3 World Series titles; AL MVP in 1914; had 3,311 career hits and 743 stolen bases.

Nadia Comaneci (b. Nov. 12, 1961): Romanian gymnast; first to record perfect 10 in Olympics; won 3 individual golds at 1976 Olympics and 2 more in '80.

Lionel Conacher (b. May 24, 1901, d. May 26, 1954): Canada's greatest all-around athlete; NHL hockey (2 Stanley Cups), CFL football (1 Grey Cup), minor league baseball, soccer, lacrosse, track, amateur boxing champion; member of Parliament (1949-54).

Tony Conigliaro (b. Jan. 7, 1945, d. Feb. 24, 1990): Baseball OF; youngest to lead the AL in HRs (32 in 1965); hit in the face with a fastball in 1967; came back to hit 36 HRs in 1970 but was never the same.

Gene Conley (b. Nov. 10, 1930): Baseball and Basketball; played for World Series and NBA champions with Milwaukee Braves (1957) and Boston Celtics (1959-61); winning pitcher in 1954 All-Star Game; 91-96 record in 11 seasons.

Billy Conn (b. Oct. 8, 1917, d. May 29, 1993): Boxer; Pittsburgh and world light heavyweight champion from 1939-41; nearly upset heavyweight champ Joe Louis in 1941 title bout, but was knocked out in 13th round; pro record 63-11-1 with 14 KOs.

Dennis Conner (b. Sept. 16, 1942): Sailing; 3-time America's Cup-winning skipper aboard *Freedom* (1980), *Stars & Stripes* (1987) and the *Stars & Stripes* catamaran (1988); only American skipper to lose Cup, first in 1983 when *Australia II* beat *Liberty* and again in '95 when New Zealand's *Black Magic* swept Conner and his *Stars & Stripes* crew aboard the borrowed *Young America*.

Maureen Connolly (b. Sept. 17, 1934, d. June 21, 1969): Tennis;.in 1953 1st woman to win Grand Slam (at age 18); riding accident ended her career in '54; won both Wimbledon and U.S. titles 3 times (1951-53); 3-time AP Female Athlete of Year (1951-53).

Jimmy Connors (b. Sept. 2, 1952): Tennis; No.1 player in world 5 times (1974-78); won 5 U.S. Opens, 2 Wimbledons and 1 Australian; rose from No. 936 at the close of 1990 to U.S. Open semifinals in 1991 at age 39; NCAA singles champ (1971); all-time leader in pro singles titles (109) and matches won at U.S. Open (98) and Wimbledon (84).

Jack Kent Cooke (b. Oct. 25, 1912, d. April 6, 1997): Football; sole owner of NFL Washington Redskins from 1985-97; teams won 2 Super Bowls (1988,92); also owned NBA Lakers and NHL Kings in LA; built LA Forum for $12 million in 1967.

Cynthia Cooper (b. April 14, 1963): Women's basketball G; won two NCAA basketball titles at USC (1983-84); won gold medal with U.S. team in 1988; 2-time WNBA MVP and 4-time league champion with Houston Comets; hired as head coach of WNBA's Phoenix Mercury in Jan. 2001.

Angel Cordero Jr. (b. Nov. 8, 1942): Jockey; retired third on all-time list with 7,057 wins in 38,646 starts; won Kentucky Derby 3 times (1974,76,85), Preakness twice and Belmont once; 2-time Eclipse Award winner (1982-83).

Howard Cosell (b. Mar. 25, 1920, d. Apr. 23, 1995): Radio-TV; former ABC commentator on *Monday Night Football* and *Wide World of Sports*, who energized TV sports journalism with abrasive "tell it like it is" style.

James (Doc) Counsilman (b. Dec. 28, 1920): Swimming; coached Indiana men's swim team to 6 NCAA championships (1968-73); coached the 1964 and '76 U.S. men's Olympic teams that won a combined 21 of 24 gold medals; in 1979 became oldest person (59) to swim English Channel; retired in 1990 with dual meet record of 287-36-1.

Fred Couples (b. Oct. 3, 1959): Golfer; 2-time PGA Tour Player of the Year (1991,92); 14 Tour victories, including 1992 Masters.

Jim Courier (b. Aug. 17, 1970): Tennis; No. 1 player in world in 1992, won 2 Australian Opens (1992-93) and 2 French Opens (1991-92); played on 1992 Davis Cup winner; Nick Bollettieri Academy classmate of Andre Agassi; announced retirement in May, 2000.

Margaret Smith Court (b. July 16, 1942): Australian tennis player; won Grand Slam in both singles (1970) and mixed doubles (with Ken Fletcher); record 24 Grand Slam singles titles—11 Australian, 5 U.S., 5 French and 3 Wimbledon.

Bob Cousy (b. Aug. 9, 1928): Basketball G; led NBA in assists 8 times; 10-time All-NBA 1st team; 1957 MVP; led Boston to 6 NBA titles (1957,59-63).

Buster Crabbe (b. Feb. 7, 1908, d. Apr. 23, 1983): Swimmer; 2-time Olympic freestyle medalist with bronze in 1928 (1500m) and gold in '32 (400m); became movie star and King of Serials as Flash Gordon and Buck Rogers.

Ben Crenshaw (b. Jan. 11, 1952): Golfer; co-NCAA champion with Tom Kite in 1972; battled Graves' disease in mid-1980s; 19 career Tour victories; won Masters for second time on April 9, 1995 and dedicated it to 90-year-old mentor Harvey Penick, who had died on April 2; captain of 1999 Ryder Cup team.

Joe Cronin (b. Oct. 12, 1906, d. Sept. 7, 1984): Baseball SS; hit over .300 and drove in over 100 runs 8 times each; player-manager in Washington and Boston (1933-47); AL president (1959-73).

Larry Csonka (b. Dec. 25, 1946): Football RB; powerful runner and blocker who gained 8,081 yards in 11 seasons in the AFL and NFL; won two consecutive Super Bowls with the Miami Dolphins (1973-74) and was named MVP in the latter, rushing for 145 yards and two TDs; member of the College and Pro Football Halls of Fame.

Ann Curtis (b. Mar. 6, 1926): Swimming; won 2 gold medals and 1 silver in 1948 Olympics; set 4 world and 18 U.S. records during career; 1st woman and swimmer to win Sullivan Award (1944).

Betty Cuthbert (b. Apr. 20, 1938): Australian runner; won gold medals in 100 and 200 meters and 4x100m relay at 1956 Olympics; also won 400m gold at 1964 Olympics.

Bjorn Dählie (b. June 19, 1967): Norwegian cross-country skier; winner of a record eight gold and 12 overall Winter Olympic medals from 1992-98.

John Daly (b. Apr. 28, 1966): Golfer; surprise winner of 1991 PGA Championship as unknown 25-year-old; battled through personal troubles in 1994 to return in '95 and win 2nd major at British Open, beating Italy's Costantino Rocca in 4-hole playoff.

Stanley Dancer (b. July 25, 1927): Harness racing; winner of 4 Hambletonians; trainer-driver of Triple Crown winners in trotting (Nevele Pride in 1968 and Super Bowl in '72) and pacing (Most Happy Fella in 1970).

Beth Daniel (b. Oct. 14, 1956): Golfer; 32 career wins, including 1 major; inducted into World Golf Hall of Fame in 1999.

Alvin Dark (b. Jan. 7, 1922): Baseball OF and MGR; hit .322 to win the NL Rookie of the Year award in 1948 with the Boston Braves; traded to the N.Y. Giants where he led the league in doubles (41) in 1951; won 994 games as a manager and led the Oakland A's to a World Series win in 1974.

Tamas Darnyi (b. June 3, 1967): Hungarian swimmer; 2-time double gold medal winner in 200m and 400m individual medley at 1988 and '92 Olympics; also won both events in 1986 and '91 world championships; set world records in both at '91 worlds; 1st swimmer to break 2 minutes in 200m IM (1:59:36).

Lindsay Davenport (b. June 8, 1976): Tennis player; first American female to be ranked No. 1 in the world (1998) since Chris Evert in 1985; won U.S. Open (1998), Wimbledon (1999) and Australian Open (2000); Olympic gold medalist at Atlanta in 1996.

Al Davis (b. July 4, 1929): Football; GM-coach of Oakland 1963-66; helped force AFL-NFL merger as AFL commissioner in 1966; returned to Oakland as managing general partner and directed club to 3 Super Bowl wins (1977,81,84); defied fellow NFL owners and moved Raiders to LA in 1982; turned down owners' 1995 offer to build him a new stadium in LA and moved back to Oakland instead.

Dwight Davis (b. July 5, 1879, d. Nov. 28, 1945): Tennis; donor of Davis Cup; played for winning U.S. team in 1st two Cup finals (1900,02); won U.S. and Wimbledon doubles titles in 1901; Secretary of War (1925-29) under President Coolidge.

Ernie Davis (b. Dec. 14, 1939, d. May 18, 1963): Football; star running back at Syracuse University; first black to win the Heisman Trophy in 1961; drafted by the Washington Redskins and traded to Cleveland but died the following year of leukemia before playing a pro game.

Glenn Davis (b. Dec. 26, 1924): Football HB; 3-time All-America; led Army to national titles in 1944-45; Doc Blanchard's running mate; won Heisman Trophy in 1946.

John Davis (b. Jan. 12, 1921, d. July 13, 1984): Weightlifting; 6-time world champion; 2-time Olympic super-heavyweight champ (1948,52); undefeated from 1938-53.

Terrell Davis (b. Oct. 28, 1972): Football RB; 1998 NFL MVP, rushing for an league-leading 2,008 yards (3rd all-time); played for two Super Bowl winners in Denver (XXXII and XXXIII), earning MVP honors in the former with Super Bowl-record 3 rushing TDs; missed most of 1999 and 2000 seasons due to injury.

Pat Day (b. Oct. 13, 1953): Jockey; 4-time Eclipse award winner; ranked 3rd all-time in career wins through 1999; won Kentucky Derby (1992), 5 Preaknesses (1985,90,94-96) and 3 Belmonts (1989,94,2000); inducted into Hall of Fame in 1991.

Dizzy Dean (b. Jan. 16 1911, d. July 17, 1974): Baseball RHP; led NL in strikeouts and complete games 4 times; last NL pitcher to win 30 games (30-7 in 1934); MVP in 1934 with St. Louis; 150-83 record.

Dave DeBusschere (b. Oct. 16, 1940): Basketball F; youngest coach in NBA history (24 in 1964); player-coach of Detroit Pistons (1964-67); played in 8 All-Star games; won 2 NBA titles as player with NY Knicks; ABA commissioner (1975-76); also pitched 2 seasons for Chicago White Sox (1962-63) with 3-4 record.

Pierre de Coubertin (b. Jan. 1, 1863, d. Sept. 2, 1937): French educator; father of the Modern Olympic Games; IOC president from 1896-1925.

Anita DeFrantz (b. Oct. 4, 1952): Olympics; attorney who became the International Olympic Committee's first female vice president in 1997; first woman to represent U.S. on IOC (elected in 1986); member of USOC Executive Committee; member of bronze medal U.S. women's eight-oared shell at Montreal in 1976.

Oscar De La Hoya (b. Feb. 4, 1973): Boxing; won 1992 Olympic gold medal (lightweight); won the IBF lightweight title in 1995; won WBC Super Lightweight title over Julio Cesar Chavez in 1996 and WBC Welterweight title over Pernell Whitaker in 1997; lost WBC Welterweight belt to Felix Trinidad in a majority decision in 1999; lost to Sugar Shane Mosley in 2000 for his 2nd career defeat.

Cedric Dempsey (b. Apr. 14, 1932): College sports; named to succeed Dick Schultz as NCAA executive director on Nov. 5, 1993; served as athletic director at Pacific (1967-79), San Diego St. (1979), Houston (1979-82) and Arizona (1983-93).

Jack Dempsey (b. June 24, 1895, d. May 31, 1983): Boxer; world heavyweight champion from 1919-26; lost title to Gene Tunney, then lost "Long Count" rematch in 1927 when he floored Tunney in 7th round but failed to retreat to neutral corner; pro record 64-6-9 with 49 KOs.

Donna de Varona (b. Apr. 26, 1947): Swimming; won gold medals in 400 IM and 400 freestyle relay at 1964 Olympics; set 18 world records during career; co-founder of Women's Sports Foundation in 1974.

Gail Devers (b. Nov. 19, 1966): Track & Field; fastest-ever woman sprinter-hurdler; overcame thyroid disorder (Graves' disease) that sidelined her in 1989-90 and nearly resulted in having both feet amputated; won Olympic gold medal in 100 meters in 1992 and '96; world champion in 100 meters (1993) and 100-meter hurdles (1993, 95).

Klaus Dibiasi (b. Oct. 6, 1947): Italian diver; won 3 consecutive Olympic gold medals in platform event (1968,72,76).

Eric Dickerson (b. Sept. 2, 1960): Football RB; led NFL in rushing 4 times (1983-84,86,88); ran for single-season record 2,105 yards in 1984; NFC Rookie of Year in 1983; All-Pro 5 times; traded from LA Rams to Indianapolis (Oct. 31, 1987) in 3-team, 10-player deal (including draft picks) that also involved Buffalo; 3rd on all-time career rushing list with 13,259 yards in 11 seasons; entered Pro Football Hall of Fame in '99, became Monday Night Football sideline reporter in 2000.

Harrison Dillard (b. July 8, 1923): Track & Field; only man to win Olympic gold medals in both sprints (100m in 1948) and hurdles (110m in 1952).

Joe DiMaggio (b. Nov. 25, 1914, d. Mar. 8, 1999): Baseball OF; hit safely in 56 straight games (1941); led AL in batting, HRs and RBI twice each; 3-time MVP (1939,41,47); hit .325 with 361 HRs over 13 seasons; led NY Yankees to 10 World Series titles.

Marcel Dionne (b. Aug. 3, 1951): Hockey C; fourth on NHL's all-time points list (1,771) and third on goals list (731); tied Wayne Gretzky for the league lead in points (137) in 1980; scored 50 goals in a season 6 times; won the Lady Byng Award for gentlemanly play in 1975 with Detroit and in 1977 with the L.A. Kings; member of the Hockey Hall of Fame.

Mike Ditka (b. Oct. 18, 1939): Football; All-America at Pitt (1960); NFL Rookie of Year (1961); 5-time Pro Bowl tight end for Chicago Bears; returned to Chicago as head coach in 1982 and won Super Bowl XX in 1986; left Bears in 1992 and worked as a broadcaster at NBC for four years; coached the New Orleans Saints from 1997-99; compiled 127-101-0 record in 14 seasons.

Larry Doby (b. Dec. 13, 1924): Baseball OF; first black player in the AL; joined the Cleveland Indians in July 1947, three months after Jackie Robinson entered the Majors with the NL's Brooklyn Dodgers; an all-star centerfielder from 1949-55; managed the Chicago White Sox in 1978, becoming the second black major league manager; inducted into the Hall of Fame in 1998.

Charlotte (Lottie) Dod (b. Sept. 24, 1871, d. June 27, 1960): British athlete; was 5-time Wimbledon singles champion (1887-88,91-93); youngest player ever to win Wimbledon (15 in 1887); archery silver medalist at 1908 Olympics; member of national field hockey team in 1899; British Amateur golf champ in 1904.

Tony Dorsett (b. Apr. 7, 1954): Football RB; won Heisman Trophy leading Pitt to national title in 1976; 3rd all-time in NCAA Div. I-A rushing with 6,082 yards; led Dallas to Super Bowl title as NFC Rookie of Year (1977); NFC Player of Year (1981); ranks 5th on all-time NFL list with 12,739 yards gained in 12 years.

James (Buster) Douglas (b. Apr. 7, 1960): Boxing; 42-1 shot who knocked out undefeated Mike Tyson in 10th round on Feb. 10, 1990 to win heavyweight title in Tokyo; 8½ months later, lost only title defense to Evander Holyfield by KO in 3rd round.

Vicki Manalo Draves (b. Dec. 31, 1924): Diving; First woman in olympic history to win gold medals in both platform diving and springboard diving; inducted into Int'l Swimming Hall of Fame in 1969.

The Dream Team Head coach Chuck Daly's "Best Ever" 12-man NBA All-Star squad that headlined the 1992 Summer Olympics in Barcelona and easily won the basketball gold medal; co-captained by Larry Bird and Magic Johnson, with veterans Charles Barkley, Clyde Drexler, Patrick Ewing, Michael Jordan, Karl Malone, Chris Mullin, Scottie Pippen, David Robinson, John Stockton and Duke's Christian Laettner.

Heike Drechsler (b. Dec. 16, 1964): German long jumper and sprinter; East German before reunification in 1991; set world long jump record (24-2¼) in 1988; won long jump gold medals at 1992 Olympics and 1983 and '93 World Championships; won silver medal in long jump and bronze medals in both 100- and 200-meter sprints at 1988 Olympics.

Ken Dryden (b. Aug. 8, 1947): Hockey G; led Montreal to 6 Stanley Cup titles; playoff MVP as rookie in 1971; won or shared 5 Vezina trophies; 2.24 career GAA; currently President of Toronto Maple Leafs.

Don Drysdale (b. July 23, 1936, d. July 3, 1993): Baseball RHP; led NL in strikeouts 3 times and games started 4 straight years; pitched record 6 shutouts in a row in 1968; won Cy Young (1962); had 209-166 record and hit 29 HRs in 14 years.

Charley Dumas (b. Feb. 12, 1937): U.S. high jumper; first man to clear 7 feet (7-0½) on June 29, 1956; won gold medal at 1956 Olympics.

Margaret Osborne du Pont (b. Mar. 4, 1918): Tennis; won 5 French, 7 Wimbledon and an unprecedented 25 U.S. national titles in singles, doubles and mixed doubles from 1941-62.

Roberto Duran (b. June 16, 1951): Panamanian boxer; one of only 4 fighters to hold 4 different world titles— lightweight (1972-79), welterweight (1980), junior middleweight (1983) and middleweight (1989-90); lost famous "No Mas" welterweight title bout when he quit in 8th round against Sugar Ray Leonard (1980); pro record of 102-14 (69 KOs).

Leo Durocher (b. July 27, 1905, d. Oct. 7, 1991): Baseball; managed in NL 24 years; won 2,015 games, including postseason; 3 pennants with Brooklyn (1941) and NY Giants (1951,54); won World Series in 1954.

Eddie Eagan (b. Apr. 26, 1898, d. June 14, 1967): Only athlete to win gold medals in both Summer and Winter Olympics (Boxing–1920, Bobsled–1932).

Alan Eagleson (b. Apr. 24, 1933): Hockey; Toronto lawyer, agent and 1st executive director of NHL Players Assn. (1967-90); midwived Team Canada vs. Soviet series (1972) and Canada Cup; charged with racketeering and defrauding NHLPA in indictment handed down by U.S. grand jury in 1994; was sentenced to 18 months in jail in Jan. 1998 after pleading guilty but only served 6 months; resigned from Hall of Fame in 1998.

Dale Earnhardt (b. Apr. 29, 1951, d. Feb. 18, 2001): Auto racer; 7-time NASCAR national champion (1980,86-87,90-91,93-94); Rookie of Year in 1979; all-time NASCAR money leader with over $34 million won and 6th on career wins list with 76; finally won Daytona 500 in 1998 on 20th attempt; died in last lap crash at the 2001 Daytona 500.

James Easton (b. July 26, 1935): Olympics; archer and sporting goods manufacturer (Easton softball bats); one of 4 American delegates to the International Olympic Committee; president of International Archery Federation (FITA); member of LA Olympic Organizing Committee in 1984.

Dennis Eckersley (b. Oct. 3, 1954): Baseball P; began his career as a starter in 1975 with Cleveland; no-hit Angels in 1977; won 20 games in 1978 with Boston; moved to the bullpen after 12 seasons as a starter and became one of the best closers of all-time with Oakland; won 1992 AL Cy Young and MVP.

Stefan Edberg (b. Jan. 19, 1966): Swedish tennis player; 2-time No.1 player (1990-91); 2-time winner of Australian Open (1985,87), Wimbledon (1988,90) and U.S. Open (1991-92).

Gertrude Ederle (b. Oct. 23, 1906): Swimmer; 1st woman to swim English Channel, breaking men's record by 2 hours in 1926; won 3 medals in 1924 Olympics.

Krisztina Egerszegi (b. Aug. 16, 1974): Hungarian swimmer; 3-time gold medal winner (100m and 200m backstroke and 400m IM) in 1992 Olympics; also won a gold (200m back) and silver (100m back) in 1988 Games; youngest (14) ever to win swimming gold. Won fifth gold medal (200m back) at '96 Games.

Lee Elder (b. July 14, 1934): Golf; in 1975, he became the first black golfer to play in the Masters Tournament; also played in the 1977 Masters; member of the 1979 U.S. Ryder Cup team; played in South Africa's first integrated tournament in 1972.

Todd Eldredge (b. Aug. 28, 1971): Figure Skater; five-time U.S. champion (1990,91,95,97,98); 1996 World Champion; has won U.S. titles at all three levels (novice, junior and senior); most decorated American figure skater without an Olympic medal.

Bill Elliott (b. Oct. 8, 1955): Auto racer; 2-time winner of Daytona 500 (1985,87); NASCAR national champ in 1988; 40 NASCAR wins as of Sept. 2001.

Herb Elliott (b. Feb. 25, 1938): Australian runner; undefeated from 1958-60; ran 17 sub-4:00 miles; 3 world records; won gold medal in 1500 meters at 1960 Olympics; retired at age 22.

John Elway (b. June 28, 1960): Football QB; All-American at Stanford; #1 overall pick in the famous quarterback draft of 1983; known for his last-minute, game-winning scoring drives; led Broncos to 3 Super Bowl losses before back-to-back wins in Super Bowl XXXII and XXXIII; 1987 NFL MVP; 4-time Pro Bowler; first QB to catch a pass in the Super Bowl (1987); one of only two QBs in NFL history (Marino) to throw for over 3,000 yards in 12 seasons.

Roy Emerson (b. Nov. 3, 1936): Australian tennis player; won 12 majors in singles— 6 Australian, 2 French, 2 Wimbledon and 2 U.S. from 1961-67.

Kornelia Ender (b. Oct. 25, 1958): East German swimmer; 1st woman to win 4 gold medals at one Olympics (1976), all in world-record time.

Julius Erving (b. Feb. 22, 1950): Basketball F; in ABA (1971-76)— 3-time MVP, 2-time playoff MVP, led NY Nets to 2 titles (1974,76); in NBA (1976-87)— 5-time All-NBA 1st team, MVP in 1981, led Philadelphia 76ers to title in 1983.

Phil Esposito (b. Feb. 20, 1942): Hockey C; 1st NHL player to score 100 points in a season (126 in 1969); 6-time All-NHL 1st team with Boston (1969-74); 2-time MVP (1969,74); 5-time scoring champ; star of 1972 Canada-Soviet series; former president-GM of Tampa Bay Lightning.

Janet Evans (b. Aug. 28, 1971): Swimmer; won 3 individual gold medals (400m & 800m freestyle, 400m IM) at 1988 Olympics; 1989 Sullivan Award winner; won 1 gold (800m) and 1 silver (400m) at 1992 Olympics.

Lee Evans (b. Feb. 25, 1947): Track & Field; dominant quarter-miler in world from 1966-72; world record in 400m set at 1968 Olympics stood 20 years.

Chris Evert (b. Dec. 21, 1954): Tennis; No.1 player in world 5 times (1975-77,80-81); won at least 1 Grand Slam singles title every year from 1974-86; 18 majors in all— 7 French, 6 U.S., 3 Wimbledon and 2 Australian; retired after 1989 season with 154 singles titles and $8,896,195 in career earnings.

Weeb Ewbank (b. May 6, 1907, d. Nov. 18, 1998): Football; only coach to win NFL and AFL titles; led Baltimore to 2 NFL titles (1958-59) and NY Jets to Super Bowl III win.

Patrick Ewing (b. Aug. 5, 1962): Basketball C; 3-time All-America; led Georgetown to 3 NCAA Finals and 1984 title; Final 4 MOP in '84; 1986 NBA Rookie of Year with New York; All-NBA (1990); on U.S. Olympic gold medal-winning teams in 1984 and '92; named one of the NBA's 50 Greatest Players; traded to Seattle in 2000 and signed with Orlando in 2001.

Ray Ewry (b. Oct. 14, 1873, d. Sept. 29, 1937): Track & Field; won 10 gold medals (although 2 are not recognized by IOC) over 4 consecutive Olympics (1900,04,06,08); all events he won (Standing HJ, LJ and TJ) were discontinued in 1912.

Nick Faldo (b. July 18, 1957): British golfer; 3-time winner of British Open (1987,90,92) and Masters (1989, 90, 96); 3-time European Golfer of Year (1989-90,92); PGA Player of Year in 1990.

Juan Manuel Fangio (b. June 24, 1911, d. July 17, 1995): Argentine auto racer; 5-time Formula One world champion (1951,54-57); 24 career wins, retired in 1958.

Brett Favre (b. Oct. 10, 1969): Football QB; Selected in the second round (33rd overall) by the Atlanta Falcons in the 1991 NFL draft; traded to Green Bay Packers in 1992; league MVP in 1995, '96 and '97; five-time Pro Bowl QB; 100th TD pass came in his 62nd game, third-fastest in league history; 39 TD passes in 1996 season broke his own NFC record of 38 set in 1995 (since broken by Kurt Warner – 41 in 1999); led Packers to Super Bowl victory in 1997.

Sergei Fedorov (b. Dec. 13, 1969): Hockey C; first Russian to win NHL Hart Trophy as 1993-94 regular season MVP; 4-time All-Star with Detroit.

Bob Feller (b. Nov. 3, 1918): Baseball RHP; led AL in strikeouts 7 times and wins 6 times with Cleveland; threw 3 no-hitters and 12 one-hitters; 266-162 record.

Tom Ferguson (b. Dec. 20, 1950): Rodeo; 6-time All-Around champion (1974-79); 1st cowboy to win $100,000 in one season (1978); 1st to win $1 million in career (1986).

Herve Filion (b. Feb. 1, 1940): Harness racing; 10-time Driver of Year; all-time leader in races won with 14,783 in 35 years.

Rollie Fingers (b. Aug. 25, 1946): Baseball RHP; relief ace with 341 career saves; won AL MVP and Cy Young awards in 1981 with Milwaukee; World Series MVP in 1974 with Oakland.

Charles O. Finley (b. Feb. 22, 1918, d. Feb, 19, 1997): Baseball owner; moved KC A's to Oakland in 1968; won 3 straight World Series from 1972-74; also owned teams in NHL and ABA.

Bobby Fischer (b. Mar. 9, 1943): Chess; at 15, became youngest international grandmaster in chess history; only American to hold world championship (1972-75); was stripped of title in 1975 after refusing to defend against Anatoly Karpov and became recluse; re-emerged to defeat old foe and former world champion Boris Spassky in 1992.

Carlton Fisk (b. Dec. 26, 1947): Baseball C; holds all-time major league record for games caught (2,229); also all-time HR leader for catchers (376); AL Rookie of Year (1972) and 10-time All-Star; hit epic, 12th-inning Game 6 homer for Boston Red Sox in 1975 World Series; inducted into the Baseball Hall of Fame in 2000.

Emerson Fittipaldi (b. Dec. 12, 1946): Brazilian auto racer; 2-time Formula One world champion (1972,74); 2-time winner of Indy 500 (1989,93); won overall IndyCar title in 1989.

Bob Fitzsimmons (b. May 26, 1863, d. Oct. 22, 1917): British boxer; held three world titles— middleweight (1881-97), heavyweight (1897-99) and light heavyweight (1903-05); pro record 40-11 with 32 KOs.

James (Sunny Jim) Fitzsimmons (b. July 23, 1874, d. Mar. 11, 1966): Horse racing; trained horses that won over 2,275 races, including 2 Triple Crown winners— Gallant Fox in 1930 and Omaha in '35.

Jim Fixx (b. Apr. 23, 1932, d. July 20, 1984): Running; author who popularized the sport of running; his 1977 bestseller The Complete Book of Running, is credited with helping start America's fitness revolution; died of a heart attack while running.

Peggy Fleming (b. July 27, 1948): Figure skating; 3-time world champion (1966-68); won Olympic gold medal in 1968.

Curt Flood (b. Jan. 18, 1938, d. Jan. 20, 1997): Baseball OF; played 15 years (1956-69,71) mainly with St. Louis; hit over .300 6 times with 7 Gold Gloves; refused trade to Phillies in 1969; lost challenge to baseball's reserve clause in Supreme Court in 1972.

Ray Floyd (b. Sept. 14, 1942): Golfer; has 22 PGA victories in 4 decades; joined Senior PGA Tour in 1992; has won Masters (1976), U.S. Open (1986), PGA twice (1969,82) and PGA Seniors Championship (1995); only player to ever win on PGA and Senior tours in same year (1992); member of 8 Ryder Cup teams and captain in 1989.

Doug Flutie (b. Oct. 23, 1962): Football QB; won Heisman Trophy with Boston College (1984); has played in USFL, NFL and CFL; 6-time CFL MVP with B.C. Lions (1991), Calgary (1992-94) and Toronto (1996-97); led Calgary (1992) and Toronto (1996-97) to Grey Cup titles; returned to NFL in 1998 with Buffalo and became part of QB controversy with Rob Johnson; signed by San Diego in 2001.

Gerald Ford (b. July 14, 1913): 38th President of the U.S.; lettered as center on undefeated Michigan football teams in 1932 and '33; MVP on 1934 squad.

Whitey Ford (b. Oct. 21, 1928): Baseball LHP; all-time leader in World Series wins (10); led AL in wins 3 times; won Cy Young and World Series MVP in 1961 with NY Yankees; 236-106 record.

George Foreman (b. Jan. 10, 1949): Boxer; Olympic heavyweight champ (1968); world heavyweight champ (1973-74 and 94-95); lost title to Muhammad Ali (KO-8th) in '74; recaptured it on Nov. 5, 1994 at age 45 with a 10-round KO of WBA/IBF champ Michael Moorer, becoming the oldest man to win heavyweight crown; named AP Male Athlete of Year 20 years after losing title to Ali; stripped of WBA title in 1995 after declining to fight No. 1 contender; successfully defended title at age 46 against 26-year-old Axel Schulz in controversial maj. decision; gave up IBF title after refusing rematch with Schulz.

Dick Fosbury (b. Mar. 6, 1947): Track & Field; revolutionized high jump with back-first "Fosbury Flop"; won gold medal at 1968 Olympics.

Greg Foster (b. Aug. 4, 1958): Track & Field; 3-time winner of World Championship in 110-m hurdles (1983,87,91); won silver in 1984 Olympics; world indoor champion in 1991.

The Four Horsemen Senior backfield that led Notre Dame to national collegiate football championship in 1924; put together as sophomores by Irish coach Knute Rockne; immortalized by sportswriter Grantland Rice, whose report of the Oct. 19, 1924, Notre Dame-Army game began: "Outlined against a blue, gray October sky the Four Horsemen rode again . . ."; HB Jim Crowley (b. Sept. 10, 1902, d. Jan. 15, 1986), FB Elmer Layden (b. May 4, 1903, d. June 30, 1973), HB Don Miller (b. May 30, 1902, d. July 28, 1979) and QB Harry Stuhldreher (b. Oct. 14, 1901, d. Jan. 26, 1965).

The Four Musketeers French quartet that dominated men's tennis in 1920s and '30s, winning 8 straight French singles titles (1925-32), 6 Wimbledons in a row (1924-29) and 6 consecutive Davis Cups (1927-32)— Jean Borotra (b. Aug. 13, 1898, d. July 17, 1994), Jacques Brugnon (b. May 11, 1895, d. Mar. 20, 1978), Henri Cochet (b. Dec. 14, 1901, d. Apr. 1, 1987), Rene Lacoste (b. July 2, 1905, d. Oct. 13, 1996).

Nellie Fox (b. Dec. 25, 1927, d. Dec. 1, 1975): Baseball 2B; batted .306 in 1959 to win the AL MVP award with the pennant-winning Chicago White Sox; led the league in fielding percentage six times, hits four times and triples once; ended his 19-year career with 2,663 hits, 1,279 runs and .288 average.

Jimmie Foxx (b. Oct. 22, 1907, d. July 21, 1967): Baseball 1B; led AL in HRs 4 times and batting twice; won Triple Crown in 1933; 3-time MVP (1932-33,38) with Philadelphia and Boston; hit 30 HRs or more 12 years in a row; 534 career HRs.

A.J. Foyt (b. Jan. 16, 1935): Auto racer; 7-time USAC-CART national champion (1960-61,63-64,67,75,79); 4-time Indy 500 winner (1961,64,67,77); only driver in history to win Indy 500, Daytona 500 (1972) and 24 Hours of LeMans (1967 with Dan Gurney); retired in 1993 as all-time CART wins leader with 67.

Bill France Sr. (b. Sept. 26, 1909, d. June 7, 1992): Stock car pioneer and promoter; founded NASCAR in 1948; guided race circuit through formative years; built both Daytona (Fla.) Int'l Speedway and Talladega (Ala.) Superspeedway.

Dawn Fraser (b. Sept. 4, 1937): Australian swimmer; won gold medals in 100m freestyle at 3 consecutive Olympics (1956,60,64).

Joe Frazier (b. Jan. 12, 1944): Boxer; 1964 Olympic heavyweight champion; world heavyweight champ (1970-73); fought Muhammad Ali 3 times and won once; pro record 32-4-1 with 27 KOs.

Walt Frazier (b. March 29, 1945): Basketball G; won the NBA championship two times (1970 and 73) with the New York Knicks; 35 points and 19 assists in the 1970 championship game vs. the Lakers; averaged 18.9 PPG and 6.1 APG over his career; four-time all-NBA and a member of the Hall of Fame; nicknamed "Clyde" after well-dressed gangster Clyde Barrow.

Cathy Freeman (b. Feb. 16, 1973): Track & Field; Australian Aborigine who lit the cauldron at the start of the 2000 Olympic Games in Sydney and provided one of the games' most memorable moments by winning gold in the 400-meters on her home soil; 2-time world champion in the 400-meters (1997,99); won silver in the 400 at the 1996 Olympics in Atlanta.

Ford Frick (b. Dec. 19, 1894, d. Apr. 8, 1978): Baseball; sportswriter and radio announcer who served as NL president (1934-51) and commissioner (1951-65); convinced record-keepers to list Roger Maris' and Babe Ruth's season records separately; major leagues moved to West Coast and expanded from 16 to 20 teams during his tenure.

Dan Gable (b. Oct. 25, 1948): Wrestling; career wrestling record of 118-1 at Iowa St., where he was a 2-time NCAA champ (1968,69) and tourney MVP in 1969 (137 lbs); won gold medal (149 lbs) at 1972 Olympics; coached U.S. freestyle team in 1988; coached Iowa to 9 straight NCAA titles (1978-86) and 15 overall in 21 years.

Eddie Gaedel (b. June 8, 1925, d. June 18, 1961): Baseball PH; St. Louis Browns' 3-foot-7 player whose career lasted one at bat (he walked) on Aug 19, 1951; hired as a publicity stunt by eccentric owner Bill Veeck.

Clarence (Big House) Gaines (b. May 21, 1924): Basketball; retired as coach of Div. II Winston-Salem after 1992-93 season with 828-447 record in 47 years; ranks 3rd on all-time NCAA list behind Dean Smith (879) and Adolph Rupp (876).

Alonzo (Jake) Gaither (b. Apr. 11, 1903, d. Feb. 18, 1994): Football; head coach at Florida A&M for 25 years; led Rattlers to 6 national black college titles; retired after 1969 season with record of 203-36-4 and a winning percentage of .844; coined phrase, "I like my boys agile, mobile and hostile."

Rulon Gardner (b. Aug. 16, 1971): Olympic wrestler; surprise winner of the super heavyweight Greco-Roman wrestling gold medal at the 2000 Sydney Games; beat unbeatable Russian legend Alexandre Kareline, 1-0; won 2000 USOC Sportsman of the Year Award.

Lou Gehrig (b. June 19, 1903, d. June 2, 1941): Baseball 1B; played in 2,130 consecutive games from 1925-39 a major league record until Cal Ripken Jr. surpassed it in 1995; led AL in RBI 5 times and HRs 3 times; drove in 100 runs or more 13 years in a row; 2-time MVP (1927,36); hit .340 with 493 HRs over 17 seasons; led NY Yankees to 6 World Series titles; died at age 37 of Amyotrophic Lateral Sclerosis (ALS), a rare and incurable disease of the nervous system now better known as Lou Gehrig's disease.

Bernie Geoffrion (b. Feb. 14, 1931): Hockey RW; credited with popularizing the slap shot, earning his nickname "Boom Boom"; scored 30 goals in 1952 to win the NHL's Calder Trophy (Rookie of the Year Award); won the MVP award (Hart) in 1955; became the second player in history to score 50 goals in one season; led the league in points in 1955 and 61; won 6 Stanley Cups with Montreal; member of the Hockey Hall of Fame.

George Gervin (b. April 27, 1952): Basketball G/F; joined the ABA in 1972 and came to the NBA with San Antonio in 1976; a five-time NBA all-star; led the league in scoring four times; scored 26,595 points with an average of 25.1 per game; known as the "Iceman" because of his cool style; elected to the Hall of Fame in 1996.

A. Bartlett Giamatti (b. Apr. 14, 1938, d. Sept. 1, 1989): Scholar and 7th commissioner of baseball; banned Pete Rose for life for betting on Major League games and associating with known gamblers; also served as president of Yale (1978-86) and National League (1986-89).

Joe Gibbs (b. Nov. 25, 1940): Football; coached Washington to 140 victories and 3 Super Bowl titles in 12 seasons before retiring in 1993; owner of NASCAR racing team that won 1993 Daytona 500 and 2000 Winston Cup title.

Althea Gibson (b. Aug. 25, 1927): Tennis; won both Wimbledon and U.S. titles in 1957 and '58; 1st black to play in either tourney and 1st to win each title.

Bob Gibson (b. Nov. 9, 1935): Baseball RHP; won 20 or more games 5 times; won 2 NL Cy Youngs (1968,70); MVP in 1968; led St. Louis to 2 World Series titles (1964,67); 251-174 record.

Josh Gibson (b. Dec. 21, 1911, d. Jan. 20, 1947): Baseball; the "Babe Ruth of the Negro Leagues"; Satchel Paige's battery mate with Pittsburgh Crawfords. The Negro Leagues did not keep accurate records but Gibson hit 84 home runs in one season and his Baseball Hall of Fame plaque says he hit "almost 800" home runs in his seventeen-year career.

Kirk Gibson (b. May 28, 1957): Baseball OF; All-America flanker at Mich. St. in 1978; chose baseball career and was AL playoff MVP with Detroit in 1984 and NL regular season MVP with Los Angeles in 1988; hit famous pinch-hit home run against Oakland's Dennis Eckersley in Game 1 of the 1988 World Series to vault the Dodgers to the title.

Frank Gifford (b. Aug. 16, 1930): Football HB; 4-time All-Pro (1955-57,59); NFL MVP in 1956; led NY Giants to 3 NFL title games; TV sportscaster since 1958, beginning career while still a player.

Sid Gillman (b. Oct. 26, 1911): Football innovator; only coach in both College and Pro Football Halls of Fame; led college teams at Miami-OH and Cincinnati to combined 81-19-2 record from 1944-54; coached LA Rams (1955-59) in NFL, then led LA-San Diego Chargers to 5 Western titles and 1 league championship in first six years of AFL.

George Gipp (b. Feb. 18, 1895, d. Dec. 14, 1920): Football FB; died of throat infection 2 weeks before he made All-America; rushed for 2,341 yards, scored 156 points and averaged 38 yards a punt in 4 years (1917-20).

Marc Girardelli (b. July 18, 1963): Luxembourg Alpine skier; Austrian native who refused to join Austrian Ski Federation because he wanted to be coached by his father; won unprecedented 5th overall World Cup title in 1993; winless at Olympics, although he won 2 silver medals in 1992.

Tom Gola (b. Jan. 13, 1933): Basketball F; 4-time All-America and 1955 Player of Year at La Salle; MOP in 1952 NIT and '54 NCAA Final 4, leading Pioneers to both titles; won NBA title as rookie with Philadelphia Warriors in 1956; 4-time NBA All-Star.

Marshall Goldberg (b. Oct. 24, 1917): Football HB; 2-time consensus All-America at Pittsburgh (1937-38); led Pitt to national championship in 1937; played with NFL champion Chicago Cardinals 10 years later.

Lefty Gomez (b. Nov. 26, 1908, d. Feb. 17, 1989): Baseball LHP; 4-time 20-game winner with NY Yankees; holds World Series record for most wins (6) without a defeat; pitched on 5 world championship clubs in 1930s.

Pancho Gonzales (b. May 9, 1928, d. July 3, 1995): Tennis; won consecutive U.S. Championships in 1947-48 before turning pro at 21; dominated pro tour from 1950-61; in 1969 at age 41, played longest Wimbledon match ever (5:12), beating Charlie Pasarell 22-24,1-6,16-14,6-3,11-9.

Gail Goodrich (b. April 23, 1943): Basketball G; starred at UCLA and won two national championships in 1964 and 1965 under legendary coach John Wooden's tutelage; won the NBA championship with the L.A. Lakers in 1972 and led the team in scoring (25.9 ppg); averaged 18.6 ppg over his 14-year career.

Jeff Gordon (b. Aug. 4, 1971): Auto racer; NASCAR Rookie of Year (1993); 3-time Winston Cup champion (1995,97,98); won inaugural Brickyard 400 in 1994; in 1997, at 25 became youngest winner of the Daytona 500; in 1998 he tied Richard Petty for the modern-era record for wins in a single season with 13.

Goose Gossage (b. July 5, 1951): Baseball RHP; Nine-time All Star (1975-78, 80-82, 84-85); intimidating relief pitcher; Fireman of the Year in 1975 with White Sox and 1978 with Yankees; led AL in saves with 26 (1975), 27 (1978); 1,002 career appearances; 310 saves.

Alf Goullet (b. Apr. 5, 1891, d. Mar. 11, 1995): Cycling; Australian who gained fame and fortune early in century as premier performer on U.S. 6-day bike race circuit; won 8 annual races at Madison Square Garden with 6 different partners from 1913-23.

Steffi Graf (b. June 14, 1969): German tennis player; won Grand Slam and Olympic gold medal in 1988 at age 19; won three of four majors in 1993, '95 and '96, won 22 Grand Slam singles titles— 7 at Wimbledon, 6 French, 5 U.S. and 4 Australian Opens, retired in 1999 as 3rd all-time with 107 career singles titles and as all-time tour leader in career earnings with over $21 million in prize money.

Otto Graham (b. Dec. 6, 1921): Football QB and basketball All-America at Northwestern; in pro ball, led Cleveland Browns to 7 league titles in 10 years, winning 4 AAFC championships (1946-49) and 3 NFL (1950,54-55); 5-time All-Pro; 2-time NFL MVP (1953,55).

Red Grange (b. June 13, 1903, d. Jan. 28, 1991): Football HB; 3-time All-America at Illinois who brought 1st huge crowds to pro football when he signed with Chicago Bears in 1925; formed 1st AFL with manager-promoter C.C. Pyle in 1926, but league folded and he returned to Bears.

Bud Grant (b. May 20, 1927): Football and Basketball; only coach to win 100 games in both CFL and NFL and only member of both CFL and U.S. Pro Football Halls of Fame; led Winnipeg to 4 Grey Cup titles (1958-59,61-62) in 6 appearances, but his Minnesota Vikings lost all 4 Super Bowl attempts in 1970s; accumulated 122 CFL wins and 168 NFL wins; also All-Big Ten at Minnesota in both football and basketball in late 1940s; a 3-time CFL All-Star offensive end; also member of 1950 NBA champion Minneapolis Lakers.

Rocky Graziano (b. June 7, 1922, d. May 22, 1990): Boxer; world middleweight champion (1946-47); fought Tony Zale for title 3 times in 21 months, losing twice; pro record 67-10-6 with 52 KOs; movie "Somebody Up There Likes Me" based on his life.

Hank Greenberg (b. Jan. 1, 1911, d. Sept. 4, 1986): Baseball 1B; led AL in HRs and RBI 4 times each; 2-time MVP (1935,40) with Detroit; 331 career HRs, including 58 in 1938.

Joe Greene (b. Sept. 24, 1946): Football DT; 5-time All-Pro (1972-74,77,79); led Pittsburgh to 4 Super Bowl titles in 1970s; nicknamed "Mean Joe".

Maurice Greene (b. July 23, 1974): Track & Field; world 100m champion in 1997, 99 and 2001 and 200m champion in 1999; current world record holder (9.79) in the 100m; injury forced him out of the 1996 Olympics in Atlanta; won the gold medal in the 100m at the 2000 Olympics in Sydney.

Bud Greenspan (b. Sept. 18, 1926): Filmmaker specializing in the Olympic Games; has won Emmy awards for 22-part "The Olympiad" (1976-77) and historical vignettes for ABC-TV's coverage of 1980 Winter Games; won 1994 Emmy award for edited special on Lillehammer Winter Olympics; won The Peabody Award in 1996 for his outstanding service in chronicling the Olympic Games.

Wayne Gretzky (b. Jan. 26, 1961): Hockey C; 10-time NHL scoring champion; 9-time regular season MVP (1979-87,89) and 9-time All-NHL first team; has scored 200 points or more in a season 4 times; led Edmonton to 4 Stanley Cups (1984-85,87-88); 2-time playoff MVP (1985,88); traded to LA Kings (Aug. 9, 1988); broke Gordie Howe's all-time NHL goal scoring record of 801 on Mar. 23, 1994; all-time NHL leader in points (2857), goals (894) and assists (1963); also all-time Stanley Cup leader in points, goals and assists; spent the end of the 1996 season with the St. Louis Blues and then signed a free agent contract with the New York Rangers; retired in 1999 at age 38 with 61 NHL scoring records in 20 seasons; became part-owner of NHL's Coyotes in 2000.

Bob Griese (b. Feb. 3, 1945): Football QB; 2-time All-Pro (1971,77); led Miami to undefeated season (17-0) in 1972 and consecutive Super Bowl titles (1973-74); father of Brian.

Ken Griffey Jr. (b. Nov. 21, 1969): Baseball OF; overall 1st pick of 1987 draft by Seattle; 10-time Gold Glove winner; 11-time All-Star; 1997 AL MVP; Mariners all-time leader in home runs and RBIs; MVP of 1992 All-Star game at age 23; hit home runs in 8 consecutive games in 1993; son of Ken Sr. and in 1990 they became the first father-son combination to appear in the same major league lineup; traded to the Cincinnati Reds before the 2000 season.

Archie Griffin (b. Aug. 21, 1954): Football RB; only college player to win two Heisman Trophies (1974-75); rushed for 5,177 yards in career at Ohio St.

Emile Griffith (b. Feb. 3, 1938): Boxer; world welterweight champion (1961,62-63,63-65); world middleweight champ (1966-67,67-68); pro record 85-24-2 with 23 KOs.

Dick Groat (b. Nov. 4, 1930): Basketball G and Baseball SS; 2-time basketball All-America at Duke and college Player of Year in 1951; won NL MVP award as shortstop with Pittsburgh in 1960; won World Series with Pirates (1960) and St. Louis (1964).

Lefty Grove (b. Mar. 6, 1900, d. May 23, 1975): Baseball LHP; won 20 or more games 8 times; led AL in ERA 9 times and strikeouts 7 times; 31-4 record and MVP in 1931 with Philadelphia; 300-141 record.

Lou Groza (b. Jan. 25, 1924, d. Nov. 29, 2000): Football T-PK; 6-time All-Pro; played in 13 championship games for Cleveland from 1946-67; kicked winning field goal in 1950 NFL title game; 1,608 career points (1,349 in NFL).

Janet Guthrie (b. Mar. 7, 1938): Auto racer; in 1977, became 1st woman to race in Indianapolis 500; placed 9th at Indy in 1978.

Tony Gwynn (b. May 9, 1960): Baseball OF; 8-time NL batting champion (1984,87-89,94-97) with San Diego, 15-time All-Star; got 3,000th career hit Aug. 6, 1999 at Montreal; played basketball at San Diego St. leaving as school's all-time assist leader; drafted in 10th round of 1981 NBA draft by San Diego Clippers.

Harvey Haddix (b. Sept. 18, 1925, d. Jan. 9; 1994): Baseball LHP; pitched 12 perfect innings for Pittsburgh, but lost to Milwaukee in the 13th, 1-0 (May 26, 1959); won Game 7 of 1960 World Series.

Walter Hagen (b. Dec. 21, 1892, d. Oct. 5, 1969): Pro golf pioneer; won 2 U.S. Opens (1914,19), 4 British Opens (1922,24,28-29), 5 PGA Championships (1921,24-27) and 5 Western Opens; retired with 40 PGA wins; 6-time U.S. Ryder Cup captain.

Marvin Hagler (b. May 23, 1954): Boxer; world middleweight champion 1980-87; enjoyed his nickname "Marvelous Marvin" so much he had his name legally changed; pro record of 62-3-2 with 52 KOs.

Mika Hakkinen (b. Sept. 28, 1968): Finnish auto racer; won two consecutive Formula One world drivers championships in 1998 and '99; recorded eight wins in '98 and five in '99, 20 career F1 wins as of Sept. 21, 2001.

George Halas (b. Feb. 2, 1895, d. Oct. 31, 1983): Football pioneer; MVP in 1919 Rose Bowl; player-coach-owner of Chicago Bears from 1920-83; signed Red Grange in 1925; coached Bears for 40 seasons and won 8 NFL titles (1921,32-33,40-41,43,46,63); 2nd on all-time career list with 324 wins; elected to NFL Hall of Fame in 1963.

Dorothy Hamill (b. July 26, 1956): Figure skater; won Olympic gold medal and world championship in 1976; Ice Capades headliner from 1977-84; bought the financially-strapped Ice Capades in 1993 and sold it several years later.

Scott Hamilton (b. Aug. 28, 1958): Figure skater; 4-time world champion (1981-84); won gold medal at 1984 Olympics.

Mia Hamm (b. Mar. 17, 1972): Soccer F; became all-time leading scorer in international soccer with her 108th goal on May 22, 1999; member of 1996 and 2000 U.S. Olympic teams, the 1991 and 1999 U.S. World Cup championship teams, and the 3rd-place 1995 World Cup team; made the U.S. National Team at 15; a three-time collegiate All-American; led UNC to 4 national titles (1989,90,92,93).

Tonya Harding (b. Nov. 12, 1970): Figure skater; 1991 U.S. women's champion; involved in bizarre plot hatched by ex-husband Jeff Gillooly to injure rival Nancy Kerrigan on Jan. 6, 1994 and keep her off Olympic team; won '94 U.S. women's title in Kerrigan's absence; denied any role in assault and sued USOC when her berth on Olympic team was threatened; finished 8th at Lillehammer (Kerrigan recovered and won silver medal); pled guilty on Mar. 16 to conspiracy to hinder investigation; stripped of 1994 title by U.S. Figure Skating Assn.

Tom Harmon (b. Sept. 28, 1919, d. Mar. 17, 1990): Football HB; 2-time All-America at Michigan; won Heisman Trophy in 1940; played with AFL NY Americans in 1941 and NFL LA Rams (1946-47); World War II fighter pilot who won Silver Star and Purple Heart; became radio-TV commentator.

Franco Harris (b. Mar. 7, 1950): Football RB; ran for over 1,000 yards a season 8 times; rushed for 12,120 yards in 13 years; led Pittsburgh to 4 Super Bowl titles.

Leon Hart (b. Nov. 2, 1928): Football E; only player to win 3 national championships in college and 3 more in the NFL; won his titles at Notre Dame (1946-47,49) and with Detroit Lions (1952-53,57); 3-time All-America and last lineman to win Heisman Trophy (1949); All-Pro on both offense and defense in 1951.

Bill Hartack (b. Dec. 9, 1932): Jockey; won Kentucky Derby 5 times (1957,60,62,64,69), Preakness 3 times (1956,64,69), and the Belmont once (1960).

Doug Harvey (b. Dec. 19, 1924, d. Dec. 26, 1989): Hockey D; 10-time All-NHL 1st team; won Norris Trophy 7 times (1955-58,60-62); led Montreal to 6 Stanley Cups.

Dominik Hasek (b. Jan. 29, 1965): Czech hockey G; 2-time NHL MVP (1997,98) with Buffalo; 6-time Vezina Trophy winner (1994,95,97,98,99,2001); led Czech Republic to Olympic gold medal in 1998 at Nagano; traded to Detroit in 2001.

Billy Haughton (b. Nov. 2, 1923, d. July 15, 1986): Harness racing; 4-time winner of Hambletonian; trainer-driver of one Pacing Triple Crown winner (1968); 4,910 career wins.

João Havelange (b. May 8, 1916): Soccer; Brazilian-born president of Federation Internationale de Football Assoc. (FIFA) 1974-98; also member of International Olympic Committee.

John Havlicek (b. Apr. 8, 1940): Basketball F; played in 3 NCAA Finals at Ohio St.; led Boston to 8 NBA titles (1963-66,68-69,74,76); Finals MVP in 1974; 4-time All-NBA 1st team.

Bob Hayes (b. Dec. 20, 1942): Track & Field and Football; won gold medal in 100m at 1964 Olympics; all-pro SE for Dallas in 1966; convicted of drug trafficking in 1979 and served 18 months of a 5-year sentence.

Elvin Hayes (b. Nov. 17, 1945): Basketball C; Known as "the Big E"; Overall number one pick of the 1968 NBA draft; three-time All-NBA first team (1975,77,79); 1978 Finals MVP; 12-time NBA all-star (1969-80); named to NBA's 50 Greatest Players; 6th leading scorer in NBA history with 27,313 points and 4th leading rebounder with 16,279; member of NBA Hall of Fame.

Woody Hayes (b. Feb. 14, 1913, d. Mar. 12, 1987): Football; coached Ohio St. to 6 national titles (1954,57,61,68,70) and 4 Rose Bowl victories; 238 career wins in 28 seasons at Denison, Miami-OH and OSU; his coaching career ended abruptly in 1978 after he attacked an opposing player on the sidelines.

Thomas Hearns (b. Oct. 18, 1958): Boxer; has held world titles as welterweight, junior middleweight, middleweight and light heavyweight; four career losses have come against Sugar Ray Leonard, Marvin Hagler and twice to Iran Barkley; pro record of 59-4-1 and 46 KOs.

Eric Heiden (b. June 14, 1958): Speedskater; 3-time overall world champion (1977-79); won all 5 men's gold medals at 1980 Olympics, setting records in each; Sullivan Award winner (1980).

John W. Heisman (b. Oct. 23, 1869, d. Oct. 3, 1936): Football; coached at 9 colleges from 1892-1927; won 185 games; Director of Athletics at Downtown Athletic Club in NYC (1928-36); DAC named Heisman Trophy after him.

Carol Heiss (b. Jan. 20, 1940): Figure skater; 5-time world champion (1956-60); won Olympic silver medal in 1956 and gold in '60; married 1956 men's gold medalist Hayes Jenkins.

Rickey Henderson (b. Dec. 25, 1958): Baseball OF; AL playoff MVP (1989) and AL regular season MVP (1990); set single-season base stealing record of 130 in 1982; has led AL in steals a record 12 times; broke Lou Brock's all-time record of 938 on May 1, 1991; all-time leader in steals, walks and HRs as leadoff batter.

Sonja Henie (b. Apr. 8, 1912, d. Oct. 12, 1969): Norwegian figure skater; 10-time world champion (1927-36); won 3 consecutive Olympic gold medals (1928,32,36); became movie star.

Foster Hewitt (b. Nov. 21, 1902, d. Apr. 21, 1985): Radio-TV; Canada's premier hockey play-by-play broadcaster from 1923-81; coined phrase, "He shoots, he scores!"

Damon Hill (b. Sept. 17, 1960): British auto racer; 1996 Formula One champion; 22 F1 wins places him 10th all-time.

Graham Hill (b. Feb. 15, 1929, d. Nov. 29, 1975): British auto racer; 2-time Formula One world champion (1962,68); won Indy 500 in 1966; killed in plane crash; father of Damon.

Phil Hill (b. Apr. 20, 1927): Auto racer; first U.S. driver to win Formula One championship (1961); 3 career wins (1958-64).

Martina Hingis (b. Sept. 30, 1980): Tennis player; in March 1997 at 16 years, 6 months, she became the youngest No. 1 ranked player since the ranking system began in 1975; has won Wimbledon (1997), U.S. Open (1997) and 3 Australian Opens (1997,98,99); first woman to surpass the $3 million mark in earnings for one season (1997).

Max Hirsch (b. July 30, 1880, d. Apr. 3, 1969): Horse racing; trained 1,933 winners from 1908-68; won Triple Crown with Assault in 1946.

Tommy Hitchcock (b. Feb. 11, 1900, d. Apr. 19, 1944): Polo; world class player at 20; achieved 10-goal rating-18 times from 1922-40.

Lew Hoad (b. Nov. 23, 1934, d. July 3, 1994): Australian tennis player; 2-time Wimbledon winner (1956-57); won Australian, French and Wimbledon titles in 1956, but missed capturing Grand Slam at Forest Hills when beaten by Ken Rosewall in 4-set final.

Gil Hodges (b. Apr. 4, 1924, d. Apr. 2, 1972): Baseball 1B-Manager; tied Major League record with four home runs in one game on Aug 31, 1950; won three Gold Gloves (1957-59); drove in 100 runs in seven consecutive seasons (1949-55); hit 370 home runs and 1,274 RBIs lifetime; won 660 games as a manager (Senators and Mets).

Ben Hogan (b. Aug. 13, 1912, d. July 25, 1997): Golfer; 4-time PGA Player of Year; one of only five players to win all four Grand Slam titles (others are Nicklaus, Player, Sarazen and Woods); won 4 U.S. Opens, 2 Masters, 2 PGAs and 1 British Open between 1946-53; one of only two players (Woods) to win three of the four current majors in one year when he won Masters, U.S. Open and British Open in 1953; nearly killed in Feb. 2, 1949 car accident, but came back to win U.S. Open in '50; third on all-time list with 63 career wins.

Chamique Holdsclaw (b. Aug. 9, 1977): Basketball F; 2-time national player of the year, leading Tennessee to 3 straight national championships (1996,97,98); 1998 Sullivan Award winner; 1999 WNBA No. 1 draft choice and Rookie of the Year.

Eleanor Holm (b. Dec. 6, 1913): Swimmer; won gold medal in 100m backstroke at 1932 Olympics; thrown off '36 U.S. team for drinking champagne in public and shooting craps on boat to Germany.

Nat Holman (b. Oct. 18, 1896, d. Feb. 12, 1995): Basketball pioneer; played with Original Celtics (1920-28); coached CCNY to both NCAA and NIT titles in 1950 (a year later, several of his players were caught up in a point-shaving scandal); 423 career wins.

Larry Holmes (b. Nov. 3, 1949): Boxer; heavyweight champion (WBC or IBF) from 1978-85; successfully defended title 20 times before losing to Michael Spinks; returned from first retirement in 1988 and was KO'd in 4th by champ Mike Tyson; launched second comeback in 1991; fought and lost title bids against Evander Holyfield in '92 and Oliver McCall in '95; pro record of 67-6 and 43 KOs.

Lou Holtz (b. Jan. 6, 1937): Football; coached Notre Dame to national title in 1988; 2-time Coach of Year (1977,88); coached six schools in all — Wm. & Mary (3 years), N.C. State (4), Arkansas (7), Minnesota (2), ND (11) and S. Carolina (3+); also coached NFL NY Jets for 13 games (3-10) in 1976.

Evander Holyfield (b. Oct. 19, 1962): Boxer; KO'd Buster Douglas in 3rd round to become world hvywt. champion in 1990; lost title to Riddick Bowe in 1992; beat Bowe to reclaim title in 1993; lost title again to Michael Moorer in 1994; defeated Mike Tyson in 1996 to win WBA belt; in 1997 rematch, Tyson was DQ'd for twice biting Holyfield's ear; escaped with controversial draw in 1999 unification bout with Lennox Lewis, then lost the rematch later that year; defeated John Ruiz in Aug. 2000 for vacant WBA belt then lost rematch and belt in 2001.

Red Holzman (b. Aug. 10, 1920, d. Nov. 13, 1998): Basketball; played for NBL and NBA champions at Rochester (1946,51); coached NY Knicks to 2 NBA titles (1970,73); Coach of Year (1970); ranks 13th on all-time NBA list with 754 wins.

Rogers Hornsby (b. Apr. 27, 1896, d. Jan. 5, 1963): Baseball 2B; hit .400 three times, including .424 in 1924; led NL in batting 7 times; 2-time MVP (1925,29); career average of .358 over 23 years is all-time highest in NL.

Paul Hornung (b. Dec. 23, 1935): Football HB-PK; only Heisman Trophy winner to play for losing team (2-8 Notre Dame in 1956); 3-time NFL scoring leader (1959-61) at Green Bay; 176 points in 1960, an all-time record; MVP in 1961; suspended by NFL for 1963 season for betting on his own team.

Gordie Howe (b. Mar. 31, 1928): Hockey RW; played 32 seasons in NHL and WHA from 1946-80; led NHL in scoring 6 times; All-NHL 1st team 12 times; MVP 6 times in NHL (1952-53,57-58,60,63) with Detroit and once in WHA (1974) with Houston; ranks 2nd on all-time NHL list in goals (801) and points (1,850) to Wayne Gretzky; played with sons Mark and Marty at Houston (1973-77) and New England-Hartford (1977-80).

Cal Hubbard (b. Oct. 31, 1900, d. Oct. 17, 1977): Member of college football, pro football and baseball halls of fame; 9 years in NFL; 4-time All-Pro at end and tackle; AL umpire (1936-51).

William DeHart Hubbard (b. Nov. 25, 1903, d. June 23, 1976): Track & Field; won the long jump at the 1924 Olympics, becoming the first black athlete to win an Olympic gold medal in an individual event; set the long jump world record in 1925 (25-10¾) and tied the 100-yard dash record (9.6) in 1926.

Carl Hubbell (b. June 22, 1903, d. Nov. 21, 1988): Baseball LHP; led NL in wins and ERA 3 times each; 2-time MVP (1933,36) with NY Giants; fanned Ruth, Gehrig, Foxx, Simmons and Cronin in succession in 1934 All-Star Game; 253-154 career record.

Sam Huff (b. Oct. 4, 1934): Football LB; glamorized NFL's middle linebacker position with NY Giants from 1956-63; subject of "The Violent World of Sam Huff" TV special in 1961; helped club win 6 division titles and a world championship (1956).

Miller Huggins (b. Mar. 27, 1878, d. Sept. 25, 1929): Baseball; managed NY Yankees from 1918 until his death late in '29 season; led Yanks to 6 pennants and 3 World Series titles from 1921-28.

Bobby Hull (b. Jan. 3, 1939): Hockey LW; led NHL in scoring 3 times; 2-time MVP (1965-66) with Chicago; All-NHL first team 10 times; jumped to WHA in 1972; 2-time MVP there (1973,75) with Winnipeg; scored 913 goals in both leagues; father of Brett.

Brett Hull (b. Aug. 9, 1964): Hockey RW; NHL MVP in 1991 with St. Louis; holds single season RW scoring record with 86 goals; he and father Bobby have both won Hart (MVP), Lady Byng (sportsmanship) and All-Star Game MVP trophies; won Stanley Cup with Dallas in 1999.

Jim (Catfish) Hunter (b. Apr. 8, 1946, d. Sept. 9, 1999): Baseball RHP; won 20 games or more 5 times (1971-75); played on 5 World Series winners with Oakland and NY Yankees; threw perfect game in 1968; won AL Cy Young Award in 1974; 224-166 career record.

Ibrahim Hussein (b. June 3, 1958): Kenyan distance runner; 3-time winner of Boston Marathon (1988,91-92) and 1st African runner to win in Boston; won New York Marathon in 1987.

Don Hutson (b. Jan. 31, 1913, d. June 24, 1997): Football E-PK; led NFL in receptions 8 times and interceptions once; 9-time All-Pro (1936,38-45) for Green Bay; 99 career TD catches.

Flo Hyman (b. July 31, 1954, d. Jan. 24, 1986): Volleyball; 3-time All-America spiker at Houston and captain of 1984 U.S. Women's Olympic team; died of heart attack caused by Marfan Syndrome during a match in Japan in 1986; namesake of award given out annually by the Women's Sports Foundation.

Hank Iba (b. Aug. 6, 1904, d. Jan. 15, 1993): Basketball; coached Oklahoma A&M to 2 straight NCAA titles (1945-46); 767 career wins in 41 years; coached U.S. Olympic team to 2 gold medals (1964,68), but lost to Soviets in controversial '72 final.

Punch Imlach (b. Mar. 15, 1918, d. Dec. 1, 1987): Hockey; directed Toronto to 4 Stanley Cups (1962-64,67) in 11 seasons as GM-coach.

Miguel Induráin (b. July 16, 1964): Spanish cyclist; won a record 5th straight Tour de France in 1995, joining legends Jacques Anquetil and Bernard Hinault of France and Eddy Merckx of Belgium as the only 5-time winners; won gold in time trial at '96 Olympics; retired in 1997.

Juli Inkster (b. June 24, 1960): Golfer; 26 career LPGA victories; winner of 6 major LPGA tournaments and 3 consecutive U.S. Women's Amateur tournaments (1980-82); inducted into the World Golf Hall of Fame in, 2000; LPGA Rookie of the Year in 1984.

Hale Irwin (b. June 3, 1945): Golfer; oldest player ever to win U.S. Open (45 in 1990); NCAA champion in 1967; 20 PGA victories, including 3 U.S. Opens (1974,79,90); 5-time Ryder Cup team member; joined senior PGA tour in 1995 and has already won 31 titles.

Bo Jackson (b. Nov. 30, 1962): Baseball OF and Football RB; won Heisman Trophy in 1985 and MVP of baseball All-Star Game in 1989; starter for both baseball's KC Royals and NFL's LA Raiders in 1988 and '89; severely injured left hip Jan. 13, 1991, in NFL playoffs; waived by Royals but signed by Chicago White Sox in 1991; missed entire 1992 season recovering from hip surgery; played for White Sox in 1993 and California in '94 before retiring.

Joe Jackson (b. July 16, 1889, d. Dec. 5, 1951): Baseball OF; hit .300 or better 11 times; nicknamed "Shoeless Joe"; career average of .356 (see Black Sox).

Phil Jackson (b. Sept. 17, 1945): Basketball; NBA champion as reserve forward with New York in 1973 (injured when Knicks won in '70); coached Chicago to six NBA titles in eight years (1991-93, 96-98); coach of the year in 1996 and 97; all-time leader in winning pct. for NBA coaches with 350 or more wins; returned to coach the LA Lakers in 1999 and has won 2 more titles (2000,01).

Reggie Jackson (b. May 18, 1946): Baseball OF; led AL in HRs 4 times; MVP in 1973; played on 5 World Series winners with Oakland, NY Yankees; 1977 Series MVP with 5 HRs; 563 career HRs; all-time strikeout leader (2,597); member of the Hall of Fame.

Helen Jacobs (b. Aug. 6, 1908, d. June 2, 1997): Tennis; 4-time winner of U.S. Championship (1932-35); Wimbledon winner in 1936; lost 4 Wimbledon finals to arch-rival Helen Wills Moody.

Jaromir Jagr (b. Feb. 15, 1972): Czech Hockey RW; fifth overall pick by Pittsburgh (1990); NHL All-Rookie team (1991); NHL MVP (1999); Won Art Ross Trophy (1995,98,99,00); NHL All-Star First Team (1995,96,97,98,99,00); NHL single season record for most points by a right wing (149); NHL single season record for most assists by a right wing (87); traded to Washington in 2001.

Dan Jansen (b. June 17, 1965): Speedskater; 1993 world record-holder in 500m; fell in 500m and 1,000m in 1988 Olympics at Calgary after learning of death of sister Jane; placed 4th in 500m and didn't attempt 1,000m 4 years later in Albertville; fell in 500m at '94 Games in Lillehammer, but finally won an Olympic medal with world record (1:12.43) effort in 1,000m, then took victory lap with baby daughter Jane in his arms; won 1994 Sullivan Award.

James J. Jeffries (b. Apr. 15, 1875, d. Mar. 3, 1953): Boxer; world heavyweight champion (1899-1905); retired undefeated but came back to fight Jack Johnson in 1910 and lost (KO, 15th).

David Jenkins (b. June 29, 1936): Figure skater; brother of Hayes; 3-time world champion (1957-59); won gold medal at 1960 Olympics.

Hayes Jenkins (b. Mat. 23, 1933): Figure skater; 4-time world champion (1953-56); won gold medal at 1956 Olympics; married 1960 women's gold medalist Carol Heiss.

Bruce Jenner (b. Oct. 28, 1949): Track & Field; won gold medal in 1976 Olympic decathlon.

Jackie Jensen (b. Mar. 9, 1927, d. July 14, 1982): Football RB and Baseball OF; All-America at California in 1948; American League MVP with Boston Red Sox in 1958.

Ben Johnson (b. Dec. 30, 1961): Canadian sprinter; set 100m world record (9.83) at 1987 World Championships; won 100m at 1988 Olympics, but flunked drug test and forfeited gold medal; 1987 world record revoked in '89 for admitted steroid use; returned drug-free in 1991, but performed poorly; banned for life by IAAF in 1993 for testing positive after a meet in Montreal.

Bob Johnson (b. Mar. 4, 1931, d. Nov. 26, 1991): Hockey; coached Pittsburgh Penguins to 1st Stanley Cup title in 1991; led Wisconsin to 3 NCAA titles (1973,77,81) in 15 years; also coached 1976 U.S. Olympic team and NHL Calgary Flames (1982-87).

Earvin (Magic) Johnson (b. Aug. 14, 1959): Basketball G; led Michigan St. to NCAA title in 1979 and was Final 4 MOP; All-NBA 1st team 9 times; 3-time MVP (1987,89-90); led LA Lakers to 5 NBA titles; 3-time Finals MVP (1980, 82, 87); 2nd all-time in NBA assists with 10,141; retired on Nov. 7, 1991 after announcing he was HIV-positive; returned to score 25 points in 1992 NBA All-Star Game; U.S. Olympic Dream Team member in '92; announced NBA comeback then retired again before start of 1992-93 season; named head coach of Lakers on Mar. 23, 1994, but finished season at 5-11 and quit; later became minority owner of team; came back a final time and played 32 games during 1995-96 season before retiring for good.

Jack Johnson (b. Mar. 31, 1878, d. June 10, 1946): Boxer; controversial heavyweight champion (1908-15) and 1st black to hold title; defeated Tommy Burns for crown at age 30; fled to Europe in 1913 after Mann Act conviction; lost title to Jess Willard in Havana, but claimed to have taken a dive; pro record 78-8-12 with 45 KOs.

Jimmy Johnson (b. July 16, 1943): Football; All-SWC defensive lineman on Arkansas' 1964 national championship team; coached Miami-FL to national title in 1987; college record of 81-34-3 in 10 years; hired by old friend and new Dallas owner Jerry Jones to succeed Tom Landry in 1989; went 1-15 in '89, then led Cowboys to consecutive Super Bowl victories in 1992 and '93 seasons; quit in 1994 after feuding with Jones; became TV analyst; replaced Don Shula as Miami Dolphins head coach from 1996-99.

Judy Johnson (b. Oct. 26, 1899, d. June 13, 1989): Baseball IF; one of the great stars of the Negro Leagues; a terrific fielding third baseman who regularly batted over .300; when baseball integrated Johnson's playing days were over but he coached and scouted for the Philadelphia Athletics, Boston Braves and Philadelphia Phillies; member of Hall of Fame.

Junior Johnson (b. 1930): Auto Racing; won the second Daytona 500 in 1960; also won 13 NASCAR races in 1965, including the Rebel 300 at Darlington; retired from racing to become a highly successful car owner; his first driver was Bobby Allison.

Michael Johnson (b. Sep 13, 1967): Track & Field; Shattered world record in 200m (19.32) and set Olympic record in 400m (43.49) to become first man to win the gold in both races in the same Olympic Games at Atlanta in 1996; two-time world champion in 200 (1991,95) and four-time world champ in 400 (1993,95,97,99); set world record in 400m (43.18) at '99 world championships in Seville; won the 400 in Sydney in 2000 to become the only man to win the event in two consecutive Olympics; retired in 2001.

Rafer Johnson (b. Aug. 18, 1935): Track & Field; won silver medal in 1956 Olympic decathlon and gold medal in 1960.

Randy Johnson (b. Sept. 10, 1963): Baseball LHP; 6'10" flamethrower; threw no-hitter June 2, 1990 for Seattle; struck out over 300 batters 5 times (1993,98,99,00,01); led majors in Ks 6 times (1993,94,98-01); struck out 20 batters in a game (5/8/01); 3-time Cy Young Award winner (AL-1995, NL-1999,00); traded to Houston in 1998 and signed as a free agent with Arizona in 1999.

Walter Johnson (b. Nov. 6, 1887, d. Dec. 10, 1946): Baseball RHP; won 20 games or more 10 straight years; led AL in ERA 5 times, wins 6 times and strikeouts 12 times; twice MVP (1913, 24) with Washington; all-time leader in shutouts (110) and 2nd in wins (417); nicknamed "Big Train."

Ben A. Jones (b. Dec. 31, 1882, d. June 13, 1961): Horse racing; Calumet Farm trainer (1939-47); saddled 6 Kentucky Derby champions, including 2 Triple Crown winners—Whirlaway in 1941 and Citation in '48.

Bobby Jones (b. Mar. 17, 1902, d. Dec. 18, 1971): Won U.S. and British Opens plus U.S. and British Amateurs in 1930 to become golf's only Grand Slam winner ever; from 1922-30, won 4 U.S. Opens, 5 U.S. Amateurs, 3 British Opens, and played in 6 Walker Cups; founded Masters tournament in 1934.

Deacon Jones (b. Dec. 9, 1938): Football DE; 5-time All-Pro (1965-69) with LA Rams; unofficially 3rd all-time in NFL sacks with 173½ in 14 years.

Marion Jones (b. Oct. 12, 1975): Track & Field; American sprinter who won 3 golds (100, 200, 4x100) at Sydney Games in 2000; 5-time world champion: 100m (1997,99), 200m (2001), 4x100m (1997,01); former college basketball star at North Carolina; voted Women's Athlete of the Year by Track & Field News in 1997,98 and 2000; 1999 Jesse Owens Award winner; 2000 AP and USOC Female Athlete of the Year.

Roy Jones Jr. (b. Jan. 16, 1969): Boxing; robbed of gold medal at 1988 Summer Olympics due to an error in scoring; still voted Outstanding Boxer of the Games; won IBF middleweight crown by beating Bernard Hopkins in 1993; moved up to super middleweight and won IBF title from James Toney in 1994; moved up to light heavyweight division winning WBC in 1997, WBA (1998) and IBF titles (1999).

Michael Jordan (b. Feb. 17, 1963): Basketball G; College Player of Year with North Carolina in 1984; NBA Rookie of the Year (1985); led NBA in scoring 7 years in a row (1987-93) and also 1996-98; 10-time All-NBA 1st team; 5-time regular season MVP (1988,91-92,96,98) and 6-time MVP of NBA Finals (1991-93,96-98); 3-time AP Male Athlete of Year; led U.S. Olympic team to gold medals in 1984 and '92; stunned sports world when he retired at age 30 on Oct. 6, 1993; signed as OF with Chi. White Sox and spent summer of '94 in AA with Birmingham; struggled with .204 average; made one of the most anticipated comebacks in sports history when he returned to the Bulls lineup on Mar. 19, 1995 but Bulls were eliminated by Orlando in second round of playoffs later that season; led Bulls to NBA titles for the next three years for 6 titles in all (1991-93,96-98); retired in 1999; became pres. of Wash. Wizards before unretiring again in 2001.

Florence Griffith Joyner (b. Dec. 21, 1959, d. Sept. 21, 1998): Track & Field; set world records in 100 and 200 meters in 1988; won 3 gold medals at '88 Olympics (100m, 200m, 4x100m relay); Sullivan Award winner (1988); retired in 1989; named as co-chairperson of President's Council on Physical Fitness and Sports in 1993; sister-in-law of Jackie Joyner-Kersee; died of suffocation during an epilectic seizure in 1998.

Jackie Joyner-Kersee (b. Mar. 3, 1962): Track & Field; 2-time world champion in both long jump (1987,91) and heptathlon (1987,93); won heptathlon gold medals at 1988 and '92 Olympics and LJ gold at '88 Games; also won Olympic silver (1984) in heptathlon and bronze (1992,96) in LJ; Sullivan Award winner (1986); only woman to receive *The Sporting News* Man of Year award.

Alberto Juantorena (b. Nov. 21, 1950): Cuban runner; won both 400m and 800m gold medals at 1976 Olympics.

Sonny Jurgensen (b. Aug. 23, 1934): Football QB; played 18 seasons with Philadelphia and Washington; led NFL in passing twice (1967,69); All-Pro in 1961; 255 career TD passes.

Duke Kahanamoku (b. Aug. 24, 1890, d. Jan. 22, 1968): Swimmer; won 3 gold medals and 2 silver over 3 Olympics (1912,20,24); also surfing pioneer.

Al Kaline (b. Dec. 19, 1934): Baseball; youngest player (at age 20) to win batting title (led AL with .340 in 1955); had 3,007 hits, 399 HRs in 22 years with Detroit.

Paul Kariya (b. Oct. 16, 1974): Hockey LW; all-time Mighty Ducks of Anaheim leader in goals, assists and points; scored 50 goals and 108 points in 1995-96; first-ever selection of Anaheim (4th overall in 1993); led Maine to an NCAA Division I national championship in 1993; won Hobey Baker Award in 1993 as a freshman.

Anatoly Karpov (b. May 23, 1951): Chess; Soviet world champion from 1975-85; regained International Chess Federation (FIDE) version of championship in 1993 when countryman Garry Kasparov was stripped of title after forming new Professional Chess Association; held FIDE title until 1999.

Garry Kasparov (b. Apr. 13, 1963): Chess; Azerbaijani who became youngest player (22 years, 210 days) ever to win world championship as Soviet in 1985; defeated countryman Anatoly Karpov for title; split with International Chess Federation (FIDE) to form Professional Chess Association (PCA) in 1993; stripped of FIDE title in '93 but successfully defended PCA title against Briton Nigel Short; beat IBM supercomputer "Deep Blue" 4 games to 2 in 1996 much-publicized match in New York; lost rematch to computer in 1997; finally lost world title to Vladimir Kramnik in 2000.

Mike Keenan (b. Oct. 21, 1949): Hockey; coach who finally led NY Rangers to Stanley Cup title in 1994 after 53 unsuccessful years; quit a month later in pay dispute and signed with St. Louis as coach-GM; later moved on to Vancouver and Boston; fired by the Bruins during 2000-01 season.

Kipchoge (Kip) Keino (b. Jan. 17, 1940): Kenyan runner; policeman who beat USA's Jim Ryun to win 1,500m gold medal at 1968 Olympics; won again in steeplechase at 1972 Summer Games; his success spawned long line of international distance champions from Kenya.

Johnny Kelley (b. Sept. 6, 1907): Distance runner; ran in his 61st and final Boston Marathon at age 84 in 1992, finishing in 5:58:36; won Boston twice (1935,45) and was 2nd 7 times.

Leroy Kelly (b. May 20, 1942): Football; replaced Jim Brown in the Cleveland Brown's backfield; in 1967, Kelly led the NFL in rushing yards (1,205), rushing average (5.1 per carry) and rushing touchdowns (11).

Jim Kelly (b. Feb. 14, 1960): Football QB; led Buffalo to four consecutive Super Bowl appearances, and is only QB to lose four times; named to AFC Pro Bowl team 5 times.

Walter Kennedy (b. June 8, 1912, d. June 26, 1977): Basketball; 2nd NBA commissioner (1963-75), league doubled in size to 18 teams during his term of office.

Nancy Kerrigan (b. Oct. 13, 1969): Figure skating; 1993 U.S. women's champion and Olympic medalist in 1992 (bronze) and '94 (silver); victim of Jan. 6, 1994 assault at U.S. nationals in Detroit when Shane Stant clubbed her in right knee with metal baton after a practice session; conspiracy hatched by Jeff Gillooly, ex-husband of rival Tonya Harding; although unable to compete in nationals, she recovered and was granted berth on Olympic team; finished 2nd in Lillehammer to Oksana Baiul of Ukraine by a 5-4 judges' vote.

Billy Kidd (b. Apr. 13, 1943): Skiing; the first great Amercian male Alpine skier; first American male to win an Olympic medal when he won a silver in the slalom and a bronze in the Alpine combined in 1964; competed respectably with the great Jean-Claude Killy; won the world Alpine combined event in 1970, which was the first world championship for an American male.

Harmon Killebrew (b. June 29, 1936): Baseball 3B-1B; led AL in HRs 6 times and RBI 3 times; MVP in 1969 with Minnesota; 573 career homers ranks him 6th all-time.

Jean-Claude Killy (b. Aug. 30, 1943): French alpine skier; 2-time World Cup champion (1967-68); won 3 gold medals at 1968 Olympics in Grenoble; co-president of 1992 Winter Games in Albertville.

Ralph Kiner (b. Oct. 27, 1922): Baseball OF; led NL in home runs 7 straight years (1946-52) with Pittsburgh; 369 career HRs and 1,015 RBI in 10 seasons; long-time NY Mets announcer.

Betsy King (b. Aug. 13, 1955): Golfer; 2-time LPGA Player of Year (1984,89); 3-time winner of Dinah Shore (1987,90,97) and 2-time winner of U.S. Open (1989,90); 34 overall Tour wins; member of LPGA Hall of Fame.

Billie Jean King (b. Nov. 22, 1943): Tennis; women's rights pioneer; Wimbledon singles champ 6 times; U.S. champ 4 times; first woman athlete to earn $100,000 in one year (1971); beat 55-year-old Bobby Riggs 6-4,6-3,6-3, in "Battle of the Sexes" to win $100,000 at Astrodome in 1973; captained the U.S. Olympic team in 1996 and 2000.

Don King (b. Aug. 20, 1931): Boxing promoter; first major black promoter who has controlled heavyweight title off and on since 1978; first big promotion was Muhammad Ali's fight against George Foreman in 1974; former numbers operator who served 4 years for manslaughter (1967-70); acquitted of tax evasion and fraud in 1985; also promoted Larry Holmes, Mike Tyson, Evander Holyfield, Roberto Duran and Julio Cesar Chavez among others; also famous for his gravity-defying hairstyle and his catchphrase "Only in America!"

Karch Kiraly (b. Nov. 3, 1960): Volleyball; USA's preeminent volleyball player; led UCLA to three NCAA championships (1979,81,82); played on US national teams that won Olympic gold medals in 1984 and '88, world championships in '82 and '86; won the inaugural gold medal for Olympic beach volleyball with Kent Steffes in 1996.

Tom Kite (b. Dec. 9, 1949): Golfer; co-NCAA champion with Ben Crenshaw (1972); PGA Rookie of Year (1973); PGA Player of Year (1989); finally won 1st major with victory in 1992 U.S. Open at Pebble Beach; captain of 1997 US Ryder Cup team; 19 career PGA wins, played on the Senior tour since 2000, winning twice.

Gene Klein (b. Jan. 29, 1921, d. Mar. 12, 1990): Horseman; won 3 Eclipse awards as top owner (1985-87); his filly Winning Colors won 1988 Kentucky Derby; also owned San Diego Chargers football team (1966-84).

Bob Knight (b. Oct. 25, 1940): Basketball; coached Indiana to 3 NCAA titles (1976,81,87); 3-time Coach of Year (1975-76,89); coached 1984 U.S. Olympic team to gold medal; his volatile temper finally cost him when he was fired from Indiana in Sept. 2000 after a string of unacceptable incidents that included choking one of his players; 5th on all-time NCAA list with 763 wins in 35 years before returning to coaching with Texas Tech in 2001.

Phil Knight (b. Feb. 24, 1938): Founder and chairman of Nike, Inc., the multi-billion dollar shoe and fitness company founded in 1972 and based in Beaverton, Ore.; ; named "The Most Powerful Man in Sports" by *The Sporting News* in 1992.

Bill Koch (b. June 7, 1955): Cross-country skiing; first highly accomplished American male in his sport; first American male to win a cross-country Olympic medal when he took home a silver in the 30-kilometer race in 1976; in 1982, he was the first American male to win the Nordic World Cup.

Olga Korbut (b. May 16, 1955): Soviet gymnast; became the media darling of the 1972 Olympics in Munich by winning 3 gold medals (balance beam, floor exercise and team all-around); came back in the 1976 Olympics in Montreal and was a part of the USSR's gold medal winning all-around team; first to perform back somersault on balance beam; was inducted into the International Women's Sports Hall of Fame in 1982, the first gymnast to be inducted.

Johann Olav Koss (b. Oct. 29, 1968): Norwegian speedskater; won three gold medals at 1994 Olympics in Lillehammer with world records in the 1,500m, 5,000m and 10,000m; also won 1,500m gold and 10,000m silver in 1992. Games; retired shortly after '94 Olympics.

Sandy Koufax (b. Dec. 30, 1935): Baseball LHP; led NL in strikeouts 4 times and ERA 5 straight years; won 3 Cy Young Awards (1963,65,66) with LA Dodgers; MVP in 1963; 2-time World Series MVP (1963, 65); threw perfect game against Chicago Cubs (1-0, Sept. 9, 1965) and had 3 other no-hitters in career.

Alvin Kraenzlein (b. Dec. 12, 1876, d. Jan. 6, 1928): Track & Field; won 4 individual gold medals in 1900 Olympics (60m, long jump and the 110m and 200m hurdles).

Jack Kramer (b. Aug. 1, 1921): Tennis; Wimbledon singles champ 1947; U.S. champ 1946-47; promoter and Open pioneer.

Lenny Krayzelburg (b. Sept. 28, 1975): Swimming; born in Ukraine but became an American citizen in 1995; won gold for U.S. in the 100m backstroke and 200m backstroke at the Sydney Games in 2000; was also part of U.S. team that set a world record in the 4x100m medley relay in Sydney; world record holder in the 50, 100 and 200 meter backstrokes.

Ingrid Kristiansen (b. Mar. 21, 1956): Norwegian runner; 2-time Boston Marathon winner (1986,89); won New York City Marathon in 1989; former world record holder in the marathon.

Julie Krone (b. July 24, 1963): Jockey; only woman to ride winning horse in a Triple Crown race when she captured Belmont Stakes aboard Colonial Affair in 1993; retired in 1999 as all-time winningest female jockey with over 3,500 wins; in 2000 became the first female jockey elected to thoroughbred racing's hall of fame.

Mike Krzyzewski (b. Feb. 13, 1947): Basketball; has coached Duke to 9 Final Four appearances and 3 NCAA titles (1991-92,2001); has coached at Army (1976-80) and Duke (1981–); inducted into Hall of Fame in 2001.

Bowie Kuhn (b. Oct. 28, 1926): Baseball Commissioner; Elected commissioner on Feb. 4, 1969 and served until Sept. 30, 1984; kept Willie Mays and Mickey Mantle out of baseball for their employment with casinos; handed down one-year suspensions of several players for drug involvement; nixed Charlie Finley's sale of three players for $3.5 million; baseball enjoyed unprecedented attendance and television contracts during his reign.

Alan Kulwicki (b. Dec. 14, 1954, d. Apr. 1, 1993): Auto racer; 1992 NASCAR national champion; 1st college grad and Northerner to win title; NASCAR Rookie of Year in 1986; famous for driving car backwards on victory lap; killed at age 38 in plane crash near Bristol, Tenn.

Michelle Kwan (b. July 7, 1980): Figure Skater; 1998 Olympic silver medalist at Nagano; 5-time U.S. Champion (1996,98,99,00,01) and 4-time World Champ (1996,98,00,01); tied an U.S. record with 6 career medals overall at the World Championships (4 gold, 2 silver); was U.S. alternate to the Olympics in 1994 as a 13-year-old.

Marion Ladewig (b. Oct. 30, 1914): Bowler; named Woman Bowler of the Year 9 times (1950-54,57-59,63).

Guy Lafleur (b. Sept. 20, 1951): Hockey RW; led NHL in scoring 3 times (1976-78); 2-time MVP (1977-78), played for 5 Stanley Cup winners in Montreal; playoff MVP in 1977; returned to NHL as player in 1988 after election to Hall of Fame; retired again in 1991 with 560 goals and 1,353 points.

Napoleon (Nap) Lajoie (b. Sept. 5, 1874, d. Feb. 7, 1959): Baseball 2B; led AL in batting 3 times (1901,03-04); batted .422 in 1901; hit .339 for career with 3,251 hits.

Jack Lambert (b. July 8, 1952): Football LB; 6-time All-Pro (1975-76,79-82); led Pittsburgh to 4 Super Bowl titles.

Kenesaw Mountain Landis (b. Nov. 20, 1866, d. Nov. 25, 1944): U.S. District Court judge who became first baseball commissioner (1920-44); banned eight Chicago Black Sox from baseball for life.

Tom Landry (b. Sept. 11, 1924, d. Feb. 12, 2000): Football; All-Pro DB for NY Giants (1954); coached Dallas for 29 years (1960-88); won 2 Super Bowls (1972,78); 3rd on NFL all-time list with 270 wins.

Steve Largent (b. Sept. 28, 1954): Football WR; retired in 1989 after 14 years in Seattle with then NFL records in passes caught (819) and TD passes caught (100); elected to U.S. House of Representatives (R, Okla.) in 1994 and Pro Football Hall of Fame in '95.

Don Larsen (b. Aug. 7, 1929): Baseball RHP; NY Yankees hurler who pitched the only perfect game in World Series history— a 2-0 victory over Brooklyn in Game 5 of the 1956 Series (Oct. 8); Series MVP that year; had career record of 81-91 in 14 seasons with 6 clubs.

Tommy Lasorda (b. Sept. 22, 1927): Baseball; managed LA Dodgers to 2 World Series titles (1981,88) in 4 appearances; retired as manager during 1996 season with 1,599 regular-season wins in 21 years; named interim GM of Dodgers in 1998; member of Baseball Hall of Fame; managed gold-medal winning U.S. Olympic team in 2000 at Sydney.

Larissa Latynina (b. Dec. 27, 1934): Soviet gymnast; won total of 18 medals, (9 gold) in 3 Olympics (1956,60,64).

Nikki Lauda (b. Feb. 22, 1949): Austrian auto racer; 3-time world Formula One champion (1975,77,84); 25 career wins from 1971-85.

Rod Laver (b. Aug. 9, 1938): Australian tennis player; only player to win Grand Slam twice (1962,69); Wimbledon champion 4 times; 1st to earn $1 million in prize money, won 11 Grand Slam singles titles.

Andrea Mead Lawrence (b. Apr. 19, 1932): Alpine skier; won 2 gold medals at 1952 Olympics.

Bobby Layne (b. Dec. 19, 1926, d. Dec. 1, 1986): Football QB; college star at Texas; master of 2-minute offense; led Detroit to 4 divisional titles and 3 NFL championships in 1950s.

Frank Leahy (b. Aug. 27, 1908, d. June 21, 1973): Football; coached Notre Dame to four national titles (1943,46-47,49); career record of 107-13-9 for a winning pct. of .864.

Sammy Lee (b. Aug. 1, 1920): Diving; won Olympic gold medals for U.S. in the platform diving event in 1948 and 1952, the first male diver in history to win 2 golds in that event; Sullivan Award winner (1953); former doctor in U.S. Army; trained Greg Louganis.

Jacques Lemaire (b. Sept. 7, 1945): Hockey C; member of 8 Stanley Cup champions in Montreal; scored 366 goals in 12 seasons; coached Canadiens (1983-85) and NJ Devils (1993-98), won 1995 Stanley Cup with New Jersey; returned to coaching with the expansion Minnesota Wild in 2000.

Mario Lemieux (b. Oct. 5, 1965): Hockey C; 6-time NHL scoring leader (1988-89,92-93,96,97); Rookie of Year (1985); 4-time All-NHL 1st team (1988-89,93,96); 3-time regular season MVP (1988,93,96); 3-time All-Star Game MVP; led Pittsburgh to consecutive Stanley Cup titles (1991 and '92) and was playoff MVP both years; won 1993 scoring title despite missing 24 games to undergo radiation treatments for Hodgkin's disease; missed 62 games during 1993-94 season and entire 94-95 season due to back injuries and fatigue; returned in 1995-96 to lead NHL in scoring and win the MVP trophy; retired after 1996-97 season and inducted into the Hall of Fame; headed group of investors that bought bankrupt Penguins in 1999; made surprising comeback with the team he owns in 2001, scoring 76 points in 43 games.

Greg LeMond (b. June 26, 1961): Cyclist; 3-time Tour de France winner (1986,89-90); only non-European to win the event until Lance Armstrong in 1999; retired in Dec. 1994 after being diagnosed with a rare muscular disease known as mitochondrial myopathy.

Ivan Lendl (b. Mar. 7, 1960): Czech tennis player; No. 1 player in world 4 times (1985-87,89); has won both French and U.S. Opens 3 times and Australian twice; owns 94 career tournament wins.

Suzanne Lenglen (b. May 24, 1899, d. July 4, 1938): French tennis player; dominated women's tennis from 1919-26; won both Wimbledon and French singles titles 6 times.

Sugar Ray Leonard (b. May 17, 1956): Boxer; light welterweight Olympic champ (1976); won world welterweight title 1979 and four more titles; retired after losing to Terry Norris on Feb. 9, 1991, with record of 36-2-1 and 25 KOs; misguided comeback in 1997 resulted in resounding defeat by Hector Camacho.

Walter (Buck) Leonard (b. Sept. 8, 1907, d. Nov. 27, 1997): Baseball 1B; won Negro League championship nine years in a row with the Homestead Grays; hit .391 in 1948 to lead the league; usually batted cleanup behind Josh Gibson; retired at the age of 48; member of the National Baseball Hall of Fame.

Lisa Leslie (b. Sept. 7, 1972): Basketball C; 2001 WNBA regular season and championship series MVP with the champion Los Angeles Sparks; WNBA All-Star Game MVP (1999); 2-time Olympic gold medalist (1996,2000); consensus National Player of the Year at USC (1994).

Marv Levy (b. Aug. 3, 1928): Football; coached Buffalo to four consecutive Super Bowls, but is one of two coaches who are 0-4 (Bud Grant is the other); won 50 games and two CFL Grey Cups with Montreal (1974,77).

Bill Lewis (b. Nov. 30, 1868, d. Jan. 1, 1949): Football; college star at Amherst College and then Harvard; first black player to be selected as an All-American (1892-93); also the first black admitted to the American Bar Association (1911); was U.S. Assistant Attorney General.

Carl Lewis (b. July 1, 1961): Track & Field; won 9 Olympic gold medals; 4 in 1984 (100m, 200m, 4x100m, LJ), 2 in '88 (100m, LJ), 2 in '92 (4x100m, LJ) and 1 in '96 (LJ); has record 8 World Championship titles and 9 medals in all; Sullivan Award winner (1981); two-time AP Athlete of the Year (1983-84).

Lennox Lewis (b. Sept. 2, 1965): British boxer; won 1988 Olympic super heavyweight gold medal for Canada; was awarded WBC heavyweight belt when Riddick Bowe tossed it in a London trash can in 1993; lost title in a 2nd round TKO loss to Oliver McCall; won rematch 3 years later when McCall suffered emotional breakdown in the ring; unified titles in his rematch with Evander Holyfield in Nov. 1999; lost belts in upset loss to Hasim Rahman in South Africa in 2001.

Nancy Lieberman (b. July 1, 1958): Basketball; 3-time All-America and 2-time Player of Year (1979-80); led Old Dominion to consecutive AIAW titles in 1979 and '80; played in defunct WPBL and WABA and became 1st woman to play in men's pro league (USBL) in 1986; played in the inaugural season of the WNBA for the Phoenix Mercury and served as coach/GM of Detroit Shock (1998-2000).

Eric Lindros (b. Feb. 28, 1973): Hockey C; No. 1 pick in 1991 NHL draft by the Nordiques; sat out 1991-92 season rather than play in Quebec; traded to Philadelphia in 1992 for 6 players, 2 No. 1 picks and $15 million; elected Flyers captain at age 22; won Hart Trophy as league MVP in 1995; suffered series of concussions in 1999-00 but was traded to NY Rangers and inked big money deal with team in 2001.

Tara Lipinski (b. June 10, 1982): Figure Skater; won the 1998 women's figure skating gold medal at the Olympics in Nagano, becoming the youngest in history (15 yrs., 7 mos.) to do so; she and Michelle Kwan gave the U.S. its first 1-2 finish in that event since 1956; 1997 U.S. and World champion; turned pro in April 1998.

Sonny Liston (b. May 8, 1932, d. Dec. 30, 1970): Boxer; heavyweight champion (1962-64), who knocked out Floyd Patterson twice in the first round, then lost title to Muhammad Ali (then Cassius Clay) in 1964; pro record of 50-4 with 39 KOs.

Vince Lombardi (b. June 11, 1913; d. Sept. 3, 1970): Football; coached Green Bay to 5 NFL titles; won first 2 Super Bowls (1967-68); died as NFL's all-time winningest coach with percentage of .740 (105-35-6); Super Bowl trophy named in his honor.

Johnny Longden (b. Feb. 14, 1907): Jockey; first to win 6,000 races; rode Count Fleet to Triple Crown in 1943.

Jeannie Longo (b. Oct. 31, 1958): French cyclist; 12-time world cycling champion and 1996 olympic road race gold medallist.

Nancy Lopez (b. Jan. 6, 1957): Golfer; 4-time LPGA Player of the Year (1978-79,85,88); Rookie of Year (1977); 3-time winner of LPGA Championship; reached Hall of Fame by age 30 with 35 victories; 48 career wins.

Donna Lopiano (b. Sept. 11, 1946): Former basketball and softball star who was women's AD at Texas for 18 years before leaving to become executive director of Women's Sports Foundation in 1992.

Greg Louganis (b. Jan. 29, 1960): U.S. diver; widely considered the greatest diver in history; won platform and springboard gold medals at both 1984 and '88 Olympics; also won a silver medal at the 1976 Olympics at the age of 16; won five world championships and 47 U.S. National Diving titles; revealed on Feb. 22, 1995 that he has AIDS.

Joe Louis (b. May 13, 1914, d. Apr. 12, 1981): Boxer; world heavyweight champion from June 22, 1937 to Mar. 1, 1949; his reign of 11 years, 8 months longest in division history; successfully defended title 25 times; retired in 1949, but returned to lose title shot against successor Ezzard Charles in 1950 and then to Rocky Marciano in '51; pro record of 63-3 with 49 KOs.

Sid Luckman (b. Nov. 21, 1916, d. July 5, 1998): Football QB; 6-time All-Pro; led Chicago Bears to 4 NFL titles (1940-41,43,46); MVP in 1943.

Hank Luisetti (b. June 16, 1916): Basketball F; 3-time All-America at Stanford (1935-38); revolutionized game with one-handed shot.

Johnny Lujack (b. Jan. 4, 1925): Football QB; led Notre Dame to three national titles (1943,46-47); won Heisman Trophy in 1947.

Darrell Wayne Lukas (b. Sept. 2, 1935): Horse racing; 4-time Eclipse-winning trainer who saddled Horses of Year Lady's Secret in 1988 and Criminal Type in 1990; first trainer to earn over $100 million in purses; led nation in earnings 14 times since 1983; Grindstone's Kentucky Derby win in 1996 gave him six Triple Crown wins in a row; has won Preakness 5 times, Kentucky Derby 4 times and Belmont 4 times, his most recent Triple Crown victory came in the 2000 Belmont with Commendable; leads all Breeders' Cup trainers with 16 victories.

Gen. Douglas MacArthur (b. Jan. 26, 1880, d. Apr. 5, 1964): Controversial U.S. general of World War II and Korea; president of U.S. Olympic Committee (1927-28); college football devotee, National Football Foundation MacArthur Bowl named after him.

Connie Mack (b. Dec. 22, 1862, d. Feb. 8, 1956): Baseball owner; managed Philadelphia A's until he was 87 (1901-50); all-time major league wins leader with 3,755, including World Series; won 9 AL pennants and 5 World Series (1910-11,13,29-30); also finished last 17 times.

Andy MacPhail (b. Apr. 5, 1953): Baseball; Chicago Cubs president/CEO and now general manager, who was GM of 2 World Series champions in Minnesota (1987,91); won first title at age 34; son of Lee, grandson of Larry.

Larry MacPhail (b. Feb. 3, 1890, d. Oct. 1, 1975): Baseball executive and innovator; introduced major leagues to night games at Cincinnati (May 24, 1935); won pennant in Brooklyn (1941) and World Series with NY Yankees (1947); father of Lee.

Lee MacPhail (b. Oct. 25, 1917): Baseball; AL president (1974-83); president of owners' Player Relations Committee (1984-85); also GM of Baltimore (1959-65) and NY Yankees (1967-74); son of Larry and father of Andy.

Wendy Macpherson (b. Jan. 28, 1968): Bowling; voted Bowler of the Decade for the 1990s; Major titles include the 1986 BPAA U.S. Open, 1988 and 2000 WIBC Queens and 1999 Sam's Town Invitational; annual PWBA money winner 3 times (1996,97,99).

John Madden (b. Apr. 10, 1936): Football and Radio-TV; won 112 games and a Super Bowl (1976 season) as coach of Oakland Raiders; has won 13 Emmy Awards since 1982 as NFL analyst; signed 4-year, $32 million deal with Fox in 1994— a richer contract than any NFL player at the time.

Greg Maddux (b. Apr. 14, 1966): Baseball RHP; won unprecedented 4 straight NL Cy Young Awards with Cubs (1992) and Atlanta (1993-95); has led NL in ERA four times (1993-95,98); won 11th straight gold glove in 2000.

Larry Mahan (b. Nov. 21, 1943): Rodeo; 6-time All-Around world champion (1966-70,73).

Phil Mahre (b. May 10, 1957): Alpine skier; 3-time World Cup overall champ (1981-83); finished 1-2 with twin brother Steve in 1984 Olympic slalom.

Karl Malone (b. July 24, 1963): Basketball F; 11-time All-NBA 1st team (1989-99) with Utah; member of the 1992 and '96 Olympic Dream Teams; 2-time NBA MVP (1997,99); all-time NBA leader in free throws made (8,636), 2nd in career points (32,919) and 3rd in field goals made (12,102) entering the 2001-02 season; named one of the NBA's 50 greatest players.

Moses Malone (b. Mar. 23, 1955): Basketball C; signed with Utah of ABA at age 19; led NBA in rebounding 6 times; 4-time All-NBA 1st team; 3-time NBA MVP (1979,82-83); Finals MVP with Philadelphia in 1983; played in 21st pro season in 1994-95.

Nigel Mansell (b. Aug. 8, 1953): British auto racer; won 1992 Formula One driving championship with record 9 victories and 14 poles; quit Grand Prix circuit to race Indy cars in 1993; 1st rookie to win IndyCar title; 3rd driver to win IndyCar and F1 titles; returned to F1 after 1994 IndyCar season and won '94 Australian Grand Prix; led again on May 23, 1995 with 31 wins and 32 poles in 15 years.

Mickey Mantle (b. Oct. 20, 1931, d. Aug. 13, 1995): Baseball OF; led AL in home runs 4 times; won Triple Crown in 1956; hit 52 HRs in 1956 and 54 in '61; 3-time MVP (1956-57,62); hit 536 career HRs; played in 12 World Series with NY Yankees and won 7 times; all-time Series leader in HRs (18), RBI (40), runs (42) and strikeouts (54).

Diego Maradona (b. Oct. 30, 1960): Soccer F; captain and MVP of 1986 World Cup champion Argentina; also led national team to 1990 World Cup final; consensus Player of Decade in 1980s; led Napoli to 2 Italian League titles (1987,90) and UEFA Cup (1989); tested positive for cocaine and suspended 15 months by FIFA in 1991; returned to World Cup as Argentine captain in 1994, but was kicked out of tournament after two games when doping test found 5 banned substances in his urine.

Pete Maravich (b. June 27, 1947, d. Jan. 5, 1988): Basketball; NCAA scoring leader 3 times at LSU (1968-70); averaged NCAA-record 44.2 points a game over career; Player of Year in 1970; NBA scoring champ in '77 with New Orleans.

Alice Marble (b. Sept. 28, 1913, d. Dec. 13, 1990): Tennis; 4-time U.S. champion (1936,38-40); won Wimbledon in 1939; swept U.S. singles, doubles and mixed doubles from 1938-40.

Gino Marchetti (b. Jan. 2, 1927): Football DE; 8-time NFL All-Pro (1957-64) with Baltimore Colts.

Rocky Marciano (b. Sept. 1, 1923, d. Aug. 31, 1969): Boxer; heavyweight champion (1952-56); retired undefeated; pro record of 49-0 with 43 KOs; killed in plane crash in Iowa.

Juan Marichal (b. Oct. 20, 1938): Baseball RHP; won 21 or more games 6 times for S.F. Giants from 1963-69; ended 16-year career at 243-142.

Dan Marino (b. Sept. 15, 1961): Football QB; 4-time leading passer in AFC (1983-84,86,89); set NFL single-season records for TD passes (48) and passing yards (5,084) with Miami in 1984; all-time leader in career TD passes, passing yards, attempts and completions.

Roger Maris (b. Sept. 10, 1934, d. Dec. 14, 1985): Baseball OF; broke Babe Ruth's season HR record with 61 in 1961 and held record until 1998; 2-time AL MVP (1960-61) with NY Yankees; 275 HRs in 12 years.

Billy Martin (b. May 16, 1928, d. Dec. 25, 1989): Baseball; 5-time manager of NY Yankees; won 2 pennants and 1 World Series (1977); also managed Minnesota, Detroit, Texas and Oakland; played on 5 Yankee world champions in 1950s.

Casey Martin (b. June 2, 1972): Golfer; suffers from a birth defect in his right leg known as Klippel-Trenauney-Webber Syndrome; won lawsuit against the PGA Tour for the right to use a golf cart during competition under the Americans with Disabilities Act.

Pedro Martinez (b. Oct. 25, 1971): Baseball RHP; one of baseball's premier pitchers; won 1997 NL Cy Young award with Montreal; traded to Boston Red Sox on Nov. 18, 1997 for pitchers Carl Pavano and Tony Armas; 2-time AL Cy Young Award winner with Boston (1999,2000).

Eddie Mathews (b. Oct. 13, 1931, d. Feb. 18, 2001): Baseball 3B; led NL in HRs twice (1953,59); hit 30 or more home runs 9 straight years; 512 career HRs.

Christy Mathewson (b. Aug. 12, 1880, d. Oct. 7, 1925): Baseball RHP; won 22 or more games 12 straight years (1903-14); 373 career wins; pitched 3 shutouts in 1905 World Series.

Bob Mathias (b. Nov. 17, 1930): Track & Field; youngest winner of decathlon with gold medal in 1948 Olympics at age 17; first to repeat as decathlon champ in 1952; Sullivan Award winner (1948); 4-term member of U.S. Congress (R, Calif.) from 1967-74.

Ollie Matson (b. May 1, 1930): Football HB; All-America at San Francisco (1951); bronze medal winner in 400m at 1952 Olympics; 4-time All-Pro for NFL Chicago Cardinals (1954-57); traded to LA Rams for 9 players in 1959; accounted for 12,884 all-purpose yards and scored 73 TDs in 14 seasons.

Don Mattingly (b. Apr. 20, 1961): Baseball 1B; American League MVP (1985); won AL batting title in 1984 (.343) and led AL with 207 hits and 44 doubles; led majors with 145 RBI in 1985; led AL with 238 hits (Yankee record), 53 doubles and a .573 slugging percentage in 1986; won 9 Gold Glove Awards (1985-89, 91-94); back injury shortened career.

Willie Mays (b. May 6, 1931): Baseball OF; nicknamed the "Say Hey Kid"; led NL in HRs and stolen bases 4 times each; 2-time MVP (1954,65) with NY-SF Giants; Hall of Famer who played in 24 All-Star Games; 660 HRs and 3,283 hits in career.

Bill Mazeroski (b. Sept. 5, 1936): Baseball 2B; career .260 hitter who won the 1960 World Series for Pittsburgh with a lead-off HR in the bottom of the 9th inning of Game 7; the pitcher was Ralph Terry of the NY Yankees, the count was 1-0 and the score was tied 9-9; also a sure-fielder, Maz won 8 Gold Gloves in 17 seasons.

Bob McAdoo (b. Sept. 25, 1951): Basketball F/C; 1972 Sporting News First Team All-American; NBA Rookie of the Year (1973); NBA MVP (1975); All-NBA First Team (1975); Led NBA in scoring three consecutive years (1974-76); 5-time All-Star (1974-78); two championships with LA Lakers (1982,85).

Joe McCarthy (b. Apr. 21, 1887, d. Jan. 13, 1978): Baseball; first manager to win pennants in both leagues (Chicago Cubs in 1929 and NY Yankees in 1932); greatest success came with Yankees when he won seven pennants and six World Series championships from 1936 to 1943; first manager to win four World Series in a row (1936-39); finished his career with the Boston Red Sox (1948-'50); lifetime record of 2125-1333; member of Baseball Hall of Fame.

Pat McCormick (b. May 12, 1930): U.S. diver; won women's platform and springboard gold medals in both 1952 and '56 Olympics.

Willie McCovey (b. Jan. 10, 1938): Baseball 1B; led NL in HRs 3 times and RBI twice; MVP in 1969 with SF; 521 career HRs; indicted for tax evasion in July 1995, pled guilty; "McCovey Cove," the bay outside the rightfield fence at San Francisco's Pacific Bell Park is named for him.

John McEnroe (b. Feb. 16, 1959): Tennis; No.1 player in the world 4 times (1981-84); 4-time U.S. Open champ (1979-81,84); 3-time Wimbledon champ (1981,83-84); played on 5 Davis Cup winners (1978,79,81,82,92); won NCAA singles title (1978); finished career with 77 singles championships, 77 more in men's doubles (including 9 Grand Slam titles), and U.S. Davis Cup records for years played (13) and singles matches won (41).

John McGraw (b. Apr. 7, 1873, d. Feb. 25, 1934): Baseball; managed NY Giants to 9 NL pennants between 1905-24; won 3 World Series (1905,21-22); 2nd on all-time career list with 2,866 wins in 33 seasons (2,840 regular season and 26 World Series).

Frank McGuire (b. Nov. 8, 1916, d. Oct. 11, 1994): Basketball; winner of 731 games as high school, college and pro coach; won at least 100 games at 3 colleges— St. John's (103), North Carolina (164) and South Carolina (283); won 550 games in 30 college seasons; 1957 UNC team went 32-0 and beat Kansas 54-53 in triple OT to win NCAA title; coached NBA Philadelphia Warriors to 49-31 record in 1961-62 season, but refused to move with team to San Francisco.

Mark McGwire (b. Oct. 1, 1963): Baseball 1B; Sporting News college player of the year (1984); Member of 1984 U.S. Olympic team; won AL Rookie of the Year and hit rookie-record 49 HRs in 1987; shattered Roger Maris' season home run record (61) in 1998 with St. Louis (70); followed that magical season with 65 HRs and 147 RBI in 1999.

Jim McKay (b. Sept. 24, 1921): Radio-TV; host and commentator of ABC's Olympic coverage and "Wide World of Sports" show since 1961; 12-time Emmy winner; also given Peabody Award in 1988 and Life Achievement Emmy in 1990; became part owner of Baltimore Orioles in 1993.

Tamara McKinney (b. Oct. 16, 1962): Skiing; first American woman to win overall Alpine World Cup championship (1983); won World Cup slalom (1984) and giant slalom titles twice (1981,83).

Denny McLain (b. Mar. 29, 1944): Baseball RHP; last pitcher to win 30 games (1968); 2-time Cy Young winner (1968-69) with Detroit; convicted of racketeering, extortion and drug possession in 1985, served 29 months of 25-year jail term, sentence overturned when court ruled he had not received a fair trial; he has faced subsequent legal troubles.

Rick Mears (b. Dec. 3, 1951): Auto racer; 3-time CART national champ (1979,81-82); 4-time winner of Indy 500 (1979,84,88,91) and only driver to win 6 Indy 500 poles; Indy 500 Rookie of Year (1978); retired after 1992 season with 29 CART wins and 40 poles.

Mark Messier (b. Jan. 18, 1961): Hockey C; 2-time NHL MVP with Edmonton (1990) and NY Rangers (1992); captain of 1994 Rangers team that won 1st Stanley Cup since 1940; ranks 2nd in all-time playoff points, goals and assists; signed free agent contract with Vancouver Canucks in 1997 but returned to the Rangers in 2000.

Anne Meyers (b. Mar. 26, 1955): Basketball G; In 1974, became first high school student to play for U.S. national team; 4-time All-American at UCLA (1976-79); member of 1976 U.S. Olympic team; Broderick Award and Cup winner (1978); Signed $50,000 no cut contract with NBA's Indiana Pacers (1980); married Dodger great Don Drysdale.

Debbie Meyer (b. Aug. 14, 1952): Swimmer; 1st swimmer to win 3 individual gold medals at one Olympics (1968).

George Mikan (b. June 18, 1924): Basketball C; 3-time All-America (1944-46); led DePaul to NIT title (1945); led Minneapolis Lakers to 5 NBA titles in 6 years (1949-54); first commissioner of ABA (1967-69).

Stan Mikita (b. May 20, 1940): Hockey C; led NHL in scoring 4 times; won both MVP and Lady Byng awards in 1967 and '68 with Chicago.

Cheryl Miller (b. Jan. 3, 1964): Basketball; 3-time College Player of Year (1984-86); led USC to NCAA title and U.S. to Olympic gold medal in 1984; coached USC to 44-14 record in 2 seasons before quitting to join Turner Sports as NBA reporter; coached WNBA's Phoenix Mercury for 4 seasons; sister of NBA star Reggie Miller.

Del Miller (b. July 5, 1913): Harness racing; driver, trainer, owner, breeder, seller and track owner; drove to 2,441 wins from 1939-90.

Marvin Miller (b. Apr. 14, 1917): Baseball labor leader; executive director of Players' Assn. from 1966-82; increased average salary from $19,000 to over $240,000; led 13-day strike in 1972 and 50-day walkout in '81.

Shannon Miller (b. Mar. 10, 1977): Gymnast; won 5 medals in 1992 Olympics and 2 golds in '96 Games; All-Around women's world champion in 1993 and '94.

Billy Mills (b. June 30, 1938): Track & Field; upset winner of 10,000m gold medal at 1964 Olympics.

Bora Milutinovic (b. Sept. 7, 1944): Soccer; Serbian who coached United States national team from 1991-95, but was fired when he refused to accept additional duties; hired 4 months later to revive Mexican national team; known as a miracle worker, has led Mexico, Costa Rica, USA and Nigeria into the 2nd round of the last four World Cups.

Tommy Moe (b. Feb. 17, 1970): Alpine skier; won Downhill gold and Super-G silver at 1994 Winter Olympics; 1st U.S. man to win 2 Olympic alpine medals in one year.

Paul Molitor (b. Aug. 22, 1956): Baseball DH-1B; All-America SS at Minnesota in 1976; signed as free agent by Toronto in 1992, after 15 years with Milwaukee; led Blue Jays to 2nd straight World Series title as MVP (1993); hit .418 in 2 Series appearances (1982,93); holds World Series record with five hits in one game.

Joe Montana (b. June 11, 1956): Football QB; led Notre Dame to national title in 1977; led San Francisco to 4 Super Bowl titles in 1980s; only 3-time Super Bowl MVP; 2-time NFL MVP (1989-90); led NFL in passing 5 times; traded to Kansas City in 1993; ranks 2nd in all-time in passing efficiency (92.3), 6th in TD passes (273) and yards passing (40,551); inducted into Pro Football Hall of Fame in 2000.

Helen Wills Moody (b. Oct. 6, 1905, d. Jan. 1, 1998): Tennis; won 8 Wimbledon singles titles, 7 U.S. and 4 French from 1923-38.

Warren Moon (b. Nov. 18, 1956): Football QB; MVP of 1978 Rose Bowl with Washington; MVP of CFL with Edmonton in 1983; led Eskimos to 5 consecutive Grey Cup titles (1978-82) and was playoff MVP twice (1980,82); entered NFL in 1984 and played for four different teams; picked for 9 Pro Bowls including a QB-record 8 straight (1988-95).

Archie Moore (b. Dec. 13, 1913, d. Dec. 9, 1998): Boxer; world light-heavyweight champion (1952-60); pro record 199-26-8 with a record 145 KOs.

Noureddine Morceli (b. Feb. 28, 1970): Algerian runner; 3-time world champion at 1,500 meters (1991,93,95); former holder of world records in several middle distance events.

Howie Morenz (b. June 21, 1902, d. Mar. 8, 1937): Hockey C; 3-time NHL MVP (1928,31,32); led Montreal Canadiens to 3 Stanley Cups; voted Outstanding Player of the Half-Century in 1950.

Joe Morgan (b. Sept. 19, 1943): Baseball 2B; led NL in walks 4 times; regular-season MVP both years he led Cincinnati to World Series titles (1975-76); 4th behind Rickey Henderson, Babe Ruth and Ted Williams in career walks with 1,865.

Bobby Morrow (b. Oct. 15, 1935): Track & Field; won 3 gold medals at 1956 Olympics (100m, 200m and 4x400m relay).

Willie Mosconi (b. June 27, 1913, d. Sept. 12, 1993): Pocket Billiards; 14-time world champion from 1941-57.

Annemarie Moser-Pröll (b. Mar. 27, 1953): Austrian alpine skier; won World Cup overall title 6 times (1971-75,79); all-time women's World Cup leader in career wins with 61; won Downhill in 1980 Olympics.

Edwin Moses (b. Aug. 31, 1955): Track & Field; won 400m hurdles at 1976 and '84 Olympics, bronze medal in '88; also winner of 122 consecutive races from 1977-87.

Stirling Moss (b. Sept. 17, 1929): Auto racer; won 194 of 466 career races and 16 Formula One events, but was never world champion.

Marion Motley (b. June 5, 1920, d. June 27, 1999): Football FB; all-time leading AAFC rusher; rushed for over 4,700 yards and 31 TDs for Cleveland Browns (1946-53).

Shirley Muldowney (b. June 19, 1940): Drag Racer; "Cha Cha"; women's racing pioneer; 3-time Winston drag racing Top Fuel champion (1977,80,82); recorded 18 career NHRA National Event Victories.

Anthony Munoz (b. Aug. 19, 1958): Football OT; drafted 3rd overall in 1980 out of USC; 11-time All Pro with Cincinnati; member of NFL 75th Anniv. All-Time Team; elected to Hall of Fame in 1998.

Calvin Murphy (b. May 9, 1948): Basketball G; NBA All-Rookie team (1971); holds NBA single season free throw percentage (.958); third all-time career free throw pct. (.892); elected to Basketball Hall of Fame in 1992; though only 5'9" and 165 pounds, he is regarded as one of the best guards ever.

Dale Murphy (b. Mar. 12, 1956): Baseball OF; led NL in RBI 3 times and HRs twice; 2-time MVP (1982-83) with Atlanta; also played with Philadelphia and Colorado; retired in 1993 with 398 HRs.

Eddie Murray (b. Feb. 24, 1956): Baseball 1B-DH; AL Rookie of Year in 1977; became 20th player in history, but only 2nd switch hitter (after Pete Rose) to get 3,000 hits; one of only 3 men (Aaron and Mays) with 500 HRs and 3,000 hits.

Jim Murray (b. Dec. 29, 1919, d. Aug. 16, 1998): Sports columnist for *LA Times* 1961-98; 14-time Sportswriter of the Year; won Pulitzer Prize for commentary in 1990.

Ty Murray (b. Oct. 11, 1969): Rodeo cowboy; 7-time All-Around world champion (1989-94,98); Rookie of Year in 1988; youngest (age 20) to win All-Around title; set single season earnings mark with $297,896 in 1993; career hampered by injury.

Stan Musial (b. Nov. 21, 1920): Baseball OF-1B; led NL in batting 7 times; 3-time MVP (1943,46,48) with St. Louis; played in 24 All-Star Games; had 3,630 career hits and a .331 average.

John Naber (b. Jan. 20, 1956): Swimmer; won 4 gold medals and a silver in 1976 Olympics.

Bronko Nagurski (b. Nov. 3, 1908, d. Jan. 7, 1990): Football FB-T; All-America at Minnesota (1929); All-Pro with Chicago Bears (1932-34); charter member of college and pro Halls of Fame.

James Naismith (b. Nov. 6, 1861, d. Nov. 28, 1939): Canadian physical education instructor who invented basketball in 1891 at the YMCA Training School (now Springfield College) in Springfield, Mass.

Joe Namath (b. May 31, 1943): Football QB; signed for unheard-of $400,000 as rookie with AFL's NY Jets in 1965; 2-time All-AFL (1968-69) and All-NFL (1972); led Jets to Super Bowl upset as MVP in '69 after making brash prediction of victory.

Ilie Nastase (b. July 19, 1946): Romanian tennis player; No.1 in the world twice (1972-73); won U.S. (1972) and French (1973) Opens; has since entered Romanian politics.

Martina Navratilova (b. Oct. 18, 1956): Tennis player; No.1 player in the world 7 times (1978-79,82-86); won her record 9th Wimbledon singles title in 1990; also won 4 U.S. Opens, 3 Australian and 2 French; in all, won 18 Grand Slam singles titles and 37 Grand Slam doubles titles; retired as all-time leader among men and women in singles titles (167) and money won ($20.3 million) over 21 years; inducted into International Tennis Hall of Fame in 2000.

Cosmas Ndeti (b. Nov. 24, 1971): Kenyan distance runner; winner of three consecutive Boston Marathons (1993-95); set what is still the course record of 2:07:15 in 1994.

Earle (Greasy) Neale (b. Nov. 5, 1891, d. Nov. 2, 1973): Baseball and Football; hit .357 for Cincinnati in 1919 World Series; also played with pre-NFL Canton Bulldogs; later coached Philadelphia Eagles to 2 NFL titles (1948-49).

Primo Nebiolo (b. July 14, 1923, d. Nov. 7, 1999): Italian president of International Amateur Athletic Federation (IAAF) since 1981; also an at-large member of International Olympic Committee; regarded as dictatorial, but credited with elevating track & field to world class financial status.

Byron Nelson (b. Feb. 4, 1912): Golfer; 2-time winner of both Masters (1937,42) and PGA (1940,45); also U.S. Open champion in 1939; won 19 tournaments in 1945, including 11 in a row; also set all-time PGA stroke average with 68.33 strokes per round over 120 rounds in '45.

Lindsey Nelson (b. May 25, 1919, d. June 10, 1995): Radio-TV; all-purpose play-by-play broadcaster for CBS, NBC and others; 4-time Sportscaster of the Year (1959-62); voice of Cotton Bowl for 25 years and NY Mets from 1962-78; given Life Achievement Emmy Award in 1991.

Ernie Nevers (b. July 11, 1903, d. May 3, 1976): Football FB; earned 11 letters in four sports at Stanford; played pro football, baseball and basketball; scored 40 points for Chicago Cardinals in one NFL game (1929).

Paula Newby-Fraser (b. June 2, 1962): Zimbabwean triathlete; 8-time winner of Ironman Triathlon in Hawaii; established women's record of 8:55:28 in 1992.

John Newcombe (b. May 23, 1944): Australian tennis player; No.1 player in world 3 times (1967,70-71); won Wimbledon 3 times and U.S. and Australian championships twice each.

Jack Nicklaus (b. Jan. 21, 1940): Golfer; all-time leader in major tournament wins with 20— including 6 Masters, 5 PGAs, 4 U.S. Opens and 3 British Opens; oldest player to win Masters (46 in 1986); PGA Player of Year 5 times (1967,72-73,75-76); named Golfer of the Century by PGA in 1988; 6-time Ryder Cup player and 2-time captain (1983,87); won NCAA title (1961) and 2 U.S. Amateurs (1959,61); 70 PGA Tour wins (2nd to Sam Snead's 81); fourth win in Tradition in 1996 gave him 8 majors on Senior PGA Tour; nicknamed "the Golden Bear."

Chuck Noll (b. Jan. 5, 1932): Football; coached Pittsburgh to 4 Super Bowl titles (1975-76,79-80); retired after 1991 season ranked 5th on all-time list with 209 wins (including playoffs) in 23 years.

Greg Norman (b. Feb. 10, 1955): Australian golfer; PGA Tour's all-time leading money winner through 1999 with $12.5 million (since passed by Tiger Woods); 73 tournament wins worldwide including 18 PGA Tour victories; 2-time British Open winner (1986,93); lost Masters by a stroke in both 1986 (to Jack Nicklaus) and '87 (to Larry Mize in sudden death); 1995 PGA Tour Player of the Year.

James D. Norris (b. Nov. 6, 1906, d. Feb. 25, 1966): Boxing promoter and NHL owner; president of International Boxing Club from 1949 until U.S. Supreme Court ordered its break-up (for anti-trust violations) in 1958; only NHL owner to win Stanley Cups in two cities: Detroit (1936-37,43) and Chicago (1961).

Paavo Nurmi (b. June 13, 1897, d. Oct. 2, 1973): Finnish runner; won 9 gold medals (6 individual) in 1920, '24 and '28 Olympics; from 1921-31 broke 23 world outdoor records in events ranging from 1,500 to 20,000 meters.

Dan O'Brien (b. July 18, 1966): Track & Field; Olympic decathlon gold medalist (1996); set former world record in decathlon (8,891 pts) in 1992, after shockingly failing to qualify for event at U.S. Olympic Trials; three-time gold medalist at World Championships (1991,93,95).

Larry O'Brien (b. July 7, 1917, d. Sept. 27, 1990): Basketball; former U.S. Postmaster General and 3rd NBA commissioner (1975-84), league absorbed 4 ABA teams and created salary cap during his term in office.

Parry O'Brien (b. Jan. 28, 1932): Track & Field; in 4 consecutive Olympics, won two gold medals, a silver and placed 4th in the shot put (1952-64).

Al Oerter (b. Sept. 19, 1936): Track & Field; his 4 discus gold medals in consecutive Olympics from 1956-68 is an unmatched Olympic record.

Sadaharu Oh (b. May 20, 1940): Baseball 1B; led Japan League in HRs 15 times; 9-time MVP for Tokyo Giants; hit 868 HRs in 22 years.

Hakeem Olajuwon (b. Jan. 21, 1963): Basketball C; Nigerian native who was All-America in 1984 and Final Four MOP in 1983 for Houston; overall 1st pick by Houston Rockets in 1984 NBA draft; led Rockets to back-to-back NBA titles (1994-95); regular season MVP (1994) and 2-time Finals MVP ('94-95); 6-time All-NBA 1st team (1987-89,93-95); all-time NBA blocks leader; traded to Toronto after 17 seasons with Houston.

Jose Maria Olazabal (b. Feb. 5, 1966): Spanish golfer; has 25 worldwide victories including 2 Masters (1994,99), played on 6 European Ryder Cup teams.

Barney Oldfield (b. Jan. 29, 1878, d. Oct. 4, 1946): Auto racing pioneer; drove cars built by Henry Ford; first man to drive car a mile per minute (1903).

Walter O'Malley (b. Oct. 9, 1903, d. Aug. 9, 1979): Baseball owner; moved Brooklyn Dodgers to Los Angeles after 1957 season; won 4 World Series (1955,59,63,65).

Shaquille O'Neal (b. Mar. 6, 1972): Basketball C; 2-time All-America at LSU (1991-92); overall 1st pick (as a junior) by Orlando in 1992 NBA draft; Rookie of Year in 1993; 2-time NBA scoring leader (1995,2000); regular season MVP (2000) and 2-time NBA Finals MVP (2000,01); named one of the NBA's 50 Greatest Players.

Bobby Orr (b. Mar. 20, 1948): Hockey D; 8-time Norris Trophy winner as best defenseman; led NHL in scoring twice and assists 5 times; All-NHL 1st team 8 times; regular season MVP 3 times (1970-72); playoff MVP twice (1970,72) with Boston.

Tom Osborne (b. Feb. 23, 1937): Football; Nebraska head coach from 1973-97; career record of 255-49-3; his win pct. of .836 is fifth all-time; finally won national championship in 1994; followed it with 2nd national title in '95 and shared national title with Michigan in '97; elected to U.S. Congress (R., Neb.) in 2000.

Mel Ott (b. Mar. 2, 1909, d. Nov. 21, 1958): Baseball OF; joined NY Giants at age 16; led NL in HRs 6 times; had 511 HRs and 1,860 RBI in 22 years.

Kristin Otto (b. Feb. 7, 1966): East German swimmer; 1st woman to win 6 gold medals (4 individual) at one Olympics (1988).

Francis Ouimet (b. May 8, 1893, d. Sept. 3, 1967): Golfer; won 1913 U.S. Open as 20-year-old amateur playing on Brookline, Mass. course where he used to caddie; won U.S. Amateur twice; 8-time Walker Cup player.

Steve Owen (b. Apr. 21, 1898, d. May 17, 1964): Football; All-Pro guard (1927); coached NY Giants for 23 years (1931-53); won 153 career games and 2 NFL titles (1934,38).

Jesse Owens (b. Sept. 12, 1913, d. Mar. 31, 1980): Track & Field; broke 5 world records in one afternoon at Big Ten Championships (May 25, 1935); a year later, he embarrassed Hitler by winning 4 gold (100m, 200m, 4x100m relay and long jump) at 1936 Olympics in Berlin.

Alan Page (b. Aug. 7, 1945): Football DE; All-America at Notre Dame in 1966 and member of two national championship teams; 6-time NFL All-Pro and 1971 Player of Year with Minnesota Vikings; later a lawyer who was elected to Minnesota Supreme Court in 1992.

Satchel Paige (b. July 7, 1906, d. June 6, 1982): Baseball RHP; pitched 55 career no-hitters over 20 seasons in Negro Leagues, entered major leagues with Cleveland in 1948 at age 42; had 28-31 record in 5 years; returned to AL at age 59 to start 1 game for Kansas City in 1965 (went 3 innings, gave up a hit and got a strikeout).

Arnold Palmer (b. Sept. 10, 1929): Golfer; winner of 4 Masters, 2 British Opens and a U.S. Open; 2-time PGA Player of Year (1960,62); 1st player to earn over $1 million in career (1968); annual PGA Tour money leader award named after him; 60 wins on PGA Tour and 10 more on Senior Tour.

Jim Palmer (b. Oct. 15, 1945): Baseball RHP; 3-time Cy Young Award winner (1973,75-76); won 20 or more games 8 times with Baltimore; 1991 comeback attempt at age 45 scrubbed in spring training.

Bill Parcells (b. Aug. 22, 1941): Football; coached NY Giants to 2 Super Bowl titles (1987,91); retired after 1990 season then returned in '93 as coach of New England; led Patriots to Super Bowl loss against Green Bay in 1997; left Patriots in 1997 to coach the New York Jets; coached three seasons with the Jets (1997-99), turning them from 1-15 doormat to AFC East champ in two years; retired from coaching again in 2000 and became director of football operations with the club for one year.

Bernie Parent (b. Apr. 3, 1945): Hockey G; led Philadelphia Flyers to 2 Stanley Cups as playoff MVP (1974,75); 2-time Vezina Trophy winner; posted 55 career shutouts and 2.55 GAA in 13 seasons.

Joe Paterno (b. Dec. 21, 1926): Football; has coached Penn St. to 2 national titles (1982,86) and 20-9-1 bowl record in 35 years; also had three unbeaten teams that didn't finish No. 1; 4-time Coach of Year (1968,78,82,86); entered 2001 season just one win behind Bear Bryant on all-time wins list.

Craig Patrick (b. May 20, 1946): Hockey; 3rd generation Patrick to have name inscribed on Stanley Cup; GM of 2 Stanley Cup champion Pittsburgh Penguins (1991-92); also captain of 1969 NCAA champion at Denver; assistant coach-GM of 1980 gold medal-winning U.S. Olympic team; scored 72 goals in 8 NHL seasons and won 69 games in 3 years as coach; grandson of Lester.

Lester Patrick (b. Dec. 30, 1883, d. June 1, 1960): Hockey; pro hockey pioneer as player, coach and general manager; led NY Rangers to 2 Stanley Cups as coach (1928,33) and GM (1940); grandfather of Craig.

Floyd Patterson (b. Jan. 4, 1935): Boxer; Olympic middleweight champ in 1952; world heavyweight champion (1956-59,60-62); 1st to regain heavyweight crown; fought Ingemar Johansson 3 times in 22 months from 1959-61 and won last two; pro record 55-8-1 with 40 KOs.

Walter Payton (b. July 25, 1954, d. Nov. 1, 1999): Football RB; NFL's all-time leading rusher with 16,726 yards; scored 125 career TDs; All-Pro 7 times with Chicago; MVP in 1977; led Bears to Super Bowl title in Jan. 1986.

Calvin Peete (b. July 18, 1943): Golf; began playing golf at the age of 23; earned over $2 million in career earnings; selected to the U.S. Ryder Cup teams in 1983 and 1985.

Pelé (b. Oct. 23, 1940): Brazilian soccer F; given name— Edson Arantes do Nascimento; led Brazil to 3 World Cup titles (1958,62,70); came to U.S. in 1975 to play for NY Cosmos in NASL; scored 1,281 goals in 22 years; currently Brazil's minister of sport.

Roger Penske (b. Feb. 20, 1937): Auto racing; national sports car driving champion (1964); established racing team in 1961; co-founder of Championship Auto Racing Teams (CART); Penske Racing has won 10 Indianapolis 500s, 9 CART points titles and the team recorded its 100th overall victory with Gil de Ferran's win at Nazareth in May, 2000.

Willie Pep (b. Sept. 19, 1922): Boxer; 2-time world featherweight champion (1942-48,49-50); pro record 230-11-1 with 65 KOs.

Marie-Jose Perec (b. 1968): Track & Field; French sprinter who became 2nd woman to win the 200m and 400m events in the same Olympics (1996); her time in the 400 (48.25) set an Olympic record; also won the 400M in 1992 Games.

Fred Perry (b. May 18, 1909, d. Feb. 2, 1995): British tennis player; 3-time Wimbledon champ (1934-36); first player to win all four Grand Slam singles titles, though not in same year; last native to win All-England men's title.

Gaylord Perry (b. Sept. 15, 1938): Baseball RHP; was only pitcher to win a Cy Young Award in both leagues until 1999 when Randy Johnson and Pedro Martinez joined him; retired in 1983 with 314-265 record, a 3,534 strikeouts over 22 years and with 8 teams; brother Jim won 215 games for family total of 529.

Bob Pettit (b. Dec. 12, 1932): Basketball F; All-NBA 1st team 10 times (1955-64); 2-time MVP (1956,59) with St. Louis Hawks; first player to score 20,000 points.

Richard Petty (b. July 2, 1937): Auto racer; 7-time winner of Daytona 500; 7-time NASCAR national champ (1964,67,71-72,74-75,79); first stock car driver to win $1 million in career; all-time NASCAR leader in races won (200), poles (127) and wins in a single season (27 in 1967); retired after 1992 season; son of Lee (54 career wins) and father of Kyle (7 career wins).

Laffit Pincay Jr. (b. Dec. 29, 1946): Jockey; 5-time Eclipse Award winner (1971,73-74,79,85); winner of 3 Belmonts and 1 Kentucky Derby (aboard Swale in 1984); with his 8834th win in Dec., 1999 he passed Bill Shoemaker to become thoroughbred racing's all-time winningest jockey.

Uta Pippig (b. Sept. 7, 1965): German marathoner; won three-straight Boston Marathons (1994,95,96); she set a new course record in '94.

Nelson Piquet (b. Aug. 17, 1952): Brazilian auto racer; 3-time Formula One world champion (1981,83, 87); left circuit in 1991 with 23 career wins.

Rick Pitino (b. Sept. 18, 1952): Basketball; won 1996 NCAA title in his 7th year at Kentucky; previously coached the New York Knicks in the NBA (96-81 overall), Providence College (42-23) and Boston University (46-24); in 1997, became coach and president of Boston Celtics; resigned from Celtics in 2001 and returned to college coaching with Louisville.

Jacques Plante (b. Jan. 17, 1929, d. Feb. 27, 1986): Hockey G; led Montreal to 6 Stanley Cups (1953,56-60); won 7 Vezina Trophies; MVP in 1962; first goalie to regularly wear a mask; posted 82 shutouts with 2.38 GAA.

Gary Player (b. Nov. 1, 1936): South African golfer; 3-time winner of Masters and British Open; only player in 20th century to win British Open in three different decades (1959,68,74); one of only five players to win all four Grand Slam titles (others are Hogan, Nicklaus, Sarazen and Woods); has also won 2 PGAs, a U.S. Open and 2 U.S. Senior Opens; owner of 21 wins on PGA Tour and 19 more on Senior Tour.

Jim Plunkett (b. Dec. 5, 1947): Football QB; Heisman Trophy winner (Stanford) in 1970; AFL Rookie of the Year in 1971; led Oakland-LA Raiders to Super Bowl wins in 1981 and '84; MVP in '81.

Maurice Podoloff (b. Aug. 18, 1890, d. Nov. 24, 1985): Basketball; engineered merger of Basketball Assn. of America and National Basketball League into NBA in 1949; NBA commissioner (1949-63); league MVP trophy named after him.

Fritz Pollard (b. Jan. 27, 1894, d. May 11, 1986): Football; 1st black All-America RB (1916 at Brown); 1st black to play in Rose Bowl; 7-year NFL pro (1920-26); 1st black NFL coach, at Milwaukee and Hammond, Ind.

Denis Potvin (b. Oct. 29, 1953): Hockey D; won Norris Trophy 3 times (1976,78-79); 5-time All-NHL 1st team; led NY Islanders to 4 Stanley Cups.

Mike Powell (b. Nov. 10, 1963): Track & Field; broke Bob Beamon's 23-year-old long jump world record by 2 inches with leap of 29-ft., 4½ in. at the 1991 World Championships; Sullivan Award winner (1991); won long jump silver medals in 1988 and '92 Olympics; repeated as world champ in 1993.

Steve Prefontaine (b. Jan. 25, 1951, d. May 30, 1975): Track & Field; All-America distance runner at Oregon; first athlete to win same event at NCAA championships 4 straight years (5,000 meters from 1970-73); finished 4th in 5,000 at 1972 Munich Olympics; first athlete to endorse Nike running shoes; killed in a one-car accident.

Nick Price (b. Jan. 28, 1957): Zimbabwean golfer; PGA Tour Player of Year in 1993 and '94; became 1st since Nick Faldo in 1990 to win 2 Grand Slam titles in same year when he took British Open and PGA Championship in 1994; also won PGA in '92.

Alain Prost (b. Feb. 24, 1955): French auto racer; 4-time Formula One world champion (1985-86,89,93); sat out 1992 then returned to win title in 1993; retired after '93 season as all-time F1 wins leader with 51 (passed by Michael Schumacher in 2001).

Kirby Puckett (b. Mar. 14, 1961): Baseball OF; led Minnesota Twins to World Series titles in 1987 and '91; retired in 1996 due to an eye ailment with a batting title (1989), 2,304 hits and a .318 career average in 12 seasons; elected to Hall of Fame in 2001.

C.C. Pyle (b. 1882, d. Feb. 3, 1939): Promoter; known as "Cash and Carry"; hyped Red Grange's pro football debut by arranging 1925 barnstorming tour with Chicago Bears; had Grange bolt NFL for new AFL in 1926 (AFL folded in '27; also staged 2 Transcontinental Races (1928-29), known as "Bunion Derbies."

Bobby Rahal (b. Jan. 10, 1953): Auto racer; 3-time PPG Cup champ (1986,87,92); 24 career Indy-Car wins, including 1986 Indy 500; current CART team owner; acted as interim president-CEO of CART until Dec., 2000 but resigned to assume position with Jaguar Formula One team.

Bill Rassmussen (b. Oct. 15, 1932): Radio-TV; unemployed radio broadcaster who founded ESPN, the nation's first 24-hour all-sports cable-TV network, in 1978; bought out by Getty Oil in 1981.

Willis Reed (b. June 25, 1942): Basketball C; led NY Knicks to NBA titles in 1970 and '73, Finals MVP both years; regular season MVP 1970. Voted one of NBA's 50 Greatest Players.

Pee Wee Reese (b. July 23, 1918, d. Aug. 14, 1999): Baseball SS; member of Brooklyn/Los Angeles Dodgers from 1940-58; led NL in runs scored (132) in 1949 and stolen bases (30) in 1952; hit over .300 in a season once (.309 in 1954); led the NL in putouts four times; real name was Harold H. Reese.

Mary Lou Retton (b. Jan. 24, 1968): Gymnast; won gold medal in women's All-Around at the 1984 Olympics; also won 2 silvers and 2 bronzes.

Grantland Rice (b. Nov. 1, 1880, d. July 13, 1954): First celebrated American sportswriter; chronicled the Golden Age of Sport in 1920s; immortalized Notre Dame's "Four Horsemen."

Jerry Rice (b. Oct. 13, 1962): Football WR; 2-time Div. I-AA All-America at Mississippi Valley St. (1983-84); 10-time All-Pro; regular season MVP in 1987 and Super Bowl MVP in 1989 with San Francisco; NFL all-time leader in touchdowns and receptions.

Henri Richard (b. Feb. 29, 1936): Hockey C; leap year baby who played on more Stanley Cup championship teams (11) than anybody else; at 5-foot-7, known as the "Pocket Rocket"; brother of Maurice.

Maurice Richard (b. Aug. 4, 1921, d. May 27, 2000): Hockey RW; the "Rocket"; 8-time NHL 1st team All-Star; MVP in 1947; 1st to score 50 goals in one season (1944-45); 544 career goals; played on 8 Stanley Cup winners in Montreal.

Bob Richards (b. Feb. 2, 1926): Track & Field; pole vaulter, ordained minister and original *Wheaties* pitchman; remains only 2-time Olympic pole vault champ (1952,56).

Nolan Richardson (b. Dec. 27, 1941): Basketball; coached Arkansas to consecutive NCAA finals, beating Duke in 1994 and losing to UCLA in '95.

Tex Rickard (b. Jan. 2, 1870, d. Jan. 6, 1929): Promoter who handled boxing's first $1 million gate (Dempsey vs. Carpentier in 1921); built Madison Square Garden in 1925; founded NY Rangers as Garden tenant in 1926 and named NHL team after himself (Tex's Rangers); also built Boston Garden in 1928.

Eddie Rickenbacker (b. Oct. 8, 1890, d. July 23, 1973): Mechanic and auto racer; became America's top flying ace (22 kills) in World War I; owned Indianapolis Speedway (1927-45) and ran Eastern Air Lines (1938-59).

Branch Rickey (b. Dec. 20, 1881, d. Dec. 9, 1965): Baseball innovator; revolutionized game with creation of modern farm system while general manager of St. Louis Cardinals (1917-42); integrated major leagues in 1947 as president-GM of Brooklyn Dodgers when he brought up Jackie Robinson (whom he had signed on Oct. 23, 1945); later GM of Pittsburgh Pirates.

Leni Riefenstahl (b. Aug. 22, 1902): German filmmaker of 1930s; directed classic sports documentary "Olympia" on 1936 Berlin Summer Olympics; infamous, however, for also making 1934 Hitler propaganda film "Triumph of the Will."

Roy Riegels (b. Apr. 4, 1908, d. Mar. 26, 1993): Football; California center who picked up fumble in 2nd quarter of 1929 Rose Bowl and raced 70 yards in the wrong direction to set up a 2-point safety in 8-7 loss to Georgia Tech.

Bobby Riggs (b. Feb. 25, 1918, d. Oct. 25, 1995): Tennis; won Wimbledon once (1939) and U.S. title twice (1939,41); legendary hustler who made his biggest score in 1973 as 55-year-old male chauvinist challenging the best women players; beat No. 1 Margaret Smith Court 6-2,6-1, but was thrashed by No. 2 Billie Jean King, 6-4,6-3,6-3 in nationally televised "Battle of the Sexes" on Sept. 20, before 30,492 at the Astrodome.

Pat Riley (b. Mar. 20, 1945): Basketball; coached LA Lakers to 4 of their 5 NBA titles in 1980s (1982,85,87-88); coached New York from 1991-95; 2-time Coach of Year (1990,93) and all-time NBA leader in playoff wins (155); quit Knicks after 1994-95 season with year left on contract; signed with Miami Heat on Sept. 2 as coach, team president and part-owner after Knicks agreed to drop tampering charges in exchange for $1 million and a conditional first round draft pick.

Cal Ripken Jr. (b. Aug. 24, 1960): Baseball SS; broke Lou Gehrig's major league Iron Man record of 2,130 consecutive games played on Sept. 6, 1995; record streak began on May 30, 1982 and ended Sept. 19, 1998 after 2,632 games; 2-time AL MVP (1983,91) for Baltimore; AL Rookie of Year (1982); AL starter in All-Star Game since 1984; holds record for career home runs by a shortstop.

Phil Rizzuto (b. Sept. 25, 1918): Baseball SS; nicknamed "the Scooter"; AL MVP with the Yankees in 1950; 5-time All-Star; retired in 1956 and became Yankees radio and television announcer; elected to the Hall of Fame in 1994.

Oscar Robertson (b. Nov. 24, 1938): Basketball G; 3-time College Player of Year (1958-60) at Cincinnati; led 1960 U.S. Olympic team to gold medal; NBA Rookie of Year (1961); 9-time All-NBA 1st team; MVP in 1964 with Cincinnati Royals; NBA champion in 1971 with Milwaukee Bucks; 3rd in career assists with 9,887.

Paul Robeson (b. Apr. 8, 1898, d. Jan. 23, 1976): Black 4-sport star and 2-time football All-America (1917-18) at Rutgers; 3-year NFL pro; also scholar, lawyer, singer, actor and political activist; long-tainted by Communist sympathies, he was finally inducted into College Football Hall of Fame in 1995.

Brooks Robinson (b. May 18, 1937): Baseball 3B; led AL in fielding 12 times from 1960-72 with Baltimore; AL MVP in 1964; World Series MVP in 1970; 16 Gold Gloves; entered Hall of Fame in 1983.

Eddie Robinson (b. Feb. 13, 1919): Football; head coach at Div. I-AA Grambling from 1941-97; winningest coach in college history (408-165-15); led Tigers to 8 national black college titles.

Frank Robinson (b. Aug. 31, 1935): Baseball OF; won MVP in NL (1961) and AL (1966); Triple Crown winner and World Series MVP in 1966 with Baltimore; 1st black manager in major leagues with Cleveland in 1975; also managed in SF and Baltimore; hired by MLB in 2000 to be the league's vice president of on-field operations.

Jackie Robinson (b. Jan. 31, 1919, d. Oct. 24, 1972): Baseball 1B-2B-3B; 4-sport athlete at UCLA (baseball, basketball, football and track); hit .387 with K.C. Monarchs of Negro Leagues in 1945; signed by Brooklyn Dodgers on Oct. 23, 1945 and broke major league baseball's color line in 1947; Rookie of Year in 1947 and NL's MVP in '49; hit .311 over 10 seasons. His #42 was retired by MLB in 1997.

Sugar Ray Robinson (b. May 3, 1921, d. Apr. 12, 1989): Boxer; arguably the greatest pound-for-pound prizefighter of all-time; world welterweight champion (1946-51); 5-time middleweight champ; retired at age 45 after 25 years in the ring; pro record 174-19-6 with 109 KOs.

Knute Rockne (b. Mar. 4, 1888, d. Mar. 31, 1931): Football; coached Notre Dame to 3 consensus national titles (1924,29,30), highest winning percentage in college history (.881) with record of 105-12-5 over 13 seasons; killed in plane crash.

Bill Rodgers (b. Dec. 23, 1947): Distance runner; won Boston and New York City marathons 4 times each from 1975-80.

Dennis Rodman (b. May 13, 1961): Basketball F; superb rebounder and defender; also known for dyeing his hair various colors and for getting suspended regularly; in 1997, he was suspended for 11 games for kicking a courtside cameraman; led NBA in rebounding 7 years in a row (1992-98); member of 5 NBA champion teams with Detroit (1989,90) and Chicago (1996-98); 2-time All Star (1990,92), 2-time defensive player of the year (1990-91) and 6-time member of the NBA All-Defensive team (1989-93,96).

Irina Rodnina (b. Sept. 12, 1949): Soviet figure skater; won 10 world championships and 3 Olympic gold medals in pairs competition from 1971-80.

Alex Rodriguez (b. July 27, 1975): Baseball SS; one of baseball's best all-around players; led AL in his first full season in the majors (1996) with .358 batting average and 141 runs; in 1998 became third player ever with 40 HRs and 40 steals in one season; signed a 10-year, $252m deal (the biggest in U.S. sports history) with Texas in 2000; has hit at least 40 homers the last four years (1998-2001).

Ronaldo (b. Sept. 22, 1976): Soccer; Brazilian forward who has been compared to the great Pele; signed with a first division club in Brazil, Cruzeiro Belo Horizonte, before he was 18 and scored 58 goals in 60 games; named to the Brazilian National Team when he was 17; named FIFA Player of the Year in 1996 and '97; European Player of the Year in '97; named 1998 World Cup MVP, but has been plagued by injuries since.

Art Rooney (b. Jan. 27, 1901, d. Aug. 25, 1988): Race track legend and pro football pioneer; bought Pittsburgh Steelers franchise in 1933 for $2,500; finally won NFL title with 1st of 4 Super Bowls in 1974 season.

Theodore Roosevelt (b. Oct. 27, 1858, d. Jan. 6, 1919): 26th President of the U.S.; physical fitness buff who boxed as undergraduate at Harvard; credited with presidential assist in forming of Intercollegiate Athletic Assn. (now NCAA) in 1905-06.

Mauri Rose (b. May 26, 1906, d. Jan. 1, 1981): Auto racer; 3-time winner of Indy 500 (1941,47-48).

Murray Rose (b. Jan. 6, 1939): Australian swimmer; won 3 gold medals at 1956 Olympics; added a gold, silver and bronze in 1960.

Pete Rose (b. Apr. 14, 1941): Baseball OF-IF; all-time hits leader with 4,256; led NL in batting 3 times; regular-season MVP in 1973; World Series MVP in 1975; had 44-game hitting streak in '78; managed Cincinnati (1984-89); banned for life in 1989 for conduct detrimental to baseball; convicted of tax evasion in 1990 and sentenced to 5 months in prison; released Jan. 7, 1991.

Ken Rosewall (b. Nov. 2, 1934): Tennis; won French and Australian singles titles at age 18; U.S. champ twice, but never won Wimbledon.

Mark Roth (b. Apr. 10, 1951): Bowler; 4-time PBA Player of Year (1977-79,84); has 34 tournament wins and over $1.5 million in career earnings; U.S. Open champ in 1984.

Alan Rothenberg (b. Apr. 10, 1939): Soccer; president of U.S. Soccer 1990-98; surprised European skeptics by directing hugely successful 1994 World Cup tournament; successfully got off-delayed outdoor Major League Soccer off ground in 1996.

Chad Rowan (Akebono) (b. May 8, 1969): Sumo Wrestling; 6-foot-9, 510-pound naturalized Japanese citizen born in Hawaii; first foreign grand champion in sumo wrestling's 2,000-year history; retired in Jan., 2001.

Patrick Roy (b. Oct. 5, 1965): Hockey G; led Montreal to 2 Stanley Cup titles; 3-time playoff MVP (as rookie in 1986, 1993, 2001); has won Vezina Trophy 3 times (1989-90,92); won 3rd and 4th Stanley Cups with Colorado (1996,2001); all-time leader in career regular season (484) and playoff wins (137).

Pete Rozelle (b. Mar. 1, 1926, d. December 6, 1996): Football; NFL Commissioner from 1960-89; presided over growth of league from 12 to 28 teams, merger with AFL, creation of Super Bowl and advent of huge TV rights fees.

Wilma Rudolph (b. June 23, 1940, d. Nov. 12, 1994): Track & Field; won 3 gold medals (100m, 200m and 4x100m relay) at 1960 Olympics; also won relay silver in '56 Games; 2-time AP Athlete of Year (1960-61) and Sullivan Award winner in 1961.

John Ruiz (b. Jan. 4, 1972): Boxer; defeated Evander Holyfield by a decision in March, 2001 to become the first-ever Hispanic heavyweight champion of the world.

Damon Runyon (b. Oct. 4, 1884, d. Dec. 10, 1946): Kansas native who gained fame as New York journalist, sports columnist and short-story writer; best known for 1932 story collection, "Guys and Dolls."

Adolph Rupp (b. Sept. 2, 1901, d. Dec. 10, 1977): Basketball; 2nd in all-time college coaching wins with 876; led Kentucky to 4 NCAA championships (1948-49,51,58) and 1 NIT title (1946).

Bill Russell (b. Feb. 12, 1934): Basketball C; won titles in college (with San Francisco in 1955,56), Olympics (1956) and pros; 5-time NBA MVP (1958,61,62, 63,65); led Boston to 11 titles from 1957-69; also became first black NBA (and major pro sports) head coach in 1966.

Babe Ruth (b. Feb. 6, 1895, d. Aug. 16, 1948): Baseball LHP-OF; two-time 20-game winner with Boston Red Sox (1916-17); had a 94-46 record with a 2.28 ERA, while he was 3-0 in the World Series with an ERA of 0.87; sold to New York Yankees for $100,000 in 1920; AL MVP in 1923; led AL in slugging average 13 times, HRs 12 times, RBI 6 times and batting once (.378 in 1924); hit 60 HRs in 1927 and at least 54 3 other times; ended career with Boston Braves in 1935 with 714 HRs, 2,211 RBI, 2,062 walks and a batting average of .342; remains all-time leader in slugging percentage (.690); member of the Hall of Fame's inaugural class of 1936.

Johnny Rutherford (b. Mar. 12, 1938): Auto racer; 3-time winner of Indy 500 (1974,76,80); CART national champion in 1980.

Nolan Ryan (b. Jan. 31, 1947): Baseball RHP; recorded 7 no-hitters against Kansas City and Detroit (1973), Minnesota (1974), Baltimore (1975), LA Dodgers (1981), Oakland A's (1990) and Toronto (1991 at age 44); 2-time 20-game winner (1973-74); 2-time NL leader in ERA (1981,87); led AL in strikeouts 9 times and NL twice in 27 years; retired after 1993 season with 324 wins, 292 losses and all-time records for strikeouts (5,714) and walks (2,795); never won Cy Young Award; had his number retired by three teams (California, Houston, Texas).

Samuel Ryder (b. Mar. 24, 1858, d. Jan. 2, 1936): Golf; English seed merchant who donated the Ryder Cup in 1927 for competition between pro golfers from Great Britain and the U.S.; made his fortune by coming up with idea of selling seeds in small packages.

Toni Sailer (b. Nov. 17, 1935): Austrian skier; 1st to win 3 alpine gold medals in Winter Olympics— taking downhill, slalom and giant slalom events in 1956.

Alberto Salazar (b. Aug. 7, 1958): Track and Field; set one world and six U.S. records during his career; broke 12-year-old record at New York Marathon in 1981 and broke Boston Marathon record in 1982; won three straight NY Marathons (1980-82); qualified for the 1980 and 1984 U.S. Olympic teams

Juan Antonio Samaranch (b. July 17, 1920): president of International Olympic Committee (1980-2001); the native of Barcelona was re-elected in 1996 after IOC's move in '95 to bump membership age limit to 80; replaced by Belgian Jacques Rogge.

Pete Sampras (b. Aug. 12, 1971): Tennis; No.1 player in world from 1993-98; youngest ever U.S. Open men's champion (19 years, 28 days) in 1990; his win at Wimbledon in 2000 gave him 13 grand slam singles titles for his career, more than any other male player; has won 2 Australian Opens (1994,97), 7 Wimbledons (1993,94,95,97,98,99,00) and 4 U.S. Opens (1990,93,95,96).

Joan Benoit Samuelson (b. May 16, 1957): Distance runner; has won Boston Marathon twice (1979,83); won first women's Olympic marathon in 1984 Games at Los Angeles; Sullivan Award recipient in 1985.

Arantxa Sanchez Vicario (b. Dec. 18, 1971): Spanish tennis player; 29 tour victories through Sept. 2001 including 3 French Opens (1989,94,98) and 1 U.S. Open (1994); finalist in three of four Grand Slam finals in '95; teamed with Conchita Martinez to win 5 Federation Cups from 1991-98.

Earl Sande (b. Nov. 13, 1898, d. Aug. 19, 1968): Jockey; rode Gallant Fox to Triple Crown in 1930; won 5 Belmonts and 3 Kentucky Derbies.

Barry Sanders (b. July 16, 1968): Football RB; won 1988 Heisman Trophy as junior at Oklahoma St.; all-time NCAA single season leader in rushing (2,628 yards), scoring (234 points) and TDs (39); 4-time NFL rushing leader with Detroit Lions (1990,94,96,97); NFC Rookie of Year (1988); 2-time NFL Player of Year (1991,97); NFC MVP (1994); rushed for 2,053 yards in 1997, second-best season total ever; No. 3 all-time rusher (15,269 yds); abruptly retired just prior to 1999 season.

Deion Sanders (b. Aug. 9, 1967): Baseball OF and Football DB-KR-WR; 2-time All-America at Florida St. in football (1987-88); 7-time NFL All-Pro CB with Atlanta, San Francisco and Dallas (1991-94,96-98); led majors in triples (14) with Atlanta in 1992 and hit .533 in World Series the same year; played on 2 Super Bowl winners (SF in XXIX, and Dallas in XXX); first 2-way starter in NFL since Chuck Bednarik in 1962; only athlete to play in both World Series and Super Bowl.

Abe Saperstein (b. July 4, 1901, d. Mar. 15, 1966): Basketball; founded all-black, Harlem Globetrotters barnstorming team in 1927; coached sharpshooting comedians to 1940 world pro title in Chicago and established troupe as game's foremost goodwill ambassadors; also served as 1st commissioner of American Basketball League (1961-62).

Gene Sarazen (b. Feb. 27, 1902, d. May 13, 1999): Golfer; one of only five players to win all four Grand Slam titles (others are Hogan, Nicklaus, Player and Woods); won Masters, British Open, 2 U.S. Opens and 3 PGA titles between 1922-35; invented sand wedge in 1930.

Glen Sather (b. Sept. 2, 1943): . Hockey; GM-coach of 4 Stanley Cup winners in Edmonton (1984-85,87-88) and GM-only for another in 1990; ranks 8th on all-time NHL coaching list with 553 wins (including playoffs); entered Hockey Hall of Fame in 1997; named pres-GM of NY Rangers in 2000.

Terry Sawchuk (b. Dec. 28, 1929, d. May 31, 1970): Hockey G; recorded 103 shutouts in 21 NHL seasons; 4-time Vezina Trophy winner; played on 4 Stanley Cup winners at Detroit and Toronto; posted career 2.52 GAA.

Gale Sayers (b. May 30, 1943): Football HB; 2-time All-America at Kansas; NFL Rookie of Year (1965) and 5-time All-Pro with Chicago; scored then-record 22 TDs in rookie year.

Vitaly Scherbo (b. Jan. 13, 1972): Russian gymnast; winner of unprecedented 6 gold medals in gymnastics, including men's All-Around, for Unified Team in 1992 Olympics; won 3 bronze in '96 Games.

Mike Schmidt (b. Sept. 27, 1949): Baseball 3B; led NL in HRs 8 times; 3-time MVP (1980,81,86) with Philadelphia; 548 career HRs and 10 Gold Gloves; inducted into Hall of Fame in 1995.

Don Schollander (b. Apr. 30, 1946): Swimming; won 4 gold medals at 1964 Olympics, plus one gold and one silver in 1968; won Sullivan Award in 1964.

Dick Schultz (b. Sept. 5, 1929): Reform-minded executive director of NCAA from 1988-93; announced resignation on May 11, 1993 in wake of special investigator's report citing Univ. of Virginia with improper student-athlete loan program during Schultz's tenure as athletic director (1981-87); executive director of USOC 1995-2000.

Michael Schumacher (b. Jan. 3, 1969): German auto racer; became Formula One's all-time win leader with his 52nd grand prix victory on Sept. 2, 2001; 4-time world champion (1994,95,00,01).

Tom Seaver (b. Nov. 17, 1944): Baseball RHP; won 3 Cy Young Awards (1969,73,75); had 311 wins, 3,640 strikeouts and 2.86 ERA over 20 years.

Monica Seles (b. Dec. 2, 1973): Tennis; No. 1 in the world in 1991 and '92 after winning Australian, French and U.S. Opens both years; won 4 Australian, 3 French and 2 US Opens; winner of 30 singles titles in just 5 years before she was stabbed in the back by Steffi Graf fan Gunter Parche on Apr. 30, 1993 during match in Hamburg, Germany; spent remainder of 1993, all of '94 and most of '95 recovering; returned to tennis with win at the 1995 Canadian Open; won 1996 Australian Open; winner of 48 WTA tournaments through Sept., 2001.

Bud Selig (b. July 30, 1934): Baseball; Milwaukee car dealer who bought AL Seattle Pilots for $10.8 million in 1970 and moved team to Midwest; as de facto comissioner, he presided over 232-day players' strike that resulted in cancellation of World Series for first time since 1904 and delayed opening of 1995 season until Apr. 25; officially named baseball's ninth commissioner on July 9, 1998.

Ayrton Senna (b. Mar. 21, 1960, d. May 1, 1994): Brazilian auto racer; 3-time Formula One champion (1988,90-91); died as all-time F1 leader in poles (65) and 2nd in wins (41, currently in 3rd place); killed in crash at Imola, Italy during '94 San Marino Grand Prix.

Patty Sheehan (b. Oct. 27, 1956): Golfer; LPGA Player of Year in 1983; clinched entry into LPGA Hall of Fame with her 30th career win in 1993; 3 LPGA titles (1983-84,93) and 2 U.S. Opens (1992,94).

Bill Shoemaker (b. Aug. 19, 1931): Jockey; ranks second all-time in career wins with 8,833 (passed by Laffit Pincay Jr. in Dec. 1999); 3-time Eclipse Award winner as jockey (1981) and special award recipient (1976,81); won Belmont 5 times, Kentucky Derby 4 times and Preakness twice; oldest jockey to win Kentucky Derby (age 54, aboard Ferdinand in 1986); retired in 1990 to become trainer; paralyzed in 1991 auto accident but continued to train horses.

Eddie Shore (b. Nov. 25, 1902, d. Mar. 16, 1985): Hockey D; only NHL defenseman to win Hart Trophy as MVP 4 times (1933,35-36,38); led Boston Bruins to Stanley Cup titles in 1929 and '39; had 105 goals and 1,047 penalty minutes in 14 seasons.

Frank Shorter (b. Oct. 31, 1947): Track & Field; won gold medal in marathon at 1972 Olympics, 1st American to win in 64 years.

Don Shula (b. Jan. 4, 1930): Football; retired after 1995 season with an NFL-record 347 career wins (including playoffs) and a winning percentage of .665; took six teams to Super Bowl and won twice with Miami (VII, VIII); 4-time Coach of Year, twice with Baltimore (1964,68) and twice with Miami (1970-71); coached 1972 Dolphins to 17-0 record, the only undefeated team in NFL history.

Charlie Sifford (b. June 2, 1922): Golf; won the Hartford Open in 1967 with a final-round 64, becoming the first black player to win a PGA event; won the PGA Seniors Championship in 1975; amassed over $1 million in career earnings; published his autobiography "Just Let Me Play" in 1992.

Al Simmons (b. May 22, 1902, d. May 26, 1956): Baseball OF; led AL in batting twice (1930-31) with Philadelphia A's and knocked in 100 runs or more 11 straight years (1924-34).

O.J. Simpson (b. July 9, 1947): Football RB; won Heisman Trophy in 1968 at USC; ran for 2,003 yards in NFL in 1973; All-Pro 5 times; MVP in 1973; rushed for 11,236 career yards; TV analyst and actor after career ended; arrested June 17, 1994 as suspect in double murder of ex-wife Nicole Brown Simpson and her friend Ronald Goldman; acquitted on Oct. 3, 1995 by a Los Angeles jury in criminal trial but forced to make financial reparations after losing wrongful death suit.

George Sisler (b. Mar. 24, 1893, d. Mar. 26, 1973): Baseball 1B; hit over .400 twice (1920,22) and batted over .300 in 13 of his 15 seasons; his 257 hits in 1920 is still a major league record; played most of his career with the St. Louis Browns; inducted into Baseball Hall of Fame in 1939.

Mary Decker Slaney (b. Aug. 4, 1958): U.S. middle distance runner; has held 7 separate American track & field records from the 800 to 10,000 meters; won both 1,500 and 3,000 meters at 1983 World Championships in Helsinki, but no Olympic medals.

Raisa Smetanina (b. Feb. 29, 1952): Russian Nordic skier; all-time Winter Olympics medalist with 10 cross-country medals (4 gold, 5 silver and a bronze) in 5 appearances (1976,80,84,88,92) for USSR and Unified Team.

Billy Smith (b. Dec. 12, 1950): Hockey G; led NY Islanders to 4 consecutive Stanley Cups (1980-83); won Vezina Trophy in 1982; Stanley Cup MVP in 1983.

Dean Smith (b. Feb. 28, 1931): Basketball; No. 1 on all-time NCAA coaches victory list (879); led North Carolina to 25 NCAA tournaments in 34 years, reaching Final Four 10 times and winning championship twice (1982,93); coached U.S. Olympic team to gold medal in 1976.

Emmitt Smith (b. May 15, 1969): Football RB; consensus All-America (1989) at Florida; 4-time NFL rushing leader (1991-93,95); regular season and Super Bowl MVP in 1993; played on three Super Bowl champions (1993,94,96); entered the 2001 season with 145 rushing TDs, more than any player in history; became 2nd all-time leading rusher (Payton) early in 2001 season.

John Smith (b. Aug. 9, 1965): Wrestler; 2-time NCAA champion for Oklahoma St. at 134 lbs (1987-88) and Most Outstanding Wrestler of '88 championships; 3-time world champion; gold medal winner at 1988 and '92 Olympics at 137 lbs; won Sullivan Award (1990); coached Oklahoma St. to 1994 NCAA title and brother Pat was Most Outstanding Wrestler.

Lee Smith (b. Dec. 4, 1957): Baseball RHP; 3-time NL saves leader (1983,91-92); retired as all-time saves leader with 478 and an ERA of 3.03; 10 seasons with 30 or more saves and 3 times saved over 40.

Michelle Smith deBruin (b. Apr. 7, 1969): Irish swimmer; won three gold medals at the 1996 Olympics; accused of using performance-enhancing drugs but passed all tests until she was suspended for 4 years by FINA in 1998 for tampering with a urine sample.

Ozzie Smith (b. Dec. 26, 1954): Baseball SS; won 13 straight Gold Gloves (1980-92); played in 12 straight All-Star Games (1981-92); MVP of 1985 NL playoffs; all-time MLB assist leader (8,375).

Walter (Red) Smith (b. Sept. 25, 1905, d. Jan. 15, 1982): Sportswriter for newspapers in Philadelphia and New York from 1936-82; won Pulitzer Prize for commentary in 1976.

Conn Smythe (b. Feb. 1, 1895, d. Nov. 18, 1980): Hockey pioneer; built Maple Leaf Gardens in 1931; managed Toronto to 7 Stanley Cups.

Sam Snead (b. May 27, 1912): Golfer; won both Masters and PGA 3 times and British Open once; runner-up in U.S. Open 4 times; PGA Player of Year in 1949; oldest player (52 years, 10 months) to win PGA event with Greater Greensboro Open title in 1965; all-time PGA Tour career victory leader with 81.

Peter Snell (b. Dec. 17, 1938): Track & Field; New Zealander who won gold medal in 800m at 1960 Olympics, then won both the 800m and 1,500m at 1964 Games.

Duke Snider (b. Sept. 19, 1926): Baseball OF; hit 40 or more home runs five straight seasons (1953-57); led the league in runs scored 1953-55; played in six World Series with the Dodgers and batted .286 with 11 home runs; nicknamed "Duke of Flatbush"; in 18 seasons hit 407 home runs, scored 1,259 runs and had 1,333 RBI.

Annika Sorenstam (b. Oct. 9, 1970): Swedish golfer; College Player of the Year and NCAA champion in 1991; won more LPGA tournaments (18) than any other player in the 1990s, including 2 U.S. Opens (1995,96); 29 tour wins through Sept., 2001; LPGA all-time leading money winner.

Sammy Sosa (b. Nov. 12, 1968): Baseball OF; slugging Chicago Cub who surpassed Roger Maris' season home run record (61), just after Mark McGwire did, in 1998 and finished the year with 66; NL MVP (1998); followed up his amazing 1998 by hitting 63 HRs in 1999 with 141 RBI; 5-time NL all-star (1995,98,99,00,01) and winner of the 2000 Home Run Derby.

Javier Sotomayor (b. Oct. 13, 1967): Cuban high jumper; first man to clear 8 feet (8-0) on July 29, 1989; won gold medal at 1992 Olympics with jump of only 7-ft. 8-in.; broke world record with leap of 8-0½ in 1993; had a controversial drug suspension reduced, which allowed him to participate in 2000 Olympics; won the silver medal in Sydney with a leap of 7-7¼.

Warren Spahn (b. Apr. 23, 1921): Baseball LHP; led NL in wins 8 times; won 20 or more games 13 times; Cy Young winner in 1957; most career wins (363) by a left-hander.

Tris Speaker (b. Apr. 4, 1888, d. Dec. 8, 1958): Baseball OF; all-time leader in outfield assists (449) and doubles (792); had .344 career BA and 3,515 hits.

J.G. Taylor Spink (b. Nov. 6, 1888, d. Dec. 7, 1962): Publisher of *The Sporting News* from 1914-62; BWAA annual meritorious service award named after him.

Leon Spinks (b. July 11, 1953): Boxing; won heavyweight crown in split decision over Muhammad Ali in Feb.1978; Ali regained title seven months later; won gold medal in light heavyweight division at 1976 Olympics; brother Michael won the heavyweight title in 1983; were the only brothers to hold world titles; known more for frequent traffic violations and lavish lifestyle than bouts late in career; filed for bankruptcy in 1986.

Mark Spitz (b. Feb. 10, 1950): Swimmer; set 23 world and 35 U.S. records; won all-time record 7 gold medals (4 individual, 3 relay) in 1972 Olympics; also won 4 medals (2 gold, a silver and a bronze) in 1968 Games for a total of 11; comeback attempt at age 41 foundered in 1991.

Lyn St. James (b. Mar. 13, 1947): Auto racer; one of just 3 women to qualify for the Indianapolis 500; best finish in the race came in 1992 when she came in 11th and won Indianapolis 500 Rookie of the Year.

Amos Alonzo Stagg (b. Aug. 16, 1862, d. Mar. 17, 1965): Football innovator; coached at U. of Chicago for 41 seasons and College of the Pacific for 14 more; 314-199-35 record; elected to both college football and basketball Halls of Fame.

Willie Stargell (b. Mar. 6, 1940, d. Apr. 9, 2001): Baseball OF-1B; led NL in home runs twice (1971,73); 475 career HRs; NL co-MVP and World Series MVP in 1979.

Bart Starr (b. Jan. 9, 1934): Football QB; led Green Bay to 5 NFL titles and 2 Super Bowl wins from 1961-67; regular season MVP in 1966; MVP of Super Bowls I and II.

Roger Staubach (b. Feb. 5, 1942): Football QB; Heisman Trophy winner as Navy junior in 1963; led Dallas to 2 Super Bowl titles (1972,78) and was Super Bowl MVP in 1972; 5-time leading passer in NFC (1971,73,77-79).

George Steinbrenner (b. July 4, 1930): Baseball; principal owner of NY Yankees since 1973; teams have won 8 pennants and 6 World Series (1977-78,96,98,99,00); has changed managers 21 times and GMs 11 times in 28 years; ordered by baseball commish Fay Vincent in 1990 to surrender control of club for dealings with small-time gambler; reinstated in 1993.

Casey Stengel (b. July 30, 1890, d. Sept. 29, 1975): Baseball; player for 14 years and manager for 25; outfielder and lifetime .284 hitter with 5 clubs (1912-25); guided NY Yankees to 10 AL pennants and 7 World Series titles from 1949-60; 1st NY Mets skipper from 1962-65.

Ingemar Stenmark (b. Mar. 18, 1956): Swedish alpine skier; 3-time World Cup overall champ (1976-78); posted 86 World Cup wins in 16 years; won 2 gold medals at 1980 Olympics.

Helen Stephens (b. Feb. 3, 1918, d. Jan. 17, 1994): Track & Field; set 3 world records in 100-yard dash and 4 more in 100 meters in 1935-36; won gold medals in 100 meters and 4x100-meter relay in 1936 Olympics; retired in 1937.

Woody Stephens (b. Sept. 1, 1913, d. Aug. 22, 1998): Horse racing; trainer who saddled an unprecedented 5 straight winners in Belmont Stakes (1982-86); also had two Kentucky Derby winners (1974,84) and one Preakness winner (1952); trained 1982 Horse of Year Conquistador Cielo; won Eclipse award as nation's top trainer in 1983.

David Stern (b. Sept. 22, 1942): Basketball; marketing expert and NBA commissioner since 1984; took office the year Michael Jordan turned pro; has presided over stunning artistic and financial success of NBA both nationally and internationally; league has grown from 23 teams to 29 during his watch and opened offices worldwide; oversaw launch of WNBA in 1997.

Teófilo Stevenson (b. Mar. 29, 1952): Cuban boxer; won 3 consecutive gold medals as Olympic heavyweight (1972,76,80); did not turn pro.

Jackie Stewart (b. June 11, 1939): Auto racer; won 27 Formula One races and 3 world driving titles from 1965-73.

John Stockton (b. Mar 26, 1962): Basketball G; all-time NBA leader in every major assist category, including most in a season (1,164), highest average in a season (14.5 per game) and most overall (14,503); also holds the NBA record for career steals (2,976); All-NBA team in '94 and '95; member of 1992 and '96 US Olympic basketball Dream Teams; 10-time All-Star.

Picabo Street (b. Apr. 3, 1971): Skiing; 2-time Olympic medalist, gold (Super G in 1998) and silver (downhill in 1994); her 1995 World Cup downhill series title first-ever by U.S. woman, she repeated the feat in 1996.

Kerri Strug (b. Nov. 19, 1977): Gymnastics; delivered the most dramatic moment of the 1996 Summer Olympics when she completed a vault (9.712) after spraining her ankle; the second vault assured the first all-around gold medal for a US Women's gymnastics team; a poor performance by the Russian team on the beam had clinched the gold medal for the US but Strug was unaware when she made the second vault; the injury prevented her from participating in any individual events.

Louise Suggs (b. Sept. 7, 1923): Golfer; won 11 majors and 50 LPGA events overall from 1949-62.

James E. Sullivan (b. Nov. 18, 1862, d. Sept. 16, 1914): Track & Field; pioneer who founded Amateur Athletic Union (AAU) in 1888; director of St. Louis Olympic Games in 1904; AAU's Sullivan Award for performance and sportsmanship named after him.

John L. Sullivan (b. Oct. 15, 1858, d. Feb. 2, 1918): Boxer; world heavyweight champion (1882-92); last of bare-knuckle champions.

Pat Summitt (b. June 14, 1952): Basketball; women's basketball coach at Tennessee (1974—); 2nd all-time in career victories to Jody Conradt of Texas; coached 1984 US women's basketball team to its first Olympic gold medal; has coached Lady Vols to 6 national championships (1987,89,91,96,97,98).

Don Sutton (b. April 2, 1945): Baseball RHP; won 324 games and tossed 58 shutouts in his 23-year career; recorded ML record five career 1-hitters; played with Dodgers, Astros, Brewers, Athletics, Angels and was a 4-time All-Star; elected to Hall of Fame in 1998.

Lynn Swann (b. Mar. 7, 1952): Football WR; played nine seasons with Pittsburgh (1974-82); appeared in four Super Bowls and had 16 catches for 364 yards and three TDs; named MVP of Super Bowl X for 4-161, 1 TD performance.

Barry Switzer (b. Oct. 5, 1937): Football; coached Oklahoma to 3 national titles (1974-75,85); 4th on all-time winning pct list at .837 (157-29-4); resigned in 1989 after OU was slapped with 3-year NCAA probation and 5 players were brought up on criminal charges; hired as Dallas Cowboys head coach in 1994 and led team to victory in Super Bowl XXX in 1996; resigned before '98 season.

Sheryl Swoopes (b. Mar. 25, 1971): Basketball; forward for WNBA's Houston Comets; WNBA regular season MVP and Defensive Player of the Year in 2000, 2-time olympic gold medalist (1996,2000); led Texas Tech to Div. I NCAA championship in 1993; consensus National Player of the Year in 1993.

Paul Tagliabue (b. Nov. 24, 1940): Football; NFL attorney who was elected league's 4th commissioner in 1989; ushered in salary cap in 1994; the league expanded by 2 teams in 1995 for 1st time since '76 (will expand to 32 by 2002).

Anatoli Tarasov (b. 1918, d. June 23, 1995): Hockey; coached Soviet Union to 9 straight world championships and 3 Olympic gold medals (1964,68,72).

Fran Tarkenton (b. Feb. 3, 1940): Football QB; 2-time NFL All-Pro (1973,75); Player of Year (1975); threw for 47,003 yards and 342 TDs (both former NFL records) in 18 seasons with Vikings and Giants.

Chuck Taylor (b. June 24, 1901, d. June 23, 1969): Converse traveling salesman whose name came to grace the classic, high-top canvas basketball sneakers known as "Chucks"; over 500 million pairs have been sold since 1917; he also ran clinics worldwide and edited Converse Basketball Yearbook (1922-68).

Lawrence Taylor (b. Feb. 4, 1959): Football LB; All-America at North Carolina (1980); only defensive player in NFL history to be consensus Player of Year (1986); led NY Giants to Super Bowl titles in 1986 and '90 seasons; played in a record 10 Pro Bowls (1981-90); retired after 1993 season with 132½ sacks and has had several drug-related arrests since; inducted into Hall of Fame in 1999.

Marshall (Major) Taylor (b. Nov. 26, 1878, d. June 21, 1932): Cyclist; Considered one of the first African-American sports heroes; held seven world cycling records at the turn of the century, racing mostly in Europe, Australia and New Zealand after being barred from many events in the U.S. due to racial prejudices; won the world 1-mile championship in 1899.

Gustavo Thoeni (b. Feb. 28, 1951): Italian alpine skier; 4-time World Cup overall champion (1971-73,75); won giant slalom at 1972 Olympics.

Isiah Thomas (b. Apr. 30, 1961): Basketball; led Indiana to NCAA title as sophomore and Final 4 MOP in 1981; consensus All-America guard in '81; led Detroit to 2 NBA titles in 1989 and '90; NBA Finals MVP in 1990; 3-time All-NBA 1st team (1984-86); retired in 1994 at age 33 after tearing right Achilles tendon; returned to NBA in 2000 as coach of the Indiana Pacers; elected to Hall of Fame in 2000.

Thurman Thomas (b. May 16, 1966): Football RB; 3-time AFC rushing leader (1990-91,93); 2-time All-Pro (1990-91); NFL Player of Year (1991); led Buffalo to 4 straight Super Bowls (1991-94).

Daley Thompson (b. July 30, 1958): British Track & Field; won consecutive gold medals in decathlon at 1980 and '84 Olympics.

Jenny Thompson (b. Feb. 26, 1973): Swimming; 8-time Olympic gold medallist (all in relays) and winner of 10 Olympic medals overall, more than any other American woman; won 3 gold (4x100 free, 4x200 free, 4x100 medley) and 1 bronze (100m freestyle) for the U.S. at the 2000 Olympics in Sydney.

John Thompson (b. Sept. 2, 1941): Basketball; coached centers Patrick Ewing, Alonzo Mourning and Dikembe Mutombo at Georgetown; reached NCAA tourney final 3 out of 4 years with Ewing, winning title in 1984; also led Hoyas to 6 Big East tourney titles; coached 1988 U.S. Olympic team to bronze medal; retired abruptly during 1999 season with 27-year mark of 596-239.

Bobby Thomson (b. Oct. 25, 1923): Baseball OF; career .270 hitter who won the 1951 NL pennant for the NY Giants with a 1-out, 3-run HR in the bottom of the 9th inning of Game 3 of a best-of-3 playoff with Brooklyn; the pitcher was Ralph Branca, the count was 0-1 and the Dodgers were ahead 4-2; the Giants had trailed Brooklyn by 13½ games on Aug. 11.

Ian Thorpe (b. Oct. 13, 1982): Swimming; Australian who won gold at Sydney Olympics in the 400m free (breaking his own world record) and silver in the 200m freestyle; was also part of relay team that won gold and broke the world record in the 4x100m and 4x200 freestyle relays; broke world records in the 200, 400 and 800m free at the 2001 world championships.

Jim Thorpe (b. May 28, 1888, d. May 28, 1953): 2-time All-America in football; won both pentathlon and decathlon at 1912 Olympics; stripped of medals a month later for playing semi-pro baseball prior to Games; medals restored in 1983; played major league baseball (1913-19) and pro football (1920-26,28); chosen "Athlete of the Half Century" by AP in 1950.

Bill Tilden (b. Feb. 10, 1893, d. June 5, 1953): Tennis; won 7 U.S. and 3 Wimbledon titles in 1920s; led U.S. to 7 straight Davis Cup victories (1920-26).

Tinker to Evers to Chance Chicago Cubs double play combination from 1903-10; immortalized in poem by New York sportswriter Franklin P. Adams— SS Joe Tinker (1880-1948), 2B Johnny Evers (1883-1947) and 1B Frank Chance (1877-1924); all 3 managed the Cubs and made the Hall of Fame.

Y.A. Tittle (b. Oct. 24, 1926): Football QB; played 17 years in AAFC and NFL; All-Pro 4 times; league MVP with San Francisco (1957) and NY Giants (1962); passed for 28,339 career yards.

Alberto Tomba (b. Dec. 19, 1966): Italian alpine skier; all-time Olympic alpine medalist with 5 (3 gold, 2 silver); became 1st alpine skier to win gold medals in 2 consecutive Winter Games when he won the slalom and giant slalom in 1988 then repeated in the GS in '92; also won silvers in slalom in 1992 and '94.

Vladislav Tretiak (b. Apr. 25, 1952): Hockey G; led USSR to Olympic gold medals in 1972 and '76; starred for Soviets against Team Canada in 1972, and again in 2 Canada Cups (1976,81).

Lee Trevino (b. Dec. 1, 1939): Golfer; 2-time winner of 3 majors—U.S. Open (1968,71), British Open (1971-72) and PGA (1974,84); Player of Year once on PGA Tour (1971) and 3 times with Seniors (1990,92,94); 27 PGA Tour and 29 Senior Tour wins.

Felix Trinidad (b. Jan. 10, 1973): Puerto Rican boxer; former WBC/IBF welterweight champion; won WBC belt with a majority decision over the slightly-favored Oscar De La Hoya in their highly-anticipated meeting in Sept., 1999; stepped up to junior middleweight and won the WBA title from David Reid in March, 2000.

Bryan Trottier (b. July 17, 1956): Hockey C; led NY Islanders to 4 straight Stanley Cups (1980-83); Rookie of Year (1976); scoring champion (134 points) and regular season MVP in 1979; playoff MVP (1980); added 5th and 6th Cups with Pittsburgh in 1991 and '92; entered Hockey Hall of Fame in 1997.

Gene Tunney (b. May 25, 1897, d. Nov. 7, 1978): Boxer; world heavyweight champion from 1926-28; beat 31-year-old champ Jack Dempsey in unanimous 10 round decision in 1926; beat him again in famous "long count" rematch in '27; quit while still champion in 1928 with 65-1-1 record and 47 KOs.

Ted Turner (b. Nov. 19, 1938): Sportsman and TV mogul; skippered *Courageous* to America's Cup win in 1977; owner of MLB Atlanta Braves, NBA Hawks and NHL Thrashers; owner of CNN, TNT and TBS; founder of Goodwill Games; 1991 *Time* Man of Year.

Mike Tyson (b. June 30, 1966): Boxer; youngest (age 19) to win heavyweight title (WBC in 1986); undisputed champ from 1987 until upset loss to 42-1 shot Buster Douglas on Feb. 10, 1990, in Tokyo; found guilty on Feb. 10, 1992, of raping 18-year-old Miss Black America contestant Desiree Washington in Indianapolis on July 19, 1991; sentenced to 6-year prison term; released May 9, 1995 after serving 3 years; reclaimed WBC and WBA belts with wins over Frank Bruno and Bruce Seldon in 1996; lost WBA title to Evander Holyfield in 1996; brought his career to a halt when he bit Holyfield twice in the ear during their WBA championship fight in 1997; returned to jail in 1999 for assaulting two motorists during a 1998 traffic dispute; see career fight record in Boxing chapter.

Wyomia Tyus (b. Aug. 29, 1945): Track & Field; 1st woman to win consecutive Olympic gold medals in 100m (1964-68).

Peter Ueberroth (b. Sept. 2, 1937): Organizer of 1984 Summer Olympics in LA; 1984 *Time* Man of Year; baseball commissioner from 1984-89; headed Rebuild Los Angeles for one year after 1992 riots.

Johnny Unitas (b. May 7, 1933): Football QB; led Baltimore Colts to 2 NFL titles (1958-59) and a Super Bowl win (1971); All-Pro 5 times; 3-time MVP (1959,64,67); passed for 40,239 career yards and 290 TDs.

Al Unser Jr. (b. Apr. 19, 1962): Auto racer; 2-time CART-IndyCar national champion (1990,94); captured Indy 500 for 2nd time in 3 years in '94, giving Unser family 9 overall titles at the Brickyard; 31 CART wins in 18 years; left CART for Indy Racing League at the start of the 2000 season; son of Al and nephew of Bobby.

Al Unser Sr. (b. May 29, 1939): Auto racer; 3-time USAC-CART national champion (1970,83,85); 4-time winner of Indy 500 (1970-71,78,87); retired in 1994 ranked 3rd on all-time CART list with 39 wins; younger brother of Bobby and father of Al Jr.

Bobby Unser (b. Feb. 20, 1934): Auto racer; 2-time USAC-CART national champion (1968,74); 3-time winner of Indy 500 (1968,75,81); retired after 1981 season; ranks 5th on all-time CART list with 35 career wins.

Gene Upshaw (b. Aug. 15, 1945): Football G; 2-time All-AFL and 3-time All-NFL selection with Oakland; helped lead Raiders to 2 Super Bowl titles in 1976 and '80 seasons; executive director of NFL Players Assn. since 1987; agreed to application of salary cap in 1994.

Jim Valvano (b. Mar. 10, 1946, d. Apr. 28, 1993): Basketball; coach at N.C. State whose team upset Houston to win national title in 1983; in 19 seasons as a coach appeared in 8 NCAA tournaments; twice voted ACC Coach of the Year; career record 346-212; AD at N.C. State (1986-89) when a recruiting and admissions scandal forced him out of the job; worked as a broadcaster for ESPN and ABC; died after a year-long battle with cancer; The V Foundation for cancer research is named for him.

Norm Van Brocklin (b. Mar. 15, 1926, d. May 2, 1983): Football QB-P; led NFL in passing 3 times and punting twice; led LA Rams (1951) and Philadelphia (1960) to NFL titles; MVP in 1960.

Amy Van Dyken (b. Feb. 17, 1973): Swimming; first American woman to win four gold medals in one Olympics (1996); won the individual 50m freestyle, 100m butterfly, and was on the US team for the 4x100 freestyle and 4x50 medley; won gold at Sydney in 2000 as part of the US 4x100 freestyle relay.

Johnny Vander Meer (b. Nov. 2, 1914, d. Oct. 6, 1997): Baseball LHP; only major leaguer to pitch consecutive no-hitters (June 11 & 15, 1938).

Harold S. Vanderbilt (b. July 6, 1884, d. July 4, 1970): Sportsman; successfully defended America's Cup 3 times (1930, 34,37); also invented contract bridge in 1926.

Glenna Collett Vare (b. June 20, 1903, d. Feb. 10, 1989): Golfer; won record 6 U.S. Women's Amateur titles from 1922-35; "the female Bobby Jones."

Bill Veeck (b. Feb. 9, 1914, d. Jan. 2, 1986): Maverick baseball executive; owned AL teams in Cleveland, St. Louis and Chicago from 1946-80; introduced ballpark giveaways, exploding scoreboards, Wrigley Field's ivy-covered walls and midget Eddie Gaedel; won World Series with Indians (1948) and pennant with White Sox (1959).

Jacques Villeneuve (b. Apr. 9, 1971): Canadian auto racer; Indianapolis 500 runner-up and IndyCar Rookie of Year in 1994; won 500 and IndyCar driving championship in 1995; jumped to Formula One racing in 1996 and won the F1 title in 1997.

Fay Vincent (b. May 29, 1938): Baseball; became 8th commissioner after death of A. Bartlett Giamatti in 1989; presided over World Series earthquake, owners' lockout and banishment of NY Yankees owner George Steinbrenner in his first year on the job; contentious relationship with owners resulted in his resignation on Sept. 7, 1992, four days after 18-9 "no confidence" vote.

Lasse Viren (b. July 22, 1949): Finnish runner; won gold medals at 5,000 and 10,000 meters in 1972 Munich Olympics; repeated 5,000/10,000 double in 1976 Games and added a 5th place in the marathon.

Dick Vitale (b. June 9, 1939): Broadcaster; Radio and television commentator for ESPN and ABC Sports known for his enthusiastic, almost spastic style; had successful college and pro basketball coaching career with the University of Detroit (1973-77) and the Detroit Pistons (1978-79); he's been nominated for a Cable ACE award eight times and won once in 1995.

Lanny Wadkins (b. Dec. 5, 1949): Golfer; member of 8 Ryder Cup teams and captain of 1995 team; 21 PGA Tour wins.

Honus Wagner (b. Feb. 24, 1874, d. Dec. 6, 1955): Baseball SS; hit .300 for 17 consecutive seasons (1897-1913) with Louisville and Pittsburgh; led NL in batting 8 times; ended career with 3,430 career hits, a .329 average and 722 stolen bases.

Lisa Wagner (b. May 19, 1961): Bowler; 4-time LPBT Player of the Year (1983,86,88,93); 1980's Bowler of Decade; first woman to earn $100,000 in a season; winner of 32 pro titles.

Grete Waitz (b. Oct. 1, 1953): Norwegian runner; 9-time winner of New York City Marathon from 1978-88; won silver medal at 1984 Olympics.

Jersey Joe Walcott (b. Jan. 31, 1914, d. Feb. 27, 1994): Boxer; oldest heavyweight (37) to ever win the championship; lost four championship bouts before knocking out Ezzard Charles in the seventh round in 1951; lost the title the following year, losing to Rocky Marciano; won 50 bouts, 30 by knockout, lost 17 and fought one draw as a professional; later became sheriff of Camden County, NJ.

Doak Walker (b. Jan. 1, 1927, d. Sept. 27, 1998): Football HB; won Heisman Trophy as SMU junior in 1948; led Detroit to 2 NFL titles (1952-53); All-Pro 4 times in 6 years.

Herschel Walker (b. Mar. 3, 1962): Football RB; led Georgia to national title as freshman in 1980; won Heisman in 1982 then jumped to upstart USFL in '83; signed by Dallas Cowboys after USFL folded; led NFL in rushing in 1988; traded to Minnesota in 1989 for 5 players and 6 draft picks.

Rusty Wallace (b. Aug. 14, 1956): Auto racing; NASCAR Winston Cup champion in 1989 and runner-up in 1980, 1988 and 1993; recorded 54 victories and has won over $25 million in earnings in 22 years of racing as of Sept. 21, 2001.

Bill Walsh (b. Nov. 30, 1931): Football; Hall of Fame coach and GM of 3 Super Bowl winners with San Francisco (1982,85,89); retired after 1989 Super Bowl; returned to college coaching in 1992 for his second stint at Stanford; retired again after 1994 season; returned as 49er GM from 1999-2001.

Bill Walton (b. Nov. 5, 1952): Basketball C; 3-time College Player of Year (1972-74); led UCLA to 2 national titles (1972-73); led Portland to NBA title as MVP in 1977; regular season MVP in 1978.

Darrell Waltrip (b. Feb. 5, 1947): Auto racing; 3-time NASCAR Winston Cup champion (1981,82,85); 84 career Winston Cup wins and 59 poles.

Arch Ward (b. Dec. 27, 1896, d. July 9, 1955): Promoter and sports editor of Chicago Tribune from 1930-55; founder of baseball All-Star Game (1933), Chicago College All-Star Football Game (1934) and the All-America Football Conference (1946-49).

Charlie Ward (b. Oct. 12, 1970): Football QB and Basketball G; first Heisman winner to play for national champs (Florida St. in 1993) since Tony Dorsett in 1976, won Sullivan Award (1993); not taken in NFL draft; 1st round pick of NY Knicks in 1994 NBA draft.

Glenn (Pop) Warner (b. Apr. 5, 1871, d. Sept. 7, 1954): Football innovator; coached at 7 colleges over 49 years; 319 career wins 2nd only to Bear Bryant's 323 in Div. I-A; produced 47 All-Americas, including Jim Thorpe and Ernie Nevers.

Tom Watson (b. Sept. 4, 1949): Golfer; 6-time PGA Player of the Year (1977-80,82,84); has won 5 British Opens, 2 Masters and a U.S. Open; 4-time Ryder Cup member and captain of 1993 team; 34 PGA tour wins.

Earl Weaver (b. Aug. 14, 1930): Baseball; managed the Baltimore Orioles to 6 Eastern Division titles, four AL pennants and a World Series victory in 1970; was ejected 91 times and suspended four times for outbursts against umpires; record of 1,480-1,060 from 1968-82 and 1985-86.

Karrie Webb (b. Dec. 21, 1974): Golfer; youngest woman to win career Grand Slam; won her second U.S. Open in 2001; recorded seven wins in 2000 and broke the LPGA record for single-season earnings with $1,876,853; has accumulated enough points to be eligible for induction to the LGPA Hall of Fame — needs only to meet the 10-year membership requirement.

Dick Weber (b. Dec. 23, 1929): Bowler; 3-time PBA Bowler of the Year (1961,63,65); won 30 PBA titles in 4 decades.

Johnny Weissmuller (b. June 2, 1904, d. Jan. 20 1984): Swimmer; won 3 gold medals at 1924 Olympics and 2 more at 1928 Games; became Hollywood's most famous Tarzan.

Jerry West (b. May 28, 1938): Basketball G; 2-time All-America and NCAA Final 4 MOP (1959) at West Virginia; led 1960 U.S. Olympic team to gold medal; 10-time All-NBA 1st-team; NBA finals MVP (1969); led LA Lakers to NBA title once as player (1972) and then 6 more times (1980,82,85,87,88, 00) as an executive in various positions with the club, most recently VP of basketball operations; retired after the 2000 season; his silhouette serves as the NBA's logo.

Pernell Whitaker (b. Jan. 2, 1964): Boxer; won Olympic gold medal as lightweight in 1984; won 4 world championships as lightweight, jr. welterweight, welterweight and jr. middleweight; outfought but failed to beat Julio Cesar Chavez when 1993 welterweight title defense ended in controversial draw; pro record of 41-3-1 (17 KOs).

Bill White (b. Jan. 28, 1934): Baseball; NL president and highest ranking black executive in sports from 1989-94; as 1st baseman, won 7 Gold Gloves and hit .286 with 202 HRs in 13 seasons.

Byron (Whizzer) White (b. June 8, 1917): Football; All-America HB at Colorado (1937); signed with Pittsburgh in 1938 for the then largest contract in pro history ($15,800); took Rhodes Scholarship in 1939; returned to NFL in 1940 to lead league in rushing and retired in 1941; named to U.S. Supreme Court by President Kennedy in 1962 and stepped down in 1993.

Reggie White (b. Dec. 19, 1961): Football DE; consensus All-America in 1983 at Tennessee; 7-time All-NFL (1986-92) with Philadelphia; signed as free agent with Green Bay in 1993 for $17 million over 4 years; played key role in Packers 1997 Super Bowl victory; made headlines in 1998 after making controversial public comments about gays and minorities; retired in 1999 but returned with the Carolina Panthers in 2000; all-time NFL leader in sacks (198).

Kathy Whitworth (b. Sept. 27, 1939): Golf; 7-time LPGA Player of the Year (1966-69,71-73); won 6 majors; 88 tour wins, most on LPGA or PGA tour.

Hazel Hotchkiss Wightman (b. Dec. 20, 1886, d. Dec. 5, 1974): Tennis; won 16 U.S. national titles; 4-time U.S. Women's champion (1909-11,19); donor of Wightman Cup.

Hoyt Wilhelm (b. July 26, 1923): Baseball RHP; Knuckleballer who is 3rd all-time in games pitched (1,070) and 1st in games finished (651) and games won in relief (123); career ERA of 2.52 and 227 saves; 1st reliever inducted into Hall of Fame (1985); threw no-hitter vs. NY Yankees (1958); also hit lone HR of career in first major league at bat (1952).

Lenny Wilkens (b. Oct. 28, 1937): Basketball; NBA's all-time winningest coach; MVP of 1960 NIT as Providence guard; played 15 years in NBA, including 4 as player-coach; MVP of 1971 All-Star Game; coached Seattle to NBA title in 1979; Coach of Year in 1994 with Atlanta; one of only two men (John Wooden) to be honored by the Hall of Fame as player and coach; left Atlanta in 2000 to coach the Toronto Raptors.

Dominique Wilkins (b. Jan. 12, 1960): Basketball F; last player to lead NBA in scoring (1986) before Michael Jordan's 7-year reign; All-NBA 1st team in 1986; elder statesman of Dream Team II.

Bud Wilkinson (b. Apr. 23, 1916, d. Feb. 9, 1994): Football; played on 1936 national championship team at Minnesota; coached Oklahoma to 3 national titles (1950, 55, 56); won 4 Orange and 2 Sugar Bowls; teams had winning streaks of 47 (1953-57) and 31 (1948-50); retired after 1963 season with 145-29-4 record in 17 years; also coached St. Louis of NFL to 9-20 record from 1978-79.

AP/Wide World Photos

Johnny Weissmuller as Tarzan.

Ricky Williams (b. May 21, 1977): Football RB; became all-time NCAA Div. I-A leader in rushing yards (6,279) and touchdowns (75) at Texas but has since been passed in both categories; 1998 Heisman Trophy winner; Mike Ditka and New Orleans Saints made history by trading their entire draft to use him fifth overall in 1999 NFL draft.

Serena Williams (b. Sept. 26, 1981): Tennis; beat Martina Hingis for 1999 U.S. Open championship becoming the first African-American woman to win a Grand Slam title since Althea Gibson in 1958; has won career doubles grand slam with sister Venus.

Ted Williams (b. Aug. 30, 1918): Baseball OF; led AL in batting 6 times, and HRs and RBI 4 times each; won Triple Crown twice (1942,47); 2-time MVP (1946,49); last player to bat .400 when he hit .406 in 1941; Marine Corps combat pilot who missed three full seasons during World War II (1943-45) and most of two others (1952-53) during Korean War; hit .344 lifetime with 521 HRs in 19 years with Boston Red Sox.

Venus Williams (b. June 17, 1980): Tennis; won career doubles grand slam with sister Serena; recorded fastest serve in WTA history with 127 mph blast; winner of 2 Wimbledon (2000,01) and 2 U.S. Open (2000,01) singles titles.

Walter Ray Williams Jr. (b. Oct. 6, 1959): Bowling and Horseshoes; 5-time PBA Bowler of Year (1986,93,96,97,98); all-time leading money winner on the PBA Tour through 2000; won 6 World Horseshoe Pitching titles.

Hack Wilson (b. Apr. 26, 1900, d. Nov. 23, 1948): Baseball; as a Chicago Cub, he produced one of baseball's most outstanding seasons in 1930 with 56 homeruns, .356 batting average, 105 walks and, most amazingly, a major league record 191 RBIs that still stands; finished with 1,461 hits, 244 homers, 1,062 RBIs; member of Baseball Hall of Fame.

Dave Winfield (b. Oct. 3, 1951): Baseball OF-DH; selected in 4 major sports league drafts in 1973 — NFL, NBA, ABA, and MLB; chose baseball and has played in 12 All-Star Games over 22-year career; at age 41, helped lead Toronto to World Series title in 1992; 3,110 hits and 465 HRs.

Katarina Witt (b. Dec. 3, 1965): East German figure skater; 4-time world champion (1984-85,87-88); won consecutive Olympic gold medals (1984,88).

John Wooden (b. Oct. 14, 1910): Basketball; College Player of Year at Purdue in 1932; coached UCLA to 10 national titles (1964-65,67-73,75); one of only two men (Lenny Wilkens) to be honored by the Hall of Fame as player and coach.

Tiger Woods (b. Dec. 30, 1975): Golfer; youngest (18) and first minority to win U.S. Amateur in 1994, won it again in '95 and '96; turned pro in Sept. of '96 and won the fifth event he entered, the Las Vegas Invitational; in first full year on the tour, he won 6 of 25 events and broke the single season money record; won 1997 Masters by a record 18 under par and 13 stroke margin of victory; won second major at 1999 PGA Championship; in 2000 won the U.S. Open at Pebble Beach by a record 15 strokes, the British Open by 8 strokes and the PGA Championship in a playoff; one of only five players to win all four Grand Slam titles (others are Hogan, Nicklaus, Player and Sarazen); held all four Major titles simultaneously after his win at 2001 Masters; is already the all-time career money leader on the PGA Tour.

Mickey Wright (b. Feb. 14, 1935): Golfer; won 3 of 4 majors (LPGA, U.S. Open, Titleholders) in 1961; 4-time winner of both U.S. Open and LPGA titles; 82 career wins including 13 majors.

Early Wynn (b. Jan. 6, 1920, d. Mar. 4, 1999): Baseball RHP; won 20 games 5 times; Cy Young winner in 1959; 300-244 record in 23 years.

Kristi Yamaguchi (b. July 12, 1971): Figure Skating; finished second in the 1991 American nationals but won the world title that year; dominated the sport in 1992 by winning the national, world and Olympic titles and then turned professional.

Cale Yarborough (b. Mar. 27, 1940): Auto racer; 3-time NASCAR national champion (1976-78); 4-time winner of Daytona 500 (1968,77,83-84); ranks 5th on NASCAR all-time list with 83 wins.

Carl Yastrzemski (b. Aug. 22, 1939): Baseball OF; led AL in batting 3 times; won Triple Crown and MVP in 1967; had 3,419 hits and 452 HRs in 23 years with Boston; member of Hall of Fame.

Cy Young (b. Mar. 29, 1867, d. Nov. 4, 1955): Baseball RHP; all-time leader in wins (511), losses (313), complete games (751) and innings pitched (7,356); had career 2.63 ERA in 22 years (1890-1911); 30-game winner 5 times and 20-game winner 11 other times; threw 3 no-hitters and perfect game (1904); AL and NL pitching awards named after him.

Sheila Young (b. Oct. 14, 1950): Speed skater and cyclist; 1st U.S. athlete to win 3 medals at Winter Olympics (1976); won speed skating overall and sprint cycling world titles in 1976.

Steve Young (b. Oct. 11, 1961): Football QB; All-America at BYU (1983); NFL Player of Year (1992) with SF 49ers; only QB to lead NFL in passer rating 4 straight years (1991-94); rating of 112.8 in 1994 was highest ever; threw record 6 TD passes in MVP performance in Super Bowl XXIX; holds NFL career records for highest passer rating (96.8) and completion percentage (64.4); retired with 232 TD passes and 33,124 yards.

Robin Yount (b. Sept. 16, 1955): Baseball SS-OF; AL MVP at 2 positions — as SS in 1982 and OF in '89; retired after 1993 season with 3,142 hits, 251 HRs and a major-league-record 123 sacrifice flies after 20 seasons with Milwaukee Brewers; inducted into Hall of Fame in 1999.

Steve Yzerman (b. May 9, 1965): Hockey C; Captained the Detroit Red Wings to back-to-back Stanley Cup sweeps in '96-97 and '97-98; took home the Conn Smythe Trophy as the playoff MVP in 1998; one of only 12 NHL players to score 600 goals; entered the 2001-02 season 6th in career scoring (1,614 points).

Mario Zagalo (b. Aug. 9, 1931): Soccer; Brazilian forward who is one of only two men (Franz Beckenbauer is the other) to serve as both captain (1962) and coach (1970,94) of World Cup champion.

Babe Didrikson Zaharias (b. June 26, 1911, d. Sept. 27, 1956): All-around athlete who was chosen AP Female Athlete of Year 6 times from 1932-54; won 2 gold medals (javelin and 80-meter hurdles) and a silver (high jump) at 1932 Olympics; played baseball and acquired the nickname "Babe" for her tape measure home runs; took up golf in 1935 and went on to win 55 pro and amateur events; won 10 majors, including 3 U.S. Opens (1948,50,54); helped found LPGA in 1949; chosen female "Athlete of the Half Century" by AP in 1950; when asked if there was anything she didn't play, she replied, "Yeah, dolls."

Tony Zale (b. May 29, 1913, d. March 20, 1997): Boxer; 2-time world middleweight champion (1941-47,48); fought Rocky Graziano for title 3 times in 21 months in 1947-48, winning twice; pro record 67-18-2 with 44 KOs.

Frank Zamboni (b. Jan. 16, 1901, d. July 27, 1988): Mechanic, ice salesman and skating rink owner in Paramount, Calif.; invented 1st ice-resurfacing machine in 1949; now there are very few skating rinks without one as over 7,000 have been sold in more than 35 countries worldwide

Emil Zatopek (b. Sept. 19, 1922, d. Nov. 22, 2000): Czech distance runner; winner of 1948 Olympic gold medal at 10,000 meters; 4 years later, won unprecedented Olympic triple crown (5,000 meters, 10,000 meters and marathon) at 1952 Games in Helsinki.

John Ziegler (b. Feb. 9, 1934): Hockey; NHL president from 1977-92; negotiated settlement with rival WHA in 1979 that led to inviting four WHA teams (Edmonton, Hartford, Quebec and Winnipeg) to join NHL; stepped down June 12, 1992, 2 months after settling 10-day players' strike.

Kim Zmeskal (b. Feb 6, 1976): Gymnastics; Won three U.S. all-around championships in a row (1990-'92); first American gymnast to win the all-around competition in the world championships (1991); only athlete to win two golds in the 1992 world championships (balance beam and floor exercise).

Pirmin Zurbriggen (b. Feb. 4, 1963): Swiss alpine skier; 4-time World Cup overall champ (1984,87-88,90) and 3-time runner-up; 40 World Cup wins in 10 years; won gold and bronze medals at 1988 Olympics.

Ballparks & Arenas

Pittsburgh's **PNC Park**, offering spectacular views
of the city's skyline, opened for business in 2001.

Ballparks and Arenas

Coming Attractions

ESPN information please®
SPORTS ALMANAC

PAGE
546

2001

BASEBALL

Milwaukee (NL): President George W. Bush threw out the first pitch at Miller Park (Miller Brewing Co. is the title sponsor) at the park's grand opening on April 6, 2001, in which the Brewers defeated the Cincinnati Reds 5-4 on a Richie Sexson home run. Located on a site adjacent to County Stadium, the retractable-roof (which takes 10 minutes to open or close) stadium has natural grass, an asymmetrical outfield and seats 42,500 including 70 luxury suites; estimated cost: $250 million plus $50-75 million to repair damage caused by a deadly construction accident which delayed the park's opening by an entire year.

Pittsburgh (NL): The Pirates' home opener at PNC Park (PNC Bank is the title sponsor), an 8-2 loss to the Cincinnati Reds, took place on April 9, 2001 in front of a crowd of 36,954. Located on the Allegheny River between the former site of Three Rivers Stadium and the Roberto Clemente Bridge (formerly Sixth Street Bridge), the baseball-only park seats 37,898, has 69 luxury suites and cost an estimated $228 million; stadium is part of city's larger construction project, including enlarged convention center and Heinz Field (new home of NFL's Steelers).

NBA BASKETBALL

Dallas (West): Grand opening of the American Airlines Center (American Airlines is also the title sponsor of American Airlines Arena in Miami) took place July 27, 2001 with a record-setting ribbon cutting. The opening, which was followed the next night with its first event (a concert by The Eagles), appears to have shattered two Guinness Book of World Records for the largest ribbon cutting (an estimated 2,000 cutters) and longest ribbon ever (three miles long). The building is located due north of Dallas' West End, east of Interstate 35E, as part of the new Victory development and seats 19,200 for the Dallas Mavericks, 18,500 for the NHL's Stars and includes 142 luxury suites; estimated cost: $420 million.

NFL FOOTBALL

Denver (AFC): INVESCO Field at Mile High (INVESCO is the title sponsor) opened on Aug. 25, 2001 with a 31-24 Broncos preseason win over the New Orleans Saints. The new open-air, grass-field stadium seats 76,125 including 124 luxury suites. The stadium is located adjacent to old Mile High Stadium and cost an estimated $401 million.

Pittsburgh (AFC): Heinz Field (H.J. Heinz Company is the title sponsor) opened Aug. 18, 2001 with an 'N Sync concert. The stadium seats 65,000 including 127 luxury suites. The Steelers' new home is part of the city's larger construction project, including enlarged convention center and PNC Park for MLB's Pirates. The park, which will also be used by the University of Pittsburgh Panthers, cost an estimated $281 million to construct.

NHL HOCKEY

Dallas (West): Grand opening of the American Airlines Center (American Airlines is also the title sponsor of American Airlines Arena in Miami) took place July 27, 2001 with a record-setting ribbon cutting. The opening, which was followed the next night with its first event (a concert by The Eagles), appears to have shattered two Guinness Book of World Records for the largest ribbon cutting (an estimated 2,000 cutters) and longest ribbon ever (three miles long). The building is located due north of Dallas' West End, east of Interstate 35E, as part of the new Victory development and seats 18,500 for hockey and 19,100 for the NBA's Mavericks and includes 142 luxury suites; estimated cost: $325 million.

2002

NBA BASKETBALL

San Antonio (West): Groundbreaking for the SBC Center (SBC Communications Inc. is the title sponsor) took place on Aug. 23, 2000. The new arena will seat 18,500 for basketball, including 54 luxury suites, and serve as the home to the Spurs as well as the annual San Antonio Livestock Exposition and Rodeo; estimated cost: $175 million; to be located adjacent to the Freeman Coliseum in East San Antonio. Opening is scheduled for September 2002.

NFL FOOTBALL

Detroit (NFC): Groundbreaking of Ford Field (Ford Motor Co., is the title sponsor) took place Nov. 16, 1999. Stadium will be located in downtown Detroit and incorporate the adjacent Old Hudson's Warehouse which will house all the stadium's suites and club level seating. Fans will have a view of the city skyline with natural light shining through the glass wall at the main entrance at Adams and Brush streets. The domed stadium will seat 65,000, including 125 luxury suites, for football; estimated cost: $300 million. The stadium is scheduled to open in August of 2002.

New England (AFC): Construction of CMGI Field (Internet company CMGI is the title sponsor) is underway next to existing Foxboro Stadium. The new open-air, grass-field stadium will have 68,000 seats and include 80 luxury suites and over 6,000 club seats; A light tower designed to evoke images of a New England lighthouse will be the stadium's signature architectural feature; estimated cost: $325 million. Earliest opening would be April 2002 for the MLS New England Revolution season.

Houston (AFC): Groundbreaking for the new Reliant Stadium (Reliant Engergy is the title sponsor) took place on March 9, 2000. The new home of the expansion Houston Texans and annual Houston Livestock Show and Rodeo will be the world's first retractable roof football stadium with a grass playing surface. The roof will be able to open or close in 10 minutes. The stadium will seat 69,500, including 147 luxury suites, but will be expandable up to 72,000 seats for events like the Super Bowl; estimated cost: $367 million. Scheduled opening is August 2002.

Seattle (NFC): Construction for the as-yet-unnamed stadium is well underway. Stadium and exhibition center will be located on old site of Kingdome, which was imploded on Mar. 26, 2000; open-air, grass-field stadium will seat 67,000 (expanded capacity: 72,000) and include 82 luxury suites and 7,000 club seats; approximately 70 percent of the seats will be protected from the elements; stadium and exhibition center will cost an estimated $400 million. The Seahawks will compete at University of Washington's Husky Stadium for two years during construction. Earliest Seahawks home opener would be August 2002.

2003

BASEBALL

Cincinnati (NL): Construction of the Great American Ballpark (Great American Insurance is the title sponsor) began Aug. 1, 2000. The stadium site overlaps the current site of Cinergy Field (formerly known as Riverfront Stadium). Part of the left and center field stands at Cinergy were removed in January 2001 to clear space for the new construction to begin. The grass-field, baseball-only park is not expected to have any unusual angles in the outfield and will seat an estimated 42,060. Home plate of the new park will be set 568 feet from the Ohio River, probably a little too far for splashdown homers that have been made famous at San Francisco's Pacific Bell Park. Estimated cost of project: $297 million. Earliest opening would be spring 2003.

San Diego (NL): Construction on the Padres new ballpark was suspended in October 2000 because of issues surrounding the financing of the new stadium. The open-air, grass-field park will be located on a one-square-block downtown lot and be part of a larger redevelopment project that will include a new hotel, office space and retail space. The park will seat approximately 46,000, including 60 luxury suites, and cost an estimated $267.5 million. The earliest Padres' home opener would be April 2003 but could be pushed back to 2004.

NBA BASKETBALL

Houston (West): Groundbreaking for the new Houston Arena (title sponsor pending) for the Rockets and WNBA Comets took place July 31, 2001. The multi-purpose complex will seat 18,500 for basketball and 17,800 for hockey including 92 luxury suites and 2,800 club seats; estimated cost: $175 million; The arena will be located in downtown Houston on a four-block site bounded by LaBranch, Jackson, Bell and Polk streets. Earliest opening would be September 2003.

NFL FOOTBALL

Green Bay (NFC): In September 2000, voters approved a plan to use a new 0.5 percent sales tax in Brown County to help fund a $295 million renovation of 43-year-old Lambeau Field. Unlike most stadium renovations, lack of luxury suites was not the issue here. The newly renovated stadium will actually have 32 fewer seats. Approximately 10,000 seats (including about 4,300 additional club seats) will be added bringing the total seating capacity to about 71,100 including 167 luxury suites. Plans also call for the team and the city of Green Bay to seek naming rights before the 2003 season. A minimum bid of $120 million would have to be considered; the team and city would split the proceeds; renovation is scheduled to be completed in September 2003.

Philadelphia (NFC): Three months after opening a $37 million corporate headquarters and training complex, the Eagles broke ground on a 66,000-seat, yet-to-be-named stadium, located at 11th Street and Pattison Avenue in South Philadelphia. The city of Philadelphia is responsible for site acquisition and preparation while the Eagles are covering construction and overrun costs. Estimated cost of $500 million includes $310 million contributed by the Eagles. Earliest Eagles' home opener could be August 2003.

NHL HOCKEY

Phoenix (West): Groundbreaking is expected in early 2002 on a 225-acre, three million square foot facility in Glendale, Ariz., featuring a new 17,500-seat multi-purpose arena that will serve as a home to the Phoenix Coyotes. The complex, to be located at 101 Freeway and Glendale Avenue, features entertainment, retail, restaurants, office, hotel and residential venues and includes 70 luxury suites. The first phase of the project, expected to open in 2003, will cost an estimated $550 million.

2004

BASEBALL

Boston (AL): New Fenway Park is in the planning stages. The current plans have the open-air, grass-field park located adjacent to the existing Fenway Park and emulating many of Fenway's features including the Green Monster and Pesky's Pole; part of the project includes preserving portions of the old ballpark as a public park; estimated cost of entire project: $627 million; would seat 44,130 and the earliest Red Sox home opener would be April 2004.

New York (NL): New ballpark for the Mets is in the planning stages. To be located adjacent to Shea Stadium in Queens. The retractable-roof stadium would seat 45,000, including 78 luxury suites and 5,000 club seats. Estimated

cost: $500 million. Earliest opening would be April 2004.

Philadelphia (NL): New ballpark is in the planning stages. Several key factors for the baseball only, grass-field park, including location and financing, need to be finalized. Ballpark would seat 45,000 and be part of a retail complex. Estimated cost of entire project: $650-675 million but could be less depending on what site is eventually chosen. Earliest Phillies home opener would be April 2004.

St. Louis (NL): New ballpark for the Cardinals is in the planning stages. The proposed site is south of the existing Busch Stadium on the south stadium parking lot. The proposed open-air, baseball-only ballpark would offer a spectacular view of the Gateway Arch. Since the new site partially overlaps the current stadium site, for the first year the park would offer about 40,000 permanent and temporary seats but by year two the stadium would be complete and the seating capacity would grow to 47,900. Estimated cost including a new Cardinals Hall of Fame and Museum is $370 million. Earliest opening would be April 2004.

NBA BASKETBALL

New Jersey (East): New arena for the Nets is in the planning stages. Arena would be located in downtown Newark near Penn Station and would house the Nets and NHL's New Jersey Devils; estimated cost: $355 million. Earliest opening would be fall 2004.

NFL FOOTBALL

Arizona (NFC): New stadium for the Cardinals is in the planning stages. The 67,000-seat (expandable to 73,000) stadium would have a partially retractable roof and wall and feature a grass field that could be rolled out into the adjoining parking lot in order to help it grow. The stadium would include 88 luxury suites and 7,000 club seats; estimated cost: $335 million. Earliest Cardinals home opener would be fall 2004.

NHL HOCKEY

New Jersey (East): New arena for the Devils is in the planning stages. Arena would be located in downtown Newark near Penn Station and would house the Devils and NBA's New Jersey Nets; estimated cost: $355 million. Earliest opening would be fall 2004.

SOCCER

England: Construction of new Wembley National Stadium is getting underway. The roof on the east, south and west sides partly retracts allowing the sunlight to help grass growth and while the roof will provide protection from the elements to all spectators, the field will be left uncovered. Instead of the twin towers, the new stadium's most distinguishing feature will be a giant 400-foot tall arch. New stadium will seat 90,000 and is scheduled to be completed in 2004. Estimated cost: £326 million ($456 million USD).

2005

BASEBALL

Florida (NL): The team is in discussions with the city of Miami involving financing for a new ballpark for the Marlins. Preliminary plans call for a $500 million ballpark to be built in downtown Miami. No realistic timetable has been set forth but the earliest Marlins home opener would likely be no earlier than April 2005.

NFL FOOTBALL

San Francisco (NFC): New stadium for the 49ers is in the early planning stages. The stadium would likely be part of a retail and entertainment complex to be located at Candlestick Point. In 1997, area voters approved a $100 million bond measure to fund a new stadium/mall. Many aspects of the project are yet to be decided including estimated costs, further financing and the actual design. The Earliest 49ers' home opener would be in the fall of 2005.

Home, Sweet Home

The home fields, home courts and home ice of the AL, NL, NBA, NFL, CFL, NHL, WNBA, NCAA Division I-A college football and Division I basketball. Also included are MLS, Formula One, CART, Indy Racing League and NASCAR auto racing tracks.

Attendance figures for the 2000 NFL regular season and the 2000-01 NBA and NHL regular seasons are provided. See Baseball chapter for 2001 AL and NL attendance figures.

MAJOR LEAGUE BASEBALL

American League

	Built	Capacity	LF	LCF	CF	RCF	RF	Field
Anaheim Angels . . . . Edison International Field of Anaheim	1966	**45,050**	365	387	400	370	365	Grass
Baltimore Orioles. . . . . Oriole Park at Camden Yards	1992	**48,262**	337	376	406	391	320	Grass
Boston Red Sox. . . . . Fenway Park	1912	**33,871**	310	379	390*	380	302	Grass
Chicago White Sox . . . . Comiskey Park	1991	**46,943**	330	377	400	372	335	Grass
Cleveland Indians. . . . . Jacobs Field	1994	**43,068**	325	370	405	375	325	Grass
Detroit Tigers . . . . Comerica Park	2000	**40,000**	345	398	420	370	330	Grass
Kansas City Royals . . . . Kauffman Stadium	1973	**40,793**	330	375	400	375	330	Grass
Minnesota Twins. . . . . Hubert H. Humphrey Metrodome	1982	**48,678**	343	385	408	367	327	Turf
New York Yankees. . . . . Yankee Stadium	1923	**57,746**	318	399	408	385	314	Grass
Oakland Athletics. . . . . . Network Associates Coliseum	1966	**43,662**	330	375	400	367	330	Grass
Seattle Mariners . . . . SAFECO Field	1999	**47,116**	331	390	405	386	327	Grass
Tampa Bay Devil Rays . . . . Tropicana Field	1990	**44,445**	315	370	404	370	322	Turf
Texas Rangers. . . . . The Ballpark in Arlington	1994	**49,115**	332	390	400	377	325	Grass
Toronto Blue Jays . . . . SkyDome	1989	**50,516**	328	375	400	375	328	Turf

*The straight-away center-field fence at Fenway Park is 390 feet from home plate but the deepest part of center-field, a.k.a. "the Triangle," is 420 feet away. The left-field fence, known as "the Green Monster," is 37 feet tall topped with a 23-foot screen.

National League

	Built	Capacity	LF	LCF	CF	RCF	RF	Field
Arizona Diamondbacks. . . . . Bank One Ballpark	1998	**49,075**	330	376	407	376	334	Grass
Atlanta Braves . . . . Turner Field	1996	**50,062**	335	380	401	385	330	Grass
Chicago Cubs. . . . . Wrigley Field	1914	**39,086**	355	368	400	368	353	Grass
Cincinnati Reds. Cinergy Field	1970	**40,043**	325	370	393*	373	325	Turf
Colorado Rockies . . . . Coors Field	1995	**50,449**	347	390	415	375	350	Grass
Florida Marlins . . . . Pro Player Stadium	1987	**42,531**	330	385	434	385	345	Grass
Houston Astros. . . . . Enron Field	2000	**40,950**	315	362	436	373	326	Grass
Los Angeles Dodgers . . . . Dodger Stadium	1962	**56,000**	330	385	395	385	330	Grass
Milwaukee Brewers . . . . Miller Park	2001	**42,500**	342	374	400	378	345	Grass
Montreal Expos. . . . . Olympic Stadium	1976	**46,620**	325	375	404	375	325	Turf
New York Mets . . . . Shea Stadium	1964	**56,516**	338	378	410	378	338	Grass
Philadelphia Phillies . . . . Veterans Stadium	1971	**62,418**	330	378	408	378	330	Turf
Pittsburgh Pirates . . . . PNC Park	2001	**37,898**	326	368	399*	375	324	Grass
St. Louis Cardinals. . . . . Busch Stadium	1966	**49,738**	330	372	402	372	330	Grass
San Diego Padres. . . . . Qualcomm Stadium	1967	**66,307**	327	370	405	370	327	Grass
San Francisco Giants . . . . Pacific Bell Park	2000	**41,341**	335	364	404	420	307	Grass

*The deepest part of PNC Park is 410 feet between straight-away center and left-center. The new dimensions of Cinergy field reflect the removal of the part of the left and center field stands to allow construction on the team's new stadium to continue. A 40-foot high wall was installed in center field.

Rank by Capacity

AL		NL	
New York. 57,746		San Diego 66,307	
Toronto. 50,516		Philadelphia 62,418	
Texas 49,115		New York. 56,516	
Minnesota 48,678		Los Angeles 56,000	
Baltimore 48,262		Colorado. 50,449	
Seattle 47,116		Atlanta 50,062	
Chicago. 46,943		St. Louis 49,738	
Anaheim 45,050		Arizona 49,075	
Tampa Bay 44,445		Montreal 46,620	
Oakland 43,662		Florida 42,531	
Cleveland 43,068		Milwaukee. 42,500	
Kansas City 40,793		San Francisco 41,341	
Detroit 40,000		Houston 40,950	
Boston 33,871		Cincinnati 40,043	
		Chicago. 39,086	
		Pittsburgh 37,898	

Rank by Age

AL		NL	
Boston 1912		Chicago. 1914	
New York 1923		Los Angeles 1962	
Anaheim 1966		New York 1964	
Oakland 1966		St. Louis 1966	
Kansas City. 1973		San Diego 1967	
Minnesota 1982		Cincinnati 1970	
Toronto. 1989		Philadelphia 1971	
Tampa Bay 1990		Montreal 1976	
Chicago. 1991		Florida 1987	
Baltimore 1992		Atlanta 1993	
Cleveland 1994		Colorado. 1995	
Texas 1994		Arizona 1998	
Seattle 1999		Houston 2000	
Detroit 2000		San Francisco 2000	
Note: New York's Yankee Stadium (AL) was rebuilt in 1976.		Milwaukee 2001	
		Pittsburgh. 2001	

Home Fields

Listed below are the principal home fields used through the years by current American and National League teams. The NL became a major league in 1876, the AL in 1901.

The capacity figures in the right-hand column indicate the largest seating capacity of the ballpark while the club played there. Capacity figures before 1915 (and the introduction of concrete grandstands) are sketchy at best and have been left blank.

American League

Anaheim Angels
1961	Wrigley Field (Los Angeles)	20,457
1962-65	Dodger Stadium	56,000
1966–	Edison International Field of Anaheim	45,050
	(1966 capacity—43,250)	

Baltimore Orioles
1901	Lloyd Street Grounds (Milwaukee)	
1902–53	Sportsman's Park II (St. Louis)	30,500
1954–91	Memorial Stadium (Baltimore)	53,371
1992–	Oriole Park at Camden Yards	48,262

Boston Red Sox
1901–11	Huntington Ave. Grounds	
1912–	Fenway Park	33,871
	(1934 capacity—27,000)	

Chicago White Sox
1901–10	Southside Park	—
1910–90	Comiskey Park I	43,931
1991–	Comiskey Park II	46,943

Cleveland Indians
1901–09	League Park I	—
1910–46	League Park II	21,414
1932–93	Cleveland Stadium	74,483
1994–	Jacobs Field	43,068

Detroit Tigers
1901–11	Bennett Park	—
1912–99	Tiger Stadium	46,945
2000–	Comerica Park	40,000
	(1912 capacity—23,000)	

Kansas City Royals
1969-72	Municipal Stadium	35,020
1973–	Kauffman Stadium	40,793
	(1973 capacity—40,762)	

Minnesota Twins
1901-02	American League Park (Washington, DC)	—
1903-60	Griffith Stadium	27,410
1960-81	Metropolitan Stadium (Bloomington, MN)	45,919
1982–	HHH Metrodome (Minneapolis)	48,678
	(1982 capacity—54,000)	

New York Yankees
1901–02	Oriole Park (Baltimore)	—
1903–12	Hilltop Park (New York)	—
1913–22	Polo Grounds II	38,000
1923–73	Yankee Stadium I	67,224
1974–75	Shea Stadium	55,101
1976–	Yankee Stadium II	57,746
	(1976 capacity—57,145)	

Oakland Athletics
1901–08	Columbia Park (Philadelphia)	—
1909–54	Shibe Park	33,608
1955–67	Municipal Stadium (Kansas City)	35,020
1968–	Network Associates Coliseum	43,662
	(1968 capacity—48,621)	

Seattle Mariners
1977–99	The Kingdome	59,166
1999–	SAFECO Field	47,116

Tampa Bay Devil Rays
1990–	Tropicana Field	44,445

Texas Rangers
1961	Griffith Stadium (Washington, DC)	27,410
1962–71	RFK Stadium	45,016
1972–93	Arlington Stadium (Texas)	43,521
1994–	The Ballpark in Arlington	49,115

Toronto Blue Jays
1977–89	Exhibition Stadium	43,737
1989–	SkyDome	50,516
	(1989 capacity—49,500)	

Ballpark Name Changes: ANAHEIM—**Edison International Field of Anaheim** originally Anaheim Stadium (1966-98); CHICAGO—**Comiskey Park I** originally White Sox Park (1910-12), then Comiskey Park in 1913, then White Sox Park again in 1962, then Comiskey Park again in 1976; CLEVELAND—**League Park** renamed Dunn Field in 1920, then League Park again in 1928; **Cleveland Stadium** originally Municipal Stadium (1932-74); DETROIT—**Tiger Stadium** originally Navin Field (1912-37), then Briggs Stadium (1938-60); KANSAS CITY—**Kauffman Stadium** originally Royals Stadium (1973-93); LOS ANGELES—**Dodger Stadium** referred to as Chavez Ravine by AL while Angels played there (1962-65); OAKLAND—**Network Associates Coliseum** originally Oakland Alameda Coliseum (1968-98); PHILADELPHIA—**Shibe Park** renamed Connie Mack Stadium in 1953; ST. LOUIS—**Sportsman's Park** renamed Busch Stadium in 1953; WASHINGTON—**Griffith Stadium** originally National Park (1892-1920), **RFK Stadium** originally D.C. Stadium (1961-68).

National League

Arizona Diamondbacks
1998–	Bank One Ballpark	49,075

Atlanta Braves
1876–94	South End Grounds I (Boston)	—
1894–1914	South End Grounds II	—
1915–52	Braves Field	40,000
1953–65	County Stadium (Milwaukee)	43,394
1966–96	Atlanta-Fulton County Stadium	52,769
	(1966 capacity—50,000)	
1997–	Turner Field	50,062

Chicago Cubs
1876–77	State Street Grounds	—
1878–84	Lakefront Park	—
1885–91	West Side Park	—
1891–93	Brotherhood Park	—
1893–1915	West Side Grounds	—
1916–	Wrigley Field	39,086
	(1916 capacity—16,000)	

Cincinnati Reds
1876–79	Avenue Grounds	—
1880	Bank Street Grounds	—
1890–1901	Redland Field I	—
1902–11	Palace of the Fans	—
1912–70	Crosley Field	29,603
1970–	Cinergy Field	40,043
	(1970 capacity—52,000)	

Colorado Rockies
1993–94	Mile High Stadium (Denver)	76,100
1995–	Coors Field	50,449

Florida Marlins
1993–	Pro Player Stadium (Miami)	42,531

Major League Baseball (Cont.)

Houston Astros

1962–64	Colt Stadium	32,601
1965–99	The Astrodome	54,370
	(1965 capacity—45,011)	
2000–	Enron Field	40,950

Los Angeles Dodgers

1890	Washington Park I (Brooklyn)	—
1891–97	Eastern Park	—
1898–1912	Washington Park II	—
1913–56	Ebbets Field	31,497
1957	Ebbets Field	31,497
	& Roosevelt Stadium (Jersey City)	24,167
1958–61	Memorial Coliseum (Los Angeles)	93,600
1962–	Dodger Stadium	56,000

Milwaukee Brewers

1969	Sick's Stadium (Seattle)	59,166
1970–	County Stadium (Milwaukee)	53,192
2000	(1970 capacity—46,620)	
2001–	Miller Park	42,500

Montreal Expos

1969–76	Jarry Park	28,000
1977–	Olympic Stadium	46,620
	(1977 capacity—58,500)	

New York Mets

1962–63	Polo Grounds	55,987
1964–	Shea Stadium	56,516
	(1964 capacity—55,101)	

Philadelphia Phillies

1883–86	Recreation Park	—
1887–94	Huntingdon Ave. Grounds	—
1895–1938	Baker Bowl	18,800
1938–70	Shibe Park	33,608
1971–	Veterans Stadium	62,418
	(1971 capacity—56,371)	

Pittsburgh Pirates

1887–90	Recreation Park	—
1891–1909	Exposition Park	—
1909–70	Forbes Field	35,000
1970–2000	Three Rivers Stadium	47,687
	(1970 capacity—50,235)	
2001–	PNC Park	37,898

St. Louis Cardinals

1876–77	Sportsman's Park I	—
1885–86	Vandeventer Lot	—
1892–1920	Robison Field	18,000
1920–66	Sportsman's Park II	30,500
1966–	Busch Stadium	49,738
	(1966 capacity—50,126)	

San Diego Padres

1969–	Qualcomm Stadium	66,307
	(1969 capacity—47,634)	

San Francisco Giants

1876	Union Grounds (Brooklyn)	—
1883–88	Polo Grounds I (New York)	—
1889–90	Manhattan Field	—
1891–1957	Polo Grounds II	55,987
1958–59	Seals Stadium (San Francisco)	22,900
1960–99	3Com Park	63,000
	(1960 capacity—42,553)	
2000–	Pacific Bell Park	41,341

Ballpark Name Changes: ATLANTA—**Atlanta-Fulton County Stadium** originally Atlanta Stadium (1966-74), **Turner Field** originally Centennial Olympic Stadium (1996); CHICAGO—**Wrigley Field** originally Weeghman Park (1914-17), then Cubs Park (1918-25); CINCINNATI—**Redland Field** originally League Park (1890-93), **Crosley Field** originally Redland Field II (1912-33) and **Cinergy Field** originally Riverfront Stadium (1970-96); FLORIDA—**Pro Player Stadium** originally Joe Robbie Stadium (1987-96); HOUSTON—**Astrodome** originally Harris County Domed Stadium before it opened in 1965; PHILADELPHIA—**Shibe Park** renamed Connie Mack Stadium in 1953; ST. LOUIS—**Robison Field** originally Vandeventer Lot, then League Park, then Cardinal Park all before becoming Robison Field in 1901, **Sportsman's Park** renamed Busch Stadium in 1953, and **Busch Stadium** originally Busch Memorial Stadium (1966-82); SAN DIEGO—**Qualcomm Stadium** originally San Diego Stadium (1967-81) and San Diego/Jack Murphy Stadium (1982-96); SAN FRANCISCO—**3Com Park** originally Candlestick Park (1960-95).

NATIONAL BASKETBALL ASSOCIATION

Western Conference

		Location	Built	Capacity
Dallas Mavericks	**American Airlines Center**	Dallas, Texas	2001	**19,200**
Denver Nuggets	**Pepsi Center**	Denver, Colo.	1999	**19,099**
Golden State Warriors	**The Arena in Oakland**	Oakland, Calif.	1997	**19,596**
Houston Rockets	**Compaq Center**	Houston, Texas	1975	**16,285**
Los Angeles Clippers	**Staples Center**	Los Angeles, Calif.	1999	**18,694**
Los Angeles Lakers	**Staples Center**	Los Angeles, Calif.	1999	**18,997**
Memphis Grizzlies	**The Pyramid**	Memphis, Tenn.	1990	**22,000**
Minnesota Timberwolves	**Target Center**	Minneapolis, Minn.	1990	**19,006**
Phoenix Suns	**America West Arena**	Phoenix, Ariz.	1992	**19,023**
Portland Trail Blazers	**Rose Garden**	Portland, Ore.	1995	**19,980**
Sacramento Kings	**ARCO Arena**	Sacramento, Calif.	1988	**17,317**
San Antonio Spurs	**The Alamodome**	San Antonio, Texas	1993	**20,557**
Seattle SuperSonics	**KeyArena at Seattle Center**	Seattle, Wash.	1962	**17,072**
Utah Jazz	**Delta Center**	Salt Lake City, Utah	1991	**19,911**

Notes: Seattle's KeyArena was originally the Seattle Coliseum before being rebuilt in 1995; San Antonio's Alamodome seating is expandable to 34,215 while Portland's Rose Garden was "downsized" from a capacity of 21,538 to 19,980 prior to the 1998-99 season. The Staples Center has different listed capacities for Clippers games and Lakers games because of different floor seating arrangements. The Pyramid's exact capacity for the Grizzlies' inaugural season in Memphis has not been finalized.

Eastern Conference

		Location	Built	Capacity
Atlanta Hawks	**Philips Arena**	Atlanta, Ga.	1999	**19,445**
Boston Celtics	**FleetCenter**	Boston, Mass.	1995	**18,624**
Charlotte Hornets	**Charlotte Coliseum**	Charlotte, N.C.	1988	**19,925**
Chicago Bulls	**United Center**	Chicago, Ill.	1994	**21,711**
Cleveland Cavaliers	**Gund Arena**	Cleveland, Ohio	1994	**20,562**
Detroit Pistons	**The Palace of Auburn Hills**	Auburn Hills, Mich.	1988	**22,076**
Indiana Pacers	**Conseco Fieldhouse**	Indianapolis, Ind.	1999	**18,345**
Miami Heat	**AmericanAirlines Arena**	Miami, Fla.	1999	**16,500**
Milwaukee Bucks	**Bradley Center**	Milwaukee, Wisc.	1988	**18,717**
New Jersey Nets	**Continental Airlines Arena**	E. Rutherford, N.J.	1981	**20,049**
New York Knicks	**Madison Square Garden**	New York, N.Y.	1968	**19,763**
Orlando Magic	**TD Waterhouse Centre**	Orlando, Fla.	1989	**17,306**
Philadelphia 76ers	**First Union Center**	Philadelphia, Penn.	1996	**20,444**
Toronto Raptors	**Air Canada Centre**	Toronto, Ont.	1999	**19,800**
Washington Wizards	**MCI Center**	Washington, D.C.	1997	**20,674**

Rank by Capacity

West		East	
Memphis	22,000	Detroit	22,076
San Antonio	20,557	Chicago	21,711
Portland	19,980	Washington	20,674
Utah	19,911	Cleveland	20,562
Golden State	19,596	Philadelphia	20,444
Dallas	19,200	New Jersey	20,049
Denver	19,099	Charlotte	19,925
Phoenix	19,023	Toronto	19,800
Minnesota	19,006	New York	19,763
LA Lakers	18,997	Atlanta	19,445
LA Clippers	18,694	Milwaukee	18,717
Sacramento	17,317	Boston	18,624
Seattle	17,072	Indiana	18,345
Houston	16,285	Orlando	17,306
		Miami	16,500

Note: Alamodome seating is expandable to 32,500. Exact capacity for the Memphis Grizzlies has yet to be determined.

Rank by Age

West		East	
Seattle	1962	New York	1968
Houston	1975	New Jersey	1981
Sacramento	1988	Charlotte	1988
Memphis	1990	Detroit	1988
Minnesota	1990	Milwaukee	1988
Utah	1991	Orlando	1989
Phoenix	1992	Chicago	1994
San Antonio	1993	Cleveland	1994
Portland	1995	Boston	1995
Golden St.	1997	Philadelphia	1996
Denver	1999	Washington	1997
LA Clippers	1999	Toronto	1999
LA Lakers	1999	Atlanta	1999
Dallas	2001	Indiana	1999
		Miami	1999

Note: The Seattle Coliseum was rebuilt and renamed KeyArena in 1995.

2000-01 NBA Attendance

Official overall attendance in the NBA for the 2000-01 season was 19,955,981 for an average per game crowd of 16,784 over 1,189 games. Teams in each conference are ranked by attendance over 41 home games based on total tickets distributed; sellouts are listed in S/O column. Numbers in parentheses indicate rank in 2000.

Western Conference

	Attendance	S/O	Average
1 San Antonio (1)	913,175	2	22,273
2 Portland (2)	831,385	41	20,278
3 Utah (3)	792,196	14	19,322
4 LA Lakers (5)	776,336	39	18,935
5 Phoenix (4)	737,586	10	17,990
6 Minnesota (7)	717,371	8	17,497
7 Sacramento (6)	709,997	41	17,317
8 Dallas (11)	680,138	20	16,589
9 Seattle (10)	640,847	17	15,630
10 Denver (8)	619,300	3	15,105
11 LA Clippers (13)	599,448	11	14,621
12 Golden St. (14)	591,981	1	14,439
13 Vancouver (12)	563,218	2	13,737
14 Houston (9)	518,555	4	12,648
TOTAL	9,691,533	213	16,884

Note: Vancouver moved to Memphis before the 2001-02 season.

Eastern Conference

	Attendance	S/O	Average
1 Chicago (1)	888,654	22	21,674
2 New York (2)	810,283	41	19,763
3 Philadelphia (3)	805,692	18	19,651
4 Toronto (4)	793,256	27	19,348
5 Indiana (5)	733,444	25	17,889
6 Milwaukee (11)	683,125	15	16,662
7 Miami (7)	677,186	20	16,517
8 Cleveland (13)	650,775	4	15,873
9 Washington (12)	638,653	7	15,577
10 Boston (8)	629,201	7	15,346
11 Charlotte (6)	615,424	3	15,010
12 Detroit (9)	607,323	3	14,813
13 Orlando (15)	605,031	6	14,757
14 New Jersey (10)	566,077	4	13,807
15 Atlanta (14)	560,324	2	13,666
TOTAL	10,264,448	204	15,700

National Basketball Association (Cont.)
Home Courts

Listed below are the principal home courts used through the years by current NBA teams. The largest capacity of each arena is noted in the right-hand column. ABA arenas (1967-76) are included for Denver, Indiana, New Jersey and San Antonio.

Western Conference

Dallas Mavericks

1980–2000	Reunion Arena	18,187
2001–	American Airlines Center	19,200

Denver Nuggets

1967–75	Auditorium Arena	6,841
1975–99	McNichols Sports Arena	17,171
	(1975 capacity—16,700)	
1999–	Pepsi Center	19,099

Golden State Warriors

1946–52	Philadelphia Arena	7,777
1952–62	Convention Hall (Philadelphia)	9,200
	& Philadelphia Arena	7,777
1962–64	Cow Palace (San Francisco)	13,862
1964–66	Civic Auditorium	7,500
	& (USF Memorial Gym)	6,000
1966–67	Cow Palace, Civic Auditorium	
	& Oakland Coliseum Arena	15,000
1967–71	Cow Palace	14,500
1971–96	Oakland Coliseum Arena	15,025
	(1971 capacity—12,905)	
1996–97	San Jose Arena	18,500
1997–	The Arena in Oakland	19,596

Houston Rockets

1967–71	San Diego Sports Arena	14,000
1971–72	Hofheinz Pavilion (Houston)	10,218
1972–73	Hofheinz Pavilion	10,218
	& HemisFair Arena (San Antonio)	10,446
1973–75	Hofheinz Pavilion	10,218
1975–	Compaq Center	16,285
	(1975 capacity—15,600)	

Los Angeles Clippers

1970–78	Memorial Auditorium (Buffalo)	17,300
1978–84	San Diego Sports Arena	12,167
1985–94	Los Angeles Sports Arena	16,005
1994–99	Los Angeles Sports Arena	16,021
	& Arrowhead Pond	18,211
1999–	Staples Center	18,694

Los Angeles Lakers

1948–60	Minneapolis Auditorium	10,000
1960–67	Los Angeles Sports Arena	14,781
1967–99	Great Western Forum (Inglewood, CA)	17,505
	(1967 capacity—17,086)	
1999–	Staples Center	18,997

Memphis Grizzlies

1995–2001	General Motors Place (Vancouver)	19,193
2001–	The Pyramid (Memphis, TN)	22,000

Minnesota Timberwolves

1989–90	Hubert H. Humphrey Metrodome	23,000
1990–	Target Center	19,006

Phoenix Suns

1968–92	Arizona Veterans' Memorial Coliseum	14,487
1992–	America West Arena	19,023

Portland Trail Blazers

1970–95	Memorial Coliseum	12,888
1995–	Rose Garden	19,980
	(1995 capacity—21,538)	

Sacramento Kings

1948–55	Edgarton Park Arena (Rochester, NY)	5,000
1955–58	Rochester War Memorial	10,000
1958–72	Cincinnati Gardens	11,438
1972–74	Municipal Auditorium (Kansas City)	9,929
	& Omaha (NE) Civic Auditorium	9,136
1974–78	Kemper Arena (Kansas City)	16,785
	& Omaha Civic Auditorium	9,136
1978–85	Kemper Arena	16,785
1985–88	ARCO Arena I	10,333
1988–	ARCO Arena II	17,317
	(1988 capacity—16,517)	

San Antonio Spurs

1967–70	Memorial Auditorium (Dallas)	8,088
	& Moody Coliseum (Dallas)	8,500
1970–71	Moody Coliseum	8,500
	Tarrant Convention Center (Ft. Worth)	13,500
	& Municipal Coliseum (Lubbock)	10,400
1971–73	Moody Coliseum	9,500
	& Memorial Auditorium	8,088
1973–93	HemisFair Arena (San Antonio)	16,057
1993–	The Alamodome	20,557

Seattle SuperSonics

1967–78	Seattle Center Coliseum	14,098
1978–85	Kingdome	40,192
1985–94	Seattle Center Coliseum	14,252
1994–95	Tacoma Dome	19,000
1995–	KeyArena at Seattle Center	17,072

Utah Jazz

1974–75	Municipal Auditorium (New Orleans)	7,853
	& Louisiana Superdome	47,284
1975–79	Superdome	47,284
1979–83	Salt Palace (Salt Lake City)	12,519
1983–84	Salt Palace	12,519
	& Thomas & Mack Center (Las Vegas)	18,500
1984–91	Salt Palace	12,616
1991–	Delta Center	19,911

Eastern Conference

Atlanta Hawks

1949–51	Wharton Field House (Moline, IL)	6,000
1951–55	Milwaukee Arena	11,000
1955–68	Kiel Auditorium (St. Louis)	10,000
1968–72	Alexander Mem. Coliseum (Atlanta)	7,166
1972–96	The Omni	16,378
1997–99	Georgia Dome	21,570
	& Alexander Mem. Coliseum	9,300
1999–	Philips Arena	19,445

Boston Celtics

1946–95	Boston Garden	14,890
1995–	FleetCenter	18,624

Note: From 1975-95 the Celtics played some regular season games at the Hartford Civic Center (15,418).

Charlotte Hornets

1988–	Charlotte Coliseum	19,925
	(1988 capacity—23,500)	

Chicago Bulls

1966–67	Chicago Amphitheater	11,002
1967–94	Chicago Stadium	18,676
1994–	United Center	21,711

Cleveland Cavaliers

1970–74	Cleveland Arena	11,000
1974–94	The Coliseum (Richfield, OH)	20,273
1994–	Gund Arena	20,562

Detroit Pistons

1948–52	North Side H.S. Gym (Ft. Wayne, IN)	3,800
1952–57	Memorial Coliseum (Ft. Wayne)	9,306
1957–61	Olympia Stadium (Detroit)	14,000
1961–78	Cobo Arena	11,147
1978–88	Silverdome (Pontiac, MI)	22,366
1988–	The Palace of Auburn Hills	22,076

Indiana Pacers

1967–74	State Fairgrounds (Indianapolis)	9,479
1974–99	Market Square Arena	16,530
	(1974 capacity—17,287)	
1999–	Conseco Fieldhouse	18,345

Miami Heat

1988–99	Miami Arena	15,200
2000–	AmericanAirlines Arena	16,500

Milwaukee Bucks

1968–88	Milwaukee Arena (The Mecca)	11,052
1988–	Bradley Center	18,717

New Jersey Nets

1967–68	Teaneck (NJ) Armory	3,500
1968–69	Long Island Arena (Commack, NY)	6,500
1969–71	Island Garden (W. Hempstead, NY)	5,200
1971–77	Nassau Coliseum (Uniondale, NY)	15,500
1977–81	Rutgers Ath. Center (Piscataway, NJ)	9,050
1981–	Continental Airlines Arena (E. Ruth., NJ)	20,049

New York Knicks

1946–68	Madison Sq. Garden III (50th St.)	18,496
1968–	Madison Sq. Garden IV (33rd St.)	19,763
	(1968 capacity—19,694)	

Orlando Magic

1989–	TD Waterhouse Centre	17,306

Philadelphia 76ers

1949–51	State Fair Coliseum (Syracuse, NY)	7,500
1951–63	Onondaga County (NY) War Memorial	8,000
1963–67	Convention Hall (Philadelphia)	12,000
	& Philadelphia Arena	7,777
1967–96	CoreStates Spectrum	18,136
1996–	First Union Center	20,444

Toronto Raptors

1995–99	SkyDome	20,125
1999–	Air Canada Centre	19,800

Washington Wizards

1961–62	Chicago Amphitheater	11,000
1962–63	Chicago Coliseum	7,100
1963–73	Baltimore Civic Center	12,289
1973–97	USAir Arena (Landover, MD)	18,756
1997–	MCI Center	20,674

Note: From 1988-96 the Wizards (then Bullets) played four regular season games at Baltimore Arena (12,756).

Building Name Changes: HOUSTON—**Compaq Center** originally The Summit (1975-97); NEW JERSEY—**Continental Airlines Arena** originally Byrne Meadowlands Arena (1981-96); ORLANDO—**TD Waterhouse Centre** originally Orlando Arena (1989-99); PHILADELPHIA—**First Union Center** originally the CoreStates Center (1996-98) and **CoreStates Spectrum** originally The Spectrum (1967-94); WASHINGTON- **USAir Arena** originally Capital Centre (1973-93).

NATIONAL FOOTBALL LEAGUE

American Football Conference

		Location	Built	Capacity	Field
Baltimore Ravens	**PSInet Stadium**	Baltimore, Md.	1998	**69,084**	Grass
Buffalo Bills	**Ralph Wilson Stadium**	Orchard Park, N.Y.	1973	**73,967**	Turf
Cincinnati Bengals	**Paul Brown Stadium**	Cincinnati, Ohio	2000	**65,393**	Grass
Cleveland Browns	**Cleveland Browns Stadium**	Cleveland, Ohio	1999	**73,200**	Grass
Denver Broncos	**INVESCO Field at Mile High**	Denver, Colo.	2001	**76,125**	Grass
Indianapolis Colts	**RCA Dome**	Indianapolis, Ind.	1984	**56,127**	Turf
Jacksonville Jaguars	**ALLTEL Stadium**	Jacksonville, Fla.	1995	**73,000**	Grass
Kansas City Chiefs	**Arrowhead Stadium**	Kansas City, Mo.	1972	**78,451**	Grass
Miami Dolphins	**Pro Player Stadium**	Miami, Fla.	1987	**74,916**	Grass
New England Patriots	**Foxboro Stadium**	Foxboro, Mass.	1971	**60,292**	Grass
New York Jets	**Giants Stadium**	E. Rutherford, N.J.	1976	**79,466**	Grass
Oakland Raiders	**Network Associates Coliseum**	Oakland, Calif.	1966	**63,142**	Grass
Pittsburgh Steelers	**Heinz Field**	Pittsburgh, Pa.	2001	**65,000**	Grass
San Diego Chargers	**Qualcomm Stadium**	San Diego, Calif.	1967	**71,000**	Grass
Seattle Seahawks	**Husky Stadium**	Seattle, Wash.	1920	**72,500**	Turf
Tennessee Titans	**Adelphia Coliseum**	Nashville, Tenn.	1999	**67,000**	Grass

National Football Conference

		Location	Built	Capacity	Field
Arizona Cardinals	**Sun Devil Stadium**	Tempe, Ariz.	1958	**73,273**	Grass
Atlanta Falcons	**Georgia Dome**	Atlanta, Ga.	1992	**71,228**	Turf
Carolina Panthers	**Ericsson Stadium**	Charlotte, N.C.	1996	**72,350**	Grass
Chicago Bears	**Soldier Field**	Chicago, Ill.	1924	**66,944**	Grass
Dallas Cowboys	**Texas Stadium**	Irving, Texas	1971	**65,675**	Turf
Detroit Lions	**Pontiac Silverdome**	Pontiac, Mich.	1975	**80,311**	Turf
Green Bay Packers	**Lambeau Field**	Green Bay, Wis.	1957	**60,790**	Grass
Minnesota Vikings	**Hubert H. Humphrey Metrodome**	Minneapolis, Minn.	1982	**64,121**	Turf
New Orleans Saints	**Louisiana Superdome**	New Orleans, La.	1975	**70,200**	Turf
New York Giants	**Giants Stadium**	E. Rutherford, N.J.	1976	**79,469**	Grass
Philadelphia Eagles	**Veterans Stadium**	Philadelphia, Pa.	1971	**65,356**	Turf
St. Louis Rams	**The Dome at America's Center**	St. Louis, Mo.	1995	**66,000**	Turf
San Francisco 49ers	**3Com Park**	San Francisco, Calif.	1960	**69,734**	Grass
Tampa Bay Buccaneers	**Raymond James Stadium**	Tampa, Fla.	1998	**66,321**	Grass
Washington Redskins	**FedEx Field**	Raljon, Md.	1997	**80,166**	Grass

National Football League (Cont.)

Rank by Capacity

AFC		NFC	
NY Jets	.79,466	Detroit	.80,311
Kansas City	.78,451	Washington	.80,166
Denver	.76,125	NY Giants	.79,469
Miami	.74,916	Arizona	.73,273
Buffalo	.73,967	Carolina	.72,350
Cleveland	.73,200	Atlanta	.71,228
Jacksonville	.73,000	New Orleans	.70,200
Seattle	.72,500	San Francisco	.69,734
San Diego	.71,000	Chicago	.66,944
Baltimore	.69,084	Tampa Bay	.66,321
Tennessee	.67,000	St. Louis	.66,000
Cincinnati	.65,393	Dallas	.65,675
Pittsburgh	.65,000	Philadelphia	.65,356
Oakland	.63,142	Minnesota	.64,121
New England	.60,292	Green Bay	.60,790
Indianapolis	.56,127		

Rank by Age

AFC		NFC	
Seattle	.1920	Chicago	.1924
Oakland	.1966	Green Bay	.1957
San Diego	.1967	Arizona	.1958
New England	.1971	San Francisco	.1960
Kansas City	.1972	Dallas	.1971
Buffalo	.1973	Philadelphia	.1971
NY Jets	.1976	New Orleans	.1975
Indianapolis	.1984	Detroit	.1975
Miami	.1987	NY Giants	.1976
Jacksonville	.1995	Minnesota	.1982
Baltimore	.1998	Atlanta	.1992
Cleveland	.1999	St. Louis	.1995
Tennessee	.1999	Carolina	.1996
Cincinnati	.2000	Washington	.1997
Denver	.2001	Tampa Bay	.1998
Pittsburgh	.2001		

2000 NFL Attendance

Official overall paid attendance in the NFL for the 2000 season was 15,866,123 for an average per game crowd of 63,971 over 248 games. Teams in each conference are ranked by attendance over eight home games. Rank column indicates rank in entire league. Numbers in parentheses indicate conference rank in 2000.

AFC

		Attendance	Rank	Average
1	Kansas City (1)	.631,365	2	78,921
2	N.Y. Jets (6)	.623,711	3	77,964
3	Denver (4)	.604,042	5	75,505
4	Miami (2)	.589,909	6	73,739
5	Cleveland (3)	.585,600	7	73,200
6	Buffalo (5)	.555,695	8	69,462
7	Tennessee (9)	.547,528	10	68,441
8	Seattle (11)	.508,367	16	63,546
9	Baltimore (7)	.482,890	19	60,361
10	Jacksonville (8)	.482,510	20	60,314
11	New England (12)	.482,336	21	60,292
12	Cincinnati (15)	.469,992	23	58,749
13	Oakland (16)	.462,515	25	57,814
14	Indianapolis (13)	.454,312	26	56,789
15	Pittsburgh (14)	.440,428	27	55,054
16	San Diego (10)	.433,459	28	54,182
	TOTAL	.8,345,659	—	65,271

NFC

		Attendance	Rank	Average
1	Washington (2)	.647,423	1	80,928
2	Detroit (3)	.607,080	4	75,885
3	NY Giants (1)	.554,395	9	69,299
4	Chicago (12)	.535,552	11	66,944
5	St. Louis (6)	.528,402	12	66,050
6	Tampa Bay (5)	.524,775	13	65,597
7	Philadelphia (7)	.523,531	14	65,441
8	Minnesota (9)	.513,322	15	64,165
9	Dallas (8)	.504,360	17	63,045
10	New Orleans (15)	.504,315	18	63,039
11	Green Bay (13)	.478,747	22	59,843
12	San Francisco (4)	.467,923	24	58,490
13	Atlanta (11)	.422,814	29	52,852
14	Arizona (14)	.359,709	30	44,964
15	Carolina (10)	.348,116	31	43,515
	TOTAL	.7,520,464	—	62,670

Home Fields

Listed below are the principal home fields used through the years by current NFL teams. The largest capacity of each stadium is noted in the right-hand column. All-America Football Conference stadiums (1946-49) are included for Cleveland and San Francisco.

AFC

Baltimore Ravens

1996–97	Memorial Stadium	.65,000
1998–	PSInet Stadium	.69,084

Buffalo Bills

1960–72	War Memorial Stadium	.45,748
1973–	Ralph Wilson Stadium (Orchard Park, NY)	.73,967
	(1973 capacity—80,020)	

Cincinnati Bengals

1968–69	Nippert Stadium (Univ. of Cincinnati)	.26,500
1970–99	Cinergy Field	.60,389
	(1970 capacity—56,200)	
2000–	Paul Brown Stadium	.65,393

Cleveland Browns

1946–95	Cleveland Stadium	.78,512
	(1946 capacity—85,703)	
1999–	Cleveland Browns Stadium	.73,200

Denver Broncos

1960–	Mile High Stadium	.76,123
2000	(1960 capacity—34,000)	
2001–	INVESCO Field at Mile High	.76,125

Indianapolis Colts

1953–83	Memorial Stadium (Baltimore)	.60,020
1984–	RCA Dome (Indianapolis)	.56,127
	(1984 capacity—60,127)	

Jacksonville Jaguars

1995–	ALLTEL Stadium	.73,000

Kansas City Chiefs

1960–62	Cotton Bowl (Dallas)	.72,000
1963–71	Municipal Stadium (Kansas City)	.47,000
1972–	Arrowhead Stadium	.78,451
	(1972 capacity—78,097)	

Miami Dolphins

1966–86	Orange Bowl	.75,206
1987–	Pro Player Stadium	.74,916
	(1987 capacity—75,500)	

New England Patriots

1960–62	Nickerson Field (Boston Univ.)	.17,369
1963–68	Fenway Park	.33,379
1969	Alumni Stadium (Boston College)	.26,000
1970	Harvard Stadium	.37,300
1971–	Foxboro Stadium	.60,292
	(1971 capacity—61,114)	

New York Jets

1960–63	Polo Grounds	.55,987
1964–83	Shea Stadium	.60,372
1984–	Giants Stadium (E. Rutherford, NJ)	.79,466

Oakland Raiders

1960	Kesar Stadium (San Francisco)	.59,636
1961	Candlestick Park	.42,500
1962–65	Frank Youell Field (Oakland)	.20,000
1966–81	Oakland-Alameda County Coliseum	.54,587
1982–94	Memorial Coliseum (Los Angeles)	.67,800
1995–	Network Associates Coliseum	.63,142

Pittsburgh Steelers

1933–57	Forbes Field	.35,000
1958–63	Forbes Field	.35,000
	& Pitt Stadium	.54,500
1964–69	Pitt Stadium	.54,500
1970–	Three Rivers Stadium	.59,600
2000	(1970 capacity—49,000)	
2001–	Heinz Field	.65,000

San Diego Chargers

1960	Memorial Coliseum (Los Angeles)	.92,604
1961–66	Balboa Stadium (San Diego)	.34,000
1967–	Qualcomm Stadium	.71,000
	(1967 capacity—54,000)	

Seattle Seahawks

1976–94	Kingdome	.66,000
1994	Kingdome	.66,400
	& Husky Stadium	.72,500
1995–99	Kingdome	.66,400
2000–	Husky Stadium	.72,500

Tennessee Titans

1960–64	Jeppesen Stadium (Houston)	.23,500
1965–67	Rice Stadium (Rice Univ.)	.70,000
1968–96	Astrodome	.59,969
1997	Liberty Bowl (Memphis)	.62,380
1998	Vanderbilt Stadium (Nashville)	.41,600
1999–	Adelphia Coliseum (Nashville)	.67,000

Ballpark Name Changes: BALTIMORE—**PSInet Stadium** originally Ravens' Stadium (1998-99); BUFFALO—**Ralph Wilson Stadium** originally Rich Stadium (1973-99); CINCINNATI—**Cinergy Field** originally Riverfront Stadium (1970-96); CLEVELAND—**Cleveland Stadium** originally Municipal Stadium (1932-74); DENVER—**Mile High Stadium** originally Bears Stadium (1948-66); INDIANAPOLIS—**RCA Dome** originally Hoosier Dome (1984-94); JACKSONVILLE—**ALLTEL Stadium** originally Jacksonville Municipal Stadium (1995-97); MIAMI—**Pro Player Stadium** originally Joe Robbie Stadium (1987-96); NEW ENGLAND—**Foxboro Stadium** originally Schaefer Stadium (1971-82), then Sullivan Stadium (1983-89); OAKLAND—**Network Associates Coliseum** originally Oakland Alameda Coliseum (1995-99); SAN DIEGO—**Qualcomm Stadium** originally San Diego Stadium (1967-81) then San Diego/Jack Murphy Stadium (1981-96).

NFC

Arizona Cardinals

1920–21	Normal Field (Chicago)	.7,500
1922–25	Comiskey Park	.28,000
1926–28	Normal Field	.7,500
1929–59	Comiskey Park	.52,000
1960–65	Busch Stadium (St. Louis)	.34,000
1966–87	Busch Memorial Stadium	.54,392
1988–	Sun Devil Stadium (Tempe, AZ)	.73,273

Atlanta Falcons

1966–91	Atlanta Fulton County Stadium	.59,643
1992–	Georgia Dome	.71,228

Carolina Panthers

1995	Memorial Stadium (Clemson, SC)	.81,473
1996–	Ericsson Stadium	.72,350

Chicago Bears

1920	Staley Field (Decatur, IL)	—
1921–70	Wrigley Field (Chicago)	.37,741
1971–	Soldier Field	.66,944
	(1971 capacity—55,049)	

Dallas Cowboys

1960–70	Cotton Bowl	.72,132
1971–	Texas Stadium (Irving, TX)	.65,675
	(1971 capacity—65,101)	

Detroit Lions

1930–33	Spartan Stadium (Portsmouth, OH)	.8,200
1934–37	Univ. of Detroit Stadium	.25,000
1938–74	Tiger Stadium	.54,468
1975–	Pontiac Silverdome	.80,311
	(1975 capacity—80,638)	

Green Bay Packers

1921–22	Hagemeister Brewery Park	—
1923–24	Bellevue Park	—
1925–56	City Stadium I	.24,800
1957–	Lambeau Field	.60,790
	(1957 capacity—32,150)	

Note: The Packers played games in Milwaukee from 1933-94: at Borchert Field, State Fair Park and Marquette Stadium (1933-52), and County Stadium (1953-94).

Minnesota Vikings

1961–81	Metropolitan Stadium (Bloomington)	.48,446
1982–	HHH Metrodome (Minneapolis)	.64,121
	(1982 capacity—62,220)	

New Orleans Saints

1967–74	Tulane Stadium	.80,997
1975–	Louisiana Superdome	.70,200
	(1975 capacity—74,472)	

New York Giants

1925–55	Polo Grounds II	.55,200
1956–73	Yankee Stadium I	.63,800
1973–74	Yale Bowl (New Haven, CT)	.70,896
1975	Shea Stadium	.60,372
1976–	Giants Stadium (E. Rutherford, NJ)	.79,469
	(1976 capacity—76,800)	

Philadelphia Eagles

1933–35	Baker Bowl	.18,800
1936–39	Municipal Stadium	.73,702
1940	Shibe Park	.33,608
1941	Municipal Stadium	.73,702
1942	Shibe Park	.33,608
1943	Forbes Field (Pittsburgh)	.34,528
1944–57	Shibe Park	.33,608
1958–70	Franklin Field (Univ. of Penn.)	.60,546
1971–	Veterans Stadium	.65,356
	(1971 capacity—65,000)	

St. Louis Rams

1937–42	Municipal Stadium (Cleveland)	.85,703
1937	League Park (Cleveland)	—
1938	Shaw Stadium (Cleveland)	—
1937	League Park	—
1943	Suspended operations for one year.	
1944–45	Municipal Stadium	.85,703
1946–79	Memorial Coliseum (Los Angeles)	.92,604
1980–94	Anaheim Stadium	.69,008
1995	Busch Stadium	.60,000
1995–	The Dome at America's Center	.66,000

San Francisco 49ers

1946–70	Kezar Stadium	.59,636
1971–	3Com Park	.69,734
	(1971 capacity—61,246)	

Tampa Bay Buccaneers

1976–97	Houlihan's Stadium	.74,300
1998–	Raymond James Stadium	.66,321

National Football League (Cont.)
Washington Redskins

1932	Braves Field (Boston)	40,000
1933–36	Fenway Park	27,000
1937–60	Griffith Stadium (Washington, DC)	35,000

1961–97	RFK Stadium	56,454
1997–	FedEx Field (Raljon, MD)	80,166

Ballpark Name Changes: ATLANTA—**Atlanta-Fulton County Stadium** originally Atlanta Stadium (1966-74); CHICAGO— **Wrigley Field** originally Cubs Park (1916-25); DETROIT—**Tiger Stadium** originally Navin Field (1912-37), then Briggs Stadium (1938-60), also, **Pontiac Silverdome** originally Pontiac Metropolitan Stadium (1975); GREEN BAY—**Lambeau Field** originally City Stadium II (1957-64); PHILADELPHIA—**Shibe Park** renamed Connie Mack Stadium in 1953; ST. LOUIS—**Busch Memorial Stadium** renamed Busch Stadium in 1983, **The Dome at America's Center** originally Trans World Dome (1995-99); SAN FRANCISCO—**3Com Park** originally Candlestick Park (1960-94); TAMPA BAY—**Raymond James Stadium** originally Tampa Stadium (1976-96), then **Houlihan's Stadium** (1996-98); WASHINGTON—**RFK Stadium** originally D.C. Stadium (1961-68), also, **FedEx Field** originally Jack Kent Cooke Stadium (1997-99).

NATIONAL HOCKEY LEAGUE
Western Conference

		Location	Built	Capacity
Anaheim, Mighty Ducks of	**Arrowhead Pond**	Anaheim, Calif.	1993	**17,174**
Calgary Flames	**Pengrowth Saddledome**	Calgary, Alb.	1983	**17,135**
Chicago Blackhawks	**United Center**	Chicago, Ill.	1994	**20,500**
Colorado Avalanche	**Pepsi Center**	Denver, Colo.	1999	**18,007**
Columbus Blue Jackets	**Nationwide Arena**	Columbus, Ohio	2000	**18,524**
Dallas Stars	**American Airlines Center**	Dallas, Texas	2001	**18,600**
Detroit Red Wings	**Joe Louis Arena**	Detroit, Mich.	1979	**19,983**
Edmonton Oilers	**Skyreach Centre**	Edmonton, Alb.	1974	**17,100**
Los Angeles Kings	**Staples Center**	Los Angeles, Calif.	1999	**18,118**
Minnesota Wild	**Xcel Energy Center**	St. Paul, Minn.	2000	**18,064**
Nashville Predators	**Gaylord Entertainment Center**	Nashville, Tenn.	1994	**17,113**
Phoenix Coyotes	**America West Arena**	Phoenix, Ariz.	1992	**16,210**
St. Louis Blues	**Savvis Center**	St. Louis, Mo.	1994	**19,022**
San Jose Sharks	**Compaq Center at San Jose**	San Jose, Calif.	1993	**17,496**
Vancouver Canucks	**General Motors Place**	Vancouver, B.C.	1995	**18,422**

Eastern Conference

		Location	Built	Capacity
Atlanta Thrashers	**Philips Arena**	Atlanta, Ga.	1999	**18,545**
Boston Bruins	**FleetCenter**	Boston, Mass.	1995	**17,565**
Buffalo Sabres	**HSBC Arena**	Buffalo, N.Y.	1996	**18,690**
Carolina Hurricanes	**Raleigh Entertainment and Sports Arena**	Raleigh, N.C.	1999	**18,730**
Florida Panthers	**National Car Rental Center**	Sunrise, Fla.	1998	**19,250**
Montreal Canadiens	**Molson Centre**	Montreal, Que.	1996	**21,273**
New Jersey Devils	**Continental Airlines Arena**	E. Rutherford, N.J.	1981	**19,040**
New York Islanders	**Nassau Veterans' Mem. Coliseum**	Uniondale, N.Y.	1972	**16,297**
New York Rangers	**Madison Square Garden**	New York, N.Y.	1968	**18,200**
Ottawa Senators	**Corel Centre**	Kanata, Ont.	1996	**18,500**
Philadelphia Flyers	**First Union Center**	Philadelphia, Penn.	1996	**19,519**
Pittsburgh Penguins	**Mellon Arena**	Pittsburgh, Penn.	1961	**16,958**
Tampa Bay Lightning	**Ice Palace**	Tampa Bay, Fla.	1996	**19,758**
Toronto Maple Leafs	**Air Canada Centre**	Toronto, Ont.	1999	**18,800**
Washington Capitals	**MCI Center**	Washington, D.C.	1997	**18,672**

Rank by Capacity

Western		Eastern	
Chicago	20,500	Montreal	21,273
Detroit	19,983	Tampa Bay	19,758
St. Louis	19,022	Philadelphia	19,519
Dallas	18,600	Florida	19,250
Columbus	18,524	New Jersey	19,040
Vancouver	18,422	Toronto	18,800
Los Angeles	18,118	Carolina	18,730
Minnesota	18,064	Buffalo	18,690
Colorado	18,007	Washington	18,672
San Jose	17,496	Atlanta	18,545
Anaheim	17,174	Ottawa	18,500
Calgary	17,135	NY Rangers	18,200
Nashville	17,113	Boston	17,565
Edmonton	17,100	Pittsburgh	16,958
Phoenix	16,210	NY Islanders	16,297

Rank by Age

Western		Eastern	
Edmonton	1974	Pittsburgh	1961
Detroit	1979	NY Rangers	1968
Calgary	1983	NY Islanders	1972
Phoenix	1992	New Jersey	1981
Anaheim	1993	Boston	1995
San Jose	1993	Montreal	1996
Chicago	1994	Ottawa	1996
St. Louis	1994	Buffalo	1996
Nashville	1994	Philadelphia	1996
Vancouver	1995	Tampa Bay	1996
Colorado	1999	Washington	1997
Los Angeles	1999	Florida	1998
Columbus	2000	Toronto	1999
Minnesota	2000	Carolina	1999
Dallas	2001	Atlanta	1999

2000-01 NHL Attendance

Official overall paid attendance for the 2000-01 season according to the NHL accounting office was 20,372,240 (paid tickets) for an average per game crowd of 16,563 over 1,230 games. Teams in each conference are ranked by attendance over 41 home games. There was one neutral site game between Nashville and Pittsburgh as part of a program to benefit school children in the Nashville community. Number of sellouts are listed in S/O column. Numbers in parentheses indicate rank in 1999-2000.

Western Conference

		Attendance	S/O	Average
1	Detroit (1)	819,303	41	19,983
2	St. Louis (2)	800,319	35	19,520
3	Minnesota (NR)	741,468	41	18,328
4	Colorado (3)	738,287	41	18,007
5	San Jose (4)	716,196	35	17,468
6	Columbus (NR)	715,740	26	17,457
7	Vancouver (12)	697,717	18	17,017
8	Dallas (5)	697,041	41	17,001
9	Calgary (10)	681,535	17	16,623
10	Los Angeles (7)	658,340	17	16,057
11	Edmonton (9)	640,085	14	15,612
12	Nashville (6)	635,775	13	15,894
13	Chicago (8)	614,875	3	14,997
14	Phoenix (11)	583,696	4	14,236
15	Anaheim (13)	553,990	3	13,512
	TOTAL	8,837,159	272	16,610

Eastern Conference

		Attendance	S/O	Average
1	Montreal (1)	824,308	13	20,105
2	Philadelphia (2)	802,595	29	19,575
3	Toronto (3)	789,467	41	19,255
4	NY Rangers (4)	746,200	41	18,200
5	Buffalo (5)	731,318	22	17,837
6	Ottawa (6)	729,515	18	17,793
7	Pittsburgh (10)	655,926	26	16,398
8	New Jersey (11)	641,340	7	15,642
9	Washington (12)	636,914	11	15,534
10	Boston (8)	632,746	10	15,433
11	Atlanta (7)	625,870	5	15,265
12	Tampa Bay (13)	611,173	10	14,907
13	Florida (9)	601,857	1	14,679
14	Carolina (14)	547,585	8	13,356
15	NY Islanders (15)	464,627	4	11,332
	TOTAL	11,525,081	246	18,870

Home Ice

Listed below are the principal home buildings used through the years by current NHL teams. The largest capacity of each arena is noted in the right hand column. World Hockey Association arenas (1972-79) are included for Edmonton, Hartford (now Carolina), Quebec (now Colorado) and Winnipeg (now Phoenix).

Western Conference

Anaheim, Mighty Ducks of

1993–	Arrowhead Pond	17,174

Calgary Flames

1972–80	The Omni (Atlanta)	15,278
1980–83	Calgary Corral	7,424
1983–	Pengrowth Saddledome	17,135
	(1983 capacity—16,674)	

Chicago Blackhawks

1926–29	Chicago Coliseum	5,000
1929–94	Chicago Stadium	17,317
1994–	United Center	20,500

Colorado Avalanche

1972–95	Le Colisee de Quebec	15,399
1995–99	McNichols Arena (Denver)	16,061
1999–	Pepsi Center	18,007

Columbus Blue Jackets

2000–	Nationwide Arena	18,524

Dallas Stars

1967–93	Met Center (Bloomington, MN)	15,174
1993–2000	Reunion Arena (Dallas)	17,001
2001–	American Airlines Center	18,600

Detroit Red Wings

1926–27	Border Cities Arena (Windsor, Ont.)	3,200
1927–79	Olympia Stadium (Detroit)	16,700
1979–	Joe Louis Arena	19,983

Edmonton Oilers

1972–74	Edmonton Gardens	7,200
1974–	Skyreach Centre	17,100
	(1974 capacity—15,513)	

Los Angeles Kings

1967–99	Great Western Forum (Inglewood)	16,005
	(1967 capacity—15,651)	
1999–	Staples Center	18,118

Note: The Kings played 17 games at Long Beach Sports Arena and LA Sports Arena at the start of the 1967-68 season.

Minnesota Wild

2000–	Xcel Energy Center (St. Paul)	18,064

Nashville Predators

1998–	Gaylord Entertainment Center	17,113

Phoenix Coyotes

1972–96	Winnipeg Arena	15,393
	(1972 capacity—10,177)	
1996–	America West (Phoenix)	16,210

St. Louis Blues

1967–94	St. Louis Arena	17,188
1994–	Savvis Center	19,022

San Jose Sharks

1991–93	Cow Palace (Daly City, CA)	11,100
1993–	Compaq Center at San Jose	17,496

Vancouver Canucks

1970–95	Pacific Coliseum	16,150
1995–	General Motors Place	18,422

Building Name Changes: CALGARY—**Pengrowth Saddledome** formerly named Canadian Airlines Saddledome (1996-2000) which was originally Olympic Saddledome (1983-95); DALLAS—**Met Center** in Minneapolis originally Metropolitan Sports Center (1967-82); EDMONTON—**Skyreach Centre** formerly named Edmonton Coliseum (1995-99) which was originally Northlands Coliseum (1974-94); LOS ANGELES—**Great Western Forum** originally The Forum (1967-88); NASHVILLE—**Gaylord Entertainment Center** originally Nashville Arena (1994-99); ST. LOUIS—**Savvis Center** originally Kiel Center (1994-2000), **St. Louis Arena** renamed The Checkerdome in 1977, then St. Louis Arena again in 1982; SAN JOSE—**Compaq Center at San Jose** originally San Jose Arena (1993-2000).

Eastern Conference

Atlanta Thrashers

1999–	Philips Arena	18,545

Boston Bruins

1924–28	Boston Arena	6,200
1928–95	Boston Garden	14,448
1995–	FleetCenter	17,565

National Hockey League (Cont.)

Buffalo Sabres

1970–96	Memorial Auditorium (The Aud)	16,284
	(1970 capacity—10,429)	
1996–	HSBC Arena	18,690

Carolina Hurricanes

1972–73	Boston Garden	14,442
1973–74	Boston Garden (regular season)	14,442
	West Springfield (MA) Big E (playoffs)	5,513
1974–75	West Springfield Big E	5,513
	& Hartford (CT) Civic Center	10,507
1975–77	Hartford Civic Center	10,507
1977–78	Hartford Civic Center	10,507
	& Springfield (MA) Civic Center	7,725
1978–79	Springfield Civic Center	7,725
1979–80	Springfield Civic Center	7,725
	& Hartford Civic Center II	14,250
1980–97	Hartford Civic Center II	15,635
1997–99	Greensboro Coliseum	21,500
1999–	Raleigh Entertainment and Sports Arena	18,730

Note: The Hartford Civic Center roof caved in January 1978, forcing the Whalers to move their home games to Springfield, MA for two years.

Florida Panthers

1993–98	Miami Arena	14,703
1998–	National Car Rental Center	19,250

Montreal Canadiens

1910–21	Jubilee Arena	3,200
1913–18	Montreal Arena (Westmount)	6,000
1918–26	Mount Royal Arena	6,750
1926–68	Montreal Forum I	15,500
1968–96	Montreal Forum II	17,959
1996–	Molson Centre	21,273

New Jersey Devils

1974–76	Kemper Arena (Kansas City)	16,300
1976–82	McNichols Arena (Denver)	15,900
1982–	Continental Airlines Arena	19,040
	(1982 capacity—19,023)	

New York Islanders

1972–	Nassau Veterans' Mem. Coliseum	16,297
	(1972 capacity—14,500)	

New York Rangers

1925–68	Madison Square Garden III	15,925
1968–	Madison Square Garden IV	18,200
	(1968 capacity—17,250)	

Ottawa Senators

1992–96	Ottawa Civic Center	10,755
1996–	Corel Centre (Kanata)	18,500

Philadelphia Flyers

1967–96	CoreStates Spectrum	17,380
	(1967 capacity—14,558)	
1996–	First Union Center	19,519

Pittsburgh Penguins

1967–	Mellon Arena	16,958
	(1967 capacity—12,508)	

Tampa Bay Lightning

1992–93	Expo Hall (Tampa)	10,500
1993–96	ThunderDome (St. Petersburg)	26,000
1996–	Ice Palace	19,758

Toronto Maple Leafs

1917–31	Mutual Street Arena	8,000
1931–99	Maple Leaf Gardens	15,746
	(1931 capacity—13,542)	
1999–	Air Canada Centre	18,800

Washington Capitals

1974–97	USAir Arena (Landover, MD)	18,130
1997–	MCI Center	18,672

Building Name Changes: BUFFALO—**HSBC Arena** originally Marine Midland Arena (1996-99); CALGARY—**Pengrowth Saddledome** originally Canadian Airlines Arena (1983-2000); DALLAS—**American Airlines Center** originally Reunion Arena (1993-2000); NEW JERSEY—**Continental Airlines Arena** originally Meadowlands Arena (1982-96); PHILADELPHIA—**First Union Center** originally the CoreStates Center (1996-98) and **CoreStates Spectrum** originally The Spectrum (1967-94); PITTSBURGH—**Mellon Arena** originally Civic Arena (1967-2000); WASHINGTON—**USAir Arena** originally Capital Centre (1974-93).

AUTO RACING

Formula One, NASCAR Winston Cup, CART and Indy Racing League (IRL) racing circuits. Qualifying records accurate as of July 16, 2001. Capacity figures for NASCAR, CART and IRL tracks are approximate and pertain to grandstand seating only. Standing room and hillside terrain seating featured at most road courses are not included.

CART

	Location	Miles	Qual.mph record	Set by	Seats
Burke Lakefront Airport	Cleveland, Ohio	2.106**	134.385	Jimmy Vasser (1998)	36,000
California Speedway	Fontana, Calif.	2.029	241.428†	Gil de Ferran (2000)	122,000
Chicago Motor Speedway	Cicero, Ill.	1.029	167.567	Juan Montoya (2000)	40,000
Concord Pacific Place	Vancouver, B.C.	1.781**	106.144	Dario Franchitti (2000)	65,000
Eurospeedway	Lausitz, Germany	2.0	210.340	Tony Kanaan (2001)	120,000
Exhibition Place	Toronto, Ont.	1.755**	110.565	Gil de Ferran (1999)	60,000
Fundidora Park	Monterrey, Mexico	2.1*	100.665	Kenny Brack (2001)	61,871
Houston Grand Prix	Houston, Texas	1.527**	93.651	Juan Montoya (1999)	60,000
Laguna Seca Raceway	Monterey, Calif.	2.238*	118.969	Helio Castro-Neves (2000)	8,000
Long Beach	Long Beach, Calif.	1.968**	104.969	Gil de Ferran (2000)	63,000
Michigan International Speedway	Brooklyn, Mich.	2.0	234.959	Paul Tracy (2000)	136,000
Mid-Ohio Sports Car Course	Lexington, Ohio	2.258*	124.394	Dario Franchitti (1999) & Gil de Ferran (2000)	6,000
The Milwaukee Mile	West Allis, Wisc.	1.032	185.500	Patrick Carpentier (1998)	36,800
Nazareth Speedway	Nazareth, Penn.	0.946	184.896	Patrick Carpentier (1998)	44,044
Portland International Raceway	Portland, Ore.	1.969*	122.768	Helio Castro-Neves (2000)	50,000
The Raceway on Belle Isle	Detroit, Mich.	2.346**	115.604	Juan Montoya (2000)	18,000
Road America	Elkhart Lake, Wisc.	4.048*	145.924	Dario Franchitti (2000)	10,000
Rockingham Motor Speedway	Corby, England	1.5	—	first race in 2001	27,500
Surfers Paradise	Queensland, Australia	2.795**	109.724	Dario Franchitti (1999)	55,000

	Location	Miles	Qual.mph record	Set by	Seats
Texas Motor Speedway	Ft. Worth, Texas	1.5	233.447	Kenny Brack (2001)	154,861
Twin Ring Motegi	Motegi, Japan	1.549	219.000	Gil de Ferran (1999)	50,000

*Road courses (not ovals). **Temporary street circuits. †Indicates world closed-course record for auto racing.

Indy Racing League

Founded by Indianapolis Motor Speedway president Tony George, the Indy Racing League competes with CART and fielded 13 races, anchored by the Indianapolis 500, in 2001. Note that the track records listed are for normally-aspirated IRL cars unless otherwise noted by an asterisk.

	Location	Miles	Qual.mph Record	Set by	Seats
Atlanta Motor Speedway	Hampton, Ga.	1.54	224.145	Billy Boat (1998)	124,000
Chicagoland Speedway	Joliet, Ill.	1.5	—	first race in 2001	75,000
Gateway International Raceway	Madison, Ill.	1.25	—	first race in 2001	35,000
Homestead-Miami Speedway	Homestead, Fla.	1.5	201.551	Jeff Ward	71,763
Indianapolis Motor Speedway	Indianapolis, Ind.	2.5	237.498	Arie Luyendyk (1996)*	250,000+
Kansas Speedway	Kansas City, Kan.	1.5	216.175	Scott Sharp	75,000
Kentucky Speedway	Sparta, Ky.	1.5	219.191	Scott Goodyear (2000)	70,000
Nashville Superspeedway	Nashville, Tenn.	1.33	199.992	Greg Ray (2001)	50,000
Phoenix International Raceway	Phoenix, Ariz.	1.0	177.139	Greg Ray (1999)	78,450
Pikes Peak Int'l. Raceway	Fountain, Colo.	1.0	179.874	Greg Ray (2000)	42,787
Richmond International Raceway	Richmond, Va.	0.75	160.417	Jaques Lazier (2001)	95,920
Texas Motor Speedway	Fort Worth, Texas	1.5	225.979	Billy Boat (1998)	154,861

NASCAR Winston Cup

	Location	Miles	Qual.mph Record	Set By	Seats
Atlanta Motor Speedway	Hampton, Ga.	1.54	197.478	Geoff Bodine (1997)	124,000
Bristol Motor Speedway	Bristol, Tenn.	0.533	126.370	Steve Park (2000)	147,000
California Speedway	Fontana, Calif.	2.0	186.061	Mike Skinner (2000)	92,000
Chicagoland Speedway	Joliet, Ill.	1.5	183.717	Todd Bodine (2001)	75,000
Darlington International Raceway	Darlington, N.C.	1.366	173.797	Ward Burton (1996)	65,000
Daytona International Speedway	Daytona Beach, Fla.	2.5	210.364	Bill Elliott (1987)	165,000
Dover Downs International Speedway	Dover, Del.	1.0	159.964	Rusty Wallace (1999)	140,000
Homestead-Miami Speedway	Homestead, Fla.	1.5	156.440	Steve Park (2000)	72,000
Indianapolis Motor Speedway	Indianapolis, Ind.	2.5	181.072	Brett Bodine (2000)	250,000+
Kansas Speedway	Kansas City, Kan.	1.5	—	first race in 2001	75,000
Las Vegas Motor Speedway	Las Vegas, Nev.	1.5	172.563	Ricky Rudd (2000)	126,000
Lowe's Motor Speedway	Concord, N.C.	1.5	186.034	Dale Earnhardt Jr. (2000)	167,000
Martinsville Speedway	Martinsville, Va.	0.526	95.371	Tony Stewart (2000)	91,000
Michigan Speedway	Brooklyn, Mich.	2.0	191.149	Dale Earnhardt Jr. (2000)	136,384
New Hampshire Int'l Speedway	Loudon, N.H.	1.058	132.089	Rusty Wallace (2000)	91,000
North Carolina Speedway	Rockingham, N.C.	1.017	158.035	Rusty Wallace (2000)	60,113
Phoenix International Raceway	Phoenix, Ariz.	1.0	134.178	Rusty Wallace (2000)	76,812
Pocono Raceway	Long Pond, Penn.	2.5	172.391	Tony Stewart (2000)	77,000
Richmond International Raceway	Richmond, Va.	0.75	126.499	Jeff Gordon (1999)	100,000+
Sears Point International Raceway	Sonoma, Calif.	1.949*	99.309	Rusty Wallace (2000)	42,500
Talladega Superspeedway	Talladega, Ala.	2.66	212.809	Bill Elliott (1987)	138,000
Texas Motor Speedway	Ft. Worth, Texas	1.5	192.137	Terry Labonte (2000)	154,861
Watkins Glen International	Watkins Glen, N.Y.	2.45*	122.698	Dale Jarret (2001)	40,000

*Road courses (not ovals).
Note: Richmond sells reserved seats only (no infield) for Winston Cup races.

Formula One
Race track capacity figures unavailable.

Grand Prix		Miles	Qual.mph Record	Set by
Australian	Albert Park (Melbourne)	3.274	136.520	Michael Schumacher (2001)
Austrian	A1-Ring (Zeltwig, Austria)	2.684	139.113	Michael Schumacher (2001)
Belgian	Spa-Francorchamps	4.333	143.418	Mika Hakkinen (1998)
Brazilian	Interlagos (Sao Paulo)	2.684	130.645	Michael Schumacher (2001)
British	Silverstone (Towcester)	3.194	148.043	Nigel Mansell (1992)
Canadian	Circuit Gilles Villeneuve (Montreal)	2.747	130.499	Michael Schumacher (2001)
European	Nürburgring (Nürburg, Germany)	2.822	135.959	Michael Schumacher (2001)
French	Magny Cours (Nevers)	2.641	130.252	Ralf Schumacher (2001)
German	Hockenheim (Germany)	4.239	156.722	Nigel Mansell (1991)
Hungarian	Hungaroring (Budapest)	2.468	120.064	Michael Schumacher (2001)
Italian	Autodromo Nazionale di Monza (Milan)	3.585	159.951	Ayrton Senna (1991)
Japanese	Suzuka (Nagoya)	3.644	138.515	Gerhard Berger (1991)
Malaysian	Sepang (Kuala Lumpur)	3.444	130.218	Michael Schumacher (2001)
Monaco	Monte Carlo (Monaco)	2.082	97.358	David Coulthard (2001)
San Marino	Autodome Enzo di Ferrari (Imola, Italy)	3.063	138.265	Ayrton Senna (1994)
Spanish	Catalunya (Barcelona)	2.937	138.205	Jacques Villeneuve (1997)
United States	Indianapolis Motor Speedway	2.606	126.355	Michael Schumacher (2000)

SOCCER

World's Premier Soccer Stadiums

(Listed alphabetically by city)

Stadium	Location	Seats	Stadium	Location	Seats
Spiros Louis	Athens, Greece	74,443	Old Trafford	Manchester, England	67,650
Eden Park	Auckland, New Zealand	50,000	Azteca	Mexico City, Mexico	106,000
Camp Nou	Barcelona, Spain	109,815	Guiseppe Meazza	Milan, Italy	85,700
Workers'	Beijing, China	72,000	Centenario	Montevideo, Uruguay	73,609
Olympiastadion	Berlin, Germany	76,243	Luzhniki Stadion	Moscow, Russia	80,840
Népstadion	Budapest, Hungary	65,000	Olympiastadion	Munich, Germany	63,000
Antonio Liberti	Buenos Aires, Argentina	76,689	San Paolo	Naples, Italy	78,210
National	Cairo, Egypt	90,000	Rungnado	Pyongyang, N. Korea	150,000
Salt Lake	Calcutta, India	120,000	Maracana	Rio de Janeiro, Brazil	122,268
Millennium	Cardiff, Wales	72,500	King Fahd II	Riyadh, Saudi Arabia	79,000
Westfalenstadion	Dortmund, Germany	68,600	Olimpico	Rome, Italy	82,922
Lansdowne Road	Dublin, Ireland	48,000	Stade de France	St. Denis, France	80,000
Celtic Park	Glasgow, Scotland	60,506	Nacional	Santiago, Chile	77,000
Hampden Park	Glasgow, Scotland	52,670	Morumbi	Sao Paulo, Brazil	80,000
FNB Stadium	Johannesburg, S. Africa	90,000	Chasmil	Seoul, S. Korea	100,000
Olympic Stadium	Kiev, Ukraine	83,160	Stadium Australia	Sydney, Australia	80,000
Estadio da Luz	Lisbon, Portugal	77,844	Olympic Stadium	Tokyo, Japan	60,000
New Wembley	London, England	90,000	Delle Alpi	Turin, Italy	69,041
Santiago Bernabeu	Madrid, Spain	87,000	Ernst Happel	Vienna, Austria	47,500

Major League Soccer

The 12-team MLS is the only U.S. Division I professional outdoor league sanctioned by FIFA and U.S. Soccer. Note that all capacity figures are approximate given the adjustments of football stadium seating to soccer.

Western Conference

	Stadium	Built	Seats	Field
Chicago Fire	Soldier Field	1924	24,955	Grass
Colorado Rapids	Mile High	1948	17,500	Grass
Dallas Burn	Cotton Bowl	1935	22,528	Grass
Kansas City Wizards	Arrowhead	1972	20,571	Grass
L.A. Galaxy	Rose Bowl	1922	30,000	Grass
San Jose Earthquakes	Spartan	1933	26,000	Grass

Eastern Conference

	Stadium	Built	Seats	Field
Columbus Crew	Columbus Crew	1999	22,500	Grass
D.C. United	RFK	1961	26,169	Grass
Metro Stars (N.Y./N.J.)	Giants	1976	25,576	Grass
Miami Fusion	Lockhart	1959	20,450	Grass
N.E. Revolution	Foxboro	1971	24,871	Grass
Tampa Bay Mutiny	Raymond James	1998	17,482	Grass

MISCELLANEOUS

Minor League Baseball

AAA Ballparks
International League

North		Built	Seats	Field
Buffalo Bisons (Indians)	Dunn Tire Park	1988	21,050	Grass
Ottawa Lynx (Expos)	JetForm Park	1993	10,332	Grass
Pawtucket Red Sox (Red Sox)	McCoy Stadium	1942	10,031	Grass
Rochester Red Wings (Orioles)	Frontier Field	1997	10,840	Grass
Scranton/Wilkes-Barre Red Barons (Phillies)	Lackawanna County Stadium	1989	11,232	Turf
Syracuse Sky Chiefs (Blue Jays)	P&C Stadium	1997	11,604	Turf
West		**Built**	**Seats**	**Field**
Columbus Clippers (Yankees)	Cooper Stadium	1932	15,000	Grass
Indianapolis Indians (Brewers)	Victory Field	1996	15,500	Grass
Louisville RiverBats (Reds)	Louisville Slugger Field	2000	13,200	Grass
Toledo Mud Hens (Tigers)	Fifth Third Field	2002	10,000	Grass
South		**Built**	**Seats**	**Field**
Charlotte Knights (White Sox)	Knights Castle	1990	10,002	Grass
Durham Bulls (Devil Rays)	Durham Bulls Athletic Park	1995	10,000	Grass
Norfolk Tides (Mets)	Harbor Park	1993	12,067	Grass
Richmond Braves (Braves)	The Diamond	1985	12,156	Grass

Pacific Coast League

East Division		Built	Seats	Field
Oklahoma RedHawks (Rangers)	**Southwestern Bell Bricktown Ballpark**	1998	13,066	Grass
Memphis Redbirds (Cardinals)	**AutoZone Park**	2000	14,300	Grass
Nashville Sounds (Pirates)	**Herschel Greer Stadium**	1978	10,700	Grass
New Orleans Zephyrs (Astros)	**Zephyr Field**	1997	11,000	Grass
North Division		**Built**	**Seats**	**Field**
Calgary Cannons (Marlins)	**Burns Stadium**	1966	8,000	Grass
Edmonton Trappers (Twins)	**TELUS Field**	1995	9,200	Grass
Tacoma Rainiers (Mariners)	**Cheney Stadium**	1960	9,600	Grass
Salt Lake Stingers (Angels)	**Franklin Covey Field**	1993	15,500	Grass
Central Division		**Built**	**Seats**	**Field**
Portland Beavers (Dodgers)	**PGE Park**	1926*	23,000	Turf
Colorado Springs Sky Sox (Rockies)	**Sky Sox Stadium**	1988	9,000	Grass
Iowa Cubs (Cubs)	**Sec Taylor Stadium**	1992	10,888	Grass
Omaha Golden Spikes (Royals)	**Johnny Rosenblatt Stadium**	1948	24,000	Turf
South Division		**Built**	**Seats**	**Field**
Las Vegas 51s (Padres)	**Cashman Field**	1983	9,334	Grass
Fresno Grizzlies (Giants)	**new Downtown Stadium**	2002	12,500	Grass
Sacramento River Cats (Athletics)	**Raley Field**	2000	14,111	Grass
Tucson Sidewinders (Diamondbacks)	**Tucson Electric Park**	1998	11,000	Grass

*PGE Park, formerly known as Civic Stadium, underwent extensive renovation prior to the 2001 season.

Japanese Baseball League

Central League

		Location	Built	Seats	Field
Chunichi Dragons	**Nagoya Dome**	Nagoya	1997	40,500	Turf
Hanshin Tigers	**Koshien Stadium**	Nisinomiya	1924	55,000	Grass
Hiroshima Carp	**Hiroshima Municipal Stadium**	Hiroshima	1957	32,000	Grass
Yakult Swallows	**Meiji Jingu Stadium**	Tokyo	1926	48,785	Turf
Yokohama BayStars	**Yokohama Stadium**	Yokohama	1978	30,000	Turf
Yomiuri Giants	**Tokyo Dome**	Tokyo	1988	48,000	Turf

Pacific League

		Location	Built	Seats	Field
Chiba Lotte Marines	**Chiba Marine Stadium**	Chiba	1991	30,000	Turf
Fukuoka Daiei Hawks	**Fukuoka Dome**	Fukuoka	1993	48,000	Turf
Kintetsu Buffaloes	**Osaka Dome**	Osaka	1997	55,000	Turf
Nippon Ham Fighters	**Tokyo Dome**	Tokyo	1988	48,000	Turf
Orix Blue Wave	**Green Stadium Kobe**	Kobe	1988	35,000	Grass
Seibu Lions	**Seibu Stadium**	Tokorozawa	1979	37,000	Turf

Canadian Football League

East Division

		Location	Built	Seats	Field
Hamilton Tiger-Cats	**Ivor Wynne Stadium**	Hamilton, Ont.	1932	28,830	Turf
Montreal Alouettes	**Percival Molson Memorial Stadium**	Montreal, Que.	1976	19,461	Turf
Toronto Argonauts	**SkyDome**	Toronto, Ont.	1989	31,600*	Turf
Winnipeg Blue Bombers	**Canad Inns Stadium**	Winnipeg, Man.	1953	29,544	Turf

*The regular season SkyDome capacity is 31,600 but it is expanded to 52,595 for postseason games.

West Division

		Location	Built	Seats	Field
British Columbia Lions	**B.C. Place Stadium**	Vancouver, B.C.	1983	40,800	Turf
Calgary Stampeders	**McMahon Stadium**	Calgary, Alb.	1960	35,967	Turf
Edmonton Eskimos	**Commonwealth Stadium**	Edmonton, Alb.	1978	60,081	Grass
Saskatchewan Roughriders	**Taylor Field**	Regina, Sask.	1948	27,732	Turf

NFL Europe

		Location	Seats
Amsterdam Admirals	**Amsterdam Arena**	Amsterdam, Netherlands	51,328
Barcelona Dragons	**Olympic Stadium**	Barcelona, Spain	54,000
Berlin Thunder	**Jahn Sportspark**	Berlin, Germany	20,000
Frankfurt Galaxy	**Waldstadion**	Frankfurt, Germany	54,000
Rhein Fire	**Rheinstadion**	Dusseldorf, Germany	57,000
Scottish Claymores	**Hampden Park**	Glasgow, Scotland	52,500

Miscellaneous (Cont.)
Arena Football League
American Conference

Western Division	Location	Built	Seats
Arizona Rattlers . . . . **America West Arena**	Phoenix, Ariz.	1992	16,923
Houston ThunderBears . . . . **Compaq Center**	Houston, Texas	1975	15,050
Los Angeles Avengers . . . . **Staples Center**	Los Angeles, Calif.	1999	16,437
Oklahoma Wranglers . . . . **Myriad Convention Center**	Oklahoma City, Okla.	1973	13,000
San Jose SaberCats . . . . **Compaq Center @ San Jose**	San Jose, Calif.	1993	16,929
Central Division	**Location**	**Built**	**Seats**
Chicago Rush . . . . **All State Arena**	Rosemont, Ill.	1979	15,700
Detroit Fury. . . . . **The Palace of Auburn Hills**	Auburn Hills, Mich.	1988	18,565
Grand Rapids Rampage . . . . **Van Andel Arena**	Grand Rapids, Mich.	1996	10,618
Indiana Firebirds . . . . **Conseco Fieldhouse**	Indianapolis, Ind.	1999	15,490
Milwaukee Mustangs . . . . **Bradley Center**	Milwaukee, Wisc.	1988	17,819

National Conference

Southern Division	Location	Built	Seats
Florida Bobcats. . . . . **National Car Rental Center**	Sunrise, Fla.	1998	17,900
Nashville Kats. . . . . **Gaylord Entertainment Center**	Nashville, Tenn.	1994	16,121
Orlando Predators . . . . **TD Waterhouse Centre**	Orlando, Fla.	1989	16,613
Tampa Bay Storm . . . . **Ice Palace**	Tampa Bay, Fla.	1996	20,282
Eastern Division	**Location**	**Built**	**Seats**
Buffalo Destroyers . . . . **HSBC Arena**	Buffalo, N.Y.	1996	18,127
Carolina Cobras . . . . **Raleigh Sports & Entertainment Arena**	Raleigh, N.C.	1999	16,985
New Jersey Gladiators . . . . **Continental Airlines Arena**	E. Rutherford, N.J.	1981	17,500
New York Dragons . . . . **Nassau Veterans' Mem. Coliseum**	Uniondale, N.Y.	1972	11,965
Toronto Phantoms. . . . . **Air Canada Centre**	Toronto, Ont.	1999	17,100

Women's Professional Basketball
Women's National Basketball Association

The WNBA teams play in the same arenas as the NBA teams in their respective cities. However, the capacities of some of the venues are "down-sized" for some games. The new, smaller capacity for WNBA games is listed below where applicable.

Eastern	Location	Built	Seats
Charlotte Sting. . . . . **Charlotte Coliseum**	Charlotte, N.C.	1988	12,843
Cleveland Rockers . . . . **Gund Arena**	Cleveland, Ohio	1994	11,751
Detroit Shock . . . . **The Palace of Auburn Hills**	Auburn Hills, Mich.	1988	11,268
Indiana Fever . . . . **Conseco Fieldhouse**	Indianapolis, Ind.	1999	18,345
Miami Sol . . . . **AmericanAirlines Arena**	Miami, Fla.	1999	10,412
New York Liberty . . . . **Madison Square Garden**	New York, N.Y.	1968	19,763
Orlando Miracle . . . . **TD Waterhouse Centre**	Orlando, Fla.	1989	17,306
Washington Mystics . . . . **MCI Center**	Washington, D.C.	1997	19,093
Western	**Location**	**Built**	**Seats**
Houston Comets. . . . . **Compaq Center**	Houston, Texas	1975	16,285
Los Angeles Sparks . . . . **Staples Center**	Inglewood, Calif.	1967	13,141
Minnesota Lynx . . . . **Target Center**	Minneapolis, Minn.	1990	11,380
Phoenix Mercury . . . . **America West Arena**	Phoenix, Ariz.	1992	10,604
Portland Fire. . . . . **Rose Garden**	Portland, Ore.	1995	19,980
Sacramento Monarchs . . . . **ARCO Arena**	Sacramento, Calif.	1988	13,500
Seattle Storm . . . . **KeyArena at Seattle Center**	Seattle, Wash.	1962	12,696
Utah Starzz . . . . **Delta Center**	Salt Lake City, Utah	1991	8,916

Horse Racing
Triple Crown race tracks

Race	Racetrack	Seats	Infield
Kentucky Derby . . . . . . Churchill Downs	48,500	65,000
Preakness. . . . . Pimlico Race Course	13,000	60,000
Belmont Stakes. . . . . Belmont Park	32,941	N/A

Record crowds: Kentucky Derby—163,628 (1974); Preakness—104,454 (2001); Belmont—85,818 (1999).

Note: Belmont Park does not open infield for Belmont Stakes.

Tennis
Grand Slam center courts

Event	Main Stadium	Seats
Australian Open . . . . Melbourne Park	15,021
French Open . . . . Stade Roland Garros	16,300
Wimbledon. Centre Court	13,813
U.S. Open . . . . Arthur Ashe Stadium	22,547

COLLEGE BASKETBALL

The 50 Largest Arenas

The 50 largest arenas in Division I for the 2001-02 NCAA regular season. Note that (*) indicates part-time home court.

		Seats	Home Team			Seats	Home Team
1	Carrier Dome	33,000	Syracuse	26	Pittsburgh Civic Arena	16,725	Pittsburgh*
2	Thompson-Boling Arena	24,535	Tennessee	27	Assembly Hall	16,450	Illinois
3	Rupp Arena	23,000	Kentucky	28	Allen Field House	16,300	Kansas
4	Marriott Center	22,700	BYU	29	Hartford Civic Center	16,294	UConn*
5	Dean Smith Center	21,750	N. Carolina	30	Erwin Center	16,175	Texas
6	First Union Center	21,000	Villanova*	31	LA Sports Arena	16,161	USC
7	MCI Center	20,600	Georgetown*	32	Carver-Hawkeye Arena	15,500	Iowa
8	The Pyramid	20,142	Memphis		Pepsi Arena	15,500	Siena*
9	Continental Airlines Arena	20,029	Seton Hall*	34	Bryce Jordan Center	15,261	Penn St.
10	Savvis Center	20,000	Saint Louis	35	Miami Arena	15,200	Miami
11	The Rose Garden	19,980	Portland St.	36	United Spirit Arena	15,050	Texas Tech
12	Ent. and Sports Arena	19,722	N.C. State	37	Coleman Coliseum	15,043	Alabama
13	HSBC Arena	19,500	Canisius* & Niagara*	38	Arena-Auditorium	15,028	Wyoming
14	Bud Walton Arena	19,200	Arkansas	39	Huntsman Center	15,000	Utah
15	Freedom Hall	18,865	Louisville	40	Joel Memorial Coliseum	14,665	Wake Forest
16	Bradley Center	18,712	Marquette	41	Breslin Events Center	14,659	Michigan St.
17	Thomas & Mack Center	18,500	UNLV	42	McKale Center	14,545	Arizona
18	Madison Square Garden	18,470	St. John's*	43	Cole Fieldhouse	14,500	Maryland
19	University Arena (The Pit)	18,018	New Mexico	44	Williams Arena	14,321	Minnesota
20	Alltel Arena	18,000	Arkansas-Little Rock	45	University Activity Center	14,198	Arizona St.
21	New Orleans Arena	17,832	Tulane	46	Memorial Gym	14,168	Vanderbilt
22	All State Arena	17,500	DePaul*	47	Maravich Assembly Ctr.	14,164	LSU
	Value City Arena	17,500	Ohio St.	48	Mackey Arena	14,123	Purdue
24	Assembly Hall	17,357	Indiana	49	Hilton Coliseum	14,092	Iowa St.
25	Kohl Center	17,142	Wisconsin	50	WVU Coliseum	14,000	West Virginia

Division I Conference Home Courts

NCAA Division I conferences for the 2001-02 season. Teams with home games in more than one arena are noted.

America East

	Home Floor	Seats
Albany	Rec & Convention Ctr.	5,000
Binghamton	West Gym	2,275
Boston University	Case Gym	1,800
Hartford	Chase Family Arena	4,475
Maine	Alfond Arena	5,712
New Hampshire	Lundholm Gym	3,500
Northeastern	Solomon Court	2,000
Stony Brook	USB Sports Complex	4,103
Vermont	Patrick Gym	3,228

Atlantic Coast

	Home Floor	Seats
Clemson	Littlejohn Coliseum	11,020
Duke	Cameron Indoor Stadium	9,314
Florida St.	Leon County Civic Center	12,200
Georgia Tech	Alexander Mem. Stadium	10,000
Maryland	Cole Field House	14,500
North Carolina	Dean Smith Center	21,750
N.C. State	Entertainment and Sports Arena	19,722
Virginia	University Hall	8,457
Wake Forest	Joel Mem. Coliseum	14,665

Atlantic Sun

	Home Floor	Seats
Belmont	Curb Event	5,000
Campbell	Carter Gym	1,050
Central Fla.	UCF Arena	5,100
Fla. Atlantic	FAU Gym	5,000
Georgia St.	GSU Sports Arena	5,500
Jacksonville	Swisher Gym	1,500
Jacksonville St.	Mathews Coliseum	5,500
Mercer	Porter Gym	1,000
Samford	Seibert Hall	4,000
Stetson	Edmunds Center	5,000
Troy St.	Trojan Arena	3,000

Atlantic 10

	Home Floor	Seats
Dayton	U. of Dayton Arena	13,455
Duquesne	Palumbo Center	6,200
Fordham	Rose Hill Gym	3,470
G. Washington	Smith Center	5,000
La Salle	Tom Gola Arena	4,000
Massachusetts	Mullins Center	9,493
Rhode Island	Keaney Gymnasium	3,385
	& Dunkin' Donuts Center	12,681
Richmond	Robins Center	9,171
St. Bonaventure	Reilly Center	6,000
St. Joseph's-PA	Alumni Mem. Fieldhouse	3,200
Temple	Liacouras Center	10,206
Xavier-OH	Cintas Center	10,200

Big East

	Home Floor	Seats
Boston College	Conte Forum	8,606
Connecticut	Gampel Pavilion	10,027
	& Hartford Civic Center	16,294
Georgetown	MCI Center	20,600
Miami-FL	Miami Arena	15,200
Notre Dame	Joyce Center	11,418
Pittsburgh	Fitzgerald Field House	6,798
	& Pittsburgh Civic Arena	16,725
Providence	Dunkin Donuts Center	12,993
Rutgers	Louis Brown Athletic Center	9,000
St. John's	Alumni Hall	6,008
	& Madison Square Garden	18,470
Seton Hall	Continental Airlines Arena	20,029
Syracuse	Carrier Dome	33,000
Villanova	The Pavilion	6,500
	First Union Center	21,000
Virginia Tech	Cassell Coliseum	10,052
West Virginia	WVU Coliseum	14,000

College Basketball (Cont.)

Big Sky

	Home Floor	Seats
CS-Sacramento	Hornet Gym	2,603
Eastern Wash	Reese Court	6,000
Idaho St	Holt Arena	8,000
Montana	Adams Center	7,500
Montana St	Worthington Arena	7,898
Northern Arizona	Walkup Skydome	7,000
Portland St	Rose Garden	19,980
	& Stott Center	1,775
Weber St	Dee Events Center	12,000

Big South

	Home Floor	Seats
Birmingham Southern	Bill Battle Coliseum	2,000
Charleston So	CSU Fieldhouse	1,500
Coastal Carolina	Kimbel Gymnasium	1,037
Elon U	Koury Center	2,000
High Point	Millis Center	2,565
Liberty	Vines Center	9,000
NC-Asheville	Justice Center	1,100
	& Asheville Civic Center	6,000
Radford	Dedmon Center	5,000
Winthrop	Winthrop Coliseum	6,100

Big Ten

	Home Floor	Seats
Illinois	Assembly Hall	16,450
Indiana	Assembly Hall	17,357
Iowa	Carver-Hawkeye Arena	15,500
Michigan	Crisler Arena	13,567
Michigan St	Breslin Events Center	14,659
Minnesota	Williams Arena	14,321
Northwestern	Welsh-Ryan Arena	8,117
Ohio St	Value City Arena	17,500
Penn St	Bryce Jordan Center	15,261
Purdue	Mackey Arena	14,123
Wisconsin	Kohl Center	17,142

Big 12

	Home Floor	Seats
Colorado	Coors Events Conference Ctr.	11,076
Iowa St	Hilton Coliseum	14,092
Kansas	Allen Fieldhouse	16,300
Kansas St	Bramlage Coliseum	13,500
Missouri	Hearnes Center	13,545
Nebraska	Devaney Sports Center	13,500
Baylor	Ferrell Center	10,284
Oklahoma	Lloyd Noble Center	11,100
Oklahoma St	Gallagher-Iba Arena	13,611
Texas	Erwin Center	16,175
Texas A&M	Reed Arena	12,700
Texas Tech	United Spirit Arena	15,050

Big West

	Home Floor	Seats
Cal Poly	Mott Gym	3,032
CS-Fullerton	Titan Gym	3,500
CS-Northridge	The Matadome	1,600
Idaho	Kibbie Dome	10,000
Long Beach St	The Pyramid	5,000
Pacific	Spanos Center	6,150
UC-Irvine	Bren Events Center	5,000
UC-Riverside	Student Rec. Center	3,168
UC-Santa Barbara	The Thunderdome	6,000
Utah St	The Smith Spectrum	10,270

Colonial

	Home Floor	Seats
Delaware	Bob Carpenter Center	5,000
Drexel	Phys. Education Center	2,300
George Mason	Patriot Center	10,000
Hofstra	Hofstra Arena	5,112
James Madison	JMU Convocation Center	7,156
NC-Wilmington	Trask Coliseum	6,100
Old Dominion	Ted Constant Convocation Ctr.	9,450
Towson	Towson Center	5,000
VCU	Siegel Center	7,500
Wm. & Mary	William & Mary Hall	8,600

Conference USA

	Home Floor	Seats
UAB	Bartow Arena	8,500
Cincinnati	Shoemaker Center	13,176
DePaul	All State Arena	17,500
East Carolina	Minges Coliseum	7,500
Houston	Hofheinz Pavilion	8,479
Louisville	Freedom Hall	18,865
Marquette	Bradley Center	18,712
Memphis	The Pyramid	20,142
UNC Charlotte	Halton Arena	9,105
Saint Louis	Savvis Center	20,000
South Florida	Sun Dome	10,411
Southern Miss	Green Coliseum	8,095
TCU	Daniel-Meyer Coliseum	7,166
Tulane	New Orleans Arena	17,832
	& Fogelman Arena	3,600

Horizon League

	Home Floor	Seats
Butler	Hinkle Fieldhouse	11,043
Cleveland St	CSU Convocation Center	13,610
Detroit Mercy	Calihan Hall	8,837
IL-Chicago	UIC Pavilion	8,000
Loyola-IL	Gentile Center	5,200
WI-Green Bay	Brown County Arena	5,600
WI-Milwaukee	Klotsche Center	5,000
Wright St	Nutter Center	10,632
Youngstown St	Beeghly Center	8,000

Ivy League

	Home Floor	Seats
Brown	Pizzitola Sports Center	2,800
Columbia	Levien Gymnasium	3,408
Cornell	Newman Arena	4,750
Dartmouth	Leede Arena	2,100
Harvard	Lavietes Pavilion	2,195
Penn	The Palestra	8,700
Princeton	Jadwin Gymnasium	6,854
Yale	Lee Amphitheater	3,100

Metro Atlantic

	Home Floor	Seats
Canisius	HSBC Arena	19,500
	& Koessler Athletic Center	1,800
Fairfield	Alumni Hall	2,479
Iona	Mulcahy Center	3,200
Loyola-MD	Reitz Arena	3,000
Manhattan	Draddy Gymnasium	3,000
Marist	McCann Center	3,944
Niagara	HSBC Arena	19,500
	& Gallagher Center	3,200
Rider	Alumni Gymnasium	1,650
St. Peter's	Yanitelli Center	3,200
Siena	Pepsi Arena	15,500

Mid American

	Home Floor	Seats
Akron	JAR Arena	5,942
Ball St.	John E. Wortham Arena	11,500
Bowling Green	Anderson Arena	5,200
Buffalo	Alumni Arena	8,500
Central Mich.	Rose Arena	5,200
Eastern Mich.	Convocation Center	8,824
Kent	MAC Center	6,327
Marshall	Henderson Center	9,043
Miami-OH	Millett Hall	9,200
Northern Illinois	Chick Evans Field House	6,044
Ohio Univ.	Convocation Center	13,000
Toledo	Savage Hall	9,000
Western Mich.	University Arena	5,800

Mid-Continent

	Home Floor	Seats
Chicago St.	Dickens Athletic Center	2,500
IU-PUI	IU-PUI Gym	2,000
Missouri-K.C.	Municipal Auditorium	9,287
Oakland	Oakland Arena	3,000
Oral Roberts	Mabee Center	10,575
Southern Utah	Centrum	5,300
Valparaiso	Athletics-Recreation Center	4,500
Western Ill.	Western Hall	5,139

Mid-Eastern Athletic

	Home Floor	Seats
Bethune-Cookman	Moore Gym	3,000
Coppin St.	Coppin Center	3,000
Delaware St.	Memorial Hall	3,000
Florida A&M	Gaither Gym	3,350
Hampton	Hampton Convocation Center	7,200
Howard	Burr Gym	3,000
MD-East.Shore	Tawes Gym	1,200
Morgan St.	Hill Fieldhouse	5,000
Norfolk St.	Echols Hall	7,600
N. Carolina A&T	Corbett Sports Center	7,500
S. Carolina St.	SHM Center	3,200

Missouri Valley

	Home Floor	Seats
Bradley	Carver Arena	11,300
Creighton	Omaha Civic Auditorium	9,377
Drake	Knapp Center	7,002
Evansville	Roberts Stadium	12,300
Illinois St.	Redbird Arena	10,200
Indiana St.	Hulman Center	10,200
Northern Iowa	UNI-Dome	10,000
Southern Ill.	SIU Arena	10,014
SW Missouri St.	Hammons Student Center	8,846
Wichita St.	Levitt Arena	10,527

Mountain West

	Home Floor	Seats
Air Force	Clune Arena	6,003
BYU	Marriott Center	22,700
Colorado St.	Moby Arena	8,754
San Diego St.	Cox Arena at the Aztec Bowl	12,000
UNLV	Thomas & Mack Center	18,500
New Mexico	The Pit	18,018
Utah	Huntsman Center	15,000
Wyoming	Arena-Auditorium	15,028

Northeast

	Home Floor	Seats
Central Conn. St.	Detrick Gym	3,200
Farleigh Dickinson	Rothman Center	5,000
LIU-Brooklyn	Schwartz Athletic Center	1,200
MD-Balt. County	Retriever Activity Center	4,024
Monmouth	Boylan Gym	2,500
Mt. St. Mary's	Knott Arena	3,196
Quinnipiac	Burt Kahn Court	1,500
Robert Morris	Sewall Center	3,056
Sacred Heart	Pitt Center	2,100
St. Francis-NY	Pope Center	1,400
St. Francis-PA	DeGol Arena	3,500
Wagner	Spiro Sports Center	2,100

Ohio Valley

	Home Floor	Seats
Austin Peay	Dunn Center	9,000
Eastern Illinois	Lantz Gym	5,300
Eastern Ky.	McBrayer Arena	6,500
Morehead St.	Johnson Arena	6,500
Murray St.	Regional Special Events Ctr.	8,600
SE Missouri St.	Show Me Center	7,000
Tennessee-Martin	Skyhawk Arena	6,700
Tennessee St.	Gentry Complex	10,500
Tennessee Tech	Eblen Center	10,152

Pacific-10

	Home Floor	Seats
Arizona	McKale Center	14,545
Arizona St.	Wells Fargo Arena	14,198
California	Haas Pavillion	12,172
Oregon	McArthur Court	9,087
Oregon St.	Gill Coliseum	10,400
Stanford	Maples Pavilion	7,500
UCLA	Pauley Pavilion	12,819
USC	LA Sports Arena	16,161
Washington	Bank of America @ Hec Edmundson Pavilion	10,000
Washington. St.	Friel Court	12,058

Patriot League

	Home Floor	Seats
American	Bender Arena	5,000
Army	Christl Arena	5,043
Bucknell	Davis Gym	2,380
Colgate	Cotterell Court	3,000
Holy Cross	Hart Recreation Center	3,600
Lafayette	Kirby Field House	3,500
Lehigh	Stabler Arena	5,600
Navy	Alumni Hall	5,710

Southeastern

Eastern	Home Floor	Seats
Florida	O'Connell Center	12,000
Georgia	Stegeman Coliseum	10,523
Kentucky	Rupp Arena	23,000
South Carolina	Frank McGuire Arena	12,401
Tennessee	Thompson-Boling Arena	24,535
Vanderbilt	Memorial Gymnasium	14,168

Western	Home Floor	Seats
Alabama	Coleman Coliseum	15,043
Arkansas	Bud Walton Arena	19,200
Auburn	Eaves-Memorial Coliseum	10,108
LSU	Maravich Assembly Center	14,164
Mississippi	Tad Smith Coliseum	8,135
Mississippi St.	Humphrey Coliseum	10,500

College Basketball (Cont.)

Southern

	Home Floor	Seats
Appalachian St.	Varsity Gymnasium	8,000
The Citadel	McAlister Field House	6,200
Coll. of Charleston	Kresse Arena	3,500
Davidson	Belk Arena	5,700
E. Tenn. St.	Memorial Center	12,000
Furman	Timmons Arena	5,000
Ga. Southern	Hanner Fieldhouse	5,500
NC-Greensboro	Fleming Gymnasium	2,320
Tenn-Chatt.	UTC Arena	11,218
VMI	Cameron Hall	5,029
W. Carolina	Ramsey Center	7,286
Wofford	Johnson Arena	3,500

Sun Belt

	Home Floor	Seats
Ark-Little Rock	Alltel Arena	18,000
Arkansas St	Convocation Center	10,563
Denver	Magness Arena	7,200
Florida International	Golden Panther Arena	5,000
LA-Lafayette	The Cajundome	12,800
Middle Tenn. St.	Murphy Center	11,520
New Mexico St.	Pan American Center	13,071
New Orleans	Lakefront Arena	10,000
North Texas	The Super Pit	10,000
South Alabama	Mitchell Center	10,000
Western Ky.	E.A. Diddle Arena	11,300

Southland

	Home Floor	Seats
Lamar	Montagne Center	10,800
McNeese St.	Burton Coliseum	8,000
Nicholls St.	Stopher Gym	3,800
Louisiana-Monroe	Ewing Coliseum	8,000
Northwestern St.	Prather Coliseum	3,900
Sam Houston St.	Johnson Coliseum	6,172
SE Louisiana	University Center	7,500
SW Texas St.	Strahan Coliseum	7,200
S.F. Austin St.	W.R. Johnson Coliseum	7,200
TX-Arlington	Texas Hall	4,200
TX-San Antonio	Convocation Center	5,100

West Coast

	Home Floor	Seats
Gonzaga	Martin Centre	4,000
Loyola Marymount	Gersten Pavilion	4,156
Pepperdine	Firestone Fieldhouse	3,104
Portland St.	Chiles Center	5,000
St. Mary's-CA	McKeon Pavilion	3,500
San Diego	Jenny Craig Pavilion	5,000
San Francisco	War Memorial Gym	5,300
Santa Clara	Leavy Center	5,000

Southwestern

	Home Floor	Seats
Alabama A&M	Elmore Healh/Science Building	6,000
Alabama St.	Joe Reed Acadome	8,000
Alcorn St.	Whitney Complex	7,000
Arkansas-Pine Bluff	HPER Complex	4,500
Grambling St.	Tiger Memorial Gym	4,500
Jackson St.	Williams Center	8,000
Miss.Valley St.	Harrison HPER Athletic Complex	6,000
Prairie View A&M	The Baby Dome	6,600
Southern-BR	Clark Activity Center	7,500
TX Southern	Health & P.E. Building	8,100

Western Athletic

	Home Floor	Seats
Boise St.	BSU Pavilion	12,380
Fresno St.	Selland Arena	10,132
Hawaii	Stan Sherif Center	10,225
Louisiana Tech	Thomas Assembly Center	8,000
Nevada	Lawlor Events Center	11,200
Rice	Autry Court	5,000
San Jose St.	The Events Center	5,000
SMU	Moody Coliseum	8,998
Tulsa	Reynolds Center	8,355
UTEP	Haskins Center	12,222

Independents

	Home Floor	Seats		Home Floor	Seats
Centenary	Gold Dome	3,000	Savannah St.	Wiley Gym	2,100
Gardner-Webb	Paul Porter Arena	5,000	Texas A&M-Corpus Christi	Memorial Coliseum	4,000
Lipscomb	Lipscomb U. Arena	5,028	Texas-Pan Am	Health/PE Fieldhouse	3,500
Morris Brown	John H. Lewis Gym	2,000			

Future NCAA Final Four Sites

Men

Year	Arena	Seats	Location
2002	Georgia Dome	40,000	Atlanta
2003	Louisiana Superdome	53,500	New Orleans
2004	Alamodome	20,557*	San Antonio
2005	The Dome at America's Center	66,000	St. Louis
2006	RCA Dome	47,100	Indianapolis
2007	Georgia Dome	40,000	Atlanta

Women

Year	Arena	Seats	Location
2002	Alamodome	20,557*	San Antonio
2003	Georgia Dome	40,000	Atlanta
2004	New Orleans Sports Arena	17,832	New Orleans
2005	Conseco Fieldhouse	18,345	Indianapolis
	or RCA Dome	56,127	Indianapolis
2006	FleetCenter	18,624	Boston
2007	Gund Arena	20,562	Cleveland

*This is the listed capacity for Spurs games at the Alamodome. It is likely that the seating will be reconfigured to fit more spectators for the Final Four.

COLLEGE FOOTBALL

The 40 Largest I-A Stadiums

The 40 largest stadiums in NCAA Division I-A college football heading into the 2001 season. Note that (*) indicates stadium not on campus.

		Location	Seats	Home Team	Conference	Built	Field
1	Michigan Stadium	Ann Arbor, Mich.	107,501	Michigan	Big Ten	1927	Grass
2	Neyland Stadium	Knoxville, Tenn.	104,079	Tennessee	SEC-East	1921	Grass
3	Ohio Stadium	Columbus, Ohio	106,537	Ohio St.	Big Ten	1922	Grass
4	Rose Bowl*	Pasadena, Calif.	98,636	UCLA	Pac-10	1922	Grass
5	Beaver Stadium	University Park, Penn.	93,967	Penn St.	Big Ten	1960	Grass
6	LA Memorial Coliseum*	Los Angeles, Calif.	92,000	USC	Pac-10	1923	Grass
7	Jordan-Hare Stadium	Auburn, Ala.	91,600	Auburn	SEC-West	1939	Grass
	Tiger Stadium	Baton Rouge, La.	91,600	LSU	SEC-West	1924	Grass
9	Sanford Stadium	Athens, Ga.	86,520	Georgia	SEC-East	1929	Grass
10	Stanford Stadium	Stanford, Calif.	85,500	Stanford	Pac-10	1921	Grass
11	Bryant-Denny Stadium	Tuscaloosa, Ala.	83,818	Alabama	SEC-West	1929	Grass
12	Legion Field*	Birmingham, Ala.	83,091	Alabama/UAB	SEC-West/USA	1927	Grass
13	Florida Field	Gainesville, Fla.	83,000	Florida	SEC-East	1929	Grass
14	Memorial Stadium	Clemson, S.C.	81,473	Clemson	ACC	1942	Grass
15	Kyle Field	College Station, Texas	80,650	Texas A&M	Big 12-South	1925	Grass
16	Williams-Brice Stadium	Columbia, S.C.	80,250	South Carolina	SEC-East	1934	Grass
17	Notre Dame Stadium	Notre Dame, Ind.	80,232	Notre Dame	Independent	1930	Grass
18	Royal-Memorial Stadium	Austin, Texas	80,082	Texas	Big 12-South	1924	Grass
19	Doak Campbell Stadium	Tallahasse, Fla.	80,000	Florida St.	ACC	1950	Grass
20	Camp Randall Stadium	Madison, Wis.	76,129	Wisconsin	Big Ten	1917	Turf
21	Memorial Stadium	Berkeley, Calif.	75,028	California	Pac-10	1923	Grass
22	Memorial Stadium	Lincoln, Neb.	74,031	Nebraska	Big 12-North	1923	Turf
23	Sun Devil Stadium	Tempe, Ariz.	73,379	Arizona St.	Pac-10	1959	Grass
24	Oklahoma Memorial Field	Norman, Okla.	72,765	Oklahoma	Big 12-South	1924	Grass
25	Husky Stadium	Seattle, Wash.	72,500	Washington	Pac-10	1920	Turf
26	Orange Bowl*	Miami, Fla.	72,314	Miami-FL	Big East	1935	Grass
27	Spartan Stadium	East Lansing, Mich.	72,027	Michigan St.	Big Ten	1957	Turf
28	Donald W. Reynolds Razorback Stadium	Fayetteville, Ark.	72,000	Arkansas	SEC-West	1938	Grass
29	Memorial Stadium	Champaign, Ill.	70,904	Illinois	Big Ten	1923	Turf
30	Kinnick Stadium	Iowa City, Iowa	70,397	Iowa	Big Ten	1929	Grass
31	Citrus Bowl*	Orlando, Fla.	70,188	Central Florida	Independent	1936	Grass
32	Rice Stadium*	Houston, Texas	70,000	Rice	WAC	1950	Turf
33	Superdome*	New Orleans, La.	69,767	Tulane	USA	1975	Turf
34	HHH Metrodome*	Minneapolis, Minn.	69,172	Minnesota	Big Ten	1982	Turf
35	Commonwealth	Lexington, Ky.	68,000	Kentucky	SEC-East	1973	Grass
36	Ross-Ade Stadium	W. Lafayette, Ind.	67,330	Purdue	Big Ten	1924	Grass
37	Veterans Stadium*	Philadelphia, Penn.	66,592	Temple	Big East	1971	Turf
38	LaVell Edwards Stadium	Provo, Utah	65,000	BYU	Mountain West	1964	Grass
	North Shore Stadium*	Pittsburgh, Penn.	65,000	Pittsburgh	Big East	2001	Grass
40	Mountaineer Field	Morgantown, W. Va.	63,500	West Virginia	Big East	1980	Turf

Note: The capacities for several stadiums including the Rose Bowl, Louisiana Superdome and Sun Devil Stadium are often listed differently for other events, such as bowl games, which they host.

2001 Conference Home Fields

NCAA Division I-A conference by conference listing includes member teams heading into the 2001 season. Note that (*) indicates stadium is not on campus.

Atlantic Coast

	Stadium	Built	Seats	Field
Clemson	Memorial	1942	81,473	Grass
Duke	Wallace Wade	1929	33,941	Grass
Florida St.	Doak Campbell	1950	80,000	Grass
Ga. Tech	Bobby Dodd	1913	46,000	Grass
Maryland	Byrd	1950	48,055	Grass
N. Carolina	Kenan Memorial	1927	60,000	Grass
N.C. State	Carter-Finley	1966	51,500	Grass
Virginia	Scott	1931	61,500	Grass
Wake Forest	Groves	1968	31,500	Grass

Big East

	Stadium	Built	Seats	Field
Boston Col.	Alumni	1957	44,500	Turf
Miami-FL	Orange Bowl*	1935	72,314	Grass
Pittsburgh	North Shore Stadium	2001	65,000	Grass
Rutgers	Rutgers	1994	41,500	Grass
Syracuse	Carrier Dome	1980	49,550	Turf
Temple	Veterans*	1971	66,592	Turf
Va. Tech	Lane	1965	50,000	Grass
West Va.	Mountaineer Fld.	1980	63,500	Turf

College Football (Cont.)

Big Ten

	Stadium	Built	Seats	Field
Illinois	Memorial	1923	70,904	Turf
Indiana	Memorial	1960	52,354	Grass
Iowa	Kinnick	1929	70,397	Grass
Michigan	Michigan	1927	107,501	Grass
Michigan St.	Spartan	1957	72,027	Turf
Minnesota	Metrodome*	1982	69,172	Turf
Northwestern	Ryan Field	1926	47,130	Grass
Ohio St.	Ohio	1922	106,537	Grass
Penn St.	Beaver	1960	93,967	Grass
Purdue	Ross-Ade	1924	67,330	Grass
Wisconsin	Camp Randall	1917	76,129	Turf

Big 12

NORTH	Stadium	Built	Seats	Field
Colorado	Folsom Field	1924	51,808	Turf
Iowa St.	Jack Trice Field	1975	43,000	Grass
Kansas	Memorial	1921	50,250	Turf
Kansas St.	Wagner Field	1968	50,000	Turf
Missouri	Faurot Field	1926	62,000	Grass
Nebraska	Memorial	1923	74,031	Turf

SOUTH	Stadium	Built	Seats	Field
Baylor	Floyd Casey	1950	50,000	Grass
Oklahoma	Memorial Stadium, Owen Field	1924	72,765	Grass
Oklahoma St.	Lewis Field	1920	48,000	Turf
Texas	Royal-Mem.	1924	80,082	Grass
Texas A&M.	Kyle Field	1925	80,650	Grass
Texas Tech	Jones-SBC	1947	50,500	Turf

Note: The annual Oklahoma-Texas game has been played at the Cotton Bowl (capacity 68,252) in Dallas since 1937.

Conference USA

	Stadium	Built	Seats	Field
UAB	Legion Field	1927	83,091	Grass
Army	Michie	1924	39,929	Turf
Cincinnati	Nippert	1924	35,000	Turf
E. Carolina	Dowdy-Ficklen	1963	43,000	Grass
Houston	Robertson	1942	31,000	Grass
Louisville	Papa John's Cardinal	1998	42,000	Turf
Memphis	Liberty Bowl*	1965	62,380	Grass
Southern Miss	M.M. Roberts	1976	33,000	Grass
TCU	Amon Carter	1929	44,008	Grass
Tulane	Superdome*	1975	69,767	Turf

Mid-American

	Stadium	Built	Seats	Field
Akron	Rubber Bowl*	1940	35,202	Turf
Ball St.	Ball State	1967	30,000	Grass
Buffalo	UB	1993	31,000	Grass
Bowling Green	Doyt Perry	1966	30,599	Grass
Central Mich.	Kelly/Shorts	1972	30,199	Turf
Eastern Mich.	Rynearson	1969	30,200	Turf
Kent	Dix	1969	30,520	Turf
Marshall	Marshall	1991	38,019	Turf
Miami-OH	Fred Yager	1983	30,012	Grass
Northern Ill.	Huskie	1965	31,000	Turf
Ohio Univ.	Peden	1929	24,000	Grass
Toledo	Glass Bowl	1937	26,248	Turf
Western Mich.	Waldo	1939	30,200	Grass

Mountain West

	Stadium	Built	Seats	Field
Air Force	Falcon	1962	52,480	Grass
BYU	LaVell Edwards	1964	65,000	Grass
Colorado St.	Hughes	1968	30,000	Grass
New Mexico	University	1960	37,000	Grass
San Diego St.	Qualcomm*	1967	54,000	Grass
UNLV	Sam Boyd*	1971	40,000	Grass
Utah	Rice-Eccles	1927†	45,634	Grass
Wyoming	War Memorial	1950	33,500	Grass

†Utah's Rice-Eccles Stadium was rebuilt in 1998.

Pacific-10

	Stadium	Built	Seats	Field
Arizona	Arizona	1928	56,002	Grass
Arizona St.	Sun Devil	1959	73,379	Grass
California	Memorial	1923	75,028	Grass
Oregon	Autzen	1967	41,698	Turf
Oregon St.	Reser's	1953	35,362	Turf
Stanford	Stanford	1921	85,500	Grass
UCLA	Rose Bowl*	1922	98,636	Grass
USC	LA Coliseum*	1923	92,000	Grass
Washington	Husky	1920	72,500	Turf
Washington St.	Martin	1972	37,600	Turf

Southeastern

EAST	Stadium	Built	Seats	Field
Florida	Florida Field	1929	83,000	Grass
Georgia	Sanford	1929	86,520	Grass
Kentucky	Commonwealth	1973	68,000	Grass
S. Carolina	Williams-Brice	1934	80,250	Grass
Tennessee	Neyland	1921	104,079	Grass
Vanderbilt	Vanderbilt	1981	41,600	Grass

WEST	Stadium	Built	Seats	Field
Alabama	Bryant-Denny & Legion	1929 1927	83,818 83,091	Grass Grass
Arkansas	Donald W. Reynolds Razorback & War Memorial*	1938 1948	72,000 53,727	Grass Grass
Auburn	Jordan-Hare	1939	91,600	Grass
LSU	Tiger	1924	91,600	Grass
Mississippi	Vaught-Hem'way	1915	50,577	Grass
Miss. St.	Scott/Davis-Wade Field	1915	45,286	Grass

Note: EAST—Vanderbilt Stadium was rebuilt in 1981.

Sun Belt

	Stadium	Built	Seats	Field
Arkansas St.	Indian	1974	33,410	Grass
Idaho	Kibbie Dome & Martin*	1975 1972	16,000 37,600	Turf Turf
UL-Lafayette	Cajun Field	1971	31,000	Grass
UL-Monroe	Malone	1978	30,427	Grass
Middle Tennessee	Johnny Red Floyd	1933	30,880	Turf
New Mexico St.	Aggie Memorial	1978	30,343	Grass
North Texas	Fouts Field	1952	30,500	Turf

Western Athletic

	Stadium	Built	Seats	Field
Boise St.	Bronco	1970	30,000	Turf
Fresno St.	Bulldog	1980	41,031	Grass
Hawaii	Aloha*	1975	50,000	Turf
Louisiana Tech	Joe Aillet	1968	30,600	Grass
Nevada	Mackay	1967	31,545	Grass
Rice	Rice	1950	70,000	Grass
San Jose St.	Spartan	1933	30,578	Grass
SMU	Gerald J. Ford Stadium	2000	32,000	Grass
Tulsa	Skelly	1930	40,385	Turf
UTEP	Sun Bowl*	1963	52,000	Turf

I-A Independents

	Stadium	Built	Seats	Field
C. Florida	Citrus Bowl	1936	70,188	Grass
Connecticut	Memorial	1953	16,200	Grass
Navy	Navy-Marine Corps Memorial	1959	30,000	Grass
Notre Dame	Notre Dame	1930	80,012	Grass
S. Florida	Raymond James*	1988	66,321	Grass
Troy State	Memorial	1950	17,500	Grass
Utah St.	Romney	1968	30,257	Grass

Business

Alex Rodriguez signed a deal worth more than the GDP
of some countries, but the Rangers still foundered in 2001.

The XFL Becomes the Ex-FL

The WWF's money and NBC's exposure aren't enough for the league to survive.

Bob Stevens *is an anchor for ESPN's SportsCenter and SportsWeekly.*

The XFL began with all the right intentions (or wrong intentions, depending on our loyalties). Vince McMahon's World Wrestling Federation, NBC and advertisers like Anheuser-Busch, Burger King and Honda—all companies used to succeeding in business—figured to cash in, literally, on America's passion for football, its love of 'rasslin, the hormones and wallets of young men and the country's fixation on "reality" television.

McMahon promised "real American football, with a lot more fun and a lot more attitude." An ESPN-commissioned poll in June 2000 found 30 percent of respondents "somewhat, or very likely to watch" the XFL. In an *ESPN the Magazine* interview in November 2000, McMahon called all NFL quarterbacks "panty-waists," and said that the NFL had become "homogenized, predictable and dull."

He also boasted, among his other juicy tidbits, that his players would be encouraged to date the cheerleaders, who will be "hot babes."

Many bought into it. Kippy Brown gave up his position as running backs coach with the Green Bay Packers for a chance to be head coach of the Memphis Maniax. Jim Skipper left his assistant coaching job with the Super Bowl-bound New York Giants to become the head coach of the San Francisco Demons.

"Naturally, I wanted to get into the Super Bowl," said Skipper. "But here was an opportunity to become a head coach and I jumped at it."

Immediately following the Super Bowl, *The Wall Street Journal* reported that NBC's goal of a 4.5 rating, or six million viewers on Saturday night, "shouldn't be too hard to attain."

And it wasn't...for one week anyway.

AP/Wide World Photos

*Well it was fun while it lasted, right? WWF Chairman **Vince McMahon**, left, tried everything, including enlisting the help of Minnesota governor and former wrestler **Jesse Ventura**.*

The season opener between the Las Vegas Outlaws and the New York/New Jersey Hitmen, featuring players with names like "He Hate Me" on their jerseys, played to a sellout crowd of over 30,000 and a national Nielsen TV rating of 9.5. The opening weekend's broadcasts were watched by 54 million viewers. McMahon and the XFL didn't know it, but it would be their crowning moment.

By Week 2, the overnight rating had fallen by 50 percent. In Week 3, "America's Most Wanted" was America's preferred Saturday night entertainment over the XFL, and Honda became the first company to pull out as a major advertiser.

By Week 7, that 9.5 rating had dropped to an NBC all-time Saturday night record low of 1.6. NBC Sports president Dick Ebersol told *The Washington Post* that he's "prepared to pull the plug on the XFL if ratings don't improve during the playoffs."

Two weeks after the league championship game, the much ballyhooed "Million Dollar Game" (Los Angeles beat San Francisco 38-6), McMahon himself pulled the plug, saying humbly, "some risks pay off, some don't."

So why. didn't it work? Because

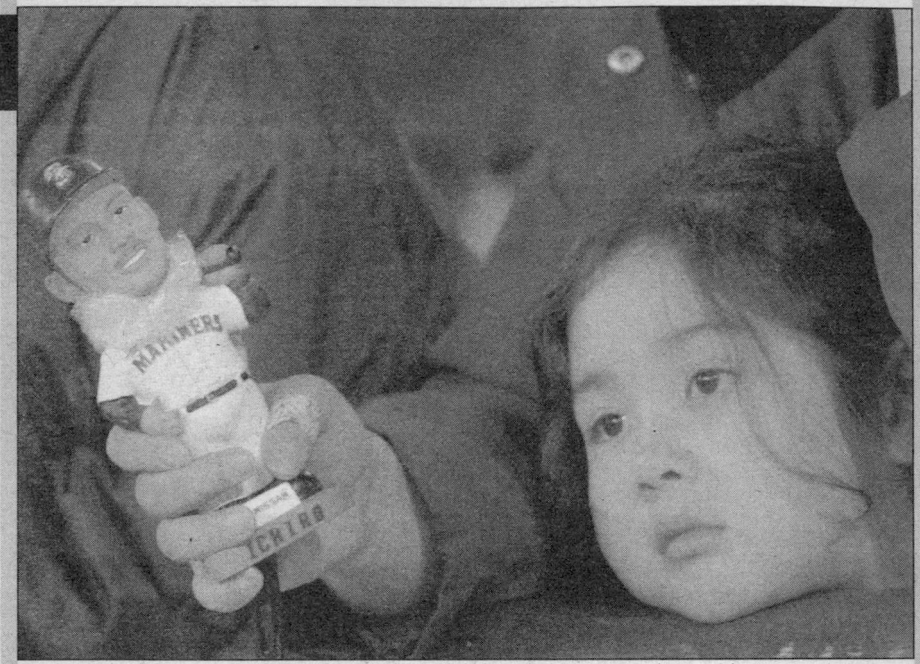

Thousands stood in line the night before the Mariners game on July 28 to be assured of receiving an Ichiro bobblehead doll. Lucky Hannah Kirihara and her mom arrived at 5:45 a.m.

McMahon, for once, couldn't deliver. The XFL's own director of football operations, Mike Keller, said it best.

"I guess we weren't wild enough or far out enough to keep the wrestling fans," said Keller. "We were neither this nor that."

It wasn't the WWF. It wasn't the NFL. And it wasn't successful. And the cost? *The Wall Street Journal* reported that the World Wrestling Federation lost $46.9 million for the year. NBC had a reported pre-tax loss of $50 million, and "He Hate Me" fled to the CFL.

Who'll bring us the Next F-L? The Arena Football League already has. And they're doing it the right way—building slowly and regionally. The league has expanded to 19 teams and has spun off a second league. They've even added NFL owners and former stars to its burgeoning future.

Bob Stevens' Ten Biggest Moments of the Year in Business

10 ▪ Hockey's Big Night—On June 18, Michigan and Michigan State officials agree to stage a hockey game between the two schools dubbed "The Cold War" to be held outdoors at East Lansing's 72,000-seat Spartan Stadium on Oct. 6. In just eight days over 56,000 tickets are sold. The previous hockey attendance world record was 55,000, set in Moscow in 1957.

9 ▪ Movers and Shakers—NBA's Vancouver Grizzlies pack up and head for Memphis, and the Seattle SuperSonics (NBA), Florida Panthers (NHL) and Montreal Canadiens (NHL) are sold to new owners—the Canadiens to George Gillett, an American businessman.

8 ▪ NBDL—The NBA enters the developmental (minor) league business in the fall of 2001 in eight southeastern markets. It already has a national cable deal.

7 ▪ Friday Night Football—As part of college football's continuing effort to saturate television, the NCAA lifts its ban and permits Friday night games for the first time. Many schools and leagues refuse to take part, citing a threat to high school football.

6 ▪ Name Games—*The Denver Post* refuses to refer to the Broncos' new stadium by its corporate sponsor, INVESCO, and instead promises to call the new venue Mile High Stadium. Also, the NHL (with Coca-Cola as a corporate sponsor) refuses to allow anyone to refer to the location of its 2001 All-Star Game in Denver as "The Pepsi Center." Instead, announcers had to refer to the arena as "the home of the Colorado Avalanche."

5 ▪ Baseball's Dual Dilemma—Bobbleheads are the new craze as thousands of fans spend the night outside Safeco Field for a chance to receive one of 20,000 Ichiro bobbleheads. Meanwhile, miserable attendance and poor prospects for stadium situations in cities like Montreal have MLB officials considering contraction.

4 ▪ D.C. Darlings—Just the rumblings of a Michael Jordan return sparks a season ticket spike for the woeful Wizards, while the Capitals' trade for Jaromir Jagr adds 800 new season tickets in just four days and well over 1,000 in the first few weeks of the summer.

3 ▪ Major League Networks—The Toronto Maple Leafs launch their own digital television network called Leafs TV, for rabid fans who crave "all Maple Leafs, all the time." The New York Yankees announce their own network that will feature Yankees, New Jersey Nets and other New York City area games.

2 ▪ Thank You Tiger—The PGA Tour inks a new television package to begin in 2003, worth an estimated $850 million through 2006, a 48 percent increase over its previous deal. ABC, CBS, NBC and USA each acquired rights to PGA tournaments, while The Golf Channel bought rights to the Buy.com tour.

1 ▪ Attack on America—In the wake of the Sept. 11 terrorist attacks in New York and Washington, the sports world is put on hold. MLB games are postponed for six days, the MLS cancels the remainder of its regular season and numerous minor league baseball leagues cancel the remainder of their playoffs. NASCAR and major golf events are postponed, the Ryder Cup is rescheduled until 2002 and the NFL pushes its schedule back a week. The cost is unknown.

$100 Million Men

A-Rod hit the jackpot in 2001 but he sure wasn't the only one. Listed are the 10 largest sports contracts (in total value) signed since November 2000.

	League	Years/$
A. Rodriguez	MLB	10/$252m
D. Jeter	MLB	10/$189m
M. Ramirez	MLB	8/$160m
T. Helton	MLB	9/$141.5m
C. Webber	NBA	7/$122.7m
M. Hampton	MLB	8/$121m
D. Bledsoe	NFL	10/$103m
M. Finley	NBA	7/$102m
B. Favre	NFL	10/$101m
A. Houston	NBA	7/$100.4m

For Richer, For Poorer

As if the New York Yankees didn't already have enough titles, *Forbes Magazine* has given them one more—baseball's most valuable team. Below are the most valuable and least valuable MLB franchises.

	Value
1. New York Yankees	$635m
2. New York Mets	454m
3. Atlanta Braves	407m
28. Florida Marlins	$128m
29. Minnesota Twins	99m
30. Montreal Expos	92m

2000-01 Top Rated TV Sports Events

Final 2000-01 network television ratings for nationally telecast sports events, according to Nielsen Media Research. Covers period from Sept. 1, 2000 through Aug. 31, 2001. Events are listed with ratings points and audience share; each ratings point represents 1,022,000 households and shares indicate percentage of TV sets in use.

Multiple entries: SPORTS—NFL Football (46); Summer Olympics (13); Major League Baseball and NBA Basketball (5); NCAA Football bowl games (3); NCAA Basketball (2). NETWORKS—FOX (21); ABC (19); NBC (18); CBS (17).

		Date	Net	Rtg/Sh
1	**Super Bowl XXXV** (Ravens vs Giants)	1/28/01	CBS	40.4/61
2	**AFC Championship Game** (Ravens at Raiders)	1/14/01	CBS	22.6/42
3	**NFC Championship Game** (Vikings at Giants)	1/14/01	FOX	20.6/44
4	**AFC Playoff Game** (Ravens at Titans)	1/7/01	CBS	19.0/42
5	**NFC Playoff Game** (Eagles at Giants)	1/7/01	FOX	18.6/34
6	**Orange Bowl** (Oklahoma vs Florida St.)	1/3/01	ABC	17.8/28
7	**NFC Playoff Game** (Buccaneers at Eagles)	12/31/00	FOX	17.3/34
8	**NFC Playoff Game** (Rams at Saints)	12/30/00	ABC	16.6/34
9	**NFL Regular Season Late Game** (Various teams)	12/10/00	FOX	16.2/30
10	**Summer Olympics** (Men's/women's gymnastics indiv. finals, women's platform diving finals)	9/24/00	NBC	16.0/26
11	**Summer Olympics** (Men's/women's gymnastics indiv. finals, T&F finals)	9/25/00	NBC	15.8/26
	AFC Playoff Game (Broncos at Ravens)	12/31/00	CBS	15.8/35
13	**NCAA Men's Basketball Championship Game** (Duke vs Arizona)	4/2/01	CBS	15.6/24
14	**Summer Olympics** (Women's gymnastics team finals, men's/women's swim finals)	9/19/00	NBC	15.5/26
15	**NFL Monday Night Football** (Broncos at Rams)	9/4/00	ABC	15.3/27
16	**NFL Monday Night Football** (Rams at Buccaneers)	12/18/00	ABC	15.2/26
17	**Summer Olympics** (Women's gymnastics indiv. all-around finals, men's/women's swim finals)	9/21/00	NBC	14.9/26
	Summer Olympics (Men's/women's swim finals, men's T&F finals)	9/22/00	NBC	14.9/27
	NFL Monday Night Football (Buccaneers at Vikings)	10/9/00	ABC	14.9/25
20	**Summer Olympics** (Men's/women's swim finals, men's gymnastics indiv. all-around final)	9/17/00	NBC	14.6/24
	Summer Olympics (Men's/women's swim finals, women's team gymnastics, men's weightlifting)	9/20/00	NBC	14.6/25
	NFL Monday Night Football (Vikings at Packers)	11/6/00	ABC	14.6/25
	AFC Playoff Game (Dolphins at Raiders)	1/6/01	CBS	14.6/31
24	**NFL Regular Season Late Game** (Various teams)	11/26/00	CBS	14.4/25
25	**NFC Playoff Game** (Saints at Vikings)	1/6/01	FOX	14.1/35
26	**Summer Olympics** (Men's/women's T&F finals, women's springboard final)	9/28/00	NBC	14.0/24
	Rose Bowl (Washington vs Purdue)	1/1/01	ABC	14.0/24

AP/Wide World Photos

*Over 41 million households watched quarterback **Trent Dilfer** and the Baltimore Ravens trounce the Giants in Super Bowl XXXV.*

		Date	Net	Rtg/Sh
28	**Summer Olympics** (Greco Roman super hvywt. finals, men's/women's T&F finals)	9/27/00	NBC	13.9/24
	NFL Monday Night Football (Redskins at Rams)	11/20/00	ABC	13.9/23
30	**Summer Olympics** (Men's gymnastics team finals, men's/women's swim finals)	9/18/00	NBC	13.8/23
	NFL Monday Night Football (Titans at Redskins)	10/30/00	ABC	13.8/23
32	**NFL Monday Night Football** (Cowboys at Redskins)	9/18/00	ABC	13.5/23
33	**Summer Olympics** (Men's women's T&F finals, men's/women's swim finals, men's sync. platform diving)	9/23/00	NBC	13.3/25
	NFL Monday Night Football — OT (Vikings at Packers)	11/6/00	ABC	13.3/35
	Masters Golf — Final Round (Tiger wins)	4/8/01	CBS	13.3/30
36	**Summer Olympics** (Men's/women's swim finals, men's team gymnastics)	9/16/00	NBC	13.1/25
	MLB World Series — Game 5 (Yankees at Mets)	10/26/00	FOX	13.1/21

2000-01 Top Rated TV Sports Events (Cont.)

		Date	Net	Rtg/Sh
38	**NFL Regular Season Late Game** (Various teams)	9/10/00	FOX	13.0/27
	Sugar Bowl (Miami-FL vs Florida)	1/2/01	ABC	13.0/21
40	**NFL Regular Season Late Game** (Various teams)	10/1/00	FOX	12.9/26
41	**NFL Regular Season Late Game** (Various teams)	11/19/00	FOX	12.8/25
	NFL Thanksgiving Day Late Game (Vikings at Cowboys)	11/23/00	FOX	12.8/34
43	**NFL Regular Season Late Game** (Various teams)	11/12/00	FOX	12.7/23
	NFL Regular Season Late Game (Various teams)	12/24/00	FOX	12.7/32
	AFC Playoff Game (Colts at Dolphins)	12/30/00	ABC	12.7/30
	NBA Finals — Game 3 (Lakers at 76ers)	6/10/01	NBC	12.7/23
47	**NFL Regular Season Late Game** (Various teams)	9/24/00	CBS	12.6/25
	MLB World Series — Game 2 (Mets at Yankees)	10/22/00	FOX	12.6/20
	MLB World Series — Game 4 (Yankees at Mets)	10/25/00	FOX	12.6/21
	NFL Regular Season Late Game (Various teams)	12/17/00	CBS	12.6/24
	NBA Finals — Game 4 (Lakers at 76ers)	6/13/01	NBC	12.6/23
52	**NFL Regular Season Late Game** (Various teams)	11/5/00	CBS	12.5/24
	NFL Monday Night Football (Packers at Panthers)	11/27/00	ABC	12.5/21
54	**Summer Olympics** (Gymnastics champions' gala, men's springboard finals)	9/26/00	NBC	12.4/21
	MLB World Series — Game 3 (Yankees at Mets)	10/24/00	FOX	12.4/21
	NFL Regular Season Early Game (Various teams)	10/29/00	FOX	12.4/29

		Date	Net	Rtg/Sh
	NFL Monday Night Football (Raiders at Broncos)	11/13/00	ABC	12.4/21
	NBA Finals — Game 1 (76ers at Lakers)	6/6/01	NBC	12.4/23
59	**NFL Regular Season Late Game** (Various teams)	10/8/00	CBS	12.3/25
60	**NFL Monday Night Football** (Patriots at Jets)	9/11/00	ABC	12.2/21
61	**NFL Monday Night Football** (Dolphins at Jets)	10/23/00	ABC	12.1/21
	NFL Thanksgiving Day Early Game (Patriots at Lions)	11/23/00	CBS	12.1/32
63	**NFL Regular Season Late Game** (Various teams)	10/29/00	CBS	11.7/23
	NFL Regular Season Early Game (Various teams)	11/19/00	CBS	11.7/26
	NFL Regular Season Early Game (Various teams)	12/17/00	FOX	11.7/26
	NBA Finals — Game 2 (76ers at Lakers)	6/8/01	NBC	11.7/22
67	**NFL Regular Season Early Game** (Various teams)	9/3/00	FOX	11.6/29
	NCAA Men's Basketball Semifinal Game (Duke vs Maryland)	3/31/01	CBS	11.6/21
69	**MLB World Series — Game 1** (Mets at Yankees)	10/21/00	FOX	11.5/22
70	**NFL Monday Night Football** (Seahawks at Chiefs)	10/2/00	ABC	11.4/19
71	**NFL Monday Night Football** (Bills at Colts)	12/11/00	ABC	11.3/18
72	**NFL Regular Season Late Game** (Various teams)	9/17/00	FOX	11.2/23
	NFL Regular Season Late Game (Various teams)	10/22/00	FOX	11.2/23
	NBA Finals — Game 5 (Lakers at 76ers)	6/15/01	NBC	11.2/22
75	**NFL Regular Season Late Game** (Various teams)	12/3/00	CBS	11.1/21

AP/Wide World Photos

With a 60.2 Nielsen rating, the final episode of M*A*S*H in February 1983 still stands as the most-watched television program of all time.

All-Time Top-Rated TV Programs

NFL Football dominates television's All-Time Top-Rated 50 Programs with 22 Super Bowls and the 1981 NFC Championship Game making the list. Rankings based on surveys taken from January 1961 through August 31, 2001; include only sponsored programs seen on individual networks; and programs under 30 minutes scheduled duration are excluded. Programs are listed with ratings points, audience share and number of households watching, according to Nielsen Media Research.

Multiple entries: The Super Bowl (22); "Roots" (7); "The Beverly Hillbillies" and "The Thorn Birds" (3); "The Bob Hope Christmas Show," "The Ed Sullivan Show," "Gone With The Wind" and 1994 Winter Olympics (2).

	Program	Episode/Game	Net	Date	Rating	Share	Households
1	M*A*S*H (series)	Final episode	CBS	2/28/83	**60.2**	77	50,150,000
2	Dallas (series)	"Who Shot J.R.?"	CBS	11/21/80	**53.3**	76	41,470,000
3	Roots (mini-series)	Part 8	ABC	1/30/77	**51.1**	71	36,380,000
4	**Super Bowl XVI**	49ers 26, Bengals 21	CBS	1/24/82	**49.1**	73	40,020,000
5	**Super Bowl XVII**	Redskins 27, Dolphins 17	NBC	1/30/83	**48.6**	69	40,480,000
6	**XVII Winter Olympics**	Women's Figure Skating	CBS	2/23/94	**48.5**	64	45,690,000
7	**Super Bowl XX**	Bears 46, Patriots 10	NBC	1/26/86	**48.3**	70	41,490,000
8	Gone With the Wind (movie)	Part 1	NBC	11/7/76	**47.7**	65	33,960,000
9	Gone With the Wind (movie)	Part 2	NBC	11/8/76	**47.4**	64	33,750,000
10	**Super Bowl XII**	Cowboys 27, Broncos 10	CBS	1/15/78	**47.2**	67	34,410,000
11	**Super Bowl XIII**	Steelers 35, Cowboys 31	NBC	1/21/79	**47.1**	74	35,090,000
12	Bob Hope Special	Christmas Show	NBC	1/15/70	**46.6**	64	27,260,000
13	**Super Bowl XVIII**	Raiders 38, Redskins 9	CBS	1/22/84	**46.4**	71	38,800,000
	Super Bowl XIX	49ers 38, Dolphins 16	ABC	1/20/85	**46.4**	63	39,390,000
15	**Super Bowl XIV**	Steelers 31, Rams 19	CBS	1/20/80	**46.3**	67	35,330,000
16	**Super Bowl XXX**	Cowboys 27, Steelers 17	NBC	1/28/96	**46.0**	68	44,115,400
	ABC Theater (special)	"The Day After"	ABC	11/20/83	**46.0**	62	38,550,000
18	Roots (mini-series)	Part 6	ABC	1/28/77	**45.9**	66	32,680,000
	The Fugitive (series)	Final episode	ABC	8/29/67	**45.9**	72	25,700,000
20	**Super Bowl XXI**	Giants 39, Broncos 20	CBS	1/25/87	**45.8**	66	40,030,000
21	Roots (mini-series)	Part 5	ABC	1/27/77	**45.7**	71	32,540,000
22	**Super Bowl XXVIII**	Cowboys 30, Bills 13	NBC	1/30/94	**45.5**	66	42,860,600
	Cheers (series)	Final episode	NBC	5/20/93	**45.5**	64	42,360,500
24	The Ed Sullivan Show	Beatles' 1st appearance	CBS	2/9/64	**45.3**	60	23,240,000
25	**Super Bowl XXVII**	Cowboys 52, Bills 17	NBC	1/31/93	**45.1**	66	41,988,100
26	Bob Hope Special	Christmas Show	NBC	1/14/71	**45.0**	61	27,050,000
27	Roots (mini-series)	Part 3	ABC	1/25/77	**44.8**	68	31,900,000
28	**Super Bowl XXXII**	Broncos 31, Packers 24	NBC	1/25/98	**44.5**	67	43,630,000
29	**Super Bowl XI**	Raiders 32, Vikings 14	NBC	1/9/77	**44.4**	73	31,610,000
	Super Bowl XV	Raiders 27, Eagles 10	NBC	1/25/81	**44.4**	63	34,540,000
31	**Super Bowl VI**	Cowboys 24, Dolphins 3	CBS	1/16/72	**44.2**	74	27,450,000
32	**XVII Winter Olympics**	Women's Figure Skating	CBS	2/25/94	**44.1**	64	41,540,000
	Roots (mini-series)	Part 2	ABC	1/24/77	**44.1**	62	31,400,000
34	The Beverly Hillbillies (series)	Regular episode	CBS	1/8/64	**44.0**	65	22,570,000
35	Roots (mini-series)	Part 4	ABC	1/26/77	**43.8**	66	31,190,000
	The Ed Sullivan Show	Beatles' 2nd appearance	CBS	2/16/64	**43.8**	60	22,445,000
37	**Super Bowl XXIII**	49ers 20, Bengals 16	NBC	1/22/89	**43.5**	68	39,320,000
38	The Academy Awards	John Wayne wins Oscar	ABC	4/7/70	**43.4**	78	25,390,000
39	**Super Bowl XXXI**	Packers 35, Patriots 21	FOX	1/26/97	**43.3**	65	42,000,000
	Super Bowl XXXIV	Rams 23, Titans 16	ABC	1/30/00	**43.3**	63	43,618,000
41	The Thorn Birds (mini-series)	Part 3	ABC	3/29/83	**43.2**	62	35,990,000
42	The Thorn Birds (mini-series)	Part 4	ABC	3/30/83	**43.1**	62	35,900,000
43	**NFC Championship Game**	49ers 28, Cowboys 27	CBS	1/10/82	**42.9**	62	34,940,000
44	The Beverly Hillbillies (series)	Regular episode	CBS	1/15/64	**42.8**	62	21,960,000
45	**Super Bowl VII**	Dolphins 14, Redskins 7	NBC	1/14/73	**42.7**	72	27,670,000
46	The Thorn Birds (mini-series)	Part 2	ABC	3/28/83	**42.5**	59	35,400,000
47	**Super Bowl IX**	Steelers 16, Vikings 6	NBC	1/12/75	**42.4**	72	29,040,000
	The Beverly Hillbillies (series)	Regular episode	CBS	2/26/64	**42.4**	60	21,750,000
49	**Super Bowl X**	Steelers 21, Cowboys 17	CBS	1/18/76	**42.3**	78	29,440,000
	ABC Sunday Night Movie	"Airport"	ABC	11/11/73	**42.3**	63	28,000,000
	ABC Sunday Night Movie	"Love Story"	ABC	10/1/72	**42.3**	62	27,410,000
	Cinderella	Musical special	CBS	2/22/65	**42.3**	59	22,250,000
	Roots (mini-series)	Part 7	ABC	1/29/77	**42.3**	65	30,120,000

All-Time Top-Rated Cable TV Sports Events

All-time cable television for sports events, according to ESPN, Turner Sports research and The Sports Business Daily. Covers period from Sept. 1, 1980 through Aug. 31, 2001.

NFL Telecasts

		Date	Net	Rtg
1	Chicago at Minnesota	12/6/87	ESPN	17.6
2	Detroit at Miami	12/25/94	ESPN	15.1
3	Chicago at Minnesota	12/3/89	ESPN	14.7
4	Cleveland at San Fran	11/29/87	ESPN	14.2
5	Pittsburgh at Houston	12/30/90	ESPN	13.8

Non-NFL Telecasts

		Date	Net	Rtg
1	MLB: Chicago (NL)-St. Louis	9/7/98	ESPN	9.5
2	NBA: Detroit-Boston	6/1/88	TBS	8.8
3	NBA: Chicago-Detroit	5/31/89	TBS	8.2
4	NBA: Detroit-Boston	5/26/88	TBS	8.1
5	MLB: Giants-Chicago (NL)	9/28/98	ESPN	8.1

Teams Bought in 2001

Three major league clubs acquired new majority owners from Sept. 11, 2000 through Sept. 10, 2001.

NBA Basketball

Seattle SuperSonics: On Jan. 11, 2001, a group of Seattle investors known as The Basketball Club of Seattle, LLC (TBCS) purchased the SuperSonics from the Ackerley Group for $200 million. The group is led by Howard Schultz, founder and chairman of the Starbucks coffee chain, and also a Sonics season ticket holder since 1982. Schultz sold 20 percent of his stock and options in Starbucks to finance the purchase. The transaction also included the WNBA's Seattle Storm. The NBA Board of Governors approved the sale, which was finalized on April 1. TBCS becomes the third owner of the Sonics since the team's NBA debut in 1967.

NHL Hockey

Florida Panthers: After an exhaustive search, original team owner H. Wayne Huizenga came to an agreement on June 5, 2001 to sell the Panthers to a group of local investors for approximately $101 million. The new ownership group consists of eight investors led by Andrx Corp. CEO Alan Cohen, former NFL quarterback Bernie Kosar, Precision Response Corp. CEO David Epstein, and Florida car magnate Mike Maroone. The estimated $101 million consists of $83.5 million in cash, a $7.5 million promissory note and the assumption of all debt. In addition, the new ownership group takes over the rights to the operating agreement of the National Car Rental Center. Huizenga stays on as a minority partner.

Montreal Canadiens: On Jan. 31, 2001, Molson Inc. sold 80.1 percent of the Canadiens and its entire stake of the Molson Centre to Colorado businessman George Gillett Jr. for $178.3 million. The deal was finalized and approved by the NHL's Board of Governors on June 19. After no significant offers came from any Canadian, Molson finally agreed to sell to Gillett, the first non-Canadian owner in the team's 91-year history, provided the team would not be moved from Montreal. The remaining 19.9 percent of the team still belongs to Molson. Gillett, 62, formerly owned the Harlem Globetrotters and had a partial stake in the Miami Dolphins in the late 1960s. He also owned the Vail Mountain ski resort in Colorado and is current owner of Booth Creek Ski Holdings.

2000-01 Team Payrolls

Team payrolls for active players during the 2000-01 season for the NBA and NHL, and the 2001 season for Major League Baseball. Figures are in millions of dollars.

Note: The NFL uses a salary cap to set payrolls. In 2000 it was $62.2 million. All 31 teams were between $42.7 million (San Francisco) and $58.6 million (Arizona). The NBA also uses a salary cap ($35.5 million in 2000-01) but it is a "soft" cap, allowing for the wider range in team payrolls. The NHL and MLB use no cap.

Sources: *Street & Smith's SportsBusiness Journal*, NHLPA and *USA Today*.

#	NBA		#	MLB		#	NHL	
1	Portland	$86.5	1	NY Yankees	$112.3	1	NY Rangers	$55.5
2	Miami	73.8	2	Boston	110.0	2	Detroit	54.1
3	New York	73.6	3	Los Angeles	109.1	3	Colorado	50.5
4	New Jersey	69.0	4	NY Mets	93.7	4	Dallas	49.7
5	Washington	59.1	5	Cleveland	93.4	5	Toronto	42.4
6	LA Lakers	58.8	6	Atlanta	91.9	6	Philadelphia	40.7
7	Milwaukee	57.3	7	Texas	88.6	7	Anaheim	38.5
8	San Antonio	57.2	8	Arizona	85.5		Florida	38.5
9	Indiana	55.2	9	St. Louis	78.5	9	Phoenix	36.5
10	Utah	53.5	10	Toronto	76.9	10	Los Angeles	35.8
	Phoenix	53.5	11	Seattle	74.7		San Jose	35.8
12	Denver	51.8	12	Baltimore	74.3		St. Louis	35.8
13	Boston	51.7	13	Colorado	71.5	13	New Jersey	35.7
14	Dallas	50.9	14	Chicago-AL	65.6	14	Buffalo	35.4
15	Seattle	50.6	15	Chicago-NL	64.7	15	Washington	34.5
	Philadelphia	50.6	16	San Francisco	63.3	16	Chicago	31.8
17	Cleveland	49.4	17	Houston	60.9	17	Carolina	31.5
18	Houston	49.3	18	Pittsburgh	57.8	18	Boston	31.1
19	Vancouver	48.2	19	Tampa Bay	57.0	19	Pittsburgh	31.0
20	Minnesota	47.1	20	Detroit	49.5	20	Montreal	30.3
21	Charlotte	46.5	21	Cincinnati	49.0	21	Calgary	28.5
22	Sacramento	46.3	22	Anaheim	47.7	22	Vancouver	28.2
23	Golden St.	41.8	23	Milwaukee	43.9	23	Ottawa	27.3
24	Detroit	40.5	24	Philadelphia	41.7	24	Edmonton	25.6
25	Atlanta	39.2	25	San Diego	38.9	25	NY Islanders	24.2
26	Toronto	37.9	26	Florida	35.8	26	Nashville	19.6
27	Orlando	37.3	27	Kansas City	35.4	27	Columbus	19.2
28	Chicago	29.7	28	Montreal	35.2	28	Atlanta	19.1
29	LA Clippers	29.6	29	Oakland	33.8	29	Tampa Bay	18.3
			30	Minnesota	24.1	30	Minnesota	15.3

Top 10 Salaries In Each Sport

The top 10 highest paid athletes over the 2000-01 season for the NBA and NHL, 2001 for Major League Baseball and the 2000 season for the NFL. Figures are in millions of dollars.

Sources: *Street & Smith's SportsBusiness Journal*, NHLPA and *USA Today*.

NFL

		Position	Team	Salary
1	Drew Bledsoe	Quarterback	N. England	$8.543
2	John Randle	Def. Lineman	Minnesota	7.750
3	Michael Strahan	Def. Lineman	NY Giants	7.603
4	Mark Brunell	Quarterback	Jacksonville	7.255
5	Peyton Manning	Quarterback	Indianapolis	6.703
6	Edgerrin James	Running Back	Indianapolis	6.692
7	Warren Sapp	Def. Lineman	Tampa Bay	6.630
8	Chris Chandler	Quarterback	Atlanta	6.201
9	Jake Plummer	Quarterback	Arizona	5.943
10	Jason Sehorn	Cornerback	NY Giants	5.650
	League Avg			1.169

NBA

		Position	Team	Salary
1	Kevin Garnett	Forward	Minnesota	$19.606
2	Shaquille O'Neal	Center	LA Lakers	19.286
3	Alonzo Mourning	Center	Miami	16.880
4	Juwan Howard	Forward	Wash/Dal	16.875
5	Hakeem Olajuwon	Center	Houston	16.700
6	Karl Malone	Forward	Utah	15.750
7	David Robinson	Center	San Antonio	14.700
8	Dikembe Mutombo	Center	Atl/Phi	14.443
9	Patrick Ewing	Center	Seattle	14.000
10	Scottie Pippen	Forward	Portland	13.750
	League Avg			4.200

MLB

		Position	Team	Salary
1	Alex Rodriguez	Shortstop	Texas	$22.000
2	Kevin Brown	Pitcher	Los Angeles	15.714
3	Carlos Delgado	First Base	Toronto	13.650
4	Mike Piazza	Catcher	NY Mets	13.571
5	Randy Johnson	Pitcher	Arizona	13.350
6	Mo Vaughn	First Base	Anaheim	13.167
7	Manny Ramirez	Left Field	Boston	13.050
8	Pedro Martinez	Pitcher	Boston	13.000
9	Derek Jeter	Shortstop	NY Yankees	12.600
10	Ken Griffey Jr.	Center Field	Cincinnati	12.500
	Greg Maddux	Pitcher	Atlanta	12.500
	Sammy Sosa	Right Field	Chicago-NL	12.500
	League Avg			2.273

NHL

		Position	Team	Salary
1	Paul Kariya	Left Wing	Anaheim	$10.000
	Peter Forsberg	Center	Colorado	10.000
3	Jaromir Jagr	Right Wing	Pittsburgh	9.533
4	Pavel Bure	Right Wing	Florida	9.000
5	Keith Tkachuk	Left Wing	Pho/St.L	8.300
6	Teemu Selanne	Right Wing	Ana/SJ	8.000
	Steve Yzerman	Center	Detroit	8.000
8	Joe Sakic	Center	Colorado	7.900
9	Brian Leetch	Defense	NY Rangers	7.680
10	Dominik Hasek	Goalie	Buffalo	7.500
	Patrick Roy	Goalie	Colorado	7.500
	Mats Sundin	Center	Toronto	7.500
	League Avg			1.484

Highest and Lowest Ticket Prices

The most expensive and least expensive average ticket prices for NFL, NBA, Major League Baseball and NHL franchises over the 2000-01 season. Note that average ticket prices for each league are as follows: **NFL** $53.64, **MLB** $18.86, **NBA** $51.27, and **NHL** $47.70.

Source: Team Marketing Report

NFL

	Highest	Venue	Avg. Price
1	Washington	FedEx Field	$81.89
2	Denver	Mile High Stadium	77.41
3	Tampa Bay	Raymond James Stad.	70.61
4	Jacksonville	ALLTEL Stadium	62.85
5	Pittsburgh	Three Rivers Stadium	62.03

	Lowest	Venue	Avg. Price
1	Arizona	Sun Devil Stadium	$37.60
2	Detroit	Pontiac Silverdome	39.05
3	Atlanta	Georgia Dome	39.14
4	Chicago	Soldier Field	42.70
5	Seattle	Husky Stadium	44.97

NBA

	Highest	Venue	Avg. Price
1	NY Knicks	Madison Sq. Garden	$91.15
2	LA Lakers	Staples Center	87.69
3	Portland	Rose Garden	70.43
4	Houston	Compaq Center	66.39
5	Seattle	KeyArena	62.19

	Lowest	Venue	Avg. Price
1	Milwaukee	Bradley Center	$33.16
2	Charlotte	Charlotte Coliseum	34.80
3	Vancouver	General Motors Place	35.31
4	Denver	Pepsi Center	37.11
5	Dallas	Reunion Arena	37.48

MLB

	Highest	Venue	Avg. Price
1	Boston	Fenway Park	$36.08
2	NY Yankees	Yankee Stadium	28.90
3	NY Mets	Shea Stadium	26.53
4	Detroit	Comerica Park	23.90
5	San Francisco	Pacific Bell Park	23.38

	Lowest	Venue	Avg. Price
1	Minnesota	HHH Metrodome	$9.55
2	Montreal	Olympic Stadium	9.70
3	Kansas City	Kaufmann Stadium	12.61
4	Anaheim	Edison Field	13.36
5	Oakland	Network Assoc. Col.	13.96

NHL

	Highest	Venue	Avg. Price
1	Toronto	Air Canada Centre	$67.01
2	NY Rangers	Madison Sq. Garden	65.82
3	Colorado	Pepsi Center	63.11
4	Philadelphia	First Union Center	62.31
5	Dallas	Reunion Arena	56.43

	Lowest	Venue	Avg. Price
1	Calgary	Pengrowth Saddledome	$32.86
2	NY Islanders	Nassau Coliseum	34.68
3	Edmonton	Skyreach Centre	34.85
4	Montreal	Molson Centre	38.36
5	Washington	MCI Center	38.42

The Rights Stuff

Major sports and their television deals as of Sept. 1, 2001.

League	Network	Yrs (Ends)	Amount	League	Network	Yrs (Ends)	Amount
NFL	ESPN	8 (2006)	$4.8 billion	NCAA Women's Hoops			
	FOX	8 (2006)	4.4 billion	Tournament	ESPN	11 (2013)	$200 million@
	ABC	8 (2006)	4.4 billion	NCAA Football BCS	ABC	8 (2006)	$930 million
	CBS	8 (2006)	4.0 billion	NASCAR	NBC/Turner	6 (2006)	$1.2 billion
NBA	NBC	4 (2002)	$1.75 billion		FOX	8 (2008)	1.6 billion
	Turner	4 (2002)	890 million	Olympics	NBC	13 (2008)	$3.5 billion#
MLB	FOX	6 (2006)	$2.5 billion	PGA Tour	ABC, CBS,		
	ESPN	6 (2005)	undisclosed*		NBC, ESPN, USA		
NHL	ESPN/ABC	5 (2004)	$600 million	and The Golf Channel		4 (2006)	$850 million%
NCAA Men's Hoops							
Tournament	CBS	11 (2013)	$6.0 billion†				

* Terms of the deal are undisclosed but estimated to be valued at more than $850 million.
† This deal doesn't begin until the 2003 tournament. CBS's current seven-year, $1.73 billion contract ends in 2002.
@ This deal doesn't begin until the 2003 tournament. ESPN's current seven-year, $19 million contract ends in 2002. Also included in the new deal are all rights to the College World Series and various other NCAA championships.
# NBC has a deal with the Olympics worth approximately $3.5 billion, which gave them exclusive rights to the 1996 Summer Games in Atlanta, the 2000 Summer Games in Sydney, the 2002 Winter Games in Salt Lake City, the 2004 Summer Games in Athens, the 2006 Winter Games in Turin (ITA), and the 2008 Summer Games (Beijing). The only Games it didn't have rights to since 1996 were the 1998 Winter Games in Nagano, which were owned by CBS.
% This deal doesn't begin until the 2003 season. In the new scheme, USA will average 33 events per year, ABC 18, CBS 17, ESPN 14 and NBC 5. The Golf Channel will broadcast no PGA events but will have exclusive rights to the Buy.com Tour.

AWARDS

The Peabody Award

Presented annually since 1940 for outstanding achievement in radio and television broadcasting. Named after Georgia banker and philanthropist George Foster Peabody, the awards are administered by the Henry W. Grady College of Journalism and Mass Communication at the University of Georgia.

Television

Year
1960 **CBS** for coverage of 1960 Winter and Summer Olympic Games
1966 ABC's **"Wide World of Sports"** (for Outstanding Achievement in Promotion of International Understanding).
1968 **ABC Sports** coverage of both the 1968 Winter and Summer Olympic Games.
1972 **ABC Sports** coverage of the 1972 Summer Olympics in Munich.
1973 **Joe Garagiola** of NBC Sports (for "The Baseball World of Joe Garagiola").
1976 **ABC Sports** coverage of both the 1976 Winter and Summer Olympic Games.
1984 **Roone Arledge**, president of ABC News & Sports (for significant contributions to news and sports programming).
1986 **WFAA-TV**, Dallas for its investigation of the Southern Methodist University football program.
1988 **Jim McKay** of ABC Sports (for pioneering efforts and career accomplishments in the world of TV sports).
1991 **CBS Sports** coverage of the 1991 Masters golf tournament
    & **HBO Sports** and **Black Canyon Productions** for the baseball special "When It Was A Game."
1995 **Kartemquin Educational Films** and **KTCA-TV** in St. Paul, MN, presented on PBS for "Hoop Dreams"
    & **Turner Original Productions** for the baseball special "Hank Aaron: Chasing the Dream."
1996 **HBO Sports** for its documentary "The Journey of the African-American Athlete."
    & **Bud Greenspan**, a personal award for excellence in chronicling the Olympic Games.
1997 **HBO Pictures** and **The Thomas Carter Company** for the original movie "Don King: Only in America."
1998 **KTVX-TV**, Salt Lake City for its investigation into the policies and practices of the IOC during the Olympic bribery scandal & **HBO Sports** for its ongoing series of sports documentaries.
1999 **WCPO-TV**, Cincinnati for its investigation of fraud and misrepresentation in the construction of new sports stadiums, **HBO Sports** for its documentary "Dare to Compete: The Struggle of Women in Sports," and its documentary "Fists of Freedom: The Story of the '68 Summer Games" & **ESPN** for its "SportsCentury" series.
2000 **HBO Sports** for its documentary "Ali-Frazier 1: One Nation...Divisible."

Radio

Year
1974 **WSB** radio in Atlanta for "Henry Aaron: A Man with a Mission."
1991 **Red Barber** of National Public Radio (for his six decades as a broadcaster and his 10 years as a commentator on NPR's "Morning Edition").

National Emmy Awards
Sports Programming

Presented by the Academy of Television Arts and Sciences since 1948. Eligibility period covered the calendar year from 1948-57 and since 1988.

Multiple major award winners: ABC "Wide World of Sports" (19), NFL Films Football coverage (11); ABC Olympics coverage (9); ABC "Monday Night Football" (8); CBS NFL Football coverage, FOX MLB coverage, NBC Olympics coverage and ESPN "Outside the Lines" series (6); CBS NCAA Basketball coverage, HBO "Real Sports with Bryant Gumbel" and CBS "NFL Today" (5); ESPN "SportsCenter" (4); ABC "The American Sportsman," ABC Indianapolis 500 coverage, ESPN "Game-Day" and Fox "NFL Sunday" (3); ABC Kentucky Derby coverage, ABC "Sportsbeat," Bud Greenspan Olympic specials, CBS Olympics coverage, CBS Golf coverage, ESPN "Speedworld," ESPN "SportsCentury" series, MTV Sports series and NBC World Series coverage (2).

1949
Coverage—"Wrestling" (KTLA, Los Angeles)

1950
Program—"Rams Football" (KNBH-TV, Los Angeles)

1954
Program—"Gillette Cavalcade of Sports" (NBC)

1965-66
Programs—"Wide World of Sports" (ABC), "Shell's Wonderful World of Golf" (NBC) and "CBS Golf Classic" (CBS)

1966-67
Program—"Wide World of Sports" (ABC)

1967-68
Program—"Wide World of Sports" (ABC)

1968-69
Program—"1968 Summer Olympics" (ABC)

1969-70
Programs—"NFL Football" (CBS) and "Wide World of Sports" (ABC)

1970-71
Program—"Wide World of Sports" (ABC)

1971-72
Program—"Wide World of Sports" (ABC)

1972-73
News Special—"Coverage of Munich Olympic Tragedy" (ABC)
Sports Programs—"1972 Summer Olympics" (ABC) and "Wide World of Sports" (ABC)

1973-74
Program—"Wide World of Sports" (ABC)

1974-75
Non-Edited Program—"Jimmy Connors vs. Rod Laver Tennis Challenge" (CBS)
Edited Program—"Wide World of Sports" (ABC)

1975-76
Live Special—"1975 World Series: Cincinnati vs. Boston" (NBC)
Live Series—"NFL Monday Night Football" (ABC)
Edited Specials—"1976 Winter Olympics" (ABC) and "Triumph and Tragedy: The Olympic Experience" (ABC)
Edited Series—"Wide World of Sports" (ABC)

1976-77
Live Special—"1976 Summer Olympics" (ABC)
Live Series—"The NFL Today/NFL Football" (CBS)
Edited Special—"1976 Summer Olympics Preview" (ABC)
Edited Series—"The Olympiad" (PBS)

1977-78
Live Special—"Muhammad Ali vs. Leon Spinks Heavyweight Championship Fight" (CBS)
Live Series—"The NFL Today/NFL Football" (CBS)
Edited Special—"The Impossible Dream: Ballooning Across the Atlantic" (CBS)
Edited Series—"The Way It Was" (PBS)

1978-79
Live Special—"Super Bowl XIII: Pittsburgh vs Dallas" (NBC)
Live Series—"NFL Monday Night Football" (ABC)
Edited Special—"Spirit of '78: The Flight of Double Eagle II" (ABC)
Edited Series—"The American Sportsman" (ABC)

1979-80
Live Special—"1980 Winter Olympics" (ABC)
Live Series—"NCAA College Football" (ABC)
Edited Special—"Gossamer Albatross: Flight of Imagination" (CBS)
Edited Series—"NFL Game of the Week" (NFL Films)

1980-81
Live Special—"1981 Kentucky Derby" (ABC)
Live Series—"PGA Golf Tour" (CBS)
Edited Special—"Wide World of Sports 20th Anniversary Show" (ABC)
Edited Series—"The American Sportsman" (ABC)

1981-82
Live Special—"1982 NCAA Basketball Final: North Carolina vs Georgetown" (CBS)
Live Series—"NFL Football" (CBS)
Edited Special—"1982 Indianapolis 500" (ABC)
Edited Series—"Wide World of Sports" (ABC)

1982-83
Live Special—"1982 World Series: St. Louis vs Milwaukee" (NBC)
Live Series—"NFL Football" (CBS)
Edited Special—"Wimbledon '83" (NBC)
Edited Series—"Wide World of Sports" (ABC)
Journalism—"ABC Sportsbeat" (ABC)

1983-84
No awards given—

1984-85
Live Special—"1984 Summer Olympics" (ABC)
Live Series—No award given
Edited Special—"Road to the Super Bowl '85" (NFL Films)
Edited Series—"The American Sportsman" (ABC)
Journalism—"ABC Sportsbeat" (ABC), "CBS Sports Sunday" (CBS), Dick Schaap features (ABC) and 1984 Summer Olympic features (ABC)

1985-86
No awards given—

National Emmy Awards (Cont.)

1986-87

Live Special—"1987 Daytona 500" (CBS)
Live Series—"NFL Football" (CBS)
Edited Special—"Wide World of Sports 25th Anniversary Special" (ABC)
Edited Series—"Wide World of Sports" (ABC)

1987-88

Live Special—"1987 Kentucky Derby" (ABC)
Live Series—"NFL Monday Night Football" (ABC)
Edited Special—"Paris-Roubaix Bike Race" (CBS)
Edited Series—"Wide World of Sports" (ABC)

1988

Live Special—"1988 Summer Olympics" (NBC)
Live Series—"1988 NCAA Basketball" (CBS)
Edited Special—"Road to the Super Bowl '88" (NFL Films)
Edited Series—"Wide World of Sports" (ABC)
Studio Show—"NFL GameDay" (ESPN)
Journalism—1988 Summer Olympic reporting (NBC)

1989

Live Special—"1989 Indianapolis 500" (ABC)
Live Series—"NFL Monday Night Football" (ABC)
Edited Special—"Trans-Antarctica! The International Expedition" (ABC)
Edited Series—"This is the NFL" (NFL Films)
Studio Show—"NFL Today" (CBS)
Journalism—1989 World Series Game 3 earthquake coverage (ABC)

1990

Live Special—"1990 Indianapolis 500" (ABC)
Live Series—"1990 NCAA Basketball Tournament" (CBS)
Edited Special—"Road to Super Bowl XXIV" (NFL Films)
Edited Series—"Wide World of Sports" (ABC)
Studio Show—"SportsCenter" (ESPN)
Journalism—"Outside the Lines: The Autograph Game" (ESPN)

1991

Live Special—"1991 NBA Finals: Chicago vs LA Lakers" (NBC)
Live Series—"1991 NCAA Basketball Tournament" (CBS)
Edited Special—"Wide World of Sports 30th Anniversary Special" (ABC)
Edited Series—"This is the NFL" (NFL Films)
Studio Show—"NFL GameDay" (ESPN) and "NFL Live" (NBC)
Journalism—"Outside the Lines: Steroids–Whatever It Takes" (ESPN)

1992

Live Special—"1992 Breeders' Cup" (NBC)
Live Series—"1992 NCAA Basketball Tournament" (CBS)
Edited Special—"1992 Summer Olympics" (NBC)
Edited Series—"MTV Sports" (MTV)
Studio Show—"The NFL Today" (CBS)
Journalism—"Outside the Lines: Portraits in Black and White" (ESPN)

1993

Live Special—"1993 World Series" (CBS)
Live Series—"Monday Night Football" (ABC)
Edited Special—"Road to the Super Bowl" (NFL Films)
Edited Series—"This is the NFL" (NFL Films)
Studio Show—"The NFL Today" (CBS)
Journalism (TIE)—"Outside the Lines: Mitch Ivey Feature" (ESPN) and "SportsCenter: University of Houston Football" (ESPN).
Feature—"Arthur Ashe: His Life, His Legacy" (NBC).

1994

Live Special—"NHL Stanley Cup Finals" (ESPN)
Live Series—"Monday Night Football" (ABC)
Edited Special—"Lillehammer '94: 16 Days of Glory" (Disney/Cappy Productions)
Edited Series—"MTV Sports" (MTV)
Studio Show—"NFL GameDay" (ESPN)
Journalism—"1994 Winter Olympic Games: Mossad feature" (CBS)
Feature (TIE)—"Heroes of Telemark" on Winter Olympic Games (CBS); and "SportsCenter: Vanderbilt running back Brad Gaines" (ESPN).

1995

Live Special—"Cal Ripken 2131" (ESPN)
Live Series—"ESPN Speedworld" (ESPN)
Edited Special (quick turn-around)—"Outside the Lines: Playball–Opening Day in America" (ESPN)
Edited Special (long turn-around)—"Lillehammer, an Olympic Diary" (CBS)
Edited Series—"NFL Films Presents" (NFL Films)
Studio Show (TIE)—"NFL GameDay" (ESPN) and "Fox NFL Sunday"(Fox)
Journalism—"Real Sports with Bryant Gumbel: Broken Promises" (HBO)
Feature (TIE)—"SportsCenter: Jerry Quarry" (ESPN) and "Real Sports with Bryant Gumbel: Coach" (HBO).

1996

Live Special—"1996 World Series" (FOX)
Live Series—"ESPN Speedworld" (ESPN)
Edited Special—"Football America" (TNT/NFL Films)
Edited Series—"NFL Films Presents" (NFL Films)
Live Event Turnaround—"The Centennial Olympic Games" (NBC)
Studio Show—"SportsCenter" (ESPN)
Journalism—"Outside the Lines: AIDS in Sports" (ESPN)
Feature—"Real Sports with Bryant Gumbel: 1966 Texas Western NCAA Champs" (HBO).

1997

Live Special—"The NBA Finals" (NBC)
Live Series—"NFL Monday Night Football" (ABC)
Edited Special—"Ironman Triathlon World Championship" (NBC/World Triathlon Corporation)
Edited Series—"NFL Films Presents" (NFL Films)
Live Event Turnaround—"Outside The Lines: Inside The Kentucky Derby" (ESPN)
Studio Show—"Fox NFL Sunday" (FOX)
Journalism—"Real Sports with Bryant Gumbel: Pros and Cons" (HBO)
Feature—"NFL Films Presents: Eddie George" (NFL Films).

1998

Live Special—"McGwire's 62nd Home Run Game" (FOX)
Live Series—"NBC Golf Tour" (NBC)
Edited Special—"A Cinderella Season: The Lady Vols Fight Back" (HBO)
Edited Series—"Real Sports with Bryant Gumbel" (HBO)
Live Event Turnaround—"Wimbledon '98" (NBC)
Studio Show—"Fox NFL Sunday" (FOX)
Journalism (TIE)—"Real Sports with Bryant Gumbel: Winning At All Costs" (HBO) and "Real Sports with Bryant Gumbel: Diamond Bucks" (HBO)
Feature—"NFL Films Presents: Steve Mariucci" (ESPN2 and NFL Films).

"Baseball" Wins Prime Time Emmy

Ken Burns's miniseries "Baseball" won the 1994 Emmy Award for Outstanding Informational Series. The nine-part documentary aired from Sept. 18-28, 1994 and ran more than 18 hours, drawing the largest audience in PBS history.

1999

Live Special—"2000 MLB All-Star Game" (FOX)
Live Series—"MLB Regular Season" (FOX)
Edited Special—"Ironman Triathlon World Championship" (NBC)
Edited Series—"SportsCentury: 50 Greatest Athletes" (ESPN)
Live Event Turnaround—"The World Track & Field Championships" (NBC)
Studio Show—"MLB Pre-Game Show" (FOX)
Journalism—"Real Sports with Bryant Gumbel: Fake Golf Clubs" (HBO)
Feature—"NFL Films Presents: Lt. Kalsu" (ESPN2)

2000

Live Special—"2000 World Series" (FOX)
Live Series—"NFL Sunday Night Football" (ESPN)
Edited Special—"Hoops and Hoosiers: The Story of the Final Four 2000" (CBS)
Edited Series—"SportsCentury: The Top 50 & Beyond" (ESPN)
Live Event Turnaround—"The Games of the XXVII Olympiad" (NBC)
Studio Show—"Fox NFL Sunday" (FOX)
Journalism—"Real Sports with Bryant Gumbel: Dominican Free-For-All" (HBO)
Feature—"The Games of the XXVII Olympiad" (NBC)

Sportscasters of the Year
National Emmy Awards

An Emmy Award for Sportscasters was first introduced in 1968 and given for Outstanding Host/Commentator for the 1967-68 TV season. Two awards, one for Outstanding Host or Play-by-Play and the other for Outstanding Analyst, were first presented in 1981 for the 1980-81 season. Three awards, for Outstanding Studio Host, Play-by-Play and Studio Analyst, have been given since the 1993 season, and one more, Sports Event Analyst, was added in 1997.

Multiple winners: John Madden (13); Bob Costas (10); Jim McKay (9); Dick Enberg and Al Michaels (4); Keith Jackson (3); James Brown and Cris Collinsworth (2). Note that Jim McKay has won a total of 12 Emmy awards: eight for Host/Commentator, one for Host/Play-by-Play, two for Sports Writing, and one for News Commentary.

Season	Host/Commentator	Season	Host/Play-by-Play	Season	Analyst
1967-68	Jim McKay, ABC	1980-81	Dick Enberg, NBC	1980-81	Dick Button, ABC
1968-69	No award	1981-82	Jim McKay, ABC	1981-82	John Madden, CBS
1969-70	No award	1982-83	Dick Enberg, NBC	1982-83	John Madden, CBS
1970-71	Jim McKay, ABC	1983-84	No award	1983-84	No award
	& Don Meredith, ABC	1984-85	George Michael, NBC	1984-85	No award
1971-72	No award	1985-86	No award	1985-86	No award
1972-73	Jim McKay, ABC	1986-87	Al Michaels, ABC	1986-87	John Madden, CBS
1973-74	Jim McKay, ABC	1987-88	Bob Costas, NBC	1987-88	John Madden, CBS
1974-75	Jim McKay, ABC	1988	Bob Costas, NBC	1988	John Madden, CBS
1975-76	Jim McKay, ABC	1989	Al Michaels, ABC	1989	John Madden, CBS
1976-77	Frank Gifford, ABC	1990	Dick Enberg, NBC	1990	John Madden, CBS
1977-78	Jack Whitaker, CBS	1991	Bob Costas, NBC	1991	John Madden, CBS
1978-79	Jim McKay, ABC	1992	Bob Costas, NBC	1992	John Madden, CBS
1979-80	Jim McKay, ABC				

Studio Host

Year		Year		Year	
1993	Bob Costas, NBC	1996	Bob Costas, NBC	1999	James Brown, FOX
1994	Bob Costas, NBC	1997	Dan Patrick, ESPN	2000	Bob Costas, NBC
1995	Bob Costas, NBC	1998	James Brown, FOX		

Play-by-Play

Year		Year		Year	
1993	Dick Enberg, NBC	1996	Keith Jackson, ABC	1999	Joe Buck, FOX
1994	Keith Jackson, ABC	1997	Bob Costas, NBC	2000	Al Michaels, ABC
1995	Al Michaels, ABC	1998	Keith Jackson, ABC		

Studio Analyst

Year		Year		Year	
1993	Billy Packer, CBS	1996	Howie Long, FOX	1999	Terry Bradshaw, FOX
1994	John Madden, FOX	1997	Cris Collinsworth, HBO/NBC	2000	Steve Lyons, FOX
1995	John Madden, FOX	1998	Cris Collinsworth, HBO/FOX		

Spec. Events Analyst

Year		Year		Year	
1997	Joe Morgan, ESPN	1999	John Madden, FOX	2000	Tim McCarver, FOX
1998	John Madden, FOX				

Lifetime Achievement Emmy Award

For outstanding work as an exemplary television sportscaster over many years.

Year		Year		Year		Year	
1989	Jim McKay	1992	Chris Schenkel	1995	Vin Scully	1998	Keith Jackson
1990	Lindsey Nelson	1993	Pat Summerall	1996	Frank Gifford	1999	Jack Buck
1991	Curt Gowdy	1994	Howard Cosell	1997	Jim Simpson	2000	Dick Enberg

National Sportscasters and Sportswriters Assn. Award

Sportscaster of the Year presented annually since 1959 by the National Sportcasters and Sportswriters Association, based in Salisbury, N.C. Voting is done by NSSA members and selected national media.

Multiple winners: Bob Costas (8); Chris Berman and Keith Jackson (5); Lindsey Nelson and Chris Schenkel (4); Dick Enberg, Al Michaels and Vin Scully (3); Curt Gowdy and Ray Scott (2).

Year		Year		Year		Year	
1959	Lindsey Nelson	1970	Chris Schenkel	1980	Dick Enberg	1990	Chris Berman
1960	Lindsey Nelson	1971	Ray Scott		& Al Michaels	1991	Bob Costas
1961	Lindsey Nelson	1972	Keith Jackson	1981	Dick Enberg	1992	Bob Costas
1962	Lindsey Nelson	1973	Keith Jackson	1982	Vin Scully	1993	Chris Berman
1963	Chris Schenkel	1974	Keith Jackson	1983	Al Michaels	1994	Chris Berman
1964	Chris Schenkel	1975	Keith Jackson	1984	John Madden	1995	Bob Costas
1965	Vin Scully	1976	Keith Jackson	1985	Bob Costas	1996	Chris Berman
1966	Curt Gowdy	1977	Pat Summerall	1986	Al Michaels	1997	Bob Costas
1967	Chris Schenkel	1978	Vin Scully	1987	Bob Costas	1998	Jim Nantz
1968	Ray Scott	1979	Dick Enberg	1988	Bob Costas	1999	Dan Patrick
1969	Curt Gowdy			1989	Chris Berman	2000	Bob Costas

American Sportscasters Association Award

Sportscaster of the Year presented annually from 1984-94, with the exception of 1988, by the New York-based American Sports-casters Association. Two awards were presented beginning in 1995 to honor top play-by-play personality and studio host. Two more were added in 1998 to honor the top color analyst and sideline reporter. Voting is done by ASA members and officials.

Multiple winners: Dick Enberg (5); Bob Costas (4); Chris Berman (3); Jim Gray, Al Michaels and Joe Morgan (2).

Sportscaster of the Year

Year		Year		Year		Year	
1984	Dick Enberg	1987	Dick Enberg	1990	Dick Enberg	1993	Bob Costas
1985	Vin Scully	1988	No award	1991	Bob Costas	1994	Pat Summerall
1986	Dick Enberg	1989	Bob Costas	1992	Bob Costas		

Play-by-Play		Studio Host		Color Analyst		Sideline Reporter	
Year		Year		Year		Year	
1995	Al Michaels	1995	Chris Berman	1998	Joe Morgan	1998	Jim Gray
1996	Marv Albert	1996	Chris Berman		& John Madden (tie)	1999	Jim Gray
1997	Dick Enberg	1997	Chris Berman	1999	Joe Morgan		
1998	Jon Miller	1998	Jim Nantz				
1999	Al Michaels	1999	James Brown				

The Pulitzer Prize

The Pulitzer Prizes for journalism, letters and music have been presented annually since 1917 in the name of Joseph Pulitzer (1847-1911), the publisher of the *New York World*. Prizes are awarded by the president of Columbia University on the recommendation of a board of review. Sixteen Pulitzers have been awarded for newspaper sports reporting, sports commentary and sports photography.

News Coverage

1935 **Bill Taylor,** *NY Herald Tribune,* for his reporting on the 1934 America's Cup yacht races.

Special Citation

1952 **Max Kase**, *NY Journal-American,* for his reporting on the 1951 college basketball point-shaving scandal.

Meritorious Public Service

1954 **Newsday** (Garden City, N.Y.) for its expose of New York State's race track scandals and labor racketeering.

General Reporting

1956 **Arthur Daley**, *NY Times,* for his 1955 columns.

Investigative Reporting

1981 **Clark Hallas** & **Robert Lowe**, *(Tucson) Arizona Daily Star,* for their 1980 investigation of the University of Arizona athletic department.

1986 **Jeffrey Marx** & **Michael York**, Lexington (Ky.) *Herald-Leader,* for their 1985 investigation of the basketball program at the University of Kentucky and other major colleges.

Specialized Reporting

1985 **Randall Savage** & **Jackie Crosby**, Macon (Ga.) *Telegraph and News,* for their 1984 investigation of athletics and academics at the University of Georgia and Georgia Tech.

Beat Reporting

2000 **George Dohrmann**, St. Paul (Min.) *Pioneer Press,* for his investigation that revealed academic fraud in the men's basketball program at the University of Minnesota.

Feature Writing

1997 **Lisa Pollak**, *Baltimore Sun,* for her story about baseball umpire John Hirschbeck dealing with the death of one son and the illness of another from the same disease.

Commentary

1976 **Red Smith**, *NY Times,* for his 1975 columns.

1981 **Dave Anderson**, *NY Times,* for his 1980 columns.

1990 **Jim Murray**, *LA Times,* for his 1989 columns.

Photography

1949 **Nat Fein,** NY Herald Tribune, for his photo, "Babe Ruth Bows Out."

1952 **John Robinson** & **Don Ultang,** Des Moines (Iowa) Register and Tribune, for their sequence of six pictures of the 1951 Drake-Oklahoma A&M football game, in which Drake's Johnny Bright had his jaw broken.

1985 **The Photography Staff** of the Orange County (Calif.) Register, for their coverage of the 1984 Summer Olympics in Los Angeles.

1993 **William Snyder** & **Ken Geiger,** The Dallas Morning News, for their coverage of the 1992 Summer Olympics in Barcelona, Spain.

Sportswriter of the Year
NSSA Award

Presented annually since 1959 by the National Sportscasters and Sportswriters Association, based in Salisbury, N.C. Voting is done by NSSA members and selected national media.

Multiple winners: Jim Murray (14); Frank Deford and Rick Reilly (6); Red Smith (5); Will Grimsley (4); Peter Gammons (3).

Year		Year		Year	
1959	Red Smith, NY Herald-Tribune	1974	Jim Murray, LA Times	1989	Peter Gammons, Sports Ill.
1960	Red Smith, NY Herald-Tribune	1975	Jim Murray, LA Times	1990	Peter Gammons, Boston Globe
1961	Red Smith, NY Herald-Tribune	1976	Jim Murray, LA Times	1991	Rick Reilly, Sports Ill.
1962	Red Smith, NY Herald-Tribune	1977	Jim Murray, LA Times	1992	Rick Reilly, Sports Ill.
1963	Arthur Daley, NY Times	1978	Will Grimsley, AP	1993	Peter Gammons, Boston Globe
1964	Jim Murray, LA Times	1979	Jim Murray, LA Times	1994	Rick Reilly, Sports Ill.
1965	Red Smith, NY Herald-Tribune	1980	Will Grimsley, AP	1995	Rick Reilly, Sports Ill.
1966	Jim Murray, LA Times	1981	Will Grimsley, AP	1996	Rick Reilly, Sports Ill.
1967	Jim Murray, LA Times	1982	Frank Deford, Sports Ill.	1997	Dave Kindred, The Sporting News
1968	Jim Murray, LA Times	1983	Will Grimsley, AP		
1969	Jim Murray, LA Times	1984	Frank Deford, Sports Ill.	1998	Mitch Albom, Detroit Free Press
1970	Jim Murray, LA Times	1985	Frank Deford, Sports Ill.	1999	Rick Reilly, Sports Ill.
1971	Jim Murray, LA Times	1986	Frank Deford, Sports Ill.	2000	Bob Ryan, Boston Globe
1972	Jim Murray, LA Times	1987	Frank Deford, Sports Ill.		
1973	Jim Murray, LA Times	1988	Frank Deford, Sports Ill.		

Best Newspaper Sports Sections of 2000

Winners of the annual Associated Press Sports Editors contest for best daily and Sunday sports sections. Awards are divided into different categories, based on circulation figures. Selections are made by a committee of APSE members.

Circulation Over 250,000

Top 10 Daily		Top 10 Sunday	
Atlanta Journal-Constitution	Daily News (NY)	Boston Globe	Daily News (NY)
Boston Globe	Orange County (CA) Register	Chicago Tribune	New York Times
Dallas Morning News	Philadelphia Daily News	Dallas Morning News	Star-Ledger (Newark, NJ)
Fort Worth Star-Telegram	USA Today	Kansas City Star	Newsday (NY)
Los Angeles Times	Washington Post	Los Angeles Times	St. Petersburg (FL) Times

Circulation 100,000-250,000

Top 10 Daily		Top 10 Sunday	
Akron-Beacon Journal (OH)	Palm Beach Post	Asbury Park Press (NJ)	Lexington (Ky.) Herald-Leader
Contra Costa Times (Walnut Creek, CA)	The Record (Hackensack, NJ)	Charlotte Observer	Palm Beach Post
	San Antonio Express-News	The State (Columbia, SC)	Pittsburgh Post-Gazette
Hartford Courant	Seattle Times	Contra Costa Times (Walnut Creek, CA)	San Antonio Express-News
Indianapolis Star	News Tribune (Tacoma, WA)	Indianapolis Star	Syracuse Newspapers
Daily News (Los Angeles)			

Best Sportswriting of 2000

Winners of the annual Associated Press Sports Editors Contest for best sportswriting in 2000. Eventual winners were chosen from five finalists in each writing division. Selections are made by a committee of APSE members. Note the investigative writing division included all circulation categories.

Circulation over 250,000

Column:	Mitch Albom, Detroit Free Press	**Feature:**	Mitch Albom, Detroit Free Press
Enterprise:	Alan Abrahamson, Randy Harvey and David Wharton, Los Angeles Times	**Game story:**	Richard Sandomir, New York Times
		News story:	Frank Fitzpatrick, Philadelphia Inquirer

Circulation 100,000-250,000

Column:	Gwen Knapp, San Francisco Examiner	**Game story:**	Geoff Calkins, The Commercial Appeal (Memphis)
Enterprise:	Jim Adams and Mike Grant, Courier-Journal (Louisville)	**News story:**	Tim Sullivan, Cincinnati Enquirer
Feature:	Hal Habib, Palm Beach Post		

All Categories

Investigative: Melissa Turner, Atlanta Journal-Constitution

Directory of Organizations

Listing of the major sports organizations, teams and media addresses and officials as of Sept. 1, 2001.

AUTO RACING

CART
(Championship Auto Racing Teams, Inc.)
755 W. Big Beaver Rd., Suite 800, Troy, MI 48084
(248) 362-8800
President-CEO .... Joseph Heitzler
Director of Publicity .... Mike Zizzo

IRL
(Indy Racing League)
4565 West 16th St., Indianapolis, IN 46222
(317) 484-6526
Founder .... Tony George
Dir. of Racing Operations .... John Lewis
Director of Public Relations .... Ron Green

FIA— Formula One
(Federation Internationale de L'Automobile)
2 Chemin de Blandonnet, 1215 Geneva 15, Switzerland
TEL: 011-41-22544-4400
President .... Max Mosley
Secretary General .... Pierre de Coninck
Director of Public Relations ...Francesco Longanesi-Cattani

NASCAR
(National Assn. for Stock Car Auto Racing)
P.O. Box 2875, Daytona Beach, FL 32120
(904) 253-0611
President .... Michael Helton
Managing Director of Communications .... John Griffin

NHRA
(National Hot Rod Association)
2035 Financial Way, Glendora, CA 91741
(626) 914-4761
President .... Tom Compton
Sr. V.P. of Racing Operations .... Graham Light
V.P. of Communications .... Jerry Archambeault

MAJOR LEAGUE BASEBALL

Office of the Commissioner
245 Park Ave., 31st Floor, New York, NY 10167
(212) 931-7800
Commissioner .... Bud Selig
President-COO .... Paul Beeston
General Counsel .... Thomas Ostertag
Senior Vice President .... Richard Levin

Player Relations Committee
245 Park Ave.
New York, NY 10160
(212) 931-7800
Chief Labor Negotiator .... Frank Coonelly
Associate Counsels .... Jennifer Gefsky
& Derek Jackson

Major League Baseball Players Association
12 East 49th St., 24th Floor
New York, NY 10017
(212) 826-0808
Exec. Director & General Counsel .... Donald Fehr
Associate General Counsel .... Gene Orza

AL

American League Office
245 Park Ave., 31st Floor, New York, NY 10167
(212) 931-7800

Anaheim Angels
P. O. Box 2000, Anaheim, CA 92803
(714) 940-2000
Chairman & CEO .... Michael Eisner
Owner .... Walt Disney Co.
President .... Tony Tavares
V.P. & General Manager .... Bill Stoneman
V.P. of Communications .... Tim Mead

Baltimore Orioles
333 West Camden St., Baltimore, MD 21201
(410) 685-9800
CEO .... Peter Angelos
Vice Chairman & COO .... Joseph Foss
V.P. of Baseball Operations .... Syd Thrift
Director of Public Relations .... Bill Stetka

Boston Red Sox
Fenway Park, 4 Yawkey Way, Boston, MA 02215
(617) 267-9440
General Partner .... Jean R. Yawkey Trust
CEO .... John Harrington
Exec. V.P./General Manager .... Dan Duquette
Director of Communications .... Kevin Shea

Chicago White Sox
Comiskey Park, 333 W. 35th St., Chicago, IL 60616
(312) 674-1000
Chairman .... Jerry Reinsdorf
Vice Chairman .... Eddie Einhorn
Senior V.P./General Manager .... Ken Williams
Director of Public Relations .... Scott Reifert

Cleveland Indians
Jacobs Field, 2401 Ontario St., Cleveland, OH 44115
(216) 420-4200
Owner-Chairman-CEO .... Lawrence Dolan
General Manager .... Mark Shapiro
V.P., Public Relations .... Bob DiBiasio

Detroit Tigers
Comerica Park, 2100 Woodward Ave., Detroit, MI 48201
(313) 962-4000
Owner and Director .... Mike Ilitch
President/CEO .... TBA
V.P. of Baseball Operations .... Randy Smith
Sr. Dir. of Marketing and Communications ....Tyler Barnes

Kansas City Royals
P.O. Box 419969, Kansas City, MO 64141
(816) 921-8000
Owner .... David Glass
Executive V.P./COO .... Herk Robinson
General Manager .... Allard Baird
Director of Media Relations .... David Witty

Minnesota Twins
Hubert H. Humphrey Metrodome
34 Kirby Puckett Place, Minneapolis, MN 55415
(612) 375-1366
Owner .... Carl Pohlad
President .... Jerry Bell
V.P./General Manager .... Terry Ryan
Director of Communications .... Brad Ruiter
Manager of Media Relations .... Sean Harlin

New York Yankees
Yankee Stadium, Bronx, NY 10451
(718) 293-4300
Principal Owner .... George Steinbrenner
General Partners ....Hal Steinbrenner & Stephen Swindal
V.P./General Manager .... Brian Cashman
Dir. of Media Relations/Publicity .... Rick Cerrone

Oakland Athletics
7677 Oakport St., Suite 200
Oakland, CA 94621
(510) 638-4900
Co-Owners . . . . .Steve Schott and Ken Hofmann
President . . . . .Mike Crowley
General Manager . . . . .Billy Beane
Baseball Information Manager . . . . .Mike Selleck

Seattle Mariners
P.O. Box 4100, Seattle, WA 98104
(206) 346-4000
Chairman-CEO . . . . .Howard Lincoln
President-COO . . . . .Chuck Armstrong
Executive V.P./General Manager . . . . .Pat Gillick
Director of Baseball Information . . . . .Tim Hevly

Tampa Bay Devil Rays
Tropicana Field, One Tropicana Dr.
St. Petersburg, FL 33705
(727) 825-3137
Managing General Partner/CEO . . . . . . .Vincent J. Naimoli
Senior V.P., Baseball Ops./GM . . . . .Chuck Lamar
V.P. of Public Relations . . . . .Rick Vaughn

Texas Rangers
1000 Ballpark Way, Arlington, TX 76011
(817) 273-5222
Owner . . . . .Thomas Hicks
President . . . . .Jim Lites
V.P., General Manager . . . . .Doug Melvin
Senior V.P. of Communications . . . . .John Blake

Toronto Blue Jays
SkyDome, One Blue Jays Way, Suite 3200
Toronto, Ontario M5V 1J1
(416) 341-1000
Majority Owner . . . . .Rogers Communications
Chairman . . . . .Herb Solway
Sr. Pres. Baseball Ops./GM . . . . .Gord Ash
V.P. of Media Relations . . . . .Howie Starkman

NL

National League Office
245 Park Ave., 31st Floor, New York, NY 10167
(212) 931-7800

Arizona Diamondbacks
Bank One Ballpark, 401 E. Jefferson St., Phoenix, AZ 85004
(602) 462-6000
Chairman/CEO . . . . .Jerry Colangelo
President . . . . .Richard H. Dozer
V.P./General Manager . . . . .Joe Garagiola Jr.
Director of Public Relations . . . . .Mike Swanson

Atlanta Braves
755 Hank Aaron Drive, Atlanta, GA 30315
(404) 522-7630
President . . . . .Stan Kasten
Exec. V.P./General Manager . . . . .John Schuerholz
Director of Public Relations . . . . .Jim Schultz

Chicago Cubs
1060 West Addison St., Chicago, IL 60613
(773) 404-2827
Owner . . . . .The Tribune Company
President-CEO-GM . . . . .Andy MacPhail
Director of Media Relations . . . . .Sharon Pannozzo

Cincinnati Reds
100 Cinergy Field, Cincinnati, OH 45202
(513) 421-4510
Majority Owner . . . . .Carl Lindner
General Manager . . . . .Jim Bowden
Director of Media Relations . . . . .Rob Butcher

Colorado Rockies
Coors Field, 2001 Blake St., Denver, CO 80205
(303) 292-0200
Chairman-President-CEO . . . . .Jerry McMorris
Executive V.P./General Manager . . . . .Dan O'Dowd
Executive V.P. . . . . .Keli McGregor
Sr. Director Comm./PR .Jay Alves

Florida Marlins
2267 N.W. 199th St., Miami, FL 33056
(305) 626-7400
Owner . . . . .John W. Henry
President/General Manager . . . . .Dave Dombrowski
Director of Media Relations . . . . .Steve Copses

Houston Astros
Enron Field, P.O. Box 288, Houston, TX 77001
(713) 259-8000
Chairman-CEO . . . . .Drayton McLane Jr.
President of Baseball Ops. . . . . .Tal Smith
General Manager . . . . .Gerry Hunsicker
Director of Media Relations . . . . .Warren Miller

Los Angeles Dodgers
1000 Elysian Park Ave., Los Angeles, CA 90012
(323) 224-1500
Owner .Bob Daly & Fox News Corp
President/COO . . . . .Bob Graziano
Interim General Manager . . . . .Dave Wallace
Director of Media Relations . . . . .John Olguin

Milwaukee Brewers
Miller Park, One Brewers Way, Milwaukee, WI 53214
(414) 902-4400
President-CEO .Wendy Selig-Prieb
Asst. to President . . . . .Sal Bando
General Manager . . . . .Dean Taylor
Director of Media Relations . . . . .Jon Greenberg

Montreal Expos
P.O. Box 500, Station M, Montreal, Quebec H1V 3P2
(514) 253-3434
General Partner-President . . . . .Jeffrey Loria
V.P./General Manager . . . . .Jim Beattie
Director of Media Relations . . . . .Peter Loyello

New York Mets
123-01 Roosevelt Ave., Flushing, NY 11368
(718) 507-6387
Chairman . . . . .Nelson Doubleday
President-CEO . . . . .Fred Wilpon
General Manager . . . . .Steve Phillips
V.P. of Media Relations . . . . .Jay Horwitz

Philadelphia Phillies
P.O. Box 7575, Philadelphia, PA 19101
(215) 463-6000
General Partner/Pres./CEO . . . . .David Montgomery
Partner/Chairman . . . . .Bill Giles
General Manager & V.P. . . . . .Ed Wade
V.P. of Public Relations . . . . .Larry Shenk

Pittsburgh Pirates
115 Federal St., Pittsburgh, PA 15212
(412) 323-5000
CEO/Managing General Partner . . . . . . .Kevin McClatchy
COO . . . . .Richard Freeman
Senior V.P. & General Manager . . . . .Dave Littlefield
Director of Media Relations . . . . .Jim Trdinich

St. Louis Cardinals
250 Stadium Plaza, St. Louis, MO 63102
(314) 421-3060
Chairman . . . . .Frederick O. Hanser
President . . . . .Mark Lamping
V.P./General Manager . . . . .Walt Jocketty
Director of Public Relations . . . . .Brian Bartow

San Diego Padres
P.O. Box 122000, San Diego, CA 92112
(619) 881-6500
Chairman ....John Moores
President-CEO ....Larry Lucchino
V.P., Baseball Operations & G.M ....Kevin Towers
Director of Media Relations ....Glenn Geffner

San Francisco Giants
Pacific Bell Park, 24 Willie Mays Plaza
San Francisco, CA 94107
(415) 972-2000
President ....Peter Magowan
Executive V.P./COO ....Laurence Baer
Senior V.P./General Manager ....Brian Sabean
V.P. of Communications ....Bob Rose

PRO BASKETBALL
NBA

League Office
Olympic Tower, 645 Fifth Ave., New York, NY 10022
(212) 407-8000
Commissioner ....David Stern
Senior V.P. of Basketball Ops. ....Stuart Jackson
Deputy Commissioner ....Russell Granik
Sr. V.P. Sports Media Relations ....Brian McIntyre
Executive V.P. Global Media ....Heidi Ueberroth

NBA Players Association
1700 Broadway, Suite 1400, New York, NY 10019
(212) 655-0880
Exec. Director ....William Hunter
General Counsel ....Robert Lanza
President ....Patrick Ewing

Atlanta Hawks
One CNN Center, South Tower, Suite 405
Atlanta, GA 30303
(404) 827-3800
Owner ....AOL/Time-Warner
President ....Stan Kasten
General Manager ....Pete Babcock
V.P. of Communications ....Arthur Triche

Boston Celtics
151 Merrimac St., 4th Floor, Boston, MA 02114
(617) 523-6050
Chairman ....Paul Gaston
President ....TBA
General Manager ....Chris Wallace
V.P. of Media Relations ....Jeff Twiss

Charlotte Hornets
100 Hive Drive, Charlotte, NC 28217
(704) 357-0252
Owners : ....George Shinn and Ray Wooldridge
Executive V.P., Basketball Operations ....Bob Bass
V.P. of Public Relations ....Harold Kaufman

Chicago Bulls
United Center, 1901 West Madison St., Chicago, IL 60612
(312) 455-4000
Chairman ....Jerry Reinsdorf
Exec. V.P., Basketball Operations ....Jerry Krause
Director of Media Services ....Tim Hallam

Cleveland Cavaliers
Gund Arena, One Centre Court, Cleveland, OH 44115
(216) 420-2000
Owner-Chairman ....Gordon Gund
Owner-Vice Chairman ....George Gund III
President & CEO ....Jim Boland
Senior V.P/General Manager ....Jim Paxson
Sr. Dir. of Communications and PR ....Bob Price

Dallas Mavericks
The Pavilion, 2909 Taylor St., Dallas, TX 75226
(214) 747-6287
Owner ....Mark Cuban
GM & Head Coach ....Don Nelson
V.P. Marketing and Communications ....Matt Fitzgerald

Denver Nuggets
1000 Chopper Cir., Denver, CO 80204
(303) 405-1100
Owner ....Stan Kroenke
President & Head Coach ....Dan Issel
General Manager ....Kiki Vandeweghe
Director of Media Services ....Tommy Sheppard

Detroit Pistons
The Palace of Auburn Hills
Two Championship Dr., Auburn Hills, MI 48326
(248) 377-0100
Managing Partner ....William Davidson
President ....Tom Wilson
President of Basketball Operations ....Joe Dumars
V.P. of Public Relations ....Matt Dobek

Golden State Warriors
1011 Broadway, Oakland, CA 94607
(510) 986-2200
Owner-CEO ....Chris Cohan
General Manager ....Garry St. Jean
Director of Public Relations ....Raymond Ridder

Houston Rockets
2 Greenway Plaza, Suite 400, Houston, TX 77046
(713) 627-3865
Owner ....Leslie L. Alexander
COO ....George Postolos
General Manager ....Carroll Dawson
Director of Team Communications ....Tim Frank

Indiana Pacers
1 Conseco Court, Indianapolis, IN 46204
(317) 917-2500
Owners ....Melvin Simon & Herb Simon
President ....Donnie Walsh
General Manager ....David Kahn
Director of Media Relations ....David Benner

Los Angeles Clippers
Staples Center
1111 S. Figueroa St., Suite 1100
Los Angeles, CA 90015
(213) 742-7500
Owner-Chairman ....Donald T. Sterling
Executive V.P. ....Andy Roeser
V.P., Basketball Operations ....Elgin Baylor
Director of Communications ....Rob Raichlen

Los Angeles Lakers
555 N. Nash St., El Segundo, CA 90245
(310) 426-6000
Owner ....Jerry Buss
General Manager ....Mitch Kupchak
Director of Public Relations ....John Black

Memphis Grizzlies
PO Box 3463
Memphis, TN 38173
(901) 205-1234
Owner ....Michael Heisley
President of Basketball Ops. ....Dick Versace
General Manager ....Billy Knight
Media Relations Assistant ....Graham Kendrick

Miami Heat
AmericanAirlines Arena, 601 Biscayne Blvd.
Miami, FL 33132
(786) 777-4328
Managing General Partner ....Micky Arison
President & Head Coach ....Pat Riley
General Manager ....Randy Pfund
V.P. of Sports Media Relations ....Tim Donovan

Milwaukee Bucks
Bradley Center, 1001 N. Fourth St., Milwaukee, WI 53203
(414) 227-0500
President ....Sen. Herb Kohl (D., Wisc.)
General Manager ....Ernie Grunfeld
Director of Public Relations ....Cheri Hanson

Minnesota Timberwolves
Target Center
600 First Ave. North, Minneapolis, MN 55403
(612) 673-1600
Owner ....Glen Taylor
President ....Rob Moor
V.P., Basketball Operations ....Kevin McHale
General Manager & Head Coach ....Flip Saunders
Dir..of Public Relations/Communications ....Kent Wipf

New Jersey Nets
390 Murray Hill Pkwy., East Rutherford, NJ 07073
(201) 935-8888
Co-Chairman/CEO ....Finn Wentworth
Co-Chair/Owner ....Lewis Katz
President/GM ....Rod Thorn
Director of Public Relations ....John Mertz

New York Knickerbockers
Madison Square Garden
2 Penn Plaza, 14th Floor, New York, NY 10121
(212) 465-6000
Owner ....Cablevision Systems Inc.
President (Cablevision) ....James Dolan
General Manager ....Scott Layden
V.P. of Public Relations ....Lori Hamamoto

Orlando Magic
2 Magic Place
8701 Maitland Summit Blvd., Orlando, FL 32810
(407) 916-2400
Owner ....Rich DeVos
President ....Bob Vander Weide
COO ....John Weisbrod
V.P., Basketball Ops. & GM ....John Gabriel
Director of Media Relations ....Joel Glass

Philadelphia 76ers
First Union Center
3601 S. Broad St., Philadelphia, PA 19148
(215) 339-7600
Owner ....Comcast-Spectacor
Chairman ....Ed Snider
General Manager ....Billy King
Director of Communications ....Karen Frascona

Phoenix Suns
P.O. Box 1369, Phoenix, AZ 85001
(602) 379-7900
Chairman-CEO/Managing Gen. Partner . Jerry Colangelo
President/General Manager ....Bryan Colangelo
Sr. V.P. of Player Personnel ....Dick Van Arsdale
V.P. of Basketball Communications ....Julie Fie

Portland Trail Blazers
One Centre Court, Suite 200, Portland, OR 97227
(503) 234-9291
Owner-Chairman ....Paul Allen
President & General Manager ....Bob Whitsitt
Assistant General Manager ....Mark Warkentein
Dir. of Sports Communications ....Sue Carpenter

Sacramento Kings
One Sports Parkway, Sacramento, CA 95834
(916) 928-0000
Controlling Partners ....Joe and Gavin Maloof
President, Basketball Operations ....Geoff Petrie
V.P., Basketball Operations ....Wayne Cooper
Director of Media Relations ....Troy Hanson

San Antonio Spurs
The Alamodome
100 Montana St., San Antonio, TX 78203
(210) 554-7700
Chairman ....Peter Holt
GM & Head Coach ....Gregg Popovich
Director of Player Personnel ....Sam Schuler
Director of Media Services ....Tom James

Seattle SuperSonics
351 Elliott Ave. West
Seattle, WA 98119
(206) 281-5800
Chairman ....Howard Schultz
President & CEO ....Wally Walker
General Manager ....Rick Sund
Executive Vice President ....Billy McKinney
Director of Public Relations ....Marc Moquin

Toronto Raptors
40 Bay St., Suite 400
Toronto, Ontario M5J 2X2
(416) 815-5600
Chairman ....Steve Stavro
President ....Richard Peddie
Sr. V.P./General Manager ....Glen Grunwald
V.P. of Communications ....John Lashway

Utah Jazz
Delta Center, 301 West South Temple
Salt Lake City, UT 84101
(801) 325-2500
Owner ....Larry Miller
President ....Dennis Haslam
V.P. of Basketball Operations ....Kevin O'Connor
Director of Media Relations ....Kim Turner

Washington Wizards
MCI Center, 601 F Street NW
Washington, D.C., 20004
(202) 661-5000
Chairman ....Abe Pollin
President ....Susan O'Malley
President, Basketball Operations ....Michael Jordan
General Manager ....Wes Unseld
Director of Public Relations ....Maureen Nasser

Other Men's Pro Leagues

United States Basketball League
46 Quirk Road, Milford, CT 06460
(203) 877-9508
Commissioner ....Daniel T. Meisenheimer III
Dir. of Public Relations ....Orville Sweeney
   Member teams (10): Atlantic City Seagulls, Brooklyn
Kings, Dodge City Legend, Florida Sea Dragons, Kansas
Cagerz, Lakeland (FL) Blue Ducks, Long Island Surf, Mary-
land Mustangs, Oklahoma Storm, Pennsylvania Valley-
Dawgs.

National Basketball Development League
645 Fifth Avenue, New York, NY 10022
(212) 407-8000
Commissioner ....David Stern
Deputy Comm. & COO ....Russell Granik
V.P., Communications ....Brian McIntyre
   Member teams (8): Asheville (NC) Altitude; Columbus
(GA) Riverdragons; Fayetteville (NC) Patriots; Greenville
(SC) Groove; Huntsville (AL) Flight; Mobile (AL) Revelers;
North Charleston (SC) Lowgators; Roanoke (VA) Dazzle.

WNBA

League Office
645 5th Ave., New York, NY 10022
(212) 826-7000
President ....Val Ackerman
Sr. Dir. of Sports Comm. ....Maureen Coyle
Director of Media Relations ....Mark Pray

Charlotte Sting
3308 Oak Lace Blvd., Ste. B, Charlotte, NC 28208
(704) 357-0252
Executive V.P. ....Sam Russo
Head Coach ....Anne Donovan
Director of Media Relations ....John Maxwell

Cleveland Rockers
Gund Arena, One Center Court
Cleveland, OH 44115
(216) 420-2000
President ....Jim Boland
Head Coach ....Dan Hughes
General Manager ....Jim Paxson
Director of Media Relations ....Amanda Ludwig

Detroit Shock
The Palace of Auburn Hills
Two Championship Dr., Auburn Hills, MI 48326
(248) 377-0100
President ....Thomas S. Wilson
Dir. of Player Personnel & Head Coach .....Greg Williams
Dir. of Public Relations & Business Ops. ....Dennis Sampier

Houston Comets
Two Greenway Plaza, Suite 400
Houston, TX 77046-3865
(713) 627-9622
Owner/President ....Leslie L. Alexander
GM/Head Coach ....Van Chancellor
Director of Media Relations ....Bob Schranz

Indiana Fever
125 S. Pennsylvania St., Indianapolis, IN 46204
(317) 917-2500
President ....Donnie Walsh
Head Coach ....Nell Fortner
Director of Media Relations ....Tom Savage

Los Angeles Sparks
555 N. Nash Street, El Segundo, CA 90245
(310) 330-2434
General Manager ....Penny Toler
Head Coach ....Michael Cooper
Director of Media Relations ....Kristal Shipp

Miami Sol
601 Biscayne Blvd., Miami, FL 33132
(786) 777-1000
Owner ....Micky Arison
President ....Pat Riley
GM/Head Coach ....Ron Rothstein
Media Relations Manager ....Alan Hancock

Minnesota Lynx
Target Center
600 First Ave. N., Minneapolis, MN 55403
(612) 673-1600
Owner ....Glen Taylor
GM/Head Coach ....Brain Agler
Manager of Media Relations ....Mike Cristaldi

New York Liberty
Madison Square Garden
Two Penn Plaza, New York, NY 10121
(212) 564-9622
General Manager ....Carol Blazejowski
Head Coach ....Richie Adubato
Manager of Public Relations ....Chris Read

Orlando Miracle
2 Magic Place
8701 Maitland Summit Blvd., Orlando, FL, 32810
(407) 916-2400
President ....Bob Vander Weide
GM/Head Coach ....Carolyn Peck
Media/Community Relations Manager ......Katherine Wu

Phoenix Mercury
America West Arena
201 E. Jefferson St.
Phoenix, AZ 85004
(602) 514-8333
President ....Brian Colangelo
General Manager ....Seth Sulka
Head Coach ....Cynthia Cooper
Director of Communications ....Tami Scott

Portland Fire
One Center Court, Suite 150
Portland, OR 97227
(503) 234-9291
Owner ....Paul Allen
GM/Head Coach ....Linda Hargrove
Director of Communications ....Jill Wiggins

Sacramento Monarchs
ARCO Arena, One Sports Pkwy.
Sacramento, CA 95834
(916) 928-0000
General Manager ....Jerry Reynolds
Head Coach ....Maura McHugh
Manager of Media Relations ....Jennifer Norris

Seattle Storm
351 Elliott Ave. W.
Seattle, WA 98119
(206) 281-5800
Chairman ....Howard Schultz
President & CEO ....Wally Walker
GM/Head Coach ....Lin Dunn
Director of Media Relations ....Valerie O'Neil

Utah Starzz
Delta Center, 301 West South Temple
Salt Lake City, UT 84101
(801) 325-2500
V.P. of Basketball Operations ....Kevin O'Connor
Head Coach ....Candi Harvey
Director of Public/Comm. Relations ....Holly Layne

Washington Mystics
MCI Center, 601 F St. NW
Washington D.C. 20004
(202) 661-5000
General Manager ....Melissa McFerrin
Head Coach ....Tom Maher
Asst. Dir. of Public Relations ....Dyani Gordon

BOWLING

ABC
(American Bowling Congress)
5301 South 76th St.
Greendale, WI 53129
(414) 421-9000
Executive Director ....Roger Dalkin
Accounting Executive ....Mark Miller

BPAA
(Bowling Proprietors' Assn. of America)
P.O. Box 5802
Arlington, TX 76005
(817) 649-5105
CEO ....Jack Kelly
President ....Michael Ducat
Director of Public Relations ....Cary Richmond

PWBA
(Professional Women's Bowling Association)
7171 Cherryvale Blvd.
Rockford, IL 61112
(815) 332-5756
President .... John Falzone
Media Director ....Lydia Rypcinski

PBA
(Professional Bowlers Association)
1720 Merriman Road, P.O. Box 5118
Akron, OH 44334
(330) 836-5568
Commissioner ....Ian Hamilton
President ....Steve Miller
Dir. of Corporate Comm. ....Beth Marshall

WIBC
(Women's International Bowling Congress, Inc.)
5301 South 76th St., Greendale, WI 53129
(414) 421-9000
President .... Joyce Deitch
Accounting Executive ....Gianna Pipino

YABA
(Young American Bowling Alliance)
5301 South 76th St., Greendale, WI 53129
(414) 421-9000
Executive Director .... Jim Zebehazy
Accounting Executive ....Kevin Gabinski

BOXING

IBF
(International Boxing Federation)
134 Evergreen Place, 9th Floor
East Orange, NJ 07018
(973) 414-0300
President ....Hiawatha Knight
Executive Secretary ....Marian Muhammad
Ratings Chairman ....Daryl Peoples

WBA
(World Boxing Association)
P.O. Box 377, Maracay 2110–A
Venezuela
TEL: 011-58-44-63-1584
President ....Gilberto Mendoza
General Counsel/U.S. Spokesman .... Jimmy Binns
1735 Market St., 39th Floor, Phila., PA 19103
(215) 557-8000
Ratings Chairman ....Bolivar Icaza
P.O. Box 1833, Panama 1, Rep. de Panama
TEL: 011-507-63-5167

WBC
(World Boxing Council)
Genova 33-503, Col. Juarez,
MEXICO, 06600, D.F., Mexico
TEL: 011-525-208-2440
President ....Jose Sulaiman
Ratings Chairman ....Frank Quill
Press Information/U.S. Spokesman ....John Brister
411 Ballentine St., Bay St. Louis, MS 39520
(209) 796-9766

WBO
(World Boxing Organization)
1st Federal Bldg.
1056 Ave Munoz Revera, Suite 711
San Juan, P.R. 00927
(787) 765-4444
President ....,.........Francisco Paco Valcarcel
Past Pres./Attorney ....Luis Batista Salas
Ratings Chairman ....Luis Perez
Public Relations Dir. ....Mario Rivera-Martino

Don King Productions, Inc.
501 Fairway Dr.
Deerfield Beach, FL 33441
(954) 418-5800
President ....Don King
V.P. of Boxing Ops. ....Bob Goodman
Director of Public Relations ....Alan Hopper

Top Rank
3980 Howard Hughes Pkwy. Ste. 580
Las Vegas, NV 89109
(702) 732-2717
Chairman ....Bob Arum
Director of Public Relations ....Lee Samuels

COLLEGE SPORTS

CCA
(Collegiate Commissioners Association)
2201 Stemmons Freeway, Dallas, TX 75207
(214) 742-1212
President .... John Steinbrecher (Mid-Continent)
Exec. V.P. ....Michael Slive (Conf. USA)
Secretary-Treasurer ....Britton Banowsky (Big 12)

NAIA
(National Assn. of Intercollegiate Athletics)
23500 W. 105th Street, Olathe, KS 66051
(913) 791-0044
President-CEO ....Steve Baker
Public Relations Director ....Darin David

NCAA
(National Collegiate Athletic Association)
P.O. Box 6222, Indianapolis, IN 46206
(317) 917-6222
Chief Operating Officer ....Daniel Boggan Jr.
President ....Cedric Dempsey
V.P. of Enforcement ....David Price
Director of Public Relations ....Wallace I. Renfro

WSF
(Women's Sports Foundation)
Eisenhower Park, East Meadow, NY 11554
(516) 542-4700
Executive Director ....Donna Lopiano
President ....Julie Foudy
Sr. Comm. Coordinators ....Kristen Conti & Ellie Seifert

Major NCAA Conferences

See pages 439-447 for football coaches, basketball
coaches, nicknames and colors of all Division I-A and I-AA
football schools and Division I basketball schools.

ATLANTIC COAST CONFERENCE
P.O. Drawer ACC
Greensboro, NC 27417-6724
(336) 854-8787   Founded: 1953
Commissioner ....John Swofford
Asst. Commis. of Media Relations ....Brian Morrison
2001-02 members: BASKETBALL & FOOTBALL (9)—
Clemson, Duke, Florida St., Georgia Tech, Maryland,
North Carolina, North Carolina St., Virginia and Wake
Forest.

Clemson University
Clemson, SC 29633   Founded: 1889
SID: (864) 656-2114   Enrollment: 16,982
President ....James F. Barker
Athletic Director ....Bobby Robinson
Sports Information Director ....Tim Baurret

Duke University
Durham, NC 27708   Founded: 1838
SID: (919) 684-2633   Enrollment: 6,246
President ....Nannerl Keohane
Athletic Director ....Joe Alleva
Sports Information Director ....John Jackson

Florida State University

Tallahassee, FL 32316   Founded: 1857
SID: (850) 644-1403   Enrollment: 34,500
President ....Talbot (Sandy) D'Alemberte
Athletic Director ....Dave Hart Jr.
Sports Information Director ....Rob Wilson

Georgia Tech

Atlanta, GA 30332   Founded: 1885
SID: (404) 894-5445   Enrollment: 14,000
President ....Wayne Clough
Athletic Director ....Dave Braine
Sports Information Director ....Mike Stamus

University of Maryland

College Park, MD 20741   Founded: 1807
SID: (301) 314-7064   Enrollment: 33,006
President ....Dr. Clayton D. Mote Jr.
Athletic Director ....Deborah Yow
Sports Information Director ....Dave Haglund

University of North Carolina

Chapel Hill, NC 27514   Founded: 1789
SID: (919) 962-2123   Enrollment: 24,635
Chancellor ....James Moeser
Athletic Director ....Dick Baddour
Sports Information Director ....Steve Kirschner

North Carolina State University

Raleigh, NC 27695   Founded: 1887
SID: (919) 515-2102   Enrollment: 28,619
Chancellor ....Mary Anne E. Fox
Athletic Director ....Lee Fowler
Asst. AD for Media Relations ....Annabelle Vaughan

University of Virginia

Charlottesville, VA 22903   Founded: 1819
SID: (804) 982-5500   Enrollment: 18,473
President ....John T. Casteen III
Athletic Director ....Craig Littlepage
Sports Information Director ....Rich Murray

Wake Forest University

Winston-Salem, NC 27109   Founded: 1834
SID: (336) 758-5640   Enrollment: 3,850
President ....Thomas K. Hearn Jr.
Athletic Director ....Ron Wellman
Athletic Media Relations ....Dean Buchan

ຂະ ຂະ ຂະ

BIG EAST CONFERENCE

222 Richmond Street, 1st Floor, Providence, RI 02903
(401) 272-9108   Founded: 1979
Commissioner ....Mike Tranghese
Assoc. Commissioner/P.R ....John Paquette
   2001-02 members: BASKETBALL (14)— Boston College, Connecticut, Georgetown, Miami-FL, Notre Dame, Pittsburgh, Providence, Rutgers, St. John's, Seton Hall, Syracuse, Villanova, Virginia Tech and West Virginia; FOOTBALL (8)— Boston College, Miami-FL, Pittsburgh, Rutgers, Syracuse, Temple, Virginia Tech and West Virginia.

Boston College

Chestnut Hill, MA 02467   Founded: 1863
SID: (617) 552-3004   Enrollment: 14,600
President ....Rev. William P. Leahy, S.J.
Athletic Director ....Gene DeFillippo
Sports Information Director ....Michael Enright

University of Connecticut

Storrs, CT 06269   Founded: 1881
SID: (860) 486-3531   Enrollment: 23,419
President ....Philip Austin
Athletic Director ....Lew Perkins
Sports Information Director ....Tim Tolokan

Georgetown University

Washington, DC 20057   Founded: 1789
SID: (202) 687-2492   Enrollment: 6,418
President ....John J. DeGioia, Ph. D.
Athletic Director ....Joseph C. Lang
Sr. Sports Communication Director ....Bill Shapland

University of Miami

Coral Gables, FL 33146   Founded: 1926
SID: (305) 284-3244   Enrollment: 13,963
President ....Dr. Donna Shalala
Athletic Director ....Paul Dee
Asst. Athletic Director/Communications ....Mark Pray

University of Notre Dame

Notre Dame, IN 46556   Founded: 1842
SID: (219) 631-7516   Enrollment: 10,301
President ....Rev. Edward (Monk) Malloy
Athletic Director ....Kevin White
Sports Information Director ....John Heisler

University of Pittsburgh

Pittsburgh, PA 15213   Founded: 1787
SID: (412) 648-8240   Enrollment: 33,112
Chancellor ....Mark A. Nordenberg
Athletic Director ....Steve Pederson
Sports Information Director ..................E.J. Borghetti

Providence College

Providence, RI 02918   Founded: 1917
SID: (401) 865-2272   Enrollment: 3,812
President ....Philip A. Smith, O.P.
Interim Athletic Director ....Marc Devine
Sports Information Director ....Arthur Parks

Rutgers University

New Brunswick, NJ 08903   Founded: 1766
SID: (732) 445-4200   Enrollment: 33,500
President ....Francis L. Lawrence
Athletic Director ....Robert E. Mulcahy III
Sports Information Director ....John Wooding

St. John's University

Jamaica, NY 11439   Founded: 1870
SID: (718) 990-6367   Enrollment: 17,250
President ....Rev. Donald J. Harrington, CM
Athletic Director ....David Wegrzyn
Sports Information Director ....Dominic Scianna

Seton Hall University

South Orange, NJ 07079   Founded: 1856
SID: (973) 761-9493   Enrollment: 9,608
President ....Monsignor Robert Sheeran
Athletic Director ....Jeff Fogelson
Sports Information Director ....Marie Wozniak

Syracuse University

Syracuse, NY 13244   Founded: 1870
SID: (315) 443-2608   Enrollment: 10,000
Chancellor ....Kenneth Shaw
Athletic Director ....Jake Crouthamel
Sports Information Director ....Sue Edson

Temple University

Philadelphia, PA 19122   Founded: 1884
SID: (215) 204-7445   Enrollment: 29,000
President ....Dr. David Adamany
Athletic Director ....David O'Brien
Sports Information Director ....Scott Cathcart

Villanova University

Villanova, PA 19085   Founded: 1842
SID: (610) 519-4120   Enrollment: 6,150
President ....Rev. Edmund J. Dobbin, OSA
Athletic Director ....Vince Nicastro
Sports Information Director ....Dean Kenefick

Virginia Tech
Blacksburg, VA 24061
SID: (540) 231-6726
President ....Charles Steger
Athletic Director ....Jim Weaver
Sports Information Director ....Dave Smith

Founded: 1872
Enrollment: 25,000

West Virginia University
Morgantown, WV 26507
SID: (304) 293-2821
President ....David Hardesty
Athletic Director ....Ed Pastilong
Sports Information Director ....Shelly Poe

Founded: 1867
Enrollment: 22,315

🐾   🐾   🐾

BIG 12 CONFERENCE
2201 Stemmons Fwy., 28th Floor
Dallas, TX 75207
(214) 742-1212
Commissioner ....Kevin Weiberg
Media Relations Director ....Bo Carter

Founded: 1996

2001-02 members: BASKETBALL & FOOTBALL (12)—
Baylor, Colorado, Iowa St., Kansas, Kansas St., Missouri,
Nebraska, Oklahoma, Oklahoma St., Texas, Texas A&M
and Texas Tech.

Baylor University
Waco, TX 76711
SID: (254) 710-2743
President ....Robert B. Sloan
Athletic Director ....Tom Stanton
Sports Information Director ....Scott Stricklin

Founded: 1845
Enrollment: 13,719

University of Colorado
Boulder, CO 80309
SID: (303) 492-5626
President ....Dr. Elizabeth Hoffman
Athletic Director ....Dick Tharp
Sports Information Director ....Dave Plati

Founded: 1876
Enrollment: 26,035

Iowa State University
Ames, IA 50011
SID: (515) 294-3372
President ....Gregory Geoffroy
Athletic Director ....Bruce Van De Velde
Sports Information Director ....Tom Kroeschell

Founded: 1858
Enrollment: 26,845

University of Kansas
Lawrence, KS 66045
SID: (785) 864-3417
Chancellor ....Robert Hemenway
Athletic Director ....Al Bohl
Asst. Athletic Director/Media Relations ....Doug Vance

Founded: 1866
Enrollment: 24,502

Kansas State University
Manhattan, KS 66502
SID: (785) 532-6735
President ....Jon Wefald
Athletic Director ....Tim Weiser
Sports Information Director ....Doug Dull

Founded: 1863
Enrollment: 21,929

University of Missouri
Columbia, MO 65205
SID: (573) 882-3241
Chancellor ....Richard Wallace
Athletic Director ....Michael Alden
Interim Sports Information Director ....Chad Moller

Founded: 1839
Enrollment: 22,898

University of Nebraska
Lincoln, NE 68588
SID: (402) 472-2263
Chancellor ....Harvey Perlman
Athletic Director ....Bill Byrne
Sports Information Director ....Chris Anderson

Founded: 1869
Enrollment: 25,000

University of Oklahoma
Norman, OK 73019
SID: (405) 325-8231
President ....David Boren
Athletic Director ....Joe Castiglione
Dir. of Athletic Media Relations ....Kenny Mossman

Founded: 1890
Enrollment: 25,000

Oklahoma State University
Stillwater, OK 74078
SID: (405) 744-7714
President ....James Halligan
Athletic Director ....Terry Don Phillips
Sports Information Director ....Steve Buzzard

Founded: 1890
Enrollment: 20,100

University of Texas
Austin, TX 78713
SID: (512) 471-7437
President ....Dr. Larry Faulkner
Athletic Director ....De Loss Dodds
Sports Information Director ....John Bianco

Founded: 1883
Enrollment: 46,484

Texas A&M University
College Station, TX 77843
SID: (979) 845-5725
President ....Ray Bowen
Athletic Director ....Wally Groff
Asst. AD for Media Relations ....Alan Cannon

Founded: 1876
Enrollment: 44,081

Texas Tech University
Lubbock, TX 79409
SID: (806) 742-2770
Chancellor ....John Montford
Athletic Director ....Gerald Myers
Sports Information Director ....Chris Cook

Founded: 1923
Enrollment: 24,558

🐾   🐾   🐾

BIG TEN CONFERENCE
1500 West Higgins Road
Park Ridge, IL 60068-6300
(847) 696-1010
Commissioner ....Jim Delany
Assistant Commissioner of Media Relations ......Sue Lister

Founded: 1895

2001-02 members: BASKETBALL & FOOTBALL (11)—
Illinois, Indiana, Iowa, Michigan, Michigan St., Minnesota,
Northwestern, Ohio St., Penn St., Purdue and Wisconsin.

University of Illinois
Champaign, IL 61820
SID: (217) 333-1390
President ....James J. Stukel
Athletic Director ....Ron Guenther
Dir. of Communications ....Kent Brown

Founded: 1867
Enrollment: 36,000

Indiana University
Bloomington, IN 47408
SID: (812) 855-9399
President ....Myles Brand
Athletic Director ....Michael McNeely
Sports Information Director ....Jeff Fanter

Founded: 1820
Enrollment: 36,000

University of Iowa
Iowa City, IA 52242
SID: (319) 335-9411
President ....Mary Sue Coleman
Athletic Director ....Bob Bowlsby
Sports Information Director ....Phil Haddy

Founded: 1847
Enrollment: 28,311

University of Michigan
Ann Arbor, MI 48109
SID: (734) 763-1381
President ....Lee Bollinger
Athletic Director ....William Martin
Sports Information Director ....Bruce Madej

Founded: 1817
Enrollment: 38,103

Michigan State University
East Lansing, MI 48824
SID: (517) 355-2271
President ....Peter McPherson
Athletic Director ....Clarence Underwood
Asst. AD for Media Relations ....John Lewandowski

Founded: 1855
Enrollment: 43,189

University of Minnesota
Minneapolis, MN 55455   Founded: 1851
SID: (612) 625-4090   Enrollment: 43,394
President .... Mark Yudof
Athletic Director .... Tom Moe
Sports Information Director .... Bill Crumley

Northwestern University
Evanston, IL 60208   Founded: 1851
SID: (847) 491-7503   Enrollment: 7,400
President .... Henry S. Bienen
Athletic Director .... Rick Taylor
Asst. Athletic Director/Media Services .... Mike Wolf

Ohio State University
Columbus, OH 43210   Founded: 1870
SID: (614) 292-6861   Enrollment: 54,989
President .... William E. Kirwan
Athletic Director .... Andy Geiger
Sports Information Director .... Steve Snapp

Penn State University
University Park, PA 16802   Founded: 1855
SID: (814) 865-1757   Enrollment: 41,050
President .... Graham Spanier
Athletic Director .... Tim Curley
Sports Information Director .... Jeff Nelson

Purdue University
West Lafayette, IN 47907   Founded: 1869
SID: (765) 494-3202   Enrollment: 36,878
President .... Martin C. Jischke
Athletic Director .... Morgan Burke
Sports Information Director .... Tom Schott

University of Wisconsin
Madison, WI 53711   Founded: 1848
SID: (608) 262-1811   Enrollment: 40,610
Chancellor .... John Wiley
Athletic Director .... Pat Richter
Sports Information Director .... Justin Doherty

      ❧   ❧   ❧

CONFERENCE USA
35 East Wacker Drive, Suite 650, Chicago, IL 60601
(312) 553-0483   Founded: 1995
Commissioner .... Mike Slive
Asst. Commissioner .... Brian Teter
    2001-02 members: BASKETBALL (14)— UAB, Charlotte, Cincinnati, DePaul, East Carolina, Houston, Louisville, Marquette, Memphis, Saint Louis, South Florida, Southern Miss, TCU and Tulane; FOOTBALL (10)— UAB, Army, Cincinnati, East Carolina, Houston, Louisville, Memphis, Southern Miss, TCU and Tulane.

University of Alabama at Birmingham
Birmingham, AL 35294   Founded: 1969
SID: (205) 934-0722   Enrollment: 16,081
President .... Dr. W. Ann Reynolds
Athletic Director .... Herman Frazier
Sports Information Director .... Grant Shingleton

Army — U.S. Military Academy
West Point, NY 10996   Founded: 1802
SID: (845) 938-3303   Enrollment: 4,000
Superintendent .... Lt. Gen. William J. Lennox, Jr.
Athletic Director .... Rick Greenspan
Media Relations .... Bob Beretta

University of Cincinnati
Cincinnati, OH 45221   Founded: 1819
SID: (513) 556-5191   Enrollment: 34,000
President .... Dr. Joseph A. Steger
Athletic Director .... Bob Goin
Sports Information Director .... Tom Hathaway

DePaul University
Chicago, IL 60614   Founded: 1898
SID: (773) 325-7525   Enrollment: 18,565
President .... Rev. John P. Minogue
Athletic Director .... Bill Bradshaw
Sports Information Director .... Scott Reed

East Carolina University
Greenville, NC 27858   Founded: 1907
SID: (252) 328-4522   Enrollment: 17,857
Chancellor .... Dr. William V. Muse
Athletic Director .... Mike Hamrick
Sports Information Director .... Jody Jones

University of Houston
Houston, TX 77204   Founded: 1927
SID: (713) 743-9404   Enrollment: 30,575
President .... Arthur K. Smith
Athletic Director .... TBA
Sports Information Director .... Chris Burkhalter

University of Louisville
Louisville, KY 40292   Founded: 1798
SID: (502) 852-6581   Enrollment: 22,000
President .... Dr. John W. Shumaker
Athletic Director .... Tom Jurich
Sports Information Director .... Kenny Klein

Marquette University
Milwaukee, WI 53233   Founded: 1881
SID: (414) 288-7447   Enrollment: 10,600
President .... Rev. Robert A. Wild S.J.
Athletic Director .... Bill Cords
Sports Information Director .... John Farina

University of Memphis
Memphis, TN 38152   Founded: 1912
SID: (901) 678-2337   Enrollment: 20,100
President .... Dr. Shirley Raines
Athletic Director .... R.C. Johnson
Sports Information Director .... Bob Winn

University of North Carolina at Charlotte
Charlotte, NC 28223   Founded: 1946
SID: (704) 547-4937   Enrollment: 16,844
Chancellor .... J. H. Woodward
Athletic Director .... Judy Rose
Sports Information Director .... Tom Whitestone

Saint Louis University
St. Louis, MO 63103   Founded: 1818
SID: (314) 977-2524   Enrollment: 11,112
President .... Rev. Lawrence Biondi, S.J.
Athletic Director .... Doug Woolard
Sport Information Director .... Doug McIlhagga

University of South Florida
Tampa, FL 33620   Founded: 1956
SID: (813) 974-4086   Enrollment: 36,000
President .... Judy Genshaft
Athletic Director .... Lee Roy Selmon
Sports Information Director .... John Gerdes

University of Southern Mississippi
Hattiesburg, MS 39406   Founded: 1910
SID: (601) 266-4503   Enrollment: 14,449
President .... Dr. Horace W. Fleming Jr.
Athletic Director .... Rich Giannini
Asst. AD for Media Relations .... Mike Montoro

TCU — Texas Christian University
Fort Worth, TX 76129   Founded: 1873
SID: (817) 257-5394   Enrollment: 7,200
Chancellor .... Dr. Michael Ferrari
Athletic Director .... Eric Hyman
Director of Media Relations .... Steve Fink

Tulane University
New Orleans, LA 70118
Founded: 1834
SID: (504) 865-5506
Enrollment: 11,300
President ....Dr. Scott S. Cowen
Athletic Director ....Rick Dickson
Sports Information Director ....Donna Turner

         ટ   ટ   ટ

MID-AMERICAN CONFERENCE
24 Public Square, 15th Floor, Cleveland, OH 44113
(216) 566-4622
Founded: 1946
Commissioner ....Rick Chryst
Director of Communications ....Gary Richter
  2001-02 members: BASKETBALL & FOOTBALL (13)—
Akron, Ball St., Bowling Green, Buffalo, Central Michigan,
Eastern Michigan, Kent, Marshall, Miami-OH, Northern
Illinois, Ohio University, Toledo and Western Michigan.

University of Akron
Akron, OH 44325
Founded: 1870
SID: (330) 972-7468
Enrollment: 23,264
President ....Luis Proenza
Athletic Director ....Michael J. Thomas
Director of Athletic Communications ....Jeff Brewer

Ball State University
Muncie, IN 47306
Founded: 1918
SID: (765) 285-8242
Enrollment: 17,529
President ....Dr. Blaine Brownell
Athletic Director ....Andrea Seger
Sports Information Director ....Joe Hernandez

Bowling Green State University
Bowling Green, OH 43403
Founded: 1910
SID: (419) 372-7075
Enrollment: 19,500
President ....Sidney Ribeau
Athletic Director ....Paul Krebs
Director of Athletic Communications .......J.D. Campbell

University of Buffalo
Buffalo, NY 14260
Founded: 1846
SID: (716) 645-6311
Enrollment: 23,000
President ....William R. Greiner
Athletic Director ....Bob Arkeilpane
Sports Information Director ....Paul Vecchio

Central Michigan University
Mt. Pleasant, MI 48859
Founded: 1892
SID: (517) 774-3277
Enrollment: 27,015
President ....Michael Rao
Athletic Director ....Herb Deromedi
Sports Information Director ....Fred Stabley Jr.

Eastern Michigan University
Ypsilanti, MI 48197
Founded: 1849
SID: (734) 487-0317
Enrollment: 23,500
President ....Dr. Samuel Kirkpatrick
Athletic Director ....Dr. David Dials
Sports Information Director ....Jim Streeter

Kent State University
Kent, OH 44242
Founded: 1910
SID: (330) 672-2110
Enrollment: 30,227
President ....Carol Cartwright
Athletic Director ....Laing Kennedy
Sports Information Director ....Will Roleson

Marshall University
Huntington, WV 25715
Founded: 1837
SID: (304) 696-4660
Enrollment: 16,000
President ....Dan Angel
Athletic Director ....Lance West
Sports Information Director ....Ricky Hazel

Miami University
Oxford, OH 45056
Founded: 1809
SID: (513) 529-4327
Enrollment: 16,000
President ....James C. Garland
Athletic Director ....Joel Maturi
Sports Information Director ....Mike Harris

Northern Illinois University
DeKalb, IL 60115
Founded: 1895
SID: (815) 753-1706
Enrollment: 23,248
President ....John G. Peters
Athletic Director ....Cary Groth
Sports Information Director ....Michael Korcek

Ohio University
Athens, OH 45701
Founded: 1804
SID: (740) 593-1298
Enrollment: 27,605
President ....Robert Glidden
Athletic Director ....Tom Boeh
Media Services Director ....Derek Scott

University of Toledo
Toledo, OH 43606
Founded: 1872
SID: (419) 530-3790
Enrollment: 20,307
President ....Dr. Daniel Johnson
Interim Athletic Director ....Mike Karabin
Sports Information Director ....Paul Helgren

Western Michigan University
Kalamazoo, MI 49008
Founded: 1903
SID: (616) 387-4138
Enrollment: 27,744
President ....Dr. Elson Floyd
Athletic Director ....Kathy Beauregard
Sports Information Director ....Dan Jankowski

         ટ   ટ   ટ

MOUNTAIN WEST CONFERENCE
15455 Gleneagle Drive, Suite 200
Colorado Springs, CO 80921
(719) 488-4040
Founded: 1999
Commissioner ....Craig Thompson
Media Relations Director ....Bob Burda
  2001-02 members: BASKETBALL & FOOTBALL (8)—
Air Force, BYU, Colorado State, UNLV, New Mexico, San
Diego St., Utah and Wyoming.

U.S. Air Force Academy
US Academy, CO 80840
Founded: 1959
SID: (719) 333-2313
Enrollment: 4,100
Superintendent ....Lt. Gen. John R. Dallager
Athletic Director ....Col. Randall W. Spetman
Sports Information Director ....Troy Garnhart

Brigham Young University
Provo, UT 84602
Founded: 1875
SID: (801) 378-4911
Enrollment: 33,132
President ....Merril J. Bateman
Athletic Director ....Val Hale
Sports Information Director ....Duff Tittle

Colorado State University
Fort Collins, CO 80523
Founded: 1870
SID: (970) 491-5067
Enrollment: 23,000
President ....Dr. Albert Yates
Athletic Director ....Jeff Hathaway
Sports Information Director ....Gary Ozzello

University of New Mexico
Albuquerque, NM 87131
Founded: 1889
SID: (505) 925-5520
Enrollment: 24,250
President ....Dr. William Gordon
Athletic Director ....Rudy Davalos
Sports Information Director ....Greg Remington

San Diego State University
San Diego, CA 92182   Founded: 1897
SID: (619) 594-5547   Enrollment: 31,500
President ....Dr. Stephen L. Weber
Athletic Director ....Rick Bay
Interim Sports Information Director ....Kevin Klintworth

UNLV — University of Nevada, Las Vegas
Las Vegas, NV 89154   Founded: 1957
SID: (702) 895-3207   Enrollment: 23,000
President ....Dr. Carol Harter
Athletic Director ....Charles Cavagnaro
Sports Information Director ....Andy Grossman

University of Utah
Salt Lake City, UT 84112   Founded: 1850
SID: (801) 581-3510   Enrollment: 25,391
President ....Dr. Bernard Machen
Athletic Director ....Dr. Chris Hill
Sports Information Director ....Liz Abel

University of Wyoming
Laramie, WY 82071   Founded: 1886
SID: (307) 766-2256   Enrollment: 10,600
President ....Philip Dubois
Athletic Director ....Lee Moon
Sports Information Director ....Kevin McKinney

       ❧   ❧   ❧

PACIFIC-10 CONFERENCE
800 South Broadway, Suite 400
Walnut Creek, CA 94596
(925) 932-4411   Founded: 1915
Commissioner ....Thomas Hansen
Asst. Commissioner, Public Relations ....Jim Muldoon
     2001-02 members: BASKETBALL & FOOTBALL (10)—
Arizona, Arizona St., California, Oregon, Oregon St.,
Stanford, UCLA, USC, Washington and Washington St.

University of Arizona
Tucson, AZ 85721   Founded: 1885
SID: (520) 621-4163   Enrollment: 35,400
President :................................Peter Likins
Athletic Director ....Jim Livengood
Sports Information Director ....Tom Duddleston

Arizona State University
Tempe, AZ 85287   Founded: 1885
SID: (480) 965-6592   Enrollment: 43,372
President ....Lattie F. Coor
Athletic Director ....Gene Smith
Sports Information Director ....Mark Brand

University of California
Berkeley, CA 94720   Founded: 1868
SID: (510) 642-5363   Enrollment: 31,000
Chancellor ....Robert Berdahl
Athletic Director ....Steve Gladstone
Sports Information Director ....Herb Benenson

University of Oregon
Eugene, OR 97401   Founded: 1876
SID: (541) 346-5488   Enrollment: 17,850
President ....David Frohnmeyer
Athletic Director ....Bill Moos
Sports Information Director ....Dave Williford

Oregon State University
Corvallis, OR 97331   Founded: 1868
SID: (541) 737-3720   Enrollment: 17,000
President ....Paul G. Risser
Athletic Director ....Mitch Barnhart
Sports Information Director ....Hal Cowan

Stanford University
Stanford, CA 94305   Founded: 1891
SID: (650) 723-4418   Enrollment: 13,075
President ....John Hennessy
Athletic Director ....Ted Leland
Sports Information Director ....Gary Migdol

UCLA — Univ. of California, Los Angeles
Los Angeles, CA 90024   Founded: 1919
SID: (310) 206-6831   Enrollment: 36,890
Chancellor ....Albert Carnesale
Athletic Director ....Pete Dalis
Sports Information Director ....Marc Dellins

USC — Univ. of Southern California
Los Angeles, CA 90089   Founded: 1880
SID: (213) 740-8480   Enrollment: 28,600
President ....Steven Sample
Athletic Director ....Mike Garrett
Sports Information Director ....Tim Tessalone

University of Washington
Seattle, WA 98195   Founded: 1861
SID: (206) 543-2230   Enrollment: 25,000
President ....Richard McCormick
Athletic Director ....Barbara Hedges
Asst. AD for Media Relations ....Jim Daves

Washington State University
Pullman, WA 99164   Founded: 1890
SID: (509) 335-2684   Enrollment: 22,000
President ....V. Lane Rawlins
Athletic Director ....Jim Sterk
Sports Information Director ....Rod Commons

       ❧   ❧   ❧

SOUTHEASTERN CONFERENCE
2201 Richard Arrington Blvd. North
Birmingham, AL 35203
(205) 458-3000   Founded: 1933
Commissioner ....Roy Kramer
Assoc. Commis. of Media Relations ....Charles Bloom
     2001-02 members: BASKETBALL & FOOTBALL (12)—
Alabama, Arkansas, Auburn, Florida, Georgia, Kentucky,
LSU, Mississippi St., Ole Miss, South Carolina, Tennessee
and Vanderbilt.

University of Alabama
Tuscaloosa, AL 35487   Founded: 1831
SID: (205) 348-6084   Enrollment: 19,400
President ....Dr. Andrew Sorensen
Athletic Director ....Mal Moore
Sports Information Director ....Larry White

University of Arkansas
Fayetteville, AR 72701   Founded: 1871
SID: (501) 575-2751   Enrollment: 15,266
Chancellor ....John White
Athletic Director ....Frank Broyles
Women's Athletic Director ....Bev Lewis
Sports Information Director ....Kevin Trainor

Auburn University
Auburn, AL 36831   Founded: 1856
SID: (334) 844-9800   Enrollment: 21,775
Interim President ....William Walker
Athletic Director ....David Housel
Sports Information Director ....Meredith Jenkins

University of Florida
Gainesville, FL 32604   Founded: 1853
SID: (352) 375-4683 ext. 6100   Enrollment: 45,114
President ....Charles Young
Athletic Director ....Jeremy Foley
Sports Information Director ....John Humenik

University of Georgia
Athens, GA 30603
SID: (706) 542-1621
President .... Michael F. Adams
Athletic Director .... Vince Dooley
Sports Information Director .... Claude Felton

Founded: 1785
Enrollment: 31,288

University of Kentucky
Lexington, KY 40506
SID: (859) 257-3838
President .... Dr. Lee Todd
Athletic Director .... Larry Ivy
Asst. Athletic Director/Media Relations .... Rena Vicini

Founded: 1865
Enrollment: 30,006

LSU — Louisiana State University
Baton Rouge, LA 70894
SID: (225) 388-8226
Chancellor .... Dr. Mark Emmert
Athletic Director .... Skip Bertman
Sports Information Director .... Michael Bonnette

Founded: 1860
Enrollment: 30,977

Mississippi State University
Starkville, MS 39762
SID: (662) 325-2703
President .... Dr. Malcolm Portera
Athletic Director .... Larry Templeton
Sports Information Director .... Mike Nemeth

Founded: 1878
Enrollment: 16,047

Ole Miss — University of Mississippi
U. of M., MS 38677
SID: (662) 915-7522
Chancellor .... Dr. Robert C. Khayat
Athletic Director .... John Shafer
Sports Information Director .... Langston Rogers

Founded: 1848
Enrollment: 13,926

University of South Carolina
Columbia, SC 29208
SID: (803) 777-5204
President .... John Palms
Athletic Director .... Mike McGee
Sports Information Director .... Kerry Tharp

Founded: 1801
Enrollment: 26,346

University of Tennessee
Knoxville, TN 37996
SID: (865) 974-1212
Interim President .... Eli Fly
Athletic Director .... Doug Dickey
Women's Athletic Director .... Joan Cronan
Sports Information Director .... Bud Ford

Founded: 1794
Enrollment: 25,474

Vanderbilt University
Nashville, TN 37212
SID: (615) 322-4121
Chancellor .... Gordon Gee
Athletic Director .... Todd Turner
Sports Information Director .... Rod Williamson

Founded: 1873
Enrollment: 5,885

≈ ≈ ≈

SUN BELT CONFERENCE
601 Poydras Street, Suite 2355
New Orleans, LA 70130
(504) 299-9066
Commissioner .... Wright Waters
Director of Media Relations .... Chris Jackson
2001-02 members: BASKETBALL (11)— Arkansas-Little Rock, Arkansas St., Denver, Florida International, LA-Lafayette, Middle Tenn. St., New Mexico St., New Orleans, North Texas, South Alabama and Western Kentucky; FOOTBALL (7)— Arkansas St., Idaho, LA-Lafayette, LA-Monroe, Middle Tenn. State, New Mexico St. and North Texas.

Founded: 1976

Arkansas-Little Rock
Little Rock, AR 72204
SID: (501) 569-3449
Chancellor .... Charles E. Hathaway
Athletic Director .... Chris Peterson
Sports Information Director .... Kevin Tankersley

Founded: 1927
Enrollment: 10,434

Arkansas State
Jonesboro, AR 72467
SID: (870) 972-2541
President .... Dr. J. Leslie Wyatt
Athletic Director .... Joe Hollis
Sports Information Director .... Bill Bowen

Founded: 1909
Enrollment: 10,461

University of Denver
Denver, CO 80208
SID: (303) 871-4990
Chancellor .... Daniel L. Ritchie
Athletic Director .... Dr. M. Dianne Murphy
Sports Information Director .... Marla Rodriguez

Founded: 1864
Enrollment: 8,870

Florida International University
Miami, FL 33199
SID: (305) 348-3164
President .... Modesto A. Maidique
Athletic Director .... Rick Mello
Asst. AD/Media Relations .... Rich Kelch

Founded: 1889
Enrollment: 31,274

University of Idaho
Modesto, ID 83844
SID: (208) 885-0211
President .... Bob Hoover
Athletic Director .... Mike Bohn
Asst. AD/Media Relations .... Becky Paull

Founded: 1889
Enrollment: 11,635

University of Louisiana at Lafayette
Lafayette, LA 70506
SID: (337) 482-6331
President .... Ray Authement
Athletic Director .... Nelson Schexnayder
Sports Information Director .... Daryl Cetnar

Founded: 1898
Enrollment: 17,000

University of Louisiana at Monroe
Monroe, LA 71209
SID: (318) 342-5460
President .... Lawson Swearingen, Jr.
Athletic Director .... Bruce Hanks
Sports Information Director .... Hank Largin

Founded: 1931
Enrollment: 9,369

Middle Tennessee State
Murfreesboro, TN 37132
SID: (615) 904-8209
President .... Dr. Sidney A. McPhee
Interim Athletic Director .... Boots Donnelly
Sports Information Director .... Mark Owens

Founded: 1911
Enrollment: 20,073

New Mexico State
Las Cruces, NM 88003
SID: (505) 646-3929
President .... Dr. Jay Gogue
Athletic Director .... Brian Faison
Asst. AD/Media Relations .... Sean Johnson

Founded: 1888
Enrollment: 14,958

University of New Orleans
New Orleans, LA 70148
SID: (504) 280-6284
Chancellor .... Dr. Gregory O'Brien
Athletic Director .... Bob Brown
Sports Information Director .... Bob Boyle

Founded: 1958
Enrollment: 16,218

University of North Texas
Denton, TX 76203
SID: (940) 565-2476
President .... Dr. Norval F. Pohl
Athletic Director .... Rick Villarreal
Asst. AD/Media Services .... Eric Capper

Founded: 1890
Enrollment: 26,500

University of South Alabama
Mobile, AL 36688
SID: (334) 460-7035
President .... V. Gordon Moulton
Athletic Director .... Joe Gottfried
Interim Dir. of Athletic Media Relations .... Matt Smith

Founded: 1963
Enrollment: 11,870

Western Kentucky University
Bowling Green, KY 42101   Founded: 1906
SID: (270) 745-4298   Enrollment: 15,113
President ....Dr. Gary Randsell
Athletic Director ....Dr. Camden Wood Selig
Sports Information Director ....Paul Just

    🐾   🐾   🐾

WESTERN ATHLETIC CONFERENCE
9250 East Costilla Ave., Suite 300
Englewood, CO 80112
(303) 799-9221   Founded: 1962
Commissioner ....Karl Benson
Directors of Communications ....Dave Chaffin & Lisa Vad
   2001-02 members: BASKETBALL & FOOTBALL (10)—
Boise St., Fresno St., Hawaii, Louisiana Tech, Nevada,
Rice, San Jose St., SMU, Tulsa and UTEP.

Boise State
Boise, ID 83725   Founded: 1932
SID: (208) 426-1515   Enrollment: 16,459
President ....Charles P. Ruch
Athletic Director ....Gene Bleymaier
Sports Information Director ....Max Corbet

Fresno State University
Fresno, CA 93740   Founded: 1911
SID: (559) 278-2509   Enrollment: 18,902
President ....Dr. John D. Welty
Interim Athletic Director ....Scott Johnson
Sports Information Director ....Steve Weakland

University of Hawaii
Honolulu, HI 96822   Founded: 1907
SID: (808) 956-7523   Enrollment: 16,356
President ....Dr. Evan Dobelle
Athletic Director ....Hugh Yoshida
Sports Information Director ....Lois Manin

Louisiana Tech University
Ruston, LA 71272   Founded: 1894
SID: (318) 257-3144   Enrollment: 10,000
President ....Dan Reneau
Athletic Director ....Jim Oakes
Sports Information Director ....Malcolm Butler

University of Nevada
Reno, NV 89557   Founded: 1874
SID: (775) 784-6900   Enrollment: 13,149
President ....Dr. John Lilley
Athletic Director ....Chris Ault
Asst. AD for Media Services ....Jamie Klund

Rice University
Houston, TX 77005   Founded: 1912
SID: (713) 348-5775   Enrollment: 4,320
President ....Dr. Malcolm Gillis
Athletic Director ....Bobby May
Sports Information Director ....Bill Cousins

San Jose State University
San Jose, CA 95192   Founded: 1857
SID: (408) 924-1217   Enrollment: 27,000
President ....Dr. Robert L. Caret
Athletic Director ....Chuck Bell
Sports Information Director ....Lawrence Fan

SMU — Southern Methodist University
Dallas, TX 75275   Founded: 1911
SID: (214) 768-2883   Enrollment: 10,038
President ....Dr. R. Gerald Turner
Athletic Director ....Jim Copeland
Sports Information Director ....Chris Walker

University of Tulsa
Tulsa, OK 74104   Founded: 1894
SID: (918) 631-2395   Enrollment: 4,200
President...........................Dr. Bob Lawless
Athletic Director ....Judy MacLeod
Sports Information Director ....Don Tomkalski

UTEP — University of Texas at El Paso
El Paso, TX 79902   Founded: 1914
SID: (915) 747-6653   Enrollment: 14,695
President ....Dr. Diana Natalicio
Athletic Director ....Bob Stull
Sports Information Director ....Jeff Darby

    🐾   🐾   🐾

Major Independents
Division I-A football independents in 2001.

University of Central Florida
Orlando, FL 32816   Founded: 1963
SID: (407) 823-2729   Enrollment: 35,000
President ....Dr. John C. Hitt
Athletic Director ....Steve Sloan
Sports Information Director ....John Marini

University of Connecticut
Storrs, CT 06269   Founded: 1881
SID: (860) 486-3531   Enrollment: 23,419
President ....Philip Austin
Athletic Director ....Lew Perkins
Sports Information Director ....Tim Tolokan

Navy — U.S. Naval Academy
Annapolis, MD 21402   Founded: 1845
SID: (410) 293-2700   Enrollment: 4,000
Superintendent ....Vice Adm. John Ryan
Athletic Director ....Chet Gladchuk
Sports Information Director ....Scott Strasemeier

University of Notre Dame
Notre Dame, IN 46556   Founded: 1842
SID: (219) 631-7516   Enrollment: 10,301
President ....Rev. Edward (Monk) Malloy
Athletic Director ....Kevin White
Sports Information Director ....John Heisler

University of South Florida
Tampa, FL 33620   Founded: 1956
SID: (813) 974-4086   Enrollment: 36,000
President ....Judy Genshaft
Athletic Director ....Lee Roy Selmon
Sports Information Director ....John Gerdes

Troy State University
Troy, AL 36082   Founded: 1887
SID: (334) 670-5665   Enrollment: 18,000
Chancellor ....Dr. Jack Hawkins Jr.
Athletic Director ....Johnny Williams
Athletics Media Relations Dir. ....Tom Strother

Utah State University
Logan, UT 84322   Founded: 1888
SID: (435) 797-1361   Enrollment: 21,490
President ....Dr. Kermit L. Hall
Athletic Director ....Rance Pugmire
Sports Information Director ....Mike Strauss

    🐾   🐾   🐾

Other Major Division I Conferences

Conferences that play either Division I basketball or Division I-AA football, or both.

America East

10 High St., Suite 860, Boston, MA 02110
(617) 695-6369   Founded: 1979
Commissioner . . . . .Chris Monasch
Director of Communications . . . . .Matt Bourque
2001-02 members: BASKETBALL (9)— Albany, Binghamton, Boston University, Hartford, Maine, New Hampshire, Northeastern, Stony Brook and Vermont.

Atlantic Sun Conference

3370 Vineville Ave., Suite 108-B
Macon, GA 31204
(912) 474-3394   Founded: 1978
Commissioner . . . . .Bill Bibb
Director of Information .Tom Snyder
2001-02 members: BASKETBALL (11)— Belmont, Campbell, Central Florida, Florida Atlantic, Georgia St., Jacksonville, Jacksonville St., Mercer, Samford, Stetson and Troy St.

Atlantic 10 Conference

2 Penn Center Plaza
Philadelphia, PA 19102   Founded: 1976
(215) 751-0500   A-10 Football founded: 1997
Commissioner . . . . .Linda Bruno
Director of Information . . . . .Ray Cella
2001-02 members: BASKETBALL (12)— Dayton, Duquesne, Fordham, George Washington, La Salle, Massachusetts, Rhode Island, Richmond, St. Bonaventure, St. Joseph's-PA, Temple and Xavier-OH. FOOTBALL (11)— Delaware, Hofstra, James Madison, Maine, Massachusetts, New Hampshire, Northeastern, Rhode Island, Richmond, Villanova and William & Mary.

Big Sky Conference

2491 Washington Blvd. Suite 201
Ogden, UT 84401
(801) 392-1978   Founded: 1963
Commissioner . . . . .Douglas Fullerton
Asst. Commissioner, Media Relations . . . . . .Dusty Clements
2001-02 members: BASKETBALL & FOOTBALL (8)— CS-Sacramento, Eastern Washington, Idaho St., Montana, Montana St., Northern Arizona, Portland St. and Weber St.

Big South Conference

6428 Bannington Dr., Ste A
Charlotte, NC 28226
(704) 341-7990   Founded: 1983
Commissioner . . . . .Kyle Kallander
Asst. Commissioner .Drew Dickerson
2001-02 members: BASKETBALL (9)— Birmingham Southern, Charleston Southern, Coastal Carolina, Elon, High Point, Liberty, NC-Asheville, Radford and Winthrop.

Big West Conference

Two Corporate Park, Suite 206
Irvine, CA 92606
(949) 261-2525   Founded: 1969
Commissioner . . . . .Dennis Farrell
Director of Information . . . . .Michael Daniels
2001-02 members: BASKETBALL (10)— CS-Fullerton, CS-Northridge, Cal Poly, Idaho, Long Beach St., Pacific, UC-Irvine, UC-Riverside, UC-Santa Barbara and Utah St

Colonial Athletic Association

8625 Patterson Ave., Richmond, VA 23229
(804) 754-1616   Founded: 1985
Commissioner . . . . .Thomas E. Yeager
Sports Information Director . . . . .Steve Vehorn
2000-01 members: BASKETBALL (10)— Delaware, Drexel, George Mason, Hofstra, James Madison, NC-Wilmington, Old Dominion, Towson, Virginia Commonwealth and William & Mary.

Gateway Football Conference

1818 Chouteau Ave.
St. Louis, MO 63103
(314) 421-2268   Founded: 1985
Commissioner . . . . .Patty Viverito
Asst. Commissioner . . . . .Mike Kern
2001 members: FOOTBALL (8)— Illinois St., Indiana St., Northern Iowa, Southern Illinois, SW Missouri St., Western Illinois, Western Kentucky and Youngstown St.

Horizon League -

201 South Capitol Ave., Suite 500
Indianapolis, IN 46225
(317) 237-5622   Founded: 1979
Commissioner . . . . .John LeCrone
Associate Commissioner . . . . .Terry Powers
2001-02 members: BASKETBALL (9)— Butler, Cleveland St., Detroit Mercy, Illinois-Chicago, Loyola-IL, Wisconsin-Green Bay, Wisconsin-Milwaukee, Wright St. and Youngstown St.

Ivy League

330 Alexander Street
Princeton, NJ 08544
(609) 258-6426   Founded: 1954
Executive Director . . . . .Jeffrey Orleans
Director of Information . . . . .Brett Hoover
2001-02 members: BASKETBALL & FOOTBALL (8)— Brown, Columbia, Cornell, Dartmouth, Harvard, Pennsylvania, Princeton and Yale.

Metro Atlantic Athletic Conference

712 Amboy Avenue
Edison, NJ 08837
(732) 738-5455   Founded: 1980
Commissioner . . . . .Richard Ensor
Director of Media Relations . . . . .Jill Skotarczak
2001-02 members: BASKETBALL (10)— Canisius, Fairfield, Iona, Loyola-MD, Manhattan, Marist, Niagara, Rider, St. Peter's and Siena. FOOTBALL (8)— Canisius, Duquesne, Fairfield, Iona, La Salle, Marist, St. Peter's and Siena.

Mid-Continent Conference

340 West Butterfield Rd., Ste 3D
Elmhurst, IL 60126
(630) 516-0661   Founded: 1982
Commissioner . . . . .Jon Steinbrecher
Director of Media Relations . . . . .Tony Hamilton
2001-02 members: BASKETBALL (8)— Chicago St., Indiana U-Purdue U Indianapolis, UMKC, Oakland, Oral Roberts, Southern Utah, Valparaiso and Western Illinois.

Mid-Eastern Athletic Conference

102 North Elm St.
SE Building, Suite 401
Greensboro, NC 27401
(336) 275-9961   Founded: 1970
Commissioner . . . . .Charles S. Harris
Asst. Commissioner, Media Relations . . .Bradford Evans, Jr.
2001-02 members: BASKETBALL (11)— Bethune-Cookman, Coppin St., Delaware St., Florida A&M, Hampton, Howard, MD-Eastern Shore, Morgan St., Norfolk St., North Carolina A&T and South Carolina St.; FOOTBALL (9)— all but Coppin St. and MD-Eastern Shore.

Missouri Valley Conference

1818 Chouteau Ave.
St. Louis, MO 63103
(314) 421-0339   Founded: 1907
Commissioner . . . . .Doug Elgin
Asst. Commiss. Media Rel. . . . . .Jack Watkins & Mike Kern
2001-02 members: BASKETBALL (10)— Bradley, Creighton, Drake, Evansville, Illinois St., Indiana St., Northern Iowa, Southern Illinois, SW Missouri St. and Wichita St.

Northeast Conference
220 Old New Brunswick Rd.
Piscataway, NJ 08854
(732) 562-0877 Founded: 1981
Commissioner . . . . .John Iamarino
Asst. Commissioner, Public Relations . . . . .Ron Ratner
   2001-02 members: BASKETBALL (12)— Cent. Conn.
St., Fairleigh Dickinson, LIU-Brooklyn, Maryland-Baltimore
County, Monmouth, Mount St. Mary's, Quinnipiac, Robert
Morris, Sacred Heart, St. Francis-NY, St. Francis-PA and
Wagner. FOOTBALL (9)—Albany, Cent. Conn. St., Mon-
mouth, Robert Morris, Sacred Heart, St. Francis-PA, St.
John's, Stony Brook and Wagner.

Ohio Valley Conference
278 Franklin Road, Suite 103
Brentwood, TN 37027
(615) 371-1698 Founded: 1948
Commissioner . . . . .Dan Beebe
Asst. Commis., Info. and Champs. . . . . Rob Washburn
   2001-02 members: BASKETBALL (9)— Austin Peay
St., Eastern Illinois, Eastern Kentucky, Morehead St., Murray St., SE Missouri St., Tennessee-Martin, Tennessee St.
and Tennessee Tech; FOOTBALL (7)— Eastern Illinois, Eastern Kentucky, Murray St., SE Missouri St., Tennessee-Martin,
Tennessee St. and Tennessee Tech.

Patriot League
3773 Corporate Pkwy, Suite 190
Center Valley, PA 18034
(610) 289-1950 Founded: 1984
Executive Director .Carolyn Femovich
Director of Media Relations . . . . .Tom Byrnes
   2001-02 members: BASKETBALL (8)— American,
Army, Bucknell, Colgate, Holy Cross, Lafayette, Lehigh and
Navy; FOOTBALL (8)— Bucknell, Colgate, Fordham, Geor-
getown, Holy Cross, Lafayette, Lehigh and Towson.

Pioneer Football League
1818 Chouteau Ave., St. Louis, MO 63103
(314) 421-2268 Founded: 1993
Commissioner . . . . .Patty Viverito
Media Relations . . . . .Cindy Kern
   2001 members: FOOTBALL (9): Austin Peay St., But-
ler, Davidson, Dayton, Drake, Jacksonville, Morehead St.,
San Diego and Valparaiso.

Southern Conference
1 West Pack Square, Suite 1508
Asheville, NC 28801
(828) 255-7872 Founded: 1921
Acting Commissioner . . . . .Geoff Cabe
Asst. Commissioner, Public Affairs . . . . .Steve Shutt
   2001-02 members: BASKETBALL (12)— Appalachian
St., The Citadel, College of Charleston, Davidson, East Ten-
nessee St., Furman, Georgia Southern, UNC-Greensboro,
Tennessee-Chattanooga, VMI, Western Carolina and Wof-
ford; FOOTBALL (9)—all except College of Charleston,
Davidson and UNC-Greensboro.

Southland Conference
1700 Alma Drive, Suite 550
Plano, TX 75075
(972) 422-9500 Founded: 1963
Commissioner . . . . .Greg Sankey
Director of Media Relations . . . . .Bruce Ludlow
   2001-02 members: BASKETBALL (11)— Lamar,
LA-Monroe, McNeese St., Nicholls St., Northwestern St.,
Sam Houston St., SE Louisiana, Southwest Texas St.,
Stephen F. Austin St., Texas-Arlington and Texas-San Anto-
nio; FOOTBALL (7)— Jacksonville St., McNeese St.,
Nicholls St., Northwestern St., Sam Houston St., Southwest
Texas St. and Stephen F. Austin St.

Southwestern Athletic Conference
1527 Fifth Ave. North
Birmingham, AL 35203
(205) 320-0263 Founded: 1920
Interim Commissioner . . . . .Dr. James Frank
Director of Publicity . . . . .TBA
   2001-02 members: BASKETBALL & FOOTBALL (10)—
Alabama A&M, Alabama St., Alcorn St., Arkansas-Pine
Bluff, Grambling St., Jackson St., Mississippi Valley St., Prai-
rie View A&M, Southern-Baton Rouge and Texas Southern.

West Coast Conference
1200 Bayhill Dr., Suite 302, San Bruno, CA 94066
(650) 873-8622 Founded: 1952
Commissioner . . . . .Michael Gilleran
Director of Communication . . . . .Brad Walker
   2001-02 members: BASKETBALL (8)— Gonzaga,
Loyola Marymount, Pepperdine, Portland, St. Mary's-CA,
San Diego, San Francisco and Santa Clara.

PRO FOOTBALL

National Football League

League Office
280 Park Ave.
New York, NY 10017
(212) 450-2000
Commissioner . . . . .Paul Tagliabue
President . . . . .Neil Austrian
Exec. Vice President . . . . .Jeff Pash
AFC Info. Coordinator . . . . .Dan Masonson
NFC Info. Coordinator . . . . .Chris McCloskey

NFL Management Council
280 Park Ave.
New York, NY 10017
(212) 450-2000
Chairman . . . . .Harold Henderson
Sr. V.P. of Broadcast/Network TV . . . . .Dennis Lewin

NFL Players Association
2021 L Street NW, Suite 600
Washington, DC 20036
(202) 463-2200
Executive Director . . . . .Gene Upshaw
Asst. Exec. Director . . . . .Doug Allen
General Counsel .Richard Berthelsen
Director of Retired Players . . . . .Frank Woschitz

AFC

Baltimore Ravens
11001 Owings Mills Blvd.
Owings Mills, MD 21117
(410) 654-6200
Owner/CEO . . . . .Arthur B. Modell
President/COO . . . . .David Modell
V.P. of Public Relations . . . . .Kevin Byrne

Buffalo Bills
One Bills Drive, Orchard Park, NY 14127
(716) 648-1800
Chairman & Owner . . . . .Ralph C. Wilson Jr.
President & GM . . . . .Tom Donahue
V.P. of Communications . . . . .Scott Berchtold

Cincinnati Bengals
One Paul Brown Stadium, Cincinnati, OH 45204
(513) 621-3550
President . . . . .Mike Brown
Sr. Vice President . . . . .Pete Brown
Public Relations Director . . . . .Jack Brennan

Cleveland Browns
76 Lou Groza Blvd., Berea, OH 44017
(440) 891-5000
Owner/Chairman ....Alfred Lerner
President/CEO ....Carmen Policy
Exec. V.P., Dir. of Football Ops. ....Dwight Clark
Exec. Dir. of Publicity/Media Relations ....Todd Stewart

Denver Broncos
13655 Broncos Parkway, Englewood, CO 80112
(303) 649-9000
Owner-President-CEO ....Pat Bowlen
General Manager ....Neal Dahlen
Sr. Dir. of Media Relations ....Jim Saccomano

Houston Texans
711 Louisiana Rd., 33rd Floor
Houston, TX 77002
(713) 336-7700
Chairman & CEO ....Robert C. McNair
Sr. V.P. & GM of Football Ops. ....Charley Casserly
V.P. of Communications ....Tony Wyllie

Indianapolis Colts
7001 W 56th St., Indianapolis, IN 46254
(317) 297-2658
Owner-CEO ....Jim Irsay
President ....Bill Polian
Dir. of Football Operations ....Dom Anile
V.P. of Public Relations ....Craig Kelley

Jacksonville Jaguars
One ALLTEL Stadium Place
Jacksonville, FL 32202
(904) 633-6000
Chairman & CEO ....Wayne Weaver
Sr. V.P., Football Operations ....Michael Huyghue
Exec. Dir. of Comm. & Broadcasting ....Dan Edwards

Kansas City Chiefs
One Arrowhead Drive, Kansas City, MO 64129
(816) 920 9300
Owner-Founder ....Lamar Hunt
Chairman ....Jack Steadman
President-CEO-General Manager ....Carl Peterson
Director of Public Relations ....Bob Moore

Miami Dolphins
7500 SW 30th St., Davie, FL 33314
(954) 452-7000
Owner-Chairman ....H. Wayne Huizenga
President & COO ....Eddie Jones
V.P. of Player Personnel ....Rick Spielman
V.P. of Media Relations ....Harvey Greene

New England Patriots
Foxboro Stadium, 60 Washington St., Foxboro, MA 02035
(508) 543-8200
Owner & Chairman ....Bob Kraft
Dir. of Player Personnel ....Scott Pioli
Director of Media Relations ....Stacey James

New York Jets
1000 Fulton Ave., Hempstead, NY 11550
(516) 560-8100
Owner & Chairman ....Robert Wood Johnson IV
President ....Jay Cross
General Manager ....Terry Bradway
Director of Public Relations ....Frank Ramos

Oakland Raiders
1220 Harbor Bay Parkway, Alameda, CA 94502
(510) 864-5000
Managing General Partner ....Al Davis
Executive Assistant ....Al LoCasale
Director of Public Relations ....Mike Taylor

Pittsburgh Steelers
3400 South Water Street, Pittsburgh, PA 15203
(412) 432-7800
Owner-President ....Dan Rooney
V.P.s ......John McGinley, Art Rooney Jr. & Art Rooney II
Communications Coordinator ....Ron Wahl

San Diego Chargers
4020 Murphy Canyon Rd.
San Diego, CA 92123
(858) 874-4500
Owner-Chairman ....Alex Spanos
President-Vice Chairman ....Dean Spanos
V.P. of Football Ops. ....Ed McGuire
Director of Public Relations ....Bill Johnston

Seattle Seahawks
11220 NE 53rd Street, Kirkland, WA 98033
(425) 827-9777
Owner ....Paul Allen
President ....Bob Whitsitt
V.P./GM/Head Coach ....Mike Holmgren
Public Relations Director ....Dave Pearson

Tennessee Titans
460 Great Circle Road, Nashville, TN 37228
(615) 565-4000
Owner .........................K.S. (Bud) Adams Jr.
President ....Jeff Diamond
Exec. V.P./General Manager ....Floyd Reese
Director of Media Services ....Robbie Bohren

NFC

Arizona Cardinals
P.O. Box 888, Phoenix, AZ 85001
(602) 379-0101
Owner-President-General Counsel ....Bill Bidwill Sr.
Vice President ....Bill Bidwill Jr.
General Manager ....Bob Ferguson
Public Relations Director ....Paul Jensen

Atlanta Falcons
4400 Falcon Pkwy
Flowery Branch, GA 30542
(770) 965-3115
Owner-President ....Taylor Smith
Exec. V.P. Football Ops./Head Coach ....Dan Reeves
Director of Communications ....Aaron Salkin

Carolina Panthers
800 South Mint St.
Charlotte, NC 28202-1502
(704) 358-7000
Founder-Owner ....Jerry Richardson
President ....Mark Richardson
Dir. of Player Personnel ....Jack Bushofsky
Director of Communications ....Charlie Dayton

Chicago Bears
1000 Football Drive, Lake Forest, IL 60045
(847) 295-6600
Owner-Chairman Emeritus ....Edward McCaskey
Chairman of the Board ....Michael McCaskey
President-CEO ....Ted Phillips
General Manager ....Jerry Angelo
Director of Public Relations ....Scott Hagel

Dallas Cowboys
Cowboys Center
One Cowboys Parkway
Irving, TX 75063
(972) 556-9900
Owner-President-GM ....Jerry Jones
V.P./Dir. of Player Personnel ....Stephen Jones
Public Relations Director ....Rich Dalrymple

Detroit Lions
Pontiac Silverdome
1200 Featherstone Rd., Pontiac, MI 48342
(248) 335-4131
Owner ....William Clay Ford
President ....Matt Millen
Dir. of Player Personnel ....Bill Tobin
Director of Media Relations ....Matt Barnhart

Green Bay Packers
1265 Lombardi Ave.
Green Bay, WI 54304
(920) 496-5700
President & CEO ....Bob Harlan
General Manager & Head Coach ....Mike Sherman
Exec. Dir. of Public Relations ....Lee Remmel

Minnesota Vikings
9520 Viking Drive, Eden Prairie, MN 55344
(952) 828-6500
Owner ....Red McCombs
President ....Gary Woods
Executive Vice President ....Michael Kelly
Director of Public Relations ....Bob Hagan

New Orleans Saints
5800 Airline Drive, Metairie, LA 70003
(504) 733-0255
Owner ....Tom Benson
General Manager ....Randy Mueller
V.P. of Football Operations ....Charles Bailey
Director of Media/Public Relations ....Greg Bensel

New York Giants
Giants Stadium
East Rutherford, NJ 07073
(201) 935-8111
President/co-CEO ....Wellington Mara
Chairman/co-CEO ....Preston Robert Tisch
V.P. & General Manager ....Ernie Accorsi
V.P. of Communications ....Pat Hanlon

Philadelphia Eagles
Veterans Stadium
3501 S. Broad St.
Philadelphia, PA 19148
(215) 463-2500
Owner ....Jeffrey Lurie
Executive V.P. & CEO ....Joe Banner
Exec. V.P. of Football Ops. & Head Coach ......Andy Reid
Dir. of Football Media Services ....Derek Boyko

St. Louis Rams
One Rams Way, St. Louis, MO 63045
(314) 982-7267
Owner-Chairman ....Georgia Frontiere
Owner-Vice Chairman ....Stan Kroenke
President ....John Shaw
Pres. of Football Operations ....Jay Zygmunt
Director of Public Relations ....Rick Smith

San Francisco 49ers
4949 Centennial Blvd.
Santa Clara, CA 95054
(408) 562-4949
Owner ....Denise DeBartolo-York
President/CEO ....Peter Harris
General Manager ....Terry Donahue
Director of Public Relations ....Kirk Reynolds

Tampa Bay Buccaneers
One Buccaneer Place, Tampa, FL 33607
(813) 870-2700
Owner-President ....Malcolm Glazer
General Manager ....Rich McKay
Director of Communications ....Reggie Roberts

Washington Redskins
Redskin Park
P.O. Box 17247, Washington D.C. 20041
(703) 478-8900
Owner ....Daniel M. Snyder
GM & Head Coach ....Marty Schottenheimer
Director of Public Relations ....Michelle Tessier

Canadian Football League

League Office
CFL Building, 110 Eglinton Avenue West, 5th Floor
Toronto, Ontario M4R 1A3
(416) 322-9650
Commissioner ....Michael Lysco
V.P. of Football Operations ....Ed Chalupka
V.P. of Communications ....Shawn Lackie

CFL Players Association
603 Argus Rd., Suite 207
Oakville, Ontario L6J 6G6
(905) 844-7852
President ....Stu Laird
Legal Counsel ....Ed Molstad

British Columbia Lions
10605 135th St.
Surrey, B.C. V3T 4C8
(604) 930-5466
Owner ....David Braley
President & CEO ....Glen Ringdal
Dir. of Media/Public Relations ....Jon Taylor

Calgary Stampeders
McMahon Stadium
1817 Crowchild Trail, NW
Calgary, Alberta T2M 4R6
(403) 289-0205
Owner ....Sig Gutsche
President ....Stan Kroenke
General Manager & Head Coach ....Wally Buono
V.P. of Marketing & Communications ....Ron Rooke

Edmonton Eskimos
9023 111th Ave.
Edmonton, Alberta T5B 0C3
(780) 448-1525
Owner ....Community-owned
President & CEO ....Hugh Campbell
GM-COO-Head Coach ....Tom Higgins
Dir. of Comm./Marketing ....Dave Jamieson

Hamilton Tiger-Cats
75 Balsam Ave. N
Hamilton, Ontario L8L 8C1
(905) 547-2418
Chairman/Owner ....David M. Macdonald
Vice Chairman/Owner/GM ....George Grant
Communications Director ....Marty Knack

Montreal Alouettes
1255 University St., Suite 120
Montreal, Quebec H3B 3A9
(514) 253-0008
Owner ....Robert Wetenhall
President & CEO ....Larry Smith
Dir. of Football Ops./GM ....Jim Popp
Dir. of Communications ....Louis-Philippe Dorais

Saskatchewan Roughriders
2940 — 10th Avenue, P.O. Box 1277
Regina, Saskatchewan S4P 3B8
(306) 569-2323
Owner ....Community-owned
President ....Tom Robinson
General Manager and Dir. of Football Ops. ....Roy Shivers
Media Coordinator ....Tony Playter

Toronto Argonauts
1100 Central Pkwy W., Suite 3, Mississauga, Ontario L5C 4E5
(416) 489-2746
Owner/Chairman . . . . .Sherwood Schwarz
General Manager . . . . .Paul Masotti
Director of Public Relations . . . . .Greg Mandziuk

Winnipeg Blue Bombers
1465 Maroons Road, Winnipeg, Manitoba R3G 0L6
(204) 784-2583
Owner . . . . .Community-owned
President . . . . .Lyle Bauer
Dir. of Football Ops./Head Coach . . . . .Dave Ritchie
Dir. of Media/Public Relations . . . . .Shawn Coates

NFL Europe

Managing Dir. of Football Ops. . . . . .John Beake
Director of Public Relations . . . . .David Tossell
Public Relations Assistant . . . . .Michael Preston

League Offices

Frankfurt
Westerbach Str. 47
Frankfurt, Germany 60489
011-49-69-978-2790

London
26A Albemarle St.
London, England W1X 3FA
011-44-171-355-1955

New York
280 Park Avenue
New York, NY 10017
(212) 450-2000

Member teams (6): Amsterdam Admirals, Barcelona Dragons, Berlin Thunder, Frankfurt Galaxy, Rhein Fire (Dusseldorf), Scottish Claymores (Edinburgh).

Arena Football League
20 North Wacker Dr., Suite 1231
Chicago, IL 60606
(312) 621-7000
Commissioner . . . . .David C. Baker
Deputy Commissioner . . . . .Ronald J. Kurpiers II
V.P. of Football Operations . . . . .Jerry Trice
V.P. of Communications . . . . .David Cooper

Member teams (19): American Conference— Arizona Rattlers, Chicago Rush, Detroit Fury, Grand Rapids Rampage, Houston Thunderbears, Indiana Firebirds, Los Angeles Avengers, Milwaukee Mustangs, Oklahoma Wranglers and San Jose Sabercats. National Conference— Buffalo Destroyers, Carolina Cobras, Florida Bobcats, Nashville Kats, New Jersey Gladiators, New York Dragons, Orlando Predators, Tampa Bay Storm and Toronto Phantoms.

GOLF

LPGA Tour
(Ladies' Professional Golf Association)
100 International Golf Drive
Daytona Beach, FL 32124
(904) 274-6200
Commissioner . . . . .Ty Votaw
Dir. of Communications . . . . .Leslie King
Manager of Public Relations . . . . .Connie Wilson

PGA of America
100 Avenue of the Champions
Palm Beach Gardens, FL 33410
(561) 624-8400
President . . . . .Jack Connelly
CEO . . . . .Jim Awtrey
Director of Public Relations . . . . .Julius Mason

PGA European Tour
Wentworth Drive, Virginia Water
Surrey, England GU25 4LX
TEL: 011-44-1344-840400
Executive Director .Ken Schofield
Director of Public Relations . . . . .Mitchell Platts

PGA Tour
112 PGA Tour Blvd.
Ponte Vedra, FL 32082
(904) 285-3700
Commissioner . . . . .Tim Finchem
Senior V.P. of Communications . . . . .Bob Combs

Royal & Ancient Golf Club of St. Andrews
St. Andrews, Fife
Scotland KY16 9JD
TEL: 011-44-1334-472112
Secretary . . . . .Peter Dawson
Press Officer . . . . .Stewart McDougall

USGA
(United States Golf Association)
P.O. Box 708, Liberty Corner Road
Far Hills, NJ 07931
(908) 234-2300
President . . . . .Trey Holland
Executive Director . . . . .David Fay
Sr. Director of Communications . . . . .Marty Parkes

PRO HOCKEY

NHL

National Hockey League

Commissioner . . . . .Gary Bettman
Pres., NHL Enterprises .Ed Horne
Exec. V.P., Dir. of Hockey Ops. . . . . .Colin Campbell
V.P. of Media Relations . . . . .Frank Brown

League Offices

Montreal
1800 McGill College Ave., Suite 2600
Montreal, Quebec H3A 3J6
(514) 841-9220

New York
1251 Sixth Ave., 47th Floor, New York, NY 10020
(212) 789-2000

Toronto
50 Bay St., 11th Floor
Toronto, Ontario M5J 2X8
(416) 981-2777

NHL Players' Association
777 Bay St., Suite 2400
P.O. Box 121
Toronto, Ontario M5G 2C8
(416) 408-4040
Executive Director . . . . .Bob Goodenow
Associate Counsel . . . . .Roland Lee,
Ian Penny, Ian Pulver
Media Relations . . . . .Jonathan Weatherdon

Anaheim, Mighty Ducks of
Arrowhead Pond of Anaheim
2695 Katella Ave.
Anaheim, CA 92806
(714) 940-2900
Owner . . . . .Walt Disney Co.
Anaheim Sports, Inc. Pres. . . . . .Tony Tavares
President/General Manager . . . . .Pierre Gauthier
Dir., Communications and Team Services . . . .Alex Gilchrist

Atlanta Thrashers
1 CNN Center
12th Floor, South Tower
Atlanta, GA 30303
(404) 584-7825
Owner . . . . .AOL-Time Warner
President/Governor .Stan Kasten
V.P./General Manager . . . . .Don Waddell
Public Relations Director . . . . .Tom Hughes

Boston Bruins

1 FleetCenter, Suite 250
Boston, MA 02114
(617) 624-1900
Owner . . . . Jeremy Jacobs
President . . . . Harry Sinden
V.P & General Manager . . . . Mike O'Connell
Director of Media Relations . . . . Heidi Holland

Buffalo Sabres

HSBC Arena
One Seymour H. Knox III Plaza
Buffalo, NY 14203-3096
(716) 855-4100
CEO . . . . Timothy Rigas
General Manager . . . . Darcy Regier
V.P. of Communications . . . . Michael Gilbert

Calgary Flames

Pengrowth Saddledome, P.O. Box 1540 Station M
Calgary, Alberta T2P 3B9
(403) 777-2177
Owners . Harley Hotchkiss, Murray Edwards, Alvin G. Libin,
    Allan P. Markin, J.R. McCaig, Byron and Daryl Seamen
President & CEO . . . . Ken King
V.P./General Manager . . . . Craig Button
Director of Communications . . . . Peter Hanlon

Carolina Hurricanes

The Raleigh Entertainment Sports Arena
1400 Edward Mill Rd., Raleigh, NC 27607
(919) 467-7825
Owner . . . . Peter Karmanos Jr.
President & COO . . . . Jim Cain
CEO & General Manager . . . . Jim Rutherford
Dir., Media Relations . . . . Jerry Higgins

Chicago Blackhawks

United Center, 1901 West Madison St.
Chicago, IL 60612
(312) 455-7000
Owner-President . . . . William Wirtz
General Manager . . . . Mike Smith
Executive Director of P.R. . . . . Jim DeMaria

Colorado Avalanche

1000 Chopper Cir., Denver, CO 80204
(303) 405-1100
Owner . . . . Stan Kroenke
President/GM/Alt. Governor . . . . Pierre Lacroix
V.P. of Comm. & Team Services . . . . Jean Martineau

Columbus Blue Jackets

150 E. Wilson Bridge Rd., Columbus, OH 43085
(614) 246-4625
Owner . . . . John H. McConnell
General Manager . . . . Doug MacLean
Director of Communications . . . . Todd Sharrock

Dallas Stars

211 Cowboys Parkway, Irving, TX 75063
(972) 831-2453
Owner . . . . Thomas O. Hicks
President . . . . Jim Lites
General Manager . . . . Bob Gainey
Director of Public Relations . . . . Larry Kelly

Detroit Red Wings

Joe Louis Arena, 600 Civic Center Drive
Detroit, MI 48226
(313) 396-7544
Owner/President . . . . Mike Ilitch
Owner/Secretary-Treasurer . . . . Marian Ilitch
General Manager . . . . Ken Holland
Director of Media Relations . . . . John Hahn

Edmonton Oilers

11230 110th St., Edmonton, Alberta, T5G 3H7
(780) 414-4000
Owners . . . . Edmonton Investors Group, Ltd.
President & CEO . . . . Patrick LaForge
General Manager . . . . Kevin Lowe
V.P./Media Relations . . . . Bill Tuele

Florida Panthers

National Car Rental Center
1 Panther Parkway, Sunrise, FL 33323
(954) 835-7000
Chairman/CEO . . . . Alan Cohen
President . . . . Bill Torrey
Dir. of Public & Media Relations . . . . Mike Hanson

Los Angeles Kings

Staples Center
1111 S. Figueroa, Los Angeles, CA 90017
(310) 535-4543
Majority Owners . . . . Philip Anschutz and Ed Roski
President . . . . Tim Leiweke
General Manager . . . . Dave Taylor
Director of Media Relations . . . . Mike Altieri

Minnesota Wild

444 Cedar Street, Suite 900
St. Paul, MN 55101
(651) 222-9453
Owner . . . . Bob Naegele Jr.
Exec. V.P./General Manager . . . . Doug Risebrough
V.P. of Comm. & Broadcast . . . . Bill Robertson

Montreal Canadiens

Molson Centre, 1260 Gauchetière St. West
Montreal, Quebec H3B 5E8
(514) 932-2582
President . . . . Pierre Boivin
General Manager . . . . Andre Savard
Director of Communications . . . . Don Beauchamp

Nashville Predators

501 Broadway, Nashville, TN 37203
(615) 770-2300
Chairman and Maj. Owner . . . . Craig Leipold
President . . . . Jack Diller
General Manager . . . . David Poile
Mgr., Team Services/Media Relations . . . . . Frank Buonomo

New Jersey Devils

Continental Airlines Arena, P.O. Box 504
East Rutherford, NJ 07073
(201) 935-6050
Owner . . . . YankeeNets
President-GM-CEO . . . . Lou Lamoriello
Director of Public Relations . . . . Jeff Altstadter

New York Islanders

Nassau Veterans' Memorial Coliseum, 1255 Hempstead Tpk,
Uniondale, NY 11553
(516) 501-6700
Owner . . . . Charles Wang & Sanjay Kumar
General Manager . . . . Mike Milbury
V.P. of Communications . . . . Chris Botta

New York Rangers

2 Penn Plaza, 14th Floor
New York, NY 10121
(212) 465-6486
Owner . . . . Cablevision Systems Inc.
President (MSG) . . . . Jim Dolan
President & General Manager . . . . Glen Sather
V.P. of Public Relations . . . . John Rosasco

Ottawa Senators
1000 Palladium Dr.
Kanata, Ontario, K2V 1A5
(613) 599-0250
Chairman & Gov. . . . . .Rod Bryden
President & CEO . . . . .Roy Mlakar
General Manager .Marshall Johnston
Director of Media Relations . . . . .Steve Keogh

Philadelphia Flyers
3601 S. Broad St., Philadelphia, PA 19148
(215) 465-4500
Chairman . . . . .Ed Snider
President & General Manager . . . . .Bob Clarke
Director of Media Relations . . . . .Zack Hill

Phoenix Coyotes
Alltel Ice Den, 9375 E. Bell Rd., Scottsdale, AZ 85260
(480) 473-5600
Chairman/CEO . . . . .Steve Ellman
President . . . . .Shawn Hunter
Executive Vice President . . . . .Cliff Fletcher
General Manager . . . . .Mike Barnett
V.P. of Media Relations . . . . .Richard Nairn

Pittsburgh Penguins
Mellon Arena, Chatham Ctr., Suite 400, Pittsburgh, PA 15219
(412) 642-1800
Owner/Chairman . . . . .Mario Lemieux
Exec. V.P. & GM . . . . .Craig Patrick
V.P. of Communications . . . . .Tom McMillan

St. Louis Blues
Savvis Center, 1401 Clark Ave.
St. Louis, MO 63103
(314) 622-2500
Owners . . . . .Bill and Nancy Laurie
General Manager . . . . .Larry Pleau
Director of Public Relations . . . . .Jeff Trammel

San Jose Sharks
525 West Santa Clara St., San Jose, CA 95113
(408) 287-7070
Owner-Chairman . . . . .George Gund III
Co-Owner . . . . .Gordon Gund
President-CEO . . . . .Greg Jamison
Exec. V.P. & GM . . . . .Dean Lombardi
Director of Media Relations . . . . .Ken Arnold

Tampa Bay Lightning
401 Channelside Drive, Tampa, FL 33602
(813) 301-6500
Owner . . . . .Palace Sports & Ent.
CEO & Governor . . . . .Tom Wilson
V.P./General Manager . . . . .Rick Dudley
Director of Public Relations . . . . .Jay Preble

Toronto Maple Leafs
Air Canada Centre
40 Bay Street, Toronto, Ontario M5J 2X2
(416) 815-5500
Owner . . . . .Steve Stavro
President . . . . .Ken Dryden
Coach/G.M. . . . . .Pat Quinn
Manager of Media Relations . . . . .Pat Park

Vancouver Canucks
General Motors Place, 800 Griffiths Way
Vancouver, B.C. V6B 6G1
(604) 899-4600
Owners . . . . .John McCaw
COO . . . . .David Cobb
President & General Manager . . . . .Brian Burke
Manager of Media Relations . . . . .Chris Brumwell

Washington Capitals
MCI Center, 401 9th St., Suite 7500
Washington, D.C. 20004
(202) 266-2200
Owners . .Raul Fernandez, Michael Jordan, Ted Leonsis and
Dick Patrick
President . . . . .Dick Patrick
V.P./General Manager . . . . .George McPhee
Manager of Media Relations . . . . .Brian Potter

AHL
American Hockey League
One Monarch Place, Springfield, MA 01144
(413) 781-2030
President . . . . .David Andrews
V.P. of Hockey Ops. . . . . .Jim Mill
Dir. of Media Relations/Communications . . . . .Brett Stothart
Member teams (27): Eastern Conference— Albany
River Rats, Bridgeport Sound Tigers, Hamilton Bulldogs,
Hartford Wolf Pack, Lowell Lock Monsters, Manchester
Monarchs, Manitoba Moose, Portland Pirates, Providence
Bruins, Quebec Citadelles, Saint John Flames, Springfield
Falcons, St. John's Maple Leafs and Worcester IceCats.
Western Conference— Chicago Wolves, Cincinnati Mighty
Ducks, Cleveland Barons, Grand Rapids Griffins, Hershey
Bears, Houston Aeros, Milwaukee Admirals, Norfolk Admi-
rals, Philadelphia Phantoms, Rochester Americans, Syra-
cuse Crunch, Utah Grizzlies and Wilkes-Barre/Scranton
Penguins.

IIHF
International Ice Hockey Federation
Parkring 11
CH-8002 Zurich, Switzerland
TEL: 011-411-289-8600
President . . . . .Rene Fasel
General Secretary . . . . .Jan-Ake Edvinsson
P.R./Marketing Mgr. . . . . .Kimmo Leinonen

HORSE RACING

Breeders' Cup Limited
PO Box 4230, Lexington, KY 40544–4230
(859) 223-5444
President . . . . .D.G. Van Clief, Jr.
Director of Marketing . . . . .Damon Thayer

National Museum of Racing and Hall of Fame
191 Union Ave.
Saratoga Springs, NY 12866
(518) 584-0400
Director . . . . .Peter Hammell
Assistant Director . . . . .Catherine Maguire
Communications Officer . . . . .Richard Hamilton

NTRA
(National Thoroughbred Racing Association)
230 Lexington Green Cir., Suite 310
Lexington, KY 40503
(859) 245-6872
CEO-Commissioner . . . . .Tim Smith
Deputy of Comm. & COO . . . . .Greg Avioli
V.P. of Communications . . . . .Chip Tuttle

TRA
(Thoroughbred Racing Associations of N. America, Inc.)
420 Fair Hill Drive, Suite 1
Elkton, MD 21921
(410) 392-9200
President . . . . .Bryan G. Krantz
Executive V.P. . . . . .Christopher N. Scherf

NTRA Communications
(National Thoroughbred Racing Association Communications)
444 Madison Ave., Suite 503
New York, NY 10022
(212) 907-9280
Commissioner & CEO ....Tim Smith
Director of Media Relations ....Eric Wing

USTA
(United States Trotting Association)
750 Michigan Ave., Columbus, OH 43215
(614) 224-2291
President ....Corwin Nixon
Executive V.P. ....Fred Noe
Director of Public Relations ....John Pawlak

MEDIA

PERIODICALS

ESPN, The Magazine
19 E 34th St., 7th Floor, New York, NY 10016
(212) 515-1000
Editor in Chief ....John Papanek
Executive Editors ....Gary Hoenig, Steve Wulf
Senior V.P./GM ....Michael Rooney
Public Relations Manager ....Kim Shapiro

Sports Illustrated
135 West 50th St., New York, NY 10020
(212) 522-9797
President/CEO ....Mike Klingensmith
Managing Editor ....Bill Colson
Executive Editors .....B. Peter Carry, Rob Fleder and David
Bauer

The Sporting News
10176 Corporate Square Dr., Suite 200
St. Louis, MO 63132
(314) 997-7111
Senior V.P./Editorial Director ....John D. Rawlings
President ....James H. Nuckols

The Sports Business Daily
120 West Morehead St., Ste. 220
Charlotte, NC 28202
(704) 973-1500
President ....Sal Schiliro
Editor ....Abe Madkour
Media Relations Mgr. ....Bill Magrath

USA Today
1000 Wilson Blvd., Arlington, VA 22229
(703) 276-3400
Owner ....Gannett Co.
President-Publisher ....Tom Curley
Managing Editor/Sports ....Monte Lorell

WIRE SERVICES

Associated Press
50 Rockefeller Plaza 5th Floor, New York, NY 10020
(212) 621-1630
Sports Editor ....Terry Taylor
Deputy Sports Editor ....Brian Friedman

United Press International
1510 H Street, Washington, DC 20005
(202) 898-8000
Sports Editor ....Ron Colbert

The Sports Network
95 James Way, Suite 107 & 109
Southampton, PA 18966
(215) 942-7890
President ....Mickey Charles
Director of Operations ....Phil Sokol
Managing Editor ....Jim Gillis

Sportsticker
800 Plaza Two, Harborside Financial Ctr., Jersey City, NJ 07311
(201) 309-1200
General Manager ....Jim Morganthaler
Dir. of New Content ....Lou Monaco

TV NETWORKS

ABC Sports
47 West 66th St., 13th Floor, New York, NY 10023
(212) 456-4867
President ....Howard Katz
Senior V.P., Production ....John Filippelli
V.P. of Media Relations ....Mark Mandel

CBC Sports
P.O. Box 500, Station A 5H 100
Toronto, Ontario M5W 1E6
(416) 205-6523
Head of Sports ....Nancy Lee
Sr. Executive Producer ....Mike Brannagan
Publicist ....Christian Hasse

CBS Sports
51 West 52nd St., 25th Floor
New York, NY 10019
(212) 975-5230
President ....Sean McManus
Executive Producer ....Terry Ewert
Sr. V.P., Programming ....Rob Correa and Mike Aresco
V.P., Communications ....Leslie Ann Wade

ESPN
ESPN Plaza, Bristol, CT 06010
(860) 585-2000
President ....George Bodenheimer
Vice President ....Chris LaPlaca
Sr. V.P. of Programming ....John Wildhack
Sr. V.P. & Exec. Editor of Internet ....John Walsh
Sr. V.P. and Managing Editor ....Bob Eaton
Director of Communications ....Mike Soltys

ESPN Classic
ESPN Plaza, Bristol, CT 06010
(860) 585-2000
Executive Producer ....Vince Doria
Communications Coordinator ....Amy Swanson

FOX Sports
10201 W. Pico Blvd., Los Angeles, CA 90035
(310) 369-1000
Chairman-CEO ....David Hill
President ....Ed Goren
V.P. of Media Relations (NYC) ....Vince Wladika

The Golf Channel
7580 Commerce Center Drive
Orlando, FL 32819
(407) 345-4653
President-CEO ....Joe Gibbs
V.P., Production ....Tony Tortorici
Director of Public Relations ....Dan Higgins

HBO Sports
1100 Ave. of the Americas
New York, NY 10036
(212) 512-1987
President-CEO ....Ross Greenberg
Sr. V.P./Exec. Producer ....Rick Bernstein
Sr. V.P., Programming ....Kery Davis
Director of Publicity ....Ray Stallone

MTV Sports
1633 Broadway, 32nd Floor
New York, NY 10019
(212) 846-8706
Executive Producer ....Alvin Patrick
Publicity Contact ....Matt Klippel

NBC Sports
30 Rockefeller Plaza, New York, NY 10112.
(212) 664-2160
Chairman ....Dick Ebersol
President ....Ken Schanzer
Executive Producer ....Tommy Roy
V.P. of Communications ....Kevin Sullivan

TSN-The Sports Network
2225 Shepherd Ave. East, Suite 100
Willowdale, Ontario, M2J-5C2
(416) 494-1212
President of Netstar ....Rick Brace
President ....Keith Pelley
Communications Manager ....Keith Marnoch

Turner Sports
One CNN Center
13th Floor, Atlanta, GA 30303
(404) 827-1735
President ....Mark Lazarus
Sr. V.P., Programming ....Kevin O'Malley
V.P., Production ....Mike Pearl
V.P. of Public Relations ....Greg Hughes

Univision (Spanish)
9405 NW 41st St., Miami, FL 33178
(305) 471-3900
V.P. of Ops./Sports ....Tony Oquendo
Publicity Coordinator ....Rosalyn Sariol

USA Network
1230 Ave. of the Americas, New York, NY 10020
(212) 664-4554
Sr. V.P., Production in Sports ....Gordon Beck
V.P., Sports Programming ....Kevin Landy
Sports Publicity ....Tom Carraccioli

OLYMPICS

IOC
(International Olympic Committee)
Chateau de Vidy
CH-1007 Lausanne, Switzerland
TEL: 011-41-21-621-6111
President ....Jacques Rogge
Director General ....Francois Carrard
Secretary General ....Francoise Zweifel
Dir. of International Cooperation ....Fekrou Kidane

2002 WINTER GAMES

Salt Lake Olympic Organizing Committee
299 South Main Street, Suite 1300
Salt Lake City, UT 84111
(801) 212-2002
Chairman ....Robert H. Garff
President & CEO ....W. Mitt Romney
COO ....Frasier Bullock
Chief Communications Officer ....Caroline Shaw
   (XIXth Olympic Winter Games, Feb. 8-24)

2004 SUMMER GAMES

Athens Olympic Organizing Committee
Zappio, Megaro, Athens, Greece
TEL: 011-30-12004-000
   Time difference: 7 hours ahead of New York (EDT)
Chairman ....Gianna Angelopoulas-Daskalaki
Managing Director ....Yannis Spanudakis
Chairmanof Coord. Commission ....Denis Oswald
   (XXVIIIth Olympic Summer Games, Aug. 13-29)

COA
(Canadian Olympic Association)
2380 Avenue Pierre Dupuy
Montreal, Quebec H3C-3R4
(514) 861-3371
Interim CEO ....Lou Ragagnin
President ....Michael Chambers
IOC members .Charmaine Crooks, Paul Henderson, Richard
       Pound, Robert Stedward, James Worrall (Honourary)
Exec. Dir. of Comm. ....Deborah Allan ....Dina Bell (Ott.)

USOC
(United States Olympic Committee)
One Olympic Plaza
Colorado Springs, CO 80909
(719) 632-5551
President ....Sandra Baldwin
Acting CEO ....Scott Blackmun
IOC members .Anita DeFrantz, James Easton, Bill Hybl & Bob
                                            Ctvrlik
Managing Director/Media Relations ....Mike Moran

2006 WINTER GAMES

Turin Olympic Organizing Committee
Via Nizza 262/58-10126
Turin, Italy
TEL: 011-39-011-63-10-511
Exec. President ....Valentino Castellini
Deputy President ....Evelina Christillin
Chairman of Coord. Commission ....Jean Claude-Killy
Media Relations Manager ....Giuseppe Gattino

U.S. OLYMPICS TRAINING CENTERS

Colorado Springs Training Center
One Olympic Plaza, Colorado Springs, CO 80909
(719) 578-4500
Director ....John Smyth

Lake Placid Training Center
421 Old Military Road, Lake Placid, NY 12946
(518) 523-2600
Director ....Jack Favro
Operations Manager ....Tracy Lumb

Arco Olympic Training Center
2800 Olympic Parkway, Chula Vista, CA 91915
(619) 656-1500
Director ....Patrice Milkovich

U.S. OLYMPIC ORGANIZATIONS

National Archery Association
One Olympic Plaza, Colorado Springs, CO 80909
(719) 578-4576
President ....Norm Graham
Executive Director ....Rick Mack
Media Contact ....Bill Kellick

U.S. Badminton Association
One Olympic Plaza, Colorado Springs, CO 80909
(719) 578-4808
President ....Don Chew
Executive Director ....Dan Cloppas
Dir. of Media & Programming ....Barb Kissick

USA Baseball
3400 E Camino Camtestre, Tucson, AZ 85716
(520) 327-9700
Executive Director & CEO ....Paul Seiler
Dir. of Media Relations ....David Fannuchi

USA Basketball
5465 Mark Dabling Blvd.
Colorado Springs, CO 80918
(719) 590-4800
President ....Tom Jernstedt
Executive Director ....James Tooley
Director of Public Relations ....Craig Miller

U.S. Biathlon Association
29 Ethan Allen Ave.
Colchester, VT 05446
(802) 654-7833
President . . . . .Lyle Nelson
Exec. Director . . . . .Stephen Sands
Director of Summer Biathlon . . . . .Marc Sheppard
Public Relations Contact . . . . Jerry Kokesh

U.S. Bobsled and Skeleton Federation
421 Old Military Road
Lake Placid, NY 12946
(518) 523-1842
President . . . . Jim Morris
Executive Director . . . . .Matt Roy
Media/P.R. Director . . . . .Julie Urbansky

USA Boxing
One Olympic Plaza, Colorado Springs, CO 80909
(719) 578-4506
President . . . . .Dr. Robert Voy
Executive Director . . . . .Mike Stone
Dir. of Media/Public Relations . . . . .Bill Kellick

U.S. Canoe and Kayak Team
15 Parkside Drive
Lake Placid, NY 12946
(518) 523-1855
Executive Director . . . . .Lisa Fish
Media & Public Relations Manager . . . . .Doug Haney

USA Curling
1100 Center Point Drive, Box 866
Stevens Point, WI 54481
(715) 344-1199
President . . . . .Peggy Hatch
Executive Director . . . . .David Garber
Media Contact . . . . .Rick Patzke

USA Cycling
One Olympic Plaza
Colorado Springs, CO 80909
(719) 578-4581
President . . . . .Mike Plant
Executive Director & CEO . . . . .Lisa Voight
Director of Communications . . . . .Patrice Quintero

United States Diving, Inc.
Pan American Plaza, Suite 430,
201 South Capitol Avenue, Indianapolis, IN 46225
(317) 237-5252
President . . . . .William Walker
Executive Director . . . . .Todd Smith
Director of Communications . . . . .Kelli Servizzi

U.S. Equestrian Team
Pottersville Road, Gladstone, NJ 07934
(908) 234-1251
President . . . . .Armand Leone, Jr.
Executive Director . . . . .Bob Standish
Director of Public Relations . . . . .Marty Bauman
(508) 698-6810

U.S. Fencing Association
One Olympic Plaza, Colorado Springs, CO 80909
(719) 578-4511
President . . . . .Stacey Johnson
Executive Director .Michael Massik
Media Relations Contact . . . . .Cindy Bent

U.S. Field Hockey Association
One Olympic Plaza, Colorado Springs, CO 80909
(719) 578-4567
President . . . . .Sharon Taylor
Executive Director . . . . .Amy Frankenstein
Director of Media/Public Relations . . . . . . .Howard Thomas

U.S. Figure Skating Association
20 First Street, Colorado Springs, CO 80906
(719) 635-5200
President . . . . .Phyllis Howard
Executive Director . . . . .John Le Fevre
Director of Events . . . . .Carrie Wolf

USA Gymnastics (Artistic & Rhythmic)
Pan American Plaza, Suite 300
201 South Capitol Avenue, Indianapolis, IN 46225
(317) 237-5050
President-Exec. Director . . . . .Robert V. Colarossi
Director of Public Relations . . . . .Courtney Caress

USA Hockey, Inc.
1775 Bob Johnson Dr., Colorado Springs, CO 80906
(719) 576-8724
President . . . . .Walter Bush Jr.
Executive Director . . . . .Doug Palazzari
Dir. of Public and Media Relations . . . . .Chuck Menke

United States Judo, Inc.
One Olympic Plaza, Suite 202
Colorado Springs, CO 80909
(719) 578-4730
President . . . . .Ron Trip
Exec. Director . . . . .William Rosenberg
Public Relations Director . . . . .John Miller

U.S. Luge Association
35 Church Street, Lake Placid, NY 12946
(518) 523-2071
President . . . . .Doug Bateman
Executive Director . . . . .Ron Rossi
Public Relations Manager . . . . John Lundin

USA Pentathlon
7330 San Pedro, Box 10, San Antonio, TX 78216
(210) 822-1206
President . . . . .Ralph Bender
Executive Director .Robert Marbit

U.S. Rowing
Pan American Plaza, Suite 400
201 South Capitol Avenue, Indianapolis, IN 46225
(317) 237-5656
President . . . . .Monk Terry
Executive Director . . . . .John Dane
Director of Communications . . . . .Brett Johnson

U.S. Sailing Association
P.O. Box 1260, 15 Maritime Drive, Portsmouth, RI 02871
(401) 683-0800
President . . . . .David Rosekrans
Interim Executive Director . . . . .William Placke
Media Liaison . . . . .Barby MacGowan (Olympics)
(401) 849-0220
Media Contact . . . . .Penny Rego

U.S. Shooting Team
One Olympic Plaza
Colorado Springs, CO 80909
(719) 578-4670
Executive Director .Robert Mitchell
Public Relations Director . . . . .TBA

U.S. Ski & Snowboard Assoc.
P.O. Box 100, 1500 Kearns Blvd.
Park City, UT 84060
(435) 649-9090
Chairman . . . . .Jim McCarthy
CEO/President . . . . .Bill Marolt
V.P. of Public Relations . . . . .Tom Kelly
Public Information Manager . . . . .Juliann Fritz

U.S. Soccer Federation
U.S. Soccer House
1801-1811 South Prairie Ave.
Chicago; IL 60616
(312) 808-1300
President ....Dr. S. Robert Contiguglia
Secretary General ....Dan Flynn
Director of Communications ....Jim Moorhouse

Amateur Softball Association
2801 N.E. 50th Street
Oklahoma City, OK 73111
(405) 424-5266
President ....Patrick Fleming
Executive Director ....Ron Radigonda
Director of Communications ....Brian McCall

U.S. Speed Skating
P.O. Box 450639, Westlake, OH 44145
(440) 899-0128
President ....Fred Benjamin
Executive Director ....Katie Marquard
Public Relations Director ....Nick Paulenich

USA Swimming
One Olympic Plaza, Colorado Springs, CO 80909
(719) 578-4578
President ....Dale Neuberger
Executive Director ....Chuck Wielgus
Dir. of Public and Media Relations ....Mary Wagner

U.S. Synchronized Swimming, Inc.
Pan American Plaza, Suite 901
201 South Capitol Avenue
Indianapolis, IN 46225
(317) 237-5700
President ....Betty Hazle
Executive Director ....Debbie Hesse
Media Relations Director ....Brian Eaton

USA Table Tennis
One Olympic Plaza
Colorado Springs, CO 80909
(719) 578-4583
President ....Sherri Pittman
Executive Director ....Dwight Johnson
Dir. of Public & Media Relations ....Debby Dohney

USA Team Handball
One Olympic Plaza
Colorado Springs, CO 80909
(719) 575-4036
President ....Bob Djokovich
Executive Director ....Mike Cavanaugh
Director of Sport Programs ....Danette Leininger

U.S. Tennis Association
70 West Red Oak Lane
White Plains, NY 10604
(914) 696-7000
President ....Merv Helleer
Executive Director ....Richard D. Fermin
Dir. of Communications ....Andrea Jayson

USA Track and Field
1 RCA Dome, Suite 140
Indianapolis, IN 46206
(317) 261-0500
President ....Bill Roe
CEO ....Craig Masback
Director of Communications ....Jill Geer

USA Triathlon
3595 East Fountain Blvd., Ste. F-1
Colorado Springs, CO 80910
(719) 597-9090
President ....Mike Highfield
Executive Director ....Steven M. Locke
Communications Director ............B.J. Hoeptner-Evans

USA Volleyball
715 S. Circle Dr., 2nd Floor
Colorado Springs, CO 80910
(719) 228-6800
President ....Al Monaco
Manager of Comm. ....Brent Buzbee

United States Water Polo
1685 W. Uintah St., Colorado Springs, CO 80904
(719) 634-0699
President ....Rich Foster
Executive Director ....Bruce Wigo
Dir. of Media/Public Relations ....Eric Tiettmeyer

USA Weightlifting
One Olympic Plaza, Colorado Springs, CO 80909
(719) 578-4508
President ....Dennis Snethen
Exec. Dir./Comm. Dir. ....James J. Fox

USA Wrestling
6155 Lehman Drive, Colorado Springs, CO 80918
(719) 598-8181
President ....Bruce Baumgartner
Executive Director ....Rich Bender
Dir. of Communications ....Gary Abbott

PAN AMERICAN SPORT ORGANIZATIONS

USA Bowling
5301 South 76th St., Greendale, WI 53129
(414) 421-9008
President ....Kevin Dornberger
Executive Director ....Gerald Koenig

USA National Karate-Do Federation, Inc.
P.O. Box 77083, 8351 15th Ave. NW, Seattle, WA 98117-7083
(206) 440-8386
President ....Julius Thiry
Executive Director ....Brian Lynch
Public/Media Information ....Howard High

United States Racquetball Association
1685 West Uintah, Colorado Springs, CO 80904
(719) 635-5396
President ....Otto Dietrich
Executive Director ....Luke Saint Onge
Associate Exec. Dir./Communications ....Linda Mojer

USA Roller Skating
P.O. Box 6579, Lincoln, NE 68506
(402) 483-7551
President ....George Kolibaba
Executive Director ....Lou Marciani
Communications Director ....Bill Wolf

U.S. Squash Racquets Association
P.O. Box 1216 (23 Cynwyd Rd.)
Bala Cynwyd, PA 19004
(610) 667-4006
President ....Kevin Jernigan
Executive Director ....Craig W. Brand

U.S. Taekwondo Union
One Olympic Plaza, Colorado Springs, CO 80909
(719) 578-4632
President ....Dr. Sang Chul Lee
Executive Director ....R. Jay Warwick

USA Water Ski Association
799 Overlook Drive, S.E., Winter Haven, FL 33884
(863) 324-4341
President ....Sherm Schraft
Executive Director ....Steve McDermett
Director of Communications ....Scott Atkinson

AFFILIATED ORGANIZATIONS

U.S. Orienteering Federation
P.O. Box 1444, Forest Park, GA 30298
(404) 363-2110
President ....Charles Ferguson
Executive Director ....Robin Shannonhouse
Media Contact ....Jon Nash

USA Rugby
3595 East Fountain Blvd., Ste. M2
Colorado Springs, CO 80910
(719) 637-1022
President ....Anne Barry
Executive V.P. ....Neal Brendel
Media/Public Relations Director ....Allison Swickard

U.S. Sports Acrobatics Federation
P.O. Box 41356, Sacramento, CA 95841-0356
(916) 488-9499
President ....Tonya Case-Patterson

SOCCER

FIFA
(Federation Internationale de Football Assn.)
P.O. Box 85, 8030 Zurich, Switzerland
TEL: 011-41-1-384-9595
President ....:. Joseph Blatter
General Secretary ....Michel Zen-Russinen
Director of Communications ....Keith Cooper

MLS

Major League Soccer
110 E. 42nd Street, 10th Floor
New York, NY 10017
(212) 450-1200
Founder ....Alan I. Rothenberg
Commissioner ....Don Garber
V.P. of Communications ....Dan Courtemanche
Director of Information & New Media ....Bob Prior

Chicago Fire
311 W Superior St., #444
Chicago, IL 60610
(312) 705-7200
Investor/Operator ....AEG
General Manager ....Peter Wilt
Director of Communications ....Diana Lopez

Colorado Rapids
555 17th Street, Suite 3350, Denver, CO 80202
(303) 299-1570
Investor/Operator ....Philip F. Anschutz
General Manager ....Dan Counce
Media Relations ....Mark Saunders

Columbus Crew
Columbus Crew Stadium
2121 Velma Ave., Columbus, OH 43211
(614) 447-2739
Investor/Operator ....Lamar Hunt and Family
President/GM ....Jim Smith
Director of Media Relations ....Jeff Wuerth

Dallas Burn
2602 McKinney, Suite 200, Dallas, TX 75204
(214) 979-0303
Investor/Operator ....League-owned
President/GM ....Andy Swift
Director of Media Relations ....Chris Ward

Kansas City Wizards
2 Arrowhead Drive
Kansas City, MO 64129
(816) 920-9300
Investor/Operator ....Lamar Hunt and Family
General Manager ....Curt Johnson
Director of Media Relations ....Rob Thomson

Los Angeles Galaxy
1010 Rose Bowl Dr., Pasadena, CA 91103
(626) 432-1540
Investor/Operator ....Philip F. Anschutz
President ....Tim Leiweke
General Manager ....Time Luse
Media Manager ....Patrick Donnelly

Miami Fusion
2200 Commercial Blvd., Ste. 104
Ft. Lauderdale, FL 33309
(954) 717-2200
Investor/Operator ....Kenneth Horowitz
V.P./General Manager ....Doug Hamilton
Director of Public Relations ....Leo Sarmiento

New England Revolution
Foxboro Stadium, 60 Washington St.
Foxboro, MA 02035
(508) 543-5001
Investor/Operator ....Robert Kraft and Family
General Manager ....Todd Smith
Director of Media Relations ....Jurgen Mainka

New York/New Jersey MetroStars
One Harmon Plaza, 3rd Floor.
Secaucus, NJ 07094
(201) 583-7000
Investor/Operator ....John Kluge and Stuart Subotnick
General Manager ....Nick Sakiewicz
Media Relations ....John Neves

San Jose Earthquakes
3550 Stevens Creek Blvd., Suite 200
San Jose, CA 95117
(408) 241-9922
Investor/Operator ....Kraft Family Sports Group
General Manager ....Tom Neale
Director of Media Relations ....Jed Mettee

Tampa Bay Mutiny
Raymond James Stadium
4042 N. Himes, Tampa, FL 33607
(813) 386-2000
Investor/Operator ....League-owned
President/GM ....Bill Manning
Director of Media Relations ....Tracey Judd

Washington D.C. United
13832 Redskin Drive, Herndon, VA 20171
(703) 478-6600
Owner ....Philip F. Anschutz
President/GM ....Kevin Payne
Director of Communications ....Doug Hicks

Other Soccer

CONCACAF
**(Confederation of North, Central American &
Caribbean Association Football)**
725 Fifth Ave., 17th Floor
New York, NY 10022
(212) 308-0044
President ....Jack Austin Warner
General Secretary ....Chuck Blazer
Senior Consultant ....Clive Toye
Press Officer ....Rick Lawes

U.S. Soccer
(United States Soccer Federation)
Soccer House, 1801-1811 South Prairie Ave.
Chicago, IL 60616
(312) 808-1300
President ....Dr. S. Robert Contiguglia
Secretary General ....Dan Flynn
Director of Communications ....Jim Moorhouse

MISL
(Major Indoor Soccer League)
1175 Post Road East.
Westport, CT 06880
(203) 222-4900
Commissioner ....Steve Ryan
V.P./Soccer Operations ....Brian Fleming
Public/Media Relations Director ....Greg Bibb
    Member teams (6): Baltimore Blast, Cleveland Crunch,
Harrisburg Heat, Kansas City Comets, Milwaukee Wave
and Philadelphia Kixx.

USL
(United Soccer Leagues)
14497 N. Dale Mabry Hwy., Ste. 201
Tampa, FL 33618
(813) 963-3909
Commissioner ....Francisco Marcos
Administrative Manager ....Maria Gomes
Director of Public Relations ....Gerald Barnhart

WUSA
(Women's United Soccer Association)
1120 Avenue of the Americas, 6th Floor
New York, NY 10036
(212) 869-8558
President ....Lynn Morgan
Commissioner ....Tony DiCicco
Director of Public Relations ....Shaun May
    Member teams (8): Atlanta Beat, Bay Area CyberRays,
Boston Breakers, Carolina Courage, New York Power, Phila-
delphia Charge, San Diego Spirit and Washington Freedom.

SWIMMING

FINA
(Federation Internationale de Natation Amateur)
4 ave de Laznte Poste
1005 Lausanne, Switzerland
TEL: 011-4121-310-4710
President ....Mustapha Larfaoui
Honorary Secretary ....Bartolo Consolu

TENNIS

ATP Tour
(Association of Tennis Professionals)
201 ATP Tour Blvd.
Ponte Vedra Beach, FL 32082
(904) 285-8000
Chief Executive Officer ....Mark Miles
V.P. of Corporate Comm. ....David Higdon
Dir. of Public Relations ....................J.J. Carter

ITF
(International Tennis Federation)
Palliser Rd., Barons Court
London, England W14 9EN
TEL: 011-44-208-878-6464
President ....Ricci Bitti
Executive V.P. ....Juan Margets
Head of Communications ....Barbara Travers

Dupont World Team Tennis
445 North Wells, Suite 404, Chicago, IL 60610
(312) 245-5300
Director/Co-Founder ....Billie Jean King
Commissioner & CEO ....Ilana Kloss
Public Relations Spokesman ....Mickey Ryan

USTA
(United States Tennis Association)
70 West Red Oak Lane, White Plains, NY 10604
(914) 696-7000
President ....Merv Heller
Executive Director ....Richard D. Fermin
Dir. of Communications ....Andrea Jayson

WTA Tour
(Women's Tennis Association)
133 First Street, St. Petersburg, FL 33701
(727) 895-5000
CEO ....Bartlett H. McGuire
COO ....Josh Ripple
V.P. of Communications/Development .....Chris De Maria

TRACK & FIELD

IAAF
(International Association of Athletics Federations)
17 Rue Princesse Florestine
BP 359, MC-98007, Monaco Cedex
TEL: 011-377-93-10-8888
President ....Lamine Diack
Senior V.P. ....Dr. Arne Ljungquist
General Secretary ....Istvan Gyulai
Director of Communications ....TBA

USA Track & Field
One RCA Dome, Suite 140
Indianapolis, IN 46225
(317) 261-0500
President ....Bill Roe
CEO ....Craig Masback
Director of Communications ....Jill Geer

MISCELLANEOUS

AAU
(Amateur Athletic Union)
c/o Walt Disney World Resorts
P.O. Box 10000
Lake Buena Vista, FL 32830-1000
(407) 934-7200
President ....Bobby Dodd
Media/Public Relations Director ....Melissa Wilson

American Powerboating Association
P.O. Box 377
Eastpointe, MI 48021
(810) 773-9700
President ....Mike Jones
Executive Administrator ....Gloria Urbin

Association of Surfing Professionals
P.O. Box 1095, Coolangatta
Queensland, Australia 4225
011-61-7-5599-1550
President/CEO ....Wayne Bartholomew
Tour Director ....Al Hunt
Media Relations ....Jesse Fein

BASS, Inc.
(Bass Anglers Sportsmen Society)
5845 Carmichael Road
Montgomery, AL 36141
(334) 272-9530
Owner ....ESPN
President ....Helen Sevier
Publicity Director ....George McNeilly

Iditarod Trail Committee
P.O. Box 870800
Wasilla, AK 99687
(907) 376-5155
Executive Director ....Stan Hooley
Race Director ....Joanne Potts

International Game Fish Association
300 Gulf Steam Way
Dania Baech, FL 33004
(954) 927-2628
Chairman ....Michael Levitt
President ....Mike Leach
Editor ....Ray Crawford

Little League Baseball Incorporated
P.O. Box 3485
Williamsport, PA 17701
(570) 326-1921
CEO-President . . . . .Stephen Keener
Director of Comm. & Media Relations . . . .Lance Van Auken

National Association for Girls and Women in Sport
1900 Association Drive, Reston, VA 20191
(703) 476-3452
Executive Director . . . . .MaryAnn Borysowicz
President . . . . .Dr. Joy Griffin
Public Relations Dir. .Shannon Tesdahl

National Lacrosse League
1212 Avenue of the Americas, 5th Floor, New York, NY 10036
(917) 510-9200
Commissioner . . . . .Jim Jennings
Dir. of Public Relations . . . . .Doug Fritts
   Member teams (13): Albany Attack, Buffalo Bandits,
Calgary Roughnecks, Columbus Landsharks, Montreal
Express, New Jersey Storm, New York Saints, Ottawa
Rebel, Philadelphia Wings, Rochester Knighthawks, Toronto
Rock, Vancouver Ravens and Washington Power.

National Sports Foundation
P.O. Box 888886, Atlanta, GA 30356
(678) 417-0041
Executive Director . . . . .Ed Harris

Professional Rodeo Cowboys Association
101 Pro Rodeo Drive
Colorado Springs, CO 80919
(719) 593-8840
Commissioner . . . . .Steve Hatchell
Director of Communications . . . . .Steve Fleming

Special Olympics
1325 G St. NW Suite 500
Washington, DC 20005
(202) 628-3630
Founder . . . . .Eunice Kennedy Shriver
Chairman . . . . .Sargent Shriver
COO . . . . .Bob Hawkins and Lee Todd
Sr. Media Relations Manager . . . . .Betty Ann Hughes

U.S. Association of Blind Athletes
33 N. Institute St.
Colorado Springs, CO 80903
(719) 630-0422
Executive Director . . . . .Charlie Huebner
Asst. Exec. Director . . . . .Mark Lucas

U.S. Polo Association
771 Corporate Dr., Suite 505
Lexington, KY 40503
(859) 219-1000
Chairman . . . . .Orrin H. Ingram
President . . . . .Robert Uihlein III

Wheelchair Sports USA
3595 East Fountain Blvd., Suite L-1
Colorado Springs, CO 80910
(719) 574-1150
Chairman . . . . .Paul DePace
Executive Director . . . . .Patricia Shepherd

Women's Professional Billiard Assoc.
6407 South Blvd.
Charlotte, NC 28217
(615) 254-3333
President . . . . .Jan McWorter
Media Contact . . . . .Andy Barton

Commissioners and Presidents
Chief Executives of Established Major Sports Organizations since 1876

Major League Baseball

Commissioner	Tenure
Kenesaw Mountain Landis*	1920–44
Albert (Happy) Chandler	1945–51
Ford Frick	1951–65
William Eckert	1965–68
Bowie Kuhn	1969–84
Peter Ueberroth	1984–89
A. Bartlett Giamatti*	1989
Fay Vincent	1989–92
Bud Selig†	1998–

*Died in office.
†Served as interim commissioner
from 1992-98.

National League

President	Tenure
Morgan G. Bulkeley	1876
William A. Hulbert*	1877–82
A.G. Mills	1883–84
Nicholas Young	1885–1902
Henry Pulliam*	1903–09
Thomas J. Lynch	1910–13
John K. Tener	1914–18
John A. Heydler	1918–34
Ford Frick	1935–51
Warren Giles	1951–69
Charles (Chub) Feeney	1970–86
A. Bartlett Giamatti	1987–89
Bill White	1989–94
Leonard Coleman	1994–99

*Died in office.
Note: League president jobs were
eliminated after the 1999 season.

American League

President	Tenure
Bancroft (Ban) Johnson	1901–27
Ernest Barnard*	1927–31
William Harridge	1931–59
Joe Cronin	1959–73
Lee McPhail	1974–83
Bobby Brown	1984–94
Gene Budig	1994–99

*Died in office.
Note: League president jobs were
eliminated after the 1999 season.

NBA

Commissioner	Tenure
Maurice Podoloff	1949–63
Walter Kennedy	1963–75
Larry O'Brien	1975–84
David Stern	1984–

NFL

President	Tenure
Jim Thorpe	1920
Joe Carr	1921–39
Carl Storck	1939–41

Commissioner	
Elmer Layden	1941–46
Bert Bell*	1946–59
Austin Gunsel	1959–60
Pete Rozelle	1960–89
Paul Tagliabue	1989–

*Died in office.

NHL

President	Tenure
Frank Calder*	1917–43
Red Dutton	1943–46
Clarence Campbell	1946–77
John Ziegler	1977–92
Gil Stein	1992–93

Commissioner	
Gary Bettman	1993–

*Died in office.

NCAA

Executive Director	Tenure
Walter Byers	1951–88
Dick Schultz	1988–93
Cedric Dempsey	1993–

IOC

President	Tenure
Demetrius Vikelas, Greece	1894–96
Baron Pierre de Coubertin, France	1896–1925
Count Henri de Baillet-Latour, Belgium	1925–42
Vacant	1942–46
J. Sigfried Edstrom, Sweden	1946–52
Avery Brundage, USA	1952–72
Lord Michael Killanin, Ireland	1972–80
Juan Antonio Samaranch, Spain	1980–2001
Jacques Rogge, Belgium	2001–

International Sports

Australian **Ian Thorpe** won six golds and broke three individual
world records at the 2001 World Swimming Championships.

King of the Mountain

Lance Armstrong scores a hat trick with his third consecutive Tour de France victory.

Jack Edwards *has been with ESPN since 1991, currently as a play-by-play announcer.*

In 1999, Lance Armstrong made a statement by winning the Tour de France after surviving testicular cancer that had traveled to both lungs and his brain.

In 2000, he won the Tour again, making the statement that '99 was no fluke. In 2001, he joined the icons of his sport...but his statement was this: Treat people the way you want them to treat you.

Armstrong's longtime friend and teammate, Kevin Livingston, had defected during the offseason. Now, not only would Armstrong be seeing Livingston in a jersey other than the US Postal Service blue, he would see him riding in support of his biggest threat, '97 Tour winner Jan Ullrich of Deutsche Telekom. In response, the Posties enlisted Roberto Heras of Spain to help protect Armstrong on the climbs.

Armstrong's climbing ability was in question early on the day of the epic L'Alpe

d'Huez stage. L'Alpe is a fearsome switchback-layered climb that is considered one of the pearls of the sport. Armstrong defined the 2001 Tour there, combining classic sandbagging with a moment that will sparkle forever as his personal manifesto.

This L'Alpe finish is the third of three back-to-back-to-back beyond-category ascents during the 130-mile 10th stage.

Up and over the Col de la Madeleine and the Col du Glandon, Livingston and the Telekom boys were controlling the front of the lead pack for Ullrich. Armstrong, frequently grimacing, was barely hanging onto the tail. Anyone getting spat out the back might never recover. Ullrich was pushing a big gear at about 80 RPM, working hard but outwardly looking stronger than Armstrong. They arrived at the bottom of the L'Alpe d'Huez and Armstrong revealed his ruse, charging until he was a wheel ahead of Ullrich.

In reviewing virtually any competition, athletes can look back and see the

AP/Wide World Photos

Lance Armstrong, right, fooled rival Jan Ullrich, left, into thinking he was exhausted, then blasted by him up the mountain en route to his third straight Tour de France win.

critical moment where victory was won. The height of sporting drama is when everyone recognizes that crux as it is happening.

Armstrong, pounding a smaller gear than Ullrich at 90-plus RPM, turned while standing in the pedals and looked his rival right in the eye for three revolutions of his legs. It was as if to say, "This is it. This is the moment that I have chosen. You and I are the strongest, and this is our contest. This is fair warning, with the Tour de France the prize. The game is on."

And then Armstrong blazed off, leaving Ullrich, leaving Livingston, leaving us all in a sea of adrenaline and awe. He won the stage by 1:59. Only

Italian Fausto Coppi—in the first year they raced to the peak, 1952—had won both L'Alpe d'Huez and the Tour. Now, Armstrong was racing history.

Three days later, in the Pyrenees, he pulled the yellow jersey over his head. He won another massive climbing stage, both individual time trials, and his third straight Tour de France. He tied Greg LeMond for most wins by an American. Only Frenchman Jacques Anquetil, Belgian Eddy Merckx (four straight, each), and Spaniard Miguel Indurain (five) have won more in succession.

Armstrong's version of history, despite its dynastic style, had a compassionate tone. When Ullrich flew into a ditch on

AP/Wide World Photos

Ukraine's **Zhanna Pintusevich-Block**, left, ended the 100-meter race winning streak of **Marion Jones**, right, at 42 with her win at the World Championships in Edmonton.

a descent a few days after L'Alpe, Armstrong waited for the German to climb out not only because it is easier to ride as a pair than alone, but also because that brand of sportsmanship is what Armstrong wants cycling to represent.

Armstrong has stood up to ridiculous bombardment by innuendo and never has tested dirty in a sport that long has been a rolling performance-enhance-ment experiment. He trains with flammable intensity, focus and unprecedented attention to a scientific method. He has forgiven detractors such as Marco Pantani and bewildering friends such as Livingston. He believes in the fair warning and the watchful wait for even his toughest foe. He has raised his game and uplifted us all.

This is the age of Lance Armstrong's Golden Rule.

Jack Edwards' Ten Biggest Moments of the Year in International Sports

10 ▪ Lee Bong-Ju of South Korea wins the 105th Boston Marathon, snapping a 10-year victory streak for Kenyan men. Kenya is represented on the winners' podium, however, as Catherine Ndereba wins the women's division for the second consecutive year.

9 ▪ Claudia Pechstein of Germany shaves almost a full second off the 3,000-meter speed skating world record at the final World Cup event in Calgary, becoming the first woman to skate 3,000 meters in less than four minutes.

8 ▪ Olympic champion pole vaulter Stacy Dragila wins gold at the IAAF Track and Field World Championships in Edmonton, clearing a meet-record 15 feet, 7 inches. For the first time in history, four women clear 14-11 in competition. Dragila would break her own outdoor world record four times during the 2001 season.

7 ▪ The IOC elects Belgian surgeon Jacques Rogge as the eighth president in its 107-year history. Rogge's principal rivals, Canadian Dick Pound and South Korea's Kim Yong-Un, accuse outgoing president Juan Antonio Samaranch of pulling strings to ensure Rogge's victory.

6 ▪ Michael Johnson announces his retirement from track and field, then goes out in style, anchoring the United States' 4x400 meter relay team to a gold medal at the Goodwill Games in his final performance.

5 ▪ Zhanna Pintusevich-Block of Ukraine defeats Marion Jones in the 100-meter race at the Track and Field World Championships, ending Jones' streak of 42 straight wins at that distance. Despite her defeat, Jones is still the only double gold medallist in Edmonton, winning the 200-meter race and anchoring the winning 4x100-meter relay.

4 ▪ At the FINA Swimming World Championships in Fukuoka, Japan, Australian Ian Thorpe breaks his own world records in the 200-, 400- and 800-meter freestyle events. He wins six gold medals in all and becomes the first swimmer in 30 years to win three individual freestyle events at one world championships.

3 ▪ Despite heated protests from human rights activists around the world, Beijing is successful in its bid to host the 2008 Olympics over Toronto, Paris, Istanbul and Osaka. The Chinese capital had lost the 2000 Sydney Games by two votes.

2 ▪ In March, Austrian skiing great Hermann Maier ties Ingemar Stenmark's record of 13 World Cup victories in a season. Five months later, he breaks a leg and damages muscle tissue in a motorcycle accident that jeopardizes his skiing career.

1 ▪ Lance Armstrong roars from behind in the mountain stages and cruises to his third straight victory in the Tour de France. His nearest competitor, Jan Ullrich, finishes 6:44 behind. He joins Greg LeMond as the only Americans with three Tour wins.

Seoul Men

By winning the 2001 Boston Marathon, South Korea's Lee Bong-Ju stopped the Kenyans' 10-year winning streak and became just the third Korean man and first in 51 years to win the event.

Year		Time
2001	Lee Bong-Ju, S. Kor.	2:09:43
1950	Kee Yonh Ham, Kor.	2:32:39
1947	Yun Bok Suh, Kor.	2:25:39

Tour de Force

All of Lance Armstrong's Tour wins have been by at least six minutes.

Year	Final Margin	Took Lead	Stages Won
2001	+6:44	13th	4
2000	+6:02	10th	1
1999	+7:37	8th	4

Note: Over the seven Tours he's participated in, he's won 11 stages and worn the yellow jersey for 35 days.

Repeat Performers

Since 1991, no woman has won the Boston Marathon and not successfully defended her title at least once.

Years	
2000-01	Catherine Ndereba, Kenya
1997-99	Fatuma Roba, Ethiopia
1994-96	Uta Pippig, Germany
1992-93	Olga Markova, CIS/Russia

Four in Store?

If history is any indication, Armstrong should win his fourth Tour in 2002. Three of the four previous winners of three consecutive also won a fourth.

Years		Following Year
1999–2001	L. Armstrong	????
1991–93	M. Indurain	Won
1969–71	E. Merckx	Won
1961–63	J. Anquetil	Won
1953–55	L. Bobet	*

* Bobet did not compete in 1956.

2000-2001 Season in Review

TRACK & FIELD

2001 IAAF World Championships

The 8th IAAF World Championships in athletics held in Edmonton, Alberta, Canada, Aug. 3-12, 2001. Note that (CR) indicates championship meet record.

Final Medal Leaders

		G	S	B	Total			G	S	B	Total
1	United States	9	5	5	19	7	Jamaica	1	2	2	5
	Russia	6	7	6	19	8	Romania	2	1	1	4
3	Ethiopia	2	2	4	8		Poland	2	0	2	4
4	Kenya	3	3	1	7		Belarus	1	3	0	4
	Germany	2	4	1	7		Greece	1	1	2	4
6	Cuba	3	1	2	6		Italy	1	1	2	4

MEN

Event		Time
100 meters	Maurice Greene, USA	9.82
200 meters	Konstantinos Kenteris, GRE	20.04
400 meters	Avard Moncur, BAH	44.64
800 meters	Andre Bucher, SWI	1:43.70
1500 meters	Hicham El Guerrouj, MOR	3:30.68
5000 meters	Richard Limo, KEN	13:00.77
10,000 meters	Charles Kamathi, KEN	27:53.25
Marathon	Gezahegne Abera, ETH	2:12:42
4x100m relay	USA (Grimes, Williams, Mitchell, Montgomery)	37.96
4x400m relay	USA (Byrd, Pettigrew, Brew, Taylor)	2:57.54
110m hurdles	Allen Johnson, USA	13.04
400m hurdles	Felix Sanchez, DOM	47.49
3000m steeple	Reuben Kosgei, KEN	8:15.16
20k walk	Roman Rasskazov, RUS	1:20:31
50k walk	Robert Korzeniowski, POL	3:42:08

Event		Hgt/Dist	
High Jump	Martin Buss, GER	7-8¾	
Pole Vault	Dmitri Markov, AUS	19-10¼	CR
Long Jump	Ivan Pedroso, CUB	27-6¾	
Triple Jump	Jonathan Edwards, GBR	58-9½	
Shot Put	John Godina, USA	71-9	
Discus	Lars Riedel, GER	228-9	CR
Hammer	Szymon Ziolkowski, POL	273-7	CR
Javelin	Jan Zelezny, CZR	304-5	CR
Decathlon	Tomas Dvorak, CZR	8902 pts	CR

WOMEN

Event		Time	
100 meters	Zhanna Pintusevich-Block, UKR	10.82	
200 meters	Marion Jones, USA	22.39	
400 meters	Amy Mbacke Thiam, SEN	49.86	
800 meters	Maria Mutola, MOZ	1:57.17	
1500 meters	Gabriela Szabo, ROM	4:00.57	
5000 meters	Olga Yegorova, RUS	15:03.39	
10,000 meters	Derartu Tulu, ETH	31:48.81	
Marathon	Lidia Simon, ROM	2:26:01	
4x100m relay	USA (White, Gaines, Miller, Jones)	41.71	
4x400m relay	Jamaica (Richards, Scott, Parris, Fenton)	3:20.65	
100m hurdles	Anjanette Kirkland, USA	12.42	
400m hurdles	Nezha Bidouane, MOR	53.34	
20k walk	Olimpiada Ivanova, RUS	1:27:48	CR

Event		Hgt/Dist	
High Jump	Hestrie Cloete, RSA	6-6¾	
Pole Vault	Stacy Dragila, USA	15-7	CR
Long Jump	Fiona May, ITA	23-0½	
Triple Jump	Tatyana Lebedeva, RUS	50-0½	
Shot Put	Yanina Korolchik, BLR	67-7½	
Discus	Natalya Sadova, RUS	224-11	
Hammer	Yipsi Moreno, CUB	231-9	
Javelin	Osleidys Menendez, CUB	228-1	CR
Heptathlon	Yelena Prokhorova, RUS	6694 pts	

2001 IAAF Mobil Grand Prix
Final Top 10 Standings

Overall Men's and Women's winners receive $100,000 (US) each; all ties broken by complex Grand Prix scoring system.

MEN

1. Andre Bucher, SWI (102 points); 2. Allen Johnson, USA (101); 3. Hicham El Guerrouj, MOR and Paul Bitok, KEN (100); 5. Anier Garcia, CUB (95); 6. Bernard Lagat, KEN (94); 7. Boris Henry, GER and Kevin Dilworth, USA (84); 9. Yuriy Borzakovskiy, RUS and Jean-Patrick Nduwimana, BDI (77).

WOMEN

1. Violeta Szekely, ROM (116 points); 2. Maria Mutola, MOZ (105); 3. Tetyana Tereshchuk, UKR (96); 4. Hestrie Cloete, RSA (93.5); 5. Kajsa Bergqvist, SWE (92.5); 6. Stacy Dragila, USA and Stephanie Graf, AUT (92); 8. Natalya Gorelova, RUS (88); 9. Debbie-Ann Parris, JAM (86); 10. Inha Babakova, UKR (85.5).

2001 IAAF World Indoor Championships

The 8th IAAF World Indoor Championships in athletics were held in Lisbon, Portugal, March 9-11, 2001. Note that (CR) indicates championship meet record.

Final Medal Leaders

		G	S	B	Total
1	United States	7	8	2	17
2	Russia	4	5	6	15
3	Jamaica	2	2	1	5
4	Great Britain	1	2	1	4
	Spain	0	1	3	4

		G	S	B	Total
6	Czech Republic	2	0	1	3
	Sweden	2	0	1	3
	Belarus	1	1	1	3
9	Nine countries tied with 2 medals each.				

MEN

Event		Time
60 meters	Tim Harden, USA	6.44
200 meters	Shawn Crawford, USA	20.63
400 meters	Daniel Caines, GBR	46.40
800 meters	Yuriy Borzakovskiy, RUS	1:44.49
1500 meters	Rui Silva, POR	3:51.06
3000 meters	Hicham El Guerrouj, MOR	7:37.74
60m hurdles	Terrence Trammell, USA	7.51
4x400m relay	Poland (Rysiukiewicz, Haczek, Bocian, Mackowiak)	3:04.47

Event		Hgt/Dist
High Jump	Stefan Holm, SWE	7-7¼
Pole Vault	Lawrence Johnson, USA	19-6¼
Long Jump	Ivan Pedroso, CUB	27-8
Triple Jump	Paolo Camossi, ITA	56-10
Shot Put	John Godina, USA	68-3¾
Heptathlon	Roman Sebrle, CZR	6420 pts

WOMEN

Event		Time
60 meters	Chandra Sturrup, BAH	7.05
200 meters	Juliet Campbell, JAM	22.64
400 meters	Sandie Richards, JAM	51.04
800 meters	Maria Mutola, MOZ	1:59.74
1500 meters	Hasna Benhassi, MOR	4:10.83
3000 meters	Olga Yegorova, RUS	8:37.48
60m hurdles	Anjanette Kirkland, USA	7.85
4x400m relay	Russia (Nosova, Zykina, Sotnikova, Kotlyarova)	3:30.00

Event		Hgt/Dist	
High Jump	Kajsa Bergqvist, SWE	6-6¾	
Pole Vault	Pávla Hamackova, CZR	14-11½	CR
Long Jump	Dawn Burrell, USA	23-0¾	
Triple Jump	Tereza Marinova, BUL	48-11	
Shot Put	Larisa Peleshenko, RUS	65-1¼	
Pentathlon	Natalya Sazanovich, BLR	4850 pts	CR

World, Olympic and American Records
As of Sept. 20, 2001

World outdoor records officially recognized by the International Amateur Athletics Federation (IAAF); (p) indicates record is pending ratification.

MEN
Running

Event		Time		Date Set	Location
100 meters:	World	9.79	**Maurice Greene**, USA	June 16, 1999	Athens
	Olympic	9.84	Donovan Bailey, Canada	July 27, 1996	Atlanta
	American	9.79	Greene (same as World)	—	—
200 meters:	World	19.32	**Michael Johnson**, USA	Aug. 1, 1996	Atlanta
	Olympic	19.32	Johnson (same as World)	—	—
	American	19.32	Johnson (same as World)	—	—
400 meters:	World	43.18	**Michael Johnson**, USA	Aug. 26, 1999	Seville
	Olympic	43.49	Michael Johnson, USA	July 29, 1996	Atlanta
	American	43.18	Johnson (same as World)	—	—
800 meters:	World	1:41.11	**Wilson Kipketer**, Denmark	Aug. 24, 1997	Cologne
	Olympic	1:42.58	Vebjoern Rodal, Norway	July 31, 1996	Atlanta
	American	1:42.60	Johnny Gray	Aug. 28, 1985	Koblenz, W. Ger.
1000 meters:	World	2:11.96	**Noah Ngeny**, Kenya	Sept. 5, 1999	Rieti, ITA
	Olympic		Not an event	—	—
	American	2:13.9	Rick Wohlhuter	July 30, 1974	Oslo
1500 meters:	World	3:26.00	**Hicham El Guerrouj**, Morocco	July 14, 1998	Rome
	Olympic	3:32.07	Noah Ngeny, Kenya	Sept. 29, 2000	Sydney
	American	3:29.77	Sydney Maree	Aug. 25, 1985	Cologne
Mile:	World	3:43.13	**Hicham El Guerrouj**, Morocco	July 7, 1999	Rome
	Olympic		Not an event	—	—
	American	3:47.69	Steve Scott	July 7, 1982	Oslo
2000 meters:	World	4:44.79	**Hicham El Guerrouj**, Morocco	Sept. 7, 1999	Berlin
	Olympic		Not an event	—	—
	American	4:52.44	Jim Spivey	Sept. 15, 1987	Lausanne, SWI
3000 meters:	World	7:20.67	**Daniel Komen**, Kenya	Sept. 1, 1996	Rieti, ITA
	Olympic		Not an event	—	—
	American	7:30.84	Bob Kennedy	Aug. 8, 1998	Monte Carlo
5000 meters:	World	12:39.36	**Haile Gebrselassie**, Ethiopia	June 13, 1998	Helsinki
	Olympic	13:05.59	Said Aouita, Morocco	Aug. 11, 1984	Los Angeles
	American	12:58.21	Bob Kennedy	Aug. 14, 1996	Zurich
10,000 meters:	World	26:22.75	**Haile Gebrselassie**, Ethiopia	June 1, 1998	Hengelo, NED
	Olympic	27:07.34	Haile Gebrselassie, Ethiopia	July 29, 1996	Atlanta
	American	27:13.98	Meb Keflezighi	May 4, 2001	Stanford, Calif.

Event		Time		Date Set	Location
20,000 meters:	**World**	..56:55.6	**Arturo Barrios**, Mexico	Mar. 30, 1991	La Fleche, FRA
	Olympic	....	Not an event	—	—
	American	..58:15.0	Bill Rodgers	Aug. 9, 1977	Boston
Marathon:	**World**	..2:05:42†	**Khalid Khannouchi**, Morocco	Oct. 24, 1999	Chicago
	Olympic	..2:09:21	Carlos Lopes, Portugal	Aug. 12, 1984	Los Angeles
	American	..2:07:01*	Khalid Khannouchi	Oct. 22, 2000	Chicago

Note: The Mile run is 1,609.344 meters and the Marathon is 42,194.988 meters (26 miles, 385 yards).
†Marathon records are not officially recognized by the IAAF.
*When Khannouchi set the world record, he was a citizen of Morocco. He became a citizen of the United States on May 2, 2000.

Relays

Event		Time		Date Set	Location
4 x 100m:	**World**	........37.40	**USA** (Marsh, Burrell, Mitchell, C. Lewis)	Aug. 8, 1992	Barcelona
		37.40	**USA** (Drummond, Cason, Mitchell, Burrell)	Aug. 21, 1993	Stuttgart
	Olympic	......37.40	USA (same as World)	—	—
	American	......37.40	USA (same as World)	—	—
4 x 200m:	**World**	......1:18.68	**USA** (Marsh, Burrell, Heard, C. Lewis)	Apr. 17, 1994	Walnut, Calif.
	Olympic	....	Not an event	—	—
	American	....1:18.68	USA (same as World)	—	—
4 x 400m:	**World**	......2:54.20	**USA** (Young, Pettigrew, Washington, Johnson)	July 22, 1998	Uniondale, N.Y.
	Olympic	....2:55.74	USA (Valmon, Watts, Johnson, S. Lewis)	Aug. 8, 1992	Barcelona
	American	....2:54.20	USA (same as World)	—	—
4 x 800m:	**World**	......7:03.89	**Great Britain** (Elliott, Cook, Cram, Coe)	Aug. 30, 1982	London
	Olympic	....	Not an event	—	—
	American	.....7:06.5	Santa Monica TC (J. Robinson, Mack, E. Jones, Gray)	Apr. 26, 1986	Walnut, Calif.
4 x 1500m:	**World**	......14:38.8	**West Germany** (Wessinghage, Hudak, Lederer, Fleschen)	Aug. 17, 1977	Cologne
	Olympic	....	Not an event	—	—
	American	....14:46.3	USA (Aldredge, Clifford, Harbour, Duits)	June 24, 1979	Bourges, FRA

Hurdles

Event		Time		Date Set	Location
110 meters:	**World**	........12.91	**Colin Jackson**, Great Britain	Aug. 20, 1993	Stuttgart
	Olympic	......12.95	Allen Johnson, USA	July 29, 1996	Atlanta
	American	......12.92	Roger Kingdom	Aug. 16, 1989	Zurich
		12.92	Allen Johnson	June 23, 1996	Atlanta
400 meters:	**World**	........46.70	**Kevin Young**, USA	Aug. 6, 1992	Barcelona
	Olympic	......46.78	Young (same as World)	—	—
	American	......46.78	Young (same as World)	—	—

Note: The 10 hurdles at 110 meters are 3 feet, 6 inches high and those at 400 meters are 3 feet.

Walking

Event		Time		Date Set	Location
20 km:	**World**	......1:17:26	**Bernardo Segura**, Mexico	May 7, 1994	Fana, NOR
	Olympic	......1:18:59	Robert Korzeniowski, Poland	Sept. 22, 2000	Sydney
	American	....1:22:17	Tim Lewis	Sept. 24, 1989	Dearborn, Mich.
50 km:	**World**	.....3:40:58	**Thierry Toutain**, France	Sept. 29, 1996	Hericourt, FRA
	Olympic	....3:38:29	Vyacheslav Ivanenko, USSR	Sept. 30, 1988	Seoul
	American	....3:48:04	Curt Clausen	May. 2, 1999	Deauville, FRA

Steeplechase

Event		Time		Date Set	Location
3000 meters:	**World**	....7:55.28p	**Brahim Boulami**, Morocco	Aug. 24, 2001	Brussels
	Olympic	...8:05.51	Julius Kariuki, Kenya	Sept. 30, 1988	Seoul
	American	..8:09.17	Henry Marsh	Aug. 28, 1985	Koblenz

Note: A men's steeplechase course consists of 28 hurdles (3 feet high) and seven water jumps (12 feet long).

Field Events

Event		Mark		Date Set	Location
High Jump:	**World**	......8-0½	**Javier Sotomayor**, Cuba	July 27, 1993	Salamanca, SPA
	Olympic	7-10	Charles Austin, USA	July 28, 1996	Atlanta
	American	....7-10½	Charles Austin	Aug. 7, 1991	Zurich
Pole Vault:	**World**	......20-1¾	**Sergey Bubka**, Ukraine	July 31, 1994	Sestriere, ITA
	Olympic	.....19-5¼	Jean Galfione, France	Aug. 2, 1996	Atlanta
		19-5¼	Igor Trandenkov, Russia	Aug. 2, 1996	Atlanta
		19-5¼	Andrei Tiwontschik, Germany	Aug. 2, 1996	Atlanta
	American	....19-9¼	Jeff Hartwig	June 14, 2000	Jonesboro, Ark.
Long Jump:	**World**	......29-4¾*	**Ivan Pedroso**, Cuba	July 29, 1995	Sestriere, ITA
		29-4½	**Mike Powell**, USA	Aug. 30, 1991	Tokyo
	Olympic	.....29-2½	Bob Beamon, USA	Oct. 18, 1968	Mexico City
	American	....29-4½	Powell (same as World)	—	—

Event		Mark		Date Set	Location
Triple Jump:	World	.....60- 0¼	**Jonathan Edwards**, GBR	Aug. 7, 1995	Göteborg, SWE
	Olympic	.....59-4¼	Kenny Harrison, USA	July 27, 1996	Atlanta
	American	.....59-4¼	Kenny Harrison (same as Olympic)	—	—
Shot Put:	World	....75-10¼	**Randy Barnes**, USA	May 20, 1990	Los Angeles
	Olympic	...73- 8¾	Ulf Timmermann, East Germany	Sept. 23, 1988	Seoul
	American	.75-10¼	Barnes (same as World)	—	—
Discus:	World	243-0	**Jurgen Schult**, East Germany	June 6, 1986	Neubrandenburg
	Olympic	227-8	Lars Riedel, Germany	July 31, 1996	Atlanta
	American	.237-4	Ben Plucknett	July 7, 1981	Stockholm
Javelin:	World	323-1	**Jan Zelezny**, Czech Republic	May 25, 1996	Jena, GER
	Olympic	.295-10	Jan Zelezny, Czech Republic	Sept. 23, 2000	Sydney
	American	.285-10	Tom Pukstys	May 25, 1997	Jena, GER
Hammer:	World	284-7	**Yuriy Sedykh**, USSR	Aug. 30, 1986	Stuttgart
	Olympic	...278-2	Sergey Litvinov, USSR	Sept. 26, 1988	Seoul
	American	..270-9	Lance Deal	Sept. 7, 1996	Milan

Note: The international weights for men—**Shot** (16 lbs); **Discus** (4 lbs/6.55 oz); **Javelin** (minimum 1 lb/12¼ oz.); **Hammer** (16 lbs).

*Apparent world record disallowed because of interference with wind gauge at altitude.

Decathlon

Ten Events:		Points		Date Set	Location
	World	9026	**Roman Sebrle**, Czech Repub.	May 26-27, 2001	Gotzis, AUT
	Olympic	8847	Daley Thompson, Great Britain	Aug. 8-9, 1984	Los Angeles
	American	8891	Dan O'Brien	Sept. 4-5, 1992	Talence, FRA

Note: Sebrle's WR times and distances, in order over two days— **100m** (10.64); **LJ** (26-7¼); **Shot** (50-3½); **HJ** (6-11½); **400m** (47.79); **110m H** (13.92); **Discus** (157-3); **PV** (15-9); **Jav** (230-2); **1500m** (4:21.98).

WOMEN
Running

Event		Time		Date Set	Location
100 meters:	World	......10.49	**Florence Griffith Joyner**, USA	July 16, 1988	Indianapolis
	Olympic	.....10.62	Florence Griffith Joyner, USA	Sept. 24, 1988	Seoul
	American	....10.49	Griffith Joyner (same as World)	—	—
200 meters:	World	......21.34	**Florence Griffith Joyner**, USA	Sept. 29, 1988	Seoul
	Olympic	.....21.34	Griffith Joyner (same as World)	—	—
	American	.....21.34	Griffith Joyner (same as World)	—	—
400 meters:	World	......47.60	**Marita Koch**, East Germany	Oct. 6, 1985	Canberra, AUS
	Olympic	....48.25	Marie-Jose Perec, France	July 29, 1996	Atlanta
	American	....48.83	Valerie Brisco	Aug. 6, 1984	Los Angeles
800 meters:	World	.....1:53.28	**Jarmila Kratochvilova**, Czech.	July 26, 1983	Munich
	Olympic	...1:53.42	Nadezhda Olizarenko, USSR	July 27, 1980	Moscow
	American	...1:56.40	Jearl Miles-Clark	Aug. 11, 1999	Zurich
1000 meters:	World	....2:28.98	**Svetlana Masterkova**, Russia	Aug. 23, 1996	Brussels
	Olympic	....	Not an event	—	—
	American	...2:31.80	Regina Jacobs	July 3, 1999	Brunswick, Me.
1500 meters:	World	....3:50.46	**Qu Yunxia**, China	Sept. 11, 1993	Beijing
	Olympic	...3:53.96	Paula Ivan, Romania	Oct. 1, 1988	Seoul
	American	...3:57.12	Mary Slaney	July 26, 1983	Stockholm
Mile:	World	....4:12.56	**Svetlana Masterkova**, Russia	Aug. 14, 1996	Zurich
	Olympic	....	Not an event	—	—
	American	...4:16.71	Mary Slaney	Aug. 21, 1985	Zurich
2000 meters:	World	....5:25.36	**Sonia O'Sullivan**, Ireland	July 8, 1994	Edinburgh
	Olympic	....	Not an event	—	—
	American	.....5:32.7	Mary Slaney	Aug. 3, 1984	Eugene
3000 meters:	World	.....8:06.11	**Wang Junxia**, China	Sept. 13, 1993	Beijing
	Olympic	...8:26.53	Tatyana Samolenko, USSR	Sept. 25, 1988	Seoul
	American	.8:25.83	Mary Slaney	Sept. 7, 1985	Rome
5000 meters:	World	...14:28.09	**Jiang Bo**, China	Oct. 23, 1997	Shanghai
	Olympic	.14:40.79	Gabriela Szabo, Romania	Sept. 25, 2000	Sydney
	American	.14:45.35	Regina Jacobs	July 27, 2000	Sacramento
10,000 meters:	World	...29:31.78	**Wang Junxia**, China	Sept. 8, 1993	Beijing
	Olympic	.30:17.49	Derartu Tulu, Ethiopia	Sept. 30, 2000	Sydney
	American	.31:19.89	Lynn Jennings	Aug. 7, 1992	Barcelona
Marathon:	World	...2:20:43†	**Tegla Loroupe**, Kenya	Sept. 26, 1999	Berlin
	Olympic	..2:23:14	Naoko Takahashi, Japan	Sept. 24, 2000	Sydney
	American	..2:21:21	Joan Benoit Samuelson	Oct. 20, 1985	Chicago

Note: The Mile run is 1,609.344 meters and the Marathon is 42,194.988 meters (26 miles, 385 yards).

†Marathon records are not officially recognized by the IAAF.

Relays

Event		Time		Date Set	Location
4 x 100m:	**World**	.......41.37	**East Germany** (Gladisch, Rieger, Auerswald, Gohr)	Oct. 6, 1985	Canberra, AUS
	Olympic	......41.60	East Germany (Muller, Wockel, Auerswald, Gohr)	Aug. 1, 1980	Moscow
	American	.....41.47	USA (Gaines, Jones, Miller, Devers)	Aug. 9, 1997	Athens
4 x 200m:	**World**	.....1:27.46	**USA** (Jenkins, Colander-Richardson, Perry, Jones)	Apr. 29, 2000	Philadelphia
	Olympic	....	Not an event	—	—
	American	...1:27.46	USA (same as World)	—	—
4 x 400m:	**World**	.....3:15.17	**USSR** (Ledovskaya, Nazarova, Pinigina, Bryzgina)	Oct. 1, 1988	Seoul
	Olympic	....3:15.17	USSR (same as World)	—	—
	American	...3:15.51	USA (Howard, Dixon, Brisco, Griffith Joyner)	Oct. 1, 1988	Seoul
4 x 800m:	**World**	.....7:50.17	**USSR** (Olizarenko, Gurina, Borisova, Podyalovskaya)	Aug. 5, 1984	Moscow
	Olympic	....	Not an event	—	—
	American	...8:17.09	Athletics West (Addison, Arbogast, Decker Slaney, Mullen)	Apr. 24, 1983	Walnut, Calif.

Hurdles

Event		Time		Date Set	Location
100 meters:	**World**	......12.21	**Yordanka Donkova**, Bulgaria	Aug. 20, 1988	Stara Zagora, BUL
	Olympic	.....12.38	Yordanka Donkova, Bulgaria	Sept. 30, 1988	Seoul
	American	....12.33	Gail Devers	July 23, 2000	Sacramento
400 meters:	**World**	......52.61	**Kim Batten**, USA	Aug. 11, 1995	Göteborg, SWE
	Olympic	.....52.82	Deon Hemmings, Jamaica	July 31, 1996	Atlanta
	American	,...52.61	Batten (same as World)	—	—

Note: The 10 hurdles at 110 meters are 3 feet, 6 inches high and those at 400 meters are 3 feet.

Walking

Event		Time		Date Set	Location
20 km:	**World**	......1:26:52p	**Olimpiada Ivanova**, Russia	Sept. 6, 2001	Brisbane
	Olympic	.....1:29:05	Wang Liping, China	Sept. 28, 2000	Sydney
	American	....1:31:51	Michelle Rohl	May 13, 2000	Kenosha, Wis.

Steeplechase

Event		Time		Date Set	Location
3000 meters:	**World**	....9:25.31p	**Justyna Bak**, Poland	July 9, 2001	Nice
	Olympic	....	Not an event	—	—
	American	..9:41.94p	Elizabeth Jackson	Sept. 4, 2001	Brisbane

Note: A women's steeplechase course consists of 28 hurdles (30 inches high) and seven water jumps (10 feet long).

Field Events

Event		Mark		Date Set	Location
High Jump:	**World**	......6-10¼	**Stefka Kostadinova**, Bulgaria	Aug. 30, 1987	Rome
	Olympic	......6-8¾	Stefka Kostadinova, Bulgaria	Aug. 3, 1996	Atlanta
	American	6-8	Louise Ritter	July 8, 1988	Austin, Texas
Pole Vault:	**World**	......15-9¼p	**Stacy Dragila**, USA	June 9, 2001	Palo Alto, Calif
	Olympic	15-1	Stacy Dragila, USA	Sept. 25, 2000	Sydney
	American	...15-9¼p	Dragila (same as World)	—	—
Long Jump:	**World**	......24-8¼	**Galina Chistyakova**, USSR	June 11, 1988	Leningrad
	Olympic	....24-3¼	Jackie Joyner-Kersee, USA	Sept. 29, 1988	Seoul
	American	24-7	Jackie Joyner-Kersee	May 22, 1994	New York
Triple Jump:	**World**	....50-10¼	**Inessa Kravets**, Ukraine	Aug. 8, 1995	Göteborg, SWE
	Olympic	....50-3½	Inessa Kravets, Ukraine	July 31, 1996	Atlanta
	American	...47-3½	Sheila Hudson	July 8, 1996	Stockholm
Shot Put:	**World**	74-3	**Natalya Lisovskaya**, USSR	June 7, 1987	Moscow
	Olympic	....73-6¼	Ilona Slupianek, E. Germany	July 24, 1980	Moscow
	American	...66-2½	Ramona Pagel	June 25, 1988	San Diego
Discus:	**World**	252-0	**Gabriele Reinsch**, E. Germany	July 9, 1988	Neubrandenburg
	Olympic	....237-2½	Martina Hellmann, E. Germany	Sept. 29, 1988	Seoul
	American	.216-10	Carol Cady	May 31, 1986	San Jose
Javelin:	**World**	...234-8*p	**Osleidys Menendez**, Cuba	July 1, 2001	Rethymno, GRE
	Olympic	...226-1*	Trine Hattestad, Norway	Sept. 30, 2000	Sydney
	American	...192-3*	Lynda Blutriech	July 1, 2000	New Haven, Conn.
Hammer:	**World**	249-7	**Mihaela Melinte**, Romania	Aug. 29, 1999	Rudlingen, SWI
	Olympic	...233-5¾	Kamila Skolimowska, Poland	Sept. 29, 2000	Sydney
	American	...231-8p	Dawn Ellerbe	Apr. 28, 2001	Philadelphia

*The IAAF changed the official design and weight for the women's javelin beginning April 1, 1999. The records shown are with the new-style javelins.

Note: The international weights for women— **Shot** (8 lbs/13 oz); **Discus** (2 lbs/3.27 oz); **Javelin** (minimum 1 lb/5.16 oz); **Hammer** (8 lbs/13 oz).

Heptathlon

	Points		Date Set	Location
Seven Events:	**World** 7291	**Jackie Joyner-Kersee**, USA	Sept. 23-24, 1988	Seoul
	Olympic 7291	Joyner-Kersee (same as World)	—	—
	American 7291	Joyner-Kersee (same as World)	—	—

Note: Joyner-Kersee's WR times and distances, in order over two days— **100m H** (12.69); **HJ** (61¼); **Shot** (51-10); **200m** (22.56); **LJ** (2310¼); **Jav** (149-10); **800m** (2:08.51).

World and American Indoor Records

As of Sept. 20, 2001

World indoor records officially recognized by the International Amateur Athletics Federation (IAAF); (p) indicates record is pending ratification by the IAAF; (a) indicates record was set at an altitude over 1000 meters.

MEN
Running

Event	Time		Date Set	Location
50 meters:	**World**........5.56a	**Donovan Bailey**, Canada	Feb. 9, 1996	Reno, Nev.
	5.56p	**Maurice Greene**, USA	Feb. 13, 1999	Los Angeles
	American......5.56	Greene (same as World)	Feb. 13, 1999	Los Angeles
60 meters:	**World**........6.39	**Maurice Greene**, USA	Feb. 3, 1998	Madrid
	6.39p	**Maurice Greene**, USA	March 3, 2001	Atlanta
	American......6.39	Greene (same as World)	—	—
200 meters:	**World** 19.92	**Frankie Fredericks**, Namibia	Feb. 18, 1996	Lievin, FRA
	American 20.26	John Capel	Mar. 11, 2000	Fayetteville, Ark.
	20.26	Shawn Crawford	Mar. 11, 2000	Fayetteville, Ark.
400 meters:	**World** 44.63	**Michael Johnson**, USA	Mar. 4, 1995	Atlanta
	American 44.63	Johnson (same as World)	—	—
800 meters:	**World**....1:42.67	**Wilson Kipketer**, Denmark	Mar. 9, 1997	Paris
	American...1:45.00	Johnny Gray	Mar. 8, 1992	Sindelfingen, GER
1000 meters:	**World**....2:14.96	**Wilson Kipketer**, Denmark	Feb. 20, 2000	Birmingham, ENG
	American..2:18.19	Ocky Clark	Feb. 12, 1989	Stuttgart
1500 meters:	**World**....3:31.18	**Hicham El Guerrouj**, Morocco	Feb. 2, 1997	Stuttgart
	American...3:38.12	Jeff Atkinson	Mar. 5, 1989	Budapest
Mile:	**World**....3:48.45	**Hicham El Guerrouj**, Morocco	Feb. 12, 1997	Ghent, BEL
	American 3:51.8	Steve Scott	Feb. 20, 1981	San Diego
3000 meters:	World......7:24.90	**Daniel Komen**, Kenya	Feb. 6, 1998	Budapest
	American...7:39.94	Steve Scott	Feb. 10, 1989	E. Rutherford, N.J.
5000 meters:	**World** ...12:50.38	**Haile Gebrselassie**, Ethiopia	Feb. 14, 1999	Birmingham, ENG
	American .13:20.55	Doug Padilla	Feb. 12, 1982	New York

Note: The Mile run is 1,609.344 meters.

Hurdles

Event	Time		Date Set	Location
50 meters:	**World**........6.25	**Mark McKoy**, Canada	Mar. 5, 1986	Kobe, JPN
	American......6.35	Greg Foster	Jan. 27, 1985	Rosemont, Ill.
	6.35	Greg Foster	Jan. 31, 1987	Ottawa
60 meters:	**World**........7.30	**Colin Jackson**, Gr. Britain	Mar. 6, 1994	Sindelfingen, GER
	American......7.36	Greg Foster	Jan. 16, 1987	Los Angeles

Note: The hurdles for both distances are 3 feet, 6 inches high. There are four hurdles in the 50 meters and five in the 60.

Relays

Event	Time		Date Set	Location
4 x 200 meters:	**World**......1:22.11	**Great Britain**	Mar. 3, 1991	Glasgow
	American....1:22.71	National Team	Mar. 3, 1991	Glasgow
4 x 400 meters:	**World**......3:02.83	**United States**	Mar. 7, 1999	Maebashi, JPN
	American...3:02.83	National Team (same as World)	Mar. 7, 1999	Maebashi, JPN
4 x 800 meters:	**World**......7:13.94	**United States**	Feb. 6, 2000	Boston
	American...7:13.94	Global Athletics (same as World)	Feb. 6, 2000	Boston

Field Events

Event	Mark		Date Set	Location
High Jump:	**World** 7-11½	**Javier Sotomayor**, Cuba	Mar. 4, 1989	Budapest
	American 7-10½	Hollis Conway	Mar. 10, 1991	Seville
Pole Vault:	**World** 20-2	**Sergey Bubka**, Ukraine	Feb. 21, 1993	Donyetsk, UKR
	American...19-6½p	Lawrence Johnson, USA	Mar. 3, 2001	Atlanta
Long Jump:	**World**......28-10¼	**Carl Lewis**, USA	Jan. 27, 1984	New York
	American....28-10¼	Lewis (same as World)		
Triple Jump:	**World** 58-6	**Aliecer Urrutia**, Cuba	Mar. 1, 1997	Sindelfingen, GER
	American 58-3¼	Mike Conley	Feb. 27, 1987	New York
Shot Put:	**World** 74-4¼	**Randy Barnes**, USA	Jan. 20, 1989	Los Angeles
	American 74-4¼	Barnes (same as World)	—	—

Note: The international shot put weight for men is 16 lbs.

Heptathlon

	Points		Date Set	Location
Seven Events:	**World** 6476	**Dan O'Brien**, USA	Mar. 13-14, 1993	Toronto
	American 6476	O'Brien (same as World)	—	—

Note: O'Brien's WR times and distances, in order over two days— **60m** (6.67); **LJ** (25-8¾); **SP** (52-6¾); **HJ** (6-11¾); **60m H** (7.85); **PV** (17-0¾); **1000m** (2:57.96).

WOMEN
Running

Event	Time		Date Set	Location
50 meters:	**World**........5.96	**Irina Privalova**, Russia	Feb. 9, 1995	Madrid
	American......6.02	Gail Devers	Feb. 21, 1999	Lievin, FRA
60 meters:	**World**........6.92	**Irina Privalova**, Russia	Feb. 11, 1993	Madrid
	6.92	**Irina Privalova**, Russia	Feb. 9, 1995	Madrid
	American......6.95	Gail Devers	Mar. 12, 1993	Toronto
	6.95	Marion Jones	Mar. 7, 1998	Maebashi, JPN
200 meters:	**World** 21.87	**Merlene Ottey**, Jamaica	Feb. 13, 1993	Lievin, FRA
	American 22.33	Gwen Torrence	Mar. 2, 1996	Atlanta
400 meters:	**World** 49.59	**Jarmila Kratochvilova**, Czech.	Mar. 7, 1982	Milan
	American 50.64	Diane Dixon	Mar. 10, 1991	Seville
800 meters:	**World**......1:56.4*	**Christine Wachtel**, E. Germany	Feb. 13, 1988	Vienna
	American ...1:58.9	Mary Slaney	Feb. 22, 1980	San Diego
	1:58.92p	Suzy Hamilton	Feb. 7, 1999	Boston
1000 meters:	**World**.....2:30.94	**Maria Mutola**, Mozambique	Feb. 25, 1999	Stockholm
	American ...2:35.29	Regina Jacobs	Feb. 6, 2000	Boston
1500 meters:	**World**....4:00.27	**Doina Melinte**, Romania	Feb. 9, 1990	E. Rutherford, N.J.
	American....4:00.8	Mary Slaney	Feb. 8, 1980	New York
Mile:	**World**....4:17.14	**Doina Melinte**, Romania	Feb. 9, 1990	E. Rutherford, N.J.
	American....4:20.5	Mary Slaney	Feb. 19, 1982	San Diego
3000 meters:	**World**....8:32.88	**Gabriela Szabo**, Romania	Feb. 18, 2001	Birmingham, ENG
	American ...8:39.14	Regina Jacobs	Mar. 7, 1999	Maebashi, JPN
5000 meters:	**World** ...14:47.35	**Gabriela Szabo**, Romania	Feb. 13, 1999	Dortmund, GER
	American .15:07.33p	Marla Runyan	Feb. 18, 2001	New York City

Note: The Mile run is 1,609.344 meters.
*Maria Mutola's apparent record of 1:56.36 in February 1998 was not ratified by the IAAF because she ran outside of her lane on the final turn.

Hurdles

Event	Time		Date Set	Location
50 meters:	**World** ,,,,,6.58	**Cornelia Oschkenat**, E. Ger.	Feb. 20, 1988	East Berlin
	American......6.67a	Jackie Joyner-Kersee	Feb. 10, 1995	Reno, Nev.
60 meters:	**World**.......7.69	**Ludmila Engquist**, USSR	Feb. 4, 1990	Chelyabinsk, USSR
	American......7.81	Jackie Joyner-Kersee	Feb. 5, 1989	Fairfax, Va.

Note: The hurdles for both distances are 2 feet, 9 inches high. There are four hurdles in the 50 meters and five in the 60.

Walking

Event	Time		Date Set	Location
3000 meters:	**World** 11:40.33	**Claudia Iovan**, Romania	Jan. 30, 1999	Bucharest
	American...12:20.79	Debbi Lawrence	Mar. 12, 1993	Toronto

Relays

Event	Time		Date Set	Location
4 x 200 meters:	**World**.....1:32.55	**West Germany**	Feb. 20, 1988	Dortmund, W. Ger.
	1:32.55	Germany	Feb. 21, 1999	Karlsruhe, GER
	American ...1:33.24	National Team	Feb. 12, 1994	Glasgow
4 x 400 meters:	**World**....3:24.25	**Russia**	Mar. 7, 1999	Maebashi, JPN
	American...3:27.59	National Team	Mar. 7, 1999	Maebashi, JPN
4 x 800 meters:	**World**....8:18.71	**Russia**	Feb. 4, 1994	Moscow
	American....8:25.5p	Villanova	Feb. 7, 1987	Gainesville, Fla.

Field Events

Event	Mark		Date Set	Location
High Jump:	**World** 6-9½	**Heike Henkel**, Germany	Feb. 9, 1992	Karlsruhe, GER
	American 6-7	Tisha Waller	Feb. 28, 1998	Atlanta
Pole Vault:	**World**........15-5p	**Stacy Dragila** USA	Feb. 17, 2001	Pocatello, Idaho
	American ...15-5p	Dragila (same as World)	—	—
Long Jump:	**World**......24-2¼	**Heike Drechsler**, E. Germany	Feb. 13, 1988	Vienna
	American ...23-4¾	Jackie Joyner-Kersee	Mar. 5, 1994	Atlanta
Triple Jump:	**World**......49-9	**Ashia Hansen**, Great Britain	Feb. 28, 1998	Valencia, SPA
	American ...46-8¼	Sheila Hudson	Mar. 4, 1995	Atlanta
Shot Put:	**World**......73-10	**Helena Fibingerova**, Czech.	Feb. 19, 1977	Jablonec, CZE
	American ...65-0¾	Ramona Pagel	Feb. 20, 1987	Inglewood, Calif.

Note: The international shotput weight for women is 8 lbs. and 13 oz.

Pentathlon

Five Events:	Points		Date Set	Location
	World 4991	**Irina Byelova**, Russia	Feb. 14-15, 1992	Berlin
	American 4753	DeDee Nathan	Mar. 4-5, 1999	Maebashi, JPN

Note: Byelova's WR times and distances, in order over two days– **60m H** (8.22); **HJ** (6-4); **SP** (43-5¾); **LJ** (21-1¾); **800m** (2:10.26).

SWIMMING

2001 FINA World Championships

The 9th FINA World Championships in swimming, diving, synchronized swimming and water polo held in Fukuoka, Japan, July 16-29, 2001. Note that (WR) indicates world record and (CR) indicates championship meet record.

Final Medal Leaders

		G	S	B	Total			G	S	B	Total
1	United States	9	9	8	26	7	Italy	2	2	2	6
2	Australia	13	3	3	19		Sweden	1	3	2	6
3	Germany	3	6	6	15		Russia	1	2	3	6
4	Netherlands	3	4	0	7	10	Ukraine	3	1	0	4
	China	2	2	3	7		Romania	1	1	2	4
	Great Britain	1	2	4	7		Japan	0	0	4	4

MEN

Event		Time	
50m free	Anthony Ervin, USA	22.09	
100m free	Anthony Ervin, USA	48.33	**CR**
200m free	Ian Thorpe, AUS	1:44.06	**WR**
400m free	Ian Thorpe, AUS	3:40.17	**WR**
800m free	Ian Thorpe, AUS	7:39.16	**WR**
1500m free	Grant Hackett, AUS	14:34.56	**WR**
50m back	Randall Bal, USA	25.34	
100m back	Matt Welsh, AUS	54.31	**CR**
200m back	Aaron Peirsol, USA	1:57.13	**CR**
50m breast	Oleg Lisogor, UKR	27.52	
100m breast	Roman Sloudnov, RUS	1:00.16	
200m breast	Brendan Hansen, USA	2:10.69	**CR**
50m fly	Geoff Huegill, AUS	23.50	
100m fly	Lars Frolander, SWE	52.10	**CR**
200m fly	Michael Phelps, USA	1:54.58	**WR**
200m I.M.	Massimiliano Rosolino, ITA	1:59.71	
400m I.M.	Alessio Boggiatto, ITA	4:13.15	

Men's Relays

Event		Time	
4x100m free	Australia (Klim, Callus, Pearson, Thorpe)	3:14.10	**CR**
4x200m free	Australia (Hackett, Klim, Kirby, Thorpe)	7:04.66	**WR**
4x100m medley	Australia (Welsh, Harrison, Huegill, Thorpe)	3:35.35	**CR**

WOMEN

Event		Time	
50m free	Inge de Bruijn, NED	24.47	
100m free	Inge de Bruijn, NED	54.18	
200m free	Giaan Rooney, AUS	1:58.57	
400m free	Yana Klochkova, UKR	4:07.30	
800m free	Hannah Stockbauer, GER	8:24.66	
1500m free	Hannah Stockbauer, GER	16:01.02	
50m back	Haley Cope, USA	28.51	
100m back	Natalie Coughlin, USA	1:00.37	
200m back	Diana Iuliana Mocanu, ROM	2:09.94	
50m breast	Xuejuan Luo, CHN	30.84	
100m breast	Xuejuan Luo, CHN	1:07.18	**CR**
200m breast	Agnes Kovacs, HUN	2:24.90	**CR**
50m fly	Inge de Bruijn, NED	25.90	
100m fly	Petria Thomas, AUS	58.27	**CR**
200m fly	Petria Thomas, AUS	2:06.73	**CR**
200m I.M.	Maggie Bowen, USA	2:11.93	
400m I.M.	Yana Klochkova, UKR	4:36.98	

Women's Relays

Event		Time	
4x100m free	Germany (Dallmann, Buschschulte, Meissmer, Volker)	3:39.58	
4x200m free	Great Britain (Jackson, Belton, Legg, Pickering)	7:58.69	
4x100m medley	Australia (Calub, Jones, Thomas, Ryan)	4:01.50	**CR**

Diving

Men

Event		Points
1-meter Springboard	Wang Feng, CHN	444.03
3-meter Springboard	Dmitri Sautin, RUS	725.82
10-meter Platform	Tian Liang, CHN	688.77
3-meter Springboard (Synchronized)	Peng Bo & Wang Kenan, CHN	342.63
10-meter Platform (Synchronized)	Tian Liang & Hu Jia, CHN	361.41

Women

Event		Points
1-meter Springboard	Blythe Hartley, CAN	300.81
3-meter Springboard	Guo Jingjing, CHN	596.67
10-meter Platform	Xu Mian, CHN	532.65
3-meter Springboard (Synchronized)	Wu Minxia & Guo Jingjing, CHN	347.31
10-meter Platform (Synchronized)	Duan Qing & Sang Xue, CHN	329.94

Synchronized Swimming

Event		Points
Solo	Olga Brousnikina, RUS	99.434
Duet	Miya Tachibana & Miho Takeda, JPN	98.910
Team	Russia	98.917

Water Polo

Men's Final: Spain 4 ....Yugoslavia 2
Women's Final: Italy 7 ....Hungary 3

World, Olympic and American Records
As of September 20, 2001

World long course records officially recognized by the Federation Internationale de Natation Amateur (FINA). Note that (p) indicates preliminary heat; (r) relay lead-off split; and (s) indicates split time. Note that (*) denotes that a record is awaiting ratification.

MEN
Freestyle

Distance		Time		Date Set	Location
50 meters:	World	21.64	Aleksandr Popov, Russia	June 16, 2000	Moscow
	Olympic	21.91	Aleksandr Popov, Unified Team	July 30, 1992	Barcelona
	American	21.76	Gary Hall Jr.	Aug. 15, 2000	Indianapolis
100 meters:	World	47.84p	P. van den Hoogenband, Netherlands	Sept. 19, 2000	Sydney
	Olympic	47.84	P. van den Hoogenband, NED (same as World)	—	—
	American	48.33	Anthony Ervin	July 27, 2001	Fukuoka, JPN
200 meters:	World	1:44.06*	Ian Thorpe, Australia	July 25, 2001	Fukuoka, JPN
	Olympic	1:45.35	P. van den Hoogenband, NED	Sept. 18, 2000	Sydney
	American	1:46.73	Josh Davis	Sept. 18, 2000	Sydney
400 meters:	World	3:40.17*	Ian Thorpe, Australia	July 22, 2001	Fukuoka, JPN
	Olympic	3:40.59	Ian Thorpe, Australia	Sept. 16, 2000	Sydney
	American	3:47.00	Klete Keller	Sept. 16, 2000	Sydney
800 meters:	World	7:39.16*	Ian Thorpe, Australia	July 24, 2001	Fukuoka, JPN
	Olympic		Not an event	—	—
	American	7:52.45	Sean Killion	July 27, 1987	Clovis, Calif.
1500 meters:	World	14:34.56*	Grant Hackett, Australia	July 29, 2001	Fukuoka, JPN
	Olympic	14:43.48	Kieren Perkins, Australia	July 31, 1992	Barcelona
	American	14:56.81	Chris Thompson	Sept. 23, 2000	Sydney

Backstroke

Distance		Time		Date Set	Location
50 meters:	World	24.99	Lenny Krayzelburg, USA	Aug. 28, 1999	Sydney
	Olympic		Not an event	—	—
	American	24.99	Krayzelburg (same as World)	—	—
100 meters:	World	53.60	Lenny Krayzelburg, USA	Aug. 24, 1999	Sydney
	Olympic	53.72	Lenny Krayzelburg, USA	Sept. 18, 2000	Sydney
	American	53.60	Krayzelburg (same as World)	—	—
200 meters:	World	1:55.87	Lenny Krayzelburg, USA	Aug. 27, 1999	Sydney
	Olympic	1:56.76	Lenny Krayzelburg, USA	Sept. 21, 2000	Sydney
	American	1:55.87	Krayzelburg (same as World)	—	—

Breaststroke

Distance		Time		Date Set	Location
50 meters:	World	27.39	Ed Moses, USA	Mar. 31, 2001	Austin, Texas
	Olympic		Not an event	—	—
	American	27.39	Moses (same as World)	—	—
100 meters:	World	59.94*	Roman Sloudnov, Russia	July 23, 2001	Fukuoka, JPN
	Olympic	1:00.46	Domenico Fioravanti, Italy	Sept. 17, 2000	Sydney
	American	1:00.29	Ed Moses	Mar. 28, 2001	Austin, Texas
200 meters:	World	2:10.16	Mike Barrowman, USA	July 29, 1992	Barcelona
	Olympic	2:10.16	Barrowman (same as World)	—	—
	American	2:10.16	Barrowman (same as World)	—	—

Butterfly

Distance		Time		Date Set	Location
50 meters:	World	23.44*	Geoff Huegill, Australia	July 26, 2001	Fukuoka, JPN
	Olympic		Not an event	—	—
	American	23.85	Ian Crocker	July 26, 2001	Fukuoka, JPN
100 meters:	World	51.81	Michael Klim, Australia	Dec. 12, 1999	Canberra, AUS
	Olympic	51.96p	Geoff Huegill, Australia	Sept. 21, 2000	Sydney
	American	52.25	Ian Crocker	July 26, 2001	Fukuoka, JPN
200 meters:	World	1:54.58*	Michael Phelps, USA	July 24, 2001	Fukuoka, JPN
	Olympic	1:55.35	Tom Malchow, USA	Sept. 19, 2000	Sydney
	American	1:54.58	Phelps (same as World)	July 24, 2001	Fukuoka, JPN

Individual Medley

Distance		Time		Date Set	Location
200 meters:	World	1:58.16	Jani Sievinen, Finland	Sept. 11, 1994	Rome
	Olympic	1:58.98	Massimiliano Rosolino, ITA	Sept. 21, 2000	Sydney
	American	1:59.77	Tom Dolan	Sept. 21, 2000	Sydney
400 meters:	World	4:11.76	Tom Dolan, USA	Sept. 17, 2000	Sydney
	Olympic	4:11.76	Dolan (same as World)	—	—
	American	4:11.76	Dolan (same as World)	—	—

Relays

Distance	Time		Date Set	Location
4x100m free:	**World**....3:13.67	**Australia** (Klim, Fydler, Callus, Thorpe)	Sept. 16, 2000	Sydney
	Olympic....3:13.67	Australia (same as world)	—	—
	American...3:13.86	USA (Ervin, Walker, Lezak, Hall Jr.)	Sept. 16, 2000	Sydney
4x200m free:	**World**....7:04.66*	**Australia** (Hackett, Klim, Kirby, Thorpe)	July 27, 2001	Fukuoka, JPN
	Olympic...7:07.05	**Australia** (Thorpe, Klim, Pearson, Kirby)	Sept. 19, 2000	Sydney
	American...7:12.51	USA (Dalbey, Cetlinski, Gjertsen, Biondi)	Sept. 21, 1988	Seoul
4x100m medley:	**World**....3:33.73	**USA** (Krayzelburg, Moses, Crocker, Hall Jr.)	Sept. 23, 2000	Sydney
	Olympic...3:33.73	USA (same as World)	—	—
	American...3:33.73	USA (same as World)	—	—

WOMEN
Freestyle

Distance	Time		Date Set	Location
50 meters:	**World** 24.13p	**Inge de Bruijn**, Netherlands	Sept. 22, 2000	Sydney
	Olympic 24.13	de Bruijn (same as World)	—	—
	American 24.63	Dara Torres	Sept. 23, 2000	Sydney
100 meters:	**World** 53.77p	**Inge de Bruijn**, Netherlands	Sept. 20, 2000	Sydney
	Olympic 53.77	de Bruijn (same as World)	—	—
	American 54.07	Jenny Thompson	Aug. 14, 2000	Indianapolis
200 meters:	**World**....1:56.78	**Franziska Van Almsick**, Ger.	Sept. 6, 1994	Rome
	Olympic...1:57.65	Heike Friedrich, E. Germany	Sept. 21, 1988	Seoul
	American...1:57.90	Nicole Haislett	July 27, 1992	Barcelona
400 meters:	**World**....4:03.85	**Janet Evans**, USA	Sept. 22, 1988	Seoul
	Olympic...4:03.85	Evans (same as World)	—	—
	American...4:03.85	Evans (same as World)	—	—
800 meters:	**World**....8:16.22	**Janet Evans**, USA	Aug. 20, 1989	Tokyo
	Olympic...8:19.67	Brooke Bennett, USA	Sept. 22, 2000	Sydney
	American...8:16.22	Evans (same as World)	—	—
1500 meters:	**World** ...15:52.10	**Janet Evans**, USA	Mar. 26, 1988	Orlando
	Olympic...........	Not an event	—	—
	American .15:52.10	Evans (same as World)	—	—

Backstroke

Distance	Time		Date Set	Location
50 meters:	**World** 28.25	**Sandra Volker**, Germany	June 17, 2000	Berlin
	Olympic...........	Not an event	—	—
	American 28.45	Natalie Coughlin	July 23, 2001	Fukuoka, JPN
100 meters:	**World** 1:00.16r	**He Cihong**, China	Sept. 10, 1994	Rome
	Olympic...1:00.21	Diana Mocanu, Romania	Sept. 18, 2000	Sydney
	American...1:00.18	Natalie Coughlin	July 28, 2001	Fukuoka, JPN
200 meters:	**World**....2:06.62	**Krisztina Egerszegi**, Hungary	Aug. 25, 1991	Athens
	Olympic...2:07.06	Krisztina Egerszegi, Hungary	July 31, 1992	Barcelona
	American...2:08.60	Betsy Mitchell	June 27, 1986	Orlando

Breaststroke

Distance	Time		Date Set	Location
50 meters:	**World** 30.83	**Penny Heyns**, South Africa	Aug. 28, 1999	Sydney
	Olympic............	Not an event	—	—
	American 31.34p	Megan Quann	Aug. 11, 2000	Indianapolis
100 meters:	**World**....1:06.52p	**Penny Heyns**, South Africa	Aug. 23, 1999	Sydney
	Olympic...1:07.02	Penny Heyns, South Africa	July 21, 1996	Atlanta
	American...1:07.05	Megan Quann	Sept. 18, 2000	Sydney
200 meters:	**World**....2:22.99*	**Hui Qi**, China	Apr. 13, 2001	Hangzhou, China
	Olympic...2:24.35	Agnes Kovacs, Hungary	Sept. 21, 2000	Sydney
	American...2:24.56	Kristy Kowal	Sept. 21, 2000	Sydney

Butterfly

Distance	Time		Date Set	Location
50 meters:	**World** 25.64	**Inge de Bruijn**, Netherlands	May 27, 2000	Sheffield, GBR
	Olympic............	Not an event	—	—
	American 25.50p	Dara Torres	Aug. 9, 2000	Indianapolis
100 meters:	**World** 56.61	**Inge de Bruijn**, Netherlands	Sept. 17, 2000	Sydney
	Olympic 56.61	de Bruijn (same as World)	—	—
	American 57.58p	Dara Torres	Aug. 9, 2000	Indianapolis

Distance	Time		Date Set	Location
200 meters:	**World**....2:05.81	**Susan O'Neill**, Australia	May 17, 2000	Sydney
	Olympic....2:05.88	Misty Hyman, USA	Sept. 20, 2000	Sydney
	American...2:05.88	Misty Hyman	Sept. 20, 2000	Sydney

Individual Medley

Distance	Time		Date Set	Location
200 meters:	**World**.....2:09.72	**Wu Yanyan**, China	Oct. 17, 1997	Shanghai
	Olympic.....2:10.68	Yana Klochkova, Ukraine	Sept. 19, 2000	Sydney
	American....2:11.91	Summer Sanders	July 30, 1992	Barcelona
400 meters:	**World**.....4:33.59	**Yana Klochkova**, Ukraine	Sept. 16, 2000	Sydney
	Olympic.....4:33.59	Klochkova, UKR (same as World)	–	–
	American....4:37.58	Summer Sanders	July 26, 1992	Barcelona

Relays

Distance	Time		Date Set	Location
4x100m free:	**World**......3:36.61	**USA** (Van Dyken, Torres, Shealy, Thompson)	Sept. 16, 2000	Sydney
	Olympic.....3:36.61	USA (same as World)	–	–
	American...3:36.61	USA (same as World)	–	–
4x200m free:	**World**.....7:55.47	**E. Germany** (Stellmach, Strauss, Mohring, Friedrich)	Aug. 18, 1987	Strasbourg, FRA
	Olympic 7:57.80	USA (Arsenault, Munz, Benko, Thompson)	Sept. 20, 2000	Sydney
	American....7:57.61	USA (Benko, Stonebraker, Thompson, Teuscher)	Aug. 26, 1999	Sydney
4x100m medley:	**World**.....3:58.30	**USA** (Bedford, Quann, Thompson, Torres)	Sept. 23, 2000	Sydney
	Olympic....3:58.30	USA (same as World)	–	–
	American...3:58.30	USA (same as World)	–	–

WINTER SPORTS

Alpine Skiing
2001 World Cup Champions

MEN

Overall	Hermann Maier, Austria
Downhill	Hermann Maier, Austria
Slalom	Benjamin Raich, Austria
Giant Slalom	Hermann Maier, Austria
Super G	Hermann Maier, Austria
Combined	Lasse Kjus, Norway

WOMEN

Overall	Janica Kostelic, Croatia
Downhill	Isolde Kostner, Italy
Slalom	Janica Kostelic, Croatia
Giant Slalom	Sonja Nef, Switzerland
Super G	Regine Cavagnoud, France
Combined	Janica Kostelic, Croatia

Top Five Standings

Overall 1. Hermann Maier, AUT (1618 pts); 2. Stephan Eberharter, AUT (875); 3. Lasse Kjus, NOR (866); 4. Benjamin Raich, AUT (865); 5. Michael Von Gruenigen, SWI (743). *Best USA—* Erik Schlopy, USA (15th, 434 pts).

Downhill 1. Hermann Maier, AUT (576 pts); 2. Stephan Eberharter, AUT (562); 3. Fritz Strobl, AUT (402); 4. Hannes Trinkl, AUT (313); 5. Lasse Kjus, NOR (301). *Best USA—* Daron Rahlves (15th, 149 pts).

Slalom 1. Benjamin Raich, AUT (545 pts); 2. Heinz Schilchegger, AUT (414); 3. Mario Matt, AUT (406); 4. Pierrick Bourgeat, FRA (368); 5. Hans-Peter Buraas, NOR (340). *Best USA—* Erik Schlopy (22nd, 84 pts).

Giant Slalom 1. Hermann Maier, AUT (622 pts); 2. Michael Von Gruenigen, SWI (612); 3. Erik Schlopy, USA (350); 4. Benjamin Raich, AUT (320); 5.Heinz Schilchegger, AUT (316).

Super G 1. Hermann Maier, AUT (420 pts); 2. Christoph Gruber, AUT (246); 3. Josef Strobl, AUT (228); 4. Stephan Eberharter, AUT (208); 5. Werner Franz, AUT (182). *Best USA—* Daron Rahlves (17th, 70 pts).

Combined 1. Lasse Kjus, NOR (100 pts); 2. Michael Walchhhofer, AUT (80); 3. Kjetil Andre Aamodt, NOR (60); 4. Casey Puckett, USA (50); 5. Paul Accola, SWI (45).

Top Five Standings

Overall 1. Janica Kostelic, CRO (1256 pts); 2. Renate Goetschl, AUT (1189); 3. Regine Cavagnoud, FRA (1105); 4. Sonja Nef, SWI (1060); 5. Michaela Dorfmeister, AUT (923). *Best USA—* Kristina Koznick (17th, 371 pts).

Downhill 1. Isolde Kostner, ITA (596 pts); 2. Renate Goetschl, AUT (455); 3. Regine Cavagnoud, FRA (360); 4. Carole Montillet, FRA (297); 5. Brigitte Obermoser, AUT (295). *Best USA—* Megan Gerety (10th, 204 pts).

Slalom 1. Janica Kostelic, CRO (824 pts); 2. Sonja Nef, SWI (384); 3. Martina Ertl, GER (346); 4. Karin Koellerer, AUT (340); 5. Kristina Koznick (7th, 300 pts). *Best USA—*

Giant Slalom 1. Sonja Nef, SWI (676 pts); 2. Anja Paerson, SWE (408); 3. Michaela Dorfmeister, AUT (341); 4. Karen Putzer, ITA (297); 5. Corinne Rey Bellet, SWI (265). *Best USA—* Sarah Schleper (21st, 106 pts).

Super G 1. Regine Cavagnoud, FRA (577 pts); 2. Renate Goetschl, AUT (466); 3. Carole Montillet, FRA (405); 4. Melanie Turgeon, CAN (364); 5. Michaela Dorfmeister, AUT (332). *Best USA—* Kirsten L. Clark (22nd, 99 pts).

Combined 1. Janica Kostelic, CRO (100 pts); 2. Caroline Lalive, USA (80); 3. Renate Goetschl, AUT (60); 4. Karen Putzer, ITA (50); 5. Pia Kaeyhkoe, FIN (45).

Alpine Skiing (Cont.)
2001 World Championships
at St. Anton, Austria (Jan. 29-Feb. 10)

MEN

Downhill — **Time**
1 Hannes Trinkl, AUT 1:38.74
2 Hermann Maier, AUT 1:38.94
3 Florian Eckert, GER 1:39.26

Slalom — **Time**
1 Mario Matt, AUT 1:39.66
2 Benjamin Raich, AUT 1:39.81
3 Mitja Kunc, SLO 1:40.36

Giant Slalom — **Time**
1 Michael Von Gruenigen, SWI 2:23.80
2 Kjetil Andre Aamodt, NOR 2:24.15
3 Frederic Covili, FRA 2:24.18

Super G — **Time**
1 Daron Rahlves, USA 1:21.46
2 Stephan Eberharter, AUT 1:21.54
3 Hermann Maier, AUT 1:21.69

Combined — **Time**
1 Kjetil Andre Aamodt, NOR 2:58.25
2 Mario Matt, AUT 2:58.93
3 Paul Accola, SWI 2:59.53

WOMEN

Downhill — **Time**
1 Michaela Dorfmeister, AUT 1:36.20
2 Renate Goetschl, AUT......................1:36.34
3 Selina Heregger, AUT......................1:36.37

Slalom — **Time**
1 Anja Paerson, SWE 1:32.95
2 Christel Saioni, FRA 1:33.56
3 Hedda Bernsten, NOR 1:33.99

Giant Slalom — **Time**
1 Sonja Nef, SWI............................2:19.01
2 Karen Putzer, ITA..........................2:20.11
3 Anja Paerson, SWE 2:20.52

Super G — **Time**
1 Regine Cavagnoud, FRA 1:23.44
2 Isolde Kostner, ITA.........................1:23.49
3 Hilde Gerg, GER...........................1:23.52

Combined — **Time**
1 Martina Ertl, GER 2:55.65
2 Christine Sponring, AUT....................2:58.23
3 Karen Putzer, ITA..........................2:58.69

Freestyle Skiing
World Cup Champions

MEN

Overall ....Mikko Ronkainen, Finland
Aerials ....Eric Bergoust, United States
Moguls ....Mikko Ronkainen, Finland

WOMEN

Overall ....Jacqui Cooper, Australia
Aerials ....Jacqui Cooper, Australia
Moguls ....Kari Traa, Norway

2001 World Championships
at Whistler, British Columbia, Canada (Jan. 17-21)

MEN

Moguls — **Pts**
1 Mikko Ronkainen, FIN 28.07
2 Pierre-Alexander Rousseau, CAN..............26.64
3 Stephane Rochon, CAN.....................26.25

Aerials — **Pts**
1 Alexei Grichin, BLR 226.46
2 Dmitri Dashinski, BLR 225.90
3 Joe Pack, USA.............................221.60

Dual Moguls
1 Stephane Yonnet, FRA
2 Patrick Sundberg, SWE
3 Johann Gregoire, FRA

WOMEN

Moguls — **Pts**
1 Kari Traa, NOR............................25.89
2 Maria Despas, AUS 24.94
3 Aiko Uemura, JPN 24.87

Aerials — **Pts**
1 Veronica Bauer, CAN 184.41
2 Michelle Rohrbach, SWI....................172.59
3 Deidra Dionne, CAN.......................172.53

Dual Moguls
1 Kari Traa, NOR
2 Corinne Bodner, SWI
3 Tami Bradley, CAN

Nordic Skiing
2001 World Championships
at Lahti, Finland (Feb. 15-25)

MEN

Sprints
1 Tor Arne Hetland, NOR
2 Cristian Zorzi, ITA
3 Haavard Solbakken, NOR

10-k Classic
		Time
1	Mika Myllyla, FIN	24:20.6
2	Per Elofsson, SWE	24:26.1
3	Janne Immonen, FIN	24:32.7

10-k Pursuit
		Time
1	Per Elofsson, SWE	47:15.5
2	Johann Muehlegg, SPA	47:42.0
3	Vitalij Denisov, RUS	47:49.5

15-k Classic
		Time
1	Per Elofsson, SWE	39:26.0
2	Mathias Fredriksson, SWE	39:42.5
3	Odd-Bjorn Hjelmeset, NOR	39:49.3

30-k Classic
		Time
1	Andrus Veerpalu, EST	1:14:17.9
2	Frode Estil, NOR	1:14:18.1
3	Mikhail Ivanov, RUS	1:14:49.1

50-k Freestyle
		Time
1	Johann Muehlegg, SPA	2:05:27.2
2	Rene Sommerfeldt, GER	2:07:23.4
3	Sergei Krianin, RUS	2:07:28.4

4 x 10-k Relay
		Time
1	Norway	1:36:42.5
2	Sweden	1:37:25.2
3	Germany	1:37:30.5

WOMEN

Sprints
1 Pirjo Manninen, FIN
2 Kati Sundqvist, FIN
3 Julija Tchepalova, RUS

5-k Classic
		Time
1	Bente Skari, NOR	14:54.3
2	Virpi Kuitunen, FIN	14:56.8
3	Larissa Lazutina, RUS	15:00.0

5-k Pursuit
		Time
1	Virpi Kuitunen, FIN	28:06.1
2	Larissa Lazutina, RUS	28:08.9
3	Olga Danilova, RUS	28:09.3

10-k Classic
		Time
1	Bente Skari, NOR	26:55.5
2	Olga Danilova, RUS	27:08.4
3	Larissa Lazutina, RUS	27:27.0

15-k Classic
		Time
1	Bente Skari, NOR	43:54.8
2	Olga Danilova, RUS	44:02.5
3	Kaisa Varis, FIN	44:57.5

4 x 5-k Relay
		Time
1	Russia	53:01.6
2	Norway	54:01.9
3	Italy	54:23.3

Note: The women's 30-k Freestyle was cancelled due to inclement weather.

Nordic Combined
90-meter jump/15-k cross country ski

Individual
		Behind
1	Bjarte Engen Vik, NOR	—
2	Samppa Lajunen, FIN	+1:04.6
3	Felix Gottwald, AUT	+1:10.3

Individual Sprint
(116-m jump/7.5 k sprint)
		Behind
1	Marco Baacke, GER	—
2	Samppa Lajunen, FIN	+6.2
3	Ronny Ackermann, GER	+9.7

Team
		Behind
1	Norway	—
2	Austria	+8.9
3	Finland	+29.4

Note: Jumping points are converted into time differences.

Ski Jumping

Large Hill (116 meters)
		Pts
1	Martin Schmitt, GER	276.3
2	Adam Malysz, POL	273.5
3	Janne Ahonen, FIN	267.4

Normal Hill (90 meters)
		Pts
1	Adam Malysz, POL	246.0
2	Martin Schmitt, GER	233.0
3	Martin Hoellwarth, AUT	223.0

Team (116 meters)
		Pts
1	Germany	939.8
2	Finland	900.2
3	Austria	880.2

Team (90 meters)
		Pts
1	Austria	953.5
2	Finland	951.5
3	Germany	911.5

Cross Country World Cup Champions

MEN

Overall
		Pts
1	Per Elofsson, Sweden	763
2	Johann Muehlegg, Spain	603
3	Thomas Alsgaard, Norway	474
4	Pietro Piller Cottrer, Italy	456
5	Odd-Bjorn Hjelmeset, Norway	439

Sprint
		Pts
1	Jan Jacob Verdenius, Norway	321
2	Cristian Zorzi, Italy	288
3	Tor Arne Hetland, Norway	239
4	Morten Broers, Norway	214
5	Trond Einar Elden, Norway	212

WOMEN

Overall
		Pts
1	Julija Tchepalova, Russia	1106
2	Bente Skari, Norway	990
3	Larissa Lazutina, Russia	893
4	Stefania Belmondo, Italy	785
5	Olga Savialova, Russia	529

Sprint
		Pts
1	Bente Skari, Norway	430
2	Pirjo Manninen, Finland	380
3	Manuela Henkel, Germany	259
4	Anita Moen, Norway	256
	Julija Tchepalova, Russia	256

Nordic Skiing (Cont.)

Nordic Combined
World Cup Champions
MEN

Overall	Pts
1 Felix Gottwald, Austria	1785
2 Ronny Ackermann, Germany	1342
3 Bjarte Engen Vik, Norway	1209
4 Kristian Hammer, Norway	1195
5 Samppa Lajunen, Finland	1010

Sprint	Pts
1 Felix Gottwald, Austria	750
2 Ronny Ackermann, Germany	572
3 Kristian Hammer, Norway	435
4 Samppa Lajunen, Finland	392
5 Marko Baacke, Germany	376

Ski Jumping
World Cup Champions
MEN

Overall	Pts
1 Adam Malysz, Poland	1531
2 Martin Schmitt, Germany	1173
3 Risto Jussilainen, Finland	938
4 Noriaki Kasai, Japan	728
5 Janne Ahonen, Finland	686

Snowboarding
World Cup Champions

MEN

Overall	Jasey Jay Anderson, Canada
Halfpipe	Magnus Sterner, Sweden
Parallel Slalom	Mathieu Bozzetto, France
Giant Slalom	Walter Feichter, Italy
Snowboardcross	Pontus Stahlkloo, Sweden

WOMEN

Overall	Karine Ruby, France
Halfpipe	Sabine Wehr-Hasler, Germany
Parallel Slalom	Carmen Ranigler, Italy
Giant Slalom	Karine Ruby, France
Snowboardcross	Karine Ruby, France

2001 World Championships
at Madonna di Campiglio, Italy (Jan. 21-28)

MEN

Halfpipe	Parallel Slalom	Giant Slalom	Parallel Giant Slalom	Snowboardcross
1 Kim Christiansen, NOR	1 Nicolas Huet, FRA	1 Jasey Jay Anderson, CAN	1 Gilles Jaquet, SWI	1 Guillaume Nantermod, SWI
2 Daniel Franck, NOR	2 Mathieu Chiquet, FRA	2 Dejan Kosir, SLO	2 Daniel Biveson, SWE	2 Markus Ebner, GER
3 Markus Hurme, FIN	3 Anton Pogue, USA	3 Walter Feichter, ITA	3 Stefan Kaltschuetz, AUT	3 Alexander Maier, AUT

WOMEN

Halfpipe	Parallel Slalom	Giant Slalom	Parallel Giant Slalom	Snowboardcross
1 Doriane Vidal, FRA	1 Karine Ruby, FRA	1 Karine Ruby, FRA	1 Ursula Bruhin, SWI	1 Karine Ruby, FRA
2 Stine B. Kjeldaas, NOR	2 Isabelle Blanc, FRA	2 Isabelle Blanc, FRA	2 Rosey Fletcher, USA	2 Emmanuelle Duboc, FRA
3 Sari Gronholm, FIN	3 Carmen Ranigler, ITA	3 D. Mair Unter Der Eggen, ITA	3 Manuela Riegler, AUT	3 Dominique Vallee, CAN

Speed Skating
World Cup Champions

MEN

500 meters	Hiroyasu Shimizu, Japan
1000 meters	Jeremy Wotherspoon, Canada
1500 meters	Aleksandr Kibalko, Russia
5000/10,000 meters	Gianni Romme, Netherlands

WOMEN

500 meters	Catriona Lemay-Doan, Canada
1000 meters	Monique Garbrecht-Enfeldt, Germany
1500 meters	Anni Friesinger, Germany
3000/5000 meters	Gunda Niemann-Stirnemann, Germany

2001 World Championships
at Budapest, Hungary (Feb. 9-11)

MEN

500 meters	Christian Breuer, Germany
1500 meters	Ids Postma, Netherlands
5000 meters	Bart Veldkamp, Belgium
10,000 meters	Bart Veldkamp, Belgium
All-Around	Rintje Ritsma, Netherlands

WOMEN

500 meters	Anni Friesinger, Germany
1500 meters	Anni Friesinger, Germany
3000 meters	Renate Groenewold, Netherlands
5000 meters	Claudia Pechstein, Germany
All-Around	Anni Friesinger, Germany

2001 World Short Track Championships
at Jeon-ju City, Korea (March 30-April 1)

MEN

500 meters	Li JiaJun, China
1000 meters	Li JiaJun, China
1500 meters	Marc Gagnon, Canada
3000 meters	Apolo Anton Ohno, USA
5000 meter relay	United States
All-Around	Li JiaJun, China

WOMEN

500 meters	Wang Chunlu, China
1000 meters	Yang Yang (A), China
1500 meters	Yang Yang (A), China
3000 meters	Yang Yang (A), China
3000 meter relay	China
All-Around	Yang Yang (A), China

Note: There are two Chinese skaters with the name Yang Yang. To differentiate, one goes by Yang Yang (A) and one by Yang Yang (S).

Figure Skating

World Championships
at Vancouver, British Columbia, Canada (March 19-25)

Men's — 1. Evgeni Plushenko, Russia; 2. Alexei Yagudin, Russia; 3. Todd Eldredge, USA; 4. Tim Goebel, USA; 5. Honda Takeshi, Japan.

Women's — 1. Michelle Kwan, USA; 2. Irina Slutskaya, Russia; 3. Sarah Hughes, USA; 4. Maria Butyrskaya, Russia; 5. Angela Nikodinov, USA.

Pairs — 1. Jamie Sale & David Pelletier, Canada; 2. Elena Berezhnaya & Anton Sikharulidze, Russia; 3. Xue Shen & Hongbo Zhao, China; 4. Maria Petrova & Alexei Tikhonov, Russia; 5. Tatiana Totmianina & Maxim Marinin, Russia.

Ice Dance — 1. Barbara Fusar Poli & Maurizio Margaglio, Italy; 2. Marina Anissina & Gwendal Peizerat, France; 3. Irina Lobacheva & Ilia Averbukh, Russia; 5. Shae-Lynn Bourne & Victor Kraatz, Canada; 5. Margarita Drobiazko & Povilas Vanagas, Lithuania.

U.S. Championships
at Boston, Mass. (Jan. 14-21)

Men's	Tim Goebel
Women's	Michelle Kwan
Pairs	Kyoko Ina & John Zimmerman
Ice Dance	Naomi Lang & Peter Tchernyshev

European Championships
at Bratislava, Slovakia (Jan. 21-28)

Men's	Evgeni Plushenko, Russia
Women's	Irina Slutskaya, Russia
Pairs	Elena Berezhnaya & Anton Sikharulidze, Russia
Ice Dance	Barbara Fusar Poli & Maurizio Margaglio, Italy

SUMMER SPORTS

Cross Country
IAAF World Championships
The 29th IAAF World Cross Country Championships held at Ostend, Belgium (March 24-25).

MEN

12 km (7.46 mi)
1. Mohammed Mourhit, Belgium 39:53
2. Sergiy Lebid, Ukraine 40:03
3. Charles Kamathi, Kenya 40:05
Best USA— Bob Kennedy, 12th, 40:43

WOMEN

8 km (4.97 mi)
1. Paula Radcliffe, Great Britain 27:49
2. Gete Wami, Ethiopia 27:52
3. Lydia Cheromei, Kenya 28:07
Best USA— Deena Drossin, 12th, 29:28

Cycling
Tour de France

The 88th Tour de France (July 7-29) ran 20 stages plus a prologue, covering 2,150 miles starting in Dunkirk, France passing through the Alps and Pyrenees in France and finishing on the Avenue des Champs-Elysees in Paris.

Lance Armstrong became the first American to win three consecutive Tours de France with another stunning victory. He finished in 86 hours, 17 minutes and 28 seconds, defeating his main competitor, Jan Ullrich of Germany, by 6 minutes and 44 seconds.

Armstrong dominated in the grueling mountain stages through the Alps and Pyrenees. After the first nine stages of relatively flat racing, he found himself in 23rd place, over 35 minutes behind the leader. Then came the mountain stages. After stage 12, he had closed the gap to nine minutes. And when stage 13 was complete, he was in the lead, grabbing the famed yellow jersey and keeping it for the rest of the race.

Less than three years before Armstrong rode down the Champs-Elysees for his first Tour de France victory in 1999, he was diagnosed with testicular cancer. The cancer then spread to his lungs and his brain and doctors gave him less than a 40 percent chance of survival. He underwent two operations and extensive chemotherapy and began his comeback in early 1998. He is only the second American to win cycling's premier event.

		Team	Behind
1	Lance Armstrong, USA	U.S. Postal	—
2	Jan Ullrich, GER	Deutche Telekom	6:44
3	Joseba Beloki, SPA	Once	9:05
4	Andrei Kivilev, KAZ	Cofidis	9:53
5	Igor Gonzalez Galdeano, SPA	Once	13:28

		Team	Behind
6	Francois Simon, FRA	Bonjour	17:22
7	Oscar Sevilla, SPA	Kelme	18:30
8	Santiago Botero, COL	Kelme	20:55
9	Marcos Serrano, SPA	Once	21:45
10	Michael Boogerd, NED	Rabobank	22:38

Cycling (Cont.)
Other Worldwide Champions

2001 Major UCI (Union Cycliste Internationale) Road results through Sept. 20. Note that in some instances, the date shown below is the final day of that particular race.

MEN

Race	Winner
Jan. 21: Tour Down Under (AUS)	Stuart O'Grady, AUS
Feb. 8: Mallorca Challenge (SPA)	Mathew Hayman, AUS
Feb. 18: Tour de Langwaki (MAS)	Paolo Lanfranchi, ITA
Feb. 18: Mediterranean Tour (FRA)	Davide Rebellin, ITA
Feb. 22: Ruta del Sol (SPA)	Erik Dekker, NED
Mar. 3: Tour de Valencia (SPA)	Fabian Jeker, SWI
Mar. 3: Omloop Het Volk (BEL)	Michele Bartoli, ITA
Mar. 18: Paris-Nice (FRA)	Dario Frigo, ITA
Mar. 21: Tirreno-Adriatico (ITA)	Davide Rebellin, ITA
Mar. 24: Milan-San Remo (ITA)	Erik Zabel, GER
Mar. 30: Semana Catalana (SPA)	Michael Boogerd, NED
Apr. 1: Criterium Int'l (FRA)	Rik Verbrugghe, BEL
Apr. 5: Three Days of de Panne (BEL)	Nico Mattan, BEL
Apr. 8: Tour de Flanders (BEL)	Gianluca Bortolami, ITA
Apr. 11: Ghent-Wevelgem (BEL)	George Hincapie, USA
Apr. 15: Paris-Roubaix (FRA)	Servais Knaven, NED
Apr. 18: Fleche Wallonne (BEL)	Rik Verbrugghe, BEL
May 13: Tour de Romandie (SWI)	Dario Frigo, ITA
May 13: Four Days of Dunkirk (FRA)	Didier Rous, FRA
June 10: Giro d'Italia (ITA)	Gilberto Simoni, ITA
June 17: Dauphine Libere (FRA)	Christophe Moreau, FRA
June 28: Tour of Switzerland (SWI)	Lance Armstrong, USA
Sept. 1: Tour of the Netherlands (NED)	Leon Van Bon, NED

WOMEN

Race	Winner
Mar. 10: Canberra World Cup (AUS)	Anna Millward, AUS
Mar. 24: Primavera Rosa (ITA)	Susanne Ljungskog, SWE
Apr. 18: Fleche Wallonne (BEL)	Fabiana Luperini, ITA
May 27: Tour de L'Aude (FRA)	Lyne Bessette, CAN
June 3: Montreal World Cup (CAN)	Genevieve Jeanson, CAN
June 10: Liberty Classic (USA)	Petra Rossner, GER
June 24: HP Women's Classic (USA)	Lyne Bessette, CAN
July 15: Giro d'Italia Femminile (ITA)	Zinaida Stahurskaia, BLR
Aug. 18: Grande Boucle Feminine (FRA)	Joane Somarriba Arrola, SPA
Sept. 9: GP de Suisse Feminin (SWI)	Susanne Ljungskog, SWE
Sept. 16: Rotterdam Tour (NED)	Judith Arndt, GER

2001 World Cyclo-cross Championships
at Tabor, Czech Republic (Feb. 3-4)

	Men's Elite	Time		Men's Juniors	Time
1	Erwin Vervecken, BEL	1:01:54	1	Martin Bina, CZR	38:54
2	Petr Dlask, CZR	1:01:55	2	Radomir Simunek, CZR	39:13
3	Mario De Clercq, BEL	1:02:08	3	Jan Kunta, CZR	39:13

	Men's Under 23	Time		Women's Race	Time
1	Sven Vanthourenhout, BEL	51:55	1	Hanka Kupfernagel, GER	28:29
2	Tomas Trunschka, CZR	52:11	2	Corine Dorland, NED	29:04
3	David Kasek, CZR	52:31	3	Daphny Van Den Brand, NED	29:10

Mountain Biking
2001 World Championships
at Vail, Colorado (Sept. 8-16)

MEN

	Cross Country (Elite)	Time
1	Roland Green, CAN	1:58.52
2	Thomas Frischknecht, SWI	1:59.36
3	Christof Sauser, SWI	1:59.42

	Downhill (Elite)	Time
1	Nicolas Vouilloz, FRA	3:35.20
2	Steve Peat, GBR	3:37.55
3	Greg Minnaar, RSA	3:37.84

	Dual (Elite)	
1	Brian Lopes, USA	
2	Cedric Gracia, FRA	
3	Wade Bootes, AUS	

	Trials – 20 inch (Elite)	
1	Rafal Kumorowski, POL	
2	Marco Hösel, GER	
3	Benito Ros Charral, SPA	

	Trials – 26 inch (Elite)	
1	Marc Caisso, FRA	
2	Daniel Comas Riera, SPA	
3	Bruno Arnold, FRA	

WOMEN

	Cross Country (Elite)	Time
1	Alison Dunlap, USA	1:51.28
2	Alison Sydor, CAN	1:51.40
3	Sabine Spitz, GER	1:52.18

	Downhill (Elite)	Time
1	Anne-Caroline Chausson, FRA	4:10.37
2	Fionn Griffiths, GBR	4:14.64
3	Leigh Donovan, USA	4:15.08

	Dual (Elite)	
1	Anne-Caroline Chausson, FRA	
2	Katrina Miller, AUS	
3	Tara Llannes, USA	

	Trials (Elite)	
1	Karin Moor, SWI	
2	Floriane Combe, FRA	
3	Celine Warther, FRA	

Marathons
2001 Boston Marathon

The 105th edition of the Boston Marathon was held Monday, April 16, 2001 and run, as always, from Hopkinton through Ashland, Framingham, Natick, Wellesley, Newton and Brookline to Boston, Mass. For the first time since 1990, a runner from a country other than Kenya won as South Korean Lee Bong-Ju was the first to break the tape in 2:09:43. He was the first Korean to win Boston since 1950. Ecuador's Silvio Guerra was runner-up in 2:10:07 while the Kenyans grabbed the next three spots.

In the women's division, 2000 champ Catherine Ndereba of Kenya successfully defended her crown, winning by almost three minutes in 2:23:53. Ndereba surged in the Newton hills to open up a commanding lead over three-time winner Fatuma Roba and the rest of the field.

In the wheelchair race, Australian ace Louise Sauvage (1:53:54) won for the fourth time, edging Switzerland's Edith Hunkeler by just four seconds. South Africa's Ernst VanDyk (1:25:12) unseated Switzerland's Franz Nietlispach in the men's wheelchair division. Nietlispach had won four in a row. Winners in the men's and women's divisions earned $80,000.

Distance: 26.2 miles.

MEN

	Time
1 Lee Bong-Ju, South Korea	2:09:43
2 Silvio Guerra, Ecuador	2:10:07
3 Joshua Chelang'a, Kenya	2:10:29
4 David Kiptum Busienei, Kenya	2:11:47
5 Mbarek Hussein, Kenya	2:12:01

Best USA: 6th— Rod DeHaven, Wisconsin, 2:12:41

WHEELCHAIR

	Time
1 Ernst VanDyk, South Africa	1:25:12
2 Franz Nietlispach, Switzerland	1:31:22
3 Heinz Frei, Switzerland	1:31:58

WOMEN

	Time
1 Catherine Ndereba, Kenya	2:23:53
2 Malgorzata Sobanska, Poland	2:26:42
3 Lyubov Morgunova, Russia	2:27:18
4 Lornah Kiplagat, Kenya	2:27:56
5 Fatuma Roba, Ethiopia	2:28:08

Best USA: 14th— Jill Gaitenby, Rhode Island, 2:36:45

WHEELCHAIR

	Time
1 Louise Sauvage, Australia	1:53:54
2 Edith Hunkeler, Switzerland	1:53:58
3 Sandra Graf, Switzerland	2:04:00

Other 2001 Winners

Tokyo

Feb. 18	Men	Kenichi Takahashi, JPN	2:10:51
	(No women's division)		

Los Angeles

Mar. 3	Men	Steven Ndungu, KEN	2:13:13
	Women	Elana Paramonova, RUS	2:35:58

Turin

Apr. 1	Men	Alemayhu Simeretu, ETH	2:07:45
	Women	Tiziana Alagia, ITA	2:27:54

Paris

Apr. 8	Men	Simon Biwott, KEN	2:09:40
	Women	Florence Barsosio, KEN	2:27:53

London

Apr. 22	Men	Abdelkhader El Mouaziz, MOR	2:07:11
	Women	Derartu Tulu, ETH	2:23:57

Rotterdam

Apr. 22	Men	Josephat Kiprono, KEN	2:06:50
	Women	Susan Chepkemei, KEN	2:25:15

Late 2000

Chicago

Nov. 5	Men	Khalid Khannouchi, USA	2:07:01
	Women	Catherine Ndereba, KEN	2:21:33

New York City

Nov. 5	Men	Abdelkhader El Mouaziz, MOR	2:10:08
	Women	Ludmila Petrova, RUS	2:25:45

Tokyo Women's

Nov. 19	Women	Joyce Chepchumba, KEN	2:24:02

Fukuoka

Dec. 3	Men	Atsushi Fujita, JPN	2:06:51
	(No women's division)		

Rowing
World Rowing Championships

at Lucerne, Switzerland (Aug. 18-26)

MEN

Eights	Romania,	5:27.48
Coxed Pairs	Great Britain,	6:49.33
Coxed Fours	France,	6:08.25
Coxless Pairs	Great Britain,	6:27.57
Coxless Fours	Great Britain,	5:48.98
Single Sculls	Olaf Tufte, NOR,	6:43.04
Double Sculls	Hungary,	6:14.16
Quad Sculls	Germany,	5:40.89

WOMEN

Eights	Australia,	6:03.66
Coxless Pairs	Romania,	7:01.27
Coxless Fours	Australia,	6:27.23
Single Sculls	Kathrin Rutschow Stomporowski, GER,	7:19.25
Double Sculls	Germany,	6:50.20
Quad Sculls	Germany,	6:12.95

1882-2001 Through the Years

TRACK & FIELD

IAAF World Championships

While the Summer Olympics have served as the unofficial world outdoor championships for track and field throughout the century, a separate World Championship meet was started in 1983 by the International Amateur Athletic Federation (IAAF). The meet was held every four years from 1983-91, but began an every-other-year cycle in 1993. World Championship sites include Helsinki (1983), Rome (1987), Tokyo (1991), Stuttgart (1993), Göteborg, Sweden (1995), Athens (1997), Seville, Spain (1999) and Edmonton (2001). Looking forward, the Championships will be held in Paris (2003) and London (2005). Note that (WR) indicates world record and (CR) indicates championship meet record.

MEN

Multiple gold medals (including relays): Michael Johnson (9); Carl Lewis (8); Sergey Bubka (6); Maurice Greene and Lars Riedel (5); Haile Gebrselassie, Ivan Pedroso, Antonio Pettigrew and Calvin Smith (4); Donovan Bailey, Tomas Dvorak, Hicham El Guerrouj, Greg Foster, John Godina, Werner Gunthor, Allen Johnson, Wilson Kipketer, Moses Kiptanui, Dennis Mitchell, Noureddine Morceli, Dan O'Brien, Butch Reynolds and Jan Zelezny (3); Andrey Abduvaliyev, Abel Anton, Leroy Burrell, Andre Cason, Maurizio Damilano, Jon Drummond, Jonathan Edwards, Colin Jackson, Ismael Kirui, Billy Konchellah, Robert Korzeniowski, Sergey Litvinov, Tim Montgomery, Edwin Moses, Mike Powell, Javier Sotomayor and Angelo Taylor (2).

100 Meters

Year		Time	
1983	Carl Lewis, USA	10.07	
1987	Carl Lewis, USA	9.93	
1991	Carl Lewis, USA	9.86	**WR**
1993	Linford Christie, GBR	9.87	
1995	Donovan Bailey, CAN	9.97	
1997	Maurice Greene, USA	9.86	
1999	Maurice Greene, USA	9.80	**CR**
2001	Maurice Greene, USA	9.82	

Note: Ben Johnson was the original winner in 1987, but was stripped of his title and world record time (9.83) following his 1989 admission of drug taking.

200 Meters

Year		Time	
1983	Calvin Smith, USA	20.14	
1987	Calvin Smith, USA	20.16	
1991	Michael Johnson, USA	20.01	
1993	Frank Fredericks, NAM	19.85	
1995	Michael Johnson, USA	19.79	**CR**
1997	Ato Boldon, USA	20.04	
1999	Maurice Greene, USA	19.90	
2001	Konstantinos Kenteris, GRE	20.04	

400 Meters

Year		Time	
1983	Bert Cameron, JAM	45.05	
1987	Thomas Schonlebe, E. Ger	44.33	
1991	Antonio Pettigrew, USA	44.57	
1993	Michael Johnson, USA	43.65	
1995	Michael Johnson, USA	43.39	
1997	Michael Johnson, USA	44.12	
1999	Michael Johnson, USA	43.18	**WR**
2001	Avard Moncur, BAH	44.64	

800 Meters

Year		Time	
1983	Willi Wülbeck, W. Ger	1:43.65	
1987	Billy Konchellah, KEN	1:43.06	**CR**
1991	Billy Konchellah, KEN	1:43.99	
1993	Paul Ruto, KEN	1:44.71	
1995	Wilson Kipketer, DEN	1:45.08	
1997	Wilson Kipketer, DEN	1:43.38	
1999	Wilson Kipketer, DEN	1:43.30	
2001	Andre Bucher, SWI	1:43.70	

1500 Meters

Year		Time	
1983	Steve Cram, GBR	3:41.59	
1987	Abdi Bile, SOM	3:36.80	
1991	Noureddine Morceli, ALG	3:32.84	
1993	Noureddine Morceli, ALG	3:34.24	
1995	Noureddine Morceli, ALG	3:33.73	
1997	Hicham El Guerrouj, MOR	3:35.83	
1999	Hicham El Guerrouj, MOR	3:27.65	**CR**
2001	Hicham El Guerrouj, MOR	3:30.68	

5000 Meters

Year		Time	
1983	Eammon Coghlan, IRL	13:28.53	
1987	Said Aouita, MOR	13:26.44	
1991	Yobes Ondieki, KEN	13:14.45	
1993	Ismael Kirui, KEN	13:02.75	
1995	Ismael Kirui, KEN	13:16.77	
1997	Daniel Komen, KEN	13:07.38	
1999	Salah Hissou, MOR	12:58.13	**CR**
2001	Richard Limo, KEN	13:00.77	

10,000 Meters

Year		Time	
1983	Alberto Cova, ITA	28:01.04	
1987	Paul Kipkoech, KEN	27:38.63	
1991	Moses Tanui, KEN	27:38.74	
1993	Haile Gebrselassie, ETH	27:46.02	
1995	Haile Gebrselassie, ETH	27:12.95	**CR**
1997	Haile Gebrselassie, ETH	27:24.58	
1999	Haile Gebrselassie, ETH	27:57.27	
2001	Charles Kamathi, KEN	27:53.25	

Marathon

Year		Time	
1983	Rob de Castella, AUS	2:10:03	**CR**
1987	Douglas Wakiihuri, KEN	2:11:48	
1991	Hiromi Taniguchi, JPN	2:14:57	
1993	Mark Plaatjes, USA	2:13:57	
1995	Martin Fíz, SPA	2:11:41	
1997	Abel Anton, SPA	2:13:16	
1999	Abel Anton, SPA	2:13:36	
2001	Gezahegne Abera, ETH	2:12:42	

110-Meter Hurdles

Year		Time	
1983	Greg Foster, USA	13.42	
1987	Greg Foster, USA	13.21	
1991	Greg Foster, USA	13.06	
1993	Colin Jackson, GBR	12.91	WR
1995	Allen Johnson, USA	13.00	
1997	Allen Johnson, USA	12.93	
1999	Colin Jackson, GBR	13.04	
2001	Allen Johnson, USA	13.04	

400-Meter Hurdles

Year		Time	
1983	Edwin Moses, USA	47.50	
1987	Edwin Moses, USA	47.46	
1991	Samuel Matete, ZAM	47.64	
1993	Kevin Young, USA	47.18	CR
1995	Derrick Adkins, USA	47.98	
1997	Stephane Diagana, FRA	47.70	
1999	Fabrizio Mori, ITA	47.72	
2001	Felix Sanchez, DOM	47.49	

3000-Meter Steeplechase

Year		Time	
1983	Patriz Ilg, W. Ger	8:15.06	
1987	Francesco Panetta, ITA	8:08.57	
1991	Moses Kiptanui, KEN	8:12.59	
1993	Moses Kiptanui, KEN	8:06.36	
1995	Moses Kiptanui, KEN	8:04.16	CR
1997	Wilson B. Kipketer, KEN	8:05.84	
1999	Christopher Koskei, KEN	8:11.76	
2001	Reuben Kosgei, KEN	8:15.16	

4 x 100-Meter Relay

Year		Time	
1983	United States	37.86	WR
1987	United States	37.90	
1991	United States	37.50	WR
1993	United States	37.48	CR
1995	Canada	38.31	
1997	Canada	37.86	
1999	United States	37.59	
2001	United States	37.96	

4 x 400-Meter Relay

Year		Time	
1983	Soviet Union	3:00.79	
1987	United States	2:57.29	
1991	Great Britain	2:57.53	
1993	United States	2:54.29	WR
1995	United States	2:57.32	
1997	United States	2:56.47	
1999	United States	2:56.45	
2001	United States	2:57.54	

20-Kilometer Walk

Year		Time	
1983	Ernesto Canto, MEX	1:20.49	
1987	Maurizio Damilano, ITA	1:20.45	
1991	Maurizio Damilano, ITA	1:19.37	CR
1993	Valentin Massana, SPA	1:22.31	
1995	Michele Didoni, ITA	1:19.59	
1997	Daniel Garcia, MEX	1:21:43	
1999	Ilya Markov, RUS	1:23:34	
2001	Roman Rasskazov, RUS	1:20:31	

50-Kilometer Walk

Year		Time	
1983	Ronald Weigel, E. Ger	3:43:08	
1987	Hartwig Gauder, E. Ger	3:40:53	CR
1991	Aleksandr Potashov, USSR	3:53:09	
1993	Jesus Angel Garcia, SPA	3:41:41	
1995	Valentin Kononen, FIN	3:43.42	
1997	Robert Korzeniowski, POL	3:44:46	
1999	German Skurygin, RUS	3:44:23	

Year		Time	
2001	Robert Korzeniowski, POL	3:42:08	

High Jump

Year		Height	
1983	Gennedy Avdeyenko, USSR	7-7¼	
1987	Patrik Sjoberg, SWE	7-9¾	
1991	Charles Austin, USA	7-9¾	
1993	Javier Sotomayor, CUB	7-10½	CR
1995	Troy Kemp, BAH	7-9¼	
1997	Javier Sotomayor, CUB	7-9¼	
1999	Vyacheslav Voronin, RUS	7-9¼	
2001	Martin Buss, GER	7-8¾	

Pole Vault

Year		Height	
1983	Sergey Bubka, USSR	18-8¼	
1987	Sergey Bubka, USSR	19-2¼	
1991	Sergey Bubka, USSR	19-6¼	CR
1993	Sergey Bubka, UKR	19-8¼	
1995	Sergey Bubka, UKR	19-5	
1997	Sergey Bubka, UKR	19-8½	CR
1999	Maksim Tarasov, RUS	19-9	CR
2001	Dmitri Markov, AUS	19-10¼	CR

Long Jump

Year		Distance	
1983	Carl Lewis, USA	28-0¾	
1987	Carl Lewis, USA	28-0¼	
1991	Mike Powell, USA	29-4½	WR
1993	Mike Powell, USA	28-2¼	
1995	Ivan Pedroso, CUB	28-6½	
1997	Ivan Pedroso, CUB	27-7½	
1999	Ivan Pedroso, CUB	28-1	
2001	Ivan Pedroso, CUB	27-6¾	

Triple Jump

Year		Distance	
1983	Zdzislaw Hoffmann, POL	57-2	
1987	Khristo Markov, BUL	58-9	
1991	Kenny Harrison, USA	58-4	
1993	Mike Conley, USA	58-7¼	
1995	Jonathan Edwards, GBR	60-0¼	WR
1997	Yoelvis Quesada, CUB	58-6¾	
1999	Charles Michael Friedek, GER	57-8½	
2001	Jonathan Edwards, GBR	58-9½	

Shot Put

Year		Distance	
1983	Edward Sarul, POL	70-2¼	
1987	Werner Günthör, SWI	72-11¼	CR
1991	Werner Günthör, SWI	71-1¼	
1993	Werner Günthör, SWI	72-1	
1995	John Godina, USA	70-5¼	
1997	John Godina, USA	70-4¼	
1999	C.J. Hunter, USA	71-6	
2001	John Godina, USA	71-9	

Discus

Year		Distance	
1983	Imrich Bugar, CZE	222-2	
1987	Jurgen Schult, E. Ger	225-6	
1991	Lars Riedel, GER	217-2	
1993	Lars Riedel, GER	222-2	
1995	Lars Riedel, GER	225-7	CR
1997	Lars Riedel, GER	224-10	
1999	Anthony Washington, USA	226-7	CR
2001	Lars Riedel, GER	228-9	CR

Hammer Throw

Year		Distance	
1983	Sergey Litvinov, USSR	271-3	
1987	Sergey Litvinov, USSR	272-6	CR
1991	Yuri Sedykh, USSR	268-0	
1993	Andrey Abduvaliyev, TAJ	267-10	
1995	Andrey Abduvaliyev, TAJ	267-7	
1997	Heinz Weis, GER	268-4	
1999	Karsten Kobs, GER	263-3	
2001	Szymon Ziolkowski, POL	273-7	CR

Track & Field (Cont.)

Javelin

Year		Distance	
1983	Detlef Michel, E. Ger	293-7	
1987	Seppo Raty, FIN	274-1	
1991	Kimmo Kinnunen, FIN	297-11	CR
1993	Jan Zelezny, CZR	282-1	
1995	Jan Zelezny, CZR	293-11	
1997	Marius Corbett, S. Afr.	290-0	
1999	Aki Parviainen, FIN	293-8	
2001	Jan Zelezny, CZR	304-5	CR

Decathlon

Year		Points	
1983	Daley Thompson, GBR	8714	
1987	Torsten Voss, E. Ger	8680	
1991	Dan O'Brien, USA	8812	CR
1993	Dan O'Brien, USA	8817	CR
1995	Dan O'Brien, USA	8695	
1997	Tomas Dvorak, CZR	8837	CR
1999	Tomas Dvorak, CZR	8744	
2001	Tomas Dvorak, CZR	8902	CR

WOMEN

Multiple gold medals (including relays): Gail Devers and Marion Jones (5), Jackie Joyner-Kersee (4); Tatyana Samolenko Dorovskikh, Chryste Gaines, Silke Gladisch, Marita Koch, Astrid Kumbernuss, Jearl Miles, Inger Miller, Merlene Ottey, Gabriela Szabo and Gwen Torrence (3); Hassiba Boulmerka, Sabine Braun, Olga Bryzgina, Mary Decker, Stacy Dragila, Heike Daute Drechsler, Lyudmila Narozhilenko Enquist, Cathy Freeman, Trine Hattestad, Martina Optiz Hellmann, Stefka Kostadinova, Katrin Krabbe, Jarmila Kratochvilova, Fiona May, Maria Mutola, Marie-José Pérec, Zhanna Pintusevich-Block, Ana Quirot and Huang Zhihong (2).

100 Meters

Year		Time	
1983	Marlies Gohr, E. Ger	10.97	
1987	Silke Gladisch, E. Ger	10.90	
1991	Katrin Krabbe, GER	10.99	
1993	Gail Devers, USA	10.81	CR
1995	Gwen Torrence, USA	10.85	
1997	Marion Jones, USA	10.83	
1999	Marion Jones, USA	10.70	CR
2001	Zhanna Pintusevich-Block, UKR	10.82	

5000 Meters
Held as 3000-meter race from 1983-93

Year		Time	
1983	Mary Decker, USA	8:34.62	
1987	Tatyana Samolenko, USSR	8:38.73	
1991	T. Samolenko Dorovskikh, USSR	8:35.82	
1993	Qu Yunxia, CHN	8:28.71	CR
1995	Sonia O'Sullivan, IRL	14:46.47	CR
1997	Gabriela Szabo, ROM	14:57.68	
1999	Gabriela Szabo, ROM	14:41.82	CR
2001	Olga Yegorova, RUS	15:03.39	

200 Meters

Year		Time	
1983	Marita Koch, E. Ger	22.13	
1987	Silke Gladisch, E. Ger	21.74	CR
1991	Katrin Krabbe, GER	22.09	
1993	Merlene Ottey, JAM	21.98	
1995	Merlene Ottey, JAM	22.12	
1997	Zhanna Pintusevich, UKR	22.32	
1999	Inger Miller, USA	21.77	
2001	Marion Jones, USA	22.39	

10,000 Meters

Year		Time	
1983	Not held		
1987	Ingrid Kristiansen, NOR	31:05.85	
1991	Liz McColgan, GBR	31:14.31	
1993	Wang Junxia, CHN	30:49.30	CR
1995	Fernanda Ribeiro, POR	31:04.99	
1997	Sally Barsosio, KEN	31:32.92	
1999	Gete Wami, ETH	30:24.56	CR
2001	Derartu Tulu, ETH	31:48.81	

400 Meters

Year		Time	
1983	Jarmila Kratochvilova, CZE	47.99	WR
1987	Olga Bryzgina, USSR	49.38	
1991	Marie-José Pérec, FRA	49.13	
1993	Jearl Miles, USA	49.82	
1995	Marie-José Pérec, FRA	49.28	
1997	Cathy Freeman, AUS	49.77	
1999	Cathy Freeman, AUS	49.67	
2001	Amy Mbacke Thiam, SEN	49.86	

Marathon

Year		Time	
1983	Grete Waitz, NOR	2:28:09	
1987	Rose Mota, POR	2:25:17	CR
1991	Wanda Panfil, POL	2:29:53	
1993	Junko Asari, JPN	2:30:03	
1995	Manuela Machado, POR	2:25:39	
1997	Hiromi Suzuki, JPN	2:29:48	
1999	Jong Song-Ok, N. Kor	2:26:59	
2001	Lidia Simon, ROM	2:26:01	

800 Meters

Year		Time	
1983	Jarmila Kratochvilova, CZE	1:54.68	CR
1987	Sigrun Wodars, E. Ger	1:55.26	
1991	Lilia Nurutdinova, USSR	1:57.50	
1993	Maria Mutola, MOZ	1:55.43	
1995	Ana Quirot, CUB	1:56.11	
1997	Ana Quirot, CUB	1:57.14	
1999	Ludmila Formanova, CZR	1:56.68	
2001	Maria Mutola, MOZ	1:57.17	

100-Meter Hurdles

Year		Time	
1983	Bettine Jahn, E. Ger	12.35^w	
1987	Ginka Zagorcheva, BUL	12.34	CR
1991	Lyudmila Narozhilenko, USSR	12.59	
1993	Gail Devers, USA	12.46	
1995	Gail Devers, USA	12.68	
1997	Ludmila Enquist, SWE	12.50	
1999	Gail Devers, USA	12.37	
2001	Anjanette Kirkland, USA	12.42	

^{w} indicates wind-aided.

1500 Meters

Year		Time	
1983	Mary Decker, USA	4:00.90	
1987	Tatiana Samolenko, USSR	3:58.56	CR
1991	Hassiba Boulmerka, ALG	4:02.21	
1993	Liu Dong, CHN	4:00.50	
1995	Hassiba Boulmerka, ALG	4:02.42	
1997	Carla Sacramento, POR	4:04.24	
1999	Svetlana Masterkova, RUS	3:59.53	
2001	Gabriela Szabo, ROM	4:00.57	

400-Meter Hurdles

Year		Time	
1983	Yekaterina Fesenko, USSR	54.14	
1987	Sabine Busch, E. Ger	53.62	
1991	Tatiana Ledovskaya, USSR	53.11	
1993	Sally Gunnell, GBR	52.74	WR
1995	Kim Batten, USA	52.61	WR
1997	Nezha Bidouane, MOR	52.97	
1999	Daima Pernia, CUB	52.89	
2001	Nezha Bidouane, MOR	53.34	

4 x 100-Meter Relay

Year		Time	
1983	East Germany	41.76	
1987	United States	41.58	
1991	Jamaica	41.94	
1993	Russia	41.49	CR
1995	United States	42.12	
1997	United States	41.47	CR
1999	Bahamas	41.92	
2001	United States	41.71	

4 x 400-Meter Relay

Year		Time	
1983	East Germany	3:19.73	
1987	East Germany	3:18.63	
1991	Soviet Union	3:18.43	
1993	United States	3:16.71	CR
1995	United States	3:22.39	
1997	Germany	3:20.92	
1999	Russia	3:21.98	
2001	Jamaica	3:20.65	

20-Kilometer Walk

Held as 10-Kilometer race from 1987-97

Year		Time	
1983	Not held		
1987	Irina Strakhova, USSR	44:12	
1991	Alina Ivanova, USSR	42:57	
1993	Sari Essayah, FIN	42:59	
1995	Irina Stankina, RUS	42:13	CR
1997	Anna Sidoti, ITA	42:55	
1999	Hongyu Liu, CHN	1:30:50	CR
2001	Olimpiada Ivanova, RUS	1:27:48	CR

High Jump

Year		Height	
1983	Tamara Bykova, USSR	6- 7	
1987	Stefka Kostadinova, BUL	6-10¼	WR
1991	Heike Henkel, GER	6- 8¾	
1993	Ioamnet Quintero, CUB	6- 6¼	
1995	Stefka Kostadinova, BUL	6- 7	
1997	Hanne Haugland, NOR	6- 6¼	
1999	Inga Babakova, UKR	6- 6¼	
2001	Hestrie Cloete, RSA	6- 6¾	

Pole Vault

Year		Height	
1999	Stacy Dragila, USA	15- 1	WR
2001	Stacy Dragila, USA	15- 7	CR

Long Jump

Year		Distance	
1983	Heike Daute, E. Ger	23-10¼ʷ	
1987	Jackie Joyner-Kersee, USA	24- 1¾	CR
1991	Jackie Joyner-Kersee, USA	24- 0¼	
1993	Heike Drechsler, GER	23- 4	
1995	Fiona May, ITA	22-10¾ʷ	
1997	Lyudmila Galkina, RUS	23- 1¾	
1999	Niurka Montalvo, SPA	23- 2	
2001	Fiona May, ITA	23- 0½	

ʷ indicates wind-aided.

Triple Jump

Year		Distance	
1993	Ana Biryukova, RUS	46- 6¼	WR
1995	Inessa Kravets, UKR	50- 10¾	WR
1997	Sarka Kasparkova, CZE	49- 10½	
1999	Paraskevi Tsiamita, GRE	48- 10	
2001	Tatyana Lebedeva, RUS	50- 0½	

Shot Put

Year		Distance	
1983	Helena Fibingerova, CZE	69- 0	
1987	Natalia Lisovskaya, USSR	69- 8	CR
1991	Huang Zhihong, CHN	68- 4	
1993	Huang Zhihong, CHN	67- 6	
1995	Astrid Kumbernuss, GER	69- 7½	
1997	Astrid Kumbernuss, GER	67- 11½	
1999	Astrid Kumbernuss, GER	65- 1½	
2001	Yanina Korolchik, BLR	67- 7½	

Discus

Year		Distance	
1983	Martina Opitz, E. Ger	226- 2	
1987	Martina Opitz Hellmann, E. Ger	235- 0	CR
1991	Tsvetanka Khristova, BUL	233- 0	
1993	Olga Burova, RUS	221- 1	
1995	Ellina Zvereva, BLR	225- 2	
1997	Beatrice Faumuina, NZE	219- 3	
1999	Franka Dietzsch, GER	223- 6	
2001	Natalya Sadova, RUS	224- 11	

Hammer Throw

Year		Distance	
1999	Mihaela Melinte, ROM	246-8¾	CR
2001	Yipsi Moreno, CUB	231-9	

Javelin

Year		Distance	
1983	Tiina Lillak, FIN	232- 4	
1987	Fatima Whitbread, GBR	251- 5	CR
1991	Xu Demei, CHN	225- 8	
1993	Trine Hattestad, NOR	227- 0	
1995	Natalya Shikolenko, BLR	221- 8	
1997	Trine Hattestad, NOR	225- 8	
1999	Mirela Manjani-Tzelili, GRE	220- 1	
2001	Osleidys Menendez, CUB	228- 1	CR

Heptathlon

Year		Points	
1983	Ramona Neubert, E. Ger	6770	
1987	Jackie Joyner-Kersee, USA	7128	CR
1991	Sabine Braun, GER	6672	
1993	Jackie Joyner-Kersee, USA	6837	
1995	Ghada Shouaa, SYR	6651	
1997	Sabine Braun, GER	6739	
1999	Eunice Barber, FRA	6861	
2001	Yelena Prokhorova, RUS	6694	

World Cross Country Championships
MEN

Multiple winners: John Ngugi and Paul Tergat (5); Carlos Lopes (3); Mohammed Mourhit, Khalid Skah, William Sigei and Craig Virgin (2).

Year	Winner	Year	Winner	Year	Winner
1973	Pekka Paivarinta, Finland	1983	Bekele Debele, Ethiopia	1993	William Sigei, Kenya
1974	Eric DeBeck, Belgium	1984	Carlos Lopes, Portugal	1994	William Sigei, Kenya
1975	Ian Stewart, Scotland	1985	Carlos Lopes, Portugal	1995	Paul Tergat, Kenya
1976	Carlos Lopes, Portugal	1986	John Ngugi, Kenya	1996	Paul Tergat, Kenya
1977	Leon Schots, Belgium	1987	John Ngugi, Kenya	1997	Paul Tergat, Kenya
1978	John Treacy, Ireland	1988	John Ngugi, Kenya	1998	Paul Tergat, Kenya
1979	John Treacy, Ireland	1989	John Ngugi, Kenya	1999	Paul Tergat, Kenya
1980	Craig Virgin, USA	1990	Khalid Skah, Morocco	2000	Mohammed Mourhit, Belgium
1981	Craig Virgin, USA	1991	Khalid Skah, Morocco	2001	Mohammed Mourhit, Belgium
1982	Mohammed Kedir, Ethiopia	1992	John Ngugi, Kenya		

Track & Field (Cont.)
WOMEN

Multiple winners: Grete Waitz (5); Lynn Jennings and Derartu Tulu (3); Zola Budd, Paola Cacchi, Maricica Puica, Annette Sergent, Carmen Valero and Gete Wami (2).

Year	Winner	Year	Winner	Year	Winner
1973	Paola Cacchi, Italy	1983	Grete Waitz, Norway	1993	Albertina Dias, Portugal
1974	Paola Cacchi, Italy	1984	Maricica Puica, Romania	1994	Helen Chepngeno, Kenya
1975	Julie Brown, USA	1985	Zola Budd, England	1995	Derartu Tulu, Ethiopia
1976	Carmen Valero, Spain	1986	Zola Budd, England	1996	Gete Wami, Ethiopia
1977	Carmen Valero, Spain	1987	Annette Sergent, France	1997	Derartu Tulu, Ethiopia
1978	Grete Waitz, Norway	1988	Ingrid Kristiansen, Norway	1998	Sonia O'Sullivan, Ireland
1979	Grete Waitz, Norway	1989	Annette Sergent, France	1999	Gete Wami, Ethiopia
1980	Grete Waitz, Norway	1990	Lynn Jennings, USA	2000	Derartu Tulu, Ethiopia
1981	Grete Waitz, Norway	1991	Lynn Jennings, USA	2001	Paula Radcliffe, Gr. Britain
1982	Maricica Puica, Romania	1992	Lynn Jennings, USA		

Marathons
Boston

America's oldest regularly contested foot race, the Boston Marathon is held on Patriots' Day every April. It has been run at four different distances: 24 miles, 1232 yards (1897-1923); 26 miles, 209 yards (1924-26); 26 miles, 385 yards (1927-52, since 1957); 25 miles, 958 yards (1953-56).

MEN

Multiple winners: Clarence DeMar (7); Gerard Cote and Bill Rodgers (4); Ibrahim Hussein, Cosmas Ndeti and Leslie Pawson (3); Tarzan Brown, Jim Caffrey, John A. Kelley, John Miles, Eino Oksanen, Toshihiko Seko, Geoff Smith, Moses Tanui and Aurele Vandendriessche (2).

Year	Winner	Time	Year	Winner	Time
1897	John McDermott, New York	2:55:10	1940	Gerard Cote, Canada	2:28:28
1898	Ronald McDonald, Massachusetts	2:42:00	1941	Leslie Pawson, Rhode Island	2:30:38
1899	Lawrence Brignolia, Massachusetts	2:54:38	1942	Joe Smith, Massachusetts	2:26:51
			1943	Gerard Cote, Canada	2:28:25
1900	Jim Caffrey, Canada	2:39:44	1944	Gerard Cote, Canada	2:31:50
1901	Jim Caffrey, Canada	2:29:23	1945	John A. Kelley, Massachusetts	2:30:40
1902	Sam Mellor, New York	2:43:12	1946	Stylianos Kyriakides, Greece	2:29:27
1903	J.C. Lorden, Massachusetts	2:41:29	1947	Yun Bok Suh, Korea	2:25:39
1904	Mike Spring, New York	2:38:04	1948	Gerard Cote, Canada	2:31:02
1905	Fred Lorz, New York	2:38:25	1949	Karle Leandersson, Sweden	2:31:50
1906	Tim Ford, Massachusetts	2:45:45			
1907	Tom Longboat, Canada	2:24:24	1950	Kee Yonh Ham, Korea	2:32:39
1908	Tom Morrissey, New York	2:25:43	1951	Shigeki Tanaka, Japan	2:27:45
1909	Henri Renaud, New Hampshire	2:53:36	1952	Doroteo Flores, Guatemala	2:31:53
			1953	Keizo Yamada, Japan	2:18:51
1910	Fred Cameron, Nova Scotia	2:28:52	1954	Veiko Karvonen, Finland	2:20:39
1911	Clarence DeMar, Massachusetts	2:21:39	1955	Hideo Hamamura, Japan	2:18:22
1912	Mike Ryan, Illinois	2:21:18	1956	Antti Viskari, Finland	2:14:14
1913	Fritz Carlson, Minnesota	2:25:14	1957	John J. Kelley, Connecticut	2:20:05
1914	James Duffy, Canada	2:25:01	1958	Franjo Mihalic, Yugoslavia	2:25:54
1915	Edouard Fabre, Canada	2:31:41	1959	Eino Oksanen, Finland	2:22:42
1916	Arthur Roth, Massachusetts	2:27:16			
1917	Bill Kennedy, New York	2:28:37	1960	Paavo Kotila, Finland	2:20:54
1918	World War relay race		1961	Eino Oksanen, Finland	2:23:39
1919	Carl Linder, Massachusetts	2:29:13	1962	Eino Oksanen, Finland	2:23:48
			1963	Aurele Vandendriessche, Belgium	2:18:58
1920	Peter Trivoulidas, New York	2:29:31	1964	Aurele Vandendriessche, Belgium	2:19:59
1921	Frank Zuna, New Jersey	2:18:57	1965	Morio Shigematsu, Japan	2:16:33
1922	Clarence DeMar, Massachusetts	2:18:10	1966	Kenji Kimihara, Japan	2:17:11
1923	Clarence DeMar, Massachusetts	2:23:37	1967	David McKenzie, New Zealand	2:15:45
1924	Clarence DeMar, Massachusetts	2:29:40	1968	Amby Burfoot, Connecticut	2:22:17
1925	Charles Mellor, Illinois	2:33:00	1969	Yoshiaki Unetani, Japan	2:13:49
1926	John Miles, Nova Scotia	2:25:40			
1927	Clarence DeMar, Massachusetts	2:40:22	1970	Ron Hill, England	2:10:30
1928	Clarence DeMar, Massachusetts	2:37:07	1971	Alvaro Mejia, Colombia	2:18:45
1929	John Miles, Nova Scotia	2:33:08	1972	Olavi Suomalainen, Finland	2:15:39
			1973	Jon Anderson, Oregon	2:16:03
1930	Clarence DeMar, Massachusetts	2:34:48	1974	Neil Cusack, Ireland	2:13:39
1931	James Henigan, Massachusetts	2:46:45	1975	Bill Rodgers, Massachusetts	2:09:55
1932	Paul deBruyn, Germany	2:33:36	1976	Jack Fultz, Pennsylvania	2:20:19
1933	Leslie Pawson, Rhode Island	2:31:01	1977	Jerome Drayton, Canada	2:14:46
1934	Dave Komonen, Canada	2:32:53	1978	Bill Rodgers, Massachusetts	2:10:13
1935	John A. Kelley, Massachusetts	2:32:07	1979	Bill Rodgers, Massachusetts	2:09:27
1936	Ellison (Tarzan) Brown, Rhode Island	2:33:40			
1937	Walter Young, Canada	2:33:20	1980	Bill Rodgers, Massachusetts	2:12:11
1938	Leslie Pawson, Rhode Island	2:35:34	1981	Toshihiko Seko, Japan	2:09:26
1939	Ellison (Tarzan) Brown, Rhode Island	2:28:51	1982	Alberto Salazar, Oregon	2:08:52

Year	Time	Year	Time
1983 Greg Meyer, New Jersey	2:09:00	1993 Cosmas Ndeti, Kenya	2:09:33
1984 Geoff Smith, England	2:10:34	1994 Cosmas Ndeti, Kenya	2:07:15*
1985 Geoff Smith, England	2:14:05	1995 Cosmas Ndeti, Kenya	2:09:22
1986 Rob de Castella, Australia	2:07:51	1996 Moses Tanui, Kenya	2:09:16
1987 Toshihiko Seko, Japan	2:11:50	1997 Lameck Aguta, Kenya	2:10:34
1988 Ibrahim Hussein, Kenya	2:08:43	1998 Moses Tanui, Kenya	2:07:34
1989 Abebe Mekonnen, Ethiopia	2:09:06	1999 Joseph Chebet, Kenya	2:09:52
1990 Gelindo Bordin, Italy	2:08:19	2000 Elijah Lagat, Kenya	2:09:47
1991 Ibrahim Hussein, Kenya	2:11:06	2001 Lee Bong-Ju, South Korea	2:09:43
1992 Ibrahim Hussein, Kenya	2:08:14	*Course record.	

WOMEN

Multiple winners: Rosa Mota, Uta Pippig and Fatuma Roba (3); Joan Benoit, Miki Gorman, Ingrid Kristiansen, Olga Markova and Catherine Ndereba (2).

Year	Time	Year	Time
1972 Nina Kuscsik, New York	3:08:58	1988 Rosa Mota, Portugal	2:24:30
1973 Jacqueline Hansen, California	3:05:59	1989 Ingrid Kristiansen, Norway	2:24:33
1974 Miki Gorman, California	2:47:11	1990 Rosa Mota, Portugal	2:25:23
1975 Liane Winter, West Germany	2:42:24	1991 Wanda Panfil, Poland	2:24:18
1976 Kim Merritt, Wisconsin	2:47:10	1992 Olga Markova, CIS	2:23:43
1977 Miki Gorman, California	2:48:33	1993 Olga Markova, Russia	2:25:27
1978 Gayle Barron, Georgia	2:44:52	1994 Uta Pippig, Germany	2:21:45*
1979 Joan Benoit, Maine	2:35:15	1995 Uta Pippig, Germany	2:25:11
1980 Jacqueline Gareau, Canada	2:34:28	1996 Uta Pippig, Germany	2:27:12
1981 Allison Roe, New Zealand	2:26:46	1997 Fatuma Roba, Ethiopia	2:26:23
1982 Charlotte Teske, West Germany	2:29:33	1998 Fatuma Roba, Ethiopia	2:23:21
1983 Joan Benoit, Maine	2:22:43	1999 Fatuma Roba, Ethiopia	2:23:25
1984 Lorraine Moller, New Zealand	2:29:28	2000 Catherine Ndereba, Kenya	2:26:11
1985 Lisa Larsen Weidenbach, Mass	2:34:06	2001 Catherine Ndereba, Kenya	2:23:53
1986 Ingrid Kristiansen, Norway	2:24:55	*Course record.	
1987 Rosa Mota, Portugal	2:25:21		

New York City

Started in 1970, the New York City Marathon is run in the fall, usually on the first Sunday in November. The route winds through all of the city's five boroughs and finishes in Central Park.

MEN

Multiple winners: Bill Rodgers (4); Alberto Salazar (3); Tom Fleming, John Kagwe, Orlando Pizzolato and German Silva (2).

Year	Time	Year	Time	Year	Time
1970 Gary Muhrcke, USA	2:31:38	1981 Alberto Salazar, USA	2:08:13	1992 Willie Mtolo, S. Afr.	2:09:29
1971 Norman Higgins, USA	2:22:54	1982 Alberto Salazar, USA	2:09:29	1993 Andres Espinosa, MEX	2:10:04
1972 Sheldon Karlin, USA	2:27:52	1983 Rod Dixon, NZ	2:08:59	1994 German Silva, MEX	2:11:21
1973 Tom Fleming, USA	2:21:54	1984 Orlando Pizzolato, ITA	2:14:53	1995 German Silva, MEX	2:11:00
1974 Norbert Sander, USA	2:26:30	1985 Orlando Pizzolato, ITA	2:11:34	1996 Giacomo Leone, ITA	2:09:54
1975 Tom Fleming, USA	2:19:27	1986 Gianni Poli, ITA	2:11:06	1997 John Kagwe, KEN	2:08:12
1976 Bill Rodgers, USA	2:10:09	1987 Ibrahim Hussein, KEN	2:11:01	1998 John Kagwe, KEN	2:08:45
1977 Bill Rodgers, USA	2:11:28	1988 Steve Jones, WAL	2:08:20	1999 Joseph Chebet, KEN	2:09:14
1978 Bill Rodgers, USA	2:12:12	1989 Juma Ikangaa, TAN	2:08:01*	2000 Abdelkhader El Mouaziz,	
1979 Bill Rodgers, USA	2:11:42	1990 Douglas Wakiihuri, KEN	2:12:39	MOR	2:10:08
1980 Alberto Salazar, USA	2:09:41	1991 Salvador Garcia, MEX	2:09:28	*Course record.	

WOMEN

Multiple winners: Grete Waitz (9); Miki Gorman, Nina Kuscsik and Tegla Loroupe (2).

Year	Time	Year	Time	Year	Time
1970 No Finisher		1981 Allison Roe, NZ	2:25:29	1992 Lisa Ondieki, AUS	2:24:40*
1971 Beth Bonner, USA	2:55:22	1982 Grete Waitz, NOR	2:27:14	1993 Uta Pippig, GER	2:26:24
1972 Nina Kuscsik, USA	3:08:41	1983 Grete Waitz, NOR	2:27:00	1994 Tegla Loroupe, KEN	2:27:37
1973 Nina Kuscsik, USA	2:57:07	1984 Grete Waitz, NOR	2:29:30	1995 Tegla Loroupe, KEN	2:28:06
1974 Katherine Switzer, USA	3:07:29	1985 Grete Waitz, NOR	2:28:34	1996 Anuta Catuna, ROM	2:28:18
1975 Kim Merritt, USA	2:46:14	1986 Grete Waitz, NOR	2:28:06	1997 F. Rochat-Moser, SWI	2:28:43
1976 Miki Gorman, USA	2:39:11	1987 Priscilla Welch, GBR	2:30:17	1998 Franca Fiacconi, ITA	2:25:17
1977 Miki Gorman, USA	2:43:10	1988 Grete Waitz, NOR	2:28:07	1999 Adriana Fernandez, MEX	2:25:06
1978 Grete Waitz, NOR	2:32:30	1989 Ingrid Kristiansen, NOR	2:25:30	2000 Ludmila Petrova, RUS	2:25:45
1979 Grete Waitz, NOR	2:27:33	1990 Wanda Panfil, POL	2:30:45	*Course record.	
1980 Grete Waitz, NOR	2:25:41	1991 Liz McColgan, SCO	2:27:23		

Track & Field (Cont.)
Annual Awards
Track & Field News Athletes of the Year

Voted on by an international panel of track and field experts and presented since 1959 for men and 1974 for women.

MEN

Multiple winners: Carl Lewis (3); Sergey Bubka, Sebastian Coe, Haile Gebrselassie, Michael Johnson, Alberto Juantorena, Noureddine Morceli, Jim Ryun and Peter Snell (2).

Year		Event	Year		Event
1959	Martin Lauer, W. Germany	110H/Decathlon	1980	Edwin Moses, USA	400 Hurdles
1960	Rafer Johnson, USA	Decathlon	1981	Sebastian Coe, Great Britain	800/1500
1961	Ralph Boston, USA	Long Jump/110 Hurdles	1982	Carl Lewis, USA	100/200/Long Jump
1962	Peter Snell, New Zealand	800/1500	1983	Carl Lewis, USA	100/200/Long Jump
1963	C.K. Yang, Taiwan	Decathlon/Pole Vault	1984	Carl Lewis, USA	100/200/Long Jump
1964	Peter Snell, New Zealand	800/1500	1985	Said Aouita, Morocco	1500/5000
1965	Ron Clarke, Australia	5000/10,000	1986	Yuri Sedykh, USSR	Hammer Throw
1966	Jim Ryun, USA	800/1500	1987	Ben Johnson, Canada	100
1967	Jim Ryun, USA	1500	1988	Sergey Bubka, USSR	Pole Vault
1968	Bob Beamon, USA	Long Jump	1989	Roger Kingdom, USA	110 Hurdles
1969	Bill Toomey, USA	Decathlon	1990	Michael Johnson, USA	200/400
1970	Randy Matson, USA	Shot Put	1991	Sergey Bubka, USSR	Pole Vault
1971	Rod Milburn, USA	110 Hurdles	1992	Kevin Young, USA	400 Hurdles
1972	Lasse Viren, Finland	5000/10,000	1993	Noureddine Morceli, Algeria	Mile/1500/3000
1973	Ben Jipcho, Kenya	1500/5000/Steeplechase	1994	Noureddine Morceli, Algeria	Mile/1500/3000
1974	Rick Wohlhuter, USA	800/1500	1995	Haile Gebrselassie, Ethiopia	5000/10,000
1975	John Walker, New Zealand	800/1500	1996	Michael Johnson, USA	200/400
1976	Alberto Juantorena, Cuba	400/800	1997	Wilson Kipketer, Denmark	800
1977	Alberto Juantorena, Cuba	400/800	1998	Haile Gebrselassie, Ethiopia	3000/5000/10,000
1978	Henry Rono, Kenya	5000/10,000/Steeplechase	1999	Hicham El Guerrouj, Morocco	Mile/1500
1979	Sebastian Coe, Great Britain	800/1500	2000	Virgilijus Alekna, Lithuania	Discus

WOMEN

Multiple winners: Marita Koch (4); Marion Jones and Jackie Joyner-Kersee (3); Evelyn Ashford (2).

Year		Event	Year		Event
1974	Irena Szewinska, Poland	100/200/400	1988	Florence Griffith Joyner, USA	100/200
1975	Faina Melnik, USSR	Shot Put/Discus	1989	Ana Quirot, Cuba	400/800
1976	Tatiana Kazankina, USSR	800/1500	1990	Merlene Ottey, Jamaica	100/200
1977	Rosemarie Ackermann, E. Germany	High Jump	1991	Heike Henkel, Germany	High Jump
1978	Marita Koch, E. Germany	100/200/400	1992	Heike Drechsler, Germany	Long Jump
1979	Marita Koch, E. Germany	100/200/400	1993	Wang Junxia, China	1500/3000/10,000
1980	Ilona Briesenick, E. Germany	Shot Put	1994	Jackie Joyner-Kersee, USA	100H/Heptathlon/LJ
1981	Evelyn Ashford, USA	100/200	1995	Sonia O'Sullivan, Ireland	1500/3000/5000
1982	Marita Koch, E. Germany	100/200/400	1996	Svetlana Masterkova, Russia	800/1500
1983	Jarmila Kratochvilova, Czech	200/400/800	1997	Marion Jones, USA	100/200
1984	Evelyn Ashford, USA	100	1998	Marion Jones, USA	100/200/LJ
1985	Marita Koch, E. Germany	100/200/400	1999	Gabriela Szabo, Romania	3000/5000
1986	Jackie Joyner-Kersee, USA	Heptathlon/Long Jump	2000	Marion Jones, USA	100/200/LJ
1987	Jackie Joyner-Kersee, USA	100H/Heptathlon/LJ			

SWIMMING & DIVING

FINA World Championships

While the Summer Olympics have served as the unofficial world championships for swimming and diving throughout the century, a separate World Championship meet was started in 1973 by the Federation Internationale de Natation Amateur (FINA). The meet was held three times between 1973-78, then every four years since then. Sites have been Belgrade (1973); Cali, COL (1975); West Berlin (1978); Guayaquil, ECU (1982); Madrid (1986); Perth (1991 & 98), Rome (1994) and Fukuoka, JPN (2001). Looking forward, the Championships will be held in Barcelona (2003) and Montreal (2005).

MEN

Most gold medals (including relays): Ian Thorpe (8); Jim Montgomery (7); Matt Biondi and Michael Klim (6); Rowdy Gaines (5); Joe Bottom, Tamas Darnyi, Michael Gross, Grant Hackett, Tom Jager, David McCagg, Vladimir Salnikov and Tim Shaw (4); Billy Forrester, Andras Hargitay, Roland Matthes, John Murphy, Aleksandr Popov, Jeff Rouse, Norbert Rozsa, Matt Welsh and David Wilkie (3).

50-Meter Freestyle

Year		Time	
1973-82	Not held		
1986	Tom Jager, USA	22.49	
1991	Tom Jager, USA	22.16	**CR**
1994	Aleksandr Popov, RUS	22.17	
1998	Bill Pilczuk, USA	22.29	
2001	Anthony Ervin, USA	22.09	

100-Meter Freestyle

Year		Time	
1973	Jim Montgomery, USA	51.70	
1975	Tim Shaw, USA	51.25	
1978	David McCagg, USA	50.24	
1982	Jorg Woithe, E. Ger	50.18	
1986	Matt Biondi, USA	48.94	
1991	Matt Biondi, USA	49.18	
1994	Aleksandr Popov, RUS	49.12	
1998	Aleksandr Popov, RUS	48.93	**CR**
2001	Anthony Ervin, USA	48.33	**CR**

200-Meter Freestyle

Year		Time	
1973	Jim Montgomery, USA	1:53.02	
1975	Tim Shaw, USA	1:52.04	
1978	Billy Forrester, USA	1:51.02	
1982	Michael Gross, W. Ger	1:49.84	
1986	Michael Gross, W. Ger	1:47.92	
1991	Giorgio Lamberti, ITA	1:47.27	
1994	Antti Kasvio, FIN	1:47.32	CR
1998	Michael Klim, AUS	1:47.41	
2001	Ian Thorpe, AUS	1:44.06	WR

400-Meter Freestyle

Year		Time	
1973	Rick DeMont, USA	3:58.18	
1975	Tim Shaw, USA	3:54.88	
1978	Vladimir Salnikov, USSR	3:51.94	
1982	Vladimir Salnikov, USSR	3:51.30	
1986	Rainer Henkel, W. Ger	3:50.05	
1991	Jorg Hoffman, GER	3:48.04	
1994	Kieren Perkins, AUS	3:43.80	WR
1998	Ian Thorpe, AUS	3:46.29	
2001	Ian Thorpe, AUS	3:40.17	WR

800-Meter Freestyle

Year		Time	
1973-98 Not held			
2001	Ian Thorpe, AUS	7:39.16	WR

1500-Meter Freestyle

Year		Time	
1973	Stephen Holland, AUS	15:31.85	
1975	Tim Shaw, USA	15:28.92	
1978	Vladimir Salnikov, USSR	15:03.99	
1982	Vladimir Salnikov, USSR	15:01.77	
1986	Rainer Henkel, W. Ger	15:05.31	
1991	Jorg Hoffman, GER	14:50.36	WR
1994	Kieren Perkins, AUS	14:50.52	
1998	Grant Hackett, AUS	14:51.70	
2001	Grant Hackett, AUS	14:34.56	WR

50-Meter Backstroke

Year		Time	
1973-98 Not held			
2001	Randall Bal, USA	25.34	

100-Meter Backstroke

Year		Time	
1973	Roland Matthes, E. Ger	57.47	
1975	Roland Matthes, E. Ger	58.15	
1978	Bob Jackson, USA	56.36	
1982	Dirk Richter, E. Ger	55.95	
1986	Igor Polianski, USSR	55.58	
1991	Jeff Rouse, USA	55.23	
1994	Martin Lopez-Zubero, SPA	55.17	CR
1998	Lenny Krayzelburg, USA	55.00	
2001	Matt Welsh, AUS	54.31	CR

200-Meter Backstroke

Year		Time	
1973	Roland Matthes, E. Ger	2:01.87	
1975	Zoltan Varraszto, HUN	2:05.05	
1978	Jesse Vassallo, USA	2:02.16	
1982	Rick Carey, USA	2:00.82	
1986	Igor Polianski, USSR	1:58.78	CR
1991	Martin Zubero, SPA	1:59.52	
1994	Vladimir Selkov, RUS	1:57.42	
1998	Lenny Krayzelburg, USA	1:58.84	
2001	Aaron Peirsol, USA	1:57.13	CR

50-Meter Breaststroke

Year		Time	
1973-98 Not held			
2001	Oleg Lisogor, UKR	27.52	

100-Meter Breaststroke

Year		Time	
1973	John Hencken, USA	1:04.02	
1975	David Wilkie, GBR	1:04.26	
1978	Walter Kusch, W. Ger	1:03.56	
1982	Steve Lundquist, USA	1:02.75	
1986	Victor Davis, CAN	1:02.71	
1991	Norbert Rozsa, HUN	1:01.45	WR
1994	Norbert Rozsa, HUN	1:01.24	
1998	Frederik deBurghgraeve, BEL	1:01.34	
2001	Roman Sloudnov, RUS	1:00.16	

200-Meter Breaststroke

Year		Time	
1973	David Wilkie, GBR	2:19.28	
1975	David Wilkie, GBR	2:18.23	
1978	Nick Nevid, USA	2:18.37	
1982	Victor Davis, CAN	2:14.77	WR
1986	Jozsef Szabo, HUN	2:14.27	
1991	Mike Barrowman, USA	2:11.23	WR
1994	Norbert Rozsa, HUN	2:12.81	
1998	Kurt Grote, USA	2:13.40	
2001	Brendan Hansen, USA	2:10.69	CR

50-Meter Butterfly

Year		Time
1973-98 Not held		
2001	Geoff Huegill, AUS.	23.50

100-Meter Butterfly

Year		Time	
1973	Bruce Robertson, CAN	55.69	
1975	Greg Jagenburg, USA	55.63	
1978	Joe Bottom, USA	54.30	
1982	Matt Gribble, USA	53.88	
1986	Pablo Morales, USA	53.54	
1991	Anthony Nesty, SUR	53.29	
1994	Rafal Szukala, POL	53.51	
1998	Michael Klim, AUS	52.25	CR
2001	Lars Frolander, SWE	52.10	CR

200-Meter Butterfly

Year		Time	
1973	Robin Backhaus, USA	2:03.32	
1975	Billy Forrester, USA	2:01.95	
1978	Mike Bruner, USA	1:59.38	
1982	Michael Gross, W. Ger	1:58.85	
1986	Michael Gross, W. Ger	1:56.53	
1991	Melvin Stewart, USA	1:55.69	WR
1994	Denis Pankratov, RUS	1:56.54	
1998	Denys Sylantyev, UKR	1:56.61	
2001	Michael Phelps, USA	1:54.58	WR

200-Meter Individual Medley

Year		Time	
1973	Gunnar Larsson, SWE	2:08.36	
1975	Andras Hargitay, HUN	2:07.72	
1978	Graham Smith, CAN	2:03.65	WR
1982	Alexander Sidorenko, USSR	2:03.30	
1986	Tamás Darnyi, HUN	2:01.57	
1991	Tamás Darnyi, HUN	1:59.36	WR
1994	Janis Sievinen, FIN	1:58.16	WR
1998	Marcel Wouda, NET	2:01.18	
2001	Massimiliano Rosolino, ITA	1:59.71	

400-Meter Individual Medley

Year		Time	
1973	Andras Hargitay, HUN	4:31.11	
1975	Andras Hargitay, HUN	4:32.57	
1978	Jesse Vassallo, USA	4:20.05	WR
1982	Ricardo Prado, BRA	4:19.78	WR
1986	Tamás Darnyi, HUN	4:18.98	
1991	Tamás Darnyi, HUN	4:12.36	WR
1994	Tom Dolan, USA	4:12.30	WR
1998	Tom Dolan, USA	4:14.95	
2001	Alessio Boggiatto, ITA	4:13.15	

Swimming & Diving (Cont.)

4 x 100-Meter Freestyle Relay

Year		Time	
1973	United States	3:27.18	
1975	United States	3:24.85	
1978	United States	3:19.74	
1982	United States	3:19.26	WR
1986	United States	3:19.98	
1991	United States	3:17.15	
1994	United States	3:16.90	
1998	United States	3:16.69	CR
2001	Australia	3:14.10	CR

4 x 200-Meter Freestyle Relay

Year		Time	
1973	United States	7:33.22	WR
1975	West Germany	7:39.44	
1978	United States	7:20.82	
1982	United States	7:21.09	
1986	East Germany	7:15.91	
1991	Germany	7:13.50	CR
1994	Sweden	7:17.34	
1998	Australia	7:12.48	
2001	Australia	7:04.66	WR

4 x 100-Meter Medley Relay

Year		Time	
1973	United States	3:49.49	
1975	United States	3:49.00	
1978	United States	3:44.63	
1982	United States	3:40.84	WR
1986	United States	3:41.25	

Year		Time	
1991	United States	3:39.66	
1994	United States	3:37.74	CR
1998	Australia	3:37.98	
2001	Australia	3:35.35	CR

WOMEN

Most gold medals (including relays): Kornelia Ender (8); Kristin Otto (7); Tracy Caulkins, Heike Friedrich, Le Jingyi, Rosemarie Kother, Ulrike Richter and Jenny Thompson (4); Hannalore Anke, Lu Bin, He Cihong, Inge De Bruijn, Janet Evans, Nicole Haislett, Lui Limin, Birgit Meineke, Joan Pennington, Manuela Stellmach, Petria Thomas, Amy Van Dyken, Renate Vogel and Cynthia Woodhead (3).

50-Meter Freestyle

Year		Time	
1973-82	Not held		
1986	Tamara Costache, ROM	25.28	WR
1991	Zhuang Yong, CHN	25.47	
1994	Le Jingyi, CHN	24.51	WR
1998	Amy Van Dyken, USA	25.15	
2001	Inge de Bruijn, NED	24.47	

100-Meter Freestyle

Year		Time	
1973	Kornelia Ender, E. Ger.	57.54	
1975	Kornelia Ender, E. Ger.	56.50	
1978	Barbara Krause, E. Ger.	55.68	
1982	Birgit Meineke, E. Ger.	55.79	
1986	Kristin Otto, E. Ger.	55.05	
1991	Nicole Haislett, USA	55.17	
1994	Le Jingyi, CHN	54.01	WR
1998	Jenny Thompson, USA	54.95	
2001	Inge de Bruijn, NED	54.18	

200-Meter Freestyle

Year		Time	
1973	Keena Rothhammer, USA	2:04.99	
1975	Shirley Babashoff, USA	2:02.50	
1978	Cynthia Woodhead, USA	1:58.53	WR
1982	Annemarie Verstappen, HOL	1:59.53	
1986	Heike Friedrich, E. Ger	1:58.26	
1991	Hayley Lewis, AUS	2:00.48	
1994	Franziska Van Almsick, GER	1:56.78	WR
1998	Claudia Poll, CRC	1:58.90	
2001	Giaan Rooney, AUS	1:58.57	

400-Meter Freestyle

Year		Time	
1973	Heather Greenwood, USA	4:20.28	
1975	Shirley Babashoff, USA	4:22.70	
1978	Tracey Wickham, AUS	4:06.28	WR
1982	Carmela Schmidt. E. Ger	4:08.98	
1986	Heike Friedrich, E. Ger	4:07.45	
1991	Janet Evans, USA	4:08.63	
1994	Yang Aihua, CHN	4:09.64	
1998	Yan Chen, CHN	4:06.72	
2001	Yana Klochkova, UKR	4:07.30	

800-Meter Freestyle

Year		Time	
1973	Novella Calligaris, ITA	8:52.97	
1975	Jenny Turrall, AUS	8:44.75	
1978	Tracey Wickham, AUS	8:25.94	
1982	Kim Linehan, USA	8:27.48	
1986	Astrid Strauss, E. Ger	8:28.24	
1991	Janet Evans, USA	8:24.05	CR
1994	Janet Evans, USA	8:29.85	
1998	Brooke Bennett, USA	8:28.71	
2001	Hannah Stockbauer, GER	8:24.66	

1500-Meter Freestyle

Year		Time	
1973-98	Not held		
2001	Hannah Stockbauer, GER	16:01.02	

50-Meter Backstroke

Year		Time	
1973-98	Not held		
2001	Haley Cope, USA	28.51	

100-Meter Backstroke

Year		Time	
1973	Ulrike Richter, E. Ger	1:05.42	
1975	Ulrike Richter, E. Ger	1:03.30	
1978	Linda Jezek, USA	1:02.55	
1982	Kristin Otto, E. Ger	1:01.30	
1986	Betsy Mitchell, USA	1:01.74	
1991	Krisztina Egerszegi, HUN	1:01.78	
1994	He Cihong, CHN	1:00.57	WR
1998	Lea Maurer, USA	1:01.16	
2001	Natalie Coughlin, USA	1:00.37	

200-Meter Backstroke

Year		Time	
1973	Melissa Belote, USA	2:20.52	
1975	Birgit Treiber, E. Ger	2:15.46	WR
1978	Linda Jezek, USA	2:11.93	WR
1982	Cornelia Sirch, E. Ger	2:09.91	WR
1986	Cornelia Sirch, E. Ger	2:11.37	
1991	Krisztina Egerszegi, HUN	2:09.15	
1994	He Cihong, CHN	2:07.40	CR
1998	Roxanna Maracineanu, FRA	2:11.26	
2001	Diana Iuliana Mocanu, ROM	2:09.94	

50-Meter Breaststroke

Year		Time	
1973-82	Not held		
2001	Xuejuan Luo, CHN	30.84	

100-Meter Breaststroke

Year		Time	
1973	Renate Vogel, E. Ger	1:13.74	
1975	Hannalore Anke, E. Ger	1:12.72	
1978	Julia Bogdanova, USSR	1:10.31	WR
1982	Ute Geweniger, E. Ger	1:09.14	
1986	Sylvia Gerasch, E. Ger	1:08.11	WR
1991	Linley Frame, AUS	1:08.81	
1994	Samantha Riley, AUS	1:07.69	WR
1998	Kristy Kowal, USA	1:08.42	
2001	Xuejuan Luo, CHN	1:07.18	CR

200-Meter Breaststroke

Year		Time	
1973	Renate Vogel, E. Ger	2:40.01	
1975	Hannalore Anke, E. Ger	2:37.25	
1978	Lina Kachushite, USSR	2:31.42	WR
1982	Svetlana Varganova, USSR	2:28.82	
1986	Silke Hoerner, E. Ger	2:27.40	WR
1991	Elena Volkova, USSR	2:29.53	
1994	Samantha Riley, AUS	2:26.87	
1998	Agnes Kovacs, HUN	2:25.45	CR
2001	Agnes Kovacs, HUN	2:24.90	CR

50-Meter Butterfly

Year		Time
1973-98	Not held	
2001	Inge de Bruijn, NED	25.90

100-Meter Butterfly

Year		Time	
1973	Kornelia Ender, E. Ger	1:02.53	
1975	Kornelia Ender, E. Ger	1:01.24	WR
1978	Joan Pennington, USA	1:00.20	
1982	Mary T. Meagher, USA	59.41	
1986	Kornelai Gressler, E. Ger	59.51	
1991	Qian Hong, CHN	59.68	
1994	Liu Limin, CHN	58.98	
1998	Jenny Thompson, USA	58.46	CR
2001	Petria Thomas, AUS	58.27	CR

200-Meter Butterfly

Year		Time	
1973	Rosemarie Kother, E. Ger	2:13.76	
1975	Rosemarie Kother, E. Ger	2:15.92	
1978	Tracy Caulkins, USA	2:09.78	WR
1982	Ines Geissler, E. Ger	2:08.66	
1986	Mary T. Meagher, USA	2:08.41	
1991	Summer Sanders, USA	2:09.24	
1994	Liu Limin, CHN	2:07.25	CR
1998	Susie O'Neill, AUS	2:07.93	
2001	Petria Thomas, AUS	2:06.73	CR

200-Meter Individual Medley

Year		Time	
1973	Andre Huebner, E. Ger	2:20.51	
1975	Kathy Heddy, USA	2:19.80	
1978	Tracy Caulkins, USA	2:19.80	WR
1982	Petra Schneider, E. Ger	2:11.79	CR
1986	Kristin Otto, E. Ger	2:15.56	
1991	Lin Li, CHN	2:13.40	
1994	Lu Bin, CHN	2:12.34	
1998	Yanyan Wu, CHN	2:10.88	CR
2001	Maggie Bowen, USA	2:11.93	

400-Meter Individual Medley

Year		Time	
1973	Gudrun Wegner, E. Ger	4:57.71	
1975	Ulrike Tauber, E. Ger	4:52.76	
1978	Tracy Caulkins, USA	4:40.83	WR
1982	Petra Schneider, E. Ger	4:36.10	WR
1986	Kathleen Nord, E. Ger	4:43.75	
1991	Lin Li, CHN	4:41.45	
1994	Dai Guohong, CHN	4:39.14	
1998	Yan Chen, CHN	4:36.66	
2001	Yana Klochkova, UKR	4:36.98	

4 x 100-Meter Freestyle Relay

Year		Time	
1973	East Germany	3:52.45	
1975	East Germany	3:49.37	
1978	United States	3:43.43	WR
1982	East Germany	3:43.97	
1986	East Germany	3:40.57	
1991	United States	3:43.26	
1994	China	3:37.91	WR
1998	United States	3:42.11	
2001	Germany	3:39.58	

4 x 200-Meter Freestyle Relay

Year		Time	
1973-82	Not held		
1986	East Germany	7:59.33	WR
1991	Germany	8:02.56	
1994	China	7:57.96	CR
1998	Germany	8:01.46	
2001	Great Britain	7:58.69	

4 x 100-Meter Medley Relay

Year		Time	
1973	East Germany	4:16.84	
1975	East Germany	4:14.74	
1978	United States	4:08.21	
1982	East Germany	4:05.80	WR
1986	East Germany	4:04.82	
1991	United States	4:06.51	
1994	China	4:01.67	CR
1998	United States	4:01.93	
2001	Australia	4:01.50	CR

Diving

Multiple Gold Medals: MEN–Greg Louganis (5); Dmitri Sautin (4); Phil Boggs (3); Klaus Dibiasi, Tian Liang and Yu Zhuocheng (2). WOMEN–Irina Kalinina and Gao Min (3); Guo Jingjing and Fu Mingxia (2).

MEN

1-Meter Springboard

Year		Pts
1991	Edwin Jongejans, NED	588.51
1994	Evan Stewart, ZIM	382.14
1998	Yu Zhuocheng, CHN	417.54
2001	Wang Feng, CHN	444.03

3-Meter Springboard

Year		Pts
1973	Phil Boggs, USA	618.57
1975	Phil Boggs, USA	597.12
1978	Phil Boggs, USA	913.95
1982	Greg Louganis, USA	752.67
1986	Greg Louganis, USA	750.06
1991	Kent Ferguson, USA	650.25
1994	Yu Zhuocheng, CHN	655.44
1998	Dmitri Sautin, RUS	746.79
2001	Dmitri Sautin, RUS	725.82

Platform

Year		Pts
1973	Klaus Dibiasi, ITA	559.53
1975	Klaus Dibiasi, ITA	547.98
1978	Greg Louganis, USA	844.11
1982	Greg Louganis, USA	634.26
1986	Greg Louganis, USA	668.58
1991	Sun Shuwei, CHN	626.79
1994	Dmitri Sautin, RUS	634.71
1998	Dmitri Sautin, RUS	750.99
2001	Tian Liang, CHN	688.77

Swimming & Diving (Cont.)

3-Meter Synchronized

Year		Pts
1973-98	Not held	
2001	Peng Bo	
	& Wang Kenan, CHN	342.63

10-Meter Synchronized

Year		Pts
1973-98	Not held	
2001	Tian Liang	
	& Hu Jia, CHN	361.41

WOMEN
1-Meter Springboard

Year		Pts
1991	Gao Min, CHN	478.26
1994	Chen Lixia, CHN	279.30
1998	Irina Lashko, RUS	296.07
2001	Blythe Hartley, CAN	300.81

3-Meter Springboard

Year		Pts
1973	Christa Koehler, E. Ger	442.17
1975	Irina Kalinina, USSR	489.81
1978	Irina Kalinina, USSR	691.43
1982	Megan Neyer, USA	501.03
1986	Gao Min, CHN	582.90

Year		Pts
1991	Gao Min, CHN	539.01
1994	Tan Shuping, CHN	548.49
1998	Yulia Pakhalina, RUS	544.52
2001	Guo Jingjing, CHN	596.67

Platform

Year		Pts
1973	Ulrike Knape, SWE	406.77
1975	Janet Ely, USA	403.89
1978	Irina Kalinina, USSR	412.71
1982	Wendy Wyland, USA	438.79
1986	Chen Lin, CHN	449.67
1991	Fu Mingxia, CHN	426.51
1994	Fu Mingxia, CHN	434.04
1998	Olena Zhupyna	550.41
2001	Xu Mian, CHN	532.65

3-Meter Synchronized

Year		Pts
1973-98	Not held	
2001	Wu Minxia	
	& Guo Jingjing, CHN	347.31

10-Meter Synchronized

Year		Pts
1973-98	Not held	
2001	Duan Qing	
	& Sang Xue, CHN	329.94

ALPINE SKIING

World Cup Overall Champions

World Cup Overall Champions (downhill and slalom events combined) since the tour was organized in 1967.

MEN

Multiple winners: Marc Girardelli (5), Gustavo Thoeni and Pirmin Zurbriggen (4); Phil Mahre, Hermann Maier and Ingemar Stenmark (3); Jean-Claude Killy, Lasse Kjus and Karl Schranz (2).

Year		Year		Year	
1967	Jean-Claude Killy, France	1979	Peter Luescher, Switzerland	1991	Marc Girardelli, Luxembourg
1968	Jean-Claude Killy, France	1980	Andreas Wenzel, Liechtenstein	1992	Paul Accola, Switzerland
1969	Karl Schranz, Austria	1981	Phil Mahre, USA	1993	Marc Girardelli, Luxembourg
		1982	Phil Mahre, USA	1994	Kjetil Andre Aamodt, Norway
1970	Karl Schranz, Austria	1983	Phil Mahre, USA	1995	Alberto Tomba, Italy
1971	Gustavo Thoeni, Italy	1984	Pirmin Zurbriggen, Switzerland	1996	Lasse Kjus, Norway
1972	Gustavo Thoeni, Italy	1985	Marc Girardelli, Luxembourg	1997	Luc Alphand, France
1973	Gustavo Thoeni, Italy	1986	Marc Girardelli, Luxembourg	1998	Hermann Maier, Austria
1974	Piero Gros, Italy	1987	Pirmin Zurbriggen, Switzerland	1999	Lasse Kjus, Norway
1975	Gustavo Thoeni, Italy	1988	Pirmin Zurbriggen, Switzerland		
1976	Ingemar Stenmark, Sweden	1989	Marc Girardelli, Luxembourg	2000	Hermann Maier, Austria
1977	Ingemar Stenmark, Sweden			2001	Hermann Maier, Austria
1978	Ingemar Stenmark, Sweden	1990	Pirmin Zurbriggen, Switzerland		

WOMEN

Multiple winners: Annemarie Moser-Proell (6); Petra Kronberger and Vreni Schneider (3); Michela Figini, Nancy Greene, Erika Hess, Katja Seizinger, Maria Walliser and Hanni Wenzel (2).

Year		Year		Year	
1967	Nancy Greene, Canada	1979	Annemarie Moser-Pröll, Austria	1990	Petra Kronberger, Austria
1968	Nancy Greene, Canada	1980	Hanni Wenzel, Liechtenstein	1991	Petra Kronberger, Austria
1969	Gertrud Gabi, Austria	1981	Marie-Therese Nadig,	1992	Petra Kronberger, Austria
			Switzerland	1993	Anita Wachter, Austria
1970	Michele Jacot, France	1982	Erika Hess, Switzerland	1994	Vreni Schneider, Switzerland
1971	Annemarie Pröll, Austria	1983	Tamara McKinney, USA	1995	Vreni Schneider, Switzerland
1972	Annemarie Pröll, Austria	1984	Erika Hess, Switzerland	1996	Katja Seizinger, Germany
1973	Annemarie Pröll, Austria	1985	Michela Figini, Switzerland	1997	Pernilla Wiberg, Sweden
1974	Annemarie Pröll, Austria	1986	Maria Walliser, Switzerland	1998	Katja Seizinger, Germany
1975	Annemarie Moser-Pröll, Austria	1987	Maria Walliser, Switzerland	1999	Alexandra Meissnitzer, Austria
1976	Rosi Mittermaier, W. Germany	1988	Michela Figini, Switzerland		
1977	Lise-Marie Morerod, Switzerland	1989	Vreni Schneider, Switzerland	2000	Renate Goetschl, Austria
1978	Hanni Wenzel, Liechtenstein			2001	Janica Kostelic, Croatia

World Cup Event Champions

World Cup Champions in each individual event since the tour was organized in 1967.

MEN

Downhill

Multiple winners: Franz Klammer (5); Luc Alphand, Franz Heinzer and Peter Muller (3); Roland Collumbin, Marc Girardelli, Helmut Hoflehner, Hermann Maier, Bernard Russi, Karl Schranz and Pirmin Zurbriggen (2).

Year		Year		Year	
1967	Jean-Claude Killy, France	1979	Peter Muller, Switzerland	1991	Franz Heinzer, Switzerland
1968	Gerhard Nenning, Austria	1980	Peter Muller, Switzerland	1992	Franz Heinzer, Switzerland
1969	Karl Schranz, Austria	1981	Harti Weirather, Austria	1993	Franz Heinzer, Switzerland
1970	Karl Schranz, Austria	1982	Steve Podborski, Canada	1994	Marc Girardelli, Luxembourg
	Karl Cordin, Austria		Peter Muller, Switzerland	1995	Luc Alphand, France
1971	Bernard Russi, Switzerland	1983	Franz Klammer, Austria	1996	Luc Alphand, France
1972	Bernard Russi, Switzerland	1984	Urs Raber, Switzerland	1997	Luc Alphand, France
1973	Roland Collumbin, Switzerland	1985	Helmut Hoflehner, Austria	1998	Andreas Schifferer, Austria
1974	Roland Collumbin, Switzerland	1986	Peter Wirnsberger, Austria	1999	Lasse Kjus, Norway
1975	Franz Klammer, Austria	1987	Pirmin Zurbriggen, Switzerland	2000	Hermann Maier, Austria
1976	Franz Klammer, Austria	1988	Pirmin Zurbriggen, Switzerland	2001	Hermann Maier, Austria
1977	Franz Klammer, Austria	1989	Marc Girardelli, Luxembourg		
1978	Franz Klammer, Austria	1990	Helmut Hoflehner, Austria		

Slalom

Multiple winners: Ingemar Stenmark (8); Alberto Tomba (4); Jean-Noel Augert and Marc Girardelli (3); Armin Bittner, Thomas Sykora and Gustavo Thoeni (2).

Year		Year		Year	
1967	Jean-Claude Killy, France	1978	Ingemar Stenmark, Sweden	1990	Armin Bittner, West Germany
1968	Domeng Giovanoli, Switzerland	1979	Ingemar Stenmark, Sweden	1991	Marc Girardelli, Luxembourg
1969	Jean-Noel Augert, France	1980	Ingemar Stenmark, Sweden	1992	Alberto Tomba, Italy
1970	Patrick Russel, France	1981	Ingemar Stenmark, Sweden	1993	Tomas Fogdof, Sweden
	Alain Penz, France	1982	Phil Mahre, USA	1994	Alberto Tomba, Italy
1971	Jean-Noel Augert, France	1983	Ingemar Stenmark, Sweden	1995	Alberto Tomba, Italy
1972	Jean-Noel Augert, France	1984	Marc Girardelli, Luxembourg	1996	Sebastien Amiez, France
1973	Gustavo Thoeni, Italy	1985	Marc Girardelli, Luxembourg	1997	Thomas Sykora, Austria
1974	Gustavo Thoeni, Italy	1986	Rok Petrovic, Yugoslavia	1998	Thomas Sykora, Austria
1975	Ingemar Stenmark, Sweden	1987	Bojan Krizaj, Yugoslavia	1999	Thomas Stangassinger, Austria
1976	Ingemar Stenmark, Sweden	1988	Alberto Tomba, Italy	2000	Kjetil Andre Aamodt, Norway
1977	Ingemar Stenmark, Sweden	1989	Armin Bittner, West Germany	2001	Benjamin Raich, Austria

Giant Slalom

Multiple winners: Ingemar Stenmark (8); Alberto Tomba (4); Michael von Gruenigen, Hermann Maier and Pirmin Zurbriggen (3); Joel Gaspoz, Jean-Claude Killy, Phil Mahre and Gustavo Thoeni (2).

Year		Year		Year	
1967	Jean-Claude Killy, France	1980	Ingemar Stenmark, Sweden	1991	Alberto Tomba, Italy
1968	Jean-Claude Killy, France	1981	Ingemar Stenmark, Sweden	1992	Alberto Tomba, Italy
1969	Karl Schranz, Austria	1982	Phil Mahre, USA	1993	Kjetil Andre Aamodt, Norway
1970	Gustavo Thoeni, Italy	1983	Phil Mahre, USA	1994	Christian Mayer, Austria
1971	Patrick Russel, France	1984	Ingemar Stenmark, Sweden	1995	Alberto Tomba, Italy
1972	Gustavo Thoeni, Italy		Pirmin Zurbriggen, Switzerland	1996	Michael von Gruenigen,
1973	Hans Hinterseer, Austria	1985	Marc Girardelli, Luxembourg		Switzerland
1974	Piero Gros, Italy	1986	Joel Gaspoz, Switzerland	1997	Michael von Gruenigen,
1975	Ingemar Stenmark, Sweden	1987	Joel Gaspoz, Switzerland		Switzerland
1976	Ingemar Stenmark, Sweden		Pirmin Zurbriggen, Switzerland	1998	Hermann Maier, Austria
1977	Heini Hemmi, Switzerland	1988	Alberto Tomba, Italy	1999	Michael von Gruenigen,
	Ingemar Stenmark, Sweden	1989	Pirmin Zurbriggen, Switzerland		Switzerland
1978	Ingemar Stenmark, Sweden	1990	Ole-Cristian Furuseth, Norway	2000	Hermann Maier, Austria
1979	Ingemar Stenmark, Sweden		Gunther Mader, Austria	2001	Hermann Maier, Austria

Super G

Multiple winners: Hermann Maier and Pirmin Zurbriggen (4).

Year		Year		Year	
1986	Markus Wasmeier,	1991	Franz Heinzer, Switzerland	1997	Luc Alphand, France
	West Germany	1992	Paul Accola, Switzerland	1998	Hermann Maier, Austria
1987	Pirmin Zurbriggen, Switzerland	1993	Kjetil Andre Aamodt, Norway	1999	Hermann Maier, Austria
1988	Pirmin Zurbriggen, Switzerland	1994	Jan Einar Thorsen, Norway	2000	Hermann Maier, Austria
1989	Pirmin Zurbriggen, Switzerland	1995	Peter Runggaldier, Italy	2001	Hermann Maier, Austria
1990	Pirmin Zurbriggen, Switzerland	1996	Atle Skaardal, Norway		

Alpine Skiing (Cont.)
Combined

Multiple winners: Marc Girardelli and Andreas Wenzel (4); Phil Mahre (3); Kjetil Andre Aamodt and Pirmin Zurbriggen (2).

Year	Year	Year
1979 Andreas Wenzel, Liechtenstein	1987 Pirmin Zurbriggen, Switzerland	1996 Gunther Mader, Austria
1980 Andreas Wenzel, Liechtenstein	1988 Hubert Strolz, Austria	1997-99 Not awarded
1981 Phil Mahre, USA	1989 Marc Girardelli, Luxembourg	2000 Kjetil Andre Aamodt, Norway
1982 Phil Mahre, USA	1990 Pirmin Zurbriggen, Switzerland	2001 Lasse Kjus, Norway
1983 Phil Mahre, USA	1991 Marc Girardelli, Luxembourg	
1984 Andreas Wenzel, Liechtenstein	1992 Paul Accola, Switzerland	
1985 Andreas Wenzel, Liechtenstein	1993 Marc Girardelli, Luxembourg	
1986 Markus Wasmeier,	1994 Kjetil Andre Aamodt, Norway	
West Germany	1995 Marc Girardelli, Luxembourg	

WOMEN
Downhill

Multiple winners: Annemarie Moser-Pröll (7), Michela Figini and Katja Seizinger (4); Renate Goetschl, Isabelle Mir, Marie-Therese Nadig, Picabo Street, Bridgitte Totschnig-Habersatter and Maria Walliser (2).

Year	Year	Year
1967 Marielle Goitschel, France	1979 Annemarie Moser-Pröll, Austria	1990 Katrin Gutensohn-Knopf,
1968 Isabelle Mir, France	1980 Marie-Therese Nadig,	Germany
Olga Pall, Austria	Switzerland	1991 Chantal Bournissen,
1969 Wiltrud Drexel, Austria	1981 Marie-Therese Nadig,	Switzerland
1970 Isabelle Mir, France	Switzerland	1992 Katja Seizinger, Germany
1971 Annemarie Pröll, Austria	1982 Marie-Cecile Gros-Gaudenier,	1993 Katja Seizinger, Germany
1972 Annemarie Pröll, Austria	France	1994 Katja Seizinger, Germany
1973 Annemarie Pröll, Austria	1983 Doris De Agostini, Switzerland	1995 Picabo Street, USA
1974 Annemarie Pröll, Austria	1984 Maria Walliser, Switzerland	1996 Picabo Street, USA
1975 Annemarie Moser-Pröll, Austria	1985 Michela Figini, Switzerland	1997 Renate Goetschl, Austria
1976 Bridgitte Totschnig-Habersatter,	1986 Maria Walliser, Switzerland	1998 Katja Seizinger, Germany
Austria	1987 Michela Figini, Switzerland	1999 Renate Goetschl, Austria
1977 Bridgitte Totschnig-Habersatter,	1988 Michela Figini, Switzerland	2000 Regina Haeusl, Germany
Austria	1989 Michela Figini, Switzerland	2001 Isolde Kostner, Italy
1978 Annemarie Moser-Pröll, Austria		

Slalom

Multiple winners: Vreni Schneider (6); Erika Hess (5); Marielle Goitschel, Britt Lafforgue, Lisa-Marie Morerod and Roswitha Steiner (2).

Year	Year	Year
1967 Marielle Goitschel, France	1978 Hanni Wenzel, Liechtenstein	1991 Petra Kronberger, Austria
1968 Marielle Goitschel, France	1979 Regina Sackl, Austria	1992 Vreni Schneider, Switzerland
1969 Gertrud Gabl, Austria	1980 Perrine Pelene, France	1993 Vreni Schneider, Switzerland
1970 Ingrid Lafforgue, France	1981 Erika Hess, Switzerland	1994 Vreni Schneider, Switzerland
1971 Britt Lafforgue, France	1982 Erika Hess, Switzerland	1995 Vreni Schneider, Switzerland
1972 Britt Lafforgue, France	1983 Erika Hess, Switzerland	1996 Elfi Eder, Austria
1973 Patricia Emonet, France	1984 Tamara McKinney, USA	1997 Pernilla Wiberg, Sweden
1974 Christa Zechmeister,	1985 Erika Hess, Switzerland	1998 Ylva Nowen, Sweden
West Germany	1986 Roswitha Steiner, Austria	1999 Sabine Egger, Austria
1975 Lisa-Marie Morerod,	Erika Hess, Switzerland	2000 Spela Pretnar, Slovenia
Switzerland	1987 Corrine Schmidhauser,	2001 Janica Kostelic, Croatia
1976 Rosi Mittermaier,	Switzerland	
West Germany	1988 Roswitha Steiner, Austria	
1977 Lisa-Marie Morerod,	1989 Vreni Schneider, Switzerland	
Switzerland	1990 Vreni Schneider, Switzerland	

Giant Slalom

Multiple winners: Vreni Schneider (5); Lisa-Marie Morerod and Annemarie Moser-Pröll (3); Martina Ertl, Nancy Greene, Carole Merle, Anita Wachter and Hanni Wenzel (2).

Year	Year	Year
1967 Nancy Greene, Canada	1978 Lisa-Marie Morerod,	1988 Mateja Svet, Yugoslavia
1968 Nancy Greene, Canada	Switzerland	1989 Vreni Schneider, Switzerland
1969 Marilyn Cochran, USA	1979 Christa Kinshofer,	1990 Anita Wachter, Austria
1970 Michele Jacot, France	West Germany	1991 Vreni Schneider, Switzerland
Francoise Macchi, France	1980 Hanni Wenzel, Liechtenstein	1992 Carole Merle, France
1971 Annemarie Pröll, Austria	1981 Marie-Therese Nadig,	1993 Carole Merle, France
1972 Annemarie Pröll, Austria	Switzerland	1994 Anita Wachter, Austria
1973 Monika Kaserer, Austria	1982 Irene Epple, West Germany	1995 Vreni Schneider, Switzerland
1974 Hanni Wenzel, Liechtenstein	1983 Tamara McKinney, USA	1996 Martina Ertl, Germany
1975 Annemarie Moser-Pröll, Austria	1984 Erika Hess, Switzerland	1997 Deborah Compagnoni, Italy
1976 Lisa-Marie Morerod,	1985 Maria Keihl, West Germany	1998 Martina Ertl, Germany
Switzerland	Michela Figini, Switzerland	1999 Alexandra Meissnitzer, Austria
1977 Lisa-Marie Morerod,	1986 Vreni Schneider, Switzerland	2000 Michaela Dorfmeister, Austria
Switzerland	1987 Vreni Schneider, Switzerland	2001 Sonja Nef, Switzerland
	Maria Walliser, Switzerland	

Super G

Multiple winners: Katja Seizinger (5); Carole Merle (4).

Year	Year	Year
1986 Maria Kiehl, West Germany	1992 Carole Merle, France	1998 Katja Seizinger, Germany
1987 Maria Walliser, Switzerland	1993 Katja Seizinger, Germany	1999 Alexandra Meissnitzer, Austria
1988 Michela Figini, Switzerland	1994 Katja Seizinger, Germany	2000 Renate Goetschl, Austria
1989 Carole Merle, France	1995 Katja Seizinger, Germany	2001 Regine Cavagnoud, France
1990 Carole Merle, France	1996 Katja Seizinger, Germany	
1991 Carole Merle, France	1997 Hilde Gerg, Germany	

Combined

Multiple winners: Brigitte Oertli (5); Anita Wachter and Hanni Wenzel (3); Sabine Ginther and Pernilla Wiberg (2).

Year	Year	Year
1979 Annemarie Moser-Pröll, Austria	1985 Brigitte Oertli, Switzerland	1992 Sabine Ginther, Austria
Hanni Wenzel, Liechtenstein	1986 Maria Walliser, Switzerland	1993 Anita Wachter, Austria
1980 Hanni Wenzel, Liechtenstein	1987 Brigitte Oertli, Switzerland	1994 Pernilla Wiberg, Sweden
1981 Maria-Therese Nadig,	1988 Brigitte Oertli, Switzerland	1995 Pernilla Wiberg, Sweden
Switzerland	1989 Brigitte Oertli, Switzerland	1996 Anita Wachter, Austria
1982 Irene Epple, West Germany	1989 Brigitte Oertli, Switzerland	1997-99 Not Awarded
1983 Hanni Wenzel, Liechtenstein	1990 Anita Wachter, Austria	2000 Renate Goetschl, Austria
1984 Erika Hess, Switzerland	1991 Sabine Ginther, Austria	2001 Janica Kostelic, Croatia

TOUR DE FRANCE

The world's premier cycling event, the Tour de France is staged throughout the country (sometimes passing through neighboring countries) over four weeks. The 1946 Tour, however, the first after World War II, was only a five-day race.

Multiple winners: Jacques Anquetil, Bernard Hinault, Miguel Induráin and Eddy Merckx (5); Lance Armstrong, Louison Bobet, Greg LeMond and Phillippe Thys (3); Gino Bartali Ottavio Bottecchia, Fausto Coppi, Laurent Fignon, Nicholas Frantz, Firmin Lambot, André Leducq, Sylvere Maes, Antonin Magne, Lucien Petit-Breton and Bernard Thevenet (2).

Year	Year	Year
1903 Maurice Garin, France	1937 Roger Lapebie, France	1973 Luis Ocana, Spain
1904 Henri Cornet, France	1938 Gino Bartali, Italy	1974 Eddy Merckx, Belgium
1905 Louis Trousselier, France	1939 Sylvere Maes, Belgium	1975 Bernard Thevenet, France
1906 René Pottier, France		1976 Lucien van Impe, Belgium
1907 Lucien Petit-Breton, France	1940-45 Not held	1977 Bernard Thevenet, France
1900 Lucien Petit Breton, France	1946 Jean Lazarides, France	1978 Bernard Hinault, France
1909 Francois Faber, Luxembourg	1947 Jean Robic, France	1979 Bernard Hinault, France
	1948 Gino Bartali, Italy	
1910 Octave Lapize, France	1949 Fausto Coppi, Italy	1980 Joop Zoetemelk, Holland
1911 Gustave Garrigou, France		1981 Bernard Hinault, France
1912 Odile Defraye, Belgium	1950 Ferdinand Kubler, Switzerland	1982 Bernard Hinault, France
1913 Philippe Thys, Belgium	1951 Hugo Koblet, Switzerland	1983 Laurent Fignon, France
1914 Philippe Thys, Belgium	1952 Fausto Coppi, Italy	1984 Laurent Fignon, France
1915-18 Not held	1953 Louison Bobet, France	1985 Bernard Hinault, France
1919 Firmin Lambot, Belgium	1954 Louison Bobet, France	1986 Greg LeMond, USA
	1955 Louison Bobet, France	1987 Stephen Roche, Ireland
1920 Philippe Thys, Belgium	1956 Roger Walkowiak, France	1988 Pedro Delgado, Spain
1921 Léon Scieur, Belgium	1957 Jacques Anquetil, France	1989 Greg LeMond, USA
1922 Firmin Lambot, Belgium	1958 Charly Gaul, Luxembourg	
1923 Henri Pelissier, France	1959 Federico Bahamontes, Spain	1990 Greg LeMond, USA
1924 Ottavio Bottecchia, Italy		1991 Miguel Induráin, Spain
1925 Ottavio Bottecchia, Italy	1960 Gastone Nencini, Italy	1992 Miguel Induráin, Spain
1926 Lucien Buysse, Belgium	1961 Jacques Anquetil, France	1993 Miguel Induráin, Spain
1927 Nicholas Frantz, Luxembourg	1962 Jacques Anquetil, France	1994 Miguel Induráin, Spain
1928 Nicholas Frantz, Luxembourg	1963 Jacques Anquetil, France	1995 Miguel Induráin, Spain
1929 Maurice Dewaele, Belgium	1964 Jacques Anquetil, France	1996 Bjarne Riis, Denmark
	1965 Felice Gimondi, Italy	1997 Jan Ullrich, Germany
1930 André Leducq, France	1966 Lucien Aimar, France	1998 Marco Pantani, Italy
1931 Antonin Magne, France	1967 Roger Pingeon, France	1999 Lance Armstrong, USA
1932 André Leducq, France	1968 Jan Janssen, Holland	
1933 Georges Speicher, France	1969 Eddy Merckx, Belgium	2000 Lance Armstrong, USA
1934 Antonin Magne, France		2001 Lance Armstrong, USA
1935 Romain Maes, Belgium	1970 Eddy Merckx, Belgium	
1936 Sylvere Maes, Belgium	1971 Eddy Merckx, Belgium	
	1972 Eddy Merckx, Belgium	

FIGURE SKATING

World Champions

Skaters who won World and Olympic championships in the same year are listed in **bold** type.

MEN

Multiple winners: Ulrich Salchow (10); Karl Schafer (7); Dick Button (5); Willy Bockl, Kurt Browning, Scott Hamilton and Hayes Jenkins (4); Emmerich Danzer, Gillis Grafstrom, Gustav Hugel, David Jenkins, Fritz Kachler, Ondrej Nepela, Elvis Stojko and Alexei Yagudin (3); Brian Boitano, Gilbert Fuchs, Jan Hoffmann, Felix Kaspar, Vladimir Kovalev and Tim Wood (2).

Year		Year		Year	
1896	Gilbert Fuchs, Germany	1934	Karl Schafer, Austria	1971	Ondrej Nepela, Czechoslovakia
1897	Gustav Hugel, Austria	1935	Karl Schafer, Austria	1972	**Ondrej Nepela**, Czechoslovakia
1898	Henning Grenander, Sweden	1936	**Karl Schafer**, Austria	1973	Ondrej Nepela, Czechoslovakia
1899	Gustav Hugel, Austria	1937	Felix Kaspar, Austria	1974	Jan Hoffmann, E. Germany
1900	Gustav Hugel, Austria	1938	Felix Kaspar, Austria	1975	Sergie Volkov, USSR
1901	Ulrich Salchow, Sweden	1939	Graham Sharp, Britain	1976	**John Curry**, Britain
1902	Ulrich Salchow, Sweden	1940-46	Not held	1977	Vladimir Kovalev, USSR
1903	Ulrich Salchow, Sweden	1947	Hans Gerschwiler, Switzerland	1978	Charles Tickner, USA
1904	Ulrich Salchow, Sweden	1948	**Dick Button**, USA	1979	Vladimir Kovalev, USSR
1905	Ulrich Salchow, Sweden	1949	Dick Button, USA	1980	Jan Hoffmann, E. Germany
1906	Gilbert Fuchs, Germany	1950	Dick Button, USA	1981	Scott Hamilton, USA
1907	Ulrich Salchow, Sweden	1951	Dick Button, USA	1982	Scott Hamilton, USA
1908	**Ulrich Salchow**, Sweden	1952	**Dick Button**, USA	1983	Scott Hamilton, USA
1909	Ulrich Salchow, Sweden	1953	Hayes Jenkins, USA	1984	**Scott Hamilton**, USA
1910	Ulrich Salchow, Sweden	1954	Hayes Jenkins, USA	1985	Alexander Fadeev, USSR
1911	Ulrich Salchow, Sweden	1955	Hayes Jenkins, USA	1986	Brian Boitano, USA
1912	Fritz Kachler, Austria	1956	**Hayes Jenkins**, USA	1987	Brian Orser, Canada
1913	Fritz Kachler, Austria	1957	David Jenkins, USA	1988	**Brian Boitano**, USA
1914	Gosta Sandhal, Sweden	1958	David Jenkins, USA	1989	Kurt Browning, Canada
1915-21	Not held	1959	David Jenkins, USA	1990	Kurt Browning, Canada
1922	Gillis Grafstrom, Sweden	1960	Alan Giletti, France	1991	Kurt Browning, Canada
1923	Fritz Kachler, Austria	1961	Not held	1992	**Viktor Petrenko**, CIS
1924	**Gillis Grafstrom,** Sweden	1962	Donald Jackson, Canada	1993	Kurt Browning, Canada
1925	Willy Bockl, Austria	1963	Donald McPherson, Canada	1994	Elvis Stojko, Canada
1926	Willy Bockl, Austria	1964	**Manfred Schnelldorfer**,	1995	Elvis Stojko, Canada
1927	Willy Bockl, Austria		W. Ger	1996	Todd Eldredge, USA
1928	Willy Bockl, Austria	1965	Alain Calmat, France	1997	Elvis Stojko, Canada
1929	Gillis Grafstrom, Sweden	1966	Emmerich Danzer, Austria	1998	Alexei Yagudin, Russia
1930	Karl Schafer, Austria	1967	Emmerich Danzer, Austria	1999	Alexei Yagudin, Russia
1931	Karl Schafer, Austria	1968	Emmerich Danzer, Austria	2000	Alexei Yagudin, Russia
1932	**Karl Schafer**, Austria	1969	Tim Wood, USA	2001	Evgeni Plushenko, Russia
1933	Karl Schafer, Austria	1970	Tim Wood, USA		

WOMEN

Multiple winners: Sonja Henie (10); Carol Heiss and Herma Planck Szabo (5); Lily Kronberger, Michelle Kwan and Katarina Witt (4); Sjoukje Dijkstra, Peggy Fleming and Meray Horvath (3); Tenley Albright, Linda Fratianne, Anett Poetzsch, Beatrix Schuba, Barbara Ann Scott, Gabriele Seyfert, Megan Taylor, Alena Vrzanova and Kristi Yamaguchi (2).

Year		Year		Year	
1906	Madge Syers, Britain	1934	Sonja Henie, Norway	1962	Sjoukje Dijkstra, Holland
1907	Madge Syers, Britain	1935	Sonja Henie, Norway	1963	Sjoukje Dijkstra, Holland
1908	Lily Kronberger, Hungary	1936	**Sonja Henie**, Norway	1964	**Sjoukje Dijkstra**, Holland
1909	Lily Kronberger, Hungary	1937	Cecilia Colledge, Britain	1965	Petra Burka, Canada
1910	Lily Kronberger, Hungary	1938	Megan Taylor, Britain	1966	Peggy Fleming, USA
1911	Lily Kronberger, Hungary	1939	Megan Taylor, Britain	1967	Peggy Fleming, USA
1912	Meray Horvath, Hungary	1940-46	Not held	1968	**Peggy Fleming**, USA
1913	Meray Horvath, Hungary	1947	Barbara Ann Scott, Canada	1969	Gabriele Seyfert, E. Germany
1914	Meray Horvath, Hungary	1948	**Barbara Ann Scott**,	1970	Gabriele Seyfert, E. Germany
1915-21	Not held		Canada	1971	Beatrix Schuba, Austria
1922	Herma Planck-Szabo, Austria	1949	Alena Vrzanova,Czechoslovakia	1972	**Beatrix Schuba**, Austria
1923	Herma Planck-Szabo, Austria	1950	Alena Vrzanova,Czechoslovakia	1973	Karen Magnussen, Canada
1924	**Herma Planck-Szabo**,	1951	Jeannette Altwegg, Britain	1974	Christine Errath, E. Germany
	Austria	1952	Jacqueline Du Bief, France	1975	Dianne DeLeeuw, Holland
1925	Herma Planck-Szabo, Austria	1953	Tenley Albright, USA	1976	**Dorothy Hamill**, USA
1926	Herma Planck-Szabo, Austria	1954	Gundi Busch, W. Germany	1977	Linda Fratianne, USA
1927	Sonja Henie, Norway	1955	Tenley Albright, USA	1978	Anett Poetzsch, E. Germany
1928	**Sonja Henie**, Norway	1956	Carol Heiss, USA	1979	Linda Fratianne, USA
1929	Sonja Henie, Norway	1957	Carol Heiss, USA	1980	**Anett Poetzsch**, E. Germany
1930	Sonja Henie, Norway	1958	Carol Heiss, USA	1981	Denise Biellmann, Switzerland
1931	Sonja Henie, Norway	1959	Carol Heiss, USA	1982	Elaine Zayak, USA
1932	**Sonja Henie**, Norway	1960	**Carol Heiss**, USA	1983	Rosalyn Sumners, USA
1933	Sonja Henie, Norway	1961	Not held	1984	**Katarina Witt**, E. Germany

Year
1985 Katarina Witt, E. Germany
1986 Debi Thomas, USA
1987 Katarina Witt, E. Germany
1988 **Katarina Witt**, E. Germany
1989 Midori Ito, Japan
1990 Jill Trenary, USA

Year
1991 Kristi Yamaguchi, USA
1992 **Kristi Yamaguchi**, USA
1993 Oksana Baiul, Ukraine
1994 Yuka Sato, Japan
1995 Lu Chen, China
1996 Michelle Kwan, USA

Year
1997 Tara Lipinski, USA
1998 Michelle Kwan, USA
1999 Maria Butyrskaya, Russia
2000 Michelle Kwan, USA
2001 Michelle Kwan, USA

PAIRS

Year
1908 **Anna Hubler**
 & Heinrich Burger, GER
1909 Phyllis Johnson
 & James H. Johnson, GBR
1910 Anna Hubler
 & Heinrich Burger, GER
1911 Ludowika Eilers, GER
 & Walter Jakobsson, FIN
1912 Phyllis Johnson
 & James H. Johnson, GBR
1913 Helene Engelmann
 & Karl Majstrik, GER
1914 Ludowika Jakobsson-Eilers
 & Walter Jakobsson-Eilers, FIN
1915-21 Not held
1922 **Helene Engelmann**
 & Alfred Berger, AUT
1923 Ludowika Jakobsson-Eilers
 & Walter Jakobsson-Eilers, FIN
1924 Helene Engelmann
 & Alfred Berger, GER
1925 Herma Jaross-Szabo
 & Ludwig Wrede, AUT
1926 Andree Joly
 & Pierre Brunet, FRA
1927 Herma Jaross-Szabo
 & Ludwig Wrede, AUT
1928 **Andree Joly**
 & Pierre Brunet, FRA
1929 Lilly Scholz
 & Otto Kaiser, AUT
1930 Andree Brunet-Joly
 & Pierre Brunet-Joly, FRA
1931 Emilie Rotter
 & Laszlo Szollas, HUN
1932 **Andree Brunet-Joly**
 & Pierre Brunet-Joly, FRA
1933 Emilie Rotter
 & Laszlo Szollas, HUN
1934 Emilie Rotter
 & Laszlo Szollas, HUN
1935 Emilie Rotter
 & Laszlo Szollas, HUN
1936 **Maxi Herber**
 & Ernst Baier, GER
1937 Maxi Herber
 & Ernst Baier, GER
1938 Maxi Herber
 & Ernst Baier, GER
1939 Maxi Herber
 & Ernst Baier, GER
1940-46 Not held
1947 Micheline Lannoy
 & Pierre Baugniet, BEL

Year
1948 **Micheline Lannoy**
 & Pierre Baugniet, BEL
1949 Phyllis Johnson
 & Ede Kiraly, HUN
1950 Karol Kennedy
 & Peter Kennedy, USA
1951 Ria Baran
 & Paul Falk, W. Ger
1952 **Ria Falk-Baran**
 & Paul Falk, W. Ger
1953 Jennifer Nicks
 & John Nicks, GBR
1954 Frances Dafoe
 & Norris Bowden, CAN
1955 Frances Dafoe
 & Norris Bowden, CAN
1956 **Elisabeth Schwarz**
 & Kurt Oppelt, AUT
1957 Barbara Wagner
 & Robert Paul, CAN
1958 Barbara Wagner
 & Robert Paul, CAN
1959 Barbara Wagner
 & Robert Paul, CAN
1960 **Barbara Wagner**
 & Robert Paul, CAN
1961 Not held
1962 Maria Jelinek
 & Otto Jelinek, CAN
1963 Marika Kilius
 & H.J. Baumler, W. Ger
1964 Marika Kilius
 & H.J. Baumler, W. Ger
1965 Ludmila Protopopov
 & Oleg Protopopov, USSR
1966 Ludmila Protopopov
 & Oleg Protopopov, USSR
1967 Ludmila Protopopov
 & Oleg Protopopov, USSR
1968 **Ludmila Protopopov**
 & Oleg Protopopov, USSR
1969 Irina Rodnina
 & Alexsei Ulanov, USSR
1970 Irina Rodnina
 & Aleksei Ulanov, USSR
1971 Irina Rodnina
 & Aleksei Ulanov, USSR
1972 **Irina Rodnina**
 & Aleksei Ulanov, USSR
1973 Irina Rodnina
 & Aleksandr Zaitsev, USSR
1974 Irina Rodnina
 & Aleksandr Zaitsev, USSR

Year
1975 Irina Rodnina
 & Aleksandr Zaitsev, USSR
1976 **Irina Rodnina**
 & Aleksandr Zaitsev, USSR
1977 Irina Rodnina
 & Aleksandr Zaitsev, USSR
1978 Irina Rodnina
 & Aleksandr Zaitsev, USSR
1979 Tai Babilonia
 & Randy Gardner, USA
1980 Maria Cherkasova
 & Sergei Shakhrai, USSR
1981 Irina Vorobieva
 & Igor Lisovsky, USSR
1982 Sabine Baess
 & Tassilio Thierbach, E. Ger
1983 Elena Valova
 & Oleg Vasiliev, USSR
1984 Barbara Underhill
 & Paul Martini, CAN
1985 Elena Valova
 & Oleg Vasiliev, USSR
1986 Ekaterina Gordeeva
 & Sergei Grinkov, USSR
1987 Ekaterina Gordeeva
 & Sergei Grinkov, USSR
1988 Elena Valova
 & Oleg Vasiliev, USSR
1989 Ekaterina Gordeeva
 & Sergei Grinkov, USSR
1990 Ekaterina Gordeeva
 & Sergei Grinkov, USSR
1991 Natalya Mishkutienok
 & Arhtur Dmitriev, USSR
1992 **Natalya Mishkutienok**
 & Arthur Dmitriev, USSR
1993 Isabelle Brasseur
 & Lloyd Eisler, CAN
1994 Evgenia Shishkova
 & Vadim Naumov, RUS
1995 Radka Kovarikova
 & Rene Novotny, CZR
1996 Marina Eltsova
 & Andrey Buskhov, RUS
1997 Mandy Wotzel
 & Ingo Steuer, GER
1998 Jenni Meno
 & Todd Sand, USA
1999 Elena Berrzhnaya
 & Anton Sikharulidze, RUS
2000 Maria Petrova
 & Alexei Tikhonov, RUS
2001 Jamie Sale
 & David Pelletier, CAN

DANCE

Year		Year		Year	
1950	Lois Waring & Michael McGean, USA	1968	Diane Towler & Bernard Ford, GBR	1985	Natalia Bestemianova & Andrei Bukin, USSR
1951	Jean Westwood & Lawrence Demmy, GBR	1969	Diane Towler & Bernard Ford, GBR	1986	Natalia Bestemianova & Andrei Bukin, USSR
1952	Jean Westwood & Lawrence Demmy, GBR	1970	Lyudmila Pakhomova & Aleksandr Gorshkov, USSR	1987	Natalia Bestemianova & Andrei Bukin, USSR
1953	Jean Westwood & Lawrence Demmy, GBR	1971	Lyudmila Pakhomova & Aleksandr Gorshkov, USSR	1988	**Natalia Bestemianova & Andrei Bukin**, USSR
1954	Jean Westwood & Lawrence Demmy, GBR	1972	Lyudmila Pakhomova & Aleksandr Gorshkov, USSR	1989	Marina Klimova & Sergei Ponomarenko, USSR
1955	Jean Westwood & Lawrence Demmy, GBR	1973	Lyudmila Pakhomova & Aleksandr Gorshkov, USSR	1990	Marina Klimova & Sergei Ponomarenko, USSR
1956	Pamela Wieght & Paul Thomas, GBR	1974	Lyudmila Pakhomova & Aleksandr Gorshkov, USSR	1991	Isabelle Duchesnay & Paul Duchesnay, FRA
1957	June Markham & Courtney Jones, GBR	1975	Irina Moiseeva & Andreij Minenkov, USSR	1992	**Marina Klimova & Sergei Ponomarenko**, USSR
1958	June Markham & Courtney Jones, GBR	1976	**Lyudmila Pakhomova & Aleksandr Gorshkov**, USSR	1993	Renee Roca & Gorsha Sur, USA
1959	Doreen D. Denny & Courtney Jones, GBR	1977	Irina Moiseeva & Andreij Minenkov, USSR	1994	**Oksana Grishuk & Evgeny Platov**, RUS
1960	Doreen D. Denny & Courtney Jones, GBR	1978	Natalia Linichuk & Gennadi Karponosov, USSR	1995	Oksana Grishuk & Evgeny Platov, RUS
1961	Not held	1979	Natalia Linichuk & Gennadi Karponosov, USSR	1996	Oksana Grishuk & Evgeny Platov, RUS
1962	Eva Romanova & Pavel Roman, CZE	1980	Krisztina Regoeczy & Andras Sallai, HUN	1997	Oksana Grishuk & Evgeny Platov, RUS
1963	Eva Romanova & Pavel Roman, CZE	1981	Jayne Torvill & Christopher Dean, GBR	1998	Anjelika Krylova & Oleg Ovsyannikov, RUS
1964	Eva Romanova & Pavel Roman, CZE	1982	Jayne Torvill & Christopher Dean, GBR	1999	Anjelika Krylova & Oleg Ovsyannikov, RUS
1965	Eva Romanova & Pavel Roman, CZE	1983	Jayne Torvill & Christopher Dean, GBR	2000	Marina Anissina & Gwendal Peizerat, FRA
1966	Diane Towler & Bernard Ford, GBR	1984	**Jayne Torvill & Christopher Dean**, GBR	2001	Barbara Fusar Poli & Maurizio Margaglio, ITA
1967	Diane Towler & Bernard Ford, GBR				

U.S. Champions

Skaters who won U.S., World and Olympic championships in same year are in **bold** type.

MEN

Multiple winners: Dick Button and Roger Turner (7); Sherwin Badger, Todd Eldredge and Robin Lee (5); Brian Boitano, Scott Hamilton, David Jenkins, Hayes Jenkins and Charles Tickner (4); Gordon McKellen, Nathaniel Niles and Tim Wood (3); Scott Allen, Christopher Bowman, Scott Davis, Eugene Turner, Gary Visconti and Michael Weiss (2).

Year		Year		Year		Year	
1914	Norman Scott	1938	Robin Lee	1961	Bradley Lord	1983	Scott Hamilton
1915-17	Not held	1939	Robin Lee	1962	Monty Hoyt	1984	**Scott Hamilton**
1918	Nathaniel Niles	1940	Eugene Turner	1963	Thomas Litz	1985	Brian Boitano
1919	Not held	1941	Eugene Turner	1964	Scott Allen	1986	Brian Boitano
1920	Sherwin Badger	1942	Robert Specht	1965	Gary Visconti	1987	Brian Boitano
1921	Sherwin Badger	1943	Arthur Vaughn	1966	Scott Allen	1988	**Brian Boitano**
1922	Sherwin Badger	1944-45	Not held	1967	Gary Visconti	1989	Christopher Bowman
1923	Sherwin Badger	1946	Dick Button	1968	Tim Wood	1990	Todd Eldredge
1924	Sherwin Badger	1947	Dick Button	1969	Tim Wood	1991	Todd Eldredge
1925	Nathaniel Niles	1948	**Dick Button**	1970	Tim Wood	1992	Christopher Bowman
1926	Chris Christenson	1949	Dick Button	1971	John (Misha) Petkevich	1993	Scott Davis
1927	Nathaniel Niles	1950	Dick Button	1972	Ken Shelley	1994	Scott Davis
1928	Roger Turner	1951	Dick Button	1973	Gordon McKellen	1995	Todd Eldredge
1929	Roger Turner	1952	**Dick Button**	1974	Gordon McKellen	1996	Rudy Galindo
1930	Roger Turner	1953	Hayes Jenkins	1975	Gordon McKellen	1997	Todd Eldredge
1931	Roger Turner	1954	Hayes Jenkins	1976	Terry Kubicka	1998	Todd Eldredge
1932	Roger Turner	1955	Hayes Jenkins	1977	Charles Tickner	1999	Michael Weiss
1933	Roger Turner	1956	**Hayes Jenkins**	1978	Charles Tickner	2000	Michael Weiss
1934	Roger Turner	1957	David Jenkins	1979	Charles Tickner	2001	Tim Goebel
1935	Robin Lee	1958	David Jenkins	1980	Charles Tickner		
1936	Robin Lee	1959	David Jenkins	1981	Scott Hamilton		
1937	Robin Lee	1960	David Jenkins	1982	Scott Hamilton		

WOMEN

Multiple winners: Maribel Vinson (9); Theresa Weld Blanchard and Gretchen Merrill (6); Tenley Albright, Peggy Fleming, Michelle Kwan and Janet Lynn (5); Linda Fratianne and Carol Heiss (4); Dorothy Hamill, Beatrix Loughran, Rosalyn Summers, Joan Tozzer and Jill Trenary (3); Yvonne Sherman and Debi Thomas (2).

Year		Year		Year		Year	
1914	Theresa Weld	1938	Joan Tozzer	1960	**Carol Heiss**	1982	Rosalyn Sumners
1915-17	Not held	1939	Joan Tozzer	1961	Laurence Owen	1983	Rosalyn Sumners
1918	Rosemary Beresford	1940	Joan Tozzer	1962	Barbara Pursley	1984	Rosalyn Sumners
1919	Not held	1941	Jane Vaughn	1963	Lorraine Hanlon	1985	Tiffany Chin
1920	Theresa Weld	1942	Jane Sullivan	1964	Peggy Fleming	1986	Debi Thomas
1921	Theresa Blanchard	1943	Gretchen Merrill	1965	Peggy Fleming	1987	Jill Trenary
1922	Theresa Blanchard	1944	Gretchen Merrill	1966	Peggy Fleming	1988	Debi Thomas
1923	Theresa Blanchard	1945	Gretchen Merrill	1967	Peggy Fleming	1989	Jill Trenary
1924	Theresa Blanchard	1946	Gretchen Merrill	1968	**Peggy Fleming**	1990	Jill Trenary
1925	Beatrix Loughran	1947	Gretchen Merrill	1969	Janet Lynn	1991	Tonya Harding
1926	Beatrix Loughran	1948	Gretchen Merrill	1970	Janet Lynn	1992	**Kristi Yamaguchi**
1927	Beatrix Loughran	1949	Yvonne Sherman	1971	Janet Lynn	1993	Nancy Kerrigan
1928	Maribel Vinson	1950	Yvonne Sherman	1972	Janet Lynn	1994	vacated*
1929	Maribel Vinson	1951	Sonya Klopfer	1973	Janet Lynn	1995	Nicole Bobek
1930	Maribel Vinson	1952	Tenley Albright	1974	Dorothy Hamill	1996	Michelle Kwan
1931	Maribel Vinson	1953	Tenley Albright	1975	Dorothy Hamill	1997	Tara Lipinski
1932	Maribel Vinson	1954	Tenley Albright	1976	**Dorothy Hamill**	1998	Michelle Kwan
1933	Maribel Vinson	1955	Tenley Albright	1977	Linda Fratianne	1999	Michelle Kwan
1934	Suzanne Davis	1956	Tenley Albright	1978	Linda Fratianne	2000	Michelle Kwan
1935	Maribel Vinson	1957	Carol Heiss	1979	Linda Fratianne	2001	Michelle Kwan
1936	Maribel Vinson	1958	Carol Heiss	1980	Linda Fratianne		
1937	Maribel Vinson	1959	Carol Heiss	1981	Elaine Zayak		

* Tonya Harding was stripped of the 1994 women's title and banned from membership in the U.S. Figure Skating Assn. for life on June 30, 1994 for violating the USFSA Code of Ethics after she pleaded guilty to a charge of conspiracy to hinder the prosecution related to the Jan. 6, 1994 attack on Nancy Kerrigan.

PAIRS

Year		Year		Year	
1914	Jeanne Chevalier & Norman M. Scott	1938	Joan Tozzer & M. Bernard Fox	1958	Nancy Rouillard Ludington & Ronald Ludington
1915-17	Not held	1939	Joan Tozzer & M. Bernard Fox	1959	Nancy Rouillard Ludington & Ronald Ludington
1918	Theresa Weld & Nathaniel W. Niles	1940	Joan Tozzer & M. Bernard Fox	1960	Nancy Rouillard Ludington & Ronald Ludington
1919	Not held	1941	Donna Atwood & Eugene Turner	1961	Maribel Y. Owen & Dudley S. Richards
1920	Theresa Weld & Nathaniel W. Niles	1942	Doris Schubach & Walter Noffke	1962	Dorothyann Nelson & Pieter Kollen
1921	Theresa Weld Blanchard & Nathaniel W. Niles	1943	Doris Schubach & Walter Noffke	1963	Judianne Fotheringill & Jerry J. Fotheringill
1922	Theresa Weld Blanchard & Nathaniel W. Niles	1944	Doris Schubach & Walter Noffke	1964	Judianne Fotheringill & Jerry J. Fotheringill
1923	Theresa Weld Blanchard & Nathaniel W. Niles	1945	Donna Jeanne Pospisil & Jean-Pierre Brunet	1965	Vivian Joseph & Ronald Joseph
1924	Theresa Weld Blanchard & Nathaniel W. Niles	1946	Donna Jeanne Pospisil & Jean-Pierre Brunet	1966	Cynthia Kauffman & Ronald Kauffman
1925	Theresa Weld Blanchard & Nathaniel W. Niles	1947	Yvonne Claire Sherman & Robert J. Swenning	1967	Cynthia Kauffman & Ronald Kauffman
1926	Theresa Weld Blanchard & Nathaniel W. Niles	1948	Karol Kennedy & Peter Kennedy	1968	Cynthia Kauffman & Ronald Kauffman
1927	Theresa Weld Blanchard & Nathaniel W. Niles	1949	Karol Kennedy & Peter Kennedy	1969	Cynthia Kauffman & Ronald Kauffman
1928	Maribel Vinson & Thornton L. Coolidge	1950	Karol Kennedy & Peter Kennedy	1970	Jo Jo Starbuck & Kenneth Shelley
1929	Maribel Vinson & Thornton L. Coolidge	1951	Karol Kennedy & Peter Kennedy	1971	Jo Jo Starbuck & Kenneth Shelley
1930	Beatrix Loughran & Sherwin C. Badger	1952	Karol Kennedy & Peter Kennedy	1972	Jo Jo Starbuck & Kenneth Shelley
1931	Beatrix Loughran & Sherwin C. Badger	1953	Carole Ann Ormaca & Robin Greiner	1973	Melissa Militano & Mark Militano
1932	Beatrix Loughran & Sherwin C. Badger	1954	Carole Ann Ormaca & Robin Greiner	1974	Melissa Militano & Johnny Johns
1933	Maribel Vinson & George E.B. Hill	1955	Carole Ann Ormaca & Robin Greiner	1975	Melissa Militano & Johnny Johns
1934	Grace E. Madden & James L. Madden	1956	Carole Ann Ormaca & Robin Greiner	1976	Tai Babilonia & Randy Gardner
1935	Maribel Vinson & George E.B. Hill	1957	Nancy Rouillard Ludington & Ronald Ludington	1977	Tai Babilonia & Randy Gardner
1936	Maribel Vinson & George E.B. Hill				
1937	Maribel Vinson & George E.B. Hill				

Year		Year		Year	
1978	Tai Babilonia & Randy Gardner	1986	Gillian Wachsman & Todd Waggoner	1994	Jenni Meno & Todd Sand
1979	Tai Babilonia & Randy Gardner	1987	Jill Watson & Peter Oppegard	1995	Jenni Meno & Todd Sand
1980	Tai Babilonia & Randy Gardner	1988	Jill Watson & Peter Oppegard	1996	Jenni Meno & Todd Sand
1981	Caitlin Carruthers & Peter Carruthers	1989	Kristi Yamaguchi & Rudy Galindo	1997	Kyoko Ina & Jason Dungjen
1982	Caitlin Carruthers & Peter Carruthers	1990	Kristi Yamaguchi & Rudy Galindo	1998	Kyoko Ina & Jason Dungjen
1983	Caitlin Carruthers & Peter Carruthers	1991	Natasha Kuchiki & Todd Sand	1999	Danielle Hartsell & Steve Hartsell
1984	Caitlin Carruthers & Peter Carruthers	1992	Calla Urbanski & Rocky Marval	2000	Kyoko Ina & John Zimmerman
1985	Jill Watson & Peter Oppegard	1993	Calla Urbanski & Rocky Marval	2001	Kyoko Ina & John Zimmerman

RUGBY

World Cup

The inaugural Rugby World Cup was held in 1987. Like soccer's World Cup, it is held every four years. Sixteen national teams were assembled for the first three tournaments but beginning in 1999, 20 teams played for the William Webb Ellis Cup, named for the game's inventor. The Rugby World Cup is now billed as the world's third largest athletic event, behind the Olympics and the soccer World Cup. Australia and New Zealand will co-host the competition in 2003.

Year	Winner	Score	Runner up	Host Country
1987	New Zealand	29-9	France	Australia & New Zealand
1991	Australia	12-6	England	United Kingdom & France
1995	South Africa	15-12	New Zealand	South Africa
1999	Australia	35-12	France	Wales

Six Nations Tournament

The annual Six Nations rugby tournament, a.k.a. the International Championship, was first contested in 1882 as a match between England and Wales. England, Ireland, Scotland and Wales competed in the early years. France made it five nations by joining the competition in 1910 and played until 1931 when they were expelled because of the sad state of French rugby. France rejoined the tournament in 1947. The Five Nations became the Six Nations in 2000 with the addition of Italy. Each team plays each other once (two points are earned for a win and one for a tie) and the team with the most points is declared the winner. (*) indicates Grand Slam, meaning team won all of its games.

In the 2001 tournament, England won its first four matches against Wales, Italy, Scotland and France. The tournament was then postponed for several months due to the onset of foot-and-mouth disease in Ireland. See the Updates chapter for final results.

Multiple winners: Wales and England (33); Scotland (21); France (19); Ireland (18).

Year		Year		Year		Year	
1882	England	1911	Wales*	1940-46	Not held—WW II	1973	Five way tie
1883	England	1912	England & Ireland	1947	Wales & England	1974	Ireland
1884	England	1913	England*	1948	Ireland*	1975	Wales
1885	Not completed	1914	England*	1949	Ireland	1976	Wales*
1886	England & Scotland	1915-19	Not held—WW I	1950	Wales*	1977	France*
1887	Scotland	1920	England, Scotland & Wales	1951	Ireland	1978	Wales*
1888	Not completed			1952	Wales*	1979	Wales
1889	Not completed	1921	England*	1953	England	1980	England*
1890	England & Scotland	1922	Wales	1954	England, France & Wales	1981	France*
1891	Scotland	1923	England*			1982	Ireland
1892	England	1924	England*	1955	France & Wales	1983	France & Ireland
1893	Wales	1925	Scotland*	1956	Wales	1984	Scotland*
1894	Ireland	1926	Scotland & Ireland	1957	England*	1985	Ireland
1895	Scotland	1927	Scotland & Ireland	1958	England	1986	France & Scotland
1896	Ireland	1928	England*	1959	France	1987	France*
1897	Not completed	1929	Scotland	1960	France & England	1988	Wales & France
1898	Not completed	1930	England	1961	France	1989	France
1899	Ireland	1931	Wales	1962	France	1990	Scotland*
1900	Wales	1932	England, Wales & Ireland	1963	England	1991	England*
1901	Scotland			1964	Scotland & Wales	1992	England*
1902	Wales	1933	Scotland	1965	Wales	1993	France
1903	Scotland	1934	England	1966	Wales	1994	Wales
1904	Scotland	1935	Ireland	1967	France	1995	England*
1905	Wales	1936	Wales	1968	France*	1996	England
1906	Ireland & Wales	1937	England	1969	Wales	1997	France*
1907	Scotland	1938	Scotland	1970	France & Wales	1998	France*
1908	Wales*	1939	England, Wales & Ireland	1971	Wales*	1999	Scotland
1909	Wales*			1972	Not completed	2000	England
1910	England						

Olympics

The IOC elected European Olympic Committees
president **Jacques Rogge** to succeed Juan Antonio
Samaranch on July 16.

Allsport UK/Allsport

1924-1998 Through the Years

The Winter Olympics

The move toward a winter version of the Olympics began in 1908 when figure skating made an appearance at the Summer Games in London. Ten-time world champion Ulrich Salchow of Sweden, who originated the backwards, one revolution jump that bears his name, and Madge Syers of Britain were the first singles champions. Germans Anna Hubler and Heinrich Berger won the pairs competition.

Organizers of the 1916 Summer Games in Berlin planned to introduce a "Skiing Olympia," featuring nordic events in the Black Forest, but the Games were cancelled after the outbreak of World War I in 1914.

The Games resumed in 1920 at Antwerp, Belgium, where figure skating returned and ice hockey was added as a medal event. Sweden's Gillis Grafstrom and Magda Julin took individual honors, while Ludovika and Walter Jakobsson were the top pair. In hockey, Canada won the gold medal with the United States second and Czechoslovakia third.

Despite the objections of Modern Olympics' founder Baron Pierre de Coubertin and the resistance of the Scandinavian countries, which had staged their own Nordic championships every four or five years from 1901-26 in Sweden, the International Olympic Committee sanctioned an "International Winter Sports Week" at Chamonix, France, in 1924. The 11-day event, which included nordic skiing, speed skating, figure skating, ice hockey and bobsledding, was a huge success and was retroactively called the first Olympic Winter Games.

Seventy years after those first cold weather Games, the 17th edition of the Winter Olympics took place in Lillehammer, Norway, in 1994. The event ended the four-year Olympic cycle of staging both Winter and Summer Games in the same year and began a new schedule that calls for the two Games to alternate every two years.

Year	No	Location	Dates	Nations	Most medals	USA medals
1924	I	Chamonix, FRA	Jan. 25-Feb. 4	16	Norway (4-7-6–17)	1-2-1– 4 (3rd)
1928	II	St. Moritz, SWI	Feb. 11-19	25	Norway (6-4-5–15)	2-2-2– 6 (2nd)
1932	III	Lake Placid, USA	Feb. 4-15	17	USA (6-4-2–12)	6-4-2–12 (1st)
1936	IV	Garmisch-Partenkirchen, GER ..	Feb. 6-16	28	Norway (7-5-3–15)	1-0-3– 4 (T-5th)
1940-a	–	Sapporo, JPN	Cancelled (WWII)			
1944	–	Cortina d'Ampezzo, ITA	Cancelled (WWII)			
1948	V	St. Moritz, SWI	Jan. 30-Feb. 8	28	Norway (4-3-3–10), Sweden (4-3-3–10) & Switzerland (3-4-3–10)	3-4-2– 9 (4th)
1952-b	VI	Oslo, NOR	Feb. 14-25	30	Norway (7-3-6–16)	4-6-1–11 (2nd)
1956-c	VII	Cortina d'Ampezzo, ITA	Jan. 26-Feb. 5	32	USSR (7-3-6–16)	2-3-2– 7 (T-4th)
1960	VIII	Squaw Valley, USA	Feb. 18-28	30	USSR (7-5-9–21)	3-4-3–10 (2nd)
1964	IX	Innsbruck, AUT	Jan. 29-Feb. 9	36	USSR (11-8-6–25)	1-2-3– 6 (7th)
1968-d	X	Grenoble, FRA	Feb. 6-18	37	Norway (6-6-2–14)	1-5-1– 7 (T-7th)
1972	XI	Sapporo, JPN	Feb. 3-13	35	USSR (8-5-3–16)	3-2-3– 8 (6th)
1976-e	XII	Innsbruck, AUT	Feb. 4-15	37	USSR (13-6-8–27)	3-3-4–10 (T-3rd)
1980	XIII	Lake Placid, USA	Feb. 14-23	37	E. Germany (9-7-7–23)	6-4-2–12 (3rd)
1984	XIV	Sarajevo, YUG	Feb. 7-19	49	USSR (6-10-9–25)	4-4-0– 8 (T-5th)
1988	XV	Calgary, CAN	Feb. 13-28	57	USSR (11-9-9–29)	2-1-3– 6 (T-8th)
1992-f	XVI	Albertville, FRA	Feb. 8-23	63	Germany (10-10-6–26)	5-4-2–11 (6th)
1994-g	XVII	Lillehammer, NOR	Feb. 12-27	67	Norway (10-11-5–26)	6-5-2–13 (T-5th)
1998	XVIII	Nagano, JPN	Feb. 7-22	72	Germany (12-9-8–29)	6-3-4–13 (5th)
2002	XIX	Salt Lake City, USA	Feb. 8-24			
2006	XX	Turin, ITA	Feb. 4-19			

a–The 1940 Winter Games are originally scheduled for Sapporo, but Japan resigns as host in 1937 when the Sino-Japanese war breaks out. St. Moritz is the next choice, but the Swiss feel that ski instructors should not be considered professionals and the IOC withdraws its offer. Finally, Garmisch-Partenkirchen is asked to serve again as host, but the Germans invade Poland in 1939 and the Games are eventually cancelled.

b–Germany and Japan are allowed to rejoin the Olympic community for the first time since World War II. Though a divided country, the Germans send a joint East-West team through 1964.

c–The Soviet Union (USSR) participates in its first Winter Olympics and takes home the most medals, including the gold medal in ice hockey.

d–East Germany and West Germany officially send separate teams for the first time and will continue to do so through 1988.

e–The IOC grants the 1976 Winter Games to Denver in May 1970, but in 1972 Colorado voters reject a $5 million bond issue to finance the undertaking. Denver immediately withdraws as host and the IOC selects Innsbruck, the site of the 1964 Games, to take over.

f–Germany sends a single team after East and West German reunification in 1990 and the USSR competes as the Unified Team after the breakup of the Soviet Union in 1991.

g–The IOC moves the Winter Games' four-year cycle ahead two years in order to separate them from the Summer Games and alternate Olympics every two years.

1924

Chamonix

The first Winter Olympic Games were actually called "The International Winter Sports Week" and went on for 11 days in the French Alps, 60 miles northeast of Grenoble.

As expected, the Scandinavians dominated the 16–nation field. Norway and Finland won 27 of the 43 medals available, including all four Nordic events and four of the five speed skating races. Speed skater Clas Thunberg of Finland and Norwegian Nordic skier and jumper Thorleif Haug each won three gold medals.

American speed skater Charles Jewtraw won the first event of the Games with an upset in the 500 meters. But the most remarkable U.S. medal was the bronze won by Anders Haugen in the ski jump. Due to a scoring error at the time he didn't receive it until 1974 – when he was 83 years old.

In its first four hockey games, Canada beat Switzerland 33–0, Czechoslovakia 30–0, Sweden 22–0 and Great Britain 19–2, before winning the tournament with a 6–1 victory over the U.S. in the final.

Top 5 Standings

National medal standings are not recognized by the IOC. The unofficial point totals are based on 3 points for a gold medal, 2 for a silver and 1 for a bronze. Total medals are in parentheses.

		Gold	Silver	Bronze	Points
1	Norway (17)	4	7	6	32
2	Finland (10)	4	3	3	21
3	Austria (3)	2	1	0	8
	USA (4)	1	2	1	8
5	Switzerland (2)	1	0	1	4
	Great Britain (3)	0	1	2	4

Leading Medal Winners

Number of individual medals won on the left; gold, silver and bronze breakdown to the right.

No		Sport	G-S-B
5	Clas Thunberg, FIN	Sp. Skate	3-1-1
5	Roald Larsen, NOR	Sp. Skate	0-2-3
3	Thorleif Haug, NOR	X-country & Nordic Combined	3-0-0
3	Julius Skutnabb, FIN	Sp. Skate	1-1-1
3	Johan Gröttumsbråten, NOR	X-country & Nordic Combined	0-1-2
2	Thoralf Strömstad, NOR	X-country & Nordic Combined	0-2-0

Bobsled

Event		Time
4-Man	SWI (Eduard Scherrer, Alfred Neveu, Alfred Schläppi, Heinrich Schläppi)	5:45.54

Figure Skating

Event		Points
Men	Gillis Grafström, SWE	367.89
Women	Herma Planck-Szabó, AUT	299.17
Pairs	Helene Engelmann & Albert Berger, AUT	10.64

Ice Hockey

Championship Round

Records include games played in two 4-team preliminary pools. Canada and Sweden qualified from one pool, the U.S. and Britain from the other.

		Gm	W-L-T	GF	GA
1	Canada	5	5-0-0	110	3
2	USA	5	4-1-0	73	6
3	Great Britain	5	3-2-0	40	38
4	Sweden	5	2-3-0	21	49

Semifinals: Canada over Britain, 19–2; USA over Sweden, 20–0. **Third place:** Britain over Sweden, 4–3 (also decided European title). **Final:** Canada over USA, 6–1.

Nordic Skiing

Cross Country

Event		Time
18km	Thorleif Haug, NOR	1:14:31
50km	Thorleif Haug, NOR	3:44:32

Ski Jumping

Event		Points
90m	Jacob Thams, NOR	18.906

Nordic Combined

Event		Points
18km/Jump	Thorleif Haug, NOR	18.906

Speed Skating

Event		Time
500m	Charles Jewtraw, USA	44.0
1500m	Clas Thunberg, FIN	2:20.8
5000m	Clas Thunberg, FIN	8:39.0
10,000m	Julius Skutnabb, FIN	18:04.8
Combined	Clas Thunberg, FIN	5.5 pts

1928

St. Moritz

Sonja Henie of Norway was only 11 years old in 1924 when she participated in her first Olympics and finished last in women's figure skating. Three years later, she won the world championship at age 14 and the year after that was Olympic champion at 15.

Henie would go on to win two more gold medals, a record that her coach, men's champion Gillis Grafstrom of Sweden, set in 1928 with his third straight victory in the Winter Games.

Otherwise, St. Moritz was plagued with warm weather that slowed bobsled and cross-country runs and cancelled the 10,000–meter speed skating race. Speed skater Bernt Evensen of Norway led the Games with three medals, sharing the 500–meter title with Finland's Clas Thunberg. Norway also got two gold medals from Johan Gröttumsbråten in cross-country and the Nordic Combined and led the 25 nations competing with six gold and 15 overall medals. The U.S. edged Sweden for second place.

Top 5 Standings

National medal standings are not recognized by the IOC. The unofficial point totals are based on 3 points for a gold medal, 2 for a silver and 1 for a bronze. Total medals are in parentheses.

		Gold	Silver	Bronze	Points
1	Norway (15)	6	4	5	31
2	USA (6)	2	2	2	12
3	Sweden (5)	2	2	1	11
4	Finland (4)	2	1	1	9
5	Austria (4)	0	3	1	7

Leading Medal Winners

Number of individual medals won on the left; gold, silver and bronze breakdown to the right.

No		Sport	G-S-B
3	Bernt Evensen, NOR	Sp. Skate	1-1-1
2	Johan Gröttumsbråten, NOR	X-country	2-0-0
2	Clas Thunberg, FIN	Sp. Skate	2-0-0
2	Jennison Heaton, USA	Bobsled & Cresta	1-1-0
2	Ivar Ballangrud, NOR	Sp. Skate	1-0-1

Note: Evensen also placed second in the 10,000–meter speed skating race that was later disallowed due to thawing ice conditions.

Bobsled

Event		Time
5-Man	USA (Billy Fiske, Nion Tucker, Geoff Mason, Clifford Gray, Richard Parke)	3:20.5

Cresta (Toboggan)

Event		Time
1-Man	Jennison Heaton, USA	3:01.8

Figure Skating

Event		Points
Men	Gillis Grafström, SWE	1630.75
Women	Sonja Henie, NOR	2452.25
Pairs	Andrée Joly & Pierre Brunet, FRA	100.50

Ice Hockey

Championship Round

(Overall record in parentheses)

		Gm	W-L-T	Pts	GF	GA
1	Canada (3-0-0)	3	3-0-0	6	38	0
2	Sweden (3-1-1)	3	2-1-0	4	7	12
3	Switzerland (2-2-1)	3	1-2-0	2	4	17
4	Britain (2-4-0)	3	0-3-0	0	1	21

Note: Canada received a bye to the 4–team championship round robin. The 10 other competing countries—not including the USA which did not send a team—were divided into three pools with the winners advancing to the final round. The Canadians routed Sweden, 11–0; Britain 14–0 and the Swiss, 13–0.

Nordic Skiing

Cross Country

Event		Time
18km	Johan Gröttumsbråten, NOR	1:37:01
50km	Per Erik Hedlund, SWE	4:52:03

Ski Jumping

Event		Points
90m	Alf Andersen, NOR	19.208

Nordic Combined

Event		Points
18km/Jump	Johan Gröttumsbråten, NOR	17.833

Speed Skating

Event		Time
500m	Bernt Evensen, NOR & Clas Thunberg, FIN	43.4 **OR**
1500m	Clas Thunberg, FIN	2:21.1
5000m	Ivar Ballangrud, NOR	8:50.5
10,000m	No decision (thawing of ice)	

Note: Irving Jaffee of USA had the fastest time in the 10,000 meters (18:36.5) before the race was cancelled.

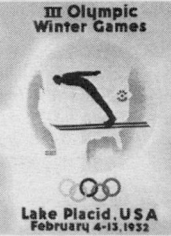

III Olympic Winter Games

Lake Placid, USA
February 4-13, 1932

1932

Lake Placid

Back in 1928, American Irving Jaffee had the fastest time in the 10,000–meter speed skating race at St. Moritz only to lose his gold medal when thawing ice made it necessary to call the event off with no official winner.

Four years later, Jaffee won the 10,000 and the 5,000–meter races and local hero Jack Shea won at 500 and 1,500 meters as the U.S. swept all four speed skating events—which were run as actual races (not timed heats) for the first time in Olympic history.

Billy Fiske, who had driven the 5–man U.S. bobsled to a gold medal at St. Moritz when he was only 16, steered the 4–man sled to victory in 1932. On board was Eddie Eagan, the 1920 Olympic light heavyweight champion, who remains the only athlete ever to win gold medals in both the Winter and Summer Games.

Canada won its fourth consecutive hockey gold medal, but 38–year-old Gillis Grafstrom of Sweden missed in his bid for a fourth straight men's figure skating title, placing second to 22–year-old Austrian Karl Schafer.

Top 5 Standings

National medal standings are not recognized by the IOC. The unofficial point totals are based on 3 points for a gold medal, 2 for a silver and 1 for a bronze. Total medals are in parentheses.

		Gold	Silver	Bronze	Points
1	USA (12)	6	4	2	28
2	Norway (10)	3	4	3	20
3	Canada (7)	1	1	5	10
4	Sweden (3)	1	2	0	7
5	Finland (3)	1	1	1	6

Leading Medal Winners

Number of individual medals won on the left; gold, silver and bronze breakdown to the right.

No		Sport	G-S-B
2	Irving Jaffee, USA	Sp. Skate	2-0-0
2	Jack Shea, USA	Sp. Skate	2-0-0
2	Veli Saarinen, FIN	X-country	1-0-1
2	Alex Hurd, CAN	Sp. Skate	0-1-1
2	William Logan, CAN	Sp. Skate	0-0-2

Bobsled

Event		Time
2-Man	USA (J.Hubert Stevens & Curtis Stevens)	8:14.74
4-Man	USA (Billy Fiske, Eddie Eagan, Clifford Gray, Jay O'Brien)	7:53.68

Figure Skating

Event		Points
Men	Karl Schäfer, AUT	2602.0
Women	Sonja Henie, NOR	2302.5
Pairs	Andrée Joly Brunet & Pierre Brunet, FRA	76.7

Ice Hockey

		Gm	W-L-T	Pts	GF	GA
1	Canada	6	5-0-1	11	32	4
2	USA	6	4-1-1	9	27	5
3	Germany	6	2-4-0	4	7	26
4	Poland	6	0-6-0	0	3	34

Note: Due to the worldwide Depression, only four teams competed. Each side played the other teams twice. Canada beat the U.S., 2–1, in their first game and tied the Americans, 2–2, in triple overtime in the second. A win by the U.S. in Game 2 would have resulted in a third contest to decide the gold medal.

Nordic Skiing

Cross Country

Event		Time
18km	Sven Utterström, SWE	1:23.07
50km	Veli Saarinen, FIN	4:28.00

Ski Jumping

Event		Points
90m	Birger Rudd, NOR	228.1

Nordic Combined

Event		Points
18km/Jump	Johan Gröttumsbråten, NOR	446.00

Speed Skating

Event		Time	
500m	Jack Shea, USA	43.4	OR
1500m	Jack Shea, USA	2:57.5	
5000m	Irving Jaffee, USA	9:40.8	
10,000m	Irving Jaffee, USA	19:13.6	

Note: For the only time in the history of the Winter Games, all events were staged as races rather than two-man heats against the clock.

1936

Garmisch-Partenkirchen

The fourth Winter Olympic Games were held in the neighboring villages of Garmisch and Partenkirchen in Germany's Bavarian Alps and included Alpine skiing for the first time.

Also featured in these Games were Norwegians Ivar Ballangrud and Sonja Henie, and Rudi Ball—the Jewish star of the German hockey team.

Ballangrud won three individual gold medals and narrowly missed a fourth in speed skating, but his heroics paled compared to the attention lavished on Henie, who won her third straight gold medal. A week later, she won the world championship for the 10th year in a row, then turned pro. Moving to the U.S., she toured in her own skating show, starred in nine Hollywood movies and was worth more than $45 million when she died in 1969 at age 57.

Ball, who had been the best player on Germany's bronze medal-winning hockey team in 1932, was invited back from voluntary exile in France to lead the 1936 German squad. He was the only Jew on the German Winter Olympic team and his presence was a token gesture by the government of Adolf Hitler to mollify anxious IOC officials who objected to the Nazis' fervent anti-Semitism.

The story of the hockey tournament, however, wasn't one German Jew, but 11 British Canadians, who led Britain to the gold medal and stopped Canada's undefeated Olympic winning streak at 20. The best of the imported Brits was goaltender Jimmy Foster, who allowed just three goals in eight games.

After winning six gold medals in 1932, the U.S. had to settle for one this time, in the two-man bobsled driven by Ivan Brown.

Top 10 Standings

National medal standings are not recognized by the IOC. The unofficial point totals are based on 3 points for a gold medal, 2 for a silver and 1 for a bronze. Total medals are in parentheses.

		Gold	Silver	Bronze	Pts
1	Norway (15)	7	5	3	34
2	Germany (6)	3	3	0	15
3	Sweden (7)	2	2	3	13
4	Finland (6)	1	2	3	10
5	Switzerland (3)	1	2	0	7
6	Austria (4)	1	1	2	7
7	Great Britain (3)	1	1	1	6
8	USA (4)	1	0	3	6
9	Canada (1)	0	1	0	2
10	France (1)	0	0	1	1
	Hungary (1)	0	0	1	1

Leading Medal Winners

Number of individual medals won on the left; gold, silver and bronze breakdown to the right.

No		Sport	G-S-B
4	Ivar Ballangrud, NOR	Sp. Skate	3-1-0
3	Oddbjörn Hagen, NOR	X-country & Nordic Combined	1-2-0
3	Birger Vasenius, FIN	Sp. Skate	0-2-1
2	Ernst Baier, GER	Fig. Skate	1-1-0
2	Joseph Beerli, SWI	Bobsled	1-1-0
2	Erik Larsson, SWE	X-country	1-0-1
2	Fritz Feierabend, SWI	Bobsled	0-2-0
2	Olaf Hoffsbakken, NOR	X-country	0-2-0
2	Sverre Brodahl, NOR	X-country	0-1-1

Alpine Skiing

MEN

Event		Pts
Combined	Franz Pfnür, GER	99.25

WOMEN

Event		Pts
Combined	Christl Cranz, GER	97.06

Bobsled

Event	Time
2-Man USA (Ivan Brown & Alan Washbond)	5:29.29
4-Man SWI (Pierre Musy, Arnold Gartmann, Charles Bouvier, Joseph Beerli)	5:19.85

Figure Skating

Event		Points
Men	Karl Schäfer, AUT	2959.0
Women	Sonja Henie, NOR	425.5
Pairs	Maxi Herber & Ernst Baier, GER	11.5

Ice Hockey

Championship Round

(Overall records in parentheses)

		Gm	W-L-T	Pts	GF	GA
1	Great Britain (5-0-2)	3	2-0-1	5	7	1
2	Canada (7-1-0)	3	2-1-0	4	9	2
3	USA (5-2-1)	3	1-1-1	3	2	1
4	Czechoslovakia (5-3-0)	3	0-3-0	0	0	14

Scores: Britain beat Canada, 2–1; Czech., 5–0; and tied the U.S., 0–0 (OT). Canada beat Czech., 7–0, and the U.S., 1–0. The U.S. beat Czech., 2–0.

Nordic Skiing
Cross Country

Event		Time
18km	Erik-August Larsson, SWE	1:14:38
50km	Elis Wiklund, SWE	3:30:11
4x10km	FIN (Sulo Nurmela, Klaes Karppinen, Matti Lähde, Kalle Jalkanen)	2:41:33

Ski Jumping

Event		Points
90m	Birger Rudd, NOR	232.0

Nordic Combined

Event		Points
18km/Jump	Oddbjörn Hagen, NOR	430.3

Speed Skating

Event		Time	
500m	Ivar Ballangrud, NOR	43.4	=OR
1500m	Charles Mathisen, NOR	2:19.2	OR
5000m	Ivar Ballangrud, NOR	8:19.6	OR
10,000m	Ivar Ballangrud, NOR	17:24.3	OR

1948
St. Moritz

JEUX OLYMPIQUES D'HIVER

The Winter Games originally scheduled for Sapporo, Japan (1940) and Cortina d'Ampezzo, Italy (1944) were cancelled because of World War II. Untouched by the war, the Swiss resort town of St. Moritz was picked to host the 1948 Games and 28 countries sent 706 athletes to compete.

The United States sent two hockey teams, one sanctioned by the American Olympic Committee and one by the American Hockey Association. The IOC ruled that the AOC team could march in the opening parade and the AHA team could play in

the tournament, but neither would be eligible for a medal. Canada and Czechoslovakia each finished with 7–0–1 records, but the Canadians won the gold medal by goal differential, 64–62. Czech team member Jaroslav Drobny later distinguished himself as a tennis player, winning the men's singles title at Wimbledon in 1954.

Dick Button of Englewood, N.J., became the first American to win a figure skating gold medal, an achievement that also earned him the Sullivan Award as U.S. amateur athlete of the year.

Alpine skier Gretchen Fraser won a gold medal in the slalom and a silver in the combined for the Americans. French Alpine skier Henri Oreiller was the men's top individual performer with two golds and a bronze.

Top 10 Standings

National medal standings are not recognized by the IOC. The unofficial point totals are based on 3 points for a gold medal, 2 for a silver and 1 for a bronze. Total medals are in parentheses.

		Gold	Silver	Bronze	Pts
1	Norway (10)	4	3	3	21
	Sweden (10)	4	3	3	21
3	Switzerland (10)	3	4	3	20
4	USA (9)	3	4	2	19
5	Austria (8)	1	3	4	13
6	Finland (6)	1	3	2	11
7	France (5)	2	1	2	10
8	Canada (3)	2	0	1	7
9	Belgium (2)	1	1	0	5
10	Italy (1)	1	0	0	3

Leading Medal Winners

Number of individual medals won on the left; gold, silver and bronze breakdown to the right.

MEN

No		Sport	G-S-B
3	Henri Oreiller, FRA	Alpine	2-0-1
2	Martin Lundström, SWE	X-country	2-0-0
2	Nils Östensson, SWE	X-country	1-1-0
2	Åke Seyffarth, SWE	Sp. Skate	1-1-0
2	Gunnar Eriksson, SWE	X-country	1-0-1
2	Karl Molitor, SWI	Alpine	1-0-1
2	James Couttet, FRA	Alpine	0-1-1
2	Odd Lundberg, NOR	Sp. Skate	0-1-1

WOMEN

No		Sport	G-S-B
2	Trude Beiser, AUT	Alpine	1-1-0
2	Gretchen Fraser, USA	Alpine	1-1-0
2	Erika Mahringer, AUT	Alpine	0-0-2

Alpine Skiing
MEN

Event		Time
Downhill	Henri Oreiller, FRA	2:55.0
Slalom	Edi Reinalter, SWI	2:10.3
Combined	Henri Oreiller, FRA	3.27 pts

WOMEN

Event		Time
Downhill	Hedy Schlunegger, SWI	2:28.3
Slalom	Gretchen Fraser, USA	1:57.2
Combined	Trude Beiser, AUT	6.58 pts

Bobsled

Event		Time
2-Man	SWI (Felix Endrich & Friedrich Waller)	5:29.2
4-Man	USA (Francis Tyler, Patrick Martin, Edward Rimkus, William D'Amico)	5:20.1

Cresta (Toboggan)

Event		Time
1-Man	Nino Bibbia, ITA	5:23.2

Figure Skating

Event		Points
Men	Dick Button, USA	191.177
Women	Barbara Ann Scott, CAN	163.077
Pairs	Micheline Lannoy & Pierre Baugniet, BEL	11.227

Ice Hockey

		Gm	W-L-T	Pts	GF	GA
1	Canada	8	7-0-1	15	69	5
2	Czechoslovakia	8	7-0-1	15	80	18
3	Switzerland	8	6-2-0	12	67	21
4	USA (AHA)	8	5-3-0	10	86	33
5	Sweden	8	4-4-0	8	55	28
6	Great Britain	8	3-5-0	6	39	47
7	Poland	8	2-6-0	4	20	97
8	Austria	8	1-7-0	2	33	77
9	Italy	8	0-8-0	0	24	156

Note: Canada won championship on goal differential, 64–62.

Nordic Skiing
Cross Country

Event		Time
18km	Martin Lundstrom, SWE	1:13:50.0
50km	Nils Karlsson, SWE	3:47:48.0
4x10km	SWE (Nils Östensson, Nils Täpp, Gunnar Eriksson, Martin Lundström)	2:32:08.0

Ski Jumping

Event		Points
90m	Peter Hugsted, NOR	228.1

Nordic Combined

Event		Points
18km/Jump	Heikki Hasu, FIN	448.80

Speed Skating

Event		Time	
500m	Finn Helgesen, NOR	43.1	OR
1500m	Sverre Farstad, NOR	2:17.6	OR
5000m	Reidar Liaklev, NOR	8:29.4	
10,000m	Åke Seyffarth, SWE	17:26.3	

1952
Oslo

Dick Button, who had revolutionized figure skating with his athletic jumps and spins at St. Moritz in 1948, repeated his gold medal performance in '52. The 22–year-old Harvard senior also won the world championship for the fifth straight year, then turned pro.

Andrea Mead Lawrence, a 19–year-old whose parents built the Pico Peak ski resort in Vermont became the first U.S. skier to win two Olympic gold

medals, taking both the slalom and giant slalom.

The star of the Games, however, was 28–year-old Norwegian truck driver Hjalmar Andersen who, urged on by his cheering countrymen, won three speed skating gold medals in three days and set Olympic records in two of the races.

The U.S. finished second to Norway in the overall medal count and was runner-up to Canada in hockey. The gold medal was the Canadians' seventh in eight Olympics and, as it turned out, their last.

Top 10 Standings

National medal standings are not recognized by the IOC. The unofficial point totals are based on 3 points for a gold medal, 2 for a silver and 1 for a bronze. Total medals are in parentheses.

		Gold	Silver	Bronze	Pts
1	Norway (16)	7	3	6	33
2	USA (11)	4	6	1	25
3	Finland (9)	3	4	2	19
4	Austria (8)	2	4	2	16
5	Germany (7)	3	2	2	15
6	Holland (3)	0	3	0	6
7	Canada (2)	1	0	1	4
	Italy (2)	1	0	1	4
	Sweden (4)	0	0	4	4
10	Great Britain (1)	1	0	0	3

Leading Medal Winners

Number of individual medals won on the left; gold, silver and bronze breakdown to the right.

MEN

No		Sport	G-S-B
3	Hjalmar Andersen, NOR	Sp. Skate	3-0-0
2	Andreas Ostler, GER	Bobsled	2-0-0
2	Lorenz Nieberl, GER	Bobsled	2-0-0
2	Hallgeir Brenden, NOR	X-country	1-1-0
2	Stein Eriksen, NOR	Alpine	1-1-0
2	Heikki Hasu, FIN	X-country & Nordic Combined	1-1-0
2	Tapio Mäkelä, FIN	X-country	1-1-0
2	Othmar Schneider, AUT	Alpine	1-1-0
2	Paavo Lonkila, FIN	X-country	1-0-1
2	Stan Benham, USA	Bobsled	0-2-0
2	Kees Broekman, NED	Sp. Skate	0-2-0
2	Patrick Martin, USA	Bobsled	0-2-0
2	Magnar Estenstad, NOR	X-country	0-1-1
2	Christian Pravda, AUT	Alpine	0-1-1
2	Fritz Feierabend, SWI	Bobsled	0-0-2
2	Stephan Waser, SWI	Bobsled	0-0-2

WOMEN

No		Sport	G-S-B
3	Annemarie Buchner, GER	Alpine	0-1-2
2	Andrea Mead Lawrence, USA	Alpine	2-0-0

Alpine Skiing
MEN

Event		Time
Downhill	Zeno Colò, ITA	2:30.8
Slalom	Othmar Schneider, AUT	2:00.0
G.Slalom	Stein Eriksen, NOR	2:25.0

WOMEN

Event		Time
Downhill	Trude Jochum-Beiser, AUT	1:47.1
Slalom	Andrea Mead Lawrence, USA	2:10.6
G.Slalom	Andrea Mead Lawrence, USA	2:06.8

Bobsled

Event		Time
2-Man	GER (Andreas Ostler & Lorenz Nieberl)	.5:24.54
4-Man	GER (Andreas Ostler, Friedrich Kuhn, Lorenz Nieberl, Franz Kemser)	5:07.84

Figure Skating

Event		Points
Men	Dick Button, USA	1730.3
Women	Jeanette Altwegg, GBR	1455.8
Pairs	Ria Falk & Paul Falk, GER	102.6

Ice Hockey

		Gm	W-L-T	Pts	GF	GA
1	Canada	8	7-0-1	15	71	14
2	USA	8	6-1-1	13	43	21
3	Sweden	8	6-2-0	12	48	19
4	Czechoslovakia	8	6-2-0	12	47	18
5	Switzerland	8	4-4-0	8	40	40
6	Poland	8	2-5-1	5	21	56
7	Finland	8	2-6-0	4	21	60
8	Germany	8	1-6-1	3	21	53
9	Norway	8	0-8-0	0	15	46

Note: Sweden defeated Czechoslovakia 5–3, in a playoff game to decide third place and the 1952 European championship.

Nordic Skiing
MEN
Cross Country

Event		Time
18km	Hallgeir Brenden, NOR	1:01:34.0
50km	Veikko Hakulinen, FIN	3:33:33.0
4x10km	FIN (Heikki Hasu, Paavo Lonkila, Urpo Korhonen, Tapio Mäkelä)	2:20:16.0

Ski Jumping

Event		Points
90m	Arnfinn Bergman, NOR	226.0

Nordic Combined

Event		Points
18km/Jump	Simon Slåttvik, NOR	51.621

WOMEN
Cross Country

Event		Time
10km	Lydia Widerman, FIN	41:40.0

Speed Skating
MEN

Event		Time	
500m	Ken Henry, USA	43.2	
1500m	Hjalmar Andersen, NOR	2:20.4	
5000m	Hjalmar Andersen, NOR	8:10.6	OR
10,000m	Hjalmar Andersen, NOR	16:45.8	OR

1956
Cortina d'Ampezzo

The Soviet Union emerged from the shadows of the Cold War in 1952 to make its Olympic debut at the Summer Games in Helsinki. Finishing a close second to the United States in overall medal count (74–71), the Russians served notice that they were an athletic superpower to be reckoned with.

In 1956, the USSR made its first appearance in the Winter Games and not only outmedaled the 32–nation field, but dethroned Canada as hockey champion. Four of the USSR's seven gold medals came in speed skating, where Yevgeny Grishin led the way with gold medals in the 500 and 1,500 meters.

Despite a shortage of snow in northern Italy, the outstanding performance of the VIIth Winter Games belonged to a skier named Sailer. By winning the downhill, slalom and giant slalom, Toni Sailer of Austria became the first skier to sweep all three Alpine events and only the fifth winter athlete to win three gold medals at one Olympics.

Swedish cross-country skier Sixten Jernberg, who would eventually participate in three Winter Games and win a total of nine medals, led all contestants in Cortina with four, including a gold at 50 kilometers.

The women's and men's figure skating titles were won by Americans Tenley Albright and Hayes Jenkins, who were both reigning world champions. Albright had won a silver medal in 1952, while Jenkins had finished fourth.

Top 10 Standings

National medal standings are not recognized by the IOC. The unofficial point totals are based on 3 points for a gold medal, 2 for a silver and 1 for a bronze. Total medals are in parentheses.

		Gold	Silver	Bronze	Pts
1	USSR (16)	7	3	6	33
2	Austria (11)	4	3	4	22
3	Sweden (10)	2	4	4	18
4	Finland (7)	3	3	1	16
5	Switzerland (6)	3	2	1	14
	USA (7)	2	3	2	14
7	Norway (4)	2	1	1	9
8	Italy (3)	1	2	0	7
9	Germany (2)	1	0	1	4
	Canada (3)	0	1	2	4

Leading Medal Winners

Number of individual medals won on the left; gold, silver and bronze breakdown to the right.

MEN

No		Sport	G-S-B
4	Sixten Jernberg, SWE	X-country	1-2-1
3	Toni Sailer, AUT	Alpine	3-0-0
3	Veikko Hakulinen, FIN	X-country	1-2-0
3	Pavel Kolchin, USSR	X-country	1-0-2
2	Yevgeny Grishin, USSR	Sp. Skate	2-0-0
2	Sigvard Ericsson, SWE	Sp. Skate	1-1-0
2	Fedor Terentyev, USSR	X-country	1-0-1
2	Renzo Alvera, ITA	Bobsled	0-2-0
2	Eugenio Monti, ITA	Bobsled	0-2-0
2	Andreas Molterer, AUT	Alpine	0-1-1
2	Oleg Goncharenko, USSR	Sp. Skate	0-0-2

WOMEN

No		Sport	G-S-B
2	Lyubov Kozyreva, USSR	X-country	1-1-0
2	Radya Eroshina, USSR	X-country	0-2-0
2	Sonja Edstrom, SWE	X-country	0-0-2

Alpine Skiing
MEN

Event		Time
Downhill	Toni Sailer, AUT	2:52.2
Slalom	Toni Sailer, AUT	3:14.7
G.Slalom	Toni Sailer, AUT	3:00.1

WOMEN

Event		Time
Downhill	Madeleine Berthod, SWI	1:40.7
Slalom	Renée Colliard, SWI	1:52.3
G.Slalom	Ossi Reichert, GER	1:56.5

Bobsled

Event		Time
2-Man	ITA (Lamberto Dalla Costa & Giacomo Conti)	5:30.14
4-Man	SWI (Franz Kapus, Gottfried Diener, Robert Alt, Heinrich Angst)	5:10.44

Figure Skating

Event		Points
Men	Hayes Jenkins, USA	166.43
Women	Tenley Albright, USA	169.67
Pairs	Elisabeth Schwartz & Kurt Oppelt, AUT	11.31

Ice Hockey

(Overall records in parentheses)

		Gm	W-L-T	Pts	GF	GA
1	USSR (7-0-0)	5	5-0-0	10	25	5
2	USA (5-2-0)	5	4-1-0	8	26	12
3	Canada (6-2-0)	5	3-2-0	6	23	11
4	Sweden (2-4-1)	5	1-3-1	3	10	22
5	Czechoslovakia (3-4-0)	5	1-4-0	2	20	30
6	Germany (1-5-2)	5	0-4-1	1	6	35

Note: The USSR beat the U.S., 4–0, and Canada, 2–0. The U.S. beat Canada, 4–1.

Nordic Skiing

MEN

Cross Country

Event		Time
15km	Hallgeir Brenden, NOR	49:39.0
30km	Veikko Hakulinen, FIN	1:44:06.0
50km	Sixten Jernberg, SWE	2:50:27.0
4x10km	USSR (Fedor Terentyev, Pavel Kolchin, Nikolai Anikin, Vladimir Kuzin)	2:15:30.0

Ski Jumping

Event		Points
90m	Antti Hyvärinen, FIN	227.0

Nordic Combined

Event		Points
15km/Jump	Sverre Stenersen, NOR	455.000

WOMEN

Cross Country

Event		Time
10km	Lyubov Kosyreva, USSR	38:11.0
3x5km	FIN (Sirkka Polkunen, Mirja Hietamies, Siira Rantanen)	1:09:01.0

Speed Skating

MEN

Event		Time	
500m	Yevgeny Grishin, USSR	40.2	WR
1500m	Yevgeny Grishin, USSR & Yuri Mikhailov, USSR	2:08.6	WR
5000m	Boris Shilkov, USSR	7:48.7	OR
10,000m	Sigvard Ericsson, SWE	16:35.9	OR

1960
Squaw Valley

The first Winter Olympics in the U.S. since 1932 was held at an obscure California ski resort near Lake Tahoe that had no bobsled run and in the days leading up to the opening ceremony, no snow. Luckily, an 11th hour drop in temperature changed a drenching rain into a much-needed blizzard and the Games got off to a wintry start.

The most exciting venue, however, was indoors at Blyth Arena where the underdog U.S. hockey team upset the Russians and Canadians to win the gold medal for the first time ever. Led by forwards Billy Cleary and Roger Christian and goaltender Jack McCartan, the Americans beat Canada 2–1, USSR 3–2, and the Czechs 9–4, in their last three games to clinch the title.

Blyth was also where Carol Heiss and David Jenkins won the women's and men's figure skating gold medals. Heiss had won a silver and Jenkins a bronze in 1956. Shortly after the Games, Heiss married Jenkins' older brother Hayes, the men's gold medalist in '56.

Outside, speed skater Yevgeny Grishin of the USSR won at 500 and 1,500 meters for the second Olympics in a row. In fact, Grishin's victory in the 1,500 was his second straight tie at that distance—sharing gold medals with teammate Yuri Mikhailov in 1956 and Norway's Roald Aas in '60. This was also the first year women could compete in speed skating and the Soviets' Lydia Skoblikova won twice, at 1,500 and 3,000 meters. She would go on to win four gold medals at Innsbruck in 1964.

At 35, three-time Olympic cross-country skier Veikko Hakulinen of Finland was the only athlete at Squaw Valley to claim three medals (for a career total of seven). He came from 20 seconds back on the anchor leg to win gold in the 40–kilometer relay.

Sweden's Klas Lestander won the first Olympic biathlon competition. A popular Scandinavian sport that combines cross-country skiing and shooting, Lestander recorded the 15th best time over the 20-kilometer course but was perfect on each of his 20 rifle shots.

Nineteen-year-old Alpine skier Penny Pitou was America's top medalist, placing second in both the downhill and slalom events. She was later married for a few years to 1964 men's downhill champion Egon Zimmermann of Austria.

Top 10 Standings

National medal standings are not recognized by the IOC. The unofficial point totals are based on 3 points for a gold medal, 2 for a silver and 1 for a bronze. Total medals are in parentheses.

		Gold	Silver	Bronze	Pts
1	USSR (21)	7	5	9	40
2	USA (10)	3	4	3	20
3	Germany (8)	4	3	1	19
4	Norway (6)	3	3	0	15
	Sweden (7)	3	2	2	15
	Finland (8)	2	3	3	15
7	Austria (6)	1	2	3	10
8	Canada (4)	2	1	1	9
9	Switzerland (2)	2	0	0	6
10	France (3)	1	0	2	5

Leading Medal Winners

Number of individual medals won on the left; gold, silver and bronze breakdown to the right.

MEN

No		Sport	G-S-B
3	Veikko Hakulinen, FIN	X-country	1-1-1
2	Yevgeny Grishin, USSR	Sp. Skate	2-0-0
2	Håkon Brusveen, NOR	X-country	1-1-0
2	Knut Johannesen, NOR	Sp. Skate	1-1-0
2	Sixten Jernberg, SWE	X-country	1-1-0
2	Viktor Kosichkin, USSR	Sp. Skate	1-1-0
2	Ernst Hinterseer, AUT	Alpine	1-0-1
2	Rolf Rämgård, SWE	X-country	0-1-1
2	Nikolai Anikin, USSR	X-country	0-0-2

WOMEN

No		Sport	G-S-B
2	Lydia Skoblikova, USSR	Sp. Skate	2-0-0
2	Maria Gusakova, USSR	X-country	1-1-0
2	Helga Haase, GER	Sp. Skate	1-1-0
2	Penny Pitou, USA	Alpine	0-2-0
2	Lyubov Baranova, USSR	X-country	0-2-0
2	Radya Eroshina, USSR	X-country	0-1-1

Alpine Skiing

MEN

Event		Time
Downhill	Jean Vuarnet, FRA	2:06.0
Slalom	Ernst Hinterseer, AUT	2:08.9
G.Slalom	Roger Staub, SWI	1:48.3

WOMEN

Event		Time
Downhill	Heidi Biebl, GER	1:37.6
Slalom	Anne Heggtveit, CAN	1:49.6
G.Slalom	Avonne Rüegg, SWI	1:39.9

Biathlon

Event		MT	Adj.Time
20 km	Klas Lestander, SWE	0	1:33:21.6

Figure Skating

Event		Points
Men	David Jenkins, USA	1440.2
Women	Carol Heiss, USA	1490.1
Pairs	Barbara Wagner & Robert Paul, CAN	80.4

Ice Hockey

Championship Round
(Overall records in parentheses)

		Gm	W-L-T	Pts	GF	GA
1	USA (7-0-0)	5	5-0-0	10	29	11
2	Canada (6-1-0)	5	4-1-0	8	31	12
3	USSR (4-2-1)	5	2-2-1	5	24	19
4	Czechoslovakia (3-4-0)	5	2-3-0	4	21	23
5	Sweden (2-4-1)	5	1-3-1	3	19	19
6	Germany (1-6-0)	5	0-5-0	0	5	45

Note: The U.S. beat Canada, 2–1, the USSR, 3–2, and Czech., 9–4, in its last three games. Canada beat the USSR, 8–5, and Sweden tied the Russians, 2–2.

Nordic Skiing
MEN
Cross Country

Event		Time
15km	Håkon Brusveen, NOR	51:55.5
30km	Sixten Jernberg, SWE	1:51:03.9
50km	Kalevi Hämäläinen, FIN	2:59:06.3
4x10km	FIN (Toimi Alatalo, Eero Mäntyranta, Väinö Huhtala, Veikko Hakulinen)	2:18:45.6

Ski Jumping

Event		Points
80m	Helmut Recknagel, GER	227.2

Nordic Combined

Event		Points
15km/Jump	Georg Thoma, GER	457.952

WOMEN
Cross Country

Event		Time
10km	Marija Gusakova, USSR	39:46.6
3x5km	SWE (Irma Johansson, Britt Strandberg, Sonja Ruthström)	1:04:21.4

Speed Skating
MEN

Event		Time	
500m	Yevgeny Grishin, USSR	40.2	=WR
1500m	Roald Aas, NOR	2:10.4	WR
	& Yevgeny Grishin, USSR	2:10.4	WR
5000m	Viktor Kosichkin, USSR	7:51.3	
10,000m	Knut Johannesen, NOR	15:46.6	

WOMEN

Event		Time	
500m	Helga Haase, GER	45.9	
1000m	Klara Guseva, USSR	1:34.1	
1500m	Lydia Skoblikova, USSR	2:25.2	WR
3000m	Lydia Skoblikova, USSR	5:14.3	

1964
Innsbruck

Death and unseasonably mild weather hung over the ninth Winter Games in the Tyrolean Alps.

Two athletes, 50–year-old British luger Kazimierz Kay-Skyszpeski and 19–year-old Australian downhill skier Ross Milne, were killed taking practice runs less than a week before the Games began. And three years before, on Feb. 15, 1961, a plane crash in Belgium had killed 18 members of the U.S. figure skating team—including America's top female skater, 16–year-old Laurence Owen.

Springlike temperatures plagued Innsbruck both before and during the Games, forcing the Austrian military to carry in over 50,000 cubic meters of snow from higher elevations.

The USSR won 11 gold medals—a combined seven by speed skater Lydia Skoblikova (4) and cross-country skier Claudia Boyarskikh (3). Other stars included the skiing Goitschel sisters, Christine and Marielle, of France; and cross-country skiers Eero Mäntyranta of Finland and 34–year-old Sixten Jernberg of Sweden.

The lone U.S. gold medal was won by 23–year-old barber Terry McDermott in speed skating.

Top 10 Standings

National medal standings are not recognized by the IOC. The unofficial point totals are based on 3 points for a gold medal, 2 for a silver and 1 for a bronze. Total medals are in parentheses.

		Gold	Silver	Bronze	Pts
1	USSR (25)	11	8	6	55
2	Norway (15)	3	6	6	27
3	Austria (12)	4	5	3	25
4	Finland (10)	3	4	3	20
5	France (7)	3	4	0	17
6	Sweden (7)	3	3	1	16
	Germany (8)	3	2	3	16
8	USA (6)	1	2	3	10
9	Holland (2)	1	1	0	5
	Canada (3)	1	0	2	5
	Italy (4)	0	1	3	5

Leading Medal Winners

Number of individual medals won on the left; gold, silver and bronze breakdown to the right.

MEN

No		Sport	G-S-B
3	Eero Mäntyranta, FIN	X-country	2-1-0
3	Sixten Jernberg, SWE	X-country	2-0-1
2	Toralf Engan, NOR	Ski Jump	1-1-0
2	Veikko Kankkonen, FIN	Ski Jump	1-1-0
2	Assar Rönnlund, SWE	X-country	1-1-0
2	Knut Johannesen, NOR	Sp. Skate	1-0-1
2	Pepi Stiegler, AUT	Alpine	1-0-1
2	Harald Grönningen, NOR	X-country	0-2-0
2	Fred Maier, NOR	Sp. Skate	0-1-1
2	Arto Tiainen, FIN	X-country	0-1-1
2	Torgeir Brandtzaeg, NOR	Ski jump	0-0-2
2	Eugenio Monti, ITA	Bobsled	0-0-2
2	Sergio Siorpaes, ITA	Bobsled	0-0-2
2	Igor Voronchikin, USSR	X-country	0-0-2

WOMEN

No		Sport	G-S-B
4	Lydia Skoblikova, USSR	Sp. Skate	4-0-0
3	Claudia Boyarskikh, USSR	X-country	3-0-0
2	Christine Goitschel, FRA	Alpine	1-1-0
2	Marielle Goitschel, FRA	Alpine	1-1-0
2	Eudokia Mekshilo, USSR	X-country	1-1-0
2	Alevtina Kolchina, USSR	X-country	1-0-1
2	Mirja Lehtonen, FIN	X-country	0-1-1
2	Kaija Mustonen, FIN	Sp. Skate	0-1-1
2	Jean Saubert, USA	Alpine	0-1-1
2	Irina Yegorova, USSR	Sp. Skate	0-2-0

Alpine Skiing

MEN

Event		Time
Downhill	Egon Zimmermann, AUT	2:18.16
Slalom	Pepi Stiegler, AUT	2:11.13
G.Slalom	Francois Bonlieu, FRA	1:46.71

Note: In the Slalom, Billy Kidd (2nd) and Jimmy Heuga (3rd) won the first U.S. men's Alpine medals ever.

WOMEN

Event		Time
Downhill	Christl Haas, AUT	1:55.39
Slalom	Christine Goitschel, FRA	1:29.86
G.Slalom	Marielle Goitschel, FRA	1:52.24

Biathlon

Event		MT	Adj.Time
20 km	Vladimir Melanin, USSR	0	1:20:26.8

Bobsled

Event		Time
2-Man	GBR (Tony Nash & Robin Dixon)	4:21.90
4-Man	CAN (Victor Emery, Peter Kirby, Doug Anakin, John Emery)	4:14.46

Figure Skating

Event		Points
Men	Manfred Schnelldorfer, GER	1916.9
Women	Sjoukje Dijkstra, NED	2018.5
Pairs	Lyudmila Belousova & Oleg Protopopov, USSR	104.4

Ice Hockey

Championship Round

(Overall records in parentheses)

		Gm	W-L-T	Pts	GF	GA
1	USSR (8-0-0)	7	7-0-0	14	54	10
2	Sweden (6-2-0)	7	5-2-0	10	47	16
3	Czechoslovakia (6-2-0)	7	5-2-0	10	38	19
4	Canada (6-2-0)	7	5-2-0	10	32	17
5	USA (3-5-0)	7	2-5-0	4	29	33
6	Finland (3-5-0)	7	2-5-0	4	10	31
7	Germany (3-5-0)	7	2-5-0	4	13	49
8	Switzerland (1-7-0)	7	0-7-0	0	9	57

Luge

MEN

Event		Time
1-Seat	Thomas Köhler, GER	3:26.77
2-Seat	Josef Feistmantl & Manfred Stengl, AUT	1:41.62

WOMEN

Event		Time
1-Seat	Ortrun Enderlein, GER	3:24.67

Nordic Skiing

MEN

Cross Country

Event		Time
15km	Eero Mäntyranta, FIN	50:54.1
30km	Eero Mäntyranta, FIN	1:30:50.7
50km	Sixten Jernberg, SWE	2:43:52.6
4x10km	SWE (Karl-Åke Asph, Sixten Jernberg Janne Stefansson, Assar Rönnlund)	2:18:34.6

Ski Jumping

Event		Points
70m	Veikko Kankkonen, FIN	229.9
80m	Toralf Engan, NOR	230.7

Nordic Combined

Event		Points
15km/Jump	Tormod Knutsen, NOR	469.28

WOMEN
Cross Country

Event		Time
5km	Claudia Boyarskikh, USSR	17:50.5
10km	Claudia Boyarskikh, USSR	40:24.3
3x5km	USSR (Alevtina Kolchina, Eudokia Mekshilo, Claudia Boyarskikh)	59:20.2

Speed Skating
MEN

Event		Time	
500m	Terry McDermott, USA	40.1	OR
1500m	Ants Antson, USSR	2:10.3	
5000m	Knut Johannesen, NOR	7:38.4	OR
10,000m	Jonny Nilsson, SWE	15:50.1	

WOMEN

Event		Time	
500m	Lydia Skoblikova, USSR	45.0	OR
1000m	Lydia Skoblikova, USSR	1:33.2	OR
1500m	Lydia Skoblikova, USSR	2:22.6	OR
3000m	Lydia Skoblikova, USSR	5:14.9	

1968
Grenoble

For the first time since they began attending the Winter Games in 1956, the Russians did not win the most medals—Norway did.

This was also the first year that the IOC permitted East and West Germany to participate as separate countries.

The host French team finished fourth in the overall standings—their best showing ever—thanks mainly to 24-year-old Jean-Claude Killy, who became the first skier to sweep all three Alpine events since Toni Sailer in 1956.

Killy was awarded his third gold medal in the slalom only after original winner Karl Schranz of Austria was disqualified for missing two gates on his second run in the two-heat race. Schranz had been allowed to retake his second heat run when a spectator interrupted his initial attempt, but officials ruled the missed gates came before the interruption.

Once again, the U.S. won only one gold medal—19-year-old Peggy Fleming in women's figure skating. Three of the five silver medals won by the U.S. came in one event—the women's 500–meter speed skating race, where Jenny Fish, Dianne Holum and Mary Myers tied for second place with a time of 46.3 seconds.

Top 10 Standings

National medal standings are not recognized by the IOC. The unofficial point totals are based on 3 points for a gold medal, 2 for a silver and 1 for a bronze. Total medals are in parentheses.

		Gold	Silver	Bronze	Pts
1	Norway (14)	6	6	2	32
2	USSR (13)	5	5	3	28
3	Austria (11)	3	4	4	21
4	France (9)	4	3	2	20
5	Holland (9)	3	3	3	18
6	Sweden (8)	3	2	3	16
7	USA (7)	1	5	1	14
8	West Germany (7)	2	2	3	13
9	Italy (4)	4	0	0	12
10	East Germany (5)	1	2	2	9
	Finland (5)	1	2	2	9

Leading Medal Winners

Number of individual medals won on the left; gold, silver and bronze breakdown to the right.

MEN

No		Sport	G-S-B
3	Jean-Claude Killy, FRA	Alpine	3-0-0
3	Eero Mäntyranta, FIN	X-country	0-1-2
2	Eugenio Monti, ITA.	Bobsled	2-0-0
2	Luciano De Paolis, ITA	Bobsled	2-0-0
2	Ole Ellefsaeter, NOR	X-country	2-0-0
2	Harald Grönningen, NOR	X-country	2-0-0
2	Thomas Köhler, E.Ger.	Luge	1-1-0
2	Fred Maier, NOR	Sp. Skate	1-1-0
2	Odd Martinsen, NOR	X-country	1-1-0
2	Jiri Raska, CZE	Ski Jump	1-1-0
2	Manfred Schmid, AUT.	Luge	1-1-0
2	Magnar Solberg, NOR	Biathlon	1-1-0
2	Aleksandr Tikhonov, USSR	Biathlon	1-1-0
2	Kees Verkerk, NED	Sp. Skate	1-1-0
2	Klaus Bonsack, E. Ger.	Luge	1-0-1
2	Vladimir Goundartsev, USSR	Biathlon	1-0-1
2	Gunnar Larsson, SWE	X-country	0-1-1

WOMEN

No		Sport	G-S-B
3	Toini Gustafsson, SWE	X-country	2-1-0
3	Carolina Geijssen, NED	Sp. Skate	1-1-0
2	Nancy Greene, CAN	Alpine	1-1-0
2	Berit Mördre, NOR	X-country	1-1-0
2	Kaija Mustonen, FIN	Sp. Skate	1-1-0
2	Lyudmila Titova, USSR.	Sp. Skate	1-1-0
2	Inger Aufles, NOR	X-country	1-0-1
2	Annie Famose, FRA	Alpine	0-1-1
2	Dianne Holum, USA	Sp. Skate	0-1-1
2	Galina Kulakova, USSR	X-country	0-1-1
2	Christina Kaiser, NED	Sp. Skate	0-0-2
2	Alevtina Kolchina, USSR	X-country	0-0-2

Alpine Skiing
MEN

Event		Time
Downhill	Jean-Claude Killy, FRA	1:59.85
Slalom	Jean-Claude Killy, FRA	1:39.73
G.Slalom	Jean-Claude Killy, FRA	3:29.28

WOMEN

Event		Time
Downhill	Olga Pall, AUT	1:40.87
Slalom	Marielle Goitschel, FRA	1:25.86
G.Slalom	Nancy Greene, CAN	1:51.97

Biathlon

Event		MT	Adj.Time
20 km	Magnar Solberg, NOR..........0		1:13:45.9
4x7.5km	USSR (Tikonov, Pousanov, Mamatov, Goundartsev).........2		2:13:02.4

Bobsled

Event		Time
2-Man	ITA (Eugenio Monti & Luciano De Paolis)..4:41.54	
4-Man	ITA (Eugenio Monti, Luciano De Paolis, Roberto Zandonella, Mario Armano).....2:17.39	

Figure Skating

Event		Points
Men	Wolfgang Schwarz, AUT 1904.1	
Women	Peggy Fleming, USA 1970.5	
Pairs	Lyudmila Belousova & Oleg Protopopov, USSR................315.2	

Ice Hockey
Group A
(Overall records in parentheses)

		Gm	W-L-T	Pts	GF	GA
1	USSR.....................7		6-1-0	12	48	10
2	Czecholslovakia 7		5-1-1	11	33	17
3	Canada.................7		5-2-0	10	28	15
4	Sweden.................7		4-2-1	9	23	18
5	Finland (4-3-1) 7		3-3-1	9	17	23
6	USA.....................7		2-4-1	5	23	28
7	West Germany (2-6-0) 7		1-6-0	2	13	39
8	East Germany (1-7-0) 7		0-7-0	0	13	48

Note: Finland and the two Germanys had to win an elimination round game to qualify for Group A.

Luge
MEN

Event		Time
1-Seat	Manfred Schmid, AUT 2:52.48	
2-Seat	Klaus Bonsack & Thomas Köhler, E. Ger ..1:35.85	

WOMEN

Event		Time
1-Seat	Erica Lechner, ITA 2:28.66	

Note: Defending champion Ortrun Enderlein and teammate Anna Maria Müller of East Germany finished 1–2, but were disqualified for heating the blades of their toboggans.

Nordic Skiing
MEN
Cross Country

Event		Time
15km	Harold Grönningen, NOR...........47:54.2	
30km	Franco Nones, ITA.................1:35:39.2	
50km	Ole Ellefsaeter, NOR..............2:28:45.8	
4x10km	NOR (Martinsen, Tyldum, Grönningen, Ellefsaeter) 2:08:33.5	

Ski Jumping

Event		Points
70m	Jiri Raska, CZE 216.5	
90m	Vladimir Beloussov, USSR 231.3	

Nordic Combined

Event		Points
15km/Jump	Franz Keller, W. Ger................449.04	

WOMEN
Cross Country

Event		Time
5km	Toini Gustafsson, SWE 16:45.2	
10km	Toini Gustafsson, SWE 36:46.5	
3x5km	NOR (Aufles, Damon-Enger, Mördre).....57:30.0	

Speed Skating
MEN

Event	Time	
500m	Erhard Keller, W. Ger. 40.3	
1500m	Kees Verkerk, NED 2:03.4	OR
5000m	Fred Maier, NOR...............7:22.4	WR
10,000m	Johnny Höglin, SWE...........15:23.6	OR

WOMEN

Event	Time	
500m	Lyudmila Titova, USSR 46.1	
1000m	Carolina Geijssen, NED........1:32.6	OR
1500m	Kaija Mustonen, FIN...........2:22.4	OR
3000m	Johanna Schut, NED...........4:56.2	OR

1972
Sapporo

The biggest controversy in the 48–year history of the Winter Games erupted just three days before the opening ceremonies were scheduled to get underway in northern Japan. That's when retiring IOC president Avery Brundage threatened to disqualify 40 Alpine skiers for professionalism.

At Grenoble in 1968, Brundage had demanded that all trademarks be removed from competitors' skis, but settled for having the offensive skis taken away from medal winners before they could be photographed. Now, the 84–year-old guardian of the Olympic flame wanted all the pros thrown out.

A compromise was reached when the IOC executive committee voted 28–14 to make an example of skiing's most commercialized star, 33-year-old Austrian World Cup champion Karl Schranz, who reportedly earned over $50,000 a year "testing" ski equipment.

All other offenders were allowed to participate.

Said Schranz after being banished: "This thing of amateur purity is something that dates back to the 19th century when amateur sportsmen were regarded as gentlemen and everyone else was an outcast. The Olympics should be a competition of skill and strength and speed—and no more."

Schranz retired after the Games, having never won an Olympic gold medal.

The amateurism question caused controversy in the ice hockey event as well. Canada refused to send a team to Sapporo, having withdrawn from international amateur competition in 1969 to protest use of "professional amateurs" by Russia and other eastern bloc countries.

Top 10 Standings

National medal standings are not recognized by the IOC. The unofficial point totals are based on 3 points for a gold medal, 2 for a silver and 1 for a bronze. Total medals are in parentheses.

		Gold	Silver	Bronze	Pts
1	USSR (16)	8	5	3	37
2	East Germany (14)	4	3	7	25
3	Switzerland (10)	4	3	3	21
	Norway (12)	2	5	5	21
5	Holland (9)	4	3	2	20
6	USA (8)	3	2	3	16
7	West Germany (5)	3	1	1	12
8	Italy (5)	2	2	1	11
9	Austria (5)	1	2	2	9
	Finland (5)	0	4	1	9

Leading Medal Winners

Number of individual medals won on the left; gold, silver and bronze breakdown to the right.

MEN

No		Sport	G-S-B
3	Ard Schenk, NED	Sp. Skate	3-0-0
3	Vyacheslav Vedenine, USSR	X-country	2-0-1
3	Pål Tyldum, NOR	X-country	1-2-0
2	Fedor Simashov, USSR	X-country	1-1-0
2	Gustav Thöni, ITA	Alpine	1-1-0
2	Wolfgang Zimmerer, W. Ger.	Bobsled	1-0-1
2	Peter Utzschneider, W. Ger.	Bobsled	1-0-1
2	Jean Wicki, SWI	Bobsled	1-0-1
2	Edy Hubacher, SWI	Bobsled	1-0-1
2	Roar Grönvold, NOR	Sp. Skate	0-2-0
2	Ivar Formo, NOR	X-country	0-1-1
2	Johs Harviken, NOR	X-country	0-1-1
2	Hansjörg Knauthe, E. Ger.	Biathlon	0-1-1
2	Wolfram Fiedler, E. Ger.	Luge	0-0-2
2	Sten Stensen, NOR	Sp. Skate	0-0-2

WOMEN

No		Sport	G-S-B
3	Galina Kulakova, USSR	X-country	3-0-0
3	Marjatta Kajosmaa, FIN	X-country	0-2-1
2	Marie-Theres Nadig, SWI	Alpine	2-0-0
2	Dianne Holum, USA	Sp. Skate	1-1-0
2	Christina Baas-Kaiser, NED	Sp. Skate	1-1-0
2	Alevtina Olunina, USSR	X-country	1-1-0
2	Anne Henning, USA	Sp. Skate	1-0-1
2	Annemarie Pröll, FRA	Alpine	0-2-0
2	Atje Keulen-Deelstra, NED	Sp. Skate	0-1-1

Alpine Skiing

MEN

Event		Time
Downhill	Bernhard Russi, SWI	1:51.43
Slalom	Francisco Ochoa, SPA	1:49.27
G.Slalom	Gustav Thöni, ITA	3:09.62

WOMEN

Event		Time
Downhill	Marie-Theres Nadig, SWI	1:36.68
Slalom	Barbara Cochran, USA	1:31.24
G.Slalom	Marie-Theres Nadig, SWI	1:29.90

Biathlon

Event		MT	Adj.Time
20 km	Magnar Solberg, NOR	2	1:15:55.50
4x7.5km	USSR (Tikonov, Safine, Biakov, Mamatov)	3	1:51:44.92

Bobsled

Event		Time
2-Man	W. Ger. (Wolfgang Zimmerer & Peter Utzschneider)	4:57.07
4-Man	SWI (Jean Wicki, Edy Hubacher, Hans Leutenegger, Werner Camichel)	4:43.07

Figure Skating

Event		Points
Men	Ondrej Nepela, CZE	2739.1
Women	Trixi Schuba, AUT.	2751.5
Pairs	Irina Rodnina & Aleksei Ulanov, USSR	420.4

Ice Hockey

Group A
(Overall records in parentheses)

		Gm	W-L-T	Pts	GF	GA
1	USSR (4-0-1)	5	4-0-1	9	33	13
2	USA (4-2-0)	5	3-2-0	6	18	15
3	Czechoslovakia (4-2-0)	5	3-2-0	6	26	13
4	Sweden (3-2-1)	5	2-2-1	5	17	13
5	Finland (3-3-0)	5	2-3-0	4	14	24
6	Poland (1-5-0)	5	0-5-0	0	9	39

Note: Pivotal game—USSR over Czech., 5–2, in final contest for both teams. The 5–1 U.S. victory over the Czechs gave the Americans second place. Also, the USSR received a bye to Group A while the other seven teams had to win a one-game elimination round to qualify.

Luge

MEN

Event		Time
1-Seat	Wolfgang Scheidel, E. Ger.	3:27.58
2-Seat	(TIE) Horst Hörnlein & Reinhard Bredow, E. Ger.	1:28.35
	Paul Hildgartner & Walter Plaikner, ITA	1:28.35

WOMEN

Event		Time
1-Seat	Anna-Maria Müller, E. Ger.	2:59.18

Nordic Skiing

MEN
Cross Country

Event		Time
15km	Sven-Ake Lundbäck, SWE	45:28.24
30km	Vyachelav Vedenine, USSR	1:36:31.15
50km	Pål Tyldum, NOR.	2:43:14.75
4x10km	USSR (Voronkov, Skobov, Simachev, Vedenine)	2:04:47.94

Ski Jumping

Event		Points
70m	Yukio Kasaya, JPN	244.2
90m	Wojciech Fortuna, POL	219.9

Nordic Combined

Event		Points
15km/Jump	Ulrich Wehling, E. Ger.	413.340

WOMEN
Cross Country

Event		Time
5km	Galina Kulakova, USSR	17:00.50
10km	Galina Kulakova, USSR	34:17.82
3x5km	USSR (Moukhatcheva, Olunina, Kulakova)	48:46.15

Speed Skating
MEN

Event		Time	
500m	Erhard Keller, W. Ger.	.39.44	OR
1500m	Ard Schenk, NED	.2:02.96	OR
5000m	Ard Schenk, NED	.7:23.61	
10,000m	Ard Schenk, NED	.15:01.35	OR

WOMEN

Event		Time	
500m	Anne Henning, USA	.43.33	OR
1000m	Monika Pflug, W. Ger.	.1:31.40	OR
1500m	Dianne Holum, USA	.2:20.85	OR
3000m	Christina Baas-Kaiser, NED	.4:52.14	OR

1976
Innsbruck

The IOC originally gave the 1976 Winter Games to Denver, but in 1972 Colorado voters rejected a $5 million bond issue to finance the undertaking. Denver immediately withdrew as host and the IOC called on Innsbruck, site of the 1964 Games.

For the second straight Winter Carnival the USSR and East Germany finished 1–2 in overall medals. In 1972, Dutch speed skater Ard Schenk and Soviet cross-country skier Galina Kulakova each won three gold medals. In '76, nobody won three, but 25–year-old West German skier Rosi Mittermaier almost did—winning two golds and a silver in the women's Alpine events.

The Russian hockey team, which had won the gold medal in 1972 and then battled the NHL's Team Canada to a virtual standoff six months later, returned with most of the same players and won its fourth straight Olympic title.

In figure skating, 19–year-old Dorothy Hamill of the U.S. and John Curry of Britain won gold medals. Both were coached by Carlo Fassi, who also coached Peggy Fleming in 1968.

Also, Bill Koch became the first U.S. skier to ever win an Olympic cross-country medal when he placed second in the 30–kilometer race.

Top 10 Standings

National medal standings are not recognized by the IOC. The unofficial point totals are based on 3 points for a gold medal, 2 for a silver and 1 for a bronze. Total medals are in parentheses.

		Gold	Silver	Bronze	Pts
1	USSR (27)	13	6	8	59
2	East Germany (19)	7	5	7	38
3	USA (10)	3	3	4	19
	West Germany (10)	2	5	3	19
5	Norway (7)	3	3	1	16
6	Finland (7)	2	4	1	15
7	Austria (6)	2	2	2	12
8	Switzerland (5)	1	3	1	10
	Holland (6)	1	2	3	10
10	Italy (4)	1	2	1	8

Leading Medal Winners

Number of individual medals won on the left; gold, silver and bronze breakdown to the right.

MEN

No		Sport	G-S-B
3	Hans van Helden, NED	Sp. Skate	0-0-3
2	Bernhard Germeshausen, E. Ger.	Bobsled	2-0-0
2	Nikolai Kruglov, USSR	Biathlon	2-0-0
2	Meinhard Nehmer, E. Ger.	Bobsled	2-0-0
2	Ivar Formo, NOR	X-country	1-1-0
2	Piet Kleine, NED	Sp. Skate	1-1-0
2	Nikolai Bazhuko, USSR	X-country	1-0-1
2	Aleksandr Elizarov, USSR	Biathlon	1-0-1
2	Arto Koivisto, FIN	X-country	1-0-1
2	Hans Rinn, E. Ger.	Luge	1-0-1
2	Sergei Saveliev, USSR	X-country	1-0-1
2	Karl Schnabl, AUT	Ski Jump	1-0-1
2	Sten Stensen, NOR	Sp. Skate	1-1-0
2	Neikki Ikola, FIN	Biathlon	0-2-0
2	Yevgeny Beliaev, USSR	X-country	0-1-1
2	Josef Benz, SWI	Bobsled	0-1-1
2	Valery Muratov, USSR	Sp. Skate	0-1-1
2	Erich Scharer, SWI	Bobsled	0-1-1
2	Manfred Schumann, W. Ger.	Bobsled	0-1-1
2	Wolfgang Zimmerer, W. Ger.	Bobsled	0-1-1
2	Ivan Garanin, USSR	X-country	0-0-2

WOMEN

No		Sport	G-S-B
4	Tatiana Averina, USSR	Sp. Skate	2-0-2
3	Rosi Mittermaier, W. Ger.	Alpine	2-1-0
3	Raisa Smetanina, USSR	X-country	2-1-0
3	Helena Takalo, FIN	X-country	1-2-0
3	Sheila Young, USA	Sp. Skate	1-1-1
2	Galina Kulakova, USSR	X-country	1-0-1

Alpine Skiing
MEN

Event		Time
Downhill	Franz Klammer, AUT	1:43.73
Slalom	Piero Gros, ITA	2:03.29
G.Slalom	Heini Hemmi, SWI	3:26.97

WOMEN

Event		Time
Downhill	Rosi Mittermaier, W. Ger.	1:46.16
Slalom	Rosi Mittermaier, W. Ger.	1:30.54
G.Slalom	Kathy Kreiner, CAN	1:29.13

Note: Mittermaier finished second in the GS, missing the first women's alpine sweep by an eighth of a second.

Biathlon

Event		MT	Adj.Time
20 km	Nikolai Kruglov, USSR	2	1:14:12.26
4x7.5km	USSR (Elizarov, Biakov, Kruglov, Tikonov)	0	1:57:55.64

Bobsled

Event		Time
2-Man	E. Ger. (Meinhard Nehmer & Bernhard Germeshausen)	3:44.42
4-Man	E. Ger. (Meinhard Nehmer, Jochen Babock, Bernhard Germeshausen, Bernhard Lehmann)	3:40.43

Figure Skating

Event		Points
Men	John Curry, GBR	192.74
Women	Dorothy Hamill, USA	193.80
Pairs	Irina Rodnina & Aleksandr Zaitsev, USSR	140.54
Dance	Lyudmila Pakhomova & Aleksandr Gorshkov, USSR	209.92

Ice Hockey
Group A
(Overall records in parentheses)

		Gm	W-L-T	Pts	GF	GA
1	USSR (6-0-0)	5	5-0-0	10	40	11
2	Czechoslovakia (3-2-0)	4	2-2-0	6	17	10
3	West Germany (3-3-0)	5	2-3-0	4	21	24
4	Finland (3-3-0)	5	2-3-0	4	19	18
5	USA (3-3-0)	5	2-3-0	4	15	21
6	Poland (1-4-0)	5	0-4-0	0	9	37

Note: Czechoslovakia's 7–1 win over Poland was disallowed when a Czech player flunked a random postgame drug test. The Czechs were given a loss and their goals vs. Poland were deleted from the records. The U.S. missed a bronze medal in its final game with a 4–1 loss to West Germany.

Luge
MEN

Event		Time
1-Seat	Dettlef Günther, E. Ger.	3:27.688
2-Seat	Hans Rinn & Norbert Hahn, E. Ger.	1:25.604

WOMEN

Event		Time
1-Seat	Margit Schumann, E. Ger.	2:50.621

Nordic Skiing
MEN
Cross Country

Event		Time
15km	Nikolai Bazhukov, USSR	43:58.47
30km	Sergei Saveliev, USSR	1:30:29.38
50km	Ivar Formo, NOR	2:37:30.05
4x10km	FIN (Pitkänen, Mieto, Teurajärvi, Koivisto)	2:07:59.72

Ski Jumping

Event		Points
70m	Hans-Goerg Aschenbach, E. Ger.	252.0
90m	Karl Schnabl, AUT	234.8

Nordic Combined

Event		Points
15km/Jump	Ulrich Wehling, E. Ger.	423.39

WOMEN
Cross Country

Event		Time
5km	Helena Takalo, FIN	15:48.69
10km	Raisa Smetanina, USSR	30:13.41
4x5km	USSR (Baldycheva, Amosova, Smetanina, Kulakova)	1:07:49.75

Speed Skating
MEN

Event		Time	
500m	Yevgeny Kulikov, USSR	39.17	**OR**
1000m	Peter Mueller, USA	1:19.32	
1500m	Jan Egil Storholt, NOR	1:59.38	**OR**
5000m	Sten Stensen, NOR	7:24.48	
10,000m	Piet Kleine, NED	14:50.59	**OR**

WOMEN

Event		Time	
500m	Sheila Young, USA	42.76	**OR**
1000m	Tatiana Averina, USSR	1:28.43	**OR**
1500m	Galina Stepanskaya, USSR	2:16.58	**OR**
3000m	Tatiana Averina, USSR	4:45.19	**OR**

XIII OLYMPIC WINTER GAMES LAKE PLACID 1980

1980
Lake Placid

Eric and the Miracles.

Over 1,100 athletes from 37 countries participated in the 1980 Winter Games, but the only ones most people will ever remember are 21-year-old American speed skater Eric Heiden, who won five individual gold medals, and the U.S. hockey team—a bunch of college kids (average age 22) who beat the unbeatable Russians.

No one before or since Heiden has won five individual gold medals in a single Olympic Games (three of swimmer Mark Spitz's seven gold medals were for relay races). And Heiden's sweep of the men's speed skating events has never been duplicated.

The hockey team, on the other hand, was a decided underdog. Seeded seventh out of 12 teams in the first round, they had also been routed, 10–3, by the Soviet Union in an exhibition game only a week before the Olympics.

Nevertheless, the Americans reached the final round with a 4–0–1 record. Playing in front of a boisterous, flag-waving home crowd, the U.S. upset the Soviets, 4–3 (captain Mike Eruzione scored the winning goal midway through the third period and goalie Jim Craig made 39 saves), then beat Finland, 4–2, to win the gold medal. "Do you believe in miracles?" asked ABC-TV announcer Al Michaels as the final seconds ticked off against the Russians. "Ye-s-s-s!"

That game was played on Feb. 22—five days short of exactly 20 years after the 1960 U.S. team beat the USSR, 3–2, on their way to the gold medal at Squaw Valley. Other links to the past included right wing Dave Christian, whose father Billy and uncle Roger were linemates on the 1960 team, and coach Herb Brooks, who had been the last player cut from the 1960 squad.

Swedish Alpine skier Ingemar Stenmark, who would retire in 1989 with 86 World Cup victories, won the slalom and GS for his only two Olympic wins.

Top 10 Standings
National medal standings are not recognized by the IOC. The unofficial point totals are based on 3 points for a gold medal, 2 for a silver and 1 for a bronze. Total medals are in parentheses.

		Gold	Silver	Bronze	Pts
1	USSR (22)	10	6	6	48
	East Germany (23)	9	7	7	48
3	USA (12)	6	4	2	28
4	Finland (9)	1	5	3	16
5	Austria (7)	3	2	2	15
	Norway (10)	1	3	6	15
7	Sweden (4)	3	0	1	10
	Liechtenstein (4)	2	2	0	10
9	Holland (4)	1	2	1	8
	Switzerland (5)	1	1	3	8

AP/Wide World Photos

▮▬▬▬▬▬▬▬▬▬▬▬▬▬▬▬▬

*The **U.S. men's hockey team** celebrates its 4-3 upset of the Soviet Union in the semifinals at the 1980 Olympic Winter Games in Lake Placid, N.Y. The team beat Finland (4-2) in the finals to win the gold medal.*

Leading Medal Winners

Number of individual medals won on the left; gold, silver and bronze breakdown to the right.

No	MEN	Sport	G-S-B
5	Eric Heiden, USA	Sp. Skating	5-0-0
3	Nikolai Zimatov, USSR	X-country	3-0-0
3	Anatoly Alyabiev, USSR	Biathlon	2-0-1
3	Frank Ullrich, E. Ger.	Biathlon	1-2-0
3	Juha Mieto, FIN	X-country	0-2-1
2	Ingemar Stenmark, SWE	Alpine	2-0-0
2	Vladimir Alikin, USSR	Biathlon	1-1-0
2	Josef Benz, SWI	Bobsled	1-1-0
2	Hans Jurgen Gerhardt, E. Ger.	Bobsled	1-1-0
2	Bernhard Germeshausen, E. Ger.	Bobsled	1-1-0
2	Vasili Rochev, USSR	X-country	1-1-0
2	Erich Schärer, SWI	Bobsled	1-1-0
2	Bogdan Musiol, E. Ger.	Bobsled	1-0-1
2	Meinhard Nehmer, E. Ger.	Bobsled	1-0-1
2	Kai Arne Stenshjemmet, NOR	Sp. Skate	0-2-0
2	Ove Aunli, NOR	X-country	0-1-1
2	Eberhard Rosch, E. Ger.	Biathlon	0-1-1
2	Tom Erik Oxholm, NOR	Sp. Skate	0-0-2

No	WOMEN	Sport	G-S-B
3	Hanni Wenzel, LIE	Alpine	2-1-0
2	Barbara Petzold, E. Ger.	X-country	2-0-0
2	Raisa Smetanina, USSR	X-country	1-1-0
2	Natalia Petruseva, USSR	Sp. Skate	1-0-1
2	Leah Mueller, USA	Sp. Skate	0-2-0
2	Hilkka Riihivuori, FIN	X-country	0-2-0
2	Sabine Becker, E. Ger.	Sp. Skate	0-1-1

Alpine Skiing

MEN

Event		Time
Downhill	Leonhard Stock, AUT	1:45.50
Slalom	Ingemar Stenmark, SWE	1:44.26
G.Slalom	Ingemar Stenmark, SWE	2:40.74

WOMEN

Event		Time
Downhill	Annemarie Moser-Pröll, AUT	1:37.52
Slalom	Hanni Wenzel, LIE	1:25.09
G.Slalom	Hanni Wenzel, LIE	2:41.66

Biathlon

Event		MT	Adj.Time
10km	Frank Ullrich, E. Ger.	2	32:10.69
20km	Anatoly Alyabiev, USSR	0	1:08:16.31
4x7.5km	USSR (Alikin, Tikonov, Barnashov, Alyabiev)	0	1:34:03.27

Bobsled

Event		Time
2-Man	SWI (Erich Schärer & Josef Benz)	4:09.36
4-Man	E. Ger (Meinhard Nehmer, Bogdan Musiol, Bernhard Germeshausen, Hans-Jürgen Gerhardt)	3:59.92

Figure Skating

Event		Points
Men	Robin Cousins, GBR	189.48
Women	Anett Pötzsch, E. Ger.	189.00
Pairs	Irina Rodnina & Aleksandr Zaitsev, USSR	147.26
Dance	Natalia Linichuk & Gennady Karponosov, USSR	205.48

Ice Hockey
Medal Round
(Overall records in parentheses)

		Gm	W-L-T	Pts	GF	GA
1	USA (6-0-1)	3	2-0-1	5	10	7
2	USSR (6-1-0)	3	2-1-0	4	16	8
3	Sweden (4-1-2)	3	0-1-2	2	7	14
4	Finland (3-3-1)	3	0-2-1	1	7	11

Note: Games against common opponents carried over from the preliminary round. FIRST ROUND—USA tied Sweden, 2–2, and USSR over Finland, 4–2. MEDAL ROUND—USA over USSR, 4–3, and Finland, 4–2; USSR over Sweden, 9–2; and Sweden tied Finland, 3–3.

Luge
MEN

Event		Time
1-Seat	Bernhard Glass, E. Ger.	2:54.796
2-Seat	Hans Rinn & Norbert Hahn, E. Ger.	1:19.331

WOMEN

Event		Time
1-Seat	Vera Zozulia, USSR	2:36.537

Nordic Skiing
MEN
Cross Country

Event		Time
15km	Thomas Wassberg, SWE	41:57.63
30km	Nikolai Zimyatov, USSR	1:27:02.80
50km	Nikolai Zimyatov, USSR	2:27:24.60
4x10km	USSR (Rochev, Bazhukov, Beliaev, Zimyatov)	1:57:03.46

Ski Jumping

Event		Points
70m	Anton Innauer, AUT	266.3
90m	Jouko Törmänen, FIN	271.0

Nordic Combined

Event		Points
15km/Jump	Ulrich Wehling, E. Ger.	432.200

WOMEN
Cross Country

Event		Time
5km	Raisa Smetanina, USSR	15:06.92
10km	Barbara Petzold, E. Ger.	30:31.54
4x5km	E. Ger. (Rostock, Anding, Hesse, Petzold)	1:02:11.10

Speed Skating
MEN

Event		Time	
500m	Eric Heiden, USA	38.03	**OR**
1000m	Eric Heiden, USA	1:15.18	**OR**
1500m	Eric Heiden, USA	1:55.44	**OR**
5000m	Eric Heiden, USA	7:02.29	**OR**
10,000m	Eric Heiden, USA	14:28.13	**WR**

WOMEN

Event		Time	
500m	Karin Enke, E. Ger.	41.78	**OR**
1000m	Natalia Petruseva, USSR	1:24.10	**OR**
1500m	Annie Borckink, NED	2:10.95	**OR**
3000m	Bjoerg Eva Jensen, NOR	4:32.13	**OR**

1984
Sarajevo

In 1980, the Soviet Union and East Germany finished the Winter Games in a virtual tie for the unofficial team championship. The USSR won more gold medals (10–9), but the GDR won more overall medals (23–22).

In 1984, the East Germans edged into the lead in the battle of state-controlled athletic programs, winning three more golds (9–6), while the Soviets won one more overall medal (25–24).

Karin Enke was the top East German performer, taking two gold medals and two silvers in the four women's speed skating events. Teammate Andrea Schöne won a gold and two silvers. Cross-country skier Marja-Liisa Hämäläinen of Finland was the only athlete to win three events and one of only three—Enke and Swedish cross-country skier Gunde Svan were the others—to win four overall medals.

The U.S. hockey team failed to qualify for the medal round, but the men's Alpine ski team, which had never won an event before, won twice. Bill Johnson took the downhill and the Mahre brothers, Phil and Steve, finished 1–2 in the slalom.

Top 10 Standings
National medal standings are not recognized by the IOC. The unofficial point totals are based on 3 points for a gold medal, 2 for a silver and 1 for a bronze. Total medals are in parentheses.

		Gold	Silver	Bronze	Pts
1	East Germany (24)	9	9	6	51
2	USSR (25)	6	10	9	47
3	Finland (13)	4	3	6	24
4	USA (8)	4	4	0	20
5	Sweden (8)	4	2	2	18
6	Norway (9)	3	2	4	17
7	Switzerland (5)	2	2	1	11
8	Canada (4)	2	1	1	9
	West Germany (4)	2	1	1	9
10	Czechoslovakia (6)	0	2	4	8

Leading Medal Winners
Number of individual medals won on the left; gold, silver and bronze breakdown to the right.

MEN

No		Sport	G-S-B
4	Gunde Svan, SWE	X-country	2-1-1
3	Gaétan Boucher, CAN	Sp. Skating	2-0-1
3	Peter Angerer, W. Ger.	Biathlon	1-1-1
3	Eirik Kvalfoss, NOR	Biathlon	1-1-1
3	Aki Karvonen, FIN	X-country	0-1-2
2	Wolfgang Hoppe, E. Ger.	Bobsled	2-0-0
2	Dietmar Schauerhammer, E. Ger.	Bobsled	2-0-0
2	Thomas Wassberg, SWE	X-country	2-0-0
2	Tomas Gustafson, SWE	Sp. Skate	1-1-0
2	Igor Malkov, USSR	Sp. Skate	1-1-0
2	Matti Nykänen, FIN	Ski Jump	1-1-0
2	Jens Weissflog, E. Ger.	Ski Jump	1-1-0
2	Nikolai Zimyatov, USSR	X-country	1-1-0
2	Sergei Khlebnikov, USSR	Sp. Skate	0-2-0

No		Sport	G-S-B
2	Bernhard Lehmann, E. Ger.	Bobsled	0-2-0
2	Bogdan Musiol, E. Ger.	Bobsled	0-2-0
2	Aleksandr Zavialov, USSR.	X-country	0-2-0
2	Harri Kirvesniemi, FIN.	X-country	0-0-2
2	Rene Schofisch, E. Ger.	Sp. Skate	0-0-2

WOMEN

No		Sport	G-S-B
4	Marja-Liisa Hämäläinen, FIN	X-country	3-0-1
4	Karin Enke, E. Ger.	Sp. Skating	2-2-0
3	Andrea Schöne, E. Ger.	Sp. Skating	1-2-0
2	Berit Aunli, NOR	X-country	1-1-0
2	Anne Jahren, NOR	X-country	1-0-1
2	Brit Pettersen, NOR	X-country	1-0-1
2	Kvetoslava Jeriova, CZE	X-country	0-1-1
2	Perrine Pelen, FRA	Alpine	0-1-1
2	Natalia Petruseva, USSR	Sp. Skate	0-0-2

Alpine Skiing
MEN

Event		Time
Downhill	Bill Johnson, USA	1:45.59
Slalom	Phil Mahre, USA	1:39.41
G.Slalom	Max Julen, SWI	2:41.18

WOMEN

Event		Time
Downhill	Michela Figini, SWI	1:13.36
Slalom	Paoletta Magoni, ITA	1:36.47
G.Slalom	Debbie Armstrong, USA	2:20.98

Biathlon

Event		MT	Adj.Time
10km	Erik Kvalfoss, NOR	2	30:53.8
20km	Peter Angerer, W. Ger	2	1:11:52.7
4x7.5km	USSR (Vasiliev, Kachkarov, Algimantas, Buligin)	2	1:38:51.7

Bobsled

Event		Time
2-Man	E. Ger. (Wolfgang Hoppe & Dietmar Schauerhammer)	3:25.56
4-Man	E. Ger. (Wolfgang Hoppe, Roland Wetzig, Dietmar Schauerhammer, Andreas Kirchner)	3:20.22

Figure Skating

Event		Points
Men	Scott Hamilton, USA	3.4
Women	Katarina Witt, E. Ger.	3.2
Pairs	Elena Valova & Oleg Vasiliev, USSR	1.4
Dance	Jayne Torvill & Christopher Dean, GBR	2.0

Ice Hockey
Medal Round
(Overall records in parentheses)

		Gm	W-L-T	Pts	GF	GA
1	USSR (7-0-0)	3	3-0-0	6	16	1
2	Czechoslovakia (6-1-0)	3	2-1-0	4	6	3
3	Sweden (4-2-1)	3	1-2-0	2	3	12
4	Canada (4-3-0)	3	0-3-0	0	0	10

Note: Games against common opponents carried over from the preliminary round. MEDAL ROUND—the USSR beat Sweden, 10–1, Canada, 4–0, and the Czechs, 2–0, the Czechs beat Canada, 4–0, and Sweden, 2–0; and Sweden beat Canada, 2–0.

Also: The U.S., featuring future NHL stars Chris Chelios and Pat LaFontaine, failed to qualify for the Medal Round, finishing 7th overall with a record of 2–2–2.

Luge
MEN

Event		Time
1-Seat	Paul Hildgartner, ITA	3:04.258
2-Seat	Hans Stanggassinger & Franz Wembacher, W. Ger.	1:23.620

WOMEN

Event		Time
1-Seat	Steffi Martin, E. Ger.	2:46.570

Nordic Skiing
MEN
Cross Country

Event		Time
15km	Gunde Svan, SWE	41:25.6
30km	Nikolai Zimyatov, USSR	1:28:56.3
50km	Thomas Wassberg, SWE	2:15:55.8
4x10km	SWE (Wassberg, Kohlberg, Ottoson, Svan)	1:55:06.3

Ski Jumping

Event		Points
70m	Jens Weissflog, E. Ger.	215.2
90m	Matti Nykänen, FIN	231.2

Nordic Combined

Event		Points
15km/Jump	Tom Sandberg, NOR	422.595

WOMEN
Cross Country

Event		Time
5km	Marja-Liisa Hämäläinen, FIN	17:04.0
10km	Marja-Liisa Hämäläinen, FIN	31:44.2
20km	Marja-Liisa Hämäläinen, FIN	1:01:45.0
4x5km	NOR (Nybråten, Jahren, Pettersen, Aunli)	1:06:49.7

Speed Skating
MEN

Event		Time
500m	Sergei Fokichev, USSR	38.19
1000m	Gaétan Boucher, CAN	1:15.80
1500m	Gaétan Boucher, CAN	1:58.36
5000m	Tomas Gustafson, SWE	7:12.28
10,000m	Igor Malkov, USSR	14:39.90

WOMEN

Event		Time	
500m	Christa Rothenburger, E. Ger.	41.02	OR
1000m	Karin Enke, E. Ger.	1:21.61	OR
1500m	Karin Enke, E. Ger.	2:03.42	WR
3000m	Andrea Schöne, E. Ger.	4:24.79	OR

1988
Calgary

A record 1,750 athletes from 57 nations came to western Canada for the first Olympics north of the U.S. border. The Games featured an indoor speed skating oval and sporadic chinook winds that sent temperatures into the unwintry 70s.

Matti Nykänen of Finland became the first pure ski jumper to capture three titles, winning gold medals at 70 and 90 meters and adding a third in the new team jumping competition.

Nykänen may have been the most decorated jumper in Calgary, but he wasn't the most celebrated. That honor belonged to Michael (Eddie the Eagle) Edwards, the accident-prone flying plasterer from Britain. Edwards finished 58th and last in the 70–meter jump and 55th and last in the 90–meter and was welcomed home after the Games by hundreds of fans at London's Heathrow Airport.

Back on the serious side, Dutch speed skater Yvonne van Gennip won three gold medals; East German figure skater Katarina Witt won her second straight women's title; and the USSR beat East Germany in both gold and overall medals in the last winterized confrontation of Communist superpowers.

Top 10 Standings

National medal standings are not recognized by the IOC. The unofficial point totals are based on 3 points for a gold medal, 2 for a silver and 1 for a bronze. Total medals in parentheses.

		Gold	Silver	Bronze	Pts
1	USSR (29)	11	9	9	60
2	East Germany (25)	9	10	6	53
3	Switzerland (15)	5	5	5	30
4	Austria (10)	3	5	2	21
5	Finland (7)	4	1	2	16
	West Germany (8)	2	4	2	16
7	Netherlands (7)	3	2	2	15
8	Sweden (6)	4	0	2	14
9	USA (6)	2	1	3	11
10	Italy (5)	2	1	2	10

Leading Medal Winners

Number of individual medals won on the left; gold, silver and bronze breakdown to the right.

MEN

No		Sport	G-S-B
3	Matti Nykänen, FIN	Ski Jump	3-0-0
3	Valery Medvedtsev, USSR	Biathlon	1-2-0
3	Vladimir Smirnov, USSR	X-country	0-2-1
2	Alberto Tomba, ITA	Alpine	2-0-0
2	Frank-Peter Rötsch, E. Ger.	Biathlon	2-0-0
2	Gunde Svan, SWE	X-country	2-0-0
2	Tomas Gustafson, SWE	Sp. Skate	2-0-0
2	Hubert Strolz, AUT	Alpine	1-1-0
2	Mikhail Deviatiarov, USSR	X-country	1-1-0
2	Hippolyt Kempf, SWI	Nordic Comb.	1-1-0
2	Jens-Uwe Mey, E. Ger.	Sp. Skate	1-1-0
2	Alexei Prokurorov, USSR	X-country	1-1-0
2	Sergei Chepikov, USSR	Biathlon	1-0-1
2	Ianis Kipours, USSR	Bobsled	1-0-1
2	Vladimir Kozlov, USSR	Bobsled	1-0-1
2	Franck Piccard, FRA	Alpine	1-0-1
2	Pirmin Zurbriggen, SWI	Alpine	1-0-1
2	Wolfgang Hoppe, E. Ger.	Bobsled	0-2-0
2	Bogdan Musiol, E. Ger.	Bobsled	0-2-0
2	Matjaz Debelak, YUG	Ski Jump	0-1-1
2	Michael Hadschieff, AUT	Sp. Skate	0-1-1
2	Erik Johnsen, NOR	Ski Jump	0-1-1
2	Klaus Sulzenbacher, AUT	Nordic Comb.	0-1-1
2	Leo Visser, NED	Sp. Skate	0-1-1
2	Johann Passler, ITA	Biathlon	0-0-2

WOMEN

No		Sport	G-S-B
3	Yvonne van Gennip, NED	Sp. Skating	3-0-0
3	Tamara Tikhonova, USSR	X-country	2-1-0
3	Marjo Matikänen, FIN	X-country	1-0-2
3	Andrea Ehrig, E. Ger.	Sp. Skating	0-2-1
3	Karin Kania, E. Ger.	Sp. Skating	0-2-1
2	Vreni Schneider, SWI	Alpine	2-0-0
2	Anfissa Reztsova, USSR	X-country	1-1-0
2	Christa Rothenburger, E. Ger.	Sp. Skate	1-1-0
2	Bonnie Blair, USA	Sp. Skate	1-0-1
2	Vida Ventsene, USSR	X-country	1-0-1
2	Brigitte Oertli, SWI	Alpine	0-2-0
2	Christa Kinshofer, W. Ger.	Alpine	0-1-1
2	Raisa Smetanina, USSR	X-country	0-1-1
2	Karen Percy, CAN	Alpine	0-0-2
2	Maria Walliser, SWI	Alpine	0-0-2
2	Gabi Zange, E. Ger.	Sp. Skate	0-0-2

Alpine Skiing
MEN

Event		Time
Downhill	Pirmin Zurbriggen, SWI	1:59.63
Slalom	Alberto Tomba, ITA	1:39.47
G.Slalom	Alberto Tomba, ITA	2:06.37
Super GS	Franck Piccard, FRA	1:39.66
Combined	Hubert Strolz, AUT	36.55 pts

WOMEN

Event		Time
Downhill	Marina Kiehl, W. Ger.	1:25.86
Slalom	Vreni Schneider, SWI	1:36.69
G.Slalom	Vreni Schneider, SWI	2:06.49
Super GS	Sigrid Wolf, AUT	1:19.03
Combined	Anita Wachter, AUT	29.25 pts

Biathlon

Event		MT	Adj.Time
10km	Frank-Peter Rötsch, E. Ger.	1	25:08.1
20km	Frank-Peter Rötsch, E. Ger.	3	56:33.3
4x7.5km	USSR (Vasiliev, Chepikov, Popov, Medvedtsev)	0	1:22:30.0

Bobsled

Event		Time
2-Man	USSR (Janis Kipours & Vladimir Kozlov)	3:53.48
4-Man	SWI (Ekkehard Fasser, Kurt Meier, Marcel Fässler, Werner Stocker)	3:47.51

Figure Skating

Event		Points
Men	Brian Boitano, USA	3.0
Women	Katarina Witt, E. Ger.	4.2
Pairs	Ekaterina Gordeeva & Sergei Grinkov, USSR	1.4
Dance	Natalya Bestemianova & Andrei Bukin, USSR	2.0

Ice Hockey

Medal Round
(Overall records in parentheses)

		Gm	W-L-T	Pts	GF	GA
1	USSR (7-1-0)	5	4-1-0	8	25	7
2	Finland (5-2-1)	5	3-1-1	7	18	10
3	Sweden (4-1-3)	5	2-1-2	6	15	16
4	Canada (5-2-1)	5	5-2-1	5	17	14
5	West Germany (4-4-0)	5	1-4-0	2	8	26
6	Czechoslovakia (4-4-0)	5	1-4-0	2	12	22

Note: Games against common opponents carried over from the preliminary round. The USSR lost its final game to Finland, 2–1, after clinching the gold medal.

Also: The U.S. finished 4th in its preliminary pool with a 2–3 record. The top three teams in each of two 6–team pools qualified for the medal round.

Luge
MEN

Event		Time
1-Seat	Jens Müller, E. Ger.	3:05.548
2-Seat	Joerg Hoffmann & Jochen Pietzsch, E. Ger.	1:31.940

WOMEN

Event		Time
1-Seat	Steffi Martin Walter, E. Ger.	3:03.973

Nordic Skiing
MEN
Cross Country

Event		Time
15 km	Mikhail Deviatiarov, USSR	41:18.9
30 km	Alexei Prokurorov, USSR	1:24:26.3
50 km	Gunde Svan, SWE	2:04:30.9
4x10 km	SWE (Ottosson, Wassberg, Svan, Mogren)	1:43:58.6

Ski Jumping

Event		Points
70m	Matti Nykänen, FIN	229.1
90m	Matti Nykänen, FIN	224.0
Team	FIN (Nikkola, Nykänen, Ylipulli, Puikkonen)	634.4

Nordic Combined

Event		Points
Indiv.	Hippolyt Kempf, SWI	432.23
Team	W. Ger. (Pohl, Schwarz, Müller)	792.08

WOMEN
Cross Country

Event		Time
5km	Marjo Matikänen, FIN	15:04.0
10km	Vida Ventsene, USSR	30:08.3
20km	Tamara Tikhonova, USSR	55:53.6
4x5km	USSR (Nagueikina, Gavriliuk, Tikhonova, Reztsova)	59:51.1

Speed Skating
MEN

Event		Time	
500m	Jens-Uwe Mey, E. Ger.	36.45	WR
1000m	Nikolai Gouliaev, USSR	1:13.03	OR
1500m	André Hoffmann, E. Ger.	1:52.06	WR
5000m	Tomas Gustafson, SWE	6:44.63	WR
10,000m	Tomas Gustafson, SWE	13:48.20	WR

WOMEN

Event		Time	
500m	Bonnie Blair, USA	39.10	WR
1000m	Christa Rothenburger, E. Ger.	1:17.65	WR
1500m	Yvonne van Gennip, NED	2:00.68	OR
3000m	Yvonne van Gennip, NED	4:11.94	WR
5000m	Yvonne van Gennip, NED	7:14.13	WR

1992
Albertville

The first Olympics since the reunification of Germany in 1990 and the breakup of the Soviet Union in 1991 resulted in a record 2,174 athletes from 65 countries as the Winter Games were staged in the French Alps for the third time. Despite all the political turmoil at home, Germany's combined East-West squad and the Unified Team of ex-Soviet athletes were again the biggest winners with the Germans edging the Unifieds in total medals, 26-23.

The female stars of the UT cross-country contingent made the most medal news as Lyubov Egorova (3 gold and 2 silver) and Elena Valbe (1 gold and 4 bronze), each won five and 39-year-old Raisa Smetanina set a Winter Games record with her 10th career medal as a member of the victorious 20-kilometer relay team.

Norway won as many gold medals (9) as the Unified Team, thanks mainly to cross-country skiers Bjorn Dählie and Vegard Ulvang, who each carried off three golds and a silver. Norwegians also won gold in alpine skiing for the first time in 40 years as Finn Christian Jagge (slalom) and Kjetil Andre Aamodt (Super G) made like Stein Eriksen in 1952.

Led by Bonnie Blair's victories at 500 and 1,000 meters in speed skating, women won all five gold medals collected by the U.S. Blair was joined by figure skater Kristi Yamaguchi, freestyle skier Donna Weinbrecht and short track speed skater Cathy Turner.

Top 10 Standings

National medal standings are not recognized by the IOC. The unofficial point totals are based on 3 points for a gold medal, 2 for a silver and 1 for a bronze. Total medals are in parentheses.

		Gold	Silver	Bronze	Points
1	Germany (26)	10	10	6	56
2	Unified Team (23)	9	6	8	47
3	Norway (20)	9	6	5	44
4	Austria (21)	6	7	8	40
5	Italy (14)	4	6	4	28
6	United States (11)	5	4	2	25
7	France (9)	3	5	1	20
8	Finland (7)	3	1	3	14
	Canada (7)	2	3	2	14
10	Japan (7)	1	2	4	11

Leading Medal Winners

Number of individual medals won on the left; gold, silver and bronze breakdown to the right.

MEN

No		Sport	G-S-B
4	Bjorn Dählie, NOR	X-country	3-1-0
4	Vegard Ulvang, NOR	X-country	3-1-0
3	Mark Kirchner, GER	Biathlon	2-1-0
3	Toni Nieminen, FIN	Ski Jump	2-0-1
3	Martin Hollwarth, AUT	Ski Jump	0-3-0
3	Giorgio Vanzetta, ITA	X-country	0-1-2
2	Kim Ki Hoon, S.Kor	ST Sp. Skate	2-0-0
2	Ricco Gross, GER	Biathlon	1-1-0
2	Johann Koss, NOR	Sp. Skate	1-1-0
2	Alberto Tomba, ITA	Alpine	1-1-0
2	Ernst Vettori, AUT	Ski Jump	1-1-0
2	Kjetil Andre Aamodt, NOR	Alpine	1-0-1
2	Donat Acklin, SWI	Bobsled	1-0-1
2	Geir Karlstad, NOR	Sp. Skate	1-0-1
2	Terje Langli, NOR	X-country	1-0-1
2	Gustav Weder, SWI	Bobsled	1-0-1
2	Lee Joon Ho, S.Kor	ST Sp. Skate	1-0-1
2	Marco Albarello, ITA	X-country	0-2-0
2	Frederic Blackburn, CAN	ST Sp. Skate	0-2-0
2	Marc Girardelli, LUX	Alpine	0-2-0
2	Heinz Kuttin, AUT	Ski Jump	0-1-1
2	Mikael Lofren, SWE	Biathlon	0-0-2
2	Klaus Sulzenbacher, AUT	Nordic Comb.	0-0-2
2	Leo Visser, NED	Sp. Skate	0-0-2

WOMEN

No		Sport	G-S-B
5	Lyubov Egorova, UT	X-country	3-2-0
5	Elena Valbe, UT	X-country	1-0-4
3	Gunda Niemann, GER	Sp. Skate	2-1-0
3	Antje Misersky, GER	Biathlon	1-2-0
3	Stefania Belmondo, ITA	X-country	1-1-1
2	Bonnie Blair, USA	Sp.Skate	2-0-0
2	Petra Kronberger, AUT	Alpine	2-0-0
2	Marjut Lukkarinen, FIN	X-country	1-1-0
2	Cathy Turner, USA	ST Sp. Skate	1-1-0
2	Anfisa Reztsova, UT	Biathlon	1-0-1
2	Ye Qiaobo, CHN	Sp. Skate	0-2-0
2	Anita Wachter, AUT	Alpine	0-2-0
2	Heike Warnicke, GER	Sp. Skate	0-2-0
2	Elena Belova, UT	Biathlon	0-0-2

Alpine Skiing

MEN

Event		Time
Downhill	Patrick Ortlieb, AUT	1:50.37
Slalom	Finn Christian Jagge, NOR	1:44.39
Giant Slalom	Alberto Tomba, ITA	2:06.98
Super G	Kjetil Andre Aamodt, NOR	1:13.04
Combined	Josef Polig, ITA	14.58 pts

WOMEN

Event		Time
Downhill	Kerrin Lee-Gartner, CAN	1:52.55
Slalom	Petra Krenberger, AUT	1:32.68
Giant Slalom	Pernilla Wiberg, SWE	2:12.74
Super G	Deborah Compagnoni, ITA	1:21.22
Combined	Petra Kronberger, AUT	2.55 pts

Biathlon
MEN

Event		MT	Time
10km	Mark Kircher, GER	0	26:02.3
20km	Yevgeny Redkine, UT	0	57:34.4
4x7.5km relay	Germany (Gross, Steinigen, Kirchner, Fischer)	0	1:24:43.5

WOMEN

Event		MT	Time
7.5km	Anfisa Reztsova, UT	3	24:29.2
15km	Antje Misersky, GER	1	51:47.2
3x7.5km relay	France (Niogret, Claudel, Briand)	0	1:15:55.6

Bobsled

Event		Time
2-Man	SWI (Gustav Weder & Donat Acklin)	4:03.26
4-Man	AUT (Ingo Appelt, Harald Winkler, Gerhard Haidacher, Thomas Schroll)	3:53.90

Figure Skating

Event		FP
Men	Viktor Petrenko, UT	1.5
Women	Kristi Yamaguchi, USA	1.5
Pairs	Natalya Mishkutienok & Artur Dmitriev, UT	1.5
Dance	Marina Klimova & Sergei Ponomarenko, UT	2.0

Freestyle Skiing

Event		Pts
Men's Moguls	Edgar Grospiron, FRA	25.81
Women's Moguls	Donna Weinbrecht, USA	23.69

Ice Hockey

Round Robin Standings

First four teams in each group advanced to medal round.

Group A	Gm	W-L-T	Pts	GF	GA
United States	5	4-0-1	9	18	7
Sweden	5	3-0-2	8	22	11
Finland	5	3-1-1	7	22	11
Germany	5	2-3-0	4	11	12
Italy	5	1-4-0	2	18	24
Poland	5	0-5-0	0	4	30

Group B	Gm	W-L-T	Pts	GF	GA
Canada	5	4-1-0	8	28	9
Unified Team	5	4-1-0	8	32	10
Czechoslovakia	5	4-1-0	8	25	15
France	5	2-3-0	4	14	22
Switzerland	5	1-4-0	2	13	25
Norway	5	0-5-0	0	7	38

Note: First place tie broken by goal differential in common games.

Quarterfinals

Canada 3 .... Germany 3
(Canada wins shootout, 3-2)
Czechoslovakia 3 .... Sweden 1
United States 4 .... France 1
Unified Team 6 .... Finland 1

Semifinals

Canada 4 .... Czechoslovakia 2
Unified Team 5 .... United States 2

Bronze Medal

Czechoslovakia 6 .... United States 1

Gold Medal

Unified Team 3 .... Canada 1

Luge
MEN

Event		Time
Singles	Georg Hackl, GER	3:02.363
Doubles	Stefan Krausse & Jan Behrendt, GER	1:32.053

WOMEN

Event		Time
Singles	Doris Neuner, AUT	3:06.696

Nordic Skiing
MEN
Cross Country

Event		Time
10km	Vegard Ulvang, NOR	27:36.0
15km	Bjorn Dählie, NOR	38:01.9
30km	Vegard Ulvang, NOR	1:22:27.8
50km	Bjorn Dählie, NOR	2:03:41.5
4x10km	NOR (Langli, Ulvang, Skjedal, Dahlie)	1:39:26.0

Ski Jumping

Event		Pts
90m	Ernst Vettori, AUT	222.8
120m	Toni Nieminen, FIN.	239.5
Team (120m)	FIN (Nikkola, Laitinen, Laakkonen, Nieminen)	644.4

Nordic Combined

Event		Pts
Indiv.	Fabrice Guy, FRA	426.47
Team	JPN (Mikata, Kono, Ogiwara)	1247.18

WOMEN
Cross Country

Event		Time
5km	Marjut Lukkarinen, FIN	14:13.8
10km	Lyubov Egorova, RUS	25:53.7
15km	Lyubov Egorova, RUS	42:20.8
30km	Stefania Belmondo, ITA	1:22:30.1
4x5km	UT (Valbe, Smetanina, Lasutina, Egorova) .	59:34.8

Speed Skating
MEN
Long Track

Event		Time
500m	Uwe-Jens Mey, GER	37.14
1000m	Olaf Zinke, GER	1:14.85
1500m	Johann Olav Koss, NOR	1:54.81
5000m	Geir Karlstad, NOR	6:59.97
10,000m	Bart Veldkamp, NED	14:12.12

Short Track

Event		Time	
1000m	Ki-Hoon Kim, S. Kor	1:30.76	**WR**
4x1250m	S.Kor (Kim, Lee, Jmo, Song) . . .	7:14.02	**WR**

WOMEN
Long Track

Event		Time
500m	Bonnie Blair, USA	40.33
1000m	Bonnie Blair, USA	1:21.90
1,500m	Jacqueline Borner, GER	2:05.87
3000m	Gunda Niemann, GER	4:19.90
5000m	Gunda Niemann, GER	7:31.57

Short Track

Event		Time
500m	Cathy Turner, USA	47.04
4x750m	CAN (Cutrone, Daigle, Lambert, Perreault)	4:36.62

1994
Lillehammer

For better or worse, the Lillehammer games may be best evoked in most people's memories by two names. Tonya and Nancy. It was an ugly attack before the U.S. Figure Skating Championships on skater Nancy Kerrigan by cohorts of teammate and rival Tonya Harding that set up the most anticipated moment of the Games. Harding's goons were arrested following the Kerrigan clubbing and charged in a plot to improve Harding's chances of medaling by removing Kerrigan from competition. The plan failed and Kerrigan did compete, finishing with the silver medal. She actually tied 16-year-old Ukrainian orphan Oksana Baiul but missed the gold on the artistic merit tiebreaker. Harding, who had to threaten a lawsuit to avoid being barred from the Games by the USOC, ended up in eighth. The broadcast of the women's skating final was the sixth highest-rated program of any sort in U.S. television history.

There are so many more names symbolic of these games, however. Norway's Johann Olav Koss set three world records and won three golds in the men's 1500-, 5000- and 10,000-meter speed skating events. American speed skaters had success as well. Dan Jansen finally caught that elusive medal, winning the 1000-meter gold with a world record in his final event. Bonnie Blair won two golds in the women's 500- and 1000-meter races. And those were just the speed skaters.

The games were the most environmentally friendly Olympics in history as well. Norway's recycling and energy-saving techniques were so successful that the IOC revised its procedure for choosing host cities as a result.

Top 10 Standings

National medal standings are not recognized by the IOC. The unofficial point totals are based on 3 points for a gold medal, 2 for a silver and 1 for a bronze. Total medals are in parentheses.

		Gold	Silver	Bronze	Points
1	Norway (26)	10	11	5	57
2	Russia (23)	11	8	4	53
3	Germany (24)	9	7	8	49
4	Italy (20)	7	5	8	39
5	United States (13)	6	5	2	30
6	Canada (13)	3	6	4	25
7	Switzerland (9)	3	4	2	19
8	Austria (9)	2	3	4	16
9	South Korea (6)	4	1	1	15
10	Japan (5)	1	2	2	9

Leading Medal Winners

Number of individual medals won on the left; gold, silver and bronze breakdown to the right.

MEN

No		Sport	G-S-B
4	Bjorn Dählie, NOR	X-country	2-2-0
3	Johann Olav Koss, NOR	Sp. Skating	3-0-0
3	Vladimir Smirnov, KAZ	X-country	1-2-0
3	Sergei Tarasov, RUS	Biathlon	1-1-1
3	Kjetil Andre Aamodt, NOR	Alpine	0-2-1
3	Mika Myllyla, FIN	X-country	0-1-2
2	Markus Wasmeier, GER	Alpine	2-0-0
2	Jens Weissflog, GER	Ski Jumping	2-0-0
2	Donat Acklin, SWI	Bobsled	1-1-0
2	Thomas Alsgaard, NOR	X-country	1-1-0
2	Espen Bredesen, NOR	Ski Jumping	1-1-0
2	Ji-Hoon Chae, S.Kor	ST Sp. Skating	1-1-0
2	Ricco Gross, GER	Biathlon	1-1-0
2	Takanori Kono, JPN	Nordic Comb.	1-1-0
2	Frank Luck, GER	Biathlon	1-1-0
2	Fred Borre Lundberg, NOR	Nordic Comb.	1-1-0
2	Tommy Moe, USA	Alpine	1-1-0
2	Sergei Chepikov, RUS	Biathlon	1-1-0
2	Mirko Vuillermin, ITA	ST. Sp. Skating	1-1-0
2	Gustav Weder, SWI	Bobsled	1-1-0
2	Marco Albarello, ITA	X-Country	1-0-1
2	Silvio Fauner, ITA	X-Country	1-0-1
2	Sven Fischer, GER	Biathlon	1-0-1
2	Dieter Thoma, GER	Ski Jumping	1-0-1
2	Kjell Storelid, NOR	Sp. Skating	0-2-0
2	Sergei Klevchenya, RUS	Sp. Skating	0-1-1
2	Rintje Ritsma, NED	Sp. Skating	0-1-1
2	Sture Sivertsen, NOR	X-Country	0-1-1
2	Bjarte Engen Vik, NOR	Nordic Comb.	0-1-1
2	Andreas Goldberger, AUT	Ski Jumping	0-0-2

WOMEN

No		Sport	G-S-B
5	Manuela Di Centa, ITA	X-Country	2-2-1
4	Lyubov Egorova, RUS	X-Country	3-1-0
3	Vreni Schneider, SWI	Alpine	1-1-1
2	Myriam Bedard, CAN	Biathlon	2-0-0
2	Bonnie Blair, USA	Sp. Skating	2-0-0
2	Lee-Kyung Chun, S. Kor	ST Sp. Skating	2-0-0
2	Emese Hunyady, AUT	Sp. Skating	1-1-0
2	Nina Gavriluk, RUS	X-Country	1-0-1
2	So-Hee Kim, S. Kor	ST Sp. Skating	1-0-1
2	Claudia Pechstein, GER	Sp. Skating	1-0-1
2	Cathy Turner, USA	ST Sp. Skating	1-0-1
2	Ann Briand, FRA	Biathlon	0-1-1
2	Ursula Disl, GER	Biathlon	0-1-1
2	Gunda Niemann, GER	Sp. Skating	0-1-1
2	Stefina Belmondo, ITA	X-Country	0-0-2
2	M.L. Kirvesniemi, FIN	X-Country	0-0-2
2	Isolde Kostner, ITA	Alpine	0-0-2
2	Amy Peterson, USA	ST Sp. Skating	0-0-2

Alpine Skiing

MEN

Event		Time
Downhill	Tommy Moe, USA	1:45.75
Slalom	Thomas Stangassinger, AUT	2:02.02
Giant Slalom	Markus Wasmeier, GER	2:52.46
Super G	Markus Wasmeier, GER	1:32.53
Combined	Lasse Kjus, NOR	3:17.53

WOMEN

Event		Time
Downhill	Katja Seizinger, GER	1:35.93
Slalom	Vreni Schneider, SWI	1:56.01
Giant Slalom	Deborah Compagnoni, ITA	2:30.97
Super G	Diann Roffe-Steinrotter, USA	1:22.15
Combined	Pernilla Wiberg, SWE	3:05.16

Biathlon

MEN

Event		MT	Time
10km	Sergei Chepikov, RUS	0	28:07.0
20km	Sergei Tarasov, RUS	3	57:25.3
4x7.5km relay	Germany	0	1:30:22.1

WOMEN

Event		MT	Time
7.5km	Myriam Bedard, CAN	2	26:08.8
15km	Myriam Bedard, CAN	2	52:06.6
4x7.5km relay	Russia	0	1:47:19.5

Bobsled

Event		Time
2-Man	SWI (Gustav Weder & Donat Acklin)	3:30.81
4-Man	GER (Harald Czudaj, Karsten Brannasch, Olaf Hampel, Alexander Szelig)	3:27.78

Freestyle Skiing

MEN

Event		Pts
Aerials	Andreas Schoenbaechler, SWI	234.67
Moguls	Jean-Luc Brassard, CAN	27.24

WOMEN

Event		Pts
Aerials	Lina Cherjazova, UZB	166.84
Moguls	Stine Lise Hattestad, NOR	25.97

Figure Skating

Event		FP
Men	Alexei Urmanov, RUS	1.5
Women	Oksana Baiul, UKR	2.0
Pairs	Ekaterina Gordeeva & Sergei Grinkov, RUS	1.5
Dance	Oksana Gritschuk & Yevgeny Platov, RUS	3.0

Ice Hockey

Round Robin Standings

First four teams in each group advanced to medal round.

Group A	Gm	W-L-T	Pts	GF	GA
Finland	5	5-0-0	10	25	4
Germany	5	3-2-0	6	11	14
Czech Republic	5	3-2-0	6	16	11
Russia	5	3-2-0	6	20	14
Austria	5	1-4-0	2	13	28
Norway	5	0-5-0	0	5	19

Note: Second place tie broken by goal differential in common games.

Group B	Gm	W-L-T	Pts	GF	GA
Slovakia	5	3-0-2	8	26	14
Canada	5	3-1-1	7	17	11
Sweden	5	3-1-1	7	23	13
United States	5	1-1-3	5	21	17
Italy	5	1-4-0	2	15	31
France	5	0-4-1	1	11	27

Note: Second place tie broken by goal differential in common games.

Quarterfinals

Sweden 3		Germany 0
Canada 3	OT	Czech Republic 2
Finland 6		United States 1
Russia 3	OT	Slovakia 2

Semifinals

Sweden 4 . . . . .Russia 3
Canada 5 . . . . .Finland 3

Bronze Medal

Finland 4 . . . . .Russia 0

Gold Medal

Sweden 2 . . . . .OT . . . . .Canada 2
(Sweden wins shootout, 3-2)

Luge
MEN

Event		Time
Singles	Georg Hackl, GER	3:21.571
Doubles	Kurt Brugger & Wilfried Huber, ITA	1:36.720

WOMEN

Event		Time
Singles	Gerda Weissensteiner, ITA	3:15.517

Nordic Skiing
MEN
Cross Country

Event		Time
10km	Bjorn Dählie, NOR	24:20.1
15km	Bjorn Dählie, NOR	1:00:08.8
30km	Thomas Alsgaard, NOR.	1:12:26.4
50km	Vladimir Smirnov, KAZ	2:07:20.3
4x10km	ITA (De Zolt, Albarello, Vanzetta, Fauner)	1:41:15.0

Ski Jumping

Event		Pts
90m	Espen Bredesen, NOR	282.0
120m	Jens Weissflog, GER	274.5
Team (120m)	GER (Jaekle, Duffner, Thoma, Weissflog)	970.1

Nordic Combined

Event		Pts
Indiv.	Fred Borre Lundberg, NOR	457.970
Team	JPN (Kono, Abe, Ogiwara)	1368.860

WOMEN
Cross Country

Event		Time
5km	Lyubov Egorova, RUS	14:08.8
10km	Lyubov Egorova, RUS	41:38.1
15km	Manuela Di Centa, ITA.	39:44.5
30km	Manuela Di Centa, ITA.	1:25:41.6
4x5km	RUS (Valbe, Lazutina, Gavriluk, Egorova).	57:12.5

Speed Skating
MEN
Long Track

Event		Time	
500m	Aleksandr Golubev, RUS	36.33	OR
1000m	Dan Jansen, USA	1:12.43	WR
1500m	Johann Olav Koss, NOR . . .	1:51.29	WR
5000m	Johann Olav Koss, NOR . .	6:34.96	WR
10,000m	Johann Olav Koss, NOR . .	13:30.55	WR

Short Track

Event		Time	
500m	Ji-Hoon Chae, S. Kor	43.45	
1000m	Ki-Hoon Kim, S. Kor	1:34.57	
5000m relay	Italy.	7:11.74	OR

WOMEN
Long Track

Event		Time
500m	Bonnie Blair, USA	39.25
1000m	Bonnie Blair, USA	1:18.74
1500m	Emese Hunyady, AUT.	2:02.19
3000m	Svetlana Bazhanova, RUS	4:17.43
5000m	Claudia Pechstein, GER	7:14.37

Short Track

Event		Time	
500m	Cathy Turner, USA	45.98	OR
1000m	Lee-Kyung Chun, S. Kor	1:36.87	
3000m Relay	South Korea	4:26.64	WR

1998
Nagano

The 18th Winter Games included a record 2,177 athletes from 72 countries and marked the Olympics first trip to Asia in 26 years. Nagano was pummeled by snow, sleet, rain and even a minor earthquake during the Games. The weather caused countless delays and rescheduling got so bad that organizers had to cram the men's super G, women's downhill, and women's combined downhill into one day—the first tripleheader in Olympic Alpine history.

Germany won the most medals (29) for the second time in its third Winter Games as a unified team. The team from host Japan surpassed expectations, winning more gold medals (five) and total medals (10) than any previous Japanese team. And the United States tied its previous best (1994), by winning 13 medals.

Austria's Hermann Maier provided the Games' most enduring image. A horrifying spill during the men's downhill spun him airborne like a rag-doll and sent him crashing through two retaining fences. Amazingly, he recovered to win two gold medals within the next six days.

For the third straight Winter Games a woman won the most medals. Russia's Larissa Lazutina medaled in all five cross-country events, earning three golds, a silver and a bronze. Cross-country veteran Bjorn Dählie, of Norway, won four medals, thus becoming the winningest Winter Games athlete ever with eight career gold medals and 12 overall.

U.S. figure skater Tara Lipinski, 15, became the youngest woman to win a gold medal at the Winter Games, and turned pro two months later. The U.S. won the first women's hockey gold medal, while the U.S. men's team—which included pros for the first time—drew ire for its disappointing sixth-place finish and room-trashing antics. The Czech Republic, which (as Czechoslovakia) had won seven Olympic hockey medals, but no golds, was a surprise winner, upsetting Russia 1-0 in the men's hockey final.

Curling and snowboarding also made their Olympic debuts in Nagano.

AP/Wide World Photos

*Norwegian cross-country skiier **Bjorn Dählie** collapses at the finish line of the 50-km race after winning his third gold medal of the Nagano Games and eighth of his career.*

Top 10 Standings

National medal standings are not recognized by the IOC. The unofficial point totals are based on 3 points for a gold medal, 2 for a silver and 1 for a bronze. Total medals are in parentheses.

		Gold	Silver	Bronze	Points
1	Germany (29)	12	9	8	62
2	Norway (25)	10	10	5	55
3	Russia (18)	9	6	3	42
4	Canada (15)	6	5	4	32
5	Austria (17)	3	5	9	28
	United States (13)	6	3	4	28
7	Netherlands (11)	5	4	2	25
8	Japan (10)	5	1	4	21
9	Finland (12)	2	4	6	20
	Italy (10)	2	6	2	20

Leading Medal Winners

Number of individual medals won on the left; gold, silver and bronze breakdown to the right.

No	MEN	Sport	G-S-B
4	Bjorn Dählie, NOR	X-country	3-1-0
3	Kazuyoshi Funaki, JPN	Ski Jumping	2-1-0
3	Rintje Ritsma, NED	Sp. Skating	0-1-2
3	Mika Myllylae, FIN	X-country	1-0-2
2	Gianni Romme, NED	Sp. Skating	2-0-0
2	Thomas Alsgaard, NOR	X-country	2-0-0
2	Hermann Maier, AUT	Alpine	2-0-0
2	Bjarte Engen Vik, NOR	Nordic Comb.	2-0-0
2	Ids Postma, NED	Sp. Skating	1-1-0
2	Jani Soininen, FIN	Ski Jumping	1-1-0
2	Erling Jevne, NOR	X-country	1-1-0
2	Ole Bjoerndalen, NOR	Biathlon	1-1-0

No		Sport	G-S-B
2	Halvard Hanevold, NOR	Biathlon	1-1-0
2	Kim Dong Sung, KOR	ST Sp. Skating	1-1-0
2	Christoph Langen, GER	Bobsled	1-0-1
2	Markus Zimmerman, GER	Bobsled	1-0-1
2	Eric Bedard, CAN	ST Sp. Skating	1-0-1
2	Masahiko Harada, JPN	Ski Jumping	1-0-1
2	Hiroyasu Shimizu, JPN	Sp. Skating	1-0-1
2	Lasse Kjus, NOR	Alpine	0-2-0
2	Samppa Lajunen, FIN	Nordic Comb.	0-2-0
2	Silvio Fauner, ITA	X-country	0-1-1
2	Li Jiajun, CHN	ST Sp. Skating	0-1-1
2	An Yulong, CHN	ST Sp. Skating	0-1-1
2	Andreas Widhoelzl, AUT	Ski Jumping	0-0-2

No	WOMEN	Sport	G-S-B
5	Larissa Lazutina, RUS	X-country	3-1-1
3	Olga Danilova, RUS	X-country	2-1-0
3	Katja Seizinger, GER	Alpine	2-0-1
3	Lee-Kyung Chun, KOR	ST Sp. Skating	2-0-1
3	G. Niemann-Stirnemann, GER	Sp. Skating	1-2-0
3	Ursula Disl, GER	Biathlon	1-1-1
3	Yang S. Yang, CHN	ST Sp. Skating	0-3-0
2	Marianne Timmer, NED	Sp. Skating	2-0-0
2	Galina Kukleva, RUS	Biathlon	1-1-0
2	Deborah Compagnoni, ITA	Alpine	1-1-0
2	Claudia Pechstein, GER	Sp. Skating	1-1-0
2	Hilde Gerg, GER	Alpine	1-0-1
2	Catriona LeMay Doan, CAN	Sp. Skating	1-0-1
2	Katrin Apel, GER	Biathlon	1-0-1
2	Annie Perreault, CAN	ST Sp. Skating	1-0-1
2	Katerina Neumannova, CZR	X-country	0-1-1
2	Bente Martinsen, NOR	X-country	0-1-1

No		Sport	G-S-B
2	Anita Moen-Guidon, NOR	X-country	0-1-1
2	Chris Witty, USA	Sp. Skating	0-1-1
2	Stefania Belmondo, ITA	X-country	0-1-1
2	Alexandra Meissnitzer, AUT	Alpine	0-1-1

Alpine Skiing
MEN

Event		Time
Downhill	Jean-Luc Cretier, FRA	1:50.11
Slalom	Hans-Petter Buraas, NOR	1:49.31
Giant Slalom	Hermann Maier, AUT	2:38.51
Super G	Hermann Maier, AUT	1:34.82
Combined	Mario Reiter, AUT	3:08.06

WOMEN

Event		Time
Downhill	Katja Seizinger, GER	1:28.89
Slalom	Hilde Gerg, GER	1:32.40
Giant Slalom	Deborah Compagnoni, ITA	2:50.59
Super G	Picabo Street, USA	1:18.02
Combined	Katja Seizinger, GER	2:40.74

Biathlon
MEN

Event		MT	Time
10km	Ole Einar Bjoerndalen, NOR	0	27:16.2
20km	Halvard Hanevold, NOR	1	56:16.4
4x7.5km relay	Germany	6	1:21:36.2

WOMEN

Event		MT	Time
7.5km	Galina Koukleva, RUS	1	23:08.0
15km	Ekaterina Dafovska, BUL	1	54:52.0
4x7.5km relay	Germany	11	1:40:13.6

Bobsled

Event		Time
2-Man	Italy I (Günther Huber & Antonio Tartaglia)	3:37.24
	Canada I (Pierre Leuders & Dave McEachern)	3:37.24
4-Man	GER II (Christoph Langen, Markus Zimmermann, Marco Jakobs, Olaf Hampel)	2:39.41

Curling
Round Robin Standings
MEN
(Overall records in parentheses)

	Gm	W-L-T	PF	PA
Canada	7	6-1-0	57	32
Switzerland	7	5-2-0	44	28
Norway	7	5-2-0	42	35
United States	7	3-4-0	34	46

Note: Japan (3-4-0), Sweden (3-4-0), Britain (2-5-0), and Germany (1-6-0) were eliminated.

Semifinals

Canada 7 .... United States 1
Switzerland 8 .... Norway 7

Bronze Medal

Norway 9 .... United States 4

Gold Medal

Switzerland 9 .... Canada 3

WOMEN

	Gm	W-L-T	PF	PA
Canada	7	6-1-0	51	34
Sweden	7	6-1-0	54	32
Denmark	7	5-2-0	46	34
Britain	7	4-3-0	38	44

Note: Japan (2-5-0), Norway (2-5-0), United States (2-5-0), and Germany (1-6-0) were eliminated.

Semifinals

Canada 6 .... Britain 5
Denmark 7 .... Sweden 5

Bronze Medal

Sweden 10 .... Britain 6

Gold Medal

Canada 7 .... Denmark 5

Figure Skating

Event		FP
Men	Ilia Kulik, RUS	1.5
Women	Tara Lipinski, USA	2.0
Pairs	Oksana Kazakova & Artur Dmitriev, RUS	1.5
Dance	Pasha Grishuk & Yevgeny Platov, RUS	2.0

Freestyle Skiing
MEN

Event		Pts
Aerials	Eric Bergoust, USA	255.64
Moguls	Jonny Moseley, USA	26.93

WOMEN

Event		Pts
Aerials	Nikki Stone, USA	193.00
Moguls	Tae Satoya, JPN	25.06

Ice Hockey
Final Round Standings
MEN
(Overall records in parentheses)

Group C	Gm	W-L-T	Pts	GF	GA
Russia	3	3-0-0	6	15	6
Czech Republic	3	2-1-0	4	12	4
Finland	3	1-2-0	2	11	9
Kazakhstan (2-4-0)	3	0-3-0	0	6	25

Group D	Gm	W-L-T	Pts	GF	GA
Canada	3	3-0-0	6	12	3
Sweden	3	2-1-0	4	11	7
United States	3	1-2-0	2	8	10
Belarus (2-3-1)	3	0-3-0	0	4	15

Note: Kazakhstan and Belarus reached the final round by winning preliminary Group A and Group B, respectively.

Quarterfinals

Czech Republic 4 .... United States 1
Russia 4 .... Belarus 1
Canada 4 .... Kazakhstan 1
Finland 2 .... Sweden 1

Semifinals

Czech Republic 2 .... Canada 1
(Czech Republic wins shootout, 1-0)
Russia 7 .... Finland 4

Bronze Medal

Finland 3 .... Canada 2

Gold Medal

Czech Republic 1 .... Russia 0

WOMEN

	Gm	W-L-T	Pts	GF	GA
United States	6	6-0-0	12	36	8
Canada	6	4-2-0	8	29	15
Finland	6	4-2-0	8	31	11
China	6	2-4-0	4	11	19
Sweden	5	1-4-0	2	10	21
Japan	5	0-5-0	0	2	45

Bronze Medal

Finland 4 .... China 1

Gold Medal

United States 3 .... Canada 1

Luge
MEN

Event		Time
Singles	Georg Hackl, GER	3:18.436
Doubles	Stefan Krausse & Jan Behrendt, GER	1:41.105

WOMEN

Event		Time
Singles	Silke Kraushaar, GER	3:23.779

Nordic Skiing
MEN
Cross Country

Event		Time
10km	Bjorn Dählie, NOR	27:24.5
15km	Thomas Alsgaard, NOR	1:07:01.7
30km	Mika Myllylae, FIN	1:33:55.8
50km	Bjorn Dählie, NOR	2:05:08.2
4x10km	NOR (Sivertsen, Jevne, Dählie, Alsgaard)	1:40:55.7

Ski Jumping

Event		Pts
90m	Jani Soininen, FIN	234.5
120m	Kazuyoshi Funaki, JPN	272.3
Team (120m)	JPN (Takanobu, Hiroya, Masahiko, Kazuyoshi)	933.0

Nordic Combined

Event		Pts
Indiv.	Bjarte Engen Vik, NOR	41:21.1
Team	NOR (Skard, Braaten, Vik, Lundberg)	54:11.5

WOMEN
Cross Country

Event		Time
5km	Larissa Lazutina, RUS	17:37.9
10km	Larissa Lazutina, RUS	46:06.9
15km	Olga Danilova, RUS	46:55.4
30km	Julija Tchepalova, RUS	1:22:01.5
4x5km	RUS (Gavryliouk, Danilova, Valbe, Lazutina)	55:13.5

Speed Skating
MEN
Long Track

Event		Time	
500m	Hiroyasu Shimizu, JPN	71.35	
1000m	Ids Postma, NED	1:10.64	OR
1500m	Aadne Sondral, NOR	1:47.87	WR
5000m	Gianni Romme, NED	6:22.20	WR
10,000m	Gianni Romme, NED	13:15.33	WR

Short Track

Event		Time
500m	Takafumi Nishitani, JPN	42.862
1000m	Dong-Sung Kim, KOR	1:32.375
5000m relay	Canada	7:06.075

WOMEN
Long Track

Event		Time	
500m	Catriona Lemay-Doan, CAN	76.60	
1000m	Marianne Timmer, NED	1:16.51	OR
1500m	Marianne Timmer, NED	1:57.58	WR
3000m	Gunda Niemann-Stirnemann, GER	4:07.29	OR
5000m	Claudia Pechstein, GER	6:59.61	WR

Short Track

Event		Time	
500m	Annie Perreault, CAN	46.568	
1000m	Lee-Kyung Chun, KOR	1:42.776	
3000m Relay	South Korea	4:16.260	WR

Snowboarding
MEN

Event		Time
Giant Slalom	Ross Rebagliati, CAN	2:03.96
Halfpipe	Gian Simmen, SWI	85.2 pts

WOMEN

Event		Time
Giant Slalom	Karine Ruby, FRA	2:17.34
Halfpipe	Nicola Thost, GER	74.6 pts

Salt Lake City, 2002

SALT LAKE 2002

By hosting the 19th Winter Games, Utah, an Indian word meaning "home on mountain top," joins California, Georgia, Missouri and New York as the only U.S. states to host the Olympics. The 2002 Games will mark the end of Salt Lake City's long quest to host the games, a story that included failed bids in 1972, 1976 and 1998.

Located in north-central Utah at the foot of the Wasatch Mountains, Salt Lake City and the surrounding towns of Heber City, Ogden, Park City and West Valley City have a combined population of 1.5 million, making it the largest urban area ever to host the Winter Games.

The sports program at Salt Lake City will be the largest in history. There will be 78 events—10 more than Nagano—occuring at five city (indoor) and five mountain (oudoor) facilities.

Here is a preview of what events have been added:

Skeleton: a Swiss sledding event similar to the luge, the men's event was last held in 1948 while the women's event is making its Olympic debut.

Bobsled: women's competition in the two-person discipline.

Biathlon: men's 12.5km pursuit and a women's 10km pursuit.

Cross Country: men's and women's sprint free.

Nordic Combined: an individual sprint event that consists of ski jumping from the large hill and a 7.5km cross-country race.

Short Track Speed Skating: men's and women's 1500m event.

Event-by-Event

Gold medal winners from 1924-98 in the following events: Alpine Skiing, Biathlon, Bobsled, Cross Country Skiing, Curling, Figure Skating, Ice Hockey, Luge, Nordic Combined, Ski Jumping, Snowboarding and Speed Skating.

ALPINE SKIING

MEN

Multiple gold medals: Jean-Claude Killy, Toni Sailer and Alberto Tomba (3); Hermann Maier, Henri Oreiller, Ingemar Stenmark and Markus Wasmeier (2).

Downhill

Year		Time	Year		Time
1948	Henri Oreiller, FRA	2:55.0	1976	Franz Klammer AUT	1:45.73
1952	Zeno Colò, ITA	2:30.8	1980	Leonhard Stock, AUS	1:45.50
1956	Toni Sailer, AUT	2:52.2	1984	Bill Johnson, USA	1:45.59
1960	Jean Vuarnet, FRA	2:06.0	1988	Pirmin Zurbriggen, SWI	1:59.63
1964	Egon Zimmermann, AUT	2:18.16	1992	Patrick Ortlieb, AUT	1:50.37
1968	Jean-Claude Killy, FRA	1:59.85	1994	Tommy Moe, USA	1:45.75
1972	Bernhard Russi, SWI	1:51.43	1998	Jean-Luc Cretier, FRA	1:50.11

Slalom

Year		Time	Year		Time
1948	Edi Reinalter, SWI	2:10.3	1976	Piero Gros, ITA	2:03.29
1952	Othmar Schneider, AUT	2:00.0	1980	Ingemar Stenmark, SWE	1:44.26
1956	Toni Sailer, AUT	3:14.7	1984	Phil Mahre, USA	1:39.41
1960	Ernst Hinterseer, AUT	2:08.9	1988	Alberto Tomba, ITA	1:39.47
1964	Pepi Stiegler, AUT	2:11.13	1992	Finn Christian Jagge, NOR	1:44.39
1968	Jean-Claude Killy, FRA	1:39.73	1994	Thomas Stangassinger, AUT	2:02.02
1972	Francisco Ochoa, SPA	1:49.27	1998	Hans-Petter Buraas, NOR	1:49.31

Giant Slalom

Year		Time	Year		Time
1952	Stein Eriksen, NOR	2:25.0	1980	Ingemar Stenmark, SWE	2:40.74
1956	Toni Sailer, AUS	3:00.1	1984	Max Julen, SWI	2:41.18
1960	Roger Staub, SWI	1:48.3	1988	Alberto Tomba, ITA	2:06.37
1964	Francois Bonlieu, FRA	1:46.71	1992	Alberto Tomba, ITA	2:06.98
1968	Jean-Claude Killy, FRA	3:29.28	1994	Markus Wasmeier, GER	2:52.46
1972	Gustav Thöni, ITA	3:09.62	1998	Hermann Maier, AUT	2:38.51
1976	Heini Hemmi, SWI	3:26.97			

Super Giant Slalom

Year		Time	Year		Time
1988	Frank Piccard, FRA	1:39.66	1994	Markus Wasmeier, GER	1:32.53
1992	Kjetil Andre Aamodt, NOR	1:13.04	1998	Hermann Maier, AUT	1:34.82

Alpine Combined

Year		Points	Year		Points
1936	Franz Pfnür, GER	99.25	1992	Josef Polig, ITA	14.58
1948	Henri Oreiller, FRA	3.27	Year		Time
1952-84	Not held		1994	Lasse Kjus, NOR	3:17.53
1988	Hubert Strolz, AUT	36.55	1998	Mario Reiter, AUT	3:08.06

WOMEN

Multiple gold medals: Deborah Compagnoni, Vreni Schneider and Katja Seizinger (3); Marielle Goitschel, Trude Jochum-Beiser, Petra Kronberger, Andrea Mead Lawrence, Rosi Mittermaier, Marie-Theres Nadig, Hanni Wenzel and Pernilla Wiberg (2).

Downhill

Year		Time	Year		Time
1948	Hedy Schlunegger, SWI	2:28.3	1976	Rosi Mittermaier, W. Ger	1:46.16
1952	Trude Jochum-Beiser, AUT	1:47.1	1980	Annemarie Moser-Pröll, AUT	1:37.52
1956	Madeleine Berthod, SWI	1:40.7	1984	Michela Figini, SWI	1:13.36
1960	Heidi Biebl, GER	1:37.6	1988	Marina Kiehl, W. Ger	1:25.86
1964	Christl Haas, AUT	1:55.39	1992	Kerrin Lee-Gartner, CAN	1:52.55
1968	Olga Pall, AUT	1:40.87	1994	Katja Seizinger, GER	1:35.93
1972	Marie-Theres Nadig, SWI	1:36.68	1998	Katja Seizinger, GER	1:28.89

Slalom

Year		Time	Year		Time
1948	Gretchen Fraser, USA	1:57.2	1960	Anne Heggtveit, CAN	1:49.6
1952	Andrea Mead Lawrence, USA	2:10.6	1964	Christine Goitschel, FRA	1:29.86
1956	Renée Colliard, SWI	1:52.3	1968	Marielle Goitschel, FRA	1:25.86

Year	Time	Year	Time
1972 Barbara Cochran, USA	1:31.24	1988 Vreni Schneider, SWI	1:36.69
1976 Rosi Mittermaier, W. Ger	1:30.54	1992 Petra Kronberger, AUT	1:32.68
1980 Hanni Wenzel, LIE	1:25.09	1994 Vreni Schneider, SWI	1:56.01
1984 Paoletta Magoni, ITA	1:36.47	1998 Hilde Gerg, GER	1:32.40

Giant Slalom

Year	Time	Year	Time
1952 Andrea Mead Lawrence, USA	2:06.8	1980 Hanni Wenzel, LIE	2:41.66
1956 Ossi Reichert, GER	1:56.5	1984 Debbie Armstrong, USA	2:20.98
1960 Yvonne Rügg, SWI	1:39.9	1988 Vreni Schneider, SWI	2:06.49
1964 Marielle Goitschel, FRA	1:52.24	1992 Pernilla Wiberg, SWE	2:12.74
1968 Nancy Greene, CAN	1:51.97	1994 Deborah Compagnoni, ITA	2:30.97
1972 Marie-Theres Nadig, SWI	1:29.90	1998 Deborah Compagnoni, ITA	2:50.59
1976 Kathy Kreiner, CAN	1:29.13		

Super Giant Slalom

Year	Time	Year	Time
1988 Sigrid Wolf, AUT	1:19.03	1994 Diann Roffe-Steinrotter, USA	1:22.15
1992 Deborah Compagnoni, ITA	1:21.22	1998 Picabo Street, USA	1:18.02

Alpine Combined

Year	Points	Year	Points
1936 Christl Cranz, GER	97.06	1992 Petra Kronberger, AUT	2.55
1948 Trude Beiser, AUT	6.58	**Year**	**Time**
1952-84 Not held		1994 Pernilla Wiberg, SWE	3:05.16
1988 Anita Wachter, AUT	29.25	1998 Katja Seizinger, GER	2:40.74

BIATHLON

MEN

Multiple gold medals (including relays): Aleksandr Tikhonov (4); Mark Kirchner and Ricco Gross (3); Anatoly Alyabyev, Ivan Biakov, Sergei Chepikov, Sven Fischer, Frank Luck, Viktor Mamatov, Frank-Peter Roetsch, Magnar Solberg and Dmitri Vasilyev (2).

10 kilometers

Year	Time	Year	Time
1980 Frank Ullrich, E. Ger	32:10.69	1992 Mark Kirchner, GER	26:02.3
1984 Erik Kvalfoss, NOR	30:53.8	1994 Sergei Chepikov, RUS	28:07.0
1988 Frank-Peter Roetsch, E. Ger	25:08.1	1998 Ole Einar Bjoerndalen, NOR	27:16.2

20 kilometers

Year	Time	Year	Time
1960 Klas Lestander, SWE	1:33:21.6	1984 Peter Angerer, W. Ger	1:11:52.7
1964 Vladimir Melanin, USSR	1:20:26.8	1988 Frank-Peter Roetsch, E. Ger	56:33.3
1968 Magnar Solberg, NOR	1:13:45.9	1992 Yevgeny Redkine, UT	57:34.4
1972 Magnar Solberg, NOR	1:15:55.50	1994 Sergei Tarasov, RUS	57:25.3
1976 Nikolai Kruglov, USSR	1:14:12.26	1998 Halvard Hanevold, NOR	56:16.4
1980 Anatoly Alyabyev, USSR	1:08:16.31		

4x7.5-kilometer Relay

Year	Time	Year	Time	Year	Time
1968 Soviet Union	2:13:02.4	1980 Soviet Union	1:34:03.27	1992 Germany	1:24:43.5
1972 Soviet Union	1:51:44.92	1984 Soviet Union	1:38:51.7	1994 Germany	1:30:22.1
1976 Soviet Union	1:57:55.64	1988 Soviet Union	1:22:30.0	1998 Germany	1:21.36.2

WOMEN

Multiple gold medals (including relays): Myriam Bedard and Anfisa Reztsova (2). Note that Reztsova won a third gold medal in 1988 in the Cross-country 4x5-kilometer Relay.

7.5 kilometers

Year	Time	Year	Time
1992 Anfisa Reztsova, UT	24:29.2	1998 Galina Koukleva, RUS	23:08.0
1994 Myriam Bedard, CAN	26:08.8		

15 kilometers

Year	Time	Year	Time
1992 Antje Misersky, GER	51:47.2	1998 Ekaterina Dafovska, BUL	54:52.0
1994 Myriam Bedard, CAN	52:06.6		

4x7.5-kilometer Relay

Year		Time	Year		Time	Year		Time
1992	France	1:15:55.6	1994	Russia	1:47:19.5	1998	Germany	1:40:13.6

Note: Event featured three skiers per team in 1992.

BOBSLED

Only drivers are listed in parentheses.

Multiple gold medals: DRIVERS–Meinhard Nehmer (3); Billy Fiske, Wolfgang Hoppe, Eugenio Monti, Andreas Ostler and Gustav Weder (2). CREW–Bernard Germeshausen (3); Donat Acklin, Luciano De Paolis, Cliff Gray, Lorenz Nieberl and Dietmar Schauerhammer (2).

Two-Man

Year		Time	Year		Time
1932	United States (Hubert Stevens)	8:14.74	1972	West Germany (Wolfgang Zimmerer)	4:57.07
1936	United States (Ivan Brown)	5:29.29	1976	East Germany (Meinhard Nehmer)	3:44.42
1948	Switzerland (Felix Endrich)	5:29.2	1980	Switzerland (Erich Schärer)	4:09.36
1952	Germany (Andreas Ostler)	5:24.54	1984	East Germany (Wolfgang Hoppe)	3:25.56
1956	Italy (Lamberto Dalla Costa)	5:30.14	1988	Soviet Union (Janis Kipurs)	3:54.19
1960	Not held		1992	Switzerland I (Gustav Weder)	4:03.26
1964	Great Britain (Anthony Nash)	4:21.90	1994	Switzerland I (Gustav Weder)	3:30.81
1968	Italy (Eugenio Monti)	4:41.54	1998	(TIE) Italy I (Guenther Huber)	3:37.24
				& Canada I (Pierre Lueders)	3:37.24

Four-Man

Year		Time	Year		Time
1924	Switzerland (Eduard Scherrer)	5:45.54	1968	Italy (Eugenio Monti)	2:17.39
1928	United States (Billy Fiske)	3:20.5	1972	Switzerland (Jean Wicki)	4:43.07
1932	United States (Billy Fiske)	7:53.68	1976	East Germany (Meinhard Nehmer)	3:40.43
1936	Switzerland (Pierre Musy)	5:19.85	1980	East Germany (Meinhard Nehmer)	3:59.92
1948	United States (Francis Tyler)	5:20.1	1984	East Germany (Wolfgang Hoppe)	3:20.22
1952	Germany (Andreas Ostler)	5:07.84	1988	Switzerland (Ekkehard Fasser)	3:47.51
1956	Switzerland (Franz Kapus)	5:10.44	1992	Austria I (Ingo Appelt)	3:53.90
1960	Not held		1994	Germany II (Harald Czudaj)	3:27.78
1964	Canada (Vic Emery)	4:14.46	1998	Germany II (Christoph Langen)	2:39.41

Note: Five-man sleds were used in 1928.

CROSS COUNTRY SKIING

There have been two significant changes in men's and women's cross country racing since the end of the 1984 Winter Games in Sarajevo. First, the classical and freestyle (i.e., skating) techniques were designated for specific events beginning in 1988, and the Pursuit race was introduced in 1992.

MEN

Multiple gold medals (including relays): Bjorn Dählie (8); Sixten Jernberg, Gunde Svan, Thomas Wassberg and Nikolai Zimyatov (4); Veikko Hakulinen, Eero Mäntyranta and Vegard Ulvang (3); Hallgeir Brenden, Harald Grönningen, Thorlief Haug, Jan Ottoson, Päl Tyldum and Vyacheslav Vedenine (2).
Multiple gold medals (including Nordic Combined): Johan Gröttumsbräten and Thorlief Haug (3).

10-kilometer Classical

Year		Time	Year		Time
1924-88	Not held		1994	Bjorn Dählie, NOR	24:20.1
1992	Vegard Ulvang, NOR	27:36.0	1998	Bjorn Dählie, NOR	27:24.5

15-kilometer Combined Pursuit

A 15-km Freestyle race in which the starting order is determined by order of finish in the 10-km Classical race. Time given is combined time of both events.

Year		Time	Year		Time
1924-88	Not held		1994	Bjorn Dählie, NOR	1:00.08.8
1992	Bjorn Dählie, NOR	1:05:37.9	1998	Thomas Alsgaard, NOR	1:07:01.7

Youngest and Oldest Gold Medalists in an Individual Event

Youngest: MEN– Toni Nieminen, Finland, Large Hill Ski Jumping, 1992 (16 years, 261 days); WOMEN–Tara Lipinski, United States, Figure Skating, 1998 (15 years, 256 days).
Oldest: MEN– Magnar Solberg, NOR, 20-km Biathlon, 1972 (35 years, 4 days); WOMEN– Christina Baas-Kaiser, Holland, 3,000m Speed Skating, 1972 (33 years, 268 days).

15-kilometer Classical (Discont.)

Discontinued in 1992 and replaced by the freestyle 15-km Combined Pursuit. Event was held over 18 kilometers from 1924-52.

Year		Time	Year		Time
1924	Thorleif Haug, NOR	1:14:31.0	1964	Eero Mäntyranta, FIN.	.50:54.1
1928	Johan Gröttumsbråten, NOR	1:37:01.0	1968	Harald Grönningen, NOR	.47:54.2
1932	Sven Utterström, SWE.	1:23:07.0	1972	Sven-Ake Lundback, SWE	.45:28.24
1936	Erik-August Larsson, SWE	1:14:38.0	1976	Nikolai Bazhukov, USSR	.43:58.47
1948	Martin Lundström, SWE	1:13:50.0	1980	Thomas Wassberg, SWE.	.41:57.63
1952	Hallgeir Brenden, NOR	1:01:34.0	1984	Gunde Svan, SWE	.41:25.6
1956	Hallgeir Brenden, NOR	.49:39.0	1988	Mikhail Devyatyarov, USSR	.41:18.9
1960	Hakon Brusveen, NOR	.51:55.5			

30-kilometer Freestyle (Discont.)
Discontinued in 1998 and replaced by the 30-kilometer Classical.

Year		Time	Year		Time
1924-52	Not held		1976	Sergei Saveliev, USSR	1:30:29.38
1956	Veikko Hakulinen, FIN	1:44:06.0	1980	Nikolai Zimyatov, USSR	1:27:02.80
1960	Sixten Jernberg, SWE.	1:51:03.9	1984	Nikolai Zimyatov, USSR	1:28:56.3
1964	Eero Mäntyranta, FIN.	1:30:50.7	1988	Alexi Prokurorov, USSR	1:24:26.3
1968	Franco Nones, ITA	1:35:39.2	1992	Vegard Ulvang, NOR.	1:22:27.8
1972	Vyacheslav Vedenine, USSR	1:36:31.15	1994	Thomas Alsgaard, NOR.	1:12:26.4

30-kilometer Classical

Year		Time
1998	Mika Myllylae, FIN.	1:33:55.8

50-kilometer Classical (Discont.)
Discontinued in 1998 and replaced by the 50-kilometer Freestyle.

Year		Time	Year		Time
1924	Thorleif Haug, NOR	3:44:32.0	1968	Ole Ellefsaeter, NOR.	2:28:45.8
1928	Per Erik Hedlund, SWE.	4:52:03.0	1972	Pål Tyldum, NOR.	2:43:14.75
1932	Veli Saarinen, FIN.	4:28:00.0	1976	Ivar Formo, NOR.	2:37:30.05
1936	Elis Wiklund, SWE	3:30:11.0	1980	Nikolai Zimyatov, USSR.	2:27:24.60
1948	Nils Karlsson, SWE.	3:47:48.0	1984	Thomas Wassberg, SWE	2:15:55.8
1952	Veikko Hakulinen, FIN	3:33:33.0	1988	Gunde Svan, SWE	2:04:30.9
1956	Sixten Jernberg, SWE.	2:50:27.0	1992	Bjorn Dählie, NOR	2:03:41.5
1960	Kalevi Hämäläinen, FIN.	2:59:06.3	1994	Vladimir Smirnov, KAZ	2:07:20.3
1964	Sixten Jernberg, SWE.	2:43:52.6			

50-kilometer Freestyle

Year		Time
1998	Bjorn Dählie, NOR	2:05:08.2

4x10-kilometer Mixed Relay
Two Classical and two Freestyle legs.

Year		Time	Year		Time	Year		Time
1936	Finland	2:41:33.0	1964	Sweden	2:18:34.6	1984	Sweden	1:55:06.3
1948	Sweden	2:32:08.0	1968	Norway	2:08:33.5	1988	Sweden	1:43:58.6
1952	Finland	2:20:16.0	1972	Soviet Union	2:04:47.94	1992	Norway	1:39:26.0
1956	Soviet Union	2:15:30.0	1976	Finland	2:07:59.72	1994	Italy	1:41:15.0
1960	Finland	2:18:45.6	1980	Soviet Union	1:57:03.46	1998	Norway	1:40:55.7

WOMEN

Multiple gold medals (including relays): Lyubov Egorova (6); Galina Kulakova and Raisa Smetanina (4); Claudia Boyarskikh and Marja-Liisa Hämäläinen (3); Manuela Di Centa, Toini Gustafsson, Larisa Lazutina, Barbara Petzold and Elena Valbe (2).

Multiple gold medals (including relays and Biathlon): Anfisa Reztsova (2).

5-kilometer Classical

Year		Time	Year		Time
1964	Claudia Boyarskikh, USSR	17:50.5	1984	Marja-Liisa Hämäläinen, FIN	17:04.0
1968	Toini Gustafsson, SWE	16:45.2	1988	Marjo Matikainen, FIN	15:04.0
1972	Galina Kulakova, USSR	17:00.50	1992	Marjut Lukkarinen, FIN	14:13.8
1976	Helena Takalo, FIN	15:48.69	1994	Lyubov Egorova, RUS	14:08.8
1980	Raisa Smetanina, USSR	15:06.92	1998	Larissa Lazutina, RUS	17:37.9

10-kilometer Combined Pursuit

A 10-km Freestyle race in which the starting order is determined by order of finish in the 5-km Classical race. Time given is combined time of both events.

Year	Time	Year	Time
1952-88 Not held		1994 Lyubov Egorova, RUS	41:38.1
1992 Lyubov Egorova, UT	40:07.7	1998 Larissa Lazutina, RUS	17:37.9

10-kilometer Classical (Discont.)

Discontinued in 1992 and replaced by the freestyle 10-km Combined Pursuit.

Year	Time	Year	Time
1952 Lydia Wideman, FIN	41:40.0	1972 Galina Kulakova, USSR	34:17.82
1956 Lyubov Kosyreva, USSR	38:11.0	1976 Raisa Smetanina, USSR	30:13.41
1960 Maria Gusakova, USSR	39:46.6	1980 Barbara Petzold, E. Ger.	30:31.54
1964 Claudia Boyarskikh, USSR	40:24.3	1984 Marja-Liisa Hämäläinen, FIN	31:44.2
1968 Toini Gustafsson, SWE	36:46.5	1988 Vida Venciene, USSR	30:08.3

15-kilometer Freestyle (Discont.)

Discontinued in 1998 and replaced by the 15-kilometer Classical.

Year	Time	Year	Time
1992 Lyubov Egorova, UT	42:20.8	1994 Manuela Di Centa, ITA	39:44.5

15-kilometer Classical

Year	Time
1998 Olga Danilova, RUS	46:55.4

20-kilometer Classical (Discont.)

Discontinued in 1992 and replaced by the 30-kilometer Freestyle.

Year	Time	Year	Time
1984 Marja-Liisa Hämäläinen, FIN	1:01:45.0	1988 Tamara Tikhonova, USSR	55:53.6

30-kilometer Freestyle

Year	Time	Year	Time
1992 Stefania Belmondo, ITA	1:22:30.1	1990 Julija Tchepalova, RUS	1:22:01.5
1994 Manuela Di Centa, ITA	1:25:41.6		

4x5-kilometer Relay

Two Classical and two Freestyle legs since 1992. Event featured three skiers per team from 1956-72.

Year	Time	Year	Time	Year	Time
1956 Finland	1:09:01.0	1972 Soviet Union	48:46.15	1988 Soviet Union	59:51.1
1960 Sweden	1:04:21.4	1976 Soviet Union	1:07:49.75	1992 Unified Team	59:34.8
1964 Soviet Union	59:20.2	1980 East Germany	1:02:11.10	1994 Russia	57:12.5
1968 Norway	57:30.0	1984 Norway	1:06:49.7	1998 Russia	55:13.5

CURLING

MEN	WOMEN

Year	Year
1998 **Switzerland**, Canada, Norway	1998 **Canada**, Denmark, Sweden

FIGURE SKATING

MEN

Multiple gold medals: Gillis Grafström (3); Dick Button and Karl Schäfer (2).

Year		Year		Year	
1908 Ulrich Salchow	SWE	1948 Dick Button	USA	1976 John Curry	GBR
1912 Not held		1952 Dick Button	USA	1980 Robin Cousins	GBR
1920 Gillis Grafström	SWE	1956 Hayes Alan Jenkins	USA	1984 Scott Hamilton	USA
1924 Gillis Grafström	SWE	1960 David Jenkins	USA	1988 Brian Boitano	USA
1928 Gillis Grafström	SWE	1964 Manfred Schnelldorfer	GER	1992 Victor Petrenko	UT
1932 Karl Schäfer	AUT	1968 Wolfgang Schwarz	AUT	1994 Alexei Urmanov	RUS
1936 Karl Schäfer	AUT	1972 Ondrej Nepela	CZE	1998 Ilia Kulik	RUS

WOMEN

Multiple gold medals: Sonja Henie (3); Katarina Witt (2).

Year			Year			Year		
1908	Madge Syers	GBR	1948	Barbara Ann Scott	CAN	1976	Dorothy Hamill	USA
1912	Not held		1952	Jeanette Altwegg	GBR	1980	Anett Pötzsch	E. Ger
1920	Magda Julin-Mauroy	SWE	1956	Tenley Albright	USA	1984	Katarina Witt	E. Ger
1924	Herma Planck-Szabö	AUT	1960	Carol Heiss	USA	1988	Katarina Witt	E. Ger
1928	Sonja Henie	NOR	1964	Sjoukje Dijkstra	NED	1992	Kristi Yamaguchi	USA
1932	Sonja Henie	NOR	1968	Peggy Fleming	USA	1994	Oksana Baiul	UKR
1936	Sonja Henie	NOR	1972	Beatrix Schuba	AUT	1998	Tara Lipinski	USA

PAIRS

Multiple gold medals: MEN–Pierre Brunet, Artur Dmitriev, Sergei Grinkov, Oleg Protopopov and Aleksandr Zaitsev (2). WOMEN–Irina Rodnina (3); Ludmila Belousova, Ekaterina Gordeeva and Andree Joly Brunet (2).

Year			Year		
1908	Anna Hübler & Heinrich Burger	Germany	1964	Ludmila Belousova & Oleg Protopopov	USSR
1912	Not held		1968	Ludmila Belousova & Oleg Protopopov	USSR
1920	Ludovika & Walter Jakobsson	Finland	1972	Irina Rodnina & Aleksei Ulanov	USSR
1924	Helene Engelmann & Alfred Berger	Austria	1976	Irina Rodnina & Aleksandr Zaitsev	USSR
1928	Andrée Joly & Pierre Brunet	France	1980	Irina Rodnina & Aleksandr Zaitsev	USSR
1932	Andrée & Pierre Brunet	France	1984	Elena Valova & Oleg Vasiliev	USSR
1936	Maxi Herber & Ernst Baier	Germany	1988	Ekaterina Gordeeva & Sergei Grinkov	USSR
1948	Micheline Lannoy & Pierre Baugniet	Belgium	1992	Natalya Mishkutienok & Arthur Dmitriev	UT
1952	Ria & Paul Falk	Germany	1994	Ekaterina Gordeeva & Sergei Grinkov	RUS
1956	Elisabeth Schwartz & Kurt Oppelt	Austria	1998	Oksana Kazakova & Artur Dmitriev	RUS
1960	Barbara Wagner & Robert Paul	Canada			

Ice Dancing

Multiple gold medals: Yevegny Platov (2).

Year			Year		
1976	Lyudmila Pakhomova & Aleksandr Gorshtkov	USSR	1992	Marina Klimova & Sergei Ponomarenko	UT
1980	Natalia Linichuk & Gennady Karponosov	USSR	1994	Oksana Gritschuk & Yevgeny Platov	RUS
1984	Jayne Torvill & Christopher Dean	Great Britain	1998	Pasha Grishuk & Yevgeny Platov	RUS
1988	Natalia Bestemianova & Andrei Bukin	USSR			

FREESTYLE SKIING

MEN
Aerials

Year		Points
1994	Andreas Schoebaechler, SWI	234.67
1998	Eric Bergoust, USA	255.6

Moguls

Year		Points
1994	Jean-Luc Brassard, CAN	27.24
1998	Jonny Moseley, USA	26.93

WOMEN
Aerials

Year		Points
1994	Lina Cherjazova, UZB	166.84
1998	Nikki Stone, USA	193.00

Moguls

Year		Points
1994	Stine Lise Hattestad, NOR	25.97
1998	Tae Satoya, JPN	25.06

ICE HOCKEY

MEN

Multiple gold medals: Soviet Union/Unified Team (8); Canada (6); United States (2).

Year		Year	
1920	**Canada**, United States Czechoslovakia	1976	**Soviet Union**, Czechoslovakia, West Germany
1924	**Canada**, United States, Great Britain	1980	**United States**, Soviet Union, Sweden
1928	**Canada**, Sweden, Switzerland	1984	**Soviet Union**, Czechoslovakia, Sweden
1932	**Canada**, United States, Germany	1988	**Soviet Union**, Finland, Sweden
1936	**Great Britain**, Canada, United States	1992	**Unified Team**, Canada, Czechoslovakia
1948	**Canada**, Czechoslovakia, Switzerland	1994	**Sweden**, Canada, Finland
1952	**Canada**, United States, Sweden	1998	**Czech Republic**, Russia, Finland
1956	**Soviet Union**, United States, Canada		
1960	**United States**, Canada, Soviet Union		
1964	**Soviet Union**, Sweden, Czechoslovakia		
1968	**Soviet Union**, Czechoslovakia, Canada		
1972	**Soviet Union**, United States, Czechoslovakia		

WOMEN

Year	
1998	**United States**, Canada, Finland

U.S. Gold Medal Hockey Teams

1960

Forwards: Billy Christian, Roger Christian, Billy Cleary, Gene Grazia, Paul Johnson, Bob McVey, Dick Meredith, Weldy Olson, Dick Rodenheiser and Tom Williams. **Defensemen:** Bob Cleary, Jack Kirrane (captain), John Mayasich, Bob Owen and Rod Paavola. **Goaltenders:** Jack McCartan and Larry Palmer. **Coach:** Jack Riley.

1980

Forwards: Neal Broten, Steve Christoff, Mike Eruzione (captain), John Harrington, Mark Johnson, Rob McClanahan, Mark Pavelich, Buzz Schneider, Dave Silk, Eric Strobel, Phil Verchota and Mark Wells. **Defensemen:** Bill Baker, Dave Christian, Ken Morrow, Jack O'Callahan, Mike Ramsey and Bob Suter. **Goaltenders:** Jim Craig and Steve Janaszak. **Coach:** Herb Brooks.

1998

Forwards: Laurie Baker, Alana Blahoski, Lisa Brown-Miller, Karen Bye, Tricia Dunn, Cammi Granato, Katie King, Shelley Looney, A.J. Mleczko, Jenny Schmidgall, Gretchen Ulion, Sandra Whyte. **Defensemen:** Chris Bailey, Colleen Coyne, Sue Mertz, Tara Mounsey, Vicki Movessian, Angela Ruggiero. **Goaltenders:** Sarah DeCosta and Sarah Tueting. **Coach:** Ben Smith.

LUGE

MEN

Multiple gold medals: (including doubles): Georg Hackl (3); Norbert Hahn, Paul Hildgartner, Thomas Köhler and Hans Rinn (2).

Singles

Year		Time	Year		Time
1964	Thomas Köhler, GER	3:26.77	1984	Paul Hildgartner, ITA	3:04.258
1968	Manfred Schmid, AUT	2:52.48	1988	Jens Müller, E. Ger	3:05.548
1972	Wolfgang Scheidel, E. Ger	3:27.58	1992	Georg Hackl, GER	3:02.363
1976	Dettlef Günther, E. Ger	3:27.688	1994	Georg Hackl, GER	3:21.571
1980	Bernhard Glass, E. Ger	2:54.796	1998	Georg Hackl, GER	3:18.436

Doubles

Year		Time	Year		Time
1964	Austria	1:41.62	1984	West Germany	1:23.620
1968	East Germany	1:35.85	1988	East Germany	1:31.940
1972	(TIE) East Germany	1:28.35	1992	Germany	1:32.053
	& Italy	1:28.35	1994	Italy	1:36.720
1976	East Germany	1:25.604	1998	Germany	1:41.105
1980	East Germany	1:19.331			

WOMEN

Multiple gold medals: Steffi Martin Walter (2).

Singles

Year		Time	Year		Time
1964	Ortrun Enderlein, GER	3:24.67	1984	Steffi Martin, E. Ger	2:46.570
1968	Erica Lechner, ITA	2:28.66	1988	Steffi Martin Walter, E. Ger	3:03.973
1972	Anna-Maria Müller, E. Ger	2:59.18	1992	Doris Neuner, AUT	3:06.696
1976	Margit Schumann, E. Ger	2:50.621	1994	Gerda Weissensteiner, ITA	3:15.517
1980	Vera Zozulya, USSR	2:36.537	1998	Silke Kraushaar, GER	3:23.779

NORDIC COMBINED

Multiple gold medals: Ulrich Wehling (3); Johan Gröttumsbråten (2).

Individual

Year		Points	Year		Points
1924	Thorleif Haug, NOR	18.906	1972	Ulrich Wehling, E. Ger	413.340
1928	Johan Gröttumsbråten, NOR	17.833	1976	Ulrich Wehling, E. Ger	423.39
1932	Johan Gröttumsbråten, NOR	446.00	1980	Ulrich Wehling, E. Ger	432.200
1936	Oddbjörn Hagen, NOR	430.3	1984	Tom Sandberg, NOR	422.595
1948	Heikki Hasu, FIN	448.80	1988	Hippolyt Kempf, SWI	432.230
1952	Simon Slattvik, NOR	451.621	1992	Fabrice Guy, FRA	426.470
1956	Sverre Stenersen, NOR	455.000	1994	Fred Borre Lundberg, NOR	457.970
1960	Georg Thoma, GER	457.952			**Time**
1964	Tormod Knutsen, NOR	469.28	1998	Bjarte Engen Vik, NOR	41:21.1
1968	Franz Keller, W. Ger	449.04			

Team

Year	Points	Year	Points
1924-84 Not held		1994 Japan	1368.860
1988 West Germany	792.08		**Time**
1992 Japan	1247.180	1998 Norway	54:11.5

SKI JUMPING

Multiple gold medals (including team jumping): Matti Nykänen (4); Jens Weissflog (3); Birger Ruud and Toni Nieminen (2).

Normal Hill–90 Meters

Year	Points	Year	Points
1924-60 Not held		1984 Jens Weissflog, E. Ger	215.2
1964 Veikko Kankkonen, FIN	229.9	1988 Matti Nykänen, FIN	229.1
1968 Jiri Raska, CZE	216.5	1992 Ernst Vettori, AUT	222.8
1972 Yukio Kasaya, JPN	244.2	1994 Espen Bredesen, NOR	282.0
1976 Hans-Georg Aschenbach, E. Ger	252.0	1998 Jani Soininen, FIN	234.5
1980 Anton Innauer, AUT	266.3	**Note:** Jump held at 70 meters from 1964-92.	

Large Hill–120 Meters

Year	Points	Year	Points
1924 Jacob Tullin Thams, NOR	18.960	1968 Vladimir Beloussov, USSR	231.3
1928 Alf Andersen, NOR	19.208	1972 Wojciech Fortuna, POL	219.9
1932 Birger Ruud, NOR	228.1	1976 Karl Schäabl, AUT	234.8
1936 Birger Ruud, NOR	232.0	1980 Jouko Törmänen, FIN	271.0
1948 Petter Hugsted, NOR	228.1	1984 Matti Nykänen, FIN	231.2
1952 Arnfinn Bergmann, NOR	226.0	1988 Matti Nykänen, FIN	224.0
1956 Antti Hyvärinen, FIN	227.0	1992 Toni Nieminen, FIN	239.5
1960 Helmut Recknagel, GER	227.2	1994 Jens Weissflog, GER	274.5
1964 Toralf Engan, NOR	230.7	1998 Kazuyoshi Funaki, JPN	272.3

Note: Jump held at various lengths from 1924-56; at 80 meters from 1960-64; and at 90 meters from 1968-88.

Team Large Hill

Year	Points	Year	Points
1924-84 Not held		1994 Germany	970.1
1988 Finland	634.4	1998 Japan	933.0
1992 Finland	644.4		

SNOWBOARDING

MEN		**WOMEN**	
Halfpipe		**Halfpipe**	
Year	Points	Year	Points
1998 Gian Simmen, SWI	85.2	1998 Nicola Thost, GER	74.6
Giant Slalom		**Giant Slalom**	
Year	Points	Year	Points
1998 Ross Rebagliati, CAN	2:03.96	1998 Karine Ruby, FRA	2:17.34

SPEED SKATING

MEN

Multiple gold medals: Eric Heiden and Clas Thunberg (5); Ivar Ballangrud, Yevgeny Grishin and Johann Olav Koss (4); Hjalmar Andersen, Tomas Gustafson, Irving Jaffee and Ard Schenk (3); Gaétan Boucher, Knut Johannesen, Erhard Keller, Uwe-Jens Mey, Gianni Romme and Jack Shea (2). Note that Thunberg's total includes the All-Around, which was contested for the only time in 1924.

500 meters

Year		Time		Year		Time	
1924 Charles Jewtraw, USA		44.0		1968 Erhard Keller, W. Ger		40.3	
1928 (TIE) Bernt Evensen, NOR		43.4	**OR**	1972 Erhard Keller, W. Ger		39.44	**OR**
& Clas Thunberg, FIN		43.4	**OR**	1976 Yevgeny Kulikov, USSR		39.17	**OR**
1932 Jack Shea, USA		43.4	**=OR**	1980 Eric Heiden, USA		38.03	**OR**
1936 Ivar Ballangrud, NOR		43.4	**=OR**	1984 Sergei Fokichev, USSR		38.19	
1948 Finn Helgesen, NOR		43.1	**OR**	1988 Uwe-Jens Mey, E. Ger		36.45	**WR**
1952 Ken Henry, USA		43.2		1992 Uwe-Jens Mey, GER		37.14	
1956 Yevgeny Grishin, USSR		40.2	**=WR**	1994 Aleksandr Golubev, RUS		36.33	**OR**
1960 Yevgeny Grishin, USSR		40.2	**=WR**	1998 Hiroyashu Shimizu, JPN		71.35	**OR**
1964 Terry McDermott, USA		40.1	**OR**				

1000 meters

Year		Time	Year		Time
1924-72	Not held		1988	Nikolai Gulyaev, USSR	1:13.03 **OR**
1976	Peter Mueller, USA	1:19.32	1992	Olaf Zinke, GER	1:14.85
1980	Eric Heiden, USA	1:15.18 **OR**	1994	Dan Jansen, USA	1:12.43 **WR**
1984	Gaétan Boucher, CAN	1:15.80	1998	Ids Postma, NED	1:10.64 **OR**

1500 meters

Year		Time	Year		Time
1924	Clas Thunberg, FIN	2:20.8	1964	Ants Antson, USSR	2:10.3
1928	Clas Thunberg, FIN	2:21.1	1968	Kees Verkerk, NED	2:03.4 **OR**
1932	Jack Shea, USA	2:57.5	1972	Ard Schenk, NED	2:02.96 **OR**
1936	Charles Mathisen, NOR	2:19.2 **OR**	1976	Jan Egil Storholt, NOR	1:59.38 **OR**
1948	Sverre Farstad, NOR	2:17.6 **OR**	1980	Eric Heiden, USA	1:55.44 **OR**
1952	Hjalmar Andersen, NOR	2:20.4	1984	Gaétan Boucher, CAN	1:58.36
1956	(TIE)Yevgeny Grishin, USSR	2:08.6 **WR**	1988	Andre Hoffman, E. Ger	1:52.06 **WR**
	& Yuri Mikhailov, USSR	2:08.6 **WR**	1992	Johann Olav Koss, NOR	1:54.81
1960	(TIE) Roald Aas, NOR	2:10.4	1994	Johann Olav Koss, NOR	1:51.29 **WR**
	& Yevgeny Grishin, USSR	2:10.4	1998	Aadne Sondral, NOR	1:47.87 **WR**

5000 meters

Year		Time	Year		Time
1924	Clas Thunberg, FIN	8:39.0	1968	Fred Anton Maier, NOR	7:22.4 **WR**
1928	Ivar Ballangrud, NOR	8:50.5	1972	Ard Schenk, NED	7:23.61
1932	Irving Jaffee, USA	9:40.8	1976	Sten Stensen, NOR	7:24.48
1936	Ivar Ballangrud, NOR	8:19.6 **OR**	1980	Eric Heiden, USA	7:02.29 **OR**
1948	Reidar Liaklev, NOR	8:29.4	1984	Tomas Gustafson, SWE	7:12.28
1952	Hjalmar Andersen, NOR	8:10.6 **OR**	1988	Tomas Gustafson, SWE	6:44.63 **WR**
1956	Boris Shilkov, USSR	7:48.7 **OR**	1992	Geir Karlstad, NOR	6:59.97
1960	Viktor Kosichkin, USSR	7:51.3	1994	Johann Olav Koss, NOR	6:34.96 **WR**
1964	Knut Johannesen, NOR	7:38.4 **OR**	1998	Gianni Romme, NED	6:22.20 **WR**

10,000 meters

Year		Time	Year		Time
1924	Julius Skutnabb, FIN	18:04.8	1968	Johnny Höglin, SWE	15:23.6 **OR**
1928	Irving Jaffee, USA*	18:36.5	1972	Ard Schenk, NED	15:01.35 **OR**
1932	Irving Jaffee, USA	19:13.6	1976	Piet Kleine, NED	14:50.59 **OR**
1936	Ivar Ballangrud, NOR	17:24.3 **OR**	1980	Eric Heiden, USA	14:28.13 **WR**
1948	Ake Seyffarth, SWE	17:26.3	1984	Igor Malkov, USSR	14:39.90
1952	Hjalmar Andersen, NOR	16:45.8 **OR**	1988	Tomas Gustafson, SWE	13:48.20 **WR**
1956	Sigvard Ericsson, SWE	16:35.9 **OR**	1992	Bart Veldkamp, NED	14:12.12
1960	Knut Johannesen, NOR	15:46.6 **WR**	1994	Johann Olav Koss, NOR	13:30.55 **WR**
1964	Jonny Nilsson, SWE	15:50.1	1998	Gianni Romme, NED	13:15.33 **WR**

*Unofficial, according to the IOC. Jaffee recorded the fastest time, but the event was called off in progress due to thawing ice.

WOMEN

Multiple gold medals: Lydia Skoblikova (6); Bonnie Blair (5); Karin Enke, Gunda Niemann-Stirnemann and Yvonne van Gennip (3); Tatiana Averina, Claudia Pechstein and Christa Rothenburger (2).

500 meters

Year		Time	Year		Time
1960	Helga Haase, GER	45.9	1984	Christa Rothenburger, E. Ger	41.02 **OR**
1964	Lydia Skoblikova, USSR	45.0 **OR**	1988	Bonnie Blair, USA	39.10 **WR**
1968	Lyudmila Titova, USSR	46.1	1992	Bonnie Blair, USA	40.33
1972	Anne Henning, USA	43.33 **OR**	1994	Bonnie Blair, USA	39.25
1976	Sheila Young, USA	42.76 **OR**	1998	Catriona Lemay-Doan, CAN	76.60 **OR**
1980	Karin Enke, E. Ger	41.78 **OR**			

1000 meters

Year		Time	Year		Time
1960	Klara Guseva, USSR	1:34.1	1984	Karin Enke, E. Ger	1:21.61 **OR**
1964	Lydia Skoblikova, USSR	1:33.2 **OR**	1988	Christa Rothenburger, E. Ger	1:17.65 **WR**
1968	Carolina Geijssen, NED	1:32.6 **OR**	1992	Bonnie Blair, USA	1:21.90
1972	Monika Pflug, W. Ger	1:31.40 **OR**	1994	Bonnie Blair, USA	1:18.74
1976	Tatiana Averina, USSR	1:28.43 **OR**	1998	Marianne Timmer, NED	1:16.51 **OR**
1980	Natalia Petruseva, USSR	1:24.10 **OR**			

1500 meters

Year		Time	
1960	Lydia Skoblikova, USSR	2:25.2	**WR**
1964	Lydia Skoblikova, USSR	2:22.6	**OR**
1968	Kaija Mustonen, FIN	2:22.4	**OR**
1972	Dianne Holum, USA	2:20.85	**OR**
1976	Galina Stepanskaya, USSR	2:16.58	**OR**
1980	Annie Borckink, NED	2:10.95	**OR**

Year		Time	
1984	Karin Enke, E. Ger	2:03.42	**WR**
1988	Yvonne van Gennip, NED	2:00.68	**OR**
1992	Jacqueline Börner, GER	2:05.87	
1994	Emese Hunyady, AUT	2:02.19	
1998	Marianne Timmer, NED	1:57.58	**WR**

3000 meters

Year		Time	
1960	Lydia Skoblikova, USSR	5:14:3	
1964	Lydia Skoblikova, USSR	5:14.9	
1968	Johanna Schut, NED	4:56.2	**OR**
1972	Christina Baas-Kaiser, NED	4:52.14	**OR**
1976	Tatiana Averina, USSR	4:45.19	**OR**
1980	Bjorg Eva Jensen, NOR	4:32.13	**OR**

Year		Time	
1984	Andrea Schöne, E. Ger	4:24.79	**OR**
1988	Yvonne van Gennip, NED	4:11.94	**WR**
1992	Gunda Niemann, GER	4:19.90	
1994	Svetlana Bazhanova, RUS	4:17.43	
1998	Gunda Niemann-Stirnemann, GER.	4:07.29	**OR**

5000 meters

Year		Time	
1960-84	Not held		
1988	Yvonne van Gennip, NED	7:14.13	**WR**
1992	Gunda Niemann, GER	7:31.57	

Year		Time	
1994	Claudia Pechstein, GER	7:14.37	
1998	Claudia Pechstein, GER	6:59.61	**WR**

All-Time Leading Medal Winners

MEN

No		Sport	G-S-B
12	Bjorn Dählie, NOR	Cross Country	8-4-0
9	Sixten Jernberg, SWE	Cross Country	4-3-2
7	Clas Thunberg, FIN	Speed Skating	5-1-1
7	Ivar Ballangrud, NOR	Speed Skating	4-2-1
7	Veikko Hakulinen, FIN	Cross Country	3-3-1
7	Eero Mäntyranta, FIN	Cross Country	3-2-2
7	Bogdan Musiol, E. Ger/GER	Bobsled	1-5-1
6	Gunde Svan, SWE	Cross Country	4-1-1
6	Vegard Ulvang, NOR	Cross Country	3-2-1
6	Johan Gröttumsbråten, NOR	Nordic	3-1-2
6	Wolfgang Hoppe, E. Ger/GER	Bobsled	2-3-1
6	Eugenio Monti, ITA	Bobsled	2-2-2
6	Vladimir Smirnov, USSR/UT/KAZ	X-country	1-4-1
6	Mika Myllylae, FIN	Cross Country	1-1-4
6	Roald Larsen, NOR	Speed Skating	0-2-4
6	Harri Kirvesniemi, FIN	Cross Country	0-0-6
5	**Eric Heiden, USA**	Speed Skating	5-0-0
5	Yevgeny Grishin, USSR	Speed Skating	4-1-0
5	Johann Olav Koss, NOR	Speed Skating	4-1-0
5	Matti Nykänen, FIN	Ski Jumping	4-1-0
5	Aleksandr Tikhonov, USSR	Biathlon	4-1-0
5	Nikolai Zimyatov, USSR	Cross Country	4-1-0
5	Alberto Tomba, ITA	Alpine	3-2-0
5	Harald Grönningen, NOR	Cross Country	2-3-0
5	Pål Tyldum, NOR	Cross Country	2-3-0
5	Knut Johannesen, NOR	Speed Skating	2-2-1
5	Kjetil André Aamodt, NOR	Alpine	1-2-2
5	Peter Angerer, W. Ger/GER	Biathlon	1-2-2
5	Juha Mieto, FIN	Cross Country	1-2-2
5	Fritz Feierabend, SWI	Bobsled	0-3-2
5	Rintje Ritsma, NED	Speed Skating	0-2-3

WOMEN

No		Sport	G-S-B
10	Raisa Smetanina, USSR/UT	Cross Country	4-5-1
9	Lyubov Egorova, UT/RUS	Cross Country	6-3-0
8	Galina Kulakova, USSR	Cross Country	4-2-2
8	Karin (Enke) Kania, E. Ger	Speed Skating	3-4-1
8	Gunda Neimann-Stirnemann, GER	Speed Skating	3-4-1
7	Larisa Lazutina, UT/RUS	Cross Country	5-1-1
7	Marja-Liisa (Hämäläinen) Kirvesniemi, FIN	Cross Country	3-0-4
7	Elena Valbe, UT/RUS	Cross Country	3-0-4
7	Andrea (Mitscherlich, Schöne) Ehrig, E. Ger	Speed Skating	1-5-1
7	Stefania Belmondo, ITA	Cross Country	1-2-4
6	Lydia Skoblikova, USSR	Speed Skating	6-0-0
6	**Bonnie Blair, USA**	Speed Skating	5-0-1
6	Manuela Di Centa, ITA	Cross Country	2-2-2
5	Lee-Kyung Chun, S. Kor	ST Sp. Skating	4-0-1
5	Anfisa Reztsova, USSR/UT	CC/Biathlon	3-1-1
5	Vreni Schneider, SWI	Alpine	3-1-1
5	Katja Seizinger, GER	Alpine	3-0-2
5	Claudia Pechstien, GER	Speed Skating	2-1-2
5	Helena Takalo, FIN	Cross Country	1-3-1
5	Ursula Disl, GER	Biathlon	1-2-2
5	Alevtina Kolchina, USSR	Cross Country	1-1-3

Games Medaled In

MEN– **Aamodt** (1992,94); **Angerer** (1980,84,88); **Ballangrud** (1928,32,36); **Dählie** (1992,94,98); **Feierabend** (1936,48,52); **Grishin** (1956,60,64); **Gröttumsbråten** (1924,28,32); **Grönningen** (1960,64,68); **Hakulinen** (1952,56,60); **Heiden** (1980); **Hoppe** (1984,88,92,94); **Jernberg** (1956,60,64); **Johannesen** (1956,60,64); **Kirvesniemi** (1980,84,92,94,98); **Koss** (1992,94). **Larsen** (1924,28); **Mäntyranta** (1960,64,68); **Mieto** (1976,80,84); **Monti** (1956,60,64,68); **Musiol** (1980,84,88,92); **Myllylae** (1994,98); **Nykänen** (1984,88); **Ritsma** (1994,98); **Smirnov** (1988,92,94,98); **Svan** (1984,88); **Thunberg** (1924,28); **Tikhonov** (1968,72,76,80); **Tomba** (1988,92,94); **Tyldum** (1968,72,76); **Ulvang** (1988,92,94); **Zimyatov** (1980,84).

WOMEN– **Belmondo** (1992,94,98); **Blair** (1988,92,94); **Chun** (1994,98); **Di Centa** (1992,94); **Disl** (1994,98); **Egorova** (1992,94); **Ehrig** (1976,80,84,88); **Kania** (1980,84,88); **Kirvesniemi** (1984,88,94); **Kolchina** (1956,64,68); **Kulakova** (1968,72,76,80); **Lazutina** (1992,94,98); **Niemann-Stirnemann** (1992,94,98); **Pechstein** (1992,94,98); **Reztsova** (1988,92,94); **Schneider** (1988,92,94); **Seizinger** (1992,94,98); **Skoblikova** (1960,64); **Smetanina** (1976,80,84,88,92); **Takalo** (1972,76,80); **Valbe** (1992,94,98).

Most Gold Medals

MEN

No		Sport	G-S-B
8	Bjorn Dählie, NOR	Cross Country	8-4-0
5	Clas Thunberg, FIN	Speed Skating	5-1-1
5	**Eric Heiden, USA**	Speed Skating	5-0-0
4	Sixten Jernberg, SWE	Cross Country	4-3-2
4	Ivar Ballangrud, NOR	Speed Skating	4-2-1
4	Gunde Svan, SWE	Cross Country	4-1-1
4	Yevgeny Grishin, USSR	Speed Skating	4-1-0
4	Johann Olav Koss, NOR	Speed Skating	4-1-0
4	Matti Nykänen, FIN	Ski Jumping	4-1-0
4	Aleksandr Tikhonov, USSR	Biathlon	4-1-0
4	Nikolai Zimyatov, USSR	Cross Country	4-1-0
4	Thomas Wassberg, SWE	Cross Country	4-0-0
3	Veikko Hakulinen, FIN	Cross Country	3-3-1
3	Eero Mäntyranta, FIN	Cross Country	3-2-2
3	Vegard Ulvang, NOR	Cross Country	3-2-1
3	Alberto Tomba, ITA	Alpine	3-2-0
3	Johan Gröttumsbråten, NOR	Nordic	3-1-2
3	Bernhard Germeshausen, E. Ger	Bobsled	3-1-0
3	Gillis Grafström, SWE	Figure Skating	3-1-0
3	Tomas Gustafson, SWE	Speed Skating	3-1-0
3	Vladislav Tretiak, USSR	Ice Hockey	3-1-0
3	Jens Weissflog, E. Ger/GER	Ski Jumping	3-1-0
3	Meinhard Nehmer, E. Ger	Bobsled	3-0-1
3	Hjalmar Andersen, NOR	Speed Skating	3-0-0
3	Vitaly Davydov, USSR	Ice Hockey	3-0-0
3	Anatoly Firsov, USSR	Ice Hockey	3-0-0
3	Thorleif Haug, NOR	Cross Country	3-0-0
3	**Irving Jaffee, USA**	Speed Skating	3-0-0
3	Andrei Khomoutov, USSR/UT	Ice Hockey	3-0-0

No		Sport	G-S-B
3	Jean-Claude Killy, FRA	Alpine	3-0-0
3	Viktor Kuzkin, USSR	Ice Hockey	3-0-0
3	Aleksandr Ragulin, USSR	Ice Hockey	3-0-0
3	Toni Sailer, AUT	Alpine	3-0-0
3	Ard Schenk, NED	Speed Skating	3-0-0
3	Ulrich Wehling, E. Ger	Ski Jumping	3-0-0

WOMEN

No		Sport	G-S-B
6	Lyubov Egorova, UT/RUS	Cross Country	6-3-0
6	Lydia Skoblikova, USSR	Speed Skating	6-0-0
5	Larissa Lazutina, UT/RUS	Cross Country	5-1-1
5	**Bonnie Blair, USA**	Speed Skating	5-0-1
4	Raisa Smetanina, USSR/UT	Cross Country	4-5-1
4	Galina Kulakova, USSR	Cross Country	4-2-2
4	Lee-Kyung Chun, S. Kor.	ST Sp. Skating	4-0-1
3	Karin (Enke) Kania, E. Ger	Speed Skating	3-4-1
3	Gunda Neimann-Stirnemann, GER	Speed Skating	3-4-1
3	Anfisa Reztsova, USSR/UT	CC/Biathlon	3-1-1
3	Vreni Schneider, SWI	Alpine	3-1-1
3	Marja-Liisa (Hämäläinen) Kirvesniemi, FIN	Cross Country	3-0-4
3	Elena Valbe, UT/RUS	Cross Country	3-0-4
3	Katja Seizinger, GER	Alpine	3-0-2
3	Claudia Boyarskikh, USSR	Cross Country	3-0-0
3	Sonja Henie, NOR	Figure Skating	3-0-0
3	Irina Rodnina, USSR	Figure Skating	3-0-0
3	Yvonne van Gennip, NED	Speed Skating	3-0-0

All-Time Leading USA Medalists

MEN

No		Sport	G-S-B
5	Eric Heiden	Speed Skating	5-0-0
3*	Irving Jaffee	Speed Skating	3-0-0
3	Pat Martin	Bobsled	1-2-0
3	John Heaton	Bobsled/Cresta	0-2-1
2	Dick Button	Figure Skating	2-0-0
2†	Eddie Eagan	Boxing/Bobsled	2-0-0
2	Billy Fiske	Bobsled	2-0-0
2	Cliff Gray	Bobsled	2-0-0
2	Jack Shea	Speed Skating	2-0-0
2	Billy Cleary	Ice Hockey	1-1-0
2	Jennison Heaton	Bobsled/Cresta	1-1-0
2	John Mayasich	Ice Hockey	1-1-0

No		Sport	G-S-B
2	Terry McDermott	Speed Skating	1-1-0
2	Dick Meredith	Ice Hockey	1-1-0
2	Tommy Moe	Alpine	1-1-0
2	Weldy Olson	Ice Hockey	1-1-0
2	Dick Rodenheiser	Ice Hockey	1-1-0
2	David Jenkins	Figure Skating	1-1-0
2	Stan Benham	Bobsled	0-2-0
2	Herb Drury	Ice Hockey	0-2-0
2	Eric Flaim	Sp. Skate/ST Sp. Skate	0-2-0
2	Frank Synott	Ice Hockey	0-2-0
2	John Garrison	Ice Hockey	0-1-1

*Jaffee is generally given credit for a third gold medal in the 10,000-meter Speed Skating race of 1928. He had the fastest time before the race was cancelled due to thawing ice. The IOC considers the race unofficial.

†Eagan won the Light Heavyweight boxing title at the 1920 Summer Games in Antwerp and the four-man Bobsled at the 1932 Winter Games in Lake Placid. He is the only athlete ever to win gold medals in both the Winter and Summer Olympics.

Athletes with Winter and Summer Medals

Only three athletes have won medals in both the Winter and Summer Olympics:
Eddie Eagan, USA– Light Heavyweight Boxing gold (1920) and Four-man Bobsled gold (1932).
Jacob Tullin Thams, Norway– Ski Jumping gold (1924) and 8-meter Yachting silver (1936).
Christa Luding-Rothenburger, East Germany– Speed Skating gold at 500 meters (1984) and 1,000m (1988), silver at 500m (1988) and bronze at 500m (1992) and Match Sprint Cycling silver (1988). Luding-Rothenburger is the only athlete to ever win medals in both Winter and Summer Games in the same year.

WOMEN

No		Sport	G-S-B	No		Sport	G-S-B
6	Bonnie Blair	Speed Skating	5-0-1	2	Carol Heiss	Figure Skating	1-1-0
4	Cathy Turner	ST Sp. Skating	2-1-1	2	Picabo Street	Alpine	1-1-0
4	Dianne Holum	Speed Skating	1-2-1	2	Diann Roffe-Steinrotter	Alpine	1-1-0
3	Sheila Young	Speed Skating	1-1-1	2	Anne Henning	Speed Skating	1-0-1
3	Leah Poulos Mueller	Speed Skating	0-3-0	2	Penny Pitou	Alpine	0-2-0
3	Beatrix Loughran	Figure Skating	0-2-1	2	Nancy Kerrigan	Figure Skating	0-1-1
3	Amy Peterson	ST Sp. Skating	0-2-1	2	Jean Saubert	Alpine	0-1-1
2	Andrea Mead Lawrence	Alpine	2-0-0	2	Chris Witty	Sp. Skating	0-1-1
2	Tenley Albright	Figure Skating	1-1-0	2	Nikki Ziegelmeyer	ST Sp. Skating	0-1-1
2	Gretchen Fraser	Alpine	1-1-0				

Notes: The Cresta run is undertaken on a heavy sled ridden head first in the prone position and has only been held at St. Moritz in 1928 and '48. Also, the term ST Sp. Skating refers to Short Track (or pack) Speed Skating.

All-Time Medal Standings, 1924-98

All-time Winter Games medal standings, according to *The Golden Book of the Olympic Games*. Medal counts include figure skating medals (1908 and '20) and hockey medals (1920) awarded at the Summer Games. National medal standings for the Winter and Summer Games are not recognized by the IOC.

		G	S	B	Total			G	S	B	Total
1	Norway	83	87	69	239	22	Liechtenstein	2	2	5	9
2	Soviet Union (1956-88)	78	57	59	194	23	Hungary	0	2	4	6
3	**United States**	59	59	41	159	24	Kazakhstan (1994–)	1	2	2	5
4	Austria	39	53	53	145		Belgium	1	1	3	5
5	Finland	38	49	48	135	26	Poland	1	1	2	4
6	East Germany (1968-88)	43	39	36	118		Yugoslavia (1924-88)	0	3	1	4
7	Sweden	39	28	35	102		Belarus (1994–)	0	2	2	4
8	Switzerland	29	31	32	92	29	Czech Republic (1998–)	1	1	1	3
9	Germany (1928-36, 52-64, 92–)	35	30	25	90		Ukraine (1994–)	1	1	1	3
							Slovenia (1992–)	0	0	3	3
10	Canada	25	25	29	79	32	Bulgaria	1	0	1	2
11	Italy	27	27	23	77		Spain	1	0	1	2
12	Netherlands	19	23	19	61		Luxembourg	0	2	0	2
	France	18	17	26	61		North Korea	0	1	1	2
14	West Germany (1968-88)	18	20	19	57		Australia	0	0	2	2
15	Russia (1994–)	21	14	7	42	37	Uzbekistan (1994–)	1	0	0	1
16	Japan	8	9	12	29		Denmark	0	1	0	1
17	Czechoslovakia (1924-92)	2	8	16	26		New Zealand	0	1	0	1
18	Great Britain	7	4	13	24		Romania	0	0	1	1
19	Unified Team (1992)	9	6	8	23						
20	South Korea	9	3	4	16	**Combined totals**		**G**	**S**	**B**	**Total**
21	China	0	10	4	14	Germany/E. Ger/W. Ger		96	89	80	265
						USSR/UT/Russia		108	77	74	259

Notes: Athletes from the USSR participated in the Winter Games from 1956-88, returned as the Unified Team in 1992 after the breakup of the Soviet Union (in 1991) and then competed for the independent republics of Belarus, Kazakhstan, Russia, Ukraine, Uzbekistan and three others in 1994. Yugoslavia divided into Croatia and Bosnia-Herzegovina in 1992, while Czechoslovakia split into Slovakia and the Czech Republic in 1993.

Germany was barred from the Olympics in 1924 and 1948 as an aggressor nation in both World Wars I and II. Divided into East and West Germany after WWII, both countries competed under one flag from 1952-64, then as separate teams from 1968-88. Germany was reunified in 1990.

1896-2000 Through the Years

information please®
SPORTS ALMANAC

Modern Olympic Games

The original Olympic Games were celebrated as a religious festival from 776 B.C. until 393 A.D., when Roman emperor Theodosius I banned all pagan festivals (the Olympics celebrated the Greek god Zeus). On June 23, 1894, French educator Baron Pierre de Coubertin, speaking at the Sorbonne in Paris to a gathering of international sports leaders, proposed that the ancient games be revived on an international scale. The idea was enthusiastically received and the Modern Olympics were born. The first Olympics were held two years later in Athens, where 245 athletes from 14 nations competed in the ancient Panathenaic stadium to large and ardent crowds. Americans captured nine out of 12 track and field events, but Greece won the most medals with 47.

The Summer Olympics

Year	No	Location	Dates	Nations	Most medals	USA medals	
1896	I	Athens, GRE	Apr. 6-15	14	Greece (10-19-18—47)	11- 6- 2 — 19	(2nd)
1900	II	Paris, FRA	May 20-Oct. 28	26	France (26-37-32—95)	18-14-15— 47	(2nd)
1904	III	St. Louis, USA.	July 1-Nov. 23	13	USA (78-84-82—244)	78-84-82—244	(1st)
1906-a	—	Athens, GRE	Apr. 22-May 2	20	France (15-9-16—40)	12- 6- 6 — 24	(3rd)
1908	IV	London, GBR	Apr. 27-Oct. 31	22	Britain (54-46-38—138)	23-12-12— 47	(2nd)
1912	V	Stockholm, SWE	May 5-July 22	28	Sweden (23-24-17—64)	25-18-20— 63	(2nd)
1916	VI	Berlin, GER	Cancelled (WWI)				
1920	VII	Antwerp, BEL	Apr. 20-Sept. 12	29	USA (41-27-27—95)	41-27-27— 95	(1st)
1924	VIII	Paris, FRA	May 4-July 27	44	USA (45-27-27—99)	45-27-27— 99	(1st)
1928	IX	Amsterdam, NED.....	May 17-Aug. 12	46	USA (22-18-16—56)	22-18-16— 56	(1st)
1932	X	Los Angeles, USA. ...	July 30-Aug. 14	37	USA (41-32-30—103)	41-32-30—103	(1st)
1936	XI	Berlin, GER	Aug. 1-16	49	Germany (33-26-30—89)	24-20-12— 56	(2nd)
1940-b	XII	Tokyo, JPN	Cancelled (WWII)				
1944	XIII	London, GBR	Cancelled (WWII)				
1948	XIV	London, GBR	July 29-Aug. 14	59	USA (38-27-19—84)	38-27-19— 84	(1st)
1952-cd	XV	Helsinki, FIN	July 19-Aug. 3	69	USA (40-19-17—76)	40-19-17— 76	(1st)
1956-e	XVI	Melbourne, AUS	Nov. 22-Dec .8	72	USSR (37-29-32—98)	32-25-17— 74	(2nd)
1960	XVII	Rome, ITA	Aug. 25-Sept. 11	83	USSR (43-29-31—103)	34-21-16— 71	(2nd)
1964	XVIII	Tokyo, JPN	Oct. 10-24	93	USSR (30-31-35—96)	36-26-28— 90	(2nd)
1968-f	XIX	Mexico City, MEX	Oct. 12-27	112	USA (45-28-34—107)	45-28-34—107	(1st)
1972	XX	Munich, W. GER	Aug. 26-Sept. 10	121	USSR (50-27-22—99)	33-31-30— 94	(2nd)
1976-g	XXI	Montreal, CAN	July 17-Aug. 1	92	USSR (49-41-35—125)	34-35-25— 94	(3rd)
1980-h	XXII	Moscow, USSR	July 19-Aug. 3	80	USSR (80-69-46—195)	Boycotted games	
1984-i	XXIII	Los Angeles, USA. ...	July 28-Aug. 12	140	USA (83-61-30—174)	83-61-30—174	(1st)
1988	XXIV	Seoul, S. KOR	Sept. 17-Oct. 2	159	USSR (55-31-46—132)	36-31-27— 94	(3rd)
1992-j	XXV	Barcelona, SPA	July 25-Aug. 9	169	UT (45-38-29—112)	37-34-37—108	(2nd)
1996	XXVI	Atlanta, USA	July 20-Aug. 4	197	USA (44-32-25—101)	44-32-25—101	(1st)
2000	XXVII	Sydney, AUS	Sept. 15-Oct. 1	199	USA (40-24-33—97)	40-24-33— 97	(1st)
2004	XXVIII	Athens, GRE	Aug. 13-29				
2008	XXIX	Beijing, CHN	TBA				

a—The 1906 Intercalated Games in Athens are considered unofficial by the IOC because they did not take place in the four-year cycle established in 1896. However, most record books include these interim games with the others.
b—The 1940 Summer Games are originally scheduled for Tokyo, but Japan resigns as host after the outbreak of the Sino-Japanese War in 1937. Helsinki is the next choice, but the IOC cancels the Games after Soviet troops invade Finland in 1939.
c—Germany and Japan are allowed to rejoin the Olympic community for the first Summer Games since 1936. Though a divided country, the Germans send a joint East-West team until 1964.
d—The Soviet Union (USSR) participates in its first Olympics, Winter or Summer, since the Russian revolution in 1917 and takes home the second most medals (22-30-19—71).
e—Due to Australian quarantine laws, the equestrian events for the 1956 Games are held in Stockholm, June 10-17.
f—East Germany and West Germany send separate teams for the first time and will continue to do so through 1988.
g—The 1976 Games are boycotted by 32 nations, most of them from black Africa, because the IOC will not ban New Zealand. Earlier that year, a rugby team from New Zealand had toured racially segregated South Africa.
h—The 1980 Games are boycotted by 64 nations, led by the USA, to protest the Soviet invasion of Afghanistan on Dec. 27, 1979.
i—The 1984 Games are boycotted by 14 Eastern Bloc nations, led by the USSR, to protest America's overcommercialization of the Games, inadequate security and an anti-Soviet attitude by the U.S. government. Most believe, however, the communist walkout is simply revenge for 1980.
j—Germany sends a single team after East and West German reunification in 1990 and the USSR competes as the Unified Team after the breakup of the Soviet Union in 1991.

Event-by-Event

Gold medal winners from 1896-2000 in the following events: Baseball, Basketball, Boxing, Diving, Field Hockey, Gymnastics, Soccer, Softball, Swimming, Tennis and Track & Field.

BASEBALL

Multiple gold medals: Cuba (2).

Year		Year	
1992	**Cuba**, Taiwan, Japan	2000	**United States**, Cuba, South Korea
1996	**Cuba**, Japan, United States		

U.S. Medal-Winning Baseball Teams

1996 (bronze medal): P–Kris Benson, R.A. Dickey, Seth Greisinger, Billy Koch, Braden Looper, Jim Parque and Jeff Weaver; C–A.J. Hinch, Matt LeCroy and Brian Lloyd; INF–Troy Glaus, Kip Harkrider, Travis Lee, Warren Morris, Augie Ojeda and Jason Williams; OF–Chad Allen, Chad Green, Jacque Jones and Mark Kotsay; Manager–Skip Bertman. Final: Cuba over Japan, 13-9

2000 (gold medal): P–Kurt Ainsworth, Ryan Franklin, Chris George, Shane Heams, Rick Krivda, Roy Oswalt, Jon Rauch, Bobby Seay, Ben Sheets, Todd Williams and Tim Young; C–Pat Borders, Marcus Jensen and Mike Kinkade; INF–Brent Abernathy, Sean Burroughs, John Cotton, Gookie Dawkins, Adam Everett and Doug Mientkiewicz; OF–Mike Neill, Anthony Sanders, Brad Wilkerson and Ernie Young; Manager–Tommy Lasorda. Final: USA over Cuba, 4-0.

BASKETBALL

MEN

Multiple gold medals: USA (12), USSR (2).

Year		Year	
1936	**United States**, Canada, Mexico	1976	**United States**, Yugoslavia, Soviet Union
1948	**United States**, France, Brazil	1980	**Yugoslavia**, Italy, Soviet Union
1952	**United States**, Soviet Union, Uruguay	1984	**United States**, Spain, Yugoslavia
1956	**United States**, Soviet Union, Uruguay	1988	**Soviet Union**, Yugoslavia, United States
1960	**United States**, Soviet Union, Brazil	1992	**United States**, Croatia, Lithuania
1964	**United States**, Soviet Union, Brazil	1996	**United States**, Yugoslavia, Lithuania
1968	**United States**, Yugoslavia, Soviet Union	2000	**United States**, France, Lithuania
1972	**Soviet Union**, United States, Cuba		

U.S. Medal-Winning Men's Basketball Teams

1936 (gold medal): Sam Balter, Ralph Bishop, Joe Fortenberry, Tex Gibbons, Francis Johnson, Carl Knowles, Frank Lubin, Art Mollner, Don Piper, Jack Ragland, Carl Shy, Willard Schmidt, Duane Swanson and William Wheatley. Coach–Jim Needles; Assistant–Gene Johnson. Final: USA over Canada, 19-8.

1948 (gold medal): Cliff Barker, Don Barksdale, Ralph Beard, Louis Beck, Vince Boryla, Gordon Carpenter, Alex Groza, Wallace Jones, Bob Kurland, Ray Lumpp, R.C. Pitts, Jesse Renick, Robert (Jackie) Robinson and Ken Rollins. Coach–Omar Browning; Assistant–Adolph Rupp. Final: USA over France, 65-21.

1952 (gold medal): Ron Bontemps, Mark Freiberger, Wayne Glasgow, Charlie Hoag, Bill Hougland, John Keller, Dean Kelley, Bob Kenney, Bob Kurland, Bill Lienhard, Clyde Lovellette, Frank McCabe, Dan Pippin and Howie Williams. Coach–Warren Womble; Assistant–Forrest (Phog) Allen. Final: USA over USSR, 36-25.

1956 (gold medal): Dick Boushka, Carl Cain, Chuck Darling, Bill Evans, Gib Ford, Burdy Haldorson, Bill Hougland, Bob Jeangerard, K.C. Jones, Bill Russell, Ron Tomsic and Jim Walsh. Coach–Gerald Tucker; Assistant–Bruce Drake. Final: USA over USSR, 89-55.

1960 (gold medal): Jay Arnette, Walt Bellamy, Bob Boozer, Terry Dischinger, Jerry Lucas, Oscar Robertson, Adrian Smith, Burdy Haldorson, Darrall Imhoff, Allen Kelley, Lester Lane and Jerry West. Coach–Pete Newell; Assistant–Warren Womble. Final round: USA defeated USSR (81-57), Italy (112-81) and Brazil (90-63) in round robin.

1964 (gold medal): Jim (Bad News) Barnes, Bill Bradley, Larry Brown, Joe Caldwell, Mel Counts, Dick Davies, Walt Hazzard, Lucious Jackson, Pete McCaffrey, Jeff Mullins, Jerry Shipp and George Wilson. Coach–Hank Iba; Assistant–Henry Vaughn. Final: USA over USSR, 73-59.

1968 (gold medal): Mike Barrett, John Clawson, Don Dee, Cal Fowler, Spencer Haywood, Bill Hosket, Jim King, Glynn Saulters, Charlie Scott, Mike Silliman, Ken Spain, and Jo Jo White. Coach–Hank Iba; Assistant–Henry Vaughn. Final: USA over Yugoslavia, 65-50.

1972 (silver medal refused): Mike Bantom, Jim Brewer, Tom Burleson, Doug Collins, Kenny Davis, Jim Forbes, Tom Henderson, Bobby Jones, Dwight Jones, Kevin Joyce, Tom McMillen and Ed Ratleff. Coach–Hank Iba; Assistants– John Bach and Don Haskins. Final: USSR over USA, 51-50.

1976 (gold medal): Tate Armstrong, Quinn Buckner, Kenny Carr, Adrian Dantley, Walter Davis, Phil Ford, Ernie Grunfeld, Phil Hubbard, Mitch Kupchak, Tommy LaGarde, Scott May and Steve Sheppard. Coach–Dean Smith; Assistants–Bill Guthridge and John Thompson. Final: USA over Yugoslavia, 95-74.

1980 (no medal): USA boycotted Moscow Games. Final: Yugoslavia over Italy, 86-77.

1984 (gold medal): Steve Alford, Patrick Ewing, Vern Fleming, Michael Jordan, Joe Kleine, Jon Koncak, Chris Mullin, Sam Perkins, Alvin Robertson, Wayman Tisdale, Jeff Turner and Leon Wood. Coach–Bobby Knight; Assistants– Don Donoher and George Raveling. Final: USA over Spain, 96-65.

1988 (bronze medal): Stacey Augmon, Willie Anderson, Bimbo Coles, Jeff Grayer, Hersey Hawkins, Dan Majerle, Danny Manning, Mitch Richmond, J.R. Reid, David Robinson, Charles D. Smith and Charles E. Smith. Coach–John Thompson; Assistants–George Raveling and Mary Fenlon. Final: USSR over Yugoslavia, 76-63.

1992 (gold medal): Charles Barkley, Larry Bird, Clyde Drexler, Patrick Ewing, Magic Johnson, Michael Jordan, Christian Laettner, Karl Malone, Chris Mullin, Scottie Pippen, David Robinson and John Stockton. Coach–Chuck Daly; Assistants–Lenny Wilkens, Mike Krzyzewski and P.J. Carlesimo. Final: USA over Croatia, 117-85.

1996 (gold medal): Charles Barkley, Anfernee Hardaway, Grant Hill, Karl Malone, Reggie Miller, Hakeem Olajuwon, Shaquille O'Neal, Gary Payton, Scottie Pippen, David Robinson and John Stockton. Coach–Lenny Wilkens; Assistants–Bobby Cremins, Clem Haskins and Jerry Sloan. Final: USA over Yugoslavia, 95-69.

2000 (gold medal): Shareef Abdur-Rahim, Ray Allen, Vin Baker, Vince Carter, Kevin Garnett, Tim Hardaway, Allan Houston, Jason Kidd, Antonio McDyess, Alonzo Mourning, Gary Payton and Steve Smith. Coach–Rudy Tomjanovich; Assistants–Larry Brown, Gene Keady and Tubby Smith. Final: USA over France, 85-75.

WOMEN

Multiple gold medals: USA (4), USSR/UT (3).

Year		Year	
1976	**Soviet Union**, United States, Bulgaria	1992	**Unified Team**, China, United States
1980	**Soviet Union**, Bulgaria, Yugoslavia	1996	**United States**, Brazil, Australia
1984	**United States**, South Korea, China	2000	**United States**, Australia, Brazil
1988	**United States**, Yugoslavia, Soviet Union		

U.S. Gold Medal-Winning Women's Basketball Teams

1984 (gold medal): Cathy Boswell, Denise Curry, Anne Donovan, Teresa Edwards, Lea Henry, Janice Lawrence, Pamela McGee, Carol Menken-Schaudt, Cheryl Miller, Kim Mulkey, Cindy Noble and Lynette Woodard. Coach–Pat Summitt; Assistant–Kay Yow. Final: USA over South Korea, 85-55.

1988 (gold medal): Cindy Brown, Vicky Bullett, Cynthia Cooper, Anne Donovan, Teresa Edwards, Kamie Ethridge, Jennifer Gillom, Bridgette Gordon, Andrea Lloyd, Katrina McClain, Suzie McConnell and Teresa Weatherspoon. Coach–Kay Yow; Assistants–Sylvia Hatchell and Susan Yow. Final: USA over Yugoslavia, 77-70.

1996 (gold medal): Jennifer Azzi, Ruthie Bolton, Teresa Edwards, Venus Lacy, Lisa Leslie, Rebecca Lobo, Katrina McClain, Nikki McCray, Carla McGee, Dawn Staley, Katy Steding and Sheryl Swoopes. Coach—Tara VanDerveer; Assistants–Ceal Barry, Nancy Darsch and Marian Washington. Final: USA over Brazil, 111-87.

2000 (gold medal): Ruthie Bolton-Holyfield, Teresa Edwards, Yolanda Griffith, Chamique Holdsclaw, Lisa Leslie, Nikki McCray, DeLisha Milton, Katie Smith, Dawn Staley, Sheryl Swoopes, Natalie Williams and Kara Wolters. Coach—Nell Fortner; Assistants–Geno Auriemma and Peggie Gillom. Final: USA over Australia, 76-54.

BOXING

Multiple gold medals: László Papp, Felix Savon and Teófilo Stevenson (3); Ariel Hernandez, Angel Herrera, Oliver Kirk, Jerzy Kulej, Boris Lagutin, Harry Mallin, Oleg Saitov and Hector Vinent (2). All fighters won titles in consecutive Olympics, except Kirk, who won both the bantamweight and featherweight titles in 1904 (he only had to fight once in each division).

Light Flyweight (106 lbs)

Year		Final Match	Year		Final Match
1968	Francisco Rodriguez, VEN	Decision, 3-2	1988	Ivailo Hristov, BUL	Decision, 5-0
1972	György Gedó, HUN	Decision, 5-0	1992	Rogelio Marcelo, CUB	Decision, 24-10
1976	Jorge Hernandez, CUB	Decision, 4-1	1996	Daniel Petrov Bojilov, BUL	Decision, 19-6
1980	Shamil Sabyrov, USSR	Decision, 3-2	2000	Brahim Asloum, FRA	Decision, 23-10
1984	Paul Gonzales, USA	Default			

Flyweight (112 lbs)

Year		Final Match	Year		Final Match
1904	George Finnegan, USA	Stopped, 1st	1964	Fernando Atzori, ITA	Decision, 4-1
1920	Frank Di Gennara, USA	Decision	1968	Ricardo Delgado, MEX	Decision, 5-0
1924	Fidel LaBarba, USA	Decision	1972	Georgi Kostadinov, BUL	Decision, 5-0
1928	Antal Kocsis, HUN	Decision	1976	Leo Randolph, USA	Decision, 3-2
1932	István Énekes, HUN	Decision	1980	Peter Lessov, BUL	Stopped, 2nd
1936	Willi Kaiser, GER	Decision	1984	Steve McCrory, USA	Decision, 4-1
1948	Pascual Perez, ARG	Decision	1988	Kim Kwang-Sun, S. Kor	Decision, 4-1
1952	Nate Brooks, USA	Decision, 3-0	1992	Su Choi-Chol, N. Kor	Decision, 12-2
1956	Terence Spinks, GBR	Decision	1996	Maikro Romero, CUB	Decision, 12-11
1960	Gyula Török, HUN	Decision, 3-2	2000	Wijan Ponlid, THA	Decision, 19-12

Bantamweight (119 lbs)

Year		Final Match	Year		Final Match
1904	Oliver Kirk, USA	Stopped, 3rd	1964	Takao Sakurai, JPN	Stopped, 2nd
1908	Henry Thomas, GBR	Decision	1968	Valery Sokolov, USSR	Stopped, 2nd
1920	Clarence Walker, RSA	Decision	1972	Orlando Martinez, CUB	Decision, 5-0
1924	William Smith, RSA	Decision	1976	Gu Yong-Ju, N. Kor	Decision, 5-0
1928	Vittorio Tamagnini, ITA	Decision	1980	Juan Hernandez, CUB	Decision, 5-0
1932	Horace Gwynne, CAN	Decision	1984	Maurizio Stecca, ITA	Decision, 4-1
1936	Ulderico Sergo, ITA	Decision	1988	Kennedy McKinney, USA	Decision, 5-0
1948	Tibor Csik, HUN	Decision	1992	Joel Casamayor, CUB	Decision, 14-8
1952	Pentti Hämäläinen, FIN	Decision, 2-1	1996	Istvan Kovacs, HUN	Decision, 14-7
1956	Wolfgang Behrendt, GER	Decision	2000	Guillermo Rigondeaux, CUB	Decision, 18-12
1960	Oleg Grigoryev, USSR	Decision			

Featherweight (125 lbs)

Year		Final Match	Year		Final Match
1904	Oliver Kirk, USA	Decision	1964	Stanislav Stepashkin, USSR	Decision, 3-2
1908	Richard Gunn, GBR	Decision	1968	Antonio Roldan, MEX	Won on Disq.
1920	Paul Fritsch, FRA	Decision	1972	Boris Kousnetsov, USSR	Decision, 3-2
1924	John Fields, USA	Decision	1976	Angel Herrera, CUB	KO, 2nd
1928	Lambertus van Klaveren, NED	Decision	1980	Rudi Fink, E. Ger	Decision, 4-1
1932	Carmelo Robledo, ARG	Decision	1984	Meldrick Taylor, USA	Decision, 5-0
1936	Oscar Casanovas, ARG	Decision	1988	Giovanni Parisi, ITA	Stopped, 1st
1948	Ernesto Formenti, ITA	Decision	1992	Andreas Tews, GER	Decision, 16-7
1952	Jan Zachara, CZE	Decision, 2-1	1996	Somluck Kamsing, THA	Decision, 8-5
1956	Vladimir Safronov, USSR	Decision	2000	Bekzat Sattarkhanov, KAZ	Decision, 22-14
1960	Francesco Musso, ITA	Decision, 4-1			

Boxing (Cont.)
Lightweight (132 lbs)

Year		Final Match	Year		Final Match
1904	Harry Spanger, USA	Decision	1964	Józef Grudzien, POL	Decision
1908	Frederick Grace, GBR	Decision	1968	Ronnie Harris, USA	Decision, 5-0
1920	Samuel Mosberg, USA	Decision	1972	Jan Szczepanski, POL	Decision, 5-0
1924	Hans Nielsen, DEN	Decision	1976	Howard Davis, USA	Decision, 5-0
1928	Carlo Orlandi, ITA	Decision	1980	Angel Herrera, CUB	Stopped, 3rd
1932	Lawrence Stevens, RSA	Decision	1984	Pernell Whitaker, USA	Foe quit, 2nd
1936	Imre Harangi, HUN	Decision	1988	Andreas Zuelow, E. Ger	Decision, 5-0
1948	Gerald Dreyer, RSA	Decision	1992	Oscar De La Hoya, USA	Decision, 7-2
1952	Aureliano Bolognesi, ITA	Decision, 2-1	1996	Hocine Soltani, ALG	Tiebreak, 3-3
1956	Richard McTaggart, GBR	Decision	2000	Mario Kindelan, CUB	Decision, 14-4
1960	Kazimierz Pazdzior, POL	Decision, 4-1			

Light Welterweight (139 lbs)

Year		Final Match	Year		Final Match
1952	Charles Adkins, USA	Decision, 2-1	1980	Patrizio Oliva, ITA	Decision, 4-1
1956	Vladimir Yengibaryan, USSR	Decision	1984	Jerry Page, USA	Decision, 5-0
1960	Bohumil Nemecek, CZE	Decision, 5-0	1988	Vyacheslav Yanovsky, USSR	Decision, 5-0
1964	Jerzy Kulej, POL	Decision, 5-0	1992	Hector Vinent, CUB	Decision, 11-1
1968	Jerzy Kulej, POL	Decision, 3-2	1996	Hector Vinent, CUB	Decision, 20-13
1972	Ray Seales, USA	Decision, 3-2	2000	Mahamadkadyz Abdullaev, UZB	Decision, 27-20
1976	Ray Leonard, USA	Decision, 5-0			

Welterweight (147 lbs)

Year		Final Match	Year		Final Match
1904	Albert Young, USA	Decision	1964	Marian Kasprzyk, POL	Decision, 4-1
1920	Bert Schneider, CAN	Decision	1968	Manfred Wolke, E. Ger	Decision, 4-1
1924	Jean Delarge, BEL	Decision	1972	Emilio Correa, CUB	Decision, 5-0
1928	Edward Morgan, NZE	Decision	1976	Jochen Bachfeld, E. Ger	Decision, 3-2
1932	Edward Flynn, USA	Decision	1980	Andrés Aldama, CUB	Decision, 4-1
1936	Sten Suvio, FIN	Decision	1984	Mark Breland, USA	Decision, 5-0
1948	Julius Torma, CZE	Decision	1988	Robert Wangila, KEN	KO, 2nd
1952	Zygmunt Chychla, POL	Decision, 3-0	1992	Michael Carruth, IRE	Decision, 13-10
1956	Nicolae Linca, ROM	Decision, 3-2	1996	Oleg Saitov, RUS	Decision, 14-9
1960	Nino Benvenuti, ITA	Decision, 4-1	2000	Oleg Saitov, RUS	Decision, 24-16

Light Middleweight (156 lbs)

Year		Final Match	Year		Final Match
1952	László Papp, HUN	Decision, 3-0	1980	Armando Martinez, CUB	Decision, 4-1
1956	László Papp, HUN	Decision	1984	Frank Tate, USA	Decision, 5-0
1960	Skeeter McClure, USA	Decision, 4-1	1988	Park Si-Hun, S. Kor	Decision, 3-2
1964	Boris Lagutin, USSR	Decision, 4-1	1992	Juan Lemus, CUB	Decision, 6-1
1968	Boris Lagutin, USSR	Decision, 5-0	1996	David Reid, USA	KO, 3rd
1972	Dieter Kottysch, W. Ger	Decision, 3-2	2000	Yermakhan Ibraimov, KAZ	Decision, 25-23
1976	Jerzy Rybicki, POL	Decision, 5-0			

Middleweight (165 lbs)

Year		Final Match	Year		Final Match
1904	Charles Mayer, USA	Stopped, 3rd	1964	Valery Popenchenko, USSR	Stopped, 1st
1908	John Douglas, GBR	Decision	1968	Christopher Finnegan, GBR	Decision, 3-2
1920	Harry Mallin, GBR	Decision	1972	Vyacheslav Lemechev, USSR	KO, 1st
1924	Harry Mallin, GBR	Decision	1976	Michael Spinks, USA	Stopped, 3rd
1928	Piero Toscani, ITA	Decision	1980	José Gomez, CUB	Decision, 4-1
1932	Carmen Barth, USA	Decision	1984	Shin Joon-Sup, S. Kor	Decision, 3-2
1936	Jean Despeaux, FRA	Decision	1988	Henry Maske, E. Ger	Decision, 5-0
1948	László Papp, HUN	Decision	1992	Ariel Hernandez, CUB	Decision, 12-7
1952	Floyd Patterson, USA	KO, 1st	1996	Ariel Hernandez, CUB	Decision, 11-3
1956	Gennady Schatkov, USSR	KO, 1st	2000	Jorge Gutierrez, CUB	Decision, 17-15
1960	Eddie Crook, USA	Decision, 3-2			

Light Heavyweight (178 lbs)

Year		Final Match	Year		Final Match
1920	Eddie Eagan, USA	Decision	1968	Dan Poznjak, USSR	Default
1924	Harry Mitchell, GBR	Decision	1972	Mate Parlov, YUG	Stopped, 2nd
1928	Victor Avendaño, ARG	Decision	1976	Leon Spinks, USA	Stopped, 3rd
1932	David Carstens, RSA	Decision	1980	Slobodan Kacar, YUG	Decision, 4-1
1936	Roger Michelot, FRA	Decision	1984	Anton Josipovic, YUG	Default
1948	George Hunter, RSA	Decision	1988	Andrew Maynard, USA	Decision, 5-0
1952	Norvel Lee, USA	Decision, 3-0	1992	Torsten May, GER	Decision, 8-3
1956	Jim Boyd, USA	Decision	1996	Vasilii Jirov, KAZ	Decision, 17-4
1960	Cassius Clay, USA	Decision, 5-0	2000	Alexander Lebziak, RUS	Decision, 20-6
1964	Cosimo Pinto, ITA	Decision, 3-2			

Note: Cassius Clay changed his name to Muhammad Ali after winning the world heavyweight championship in 1964.

Heavyweight (201 lbs)

Year		Final Match	Year		Final Match
1984	Henry Tillman, USA	Decision, 5-0	1996	Felix Savon, CUB	Decision, 20-2
1988	Ray Mercer, USA	KO, 1st	2000	Felix Savon, CUB	Decision, 21-13
1992	Felix Savon, CUB	Decision, 14-1			

Super Heavyweight (Unlimited)

Year		Final Match	Year		Final Match
1904	Samuel Berger, USA	Decision	1964	Joe Frazier, USA	Decision, 3-2
1908	Albert Oldham, GBR	KO, 1st	1968	George Foreman, USA	Stopped, 2nd
1920	Ronald Rawson, GBR	Decision	1972	Teófilo Stevenson, CUB	Default
1924	Otto von Porat, NOR	Decision	1976	Teófilo Stevenson, CUB	KO, 3rd
1928	Arturo Rodriguez Jurado, ARG	Stopped, 1st	1980	Teófilo Stevenson, CUB	Decision, 4-1
1932	Santiago Lovell, ARG	Decision	1984	Tyrell Biggs, USA	Decision, 4-1
1936	Herbert Runge, GER	Decision	1988	Lennox Lewis, CAN	Stopped, 2nd
1948	Rafael Iglesias, ARG	KO, 2nd	1992	Roberto Balado, CUB	Decision, 13-2
1952	Ed Sanders, USA	Won on Disq.*	1996	Vladimir Klichko, UKR	Decision, 7-3
1956	Pete Rademacher, USA	Stopped, 1st	2000	Audley Harrison, GBR	Decision, 30-16
1960	Franco De Piccoli, ITA	KO, 1st			

*Sanders' opponent, Ingemar Johansson, was disqualified in 2nd round for not trying.
Note: Called heavyweight through 1980.

DIVING

MEN

Multiple gold medals: Greg Louganis (4); Klaus Dibiasi (3); Pete Desjardins, Sammy Lee, Xiong Ni, Bob Webster and Albert White (2).

Springboard

Year		Points	Year		Points
1908	Albert Zürner, GER	85.5	1964	Ken Sitzberger, USA	159.90
1912	Paul Günther, GER	79.23	1968	Bernie Wrightson, USA	170.15
1920	Louis Kuehn, USA	675.4	1972	Vladimir Vasin, USSR	594.09
1924	Albert White, USA	696.4	1976	Phil Boggs, USA	619.05
1928	Pete Desjardins, USA	185.04	1980	Aleksandr Portnov, USSR	905.03
1932	Michael Galitzen, USA	161.38	1984	Greg Louganis, USA	754.41
1936	Richard Degener, USA	163.57	1988	Greg Louganis, USA	730.80
1948	Bruce Harlan, USA	163.64	1992	Mark Lenzi, USA	676.53
1952	David Browning, USA	205.29	1996	Xiong Ni, CHN	701.46
1956	Bob Clotworthy, USA	159.56	2000	Xiong Ni, CHN	708.72
1960	Gary Tobian, USA	170.00			

Platform

Year		Points	Year		Points
1904	George Sheldon, USA	12.66	1960	Bob Webster, USA	165.56
1906	Gottlob Walz, GER	156.0	1964	Bob Webster, USA	148.58
1908	Hjalmar Johansson, SWE	83.75	1968	Klaus Dibiasi, ITA	164.18
1912	Erik Adlerz, SWE	73.94	1972	Klaus Dibiasi, ITA	504.12
1920	Clarence Pinkston, USA	100.67	1976	Klaus Dibiasi, ITA	600.51
1924	Albert White, USA	97.46	1980	Falk Hoffmann, E. Ger	835.65
1928	Pete Desjardins, USA	98.74	1984	Greg Louganis, USA	710.91
1932	Harold Smith, USA	124.80	1988	Greg Louganis, USA	638.61
1936	Marshall Wayne, USA	113.58	1992	Sun Shuwei, CHN	677.31
1948	Sammy Lee, USA	130.05	1996	Dmitri Sautin, RUS	692.34
1952	Sammy Lee, USA	156.28	2000	Tian Liang, CHN	724.53
1956	Joaquin Capilla, MEX	152.44			

WOMEN

Multiple gold medals: Pat McCormick and Fu Mingxia (4); Ingrid Engel-Krämer (3); Vicki Draves, Dorothy Poynton Hill and Gao Min (2).

Springboard

Year		Points	Year		Points
1920	Aileen Riggin, USA	539.9	1968	Sue Gossick, USA	150.77
1924	Elizabeth Becker, USA	474.5	1972	Micki King, USA	450.03
1928	Helen Meany, USA	78.62	1976	Jennifer Chandler, USA	506.19
1932	Georgia Coleman, USA	87.52	1980	Irina Kalinina, USSR	725.91
1936	Marjorie Gestring, USA	89.27	1984	Sylvie Bernier, CAN	530.70
1948	Vicki Draves, USA	108.74	1988	Gao Min, CHN	580.23
1952	Pat McCormick, USA	147.30	1992	Gao Min, CHN	572.40
1956	Pat McCormick, USA	142.36	1996	Fu Mingxia, CHN	547.68
1960	Ingrid Krämer, GER	155.81	2000	Fu Mingxia, CHN	609.42
1964	Ingrid Engel-Kräamer, GER	145.00			

Platform

Year		Points	Year		Points
1912	Greta Johansson, SWE	39.9	1964	Lesley Bush, USA	99.80
1920	Stefani Fryland-Clausen, DEN	34.6	1968	Milena Duchková, CZE	109.59
1924	Caroline Smith, USA	33.2	1972	Ulrika Knape, SWE	390.00
1928	Elizabeth Becker Pinkston, USA	31.6	1976	Elena Vaytsekhovskaya, USSR	406.59
1932	Dorothy Poynton, USA	40.26	1980	Martina Jäschke, E. Ger	596.25
1936	Dorothy Poynton Hill, USA	33.93	1984	Zhou Jihong, CHN	435.51
1948	Vicki Draves, USA	68.87	1988	Xu Yanmei, CHN	445.20
1952	Pat McCormick, USA	79.37	1992	Fu Mingxia, CHN	461.43
1956	Pat McCormick, USA	84.85	1996	Fu Mingxia, CHN	521.58
1960	Ingrid Krämer, GER	91.28	2000	Laura Wilkinson, USA	543.75

FIELD HOCKEY

MEN

Multiple gold medals: India (8); Great Britain and Pakistan (3); West Germany/Germany and Netherlands (2).

Year		Year	
1908	**Great Britain**, Ireland, Scotland	1968	**Pakistan**, Australia, India
1920	**Great Britain**, Denmark, Belgium	1972	**West Germany**, Pakistan, India
1928	**India**, Netherlands, Germany	1976	**New Zealand**, Australia, Pakistan
1932	**India**, Japan, United States	1980	**India**, Spain, Soviet Union
1936	**India**, Germany, Netherlands	1984	**Pakistan**, West Germany, Great Britain
1948	**India**, Great Britain, Netherlands	1988	**Great Britain**, West Germany, Netherlands
1952	**India**, Netherlands, Great Britain	1992	**Germany**, Australia, Pakistan
1956	**India**, Pakistan, Germany	1996	**Netherlands**, Spain, Australia
1960	**Pakistan**, India, Spain	2000	**Netherlands**, South Korea, Australia
1964	**India**, Pakistan, Australia		

WOMEN

Multiple gold medals: Australia (3).

Year		Year	
1980	**Zimbabwe**, Czechoslovakia, Soviet Union	1992	**Spain**, Germany, Great Britain
1984	**Netherlands**, West Germany, United States	1996	**Australia**, South Korea, Netherlands
1988	**Australia**, South Korea, Netherlands	2000	**Australia**, Argentina, Netherlands

GYMNASTICS

MEN

At least 4 gold medals (including team events): Sawao Kato (8); Nikolai Andrianov, Viktor Chukarin and Boris Shakhlin (7); Akinori Nakayama and Vitaly Scherbo (6); Yukio Endo, Anton Heida, Mitsuo Tsukahara and Takashi Ono (5); Vladimir Artemov, Georges Miez, Valentin Muratov and Alexei Nemov (4).

All-Around

Year		Points	Year		Points
1900	Gustave Sandras, FRA	302	1956	Viktor Chukarin, USSR	114.25
1904	Julius Lenhart, AUT	69.80	1960	Boris Shakhlin, USSR	115.95
1906	Pierre Payssé, FRA	97.0	1964	Yukio Endo, JPN	115.95
1908	Alberto Braglia, ITA	317.0	1968	Sawao Kato, JPN	115.9
1912	Alberto Braglia, ITA	135.0	1972	Sawao Kato, JPN	114.650
1920	Giorgio Zampori, ITA	88.35	1976	Nikolai Andrianov, USSR	116.65
1924	Leon Stukelj, YUG	110.340	1980	Aleksandr Dityatin, USSR	118.65
1928	Georges Miez, SWI	247.500	1984	Koji Gushiken, JPN	118.7
1932	Romeo Neri, ITA	140.625	1988	Vladimir Artemov, USSR	119.125
1936	Alfred Schwarzmann, GER	113.100	1992	Vitaly Scherbo, UT	59.025
1948	Veikko Huhtanen, FIN	229.7	1996	Li Xiaoshuang, CHN	58.423
1952	Viktor Chukarin, USSR	115.7	2000	Alexei Nemov, RUS	58.474

Horizontal Bar

Year		Points	Year		Points
1896	Hermann Weingärtner, GER	–	1968	(TIE) Akinori Nakayama, JPN	19.55
1904	(TIE) Anton Heida, USA	40		& Mikhail Voronin, USSR	19.55
	& Edward Hennig, USA	40	1972	Mitsuo Tsukahara, JPN	19.725
1924	Leon Stukelj, YUG	19.73	1976	Mitsuo Tsukahara, JPN	19.675
1928	Georges Miez, SWI	19.17	1980	Stoyan Deltchev, BUL	19.825
1932	Dallas Bixler, USA	18.33	1984	Shinji Morisue, JPN	20.00
1936	Aleksanteri Saarvala, FIN	19.367	1988	(TIE) Vladimir Artemov, USSR	19.900
1948	Josef Stalder, SWI	19.85		& Valeri Lyukin, USSR	19.900
1952	Jack Günthard, SWI	19.55	1992	Trent Dimas, USA	9.875
1956	Takashi Ono, JPN	19.60	1996	Andreas Wecker, GER	9.850
1960	Takashi Ono, JPN	19.60	2000	Alexei Nemov, RUS	9.787
1964	Boris Shakhlin, USSR	19.625			

Parallel Bars

Year		Points	Year		Points
1896	Alfred Flatow, GER	–	1964	Yukio Endo, JPN	19.675
1904	George Eyser, USA	44	1968	Akinori Nakayama, JPN	19.475
1924	August Güttinger, SWI	21.63	1972	Sawao Kato, JPN	19.475
1928	Ladislav Vácha, CZE	18.83	1976	Sawao Kato, JPN	19.675
1932	Romeo Neri, ITA	18.97	1980	Aleksandr Tkachyov, USSR	19.775
1936	Konrad Frey, GER	19.067	1984	Bart Conner, USA	19.95
1948	Michael Reusch, SWI	19.75	1988	Vladimir Artemov, USSR	19.925
1952	Hans Eugster, SWI	19.65	1992	Vitaly Scherbo, UT	9.900
1956	Viktor Chukarin, USSR	19.20	1996	Rustam Sharipov, UKR	9.837
1960	Boris Shakhlin, USSR	19.40	2000	Li Xiaopeng, CHN	9.825

Vault

Year		Points	Year		Points
1896	Karl Schumann, GER	–	1964	Haruhiro Yamashita, JPN	19.60
1904	(TIE) George Eyser, USA	36	1968	Mikhail Voronin, USSR	19.00
	& Anton Heida, USA	36	1972	Klaus Köste, E. Ger	18.85
1924	Frank Kriz, USA	9.98	1976	Nikolai Andrianov, USSR	19.45
1928	Eugen Mack, SWI	9.58	1980	Nikolai Andrianov, USSR	19.825
1932	Savino Guglielmetti, ITA	18.03	1984	Lou Yun, CHN	19.95
1936	Alfred Schwarzmann, GER	19.20	1988	Lou Yun, CHN	19.875
1948	Paavo Aaltonen, FIN	19.55	1992	Vitaly Scherbo, UT	9.856
1952	Viktor Chukarin, USSR	19.20	1996	Alexei Nemov, RUS	9.787
1956	(TIE) Helmut Bantz, GER	18.85	2000	Gervasio Deferr, SPA	9.712
	& Valentin Muratov, USSR	18.85			
1960	(TIE) Takashi Ono, JPN	19.35			
	& Boris Shakhlin, USSR	19.35			

Pommel Horse

Year		Points	Year		Points
1896	Louis Zutter, SWI	–	1968	Miroslav Cerar, YUG	19.325
1904	Anton Heida, USA	42	1972	Viktor Klimenko, SOV	19.125
1924	Josef Wilhelm, SWI	21.23	1976	Zoltán Magyar, HUN	19.70
1928	Hermann Hänggi, SWI	19.75	1980	Zoltán Magyar, HUN	19.925
1932	István Pelle, HUN	19.07	1984	(TIE) Li Ning, CHN	19.95
1936	Konrad Frey, GER	19.333		& Peter Vidmar, USA	19.95
1948	(TIE) Paavo Aaltonen, FIN	19.35	1988	(TIE) Dmitri Bilozerchev, USSR,	19.95
	Veikko Huhtanen, FIN	19.35		Zsolt Borkai, HUN	19.95
	& Heikki Savolainen, FIN	19.35		& Lyubomir Geraskov, BUL	19.95
1952	Viktor Chukarin, USSR	19.50	1992	(TIE) Pae Gil-Su, N. Kor	9.925
1956	Boris Shakhlin, USSR	19.25		& Vitaly Scherbo, UT	9.925
1960	(TIE) Eugen Ekman, FIN	19.375	1996	Li Donghua, SWI	9.875
	& Boris Shakhlin, USSR	19.375	2000	Marius Urzica, ROM	9.862
1964	Miroslav Cerar, YUG	19.525			

Rings

Year		Points	Year		Points
1896	Ioannis Mitropoulos, GRE	–	1968	Akinori Nakayama, JPN	19.45
1904	Hermann Glass, USA	45	1972	Akinori Nakayama, JPN	19.35
1924	Francesco Martino, ITA	21.553	1976	Nikolai Andrianov, USSR	19.65
1928	Leon Stukelj, YUG	19.25	1980	Aleksandr Dityatin, USSR	19.875
1932	George Gulack, USA	18.97	1984	(TIE) Koji Gushiken, JPN	19.85
1936	Alois Hudec, CZE	19.433		& Li Ning, CHN	19.85
1948	Karl Frei, SWI	19.80	1988	(TIE) Holger Behrendt, E. Ger	19.925
1952	Grant Shaginyan, USSR	19.75		& Dmitri Bilozerchev, USSR	19.925
1956	Albert Azaryan, USSR	19.35	1992	Vitaly Scherbo, UT	9.937
1960	Albert Azaryan, USSR	19.725	1996	Yuri Chechi, ITA	9.887
1964	Takuji Haytta, JPN	19.475	2000	Szilveszter Csollany, HUN	9.850

Floor Exercise

Year		Points	Year		Points
1932	Istvan Pelle, HUN	9.60	1972	Nikolai Andrianov, USSR	19.175
1936	Georges Miez, SWI	18.666	1976	Nikolai Andrianov, USSR	19.45
1948	Ferenc Pataki, HUN	19.35	1980	Roland Brückner, E. Ger	19.75
1952	William Thoresson, SWE	19.25	1984	Li Ning, CHN	19.925
1956	Valentin Muratov, USSR	19.20	1988	Sergei Kharkov, USSR	19.925
1960	Nobuyuki Aihara, JPN	19.45	1992	Li Xiaosahuang, CHN	9.925
1964	Franco Menichelli, ITA	19.45	1996	Ioannis Melissanidis, GRE	9.850
1968	Sawao Kato, JPN	19.475	2000	Igors Vihrovs, LAT	9.812

Gymnastics (Cont.)
Team Combined Exercises

Year	Points	Year	Points
1904 United States	374.43	1960 Japan	575.20
1906 Norway	19.00	1964 Japan	577.95
1908 Sweden	438	1968 Japan	575.90
1912 Italy	265.75	1972 Japan	571.25
1920 Italy	359.855	1976 Japan	576.85
1924 Italy	839.058	1980 Soviet Union	598.60
1928 Switzerland	1718.625	1984 United States	591.40
1932 Italy	541.850	1988 Soviet Union	593.35
1936 Germany	657.430	1992 Unified Team	585.45
1948 Finland	1358.30	1996 Russia	576.778
1952 Soviet Union	574.40	2000 China	231.919
1956 Soviet Union	568.25		

WOMEN

At least 4 gold medals (including team events): Larissa Latynina (9); Vera Cáslavská (7); Polina Astakhova, Nadia Comaneci, Agnes Keleti and Nelli Kim (5); Olga Korbut, Ecaterina Szabó and Lyudmila Tourischeva (4).

All-Around

Year	Points	Year	Points
1952 Maria Gorokhovskaya, USSR	76.78	1980 Yelena Davydova, USSR	79.15
1956 Larissa Latynina, USSR	74.933	1984 Mary Lou Retton, USA	79.175
1960 Larissa Latynina, USSR	77.031	1988 Yelena Shushunova, USSR	79.662
1964 Vera Cáslavská, CZE	77.564	1992 Tatiana Gutsu, UT	39.737
1968 Vera Cáslavská, CZE	78.25	1996 Lilia Podkopayeva, UKR	39.255
1972 Lyudmila Tourischeva, USSR	77.025	2000 Simona Amanar, ROM*	38.642
1976 Nadia Comaneci, ROM	79.275		

*Amanar finished second to Andreea Raducan, Romania, who was disqualified for testing positive for pseudo-ephedrine, a drug banned by the IOC and found in Nurofen—an over-the-counter medicine she purportedly took to treat a cold.

Vault

Year	Points	Year	Points
1952 Yekaterina Kalinchuk, USSR	19.20	1980 Natalia Shaposhnikova, USSR	19.725
1956 Larissa Latynina, USSR	18.833	1984 Ecaterina Szabó, ROM	19.875
1960 Margarita Nikolayeva, USSR	19.316	1988 Svetlana Boginskaya, USSR	19.905
1964 Vera Cáslavská, CZE	19.483	1992 (TIE) Henrietta Onodi, HUN	9.925
1968 Vera Cáslavská, CZE	19.775	& Lavinia Milosovici, ROM	9.925
1972 Karin Janz, E. Ger	19.525	1996 Simona Amanar, ROM	9.775
1976 Nelli Kim, USSR	19.80	2000 Elena Zamolodtchikova, RUS	9.731

Uneven Bars

Year	Points	Year	Points
1952 Margit Korondi, HUN	19.40	1980 Maxi Gnauck, E. Ger	19.875
1956 Agnes Keleti, HUN	18.966	1984 (TIE) Julianne McNamora, USA	19.95
1960 Polina Astakhova, USSR	19.616	& Ma Yanhong, CHN	19.95
1964 Polina Astakhova, USSR	19.332	1988 Daniela Silivas, ROM	20.00
1968 Vera Cáslavská, CZE	19.65	1992 Lu Li, CHN	10.00
1972 Karin Janz, E. Ger	19.675	1996 Svetlana Khorkina, RUS	9.850
1976 Nadia Comaneci, ROM	20.00	2000 Svetlana Khorkina, RUS	9.862

Balance Beam

Year	Points	Year	Points
1952 Nina Bocharova, USSR	19.22	1980 Nadia Comaneci, ROM	19.80
1956 Agnes Keleti, HUN	18.80	1984 (TIE) Simona Pauca, ROM	19.80
1960 Eva Bosakova, CZE	19.283	& Ecaterina Szabó, ROM	19.80
1964 Vera Cáslavská, CZE	19.449	1988 Daniela Silivas, ROM	19.924
1968 Natalya Kuchinskaya, USSR	19.65	1992 Tatiana Lyssenko, UT	9.975
1972 Olga Korbut, USSR	19.40	1996 Shannon Miller, USA	9.862
1976 Nadia Comaneci, ROM	19.95	2000 Liu Xuan, CHN	9.825

Floor Exercise

Year	Points	Year	Points
1952 Agnes Keleti, HUN	19.36	1976 Nelli Kim, USSR	19.85
1956 (TIE) Agnes Keleti, HUN	18.733	1980 (TIE) Nadia Comaneci, ROM	19.875
& Larissa Latynina, USSR	18.733	& Nelli Kim, USSR	19.875
1960 Larissa Latynina, USSR	19.583	1984 Ecaterina Szabó, ROM	19.975
1964 Larissa Latynina, USSR	19.599	1988 Daniela Silivas, ROM	19.937
1968 (TIE) Vera Cáslavská, CZE	19.675	1992 Lavinia Milosovici, ROM	10.000
& Larissa Petrik, USSR	19.675	1996 Lilia Podkopayeva, UKR	9.887
1972 Olga Korbut, USSR	19.575	2000 Elena Zamolodtchikova, RUS	9.850

Team Combined Exercises

Year		Points	Year		Points
1928	Netherlands	.316.75	1972	Soviet Union	.380.50
1936	Germany	.506.50	1976	Soviet Union	.466.00
1948	Czechoslovakia	.445.45	1980	Soviet Union	.394.90
1952	Soviet Union	.527.03	1984	Romania	.392.02
1956	Soviet Union	.444.800	1988	Soviet Union	.395.475
1960	Soviet Union	.382.320	1992	Unified Team	.395.666
1964	Soviet Union	.280.890	1996	United States	.389.225
1968	Soviet Union	.382.85	2000	Romania	.154.608

SOCCER

MEN

Multiple gold medals: Great Britain and Hungary (3); Uruguay and USSR (2).

Year		Year	
1900	**Great Britain**, France, Belgium	1960	**Yugoslavia**, Denmark, Hungary
1904	**Canada**, USA I, USA II	1964	**Hungary**, Czechoslovakia, Germany
1906	**Denmark**, Smyrna (Int'l entry), Greece	1968	**Hungary**, Bulgaria, Japan
1908	**Great Britain**, Denmark, Netherlands	1972	**Poland**, Hungary, East Germany & Soviet Union
1912	**Great Britain**, Denmark, Netherlands	1976	**East Germany**, Poland, Soviet Union
1920	**Belgium**, Spain, Netherlands	1980	**Czechoslovakia**, East Germany, Soviet Union
1924	**Uruguay**, Switzerland, Sweden	1984	**France**, Brazil, Yugoslavia
1928	**Uruguay**, Argentina, Italy	1988	**Soviet Union**, Brazil, West Germany
1936	**Italy**, Austria, Norway	1992	**Spain**, Poland, Ghana
1948	**Sweden**, Yugoslavia, Denmark	1996	**Nigeria**, Argentina, Brazil
1952	**Hungary**, Yugoslavia, Sweden	2000	**Cameroon**, Spain, Chile
1956	**Soviet Union**, Yugoslavia, Bulgaria		

WOMEN

Year		Year	
1996	**United States**, China, Norway	2000	**Norway**, United States, Germany

SOFTBALL

Multiple gold medals: United States (2).

Year		Year	
1996	**United States**, China, Australia	2000	**United States**, Japan, Australia

U.S. Medal-Winning Softball Teams

1996 (gold medal): P–Lisa Fernandez, Michele Granger, Lori Harrigan and Michele Smith; C–Gillian Boxx and Shelly Stokes; INF–Sheila Cornell, Kim Maher, Leah O'Brien, Dot Richardson, Julie Smith and Dani Tyler; OF–Laura Berg, Dionna Harris; Manager–Ralph Raymond. Final: USA over China, 3-1.

2000 (gold medal): P–Lisa Fernandez, Lori Harrigan, Danielle Henderson, Michele Smith and Christa Williams; C–Stacey Nuveman and Michelle Venturella; INF–Jennifer Brundage, Crystl Bustos, Sheila Douty, Jennifer McFalls and Dot Richardson; OF–Christie Ambrosi, Laura Berg, Leah O'Brien-Amico; Manager–Ralph Raymond. Final: USA over Japan, 2-1.

SWIMMING

World and Olympic records below that appear to be broken or equaled by winning times in subsequent years, but are not so indicated, were all broken in preliminary heats leading up to the finals. Some events were not held at every Olympics.

MEN

At least 4 gold medals (including relays): Mark Spitz (9); Matt Biondi (8); Charles Daniels, Tom Jager, Don Schollander, and Johnny Weissmuller (5); Tamás Darnyi, Gary Hall Jr., Roland Matthes, John Naber, Aleksandr Popov, Murray Rose, Vladimir Salnikov and Henry Taylor (4).

50-meter Freestyle

Year		Time		Year		Time	
1904	Zoltán Halmay, HUN (50 yds)	.28.0		1996	Aleksandr Popov, RUS	.22.13	
1906-84	Not held			2000	(TIE) Anthony Ervin, USA	.21.98	
1988	Matt Biondi, USA	.22.14	**WR**		& Gary Hall Jr., USA	.21.98	
1992	Aleksandr Popov, UT	.21.91	**OR**				

100-meter Freestyle

Year		Time		Year		Time	
1896	Alfréd Hajós, HUN	1:22.2	**OR**	1936	Ferenc Csik, HUN	.57.6	
1904	Zoltán Halmay, HUN (100 yds)	1:02.8		1948	Wally Ris, USA	.57.3	**OR**
1906	Charles Daniels, USA	1:13.4		1952	Clarke Scholes, USA	.57.4	
1908	Charles Daniels, USA	1:05.6	**WR**	1956	Jon Henricks, AUS	.55.4	**OR**
1912	Duke Kahanamoku, USA	1:03.4		1960	John Devitt, AUS	.55.2	**OR**
1920	Duke Kahanamoku, USA	1:00.4	**WR**	1964	Don Schollander, USA	.53.4	**OR**
1924	Johnny Weissmuller, USA	.59.0	**OR**	1968	Michael Wenden, AUS	.52.2	**WR**
1928	Johnny Weissmuller, USA	.58.6	**OR**	1972	Mark Spitz, USA	.51.22	**WR**
1932	Yasuji Miyazaki, JPN	.58.2		1976	Jim Montgomery, USA	.49.99	**WR**

Swimming (Cont.)

Year		Time		Year		Time	
1980	Jorg Woithe, E. Ger	.50.40		1992	Aleksandr Popov, UT	.49.02	
1984	Rowdy Gaines, USA	.49.80	**OR**	1996	Aleksandr Popov, RUS	.48.74	
1988	Matt Biondi, USA	.48.63	**OR**	2000	Pieter van den Hoogenband, NED	.48.30	

200-meter Freestyle

Year		Time		Year		Time	
1900	Frederick Lane, AUS (220 yds)	.2:25.2	**OR**	1984	Michael Gross, W. Ger	1:47.44	**WR**
1904	Charles Daniels, USA (220 yds)	.2:44.2		1988	Duncan Armstrong, AUS	1:47.25	**WR**
1968	Michael Wenden, AUS	1:55.2	**OR**	1992	Yevgeny Sadovyi, UT	1:46.70	**OR**
1972	Mark Spitz, USA	1:52.78	**WR**	1996	Danyon Loader, NZE	1:47.63	
1976	Bruce Furniss, USA	1:50.29	**WR**	2000	Pieter van den Hoogenband, NED	1:45.35	**WR**
1980	Sergei Kopliakov, USSR	1:49.81	**OR**				

400-meter Freestyle

Year		Time		Year		Time	
1896	Paul Neumann, AUT (550m)	8:12.6		1956	Murray Rose, AUS	4:27.3	**OR**
1904	Charles Daniels, USA (440 yds)	.6:16.2		1960	Murray Rose, AUS	4:18.3	**OR**
1906	Otto Scheff, AUT	.6:23.8		1964	Don Schollander, USA	4:12.2	**WR**
1908	Henry Taylor, GBR	5:36.8		1968	Mike Burton, USA	4:09.0	**OR**
1912	George Hodgson, CAN	5:24.4		1972	Bradford Cooper, AUS*	4:00.27	**OR**
1920	Norman Ross, USA	5:26.8		1976	Brian Goodell, USA	3:51.93	**WR**
1924	Johnny Weissmuller, USA	5:04.2	**OR**	1980	Vladimir Salnikov, USSR	3:51.31	**OR**
1928	Alberto Zorilla, ARG	5:01.6	**OR**	1984	George DiCarlo, USA	3:51.23	**OR**
1932	Buster Crabbe, USA	4:48.4	**OR**	1988	Uwe Dassler, E. Ger	3:46.95	**WR**
1936	Jack Medica, USA	4:44.5	**OR**	1992	Yevgeny Sadovyi, UT	3:45.00	**WR**
1948	Bill Smith, USA	4:41.0	**OR**	1996	Danyon Loader, NZE	3:47.97	
1952	Jean Boiteux, FRA	4:30.7	**OR**	2000	Ian Thorpe, AUS	3:40.59	**WR**

*Cooper finished second to Rick DeMont of the U.S., who was disqualified when he flunked the post-race drug test (his asthma medication was on the IOC's banned list).

1500-meter Freestyle

Year		Time		Year		Time	
1896	Alfréd Hajós, HUN (1200m)	18:22.2	**OR**	1956	Murray Rose, AUS	17:58.9	
1900	John Arthur Jarvis, GBR (1000m)	13:40.2		1960	Jon Konrads, AUS	17:19.6	**OR**
1904	Emil Rausch, GER (1 mile)	27:18.2		1964	Robert Windle, AUS	17:01.7	**OR**
1906	Henry Taylor, GBR (1 mile)	28:00.0		1968	Mike Burton, USA	16:38.9	**OR**
1908	Henry Taylor, GBR	22:48.4	**WR**	1972	Mike Burton, USA	15:52.58	**WR**
1912	George Hodgson, CAN	22:00.0	**WR**	1976	Brian Goodell, USA	15:02.40	**WR**
1920	Norman Ross, USA	22:23.2		1980	Vladimir Salnikov, USSR	14:58.27	**WR**
1924	Andrew (Boy) Charlton, AUS	20:06.6	**WR**	1984	Mike O'Brien, USA	15:05.20	
1928	Arne Borge, SWE	19:51.8	**OR**	1988	Vladimir Salnikov, USSR	15:00.40	
1932	Kusuo Kitamura, JPN	19:12.4	**OR**	1992	Kieren Perkins, AUS	14:43.48	**WR**
1936	Noboru Terada, JPN	19:13.7		1996	Kieren Perkins, AUS	14:56.40	
1948	James McLane, USA	19:18.5		2000	Grant Hackett, AUS	14:48.33	
1952	Ford Konno, USA	18:30.3	**OR**				

100-meter Backstroke

Year		Time		Year		Time	
1904	Walter Brack, GER (100 yds)	1:16.8		1960	David Theile, AUS	1:01.9	**OR**
1908	Arno Bieberstein, GER	1:24.6	**WR**	1968	Roland Matthes, E. Ger	.58.7	**OR**
1912	Harry Hebner, USA	1:21.2		1972	Roland Matthes, E. Ger	.56.58	**OR**
1920	Warren Kealoha, USA	1:15.2		1976	John Naber, USA	.55.49	**WR**
1924	Warren Kealoha, USA	1:13.2	**OR**	1980	Bengt Baron, SWE	.56.33	
1928	George Kojac, USA	1:08.2	**WR**	1984	Rick Carey, USA	.55.79	
1932	Masaji Kiyokawa, JPN	1:08.6		1988	Daichi Suzuki, JPN	.55.05	
1936	Adolf Kiefer, USA	1:05.9	**OR**	1992	Mark Tewksbury, CAN	.53.98	**OR**
1948	Allen Stack, USA	1:06.4		1996	Jeff Rouse, USA	.54.10	
1952	Yoshinobu Oyakawa, USA	1:05.4	**OR**	2000	Lenny Krayzelburg, USA	.53.72	**OR**
1956	David Theile, AUS	1:02.2	**OR**				

200-meter Backstroke

Year		Time		Year		Time	
1900	Ernst Hoppenberg, GER	2:47.0		1984	Rick Carey, USA	2:00.23	
1964	Jed Graef, USA	2:10.3	**WR**	1988	Igor Poliansky, USSR	1:59.37	
1968	Roland Matthes, E. Ger	2:09.6	**OR**	1992	Martin Lopez-Zubero, SPA	1:58.47	**OR**
1972	Roland Matthes, E. Ger	2:02.82	**=WR**	1996	Brad Bridgewater, USA	1:58.54	
1976	John Naber, USA	1:59.19	**WR**	2000	Lenny Krayzelburg, USA	1:56.76	**OR**
1980	Sándor Wládar, HUN	2:01.93					

100-meter Breaststroke

Year		Time		Year		Time	
1968	Don McKenzie, USA	1:07.7	OR	1988	Adrian Moorhouse, GBR	1:02.04	
1972	Nobutaka Taguchi, JPN	1:04.94	WR	1992	Nelson Diebel, USA	1:01.50	OR
1976	John Hencken, USA	1:03.11	WR	1996	Fred deBurghgraeve, BEL	1:00.60	
1980	Duncan Goodhew, GBR	1:03.44		2000	Domenico Fioravanti, ITA	1:00.46	OR
1984	Steve Lundquist, USA	1:01.65	WR				

200-meter Breaststroke

Year		Time		Year		Time	
1908	Frederick Holman, GBR	3:09.2	WR	1964	Ian O'Brien, AUS	2:27.8	WR
1912	Walter Bathe, GER	3:01.8	OR	1968	Felipe Muñoz, MEX	2:28.7	
1920	Hakan Malmroth, SWE	3:04.4		1972	John Hencken, USA	2:21.55	WR
1924	Robert Skelton, USA	2:56.6		1976	David Wilkie, GBR	2:15.11	WR
1928	Yoshiyuki Tsuruta, JPN	2:48.8	OR	1980	Robertas Zhulpa, USSR	2:15.85	
1932	Yoshiyuki Tsuruta, JPN	2:45.4		1984	Victor Davis, CAN	2:13.34	WR
1936	Tetsuo Hamuro, JPN	2:41.5	OR	1988	József Szabó, HUN	2:13.52	
1948	Joseph Verdeur, USA	2:39.3	OR	1992	Mike Barrowman, USA	2:10.16	WR
1952	John Davies, AUS	2:34.4	OR	1996	Norbert Rozsa, HUN	2:12.57	
1956	Masaru Furukawa, JPN	2:34.7*	OR	2000	Domenico Fioravanti, ITA	2:10.87	
1960	Bill Mulliken, USA	2:37.4					

*In 1956, the butterfly stroke and breaststroke were separated into two different events.

100-meter Butterfly

Year		Time		Year		Time	
1968	Doug Russell, USA	55.9	OR	1988	Anthony Nesty, SUR	53.0	OR
1972	Mark Spitz, USA	54.27	WR	1992	Pablo Morales, USA	53.32	
1976	Matt Vogel, USA	54.35		1996	Dennis Pankratov, RUS	52.27	
1980	Pär Arvidsson, SWE	54.92		2000	Lars Frolander, SWE	52.00	
1984	Michael Gross, W. Ger	53.08	WR				

200-meter Butterfly

Year		Time		Year		Time	
1956	Bill Yorzyk, USA	2:19.3	OR	1980	Sergei Fesenko, USSR	1:59.76	
1960	Mike Troy, USA	2:12.8	WR	1984	Jon Sieben, AUS	1:57.04	WR
1964	Kevin Berry, AUS	2:06.6	WR	1988	Michael Gross, W. Ger	1:56.94	OR
1968	Carl Robie, USA	2:08.7		1992	Melvin Stewart, USA	1:56.26	OR
1972	Mark Spitz, USA	2:00.70	WR	1996	Dennis Pankratov, RUS	1:56.51	
1976	Mike Bruner, USA	1:59.23	WR	2000	Tom Malchow, USA	1:55.35	OR

200-meter Individual Medley

Year		Time		Year		Time	
1968	Charles Hickcox, USA	2:12.0	OR	1992	Tamás Darnyi, HUN	2:00.76	
1972	Gunnar Larsson, SWE	2:07.17	WR	1996	Attila Czene, HUN	1:59.91	
1984	Alex Baumann, CAN	2:01.42	WR	2000	Massimiliano Rosolino, ITA	1:58.98	OR
1988	Tamás Darnyi, HUN	2:00.17	WR				

400-meter Individual Medley

Year		Time		Year		Time	
1964	Richard Roth, USA	4:45.4	WR	1984	Alex Baumann, CAN	4:17.41	WR
1968	Charles Hickcox, USA	4:48.4		1988	Tamás Darnyi, HUN	4:14.75	WR
1972	Gunnar Larsson, SWE	4:31.98	OR	1992	Tamás Darnyi, HUN	4:14.23	OR
1976	Rod Strachan, USA	4:23.68	WR	1996	Tom Dolan, USA	4:14.90	
1980	Aleksandr Sidorenko, USSR	4:22.89	OR	2000	Tom Dolan, USA	4:11.76	WR

4x100-meter Freestyle Relay

Year		Time		Year		Time	
1964	United States	3:32.2	WR	1988	United States	3:16.53	WR
1968	United States	3:31.7	WR	1992	United States	3:16.74	
1972	United States	3:26.42	WR	1996	United States	3:15.41	
1976-80 Not held				2000	Australia	3:13.67	WR
1984	United States	3:19.03	WR				

4x200-meter Freestyle Relay

Year		Time		Year		Time	
1906	Hungary (x250m)	16:52.4		1948	United States	8:46.0	WR
1908	Great Britain	10:55.6	WR	1952	United States	8:31.1	OR
1912	Australia/New Zealand	10:11.6	WR	1956	Australia	8:23.6	WR
1920	United States	10:04.4	WR	1960	United States	8:10.2	WR
1924	United States	9:53.4	WR	1964	United States	7:52.1	WR
1928	United States	9:36.2	WR	1968	United States	7:52.33	
1932	Japan	8:58.4	WR	1972	United States	7:35.78	WR
1936	Japan	8:51.5	WR	1976	United States	7:23.22	WR

Swimming (Cont.)

Year		Time		Year		Time	
1980	Soviet Union	7:23.50		1992	Unified Team	7:11.95	WR
1984	United States	7:15.69	WR	1996	United States	7:14.84	
1988	United States	7:12.51	WR	2000	Australia	7:07.05	WR

4x100-meter Medley Relay

Year		Time		Year		Time	
1960	United States	4:05.4	WR	1984	United States	3:39.30	WR
1964	United States	3:58.4	WR	1988	United States	3:36.93	WR
1968	United States	3:54.9	WR	1992	United States	3:36.93	=WR
1972	United States	3:48.16	WR	1996	United States	3:34.84	
1976	United States	3:42.22	WR	2000	United States	3:33.73	WR
1980	Australia	3:45.70					

WOMEN

At least 4 gold medals (including relays): Jenny Thompson (8); Kristin Otto and Amy Van Dyken (6); Krisztina Egerszegi (5), Kornelia Ender, Janet Evans, Dawn Fraser and Dara Torres (4).

50-meter Freestyle

Year		Time		Year		Time	
1988	Kristin Otto, E. Ger	25.49	OR	1996	Amy Van Dyken, USA	24.87	
1992	Yang Wenyi, CHN	24.79	WR	2000	Inge de Bruijn, NED	24.32	

100-meter Freestyle

Year		Time		Year		Time	
1912	Fanny Durack, AUS	1:22.2		1968	Jan Henne, USA	1:00.0	
1920	Ethelda Bleibtrey, USA	1:13.6	WR	1972	Sandra Neilson, USA	58.59	OR
1924	Ethel Lackie, USA	1:12.4		1976	Kornelia Ender, E. Ger	55.65	WR
1928	Albina Osipowich, USA	1:11.0	OR	1980	Barbara Krause, E. Ger	54.79	WR
1932	Helene Madison, USA	1:06.8	OR	1984	(TIE) Nancy Hogshead, USA	55.92	
1936	Rie Mastenbroek, NED	1:05.9	OR		& Carrie Steinseifer, USA	55.92	
1948	Greta Andersen, DEN	1:06.3		1988	Kristin Otto, E. Ger	54.93	
1952	Katalin Szöke, HUN	1:06.8		1992	Zhuang Yong, CHN	54.65	OR
1956	Dawn Fraser, AUS	1:02.0	WR	1996	Le Jingyi, CHN	54.50	
1960	Dawn Fraser, AUS	1:01.2	OR	2000	Inge de Bruijn, NED	53.83	
1964	Dawn Fraser, AUS	59.5	OR				

200-meter Freestyle

Year		Time		Year		Time	
1968	Debbie Meyer, USA	2:10.5	OR	1988	Heike Friedrich, E. Ger	1:57.65	OR
1972	Shane Gould, AUS	2:03.56	WR	1992	Nicole Haislett, USA	1:57.90	
1976	Kornelia Ender, E. Ger	1:59.26	WR	1996	Claudia Poll, CRC	1:58.16	
1980	Barbara Krause, E. Ger	1:58.33	OR	2000	Susie O'Neill, AUS	1:58.24	
1984	Mary Wayte, USA	1:59.23					

400-meter Freestyle

Year		Time		Year		Time	
1920	Ethelda Bleibtrey, USA (300m)	4:34.0	WR	1968	Debbie Meyer, USA	4:31.8	OR
1924	Martha Norelius, USA	6:02.2	OR	1972	Shane Gould, AUS	4:19.44	WR
1928	Martha Norelius, USA	5:42.8	WR	1976	Petra Thümer, E. Ger	4:09.89	WR
1932	Helene Madison, USA	5:28.5	WR	1980	Ines Diers, E. Ger	4:08.76	OR
1936	Rie Mastenbroek, NED	5:26.4	OR	1984	Tiffany Cohen, USA	4:07.10	OR
1948	Ann Curtis, USA	5:17.8	OR	1988	Janet Evans, USA	4:03.85	WR
1952	Valéria Gyenge, HUN	5:12.1	OR	1992	Dagmar Hase, GER	4:07.18	
1956	Lorraine Crapp, AUS	4:54.6	OR	1996	Michelle Smith, IRE	4:07.25	
1960	Chris von Saltza, USA	4:50.6	OR	2000	Brooke Bennett, USA	4:05.80	
1964	Ginny Duenkel, USA	4:43.3	OR				

800-meter Freestyle

Year		Time		Year		Time	
1968	Debbie Meyer, USA	9:24.0	OR	1988	Janet Evans, USA	8:20.20	OR
1972	Keena Rothhammer, USA	8:53.68	WR	1992	Janet Evans, USA	8:25.52	
1976	Petra Thümer, E. Ger	8:37.14	WR	1996	Brooke Bennett, USA	8:27.89	
1980	Michelle Ford, AUS	8:28.90	OR	2000	Brooke Bennett, USA	8:19.67	OR
1984	Tiffany Cohen, USA	8:24.95	OR				

100-meter Backstroke

Year		Time		Year		Time	
1924	Sybil Bauer, USA	1:23.2	OR	1968	Kaye Hall, USA	1:06.2	WR
1928	Maria Braun, NED	1:22.0		1972	Melissa Belote, USA	1:05.78	OR
1932	Eleanor Holm, USA	1:19.4		1976	Ulrike Richter, E. Ger	1:01.83	OR
1936	Dina Senff, NED	1:18.9		1980	Rica Reinisch, E. Ger	1:00.86	WR
1948	Karen-Margrete Harup, DEN	1:14.4	OR	1984	Theresa Andrews, USA	1:02.55	
1952	Joan Harrison, S. Afr.	1:14.3		1988	Kristin Otto, E. Ger	1:00.89	
1956	Judy Grinham, GBR	1:12.9	OR	1992	Krisztina Egerszegi, HUN	1:00.68	OR
1960	Lynn Burke, USA	1:09.3	OR	1996	Beth Botsford, USA	1:01.19	
1964	Cathy Ferguson, USA	1:07.7	WR	2000	Diana Mocanu, ROM	1:00.21	OR

200-meter Backstroke

Year		Time		Year		Time	
1968	Pokey Watson, USA	2:24.8	OR	1988	Krisztina Egerszegi, HUN	2:09.29	OR
1972	Melissa Belote, USA	2:19.19	WR	1992	Krisztina Egerszegi, HUN	2:07.06	OR
1976	Ulrike Richter, E. Ger	2:13.43	OR	1996	Krisztina Egerszegi, HUN	2:07.83	
1980	Rica Reinisch, E. Ger	2:11.77	WR	2000	Diana Mocanu, ROM	2:08.16	
1984	Jolanda de Rover, NED	2:12.38					

100-meter Breaststroke

Year		Time		Year		Time	
1968	Djurdjica Bjedov, YUG	1:15.8	OR	1988	Tania Dangalakova, BUL	1:07.95	OR
1972	Cathy Carr, USA	1:13.58	WR	1992	Yelena Rudkovskaya, UT	1:08.00	
1976	Hannelore Anke, E. Ger	1:11.16		1996	Penny Heyns, RSA	1:07.73	
1980	Ute Geweniger, E. Ger	1:10.22		2000	Megan Quann, USA	1:07.05	
1984	Petra van Staveren, NED	1:09.88	OR				

200-meter Breaststroke

Year		Time		Year		Time	
1924	Lucy Morton, GBR	3:33.2	OR	1968	Sharon Wichman, USA	2:44.4	OR
1928	Hilde Schrader, GER	3:12.6		1972	Beverley Whitfield, AUS	2:41.71	OR
1932	Clare Dennis, AUS	3:06.3	OR	1976	Marina Koshevaya, USSR	2:33.35	WR
1936	Hideko Maehata, JPN	3:03.6		1980	Lina Kaciusyte, USSR	2:29.54	OR
1948	Petronella van Vliet, NED	2:57.2		1984	Anne Ottenbrite, CAN	2:30.38	
1952	Éva Székely, HUN	2:51.7	OR	1988	Silke Hörner, E. Ger	2:26.71	WR
1956	Ursula Happe, GER	2:53.1	OR	1992	Kyoko Iwasaki, JPN	2:26.65	OR
1960	Anita Lonsbrough, GBR	2:49.5	WR	1996	Penny Heyns, RSA	2:25.41	
1964	Galina Prozumenshikova, USSR	2:46.4	OR	2000	Agnes Kovacs, HUN	2:24.35	

100-meter Butterfly

Year		Time		Year		Time	
1956	Shelly Mann, USA	1:11.0	OR	1980	Caren Metschuck, E. Ger	1:00.42	
1960	Carolyn Schuler, USA	1:09.5	OR	1984	Mary T. Meagher, USA	.59.26	
1964	Sharon Stouder, USA	1:04.7	WR	1988	Kristin Otto, E. Ger	.59.00	OR
1968	Lynn McClements, AUS	1:05.5		1992	Qian Hong, CHN	.58.62	OR
1972	Mayumi Aoki, JPN	1:03.34	WR	1996	Amy Van Dyken, USA	.59.13	
1976	Kornelia Ender, E. Ger	1:00.13	=WR	2000	Inge de Bruijn, NED	.56.61	WR

200-meter Butterfly

Year		Time		Year		Time	
1968	Ada Kok, NED	2:24.7	OR	1988	Kathleen Nord, E. Ger	2:09.51	
1972	Karen Moe, USA	2:15.57	WR	1992	Summer Sanders, USA	2:08.67	
1976	Andrea Pollack, E. Ger	2:11.41	OR	1996	Susie O'Neill, AUS	2:07.76	
1980	Ines Geissler, E. Ger	2:10.44	OR	2000	Misty Hyman, USA	2:05.88	OR
1984	Mary T. Meagher, USA	2:06.90	OR				

200-meter Individual Medley

Year		Time		Year		Time	
1968	Claudia Kolb, USA	2:24.7	OR	1992	Lin Li, CHN	2:11.65	WR
1972	Shane Gould, AUS	2:23.07	WR	1996	Michelle Smith, IRE	2:13.93	
1984	Tracy Caulkins, USA	2:12.64	OR	2000	Yana Klochkova, UKR	2:10.68	OR
1988	Daniela Hunger, E. Ger	2:12.59	OR				

400-meter Individual Medley

Year		Time		Year		Time	
1964	Donna de Varona, USA	5:18.7	OR	1984	Tracy Caulkins, USA	4:39.24	
1968	Claudia Kolb, USA	5:08.5	OR	1988	Janet Evans, USA	4:37.76	
1972	Gail Neall, AUS	5:02.97	WR	1992	Krisztina Egerszegi, HUN	4:36.54	
1976	Ulrike Tauber, E. Ger	4:42.77	WR	1996	Michelle Smith, IRE	4:39.18	
1980	Petra Schneider, E. Ger	4:36.29	WR	2000	Yana Klochkova, UKR	4:33.59	WR

4x100-meter Freestyle Relay

Year		Time		Year		Time	
1912	Great Britain	5:52.8	WR	1964	United States	4:03.8	WR
1920	United States	5:11.6	WR	1968	United States	4:02.5	OR
1924	United States	4:58.8	WR	1972	United States	3:55.19	WR
1928	United States	4:47.6	WR	1976	United States	3:44.82	WR
1932	United States	4:38.0	WR	1980	East Germany	3:42.71	WR
1936	Netherlands	4:36.0	OR	1984	United States	3:43.43	
1948	United States	4:29.2	OR	1988	East Germany	3:40.63	OR
1952	Hungary	4:24.4	WR	1992	United States	3:39.46	WR
1956	Australia	4:17.1	WR	1996	United States	3:39.29	
1960	United States	4:08.9	WR	2000	United States	3:36.61	WR

4x200-meter Freestyle Relay

Year		Time		Year		Time	
1996	United States	7:59.87		2000	United States	7:57.80	OR

Swimming (Cont.)
4x100-meter Medley Relay

Year		Time		Year		Time	
1960	United States	4:41.1	WR	1984	United States	4:08.34	
1964	United States	4:33.9	WR	1988	East Germany	4:03.74	OR
1968	United States	4:28.3	OR	1992	United States	4:02.54	WR
1972	United States	4:20.75	WR	1996	United States	4:02.88	
1976	East Germany	4:07.95	WR	2000	United States	3:58.30	WR
1980	East Germany	4:06.67	WR				

TENNIS

MEN

Multiple gold medals (including men's doubles): John Boland, Max Decugis, Laurie Doherty, Reggie Doherty, Arthur Gore, Andre Grobert, Vincent Richards, Charles Winslow and Beals Wright (2).

Singles

Year			Year		
1896	John Boland	Great Britain/Ireland	1920	Louis Raymond	South Africa
1900	Laurie Doherty,	Great Britain	1924	Vincent Richards	United States
1904	Beals Wright	United States	1928-84	Not held	
1906	Max Decugis	France	1988	Miloslav Mecir	Czechoslovakia
1908	Josiah Ritchie	Great Britain	1992	Marc Rosset	Switzerland
	(Indoor) Arthur Gore	Great Britain	1996	Andre Agassi	United States
1912	Charles Winslow	South Africa	2000	Yevgeny Kafelnikov	Russia
	(Indoor) André Gobert	France			

Doubles

Year		Year	
1896	John Boland, IRE & Fritz Traun, GER	1920	Noel Turnbull & Max Woosnam, GBR
1900	Laurie and Reggie Doherty, GBR	1924	Vincent Richards & Frank Hunter, USA
1904	Edgar Leonard & Beals Wright, USA	1928-84	Not held
1906	Max Decugis & Maurice Germot, FRA	1988	Ken Flach & Robert Seguso, USA
1908	George Hillyard & Reggie Doherty, GBR	1992	Boris Becker & Michael Stich, GER
	(Indoor) Arthur Gore & Herbert Barrett, GBR	1996	Todd Woodbridge & Mark Woodforde, AUS
1912	Charles Winslow & Harold Kitson, S. Afr.	2000	Sebastien Lareau & Daniel Nestor, CAN
	(Indoor) Andre Gobert & Maurice Germot, FRA		

WOMEN

Multiple gold medals (including women's doubles): Helen Wills, Gigi Fernandez, Mary Joe Fernandez and Venus Williams (2).

Singles

Year			Year		
1900	Charlotte Cooper	Great Britain	1924	Helen Wills	United States
1906	Esmee Simiriotou	Greece	1928-84	Not held	
1908	Dorothea Chambers	Great Britain	1988	Steffi Graf	West Germany
	(Indoor) Gwen Eastlake-Smith	Great Britain	1992	Jennifer Capriati	United States
1912	Marguerite Broquedis	France	1996	Lindsay Davenport	United States
	(Indoor) Edith Hannam	Great Britain	2000	Venus Williams	United States
1920	Suzanne Lenglen	France			

Doubles

Year		Year	
1920	Winifred McNair & Kitty McKane, GBR	1992	Gigi Fernandez & Mary Joe Fernandez, USA
1924	Hazel Wightman & Helen Wills, USA	1996	Gigi Fernandez & Mary Joe Fernandez, USA
1928-84	Not held	2000	Serena Williams & Venus Williams, USA
1988	Pam Shriver & Zina Garrison, USA		

TRACK & FIELD

World and Olympic records below that appear to be broken or equaled by winning times, heights and distances in subsequent years, but are not so indicated, were all broken in preliminary races and field events leading up to the finals.

MEN

At least 4 gold medals (including relays and discontinued events): Ray Ewry (10); Carl Lewis and Paavo Nurmi (9); Ville Ritola and Martin Sheridan (5); Harrison Dillard, Archie Hahn, Michael Johnson, Hannes Kolehmainen, Alvin Kraenzlein, Eric Lemming, Jim Lightbody, Al Oerter, Jesse Owens, Meyer Prinstein, Mel Sheppard, Lasse Viren and Emil Zátopek (4). Note that all of Ewry's gold medals came before 1912, in the Standing High Jump, Standing Long Jump and Standing Triple Jump.

100 meters

Year		Time		Year		Time	
1896	Tom Burke, USA	12.0		1920	Charley Paddock, USA	10.8	
1900	Frank Jarvis, USA	11.0		1924	Harold Abrahams, GBR	10.6	=OR
1904	Archie Hahn, USA	11.0		1928	Percy Williams, CAN	10.8	
1906	Archie Hahn, USA	11.2		1932	Eddie Tolan, USA	10.3	OR
1908	Reggie Walker, S. Afr.	10.8	=OR	1936	Jesse Owens, USA	10.3ʷ	
1912	Ralph Craig, USA	10.8		1948	Harrison Dillard, USA	10.3	=OR

Year		Time		Year		Time	
1952	Lindy Remigino, USA	10.4		1980	Allan Wells, GBR	10.25	
1956	Bobby Morrow, USA	10.5		1984	Carl Lewis, USA	9.99	
1960	Armin Hary, GER	10.2	OR	1988	Carl Lewis, USA*	9.92	WR
1964	Bob Hayes, USA	10.0	=WR	1992	Linford Christie, GBR	9.96	
1968	Jim Hines, USA	9.95	WR	1996	Donovan Bailey, CAN	9.84	WR
1972	Valery Borzov, USSR	10.14		2000	Maurice Greene, USA	9.87	
1976	Hasely Crawford, TRI	10.06					

ᵂindicates wind-aided.

*Lewis finished second to Ben Johnson of Canada, who set a world record of 9.79 seconds. Two days later, Johnson was stripped of his gold medal and his record when he tested positive for steroid use in a post-race drug test.

200 meters

Year		Time		Year		Time	
1900	Walter Tewksbury, USA	22.2		1960	Livio Berruti, ITA	20.5	=WR
1904	Archie Hahn, USA	21.6	OR	1964	Henry Carr, USA	20.3	OR
1908	Bobby Kerr, CAN	22.6		1968	Tommie Smith, USA	19.83	WR
1912	Ralph Craig, USA	21.7		1972	Valery Borzov, USSR	20.00	
1920	Allen Woodring, USA	22.0		1976	Donald Quarrie, JAM	20.23	
1924	Jackson Scholz, USA	21.6		1980	Pietro Mennea, ITA	20.19	
1928	Percy Williams, CAN	21.8		1984	Carl Lewis, USA	19.80	OR
1932	Eddie Tolan, USA	21.2	OR	1988	Joe DeLoach, USA	19.75	OR
1936	Jesse Owens, USA	20.7	⌣ OR	1992	Mike Marsh, USA	20.01	
1948	Mel Patton, USA	21.1		1996	Michael Johnson, USA	19.32	WR
1952	Andy Stanfield, USA	20.7		2000	Konstantinos Kenteris, GRE	20.09	
1956	Bobby Morrow, USA	20.6	OR				

400 meters

Year		Time		Year		Time	
1896	Tom Burke, USA	54.2		1956	Charley Jenkins, USA	46.7	
1900	Maxey Long, USA	49.4	OR	1960	Otis Davis, USA	44.9	WR
1904	Harry Hillman, USA	49.2	OR	1964	Mike Larrabee, USA	45.1	
1906	Paul Pilgrim, USA	53.2		1968	Lee Evans, USA	43.86	WR
1908	Wyndham Halswelle, GBR	50.0		1972	Vince Matthews, USA	44.66	
1912	Charlie Reidpath, USA	48.2	OR	1976	Alberto Juantorena, CUB	44.26	
1920	Bevil Rudd, S. Afr.	49.6		1980	Viktor Markin, USSR	44.60	
1924	Eric Liddell, GBR	47.6	OR	1984	Alonzo Babers, USA	44.27	
1928	Ray Barbuti, USA	47.8		1988	Steve Lewis, USA	43.87	
1932	Bill Carr, USA	46.2	WR	1992	Quincy Watts, USA	43.50	OR
1936	Archie Williams, USA	46.5		1996	Michael Johnson, USA	43.49	OR
1948	Arthur Wint, JAM	46.2		2000	Michael Johnson, USA	43.84	
1952	George Rhoden, JAM	45.9	OR				

800 meters

Year		Time		Year		Time	
1896	Teddy Flack, AUS	2:11.0		1956	Tom Courtney, USA	1:47.7	OR
1900	Alfred Tysoe, GBR	2:01.2		1960	Peter Snell, NZE	1:46.3	OR
1904	Jim Lightbody, USA	1:56.0	OR	1964	Peter Snell, NZE	1:45.1	OR
1906	Paul Pilgrim, USA	2:01.5		1968	Ralph Doubell, AUS	1:44.3	=WR
1908	Mel Sheppard, USA	1:52.8	WR	1972	Dave Wottle, USA	1:45.9	
1912	Ted Meredith, USA	1:51.9	WR	1976	Alberto Juantorena, CUB	1:43.50	WR
1920	Albert Hill, GBR	1:53.4		1980	Steve Ovett, GBR	1:45.4	
1924	Douglas Lowe, GBR	1:52.4		1984	Joaquim Cruz, BRA	1:43.00	OR
1928	Douglas Lowe, GBR	1:51.8	OR	1988	Paul Ereng, KEN	1:43.45	
1932	Tommy Hampson, GBR	1:49.7	WR	1992	William Tanui, KEN	1:43.66	
1936	John Woodruff, USA	1:52.9		1996	Vebjoern Rodal, NOR	1:42.58	OR
1948	Mal Whitfield, USA	1:49.2	OR	2000	Nils Schumann, GER	1:45.08	
1952	Mal Whitfield, USA	1:49.2	=OR				

1500 meters

Year		Time		Year		Time	
1896	Teddy Flack, AUS	4:33.2		1956	Ron Delany, IRE	3:41.2	OR
1900	Charles Bennett, GBR	4:06.2	WR	1960	Herb Elliott, AUS	3:35.6	WR
1904	Jim Lightbody, USA	4:05.4	WR	1964	Peter Snell, NZE	3:38.1	
1906	Jim Lightbody, USA	4:12.0		1968	Kip Keino, KEN	3:34.9	OR
1908	Mel Sheppard, USA	4:03.4	OR	1972	Pekka Vasala, FIN	3:36.3	
1912	Arnold Jackson, GBR	3:56.8	OR	1976	John Walker, NZE	3:39.17	
1920	Albert Hill, GBR	4:01.8		1980	Sebastian Coe, GBR	3:38.4	
1924	Paavo Nurmi, FIN	3:53.6	OR	1984	Sebastian Coe, GBR	3:32.53	OR
1928	Harry Larva, FIN	3:53.2	OR	1988	Peter Rono, KEN	3:35.96	
1932	Luigi Beccali, ITA	3:51.2	OR	1992	Fermin Cacho, SPA	3:40.12	
1936	John Lovelock, NZE	3:47.8	WR	1996	Noureddine Morceli, ALG	3:35.78	
1948	Henry Eriksson, SWE	3:49.8		2000	Noah Ngeny, KEN	3:32.07	OR
1952	Josy Barthel, LUX	3:45.1	OR				

Track & Field (Cont.)

5000 meters

Year		Time		Year		Time	
1912	Hannes Kolehmainen, FIN	14:36.6	WR	1964	Bob Schul, USA	13:48.8	
1920	Joseph Guillemot, FRA	14:55.6		1968	Mohamed Gammoudi, TUN	14:05.0	
1924	Paavo Nurmi, FIN	14:31.2	OR	1972	Lasse Viren, FIN	13:26.4	OR
1928	Ville Ritola, FIN	14:38.0		1976	Lasse Viren, FIN	13:24.76	
1932	Lauri Lehtinen, FIN	14:30.0	OR	1980	Miruts Yifter, ETH	13:21.0	
1936	Gunnar Höckert, FIN	14:22.2	OR	1984	Said Aouita, MOR	13:05.59	OR
1948	Gaston Reiff, BEL	14:17.6	OR	1988	John Ngugi, KEN	13:11.70	
1952	Emil Zátopek, CZE	14:06.6	OR	1992	Dieter Baumann, GER	13:12.52	
1956	Vladimir Kuts, USSR	13:39.6	OR	1996	Venuste Niyongabo, BUR	13:07.96	
1960	Murray Halberg, NZE	13:43.4		2000	Millon Wolde, ETH	13:35.49	

10,000 meters

Year		Time		Year		Time	
1912	Hannes Kolehmainen, FIN	31:20.8		1964	Billy Mills, USA	28:24.4	OR
1920	Paavo Nurmi, FIN	31:45.8		1968	Naftali Temu, KEN	29:27.4	
1924	Ville Ritola, FIN	30:23.2	WR	1972	Lasse Viren, FIN	27:38.4	WR
1928	Paavo Nurmi, FIN	30:18.8	OR	1976	Lasse Viren, FIN	27:40.38	
1932	Janusz Kusocinski, POL	30:11.4	OR	1980	Miruts Yifter, ETH	27:42.7	
1936	Ilmari Salminen, FIN	30:15.4		1984	Alberto Cova, ITA	27:47.54	
1948	Emil Zátopek, CZE	29:59.6	OR	1988	Brahim Boutaib, MOR	27:21.46	OR
1952	Emil Zátopek, CZE	29:17.0	OR	1992	Khalid Skah, MOR	27:46.70	
1956	Vladimir Kuts, USSR	28:45.6	OR	1996	Haile Gebrselassie, ETH	27:07.34	OR
1960	Pyotr Bolotnikov, USSR	28:32.2	OR	2000	Haile Gebrselassie, ETH	27:18.20	

Marathon

Year		Time		Year		Time	
1896	Spiridon Louis, GRE	2:58:50		1956	Alain Mimoun, FRA	2:25:00.0	
1900	Michel Théato, FRA	2:59:45		1960	Abebe Bikila, ETH	2:15:16.2	WB
1904	Thomas Hicks, USA	3:28:53		1964	Abebe Bikila, ETH	2:12:11.2	WB
1906	Billy Sherring, CAN	2:51:23.6		1968	Mamo Wolde, ETH	2:20:26.4	
1908	Johnny Hayes, USA*	2:55:18.4	OR	1972	Frank Shorter, USA	2:12:19.8	
1912	Kenneth McArthur, S. Afr.	2:36:54.8		1976	Waldemar Cierpinski, E. Ger	2:09:55.0	OR
1920	Hannes Kolehmainen, FIN	2:32:35.8	WB	1980	Waldemar Cierpinski, E. Ger	2:11:03.0	
1924	Albin Stenroos, FIN	2:41:22.6		1984	Carlos Lopes, POR	2:09:21.0	OR
1928	Boughèra El Ouafi, FRA	2:32:57.0		1988	Gelindo Bordin, ITA	2:10:32	
1932	Juan Carlos Zabala, ARG	2:31:36.0	OR	1992	Hwang Young-Cho, S. Kor	2:13:23	
1936	Sohn Kee-Chung, JPN†	2:29:19.2	OR	1996	Josia Thugwane, RSA	2:12:36	
1948	Delfo Cabrera, ARG	2:34:51.6		2000	Gezahenge Abera, ETH	2:10.11	
1952	Emil Zátopek, CZE	2:23:03.2	OR				

*Dorando Pietri of Italy placed first, but was disqualified for being helped across the finish line.

†Sohn was a Korean, but he was forced to compete under the name Kitei Son by Japan, which occupied Korea at the time.

Note: Marathon distances—40,000 meters (1896,1904); 40,260 meters (1900); 41,860 meters (1906); 42,195 meters (1908 and since 1924); 40,200 meters (1912); 42,750 meters (1920). Current distance of 42,195 meters measures 26 miles, 385 yards.

110-meter Hurdles

Year		Time		Year		Time	
1896	Tom Curtis, USA	17.6		1956	Lee Calhoun, USA	13.5	OR
1900	Alvin Kraenzlein, USA	15.4	OR	1960	Lee Calhoun, USA	13.8	
1904	Frederick Schule, USA	16.0		1964	Hayes Jones, USA	13.6	
1906	Robert Leavitt, USA	16.2		1968	Willie Davenport, USA	13.3	OR
1908	Forrest Smithson, USA	15.0	WR	1972	Rod Milburn, USA	13.24	=WR
1912	Frederick Kelly, USA	15.1		1976	Guy Drut, FRA	13.30	
1920	Earl Thomson, CAN	14.8	WR	1980	Thomas Munkelt, E. Ger	13.39	
1924	Daniel Kinsey, USA	15.0		1984	Roger Kingdom, USA	13.20	OR
1928	Syd Atkinson, S. Afr.	14.8		1988	Roger Kingdom, USA	12.98	OR
1932	George Saling, USA	14.6		1992	Mark McKoy, CAN	13.12	
1936	Forrest (Spec) Towns, USA	14.2		1996	Allen Johnson, USA	12.95	OR
1948	William Porter, USA	13.9	OR	2000	Anier Garcia, CUB	13.00	
1952	Harrison Dillard, USA	13.7	OR				

400-meter Hurdles

Year		Time		Year		Time	
1900	Walter Tewksbury, USA	57.6		1960	Glenn Davis, USA	49.3	OR
1904	Harry Hillman, USA	53.0		1964	Rex Cawley, USA	49.6	
1908	Charley Bacon, USA	55.0	WR	1968	David Hemery, GBR	48.12	WR
1920	Frank Loomis, USA	54.0	WR	1972	John Akii-Bua, UGA	47.82	WR
1924	Morgan Taylor, USA	52.6		1976	Edwin Moses, USA	47.64	WR
1928	David Burghley, GBR	53.4	OR	1980	Volker Beck, E. Ger	48.70	
1932	Bob Tisdall, IRE	51.7		1984	Edwin Moses, USA	47.75	
1936	Glenn Hardin, USA	52.4		1988	Andre Phillips, USA	47.19	OR
1948	Roy Cochran, USA	51.1	OR	1992	Kevin Young, USA	46.78	WR
1952	Charley Moore, USA	50.8	OR	1996	Derrick Adkins, USA	47.54	
1956	Glenn Davis, USA	50.1	=OR	2000	Angelo Taylor, USA	47.50	

3000-meter Steeplechase

Year		Time		Year		Time	
1900	George Orton, CAN	7:34.4		1960	Zdzislaw Krzyszkowiak, POL	8:34.2	OR
1904	Jim Lightbody, USA	7:39.6		1964	Gaston Roelants, BEL	8:30.8	OR
1908	Arthur Russell, GBR	10:47.8		1968	Amos Biwott, KEN	8:51.0	
1920	Percy Hodge, GBR	10:00.4	OR	1972	Kip Keino, KEN	8:23.6	OR
1924	Ville Ritola, FIN	9:33.6	OR	1976	Anders Gärderud, SWE	8:08.2	WR
1928	Toivo Loukola, FIN	9:21.8	WR	1980	Bronislaw Malinowski, POL	8:09.7	
1932	Volmari Iso-Hollo, FIN	10:33.4*		1984	Julius Korir, KEN	8:11.80	
1936	Volmari Iso-Hollo, FIN	9:03.8	WR	1988	Julius Kariuki, KEN	8:05.51	OR
1948	Thore Sjöstrand, SWE	9:04.6		1992	Matthew Birir, KEN	8:08.84	
1952	Horace Ashenfelter, USA	8:45.4	WR	1996	Joseph Keter, KEN	8:07.12	
1956	Chris Brasher, GBR	8:41.2	OR	2000	Reuben Kosgei, KEN	8:21.43	

*Iso-Hollo ran one extra lap due to lap counter's mistake.
Note: Other steeplechase distances– 2500 meters (1900); 2590 meters (1904); 3200 meters (1908) and 3460 meters (1932).

4x100-meter Relay

Year		Time		Year		Time	
1912	Great Britain	42.4		1964	United States	39.0	WR
1920	United States	42.2	WR	1968	United States	38.23	WR
1924	United States	41.0	=WR	1972	United States	38.19	WR
1928	United States	41.0	=WR	1976	United States	38.33	
1932	United States	40.0	WR	1980	Soviet Union	38.26	
1936	United States	39.8	WR	1984	United States	37.83	WR
1948	United States	40.6		1988	Soviet Union	38.19	
1952	United States	40.1		1992	United States	37.40	WR
1956	United States	39.5	WR	1996	Canada	37.69	
1960	Germany	39.5	=WR	2000	United States	37.61	

4x400-meter Relay

Year		Time		Year		Time	
1908	United States	3:29.4		1964	United States	3:00.7	WR
1912	United States	3:16.6	WR	1968	United States	2:56.16	WR
1920	Great Britain	3:22.2		1972	Kenya	2:59.8	
1924	United States	3:16.0	WR	1976	United States	2:58.65	
1928	United States	3:14.2	WR	1980	Soviet Union	3:01.1	
1932	United States	3:08.2	WR	1984	United States	2:57.91	
1936	Great Britain	3:09.0		1988	United States	2:56.16	=WR
1948	United States	3:10.4		1992	United States	2:55.74	WR
1952	Jamaica	3:03.9	WR	1996	United States	2:55.99	
1956	United States	3:04.8		2000	United States	2:56.35	
1960	United States	3:02.2	WR				

20-kilometer Walk

Year		Time		Year		Time	
1956	Leonid Spirin, USSR	1:31:27.4		1980	Maurizio Damilano, ITA	1:23:35.5	OR
1960	Vladimir Golubnichiy, USSR	1:34:07.2		1984	Ernesto Canto, MEX	1:23:13	OR
1964	Ken Matthews, GBR	1:29:34.0	OR	1988	Jozef Pribilinec, CZE	1:19:57	OR
1968	Vladimir Golubnichiy, USSR	1:33:58.4		1992	Daniel Plaza Montero, SPA	1:21:45	
1972	Peter Frenkel, E. Ger	1:26:42.4	OR	1996	Jefferson Perez, ECU	1:20:07	
1976	Daniel Bautista, MEX	1:24:40.6	OR	2000	Robert Korzeniowski, POL	1:18.59	OR

50-kilometer Walk

Year		Time		Year		Time	
1932	Thomas Green, GBR	4:50:10		1972	Bernd Kannenberg, W. Ger	3:56:11.6	OR
1936	Harold Whitlock, GBR	4:30:41.4	OR	1976	Not held		
1948	John Ljunggren, SWE	4:41:52		1980	Hartwig Gauder, E. Ger	3:49:24.0	OR
1952	Giuseppe Dordoni, ITA	4:28:07.8	OR	1984	Raul Gonzalez, MEX	3:47:26	OR
1956	Norman Read, NZE	4:30:42.8		1988	Vyacheslav Ivanenko, USSR	3:38:29	OR
1960	Don Thompson, GBR	4:25:30.0	OR	1992	Andrei Perlov, UT	3:50:13	
1964	Abdon Pamich, ITA	4:11:12.4	OR	1996	Robert Korzeniowski, POL	3:43:30	
1968	Christoph Höhne, E. Ger	4:20:13.6		2000	Robert Korzeniowski, POL	3:42.22	

High Jump

Year		Height		Year		Height	
1896	Ellery Clark, USA	5-11¼		1956	Charley Dumas, USA	6-11½	OR
1900	Irving Baxter, USA	6-2¾	OR	1960	Robert Shavlakadze, USSR	7-1	OR
1904	Sam Jones, USA	5-11		1964	Valery Brumel, USSR	7-1¾	OR
1906	Cornelius Leahy, GBR/IRE	5-10		1968	Dick Fosbury, USA	7-4¼	OR
1908	Harry Porter, USA	6-3	OR	1972	Yuri Tarmak, USSR	7-3¾	
1912	Alma Richards, USA	6-4	OR	1976	Jacek Wszola, POL	7-4½	OR
1920	Richmond Landon, USA	6-4	=OR	1980	Gerd Wessig, E. Ger	7-8¾	WR
1924	Harold Osborn, USA	6-6		1984	Dietmar Mögenburg, W. Ger	7-8½	
1928	Bob King, USA	6-4½		1988	Gennady Avdeyenko, USSR	7-9¾	OR
1932	Duncan McNaughton, CAN	6-5½		1992	Javier Sotomayor, CUB	7-8	
1936	Cornelius Johnson, USA	6-8	OR	1996	Charles Austin, USA	7-10	OR
1948	John Winter, AUS	6-6		2000	Sergey Klugin, RUS	7-8½	
1952	Walt Davis, USA	6-8½	OR				

Track & Field (Cont.)

Pole Vault

Year		Height		Year		Height	
1896	William Hoyt, USA	10-10		1952	Bob Richards, USA	14-11	OR
1900	Irving Baxter, USA	10-10		1956	Bob Richards, USA	14-11½	OR
1904	Charles Dvorak, USA	11-5¾		1960	Don Bragg, USA	15- 5	OR
1906	Fernand Gonder, FRA	11-5¾		1964	Fred Hansen, USA	16-8¾	OR
1908	(TIE) Edward Cooke, USA	12- 2		1968	Bob Seagren, USA	17-8½	OR
	Alfred Gilbert, USA	12- 2	OR	1972	Wolfgang Nordwig, E. Ger	18- 0½	OR
1912	Harry Babcock, USA	12-11½	OR	1976	Tadeusz Slusarski, POL	18- 0½	=OR
1920	Frank Foss, USA	13- 5	WR	1980	Wladyslaw Kozakiewicz, POL	18-11½	WR
1924	Lee Barnes, USA	12-11½		1984	Pierre Quinon, FRA	18-10¼	
1928	Sabin Carr, USA	13- 9¼		1988	Sergey Bubka, USSR	19- 4¼	OR
1932	Bill Miller, USA	14- 1¾	OR	1992	Maksim Tarasov, UT	19- 0¼	
1936	Earle Meadows, USA	14- 3¼	OR	1996	Jean Galfione, FRA	19- 5¼	OR
1948	Guinn Smith, USA	14- 1¼		2000	Nick Hysong, USA	19- 4¼	

Long Jump

Year		Distance		Year		Distance	
1896	Ellery Clark, USA	20-10		1956	Greg Bell, USA	25- 8¼	
1900	Alvin Kraenzlein, USA	23- 6¾	OR	1960	Ralph Boston, USA	26- 7¾	OR
1904	Meyer Prinstein, USA	24- 1	OR	1964	Lynn Davies, GBR	26- 5¾	
1906	Meyer Prinstein, USA	23- 7½		1968	Bob Beamon, USA	29- 2½	WR
1908	Frank Irons, USA	24- 6½	OR	1972	Randy Williams, USA	27- 0½	
1912	Albert Gutterson, USA	24-11¼	OR	1976	Arnie Robinson, USA	27- 4¾	
1920	William Petersson, SWE	23- 5½		1980	Lutz Dombrowski, E. Ger	28- 0¼	
1924	De Hart Hubbard, USA	24- 5		1984	Carl Lewis, USA	28- 0¼	
1928	Ed Hamm, USA	25- 4½	OR	1988	Carl Lewis, USA	28- 7¼	
1932	Ed Gordon, USA	25- 0¾		1992	Carl Lewis, USA	28- 5½	
1936	Jesse Owens, USA	26- 5½	OR	1996	Carl Lewis, USA	27- 10¾	
1948	Willie Steele, USA	25- 8		2000	Ivan Pedroso, CUB	28- 0¾	
1952	Jerome Biffle, USA	24-10					

Triple Jump

Year		Distance		Year		Distance	
1896	James Connolly, USA	44-11¾		1956	Adhemar da Silva, BRA	53- 7¾	OR
1900	Meyer Prinstein, USA	47- 5¾	OR	1960	Józef Schmidt, POL	55- 2	
1904	Meyer Prinstein, USA	47- 1		1964	Józef Schmidt, POL	55- 3½	OR
1906	Peter O'Connor, GBR/IRE	46- 2¼		1968	Viktor Saneyev, USSR	57- 0¾	WR
1908	Timothy Ahearne, GBR/IRE	48-11¼	OR	1972	Viktor Saneyev, USSR	56-11¼	
1912	Gustaf Lindblom, SWE	48- 5¼		1976	Viktor Saneyev, USSR	56- 8¾	
1920	Vilho Tuulos, FIN	47- 7		1980	Jaak Uudmäe, USSR	56-11¼	
1924	Nick Winter, AUS	50-11¼	WR	1984	Al Joyner, USA	56- 7½	
1928	Mikio Oda, JPN	49-11		1988	Khristo Markov, BUL	57- 9¼	OR
1932	Chuhei Nambu, JPN	51- 7	WR	1992	Mike Conley, USA	59- 7½ ʷ	OR
1936	Naoto Tajima, JPN	52- 6	WR	1996	Kenny Harrison, USA	59- 4¼	OR
1948	Arne Ahman, SWE	50- 6¼		2000	Jonathan Edwards, GBR	58- 1¼	
1952	Adhemar da Silva, BRA	53- 2¾	WR		ʷindicates wind-aided.		

Shot Put

Year		Distance		Year		Distance	
1896	Bob Garrett, USA	36- 9¾		1956	Parry O'Brien, USA	60-11¼	OR
1900	Richard Sheldon, USA	46- 3¼	OR	1960	Bill Nieder, USA	64- 6¾	OR
1904	Ralph Rose, USA	48- 7	WR	1964	Dallas Long, USA	66- 8½	OR
1906	Martin Sheridan, USA	40- 5¼		1968	Randy Matson, USA	67- 4¾	
1908	Ralph Rose, USA	46- 7½		1972	Wladyslaw Komar, POL	69- 6	OR
1912	Patrick McDonald, USA	50- 4	OR	1976	Udo Beyer, E. Ger	69- 0¾	
1920	Ville Pörhölä, FIN	48- 7¼		1980	Vladimir Kiselyov, USSR	70- 0½	OR
1924	Bud Houser, USA	49- 2¼		1984	Alessandro Andrei, ITA	69- 9	
1928	John Kuck, USA	52- 0¾	WR	1988	Ulf Timmermann, E. Ger	73- 8¾	OR
1932	Leo Sexton, USA	52- 6	OR	1992	Mike Stulce, USA	71- 2½	
1936	Hans Woellke, GER	53- 1¾	OR	1996	Randy Barnes, USA	70- 11¼	
1948	Wilbur Thompson, USA	56- 2	OR	2000	Arsi Harju, FIN	69- 10¼	
1952	Parry O'Brien, USA	57- 1½	OR				

Discus Throw

Year		Distance		Year		Distance	
1896	Bob Garrett, USA	95- 7½		1956	Al Oerter, USA	184-11	OR
1900	Rudolf Bauer, HUN	118- 3	OR	1960	Al Oerter, USA	194- 2	OR
1904	Martin Sheridan, USA	128-10½	OR	1964	Al Oerter, USA	200- 1	OR
1906	Martin Sheridan, USA	136- 0		1968	Al Oerter, USA	212- 6	OR
1908	Martin Sheridan, USA	134- 2	OR	1972	Ludvik Danek, CZE	211- 3	
1912	Armas Taipale, FIN	148- 3	OR	1976	Mac Wilkins, USA	221- 5	
1920	Elmer Niklander, FIN	146- 7		1980	Viktor Rashchupkin, USSR	218- 8	
1924	Bud Houser, USA	151- 4	OR	1984	Rolf Danneberg, W. Ger	218- 6	
1928	Bud Houser, USA	155- 3	OR	1988	Jürgen Schult, E. Ger	225- 9	OR
1932	John Anderson, USA	162- 4	OR	1992	Romas Ubartas, LIT	213- 8	
1936	Ken Carpenter, USA	165- 7	OR	1996	Lars Riedel, GER.	227- 8	
1948	Adolfo Consolini, ITA	173- 2	OR	2000	Virgilijus Alekna, LIT	227- 4	
1952	Sim Iness, USA	180- 6	OR				

Hammer Throw

Year		Distance		Year		Distance	
1900	John Flanagan, USA	163- 1		1960	Vasily Rudenkov, USSR	220- 2	OR
1904	John Flanagan, USA	168- 1	OR	1964	Romuald Klim, USSR	228-10	OR
1908	John Flanagan, USA	170- 4	OR	1968	Gyula Zsivótzky, HUN	240- 8	OR
1912	Matt McGrath, USA	179- 7	OR	1972	Anatoly Bondarchuk, USSR	247- 8	OR
1920	Pat Ryan, USA	173- 5		1976	Yuri Sedykh, USSR	254- 4	OR
1924	Fred Tootell, USA	174-10		1980	Yuri Sedykh, USSR	268- 4	WR
1928	Pat O'Callaghan, IRE	168- 7		1984	Juha Tiainen, FIN	256- 2	
1932	Pat O'Callaghan, IRE	176-11		1988	Sergey Litvinov, USSR	278- 2	OR
1936	Karl Hein, GER	185- 4	OR	1992	Andrei Abduvaliyev, UT	270- 9	
1948	Imre Németh, HUN	183-11		1996	Balazs Kiss, HUN.	266- 6	
1952	József Csérmák, HUN	197-11	WR	2000	Szymon Ziolkowski, POL.	262- 6	
1956	Harold Connolly, USA	207- 3	OR				

Javelin Throw

Year		Distance		Year		Distance	
1908	Eric Lemming, SWE	179-10	WR	1964	Pauli Nevala, FIN	271- 2	
1912	Eric Lemming, SWE	198-11	WR	1968	Jānis Lūsis, USSR	295- 7	OR
1920	Jonni Myyrä, FIN	215-10	OR	1972	Klaus Wolfermann, W. Ger	296-10	OR
1924	Jonni Myyrä, FIN	206- 7		1976	Miklos Németh, HUN	310- 4	WR
1928	Erik Lundkvist, SWE	218- 6	OR	1980	Dainis Kula, USSR	299- 2	
1932	Matti Järvinen, FIN	238- 6	OR	1984	Arto Härkönen, FIN	284- 8	
1936	Gerhard Stöck, GER	235- 8		1988	Tapio Korjus, FIN	276- 6	
1948	Kai Tapio Rautavaara, FIN	228-10		1992	Jan Zelezny, CZE	294- 2*	OR
1952	Cy Young, USA	242- 1	OR	1996	Jan Zelezny, CZR	289- 3	
1956	Egil Danielson, NOR	281- 2	WR	2000	Jan Zelezny, CZR	295- 10	OR
1960	Viktor Tsibulenko, USSR	277- 8					

*In 1986 the balance point of the javelin was modified and new records have been kept since.

Decathlon

Year		Points		Year		Points	
1904	Thomas Kiely, IRE	6036		1960	Rafer Johnson, USA	8392	OR
1906-08 Not held				1964	Willi Holdorf, GER	7887	
1912	Jim Thrope, USA	8412	WR	1968	Bill Toomey, USA	8193	OR
1920	Helge Lövland, NOR	6803		1972	Nikolai Avilov, USSR	8454	WR
1924	Harold Osborn, USA	7711	WR	1976	Bruce Jenner, USA	8617	WR
1928	Paavo Yrjölä, FIN	8053	WR	1980	Daley Thompson, GBR	8495	
1932	Jim Bausch, USA	8462	WR	1984	Daley Thompson, GBR	8798	=WR
1936	Glenn Morris, USA	7900	WR	1988	Christian Schenk, E. Ger	8488	
1948	Bob Mathias, USA	7139		1992	Robert Zmelik, CZE	8611	
1952	Bob Mathias, USA	7887	WR	1996	Dan O'Brien, USA	8824	
1956	Milt Campbell, USA	7937	OR	2000	Erki Nool, EST	8641	

WOMEN

At least 4 gold medals (including relays): Evelyn Ashford, Fanny Blankers-Koen, Betty Cuthbert and Bärbel Eckert Wöckel (4).

100 meters

Year		Time		Year		Time	
1928	Betty Robinson, USA	12.2	=WR	1972	Renate Stecher, E. Ger	11.07	
1932	Stella Walsh, POL*	11.9	=WR	1976	Annegret Richter, W. Ger	11.08	
1936	Helen Stephens, USA	11.5ʷ		1980	Lyudmila Kondratyeva, USSR	11.06	
1948	Fanny Blankers-Koen, NED	11.9		1984	Evelyn Ashford, USA	10.97	OR
1952	Marjorie Jackson, AUS	11.5	=WR	1988	Florence Griffith Joyner, USA	10.54ʷ	
1956	Betty Cuthbert, AUS	11.5		1992	Gail Devers, USA	10.82	OR
1960	Wilma Rudolph, USA	11.0ʷ		1996	Gail Devers, USA.	10.94	
1964	Wyomia Tyus, USA	11.4		2000	Marion Jones, USA	10.75	
1968	Wyomia Tyus, USA	11.08	WR				

*An autopsy performed after Walsh's death in 1980 revealed that she was a man.
ʷindicates wind-aided.

Track & Field (Cont.)

200 meters

Year		Time		Year		Time	
1948	Fanny Blankers-Koen, NED	24.4		1976	Bärbel Eckert, E. Ger	22.37	OR
1952	Marjorie Jackson, AUS	23.7	OR	1980	Bärbel Eckert Wockel, E. Ger	22.03	OR
1956	Betty Cuthbert, AUS	23.4	=OR	1984	Valerie Brisco-Hooks, USA	21.81	OR
1960	Wilma Rudolph, USA	24.0		1988	Florence Griffith Joyner, USA	21.34	WR
1964	Edith McGuire, USA	23.0	OR	1992	Gwen Torrence, USA	21.81	
1968	Irena Szewinska, POL	22.5	WR	1996	Marie-Jose Perec, FRA	22.12	
1972	Renate Stecher, E. Ger	22.40	=WR	2000	Marion Jones, USA	21.84	

400 meters

Year		Time		Year		Time	
1964	Betty Cuthbert, AUS	52.0		1984	Valerie Brisco-Hooks, USA	48.83	OR
1968	Colette Besson, FRA	52.03	=OR	1988	Olga Bryzgina, USSR	48.65	OR
1972	Monika Zehrt, E. Ger	51.08	OR	1992	Marie-Jose Perec, FRA	48.83	
1976	Irena Szewinska, POL	49.29	WR	1996	Marie-Jose Perec, FRA	48.25	OR
1980	Marita Koch, E. Ger	48.88	OR	2000	Cathy Freeman, AUS	49.11	

800 meters

Year		Time		Year		Time	
1928	Lina Radke, GER	2:16.8	WR	1980	Nadezhda Olizarenko, USSR	1:53.42	WR
1932-56	Not held			1984	Doina Melinte, ROM	1:57.60	
1960	Lyudmila Shevtsova, USSR	2:04.3	=WR	1988	Sigrun Wodars, E. Ger	1:56.10	
1964	Ann Packer, GBR	2:01.1	OR	1992	Ellen van Langen, NED	1:55.54	
1968	Madeline Manning, USA	2:00.9	OR	1996	Svetlana Masterkova, RUS	1:57.73	
1972	Hildegard Falck, W. Ger	1:58.55	OR	2000	Maria Mutola, MOZ	1:56.15	
1976	Tatyana Kazankina, USSR	1:54.94	WR				

1500 meters

Year		Time		Year		Time	
1972	Lyudmila Bragina, USSR	4:01.4	WR	1988	Paula Ivan, ROM	3:53.96	OR
1976	Tatyana Kazankina, USSR	4:05.48		1992	Hassiba Boulmerka, ALG	3:55.30	
1980	Tatyana Kazankina, USSR	3:56.6	OR	1996	Svetlana Masterkova, RUS	4:00.83	
1984	Gabriella Dorio, ITA	4:03.25		2000	Nouria Merah-Benida, ALG	4:05.10	

5000 meters

Year		Time		Year		Time	
1984	Maricica Puica, ROM	8:35.96		1996	Wang Junxia, CHN	14:59.88	
1988	Tatyana Samolenko, USSR	8:26.53	OR	2000	Gabriela Szabo, ROM	14:40.79	OR
1992	Elena Romanova, UT	8:46.04			Note: Event held over 3000 meters from 1984-92.		

10,000 meters

Year		Time		Year		Time	
1988	Olga Bondarenko, USSR	31:05.21	OR	1996	Fernanda Ribeiro, POR	31:01.63	OR
1992	Derartu Tulu, ETH	31:06.02		2000	Derartu Tulu, ETH	30:17.49	OR

Marathon

Year		Time		Year		Time	
1984	Joan Benoit, USA	2:24:52		1996	Fatuma Roba, ETH	2:26:05	
1988	Rosa Mota, POR	2:25:40		2000	Naoko Takahashi, JPN	2:23:14	
1992	Valentina Yegorova, UT	2:32:41					

100-meter Hurdles

Year		Time		Year		Time	
1932	Babe Didrikson, USA	11.7	WR	1976	Johanna Schaller, E. Ger	12.77	
1936	Trebisonda Valla, ITA	11.7		1980	Vera Komisova, USSR	12.56	OR
1948	Fanny Blankers-Koen, NED	11.2	OR	1984	Benita Fitzgerald-Brown, USA	12.84	
1952	Shirley Strickland, AUS	10.9	WR	1988	Yordanka Donkova, BUL	12.38	OR
1956	Shirley Strickland, AUS	10.7	OR	1992	Paraskevi Patoulidou, GRE	12.64	
1960	Irina Press, USSR	10.8		1996	Ludmila Enquist, SWE	12.58	
1964	Karin Balzer, GER	10.5ʷ		2000	Olga Shishigina, KAZ	12.65	
1968	Maureen Caird, AUS	10.3	OR		ʷindicates wind-aided.		
1972	Annelie Ehrhardt, E. Ger	12.59	WR		Note: Event held over 80 meters from 1932-68.		

400-meter Hurdles

Year		Time		Year		Time	
1984	Nawal El Moutawakel, MOR	54.61	OR	1996	Deon Hemmings, JAM	52.82	OR
1988	Debra Flintoff-King, AUS	53.17	OR	2000	Irina Privalova, RUS	53.02	
1992	Sally Gunnell, GBR	53.23					

4x100-meter Relay

Year		Time		Year		Time	
1928	Canada	48.4	WR	1972	West Germany	42.81	WR
1932	United States	46.9	WR	1976	East Germany	42.55	OR
1936	United States	46.9		1980	East Germany	41.60	WR
1948	Holland	47.5		1984	United States	41.65	
1952	United States	45.9	WR	1988	United States	41.98	
1956	Australia	44.5	WR	1992	United States	42.11	
1960	United States	44.5		1996	United States	41.95	
1964	Poland	43.6		2000	Bahamas	42.20	
1968	United States	42.87	WR				

4x400-meter Relay

Year		Time		Year		Time	
1972	East Germany	3:23.0	WR	1988	Soviet Union	3:15.18	WR
1976	East Germany	3:19.23	WR	1992	Unified Team	3:20.20	
1980	Soviet Union	3:20.2		1996	United States	3:20.91	
1984	United States	3:18.29	OR	2000	United States	3:22.62	

20-kilometer Walk

Year		Time	Year		Time
1992	Chen Yueling, CHN	44:32	2000	Wang Liping, CHN	1:29.05
1996	Yelena Ninikolayeva, RUS	41:49			

Note: Event was held over 10 kilometers from 1992-96.

High Jump

Year		Height		Year		Height	
1928	Ethel Catherwood, CAN	5- 2½		1972	Ulrike Meyfarth, W. Ger	6- 3½	=WR
1932	Jean Shiley, USA	5- 5¼	WR	1976	Rosemarie Ackermann, E. Ger	6- 4	OR
1936	Ibolya Csák, HUN	5- 3		1980	Sara Simeoni, ITA	6- 5½	OR
1948	Alice Coachman, USA	5- 6	OR	1984	Ulrike Meyfarth, W. Ger	6- 7½	OR
1952	Esther Brand, RSA	5- 5¾		1988	Louise Ritter, USA	6- 8	OR
1956	Mildred McDaniel, USA	5- 9¼	WR	1992	Heike Henkel, GER	6- 7½	
1960	Iolanda Balas, ROM	6- 0¾	OR	1996	Stefka Kostadinova, BUL	6- 8¾	
1964	Iolanda Balas, ROM	6- 2¾	OR	2000	Yelena Yelesina, RUS	6- 7	
1968	Miloslava Rezkova, CZE	5-11½					

Pole Vault

Year		Height	
2000	Stacy Draglia, USA	15- 1	OR

Long Jump

Year		Distance		Year		Distance	
1948	Olga Gyarmati, HUN	18- 8¼		1976	Angela Voigt, E. Ger	22- 0¾	
1952	Yvette Williams, NZE	20- 5¾	OR	1980	Tatyana Kolpakova, USSR	23- 2	OR
1956	Elzbieta Krzesinska, POL	20-10	=WR	1984	Anisoara Cusmir-Stanciu, ROM	22- 10	
1960	Vyera Krepkina, USSR	20-10¾	OR	1988	Jackie Joyner-Kersee, USA	24- 3¼	OR
1964	Mary Rand, GBR	22- 2¼	WR	1992	Heike Drechsler, GER	23- 5¼	
1968	Viorica Viscopoleanu, ROM	22- 4½	WR	1996	Chioma Ajunwa, NGR	23- 4½	
1972	Heidemarie Rosendahl, W. Ger	22- 3		2000	Heike Drechsler, GER	22- 11¼	

Triple Jump

Year		Distance	Year		Distance
1996	Inessa Kravets, UKR	50- 3½	2000	Tereza Marinova, BUL	49- 10½

Shot Put

Year		Distance		Year		Distance	
1948	Micheline Ostermeyer, FRA	45- 1½		1976	Ivanka Hristova, BUL	69- 5¼	OR
1952	Galina Zybina, USSR	50- 1¾	WR	1980	Ilona Slupianek, E. Ger	73- 6¼	OR
1956	Tamara Tyshkevich, USSR	54- 5	OR	1984	Claudia Losch, W. Ger	67- 2¼	
1960	Tamara Press, USSR	56- 10	OR	1988	Natalia Lisovskaya, USSR	72- 11¾	
1964	Tamara Press, USSR	59- 6¼	OR	1992	Svetlana Krivaleva, UT	69- 1¼	
1968	Margitta Gummel, E. Ger	64- 4	WR	1996	Astrid Kumbernuss, GER	67- 5½	
1972	Nadezhda Chizhova, USSR	69- 0	WR	2000	Yanina Korolchik, BLR	67- 5½	

Track & Field (Cont.)
Discus Throw

Year		Distance		Year		Distance	
1928	Halina Konopacka, POL	129-11¾	WR	1972	Faina Melnik, USSR	218-7	OR
1932	Lillian Copeland, USA	133-2	OR	1976	Evelin Schlaak, E. Ger	226-4	OR
1936	Gisela Mauermayer, GER	156-3	OR	1980	Evelin Schlaak Jahl, E. Ger	229-6	OR
1948	Micheline Ostermeyer, FRA	137-6		1984	Ria Stalman, NED	214-5	
1952	Nina Romaschkova, USSR	168-8	OR	1988	Martina Hellmann, E. Ger	237-2½	OR
1956	Olga Fikotová, CZE	176-1	OR	1992	Maritza Marten, CUB	229-10	
1960	Nina Ponomaryeva, USSR	180-9	OR	1996	Ilke Wyludda, GER	228-6	
1964	Tamara Press, USSR	187-10	OR	2000	Ellina Zvereva, BLR	224-5	
1968	Lia Manoliu, ROM	191-2	OR				

Hammer Throw

Year		Distance	
2000	Kamila Skolimowska, POL	233-5¾	OR

Javelin Throw

Year		Distance		Year		Distance	
1932	Babe Didrikson, USA	143-4		1972	Ruth Fuchs, E. Ger	209-7	OR
1936	Tilly Fleischer, GER	148-3	OR	1976	Ruth Fuchs, E. Ger	216-4	OR
1948	Herma Bauma, AUT	149-6	OR	1980	Maria Colon Rueñes, CUB	224-5	OR
1952	Dana Zátopková, CZE	165-7	OR	1984	Tessa Sanderson, GBR	228-2	OR
1956	Ineze Jaunzeme, USSR	176-8	OR	1988	Petra Felke, E. Ger	245-0	OR
1960	Elvira Ozolina, USSR	183-8	OR	1992	Silke Renk, GER	224-2	
1964	Mihaela Penes, ROM	198-7	OR	1996	Heli Rantanen, FIN	222-11	
1968	Angéla Németh, HUN	198-0		2000	Trine Hattestad, NOR	226-1	OR

Heptathlon

Year		Points		Year		Points	
1964	Irina Press, USSR	5246	WR	1984	Glynis Nunn, AUS	6390	OR
1968	Ingrid Becker, W. Ger	5098		1988	Jackie Joyner-Kersee, USA	7291	WR
1972	Mary Peters, GBR	4801	WR	1992	Jackie Joyner-Kersee, USA	7044	
1976	Siegrun Siegl, E. Ger	4745		1996	Ghada Shouaa, SYR	6780	
1980	Nadezhda Tkachenko, USSR	5083	WR	2000	Denise Lewis, GBR	6584	

Note: Seven-event Heptathlon replaced five-event Pentathlon in 1984.

All-Time Leading Medal Winners – Single Games

Athletes who have won the most medals in a single Summer Olympics. Totals include individual, relay and team medals. U.S. athletes are in **bold** type.

MEN

No		Sport	G-S-B	No		Sport	G-S-B
8	Aleksandr Dityatin, USSR (1980)	Gym	3-4-1	6	Viktor Chukarin, USSR (1956)	Gym	4-2-0
7	**Mark Spitz**, USA (1972)	Swim	7-0-0	6	Konrad Frey, GER (1936)	Gym	3-1-2
7	**Willis Lee**, USA (1920)	Shoot	5-1-1	6	Ville Ritola, FIN (1924)	Track	4-2-0
7	**Matt Biondi**, USA (1988)	Swim	5-1-1	6	Hubert Van Innis, BEL (1920)	Arch	4-2-0
7	Boris Shakhlin, USSR (1960)	Gym	4-2-1	6	**Carl Osburn**, USA (1920)	Shoot	4-1-1
7	**Lloyd Spooner**, USA (1920)	Shoot	4-1-2	6	Louis Richardet, SWI (1906)	Shoot	3-3-0
7	Mikhail Voronin, USSR (1968)	Gym	2-4-1	6	**Anton Heida**, USA (1904)	Gym	5-1-0
7	Nikolai Andrianov, USSR (1976)	Gym	2-4-1	6	**George Eyser**, USA (1904)	Gym	3-2-1
6	Vitaly Scherbo, UT (1992)	Gym	6-0-0	6	**Burton Downing**, USA (1904)	Cycle	2-3-1
6	Li Ning, CHN (1984)	Gym	3-2-1	6	Alexei Nemov, RUS (1996)	Gym	2-1-3
6	Akinori Nakayama, JPN (1968)	Gym	4-1-1	6	Alexei Nemov, RUS (2000)	Gym	2-1-3
6	Takashi Ono, JPN (1960)	Gym	3-1-2				

WOMEN

No		Sport	G-S-B	No		Sport	G-S-B
7	Maria Gorokhovskaya, USSR (1952)	Gym	2-5-0	5	Ecaterina Szabó, ROM (1984)	Gym	4-1-0
6	Kristin Otto, E. Ger (1988)	Swim	6-0-0	5	Shane Gould, AUS (1972)	Swim	3-1-1
6	Agnes Keleti, HUN (1956)	Gym	4-2-0	5	Nadia Comaneci, ROM (1976)	Gym	3-1-1
6	Vera Cáslavská, CZE (1968)	Gym	4-2-0	5	Karin Janz, E. Ger (1972)	Gym	2-2-1
6	Larisa Latynina, USSR (1956)	Gym	4-1-1	5	Ines Diers, E. Ger (1980)	Swim	2-2-1
6	Larisa Latynina, USSR (1960)	Gym	3-2-1	5	**Shirley Babashoff**, USA (1976)	Swim	1-4-0
6	Daniela Silivas, ROM (1988)	Gym	3-2-1	5	**Mary Lou Retton**, USA (1984)	Gym	1-2-2
6	Larisa Latynina, USSR (1964)	Gym	2-2-2	5	**Shannon Miller**, USA (1992)	Gym	0-2-3
6	Margit Korondi, HUN, (1956)	Gym	1-1-4	5	**Marion Jones**, USA (2000)	Track	3-0-2
5	Kornelia Ender, E. Ger (1976)	Swim	4-1-0	5	**Dara Torres**, USA (2000)	Swim	2-0-3

All-Time Leading Medal Winners – Career

MEN

No		Sport	G-S-B	No		Sport	G-S-B
15	Nikolai Andrianov, USSR	Gymnastics	7-5-3	10	Carl Lewis, USA	Track/Field	9-1-0
13	Boris Shakhlin, USSR	Gymnastics	7-4-2	10	Aladár Gerevich, HUN	Fencing	7-1-2
13	Edoardo Mangiarotti, ITA	Fencing	6-5-2	10	Akinori Nakayama, JPN	Gymnastics	6-2-2
13	Takashi Ono, JPN	Gymnastics	5-4-4	10	Aleksandr Dityatin, USSR	Gymnastics	3-6-1
12	Paavo Nurmi, FIN	Track/Field	9-3-0	9	Vitaly Scherbo, BLR	Gymnastics	6-0-3
12	Sawao Kato, JPN	Gymnastics	8-3-1	9*	**Martin Sheridan**, USA	Track/Field	5-3-1
12	Alexei Nemov, RUS	Gymnastics	4-2-6	9*	Zoltán Halmay, HUN	Swimming	3-5-1
11	**Mark Spitz**, USA	Swimming	9-1-1	9	Giulio Gaudini, ITA	Fencing	3-4-2
11†	**Matt Biondi**, USA	Swimming	8-2-1	9	Mikhail Voronin, USSR	Gymnastics	2-6-1
11	Viktor Chukarin, USSR	Gymnastics	7-3-1	9	Heikki Savolainen, FIN	Gymnastics	2-1-6
11	**Carl Osburn**, USA	Shooting	5-4-2	9	Yuri Titov, USSR	Gymnastics	1-5-3
10*	**Ray Ewry**, USA	Track/Field	10-0-0				

†Includes gold medal as preliminary member of 1st-place relay team.
*Medals won by Ewry (2-0-0), Sheridan (2-3-0) and Halmay (1-1-0) at the 1906 Intercalated games are not officially recognized by the IOC.

Games Participated In

Andrianov (1972,76,80); **Biondi** (1984,88,92); **Chukarin** (1952,56); **Dityatin** (1976,80); **Ewry** (1900,04,06,08); **Gerevich** (1932,36,48,52,56,60); **Gaudini** (1928,32,36); **Halmay** (1900,04,06,08); **Kato** (1968,72,76); **Lewis** (1984,88,92,96); **Mangiarotti** (1936,48,52,56,60); **Nakayama** (1968,72); **Nemov** (1996,2000) **Nurmi** (1920,24,28); **Ono** (1952,56,60,64); **Osburn** (1912,20, 24); **Savolainen** (1928,32,36,48,52); **Scherbo** (1992,96); **Shakhlin** (1956,60,64); **Sheridan** (1904,06,08); **Spitz** (1968,72); **Titov** (1956,60,64); **Voronin** (1968,72).

WOMEN

No		Sport	G-S-B
18	Larissa Latynina, USSR	Gymnastics	9-5-4
11	Vera Cáslavská, CZE	Gymnastics	7-4-0
10	Birgit Fischer, GER	Canoe/Kayak	7-3-0
10	**Jenny Thompson**, USA	Swimming	8-1-1
10	Agnes Keleti, HUN	Gymnastics	5-3-2
10	Polina Astaknova, USSR	Gymnastics	5-2-3
9	Nadia Comaneci, ROM	Gymnastics	5-3-1
9	Lyudmila Tourischeva, USSR	Gymnastics	4-3-2
8	**Dara Torres**, USA	Swimming	4-1-4
8	Kornelia Ender, E. Ger	Swimming	4-4-0
8	Dawn Fraser, AUS	Swimming	4-4-0
8	**Shirley Babashoff**, USA	Swimming	2-6-0
8	Sofia Muratova, USSR	Gymnastics	2-2-4
7	Krisztina Egerszegi, HUN	Swimming	5-1-1
7	Irena Kirszenstein Szewinska, POL	Track/Field	3-2-2
7	Shirley Strickland, AUS	Track/Field	3-1-3
7	Maria Gorokhovskaya, USSR	Gymnastics	2-5-0
7	Ildikó Ságiné-Ujlaki-Rejtö, HUN	Fencing	2-3-2
7	**Shannon Miller**, USA	Gymnastics	2-2-3
7	Susie O'Neill, AUS	Swimming	2-4-1
7	Merlene Ottey, JAM	Track/Field	0-2-5

Games Participated In

Astaknova (1956,60,64); **Babashoff** (1972,76); **Cáslavská** (1960,64,68); **Comaneci** (1976,80); **Egerszegi** (1988,92,96); **Ender** (1972,76); **Fischer** (1980,92,96,2000); **Fraser** (1956,60,64); **Gorokhovskaya** (1952); **Keleti** (1952,56); **Latynina** (1956,60,64); **Miller** (1992,96); **Muratova** (1956,60); **O'Neill** (1996,2000) **Ottey** (1980,84,88,92,96) **Ságiné-Ujlaki-Rejtä** (1960,64, 68,72,76); **Strickland** (1948,52,56); **Szewinska** (1964,68,72,76,80); **Thompson** (1992,96,2000); **Torres** (1984,88,92,2000) **Tourischeva** (1968, 72,76).

Most Individual Medals
Not including team competition.

	Sport	G-S-B
Men: 12-Nikolai Andrianov, USSR	Gym	6-3-3
Women: 15-Larissa Latynina, USSR	Gym	7-5-3

Most Gold Medals

MEN

No		Sport	G-S-B	No		Sport	G-S-B
10*	**Ray Ewry**, USA	Track/Field	10-0-0	7	Boris Shakhlin, USSR	Gymnastics	7-4-2
9	Paavo Nurmi, FIN	Track/Field	9-3-0	7	Viktor Chukarin, USSR	Gymnastics	7-3-1
9	**Mark Spitz**, USA	Swimming	9-1-1	7	Aladar Gerevich, HUN	Fencing	7-1-2
9	**Carl Lewis**, USA	Track/Field	9-1-0				
8	Sawao Kato, JPN	Gymnastics	8-3-1				
8†	**Matt Biondi**, USA	Swimming	8-2-1				
7	Nikolai Andrianov, USSR	Gymnastics	7-5-3				

*Medals won by Ewry (2-0-0) at the 1906 Intercalated games are not officially recognized by the IOC.
†Includes gold medal as preliminary member of 1st-place relay team.

WOMEN

No		Sport	G-S-B	No		Sport	G-S-B
9	Larissa Latynina, USSR	Gymnastics	9-5-4	4	Lyudmila Tourischeva, USSR	Gymnastics	4-3-2
8	**Jenny Thompson**, USA	Swimming	8-1-1	4	**Dara Torres**, USA	Swimming	4-1-4
7	Vera Cáslavská, CZE	Gymnastics	7-4-0	4	**Evelyn Ashford**, USA	Track/Field	4-1-0
7	Birgit Fischer, GER	Canoe/Kayak	7-3-0	4	Janet Evans, USA	Swimming	4-1-0
6	Kristin Otto, E. Ger	Swimming	6-0-0	4	Fu Mingxia, CHN	Diving	4-1-0
6†	**Amy Van Dyken**, USA	Swimming	6-0-0	4	Fanny Blankers-Koen, NED	Track/Field	4-0-0
5	Agnes Keleti, HUN	Gymnastics	5-3-2	4	Betty Cuthbert, AUS	Track/Field	4-0-0
5	Nadia Comaneci, ROM	Gymnastics	5-3-1	4	**Pat McCormick**, USA	Diving	4-0-0
5	Polina Astaknova, USSR	Gymnastics	5-2-3	4	Bärbel Eckert Wäckel, E. Ger	Track/Field	4-0-0
5	Krisztina Egerszegi, HUN	Swimming	5-1-1				
4	Kornelia Ender, E. Ger	Swimming	4-4-0				
4	Dawn Fraser, AUS	Swimming	4-4-0				

†Includes gold medal as preliminary member of 1st-place relay team.

All-Time Leading Medal Winners – Career (Cont.)
Most Silver Medals

MEN

No		Sport	G-S-B
6	Alexandr Dityatin, USSR	Gymnastics	3-6-1
6	Mikhail Voronin, USSR	Gymnastics	2-6-1
5	Nikolai Andrianov, USSR	Gymnastics	7-5-3
5	Edoardo Mangiarotti, ITA	Fencing	6-5-2
5	Zoltán Halmay, HUN	Swimming	3-5-1
5	Gustavo Marzi, ITA	Fencing	2-5-0
5	Yuri Titov, USSR	Gymnastics	1-5-3
5	Viktor Lisitsky, USSR	Gymnastics	0-5-0

WOMEN

No		Sport	G-S-B
6	**Shirley Babashoff**, USA	Swimming	2-6-0
5	Larissa Latynina, USSR	Gymnastics	9-5-4
5	Maria Gorokhovskaya, USSR	Gymnastics	2-5-0
4	Vera Cáslavská, CZE	Gymnastics	7-4-0
4	Kornelia Ender, E. Ger	Swimming	4-4-0
4	Dawn Fraser, AUS	Swimming	4-4-0
4	Erica Zuchold, E. Ger	Gymnastics	0-4-1

Most Bronze Medals

MEN

No		Sport	G-S-B
6	Alexei Nemov, RUS	Gymnastics	4-2-6
6	Heikki Savolainen, FIN	Gymnastics	2-1-6
5	Daniel Revenu, FRA	Fencing	1-0-5
5	Philip Edwards, CAN	Track/Field	0-0-5
5	Adrianus Jong, NED	Fencing	0-0-5

WOMEN

No		Sport	G-S-B
5	Merlene Ottey, JAM	Track/Field	0-2-5
4	Larissa Latynina, USSR	Gymnastics	9-5-4
4	**Dara Torres**, USA	Swimming	4-1-4
4	Sofia Muratova, USSR	Gymnastics	2-2-4

All-Time Leading USA Medal Winners
Most Overall Medals

MEN

No		Sport	G-S-B
11	Mark Spitz	Swimming	9-1-1
11†	Matt Biondi	Swimming	8-2-1
11	Carl Osburn	Shooting	5-4-2
10*	Ray Ewry	Track/Field	10-0-0
10	Carl Lewis	Track/Field	9-1-0
9*	Martin Sheridan	Track/Field	5-3-1
8	Charles Daniels	Swimming	5-1-2
8	Gary Hall Jr.	Swimming	4-3-1
7†	Tom Jager	Swimming	5-1-1
7	Willis Lee	Shooting	5-1-1
7	Lloyd Spooner	Shooting	4-1-2
6	Anton Heida	Gymnastics	5-1-0
6	Don Schollander	Swimming	5-1-0
6	Johnny Weissmuller	Swim/Water Polo	5-0-1
6	Alfred Lane	Shooting	5-0-1
6	Jim Lightbody	Track/Field	4-2-0
6	George Eyser	Gymnastics	3-2-1
6	Ralph Rose	Track/Field	3-2-1
6	Michael Plumb	Equestrian	2-4-0
6	Burton Downing	Cycling	2-3-1
6	Bob Garrett	Track/Field	2-2-2

†Includes gold medal as prelim. member of 1st-place relay team.
*Medals won by Ewry (2-0-0) and Sheridan (2-3-0) at the 1906 Intercalated games are not officially recognized by the IOC.
‡Includes 3 gold medals as prelim. member of 1st-place relay teams.

Games Participated In
Biondi (1984,88,92); **Daniels** (1904,06,08); **Downing** (1904); **Ewry** (1900,04,06,08); **Eyser** (1904); **Garrett** (1896,1900); **Hall** (1996,2000) **Heida** (1904); **Jager** (1984,88,92); **Lane** (1912,20); **Lee** (1920); **Lewis** (1984,88,92,96); **Lightbody** (1904,06); **Osburn** (1912,20,24); **Plumb** (1960, 64,68,72,76,84); **Rose** (1904,08,12); **Schollander** (1964, 68); **Sheridan** (1904,06,08); **Spitz** (1968,72); **Spooner** (1920); **Weissmuller** (1924,28).

WOMEN

No		Sport	G-S-B
10	Jenny Thompson	Swimming	8-1-1
9	Dara Torres	Swimming	4-1-4
8	Shirley Babashoff	Swimming	2-6-0
7	Shannon Miller	Gymnastics	2-2-3
6†	Amy Van Dyken	Swimming	6-0-0
6	Jackie Joyner-Kersee	Track/Field	3-1-2
6	Angel Martino	Swimming	3-0-3
5	Evelyn Ashford	Track/Field	4-1-0
5	Janet Evans	Swimming	4-1-0
5	Florence Griffith Joyner	Track/Field	3-2-0
5†	Mary T. Meagher	Swimming	3-1-1
5	Gwen Torrence	Track/Field	3-2-0
5	Marion Jones	Track/Field	3-0-2
5	Mary Lou Retton	Gymnastics	1-2-2
4	Pat McCormick	Diving	4-0-0
4	Valerie Brisco-Hooks	Track/Field	3-1-0
4	Nancy Hogshead	Swimming	3-1-0
4	Sharon Stouder	Swimming	3-1-0
4	Wyomia Tyus	Track/Field	3-1-0
4	Wilma Rudolph	Track/Field	3-0-1
4	Chris von Saltza	Swimming	3-1-0
4	Sue Pedersen	Swimming	2-2-0
4	Eleanor Garatti Saville	Swimming	2-1-1
4	Jan Henne	Swimming	2-1-1
4	Mary Wayte	Swimming	2-1-1
4	Dorothy Poynton Hill	Diving	2-1-1
4†	Summer Sanders	Swimming	2-1-1
4	Kathy Ellis	Swimming	2-0-2
4	Jill Sterkel	Swimming	2-0-2
4	Amanda Beard	Swimming	1-2-1
4	Georgia Coleman	Diving	1-2-1
4	Ellie Daniel	Swimming	1-1-2

†Includes gold medal as prelim. member of 1st-place relay team.

Games Participated In
Ashford (1976,84,88,92); **Babashoff** (1972,76); **Beard** (1996,2000); **Brisco-Hooks** (1984,88); **Coleman** (1928,32); **Daniel** (1968,72); **Ellis** (1964); **Evans** (1988,92,96); **Garatti Saville** (1928,32); **Griffith Joyner** (1984,88); **Henne** (1968); **Hogshead** (1984); **Jones** (2000); **Joyner-Kersee** (1984,88,92,96); **Martino** (1992,96); **McCormick** (1952,56); **Meagher** (1984,88); **Miller** (1992, 96); **Pedersen** (1968); **Poynton Hill** (1928,32,36); **Retton** (1984); **Rudolph** (1956,60); **Sanders** (1992); **Sterkel** (1976,84,88); **Stouder** (1964); **Thompson** (1988,92,96,2000); **Torrence** (1988,92,96); **Torres** (1984,88,92,2000); **Tyus** (1964,68); **Van Dyken** (1996,2000); **von Saltza** (1960); **Wayte** (1984,88).

Most Gold Medals

	MEN				WOMEN		
No		Sport	G-S-B	No		Sport	G-S-B
10*	Raymond Ewry	Track/Field	10-0-0	8	Jenny Thompson	Swimming	8-1-1
9	Mark Spitz	Swimming	9-1-1	6†	Amy Van Dyken	Swimming	6-0-0
9	Carl Lewis	Track/Field	9-1-1	4	Dara Torres	Swimming	4-1-4
8†	Matt Biondi	Swimming	8-2-1	4	Evelyn Ashford	Track/Field	4-1-0
5	Carl Osburn	Shooting	5-4-2	4	Janet Evans	Swimming	4-1-0
5*	Martin Sheridan	Track/Field	5-3-1	4	Pat McCormick	Diving	4-0-0
5	Charles Daniels	Swimming	5-1-2	3	Florence Griffith Joyner	Track/Field	3-2-0
5‡	Tom Jager	Swimming	5-1-1	3	Jackie Joyner-Kersee	Track/Field	3-1-2
5	Willis Lee	Shooting	5-1-1	3†	Mary T. Meagher	Swimming	3-1-1
5	Anton Heida	Gymnastics	5-1-0	3	Gwen Torrence	Track/Field	3-1-1
5	Don Schollander	Swimming	5-1-0	3	Valerie Brisco-Hooks	Track/Field	3-1-0
5	Johnny Weissmuller	Swim/Water Polo	5-0-1	3	Nancy Hogshead	Swimming	3-1-0
5	Alfred Lane	Shooting	5-0-1	3	Sharon Stouder	Swimming	3-1-0
5	Morris Fisher	Shooting	5-0-0	3	Wyomia Tyus	Track/Field	3-1-0
4	Gary Hall Jr.	Swimming	4-3-1	3	Chris von Saltza	Swimming	3-1-0
4	Jim Lightbody	Track/Field	4-2-0	3	Wilma Rudolph	Track/Field	3-0-1
4	Lloyd Spooner	Shooting	4-1-2	3	Melissa Belote	Swimming	3-0-0
4	Greg Louganis	Diving	4-1-0	3	Ethelda Bleibtrey	Swimming	3-0-0
4	John Naber	Swimming	4-1-0	3	Tracy Caulkins	Swimming	3-0-0
4	Meyer Prinstein	Track/Field	4-1-0	3†	Nicole Haislett	Swimming	3-0-0
4	Mel Sheppard	Track/Field	4-1-0	3	Helen Madison	Swimming	3-0-0
4	Marcus Hurley	Cycling	4-0-1	3	Debbie Meyer	Swimming	3-0-0
4	Marcus Hurley	Cycling	4-0-1	3	Sandra Neilson	Swimming	3-0-0
4†	Jon Olsen	Swimming	4-0-1	3	Martha Norelius	Swimming	3-0-0
4	Archie Hahn	Track/Field	4-0-0	3†	Carrie Steinseifer	Swimming	3-0-0
4	Alvin Kraenzlein	Track/Field	4-0-0	3‡	Ashley Tappin	Swimming	3-0-0
4	Al Oerter	Track/Field	4-0-0				
4	Jesse Owens	Track/Field	4-0-0				

*Medals won by Ewry (2-0-0) and Sheridan (2-3-0) at the 1906 Intercalated games are not officially recognized by the IOC.
†Includes gold medal as prelim. member of 1st-place relay team.
‡ Includes 3 gold medals as prelim. member of 1st-place relay teams.

†Includes gold medal as prelim. member of 1st-place relay team.
‡ Includes 3 gold medals as prelim. member of 1st-place relay teams.

Most Silver Medals

	MEN						Sport	G-S-B
No		Sport	G-S-B	No				
4	Carl Osburn	Shooting	5-4-2	3	Earl Thomson		Equestrian	2-3-0
4	Michael Plumb	Equestrian	2-4-0	3	Alexander McKee		Swimming	0-3-0
3	Martin Sheridan	Track/Field	5-3-1					
3	Burton Downing	Cycling	2-3-1		WOMEN		Sport	G-S-B
3	Irving Baxter	Track/Field	2-3-0	No				
				6	Shirley Babashoff		Swimming	2-6-0

All-Time Medal Standings, 1896-2000

All-time Summer Games medal standings, based on *The Golden Book of the Olympic Games*. Medal counts include the 1906 Intercalated Games, which are not recognized by the IOC.

		G	S	B	Total			G	S	B	Total
1	**United States**	872	658	586	2116	18	Netherlands	61	67	85	213
2	USSR (1952-88)	395	319	296	1010	19	Bulgaria	48	82	65	195
3	Great Britain	180	233	225	638	20	Switzerland	47	75	61	183
4	France	188	193	217	598	21	Denmark	40	63	58	161
5	Italy	179	143	157	479	22	Russia (1896-1912, 96–)	58	52	46	156
6	Sweden	136	156	177	469	23	South Korea	46	52	56	154
7	East Germany (1968-88)	159	150	136	445	24	Czechoslovakia (1924-92)	49	49	44	142
8	Hungary	150	135	158	443	25	Belgium	37	51	52	140
9	Germany (1896-64,92–)	137	138	160	435	26	Cuba	55	44	38	137
10	Australia	102	110	138	350	27	Norway	49	44	41	134
11	West Germany (1968-88)	77	104	120	301	28	Greece	32	48	46	126
12	Finland	101	81	114	296	29	Unified Team (1992)	45	38	29	112
	Japan	97	97	102	296	30	Yugoslavia (1924-88, 96–)	28	32	33	93
14	Romania	74	83	108	265	31	Austria	20	32	34	86
15	Poland	56	72	113	241	32	Spain	25	28	22	75
16	Canada	51	81	98	230	33	New Zealand	30	12	32	74
17	China	80	79	64	223	34	Brazil	12	19	35	66

All-Time Medal Standings, 1896-2000 (Cont.)

		G	S	B	Total
35	Turkey	33	16	15	64
36	Rep. of S. Africa (1904-60, 92–)	19	20	24	63
37	Argentina	13	23	18	54
	Kenya	16	20	18	54
39	Mexico	10	15	22	47
40	Iran	8	13	19	40
41	Jamaica	5	20	12	37
42	North Korea	8	7	15	30
43	Estonia	8	6	12	26
44	Ethiopia	12	2	10	24
45	Ukraine	3	10	10	23
46	Great Britain/Ireland	6	11	3	20
	Ireland	8	6	6	20
48	Czech Republic	6	6	7	19
49	Portugal	3	4	10	17
	Belarus	3	3	11	17
	Nigeria	2	8	7	17
52	India	8	3	5	16
	Egypt	6	5	5	16
	Indonesia	4	7	5	16
	Morocco	4	3	9	16
56	Mongolia	0	5	9	14
57	Algeria	4	1	7	12
58	Trinidad & Tobago	1	3	7	11
59	Pakistan	3	3	4	10
	Uruguay	2	2	6	10
	Latvia	1	6	3	10
	Chinese Taipei	0	4	6	10
63	Lithuania	3	0	6	9
	Thailand	2	1	6	9
	Chile	0	6	3	9
	Philippines	0	2	7	9
67	Slovakia	2	4	2	8
	Venezuela	1	2	5	8
	Georgia	0	0	8	8
70	Kazakhstan	3	4	0	7
	Croatia	2	2	3	7
	Colombia	1	2	4	7
73	Bahamas	2	2	2	6
	Slovenia	2	2	2	6
	Uganda	1	3	2	6
	Tunisia	1	2	3	6
	Uzbekistan	1	2	3	6
	Bohemia	0	1	5	6
	Puerto Rico	0	1	5	6
80	Azerbaijan	2	1	1	4
	Peru	1	3	0	4
	Costa Rica	1	1	2	4
	Namibia	0	4	0	4
	Lebanon	0	2	2	4
	Moldova	0	2	2	4
	Ghana	0	1	3	4
	Israel	0	1	3	4
88	Luxembourg	2	1	0	3
	Armenia	1	1	1	3
	Cameroon	1	1	1	3
	Iceland	0	1	2	3
	Malaysia	0	1	2	3

		G	S	B	Total
93	Syria	1	1	0	2
	Japan/Korea	1	0	1	2
	Mozambique	1	0	1	2
	Surinam	1	0	1	2
	Tanzania	0	2	0	2
	Great Britain/USA	0	1	1	2
	Haiti	0	1	1	2
	Russia/Estonia	0	1	1	2
	Saudi Arabia	0	1	1	2
	United Arab Republic	0	1	1	2
	Zambia	0	1	1	2
	The Antilles	0	0	2	2
	Panama	0	0	2	2
	Qatar	0	0	2	2
107	Australia/New Zealand	1	0	0	1
	Burkina Faso	1	0	0	1
	Cuba/USA	1	0	0	1
	Denmark/Sweden	1	0	0	1
	Ecuador	1	0	0	1
	Gr. Britain/Ireland/Germany	1	0	0	1
	Gr. Britain/Ireland/USA	1	0	0	1
	Hong Kong	1	0	0	1
	Ireland/USA	1	0	0	1
	Zimbabwe	1	0	0	1
	Belgium/Greece	0	1	0	1
	Ceylon	0	1	0	1
	France/USA	0	1	0	1
	France/Gr. Britain/Ireland	0	1	0	1
	Ivory Coast	0	1	0	1
	Netherlands Antilles	0	1	0	1
	Senegal	0	1	0	1
	Singapore	0	1	0	1
	Smyrna	0	1	0	1
	Tonga	0	1	0	1
	Vietnam	0	1	0	1
	Virgin Islands	0	1	0	1
	Australia/Great Britain	0	0	1	1
	Barbados	0	0	1	1
	Bermuda	0	0	1	1
	Bohemia/Great Britain	0	0	1	1
	Djibouti	0	0	1	1
	Dominican Republic	0	0	1	1
	France/Great Britain	0	0	1	1
	Guyana	0	0	1	1
	Iraq	0	0	1	1
	Kuwait	0	0	1	1
	Kyrgyzstan	0	0	1	1
	Macedonia	0	0	1	1
	Mexico/Spain	0	0	1	1
	Niger	0	0	1	1
	Scotland	0	0	1	1
	Sri Lanka	0	0	1	1
	Thessalonika	0	0	1	1
	Wales	0	0	1	1

Combined totals:	G	S	B	Total
USSR/UT/Russia	498	409	371	1278
Germany/E. Ger/W. Ger	374	392	416	1182

Notes: Athletes from the USSR participated in the Summer Games from 1952-88, returned as the Unified Team in 1992 after the breakup of the Soviet Union (in 1991) and have competed as independent republics since the 1994 Winter Games. Germany was barred from the Olympics in 1924 and 1948 following World Wars I and II. Divided into East and West Germany after WWII, both countries competed together from 1952-64, then separately from 1968-88. Germany was reunified in 1990. Czechoslovakia split into Slovakia and the Czech Republic in 1993. Croatia and Bosnia-Herzegovina gained independence from Yugoslavia in 1991. Yugoslavia was not invited to the 1992 games (though Serbian and Montenegrin athletes were allowed to compete as independent athletes) but returned in 1996. South Africa was banned from 1964-88 for using the apartheid policy in the selection of its teams. It returned in 1992 as the Republic of South Africa (RSA).

Soccer

The U.S. national team celebrates its 2–1 win over Jamaica in their 2002 World Cup Qualifying match at Foxboro Stadium on October 7.

Cup Fever

Jack Edwards
is the lead play-by-play announcer for MLS and
U.S. national team games on ESPN and ABC.

*In a surprising turn, the U.S. qualifies
for its fourth straight World Cup with
a win over Jamaica and a little help.*

The reckless kid from Tulsa, Oklahoma, Joe-Max Moore, stood at the top of the penalty area with the ball on the spot. All that rode on the next few moments was the future of American soccer.

The U.S. had bolted from the gate in the final round of regional World Cup qualifying, compiling a 4-0-1 mark in its first five games, tallying 13 points out of a possible 15. But en route to that sparkling record, Clint Mathis went down with a blown ACL, Josh Wolff was sidelined with a stress fracture and Brian McBride was on the bench with a recurrence of a blood clot problem. All were out for the year. To make matters even worse, team captain and catalyst Claudio Reyna was limited by nagging groin injuries.

Staggered, the U.S. lost three in a row—at Mexico, home against Honduras, and at Costa Rica. Three teams from the final six would reach the 2002 World Cup. The U.S. had sunk from leading their group on June 20...to fourth place by September 5.

Beneath the surface of that, things weren't going well on the domestic front either. Major League Soccer had entered its playoffs without a network television deal for the 2002 season. No network equals no growth. No growth means a limited life for the league. Without an ever-improving MLS, the national team will have no depth. No depth means saying goodbye to this unprecedented period of national-team improvement. It was no stretch to conceive that American soccer, on the morning of Oct. 7, 2001, was on the precipice of a nightmarish spiral toward oblivion.

Still, if the U.S. beat Jamaica on October 7 and Trinidad & Tobago, on the road, in November, it would qualify for the 2002 World Cup. The U.S.

AP/Wide World Photos

Sam's Army, the U.S. national team's ardent supporters, helped root the team to a spot in the 32-team field of the 2002 World Cup.

would still be mathematically alive after the Jamaica game—no matter what—and could actually qualify for 2002 via an improbable scenario.

The feeling in Foxboro Stadium was certainly patriotic but also uneasy. The U.S. and Britain had just commenced bombing Afghanistan two hours before game time. Security was on high alert, and thousands of fans missed the kickoff because of the bag-search backup at the gates. Fans watching at home missed out entirely, as ABC stayed with its news coverage of the air strikes over Afghanistan instead of the regularly scheduled broadcast of the game.

Just three minutes in, Reyna, who had played just 3½ of the team's eight previous qualifiers, showed his genius with a low, hard, curling free kick from the left wing. Moore dove and deflected it in. The crowd boiled. The air sizzled. Then the tire went flat. Eleven minutes later, a marking error left Jamaican midfielder James Lawrence wide open at the top of the U.S. box. He slid one into the low corner beyond American goalkeeper Brad Friedel's left hand.

AP/Wide World Photos

*Sissi, Katia and Thori Staples Bryan of the **Bay Area CyberRays** hoist the Founders Cup following their victory over Atlanta in the inaugural WUSA Championship Game.*

The U.S. answered by storming the Jamaican goal, trying one route of entry after another without success. In the 80th minute, Reyna pushed the ball down the right side of the penalty area for Landon Donovan. The 19-year-old sped past Jamaican substitute fullback Tyrone Marshall. Marshall chopped him. Penalty kick.

Moore stepped up. He fired with the inside of his right foot, and buried the ball in the right side panel of the goal. The U.S. was happy. It had done its part by beating Jamaica, 2-1. Now, for Trinidad & Tobago in November…only…

Word crackled in, by cell phone and the internet, checked and double-checked because it was so preposterous: Mexico had been held to a scoreless tie in Costa Rica (believable) AND previously winless Trinidad & Tobago had won, 1-0, at Honduras.

The improbable scenario had played out exactly as it had to for the United States to qualify. A day that began with doubt ended in players embracing in front of a sea of delirious red-clad Sam's Army fans. They wouldn't have to wait for November and Trinidad & Tobago after all.

The U.S. was in!

Jack Edwards' Ten Biggest Stories of the Year in Soccer

10 ▪ Major League Soccer averages nearly 15,000 in paid attendance, an increase of more than 8 percent over the 2000 season.

9 ▪ Columbus Crew Stadium in Columbus, Ohio, becomes the de facto national soccer stadium, hosting the U.S. vs. Mexico match in February, the MLS Cup in October and the NCAA College Cup in December.

8 ▪ The Los Angeles Galaxy (with Cobi Jones and Alexi Lalas) wins the CONCACAF Champions' Cup, the regional club championship. Then the Galaxy gets hosed by FIFA, soccer's world governing body, when its Club World Championship, for which L.A. re-arranged its MLS schedule, gets postponed until at least 2003.

7 ▪ Sixteen-year-old Santino Quaranta of Baltimore, becomes the youngest professional athlete in a U.S. team sport and scores five goals as an MLS all-star for the D.C. United.

6 ▪ Clint Mathis emerges as an elite player, setting up Josh Wolff against Mexico, scoring vs. Brazil, and leading the MetroStars in scoring despite playing just 10 games before blowing out his ACL.

5 ▪ D.C. United trades Jeff Agoos to the San Jose Earthquakes and Carlos Llamosa to the Miami Fusion. D.C. misses the playoffs for the second straight year, while Miami and San Jose finish first and second, respectively, in their divisions en route to meeting in the MLS semifinals.

4 ▪ The L.A. Galaxy begins work on a new soccer-specific stadium and training center on the campus of Cal State at Dominguez Hills. It is Major League Soccer's second soccer-only venue, after Crew Stadium in Columbus (see #9).

3 ▪ Speedy forward and teenage phenom Landon Donovan signs with the San Jose Earthquakes of Major League Soccer and becomes a fixture with the U.S. national team.

2 ▪ WUSA (Women's United Soccer Association), the women's eight-team pro league, stocked with some of the best players in the world, has a very solid first season.

1 ▪ The United States men's national team qualifies for its fourth straight World Cup thanks to a win over Jamaica, a tie between Mexico and Costa Rica and a loss by Honduras on October 7.

Orange Crushed

The Netherlands had a strong showing at the last World Cup in 1998, finishing the tournament in fourth place overall. Four years later, the Dutch have been shut out of the party, having failed to qualify for the 2002 World Cup finals in South Korea/Japan. Here is a look at the highest finishers that failed to qualify for the World Cup finals the next time around.

Team	Place	Year
Uruguay	1st*	1930
Hungary	2nd	1938†
Sweden	2nd	1958
Czechoslovakia	2nd	1962
Netherlands	2nd	1978
Yugoslavia	3rd	1930
Sweden	3rd	1950
France	3rd	1958
France	3rd	1986
Sweden	3rd	1994
Portugal	3rd	1966
Austria	4th	1934
Spain	4th	1950
Uruguay	4th	1954
Yugoslavia	4th	1962
England	4th	1990
Netherlands	4th	1998

*Uruguay chose not to compete in 1934. Since 1938, the defending champion has automatically received a spot in the World Cup finals.
†The 1938 was the last World Cup until 1950.

Attaboy Roy

Roy Lassiter is Major League Soccer's all-time leading goal scorer. The current Kansas City Wizard has tallied 88 goals in 165 games with Tampa Bay, D.C. United, Miami and Kansas City. Here is a look at the all-time MLS top five goal scorers:

Name	Games	Goals
Roy Lassiter	165	88
Raul Diaz Arce	150	82
Jaime Moreno	134	66
Jason Kreis	177	66
Preki	169	58

WUSAttendance

Thanks to the drawing power of U.S. national team star Mia Hamm, the Washington Freedom led the WUSA in attendance in their 2001 inaugural season. Here is a look at the first-year attendance figures for the upstart women's professional soccer league.

Team	Avg Attendance
Washington	14,421
Atlanta	11,092
Boston	8,012
Bay Area	7,692
Philadelphia	7,154
New York	5,724
San Diego	5,714
Carolina	5,255
League Average	**8,104**

2000-2001 Season in Review

FIFA Top 50 World Rankings

FIFA announced a new monthly world ranking system on Aug. 13, 1993 designed to "provide a constant international comparison of national team performances." The rankings are based on a mathematical formula that weighs strength of schedule, importance of matches and goals scored for and against. Games considered include World Cup qualifying and final rounds, Continental championship qualifying and final rounds, and friendly matches.

The formula was altered slightly in January 1999. Now the rankings annually take into account a team's seven best matches of the last eight years. Thereby favoring some teams that have been consistent over a long period of time but that may have stumbled just recently. At the end of the year, FIFA designates a Team of the Year. Teams of the Year so far have been Germany (1993) and Brazil (1994-2000).

2000

		Points	1999 Rank				Points	1999 Rank				Points	1999 Rank
1	Brazil	.821	11		18	Croatia	.656	9		35	Slovenia	.586	40
2	France	.801	3		19	Chile	.639	23		36	Saudi Arabia	.585	38
3	Argentina	.773	6		20	South Africa	.635	30			Iran	.585	48
4	Italy	.742	14		21	Russia	.634	18		38	Japan	.584	57
	Czech Republic	.742	2		22	Denmark	.625	11		39	Cameroon	.581	58
6	Portugal	.738	15			Sweden	.625	16		40	Korea Republic	.579	51
7	Spain	.735	4		24	Slovakia	.614	21		41	Israel	.578	26
8	Netherlands	.709	19		25	Scotland	.613	20		42	Greece	.574	34
9	Yugoslavia	.707	13		26	Tunisia	.611	31		43	Poland	.573	32
	Paraguay	.707	17		27	Belgium	.610	33		44	Austria	.572	28
11	Germany	.705	5		28	Morocco	.602	24		45	Peru	.560	42
12	Mexico	.693	10		29	Trinidad & Tobago	.600	43		46	Honduras	.557	69
13	Romania	.683	8		30	Turkey	.599	29		47	Hungary	.556	45
14	Norway	.675	7		31	Ireland Republic	.596	35		48	Jamaica	.555	41
15	Colombia	.672	25		32	Uruguay	.590	45			Zambia	.555	36
16	**USA**	.659	22		33	Egypt	.589	38		50	Iceland	.554	43
17	England	.657	12		34	Ukraine	.587	26					

2001 (as of Sept. 19)

		Points	2000 Rank				Points	2000 Rank				Points	2000 Rank
1	France	.810	2		18	Denmark	.664	22		35	Saudi Arabia	.615	36
2	Brazil	.799	1		19	**USA**	.660	16			Trinidad and Tobago	.615	29
3	Argentina	.794	3		20	Honduras	.656	46		37	Chile	.612	19
4	Italy	.737	4		21	Uruguay	.653	32		38	Iran	.610	36
5	Portugal	.732	6			Ireland	.653	31		39	Cameroon	.608	39
6	Spain	.730	7		23	Norway	.650	14		40	Nigeria	.604	52
7	Colombia	.719	15		24	Russia	.648	21			Egypt	.604	33
8	Netherlands	.717	8		25	Tunisia	.645	26		42	Slovakia	.598	24
9	England	.712	17		26	Belgium	.643	27		43	South Korea	.597	40
10	Mexico	.711	12		27	Poland	.634	27		44	Peru	.594	45
11	Paraguay	.710	9		28	Japan	.633	38		45	Ivory Coast	.593	51
12	Germany	.708	11		29	Costa Rica	.630	60		46	Ecuador	.591	53
13	Yugoslavia	.705	9		30	South Africa	.628	20		47	Israel	.590	41
14	Czech Republic	.704	4		31	Slovenia	.622	35		48	Bulgaria	.586	53
15	Romania	.695	13		32	Morocco	.621	28			Scotland	.586	25
16	Croatia	.674	18		33	Ukraine	.617	34		50	Austria	.585	44
17	Sweden	.673	22		34	Turkey	.616	30					

Countdown to 2002 World Cup

Date	Activity
Nov. 15, 2001	End of preliminary competition
Nov. 25, 2001	Completion of any necessary playoffs
Dec. 1, 2001	Draw for final competition held in Busan, South Korea
May 31, 2002	Final 32-team tournament begins in Seoul, South Korea
June 30, 2002	Championship match played at Yokohama International Sports Stadium in Yokohama, Japan.

2001 World Youth Championship

The FIFA World Youth Championship is held every two years to determine the best under-20 national team in the world. In 2001 it was contested for the 11th time since its inception in 1977. Held June 17-July 8 in Argentina.

First Round

Round robin; each team played the other three teams in its group once. Note that three points were awarded for a win and one point for a tie. (*) indicates team advanced to second round.

Group A	Gm	W	L	T	Pts	GF	GA
*Argentina	3	3	0	0	9	14	2
*Egypt	3	1	1	1	4	3	8
Finland	3	1	2	0	3	2	4
Jamaica	3	0	2	1	1	1	6

RESULTS: **June 17**—Argentina 2, Finland 0; Egypt 0, Jamaica 0. **June 20**—Finland 1, Jamaica 0; Argentina 7, Egypt 1; **June 23**—Argentina 5, Jamaica 1; Egypt 2, Finland 1.

Group B	Gm	W	L	T	Pts	GF	GA
*Brazil	3	3	0	0	9	10	1
*Germany	3	2	1	0	6	7	3
Iraq	3	1	2	0	3	5	9
Canada	3	0	3	0	0	0	9

RESULTS: **June 17**—Brazil 2, Germany 0; Iraq 3, Canada 0. **June 20**—Germany 4, Canada 0; Brazil 6, Iraq 1. **June 23**—Brazil 2, Canada 0; Germany 3, Iraq 1.

Group C	Gm	W	L	T	Pts	GF	GA
*Ukraine	3	1	0	2	5	5	3
*United States	3	1	1	1	4	5	3
*China	3	1	1	1	4	1	1
Chile	3	1	2	0	3	4	8

RESULTS: **June 17**—China 1, United State 0; Ukraine 4, Chile 2. **June 20**—Ukraine 0, China 0; United States 4, Chile 1; **June 23**—United States 1, Ukraine 1; Chile 1, China 0.

Group D	Gm	W	L	T	Pts	GF	GA
*Angola	3	1	0	2	5	3	2
*Czech Republic	3	1	1	1	4	3	3
*Australia	3	1	1	1	4	3	4
Japan	3	1	2	0	3	4	4

RESULTS: **June 18**—Angola 0, Czech Republic 0; Australia 2, Japan 0. **June 21**—Czech Republic 3, Australia 0; Angola 2, Japan 1. **June 24**—Angola 1, Australia 1; Japan 3, Czech Republic 0.

Group E	Gm	W	L	T	Pts	GF	GA
*Costa Rica	3	3	0	0	9	7	2
*Ecuador	3	1	1	1	4	3	3
*Netherlands	3	1	1	1	4	5	6
Ethiopia	3	0	3	0	0	4	8

RESULTS: **June 18**—Ecuador 2, Ethiopia 1; Costa Rica 3, Netherlands 1; **June 21**—Costa Rica 3, Ethiopia 1; Netherlands 1, Ecuador 1. **June 24**—Costa Rica 1, Ecuador 0; Netherlands 3, Ethiopia 2.

Group F	Gm	W	L	T	Pts	GF	GA
*Ghana	3	2	0	1	7	3	1
*France	3	1	0	2	5	7	2
*Paraguay	3	1	1	1	4	5	4
Iran	3	0	3	0	0	0	8

RESULTS: **June 18**—Ghana 2, Paraguay 1; France 5, Iran 0. **June 21**—France 2, Paraguay 2; Ghana 1, Iran 0; **June 24**—Ghana 0, France 0; Paraguay 2, Iran 0.

Round of 16

Single elimination with a 30 minute "golden goal" overtime period. If still tied, games are decided by shoot-out.

June 27	Egypt 2	United States 0
June 27	Argentina 2	China 1
June 27	France 3	Germany 1
June 27	Brazil 4	Australia 0
June 28	Paraguay 2	Ukraine 1
June 28	Netherlands 2	Angola 0
June 28	Czech Republic 2	Costa Rica 1
June 28	Ghana 1	Ecuador 0

Quarterfinals

July 1	Argentina 3	France 1
July 1	Ghana 2	OT	Brazil 1
July 1	Paraguay 1	Czech Republic 0
July 1	Egypt 2	Netherlands 1

Semifinals

July 4	Ghana 2	Egypt 0
July 4	Argentina 5	Paraguay 0

Final

July 8, 2001 in Buenos Aires. Attendance: 32,000.

Argentina 3...................................Ghana 0

Scoring: Argentina— Diego Colotto (6th), Javier Saviola (14th), Maximiliano Rodriguez (73rd).

Referee: Manuel Enrique Mejuto Gonzalez, Spain.

2001 Copa America

Contested for the 40th time in 2001 since its inception in 1916. Played July 11-July 29 and hosted by Colombia.

First Round

Round Robin; each team plays the other teams in its group once. Note that three points are awarded for a win and one for a tie. (*) indicates team advanced to the quarterfinals.

Group A	W	L	T	GF	GA	Pts
*Colombia	3	0	0	5	0	9
*Chile	2	1	0	5	3	6
Ecuador	1	2	0	5	5	3
Venezuela	0	3	0	0	7	0

RESULTS: **July 11**—Chile 4, Ecuador 1; Colombia 2, Venezuela 0. **July 14**—Chile 1, Venezuela 0; Colombia 1, Ecuador 0. **July 17**—Ecuador 4, Venezuela 0; Colombia 2, Chile 0.

Group B	W	L	T	GF	GA	Pts
*Brazil	2	1	0	5	2	6
*Mexico	1	1	1	1	1	4
*Peru	1	1	1	4	5	4
Paraguay	0	1	2	4	6	2

RESULTS: **July 12**—Peru 3, Paraguay 3; Mexico 1, Brazil 0; **July 15**—Brazil 2, Peru 0; Paraguay 0, Mexico 0. **July 18**—Peru 1, Mexico 0; Brazil 3, Paraguay 1.

Group C	W	L	T	GF	GA	Pts
*Costa Rica	2	0	1	6	1	7
*Honduras	2	0	1	3	1	6
*Uruguay	1	1	1	2	2	4
Bolivia	0	3	0	0	7	0

RESULTS: **July 13**—Uruguay 1, Bolivia 0; Costa Rica 1, Honduras 0. **July 16**—Uruguay 1, Costa Rica 1; Honduras 2, Bolivia 0 **July 19**—Costa Rica 4, Bolivia 0; Honduras 1, Uruguay 0.

Quarterfinals

Date	Site	Result
June 22	Pereira	Mexico 2, Chile 0
June 22	Armenia	Uruguay 2, Costa Rica 1
June 23	Armenia	Colombia 3, Peru 0
June 23	Manizales	Honduras 2, Brazil 0

Third Place

July 29	Bogota	Honduras 2, Uruguay 2

Honduras won the shootout, 5-4

Semifinals

Date	Site	Result
June 25	Pereira	Mexico 2, Uruguay 1
June 26	Manizales	Colombia 2, Honduras 0

Final

July 29, 2001 in Bogota.

Colombia 1 .... Mexico 0

Scoring: Colombia– Ivan Cordoba (65th).

FIFA Confederations Cup

Contested by the continental champions of Africa, Asia, Europe, North America, Oceania, and South America. Played in Japan and South Korea May 30-June 10, 2001.

First Round

Round Robin; each team plays the other teams in its group once. Note that three points are awarded for a win and one for a tie. (*) indicates team advanced to quarterfinals.

Group A	W	L	T	GF	GA	Pts
*France	2	1	0	9	1	6
*Australia	2	1	0	3	1	6
South Korea	2	1	0	3	6	6
Mexico	0	3	0	1	8	0

RESULTS: **May 30**–France 5, South Korea 0; Australia 2, Mexico 0. **June 1**–Australia 1, France 0; South Korea 2, Mexico 1; **June 3**–France 4, Mexico 0; South Korea 1, Australia 0.

Group B	W	L	T	GF	GA	Pts
*Japan	2	0	1	5	0	7
*Brazil	1	0	2	2	0	5
Cameroon	1	2	0	2	4	3
Canada	0	2	1	0	5	1

RESULTS: **May 31**–Brazil 2, Cameroon 0; Japan 3, Canada 0; **June 2**–Canada 0, Brazil 0; Japan 2, Cameroon 0; **June 4**–Brazil 0, Japan 0; Cameroon 2, Canada 0.

Semifinals

		Result
June 7		Japan 1, Australia 0
June 7		France 2, Brazil 1

Third Place Match

Date	Site	Result
June 9	Ulsan, S. Korea	Australia 1, Brazil 0

Final

Attendance: 65,335

Date	Site	Result
June 10	Yokohama, Japan	France 1, Japan 0

Scoring: FRA–Patrick Viera (30th minute).
Referee: Ali Bujsaim, UAE

2001 FIFA Under-17 World Championship

The World Cup for Under-17 national teams. Held in Trinidad & Tobago from Sept. 13-30, 2001. In the first round, 16 teams were separated into four groups of four for round robin play. The top two finishers from each group advanced to the quarterfinals.

Quarterfinals

Date		Result
Sept. 23		France 2, Brazil 1
Sept. 23		Nigeria 4, Australia 1
Sept. 24		Argentina 2, Mali 1 (OT)
Sept. 24		Burkina Faso 2, Costa Rica 0

Semifinals

Date		Result
Sept. 27		France 2, Argentina 1
Sept. 27		Nigeria 1, Burkina Faso 0

Third Place Match

Date	Site	Result
Sept. 30	Port of Spain	Burkina Faso 2, Argentina 0

Final

Attendance: 20,790

Date	Site	Result
Sept. 30	Port of Spain	France 3, Nigeria 0

Scoring: SPA–Florent Sinama Pongolle (34th minute), Anthony Le Tallec (53rd), Samuel Pietre (81st).
Referee: Lucillo Cardoso Cortez Batista, Portugal

U.S. Men's National Team
2001 Schedule and Results

Through Oct. 7, 2001. Games in **bold** type are CONCACAF Final Round Qualifying matches.

Date		Result	USA Goals	Site
Jan. 27	China	W, 2-1	McBride, own goal	Oakland, Calif.
Feb. 3	Colombia	L, 0-1	—	Miami, Fla.
Feb. 28	**Mexico**	W, 2-0	Wolff, Stewart	Columbus, Ohio
Mar. 3	Brazil	L, 1-2	Mathis	Pasadena, Calif.
Mar. 28	**Honduras**	W, 2-1	Stewart, Mathis	San Pedro Sulas, Honduras
Apr. 25	**Costa Rica**	W, 1-0	Wolff	Kansas City, Mo.
June 7	Ecuador	T, 0-0	—	Columbus, Ohio
June 16	**Jamaica**	T, 0-0	—	Kingston, Jamaica
June 20	**Trinidad & Tobado**	W, 2-0	Razov, Stewart	Foxboro, Mass.
July 1	**Mexico**	L, 0-1	—	Mexico City
Sept. 1	**Honduras**	L, 2-3	Stewart (2)	Washington, D.C.
Sept. 5	**Costa Rica**	L, 0-2	—	San Jose, Costa Rica
Oct. 7	**Jamaica**	W, 2-1	Moore (2)	Foxboro, Mass.
Nov. 11	**Trinidad & Tobago**			Port of Spain, Trinidad

Overall record: 6-5-2. **Team scoring:** Goals For–14; Goals Against–12.

2001 U.S. Men's National Team Statistics

Individual records for season through Oct. 1, 2001. Note that the column labeled "Career C/G" refers to career caps and goals.

Forwards	GP	GS	Mins	G	A	Pts	Career C/G
Chris Albright	3	1	133	0	0	0	7/1
Landon Donovan	5	4	388	0	1	1	6/1
Jovan Kirovski	6	5	406	0	0	0	51/7
Brian McBride	4	3	183	1	0	2	49/14
Joe-Max Moore	7	4	353	0	0	0	90/22
Ante Razov	5	3	254	1	0	2	18/5
Josh Wolff	5	3	329	2	1	5	8/3

Defenders	GP	GS	Mins	G	A	Pts	Career C/G
Jeff Agoos	10	10	900	0	1	1	114/3
Gregg Berhalter	4	2	92	0	0	0	21/0
Steve Cherundolo	7	7	587	0	1	1	8/0
Robin Fraser	1	1	90	0	0	0	28/0
Carlos Llamosa	9	8	731	0	0	0	2/0
Pablo Mastroeni	1	0	45	0	0	0	1/0
Mike Petke	1	1	90	0	0	0	1/0
Eddie Pope	7	7	630	0	0	0	42/4
David Regis	7	7	617	0	0	0	22/0
Tony Sanneh	10	9	800	0	1	1	2/0
Greg Vanney	4	3	270	0	0	0	14/0

Midfielders	GP	GS	Mins	G	A	Pts	Career C/G
Chris Armas	11	11	990	0	1	1	33/2
DaMarcus Beasley	2	2	162	0	0	0	2/0
Bobby Convey	1	1	64	0	0	0	2/0
Joe Enochs	1	0	28	0	0	0	1/0

Midfielders	GP	GS	Mins	G	A	Pts	Career C/G
Frankie Hejduk	1	1	61	0	0	0	30/5
Chris Henderson	1	0	13	0	0	0	79/3
Cobi Jones	6	3	363	0	0	0	142/14
Chris Klein	4	0	57	0	0	0	6/0
Eddie Lewis	2	1	100	0	0	0	29/2
Clint Mathis	6	5	439	2	3	7	11/3
John O'Brien	2	0	113	0	0	0	9/1
Ben Olsen	1	1	85	0	0	0	19/3
Preki Radosavljevic	2	0	44	0	0	0	28/4
Claudio Reyna	5	5	402	0	0	0	83/8
Earnie Stewart	8	8	720	5	0	10	1/0
John Thorrington	1	0	19	0	0	0	1/0
Richie Williams	4	2	134	0	0	0	17/0
Kerry Zavagnin	1	0	20	0	0	0	2/0

Goalkeepers	GP	GS	Mins	W-L-T	SO	GAA	Caps
Brad Friedel	5	5	450	2-2-1	2	1.20	71
Kasey Keller	4	4	360	2-1-1	3	0.25	50
Tony Meola	3	3	270	1-2-0	1	1.33	97

Yellow cards: Mathis (3), Llamosa, Reyna, Sanneh (2), Cherundolo, Friedel, Kirovski, Moore, Razov, Regis, Stewart, Wolff. **Red cards:** Jones.

Head coach: Bruce Arena; **Assistant coach:** Dave Sarachan; **Goal coach:** Milutin Soskic; **General manager:** Pam Perkins.

U.S. Women's National Team
2001 Schedule and Results
Through Oct. 1, 2001.

Date		Result	USA Goals	Site
Jan. 11	China	L, 0-1	—	Panyu, China
Jan. 14	China	T, 1-1	Lalor	Hangzhou, China
Mar. 7	Italy	L, 0-1	—	Rieti, Italy
Mar. 11	Canada	L, 0-3	—	Lagos, Portugal
Mar. 13	Portugal	W, 2-0	Welsh, Rigamat	Silves, Portugal
Mar. 15	Sweden	L, 0-2	—	Albufeira, Portugal
Mar. 17	Norway	L, 3-4	Marquand, Schott, Reddick	Quarteira, Portugal
June 30	Canada	T, 2-2	MacMillan, Milbrett	Toronto, Ontario
July 3	Canada	W, 1-0	Milbrett	Blaine, Minn.

Overall record: 2-5-2.
Team Scoring: Goals for–9; Goals against–14.

2001 U.S. Women's National Team Statistics
Individual records through Oct. 1, 2001. Note that the column labeled "Career C/G" refers to career caps and goals.

Forwards	GP	GS	Mins	G	A	Pts	Career C/G
Meredith Florance	2	2	134	0	0	0	3/0
Mia Hamm	2	1	79	0	1	1	218/127
Shannon MacMillan	2	2	101	1	0	2	126/35
Tiffeny Milbrett	4	3	315	2	1	5	168/85
Cindy Parlow	2	2	180	0	0	0	100/45
Alyssa Ramsey	3	3	220	0	0	0	8/0
Laura Schott	5	4	323	1	0	2	5/1
Kristen Weiss	4	1	146	0	0	0	4/0
Christie Welsh	5	4	302	1	1	3	19/12

Defenders	GP	GS	Mins	G	A	Pts	Career C/G
Keisha Bell	2	1	101	0	0	0	2/0
Thori Bryan	2	2	90	0	0	0	56/0
Lori Chalupny	4	1	175	0	0	0	4/0
Brandi Chastain	2	2	161	0	0	0	142/25
Michelle French	3	3	204	0	0	0	13/0
Anna Kraus	5	4	372	0	0	0	5/0
Ally Marquand	4	4	245	1	0	2	4/1
Lauren Orlandos	1	1	28	0	0	0	1/0
Christie Pearce	4	2	242	0	0	0	91/4

Defenders	GP	GS	Mins	G	A	Pts	Career C/G
Sara Randolph	2	1	86	0	0	0	2/0
Keri Raygor	4	1	170	0	0	0	13/0
Catherine Reddick	7	7	630	1	1	3	9/1
Kate Sobrero	3	3	270	0	0	0	66/0
Amy Steadman	4	1	159	0	0	0	4/0

Midfielders	GP	GS	Mins	G	A	Pts	Career C/G
Jenny Benson	1	0	21	0	0	0	1/0
Aleisha Cramer	8	4	452	0	1	1	15/0
Lorrie Fair	4	4	270	0	0	0	88/7
Julie Foudy	2	2	180	0	1	1	201/38
Devvyn Hawkins	5	4	327	0	0	0	5/0
Jena Kluegel	9	6	647	0	0	0	12/0
Jennifer Lalor	2	1	104	1	0	2	23/2
Kristine Lilly	2	1	128	0	0	0	227/87
Joanna Lohman	4	2	168	0	0	0	4/0
M.F. Monroe	6	5	414	0	0	0	9/0
Nikki Serlenga	4	2	206	0	0	0	30/6
Marcie Ward	3	2	124	0	0	0	3/0

Goalkeepers	GP	GS	Mins	W-L-T	SO	GAA	Career Caps	Goalkeepers	GP	GS	Mins	W-L-T	SO	GAA	Career Caps
Siri Mullinix	1	1	90	1-0-0	1	0.00	31	Jaime Pagliarulo	2	2	180	0-1-1	0	1.50	3
Emily Oleksiuk	2	2	180	1-1-0	1	2.00	2	Hope Solo	4	4	360	0-3-1	0	1.75	7

Yellow Cards: Hawkins, Lohman, Marquand, Milbrett, Reddick, Sobrero, Steadman. **Red Cards:** none.
Head coach: April Heinrichs; **General Manager:** Nils Krumins.

U.S. Under-20 Men's National Team
2001 Schedule and Results
Through Oct. 1, 2001. FIFA World Youth Championship games in **bold** type.

Date		Result	USA Goals	Site
Jan. 5	LA Galaxy (MLS)	L, 0-5	—	Chula Vista, Calif.
Jan. 7	D.C. United (MLS)	L, 0-1	—	Chula Vista, Calif.
Jan. 13	Hyang Hee University	W, 2-1	Buddle, Gray	Chula Vista, Calif.
Jan. 14	San Diego Flash (A-League)	T, 0-0	—	Chula Vista, Calif.
Jan. 23	Hyang Hee University	L, 1-2	Davis	Chula Vista, Calif.
Jan. 24	La Jolla Nomads	W, 5-1	Eskandarian, Barclay (2), Martino, Trembly	Chula Vista, Calif.
Jan. 28	Chivas	T, 0-0	—	Guadalajara, Mexico
Jan. 30	Mexico	W, 1-0	Martino	Guadalajara, Mexico
Feb. 1	Mexico	W, 2-1	Buddle, Trembly	Guadalajara, Mexico
Feb. 17	CSEPEL Auto Traders	W, 4-1	Martino, Buddle (2), Trembly	Chula Vista, Calif.
Feb. 20	San Diego St.	W, 2-1	Burciaga, Beckerman	Chula Vista, Calif.
Feb. 23	CSEPEL Auto Traders	T, 1-1	Buddle	Chula Vista, Calif.
Feb. 25	Univ. of San Francisco	W, 4-0	n/a	Chula Vista, Calif.
Mar. 9	NY/NJ MetroStars	L, 1-2	Cutler	Sunrise, Fla.
Mar. 11	Haiti Select	W, 5-1	Beasley, Gray, Martino, Donovan (2)	Ft. Lauderdale, Fla.
Mar. 13	Miami Fusion (MLS)	W, 2-0	Donovan (2)	Ft. Lauderdale, Fla.
Mar. 18	Guatemala	W, 5-0	Casey, Convey (2), Beasley, Davis	Tunapuna, Trinidad
Mar. 20	Trinidad & Tobago	W, 5-1	Beasley (2), Donovan, Convey, Davis	Tunapuna, Trinidad
Mar. 22	Costa Rica	T, 1-1	Martino	Tunapuna, Trinidad
April 11	LA Galaxy (MLS)	L, 1-4	n/a	Pasadena, Calif.
April 17	UCLA	L, 1-2	n/a	Chula Vista, Calif.
May 12	Costa Rica	T, 1-1	Gray	Chula Vista, Calif.
May 24	Italy	W, 2-1	Onyewu, Eskandarian	Toulon, France
May 26	Colombia	L, 1-3	Eskandarian	Le Pontet, France
May 28	Netherlands	T, 0-0	—	Aubagne, France
June 17	**China**	L, 0-1	—	Mendoza, Argentina
June 20	**Chile**	W, 4-1	Beasley (2), Davis, Buddle	Mendoza, Argentina
June 23	**Ukraine**	T, 1-1	Arena	Mendoza, Argentina
June 27	**Egypt**	L, 0-2	—	Buenos Aires

Overall record: 13-9-7. **Team scoring:** Goals For–52; Goals Against–35.

Club Team Competition
2000 Toyota Cup
Also known as the Intercontinental Cup; a year-end match for the Club World Championship between the European Cup and Copa Libertadores winners. Played on Nov. 28 in front of 51,000 at Tokyo's National Stadium. Its winner is generally recognized as the Club World Champion but with the recent advent of FIFA's Club World Championship that could change. Note that the 2001 FIFA Club World Championship was postponed until 2003 (see below).

Final
Boca Juniors (Argentina) 2 . . . . Real Madrid (Spain) 1
Scoring: Boca Juniors–Martin Palermo (3rd, 6th); Real Madrid–Roberto Carlos (12th).
Referee: Julian Oscar Ruiz Acosta (Colombia)

FIFA Club World Championship
The 2001 FIFA Club World Championship that was scheduled to be held in Spain from July 28-August 12 was postponed by FIFA until 2003. The reasons for the postponement on May 18 (just two months before the 12-team tournament was to start) given by FIFA were as follows: the timing of the originally scheduled tournament was inconvenient from the perspective of national and international fixtures (national leagues and Champions League qualifiers are in progress), the economic crises affecting some of the countries made some teams less eager to participate and FIFA's marketing partner for the event, Traffic, was having severe financial problems which would have negatively affected its ability to market the tournament to sponsors and broadcasters.

SOUTH AMERICA

2001 Liberatadores Cup

Contested by the league champions of South America's football union. Two-leg Semifinals and two-leg Final; home teams listed first. Winner Boca Juniors of Argentina plays European Champions League winner Bayern Munich in the 2001 Toyota Cup in Tokyo in November.

Final Four: Boca Juniors (Argentina), Cruz Azul (Mexico), Palmeiras (Brazil) and Rosario Central (Argentina)

Semifinals

Cruz Azul vs. Rosario Central

Cruz Azul 2 . . . . Rosario Central 0
Rosario Central 3 . . . . Cruz Azul 3
Cruz Azul wins 5-3 on aggregate

Boca Juniors vs. Palmeiras

Boca Juniors 2 . . . . Palmeiras 2
Palmeiras 2 . . . . Boca Juniors 2
Aggregate tied 4-4, Boca Juniors won shootout, 3-2

Final

Cruz Azul 1 . . . . Boca Juniors 0
Boca Juniors 1 . . . . Cruz Azul 0
Aggregate tied 1-1, Boca Juniors won shootout, 3-1

EUROPE

There are two major European club competitions sanctioned by the Union of European Football Associations (UEFA). The newly devised **Champions League** is a 72-team tournament made up from UEFA member countries. The teams are ranked 1-72 depending on how they finish in their own domestic leagues. UEFA ranks the quality of the 50 European national football associations (from number one Italy to number 50 Bosnia-Herzegovina) and assigns each association a number weighted by their respective ranking (UEFA calls this number a coefficient). Each team's domestic league finish is then multiplied by the coefficient and the teams are finally ranked (countries can enter a maximum of four teams).

The defending champions Real Madrid (from the UEFA Champions' Cup) and the other 15 highest-ranked teams form Group 1 and are given a direct entry into the League but the remaining 16 teams are determined by dividing teams 17-72 into three groups–Group 2 (teams 17-34), Group 3 (35-52) and Group 4 (53-72). The 22 teams in the lowest Group (Group 4) play two-leg, total goal elimination series. The 11 survivors advance to the Second Qualifying Phase and join the 17 teams from Group 3 to play 14 two-leg, total goal elimination series. The 14 clubs that survive this phase join the 18 teams from Group 2 to play in the Third Qualifying Phase. The winning clubs from the 16 two-leg, total goal elimination series advance to the Champions League for the right to play against the top-ranked 16 teams in Europe.

The 32 teams are separated into eight groups of four and play a round-robin series of home-and-home matches. The eight group winners and eight group runners-up advance to the next round where they are split up into four groups of four. The four group winners and runners-up then advance to the quarterfinals where home-and-home series are played through the semifinals until ultimately a single championship match for the European club championship is held. Winner Bayern Munich plays Libertadores Cup champion Boca Juniors of Argentina in the 2001 Toyota Cup this November in Tokyo.

The updated **UEFA Cup,** which is basically a combination of the what was known as the Cup Winners' Cup (played between national cup champions) and the old UEFA Cup (sort of a "best of the rest" tournament), is single-elimination throughout and features 121 additional teams plus 24 teams that have been already eliminated from the Champions League.

2000-01 Champions League

Following the first three qualifying phases, the first group phase starts with six-game double round robin in eight four-team groups (Sept. 9-Nov. 7) where two teams in each group advance to second group phase (Nov. 7-Mar. 22) where four four-team groups compete in the same format. Group winners and runners-up advance to the quarterfinals. (*) indicates team advanced to the next round. Note that in results listing under each table that the home team is listed first.

First Group Phase

Group A	W	T	L	GF	GA	Pts
*Real Madrid (Spain)	4	1	1	15	8	13
*Spartak Moscow (Russia)	4	0	2	9	3	12
Bayer Leverkusen (Germany)	2	1	3	9	12	7
Sporting Lisbon (Portugal)	0	2	4	5	15	2

RESULTS: **Sept. 12**–Spartak Moscow 2, Bayer Leverkusen 0; **Sept. 20**–Bayer Leverkusen 3, Sporting Lisbon 2; Real Madrid 1, Spartak Moscow 0; **Sept. 27**–Real Madrid 3, Bayer Leverkusen 2; Spartak Moscow 3, Sporting Lisbon 1; **Oct. 17**–Spartak Moscow 3, Sporting Lisbon 0; Real Madrid 5, Bayer Leverkusen 3; **Oct. 25**–Bayer Leverkusen 1, Spartak Moscow 0; Real Madrid 4, Sporting Lisbon 0; **Nov. 7**–Spartak Moscow 1, Real Madrid 0; Sporting Lisbon 0, Bayer Leverkusen 0.

Group B	W	T	L	GF	GA	Pts
*Arsenal (England)	4	1	1	11	8	13
*Lazio (Italy)	4	1	1	13	4	13
Shakhtar Donetsk (Ukraine)	2	0	4	10	15	6
Sparta Prague (Czech. Rep.)	1	0	5	6	13	3

RESULTS: **Sept. 9**–Lazio 3, Shakhtar Donetsk 0; **Sept. 11**–Arsenal 1, Sparta Prague 0; **Sept. 20**–Arsenal 3, Shakhtar Donetsk 2; Lazio 3, Sparta Prague 0; **Sept. 27**–Sparta Prague 3, Shakhtar Donetsk 2; Arsenal 2, Lazio 0; **Oct. 17**–Lazio 1, Arsenal 1; Shakhtar Donetsk 2, Sparta Prague 1; **Oct. 25**–Arsenal 4, Sparta Prague 2; Lazio 5, Shakhtar Donetsk 1; **Nov. 7**–Shakhtar Donetsk 0, Arsenal 0; Lazio 1, Sparta Prague 0.

Group C	W	T	L	GF	GA	Pts
*Valencia (Spain)	4	1	1	7	4	13
*Lyon (France)	1	0	3	8	6	9
Olympiakos (Greece)	3	0	3	6	5	9
Heerenveen (Netherlands)	1	1	4	3	9	4

RESULTS: **Sept. 9**–Lyon 3, Heerenveen 1; **Sept. 11**–Valencia 2, Olympiakos 1; **Sept. 20**–Valencia 1, Heerenveen 0; Olympiakos 1, Lyon 0; **Sept. 27**–Olympiakos 2, Heerenveen 0; Valencia 1, Lyon 0; **Oct. 17**– Heerenveen 1, Olympiakos 0; Valencia 2, Lyon 1; **Oct. 25**–Lyon 2, Heerenveen 0; Olympiakos 1, Valencia 0; **Nov. 7**–Lyon 1, Olympiakos 0; Valencia 1, Heerenveen 1.

Group D	W	T	L	GF	GA	Pts
*SK Sturm Graz (Austria) 3	1	2	8	11	10
*Galatasaray (Turkey) 2	2	2	10	13	8
Glasgow Rangers (Scotland) ..2	2	2	10	7	8
Monaco (France) 2	1	3	13	10	7

RESULTS: **Sept. 11**–Glasgow Rangers 5, SK Sturm Graz 0; **Sept. 12**–Galatasaray 3, Monaco 2; **Sept. 20**–Glasgow Rangers 1, Monaco 0; SK Sturm Graz 3, Galatasaray 0; **Sept. 27**–Monaco 5, SK Sturm Graz 0; Galatasaray 3, Glasgow Rangers 2; **Oct. 17**–Glasgow Rangers 0, Galatasaray 0; SK Sturm Graz 2, Monaco 0; **Oct. 25**–Monaco 4, Galatasaray 2; SK Sturm Graz 2, Glasgow Rangers 0; **Nov. 7**–Galatasaray 2, SK Sturm Graz 2; Glasgow Rangers 2, Monaco 2.

Group E	W	T	L	GF	GA	Pts
*Deportivo la Coruna (Spain) ..2	4	0	6	4	10
*Panathinaikos (Greece).......2	2	2	6	5	8
Hamburg (Germany).........1	3	2	9	6	6
Juventus (Italy)..............1	3	2	9	12	6

RESULTS: **Sept. 13**–Hamburg 4, Juventus 4; Panathinaikos 1, Deportivo la Coruna 1; **Sept. 19**–Juventus 2, Panathinaikos 1; Deportivo 2, Hamburg 1; **Sept. 26**–Panathinaikos 1, Hamburg 0; Juventus 0, Deportivo la Coruna 0; **Oct. 18**–Deportivo la Coruna 1, Juventus 1; Hamburg 1, Panathinaikos 0; **Oct. 24**–Deportivo la Coruna 1, Panathinaikos 0; Hamburg 3, Juventus 1; **Nov. 8**–Hamburg 1, Deportivo la Coruna 1; Panathinaikos 3, Juventus 1.

Group F	W	T	L	GF	GA	Pts
*Bayern Munich (Germany) ...3	2	1	9	4	11
*Paris St. Germain (France) 3	1	2	14	9	10
Rosenborg Trondheim (Norway) .2	1	3	13	15	7
Helsingborgs (Sweden).......1	2	3	6	14	5

RESULTS: **Sept. 13**–Bayern Munich 3, Helsingborgs 1; Rosenborg 3, Paris St. Germain 1; **Sept. 19**–Bayern Munich 3, Rosenborg 1; Paris St. Germain 4, Helsingborgs 1; **Sept. 26**–Paris St. Germain 1, Bayern Munich 0; Rosenborg 6, Helsingborgs 1; **Oct. 18**–Bayern Munich 2, Paris St. Germain 0; Helsingborgs 2, Rosenborg 0; **Oct. 24**–Bayern Munich 0, Helsingborgs 0; Paris St. Germain 7, Rosenborg 2; **Nov. 8**–Helsingborgs 1, Paris St. Germain 1; Rosenborg 1, Bayern Munich 1.

Group G	W	T	L	GF	GA	Pts
*Anderlecht (Belgium)........4	0	2	11	14	12
*Manchester United (England)..3	1	2	11	7	10
PSV Eindhoven (Netherlands) .3	0	3	9	9	9
Dynamo Kiev (Ukraine).......1	1	4	7	8	4

RESULTS: **Sept. 13**–Manchester United 5, Anderlecht 1; PSV Eindhoven 2, Dynamo Kiev 1; **Sept. 19**–Anderlecht 1, PSV Eindhoven 0; Dynamo Kiev 0, Manchester United 0; **Sept. 26**– Dynamo Kiev 4, Anderlecht 0; PSV Eindhoven 3, Manchester United 1; **Oct. 18**–Anderlecht 4, Dynamo Kiev 2; Manchester United 3, PSV Eindhoven 1; **Oct. 24**–Anderlecht 2, Manchester United 1; PSV Eindhoven 1, Dynamo Kiev 0; **Nov. 8**–Manchester United 1, Dynamo Kiev 0; Anderlecht 3, PSV Eindhoven 2.

Group H	W	T	L	GF	GA	Pts
*AC Milan (Italy).............3	2	1	12	6	11
*Leeds United (England) 2	3	1	9	6	9
Barcelona (Spain) 2	2	2	13	9	8
Besiktas (Turkey)............1	1	4	4	17	4

RESULTS: **Sept. 13**–AC Milan 4, Besiktas 1; Barcelona 4, Leeds United 0; **Sept. 19**–Besiktas 3, Barcelona 0; Leeds United 1, AC Milan 0; **Sept. 26**–AC Milan 2, Barcelona 0; Leeds United 6, Besiktas 0; **Oct. 18**–AC Milan 3, Barcelona 3; Besiktas 0, Leeds United 0; **Oct. 24**–AC Milan 2, Besiktas 1; Leeds United 1, Barcelona 1; **Nov. 8**–AC Milan 1, Leeds United 1; Barcelona 5, Besiktas 0.

Second Group Phase

Group A	W	T	L	GF	GA	Pts
*Valencia 3	3	0	10	2	12
*Manchester United..........3	3	0	10	3	12
SK Sturm Graz 2	0	4	4	13	6
Panathinaikos...............0	2	4	4	10	2

RESULTS: **Nov. 21**–Manchester United 3, Panathinaikos 1; Valencia 2, SK Sturm Graz 0; **Dec. 6**–Panathinaikos 0, Valencia 0; Manchester United 2, SK Sturm Graz 0; **Feb. 14**–SK Sturm Graz 2, Panathinaikos 0; Valencia 0, Manchester United 0; **Feb. 20**– SK Sturm Graz 2, Panathinaikos 1; Manchester United 1, Valencia 1; **Mar. 7**–Manchester United 1, Panathinaikos 1; Valencia 5, SK Sturm Graz 0; **Mar 13**– Manchester United 3, SK Sturm Graz 0; Valencia 2, Panathinaikos 1.

Group B	W	T	L	GF	GA	Pts
*Deportivo la Coruna 3	1	2	10	7	10
*Galatasaray 3	1	2	6	6	10
AC Milan 1	4	1	5	6	7
Paris St. Germain 1	2	3	8	10	5

RESULTS: **Nov. 21**–AC Milan 2, Galatasaray 2; Deportivo la Coruna 3, Paris St. Germain 1; **Dec. 6**–AC Milan 1, Deportivo la Coruna 0; Galatasaray 2, Paris St. Germain 0; **Feb. 14**–AC Milan 1, Paris St. Germain 1; Galatasaray 1, Deportivo la Coruna 0; **Feb. 20**–Deportivo la Coruna 2, Galatasaray 0; Paris St. Germain 1, AC Milan 1; **Mar. 7**–Deportivo la Coruna 4, Paris St. Germain 3; Galatasaray 2, AC Milan 0; **Mar. 13**–AC Milan 1, Deportivo la Coruna 1; Paris St. Germain 2, Galatasaray 0.

Group C	W	T	L	GF	GA	Pts
*Bayern Munich 4	1	1	8	5	13
*Arsenal 2	2	2	6	8	8
Lyon 2	2	2	8	4	8
Spartak Moscow 1	1	4	5	10	4

RESULTS: **Nov. 22**–Bayern Munich 1, Lyon 0; Spartak Moscow 4, Arsenal 1; **Dec. 5**–Arsenal 2, Bayern Munich 2; Lyon 3, Spartak Moscow 0; **Feb. 13**–Bayern Munich 1, Spartak Moscow 0; Arsenal 1, Lyon 0; **Feb. 21**–Arsenal 1, Lyon 1; Bayern Munich 3, Spartak Moscow 0; **Mar. 6**–Arsenal 1, Spartak Moscow 0; Lyon 3, Bayern Munich 0; **Mar. 14**–Bayern Munich 1, Arsenal 0; Spartak Moscow 1, Lyon 1.

Group D	W	T	L	GF	GA	Pts
*Real Madrid................4	1	1	14	9	13
*Leeds United 3	1	2	12	10	10
Anderlecht.................2	0	4	7	12	6
Lazio 1	2	3	9	11	5

RESULTS: **Nov. 22**–Anderlecht 1, Lazio 0; Real Madrid 2, Leeds United 0; **Dec. 5**–Leeds United 1, Lazio 0; Real Madrid 4, Anderlecht 1; **Feb. 13**–Leeds United 2, Anderlecht 1; Real Madrid 3, Lazio 2; **Feb. 21**–Leeds United 4, Anderlecht 1; Lazio 2, Real Madrid 1; **Mar. 6**–Lazio 2, Anderlecht 1; Real Madrid 3, Leeds United 2; **Mar. 14**–Anderlecht 2, Real Madrid 0; Leeds United 3, Lazio 3.

Quarterfinals
Two legs, total goals; home team listed first.

Real Madrid vs. Galatasaray

Apr. 3– Galatasaray 3...................Real Madrid 2
Apr. 18– Real Madrid 3.................Galatasaray 0
Real Madrid wins 5-3 on aggregate

Bayern Munich vs. Manchester United

Apr. 3– Manchester United 0.........Bayern Munich 1
Apr. 18– Bayern Munich 2..........Manchester United 1
Bayern Munich wins 3-1 on aggregate

EUROPE (Cont.)

Arsenal vs. Valencia

Apr. 4	Arsenal 2	Valencia 1
Apr. 17	Valencia 1	Arsenal 0

Valencia wins on away goals

Leeds United vs. Deportivo la Coruna

Apr. 4	Leeds United 3	Deportivo la Coruna 0
Apr. 17	Deportivo la Coruna 2	Leeds United 0

Leeds United wins 3-2 on aggregate

Semifinals

Two legs, total goals; home team listed first.

Real Madrid vs. Bayern Munich

May 1	Real Madrid 0	Bayern Munich 1
May 9	Bayern Munich 2	Real Madrid 1

Bayern Munich wins 3-1 on aggregate

Leeds United vs. Valencia

May 2	Leeds United 0	Valencia 0
May 8	Valencia 3	Leeds United 0

Valencia wins 3-0 on aggregate

Final

May 23 at the San Siro Stadium, Milan, Italy.
Attendance: 71,500

Bayern Munich 1 .... Valencia 1
Bayern Munich wins shootout, 5-4

Scoring: Valencia– Gaiska Mendieta (pen 3rd); Bayern Munich– Stefan Effenberg (pen 51st).
Shootout: BAYERN-Paulo Sergio (Miss), Salihamidzic (Goal), Zickler (Goal), Andersson (Miss), Effenberg (Goal), Lizarazu (Goal), Linke (Goal). VALENCIA-Mendieta (Goal), Carew (Goal), Zahovic (Miss), Carboni (Miss), Baraja (Goal), Kily Gonzazles (Goal), Pellegrino (Miss).

Referee: Dick Jol, Netherlands

2001 UEFA Cup

Two-leg Quarterfinals and Semifinals, one-game Final; home team listed first.
Final Eight: Alaves (Spain), Barcelona (Spain), Celta Vigo (Spain), Kaiserslautern (Germany), Liverpool (England), PSV Eindhoven (Netherlands), FC Porto (Portugal), Rayo Vallecano (Spain).

Quarterfinals

Kaiserslautern vs. PSV Eindhoven

Mar. 8	Kaiserslautern 1	PSV Eindhoven 0
Mar. 15	PSV Eindhoven 0	Kaiserslautern 1

Kaiserslautern wins 2-0 on aggregate

Barcelona vs. Celta Vigo

Mar. 8	Barcelona 2	Celta Vigo 1
Mar. 15	Celta Vigo 3	Barcelona 2

Barcelona wins on away goals

FC Porto vs. Liverpool

Mar. 8	FC Porto 0	Liverpool 0
Mar. 15	Liverpool 2	FC Porto 0

Liverpool wins 2-0 on aggregate

Alaves vs. Rayo Vallecano

Mar. 8	Alaves 3	Rayo Vallecano 0
Mar. 15	Rayo Vallecano 2	Alaves 1

Alaves wins 4-2 on aggregate

Semifinals

Barcelona vs. Liverpool

Apr. 5	Barcelona 0	Liverpool 0
Apr. 19	Liverpool 1	Barcelona 0

Liverpool wins 1-0 on aggregate

Alaves vs. Kaiserslautern

Apr. 5	Alaves 5	Kaiserslautern 1
Apr. 19	Kaiserslautern 1	Alaves 4

Alaves wins 9-2 on aggregate

Final

May 16 in Dortmund, Germany. **Attendance:** 65,000

Liverpool 5 .... OT .... Alaves 4

Scoring: Liverpool-Markus Babbel (3rd), Steven Gerrard (16th), Gary McAllister (pen 41st), Robbie Fowler (73rd), Delifi Geli (own goal 117th). Alaves-Ivan Alonso (27th), Javi Moreno (48th, 51st), Jordi Cruyff (88th).
Referee: G. Veissiere, France

2001 CONCACAF Giants' Cup

The Confederation of North, Central America and Caribbean Association Football (CONCACAF) instituted a new tournament in 2001. The all-new Giants' Cup joins the Champions' Series as CONCACAF club competitions set to be played each year. The Champions' Series has served as CONCACAF's premier club competition since its inception in 1962 and features the champions and runners-up of the domestic competitions within each of CONCACAF's 38 member nations.

The Giants' Series will include those clubs which are the most popular in each country, as determined by highest attendance. In addition, every two years the winners and runners-up of both the Giants' and Champions' Series (formerly known as the Champions' Cup) of the previous two years will meet in the eight-team FC Clubs' Cup (the inaugural edition is set for January 2003), a qualifying tournament to determine the representatives for the biennial FIFA Club World Championship (the next of which will be held in Spain in 2003).

Semifinals (Aug. 3)
D.C. United (MLS) def. CSD Communicaciones
(Guatemala), 2-1
CF America (Mexico) def. CD Saprissa
(Costa Rica), 2-1

Final (Aug. 5)
CF America def. D.C. United, 2-0

Major League Soccer
2001 Final Regular Season Standings

Conference champions (*) and playoff qualifiers (†) are noted. Teams receive three points for a win. The GF and GA columns refer to Goals For and Goals Against in regulation play. Number of seasons listed after each head coach refers to current tenure with club through the 2001 season. Note that the regular season was cut short in the wake of the September 11 terrorist attack.

Eastern Conference

Team	W	L	T	Pts	GF	GA
*Miami Fusion	16	5	5	53	57	36
†NY/NJ MetroStars	13	10	3	42	38	35
N.E. Revolution	7	14	6	27	35	52
D.C. United	8	16	2	26	42	50

Head Coaches: Mia— Ray Hudson (2nd season); **NY/NJ—** Octavio Zambrano (2nd); **NE—** Fernando Clavijo (2nd); **DC—** Thomas Rongen (3rd).

Central Conference

Team	W	L	T	Pts	GF	GA
*Chicago Fire	16	6	5	53	50	30
†Columbus Crew	13	7	6	45	49	36
†Dallas Burn	10	11	5	35	48	47
Tampa Bay Mutiny	4	21	2	14	32	68

Head Coaches: Chi— Bob Bradley (4th season); **Clb—** Tom Fitzgerald (6th, 1-3-2) fired on May 17 and replaced by assistant Greg Andrulis (12-4-4); **Dal—** Mike Jeffries (1st); **TB—** Alfonso Mondelo (1st, 3-13-1) resigned on July 5 and was replaced by assistant Perry Van Der Beck (1-8-1).

Western Conference

Team	W	L	T	Pts	GF	GA
*Los Angeles Galaxy	14	7	5	47	52	36
†San Jose Earthqaukes	13	7	6	45	47	29
†Kansas City Wizards	11	13	3	36	33	53
Colorado Rapids	5	13	8	23	36	47

Head Coaches: LA— Sigi Schmid (3rd season); **SJ—** Frank Yallop (1st); **KC—** Bob Gansler (3rd); **Colo—** Tim Hankinson (1st).

MLS All-Star Game

East 6, West 6

Date: Saturday, July 28, 2001 at Spartan Stadium in San Jose; **Attendance:** 23,512; **Coaches:** Ray Hudson, Miami (East) and Bob Bradley, Chicago (West); **MVP:** Landon Donovan, San Jose forward (West) — four goals.

	1	2	Final
East	3	3	— 6
West	4	2	— 6

Scoring

1st Half: WEST— Landon Donovan (Joe Cannon, Marcelo Balboa) 3; WEST— Donovan (Ariel Graziani, Mauricio Cienfuegos) 7; WEST— Donovan (Manny Lagos, Balboa) 19; WEST— Graziani (Ronald Cerritos, Jeff Agoos) 26; EAST— Alex Pineda Chacon (Brian McBride, Marco Etcheverry) 28; EAST— McBride (Preki, Santino Quaranta) 34; EAST— McBride (Preki, Quaranta) 39.

2nd Half: EAST— Mamadou Diallo (Pablo Mastroeni) 53; WEST— Dema Kovalenko (Cobi Jones, John Spencer) 69; EAST— Jim Rooney (unassisted) 84; EAST— Cate (Ian Bishop, Etcheverry) 87; WEST— Donovan (Matt McKeon, C.J. Brown) 92.

Goaltenders

Saves: EAST— Tim Howard 11, Nick Rimando 3; WEST— Joe Cannon 6, Zach Thornton 6.

Leading Scorers

Points

	Gm	G	A	Pts
Alex Pineda Chacon, Mia	25	19	9	47
Diego Serna, Mia	22	15	15	45
John Spencer, Col	23	14	7	35
Jeff Cunningham, Clb	22	10	13	33
John Wilmar Perez, Clb	25	8	15	31
Preki, Mia	24	8	14	30
Ariel Graziani, Dal	25	11	8	30
Abdul Thompson Conteh, DC	25	14	1	29
Ronald Cerritos, SJ	25	11	6	28
Eric Wynalda, Chi	21	11	6	28

Goals

	Gm	No
Alex Pineda Chacon, Mia	25	19
Diego Serna, Mia	22	15
John Spencer, Col	23	14
Abdul Thompson Conteh, DC	25	14
Ronald Cerritos, SJ	25	11
Ariel Graziani, Dal	25	11
Jeff Cunningham, Clb	22	10
Eric Wynalda, Chi	24	10
Mamadou Diallo, TB	22	9
Jaime Moreno, DC	24	9

Assists

	Gm	No
Diego Serna, Mia	22	15
John Wilmar Perez, Clb	25	15
Preki, Mia	24	14
Jeff Cunningham, Clb	22	13
Ian Bishop, Mia	23	13
Marco Etcheverry, DC	23	12
Oscar Pareja, Dal	24	12
Simon Elliott, LA	21	11
Ross Paule, NY/NJ	25	11

Four players tied with 10 each.

2001 MLS Attendance

Number in parentheses indicates last year's rank.

	Gm	Total	Avg
Wash. D.C. (2)	12	258,213	21,518
N.Y./N.J.(3)	13	270,487	20,807
Columbus (5)	13	227,644	17,511
Los Angeles (1)	13	226,035	17,387
Colorado (8)	13	214,249	16,481
Chicago (6)	14	229,438	16,388
New England (4)	13	203,501	15,654
Dallas (7)	13	163,465	12,574
Miami (12)	14	156,481	11,177
Kansas City (11)	13	142,402	10,954
Tampa Bay (10)	14	147,164	10,512
San Jose (9)	13	125,250	9,635
TOTAL	158	2,364,329	14,964

Major League Soccer (Cont.)

Shots

	Gm	No
Mamadou Diallo, TB.	22	94
Diego Serna, Mia.	22	90
Ariel Graziani, Dal.	25	83
Preki, Mia.	24	80
Jason Kreis, Dal.	25	77

Shots on Goal

	Gm	No
Abdul Thompson Conteh, DC	25	45
Mamadou Diallo, TB.	22	41
Jaime Moreno, DC	24	40
Preki, Mia.	24	40
Ariel Graziani, Dal.	25	40
Manny Lagos, SJ	26	39
Diego Serna, Mia	22	37

Game-Winning Goals

	Gm	GWG
Alex Pineda Chacon, Mia	25	7
Jeff Cunningham, Clb	22	5
Ezra Hendrickson, LA	23	5
Abdul Thompson Conteh, DC	25	5
Dema Kovalenko, Chi	25	4

Hat Tricks

	Gm	Hats
Clint Mathis, NY/NJ.	10	1
Dante Washington, Clb	21	1
Diego Serna, Mia.	22	1
Mamadou Diallo, TB.	22	1
John Spencer, Col.	23	1
Alex Pineda Chacon, Mia	25	1
Abdul Thompson Conteh, DC	25	1

Fouls Committed

	Gm	No
Matt McKeon, KC.	26	76
Diego Serna, Mia.	22	73
Oscar Pareja, Dal.	24	59
Danny Califf, LA	24	58
Brian Maisonneuve, Clb	25	57
Carey Talley, DC.	22	55
Diego Gutierrez, Chi	24	52
Peter Vagenas, LA.	26	52

Fouls Suffered

	Gm	No
Jaime Moreno, DC	24	87
DaMarcus Beasley, Chi	24	82
Jason Moore, Col	26	77
Diego Serna, Mia.	22	72
Mark Chung, NY/NJ	26	71
Manny Lagos, SJ	26	64
Andy Williams, NE.	20	63
Marco Etcheverry, DC	23	63

Offsides

	Gm	Offs
Mamadou Diallo, TB.	22	56
Junior Agogo, SJ	24	37
Ariel Graziani, Dal.	25	37
Abdul Thompson Conteh, DC	25	30
Diego Serna, Mia.	22	27
Chris Henderson, Mia	25	26

Corner Kicks

	Gm	CKs
Marco Etcheverry, DC	23	115
Richard Mulrooney, SJ	21	72
Cate, NE	22	70
Francisco Gomez, KC	24	66
Cobi Jones, LA.	22	64
John Wilmar Perez, Clb.	25	60

Minutes Played

	Mins
Zach Thornton, Chi	2496
Kerry Zavagnin, KC.	2472
Jesse Marsch, Chi	2429
Scott Garlick, Col.	2400
Matt Jordan, Dal	2388
Matt McKeon, KC	2372
Tim Howard, NY/NJ	2370
Steve Jolley, NY/NJ	2370

Leading Goaltenders

Goals Against Average

	Gm	Min	Shts	Svs	GAA	W-L-T
Zach Thornton, Chi	27	2496	145	111	1.08	16-6-5
Joe Cannon, SJ	25	2306	134	101	1.09	13-6-6
Nick Rimando, Mia	25	2300	155	116	1.29	14-5-5
Tim Howard, NY	26	2370	190	146	1.33	13-10-3
Tom Presthus, Clb	25	2309	178	136	1.36	12-7-6
Matt Reis, LA	16	1405	76	52	1.41	8-3-4
Tony Meola, KC	17	1534	111	80	1.64	7-8-2
Matt Jordan, Dal	26	2388	138	91	1.70	10-11-5
Mike Ammann, DC	19	1739	111	73	1.97	3-14-2
Scott Garlick, Col	26	2400	205	138	2.10	6-15-5

Saves

	Gm	No
Tim Howard, NY/NJ	26	146
Scott Garlick, Col	26	138
Tom Presthus, Clb	25	136
Adin Brown, TB.	22	118
Nick Rimando, Mia	25	116
Zach Thornton, Chi.	27	111

Shutouts

	Gm	No
Matt Jordan, Dal.	26	9
Zach Thornton, Chi.	27	9
Joe Cannon, SJ	25	7
Matt Reis, LA	16	6
Tom Presthus, Clb	25	5
Nick Rimando, Mia	25	5

Save Percentage

	Svs	SOG	SV Pct
Tim Howard, NY/NJ	146	190	.768
Zach Thornton, Chi	111	145	.766
Tom Presthus, Clb.	136	178	.764
Joe Cannon, SJ	101	134	.754
Nick Rimando, Mia	116	155	.748
Tony Meola, KC	80	111	.721

Team-by-Team Statistics

Players who played with more than one club during the season are listed with final team.

Eastern Conference

D.C. United

	Pos	Gm	Min	G	A	Pts
Abdul Thompson Conteh	.F	25	1676	14	1	29
Jaime Moreno	.F	24	1888	9	6	24
Mark Lisi	.M	25	1720	4	5	13
Marco Etcheverry	.M	23	2024	0	12	12
Santino Quaranta	.F	16	949	5	1	11
Bobby Convey	.M	12	992	1	7	9
Carey Talley	.D	22	1890	2	3	7
Bryan Namoff	.M	15	1152	0	7	7
Stephen Armstrong	.M	15	1112	3	0	6
Chris Albright	.F	23	1411	1	1	3
Craig Ziadie	.D	18	1307	0	3	3
Jose Alegria	.M	7	277	1	1	3
Ryan Nelsen	.M	19	1643	0	2	2
Brian Kamler	.M/D	17	1094	0	2	2
Eddie Pope	.D	19	1528	0	2	2
Mark Watson	.D	11	923	0	2	2
Scott Vermillion	.D	21	1546	0	1	1
Mark Simpson	.G	7	630	0	1	1
A.J. Wood	.D	7	180	0	0	0
Micah Cooks	.D	1	2	0	0	0

Goalkeepers	Gm	Min	W-L-T	Shts	Svs	GAA
Mark Simpson	7	630	5-2-0	44	30	1.71
Mike Amman	19	1739	3-14-2	111	73	1.97

New England Revolution

	Pos	Gm	Min	G	A	Pts
Cate	.M	22	1807	8	8	24
Matt Okoh	.F	18	885	6	2	14
Andy Williams	.F	20	1465	3	7	13
Wolde Harris	.F	21	1584	3	5	11
Ted Chronopoulos	.D	16	1314	5	1	11
William Sunsing	.M/F	22	1100	3	1	7
Mauricio Wright	.D	24	2156	2	0	4
Jay Heaps	.M/D	28	1917	0	4	4
Leonel Alvarez	.M	22	1849	1	1	3
Braden Cloutier	.M	13	1057	0	3	3
John Wolyniec	.F	5	330	1	0	2
Joe Franchino	.M	23	2027	0	1	1
Yari Allnut	.F	9	707	0	1	1
Leo Cullen	.D	14	794	0	1	1
Rusty Pierce	.D	23	1988	0	0	0
Alan Woods	.D	18	1475	0	0	0
Roland Aguilera	.M	3	76	0	0	0
Nick Downing	.D	5	279	0	0	0

Goalkeepers	Gm	Min	W-L-T	Shts	Svs	GAA
Nick Downing	1	3	0-0-0	1	1	0.00
Wolde Harris	1	1	0-0-0	0	0	0.00
Juergen Sommer	10	911	3-6-1	50	1	1.68
Jose Fernandez	7	578	1-3-2	45	30	1.87
Jeff Causey	11	1000	3-4-3	91	58	2.07

Miami Fusion

	Pos	Gm	Min	G	A	Pts
Alex Pineda Chacon	.M	25	2055	19	9	47
Diego Serna	.F	22	1978	15	15	45
Preki	.M	24	2139	8	14	30
Jim Rooney	.M	25	2294	6	9	21
Chris Henderson	.M	25	2184	3	8	14
Ian Bishop	.M	23	2115	0	13	13
Johnny Torres	.M	23	1446	2	5	9
Tyrone Marshall	.M/D	23	1831	3	2	8
Pablo Mastroeni	.M	25	2290	2	2	6
Shaker Asad	.M	20	978	1	2	4
Lazo Alavanja	.M	16	896	0	3	3
Greg Simmonds	.F	9	415	0	2	2
Ivan McKinley	.M/D	19	1250	0	2	2
Ian Woan	.M	4	107	0	2	2
Nick Rimando	.G	25	2300	0	2	2
Brian Dunseth	.D	18	1066	0	1	1
Jeff Bilyk	.M	15	535	0	1	1
Carlos Llamosa	.D	20	1827	0	0	0
Tim Sahaydak	.D	4	171	0	0	0
Pete Marino	.F	2	19	0	0	0
Judah Cooks	.M	2	24	0	0	0
Kyle Beckerman	.M	1	14	0	0	0
Randy Merkel	.D	1	6	0	0	0

Goalkeepers	Gm	Min	W-L-T	Shts	Svs	GAA
Nick Rimando	25	2300	14-5-5	155	116	1.29
Jeff Cassar	1	90	1-0-0	9	5	3.00

New York/New Jersey MetroStars

	Pos	Gm	Min	G	A	Pts
Clint Mathis	.M/F	10	905	7	5	19
Rodrigo Faria	F	21	1344	8	2	18
Petter Villegas	.M	22	1798	5	5	15
Adolfo Valencia	.F	17	1155	5	4	14
Ross Paule	.M	25	1481	1	11	13
Mark Chung	.M	26	2226	3	6	12
Daniel Hernandez	.D	16	1358	1	7	9
Alex Comas	.F	12	748	2	2	6
Billy Walsh	.M	18	756	3	0	6
Tab Ramos	.M	18	1459	0	5	5
Pedro Alvarez	.M	21	1494	1	1	3
Steve Jolley	.D	26	2370	0	3	3
Richie Williams	.M	21	1868	0	2	2
Michael Butler	.F	1	24	1	0	2
Mike Petke	.D	25	2194	0	1	1
Gilmar	.M/F	4	191	0	1	1
Martin Klinger	.F	9	272	0	0	0
Roy Myers	.M/F	3	168	0	0	0
Orlando Perez	.M	24	1948	0	0	0
Mark Semioli	.D	14	549	0	0	0
Cordt Weinstein	.F	2	41	0	0	0
Fausto Klinger	.M	1	14	0	0	0
Mersim Beskovic	.D	3	11	0	0	0

Goalkeepers	Gm	Min	W-L-T	Shts	Svs	GAA
Tim Howard	26	2370	13-10-3	190	146	1.33

Major League Soccer (Cont.)
Central Conference

Chicago Fire

	Pos	Gm	Min	G	A	Pts
Eric Wynalda	F	24	1349	10	5	25
Dema Kovalenko	M	25	2311	8	7	23
Peter Nowak	M	18	1560	6	10	22
Hristo Stoitchkov	F	17	916	6	5	17
Jesse Marsch	M	27	2429	3	6	12
Jamar Beasley	M/F	19	746	4	3	11
DaMarcus Beasley	M	24	2156	2	6	10
Sergi Daniv	M	14	813	2	3	7
Diego Gutierrez	M	24	2123	1	5	7
Ante Razov	F	7	541	2	0	4
Josh Wolff	F	3	244	2	0	4
Carlos Bocanegra	D	15	1250	1	2	4
Evan Whitfield	D	26	1882	0	3	3
David Vaudreuil	M/D	9	415	0	3	3
David Hayes	F	3	80	1	0	2
Andrew Lewis	D	13	502	1	0	2
Chris Armas	M	21	1940	0	1	1
C.J. Brown	D	22	1882	0	1	1
Jim Curtin	D	18	1194	0	1	1
Matt Chulis	D	1	71	0	0	0
Chad Prince	D	1	5	0	0	0
Amos Magee	F	1	2	0	0	0

Goalkeepers	Gm	Min	W-L-T	Shts	Svs	GAA
Zach Thornton	27	2496	16-6-5	145	111	1.08

Dallas Burn

	Pos	Gm	Min	G	A	Pts
Ariel Graziani	F	25	2208	11	8	30
Jason Kreis	F	25	2175	7	10	24
Bobby Rhine	F	18	972	5	8	18
Jorge Rodriguez	M/D	24	2232	6	5	17
Oscar Pareja	M	24	2113	2	12	16
Antonio Martinez	M	17	1011	1	9	11
Chad Deering	M	25	2317	2	4	8
Joselito Vaca	M	21	1461	2	4	8
Ryan Suarez	D	20	1666	2	3	7
Richard Farrer	D	25	2108	2	3	7
Aleksey Korol	F	15	372	2	1	5
Lubos Kubik	D	11	998	1	2	4
Edward Johnson	F	10	263	2	0	4
Paul Broome	M	22	1513	1	2	4
Eric Dade	D	21	1639	0	1	1
Miles Joseph	M	9	389	0	1	1
Ted Eck	M	9	323	0	0	0
Josue Mayard	D	3	27	0	0	0
Justin Evans	M	15	622	0	0	0

Goalkeepers	Gm	Min	W-L-T	Shts	Svs	GAA
Matt Jordan	26	2388	10-11-5	138	91	1.70
Chris Snitko	1	24	0-0-0	2	0	7.50

Columbus Crew

	Pos	Gm	Min	G	A	Pts
Jeff Cunningham	F	22	1770	10	13	33
John Wilmar Perez	M	25	2105	8	15	31
Brian Maisonneuve	M	25	2184	8	5	21
Dante Washington	F	21	1203	7	3	17
Brian West	M/F	21	1657	5	5	15
Brian McBride	F	15	1326	1	6	8
Edson Buddle	F	17	556	3	2	8
Robert Warzycha	M	11	710	3	2	8
Mike Lapper	D	24	1929	1	3	5
Mike Duhaney	D	25	2164	1	2	4
John Harkes	M	23	1793	0	3	3
Tenywa Bonseu	D	24	2160	0	3	3
Ansil Elcock	M/D	15	725	1	0	2
Duncan Oughton	D	20	1233	0	1	1
Mike Clark	D	25	2280	0	1	1
Mario Longo	M	4	32	0	1	1
Todd Yeagley	M/D	5	254	0	1	1
John DeBrito	M	2	48	0	0	0
Kevin Adams	D	5	42	0	0	0

Goalkeepers	Gm	Min	W-L-T	Shts	Svs	GAA
Mark Dougherty	2	100	1-0-0	6	5	0.90
Tom Presthus	25	2309	12-7-6	178	136	1.36

Tampa Bay Mutiny

	Pos	Gm	Min	G	A	Pts
Mamadou Diallo	F	22	1818	9	5	23
Steve Ralston	M	25	2221	7	6	20
Eric Quill	F	24	1840	2	8	12
Jair	M	25	1565	1	6	8
Devin Barclay	F	23	1324	3	2	8
Josh Keller	M	22	1952	3	1	7
Eric Denton	M/D	24	1884	1	4	6
Ali Curtis	F	20	1211	2	1	5
Steve Trittschuh	D	18	1600	1	2	4
John Maessner	M	24	1707	1	2	4
Joseph Addo	D	20	1467	1	1	3
Danny Pena	D	16	1117	1	0	2
Craig Demmin	D	19	1702	0	1	1
Kevin Anderson	M	10	443	0	1	1
Gus Kartes	M	18	516	0	0	0
Scott Cannon	D	9	681	0	0	0
Diego Sonora	M/D	4	353	0	0	0
Brian Kelly	M	2	13	0	0	0
Chad McCarty	D	2	79	0	0	0
Kalin Bankov	M	1	45	0	0	0
Albert Munoz	M	2	21	0	0	0
Paul Schneider	F	1	10	0	0	0
Don Gramenz	D	1	1	0	0	0

Goalkeepers	Gm	Min	W-L-T	Shts	Svs	GAA
Adin Brown	22	2018	3-16-3	179	118	2.27

Western Conference

Colorado Rapids

	Pos	Gm	Min	G	A	Pts
John Spencer	M/F	23	2083	14	7	35
Marcelo Balboa	D	24	2119	5	6	16
Chris Carrieri	F	19	1081	5	4	14
Paul Bravo	M	23	1352	6	0	12
Raul Diaz Arce	F	14	944	4	4	12
Carlos Valderrama	M	24	2142	1	9	11
Imad Baba	M	22	1631	1	6	8
Jason Moore	M	26	1798	0	4	4
Robin Fraser	D	20	1714	0	2	2
Scott Garlick	GK	24	2400	0	2	2
Lance Key	D	13	1193	0	1	1
Steve Shak	D	14	806	0	1	1
Ritchie Kotschau	D	22	2000	0	1	1
Wes Hart	M	5	178	0	1	1
Chris Martinez	D	26	2189	0	0	0
Steven Herdsman	D	20	1276	0	0	0
Chris Dawes	D	16	1478	0	0	0
Neathen Gibson	F	8	154	0	0	0
Seth Trembly	M/D	4	198	0	0	0
Geoff Aunger	D	1	82	0	0	0
Rivers Guthrie	M	1	10	0	0	0

Goalkeepers	Gm	Min	W-L-T	Shts	Svs	GAA
David Kramer	5	466	0-3-2	34	25	1.55
Scott Garlick	26	2400	6-15-6	205	138	2.10

Kansas City Wizards

	Pos	Gm	Min	G	A	Pts
Roy Lassiter	F	23	1648	7	1	15
Francisco Gomez	M	24	1320	4	6	14
Matt McKeon	M	26	2372	5	2	12
Chris Brown	M/F	27	2034	5	2	12
Chris Klein	M	24	2039	3	6	12
Onandi Lowe	F	13	1034	4	3	11
Gary Glasgow	F	18	1124	2	5	9
Kerry Zavagnin	M	27	2472	1	5	7
Mo Johnston	F	11	864	1	3	5
Mike Burns	D	19	1179	0	3	3
Mark Santel	M	21	813	1	1	3
Peter Vermes	D	20	1826	0	2	2
Andrew Gregor	M	13	812	0	2	2
Michael Green	D	3	154	0	1	1
Brandon Prideaux	D	23	2028	0	1	1
Tahj Jakins	D	10	604	0	0	0
Brian Johnson	M	3	62	0	0	0
Nick Garcia	D	24	2142	0	0	0
Jose Burciaga Jr.	D	3	93	0	0	0
Narciso Fernandes	M/F	1	6	0	0	0

Goalkeepers	Gm	Min	W-L-T	Shts	Svs	GAA
Tony Meola	17	1534	7-8-2	111	80	1.64
Bo Oshoniyi	11	938	4-5-1	74	48	2.40

Los Angeles Galaxy

	Pos	Gm	Min	G	A	Pts
Cobi Jones	M/F	22	1890	6	10	22
Sasha Victorine	M	24	1758	7	5	19
Luis Hernandez	F	14	1189	8	3	19
Greg Vanney	D	22	2032	6	3	15
Simon Elliott	M	21	1909	1	11	13
Ezra Hendrickson	D	23	2132	5	3	13
Mauricio Cienfuegos	M	25	2229	2	7	11
Peter Vagenas	M	26	2197	0	0	0
Danny Califf	D	24	2161	3	1	7
Brian Mullan	F	10	809	2	2	6
Adam Frye	D	22	1065	2	2	6
Marvin Quijano	F	12	730	2	2	6
Alexi Lalas	D	11	764	2	2	6
Paul Caligiuri	D	24	1854	0	4	4
Brian Ching	F	8	228	1	1	3
Craig Waibel	D	9	279	0	1	1
Isaias Bardales Jr.	F	12	270	0	0	0
Alex Bengard	M	3	56	0	0	0

Goalkeepers	Gm	Min	W-L-T	Shts	Svs	GAA
Kevin Hartman	11	1007	6-4-1	66	48	1.25
Matt Reis	16	1405	8-3-4	76	52	1.41

San Jose Earthquakes

	Pos	Gm	Min	G	A	Pts
Ronald Cerritos	F	25	1954	11	6	28
Manny Lagos	M	26	2310	8	8	24
Landon Donovan	F	22	1666	7	10	24
Ian Russell	M	26	2216	3	9	15
Dwayne DeRosario	F	21	1072	5	4	14
Richard Mulrooney	M	21	1878	1	9	11
Junior Agogo	F	24	1186	5	3	13
Wade Barrett	M	24	2125	1	6	8
Zak Ibsen	D	24	2137	2	3	7
Jeff Agoos	D	20	1765	2	2	6
Troy Dayak	D	25	2236	2	0	4
Ramiro Corrales	D	14	1058	1	1	3
Scott Bower	M	12	391	0	3	3
Ronnie Ekelund	M	16	1421	0	2	2
Jimmy Conrad	D	16	928	0	0	0
Eddie Robinson	M/D	1	88	0	0	0
Dario Brose	M	1	3	0	0	0

Goalkeepers	Gm	Min	W-L-T	Shts	Svs	GAA
Jon Conway	1	90	0-1-0	5	3	1.00
Joe Cannon	25	2306	13-6-6	134	101	1.09

2001 U.S. Open Cup

Dating back to 1914, the U.S. Open Cup is the oldest soccer competition in the United States and is among the oldest in the world. The U.S. Open Cup is a single-elimination tournament open to all amateur and professional teams in the United States. Thirty-two teams competed for the 87-year-old Dewar Cup trophy in the 2001 U.S. Open Cup.

Quarterfinals

June 24, 2001

Chicago Fire (MLS) def. Pittsburgh Riverhounds (A-League), 3-2 (OT)

Los Angeles Galaxy (MLS) def. San Jose Earthquakes (MLS), 1-1 (10-9 on PKs)

New England Revolution (MLS) def. Columbus Crew (MLS), 2-1

D.C. United (MLS) def. Richmond Kickers (A-League), 2-1

Semifinals

August 22, 2001

Los Angeles Galaxy def. Chicago Fire, 2-1 (OT)

New England Revolution def. D.C. United, 2-0

Final

October 27, 2001

New England Revolution at Los Angeles Galaxy (see Updates chapter)

Major League Soccer (Cont.)
MLS Playoffs

Instead of a standard best-of-three series, each quarterfinal and semifinal of the MLS playoffs is won by the first team to accumulate five points. Just like in the regular season, three points were awarded for a win and one for a tie. The standard 10-minute, sudden-death overtime is played following each game in the event the score is tied. The winner of the series is the first team to reach or exceed five points within the three games. Should the series remain even on points following regulation or overtime of the third game (3-3, or 4-4) the two clubs would move directly to an additional 20-minute "golden-goal" overtime period (two 10-minute halves). If neither team scores during the 20-minute period, the game would be decided on penalty kicks.

Quarterfinals

Date	Result
Sept. 22	.....................at Miami 2, Kansas City 0
Sept. 26	.................at Kansas City 3, Miami 0
Sept. 29	.....................at Miami 2, Kansas City 1

Miami wins series, 6-3

Date	Result
Sept. 22	.....................San Jose 3, at Columbus 1
Sept. 26	.....................at San Jose 3, Columbus 0

San Jose wins series, 6-0

Date	Result
Sept. 23	..................at Los Angeles 1, N.Y./N.J. 1
Sept. 26	..................at N.Y./N.J. 4, Los Angeles 1
Sept. 29	............at Los Angeles 3, N.Y./N.J. 2 (OT)

Series tied 4-4, Los Angeles wins series in tiebreaker

Date	Result
Sept. 20	.......................at Chicago 2, Dallas 0
Sept. 23	.......................at Dallas 1, Chicago 1
Sept. 29	.,.....................at Chicago 2, Dallas 0

Chicago wins series, 7-1

Semifinals and MLS Cup 2001
See Updates chapter.

A-League

2001 Final Standings

The A-League serves as a minor league system for Major League Soccer. The division II outdoor league is part of the United Systems of Independent Soccer Leagues (USISL) and is recognized by U.S. Soccer. MLS and the USISL have an agreement where MLS teams can assign players to the A-League and call-up A-League players when desired. Conference champions (*) and playoff qualifiers (†) are noted.

Northern Conference

Team	W	T	L	Pts	GF	GA
* Hershey Wildcats	16	3	7	75	45	20
† Rochester Raging Rhinos	16	4	6	74	43	27
† Pittsburgh Riverhounds	10	4	12	50	39	39
Montreal Impact	10	2	14	45	29	37
Connecticut Wolves	9	6	11	43	30	37
Long Island Rough Riders	6	4	16	33	31	50
Toronto Lynx	7	3	16	32	20	41

Western Conference

Team	W	L	T	Pts	GF	GA
* Vancouver Whitecaps	16	2	8	74	44	33
† San Diego Flash F.C.	14	1	11	68	55	42
† Milwaukee Rampage	14	2	10	63	45	40
† Portland Timbers	13	3	10	62	41	38
Seattle Sounders	13	1	12	57	40	39
Minnesota Thunder	9	2	15	41	29	34
El Paso Patriots	8	4	14	40	39	42

Central Conference

Team	W	L	T	Pts	GF	GA
* Richmond Kickers	16	3	7	76	47	34
† Charleston Battery	16	1	9	73	51	34
† Charlotte Eagles	14	2	10	66	50	41
† Nashville Metros	14	2	10	63	47	48
† Atlanta Silverbacks	13	1	12	59	48	39
Indiana Blast	8	0	18	35	38	55
Cincinnati Riverhawks	6	0	20	27	39	80

Note: Three points are awarded for a victory in regulation or overtime. One point is awarded for a shootout win. Shootouts occur if a game is tied after a 15-minute sudden-death overtime

Playoffs
First Round (Total Goals)
Pittsburgh vs. Charleston

Sept. 20	Pittsburgh 2, Charleston 1	at Pittsburgh
Sept. 22	Pittsburgh 3, Charleston 1	at Charleston

Pittsburgh wins 5-2 on aggregate

San Diego vs. Atlanta

Sept. 19	San Diego 2, Atlanta 0	at Atlanta
Sept. 23	Atlanta 2, San Diego 2	at San Diego

San Diego wins 4-2 on aggregate

Portland vs. Charlotte

Sept. 21	Portland 2, Charlotte 0	at Portland
Sept. 22	Portland 3, Charlotte 2	at Charlotte

Portland wins 5-2 on aggregate

Milwaukee vs. Nashville

Sept. 19	Milwaukee 3, Nashville 2	at Nashville
Sept. 22	Nashville 1, Milwaukee 0	at Milwaukee

Aggregate tied 3-3, Milwaukee advances 4-3 on penalty kicks

Quarterfinals (Total Goals)
Richmond vs. Milwaukee

Sept. 29	Richmond 2, Milwaukee 2	at Milwaukee
Sept. 30	Milwaukee 2, Richmond 1	at Richmond

Milwaukee wins 4-3 on aggregate

Hershey vs. Portland

Sept. 27	Hershey 2, Portland 0	at Portland
Sept. 29	Hershey 1, Portland 0	at Hershey

Hershey wins 3-0 on aggregate .

Vancouver vs. San Diego

Sept. 26	San Diego 2, Vancouver 0	at San Diego
Sept. 29	Vancouver 4, San Diego 1	at Vancouver

Vancouver wins 4-3 on aggregate

Rochester vs. Pittsburgh

Sept. 26	Pittsburgh 2, Rochester 1	at Pittsburgh
Sept. 29	Rochester 3, Pittsburgh 0	at Rochester

Rochester wins 4-2 on aggregate

Semifinals and Finals
see Updates chapter.

2001 WUSA Final Standings

The WUSA (Women's United Soccer Association) is the top women's outdoor professional league. The league was formed in 2000 and began play in 2001. Three points awarded for a win, one point for a tie; (*) indicates team advanced to semifinals.

	W	L	T	Pts	GF	GA
*Atlanta	10	4	7	37	31	21
*Bay Area	11	6	4	37	27	23
*New York	9	7	5	32	30	25
*Philadelphia	9	8	4	31	35	28
San Diego	7	7	7	28	29	28
Boston	8	10	3	27	29	35
Washington	6	12	3	21	26	35
Carolina	6	12	3	21	28	40

Semifinals

Aug. 18 .at Bay Area 3, New York 2
Aug. 18 . . . . .at Atlanta 3, Philadelphia 2 (OT)

Final

Held Aug. 25, 2001 at Foxboro Stadium, Foxboro, Mass.
Attendance: 21,078
Bay Area 3 . . . . .Atlanta 3

Scoring

First Half: BAY–Brandi Chastain (Kelly Lindsey) 6th; ATL–Kylie Bivens (Homare Sawa, Nancy Augustyniak) 11th; ATL–Charmaine Hooper (Cindy Parlow, Briana Scurry) 14th; BAY–Julie Murray (Christina Bell) 43rd.
Second Half: ATL–Sun Wen (Parlow, Nikki Serlenga) 83rd; BAY–Tisha Venturini (Sissi, Katia) 86th.
Bay Area won WUSA championship on penalty kicks, 4-2

Colleges

MEN

2000 Final *Soccer America* Top 20

Final 2000 regular season poll including games through Nov. 12. Conducted by the national weekly *Soccer America* and released in the Nov. 27 issue. Listing includes records through conference playoffs as well as NCAA tournament record and team lost to. Teams in **bold** type went on to reach NCAA Final Four. All tournament games decided by penalty kicks are considered ties.

		Nov. 12 Record	NCAA Recap			Nov. 12 Record	NCAA Recap
1	North Carolina	19-2-0	2-1 (Indiana)	11	SMU	17-4-0	3-1 (Connecticut)
2	San Jose State	20-0-1	0-1 (Indiana)	12	Furman	17-3-2	0-1 (Clemson)
3	San Diego	15-1-2	1-1 (Creighton)	13	CS-Fullerton	15-5-1	0-1 (Stanford)
4	Stanford	16-2-1	2-1 (SMU)	14	UCLA	12-6-0	0-1 (San Diego)
5	**Connecticut**	15-3-2	5-0	15	Saint Louis	13-3-2	0-1 (Kentucky)
6	Virginia	15-5-1	2-1 (Creighton)	16	St. John's	13-4-2	1-1 (Virginia)
7	**Creighton**	18-3-0	4-1 (Connecticut)	17	Rhode Island	16-5-1	1-1 (North Carolina)
8	Clemson	13-3-2	1-1 (Connecticut)				
9	Duke	14-5-0	1-1 (Brown)	18	**Indiana**	13-6-0	3-1 (Creighton)
10	Washington	17-4-0	0-1 (UAB)	19	South Carolina	12-3-3	0-1 (Duke)
				20	Ohio State	11-5-1	0-1 (Creighton)

NCAA Division I Tournament

First Round (Nov. 17-19)

Kentucky 1 . . . . .at St. Louis 0
Kentucky won shootout 4-2
UAB 0 . . . . .4 OT . . . . .at Washington 1
at North Carolina 3 . . . . . .OT . . . . . . .William & Mary 2
at San Diego 1 . . . . .OT . . . . .UCLA 0
St John's 1 .at James Madison 0
Indiana 4 .at San Jose State 0
at Southern Methodist 2 .IUPUI 0
at Stanford 4 . . . . .California St.-Fullerton 0
at Connecticut 3 . . . . .Dartmouth 0
Duke 1 .at South Carolina 0
at Brown 2 . . . . .Vermont 0
at Rhode Island 3 . . . . .Boston College 0
Creighton 1 . . . . .at Ohio State 0
at Virginia 5 . . . . .Lehigh 0
at Clemson 3 . . . . .Furman 2
Illinois-Chicago 1 . . . . .at Bradley 0

Second Round (Nov. 25-26)

Connecticut 2 . . . . .OT . . . . .at Clemson 1
Creighton 3 . . . . .at San Diego 0
at Southern Methodist 3 . . . . .Kentucky 1
Indiana 2 . . . . .at Washington 1
at Stanford 6 .Illinois-Chicago 0
at Brown 1 . . . . .Duke 0
at North Carolina 3 . . . . .Rhode Island 1
at Virginia 2 . . . . .St. John's 1

Quarterfinals (Dec. 2-3)

Indiana 1 . . . . .at North Carolina 0
Creighton 3 . . . . .at Virginia 0
Southern Methodist 2 . . . . .at Stanford 1
at Connecticut 1 . . . . .Brown 0

2000 College Cup

at Charlotte, N.C. (Dec. 8 & 10)

Semifinals

Creighton 2 . . . . .3 OT . . . . .Indiana 1
Connecticut 2 . . . . .SMU 0

Championship

Connecticut 2 . . . . .Creighton 0
Scoring: UConn—Chris Gbandi, 15:00; Darin Lewis, 85:00.
Attendance: 11,421

Final records: Connecticut (20-3-2), Creighton (22-4-0).
Most Outstanding Offensive Player: Darin Lewis, UConn. **Most Outstanding Defensive Player:** Chris Gbandi, UConn.
All-Tournament Team: Chris Gbandi, Bryhemm Hancock, Darin Lewis, Brent Raahim and Max Zieky from UConn; Mike Gabb, Ishmael Mintah, Brian Mullan and Mike Tranchilla from Creighton; Diego Walsh from Southern Methodist; Pat Noonan from Indiana.

WOMEN

2000 Final *Soccer America* Top 20

Final 2000 regular season poll including games through Nov. 5. Conducted by the national weekly *Soccer America* and released in the Nov. 20 issue. Listing includes records through conference playoffs as well as NCAA tournament record and team lost to. Teams in **bold** type went on to reach NCAA Final Four. All tournament games decided by penalty kicks are considered ties.

		Nov. 5 Record	NCAA Recap			Nov. 5 Record	NCAA Recap
1	**Notre Dame**	20-0-1	3-1 (North Carolina)	11	Stanford	13-5-1	1-1 (BYU)
2	Penn State	20-2-1	2-1 (Portland)	12	Texas A&M	17-6-0	1-1 (UCLA)
3	Nebraska	21-1-0	1-1 (Connecticut)	13	Soutern California	13-5-2	1-1 (UCLA)
4	California	17-2-1	0-1 (Santa Clara)	14	Florida State	12-7-2	1-1 (Clemson)
5	Washington	17-2-0	1-1 (Portland)	15	Wake Forest	10-7-2	1-1 (North Carolina)
6	**UCLA**	15-3-1	4-1 (North Carolina)	16	Florida	16-7-0	0-1 (Florida)
7	Clemson	17-2-1	2-1 (UCLA)	17	Dartmouth	13-4-0	1-1 (Penn State)
8	**North Carolina**	16-3-0	5-0	18	Connecticut	15-6-2	2-1 (North Carolina)
9	Brigham Young	18-3-1	1-1 (Santa Clara)	19	Washington State	13-6-0	0-1 (Montana)
10	**Portland**	15-3-0	3-1 (UCLA)	20	Boston	15-6-0	1-1 (Dartmouth)

NCAA Division I Tournament

First Round (Nov. 8)

at Michigan 4 .... 2 OT .... Miami U. 3
at UNC-Greensboro 3 .... 2 OT .... William & Mary 2
at Wisconsin 1 .... 2 OT .... Princeton 0
at Marquette 2 .... 2 OT .... Wright State 1
at Harvard 2 .... Quinnipiac 1
at Stanford 4 .... San Jose State 1
at Santa Clara 3 .... Cal Poly 1
at Wake Forest 6 .... Liberty 1
at Richmond 5 .... West Virginia 1
at Duke 3 .... Furman 1
at Florida State 4 .... Jacksonville 1
at Southern California 2 .... San Diego 1
at Illinois 2 .... Xavier 0
Boston U. 1 .... at Holy Cross 0
Arizona State 2 .... SW Missouri St. 0
Montana 1 .... at Washington State 0

Second Round (Nov. 11-12)

Harvard 3 .... at Hartford 1
at Clemson 2 .... Duke 1
Santa Clara 2 .... at California 0
at UCLA 3 .... Southern California 0
at Portland 3 .... Arizona State 1
at Virginia 6 .... UNC-Greensboro 1

at Brigham Young 5 .... Stanford 0
at Nebraska 4 .... Richmond 0
at Notre Dame 3 .... Michigan 1
at Connecticut 1 .... Wisconsin 0
at Dartmouth 4 .... Boston U. 1
at North Carolina 5 .... Wake Forest 0
at Texas A&M 4 .... Marquette 0
Florida State 2 .... at Florida 1
at Washington 5 .... Montana 0
at Penn State 1 .... Illinois 0

Third Round (Nov. 17-19)

Santa Clara 2 .... OT ...... at Brigham Young 1
at Penn State 4 .... Dartmouth 1
at Clemson 2 .... Florida State 0
at Notre Dame 2 .... Harvard 0
Connecticut 1 .... at Nebraska 0
at North Carolina 2 .... Virginia 1
Portland 1 .... at Washington 0
at UCLA 4 .... Texas A&M 0

Quarterfinals (Nov. 24-25)

at Notre Dame 2 .... OT .... Santa Clara 1
Portland 1 .... OT .... at Penn State 0
at North Carolina 3 .... Connecticut 1
UCLA 2 .... at Clemson 1

2000 College Cup

at San Jose, Calif. (Dec. 1 and 3)

Semifinals

North Carolina 2 .... Notre Dame 1
UCLA 1 .... Portland 0

Championship

North Carolina 2 .... UCLA 1
Scoring: UNC—Meredith Florance (Alyssa Ramsey, Danielle Borgman) 75:11, Own goal 82:18; UCLA—Lindsay Greco (unassisted) 53:37.
Attendance: 9,566

Final records: North Carolina (21-3), UCLA (19-4-1).
Most Outstanding Offensive Player: Meredith Florance, North Carolina, F; **Most Outstanding Defensive Player:** Catherine Reddick, North Carolina, D.
All Tournament Team: Danielle Borgman, Meredith Florance, Jena Kluegel, Kim Patrick, Catherine Reddick, Jordan Walker from North Carolina; Meotis Erikson, Liz Wagner and Amy Warner from Notre Dame; Karissa Hampton and Venus James from UCLA; Lauren Orlandos from Portland.

AP/Wide World Photos

North Carolina players celebrate following the victory over UCLA in the NCAA Division I women's soccer championship game.

2000 Annual Awards
Men's Players of the Year

Hermann Trophy............Chris Gbandi, Connecticut, D
MAC Award/NSCAA.................Ali Curtis, Duke, F
Soccer America..........Alecko Eskandarian, Virginia, F

Women's Player of the Year

Hermann Trophy........Anne Makinen, Notre Dame, MF
MAC Award/NSCAA ...Anne Makinen, Notre Dame, MF
Soccer America......Anne Makinen, Notre Dame, MF

NSCAA Coaches of the Year

Division I: Women's....................Jillian Ellis, UCLA
Men's......................Ray Reid, UConn

Division I All-America Teams
MEN

The 2000 first team All-America selections of the National Soccer Coaches Association of America (NSCAA). Holdovers from the 1999 NSCAA All-America team are in **bold** type.

GOALKEEPER—Chris Hamblin, Boston College, Sr.

DEFENDERS—**Chris Gbandi**, Connecticut, Jr.; Cory Gibbs, Brown, Sr.; Ryan Suarez, San Jose State, Sr.

MIDFIELDERS—Mark Lisi, Clemson, Sr.; Jorge Martinez, San Jose State, Sr.; Ryan Nelson, Stanford, Sr.

FORWARDS—**Carl Bussey**, SMU, Jr.; **Chris Carrieri**, North Carolina, Jr.; **Ali Curtis**, Duke, Sr.; **John Barry Nusum**, Furman, Jr.

WOMEN

The 2000 first team All-America selections of the National Soccer Coaches Association of America (NSCAA). Holdovers from the combined 1999 All-America team are in **bold** type.

GOALKEEPER—**Emily Oleksiuk**, Penn St., Jr.

DEFENDERS—Jenny Benson, Nebraska, Jr.; Rhegan Hypio, Marquette, Sr.; Jaclyn Ravenia, Richmond, Sr.; **Danielle Slaton**, Santa Clara, Jr.

MIDFIELDERS—Meghan Anderson, Nebraska, Jr.; Aleisha Cramer, BYU, Fr.; Katherine Linder, Hartford, So.; **Anne Makinen**, Notre Dame, Sr.

FORWARDS—Andrea Cunningham, Miami (Ohio), So.; Laura Schott, Cal-Berkley, So.; **Christie Welch**, Penn State, So.

Small College Final Fours
MEN
NCAA Division II

at Barry University, Miami Shores, Fla. (Dec. 1-3)

Semifinals: Cal.St. Dom. Hills def. Fort Lewis (Colo.), 1-0; Barry (Fla.) def. East Stroudsburg (Penn.), 2-1.

Championship: Cal.St. Dom. Hills def. Barry, 2-1 (4OT). Final records: Cal.St. Dom. Hills (23-1-1), Barry (17-4-0).

NCAA Division III

at Glassboro, NJ (Nov. 24-25)

Semifinals: Rowan (NJ) def. Wisconsin-Oshkosh, 2-0; Messiah (Penn.) def. Linfield (Oreg.), 3-2.

Championship: Messiah def. Rowan, 2-0; Final records: Messiah (22-2-1), Rowan (24-2-0).

NAIA

at Albuquerque, N.M. (Nov. 19-21)

Semifinals: Lindsey Wilson (Ky.) def. Harris-Stowe (Mon.), 3-0; Auburn-Montgomery def. Mobile (Ala.), 1-0.

Championship: Lindsey Wilson def. Auburn-Montgomery, 2-1 (OT); Final records: Lindsey Wilson (22-4-0), Auburn-Montgomery (23-2-0).

WOMEN
NCAA Division II

at Barry University, Miami Shores, Fla. (Dec. 30-2)

Semifinals: UC-San Diego def. Franklin Pierce (NH), 2-1 (OT); Northern Kentucky def. Barry, 5-1.

Championship: UC-San Diego def. Northern Kentucky, 2-1. Final records: UC-San Diego (21-2-0), Northern Kentucky. (21-2-2).

NCAA Division III

at Medford, Mass. (Nov. 18-19)

Semifinals: Tufts (Mass.) def. Wisconsin-Stevens Point, 1-0 (OT); Col. of New Jersey def. Trinity (Conn.), 1-0 (OT).

Championship: Col. of New Jersey def. Tufts, 2-1. Final records: Col. of New Jersey (23-1-0), Tufts (18-4-1).

NAIA

at Miami, Fla. (Nov. 19-21)

Semifinals: Lindenwood (Mon.) def. Azusa Pacific (Cal.), 1-0; Simon Fraser (B.C.) def. Madonna (Mich.), 3-0.

Championship: Simon Fraser def. Lindenwood, 1-0 (5OT); Final records: Simon Fraser (16-4-1), Lindenwood (24-1-0).

1900-2001 Through the Years

information please® SPORTS ALMANAC

The World Cup

The Federation Internationale de Football Association (FIFA) began the World Cup championship tournament in 1930 with a 13-team field in Uruguay. Sixty-four years later, 138 countries competed in qualifying rounds to fill 24 berths in the 1994 World Cup finals. FIFA increased the World Cup '98 tournament field from 24 to 32 teams, and it will remain at 32 in 2002 including automatic berths for defending champion France and co-hosts Japan and South Korea. The other 29 slots will be allotted by region: Europe (13), Africa (5), South America (4), CONCACAF (3), Asia (2), the two remaining positions will be determined via two home-and-away playoff series. One will be between the #14 European team and the #3 Asian team and the other will be between the #5 South American team and the champion of Oceania.

Tournaments have been played three times in North America (Mexico 2 and U.S.), four times in South America (Argentina, Chile, Brazil and Uruguay) and nine times in Europe (France 2, Italy 2, England, Spain, Sweden, Switzerland and West Germany). Following an outcry when Germany was awarded the 2006 World Cup over South Africa, FIFA announced that, starting in 2010, the World Cup will be rotated among six continents.

Brazil retired the first World Cup (called the Jules Rimet Trophy after FIFA's first president) in 1970 after winning it for the third time. The new trophy, first presented in 1974, is known as simply the World Cup.

Multiple winners: Brazil (4); Italy and West Germany (3); Argentina and Uruguay (2).

Year	Champion	Manager	Score	Runner-up	Host Country	Third Place
1930	Uruguay	Alberto Suppici	4-2	Argentina	Uruguay	No game
1934	Italy	Vittório Pozzo	2-1*	Czechoslovakia	Italy	Germany 3, Austria 2
1938	Italy	Vittório Pozzo	4-2	Hungary	France	Brazil 4, Sweden 2
1942-46 Not held						
1950	Uruguay	Juan Lopez	2-1	Brazil	Brazil	No game
1954	West Germany	Sepp Herberger	3-2	Hungary	Switzerland	Austria 3, Uruguay 1
1958	Brazil	Vicente Feola	5-2	Sweden	Sweden	France 6, W. Ger. 3
1962	Brazil	Aimoré Moreira	3-1	Czechoslovakia	Chile	Chile 1, Yugoslavia 0
1966	England	Alf Ramsey	4-2*	W. Germany	England	Portugal 2, USSR 1
1970	Brazil	Mario Zagalo	4-1	Italy	Mexico	W. Ger. 1, Uruguay 0
1974	West Germany	Helmut Schoen	2-1	Netherlands	W. Germany	Poland 1, Brazil 0
1978	Argentina	Cesar Menotti	3-1*	Netherlands	Argentina	Brazil 2, Italy 1
1982	Italy	Enzo Bearzot	3-1	W. Germany	Spain	Poland 3, France 2
1986	Argentina	Carlos Bilardo	3-2	W. Germany	Mexico	France 4, Belgium 2*
1990	West Germany	Franz Beckenbauer	1-0	Argentina	Italy	Italy 2, England 1
1994	Brazil	Carlos Parreira	0-0†	Italy	USA	Sweden 4, Bulgaria 0
1998	France	Aimé Jacquet	3-0	Brazil	France	Croatia 2, Netherlands 1
2002	at Japan/South Korea (May 31-June 30)					
2006	at Germany					

*Winning goals scored in overtime (no sudden death); †Brazil defeated Italy in shootout (3-2) after scoreless overtime period.

All-Time World Cup Leaders

Career Goals

World Cup scoring leaders through 1998. Years listed are years played in World Cup.

	No
Gerd Müller, West Germany (1970, 74)	14
Just Fontaine, France (1958)	13
Pelé, Brazil (1958, 62, 66, 70)	12
Sandor Kocsis, Hungary (1954)	11
Juergen Klinsmann, Germany (1990, 94, 98)	11
Helmut Rahn, West Germany (1954, 58)	10
Teofilo Cubillas, Peru (1970, 78)	10
Gregorz Lato, Poland (1974, 78, 82)	10
Gary Lineker, England (1986, 90)	10

Most Valuable Player

Officially, the Golden Ball Award, the Most Valuable Player of the World Cup tournament has been selected since 1982 by a panel of international soccer journalists.

Year		Year	
1982	Paolo Rossi, Italy	1994	Romario, Brazil
1986	Diego Maradona, Arg.	1998	Ronaldo, Brazil
1990	Toto Schillaci, Italy		

Single Tournament Goals

World Cup tournament scoring leaders through 1998.

Year		Gm	No
1930	Guillermo Stabile, Argentina	4	8
1934	Angelo Schiavio, Italy	3	4
	Oldrich Nejedly, Czechoslovakia	4	4
	Edmund Conen, Germany	4	4
1938	Leônidas, Brazil	3	8
1950	Ademir, Brazil	6	7
1954	Sandor Kocsis, Hungary	5	11
1958	Just Fontaine, France	6	13
1962	Drazen Jerkovic, Yugoslavia	6	5
1966	Eusébio, Portugal	6	9
1970	Gerd Müller, West Germany	6	10
1974	Grzegorz Lato, Poland	7	7
1978	Mario Kempes, Argentina	7	6
1982	Paolo Rossi, Italy	7	6
1986	Gary Lineker, England	5	6
1990	Toto Schillaci, Italy	7	6
1994	Oleg Salenko, Russia	3	6
	Hristo Stoitchkov, Bulgaria	7	6
1998	Davor Suker, Croatia	7	6

All-Time World Cup Ranking Table

Since the first World Cup in 1930, Brazil is the only country to play in all 16 final tournaments. The FIFA all-time table below ranks all nations that have ever qualified for a World Cup final tournament by points earned through 1998. Victories, which earned two points from 1930-90, were awarded three points starting in 1994. Note that Germany's appearances include 10 made by West Germany from 1954-90. Participants in the 1998 World Cup final are in **bold** type.

		App	Gm	W	L	T	Pts	GF	GA
1	**Brazil**	16	80	53	13	14	120	173	78
2	**Germany**	14	78	45	16	17	107	162	103
3	**Italy**	14	66	38	12	16	92	105	62
4	**Argentina**	12	57	29	18	10	68	100	69
5	**England**	10	45	20	12	13	53	62	42
6	**France**	10	41	21	14	6	48	86	58
7	**Spain**	10	40	16	14	10	42	61	48
8	**Yugoslavia**	9	37	16	13	8	40	60	46
9	Uruguay	9	37	15	14	8	38	61	52
	Russia	8	34	16	12	6	38	60	40
11	Sweden	9	38	14	15	9	37	66	60
	Netherlands	7	31	14	9	9	37	56	36
13	Hungary	9	32	15	14	3	33	87	57
14	Poland	5	25	13	7	5	31	39	29
15	**Austria**	7	29	12	13	4	28	43	47
16	Czech Republic	8	30	11	14	5	27	44	45
17	**Mexico**	11	37	8	19	10	26	39	75
18	**Belgium**	10	32	9	16	7	25	40	56
19	**Romania**	7	21	8	8	5	21	30	32
20	**Chile**	7	25	7	12	6	20	31	40
21	Scotland	8	23	4	12	7	15	25	41
	Switzerland	7	22	6	13	3	15	33	51
23	**Bulgaria**	7	26	3	15	8	14	22	53
	Paraguay	5	15	4	6	5	14	19	27
25	**Cameroon**	4	14	3	5	6	12	13	26
26	Portugal	2	9	6	3	0	12	19	12
27	Peru	4	15	4	8	3	11	19	31
	No. Ireland	3	13	3	5	5	11	13	23
	Denmark	2	9	5	3	1	11	19	13
30	**Croatia**	1	7	5	2	0	10	11	5
31	**USA**	6	17	4	12	1	9	18	38
32	Morocco	4	13	2	7	4	8	12	18
	Colombia	4	13	3	0	2	8	14	23

		App	Gm	W	L	T	Pts	GF	GA
	Nigeria	2	8	4	4	0	8	13	13
35	Ireland	2	9	1	3	5	7	4	7
	Norway	2	8	2	3	3	7	7	8
37	East Germany	1	6	2	2	2	6	5	5
38	**Saudi Arabia**	2	7	2	4	1	5	7	13
	Algeria	2	6	2	3	1	5	6	10
	Wales	1	5	1	3	1	5	4	4
41	**South Korea**	5	14	0	10	4	4	11	43
	Tunisia	2	6	1	3	2	4	4	6
	Costa Rica	1	4	2	2	0	4	4	6
44	**Iran**	2	6	1	4	1	3	4	12
	North Korea	1	4	1	2	1	3	5	9
	Cuba	1	3	1	1	1	3	5	12
	Jamaica	1	3	1	2	0	3	3	9
48	Egypt	2	4	0	2	2	2	3	6
	Honduras	1	3	0	1	2	2	2	3
	Israel	1	3	0	1	2	2	1	3
	Turkey	1	3	1	2	0	2	10	11
	South Africa	1	3	0	1	2	2	3	6
53	Bolivia	3	6	0	5	1	1	1	20
	Australia	1	3	0	2	1	1	0	5
	Kuwait	1	3	0	2	1	1	2	6
56	El Salvador	2	6	0	6	0	0	1	22
	Canada	1	3	0	3	0	0	0	5
	East Indies	1	1	0	1	0	0	0	6
	Greece	1	3	0	3	0	0	0	10
	Haiti	1	3	0	3	0	0	2	14
	Iraq	1	3	0	3	0	0	1	4
	Japan	1	3	0	3	0	0	1	4
	New Zealand	1	3	0	3	0	0	2	12
	UAE	1	3	0	3	0	0	2	11
	Zaire	1	3	0	3	0	0	0	14

The United States in the World Cup

While the United States has fielded a national team every year of the World Cup, only five of those teams have been able to make it past the preliminary competition and qualify for the final World Cup tournament. The 1994 national team automatically qualified because the U.S. served as host of the event for the first time. The U.S. played in three of the first four World Cups (1930, '34 and '50) and each of the last three (1990, '94 and '98). The Americans have a record of 4-12-1 in 17 World Cup matches, with two victories in 1930, a 1-0 upset of England in 1950, and a 2-1 shocker over Colombia in 1994.

1930

1st Round Matches

United States 3 . . . . Belgium 0
United States 3 . . . . Paraguay 0

Semifinals

Argentina 6 . . . . United States 1
U.S. Scoring—Bert Patenaude (3), Bart McGhee (2), James Brown and Thomas Florie.

1934

1st Round Match

Italy 7 . . . . United States 1
U.S. Scoring—Buff Donelli (who later became a noted college and NFL football coach).

1950

1st Round Matches

Spain 3 . . . . United States 1
United States 1 . . . . England 0
Chile 5 . . . . United States 2
U.S. Scoring—Joe Gaetjens, Joe Maca, John Souza and Frank Wallace.

1990

1st Round Matches

Czechoslovakia 5 . . . . United States 1
Italy 1 . . . . United States 0
Austria 2 . . . . United States 1
U.S. Scoring—Paul Caligiuri and Bruce Murray.

1994

1st Round Matches

United States 1 . . . . Switzerland 1
United States 2 . . . . Colombia 1
Romania 1 . . . . United States 0

Round of 16

Brazil 1 . . . . United States 0
U.S. Scoring— Eric Wynalda, Earnie Stewart and own goal (Colombia defender Andres Escobar).

1998

1st Round Matches

Germany 2 . . . . United States 0
Iran 2 . . . . United States 1
Yugoslavia 1 . . . . United States 0
U.S. Scoring— Brian McBride.

World Cup Finals

Brazil and West Germany (now Germany) have played in the most Cup finals with six. Note that a four-team round robin determined the 1950 championship–the deciding game turned out to be the last one of the tournament between Uruguay and Brazil.

1930

Uruguay 4, Argentina 2
(at Montevideo, Uruguay)

	1	2–T
July 30 Uruguay (4-0)	1	3–4
Argentina (4-1)	2	0–2

Goals: Uruguay–Pablo Dorado (12th minute), Pedro Cea (54th), Santos Iriarte (68th), Castro (89th); Argentina–Carlos Peucelle (20th), Guillermo Stabile (37th).
Uruguay–Ballesteros, Nasazzi, Mascheroni, Andrade, Fernandez, Gestido, Dorado, Scarone, Castro, Cea, Iriarte.
Argentina–Botasso, Della Torre, Paternoster, J. Evaristo, Monti, Suarez, Peucelle, Varallo, Stabile, Ferreira, M. Evaristo.
Attendance: 90,000. **Referee:** Langenus (Belgium).

1934

Italy 2, Czechoslovakia 1 (OT)
(at Rome)

	1	2	OT–T
June 10 Italy (4-0-1)	0	1	1–2
Czechoslovakia (3-1)	0	1	0–1

Goals: Italy–Raimondo Orsi (80th minute), Angelo Schiavio (95th); Czechoslovakia–Puc (70th).
Italy–Combi, Monzeglio, Allemandi, Ferraris IV, Monti, Bertolini, Guaita, Meazza, Schiavio, Ferrari, Orsi.
Czechoslovakia–Planicka, Zenisek, Ctyroky, Kostalek, Cambal, Krcil, Junek, Svoboda, Sobotka, Nejedly, Puc.
Attendance: 55,000. **Referee:** Eklind (Sweden).

1938

Italy 4, Hungary 2
(at Paris)

	1	2–T
June 19 Italy (4-0)	3	1–4
Hungary (3-1)	1	1–2

Goals: Italy–Gino Colaussi (5th minute), Silvio Piola (16th), Colaussi (35th), Piola (82nd); Hungary–Titkos (7th), Georges Sarosi (70th).
Italy–Olivieri, Foni, Rava, Serantoni, Andreolo, Locatelli, Biavati, Meazza, Piola, Ferrari, Colaussi.
Hungary–Szabo, Polgar, Biro, Szalay, Szucs, Lazar, Sas, Vincze, G. Sarosi, Szengeller, Titkos.
Attendance: 65,000. **Referee:** Capdeville (France).

1950

Uruguay 2, Brazil 1
(at Rio de Janeiro)

	1	2–T
July 16 Uruguay (3-0-1)	0	2–2
Brazil (4-1-1)	0	1–1

Goals: Uruguay–Juan Schiaffino (66th minute), Chico Ghiggia (79th); Brazil–Friaca (47th).
Uruguay–Maspoli, M. Gonzales, Tejera, Gambetta, Varela, Andrade, Ghiggia, Perez, Miguez, Schiaffino, Moran.
Brazil–Barbosa, Augusto, Juvenal, Bauer, Danilo, Bigode, Friaça, Zizinho, Ademir, Jair, Chico.
Attendance: 199,854. **Referee:** Reader (England).

1954

West Germany 3, Hungary 2
(at Berne, Switzerland)

	1	2–T
July 4 West Germany (4-1)	2	1–3
Hungary (4-1)	2	0–2

Goals: West Germany–Max Morlock (10th minute), Helmut Rahn (18th), Rahn (84th); Hungary–Ferenc Puskas (4th), Zoltan Czibor (9th).
West Germany–Turek, Posipal, Liebrich, Kohlmeyer, Eckel, Mai, Rahn, Morlock, O. Walter, F. Walter, Schaefer.
Hungary–Grosics, Buzansky, Lorant, Lantos, Bozsik, Zakarias, Czibor, Kocsis, Hidegkuti, Puskas, J. Toth.
Attendance: 60,000. **Referee:** Ling (England).

1958

Brazil 5, Sweden 2
(at Stockholm)

	1	2–T
June 29 Brazil (5-0-1)	2	3–5
Sweden (4-1-1)	1	1–2

Goals: Brazil–Vava (9th minute), Vava (32nd), Pelé (55th), Mario Zagalo (68th), Pelé (90th); Sweden–Nils Liedholm (3rd), Agne Simonsson (80th).
Brazil–Gilmar, D. Santos, N. Santos, Zito, Bellini, Orlando, Garrincha, Didi, Vava, Pelé, Zagalo.
Sweden–Svensson, Bergmark, Axbom, Boerjesson, Gustavsson, Parling, Hamrin, Gren, Simonsson, Liedholm, Skoglund.
Attendance: 49,737. **Referee:** Guigue (France).

1962

Brazil 3, Czechoslovakia 1
(at Santiago, Chile)

	1	2–T
June 17 Brazil (5-0-1)	1	2–3
Czechoslovakia (3-2-1)	1	0–1

Goals: Brazil–Amarildo (17th minute), Zito (68th), Vava (77th); Czechoslovakia–Josef Masopust (15th).
Brazil–Gilmar, D. Santos, N. Santos, Zito, Mauro, Zozimo, Garrincha, Didi, Vava, Amarildo, Zagalo.
Czechoslovakia–Schroiff, Tichy, Novak, Pluskal, Popluhar, Masopust, Pospichal, Scherer, Kvasniak, Kadraba, Jelinek.
Attendance: 68,679. **Referee:** Latishev (USSR).

1966

England 4, West Germany 2 (OT)
(at London)

	1	2	OT–T
July 30 England (5-0-1)	1	1	2–4
West Germany (4-1-1)	1	1	0–2

Goals: England–Geoff Hurst (18th minute), Martin Peters (78th), Hurst (101st), Hurst (120th); West Germany–Helmut Haller (12th), Wolfgang Weber (90th).
England–Banks, Cohen, Wilson, Stiles, J. Charlton, Moore, Ball, Hurst, B. Charlton, Hunt, Peters.
West Germany–Tilkowski, Hottges, Schnellinger, Beckenbauer, Schulz, Weber, Haller, Seeler, Held, Overath, Emmerich.
Attendance: 93,802. **Referee:** Dienst (Switzerland).

1970
Brazil 4, Italy 1
(at Mexico City)

	1	2–T
June 21 Brazil (6-0)	1	3–4
Italy (3-1-2)	1	0–1

Goals: Brazil–Pelé (18th minute), Gerson (65th), Jairzinho (70th), Carlos Alberto (86th); Italy–Roberto Boninsegna (37th).
Brazil–Felix, C. Alberto, Everaldo, Clodoaldo, Brito, Piazza, Jairzinho, Gerson, Tostão, Pelé, Rivelino.
Italy–Albertosi, Burgnich, Facchetti, Bertini (Juliano, 73rd), Rosato, Cera, Domenghini, Mazzola, Boninsegna (Rivera, 84th), De Sisti, Riva.
Attendance: 107,412. **Referee:** Glockner (E. Germany).

1974
West Germany 2, Netherlands 1
(at Munich)

	1	2–T
July 7 West Germany (6-1)	2	0–2
Netherlands (5-1-1)	1	0–1

Goals: West Germany–Paul Breitner (25th minute, penalty kick), Gerd Müller (43rd); Netherlands–Johan Neeskens (1st, penalty kick).
West Germany–Maier, Beckenbauer, Vogts, Breitner, Schwarzenbeck, Overath, Bonhof, Hoeness, Grabowski, Muller, Holzenbein.
Netherlands–Jongbloed, Suurbier, Rijsbergen (De Jong, 58th), Krol, Haan, Jansen, Van Hanegem, Neeskens, Rep, Cruyff, Rensenbrink (R. Van de Kerkhof, 46th).
Attendance: 77,833. **Referee:** Taylor (England).

1978
Argentina 3, Netherlands 1 (OT)
(at Buenos Aires)

	1	2	OT–T
June 25 Argentina (5-1-1)	1	0	2–3
Netherlands (3-2-2)	0	1	0–1

Goals: Argentina–Mario Kempes (37th minute), Kempes (104th), Daniel Bertoni (114th); Netherlands–Dirk Nanninga (81st).
Argentina–Fillol, Olguin, L. Galvan, Passarella, Tarantini, Ardiles (Larrosa, 65th), Gallego, Kempes, Luque, Bertoni, Ortiz (Houseman, 77th).
Netherlands–Jongbloed, Jansen (Suurbier, 72nd), Brandts, Krol, Poortvliet, Haan, Neeskens, W. Van de Kerkhof, R. Van de Kerkhof, Rep (Nanninga, 58th), Rensenbrink.
Attendance: 77,260. **Referee:** Gonella (Italy).

1982
Italy 3, West Germany 1
(at Madrid)

	1	2–T
July 11 Italy (4-0-3)	0	3–3
West Germany (4-2-1)	0	1–1

Goals: Italy–Paolo Rossi (57th minute), Marco Tardelli (68th), Alessandro Altobelli (81st); West Germany–Paul Breitner (83rd).
Italy–Zoff, Scirea, Gentile, Cabrini, Collovati, Bergomi, Tardelli, Oriali, Conti, Rossi, Graziani (Altobelli, 8th, and Causio, 89th).
West Germany–Schumacher, Stielike, Kaltz, Briegel, K.H. Forster, B. Forster, Breitner, Dremmler (Hrubesch, 61st), Littbarski, Fischer, Rummenigge (Muller, 69th).
Attendance: 90,080. **Referee:** Coelho (Brazil).

1986
Argentina 3, West Germany 2
(at Mexico City)

	1	2–T
June 29 Argentina (6-0-1)	1	2–3
West Germany (4-2-1)	0	2–2

Goals: Argentina–Jose Brown (22nd minute), Jorge Valdano (55th), Jorge Burruchaga (83rd); West Germany–Karl-Heinz Rummenigge (73rd), Rudi Voller (81st).
Argentina–Pumpido, Cuciuffo, Olarticoechea, Ruggeri, Brown, Batista, Burruchaga (Trobbiani, 89th), Giusti, Enrique, Maradona, Valdano.
West Germany–Schumacher, Jakobs, B. Forster, Berthold, Briegel, Eder, Brehme, Matthaus, Rummenigge, Magath (Hoeness, 61st), Allofs (Voller, 46th).
Attendance: 114,590. **Referee:** Filho (Brazil).

1990
West Germany 1, Argentina 0
(at Rome)

	1	2–T
July 8 West Germany (6-0-1)	0	1–1
Argentina (4-2-1)	0	0–0

Goals: West Germany–Andreas Brehme (85th minute, penalty kick).
West Germany–Illgner, Berthold (Reuter, 73rd), Kohler, Augenthaler, Buchwald, Brehme, Haessler, Matthaus, Littbarski, Klinsmann, Voller.
Argentina–Goycoechea, Ruggeri (Monzon, 46th), Simon, Serrizuela, Lorenzo, Basualdo, Troglio, Burruchaga (Calderon, 53rd), Sensini, Dezotti, Maradona.
Attendance: 73,603. **Referee:** Codesal (Mexico).

1994
Brazil 0, Italy 0 (Shootout)
(at Pasadena, Calif.)

	1	2	OT–T
July 17 Brazil (6-0-1)	0	0	0–0*
Italy (4-2-1)	0	0	0–0

*Brazil wins shootout, 3-2.
Shootout (five shots each, alternating): ITA–Baresi (miss, 0-0); BRA–Santos (blocked, 0-0); ITA– Albertini (goal, 1-0); BRA–Romario (goal, 1-1); ITA–Evani (goal, 2-1); BRA–Branco (goal, 2-2); ITA–Massaro (blocked, 2-2); BRA–Dunga (goal, 2-3); ITA–R. Baggio (miss, 2-3).
Brazil– Taffarel, Jorginho (Cafu, 21st minute), Branco, Aldair, Santos, Mazinho, Silva, Dunga, Zinho (Viola, 106th), Bebeto, Romario.
Italy– Pagliuca, Mussi (Apolloni, 35th minute), Baresi, Benarrivo, Maldini, Albertini, D. Baggio (Evani, 95th), Berti, Donadoni, R. Baggio, Massaro.
Attendance: 94,194. **Referee:** Puhl (Hungary).

1998
France 3, Brazil 0
(at Paris)

	1	2–T
July 12 Brazil (6-1)	0	0–0
France (7-0)	2	1–3

Goals: France– Zinédine Zidane (27th and 46th minutes), Petit (92).
Brazil– Taffarel, Cafu, Aldair, Baiano, Carlos, Sampaio (Edmundo, 74th minute), Dunga, Rivaldo, Leonardo (Denilson, 46th minute), Bebeto, Ronaldo.
France– Barthez, Lizarazu, Desailly, Thuram, Leboeuf, Djorkaeff (Viera, 75th minute), Deschamps, Zidane, Petit, Karembeu (Boghossian, 57th minute), Guivarc'h, Dugarry.
Attendance: 75,000. **Referee:** Belqola (Morocco).

Year-by-Year Comparisons

How the 16 World Cup tournaments have compared in nations qualifying, matches played, players participating, goals scored, average goals per game, overall attendance and attendance per game.

Year	Host	Continent	Nations	Matches	Players	Scored	Goals Per Game	Overall	Attendance Per Game
1930	Uruguay	So. America	13	18	189	70	3.8	589,300	32,739
1934	Italy	Europe	16	17	208	70	4.1	361,000	21,235
1938	France	Europe	15	18	210	84	4.7	376,000	20,889
1942-46	Not held								
1950	Brazil	So. America	13	22	192	88	4.0	1,044,763	47,489
1954	Switzerland	Europe	16	26	233	140	5.3	872,000	33,538
1958	Sweden	Europe	16	35	241	126	3.6	819,402	23,411
1962	Chile	So. America	16	32	252	89	2.8	892,812	27,900
1966	England	Europe	16	32	254	89	2.8	1,464,944	45,780
1970	Mexico	No. America	16	32	270	95	3.0	1,690,890	52,840
1974	West Germany	Europe	16	38	264	97	2.6	1,809,953	47,630
1978	Argentina	So. America	16	38	277	102	2.7	1,685,602	44,358
1982	Spain	Europe	24	52	396	146	2.8	2,108,723	40,552
1986	Mexico	No. America	24	52	414	132	2.5	2,393,031	46,020
1990	Italy	Europe	24	52	413	115	2.2	2,516,354	48,391
1994	United States	No. America	24	52	437	140	2.7	3,587,088	68,982
1998	France	Europe	32	64	704	171	2.7	2,775,400	43,366

World Team of the 20th Century

The team, comprised of the century's best players, was voted on by a panel that included 250 international soccer journalists and released on June 10, 1998 in conjunction with the opening of the 1998 World Cup. The panel first selected the European and South American Teams of the Century and then chose the World Team from those two lists.

World Team

Pos		Pos	
GK	Lev Yashin, Soviet Union	MF	Alfredo Di Stefano, Argentina
D	Carlos Alberto, Brazil	MF	Michel Platini, France
D	Franz Beckenbauer, West Germany	F	Pele, Brazil
D	Bobby Moore, England	F	Garrincha, Brazil
D	Nilton Santos, Brazil	F	Diego Maradona, Argentina
MF	Johan Cruyff, Netherlands		

European Team

Pos	
GK	Lev Yashin, Soviet Union
D	Paolo Maldini, Italy
D	Franz Beckenbauer, West Germany
D	Bobby Moore, England
D	Franco Baresi, Italy
MF	Johan Cruyff, Netherlands
MF	Eusebio, Portugal
MF	Michel Platini, France
F	Ferenc Puskas, Hungary
F	Bobby Charlton, England
F	Marco Van Basten, Netherlands

South American Team

Pos	
GK	Ubaldo Fillol, Argentina
D	Carlos Alberto, Brazil
D	Elias Figueroa, Chile
D	Daniel Passarella, Argentina
D	Nilton Santos, Brazil
MF	Didi, Brazil
MF	Alfredo Di Stefano, Argentina
MF	Rivelino, Brazil
F	Pele, Brazil
F	Garrincha, Brazil
F	Diego Maradona, Argentina

World Cup Shootouts

Introduced in 1982; winning sides in **bold** type.

Year	Round		Final	SO	Year	Round		Final	SO
1982	Semi	**W. Germany** vs. France	3-3	(5-4)		Semi	**W. Germany** vs. England	1-1	(4-3)
1986	Quarter	**Belgium** vs. Spain	1-1	(5-4)					
	Quarter	**France** vs. Brazil	1-1	(4-3)	1994	Second	**Bulgaria** vs. Mexico	1-1	(3-1)
	Quarter	**W. Germany** vs. Mexico	0-0	(4-1)		Quarter	**Sweden** vs. Romania	2-2	(5-4)
1990	Second	**Ireland** vs. Romania	0-0	(5-4)		Final	**Brazil** vs. Italy	0-0	(3-2)
	Quarter	**Argentina** vs. Yugoslavia	0-0	(3-2)	1998	Second	**Argentina** vs. England	2-2	(4-3)
	Semi	**Argentina** vs. Italy	1-1	(4-3)		Quarter	**France** vs. Italy	0-0	(4-3)

OTHER WORLDWIDE COMPETITION

The Olympic Games

Held every four years since 1896, except during World War I (1916) and World War II (1940-44). Soccer was not a medal sport in 1896 at Athens or in 1932 at Los Angeles. By agreement between FIFA and the IOC, Olympic soccer competition is currently limited to players 23 years old and under with a few exceptions.
Multiple winners: England and Hungary (3); Soviet Union and Uruguay (2).

MEN

Year		Year	
1900	**England**, France, Belgium	1960	**Yugoslavia**, Denmark, Hungary
1904	**Canada**, USA I, USA II	1964	**Hungary**, Czechoslovakia, Germany
1906	**Denmark**, Smyrna (Int'l entry), Greece	1968	**Hungary**, Bulgaria, Japan
1908	**England**, Denmark, Netherlands	1972	**Poland**, Hungary, East Germany & Soviet Union
1912	**England**, Denmark, Netherlands	1976	**East Germany**, Poland, Soviet Union
1920	**Belgium**, Spain, Netherlands	1980	**Czechoslovakia**, East Germany, Soviet Union
1924	**Uruguay**, Switzerland, Sweden	1984	**France**, Brazil, Yugoslavia
1928	**Uruguay**, Argentina, Italy	1988	**Soviet Union**, Brazil, West Germany
1936	**Italy**, Austria, Norway	1992	**Spain**, Poland, Ghana
1948	**Sweden**, Yugoslavia, Denmark	1996	**Nigeria**, Argentina, Brazil
1952	**Hungary**, Yugoslavia, Sweden	2000	**Cameroon**, Spain, Chile
1956	**Soviet Union**, Yugoslavia, Bulgaria		

WOMEN

Year		Year	
1996	**USA**, China, Norway	2000	**Norway**, USA, Germany

The Under-20 World Cup

Held every two years since 1977. Officially, the World Youth Championship for the FIFA/Coca-Cola Cup.
Multiple winners: Argentina (4); Brazil (3); Portugal (2).

Year		Year	
1977	Soviet Union	1991	Portugal
1979	Argentina	1993	Brazil
1981	West Germany	1995	Argentina
1983	Brazil	1997	Argentina
1985	Brazil	1999	Spain
1987	Yugoslavia	2001	Argentina
1989	Portugal		

The Under-17 World Cup

Held every two years since 1985. Officially, the U-17 World Championship for the FIFA/JVC Cup. See Updates chapter for 2001 results.
Multiple winners: Brazil, Ghana and Nigeria (2).

Year		Year	
1985	Nigeria	1995	Ghana
1987	Soviet Union	1997	Brazil
1989	Saudi Arabia	1999	Brazil
1991	Ghana	2001	France
1993	Nigeria		

Indoor World Championship

First held in 1989. FIFA's only Five-a-Side tournament.
Multiple winner: Brazil (3).

Year		Year	
1989	Brazil	1996	Brazil
1992	Brazil	2000	Spain

Women's World Cup

First held in 1991. Officially, the FIFA Women's World Championship.
Multiple winner: United States (2).

Year		Year	
1991	United States	1999	United States
1995	Norway		

Confederations Cup

First held in 1992. Contested by the Continental champions of Africa, Asia, Europe, North America and South America and originally called the Intercontinental Championship for the King Fahd Cup until it was redubbed the FIFA/Confederations Cup for the King Fahd Trophy in 1997.

Year		Year	
1992	Argentina	1999	Mexico
1995	Denmark	2001	France
1997	Brazil		

CONTINENTAL COMPETITION

European Championship

Held every four years since 1960. Officially, the European Football Championship. Winners receive the Henri Delaunay trophy, named for the Frenchman who first proposed the idea of a European Soccer Championship in 1927. The first one would not be played until five years after his death in 1955.
Multiple winners: France and West Germany (2).

Year		Year		Year		Year	
1960	Soviet Union	1972	West Germany	1984	France	1996	Germany
1964	Spain	1976	Czechoslovakia	1988	Netherlands	2000	France
1968	Italy	1980	West Germany	1992	Denmark	2004	(at Portugal)

Continental Competition (Cont.)
Copa America

Held irregularly since 1916. Unofficially, the Championship of South America.

Multiple winners: Argentina and Uruguay (14); Brazil (6); Paraguay and Peru (2).

Year		Year		Year		Year		Year	
1916	Uruguay	1925	Argentina	1942	Uruguay	1957	Argentina	1987	Uruguay
1917	Uruguay	1926	Uruguay	1945	Argentina	1958	Argentina	1989	Brazil
1919	Brazil	1927	Argentina	1946	Argentina	1959	Uruguay	1991	Argentina
1920	Uruguay	1929	Argentina	1947	Argentina	1963	Bolivia	1993	Argentina
1921	Argentina	1935	Uruguay	1949	Brazil	1967	Uruguay	1995	Uruguay
1922	Brazil	1937	Argentina	1953	Paraguay	1975	Peru	1997	Brazil
1923	Uruguay	1939	Peru	1955	Argentina	1979	Paraguay	1999	Brazil
1924	Uruguay	1941	Argentina	1956	Uruguay	1983	Uruguay	2001	Colombia

African Nations Cup

Contested since 1957 and held every two years since 1968.

Multiple winners: Egypt and Ghana (4); Cameroon and Congo/Zaire (3); Nigeria (2).

Year		Year		Year		Year		Year	
1957	Egypt	1968	Zaire	1978	Ghana	1988	Cameroon	1998	Egypt
1959	Egypt	1970	Sudan	1980	Nigeria	1990	Algeria	2000	Cameroon
1962	Ethiopia	1972	Congo	1982	Ghana	1992	Ivory Coast	2002	(at Mali)
1963	Ghana	1974	Zaire	1984	Cameroon	1994	Nigeria	2004	(at Tunisia)
1965	Ghana	1976	Morocco	1986	Egypt	1996	South Africa		

CONCACAF Gold Cup

The Confederation of North, Central American and Caribbean Football Championship. Contested irregularly from 1963-81 and revived as CONCACAF Gold Cup in 1991.

Multiple winners: Mexico (6); Costa Rica (2).

Year		Year		Year		Year		Year	
1963	Costa Rica	1969	Costa Rica	1977	Mexico	1993	Mexico	2000	Canada
1965	Mexico	1971	Mexico	1981	Honduras	1996	Mexico		
1967	Guatemala	1973	Haiti	1991	United States	1998	Mexico		

CLUB COMPETITION

Toyota Cup

Also known as the Intercontinental Cup. Contested annually in December between the winners of the European Champions League (formerly European Cup) and South America's Copa Libertadores for the unofficial World Club Championship. Four European Cup winners refused to participate in the championship match in the 1970s and were replaced each time by the European Cup runner-up: Panathinaikos (Greece) for Ajax Amsterdam (Netherlands) in 1971; Juventus (Italy) for Ajax in 1973; Atlético Madrid (Spain) for Bayern Munich (West Germany) in 1974; and Malmo (Sweden) for Nottingham Forest (England) in 1979. Another European Cup winner, Marseille of France, was prohibited by the Union of European Football Associations (UEFA) from playing for the 1993 Toyota Cup because of its involvement in the match-rigging scandal.

Best-of-three game format from 1960-68, then a two-game/total goals format from 1969-79. Toyota became Cup sponsor in 1980, changed the format to a one-game championship and moved it to Toyko.

Multiple winners: AC Milan, Nacional and Penarol (3); Ajax Amsterdam, Boca Juniors, Independiente, Inter Milan, Juventus, Real Madrid, Santos and Sao Paulo (2).

Year		Year		Year	
1960	Real Madrid (Spain)	1975	Not held	1990	AC Milan (Italy)
1961	Peñarol (Uruguay)	1976	Bayern Munich (W. Germany)	1991	Red Star (Yugoslavia)
1962	Santos (Brazil)	1977	Boca Juniors (Argentina)	1992	Sao Paulo (Brazil)
1963	Santos (Brazil)	1978	Not held	1993	Sao Paulo (Brazil)
1964	Inter Milan (Italy)	1979	Olimpia (Paraguay)	1994	Velez Sarsfield (Argentina)
1965	Inter Milan (Italy)	1980	Nacional (Uruguay)	1995	Ajax Amsterdam (Netherlands)
1966	Penarol (Uruguay)	1981	Flamengo (Brazil)	1996	Juventus (Italy)
1967	Racing Club (Argentina)	1982	Peñarol (Uruguay)	1997	Borussia Dortmund (Germany)
1968	Estudiantes (Argentina)	1983	Gremio (Brazil)	1998	Real Madrid (Spain)
1969	AC Milan (Italy)	1984	Independiente (Argentina)	1999	Manchester United (England)
1970	Feyenoord (Netherlands)	1985	Juventus (Italy)	2000	Boca Juniors (Argentina)
1971	Nacional (Uruguay)	1986	River Plate (Argentina)		
1972	Ajax Amsterdam (Netherlands)	1987	FC Porto (Portugal)		
1973	Independiente (Argentina)	1988	Nacional (Uruguay)		
1974	Atlético Madrid (Spain)	1989	AC Milan (Italy)		

European Cup/Champions League

Contested annually since the 1955-56 season by the league champions of the member countries of the Union of European Football Associations (UEFA). In 1999, UEFA announced the formation of a new competition called the UEFA Champions League to take the place of the Cup competition.

Multiple winners: Real Madrid (8); AC Milan (5); Ajax Amsterdam, Bayern Munich and Liverpool (4); Benfica, Inter-Milan, Juventus and Nottingham Forest (2).

Year		Year		Year	
1956	Real Madrid (Spain)	1958	Real Madrid (Spain)	1960	Real Madrid (Spain)
1957	Real Madrid (Spain)	1959	Real Madrid (Spain)	1961	Benfica (Portugal)

Year		Year		Year	
1962	Benfica (Portugal)	1976	Bayern Munich (W. Germany)	1990	AC Milan (Italy)
1963	AC Milan (Italy)	1977	Liverpool (England)	1991	Red Star Belgrade (Yugo.)
1964	Inter Milan (Italy)	1978	Liverpool (England)	1992	Barcelona (Spain)
1965	Inter Milan (Italy)	1979	Nottingham Forest (England)	1993	Marseille (France)*
1966	Real Madrid (Spain)	1980	Nottingham Forest (England)	1994	AC Milan (Italy)
1967	Glasgow Celtic (Scotland)	1981	Liverpool (England)	1995	Ajax Amsterdam (Netherlands)
1968	Manchester United (England)	1982	Aston Villa (England)	1996	Juventus (Italy)
1969	AC Milan (Italy)	1983	SV Hamburg (W. Germany)	1997	Borussia Dortmund (Germany)
1970	Feyenoord (Netherlands)	1984	Liverpool (England)	1998	Real Madrid (Spain)
1971	Ajax Amsterdam (Netherlands)	1985	Juventus (Italy)	1999	Manchester United (England)
1972	Ajax Amsterdam (Netherlands)	1986	Steaua Bucharest (Romania)	2000	Real Madrid (Spain)
1973	Ajax Amsterdam (Netherlands)	1987	FC Porto (Portugal)	2001	Bayern Munich (Germany)
1974	Bayern Munich (W. Germany)	1988	PSV Eindhoven (Netherlands)	*title vacated	
1975	Bayern Munich (W. Germany)	1989	AC Milan (Italy)		

European Cup Winner's Cup

Contested annually from the 1960-61 season through the 1999-2000 season by the cup winners of the member countries of the Union of European Football Associations (UEFA). The Cup Winner's Cup was absorbed by the UEFA Cup in 2000.

Multiple winners: Barcelona (4); AC Milan, RSC Anderlecht, Chelsea and Dinamo Kiev (2).

Year		Year		Year	
1961	Fiorentina (Italy)	1975	Dinamo Kiev (USSR)	1989	Barcelona (Spain)
1962	Atletico Madrid (Spain)	1976	RSC Anderlecht (Belgium)	1990	Sampdoria (Italy)
1963	Tottenham Hotspur (England)	1977	SV Hamburg (W. Germany)	1991	Manchester United (England)
1964	Sporting Lisbon (Portugal)	1978	RSC Anderlecht (Belgium)	1992	Werder Bremen (Germany)
1965	West Ham United (England)	1979	Barcelona (Spain)	1993	Parma (Italy)
1966	Borussia Dortmund (W.Germany)	1980	Valencia (Spain)	1994	Arsenal (England)
1967	Bayern Munich (W. Germany)	1981	Dinamo Tbilisi (USSR)	1995	Real Zaragoza (Spain)
1968	AC Milan (Italy)	1982	Barcelona (Spain)	1996	Paris St. Germain (France)
1969	Slovan Bratislava (Czech.)	1983	Aberdeen (Scotland)	1997	Barcelona (Spain)
1970	Manchester City (England)	1984	Juventus (Italy)	1998	Chelsea (England)
1971	Chelsea (England)	1985	Everton (England)	1999	Lazio (Italy)
1972	Glasgow Rangers (Scotland)	1986	Dinamo Kiev (USSR)	2000	discontinued
1973	AC Milan (Italy)	1987	Ajax Amsterdam (Netherlands)		
1974	FC Magdeburg (E. Germany)	1988	Mechelen (Belgium)		

UEFA Cup

Contested annually since the 1957-58 season by teams other than league champions and cup winners of the Union of European Football Associations (UEFA). Teams selected by UEFA based on each country's previous performance in the tournament. Teams from England were banned from UEFA Cup play from 1985-90 for the criminal behavior of their supporters. In 1999, with the formation of the new Champions League, UEFA announced that the UEFA Cup would be expanded and include any teams that would have normally played in the Cup Winner's Cup.

Multiple winners: Barcelona, Inter Milan, Juventus and Liverpool (3); Borussia Mönchengladbach, IFK Göteborg, Leeds United, Parma, Real Madrid, Tottenham Hotspur and Valencia (2).

Year		Year		Year	
1958	Barcelona (Spain)	1974	Feyenoord (Netherlands)	1988	Bayer Leverkusen (W. Germany)
1959	Not held	1975	Borussia Mönchengladbach (W. Germany)	1989	Napoli (Italy)
1960	Barcelona (Spain)	1976	Liverpool (England)	1990	Juventus (Italy)
1961	AS Roma (Italy)	1977	Juventus (Italy)	1991	Inter Milan (Italy)
1962	Valencia (Spain)	1978	PSV Eindhoven (Netherlands)	1992	Ajax Amsterdam (Netherlands)
1963	Valencia (Spain)	1979	Borussia Mönchengladbach (W. Germany)	1993	Juventus (Italy)
1964	Real Zaragoza (Spain)	1980	Eintracht Frankfurt (W. Germany)	1994	Inter Milan (Italy)
1965	Ferencvaros (Hungary)	1981	Ipswich Town (England)	1995	Parma (Italy)
1966	Barcelona (Spain)	1982	IFK Göteborg (Sweden)	1996	Bayern Munich (Germany)
1967	Dinamo Zagreb (Yugoslavia)	1983	RSC Anderlecht (Belgium)	1997	Schalke 04 (Germany)
1968	Leeds United (England)	1984	Tottenham Hotspur (England)	1998	Inter Milan (Italy)
1969	Newcastle United (England)	1985	Real Madrid (Spain)	1999	Parma (Italy)
1970	Arsenal (England)	1986	Real Madrid (Spain)	2000	Galatasaray (Turkey)
1971	Leeds United (England)	1987	IFK Göteborg (Sweden)	2001	Liverpool (England)
1972	Tottenham Hotspur (England)				
1973	Liverpool (England)				

Copa Libertadores

Contested annually since the 1955-56 season by the league champions of South America's football union.

Multiple winners: Independiente (7); Peñarol (5); Boca Juniors, Estudiantes and Nacional-Uruguay (3); Cruzeiro, Gremio, Olimpia, River Plate, Santos and São Paulo (2).

Year		Year		Year	
1960	Peñarol (Uruguay)	1966	Peñarol (Uruguay)	1972	Independiente (Argentina)
1961	Peñarol (Uruguay)	1967	Racing Club (Argentina)	1973	Independiente (Argentina)
1962	Santos (Brazil)	1968	Estudiantes de la Plata (Argentina)	1974	Independiente (Argentina)
1963	Santos (Brazil)	1969	Estudiantes de la Plata (Argentina)	1975	Independiente (Argentina)
1964	Independiente (Argentina)	1970	Estudiantes de la Plata (Argentina)	1976	Cruzeiro (Brazil)
1965	Independiente (Argentina)	1971	Nacional (Uruguay)	1977	Boca Juniors (Argentina)

Club Competition (Cont.)

Year		Year		Year	
1978	Boca Juniors (Argentina)	1985	Argentinos Jrs. (Argentina)	1992	São Paulo (Brazil)
1979	Olimpia (Paraguay)	1986	River Plate (Argentina)	1993	São Paulo (Brazil)
1980	Nacional (Uruguay)	1987	Peñarol (Uruguay)	1994	Velez Sarsfield (Argentina)
1981	Flamengo (Brazil)	1988	Nacional (Uruguay)	1995	Gremio (Brazil)
1982	Peñarol (Uruguay)	1989	Nacional Medellin (Colombia)	1996	River Plate (Argentina)
1983	Gremio (Brazil)			1997	Cruzeiro (Brazil)
1984	Independiente (Argentina)	1990	Olimpia (Paraguay)	1998	Vasco da Gama (Brazil)
		1991	Colo Colo (Chile)	1999	Palmeiras (Brazil)
				2000	Boca Juniors (Argentina)

Annual Awards
World Player of the Year

Presented by FIFA, the European Sports Magazine Association (ESM) and Adidas, the sports equipment manufacturer, since 1991. Winners are selected by national team coaches from around the world.

Multiple winners: Ronaldo and Zinedine Zidane (2).

Year		Nat'l Team	Year		Nat'l Team
1991	Lothar Matthäus, Inter Milan	Germany	1996	Ronaldo, Barcelona	Brazil
1992	Marco Van Basten, AC Milan	Netherlands	1997	Ronaldo, Inter Milan	Brazil
1993	Roberto Baggio, Juventus	Italy	1998	Zinedine Zidane, Juventus	France
1994	Romario, Barcelona	Brazil	1999	Rivaldo, Barcelona	Brazil
1995	George Weah, AC Milan	Liberia	2000	Zinedine Zidane, Juventus	France

European Player of the Year

Officially, the "Ballon d'Or," or "Golden Ball," and presented by *France Football* magazine since 1956. Candidates are limited to European players in European leagues and winners are selected by a poll of European soccer journalists.

Multiple winners: Johan Cruyff, Michel Platini and Marco Van Basten (3); Franz Beckenbauer, Alfredo di Stéfano, Kevin Keegan and Karl-Heinz Rummenigge (2).

Year		Nat'l Team	Year		Nat'l Team
1956	Stanley Matthews, Blackpool	England	1979	Kevin Keegan, SV Hamburg	England
1957	Alfredo di Stéfano, Real Madrid	Arg./Spain	1980	K.H. Rummenigge, Bayern Munich	W. Ger.
1958	Raymond Kopa, Real Madrid	France	1981	K.H. Rummenigge, Bayern Munich	W. Ger.
1959	Alfredo di Stéfano, Real Madrid	Arg./Spain	1982	Paolo Rossi, Juventus	Italy
1960	Luis Suarez, Barcelona	Spain	1983	Michel Platini, Juventus	France
1961	Enrique Sivori, Juventus	Arg./Italy	1984	Michel Platini, Juventus	France
1962	Josef Masopust, Dukla Prague	Czech.	1985	Michel Platini, Juventus	France
1963	Lev Yashin, Dinamo Moscow	Soviet Union	1986	Igor Belanov, Dinamo Kiev	Soviet Union
1964	Denis Law, Manchester United	Scotland	1987	Ruud Gullit, AC Milan	Netherlands
1965	Eusébio, Benfica	Portugal	1988	Marco Van Basten, AC Milan	Netherlands
1966	Bobby Charlton, Manchester United	England	1989	Marco Van Basten, AC Milan	Netherlands
1967	Florian Albert, Ferencvaros	Hungary	1990	Lothar Matthäus, Inter Milan	W. Ger.
1968	George Best, Manchester United	No. Ireland	1991	Jean-Pierre Papin, Marseille	France
1969	Gianni Rivera, AC Milan	Italy	1992	Marco Van Basten, AC Milan	Netherlands
1970	Gerd Müller, Bayern Munich	W. Ger.	1993	Roberto Baggio, Juventus	Italy
1971	Johan Cruyff, Ajax Amsterdam	Netherlands	1994	Hristo Stoitchkov, Barcelona	Bulgaria
1972	Franz Beckenbauer, Bayern Munich	W. Ger.	1995	George Weah, AC Milan	Liberia
1973	Johan Cruyff, Barcelona	Netherlands	1996	Matthias Sammer, Bor. Dortmund	Germany
1974	Johan Cruyff, Barcelona	Netherlands	1997	Ronaldo, Inter Milan	Brazil
1975	Oleg Blokhin, Dinamo Kiev	Soviet Union	1998	Zinedine Zidane, Juventus	France
1976	Franz Beckenbauer, Bayern Munich	W. Ger.	1999	Rivaldo, Barcelona	Brazil
1977	Allan Simonsen, B. Mönchengladbach	Denmark	2000	Luis Figo, Real Madrid	Portugal
1978	Kevin Keegan, SV Hamburg	England			

South American Player of the Year

Presented by El Pais of Uruguay since 1971. Candidates are limited to South American players in South American leagues and winners are selected by a poll of South American sports editors.

Multiple winners: Elias Figueroa and Zico (3); Enzo Francescoli, Diego Maradona and Carlos Valderrama (2).

Year		Nat'l Team	Year		Nat'l Team
1971	Tostao, Cruzeiro	Brazil	1986	Antonio Alzamendi, River Plate	Uruguay
1972	Teofilo Cubillas, Alianza Lima	Peru	1987	Carlos Valderrama, Deportivo Cali	Colombia
1973	Pelé, Santos	Brazil	1988	Ruben Paz, Racing Buenos Aires	Uruguay
1974	Elias Figueroa, Internacional	Chile	1989	Bebeto, Vasco da Gama	Brazil
1975	Elias Figueroa, Internacional	Chile	1990	Raul Amarilla, Olimpia	Paraguay
1976	Elias Figueroa, Internacional	Chile	1991	Oscar Ruggeri, Velez Sarsfield	Argentina
1977	Zico, Flamengo	Brazil	1992	Rai, Sao Paulo	Brazil
1978	Mario Kempes, Valencia	Argentina	1993	Carlos Valderrama, Atl. Junior	Colombia
1979	Diego Maradona, Argentinos Juniors	Argentina	1994	Cafu, Sao Paulo	Brazil
1980	Diego Maradona, Boca Juniors	Argentina	1995	Enzo Francescoli, River Plate	Uruguay
1981	Zico, Flamengo	Brazil	1996	Jose Luis Chilavert, Velez Sarsfield	Paraguay
1982	Zico, Flamengo	Brazil	1997	Marcelo Salas, River Plate	Chile
1983	Socrates, Corinthians	Brazil	1998	Martin Palermo, Boca Juniors	Argentina
1984	Enzo Francescoli, River Plate	Uruguay	1999	Javier Saviola, River Plate	Argentina
1985	Julio Cesar Romero, Fluminense	Paraguay	2000	Romario, Vasco da Gama	Brazil

African Player of the Year

Officially, the African "Ballon d'Or" and presented by *France Football* magazine from 1970-96. The Arican Player of the Year award has been presented by the CAF (African Football Confederation) since 1997. All African players are eligible for the award.

Multiple winners: George Weah and Abedi Pelé (3); Nwankwo Kanu, Roger Milla and Thomas N'Kono (2).

Year		Year		Year	
1970	Salif Keita, Mali	1981	Lakhdar Belloumi, Algeria	1992	Abedi Pelé, Ghana
1971	Ibrahim Sunday, Ghana	1982	Thomas N'Kono, Cameroon	1993	Abedi Pelé, Ghana
1972	Cherif Souleymane, Guinea	1983	Mahmoud Al-Khatib, Egypt	1994	George Weah, Liberia
1973	Tshimimu Bwanga, Zaire	1984	Theophile Abega, Cameroon	1995	George Weah, Liberia
1974	Paul Moukila, Congo	1985	Mohamed Timoumi, Morocco	1996	Nwankwo Kanu, Nigeria
1975	Ahmed Faras, Morocco	1986	Badou Zaki, Morocco	1997	Victor Ikpeba, Nigeria
1976	Roger Milla, Cameroon	1987	Rabah Madjer, Algeria	1998	Mustapha Hadji, Morocco
1977	Dhiab Tarak, Tunisia	1988	Kalusha Bwalya, Zambia	1999	Nwankwo Kanu, Nigeria
1978	Abdul Razak, Ghana	1989	George Weah, Liberia	2000	Patrick Mboma, Cameroon
1979	Thomas N'Kono, Cameroon	1990	Roger Milla, Cameroon		
1980	Jean Manga Onguene, Cameroon	1991	Abedi Pelé, Ghana		

U.S. Player of the Year

Presented by Honda and the Spanish-speaking radio show "Futbol de Primera" since 1991. Candidates are limited to American players who have played with the U.S. National Team and winners are selected by a panel of U.S. soccer journalists.

Multiple winner: Eric Wynalda (2).

Year		Year		Year		Year		Year	
1991	Hugo Perez	1993	Thomas Dooley	1995	Alexi Lalas	1997	Eddie Pope	1999	Kasey Keller
1992	Eric Wynalda	1994	Marcelo Balboa	1996	Eric Wynalda	1998	Cobi Jones	2000	Claudio Reyna

U.S. PRO LEAGUES

OUTDOOR

Major League Soccer

Sanctioned by U.S. Soccer and FIFA, the international soccer federation. MLS was founded on the heels of the successful 1994 World Cup tournament hosted by the United States and it remains the only FIFA-sanctioned division I outdoor league in the United States. The annual MLS title game is known as the MLS Cup.

Multiple Winner: D.C. United (3).

MLS Cup

Year	Winner	Head Coach	Score	Loser	Head Coach	Site
1996	D.C. United	Bruce Arena	3-2	Los Angeles Galaxy	Lothar Osiander	Foxboro, Mass.
1997	D.C. United	Bruce Arena	2-1	Colorado Rapids	Glen Myernick	Washington, D.C.
1998	Chicago Fire	Bob Bradley	2-0	D.C. United	Bruce Arena	Pasadena, Calif.
1999	D.C. United	Thomas Rongen	2-0	Los Angeles Galaxy	Sigi Schmid	Foxboro, Mass.
2000	K.C. Wizards	Bob Gansler	1-0	Chicago Fire	Bob Bradley	Washington, D.C.
2001	See Updates Chapter					

MLS Cup '96
D.C. United, 3-2 (OT)
Oct. 20 at Foxboro Stadium, Foxboro, Mass.
Attendance: 34,643

	1	2	OT	
Los Angeles Galaxy	1	1	0	—2
D.C. United	0	2	1	—3

First Half: LA—Eduardo Hurtado (Mauricio Cienfuegos), 5th minute.
Second Half: LA—Chris Armas (unassisted), 56th; DC—Tony Sanneh (Marco Etcheverry), 73rd; DC—Shawn Medved (unassisted), 82nd.
Overtime: DC—Eddie Pope (Etcheverry), 94th.
MVP: Marco Etcheverry, D.C. United, Midfielder

MLS Cup '97
D.C. United, 2-1
Oct. 26 at RFK Stadium, Washington, D.C.
Attendance: 57,431

	1	2	
Colorado Rapids	0	1	—1
D.C. United	1	1	—2

First Half: DC—Jaime Moreno (Tony Sanneh, David Vaudreuil), 37th minute.
Second Half: DC—Sanneh (John Harkes, Richie Williams), 68th; COL—Adrian Paz (David Patino, Matt Kmosko), 75th.
MVP: Jaime Moreno, D.C. United, Forward

MLS Cup '98
Chicago Fire, 2-0
Oct. 25 at the Rose Bowl, Pasadena, Calif.
Attendance: 51,350

	1	2	
D.C. United	0	0	—0
Chicago	2	0	—2

First Half: CHI—Jerzy Podbrozny (Peter Nowak, Ante Razov), 29th minute; CHI—Diego Gutierrez (Nowak), 45th.
MVP: Nowak, Chicago, Midfielder

MLS Cup '99
D.C. United, 2-0
Nov. 21 at Foxboro Stadium, Foxboro, Mass.
Attendance: 44,910

	1	2	
D.C. United	2	0	—2
Los Angeles	0	0	—0

First Half: DC— Jaime Moreno (Roy Lassiter), 19th minute; DC—Ben Olsen (unassisted), 48th
MVP: Olsen, D.C. United, Midfielder

U.S. Pro Leagues (Cont.)

MLS Cup 2000
Kansas City Wizards, 1-0
Oct. 15 at RFK Stadium, Washington, D.C.
Attendance: 39,159

	1	**2**	
Chicago	0	0	**-0**
Kansas City	1	0	**-1**

First Half: DC– Miklos Molnar (Chris Klein), 11th minute.
MVP: Tony Meola, Kansas City, Goalkeeper

Regular Season

Most Valuable Player

1996	Carlos Valderrama, Tampa Bay
1997	Preki, Kansas City
1998	Marco Etcheverry, D.C.
1999	Jason Kreis, Dallas
2000	Tony Meola, Kansas City

Leading Scorer

		G	**A**	**Pts**
1996	Roy Lassiter, Tampa Bay	27	4	58
1997	Preki, Kansas City	12	17	41
1998	Stern John, Columbus	26	5	57
1999	Jason Kreis, Dallas	18	15	51
2000	Mamadou Diallo, Tampa Bay	26	4	56

National Professional Soccer League (1967)

Not sanctioned by FIFA, the international soccer federation. The NPSL recruited individual players to fill the rosters of its 10 teams. The league lasted only one season.

	Playoff Final			**Regular Season**			
Year	**Winner**	**Scores**	**Loser**	**Leading Scorer**	**G**	**A**	**Pts**
1967	Oakland Clippers	0-1, 4-1	Baltimore Bays	Yanko Daucik, Toronto	20	8	48

United Soccer Association (1967)

Sanctioned by FIFA. Originally called the North American Soccer League, it became the USA to avoid being confused with the National Professional Soccer League (see above). Instead of recruiting individual players, the USA imported 12 entire teams from Europe to represent its 12 franchises. It, too, only lasted a season. The league champion Los Angeles Wolves were actually Wolverhampton of England and the runner-up Washington Whips were Aberdeen of Scotland.

	Playoff Final			**Regular Season**			
Year	**Winner**	**Score**	**Loser**	**Leading Scorer**	**G**	**A**	**Pts**
1967	Los Angeles Wolves	6-5 (OT)	Washington Whips	Roberto Boninsegna, Chicago	10	1	21

North American Soccer League (1968-84)

The NPSL and USA merged to form the NASL in 1968 and the new league lasted through 1984. The NASL championship was known as the Soccer Bowl from 1975-84. One game decided the NASL title every year but five. There were no playoffs in 1969; a two-game/aggregate goals format was used in 1968 and '70; and a best-of-three games format was used in 1971 and '84; (*) indicates overtime and (†) indicates game decided by shootout.
Multiple winners: NY Cosmos (5); Chicago (2).

	Playoff Final			**Regular Season**			
Year	**Winner**	**Score(s)**	**Loser**	**Leading Scorer**	**G**	**A**	**Pts**
1968	Atlanta Chiefs	0-0, 3-0	San Diego Toros	John Kowalik, Chicago	30	9	69
1969	Kansas City Spurs	No game	Atlanta Chiefs	Kaiser Motaung, Atlanta	16	4	36
1970	Rochester Lancers	3-0, 1-3	Washington Darts	Kirk Apostolidis, Dallas	16	3	35
1971	Dallas Tornado	1-2*, 4-1, 2-0	Atlanta Chiefs	Carlos Metidieri, Rochester	19	8	46
1972	New York Cosmos	2-1	St. Louis Stars	Randy Horton, New York	9	4	22
1973	Philadelphia Atoms	2-0	Dallas Tornado	Kyle Rote Jr., Dallas	10	10	30
1974	Los Angeles Aztecs	3-3†	Miami Toros	Paul Child, San Jose	15	6	36
1975	Tampa Bay Rowdies	2-0	Portland Timbers	Steve David, Miami	23	6	52
1976	Toronto Metros	3-0	Minnesota Kicks	Giorgio Chinaglia, New York	19	11	49
1977	New York Cosmos	2-1	Seattle Sounders	Steve David, Los Angeles	26	6	58
1978	New York Cosmos	3-1	Tampa Bay Rowdies	Giorgio Chinaglia, New York	34	11	79
1979	Vancouver Whitecaps	2-1	Tampa Bay Rowdies	Oscar Fabbiani, Tampa Bay	25	8	58
1980	New York Cosmos	3-0	Ft. Laud. Strikers	Giorgio Chinaglia, New York	32	13	77
1981	Chicago Sting	0-0†	New York Cosmos	Giorgio Chinaglia, New York	29	16	74
1982	New York Cosmos	1-0	Seattle Sounders	Giorgio Chinaglia, New York	20	15	55
1983	Tulsa Roughnecks	2-0	Toronto Blizzard	Roberto Cabanas, New York	25	16	66
1984	Chicago Sting	2-1, 3-2	Toronto Blizzard	Steve Zungul, Golden Bay	20	10	50

Note: In 1969, Kansas City won the NASL regular season championship with 110 points to 109 for Atlanta. There were no playoffs.

Regular Season MVP
Regular season Most Valuable Player as designated by the NASL.
Multiple winner: Carlos Metidieri (2).

Year	**Year**	**Year**
1967 Rueben Navarro, Phila (NPSL)	1973 Warren Archibald, Miami	1979 Johan Cruyff, Los Angeles
1968 John Kowalik, Chicago	1974 Peter Silvester, Baltimore	1980 Roger Davies, Seattle
1969 Cirilio Fernandez, KC	1975 Steve David, Miami	1981 Giorgio Chinaglia, New York
1970 Carlos Metidieri, Rochester	1976 Pelé, New York	1982 Peter Ward, Seattle
1971 Carlos Metidieri, Rochester	1977 Franz Beckenbauer, New York	1983 Roberto Cabanas, New York
1972 Randy Horton, New York	1978 Mike Flanagan, New England	1984 Steve Zungul, Golden Bay

A-League (American Professional Soccer League)

The American Professional Soccer League was formed in 1990 with the merger of the Western Soccer League and the New American Soccer League. The APSL was officially sanctioned as an outdoor pro league in 1992 and changed its name to the A-League in 1995.

Multiple winners: Colorado, Rochester and Seattle (2).

Year		Year		Year		Year	
1990	Maryland Bays	1993	Colorado Foxes	1996	Seattle Sounders	1999	Minnesota Thunder
1991	SF Bay Blackhawks	1994	Montreal Impact	1997	Milwaukee Rampage	2000	Rochester Rhinos
1992	Colorado Foxes	1995	Seattle Sounders	1998	Rochester Rhinos		

INDOOR

Major Soccer League (1978-92)

Originally the Major Indoor Soccer League from 1978-79 season through 1989-90. The MISL championship was decided by one game in 1980 and 1981; a best-of-three games series in 1979, best-of-five games in 1982 and 1983; and best-of-seven games since 1984. The MSL folded after the 1991-92 season.

Multiple winners: San Diego (8); New York (4).

	Playoff Final			Regular Season			
Year	Winner	Series	Loser	Leading Scorer	G	A	Pts
1979	New York Arrows	2-0	Philadelphia	Fred Grgurev, Philadelphia 46	28	74	
1980	New York Arrows	7-4 (1 game)	Houston	Steve Zungul, New York 90	46	136	
1981	New York Arrows	6-5 (1 game)	St. Louis	Steve Zungul, New York 108	44	152	
1982	New York Arrows	3-2 (LWWLW)	St. Louis	Steve Zungul, New York 103	60	163	
1983	San Diego Sockers	3-2 (WWLLW)	Baltimore	Steve Zungul, NY/Golden Bay 75	47	122	
1984	Baltimore Blast	4-1 (LWWWW)	St. Louis	Stan Stamenkovic, Baltimore 34	63	97	
1985	San Diego Sockers	4-1 (WWLWW)	Baltimore	Steve Zungul, San Diego 68	68	136	
1986	San Diego Sockers	4-3 (WLLLWWW)	Minnesota	Steve Zungul, Tacoma 55	60	115	
1987	Dallas Sidekicks	4-3 (LLWWLWW)	Tacoma	Tatu, Dallas 73	38	111	
1988	San Diego Sockers	4-0	Cleveland	Eric Rasmussen, Wichita 55	57	112	
1989	San Diego Sockers	4-3 (LWWWLLW)	Baltimore	Preki, Tacoma 51	53	104	
1990	San Diego Sockers	4-2 (LWWWLW)	Baltimore	Tatu, Dallas 64	49	113	
1991	San Diego Sockers	4-2 (WLWLWW)	Cleveland	Tatu, Dallas 78	66	144	
1992	San Diego Sockers	4-2 (WWWLLW)	Dallas	Zoran Karic, Cleveland 39	63	102	

Playoff MVPs

MSL playoff Most Valuable Players, selected by a panel of soccer media covering the playoffs.

Multiple winners: Steve Zungul (4); Brian Quinn (2).

Year		Year	
1979	Shep Messing, NY	1986	Brian Quinn, SD
1980	Steve Zungul, NY	1987	Tatu, Dallas
1981	Steve Zungul, NY	1988	Hugo Perez, SD
1982	Steve Zungul, NY	1989	Victor Nogueira, SD
1983	Juli Veee, SD	1990	Brian Quinn, SD
1984	Scott Manning, Bal.	1991	Ben Collins, SD
1985	Steve Zungul, SD	1992	Thompson Usiyan, SD

Regular Season MVPs

MSL regular season Most Valuable Players, selected by a panel of soccer media from every city in the league.

Multiple winners: Steve Zungul (6); Victor Nogueira and Tatu (2).

Year		Year	
1979	Steve Zungul, NY	1986	Steve Zungul, SD/Tac.
1980	Steve Zungul, NY	1987	Tatu, Dallas
1981	Steve Zungul, NY	1988	Erik Rasmussen, Wich.
1982	Steve Zungul, NY & Stan Terlecki, Pit.	1989	Preki, Tacoma
1983	Alan Mayer, SD	1990	Tatu, Dallas
1984	Stan Stamenkovic, Bal.	1991	Victor Nogueira, SD
1985	Steve Zungul, SD	1992	Victor Nogueira, SD

NASL Indoor Champions (1980-84)

The North American Soccer League started an indoor league in the fall of 1979. The indoor NASL, which featured many of the same teams and players who played in the outdoor NASL, crowned champions from 1980-82 before suspending play. It was revived for the 1983-84 indoor season but folded for good in 1984. The NASL held indoor tournaments in 1975 (San Jose Earthquakes won) and 1976 (Tampa Bay Rowdies won) before the indoor league was started.

Multiple winner: San Diego (2).

Year		Year		Year		Year	
1980	Tampa Bay Rowdies	1982	San Diego Sockers	1983	Play suspended	1984	San Diego Sockers
1981	Edmonton Drillers						

Major Indoor Soccer League

The winter indoor MISL began as the American Indoor Soccer Association in 1984-85, then changed its name to the National Professional Soccer League in 1989-90 and was known as the NPSL until 2001 when the name was changed again to the MISL.

Multiple winners: Canton (5); Cleveland (3); Kansas City and Milwaukee (2).

Year		Year		Year		Year	
1985	Canton (OH) Invaders	1989	Canton Invaders	1993	Kansas City Attack	1997	Kansas City Attack
1986	Canton Invaders	1990	Canton Invaders	1994	Cleveland Crunch	1998	Milwaukee Wave
1987	Louisville Thunder	1991	Chicago Power	1995	St. Louis Ambush	1999	Cleveland Crunch
1988	Canton Invaders	1992	Detroit Rockers	1996	Cleveland Crunch	2000	Milwaukee Wave

U.S. Pro Leagues (Cont.)
Continental Indoor Soccer League (1993-97)

The summer indoor CISL played its first season in 1993 and folded following the 1997 season.

Multiple winner: Monterrey (2).

Year		Year		Year	
1993	Dallas Sidekicks	1995	Monterrey La Raza	1997	Seattle Seadogs
1994	Las Vegas Dustdevils	1996	Monterrey La Raza		

U.S. COLLEGES

NCAA Men's Division I Champions

NCAA Division I champions since the first title was contested in 1959. The championship has been shared three times—in 1967, 1968 and 1989. There was a playoff for third place from 1974-81.

Multiple winners: Saint Louis (10); Indiana, San Francisco and Virginia (5); UCLA (3); Clemson, Connecticut, Howard and Michigan St. (2).

Year	Winner	Head Coach	Score	Runner-up	Host/Site	Semifinalists
1959	Saint Louis	Bob Guelker	5-2	Bridgeport	Connecticut	West Chester, CCNY
1960	Saint Louis	Bob Guelker	3-2	Maryland	Brooklyn	West Chester, Connecticut
1961	West Chester	Mel Lorback	2-0	Saint Louis	Saint Louis	Bridgeport, Rutgers
1962	Saint Louis	Bob Guelker	4-3	Maryland	Saint Louis	Mich. St., Springfield
1963	Saint Louis	Bob Guelker	3-0	Navy	Rutgers	Army, Maryland
1964	Navy	F.H. Warner	1-0	Michigan St.	Brown	Army, Saint Louis
1965	Saint Louis	Bob Guelker	1-0	Michigan St.	Saint Louis	Army, Navy
1966	San Francisco	Steve Negoesco	5-2	LIU-Brooklyn	California	Army, Mich. St.
1967-a	Michigan St. & Saint Louis	Gene Kenney, Harry Keough	0-0	–	Saint Louis	LIU-Bklyn, Navy
1968-b	Michigan St. & Maryland	Gene Kenney, Doyle Royal	2-2 (2 OT)	–	Ga. Tech	Brown, San Jose St.
1969	Saint Louis	Harry Keough	4-0	San Francisco	San Jose St.	Harvard, Maryland
1970	Saint Louis	Harry Keough	1-0	UCLA	SIU-Ed'sville	Hartwick, Howard
1971-c	Howard	Lincoln Phillips	3-2	Saint Louis	Miami	Harvard, San Fran.
1972	Saint Louis	Harry Keough	4-2	UCLA	Miami	Cornell, Howard
1973	Saint Louis	Harry Keough	2-1 (OT)	UCLA	Miami	Brown, Clemson

Year	Winner	Head Coach	Score	Runner-up	Host/Site	Third Place
1974	Howard	Lincoln Phillips	2-1 (4OT)	Saint Louis	Saint Louis	Hartwick 3, UCLA 1
1975	San Francisco	Steve Negoesco	4-0	SIU-Ed'sville	SIU-Ed'sville	Brown 2, Howard 0
1976	San Francisco	Steve Negoesco	1-0	Indiana	Penn	Hartwick 4, Clemson 3
1977	Hartwick	Jim Lennox	2-1	San Francisco	California	SIU-Ed'sville 3, Brown 2
1978-d	San Francisco	Steve Negoesco	4-3 (OT)	Indiana	Tampa	Clemson 6, Phi. Textile 2
1979	SIU-Ed'sville	Bob Guelker	3-2	Clemson	Tampa	Penn St. 2, Columbia 1
1980	San Francisco	Steve Negoesco	4-3 (OT)	Indiana	Tampa	Ala. A&M 2, Hartwick 0
1981	Connecticut	Joe Morrone	2-1 (OT)	Alabama A&M	Stanford	East. Ill. 4, Phi. Textile 2

Year	Winner	Head Coach	Score	Runner-up	Host/Site	Semifinalists
1982	Indiana	Jerry Yeagley	2-1 (8 OT)	Duke	Ft. Lauderdale	Connecticut, SIU-Ed'sville
1983	Indiana	Jerry Yeagley	1-0 (2 OT)	Columbia	Ft. Lauderdale	Connecticut, Virginia
1984	Clemson	I.M. Ibrahim	2-1	Indiana	Seattle	Hartwick, UCLA
1985	UCLA	Sigi Schmid	1-0 (8 OT)	American	Seattle	Evansville, Hartwick
1986	Duke	John Rennie	1-0	Akron	Tacoma	Fresno St., Harvard
1987	Clemson	I.M. Ibrahim	2-0	San Diego St.	Clemson	Harvard, N. Carolina
1988	Indiana	Jerry Yeagley	1-0	Howard	Indiana	Portland, S. Carolina
1989-e	Santa Clara & Virginia	Steve Sampson, Bruce Arena	1-1 (2 OT)	–	Rutgers	Indiana, Rutgers
1990-f	UCLA	Sigi Schmid	0-0 (PKs)	Rutgers	South Fla.	Evansville, N.C. State
1991-g	Virginia	Bruce Arena	0-0 (PKs)	Santa Clara	Tampa	Indiana, Saint Louis
1992	Virginia	Bruce Arena	2-0	San Diego	Davidson	Davidson, Duke
1993	Virginia	Bruce Arena	2-0	South Carolina	Davidson	CS-Fullerton, Princeton
1994	Virginia	Bruce Arena	1-0	Indiana	Davidson	Rutgers, UCLA
1995	Wisconsin	Jim Launder	2-0	Duke	Richmond	Portland, Virginia
1996	St. John's	Dave Masur	4-1	Fla. International	Richmond	Creighton, NC-Charlotte
1997	UCLA	Sigi Schmid	2-0	Virginia	Richmond	Indiana, Saint Louis
1998	Indiana	Jerry Yeagley	3-1	Stanford	Richmond	Maryland, Santa Clara
1999	Indiana	Jerry Yeagley	1-0	Santa Clara	Charlotte	Connecticut, UCLA
2000	Connecticut	Ray Reid	2-0	Creighton	Charlotte	Indiana, Southern Method

a–game declared a draw due to inclement weather after regulation time; **b**–game declared a draw after two overtimes; **c**–Howard vacated title for using ineligible player; **d**–San Francisco vacated title for using ineligible player; **e**–game declared a draw due to inclement weather after two overtimes. **f**–UCLA wins on penalty kicks (4-3) after four overtimes; **g**–Virginia wins on penalty kicks (3-1) after four overtimes.

Women's NCAA Division I Champions

NCAA Division I women's champions since the first tournament was contested in 1982.

Multiple winner: North Carolina (16).

Year	Winner	Coach	Score	Runner-up	Host/Site
1982	North Carolina	Anson Dorrance	2-0	Central Florida	Central Florida
1983	North Carolina	Anson Dorrance	4-0	George Mason	Central Florida
1984	North Carolina	Anson Dorrance	2-0	Connecticut	North Carolina
1985	George Mason	Hank Leung	2-0	North Carolina	George Mason
1986	North Carolina	Anson Dorrance	2-0	Colorado College	George Mason
1987	North Carolina	Anson Dorrance	1-0	Massachusetts	Massachusetts
1988	North Carolina	Anson Dorrance	4-1	N.C. State	North Carolina
1989	North Carolina	Anson Dorrance	2-0	Colorado College	N.C. State
1990	North Carolina	Anson Dorrance	6-0	Connecticut	North Carolina
1991	North Carolina	Anson Dorrance	3-1	Wisconsin	North Carolina
1992	North Carolina	Anson Dorrance	9-1	Duke	North Carolina
1993	North Carolina	Anson Dorrance	6-0	George Mason	North Carolina
1994	North Carolina	Anson Dorrance	5-0	Notre Dame	Portland
1995	Notre Dame	Chris Petrucelli	1-0 (3OT)	Portland	North Carolina
1996	North Carolina	Anson Dorrance	1-0 (2OT)	Notre Dame	Santa Clara
1997	North Carolina	Anson Dorrance	2-0	Connecticut	NC-Greensboro
1998	Florida	Becky Burleigh	1-0	North Carolina	NC-Greensboro
1999	North Carolina	Anson Dorrance	2-0	Notre Dame	San Jose, Calif.
2000	North Carolina	Anson Dorrance	2-1	UCLA	San Jose, Calif.

Annual Awards
MEN
Hermann Trophy

College Player of the Year. Voted on by Division I college coaches and selected sportswriters and first presented in 1967 in the name of Robert Hermann, one of the founders of the North American Soccer League.

Multiple winners: Mike Fisher, Mike Seerey, Ken Snow and Al Trost (2).

Year		
1967 Dov Markus, LIU	1979 Jim Stamatis, Penn St.	1991 Alexi Lalas, Rutgers
1968 Manuel Hernandez, San Jose St.	1980 Joe Morrone, Jr. Connecticut	1992 Brad Friedel, UCLA
1969 Al Trost, Saint Louis	1981 Armando Betancourt, Indiana	1993 Claudio Reyna, Virginia
1970 Al Trost, Saint Louis	1982 Joe Ulrich, Duke	1994 Brian Maisonneuve, Indiana
1971 Mike Seerey, Saint Louis	1983 Mike Jeffries, Duke	1995 Mike Fisher, Virginia
1972 Mike Seerey, Saint Louis	1984 Amr Aly, Columbia	1996 Mike Fisher, Virginia
1973 Dan Counce, Saint Louis	1985 Tom Kain, Duke	1997 Johnny Torres, Creighton
1974 Farrukh Quraishi, Oneonta St.	1986 John Kerr, Duke	1998 Wojtek Krakowiak, Clemson
1975 Steve Ralbovsky, Brown	1987 Bruce Murray, Clemson	1999 Ali Curtis, Duke
1976 Glenn Myernick, Hartwick	1988 Ken Snow, Indiana	2000 Chris Gbandi, Connecticut
1977 Billy Gazonas, Hartwick	1989 Tony Meola, Virginia	
1978 Angelo DiBernardo, Indiana	1990 Ken Snow, Indiana	

Missouri Athletic Club Award

College Player of the Year. Voted on by men's team coaches around the country from Division I to junior college level and first presented in 1986 by the Missouri Athletic Club of St. Louis.

Multiple winners: Claudio Reyna and Ken Snow (2).

Year		
1986 John Kerr, Duke	1991 Alexi Lalas, Rutgers	1996 Mike Fisher, Virginia
1987 John Harkes, Virginia	1992 Claudio Reyna, Virginia	1997 Johnny Torres, Creighton
1988 Ken Snow, Indiana	1993 Claudio Reyna, Virginia	1998 Jay Heaps, Duke
1989 Tony Meola, Virginia	1994 Todd Yeagley, Indiana	1999 Sasha Victorine, UCLA
1990 Ken Snow, Indiana	1995 Matt McKeon, St. Louis	2000 Ali Curtis, Duke

Coach of the Year

Men's Coach of the Year. Voted on by the National Soccer Coaches Association of America. From 1973-81 all Senior College coaches were eligible. In 1982, the award was split into several divisions. The Division I Coach of the Year is listed since 1982.

Multiple winner: Jerry Yeagley (5).

Year		
1973 Robert Guelker, SIU-Edwardsville	1983 Dieter Ficken, Columbia	1993 Bob Bradley, Princeton
1974 Jack MacKenzie, Quincy College	1984 James Lennox, Hartwick	1994 Jerry Yeagley, Indiana
1975 Paul Reinhardt, Vermont	1985 Peter Mehlert, American	1995 Jim Launder, Wisconsin
1976 Jerry Yeagley, Indiana	1986 Steve Parker, Akron	1996 Dave Masur, St. John's
1977 Klass Deboer, Cleveland St.	1987 Anson Dorrance, N. Carolina	1997 Sigi Schmid, UCLA
1978 Cliff McCrath, Seattle Pacific	1988 Keith Tucker, Howard	1998 Jerry Yeagley, Indiana
1979 Walter Bahr, Penn St.	1989 Steve Sampson, Santa Clara	1999 Jerry Yeagley, Indiana
1980 Jerry Yeagley, Indiana	1990 Bob Reasso, Rutgers	2000 Ray Reid, Connecticut
1981 Schellas Hyndman, E. Illinois	1991 Mitch Murray, Santa Clara	
1982 John Rennie, Duke	1992 Charles Slagle, Davidson	

U.S. Colleges (Cont.)
WOMEN

Hermann Trophy

Women's College Player of the year. Voted on by Division I college coaches and selected sportswriters and first presented in 1988 in the name of Robert Hermann, one of the founders of the North American Soccer League.

Multiple winners: Mia Hamm and Cindy Parlow (2).

Year	Year	Year
1988 Michelle Akers, Central Fla.	1993 Mia Hamm, N. Carolina	1998 Cindy Parlow, N. Carolina
1989 Shannon Higgins, N. Carolina	1994 Tisha Venturini, N. Carolina	1999 Mandy Clemens, Santa Clara
1990 April Kater, Massachusetts	1995 Shannon McMillan, Portland	2000 Anne Makinen, Notre Dame
1991 Kristine Lilly, N. Carolina	1996 Cindy Daws, Notre Dame	
1992 Mia Hamm, N. Carolina	1997 Cindy Parlow, N. Carolina	

Missouri Athletic Club Award

Women's College Player of the Year. Voted on by women's team coaches around the country from Division I to junior college level and first presented in 1991 by the Missouri Athletic Club of St. Louis.

Multiple winners: Mia Hamm and Cindy Parlow (2).

Year	Year	Year
1991 Kristine Lilly, N. Carolina	1995 Shannon McMillan, Portland	1999 Mandy Clemens, Santa Clara
1992 Mia Hamm, N. Carolina	1996 Cindy Daws, Notre Dame	2000 Anne Makinen, Notre Dame
1993 Mia Hamm, N. Carolina	1997 Cindy Parlow, N. Carolina	
1994 Tisha Venturini, N. Carolina	1998 Cindy Parlow, N. Carolina	

Coach of the Year

Women's Coach of the Year. Voted on by the National Soccer Coaches Association of America. From 1982-87 all Senior College coaches were eligible. In 1988, the award was split into several divisions. The Division I Coach of the Year is listed since 1988.

Multiple winners: Kalenkeni M. Banda, Anson Dorrance and Chris Petrucelli (2).

Year	Year	Year
1982 Anson Dorrance, N. Carolina	1989 Austin Daniels, Hartford	1996 John Walker, Nebraska
1983 David Lombardo, Keene St.	1990 Lauren Gregg, Virginia	1997 Len Tsantiris, Connecticut
1984 Phillip Picince, Brown	1991 Greg Ryan, Wisc-Madison	1998 Becky Burleigh, Florida
1985 Kalenkeni M. Banda, UMass	1992 Bell Hempen, Duke	1999 Patrick Farmer, Penn St.
1986 Anson Dorrance, N. Carolina	1993 Jac Cicala, George Mason	2000 Jillian Ellis, UCLA
1987 Kalenkeni M. Banda, UMass	1994 Chris Petrucelli, Norte Dame	
1988 Larry Gross, N.C. State	1995 Chris Petrucelli, Norte Dame	

All-Century Teams

Soccer America named their Men's and Women's Collegiate All-Century Teams as well as their Men's Player of the Century (Claudio Reyna) and Women's Player of the Century (Mia Hamm) in their Jan. 17, 2000 issue.

Men

Pos	Player	Years Played
GK	Brad Friedel, UCLA	1990-95
D	Erik Imler, Virginia	1989-92
D	Paul Caligiuri, UCLA	1982-83, 85-86
D	Adubarie Otorubio, Clemson	1981-84
M	Andy Atuegbu, San Francisco	1974-77
M	Claudio Reyna, Virginia	1991-93
M	Mike Fisher, Virginia	1993-96
M	Bruce Murray, Clemson	1984-87
F ·	Angelo DiBernardo, Indiana	1976-78
F	Ken Snow, Indiana	1987-89
F	Armando Betancourt, Indiana	1979-81

Women

Pos	Player	Years Played
GK	Kim Maslin, George Mason	1983-86
D	Carla Werden, North Carolina	1986-89
D	Debbie Belkin, Massachusetts	1984-87
D	Sara Whalen, Connecticut	1994-97
M	Kristine Lilly, North Carolina	1989-92
M	Shannon Higgins, North Carolina	1986-89
M	Michelle Akers, Central Florida	1984-89
M	Julie Foudy, Stanford	1989-92
F	April Heinrichs, North Carolina	1983-86
F	Carin Jennings, UC-Santa Barbara	1983-86
F	Mia Hamm, North Carolina	1989-90, 92-93

Bowling

The PBA lost one of its greats in 2001 when **Earl Anthony** died after a fall in August.

Bowling Gets a Makeover

New PBA owners begin to put their stamp on the sport in 2001.

Dick Evans writes for the Miami Herald and the Daytona Beach News-Journal and is a member of the PBA Hall of Fame.

The face of bowling was changing on almost every front in 2001 but nowhere was it more evident than the "new" Professional Bowlers Association, which was purchased in early 2000 by three former Microsoft executives.

After hiring two former Nike executives, Ian Hamilton as commissioner and Steve Miller as president, the PBA made some major policy changes to save a sinking ship. The five major changes were:

A guaranteed $4.5 million prize fund (a 140 percent increase over the previous season) for 20 tournaments to run from September through March. The winner of each event is guaranteed $40,000, with the winners of the four majors guaranteed to receive a championship check worth between $100,000 and a PBA record $120,000.

A new tournament format that calls for qualifying games to determine the 32 bowlers who meet in the best-of-five game matches. The winner of those matches then advances while the loser heads home.

A three-year deal with ESPN that is more fan friendly since most of the live 90-minute telecasts will follow a regular time pattern.

The elimination of coaching during actual competition. Things had gotten so bad that paying spectators could not see the participants through all the ball reps on the lanes. This rule evens the playing field since the tour stars got most of the coaching expertise.

The hiring of Jim Kelly, a highly respected ESPN sports announcer, to become the voice of the PBA, and 12-time tour champion Randy Pedersen to be the color commentator on the 20 ESPN telecasts.

On the women's tour, the Professional Women's Bowling Association made a daring decision to boycott the 2001

AP/Wide World Photos

*The PBA took major strides in 2001 under the guidance of former high-tech entrepreneurs and new league owners **Mike Slade**, **Chris Peters** and **Rob Glaser** (left to right).*

BPAA U.S. Open, and it paid major dividends. The touring PWBA players were irate when they found that the tournament had two different prize funds— $350,000 for the men and $187,500 for the women—although the event was going to be held at the same time at the same bowling center. They also were disenchanted with the fact that the men had a 90-minute live telecast and the women had no TV.

The Women's Sports Foundation came out with vocal support for the boycott, mainly from founder Billie Jean King. The end result—the PWBA wound up with a record $300,000 prize fund featuring a record $50,000 check for the winner, and a 90-minute live ESPN telecast.

Meanwhile, the bowling industry got a big shot in the arm when NBC decided to introduce a new comedy series called "Ed" that centered around a lovesick lawyer who buys a bowling center in order to charm his old high-school sweetheart. The hour-long series proved popular and was named the best new comedy series of the season. It didn't hurt when the NBC executives decided to move "Ed" from Sunday night to the lead-in show to the popular "West Wing" and "Law and Order" on Wednesday nights. Anyone who can remember dismal bowl-

PWBA Tour

With five titles in 12 tournaments on the PWBA Spring/Summer Tour, **Carolyn Dorin-Ballard** *is out to shed her label as perennial Player of the Year bridesmaid.*

ing movies like "Dreamer" and "Greedy" fell in love with the way bowling was depicted in "Ed."

But not all news was positive. On Feb. 19, the legendary Joe Norris died in San Diego at the age of 93. Norris, who bowled before Hitler during the 1936 Olympic Games in Berlin, was considered the greatest team bowler in history. He was scheduled to bowl in the giant ABC Championships Tournament in Reno in March for a record 72nd time. During that 71-year period, the former Detroit phenom knocked down a record 123,770 pins in 642 games, which figures out to an amazing 192.78 average.

Still more startling to the bowling world was the death on Aug. 14 of the fabled Earl Anthony, 63, following a fall down the stairs at a friend's home. The Bowler of the Decade in the 70s, Anthony was considered the greatest bowler in history and a well-respected TV color commentator. He won a record 41 PBA regular-tour titles, two ABC Masters championships and was selected BWAA and PBA Bowler of the Year six times. He was the first bowler to win $100,000 in a season and $1 million in a career.

For one of the few times in history, bowling grabbed front page headlines as major newspapers around the country ran stories about Anthony.

Dick Evans' Ten Biggest Stories of the Year in Bowling

10 The NCAA, which currently recognizes women's bowling as an "emerging sport," announces that 15 schools have added women's collegiate bowling to their athletic programs (In order to become an official NCAA championship sport, 40 schools must be on board by 2003-04).

9 Carolyn Dorin-Ballard, a four-time bridesmaid in the voting for PWBA Player of the Year, opens the 2001 season with a victory in the prestigious WIBC Queens Tournament en route to five victories in 12 spring/summer stops.

8 World bowling leaders are elated when Beijing lands the 2008 Olympic Summer Games and Belgium's Jacques Rogge is named new IOC president. China and Rogge could be instrumental in bowling becoming a medal sport for the first time in history.

7 "Sport Bowling," a new program developed by the ABC and WIBC, is introduced to put a challenge back into a game that is often ridiculed for its soft scoring conditions (there were 43,431 perfect games in 2000-01). Lane conditions and equipment are controlled to emphasize a bowler's skills, rather than technology.

6 Retired New York City fireman Thomas DeChalus becomes the first black president of the 106-year-old American Bowling Congress—an organization that did not accept black members until 1950. In other administrative news, Joyce Deitch announces she will step down as president of the WIBC after serving for nine years.

5 AMF, which operates 518 bowling centers worldwide (400 in the U.S.), files a voluntary Chapter 11 petition to facilitate major financial restructuring. The filing should enable the company to "maintain ordinary course operations."

4 Earl Anthony, the greatest champion in pro-tour history, dies on Aug. 14 at the age of 63 from head injuries sustained after a fall. The legendary Joe Norris, the greatest team player in league history and the one time "Boy Wonder of Bowling," dies of pneumonia on Feb. 19 at the age of 93.

3 "Ed," a romantic comedy about a lawyer who buys a bowling center, scores a strike for bowling and NBC by receiving three Emmy nominations and being awarded a People's Choice Award for best new comedy series.

2 ▪ After threatening to boycott the BPAA U.S. Open, the Professional Women's Bowling Association lands a 90-minute live ESPN telecast of its own Open at a separate venue with a $300,000 prize fund.

1 ▪ The new Professional Bowlers Association unveils a three-year deal with ESPN, a revolutionary new format, an improved prize fund and new rules that prevent coaching during competition.

Earl the Pearl

Earl Anthony was truly a pioneer of his sport. He was the first to reach the $100,000 plateau in a single season ($107,585 in 1975) and the first to reach $1 million in a career. He was selected Bowler of the Decade for the 1970s. Listed are his career accomplishments.

Career titles	41
Second place finishes	42
Championship round app.	144
Major titles*	10
Career Earnings	$1,441,061
Years with highest scoring avg.	5
PBA Player of the Year awards	6

*Two Tournaments of Champions, six PBA National Championships and two ABC Masters. He never won the BPAA U.S. Open but finished runner-up three times.

Loaded Lefties

Earl Anthony's $1.4 million in career earnings is good for 11th on the all-time PBA list, but he's third on the all-time list of lefties.

	Titles	Earnings
Mike Aulby	26	$1,999,685
Parker Bohn III	24	1,949,401
Earl Anthony	41	1,441,061
Johnny Petraglia	14	1,032,893

Model of Consistency

Earl Anthony won at least one tournament each year from 1970–83, setting yet another PBA mark.

	Years
Earl Anthony (1970–83)	14
Don Johnson (1966–77)	12
Brian Voss (1987–98)	12
Pete Weber (1984–93)	10
Mark Roth (1975–84)	10

2000-2001 Season in Review

ESPN information please®
SPORTS ALMANAC

Tournament Results

Winners of stepladder finals in all PBA, Seniors and PWBA tournaments from Sept. 7, 2000, through July 26, 2001; major tournaments in **bold** type.

PBA

Late 2000 Fall Tour

Final	Event	Winner	Earnings	Score	Runner-up
Sept. 17	Japan Cup	Parker Bohn III	$50,000	235-206	Yasuyki Sadamatsu
Oct. 10	Track Canandaigua Open	Walter Ray Williams Jr.	20,000	225-217	Patrick Healey Jr.
Oct. 17	Johnny Petraglia Open	Walter Ray Williams Jr.	26,000	215-177	Bob Learn Jr.
Oct. 24	Flagship Open	Robert Smith	19,000	239-233	Walter Ray Williams Jr.
Oct. 31	Indianapolis Open	Doug Kent	19,000	253-236	Jeff Zaffino
Nov. 7	**Brunswick World TOC**	Jason Couch	60,000	198-166	Ryan Shafer
Nov. 14	Columbia 300 Open	Danny Wiseman	20,000	252-232	Chris Barnes
Nov. 21	Lone Star Open	Steve Hoskins	19,000	246-236	Doug Kent

2001 Winter/Spring Tour

Final	Event	Winner	Earnings	Score	Runner-up
Jan. 14	National/Senior Doubles	Parker Bohn III/ Rohn Morton	$15,000 (each)	248-185	Mika Koivuniemi/ Junichi Yajima
Jan. 21	Silicon Valley Open	Mike Aulby	19,000	257-211	Jason Couch
Jan. 25	Orleans Casino Open	Ryan Shafer	25,000	210-200	Jeff Lizzi
Feb. 4	**PBA National Championship**	Walter Ray Williams Jr.	25,000	258-204	Jeff Lizzi
Feb. 11	Empire State Open	Parker Bohn III	20,000	210-187	Chris Barnes
Feb. 18	Tarheel Open	Ricky Ward	20,000	269-237	Jason Couch
Feb. 24	The Villages PBA Open	Jason Couch	25,000	223-201	Chris Barnes
Mar. 4	Battle at Little Creek	Steve Wilson	20,000	246-228	Jason Couch

2001 Summer Tour

Final	Event	Winner	Earnings	Score	Runner-up
June 17	**ABC Masters**	Parker Bohn III	$40,000	248-237	Jason Couch

Note: The American Bowling Congress Masters tournament is not a PBA Tour event.

SENIOR PBA

Late 2000 Fall Tour

Final	Event	Winner	Earnings	Score	Runner-up
Sept. 27	Columbia 300 Open	Johnny Petraglia	$12,000	258-211	Barry Gurney
Oct. 5	Gastonia Senior Classic	Roger Workman	8,000	266-191	Gary Dickinson
Oct. 13	**Senior National Championship**	Bob Glass	20,000	246-236	Rohn Morton
Oct. 20	Hammond Open	Mike Pullin	8,000	190-171	Roger Workman

2001 Winter Tour

Final	Event	Winner	Earnings	Score	Runner-up
Jan. 7	ABC Senior Masters	Bob Glass	$18,000	696-616	Dave Soutar
Jan. 14	National/Senior Doubles	Parker Bohn III/ Rohn Morton	15,000 (each)	248-185	Mika Koivuniemi/ Junichi Yajima

Note: The American Bowling Congress Senior Masters tournament is not a PBA Senior Tour event.

2001 Spring/Summer Tour

Final	Event	Winner	Earnings	Score	Runner-up
May 10	Greater Syracuse Open	Bob Glass	$8,000	228-203	Bob Chamberlain
May 17	Senior Open	Bob Glass	8,000	235-213	George Pappas
May 24	Hawthorn Lanes Open	Chuck Pierce	8,000	245-234	Dale Eagle
June 1	Seattle Open	Mark Roth	10,000	234-204	Steve Neff
June 7	Northwest Classic	Bob Chamberlain	10,000	268-202	Sal Bongiorno
June 14	Epicenter Classic	Johnny Petraglia	10,000	237-237*	Bob Glass
June 20	Orleans Casino Open	Steve Neff	20,000	214-196	Bob Chamberlain
June 28	Tucson Open	Dave Soutar	8,000	233-190	Larry Laub
July 5	Northern California Classic	Larry Laub	10,000	279-223	Rohn Morton

*Petraglia def. Glass in a one-ball rolloff, 10-9.

PWBA
Late 2000 Fall Tour

Final	Event	Winner	Earnings	Score	Runner-up
Sept. 7	Greater Orlando Classic	Cara Honeychurch	$11,000	218-184	Dede Davidson
Sept. 14	Paula Carter Classic	Debbie McMullen	11,000	234-228	Michelle Feldman
Sept. 21	The Foundation Games II	Lisa Bishop	11,000	257-193	Cara Honeychurch
Sept. 28	Brunswick Women's World Open	Cara Honeychurch	14,400	179-160	Marianne DiRupo
Oct. 5	North Myrtle Beach Classic	Tish Johnson	11,000	229-200	Cara Honeychurch
Oct. 12	Columbia 300 Open	Carol Gianotti-Block	14,400	211-198	Wendy Macpherson
Oct. 19	Three Rivers Open	Carolyn Dorin-Ballard	11,000	213-161	Cheryl Daniels
Oct. 26	Greater Harrisburg Open	Dede Davidson	11,000	234-214	Leanne Barrette
Nov. 2	Hammer Players Championship	Tennelle Grijalva	16,000	248-171	Wendy Macpherson
Nov. 11	**Sam's Town Invitational**	Dede Davidson	14,400	182-179	Tiffany Stanbrough

2001 Spring/Summer Tour

Final	Event	Winner	Earnings	Score	Runner-up
May 11	**WIBC Queens**	Carolyn Dorin-Ballard	$18,000	213-197	Kelly Kulick
May 17	St. Clair Classic	Liz Johnson	9,000	268-179	Cara Honeychurch
May 24	Miller High Life Open	Michelle Feldman	15,000	257-224	Cara Honeychurch
May 31	Albuquerque Open	Carolyn Dorin-Ballard	9,000	248-184	Lisa Bishop
June 7	Wheelchair Awareness Classic	Tish Johnson	9,000	210-150	Kim Adler
June 14	Greater San Diego Open	Cara Honeychurch	9,000	200-165	Anne Marie Duggan
June 21	Fort Worth Classic	Carolyn Dorin-Ballard	9,000	217-213	Dede Davidson
June 28	Greater Memphis Open	Carolyn Dorin-Ballard	9,000	225-196	Marianne DiRupo
July 6	Southern Virginia Open	Carolyn Dorin-Ballard	9,000	226-195	Wendy Macpherson
July 12	Sport Bowling Challenge	Cara Honeychurch	50,000	206-189	Brenda Norman
July 19	Lady Ebonite Kentucky Classic	Leanne Barrette	11,000	204-177	Cara Honeychurch
July 26	Clabber Girl Greater Terre Haute Open .	Cara Honeychurch	10,000	279-208	Carol Gianotti-Block

Note: The Women's International Bowling Congress Queens tournament is not an official PWBA Tour event.

2001 Fall Tour Schedules
PBA Tour

September—Columbia 300 Open, Wichita, Kan. (Sept. 13-18); Peoria (Ill.) Open (Sept. 20-25).

October—Greater Nashville Open, Hendersonville, Tenn. (Sept. 27-Oct. 2); Miller High Life Open, Indianapolis, Ind. (Oct. 4-9); Great Lakes Classic, Grand Rapids, Mich. (Oct. 11-16); Greater Detroit Open, Taylor, Mich. (Oct. 18-23); Johnny Petraglia Open, North Brunswick, N.J. (Oct. 25-30).

November—Greater Cincinnati Classic, Erlanger, Ky. (Nov. 6-11); Long Island Open, Syosset, N.Y. with TV finals at Uncasville, Conn. (Nov. 13-18).

December—BPAA U.S. Open, Fountain Valley, Calif. (Dec. 1-9).

Senior PBA Tour

September—Senior Tarheel Open, Huntersville, N.C. (Sept. 23-27).

October—Senior National Championship, Jackson, Mich. (Oct. 13-18); Senior Hammond Open, Hammond, Ind. (Oct. 22-26).

PWBA Tour

September—Foundation Games V, Sebring, Fla. (Sept. 1-6); Paula Carter Classic, Davie, Fla. (Sept. 8-13); Storm Challenge, Cape Coral, Fla. (Sept. 16-21); Jacksonville Open, Jacksonville, Fla. (Sept. 23-28).

October—North Myrtle Beach (S.C.) Classic (Sept. 30-Oct. 4); Columbia 300 Open, Lancaster, Ohio (Oct. 7-11); Three Rivers Open, Pittsburgh, Penn. (Oct. 14-18); Hammer Players Championship, Rockford, Ill. (Oct. 20-24).

November—Las Cruces New Mexico Open (Oct. 28-Nov. 1); Brunswick Women's World Open, Las Vegas, Nev. (Nov. 4-10).

December—BPAA U.S. Open, TBA (Dec. 1-9).

Tour Leaders

Official standings for 2000 and unofficial standings for 2001. Note that (TB) indicates Tournaments Bowled; (CR) Championship Rounds as Stepladder Finalist; and (1st) Titles Won.

FINAL 2000
PBA

Top 10 Money Winners

		TB	CR	1st	Earnings
1	Norm Duke	17	7	3	$136,900
2	Ryan Shafer	19	11	2	123,600
3	Jason Couch	19	4	1	111,715
4	Parker Bohn III	19	5	2	108,105
5	Chris Barnes	19	5	0	103,900
6	Walter Ray Williams Jr.	18	7	2	102,693
7	Robert Smith	16	3	2	74,180
8	Danny Wiseman	19	5	1	72,700
9	Doug Kent	17	5	1	67,075
10	Mika Koivuniemi	18	2	1	63,125

Top 10 Averages

		TB	Games	Avg
1	Chris Barnes	19	785	220.93
2	Ryan Shafer	19	662	219.50
3	Walter Ray Williams Jr.	18	680	219.00
4	Norm Duke	17	658	218.77
5	Danny Wiseman	19	717	218.05
6	Patrick Healey Jr.	17	551	217.98
7	Doug Kent	17	599	217.64
8	Parker Bohn III	19	608	217.44
9	Jason Couch	19	644	217.32
10	Brian Voss	18	642	217.19

Note: Earnings include ABC Masters and BPAA U.S. Open.

SENIOR PBA

Top 5 Money Winners

		TB	CR	1st	Earnings
1	Roger Workman	12	4	2	$145,275
2	Bob Glass	12	8	2	66,650
3	Dave Soutar	12	5	1	36,985
4	Steve Neff	10	3	0	32,525
5	Dave Davis	9	3	1	31,995

Note: Earnings include ABC Senior Masters.

Top 5 Averages

		TB	Games	Avg
1	Bob Glass	12	537	222.69
2	Gary Dickinson	7	250	220.08
3	Dave Soutar	12	438	219.69
4	Roger Workman	12	483	219.26
5	John Bennett	8	310	218.93
	Johnny Petraglia	8	280	218.93

PWBA

Top 10 Money Winners

		TB	CR	1st	Earnings
1	Wendy Macpherson	23	15	2	$108,525
2	Cara Honeychurch	22	9	2	100,950
3	Michelle Feldman	23	9	3	92,925
4	Carolyn Dorin-Ballard	23	8	3	88,677
5	Tennelle Grijalva	21	4	2	84,575
6	Carol Gianotti-Block	21	4	2	77,025
7	Kim Adler	23	8	2	68,562
8	Marianne DiRupo	23	6	0	58,315
9	Anne Marie Duggan	23	5	0	57,340
10	Leanne Barrette	22	5	0	54,735

Note: Earnings include WIBC Queens and BPAA U.S. Open.

Top 10 Averages

		TB	Games	Avg
1	Cara Honeychurch	22	774	215.18
2	Wendy Macpherson	23	936	214.90
3	Michelle Feldman	23	856	214.38
4	Carolyn Dorin-Ballard	23	953	213.87
5	Carol Gianotti-Block	21	815	213.75
6	Kim Adler	23	835	211.24
7	Dede Davidson	19	597	211.18
8	Tish Johnson	23	691	210.81
9	Leanne Barrette	22	809	210.62
10	Kim Terrell	23	799	210.03

2001 (through July 26)

PBA

Top 10 Money Winners

		TB	CR	1st	Earnings
1	Parker Bohn III	9	4	3	$91,200
2	Jason Couch	9	6	1	88,025
3	Mike Aulby	9	3	1	38,675
4	Ricky Ward	8	2	1	37,150
5	Ryan Shafer	9	1	1	33,100
6	Walter Ray Williams Jr.	9	2	1	31,900
7	Chris Barnes	9	2	0	29,275
8	Tony Reyes	9	2	0	29,264
9	Steve Wilson	8	1	1	29,225
10	Jeff Lizzi	9	2	0	27,835

Note: Earnings include ABC Masters.

Top 10 Averages

		TB	Games	Avg
1	Jason Couch	9	339	226.12
2	Parker Bohn III	9	340	222.94
3	Mike Aulby	9	292	219.95
4	Ricky Ward	8	303	218.75
5	Patrick Healey Jr.	8	206	217.32
6	Joe Salvemini	4	114	216.96
7	Chris Barnes	9	224	216.31
8	Chris Hayden	8	252	215.82
9	Dennis Horan Jr.	8	233	215.14
10	Norm Duke	9	283	214.95

SENIOR PBA

Top 5 Money Winners

		TB	CR	1st	Earnings
1	Bob Glass	10	7	3	$62,900
2	Bob Chamberlain	11	6	1	40,750
3	Steve Neff	9	3	1	40,310
4	Dave Soutar	11	2	1	33,940
5	Rohn Morton	11	3	1	32,423

Note: Earnings include ABC Senior Masters.

Top 5 Averages

		TB	Games	Avg
1	Steve Neff	9	325	221.90
2	Larry Laub	5	200	221.54
3	Bob Glass	10	385	221.00
4	Bob Chamberlain	11	385	219.20
5	Mark Roth	8	319	218.59

PWBA

Top 10 Money Winners

		TB	CR	1st	Earnings
1	Carolyn Dorin-Ballard	12	10	5	$75,870
2	Cara Honeychurch	12	8	3	58,250
3	Kelly Kulick	12	2	0	29,283
4	Leanne Barrette	12	4	1	27,930
5	Michelle Feldman	12	1	1	26,545
6	Wendy Macpherson	12	3	0	23,790
7	Kim Terrell	12	2	0	23,685
8	Liz Johnson	12	3	1	22,248
9	Anne Marie Duggan	12	2	0	21,810
10	Kendra Gaines	12	5	0	21,360

Note: Earnings include WIBC Queens.

Top 10 Averages

		TB	Games	Avg
1	Carolyn Dorin-Ballard	12	473	215.17
2	Cara Honeychurch	12	453	214.43
3	Wendy Macpherson	12	442	209.71
4	Liz Johnson	10	333	209.48
5	Leanne Barrette	12	420	208.41
6	Kendra Gaines	12	420	208.24
7	Kim Adler	12	414	208.10
8	Anne Marie Duggan	12	440	207.23
9	Lisa Bishop	10	334	206.98
10	Michelle Feldman	12	404	206.44

1942-2001 Through the Years

Major Championships
MEN
BPAA U.S. Open

Started in 1941 by the Bowling Proprietors' Association of America, 18 years before the founding of the Professional Bowlers Association. Originally the BPAA All-Star Tournament, it became the U.S. Open in 1971.

Multiple winners: Don Carter and Dick Weber (4); Dave Husted (3); Del Ballard Jr., Marshall Holman, Junie McMahon, Connie Schwoegler, Andy Varipapa and Pete Weber (2).

Year		Year		Year		Year	
1942	John Crimmins	1957	Don Carter	1972	Don Johnson	1987	Del Ballard Jr.
1943	Connie Schwoegler	1958	Don Carter	1973	Mike McGrath	1988	Pete Weber
1944	Ned Day	1959	Billy Welu	1974	Larry Laub	1989	Mike Aulby
1945	Buddy Bomar			1975	Steve Neff		
1946	Joe Wilman	1960	Harry Smith	1976	Paul Moser	1990	Ron Palombi Jr.
1947	Andy Varipapa	1961	Bill Tucker	1977	Johnny Petraglia	1991	Pete Weber
1948	Andy Varipapa	1962	Dick Weber	1978	Nelson Burton Jr.	1992	Robert Lawrence
1949	Connie Schwoegler	1963	Dick Weber	1979	Joe Berardi	1993	Del Ballard Jr.
		1964	Bob Strampe			1994	Justin Hromek
1950	Junie McMahon	1965	Dick Weber	1980	Steve Martin	1995	Dave Husted
1951	Dick Hoover	1966	Dick Weber	1981	Marshall Holman	1996	Dave Husted
1952	Junie McMahon	1967	Les Schissler	1982	Dave Husted	1997	Not held
1953	Don Carter	1968	Jim Stefanich	1983	Gary Dickinson	1998	Walter Ray Williams Jr.
1954	Don Carter	1969	Billy Hardwick	1984	Mark Roth	1999	Bob Learn Jr.
1955	Steve Nagy			1985	Marshall Holman		
1956	Bill Lillard	1970	Bobby Cooper	1986	Steve Cook	2000	Robert Smith
		1971	Mike Limongello				

PBA National Championship

The Professional Bowlers Association was formed in 1958 and its first national championship tournament was held in Memphis in 1960. The tournament has been held in Toledo, Ohio, since 1981.

Multiple winners: Earl Anthony (6); Mike Aulby, Dave Davis, Mike McGrath, Pete Weber and Wayne Zahn (2).

Year		Year		Year		Year	
1960	Don Carter	1971	Mike Limongello	1982	Earl Anthony	1993	Ron Palombi Jr.
1961	Dave Soutar	1972	Johnny Guenther	1983	Earl Anthony	1994	David Traber
1962	Carmen Salvino	1973	Earl Anthony	1984	Bob Chamberlain	1995	Scott Alexander
1963	Billy Hardwick	1974	Earl Anthony	1985	Mike Aulby	1996	Butch Soper
1964	Bob Strampe	1975	Earl Anthony	1986	Tom Crites	1997	Rick Steelsmith
1965	Dave Davis	1976	Paul Colwell	1987	Randy Pedersen	1998	Pete Weber
1966	Wayne Zahn	1977	Tommy Hudson	1988	Brian Voss	1999	Tim Criss
1967	Dave Davis	1978	Warren Nelson	1989	Pete Weber		
1968	Wayne Zahn	1979	Mike Aulby			2000	Norm Duke
1969	Mike McGrath			1990	Jim Pencak	2001	Walter Ray Williams Jr.
		1980	Johnny Petraglia	1991	Mike Miller		
1970	Mike McGrath	1981	Earl Anthony	1992	Eric Forkel		

Brunswick World Tournament of Champions

Originally the Firestone Tournament of Champions (1965-93), the tournament has also been sponsored by General Tire (1994) and Brunswick Corp. (since 1995). Held in Akron, Ohio in 1965, then Fairlawn, Ohio (1966-94), Lake Zurich, Ill. (1995-96), Reno, N.V. (1997) and Overland Park, Kan. (since 1998).

Multiple winners: Mike Durbin (3); Earl Anthony, Jason Couch, Dave Davis, Jim Godman, Marshall Holman and Mark Williams (2).

Year		Year		Year		Year	
1965	Billy Hardwick	1974	Earl Anthony	1983	Joe Berardi	1992	Marc McDowell
1966	Wayne Zahn	1975	Dave Davis	1984	Mike Durbin	1993	George Branham III
1967	Jim Stefanich	1976	Marshall Holman	1985	Mark Williams	1994	Norm Duke
1968	Dave Davis	1977	Mike Berlin	1986	Marshall Holman	1995	Mike Aulby
1969	Jim Godman	1978	Earl Anthony	1987	Pete Weber	1996	Dave D'Entremont
		1979	George Pappas	1988	Mark Williams	1997	John Gant
1970	Don Johnson			1989	Del Ballard Jr.	1998	Bryan Goebel
1971	Johnny Petraglia	1980	Wayne Webb			1999	Jason Couch
1972	Mike Durbin	1981	Steve Cook	1990	Dave Ferraro		
1973	Jim Godman	1982	Mike Durbin	1991	David Ozio	2000	Jason Couch

ABC Masters Tournament

Sponsored by the American Bowling Congress. The Masters is not a PBA event, but is considered one of the four major tournaments on the men's tour and is open to qualified pros and amateurs.

Multiple winners: Mike Aulby (3); Earl Anthony, Billy Golembiewski, Dick Hoover and Billy Welu (2).

Year		Year		Year		Year	
1951	Lee Jouglard	1964	Billy Welu	1977	Earl Anthony	1990	Chris Warren
1952	Willard Taylor	1965	Billy Welu	1978	Frank Ellenburg	1991	Doug Kent
1953	Rudy Habetler	1966	Bob Strampe	1979	Doug Myers	1992	Ken Johnson
1954	Red Elkins	1967	Lou Scalia	1980	Neil Burton	1993	Norm Duke
1955	Buzz Fazio	1968	Pete Tountas	1981	Randy Lightfoot	1994	Steve Fehr
1956	Dick Hoover	1969	Jim Chestney	1982	Joe Berardi	1995	Mike Aulby
1957	Dick Hoover	1970	Don Glover	1983	Mike Lastowski	1996	Ernie Schlegel
1958	Tom Hennessey	1971	Jim Godman	1984	Earl Anthony	1997	Jason Queen
1959	Ray Bluth	1972	Bill Beach	1985	Steve Wunderlich	1998	Mike Aulby
1960	Billy Golembiewski	1973	Dave Soutar	1986	Mark Fahy	1999	Brian Boghosian
1961	Don Carter	1974	Paul Colwell	1987	Rick Steelsmith	2000	Mika Koivuniemi
1962	Billy Golembiewski	1975	Eddie Ressler Jr.	1988	Del Ballard Jr.	2001	Parker Bohn III
1963	Harry Smith	1976	Nelson Burton Jr.	1989	Mike Aulby		

WOMEN

BPAA U.S. Open

Started by the Bowling Proprietors' Association of America in 1949. Originally the BPAA Women's All-Star Tournament (1949-70); and U.S. Open since 1971. There were two BPAA All-Star tournaments in 1955, in January and December. Note that (a) indicates amateur.

Multiple winners: Marion Ladewig (8); Donna Adamek, Paula Sperber Carter, Pat Costello, Dotty Fothergill, Dana Miller-Mackie, Aleta Sill and Sylvia Wene (2).

Year		Year		Year		Year	
1949	Marion Ladewig	1962	Shirley Garms	1976	Patty Costello	1990	Dana Miller-Mackie
1950	Marion Ladewig	1963	Marion Ladewig	1977	Betty Morris	1991	Anne Marie Duggan
1951	Marion Ladewig	1964	LaVerne Carter	1978	Donna Adamek	1992	Tish Johnson
1952	Marion Ladewig	1965	Ann Slattery	1979	Diana Silva	1993	Dede Davidson
1953	Not held	1966	Joy Abel	1980	Patty Costello	1994	Aleta Sill
1954	Marion Ladewig	1967	Gloria Simon	1981	Donna Adamek	1995	Cheryl Daniels
1955	Sylvia Wene	1968	Dotty Fothergill	1982	Shinobu Saitoh	1996	Liz Johnson
1955	Anita Cantaline	1969	Dotty Fothergill	1983	Dana Miller	1997	Not held
1956	Marion Ladewig	1970	Mary Baker	1984	Karen Ellingsworth	1998	Aleta Sill
1957	Not held	1971	a-Paula Sperber	1985	Pat Mercatanti	1999	Kim Adler
1958	Merle Matthews	1972	a-Lorrie Koch	1986	Wendy Macpherson	2000	Tennelle Grijalva
1959	Marion Ladewig	1973	Millie Martorella	1987	Carol Norman		
1960	Sylvia Wene	1974	Patty Costello	1988	Lisa Wagner		
1961	Phyllis Notaro	1975	Paula Sperber Carter	1989	Robin Romeo		

WIBC Queens

Sponsored by the Women's International Bowling Congress, the Queens is a double elimination, match play tournament. It is not a PWBA event, but is open to qualified pros and amateurs. Note that (a) indicates amateur.

Multiple winners: Millie Martorella (3); Donna Adamek, Dotty Fothergill, Wendy Macpherson, Aleta Sill and Katsuko Sugimoto (2).

Year		Year		Year		Year	
1961	Janet Harman	1971	Millie Martorella	1981	Katsuko Sugimoto	1991	Dede Davidson
1962	Dorothy Wilkinson	1972	Dotty Fothergill	1982	Katsuko Sugimoto	1992	Cindy Coburn-Carroll
1963	Irene Monterosso	1973	Dotty Fothergill	1983	Aleta Sill	1993	Jan Schmidt
1964	D.D. Jacobson	1974	Judy Soutar	1984	Kazue Inahashi	1994	Anne Marie Duggan
1965	Betty Kuczynski	1975	Cindy Powell	1985	Aleta Sill	1995	Sandra Postma
1966	Judy Lee	1976	Pam Rutherford	1986	Cora Fiebig	1996	Lisa Wagner
1967	Millie Martorella	1977	Dana Stewart	1987	Cathy Almeida	1997	Sandra Jo Odom
1968	Phyllis Massey	1978	Loa Boxberger	1988	Wendy Macpherson	1998	Lynda Norry
1969	Ann Feigel	1979	Donna Adamek	1989	Carol Gianotti	1999	Leanne Barrette
1970	Millie Martorella	1980	Donna Adamek	1990	a-Patty Ann	2000	Wendy Macpherson
						2001	Carolyn Dorin-Ballard

Sam's Town Invitational

Originally held in Milwaukee as the Pabst Tournament of Champions, but discontinued after one year (1981). Revived in 1984, moved to Las Vegas and renamed the Sam's Town Tournament of Champions (1984); LPBT Tournament of Champions (1985); the Sam's Town National Pro/Am (1986-88); and the Sam's Town Invitational (since 1989).

Multiple winners: Tish Johnson (3); Wendy Macpherson and Aleta Sill (2).

Year	Winners	Year	Winners	Year	Winners	Year	Winners
1981	Cindy Coburn	1987	Debbie Bennett	1992	Tish Johnson	1997	Kim Adler
1982-83	Not held	1988	Donna Adamek	1993	Robin Romeo	1998	Julie Gardner
1984	Aleta Sill	1989	Tish Johnson	1994	Tish Johnson	1999	Wendy Macpherson
1985	Patty Costello	1990	Wendy Macpherson	1995	Michelle Mullen	2000	Dede Davidson
1986	Aleta Sill	1991	Lorrie Nichols	1996	Carol Gianotti-Block		

WPBA National Championship (1960-1980)

The Women's Professional Bowling Association National Championship tournament was discontinued when the WPBA broke up in 1981. The WPBA changed its name from the Professional Women Bowlers Association (PWBA) in 1978.

Multiple winners: Patty Costello (3); Dotty Fothergill (2).

Year		Year		Year		Year	
1960	Marion Ladewig	1966	Judy Lee	1972	Patty Costello	1978	Toni Gillard
1961	Shirley Garms	1967	Betty Mivelaz	1973	Betty Morris	1979	Cindy Coburn
1962	Stephanie Balogh	1968	Dotty Fothergill	1974	Pat Costello	1980	Donna Adamek
1963	Janet Harman	1969	Dotty Fothergill	1975	Pam Buckner		
1964	Betty Kuczynski	1970	Bobbe North	1976	Patty Costello		
1965	Helen Duval	1971	Patty Costello	1977	Vesma Grinfelds		

Annual Leaders
Average
PBA Tour

The George Young Memorial Award, named after the late ABC Hall of Fame bowler. Based on at least 16 national PBA tournaments from 1959-78, and at least 400 games of tour competition since 1979.

Multiple winners: Mark Roth (6); Earl Anthony (5); Walter Ray Williams Jr. (4); Marshall Holman (3); Norm Duke, Billy Hardwick, Don Johnson and Wayne Zahn (2).

Year		Avg	Year		Avg	Year		Avg
1962	Don Carter	212.84	1975	Earl Anthony	219.06	1988	Mark Roth	218.04
1963	Billy Hardwick	210.35	1976	Mark Roth	215.97	1989	Pete Weber	215.43
1964	Ray Bluth	210.51	1977	Mark Roth	218.17	1990	Amleto Monacelli	218.16
1965	Dick Weber	211.90	1978	Mark Roth	219.83	1991	Norm Duke	218.21
1966	Wayne Zahn	208.63	1979	Mark Roth	221.66	1992	Dave Ferraro	219.70
1967	Wayne Zahn	212.14	1980	Earl Anthony	218.54	1993	Walter Ray Williams Jr.	222.98
1968	Jim Stefanich	211.90	1981	Mark Roth	216.70	1994	Norm Duke	222.83
1969	Billy Hardwick	212.96	1982	Marshall Holman	216.15	1995	Mike Aulby	225.49
1970	Nelson Burton Jr.	214.91	1983	Earl Anthony	216.65	1996	Walter Ray Williams Jr.	225.37
1971	Don Johnson	213.98	1984	Marshall Holman	213.91	1997	Walter Ray Williams Jr.	222.00
1972	Don Johnson	215.29	1985	Mark Baker	213.72	1998	Walter Ray Williams Jr.	226.13
1973	Earl Anthony	215.80	1986	John Gant	214.38	1999	Parker Bohn III	228.04
1974	Earl Anthony	219.34	1987	Marshall Holman	216.80	2000	Chris Barnes	220.93

PWBA Tour

The Professional Women's Bowling Association (PWBA) went by the name Ladies Professional Bowling Tour (LPBT) from 1981-1997 and the Women's Professional Bowling Association prior to that. This table is based on at least 282 games of tour competition.

Multiple winners: Leanne Barrette, Nikki Gianulias, Wendy Macpherson and Lisa Rathgeber Wagner (3); Anne Marie Duggan and Aleta Sill (2).

Year		Avg	Year		Avg	Year		Avg
1981	Nikki Gianulias	213.71	1988	Lisa Wagner	213.02	1995	Anne Marie Duggan	215.79
1982	Nikki Gianulias	210.63	1989	Lisa Wagner	211.87	1996	Tammy Turner	215.23
1983	Lisa Rathgeber	208.50	1990	Leanne Barrette	211.53	1997	Wendy Macpherson	214.68
1984	Aleta Sill	210.68	1991	Leanne Barrette	211.48	1998	Dede Davidson	217.25
1985	Aleta Sill	211.10	1992	Leanne Barrette	211.36	1999	Wendy Macpherson	218.85
1986	Nikki Gianulias	213.89	1993	Tish Johnson	215.39	2000	Cara Honeychurch	215.18
1987	Wendy Macpherson	211.11	1994	Anne Marie Duggan	213.47			

Money Won
PBA Tour

Since 1998 annual totals have included two non-PBA Tour events: BPAA U.S. Open and ABC Masters.

Multiple winners: Earl Anthony (6); Walter Ray Williams Jr. (5); Mark Roth and Dick Weber (4); Mike Aulby (3); Don Carter and Norm Duke (2).

Year		Earnings	Year		Earnings	Year		Earnings
1959	Dick Weber	$7,672	1973	Don McCune	$69,000	1987	Pete Weber	$179,516
1960	Don Carter	22,525	1974	Earl Anthony	99,585	1988	Brian Voss	225,485
1961	Dick Weber	26,280	1975	Earl Anthony	107,585	1989	Mike Aulby	298,237
1962	Don Carter	49,972	1976	Earl Anthony	110,833	1990	Amleto Monacelli	204,775
1963	Dick Weber	46,333	1977	Mark Roth	105,583	1991	David Ozio	225,585
1964	Bob Strampe	33,592	1978	Mark Roth	134,500	1992	Marc McDowell	176,215
1965	Dick Weber	47,675	1979	Mark Roth	124,517	1993	Walter Ray Williams Jr.	296,370
1966	Wayne Zahn	54,720	1980	Wayne Webb	116,700	1994	Norm Duke	273,752
1967	Dave Davis	54,165	1981	Earl Anthony	164,735	1995	Mike Aulby	219,792
1968	Jim Stefanich	67,375	1982	Earl Anthony	134,760	1996	Walter Ray Williams Jr.	244,630
1969	Billy Hardwick	64,160	1983	Earl Anthony	135,605	1997	Walter Ray Williams Jr.	240,544
1970	Mike McGrath	52,049	1984	Mark Roth	158,712	1998	Walter Ray Williams Jr.	238,225
1971	Johnny Petraglia	85,065	1985	Mike Aulby	201,200	1999	Parker Bohn III	232,595
1972	Don Johnson	56,648	1986	Walter Ray Williams Jr.	145,550	2000	Norm Duke	136,900

WPBA and PWBA Tours

WPBA leaders through 1980; PWBA leaders since 1981. Totals include the WIBC Queens, but do not include TV incentives.

Multiple winners: Aleta Sill (6); Donna Adamek and Wendy Macpherson (4); Patty Costello, Tish Johnson and Betty Morris (3); Dotty Fothergill (2).

Year		Earnings	Year		Earnings	Year		Earnings
1965	Betty Kuczynski	$ 3,792	1977	Betty Morris	$23,802	1989	Robin Romeo	$113,750
1966	Joy Abel	5,795	1978	Donna Adamek	31,000	1990	Tish Johnson	94,420
1967	Shirley Garms	4,920	1979	Donna Adamek	26,280	1991	Leanne Barrette	87,618
1968	Dotty Fothergill	16,170	1980	Donna Adamek	31,907	1992	Tish Johnson	96,872
1969	Dotty Fothergill	9,220	1981	Donna Adamek	41,270	1993	Aleta Sill	57,995
1970	Patty Costello	9,317	1982	Nikki Gianulias	45,875	1994	Aleta Sill	126,325
1971	Vesma Grinfelds	4,925	1983	Aleta Sill	42,525	1995	Tish Johnson	123,440
1972	Patty Costello	11,350	1984	Aleta Sill	81,452	1996	Wendy Macpherson	107,230
1973	Judy Cook	11,200	1985	Aleta Sill	52,655	1997	Wendy Macpherson	165,425
1974	Betty Morris	30,037	1986	Aleta Sill	36,962	1998	Carol Gianotti-Block	150,350
1975	Judy Soutar	20,395	1987	Betty Morris	63,735	1999	Wendy Macpherson	86,265
1976	Patty Costello	39,585	1988	Lisa Wagner	105,500	2000	Wendy Macpherson	108,525

All-Time Leaders

All-time leading money winners on the PBA and PWBA tours, through 2000. PBA figures date back to 1959, while PWBA figures include Women's Pro Bowlers Association (WPBA) earnings through 1980. National tour titles are also listed.

Money Won

PBA Top 20

		Titles	Earnings
1	Walter Ray Williams Jr.	32	$2,516,551
2	Pete Weber	25	2,216,348
3	Mike Aulby	26	1,999,685
4	Parker Bohn III	24	1,949,401
5	Amleto Monacelli	18	1,767,209
6	Brian Voss	20	1,760,745
7	Marshall Holman	22	1,694,555
8	Norm Duke	19	1,618,531
9	Dave Husted	14	1,575,783
10	Mark Roth	34	1,533,277
11	Earl Anthony	41	1,441,061
12	Wayne Webb	20	1,358,806
13	David Ozio	11	1,322,549
14	Gary Dickinson	8	1,275,026
15	Mark Williams	7	1,134,902
16	Tom Baker	9	1,133,695
17	Del Ballard Jr.	12	1,114,977
18	Dave Soutar	17	1,047,498
19	Dave Ferraro	10	1,044,176
20	Johnny Petraglia	14	1,032,893

WPBA-PWBA Top 10

		Titles	Earnings
1	Aleta Sill	31	$1,057,112
2	Wendy Macpherson	18	1,020,795
3	Tish Johnson	23	980,850
4	Anne Marie Duggan	15	855,558
5	Leanne Barrette	21	847,928
6	Carol Gianotti-Block	16	841,269
7	Lisa Wagner	32	827,226
8	Robin Mossontte	17	709,344
9	Kim Adler	14	703,892
10	Cheryl Daniels	10	703,677

Senior PBA Top 5

		Titles	Earnings
1	John Handegard	14	$442,726
2	Gene Stus	10	436,880
3	Gary Dickinson	10	410,115
4	Dave Soutar	4	400,850
5	John Hricsina	7	400,195

Annual Awards
MEN
BWAA Bowler of the Year

Winners selected by Bowling Writers Association of America.

Multiple winners: Earl Anthony and Don Carter (6); Walter Ray Williams Jr. (5); Mark Roth (4); Mike Aulby and Dick Weber (3); Buddy Bomar, Ned Day, Norm Duke, Billy Hardwick, Don Johnson and Steve Nagy (2).

Year		Year		Year		Year	
1942	John Crimmins	1957	Don Carter	1972	Don Johnson	1987	Marshall Holman
1943	Ned Day	1958	Don Carter	1973	Don McCune	1988	Brian Voss
1944	Ned Day	1959	Ed Lubanski	1974	Earl Anthony	1989	Mike Aulby
1945	Buddy Bomar	1960	Don Carter	1975	Earl Anthony	1990	Amleto Monacelli
1946	Joe Wilman	1961	Dick Weber	1976	Earl Anthony	1991	David Ozio
1947	Buddy Bomar	1962	Don Carter	1977	Mark Roth	1992	Marc McDowell
1948	Andy Varipapa	1963	Dick Weber	1978	Mark Roth	1993	Walter Ray Williams Jr.
1949	Connie Schwoegler	1964	Billy Hardwick	1979	Mark Roth	1994	Norm Duke
1950	Junie McMahon	1965	Dick Weber	1980	Wayne Webb	1995	Mike Aulby
1951	Lee Jouglard	1966	Wayne Zahn	1981	Earl Anthony	1996	Walter Ray Williams Jr.
1952	Steve Nagy	1967	Dave Davis	1982	Earl Anthony	1997	Walter Ray Williams Jr.
1953	Don Carter	1968	Jim Stefanich	1983	Earl Anthony	1998	Walter Ray Williams Jr.
1954	Don Carter	1969	Billy Hardwick	1984	Mark Roth	1999	Parker Bohn III
1955	Steve Nagy	1970	Nelson Burton Jr.	1985	Mike Aulby	2000	Norm Duke
1956	Bill Lillard	1971	Don Johnson	1986	Walter Ray Williams Jr.		

Annual Awards (Cont.)
PBA Player of the Year

Named after longtime broadcaster Chris Schenkel, winners are selected by members of Professional Bowlers Association. The PBA Player of the Year has differed from the BWAA Bowler of the Year four times–in 1963, '64, '89 and '92.

Multiple winners: Earl Anthony (6); Walter Ray Williams Jr. (5); Mark Roth (4); Mike Aulby, Norm Duke, Billy Hardwick, Don Johnson and Amleto Monacelli (2).

Year		Year		Year		Year	
1963	Billy Hardwick	1973	Don McCune	1983	Earl Anthony	1993	Walter Ray Williams Jr.
1964	Bob Strampe	1974	Earl Anthony	1984	Mark Roth	1994	Norm Duke
1965	Dick Weber	1975	Earl Anthony	1985	Mike Aulby	1995	Mike Aulby
1966	Wayne Zahn	1976	Earl Anthony	1986	Walter Ray Williams Jr.	1996	Walter Ray Williams Jr.
1967	Dave Davis	1977	Mark Roth	1987	Marshall Holman	1997	Walter Ray Williams Jr.
1968	Jim Stefanich	1978	Mark Roth	1988	Brian Voss	1998	Walter Ray Williams Jr.
1969	Billy Hardwick	1979	Mark Roth	1989	Amleto Monacelli	1999	Parker Bohn III
1970	Nelson Burton Jr.	1980	Wayne Webb	1990	Amleto Monacelli	2000	Norm Duke
1971	Don Johnson	1981	Earl Anthony	1991	David Ozio		
1972	Don Johnson	1982	Earl Anthony	1992	Dave Ferraro		

PBA Rookie of the Year

Named after PBA Hall of Famer Harry Golden, who was the PBA's national tournament director for 30 years. Winners selected by members of Professional Bowlers Association.

Year		Year		Year		Year	
1964	Jerry McCoy	1974	Cliff McNealy	1984	John Gant	1994	Tony Ament
1965	Jim Godman	1975	Guy Rowbury	1985	Tom Crites	1995	Billy Myers Jr.
1966	Bobby Cooper	1976	Mike Berlin	1986	Marc McDowell	1996	C.K. Moore
1967	Mike Durbin	1977	Steve Martin	1987	Ryan Shafer	1997	Anthony Lombardo
1968	Bob McGregor	1978	Joseph Groskind	1988	Rick Steelsmith	1998	Chris Barnes
1969	Larry Lichstein	1979	Mike Aulby	1989	Steve Hoskins	1999	Paul Fleming
1970	Denny Krick	1980	Pete Weber	1990	Brad Kiszewski	2000	Joe Ciccone
1971	Tye Critchlow	1981	Mark Fahy	1991	Ricky Ward		
1972	Tommy Hudson	1982	Mike Steinbach	1992	Jason Couch		
1973	Steve Neff	1983	Toby Contreras	1993	Mark Scroggins		

WOMEN
BWAA Bowler of the Year

Winners selected by Bowling Writers Association of America.

Multiple winners: Marion Ladewig (9); Donna Adamek, Lisa Rathgeber Wagner and Wendy Macpherson (4); Tish Johnson and Betty Morris (3); Patty Costello, Dotty Fothergill, Shirley Garms, Val Mikiel, Aleta Sill, Judy Soutar and Sylvia Wene (2).

Year		Year		Year		Year	
1948	Val Mikiel	1962	Shirley Garms	1976	Patty Costello	1990	Tish Johnson
1949	Val Mikiel	1963	Marion Ladewig	1977	Betty Morris	1991	Leanne Barrette
1950	Marion Ladewig	1964	LaVerne Carter	1978	Donna Adamek	1992	Tish Johnson
1951	Marion Ladewig	1965	Betty Kuczynski	1979	Donna Adamek	1993	Lisa Wagner
1952	Marion Ladewig	1966	Joy Abel	1980	Donna Adamek	1994	Anne Marie Duggan
1953	Marion Ladewig	1967	Millie Martorella	1981	Donna Adamek	1995	Tish Johnson
1954	Marion Ladewig	1968	Dotty Fothergill	1982	Nikki Gianulias	1996	Wendy Macpherson
1955	Sylvia Wene	1969	Dotty Fothergill	1983	Lisa Rathgeber	1997	Wendy Macpherson
1956	Anita Cantaline	1970	Mary Baker	1984	Aleta Sill	1998	Carol Gianotti-Block
1957	Marion Ladewig	1971	Paula Sperber	1985	Aleta Sill	1999	Wendy Macpherson
1958	Marion Ladewig	1972	Patty Costello	1986	Lisa Wagner	2000	Wendy Macpherson
1959	Marion Ladewig	1973	Judy Soutar	1987	Betty Morris		
1960	Sylvia Wene	1974	Betty Morris	1988	Lisa Wagner		
1961	Shirley Garms	1975	Judy Soutar	1989	Robin Romeo		

PWBA Player of the Year

Winners selected by members of Professional Women's Bowling Association. The PWBA Player of the Year has differed from the BWAA Bowler of the Year three times–in 1985, '86 and '90.

Multiple winners: Wendy Macpherson (4); Lisa Rathgeber Wagner (3); Leanne Barrette and Tish Johnson (2).

Year		Year		Year		Year	
1983	Lisa Rathgeber	1988	Lisa Wagner	1993	Lisa Wagner	1998	Carol Gianotti-Block
1984	Aleta Sill	1989	Robin Romeo	1994	Anne Marie Duggan	1999	Wendy Macpherson
1985	Patty Costello	1990	Leanne Barrette	1995	Tish Johnson	2000	Wendy Macpherson
1986	Jeanne Maiden	1991	Leanne Barrette	1996	Wendy Macpherson		
1987	Betty Morris	1992	Tish Johnson	1997	Wendy Macpherson		

Note: This award was known as the LPBT Player of the Year Award from 1983-97.

Horse Racing

Trainer **Bob Baffert** and jockey **Gary Stevens** made a formidable pair in 2001.

Point Taken

After stumbling in the Kentucky Derby, Point Given shows his dominance.

Steve Cyphers *covers horse racing for ESPN.*

Trainer Howard Zucker said it out loud, just after his colt, Crafty CT ran second in the Santa Anita Derby in April. It was on TV, and in all the papers.

"If that horse doesn't win the Triple Crown," said Zucker, "something's wrong." Considering it had been 23 years since Affirmed swept the Kentucky Derby, the Preakness and the Belmont Stakes, it was quite a statement. But then, "that horse" was quite a horse. Point Given had just left Zucker's speedy colt in the Santa Anita dust.

A son of Thunder Gulch (the 1995 Kentucky Derby winner), Point Given stood a huge 17 hands high while carrying a massive 1,265 pounds of muscle beneath a radiant chestnut coat. Had an artist imagined the perfect thoroughbred and conveyed that image to canvas, it would have been Point Given.

And he could run. He served notice as a 2-year-old in the Breeders' Cup Juvenile when he charged from behind to close within a nose

of the winner, Macho Uno. Six months later, during the week leading up to the 127th Kentucky Derby, "The Big Red Machine" (nicknamed by trainer Bob Baffert) was the buzz of the backside at Churchill Downs in Louisville.

In horse racing, it's fashionable to look for a flaw, or a "hole" in a horse—something that might diminish his/her chance for victory. It could be the pedigree...the conformation...anything. Point Given had no such holes.

His blood was blue, his legs straight, his body balanced. He was trained by the experienced Baffert, who had led Silver Charm and Real Quiet to the winner's circle in back-to-back Derbys in 1997-98.

The draw for post position did provide some fodder for the "flaw finders." Point Given would start on the far outside—the 17th gate in a field of 17. No horse had won the Run for the Roses from that position in its 126-year history. Baffert and jockey Gary Stevens shrugged it off, saying that in the course

Jamie Squire/Allsport

Point Given *cruises to a 12¼-length romp in the Belmont Stakes, giving him victories in two of the three Triple Crown events.*

of a mile-and-a-quarter race on a wide track such as Churchill, starting position wouldn't affect their finish.

The day before the first Saturday in May, Point Given went to the track for his morning gallop. It's routine. Nothing special. Every spring morning at Churchill you can see hundreds of horses under their exercise riders. But this morning was different. With hundreds of fans and media lining the rail on the backside, the majestic chestnut came out of the first turn in an effortless, yet powerful, gait as if to grace them with his presence—to show off his magnificence. His color danced through the early sun streaming through the trees. His mane caught the air and flowed in cinematic style. His head cocked toward the crowd. Point Given watched everyone who watched him. And all eyes approved. No doubt many believed Zucker might be right.

The number 17 post proved to be no problem. Stevens guided his horse into second place after a mile. Down the backstretch, the traffic was tolerable but the pace was blistering. Already that day, four track records had fallen on what horsemen were calling a "souped up" track.

Point Given made his move when everyone expected, and when he pulled even with his stablemate Congaree with

AP/Wide World Photos

Jockey **Jorge Chavez** smiles aboard **Monarchos** as he is draped with a blanket of roses after winning the Kentucky Derby on May 5.

a quarter mile to go, it looked to be his race. But it wasn't to be. The post-time favorite was on empty, though Stevens asked for more. It wasn't the same colt he'd ridden before.

Down the long stretch for home, Monarchos charged, picking off the front runners who were now tiring. Ridden by Jorge Chavez, he hit the wire in just under two minutes, a time bettered only by Secretariat in 1973—this from a colt that was rumored to be sore and not fit enough to go the entire mile and a quarter.

Invisible Ink had closed with Monarchos to place second while the gutty Congaree held on for third. Point Given finished a disappointing fifth.

Monarchos trainer John Ward Jr., a Kentucky hardboot, spent the rest of the night and most of the next day explaining that his horse was always fit and never sore, as his doubters had implied.

Baffert had no explanation. Nor did Stevens. Point Given simply did not run his race.

continued on page 778 ▶

Steve Cyphers' Ten Biggest Stories of the Year in Horse Racing

10 ▪ Jerry Bailey rides Captain Steve to victory in late March at the world's richest race, the $6 million Dubai World Cup.

9 ▪ Bob Baffert is slapped with a 60-day suspension by the California Horse Racing Board after one of his horses, Nautical Look, tested positive for morphine in May 2000. The case is still pending.

8 ▪ Hall of Famer and Eclipse Award-winning trainer Bobby Frankel has an incredible summer—on both coasts. Among his 73 victories through mid-September are wins at Saratoga (N.Y.), Belmont (N.Y.), Hollywood Park (Calif.) and Monmouth (N.J.).

7 ▪ Despite riding three other Kentucky Derby entrants at one point, one of the world's top jockeys, Jerry Bailey, ends up riding 50-1 longshot Talk is Money on Derby day. In eighth place after a half mile, the horse is pulled up and doesn't finish.

6 ▪ Apprentice jockey Kris Prather, 22, is leading the nation in wins (110) and winning percentage until an accident on St. Patrick's Day forces her off the track and into rehab with injuries to both knees. She returns to action in June but continues to be plagued by injuries.

5 ▪ A strained tendon in his left foreleg causes Point Given to retire from racing in August. He leaves with nine wins and close to $4 million in career earnings.

4 ▪ Monarchos makes a breathtaking move on the second turn of the Florida Derby on March 10, stamping him as one of the favorites to win the Kentucky Derby. His dull performance at the Wood Memorial a month later, however, gives rise to rumors that he is too sore to effectively compete at Churchill.

3 ▪ A mysterious equine epidemic sweeps through Kentucky in April, killing more than 500 foals and causing the abortion of an estimated 3,000 fetuses, costing farms millions of dollars in potential earnings.

2 ▪ With his Eclipse Award and Breeders' Cup win in November 2000, Kona Gold makes it known he is horse racing's premier sprinter. Through September 2001 he had started three races and won them all.

1 ▪ Despite chronic knee problems, Hall of Famer Gary Stevens comes out of retirement (with the help of arthritis medications glucosamine and chondroitin) to win two Triple Crown races and $10.3 million in purses through mid-September.

The queries lasted all of two weeks. At the Preakness, Point Given was now being called "T-Rex" around his barn, and Baffert sounded more confident than ever. The confidence was justified with Point Given's 2¼-length win.

The final leg of the Triple Crown, the Belmont Stakes, looked a lot like that Friday before the Derby. Again, Point Given graced onlookers with his presence. The field was no match. He ran as if redemption was the prize, carrying Stevens to a 12¼-length victory.

Still, no margin of victory could erase that race in Kentucky. Nothing could undo what was done that first Saturday in May. Something went wrong. "That horse" didn't win the Triple Crown.

In Select Company

In 2001, Monarchos ran the second fastest Kentucky Derby in history, trailing only the legendary Secretariat. Listed are the top five Derby times

Horse	Year	Time
Secretariat	1973	1:59²/₅
Monarchos	2001	1:59⁴/₅
Northern Dancer	1964	2:00
Spend A Buck	1985	2:00¹/₅
Decidedly	1962	2:00²/₅

Triple Crossed

No thoroughbred horse has won the Triple Crown (Kentucky Derby, Preakness, Belmont Stakes) since Affirmed in 1978. It is the second-longest drought in history.

Drought (Years)	Ended By
25 (1948–73)	Secretariat
23 (1978–)	?????
11 (1919–30)	Gallant Fox
5 (1930–35)	Omaha

Two Legs Aren't Enough

Point Given is the sixth horse in the last 45 years to lose the Kentucky Derby, then go on to win the Preakness and the Belmont Stakes.

Horse	Year	Derby Fin.
Point Given	2001	5th
Tabasco Cat	1994	6th
Hansel	1991	10th
Risen Star	1988	3rd
Little Current	1974	5th
Damascus	1967	3rd

Proper Positioning

Monarchos won the 2001 Kentucky Derby from the 16th post position, the third horse to do so. Below are the most successful Derby starting spots.

PP	Wins	PP	Wins
1	12	10	9
4	10	8	8
5	10	3	8
2	9	7	7

2000-2001 Season in Review

information please®
SPORTS ALMANAC

Thoroughbred Racing
Major Stakes Races
Winners of major stakes races from Oct. 7, 2000 through Sept. 22, 2001; (T) indicates turf race course; F indicates furlongs.

LATE 2000

Date	Race	Track	Miles	Winner	Jockey	Purse
Oct. 7	Hawthorne Gold Cup Handicap	Hawthorne	1 1/16	Dust on the Bottle	Tim Doocy	$500,000
Nov. 4	Breeders' Cup - Juv. Fillies	Churchill Downs	1 1/16	Caressing	John Velazquez	1,000,000
Nov. 4	Breeders' Cup - Sprint	Churchill Downs	6 F	Kona Gold	Alex Solis	1,000,000
Nov. 4	Breeders' Cup - Distaff	Churchill Downs	1 1/8	Spain	Victor Espinoza	2,000,000
Nov. 4	Breeders' Cup - Mile	Churchill Downs	1	War Chant	Gary Stevens	1,000,000
Nov. 4	Breeders' Cup - Juvenile	Churchill Downs	1 1/16	Macho Uno	Jerry Bailey	1,000,000
Nov. 4	Breeders' Cup - Turf	Churchill Downs	1 1/2 (T)	Kalanisi	John Murtagh	2,000,000
Nov. 4	Breeders' Cup - Filly & Mare Turf	Churchill Downs	1 3/8 (T)	Perfect Sting	Jerry Bailey	1,000,000
Nov. 4	Breeders' Cup - Classic	Churchill Downs	1 1/4	Tiznow	Chris McCarron	4,000,000
Nov. 26	Japan Cup	Tokyo Racecourse	1 1/2	T.M. Opera O	Ryuji Wada	4,284,000
Nov. 26	Matriarch Stakes	Hollywood	1 1/4 (T)	Tout Charmant	Chris McCarron	500,000
Nov. 26	Hollywood Derby	Hollywood	1 1/8 (T)	Brahms	Pat Day	500,000
Dec. 2	Hollywood Futurity	Hollywood	1 1/16	Point Given	Gary Stevens	345,690
Dec. 16	Hollywood Turf Cup	Hollywood	1 1/2 (T)	Bienamado	Chris McCarron	400,000

2001 (through Sept. 22)

Date	Race	Track	Miles	Winner	Jockey	Purse
Jan. 3	Spectacular Bid Stakes	Gulfstream	6 F	Icanseetherain	Jose Santos	$100,000
Jan. 13	San Miguel Stakes	Santa Anita	6 F	Lasersport	Corey Nakatani	107,500
Jan. 13	Golden Gate Derby	Golden Gate	1 1/16	Hoovergethekeys	Ronald Warren Jr.	150,000
Jan. 20	Holy Bull Stakes	Gulfstream	1 1/16	Radical Riley	Eduardo Nunez	100,000
Jan. 21	Santa Catalina Stakes	Santa Anita	1 1/16	Millennium Wind	Chris McCarron	107,700
Jan. 27	Hutcheson Stakes	Gulfstream	7 F	Yonaguska	Jerry Bailey	150,000
Feb. 3	Donn Handicap	Gulfstream	1 1/8	Captain Steve	Jerry Bailey	500,000
Feb. 3	Charles H. Strub Stakes	Santa Anita	1 1/8	Wooden Phone	Corey Nakatani	500,000
Feb. 3	San Vicente Stakes	Santa Anita	7 F	Early Flyer	Chris McCarron	150,000
Feb. 17	Fountain of Youth Stakes	Gulfstream	1 1/16	Songandaprayer	Edgar Prado	200,000
Mar. 3	Gulfstream Park Handicap	Gulfstream	1 1/4	Sir Bear	Eibar Coa	200,000
Mar. 3	San Rafael Stakes	Santa Anita	1	Crafty CT	Eddie Delahoussaye	200,000
Mar. 3	The Southwest	Oaklawn	1	Son of Rocket	Terry Thompson	75,000
Mar. 3	Santa Anita Handicap	Santa Anita	1 1/4	Tiznow	Chris McCarron	1,000,000
Mar. 4	Rampart Handicap	Gulfstream	1 1/16	De Bertie	Jorge Chavez	200,000
Mar. 10	Santa Margarita Handicap	Santa Anita	1 1/8	Lazy Slusan	David Flores	300,000
Mar. 10	El Camino Real Derby	Golden Gate	1 1/16	Hoovergethekeys	Ronald Warren Jr.	200,000
Mar. 10	Swale Stakes	Gulfstream	7 F	D'wildcat	Corey Nakatani	150,000
Mar. 10	Florida Derby	Gulfstream	1 1/8	Monarchos	Jorge Chavez	1,000,000
Mar. 10	Santa Anita Oaks	Santa Anita	1 1/16	Golden Ballet	Chris McCarron	300,000
Mar. 11	Louisiana Derby	Fairgrounds	1 1/16	Fifty Stars	Donnie Meche	750,000
Mar. 17	San Felipe Stakes	Santa Anita	1 1/16	Point Given	Gary Stevens	250,000
Mar. 18	Gotham Stakes	Aqueduct	1	Richly Blended	Rick Wilson	200,000
Mar. 18	Tampa Bay Derby	Tampa Bay	1 1/16	Burning Roma	Richard Migliore	200,000
Mar. 24	Rebel Stakes	Oaklawn	1 1/16	Crafty Shaw	Joe Johnson	100,000
Mar. 24	Spiral Stakes	Turfway	1 1/16	Balto Star	Mark Guidry	600,000
Mar. 24	Dubai World Cup*	Nad al-Sheba	1 1/4	Captain Steve	Jerry Bailey	6,000,000
Apr. 7	Santa Anita Derby	Santa Anita	1 1/8	Point Given	Gary Stevens	750,000
Apr. 7	Flamingo Stakes	Hialeah	1 1/8	Thunder Blitz	Edgar Prado	250,000
Apr. 7	Ashland Stakes	Keeneland	1 1/16	Fleet Renee	John Velazquez	500,000
Apr. 7	The Oaklawn Handicap	Oaklawn	1 1/8	Traditionally	Pat Day	600,000
Apr. 7	Lone Star Derby	Lone Star	1 1/16	Percy Hope	Jon Court	500,000
Apr. 7	Illinois Derby	Sportsman's Park	1 1/8	Distilled	Mike Smith	500,000
Apr. 8	Apple Blossom Handicap	Oaklawn	1 1/16	Gourmet Girl	Calvin Borel	500,000
Apr. 11	Lafayette Stakes	Keeneland	7 F	Griffinite	Jose Santos	100,000
Apr. 14	Blue Grass Stakes	Keeneland	1 1/8	Millennium Wind	Laffit Pincay Jr.	750,000

Major Stakes Races (Cont.)

Date	Race	Track	Miles	Winner	Jockey	Purse
Apr. 14	Bay Shore Stakes	Aqueduct	7 F	Skip to the Stone	Victor Espinoza	$150,000
Apr. 14	San Juan Capistrano Handicap	Santa Anita	1¾	Bienamado	Chris McCarron	400,000
Apr. 14	Wood Memorial	Aqueduct	1⅛	Congaree	Victor Espinoza	750,000
Apr. 21	Federico Tesio Stakes	Pimlico	1⅛	Marciano	Mark Johnston	100,000
Apr. 21	Lexington Stakes	Keeneland	1¹⁄₁₆	Keats	Larry Melancon	350,000
Apr. 28	Derby Trial	Churchill Downs	1	Meetyouathebrig	Robby Albarado	117,100
Apr. 28	Snow Chief Stakes	Hollywood	1⅛	Romanceishope	Chris McCarron	250,000
May 4	Kentucky Oaks	Churchill Downs	1⅛	Flute	Jerry Bailey	609,200
May 5	**Kentucky Derby**	Churchill Downs	1¼	Monarchos	Jorge Chavez	1,112,000
May 5	Withers Stakes	Aqueduct	1	Richly Blended	Rick Wilson	150,000
May 12	Pimlico Special	Pimlico	1³⁄₁₆	Include	Jerry Bailey	750,000
May 18	Black-Eyed Susan Stakes	Pimlico	1⅛	Two Item Limit	Richard Migliore	200,000
May 19	**Preakness Stakes**	Pimlico	1³⁄₁₆	Point Given	Gary Stevens	1,000,000
May 26	Peter Pan Stakes	Belmont	1⅛	Hero's Tribute	Jorge Chavez	200,000
May 28	Shoemaker BC Mile	Hollywood	1 (T)	Irish Prize	Gary Stevens	475,000
May 28	Metropolitan Mile	Belmont	1	Exciting Story	Patrick Husbands	750,000
June 2	Massachusetts Handicap	Suffolk Downs	1⅛	Include	Jerry Bailey	500,000
June 8	Acorn Stakes	Belmont	1	Forest Secrets	Chris McCarron	200,000
June 9	**Belmont Stakes**	Belmont	1½	Point Given	Gary Stevens	1,000,000
June 9	Riva Ridge Stakes	Belmont	7 F	Put It Back	Noel Wynter	150,000
June 9	Vodafone English Derby	Epsom Downs	1½ (T)	Galileo	Michael Kinane	1,400,000
June 10	Charles Whittingham Handicap	Hollywood Park	1¼ (T)	Bienamado	Chris McCarron	350,000
June 10	The Californian	Hollywood Park	1⅛	Skimming	Garrett Gomez	500,000
June 16	Stephen Foster Handicap	Churchill Downs	1⅛	Guided Tour	Larry Melancon	831,000
June 17	Affirmed Handicap	Hollywood Park	1¹⁄₁₆	Until Sundown	Gary Stevens	100,000
June 17	Leonard Richards Stakes	Delaware	1¹⁄₁₆	Burning Roma	Rick Wilson	200,000
June 24	Beverly Hills Handicap	Hollywood Park	1¼ (T)	Astra	Kent Desormeaux	200,000
June 24	Queen's Plate	Woodbine	1¼	Dancethruthedawn	Gary Boulanger	1,000,000
June 30	Vanity Handicap	Hollywood Park	1⅛	Gourmet Girl	Gary Stevens	250,000
June 30	Mother Goose Stakes	Belmont	1⅛	Fleet Renee	John Velazquez	250,000
July 1	Hollywood Gold Cup	Hollywood Park	1¼	Aptitude	Laffit Pincay Jr.	750,000
July 1	Suburban Handicap	Belmont	1¼	Albert the Great	Jorge Chavez	500,000
July 1	Irish Derby	Curragh	1½ (T)	Galileo	Michael Kinane	1,550,000
July 4	Jersey Shore BC	Monmouth	6 F	City Zip	Jose Ferrer	95,000
July 8	Dwyer Stakes	Belmont	1¹⁄₁₆	E Dubai	Jerry Bailey	145,500
July 14	Carry Back Stakes	Calder	6 F	Illusioned	Jorge Chavez	250,000
July 14	Hollywood Oaks	Hollywood Park	1⅛	Affluent	Eddie Delahoussaye	150,000
July 15	Swaps Stakes	Hollywood Park	1⅛	Congaree	Gary Stevens	500,000
July 21	Coaching Club Am. Oaks	Belmont	1½	Tweedside	John Velazquez	350,000
July 28	Round Table Stakes	Arlington	1⅛	Discreet Hero	Shane Laviolette	125,000
July 28	K. George VI and Q. Elizabeth Diamond Stakes*	Ascot	1½ (T)	Galileo	Michael Kinane	1,084,274
July 28	Whitney Handicap	Saratoga	1⅛	Lido Palace	Jerry Bailey	1,008,000
July 28	Eddie Read Handicap	Del Mar	1⅛ (T)	Redattore	Alex Solis	400,000
July 29	Go for Wand Handicap	Saratoga	1⅛	Serra Lake	Edgar Prado	250,000
Aug. 3	Amsterdam Stakes	Saratoga	6 F	City Zip	Jorge Chavez	135,700
Aug. 4	Jim Dandy Stakes	Saratoga	1⅛	Scorpion	Jerry Bailey	600,000
Aug. 5	Haskell Invitational	Monmouth	1⅛	Point Given	Gary Stevens	1,500,000
Aug. 12	Oklahoma Derby†	Remington	1¹⁄₁₆	Top Hit	Garrett Gomez	300,000
Aug. 18	Arlington Million*	Arlington	1¼ (T)	Silvano	Andreas Suborics	1,000,000
Aug. 18	Alabama Stakes	Saratoga	1¼	Flute	Edgar Prado	750,000
Aug. 19	Pacific Classic	Del Mar	1¼	Skimming	Garrett Gomez	1,000,000
Aug. 19	Saratoga BC Handicap	Saratoga	1¼	Aptitude	Jerry Bailey	291,000
Aug. 24	Personal Ensign Handicap	Saratoga	1¼	Pompeii	Richard Migliore	400,000
Aug. 25	Travers Stakes	Saratoga	1¼	Point Given	Gary Stevens	1,000,000
Aug. 25	King's Bishop Stakes	Saratoga	7 F	Squirtle Squirt	Jerry Bailey	200,000
Aug. 26	Philip H. Iselin Handicap	Monmouth	1⅛	Broken Vow	Ramon Dominguez	350,000
Sept. 8	Man o' War Stakes	Belmont	1⅜ (T)	With Anticipation	Pat Day	500,000
Sept. 8	The Woodward Stakes	Belmont	1⅛	Lido Palace	Jerry Bailey	500,000
Sept. 9	Atto Mile	Woodbine	1 (T)	Numerous Times	Patrick Husbands	1,000,000
Sept. 9	UAE Grosser Preis von Baden*	Baden-Baden	1½ (T)	Morshdi	Philip Robinson	745,000
Sept. 16	Irish Champion Stakes*	Leopardstown	1¼	Fantastic Light	Frankie Dettori	928,620
Sept. 22	Jerome Handicap	Belmont	1	Express Tour	John Velazquez	150,000
Sept. 22	Vosburgh Stakes	Belmont	7 F	Left Bank	John Velazquez	300,000
Sept. 22	Mazarine B.C. Stakes	Woodbine	1¹⁄₁₆	Lady Shari	Constant Montpellier	275,000
Sept. 22	Kentucky Cup Classic	Turfway	1⅛	Guided Tour	Larry Melancon	500,000

*Emirates World Series race (see table on page 782).
†formerly known as Remington Park Derby.

The 2001 Triple Crown

Thoroughbred racing's Triple Crown for three-year-olds consists of the Kentucky Derby, Preakness Stakes and Belmont Stakes run over six weeks on May 5, May 19 and June 9, respectively.

127th KENTUCKY DERBY

Grade I for three-year-olds; 8th race at Churchill Downs in Louisville. **Date**—May 5, 2001; **Distance**—1¼ miles; **Stakes Purse**—$1,112,000 ($812,000 to winner; $170,000 for 2nd; $85,000 for 3rd; $45,000 for 4th); **Track**—Fast; **Off**—6:11 p.m. EDT; **Favorite**—Point Given (9-5 odds).

Winner—Monarchos; **Field**—17 horses; **Time**—1:59.97; **Start**—Good for all; **Won**—Driving; **Sire**—Maria's Mon; **Dam**—Regal Band; **Record** (going into race)—6 starts, 3 wins, 1 second, 1 third; **Last start**—2nd in Wood Memorial (Apr. 14); **Breeder**—J.D. Squires (Ky.).

Order of Finish	Jockey	PP	1/4	1/2	3/4	Mile	Stretch	Finish	To $1
Monarchos	Jorge Chavez	16	13-2	13-½	10-1½	6-hd	2-3	1-4¾	10.50
Invisible Ink	John Velazquez	13	9-hd	9-2½	9-2½	5-hd	3-1	2-ns	55.00
Congaree	Victor Espinoza	8	5-2½	5-1½	5-½	1-1½	1-½	3-4	7.20
Thunder Blitz	Edgar Prado	4	11-hd	10-hd	8-hd	7-hd	6-2	4-2¾	25.40
Point Given	Gary Stevens	17	6-hd	7-hd	7-1	2-hd	4-1½	5-1¼	1.80
Jamaican Rum	Eddie Delahoussaye	15	17	16-1	15-2½	12-1	7-2½	6-nk	20.20
A P Valentine	Corey Nakatani	9	12-3	12-1½	13-1	13-2	9-hd	7-1¼	19.90
Express Tour	David Flores	6	8-4	6-1½	6-hd	3-hd	5-hd	8-¾	18.10
Fifty Stars	Donnie Meche	5	16-1½	17	16-3	14-3	11-1	9-1¼	43.60
Startac	Alex Solis	12	10-1½	11-1½	11-½	10-1	10-1½	10-4	102.40
Millennium Wind	Laffit Pincay Jr.	2	4-½	4-1½	3-1½	8-hd	8-hd	11-nk	9.90
Arctic Boy	Calvin Borel	7	15-4	14-1½	12-½	11-hd	12-2½	12-6½	101.20
Songandaprayer	Aaron Gryder	1	1-hd	1-1½	1-1½	4-½	13-4	13-5	35.90
Balto Star	Mark Guidry	3	2-1	2-hd	2-hd	9-1	14-6	14-2¼	8.30
Dollar Bill	Pat Day	10	14-hd	15-4	14-hd	16	15-4	15-17	6.60
Keats	Larry Melancon	14	3-½	3-hd	4-hd	15-1½	16	16	95.00
Talk is Money	Jerry Bailey	11	7-hd	8-4	17	17	17	17-DNF	47.10

Times— 22⅕; 44⅘; 1:09⅕; 1:35; 1:59⅘.

$2 Mutual Prices—#16 Monarchos ($23.00, $11.80, $8.80); #13 Invisible Ink ($46.60, $21.20); #8 Congaree ($7.20). **Exacta**—(16-13) for $1,229.00; **Trifecta**—(16-13-8) for $12,238.00; **Superfecta**—(16-13-8-4) for $62,986.90; **Pick Six**—(5-1/2-2/8-2-1-16) for $16,245.00 (5-correct) $117.20; **Scratched**—none; **Overweights**—none; **Attendance**—154,210; **TV Rating**—8.3/20 share (NBC).

Trainers & Owners (by finish): **1**—John Ward Jr. & John Oxley; **2**—Todd Pletcher & Peachtree Stable; **3**—Bob Baffert & Stonerside Stable; **4**—Joe Orseno & Stronach Stable; **5**—Bob Baffert & The Thoroughbred Corp.; **6**—James Cassidy & Southern Nevada Racing Stables, Inc.; **7**—Nick Zito & Ol Memorial Stable (Michael Tabor/Rick Pitino); **8**—Saeed bin Suroor & Godolphin Racing, Inc.; **9**—Steve Asmussen & James Cassels/Bob Zollars; **10**—Simon Bray & Allen Paulson; **11**—David Hofmans & David/Jill Heerensperger; **12**—Tony Richey & Royce Roberts; **13**—John Dowd & Devil Eleven Stable (Leslie/Bobby Hurley)/ DJ Stable; **14**—Todd Pletcher & Anstu Stables, Inc.; **15**—Dallas Stewart & Gary/Mary West; **16**—Niall O'Callaghan & Henry Pabst; **17**—John Scanlan & Dan Borislow.

126th PREAKNESS STAKES

Grade I for three-year-olds; 11th race at Pimlico in Baltimore. **Date**— May 19, 2001; **Distance**—1³⁄₁₆ miles; **Stakes Purse**—$1,000,000 ($650,000 to winner; $200,000 for 2nd; $100,000 for 3rd; $50,000 for 4th); **Track**—Fast; **Off**—6:09 p.m. EDT; **Favorite**—Monarchos (2-1 odds).

Winner—Point Given; **Field**—11 horses; **Time**—1:55.51; **Start**—Good for all; **Won**—Driving; **Sire**—Thunder Gulch; **Dam**—Turko's Turn; **Record** (going into race)—9 starts, 5 wins, 3 second, 1 fifth; **Last start**—5th in Kentucky Derby (May 5); **Breeder**—The Thoroughbred Corp.

Order of Finish	Jockey	PP	1/4	1/2	3/4	Stretch	Finish	To $1
Point Given	Gary Stevens	11	9-1½	6-hd	3-1	1-½	1-2¼	2.30
A P Valentine	Victor Espinoza	4	6-2	7-1	7-1	3-2	2-nk	10.20
Congaree	Jerry Bailey	5	2-½	2-½	2-hd	2-2½	3-1¼	2.80
Dollar Bill	Pat Day	10	8-1	9-2	11	5-1	4-2¼	8.30
Griffinite	Shaun Bridgmohan	3	7-½	8-hd	9-hd	7-½	5-1½	59.10
Monarchos	Jorge Chavez	7	11	11	8-1½	6-hd	6-1	2.30
Marciano	Mark Johnston	1	4-hd	4-½	4-2	4-1½	7-1¼	46.30
Bay Eagle	Raymond Dominguez	9	10-3½	10-1½	10-3	9-10	8-no	88.30
Percy Hope	Jon Court	8	5-2	5-1½	5-hd	8-2	9-17½	52.60
Richly Blended	Rick Wilson	6	1-2½	1-2½	1-hd	10-4	10-9¾	17.90
Mr. John	Corey Nakatani	2	3-1½	3-2½	6-½	11	11	20.20

Times—23⅘; 47⅕; 1:11⅘; 1:36⅖; 1:55⅖.

$2 Mutual Prices—#11 Point Given ($6.60, $5.00, $4.00); #4 A P Valentine ($8.20, $5.20); #5 Congaree ($3.40). **Exacta**—(11-4) for $81.40; **Trifecta**—(11-4-5) for $279.00; **Pick Six**—none; **Scratched**—none; **Overweights**—none; **Attendance**—104,454; **TV Rating**—6.0/15 share (NBC).

Trainers & Owners (by finish): **1**—Bob Baffert & The Thoroughbred Corp.; **2**—Nick Zito & Ol Memorial Stable (Michael Tabor/Rick Pitino); **3**—Bob Baffert & Stonerside Stable; **4**—Dallas Stewart & Gary/Mary West; **5**—Jennifer Pedersen & Paraneck Stable; **6**—John Ward Jr. & John Oxley; **7**—Tim Ritchey & Win More Stable, Inc.; **8**—Graham Motion & Lazy Lane Farms, Inc.; **9**—Anthony Reinstedler & Waterfall Stable; **10**—Ben Perkins Jr. & Raymond Dweck; **11**—Elliott Walden & Thomas Van Meter II.

The 2001 Triple Crown (Cont.)

133rd BELMONT STAKES

Grade I for three-year-olds; 10th race at Belmont Park in Elmont, N.Y. **Date**—June 9, 2001; **Distance**—1½ miles; **Stakes Purse**—$1,000,000 ($600,000 to winner; $200,000 for 2nd; $110,000 for 3rd; $60,000 for 4th; $30,000 for 5th); **Track**—Fast; **Off**—6:10 p.m. EDT; **Favorite**—Point Given (8-5 odds).

Winner—Point Given; **Field**—9 horses; **Time**—2:26⅖; **Start**—Good for all; **Won**—Driving; **Sire**—Thunder Gulch; **Dam**—Turko's Turn; **Record** (going into race): 10 starts, 6 wins, 3 seconds; **Last Start**—1st in Preakness (May 19); **Breeder**—The Thoroughbred Corp.

Order of Finish	Jockey	PP	1/4	1/2	3/4	Mile	Stretch	Finish	To $1
Point Given	Gary Stevens	9	3-hd	3-1½	1-hd	1-2	1-7	1-12¼	1.35
A P Valentine	Victor Espinoza	8	7-1½	4-hd	4-6	2-3	2-1	2-¾	5.90
Monarchos	Jorge Chavez	5	6-hd	7-2½	6-5	3-hd	3-½	3-1	5.00
Dollar Bill	Pat Day	3	8-hd	9	8-8	5-hd	5-8	4-2½	6.60
Invisible Ink	John Velazquez	1	4-1½	5-2½	5-½	4-3½	4-2½	5-7½	10.10
Thunder Blitz	Jerry Bailey	4	5-hd	6-hd	7-½	7-5	6-½	6-5¾	12.70
Buckle Down Ben	Corey Nakatani	6	2-½	2-½	2-hd	6-3	7-15	7-15½	28.75
Balto Star	Chris McCarron	2	1-1½	1-½	3-hd	8-12	8-20	8-28¾	12.00
Dr. Greenfield	Edgar Prado	7	9	8-hd	9	9	9	9	19.60

Times—23⅘; 48; 1:11⅗; 1:35⅖; 2:00⅗; 2:26⅖.

$2 Mutual Prices—#9 Point Given ($4.70, $3.70, $3.00); #8 A P Valentine ($5.00, $3.90); #5 Monarchos ($4.20).

Exacta—(9-8) for $20.60; **Trifecta**—(9-8-5) for $76.00; **Pick Three**—None; **Scratched**—None; **Overweights**—None; **Attendance**—73,857; **TV Rating**—4.9/14 share (NBC).

Trainers & Owners (by finish): 1—Bob Baffert & The Thoroughbred Corp; 2—Nick Zito & Ol Memorial Stable (Michael Tabor/Rick Pitino); 3—John Ward Jr. & John Oxley; 4—Dallas Stewart & Gary/Mary West; 5—Todd Pletcher & Peachtree Stable; 6—Joe Orseno & Stronach Stable; 7—D. Wayne Lukas & Michael Tabor; 8—Todd Pletcher & Anstu Stables, Inc.; 9—Gerard Butler & Team Valor.

NTRA National Thoroughbred Poll

The NTRA Thoroughbred Poll conducted by National Thoroughbred Racing Association, covering races through Sept. 16, 2001. Rankings are based on the votes of sports and thoroughbred media representatives on a 10-9-8-7-6-5-4-3-2-1 basis. First place votes are in parentheses.

		Pts	Age	Sex	'01 Record Sts—1-2-3	Owner	Trainer
1	Kona Gold (11)	168	7	Gelding	3-3-0-0	Irwin/Andrew Molasky & Michael Singh*	Bruce Headley
2	Lido Palace (6)	164	4	Colt	5-2-2-1	John Amerman	Bobby Frankel
3	Albert The Great	116	4	Colt	7-3-4-0	Tracy Farmer	Nick Zito
4	Tiznow	114	4	Colt	4-2-1-1	Cee's Stable	Jay Robbins
5	Flute (1)	102	3	Filly	5-4-1-0	Juddmonte Farms	Bobby Frankel
6	With Anticipation	68	6	Gelding	7-4-1-0	Augustine Stable	Jonathan Sheppard
7	Skimming	46	5	Horse	5-3-2-0	Juddmonte Farms	Bobby Frankel
8	Include	43	4	Colt	6-5-0-1	Robert Meyerhoff	Bud Delp
9	Officer	36	2	Colt	4-4-0-0	The Thoroughbred Corp.	Bob Baffert
10	Guided Tour	23	5	Gelding	6-3-1-1	Morton Fink	Niall O'Callaghan

*Kona Gold is also co-owned by trainer Bruce Headley.

Others receiving votes: 11. Aptitude (19 points); **12.** England's Legend (16); **13.** Xtra Heat (11); **14.** Came Home (9); **15.** Macho Uno (8); **16.** Bienamado (7); **17.** Silvano, Bet On Sunshine, Caller One and Touch Tone (5); **21.** Broken Vow and Tranquility Lake (4); **23.** Captain Steve, E Dubai, Hap (3); **26.** Fleet Renee (2); **27.** Dixie Dot Com (1).

2001 Emirates World Series Current Points Rankings

Sponsored by Emirates, international airline of the United Arab Emirates, the World Series includes 12 prestigious thoroughbred races in 10 countries on four continents. Points are awarded to the top six finishers in each race as follows: 12–6–4–3–2–1. Top horses, jockeys and trainers are listed below. Through Sept. 16, 2001 and five series races.

	Horses	Pts		Jockeys	Pts		Trainers	Pts
1	Fantastic Light	18	1	Jerry Bailey	18	1	Aidan O'Brien	24
2	Galileo	16		Frankie Dettori	18	2	Saeed bin Suroor	20
3	Captain Steve	12		Michael Kinane	18	3	Andreas Wohler	19
	Silvano	12	4	Andreas Suborics	16	4	Bob Baffert	12
	Morshdi	12	5	Philip Robinson	12		Michael Jarvis	12
6	Hightori	8	6	Gerald Mosse	8	6	Philippe Demercastel	8
7	To The Victory	6	7	Yutaka Take	6	7	Yasuo Ikee	6
	Hap	6		John Reid	6		Bill Mott	6
	Boreal	6	9	Alex Solis	4		Peter Schiergen	6
10	Redattore	4		Seamus Heffernan	4	10	Richard Mandella	4
	Sabiango	4						
	Bach	4						

Remaining 2001 Emirates World Series races: Canadian International (Canada), Sept. 30; Prix de l'Arc de Triomphe (France), Oct. 7; Breeders' Cup Turf (United States), Oct. 27; Breeders' Cup Classic (United States), Oct. 27; Carlton Draught Cox Plate (Australia), Oct. 27; Japan Cup (Japan), Nov. 25; Hong Kong Cup (China), Dec. 16.

2000-01 Money Leaders

Official Top 10 standings for 2000 and unofficial Top 10 standings for 2001, through Sept. 16, 2001.

FINAL 2000 HORSES	Age	Sts	1-2-3	Earnings	2001 (through Sept. 16) HORSES	Age	Sts	1-2-3	Earnings
Dubai Millennium	4	1	1-0-0	$3,600,000	Captain Steve	4	6	2-1-1	$4,201,200
Tiznow	3	9	5-3-0	3,445,950	Point Given	3	7	6-0-0	3,350,000
Fantastic Light	4	6	2-2-1	3,238,998	Monarchos	3	7	4-1-1	1,711,600
T.M. Opera O (JPN)	4	1	1-0-0	2,278,332	Include	4	6	5-0-1	1,290,000
Fusaichi Pegasus	3	8	6-1-0	1,987,800	Skimming	5	5	3-2-0	1,230,000
Spain	3	13	5-3-1	1,979,500	Albert the Great	4	7	3-4-0	1,200,000
Captain Steve	3	11	3-2-4	1,882,276	To the Victory (JPN)	5	1	0-1-0	1,200,000
Behrens	6	7	1-3-2	1,764,500	Congaree	3	7	4-0-3	1,063,400
Lemon Drop Kid	4	9	5-0-1	1,673,900	Guided Tour	5	6	3-1-1	1,050,220
Giant's Causeway	3	3	1-2-0	1,600,593	Dancethruthedawn	3	6	3-1-0	1,045,039
JOCKEYS		Mts	1st	Earnings	**JOCKEYS**		Mts	1st	Earnings
Pat Day		1219	267	$17,479,838	Jerry Bailey		749	185	$17,656,630
Jerry Bailey		908	246	17,468,690	Jorge Chavez		1006	190	10,310,279
Shane Sellers		1109	192	14,881,680	Gary Stevens		421	86	10,256,452
Jorge Chavez		1447	261	14,440,907	John Velazquez		1072	224	10,179,407
Kent Desormeaux		887	177	13,460,166	Pat Day		918	187	9,750,879
Chris McCarron		563	115	13,405,170	Edgar Prado		1187	189	9,610,927
Victor Espinoza		1325	243	13,286,705	Chris McCarron		452	89	8,282,896
Corey Nakatani		889	185	12,670,504	Alex Solis		869	155	8,276,331
Edgar Prado		1642	255	12,375,107	Victor Espinoza		868	121	8,040,376
John Velazquez		1083	200	10,794,003	Laffit Pincay Jr.		901	167	7,912,916
TRAINERS		Sts	1st	Earnings	**TRAINERS**		Sts	1st	Earnings
Bob Baffert		678	146	$11,831,605	Bob Baffert		473	103	$14,269,473
Bobby Frankel		371	96	10,839,071	Bobby Frankel		282	73	9,497,761
D. Wayne Lukas		815	112	10,490,292	Bill Mott		554	112	6,855,624
Bill Mott		733	155	8,591,389	Steve Asmussen		1018	206	5,901,305
Saeed bin Suroor		28	5	8,065,104	Scott Lake		1069	302	5,725,203
Todd Pletcher		661	114	7,058,280	Todd Pletcher		373	84	5,085,228
Joe Orseno		245	52	6,673,714	D. Wayne Lukas		517	80	4,245,954
Neil Drysdale		197	48	6,111,440	Christophe Clement		255	60	4,235,152
Steve Asmussen		1119	234	5,872,931	John Kimmel		370	86	4,067,669
Scott Lake		1045	336	5,731,522	Nick Zito		326	54	3,769,872

Harness Racing

2000-01 Major Stakes Races

Winners of major stakes races from Nov. 10, 2000 through Sept. 20, 2001; all paces and trots cover one mile; (BC) indicates year-end Breeders' Crown series.

LATE 2000

Date	Race	Raceway	Winner	Time	Driver	Purse
Nov. 10	Windy City Pace	Maywood	Camotion	1:51 4/5	Dale Hiteman	$300,000
Nov. 18	Three Diamonds Pace	Garden St.	Electrical Art	1:53 3/5	Ron Pierce	456,100
Nov. 18	Valley Victory	Garden St.	Chasing Tail	1:56	John Campbell	464,100
Nov. 18	Governor's Cup	Garden St.	Bettor's Delight	1:52 2/5	Mike Lachance	545,300

2001 (through Sept. 20)

Date	Race	Raceway	Winner	Time	Driver	Purse
May 12	Berry's Creek	Meadowlands	Gunthatwonthewest	1:52	George Brennan	$300,000
June 2	New Jersey Classic	Meadowlands	Bettor's Delight	1:50	Mike Lachance	500,000
June 23	North America Cup	Woodbine	LCB	1:50	Luc Ouellette	100,000
July 13	Del Miller Memorial	Meadowlands	Syrinx Hanover	1:54 2/5	John Campbell	400,500
July 13	Budweiser Beacon Course	Meadowlands	SJ's Caviar	1:54 1/5	Bob Blanton Jr.	401,500
July 14	Meadowlands Pace	Meadowlands	Real Desire	1:49 3/5	John Campbell	1,009,500
July 28	BC Open Pace	Meadowlands	Goliath Bayama	1:48 4/5	Sylvain Filion	500,000
July 28	BC Open Trot	Meadowlands	Varenne	1:51 1/5	Minnucci	1,000,000
July 28	BC Mare Pace	Meadowlands	Eternal Camnation	1:50 1/5	Eric Ledford	332,500
Aug. 2	Peter Haughton Memorial	Meadowlands	Civil Action	1:56 4/5	Mike Lachance	460,000
Aug. 2	Merrie Annabelle Final	Meadowlands	Fluttering Wings	1:58 2/5	Berndt Linstedt	417,000
Aug. 3	Sweetheart Pace	Meadowlands	Sing Fat Lady	1:53 2/5	Mike Lachance	500,000
Aug. 3	Woodrow Wilson Pace	Meadowlands	Allamerican Ingot	1:51 3/5	John Campbell	700,000
Aug. 4	**Hambletonian**	Meadowlands	Scarlet Knight	1:53 4/5	Stefan Melander	1,000,000
Aug. 4	Hambletonian Oaks	Meadowlands	Syrinx Hanover	1:55 1/5	John Campbell	500,000
Aug. 4	Nat Ray	Meadowlands	Fool's Goal	1:53	Jack Moiseyev	500,000
Aug. 11	Adios Final	Ladbroke	Pine Valley	1:51 4/5	Brian Sears	272,547
Aug. 18	Hoosier Cup	Hoosier Park	Real Desire	1:53	John Campbell	450,000
Aug. 19	Confederation Cup XXV	Flamboro	Ring of Life	1:54 2/5	Sylvain Filion	531,500
Aug. 25	Maple Leaf Trot	Woodbine	Plesac	1:53 2/5	Doug Brown	838,500
Aug. 25	**Yonkers Trot**	Yonkers	Banker Hall	1:59 1/5	Trevor Ritchie	454,150
Sept. 1	Metro Pace	Woodbine	Mach Three	1:51 4/5	Mike Lachance	1,123,400

Date	Race	Raceway	Winner	Time	Driver	Purse
Sept. 1	World Trotting Derby	Du Quoin	Cobol	2:01⅖	Mike Lachance	$550,000
Sept. 3	**Cane Pace**	Freehold	Four Starzzz Shark	1:53⅗	David Miller	345,694
Sept. 20	**Little Brown Jug**	Delaware	Bettor's Delight	1:51⅘	Mike Lachance	646,050

2000-01 Money Leaders

Official Top 10 standings for 2000 and unofficial Top 10 standings for 2001 through Sept. 20, 2001.

FINAL 2000

HORSES	Age	Sts	1-2-3	Earnings
Gallo Blue Chip	3pg	29	19-5-1	$2,428,816
Yankee Paco	3tc	16	10-2-0	1,361,421
Western Ideal	5ph	14	10-3-0	1,220,000
Magician	5tg	17	11-2-2	1,200,190
Moni Maker	7tm	14	7-4-1	1,173,273
Credit Winner	3tc	14	6-5-1	1,136,088
Dragon Again	5ph	24	13-5-4	891,740
Bettor's Delight	2pc	10	6-1-1	804,661
Astreos	3pc	17	5-4-2	764,597
Casual Breeze	3tf	19	12-3-3	752,567

DRIVERS	Mts	1st	Earnings
John Campbell	1635	292	$11,160,482
Luc Ouellette	2383	409	9,566,305
Mike Lachance	2041	257	9,070,680
Chris Christoforou	2632	571	8,986,409
David Miller	2658	401	7,594,003
Ron Pierce	2051	271	6,992,328
Daniel Dube	2260	288	6,921,164
Eric Ledford	1977	427	6,523,727
Randy Waples	2115	352	6,380,157
Andy Miller	3303	613	5,623,134

2001 (through Sept. 20)

HORSES	Age	Sts	1-2-3	Earnings
Bettor's Delight	3pc	13	8-4-0	$1,503,853
Gallo Blue Chip	4pg	16	9-3-1	1,082,690
SJ's Caviar	3tc	15	13-1-0	1,032,943
Real Desire	3pc	12	5-5-1	1,015,225
Plesac	4th	17	7-4-2	836,675
Magician	6tg	17	9-2-1	762,575
Mach Three	2pc	7	6-1-0	693,057
Eternal Carnation	4pm	15	6-5-0	639,785
Royalflush Hanover	5pg	22	7-5-3	632,156
Goliath Bayama	5ph	16	5-2-2	629,400

DRIVERS	Mts	1st	Earnings
John Campbell	1489	258	$10,276,779
Mike Lachance	1694	189	8,052,312
David Miller	2146	364	7,846,158
Randy Waples	2084	440	7,630,726
Luc Ouellette	1705	293	7,159,078
Chris Christoforou	2187	440	6,806,829
Mario Baillargeon	1586	219	5,285,015
Daniel Dube	1571	188	4,723,946
Sylvain Filion	1533	332	4,429,504
Mike Saftic	1511	158	4,316,603

Hambletonian Society/Breeders Crown Standardbred Poll

Final Poll conducted by Harness Racing Communications as of Sept. 17, 2001 and based on the votes of 35 harness racing media representatives. First place votes are in parentheses. (p-pacer, t-trotter, h-horse, f-filly, m-mare, c-colt, g-gelding).

		Pts	Age/Gait/Sex	'01 Sts—1-2-3	Earnings
1	SJ's Caviar (27)	341	3tc	14–12-1-0	$1,011,168
2	Real Desire (1)	269	3pc	10–5-3-1	908,628
3	Gallo Blue Chip (3)	255	4pg	16–9-3-1	1,082,690
4	Syrinx Hanover	199	3tf	6–6-0-0	493,933
5	Bettor's Delight	185	3pc	11–6-4-0	1,247,372
6	Varenne* (4)	156	6th	11–10-1-0	1,454,685
7	Bunny Lake	134	3pf	14–12-2-0	517,185
8	Eternal Carnation	118	4pm	15–6-5-0	639,785
9	Plesac	69	4th	17–7-4-2	836,675
10	Goliath Bayama	53	5ph	16–5-2-2	629,400

*Varenne's totals include foreign starts and earnings.
Others receiving votes: **11.** Mach Three (38 points); **12.** Magician (33); **13.** Scarlet Knight (28); **14.** Mini Me (18); **15.** Rama's Pleasure (8); **16.** Determination Plus (6); **17.** Cathedra Dot Com (5); **18.** Cobol (4); **19.** Hez Striking and Worldly Beauty (1).

Steeplechase Racing
2000-01 Major Stakes Races

Winners of major steeplechase races from Nov. 19, 2000 through Aug. 30, 2001.

LATE 2000

Date	Race	Location	Miles	Winner	Jockey	Purse
Nov. 19	Colonial Cup	Camden, S.C.	2 ¾	Romantic	Arch Kingsley, Jr.	$100,000

2001 (through Aug. 30)

Date	Race	Location	Miles	Winner	Jockey	Purse
Apr. 14	Atlanta Cup	Kingston, Ga.	2	Electron	Craig Thornton	$100,000
Apr. 21	Grand National	Butler, Md.	3	Welterweight	Alfred Smithwick Jr.	30,000
Apr. 28	Maryland Hunt Cup	Glyndon, Md.	4	Solo Lord	Michael Hoffman	65,000
May 5	Virginia Gold Cup	The Plains, Va.	4	Ironfist	Roger Horgan	50,000
May 12	Iroquois	Nashville, Tenn.	3	Rand (NZ)	Eddie Lamb	100,000
Aug. 30	N.Y. Turf Writers Cup	Saratoga, N.Y.	2 ⅜	It's a Giggle	Blythe Miller	107,700

1867-2001 Through the Years

information please®
SPORTS ALMANAC

Thoroughbred Racing
The Triple Crown

The term "Triple Crown" was coined by sportswriter Charles Hatton while covering the 1930 victories of Gallant Fox in the Kentucky Derby, Preakness Stakes and Belmont Stakes. Before then, only Sir Barton (1919) had won all three races in the same year. Since then, nine horses have won the Triple Crown. Two trainers, James (Sunny Jim) Fitzsimmons and Ben A. Jones, have saddled two Triple Crown champions, while Eddie Arcaro is the only jockey to ride two champions.

Year		Jockey	Trainer	Owner	Sire/Dam
1919	**Sir Barton**	Johnny Loftus	H. Guy Bedwell	J.K.L. Ross	Star Shoot/Lady Sterling
1930	**Gallant Fox**	Earl Sande	J.E. Fitzsimmons	Belair Stud	Sir Gallahad III/Marguerite
1935	**Omaha**	Willie Saunders	J.E. Fitzsimmons	Belair Stud	Gallant Fox/Flambino
1937	**War Admiral**	Charley Kurtsinger	George Conway	Samuel Riddle	Man o' War/Brushup
1941	**Whirlaway**	Eddie Arcaro	Ben A. Jones	Calumet Farm	Blenheim II/Dustwhirl
1943	**Count Fleet**	Johnny Longden	Don Cameron	Mrs. J.D. Hertz	Reigh Count/Quickly
1946	**Assault**	Warren Mehrtens	Max Hirsch	King Ranch	Bold Venture/Igual
1948	**Citation**	Eddie Arcaro	Ben A. Jones	Calumet Farm	Bull Lea/Hydroplane II
1973	**Secretariat**	Ron Turcotte	Lucien Laurin	Meadow Stable	Bold Ruler/Somethingroyal
1977	**Seattle Slew**	Jean Cruguet	Billy Turner	Karen Taylor	Bold Reasoning/My Charmer
1978	**Affirmed**	Steve Cauthen	Laz Barrera	Harbor View Farm	Exclusive Native/Won't Tell You

Note: Gallant Fox (1930) is the only Triple Crown winner to sire another Triple Crown winner, Omaha (1935). Wm. Woodward Sr., owner of Belair Stud, was breeder-owner of both horses and both were trained by Sunny Jim Fitzsimmons.

Triple Crown Near Misses

Forty-five horses have won two legs of the Triple Crown. Of those, fifteen won the Kentucky Derby (KD) and Preakness Stakes (PS) only to be beaten in the Belmont Stakes (BS). Two others, Burgoo King (1932) and Bold Venture (1936), won the Derby and Preakness, but were forced out of the Belmont with the same injury—a bowed tendon—that effectively ended their racing careers. In 1978, Alydar finished second to Affirmed in all three races, the only time that has happened. Note that the Preakness preceded the Kentucky Derby in 1922, '23 and '31; (*) indicates won on disqualification.

Year		KD	PS	BS	Year		KD	PS	BS
1877	**Cloverbrook**	DNS	won	won	1964	**Northern Dancer**	won	won	3rd
1878	**Duke of Magenta**	DNS	won	won	1966	**Kauai King**	won	won	4th
1880	**Grenada**	DNS	won	won	1967	**Damascus**	3rd	won	won
1881	**Saunterer**	DNS	won	won	1968	**Forward Pass**	won*	won	2nd
1895	**Belmar**	DNS	won	won	1969	**Majestic Prince**	won	won	2nd
1920	**Man o' War**	DNS	won	won	1971	**Canonero II**	won	won	4th
1922	**Pillory**	DNS	won	won	1972	**Riva Ridge**	won	4th	won
1923	**Zev**	won	12th	won	1974	**Little Current**	5th	won	won
1931	**Twenty Grand**	won	2nd	won	1976	**Bold Forbes**	won	3rd	won
1932	**Burgoo King**	won	won	DNS	1979	**Spectacular Bid**	won	won	3rd
1936	**Bold Venture**	won	won	DNS	1981	**Pleasant Colony**	won	won	3rd
1939	**Johnstown**	won	5th	won	1984	**Swale**	won	7th	won
1940	**Bimelech**	2nd	won	won	1987	**Alysheba**	won	won	4th
1942	**Shut Out**	won	5th	won	1988	**Risen Star**	3rd	won	won
1944	**Pensive**	won	won	2nd	1989	**Sunday Silence**	won	won	2nd
1949	**Capot**	2nd	won	won	1991	**Hansel**	10th	won	won
1950	**Middleground**	won	2nd	won	1994	**Tabasco Cat**	6th	won	won
1953	**Native Dancer**	2nd	won	won	1995	**Thunder Gulch**	won	3rd	won
1955	**Nashua**	2nd	won	won	1997	**Silver Charm**	won	won	2nd
1956	**Needles**	won	2nd	won	1998	**Real Quiet**	won	won	2nd
1958	**Tim Tam**	won	won	2nd	1999	**Charismatic**	won	won	3rd
1961	**Carry Back**	won	won	7th	2001	**Point Given**	5th	won	won
1963	**Chateaugay**	won	2nd	won					

The Triple Crown Challenge (1987-93)

Seeking to make the Triple Crown more than just a media event and to insure that owners would not be attracted to more lucrative races, officials at Churchill Downs, the Maryland Jockey Club and the New York Racing Association created Triple Crown Productions in 1985 and announced that a $1 million bonus would be given to the horse that performs best in the Kentucky Derby, Preakness Stakes and Belmont Stakes. Furthermore, a bonus of $5 million would be presented to any horse winning all three races.

Revised in 1991, the rules stated that the winning horse must: 1. finish all three races; 2. earn points by finishing first, second, third or fourth in at least one of the three races; and 3. earn the highest number of points based on the following system–10 points to win, five to place, three to show and one to finish fourth. In the event of a tie, the $1 million is distributed equally among the top point-getters. From 1987-90, the system was five points to win, three to place and one to show. The Triple Crown Challenge was discontinued in 1994.

Year	Winner	KD	PS	BS	Pts	Year	Winner	KD	PS	BS	Pts
1987	1 **Bet Twice**	2nd	2nd	1st —	11	1991	1 **Hansel**	10th	1st	1st —	20
	2 Alysheba	1st	1st	4th —	10		2 Strike the Gold	1st	6th	2nd —	15
	3 Cryptoclearance	4th	3rd	2nd —	4		3 Mane Minister	3rd	3rd	3rd —	9
1988	1 **Risen Star**	3rd	1st	1st —	11	1992	1 **Pine Bluff**	5th	1st	3rd —	13
	2 Winning Colors	1st	3rd	6th —	6		2 Casual Lies	2nd	3rd	5th —	8
	3 Brian's Time	6th	2nd	3rd —	4		(No other horses ran all three races.)				
1989	1 **Sunday Silence**	1st	1st	2nd —	13	1993	1 **Sea Hero**	1st	5th	7th —	10
	2 Easy Goer	2nd	2nd	1st —	11		2 Wild Gale	3rd	8th	3rd —	6
	3 Hawkster	5th	5th	5th —	0		(No other horses ran all three races.)				
1990	1 **Unbridled**	1st	2nd	4th —	8						
	2 Summer Squall	2nd	1st	DNR —	8						
	3 Go and Go	DNR	DNR	1st —	5						
(Unbridled was only horse to run all three races.)											

Kentucky Derby

For three-year-olds. Held the first Saturday in May at Churchill Downs in Louisville, Ky. Inaugurated in 1875. Originally run at 1½ miles (1875-95), shortened to present 1¼ miles in 1896.

Trainers with most wins: Ben Jones (6); D. Wayne Lukas and Dick Thompson (4); Sunny Jim Fitzsimmons and Max Hirsch (3).

Jockeys with most wins: Eddie Arcaro and Bill Hartack (5); Bill Shoemaker (4); Angel Cordero Jr., Issac Murphy, Earl Sande and Gary Stevens (3).

Winning fillies: Regret (1915), Genuine Risk (1980) and Winning Colors (1988).

Year	Winner (Margin)	Time	Jockey	Trainer	2nd place	3rd place
1875	**Aristides** (1)	2:37¾	Oliver Lewis	Ansel Anderson	Volcano	Verdigris
1876	**Vagrant** (2)	2:38¼	Bobby Swim	James Williams	Creedmore	Harry Hill
1877	**Baden-Baden** (2)	2:38	Billy Walker	Ed Brown	Leonard	King William
1878	**Day Star** (2)	2:37¼	Jimmy Carter	Lee Paul	Himyar	Leveler
1879	**Lord Murphy** (1)	2:37	Charlie Shauer	George Rice	Falsetto	Strathmore
1880	**Fonso** (1)	2:37½	George Lewis	Tice Hutsell	Kimball	Bancroft
1881	**Hindoo** (4)	2:40	Jim McLaughlin	James Rowe Sr.	Lelex	Alfambra
1882	**Apollo** (½)	2:40¼	Babe Hurd	Green Morris	Runnymede	Bengal
1883	**Leonatus** (3)	2:43	Billy Donohue	John McGinty	Drake Carter	Lord Raglan
1884	**Buchanan** (2)	2:40¼	Isaac Murphy	William Bird	Loftin	Audrain
1885	**Joe Cotton** (nk)	2:37¼	Babe Henderson	Alex Perry	Bersan	Ten Booker
1886	**Ben Ali** (½)	2:36½	Paul Duffy	Jim Murphy	Blue Wing	Free Knight
1887	**Montrose** (2)	2:39¼	Isaac Lewis	John McGinty	Jim Gore	Jacobin
1888	**MacBeth II** (1)	2:38¼	George Covington	John Campbell	Gallifet	White
1889	**Spokane** (ns)	2:34½	Thomas Kiley	John Rodegap	Proctor Knott	Once Again
1890	**Riley** (2)	2:45	Isaac Murphy	Edward Corrigan	Bill Letcher	Robespierre
1891	**Kingman** (1)	2:52¼	Isaac Murphy	Dud Allen	Balgowan	High Tariff
1892	**Azra** (ns)	2:41½	Lonnie Clayton	John Morris	Huron	Phil Dwyer
1893	**Lookout** (5)	2:39¼	Eddie Kunze	Wm. McDaniel	Plutus	Boundless
1894	**Chant** (2)	2:41	Frank Goodale	Eugene Leigh	Pearl Song	Sigurd
1895	**Halma** (3)	2:37½	Soup Perkins	Byron McClelland	Basso	Laureate
1896	**Ben Brush** (ns)	2:07¾	Willie Simms	Hardy Campbell	Ben Eder	Semper Ego
1897	**Typhoon II** (hd)	2:12½	Buttons Garner	J.C. Cahn	Ornament	Dr. Catlett
1898	**Plaudit** (nk)	2:09	Willie Simms	John E. Madden	Lieber Karl	Isabey
1899	**Manuel** (2)	2:12	Fred Taral	Robert Walden	Corsini	Mazo
1900	**Lieut. Gibson** (4)	2:06¼	Jimmy Boland	Charles Hughes	Florizar	Thrive
1901	**His Eminence** (2)	2:07¾	Jimmy Winkfield	F.B. Van Meter	Sannazarro	Driscoll
1902	**Alan-a-Dale** (ns)	2:08¾	Jimmy Winkfield	T.C. McDowell	Inventor	The Rival
1903	**Judge Himes** (¾)	2:09	Hal Booker	J.P. Mayberry	Early	Bourbon
1904	**Elwood** (½)	2:08½	Shorty Prior	C.E. Durnell	Ed Tierney	Brancas
1905	**Agile** (3)	2:10¾	Jack Martin	Robert Tucker	Ram's Horn	Layson
1906	**Sir Huon** (2)	2:08⅘	Roscoe Troxler	Pete Coyne	Lady Navarre	James Reddick
1907	**Pink Star** (2)	2:12⅗	Andy Minder	W.H. Fizer	Zal	Ovelando
1908	**Stone Street** (1)	2:15⅕	Arthur Pickens	J.W. Hall	Sir Cleges	Dunvegan
1909	**Wintergreen** (4)	2:08⅕	Vincent Powers	Charles Mack	Miami	Dr. Barkley

Year	Winner (Margin)	Time	Jockey	Trainer	2nd place	3rd place
1910	**Donau** (½)	2:06⅖	Fred Herbert	George Ham	Joe Morris	Fighting Bob
1911	**Meridian** (¾)	2:05	George Archibald	Albert Ewing	Governor Gray	Colston
1912	**Worth** (nk)	2:09⅖	C.H. Shilling	Frank Taylor	Duval	Flamma
1913	**Donerail** (½)	2:04⅘	Roscoe Goose	Thomas Hayes	Ten Point	Gowell
1914	**Old Rosebud** (8)	2:03⅖	John McCabe	F.D. Weir	Hodge	Bronzewing
1915	**Regret** (2)	2:05⅖	Joe Notter	James Rowe Sr.	Pebbles	Sharpshooter
1916	**George Smith** (nk)	2:04	Johnny Loftus	Hollie Hughes	Star Hawk	Franklin
1917	**Omar Khayyam** (2)	2:04⅗	Charles Borel	C.T. Patterson	Ticket	Midway
1918	**Exterminator** (1)	2:10⅘	William Knapp	Henry McDaniel	Escoba	Viva America
1919	**SIR BARTON** (5)	2:09⅘	Johnny Loftus	H. Guy Bedwell	Billy Kelly	Under Fire
1920	**Paul Jones** (hd)	2:09	Ted Rice	Billy Garth	Upset	On Watch
1921	**Behave Yourself** (hd)	2:04⅕	Charles Thompson	Dick Thompson	Black Servant	Prudery
1922	**Morvich** (1½)	2:04⅗	Albert Johnson	Fred Burlew	Bet Mosie	John Finn
1923	**Zev** (1½)	2:05⅖	Earl Sande	David Leary	Martingale	Vigil
1924	**Black Gold** (½)	2:05⅕	John Mooney	Hanly Webb	Chilhowee	Beau Butler
1925	**Flying Ebony** (1½)	2:07⅗	Earl Sande	William Duke	Captain Hal	Son of John
1926	**Bubbling Over** (5)	2:03⅘	Albert Johnson	Dick Thompson	Bagenbaggage	Rock Man
1927	**Whiskery** (hd)	2:06	Linus McAtee	Fred Hopkins	Osmand	Jock
1928	**Reigh Count** (3)	2:10⅖	Chick Lang	Bert Michell	Misstep	Toro
1929	**Clyde Van Dusen** (2)	2:10⅘	Linus McAtee	Clyde Van Dusen	Naishapur	Panchio
1930	**GALLANT FOX** (2)	2:07⅗	Earl Sande	Jim Fitzsimmons	Gallant Knight	Ned O.
1931	**Twenty Grand** (4)	2:01⅘	Charley Kurtsinger	James Rowe Jr.	Sweep All	Mate
1932	**Burgoo King** (5)	2:05⅕	Eugene James	Dick Thompson	Economic	Stepenfetchit
1933	**Brokers Tip** (ns)	2:06⅘	Don Meade	Dick Thompson	Head Play	Charley O.
1934	**Cavalcade** (2½)	2:04	Mack Garner	Bob Smith	Discovery	Agrarian
1935	**OMAHA** (1½)	2:05	Willie Saunders	Jim Fitzsimmons	Roman Soldier	Whiskolo
1936	**Bold Venture** (hd)	2:03⅗	Ira Hanford	Max Hirsch	Brevity	Indian Broom
1937	**WAR ADMIRAL** (1¾)	2:03⅕	Charley Kurtsinger	George Conway	Pompoon	Reaping Reward
1938	**Lawrin** (1)	2:04⅘	Eddie Arcaro	Ben Jones	Dauber	Can't Wait
1939	**Johnstown** (8)	2:03⅖	James Stout	Jim Fitzsimmons	Challedon	Heather Broom
1940	**Gallahadion** (1½)	2:05	Carroll Bierman	Roy Waldron	Bimelech	Dit
1941	**WHIRLAWAY** (8)	2:01⅖	Eddie Arcaro	Ben Jones	Staretor	Market Wise
1942	**Shut Out** (2½)	2:04⅖	Wayne Wright	John Gaver	Alsab	Valdina Orphan
1943	**COUNT FLEET** (3)	2:04	Johnny Longden	Don Cameron	Blue Swords	Slide Rule
1944	**Pensive** (4½)	2:04⅕	Conn McCreary	Ben Jones	Broadcloth	Stir Up
1945	**Hoop Jr** (6)	2:07	Eddie Arcaro	Ivan Parke	Pot O'Luck	Darby Dieppe
1946	**ASSAULT** (8)	2:06⅗	Warren Mehrtens	Max Hirsch	Spy Song	Hampden
1947	**Jet Pilot** (hd)	2:06⅘	Eric Guerin	Tom Smith	Phalanx	Faultless
1948	**CITATION** (3½)	2:05⅖	Eddie Arcaro	Ben Jones	Coaltown	My Request
1949	**Ponder** (3)	2:04⅕	Steve Brooks	Ben Jones	Capot	Palestinian
1950	**Middleground** (1¼)	2:01⅗	William Boland	Max Hirsch	Hill Prince	Mr. Trouble
1951	**Count Turf** (4)	2:02⅗	Conn McCreary	Sol Rutchick	Royal Mustang	Ruhe
1952	**Hill Gail** (2)	2:01⅗	Eddie Arcaro	Ben Jones	Sub Fleet	Blue Man
1953	**Dark Star** (hd)	2:02	Hank Moreno	Eddie Hayward	Native Dancer	Invigorator
1954	**Determine** (1½)	2:03	Raymond York	Willie Molter	Hasty Road	Hasseyampa
1955	**Swaps** (1½)	2:01⅘	Bill Shoemaker	Mesh Tenney	Nashua	Summer Tan
1956	**Needles** (¾)	2:03⅖	David Erb	Hugh Fontaine	Fabius	Come On Red
1957	**Iron Liege** (ns)	2:02⅕	Bill Hartack	Jimmy Jones	Gallant Man	Round Table
1958	**Tim Tam** (½)	2:05	Ismael Valenzuela	Jimmy Jones	Lincoln Road	Noureddin
1959	**Tomy Lee** (ns)	2:02⅕	Bill Shoemaker	Frank Childs	Sword Dancer	First Landing
1960	**Venetian Way** (3½)	2:02⅖	Bill Hartack	Victor Sovinski	Bally Ache	Victoria Park
1961	**Carry Back** (¾)	2:04	John Sellers	Jack Price	Crozier	Bass Clef
1962	**Decidedly** (2¼)	2:00⅖	Bill Hartack	Horatio Luro	Roman Line	Ridan
1963	**Chateaugay** (1¼)	2:01⅘	Braulio Baeza	James Conway	Never Bend	Candy Spots
1964	**Northern Dancer** (nk)	2:00	Bill Hartack	Horatio Luro	Hill Rise	The Scoundrel
1965	**Lucky Debonair** (nk)	2:01⅕	Bill Shoemaker	Frank Catrone	Dapper Dan	Tom Rolfe
1966	**Kauai King** (½)	2:02	Don Brumfield	Henry Forrest	Advocator	Blue Skyer
1967	**Proud Clarion** (1)	2:00⅗	Bobby Ussery	Loyd Gentry	Barbs Delight	Damascus
1968	**Forward Pass*** (nk)	—	Ismael Valenzuela	Henry Forrest	Francie's Hat	T.V. Commercial
1969	**Majestic Prince** (nk)	2:01⅘	Bill Hartack	Johnny Longden	Arts and Letters	Dike
1970	**Dust Commander** (5)	2:03⅖	Mike Manganello	Don Combs	My Dad George	High Echelon
1971	**Canonero II** (3¼)	2:03⅕	Gustavo Avila	Juan Arias	Jim French	Bold Reason
1972	**Riva Ridge** (3¼)	2:01⅘	Ron Turcotte	Lucien Laurin	No Le Hace	Hold Your Peace
1973	**SECRETARIAT** (2½)	1:59⅖	Ron Turcotte	Lucien Laurin	Sham	Our Native
1974	**Cannonade** (2¼)	2:04	Angel Cordero Jr.	Woody Stephens	Hudson County	Agitate
1975	**Foolish Pleasure** (1¾)	2:02	Jacinto Vasquez	LeRoy Jolley	Avatar	Diabolo
1976	**Bold Forbes** (1)	2:01⅗	Angel Cordero Jr.	Laz Barrera	Honest Pleasure	Elocutionist
1977	**SEATTLE SLEW** (1¾)	2:02⅕	Jean Cruguet	Billy Turner	Run Dusty Run	Sanhedrin
1978	**AFFIRMED** (1½)	2:01⅕	Steve Cauthen	Laz Barrera	Alydar	Believe It

Kentucky Derby (Cont.)

Year	Winner (Margin)	Time	Jockey	Trainer	2nd place	3rd place
1979	**Spectacular Bid** (2¾)	2:02⅖	Ron Franklin	Bud Delp	General Assembly	Golden Act
1980	**Genuine Risk** (1)	2:02	Jacinto Vasquez	LeRoy Jolley	Rumbo	Jaklin Klugman
1981	**Pleasant Colony** (¾)	2:02	Jorge Velasquez	John Campo	Woodchopper	Partez
1982	**Gato Del Sol** (2½)	2:02⅖	E. Delahoussaye	Eddie Gregson	Laser Light	Reinvested
1983	**Sunny's Halo** (2)	2:02⅕	E. Delahoussaye	David Cross Jr.	Desert Wine	Caveat
1984	**Swale** (3¼)	2:02⅖	Laffit Pincay Jr.	Woody Stephens	Coax Me Chad	At The Threshold
1985	**Spend A Buck** (5¼)	2:00⅕	Angel Cordero Jr.	Cam Gambolati	Stephan's Odyssey	Chief's Crown
1986	**Ferdinand** (2¼)	2:02⅘	Bill Shoemaker	Chas. Whittingham	Bold Arrangement	Broad Brush
1987	**Alysheba** (¾)	2:03⅖	Chris McCarron	Jack Van Berg	Bet Twice	Avies Copy
1988	**Winning Colors** (nk)	2:02⅕	Gary Stevens	D. Wayne Lukas	Forty Niner	Risen Star
1989	**Sunday Silence** (2½)	2:05	Pat Valenzuela	Chas. Whittingham	Easy Goer	Awe Inspiring
1990	**Unbridled** (3½)	2:02	Craig Perret	Carl Nafzger	Summer Squall	Pleasant Tap
1991	**Strike the Gold** (1¾)	2:03	Chris Antley	Nick Zito	Best Pal	Mane Minister
1992	**Lil E. Tee** (1)	2:03	Pat Day	Lynn Whiting	Casual Lies	Dance Floor
1993	**Sea Hero** (2½)	2:02⅖	Jerry Bailey	Mack Miller	Prairie Bayou	Wild Gale
1994	**Go For Gin** (2)	2:03⅗	Chris McCarron	Nick Zito	Strodes Creek	Blumin Affair
1995	**Thunder Gulch** (2¼)	2:01⅕	Gary Stevens	D. Wayne Lukas	Tejano Run	Timber Country
1996	**Grindstone** (ns)	2:01	Jerry Bailey	D. Wayne Lukas	Cavonnier	Prince of Thieves
1997	**Silver Charm** (hd)	2:02⅖	Gary Stevens	Bob Baffert	Captain Bodgit	Free House
1998	**Real Quiet** (½)	2:02⅕	Kent Desormeaux	Bob Baffert	Victory Gallop	Indian Charlie
1999	**Charismatic** (nk)	2:03⅕	Chris Antley	D. Wayne Lukas	Menifee	Cat Thief
2000	**Fusaichi Pegasus** (1½)	2:01⅕	Kent Desormeaux	Neil Drysdale	Aptitude	Impeachment
2001	**Monarchos** (4¾)	1:59⅘	Jorge Chavez	John Ward Jr.	Invisible Ink	Congaree

*Dancer's Image finished first (in 2:02⅕), but was disqualified after traces of prohibited medication were found in his system.

Preakness Stakes

For three-year-olds. Held two weeks after the Kentucky Derby at Pimlico Race Course in Baltimore. Inaugurated 1873. Note that the 1918 race was held over two divisions. Originally run at 1½ miles (1873-88), then at 1¼ miles (1889), 1½ miles (1890), 1 1/16 miles (1894-1900), 1 mile & 70 yards (1901-07), 1 1/16 miles (1908), 1 mile (1909-1910), 1⅛ miles (1911-24), and the present 1 3/16 miles since 1925.

Trainers with most wins: Robert W. Walden (7); T.J. Healey and D. Wayne Lukas (5); Sunny Jim Fitzsimmons and Jimmy Jones (4); Bob Baffert and J. Whalen (3).

Jockeys with most wins: Eddie Arcaro (6); Pat Day (5); G. Barbee, Bill Hartack and Lloyd Hughes (3).

Winning fillies: Flocarline (1903), Whimsical (1906), Rhine Maiden (1915) and Nellie Morse (1924).

Year	Winner (Margin)	Time	Jockey	Trainer	2nd place	3rd place
1873	**Survivor** (10)	2:43	G. Barbee	A.D. Pryor	John Boulger	Artist
1874	**Culpepper** (¾)	2:56½	W. Donohue	H. Gaffney	King Amadeus	Scratch
1875	**Tom Ochiltree** (2)	2:43½	L. Hughes	R.W. Walden	Viator	Bay Final
1876	**Shirley** (4)	2:44¾	G. Barbee	W. Brown	Rappahannock	Compliment
1877	**Cloverbrook** (2)	2:45½	C. Holloway	J. Walden	Bombast	Lucifer
1878	**Duke of Magenta** (2)	2:41¾	C. Holloway	R.W. Walden	Bayard	Albert
1879	**Harold** (1)	2:40½	L. Hughes	R.W. Walden	Jericho	Rochester
1880	**Grenada** (¾)	2:40½	L. Hughes	R.W. Walden	Oden	Emily F.
1881	**Saunterer** (½)	2:40½	T. Costello	R.W. Walden	Compensation	Baltic
1882	**Vanguard** (nk)	2:44½	T. Costello	R.W. Walden	Heck	Col. Watson
1883	**Jacobus** (4)	2:42½	G. Barbee	R. Dwyer	Parnell	(2-horse race)
1884	**Knight of Ellerslie** (2)	2:39½	S. Fisher	T.B. Doswell	Welcher	(2-horse race)
1885	**Tecumseh** (2)	2:49	Jim McLaughlin	C. Littlefield	Wickham	John C.
1886	**The Bard** (3)	2:45	S. Fisher	J. Huggins	Eurus	Elkwood
1887	**Dunboyne** (1)	2:39½	W. Donohue	W. Jennings	Mahoney	Raymond
1888	**Refund** (3)	2:49	F. Littlefield	R.W. Walden	Bertha B.*	Glendale
1889	**Buddhist** (8)	2:17½	W. Anderson	J. Rogers	Japhet	(2-horse race)
1890	**Montague** (3)	2:36¾	W. Martin	E. Feakes	Philosophy	Barrister
1891-93	Not held					
1894	**Assignee** (3)	1:49¼	F. Taral	W. Lakeland	Potentate	Ed Kearney
1895	**Belmar** (1)	1:50½	F. Taral	E. Feakes	April Fool	Sue Kittie
1896	**Margrave** (1)	1:51	H. Griffin	Byron McClelland	Hamilton II	Intermission
1897	**Paul Kauvar** (1½)	1:51¼	T. Thorpe	T.P. Hayes	Elkins	On Deck
1898	**Sly Fox** (2)	1:49¾	W. Simms	H. Campbell	The Huguenot	Nuto
1899	**Half Time** (1)	1:47	R. Clawson	F. McCabe	Filigrane	Lackland
1900	**Hindus** (hd)	1:48⅖	H. Spencer	J.H. Morris	Sarmatian	Ten Candles
1901	**The Parader** (2)	1:47⅕	F. Landry	T.J. Healey	Sadie S.	Dr. Barlow
1902	**Old England** (ns)	1:45⅘	L. Jackson	G.B. Morris	Maj. Daingerfield	Namtor
1903	**Flocarline** (½)	1:44⅘	W. Gannon	H.C. Riddle	Mackey Dwyer	Rightful
1904	**Bryn Mawr** (1)	1:44⅕	E. Hildebrand	W.F. Presgrave	Wotan	Dolly Spanker
1905	**Cairngorm** (hd)	1:45⅘	W. Davis	A.J. Joyner	Kiamesha	Coy Maid
1906	**Whimsical** (4)	1:45	Walter Miller	T.J. Gaynor	Content	Larabie

Year	Winner (Margin)	Time	Jockey	Trainer	2nd place	3rd place
1907	**Don Enrique** (1)	1:45⅖	G. Mountain	J. Whalen	Ethon	Zambesi
1908	**Royal Tourist** (4)	1:46⅖	Eddie Dugan	A.J. Joyner	Live Wire	Robert Cooper
1909	**Effendi** (1)	1:39⅘	Willie Doyle	F.C. Frisbie	Fashion Plate	Hill Top
1910	**Layminster** (½)	1:40⅗	R. Estep	J.S. Healy	Dalhousie	Sager
1911	**Watervale** (1)	1:51	Eddie Dugan	J. Whalen	Zeus	The Nigger
1912	**Colonel Holloway** (5)	1:56⅗	C. Turner	D. Woodford	Bwana Tumbo	Tipsand
1913	**Buskin** (nk)	1:53⅖	James Butwell	J. Whalen	Kleburne	Barnegat
1914	**Holiday** (¾)	1:53⅘	A. Schuttinger	J.S. Healy	Brave Cunarder	Defendum
1915	**Rhine Maiden** (1½)	1:58	Douglas Hoffman	F. Devers	Half Rock	Runes
1916	**Damrosch** (1½)	1:54⅘	Linus McAtee	A.G. Weston	Greenwood	Achievement
1917	**Kalitan** (2)	1:54⅖	E. Haynes	Bill Hurley	Al M. Dick	Kentucky Boy
1918	**War Cloud** (¾)	1:53⅗	Johnny Loftus	W.B. Jennings	Sunny Slope	Lanius
1918	**Jack Hare Jr** (2)	1:53⅖	Charles Peak	F.D. Weir	The Porter	Kate Bright
1919	**SIR BARTON** (4)	1:53	Johnny Loftus	H. Guy Bedwell	Eternal	Sweep On
1920	**Man o' War** (1½)	1:51⅗	Clarence Kummer	L. Feustel	Upset	Wildair
1921	**Broomspun** (¾)	1:54⅕	F. Coltiletti	James Rowe Sr.	Polly Ann	Jeg
1922	**Pillory** (hd)	1:51⅗	L. Morris	Thomas Healey	Hea	June Grass
1923	**Vigil** (1¼)	1:53⅗	B. Marinelli	Thomas Healey	General Thatcher	Rialto
1924	**Nellie Morse** (1½)	1:57⅕	John Merimee	A.B. Gordon	Transmute	Mad Play
1925	**Coventry** (4)	1:59	Clarence Kummer	William Duke	Backbone	Almadel
1926	**Display** (hd)	1:59⅘	John Maiben	Thomas Healey	Blondin	Mars
1927	**Bostonian** (½)	2:01⅗	Whitey Abel	Fred Hopkins	Sir Harry	Whiskery
1928	**Victorian** (ns)	2:00⅕	Sonny Workman	James Rowe Jr.	Toro	Solace
1929	**Dr. Freeland** (1)	2:01⅗	Louis Schaefer	Thomas Healey	Minotaur	African
1930	**GALLANT FOX** (¾)	2:00⅗	Earl Sande	Jim Fitzsimmons	Crack Brigade	Snowflake
1931	**Mate** (1½)	1:59	George Ellis	J.W. Healy	Twenty Grand	Ladder
1932	**Burgoo King** (hd)	1:59⅘	Eugene James	Dick Thompson	Tick On	Boatswain
1933	**Head Play** (4)	2:02	Charley Kurtsinger	Thomas Hayes	Ladysman	Utopian
1934	**High Quest** (ns)	1:58⅕	Robert Jones	Bob Smith	Cavalcade	Discovery
1935	**OMAHA** (6)	1:58⅖	Willie Saunders	Jim Fitzsimmons	Firethorn	Psychic Bid
1936	**Bold Venture** (ns)	1:59	George Woolf	Max Hirsch	Granville	Jean Bart
1937	**WAR ADMIRAL** (hd)	1:58⅖	Charley Kurtsinger	George Conway	Pompoon	Flying Scot
1938	**Dauber** (7)	1:59⅘	Maurice Peters	Dick Handlen	Cravat	Menow
1939	**Challedon** (1¼)	1:59⅘	George Seabo	Louis Schaefer	Gilded Knight	Volitant
1940	**Bimelech** (3)	1:58⅗	F.A. Smith	Bill Hurley	Mioland	Gallahadion
1941	**WHIRLAWAY** (5½)	1:58⅘	Eddie Arcaro	Ben Jones	King Cole	Our Boots
1942	**Alsab** (1)	1:57	Basil James	Sarge Swenke	Requested & Sun Again (dead heat)	
1943	**COUNT FLEET** (8)	1:57⅖	Johnny Longden	Don Cameron	Blue Swords	Vincentive
1944	**Pensive** (¾)	1:59⅕	Conn McCreary	Ben Jones	Platter	Stir Up
1945	**Polynesian** (2½)	1:58⅘	W.D. Wright	Morris Dixon	Hoop Jr.	Darby Dieppe
1946	**ASSAULT** (nk)	2:01⅖	Warren Mehrtens	Max Hirsch	Lord Boswell	Hampden
1947	**Faultless** (1¼)	1:59	Doug Dodson	Jimmy Jones	On Trust	Phalanx
1948	**CITATION** (5½)	2:02⅖	Eddie Arcaro	Jimmy Jones	Vulcan's Forge	Bovard
1949	**Capot** (hd)	1:56	Ted Atkinson	J.M. Gaver	Palestinian	Noble Impulse
1950	**Hill Prince** (5)	1:59⅕	Eddie Arcaro	Casey Hayes	Middleground	Dooly
1951	**Bold** (7)	1:56⅖	Eddie Arcaro	Preston Burch	Counterpoint	Alerted
1952	**Blue Man** (3½)	1:57⅖	Conn McCreary	Woody Stephens	Jampol	One Count
1953	**Native Dancer** (nk)	1:57⅘	Eric Guerin	Bill Winfrey	Jamie K.	Royal Bay Gem
1954	**Hasty Road** (nk)	1:57⅖	Johnny Adams	Harry Trotsek	Correlation	Hasseyampa
1955	**Nashua** (1)	1:54⅗	Eddie Arcaro	Jim Fitzsimmons	Saratoga	Traffic Judge
1956	**Fabius** (¾)	1:58⅖	Bill Hartack	Jimmy Jones	Needles	No Regrets
1957	**Bold Ruler** (2)	1:56⅕	Eddie Arcaro	Jim Fitzsimmons	Iron Liege	Inside Tract
1958	**Tim Tam** (1½)	1:57⅕	Ismael Valenzuela	Jimmy Jones	Lincoln Road	Gone Fishin'
1959	**Royal Orbit** (4)	1:57	William Harmatz	R. Cornell	Sword Dancer	Dunce
1960	**Bally Ache** (4)	1:57⅗	Bobby Ussery	Jimmy Pitt	Victoria Park	Celtic Ash
1961	**Carry Back** (¾)	1:57⅗	Johnny Sellers	Jack Price	Globemaster	Crozier
1962	**Greek Money** (ns)	1:56⅕	John Rotz	V.W. Raines	Ridan	Roman Line
1963	**Candy Spots** (3½)	1:56⅕	Bill Shoemaker	Mesh Tenney	Chateaugay	Never Bend
1964	**Northern Dancer** (2¼)	1:56⅘	Bill Hartack	Horatio Luro	The Scoundrel	Hill Rise
1965	**Tom Rolfe** (nk)	1:56⅕	Ron Turcotte	Frank Whiteley	Dapper Dan	Hail To All
1966	**Kauai King** (1¾)	1:55⅖	Don Brumfield	Henry Forrest	Stupendous	Amberoid
1967	**Damascus** (2¼)	1:55⅕	Bill Shoemaker	Frank Whiteley	In Reality	Proud Clarion
1968	**Forward Pass** (6)	1:56⅘	Ismael Valenzuela	Henry Forrest	Out Of the Way	Nodouble
1969	**Majestic Prince** (hd)	1:55⅗	Bill Hartack	Johnny Longden	Arts and Letters	Jay Ray
1970	**Personality** (nk)	1:56⅕	Eddie Belmonte	John Jacobs	My Dad George	Silent Screen
1971	**Canonero II** (1½)	1:54	Gustavo Avila	Juan Arias	Eastern Fleet	Jim French
1972	**Bee Bee Bee** (1¼)	1:55⅗	Eldon Nelson	Red Carroll	No Le Hace	Key To The Mint
1973	**SECRETARIAT** (2½)	1:54⅖	Ron Turcotte	Lucien Laurin	Sham	Our Native
1974	**Little Current** (7)	1:54⅗	Miguel Rivera	Lou Rondinello	Neapolitan Way	Cannonade

Preakness Stakes (Cont.)

Year	Winner (Margin)	Time	Jockey	Trainer	2nd place	3rd place
1975	**Master Derby** (1)	1:56⅖	Darrel McHargue	Smiley Adams	Foolish Pleasure	Diabolo
1976	**Elocutionist** (3½)	1:55	John Lively	Paul Adwell	Play The Red	Bold Forbes
1977	**SEATTLE SLEW** (1½)	1:54⅖	Jean Cruguet	Billy Turner	Iron Constitution	Run Dusty Run
1978	**AFFIRMED** (nk)	1:54⅖	Steve Cauthen	Laz Barrera	Alydar	Believe It
1979	**Spectacular Bid** (3½)	1:54⅕	Ron Franklin	Bud Delp	Golden Act	Screen King
1980	**Codex** (4¾)	1:54⅕	Angel Cordero Jr.	D. Wayne Lukas	Genuine Risk	Colonel Moran
1981	**Pleasant Colony** (1)	1:54⅗	Jorge Velasquez	John Campo	Bold Ego	Paristo
1982	**Aloma's Ruler** (½)	1:55⅖	Jack Kaenel	John Lenzini Jr.	Linkage	Cut Away
1983	**Deputed Testamony** (2¾)	1:55⅖	Donald Miller Jr.	Bill Boniface	Desert Wine	High Honors
1984	**Gate Dancer** (1½)	1:53⅗	Angel Cordero Jr.	Jack Van Berg	Play On	Fight Over
1985	**Tank's Prospect** (hd)	1:53⅖	Pat Day	D. Wayne Lukas	Chief's Crown	Eternal Prince
1986	**Snow Chief** (4)	1:54⅘	Alex Solis	Melvin Stute	Ferdinand	Broad Brush
1987	**Alysheba** (½)	1:55⅘	Chris McCarron	Jack Van Berg	Bet Twice	Cryptoclearance
1988	**Risen Star** (1¼)	1:56⅕	E. Delahoussaye	Louie Roussel III	Brian's Time	Winning Colors
1989	**Sunday Silence** (ns)	1:53⅘	Pat Valenzuela	Chas. Whittingham	Easy Goer	Rock Point
1990	**Summer Squall** (2¼)	1:53⅗	Pat Day	Neil Howard	Unbridled	Mister Frisky
1991	**Hansel** (7)	1:54	Jerry Bailey	Frank Brothers	Corporate Report	Mane Minister
1992	**Pine Bluff** (¾)	1:55⅗	Chris McCarron	Tom Bohannan	Alydeed	Casual Lies
1993	**Prairie Bayou** (½)	1:56⅗	Mike Smith	Tom Bohannan	Cherokee Run	El Bakan
1994	**Tabasco Cat** (¾)	1:56⅖	Pat Day	D. Wayne Lukas	Go For Gin	Concern
1995	**Timber Country** (½)	1:54⅖	Pat Day	D. Wayne Lukas	Oliver's Twist	Thunder Gulch
1996	**Louis Quatorze** (3¼)	1:53⅖	Pat Day	Nick Zito	Skip Away	Editor's Note
1997	**Silver Charm** (hd)	1:54⅖	Gary Stevens	Bob Baffert	Free House	Captain Bodgit
1998	**Real Quiet** (2¼)	1:54⅘	Kent Desormeaux	Bob Baffert	Victory Gallop	Classic Cat
1999	**Charismatic** (1½)	1:55⅕	Chris Antley	D. Wayne Lukas	Menifee	Badge
2000	**Red Bullet** (3¾)	1:56	Jerry Bailey	Joe Orseno	Fusaichi Pegasus	Impeachment
2001	**Point Given** (2¼)	1:55⅖	Gary Stevens	Bob Baffert	A P Valentine	Congaree

* Later named Judge Murray.

Belmont Stakes

For three-year-olds. Held three weeks after Preakness Stakes at Belmont Park in Elmont, N.Y. Inaugurated in 1867 at Jerome Park, moved to Morris Park in 1890 and then to Belmont Park in 1905.

Originally run at 1 mile and 5 furlongs (1867-89), then 1¼ miles (1890-1905), 1⅜ miles (1906-25), and the present 1½ miles since 1926.

Trainers with most wins: James Rowe Sr. (8); Sam Hildreth (7); Sunny Jim Fitzsimmons (6); Woody Stephens (5); Max Hirsch, D. Wayne Lukas and Robert W. Walden (4); Elliott Burch, Lucien Laurin, F. McCabe and D. McDaniel (3).

Jockeys with most wins: Eddie Arcaro and Jim McLaughlin (6); Earl Sande and Bill Shoemaker (5); Braulio Baeza, Pat Day, Laffit Pincay Jr., Gary Stevens and James Stout (4).

Winning fillies: Ruthless (1867) and Tanya (1905).

Year	Winner (Margin)	Time	Jockey	Trainer	2nd place	3rd place
1867	**Ruthless** (½)	3:05	J. Gilpatrick	A.J. Minor	DeCourcey	Rivoli
1868	**General Duke** (2)	3:02	Bobby Swim	A. Thompson	Northumberland	Fanny Ludlow
1869	**Fenian** (6)	3:04¼	C. Miller	J. Pincus	Glenelg	Invercauld
1870	**Kingfisher** (nk)	2:59½	W. Dick	R. Colston	Foster	Midday
1871	**Harry Bassett** (3)	2:56	W. Miller	D. McDaniel	Stockwood	By the Sea
1872	**Joe Daniels** (¾)	2:58¼	James Roe	D. McDaniel	Meteor	Shylock
1873	**Springbok** (¾)	3:01¾	James Roe	D. McDaniel	Count d'Orsay	Strachino
1874	**Saxon** (nk)	2:39½	G. Barbee	W. Prior	Grinstead	Aaron Pennington
1875	**Calvin** (2)	2:42¼	Bobby Swim	A. Williams	Aristides	Milner
1876	**Algerine** (½)	2:40½	Billy Donohue	Major Doswell	Fiddlesticks	Barricade
1877	**Cloverbrook** (1)	2:46	C. Holloway	J. Walden	Loiterer	Baden-Baden
1878	**Duke of Magenta** (2)	2:43½	L. Hughes	R.W. Walden	Bramble	Sparta
1879	**Spendthrift** (6)	2:42¾	George Evans	T. Puryear	Monitor	Jericho
1880	**Grenada** (nk)	2:47	L. Hughes	R.W. Walden	Ferncliffe	Turenne
1881	**Saunterer** (nk)	2:47	T. Costello	R.W. Walden	Eole	Baltic
1882	**Forester** (5)	2:43	Jim McLaughlin	L. Stuart	Babcock	Wyoming
1883	**George Kinney** (3)	2:42½	Jim McLaughlin	James Rowe Sr.	Trombone	Renegade
1884	**Panique** (nk)	2:42	Jim McLaughlin	James Rowe Sr.	Knight of Ellerslie	Himalaya
1885	**Tyrant** (3)	2:43	Paul Duffy	W. Claypool	St. Augustine	Tecumseh
1886	**Inspector B** (1)	2:41	Jim McLaughlin	F. McCabe	The Bard	Linden
1887	**Hanover** (15)	2:43½	Jim McLaughlin	F. McCabe	Oneko	(2-horse race)
1888	**Sir Dixon** (15)	2:40¼	Jim McLaughlin	F. McCabe	Prince Royal	(2-horse race)
1889	**Eric** (½)	2:47¼	W. Hayward	J. Huggins	Diablo	Zephyrus
1890	**Burlington** (2)	2:07¾	Pike Barnes	A. Cooper	Devotee	Padishah
1891	**Foxford** (nk)	2:08¾	Ed Garrison	M. Donavan	Montana	Laurestan
1892	**Patron** (6)	2:12	W. Hayward	L. Stuart	Shellbark	(2-horse race)

Year	Winner (Margin)	Time	Jockey	Trainer	2nd place	3rd place
1893	**Commanche** (hd)	1:53¼	Willie Simms	G. Hannon	Dr. Rice	Rainbow
1894	**Henry of Navarre** (1½)	1:56½	Willie Simms	B. McClelland	Prig	Assignee
1895	**Belmar** (hd)	2:11½	Fred Taral	E. Feakes	Counter Tenor	Nanki Poo
1896	**Hastings** (hd)	2:24½	H. Griffin	J.J. Hyland	Handspring	Hamilton II
1897	**Scottish Chieftain** (1)	2:23¼	J. Scherrer	M. Byrnes	On Deck	Octagon
1898	**Bowling Brook** (6)	2:32	F. Littlefield	R.W. Walden	Previous	Hamburg
1899	**Jean Beraud** (hd)	2:23	R. Clawson	Sam Hildreth	Half Time	Glengar
1900	**Ildrim** (ns)	2:21¼	Nash Turner	H.E. Leigh	Petruchio	Missionary
1901	**Commando** (2)	2:21	H. Spencer	James Rowe Sr.	The Parader	All Green
1902	**Masterman** (2)	2:22⅗	John Bullman	J.J. Hyland	Renald	King Hanover
1903	**Africander** (2)	2:21¾	John Bullman	R. Miller	Whorler	Red Knight
1904	**Delhi** (4)	2:06⅗	George Odom	James Rowe Sr.	Graziallo	Rapid Water
1905	**Tanya** (½)	2:08	E. Hildebrand	J.W. Rogers	Blandy	Hot Shot
1906	**Burgomaster** (4)	2:20	Lucien Lyne	J.W. Rogers	The Quail	Accountant
1907	**Peter Pan** (1)	N/A	G. Mountain	James Rowe Sr.	Superman	Frank Gill
1908	**Colin** (hd)	N/A	Joe Notter	James Rowe Sr.	Fair Play	King James
1909	**Joe Madden** (8)	2:21⅗	E. Dugan	Sam Hildreth	Wise Mason	Donald MacDonald
1910	**Sweep** (6)	2:22	James Butwell	James Rowe Sr.	Duke of Ormonde	(2-horse race)
1911-12	Not held					
1913	**Prince Eugene** (½)	2:18	Roscoe Troxler	James Rowe Sr.	Rock View	Flying Fairy
1914	**Luke McLuke** (8)	2:20	Merritt Buxton	J.F. Schorr	Gainer	Charlestonian
1915	**The Finn** (4)	2:18⅖	George Byrne	E.W. Heffner	Half Rock	Pebbles
1916	**Friar Rock** (3)	2:22	E. Haynes	Sam Hildreth	Spur	Churchill
1917	**Hourless** (10)	2:17⅘	James Butwell	Sam Hildreth	Skeptic	Wonderful
1918	**Johren** (2)	2:20⅖	Frank Robinson	A. Simons	War Cloud	Cum Sah
1919	**SIR BARTON** (5)	2:17⅖	John Loftus	H. Guy Bedwell	Sweep On	Natural Bridge
1920	**Man o' War** (20)	2:14⅕	Clarence Kummer	L. Feustel	Donnacona	(2-horse race)
1921	**Grey Lag** (3)	2:16⅘	Earl Sande	Sam Hildreth	Sporting Blood	Leonardo II
1922	**Pillory** (2)	2:18⅘	C.H. Miller	T.J. Healey	Snob II	Hea
1923	**Zev** (1½)	2:19	Earl Sande	Sam Hildreth	Chickvale	Rialto
1924	**Mad Play** (2)	2:18⅘	Earl Sande	Sam Hildreth	Mr. Mutt	Modest
1925	**American Flag** (8)	2:16⅘	Albert Johnson	G.R. Tompkins	Dangerous	Swope
1926	**Crusader** (1)	2:32⅕	Albert Johnson	George Conway	Espino	Haste
1927	**Chance Shot** (1½)	2:32⅖	Earl Sande	Pete Coyne	Bois de Rose	Flambino
1928	**Vito** (3)	2:33⅕	Clarence Kummer	Max Hirsch	Genie	Diavolo
1929	**Blue Larkspur** (¾)	2:32⅘	Mack Garner	C. Hastings	African	Jack High
1930	**GALLANT FOX** (3)	2:31⅗	Earl Sande	Jim Fitzsimmons	Whichone	Questionnaire
1931	**Twenty Grand** (10)	2:29⅗	Charley Kurtsinger	James Rowe Jr.	Sun Meadow	Jamestown
1932	**Faireno** (1½)	2:32⅘	Tom Malley	Jim Fitzsimmons	Osculator	Flag Pole
1933	**Hurryoff** (1½)	2:32⅗	Mack Garner	H. McDaniel	Nimbus	Union
1934	**Peace Chance** (6)	2:29⅕	W.D. Wright	Pete Coyne	High Quest	Good Goods
1935	**OMAHA** (1½)	2:30⅗	Willie Saunders	Jim Fitzsimmons	Firethorn	Rosemont
1936	**Granville** (ns)	2:30	James Stout	Jim Fitzsimmons	Mr. Bones	Hollyrood
1937	**WAR ADMIRAL** (3)	2:28⅗	Charley Kurtsinger	George Conway	Sceneshifter	Vamoose
1938	**Pasteurized** (nk)	2:29⅖	James Stout	George Odom	Dauber	Cravat
1939	**Johnstown** (5)	2:29⅗	James Stout	Jim Fitzsimmons	Belay	Gilded Knight
1940	**Bimelech** (¾)	2:29⅗	Fred Smith	Bill Hurley	Your Chance	Andy K.
1941	**WHIRLAWAY** (2½)	2:31	Eddie Arcaro	Ben Jones	Robert Morris	Yankee Chance
1942	**Shut Out** (2)	2:29⅕	Eddie Arcaro	John Gaver	Alsab	Lochinvar
1943	**COUNT FLEET** (25)	2:28⅕	Johnny Longden	Don Cameron	Fairy Manhurst	Deseronto
1944	**Bounding Home** (½)	2:32⅕	G.L. Smith	Matt Brady	Pensive	Bull Dandy
1945	**Pavot** (5)	2:30⅕	Eddie Arcaro	Oscar White	Wildlife	Jeep
1946	**ASSAULT** (3)	2:30⅘	Warren Mehrtens	Max Hirsch	Natchez	Cable
1947	**Phalanx** (5)	2:29⅖	R. Donoso	Syl Veitch	Tide Rips	Tailspin
1948	**CITATION** (8)	2:28⅕	Eddie Arcaro	Jimmy Jones	Better Self	Escadru
1949	**Capot** (½)	2:30⅕	Ted Atkinson	John Gaver	Ponder	Palestinian
1950	**Middleground** (1)	2:28⅗	William Boland	Max Hirsch	Lights Up	Mr. Trouble
1951	**Counterpoint** (4)	2:29	David Gorman	Syl Veitch	Battlefield	Battle Morn
1952	**One Count** (2½)	2:30⅕	Eddie Arcaro	Oscar White	Blue Man	Armageddon
1953	**Native Dancer** (nk)	2:28⅗	Eric Guerin	Bill Winfrey	Jamie K.	Royal Bay Gem
1954	**High Gun** (nk)	2:30⅘	Eric Guerin	Max Hirsch	Fisherman	Limelight
1955	**Nashua** (9)	2:29	Eddie Arcaro	Jim Fitzsimmons	Blazing Count	Portersville
1956	**Needles** (nk)	2:29⅘	David Erb	Hugh Fontaine	Career Boy	Fabius
1957	**Gallant Man** (8)	2:26⅗	Bill Shoemaker	John Nerud	Inside Tract	Bold Ruler
1958	**Cavan** (6)	2:30⅕	Pete Anderson	Tom Barry	Tim Tam	Flamingo
1959	**Sword Dancer** (¾)	2:28⅖	Bill Shoemaker	Elliott Burch	Bagdad	Royal Orbit
1960	**Celtic Ash** (5½)	2:29⅕	Bill Hartack	Tom Barry	Venetian Way	Disperse
1961	**Sherluck** (2¼)	2:29⅕	Braulio Baeza	Harold Young	Globemaster	Guadalcanal
1962	**Jaipur** (ns)	2:28⅘	Bill Shoemaker	B. Mulholland	Admiral's Voyage	Crimson Satan

Belmont Stakes (Cont.)

Year	Winner (Margin)	Time	Jockey	Trainer	2nd place	3rd place
1963	**Chateaugay** (2½)	2:30⅕	Braulio Baeza	James Conway	Candy Spots	Choker
1964	**Quadrangle** (2)	2:28⅖	Manuel Ycaza	Elliott Burch	Roman Brother	Northern Dancer
1965	**Hail to All** (nk)	2:28⅖	John Sellers	Eddie Yowell	Tom Rolfe	First Family
1966	**Amberoid** (2½)	2:29⅗	William Boland	Lucien Laurin	Buffle	Advocator
1967	**Damascus** (2½)	2:28⅘	Bill Shoemaker	F.Y. Whiteley Jr.	Cool Reception	Gentleman James
1968	**Stage Door Johnny** (1¼)	2:27⅕	Gus Gustines	John Gaver	Forward Pass	Call Me Prince
1969	**Arts and Letters** (5½)	2:28⅘	Braulio Baeza	Elliott Burch	Majestic Prince	Dike
1970	**High Echelon** (¾)	2:34	John Rotz	John Jacobs	Needles N Pens	Naskra
1971	**Pass Catcher** (¾)	2:30⅖	Walter Blum	Eddie Yowell	Jim French	Bold Reason
1972	**Riva Ridge** (7)	2:28	Ron Turcotte	Lucien Laurin	Ruritania	Cloudy Dawn
1973	**SECRETARIAT** (31)	2:24	Ron Turcotte	Lucien Laurin	Twice A Prince	My Gallant
1974	**Little Current** (7)	2:29⅕	Miguel Rivera	Lou Rondinello	Jolly Johu	Cannonade
1975	**Avatar** (nk)	2:28⅕	Bill Shoemaker	Tommy Doyle	Foolish Pleasure	Master Derby
1976	**Bold Forbes** (nk)	2:29	Angel Cordero Jr.	Laz Barrera	McKenzie Bridge	Great Contractor
1977	**SEATTLE SLEW** (4)	2:29⅗	Jean Cruguet	Billy Turner	Run Dusty Run	Sanhedrin
1978	**AFFIRMED** (hd)	2:26⅘	Steve Cauthen	Laz Barrera	Alydar	Darby Creek Road
1979	**Coastal** (3¼)	2:28⅗	Ruben Hernandez	David Whiteley	Golden Act	Spectacular Bid
1980	**Temperence Hill** (2)	2:29⅘	Eddie Maple	Joseph Cantey	Genuine Risk	Rockhill Native
1981	**Summing** (nk)	2:29	George Martens	Luis Barerra	Highland Blade	Pleasant Colony
1982	**Conquistador Cielo** (14)	2:28⅕	Laffit Pincay Jr.	Woody Stephens	Gato Del Sol	Illuminate
1983	**Caveat** (3½)	2:27⅘	Laffit Pincay Jr.	Woody Stephens	Slew o' Gold	Barberstown
1984	**Swale** (4)	2:27⅕	Laffit Pincay Jr.	Woody Stephens	Pine Circle	Morning Bob
1985	**Creme Fraiche** (½)	2:27	Eddie Maple	Woody Stephens	Stephan's Odyssey	Chief's Crown
1986	**Danzig Connection** (1¼)	2:29⅘	Chris McCarron	Woody Stephens	Johns Treasure	Ferdinand
1987	**Bet Twice** (14)	2:28⅕	Craig Perret	Jimmy Croll	Cryptoclearance	Gulch
1988	**Risen Star** (14¾)	2:26⅖	E. Delahoussaye	Louie Roussel III	Kingpost	Brian's Time
1989	**Easy Goer** (8)	2:26	Pat Day	Shug McGaughey	Sunday Silence	Le Voyageur
1990	**Go And Go** (8¼)	2:27⅕	Michael Kinane	Dermot Weld	Thirty Six Red	Baron de Vaux
1991	**Hansel** (hd)	2:28	Jerry Bailey	Frank Brothers	Strike the Gold	Mane Minister
1992	**A.P. Indy** (¾)	2:26	E. Delahoussaye	Neil Drysdale	My Memoirs	Pine Bluff
1993	**Colonial Affair** (2)	2:29⅘	Julie Krone	Scotty Schulhofer	Kissin Kris	Wild Gale
1994	**Tabasco Cat** (2)	2:26⅘	Pat Day	D. Wayne Lukas	Go For Gin	Strodes Creek
1995	**Thunder Gulch** (2)	2:32	Gary Stevens	D. Wayne Lukas	Star Standard	Citadeed
1996	**Editor's Note** (1)	2:28⅘	Rene Douglas	D. Wayne Lukas	Skip Away	My Flag
1997	**Touch Gold** (¾)	2:28⅘	Chris McCarron	David Hofmans	Silver Charm	Free House
1998	**Victory Gallop** (ns)	2:29	Gary Stevens	Elliott Walden	Real Quiet	Thomas Jo
1999	**Lemon Drop Kid** (hd)	2:27⅘	Jose Santos	Scotty Schulhofer	Vision and Verse	Charismatic
2000	**Commendable** (1½)	2:31⅕	Pat Day	D. Wayne Lukas	Aptitude	Unshaded
2001	**Point Given** (12¼)	2:26⅖	Gary Stevens	Bob Baffert	A P Valentine	Monarchos

Breeders' Cup Championship

Inaugurated on Nov. 10, 1984, the Breeders' Cup World Thoroughbred Championships consists of eight races on one track on one day late in the year to determine thoroughbred racing's principle champions.

The Breeders' Cup has been held at the following tracks (in alphabetical order): Aqueduct Racetrack (N.Y.) in 1985; Belmont Park (N.Y.) in 1990, '95 and 2001; Churchill Downs (Ky.) in 1988, '91, '94, '98 and 2000; Gulfstream Park (Fla.) in 1989, '92 and '99; Hollywood Park (Calif.) in 1984, '87 and '97; Santa Anita Park (Calif.) in 1986 and '93 and Woodbine (Toronto) in 1996. See Updates chapter for 2001 results.

Trainers with most wins: D. Wayne Lukas (16); Shug McGaughey (7); Neil Drysdale (6); Bill Mott (5); Ron McAnally (4); Francois Boutin and Patrick Byrne (3).

Jockeys with most wins: Jerry Bailey and Pat Day (11); Chris McCarron, Mike Smith and Gary Stevens (8); Eddie Delahoussaye and Laffit Pincay Jr. (7); Jose Santos and Pat Valenzuela (6); Corey Nakatani (5); Angel Cordero Jr. and Craig Perret (4); Randy Romero (3).

Juvenile

Distances: one mile (1984-85, 87); 1 1/16 miles (1986 and since 1988).

Year	Winner (Margin)	Time	Jockey	Trainer	2nd place	3rd place
1984	**Chief's Crown** (¾)	1:36⅕	Don MacBeth	Roger Laurin	Tank's Prospect	Spend A Buck
1985	**Tasso** (ns)	1:36⅕	Laffit Pincay Jr.	Neil Drysdale	Storm Cat	Scat Dancer
1986	**Capote** (1¼)	1:43⅘	Laffit Pincay Jr.	D. Wayne Lukas	Qualify	Alysheba
1987	**Success Express** (1¾)	1:35⅕	Jose Santos	D. Wayne Lukas	Regal Classic	Tejano
1988	**Is It True** (1¼)	1:46⅗	Laffit Pincay Jr.	D. Wayne Lukas	Easy Goer	Tagel
1989	**Rhythm** (2)	1:43⅗	Craig Perret	Shug McGaughey	Grand Canyon	Slavic
1990	**Fly So Free** (3)	1:43⅖	Jose Santos	Scotty Schulhofer	Take Me Out	Lost Mountain
1991	**Arazi** (4¾)	1:44⅗	Pat Valenzuela	Francois Boutin	Bertrando	Snappy Landing
1992	**Gilded Time** (¾)	1:43⅖	Chris McCarron	Darrell Vienna	It'sali'lknownfact	River Special
1993	**Brocco** (5)	1:42⅘	Gary Stevens	Randy Winick	Blumin Affair	Tabasco Cat
1994	**Timber Country** (½)	1:44⅖	Pat Day	D. Wayne Lukas	Eltish	Tejano Run
1995	**Unbridled's Song** (nk)	1:41⅗	Mike Smith	James Ryerson	Hennessy	Editor's Note
1996	**Boston Harbor** (nk)	1:43⅖	Jerry Bailey	D. Wayne Lukas	Acceptable	Ordway

Year	Winner (Margin)	Time	Jockey	Trainer	2nd place	3rd place
1997	**Favorite Trick** (5½)	1:41⅖	Pat Day	Patrick Byrne	Dawson's Legacy	Nationalore
1998	**Answer Lively** (hd)	1:44	Jerry Bailey	Bobby Barnett	Aly's Alley	Cat Thief
1999	**Anees** (2½)	1:42⅕	Gary Stevens	Alex Hassinger Jr.	Chief Seattle	High Yield
2000	**Macho Uno** (ns)	1:42	Jerry Bailey	Joe Orseno	Point Given	Street Cry

Juvenile Fillies

Distances: one mile (1984-85, 87); 1¹⁄₁₆ miles (1986 and since 1988).

Year	Winner (Margin)	Time	Jockey	Trainer	2nd place	3rd place
1984	**Outstandingly***	1:37⅘	Walter Guerra	Pancho Martin	Dusty Heart	Fine Spirit
1985	**Twilight Ridge** (1)	1:35⅘	Jorge Velasquez	D. Wayne Lukas	Family Style	Steal A Kiss
1986	**Brave Raj** (5½)	1:43⅕	Pat Valenzuela	Melvin Stute	Tappiano	Saros Brig
1987	**Epitome** (ns)	1:36⅖	Pat Day	Phil Hauswald	Jeanne Jones	Dream Team
1988	**Open Mind** (1¾)	1:46⅗	Angel Cordero Jr.	D. Wayne Lukas	Darby Shuffle	Lea Lucinda
1989	**Go for Wand** (2¾)	1:44⅕	Randy Romero	Wm. Badgett Jr.	Sweet Roberta	Stella Madrid
1990	**Meadow Star** (5)	1:44	Jose Santos	LeRoy Jolley	Private Treasure	Dance Smartly
1991	**Pleasant Stage** (nk)	1:46⅖	Eddie Delahoussaye	Chris Speckert	La Spia	Cadillac Women
1992	**Eliza** (nk)	1:42⅘	Pat Valenzuela	Alex Hassingfer	Educated Risk	Boots 'n Jackie
1993	**Phone Chatter** (hd)	1:43	Laffit Pincay Jr.	Richard Mandella	Sardula	Heavenly Prize
1994	**Flanders** (hd)	1:45⅕	Pat Day	D. Wayne Lukas	Serena's Song	Stormy Blues
1995	**My Flag** (½)	1:42⅖	Jerry Bailey	Shug McGaughey	Cara Rafaela	Golden Attraction
1996	**Storm Song** (4½)	1:43⅗	Craig Perret	Nick Zito	Love That Jazz	Critical Factor
1997	**Countess Diana** (8½)	1:42⅕	Shane Sellers	Patrick Byrne	Career Collection	Primaly
1998	**Silverbulletday** (½)	1:43⅗	Gary Stevens	Bob Baffert	Excellent Meeting	Three Ring
1999	**Cash Run** (1¼)	1:43⅕	Jerry Bailey	D. Wayne Lukas	Chilukki	Surfside
2000	**Caressing** (½)	1:42⅗	John Velazquez	David Vance	Platinum Tiara	She's a Devil Due

*In 1984, winner Fran's Valentine was disqualified for interference in the stretch and placed 10th.

Sprint

Distance: six furlongs (since 1984).

Year	Winner (Margin)	Time	Jockey	Trainer	2nd place	3rd place
1984	**Eillo** (ns)	1:10⅕	Craig Perret	Budd Lepman	Commemorate	Fighting Fit
1985	**Precisionist** (¾)	1:08⅖	Chris McCarron	L.R. Fenstermaker	Smile	Mt. Livermore
1986	**Smile** (1¼)	1:08⅖	Jacinto Vasquez	Scotty Schulhofer	Pine Tree Lane	Bedside Promise
1987	**Very Subtle** (4)	1:08⅘	Pat Valenzuela	Melvin Stute	Groovy	Exclusive Enough
1988	**Gulch** (¾)	1:10⅖	Angel Cordero Jr.	D. Wayne Lukas	Play The King	Afleet
1989	**Dancing Spree** (nk)	1:09	Angel Cordero Jr.	Shug McGaughey	Safely Kept	Dispersal
1990	**Safely Kept** (nk)	1:09⅗	Craig Perret	Alan Goldberg	Dayjur	Black Tie Affair
1991	**Sheikh Albadou** (nk)	1:09⅕	Pat Eddery	Alexander Scott	Pleasant Tap	Robyn Dancer
1992	**Thirty Slews** (nk)	1:08⅕	Eddie Delahoussaye	Bob Baffert	Meafara	Rubiano
1993	**Cardmania** (nk)	1:08⅗	Eddie Delahoussaye	Derek Meredith	Meafara	Gilded Time
1994	**Cherokee Run** (nk)	1:09⅗	Mike Smith	Frank Alexander	Soviet Problem	Cardmania
1995	**Desert Stormer** (nk)	1:09	Kent Desormeaux	Frank Lyons	Mr. Greeley	Lit de Justice
1996	**Lit de Justice** 1¼)	1:08⅗	Corey Nakatani	Jenine Sahadi	Paying Dues	Honour and Glory
1997	**Elmhurst** ½)	1:08⅕	Corey Nakatani	Jenine Sahadi	Hesabull	Bet On Sunshine
1998	**Reraise** (2)	1:09	Corey Nakatani	Craig Dollase	Grand Slam	Kona Gold
1999	**Artax** (½)	1:07⅘	Jorge Chavez	Louis Albertrani	Kona Gold	Big Jag
2000	**Kona Gold** (½)	1:07⅗	Alex Solis	Bruce Headley	Honest Lady	Bet On Sunshine

Mile

Year	Winner (Margin)	Time	Jockey	Trainer	2nd place	3rd place
1984	**Royal Heroine** (1½)	1:32⅗	Fernando Toro	John Gosden	Star Choice	Cozzene
1985	**Cozzene** (2¼)	1:35	Walter Guerra	Jan Nerud	Al Mamoon*	Shadeed
1986	**Last Tycoon** (hd)	1:35⅕	Yves St.-Martin	Robert Collet	Palace Music	Fred Astaire
1987	**Miesque** (3½)	1:32⅘	Freddie Head	Francois Boutin	Show Dancer	Sonic Lady
1988	**Miesque** (4)	1:38⅗	Freddie Head	Francois Boutin	Steinlen	Simply Majestic
1989	**Steinlen** (¾)	1:37⅕	Jose Santos	D. Wayne Lukas	Sabona	Most Welcome
1990	**Royal Academy** (nk)	1:35⅕	Lester Piggott	M.V. O'Brien	Itsallgreektome	Priolo
1991	**Opening Verse** (2¼)	1:37⅖	Pat Valenzuela	Dick Lundy	Val des Bois	Star of Cozzene
1992	**Lure** (3)	1:32⅘	Mike Smith	Shug McGaughey	Paradise Creek	Brief Truce
1993	**Lure** (2¼)	1:33⅖	Mike Smith	Shug McGaughey	Ski Paradise	Fourstars Allstar
1994	**Barathea** (hd)	1:34⅖	Frankie Dettori	Luca Cumani	Johann Quatz	Unfinished Symph
1995	**Ridgewood Pearl** (2)	1:43⅗	John Murtagh	John Oxx	Fastness	Sayyedati
1996	**Da Hoss** (1½)	1:35⅘	Gary Stevens	Michael Dickinson	Spinning World	Same Old Wish
1997	**Spinning World** (2)	1:32⅗	Cash Asmussen	Jonathan Pease	Geri	Decorated Hero
1998	**Da Hoss** (hd)	1:35⅕	John Velazquez	Michael Dickinson	Hawksley Hill	Labeeb
1999	**Silic** (nk)	1:34⅕	Corey Nakatani	Julio Canani	Tuzla	Docksider
2000	**War Chant** (nk)	1:34⅗	Gary Stevens	Neil Drysdale	North East Bound	Dansili

*In 1985, 2nd place finisher Palace Music was disqualified for interference and placed 9th.

Breeders' Cup Championship (Cont.)

Distaff

Distances: 1¼ miles (1984-87); 1⅛ miles (since 1988).

Year	Winner (Margin)	Time	Jockey	Trainer	2nd place	3rd place
1984	**Princess Rooney** (7)	2:02⅖	Eddie Delahoussaye	Neil Drysdale	Life's Magic	Adored
1985	**Life's Magic** (6¼)	2:02	Angel Cordero Jr.	D. Wayne Lukas	Lady's Secret	DontstopThemusic
1986	**Lady's Secret** (2½)	2:01⅕	Pat Day	D. Wayne Lukas	Fran's Valentine	Outstandingly
1987	**Sacahuista** (2¼)	2:02⅘	Randy Romero	D. Wayne Lukas	Clabber Girl	Oueee Bebe
1988	**Personal Ensign** (ns)	1:52	Randy Romero	Shug McGaughey	Winning Colors	Goodbye Halo
1989	**Bayakoa** (1½)	1:47⅖	Laffit Pincay Jr.	Ron McAnally	Gorgeous	Open Mind
1990	**Bayakoa** (6¾)	1:49⅕	Laffit Pincay Jr.	Ron McAnally	Colonial Waters	Valay Maid
1991	**Dance Smartly** (½)	1:50⅘	Pat Day	Jim Day	Versailles Treaty	Brought to Mind
1992	**Paseana** (4)	1:48	Chris McCarron	Ron McAnally	Versailles Treaty	Magical Maiden
1993	**Hollywood Wildcat** (ns)	1:48⅕	Eddie Delahoussaye	Neil Drysdale	Paseana	Re Toss
1994	**One Dreamer** (nk)	1:50⅗	Gary Stevens	Thomas Proctor	Heavenly Prize	Miss Dominique
1995	**Inside Information** (13½)	1:46	Mike Smith	Shug McGaughey	Heavenly Prize	Lakeway
1996	**Jewel Princess** (1½)	1:48⅕	Corey Nakatani	Wallace Dollase	Serena's Song	Different
1997	**Ajina** (2)	1:47⅕	Mike Smith	Bill Mott	Sharp Cat	Escena
1998	**Escena** (ns)	1:49⅘	Gary Stevens	Bill Mott	Banshee Breeze	Keeper Hill
1999	**Beautiful Pleasure** (¾)	1:47⅖	Jorge Chavez	John Ward Jr.	Banshee Breeze	Heritage of Gold
2000	**Spain** (1½)	1:47⅗	Victor Espinoza	D. Wayne Lukas	Surfside	Heritage of Gold

Turf

Distance: 1½ miles (since 1984).

Year	Winner (Margin)	Time	Jockey	Trainer	2nd place	3rd place
1984	**Lashkari** (nk)	2:25⅕	Yves St.-Martin	de Royer-Dupre	All Along	Raami
1985	**Pebbles** (nk)	2:27	Pat Eddery	Clive Brittain	StrawberryRoad II	Mourjane
1986	**Manila** (nk)	2:25⅖	Jose Santos	Leroy Jolley	Theatrical	Estrapade
1987	**Theatrical** (½)	2:24⅖	Pat Day	Bill Mott	Trempolino	Village Star II
1988	**Gt. Communicator** (½)	2:35⅕	Ray Sibille	Thad Ackel	Sunshine Forever	Indian Skimmer
1989	**Prized** (hd)	2:28	Eddie Delahoussaye	Neil Drysdale	Sierra Roberta	Star Lift
1990	**In The Wings** (½)	2:29⅗	Gary Stevens	Andre Fabre	With Approval	El Senor
1991	**Miss Alleged** (2)	2:30⅘	Eric Legrix	Pascal Bary	Itsallgreektome	Quest for Fame
1992	**Fraise** (ns)	2:24	Pat Valenzuela	Bill Mott	Sky Classic	Quest for Fame
1993	**Kotashaan** (½)	2:25	Kent Desormeaux	Richard Mandella	Bien Bien	Luazur
1994	**Tikkanen** (1½)	2:26⅖	Mike Smith	Jonathan Pease	Hatoof	Paradise Creek
1995	**Northern Spur** (nk)	2:42	Chris McCarron	Ron McAnally	Freedom Cry	Carnegie
1996	**Pilsudski** (1¼)	2:30⅕	Walter Swinburn	Michael Stoute	Singspiel	Swain
1997	**Chief Bearhart** (¾)	2:24	Jose Santos	Mark Frostad	Borgia	Flag Down
1998	**Buck's Boy** (1¼)	2:28⅗	Shane Sellers	Noel Hickey	Yagli	Dushyantor
1999	**Daylami** (2½)	2:24⅗	Frankie Dettori	Saeed bin Suroor	Royal Anthem	Buck's Boy
2000	**Kalanisi** (½)	2:26⅘	John Murtagh	Sir Michael Stoute	Quiet Resolve	John's Call

Filly & Mare Turf

Distance: 1⅜ miles (since 1999).

Year	Winner (Margin)	Time	Jockey	Trainer	2nd place	3rd place
1999	**Soaring Softly** (¾)	2:13⅘	Jerry Bailey	James J. Toner	Coretta	Zomarradah
2000	**Perfect Sting** (¾)	2:13	Jerry Bailey	Joe Orseno	Tout Charmant	Catella

Classic

Distance: 1¼ miles (since 1984).

Year	Winner (Margin)	Time	Jockey	Trainer	2nd place	3rd place
1984	**Wild Again** (hd)	2:03⅖	Pat Day	Vincent Timphony	Slew o' Gold	Gate Dancer*
1985	**Proud Truth** (hd)	2:00⅘	Jorge Velasquez	John Veitch	Gate Dancer	Turkoman
1986	**Skywalker** (1¼)	2:00⅖	Laffit Pincay Jr.	M. Whittingham	Turkoman	Precisionist
1987	**Ferdinand** (ns)	2:01⅖	Bill Shoemaker	C. Whittingham	Alysheba	Judge Angelucci
1988	**Alysheba** (ns)	2:04⅘	Chris McCarron	Jack Van Berg	Seeking the Gold	Waquoit
1989	**Sunday Silence** (½)	2:00⅕	Chris McCarron	C. Whittingham	Easy Goer	Blushing John
1990	**Unbridled** (1)	2:02⅕	Pat Day	Carl Nafzger	Ibn Bey	Thirty Six Red
1991	**Black Tie Affair** (1¼)	2:02⅘	Jerry Bailey	Ernie Poulos	Twilight Agenda	Unbridled
1992	**A.P. Indy** (2)	2:00⅕	Eddie Delahoussaye	Neil Drysdale	Pleasant Tap	Jolypha
1993	**Arcangues** (2)	2:00⅘	Jerry Bailey	Andre Fabre	Bertrando	Kissin Kris
1994	**Concern** (nk)	2:02⅖	Jerry Bailey	Richard Small	Tabasco Cat	Dramatic Gold
1995	**Cigar** (2½)	1:59⅖	Jerry Bailey	Bill Mott	L'Carriere	Unaccounted For
1996	**Alphabet Soup** (ns)	2:01	Chris McCarron	David Hofmans	Louis Quatorze	Cigar
1997	**Skip Away** (6)	1:59⅕	Mike Smith	Hubert Hine	Deputy Commander	Dowty
1998	**Awesome Again** (¾)	2:02	Pat Day	Patrick Byrne	Silver Charm	Swain
1999	**Cat Thief** (1¼)	1:59⅖	Pat Day	D. Wayne Lukas	Budroyale	Golden Missile
2000	**Tiznow** (nk)	2:00⅗	Chris McCarron	Jay Robbins	Giant's Causeway	Captain Steve

*In 1984, 2nd place finisher Gate Dancer was disqualified for interference and placed 3rd.

Breeders' Cup Leaders

The all-time money-winning horses and jockeys in the history of the Breeders' Cup through 2000.

Top 10 Horses

		Sts	1-2-3	Earnings
1	Awesome Again	1	1-0-0	$2,662,400
2	Tiznow	1	1-0-0	2,480,400
3	Skip Away	2	1-0-0	2,288,000
4	Cat Thief	2	1-0-1	2,200,000
5	Alysheba	3	1-1-1	2,133,000
6	Alphabet Soup	1	1-0-0	2,080,000
7	Cigar	2	1-0-1	2,040,000
8	Unbridled	2	1-0-1	1,710,000
9	Black Tie Affair (IRE)	3	1-0-1	1,668,000
10	A.P. Indy	1	1-0-0	1,560,000
	Arcangues	1	1-0-0	1,560,000
	Concern	1	1-0-0	1,560,000

Top 10 Jockeys

		Sts	1-2-3	Earnings
1	Pat Day	95	11-15-10	$20,412,760
2	Chris McCarron	96	8-11-7	15,542,320
3	Jerry Bailey	67	11-5-6	13,008,200
4	Gary Stevens	81	8-15-9	12,916,880
5	Mike Smith	40	8-3-3	7,860,200
6	Eddie Delahoussaye	66	7-3-6	7,719,000
7	Laffit Pincay Jr.	61	7-4-9	6,811,000
8	Angel Cordero Jr.	48	4-7-7	6,020,000
9	Corey Nakatani	39	5-5-5	5,972,520
10	Jose Santos	52	6-2-4	5,801,000

Annual Money Leaders
Horses

Annual money-leading horses since 1910, according to *The American Racing Manual*.

Multiple leaders: Round Table, Buckpasser, Alysheba and Cigar (2).

Year		Age	Sts	1-2-3	Earnings
1910	Novelty	2	16	11—	$72,630
1911	Worth	2	13	10—	16,645
1912	Star Charter	4	17	6—	14,655
1913	Old Rosebud	2	14	12—	19,057
1914	Roamer	3	16	12—	29,105
1915	Borrow	7	9	4—	20,195
1916	Campfire	2	9	6—	49,735
1917	Sun Briar	2	9	5—	59,505
1918	Eternal	2	8	6—	56,173
1919	Sir Barton	3	13	8-3-2	88,250
1920	Man o' War	3	11	11-0-0	166,140
1921	Morvich	2	11	11-0-0	115,234
1922	Pillory	3	7	4-1-1	95,654
1923	Zev	3	14	12-1-0	272,008
1924	Sarzen	3	12	8-1-1	95,640
1925	Pompey	2	10	7-2-0	121,630
1926	Crusader	3	15	9-4-0	166,033
1927	Anita Peabody	2	7	6-0-1	111,905
1928	High Strung	2	6	5-0-0	153,590
1929	Blue Larkspur	3	6	4-1-0	153,450
1930	Gallant Fox	3	10	9-1-0	308,275
1931	Gallant Flight	2	7	7-0-0	219,000
1932	Gusto	3	16	4-3-2	145,940
1933	Singing Wood	2	9	3-2-2	88,050
1934	Cavalcade	3	7	6-1-0	111,235
1935	Omaha	3	9	6-1-2	142,255
1936	Granville	3	11	7-3-0	110,295
1937	Seabiscuit	4	15	11-2-2	168,580
1938	Stagehand	3	15	8-2-3	189,710
1939	Challedon	3	15	9-2-3	184,535
1940	Bimelech	3	7	4-2-1	110,005
1941	Whirlaway	3	20	13-5-2	272,386
1942	Shut Out	3	12	8-2-0	238,872
1943	Count Fleet	3	6	6-0-0	174,055
1944	Pavot	2	8	8-0-0	179,040
1945	Busher	3	13	10-2-1	273,735
1946	Assault	3	15	8-2-3	424,195
1947	Armed	6	17	11-4-1	376,325
1948	Citation	3	20	19-1-0	709,470
1949	Ponder	3	21	9-5-2	321,825
1950	Noor	5	12	7-4-1	346,940
1951	Counterpoint	3	15	7-2-1	250,525
1952	Crafty Admiral	4	16	9-4-1	277,225
1953	Native Dancer	3	10	9-1-0	513,425
1954	Determine	3	15	10-3-2	328,700
1955	Nashua	3	12	10-1-1	752,550
1956	Needles	3	8	4-2-0	$440,850
1957	Round Table	3	22	15-1-3	600,383
1958	Round Table	4	20	14-4-0	662,780
1959	Sword Dancer	3	13	8-4-0	537,004
1960	Bally Ache	3	15	10-3-1	445,045
1961	Carry Back	3	16	9-1-3	565,349
1962	Never Bend	2	10	7-1-2	402,969
1963	Candy Spots	3	12	7-2-1	604,481
1964	Gun Bow	4	16	8-4-2	580,100
1965	Buckpasser	2	11	9-1-0	568,096
1966	Buckpasser	3	14	13-1-0	669,078
1967	Damascus	3	16	12-3-1	817,941
1968	Forward Pass	3	13	7-2-0	546,674
1969	Arts and Letters	3	14	8-5-1	555,604
1970	Personality	3	18	8-2-1	444,049
1971	Riva Ridge	2	9	7-0-0	503,263
1972	Droll Role	4	19	7-3-4	471,633
1973	Secretariat	3	12	9-2-1	860,404
1974	Chris Evert	3	8	5-1-2	551,063
1975	Foolish Pleasure	3	11	5-4-1	716,278
1976	Forego	6	8	6-1-1	401,701
1977	Seattle Slew	3	7	6-1-1	641,370
1978	Affirmed	3	11	8-2-0	901,541
1979	Spectacular Bid	3	12	10-1-1	1,279,334
1980	Temperence Hill	3	17	8-3-1	1,130,452
1981	John Henry	6	10	8-0-0	1,798,030
1982	Perrault (GBR)	5	8	4-1-2	1,197,400
1983	All Along (FRA)	4	7	4-1-1	2,138,963
1984	Slew o' Gold	4	6	5-1-0	2,627,944
1985	Spend A Buck	3	7	5-1-1	3,552,704
1986	Snow Chief	3	9	6-1-1	1,875,200
1987	Alysheba	3	10	3-3-1	2,511,156
1988	Alysheba	4	9	7-1-0	3,808,600
1989	Sunday Silence	3	9	7-2-0	4,578,454
1990	Unbridled	3	11	4-3-2	3,718,149
1991	Dance Smartly	3	8	8-0-0	2,876,821
1992	A.P. Indy	3	7	5-0-1	2,622,560
1993	Kotashaan (FRA)	5	10	6-2-0	2,619,014
1994	Paradise Creek	5	11	8-2-1	2,610,187
1995	Cigar	5	10	10-0-0	4,819,800
1996	Cigar	6	8	5-2-1	4,910,000
1997	Skip Away	4	11	4-5-2	4,089,000
1998	Silver Charm	4	9	6-2-0	4,696,506
1999	Almutawakel	4	4	1-1-1	3,290,000
2000	Dubai Millennium (GBR)	4	1	1-0-0	3,600,000

Annual Money Leaders (Cont.)
Jockeys

Annual money-leading jockeys since 1910, according to *The American Racing Manual*.

Multiple leaders: Bill Shoemaker (10); Laffit Pincay Jr. (7); Eddie Arcaro (6); Braulio Baeza (5); Chris McCarron and Jose Santos (4); Jerry Bailey, Angel Cordero Jr. and Earl Sande (3); Ted Atkinson, Pat Day, Laverne Fator, Mack Garner, Bill Hartack, Charles Kurtsinger, Johnny Longden, Mike Smith, Gary Stevens, Sonny Workman and Wayne Wright (2).

Year		Mts	Wins	Earnings	Year		Mts	Wins	Earnings
1910	Carroll Shilling	.506	172	$176,030	1956	Bill Hartack	.1387	347	$2,343,955
1911	Ted Koerner	.813	162	88,308	1957	Bill Hartack	.1238	341	3,060,501
1912	Jimmy Butwell	.684	144	79,843	1958	Bill Shoemaker	.1133	300	2,961,693
1913	Merritt Buxton	.887	146	82,552	1959	Bill Shoemaker	.1285	347	2,843,133
1914	J. McCahey	.824	155	121,845					
1915	Mack Garner	.775	151	96,628	1960	Bill Shoemaker	.1227	274	2,123,961
1916	John McTaggart	.832	150	155,055	1961	Bill Shoemaker	.1256	304	2,690,819
1917	Frank Robinson	.731	147	148,057	1962	Bill Shoemaker	.1126	311	2,916,844
1918	Lucien Luke	.756	178	201,864	1963	Bill Shoemaker	.1203	271	2,526,925
1919	John Loftus	.177	65	252,707	1964	Bill Shoemaker	.1056	246	2,649,553
					1965	Braulio Baeza	.1245	270	2,582,702
1920	Clarence Kummer	.353	87	292,376	1966	Braulio Baeza	.1341	298	2,951,022
1921	Earl Sande	.340	112	263,043	1967	Braulio Baeza	.1064	256	3,088,888
1922	Albert Johnson	.297	43	345,054	1968	Braulio Baeza	.1089	201	2,835,108
1923	Earl Sande	.430	122	569,394	1969	Jorge Velasquez	.1442	258	2,542,315
1924	Ivan Parke	.844	205	290,395					
1925	Laverne Fator	.315	81	305,775	1970	Laffit Pincay Jr.	.1328	269	2,626,526
1926	Laverne Fator	.511	143	361,435	1971	Laffit Pincay Jr.	.1627	380	3,784,377
1927	Earl Sande	.179	49	277,877	1972	Laffit Pincay Jr.	.1388	289	3,225,827
1928	Linus McAtee	.235	55	301,295	1973	Laffit Pincay Jr.	.1444	350	4,093,492
1929	Mack Garner	.274	57	314,975	1974	Laffit Pincay Jr.	.1278	341	4,251,060
					1975	Braulio Baeza	.1190	196	3,674,398
1930	Sonny Workman	.571	152	420,438	1976	Angel Cordero Jr.	.1534	274	4,709,500
1931	Charley Kurtsinger	.519	93	392,095	1977	Steve Cauthen	.2075	487	6,151,750
1932	Sonny Workman	.378	87	385,070	1978	Darrel McHargue	.1762	375	6,188,353
1933	Robert Jones	.471	63	226,285	1979	Laffit Pincay Jr.	.1708	420	8,183,535
1934	Wayne Wright	.919	174	287,185					
1935	Silvio Coucci	.749	141	319,760	1980	Chris McCarron	.1964	405	7,666,100
1936	Wayne Wright	.670	100	264,000	1981	Chris McCarron	.1494	326	8,397,604
1937	Charley Kurtsinger	.765	120	384,202	1982	Angel Cordero Jr.	.1838	397	9,702,520
1938	Nick Wall	.658	97	385,161	1983	Angel Cordero Jr.	.1792	362	10,116,807
1939	Basil James	.904	191	353,333	1984	Chris McCarron	.1565	356	12,038,213
					1985	Laffit Pincay Jr.	.1409	289	13,415,049
1940	Eddie Arcaro	.783	132	343,661	1986	Jose Santos	.1636	329	11,329,297
1941	Don Meade	.1164	210	398,627	1987	Jose Santos	.1639	305	12,407,355
1942	Eddie Arcaro	.687	123	481,949	1988	Jose Santos	.1867	370	14,877,298
1943	Johnny Longden	.871	173	573,276	1989	Jose Santos	.1459	285	13,847,003
1944	Ted Atkinson	.1539	287	899,101					
1945	Johnny Longden	.778	180	981,977	1990	Gary Stevens	.1504	283	13,881,198
1946	Ted Atkinson	.1377	233	1,036,825	1991	Chris McCarron	.1440	265	14,456,073
1947	Douglas Dodson	.646	141	1,429,949	1992	Kent Desormeaux	.1568	361	14,193,006
1948	Eddie Arcaro	.726	188	1,686,230	1993	Mike Smith	.1510	343	14,024,815
1949	Steve Brooks	.906	209	1,316,817	1994	Mike Smith	.1484	317	15,979,820
					1995	Jerry Bailey	.1367	287	16,311,876
1950	Eddie Arcaro	.888	195	1,410,160	1996	Jerry Bailey	.1187	298	19,465,376
1951	Bill Shoemaker	.1161	257	1,329,890	1997	Jerry Bailey	.1136	269	18,206,013
1952	Eddie Arcaro	.807	188	1,859,591	1998	Gary Stevens	.869	178	19,358,840
1953	Bill Shoemaker	.1683	485	1,784,187	1999	Pat Day	.1265	254	18,092,845
1954	Bill Shoemaker	.1251	380	1,876,760	2000	Pat Day	.1219	267	17,479,838
1955	Eddie Arcaro	.820	158	1,864,796					

Trainers

Annual money-leading trainers since 1908, according to *The American Racing Manual*.

Multiple Leaders: D. Wayne Lukas (14); Sam Hildreth (9); Charlie Whittingham (7); Sunny Jim Fitzsimmons and Jimmy Jones (5); Laz Barrera, Ben Jones and Willie Molter (4); Bob Baffert, Hirsch Jacobs, Eddie Neloy and James Rowe Sr. (3); H. Guy Bedwell, Jack Gaver, John Schorr, Humming Bob Smith, Silent Tom Smith and Mesh Tenney (2).

Year		Wins	Earnings	Year		Wins	Earnings
1908	James Rowe Sr.	.50	$284,335	1916	Sam Hildreth	.39	$70,950
1909	Sam Hildreth	.73	123,942	1917	Sam Hildreth	.23	61,698
				1918	H. Guy Bedwell	.53	80,296
1910	Sam Hildreth	.84	148,010	1919	H. Guy Bedwell	.63	208,728
1911	Sam Hildreth	.67	49,418	1920	Louis Feustel	.22	186,087
1912	John Schorr	.63	58,110	1921	Sam Hildreth	.85	262,768
1913	James Rowe Sr.	.18	45,936	1922	Sam Hildreth	.74	247,014
1914	R.C. Benson	.45	59,315	1923	Sam Hildreth	.75	392,124
1915	James Rowe Sr.	.19	75,596				

Year		Wins	Earnings	Year		Sts	Wins	Earnings
1924	Sam Hildreth	77	$255,608	1963	Mesh Tenney	192	40	$860,703
1925	G.R. Tompkins	30	199,245	1964	Bill Winfrey	287	61	1,350,534
1926	Scott Harlan	21	205,681	1965	Hirsch Jacobs	610	91	1,331,628
1927	W.H. Bringloe	63	216,563	1966	Eddie Neloy	282	93	2,456,250
1928	John Schorr	65	258,425	1967	Eddie Neloy	262	72	1,776,089
1929	James Rowe Jr.	25	314,881	1968	Eddie Neloy	212	52	1,233,101
1930	Sunny Jim Fitzsimmons	47	397,355	1969	Elliott Burch	156	26	1,067,936
1931	Big Jim Healy	33	297,300	1970	Charlie Whittingham	551	82	1,302,354
1932	Sunny Jim Fitzsimmons	68	266,650	1971	Charlie Whittingham	393	77	1,737,115
1933	Humming Bob Smith	53	135,720	1972	Charlie Whittingham	429	79	1,734,020
1934	Humming Bob Smith	43	249,938	1973	Charlie Whittingham	423	85	1,865,385
1935	Bud Stotler	87	303,005	1974	Pancho Martin	846	166	2,408,419
1936	Sunny Jim Fitzsimmons	42	193,415	1975	Charlie Whittingham	487	3	2,437,244
1937	Robert McGarvey	46	209,925	1976	Jack Van Berg	2362	496	2,976,196
1938	Earl Sande	15	226,495	1977	Laz Barrera	781	127	2,715,848
1939	Sunny Jim Fitzsimmons	45	266,205	1978	Laz Barrera	592	100	3,307,164
1940	Silent Tom Smith	14	269,200	1979	Laz Barrera	492	98	3,608,517
1941	Ben Jones	70	475,318	1980	Laz Barrera	559	99	2,969,151
1942	Jack Gaver	48	406,547	1981	Charlie Whittingham	376	74	3,993,302
1943	Ben Jones	73	267,915	1982	Charlie Whittingham	410	63	4,587,457
1944	Ben Jones	60	601,660	1983	D. Wayne Lukas	595	78	4,267,261
1945	Silent Tom Smith	52	510,655	1984	D. Wayne Lukas	805	131	5,835,921
1946	Hirsch Jacobs	99	560,077	1985	D. Wayne Lukas	1140	218	11,155,188
1947	Jimmy Jones	85	1,334,805	1986	D. Wayne Lukas	1510	259	12,345,180
1948	Jimmy Jones	81	1,118,670	1987	D. Wayne Lukas	1735	343	17,502,110
1949	Jimmy Jones	76	978,587	1988	D. Wayne Lukas	1500	318	17,842,358
1950	Preston Burch	96	637,754	1989	D. Wayne Lukas	1398	305	16,103,998
1951	Jack Gaver	42	616,392	1990	D. Wayne Lukas	1396	267	14,508,871
1952	Ben Jones	29	662,137	1991	D. Wayne Lukas	1497	289	15,942,223
1953	Harry Trotsek	54	1,028,873	1992	D. Wayne Lukas	1349	230	9,806,436
1954	Willie Molter	136	1,107,860	1993	Bobby Frankel	345	79	8,933,252
1955	Sunny Jim Fitzsimmons	66	1,270,055	1994	D. Wayne Lukas	693	147	9,247,457
1956	Willie Molter	142	1,227,402	1995	D. Wayne Lukas	837	194	12,834,483
1957	Jimmy Jones	70	1,150,910	1996	D. Wayne Lukas	1006	192	15,966,344
1958	Willie Molter	69	1,116,544	1997	D. Wayne Lukas	824	169	9,993,569
1959	Willie Molter	71	847,290	1998	Bob Baffert	538	139	15,000,870
1960	Hirsch Jacobs	97	748,349	1999	Bob Baffert	735	169	16,934,607
1961	Jimmy Jones	62	759,856	2000	Bob Baffert	678	146	11,831,605
1962	Mesh Tenney	58	1,099,474					

All-Time Leaders

The all-time money-winning horses and race-winning jockeys through 2000, according to the *National Thoroughbred Racing Association*. Records include all available information on races in foreign countries.

Top 35 Horses — Money Won

Note that horses who raced in 2000 are in **bold** type.

		Sts	1st	2nd	3rd	Earnings			Sts	1st	2nd	3rd	Earnings
1	Cigar	33	19	4	5	$9,999,815	19	Sunline	29	21	5	0	$4,553,775
2	Skip Away	38	18	10	6	9,616,360	20	Unbridled	24	8	6	6	4,489,475
3	Hokuto Vega	42	16	5	4	8,337,603	21	**Dubai Millennium**	10	9	0	0	4,452,047
4	Silver Charm	24	12	7	2	6,944,369	22	Pilsudski	22	10	6	2	4,389,167
5	Alysheba	26	11	8	2	6,679,242	23	Awesome Again	12	9	0	2	4,374,590
6	John Henry	83	39	15	9	6,597,947	24	Lively Mount	22	10	4	2	4,332,104
7	Singspiel	20	9	8	0	5,950,217	25	Indigenous	46	15	6	4	4,283,092
8	Sakura Laurel	22	9	5	4	5,763,926	26	Spend A Buck	15	10	3	2	4,220,689
9	Best Pal	47	18	11	4	5,668,245	27	Creme Fraiche	64	17	12	13	4,024,727
10	Taiki Blizzard	22	6	8	2	5,544,484	28	Seeking the Pearl	21	8	2	3	4,022,286
11	Taiki Shuttle	13	11	1	1	4,981,132	29	**Cat Thief**	30	4	9	8	3,991,012
12	Sunday Silence	14	9	5	0	4,968,554	30	Devil His Due	41	11	12	3	3,920,405
13	Easy Goer	20	14	5	1	4,873,770	31	Sandpit	40	14	11	6	3,802,971
14	**Fantastic Light**	19	8	3	3	4,850,318	32	Ferdinand	29	8	9	6	3,777,978
15	Hishi Amazon	12	8	4	0	4,702,968	33	Swain	22	10	4	6	3,777,115
16	Kyoto City	44	11	11	5	4,683,897	34	**Almutwakel**	19	4	4	1	3,642,698
17	Daylami	21	11	3	4	4,594,647	35	Gentlemen	24	13	4	2	3,608,598
18	**Behrens**	27	9	8	3	4,585,500							

Top 35 Jockeys — Races Won

Note that jockeys active in 2000 are in **bold** type.

		Yrs	Wins	Earnings			Yrs	Wins	Earnings
1	**Laffit Pincay Jr.**	.35	9050	$215,524,691	19	Eddie Arcaro	.31	4779	$30,039,543
2	Bill Shoemaker	.42	8833	123,375,524	20	**Rick Wilson**	.28	4660	69,000,141
3	**Pat Day**	.28	7883	241,499,902	21	Don Brumfield	.37	4573	43,567,861
4	David Gall	.43	7396	24,972,821	22	**Gary Stevens**	.22	4547	190,344,539
5	**Russell Baze**	.27	7220	103,632,774	23	**Mario Pino**	.23	4480	64,791,301
6	Angel Cordero Jr.	.35	7057	164,561,227	24	Steve Brooks	.34	4451	18,239,817
7	**Chris McCarron**	.27	6961	247,130,197	25	Eddie Maple	.34	4398	105,338,573
8	Jorge Velasquez	.33	6795	125,544,379	26	Walter Blum	.22	4302	26,497,189
9	Sandy Hawley	.31	6449	88,681,292	27	Randy Romero	.26	4294	75,264,198
10	Larry Snyder	.35	6388	47,207,289	28	**Jeffrey Lloyd**	.24	4276	34,199,413
11	Carl Gambardella	.39	6349	29,389,041	29	Bill Hartack	.22	4272	26,466,758
12	**E. Delahoussaye**	.33	6200	182,006,473	30	**Craig Perret**	.34	4269	104,095,089
13	**Earlie Fires**	.36	6150	77,157,863	31	**Anthony Black**	.31	4218	40,881,313
14	John Longden	.41	6032	24,665,800	32	**Edgar Prado**	.14	4143	79,983,504
15	Jacinto Vasquez	.37	5231	80,764,853	33	**Mark Guidry**	.27	4119	59,546,094
16	**Ron Ardoin**	.28	5039	55,561,463	34	**Ray Sibille**	.32	4088	63,579,447
17	**Jerry Bailey**	.26	4922	199,325,433	35	Avelino Gomez	.34	4081	11,777,297
18	Rudy Baez	.25	4875	30,474,225					

Eclipse Awards

The Eclipse Awards, honoring the Horse of the Year and other champions of the sport, are sponsored by the National Thoroughbred Racing Association (NTRA), *Daily Racing Form* and the National Turf Writers Assn. In 1998, the NTRA replaced the Thoroughbred Racing Associations of North America as co-sponsor.

The awards are named after the 18th century racehorse and sire, Eclipse, who began racing at age five and was unbeaten in 18 starts (eight wins were walkovers). As a stallion, Eclipse sired winners of 344 races, including three Epsom Derby champions.

Horses listed in CAPITAL letters won the Triple Crown that year. Age of horse in parentheses where necessary.

Multiple winners: (horses): Forego (8); John Henry (7); Affirmed, Lonesome Glory and Secretariat (5); Cigar, Flatterer, Seattle Slew, Skip Away and Spectacular Bid (4); Ack Ack, Susan's Girl and Zaccio (3); All Along, Alysheba, Bayakoa, Black Tie Affair, Cafe Prince, Charismatic, Conquistador Cielo, Desert Vixen, Favorite Trick, Ferdinand, Flawlessly, Go for Wand, Holy Bull, Housebuster, Kotashaan, Lady's Secret, Life's Magic, Miesque, Morley Street, Open Mind, Paseana, Riva Ridge, Silverbulletday, Slew o' Gold, Spend A Buck and Tiznow (2).

Multiple winners: (people): Laffit Pincay Jr. (6); Jerry Bailey, Laz Barrera, Pat Day, John Franks, D. Wayne Lukas, Allen Paulson and Frank Stronach (4); Bob Baffert, Steve Cauthen, Harbor View Farm, Fred W. Hooper, Nelson Bunker Hunt, Mr. & Mrs. Gene Klein, Dan Lasater, John & Betty Mabee, Paul Mellon, Ogden Phipps, Bill Shoemaker, Edward Taylor and Charlie Whittingham (3); Braulio Baeza, C.T. Chenery, Claiborne Farm, Angel Cordero Jr., Kent Desormeaux, William S. Farish, Bobby Frankel, John W. Galbreath, Chris McCarron, Bill Mott and Mike Smith (2).

Horse of the Year

Year		Year		Year		Year	
1971	Ack Ack (5)	1979	Affirmed (4)	1987	Ferdinand (4)	1995	Cigar (5)
1972	Secretariat (2)	1980	Spectacular Bid (4)	1988	Alysheba (4)	1996	Cigar (6)
1973	SECRETARIAT (3)	1981	John Henry (6)	1989	Sunday Silence (3)	1997	Favorite Trick (2)
1974	Forego (4)	1982	Conquistador Cielo (3)	1990	Criminal Type (5)	1998	Skip Away (5)
1975	Forego (5)	1983	All Along (4)	1991	Black Tie Affair (5)	1999	Charismatic (3)
1976	Forego (6)	1984	John Henry (9)	1992	A.P. Indy (3)	2000	Tiznow (3)
1977	SEATTLE SLEW (3)	1985	Spend A Buck (3)	1993	Kotashaan (5)		
1978	AFFIRMED (3)	1986	Lady's Secret (4)	1994	Holy Bull (3)		

Horse of the Year (1936-70)

In 1971, the *Daily Racing Form*, the Thoroughbred Racing Associations, and the National Turf Writers Assn. joined forces to create the Eclipse Awards. Before then, however, the *Racing Form* (1936-70) and the TRA (1950-70) issued separate selections for Horse of the Year. Their picks differed only four times from 1950-70 and are so noted. Horses listed in CAPITAL letters are Triple Crown winners; (f) indicates female.

Multiple winners: Kelso (5); Challedon, Native Dancer and Whirlaway (2).

Year		Year		Year		Year	
1936	Granville	1946	ASSAULT	1955	Nashua	1964	Kelso
1937	WAR ADMIRAL	1947	Armed	1956	Swaps	1965	Roman Brother (DRF)
1938	Seabiscuit	1948	CITATION	1957	Bold Ruler (DRF)		Moccasin (TRA)
1939	Challedon	1949	Capot		Dedicate (TRA)	1966	Buckpasser
1940	Challedon	1950	Hill Prince	1958	Round Table	1967	Damascus
1941	WHIRLAWAY	1951	Counterpoint	1959	Sword Dancer	1968	Dr. Fager
1942	Whirlaway	1952	One Count (DRF)	1960	Kelso	1969	Arts and Letters
1943	COUNT FLEET		Native Dancer (TRA)	1961	Kelso	1970	Fort Marcy (DRF)
1944	Twilight Tear (f)	1953	Tom Fool	1962	Kelso		Personality (TRA)
1945	Busher (f)	1954	Native Dancer	1963	Kelso		

Older Male

Year		Year		Year		Year	
1971	Ack Ack (5)	1979	Affirmed (4)	1987	Ferdinand (4)	1995	Cigar (5)
1972	Autobiography (4)	1980	Spectacular Bid (4)	1988	Alysheba (4)	1996	Cigar (6)
1973	Riva Ridge (4)	1981	John Henry (6)	1989	Blushing John (4)	1997	Skip Away (4)
1974	Forego (4)	1982	Lemhi Gold (4)	1990	Criminal Type (5)	1998	Skip Away (5)
1975	Forego (5)	1983	Bates Motel (4)	1991	Black Tie Affair (5)	1999	Victory Gallop (4)
1976	Forego (6)	1984	Slew o' Gold (4)	1992	Pleasant Tap (5)	2000	Lemon Drop Kid (4)
1977	Forego (7)	1985	Vanlandingham (4)	1993	Bertrando (4)		
1978	Seattle Slew (4)	1986	Turkoman (4)	1994	The Wicked North (4)		

Older Filly or Mare

Year		Year		Year		Year	
1971	Shuvee (5)	1979	Waya (5)	1987	North Sider (5)	1995	Inside Information (4)
1972	Typecast (6)	1980	Glorious Song (4)	1988	Personal Ensign (4)	1996	Jewel Princess (4)
1973	Susan's Girl (4)	1981	Relaxing (5)	1989	Bayakoa (5)	1997	Hidden Lake (4)
1974	Desert Vixen (4)	1982	Track Robbery (6)	1990	Bayakoa (6)	1998	Escena (5)
1975	Susan's Girl (6)	1983	Amb. of Luck (4)	1991	Queena (5)	1999	Beautiful Pleasure (4)
1976	Proud Delta (4)	1984	Princess Rooney (4)	1992	Paseana (5)	2000	Riboletta (5)
1977	Cascapedia (4)	1985	Life's Magic (4)	1993	Paseana (6)		
1978	Late Bloomer (4)	1986	Lady's Secret (4)	1994	Sky Beauty (4)		

3-Year-Old Colt or Gelding

Year		Year		Year		Year	
1971	Canonero II	1979	Spectacular Bid	1987	Alysheba	1995	Thunder Gulch
1972	Key to the Mint	1980	Temperence Hill	1988	Risen Star	1996	Skip Away
1973	SECRETARIAT	1981	Pleasant Colony	1989	Sunday Silence	1997	Silver Charm
1974	Little Current	1982	Conquistador Cielo	1990	Unbridled	1998	Real Quiet
1975	Wajima	1983	Slew o' Gold	1991	Hansel	1999	Charismatic
1976	Bold Forbes	1984	Swale	1992	A.P. Indy	2000	Tiznow
1977	SEATTLE SLEW	1985	Spend A Buck	1993	Prairie Bayou		
1978	AFFIRMED	1986	Snow Chief	1994	Holy Bull		

3-Year-Old Filly

Year		Year		Year		Year	
1971	Turkish Trousers	1979	Davona Dale	1987	Sacahuista	1995	Serena's Song
1972	Susan's Girl	1980	Genuine Risk	1988	Winning Colors	1996	Yanks Music
1973	Desert Vixen	1981	Wayward Lass	1989	Open Mind	1997	Ajina
1974	Chris Evert	1982	Christmas Past	1990	Go for Wand	1998	Banshee Breeze
1975	Ruffian	1983	Heartlight No. One	1991	Dance Smartly	1999	Silverbulletday
1976	Revidere	1984	Life's Magic	1992	Saratoga Dew	2000	Surfside
1977	Our Mims	1985	Mom's Command	1993	Hollywood Wildcat		
1978	Tempest Queen	1986	Tiffany Lass	1994	Heavenly Prize		

2-Year-Old Colt or Gelding

Year		Year		Year		Year	
1971	Riva Ridge	1979	Rockhill Native	1987	Forty Niner	1995	Maria's Mon
1972	Secretariat	1980	Lord Avie	1988	Easy Goer	1996	Boston Harbor
1973	Protagonist	1981	Deputy Minister	1989	Rhythm	1997	Favorite Trick
1974	Foolish Pleasure	1982	Roving Boy	1990	Fly So Free	1998	Answer Lively
1975	Honest Pleasure	1983	Devil's Bag	1991	Arazi	1999	Anees
1976	Seattle Slew	1984	Chief's Crown	1992	Gilded Time	2000	Macho Uno
1977	Affirmed	1985	Tasso	1993	Dehere		
1978	Spectacular Bid	1986	Capote	1994	Timber Country		

2-Year-Old Filly

Year		Year		Year		Year	
1971	Numbered Account	1978	(TIE) Candy Eclair	1985	Family Style	1993	Phone Chatter
1972	La Prevoyante		& It's in the Air	1986	Brave Raj	1994	Flanders
1973	Talking Picture	1979	Smart Angle	1987	Epitome	1995	Golden Attraction
1974	Ruffian	1980	Heavenly Cause	1988	Open Mind	1996	Storm Song
1975	Dearly Precious	1981	Before Dawn	1989	Go for Wand	1997	Countess Diana
1976	Sensational	1982	Landaluce	1990	Meadow Star	1998	Silverbulletday
1977	Lakeville Miss	1983	Althea	1991	Pleasant Stage	1999	Chilukki
		1984	Outstandingly	1992	Eliza	2000	Caressing

Champion Turf Horse

Year		Year		Year		Year	
1971	Run the Gantlet (3)	1973	SECRETARIAT (3)	1975	Snow Knight (4)	1977	Johnny D (3)
1972	Cougar II (6)	1974	Dahlia (4)	1976	Youth (3)	1978	Mac Diarmida (3)

Eclipse Awards (Cont.)
Champion Male Turf Horse

Year		Year		Year		Year	
1979	Bowl Game (5)	1985	Cozzene (4)	1990	Itsallgreektome (3)	1995	Northern Spur (4)
1980	John Henry (5)	1986	Manila (3)	1991	Tight Spot (4)	1996	Singspiel (4)
1981	John Henry (6)	1987	Theatrical (5)	1992	Sky Classic (5)	1997	Chief Bearhart (4)
1982	Perrault (5)	1988	Sunshine Forever (3)	1993	Kotashaan (5)	1998	Buck's Boy (5)
1983	John Henry (8)	1989	Steinlen (6)	1994	Paradise Creek (5)	1999	Daylami (5)
1984	John Henry (9)					2000	Kalanisi (4)

Champion Female Turf Horse

Year		Year		Year		Year	
1979	Trillion (5)	1985	Pebbles (4)	1990	Laugh and Be Merry (5)	1995	Possibly Perfect (5)
1980	Just A Game II (4)	1986	Estrapade (6)	1991	Miss Alleged (4)	1996	Wandesta (5)
1981	De La Rose (3)	1987	Miesque (3)	1992	Flawlessly (4)	1997	Ryafan (3)
1982	April Run (4)	1988	Miesque (4)	1993	Flawlessly (5)	1998	Fiji (4)
1983	All Along (4)	1989	Brown Bess (7)	1994	Hatoof (5)	1999	Soaring Softly (4)
1984	Royal Heroine (4)					2000	Perfect Sting (4)

Sprinter

Year		Year		Year		Year	
1971	Ack Ack (5)	1979	Star de Naskra (4)	1987	Groovy (4)	1995	Not Surprising (4)
1972	Chou Croute (4)	1980	Plugged Nickle (3)	1988	Gulch (4)	1996	Lit de Justice (6)
1973	Shecky Greene (3)	1981	Guilty Conscience (5)	1989	Safely Kept (3)	1997	Smoke Glacken (3)
1974	Forego (4)	1982	Gold Beauty (3)	1990	Housebuster (3)	1998	Reraise (3)
1975	Gallant Bob (3)	1983	Chinook Pass (4)	1991	Housebuster (4)	1999	Artax (4)
1976	My Juliet (4)	1984	Eillo (4)	1992	Rubiano (5)	2000	Kona Gold (6)
1977	What a Summer (4)	1985	Precisionist (4)	1993	Cardmania (7)		
1978	(TIE) Dr. Patches (4) & J.O. Tobin (4)	1986	Smile (5)	1994	Cherokee Run (4)		

Steeplechase or Hurdle Horse

Year		Year		Year		Year	
1971	Shadow Brook (7)	1979	Martie's Anger (4)	1986	Flatterer (7)	1993	Lonesome Glory (5)
1972	Soothsayer (5)	1980	Zaccio (4)	1987	Inlander (6)	1994	Warm Spell (6)
1973	Athenian Idol (5)	1981	Zaccio (5)	1988	Jimmy Lorenzo (6)	1995	Lonesome Glory (7)
1974	Gran Kan (8)	1982	Zaccio (6)	1989	Highland Bud (4)	1996	Correggio (5)
1975	Life's Illusion (4)	1983	Flatterer (4)	1990	Morley Street (6)	1997	Lonesome Glory (9)
1976	Straight and True (6)	1984	Flatterer (5)	1991	Morley Street (7)	1998	Flat Top (5)
1977	Cafe Prince (7)	1985	Flatterer (6)	1992	Lonesome Glory (4)	1999	Lonesome Glory (11)
1978	Cafe Prince (8)					2000	All Gong (6)

Outstanding Jockey

Year		Year		Year		Year	
1971	Laffit Pincay Jr.	1979	Laffit Pincay Jr.	1986	Pat Day	1993	Mike Smith
1972	Braulio Baeza	1980	Chris McCarron	1987	Pat Day	1994	Mike Smith
1973	Laffit Pincay Jr.	1981	Bill Shoemaker	1988	Jose Santos	1995	Jerry Bailey
1974	Laffit Pincay Jr.	1982	Angel Cordero Jr.	1989	Kent Desormeaux	1996	Jerry Bailey
1975	Braulio Baeza	1983	Angel Cordero Jr.	1990	Craig Perret	1997	Jerry Bailey
1976	Sandy Hawley	1984	Pat Day	1991	Pat Day	1998	Gary Stevens
1977	Steve Cauthen	1985	Laffit Pincay Jr.	1992	Kent Desormeaux	1999	Jorge Chavez
1978	Darrel McHargue					2000	Jerry Bailey

Outstanding Apprentice Jockey

Year		Year		Year		Year	
1971	Gene St. Leon	1979	Cash Asmussen	1987	Kent Desormeaux	1995	Ramon B. Perez
1972	Thomas Wallis	1980	Frank Lovato Jr.	1988	Steve Capanas	1996	Neil Poznansky
1973	Steve Valdez	1981	Richard Migliore	1989	Michael Luzzi	1997	Roberto Rosado
1974	Chris McCarron	1982	Alberto Delgado	1990	Mark Johnston		& Philip Teator
1975	Jimmy Edwards	1983	Declan Murphy	1991	Mickey Walls	1998	Shaun Bridgmohan
1976	George Martens	1984	Wesley Ward	1992	Rosemary Homeister	1999	Ariel Smith
1977	Steve Cauthen	1985	Art Madrid Jr.	1993	Juan Umana	2000	Tyler Baze
1978	Ron Franklin	1986	Allen Stacy	1994	Dale Beckner		

Outstanding Trainer

Year		Year		Year		Year	
1971	Charlie Whittingham	1979	Laz Barrera	1987	D. Wayne Lukas	1995	Bill Mott
1972	Lucien Laurin	1980	Bud Delp	1988	Shug McGaughey	1996	Bill Mott
1973	H. Allen Jerkens	1981	Ron McAnally	1989	Charlie Whittingham	1997	Bob Baffert
1974	Sherill Ward	1982	Charlie Whittingham	1990	Carl Nafzger	1998	Bob Baffert
1975	Steve DiMauro	1983	Woody Stephens	1991	Ron McAnally	1999	Bob Baffert
1976	Laz Barrera	1984	Jack Van Berg	1992	Ron McAnally	2000	Bobby Frankel
1977	Laz Barrera	1985	D. Wayne Lukas	1993	Bobby Frankel		
1978	Laz Barrera	1986	D. Wayne Lukas	1994	D. Wayne Lukas		

Outstanding Owner

Year		Year		Year		Year	
1971	Mr. & Mrs. E.E. Fogleson	1979	Harbor View Farm	1986	Mr. & Mrs. Gene Klein	1994	John Franks
1972-73	No award	1980	Mr. & Mrs. Bertram Firestone	1987	Mr. & Mrs. Gene Klein	1995	Allen Paulson
1974	Dan Lasater	1981	Dotsam Stable	1988	Ogden Phipps	1996	Allen Paulson
1975	Dan Lasater	1982	Viola Sommer	1989	Ogden Phipps	1997	Carolyn Hine
1976	Dan Lasater	1983	John Franks	1990	Frances Genter	1998	Frank Stronach
1977	Maxwell Gluck	1984	John Franks	1991	Sam-Son Farms	1999	Frank Stronach
1978	Harbor View Farm	1985	Mr. & Mrs. Gene Klein	1992	Juddmonta Farms	2000	Frank Stronach
				1993	John Franks		

Outstanding Breeder

Year		Year		Year		Year	
1971	Paul Mellon	1979	Claiborne Farm	1987	Nelson Bunker Hunt	1995	Juddmonte Farms
1972	C.T. Chenery	1980	Mrs. Henry Paxson	1988	Ogden Phipps	1996	Farnsworth Farms
1973	C.T. Chenery	1981	Golden Chance Farm	1989	North Ridge Farm	1997	John & Betty Mabee
1974	John W. Galbreath	1982	Fred W. Hooper	1990	Calumet Farm	1998	John & Betty Mabee
1975	Fred W. Hooper	1983	Edward P. Taylor	1991	John & Betty Mabee	1999	William S. Farish
1976	Nelson Bunker Hunt	1984	Claiborne Farm	1992	William S. Farish	2000	Frank Stronach
1977	Edward P. Taylor	1985	Nelson Bunker Hunt	1993	Allan Paulson		
1978	Harbor View Farm	1986	Paul Mellon	1994	William T. Young		

Award of Merit

Year		Year		Year		Year	
1976	Jack J. Dreyfus	1984	John Gaines	1990	Warner L. Jones	1995	Ted Bassett III
1977	Steve Cauthen	1985	Keene Daingerfield	1991	Fred W. Hooper	1996	Allen Paulson
1978	Dinny Phipps	1986	Herman Cohen	1992	Joe Hirsch	1997	Robert & Beverly Lewis
1979	Jimmy Kilroe	1987	J.B. Faulconer		& Robert P. Strub	1998	D.G. Van Clief Jr.
1980	John D. Shapiro	1988	John Forsythe	1993	Paul Mellon	2000	Jim McKay
1981	Bill Shoemaker	1989	Michael Sandler	1994	Alfred G. Vanderbilt		

Special Award

Year		Year		Year		Year	
1971	Robert J. Kleberg	1984	C.V. Whitney	1994	Eddie Arcaro & John Longden	1999	Laffit Pincay Jr.
1974	Charles Hatton	1985	Arlington Park			2000	John Hettinger
1976	Bill Shoemaker	1987	Anheuser-Busch	1995	Russell Baze		
1980	John T. Landry & Pierre E. Bellocq	1988	Edward J. DeBartolo Sr.	1998	Oak Tree Racing Assoc.		
		1989	Richard Duchossois				

HARNESS RACING

Triple Crown Winners
PACERS

Nine three-year-olds have won the Cane Pace, Little Brown Jug and Messenger Stakes in the same year since the Pacing Triple Crown was established in 1956. No trainer or driver has won it more than once.

Year		Driver	Trainer	Owner
1959	**Adios Butler**	Clint Hodgins	Paige West	Paige West & Angelo Pellillo
1965	**Bret Hanover**	Frank Ervin	Frank Ervin	Richard Downing
1966	**Romeo Hanover**	Bill Myer & George Sholty*	Jerry Silverman	Lucky Star Stables & Morton Finder
1968	**Rum Customer**	Billy Haughton	Billy Haughton	Kennilworth Farms & L.C. Mancuso
1970	**Most Happy Fella**	Stanley Dancer	Stanley Dancer	Egyptian Acres Stable
1980	**Niatross**	Clint Galbraith	Clint Galbraith	Niagara Acres, Niatross Stables & Clint Galbraith
1983	**Ralph Hanover**	Ron Waples	Stew Firlotte	Waples Stable, Pointsetta Stable, Grant's Direct Stable & P.J. Baugh
1997	**Western Dreamer**	Mike Lachance	Bill Robinson Stable	Matthew, Daniel and Patrick Daly
1999	**Blissful Hall**	Ron Pierce	Benn Wallace	Daniel Plouffe

*Myer drove Romeo Hanover in the Cane, Sholty in the other two races.

TROTTERS

Six three-year-olds have won the Yonkers Trot, Hambletonian and Kentucky Futurity in the same year since the Trotting Triple Crown was established in 1955. Stanley Dancer is the only driver/trainer to win it twice.

Year		Driver/Trainer	Owner
1955	**Scott Frost**	Joe O'Brien	S.A. Camp Farms
1963	**Speedy Scot**	Ralph Baldwin	Castleton Farms
1964	**Ayres**	John Simpson Sr.	Charlotte Sheppard
1968	**Nevele Pride**	Stanley Dancer	Nevele Acres & Lou Resnick
1969	**Lindy's Pride**	Howard Beissinger	Lindy Farms
1972	**Super Bowl**	Stanley Dancer	Rachel Dancer & Rose Hild Breeding Farm

Harness Racing (Cont.)
Triple Crown Near Misses

PACERS

Nine horses have won the first two legs of the Triple Crown, but not the third. The Cane Pace (CP), Little Brown Jug (LBJ), and Messenger Stakes (MS) have not always been run in the same order so numbers after races won indicate sequence for that year.

Year		CP	LBJ	MS
1957	**Torpid**	won, 1	won, 2	DNF*
1960	**Countess Adios**	won, 2	NE	won, 1
1971	**Albatross**	won, 2	2nd*	won, 1
1976	**Keystone Ore**	won, 1	won, 2	2nd*
1986	**Barberry Spur**	won, 1	won, 2	2nd*
1990	**Jake and Elwood** ...	won, 1	NE	won, 2
1992	**Western Hanover** ...	won, 1	2nd*	won, 2
1993	**Rijadh**	won, 1	2nd*	won, 2
1998	**Shady Character**	won, 1	won, 2	6th*

*Winning horses: Meadow Lands (1957), Nansemond (1971), Windshield Wiper (1976), Amity Chef (1986), Fake Left (1992), Life Sign (1993), Fit for Life (1998).

Note: Torpid (1957) scratched before the final heat; Countess Adios (1960) and Jake and Elwood (1990) not eligible for Little Brown Jug.

TROTTERS

Eight horses have won the first two legs of the Triple Crown—the Yonkers Trot (YT) and the Hambletonian (Ham)—but not the third. The winner of the Ky. Futurity (KF) is listed.

Year		YT	Ham	KF
1962	**A.C.'s Viking**	won	won	Safe Mission
1976	**Steve Lobell**	won	won	Quick Pay
1977	**Green Speed**	won	won	Texas
1978	**Speedy Somolli**	won	won	Doublemint
1987	**Mack Lobell**	won	won	Napoletano
1993	**American Winner** ...	won	won	Pine Chip
1996	**Continentalvictory** ..	won	won	Running Sea
1998	**Muscles Yankee**	won	won	Trade Balance

Note: Green Speed (1977) not eligible for Ky. Futurity; Continentalvictory (1996) was withdrawn from the Ky. Futurity due to a leg injury.

The Hambletonian

For three-year-old trotters. Inaugurated in 1926 and has been held in Syracuse, N.Y.; Lexington, Ky.; Goshen, N.Y.; Yonkers, N.Y.; Du Quoin, Ill.; and since 1981 at The Meadowlands in East Rutherford, N.J.

Run at one mile since 1947. Winning horse must win two heats.

Drivers with most wins: John Campbell (5); Stanley Dancer, Billy Haughton and Ben White (4); Howard Beissinger, Del Cameron, Mike Lachance and Henry Thomas (3).

Year		Driver	Fastest Heat	Year		Driver	Fastest Heat
1926	**Guy McKinney** ...	Nat Ray	2:04¾	1965	**Egyptian Candor** ..	Del Cameron	2:03⅘
1927	**Iosola's Worthy** ..	Marvin Childs	2:03¾	1966	**Kerry Way**	Frank Ervin	1:58⅘
1928	**Spencer**	W.H. Lessee	2:02½	1967	**Speedy Streak**	Del Cameron	2:00
1929	**Walter Dear**	Walter Cox	2:02¾	1968	**Nevele Pride**	Stanley Dancer	1:59⅖
				1969	**Lindy's Pride**	Howard Beissinger	1:57⅗
1930	**Hanover's Bertha** .	Tom Berry	2:03				
1931	**Calumet Butler** ...	R.D. McMahon	2:03¼	1970	**Timothy T**	John Simpson Jr.	1:58⅖
1932	**The Marchioness** ..	Will Caton	2:01¼	1971	**Speedy Crown**	Howard Beissinger	1:57⅖
1933	**Mary Reynolds** ...	Ben White	2:03¾	1972	**Super Bowl**	Stanley Dancer	1:56⅖
1934	**Lord Jim**	Doc Parshall	2:02¾	1973	**Flirth**	Ralph Baldwin	1:57⅕
1935	**Greyhound**	Sep Palin	2:02¼	1974	**Christopher T**	Billy Haughton	1:58⅗
1936	**Rosalind**	Ben White	2:01¾	1975	**Bonefish**	Stanley Dancer	1:59
1937	**Shirley Hanover** ..	Henry Thomas	2:01½	1976	**Steve Lobell**	Billy Haughton	1:56⅖
1938	**McLin Hanover** ...	Henry Tomas	2:02¼	1977	**Green Speed**	Billy Haughton	1:55⅗
1939	**Peter Astra**	Doc Parshall	2:04¼	1978	**Speedy Somolli** ...	Howard Beissinger	1:55
				1979	**Legend Hanover** ..	George Sholty	1:56⅕
1940	**Spencer Scott**	Fred Egan	2:02				
1941	**Bill Gallon**	Lee Smith	2:05	1980	**Burgomeister**	Billy Haughton	1:56⅗
1942	**The Ambassador** ..	Ben White	2:04	1981	**Shiaway St. Pat** ...	Ray Remmen	2:01⅕
1943	**Volo Song**	Ben White	2:02½	1982	**Speed Bowl**	Tommy Haughton	1:56⅘
1944	**Yankee Maid**	Henry Thomas	2:04	1983	**Duenna**	Stanley Dancer	1:57⅖
1945	**Titan Hanover**	Harry Pownall Sr.	2:04	1984	**Historic Freight** ...	Ben Webster	1:56⅖
1946	**Chestertown**	Thomas Berry	2:02½	1985	**Prakas**	Bill O'Donnell	1:54⅗
1947	**Hoot Mon**	Sep Palin	2:00	1986	**Nuclear Kosmos** ..	Ulf Thoresen	1:55⅖
1948	**Demon Hanover** ..	Harrison Hoyt	2:02	1987	**Mack Lobell**	John Campbell	1:53⅗
1949	**Miss Tilly**	Fred Egan	2:01⅖	1988	**Armbro Goal**	John Campbell	1:54⅗
				1989	**Park Avenue Joe** ..	Ron Waples	1:54⅗
1950	**Lusty Song**	Del Miller	2:02		**& Probe** *	Bill Fahy	
1951	**Mainliner**	Guy Crippen	2:02⅗				
1952	**Sharp Note**	Bion Shively	2:02⅗	1990	**Harmonious**	John Campbell	1:54⅕
1953	**Helicopter**	Harry Harvey	2:01⅗	1991	**Giant Victory**	Jack Moiseyev	1:54⅘
1954	**Newport Dream** ..	Del Cameron	2:02⅘	1992	**Alf Palema**	Mickey McNichol	1:56⅖
1955	**Scott Frost**	Joe O'Brien	2:00⅗	1993	**American Winner** .	Ron Pierce	1:53⅕
1956	**The Intruder**	Ned Bower	2:01⅖	1994	**Victory Dream**	Mike Lachance	1:54⅕
1957	**Hickory Smoke** ...	John Simpson Sr.	2:00⅕	1995	**Tagliabue**	John Campbell	1:54⅘
1958	**Emily's Pride**	Flave Nipe	1:59⅘	1996	**Continentalvictory**	Mike Lachance	1:52⅘
1959	**Diller Hanover**	Frank Ervin	2:01⅕	1997	**Malabar Man**	Mal Burroughs	1:55
				1998	**Muscles Yankee** ...	John Campbell	1:52⅖
1960	**Blaze Hanover** ...	Joe O'Brien	1:59⅗	1999	**Self Possessed**	Mike Lachance	1:51⅗
1961	**Harlan Dean**	James Arthur	1:58⅖				
1962	**A.C.'s Viking**	Sanders Russell	1:59⅗	2000	**Yankee Paco**	Trevor Ritchie	1:53⅗
1963	**Speedy Scot**	Ralph Baldwin	1:57⅗	2001	**Scarlet Knight**	Stefan Melander	1:53⅘
1964	**Ayres**	John Simpson Sr.	1:56⅘				

*In 1989, Park Avenue Joe and Probe finished in a dead heat in the race-off. They were later declared co-winners, but Park Avenue Joe was awarded 1st place money because his three-race summary (2-1-1) was better than Probe's (1-9-1).

The Little Brown Jug

Harness racing's most prestigious race for three-year-old pacers. Inaugurated in 1946 and held annually at the Delaware, Ohio County Fairgrounds. Winning horse must win two heats.

Drivers with most wins: Billy Haughton and Mike Lachance (5); Stanley Dancer (4); John Campbell, Frank Ervin and John Simpson Sr. (3); Adelbert Cameron, Herve Filion, Jack Moiseyev, Joe O'Brien, Bill O'Donnell, Ron Pierce, "Curly" Smart and Ron Waples (2).

Year	Horse	Driver	Fastest Heat	Year	Horse	Driver	Fastest Heat
1946	**Ensign Hanover**	"Curly" Smart	2:02	1974	**Armbro Omaha**	Billy Haughton	1:57
1947	**Forbes Chief**	Adelbert Cameron	2:05	1975	**Seatrain**	Ben Webster	1:56⅘
1948	**Knight Dream**	Frank Safford	2:07	1976	**Keystone Ore**	Stanley Dancer	1:56⅘
1949	**Good Time**	Frank Ervin	2:03⅖	1977	**Governor Skipper**	John Chapman	1:56⅕
				1978	**Happy Escort**	Bill Popfinger	1:55⅖
1950	**Dudley Hanover**	Delvin Miller	2:02⅗	1979	**Hot Hitter**	Herve Filion	1:55⅗
1951	**Tar Heel**	Adelbert Cameron	2:00				
1952	**Meadow Rice**	"Curly" Smart	2:01⅗	1980	**Niatross**	Clint Galbraith	1:54⅘
1953	**Keystoner**	Frank Ervin	2:01⅕	1981	**Fan Hanover** (f)	Glen Garnsey	1:56
1954	**Adios Harry**	Morris MacDonald	2:02⅘	1982	**Merger**	John Campbell	1:54⅗
1955	**Quick Chief**	Billy Haughton	2:00	1983	**Ralph Hanover**	Ron Waples	1:55⅗
1956	**Noble Adios**	John Simpson Sr.	2:00⅘	1984	**Colt Fortysix**	Chris Boring	1:53⅗
1957	**Torpid**	John Simpson Sr.	2:00⅘	1985	**Nihilator**	Bill O'Donnell	1:52⅕
1958	**Shadow Wave**	Joe O'Brien	2:01	1986	**Barberry Spur**	Bill O'Donnell	1:52⅘
1959	**Adios Butler**	Clint Hodgkins	1:59⅖	1987	**Jaguar Spur**	Dick Stillings	1:54
				1988	**B.J. Scoot**	Mike Lachance	1:52⅗
1960	**Bullet Hanover**	John Simpson Sr.	1:58⅗	1989	**Goalie Jeff**	Mike Lachance	1:54⅕
1961	**Henry T. Adios**	Stanley Dancer	1:58⅘				
1962	**Lehigh Hanover**	Stanley Dancer	1:58⅘	1990	**Beach Towel**	Ray Remmen	1:53⅗
1963	**Overtrick**	John Patterson Sr.	1:57⅕	1991	**Precious Bunny**	Jack Moiseyev	1:53⅘
1964	**Vicar Hanover**	Billy Haughton	2:00⅘	1992	**Fake Left**	Ron Waples	1:53⅗
1965	**Bret Hanover**	Frank Ervin	1:57	1993	**Life Sign**	John Campbell	1:52
1966	**Romeo Hanover**	George Sholty	1:59⅗	1994	**Magical Mike**	Mike Lachance	1:52⅗
1967	**Best Of All**	Jim Hackett	1:59	1995	**Nick's Fantasy**	John Campbell	1:51⅖
1968	**Rum Customer**	Billy Haughton	1:59⅗	1996	**Armbro Operative**	Jack Moiseyev	1:52⅗
1969	**Laverne Hanover**	Billy Haughton	2:00⅖	1997	**Western Dreamer**	Mike Lachance	1:51⅕
				1998	**Shady Character**	Ron Pierce	1:52⅗
1970	**Most Happy Fella**	Stanley Dancer	1:57⅕	1999	**Blissfull Hall**	Ron Pierce	1:55⅗
1971	**Nansemond**	Herve Filion	1:57⅖				
1972	**Strike Out**	Keith Waples	1:56⅗	2000	**Astreos**	Chris Christoforou	1:55⅗
1973	**Melvin's Woe**	Joe O'Brien	1:57⅗	2001	**Bettor's Delight**	Mike Lachance	1:51⅘

All-Time Leaders

The all-time winning trotters, pacers and drivers through 2000, according to *The Trotting and Pacing Guide*. Purses for horses include races in foreign countries. Earnings and wins for drivers include only races held in North America.

Top 10 Horses — Money Won

		T/P	Sts	1st	Earnings
1	Moni Maker	T	91	60	$5,589,256
2	Peace Corps	T	42	35	4,137,737
3	Ourasi (FRA)	T	N/A	32	4,010,105
4	Mack Lobell	T	86	65	3,917,594
5	Reve d'Udon	T	23	18	3,611,351
6	Zoogin	T	N/A	N/A	3,513,324
7	Nihilator	P	38	35	3,225,653
8	Sea Cove	T	N/A	N/A	3,138,986
9	Artsplace	P	49	37	3,085,083
10	Presidential Ball	P	38	26	3,021,363

Top 10 Drivers — Races Won

		Yrs	1st	Earnings
1	Herve Filion	35	14,783	$85,044,653
2	Walter Case Jr.	23	9,323	37,135,766
3	Cat Manzi	33	8,835	79,678,704
4	Mike Lachance	33	8,806	128,696,540
5	Dave Magee	28	8,617	64,798,245
6	John Campbell	29	8,484	187,626,804
7	Jack Moiseyev	25	7,947	81,893,475
8	Dave Palone	19	7,592	30,338,628
9	Doug Brown	28	7,535	75,209,452
10	Eddie Davis	37	7,534	39,947,212

Annual Awards

Harness Horse of the Year

Selected since 1947 by U.S. Trotting Association and the U.S. Harness Writers Association; age of winning horse is noted; (t) indicates trotter and (p) indicates pacer.

Multiple winners: Bret Hanover and Nevele Pride (3); Adios Butler, Albatross, Cam Fella, Good Time, Mack Lobell, Moni Maker, Niatross and Scott Frost (2).

Year		Year		Year		Year	
1947	Victory Song (4t)	1953	Hi Lo's Forbes (5p)	1960	Adios Butler (4p)	1967	Nevele Pride (2t)
1948	Rodney (4t)	1954	Stenographer (3t)	1961	Adios Butler (5p)	1968	Nevele Pride (3t)
1949	Good Time (3p)	1955	Scott Frost (3t)	1962	Su Mac Lad (8t)	1969	Nevele Pride (4t)
		1956	Scott Frost (4t)	1963	Speedy Scot (3t)		
1950	Proximity (8t)	1957	Torpid (3p)	1964	Bret Hanover (2p)	1970	Fresh Yankee (7t)
1951	Pronto Don (6t)	1958	Emily's Pride (3t)	1965	Bret Hanover (3p)	1971	Albatross (3p)
1952	Good Time (6p)	1959	Bye Bye Byrd (4p)	1966	Bret Hanover (4p)	1972	Albatross (4p)

Annual Awards (Cont.)

Year		Year		Year		Year	
1973	Sir Dalrae (4p)	1980	Niatross (3p)	1987	Mack Lobell (3t)	1993	Staying Together (4p)
1974	Delmonica Hanover (5t)	1981	Fan Hanover (3p)	1988	Mack Lobell (4t)	1994	Cam's Card Shark (3p)
1975	Savoir (7t)	1982	Cam Fella (3p)	1989	Matt's Scooter (4p)	1995	CR Kay Suzie (3t)
1976	Keystone Ore (3p)	1983	Cam Fella (4p)	1990	Beach Towel (3p)	1996	Continentalvictory (3t)
1977	Green Speed (3t)	1984	Fancy Crown (3t)	1991	Precious Bunny (3p)	1997	Malabar Man (3t)
1978	Abercrombie (3p)	1985	Nihilator (3p)	1992	Artsplace (4p)	1998	Moni Maker (5t)
1979	Niatross (2p)	1986	Forrest Skipper (4p)			1999	Moni Maker (6t)
						2000	Gallo Blue Chip (3p)

Driver of the Year

Determined by Universal Driving Rating System (UDR) and presented by the Harness Tracks of America since 1968. Eligible drivers must have at least 1,000 starts for the season.

Multiple winners: Herve Filion (10); John Campbell, Walter Case Jr. and Mike Lachance (3); Tony Morgan, Bill O'Donnell, Luc Ouellette, Dave Palone and Ron Waples (2).

Year		Year		Year		Year	
1968	Stanley Dancer	1977	Donald Dancer	1985	Mike Lachance	1994	Dave Magee
1969	Herve Filion	1978	Carmine Abbatiello	1986	Mike Lachance	1995	Luc Ouellette
			& Herve Filion	1987	Mike Lachance	1996	Tony Morgan
1970	Herve Filion	1979	Ron Waples	1988	John Campbell		& Luc Ouellette
1971	Herve Filion			1989	Herve Filion	1997	Tony Morgan
1972	Herve Filion	1980	Ron Waples			1998	Walter Case Jr.
1973	Herve Filion	1981	Herve Filion	1990	John Campbell	1999	Dave Palone
1974	Herve Filion	1982	Bill O'Donnell	1991	Walter Case Jr.		
1975	Joe O'Brien	1983	John Campbell	1992	Walter Case Jr.	2000	Dave Palone
1976	Herve Filion	1984	Bill O'Donnell	1993	Jack Moiseyev		

STEEPLECHASE RACING

Champion Horses

Annual horse of the year since 1956 based on vote of the National Turf Writers Association and other selected media.

Multiple winners: Lonesome Glory (5); Flatterer (4); Bon Nouvel and Zaccio (3); Café Prince, Morley Street and Neji (2).

Year		Year		Year		Year	
1956	Shipboard	1968	Bon Nouvel	1979	Martie's Anger	1990	Morley Street
1957	Neji	1969	L'Escargot			1991	Morley Street
1958	Neji			1980	Zaccio	1992	Lonesome Glory
1959	Ancestor	1970	Top Bid	1981	Zaccio	1993	Lonesome Glory
		1971	Shadow Brok	1982	Zaccio	1994	Warm Spell
1960	Benguala	1972	Soothsayer	1983	Flatterer	1995	Lonesome Glory
1961	Peal	1973	Athenian Idol	1984	Flatterer	1996	Correggio
1962	Barnaby's Bluff	1974	Gran Kan	1985	Flatterer	1997	Lonesome Glory
1963	Amber Diver	1975	Life's Illusion	1986	Flatterer	1998	Flat Top
1964	Bon Nouvel	1976	Fire Control	1987	Inlander	1999	Lonesome Glory
1965	Bon Nouvel		& Straight and True	1988	Jimmy Lorenzo		
1966	Tuscalee & Mako	1977	Café Prince	1989	Highland Bud	2000	All Gong
1967	Quick Pitch	1978	Café Prince				

Champion Jockeys

Annual leading jockeys by races won since 1956, according to the National Steeplechase Association.

Multiple winners: Joe Aitcheson Jr. (7); Jerry Fishback (5); John Cushman and Alfred P. Smithwick (4); Tom Skiffington and Jeff Teter (3); Ricky Hendriks, Jonathan Kiser, James Lawrence, Blythe Miller, Chip Miller and Thomas Walsh (2).

Year		Year		Year		Year	
1956	Alfred P. Smithwick	1968	Joe Aitcheson Jr.	1980	John Cushman	1992	Craig Thornton
1957	Alfred P. Smithwick	1969	Joe Aitcheson Jr.	1981	John Cushman	1993	James Lawrence
1958	Alfred P. Smithwick			1982	John Cushman	1994	Blythe Miller
1959	James Murphy	1970	Joe Aitcheson Jr.	1983	John Cushman	1995	Blythe Miller
		1971	Jerry Fishback	1984	Jeff Teter	1996	Chip Miller
1960	Thomas Walsh	1972	Michael O'Brien	1985	Bernie Houghton	1997	Arch Kingsley Jr.
1961	Joe Aitcheson Jr.	1973	Jerry Fishback	1986	Ricky Hendriks		& Jonathan Kiser
1962	Alfred P. Smithwick	1974	Jerry Fishback	1987	Ricky Hendriks	1998	Chip Miller
1963	Joe Aitcheson Jr.	1975	Jerry Fishback	1988	Jonathan Smart		& Sean Clancy
1964	Joe Aitcheson Jr.	1976	Tom Skiffington	1989	James Lawrence	1999	Jonathan Kiser
1965	Doug Small Jr.	1977	Jerry Fishback			2000	Gus Brown
1966	Thomas Walsh	1978	Tom Skiffington	1990	Jeff Teter		
1967	Joe Aitcheson Jr.	1979	Tom Skiffington	1991	Jeff Teter		

Tennis

Jennifer Capriati cradles her trophy after winning the
2001 French Open, her second major title of the year.

Sister Act

Sal Paolantonio is a tennis analyst for ESPN.

Big sister prevails when Venus and Serena meet for the U.S. Open title.

Venus and Serena Williams walked together onto center court at Arthur Ashe Stadium, holding two sparkling bouquets of yellow flowers. The stadium was full. Flash bulbs sparkled like a thousand fireflies in the New York night. A huge American flag was unfurled and a national television audience waited for this moment in history.

Two sisters, who grew up in the Los Angeles ghetto of Compton, were about to play for the U.S. Open championship. It was a grand moment, perhaps the biggest splash caused by the game of tennis since Billie Jean King spanked Bobby Riggs at the Astrodome in what seems like a lifetime ago.

Two sisters had not played in the final of a major championship in 117 years. And the fact that they were African-Americans playing in a stadium named for another great black champion made it all the more significant.

That's the memory we will have of the 2001 tennis season—the spectacular moments before the beginning of the U.S. Open women's final. Diana Ross sang the national anthem, then she gave Venus a kiss and Serena a big hug. It had a Super Bowl feel.

And then it was time for tennis. Unfortunately that had a Super Bowl feel as well. It was a blowout. Venus beat her younger sister easily. Indeed, in the nine previous matches pitting sisters against one another at a Grand Slam event, the older sister had prevailed in all nine of them.

This would be no different. Serena sprayed the ball all over the court. Venus responded with little strategy of her own, but she had enough to win easily.

"Super Bowl coaches have Super Bowl game plans," said my SportsCenter partner, Luke Jensen. "Venus and Serena had no game plans. They went for everything on every shot."

Venus' sloppy victory over her sister, however, will not diminish her accomplishments over the last two years.

AP/Wide World Photos

Venus Williams, right, had no trouble with sister Serena in the U.S. Open, where for the first time since 1884, sisters faced each other in the final of a Grand Slam event.

Winning the 2001 Wimbledon title gave her two straight at the All-England Club. And the 2001 U.S. Open championship gave her two straight in Flushing Meadows. Without a doubt, Venus is the grand dame of the game right now.

That's not to take anything away from Jennifer Capriati. She began the year by winning the Australian Open, the first Grand Slam singles win of her long, tortuous career. No one will ever forget Capriati's joyous celebration Down Under, hugging her father, Stefano, who stood by her through all the troubled teenage years.

Four months later, Capriati added the French Open title, creating a storm of anticipation that she might win Wimbledon and ultimately the Grand Slam. But she fell in the semifinals at Wimbledon to Justine Henin.

Capriati never believed that she was on a personal mission to claim all four major titles in one year. For the first time in her career she seemed to be at peace with her game and, perhaps more importantly, herself.

"I don't feel like I have to prove anything to anyone anymore," she said at Wimbledon.

Neither does Pete Sampras. And yet the talk of his retirement persists. At age 30, after getting married to actress Bridgette Wilson and beginning to con-

AP/Wide World Photos

Goran Ivanisevic of Croatia raises his arms in celebration and disbelief after his improbable Wimbledon victory.

centrate more on his business interests in Los Angeles, Sampras has, at times, not looked like the dominant Pistol Pete of old.

He was unceremoniously blasted out of Wimbledon by Roger Federer—after winning seven of the eight previous titles. After leaving England in July, he rested and prepared for one last spectacular run at the U.S. Open.

In four glorious tie-breakers under the lights at Ashe Stadium, Sampras prevailed over fellow legend and old foe Andre Agassi in the quarterfinals. Prior to the fourth-set tie-break, the New York

crowd gave both players a standing ovation.

Then Sampras vanquished the defending champ, Russian Marat Safin in the semis. Safin had embarrassed Sampras in the 2000 U.S. Open final, so a bit of revenge was in order. Prior to beating Agassi and Safin, Sampras beat Australian Patrick Rafter. So, to get to the final, Sampras beat the three previous U.S. Open champions.

And that's where he ran out of gas. His opponent in the final was Lleyton Hewitt, a 20-year-old human pinball from

continued on page 810 ▶

Sal Paolantonio's Ten Biggest Stories of the Year in Tennis

10 ■ In July, retired star Steffi Graf and the world's #1 ranked player Andre Agassi announce they are expecting a baby boy in December 2001.

9 ■ With his come-from-behind four-set victory over Alex Corretja, clay court artist Gustavo Kuerten of Brazil wins the French Open for the second year in a row and third time in the last five years.

8 ■ Jennifer Capriati, 24, wins the Australian Open, the first Grand Slam title of her career, completing her long road back. A heavy underdog, Capriati beat defending champ Lindsay Davenport, four-time champ Monica Seles and then top-seeded Martina Hingis 6-4, 6-3 for the title.

7 ■ Venus and Serena Williams meet in the women's finals of the U.S. Open. They are the first sisters to meet in a Grand Slam championship match since 1884 when Maud Watson beat Lillian Watson at Wimbledon, the first official year of women's play at Wimbledon.

6 ■ Twenty-year-old Australian Lleyton Hewitt thrashes Pete Sampras in straight sets 7-6 (4), 6-1, 6-1 in the U.S. Open finals to win his first major title. Hewitt commits just 13 unforced errors in the entire match.

5 ■ Pete Sampras defeats Andre Agassi in four sets, all of which extend to a tiebreaker, in the thrilling U.S. Open quarterfinals. The match lasts over three and a half hours and is viewed by more than 23,000 spectators in Arthur Ashe Stadium. The win gives Sampras an 18-14 edge in their head-to-head history.

4 ■ Jennifer Capriati continues to impress, winning the French Open 1-6, 6-4, 12-10 over Belgian Kim Clijsters. It is her second Grand Slam title of the year.

3 ■ With her 6-1, 3-6, 6-0 win over Belgian Justine Henin, Venus Williams wins her second consecutive Wimbledon women's singles title.

2 ■ Goran Ivanisevic defeats Patrick Rafter in five gripping sets 6-3, 3-6, 6-3, 2-6, 9-7, in the finals of Wimbledon, to win his first major singles championship. He becomes the first wild card ever to win a Wimbledon title.

1 ■ Venus Williams claims her second consecutive U.S. Open championship with an easy 6-2, 6-4 finals win over sister Serena. Neither player is at her best, but Serena's 36 unforced errors prove to be the difference. The two have now combined to win the past three U.S. Opens.

Australia. Hewitt won the first set in a tie-break, then swept the next two sets 6-1, 6-1, as Sampras looked tired, distracted and demoralized that his body would not do what his mind commanded.

Is Sampras done? The easy answer to that question is yes. He has not won a major championship since Wimbledon in 2000, which gave him a record 13 Grand Slam titles.

But he continues to show tremendous competitive spirit and determination. And he still possesses the Big Hammer—his powerful first serve that reaches speeds of up to 135 mph, and an elusive, very accurate second serve that hits the corners at 120 mph.

Until those are gone, Sampras will not go away.

Two Timers

Jennifer Capriati became just the fifth woman to win the Australian Open and the French Open in the same year. If she does it four more times, she'll match Margaret Smith Court's five.

	Years
J. Capriati	2001
M. Seles	'91,'92
S. Graf	'88
M. Smith Court	'62,'64,'69,'70,'73
M. Connolly	'53

Out of Nowhere

Goran Ivanisevic is the first wild card to win a Wimbledon men's singles title. Listed are the lowest-ranked men to win any Grand Slam event.

	Rank	Event
M. Edmondson, '76	212	Aus
G. Ivanisevic, '01	125	Wim
G. Kuerten, '97	66	Fre
A. Agassi, '94	20	U.S.
B. Becker, '85	20	Wim
M. Wilander, '82	18	Fre

Baby Boomers

Lleyton Hewitt tied John McEnroe as the second-youngest U.S. Open champ.

(Men's)	Yrs	Mo's	Days
P. Sampras, '90	19	0	28
McEnroe, '79	20	6	13
Hewitt, '01	20	6	13
Safin, '00	20	7	13

Major League

After her U.S. Open win, Venus Williams is now tied for third on the active women's Grand Slam titles list.

Monica Seles	9
Martina Hingis	5
Venus Williams	4
Arantxa Sanchez Vicario	4

2000-2001 Season in Review

Tournament Results

Winners of men's and women's pro singles championships from Oct. 29, 2000 through Sept. 16, 2001.

Men's ATP Tour

LATE 2000

Finals	Tournament	Winner	Earnings	Runner-Up	Score
Oct. 29	Kremlin Cup (Moscow)	Yevgeny Kafelnikov	$137,000	D. Prinosil	62 75
Oct. 29	Swiss Indoors (Basel)	Thomas Enqvist	137,000	R. Federer	62 46 76 16 61
Nov. 5	TMS—Stuttgart	Wayne Ferreira	434,000	L. Hewitt	76 36 67 76 62
Nov. 12	Grand Prix de Tennis (Lyon)	Arnaud Clement	109,000	P. Rafter	76 76
Nov. 19	TMS—Paris	Marat Safin	434,000	M. Philippoussis	36 76 64 36 76
Nov. 26	Stockholm Open	Thomas Johansson	109,000	Y. Kafelnikov	62 64 64
Nov. 26	Samsung Open (Brighton)	Tim Henman	54,000	D. Hrbaty	62 62
Dec. 3	Tennis Masters Cup (Lisbon)	Gustavo Kuerten	1,400,000	A. Agassi	64 64 64
Dec. 10	ATP World Doubles Champs	Donald Johnson/ Piet Norval	150,000	L. Paes/M. Bhupathi	76 63 64

2001

Finals	Tournament	Winner	Earnings	Runner-Up	Score
Jan. 7	AAPT Championships (Adelaide)	Tommy Haas	$49,500	N. Massu	63 61
Jan. 7	Qatar Open (Doha)	Marcelo Rios	137,000	B. Uihrach	63 26 63
Jan. 7	Gold Flake Open (Chennai)	Michal Tabara	54,000	A. Stoliarov	62 76
Jan. 14	adidas International (Sydney)	Lleyton Hewitt	54,000	M. Norman	64 61
Jan. 14	Heineken Open (Auckland)	Dominik Hrbaty	49,500	F. Clavet	46 62 63
Jan. 28	**Australian Open** (Melbourne)	Andre Agassi	462,887	A. Clement	64 62 62
Feb. 4	Milan Indoors	Roger Federer	54,000	J. Boutter	64 67 64
Feb. 4	Colombia Open (Bogota)	Fernando Vicente	49,500	J.I. Chela	64 76
Feb. 18	Marseille Open	Yevgeny Kafelnikov	34,000	S. Grosjean	76 62
Feb. 18	Copenhagen Open	Tim Henman	22,600	A. Vinciguerra	63 64
Feb. 25	Kroger St. Jude (Memphis)	Mark Philippoussis	120,000	D. Sanguintti	63 67 63
Feb. 25	ABN/AMRO World Tennis Tournament (Rotterdam)	Nicolas Escude	139,300	R. Federer	75 36 76
Feb. 25	AT&T Cup (Buenos Aires)	Gustavo Kuerten	84,000	J. Acasuso	61 63
Mar. 4	Mexican Open (Acapulco)	Gustavo Kuerten	130,000	G. Blanco	64 62
Mar. 4	Dubai Open	Juan Carlos Ferrero	167,000	M. Safin	62 31 ret.
Mar. 4	Sybase Open (San Jose)	Greg Rusedski	54,000	A. Agassi	63 64
Mar. 11	Citrix Tennis Championships (Delray Beach)	Jan-Michael Gambill	46,000	X. Malisse	75 64
Mar. 11	Franklin Templeton Tennis Classic (Scottsdale)	Francisco Clavet	54,000	M. Norman	64 62
Mar. 18	TMS—Indian Wells	Andre Agassi	400,000	P. Sampras	76 75 61
Apr. 1	TMS—Ericsson Open (Miami)	Andre Agassi	444,000	J. Gambill	76 61 60
Apr. 15	Estoril Open	Juan Carlos Ferrero	180,000	F. Mantilla	76 46 63
Apr. 22	TMS—Monte Carlo	Gustavo Kuerten	400,000	H. Arazi	63 62 64
Apr. 29	Open Seat Godo (Barcelona)	Juan Carlos Ferrero	148,000	C. Moya	46 75 63 36 75
Apr. 29	Verizon Tennis Challenge (Atlanta)	Andy Roddick	54,000	X. Malisse	62 64
May 6	BMW Open (Munich)	Jiri Novak	54,000	A. Dupuis	64 75
May 6	U.S. Men's Clay Court Champs (Houston)	Andy Roddick	46,000	H. Lee	75 63
May 6	Mallorca Open	Alberto Martin	66,400	G. Coria	63 36 62
May 13	TMS—Rome	Juan Carlos Ferrero	400,000	G. Kuerten	36 61 26 64 62
May 20	TMS—Hamburg	Albert Portas	400,000	J. C. Ferrero	46 62 06 76 75
May 27	ATP World Team Championship (Dusseldorf)	Australia	500,000	Russia	2-1
May 27	International Raiffeisen Grand Prix (St. Poelten)	Andrea Gaudenzi	57,000	M. Hipfl	60 75
June 10	**French Open** (Paris)	Gustavo Kuerten	588,664	A. Corretja	67 75 62 60
June 17	Gerry Weber Open (Halle)	Thomas Johansson	137,000	F. Santoro	63 67 62
June 17	Stella Artois Championships (London)	Lleyton Hewitt	91,000	T. Henman	76 76
June 24	Heineken Trophy (s'Hertogenbosch)	Lleyton Hewitt	54,000	G. Canas	63 64
June 24	Nottingham Open	Thomas Johansson	54,000	H. Levy	75 63
July 9	**Wimbledon** (London)	Goran Ivanisevic	705,310	P. Rafter	63 36 63 26 97

Tournament Results (Cont.)

Finals	Tournament	Winner	Earnings	Runner-Up	Score
July 15	Swedish Open (Bastad)	Andrea Gaudenzi	$54,000	B. Uihrach	75 63
July 15	Gstaad Open	Jiri Novak	81,000	J.C. Ferrero	61 67 75
July 15	Hall of Fame Championships (Newport)	Neville Godwin	54,000	M. Lee	61 64
July 22	Mercedes Cup (Stuttgart)	Gustavo Kuerten	120,000	G. Canas	63 62 64
July 22	Dutch Open (Amsterdam)	Alex Corretja	54,000	Y. El Aynaoui	36 63 57 76 64
July 22	Croatian Open (Umag)	Carlos Moya	54,000	J. Golmard	64 36 76
July 29	Generali Open (Kitzbuhel)	Nicolas Lapentti	137,000	A. Costa	16 64 75 75
July 29	Idea Prokom Open (Sopot)	Tommy Robredo	54,000	A. Portas	16 75 76
July 29	Mercedes-Benz Cup (Los Angeles)	Andre Agassi	54,000	P. Sampras	64 62
Aug. 5	TMS—Montreal	Andrei Pavel	54,000	P. Rafter	76 26 63
Aug. 12	TMS—Cincinnati	Gustavo Kuerten	400,000	P. Rafter	61 63
Aug. 19	RCA Championships (Indianapolis)	Patrick Rafter	115,000	G. Kuerten	42 ret.
Aug. 19	Legg Mason Classic (Washington D.C.)	Andy Roddick	115,000	S. Schalken	63 62
Aug. 26	Hamlet Cup (Commack)	Tommy Haas	54,000	P. Sampras	63 36 62
Sept. 9	**U.S. Open** (Flushing)	Lleyton Hewitt	850,000	P. Sampras	76 61 61
Sept. 16	Gelsor Open (Bucharest)	Younes El Aynaoui	54,000	A. Montanes	76 76
Sept. 16	President's Cup (Tashkent)	Marat Safin	74,000	Y. Kafelnikov	62 62
Sept. 16	Brasil Open (Salvador)	Jan Vacek	54,000	F. Meligeni	26 76 63

Note: In 2000, the ATP Tour replaced the prestigious Mercedes Super 9 and the ATP Championship tournaments with the Tennis Masters Series and the Tennis Masters Cup. Tennis Masters Series tournaments are identified by TMS.

Women's WTA Tour

LATE 2000

Finals	Tournament	Winner	Earnings	Runner-Up	Score
Oct. 29	Ladies Kremlin Cup (Moscow)	Martina Hingis	$166,000	A. Kournikova	63 61
Oct. 29	Slovak Indoor (Bratislava)	Daniela Bedanova	16,000	M. Oremans	61 57 63
Nov. 5	Sparkassen Cup (Leipzig)	Kim Clijsters	87,000	E. Likhovtseva	76 46 64
Nov. 5	Bell Challenge (Quebec City)	Chanda Rubin	27,000	J. Capriati	64 62
Nov. 12	Advanta Championships (Philadelphia)	Lindsay Davenport	87,000	M. Hingis	76 64
Nov. 12	Wismilak International (Kuala Lumpur)	Henrieta Nagyova	27,573	I. Majoli	64 62
Nov. 19	Chase Championships (New York)	Martina Hingis	500,000	M. Seles	67 64 64
Nov. 19	Volvo Women's Open (Pattaya)	Anne Kremer	16,000	T. Panova	61 64

2001

Finals	Tournament	Winner	Earnings	Runner-Up	Score
Jan. 6	Australian Hardcourt Champs (Gold Coast)	Justine Henin	$27,000	S. Farina Elia	76 64
Jan. 6	ASB Bank Classic (Auckland)	Meilen Tu	16,000	P. Suarez	76 62
Jan. 13	adidas International (Sydney)	Martina Hingis	81,000	L. Davenport	63 46 75
Jan. 13	ANZ Tasmanian Int'l (Hobart)	Rita Grande	16,000	J. Hopkins	06 63 63
Jan. 13	Canberra International	Justine Henin	27,000	S. Testud	62 62
Jan. 28	**Australian Open** (Melbourne)	Jennifer Capriati	462,887	M. Hingis	64 63
Feb. 4	Pan Pacific Open (Tokyo)	Lindsay Davenport	175,000	M. Hingis	67 64 62
Feb. 11	Open Gaz de France (Paris)	Amelie Mauresmo	90,000	A. Huber	76 61
Feb. 18	Terazura 2001 (Nice)	Amelie Mauresmo	90,000	M. Maleeva	62 60
Feb. 18	Qatar Open (Doha)	Martina Hingis	27,000	S. Testud	63 62
Feb. 25	Dubai Open	Martina Hingis	80,000	N. Tauziat	64 64
Feb. 25	IGA U.S. Indoors (Oklahoma City)	Monica Seles	27,000	J. Capriati	63 57 62
Feb. 25	Copa Colsanitas (Bogota)	Paola Suarez	27,000	R. Kuti Kis	62 64
Mar. 4	State Farm Tennis Classic (Scottsdale)	Lindsay Davenport	90,000	M. Shaughnessy	62 63
Mar. 4	Mexican Open (Acapulco)	Amanda Coetzer	27,000	E. Dementieva	26 61 62
Mar. 18	Tennis Masters Series—Indian Wells	Serena Williams	330,000	K. Clijsters	46 64 62
Apr. 1	Ericsson Open (Miami)	Venus Williams	375,000	J. Capriati	46 61 76
Apr. 8	Porto Ladies Open	Arantxa Sanchez Vicario	22,000	M. Serna	63 61
Apr. 15	Bausch & Lomb Championships (Amelia Island)	Amelie Mauresmo	90,000	A. Coetzer	64 75
Apr. 15	Estoril Open	Angeles Montolio	22,000	E. Bovina	36 63 62
Apr. 22	Family Circle Cup (Charleston)	Jennifer Capriati	178,000	M. Hingis	60 46 64
Apr. 22	Budapest Open	Magdalena Maleeva	16,000	A. Kremer	36 62 64
May 6	Betty Barclay Cup (Hamburg)	Venus Williams	90,000	M. Shaughnessy	63 60
May 6	Croatian Bol Open	Angeles Montolio	27,000	M. Diaz Oliva	63 62 64
May 13	German Open (Berlin)	Amelie Mauresmo	175,000	J. Capriati	64 26 63
May 20	Benelux Open (Antwerp)	Barbara Rittner	16,000	K. Koukalova	63 62
May 27	Strasbourg International	Silvia Farina Elia	27,000	A. Huber	75 06 64
May 27	Madrid Open	Arantxa Sanchez Vicario	27,000	A. Montolio	75 60
June 10	**French Open** (Paris)	Jennifer Capriati	557,000	K. Clijsters	16 64 1210

Finals	Tournament	Winner	Earnings	Runner-Up	Score
June 17	DFS Classic (Birmingham)	Nathalie Tauziat	$27,000	M. Oremans	63 75
June 17	Tashkent Open	Bianka Lamade	22,000	S. Noorlander	63 26 62
June 24	Heineken Trophy ('s-Hertogenbosch)	Justine Henin	27,000	K. Clijsters	64 36 63
June 24	Britannic Asset Management (Eastbourne)	Lindsay Davenport	90,000	M. Serna	62 60
July 8	**Wimbledon** (London)	Venus Williams	647,500	J. Henin	61 36 60
July 15	Palermo International	Ana Isabel Medina Garrigues	16,000	C. Torrens Valero	64 64
July 15	UNIQA Grand Prix (Klagenfurt)	Iroda Tulyaganova	23,500	P. Schnyder	63 62
July 22	Sanex Trophy (Knokke-Heist)	Iroda Tulyaganova	23,500	G. Leon Garcia	62 63
July 29	Idea Prokom Open (Sopot)	Cristina Torrens Valero	27,000	G. Leon Garcia	62 62
July 29	Bank of the West Classic (Stanford)	Kim Clijsters	90,000	L. Davenport	64 67 61
July 29	Grand Prix De S.A.R. (Casablanca)	Zsofia Gubacsi	16,000	M. Elena Camerin	16 63 76
Aug. 5	Acura Classic (San Diego)	Venus Williams	125,000	M. Seles	62 63
Aug. 5	PreCon Open (Basel)	Adriana Gersi	22,000	M. Mikaelian	64 61
Aug. 12	estyle.com Classic (Los Angeles)	Lindsay Davenport	90,000	M. Seles	63 75
Aug. 19	Rogers AT&T Cup (Toronto)	Serena Williams	178,000	J. Capriati	61 67 63
Aug. 26	Pilot Pen Tennis (New Haven)	Venus Williams	90,000	L. Davenport	76 64
Sept. 9	**U.S. Open** (Flushing)	Venus Williams	850,000	S. Williams	62 64
Sept. 16	Brasil Open (Costa Do Sauipe)	Monica Seles	100,000	J. Dokic	63 63
Sept. 16	Big Island Championships (Waikoloa)	Sandrine Testud	22,000	J. Henin	63 20 ret.

2001 Grand Slam Tournaments

Australian Open

MEN'S SINGLES

FINAL EIGHT—#5 Yevgeny Kafelnikov; #6 Andre Agassi; #12 Patrick Rafter; #14 Dominik Hrbaty; #15 Arnaud Clement; #16 Sebastien Grosjean; plus unseeded Todd Martin and Carlos Moya.

Quarterfinals

Clement def. Kafelnikov . . . . .64 57 76(3) 76(3)
Grosjean def. Moya 61 64 62
Agassi def. Martin 75 63 64
Rafter def. Hrbaty . . . . .62 67(4) 75 60

Semifinals

Clement def. Grosjean . . . . .57 26 76(4) 75 62
Agassi def. Rafter . . . . .75 26 67(5) 62 63

Final

Agassi def. Clement .64 62 62

WOMEN'S SINGLES

FINAL EIGHT—#1 Martina Hingis; #2 Lindsay Davenport; #3 Venus Williams; #4 Monica Seles; #6 Serena Williams; #8 Anna Kournikova; #10 Amanda Coetzer; #12 Jennifer Capriati.

Quarterfinals

Hingis def. S. Williams 62 36 86
V. Williams def. Coetzer 26 61 86
Capriati def. Seles 57 64 63
Davenport def. Kournikova 64 62

Semifinals

Hingis def. V. Williams 61 61
Capriati def. Davenport 63 64

Final

Capriati def. Hingis 64 63

DOUBLES FINALS

Men—#4 Jonas Bjorkman & Todd Woodbridge def. #14 Byron Black & David Prinosil, 6-1, 5-7, 6-4, 6-4.

Women—Serena Williams & Venus Williams def. #7 Lindsay Davenport & Corina Morariu, 6-2, 4-6, 6-4.

Mixed—#3 Ellis Ferreira & Corina Morariu def. #4 Joshua Eagle & Barbara Schett, 6-1, 6-3.

French Open

MEN'S SINGLES

FINAL EIGHT—#1 Gustavo Kuerten; #3 Andre Agassi; #4 Juan Carlos Ferrero; #6 Lleyton Hewitt; #7 Yevgeny Kafelnikov; #10 Sebastien Grosjean and #13 Alex Corretja; plus unseeded Roger Federer.

Quarterfinals

Kuerten def. Kafelnikov . . . . .61 36 76(3) 64
Ferrero def. Hewitt .64 62 61
Grosjean def. Agassi 16 61 61 63
Federer def. Corretja 57 46 57

Semifinals

Kuerten def. Ferrero 64 64 63
Grosjean def. Corretja . . . . .76(2) 64 64

Final

Kuerten def. Corretja . . . . .67(3) 75 62 60

WOMEN'S SINGLES

FINAL EIGHT—#1 Martina Hingis; #4 Jennifer Capriati; #6 Serena Williams; #12 Kim Clijsters; #14 Justine Henin; plus unseeded Lina Krasnoroutskaya, Petra Mandula and Francesca Schiavone.

Quarterfinals

Hingis def. Schiavone .61 64
Capriati def. Williams 62 57 62
Clijsters def. Mandula .61 63
Henin def. Krasnoroutskaya 61 62

Semifinals

Capriati def. Hingis 64 63
Clijsters def. Henin 26 75 63

Final

Capriati def. Clijsters 16 64 1210

DOUBLES FINALS

Men—Mahesh Bhupathi & Leander Paes def. #13 Petr Pala & Pavel Vizner, 7-6 (7-5), 6-3.

Women—#2 Virginia Ruano-Pascual & Paola Suarez def. #16 Jelena Dokic & Conchita Martinez, 6-2, 6-1.

Mixed—Virginia Ruano-Pascual & Tomas Carbonell def. Paola Suarez & Jaime Oncins, 7-5, 6-3.

Wimbledon

MEN'S SINGLES

FINAL EIGHT—#2 Andre Agassi; #3 Patrick Rafter; #4 Marat Safin; #6 Tim Henman; #10 Thomas Enqvist; #15 Roger Federer; #24 Nicolas Escude; plus unseeded Goran Ivanisevic.

Quarterfinals

Henman def. Federer .... 75 76(6) 26 76(6)
Ivanisevic def. Safin .... 76(2) 75 36 76(3)
Rafter def. Enqvist .... 61 63 76(5)
Agassi def. Escude .... 67(3) 63 64 62

Semifinals

Ivanisevic def. Henman .... 75 67(6) 06 76(5) 63
Rafter def Agassi 26 63 36 62 86

Final

Ivanisevic def. Rafter 63 36 63 26 97

WOMEN'S SINGLES

FINAL EIGHT—#2 Venus Williams; #3 Lindsay Davenport; #4 Jennifer Capriati; #5 Serena Williams; #7 Kim Clijsters; #8 Justine Henin; #9 Nathalie Tauziat; #19 Conchita Martinez.

Quarterfinals

Henin def. Martinez 61 60
Capriati def. S. Williams .... 67(4) 75 63
Davenport def. Clijsters 61 62
V. Williams def. Tauziat 75 61

Semifinals

Henin def. Capriati 26 64 62
V. Williams def. Davenport .... 62 67(1) 61

Final

V. Williams def. Henin 61 36 60

DOUBLES FINALS

Men—#3 Jiri Novak & David Rikl def. #4 Donald Johnson & Jared Palmer 6-4, 4-6, 6-3, 7-6 (8-6).

Women—#1 Lisa Raymond & Rennae Stubbs def. #9 Kim Clijsters & Ai-Sugiyama 6-4, 6-3.

Mixed—Leos Friedl & Daniela Hantuchova def. Mike Bryan & Liezel Huber 4-6, 6-3, 6-2.

U.S. Open

MEN'S SINGLES

FINAL EIGHT—#1 Gustavo Kuerten, #2 Andre Agassi, #3 Marat Safin, #4 Lleyton Hewitt, #7 Yevgeny Kafelnikov, #10 Pete Sampras, #18 Andy Roddick; plus unseeded Mariano Zabaleta.

Quarterfinals

Kafelnikov def. Kuerten 64 60 63
Hewitt def. Roddick................. 67(5) 63 64 36 64
Safin def. Zabaleta....................... 64 64 62
Sampras def. Agassi............ 67(7) 76(2) 76(2) 76(5)

Semifinals

Hewitt def. Kafelnikov 61 62 61
Sampras def. Safin .... 63 76(5) 63

Final

Hewitt def. Sampras .... 76(4) 61 61

WOMEN'S SINGLES

FINAL EIGHT—#1 Martina Hingis; #2 Jennifer Capriati; #3 Lindsay Davenport, #4 Venus Williams, #5 Kim Clijsters, #8 Amelie Mauresmo, #10 Serena Williams; plus unseeded Daja Bedanova.

Quarterfinals

Hingis def. Bedanova 62 60
S. Williams def. Davenport .... 63 76(7) 75
V. Williams def. Clijsters 63 61
Capriati def. Mauresmo....................... 63 64

Semifinals

S. Williams def. Hingis 63 62
V. Williams def. Capriati 64 62

Final

V. Williams def. S. Williams 62 64

DOUBLES FINALS

Men—#14 Wayne Black & Kevin Ullyett def. #2 Donald Johnson & Jared Palmer 7-6 (11-9), 2-6, 6-3.

Women—#1 Lisa Raymond & Rennae Stubbs def. #4 Kimberly Po-Messerli & Nathalie Tauziat 6-2, 5-7, 7-5.

Mixed—#1 Rennae Stubbs & Todd Woodbridge def. #2 Lisa Raymond & Leander Paes 6-4, 5-7, 7-6 (11-9).

Fed Cup

Originally the Federation Cup and started in 1963 by the International Tennis Federation as the Davis Cup of women's tennis.

2000 FINAL

United States 5, Spain 0

at Las Vegas, Nev. (Nov. 24-25)

Day One (singles)—Monica Seles (USA) def. Conchita Martinez (SPA) 6-2, 6-3; Lindsay Davenport (USA) def. Arantxa Sanchez Vicario (SPA), 6-2, 1-6, 6-3.

Day Two (s)—Davenport (USA) def. Martinez (SPA) 6-1, 6-2; Capriati (USA) def. Sanchez Vicario 6-1, 1-0 ret.

Day Two (doubles)—Jennifer Capriati & Lisa Raymond (USA) def. Virginia Ruano-Pascual & Magui Serna (SPA) 4-6, 6-4, 6-2.

SEMIFINALS

Spain 2, Czech Republic 1

at Las Vegas, Nev. (Nov. 21)

Day One (s)—Arantxa Sanchez Vicario (SPA) def. Daja Bedanova (CZR) 5-7, 6-4, 6-3; Conchita Martinez (SPA) def. Kveta Hrdlickova (CZR) 7-6 (7-3), 6-7 (7-2), 6-4.

Day One (d)—Bedanova & Hrdlickova (CZR) def. Virginia Ruano-Pascual & Magui Serna (SPA) 1-6, 6-3, 7-6 (7-5).

United States 2, Belgium 1

at Las Vegas, Nev. (Nov. 22)

Day One (s)—Monica Seles (USA) def. Justine Henin (BEL) 7-6 (7-1), 6-2; Lindsay Davenport (USA) def. Kim Clijsters (BEL) 7-6 (7-4), 4-6, 6-3.

Day One (d)—Els Callens & Dominique Van Roost (BEL) def. Jennifer Capriati & Lisa Raymond (USA) 6-3, 7-5.

2001 Early Rounds

FIRST ROUND

(April 28-29)

Winner	Loser
at Italy 4	Croatia 1
Argentina 4	at Japan 1
at Slovakia 4	Hungary 1
at Australia 5	Austria 0

SECOND ROUND

(July 21-22)

Winner	Loser
at France 4	Italy 1
Argentina 4	at Germany 1
Russia 3	at Slovakia 2
at Australia 4	Switzerland 1

SEMIFINALS & FINAL

The 2001 Fed Cup semifinal round-robin tournament and final will be held from Nov. 7-11 in Madrid, Spain. The following eight teams have qualified: **Group A**—United States, France, Czech Republic, Argentina; **Group B**—Belgium, Spain, Russia, Australia.

Singles Leaders

Official Top 20 rankings and money leaders of men's and women's tours for 2000 and unofficial rankings for 2001 (through Sept. 16), as compiled by the ATP Tour (Association of Tennis Professionals) and WTA (Women's Tennis Association). Note that money lists include doubles earnings.

Final 2000 Rankings and Money Won

Listed are events won and times a finalist and semifinalist (Finish, 1-2-SF), match record (W-L), and earnings for the year.

MEN

		Finish 1-2-SF	W-L	Earnings
1	Gustavo Kuerten	5-2-3	63-22	$4,701,610
2	Marat Safin	7-2-3	73-27	3,524,959
3	Pete Sampras	2-2-2	42-13	2,254,598
4	Magnus Norman	5-1-4	67-25	1,846,269
5	Yevgeny Kafelnikov	2-3-4	66-35	3,755,599
6	Andre Agassi	1-2-3	40-15	1,884,443
7	Lleyton Hewitt	4-1-5	61-19	1,642,572
8	Alex Corretja	5-0-2	54-19	1,530,062
9	Thomas Enqvist	2-3-2	51-23	2,381,060
10	Tim Henman	2-3-3	57-25	1,057,823
11	Mark Philippoussis	1-2-1	43-22	839,567
12	Juan Carlos Ferrero	0-2-3	46-26	812,636
13	Wayne Ferreira	1-0-2	43-22	1,237,864
14	Franco Squillari	2-0-2	34-24	754,458
15	Patrick Rafter	1-2-1	34-19	814,586
16	Cedric Pioline	2-0-2	32-20	888,789
17	Dominik Hrbaty	0-3-1	44-29	1,195,760
18	Arnaud Clement	1-0-3	36-27	671,815
19	Sebastien Grosjean	1-1-2	44-26	655,280
20	Nicolas Kiefer	2-0-2	30-16	591,749

WOMEN

		Finish 1-2-SF	W-L	Earnings
1	Martina Hingis	9-4-5	77-10	$3,457,049
2	Lindsay Davenport	4-8-0	60-12	2,444,734
3	Venus Williams	6-1-0	41-4	2,074,150
4	Monica Seles	3-3-5	58-13	1,140,850
5	Conchita Martinez	1-3-4	51-23	1,067,930
6	Serena Williams	3-2-1	37-8	1,026,818
7	Mary Pierce	2-0-2	29-11	1,208,018
8	Anna Kournikova	0-1-8	47-29	984,930
9	Arantxa Sanchez Vicario	0-2-4	45-19	819,689
10	Nathalie Tauziat	1-0-5	36-26	761,211
11	Amanda Coetzer	1-1-3	46-23	593,357
12	Elena Dementieva	0-0-4	40-22	613,627
13	Chanda Rubin	1-1-3	42-21	528,020
14	Jennifer Capriati	1-1-3	36-19	488,861
15	Julie Halard-Decugis	2-1-1	32-23	879,570
16	Amelie Mauresmo	1-2-2	24-13	365,074
17	Sandrine Testud	0-1-1	31-21	547,384
18	Kim Clijsters	2-1-0	30-17	559,245
19	Anke Huber	2-0-1	32-16	447,441
20	Amy Frazier	0-1-3	30-22	306,059

2001 Tour Rankings (through Sept. 16)

Listed are tournaments won and times a finalist and semifinalist (Finish, 1-2-SF), match record (W-L), and points earned (Pts). The **ATP Champions Race** replaced the men's pro tennis tour's 27-year-old computer ranking system in 2000. Under the new system players start from zero on Jan. 1 and accumulate points during the calendar year with the player accumulating the most points becoming the World No. 1. Points are awarded in 18 tournaments: nine Tennis Masters Series events, four Grand Slams and five other International Series events.

MEN

Final ATP Tour singles rankings will be based on points earned from 18 tournaments played in 2001. Tournaments, titles and match won-lost records are for 2001 only.

Rank 01	(00)		Finish 1-2-SF	W-L	Pts
1	1	Gustavo Kuerten	6-2-1	59-11	755
2	6	Andre Agassi	4-1-2	44-11	683
3	7	Lleyton Hewitt	4-0-5	64-15	635
4	15	Patrick Rafter	1-3-3	46-14	557
5	12	Juan Carlos Ferrero	4-2-1	49-14	552
6	5	Yevgeny Kafelnikov	1-1-4	51-23	400
7	3	Pete Sampras	0-4-1	33-15	363
8	19	Sebastien Grosjean	0-1-5	38-18	360
9	10	Tim Henman	1-1-3	42-17	352
10	29	Roger Federer	1-1-2	43-16	324
11	2	Marat Safin	1-2-2	34-22	315
12	8	Alex Corretja	1-1-1	32-15	303
13	96	Goran Ivanisevic	1-1-1	24-15	296
14	18	Arnaud Clement	0-1-1	34-23	293
15	160	Andy Roddick	3-0-1	37-12	275
16	23	Tommy Haas	2-0-2	41-18	256
17	130	Guillermo Canas	1-2-2	35-16	246
18	38	Thomas Johansson	2-0-2	39-20	245
19	33	Jan-Michael Gambill	1-1-1	35-23	242
20	41	Carlos Moya	1-1-2	32-19	241

WOMEN

Sanex WTA Tour singles ranking system based on total Round and Quality Points for each tournament played during the last 12 months. Tournaments, titles and match won-lost records, however, are for 2001 only.

Rank 01	(00)		Finish 1-2-SF	W-L	Pts
1	1	Martina Hingis	3-3-8	57-13	5256
2	14	Jennifer Capriati	3-4-4	52-11	5123
3	2	Lindsay Davenport	4-3-3	47-9	4345
4	3	Venus Williams	6-0-3	46-5	4333
5	18	Kim Clijsters	1-3-3	42-15	3176
6	16	Amelie Mauresmo	4-1-1	42-8	2842
7	6	Serena Williams	2-1-0	35-7	2753
8	48	Justine Henin	3-2-3	51-14	2742
9	4	Monica Seles	2-2-3	31-10	2414
10	10	Nathalie Tauziat	1-1-3	28-15	2083
11	26	Jelena Dokic	1-1-3	37-19	1808
12	39	Meghann Shaughnessy	0-2-2	41-21	1756
13	11	Amanda Coetzer	1-1-1	28-17	1603
14	17	Sandrine Testud	1-2-1	46-22	1580
15	63	Silvia Farina Elia	1-1-2	38-21	1535
16	22	Magdalena Maleeva	1-1-2	26-18	1522
17	12	Elena Dementieva	0-1-1	27-16	1515
18	23	Barbara Schett	0-0-1	26-20	1389
19	9	Arantxa Sanchez Vicario	2-0-1	26-16	1286
20	8	Anna Kournikova	0-0-1	8-5	1258

2001 Money Winners

Amounts include singles and doubles earnings through Sept. 16, 2001.

MEN

		Earnings			Earnings			Earnings
1	Gustavo Kuerten	$2,271,514	11	Jan-Michael Gambill	$746,976	21	Tommy Haas	$609,230
2	Lleyton Hewitt	1,998,118	12	Alex Corretja	737,112	22	Nicolas Escude	596,929
3	Andre Agassi	1,854,896	13	Andrei Pavel	721,514	23	Nicolas Lapentti	588,257
4	Patrick Rafter	1,580,592	14	Roger Federer	713,555	24	Fabrice Santoro	582,911
5	Juan Carlos Ferrero	1,443,221	15	Jonas Bjorkman	711,596	25	Thomas Johansson	562,072
6	Yevgeny Kafelnikov	1,243,699	16	Sebastien Grosjean	697,434	26	Sjeng Schalken	529,740
7	Pete Sampras	931,281	17	Tim Henman	691,149	27	Hicham Arazi	504,378
8	Goran Ivanisevic	925,350	18	Arnaud Clement	680,190	28	Carlos Moya	474,002
9	Marat Safin	882,102	19	Andy Roddick	663,314	29	Todd Woodbridge	473,430
10	Albert Portas	752,354	20	Jiri Novak	614,938	30	Dominik Hrbaty	470,713

WOMEN

		Earnings			Earnings			Earnings
1	Venus Williams	$2,522,610	11	Nathalie Tauziat	$603,585	21	Virginia Ruano-Pascual	$373,221
2	Jennifer Capriati	2,073,024	12	Rennae Stubbs	536,554	22	Ai Sugiyama	371,814
3	Martina Hingis	1,382,029	13	Monica Seles	503,211	23	Elena Dementieva	357,439
4	Serena Williams	1,336,263	14	Meghann Shaughnessy	498,926	24	Anke Huber	356,122
5	Lindsay Davenport	1,154,492	15	Sandrine Testud	461,376	25	Cara Black	348,589
6	Kim Clijsters	961,809	16	Elena Likhovtseva	451,577	26	Magdalena Maleeva	332,384
7	Justine Henin	821,004	17	Arantxa Sanchez Vicario	428,642	27	Barbara Schett	326,734
8	Amelie Mauresmo	794,602	18	Paola Suarez	421,552	28	Silvia Farina Elia	321,276
9	Lisa Raymond	722,085	19	Amanda Coetzer	420,319	29	Magui Serna	259,114
10	Jelena Dokic	625,891	20	Conchita Martinez	374,517	30	Henrieta Nagyova	255,862

Davis Cup

With Spain's King Juan Carlos watching in the stands, 20-year-old Juan Carlos Ferrero captured a four-set victory over Australian star Lleyton Hewitt that earned Spain a 3-1 victory in the 2000 final and its first-ever Davis Cup title. Here is a recap of the 2000 final, plus a summary of the 2001 Davis Cup tournament.

2000 FINAL
Spain 3, Australia 1
at Barcelona, Spain (Dec. 8-10)

Day One—Lleyton Hewitt (AUS) def. Albert Costa (SPA), 3-6, 6-1, 2-6, 6-4, 6-4; Juan Carlos Ferrero (SPA) def. Patrick Rafter (AUS), 6-7 (4-7), 7-6 (7-2), 6-2, 3-1 ret.

Day Two—Juan Balcells & Alex Corretja (SPA) def. Mark Woodforde & Sandon Stolle (AUS), 6-4, 6-4, 6-4.

Day Three—Ferrero (SPA) def. Hewitt (AUS), 6-2, 7-6 (7-5), 4-6, 6-4; Corretja (SPA) vs. Rafter (AUS), cancelled.

2001 Early Rounds
FIRST ROUND
(Feb. 9-11)

Winner	Loser
at Australia 4	Ecuador 1
at Brazil 4	Morocco 1
at Sweden 3	Czech Republic 2
Russia 5	at Slovakia 0
France 5	at Belgium 0
at Switzerland 3	United States 2
Germany 3	at Romania 2
at Netherlands 4	Spain 1

QUARTERFINALS
(Apr. 6-8)

Winner	Loser
Australia 3	at Brazil 1
at Sweden 4	Russia 1
France 3	at Switzerland 2
at Netherlands 4	Germany 1

2001 SEMIFINALS
Australia 4, Sweden 1
at Sydney, Australia (Sept. 21-23)

Day One—Thomas Johansson (SWE) def. Patrick Rafter (AUS) 3-6, 6-7 (8-10), 6-3, 6-2, 6-3; Lleyton Hewitt (AUS) def. Jonas Bjorkman (SWE) 4-6, 6-4, 7-6 (7-5), 7-6 (7-2).

Day Two—Wayne Arthurs & Todd Woodbridge (AUS) def. Bjorkman & Magnus Larsson (SWE) 6-7 (3-7), 7-6 (7-2), 7-6 (7-5), 7-6 (7-3).

Day Three—Rafter (AUS) def. Bjorkman (SWE) 6-3, 6-1; Hewitt (AUS) def. Johansson (SWE) 7-6 (7-3), 5-7, 6-2, 6-1.

France 3, Netherlands 2
at Rotterdam, Netherlands (Sept. 21-23)

Day One—Arnaud Clement (FRA) def. Raemon Sluiter (NED) 3-6, 6-2, 2-1, ret.; Nicolas Escude (FRA) def. Sjeng Schalken (NED) 6-7 (5-7), 7-6 (7-4), 4-6, 7-6 (7-4), 8-6.

Day Two—Cedric Pioline & Fabrice Santoro (FRA) def. Paul Haarhuis & Schalken (NED) 7-5, 6-1, 7-5.

Day Three—Jan Siemerink (NED) def. Fabrice Santoro (FRA) 6-4, 6-4; Schalken (NED) def. Clement (FRA) 7-6 (8-6), 7-6 (7-4).

2001 FINAL

Australia, which is making its third straight trip to the finals, will host France from Nov. 30 to Dec. 2 in Melbourne. Australia beat France in 1999 to win its 27th title. This is the fourth time in the past 10 years that France has reached the final. France will be chasing its ninth Davis Cup title. The two nations have met 13 times in Davis Cup competition, Australia leading the head-to-head tally 10-3.

1877-2001 Through the Years

Grand Slam Championships
Australian Open
MEN

Became an Open Championship in 1969. Two tournaments were held in 1977; the first in January, the second in December. Tournament moved back to January in 1987, so no championship was decided in 1986.

Surface: Synpave Rebound Ace (hardcourt surface composed of polyurethane and synthetic rubber).

Multiple winners: Roy Emerson (6); Jack Crawford and Ken Rosewall (4); Andre Agassi, James Anderson, Rod Laver, Adrian Quist, Mats Wilander and Pat Wood (3); Boris Becker, Jack Bromwich, Ashley Cooper, Jim Courier, Stefan Edberg, Rodney Heath, Johan Kriek, Ivan Lendl, John Newcombe, Pete Sampras, Frank Sedgman, Guillermo Vilas and Tony Wilding (2).

Year	Winner	Loser	Score	Year	Winner	Loser	Score
1905	Rodney Heath	A. Curtis	46 63 64 64	1957	Ashley Cooper	N. Fraser	63 9-11 64 62
1906	Tony Wilding	H. Parker	60 64 64	1958	Ashley Cooper	M. Anderson	75 63 64
1907	Horace Rice	H. Parker	63 64 64	1959	Alex Olmedo	N. Fraser	61 62 36 63
1908	Fred Alexander	A. Dunlop	36 36 60 62 63	1960	Rod Laver	N. Fraser	57 36 63 86 86
1909	Tony Wilding	E. Parker	61 75 62	1961	Roy Emerson	R. Laver	16 63 75 64
1910	Rodney Heath	H. Rice	64 63 62	1962	Rod Laver	R. Emerson	86 06 64 64
1911	Norman Brookes	H. Rice	61 62 63	1963	Roy Emerson	K. Fletcher	63 63 61
1912	J. Cecil Parke	A. Beamish	36 63 16 61 75	1964	Roy Emerson	F. Stolle	63 64 62
1913	Ernie Parker	H. Parker	26 61 62 63	1965	Roy Emerson	F. Stolle	79 26 64 75 61
1914	Pat Wood	G. Patterson	64 63 57 61	1966	Roy Emerson	A. Ashe	64 68 62 63
1915	Francis Lowe	H. Rice	46 61 61 64	1967	Roy Emerson	A. Ashe	64 61 61
1916-18	Not held	World War I		1968	Bill Bowrey	J. Gisbert	75 26 97 64
1919	A.R.F. Kingscote	E. Pockley	64 60 63	1969	Rod Laver	A. Gimeno	63 64 75
1920	Pat Wood	R. Thomas	63 46 68 61 63	1970	Arthur Ashe	D. Crealy	64 97 62
1921	Rhys Gemmell	A. Hedeman	75 61 64	1971	Ken Rosewall	A. Ashe	61 75 63
1922	James Anderson	G. Patterson	60 36 36 63 62	1972	Ken Rosewall	M. Anderson	76 63 75
1923	Pat Wood	C.B. St. John	61 61 63	1973	John Newcombe	O. Parun	63 67 75 61
1924	James Anderson	R. Schlesinger	63 64 36 57 63	1974	Jimmy Connors	P. Dent	76 64 46 63
1925	James Anderson	G. Patterson	11-9 26 62 63	1975	John Newcombe	J. Connors	75 36 64 75
1926	John Hawkes	J. Willard	61 63 61	1976	Mark Edmondson	J. Newcombe	67 63 76 61
1927	Gerald Patterson	J. Hawkes	36 64 36 18 16 63	1977	Roscoe Tanner	G. Vilas	63 63 63
1928	Jean Borotra	R.O. Cummings	64 61 46 57 63		Vitas Gerulaitis	J. Lloyd	63 76 57 36 62
1929	John Gregory	R. Schlesinger	62 62 57 75	1978	Guillermo Vilas	J. Marks	64 64 36 63
				1979	Guillermo Vilas	J. Sadri	76 63 62
1930	Gar Moon	H. Hopman	63 61 63	1980	Brian Teacher	K. Warwick	75 76 63
1931	Jack Crawford	H. Hopman	64 62 26 61	1981	Johan Kriek	S. Denton	62 76 67 64
1932	Jack Crawford	H. Hopman	46 63 36 63 61	1982	Johan Kriek	S. Denton	63 63 62
1933	Jack Crawford	K. Gledhill	26 75 63 62	1983	Mats Wilander	I. Lendl	61 64 64
1934	Fred Perry	J. Crawford	63 75 61	1984	Mats Wilander	K. Curren	67 64 76 62
1935	Jack Crawford	F. Perry	26 64 64 64	1985	Stefan Edberg	M. Wilander	64 63 63
1936	Adrian Quist	J. Crawford	62 63 46 36 97	1986	Not held		
1937	Viv McGrath	J. Bromwich	63 16 60 26 61	1987	Stefan Edberg	P. Cash	63 64 36 57 63
1938	Don Budge	J. Bromwich	64 62 61	1988	Mats Wilander	P. Cash	63 67 36 61 86
1939	Jack Bromwich	A. Quist	64 61 63	1989	Ivan Lendl	M. Mecir	62 62 62
1940	Adrian Quist	J. Crawford	63 61 62	1990	Ivan Lendl	S. Edberg	46 76 52 (ret.)
1941-45	Not held	World War II		1991	Boris Becker	I. Lendl	16 64 64 64
1946	Jack Bromwich	D. Pails	57 63 75 36 62	1992	Jim Courier	S. Edberg	63 36 64 62
1947	Dinny Pails	J. Bromwich	46 64 36 75 86	1993	Jim Courier	S. Edberg	62 61 26 75
1948	Adrian Quist	J. Bromwich	64 36 63 26 63	1994	Pete Sampras	T. Martin	76 64 64
1949	Frank Sedgman	J. Bromwich	63 63 62	1995	Andre Agassi	P. Sampras	46 61 76 64
1950	Frank Sedgman	K. McGregor	63 64 46 61	1996	Boris Becker	M. Chang	62 64 26 62
1951	Dick Savitt	K. McGregor	63 26 63 61	1997	Pete Sampras	C. Moya	62 63 63
1952	Ken McGregor	F. Sedgman	75 12-10 26 62	1998	Petr Korda	M. Rios	62 62 62
1953	Ken Rosewall	M. Rose	60 63 64	1999	Yevgeny Kafelnikov	T. Enqvist	46 60 63 76
1954	Mervyn Rose	R. Hartwig	62 06 64 62	2000	Andre Agassi	Y. Kafelnikov	36 63 62 64
1955	Ken Rosewall	L. Hoad	97 64 64	2001	Andre Agassi	A. Clement	64 62 62
1956	Lew Hoad	K. Rosewall	64 36 64 75				

WOMEN

Became an Open Championship in 1969. Two tournaments were held in 1977, the first in January, the second in December. Tournament moved back to January in 1987, so no championship was decided in 1986.

Multiple winners: Margaret Smith Court (11); Nancye Wynne Bolton (6); Daphne Akhurst (5); Evonne Goolagong Cawley, Steffi Graf and Monica Seles (4); Joan Hartigan, Martina Hingis and Martina Navratilova (3); Coral Buttsworth, Chris Evert Lloyd, Thelma Long, Hana Mandlikova, Mall Molesworth and Mary Carter Reitano (2).

Year	Winner	Loser	Score	Year	Winner	Loser	Score
1922	Mall Molesworth	E. Boyd	63 10-8	1965	Margaret Smith	M. Bueno	57 64 52 (ret)
1923	Mall Molesworth	E. Boyd	61 75	1966	Margaret Smith	N. Richey	walkover
1924	Sylvia Lance	E. Boyd	63 36 64	1967	Nancy Richey	L. Turner	61 64
1925	Daphne Akhurst	E. Boyd	16 86 64	1968	Billie Jean King	M. Smith	61 62
1926	Daphne Akhurst	E. Boyd	61 63	1969	Margaret Court	B.J. King	64 61
1927	Esna Boyd	S. Harper	57 61 62				
1928	Daphne Akhurst	E. Boyd	75 62	1970	Margaret Court	K. Melville	61 63
1929	Daphne Akhurst	L. Bickerton	61 57 62	1971	Margaret Court	E. Goolagong	26 76 75
				1972	Virginia Wade	E. Goolagong	64 64
1930	Daphne Akhurst	S. Harper	10-8 26 75	1973	Margaret Court	E. Goolagong	64 75
1931	Coral Buttsworth	M. Crawford	16 63 64	1974	Evonne Goolagong	C. Evert	76 46 60
1932	Coral Buttsworth	K. Le Messurier	97 64	1975	Evonne Goolagong	M. Navratilova	63 62
1933	Joan Hartigan	C. Buttsworth	64 63	1976	Evonne Cawley	R. Tomanova	62 62
1934	Joan Hartigan	M. Molesworth	61 64	1977	Kerry Reid	D. Balestrat	75 62
1935	Dorothy Round	N. Lyle	16 61 63		Evonne Cawley	H. Gourlay	63 60
1936	Joan Hartigan	N. Bolton	64 64	1978	Chris O'Neil	B. Nagelsen	63 76
1937	Nancye Wynne	E. Westacott	63 57 64	1979	Barbara Jordan	S. Walsh	63 63
1938	Dorothy Bundy	D. Stevenson	63 62				
1939	Emily Westacott	N. Hopman	61 62	1980	Hana Mandlikova	W. Turnbull	60 75
				1981	Martina Navratilova	C. Evert Lloyd	67 64 75
1940	Nancye Wynne	T. Coyne	57 64 60	1982	Chris Evert Lloyd	M. Navratilova	63 26 63
1941-45	Not held	World War II		1983	Martina Navratilova	K. Jordan	62 76
1946	Nancye Bolton	J. Fitch	64 64	1984	Chris Evert Lloyd	H. Sukova	67 61 63
1947	Nancye Bolton	N. Hopman	63 62	1985	Martina Navratilova	C. Evert Lloyd	62 46 62
1948	Nancye Bolton	M. Toomey	63 61	1986	Not held		
1949	Doris Hart	N. Bolton	63 64	1987	Hana Mandlikova	M. Navratilova	75 76
				1988	Steffi Graf	C. Evert	61 76
1950	Louise Brough	D. Hart	64 36 64	1989	Steffi Graf	H. Sukova	64 64
1951	Nancye Bolton	T. Long	61 75				
1952	Thelma Long	H. Angwin	62 63	1990	Steffi Graf	M.J. Fernandez	63 64
1953	Maureen Connolly	J. Sampson	63 64	1991	Monica Seles	J. Novotna	57 63 61
1954	Thelma Long	J. Staley	63 64	1992	Monica Seles	M.J. Fernandez	62 63
1955	Beryl Penrose	T. Long	64 63	1993	Monica Seles	S. Graf	46 63 62
1956	Mary Carter	T. Long	36 62 97	1994	Steffi Graf	A.S. Vicario	60 62
1957	Shirley Fry	A. Gibson	63 64	1995	Mary Pierce	A.S. Vicario	63 62
1958	Angela Mortimer	L. Coghlan	63 64	1996	Monica Seles	A. Huber	64 61
1959	Mary Reitano	T. Schuurman	62 63	1997	Martina Hingis	M. Pierce	62 62
				1998	Martina Hingis	C. Martinez	63 63
1960	Margaret Smith	J. Lehane	75 62	1999	Martina Hingis	A. Mauresmo	62 63
1961	Margaret Smith	J. Lehane	61 64				
1962	Margaret Smith	J. Lehane	60 62	2000	Lindsay Davenport	M. Hingis	61 75
1963	Margaret Smith	J. Lehane	62 62	2001	Jennifer Capriati	M. Hingis	64 63
1964	Margaret Smith	L. Turner	63 62				

French Open

MEN

Prior to 1925, entry was restricted to members of French clubs. Became an Open Championship in 1968, but closed to contract pros in 1972.

Surface: Red clay.

First year: 1891. **Most wins:** Max Decugis (8).

Multiple winners (since 1925): Bjorn Borg (6); Henri Cochet (4); Gustavo Kuerten, Rene Lacoste, Ivan Lendl and Mats Wilander (3); Sergi Bruguera, Jim Courier, Jaroslav Drobny, Roy Emerson, Jan Kodes, Rod Laver, Frank Parker, Nicola Pietrangeli, Ken Rosewall, Manuel Santana, Tony Trabert and Gottfried von Cramm (2).

Year	Winner	Loser	Score	Year	Winner	Loser	Score
1925	Rene Lacoste	J. Borotra	75 61 64	1938	Don Budge	R. Menzel	63 62 64
1926	Henri Cochet	R. Lacoste	62 64 63	1939	Don McNeill	B. Riggs	75 60 63
1927	Rene Lacoste	B. Tilden	64 46 57 63 11-9				
1928	Henri Cochet	R. Lacoste	57 63 61 63	1941-45	Not held	World War II	
1929	Rene Lacoste	J. Borotra	63 26 60 26 86	1946	Marcel Bernard	J. Drobny	36 26 61 64 63
				1947	Joseph Asboth	E. Sturgess	86 75 64
1930	Henri Cochet	B. Tilden	36 86 63 61	1948	Frank Parker	J. Drobny	64 75 57 86
1931	Jean Borotra	C. Boussus	26 64 75 64	1949	Frank Parker	B. Patty	63 16 61 64
1932	Henri Cochet	G. de Stefani	60 64 46 63				
1933	Jack Crawford	H. Cochet	86 61 63	1950	Budge Patty	J. Drobny	61 62 36 57 75
1934	Gottfried von Cramm	J. Crawford	64 79 36 75 63	1951	Jaroslav Drobny	E. Sturgess	63 63 63
1935	Fred Perry	G. von Cramm	63 36 61 63	1952	Jaroslav Drobny	F. Sedgman	62 60 36 64
1936	Gottfried von Cramm	F. Perry	60 26 62 26 60	1953	Ken Rosewall	V. Seixas	63 64 16 62
1937	Henner Henkel	H. Austin	61 64 63	1954	Tony Trabert	A. Larsen	64 75 61

Year	Winner	Loser	Score
1955	Tony Trabert	S. Davidson	26 61 64 62
1956	Lew Hoad	S. Davidson	64 86 63
1957	Sven Davidson	H. Flam	63 64 64
1958	Mervyn Rose	L. Ayala	63 64 64
1959	Nicola Pietrangeli	I. Vermaak	36 63 64 61
1960	Nicola Pietrangeli	L. Ayala	36 63 64 46 63
1961	Manuel Santana	N. Pietrangeli	46 61 36 60 62
1962	Rod Laver	R. Emerson	36 26 63 97 62
1963	Roy Emerson	P. Darmon	36 61 64 64
1964	Manuel Santana	N. Pietrangeli	63 61 46 75
1965	Fred Stolle	T. Roche	36 60 62 63
1966	Tony Roche	I. Gulyas	61 64 75
1967	Roy Emerson	T. Roche	61 64 26 62
1968	Ken Rosewall	R. Laver	63 61 26 62
1969	Rod Laver	K. Rosewall	64 63 64
1970	Jan Kodes	Z. Franulovic	62 64 60
1971	Jan Kodes	I. Nastase	86 62 26 75
1972	Andres Gimeno	P. Proisy	46 63 61 61
1973	Ilie Nastase	N. Pilic	63 63 60
1974	Bjorn Borg	M. Orantes	26 67 60 61 61
1975	Bjorn Borg	G. Vilas	62 63 64
1976	Adriano Panatta	H. Solomon	61 64 46 76
1977	Guillermo Vilas	B. Gottfried	60 63 60
1978	Bjorn Borg	G. Vilas	61 61 63
1979	Bjorn Borg	V. Pecci	63 61 67 64
1980	Bjorn Borg	V. Gerulaitis	64 61 62
1981	Bjorn Borg	I. Lendl	61 46 62 36 61
1982	Mats Wilander	G. Vilas	16 76 60 64
1983	Yannick Noah	M. Wilander	62 75 76
1984	Ivan Lendl	J. McEnroe	36 26 64 75 75
1985	Mats Wilander	I. Lendl	36 64 62 62
1986	Ivan Lendl	M. Pernfors	63 62 64
1987	Ivan Lendl	M. Wilander	75 62 36 76
1988	Mats Wilander	H. Leconte	75 62 61
1989	Michael Chang	S. Edberg	61 36 46 64 62
1990	Andres Gomez	A. Agassi	63 26 64 64
1991	Jim Courier	A. Agassi	36 64 26 61 64
1992	Jim Courier	P. Korda	75 62 61
1993	Sergi Bruguera	J. Courier	64 26 62 36 63
1994	Sergi Bruguera	A. Berasategui	63 75 26 61
1995	Thomas Muster	M. Chang	75 62 64
1996	Yevgeny Kafelnikov	M. Stich	76 75 76
1997	Gustavo Kuerten	S. Bruguera	63 64 62
1998	Carlos Moya	A. Corretja	63 75 63
1999	Andre Agassi	A. Medvedev	16 26 64 63 64
2000	Gustavo Kuerten	M. Norman	62 63 26 76
2001	Gustavo Kuerten	A. Corretja	67 75 62 60

WOMEN

Prior to 1925, entry was restricted to members of French clubs. Became an Open Championship in 1968, but closed to contract pros in 1972.

First year: 1897. **Most wins:** Chris Evert Lloyd (7); Suzanne Lenglen and Steffi Graf (6).

Multiple winners (since 1925): Chris Evert Lloyd (7); Steffi Graf (6); Margaret Smith Court (5); Helen Wills Moody (4); Arantxa Sanchez Vicario, Monica Seles and Hilde Sperling (3); Maureen Connolly, Margaret Osborne duPont, Doris Hart, Ann Haydon Jones, Suzanne Lenglen, Simone Mathieu, Margaret Scriven, Martina Navratilova and Lesley Turner (2).

Year	Winner	Loser	Score
1925	Suzanne Lenglen	K. McKane	61 62
1926	Suzanne Lenglen	M. Browne	61 60
1927	Kea Bouman	I. Peacock	62 64
1928	Helen Wills	E. Bennett	61 62
1929	Helen Wills	S. Mathieu	63 64
1930	Helen Moody	H. Jacobs	62 61
1931	Cilly Aussem	B. Nuthall	86 61
1932	Helen Moody	S. Mathieu	75 61
1933	Margaret Scriven	S. Mathieu	62 46 64
1934	Margaret Scriven	H. Jacobs	75 46 61
1935	Hilde Sperling	S. Mathieu	62 61
1936	Hilde Sperling	S. Mathieu	63 64
1937	Hilde Sperling	S. Mathieu	62 64
1938	Simone Mathieu	N. Landry	60 63
1939	Simone Mathieu	J. Jedrzejowska	63 86
1940-45	Not held	World War II	
1946	Margaret Osborne	P. Betz	16 86 75
1947	Patricia Todd	D. Hart	63 36 64
1948	Nelly Landry	S. Fry	62 06 60
1949	Margaret duPont	N. Adamson	75 62
1950	Doris Hart	P. Todd	64 46 62
1951	Shirley Fry	D. Hart	63 36 63
1952	Doris Hart	S. Fry	64 64
1953	Maureen Connolly	D. Hart	62 64
1954	Maureen Connolly	G. Bucaille	64 61
1955	Angela Mortimer	D. Knode	26 75 10-8
1956	Althea Gibson	A. Mortimer	60 12-10
1957	Shirley Bloomer	D. Knode	61 63
1958	Susi Kormoczi	S. Bloomer	64 16 62
1959	Christine Truman	S. Kormoczi	64 75
1960	Darlene Hard	Y. Ramirez	63 64
1961	Ann Haydon	Y. Ramirez	62 61
1962	Margaret Smith	L. Turner	63 36 75
1963	Lesley Turner	A. Jones	26 63 75
1964	Margaret Smith	M. Bueno	57 61 62
1965	Lesley Turner	M. Smith	63 64
1966	Ann Jones	N. Richey	63 61
1967	Francoise Durr	L. Turner	46 63 64
1968	Nancy Richey	A. Jones	57 64 61
1969	Margaret Court	A. Jones	61 46 63
1970	Margaret Court	H. Niessen	62 64
1971	Evonne Goolagong	H. Gourlay	63 75
1972	Billie Jean King	E. Goolagong	63 63
1973	Margaret Court	C. Evert	67 76 64
1974	Chris Evert	O. Morozova	61 62
1975	Chris Evert	M. Navratilova	26 62 61
1976	Sue Barker	R. Tomanova	62 06 62
1977	Mima Jausovec	F. Mihai	62 67 61
1978	Virginia Ruzici	M. Jausovec	62 62
1979	Chris Evert Lloyd	W. Turnbull	62 60
1980	Chris Evert Lloyd	V. Ruzici	60 63
1981	Hana Mandlikova	S. Hanika	62 64
1982	Martina Navratilova	A. Jaeger	76 61
1983	Chris Evert Lloyd	M. Jausovec	61 62
1984	Martina Navratilova	C. Evert Lloyd	63 61
1985	Chris Evert Lloyd	M. Navratilova	63 67 75
1986	Chris Evert Lloyd	M. Navratilova	26 63 63
1987	Steffi Graf	M. Navratilova	64 46 86
1988	Steffi Graf	N. Zvereva	60 60
1989	A. Sanchez Vicario	S. Graf	76 36 75
1990	Monica Seles	S. Graf	76 64
1991	Monica Seles	A.S. Vicario	63 64
1992	Monica Seles	S. Graf	62 36 10-8
1993	Steffi Graf	M.J. Fernandez	46 62 64
1994	A. Sanchez Vicario	M. Pierce	64 64
1995	Steffi Graf	A.S. Vicario	76 46 60
1996	Steffi Graf	A.S. Vicario	63 61
1997	Iva Majoli	M. Hingis	64 62
1998	A. Sanchez Vicario	M. Seles	76 06 62
1999	Steffi Graf	M. Hingis	46 75 62
2000	Mary Pierce	C. Martinez	62 75
2001	Jennifer Capriati	K. Clijsters	16 64 1210

Wimbledon

MEN

Officially called "The Lawn Tennis Championships" at the All England Club, Wimbledon. Challenge round system (defending champion qualified for following year's final) used from 1877-1921. Became an Open Championship in 1968, but closed to contract pros in 1972.

Surface: Grass.

Multiple winners: Willie Renshaw and Pete Sampras (7); Bjorn Borg and Laurie Doherty (5); Reggie Doherty, Rod Laver and Tony Wilding (4); Wilfred Baddeley, Boris Becker, Arthur Gore, John McEnroe, John Newcombe, Fred Perry and Bill Tilden (3); Jean Borotra, Norman Brookes, Don Budge, Henri Cochet, Jimmy Connors, Stefan Edberg, Roy Emerson, John Hartley, Lew Hoad, Rene Lacoste, Gerald Patterson and Joshua Pim (2).

Year	Winner	Loser	Score
1877	Spencer Gore	W. Marshall	61 62 64
1878	Frank Hadow	S. Gore	75 61 97
1879	John Hartley	V. St. L. Gould	62 64 62
1880	John Hartley	H. Lawford	60 62 26 63
1881	Willie Renshaw	J. Hartley	60 62 61
1882	Willie Renshaw	E. Renshaw	61 26 46 62 62
1883	Willie Renshaw	E. Renshaw	26 63 63 46 63
1884	Willie Renshaw	H. Lawford	60 64 97
1885	Willie Renshaw	H. Lawford	75 62 46 75
1886	Willie Renshaw	H. Lawford	60 57 63 64
1887	Herbert Lawford	E. Renshaw	16 63 36 64 64
1888	Ernest Renshaw	H. Lawford	63 75 60
1889	Willie Renshaw	E. Renshaw	64 61 36 60
1890	William Hamilton	W. Renshaw	68 62 36 61 61
1891	Wilfred Baddeley	J. Pim	64 16 75 60
1892	Wilfred Baddeley	J. Pim	46 63 63 62
1893	Joshua Pim	W. Baddeley	36 61 63 62
1894	Joshua Pim	W. Baddeley	10-8 62 86
1895	Wilfred Baddeley	W. Eaves	46 26 86 62 63
1896	Harold Mahony	W. Baddeley	62 68 57 86 63
1897	Reggie Doherty	H. Mahony	64 64 63
1898	Reggie Doherty	L. Doherty	63 63 26 57 61
1899	Reggie Doherty	A. Gore	16 46 62 63 63
1900	Reggie Doherty	S. Smith	68 63 61 62
1901	Arthur Gore	R. Doherty	46 75 64 64
1902	Laurie Doherty	A. Gore	64 63 36 60
1903	Laurie Doherty	F. Riseley	75 63 60
1904	Laurie Doherty	F. Riseley	61 75 86
1905	Laurie Doherty	N. Brookes	86 62 64
1906	Laurie Doherty	F. Riseley	64 46 62 63
1907	Norman Brookes	A. Gore	64 62 62
1908	Arthur Gore	R. Barrett	63 62 46 36 64
1909	Arthur Gore	M. Ritchie	68 16 62 62 62
1910	Tony Wilding	A. Gore	64 75 46 62
1911	Tony Wilding	R. Barrett	64 46 26 62 (ret)
1912	Tony Wilding	A. Gore	64 64 46 64
1913	Tony Wilding	M. McLoughlin	86 63 10-8
1914	Norman Brookes	T. Wilding	64 64 75
1915-18	Not held	World War I	
1919	Gerald Patterson	N. Brookes	63 75 62
1920	Bill Tilden	G. Patterson	26 63 62 64
1921	Bill Tilden	B. Norton	46 26 61 60 75
1922	Gerald Patterson	R. Lycett	63 64 62
1923	Bill Johnston	F. Hunter	60 63 61
1924	Jean Borotra	R. Lacoste	61 36 61 36 64
1925	Rene Lacoste	J. Borotra	63 63 46 86
1926	Jean Borotra	H. Kinsey	86 61 63
1927	Henri Cochet	J. Borotra	46 46 63 64 75
1928	Rene Lacoste	H. Cochet	61 46 64 62
1929	Henri Cochet	J. Borotra	64 63 64
1930	Bill Tilden	W. Allison	63 97 64
1931	Sidney Wood	F. Shields	walkover
1932	Ellsworth Vines	H. Austin	64 62 60
1933	Jack Crawford	E. Vines	46 11-9 62 26 64
1934	Fred Perry	J. Crawford	63 60 75
1935	Fred Perry	G. von Cramm	62 64 64
1936	Fred Perry	G. von Cramm	61 61 60
1937	Don Budge	G. von Cramm	63 64 62
1938	Don Budge	H. Austin	61 60 63

Year	Winner	Loser	Score
1939	Bobby Riggs	E. Cooke	26 86 36 63 62
1940-45	Not held	World War II	
1946	Yvon Petra	G. Brown	62 64 79 57 64
1947	Jack Kramer	T. Brown	61 63 62
1948	Bob Falkenburg	J. Bromwich	75 06 62 36 75
1949	Ted Schroeder	J. Drobny	36 60 63 46 64
1950	Budge Patty	F. Sedgman	61 8-10 62 63
1951	Dick Savitt	K. McGregor	64 64 64
1952	Frank Sedgman	J. Drobny	46 62 63 62
1953	Vic Seixas	K. Nielsen	97 63 64
1954	Jaroslav Drobny	K. Rosewall	13-11 46 62 97
1955	Tony Trabert	K. Nielsen	63 75 61
1956	Lew Hoad	K. Rosewall	62 46 75 64
1957	Lew Hoad	A. Cooper	62 61 62
1958	Ashley Cooper	N. Fraser	36 63 64 13-11
1959	Alex Olmedo	R. Laver	64 63 64
1960	Neale Fraser	R. Laver	64 36 97 75
1961	Rod Laver	C. McKinley	63 61 64
1962	Rod Laver	M. Mulligan	62 62 61
1963	Chuck McKinley	F. Stolle	97 61 64
1964	Roy Emerson	F. Stolle	64 12-10 46 63
1965	Roy Emerson	F. Stolle	62 64 64
1966	Manuel Santana	D. Ralston	64 11-9 64
1967	John Newcombe	W. Bungert	63 61 61
1968	Rod Laver	T. Roche	63 64 62
1969	Rod Laver	J. Newcombe	64 57 64 64
1970	John Newcombe	K. Rosewall	57 63 62 36 61
1971	John Newcombe	S. Smith	63 57 26 64 64
1972	Stan Smith	I. Nastase	46 63 63 46 75
1973	Jan Kodes	A. Metreveli	61 98 63
1974	Jimmy Connors	K. Rosewall	61 61 64
1975	Arthur Ashe	J. Connors	61 61 57 64
1976	Bjorn Borg	I. Nastase	64 62 97
1977	Bjorn Borg	J. Connors	36 62 61 57 64
1978	Bjorn Borg	J. Connors	62 62 63
1979	Bjorn Borg	R. Tanner	67 61 36 63 64
1980	Bjorn Borg	J. McEnroe	16 75 63 67 86
1981	John McEnroe	B. Borg	46 76 76 64
1982	Jimmy Connors	J. McEnroe	36 63 67 76 64
1983	John McEnroe	C. Lewis	62 62 62
1984	John McEnroe	J. Connors	61 61 62
1985	Boris Becker	K. Curren	63 67 76 64
1986	Boris Becker	I. Lendl	64 63 75
1987	Pat Cash	I. Lendl	76 62 75
1988	Stefan Edberg	B. Becker	46 76 64 62
1989	Boris Becker	S. Edberg	60 76 64
1990	Stefan Edberg	B. Becker	62 62 36 36 64
1991	Michael Stich	B. Becker	64 76 64
1992	Andre Agassi	G. Ivanisevic	67 64 64 16 64
1993	Pete Sampras	J. Courier	76 76 36 63
1994	Pete Sampras	G. Ivanisevic	76 76 60
1995	Pete Sampras	B. Becker	67 62 64 62
1996	Richard Krajicek	M. Washington	63 64 63
1997	Pete Sampras	C. Pioline	64 62 64
1998	Pete Sampras	G. Ivanisevic	67 76 64 36 62
1999	Pete Sampras	A. Agassi	63 64 75
2000	Pete Sampras	P. Rafter	67 76 64 62
2001	Goran Ivanisevic	P. Rafter	63 36 63 26 97

WOMEN

Officially called "The Lawn Tennis Championships" at the All England Club, Wimbledon. Challenge round system (defending champion qualified for following year's final) used from 1877-1921. Became an Open Championship in 1968, but closed to contract pros in 1972.

Multiple winners: Martina Navratilova (9); Helen Wills Moody (8); Dorothea Douglass Chambers and Steffi Graf (7); Blanche Bingley Hillyard, Billie Jean King and Suzanne Lenglen (6); Lottie Dod and Charlotte Cooper Sterry (5); Louise Brough (4); Maria Bueno, Maureen Connolly, Margaret Smith Court and Chris Evert Lloyd (3); Evonne Goolagong Cawley, Althea Gibson, Kathleen McKane Godfrey, Dorothy Round, May Sutton, Maud Watson and Venus Williams (2).

Year	Winner	Loser	Score	Year	Winner	Loser	Score
1884	Maud Watson	L. Watson	68 63 63	1948	Louise Brough	D. Hart	63 86
1885	Maud Watson	B. Bingley	61 75	1949	Louise Brough	M. duPont	10-8 16 10-8
1886	Blanche Bingley	M. Watson	63 63	1950	Louise Brough	M. duPont	61 36 61
1887	Lottie Dod	B. Bingley	62 60	1951	Doris Hart	S. Fry	61 60
1888	Lottie Dod	B. Hillyard	63 63	1952	Maureen Connolly	L. Brough	75 63
1889	Blanche Hillyard	L. Rice	46 86 64	1953	Maureen Connolly	D. Hart	86 75
1890	Lena Rice	M. Jacks	64 61	1954	Maureen Connolly	L. Brough	62 75
1891	Lottie Dod	B. Hillyard	62 61	1955	Louise Brough	B. Fleitz	75 86
1892	Lottie Dod	B. Hillyard	61 61	1956	Shirley Fry	A. Buxton	63 61
1893	Lottie Dod	B. Hillyard	68 61 64	1957	Althea Gibson	D. Hard	63 62
1894	Blanche Hillyard	E. Austin	61 61	1958	Althea Gibson	A. Mortimer	86 62
1895	Charlotte Cooper	H. Jackson	75 86	1959	Maria Bueno	D. Hard	64 63
1896	Charlotte Cooper	W. Pickering	62 63	1960	Maria Bueno	S. Reynolds	86 60
1897	Blanche Hillyard	C. Cooper	57 75 62	1961	Angela Mortimer	C. Truman	46 64 75
1898	Charlotte Cooper	L. Martin	64 64	1962	Karen Susman	V. Sukova	64 64
1899	Blanche Hillyard	C. Cooper	62 63	1963	Margaret Smith	B.J. Moffitt	63 64
1900	Blanche Hillyard	C. Cooper	46 64 64	1964	Maria Bueno	M. Smith	64 79 63
1901	Charlotte Sterry	B. Hillyard	62 62	1965	Margaret Smith	M. Bueno	64 75
1902	Muriel Robb	C. Sterry	75 61	1966	Billie Jean King	M. Bueno	63 36 61
1903	Dorothea Douglass	E. Thomson	46 64 62	1967	Billie Jean King	A. Jones	63 64
1904	Dorothea Douglass	C. Sterry	60 63	1968	Billie Jean King	J. Tegart	97 75
1905	May Sutton	D. Douglass	63 64	1969	Ann Jones	B.J. King	36 63 62
1906	Dorothea Douglass	M. Sutton	63 97	1970	Margaret Court	B.J. King	14-12 11-9
1907	May Sutton	D. Chambers	61 64	1971	Evonne Goolagong	M. Court	64 61
1908	Charlotte Sterry	A. Morton	64 64	1972	Billie Jean King	E. Goolagong	63 63
1909	Dora Boothby	A. Morton	64 46 86	1973	Billie Jean King	C. Evert	60 75
1910	Dorothea Chambers	D. Boothby	62 62	1974	Chris Evert	O. Morozova	60 64
1911	Dorothea Chambers	D. Boothby	60 60	1975	Billie Jean King	E. Cawley	60 61
1912	Ethel Larcombe	C. Sterry	63 61	1976	Chris Evert	E. Cawley	63 46 86
1913	Dorothea Chambers	R. McNair	60 64	1977	Virginia Wade	B. Stove	46 63 61
1914	Dorothea Chambers	E. Larcombe	75 64	1978	Martina Navratilova	C. Evert	26 64 75
1915-18	Not held	World War I		1979	Martina Navratilova	C. Evert Lloyd	64 64
1919	Suzanne Lenglen	D. Chambers	10-8 46 97	1980	Evonne Cawley	C. Evert Lloyd	61 76
1920	Suzanne Lenglen	D. Chambers	63 60	1981	Chris Evert Lloyd	H. Mandlikova	62 62
1921	Suzanne Lenglen	E. Ryan	62 60	1982	Martina Navratilova	C. Evert Lloyd	61 36 62
1922	Suzanne Lenglen	M. Mallory	62 60	1983	Martina Navratilova	A. Jaeger	60 63
1923	Suzanne Lenglen	K. McKane	62 62	1984	Martina Navratilova	C. Evert Lloyd	76 62
1924	Kathleen McKane	H. Wills	46 64 64	1985	Martina Navratilova	C. Evert Lloyd	46 63 62
1925	Suzanne Lenglen	J. Fry	62 60	1986	Martina Navratilova	H. Mandlikova	76 63
1926	Kathleen Godfrey	L. de Alvarez	62 46 63	1987	Martina Navratilova	S. Graf	75 63
1927	Helen Wills	L. de Alvarez	62 64	1988	Steffi Graf	M. Navratilova	57 62 61
1928	Helen Wills	L. de Alvarez	62 63	1989	Steffi Graf	M. Navratilova	62 67 61
1929	Helen Wills	H. Jacobs	61 62	1990	Martina Navratilova	Z. Garrison	64 61
1930	Helen Moody	E. Ryan	62 62	1991	Steffi Graf	G. Sabatini	64 36 86
1931	Cilly Aussem	H. Kranwinkel	62 75	1992	Steffi Graf	M. Seles	62 61
1932	Helen Moody	H. Jacobs	63 61	1993	Steffi Graf	J. Novotna	76 16 64
1933	Helen Moody	D. Round	64 68 63	1994	Conchita Martinez	M. Navratilova	64 36 63
1934	Dorothy Round	H. Jacobs	62 57 63	1995	Steffi Graf	A.S. Vicario	46 61 75
1935	Helen Moody	H. Jacobs	63 36 75	1996	Steffi Graf	A.S. Vicario	63 75
1936	Helen Jacobs	H.K. Sperling	62 46 75	1997	Martina Hingis	J. Novotna	26 63 63
1937	Dorothy Round	J. Jedrzejowska	62 26 75	1998	Jana Novotna	N. Tauziat	64 76
1938	Helen Moody	H. Jacobs	64 60	1999	Lindsay Davenport	S. Graf	64 75
1939	Alice Marble	K. Stammers	62 60	2000	Venus Williams	L. Davenport	63 76
1940-45	Not held	World War II		2001	Venus Williams	J. Henin	61 36 60
1946	Pauline Betz	L. Brough	62 64				
1947	Margaret Osborne	D. Hart	62 64				

U.S. Open

MEN

Challenge round system (defending champion qualified for following year's final) used from 1884-1911. Known as the Patriotic Tournament in 1917 during World War I. Amateur and Open Championships held in 1968 and '69. Became an exclusively Open Championship in 1970.

Surface: Decoturf II (acrylic cement).

Multiple winners: Bill Larned, Richard Sears and Bill Tilden (7); Jimmy Connors (5); John McEnroe, Pete Sampras and Robert Wrenn (4); Oliver Campbell, Ivan Lendl, Fred Perry and Malcolm Whitman (3); Andre Agassi, Don Budge, Stefan Edberg, Roy Emerson, Neale Fraser, Pancho Gonzales, Bill Johnston, Jack Kramer, Rene Lacoste, Rod Laver, Maurice McLoughlin, Lindley Murray, John Newcombe, Frank Parker, Patrick Rafter, Bobby Riggs, Ken Rosewall, Frank Sedgman, Henry Slocum Jr., Tony Trabert, Ellsworth Vines and Dick Williams (2).

Year	Winner	Loser	Score	Year	Winner	Loser	Score
1881	Richard Sears	W. Glyn	60 63 62	1943	Joe Hunt	J. Kramer	63 68 10-8 60
1882	Richard Sears	C. Clark	61 64 60	1944	Frank Parker	B. Talbert	64 36 63 63
1883	Richard Sears	J. Dwight	62 60 97	1945	Frank Parker	B. Talbert	14-12 61 62
1884	Richard Sears	H. Taylor	60 16 60 62	1946	Jack Kramer	T. Brown, Jr.	97 63 60
1885	Richard Sears	G. Brinley	63 46 60 63	1947	Jack Kramer	F. Parker	46 26 61 60 63
1886	Richard Sears	R. Beeckman	46 61 63 64	1948	Pancho Gonzales	E. Sturgess	62 63 14-12
1887	Richard Sears	H. Slocum Jr.	61 63 62	1949	Pancho Gonzales	F. Schroeder 16-18 26 61 62 64
1888	Henry Slocum Jr.	H. Taylor	64 61 60	1950	Arthur Larsen	H. Flam	63 46 57 64 63
1889	Henry Slocum Jr.	Q. Shaw	63 61 46 62	1951	Frank Sedgman	V. Seixas	64 61 61
1890	Oliver Campbell	H. Slocum Jr.	62 46 63 61	1952	Frank Sedgman	G. Mulloy	61 62 63
1891	Oliver Campbell	C. Hobart	26 75 79 61 62	1953	Tony Trabert	V. Seixas	63 62 63
1892	Oliver Campbell	F. Hovey	75 36 63 75	1954	Vic Seixas	R. Hartwig	36 62 64 64
1893	Robert Wrenn	F. Hovey	64 36 64 64	1955	Tony Trabert	K. Rosewall	97 63 63
1894	Robert Wrenn	M. Goodbody	68 61 64 64	1956	Ken Rosewall	L. Hoad	46 62 63 63
1895	Fred Hovey	R. Wrenn	63 62 64	1957	Mal Anderson	A. Cooper	10-8 75 64
1896	Robert Wrenn	F. Hovey	75 36 60 16 61	1958	Ashley Cooper	M. Anderson 62 36 46 10-8 86
1897	Robert Wrenn	W. Eaves	46 86 63 26 62	1959	Neale Fraser	A. Olmedo	63 57 62 64
1898	Malcolm Whitman	D. Davis	36 62 62 61	1960	Neale Fraser	R. Laver	64 64 97
1899	Malcolm Whitman	P. Paret	61 62 36 75	1961	Roy Emerson	R. Laver	75 63 62
1900	Malcolm Whitman	B. Larned	61 16 62 62	1962	Rod Laver	R. Emerson	62 64 57 64
1901	Bill Larned	B. Wright	62 68 64 64	1963	Rafael Osuna	F. Froehling	75 64 62
1902	Bill Larned	R. Doherty	46 62 64 86	1964	Roy Emerson	F. Stolle	64 62 64
1903	Laurie Doherty	B. Larned	60 63 10-8	1965	Manuel Santana	C. Drysdale	62 79 75 61
1904	Holcombe Ward	B. Clothier	10-8 64 97	1966	Fred Stolle	J. Newcombe 46 12-10 63 64
1905	Beals Wright	H. Ward	62 61 11-9	1967	John Newcombe	C. Graebner	64 64 86
1906	Bill Clothier	B. Wright	63 60 64	1968	Am-Arthur Ashe	B. Lutz	46 63 8-10 60 64
1907	Bill Larned	R. LeRoy	62 62 64		Op-Arthur Ashe	T. Okker	14-12 57 63 36 63
1908	Bill Larned	B. Wright	61 62 86	1969	Am-Stan Smith	B. Lutz	97 63 61
1909	Bill Larned	B. Clothier	61 62 57 16 61		Op-Rod Laver	T. Roche	79 61 63 62
1910	Bill Larned	T. Bundy	61 57 60 68 61	1970	Ken Rosewall	T. Roche	26 64 76 63
1911	Bill Larned	M. McLoughlin	64 64 62	1971	Stan Smith	J. Kodes	36 63 62 76
1912	Maurice McLoughlin	W.F. Johnson	36 26 62 64 62	1972	Ilie Nastase	A. Ashe	36 63 67 64 63
1913	Maurice McLoughlin	R. Williams	64 57 63 61	1973	John Newcombe	J. Kodes	64 16 46 62 63
1914	Dick Williams	M. McLoughlin	63 86 10-8	1974	Jimmy Connors	K. Rosewall	61 60 61
1915	Bill Johnston	M. McLoughlin	16 60 75 10-8	1975	Manuel Orantes	J. Connors	64 63 63
1916	Dick Williams	B. Johnston	46 64 06 62 64	1976	Jimmy Connors	B. Borg	64 36 76 64
1917	Lindley Murray	N. Niles	57 86 63 63	1977	Guillermo Vilas	J. Connors	26 63 76 60
1918	Lindley Murray	B. Tilden	63 61 75	1978	Jimmy Connors	B. Borg	64 62 62
1919	Bill Johnston	B. Tilden	64 64 63	1979	John McEnroe	V. Gerulaitis	75 63 63
1920	Bill Tilden	B. Johnston	61 16 75 57 63	1980	John McEnroe	B. Borg	76 61 67 57 64
1921	Bill Tilden	W. Johnson	61 63 61	1981	John McEnroe	B. Borg	46 62 64 63
1922	Bill Tilden	B. Johnston	46 36 62 63 64	1982	Jimmy Connors	I. Lendl	63 62 46 64
1923	Bill Tilden	B. Johnston	64 61 64	1983	Jimmy Connors	I. Lendl	63 67 75 60
1924	Bill Tilden	B. Johnston	61 97 62	1984	John McEnroe	I. Lendl	63 64 61
1925	Bill Tilden	B. Johnston	46 11-9 63 46 63	1985	Ivan Lendl	J. McEnroe	76 63 64
1926	Rene Lacoste	J. Borotra	64 60 64	1986	Ivan Lendl	M. Mecir	64 62 60
1927	Rene Lacoste	B. Tilden	11-9 63 11-9	1987	Ivan Lendl	M. Wilander	67 60 76 64
1928	Henri Cochet	F. Hunter	46 64 36 75 63	1988	Mats Wilander	I. Lendl	64 46 63 57 64
1929	Bill Tilden	F. Hunter	36 63 46 62 64	1989	Boris Becker	I. Lendl	76 16 63 76
1930	John Doeg	F. Shields	10-8 16 64 16-14	1990	Pete Sampras	A. Agassi	64 63 62
1931	Ellsworth Vines	G. Lott Jr.	79 63 97 75	1991	Stefan Edberg	J. Courier	62 64 60
1932	Ellsworth Vines	H. Cochet	64 64 64	1992	Stefan Edberg	P. Sampras	36 64 76 62
1933	Fred Perry	J. Crawford 63 11-13 46 60 61	1993	Pete Sampras	C. Pioline	64 64 63
1934	Fred Perry	W. Allison	64 63 16 86	1994	Andre Agassi	M. Stich	61 76 75
1935	Wilmer Allison	S. Wood	62 62 63	1995	Pete Sampras	A. Agassi	64 63 46 75
1936	Fred Perry	D. Budge	26 62 86 16 10-8	1996	Pete Sampras	M. Chang	61 64 76
1937	Don Budge	G. von Cramm	61 79 61 36 61	1997	Patrick Rafter	G. Rusedski	63 62 46 75
1938	Don Budge	G. Mako	63 68 62 61	1998	Patrick Rafter	M. Philippoussis	63 36 62 60
1939	Bobby Riggs	S.W. van Horn	64 62 64	1999	Andre Agassi	T. Martin	64 67 67 62 62
1940	Don McNeill	B. Riggs	46 68 63 63 75	2000	Marat Safin	P. Sampras	64 63 63
1941	Bobby Riggs	F. Kovacs	57 61 63 63	2001	Lleyton Hewitt	P. Sampras	76 61 61
1942	Fred Schroeder	F. Parker	86 75 36 46 62				

WOMEN

Challenge round system used from 1887-1918. Five set final played from 1887-1901. Amateur and Open Championships held in 1968 and '69. Became an exclusively Open Championship in 1970.

Multiple winners: Molla Mallory Bjurstedt (8); Helen Wills Moody (7); Chris Evert Lloyd (6); Margaret Smith Court and Steffi Graf (5); Pauline Betz, Maria Bueno, Helen Jacobs, Billie Jean King, Alice Marble, Elisabeth Moore, Martina Navratilova and Hazel Hotchkiss Wightman (4); Juliette Atkinson, Mary Browne, Maureen Connolly and Margaret Osborne duPont (3); Tracy Austin, Mabel Cahill, Sarah Palfrey Cooke, Althea Gibson, Darlene Hard, Doris Hart, Marion Jones, Monica Seles, Bertha Townsend and Venus Williams (2).

Year	Winner	Loser	Score
1887	Ellen Hansell	L. Knight	61 60
1888	Bertha Townsend	E. Hansell	63 65
1889	Bertha Townsend	L. Voorhes	75 62
1890	Ellen Roosevelt	B. Townsend	62 62
1891	Mabel Cahill	E. Roosevelt	64 61 46 63
1892	Mabel Cahill	E. Moore	57 63 64 46 62
1893	Aline Terry	A. Schultz	61 63
1894	Helen Hellwig	A. Terry	75 36 60 36 63
1895	Juliette Atkinson	H. Hellwig	64 62 61
1896	Elisabeth Moore	J. Atkinson	64 46 62 62
1897	Juliette Atkinson	E. Moore	63 63 46 36 63
1898	Juliette Atkinson	M. Jones	63 57 64 26 75
1899	Marion Jones	M. Banks	61 61 75
1900	Myrtle McAteer	E. Parker	62 62 60
1901	Elizabeth Moore	M. McAteer	64 36 75 26 62
1902	Marion Jones	E. Moore	61 10(ret)
1903	Elizabeth Moore	M. Jones	75 86
1904	May Sutton	E. Moore	61 62
1905	Elizabeth Moore	H. Homans	64 57 61
1906	Helen Homans	M. Barger-Wallach	64 63
1907	Evelyn Sears	C. Neely	63 62
1908	Maud B. Wallach	Ev. Sears	63 16 63
1909	Hazel Hotchkiss	M. Wallach	60 61
1910	Hazel Hotchkiss	L. Hammond	64 62
1911	Hazel Hotchkiss	F. Sutton	8-10 61 97
1912	Mary Browne	E. Sears	64 62
1913	Mary Browne	D. Green	62 75
1914	Mary Browne	M. Wagner	62 16 61
1915	Molla Bjurstedt	H. Wightman	46 62 60
1916	Molla Bjurstedt	L. Raymond	60 61
1917	Molla Bjurstedt	M. Vanderhoef	46 60 62
1918	Molla Bjurstedt	E. Goss	64 63
1919	Hazel Wightman	M. Zinderstein	61 62
1920	Molla Mallory	M. Zinderstein	63 61
1921	Molla Mallory	M. Browne	46 64 62
1922	Molla Mallory	H. Wills	63 61
1923	Helen Wills	M. Mallory	62 61
1924	Helen Wills	M. Mallory	61 63
1925	Helen Wills	K. McKane	36 60 62
1926	Molla Mallory	E. Ryan	46 64 97
1927	Helen Wills	B. Nuthall	61 64
1928	Helen Wills	H. Jacobs	62 61
1929	Helen Wills	P. Watson	64 62
1930	Betty Nuthall	A. Harper	61 64
1931	Helen Moody	E. Whitingstall	64 61
1932	Helen Jacobs	C. Babcock	62 62
1933	Helen Jacobs	H. Moody	86 36 30(ret)
1934	Helen Jacobs	S. Palfrey	61 64
1935	Helen Jacobs	S. Fabyan	62 64
1936	Alice Marble	H. Jacobs	46 63 62
1937	Anita Lizana	J. Jedrzejowska	64 62
1938	Alice Marble	N. Wynne	60 63
1939	Alice Marble	H. Jacobs	60 8-10 64
1940	Alice Marble	H. Jacobs	62 63
1941	Sarah Cooke	P. Betz	75 62
1942	Pauline Betz	L. Brough	46 61 64
1943	Pauline Betz	L. Brough	63 57 63
1944	Pauline Betz	M. Osborne	63 86
1945	Sarah Cooke	P. Betz	36 86 64

Year	Winner	Loser	Score
1946	Pauline Betz	P. Canning	11-9 63
1947	Louise Brough	M. Osborne	86 46 61
1948	Margaret duPont	L. Brough	46 64 15-13
1949	Margaret duPont	D. Hart	64 61
1950	Margaret duPont	D. Hart	64 63
1951	Maureen Connolly	S. Fry	63 16 64
1952	Maureen Connolly	D. Hart	63 75
1953	Maureen Connolly	D. Hart	62 64
1954	Doris Hart	L. Brough	68 61 86
1955	Doris Hart	P. Ward	64 62
1956	Shirley Fry	A. Gibson	63 64
1957	Althea Gibson	L. Brough	63 62
1958	Althea Gibson	D. Hard	36 61 62
1959	Maria Bueno	C. Truman	61 64
1960	Darlene Hard	M. Bueno	64 10-12 64
1961	Darlene Hard	A. Haydon	63 64
1962	Margaret Smith	D. Hard	97 64
1963	Maria Bueno	M. Smith	75 64
1964	Maria Bueno	C. Graebner	61 60
1965	Margaret Smith	B.J. Moffitt	86 75
1966	Maria Bueno	N. Richey	63 61
1967	Billie Jean King	A. Jones	11-9 64
1968	Am-Margaret Court	M. Bueno	62 62
	Op-Virginia Wade	B.J. King	64 62
1969	Am-Margaret Court	V. Wade	46 63 60
	Op-Margaret Court	N. Richey	62 62
1970	Margaret Court	R. Casals	62 26 61
1971	Billie Jean King	R. Casals	64 76
1972	Billie Jean King	K. Melville	63 75
1973	Margaret Court	E. Goolagong	76 57 62
1974	Billie Jean King	E. Goolagong	36 63 75
1975	Chris Evert	E. Cawley	57 64 62
1976	Chris Evert	E. Cawley	63 60
1977	Chris Evert	W. Turnbull	76 62
1978	Chris Evert	P. Shriver	75 64
1979	Tracy Austin	C. Evert Lloyd	64 63
1980	Chris Evert Lloyd	H. Mandlikova	57 61 61
1981	Tracy Austin	M. Navratilova	16 76 76
1982	Chris Evert Lloyd	H. Mandlikova	63 61
1983	Martina Navratilova	C. Evert Lloyd	61 63
1984	Martina Navratilova	C. Evert Lloyd	46 64 64
1985	Hana Mandlikova	M. Navratilova	76 16 76
1986	Martina Navratilova	H. Sukova	63 62
1987	Martina Navratilova	S. Graf	76 61
1988	Steffi Graf	G. Sabatini	63 36 61
1989	Steffi Graf	M. Navratilova	36 75 61
1990	Gabriela Sabatini	S. Graf	62 76
1991	Monica Seles	M. Navratilova	76 61
1992	Monica Seles	A.S. Vicario	63 63
1993	Steffi Graf	H. Sukova	63 63
1994	A. Sanchez Vicario	S. Graf	16 76 64
1995	Steffi Graf	M. Seles	76 06 63
1996	Steffi Graf	M. Seles	75 64
1997	Martina Hingis	V. Williams	60 64
1998	Lindsay Davenport	M. Hingis	63 75
1999	Serena Williams	M. Hingis	63 76
2000	Venus Williams	L. Davenport	64 75
2001	Venus Williams	S. Williams	62 64

Grand Slam Summary

Singles winners of the four Grand Slam tournaments—Australian, French, Wimbledon and United States—since the French was opened to all comers in 1925. Note that there were two Australian Opens in 1977 and none in 1986.

MEN

Three wins in one year: Jack Crawford (1933); Fred Perry (1934); Tony Trabert (1955); Lew Hoad (1956); Ashley Cooper (1958); Roy Emerson (1964); Jimmy Connors (1974); Mats Wilander (1988).

Two wins in one year: Roy Emerson and Pete Sampras (4 times); Bjorn Borg (3 times); Rene Lacoste, Ivan Lendl, John Newcombe and Fred Perry (twice); Andre Agassi, Boris Becker, Don Budge, Henri Cochet, Jimmy Connors, Jim Courier, Neale Fraser, Jack Kramer, John McEnroe, Alex Olmedo, Budge Patty, Bobby Riggs, Ken Rosewall, Dick Savitt, Frank Sedgman and Guillermo Vilas (once).

Year	Australian	French	Wimbledon	U.S.	Year	Australian	French	Wimbledon	U.S.
1925	Anderson	Lacoste	Lacoste	Tilden	1965	Emerson	Stolle	Emerson	Santana
1926	Hawkes	Cochet	Borotra	Lacoste	1966	Emerson	Roche	Santana	Stolle
1927	Patterson	Lacoste	Cochet	Lacoste	1967	Emerson	Emerson	Newcombe	Newcombe
1928	Borotra	Cochet	Lacoste	Cochet	1968	Bowrey	Rosewall	Laver	Ashe
1929	Gregory	Lacoste	Cochet	Tilden	1969	**Laver**	**Laver**	**Laver**	**Laver**
1930	Moon	Cochet	Tilden	Doeg	1970	Ashe	Kodes	Newcombe	Rosewall
1931	Crawford	Borotra	Wood	Vines	1971	Rosewall	Kodes	Newcombe	Smith
1932	Crawford	Cochet	Vines	Vines	1972	Rosewall	Gimeno	Smith	Nastase
1933	Crawford	Crawford	Crawford	Perry	1973	Newcombe	Nastase	Kodes	Newcombe
1934	Perry	von Cramm	Perry	Perry	1974	Connors	Borg	Connors	Connors
1935	Crawford	Perry	Perry	Allison	1975	Newcombe	Borg	Ashe	Orantes
1936	Quist	von Cramm	Perry	Perry	1976	Edmondson	Panatta	Borg	Connors
1937	McGrath	Henkel	Budge	Budge	1977	Tanner	Vilas	Borg	Vilas
1938	**Budge**	**Budge**	**Budge**	**Budge**		& Gerulaitis			
1939	Bromwich	McNeill	Riggs	Riggs	1978	Vilas	Borg	Borg	Connors
1940	Quist	—	—	McNeill	1979	Vilas	Borg	Borg	McEnroe
1941	—	—	—	Riggs	1980	Teacher	Borg	Borg	McEnroe
1942	—	—	—	Schroeder	1981	Kriek	Borg	McEnroe	McEnroe
1943	—	—	—	Hunt	1982	Kriek	Wilander	Connors	Connors
1944	—	—	—	Parker	1983	Wilander	Noah	McEnroe	Connors
1945	—	—	—	Parker	1984	Wilander	Lendl	McEnroe	McEnroe
1946	Bromwich	Bernard	Petra	Kramer	1985	Edberg	Wilander	Becker	Lendl
1947	Pails	Asboth	Kramer	Kramer	1986	—	Lendl	Becker	Lendl
1948	Quist	Parker	Falkenburg	Gonzales	1987	Edberg	Lendl	Cash	Lendl
1949	Sedgman	Parker	Schroeder	Gonzales	1988	Wilander	Wilander	Edberg	Wilander
1950	Sedgman	Patty	Patty	Larsen	1989	Lendl	Chang	Becker	Becker
1951	Savitt	Drobny	Savitt	Sedgman	1990	Lendl	Gomez	Edberg	Sampras
1952	McGregor	Drobny	Sedgman	Sedgman	1991	Becker	Courier	Stich	Edberg
1953	Rosewall	Rosewall	Seixas	Trabert	1992	Courier	Courier	Agassi	Edberg
1954	Rose	Trabert	Drobny	Seixas	1993	Courier	Bruguera	Sampras	Sampras
1955	Rosewall	Trabert	Trabert	Trabert	1994	Sampras	Bruguera	Sampras	Agassi
1956	Hoad	Hoad	Hoad	Rosewall	1995	Agassi	Muster	Sampras	Sampras
1957	Cooper	Davidson	Hoad	Anderson	1996	Becker	Kafelnikov	Krajicek	Sampras
1958	Cooper	Rose	Cooper	Cooper	1997	Sampras	Kuerten	Sampras	Rafter
1959	Olmedo	Pietrangeli	Olmedo	Fraser	1998	Korda	Moya	Sampras	Rafter
1960	Laver	Pietrangeli	Fraser	Fraser	1999	Kafelnikov	Agassi	Sampras	Agassi
1961	Emerson	Santana	Laver	Emerson	2000	Agassi	Kuerten	Sampras	Safin
1962	**Laver**	**Laver**	**Laver**	**Laver**	2001	Agassi	Kuerten	Ivanisevic	Hewitt
1963	Emerson	Emerson	McKinley	Osuna					
1964	Emerson	Santana	Emerson	Emerson					

WOMEN

Three in one year: Helen Wills Moody (1928 and '29); Margaret Smith Court (1962, '65, '69 and '73); Billie Jean King (1972); Martina Navratilova (1983 and '84); Steffi Graf (1989, '93, '95 and '96); Monica Seles (1991 and '92); and Martina Hingis (1997).

Two in one year: Chris Evert Lloyd (5 times); Helen Wills Moody and Martina Navratilova (3 times); Maria Bueno, Maureen Connolly, Margaraet Smith Court, Althea Gibson, Billie Jean King and Venus Williams (twice); Cilly Aussem, Pauleen Betz, Louise Brough, Jennifer Capriati, Evonne Goolagong Cawley, Shirley Fry, Darlene Hard, Margaret Osborne duPont, Suzanne Lenglen, Alice Marble and Arantxa Sanchez Vicario (once).

Year	Australian	French	Wimbledon	U.S.	Year	Australian	French	Wimbledon	U.S.
1925	Akhurst	Lenglen	Lenglen	Wills	1936	Hartigan	Sperling	Jacobs	Marble
1926	Akhurst	Lenglen	Godfree	Mallory	1937	Bolton	Sperling	Round	Lizana
1927	Boyd	Bouman	Wills	Wills	1938	Bundy	Mathieu	Moody	Marble
1928	Akhurst	Wills	Wills	Wills	1939	Westacott	Mathieu	Marble	Marble
1929	Akhurst	Wills	Wills	Wills	1940	Bolton	—	—	Marble
1930	Akhurst	Moody	Moody	Nuthall	1941	—	—	—	Cooke
1931	Buttsworth	Aussem	Aussem	Moody	1942	—	—	—	Betz
1932	Buttsworth	Moody	Moody	Jacobs	1943	—	—	—	Betz
1933	Hartigan	Scriven	Moody	Jacobs	1944	—	—	—	Betz
1934	Hartigan	Scriven	Round	Jacobs	1945	—	—	—	Cooke
1935	Round	Sperling	Moody	Jacobs	1946	Bolton	Osborne	Betz	Betz

Year	Australian	French	Wimbledon	U.S.	Year	Australian	French	Wimbledon	U.S.
1947	Bolton	Todd	Osborne	Brough	1975	Goolagong	Evert	King	Evert
1948	Bolton	Landry	Brough	du Pont	1976	Cawley	Barker	Evert	Evert
1949	Hart	du Pont	Brough	du Pont	1977	Reid	Jausovec	Wade	Evert
1950	Brough	Hart	Brough	du Pont		& Cawley			
1951	Bolton	Fry	Hart	Connolly	1978	O'Neil	Ruzici	Navratilova	Evert
1952	Long	Hart	Connolly	Connolly	1979	Jordan	Evert Lloyd	Navratilova	Austin
1953	**Connolly**	**Connolly**	**Connolly**	**Connolly**	1980	Mandlikova	Evert Lloyd	Cawley	Evert Lloyd
1954	Long	Connolly	Connolly	Hart	1981	Navratilova	Mandlikova	Evert Lloyd	Austin
1955	Penrose	Mortimer	Brough	Hart	1982	Evert Lloyd	Navratilova	Navratilova	Evert Lloyd
1956	Carter	Gibson	Fry	Fry	1983	Navratilova	Evert Lloyd	Navratilova	Navratilova
1957	Fry	Bloomer	Gibson	Gibson	1984	Evert Lloyd	Navratilova	Navratilova	Navratilova
1958	Mortimer	Kormoczi	Gibson	Gibson	1985	Navratilova	Evert Lloyd	Navratilova	Mandlikova
1959	Reitano	Truman	Bueno	Bueno	1986	–	Evert Lloyd	Navratilova	Navratilova
1960	Smith	Hard	Bueno	Hard	1987	Mandlikova	Graf	Navratilova	Navratilova
1961	Smith	Haydon	Mortimer	Hard	1988	**Graf**	**Graf**	**Graf**	**Graf**
1962	Smith	Smith	Susman	Smith	1989	Graf	Vicario	Graf	Graf
1963	Smith	Turner	Smith	Bueno	1990	Graf	Seles	Navratilova	Sabatini
1964	Smith	Smith	Bueno	Bueno	1991	Seles	Seles	Graf	Seles
1965	Smith	Turner	Smith	Smith	1992	Seles	Seles	Graf	Seles
1966	Smith	Jones	King	Bueno	1993	Seles	Graf	Graf	Graf
1967	Richey	Durr	King	King	1994	Graf	Vicario	Martinez	Vicario
1968	King	Richey	King	Wade	1995	Pierce	Graf	Graf	Graf
1969	Court	Court	Jones	Court	1996	Seles	Graf	Graf	Graf
1970	**Court**	**Court**	**Court**	**Court**	1997	Hingis	Majoli	Hingis	Hingis
1971	Court	Goolagong	Goolagong	King	1998	Hingis	Vicario	Novotna	Davenport
1972	Wade	King	King	King	1999	Hingis	Graf	Davenport	S. Williams
1973	Court	Court	King	Court	2000	Davenport	Pierce	V. Williams	V. Williams
1974	Goolagong	Evert	Evert	King	2001	Capriati	Capriati	V. Williams	V. Williams

Overall Leaders

All-Time Grand Slam titleists including all singles and doubles championships at the four major tournaments. Titles listed under each heading are singles, doubles and mixed doubles. Players active in 2001 are in **bold** type.

MEN

		Career	Australian	French	Wimbledon	U.S.	S-D-M	Total Titles
1	Roy Emerson	1959-71	6-3-0	2-6-0	2-3-0	2-4-0	12-16-0	28
2	John Newcombe	1965-76	2-5-0	0-3-0	3-6-0	2-3-1	7-17-1	25
3	Frank Sedgman	1949-52	?-?-?	0-?-?	1-3-?	?-?-?	5-9-8	22
4	Bill Tilden	1913-30	*	0-0-1	3-1-0	7-5-4	10-6-5	21
5	Rod Laver	1959-71	3-4-0	2-1-1	4-1-2	2-0-0	11-6-3	20
6	Jack Bromwich	1938-50	2-8-1	0-0-0	0-2-2	0-3-1	2-13-4	19
	Neale Fraser	1957-62	0-3-1	0-3-0	1-2-1	2-3-3	3-11-5	19
8	**Todd Woodbridge**	1988–	0-3-1	0-1-1	0-6-1	0-2-3	0-12-6	18
	Ken Rosewall	1953-72	4-3-0	2-2-0	0-2-0	2-2-1	8-9-1	18
	Jean Borotra	1925-36	1-1-1	1-5-2	2-3-1	0-0-1	4-9-5	18
	Fred Stolle	1962-69	0-3-1	1-2-0	0-2-3	1-3-2	2-10-6	18
12	John McEnroe	1977-93	0-0-0	0-0-1	3-5-0	4-4-0	7-9-1	17
	Jack Crawford	1929-35	4-4-3	1-1-1	1-1-1	0-0-0	6-6-5	17
	Mark Woodforde	1985-2000	0-2-2	0-1-1	0-6-1	0-3-1	0-12-5	17
	Adrian Quist	1936-50	3-10-0	0-1-0	0-2-0	0-1-0	3-14-0	17

WOMEN

		Career	Australian	French	Wimbledon	U.S.	S-D-M	Total Titles
1	Margaret Smith Court	1960-75	11-8-2	5-4-4	3-2-5	5-5-8	24-19-19	62
2	**Martina Navratilova**	1974-95, 2000–	3-8-0	2-7-2	9-7-3	4-9-2	18-31-7	56
3	Billie Jean King	1961-81	1-0-1	1-1-2	6-10-4	4-5-4	12-16-11	39
4	Margaret du Pont	1941-60	*	2-3-0	1-5-1	3-13-9	6-21-10	37
5	Louise Brough	1942-57	1-1-0	0-3-0	4-5-4	1-12-4	6-21-8	35
	Doris Hart	1948-55	1-1-2	2-5-3	1-4-5	2-4-5	6-14-15	35
7	Helen Wills Moody	1923-38	*	4-2-0	8-3-1	7-4-2	19-9-3	31
8	Elizabeth Ryan	1914-34	*	0-4-0	0-12-7	0-1-2	0-17-9	26
9	Suzanne Lenglen	1919-26	*	6-2-2	6-6-3	0-0-0	12-8-5	25
10	Steffi Graf	1982-99	4-0-0	6-0-0	7-1-0	5-0-0	22-1-0	23
11	Pam Shriver	1981-97	0-7-0	0-4-1	0-5-0	0-5-0	0-21-1	22
12	Chris Evert	1974-89	2-0-0	7-2-0	3-1-0	6-0-0	18-3-0	21
	Darlene Hard	1958-69	*	1-3-2	0-4-3	2-6-0	3-13-5	21
14	**Natasha Zvereva**	1989–	0-3-2	0-6-0	0-5-0	0-4-0	0-18-2	20
	Nancye Wynne Bolton	1935-52	6-10-4	0-0-0	0-0-0	0-0-0	6-10-4	20
	Maria Bueno	1958-68	0-1-0	0-1-1	3-5-0	4-5-0	7-12-1	20

Men's, Women's & Mixed Doubles Grand Slam

The tennis Grand Slam has only been accomplished in doubles competition six times in the same calendar year. Here are the doubles teams to accomplish the feat. The two men and three women to win the singles Grand Slam are noted in the Grand Slam Summary tables beginning on page 824.

Men's Doubles

1951 . . . . .Frank Sedgman, Australia
& Ken McGregor, Australia

Mixed Doubles

1963 . . . . .Ken Fletcher, Australia
& Margaret Smith, Australia
1967 . . . . .Owen Davidson and two partners*
*Davidson's partners: AUS–Lesley Turner; FR, WIM, U.S.–
Billie Jean King.

Women's Doubles

1960 . . . . .Maria Bueno, Brazil & two partners†
1984. .Martina Navratilova, USA
& Pam Shriver, USA
1998 . . . .Martina Hingis, Switzerland & two partners#
†Bueno's partners: AUS–Christine Truman; FR, WIM,
U.S.–Darlene Hard.
#Hingis' partners: AUS–Mirjana Lucic; FR, WIM, U.S.–
Jana Novotna.

All-Time Grand Slam Singles Titles

Men and women with the most singles championships in the Australian, French, Wimbledon and U.S. championships, through 2001. Note that (*) indicates player never played in that particular Grand Slam event; and players active in singles play in 2001 are in **bold** type.

Top 10 Men

		Aus	Fre	Wim	US	Total
1	**Pete Sampras**	2	0	7	4	13
2	Roy Emerson	6	2	2	2	12
3	Bjorn Borg	0	6	5	0	11
	Rod Laver	3	2	4	2	11
5	Bill Tilden	*	0	3	7	10
6	Jimmy Connors	1	0	2	5	8
	Ivan Lendl	2	3	0	3	8
	Fred Perry	1	1	3	3	8
	Ken Rosewall	4	2	0	2	8
10	**Andre Agassi**	3	1	1	2	7
	Henri Cochet	*	4	2	1	7
	Rene Lacoste	*	3	2	2	7
	Bill Larned	*	*	0	7	7
	John McEnroe	0	0	3	4	7
	John Newcombe	2	0	3	2	7
	Willie Renshaw	*	*	7	*	7
	Dick Sears	*	*	0	7	7

Top 15 Women

		Aus	Fre	Wim	US	Total
1	Margaret Smith Court	11	5	3	5	24
2	Steffi Graf	4	6	7	5	22
3	Helen Wills Moody	*	4	8	7	19
4	Chris Evert	2	7	3	6	18
	Martina Navratilova	3	2	9	4	18
6	Billie Jean King	1	1	6	4	12
	Suzanne Lenglen	*	6	6	0	12
8	Maureen Connolly	1	2	3	3	9
	Monica Seles	4	3	0	2	9
10	Molla Bjurstedt Mallory	*	*	0	8	8
11	Maria Bueno	0	0	3	4	7
	Evonne Goolagong	4	1	2	0	7
	Dorothea D. Chambers	*	*	7	0	7
14	Nancy Bolton	6	0	0	0	6
	Louise Brough	1	0	4	1	6
	Margaret du Pont	*	2	1	3	6
	Doris Hart	1	2	1	2	6
	Blanche Bingley Hillyard	*	*	6	*	6

Annual Number One Players

Unofficial world rankings for men and women determined by the *London Daily Telegraph* from 1914-72. Since then, official world rankings computed by men's and women's tours. Rankings included only amateur players from 1914 until the arrival of open (professional) tennis in 1968. No rankings were released during World Wars I and II.

MEN

Multiple winners: Pete Sampras and Bill Tilden (6); Jimmy Connors (5); Henri Cochet, Rod Laver, Ivan Lendl and John McEnroe (4); John Newcombe and Fred Perry (3); Bjorn Borg, Don Budge, Ashley Cooper, Stefan Edberg, Roy Emerson, Neale Fraser, Jack Kramer, Rene Lacoste, Ilie Nastase, Frank Sedgman and Tony Trabert (2).

Year		Year		Year		Year	
1914	Maurice McLoughlin	1937	Don Budge	1962	Rod Laver	1982	John McEnroe
1915-18	No rankings	1938	Don Budge	1963	Rafael Osuna	1983	John McEnroe
1919	Gerald Patterson	1939	Bobby Riggs	1964	Roy Emerson	1984	John McEnroe
1920	Bill Tilden	1940-45	No rankings	1965	Roy Emerson	1985	Ivan Lendl
1921	Bill Tilden	1946	Jack Kramer	1966	Manuel Santana	1986	Ivan Lendl
1922	Bill Tilden	1947	Jack Kramer	1967	John Newcombe	1987	Ivan Lendl
1923	Bill Tilden	1948	Frank Parker	1968	Rod Laver	1988	Mats Wilander
1924	Bill Tilden	1949	Pancho Gonzales	1969	Rod Laver	1989	Ivan Lendl
1925	Bill Tilden	1950	Budge Patty	1970	John Newcombe	1990	Stefan Edberg
1926	Rene Lacoste	1951	Frank Sedgman	1971	John Newcombe	1991	Stefan Edberg
1927	Rene Lacoste	1952	Frank Sedgman	1972	Ilie Nastase	1992	Jim Courier
1928	Henri Cochet	1953	Tony Trabert	1973	Ilie Nastase	1993	Pete Sampras
1929	Henri Cochet	1954	Jaroslav Drobny	1974	Jimmy Connors	1994	Pete Sampras
1930	Henri Cochet	1955	Tony Trabert	1975	Jimmy Connors	1995	Pete Sampras
1931	Henri Cochet	1956	Lew Hoad	1976	Jimmy Connors	1996	Pete Sampras
1932	Ellsworth Vines	1957	Ashley Cooper	1977	Jimmy Connors	1997	Pete Sampras
1933	Jack Crawford	1958	Ashley Cooper	1978	Jimmy Connors	1998	Pete Sampras
1934	Fred Perry	1959	Neale Fraser	1979	Bjorn Borg	1999	Andre Agassi
1935	Fred Perry	1960	Neale Fraser	1980	Bjorn Borg	2000	Gustavo Kuerten
1936	Fred Perry	1961	Rod Laver	1981	John McEnroe		

WOMEN

Multiple winners: Helen Wills Moody (9); Steffi Graf (8); Margaret Smith Court and Martina Navratilova (7); Chris Evert Lloyd (5); Margaret Osborne duPont and Billie Jean King (4); Maureen Connolly, Martina Hingis and Monica Seles (3); Maria Bueno, Althea Gibson and Suzanne Lenglen (2).

Year		Year		Year		Year	
1925	Suzanne Lenglen	1948	Margaret duPont	1966	Billie Jean King	1984	Martina Navratilova
1926	Suzanne Lenglen	1949	Margaret duPont	1967	Billie Jean King	1985	Martina Navratilova
1927	Helen Wills	1950	Margaret duPont	1968	Billie Jean King	1986	Martina Navratilova
1928	Helen Wills	1951	Doris Hart	1969	Margaret Court	1987	Steffi Graf
1929	Helen Wills Moody	1952	Maureen Connolly			1988	Steffi Graf
1930	Helen Wills Moody	1953	Maureen Connolly	1970	Margaret Court	1989	Steffi Graf
1931	Helen Wills Moody	1954	Maureen Connolly	1971	Evonne Goolagong		
1932	Helen Wills Moody	1955	Louise Brough	1972	Billie Jean King	1990	Steffi Graf
1933	Helen Wills Moody	1956	Shirley Fry	1973	Margaret Court	1991	Monica Seles
1934	Dorothy Round	1957	Althea Gibson	1974	Billie Jean King	1992	Monica Seles
1935	Helen Wills Moody	1958	Althea Gibson	1975	Chris Evert	1993	Steffi Graf
1936	Helen Jacobs	1959	Maria Bueno	1976	Chris Evert	1994	Steffi Graf
1937	Anita Lizana			1977	Chris Evert	1995	Steffi Graf
1938	Helen Wills Moody	1960	Maria Bueno	1978	Martina Navratilova		& Monica Seles*
1939	Alice Marble	1961	Angela Mortimer	1979	Martina Navratilova	1996	Steffi Graf
		1962	Margaret Smith	1980	Chris Evert Lloyd	1997	Martina Hingis
1940-45	No rankings	1963	Margaret Smith	1981	Chris Evert Lloyd	1998	Lindsay Davenport
1946	Pauline Betz	1964	Margaret Smith	1982	Martina Navratilova	1999	Martina Hingis
1947	Margaret Osborne	1965	Margaret Smith	1983	Martina Navratilova	2000	Martina Hingis

*Upon her return to the WTA Tour on Aug. 15, 1995, Seles retained her #1 ranking and was co-ranked at #1 through her first six tournaments (August '95–May '96). Seles was on leave since April 1993 when she was stabbed by a fan during a match.

Annual Top 10 World Rankings (since 1968)

Year by year Top 10 world computer rankings for men (ATP Tour) and women (WTA Tour) since the arrival of open tennis in 1968. Rankings from 1968-72 made by Lance Tingay of the *London Daily Telegraph*. Since 1973 the WTA Tour and ATP tour had compiled its own computer rankings. Since 2000, however, the ATP Tour rankings below reflect the final standings of the ATP Champions Race.

MEN

1968
1 Rod Laver
2 Arthur Ashe
3 Ken Rosewall
4 Tom Okker
5 Tony Roche
6 John Newcombe
7 Clark Graebner
8 Dennis Ralston
9 Cliff Drysdale
10 Pancho Gonzales

1969
1 Rod Laver
2 Tony Roche
3 John Newcombe
4 Tom Okker
5 Ken Rosewall
6 Arthur Ashe
7 Cliff Drysdale
8 Pancho Gonzales
9 Andres Gimeno
10 Fred Stolle

1970
1 John Newcombe
2 Ken Rosewall
3 Tony Roche
4 Rod Laver
5 Arthur Ashe
6 Ilie Nastase
7 Tom Okker
8 Roger Taylor
9 Jan Kodes
10 Cliff Richey

1971
1 John Newcombe
2 Stan Smith
3 Rod Laver
4 Ken Rosewall
5 Jan Kodes
6 Arthur Ashe
7 Tom Okker
8 Marty Riessen
9 Cliff Drysdale
10 Ilie Nastase

1972
1 Stan Smith
2 Ken Rosewall
3 Ilie Nastase
4 Rod Laver
5 Arthur Ashe
6 John Newcombe
7 Bob Lutz
8 Tom Okker
9 Marty Riessen
10 Andres Gimeno

1973
1 Ilie Nastase
2 John Newcombe
3 Jimmy Connors
4 Tom Okker
5 Stan Smith
6 Ken Rosewall
7 Manuel Orantes
8 Rod Laver
9 Jan Kodes
10 Arthur Ashe

1974
1 Jimmy Connors
2 John Newcombe
3 Bjorn Borg
4 Rod Laver
5 Guillermo Vilas
6 Tom Okker
7 Arthur Ashe
8 Ken Rosewall
9 Stan Smith
10 Ilie Nastase

1975
1 Jimmy Connors
2 Guillermo Vilas
3 Bjorn Borg
4 Arthur Ashe
5 Manuel Orantes
6 Ken Rosewall
7 Ilie Nastase
8 John Alexander
9 Roscoe Tanner
10 Rod Laver

1976
1 Jimmy Connors
2 Bjorn Borg
3 Ilie Nastase
4 Manuel Orantes
5 Raul Ramirez
6 Guillermo Vilas
7 Adriano Panatta
8 Harold Solomon
9 Eddie Dibbs
10 Brian Gottfried

1977
1 Jimmy Connors
2 Guillermo Vilas
3 Bjorn Borg
4 Vitas Gerulaitis
5 Brian Gottfried
6 Eddie Dibbs
7 Manuel Orantes
8 Raul Ramirez
9 Ilie Nastase
10 Dick Stockton

1978
1 Jimmy Connors
2 Bjorn Borg
3 Guillermo Vilas
4 John McEnroe
5 Vitas Gerulaitis
6 Eddie Dibbs
7 Brian Gottfried
8 Raul Ramirez
9 Harold Solomon
10 Corrado Barazzutti

1979
1 Bjorn Borg
2 Jimmy Connors
3 John McEnroe
4 Vitas Gerulaitis
5 Roscoe Tanner
6 Guillermo Vilas
7 Arthur Ashe
8 Harold Solomon
9 Jose Higueras
10 Eddie Dibbs

Annual Top 10 World Rankings (since 1968) (Cont.)
MEN

1980
1 Bjorn Borg
2 John McEnroe
3 Jimmy Connors
4 Gene Mayer
5 Guillermo Vilas
6 Ivan Lendl
7 Harold Solomon
8 Jose-Luis Clerc
9 Vitas Gerulaitis
10 Eliot Teltscher

1981
1 John McEnroe
2 Ivan Lendl
3 Jimmy Connors
4 Bjorn Borg
5 Jose-Luis Clerc
6 Guillermo Vilas
7 Gene Mayer
8 Eliot Teltscher
9 Vitas Gerulaitis
10 Peter McNamara

1982
1 John McEnroe
2 Jimmy Connors
3 Ivan Lendl
4 Guillermo Vilas
5 Vitas Gerulaitis
6 Jose-Luis Clerc
7 Mats Wilander
8 Gene Mayer
9 Yannick Noah
10 Peter McNamara

1983
1 John McEnroe
2 Ivan Lendl
3 Jimmy Connors
4 Mats Wilander
5 Yannick Noah
6 Jimmy Arias
7 Jose Higueras
8 Jose-Luis Clerc
9 Kevin Curren
10 Gene Mayer

1984
1 John McEnroe
2 Jimmy Connors
3 Ivan Lendl
4 Mats Wilander
5 Andres Gomez
6 Anders Jarryd
7 Henrik Sundstrom
8 Pat Cash
9 Eliot Teltscher
10 Yannick Noah

1985
1 Ivan Lendl
2 John McEnroe
3 Mats Wilander
4 Jimmy Connors
5 Stefan Edberg
6 Boris Becker
7 Yannick Noah
8 Anders Jarryd
9 Miloslav Mecir
10 Kevin Curren

1986
1 Ivan Lendl
2 Boris Becker
3 Mats Wilander
4 Yannick Noah
5 Stefan Edberg
6 Henri Leconte
7 Joakim Nystrom
8 Jimmy Connors
9 Miloslav Mecir
10 Andres Gomez

1987
1 Ivan Lendl
2 Stefan Edberg
3 Mats Wilander
4 Jimmy Connors
5 Boris Becker
6 Miloslav Mecir
7 Pat Cash
8 Yannick Noah
9 Tim Mayotte
10 John McEnroe

1988
1 Mats Wilander
2 Ivan Lendl
3 Andre Agassi
4 Boris Becker
5 Stefan Edberg
6 Kent Carlsson
7 Jimmy Connors
8 Jakob Hlasek
9 Henri Leconte
10 Tim Mayotte

1989
1 Ivan Lendl
2 Boris Becker
3 Stefan Edberg
4 John McEnroe
5 Michael Chang
6 Brad Gilbert
7 Andre Agassi
8 Aaron Krickstein
9 Alberto Mancini
10 Jay Berger

1990
1 Stefan Edberg
2 Boris Becker
3 Ivan Lendl
4 Andre Agassi
5 Pete Sampras
6 Andres Gomez
7 Thomas Muster
8 Emilio Sanchez
9 Goran Ivanisevic
10 Brad Gilbert

1991
1 Stefan Edberg
2 Jim Courier
3 Boris Becker
4 Michael Stich
5 Ivan Lendl
6 Pete Sampras
7 Guy Forget
8 Karel Novacek
9 Petr Korda
10 Andre Agassi

1992
1 Jim Courier
2 Stefan Edberg
3 Pete Sampras
4 Goran Ivanisevic
5 Boris Becker
6 Michael Chang
7 Petr Korda
8 Ivan Lendl
9 Andre Agassi
10 Richard Krajicek

1993
1 Pete Sampras
2 Michael Stich
3 Jim Courier
4 Sergi Bruguera
5 Stefan Edberg
6 Andrei Medvedev
7 Goran Ivanisevic
8 Michael Chang
9 Thomas Muster
10 Cedric Pioline

1994
1 Pete Sampras
2 Andre Agassi
3 Boris Becker
4 Sergi Bruguera
5 Goran Ivanisevic
6 Michael Chang
7 Stefan Edberg
8 Alberto Berasategui
9 Michael Stich
10 Todd Martin

1995
1 Pete Sampras
2 Andre Agassi
3 Thomas Muster
4 Boris Becker
5 Michael Chang
6 Yevgeny Kafelnikov
7 Thomas Enqvist
8 Jim Courier
9 Wayne Ferreira
10 Goran Ivanisevic

1996
1 Pete Sampras
2 Michael Chang
3 Yevgeny Kafelnikov
4 Goran Ivanisevic
5 Thomas Muster
6 Boris Becker
7 Richard Krajicek
8 Andre Agassi
9 Thomas Enqvist
10 Wayne Ferreira

1997
1 Pete Sampras
2 Patrick Rafter
3 Michael Chang
4 Jonas Bjorkman
5 Yevgeny Kafelnikov
6 Greg Rusedski
7 Carlos Moya
8 Sergi Bruguera
9 Thomas Muster
10 Marcelo Rios

1998
1 Pete Sampras
2 Marcelo Rios
3 Alex Corretja
4 Patrick Rafter
5 Carlos Moya
6 Andre Agassi
7 Tim Henman
8 Karol Kucera
9 Greg Rusedski
10 Richard Krajicek

1999
1 Andre Agassi
2 Yevgeny Kafelnikov
3 Pete Sampras
4 Thomas Enqvist
5 Gustavo Kuerten
6 Nicolas Kiefer
7 Todd Martin
8 Nicolas Lapentti
9 Marcelo Rios
10 Richard Krajicek

2000
1 Gustavo Kuerten
2 Marat Safin
3 Pete Sampras
4 Magnus Norman
5 Yevgeny Kafelnikov
6 Andre Agassi
7 Lleyton Hewitt
8 Alex Corretja
9 Thomas Enqvist
10 Tim Henman

WOMEN

1968
1 Billie Jean King
2 Virginia Wade
3 Nancy Richey
4 Maria Bueno
5 Margaret Court
6 Ann Jones
7 Judy Tegart
8 Annette du Plooy
9 Leslie Bowrey
10 Rosie Casals

1969
1 Margaret Court
2 Ann Jones
3 Billie Jean King
4 Nancy Richey
5 Julie Heldman
6 Rosie Casals
7 Kerry Melville
8 Peaches Bartkowicz
9 Virginia Wade
10 Leslie Bowrey

1970
1 Margaret Court
2 Billie Jean King
3 Rosie Casals
4 Virginia Wade
5 Helga Niessen
6 Kerry Melville
7 Julie Heldman
8 Karen Krantczke
9 Francoise Durr
10 Nancy R. Gunter

1971
1 Evonne Goolagong
2 Billie Jean King
3 Margaret Court
4 Rosie Casals
5 Kerry Melville
6 Virginia Wade
7 Judy Tagert
8 Francoise Durr
9 Helga N. Masthoff
10 Chris Evert

1972
1 Billie Jean King
2 Evonne Goolagong
3 Chris Evert
4 Margaret Court
5 Kerry Melville
6 Virginia Wade
7 Rosie Casals
8 Nancy R. Gunter
9 Francoise Durr
10 Linda Tuero

1973
1 Margaret S. Court
2 Billie Jean King
3 Evonne G. Cawley
4 Chris Evert
5 Rosie Casals
6 Virginia Wade
7 Kerry Reid
8 Nancy Richey
9 Julie Heldman
10 Helga Masthoff

1974
1 Billie Jean King
2 Evonne G. Cawley
3 Chris Evert
4 Virginia Wade
5 Julie Heldman
6 Rosie Casals
7 Kerry Reid
8 Olga Morozova
9 Lesley Hunt
10 Francoise Durr

1975
1 Chris Evert
2 Billie Jean King
3 Evonne G. Cawley
4 Martina Navratilova
5 Virginia Wade
6 Margaret S. Court
7 Olga Morozova
8 Nancy Richey
9 Francoise Durr
10 Rosie Casals

1976
1 Chris Evert
2 Evonne G. Cawley
3 Virginia Wade
4 Martina Navratilova
5 Sue Barker
6 Betty Stove
7 Dianne Balestrat
8 Mima Jausovec
9 Rosie Casals
10 Francoise Durr

1977
1 Chris Evert
2 Billie Jean King
3 Martina Navratilova
4 Virginia Wade
5 Sue Barker
6 Rosie Casals
7 Betty Stove
8 Dianne Balestrat
9 Wendy Turnbull
10 Kerry Reid

1978
1 Martina Navratilova
2 Chris Evert Lloyd
3 Evonne G. Cawley
4 Virginia Wade
5 Billie Jean King
6 Tracy Austin
7 Wendy-Turnbull
8 Kerry Reid
9 Betty Stove
10 Dianne Balestrat

1979
1 Martina Navratilova
2 Chris Evert Lloyd
3 Tracy Austin
4 Evonne G. Cawley
5 Billie Jean King
6 Dianne Balestrat
7 Wendy Turnbull
8 Virginia Wade
9 Kerry Reid
10 Sue Barker

1980
1 Chris Evert Lloyd
2 Tracy Austin
3 Martina Navratilova
4 Hana Mandlikova
5 Evonne G. Cawley
6 Billie Jean King
7 Andrea Jaeger
8 Wendy Turnbull
9 Pam Shriver
10 Greer Stevens

1981
1 Chris Evert Lloyd
2 Tracy Austin
3 Martina Navratilova
4 Andrea Jaeger
5 Hana Mandlikova
6 Sylvia Hanika
7 Pam Shriver
8 Wendy Turnbull
9 Bettina Bunge
10 Barbara Potter

1982
1 Martina Navratilova
2 Chris Evert Lloyd
3 Andrea Jaeger
4 Tracy Austin
5 Wendy Turnbull
6 Pam Shriver
7 Hana Mandlikova
8 Barbara Potter
9 Bettina Bunge
10 Sylvia Hanika

1983
1 Martina Navratilova
2 Chris Evert Lloyd
3 Andrea Jaeger
4 Pam Shriver
5 Sylvia Hanika
6 Jo Durie
7 Bettina Bunge
8 Wendy Turnbull
9 Tracy Austin
10 Zina Garrison

1984
1 Martina Navratilova
2 Chris Evert Lloyd
3 Hana Mandlikova
4 Pam Shriver
5 Wendy Turnbull
6 Manuela Maleeva
7 Helena Sukova
8 Claudia Kohde-Kilsch
9 Zina Garrison
10 Kathy Jordan

1985
1 Martina Navratilova
2 Chris Evert Lloyd
3 Hana Mandlikova
4 Pam Shriver
5 Claudia Kohde-Kilsch
6 Steffi Graf
7 Manuela Maleeva
8 Zina Garrison
9 Helena Sukova
10 Bonnie Gadusek

1986
1 Martina Navratilova
2 Chris Evert Lloyd
3 Steffi Graf
4 Hana Mandlikova
5 Helena Sukova
6 Pam Shriver
7 Claudia Kohde-Kilsch
8 M. Maleeva-Fragniere
9 Zina Garrison
10 Gabriela Sabatini

1987
1 Steffi Graf
2 Martina Navratilova
3 Chris Evert
4 Pam Shriver
5 Hana Mandlikova
6 Gabriela Sabatini
7 Helena Sukova
8 M. Maleeva-Fragniere
9 Zina Garrison
10 Claudia Kohde-Kilsch

1988
1 Steffi Graf
2 Martina Navratilova
3 Chris Evert
4 Gabriela Sabatini
5 Pam Shriver
6 M. Maleeva-Fragniere
7 Natalia Zvereva
8 Helena Sukova
9 Zina Garrison
10 Barbara Potter

1989
1 Steffi Graf
2 Martina Navratilova
3 Gabriela Sabatini
4 Z. Garrison-Jackson
5 A. Sanchez Vicario
6 Monica Seles
7 Conchita Martinez
8 Helena Sukova
9 M. Maleeva-Fragniere
10 Chris Evert

1990
1 Steffi Graf
2 Monica Seles
3 Martina Navratilova
4 Mary Joe Fernandez
5 Gabriela Sabatini
6 Katerina Maleeva
7 A. Sanchez Vicario
8 Jennifer Capriati
9 M. Maleeva-Fragniere
10 Z. Garrison-Jackson

1991
1 Monica Seles
2 Steffi Graf
3 Gabriela Sabatini
4 Martina Navratilova
5 A. Sanchez Vicario
6 Jennifer Capriati
7 Jana Novotna
8 Mary Joe Fernandez
9 Conchita Martinez
10 M. Maleeva-Fragniere

1992
1 Monica Seles
2 Steffi Graf
3 Gabriela Sabatini
4 A. Sanchez Vicario
5 Martina Navratilova
6 Mary Joe Fernandez
7 Jennifer Capriati
8 Conchita Martinez
9 M. Maleeva-Fragniere
10 Jana Novotna

1993
1 Steffi Graf
2 A. Sanchez Vicario
3 Martina Navratilova
4 Conchita Martinez
5 Gabriela Sabatini
6 Jana Novotna
7 Mary Joe Fernandez
8 Monica Seles
9 Jennifer Capriati
10 Anke Huber

1994
1 Steffi Graf
2 A. Sanchez Vicario
3 Conchita Martinez
4 Jana Novotna
5 Mary Pierce
6 Lindsay Davenport
7 Gabriela Sabatini
8 Martina Navratilova
9 Kimiko Date
10 Natasha Zvereva

1995
1 Steffi Graf
  Monica Seles*
2 Conchita Martinez
3 A. Sanchez Vicario
4 Kimiko Date
5 Mary Pierce
6 Magdalena Maleeva
7 Gabriela Sabatini
8 Mary Joe Fernandez
9 Iva Majoli
10 Anke Huber

1996
1 Steffi Graf
2 Monica Seles†
  A. Sanchez Vicario
3 Jana Novotna
4 Martina Hingis
5 Conchita Martinez
6 Anke Huber
7 Iva Majoli
8 Kimiko Date
9 Lindsay Davenport
10 Barbara Paulus

Annual Top 10 World Rankings (since 1968) (Cont.)
WOMEN

1997	1998	1999	2000
1 Martina Hingis	1 Lindsay Davenport	1 Martina Hingis	1 Martina Hingis
2 Jana Novotna	2 Martina Hingis	2 Lindsay Davenport	2 Lindsay Davenport
3 Lindsay Davenport	3 Jana Novotna	3 Venus Williams	3 Venus Williams
4 Amanda Coetzer	4 A. Sanchez Vicario	4 Serena Williams	4 Monica Seles
5 Monica Seles	5 Venus Williams	5 Mary Pierce	5 Conchita Martinez
6 Iva Majoli	6 Monica Seles	6 Monica Seles	6 Serena Williams
7 Mary Pierce	7 Mary Pierce	7 Nathalie Tauziat	7 Mary Pierce
8 Irina Spirlea	8 Conchita Martinez	8 Barbara Schett	8 Anna Kournikova
9 A. Sanchez Vicario	9 Steffi Graf	9 Julie Halard-Decugis	9 A. Sanchez Vicario
10 Mary Joe Fernandez	10 Nathalie Tauziat	10 Amelie Mauresmo	10 Nathalie Tauziat

*Returning to the WTA Tour on Aug. 15, 1995, Seles was co-ranked #1 for her first six tournaments. Seles had been absent from the Tour since April 1993 when she was stabbed by a fan during a match. She was ranked #1 at the time of the stabbing.
†Seles' ranking was revised in May 1996. The revision stipulated that her new modified ranking average would be calculated using a divisor of the acutal number of tournaments she had played (13), and she would be co-ranked with the player whose average is immediately below her average (Sanchez Vicario).

Maiden and Married Names of Women's Champions

Maiden Name	Married Name	Maiden Name	Married Name
Blanche Bingley	Blanche Hillyard	Hazel Hotchkiss	Hazel Wightman
Molla Bjurstedt	Molla Mallory	Hilde Krahwinkel	Hilde Sperling
Patricia Canning	Patricia Todd	Kerry Melville	Kerry Reid
Mary Carter	Mary Raitano	Kathleen McKane	Kathleen Godfrey
Charlotte Cooper	Charlotte Sterry	Billie Jean Moffitt	Billie Jean King
Thelma Coyne	Thelma Long	Margaret Osborne	Margaret duPont
Dorothea Douglass	Dorothea Lambert Chambers	Sarah Palfrey	Sarah Fabyan Cooke
Chris Evert	Chris Evert Lloyd*	Margaret Smith	Margaret Smith Court
Evonne Goolagong	Evonne Cawley	Helen Wills	Helen Wills Moody
Louise Hammond	Louise Raymond	Nancye Wynne	Nancye Bolton
Ann Haydon	Ann Haydon Jones		

*Chris Evert Lloyd divorced husband John Lloyd in 1987, and has since gone by the name Chris Evert.

All-Time Singles Leaders
Tournaments Won

All-time tournament wins from the arrival of open tennis in 1968 through 2000. Men's totals include ATP Tour, Grand Prix and WCT tournaments. Players active in singles play in 2001 are in **bold** type.

MEN

		Total			Total			Total
1	Jimmy Connors	109	11	Thomas Muster	44	21	Vitas Gerulaitis	27
2	Ivan Lendl	94	12	Stefan Edberg	41	22	Jose-Luis Clerc	25
3	John McEnroe	77	13	Stan Smith	39		Brian Gottfried	25
4	**Pete Sampras**	63	14	**Michael Chang**	34	24	Jim Courier	23
5	Bjorn Borg	62	15	Arthur Ashe	33		Yannick Noah	23
	Guillermo Vilas	62		Mats Wilander	33	26	Eddie Dibbs	22
7	Ilie Nastase	57	17	John Newcombe	32		**Yevgeny Kafelnikov**	22
8	Boris Becker	49		Manuel Orantes	32		Harold Solomon	22
9	Rod Laver	47		Ken Rosewall	32	29	Andres Gomez	21
10	**Andre Agassi**	45	20	Tom Okker	31		**Goran Ivanisevic**	21

WOMEN

		Total			Total			Total
1	Martina Navratilova	167	10	**Conchita Martinez**	32	19	Kerry Melville Reid	22
2	Chris Evert	154	11	Olga Morozova	31	20	Pam Shriver	21
3	Steffi Graf	107	12	**Lindsay Davenport**	30	21	Julie Heldman	20
4	Margaret Court	92	13	Tracy Austin	29	22	M. Maleeva-Fragniere	19
5	Billie Jean King	67	14	Hana Mandlikova	27	23	Virginia Ruzici	17
6	E. Goolagong Cawley	65		Gabriela Sabatini	27		Regina Marsikova	17
7	Virginia Wade	55		**A. Sanchez Vicario**	27	25	Sue Barker	15
8	**Monica Seles**	47	17	Nancy Richey	25		**Mary Pierce**	15
9	**Martina Hingis**	35	18	Jana Novotna	24		**Venus Williams**	15

Money Won

All-time money winners from the arrival of open tennis in 1968 through 2000. Totals include doubles earnings.

MEN

		Earnings			Earnings			Earnings
1	Pete Sampras	$41,063,159	11	John McEnroe	$12,539,622	21	Mark Woodforde	$8,324,401
2	Boris Becker	25,079,456	12	Thomas Muster	12,224,410	22	Wayne Ferreira	8,189,242
3	Ivan Lendl	21,262,417	13	Sergi Bruguera	11,421,046	23	Alex Corretja	8,150,134
4	Andre Agassi	21,140,724	14	Petr Korda	10,448,085	24	Mats Wilander	7,976,256
5	Stefan Edberg	20,630,941	15	Richard Krajicek	9,814,581	25	Todd Woodbridge	7,715,042
6	Michael Chang	18,651,206	16	Patrick Rafter	9,432,719	26	Jonas Bjorkman	7,502,600
7	Goran Ivanisevic	18,437,580	17	Gustavo Kuerten	8,923,321	27	Paul Haarhuis	7,264,084
8	Yevgeny Kafelnikov	18,184,646	18	Thomas Enqvist	8,680,378	28	Todd Martin	7,153,598
9	Jim Courier	14,033,132	19	Jimmy Connors	8,641,040	29	Greg Rusedski	6,937,169
10	Michael Stich	12,590,152	20	Marcelo Rios	8,423,663	30	Andrei Medvedev	6,580,136

WOMEN

		Earnings			Earnings			Earnings
1	Steffi Graf	$21,895,277	11	Natasha Zvereva	$7,714,430	21	Anke Huber	$4,251,770
2	Mart. Navratilova	20,396,399	12	Venus Williams	6,656,727	22	Larisa Neiland	4,083,936
3	A. Sanchez Vicario	15,747,252	13	Helena Sukova	6,391,245	23	Serena Williams	3,995,061
4	Martina Hingis	15,080,325	14	Mary Pierce	6,169,661	24	Iva Majoli	3,604,806
5	Monica Seles	12,891,708	15	Nathalie Tauziat	5,707,942	25	Lori McNeil	3,475,690
6	Lindsay Davenport	11,934,628	16	Pam Shriver	5,460,566	26	Hana Mandlikova	3,340,959
7	Jana Novotna	11,249,134	17	Mary Joe Fernandez	5,258,471	27	M. Maleeva-Fragniere	3,244,811
8	Conchita Martinez	9,335,263	18	Gigi Fernandez	4,681,906	28	Julie Halard-Decugis	3,096,734
9	Chris Evert	8,896,195	19	Z. Garrison Jackson	4,590,816	29	Lisa Raymond	2,797,956
10	Gabriela Sabatini	8,785,850	20	Amanda Coetzer	4,252,428	30	Wendy Turnbull	2,769,024

Year-end Tournaments

MEN

Tennis Masters Cup

The year-end championship featuring the top eight players in the Tennis Masters Series rankings. Two groups of four players square off in a round-robin tournament followed by a single-elimination semifinals and finals. Originally called the Masters in 1970, the tournament followed a round-robin format, but was revised in 1972 to include a round-robin to decide the four semi-finalists then a single elimination format after that. Replaced by ATP Tour World Championship in 1990 through 1999.

Multiple Winners: Ivan Lendl and Pete Sampras (5); Ilie Nastase (4); Boris Becker and John McEnroe (3); Bjorn Borg (2).

Year	Winner	Runner-Up
1970	Stan Smith (4-1) *	Rod Laver (4-1)
1971	Ilie Nastase (6-0)	Stan Smith (4-2)

Year	Winner	Loser	Score
1972	Ilie Nastase	S. Smith	63 62 36 26 63
1973	Ilie Nastase	T. Okker	63 75 46 63
1974	Guillermo Vilas	I. Nastase	76 62 36 36 64
1975	Ilie Nastase	B. Borg	62 62 61
1976	Manuel Orantes	W. Fibak	57 62 06 76 61
1978	Jimmy Connors	B. Borg	64 16 64
1979	John McEnroe	A. Ashe	67 63 75
1980	Bjorn Borg	V. Gerulaitis	62 62
1981	Bjorn Borg	I. Lendl	64 62 62
1982	Ivan Lendl	V. Gerulaitis	67 26 76 62 62
1983	Ivan Lendl	J. McEnroe	64 64 62
1984	John McEnroe	I. Lendl	63 64 64
1985	John McEnroe	I. Lendl	75 60 64

Year	Winner	Loser	Score
1986	Ivan Lendl	B. Becker	62 76 63
1986	Ivan Lendl	B. Becker	64 64 64
1987	Ivan Lendl	M. Wilander	62 62 63
1988	Boris Becker	I. Lendl	57 76 36 62 76
1989	Stefan Edberg	B. Becker	46 76 63 61
1990	Andre Agassi	S. Edberg	57 76 75 62
1991	Pete Sampras	J. Courier	36 76 63 64
1992	Boris Becker	J. Courier	64 63 75
1993	Michael Stich	P. Sampras	76 26 76 62
1994	Pete Sampras	B. Becker	46 63 75 64
1995	Boris Becker	M. Chang	76 60 76
1996	Pete Sampras	B. Becker	36 76 76 67 64
1997	Pete Sampras	Y. Kafelnikov	63 62 62
1998	Alex Corretja	C. Moya	36 36 75 63 75
1999	Pete Sampras	A. Agassi	61 75 64
2000	Gustavo Kuerten	A. Agassi	64 64 64

*Smith was declared the winner because he beat Laver in their round-robin match (4-6, 6-3, 6-4).
Note: The tournament switched from December to January in 1977-78, then back to December in 1986.

Playing Sites

1970—Tokyo; **1971**—Paris; **1972**—Barcelona; **1973**—Boston; **1974**—Melbourne; **1975**—Stockholm; **1976**—Houston; **1977-89**—New York City; **1990-95**—Frankfurt, GER; **1996-99**—Hannover, GER; **2000**—Lisbon, POR; **2001**—Sydney, AUS.

WCT Championship (1971-89)

World Championship Tennis was established in 1967 to promote professional tennis and led the way into the open era. It's major singles and doubles championships were held every May among the top eight regular season finishers on the circuit from 1971 until the WCT folded in 1989.

Multiple winners: John McEnroe (5), Jimmy Connors, Ivan Lendl and Ken Rosewall (2).

Year	Winner	Loser	Score	Year	Winner	Loser	Score
1971	Ken Rosewall	R. Laver	64 16 76 76	1973	Stan Smith	A. Ashe	63 63 46 64
1972	Ken Rosewall	R. Laver	46 60 63 67 76	1974	John Newcombe	B. Borg	46 63 63 62

Year-end Tournaments (Cont.)

Year	Winner	Loser	Score	Year	Winner	Loser	Score
1975	Arthur Ashe	B. Borg	36 64 64 60	1983	John McEnroe	I. Lendl	62 46 63 67 76
1976	Bjorn Borg	G. Vilas	16 61 75 61	1984	John McEnroe	J. Connors	61 62 63
1977	Jimmy Connors	D. Stockton	67 61 64 63	1985	Ivan Lendl	T. Mayotte	76 64 61
1978	Vitas Gerulaitis	E. Dibbs	63 62 61	1986	Anders Jarryd	B. Becker	67 61 61 64
1979	John McEnroe	B. Borg	75 46 62 76	1987	Miloslav Mercir	J. McEnroe	60 36 62 62
1980	Jimmy Connors	J. McEnroe	26 76 61 62	1988	Boris Becker	S. Edberg	64 16 75 62
1981	John McEnroe	J. Kriek	61 62 64	1989	John McEnroe	B. Gilbert	63 63 76
1982	Ivan Lendl	J. McEnroe	62 36 63 63				

WOMEN
WTA Tour Championship

Originally the Virginia Slims Championships from 1971-94. The WTA Tour's year-end tournament took place in March from 1972 until 1986 when the WTA decided to adopt a January-to-November playing season. Given the changeover, two championships were held in 1986. Held every year since 1979 at Madison Square Garden in New York.

Multiple winners: Martina Navratilova (8); Steffi Graf (5); Chris Evert (4); Monica Seles (3); Evonne Goolagong, Martina Hingis and Gabriela Sabatini (2).

Year	Winner	Loser	Score	Year	Winner	Loser	Score
1972	Chris Evert	K. Reid	75 64	1988	Gabriela Sabatini	P. Shriver	75 62 62
1973	Chris Evert	N. Richey	63 63	1989	Steffi Graf	M. Navratilova	64 75 26 62
1974	Evonne Goolagong	C. Evert	63 64	1990	Monica Seles	G. Sabatini	64 57 36 64 62
1975	Chris Evert	M. Navratilova	64 62	1991	Monica Seles	M. Navratilova	64 36 75 60
1976	Evonne Goolagong	C. Evert	63 57 63	1992	Monica Seles	M. Navratilova	75 63 61
1977	Chris Evert	S. Barker	26 61 61	1993	Steffi Graf	A. S. Vicario	61 64 36 61
1978	M. Navratilova	E. Goolagong	76 64	1994	Gabriela Sabatini	L. Davenport	63 62 64
1979	M. Navratilova	T. Austin	63 36 62	1995	Steffi Graf	A. Huber	61 26 61 46 63
1980	Tracy Austin	M. Navratilova	62 26 62	1996	Steffi Graf	M. Hingis	63 46 60 46 60
1981	M. Navratilova	A. Jaeger	63 76	1997	Jana Novotna	M. Pierce	76 62 63
1982	Sylvia Hanika	M. Navratilova	16 63 64	1998	Martina Hingis	L. Davenport	75 64 46 62
1983	M. Navratilova	C. Evert	62 60	1999	Lindsay Davenport	M. Hingis	64 62
1984	M. Navratilova	C. Evert	63 75 61	2000	Martina Hingis	M. Seles	67 64 64
1985	M. Navratilova	H. Sukova	63 75 64				
1986	M. Navratilova	H. Mandlikova	62 60 36 61	**Notes:** Two tournaments were held in 1986 due to change			
1986	M. Navratilova	S. Graf	76 63 62	in playing season. The final was best-of-five sets from			
1987	Steffi Graf	G. Sabatini	46 64 60 64	1984-98 and best-of-three sets from 1972-83 and since 1999.			

Davis Cup

Established in 1900 as an annual international tournament by American player Dwight Davis. Originally called the International Lawn Tennis Challenge Trophy. Challenge round system until 1972. Since 1981, the top 16 nations in the world have played a straight knockout tournament over the course of a year. The format is a best-of-five match of five singles, one doubles and two singles over three days. Note that from 1900-24 Australia and New Zealand competed together as Australasia.

Multiple winners: USA (31); Australia (21); France (8); Sweden (7); Australasia (6); British Isles (5); Britain (4); Germany (3).

Challenge Rounds

Year	Winner	Loser	Score	Site	Year	Winner	Loser	Score	Site
1900	USA	British Isles	3-0	Boston	1927	France	USA	3-2	Philadelphia
1901	Not held				1928	France	USA	4-1	Paris
1902	USA	British Isles	3-2	New York	1929	France	USA	3-2	Paris
1903	British Isles	USA	4-1	Boston	1930	France	USA	4-1	Paris
1904	British Isles	Belgium	5-0	Wimbledon	1931	France	Britain	3-2	Paris
1905	British Isles	USA	5-0	Wimbledon	1932	France	USA	3-2	Paris
1906	British Isles	USA	5-0	Wimbledon	1933	Britain	France	3-2	Paris
1907	Australasia	British Isles	3-2	Wimbledon	1934	Britain	USA	4-1	Wimbledon
1908	Australasia	USA	3-2	Melbourne	1935	Britain	USA	5-0	Wimbledon
1909	Australasia	USA	5-0	Sydney	1936	Britain	Australia	3-2	Wimbledon
1910	Not held				1937	USA	Britain	4-1	Wimbledon
1911	Australasia	USA	5-0	Christchurch, NZ	1938	USA	Australia	3-2	Philadelphia
1912	British Isles	Australasia	3-2	Melbourne	1939	Australia	USA	3-2	Philadelphia
1913	USA	British Isles	3-2	Wimbledon	1940-45	Not held	World War II		
1914	Australasia	USA	3-2	New York	1946	USA	Australia	5-0	Melbourne
1915-18	Not held	World War I			1947	USA	Australia	4-1	New York
1919	Australasia	British Isles	4-1	Sydney	1948	USA	Australia	5-0	New York
1920	USA	Australasia	5-0	Auckland, NZ	1949	USA	Australia	4-1	New York
1921	USA	Japan	5-0	New York	1950	Australia	USA	4-1	New York
1922	USA	Australasia	4-1	New York	1951	Australia	USA	3-2	Sydney
1923	USA	Australasia	4-1	New York	1952	Australia	USA	4-1	Adelaide
1924	USA	Australia	5-0	Philadelphia	1953	Australia	USA	3-2	Melbourne
1925	USA	France	5-0	Philadelphia	1954	USA	Australia	3-2	Sydney
1926	USA	France	4-1	Philadelphia					

Year	Winner	Loser	Score	Site	Year	Winner	Loser	Score	Site
1955	Australia	USA	5-0	New York	1962	Australia	Mexico	5-0	Brisbane
1956	Australia	USA	5-0	Adelaide	1963	USA	Australia	3-2	Adelaide
1957	Australia	USA	3-2	Melbourne	1964	Australia	USA	3-2	Cleveland
1958	USA	Australia	3-2	Brisbane	1965	Australia	Spain	4-1	Sydney
1959	Australia	USA	3-2	New York	1966	Australia	India	4-1	Melbourne
1960	Australia	Italy	4-1	Sydney	1967	Australia	Spain	4-1	Brisbane
1961	Australia	Italy	5-0	Melbourne					

Final Rounds

Year	Winner	Loser	Score	Site	Year	Winner	Loser	Score	Site
1968	USA	Australia	4-1	Adelaide	1985	Sweden	W. Germany	3-2	Munich
1969	USA	Romania	5-0	Cleveland	1986	Australia	Sweden	3-2	Melbourne
1970	USA	W. Germany	5-0	Cleveland	1987	Sweden	India	5-0	Göteborg
1971	USA	Romania	3-2	Charlotte	1988	W. Germany	Sweden	4-1	Göteborg
1972	USA	Romania	3-2	Bucharest	1989	W. Germany	Sweden	3-2	Stuttgart
1973	Australia	USA	5-0	Cleveland	1990	USA	Australia	3-2	St. Petersburg
1974	So. Africa	India	walkover	Not held	1991	France	USA	3-1	Lyon
1975	Sweden	Czech.	3-2	Stockholm	1992	USA	Switzerland	3-1	Ft. Worth
1976	Italy	Chile	4-1	Santiago	1993	Germany	Australia	4-1	Dusseldorf
1977	Australia	Italy	3-1	Sydney	1994	Sweden	Russia	4-1	Moscow
1978	USA	Britain	4-1	Palm Springs	1995	USA	Russia	3-2	Moscow
1979	USA	Italy	5-0	San Francisco	1996	France	Sweden	3-2	Malmo
1980	Czech.	Italy	4-1	Prague	1997	Sweden	USA	5-0	Göteborg
1981	USA	Argentina	3-1	Cincinnati	1998	Sweden	Italy	4-1	Milan
1982	USA	France	4-1	Grenoble	1999	Australia	France	3-2	Nice
1983	Australia	Sweden	3-2	Melbourne	2000	Spain	Australia	3-1	Barcelona
1984	Sweden	USA	4-1	Göteborg					

Note: In 1974, India refused to play the final as a protest against the South African government's policies of apartheid.

Fed Cup

Originally the Federation Cup started by the International Tennis Federation as the Davis Cup of women's tennis. Played by 32 teams over one week at one site from 1963-94. Tournament changed to Davis Cup-style format of four rounds and home site from 1995-99. In 2000, a 12-nation, round-robin tournament was played over two weeks, with the previous year's winner hosting the semifinals and finals.

Multiple winners: USA (17); Australia (7); Czechoslovakia and Spain (5); Germany (2).

Year	Winner	Loser	Score	Site	Year	Winner	Loser	Score	Site
1963	USA	Australia	2-1	London	1982	USA	W. Germany	3-0	Santa Clara
1964	Australia	USA	2-1	Philadelphia	1983	Czech.	W. Germany	2-1	Zurich
1965	Australia	USA	2-1	Melbourne	1984	Czech.	Australia	2-1	Brazil
1966	USA	W. Germany	3-0	Italy	1985	Czech.	USA	2-1	Japan
1967	USA	Britain	2-0	W. Germany	1986	USA	Czech.	3-0	Prague
1968	Australia	Holland	3-0	Paris	1987	W. Germany	USA	2-1	Vancouver
1969	USA	Australia	2-1	Athens	1988	Czech.	USSR	2-1	Melbourne
1970	Australia	Britain	3-0	W. Germany	1989	USA	Spain	3-0	Tokyo
1971	Australia	Britain	3-0	Perth	1990	USA	USSR	2-1	Atlanta
1972	So. Africa	Britain	2-1	Africa	1991	Spain	USA	2-1	Nottingham
1973	Australia	So. Africa	3-0	W. Germany	1992	Germany	Spain	2-1	Frankfurt
1974	Australia	USA	2-1	Italy	1993	Spain	Australia	3-0	Frankfurt
1975	Czech.	Australia	3-0	France	1994	Spain	USA	3-0	Frankfurt
1976	USA	Australia	2-1	Philadelphia	1995	Spain	USA	3-2	Valencia
1977	USA	Australia	2-1	Eastbourne	1996	USA	Spain	5-0	Atlantic City
1978	USA	Australia	2-1	Melbourne	1997	France	Netherlands	4-1	Nice, France
1979	USA	Australia	3-0	Spain	1998	Spain	Switzerland	3-2	Geneva
1980	USA	Australia	3-0	W. Germany	1999	USA	Russia	4-1	Palo Alto
1981	USA	Britain	3-0	Tokyo	2000	USA	Spain	5-0	Las Vegas

COLLEGES

NCAA team titles were not sanctioned until 1946. NCAA women's individual and team championships started in 1982.

Men's NCAA Individual Champions (1883-1945)

Multiple winners: Malcolm Chace and Pancho Segura (3); Edward Chandler, George Church, E.B. Dewhurst, Fred Hovey, Frank Guernsey, W.P. Knapp, Robert LeRoy, P.S. Sears, Cliff Sutter, Ernest Sutter and Richard Williams (2).

Year		Year		Year	
1883	J. Clark, Harvard (spring)	1886	G.M. Brinley, Trinity, CT	1890	Fred Hovey, Harvard
	H. Taylor, Harvard (fall)	1887	P.S. Sears, Harvard	1891	Fred Hovey, Harvard
1884	W.P. Knapp, Yale	1888	P.S. Sears, Harvard	1892	William Larned, Cornell
1885	W.P. Knapp, Yale	1889	R.P. Huntington Jr., Yale	1893	Malcolm Chace, Brown

Colleges (Cont.)

Year		Year		Year	
1894	Malcolm Chace, Yale	1911	E.H. Whitney, Harvard	1929	Berkeley Bell, Texas
1895	Malcolm Chace, Yale	1912	George Church, Princeton		
1896	Malcolm Whitman, Harvard	1913	Richard Williams, Harv.	1930	Cliff Sutter, Tulane
1897	S.G. Thompson, Princeton	1914	George Church, Princeton	1931	Keith Gledhill, Stanford
1898	Leo Ware, Harvard	1915	Richard Williams, Harv.	1932	Cliff Sutter, Tulane
1899	Dwight Davis, Harvard	1916	G.C. Caner, Harvard	1933	Jack Tidball, UCLA
		1917-1918	Not held	1934	Gene Mako, USC
1900	Ray Little, Princeton	1919	Charles Garland, Yale	1935	Wilbur Hess, Rice
1901	Fred Alexander, Princeton			1936	Ernest Sutter, Tulane
1902	William Clothier, Harvard	1920	Lascelles Banks, Yale	1937	Ernest Sutter, Tulane
1903	E.B. Dewhurst, Penn	1921	Philip Neer, Stanford	1938	Frank Guernsey, Rice
1904	Robert LeRoy, Columbia	1922	Lucien Williams, Yale	1939	Frank Guernsey, Rice
1905	E.B. Dewhurst, Penn	1923	Carl Fischer, Phi. Osteo.		
1906	Robert LeRoy, Columbia	1924	Wallace Scott, Wash.	1940	Don McNeill, Kenyon
1907	G.P. Gardner Jr., Harvard	1925	Edward Chandler, Calif.	1941	Joseph Hunt, Navy
1908	Nat Niles, Harvard	1926	Edward Chandler, Calif.	1942	Fred Schroeder, Stanford
1909	Wallace Johnson, Penn	1927	Wilmer Allison, Texas	1943	Pancho Segura, Miami-FL
		1928	Julius Seligson, Lehigh	1944	Pancho Segura, Miami-FL
1910	R.A. Holden Jr., Yale			1945	Pancho Segura, Miami-FL

NCAA Men's Division I Champions

Multiple winners (Teams): Stanford (17); UCLA and USC (15); Georgia (4); William & Mary (2). (Players): Alex Olmedo, Mikael Pernfors, Dennis Ralston and Ham Richardson (2).

Year	Team winner	Individual Champion	Year	Team winner	Individual Champion
1946	USC	Bob Falkenburg, USC	1974	Stanford	John Whitlinger, Stanford
1947	Wm. & Mary	Garner Larned, Wm.& Mary	1975	UCLA	Bill Martin, UCLA
1948	Wm. & Mary	Harry Likas, San Francisco	1976	USC & UCLA	Bill Scanlon, Trinity-TX
1949	San Francisco	Jack Tuero, Tulane	1977	Stanford	Matt Mitchell, Stanford
			1978	Stanford	John McEnroe, Stanford
1950	UCLA	Herbert Flam, UCLA	1979	UCLA	Kevin Curren, Texas
1951	USC	Tony Trabert, Cincinnati			
1952	UCLA	Hugh Stewart, USC	1980	Stanford	Robert Van't Hof, USC
1953	UCLA	Ham Richardson, Tulane	1981	Stanford	Tim Mayotte, Stanford
1954	UCLA	Ham Richardson, Tulane	1982	UCLA	Mike Leach, Michigan
1955	USC	Jose Aguero, Tulane	1983	Stanford	Greg Holmes, Utah
1956	UCLA	Alex Olmedo, USC	1984	UCLA	Mikael Pernfors, Georgia
1957	Michigan	Barry MacKay, Michigan	1985	Georgia	Mikael Pernfors, Georgia
1958	USC	Alex Olmedo, USC	1986	Stanford	Dan Goldie, Stanford
1959	Tulane & Notre Dame	Whitney Reed, San Jose St.	1987	Georgia	Andrew Burrow, Miami-FL
			1988	Stanford	Robby Weiss, Pepperdine
1960	UCLA	Larry Nagler, UCLA	1989	Stanford	Donni Leaycraft, LSU
1961	UCLA	Allen Fox, UCLA			
1962	USC	Rafael Osuna, USC	1990	Stanford	Steve Bryan, Texas
1963	USC	Dennis Ralston, USC	1991	USC	Jared Palmer, Stanford
1964	USC	Dennis Ralston, USC	1992	Stanford	Alex O'Brien Stanford
1965	UCLA	Arthur Ashe, UCLA	1993	USC	Chris Woodruff, Tennessee
1966	USC	Charlie Pasarell, UCLA	1994	USC	Mark Merklein, Florida
1967	USC	Bob Lutz, USC	1995	Stanford	Sargis Sargisian, Ariz. St.
1968	USC	Stan Smith, USC	1996	Stanford	Cecil Mamiit, USC
1969	USC	Joaquin Loyo-Mayo, USC	1997	Stanford	Luke Smith, UNLV
			1998	Stanford	Bob Bryan, Stanford
1970	UCLA	Jeff Borowiak, UCLA	1999	Georgia	Jeff Morrison, Florida
1971	UCLA	Jimmy Connors, UCLA			
1972	Trinity-TX	Dick Stockton, Trinity-TX	2000	Stanford	Alex Kim, Stanford
1973	Stanford	Alex Mayer, Stanford	2001	Georgia	Matias Boeker, Georgia

NCAA Women's Division I Champions

Multiple winners (Teams): Stanford (11); Florida (3); Georgia, Texas and USC (2). (Players): Sandra Birch, Patty Fendick, Laura Granville and Lisa Raymond (2).

Year	Team winner	Individual Champion	Year	Team winner	Individual Champion
1982	Stanford	Alycia Moulton, Stanford	1993	Texas	Lisa Raymond, Florida
1983	USC	Beth Herr, USC	1994	Georgia	Angela Lettiere, Georgia
1984	Stanford	Lisa Spain, Georgia	1995	Texas	Keri Phoebus, UCLA
1985	USC	Linda Gates, Stanford	1996	Florida	Jill Craybas, Florida
1986	Stanford	Patty Fendick, Stanford	1997	Stanford	Lilia Osterloh, Stanford
1987	Stanford	Patty Fendick, Stanford	1998	Florida	Vanessa Webb, Duke
1988	Stanford	Shaun Stafford, Florida	1999	Stanford	Zuzana Lesenarova, S. Diego
1989	Stanford	Sandra Birch, Stanford			
1990	Stanford	Debbie Graham, Stanford	2000	Georgia	Laura Granville, Stanford
1991	Stanford	Sandra Birch, Stanford	2001	Stanford	Laura Granville, Stanford
1992	Florida	Lisa Raymond, Florida			

Golf

Tiger Woods is all smiles after donning the famed green jacket after his 2001 Masters win.

Major Breakthrough

David tames Goliath as Duval wins his first major title at the British Open.

Karl Ravech
is an analyst for ESPN's golf coverage.

According to the Chinese calendar, the Year of the Tiger is followed by the Year of the Rabbit. This is also fitting in golf terms as last year was all about Tiger Woods. This year failed on many levels to match the drama of 2000 but it did, as rabbits have been known to do, produce a variety of story lines.

Like all facets of life in this country and abroad, the terrorist attacks affected golf. The Ryder Cup, which has become golf's biggest event, was postponed until September 2002 at the Belfry. This year's cancellation marked the first in the event's history for reasons other than a World War. Curtis Strange, the captain of the United States team, vowed not only to bring back the same team but to have them wear the uniforms that had been selected for this competition with the year 2001 displayed on them.

Next year will also be the final year of the PGA Tour's current television contract. In July, the Tour agreed to new deals with all of its partners that will increase its take by hundreds of millions of dollars. Those of us who watch golf on television will see very little difference, as all the major networks will still be in the golf business. And the golf business has changed dramatically, thanks to Woods. Television ratings consistently rise when Woods is playing, and if he's in contention on the weekend, ratings can increase by as much as 50 percent. It's Tiger's world and everyone else has him to thank for the increased purses and popularity.

One of Woods' lesser celebrated but equally recognizable college teammates at Stanford, is Casey Martin. For 3½ years Martin, who suffers from a rare circulatory disease that makes it virtually impossible for him to walk 18 holes, has been battling the PGA Tour to gain the right to drive a golf cart during competition. His case was heard by the U.S.

AP/Wide World Photos

*After his British Open win, an ecstatic and relieved **David Duval**, left, accepts the Claret Jug from Royal Lytham and St. Annes GC captain Alan Halsall.*

Supreme Court and on the morning of May 29, Martin was awoken by the ring of his cell phone. In Eugene, Ore., his hometown, it was 7:25 a.m. On the East Coast it was three hours later and about the time the court was to release its decision. On the phone was PGA Tour Commissioner Tim Finchem telling Martin simply, "You prevailed."

On the course, the first 11 events produced 10 different winners, with only Joe Durant winning twice. As the tour moved to Florida, Woods began to warm up. He won the Bay Hill Invitational, edging Phil Mickelson by a shot. In this case, Woods' success was due to luck as much as skill. His drive on the finishing hole was headed out of bounds when it struck a spectator in the neck. He got a free drop, hit a remarkable second shot to the green and made a curling 20-foot putt to win. The following week, he took home the $1,080,000 first-prize paycheck at The Players Championship, serving notice that he'd be his usual force to be reckoned with at the Masters.

And he was—winning with a picture perfect back nine at Augusta. He lost both David Duval and Mickelson on the par-3, 16th hole. With the win, Woods accomplished something no one in the history of the game ever had. He held the four major championship trophies all

*With four consecutive tournament wins during the spring, **Annika Sorenstam** put on a magnificent show on the LPGA Tour in 2001.*

at once. Not even his idol Jack Nicklaus can make the same claim. Amazingly, Tiger's combined score in those four majors was 65-under par. He'd win twice more in 2001 but would add no more majors to his resume. Goliath had been tamed, at least by his standards, but there was still David to contend with.

Having come to the same conclusion that most mortals do, "if you can't beat 'em you may as well join 'em," Duval had gone through a messy legal battle with his club manufacturer because he wanted to become a "Nike guy" like Tiger. In July he played like one, winning the British Open in impressive fashion. His scores on the weekend at Royal Lytham were 65-67. He beat Niclas Fasth by three shots but was never really challenged. Making it doubly sweet was the fact that the year before at the British Open he had come close to knocking Woods off the top of the leaderboard only to falter late. It was Duval's first major title—and the monkey that had taken residence on his back had vacated and landed squarely on Mickelson.

In August, the Tour made its last major stop of the year at the PGA Championship. Once again Mickelson was in contention. On the final hole, it appeared as if he'd finally tasted victory. Playing with

continued on page 840 ▶

Karl Ravech's Ten Biggest Stories of the Year in Golf

10 ■ David Toms drains a 15-foot putt on the 72nd hole of the PGA Championship to defeat a distraught Phil Mickelson by one stroke. It is the first major title of Toms' career and second time Mickelson has placed second at a major.

9 ■ Tiger Woods and Jim Furyk stage an epic battle at the NEC Invitational in late August. The match goes into the seventh sudden death playoff hole, when Woods finally wins by tapping in a two-footer for a birdie, after a bogey by Furyk. It is the longest PGA playoff in 10 years.

8 ■ Retief Goosen three-putts from just 12 feet away on the 72nd hole of the U.S. Open, forcing an unexpected 18-hole playoff with Mark Brooks. Stewart Cink blows a putt from 18 inches that would have ultimately put him in the playoff round as well. Goosen, however, redeems himself the next day, besting Brooks, 70-72, for his first major title.

7 ■ By a 7-2 majority, the Supreme Court rules in May that golfer Casey Martin, who suffers from a degenerative leg ailment, may use a cart to ride in PGA tournaments. The decision states that allowing Martin to use a cart "will not fundamentally change the game."

6 ■ The PGA Tour signs a whopper of a television deal with five networks worth $850 million over four years, beginning in 2003.

5 ■ Annika Sorenstam overcomes a 10-stroke, final-day deficit to win The Office Depot tourney in April. It is the biggest comeback in LPGA history and the win is her fourth consecutive, tying an LPGA record. Just four weeks earlier in Phoenix, she became the first woman to card a 59.

4 ■ David Duval records a third-round 65 and then holds off Swede Niclas Fasth with a final-round 67 to win the 2001 British Open, his first major tournament title.

3 ■ With her win at the LPGA Championship, Karrie Webb, 26, becomes the youngest golfer in LPGA history to win the career Grand Slam. The victory gives her five victories in the last eight major tournaments.

2 ■ All of the Tours cancel their scheduled tournaments during the week following the Sept. 11 attacks on America. In addition, The Ryder Cup is postponed until Sept. 2002.

1 ■ Tiger Woods wins his second Masters, the sixth major championship of his career, and becomes the only golfer to claim possession of all four PGA major titles simultaneously.

David Toms, Mickelson landed his second shot on the green on the 18th, leaving himself a 20-foot putt for birdie. Toms had been forced to lay up on his second shot, and his third shot landed about 15 feet left of the hole. A par would force Mickelson to make his putt to force a playoff. As has become Mickelson's calling card, Toms made his par putt, and Mickelson missed his birdie attempt. Another second place finish for the anointed "best player never to have won a major." Making bad news even worse for Mickelson, according to the Chinese calendar, the year of the monkey won't occur until 2004.

Five Year Anniversary

Tiger Woods celebrated his five-year anniversary as a PGA Tour professional on Aug. 27, 2001. Below is a comparison of his accomplishments thus far with those of Jack Nicklaus in his first five years on the Tour.

	Nicklaus	Woods
Events	113	107
Major Wins	6	6
Wins	19	29
Top 10s	79	69
Earnings	$527,365	$26,021,227

Note: Figures as of Aug. 27, 2001.

That 70's Show

Tiger Woods' 29th place finish at the 2001 PGA Championship marked the eighth major he has played as a pro on a par-70 course—with no wins.

	Starts	Wins	Avg. Score
Par 72s	8	5	69.3
Par 71s	4	1	70.8
Par 70s	8	0	70.8

Major Bust

The dreaded monkey on the back of Phil Mickelson grew a little heavier in 2001. Using the official World Golf Rankings (as of Oct. 14, 2001), below are the best active players without a major win.

Rank	Majors	Best Finish
2. Phil Mickelson	38	2nd
7. Sergio Garcia	13	2nd
9. Darren Clarke	26	t-2nd
10. C. Montgomerie	42	2nd

Prime Numbers

Nielsen ratings for ABC's annual prime-time golf event (see pg. 849) took a 20 percent dip in 2001.

	Ratings/Share
'01 Battle at Bighorn II	6.1/11
'00 Battle at Bighorn	7.6/13
'99 Showdown at Sherwood	6.9/12

Note: Each ratings point represents 1,022,000 households. Share indicates percentage of TV sets in use.

2000-2001 Season in Review

Tournament Results

Schedules and results of PGA, European PGA, PGA Seniors and LPGA tournaments from Oct. 29, 2000 through Oct. 14, 2001.

PGA Tour

LATE 2000

Last Rd	Tournament	Winner	Earnings	Runner-Up
Oct. 29	National Car Rental Classic	Duffy Waldorf (262)	$540,000	S. Flesch (263)
Nov. 5	Southern Farm Bureau Classic	Steve Lowery (266)*	396,000	S. Kendall (266)
Nov. 5	The Tour Championship	Phil Mickelson (267)	900,000	T. Woods (269)
Nov. 12	WGC: American Express Championship	Mike Weir (277)	1,000,000	L. Westwood (279)
Nov. 19@	Franklin Templeton Shootout	Brad Faxon/ Scott McCarron (190)*	200,000 (each)	C. Franco/ S. Hoch (190)
Nov. 26@	Skins Game	Colin Montgomerie (6 skins)	415,000	V. Singh (4 skins)
Dec. 3@	Williams World Challenge	Davis Love III (266)	1,000,000	T. Woods (268)
Dec. 10@	WGC: EMC World Cup	United States (254)	1,000,000	Argentina (257)
Dec. 17@	Hyundai Team Matches	Tom Lehman (277)/ Duffy Waldorf (20th hole)	100,000 (each)	M. Calcavecchia/ F. Couples

@ Unofficial PGA Tour event.

***Playoffs: Southern Farm Bureau**—Lowery won on 1st hole; **Franklin Templeton**—Faxon/McCarron won on 1st hole.

2001

Last Rd	Tournament	Winner	Earnings	Runner-Up
Jan. 7@	WGC: Accenture Match Play Championship	Steve Stricker (2&1)	$1,000,000	P. Fulke
Jan. 14	Mercedes Championships	Jim Furyk (274)	630,000	R. Sabbatini (275)
Jan. 14	Tucson Open	Garrett Willis (273)	540,000	K. Sutherland (274)
Jan. 21	Sony Open	Brad Faxon (260)	720,000	T. Lehman (264)
Jan. 28	Phoenix Open	Mark Calcavecchia (256)	720,000	R. Mediate (264)
Feb. 4	AT&T Pebble Beach Pro-Am	Davis Love III (272)	720,000	V. Singh (273)
Feb. 11	Buick Invitational	Phil Mickelson (269)*	630,000	F. Lickliter & D. Love III (269)
Feb. 18	Bob Hope Chrysler Classic	Joe Durant (324)+	630,000	P. Stankowski (328)
Feb. 25	Nissan Open	Robert Allenby (276)*	612,000	5-way tie (276)
Mar. 4	Genuity Championship	Joe Durant (270)	810,000	M. Weir (272)
Mar. 11	Honda Classic	Jesper Parnevik (270)	576,000	3-way tie (271)
Mar. 18	Bay Hill Invitational	Tiger Woods (273)	630,000	P. Mickelson (274)
Mar. 25	The Players Championship	Tiger Woods (274)	1,080,000	V. Singh (275)
Apr. 1	BellSouth Classic	Scott McCarron (280)	594,000	M. Weir (283)
Apr. 8	**The Masters** (Augusta, Ga.)	Tiger Woods (272)	1,008,000	D. Duval (274)
Apr. 15	Worldcom Classic	Jose Coceres (273)*	630,000	B. Mayfair (273)
Apr. 22	Shell Houston Open	Hal Sutton (278)	614,000	J. Durant & L. Janzen (281)
Apr. 29	Greater Greensboro Chrysler Classic	Scott Hoch (272)	630,000	B. Quigley & S. Simpson (273)
May 6	Compaq Classic of New Orleans	David Toms (266)	720,000	P. Mickelson (268)
May 13	Byron Nelson Classic	Robert Damron (263)*	810,000	S. Verplank (263)
May 20	MasterCard Colonial	Sergio Garcia (267)	720,000	B. Gay & P. Mickelson (269)
May 27	Kemper Insurance Open	Frank Lickliter (268)	630,000	J.J. Henry (269)
June 3	Memorial Tournament	Tiger Woods (271)	738,000	P. Azinger & S. Garcia (278)
June 10	FedEx St. Jude Classic	Bob Estes (267)	630,000	B. Langer (268)
June 17	**U.S. Open** (Tulsa, Okla.)	Retief Goosen (276)*	900,000	M. Brooks (276)
June 24	Buick Classic	Sergio Garcia (268)	630,000	S. Hoch (271)
July 1	Greater Hartford Open	Phil Mickelson (264)	558,000	B. Andrade (265)
July 8	Western Open	Scott Hoch (267)	648,000	D. Love III (268)
July 15	Greater Milwaukee Open	Shigeki Maruyama (266)*	558,000	C. Howell III (266)
July 22	**British Open** (Lytham, ENG)	David Duval (274)	858,000	N. Fasth (277)
July 22	B.C. Open	Jeff Sluman (266)*	360,000	P. Gow (266)
July 29	John Deere Classic	David Gossett (265)	504,000	B. Baird (266)
Aug. 5	The International†	Tom Pernice Jr. (34 pts)	720,000	C. Riley (33 pts)
Aug. 12	Buick Open	Kenny Perry (266)	558,000	C. DiMarco & J. Furyk (265)
Aug. 19	**PGA Championship** (Duluth, Ga.)	David Toms (265)	936,000	P. Mickelson (266)

Tournament Results (Cont.)

Last Rd	Tournament	Winner	Earnings	Runner-Up
Aug. 26	WGC: NEC Invitational	Tiger Woods (268)*	$1,000,000	J. Furyk (268)
Aug. 26	Reno-Tahoe Open	John Cook (271)	540,000	J. Kelly (272)
Sept. 2	Air Canada Championship	Joel Edwards (265)	612,000	S. Lowery (272)
Sept. 9	Bell Canadian Open	Scott Verplank (266)	684,000	B. Estes & J. Sindelar (269)
Sept. 16	WGC: American Express Championship	cancelled		
Sept. 16	Tampa Bay Classic	cancelled		
Sept. 23	Marconi Pennsylvania Classic	Robert Allenby (269)	594,000	R. Mediate & L. Mize (272)
Sept. 30	The Ryder Cup	postponed until 2002		
Sept. 30	Texas Open at LaCantera	Justin Leonard (266)	540,000	J.J. Henry & M. Kuchar (268)
Oct. 7	Michelob Championship at Kingsmill	David Toms (269)	630,000	K. Triplett (270)
Oct. 14	Invensys Classic at Las Vegas	Bob Estes (329)+	810,000	T. Lehman & R. Sabbatini (330)

@ Unofficial PGA Tour money event.

+This is a five-round, 90-hole event played over five days.

†The scoring for The International is based on a modified Stableford system (8 points for a double eagle, 5 for an eagle, 2 for a birdie, 0 for a par, –1 for a bogey, –3 for double bogey or worse).

*Playoffs: Buick— Mickelson won on 3rd hole; **Nissan—** Allenby won on 1st hole; **Worldcom—** Coceres won on 5th hole; **Byron Nelson—** Damron won on 4th hole; **U.S. Open—** Goosen won after 18 holes (70-72); **Greater Milwaukee—** Maruyama won on 1st hole; **B.C. Open—** Sluman won on 2nd hole; **NEC Invitational—** Woods won on 7th hole.

Second place ties (3 players or more): 5-WAY—**Nissan** (T. Izawa, B. Chamblee, B. Tway, J. Sluman, D. Paulson); 3-WAY—**Honda** (M. Calcavecchia, G. Ogilvy, C. Perks).

PGA Majors

The Masters

Edition: 65th   **Dates:** April 5–8
Site: Augusta National GC, Augusta, Ga.
Par: 36-36—72 (6985 yards)   **Purse:** $5,600,000

		1	2	3	4	Tot	Earnings
1	Tiger Woods	70	66	68	68	272	$1,008,000
2	David Duval	71	66	70	67	274	604,800
3	Phil Mickelson	67	69	69	70	275	380,800
4	Mark Calcavecchia	72	66	68	72	278	246,400
	Toshi Izawa	71	66	74	67	278	246,400
6	Ernie Els	71	68	68	72	279	181,300
	Jim Furyk	69	71	70	69	279	181,300
	Bernhard Langer	73	69	68	69	279	181,300
	Kirk Triplett	68	70	70	71	279	181,300
10	Angel Cabrera	66	71	70	73	280	128,800
	Chris DiMarco	65	69	72	74	280	128,800
	Brad Faxon	73	68	68	71	280	128,800
	Miguel A. Jimenez	68	72	71	69	280	128,800
	Steve Stricker	66	71	72	71	280	128,800
15	Paul Azinger	70	71	71	69	281	95,200
	Rocco Mediate	72	70	66	73	281	95,200
	Jose Maria Olazabal	70	68	71	72	281	95,200
18	Tom Lehman	75	68	71	68	282	81,200
	Vijay Singh	69	71	73	69	282	81,200
20	John Huston	67	75	72	69	283	65,240
	Jeff Maggert	72	70	70	71	283	65,240
	Mark O'Meara	69	74	72	68	283	65,240
	Jesper Parnevik	71	71	72	69	283	65,240

Early round leaders: 1st—DiMarco (65); 2nd—DiMarco (134); 3rd—Woods (204).
Top amateur: none.

U.S. Open

Edition: 101st   **Dates:** June 14–17
Site: Southern Hills CC, Tulsa, Okla.
Par: 35-35—70 (6973 yards)   **Purse:** $5,000,000

		1	2	3	4	Tot	Earnings
1	Retief Goosen*	66	70	69	71	276	$900,000
	Mark Brooks	72	64	70	70	276	530,000
3	Stewart Cink	69	69	67	72	277	325,310
4	Rocco Mediate	71	68	67	72	278	226,777
5	Tom Kite	73	72	72	64	281	172,912
	Paul Azinger	74	67	69	71	281	172,912
7	Vijay Singh	74	70	74	64	282	125,172
	Angel Cabrera	70	71	72	69	282	125,172
	Davis Love III	72	69	71	70	282	125,172
	Kirk Triplett	72	69	71	70	282	125,172
	Phil Mickelson	70	69	68	75	282	125,172
12	Tiger Woods	74	71	69	69	283	91,733
	Matt Gogel	70	69	74	70	283	91,733
	Michael Allen	77	68	67	71	283	91,733
	Sergio Garcia	70	68	68	77	283	91,733
16	Scott Hoch	73	73	69	69	284	75,337
	Chris DiMarco	69	73	70	72	284	75,337
	David Duval	70	69	71	74	284	75,337
19	Chris Perry	72	71	73	69	285	63,425
	Corey Pavin	70	75	68	72	285	63,425
	Mike Weir	67	76	68	74	285	63,425

*Goosen won an 18-hole playoff on June 18 over Brooks (70-72).

Early round leaders: 1st—Goosen (66); 2nd—Goosen, Brooks and J.L. Lewis (136); 3rd—Goosen and Cink (205).
Top amateur: Bryce Molder (288).

The Official World Golf Ranking

Begun in 1986, the Official World Golf Ranking (formerly the Sony World Ranking) combines the best golfers on the world's leading professional tours—Asian, PGA Tour of Australia, European, European Challenge, Japan Golf Tour, Southern African and U.S. (PGA Tour, Buy.com). Rankings are based on a rolling two-year period and weighted in favor of more recent results. Points are awarded after each worldwide tournament according to finish. Final points-per-tournament averages are determined by dividing a player's total points by the number of tournaments played over that two-year period (through Oct. 14, 2001).

		Avg			Avg			Avg
1	Tiger Woods, USA	18.91	6	Vijay Singh, FIJ	6.08	11	Bernhard Langer, GER	4.81
2	Phil Mickelson, USA	10.28	7	Sergio Garcia, SPA	5.98	12	Jim Furyk, USA	4.69
3	David Duval, USA	7.47	8	David Toms, USA	5.92	13	Scott Verplank, USA	4.68
4	Ernie Els, RSA	6.27	9	Darren Clarke, N.IRE	5.44	15	Retief Goosen, RSA	4.59
5	Davis Love III, USA	6.08	10	Colin Montgomerie, SCO	4.88	15	Padraig Harrington, IRE	4.55

British Open

Edition: 130th **Dates:** July 19–22
Site: Royal Lytham & St. Annes GC, Lytham, England
Par: 35-36–71 (6905 yards) **Purse:** $4,620,000

		1 2 3 4	Tot	Earnings
1	David Duval	69-73-65-67	274	$858,000
2	Niclas Fasth	69-72-67–277		514,800
3	Ernie Els	71-71-67-69	278	202,584
	Darren Clarke	70-69-69-70	278	202,584
	Miguel A. Jimenez	69-72-67-70	278	202,584
	Billy Mayfair	69-72-67-70	278	202,584
	Ian Woosnam	72-68-67-71	278	202,584
	Bernhard Langer	71-69-67-71	278	202,584
9	Mikko Ilonen	68-75-70-66	279	91,163
	Kevin Sutherland	75-69-68-67	279	91,163
	Sergio Garcia	70-72-67-70	279	91,163
	Jesper Parnevik	69-68-71-71	279	91,163
13	Vijay Singh	70-70-71-69	280	57,290
	Loren Roberts	70-70-70-70	280	57,290
	Des Smyth	74-65-70-71	280	57,290
	Billy Andrade	69-70-70-71	280	57,290
	Retief Goosen	74-68-67-71	280	57,290
	Colin Montgomerie	65-70-73-72	280	57,290
	Raphael Jacquelin	71-68-69-72	280	57,290
	Alex Cejka	69-69-69-73	280	57,290

Early round leaders: 1st— Montgomerie (65); 2nd— Montgomerie (135); 3rd— Duval, Woosnam, Langer and Cejka (207).

Top amateur: David Dixon (285).

PGA Championship

Edition: 83rd **Dates:** Aug. 16–19
Site: Atlanta Athletic Club, Duluth, Ga.
Par: 35-35–70 (7213 yards) **Purse:** $5,000,000

		1 2 3 4	Tot	Earnings
1	David Toms	66-65-65-69	265	$936,000
2	Phil Mickelson	66-66-66-68	266	562,000
3	Steve Lowery	67-67-66-68	268	354,000
4	Mark Calcavecchia	71-68-66-65	270	222,500
	Shingo Katayama	67-64-69-70	270	222,500
6	Billy Andrade	68-70-68-66	272	175,000
7	Scott Hoch	68-70-69-67	274	152,333
	Scott Verplank	69-68-70-67	274	152,333
	Jim Furyk	70-64-71-69	274	152,333
10	Kirk Triplett	68-70-71-66	275	122,000
	Justin Leonard	70-69-67-69	275	122,000
	David Duval	66-68-67-74	275	122,000
13	Steve Flesch	73-67-70-66	276	94,666
	Jesper Parnevik	70-68-70-68	276	94,666
	Ernie Els	67-67-70-72	276	94,666
16	Jose Coceres	69-68-73-67	277	70,666
	Robert Allenby	69-67-73-68	277	70,666
	Dudley Hart	66-68-73-70	277	70,666
	Mike Weir	69-72-66-70	277	70,666
	Chris DiMarco	68-67-71-71	277	70,666
	Stuart Appleby	66-70-68-73	277	70,666

Early round leaders: 1st— Grant Waite (64); 2nd— Toms and Katayama (131); 3rd— Toms (196).

Top amateur: none.

European PGA Tour

Official money won on the European Tour is presented in euros (€).

LATE 2000

Last Rd	Tournament	Winner	Earnings	Runner-Up
Oct. 29	Italian Open	Ian Poulter (267)	€166,660	G. Brand Jr. (268)
Nov. 5	Volvo Masters	Pierre Fulke (272)	575,654	D. Clarke (273)
Nov. 19	Johnnie Walker Classic	Tiger Woods (263)	221,134	G. Ogilvy (266)

2001

Last Rd	Tournament	Winner	Earnings	Runner-Up
Jan. 7	WGC: Accenture Match Play Championship	Steve Stricker (2&1)	€1,065,188	P. Fulke
Jan. 21	Alfred Dunhill Championship	Adam Scott (267)	123,071	J. Rose (268)
Jan. 28	South African Open	Mark McNulty (280)	169,283	J. Rose (281)
Feb. 4	Heineken Classic	Michael Campbell (270)	195,498	D. Smail (275)
Feb. 11	Greg Norman Holden Int'l	Aaron Baddeley (271)*	223,593	S. Garcia (271)
Feb. 18	Malaysian Open	Vijay Singh (274)*	163,655	P. Harrington (274)
Feb. 25	Singapore Masters	Vijay Singh (263)	154,616	W. Bennett (265)
Mar. 4	Dubai Desert Classic	Thomas Björn (266)	265,152	T. Woods & P. Harrington (268)
Mar. 11	Qatar Masters	Tony Johnstone (274)	133,832	R. Karlsson (276)
Mar. 18	Madeira Island Open	Des Smyth (270)	91,660	J. Bickerton (272)
Mar. 25	Sao Paolo Brazil Open	Darren Fichardt (195)#	125,000	3-way tie (200)
Apr. 1	Argentina Open	Angel Cabrera (268)	130,697	C. Petterson (270)
Apr. 8	The Masters	Tiger Woods (272)	1,146,236	D. Duval (274)
Apr. 15	Moroccan Open	Ian Poulter (277)	106,506	D. Lynn (279)
Apr. 22	Via Digital Open of Spain	Robert Karlsson (277)	200,000	J.F. Remesy (279)
Apr. 29	Portuguese Open	Phillip Price (273)	166,660	P. Harrington & S. Strüver (275)
May 6	French Open	Jose Maria Olazabal (268)	216,660	C. Rocca & G. Turner (270)
May 13	Benson & Hedges International	Henrik Stenson (275)	267,918	P. McGinley & A. Cabrera (278)
May 20	Deutsche Bank-SAP Open	Tiger Woods (266)	450,000	M. Campbell (270)
May 28	Volvo PGA Championship	Andrew Oldcorn (272)	544,521	A. Cabrera (274)
June 3	British Masters	Thomas Levet (274)*	345,080	3-way tie (274)
June 10	English Open	Peter O'Malley (274)	223,373	R. Jacquelin (274)
June 17	U.S. Open	Retief Goosen (276)*	1,058,198	M. Brooks (276)
June 24	The Great North Open	Andrew Coltart (277)	217,209	S. Gallacher (278)
July 1	Murphy's Irish Open	Colin Montgomerie (266)	266,660	3-way tie (271)
July 8	European Open	Darren Clarke (273)	553,722	3-way tie (276)
July 15	Scottish Open at Loch Lomond	Retief Goosen (268)	610,998	T. Björn (271)
July 22	British Open	David Duval (274)	984,756	N. Fasth (277)
July 29	The TNT Open	Bernhard Langer (269)*	300,000	W. Bennett (269)

Tournament Results (Cont.)

Last Rd	Tournament	Winner	Earnings	Runner-Up
Aug. 5	Scandinavian Masters.............	Colin Montgomerie (274)	€300,000	I. Poulter & L. Westwood (275)
Aug. 12	Wales Open......................	Paul McGinley (138)#*	201,685	P. Lawrie & D. Lee (138)
Aug. 19	PGA Championship...............	David Toms (265)	1,024,347	P. Mickelson (266)
Aug. 19	North West of Ireland Open	Tobias Dier (271)	58,330	S. Dodd (272)
Aug. 26	WGC: NEC Invitational	Tiger Woods (268)*	1,091,096	J. Furyk (268)
Aug. 26	Scottish PGA Championship........	Paul Casey (274)	263,034	A. Cejka (275)
Sept. 2	BMW International Open..........	John Daly (261)	300,000	P. Harrington (262)
Sept. 9	European Masters	Ricardo Gonzalez (268)	250,000	S. Hansen (271)
Sept. 16	WGC: American Express Championship	cancelled		
Sept. 23	Trophee Lancome	Sergio Garcia (266)	239,782	R. Goosen (267)
Sept. 30	The Ryder Cup	postponed until 2002		
Oct. 7	German Masters	Bernhard Langer (266)	450,000	F. Jacobson & J. Daly (267)
Oct. 14	Cisco World Match Play Championship	Ian Woosnam (2&1)	403,400	P. Harrington
Oct. 14	Cannes Open....................	Jorge Berendt (268)	92,500	J. Van de Velde (269)

#Weather-shortened

*Playoffs: Holden International— Baddeley won on 1st hole; **Malaysian—** Singh won on 3rd hole; **British Masters—** Levet won on 3rd hole; **U.S. Open—** Goosen won after 18 holes (70-72); **TNT—** Langer won on 1st hole; **Wales—** McGinley won on fifth hole; **NEC Invitational—** Woods won on 7th hole.

Second place ties (3 players or more): 3-WAY—**Sao Paolo Open** (R. Johnson, J. Coceres, B. Rumford); **British Masters** (D. Howell, R. Karlsson, M. Grönberg); **Irish Open** (P. Harrington, D. Clarke, N. Fasth); **European Open** (I. Woosnam, P. Harrington, T. Björn).

Senior PGA Tour

LATE 2000

Last Rd	Tournament	Winner	Earnings	Runner-Up
Oct. 29	SBC Senior Classic	Joe Inman (198)	$210,000	L. Nelson (201)
Nov. 5	Senior Tour Championship	Tom Watson (270)	365,000	J. Jacobs (271)
Nov. 12@	Chrysler Senior Match Play Challenge ...	Vicente Fernandez (19th hole)	240,000	L. Thompson
Dec. 3@	Senior Slam	Hale Irwin (135)	300,000	T. Kite (137)
Dec. 10@	Office Depot Father/Son Challenge	Ray/Robert Floyd (122)*	75,000 (each)	J./S. Miller (122)

*Playoffs: Office Depot Father/Son— Ray/Robert Floyd won on 1st hole.

2001

Last Rd	Tournament	Winner	Earnings	Runner-Up
Jan. 21	MasterCard Championship	Larry Nelson (197)	$240,000	J. Thorpe (198)
Jan. 28@	Senior Skins Game	Hale Irwin (7 skins)	320,000	J. Nicklaus (10 skins)
Feb. 4	Royal Caribbean Classic†	Larry Nelson (29 pts)	210,000	I. Aoki (28 pts)
Feb. 11	Ace Group Classic.................	Gil Morgan (204)	210,000	D. Quigley (206)
Feb. 18	Verizon Classic...................	Bob Gilder (205)	210,000	4-way tie (208)
Feb. 25	Mexico Senior Classic...............	Mike McCullough (204)	225,000	J. Colbert & B. Eastwood (205)
Mar. 4	Toshiba Senior Classic	Jose M. Canizares (202)*	210,000	G. Morgan (202)
Mar. 11	SBC Senior Classic	Jim Colbert (204)	210,000	J.M. Canizares (205)
Mar. 18	Siebel Classic in Silicon Valley	Hale Irwin (206)	210,000	A. Doyle & T. Watson (211)
Mar. 25	Emerald Coast Classic	Mike McCullough (200)*	210,000	A. North (200)
Apr. 1@	Liberty Mutual Legends of Golf	Jim Colbert/ Andy North (124)#	170,000 (each)	B. Fleisher/ D. Graham (127)
Apr. 15	**Countrywide Tradition** (Scottsdale, Ariz.).....................	Doug Tewell (265)	255,000	M. McCullough (274)
Apr. 22	Las Vegas Senior Classic	Bruce Fleisher (208)	210,000	5-way tie (211)
Apr. 29	Bruno's Memorial Classic	Hale Irwin (195)	210,000	S. Ginn (199)
May 6	Home Depot Invitational	Bruce Fleisher (201)	195,000	J. Bland (204)
May 13	Enterprise Rent-A-Car Match Play Championship	Leonard Thompson (2-up)	300,000	V. Fernandez
May 20	TD Waterhouse Championship	Ed Dougherty (194)	225,000	3-way tie (202)
May 27	**Senior PGA Championship** (Paramus, N.J.)......................	Tom Watson (274)	360,000	J. Thorpe (275)
June 3	BellSouth Senior Classic at Opryland	Sammy Rachels (199)	240,000	H. Irwin (203)
June 10	NFL Golf Classic	John Schroeder (207)*	180,000	A. Doyle (207)

Last Rd	Tournament	Winner	Earnings	Runner-Up
June 17	Instinet Classic	Gil Morgan (201)	$225,000	T. Jenkins & J.C. Snead (203)
June 24	FleetBoston Classic	Larry Nelson (201)	210,000	B. Fleisher (204)
July 1	**U.S. Senior Open** (Peabody, Mass.)	Bruce Fleisher (280)	430,000	I. Aoki & G. Morgan (281)
July 8	Farmers Charity Classic	Larry Nelson (202)	210,000	J. Ahern (203)
July 15	**Ford Senior Players Championship** (Dearborn, Mich.)	Allen Doyle (273)*	375,000	D. Tewell (273)
July 22	SBC Senior Open	Dana Quigley (200)	210,000	J. Sigel (205)
July 29	State Farm Senior Classic	Allen Doyle (205)*	217,500	B. Fleisher (205)
Aug. 5	Lightpath Long Island Classic	Bobby Wadkins (202)	255,000	A. Doyle & L. Nelson (203)
Aug. 12	3M Championship	Bruce Lietzke (207)	262,500	D. Tewell (209)
Aug. 19	Novell Utah Showdown	Steve Veriato (204)	225,000	4-way tie (205)
Aug. 26	AT&T Canada Senior Open	Walter Hall (273)*	240,000	E. Dougherty (273)
Sept. 2	Kroger Senior Classic	Jim Thorpe (130)#*	225,000	T. Jenkins (130)
Sept. 9	Allianz Championship	Jim Thorpe (199)	262,500	G. Morgan (201)
Sept. 16	Vantage Championship	cancelled		
Sept. 23	SAS Championship	Bruce Lietzke (201)	240,000	A. Doyle & G. McCord (204)
Sept. 30	Gold Rush Classic	Tom Kite (194)	195,000	A. Doyle (195)
Oct. 7	Turtle Bay Championship	Hale Irwin (205)	225,000	J. Jacobs (208)
Oct. 14	The Transamerica	Sammy Rachels (202)	195,000	R. Floyd & D. Tewell (203)

#Weather-shortened.

@ Unofficial Senior PGA Tour money event.

†The scoring for the Royal Caribbean Classic is based on a modified Stableford system (8 points for a double eagle, 5 for an eagle, 2 for a birdie, 0 for a par, −1 for a bogey, −3 for double bogey or worse).

Playoffs: Toshiba—Canizares won on 9th hole; **Emerald Coast**—McCullough won on 1st hole; **NFL Golf**—Schroeder won on 2nd hole; **Ford Senior Players**—Doyle won on 1st hole; **State Farm**—Doyle won on 3rd hole; **Canada**—Hall won on 1st hole; **Kroger**—Thorpe won on 1st hole.

Second place ties (3 players or more): 5-WAY—**Las Vegas** (J.M. Canizares, V. Fernandez, W. Hall, H. Irwin, D. Tewell); 4-WAY—**Verizon** (B. Fleisher, R. Floyd, G. Morgan, B. Walzel), **Utah Showdown** (T. Jenkins, B. Lietzke, G. Marsh, J. Patino); 3-WAY—**TD Waterhouse** (H. Baiocchi, D. Quigley, W. Morgan).

Senior PGA Majors

The Tradition

Edition: 13th   **Dates:** April 12–15
Site: Desert Mt. Cochise Course, Scottsdale, Ariz.
Par: 36-36—72 (6961 yards)   **Purse:** $1,700,000

		1	2	3	4	Tot	Earnings
1	Doug Tewell	66	67	70	62	265	$255,000
2	Mike McCullough	67	69	69	69	274	149,600
3	Hale Irwin	70	68	70	67	275	122,400
4	Gil Morgan	69	69	73	66	277*	102,000
5	J.C. Snead	70	71	69	70	280	74,800
	Larry Nelson	72	64	69	75	280	74,800
7	John Bland	73	66	71	71	281	54,400
	Bruce Fleisher	71	67	72	71	281	54,400
	Howard Twitty	73	68	69	71	281	54,400
10	Hubert Green	70	69	72	71	282	42,500
	Allen Doyle	71	66	73	72	282	42,500
12	Bill Brask	71	79	65	68	283	33,575
	Walter Hall	72	70	71	70	283	33,575
	Jose M. Canizares	69	73	71	70	283	33,575
	Jim Ahern	69	74	66	74	283	33,575
16	Ray Floyd	76	71	68	69	284	27,200
	Terry Dill	68	72	71	73	284	27,200
	John Jacobs	69	71	70	74	284	27,200
19	Stewart Ginn	71	70	75	69	285	21,182
	Gary Player	72	72	72	69	285	21,182
	Jim Holtgrieve	68	72	72	73	285	21,182
	Jim Thorpe	69	77	66	73	285	21,182
	Tom Wargo	67	69	71	78	285	21,182

Early round leaders: 1st—Tewell (66); 2nd—Tewell (133); 3rd—Tewell (203).

Top amateur: none.

Senior PGA Championship

Edition: 64th   **Dates:** May 24–27
Site: Ridgewood Country Club, Paramus, N.J.
Par: 36-36—72 (6904 yards)   **Purse:** $1,800,000

		1	2	3	4	Tot	Earnings
1	Tom Watson	72	69	66	67	274	$360,000
2	Jim Thorpe	67	69	71	68	275	216,000
3	Bob Gilder	68	69	70	70	277	136,000
4	Allen Doyle	70	70	68	70	278	96,000
5	Hale Irwin	69	75	71	66	281	71,000
	Stewart Ginn	73	68	71	69	281	71,000
7	Bruce Fleisher	70	69	72	71	282	62,000
8	Doug Tewell	70	75	69	69	283	56,000
	Gary Player	70	73	71	69	283	56,000
10	Bruce Summerhays	73	69	75	67	284	48,000
	Walter Hall	73	73	69	69	284	48,000
12	Jack Nicklaus	68	75	71	71	285	42,000
13	Bob Murphy	71	72	73	70	286	37,500
	Howard Twitty	71	70	73	72	286	37,500
15	Lanny Wadkins	73	75	71	68	287	33,000
	Dana Quigley	70	71	75	71	287	33,000
17	Seiji Ebihara	74	71	74	69	288	28,000
	John Bland	74	73	70	71	288	28,000
	Terry Dill	73	73	71	71	288	28,000
20	Isao Aoki	71	76	73	69	289	22,000
	Tom Wargo	71	75	72	71	289	22,000
	Joe Inman	74	74	67	74	289	22,000

Early round leaders: 1st—Thorpe (67); 2nd—Thorpe (136); 3rd—Thorpe, Watson and Gilder (207).

Top amateur: none.

Senior PGA Majors (Cont.)

U.S. Senior Open

Edition: 22nd **Dates:** June 28–July 1
Site: Salem CC, Peabody, Mass.
Par: 35-35—70 (6709 yards) **Purse:** $2,400,000

		1 2 3 4	Tot	Earnings
1	Bruce Fleisher	69-71-72-68	280	$430,000
2	Gil Morgan	70-70-71-70	281	209,799
	Isao Aoki	71-68-69-73	281	209,799
4	Allen Doyle	78-67-68-69	282	96,655
	Jack Nicklaus	71-72-69-70	282	96,655
	Jim Colbert	75-67-67-73	282	96,655
7	Dave Stockton	73-70-74-67	284	65,735
	John Mahaffey	78-69-69-68	284	65,735
	Jim Ahern	72-70-71-71	284	65,735
	Larry Nelson	74-67-68-75	284	65,735
11	Jay Sigel	77-72-64-72	285	49,436
	Bob Gilder	74-69-69-73	285	49,436
	Hale Irwin	73-70-69-73	285	49,436
	Dana Quigley	71-70-70-74	285	49,436
15	Tom Kite	73-70-74-69	286	42,416
16	Ted Goin	75-70-74-68	287	38,177
	Tom Watson	74-73-70-70	287	38,177
	Raymond Floyd	72-70-73-72	287	38,177
19	Leonard Thompson	72-77-69-70	288	33,042
	Walter Hall	71-74-70-73	288	33,042

Early round leaders: 1st—Fleisher (69); 2nd—Aoki (139); 3rd—Aoki (208).

Top amateur: Paul Simson (294).

PGA Sr. Players Championship

Edition: 19th **Dates:** July 12–15
Site: TPC of Michigan, Dearborn, Mich.
Par: 36-36—72 (6986 yards) **Purse:** $2,400,000

		1 2 3 4	Tot	Earnings
1	Allen Doyle*	67-69-70-67	273	$375,000
	Doug Tewell	74-66-67-66	273	220,000
3	Hale Irwin	70-65-75-66	276	180,000
4	Bruce Fleisher	69-69-72-68	278	135,000
	Ed Dougherty	67-70-68-73	278	135,000
6	Ray Floyd	67-73-69-70	279	95,000
	Mike McCullough	69-73-68-69	279	95,000
8	Tom Watson	67-68-72-73	280	75,000
	Jay Sigel	68-70-70-72	280	75,000
10	Jim Albus	72-70-72-68	282	60,000
	Bobby Walzel	75-74-66-67	282	60,000
	Tom Kite	71-68-71-72	282	60,000
13	Gil Morgan	72-68-69-74	283	50,000
14	Gary McCord	74-74-67-69	284	46,250
	Hugh Baiocchi	71-67-74-72	284	46,250
16	J.C. Snead	69-74-70-72	285	42,500
17	Vicente Fernandez	71-69-78-68	286	37,583
	Joe Inman	72-70-71-73	286	37,583
	Isao Aoki	69-69-73-75	286	37,583
20	Hubert Green	77-69-73-68	287	31,000
	Mike Hill	77-72-68-70	287	31,000
	John Jacobs	74-68-72-73	287	31,000

*Doyle won on the 1st playoff hole.

Early round leaders: 1st—Watson, Nelson, Floyd, Doyle and Dougherty (67); 2nd—Irwin and Watson (135); 3rd—Dougherty (205).

Top amateur: none.

LPGA Tour

LATE 2000

Last Rd	Tournament	Winner	Earnings	Runner-Up
Oct. 29	Cisco World Ladies Challenge	Japan (13½)	$40,000 (each)	United States (10½)
Nov. 5	Mizuno Classic	Lorie Kane (204)*	127,500	S. Gustafson (204)
Nov. 19	ARCH Tour Championship	Dottie Pepper (279)	215,000	R. Hetherington (282)
Dec. 3@	Women's World Cup	Australia (275)	100,000 (each)	Sweden (277)
Dec. 17@	Hyundai Team Matches	Juli Inkster/ Dottie Pepper (21st hole)	100,000 (each)	L. Kane/ A. Sorenstam

*Playoffs: Mizuno— Kane won on 1st hole.

2001

Last Rd	Tournament	Winner	Earnings	Runner-Up
Jan. 14	YourLife Vitamins Classic	Se Ri Pak (203)	$150,000	P. Hammel & C. Koch (207)
Jan. 21	Subaru Memorial of Naples	Sophie Gustafson (272)	150,000	K. Webb (275)
Jan. 28	The Office Depot	Grace Park (280)	123,750	K. Webb (281)
Feb. 10	Takefuji Classic	Lorie Kane (205)	127,500	A. Sorenstam (207)
Feb. 17	Hawaiian Ladies Open	Catriona Matthew (210)	112,500	A. Sorenstam (213)
Mar. 11	Welch's/Circle K Championship	Annika Sorenstam (265)	112,500	4-way tie (271)
Mar. 18	Standard Register Ping	Annika Sorenstam (261)	150,000	S. Ri Pak (263)
Mar. 25	**Nabisco Championship** (Rancho Mirage, Calif.)	Annika Sorenstam (281)	225,000	5-way tie (284)
Apr. 15	Office Depot Hosted by Amy Alcott	Annika Sorenstam (210)*	120,000	M. Hyun Kim (210)
Apr. 22	Longs Drugs Challenge	Se Ri Pak (208)#	120,000	L. Diaz (210)
Apr. 29	Kathy Ireland Championship	Rosie Jones (268)*	135,000	M. Hyun Kim (268)
May 6	Chick-fil-A Charity Championship	Annika Sorenstam (208)*	180,000	S. Gustafson (208)
May 13	Electrolux USA Championship	Juli Inkster (274)	120,000	C. Matthew (275)
May 20	Champions Classic	Wendy Doolan (132)*#	112,500	W. Ward (132)
May 27	Corning Classic	Carin Koch (270)	135,000	M. Hjorth & M. McKay (272)
June 3	**U.S. Women's Open** (Southern Pines, N.C.)	Karrie Webb (273)	520,000	S. Ri Pak (281)

Last Rd	Tournament	Winner	Earnings	Runner-Up
June 10	Wegmans Rochester International	Laura Davies (279)	$150,000	M. Hjorth & W. Ward (282)
June 16	Evian Masters	Rachel Teske (273)	315,000	M. Hjorth (274)
June 24	**McDonald's LPGA Championship**			
	(Wilmington, Del.)....................	Karrie Webb (270)	225,000	L. Diaz (272)
July 1	ShopRite Classic	Betsy King (201)	180,000	L. Kane (203)
July 8	Jamie Farr Kroger Classic	Se Ri Pak (269)	150,000	M. Hjorth (271)
July 15	Michelob Light Classic	Emilee Klein (205)	120,000	J. McGill & A. Sorenstam (210)
July 22	Big Apple Classic	Rosie Jones (272)	142,500	L. Diaz (273)
July 29	Giant Eagle Classic	Dorothy Delasin (203)	150,000	T. Green (204)
Aug. 5	**Weetabix Women's British Open**			
	(Sunningdale, ENG)	Se Ri Pak (277)	221,650	M. Hyun Kim (279)
Aug. 12	Wendy's Championship for Children	Wendy Ward (195)	150,000	M. Dunn & A. Sorenstam (198)
Aug. 19	Bank of Montreal Canadian Open	Annika Sorenstam (272)	180,000	K. Robbins (274)
Aug. 26	First Union Betsy King Classic	Heather Daly-Donofrio (273)	120,000	M. Dunn & M. McKay (274)
Sept. 2	State Farm Rail Classic................	Kate Golden (267)	150,000	A. Sorenstam (268)
Sept. 9	Williams Championship................	Gloria Park (201)	150,000	D. Andrews (202)
Sept. 16	Safeway Championship................	cancelled		
Sept. 23	Asahi Ryokuken International...........	Tina Fischer (206)	180,000	E. Klein & T. Hanson (207)
Sept. 30	AFLAC Champions	Se Ri Pak (272)	122,000	L. Kane (277)
Oct. 7	Samsung World Championship.........	Dorothy Delasin (277)	157,000	S. Ri Pak & K. Webb (281)

Weather-shortened

*Playoffs: Office Depot— Sorenstam won on 1st hole; **Kathy Ireland—** Jones won on 1st hole; **Chick-fil-A—** Sorenstam won on 2nd hole; **Champions—** Doolan won on 5th hole.

Second place ties (3 players or more): 5-WAY—**Nabisco** (K. Webb, J. Moodie, D. Pepper, A. Fukushima, R. Teske); 4-WAY—**Welch's** (L. Diaz, M. McGann, S. Pak, D. Pepper).

LPGA Majors

Nabisco Championship

Edition: 30th   **Dates:** March 22-25
Site: Mission Hills CC, Rancho Mirage, Calif.
Par: 36-36—72 (6520 yards)   **Purse:** $1,500,000

		1	2	3	4	Tot	Earnings
1	Annika Sorenstam ...	72	70	70	69	—281	$225,000
2	Karrie Webb........	73	72	70	69	—284	87,557
	Janice Moodie	72	72	70	70	—284	87,557
	Dottie Pepper	71	71	71	71	—284	87,557
	Akiko Fukushima	74	68	70	72	—284	87,557
	Rachel Teske	72	73	66	73	—284	87,557
7	Sophie Gustafson....	72	74	70	69	—285	41,891
	Brandie Burton	74	69	72	70	—285	41,891
9	Laura Diaz	71	74	69	72	—286	33,589
	Pat Hurst	70	68	74	74	—286	33,589
11	Laura Davies........	71	73	75	68	—287	25,957
	Dorothy Delasin	73	70	74	70	—287	25,957
	Se Ri Pak...........	73	69	73	72	—287	25,957
	Tina Barrett	71	73	70	73	—287	25,957
15	Mi Hyun Kim........	74	71	70	73	—288	20,736
	Carin Koch	70	69	75	74	—288	20,736
	Juli Inkster	70	75	68	75	—288	20,736
18	Liselotte Neumann ...	70	74	74	71	—289	18,220
	Jeong Jang	74	71	71	73	—289	18,220
	Michele Redman	71	72	71	75	—289	18,220

Early round leaders: 1st—Penny Hammel, Hurst, Inkster, Koch and Neumann (70); 2nd—Hurst (138); 3rd—Teske (211).

Top amateur: Lorena Ochoa (290).

U.S. Women's Open

Edition: 56th   **Dates:** May 31– June 3
Site: Pine Needles Lodge and GC, Southern Pines, N.C.
Par: 35-35—70 (6256 yards)   **Purse:** $2,900,000

		1	2	3	4	Tot	Earnings
1	Karrie Webb........	70	65	69	69	—273	$520,000
2	Se Ri Pak,..........	69	70	70	72	—281	310,000
3	Dottie Pepper	74	69	70	69	—283	202,580
4	Cristie Kerr	69	73	71	70	—283	118,697
	Sherri Turner	72	70	71	70	—283	118,697
	Catriona Matthew	72	68	70	73	—283	118,697
7	Lorie Kane..........	75	68	72	69	—284	80,726
	Kristi Albers........	71	69	74	70	—284	80,726
	Kelli Kuehne........	70	71	72	71	—284	80,726
	Wendy Doolan......	71	70	70	73	—284	80,726
11	Sophie Gustafson....	74	66	74	71	—285	66,581
12	Kelly Robbins	72	68	76	70	—286	57,088
	A.J. Eathorne.......	67	71	75	73	—286	57,088
	Juli Inkster	68	72	71	75	—286	57,088
	Yuri Fudoh.........	73	68	70	75	—286	57,088
16	Emilee Klein	72	69	75	71	—287	46,885
	Michele Redman	70	72	73	72	—287	46,885
	Annika Sorenstam ...	70	72	73	72	—287	46,885
19	Maria Hjorth	70	71	77	70	—288	37,327
	Marisa Baena.......	71	72	75	70	—288	37,327
	Jill McGill	68	76	72	72	—288	37,327
	Wendy Ward	70	71	74	73	—288	37,327
	Dorothy Delasin	75	72	72	73	—288	37,327

Early round leaders: 1st—Cindy Figg-Currier and Eathorne (67); 2nd—Webb (135); 3rd—Webb (204).

Top amateur: Candy Hannemann (291).

LPGA Majors (Cont.)

LPGA Championship

Edition: 47th   **Dates:** June 21–24
Site: DuPont CC, Wilmington, Del.
Par: 35-36–71 (6408 yards)   **Purse:** $1,500,000

		1 2 3 4	Tot	Earnings
1	Karrie Webb	67-64-70-69	270	$225,000
2	Laura Diaz	67-71-66-68	272	139,639
3	Wendy Ward	65-69-71-69	274	90,577
	Maria Hjorth	71-67-66-70	274	90,577
5	Annika Sorenstam	68-69-71-67	275	64,157
6	Becky Iverson	66-73-67-70	276	48,684
	Laura Davies	67-68-70-71	276	48,684
8	Mi Hyun Kim	70-70-68-69	277	39,250
9	Helen Alfredsson	68-66-74-70	278	35,476
10	Maggie Will	68-74-67-70	279	30,245
	Michele Redman	69-66-73-71	279	30,245
12	Rosie Jones	71-69-71-69	280	25,013
	Lorie Kane	69-71-71-69	280	25,013
	Liselotte Neumann	69-72-68-71	280	25,013
15	Wendy Doolan	70-71-72-68	281	21,239
	Juli Inkster	71-71-69-70	281	21,239
17	Dottie Pepper	71-72-71-68	282	16,819
	Kelly Robbins	69-74-71-68	282	16,819
	Carin Koch	69-73-71-69	282	16,819
	Meg Mallon	71-74-67-70	282	16,819
	Leta Lindley	71-71-70-70	282	16,819
	Pat Hurst	72-68-72-70	282	16,819
	Terry-Jo Myers	70-71-69-72	282	16,819
	Rachel Teske	68-72-70-72	282	16,819
	Mhairi McKay	68-72-70-72	282	16,819

Early round leaders: 1st—Ward (65); 2nd—Webb (131); 3rd—Webb (201).

Top amateur: none.

Women's British Open

Edition: 8th   **Dates:** Aug. 2–5
Site: Sunningdale GC, Sunningdale, England
Par: 36-36–72 (6277 yards)   **Purse:** $1,500,000

		1 2 3 4	Tot	Earnings
1	Se Ri Pak	71-70-70-66	277	$221,650
2	Mi Hyun Kim	72-65-71-71	279	143,000
3	Laura Diaz	74-70-69-67	280	74,092
	Iben Tinning	71-69-72-68	280	74,092
	Janice Moodie	67-70-71-72	280	74,092
	Catriona Matthew	70-65-72-73	280	74,092
7	Kathryn Marshall	75-71-68-67	281	36,608
	Marina Arruti	71-73-70-67	281	36,608
	Kristal Parker	72-71-71-67	281	36,608
	Kelli Kuehne	71-70-71-69	281	36,608
	Kasumi Fujii	71-71-69-70	281	36,608
12	Raquel Carriedo	73-70-70-69	282	25,382
	Tracy Hanson	72-69-70-71	282	25,382
	Rosie Jones	70-69-71-72	282	25,382
15	Pearl Sinn	74-70-72-67	283	20,592
	Brandie Burton	72-71-73-67	283	20,592
	Jill McGill	70-70-72-71	283	20,592
	Karrie Webb	74-67-68-74	283	20,592
19	Becky Morgan	73-68-71-72	284	17,982
	Trish Johnson	70-67-72-75	284	17,982

Early round leaders: 1st—Moodie (67); 2nd—Matthew (135); 3rd—Matthew (207).

Top amateur: Rebecca Hudson (287).

2001 Statistics (through Oct. 14)

Statistical leaders on the PGA, European PGA, Senior PGA and LPGA tours.

PGA

	Scoring	Avg.
1	Tiger Woods	68.61
2	Sergio Garcia	68.99
	Davis Love III	68.99
4	Vijay Singh	69.05
5	Phil Mickelson	69.21

	Putting	Putts
1	David Frost	1.708
2	Phil Mickelson	1.717
3	Vijay Singh	1.719
4	Jeff Sluman	1.720
5	Brian Gay	1.721

	Greens Hit	Pct.
1	Tom Lehman	73.9
2	Charles Howell III	72.5
3	John Cook	72.4
	Joe Durant	72.4
5	Tiger Woods	71.5

	Sand Saves	Pct.
1	Franklin Langham	68.9
2	Brad Faxon	65.7
3	Scott Verplank	64.5
4	Nick Price	63.5
5	Kevin Sutherland	63.4

	Driving Accuracy	Pct.
1	Joe Durant	81.2
2	Glen Hnatiuk	78.1
3	John Cook	77.1
	Fred Funk	77.1
5	Billy Mayfair	76.7

	Driving Distance	Avg.
1	John Daly	306.9
2	Brett Quigley	298.6
3	Davis Love III	298.2
4	Tiger Woods	296.8
5	Charles Howell III	295.7

European PGA

	Scoring	Avg.
1	Padraig Harrington	69.38
2	Sergio Garcia	69.53
	Retief Goosen	69.53
4	Colin Montgomerie	69.83
5	Bernhard Langer	69.85

	Putting	Putts
1	Michael Campbell	1.719
2	Thomas Björn	1.722
3	Padraig Harrington	1.727
4	Seve Ballesteros	1.734
5	Pierre Fulke	1.735

	Greens Hit	Pct.
1	Padraig Harrington	77.7
2	Sergio Garcia	77.1
3	Greg Owen	76.9
4	Peter O'Malley	76.7
5	Retief Goosen	75.6

	Sand Saves	Pct.
1	Brett Rumford	82.0
2	Tony Johnstone	81.6
3	John Senden	75.7
4	Bernhard Langer	75.0
5	Jose Maria Olazabal	74.1

	Driving Accuracy	Pct.
1	Peter O'Malley	84.1
2	Richard Green	81.7
3	John Bickerton	78.1
4	Mark Pilkington	76.9
5	Gary Orr	76.7

	Driving Distance	Avg.
1	Ricardo Gonzalez	303.8
2	Angel Cabrera	301.8
3	Emanuele Canonica	298.1
4	Jean Hugo	298.0
5	Adam Scott	297.5

Senior PGA

Scoring	Avg.
1 Gil Morgan	.69.06
2 Hale Irwin	.69.17
3 Allen Doyle	.69.23
4 Bruce Fleisher	.69.40
5 Tom Kite	.69.72

Putting	Putts
1 Hale Irwin	.1.721
2 Larry Nelson	.1.728
3 Bruce Fleisher	.1.732
4 Gil Morgan	.1.737
5 Terry Mauney	.1.738

Greens Hit	Pct.
1 Tom Kite	.75.4
2 Bruce Fleisher	.74.4
3 Allen Doyle	.73.7
Hale Irwin	.73.7
5 Doug Tewell	.73.5

Sand Saves	Pct.
1 Jose Maria Canizares	.61.5
Bob Eastwood	.61.5
3 Steven Veriato	.59.3
4 Isao Aoki	.57.9
5 Gary Player	.57.1

Driving Accuracy	Pct.
1 Doug Tewell	.83.1
2 John Bland	.82.7
3 Bruce Fleisher	.81.3
4 Allen Doyle	.81.1
5 Bob Murphy	.80.0

Driving Distance	Avg.
1 Lon Hinkle	.289.3
2 Jim Ahern	.285.9
3 Bobby Walzel	.285.2
4 Terry Dill	.284.1
5 Tom Kite	.283.6

LPGA

Scoring	Avg.
1 Annika Sorenstam	.69.44
2 Se Ri Pak	.69.69
3 Karrie Webb	.70.19
4 Lorie Kane	.70.37
5 Rosie Jones	.70.43

Putting	Putts
1 Vicki Goetze-Ackerman	.28.65
2 Laura Davies	.28.83
3 Rosie Jones	.29.17
4 Dottie Pepper	.29.18
5 Mi Hyun Kim	.29.23

Note: Putts per round.

Greens Hit	Pct.
1 Annika Sorenstam	.79.8
2 Karrie Webb	.74.4
3 Se Ri Pak	.73.7
4 Sherri Steinhauer	.72.8
5 Donna Andrews	.72.6

Sand Saves	Pct.
1 Michelle Louviere	.80.0
2 Karen Pearce	.63.1
3 Becky Morgan	.56.1
4 Rachel Teske	.54.1
5 Lisa Hackney	.52.8
Carin Koch	.52.8

Driving Accuracy	Pct.
1 Donna Andrews	.85.3
2 Amy Fruhwirth	.81.4
3 Luciana Bemvenuti	.80.9
4 Patti Liscio	.80.7
5 Dodie Mazzuca	.79.9

Driving Distance	Avg.
1 Wendy Doolan	.265.3
2 Maria Hjorth	.264.1
3 Akiko Fukushima	.263.5
4 Kelly Robbins	.262.2
Sophie Gustafson	.262.2

Key: Scoring—average strokes per round adjusted to the average score of the field each week. If the field is under par, each player's score is adjusted upward a corresponding amount and vice-versa if the field is over par. This keeps a player from receiving an advantage for playing easier-than-average courses; **Putting**—average number of putts taken on greens hit in regulation; **Greens Hit**—or Greens in Regulation, percentage based on number of greens reached in regulation out of total holes played. A green is considered hit in regulation if any portion of the ball rests on the putting surface in two shots less than par; **Sand Saves**—percentage of up-and-down efforts from greenside sand traps; **Driving Accuracy**—percentage of fairways hit on par-4 and par-5 holes; **Driving Distance**—average computed by charting exact distances of two tee shots on the most open par four or five holes on both front and back nine.

Battle at Bighorn

July 30 at Bighorn Golf Club, Palm Desert, Calif.

This 18-hole match-play exhibition featured Tiger Woods & Annika Sorenstam taking on David Duval & Karrie Webb and was broadcast live during primetime on ABC. It was an alternate-shot contest with Woods and Duval teeing off on odd-numbered holes and Sorenstam and Webb teeing off on even-numbered holes. Sorenstam drained a 15-foot birdie putt on the 18th hole to push the match into a sudden death playoff round, which her team won on the first hole. **Purse:** $2.0 million ($1.2 million divided by winners, $500,000 divided by losers, $300,000 to charity); **Sponsored by:** Lincoln Financial Group; **TV Rating:** 6.1/11 (ABC).

SCORECARD

	Hole	1	2	3	4	5	6	7	8	9		
	Par	4	4	5	4	4	3	5	3	4	36	
	Yards	429	416	531	447	367	175	519	202	449	3535	
Woods/ Sorenstam		5	4	5	4	3	3	4	3	5	1-up	
Duval/ Webb		5	5	4	4	5	3	5	3	4		
	Hole	10	11	12	13	14	15	16	17	18		
	Par	4	4	5	3	4	5	3	4	4	36	72
	Yards	397	434	550	227	351	528	153	443	355	3438	6973
Woods/ Sorenstam		6	6	5	3	5	5	3	5	3		
Duval/ Webb		4	6	3	4	4	4	4	5	4	1-up	even

Playoff: First hole (No. 18, par 4, 355 yards) — After Duval missed a 12-foot putt for par, Woods sank a two-foot putt for par and the victory.

Money Leaders

Official money leaders of PGA, European PGA, Senior PGA and LPGA tours for 2000 and unofficial money leaders for 2001, as compiled by the PGA, European PGA and LPGA. All European amounts are in euros (€).

PGA

Arnold Palmer Award standings: listed are tournaments played (TP); cuts made (CM); 1st, 2nd and 3rd place finishes; and earnings for the year.

FINAL 2000	TP	CM	Finish 1-2-3	Earnings	2001 (through Oct. 14)	TP	CM	Finish 1-2-3	Earnings
1 Tiger Woods	20	20	9-4-1	$9,188,321	1 Tiger Woods	17	17	5-0-1	$5,517,777
2 Phil Mickelson	23	21	4-3-0	4,746,457	2 Phil Mickelson	23	20	2-4-4	4,403,883
3 Ernie Els	19	19	1-5-2	3,469,405	3 David Toms	25	21	3-0-0	3,307,267
4 Hal Sutton	25	20	2-0-1	3,061,444	4 Vijay Singh	23	21	0-2-4	3,151,100
5 Vijay Singh	25	23	1-1-2	2,573,835	5 Scott Hoch	22	16	2-1-0	2,794,319
6 Mike Weir	28	23	1-1-0	2,547,829	6 Scott Verplank	24	22	1-1-1	2,571,262
7 David Duval	19	18	1-1-3	2,462,846	7 Davis Love III	17	14	1-2-0	2,558,263
8 Jesper Parnevik	20	17	2-1-1	2,413,345	8 Sergio Garcia	16	13	2-1-0	2,513,635
9 Davis Love III	25	22	0-3-1	2,337,765	9 Bob Estes	24	18	2-1-0	2,431,610
10 Stewart Cink	23	27	1-1-1	2,169,727	10 Jim Furyk	22	18	1-2-0	2,374,067

EUROPEAN PGA

Volvo Order of Merit standings: listed are tournaments played (TP); cuts made (CM); 1st, 2nd and 3rd place finishes; and earnings for the year.

FINAL 2000	TP	CM	Finish 1-2-3	Earnings	2001 (through Oct. 14)	TP	CM	Finish 1-2-3	Earnings
1 Lee Westwood	23	22	5-2-2	€3,125,147	1 Retief Goosen	18	15	2-1-0	€2,464,915
2 Darren Clarke	22	21	2-3-2	2,717,965	2 Darren Clarke	19	17	1-1-2	1,756,368
3 Ernie Els	11	11	1-3-1	2,017,248	3 Bernhard Langer	13	11	2-0-1	1,493,680
4 Michael Campbell	21	20	3-3-1	1,993,550	4 Padraig Harrington	17	16	0-6-0	1,362,565
5 Thomas Björn	27	23	1-3-1	1,929,657	5 Thomas Björn	19	17	1-2-1	1,352,173
6 Colin Montgomerie	23	22	2-0-3	1,740,917	6 Colin Montgomerie	20	16	2-0-1	1,320,210
7 Padraig Harrington	24	20	2-2-2	1,350,921	7 Niclas Fasth	21	17	0-2-1	1,186,097
8 Phillip Price	26	24	0-4-0	1,331,591	8 Ernie Els	9	9	0-0-1	1,128,791
9 Jose Maria Olazabal	21	18	1-0-0	1,174,564	9 Angel Cabrera	14	12	1-2-0	1,108,157
10 Gary Orr	26	24	2-2-0	1,009,473	10 Michael Campbell	17	12	1-1-1	1,036,354

SENIOR PGA

FINAL 2000	TP	CM	Finish 1-2-3	Earnings	2001 (through Oct. 14)	TP	CM	Finish 1-2-3	Earnings
1 Larry Nelson	30	30	6-7-1	$2,708,005	1 Allen Doyle	32	32	2-5-3	$2,491,742
2 Bruce Fleisher	30	30	4-5-3	2,373,977	2 Bruce Fleisher	29	29	3-3-4	2,313,177
3 Hale Irwin	24	24	4-4-1	2,128,968	3 Hale Irwin	24	24	3-2-4	2,037,958
4 Gil Morgan	23	23	3-5-0	1,873,216	4 Larry Nelson	26	25	4-1-2	1,771,436
5 Dana Quigley	39	39	1-5-2	1,802,063	5 Jim Thorpe	33	33	2-2-2	1,747,804
6 Jim Thorpe	37	37	2-3-2	1,656,747	6 Gil Morgan	22	22	2-4-1	1,736,908
7 Allen Doyle	33	33	1-0-4	1,505,471	7 Dana Quigley	35	35	1-2-2	1,479,091
8 Doug Tewell	27	26	3-1-1	1,408,194	8 Doug Tewell	26	25	1-4-0	1,383,339
9 Hubert Green	28	28	2-1-0	1,308,784	9 Tom Kite	21	21	1-0-4	1,289,338
10 Tom Jenkins	36	36	1-1-1	1,298,244	10 Ed Dougherty	34	33	1-1-4	1,289,233

LPGA

FINAL 2000	TP	CM	Finish 1-2-3	Earnings	2001 (through Oct. 14)	TP	CM	Finish 1-2-3	Earnings
1 Karrie Webb	22	22	7-3-1	$1,876,853	1 Annika Sorenstam	23	23	6-5-1	$1,684,868
2 Annika Sorenstam	22	22	5-2-4	1,404,948	2 Se Ri Pak	20	19	5-4-1	1,533,009
3 Meg Mallon	26	24	2-4-2	1,146,360	3 Karrie Webb	21	21	2-4-0	1,320,404
4 Juli Inkster	19	18	3-3-2	980,330	4 Lorie Kane	24	23	1-2-1	851,134
5 Lorie Kane	30	26	3-1-1	929,189	5 Maria Hjorth	26	21	0-4-2	797,715
6 Pat Hurst	26	25	1-4-2	840,161	6 Mi Hyun Kim	29	28	0-3-0	762,363
7 Mi Hyun Kim	27	26	1-2-1	825,720	7 Dottie Pepper	22	21	0-2-4	754,832
8 Dottie Pepper	19	17	1-3-1	786,695	8 Laura Diaz	26	25	0-4-1	741,316
9 Rosie Jones	25	23	0-2-1	643,054	9 Rosie Jones	22	22	2-0-1	728,010
10 Michele Redman	28	25	1-1-1	585,694	10 Catriona Matthew	26	23	1-1-2	704,123

1860-2001 Through the Years

Major Golf Championships
MEN
The Masters

The Masters has been played every year (except during World War II) since 1934 at the Augusta National Golf Club in Augusta, Ga. Both the course (6905 yards, par 72) and the tournament were created by Bobby Jones; (*) indicates playoff winner.

Multiple winners: Jack Nicklaus (6); Arnold Palmer (4); Jimmy Demaret, Nick Faldo, Gary Player and Sam Snead (3); Seve Ballesteros, Ben Crenshaw, Ben Hogan, Bernhard Langer, Byron Nelson, Jose Maria Olazabal, Horton Smith, Tom Watson and Tiger Woods (2).

Year	Winner	Score	Runner-up
1934	Horton Smith	284	Craig Wood (285)
1935	Gene Sarazen*	282	Craig Wood (282)
1936	Horton Smith	285	Harry Cooper (286)
1937	Byron Nelson	283	Ralph Guldahl (285)
1938	Henry Picard	285	Ralph Guldahl & Harry Cooper (287)
1939	Ralph Guldahl	279	Sam Snead (280)
1940	Jimmy Demaret	280	Lloyd Mangrum (284)
1941	Craig Wood	280	Byron Nelson (283)
1942	Byron Nelson*	280	Ben Hogan (280)
1943-45	Not held		World War II
1946	Herman Keiser	282	Ben Hogan (283)
1947	Jimmy Demaret	281	Frank Stranahan & Byron Nelson (283)
1948	Claude Harmon	279	Cary Middlecoff (284)
1949	Sam Snead	282	Lloyd Mangrum & Johnny Bulla (285)
1950	Jimmy Demaret	283	Jim Ferrier (285)
1951	Ben Hogan	280	Skee Riegel (282)
1952	Sam Snead	286	Jack Burke Jr. (290)
1953	Ben Hogan	274	Porky Oliver (279)
1954	Sam Snead*	289	Ben Hogan (289)
1955	Cary Middlecoff	279	Ben Hogan (286)
1956	Jack Burke Jr.	289	Ken Venturi (290)
1957	Doug Ford	283	Sam Snead (286)
1958	Arnold Palmer	284	Doug Ford & Fred Hawkins (285)
1959	Art Wall Jr.	284	Cary Middlecoff (285)
1960	Arnold Palmer	282	Ken Venturi (283)
1961	Gary Player	280	Arnold Palmer & Charles R. Coe (281)
1962	Arnold Palmer*	280	Dow Finsterwald & Gary Player (280)
1963	Jack Nicklaus	286	Tony Lema (287)
1964	Arnold Palmer	276	Jack Nicklaus & Dave Marr (282)
1965	Jack Nicklaus	271	Arnold Palmer & Gary Player (280)
1966	Jack Nicklaus*	288	Gay Brewer Jr. & Tommy Jacobs (288)
1967	Gay Brewer Jr.	280	Bobby Nichols (281)
1968	Bob Goalby	277	Roberto DeVicenzo (278)
1969	George Archer	281	Billy Casper, George Knudson & Tom Weiskopf (282)
1970	Billy Casper*	279	Gene Littler (279)
1971	Charles Coody	279	Jack Nicklaus & Johnny Miller (281)
1972	Jack Nicklaus	286	Bruce Crampton, Bobby Mitchell & Tom Weiskopf (289)
1973	Tommy Aaron	283	J.C. Snead (284)
1974	Gary Player	278	Tom Weiskopf, & Dave Stockton (280)
1975	Jack Nicklaus	276	Johnny Miller & Tom Weiskopf (277)
1976	Ray Floyd	271	Ben Crenshaw (279)
1977	Tom Watson	276	Jack Nicklaus (278)
1978	Gary Player	277	Hubert Green, Rod Funseth & Tom Watson (278)
1979	Fuzzy Zoeller*	280	Ed Sneed & Tom Watson (280)
1980	Seve Ballesteros	275	Gibby Gilbert & Jack Newton (279)
1981	Tom Watson	280	Jack Nicklaus & Johnny Miller (282)
1982	Craig Stadler*	284	Dan Pohl (284)
1983	Seve Ballesteros	280	Ben Crenshaw & Tom Kite (284)
1984	Ben Crenshaw	277	Tom Watson (279)
1985	Bernhard Langer	282	Curtis Strange, Seve Ballesteros & Ray Floyd (284)
1986	Jack Nicklaus	279	Greg Norman & Tom Kite (280)
1987	Larry Mize*	285	Seve Ballesteros & Greg Norman (285)
1988	Sandy Lyle	281	Mark Calcavecchia (282)
1989	Nick Faldo*	283	Scott Hoch (283)
1990	Nick Faldo*	278	Ray Floyd (278)
1991	Ian Woosnam	277	J.M. Olazabal (278)
1992	Fred Couples	275	Ray Floyd (277)
1993	Bernhard Langer	277	Chip Beck (281)
1994	J.M. Olazabal	279	Tom Lehman (281)
1995	Ben Crenshaw	274	Davis Love III (275)
1996	Nick Faldo	276	Greg Norman (281)
1997	Tiger Woods	270	Tom Kite (282)
1998	Mark O'Meara	279	Fred Couples & David Duval (280)
1999	J.M. Olazabal	280	Davis Love III (282)
2000	Vijay Singh	278	Ernie Els (281)
2001	Tiger Woods	272	David Duval (274)

The Masters (Cont.)
*PLAYOFFS:

1935: Gene Sarazen (144) def. Craig Wood (149) in 36 holes. **1942:** Byron Nelson (69) def. Ben Hogan (70) in 18 holes. **1954:** Sam Snead (70) def. Ben Hogan (71) in 18 holes. **1962:** Arnold Palmer (68) def. Gary Player (71) and Dow Finsterwald (77) in 18 holes. **1966:** Jack Nicklaus (70) def. Tommy Jacobs (72) and Gay Brewer Jr. (78) in 18 holes. **1970:** Billy Casper (69) def. Gene Littler (74) in 18 holes. **1979:** Fuzzy Zoeller (4-3) def. Ed Sneed (4-4) and Tom Watson (4-4) on 2nd hole of sudden death. **1982:** Craig Stadler (4) def. Dan Pohl (5) on 1st hole of sudden death. **1987:** Larry Mize (4-3) def. Greg Norman (4-4) and Seve Ballesteros (5) on 2nd hole of sudden death. **1989:** Nick Faldo (5-3) def. Scott Hoch (5-4) on 2nd hole of sudden death. **1990:** Nick Faldo (4-4) def. Raymond Floyd (4) on second hole of sudden death.

U.S. Open

Played at a different course each year, the U.S. Open was launched by the new U.S. Golf Association in 1895. The Open was a 36-hole event from 1895-97 and has been 72 holes since then. It switched from a 3-day, 36-hole Saturday finish to 4 days of play in 1965. Note that (*) indicates playoff winner and (a) indicates amateur winner.

Multiple winners: Willie Anderson, Ben Hogan, Bobby Jones and Jack Nicklaus (4); Hale Irwin (3); Julius Boros, Billy Casper, Ernie Els, Ralph Guldahl, Walter Hagen, Lee Janzen, John McDermott, Cary Middlecoff, Andy North, Gene Sarazen, Alex Smith, Payne Stewart, Curtis Strange and Lee Trevino (2).

Year	Winner	Score	Runner-up	Course	Location
1895	Horace Rawlins	173	Willie Dunn (175)	Newport GC	Newport, R.I.
1896	James Foulis	152	Horace Rawlins (155)	Shinnecock Hills GC	Southampton, N.Y.
1897	Joe Lloyd	162	Willie Anderson (163)	Chicago GC	Wheaton, Ill.
1898	Fred Herd	328	Alex Smith (335)	Myopia Hunt Club	Hamilton, Mass.
1899	Willie Smith	315	George Low, W.H. Way & Val Fitzjohn (326)	Baltimore CC	Baltimore
1900	Harry Vardon	313	J.H. Taylor (315)	Chicago GC	Wheaton, Ill.
1901	Willie Anderson*	331	Alex Smith (331)	Myopia Hunt Club	Hamilton, Mass.
1902	Laurie Auchterlonie	307	Stewart Gardner (313)	Garden City GC	Garden City, N.Y.
1903	Willie Anderson*	307	David Brown (307)	Baltusrol GC	Springfield, N.J.
1904	Willie Anderson*	303	Gil Nicholls (308)	Glen View Club	Golf, Ill.
1905	Willie Anderson	314	Alex Smith (316)	Myopia Hunt Club	Hamilton, Mass.
1906	Alex Smith	295	Willie Smith (302)	Onwentsia Club	Lake Forest, Ill.
1907	Alec Ross	302	Gil Nicholls (304)	Phila. Cricket Club	Chestnut Hill, Pa.
1908	Fred McLeod*	322	Willie Smith (322)	Myopia Hunt Club	Hamilton, Mass.
1909	George Sargent	290	Tom McNamara (294)	Englewood GC	Englewood, N.J.
1910	Alex Smith*	298	Macdonald Smith & John McDermott (298)	Phila. Cricket Club	Chestnut Hill, Pa.
1911	John McDermott*	307	George Simpson & Mike Brady (307)	Chicago GC	Wheaton, Ill.
1912	John McDermott	294	Tom McNamara (296)	CC of Buffalo	Buffalo
1913	a-Francis Ouimet*	304	Harry Vardon & Ted Ray (304)	The Country Club	Brookline, Mass.
1914	Walter Hagen	290	a-Chick Evans (291)	Midlothian CC	Blue Island, Ill.
1915	a-John Travers	297	Tom McNamara (298)	Baltusrol GC	Springfield, N.J.
1916	a-Chick Evans	286	Jock Hutchinson (288)	Minikahda Club	Minneapolis
1917-18 Not held			World War I		
1919	Walter Hagen*	301	Mike Brady (301)	Brae Burn CC	West Newton, Mass.
1920	Ted Ray	295	Jock Hutchinson, Jack Burke, Leo Diegel & Harry Vardon (296)	Inverness Club	Toledo, Ohio
1921	Jim Barnes	289	Walter Hagen & Fred McLeod (298)	Columbia CC	Chevy Chase, Md.
1922	Gene Sarazen	288	a-Bobby Jones & John Black (289)	Skokie CC	Glencoe, Ill.
1923	a-Bobby Jones*	296	Bobby Cruickshank (296)	Inwood CC	Inwood, N.Y.
1924	Cyril Walker	297	a-Bobby Jones (300)	Oakland Hills CC	Birmingham, Mich.
1925	Willie Macfarlane*	291	a-Bobby Jones (291)	Worcester CC	Worcester, Mass.
1926	a-Bobby Jones	293	Joe Turnesa (294)	Scioto CC	Columbus, Ohio
1927	Tommy Armour*	301	Harry Cooper (301)	Oakmont CC	Oakmont, Pa.
1928	Johnny Farrell*	294	a-Bobby Jones (294)	Olympia Fields CC	Matteson, Ill.
1929	a-Bobby Jones*	294	Al Espinosa (294)	Winged Foot CC	Mamaroneck, N.Y.
1930	a-Bobby Jones	287	Macdonald Smith (289)	Interlachen CC	Hopkins, Minn.
1931	Billy Burke*	292	George Von Elm (292)	Inverness Club	Toledo, Ohio
1932	Gene Sarazen	286	Bobby Cruickshank & Phil Perkins (289)	Fresh Meadow CC	Flushing, N.Y.
1933	a-Johnny Goodman	287	Ralph Guldahl (288)	North Shore CC	Glenview, Ill.
1934	Olin Dutra	293	Gene Sarazen (294)	Merion Cricket Club	Ardmore, Pa.
1935	Sam Parks Jr.	299	Jimmy Thomson (301)	Oakmont CC	Oakmont, Pa.
1936	Tony Manero	282	Harry E. Cooper (284)	Baltusrol GC	Springfield, N.J.
1937	Ralph Guldahl	281	Sam Snead (283)	Oakland Hills CC	Birmingham, Mich.
1938	Ralph Guldahl	284	Dick Metz (290)	Cherry Hills CC	Denver
1939	Byron Nelson*	284	Craig Wood & Denny Shute (284)	Philadelphia CC	Philadelphia

Year	Winner	Score	Runner-up	Course	Location
1940	Lawson Little*	287	Gene Sarazen (287)	Canterbury GC	Cleveland
1941	Craig Wood	284	Denny Shute (287)	Colonial Club	Ft. Worth
1942-45 Not held			World War II		
1946	Lloyd Mangrum*	284	Byron Nelson & Vic Ghezzi (284)	Canterbury GC	Cleveland
1947	Lew Worsham*	282	Sam Snead (282)	St. Louis CC	Clayton, Mo.
1948	Ben Hogan	276	Jimmy Demaret (278)	Riviera CC	Los Angeles
1949	Cary Middlecoff	286	Clayton Heafner & Sam Snead (287)	Medinah CC	Medinah, Ill.
1950	Ben Hogan*	287	Lloyd Mangrum & George Fazio (287)	Merion Golf Club	Ardmore, Pa.
1951	Ben Hogan	287	Clayton Heafner (289)	Oakland Hills CC	Birmingham, Mich.
1952	Julius Boros	281	Porky Oliver (285)	Northwood Club	Dallas
1953	Ben Hogan	283	Sam Snead (289)	Oakmont CC	Oakmont, Pa.
1954	Ed Furgol	284	Gene Littler (285)	Baltusrol GC	Springfield, N.J.
1955	Jack Fleck*	287	Ben Hogan (287)	Olympic CC	San Francisco
1956	Cary Middlecoff	281	Ben Hogan & Julius Boros (282)	Oak Hill CC	Rochester, N.Y.
1957	Dick Mayer*	282	Cary Middlecoff (282)	Inverness Club	Toledo, Ohio
1958	Tommy Bolt	283	Gary Player (287)	Southern Hills CC	Tulsa
1959	Billy Casper	282	Bob Rosburg (283)	Winged Foot GC	Marmaroneck, N.Y.
1960	Arnold Palmer	280	Jack Nicklaus (282)	Cherry Hills CC	Denver
1961	Gene Littler	281	Doug Sanders & Bob Goalby (282)	Oakland Hills CC	Birmingham, Mich.
1962	Jack Nicklaus*	283	Arnold Palmer (283)	Oakmont CC	Oakmont, Pa.
1963	Julius Boros*	293	Arnold Palmer & Jacky Cupit (293)	The Country Club	Brookline, Mass.
1964	Ken Venturi	278	Tommy Jacobs (282)	Congressional CC	Bethesda, Md.
1965	Gary Player*	282	Kel Nagle (282)	Bellerive CC	St. Louis
1966	Billy Casper*	278	Arnold Palmer (278)	Olympic CC	San Francisco
1967	Jack Nicklaus	275	Arnold Palmer (279)	Baltusrol GC	Springfield, N.J.
1968	Lee Trevino	275	Jack Nicklaus (279)	Oak Hill CC	Rochester, N.Y.
1969	Orville Moody	281	Al Geiberger, Deane Beman & Bob Rosburg (282)	Champions GC	Houston
1970	Tony Jacklin	281	Dave Hill (288)	Hazeltine National GC	Chaska, Minn.
1971	Lee Trevino*	280	Jack Nicklaus (280)	Merion GC	Ardmore, Pa.
1972	Jack Nicklaus	290	Bruce Crampton (293)	Pebble Beach GL	Pebble Beach, Calif.
1973	Johnny Miller	279	John Schlee (280)	Oakmont CC	Oakmont, Pa
1974	Hale Irwin	287	Forest Fezler (289)	Winged Foot GC	Mamaroneck, N.Y.
1975	Lou Graham*	287	John Mahaffey (287)	Medinah CC	Medinah, Ill.
1976	Jerry Pate	277	Al Geiberger & Tom Weiskopf (279)	Atlanta AC	Duluth, Ga.
1977	Hubert Green	278	Lou Graham (279)	Southern Hills CC	Tulsa
1978	Andy North	285	Dave Stockton & J.C. Snead (286)	Cherry Hills CC	Denver
1979	Hale Irwin	284	Gary Player & Jerry Pate (286)	Inverness Club	Toledo, Ohio
1980	Jack Nicklaus	272	Isao Aoki (274)	Baltusrol GC	Springfield, N.J.
1981	David Graham	273	George Burns & Bill Rogers (276)	Merion GC	Ardmore, Pa.
1982	Tom Watson	282	Jack Nicklaus (284)	Pebble Beach GL	Pebble Beach, Calif.
1983	Larry Nelson	280	Tom Watson (281)	Oakmont CC	Oakmont, Pa.
1984	Fuzzy Zoeller*	276	Greg Norman (276)	Winged Foot GC	Mamaroneck, N.Y.
1985	Andy North	279	Dave Barr, T.C. Chen & Denis Watson (280)	Oakland Hills CC	Birmingham, Mich.
1986	Ray Floyd	279	Lanny Wadkins & Chip Beck (281)	Shinnecock Hills GC	Southampton, N.Y.
1987	Scott Simpson	277	Tom Watson (278)	Olympic Club	San Francisco
1988	Curtis Strange*	278	Nick Faldo (278)	The Country Club	Brookline, Mass.
1989	Curtis Strange	278	Chip Beck, Ian Woosnam & Mark McCumber (279)	Oak Hill CC	Rochester, N.Y.
1990	Hale Irwin*	280	Mike Donald (280)	Medinah CC	Medinah, Ill.
1991	Payne Stewart*	282	Scott Simpson (282)	Hazeltine National GC	Chaska, Minn.
1992	Tom Kite	285	Jeff Sluman (287)	Pebble Beach GL	Pebble Beach, Calif.
1993	Lee Janzen	272	Payne Stewart (274)	Baltusrol GC	Springfield, N.J.
1994	Ernie Els*	279	Colin Montgomerie (279) & Loren Roberts (279)	Oakmont CC	Oakmont, Pa.
1995	Corey Pavin	280	Greg Norman (282)	Shinnecock Hills GC	Southampton, N.Y.
1996	Steve Jones	278	Davis Love III & Tom Lehman (279)	Oakland Hills CC	Bloomfield Hills, Mich.

U.S. Open (Cont.)

Year	Winner	Score	Runner-up	Course	Location
1997	Ernie Els..............	276	Colin Montgomerie (277)	Congressional CC	Bethesda, Md.
1998	Lee Janzen.............	280	Payne Stewart (281)	Olympic Club	San Francisco
1999	Payne Stewart.........	279	Phil Mickelson (280)	Pinehurst CC	Pinehurst, N.C.
2000	Tiger Woods	272	Miguel Angel Jimenez & Ernie Els (287)	Pebble Beach GL	Pebble Beach, Calif.
2001	Retief Goosen*	276	Mark Brooks (276)	Southern Hills CC	Tulsa

*PLAYOFFS:

1901: Willie Anderson (85) def. Alex Smith (86) in 18 holes. **1903:** Willie Anderson (82) def. David Brown (84) in 18 holes. **1908:** Fred McLeod (77) def. Willie Smith (83) in 18 holes. **1910:** Alex Smith (71) def. John McDermott (75) & Macdonald Smith (77) in 18 holes. **1911:** John McDermott (80) def. Mike Brady (82) & George Simpson (85) in 18 holes. **1913:** Francis Ouimet (72) def. Harry Vardon (77) & Edward Ray (78) in 18 holes. **1919:** Walter Hagen (77) def. Mike Brady (78) in 18 holes. **1923:** Bobby Jones (76) def. Bobby Cruickshank (78) in 18 holes. **1925:** Willie Macfarlane (75-72—147) def. Bobby Jones (75-73—148) in 36 holes. **1927:** Tommy Armour (76) def. Harry Cooper (79) in 18 holes. **1928:** Johnny Farrell (70-73—143) def. Bobby Jones (73-71—144) in 36 holes. **1929:** Bobby Jones (141) def. Al Espinosa (164) in 36 holes. **1931:** Billy Burke (149-148) def. George Von Elm (149-149) in 72 holes. **1939:** Byron Nelson (68-70) def. Craig Wood (68-73) and Denny Shute (76) in 36 holes. **1940:** Lawson Little (70) def. Gene Sarazen (73) in 18 holes. **1946:** Lloyd Mangrum (72-72—144) def. Byron Nelson (72-73—145) and Vic Ghezzi (72-73—145) in 36 holes. **1947:** Lew Worsham (69) def. Sam Snead (70) in 18 holes. **1950:** Ben Hogan (69) def. Lloyd Mangrum (73) & George Fazio (75) in 18 holes. **1955:** Jack Fleck (69) def. Ben Hogan (72) in 18 holes. **1957:** Dick Mayer (72) def. Cary Middlecoff (79) in 18 holes. **1962:** Jack Nicklaus (71) def. Arnold Palmer (74) in 18 holes. **1963:** Julius Boros (70) def. Jacky Cupit (73) & Arnold Palmer (76) in 18 holes. **1965:** Gary Player (71) def. Kel Nagle (74) in 18 holes. **1966:** Billy Casper (69) def. Arnold Palmer (73) in 18 holes. **1971:** Lee Trevino (68) def. Jack Nicklaus (71) in 18 holes. **1975:** Lou Graham (71) def. John Mahaffey (73) in 18 holes. **1984:** Fuzzy Zoeller (67) def. Greg Norman (75) in 18 holes. **1988:** Curtis Strange (71) def. Nick Faldo (75) in 18 holes. **1990:** Hale Irwin (74-3) def. Mike Donald (74-4) on 1st hole of sudden death after 18 holes. **1991:** Payne Stewart (75) def. Scott Simpson (77) in 18 holes. **1994:** Ernie Els (74-4-4) def. Loren Roberts (74-4-5) and Colin Montgomerie (78) on 2nd hole of sudden death after 18 holes; **2001:** Goosen (70) def. Brooks (72) in 18 holes.

British Open

The oldest of the Majors, the Open began in 1860 to determine "the champion golfer of the world." While only professional golfers participated in the first year of the tournament, amateurs have been invited ever since. Competition was extended from 36 to 72 holes in 1892. Conducted by the Royal and Ancient Golf Club of St. Andrews, the Open is rotated among select golf courses in England and Scotland. Note that (*) indicates playoff winner and (a) indicates amateur winner.

Multiple winners: Harry Vardon (6); James Braid, J.H. Taylor, Peter Thomson and Tom Watson (5); Walter Hagen, Bobby Locke, Tom Morris Sr., Tom Morris Jr. and Willie Park (4); Jamie Anderson, Seve Ballesteros, Henry Cotton, Nick Faldo, Bob Ferguson, Bobby Jones, Jack Nicklaus and Gary Player (3); Harold Hilton, Bob Martin, Greg Norman, Arnold Palmer, Willie Park Jr. and Lee Trevino (2).

Year	Winner	Score	Runner-up	Course	Location
1860	Willie Park.............	174	Tom Morris Sr. (176)	Prestwick Club	Ayrshire, Scotland
1861	Tom Morris Sr..........	163	Willie Park (167)	Prestwick Club	Ayrshire, Scotland
1862	Tom Morris Sr..........	163	Willie Park (176)	Prestwick Club	Ayrshire, Scotland
1863	Willie Park.............	168	Tom Morris Sr. (170)	Prestwick Club	Ayrshire, Scotland
1864	Tom Morris Sr..........	167	Andrew Strath (169)	Prestwick Club	Ayrshire, Scotland
1865	Andrew Strath	162	Willie Park (164)	Prestwick Club	Ayrshire, Scotland
1866	Willie Park.............	169	David Park (171)	Prestwick Club	Ayrshire, Scotland
1867	Tom Morris Sr..........	170	Willie Park (172)	Prestwick Club	Ayrshire, Scotland
1868	Tom Morris Jr..........	157	Robert Andrew (159)	Prestwick Club	Ayrshire, Scotland
1869	Tom Morris Jr..........	154	Tom Morris Sr. (157)	Prestwick Club	Ayrshire, Scotland
1870	Tom Morris Jr.	149	Bob Kirk (161)	Prestwick Club	Ayrshire, Scotland
1871	Not held				
1872	Tom Morris Jr..........	166	David Strath (169)	Prestwick Club	Ayrshire, Scotland
1873	Tom Kidd	179	Jamie Anderson (180)	St. Andrews	St. Andrews, Scotland
1874	Mungo Park...........	159	Tom Morris Jr. (161)	Musselburgh	Musselburgh, Scotland
1875	Willie Park.............	166	Bob Martin (168)	Prestwick Club	Ayrshire, Scotland
1876	Bob Martin*...........	176	David Strath (176)	St. Andrews	St. Andrews, Scotland
1877	Jamie Anderson	160	Bob Pringle (162)	Musselburgh	Musselburgh, Scotland
1878	Jamie Anderson	157	Bob Kirk (159)	Prestwick Club	Ayrshire, Scotland
1879	Jamie Anderson	169	Andrew Kirkaldy & James Allan (172)	St. Andrews	St. Andrews, Scotland
1880	Bob Ferguson	162	Peter Paxton (167)	Musselburgh	Musselburgh, Scotland
1881	Bob Ferguson	170	Jamie Anderson (173)	Prestwick Club	Ayrshire, Scotland
1882	Bob Ferguson	171	Willie Fernie (174)	St. Andrews	St. Andrews, Scotland
1883	Willie Fernie*..........	159	Bob Ferguson (159)	Musselburgh	Musselburgh, Scotland
1884	Jack Simpson...........	160	David Rollan & Willie Fernie (164)	Prestwick Club	Ayrshire, Scotland
1885	Bob Martin	171	Archie Simpson (172)	St. Andrews	St. Andrews, Scotland
1886	David Brown............	157	Willie Campbell (159)	Musselburgh	Musselburgh, Scotland
1887	Willie Park Jr...........	161	Bob Martin (162)	Prestwick Club	Ayrshire, Scotland
1888	Jack Burns	171	David Anderson & Ben Sayers (172)	St. Andrews	St. Andrews, Scotland
1889	Willie Park Jr.*	155	Andrew Kirkaldy (155)	Musselburgh	Musselburgh, Scotland
1890	a-John Ball	164	Willie Fernie (167) & A. Simpson (167)	Prestwick Club	Ayrshire, Scotland

Year	Winner	Score	Runner-up	Course	Location
1891	Hugh Kirkaldy	166	Andrew Kirkaldy & Willie Fernie (168)	St. Andrews	St. Andrews, Scotland
1892	a-Harold Hilton	305	John Ball, Sandy Herd & Hugh Kirkaldy (308)	Muirfield	Gullane, Scotland
1893	Willie Auchterlonie	322	Johnny Laidley (324)	Prestwick Club	Ayrshire, Scotland
1894	J.H. Taylor	326	Douglas Rolland (331)	Royal St. George's	Sandwich, England
1895	J.H. Taylor	322	Sandy Herd (326)	St. Andrews	St. Andrews, Scotland
1896	Harry Vardon*	316	J.H. Taylor (316)	Muirfield	Gullane, Scotland
1897	a-Harold Hilton	314	James Braid (315)	Hoylake	Hoylake, England
1898	Harry Vardon	307	Willie Park Jr. (308)	Prestwick Club	Ayrshire, Scotland
1899	Harry Vardon	310	Jack White (315)	Royal St. George's	Sandwich, England
1900	J.H. Taylor	309	Harry Vardon (317)	St. Andrews	St. Andrews, Scotland
1901	James Braid	309	Harry Vardon (312)	Muirfield	Gullane, Scotland
1902	Sandy Herd	307	Harry Vardon (308)	Hoylake	Hoylake, England
1903	Harry Vardon	300	Tom Vardon (306)	Prestwick Club	Ayrshire, Scotland
1904	Jack White	296	James Braid (297)	Royal St. George's	Sandwich, England
1905	James Braid	318	J.H. Taylor (323) & Rolland Jones (323)	St. Andrews	St. Andrews, Scotland
1906	James Braid	300	J.H. Taylor (304)	Muirfield	Gullane, Scotland
1907	Arnaud Massy	312	J.H. Taylor (314)	Hoylake	Hoylake, England
1908	James Braid	291	Tom Ball (299)	Prestwick Club	Ayrshire, Scotland
1909	J.H. Taylor	295	James Braid (299)	Deal	Deal, England
1910	James Braid	299	Sandy Herd (303)	St. Andrews	St. Andrews, Scotland
1911	Harry Vardon*	303	Arnaud Massy (303)	Royal St. George's	Sandwich, England
1912	Ted Ray	295	Harry Vardon (299)	Muirfield	Gullane, Scotland
1913	J.H. Taylor	304	Ted Ray (312)	Hoylake	Hoylake, England
1914	Harry Vardon	306	J.H. Taylor (309)	Prestwick Club	Ayrshire, Scotland
1915-19 Not held			World War I		
1920	George Duncan	303	Sandy Herd (305)	Deal	Deal, England
1921	Jock Hutchison*	296	Roger Wethered (296)	St. Andrews	St. Andrews, Scotland
1922	Walter Hagen	300	George Duncan & Jim Barnes (301)	Royal St. George's	Sandwich, England
1923	Arthur Havers	295	Walter Hagen (296)	Royal Troon	Troon, Scotland
1924	Walter Hagen	301	Ernest Whitcombe (302)	Hoylake	Hoylake, England
1925	Jim Barnes	300	Archie Compston & Ted Ray (301)	Prestwick Club	Ayrshire, Scotland
1926	a-Bobby Jones	291	Al Watrous (293)	Royal Lytham	Lytham, England
1927	a-Bobby Jones	285	Aubrey Boomer (291)	St. Andrews	St. Andrews, Scotland
1928	Walter Hagen	292	Gene Sarazen (294)	Royal St. George's	Sandwich, England
1929	Walter Hagen	292	Johnny Farrell (298)	Muirfield	Gullane, Scotland
1930	a-Bobby Jones	291	Macdonald Smith & Leo Diegel (293)	Hoylake	Hoylake, England
1931	Tommy Armour	296	Jose Jurado (297)	Carnoustie	Carnoustie, Scotland
1932	Gene Sarazen	283	Macdonald Smith (288)	Prince's	Prince's, England
1933	Denny Shute*	292	Craig Wood (292)	St. Andrews	St. Andrews, Scotland
1934	Henry Cotton	283	Sid Brews (288)	Royal St. George's	Sandwich, England
1935	Alf Perry	283	Alf Padgham (287)	Muirfield	Gullane, Scotland
1936	Alf Padgham	287	Jimmy Adams (288)	Hoylake	Hoylake, England
1937	Henry Cotton	290	Reg Whitcombe (292)	Carnoustie	Carnoustie, Scotland
1938	Reg Whitcombe	295	Jimmy Adams (297)	Royal St. George's	Sandwich, England
1939	Dick Burton	290	Johnny Bulla (292)	St. Andrews	St. Andrews, Scotland
1940-45 Not held			World War II		
1946	Sam Snead	290	Bobby Locke (294) & Johnny Bulla (294)	St. Andrews	St. Andrews, Scotland
1947	Fred Daly	293	Frank Stranahan & Reg Horne (294)	Hoylake	Hoylake, England
1948	Henry Cotton	284	Fred Daly (289)	Muirfield	Gullane, Scotland
1949	Bobby Locke*	283	Harry Bradshaw (283)	Royal St. George's	Sandwich, England
1950	Bobby Locke	279	Roberto de Vicenzo (281)	Royal Troon	Troon, Scotland
1951	Max Faulkner	285	Tony Cerda (287)	Royal Portrush	Portrush, Ireland
1952	Bobby Locke	287	Peter Thomson (288)	Royal Lytham	Lytham, England
1953	Ben Hogan	282	Frank Stranahan, Dai Rees, Tony Cerda & Peter Thomson (286)	Carnoustie	Carnoustie, Scotland
1954	Peter Thomson	283	Sid Scott, Dai Rees & Bobby Locke (284)	Royal Birkdale	Southport, England
1955	Peter Thomson	281	Johny Fallon (283)	St. Andrews	St. Andrews, Scotland
1956	Peter Thomson	286	Flory Van Donck (289)	Hoylake	Hoylake, England
1957	Bobby Locke	279	Peter Thomson (282)	St. Andrews	St. Andrews, Scotland
1958	Peter Thomson*	278	Dave Thomas (278)	Royal Lytham	Lytham, England

British Open (Cont.)

Year	Winner	Score	Runner-up	Course	Location
1959	Gary Player	284	Flory Van Donck & Fred Bullock (286)	Muirfield	Gullane, Scotland
1960	Kel Nagle	278	Arnold Palmer (279)	St. Andrews	St. Andrews, Scotland
1961	Arnold Palmer	284	Dai Rees (285)	Royal Birkdale	Southport, England
1962	Arnold Palmer	276	Kel Nagle (282)	Royal Troon	Troon, Scotland
1963	Bob Charles*	277	Phil Rodgers (277)	Royal Lytham	Lytham, England
1964	Tony Lema	279	Jack Nicklaus (284)	St. Andrews	St. Andrews, Scotland
1965	Peter Thomson	285	Christy O'Connor & Brian Huggett (287)	Royal Birkdale	Southport, England
1966	Jack Nicklaus	282	Doug Sanders & Dave Thomas (283)	Muirfield	Gullane, Scotland
1967	Roberto de Vicenzo	278	Jack Nicklaus (280)	Hoylake	Hoylake, England
1968	Gary Player	289	Jack Nicklaus & Bob Charles (291)	Carnoustie	Carnoustie, Scotland
1969	Tony Jacklin	280	Bob Charles (282)	Royal Lytham	Lytham, England
1970	Jack Nicklaus*	283	Doug Sanders (283)	St. Andrews	St. Andrews, Scotland
1971	Lee Trevino	278	Lu Liang Huan (279)	Royal Birkdale	Southport, England
1972	Lee Trevino	278	Jack Nicklaus (279)	Muirfield	Gullane, Scotland
1973	Tom Weiskopf	276	Johnny Miller & Neil Coles (279)	Royal Troon	Troon, Scotland
1974	Gary Player	282	Peter Oosterhuis (286)	Royal Lytham	Lytham, England
1975	Tom Watson*	279	Jack Newton (279)	Carnoustie	Carnoustie, Scotland
1976	Johnny Miller	279	Seve Ballesteros & Jack Nicklaus (285)	Royal Birkdale	Southport, England
1977	Tom Watson	268	Jack Nicklaus (269)	Turnberry	Turnberry, Scotland
1978	Jack Nicklaus	281	Tom Kite, Ray Floyd, Ben Crenshaw & Simon Owen (283)	St. Andrews	St. Andrews, Scotland
1979	Seve Ballesteros	283	Jack Nicklaus & Ben Crenshaw (286)	Royal Lytham	Lytham, England
1980	Tom Watson	271	Lee Trevino (275)	Muirfield	Gullane, Scotland
1981	Bill Rogers	276	Bernhard Langer (280)	Royal St. George's	Sandwich, England
1982	Tom Watson	284	Peter Oosterhuis & Nick Price (285)	Royal Troon	Troon, Scotland
1983	Tom Watson	275	Hale Irwin & Andy Bean (276)	Royal Birkdale	Southport, England
1984	Seve Ballesteros	276	Bernhard Langer & Tom Watson (278)	St. Andrews	St. Andrews, Scotland
1985	Sandy Lyle	282	Payne Stewart (283)	Royal St. George's	Sandwich, England
1986	Greg Norman	280	Gordon J. Brand (285)	Turnberry	Turnberry, Scotland
1987	Nick Faldo	279	Paul Azinger & Rodger Davis (280)	Muirfield	Gullane, Scotland
1988	Seve Ballesteros	273	Nick Price (275)	Royal Lytham	Lytham, England
1989	Mark Calcavecchia*	275	Greg Norman & Wayne Grady (275)	Royal Troon	Troon, Scotland
1990	Nick Faldo	270	Payne Stewart & Mark McNulty (275)	St. Andrews	St. Andrews, Scotland
1991	Ian Baker-Finch	272	Mike Harwood (274)	Royal Birkdale	Southport, England
1992	Nick Faldo	272	John Cook (273)	Muirfield	Gullane, Scotland
1993	Greg Norman	267	Nick Faldo (269)	Royal St. George's	Sandwich, England
1994	Nick Price	268	Jesper Parnevik (269)	Turnberry	Turnberry, Scotland
1995	John Daly*	282	Costantino Rocca (282)	St. Andrews	St. Andrews, Scotland
1996	Tom Lehman	271	Mark McCumber & Ernie Els (273)	Royal Lytham	Lytham, England
1997	Justin Leonard	272	Jesper Parnevik & Darren Clarke (275)	Royal Troon	Troon, Scotland
1998	Mark O'Meara*	280	Brian Watts (280)	Royal Birkdale	Southport, England
1999	Paul Lawrie*	290	Justin Leonard & Jean Van de Velde (290)	Carnoustie	Carnoustie, Scotland
2000	Tiger Woods	269	Thomas Bjorn & Ernie Els (277)	St. Andrews	St. Andrews, Scotland
2001	David Duval	274	Niclas Fasth (277)	Royal Lytham	Lytham, England

*PLAYOFFS:

1876: Bob Martin awarded title when David Strath refused playoff. **1883:** Willie Fernie (158) def. Robert Ferguson (159) in 36 holes. **1889:** Willie Park Jr. (158) def. Andrew Kirkaldy (163) in 36 holes. **1896:** Harry Vardon (157) def. John H. Taylor (161) in 36 holes. **1911:** Harry Vardon won when Arnaud Massy conceded at 35th hole. **1921:** Jock Hutchison (150) def. Roger Wethered (159) in 36 holes. **1933:** Denny Shute (149) def. Craig Wood (154) in 36 holes. **1949:** Bobby Locke (135) def. Harry Bradshaw (147) in 36 holes. **1958:** Peter Thomson (139) def. Dave Thomas (143) in 36 holes. **1963:** Bob Charles (140) def. Phil Rodgers (148) in 36 holes. **1970:** Jack Nicklaus (72) def. Doug Sanders (73) in 18 holes. **1975:** Tom Watson (71) def. Jack Newton (72) in 18 holes. **1989:** Mark Calcavecchia (4-3-3-3—13) def. Wayne Grady (4-4-4-4—16) and Greg Norman (3-3-4) in 4 holes. **1995:** John Daly (3-4-4-4—15) def. Costantino Rocca (4-5-7-3—19) in 4 holes. **1998:** Mark O'Meara (4-4-5-4—17) def. Brian Watts (5-4-5-5—19) in 4 holes **1999:** Paul Lawrie (5-4-3-3—15) def. Justin Leonard (5-4-4-5—18) and Jean Van de Velde (6-4-3-5—18) in 4 holes.

PGA Championship

The PGA Championship began in 1916 as a professional golfers match play tournament, but switched to stroke play in 1958. Conducted by the PGA of America, the tournament is played on a different course each year.

Multiple winners: Walter Hagen and Jack Nicklaus (5); Gene Sarazen and Sam Snead (3); Jim Barnes, Leo Diegel, Ray Floyd, Ben Hogan, Byron Nelson, Larry Nelson, Gary Player, Nick Price, Paul Runyan, Denny Shute, Dave Stockton, Lee Trevino and Tiger Woods (2).

Year	Winner	Score	Runner-up	Course	Location
1916	Jim Barnes	1-up	Jock Hutchison	Siwanoy CC	Bronxville, N.Y.
1917-18	Not held		World War I		
1919	Jim Barnes	6 & 5	Fred McLeod	Engineers CC	Roslyn, N.Y.
1920	Jock Hutchison	1-up	J. Douglas Edgar	Flossmoor CC	Flossmoor, Ill.
1921	Walter Hagen	3 & 2	Jim Barnes	Inwood CC	Inwood, N.Y.
1922	Gene Sarazen	4 & 3	Emmet French	Oakmont CC	Oakmont, Pa.
1923	Gene Sarazen*	1-up/38	Walter Hagen	Pelham CC	Pelham, N.Y.
1924	Walter Hagen	2-up	Jim Barnes	French Lick CC	French Lick, Ind.
1925	Walter Hagen	6 & 5	Bill Mehlhorn	Olympia Fields CC	Matteson, Ill.
1926	Walter Hagen	5 & 3	Leo Diegel	Salisbury GC	Westbury, N.Y.
1927	Walter Hagen	1-up	Joe Turnesa	Cedar Crest CC	Dallas
1928	Leo Diegel	6 & 5	Al Espinosa	Five Farms CC	Baltimore
1929	Leo Diegel	6 & 4	John Farrell	Hillcrest CC	Los Angeles
1930	Tommy Armour	1-up	Gene Sarazen	Fresh Meadow CC	Flushing, N.Y.
1931	Tom Creavy	2 & 1	Denny Shute	Wannamoisett CC	Rumford, R.I.
1932	Olin Dutra	4 & 3	Frank Walsh	Keller GC	St. Paul, Minn.
1933	Gene Sarazen	5 & 4	Willie Goggin	Blue Mound CC	Milwaukee
1934	Paul Runyan*	1-up/38	Craig Wood	Park CC	Williamsville, N.Y.
1935	Johnny Revolta	5 & 4	Tommy Armour	Twin Hills CC	Oklahoma City
1936	Denny Shute	3 & 2	Jimmy Thomson	Pinehurst CC	Pinehurst, N.C.
1937	Denny Shute*	1-up/37	Harold McSpaden	Pittsburgh FC	Aspinwall, Pa.
1938	Paul Runyan	8 & 7	Sam Snead	Shawnee CC	Shawnee-on-Del, Pa.
1939	Henry Picard*	1-up/37	Byron Nelson	Pomonok CC	Flushing, N.Y.
1940	Byron Nelson	1-up	Sam Snead	Hershey CC	Hershey, Pa.
1941	Vic Ghezzi*	1-up/38	Byron Nelson	Cherry Hills CC	Denver
1942	Sam Snead	2 & 1	Jim Turnesa	Seaview CC	Atlantic City, N.J.
1943	Not held		World War II		
1944	Bob Hamilton	1-up	Byron Nelson	Manito G & CC	Spokane, Wash.
1945	Byron Nelson	4 & 3	Sam Byrd	Morraine CC	Dayton, Ohio
1946	Ben Hogan	6 & 4	Porky Oliver	Portland GC	Portland, Ore.
1947	Jim Ferrier	2 & 1	Chick Harbert	Plum Hollow CC	Detroit
1948	Ben Hogan	7 & 6	Mike Turnesa	Norwood Hills CC	St. Louis
1949	Sam Snead	3 & 2	John Palmer	Hermitage CC	Richmond, Va.
1950	Chandler Harper	4 & 3	Henry Williams Jr.	Scioto CC	Columbus, Ohio
1951	Sam Snead	7 & 6	Walter Burkemo	Oakmont CC	Oakmont, Pa.
1952	Jim Turnesa	1-up	Chick Harbert	Big Spring CC	Louisville
1953	Walter Burkemo	2 & 1	Felice Torza	Birmingham CC	Birmingham, Mich.
1954	Chick Harbert	4 & 3	Walter Burkemo	Keller GC	St. Paul, Minn.
1955	Doug Ford	4 & 3	Cary Middlecoff	Meadowbrook CC	Detroit
1956	Jack Burke	3 & 2	Ted Kroll	Blue Hill CC	Boston
1957	Lionel Hebert	2 & 1	Dow Finsterwald	Miami Valley GC	Dayton, Ohio
1958	Dow Finsterwald	276	Billy Casper (278)	Llanerch CC	Havertown, Pa.
1959	Bob Rosburg	277	Jerry Barber & Doug Sanders (278)	Minneapolis GC	St. Louis Park, Minn.
1960	Jay Hebert	281	Jim Ferrier (282)	Firestone CC	Akron, Ohio
1961	Jerry Barber**	277	Don January (277)	Olympia Fields CC	Matteson, Ill.
1962	Gary Player	278	Bob Goalby (279)	Aronimink GC	Newtown Square, Pa.
1963	Jack Nicklaus	279	Dave Ragan (281)	Dallas AC	Dallas
1964	Bobby Nichols	271	Jack Nicklaus & Arnold Palmer (274)	Columbus CC	Columbus, Ohio
1965	Dave Marr	280	Jack Nicklaus & Billy Casper (282)	Laurel Valley GC	Ligonier, Pa.
1966	Al Geiberger	280	Dudley Wysong (284)	Firestone CC	Akron, Ohio
1967	Don January**	281	Don Massengale (281)	Columbine CC	Littleton, Colo.
1968	Julius Boros	281	Arnold Palmer & Bob Charles (282)	Pecan Valley CC	San Antonio
1969	Ray Floyd	276	Gary Player (277)	NCR GC	Dayton, Ohio
1970	Dave Stockton	279	Arnold Palmer & Bob Murphy (281)	Southern Hills CC	Tulsa
1971	Jack Nicklaus	281	Billy Casper (283)	PGA National GC	Palm Beach Gardens, Fla.
1972	Gary Player	281	Jim Jamieson & Tommy Aaron (283)	Oakland Hills GC	Birmingham, Mich.

PGA Championship (Cont.)

Year	Winner	Score	Runner-up	Course	Location
1973	Jack Nicklaus	277	Bruce Crampton (281)	Canterbury GC	Cleveland
1974	Lee Trevino	276	Jack Nicklaus (277)	Tanglewood GC	Winston-Salem, N.C.
1975	Jack Nicklaus	276	Bruce Crampton (278)	Firestone CC	Akron, Ohio
1976	Dave Stockton	281	Don January & Ray Floyd (282)	Congressional CC	Bethesda, Md.
1977	Lanny Wadkins**	282	Gene Littler (282)	Pebble Beach GL	Pebble Beach, Calif.
1978	John Mahaffey**	276	Jerry Pate & Tom Watson (276)	Oakmont CC	Oakmont, Pa.
1979	David Graham**	272	Ben Crenshaw (272)	Oakland Hills CC	Birmingham, Mich.
1980	Jack Nicklaus	274	Andy Bean (281)	Oak Hill CC	Rochester, N.Y.
1981	Larry Nelson	273	Fuzzy Zoeller (277)	Atlanta AC	Duluth, Ga.
1982	Ray Floyd	272	Lanny Wadkins (275)	Southern Hills CC	Tulsa
1983	Hal Sutton	274	Jack Nicklaus (275)	Riviera CC	Los Angeles
1984	Lee Trevino	273	Lanny Wadkins & Gary Player (277)	Shoal Creek	Birmingham, Ala.
1985	Hubert Green	278	Lee Trevino (280)	Cherry Hills CC	Denver
1986	Bob Tway	276	Greg Norman (278)	Inverness Club	Toledo, Ohio
1987	Larry Nelson**	287	Lanny Wadkins (287)	PGA National	Palm Beach Gardens, Fla.
1988	Jeff Sluman	272	Paul Azinger 275)	Oak Tree GC	Edmond, Okla.
1989	Payne Stewart	276	Andy Bean, Mike Reid & Curtis Strange (277)	Kemper Lakes GC	Hawthorn Woods, Ill.
1990	Wayne Grady	282	Fred Couples (285)	Shoal Creek	Birmingham, Ala.
1991	John Daly	276	Bruce Lietzke (279)	Crooked Stick GC	Carmel, Ind.
1992	Nick Price	278	Nick Faldo, John Cook, Jim Gallagher & Gene Sauers (281)	Bellerive CC	St. Louis
1993	Paul Azinger**	272	Greg Norman (272)	Inverness Club	Toledo, Ohio
1994	Nick Price	269	Corey Pavin (275)	Southern Hills CC	Tulsa
1995	Steve Elkington**	267	Colin Montgomerie (267)	Riviera CC	Pacific Palisades, Calif.
1996	Mark Brooks**	277	Kenny Perry (277)	Valhalla GC	Louisville, Ky.
1997	Davis Love III	269	Justin Leonard (274)	Winged Foot GC	Mamaroneck, N.Y.
1998	Vijay Singh	271	Steve Stricker (273)	Sahalee CC	Redmond, Wash.
1999	Tiger Woods	277	Sergio Garcia (278)	Medinah CC	Medinah, Ill.
2000	Tiger Woods**	270	Bob May (270)	Valhalla GC	Louisville, Ky.
2001	David Toms	265	Phil Mickelson (266)	Atlanta AC	Duluth, Ga.

*While the PGA Championship was a match play tournament from 1916-57, the two finalists played 36 holes for the title. In the five years that a playoff was necessary, the match was decided on the 37th or 38th hole.

PLAYOFFS:

1961: Jerry Barber (67) def. Don January (68) in 18 holes. **1967:** Don January (69) def. Don Massengale (71) in 18 holes. **1977:** Lanny Wadkins (4-4-4) def. Gene Littler (4-4-5) on 3rd hole of sudden death. **1978:** John Mahaffey (4-3) def. Jerry Pate (4-4) and Tom Watson (4-5) on 2nd hole of sudden death. **1979:** David Graham (4-4-2) def. Ben Crenshaw (4-4-4) on 3rd hole of sudden death. **1987:** Larry Nelson (4) def. Lanny Wadkins (5) on 1st hole of sudden death. **1993:** Paul Azinger (4-4) def. Greg Norman (4-5) on 2nd hole of sudden death. **1995:** Steve Elkington (3) def. Colin Montgomerie (4) on 1st hole of sudden death. **1996:** Mark Brooks (4) def. Kenny Perry (5) on 1st hole of sudden death. **2000:** Tiger Woods (3-4-5—12) won a three-hole playoff over Bob May (4-4-5—13).

Major Championship Leaders

Through 2001; active PGA players in **bold** type.

	US Open	British Open	PGA	Masters	US Am	British Am	Total
Jack Nicklaus	4	3	5	6	2	0	**20**
Bobby Jones	4	3	0	0	5	1	**13**
Walter Hagen	2	4	5	0	0	0	**11**
Ben Hogan	4	1	2	2	0	0	**9**
Gary Player	1	3	2	3	0	0	**9**
Tiger Woods	1	1	2	2	3	0	**9**
John Ball	0	1	0	0	0	8	**9**
Arnold Palmer	1	2	0	4	1	0	**8**
Tom Watson	1	5	0	2	0	0	**8**
Harold Hilton	0	2	0	0	1	4	**7**
Gene Sarazen	2	1	3	1	0	0	**7**
Sam Snead	0	1	3	3	0	0	**7**
Harry Vardon	1	6	0	0	0	0	**7**
Nick Faldo	0	3	0	3	0	0	**6**
Lee Trevino	2	2	2	0	0	0	**6**

Tournaments: U.S. Open, British Open, PGA Championship, Masters, U.S. Amateur and British Amateur.

Grand Slam Summary

The only golfer ever to win a recognized Grand Slam—four major championships in a single season—was Bobby Jones in 1930. That year, Jones won the U.S. and British Opens as well as the U.S. and British Amateurs.

The men's professional Grand Slam—the Masters, U.S. Open, British Open and PGA Championship—did not gain acceptance until 30 years later when Arnold Palmer won the 1960 Masters and U.S. Open. The media wrote that the popular Palmer was chasing the "new" Grand Slam and would have to win the British Open and the PGA to claim it. He did not, but then nobody has before or since.

Three wins in one year: Ben Hogan (1953) and Tiger Woods (2000). **Two wins in one year** (18): Jack Nicklaus (5 times); Ben Hogan, Arnold Palmer and Tom Watson (twice); Nick Faldo, Mark O'Meara, Gary Player, Nick Price, Sam Snead, Lee Trevino and Craig Wood (once).

Year	Masters	US Open	Brit. Open	PGA	Year	Masters	US Open	Brit. Open	PGA
1934	H. Smith	Dutra	Cotton	Runyan	1968	Goalby	Trevino	Player	Boros
1935	Sarazen	Parks	Perry	Revolta	1969	Archer	Moody	Jacklin	Floyd
1936	H. Smith	Manero	Padgham	Shute	1970	Casper	Jacklin	Nicklaus	Stockton
1937	B. Nelson	Guldahl	Cotton	Shute	1971	Coody	Trevino	Trevino	Nicklaus
1938	Picard	Guldahl	Whitcombe	Runyan	1972	Nicklaus	Nicklaus	Trevino	Player
1939	Guldahl	B. Nelson	Burton	Picard	1973	Aaron	J. Miller	Weiskopf	Nicklaus
1940	Demaret	Little	—	B. Nelson	1974	Player	Irwin	Player	Trevino
1941	Wood	Wood	—	Ghezzi	1975	Nicklaus	L. Graham	T. Watson	Nicklaus
1942	B. Nelson	—	—	Snead	1976	Floyd	J. Pate	Miller	Stockton
1943	—	—	—	—	1977	T. Watson	H. Green	T. Watson	L. Wadkins
1944	—	—	—	Hamilton	1978	Player	North	Nicklaus	Mahaffey
1945	—	—	—	B. Nelson	1979	Zoeller	Irwin	Ballesteros	D. Graham
1946	Keiser	Mangrum	Snead	Hogan	1980	Ballesteros	Nicklaus	T. Watson	Nicklaus
1947	Demaret	Worsham	F. Daly	Ferrier	1981	T. Watson	D. Graham	Rogers	L. Nelson
1948	Harmon	Hogan	Cotton	Hogan	1982	Stadler	T. Watson	T. Watson	Floyd
1949	Snead	Middlecoff	Locke	Snead	1983	Ballesteros	L. Nelson	T. Watson	Sutton
1950	Demaret	Hogan	Locke	Harper	1984	Crenshaw	Zoeller	Ballesteros	Trevino
1951	Hogan	Hogan	Faulkner	Snead	1985	Langer	North	Lyle	H. Green
1952	Snead	Boros	Locke	Turnesa	1986	Nicklaus	Floyd	Norman	Tway
1953	Hogan	Hogan	Hogan	Burkemo	1987	Mize	S. Simpson	Faldo	L. Nelson
1954	Snead	Furgol	Thomson	Harbert	1988	Lyle	Strange	Ballesteros	Sluman
1955	Middlecoff	Fleck	Thomson	Ford	1989	Faldo	Strange	Calcavecchia	Stewart
1956	Burke	Middlecoff	Thomson	Burke	1990	Faldo	Irwin	Faldo	Grady
1957	Ford	Mayer	Locke	L. Hebert	1991	Woosnam	Stewart	Baker-Finch	J. Daly
1958	Palmer	Bolt	Thomson	Finsterwald	1992	Couples	Kite	Faldo	Price
1959	Wall	Casper	Player	Rosburg	1993	Langer	Janzen	Norman	Azinger
1960	Palmer	Palmer	Nagle	J. Hebert	1994	Olazabal	Els	Price	Price
1961	Player	Littler	Palmer	J. Barber	1995	Crenshaw	Pavin	Daly	Elkington
1962	Palmer	Nicklaus	Palmer	Player	1996	Faldo	S. Jones	Lehman	Brooks
1963	Nicklaus	Boros	Charles	Nicklaus	1997	Woods	Els	Leonard	Love
1964	Palmer	Venturi	Lema	Nichols	1998	O'Meara	Janzen	O'Meara	Singh
1965	Nicklaus	Player	Thomson	Marr	1999	Olazabal	Stewart	Lawrie	Woods
1966	Nicklaus	Casper	Nicklaus	Geiberger	2000	Singh	Woods	Woods	Woods
1967	Brewer Jr.	Nicklaus	De Vicenzo	January	2001	Woods	Goosen	Duval	Toms

Vardon Trophy

Awarded since 1937 by the PGA of America to the PGA Tour regular with the lowest adjusted scoring average. The award is named after Harry Vardon, the six-time British Open champion who also won the U.S. Open in 1900. A point system was used from 1937-41.

Multiple winners: Billy Casper and Lee Trevino (5); Arnold Palmer and Sam Snead (4); Ben Hogan, Greg Norman and Tom Watson (3); Fred Couples, Bruce Crampton, Tom Kite, Lloyd Mangrum, Nick Price and Tiger Woods (2).

Year	Pts	Year	Avg	Year	Avg
1937	Harry Cooper 500	1961	Arnold Palmer 69.85	1982	Tom Kite 70.21
1938	Sam Snead 520	1962	Arnold Palmer 70.27	1983	Ray Floyd 70.61
1939	Byron Nelson 473	1963	Billy Casper 70.58	1984	Calvin Peete........70.56
1940	Ben Hogan 423	1964	Arnold Palmer 70.01	1985	Don Pooley 70.36
1941	Ben Hogan 494	1965	Billy Casper 70.85	1986	Scott Hoch........70.08
1942-46	No award	1966	Billy Casper 70.27	1987	Dan Pohl.........70.25
Year	**Avg**	1967	Arnold Palmer 70.18	1988	Chip Beck 69.46
1947	Jimmy Demaret 69.90	1968	Billy Casper 69.82	1989	Greg Norman 69.49
1948	Ben Hogan.........69.30	1969	Dave Hill 70.34	1990	Greg Norman 69.10
1949	Sam Snead 69.37	1970	Lee Trevino 70.64	1991	Fred Couples 69.59
1950	Sam Snead 69.23	1971	Lee Trevino 70.27	1992	Fred Couples 69.38
1951	Lloyd Mangrum 70.05	1972	Lee Trevino 70.89	1993	Nick Price 69.11
1952	Jack Burke 70.54	1973	Bruce Crampton 70.57	1994	Greg Norman 68.81
1953	Lloyd Mangrum 70.22	1974	Lee Trevino 70.53	1995	Steve Elkington ...69.62
1954	E.J. Harrison 70.41	1975	Bruce Crampton 70.51	1996	Tom Lehman.......69.32
1955	Sam Snead 69.86	1976	Don January 70.56	1997	Nick Price 68.98
1956	Cary Middlecoff 70.35	1977	Tom Watson 70.32	1998	David Duval.......69.13
1957	Dow Finsterwald ...70.30	1978	Tom Watson 70.16	1999	Tiger Woods 68.43
1958	Bob Rosburg 70.11	1979	Tom Watson 70.27	2000	Tiger Woods 67.79
1959	Art Wall 70.35	1980	Lee Trevino 69.73		
1960	Billy Casper 69.95	1981	Tom Kite 69.80		

U.S. Amateur

Match play from 1895-64, stroke play from 1965-72, match play 1973-79, 36-hole stroke-play qualifying before match play since 1979.

Multiple winners: Bobby Jones (5); Jerry Travers (4); Walter Travis and Tiger Woods (3); Deane Beman, Charles Coe, Gary Cowan, H. Chandler Egan, Chick Evans, Lawson Little, Jack Nicklaus, Francis Ouimet, Jay Sigel, William Turnesa, Bud Ward, Harvie Ward, and H.J. Whigham (2).

Year		Year		Year		Year	
1895	Charles Macdonald	1922	Jess Sweetser	1951	Billy Maxwell	1977	John Fought
1896	H.J. Whigham	1923	Max Marston	1952	Jack Westland	1978	John Cook
1897	H.J. Whigham	1924	Bobby Jones	1953	Gene Littler	1979	Mark O'Meara
1898	Findlay Douglas	1925	Bobby Jones	1954	Arnold Palmer	1980	Hal Sutton
1899	H.M. Harriman	1926	George Von Elm	1955	Harvie Ward	1981	Nathaniel Crosby
1900	Walter Travis	1927	Bobby Jones	1956	Harvie Ward	1982	Jay Sigel
1901	Walter Travis	1928	Bobby Jones	1957	Hillman Robbins	1983	Jay Sigel
1902	Louis James	1929	Harrison Johnston	1958	Charles Coe	1984	Scott Verplank
1903	Walter Travis	1930	Bobby Jones	1959	Jack Nicklaus	1985	Sam Randolph
1904	H. Chandler Egan	1931	Francis Ouimet	1960	Deane Beman	1986	Buddy Alexander
1905	H. Chandler Egan	1932	Ross Somerville	1961	Jack Nicklaus	1987	Billy Mayfair
1906	Eben Byers	1933	George Dunlap	1962	Labron Harris	1988	Eric Meeks
1907	Jerry Travers	1934	Lawson Little	1963	Deane Beman	1989	Chris Patton
1908	Jerry Travers	1935	Lawson Little	1964	Bill Campbell	1990	Phil Mickelson
1909	Robert Gardner	1936	John Fischer	1965	Bob Murphy	1991	Mitch Voges
1910	W.C. Fownes Jr.	1937	John Goodman	1966	Gary Cowan	1992	Justin Leonard
1911	Harold Hilton	1938	William Turnesa	1967	Bob Dickson	1993	John Harris
1912	Jerry Travers	1939	Bud Ward	1968	Bruce Fleisher	1994	Tiger Woods
1913	Jerry Travers	1940	Richard Chapman	1969	Steve Melnyk	1995	Tiger Woods
1914	Francis Ouimet	1941	Bud Ward	1970	Lanny Wadkins	1996	Tiger Woods
1915	Robert Gardner	1942-45	Not held	1971	Gary Cowan	1997	Matt Kuchar
1916	Chick Evans	1946	Ted Bishop	1972	Vinny Giles	1998	Hank Kuehne
1917-18	Not held	1947	Skee Riegel	1973	Craig Stadler	1999	David Gossett
1919	Davidson Herron	1948	William Turnesa	1974	Jerry Pate	2000	Jeff Quinney
1920	Chick Evans	1949	Charles Coe	1975	Fred Ridley	2001	Bubba Dickerson
1921	Jesse Guilford	1950	Sam Urzetta	1976	Bill Sander		

British Amateur

Match play since 1885.

Multiple winners: John Ball (8); Michael Bonallack (5); Harold Hilton (4); Joe Carr (3); Horace Hutchinson, Ernest Holderness, Trevor Homer, Johnny Laidley, Lawson Little, Peter McEvoy, Dick Siderowf, Frank Stranahan, Freddie Tait and Cyril Tolley (2).

Year		Year		Year		Year	
1885	Allen MacFie	1912	John Ball	1948	Frank Stranahan	1975	Vinny Giles
1886	Horace Hutchinson	1913	Harold Hilton	1949	Samuel McCready	1976	Dick Siderowf
1887	Horace Hutchinson	1914	J.L.C. Jenkins	1950	Frank Stranahan	1977	Peter McEvoy
1888	John Ball	1915-19	Not held	1951	Richard Chapman	1978	Peter McEvoy
1889	Johnny Laidley	1920	Cyril Tolley	1952	Harvie Ward	1979	Jay Sigel
1890	John Ball	1921	William Hunter	1953	Joe Carr	1980	Duncan Evans
1891	Johnny Laidley	1922	Ernest Holderness	1954	Douglas Bachli	1981	Phillipe Ploujoux
1892	John Ball	1923	Roger Wethered	1955	Joe Conrad	1982	Martin Thompson
1893	Peter Anderson	1924	Ernest Holderness	1956	John Beharrell	1983	Philip Parkin
1894	John Ball	1925	Robert Harris	1957	Reid Jack	1984	Jose-Maria Olazabal
1895	Leslie Balfour-Melville	1926	Jess Sweetser	1958	Joe Carr	1985	Garth McGimpsey
1896	Freddie Tait	1927	William Tweddell	1959	Deane Beman	1986	David Curry
1897	Jack Allan	1928	Thomas Perkins	1960	Joe Carr	1987	Paul Mayo
1898	Freddie Tait	1929	Cyril Tolley	1961	Michael Bonallack	1988	Christian Hardin
1899	John Ball	1930	Bobby Jones	1962	Richard Davies	1989	Stephen Dodd
1900	Harold Hilton	1931	Eric Smith	1963	Michael Lunt	1990	Rolf Muntz
1901	Harold Hilton	1932	John deForest	1964	Gordon Clark	1991	Gary Wolstenholme
1902	Charles Hutchings	1933	Michael Scott	1965	Michael Bonallack	1992	Stephen Dundas
1903	Robert Maxwell	1934	Lawson Little	1966	Bobby Cole	1993	Ian Pyman
1904	Walter Travis	1935	Lawson Little	1967	Bob Dickson	1994	Lee James
1905	Arthur Barry	1936	Hector Thomson	1968	Michael Bonallack	1995	Gordon Sherry
1906	James Robb	1937	Robert Sweeny Jr.	1969	Michael Bonallack	1996	Warren Bledon
1907	John Ball	1938	Charles Yates	1970	Michael Bonallack	1997	Craig Watson
1908	E.A. Lassen	1939	Alexander Kyle	1971	Steve Melnyk	1998	Sergio Garcia
1909	Robert Maxwell	1940-45	Not held	1972	Trevor Homer	1999	Graeme Storm
1910	John Ball	1946	James Bruen	1973	Dick Siderowf	2000	Mikko Ilonen
1911	Harold Hilton	1947	William Turnesa	1974	Trevor Homer	2001	Michael Hoey

WOMEN
Nabisco Championship

Formerly known as the Colgate Dinah Shore (1972-81) and the Nabisco Dinah Shore (1982-99), the tournament became the LPGA's fourth designated major championship in 1983. Shore's name, which was dropped from the tournament in 2000, is preserved with the Nabisco Dinah Shore Trophy, which is awarded to the winner. The tourney has been played at Mission Hills CC in Rancho Mirage, Calif., since it began; (*) indicates playoff winner.

Multiple winners: (as a major): Amy Alcott and Betsy King (3); Juli Inkster and Dottie Pepper (2).

Year	Winner	Score	Runner-up
1972	Jane Blalock	213	Carol Mann & Judy Rankin (216)
1973	Mickey Wright	284	Joyce Kazmierski (286)
1974	Jo Anne Prentice*	289	Jane Blalock & Sandra Haynie (289)
1975	Sandra Palmer	283	Kathy McMullen (284)
1976	Judy Rankin	285	Betty Burfeindt (288)
1977	Kathy Whitworth	289	JoAnne Carner & Sally Little (290)
1978	Sandra Post*	283	Penny Pulz (283)
1979	Sandra Post	276	Nancy Lopez (277)
1980	Donna Caponi	275	Amy Alcott (277)
1981	Nancy Lopez	277	Carolyn Hill (279)
1982	Sally Little	278	Hollis Stacy & Sandra Haynie (281)
1983	Amy Alcott	282	Beth Daniel & Kathy Whitworth (284)
1984	Juli Inkster*	280	Pat Bradley (280)
1985	Alice Miller	275	Jan Stephenson (278)
1986	Pat Bradley	280	Val Skinner (282)
1987	Betsy King*	283	Patty Sheehan (283)
1988	Amy Alcott	274	Colleen Walker (276)
1989	Juli Inkster	279	Tammie Green & JoAnne Carner (284)
1990	Betsy King	283	Kathy Postlewait & Shirley Furlong (285)
1991	Amy Alcott	273	Dottie Pepper (281)
1992	Dottie Pepper*	279	Juli Inkster (279)
1993	Helen Alfredsson	284	Amy Benz & Tina Barrett (286)
1994	Donna Andrews	276	Laura Davies (277)
1995	Nanci Bowen	285	Susie Redman (286)
1996	Patty Sheehan	281	Kelly Robbins, Meg Mallon & Annika Sorenstam (276)
1997	Betsy King	276	Kris Tschetter (278)
1998	Pat Hurst	281	Helen Dobson (282)
1999	Dottie Pepper	269	Meg Mallon (275)
2000	Karrie Webb	274	Dottie Pepper (284)
2001	Annika Sorenstam	281	Akiko Fukushima, Janice Moodie, Dottie Pepper, Rachel Teske & Karrie Webb (284)

*PLAYOFFS:

1974: Jo Ann Prentice def. Jane Blalock in sudden death. **1978:** Sandra Post def. Penny Pulz in sudden death. **1984:** Juli Inkster def. Pat Bradley in sudden death. **1987:** Betsy King def. Patty Sheehan in sudden death. **1992:** Dottie Pepper def. Juli Inkster in sudden death.

U.S. Women's Open

The U.S. Women's Open began under the direction of the defunct Women's Professional Golfers Assn. In 1946, passed to the LPGA in 1949 and to the USGA in 1953. The tournament used a match play format its first year then switched to stroke play; (*) indicates playoff winner and (a) indicates amateur winner.

Multiple winners: Betsy Rawls and Mickey Wright (4); Susie Maxwell Berning, Hollis Stacy and Babe Zaharias (3); JoAnne Carner, Donna Caponi, Betsy King, Patty Sheehan, Annika Sorenstam, Louise Suggs and Karrie Webb (2).

Year	Winner	Score	Runner-up	Course	Location
1946	Patty Berg	5&4	Betty Jameson	Spokane CC	Spokane, Wash.
1947	Betty Jameson	295	a-Sally Sessions & a-Rolly Riley (301)	Starmount Forest CC	Greensboro, N.C.
1948	Babe Zaharias	300	Betty Hicks (308)	Atlantic City CC	Northfield, N.J.
1949	Louise Suggs	291	Babe Zaharias (305)	Prince Georges CC	Landover, Md.
1950	Babe Zaharias	291	a-Betsy Rawls (300)	Rolling Hills CC	Wichita, Kan.
1951	Betsy Rawls	293	Louise Suggs (298)	Druid Hills GC	Atlanta, Ga.
1952	Louise Suggs	284	Marlene Hagge (291)	Bala GC	Philadelphia, Penn.
1953	Betsy Rawls*	302	Jackie Pung (302)	CC of Rochester	Rochester, N.Y.
1954	Babe Zaharias	291	Betty Hicks (303)	Salem CC	Peabody, Mass.
1955	Fay Crocker	299	Mary Lena Faulk (303)	Wichita CC	Wichita, Kan.
1956	Kathy Cornelius*	302	Barbara McIntire (302)	Northland CC	Duluth, Minn.
1957	Betsy Rawls	299	Patty Berg (305)	Winged Foot GC	Mamaroneck, N.Y.
1958	Mickey Wright	290	Louise Suggs (295)	Forest Lake CC	Detroit, Mich.
1959	Mickey Wright	287	Louise Suggs (289)	Chuchill Valley CC	Pittsburgh, Penn.
1960	Betsy Rawls	292	Joyce Ziske (293)	Worcester CC	Worcester, Mass.
1961	Mickey Wright	293	Betsy Rawls (299)	Baltusrol GC	Springfield, N.J.
1962	Murle Breer	301	Jo Anne Prentice & Ruth Jessen (303)	Dunes GC	Myrtle Beach, S.C.
1963	Mary Mills	289	Sandra Haynie & Louise Suggs (292)	Kenwood CC	Cincinnati, Ohio
1964	Mickey Wright*	290	Ruth Jessen (290)	San Diego CC	Chula Vista, Calif.
1965	Carol Mann	290	Kathy Cornelius (292)	Atlantic City CC	Northfield, N.J.
1966	Sandra Spuzich	297	Carol Mann (298)	Hazeltine National GC	Chaska, Minn.
1967	a-Catherine LaCoste	294	Susie Berning & Beth Stone (296)	Hot Springs GC	Hot Springs, Va.

U.S. Women's Open (Cont.)

Year	Winner	Score	Runner-up	Course	Location
1968	Susie Berning	289	Mickey Wright (292)	Moselem Springs GC	Fleetwood, Penn.
1969	Donna Caponi	294	Peggy Wilson (295)	Scenic Hills CC	Pensacola, Fla.
1970	Donna Caponi	287	Sandra Haynie (288)	Muskogee CC	Muskogee, Okla.
1971	JoAnne Carner	288	Kathy Whitworth (295)	Kahkwa CC	Erie, Penn.
1972	Susie Berning	299	Kathy Ahern, Pam Barnett & Judy Rankin (300)	Winged Foot GC	Mamaroneck, N.Y.
1973	Susie Berning	290	Gloria Ehret (295)	CC of Rochester	Rochester, N.Y.
1974	Sandra Haynie	295	Carol Mann & Beth Stone (296)	La Grange CC	La Grange, Ill.
1975	Sandra Palmer	295	JoAnne Carner, a-Nancy Lopez & Sandra Post (299)	Atlantic City CC	Northfield, N.J.
1976	JoAnne Carner*	292	Sandra Palmer (292)	Rolling Green CC	Springfield, Penn.
1977	Hollis Stacy	292	Nancy Lopez (294)	Hazeltine National GC	Chaska, Minn.
1978	Hollis Stacy	289	JoAnne Carner & Sally Little (290)	CC of Indianapolis	Indianapolis, Ind.
1979	Jerilyn Britz	284	Debbie Massey & Sandra Palmer (286)	Brooklawn CC	Fairfield, Conn.
1980	Amy Alcott	280	Hollis Stacy (289)	Richland CC	Nashville, Tenn.
1981	Pat Bradley	279	Beth Daniel (280)	La Grange CC	La Grange, Ill.
1982	Janet Anderson	283	Beth Daniel, Sandra Haynie & Donna White (289)	Del Paso CC	Sacramento, Calif.
1983	Jan Stephenson	290	JoAnne Carner (291)	Cedar Ridge CC	Tulsa, Okla.
1984	Hollis Stacy	290	Rosie Jones (291)	Salem CC	Peabody, Mass.
1985	Kathy Baker	280	Judy Dickenson (283)	Baltusrol GC	Springfield, N.J.
1986	Jane Geddes*	287	Sally Little (287)	NCR GC	Dayton, Ohio
1987	Laura Davies*	285	Ayako Okamoto & JoAnne Carner (285)	Plainfield CC	Plainfield, N.J.
1988	Liselotte Neumann	277	Patty Sheehan (280)	Baltimore CC	Baltimore, Md.
1989	Betsy King	278	Nancy Lopez (282)	Indianwood GC	Lake Orion, Mich.
1990	Betsy King	284	Patty Sheehan (285)	Atlanta Athletic Club	Duluth, Ga.
1991	Meg Mallon	283	Pat Bradley (285)	Colonial CC	Ft. Worth, Texas
1992	Patty Sheehan*	280	Juli Inkster (280)	Oakmont CC	Oakmont, Penn.
1993	Lauri Merten	280	Donna Andrews & Helen Alfredsson (281)	Crooked Stick GC	Carmel, Ind.
1994	Patty Sheehan	277	Tammie Green (278)	Indianwood CC	Lake Orion, Mich.
1995	Annika Sorenstam	278	Meg Mallon (279)	The Broadmoor	Colorado Springs, Colo.
1996	Annika Sorenstam	272	Kris Tschetter (278)	Pine Needles Lodge & GC	Southern Pines, N.C.
1997	Alison Nicholas	274	Nancy Lopez (275)	Pumpkin Ridge GC	Cornelius, Ore.
1998	Se Ri Pak*	290	a-Jenny Chuasiriporn (290)	Blackwolf Run GC	Kohler, Wis.
1999	Juli Inkster	272	Sherri Turner (277)	Old Waverly GC	West Point, Miss.
2000	Karrie Webb	282	Cristie Kerr & Meg Mallon (287)	Merit Club	Libertyville, Ill.
2001	Karrie Webb	273	Se Ri Pak (281)	Pine Needles Lodge & GC	Southern Pines, N.C.

*PLAYOFFS:

1953: Betsy Rawls (70) def. Jackie Pung (77) in 18 holes. **1956:** Kathy Cornelius (75) def. Barbara McIntire (82) in 18 holes. **1964:** Mickey Wright (70) def. Ruth Jessen (72) in 18 holes. **1976:** JoAnne Carner (76) def. Sandra Palmer (78) in 18 holes. **1986:** Jane Geddes (71) def. Sally Little (73) in 18 holes. **1987:** Laura Davies (71) def. Ayako Okamoto (73) and JoAnne Carner (74) in 18 holes. **1992:** Patty Sheehan (72) def. Juli Inkster (74) in 18 holes. **1998:** Se Ri Pak def. Jenny Chuasiriporn on the second sudden death hole after both players were tied after an 18-hole playoff.

LPGA Championship

Officially the McDonald's LPGA Championship since 1994 (Mazda sponsored from 1987-93), the tournament began in 1955 and has had extended stays at the Stardust CC in Las Vegas (1961-66), Pleasant Valley CC in Sutton, Mass. (1967-68, 70-74), the Jack Nicklaus Sports Center at Kings Island, Ohio (1978-89), Bethesda CC in Maryland (1990-93) and DuPont CC in Wilmington, Del. (since 1994); (*) indicates playoff winner and (#) weather-shortened.

Multiple winners: Mickey Wright (4); Nancy Lopez, Patty Sheehan and Kathy Whitworth (3); Donna Caponi, Laura Davies, Sandra Haynie, Juli Inkster, Mary Mills and Betsy Rawls (2).

Year	Winner	Score	Runner-up	Year	Winner	Score	Runner-up
1955	Beverly Hanson	220	Louise Suggs (223)	1963	Mickey Wright	294	Mary Lena Faulk & Mary Mills (296)
1956	Marlene Hagge*	291	Patty Berg (291)				
1957	Louise Suggs	285	Wiffi Smith (288)	1964	Mary Mills	278	Mickey Wright (280)
1958	Mickey Wright	288	Fay Crocker (294)	1965	Sandra Haynie	279	Clifford A. Creed (280)
1959	Betsy Rawls	288	Patty Berg (289)	1966	Gloria Ehret	282	Mickey Wright (285)
				1967	Kathy Whitworth	284	Shirley Englehorn (285)
1960	Mickey Wright	292	Louise Suggs (295)	1968	Sandra Post	294	Kathy Whitworth (294)
1961	Mickey Wright	287	Louise Suggs (296)	1969	Betsy Rawls	293	Susie Berning & Carol Mann (297)
1962	Judy Kimball	282	Shirley Spork (286)				

Year	Winner	Score	Runner-up
1970	Shirley Englehorn	.285	Kathy Whitworth (285)
1971	Kathy Whitworth	.288	Kathy Ahern (292)
1972	Kathy Ahern	.293	Jane Blalock (299)
1973	Mary Mills	.288	Betty Burfeindt (289)
1974	Sandra Haynie	.288	JoAnne Carner (290)
1975	Kathy Whitworth	.288	Sandra Haynie (289)
1976	Betty Burfeindt	.287	Judy Rankin (288)
1977	Chako Higuchi	.279	Pat Bradley, Sandra Post & Judy Rankin (282)
1978	Nancy Lopez	.275	Amy Alcott (281)
1979	Donna Caponi	.279	Jerilyn Britz (282)
1980	Sally Little	.285	Jane Blalock (288)
1981	Donna Caponi	.280	Jerilyn Britz & Pat Meyers (281)
1982	Jan Stephenson	.279	JoAnne Carner (281)
1983	Patty Sheehan	.279	Sandra Haynie (281)
1984	Patty Sheehan	.272	Beth Daniel & Pat Bradley (282)
1985	Nancy Lopez	.273	Alice Miller (281)
1986	Pat Bradley	.277	Patty Sheehan (278)

Year	Winner	Score	Runner-up
1987	Jane Geddes	.275	Betsy King (275)
1988	Sherri Turner	.281	Amy Alcott (282)
1989	Nancy Lopez	.274	Ayako Okamoto (277)
1990	Beth Daniel	.280	Rosie Jones (281)
1991	Meg Mallon	.274	Pat Bradley & Ayako Okamoto (275)
1992	Betsy King	.267	JoAnne Carner, Karen Noble & Liselotte Neumann (278)
1993	Patty Sheehan	.275	Lauri Merten (276)
1994	Laura Davies	.279	Alice Ritzman (280)
1995	Kelly Robbins	.274	Laura Davies (275)
1996	Laura Davies#	.213	Julie Piers (214)
1997	Chris Johnson*	.281	Leta Lindley (281)
1998	Se Ri Pak	.273	Donna Andrews & Lisa Hackney (276)
1999	Juli Inkster	.268	Liselotte Neumann (272)
2000	Juli Inkster*	.281	Stefania Croce (281)
2001	Karrie Webb	.270	Laura Diaz (272)

*PLAYOFFS:

1956: Marlene Hagge def. Patti Berg in sudden death. **1968:** Sandra Post (68) def. Kathy Whitworth (75) in 18 holes. **1970:** Shirley Englehorn def. Kathy Whitworth in sudden death. **1997:** Chris Johnson def. Leta Lindley in sudden death. **2000:** Juli Inkster def. Stefania Croce in sudden death.

Women's British Open

Sponsored by Weetabix, this has been an official stop on the LPGA Tour since 1994, and it became the fourth designated major championship in 2001 when it replaced the du Maurier Classic.

Multiple winners Sherri Steinhauer and Karrie Webb (2); (as a major): none.

Year	Winner	Score	Runner-up	Course	Location
1994	Liselotte Neumann	.280	Dottie Mochrie & Annika Sorenstam (283)	Woburn G&CC	Milton Keynes, England
1995	Karrie Webb	.278	Annika Sorenstam & Jill McGill (284)	Woburn G&CC	Milton Keynes, England
1996	Emilee Klein	.277	Penny Hammel & Amy Alcott (284)	Woburn G&CC	Milton Keynes, England
1997	Karrie Webb	.269	Rosie Jones (277)	Sunningdale GC	Berkshire, England
1998	Sherri Steinhauer	.292	Sophie Gustafson & Brandie Burton (293)	Royal Lytham	Lytham, England
1999	Sherri Steinhauer	.283	Annika Sorenstam (284)	Woburn G&CC	Milton Keynes, England
2000	Sophie Gustafson	.282	Kirsty Taylor, Liselotte Neumann, Becky Iverson & Meg Mallon (284)	Royal Birkdale	Southport, England
2001	Se Ri Pak	.277	Mi Hyun Kim (279)	Sunningdale GC	Berkshire, England

du Maurier Classic (1979-2000)

This Canadian stop on the LPGA Tour was considered a major title from 1979-2000; (*) indicates playoff winner.

Multiple winners (as a major): Pat Bradley (3); Brandie Burton (2).

Year	Winner	Year	Winner	Year	Winner	Year	Winner
1973	Jocelyne Bourassa	1981	Jan Stephenson	1989	Tammie Green	1997	Colleen Walker
1974	Carole Jo Skala	1982	Sandra Haynie	1990	Cathy Johnston	1998	Brandie Burton
1975	JoAnne Carner	1983	Hollis Stacy	1991	Nancy Scranton	1999	Karrie Webb
1976	Donna Caponi	1984	Juli Inkster	1992	Sherri Steinhauer	2000	Meg Mallon
1977	Judy Rankin	1985	Pat Bradley	1993	Brandie Burton*		
1978	JoAnne Carner	1986	Pat Bradley*	1994	Martha Nause		
1979	Amy Alcott	1987	Jody Rosenthal	1995	Jenny Lidback		
1980	Pat Bradley	1988	Sally Little	1996	Laura Davies		

Titleholders Championship (1937-72)

The Titleholders was considered a major title on the women's tour until it was discontinued after the 1972 tournament.

Multiple winners: Patty Berg (7); Louise Suggs (4); Babe Zaharias (3); Dorothy Kirby, Marilynn Smith, Kathy Whitworth and Mickey Wright (2).

Year		Year		Year		Year	
1937	Patty Berg	1947	Babe Zaharias	1955	Patty Berg	1963	Marilynn Smith
1938	Patty Berg	1948	Patty Berg	1956	Louise Suggs	1964	Marilynn Smith
1939	Patty Berg	1949	Peggy Kirk	1957	Patty Berg	1965	Kathy Whitworth
1940	Betty Hicks	1950	Babe Zaharias	1958	Beverly Hanson	1966	Kathy Whitworth
1941	Dorothy Kirby	1951	Pat O'Sullivan	1959	Louise Suggs	1967-71	Not held
1942	Dorothy Kirby	1952	Babe Zaharias	1960	Fay Crocker	1972	Sandra Palmer
1943-45	Not held	1953	Patty Berg	1961	Mickey Wright		
1946	Louise Suggs	1954	Louise Suggs	1962	Mickey Wright		

Western Open (1930-67)

The Western Open was considered a major title on the women's tour until it was discontinued after the 1967 tournament.

Multiple winners: Patty Berg (7); Louise Suggs and Babe Zaharias (4); Mickey Wright (3); June Beebe, Opal Hill, Betty Jameson and Betsy Rawls (2).

Year		Year		Year		Year	
1930	Mrs. Lee Mida	1940	Babe Zaharias	1950	Babe Zaharias	1960	Joyce Ziske
1931	June Beebe	1941	Patty Berg	1951	Patty Berg	1961	Mary Lena Faulk
1932	Jane Weiller	1942	Betty Jameson	1952	Betsy Rawls	1962	Mickey Wright
1933	June Beebe	1943	Patty Berg	1953	Louise Suggs	1963	Mickey Wright
1934	Marian McDougall	1944	Babe Zaharias	1954	Betty Jameson	1964	Carol Mann
1935	Opal Hill	1945	Babe Zaharias	1955	Patty Berg	1965	Susie Maxwell
1936	Opal Hill	1946	Louise Suggs	1956	Beverly Hanson	1966	Mickey Wright
1937	Betty Hicks	1947	Louise Suggs	1957	Patty Berg	1967	Kathy Whitworth
1938	Bea Barrett	1948	Patty Berg	1958	Patty Berg		
1939	Helen Dettweiler	1949	Louise Suggs	1959	Betsy Rawls		

Grand Slam Summary

From 1955-66, the U.S. Open, LPGA Championship, Western Open and Titleholders tournaments served as the Women's Grand Slam. From 1983-2000, however, the U.S. Open, LPGA, du Maurier Classic in Canada and Nabisco Championship were the major events. In 2001, the Weetabix Women's British Open replaced the du Maurier Classic as the tour's fourth major. No one has won a four-event Grand Slam on the women's tour.

Three wins in one year (3): Babe Zaharias (1950), Mickey Wright (1961) and Pat Bradley (1986).

Two wins in one year (16): Patty Berg and Mickey Wright (3 times); Juli Inkster, Louise Suggs and Karrie Webb (twice); Laura Davies, Sandra Haynie, Betsy King, Meg Mallon, Se Ri Pak, Betsy Rawls and Kathy Whitworth (once).

Year	LPGA	US Open	T'holders	Western	Year	LPGA	US Open	T'holders	Western
1937	—	—	Berg	Hicks	1964	Mills	Wright	M. Smith	Mann
1938	—	—	Berg	Barrett	1965	Haynie	Mann	Whitworth	Maxwell
1939	—	—	Berg	Dettweiler	1966	Ehret	Spuzich	Whitworth	Wright
1940	—	—	Hicks	Zaharias	1967	Whitworth	a-LaCoste	—	Whitworth
1941	—	—	Kirby	Berg	1968	Post	Berning	—	
1942	—	—	Kirby	Jameson	1969	Rawls	Caponi	—	
1943	—	—	—	Berg	1970	Englehorn	Caponi	—	
1944	—	—	—	Zaharias	1971	Whitworth	Carner	—	
1945	—	—	—	Zaharias	1972	Ahern	Berning	Palmer	—
1946	—	Berg	Suggs	Suggs	1973	Mills	Berning	—	
1947	—	Jameson	Zaharias	Suggs	1974	Haynie	Haynie	—	
1948	—	Zaharias	Berg	Berg	1975	Whitworth	Palmer	—	
1949	—	Suggs	Kirk	Suggs	1976	Burfeindt	Carner	—	
1950	—	Zaharias	Zaharias	Zaharias	1977	Higuchi	Stacy	—	
1951	—	Rawls	O'Sullivan	Berg	1978	Lopez	Stacy	—	

Year	LPGA	US Open	T'holders	Western
1952	—	Suggs	Zaharias	Rawls
1953	—	Rawls	Berg	Suggs
1954	—	Zaharias	Suggs	Jameson
1955	Hanson	Crocker	Berg	Berg
1956	Hagge	Cornelius	Suggs	Hanson
1957	Suggs	Rawls	Berg	Berg
1958	Wright	Wright	Hanson	Berg
1959	Rawls	Wright	Suggs	Rawls
1960	Wright	Rawls	Crocker	Ziske
1961	Wright	Wright	Wright	Faulk
1962	Kimball	Lindstrom	Wright	Wright
1963	Wright	Mills	M. Smith	Wright

Year	LPGA	US Open	duMaurier	Nabisco
1979	Caponi	Britz	Alcott	
1980	Little	Alcott	Bradley	—
1981	Caponi	Bradley	Stephenson	—
1982	Stephenson	Anderson	Haynie	—
1983	Sheehan	Stephenson	Stacy	Alcott
1984	Sheehan	Stacy	Inkster	Inkster
1985	Lopez	Baker	Bradley	Miller
1986	Bradley	Geddes	Bradley	Bradley
1987	Geddes	Davies	Rosenthal	King
1988	Turner	Neumann	Little	Alcott
1989	Lopez	King	Green	Inkster

Year	LPGA	US Open	duMaurier	Nabisco
1990	Daniel	King	Johnston	King
1991	Mallon	Mallon	Scranton	Alcott
1992	King	Sheehan	Steinhauer	Pepper
1993	Sheehan	Merten	Burton	Alfredsson
1994	Davies	Sheehan	Nause	Andrews
1995	Robbins	Sorenstam	Lidback	Bowen
1996	Davies	Sorenstam	Davies	Sheehan

Year	LPGA	US Open	duMaurier	Nabisco
1997	Johnson	Nicholas	Walker	King
1998	Pak	Pak	Burton	Hurst
1999	Inkster	Inkster	Webb	Pepper
2000	Inkster	Webb	Mallon	Webb
Year	**LPGA**	**US Open**	**Brit. Open**	**Nabisco**
2001	Webb	Webb	Pak	Sorenstam

Major Championship Leaders

Through 2001; active LPGA players in **bold** type.

	US Open	LPGA	Nabisco	British Open	duM	Title	Western	US Am	Brit Am	Total
Patty Berg	1	0	0	0	0	7	7	1	0	**16**
Mickey Wright	4	4	0	0	0	2	3	0	0	**13**
Louise Suggs	2	1	0	0	0	4	4	1	1	**13**
Babe Zaharias	3	0	0	0	0	3	4	1	1	**12**
Juli Inkster	1	2	2	0	1	0	0	3	0	**9**
Betsy Rawls	4	2	0	0	0	0	2	0	0	**8**
JoAnne Carner	2	0	0	0	0	0	0	5	0	**7**
Kathy Whitworth	0	3	0	0	0	2	1	0	0	**6**
Pat Bradley	1	1	1	0	3	0	0	0	0	**6**
Betsy King	2	1	3	0	0	0	0	0	0	**6**
Patty Sheehan	2	3	1	0	0	0	0	0	0	**6**
Glenna C. Vare	0	0	0	0	0	0	0	6	0	**6**

Tournaments: U.S. Open, LPGA Championship, British Open, Nabisco Championship, du Maurier Classic (1979-2000), Titleholders (1930-72), Western Open (1937-67), U.S. Amateur, and British Amateur.

U.S. Women's Amateur

Stroke play in 1895, match play since 1896.

Multiple winners: Glenna Collett Vare (6); JoAnne Gunderson Carner (5); Margaret Curtis, Beatrix Hoyt, Dorothy Campbell Hurd, Juli Inkster, Alexa Stirling, Virginia Van Wie, Anne Quast Decker Welts (3); Kay Cockerill, Beth Daniel, Vicki Goetze, Katherine Harley, Genevieve Hecker, Betty Jameson, Kelli Kuehne and Barbara McIntire (2).

Year		Year		Year		Year	
1895	Mrs. C.S. Brown	1922	Glenna Collett	1951	Dorothy Kirby	1977	Beth Daniel
1896	Beatrix Hoyt	1923	Edith Cummings	1952	Jacqueline Pung	1978	Cathy Sherk
1897	Beatrix Hoyt	1924	Dorothy C. Hurd	1953	Mary Lena Faulk	1979	Carolyn Hill
1898	Beatrix Hoyt	1925	Glenna Collett	1954	Barbara Romack		
1899	Ruth Underhill	1926	Helen Stetson	1955	Patricia Lesser	1980	Juli Inkster
		1927	Miriam Burns Horn	1956	Marlene Stewart	1981	Juli Inkster
1900	Frances Griscom	1928	Glenna Collett	1957	JoAnne Gunderson	1982	Juli Inkster
1901	Genevieve Hecker	1929	Glenna Collett	1958	Anne Quast	1983	Joanne Pacillo
1902	Genevieve Hecker			1959	Barbara McIntire	1984	Deb Richard
1903	Bessie Anthony	1930	Glenna Collett			1985	Michiko Hattori
1904	Georgianna Bishop	1931	Helen Hicks	1960	JoAnne Gunderson	1986	Kay Cockerill
1905	Pauline Mackay	1932	Virginia Van Wie	1961	Anne Quast Decker	1987	Kay Cockerill
1906	Harriot Curtis	1933	Virginia Van Wie	1962	JoAnne Gunderson	1988	Pearl Sinn
1907	Margaret Curtis	1934	Virginia Van Wie	1963	Anne Quast Welts	1989	Vicki Goetze
1908	Katherine Harley	1935	Glenna Collett Vare	1964	Barbara McIntire		
1909	Dorothy Campbell	1936	Pamela Barton	1965	Jean Ashley	1990	Pat Hurst
		1937	Estelle Lawson	1966	JoAnne G. Carner	1991	Amy Fruhwirth
1910	Dorothy Campbell	1938	Patty Berg	1967	Mary Lou Dill	1992	Vicki Goetze
1911	Margaret Curtis	1939	Betty Jameson	1968	JoAnne G. Carner	1993	Jill McGill
1912	Margaret Curtis			1969	Catherine Lacoste	1994	Wendy Ward
1913	Gladys Ravenscroft	1940	Betty Jameson			1995	Kelli Kuehne
1914	Katherine Harley	1941	Elizabeth Hicks	1970	Martha Wilkinson	1996	Kelli Kuehne
1915	Florence Vanderbeck	1942-45	Not held	1971	Laura Baugh	1997	Silvia Cavalleri
1916	Alexa Stirling	1946	Babe D. Zaharias	1972	Mary Budke	1998	Grace Park
1917-18	Not held	1947	Louise Suggs	1973	Carol Semple	1999	Dorothy Delasin
1919	Alexa Stirling	1948	Grace Lenczyk	1974	Cynthia Hill		
		1949	Dorothy Porter	1975	Beth Daniel	2000	Marcy Newton
1920	Alexa Stirling	1950	Beverly Hanson	1976	Donna Horton	2001	Meredith Duncan
1921	Marion Hollins						

British Women's Amateur
Match play since 1893.

Multiple winners: Cecil Leitch and Joyce Wethered (4); May Hezlet, Lady Margaret Scott, Brigitte Varangot and Enid Wilson (3); Rhone Adair, Pam Barton, Dorothy Campbell, Elizabeth Chadwick, Helen Holm, Marley Spearman, Frances Stephens, Jessie Valentine and Michelle Walker (2).

Year		Year		Year		Year	
1893	Lady Margaret Scott	1926	Cecil Leitch	1960	Barbara McIntire	1989	Helen Dobson
1894	Lady Margaret Scott	1927	Simone de la Chaume	1961	Marley Spearman	1990	Julie Wade Hall
1895	Lady Margaret Scott	1928	Nanette le Blan	1962	Marley Spearman	1991	Valerie Michaud
1896	Amy Pascoe	1929	Joyce Wethered	1963	Brigitte Varangot	1992	Bernille Pedersen
1897	Edith Orr			1964	Carol Sorenson	1993	Catriona Lambert
1898	Lena Thomson	1930	Diana Fishwick	1965	Brigitte Varangot	1994	Emma Duggleby
1899	May Hezlet	1931	Enid Wilson	1966	Elizabeth Chadwick	1995	Julie Wade Hall
		1932	Enid Wilson	1967	Elizabeth Chadwick	1996	Kelli Kuehne
1900	Rhona Adair	1933	Enid Wilson	1968	Brigitte Varangot	1997	Alison Rose
1901	Mary Graham	1934	Helen Holm	1969	Catherine Lacoste	1998	Kim Rostron
1902	May Hezlet	1935	Wanda Morgan			1999	Marine Monnet
1903	Rhona Adair	1936	Pam Barton	1970	Dinah Oxley		
1904	Lottie Dod	1937	Jessie Anderson	1971	Michelle Walker	2000	Rebecca Hudson
1905	Bertha Thompson	1938	Helen Holm	1972	Michelle Walker	2001	Marta Prieto
1906	Mrs. W. Kennion	1939	Pam Barton	1973	Ann Irvin		
1907	May Hezlet			1974	Carol Semple		
1908	Maud Titterton	1940-45	Not held	1975	Nancy Roth Syms		
1909	Dorothy Campbell	1946	Jean Hetherington	1976	Cathy Panton		
		1947	Babe Zaharias	1977	Angela Uzielli		
1910	Elsie Grant-Suttie	1948	Louise Suggs	1978	Edwina Kennedy		
1911	Dorothy Campbell	1949	Frances Stephens	1979	Maureen Madill		
1912	Gladys Ravenscroft						
1913	Muriel Dodd	1950	Lally de St. Sauveur	1980	Anne Quast Sander		
1914	Cecil Leitch	1951	Catherine MacCann	1981	Belle Robertson		
1915-19	Not held	1952	Moira Paterson	1982	Kitrina Douglas		
		1953	Marlene Stewart	1983	Jill Thornhill		
1920	Cecil Leitch	1954	Frances Stephens	1984	Jody Rosenthal		
1921	Cecil Leitch	1955	Jessie Valentine	1985	Lillian Behan		
1922	Joyce Wethered	1956	Wiffi Smith	1986	Marnie McGuire		
1923	Doris Chambers	1957	Philomena Garvey	1987	Janet Collingham		
1924	Joyce Wethered	1958	Jessie Valentine	1988	Joanne Furby		
1925	Joyce Wethered	1959	Elizabeth Price				

Vare Trophy

The Vare Trophy for best scoring average by a player on the LPGA Tour has been awarded since 1937 by the LPGA. The award is named after Glenna Collett Vare, winner of six U.S. women's amateur titles from 1922-35.

Multiple winners: Kathy Whitworth (7); JoAnne Carner and Mickey Wright (5); Patty Berg, Beth Daniel, Nancy Lopez, Judy Rankin, Annika Sorenstam and Karrie Webb (3); Pat Bradley and Betsy King (2).

Year		Avg	Year		Avg	Year		Avg
1953	Patty Berg	75.00	1970	Kathy Whitworth	72.26	1987	Betsy King	71.14
1954	Babe Zaharias	75.48	1971	Kathy Whitworth	72.88	1988	Colleen Walker	71.26
1955	Patty Berg	74.47	1972	Kathy Whitworth	72.38	1989	Beth Daniel	70.38
1956	Patty Berg	74.57	1973	Judy Rankin	73.08			
1957	Louise Suggs	74.64	1974	JoAnne Carner	72.87	1990	Beth Daniel	70.54
1958	Beverly Hanson	74.92	1975	JoAnne Carner	72.40	1991	Pat Bradley	70.66
1959	Betsy Rawls	74.03	1976	Judy Rankin	72.25	1992	Dottie Pepper	70.80
			1977	Judy Rankin	72.16	1993	Betsy King	70.85
1960	Mickey Wright	73.25	1978	Nancy Lopez	71.76	1994	Beth Daniel	70.90
1961	Mickey Wright	73.55	1979	Nancy Lopez	71.20	1995	Annika Sorenstam	71.00
1962	Mickey Wright	73.67				1996	Annika Sorenstam	70.47
1963	Mickey Wright	72.81	1980	Amy Alcott	71.51	1997	Karrie Webb	70.00
1964	Mickey Wright	72.46	1981	JoAnne Carner	71.75	1998	Annika Sorenstam	69.99
1965	Kathy Whitworth	72.61	1982	JoAnne Carner	71.49	1999	Karrie Webb	69.43
1966	Kathy Whitworth	72.60	1983	JoAnne Carner	71.41			
1967	Kathy Whitworth	72.74	1984	Patty Sheehan	71.40	2000	Karrie Webb	70.05
1968	Carol Mann	72.04	1985	Nancy Lopez	70.73			
1969	Kathy Whitworth	72.38	1986	Pat Bradley	71.10			

Senior PGA
The Tradition

First played in 1989 and played every year since at the Golf Club at Desert Mountain in Scottsdale, Ariz.
Multiple winners: Jack Nicklaus (4); Gil Morgan (2).

Year		Year		Year		Year	
1989	Don Bies	1993	Tom Shaw	1997	Gil Morgan	2001	Doug Tewell
1990	Jack Nicklaus	1994	Ray Floyd*	1998	Gil Morgan		
1991	Jack Nicklaus	1995	Jack Nicklaus*	1999	Graham Marsh		
1992	Lee Trevino	1996	Jack Nicklaus	2000	Tom Kite		

*PLAYOFFS:

1994: Ray Floyd def. Dale Douglas on 1st extra hole. **1995:** Jack Nicklaus def. Isao Aoki on 3rd extra hole.

Senior PGA Championship

First played in 1937. Two championships played in 1979 and 1984.
Multiple winners: Sam Snead (6); Hale Irwin, Gary Player, Al Watrous and Eddie Williams (3); Julius Boros, Jock Hutchison, Don January, Arnold Palmer, Paul Runyan, Gene Sarazen and Lee Trevino (2).

Year		Year		Year		Year	
1937	Jock Hutchison	1955	Mortie Dutra	1972	Sam Snead	1987	Chi Chi Rodriguez
1938	Fred McLeod*	1956	Pete Burke	1973	Sam Snead	1988	Gary Player
1939	Not held	1957	Al Watrous	1974	Roberto De Vicenzo	1989	Larry Mowry
1940	Otto Hackbarth*	1958	Gene Sarazen	1975	Charlie Sifford*	1990	Gary Player
1941	Jack Burke	1959	Willie Goggin	1976	Pete Cooper	1991	Jack Nicklaus
1942	Eddie Williams	1960	Dick Metz	1977	Julius Boros	1992	Lee Trevino
1943-44	Not held	1961	Paul Runyan	1978	Joe Jiminez*	1993	Tom Wargo*
1945	Eddie Williams	1962	Paul Runyan	1979	Jack Fleck*	1994	Lee Trevino
1946	Eddie Williams*	1963	Herman Barron	1979	Don January	1995	Ray Floyd
1947	Jock Hutchison	1964	Sam Snead	1980	Arnold Palmer*	1996	Hale Irwin
1948	Charles McKenna	1965	Sam Snead	1981	Miller Barber	1997	Hale Irwin
1949	Marshall Crichton	1966	Fred Haas	1982	Don January	1998	Hale Irwin
1950	Al Watrous	1967	Sam Snead	1983	Not held	1999	Allen Doyle
1951	Al Watrous*	1968	Chandler Harper	1984	Arnold Palmer	2000	Doug Tewell
1952	Ernest Newnham	1969	Tommy Bolt	1984	Peter Thomson	2001	Tom Watson
1953	Harry Schwab	1970	Sam Snead	1985	Not held		
1954	Gene Sarazen	1971	Julius Boros	1986	Gary Player		

*PLAYOFFS:

1938: Fred McLeod def. Otto Hackbarth in 18 holes. **1940:** Otto Hackbarth def. Jock Hutchison in 36 holes. **1946:** Eddie Williams def. Jock Hutchison in 18 holes. **1951:** Al Watrous def. Jock Hutchison in 18 holes. **1975:** Charlie Sifford def. Fred Wampler on 1st extra hole **1978:** Joe Jiminez def. Paul Harney on 1st extra hole **1979:** Jack Fleck def. Bill Johnston on 1st extra hole. **1980:** Arnold Palmer def. Paul Harney on 1st extra hole. **1993:** Tom Wargo def. Bruce Crampton on 2nd extra hole.

U.S. Senior Open

Established in 1980 for senior players 55 years old and over, the minimum age was dropped to 50 (the PGA Seniors Tour entry age) in 1981. Arnold Palmer, Billy Casper, Hale Irwin, Orville Moody, Jack Nicklaus and Lee Trevino are the only golfers who have won both the U.S. Open and U.S. Senior Open.
Multiple winners: Miller Barber (3); Hale Irwin, Jack Nicklaus and Gary Player (2).

Year		Year		Year		Year	
1980	Roberto De Vicenzo	1986	Dale Douglass	1992	Larry Laoretti	1998	Hale Irwin
1981	Arnold Palmer*	1987	Gary Player	1993	Jack Nicklaus	1999	Dave Eichelberger
1982	Miller Barber	1988	Gary Player*	1994	Simon Hobday	2000	Hale Irwin
1983	Bill Casper*	1989	Orville Moody	1995	Tom Weiskopf	2001	Bruce Fleisher
1984	Miller Barber	1990	Lee Trevino	1996	Dave Stockton		
1985	Miller Barber	1991	Jack Nicklaus*	1997	Graham Marsh		

*PLAYOFFS:

1981: Arnold Palmer (70) def. Bob Stone (74) and Billy Casper (77) in 18 holes. **1983:** Tied at 75 after 18-hole playoff, Casper def. Rod Funseth with a birdie on the 1st extra hole. **1988:** Gary Player (68) def. Bob Charles (70) in 18 holes. **1991:** Jack Nicklaus (65) def. Chi Chi Rodriguez (69) in 18 holes.

Senior Players Championship

First played in 1983 and contested in Cleveland (1983-86), Ponte Vedra, Fla. (1987-89) and Dearborn, Mich. (since 1990).
Multiple winners: Ray Floyd, Arnold Palmer and Dave Stockton (2).

Year		Year		Year		Year	
1983	Miller Barber	1988	Billy Casper	1993	Jim Colbert	1998	Gil Morgan
1984	Arnold Palmer	1989	Orville Moody	1994	Dave Stockton	1999	Hale Irwin
1985	Arnold Palmer	1990	Jack Nicklaus	1995	J.C. Snead*	2000	Ray Floyd
1986	Chi Chi Rodriguez	1991	Jim Albus	1996	Ray Floyd	2001	Allen Doyle*
1987	Gary Player	1992	Dave Stockton	1997	Larry Gilbert		

*PLAYOFF:

1995: J.C. Snead def. Jack Nicklaus on 1st extra hole. **2001:** Allen Doyle def. Doug Tewell on 1st extra hole.

Major Senior Championship Leaders

Through 2001. All players are still active.

	Senior PGA	US Open	Senior Players	Trad	Total			Senior PGA	US Open	Senior Players	Trad	Total
1 Jack Nicklaus	1	2	1	4	8	6 Miller Barber	0	2	1	0	3
2 Hale Irwin	3	2	1	0	6	Gil Morgan	0	0	1	2	3
Gary Player	3	2	1	0	6	Arnold Palmer	1	0	2	0	3
4 Ray Floyd	1	0	2	1	4	Dave Stockton	0	1	2	0	3
Lee Trevino	2	1	0	1	4						

Grand Slam Summary

The Senior Grand Slam has officially consisted of The Tradition, the Senior PGA Championship, the Senior Players Championship and the U.S. Senior Open since 1990. Jack Nicklaus won three of the four events in 1991, but no one has won all four in one season.

Three wins in one year: Jack Nicklaus (1991). **Two wins in one year:** Gary Player (twice); Hale Irwin, Gil Morgan, Orville Moody, Jack Nicklaus, Arnold Palmer and Lee Trevino (once).

Year	Tradition	Sr. PGA	Players	US Open	Year	Tradition	Sr. PGA	Players	US Open
1983	—	—	M. Barber	Casper	1993	Shaw	Wargo	Colbert	Nicklaus
1984	—	Palmer	Palmer	M. Barber	1994	Floyd	Trevino	Stockton	Hobday
1985	—	Thomson	Palmer	M. Barber	1995	Nicklaus	Floyd	Snead	Weiskopf
1986	—	Player	Rodriguez	Douglass	1996	Nicklaus	Irwin	Floyd	Stockton
1987	—	Rodriguez	Player	Player	1997	Morgan	Irwin	Gilbert	Marsh
1988	—	Player	Casper	Player	1998	Morgan	Irwin	Morgan	Irwin
1989	Bies	Mowry	Moody	Moody	1999	Marsh	Doyle	Irwin	Eichelberger
1990	Nicklaus	Player	Nicklaus	Trevino	2000	Kite	Tewell	Floyd	Irwin
1991	Nicklaus	Nicklaus	Albus	Nicklaus	2001	Tewell	Watson	Doyle	Fleisher
1992	Trevino	Trevino	Stockton	Laoretti					

Annual Money Leaders

Official annual money leaders on the PGA, European PGA, Senior PGA and LPGA tours.

PGA

Multiple leaders: Jack Nicklaus (8); Ben Hogan and Tom Watson (5); Arnold Palmer (4); Greg Norman, Sam Snead, Curtis Strange and Tiger Woods (3); Julius Boros, Billy Casper, Tom Kite, Byron Nelson and Nick Price (2).

Year		Earnings	Year		Earnings	Year		Earnings
1934	Paul Runyan	$6,767	1957	Dick Mayer	$65,835	1980	Tom Watson	$530,808
1935	Johnny Revolta	9,543	1958	Arnold Palmer	42,608	1981	Tom Kite	375,699
1936	Horton Smith	7,682	1959	Art Wall	53,168	1982	Craig Stadler	446,462
1937	Harry Cooper	14,139	1960	Arnold Palmer	75,263	1983	Hal Sutton	426,668
1938	Sam Snead	19,534	1961	Gary Player	64,540	1984	Tom Watson	476,260
1939	Henry Picard	10,303	1962	Arnold Palmer	81,448	1985	Curtis Strange	542,321
1940	Ben Hogan	10,655	1963	Arnold Palmer	128,230	1986	Greg Norman	653,296
1941	Ben Hogan	18,358	1964	Jack Nicklaus	113,285	1987	Curtis Strange	925,941
1942	Ben Hogan	13,143	1965	Jack Nicklaus	140,752	1988	Curtis Strange	1,147,644
1943	No records kept		1966	Billy Casper	121,945	1989	Tom Kite	1,395,278
1944	Byron Nelson	37,968	1967	Jack Nicklaus	188,998	1990	Greg Norman	1,165,477
1945	Byron Nelson	63,336	1968	Billy Casper	205,169	1991	Corey Pavin	979,430
1946	Ben Hogan	42,556	1969	Frank Beard	164,707	1992	Fred Couples	1,344,188
1947	Jimmy Demaret	27,937	1970	Lee Trevino	157,037	1993	Nick Price	1,478,557
1948	Ben Hogan	32,112	1971	Jack Nicklaus	244,491	1994	Nick Price	1,499,927
1949	Sam Snead	31,594	1972	Jack Nicklaus	320,542	1995	Greg Norman	1,654,959
1950	Sam Snead	35,759	1973	Jack Nicklaus	308,362	1996	Tom Lehman	1,780,159
1951	Lloyd Mangrum	26,089	1974	Johnny Miller	353,022	1997	Tiger Woods	2,066,833
1952	Julius Boros	37,033	1975	Jack Nicklaus	298,149	1998	David Duval	2,591,031
1953	Lew Worsham	34,002	1976	Jack Nicklaus	266,439	1999	Tiger Woods	6,616,585
1954	Bob Toski	65,820	1977	Tom Watson	310,653	2000	Tiger Woods	9,188,321
1955	Julius Boros	63,122	1978	Tom Watson	362,429			
1956	Ted Kroll	72,836	1979	Tom Watson	462,636			

Note: In 1944-45, Nelson's winnings were in War Bonds.

Senior PGA

Multiple leaders: Don January (3); Miller Barber, Bob Charles, Jim Colbert, Hale Irwin, Dave Stockton and Lee Trevino (2).

Year		Earnings	Year		Earnings	Year		Earnings
1980	Don January	$44,100	1987	Chi Chi Rodriguez	$509,145	1994	Dave Stockton	$1,402,519
1981	Miller Barber	83,136	1988	Bob Charles	533,929	1995	Jim Colbert	1,444,386
1982	Miller Barber	106,890	1989	Bob Charles	725,887	1996	Jim Colbert	1,627,890
1983	Don January	237,571	1990	Lee Trevino	1,190,518	1997	Hale Irwin	2,343,36
1984	Don January	328,597	1991	Mike Hill	1,065,657	1998	Hale Irwin	2,861,94
1985	Peter Thomson	386,724	1992	Lee Trevino	1,027,002	1999	Bruce Fleisher	2,515,70
1986	Bruce Crampton	454,299	1993	Dave Stockton	1,175,944	2000	Larry Nelson	2,708,00

European PGA

Official money in the Volvo Order of Merit was awarded in British pounds from 1961-98 and euros since 1999.
Multiple leaders: Colin Montgomerie (7); Seve Ballesteros (6); Sandy Lyle (3); Gay Brewer Jr., Nick Faldo, Bernard Hunt, Bernhard Langer, Peter Thomson and Ian Woosnam (2).

Year		Earnings	Year		Earnings	Year		Earnings
1961	Bernard Hunt	£4,492	1975	Dale Hayes	£20,507	1989	Ronan Rafferty	£465,981
1962	Peter Thomson	5,764	1976	Seve Ballesteros	39,504	1990	Ian Woosnam	737,977
1963	Bernard Hunt	7,209	1977	Seve Ballesteros	46,436	1991	Seve Ballesteros	790,811
1964	Neil Coles	7,890	1978	Seve Ballesteros	54,348	1992	Nick Faldo	1,220,540
1965	Peter Thomson	7,011	1979	Sandy Lyle	49,233	1993	Colin Montgomerie	798,145
1966	Bruce Devlin	13,205	1980	Greg Norman	74,829	1994	Colin Montgomerie	920,647
1967	Gay Brewer Jr.	20,235	1981	Bernhard Langer	95,991	1995	Colin Montgomerie	1,038,718
1968	Gay Brewer Jr.	23,107	1982	Sandy Lyle	£86,141	1996	Colin Montgomerie	1,034,752
1969	Billy Casper	23,483	1983	Nick Faldo	140,761	1997	Colin Montgomerie	1,583,904
1970	Christy O'Connor	31,532	1984	Bernhard Langer	160,883	1998	Colin Montgomerie	1,082,833
1971	Gary Player	11,281	1985	Sandy Lyle	254,711	1999	C. Montgomerie	€2,066,885
1972	Bob Charles	18,538	1986	Seve Ballesteros	259,275	2000	Lee Westwood	3,125,147
1973	Tony Jacklin	24,839	1987	Ian Woosnam	439,075			
1974	Peter Oosterhuis	32,127	1988	Seve Ballesteros	502,000			

LPGA

Multiple leaders: Kathy Whitworth (8); Mickey Wright (4); Patty Berg, JoAnne Carner, Beth Daniel, Betsy King, Nancy Lopez, Annika Sorenstam and Karrie Webb (3); Pat Bradley, Judy Rankin, Betsy Rawls, Louise Suggs and Babe Zaharias (2).

Year		Earnings	Year		Earnings	Year		Earnings
1950	Babe Zaharias	$14,800	1967	Kathy Whitworth	$32,937	1984	Betsy King	$266,771
1951	Babe Zaharias	15,087	1968	Kathy Whitworth	48,379	1985	Nancy Lopez	416,472
1952	Betsy Rawls	14,505	1969	Carol Mann	49,152	1986	Pat Bradley	492,021
1953	Louise Suggs	19,816	1970	Kathy Whitworth	30,235	1987	Ayako Okamoto	466,034
1954	Patty Berg	16,011	1971	Kathy Whitworth	41,181	1988	Sherri Turner	350,851
1955	Patty Berg	16,492	1972	Kathy Whitworth	65,063	1989	Betsy King	654,132
1956	Marlene Hagge	20,235	1973	Kathy Whitworth	82,864	1990	Beth Daniel	863,578
1957	Patty Berg	16,272	1974	JoAnne Carner	87,094	1991	Pat Bradley	763,118
1958	Beverly Hanson	12,639	1975	Sandra Palmer	76,374	1992	Dottie Pepper	693,335
1959	Betsy Rawls	26,774	1976	Judy Rankin	150,734	1993	Betsy King	595,992
1960	Louise Suggs	16,892	1977	Judy Rankin	122,890	1994	Laura Davies	687,201
1961	Mickey Wright	22,236	1978	Nancy Lopez	189,814	1995	Annika Sorenstam	666,533
1962	Mickey Wright	21,641	1979	Nancy Lopez	197,489	1996	Karrie Webb	1,002,000
1963	Mickey Wright	31,269	1980	Beth Daniel	231,000	1997	Annika Sorenstam	1,236,789
1964	Mickey Wright	29,800	1981	Beth Daniel	206,998	1998	Annika Sorenstam	1,092,748
1965	Kathy Whitworth	28,658	1982	JoAnne Carner	310,400	1999	Karrie Webb	1,591,959
1966	Kathy Whitworth	33,517	1983	JoAnne Carner	291,404	2000	Karrie Webb	1,876,853

All-Time Leaders

PGA, Senior PGA and LPGA leaders through 2000.

Tournaments Won

PGA

		No			No			No
1	Sam Snead	81	9	Gene Sarazen	38		Paul Runyan	29
2	Jack Nicklaus	70	10	Lloyd Mangrum	36	18	Lee Trevino	27
3	Ben Hogan	63	11	Tom Watson	34	19	Henry Picard	26
4	Arnold Palmer	60	12	Horton Smith	32	20	Tommy Armour	24
5	Byron Nelson	52	13	Harry Cooper	31		Macdonald Smith	24
6	Billy Casper	51		Jimmy Demaret	31		Johnny Miller	24
7	Walter Hagen	40	15	Leo Diegel	30		Tiger Woods	24
	Cary Middlecoff	40	16	Gene Littler	29			

Senior PGA

		No			No			No
1	Lee Trevino	29	8	George Archer	19	15	Jim Dent	12
	Hale Irwin	29		Jim Colbert	19	16	Dale Douglass	11
3	Miller Barber	24		Gary Player	19		Bruce Fleisher	11
4	Bob Charles	23	11	Mike Hill	18		Orville Moody	11
5	Don January	22		Gil Morgan	18		Bob Murphy	11
	Chi Chi Rodriguez	22	13	Dave Stockton	14		Larry Nelson	11
7	Bruce Crampton	20		Raymond Floyd	14		Peter Thomson	11

All-Time Leaders (Cont.)
LPGA

		No				No				No
1	Kathy Whitworth	88	9	Babe Zaharias	41		16	Jane Blalock	27
2	Mickey Wright	82	10	Carol Mann	38		17	Judy Rankin	26
3	Patty Berg	60	11	Patty Sheehan	35		18	Marlene Hagge	25
4	Louise Suggs	58	12	Betsy King	33			Juli Inkster	25
5	Betsy Rawls	55	13	Beth Daniel	32		20	Donna Caponi	24
6	Nancy Lopez	48	14	Pat Bradley	31				
7	JoAnne Carner	43	15	Amy Alcott	29				
8	Sandra Haynie	42							

Money Won
PGA
All-time earnings through 2000.

		Earnings				Earnings				Earnings
1	Tiger Woods	$20,503,450	10	Scott Hoch	$11,667,883		19	Loren Roberts	$9,282,413
2	Davis Love III	14,825,227	11	Mark O'Meara	11,586,578		20	Justin Leonard	9,136,157
3	Phil Mickelson	13,434,115	12	Mark Calcavecchia	11,417,773		21	Corey Pavin	9,077,769
4	Nick Price	13,190,669	13	Vijay Singh	11,083,624		22	Jim Furyk	8,952,859
5	Greg Norman	13,087,832	14	Tom Kite	10,654,707		23	Jeff Sluman	8,792,621
6	David Duval	12,510,792	15	Tom Lehman	10,180,736		24	John Huston	8,762,277
7	Fred Couples	12,295,284	16	Paul Azinger	10,178,834		25	Jeff Maggert	8,559,214
8	Hal Sutton	12,162,000	17	Ernie Els	9,680,179				
9	Payne Stewart	11,737,008	18	Tom Watson	9,583,681				

Senior PGA
All-time earnings through 2000.

		Earnings				Earnings				Earnings
1	Hale Irwin	$11,774,453	10	Mike Hill	$7,023,822		19	Tom Wargo	$5,626,463
2	Jim Colbert	9,623,844	11	Isao Aoki	6,881,214		20	Gary Player	5,368,573
3	Lee Trevino	9,211,216	12	Chi Chi Rodriguez	6,526,164		21	Jim Albus	5,340,502
4	Dave Stockton	8,618,426	13	Bob Murphy	6,298,039		22	Al Geiberger	5,133,466
5	Bob Charles	8,284,081	14	Dale Douglass	6,285,059		23	Bruce Summerhays	5,018,068
6	Gil Morgan	7,863,446	15	Larry Nelson	5,976,461		24	Bruce Fleisher	4,889,682
7	George Archer	7,783,007	16	Jay Sigel	5,906,834		25	Dana Quigley	4,661,376
8	Ray Floyd	7,683,314	17	Graham Marsh	5,797,394				
9	Jim Dent	7,540,494	18	J.C. Snead	5,791,293				

European PGA
All-time earnings through 2000.

		Earnings				Earnings				Earnings
1	C. Montgomerie	€15,119,827	10	Seve Ballesteros	€6,659,360		19	Barry Lane	€4,307,432
2	Bernhard Langer	10,390,824	11	Sam Torrance	6,552,669		20	Thomas Björn	4,254,937
3	Ian Woosnam	9,174,224	12	M. A. Jimenez	6,305,746		21	Padraig Harrington	4,201,295
4	Tiger Woods	9,163,264	13	Vijay Singh	5,403,154		22	Fred Couples	4,102,064
5	Nick Faldo	8,278,557	14	Mark McNulty	5,192,848		23	Gordon Brand Jr.	4,050,379
6	Lee Westwood	8,160,645	15	Mark James	4,835,494		24	Ronan Rafferty	3,816,081
7	Darren Clarke	7,789,153	16	Eduardo Romero	4,722,056		25	Per-Ulrik Johansson	3,783,393
8	Ernie Els	7,766,194	17	Costantino Rocca	4,652,478				
9	Jose Maria Olazabal	7,740,529	18	Retief Goosen	4,382,783				

LPGA
All-time earnings through 2000.

		Earnings				Earnings				Earnings
1	Betsy King	$6,828,688	10	Nancy Lopez	$5,297,955		19	Chris Johnson	$3,360,592
2	Annika Sorenstam	6,200,596	11	Laura Davies	5,203,382		20	Brandie Burton	3,176,389
3	Karrie Webb	6,162,895	12	Rosie Jones	4,898,924		21	Jan Stephenson	2,987,515
4	Juli Inkster	6,057,400	13	Liselotte Neumann	4,048,629		22	JoAnne Carner	2,941,552
5	Beth Daniel	6,022,461	14	Kelly Robbins	3,956,643		23	Michelle McGann	2,915,291
6	Dottie Pepper	5,882,131	15	Jane Geddes	3,705,450		25	Ayako Okamoto	2,749,508
7	Pat Bradley	5,743,605	16	Sherri Steinhauer	3,627,096		25	Colleen Walker	2,747,277
8	Patty Sheehan	5,500,983	17	Tammie Green	3,386,308				
9	Meg Mallon	5,466,338	18	Amy Alcott	3,368,340				

Official World Rankings

Begun in 1986, the Official World Golf Ranking (formerly the Sony World Ranking) combines the best golfers on the five PGA men's tours throughout the world. Rankings are based on a rolling two-year period and weighed in favor of more recent results. While annual winners are not announced, certain players reaching No. 1 have dominated each year.

Multiple winners (at year's end): Greg Norman (6); Tiger Woods (4); Nick Faldo (3); Seve Ballesteros (2).

Year		Year		Year		Year	
1986	Seve Ballesteros	1990	Nick Faldo	1993	Nick Faldo	1998	Tiger Woods
1987	Greg Norman		& Greg Norman	1994	Nick Price	1999	Tiger Woods
1988	Greg Norman	1991	Ian Woosnam	1995	Greg Norman	2000	Tiger Woods
1989	Seve Ballesteros	1992	Fred Couples	1996	Greg Norman		
	& Greg Norman		& Nick Faldo	1997	Tiger Woods		

Annual Awards
PGA of America Player of the Year

Awarded by the PGA of America; based on points scale that weighs performance in major tournaments, regular events, money earned and scoring average.

Multiple winners: Tom Watson (6); Jack Nicklaus (5); Ben Hogan (4); Tiger Woods (3); Julius Boros, Billy Casper, Arnold Palmer and Nick Price.

Year		Year		Year		Year	
1948	Ben Hogan	1962	Arnold Palmer	1976	Jack Nicklaus	1990	Nick Faldo
1949	Sam Snead	1963	Julius Boros	1977	Tom Watson	1991	Corey Pavin
1950	Ben Hogan	1964	Ken Venturi	1978	Tom Watson	1992	Fred Couples
1951	Ben Hogan	1965	Dave Marr	1979	Tom Watson	1993	Nick Price
1952	Julius Boros	1966	Billy Casper	1980	Tom Watson	1994	Nick Price
1953	Ben Hogan	1967	Jack Nicklaus	1981	Bill Rogers	1995	Greg Norman
1954	Ed Furgol	1968	No award	1982	Tom Watson	1996	Tom Lehman
1955	Doug Ford	1969	Orville Moody	1983	Hal Sutton	1997	Tiger Woods
1956	Jack Burke	1970	Billy Casper	1984	Tom Watson	1998	Mark O'Meara
1957	Dick Mayer	1971	Lee Trevino	1985	Lanny Wadkins	1999	Tiger Woods
1958	Dow Finsterwald	1972	Jack Nicklaus	1986	Bob Tway	2000	Tiger Woods
1959	Art Wall	1973	Jack Nicklaus	1987	Paul Azinger		
1960	Arnold Palmer	1974	Johnny Miller	1988	Curtis Strange		
1961	Jerry Barber	1975	Jack Nicklaus	1989	Tom Kite		

PGA Tour Player of the Year

Award by the PGA Tour starting in 1990. Winner voted on by tour members from list of nominees. Winner receives the Jack Nicklaus Trophy, which originated in 1997.

Multiple winners: Tiger Woods (3); Fred Couples and Nick Price (2).

Year		Year		Year		Year	
1990	Wayne Levi	1993	Nick Price	1996	Tom Lehman	1999	Tiger Woods
1991	Fred Couples	1994	Nick Price	1997	Tiger Woods	2000	Tiger Woods
1992	Fred Couples	1995	Greg Norman	1998	Mark O'Meara		

PGA Tour Rookie of the Year

Awarded by the PGA Tour in 1990. Winner voted on by tour members from list of first-year nominees.

Year		Year		Year		Year	
1990	Robert Gamez	1993	Vijay Singh	1996	Tiger Woods	1999	Carlos Franco
1991	John Daly	1994	Ernie Els	1997	Stewart Cink	2000	Michael Clark II
1992	Mark Carnevale	1995	Woody Austin	1998	Steve Flesch		

PGA Senior Player of the Year

Awarded by th PGA Seniors Tour starting in 1990. Winner voted on by tour members from list of nominees.
Multiple winner: Lee Trevino (3); Jim Colbert and Hale Irwin (2).

Year		Year		Year		Year	
1990	Lee Trevino	1992	Lee Trevino	1995	Jim Colbert	1998	Hale Irwin
1991	George Archer	1993	Dave Stockton	1996	Jim Colbert	1999	Bruce Fleisher
	& Mike Hill	1994	Lee Trevino	1997	Hale Irwin	2000	Larry Nelson

PGA Senior Tour Rookie of the Year

Awarded by th PGA Tour starting in 1990. Winner voted on by tour members from list of first-year nominees.

Year		Year		Year		Year	
1990	Lee Trevino	1993	Bob Murphy	1996	John Bland	1999	Bruce Fleisher
1991	Jim Colbert	1994	Jay Sigel	1997	Gil Morgan	2000	Doug Tewell
1992	Dave Stockton	1995	Hale Irwin	1998	Joe Inman		

Annual Awards (Cont.)
European Golfer of the Year

Officially, the Ritz Club Trophy (1985-92), Johnnie Walker Trophy (1993-97) and Asprey and Garrard Golfer of the Year (1998-present); voting done by panel of European golf writers and tour members.

Multiple winners: Colin Montgomerie (4); Seve Ballesteros and Nick Faldo (3); Bernhard Langer and Lee Westwood (2).

Year		Year		Year		Year	
1985	Bernhard Langer	1989	Nick Faldo	1993	Bernhard Langer	1997	Colin Montgomerie
1986	Seve Ballesteros	1990	Nick Faldo	1994	Ernie Els	1998	Lee Westwood
1987	Ian Woosnam	1991	Seve Ballesteros	1995	Colin Montgomerie	1999	Colin Montgomerie
1988	Seve Ballesteros	1992	Nick Faldo	1996	Colin Montgomerie	2000	Lee Westwood

LPGA Player of the Year

Awarded by the LPGA; based on performance points accumulated during the year.

Multiple winners: Kathy Whitworth (7); Nancy Lopez (4); JoAnne Carner, Beth Daniel, Betsy King and Annika Sorenstam (3); Pat Bradley, Judy Rankin and Karrie Webb (2).

Year		Year		Year		Year	
1966	Kathy Whitworth	1975	Sandra Palmer	1984	Betsy King	1993	Betsy King
1967	Kathy Whitworth	1976	Judy Rankin	1985	Nancy Lopez	1994	Beth Daniel
1968	Kathy Whitworth	1977	Judy Rankin	1986	Pat Bradley	1995	Annika Sorenstam
1969	Kathy Whitworth	1978	Nancy Lopez	1987	Ayako Okamoto	1996	Laura Davies
1970	Sandra Haynie	1979	Nancy Lopez	1988	Nancy Lopez	1997	Annika Sorenstam
1971	Kathy Whitworth	1980	Beth Daniel	1989	Betsy King	1998	Annika Sorenstam
1972	Kathy Whitworth	1981	JoAnne Carner	1990	Beth Daniel	1999	Karrie Webb
1973	Kathy Whitworth	1982	JoAnne Carner	1991	Pat Bradley	2000	Karrie Webb
1974	JoAnne Carner	1983	Patty Sheehan	1992	Dottie Mochrie		

LPGA Rookie of the Year

Awarded by the LPGA; based on performance points accumulated during the year.

Year		Year		Year		Year	
1962	Mary Mills	1972	Jocelyne Bourassa	1982	Patti Rizzo	1992	Helen Alfredsson
1963	Clifford Ann Creed	1973	Laura Baugh	1983	Stephanie Farwig	1993	Suzanne Strudwick
1964	Susie Berning	1974	Jan Stephenson	1984	Juli Inkster	1994	Annika Sorenstam
1965	Margie Masters	1975	Amy Alcott	1985	Penny Hammel	1995	Pat Hurst
1966	Jan Ferraris	1976	Bonnie Lauer	1986	Jody Rosenthal	1996	Karrie Webb
1967	Sharron Moran	1977	Debbie Massey	1987	Tammie Green	1997	Lisa Hackney
1968	Sandra Post	1978	Nancy Lopez	1988	Liselotte Neumann	1998	Se Ri Pak
1969	Jane Blalock	1979	Beth Daniel	1989	Pamela Wright	1999	Mi Hyun Kim
1970	JoAnne Carner	1980	Myra Van Hoose	1990	Hiromi Kobayashi	2000	Dorothy Delasin
1971	Sally Little	1981	Patty Sheehan	1991	Brandie Burton		

National Team Competition
MEN
Ryder Cup

The Ryder Cup was presented by British seed merchant and businessman Samuel Ryder in 1927 for competition between professional golfers from Great Britain and the United States. The British team was expanded to include Irish players in 1973 and the rest of Europe in 1979. The United States leads the series 24-7-2 after 33 matches.

Year		Year		Year		Year	
1927	USA, 9½-2½	1951	USA, 9½-2½	1969	Draw, 16-16	1987	Europe, 15-13
1929	Britain-Ireland, 7-5	1953	USA, 6½-5½	1971	USA, 18½-13½	1989	Draw, 14-14
1931	USA, 9-3	1955	USA, 8-4	1973	USA, 19-13	1991	USA, 14½-13½
1933	Great Britain, 6½-5½	1957	Britain-Ireland, 7½-4½	1975	USA, 21-11	1993	USA, 15-13
1935	USA, 9-3	1959	USA, 8½-3½	1977	USA, 12½-13½	1995	Europe, 14½-13½
1937	USA, 8-4	1961	USA, 14½-9½	1979	USA, 17-11	1997	Europe, 14½-13½
1939-45	Not held	1963	USA, 23-9	1981	USA, 18½-9½	1999	USA, 14½-13½
1947	USA, 11-1	1965	USA, 19½-12½	1983	USA, 14½-13½	2001	Postponed until 2002
1949	USA, 7-5	1967	USA, 23½-8½	1985	Europe, 16½-11½		

Playing Sites

1927—Worcester CC (Mass.); **1929**—Moortown, England; **1931**—Scioto CC (Ohio); **1933**—Southport & Ainsdale, England; **1935**—Ridgewood CC (N.J.); **1937**—Southport & Ainsdale, England; **1939-45**—Not held; **1947**—Portland CC (Ore.); **1949**—Ganton GC, England; **1951**—Pinehurst CC (N.C.); **1953**—Wentworth, England; **1955**—Thunderbird Ranch &CC (Calif.); **1957**—Lindrick GC, England; **1959**—Eldorado CC (Calif.); **1961**—Royal Lytham & St. Annes, England; **1963**—East Lake CC (Ga.); **1965**—Royal Birkdale, England; **1967**—Champions GC (Tex.); **1969**—Royal Birkdale, England; **1971**—Old Warson CC (Mo.); **1973**—Muirfield, Scotland; **1975**—Laurel Valley GC (Pa.); **1977**—Royal Lytham & St. Annes, England; **1979**—The Greenbrier (W.Va.); **1981**—Walton Heath GC, England; **1983**—PGA National GC (Fla.); **1985**—The Belfry, England; **1987**—Muirfield Village GC (Ohio); **1989**—The Belfry, England; **1991**—Ocean Course (S.C.); **1993**—The Belfry, England; **1995**—Oak Hill CC (N.Y.); **1997**—Valderrama, Costa del Sol, Spain; **1999**—The Country Club (Mass.); **2002**—The Belfry, England; **2004**—Oakland Hills CC (Mich.).

Walker Cup

The Walker Cup was presented by American businessman George Herbert Walker in 1922 for competition between amateur golfers from Great Britain, Ireland and the United States. The U.S. leads the series against the combined Great Britain-Ireland team, 31-6-1, after 38 matches.

Year		Year		Year		Year	
1922	USA, 8-4	1940-46	Not held	1965	Draw, 12-12	1985	USA, 13-11
1923	USA, 6½-5½	1947	USA, 8-4	1967	USA, 15-9	1987	USA, 16½-7½
1924	USA, 9-3	1949	USA, 10-2	1969	USA, 13-11	1989	Britain-Ireland,
1926	USA, 6½-5½	1951	USA, 7½-4½	1971	Britain-Ireland, 13-11		12½-11½
1928	USA, 11-1	1953	USA, 9-3	1973	USA, 14-10	1991	USA, 14-10
1930	USA, 10-2	1955	USA, 10-2	1975	USA, 15½-8½	1993	USA, 19-5
1932	USA, 9½-2½	1957	USA, 8½-3½	1977	USA, 16-8	1995	Britain-Ireland, 14-10
1934	USA, 9½-2½	1959	USA, 9-3	1979	USA, 15½-8½	1997	USA, 18-6
1936	USA, 10½-1½	1961	USA, 11-1	1981	USA, 15-9	1999	Britain-Ireland, 15-9
1938	Britain-Ireland, 7½-4½	1963	USA, 14-10	1983	USA, 13½-10½	2001	Britain-Ireland, 15-9

Presidents Cup

The Presidents Cup is a biennial event played in non-Ryder Cup years in which the world's best non-European players compete against players from the United States. The U.S. leads the series, 3-1.

Year		Year	
1994	USA, 20-12	1998	International, 20½-11½
1996	USA, 16½-15½	2000	USA, 21½-10½

WOMEN

Solheim Cup

The Solheim Cup was presented by the Karsten Manufacturing Co. in 1990 for competition between women professional golfers from Europe and the United States. The U.S. leads the series, 4-2.

Year		Year		Year	
1990	USA, 11½-4½	1994	USA, 13-7	1998	USA, 16-12
1992	Europe, 11½-6½	1996	USA, 17-11	2000	Europe, 14½-11½

Playing Sites

1990—Lake Nona CC (Fla.); **1992**—Dalmahoy CC, Scotland; **1994**—The Greenbrier (W. Va.); **1996**—Marriott St. Pierre Hotel G&CC, Wales; **1998**—Muirfield Village GC (Ohio); **2000**—Loch Lomond GC, Scotland; **2002**—Interlachen CC (Minn.); **2004**—Barseback G&CC, Sweden.

Curtis Cup

Named after British golfing sisters Harriot and Margaret Curtis, the Curtis Cup was first contested in 1932 between teams of women amateurs from the United States and the British Isles.

Competed for every other year since 1932 (except during WWII). The U.S. leads the series, 22-6-3, after 31 matches.

Year		Year		Year		Year	
1932	USA, 5½-3½	1954	USA, 6-3	1970	USA, 11½-6½	1986	British Isles, 13-5
1934	USA, 6½-2½	1956	British Isles, 5-4	1972	USA, 10-8	1988	British Isles, 11-7
1936	Draw, 4½-4½	1958	Draw, 4½-4½	1974	USA, 13-5	1990	USA, 14-4
1938	USA, 5½-3½	1960	USA, 6½-2½	1976	USA, 11½-6½	1992	British Isles, 10-8
1940-46	Not held	1962	USA, 8-1	1978	USA, 12-6	1994	Draw, 9-9
1948	USA, 6½-2½	1964	USA, 10½-7½	1980	USA, 13-5	1996	British Isles, 11½-6½
1950	USA, 7½-1½	1966	USA, 13-5	1982	USA, 14½-3½	1998	USA, 10-8
1952	British Isles, 5-4	1968	USA, 10½-7½	1984	USA, 9½-8½	2000	USA, 10-8

<hr>

COLLEGES

Men's NCAA Division I Champions

College championships decided by match play from 1897-1964 and stroke play since 1965.

Multiple winners (Teams): Yale (21); Houston (16); Oklahoma St. (9); Stanford (7); Harvard (6); Florida, LSU and North Texas (4); Wake Forest (3); Arizona St., Michigan, Ohio St. and Texas (2).

Multiple winners (Individuals): Ben Crenshaw and Phil Mickelson (3); Dick Crawford, Dexter Cummings, G.T. Dunlop, Fred Lamprecht and Scott Simpson (2).

Year	Team winner	Individual champion	Year	Team winner	Individual champion
1897	Yale	Louis Bayard, Princeton	1902	Yale (spring)	Chas. Hitchcock Jr., Yale
1898	Harvard (spring)	John Reid, Yale	1902	Harvard (fall)	Chandler Egan, Harvard
1898	Yale (fall)	James Curtis, Harvard	1903	Harvard	F.O. Reinhart, Princeton
1899	Harvard	Percy Pyne, Princeton	1904	Harvard	A.L. White, Harvard
1900	Not held		1905	Yale	Robert Abbott, Yale
1901	Harvard	H. Lindsley, Harvard	1906	Yale	W.E. Clow Jr., Yale
			1907	Yale	Ellis Knowles, Yale

Year	Team winner	Individual champion
1908	Yale	H.H. Wilder, Harvard
1909	Yale	Albert Seckel, Princeton
1910	Yale	Robert Hunter, Yale
1911	Yale	George Stanley, Yale
1912	Yale	F.C. Davison, Harvard
1913	Yale	Nathaniel Wheeler, Yale
1914	Princeton	Edward Allis, Harvard
1915	Yale	Francis Blossom, Yale
1916	Princeton	J.W. Hubbell, Harvard
1917-18 Not held		
1919	Princeton	A.L. Walker Jr., Columbia
1920	Princeton	Jess Sweetser, Yale
1921	Dartmouth	Simpson Dean, Princeton
1922	Princeton	Pollack Boyd, Dartmouth
1923	Princeton	Dexter Cummings, Yale
1924	Yale	Dexter Cummings, Yale
1925	Yale	Fred Lamprecht, Tulane
1926	Yale	Fred Lamprecht, Tulane
1927	Princeton	Watts Gunn, Georgia Tech
1928	Princeton	Maurice McCarthy, G'town
1929	Princeton	Tom Aycock, Yale
1930	Princeton	G.T. Dunlap Jr., Princeton
1931	Yale	G.T. Dunlap Jr., Princeton
1932	Yale	J.W. Fischer, Michigan
1933	Yale	Walter Emery, Oklahoma
1934	Michigan	Charles Yates, Ga.Tech
1935	Michigan	Ed White, Texas
1936	Yale	Charles Kocsis, Michigan
1937	Princeton	Fred Haas Jr., LSU
1938	Stanford	John Burke, Georgetown
1939	Stanford	Vincent D'Antoni, Tulane
1940	Princeton & LSU	Dixon Brooke, Virginia
1941	Stanford	Earl Stewart, LSU
1942	LSU & Stanford	Frank Tatum Jr., Stanford
1943	Yale	Wallace Ulrich, Carleton
1944	Notre Dame	Louis Lick, Minnesota
1945	Ohio State	John Lorms, Ohio St.
1946	Stanford	George Hamer, Georgia
1947	LSU	Dave Barclay, Michigan
1948	San Jose St.	Bob Harris, San Jose St.
1949	North Texas	Harvie Ward, N.Carolina
1950	North Texas	Fred Wampler, Purdue
1951	North Texas	Tom Nieporte, Ohio St.
1952	North Texas	Jim Vichers, Oklahoma
1953	Stanford	Earl Moeller, Oklahoma St.
1954	SMU	Hillman Robbins, Memphis St.
1955	LSU	Joe Campbell, Purdue

Year	Team winner	Individual champion
1956	Houston	Rick Jones, Ohio St.
1957	Houston	Rex Baxter Jr., Houston
1958	Houston	Phil Rodgers, Houston
1959	Houston	Dick Crawford, Houston
1960	Houston	Dick Crawford, Houston
1961	Purdue	Jack Nicklaus, Ohio St.
1962	Houston	Kermit Zarley, Houston
1963	Oklahoma St.	R.H. Sikes, Arkansas
1964	Houston	Terry Small, San Jose St.
1965	Houston	Marty Fleckman, Houston
1966	Houston	Bob Murphy, Florida
1967	Houston	Hale Irwin, Colorado
1968	Florida	Grier Jones, Oklahoma St.
1969	Houston	Bob Clark, Cal St.-LA
1970	Houston	John Mahaffey, Houston
1971	Texas	Ben Crenshaw, Texas
1972	Texas	Ben Crenshaw, Texas
		& Tom Kite, Texas
1973	Florida	Ben Crenshaw, Texas
1974	Wake Forest	Curtis Strange, W.Forest
1975	Wake Forest	Jay Haas, Wake Forest
1976	Oklahoma St.	Scott Simpson, USC
1977	Houston	Scott Simpson, USC
1978	Oklahoma St.	David Edwards, Okla. St.
1979	Ohio St.	Gary Hallberg, Wake Forest
1980	Oklahoma St.	Jay Don Blake, Utah St.
1981	Brigham Young	Ron Commans, USC
1982	Houston	Billy Ray Brown, Houston
1983	Oklahoma St.	Jim Carter, Arizona St.
1984	Houston	John Inman, N.Carolina
1985	Houston	Clark Burroughs, Ohio St.
1986	Wake Forest	Scott Verplank, Okla. St.
1987	Oklahoma St.	Brian Watts, Oklahoma St.
1988	UCLA	E.J. Pfister, Oklahoma St.
1989	Oklahoma	Phil Mickelson, Ariz. St.
1990	Arizona St.	Phil Mickelson, Ariz. St.
1991	Oklahoma St.	Warren Schuette, UNLV
1992	Arizona	Phil Mickelson, Ariz. St.
1993	Florida	Todd Demsey, Ariz. St.
1994	Stanford	Justin Leonard, Texas
1995	Oklahoma St.	Chip Spratlin, Auburn
1996	Arizona St.	Tiger Woods, Stanford
1997	Pepperdine	Charles Warren, Clemson
1998	UNLV	James McLean, Minnesota
1999	Georgia	Luke Donald, Northwestern
2000	Oklahoma St.	Charles Howell, Oklahoma St.
2001	Florida	Nick Gilliam, Florida

Women's NCAA Division I Champions

College championships decided by stroke play since 1982.

Multiple winners (teams): Arizona St. (6); Arizona, Florida, San Jose St. and Tulsa (2).

Year	Team winner	Individual champion
1982	Tulsa	Kathy Baker, Tulsa
1983	TCU	Penny Hammel, Miami
1984	Miami-FL	Cindy Schreyer, Georgia
1985	Florida	Danielle Ammaccapane, Ariz.St.
1986	Florida	Page Dunlap, Florida
1987	San Jose St.	Caroline Keggi, New Mexico
1988	Tulsa	Melissa McNamara, Tulsa
1989	San Jose St.	Pat Hurst, San Jose St.
1990	Arizona St.	Susan Slaughter, Arizona
1991	UCLA	Annika Sorenstam, Arizona

Year	Team winner	Individual champion
1992	San Jose St.	Vicki Goetze, Georgia
1993	Arizona St.	Charlotta Sorenstam, Ariz. St.
1994	Arizona St.	Emilee Klein, Ariz. St.
1995	Arizona St.	K. Mourgue d'Algue, Ariz. St.
1996	Arizona	Marisa Baena, Arizona
1997	Arizona St.	Heather Bowie, Texas
1998	Arizona St.	Jennifer Rosales, USC
1999	Duke	Grace Park, Arizona St.
2000	Arizona	Jenna Daniels, Arizona
2001	Georgia	Candy Hannemann, Duke

Auto Racing

An American flag flies at half-mast in memory of Dale
Earnhardt, who was killed at the 2001 Daytona 500.

AP/Wide World Photos

Fallen Star

Racing fans mourn the loss of Dale Earnhardt after NASCAR's premier driver is killed at its premier event.

John Kernan *is host of RPM 2Night on ESPN2 and a pit reporter for ESPN's NASCAR coverage.*

Without a doubt, auto racing in 2001 will forever be remembered for the way the sport changed. Perhaps the most important change is the way those of us who have been around the sport for a long time perceive its safety issues.

For someone who has been covering motor sports since the early 1980's and has covered more than his share of driver deaths, I was initially shocked at the way most of the competitors seemingly took the ever-present risk of tragedy in stride. Quite simply, racing was dangerous. It was just part of the game.

But after the deaths of three young drivers during the 2000 NASCAR season, questions started forming in everyone's mind.

"Why did they have to die? What can be done to make racing safer?"

Then the 2001 season began with the Daytona 500. Dale Earnhardt crashed on the last lap while running third. It didn't look that bad. We'd seen Dale walk away from much worse looking accidents. Only this time he didn't walk away.

Perhaps the most beloved and well-known figure in the history of the sport, the man we'd all seen drive with broken bones, was gone. For racing fans, it was the day the music died. But none of us were singing. Instead, we were questioning.

There was an outcry from the public and from the news media.

"How could this have happened?"

The finger pointing started almost immediately. NASCAR said a few days after the accident that it had found that the left lap belt in Earnhardt's car had separated. That comment began a game of verbal jousting that could well

Dale Earnhardt, in his infamous No. 3 car, slams into the restraining wall on the final lap of the Daytona 500. The crash didn't appear to be serious at first, but turned out to be devastating.

bring about legal action against NASCAR by Bill Simpson, founder of the company that manufactured Earnhardt's belts.

Earnhardt was not wearing a head and neck restraint system, something that most of us had not even heard of until the middle of 2000. The most commonly used system is the HANS Device. After the crash at Daytona, almost every NASCAR driver began to wear either a HANS or a Hutchens device. But they were doing it on their own volition, not because NASCAR told them to.

Many members of the news media criticized NASCAR for not making it a mandatory piece of equipment, and finally on Oct. 17, NASCAR seemingly yielded to the criticism and made it a requirement. Also, in its report on Earnhardt's death, the sanctioning body

AP/Wide World Photos

*Germany's **Michael Schumacher** pumps his fist to his adoring fans after winning the Hungarian Grand Prix on Aug. 19, becoming Formula One world champ for the fourth time.*

announced that it would start using crash data recorders in the cars, something the open wheel series like CART and Formula One have done for years.

It also announced that it would employ a medical liaison to work with the local doctors and EMTs assigned to its races beginning with the 2002 season. Again, NASCAR could learn from both CART and the IRL, which have traveling medical teams, meaning the same doctors and technicians are at every race. As an example of the success of this plan, many credit CART's medical crew with saving the life of Alex Zanardi, who lost his legs in a horrific crash in Germany in September.

If there's anything positive to come from that horrible day at Daytona, it's that NASCAR is taking small steps toward improving safety. Personally, I'm glad because I have a lot of friends who drive those cars. And quite honestly, I'm tired of having to talk about their deaths.

John Kernan's Ten Biggest Stories of the Year in Auto Racing

10 • Tragedy for Alex the Great—Two-time CART champ Alex Zanardi returns to the series for one last hurrah, but unfortunately the cheers turn into gasps. Zanardi loses his legs in a horrific crash in Germany. But in typical Zanardi style, he says that doesn't matter as long as he's alive and he has his family—wife Daniela and son Niccolo.

9 • A Star is Born—Johnny Sauter comes from a racing family. His father, Jim, was a stock car veteran and his older brother, Jay, has raced in NASCAR's Craftsman Truck and Busch divisions. So, it was only fitting that he follow in the family footsteps. Actually he stomped on those footsteps, winning a record 10 races to become the first rookie to win the American Speed Association Championship. That has earned him a part-time Busch Series ride with Richard Childress in 2002.

8 • Rusty Wallace vs. Ricky Rudd—These two veteran NASCAR drivers were never best friends, but they were never considered bitter rivals either. That changed on a Saturday night in August in Bristol, Tenn. While racing for position, Rudd gave Wallace a nudge to move him out of the way. Wallace retaliated with a bump of his own on the cool-down lap. A few weeks later, while Rudd was leading at Dover, Wallace bumped him out of the way, leading to a harsh verbal exchange afterwards.

7 • Make Mine a BMW—The German carmaker beat up on all the competition in the GT Class of the American Le Mans Series. With its somewhat controversial V-8 engine, something not offered in the stock version of the racing car, BMW has won the last seven races, capturing the driver, team and manufacturer titles with ease.

6 • Passing the Torch—After dominating motocross for nearly a decade, the tables are turned and Jeremy McGrath becomes the one doing all the chasing. Ricky Carmichael, a red-haired freckle-faced kid from Florida hit his stride in 2001 and by the end of the season had knocked McGrath from the top spot.

5 • CART Decisions—With a new leader in CEO Joe Heitzler, the CART FedEx Championship Series turned a lot of heads in 2001, mostly in the wrong direction. Races in Brazil and Ft. Worth, Texas were cancelled. Then late in the year came the decision to give up on turbocharged engines in 2003 in favor of an engine package very similar to that of the rival Indy Racing League.

4 • Sam's the Man—Before the 2001 Indy Racing League season Sam Hornish Jr. had made just eight starts in the series. He was then handed keys to one of the top rides in the series, and he responded right away, driving the Panther Racing car to victory in his first two races en route to the IRL title.

3 • Big Shoes to Fill—The tragic death of Dale Earnhardt left one of the best rides in NASCAR open. Enter young Kevin Harvick. The 25-year-old Bakersfield, Calif. native was suddenly thrust into the limelight, chosen to take over Earnhardt's spot. He won his first Winston Cup race in his third start, beating Jeff Gordon in one of the closest finishes in NASCAR history.

2 • The Right Formula—After winning two Formula One titles with Benetton, Michael Schumacher moved over to Ferrari where he was charged with bringing the famed automaker back to the top of the sport. He delivered. In 2001 he locked up his second straight championship, but more importantly set a mark that might never be broken. His victory in Belgium gave him 52 career Grand Prix wins, surpassing the legendary Alain Prost for the most all-time.

1 • The Death of a Legend—Dale Earnhardt's tragic death on the closing lap of the Daytona 500 changed the way everyone in and around the sport looks at Winston Cup racing. The seven-time series champion's death, in addition to the three deaths NASCAR experienced in 2000, raised safety consciousness to a new level. No longer do those involved with racing simply accept the fact that it is a very dangerous business. The public outcry from the news media to make the sport safer was something rarely seen in prior years.

inside the **numbers**

Thirty Something

Jeff Gordon turned 30 on Aug. 4, 2001 and gave himself a present the following day by winning the Brickyard 400. He's just behind the pace set by legend Richard Petty, the all-time career leader with 200 wins.

	Gordon	Petty
Turned 30	8/4/01	7/2/67
Starts*	278	360
Wins*	56	60
Win Pct.	20.1	16.7

*Totals are as of the week of their birthdays.

Year After Year

In 2001 CART driver Michael Andretti extended his streak of consecutive years with at least one victory to eight. Listed are the longest streaks.

	Years
Emerson Fittipaldi, '85-95	11
Michael Andretti, '94-01	8
Al Unser Jr., '88-95	8
Bobby Rahal, '82-89	8
Rick Mears, '79-85	7

King of the Road

Jeff Gordon became the all-time leader in road-course wins in 2001 with his seventh. And he needed just 18 starts.

	Wins
Jeff Gordon	7
Rusty Wallace	6
Richard Petty	6
Bobby Allison	6

2000-2001 Season in Review

**information please®
SPORTS ALMANAC**

NASCAR RESULTS

Winston Cup Series

Winners of NASCAR Winston Cup races from Nov. 5, 2000 through Oct. 21, 2001. Note that earnings include bonus money.

LATE 2000

Date	Event	Location	Winner (Pos.)	Avg.mph	Earnings	Pole	Qual.mph
Nov. 5	Checker/Dura Lube 500K	Phoenix	Jeff Burton (2)	105.041	$197,345	R. Wallace	134.178
Nov. 12	Pennzoil 400	Homestead	Tony Stewart (13)	127.480	291,325	S. Park	156.440
Nov. 19	NAPA 500	Atlanta	Jerry Nadeau (2)	141.295	180,550	J. Gordon	194.274

Winning cars (2000 season): FORD TAURUS (14)—J. Burton (4), Wallace (4), Jarrett (2), Mayfield (2), Kenseth, Martin; PONTIAC GRAND PRIX (11)—T. Stewart (6), B. Labonte (4), W. Burton; CHEVY MONTE CARLO (10)—Earnhardt Jr. (3), Earnhardt (2), Gordon (3), Nadeau, Park.

2001 SEASON

Date	Event	Location	Winner (Pos.)	Avg.mph	Earnings	Pole	Qual.mph
Feb. 18	**Daytona 500**	Daytona	Michael Waltrip (19)	161.783	$1,331,185+	B. Elliott	183.565
Feb. 26†	Dura Lube 400	Rockingham	Steve Park (2)	111.966	144,580	J. Gordon	156.455
Mar. 4	UAW-DaimlerChrysler 400	Las Vegas	Jeff Gordon (24)	135.546	1,369,600*	D. Jarrett	172.106
Mar. 11	Cracker Barrel 500	Atlanta	Kevin Harvick (5)	143.416	158,427	D. Jarrett	192.748
Mar. 18	Dodge Dealers 400	Darlington	Dale Jarrett (2)	126.558	214,612+	J. Gordon	—**
Mar. 25	Food City 500	Bristol	Elliott Sadler (38)	86.949	124,700	M. Martin	126.303
Apr. 11	Harrah's 500	Ft. Worth	Dale Jarrett (3)	141.804	444,527+	D. Earnhardt Jr.	190.678
Apr. 8	Virginia 500	Martinsville	Dale Jarrett (13)	70.799	170,027+	J. Gordon	94.087
Apr. 22	Talladega 500	Talladega	Bobby Hamilton (14)	184.003	173,855	S. Compton	184.861
Apr. 29	NAPA Auto Parts 500	Fontana	Rusty Wallace (19)	143.118	195,090	B. Labonte	182.635
May 5	Pontiac Excitement 400	Richmond	Tony Stewart (7)	95.872	150,175	M. Martin	124.614
May 19@	The Winston	Charlotte	Jeff Gordon (10)	185.002	515,000	R. Wallace	115.337
May 27	**Coca-Cola 600**	Charlotte	Jeff Burton (18)	138.107	258,846	R. Newman	185.217
June 3	MBNA Platinum 400	Dover	Jeff Gordon (2)	120.361	183,907	D. Jarrett	—**
June 10	Kmart 400	Brooklyn	Jeff Gordon (1)	134.197	240,137+	J. Gordon	188.250
June 17	Pocono 500	Long Pond	Ricky Rudd (1)	134.389	189,542	R. Rudd	170.503
June 24	Dodge/Save Mart 350	Sonoma	Tony Stewart (3)	75.889	139,875	J. Gordon	93.698
July 7	Pepsi 400	Daytona	Dale Earnhardt Jr. (13)	157.601	185,873	S. Marlin	183.778
July 15	Tropicana 400	Joliet	Kevin Harvick (6)	121.200	162,500	T. Bodine	183.717
July 22	New England 300	Loudon	Dale Jarrett (9)	102.131	238,027+	J. Gordon	131.769
July 29	Pennsylvania 500	Long Pond	Bobby Labonte (11)	134.590	189,427	T. Bodine	170.325
Aug. 5	**Brickyard 400**	Indianapolis	Jeff Gordon (27)	130.790	428,452+	J. Spencer	179.665
Aug. 12	Global Crossing at The Glen	Watkins Glen	Jeff Gordon (13)	89.081	173,402+	D. Jarrett	122.697
Aug. 19	Pepsi 400	Brooklyn	Sterling Marlin (15)	140.513	157,830	R. Craven	188.127
Aug. 25	Sharpie 500	Bristol	Tony Stewart (18)	85.106	189,415	J. Green	123.673
Sept. 2	**Southern 500**	Darlington	Ward Burton (37)	122.773	181,435	K. Busch	168.048
Sept. 8	Monte Carlo 400	Richmond	Ricky Rudd (9)	95.146	171,992	J. Gordon	124.901
Sept. 23	MBNA/Cal Ripken Jr. 400	Dover	Dale Earnhardt Jr. (3)	101.559	168,858	D. Jarrett	154.918
Sept. 30	Protection One 400	Kansas City	Jeff Gordon (2)	110.576	254,377+	J. Leffler	176.499
Oct. 7	UAW-GM Quality 500	Charlotte	Sterling Marlin (13)	139.006	196,360	J. Spencer	185.147
Oct. 14	Old Dominion 500	Martinsville	Ricky Craven (6)	75.750	130,475	T. Bodine	93.724
Oct. 21	EA Sports 500	Talladega	Dale Earnhardt Jr. (6)	185.240	1,165,773*	S. Compton	185.240

†The Dura-Lube 400 was postponed one day (Feb. 26) due to rain.
*Includes $1 million Winston "No Bull 5" bonus.
**Qualifying was cancelled due to inclement weather and the pole was awarded to the current Winston Cup points leader.
@ Non-points exhibition event
+Includes carryover Winston Cup leader bonus ($10,000 per race): **Daytona 500**–Waltrip ($10,000); **Dodge Dealers 400**–Jarrett ($40,000); **Harrah's 500**–Jarrett ($20,000); **Virginia 500**–Jarrett ($10,000); **Kmart 400**–Gordon ($70,000); **New England 300**–Jarrett ($50,000); **Brickyard 400**–Gordon ($20,000); **Global Crossing**–Gordon ($10,000); **Protection One 400**–Gordon ($60,000).
Note: The New Hampshire 300, scheduled for Sept. 16, was postponed due to the Sept. 11 attacks and rescheduled for Nov. 23.
Winning Cars: CHEVY MONTE CARLO (14)—Gordon (6), Earnhardt Jr. (3), Harvick (2), Hamilton, Park, Waltrip; FORD TAURUS (10)—Jarrett (4), Rudd (2), J. Burton, Craven, Sadler, Wallace. PONTIAC GRAND PRIX (4)—Stewart (3), B. Labonte; DODGE INTREPID (3)—Marlin (2), W. Burton.

2001 NASCAR Winston Cup Race Locations

February—DAYTONA 500 at Daytona International Speedway in Daytona Beach, Fla.; DURA LUBE 400 at North Carolina Motor Speedway in Rockingham, N.C.

March—UAW-DAIMLERCHRYSLER 400 at Las Vegas (Nev.) Motor Speedway; CRACKER BARREL 500 at Atlanta (Ga.) Motor Speedway; CAROLINA DODGE DEALERS 400 at Darlington (S.C.) International Raceway; FOOD CITY 500 at Bristol (Tenn.) Motor Speedway.

April—HARRAH'S 500 at Texas Motor Speedway in Ft. Worth, Texas; VIRGINIA 500 at Martinsville (Va.) Speedway; TALLADEGA 500 at Talladega (Ala.) Superspeedway; NAPA 500 at California Speedway in Fontana, Calif.

May—PONTIAC EXCITEMENT 400 at Richmond (Va.) International Speedway; THE WINSTON at Lowe's Motor Speedway in Charlotte, N.C.; COCA-COLA 600 at Lowe's.

June—MBNA PLATINUM 400 at Dover (Del.) Downs International Speedway; KMART 400 at Michigan Speedway in Brooklyn, Mich.; POCONO 500 at Pocono International Raceway in Long Pond, Penn.; SAVE MART/KRAGEN 350K at Sears Point International Raceway in Sonoma, Calif.

July—PEPSI 400 at Daytona; TROPICANA 400 at Chicagoland Speedway in Joliet, Ill.; NEW ENGLAND 300 at New Hampshire International Speedway in Loudon, N.H.; PENNSYLVANIA 500 at Pocono.

August—BRICKYARD 400 at Indianapolis (Ind.) Motor Speedway; GLOBAL CROSSING AT THE GLEN at Watkins Glen (N.Y.) International; PEPSI 400 at Michigan; SHARPIE 500 at Bristol.

September—MOUNTAIN DEW SOUTHERN 500 at Darlington; CHEVROLET MONTE CARLO 400 at Richmond; MBNA.COM/CAL RIPKEN JR. 400 at Dover Downs; PROTECTION ONE 400 at Kansas Speedway in Kansas City, Mo.

October—UAW-GM QUALITY 500 at Lowe's; OLD DOMINION 500 at Martinsville; EA SPORTS 500 at Talladega; CHECKER AUTO PARTS 500 at Phoenix (Ariz.) International Raceway.

November—POP SECRET MICROWAVE POPCORN 400 at North Carolina; PENNZOIL 400 at Miami-Dade Homestead Motorsports Complex in Homestead, Fla.; NAPA 500 at Atlanta; NEW HAMPSHIRE 300 at New Hampshire.

2001 Daytona 500

Date—Sunday, Feb. 18, 2001, at Daytona International Speedway. **Distance**—500 miles; **Course**—2.5 miles; **Field**—43 cars; **Average speed**—161.783 mph; **Margin of victory**—0.124 seconds; **Time of race**—3 hours, 5 minutes, 26 seconds; **Caution flags**—3 for 14 laps; **Lead changes**—49 among 14 drivers; **Lap leaders**—W. Burton (53), Marlin (40), Waltrip (27), Skinner (24), Earnhardt (16), Earnhardt Jr. (13), Gordon (11), Schrader (7), B. Labonte (3), Park (2), Elliott, Bodine, Martin and Jarrett (1). **Pole sitter**—Bill Elliott 183.565 mph; **Attendance**—150,000 (estimated). **Rating**—10.0/24 share (FOX).

	Driver (start pos.)	Team	Car	Laps	Ended	Earnings
1	Michael Waltrip (19)	NAPA	Chevrolet Monte Carlo	200	Running	$1,331,185
2	Dale Earnhardt Jr. (6)	Budweiser	Chevrolet Monte Carlo	200	Running	975,907
3	Rusty Wallace (12)	Miller Lite	Ford Taurus	200	Running	676,224
4	Ricky Rudd (30)	Texaco/Havoline	Ford Taurus	200	Running	517,831
5	Bill Elliott (1)	Dodge Dealers	Dodge Intrepid	200	Running	392,582
6	Mike Wallace (27)	Nations Rent	Ford Taurus	200	Running	275,269
7	Sterling Marlin (3)	Coors Light	Dodge Intrepid	200	Running	262,354
8	Bobby Hamilton (35)	Square D	Chevrolet Monte Carlo	200	Running	189,259
9	Jeremy Mayfield (38)	Mobil 1	Ford Taurus	200	Running	207,168
10	Stacy Compton (2)	Kodiak	Dodge Intrepid	200	Running	168,770
11	Joe Nemechek (32)	Oakwood Homes	Chevrolet Monte Carlo	200	Running	174,754
12	Dale Earnhardt (7)	GM Goodwrench Service Plus	Chevrolet Monte Carlo	199	Accident	194,111
13	Ken Schrader (14)	M & M's	Pontiac Grand Prix	199	Accident	154,874
14	Robert Pressley (39)	Jasper Engines	Ford Taurus	199	Running	142,809
15	Brett Bodine (43)	Ralphs Supermarkets	Ford Taurus	199	Running	133,509
16	Kyle Petty (28)	Sprint/Dodge	Dodge Intrepid	199	Running	125,909
17	Ron Hornaday (42)	Conseco	Pontiac Grand Prix	199	Running	129,534
18	Elliott Sadler (40)	Motorcraft	Ford Taurus	199	Running	127,909
19	Jeff Burton (8)	Citgo	Ford Taurus	199	Running	155,884
20	Casey Atwood (21)	Dodge/UAW	Dodge Intrepid	198	Running	128,034
21	Matt Kenseth (16)	DeWalt Power Tools	Ford Taurus	196	Running	136,584
22	Dale Jarrett (31)	UPS	Ford Taurus	186	Accident	167,711
23	Ricky Craven (37)	Tide	Ford Taurus	185	Running	122,484
24	Terry Labonte (34)	Kellogg's	Chevrolet Monte Carlo	184	Accident	157,589
25	Kenny Wallace (23)	Unsponsored	Pontiac Grand Prix	184	Accident	124,509
26	Mike Skinner (4)	Lowe's	Chevrolet Monte Carlo	183	Running	187,358
27	Jimmy Spencer (11)	Kmart	Ford Taurus	183	Running	135,134
28	Johnny Benson (33)	Valvoline	Pontiac Grand Prix	181	Engine	129,009
29	Buckshot Jones (29)	Georgia Pacific	Dodge Intrepid	181	Accident	126,234
30	Jeff Gordon (13)	Dupont	Chevrolet Monte Carlo	178	Accident	166,411
31	Steve Park (25)	Pennzoil	Chevrolet Monte Carlo	177	Running	144,027
32	Jerry Nadeau (5)	UAW	Chevrolet Monte Carlo	176	Accident	141,384
33	Mark Martin (22)	Pfizer/Viagra	Ford Taurus	175	Accident	160,685
34	Jason Leffler (15)	Cingular Wireless	Dodge Intrepid	174	Accident	124,884
35	Ward Burton (22)	Caterpillar	Dodge Intrepid	173	Accident	165,019
36	Tony Stewart (24)	Home Depot	Pontiac Grand Prix	173	Accident	135,009
37	Robby Gordon (41)	Kodak Film	Chevrolet Monte Carlo	173	Accident	113,959
38	Andy Houston (9)	McDonald's	Ford Taurus	173	Accident	120,384
39	John Andretti (36)	Cheerios	Dodge Intrepid	173	Accident	148,136
40	Bobby Labonte (37)	Interstate Batteries	Pontiac Grand Prix	173	Accident	164,611
41	Kurt Busch (26)	Unsponsored	Ford Taurus	169	Running	120,284
42	Dave Blaney (20)	Amoco	Dodge Intrepid	135	Engine	111,859
43	Jeff Purvis (17)	Phoenix Construction	Ford Taurus	47	Accident	111,384

Winston Cup Point Standings

Official Top 10 NASCAR Winston Cup point leaders and Top 10 money leaders for 2000 and unofficial leaders for 2001. Points awarded for all qualifying drivers (winner receives 175) and lap leaders. Earnings include bonuses. Listed are starts (Sts), top-5 finishes (1-2-3-4-5), poles won (PW) and points (Pts).

FINAL 2000

		Sts	Finishes 1-2-3-4-5	PW	Pts
1	Bobby Labonte	34	4-4-4-2-6	2*	5130
2	Dale Earnhardt	34	2-5-4-2-1	0	4865
3	Jeff Burton	34	4-5-2-1-3	1	4836
4	Dale Jarrett	34	2-3-1-5-3	3	4684
5	Ricky Rudd	34	0-1-5-3-3	2	4575
6	Tony Stewart	34	6-2-0-3-1	2	4570
7	Rusty Wallace	34	4-1-1-3-3	9	4544
8	Mark Martin	34	1-2-6-1-3	0	4410
9	Jeff Gordon	34	3-1-1-3-3	3	4361
10	Ward Burton	34	1-0-3-0-0	0	4152

*Doesn't include pole awarded at Global Crossing.
Other wins (7): Dale Earnhardt Jr. and Jeremy Mayfield (2); Matt Kenseth, Jerry Nadeau and Steve Park.

2001 (through Oct. 21)

		Sts	Finishes 1-2-3-4-5	PW	Pts
1	Jeff Gordon	31	6-6-3-2-1	6*	4512
2	Ricky Rudd	31	2-2-4-4-1	1	4117
3	Tony Stewart	31	3-3-2-3-2	0	4043
4	Sterling Marlin	31	2-1-2-1-3	1	4040
5	Dale Jarrett	31	4-2-1-3-1	4†	3998
6	Dale Earnhardt Jr.	31	3-2-3-1-0	1	3925
7	Rusty Wallace	31	1-0-2-2-3	0	3904
8	Kevin Harvick	30	2-3-0-0-0	0	3806
9	Bobby Labonte	31	1-1-1-1-2	1	3799
10	Jeff Burton	31	1-1-2-0-3	0	3689

*Doesn't include Dodge Dealers 400 (see page 881).
†Doesn't include MBNA Platinum 400 (see page 881).
Other wins (6): Ward Burton, Ricky Craven, Bobby Hamilton, Steve Park, Elliott Sadler and Michael Waltrip.

Top 5 Finishing Order + Pole
2001 SEASON

No. Event	Winner	2nd	3rd	4th	5th	Pole
1 Daytona 500	M. Waltrip	D. Earnhardt Jr.	R. Wallace	R. Rudd	B. Elliott	B. Elliott
2 Dura Lube 400	S. Park	B. Labonte	J. Gordon	T. Stewart	R. Craven	J. Gordon
3 UAW-DaimlerChrysler 400	J. Gordon	D. Jarrett	S. Marlin	J. Benson	T. Bodine	D. Jarrett
4 Cracker Barrel 500	K. Harvick	J. Gordon	J. Nadeau	D. Jarrett	T. Labonte	D. Jarrett
5 Dodge Dealers 400	D. Jarrett	S. Park	J. Mayfield	J. Spencer	S. Marlin	J. Gordon
6 Food City 500	E. Sadler	J. Andretti	J. Mayfield	J. Gordon	W. Burton	M. Martin
7 Harrah's 500	D. Jarrett	S. Park	J. Benson	K. Busch	J. Gordon	D. Earnhardt Jr.
8 Virginia 500	D. Jarrett	R. Rudd	J. Burton	B. Hamilton	S. Marlin	J. Gordon
9 Talladega 500	B. Hamilton	T. Stewart	K. Busch	M. Martin	B. Labonte	S. Compton
10 NAPA Auto Parts 500	R. Wallace	J. Gordon	D. Earnhardt Jr.	T. Stewart	J. Mayfield	B. Labonte
11 Pontiac Excitement 400	T. Stewart	J. Gordon	R. Wallace	S. Park	R. Rudd	M. Martin
12 Coca-Cola 600	J. Burton	K. Harvick	T. Stewart	M. Martin	B. Labonte	R. Newman
13 MBNA Platinum 400	J. Gordon	S. Park	D. Earnhardt Jr.	R. Craven	D. Jarrett	D. Jarrett
14 Kmart 400	J. Gordon	R. Rudd	S. Marlin	J. Mayfield	R. Newman	J. Gordon
15 Pocono 500	R. Rudd	J. Gordon	D. Jarrett	S. Marlin	M. Martin	R. Rudd
16 Dodge/Save Mart 350	T. Stewart	R. Gordon	J. Gordon	R. Rudd	R. Wallace	J. Gordon
17 Pepsi 400	D. Earnhardt Jr.	M. Waltrip	E. Sadler	W. Burton	J. Burton	S. Marlin
18 Tropicana 400	K. Harvick	R. Pressley	R. Rudd	D. Jarrett	J. Spencer	T. Bodine
19 New England 300	D. Jarrett	J. Gordon	R. Rudd	J. Spencer	T. Stewart	T. Bodine
20 Pennsylvania 500	B. Labonte	D. Earnhardt Jr.	T. Stewart	B. Elliott	J. Benson	T. Bodine
21 Brickyard 400	J. Gordon	S. Marlin	J. Benson	R. Wallace	K. Busch	J. Spencer
22 Global Crossing at The Glen	J. Gordon	J. Burton	J. Mayfield	R. Rudd	T. Bodine	D. Jarrett
23 Pepsi 400	S. Marlin	R. Craven	B. Elliott	M. Kenseth	J. Benson	R. Craven
24 Sharpie 500	T. Stewart	K. Harvick	J. Gordon	R. Rudd	R. Wallace	J. Green
25 Southern 500	W. Burton	J. Gordon	B. Labonte	T. Stewart	B. Elliott	K. Busch
26 Monte Carlo 400	R. Rudd	K. Harvick	D. Earnhardt Jr.	D. Jarrett	R. Wallace	J. Andretti
27 MBNA/Cal Ripken Jr. 400	D. Earnhardt Jr.	J. Nadeau	R. Rudd	J. Gordon	T. Stewart	D. Jarrett
28 Protection One 400	J. Gordon	R. Newman	R. Rudd	R. Wallace	S. Marlin	J. Leffler
29 UAW-GM Quality 500	S. Marlin	T. Stewart	W. Burton	D. Earnhardt Jr.	J. Burton	J. Spencer
30 Old Dominion 500	R. Craven	D. Jarrett	W. Burton	B. Labonte	J. Burton	T. Bodine
31 EA Sports 500	D. Earnhardt Jr.	T. Stewart	J. Burton	M. Kenseth	B. Hamilton	S. Compton

Money Leaders

FINAL 2000

		Earnings
1	Dale Jarrett	$5,225,499
2	Jeff Burton	5,121,354
3	Bobby Labonte	4,041,746
4	Dale Earnhardt	3,701,391
5	Tony Stewart	3,200,191
6	Rusty Wallace	3,037,721
7	Mark Martin	2,763,536
8	Jeff Gordon	2,703,586
9	Dale Earnhardt Jr.	2,610,396
10	Bill Elliott	2,447,788

2001 (through Oct. 21)

		Earnings
1	Jeff Gordon	$6,148,590
2	Dale Jarrett	4,128,760
3	Dale Earnhardt Jr.	3,963,710
4	Rusty Wallace	3,823,610
5	Ricky Rudd	3,533,370
6	Bobby Labonte	3,474,290
7	Jeff Burton	3,226,580
8	Kevin Harvick	3,222,150
9	Tony Stewart	3,114,060
10	Mark Martin	3,083,260

AP/Wide World Photos

CART driver and Indianapolis 500 champ **Helio Castroneves,** *center, climbs the fence with his crew at the Indianapolis Motor Speedway start/finish line, recreating the post-race celebration which has helped earn him the nickname, "Spiderman" (See Indy 500 results on pg. 886).*

CART RESULTS

Schedule and results of CART races from Oct. 29, 2000 through Oct. 14, 2001. Note that CART does not release per-race winnings.

FedEx Championship Series
LATE 2000

Date	Event	Location	Winner (Pos.)	Time	Avg.mph	Pole	Qual.mph
Oct. 30#	Marlboro 500	Fontana	Christian Fittipaldi (3)	3:38:04.376	139.563	G. de Ferran	241.428

#Race started Oct. 29 but had to be finished on Oct. 30 due to rain.

Winning cars (2000 season): REYNARD/HONDA (9)—Castroneves (3), de Ferran (3), Tracy (3); REYNARD/FORD (4)—Fernandez (2), Moreno, Papis; LOLA/TOYOTA (4)—Montoya (3), Vasser; LOLA/FORD (3)—Andretti (2), Fittipaldi; REYNARD/TOYOTA (1)—da Matta.

2001 SEASON

Date	Event	Location	Winner (Pos.)	Time	Avg.mph	Pole	Qual.mph
Mar. 11	Monterrey GP	Monterrey	Cristiano da Matta (2)	2:00:44.850	81.548	K. Brack	100.665
Apr. 8	Toyota GP	Long Beach	Helio Castroneves (1)	1:52:17.779	86.223	H. Castroneves	103.343
Apr. 29	Firestone Firehawk 600	Ft. Worth	cancelled	—	—	K. Brack	233.447
May 6	Lehigh Valley GP	Nazareth	Scott Dixon (23)	1:51:12.419	114.840	B. Junqueira	172.873
May 19	Firestone Firehawk 500	Montegi	Kenny Brack (6)	1:44:48.888	178.113	H. Castroneves	215.591
June 3	Miller Lite 225	West Allis	Kenny Brack (1)	1:54:08.097	122.066	K. Brack	—*
June 17	GP of Detroit	Detroit	Helio Castroneves (1)	1:53:51.815	89.008	H. Castroneves	114.908
June 24	Freightliner/ G.I. Joe's 200	Portland	Max Papis (1)	2:00:20.836	74.606	M. Papis	122.669
July 1	GP of Cleveland	Cleveland	Dario Franchitti (14)	1:47:04.723	118.007	M. Gugelmin	132.185
July 15	Molson Indy	Toronto	Michael Andretti (13)	1:59:58.904	83.375	G. de Ferran	109.492
July 22	**Harrah's 500**	Brooklyn	Patrick Carpentier (21)	2:54:55.757	171.498	K. Brack	229.812
July 29	Target GP	Cicero	Kenny Brack (8)	1:54:12.835	132.031	T. Kanaan	160.052
Aug. 12	Miller Lite 200	Lexington	Helio Castroneves (2)	1:44:54.931	106.627	G. de Ferran	124.214
Aug. 19	Motorola 220	Elkhart Lake	Bruno Junqueira (10)	2:00:28.453	90.721	K. Brack	117.969
Sept. 2	Molson Indy	Vancouver	Roberto Moreno (7)	2:10:01.276	80.543	A. Tagliani	105.329
Sept. 15	The American Memorial†	Lausitz	Kenny Brack (2)	2:00:20.940	155.319	G. de Ferran	—*
Sept. 22	Rockingham 500	Corby	Gil de Ferran (2)	1:20:59.050	153.406	K. Brack	—*
Oct. 7	GP of Houston	Houston	Gil de Ferran (1)	1:54:42.336	79.521	G. de Ferran	92.513
Oct. 14	GP of Monterey	Monterey	Max Papis (25)	2:00:10.589	84.919	G. de Ferran	117.453

*Qualifying was cancelled and the starting lineup was determined by the current FedEx Series drivers points standings.
†Originally called the German 500, CART officials changed the race's name on Sept. 14 to The American Memorial to honor those killed in the Sept. 11 attacks on the United States.
Note: The inaugural Firestone Firehawk 600 at Texas Motor Speedway in Ft. Worth, Texas, scheduled for April 29, was cancelled the day of the race after officials determined the track was unfit for CART racing.
Winning cars: REYNARD/HONDA (7)—Castroneves (3), de Ferran (2), Andretti, Franchitti; LOLA/FORD (6)—Brack (4), Papis (2); LOLA/TOYOTA (2)—da Matta, Junqueira; REYNARD/TOYOTA (2)—Dixon, Moreno; REYNARD/FORD (1)—Carpentier.

CART Point Standings

Official Top 10 FedEx Championship Series point leaders and Top 15 money leaders for 2000 and unoffical leaders for 2001. Points awarded for places 1 to 12, fastest qualifier and overall lap leader. Listed are starts (Sts), top-5 finishes, poles won (PW) and points (Pts).

FINAL 2000

		Sts	Finishes 1-2-3-4-5	PW	Pts
1	Gil de Ferran	20	2-2-3-0-1	5	168
2	Adrian Fernandez	20	2-2-1-0-3	0	158
3	Roberto Moreno	20	1-3-2-1-1	1	147
4	Kenny Brack	20	0-2-2-2-3	0	135
5	Paul Tracy	20	3-0-3-1-0	1	134
6	Jimmy Vasser	20	1-1-2-1-1	0	131
7	Helio Castroneves	20	3-1-0-0-2	3	129
8	Michael Andretti	20	2-3-0-2-0	0	127
9	Juan Montoya	20	3-1-0-1-0	7	126
10	Cristiano da Matta	20	1-0-1-5-1	0	112

Other wins (2): Christian Fittipaldi and Max Papis.

2001 (through Oct. 14)

		Sts	Finishes 1-2-3-4-5	PW	Pts
1	Gil de Ferran	18	2-3-3-1-1	4*	179
2	Kenny Brack	18	4-2-0-0-1	4†	153
3	Helio Castroneves	18	3-1-0-1-1	3	141
4	Michael Andretti	18	1-2-1-3-1	0	125
5	Dario Franchitti	18	1-3-0-0-0	0	105
6	Cristiano da Matta	18	1-1-1-1-0	0	100
7	Scott Dixon	18	1-0-1-3-1	0	98
8	Max Papis	18	2-1-0-0-0	1	86
9	Patrick Carpentier	18	1-1-2-0-1	0	86
10	Tony Kanaan	18	0-0-1-1-1	1	83

*Doesn't include The American Memorial (See page 884).
†Doesn't include Miller Lite 225 or Rockingham 500, but does include Firehawk 600, which was cancelled after qualifying (See page 884).

Other wins (2): Bruno Junqueira and Roberto Moreno.

Top 5 Finishing Order + Pole
2001 Season

No.	Event	Winner	2nd	3rd	4th	5th	Pole
1	Monterrey GP	C. da Matta	G. de Ferran	P. Tracy	M. Andretti	K. Brack	K. Brack
2	Toyota GP	H. Castroneves	C. da Matta	G. de Ferran	P. Tracy	J. Vasser	H. Castroneves
3	Lehigh Valley GP	S. Dixon	K. Brack	P. Tracy	J. Vasser	C. Fittipaldi	B. Junqueira
4	Firestone Firehawk 500	K. Brack	H. Castroneves	T. Kanaan	C. Fittipaldi	J. Vasser	H. Castroneves
5	Miller Lite 225	K. Brack	M. Andretti	S. Dixon	B. Junqueira	A. Fernandez	K. Brack
6	GP of Detroit	H. Castroneves	D. Franchitti	R. Moreno	M. Andretti	C. Fittipaldi	H. Castroneves
7	Freightliner/G.I. Joe's 200	M. Papis	R. Moreno	C. Fittipaldi	M. Wilson	P. Carpentier	M. Papis
8	GP of Cleveland	D. Franchitti	M. Gidley	B. Herta	G. de Ferran	J. Vasser	M. Gugelmin
9	Molson Indy (Tor.)	M. Andretti	A. Tagliani	A. Fernandez	A. Zanardi	S. Dixon	G. de Ferran
10	Harrah's 500	P. Carpentier	D. Franchitti	M. Jourdain	C. da Matta	B. Herta	K. Brack
11	Target GP	K. Brack	P. Carpentier	G. de Ferran	S. Dixon	M. Gidley	T. Kanaan
12	Miller Lite 200	H. Castroneves	G. de Ferran	P. Carpentier	P. Tracy	T. Kanaan	G. de Ferran
13	Motorola 220	B. Junqueira	M. Andretti	A. Fernandez	S. Dixon	G. de Ferran	K. Brack
14	Molson Indy (Van.)	R. Moreno	G. de Ferran	M. Andretti	T. Kanaan	O. Servia	A. Tagliani
15	The American Memorial	K. Brack	M. Papis	P. Carpentier	M. Andretti	O. Servia	G. de Ferran
16	Rockingham 500	G. de Ferran	K. Brack	C. da Matta	H. Castroneves	M. Andretti	K. Brack
17	GP of Houston	G. de Ferran	D. Franchitti	M. Gidley	T. Takagi	H. Castroneves	G. de Ferran
18	GP of Monterey	M. Papis	M. Gidley	G. de Ferran	S. Dixon	J. Vasser	G. de Ferran

Money Leaders

FINAL 2000

		Earnings
1	Gil de Ferran	$1,677,000
2	Christian Fittipaldi	1,373,500
3	Adrian Fernandez	1,136,500
4	Roberto Moreno	907,750
5	Paul Tracy	804,750
6	Michael Andretti	724,500
7	Kenny Brack	718,750
8	Helio Castroneves	709,250
9	Juan Montoya	665,500
10	Jimmy Vasser	648,250
11	Cristiano da Matta	565,000
12	Max Papis	414,000
13	Patrick Carpentier	390,750
14	Dario Franchitti	366,250
15	Oriol Servia	317,250

2001 (through Oct. 14)

		Earnings
1	Gil de Ferran	$701,500
2	Kenny Brack	695,750
3	Helio Castroneves	612,500
4	Michael Andretti	485,500
5	Dario Franchitti	477,250
6	Max Papis	446,750
7	Cristiano da Matta	434,000
8	Scott Dixon	432,750
9	Patrick Carpentier	390,000
10	Roberto Moreno	381,750
11	Tony Kanaan	336,000
12	Paul Tracy	308,250
13	Christian Fittipaldi	302,750
14	Bruno Junqueira	293,500
15	Memo Gidley	290,250

Note: The 2001 totals don't include Performance Award earnings.

INDY RACING LEAGUE RESULTS

Results of Indy Racing Northern Light Series events during the 2001 season.

2001 SEASON

Date	Event	Location	Winner (Pos.)	Time	Avg.mph	Pole	Qual.mph
Mar. 18	Pennzoil Copper World 200	Phoenix	Sam Hornish Jr. (2)	1:36:56.705	125.072	G. Ray	177.663
Apr. 8	Infiniti GP of Miami	Miami	Sam Hornish Jr. (5)	2:01:12.336	148.508	J. Ward	201.551
Apr. 28	zMAX 500	Atlanta	Greg Ray (1)	2:14:40.989	133.647	G. Ray	218.265
May 27	**Indianapolis 500** . . .	Indianapolis	Helio Castroneves (11)	3:31:54.180	141.574	S. Sharp	226.037
June 9	Casino Magic 500	Ft. Worth	Scott Sharp (2)	1:55:43.577	150.837	M. Dismore	215.508
June 17	Radisson 200	Pikes Peak	Buddy Lazier (5)	1:23:55.426	142.987	G. Ray	176.585
June 30	Sun Trust Challenge	Richmond	Buddy Lazier (4)	1:55:27.730	97.435	J. Lazier	160.417
July 8	Ameristar Casino 200 . .	Kansas City	Eddie Cheever Jr. (2)	2:02:29.203	148.914	S. Sharp	216.175
July 21	Harrah's 200	Nashville	Buddy Lazier (6)	1:47:43.682	144.809	G. Ray	199.922
Aug. 12	Belterra Casino 300	Sparta	Buddy Lazier (11)	1:42:54.593	174.910	S. Sharp	214.598
Aug. 26	Gateway 250	St. Louis	Al Unser Jr. (8)	1:49:59.268	136.379	S. Hornish Jr.	—*
Sept. 2	Delphi 300	Joliet	Jaques Lazier (1)	1:45:57.403	172.146	J. Lazier	221.740
Oct. 6	Chevy 500	Ft. Worth	Sam Hornish Jr. (1)	1:47:43.682	168.523	S. Hornish Jr.	—*

*Qualifying was cancelled due to inclement weather and the starting lineup was determined by current Indy Racing Northern Lights Series drivers' points standings.
Winning cars: DALLARA/OLDS AURORA (11)—B. Lazier (4), Hornish Jr. (3), J. Lazier, Castroneves, Ray, Sharp; G-FORCE/ OLDS AURORA (1)—Unser Jr.; DALLARA/INFINITI (1)—Cheever Jr.

85th Indianapolis 500

Date—Sunday, May 27, 2001, at Indianapolis Motor Speedway. **Distance**—500 miles; **Course**—2.5 mile oval; **Field**—33 cars; **Winner's average speed**—141.574 mph; **Margin of victory**—1.737 seconds; **Time of race**—3 hours, 31 minutes, 54.180 seconds; **Caution flags**—8 for 56 laps; **Lead changes**—13 by 8 drivers; **Lap leaders**— Castroneves (52), Ray (40), Dismore (29), de Ferran (27), Gordon (22), Andretti (16), Stewart (13), Luyendyk (1); **Pole Sitter**—Scott Sharp at 226.037 mph; **Attendance**—400,000 (est.); **TV Rating**—5.3/14 share (ABC). Note that (r) indicates rookie driver.

	Driver (start pos.)	Country	Car	Laps	Ended	Earnings
1	r-Helio Castroneves (11)	Brazil	D/A/F	200	Running	$1,270,475
2	Gil de Ferran (5)	Brazil	D/A/F	200	Running	482,775
3	Michael Andretti (21)	United States	D/A/F	200	Running	346.225
4	Jimmy Vasser (12)	United States	G/A/F	200	Running	233,325
5	r-Bruno Junqueira (20)	Brazil	G/A/F	200	Running	255,825
6	Tony Stewart (7)	United States	G/A/F	200	Running	218.850
7	Eliseo Salazar (28)	Chile	D/A/F	199	Running	355,300
8	Airton Daré (30)	Brazil	G/A/F	199	Running	319.325
9	Billy Boat (32)	United States	D/A/F	199	Running	336,325
10	r-Felipe Giaffone (33)	Brazil	G/A/F	199	Running	211.575
11	Robby McGehee (14)	United States	D/A/F	199	Running	290,825
12	Buzz Calkins (24)	United States	D/A/F	198	Running	285,025
13	Arie Luyendyk (6)	Netherlands	G/A/F	198	Running	182,275
14	Sam Hornish Jr. (13)	United States	D/A/F	196	Running	307,825
15	Robbie Buhl (9)	United States	G/I/F	196	Running	300,325
16	Mark Dismore (4)	United States	D/A/F	195	Running	287,375
17	Greg Ray (2)	United States	D/A/F	192	Running	335,325
18	Buddy Lazier (10)	United States	D/A/F	192	Running	262,325
19	r-Cory Witherill (31)	United States	G/A/F	187	Running	159,575
20	Jeret Schroeder (23)	United States	D/A/F	187	Running	256,325
21	Robby Gordon (3)	United States	D/A/F	184	Running	173,225
22	Jaques Lazier (17)	United States	G/A/F	183	Running	161,325
23	Davey Hamilton (26)	United States	D/A/F	182	Engine	255,325
24	Jeff Ward (8)	United States	G/A/F	168	Running	248,325
25	Donnie Beechler (27)	United States	D/A/F	160	Oil Leak	172,325
26	Eddie Cheever Jr. (25)	United States	D/I/F	108	Electrical	247,325
27	r-Jon Herb (18)	United States	D/A/F	104	Accident	245,575
28	Stephan Gregoire (29)	France	G/A/F	86	Oil Leak	154,325
29	r-Nicolas Minassian (22)	France	G/A/F	74	Gearbox	149,575
30	Al Unser Jr. (19)	United States	D/A/F	16	Accident	255,825
31	Sarah Fisher (15)	United States	D/A/F	7	Accident	247,325
32	Scott Goodyear (16)	Canada	D/I/F	7	Accident	143,325
33	Scott Sharp (1)	United States	D/A/F	0	Accident	427,325

Car Legend: Chassis/Engine/Tires. D—Dallara; G—G Force (chassis); A—Oldsmobile Aurora V-8; I—Nissan Infiniti V-8 (engine); F—Firestone (tires).

Indy Racing League Point Standings

Official Top 10 Indy Racing Northern Light Series driver points leaders and Top 10 money leaders for 2000 and 2001. Listed are starts (Sts), top-5 finishes, poles won (PW) and points (Pts).

FINAL 2000

		Sts	Finishes 1-2-3-4-5	PW	Pts
1	Buddy Lazier	9	2-3-0-1-0	0*	290
2	Scott Goodyear	9	1-2-0-1-1	1	272
3	Eddie Cheever Jr.	9	1-1-1-1-1	0	257
4	Eliseo Salazar	9	0-0-1-1-2	0	210
5	Mark Dismore	9	0-1-0-1-1	1	202
6	Donnie Beechler	9	0-0-1-0-2	0	202
7	Scott Sharp	9	1-0-1-0-1	0	196
8	Robbie Buhl	9	1-0-0-0-1	0	190
9	Al Unser Jr.	9	1-0-2-0-0	0	188
10	Billy Boat	9	0-0-1-0-0	0	181

*Doesn't include Casino Magic 500.
Other wins (2): Juan Montoya and Greg Ray.

FINAL 2001

		Sts	Finishes 1-2-3-4-5	PW	Pts
1	Sam Hornish Jr.	13	3-4-3-1-0	0*	503
2	Buddy Lazier	13	4-0-1-1-1	0	398
3	Scott Sharp	13	1-3-0-1-2	3	355
4	Billy Boat	13	0-1-0-1-2	0	313
5	Eliseo Salazar	13	0-1-1-1-1	0	308
6	Felipe Giaffone	13	0-1-0-2-0	0	304
7	Al Unser Jr.	13	1-0-1-1-0	0	287
8	Eddie Cheever Jr.	13	1-0-1-1-0	0	261
9	Buzz Calkins	13	0-0-1-0-0	0	242
10	Airton Dare	13	0-0-0-0-1	0	239

*Doesn't include Gateway 250 and Chevy 500 (See page 886).
Other wins (3): Helio Castroneves, Jaques Lazier and Greg Ray.

Top 5 Finishing Order + Pole

2001 Season

No.	Event	Winner	2nd	3rd	4th	5th	Pole
1	Pennzoil 200	S. Hornish Jr.	E. Salazar	B. Lazier	S. Sharp	B. Boat	G. Ray
2	GP of Miami	S. Hornish Jr.	S. Fisher	E. Salazar	F. Giaffone	J. Ward	J. Ward
3	Atlanta	G. Ray	S. Sharp	B. Calkins	S. Hornish Jr.	E. Salazar	G. Ray
4	Indy 500	H. Castroneves	G. de Ferran	M. Andretti	J. Vasser	B. Junqueira	S. Sharp
5	Casino Magic 500	S. Sharp	F. Giaffone	S. Hornish Jr.	B. Lazier	B. Boat	M. Dismore
6	Radisson 200	B. Lazier	S. Hornish Jr.	R. Buhl	B. Boat	A. Dare	G. Ray
7	Sun Trust Challenge	B. Lazier	S. Hornish Jr.	A. Unser Jr.	D. Andre	S. Sharp	J. Lazier
8	Ameristar Casino 200	E. Cheever Jr.	S. Hornish Jr.	D. Beechler	F. Giaffone	B. Lazier	S. Sharp
9	Harrah's 200	B. Lazier	B. Boat	J. Lazier	R. McGehee	S. Sharp	G. Ray
10	Belterra Casino 300	B. Lazier	S. Sharp	S. Hornish Jr.	A. Unser Jr.	D. Beechler	S. Sharp
11	Gateway 250	A. Unser Jr.	M. Dismore	S. Hornish Jr.	E. Cheever Jr.	R. Buhl	S. Hornish Jr.
12	Delphi 300	J. Lazier	S. Hornish Jr.	E. Cheever Jr.	J. Ward	D. Beechler	J. Lazier
13	Chevy 500	S. Hornish Jr.	S. Sharp	R. Buhl	E. Salazar	R. Treadway	S. Hornish Jr.

Money Leaders

FINAL 2000

		Earnings
1	Juan Montoya	$1,235,690
2	Buddy Lazier	1,168,700
3	Scott Goodyear	884,900
4	Eddie Cheever Jr.	876,200
5	Greg Ray	821,700
6	Eliseo Salazar	820,000
7	Scott Sharp	767,050
8	Al Unser Jr.	730,300
9	Mark Dismore	712,950
10	Robbie Buhl	685,500

FINAL 2001

		Earnings
1	Sam Hornish Jr.	$2,477,025
2	Helio Castroneves	1,305,075
3	Scott Sharp	1,234,425
4	Buddy Lazier	1,196,525
5	Eliseo Salazar	949,900
6	Billy Boat	925,025
7	Eddie Cheever Jr.	881,275
8	Robbie Buhl	873,375
9	Greg Ray	859,875
10	Al Unser Jr.	844,525

FORMULA ONE RESULTS

Results of Formula One Grand Prix races in 2001.

2001 SEASON

Date	Grand Prix	Location	Winner (Pos.)	Time	Avg.mph	Pole	Qual.mph
Mar. 3	Australian	Melbourne	Michael Schumacher (1)	1:38:26.533	116.485	M. Schumacher	136.520
Mar. 18	Malaysian	Kuala Lumpur	Michael Schumacher (1)	1:47:34.801	105.652	M. Schumacher	130.218
Apr. 1	Brazilian	Sao Paulo	David Coulthard (5)	1:39:00.384	115.185	M. Schumacher	130.645
Apr. 15	San Marino	Imola	Ralf Schumacher (3)	1:30:44.817	125.556	D. Coulthard	132.863
Apr. 29	Spanish	Barcelona	Michael Schumacher (1)	1:31:03.305	125.832	M. Schumacher	135.302
May 13	Austrian	Spielberg	David Coulthard (7)	1:27:45.927	130.474	M. Schumacher	139.113
May 27	Monaco	Monaco	Michael Schumacher (2)	1:47:22.561	91.247	D. Coulthard	97.358
June 10	Canadian	Montreal	Ralf Schumacher (2)	1:34:31.522	120.315	M. Schumacher	130.499
June 24	European	Nürburgring	Michael Schumacher (1)	1:29:42.724	126.848	M. Schumacher	135.959
July 1	French	Magny-Cours	Michael Schumacher (2)	1:33:35.636	121.846	R. Schumacher	130.252
July 15	Great Britain	Silverstone	Mika Hakkinen (2)	1:25:33.770	134.359	M. Schumacher	142.952
July 29	German	Hockenheim	Ralf Schumacher (2)	1:18:17.873	146.240	J. Montoya	155.600
Aug. 19	Hungarian	Budapest	Michael Schumacher (1)	1:41:49.675	112.063	M. Schumacher	120.064
Sept. 2	Belgian	Spa	Michael Schumacher (3)	1:15:31.935	137.354	J. Montoya	139.080

FORMULA ONE RESULTS (Cont.)

Date	Grand Prix	Location	Winner (Pos.)	Time	Avg.mph	Pole	Qual.mph
Sept. 16	Italian	Monza	Juan Montoya (1)	1:16:58.493	148.571	J. Montoya	157.270
Sept. 30	U.S.	Indianapolis	Mika Hakkinen (4)	1:32:42.840	123.055	M. Schumacher	130.770
Oct. 14	Japan	Suzuka	Michael Schumacher (1)	1:27:33.298	132.143	M. Schumacher	141.713

Winning Constructors: FERRARI (9)—M. Schumacher (9); MCLAREN/MERCEDES (4)—Coulthard (2), Hakkinen (2); WILLIAMS/BMW (4)—R. Schumacher (3), J. Montoya.

Formula One Point Standings

Official Top 10 Formula One World Championship point leaders for 2000 and 2001. Points awarded for places 1 through 6 only (i.e., 10-6-4-3-2-1). Listed are starts (Sts), top-6 finishes, poles won (PW) and points (Pts). **Note:** Formula One does not keep Money Leader standings.

FINAL 2000

		Sts	Finishes 1-2-3-4-5-6	PW	Pts
1	Michael Schumacher	17	9-2-1-0-1-0	9	108
2	Mika Hakkinen	17	4-7-0-2-0-1	5	89
3	David Coulthard	17	3-3-5-1-1-0	2	73
4	Rubens Barrichello	17	1-4-4-4-0-0	1	62
5	Ralf Schumacher	17	0-0-3-2-3-0	0	24
6	Giancarlo Fisichella	17	0-1-2-0-2-0	0	18
7	Jacques Villeneuve	17	0-0-0-4-2-1	0	17
8	Jenson Button	17	0-0-0-1-4-1	0	12
9	Heinz-Harald Frentzen	17	0-0-2-0-0-3	0	11
10	Jarno Trulli	17	0-0-0-1-0-3	0	6
	Mika Salo	17	0-0-0-0-2-2	0	6

FINAL 2001

		Sts	Finishes 1-2-3-4-5-6	PW	Pts
1	Michael Schumacher	17	9-5-0-1-0-0	11	123
2	David Coulthard	17	2-3-5-1-2-0	2	65
3	Rubens Barrichello	17	0-3-5-0-3-0	0	56
4	Ralf Schumacher	17	3-1-1-2-1-1	1	49
5	Mika Hakkinen	17	2-0-1-3-1-2	0	37
6	Juan Montoya	17	1-3-0-1-0-0	3	31
7	Jacques Villeneuve	17	0-0-2-1-0-1	0	12
	Nick Heidfeld	17	0-0-1-1-1-4	0	12
	Jarno Trulli	17	0-0-2-1-0-1	0	12
10	Kimi Raikkonen	17	0-0-0-2-1-1	0	9

Top 5 + Pole Finishing Order

No.	Event	Winner	2nd	3rd	4th	5th	Pole
1	Australian	M. Schumacher	D. Coulthard	R. Barrichello	N. Heidfeld	H.H. Frentzen	M. Schumacher
2	Malaysian	M. Schumacher	R. Barrichello	D. Coulthard	H.H. Frentzen	R. Schumacher	M. Schumacher
3	Brazilian	D. Coulthard	M. Schumacher	N. Heidfeld	O. Panis	J. Trulli	M. Schumacher
4	San Marino	R. Schumacher	M. Schumacher	D. Coulthard	R. Barrichello	M. Hakkinen	D. Coulthard
5	Spanish	M. Schumacher	J. Montoya	J. Villeneuve	J. Trulli	D. Coulthard	M. Schumacher
6	Austrian	D. Coulthard	M. Schumacher	R. Barrichello	K. Raikkonen	O. Panis	M. Schumacher
7	Monaco	M. Schumacher	R. Barrichello	E. Irvine	J. Villeneuve	D. Coulthard	D. Coulthard
8	Canadian	R. Schumacher	M. Schumacher	M. Hakkinen	K. Raikkonen	J. Alesi	M. Schumacher
9	European	M. Schumacher	J. Montoya	D. Coulthard	R. Schumacher	R. Barrichello	M. Schumacher
10	French	M. Schumacher	R. Schumacher	R. Barrichello	D. Coulthard	J. Trulli	R. Schumacher
11	British	M. Hakkinen	M. Schumacher	R. Barrichello	J. Montoya	K. Hakkinen	R. Schumacher
12	German	R. Schumacher	R. Barrichello	J. Villeneuve	G. Fisichella	J. Button	J. Montoya
13	Hungarian	M. Schumacher	R. Barrichello	D. Coulthard	R. Schumacher	M. Hakkinen	M. Schumacher
14	Belgian	M. Schumacher	D. Coulthard	G. Fisichella	M. Hakkinen	R. Barrichello	J. Montoya
15	Italian	J. Montoya	R. Barrichello	R. Schumacher	M. Schumacher	P. de la Rosa	J. Montoya
16	U.S.	M. Hakkinen	M. Schumacher	D. Coulthard	E. Irvine	N. Heidfeld	M. Schumacher
17	Japan	M. Schumacher	J. Montoya	D. Coulthard	M. Hakkinen	R. Barrichello	M. Schumacher

Major 2001 Endurance Races

24 Hours of Daytona
Feb. 3-4, at Daytona Beach, Fla.

Officially the Rolex 24 at Daytona and first held in 1962 (as a 3-hour race). An IMSA Camel GT race for exotic prototype sports cars and contested over a 3.56-mile road course at Daytona International Speedway. Listed are qualifying position, drivers, chassis, class and laps completed.
1 (14) Ron Fellows, Chris Kneifel, Frank Freon, Johnny O'Connell; CHEVROLET CORVETTE; 656 laps (2,573.88 miles) at 97.293 mph; margin of victory eight laps.
2 (39) Lucas Luhr, Mike Fitzgerald, Randy Pobst; PORSCHE GT3R, 648 laps.
3 (57) Wolfgang Kaufmann, Lance Stewart, Ciril Chateau, PORSCHE GT3RS, 644 laps.
4 (19) Andy Pilgrim, Dale Earnhardt, Dale Earnhardt Jr., Kelly Collins, CHEVROLET CORVETTE; 642 laps.
5 (40) Fabio Babini, Fabio Rosa, Alex Caffi, Gabrio Rosa; PORSCHE GT3RS; 637 laps.
Top qualifier: James Weaver, RILEY & SCOTT FORD, 119.351 mph (1:47.361).
Weather: Rain. **Attendance:** 40,000 (est.).

24 Hours of Le Mans
June 16-17, at Le Mans, France

Officially the Le Mans Grand Prix d'Endurance and first held in 1923. Contested over the 8.456-mile Circuit de la Sarthe in Le Mans, France. Listed are qualifying position, drivers, car, and laps completed.
1 (2) Frank Biela, Tom Kristensen and Emanuele Pirro; AUDI R8; 321 laps (2,712.711 miles) at 129.659.
2 (1) Laurent Aiello, Rinaldo Capelo and Christian Pescatori; AUDI R8; 320 laps.
3 (9) Andy Wallace, Butch Leitzinger, Eric Van De Poele; BENTLEY EXP SPEED 8; 306 laps.
4 (6) Oliver Baretta, Karl Wendlinger, Pedro Lamy; CHRYSLER LMP 2001 MOPAR; 298 laps.
5 (23) Jean Denis Deletraz, Pascal Fabre, Jordi Gene; REYNARD 2KQ LEHMANN; 284 laps.
Top qualifier: Rinaldo Capelo, AUDI R8, 143.264 mph (3:32.429).
Weather: Rain. **Attendance:** 200,000 (est.).

NHRA RESULTS

Winners of National Hot Rod Association Drag Racing events in the Top Fuel, Funny Car and Pro Stock divisions through Oct. 21, 2001. All times are based on two cars racing head-to-head from a standing start over a straight line, quarter-mile course. Differences in reaction time account for apparently faster losing times.

2001 Season

Date	Event	Event	Winner	Time	MPH	2nd Place	Time	MPH
Feb. 4	AutoZone Winternationals . .	Top Fuel	Darrell Russell	4.665	309.77	M. Dunn	5.560	231.44
		Funny Car	Bruce Sarver	4.887	308.35	T. Pedregon	4.957	284.39
		Pro Stock	Kurt Johnson	6.912	200.44	D. Alderman	6.936	200.41
Feb. 18	Kragen Nationals	Top Fuel	Doug Kalitta	4.628	309.84	D. Russell	7.416	111.94
		Funny Car	John Force	4.929	285.77	B. Sarver	6.956	121.91
		Pro Stock	Warren Johnson	6.924	199.20	B. Jeter	6.967	198.23
Mar. 18	Gatornationals	Top Fuel	Larry Dixon	4.661	313.95	G. Scelzi	4.727	313.95
		Funny Car	John Force	5.310	273.27	D. Skuza	10.728	79.11
		Pro Stock	Jeg Coughlin	6.935	199.40	M. Osborne	6.928	199.58
Apr. 8	SummitRacing.com Nationals .	Top Fuel	Kenny Bernstein	4.533	325.53	A. Cowin	4.615	322.73
		Funny Car	Tommy Johnson Jr.	4.856	310.77	W. Bazemore	4.965	291.07
		Pro Stock	Jeg Coughlin	6.959	197.62	J. Yates	6.940	197.71
Apr. 29	Thunder Valley Nationals . . .	Top Fuel	Doug Kalitta	4.690	300.73	T. Schumacher	5.065	217.14
		Funny Car	Ron Capps	5.045	288.52	A. Hofmann	5.154	283.79
		Pro Stock	Greg Anderson	6.993	196.85	J. Yates	6.985	197.51
May 6	Southern Nationals	Top Fuel	Mike Dunn	4.591	325.06	D. Russell	broke	broke
		Funny Car	Frank Pedregon	4.902	305.98	R. Capps	5.566	180.07
		Pro Stock	Jim Yates	6.959	199.43	G. Anderson	6.957	198.17
May 20	Matco Tools SuperNationals .	Top Fuel	Kenny Bernstein	4.532	321.35	D. Kalitta	9.169	87.98
		Funny Car	Tony Pedregon	4.936	316.23	J. Force	6.117	147.58
		Pro Stock	Richie Stevens	6.892	200.14	M. Pawuk	8.504	113.81
May 27	Advance Auto Parts Nationals	Top Fuel	Kenny Bernstein	4.625	317.94	L. Dixon	4.648	313.73
		Funny Car	Tony Pedregon	4.912	309.77	J. Force	6.032	246.62
		Pro Stock	Ron Krisher	6.963	198.73	M. Pawuk	7.076	197.19
June 3	Lucas Nationals	Top Fuel	Kenny Bernstein	4.546	322.81	G. Scelzi	7.197	109.25
		Funny Car	Del Worsham	4.811	314.39	J. Force	4.805	321.19
		Pro Stock	Mike Edwards	6.848	200.23	J. Yates	6.888	200.11
June 17	Pontiac Excitement Nationals .	Top Fuel	Larry Dixon	4.700	306.53	D. Russell	4.929	230.37
		Funny Car	John Force	4.963	308.00	D. Worsham	6.204	160.79
		Pro Stock	Warren Johnson	6.948	198.00	M. Osborne	6.985	198.58
June 24	Sears Craftsman Nationals . .	Top Fuel	Doug Kalitta	4.772	302.82	K. Bernstein	4.756	309.13
		Funny Car	Tony Pedregon	5.006	296.31	T. Johnson Jr.	4.989	293.54
		Pro Stock	Warren Johnson	6.908	200.74	J. Yates	6.930	200.62
July 7	Pep Boys NHRA 50th Anniversary Nationals	Top Fuel	Doug Herbert	4.600	320.58	G. Scelzi	5.574	305.42
		Funny Car	John Force	4.853	317.64	W. Bazemore	5.691	168.51
		Pro Stock	Jeg Coughlin	6.911	199.26	M. Edwards	6.923	200.05
July 22	Mile-High Nationals	Top Fuel	Larry Dixon	4.844	298.47	D. Kalitta	5.364	257.24
		Funny Car	John Force	5.225	288.39	B. Gilbertson	8.834	288.39
		Pro Stock	Warren Johnson	7.347	188.28	K. Johnson	7.335	188.73
July 29	Northwest Nationals	Top Fuel	Gary Scelzi	4.556	319.29	K. Bernstein	4.881	264.91
		Funny Car	Whit Bazemore	5.049	284.56	R. Capps	5.086	277.43
		Pro Stock	Mark Osborne	6.893	201.43	D. Alderman	6.894	201.73
Aug. 5	Autolite Nationals	Top Fuel	Kenny Bernstein	4.819	298.40	D. Grubnic	5.843	153.54
		Funny Car	Del Worsham	5.044	301.60	J. Epler	6.222	156.88
		Pro Stock	Tom Martino	7.037	196.50	M. Edwards	13.853	59.64
Aug. 19	Colonel's Nationals	Top Fuel	Larry Dixon	4.609	316.90	D. Russell	4.709	317.42
		Funny Car	Ron Capps	4.939	306.53	W. Bazemore	5.991	201.70
		Pro Stock	Bruce Allen	6.962	197.28	R. Krisher	6.985	198.17
Sept. 3	U.S. Nationals	Top Fuel	Larry Dixon	4.609	315.93	M. Dunn	5.149	199.79
		Funny Car	Whit Bazemore	4.971	298.14	T. Pedregon	5.123	275.06
		Pro Stock	Greg Anderson	6.958	198.58	M. Osborne	7.016	198.70
Sept. 23	AutoZone Nationals	Top Fuel	Kenny Bernstein	4.682	308.78	L. Dixon	4.753	304.05
		Funny Car	Gary Densham	5.070	290.01	J. Force	5.111	283.73
		Pro Stock	George Marnell	6.974	198.12	M. Pawuk	6.950	198.00
Sept. 30	NHRA Nationals at Route 66 Raceway	Top Fuel	Kenny Bernstein	4.569	322.04	D. Russell	8.731	89.05
		Funny Car	Whit Bazemore	4.823	320.97	J. Force	4.875	312.93
		Pro Stock	Warren Johnson	6.832	201.70	D. Alderman	6.852	201.97
Oct. 7	Pep Boys Nationals	Top Fuel	Gary Scelzi	4.511	317.19	K. Bernstein	4.528	319.67
		Funny Car	John Force	4.792	312.06	W. Bazemore	4.832	318.54
		Pro Stock	Troy Coughlin	6.768	203.40	T. Martino	6.847	200.59
Oct. 21	O'Reilly Nationals	Top Fuel	Larry Dixon	4.553	320.05	D. Kalitta	7.908	105.64
		Funny Car	Gary Densham	4.832	318.13	J. Force	4.852	318.69
		Pro Stock	V. Gaines	6.929	199.77	T. Hammonds	6.961	200.00

Note: The Keystone Nationals, scheduled for Sept. 13-16, was postponed due to the Sept. 11 attacks and run from Oct. 4-7 with a new title sponsor, Pep Boys.

2000-2001 Through the Years

NASCAR Circuit
The Crown Jewels

The five biggest races on the NASCAR (National Association for Stock Car Auto Racing) circuit are the Daytona 500, the EA Sports 500, the Coca-Cola 600, the Mountain Dew Southern 500, and the Brickyard 400 (Indianapolis). They are the Winston Cup Series' biggest (Daytona), fastest (EA Sports), longest (Coca-Cola), oldest (Southern) and richest (Brickyard) races. The only drivers to win three of the races in a year are Lee Roy Yarbrough (1969), David Pearson (1976), Bill Elliott (1985) Dale Jarrett (1996) and Jeff Gordon (1997-98).

Daytona 500

Held early in the NASCAR season; 200 laps around a 2.5-mile high-banked oval at Daytona International Speedway in Daytona Beach, Fla. First race in 1959, although stock car racing at Daytona dates back to 1936. Winning drivers who started from pole positions are in **bold** type.

Multiple winners: Richard Petty (7); Cale Yarborough (4); Bobby Allison and Dale Jarrett (3); Bill Elliott, Jeff Gordon and Sterling Marlin (2). **Multiple poles:** Buddy Baker and Cale Yarborough (4); Bill Elliott, Dale Jarrett, Fireball Roberts and Ken Schrader (3); Donnie Allison (2).

Year	Winner	Car	Owner	MPH	Pole Sitter	MPH
1959	Lee Petty	Oldsmobile	Petty Enterprises	135.521	Bob Welborn	140.121
1960	Junior Johnson	Chevrolet	Ray Fox	124.740	Cotton Owens	149.892
1961	Marvin Panch	Pontiac	Smokey Yunick	149.601	Fireball Roberts	155.709
1962	**Fireball Roberts**	Pontiac	Smokey Yunick	152.529	Fireball Roberts	156.999
1963	Tiny Lund	Ford	Wood Brothers	151.566	Fireball Roberts	160.943
1964	Richard Petty	Plymouth	Petty Enterprises	154.334	Paul Goldsmith	174.910
1965-a	Fred Lorenzen	Ford	Holman-Moody	141.539	Darel Dieringer	171.151
1966-b	**Richard Petty**	Plymouth	Petty Enterprises	160.627	Richard Petty	175.165
1967	Mario Andretti	Ford	Holman-Moody	149.926	Curtis Turner	180.831
1968	**Cale Yarborough**	Mercury	Wood Brothers	143.251	Cale Yarborough	189.222
1969	Lee Roy Yarbrough	Ford	Junior Johnson	157.950	Buddy Baker	188.901
1970	Pete Hamilton	Plymouth	Petty Enterprises	149.601	Cale Yarborough	194.015
1971	Richard Petty	Plymouth	Petty Enterprises	144.462	A.J. Foyt	182.744
1972	A.J. Foyt	Mercury	Wood Brothers	161.550	Bobby Isaac	186.632
1973	Richard Petty	Dodge	Petty Enterprises	157.205	Buddy Baker	185.662
1974-c	Richard Petty	Dodge	Petty Enterprises	140.894	David Pearson	185.017
1975	Benny Parsons	Chevrolet	L.G. DeWitt	153.649	Donnie Allison	185.827
1976	David Pearson	Mercury	Wood Brothers	152.181	Ramo Stott	183.456
1977	Cale Yarborough	Chevrolet	Junior Johnson	153.218	Donnie Allison	188.048
1978	Bobby Allison	Ford	Bud Moore	159.730	Cale Yarborough	187.536
1979	Richard Petty	Oldsmobile	Petty Enterprises	143.977	Buddy Baker	196.049
1980	**Buddy Baker**	Oldsmobile	Ranier Racing	177.602*	Buddy Baker	194.099
1981	Richard Petty	Buick	Petty Enterprises	169.651	Bobby Allison	194.624
1982	Bobby Allison	Buick	DiGard Racing	153.991	Benny Parsons	196.317
1983	Cale Yarborough	Pontiac	Ranier Racing	155.979	Ricky Rudd	198.864
1984	**Cale Yarborough**	Chevrolet	Ranier Racing	150.994	Cale Yarborough	201.848
1985	**Bill Elliott**	Ford	Melling Racing	172.265	Bill Elliott	205.114
1986	Geoff Bodine	Chevrolet	Hendrick Motorsports	148.124	Bill Elliott	205.039
1987	**Bill Elliott**	Ford	Melling Racing	176.263	Bill Elliott	210.364†
1988	Bobby Allison	Buick	Stavola Brothers	137.531	Ken Schrader	198.823
1989	Darrell Waltrip	Chevrolet	Hendrick Motorsports	148.466	Ken Schrader	196.996
1990	Derrike Cope	Chevrolet	Bob Whitcomb	165.761	Ken Schrader	196.515
1991	Ernie Irvan	Chevrolet	Morgan-McClure	148.148	Davey Allison	195.955
1992	Davey Allison	Ford	Robert Yates	160.256	Sterling Martin	192.213
1993	Dale Jarrett	Chevrolet	Joe Gibbs Racing	154.972	Kyle Petty	189.426
1994	Sterling Marlin	Chevrolet	Morgan-McClure	156.931	Loy Allen	190.158
1995	Sterling Marlin	Chevrolet	Morgan-McClure	141.710	Dale Jarrett	193.498
1996	Dale Jarrett	Ford	Robert Yates	154.308	Dale Earnhardt	189.510
1997	Jeff Gordon	Chevrolet	Rick Hendrick	148.295	Mike Skinner	189.813
1998	Dale Earnhardt	Chevrolet	Richard Childress	172.712	Bobby Labonte	192.415
1999	**Jeff Gordon**	Chevrolet	Rick Hendrick	161.551	Jeff Gordon	195.067
2000	**Dale Jarrett**	Ford	Robert Yates	155.669	Dale Jarrett	191.091
2001	Michael Waltrip	Chevrolet	Dale Earnhardt, Inc.	161.783	Bill Elliott	183.565

*Track and race record for winning speed. †Track and race record for qualifying speed.
Notes: a—rain shortened 1965 to 332+ miles; **b**—rain shortened 1966 race to 495 miles; **c**—in 1974, race shortened 50 miles due to energy crisis. **Also:** Pole sitters determined by pole qualifying race (1959-65); by two-lap average (1966-68); by fastest single lap (since 1969).

EA Sports 500

Held at Talladega (Ala.) Superspeedway. Previously called Winston 500. **Multiple winners:** Dale Earnhardt (4); Bobby Allison, Davey Allison, Buddy Baker and David Pearson (3); Mark Martin, Darrell Waltrip and Cale Yarborough (2).

Year		Year		Year		Year	
1970	Pete Hamilton	1978	Cale Yarborough	1986	Bobby Allison	1994	Dale Earnhardt
1971	Donnie Allison	1979	Bobby Allison	1987	Davey Allison	1995	Mark Martin
1972	David Pearson	1980	Buddy Baker	1988	Phil Parsons	1996	Sterling Marlin
1973	David Pearson	1981	Bobby Allison	1989	Davey Allison	1997	Mark Martin
1974	David Pearson	1982	Darrell Waltrip	1990	Dale Earnhardt	1998	Dale Jarrett
1975	Buddy Baker	1983	Richard Petty	1991	Harry Gant	1999	Dale Earnhardt
1976	Buddy Baker	1984	Cale Yarborough	1992	Davey Allison	2000	Dale Earnhardt
1977	Darrell Waltrip	1985	Bill Elliott	1993	Ernie Irvan	2001	Dale Earnhardt Jr.

Coca-Cola 600

Held at Lowe's Motor Speedway. **Multiple winners:** Darrell Waltrip (5); Bobby Allison, Buddy Baker, Dale Earnhardt, Jeff Gordon and David Pearson (3); Neil Bonnett, Jeff Burton, Fred Lorenzen, Jim Paschal and Richard Petty (2).

Year		Year		Year		Year	
1960	Joe Lee Johnson	1971	Bobby Allison	1982	Neil Bonnett	1993	Dale Earnhardt
1961	David Pearson	1972	Buddy Baker	1983	Neil Bonnett	1994	Jeff Gordon
1962	Nelson Stacy	1973	Buddy Baker	1984	Bobby Allison	1995	Bobby Labonte
1963	Fred Lorenzen	1974	David Pearson	1985	Darrell Waltrip	1996	Dale Jarrett
1964	Jim Paschal	1975	Richard Petty	1986	Dale Earnhardt	1997	Jeff Gordon
1965	Fred Lorenzen	1976	David Pearson	1987	Kyle Petty	1998	Jeff Gordon
1966	Marvin Panch	1977	Richard Petty	1988	Darrell Waltrip	1999	Jeff Burton
1967	Jim Paschal	1978	Darrell Waltrip	1989	Darrell Waltrip	2000	Matt Kenseth
1968	Buddy Baker	1979	Darrell Waltrip	1990	Rusty Wallace	2001	Jeff Burton
1969	Lee Roy Yarbrough	1980	Benny Parsons	1991	Davey Allison		
1970	Donnie Allison	1981	Bobby Allison	1992	Dale Earnhardt		

Mountain Dew Southern 500

Held at Darlington (S.C.) International Raceway. **Multiple winners:** Cale Yarborough (5); Bobby Allison and Jeff Gordon (4); Buck Baker, Dale Earnhardt, Bill Elliott, David Pearson and Herb Thomas (3); Harry Gant and Fireball Roberts (2).

Year		Year		Year		Year	
1950	Johnny Mantz	1963	Fireball Roberts	1976	David Pearson	1989	Dale Earnhardt
1951	Herb Thomas	1964	Buck Baker	1977	David Pearson	1990	Dale Earnhardt
1952	Fonty Flock	1965	Ned Jarrett	1978	Cale Yarborough	1991	Harry Gant
1953	Buck Baker	1966	Darel Dieringer	1979	David Pearson	1992	Darrell Waltrip
1954	Herb Thomas	1967	Richard Petty	1980	Terry Labonte	1993	Mark Martin
1955	Herb Thomas	1968	Cale Yarborough	1981	Neil Bonnett	1994	Bill Elliott
1956	Curtis Turner	1969	Lee Roy Yarbrough	1982	Cale Yarborough	1995	Jeff Gordon
1957	Speedy Thompson	1970	Buddy Baker	1983	Bobby Allison	1996	Jeff Gordon
1958	Fireball Roberts	1971	Bobby Allison	1984	Harry Gant	1997	Jeff Gordon
1959	Jim Reed	1972	Bobby Allison	1985	Bill Elliott	1998	Jeff Gordon
1960	Buck Baker	1973	Cale Yarborough	1986	Tim Richmond	1999	Jeff Burton
1961	Nelson Stacy	1974	Cale Yarborough	1987	Dale Earnhardt	2000	Bobby Labonte
1962	Larry Frank	1975	Bobby Allison	1988	Bill Elliott	2001	Ward Burton

Brickyard 400

Held at Indianapolis (Ind.) Motor Speedway. **Multiple winners:** Jeff Gordon (3); Dale Jarrett (2).

Year		Year		Year		Year	
1994	Jeff Gordon	1996	Dale Jarrett	1998	Jeff Gordon	2000	Bobby Labonte
1995	Dale Earnhardt	1997	Ricky Rudd	1999	Dale Jarrett	2001	Jeff Gordon

All-Time Leaders

NASCAR's all-time Top 20 drivers in victories, pole positions and earnings based on records through 2000. Drivers active in 2001 are in **bold** type.

Victories

1 Richard Petty 200	8 **Rusty Wallace** 53		Tim Flock 40
2 David Pearson 105	9 **Jeff Gordon** 52	16 Bobby Isaac 37
3 Bobby Allison 84	10 Ned Jarrett 50	17 Fireball Roberts 32
Darrell Waltrip 84	Junior Johnson 50	**Mark Martin** 32
5 Cale Yarborough 83	12 Herb Thomas 48	19 Fred Lorenzen 26
6 Dale Earnhardt 76	13 Buck Baker 46	Rex White 26
7 Lee Petty 55	14 **Bill Elliott** 40	

Pole Positions

1 Richard Petty 126	8 Junior Johnson 47	15 Ned Jarrett 35
2 David Pearson 113	9 Buck Baker 44	Fireball Roberts 35
3 Cale Yarborough 70	10 Buddy Baker 40	**Rusty Wallace** 35
4 Darrell Waltrip 59	11 Tim Flock 39	Rex White 35
5 Bobby Allison 57	**Mark Martin** 39	19 Fonty Flock 34
6 Bobby Isaac 51	Herb Thomas 39	20 Fred Lorenzen 33
7 **Bill Elliott** 49	14 **Geoff Bodine** 37	**Jeff Gordon** 33

NASCAR Circuit (Cont.)
Earnings

1	Dale Earnhardt	$41,445,551	8	Bobby Labonte	$23,524,792	15	Kyle Petty	$12,322,649
2	Jeff Gordon	34,868,823	9	Ricky Rudd	19,652,196	16	Ernie Irvan	11,625,817
3	Dale Jarrett	27,897,090	10	Darrell Waltrip	19,416,618	17	Michael Waltrip	11,416,832
4	Mark Martin	25,368,316	11	Jeff Burton	18,727,762	18	Bobby Hamilton	10,462,749
5	Rusty Wallace	24,869,068	12	Ken Schrader	15,682,101	19	Jimmy Spencer	10,077,744
6	Bill Elliott	23,688,157	13	Sterling Marlin	15,381,905	20	Brett Bodine	9,684,927
7	Terry Labonte	23,668,157	14	Geoff Bodine	14,749,414			

Winston Cup Champions

Originally the Grand National Championship, 1949-70, and based on official NASCAR records. Note that earnings totals include bonus awards.

Multiple winners: Dale Earnhardt and Richard Petty (7); Jeff Gordon, David Pearson, Lee Petty, Darrell Waltrip and Cale Yarborough (3); Buck Baker, Tim Flock, Ned Jarrett, Terry Labonte, Herb Thomas and Joe Weatherly (2).

Year	Car No.	Driver	Owner	Car	Wins	Poles	Earnings
1949	22	Red Byron	Raymond Parks	Oldsmobile	2	1	$5,800
1950	60	Bill Rexford	Julian Buesink	Oldsmobile	1	0	6,175
1951	92	Herb Thomas	Herb Thomas	Hudson	7	4	18,200
1952	91	Tim Flock	Ted Chester	Hudson	8	4	20,210
1953	92	Herb Thomas	Herb Thomas	Hudson	11	10	27,300
1954	92	Herb Thomas	Herb Thomas	Hudson	12	8	27,540
1954	42	Lee Petty	Herb Thomas	Chrysler	7	3	26,706
1955	300	Tim Flock	Carl Kiekhaefer	Chrysler	18	19	33,750
1956	300B	Buck Baker	Carl Kiekhaefer	Chevrolet	14	12	29,790
1957	87	Buck Baker	Buck Baker	Chevrolet	10	5	24,712
1958	42	Lee Petty	Petty Ent.	Oldsmobile	7	4	20,600
1959	42	Lee Petty	Petty Ent.	Plymouth	10	2	45,570
1960	4	Rex White	White-Clements	Chevrolet	6	3	45,260
1961	11	Ned Jarrett	W.G. Holloway Jr.	Chevrolet	1	4	27,285
1962	8	Joe Weatherly	Bud Moore	Pontiac	9	6	56,110
1963	21	Joe Weatherly	Wood Brothers	Ford	3	5	77,636
1963	8	Joe Weatherly	Wood Brothers	Mercury	3	6	58,110
1964	43	Richard Petty	Petty Ent.	Plymouth	9	8	98,810
1965	11	Ned Jarrett	Bondy Long	Ford	13	9	77,960
1966	6	David Pearson	Cotton Owens	Dodge	14	7	59,205
1967	43	Richard Petty	Petty Ent.	Plymouth	27	18	130,275
1968	17	David Pearson	Holman-Moody	Ford	16	12	118,842
1969	17	David Pearson	Holman-Moody	Ford	11	14	183,700
1970	71	Bobby Isaac	Nord Krauskopf	Dodge	11	13	121,470
1971	43	Richard Petty	Petty Ent.	Plymouth	21	9	309,225
1972	43	Richard Petty	Petty Ent.	Plymouth	8	3	227,015
1973	72	Benny Parsons	L.G. DeWitt	Chevrolet	1	0	114,345
1974	43	Richard Petty	Petty Ent.	Dodge	10	7	299,175
1975	43	Richard Petty	Petty Ent.	Dodge	13	3	378,865
1976	11	Cale Yarborough	Junior Johnson	Chevrolet	9	2	387,173
1977	11	Cale Yarborough	Junior Johnson	Chevrolet	9	3	477,499
1978	11	Cale Yarborough	Junior Johnson	Oldsmobile	10	8	530,751
1979	43	Richard Petty	Petty Ent.	Chevrolet	5	1	531,292
1980	2	Dale Earnhardt	Rod Osterlund	Chevrolet	5	0	588,926
1981	11	Darrell Waltrip	Junior Johnson	Buick	12	11	693,342
1982	11	Darrell Waltrip	Junior Johnson	Buick	12	7	873,118
1983	22	Bobby Allison	Bill Gardner	Buick	6	0	828,355
1984	44	Terry Labonte	Billy Hagan	Chevrolet	2	2	713,010
1985	11	Darrell Waltrip	Junior Johnson	Chevrolet	3	4	1,318,735
1986	3	Dale Earnhardt	Richard Childress	Chevrolet	5	1	1,783,880
1987	3	Dale Earnhardt	Richard Childress	Chevrolet	11	1	2,099,243
1988	9	Bill Elliott	Harry Meling	Ford	6	6	1,574,639
1989	27	Rusty Wallace	Raymond Beadle	Pontiac	6	4	2,247,950
1990	3	Dale Earnhardt	Richard Childress	Chevrolet	9	4	3,083,056
1991	3	Dale Earnhardt	Richard Childress	Chevrolet	4	0	2,396,685
1992	7	Alan Kulwicki	Alan Kulwicki	Ford	2	6	2,322,561
1993	3	Dale Earnhardt	Richard Childress	Chevrolet	6	2	3,353,789
1994	3	Dale Earnhardt	Richard Childress	Chevrolet	4	2	3,400,733
1995	24	Jeff Gordon	Rick Hendrick	Chevrolet	7	8	4,347,343
1996	5	Terry Labonte	Rick Hendrick	Chevrolet	2	4	4,030,648
1997	24	Jeff Gordon	Rick Hendrick	Chevrolet	10	1	6,375,658
1998	24	Jeff Gordon	Rick Hendrick	Chevrolet	13	7	9,306,584
1999	88	Dale Jarrett	Robert Yates	Ford	4	0	6,649,596
2000	18	Bobby Labonte	Joe Gibbs	Pontiac	4	2	7,361,387

NASCAR Rookie of the Year

Sponsored by Raybestos and presented to rookie driver who accumulates the most Winston Cup points based on his best 15 finishes.

Year		Year		Year		Year	
1958	Shorty Rollins	1969	Dick Brooks	1980	Jody Ridley	1991	Bobby Hamilton
1959	Richard Petty	1970	Bill Dennis	1981	Ron Bouchard	1992	Jimmy Hensley
1960	David Pearson	1971	Walter Ballard	1982	Geoff Bodine	1993	Jeff Gordon
1961	Woodie Wilson	1972	Larry Smith	1983	Sterling Marlin	1994	Jeff Burton
1962	Tom Cox	1973	Lennie Pond	1984	Rusty Wallace	1995	Ricky Craven
1963	Billy Wade	1974	Earl Ross	1985	Ken Schrader	1996	Johnny Benson
1964	Doug Cooper	1975	Bruce Hill	1986	Alan Kulwicki	1997	Mike Skinner
1965	Sam McQuagg	1976	Skip Manning	1987	Davey Allison	1998	Kenny Irwin
1966	James Hylton	1977	Ricky Rudd	1988	Ken Bouchard	1999	Tony Stewart
1967	Donnie Allison	1978	Ronnie Thomas	1989	Dick Trickle	2000	Matt Kenseth
1968	Pete Hamilton	1979	Dale Earnhardt	1990	Rob Moroso		

CART Circuit
FedEx Series Champions

Officially the FedEx Championship Series since 1997. Formerly, AAA (American Automobile Assn., 1909-55), USAC (U.S. Auto Club, 1956-78), CART (Championship Auto Racing Teams, 1979-91). CART was renamed IndyCar in 1992 and then lost use of the name in 1997.

Multiple titles: A.J. Foyt (7); Mario Andretti (4); Jimmy Bryan, Earl Cooper, Ted Horn, Rick Mears, Louie Meyer, Bobby Rahal, Al Unser (3); Tony Bettenhausen, Ralph DePalma, Peter DePaolo, Joe Leonard, Rex Mays, Tommy Milton, Jimmy Murphy, Wilbur Shaw, Tom Sneva, Al Unser Jr., Bobby Unser, Rodger Ward and Alex Zanardi (2).

AAA

Year		Year		Year		Year	
1909	George Robertson	1920	Tommy Milton	1931	Louis Schneider	1942-45	No racing
1910	Ray Harroun	1921	Tommy Milton	1932	Bob Carey	1946	Ted Horn
1911	Ralph Mulford	1922	Jimmy Murphy	1933	Louie Meyer	1947	Ted Horn
1912	Ralph DePalma	1923	Eddie Hearne	1934	Bill Cummings	1948	Ted Horn
1913	Earl Cooper	1924	Jimmy Murphy	1935	Kelly Petillo	1949	Johnnie Parsons
1914	Ralph DePalma	1925	Peter DePaolo	1936	Mauri Rose	1950	Henry Banks
1915	Earl Cooper	1926	Harry Hartz	1937	Wilbur Shaw	1951	Tony Bettenhausen
1916	Dario Resta	1927	Peter DePaolo	1938	Floyd Roberts	1952	Chuck Stevenson
1917	Earl Cooper	1928	Louie Meyer	1939	Wilbur Shaw	1953	Sam Hanks
1918	Ralph Mulford	1929	Louie Meyer	1940	Rex Mays	1954	Jimmy Bryan
1919	Howard Wilcox	1930	Billy Arnold	1941	Rex Mays	1955	Bob Sweikert

USAC

Year		Year		Year		Year	
1956	Jimmy Bryan	1962	Rodger Ward	1968	Bobby Unser	1974	Bobby Unser
1957	Jimmy Bryan	1963	A.J. Foyt	1969	Mario Andretti	1975	A.J. Foyt
1958	Tony Bettenhausen	1964	A.J. Foyt	1970	Al Unser	1976	Gordon Johncock
1959	Rodger Ward	1965	Mario Andretti	1971	Joe Leonard	1977	Tom Sneva
1960	A.J. Foyt	1966	Mario Andretti	1972	Joe Leonard	1978	A.J. Foyt
1961	A.J. Foyt	1967	A.J. Foyt	1973	Roger McCluskey		

CART

Year		Year		Year		Year	
1979	Rick Mears	1985	Al Unser	1991	Michael Andretti	1997	Alex Zanardi
1980	Johnny Rutherford	1986	Bobby Rahal	1992	Bobby Rahal	1998	Alex Zanardi
1981	Rick Mears	1987	Bobby Rahal	1993	Nigel Mansell	1999	Juan Montoya
1982	Rick Mears	1988	Danny Sullivan	1994	Al Unser Jr.	2000	Gil de Ferran
1983	Al Unser	1989	Emerson Fittipaldi	1995	Jacques Villeneuve		
1984	Mario Andretti	1990	Al Unser Jr.	1996	Jimmy Vasser		

All-Time CART Leaders

CART's all-time Top 20 drivers in victories, pole positions and earnings, based on records through 2000. Drivers active in 2001 are in **bold** type. Totals include victories, poles and earnings before CART was established in 1979.

Victories

1 A.J. Foyt 67	8	Johnny Rutherford 27		Emerson Fittipaldi 22
2 Mario Andretti.............52	9	Roger Ward 26	16	Earl Cooper 20
3 **Michael Andretti** 40	10	Gordon Johncock 25	17	Jimmy Bryan.................19
4 Al Unser..................39	11	Ralph DePalma 24		Jimmy Murphy 19
5 Bobby Unser 35		Bobby Rahal 24	19	**Paul Tracy** 18
6 Al Unser Jr.* 31	13	Tommy Milton................23	20	Ralph Mulford 17
7 Rick Mears................29	14	Tony Bettenhausen..........22		Danny Sullivan 17

CART Circuit (Cont.)

Pole Positions

1 Mario Andretti 67	9 Rex Mays 19	16 **Paul Tracy** 13
2 A.J. Foyt 53	Danny Sullivan 19	17 Parnelli Jones 12
3 Bobby Unser 49	11 Bobby Rahal 18	18 Gil de Ferran 11
4 Rick Mears 40	12 Emerson Fittipaldi 17	Danny Ongais 11
5 **Michael Andretti** 32	13 Tony Bettenhausen 14	Rodger Ward 11
6 Al Unser 27	Don Branson 14	
7 Johnny Rutherford 23	Tom Sneva 14	
8 Gordon Johncock : 20		

Earnings

1 Al Unser Jr.* $18,828,406	8 Danny Sullivan $8,884,126	15 Gil de Ferran $5,629,203
2 **Michael Andretti** . .16,841,369	9 **Paul Tracy** 8,010,770	16 Scott Pruett 5,440,144
3 Bobby Rahal 16,344,008	10 Arie Luyendyk 7,732,188	17 A.J. Foyt 5,357,589
4 Emerson Fittipaldi 14,293,625	11 Raul Boesel 6,971,887	18 Teo Fabi 5,045,881
5 Mario Andretti 11,552,154	12 Al Unser 6,740,843	19 Scott Brayton 4,807,274
6 Rick Mears 11,050,807	13 **Adrian Fernandez** .6,036,765	20 Christian Fittipaldi 4,655,668
7 **Jimmy Vasser** 9,809,994	14 **Alex Zanardi** 5,733,750	*Driver active, but in IRL not CART.

CART Rookie of the Year

Award presented to rookie who accumulates the most FedEx Championship Series points among first year drivers. Originally the CART Rookie of the Year; CART was renamed IndyCar in 1992 and then lost use of the name in 1997.

Year	Year	Year	Year
1979 Bill Alsup	1985 Arie Luyendyk	1991 Jeff Andretti	1997 Patrick Carpentier
1980 Dennis Firestone	1986 Dominic Dobson	1992 Stefan Johansson	1998 Tony Kanaan
1981 Bob Lazier	1987 Fabrizio Barbazza	1993 Nigel Mansell	1999 Juan Montoya
1982 Bobby Rahal	1988 John Jones	1994 Jacques Villeneuve	2000 Kenny Brack
1983 Teo Fabi	1989 Bernard Jourdain	1995 Gil de Ferran	
1984 Roberto Guerrero	1990 Eddie Cheever	1996 Alex Zanardi	

Indy Racing League Circuit

Indianapolis 500

Held every Memorial Day weekend; 200 laps around a 2.5-mile oval at Indianapolis Motor Speedway. First race was held in 1911. The Indy Racing League began in 1996 and made the Indianapolis 500 its cornerstone event. Winning drivers are listed with starting positions. Winners who started from pole position are in **bold** type.

Multiple wins: A.J. Foyt, Rick Mears and Al Unser (4); Louis Meyer, Mauri Rose, Johnny Rutherford, Wilbur Shaw and Bobby Unser (3); Emerson Fittipaldi, Gordon Johncock, Arie Luyendyk, Tommy Milton, Al Unser Jr., Bill Vukovich and Rodger Ward (2).

Multiple poles: Rick Mears (6); A.J. Foyt and Rex Mays (4); Mario Andretti, Arie Luyendyk, Johnny Rutherford and Tom Sneva (3); Scott Brayton, Bill Cummings, Ralph DePalma, Leon Duray, Parnelli Jones, Jimmy Murphy, Duke Nalon, Eddie Sachs and Bobby Unser (2).

Year	Winner (Pos.)	Car	MPH	Pole Sitter	MPH
1911	Ray Harroun (28)	Marmon Wasp	74.602	Lewis Strang	–
1912	Joe Dawson (7)	National	78.719	Gil Anderson	–
1913	Jules Goux (7)	Peugeot	75.933	Caleb Bragg	–
1914	Rene Thomas (15)	Delage	82.474	Jean Chassagne	–
1915	Ralph DePalma (2)	Mercedes	89.840	Howard Wilcox	98.90
1916-**a**	Dario Resta (4)	Peugeot	84.001	John Aitken	96.69
1917-18	Not held	World War I			
1919	Howdy Wilcox (2)	Peugeot	88.050	Rene Thomas	104.78
1920	Gaston Chevrolet (6)	Monroe	88.618	Ralph DePalma	99.15
1921	Tommy Milton (20)	Frontenac	89.621	Ralph DePalma	100.75
1922	**Jimmy Murphy** (1)	Murphy Special	94.484	Jimmy Murphy	100.50
1923	**Tommy Milton** (1)	H.C.S. Special	90.954	Tommy Milton	108.17
1924	L.L. Corum				
	& Joe Boyer (21)	Duesenberg Special	98.234	Jimmy Murphy	108.037
1925	Peter DePaolo (2)	Duesenberg Special	101.127	Leon Duray	113.196
1926-**b**	Frank Lockhart (20)	Miller Special	95.904	Earl Cooper	111.735
1927	George Souders (22)	Duesenberg	97.545	Frank Lockhart	120.100
1928	Louie Meyer (13)	Miller Special	99.482	Leon Duray	122.391
1929	Ray Keech (6)	Simplex Piston Ring Special	97.585	Cliff Woodbury	120.599
1930	**Billy Arnold** (1)	Miller-Hartz Special	100.448	Billy Arnold	113.268
1931	Louis Schneider (13)	Bowes Seal Fast Special	96.629	Russ Snowberger	112.796
1932	Fred Frame (27)	Miller-Hartz Special	104.144	Lou Moore	117.363
1933	Louie Meyer (6)	Tydol Special	104.162	Bill Cummings	118.530
1934	Bill Cummings (10)	Boyle Products Special	104.863	Kelly Petillo	119.329
1935	Kelly Petillo (22)	Gilmore Speedway Special	106.240	Rex Mays	120.736
1936	Louie Meyer (28)	Ring Free Special	109.069	Rex Mays	119.644
1937	Wilbur Shaw (2)	Shaw-Gilmore Special	113.580	Bill Cummings	123.343
1938	**Floyd Roberts** (1)	Burd Piston Ring Special	117.200	Floyd Roberts	125.681

Year	Winner (Pos.)	Car	MPH	Pole Sitter	MPH
1939	Wilbur Shaw (3)	Boyle Special	115.035	Jimmy Snyder	130.138
1940	Wilbur Shaw (2)	Boyle Special	114.277	Rex Mays	127.850
1941	Floyd Davis & Mauri Rose (17)	Noc-Out Hose Clamp Special	115.117	Mauri Rose	128.691
1942-45	Not held	World War II			
1946	George Robson (15)	Thorne Engineering Special	114.820	Cliff Bergere	126.471
1947	Mauri Rose (3)	Blue Crown Spark Plug Special	116.338	Ted Horn	126.564
1948	Mauri Rose (3)	Blue Crown Spark Plug Special	119.814	Rex Mays	130.577
1949	Bill Holland (4)	Blue Crown Spark Plug Special	121.327	Duke Nalon	132.939
1950-c	Johnnie Parsons (5)	Wynn's Friction Proofing	124.002	Walt Faulkner	134.343
1951	Lee Wallard (2)	Belanger Special	126.244	Duke Nalon	136.498
1952	Troy Ruttman (7)	Agajanian Special	128.922	Fred Agabashian	138.010
1953	**Bill Vukovich (1)**	Fuel Injection Special	128.740	Bill Vukovich	138.392
1954	Bill Vukovich (19)	Fuel Injection Special	130.840	Jack McGrath	141.033
1955	Bob Sweikert (14)	John Zink Special	128.213	Jerry Hoyt	140.045
1956	**Pat Flaherty (1)**	John Zink Special	128.490	Pat Flaherty	145.596
1957	Sam Hanks (13)	Belond Exhaust Special	135.601	Pat O'Connor	143.948
1958	Jimmy Bryan (7)	Belond AP Parts Special	133.791	Dick Rathmann	145.974
1959	Rodger Ward (6)	Leader Card 500 Roadster	135.857	Johnny Thomson	145.908
1960	Jim Rathmann (2)	Ken-Paul Special	138.767	Eddie Sachs	146.592
1961	A.J. Foyt (7)	Bowes Seal Fast Special	139.130	Eddie Sachs	147.481
1962	Rodger Ward (2)	Leader Card 500 Roadster	140.293	Parnelli Jones	150.370
1963	**Parnelli Jones (1)**	Agajanian-Willard Special	143.137	Parnelli Jones	151.153
1964	A.J. Foyt (5)	Sheraton-Thompson Special	147.350	Jim Clark	158.828
1965	Jim Clark (2)	Lotus Ford	150.686	A.J. Foyt	161.233
1966	Graham Hill (15)	American Red Ball Special	144.317	Mario Andretti	165.899
1967-d	A.J. Foyt (4)	Sheraton-Thompson Special	151.207	Mario Andretti	168.982
1968	Bobby Unser (3)	Rislone Special	152.882	Joe Leonard	171.559
1969	Mario Andretti (2)	STP Oil Treatment Special	156.867	A.J. Foyt	170.568
1970	**Al Unser (1)**	Johnny Lightning Special	155.749	Al Unser	170.221
1971	Al Unser (5)	Johnny Lightning Special	157.735	Peter Revson	178.696
1972	Mark Donohue (3)	Sunoco McLaren	162.962	Bobby Unser	195.940
1973-e	Gordon Johncock (11)	STP Double Oil Filters	159.036	Johnny Rutherford	198.413
1974	Johnny Rutherford (25)	McLaren	158.589	A.J. Foyt	191.632
1975-f	Bobby Unser (3)	Jorgensen Eagle	149.213	A.J. Foyt	193.976
1976-g	**Johnny Rutherford (1)**	Hy-Gain McLaren/Goodyear	148.725	Johnny Rutherford	188.957
1977	A.J. Foyt (4)	Gilmore Racing Team	161.331	Tom Sneva	198.884
1978	Al Unser (5)	FNCTC Chaparral Lola	161.363	Tom Sneva	202.156
1979	**Rick Mears (1)**	The Gould Charge	158.899	Rick Mears	193.736
1980	**Johnny Rutherford (1)**	Pennzoil Chaparral	142.862	Johnny Rutherford	192.256
1981-h	**Bobby Unser (1)**	Norton Spirit Penske PC-9B	139.084	Bobby Unser	200.546
1982	Gordon Johncock (5)	STP Oil Treatment	162.029	Rick Mears	207.004
1983	Tom Sneva (4)	Texaco Star	162.117	Teo Fabi	207.395
1984	Rick Mears (3)	Pennzoil Z-7	163.612	Tom Sneva	210.029
1985	Danny Sullivan (8)	Miller American Special	152.982	Pancho Carter	212.583
1986	Bobby Rahal (4)	Budweiser/Truesports/March	170.722	Rick Mears	216.828
1987	Al Unser (20)	Cummins Holset Turbo	162.175	Mario Andretti	215.390
1988	**Rick Mears (1)**	Pennzoil Z-7/Penske Chevy V-8	144.809	Rick Mears	219.198
1989	Emerson Fittipaldi (3)	Marlboro/Penske Chevy V-8	167.581	Rick Mears	223.885
1990	Arie Luyendyk (3)	Domino's Pizza Chevrolet	185.981*	Emerson Fittipaldi	225.301
1991	**Rick Mears (1)**	Marlboro Penske Chevy	176.457	Rick Mears	224.113
1992	Al Unser Jr. (12)	Valvoline Galmer '92	134.477	Roberto Guerrero	232.482
1993	Emerson Fittipaldi (9)	Marlboro Penske Chevy	157.207	Arie Luyendyk	223.967
1994	**Al Unser Jr. (1)**	Marlboro Penske Mercedes	160.872	Al Unser Jr.	228.011
1995	Jacques Villeneuve (5)	Player's Ltd. Reynard Ford	153.616	Scott Brayton	231.604
1996	Buddy Lazier (5)	Reynard Ford	147.956	Tony Stewart	233.100&
1997	**Arie Luyendyk (1)**	G-Force Olds Aurora	145.827	Arie Luyendyk	218.263
1998	Eddie Cheever Jr. (17)	Dallara Olds Aurora	145.155	Billy Boat	223.503
1999	Kenny Brack (8)	Dallara Olds Aurora	153.176	Arie Luyendyk	225.179
2000	Juan Montoya (2)	G-Force Olds Aurora	167.607	Greg Ray	223.471
2001	Helio Castroneves (11)	Dallara Olds Aurora	153.601	Scott Sharp	226.037

*Track record for winning time.

& Scott Brayton won the pole position with an avg. mph of 233.718 but was killed in a practice run. Stewart was given pole position with the next fastest speed.

Notes: a—1916 race scheduled for 300 miles; **b**—rain shortened 1926 race to 400 miles; **c**—rain shortened 1950 race to 345 miles; **d**—1967 race postponed due to rain after 18 laps (May 30), resumed next day (May 31); **e**—rain shortened 1973 race to 332.5 miles; **f**—rain shortened 1975 race to 435 miles; **g**—rain shortened 1976 race to 255 miles; **h**—in 1981, runner-up Mario Andretti was awarded 1st place when winner Bobby Unser was penalized a lap after the race was completed for passing cars illegally under the caution flag. Unser and car-owner Roger Penske appealed the race stewards' decision to the U.S. Auto Club. Four months later, USAC overturned the ruling, saying that the penalty was too harsh and Unser should be fined $40,000 rather than stripped of his championship.

Indy Racing League Circuit (Cont.)
Indy 500 Rookie of the Year

Voted on by a panel of auto racing media. Award does not necessarily go to highest-finishing first-year driver. Graham Hill won the race on his first try in 1966, but the rookie award went to Jackie Stewart, who led with 10 laps to go only to lose oil pressure and finish 6th.

Father and son winners: Mario and Michael Andretti (1965 and 1984); Bill and Billy Vukovich III (1968 and 1988).

Year		Year		Year		Year	
1952	Art Cross	1965	Mario Andretti		& Larry Rice	1990	Eddie Cheever
1953	Jimmy Daywalt	1966	Jackie Stewart	1979	Howdy Holmes	1991	Jeff Andretti
1954	Larry Crockett	1967	Denis Hulme	1980	Tim Richmond	1992	Lyn St. James
1955	Al Herman	1968	Bill Vukovich	1981	Josele Garza	1993	Nigel Mansell
1956	Bob Veith	1969	Mark Donohue	1982	Jim Hickman	1994	Jacques Villeneuve
1957	Don Edmunds	1970	Donnie Allison	1983	Teo Fabi	1995	Christian Fittipaldi
1958	George Amick	1971	Denny Zimmerman	1984	Michael Andretti	1996	Tony Stewart
1959	Bobby Grim	1972	Mike Hiss		& Roberto Guerrero	1997	Jeff Ward
1960	Jim Hurtubise	1973	Graham McRae	1985	Arie Luyendyk	1998	Steve Knapp
1961	Parnelli Jones	1974	Pancho Carter	1986	Randy Lanier	1999	Robby McGehee
	& Bobby Marshman	1975	Bill Puterbaugh	1987	Fabrizio Barbazza	2000	Juan Montoya
1962	Jimmy McElreath	1976	Vern Schuppan	1988	Billy Vukovich III	2001	Helio Castroneves
1963	Jim Clark	1977	Jerry Sneva	1989	Bernard Jourdain		
1964	Johnny White	1978	Rick Mears		& Scott Pruett		

IRL Champions

Year		Year		Year		Year	
1996	Buzz Calkins	1997	Tony Stewart	1999	Greg Ray	2001	Sam Hornish Jr.
	& Scott Sharp	1998	Kenny Brack	2000	Buddy Lazier		

IRL Rookie of the Year

Officially the Chevy Rookie of the Year Award, presented to rookie driver who accumulates the most points in the IRL standings.

Year		Year		Year		Year	
1996	None	1998	Robby Unser	1999	Scott Harrington	2000	Airton Dare
1997	Jim Guthrie					2001	Felipe Giaffone

Formula One Circuit

United States Grand Prix

There have been 55 official Formula One races held in the United States since 1950, including the Indianapolis 500 from 1950-60. FISA sanctioned two annual U.S. Grand Prix–USA/East and USA/West–from 1976-80 and 1983-84. Phoenix was the site of the U.S. Grand Prix from 1989-91. Indianapolis hosted the U.S. Grand Prix starting in 2000.

Indianapolis 500

Officially sanctioned as Grand Prix race from 1950-60 only. See IRL Circuit for details.

U.S. Grand Prix—East

Held from 1959-80 and 1981-88 at the following locations: Sebring, Fla. (1959); Riverside, Calif. (1960); Watkins Glen, N.Y. (1961-80); and Detroit (1982-88). There was no race in 1981. Race discontinued in 1989.

Multiple winners: Jim Clark, Graham Hill and Ayrton Senna (3); James Hunt, Carlos Reutemann and Jackie Stewart (2).

Year		Car	Year		Car
1959	Bruce McLaren, NZE	Cooper Climax	1974	Carlos Reutemann, ARG	Brabham Ford
1960	Stirling Moss, GBR	Lotus Climax	1975	Niki Lauda, AUT	Ferrari
1961	Innes Ireland, GBR	Lotus Climax	1976	James Hunt, GBR	McLaren Ford
1962	Jim Clark, GBR	Lotus Climax	1977	James Hunt, GBR	McLaren Ford
1963	Graham Hill, GBR	BRM	1978	Carlos Reutemann, ARG	Ferrari
1964	Graham Hill, GBR	BRM	1979	Gilles Villeneuve, CAN	Ferrari
1965	Graham Hill, GBR	BRM	1980	Alan Jones, AUS	Williams Ford
1966	Jim Clark, GBR	Lotus BRM	1981	Not held	
1967	Jim Clark, GBR	Lotus Ford	1982	John Watson, GBR	McLaren Ford
1968	Jackie Stewart, GBR	Matra Ford	1983	Michele Alboreto, ITA	Tyrrell Ford
1969	Jochen Rindt, AUT	Lotus Ford	1984	Nelson Piquet, BRA	Brabham BMW Turbo
1970	Emerson Fittipaldi, BRA	Lotus Ford	1985	Keke Rosberg, FIN	Williams Honda Turbo
1971	Francois Cevert, FRA	Tyrrell Ford	1986	Ayrton Senna, BRA	Lotus Renault Turbo
1972	Jackie Stewart, GBR	Tyrrell Ford	1987	Ayrton Senna, BRA	Lotus Honda Turbo
1973	Ronnie Peterson, SWE	Lotus Ford	1988	Ayrton Senna, BRA	McLaren Honda Turbo

U.S. Grand Prix—West

Held from 1976-83 at Long Beach, Calif. Races also held in Las Vegas (1981-82), Dallas (1984) and Phoenix (1989-91). Race discontinued in 1992.

Multiple winners: Alan Jones and Ayrton Senna (2).

Year		Car	Year		Car
1976	Clay Regazzoni, SWI	Ferrari	1983	John Watson, GBR	McLaren Ford
1977	Mario Andretti, USA	Lotus Ford	1984	Keke Rosberg, FIN	Williams Honda Turbo
1978	Carlos Reutemann, ARG	Ferrari	1985-88	Not held	
1979	Gilles Villeneuve, CAN	Ferrari	1989	Alain Prost, FRA	McLaren Honda
1980	Nelson Piquet, BRA	Brabham Ford	1990	Ayrton Senna, BRA	McLaren Honda
1981	Alan Jones, AUS	Williams Ford	1991	Ayrton Senna, BRA	McLaren Honda
1982	Niki Lauda, AUT	McLaren Ford			

U.S. Grand Prix

Held since 2000 at Indianapolis Motor Speedway.

Year		Car	Year		Car
2000 Michael Schumacher, GER		Ferrari	2001 Mika Hakkinen		McLaren Mercedes

All-Time Leaders

The all-time Top 15 Grand Prix winning drivers, based on records through 2000. Listed are starts (Sts), poles won (Pole), wins (1st), second place finishes (2nd), and third (3rd). Drivers active in 2001 and career victories in **bold** type.

	Sts	Pole	1st	2nd	3rd			Sts	Pole	1st	2nd	3rd
1 Alain Prost	199	33	**51**	35	20	9	Nelson Piquet	204	24	**23**	20	17
2 **M. Schumacher**	134	32	**44**	23	15	10	Damon Hill	99	20	**22**	15	5
3 Ayrton Senna	161	65	**41**	23	16	11	**Mika Hakkinen**	146	27	**18**	14	16
4 Nigel Mansell	187	32	**31**	17	11	12	Stirling Moss	66	16	**16**	5	3
5 Jackie Stewart	99	17	**27**	11	5	13	Jack Brabham	126	13	**14**	10	7
6 Jim Clark	72	33	**25**	1	6		Emerson Fittipaldi	144	6	**14**	13	8
Niki Lauda	171	24	**25**	20	9		Graham Hill	176	13	**14**	15	7
8 Juan-Manuel Fangio	51	28	**24**	10	1	16	Alberto Ascari	32	14	**13**	4	0

World Champions

Officially called the World Championship of Drivers and based on Formula One (Grand Prix) records through the 1998 racing season.

Multiple winners: Juan-Manuel Fangio (5); Alain Prost and Michael Schumacher (4); Jack Brabham, Niki Lauda, Nelson Piquet, Ayrton Senna and Jackie Stewart (3); Alberto Ascari, Jim Clark, Emerson Fittipaldi, Mika Hakkinen and Graham Hill (2).

Year		Car	Year		Car
1950 Guiseppe Farina, ITA		Alfa Romeo	1976 James Hunt, GBR		McLaren Ford
1951 Juan-Manuel Fangio, ARG		Alfa Romeo	1977 Niki Lauda, AUT		Ferrari
1952 Alberto Ascari, ITA		Ferrari	1978 Mario Andretti, USA		Lotus Ford
1953 Alberto Ascari, ITA		Ferrari	1979 Jody Scheckter, SAF		Ferrari
1954 Juan-Manuel Fangio, ARG		Maserati/Mercedes	1980 Alan Jones, AUS		Williams Ford
1955 Juan-Manuel Fangio, ARG		Mercedes	1981 Nelson Piquet, BRA		Brabham Ford
1956 Juan-Manuel Fangio, ARG		Ferrari	1982 Keke Rosberg, FIN		Williams Ford
1957 Juan-Manuel Fangio, ARG		Maserati	1983 Nelson Piquet, BRA		Brabham BMW Turbo
1958 Mike Hawthorn, GBR		Ferrari	1984 Niki Lauda, AUT		McL. TAG Porsche Turbo
1959 Jack Brabham, AUS		Cooper Climax	1985 Alain Prost, FRA		McL. TAG Porsche Turbo
1960 Jack Brabham, AUS		Cooper Climax	1986 Alain Prost, FRA		McL. TAG Porsche Turbo
1961 Phil Hill, USA		Ferrari	1987 Nelson Piquet, BRA		Williams Honda Turbo
1962 Graham Hill, GBR		BRM	1988 Ayrton Senna, BRA		McLaren Honda Turbo
1963 Jim Clark, GBR		Lotus Climax	1989 Alain Prost, FRA		McLaren Honda
1964 John Surtees, GBR		Ferrari	1990 Ayrton Senna, BRA		McLaren Honda
1965 Jim Clark, GBR		Lotus Climax	1991 Ayrton Senna, BRA		McLaren Honda
1966 Jack Brabham, AUS		Brabham Repco	1992 Nigel Mansell, GBR		Williams-Renault
1967 Denis Hulme, NZE		Brabham Repco	1993 Alain Prost, FRA		Williams-Renault
1968 Graham Hill, GBR		Lotus Ford	1994 Michael Schumacher, GER		Benetton Ford
1969 Jackie Stewart, GBR		Matra Ford	1995 Michael Schumacher, GER		Benetton Renault
1970 Jochen Rindt, AUT		Lotus Ford	1996 Damon Hill, GBR		Williams-Renault
1971 Jackie Stewart, GBR		Tyrrell Ford	1997 Jacques Villeneuve, CAN		Williams-Renault
1972 Emerson Fittipaldi, BRA		Lotus Ford	1998 Mika Hakkinen, FIN		McLaren-Mercedes
1973 Jackie Stewart, GBR		Tyrrell Ford	1999 Mika Hakkinen, FIN		McLaren-Mercedes
1974 Emerson Fittipaldi, BRA		McLaren Ford	2000 Michael Schumacher, GER		Ferrari
1975 Niki Lauda, AUT		Ferrari	2001 Michael Schumacher, GER		Ferrari

ENDURANCE RACES

The 24 Hours of Le Mans

Multiple winners: Jacky Ickx (6); Derek Bell (5); Yannick Dalmas, Oliver Gendebien and Henri Pescarolo (4); Woolf Barnato, Luigi Chinetti, Hurley Haywood, Phil Hill, Al Holbert, Tom Kristensen and Klaus Ludwig (3); Frank Biela, Sir Henry Birkin, Ivoe Bueb, Ron Flockhart, Jean-Pierre Jaussaud, Gerard Larrousse, Emanuele Pirro, Andre Rossignol, Raymond Sommer, Hans Stuck, Gijs van Lennep and Jean-Pierre Wimille (2).

Year	Drivers	Car	MPH	Year	Drivers	Car	MPH
1923	Andre Lagache & Rene Leonard	Chenard & Walcker	57.21	1930	Woolf Barnato & Glen Kidston	Bentley Speed 6	75.88
1924	John Duff & Francis Clement	Bentley	53.78	1931	Earl Howe & Sir Henry Birkin	Alfa Romeo	78.13
1925	Gerard de Courcelles & Andre Rossignol	La Lorraine	57.84	1932	Raymond Sommer & Luigi Chinetti	Alfa Romeo	76.48
1926	Robert Bloch & Andre Rossignol	La Lorraine	66.08	1933	Raymond Sommer & Tazio Nuvolari	Alfa Romeo	81.40
1927	J.D. Benjafield & Sammy Davis	Bentley	61.35	1934	Luigi Chinetti & Philippe Etancelin	Alfa Romeo	74.74
1928	Woolf Barnato & Bernard Rubin	Bentley	69.11	1935	John Hindmarsh & Louis Fontes	Lagonda	77.85
1929	Woolf Barnato & Sir Henry Birkin	Bentley Speed 6	73.63	1936	Not held		

ENDURANCE RACES (Cont.)

Year	Drivers	Car	MPH	Year	Drivers	Car	MPH
1937	Jean-Pierre Wimille & Robert Benoist	Bugatti 57G	85.13	1979	Klaus Ludwig, Bill Wittington & Don Whittington	Porsche 935	108.10
1938	Eugene Chaboud & Jean Tremoulet	Delahaye	82.36	1980	Jean-Pierre Jaussaud & Jean Rondeau	Rondeau-Cosworth	119.23
1939	Jean-Pierre Wimille & Pierre Veyron	Bugatti 57G	86.86	1981	Jacky Ickx & Derek Bell	Porsche 936	124.94
1940-48	Not held			1982	Jacky Ickx & Derek Bell	Porsche 956	126.85
1949	Luigi Chinetti & Lord Selsdon	Ferrari	82.28	1983	Vern Schuppan, Hurley Haywood & Al Holbert	Porsche 956	130.70
1950	Louis Rosier & Jean-Louis Rosier	Talbot-Lago	89.71	1984	Klaus Ludwig & Henri Pescarolo	Porsche 956	126.88
1951	Peter Walker & Peter Whitehead	Jaguar C	93.50	1985	Klaus Ludwig, Paolo Barilla & John Winter	Porsche 956	131.75
1952	Hermann Lang & Fritz Reiss	Mercedes-Benz	96.67	1986	Derek Bell, Hans Stuck & Al Holbert	Porsche 962	128.75
1953	Tony Rolt & Duncan Hamilton	Jaguar C	98.65	1987	Derek Bell, Hans Stuck & Al Holbert	Porsche 962	124.06
1954	Froilan Gonzalez & Maurice Trintignant	Ferrari 375	105.13	1988	Jan Lammers, Johnny Dumfries & Andy Wallace	Jaguar XJR	137.75
1955	Mike Hawthorn & Ivor Bueb	Jaguar D	107.05	1989	Jochen Mass, Manuel Reuter & Stanley Dickens	Sauber-Mercedes	136.39
1956	Ron Flockhart & Ninian Sanderson	Jaguar D	104.47	1990	John Nielsen, Price Cobb & Martin Brundle	Jaguar XJR-12	126.71
1957	Ron Flockhart & Ivor Bueb	Jaguar D	113.83	1991	Volker Weider, Johnny Herbert & Bertrand Gachot	Mazda 787B	127.31
1958	Oliver Gendebien & Phil Hill	Ferrari 250	106.18	1992	Derek Warwick, Yannick Dalmas & Mark Blundell	Peugeot 905B	123.89
1959	Roy Salvadori & Carroll Shelby	Aston Martin	112.55	1993	Geoff Brabham, Christophe Bouchut & Eric Helary	Peugeot 905	132.58
1960	Oliver Gendebien & Paul Fräre	Ferrari 250	109.17	1994	Yannick Dalmas, Hurley Haywood & Mauro Baldi	Porsche 962LM	129.82
1961	Oliver Gendebien & Phil Hill	Ferrari 250	115.88	1995	Yannick Dalmas, J.J. Lehto & Masanori Sekiya	McLaren BMW	105.00
1962	Oliver Gendebien & Phil Hill	Ferrari 250	115.22	1996	Davy Jones, Manuel Reuter & Alexander Wurz	TWR Porsche	124.65
1963	Lodovico Scarfiotti & Lorenzo Bandini	Ferrari 250	118.08	1997	Michele Alberto, Stefan Johansson & Tom Kristensen	TWR Porsche	126.88
1964	Jean Guichel & Nino Vaccarella	Ferrari 275	121.54	1998	Laurent Aiello, Allan McNish & Stephane Ortelli	Porsche 911 GT1	123.86
1965	Masten Gregory & Jochen Rindt	Ferrari 250	121.07	1999	Yannick Dalmas, Joachim Winkelhock & Pierluigi Martini	BMW V-12 LMR	129.38
1966	Bruce McLaren & Chris Amon	Ford Mk. II	125.37	2000	Frank Biela, Tom Kristensen & Emanuele Pirro	Audi R8	128.34
1967	A.J. Foyt & Dan Gurney	Ford Mk. IV	135.46	2001	Frank Biela, Tom Kristensen & Emanuele Pirro	Audi R8	129.66
1968	Pedro Rodriguez & Lucien Bianchi	Ford GT40	115.27				
1969	Jacky Ickx & Jackie Oliver	Ford GT40	129.38				
1970	Hans Herrmann & Richard Attwood	Porsche 917	119.28				
1971	Gijs van Lennep & Helmut Marko	Porsche 917	138.13				
1972	Graham Hill & Henri Pescarolo	Matra-Simca	121.45				
1973	Henri Pescarolo & Gerard Larrousse	Matra-Simca	125.67				
1974	Henri Pescarolo & Gerard Larrousse	Matra-Simca	119.27				
1975	Derek Bell & Jacky Ickx	Mirage-Ford	118.98				
1976	Jacky Ickx & Gijs van Lennep	Porsche 936	123.49				
1977	Jacky Ickx, Jurgen Barth & Hurley Haywood	Porsche 936	120.95				
1978	Jean-Pierre Jaussaud & Didier Pironi	Renault-Alpine	130.60				

The 24 Hours of Daytona

Officially, the Rolex 24 at Daytona. First run in 1962 as a three-hour race and won by Dan Gurney in a Lotus 19 Ford. Contested over a 3.56-mile course at Daytona (Fla.) International Speedway. There have been several distance changes since 1962: the event was a three-hour race (1962-63); a 2,000-kilometer race (1964-65); a 24-hour race (1966-71); a six-hour race (1972) and a 24-hour race again since 1973. The race was canceled in 1974 due to a national energy crisis.

Multiple winners: Hurley Haywood (5); Peter Gregg, Pedro Rodriguez and Bob Wollek (4); Derek Bell, Butch Leitzinger and Rolf Stommelen (3); A.J. Foyt, Al Holbert, Ken Miles, Brian Redman, Elliott Forbes-Robinson, Lloyd Ruby, Al Unser Jr. and Andy Wallace (2).

Year	Drivers	Car	MPH
1962	Dan Gurney	Lotus 19 Ford	104.101
1963	Pedro Rodriguez	Ferrari GTO	102.074
1964	Pedro Rodriguez & Phil Hill	Ferrari GTO	98.230
1965	Ken Miles & Lloyd Ruby	Ford GT	99.944
1966	Ken Miles & Lloyd Ruby	Ford Mk. II	108.020
1967	Lorenzo Bandini & Chris Amon	Ferrari 330	105.688
1968	Vic Elford & Jochen Neerpasch	Porsche 907	106.697
1969	Mark Donohue & Chuck Parsons	Lola Chevrolet	99.268
1970	Pedro Rodriguez & Leo Kinnunen	Porsche 917	114.866
1971	Pedro Rodriguez & Jackie Oliver	Porsche 917K	109.203
1972	Mario Andretti & Jacky Ickx	Ferrari 312P	122.573
1973	Peter Gregg & Hurley Haywood	Porsche Carrera	106.225
1974	Not held		
1975	Peter Gregg & Hurley Haywood	Porsche Carrera	108.531
1976	Peter Gregg, Brian Redman & John Fitzpatrick	BMW CSL	104.040
1977	Hurley Haywood, John Graves & Dave Helmick	Porsche Carrera	108.801
1978	Peter Gregg, Rolf Stommelen & Antoine Hezemans	Porsche Turbo	108.743
1979	Hurley Haywood, Ted Field & Danny Ongais	Porsche Turbo	109.249
1980	Rolf Stommelen, Volkert Merl & Reinhold Joest	Porsche Turbo	114.303
1981	Bobby Rahal, Brian Redman & Bob Garretson	Porsche Turbo	113.153
1982	John Paul Sr., John Paul Jr. & Rolf Stommelen	Porsche Turbo	114.794
1983	A.J. Foyt, Preston Henn, Bob Wollek & Claude Ballot-Lena	Porsche Turbo	98.781
1984	Sarel van der Merwe, Tony Martin & Graham Duxbury	March Porsche	103.119
1985	A.J. Foyt, Bob Wollek, Al Unser Sr. & Thierry Boutsen	Porsche 962	104.162
1986	Al Holbert, Derek Bell & Al Unser Jr	Porsche 962	105.484
1987	Al Holbert, Derek Bell, Chip Robinson & Al Unser Jr	Porsche 962	111.599
1988	Raul Boesel, Martin Brundle & John Nielsen	Jaguar XJR-9	107.943
1989	John Andretti, Derek Bell & Bob Wollek	Porsche 962	92.009
1990	Davy Jones, Jan Lammers & Andy Wallace	Jaguar XJR-12	112.857
1991	Hurley Haywood, John Winter, Frank Jelinski, Henri Pescarolo & Bob Wollek	Porsche 962-C	106.633
1992	Masahiro Hasemi, Kazuyoshi Hoshino & Toshio Suzuki	Nissan R-91	112.897
1993	P.J. Jones, Mark Dismore & Rocky Moran	Toyota Eagle	103.537
1994	Paul Gentilozzi, Scott Pruett, Butch Leitzinger & Steve Millen	Nissan 300 ZXT	104.80
1995	Jurgen Lassig, Christophe Bouchut, Giovanni Lavaggi & Marco Werner	Porsche Spyder	102.280
1996	Wayne Taylor, Scott Sharp & Jim Pace	Oldsmobile Arness MK-III	103.32
1997	Rob Dyson, James Weaver, Butch Leitzinger, Andy Wallace, John Paul Jr., Eliot Forbes-Robinson & John Schneider	Ford R&S MK-III	102.29
1998	Mauro Baldi, Arie Luyendyk & Gianpiero Moretti		
1999	Elliot Forbes-Robinson, Butch Leitzinger & Andy Wallace	Riley & Scott Ford	104.957
2000	Olivier Beretta, Dominique Dupuy & Karl Wendlinger	Dodge Viper	107.207
2001	Ron Fellows, Franck Freon, Chris Kneifel & Johnny O'Connell	Chevy Corvette	97.293

˙NHRA Drag Racing
NHRA Winston Champions

Based on points earned during the NHRA Winston Drag Racing series. The series began for Top Fuel, Funny Car and Pro Stock in 1975.

Top Fuel

Multiple winners: Joe Amato (5); Don Garlits, Shirley Muldowney and Gary Scelzi (3); Scott Kalitta (2).

Year		Year		Year		Year	
1975	Don Garlits	1982	Shirley Muldowney	1989	Gary Ormsby	1996	Kenny Bernstein
1976	Richard Tharp	1983	Gary Beck	1990	Joe Amato	1997	Gary Scelzi
1977	Shirley Muldowney	1984	Joe Amato	1991	Joe Amato	1998	Gary Scelzi
1978	Kelly Brown	1985	Don Garlits	1992	Joe Amato	1999	Tony Schumacher
1979	Rob Bruins	1986	Don Garlits	1993	Eddie Hill	2000	Gary Scelzi
1980	Shirley Muldowney	1987	Dick LaHaie	1994	Scott Kalitta		
1981	Jeb Allen	1988	Joe Amato	1995	Scott Kalitta		

Funny Car

Multiple winners: John Force (10); Don Prudhomme, Kenny Bernstein (4); Raymond Beadle (3); Frank Hawley (2).

Year		Year		Year		Year	
1975	Don Prudhomme	1982	Frank Hawley	1989	Bruce Larson	1996	John Force
1976	Don Prudhomme	1983	Frank Hawley	1990	John Force	1997	John Force
1977	Don Prudhomme	1984	Mark Oswald	1991	John Force	1998	John Force
1978	Don Prudhomme	1985	Kenny Bernstein	1992	Cruz Pedregon	1999	John Force
1979	Raymond Beadle	1986	Kenny Bernstein	1993	John Force	2000	John Force
1980	Raymond Beadle	1987	Kenny Bernstein	1994	John Force		
1981	Raymond Beadle	1988	Kenny Bernstein	1995	John Force		

Pro Stock

Multiple winners: Bob Glidden (9); Warren Johnson (5); Lee Shepherd (4); Darrell Alderman and Jim Yates (2).

Year		Year		Year		Year	
1975	Bob Glidden	1982	Lee Shepherd	1989	Bob Glidden	1996	Jim Yates
1976	Larry Lombardo	1983	Lee Shepherd	1990	John Myers	1997	Jim Yates
1977	Don Nicholson	1984	Lee Shepherd	1991	Darrell Alderman	1998	Warren Johnson
1978	Bob Glidden	1985	Bob Glidden	1992	Warren Johnson	1999	Warren Johnson
1979	Bob Glidden	1986	Bob Glidden	1993	Warren Johnson	2000	Jeg Coughlin Jr.
1980	Bob Glidden	1987	Bob Glidden	1994	Darrell Alderman		
1981	Lee Shepherd	1988	Bob Glidden	1995	Warren Johnson		

All-Time Leaders
Career Victories

All-time leaders through 2000. Drivers active in 2001 are in **bold**.

	Top Fuel			Funny Car			Pro Stock	
1	Joe Amato	52	1	**John Force**	92	1	Bob Glidden	85
2	Don Garlits	35	2	Don Prudhomme	35	2	**Warren Johnson**	81
3	**Cory McClenathan**	26	3	**Kenny Bernstein**	30	3	**Darrell Alderman**	27
4	**Kenny Bernstein**	23	4	**Cruz Pedregon**	22	4	Lee Shepherd	26
	Gary Scelzi	23	5	Ed McCulloch	18	5	**Jim Yates**	22
				Mark Oswald	18			

National-Event Victories (pro categories)

1	**John Force**	92	8	Don Garlits	35	15	**Gary Scelzi**	23
2	Bob Glidden	85	9	John Myers	33	16	Ed McCulloch	22
3	**Warren Johnson**	81	10	Terry Vance	29		**Jim Yates**	22
4	**Kenny Bernstein**	53	11	**Darrell Alderman**	27		Cruz Pedregon	22
5	Joe Amato	52	12	Lee Shepherd	26	19	**Kurt Johnson**	21
6	Don Prudhomme	49		**Cory McClenathan**	26	20	**Jeg Coughlin Jr.**	20
7	**Dave Schultz**	45	14	**Matt Hines**	25		Mark Oswald	20

Fastest Mile-Per-Hour Speeds

Fastest performances in NHRA major event history through 2000.

Top Fuel	Funny Car	Pro Stock
MPH	**MPH**	**MPH**
330.23 . . Tony Schumacher, 2/28/99	324.05 . . . . John Force, 3/21/99	202.36 . Warren Johnson, 10/31/99
327.90 . . Tony Schumacher, 10/3/99	324.05 . . . . John Force, 3/21/99	202.33 . Warren Johnson, 10/23/99
327.27 . . Tony Schumacher, 4/25/99	323.89 . . . . John Force, 5/17/98	202.24 . . Warren Johnson, 4/30/99
327.03 . Tony Schumacher, 11/13/99	323.35 . . . . John Force, 5/15/98	202.15 . Warren Johnson, 10/23/99
326.91 . Tony Schumacher, 10/22/99	322.81 . . . . . . John Force, 10/25/98	202.02 . . . . . Kurt Johnson, 10/23/99
	322.81 . . . . Tony Pedregon, 4/25/99	

Boxing

Hasim Rahman shocked Lennox Lewis for the
WBC/IBF World Heavyweight Championship in 2001.

John Gichigi/Allsport

Not Enough To Go Around

Despite a slew of high-profile fighters in the mix, there were a disappointing number of big match-ups in 2001.

Al Bernstein
has been ESPN's boxing analyst since 1980.

This year was supposed to be the year of the big fight. With a few notable exceptions, it just wasn't. Instead, for the most part, boxing fans were deprived of the matches they yearned to see.

For instance, a funny thing happened on the way to the expected Lennox Lewis-Mike Tyson match—Lewis lost to Hasim Rahman. In the biggest upset of the year, the unheralded Rahman stopped Lewis with a huge right hand in the fifth round in South Africa.

Lewis had taken time out of his training to film a scene in the remake of *Ocean's Eleven* and didn't arrive in Johannesburg to acclimate himself to the thin air until just 11 days before the fight. After the surprising KO, talk that Lewis may have looked past Rahman began.

This set up a series of legal battles involving managers, promoters and TV networks. The result was a scheduled November rematch.

Tyson, meanwhile, stayed inactive for virtually the entire year, with fights being cancelled, until he beat up the lightly regarded Dane Brian Nielsen. Though still a marquee name, at 35, Tyson is not a very active participant in the sport.

The WBA heavyweight title changed hands in March when John Ruiz avenged a controversial loss to Evander Holyfield with an exciting decision win, in which Holyfield's skills appeared to have eroded even further. A third fight between the two men was postponed in China, then finally rescheduled.

One big fight that lived up to its hype was the middleweight title unification match between Bernard Hopkins and Felix Trinidad. The 36-year-old Hopkins fought a brilliant tactical fight and showed more than enough power in upsetting Trinidad with a 12th round TKO. More than 19,000 fans (mostly rooting for Trinidad) packed Madison Square Garden only weeks after the World Trade Center attack. And they were treated to a coming out party for Hopkins who showed that, as he had been claiming all along, he is one of the best fighters in the world.

Al Bello/Allsport

Bernard Hopkins knocked out Felix Trinidad in the final round
to unify the middleweight belts for the first time since 1987.

The most dramatic win of the year came in a non-title fight. Marco Antonio Barrera moved up in weight and beat the flamboyant featherweight Naseem Hamed. The usually aggressive Barrera stepped out of character to out wit and out box the arrogant Hamed, handing him his first defeat. Barrera went back down to his normal junior featherweight division to defend his title as he planned for a 2002 rematch with Erik Morales, while Hamed stayed idle the rest of the year.

Fans had hoped to see an Oscar De La Hoya-Shane Mosley rematch in 2001, but instead saw each man win convincingly over others. De Le Hoya dominated former junior lightweight champ Arturo Gatti and then won the WBC Super Welterweight title from Javier Castillejo. An anticipated match with Fernando Vargas was all but agreed upon when De La Hoya nixed the deal.

Mosley, who might deserve the mantle of best pound-for-pound fighter in the sport, spent his time successfully defending his WBC Welterweight title against Shannan Taylor and Adrian Stone. He is eyeing a title unification bout with IBF champ Vernon Forrest for early 2002—that should be a good one.

Floyd Mayweather Jr. made a huge statement with his demolition of Diego Corrales in what was supposed to be a

John Gichigi/Allsport

Mike Tyson eventually got back in business in 2001
with a KO of puffy Danish fighter Brian Nielsen.

war of the two best junior lightweights in the world. Instead Mayweather delivered one of the best exhibitions of boxing in the last several years. Mayweather firmly planted himself in the top five best pound-for-pound fighters in the world.

The last time the cruiserweight division produced a boxing superstar was Evander Holyfield in the 1980's. But a new one may be emerging. Former Olympic champion Vassiliy Jirov won four fights in 2001 and three were defenses of his IBF Cruiserweight title. He may be poised to challenge heavyweights—or meet Roy Jones Jr., coming up from light heavyweight.

One surprisingly successful fight came on the women's side, when Laila Ali and Jackie Frazier Lyde, the daughters of former champions Muhammad Ali and Joe Frazier, battled in a pay-per-view event. Not only was the match competitive and exciting, it surprised almost everyone by garnering national publicity and over 100,000 pay-per-view sales.

Boxing concluded 2001 as it has most other recent years—with a handful of marquee names driving the sport economically. And those fighters are like actors searching for the right roles. In 2001, those roles seldom produced big match-ups. Everyone hopes 2002 will be different.

Al Bernstein's Ten Biggest Stories of the Year in Boxing

10 ▪ Laila Ali vs. Jackie Frazier Lyde—Say what you want, this fight between the daughters of legends Muhammad Ali and Joe Frazier produced excitement and over 100,000 pay-per-view buys.

9 ▪ Manny Pacquiao Upsets Lehlohonolo Ledwaba—Pacquiao shocks boxing experts by taking the IBF junior featherweight crown and stamping himself as a rising star in the process.

8 ▪ Joel Casamayor and Acelino Freitas Won't Fight—The two lightweight champions find every excuse to not hold their agreed upon bout, dissapointing fight fans by denying them this highly anticipated match-up.

7 ▪ Paulie Ayala Over Clarence "Bones" Adams—This junior featherweight fight, in which Ayala got the controversial decision, is one of the best of the year. More good news for fight fans is that they will meet in a rematch in 2002.

6 ▪ Chris Byrd Beats David Tua—This upset returns Byrd to the ranks of the legitimate heavyweight contenders and may have permanently derailed Tua's future hopes for another title shot.

5 ▪ Floyd Mayweather Jr. Dominates Diego Corrales—Mayweather gives the performance of his life against a man many said could beat him.

4 ▪ Legal Battles in the Heavyweight Division— After lightly regarded Hasim Rahman beats World Heavyweight Champion Lennox Lewis, all the ensuing legal wrangling changes the landscape of the division temporarily and gives promoter Don King a chance to control the division again.

3 ▪ Marco Antonio Barrera Whips Naseem Hamed—Barrera shuts up "The Prince" with a brilliant performance in this meeting of top lightweights.

2 ▪ Bernard Hopkins Unifies Middleweight Title—In a superb performance, he soundly beats Felix Trinidad in front of a hostile New York crowd to unify the middleweight belt for the first time since Marvelous Marvin Hagler in 1987.

1 ▪ Rahman Shocks Lewis, World—It was shades of Douglas-Tyson and one of the biggest upsets in years. This early-morning fifth-round TKO near Johannesburg, South Africa, turned the heavyweight division upside down.

Title Runs

Until his upset loss to Bernard Hopkins in September 2001, Felix Trinidad was steadily climbing the list of most consecutive wins in title fights. Trinidad, who is now 20-1 in title fights, began the streak as a welterweight, then moved up to junior middleweight and eventually to middleweight before suffering his first defeat.

Fighter, Streak	Fights
Joe Louis, 1937-48	26
Julio Cesar Chavez, 1984-93	25
Ricardo Lopez, 1990-97	21
Larry Holmes, 1978-85	21
Felix Trinidad, 1993-2001	20
Khaosai Galaxy, 1984-91	20

Heavy Duty

Hasim Rahman's upset of Lennox Lewis in their April heavyweight title bout was similar in scope to Buster Douglas' monumental upset of Mike Tyson in 1990. Both challengers were substantial underdogs to champions riding unbeaten streaks of 10 straight title bouts and both fights took place overseas, each ending with a dramatic knockout.

Fighter:	Rahman	Douglas
Date:	4/21/01	2/10/90
Location:	S. Africa	Japan
Odds:	20-1	42-1
Result:	KO 5	KO 10

Unified Champs

Bernard Hopkins joined Roy Jones Jr. as the only active unified champions in boxing with his win over Felix Trinidad on Sept. 29, 2001. Here is a look at the most recent unified champions (in the traditional weight classes):

Division: Fighter	Year
Middleweight: Bernard Hopkins	2001
Lt. Heavyweight: Roy Jones Jr.	2001
Heavyweight: Lennox Lewis	2000
Lightweight: Pernell Whitaker	1992
Middleweight: Marvin Hagler	1987
Welterweight: Lloyd Honeyghan	1987
Bantamweight: Romeo Anaya	1973
Featherweight: Vicente Saldivar	1967
Flyweight: Salvatore Burruni	1966

Two Sweet

A comparison of "Sugar" Shane Mosley and Hall of Famer "Sugar" Ray Robinson over their first 38 career bouts shows how boxing has changed over the years. While both fighters went 38-0, Mosley was 13-0 in title fights during that stretch in the lightweight and welterweight divisions. Robinson didn't even see his first title fight until his 76th pro bout.

Fighter:	Mosley	Robinson
Pro Debut:	1993	1940
Nickname:	Sugar	Sugar
W-L (KO)	38-0 (35)	38-0 (27)
Title bouts	13-0	0-0

2000-2001 Season in Review

information please®
SPORTS ALMANAC

Current Champions
WBA, WBC and IBF Titleholders (through Oct. 31, 2001)

The champions of professional boxing's 17 principal weight divisions, as recognized by the Word Boxing Association (WBA), World Boxing Council (WBC) and International Boxing Federation (IBF).

	Weight Limit	WBA Champion	WBC Champion	IBF Champion
Heavyweight	—	John Ruiz 37-4-0, 27 KOs	Hasim Rahman 35-2-0, 29 KOs	Hasim Rahman 35-2-0, 29 KOs
Cruiserweight	190 lbs	Virgil Hill 46-3-0, 22 KOs	Juan Carlos Gomez 33-0-0, 27 KOs	Vassiliy Jirov 30-0-0, 27 KOs
Light Heavyweight	175 lbs	Roy Jones Jr.* 45-1-0, 36 KOs	Roy Jones Jr. 45-1-0, 36 KOs	Roy Jones Jr. 45-1-0, 36 KOs
Super Middleweight	168 lbs	Byron Mitchell 24-1-1, 17KOs	Eric Lucas 33-4-3, 12 KOs	Sven Ottke 24-0-0, 4 KOs
Middleweight	160 lbs	Bernard Hopkins 40-2-1, 29 KOs	Bernard Hopkins 40-2-1, 29 KOs	Bernard Hopkins 40-2-1, 29 KOs
Jr. Middleweight	154 lbs	Fernando Vargas 22-1-0, 20 KOs	Oscar De La Hoya 34-2-0, 27 KOs	Ronald Wright 42-3-0, 24 KOs
Welterweight	147 lbs	Andrew Lewis 21-0-1, 19 KOs	Shane Mosley 38-0-0, 35 KOs	Vernon Forrest 33-0-1, 26 KOs
Jr. Welterweight	140 lbs	Kostya Tszyu* 27-1-1, 22 KOs	Kostya Tszyu 27-1-1, 22 KOs	Zab Judah 27-0-0, 20 KOs
Lightweight	135 lbs	Raul Balbi 48-4-1, 33 KOs	Jose Luis Castillo 44-4-0, 40 KOs	Paul Spadafora 33-0-0, 14 KOs
Jr. Lightweight	130 lbs	Joel Casamayor 26-0-0, 16 KOs	Floyd Mayweather Jr. 26-0-0, 19 KOs	Steve Forbes 20-1-0, 5 KOs
Featherweight	126 lbs	Derrick Gainer 37-5-0, 23 KOs	Erik Morales 41-0-0, 31 KOs	Frankie Toledo 40-5-1, 16 KOs
Jr. Featherweight	122 lbs	Vacant*	Willie Jorrin 27-0-0, 12 KOs	Manny Pacquiao 32-2-0, 23 KOs
Bantamweight	118 lbs	Eidy Moya 15-1-0, 8 KOs	Veerapol Sahaprom 30-1-0, 21 KOs	Tim Austin 23-0-1, 21 KOs
Jr. Bantamweight	115 lbs	Celes Kobayashi 24-4-3, 0 KOs	Masanori Tokuyama 24-2-1, 6 KOs	Felix Machado 21-3-1, 12 KOs
Flyweight	112 lbs	Eric Morel 30-0-0, 17 KOs	Pongsaklek Wonjongkam 41-2-0, 24 KOs	Irene Pacheco 25-0-0, 19 KOs
Jr. Flyweight	108 lbs	Rosendo Alvarez 28-2-1, 17 KOs	Choi Yo-Sam 23-1-0, 12 KOs	Ricardo Lopez 50-0-1, 37 KOs
Minimumweight	105 lbs	Yutaka Niida 14-0-3, 7 KOs	Jose Antonio Aguirre 26-1-1, 16 KOs	Robert Leyva 18-0-0, 16 KOs

Note: The following weight divisions are also known by these names—**Cruiserweight** as Jr. Heavyweight; **Jr. Middleweight** as Super Welterweight; **Jr. Welterweight** as Super Lightweight; **Jr. Lightweight** as Super Featherweight; **Jr. Featherweight** as Super Bantamweight; **Jr. Bantamweight** as Super Flyweight; **Jr. Flyweight** as Light Flyweight; and **Minimum** as Strawweight or Mini-Flyweights.

*Roy Jones Jr. is the WBA light heavyweight "super world champion;" Kostya Tszyu is the WBA super lightweight "super world champion;" Yober Ortega (31-3-0, 21 KOs) is currently the interim WBA junior featherweight champ.

Major Bouts, 2000–01

Division by division, from Oct. 24, 2000 through Oct. 31, 2001.

WBA, WBC and IBF champions are listed in **bold** type. Note the following Result column abbreviations (in alphabetical order): **Disq.** (won by disqualification); **KO** (knockout); **MDraw** (majority draw); **NC** (no contest); **SDraw** (split draw); **TDraw** (technical draw); **TKO** (technical knockout); **TWm** (won by technical majority decision); **TWs** (won by technical split decision); **TWu** (won by technical unanimous decision); **Wm** (won by majority decision); **Ws** (won by split decision) and **Wu** (won by unanimous decision).

Heavyweights

Date	Winner	Loser	Result	Title	Site
Nov. 11	Clifford Etienne	Lawrence Clay-Bey	Wu 10	—	Las Vegas
Nov. 11	**Lennox Lewis**	David Tua	Wu 12	**IBF/WBC**	Las Vegas
Nov. 17	Michael Moorer	Lorenzo Boyd	TKO 4	—	Burlington, Iowa
Nov. 25	Vitali Klitschko	Timo Hoffmann	Wu 12	—	Hannover, Germany
Nov. 28	Larry Donald	Obed Sullivan	Draw 12	—	Las Vegas
Dec. 8	Henry Akinwande	Kenny Craven	KO 1	—	Tallahassee, Fla.
Jan. 12	Michael Moorer	Terrance Lewis	TKO 2	—	Concho, Okla.
Jan. 19	Chris Byrd	David Vedder	Wu 10	—	Mt. Pleasant, Mich.
Jan. 27	Vitali Klitschko	Orlin Norris	KO 1	—	Munich
Jan. 24	Jameel McCline	King Ipitan	KO 1	—	Las Vegas
Feb. 11	Ray Mercer	Jeff Pegues	KO 2	—	Elgin, Ill.
Feb. 22	Tim Witherspoon	David Bostice	TKO.1	—	Harrisburg, Penn.
Mar. 3	John Ruiz	**Evander Holyfield**	Wu 12	**WBA**	Las Vegas
Mar. 10	Lance "Mount" Whitaker	Oleg Maskaev	KO 2	—	Las Vegas
Mar. 17	Henry Akinwande	Peter McNeeley	KO 2	—	Tallahassee, Fla.
Mar. 17	Ray Mercer	Don Steele	KO 5	—	Philadelphia, Miss.
Mar. 17	Lawrence Clay-Bey	Ken Murphy	TKO 5	—	Philadelphia, Miss.
Mar. 23	David Tua	Dannell Nicholson	KO 6	—	Las Vegas
Mar. 23	Fres Oquendo	Clifford Etienne	TKO 8	—	Las Vegas
Mar. 24	Wladimir Klitschko	Derrick Jefferson	TKO 2	WBO	Munich, Germany
Mar. 31	Tim Witherspoon	Eliecer Castillo	Wm 10	—	Atlantic City
Apr. 1	Pea Wolfgramm	Jimmy Thunder	TWu 7	—	Las Vegas
Apr. 22	Hasim Rahman	**Lennox Lewis**	KO 5	**IBF/WBC**	Johannesburg, S. Africa
May 12	Chris Byrd	Maurice Harris	Wu 12	—	New York City
May 20	Obed Sullivan	Sherman Williams	Ws 12	—	Belterra, Ind.
May 22	Terrance Lewis	Robert Davis	TKO 9	—	San Francisco
June 5	Frans Botha	David Bostice	Wu 10	—	Las Vegas
June 8	Monte Barrett	Tim Witherspoon	Ws 10	—	Verona, N.Y.
June 12	Lou Savarese	Tom Glesby	TKO 3	—	Galveston, Texas
July 7	Kirk Johnson	Larry Donald	Wu 12	—	Brooklyn, N.Y.
July 13	Frans Botha	Russell Chasteen	KO 2	—	Palm Springs, Calif.
July 20	Vassiliy Jirov	Adolpho Washington	Wu 10	—	Canton, Ohio
July 21	Jameel McCline	Michael Grant	TKO 1	—	Las Vegas
July 27	Michael Moorer	Dale Crow	TDraw 5	—	Mt. Pleasant, Mich.
Aug. 4	Wladimir Klitschko	Charles Shufford	TKO 6	WBO	Las Vegas
Aug. 18	Chris Byrd	David Tua	Wu 12	—	Las Vegas
Sept. 2	Fres Oquendo	Obed Sullivan	KO 11	—	Choctaw, Miss.
Oct. 12	Razor Ruddock	Egerton Marcus	KO 10	—	Niagara Falls, N.Y.
Oct. 13	Ray Mercer	Brian Scott	KO 2	—	Copenhagen, Denmark
Oct. 13	Mike Tyson	Brian Nielsen	KO 7	—	Copenhagen, Denmark

Cruiserweights (190 lbs)
(Jr. Heavyweights)

Date	Winner	Loser	Result	Title	Site
Dec. 9	Virgil Hill	**Fabrice Tiozzo**	TKO 1	**WBA**	Lyon, France
Dec. 16	**Juan Carlos Gomez**	Jorge Castro	KO 10	**WBC**	Essen, Germany
Jan. 27	Johnny Nelson	George Arias	Wu 12	WBO	London
Feb. 6	**Vassiliy Jirov**	Alex Gonzales	KO 1	**IBF**	Almaty, Kazakstan
Mar. 24	**Vassiliy Jirov**	Terry McGroom	TKO 1	**IBF**	Las Vegas
July 21	Johnny Nelson	Marcelo Dominguez	Wu 12	WBO	Sheffield, England
Sept. 7	O'Neill Bell	King Arthur Williams	TKO 11	—	Hankinson, N.D.
Sept. 8	**Vassiliy Jirov**	Julian Letterlough	TKO 8	**IBF**	Reno, Nev.

Light Heavyweights (175 lbs)

Date	Winner	Loser	Result	Title	Site
Dec. 16	Dariusz Michalczewski	Ka-Dy King	TKO 7	WBO	Essen, Germany
Jan. 5	Reggie Johnson	Chris Johnson	Wu 12	—	Biloxi, Miss.
Jan. 17	Lou Del Valle	Earl Butler	KO 3	—	Yonkers, N.Y.
Feb. 24	**Roy Jones Jr.**	Derrick Harmon	TKO 10	**IBF/WBA/WBC**	Tampa, Fla.
May 5	Dariusz Michalczewski	Venti Lakatus	KO 9	WBO	Gdansk, Poland
May 17	Lou Del Valle	Dennis McKinney	Wu 8	—	New York City
May 17	David Telesco	Tom Cameron	KO 1	—	New York City
May 25	Reggie Johnson	Will Taylor	Wu 12	—	Prior Lake, Minn.
July 28	**Roy Jones Jr.**	Julio Gonzalez	Wu 12	**IBF/WBA/WBC**	Los Angeles
Aug. 5	Lou Del Valle	Bruno Girard	Draw 12	WBA*	Marseille, France

*Roy Jones Jr. is the WBA light heavyweight "super world champion."

Super Middleweights (168 lbs)

Date	Winner	Loser	Result	Title	Site
Dec. 8	Charles Brewer	Esteban Cervantes	TKO 1	—	Philadelphia
Dec. 15	Davey Hilton	**Dingaan Thobela**	Ws 12	**WBC**	Montreal
Dec. 16	**Sven Ottke**	Silvio Branco	Wu 12	**IBF**	Karlsruhe, Germany
Dec. 16	Joe Calzaghe	Richie Woodhall	TKO 10	WBO	Sheffield, England
Jan. 27	Danilo Haussler	Andrei Shkalikov	Ws 12	—	Riesa, Germany
Mar. 3	Byron Mitchell	Manuel Siaca	TKO 12	**WBA**	Las Vegas
Mar. 24	**Sven Ottke**	James Crawford	TKO 8	**IBF**	Magdeburg, Germany
Apr. 28	Joe Calzaghe	Mario Veit	TKO 1	WBO	Cardiff, Wales
May 4	Thomas Tate	Fernando Zuniga	Ws 12	—	Uncasville, Conn.
May 19	Antwun Echols	Charles Brewer	TKO 3	—	Uncasville, Conn.
June 9	**Sven Ottke**	Ali Ennebati	TKO 11	**IBF**	Nuremberg, Germany
July 10	Eric Lucas	Glenn Catley	KO 7	**WBC***	Montreal
July 14	Hector Camacho	Roberto Duran	Wu 12	—	Denver
Sept. 1	**Sven Ottke**	James Butler	Wu 12	**IBF**	Magdeburg, Germany
Sept. 29	**Byron Mitchell**	Manuel Siaca	Ws 12	WBA	New York City
Oct. 13	Joe Calzaghe	Will McIntyre	TKO 4	WBO	Copenhagen, Denmark

*Eric Lucas won the vacant WBC super middleweight title. Former champion Davey Hilton was stripped of the title following a conviction on sexual assault charges.

Middleweights (160 lbs)

Date	Winner	Loser	Result	Title	Site
Dec. 1	**Bernard Hopkins**	Antwun Echols	TKO 10	IBF	Las Vegas
Dec. 2	**William Joppy**	Johnathan Reid	TKO 4	**WBA**	Las Vegas
Apr. 14	**Bernard Hopkins**	Keith Holmes	Wu 12	**IBF/WBC**	New York City
May 12	Felix Trinidad	**William Joppy**	TKO 5	**WBA**	New York City
July 21	Harry Simon	Hassine Cherifi	Wu 12	WBO	Bayomon, P.R.
Sept. 29	**Bernard Hopkins**	**Felix Trinidad**	TKO 12	**IBF/WBA/WBC**	New York City

Junior Middleweights (154 lbs)
(Super Welterweights)

Date	Winner	Loser	Result	Title	Site
Dec. 2	**Felix Trinidad**	**Fernando Vargas**	TKO 12	**WBA/IBF**	Las Vegas
Dec. 16	Ronald "Winky" Wright	Keith Mullings	Wu 12	—	Pittsburgh
Feb. 3	Hector Camacho Sr.	Troy Lowry	Wu 10	—	Miami
Feb. 12	Harry Simon	Wayne Alexander	TKO 5	—	Widnes, England
Apr. 1	David Reid	Urbano Gurrola	Wu 10	—	Las Vegas
Apr. 20	Bronco McKart	Michael Lerma	Wu 10	—	Cincinnati
Apr. 27	Carlos Bojorquez	Pernell Whitaker	TKO 4	—	Stateline, Nev.
May 5	Fernando Vargas	Wilfredo Rivera	TKO 6	—	El Paso, Texas
June 23	Oscar De La Hoya	**Javier Castillejo**	Wu 12	**WBC**	Las Vegas
Aug. 24	Vernon Forrest	Edgar Ruiz	TKO 4	—	Baltimore
Sept. 21	Nick Acevedo	Carlos Bojorquez	Ws 10	—	Philadelphia, Penn.
Sept. 22	Fernando Vargas	Shibata Flores	KO 7	**WBA**	Las Vegas
Oct. 12	Ronald "Winky" Wright	Robert Frazier	Wu 12	**IBF**	Indio, Calif.

Note: Felix Trinidad vacated the WBA and IBF junior middleweight titles in order to move up in weight to middleweight.

Major Bouts, 2000–01 (Cont.)
Welterweights (147 lbs)

Date	Winner	Loser	Result	Title	Site
Nov. 4	**Shane Mosley**	Antonio Diaz	TKO 6	**WBC**	New York City
Dec. 15	Oba Carr	Agustine Caballero	KO 6	—	Fresno, Calif.
Dec. 16	Daniel Santos	Neil Sinclair	KO 2	WBO	Sheffield, England
Feb. 17	Andrew Lewis	James Page	TKO 7	**WBA**	Las Vegas
Mar. 10	**Shane Mosley**	Shannan Taylor	TKO 5	**WBC**	Las Vegas
Mar. 24	Oscar De La Hoya	Arturo Gatti	TKO 5	—	Las Vegas
Mar. 24	Rafael Pineda	Oba Carr	TKO 6	—	Las Vegas
Apr. 28	**Andrew Lewis**	Larry Marks	Wu 12	**WBA**	New York City
May 12	Vernon Forrest	Raul Frank	Wu 12	**IBF**	New York City
June 15	Vivian Harris	Golden Johnson	KO 3	—	Philadelphia
July 14	Oba Carr	Norberto Sandoval	Wu 10	—	Denver
July 21	**Shane Mosley**	Adrian Stone	KO 3	**WBC**	Las Vegas
July 28	**Andrew Lewis**	Ricardo Mayorga	NC 2*	**WBA**	Los Angeles
Aug. 17	Cory Spinks	Larry Marks	Wu 12	—	Chicago
Sept. 29	Michele Piccirillo	Rafael Pineda	Wu 12	—	New York City
Oct. 13	Thomas Damgaard	Freddy Italo Rojas	TKO 3	—	Copenhagen, Denmark

*Andrew Lewis was unable to continue due to a cut from an accidental head butt in the second round.

Junior Welterweights (140 lbs)
(Super Lightweights)

Date	Winner	Loser	Result	Title	Site
Nov. 4	Hector Camacho Jr.	Joe Hutchinson	Wu 10	—	New York City
Nov. 11	John-John Molina	Ben Tackie	Ws 10	—	Las Vegas
Nov. 11	Jesse James Leija	Ivan Robinson	Wu 10	—	Las Vegas
Jan. 7	Jesse James Leija	Fred Ladd	TKO 3	—	Las Vegas
Jan. 13	**Zab Judah**	Reggie Green	TKO 10	**IBF**	Uncasville, Conn.
Feb. 3	**Kostya Tszyu**	**Sharmba Mitchell**	TKO 8	**WBA/WBC**	Las Vegas
Feb. 3	Hector Camacho Jr.	Rocky Martinez	Wu 12	—	Miami
May 11	Terronn Millett	Luis Perez	Wu 10	—	Savannah, Ga.
May 18	Mickey Ward	Steve Quinonez	KO 1	—	Ledyard, Conn.
June 23	**Zab Judah**	Allan Vester	KO 3	**IBF**	Uncasville, Conn.
June 23	**Kostya Tszyu**	Oktay Urkal	Wu 12	**WBA/WBC**	Uncasville, Conn.
July 7	Hector Camacho Jr.	Jesse James Leija	TWu 5*	—	Brooklyn, N.Y.
July 10	Mickey Ward	Emmanuel Burton	Wu 10	—	Ledyard, Conn.
Aug. 10	Ben Tackie	Ray Oliveira	Wm 12	—	Ledyard, Conn.
Aug. 14	Paul Spadafora	Chucky Tschorniawsky	Wu 10	—	Chester, Va.
Aug. 31	Teddy Reid	Joe Hutchinson	TKO 1	—	Baltimore

*Hector Camacho Jr. was awarded the technical decision after he was cut over his right eye and was unable to continue. The bout was stopped between the fifth and sixth rounds by referee Steve Smoger. Under New York State rules, the bout went to the scorecards since five rounds were completed.

Lightweights (135 lbs)

Date	Winner	Loser	Result	Title	Site
Dec. 1	Angel Manfredy	Carlos Ramirez	TKO 5	—	Las Vegas
Dec. 3	Julio Diaz	Eduardo Perez	TKO 6	—	Las Vegas
Dec. 16	**Paul Spadafora**	Billy Irwin	Wu 12	**IBF**	Pittsburgh
Jan. 18	Angel Manfredy	Juan Polo Perez	TKO 4	—	Biloxi, Miss.
Jan. 20	**Jose Luis Castillo**	Cesar Bazan	TKO 6	**WBC**	Las Vegas
Jan. 21	Julio Diaz	Juan Macias	Wu 10	—	Reno, Nev.
Jan. 29	Julien Lorcy	Wilson Galli	TKO 6	—	Paris
Feb. 17	**Takanori Hatakeyama**	Rick Yoshimura	Draw 12	**WBA**	Tokyo
Feb. 24	Artur Grigorian	Jose Angel Perez	KO 6	WBO	Hamburg, Germany
Mar. 4	Julio Diaz	Bernard Harris	Wu 10	—	Reno, Nev.
Apr. 28	Julio Diaz	Justo Sencion	KO 9	—	New York City
May 5	Juan Lazcano	John-John Molina	TKO 11	—	El Paso, Texas
May 8	**Paul Spadafora**	Joel Perez	Wu 12	**IBF**	Pittsburgh
June 1	Stevie Johnston	James Crayton	TWu 9	—	Galveston, Texas
June 16	**Jose Luis Castillo**	Sung Ho-Yuh	TKO 1	**WBC**	Hermosillo, Mexico
July 1	Julien Lorcy	**Takanori Hatakeyama**	Wu 12	**WBA**	Tokyo
Aug. 3	Angel Manfredy	Lamar Murphy	Wu 10	—	Toppenish, Wash.
Aug. 7	Julio Diaz	Dario Esalas	KO 4	—	Florence, Ind.
Sept. 1	Juan Lazcano	Julio Alvarez	KO 4	—	El Paso, Texas
Oct. 6	Angel Manfredy	Julio Diaz	Ws 12	—	Corpus Christi, Texas
Oct. 8	Raul Balbi	**Julien Lorcy**	Wm 12	**WBA**	Paris

Junior Lightweights (130 lbs)
(Super Featherweights)

Date	Winner	Loser	Result	Title	Site
Oct. 21	Floyd Mayweather Jr.	Emanuel Barton	TKO 9	**WBC**	Detroit
Dec. 3	Steve Forbes	John Brown	TKO 8	**IBF**	Miami
Dec. 16	Acelino Freitas	Daniel Alicea	TKO 1	—	Sheffield, England
Jan. 4	Jesus Chavez	Benito Rodriguez	TKO 6	—	Houston
Jan. 6	**Joel Casamayor**	Roberto Garcia	TKO 9	**WBA**	Las Vegas
Jan. 20	**Floyd Mayweather Jr.**	Diego Corrales	TKO 10	**WBC**	Las Vegas
Jan. 27	Acelino Freitas	Orlando Soto	KO 1	WBO	Brasilia, Brazil
Feb. 23	Jesus Chavez	Tom Johnson	TKO 8	—	Austin, Texas
May 5	**Joel Casamayor**	Edwin Santana	Wu 12	**WBA**	Philadelphia, Miss.
May 26	Jesus Chavez	Juan Arias	Wu 12	—	Grand Rapids, Mich.
May 26	**Floyd Mayweather Jr.**	Carlos Hernandez	Wu 12	**WBC**	Grand Rapids, Mich.
June 3	Lamont Pearson	Carlos Navarro	TKO 9	—	Chicago
Sept. 29	**Joel Casamayor**	Joe Morales	TKO 8	**WBA**	Miami
Sept. 29	Acelino Freitas	Alfred Kotey	Wu 10	—	Miami
Sept. 29	**Steve Forbes**	John Brown	Wu 12	**IBF**	Miami

Featherweights (126 lbs)

Date	Winner	Loser	Result	Title	Site
Dec. 9	Erik Morales	Rodney Jones	KO 3	—	Tijuana, Mexico
Dec. 16	Mbulelo Botile	**Paul Ingle**	KO 12	**IBF**	Sheffield, England
Dec. 16	Julio Pablo Chacon	Sergio Rafael Liendo	TKO 4	—	Buenos Aires
Jan. 27	Istvan Kovacs	Antonio Diaz	TKO 12	WBO	Munich, Germany
Feb. 17	Erik Morales	**Guty Espadas**	Wu 12	**WBC**	Las Vegas
Feb. 24	**Derrick Gainer**	Victor Polo	Ws 12	**WBA**	Tampa, Fla.
Apr. 6	Frankie Toledo	**Mbulelo Botile**	Wu 12	**IBF**	Las Vegas
Apr. 7	Marco Antonio Barrera	Naseem Hamed	Wu 12	—	Las Vegas
June 16	Julio Pablo Chacon	Istvan Kovacs	TKO 6	WBO	Budapest, Hungary
June 26	Victor Polo	David Toledo	Wu 12	—	New York City
June 30	Johnny Tapia	Cesar Soto	TKO 3	—	Las Vegas
July 28	**Erik Morales**	InJin Chi	Wu 12	**WBC**	Los Angeles
Aug. 11	Julio Pablo Chacon	Edward Barrios	TKO 5	WBO	Mendoza, Argentina
Aug. 18	Robbie Peden	Sergio Perez	Wu 12	—	Las Vegas
Sept. 8	Marco Antonio Barrera	Enrique Sanchez	TKO 6	—	Reno, Nev.

Note: Naseem Hamed vacated the WBO belt when he refused to fight the WBO's No. 1 contender Istvan Kovacs and signed to fight Marco Antonio Barrera instead, so the April 7 Hamed-Barrera fight was a non-title bout.

Junior Featherweights (122 lbs)
(Super Bantamweights)

Date	Winner	Loser	Result	Title	Site
Nov. 22	Yober Ortega	Kozo Ishii	TKO 11	**WBA†**	Nagoya, Japan
Dec. 1	Marco Antonio Barrera	Jesus Salad	TKO 6	WBO	Las Vegas
Jan. 19	**Willie Jorrin**	Oscar Larios	Wu 12	**WBC**	Sacramento, Calif.
Feb. 17	**Lehlohonolo Ledwaba**	Arnel Barotillo	TKO 8	**IBF**	Johannesburg, S. Africa
Feb. 24	Manny Pacquiao	Tetsutora Senrima	TKO 5	—	Manila, Phillipines
Mar. 23	**Clarence Adams**	Ivan Alvarez	Wu 12	**WBA**	Owensboro, Ky.
Mar. 23	Johnny Tapia	Cuauhtemoc Gomez	TKO 6	—	Albuquerque
Apr. 22	**Lehlohonolo Ledwaba**	Carlos Contreras	Wu 12	**IBF**	Johannesburg, S. Africa
June 23	Manny Pacquiao	**Lehlohonolo Ledwaba**	TKO 6	**IBF**	Las Vegas
June 23	Agapito Sanchez	Jorge Monsalvo	TKO 7	WBO	Las Vegas
Aug. 4	Paulie Ayala	Clarence Adams	Ws 12	—	Las Vegas
Sept. 29	Ratanachai Vorapin	Danny Romero	Wm 10	—	New York City

Note: Clarence Adams had his title stripped by the WBA for not defending his title properly before signing to fight Paulie Ayala. As a result, the Adams-Ayala meeting on Aug. 4, 2001 was a non-title bout. Adams was originally scheduled to fight interim champion Yober Ortega on March 23 but Ortega refused the fight, as did the No. 2 and No. 3 WBA contenders. Adams was forced to settle for Ivan Alvarez, the No. 4 contender.

†interim title

Major Bouts, 2000–01 (Cont.)
Bantamweights (118 lbs)

Date	Winner	Loser	Result	Title	Site
Dec. 5	**Veerapol Sahaprom**	Oscar Arciniega	TKO 5	**WBC**	Bangkok, Thailand
Dec. 16	Mauricio Martinez	Esham Pickering	KO 1	WBO	Sheffield, England
Mar. 3	**Tim Austin**	Jesus Perez	TKO 6	**IBF**	Las Vegas
Mar. 30	**Paulie Ayala**	Hugo Dianzo	Wu 12	**WBA**	Fort Worth, Texas
May 14	**Veerapol Sahaprom**	Ricardo Barajas	KO 3	**WBC**	Paris
June 8	Mark Johnson	Sergio Perez	Wu 10	—	Madison, Wis.
June 16	**Tim Austin**	Steve Dotse	TKO 6	**IBF**	Cincinnati
Sept. 1	**Veerapol Sahaprom**	Toshiaki Nishioka	MDraw 12	**WBC**	Yokohama, Japan
Oct. 14	Eidy Moya	Adan Vargas	KO 11	**WBA**	McAllen, Texas

Note: Paulie Ayala vacated his WBA belt to move up in weight and fight Clarence Adams on Aug. 4, 2001.

Junior Bantamweights (115 lbs)
(Super Flyweights)

Date	Winner	Loser	Result	Title	Site
Dec. 12	**Masanori Tokuyama**	Akihiko Nago	Wu 12	**WBC**	Osaka, Japan
Dec. 16	**Felix Machado**	William de Souza	TKO 3	**IBF**	Maracay, Venezuela
Mar. 11	Celes Kobayashi	**Leo Gamez**	TKO 10	**WBA**	Yokohama, Japan
May 20	**Masanori Tokuyama**	Choi In-Joo	KO 5	**WBC**	Seoul, S. Korea
June 16	**Felix Machado**	Mauricio Pastrana	Wu 12	**IBF**	Cincinnati
Sept. 1	**Celes Kobayashi**	Jesus Rojas	Ws 12	**WBA**	Yokohama, Japan
Sept. 24	**Masanori Tokuyama**	Gerry Penalosa	Wu 12	**WBC**	Yokohama, Japan

Flyweights (112 lbs)

Date	Winner	Loser	Result	Title	Site
Nov. 10	**Irene Pacheco**	Masibulele Makepula	Wm 12	**IBF**	Las Vegas
Dec. 15	Fernando Montiel	Isidro Garcia	KO 7	WBO	Obregon, Mexico
Dec. 15	**Eric Morel**	Gilberto Keb-Baas	Wu 12	**WBA**	Madison, Wis.
Mar. 2	Pongsaklek Wonjongkam	Malcolm Tunacao	KO 1	**WBC**	Pichit, Thailand
Mar. 24	Fernando Montiel	Zoltan Lunka	TKO 7	WBO	Munich
June 8	**Eric Morel**	Jose Jesus Luis Lopez	TKO 9	**WBA**	Baraboo, Wis.
July 15	**Pongsaklek Wonjongkam**	Hayato Asai	TKO 5	**WBC**	Nagoya, Japan
Sept. 7	Fernando Montiel	Jose Carita Lopez	Wu 12	WBO	Reno, Nev.

Junior Flyweights (108 lbs)
(Light Flyweights)

Date	Winner	Loser	Result	Title	Site
Dec. 2	**Ricardo Lopez**	Ratanapol Vorapin	TKO 3	**IBF**	Las Vegas
Jan. 30	**Choi Yo-Sam**	Saman Sorjaturong	KO 7	**WBC**	Seoul, S. Korea
Mar. 3	Rosendo Alvarez	**Bebis Mendoza**	Ws 12	**WBA**	Las Vegas
Sept. 29	**Ricardo Lopez**	Zolani Petelo	KO 8	**IBF**	New York City
Sept. 29	Nelson Dieppa	Fahlan Sakreerin	Wu 12	WBO	New York City

Minimumweights (105 lbs)
(Strawweights or Mini-Flyweights)

Date	Winner	Loser	Result	Title	Site
Dec. 6	Keitaro Hoshino	**Joma Gamboa**	Wu 12	**WBA**	Yokohama, Japan
Feb. 2	**Jose Antonio Aguirre**	Manny Melchor	Wu 12	**WBC**	Tijuana, Mexico
Apr. 16	Chana Porpaoin	**Keitaro Hoshino**	Ws 12	**WBA**	Yokohama, Japan
Apr. 29	Robert Leyva	Daniel Reyes	Wu 12	**IBF**	Jamaica, N.Y.
Aug. 25	Yutaka Niida	**Chana Porpaoin**	Wu 12	**WBA**	Yokohama, Japan
Sept. 29	**Robert Leyva**	Miguel Barrera	TDraw 3*	**IBF**	Ensenada, Mexico

*The Leyva-Barrera fight was ruled a technical draw in the third round following an accidental head butt. Leyva retained the IBF belt.

1884-2001 Through the Years

ESPN information please®
SPORTS ALMANAC

World Heavyweight Championship Fights

Widely accepted world champions in **bold** type. Note following result abbreviations: KO (knockout), TKO (technical knockout), Wu (unanimous decision), Wm (majority decision), Ws (split decision), Ref (referee's decision), ND (no decision), Disq. (won on disqualification).

Year	Date	Winner	Age	Wgt	Loser	Wgt	Result	Location
1892	Sept. 7	James J. Corbett	26	178	John L. Sullivan	212	KO 21	New Orleans
1894	Jan. 25	**James J. Corbett**	27	184	Charley Mitchell	158	KO 3	Jacksonville, Fla.
1897	Mar. 17	Bob Fitzsimmons	34	167	**James J. Corbett**	183	KO 14	Carson City, Nev.
1899	June 9	James J. Jeffries	24	206	**Bob Fitzsimmons**	167	KO 11	Coney Island, N.Y.
1899	Nov. 3	**James J. Jeffries**	24	215	Tom Sharkey	183	Ref 25	Coney Island, N.Y.
1900	Apr. 6	**James J. Jeffries**	24	NA	Jack Finnegan	NA	KO 1	Detroit
1900	May 11	**James J. Jeffries**	25	218	James J. Corbett	188	KO 23	Coney Island, N.Y.
1901	Nov. 15	**James J. Jeffries**	26	211	Gus Ruhlin	194	TKO 6	San Francisco
1902	July 25	**James J. Jeffries**	27	219	Bob Fitzsimmons	172	KO 8	San Francisco
1903	Aug. 14	**James J. Jeffries**	28	220	James J. Corbett	190	KO 10	San Francisco
1904	Aug. 25	**James J. Jeffries***	29	219	Jack Munroe	186	TKO 2	San Francisco
1905	July 3	Marvin Hart	28	190	Jack Root	171	KO 12	Reno, Nev.
1906	Feb. 23	Tommy Burns	24	~180	**Marvin Hart**	188	Ref 20	Los Angeles
1906	Oct. 2	**Tommy Burns**	25	NA	Jim Flynn	NA	KO 15	Los Angeles
1906	Nov. 28	**Tommy Burns**	25	172	Phila. Jack O'Brien	163½	Draw 20	Los Angeles
1907	May 8	**Tommy Burns**	25	180	Phila. Jack O'Brien	167	Ref 20	Los Angeles
1907	July 4	**Tommy Burns**	26	181	Bill Squires	180	KO 1	Colma, Calif.
1907	Dec. 2	**Tommy Burns**	26	177	Gunner Moir	204	KO 10	London
1908	Feb. 10	**Tommy Burns**	26	NA	Jack Palmer	NA	KO 4	London
1908	Mar. 17	**Tommy Burns**	26	NA	Jem Roche	NA	KO 1	Dublin
1908	Apr. 18	**Tommy Burns**	26	NA	Jewey Smith	NA	KO 5	Paris
1908	June 13	**Tommy Burns**	26	184	Bill Squires	183	KO 8	Paris
1908	Aug. 24	**Tommy Burns**	27	181	Bill Squires	184	KO 13	Sydney
1908	Sept. 2	**Tommy Burns**	27	183	Bill Lang	187	KO 6	Melbourne
1908	Dec. 26	Jack Johnson	30	192	**Tommy Burns**	168	TKO 14	Sydney
1909	Mar. 10	**Jack Johnson**	30	NA	Victor McLaglen	NA	ND 6	Vancouver
1909	May 19	**Jack Johnson**	31	205	Phila. Jack O'Brien	161	ND 6	Philadelphia
1909	June 30	**Jack Johnson**	31	207	Tony Ross	214	ND 6	Pittsburgh
1909	Sept. 9	**Jack Johnson**	31	209	Al Kaufman	191	ND 10	San Francisco
1909	Oct. 16	**Jack Johnson**	31	205½	Stanley Ketchel	170¼	KO 12	Colma, Calif.
1910	July 4	**Jack Johnson**	32	208	James J. Jeffries	227	KO 15	Reno, Nev.
1912	July 4	**Jack Johnson**	34	195½	Jim Flynn	175	TKO 9	Las Vegas, Nev.
1913	Dec. 19	**Jack Johnson**	35	NA	Jim Johnson	NA	Draw 10	Paris
1914	June 27	**Jack Johnson**	36	221	Frank Moran	203	Ref 20	Paris
1915	Apr. 5	Jess Willard	33	230	**Jack Johnson**	205½	KO 26	Havana
1916	Mar. 25	**Jess Willard**	34	225	Frank Moran	203	ND 10	NYC (Mad.Sq. Garden)
1919	July 4	Jack Dempsey	24	187	**Jess Willard**	245	TKO 4	Toledo, Ohio
1920	Sept. 6	**Jack Dempsey**	25	185	Billy Miske	187	KO 3	Benton Harbor, Mich.
1920	Dec. 14	**Jack Dempsey**	25	188¼	Bill Brennan	197	KO 12	NYC (Mad. Sq. Garden)
1921	July 2	**Jack Dempsey**	26	188	Georges Carpentier	172	KO 4	Jersey City, N.J.
1923	July 4	**Jack Dempsey**	28	188	Tommy Gibbons	175½	Ref 15	Shelby, Mont.
1923	Sept. 14	**Jack Dempsey**	28	192½	Luis Firpo	216½	KO 2	NYC (Polo Grounds)
1926	Sept. 23	Gene Tunney	29	189½	**Jack Dempsey**	190	Wu 10	Philadelphia
1927	Sept. 22	**Gene Tunney**	30	189½	Jack Dempsey	192½	Wu 10	Chicago
1928	July 26	**Gene Tunney******	31	192	Tom Heeney	203	TKO 11	NYC (Yankee Stadium)

*James J. Jeffries retired as champion on May 13, 1905, then came out of retirement to fight Jack Johnson for the title in 1910.
**Gene Tunney retired as champion in 1928.

World Heavyweight Championship Fights (Cont.)

Year	Date	Winner	Age	Wgt	Loser	Wgt	Result	Location
1930	June 12	Max Schmeling	24	188	Jack Sharkey	197	Disq. 4	NYC (Yankee Stadium)
1931	July 3	**Max Schmeling**	25	189	Young Stribling	186½	TKO 15	Cleveland
1932	June 21	Jack Sharkey	29	205	**Max Schmeling**	188	Ws 15	Long Island City, N.Y.
1933	June 29	Primo Carnera	26	260½	**Jack Sharkey**	201	KO 6	Long Island City, N.Y.
1933	Oct. 22	**Primo Carnera**	26	259½	Paulino Uzcudun	229¼	Wu 15	Rome
1934	Mar. 1	**Primo Carnera**	27	270	Tommy Loughran	184	Wu 15	Miami
1934	June 14	Max Baer	25	209½	**Primo Carnera**	263¼	TKO 11	Long Island City, N.Y.
1935	June 13	James J. Braddock	29	193¾	**Max Baer**	209	Wu 15	Long Island City, N.Y.
1937	June 22	Joe Louis	23	197¼	**James J. Braddock**	197	KO 8	Chicago
1937	Aug. 30	**Joe Louis**	23	197	Tommy Farr	204¼	Wu 15	NYC (Yankee Stadium)
1938	Feb. 23	**Joe Louis**	23	200	Nathan Mann	193½	KO 3	NYC (Mad. Sq. Garden
1938	Apr. 1	**Joe Louis**	23	202½	Harry Thomas	196	KO 5	Chicago
1938	June 22	**Joe Louis**	24	198¾	Max Schmeling	193	KO 1	NYC (Yankee Stadium)
1939	Jan. 25	**Joe Louis**	24	200¼	John Henry Lewis	180¾	KO 1	NYC (Mad. Sq. Garden
1939	Apr. 17	**Joe Louis**	24	201¼	Jack Roper	204¾	KO 1	Los Angeles
1939	June 28	**Joe Louis**	25	200¾	Tony Galento	233¾	TKO 4	NYC (Yankee Stadium)
1939	Sept. 20	**Joe Louis**	25	200	Bob Pastor	183	KO 11	Detroit
1940	Feb. 9	**Joe Louis**	25	203	Arturo Godoy	202	Ws 15	NYC (Mad. Sq. Garden
1940	Mar. 29	**Joe Louis**	25	201½	Johnny Paychek	187½	KO 2	NYC (Mad. Sq. Garden
1940	June 20	**Joe Louis**	26	199	Arturo Godoy	201¼	TKO 8	NYC (Yankee Stadium)
1940	Dec. 16	**Joe Louis**	26	202¼	Al McCoy	180¾	TKO 6	Boston
1941	Jan. 31	**Joe Louis**	26	202½	Red Burman	188	KO 5	NYC (Mad. Sq. Garden
1941	Feb. 17	**Joe Louis**	26	203½	Gus Dorazio	193½	KO 2	Philadelphia
1941	Mar. 21	**Joe Louis**	26	202	Abe Simon	254½	TKO 13	Detroit
1941	Apr. 8	**Joe Louis**	26	203½	Tony Musto	199½	TKO 9	St. Louis
1941	May 23	**Joe Louis**	27	201½	Buddy Baer	237½	Disq. 7	Washington, D.C.
1941	June 18	**Joe Louis**	27	199½	Billy Conn	174	KO 13	NYC (Polo Grounds)
1941	Sept. 29	**Joe Louis**	27	202¼	Lou Nova	202½	TKO 6	NYC (Polo Grounds)
1942	Jan. 9	**Joe Louis**	27	206¾	Buddy Baer	250	KO 1	NYC (Mad. Sq. Garden
1942	Mar. 27	**Joe Louis**	27	207½	Abe Simon	255½	KO 6	NYC (Mad. Sq. Garden
1942-45 World War II								
1946	June 9	**Joe Louis**	32	207	Billy Conn	187	KO 8	NYC (Yankee Stadium)
1946	Sept. 18	**Joe Louis**	32	211	Tami Mauriello	198½	KO 1	NYC (Yankee Stadium)
1947	Dec. 5	**Joe Louis**	33	211½	Jersey Joe Walcott	194½	Ws 15	NYC (Mad. Sq. Garden
1948	June 25	**Joe Louis***	34	213½	Jersey Joe Walcott	194¾	KO 11	NYC (Yankee Stadium)
1949	June 22	**Ezzard Charles**	27	181¾	Jersey Joe Walcott	195½	Wu 15	Chicago
1949	Aug. 10	**Ezzard Charles**	28	180	Gus Lesnevich	182	TKO 8	NYC (Yankee Stadium)
1949	Oct. 14	**Ezzard Charles**	28	182	Pat Valentino	188½	KO 8	San Francisco
1950	Aug. 15	**Ezzard Charles**	29	183¼	Freddie Beshore	184½	TKO 14	Buffalo
1950	Sept. 27	**Ezzard Charles**	29	184½	Joe Louis	218	Wu 15	NYC (Yankee Stadium)
1950	Dec. 5	**Ezzard Charles**	29	185	Nick Barone	178½	KO 11	Cincinnati
1951	Jan. 12	**Ezzard Charles**	29	185	Lee Oma	193	TKO 10	NYC (Mad. Sq. Garden
1951	Mar. 7	**Ezzard Charles**	29	186	Jersey Joe Walcott	193	Wu 15	Detroit
1951	May 30	**Ezzard Charles**	29	182	Joey Maxim	181½	Wu 15	Chicago
1951	July 18	Jersey Joe Walcott	37	194	**Ezzard Charles**	182	KO 7	Pittsburgh
1952	June 5	**Jersey Joe Walcott**	38	196	Ezzard Charles	191½	Wu 15	Philadelphia
1952	Sept. 23	Rocky Marciano	29	184	**Jersey Joe Walcott**	196	KO 13	Philadelphia
1953	May 15	**Rocky Marciano**	29	184½	Jersey Joe Walcott	197¾	KO 1	Chicago
1953	Sept. 24	**Rocky Marciano**	30	185	Roland LaStarza	184¾	TKO 11	NYC (Polo Grounds)
1954	June 17	**Rocky Marciano**	30	187½	Ezzard Charles	185½	Wu 15	NYC (Yankee Stadium)
1954	Sept. 17	**Rocky Marciano**	31	187	Ezzard Charles	192½	KO 8	NYC (Yankee Stadium)
1955	May 16	**Rocky Marciano**	31	189	Don Cockell	205	TKO 9	San Francisco
1955	Sept. 21	**Rocky Marciano****	32	188¼	Archie Moore	188	KO 9	NYC (Yankee Stadium)
1956	Nov. 30	Floyd Patterson	21	182¼	Archie Moore	187¾	KO 5	Chicago
1957	July 29	**Floyd Patterson**	22	184	Tommy Jackson	192½	TKO 10	NYC (Polo Grounds)
1957	Aug. 22	**Floyd Patterson**	22	187¼	Pete Rademacher	202	KO 6	Seattle
1958	Aug. 18	**Floyd Patterson**	23	184½	Roy Harris	194	TKO 13	Los Angeles
1959	May 1	**Floyd Patterson**	24	182½	Brian London	206	KO 11	Indianapolis
1959	June 26	Ingemar Johansson	26	196	**Floyd Patterson**	182	TKO 3	NYC (Yankee Stadium)
1960	June 20	Floyd Patterson	25	190	**Ingemar Johansson**	194¾	KO 5	NYC (Polo Grounds)

*Joe Louis retired as champion on Mar. 1, 1949, then came out of retirement to fight Ezzard Charles for the title in 1950.

**Rocky Marciano retired as undefeated champion on Apr. 27, 1956.

Year	Date	Winner	Age	Wgt	Loser	Wgt	Result	Location
1961	Mar. 13	**Floyd Patterson**	26	194¾	Ingemar Johansson	206½	KO 6	Miami Beach
1961	Dec. 4	**Floyd Patterson**	26	188½	Tom McNeeley	197	KO 4	Toronto
1962	Sept. 25	Sonny Liston	30	214	**Floyd Patterson**	189	KO 1	Chicago
1963	July 22	**Sonny Liston**	31	215	Floyd Patterson	194½	KO 1	Las Vegas
1964	Feb. 25	Cassius Clay**	22	210½	**Sonny Liston**	218	TKO 7	Miami Beach
1965	Mar. 5	Ernie Terrell WBA	25	199	Eddie Machen	192	Wu 15	Chicago
1965	May 25	**Muhammad Ali**	23	206	Sonny Liston	215¼	KO 1	Lewiston, Maine
1965	Nov. 1	Ernie Terrell WBA	26	206	George Chuvalo	209	Wu 15	Toronto
1965	Nov. 22	**Muhammad Ali**	23	210	Floyd Patterson	196¾	TKO 12	Las Vegas
1966	Mar. 29	**Muhammad Ali**	24	214½	George Chuvalo	216	Wu 15	Toronto
1966	May 21	**Muhammad Ali**	24	201½	Henry Cooper	188	TKO 6	London
1966	June 28	Ernie Terrell WBA	27	209½	Doug Jones	187½	Wu 15	Houston
1966	Aug. 6	**Muhammad Ali**	24	209½	Brian London	201½	KO 3	London
1966	Sept. 10	**Muhammad Ali**	24	203½	Karl Mildenberger	194¼	TKO 12	Frankfurt, W. Ger.
1966	Nov. 14	**Muhammad Ali**	24	212¾	Cleveland Williams	210½	TKO 3	Houston
1967	Feb. 6	**Muhammad Ali**	25	212¼	Ernie Terrell WBA	212¼	Wu 15	Houston
1967	Mar. 22	**Muhammad Ali**	25	211½	Zora Folley	202½	KO 7	NYC (Mad. Sq. Garden)
1968	Mar. 4	Joe Frazier	24	204½	Buster Mathis	243½	TKO 11	NYC (Mad. Sq. Garden)
1968	Apr. 27	Jimmy Ellis	28	197	Jerry Quarry	195	Wm 15	Oakland
1968	June 24	Joe Frazier NY	24	203½	Manuel Ramos	208	TKO 2	NYC (Mad. Sq. Garden)
1968	Aug. 14	Jimmy Ellis WBA	28	198	Floyd Patterson	188	Ref 15	Stockholm
1968	Dec. 10	Joe Frazier NY	24	203	Oscar Bonavena	207	Wu 15	Philadelphia
1969	Apr. 22	Joe Frazier NY	25	204½	Dave Zyglewicz	190½	KO 1	Houston
1969	June 23	Joe Frazier NY	25	203½	Jerry Quarry	198½	TKO 8	NYC (Mad. Sq. Garden)
1970	Feb. 16	Joe Frazier NY	26	205	Jimmy Ellis WBA	201	TKO 5	NYC (Mad. Sq. Garden)
1970	Nov. 18	**Joe Frazier**	26	209	Bob Foster	188	KO 2	Detroit
1971	Mar. 8	**Joe Frazier**	27	205½	Muhammad Ali	215	Wu 15	NYC (Mad. Sq. Garden)
1972	Jan. 15	**Joe Frazier**	28	215½	Terry Daniels	195	TKO 4	New Orleans
1972	May 26	**Joe Frazier**	28	217½	Ron Stander	218	TKO 5	Omaha, Neb.
1973	Jan. 22	George Foreman	24	217½	**Joe Frazier**	214	TKO 2	Kingston, Jamaica
1973	Sept. 1	**George Foreman**	24	219½	Jose (King) Roman	196½	KO 1	Tokyo
1974	Mar. 26	**George Foreman**	25	224¾	Ken Norton	212¾	TKO 2	Caracas, Venezuela
1974	Oct. 30	Muhammad Ali	32	216½	**George Foreman**	220	KO 8	Kinshasa, Zaire
1975	Mar. 24	**Muhammad Ali**	33	223½	Chuck Wepner	225	TKO 15	Cleveland
1975	May 16	**Muhammad Ali**	33	224½	Ron Lyle	219	TKO 11	Las Vegas
1975	June 30	**Muhammad Ali**	33	224½	Joe Bugner	230	Wu 15	Kuala Lumpur, Malaysia
1975	Oct. 1	**Muhammad Ali**	33	224½	Joe Frazier	215	TKO 14	Manila, Philippines
1976	Feb. 20	**Muhammad Ali**	34	226	Jean Pierre Coopman	206	KO 5	San Juan, P.R.
1976	Apr. 30	**Muhammad Ali**	34	230	Jimmy Young	209	Wu 15	Landover, Md.
1976	May 24	**Muhammad Ali**	34	220	Richard Dunn	206½	TKO 5	Munich, W. Ger.
1976	Sept. 28	**Muhammad Ali**	34	221	Ken Norton	217½	Wu 15	NYC (Yankee Stadium)
1977	May 16	**Muhammad Ali**	35	221¼	Alfredo Evangelista	209¼	Wu 15	Landover, Md.
1977	Sept. 29	**Muhammad Ali**	35	225	Earnie Shavers	211¼	Wu 15	NYC (Mad. Sq. Garden)
1978	Feb. 15	Leon Spinks	24	197¼	**Muhammad Ali**	224¼	Ws 15	Las Vegas
1978	June 9	Larry Holmes	28	209	Ken Norton WBC††	220	Ws 15	Las Vegas
1978	Sept. 15	Muhammad Ali†	36	221	**Leon Spinks**	201	Wu 15	New Orleans
1978	Nov. 10	Larry Holmes WBC	29	214	Alfredo Evangelista	208¼	KO 7	Las Vegas
1979	Mar. 23	Larry Holmes WBC	29	214	Osvaldo Ocasio	207	TKO 7	Las Vegas
1979	June 22	Larry Holmes WBC	29	215	Mike Weaver	202	TKO 12	NYC (Mad. Sq. Garden)
1979	Sept. 28	Larry Holmes WBC	29	210	Earnie Shavers	211	TKO 11	Las Vegas
1979	Oct. 20	John Tate	24	240	Gerrie Coetzee	222	Wu 15	Pretoria, S. Africa
1980	Feb. 3	Larry Holmes WBC	30	213½	Lorenzo Zanon	215	TKO 6	Las Vegas
1980	Mar. 31	Mike Weaver	27	232	John Tate WBA	232	KO 15	Knoxville, Tenn.
1980	Mar. 31	Larry Holmes WBC	30	211	Leroy Jones	254½	TKO 8	Las Vegas
1980	July 7	Larry Holmes WBC	30	214¼	Scott LeDoux	226	TKO 7	Minneapolis
1980	Oct. 2	Larry Holmes WBC	30	211½	Muhammad Ali	217½	TKO 11	Las Vegas
1980	Oct. 25	Mike Weaver WBA	28	210	Gerrie Coetzee	226½	KO 13	Sun City, S. Africa
1981	Apr. 11	**Larry Holmes**	31	215	Trevor Berbick	215½	Wu 15	Las Vegas
1981	June 12	**Larry Holmes**	31	212½	Leon Spinks	200¼	TKO 3	Detroit
1981	Oct. 3	Mike Weaver WBA	29	215	James (Quick) Tillis	209	Wu 15	Rosemont, Ill.

**After defeating Liston, Cassius Clay announced that he had changed his name to Muhammad Ali. He was later stripped of his title by the WBA and most state boxing commissions after refusing induction into the U.S. Army on Apr. 28, 1967.

† Muhammad Ali retired as champion on June 27, 1979, then came out of retirement to fight Larry Holmes for the title in 1980.

†† WBC recognized Ken Norton as world champion when Leon Spinks refused to meet Norton before Spinks' rematch with Muhammad Ali. Norton had scored a 15-round split decision over Jimmy Young on Nov. 5, 1977 in Las Vegas.

World Heavyweight Championship Fights (Cont.)

Year	Date	Winner	Age	Wgt	Loser	Wgt	Result	Location
1981	Nov. 6	**Larry Holmes**	32	213¼	Renaldo Snipes	215¾	TKO 11	Pittsburgh
1982	June 11	**Larry Holmes**	32	212½	Gerry Cooney	225½	TKO 13	Las Vegas
1982	Nov. 26	**Larry Holmes**	33	217½	Randall (Tex) Cobb	234¼	Wu 15	Houston
1982	Dec. 10	Michael Dokes	24	216	Mike Weaver WBA	209¾	TKO 1	Las Vegas
1983	Mar. 27	**Larry Holmes**	33	221	Lucien Rodriguez	209	Wu 12	Scranton, Pa.
1983	May 20	Michael Dokes WBA	24	223	Mike Weaver	218½	Draw 15	Las Vegas
1983	May 20	**Larry Holmes**	33	213	Tim Witherspoon	219½	Ws 12	Las Vegas
1983	Sept. 10	**Larry Holmes**	33	223	Scott Frank	211¼	TKO 5	Atlantic City
1983	Sept. 23	Gerrie Coetzee	28	215	Michael Dokes WBA	217	KO 10	Richfield, Ohio
1983	Nov. 25	**Larry Holmes**	34	219	Marvis Frazier	200	TKO 1	Las Vegas
1984	Mar. 9	Tim Witherspoon*	26	220¼	Greg Page	239½	Wm 12	Las Vegas
1984	Aug. 31	Pinklon Thomas	26	216	Tim Witherspoon	217	Wm 12	Las Vegas
1984	Nov. 9	**Larry Holmes** IBF	35	221½	Bonecrusher Smith	227	TKO 12	Las Vegas
1984	Dec. 1	Greg Page	26	236½	Gerrie Coetzee WBA	218	KO 8	Sun City, S. Africa
1985	Mar. 15	**Larry Holmes** IBF	35	223½	David Bey	233¼	TKO 10	Las Vegas
1985	Apr. 29	Tony Tubbs	26	229	Greg Page WBA	239½	Wu 15	Buffalo
1985	May 20	**Larry Holmes** IBF	35	224¼	Carl Williams	215	Wu 15	Las Vegas
1985	June 15	Pinklon Thomas WBC	27	220¼	Mike Weaver	221¼	KO 8	Las Vegas
1985	Sept. 21	Michael Spinks	29	200	**Larry Holmes** IBF	221½	Wu 15	Las Vegas
1986	Jan. 17	Tim Witherspoon	28	227	Tony Tubbs WBA	229	Wm 15	Atlanta
1986	Mar. 22	Trevor Berbick	33	218½	Pinklon Thomas WBC	222¾	Wu 15	Las Vegas
1986	Apr. 19	**Michael Spinks** IBF	29	205	Larry Holmes	223	Ws 15	Las Vegas
1986	July 19	Tim Witherspoon WBA	28	234¾	Frank Bruno	228	TKO 11	Wembley, England
1986	Sept. 6	**Michael Spinks** IBF	30	201	Steffen Tangstad	214¾	TKO 4	Las Vegas
1986	Nov. 22	Mike Tyson	20	221¼	Trevor Berbick WBC	218½	TKO 2	Las Vegas
1986	Dec. 12	Bonecrusher Smith	33	228½	Tim Witherspoon WBA	233½	TKO 1	NYC (Mad. Sq. Garden)
1987	Mar. 7	Mike Tyson WBC	20	219	Bonecrusher Smith WBA	233	Wu 12	Las Vegas
1987	May 30	Mike Tyson	20	218¾	Pinklon Thomas	217¾	TKO 6	Las Vegas
1987	May 30	Tony Tucker**	28	222¼	Buster Douglas	227¼	TKO 10	Las Vegas
1987	June 15	**Michael Spinks**†	30	208¾	Gerry Cooney	238	TKO 5	Atlantic City
1987	Aug. 1	Mike Tyson	21	221	Tony Tucker IBF	221	Wu 12	Las Vegas
1987	Oct. 16	Mike Tyson	21	216	Tyrell Biggs	228¾	TKO 7	Atlantic City
1988	Jan. 22	Mike Tyson	21	215¾	Larry Holmes	225¾	TKO 4	Atlantic City
1988	Mar. 20	Mike Tyson	21	216¼	Tony Tubbs	238¼	KO 2	Tokyo
1988	June 27	Mike Tyson	21	218¼	**Michael Spinks**	212¼	KO 1	Atlantic City
1989	Feb. 25	**Mike Tyson**	22	218	Frank Bruno	228	TKO 5	Las Vegas
1989	July 21	**Mike Tyson**	23	219¼	Carl Williams	218	TKO 1	Atlantic City
1990	Feb. 10	Buster Douglas	29	231½	**Mike Tyson**	220½	KO 10	Tokyo
1990	Oct. 25	Evander Holyfield	28	208	**Buster Douglas**	246	KO 3	Las Vegas
1991	Apr. 19	**Evander Holyfield**	28	208	George Foreman	257	Wu 12	Atlantic City
1991	Nov. 23	**Evander Holyfield**	29	210	Bert Cooper	215	TKO 7	Atlanta
1992	June 19	**Evander Holyfield**	29	210	Larry Holmes	233	Wu 12	Las Vegas
1992	Nov. 13	Riddick Bowe	25	235	**Evander Holyfield**	205	Wu 12	Las Vegas
1993	Feb. 6	**Riddick Bowe**	25	243	Michael Dokes	244	TKO 1	NYC (Mad. Sq. Garden)
1993	May 8	Lennox Lewis WBC‡	27	235	Tony Tucker	235	Wu 12	Las Vegas
1993	May 22	**Riddick Bowe**	25	244	Jesse Ferguson	224	TKO 2	Washington, D.C.
1993	Oct. 1	Lennox Lewis WBC	28	233	Frank Bruno	238	TKO 7	Cardiff, Wales
1993	Nov. 6	Evander Holyfield	31	217	**Riddick Bowe** WBA/IBF	246	Wm 12	Las Vegas
1994	Apr. 22	Michael Moorer	26	214	**Evander Holyfield**	214	Wm 12	Las Vegas
1994	May 6	Lennox Lewis WBC	28	235	Phil Jackson	218	TKO 8	Atlantic City
1994	Sept. 25	Oliver McCall	29	231¼	**Lennox Lewis** WBC	238	TKO 2	London
1994	Nov. 5	George Foreman!	45	250	**Michael Moorer**	222	KO 10	Las Vegas
1995	Apr. 8	Oliver McCall WBC	29	231	Larry Holmes	236	Wu 12	Las Vegas
1995	Apr. 8	Bruce Seldon!	28	236	Tony Tucker	240	TKO 7	Las Vegas
1995	Apr. 22	**George Foreman**!	46	256	Axel Schulz	221	Wu 12	Las Vegas

*WBC recognized winner of Mar. 9, 1984 fight between Tim Witherspoon and Greg Page as world champion after Larry Holmes relinquished title in dispute. IBF then recognized Holmes.

**IBF recognized winner of May 30, 1987 fight between Tony Tucker and James (Buster) Douglas as world champion after Michael Spinks relinquished title in dispute.

†The July 15, 1987 Spinks-Cooney fight was not an official championship bout because it was not sanctioned by any boxing associations, councils or federations.

‡WBC recognized Lennox Lewis as world champion when Riddick Bowe gave up that portion of his title on Dec. 14, 1992, rather than fight Lewis, the WBC's mandatory challenger.

!George Foreman won WBA and IBF championships when he beat Michael Moorer on Nov. 5, 1994. He was stripped of WBA title on Mar. 4, 1995, when he refused to fight No. 1 contender Tony Tucker, and he relinquished IBF title on June 29, 1995, rather than give Axel Schulz a rematch. Tucker lost to Bruce Seldon in their April 8, 2001 fight for vacant WBA title.

Year	Date	Winner	Age	Wgt	Loser	Wgt	Result	Location
1995	Aug. 19	Bruce Seldon WBA	28	234	Joe Hipp	223	TKO 10	Las Vegas
1995	Sept. 2	Frank Bruno	33	248	Oliver McCall WBC	235	Wu 12	London
1995	Dec. 9	Frans Botha*	27	237	Axel Schulz	222	Wu 12	Stuttgart, GER
1996	Mar. 16	Mike Tyson	29	220	Frank Bruno WBC	247	TKO 3	Las Vegas
1996	June 22	Michael Moorer*	28	222	Axel Schulz	223	Ws 12	Dortmund, GER
1996	Sept. 7	Mike Tyson WBC†	30	219	Bruce Seldon WBA	229	TKO 1	Las Vegas
1996	Nov. 9	Evander Holyfield	34	215	**Mike Tyson** WBA	222	TKO 11	Las Vegas
1997	Feb. 7	Lennox Lewis†	31	251	Oliver McCall	237	TKO 5	Las Vegas
1997	Mar. 29	Michael Moorer IBF	29	212	Vaughn Bean	212	Wm 12	Las Vegas
1997	June 28	**Evander Holyfield** WBA‡	34	218	Mike Tyson	218	Disq. 3	Las Vegas
1997	July 12	Lennox Lewis WBC	31	242	Henry Akinwande	237½	Disq. 5	Stateline, Nev.
1997	Oct. 4	Lennox Lewis WBC	32	244	Andrew Golota	244	TKO 1	Atlantic City
1997	Nov. 8	Evander Holyfield WBA	35	214	Michael Moorer IBF	223	TKO 8	Las Vegas
1998	Mar. 28	Lennox Lewis WBC	32	243	Shannon Briggs	228	TKO 5	Atlantic City
1998	Sept. 19	**Evander Holyfield** WBA/IBF	35	217	Vaughn Bean	231	Wu 12	Atlanta
1998	Sept. 26	Lennox Lewis WBC	33	250	Zeljko Mavrovic	220	Wu 12	Uncasville, Conn.
1999	Mar. 13	Lennox Lewis WBC	33	246	**Evander Holyfield** WBA/IBF	215	Draw 12	NYC (Mad. Sq. Garden)
1999	Nov. 13	Lennox Lewis WBC	34	240	**Evander Holyfield** WBA/IBF	218	Wu 12	Las Vegas
2000	Apr. 29	**Lennox Lewis** WBC/IBF!	34	247	Michael Grant	250	KO 2	NYC (Mad. Sq. Garden)
2000	July 15	**Lennox Lewis** WBC/IBF	34	250	Frans Botha	237	TKO 2	London
2000	Aug. 12	Evander Holyfield	37	221	John Ruiz	224	Wu 12	Las Vegas
2000	Nov. 11	**Lennox Lewis** WBC/IBF	35	249	David Tua	245	Wu 12	Las Vegas
2001	Mar. 3	John Ruiz	29	227	Evander Holyfield	217	Wu 12	Las Vegas
2001	Apr. 22	Hasim Rahman	28	237	**Lennox Lewis** WBC/IBF	253	KO 5	Johannesburg, S. Africa

*Frans Botha won the vacant IBF title with a controversial 12-round decision over Axel Schulz on Dec. 9, 1995, but after legal sparring, was eventually stripped of the IBF belt for using anabolic steroids. Moorer then claimed the revacated title with his June 22, 1996 win over Schulz.

†Mike Tyson won the WBC belt from Frank Bruno on Mar. 16, 1996 and still held it at the time of his Sept. 7, 1996 win over Bruce Seldon (although it was not at risk for that fight) but was forced to relinquish the title after the bout for not fighting mandatory challenge Lennox Lewis. Tyson also paid Lewis $4 million to step aside and allow the Tyson-Seldon bout to take place. Lewis then fought Oliver McCall for the vacant WBC belt. The fight was stopped 55 seconds into round 5 because, inexplicably, McCall was visibly distraught and stopped throwing punches.

‡Holyfield won the bout by disqualification and retained the WBA belt after Tyson spit out his mouthpiece and bit off a piece of Holyfield's ear. Tyson had received a two-point deduction from referee Mills Lane and after a stern warning and a short delay the fight was allowed to continue. Later in round 3, he bit Holyfield's other ear and Tyson was disqualified.

!Lewis was stripped of the WBA title for choosing to fight Michael Grant instead of John Ruiz, the WBA's #1 challenger. The WBA sanctioned the Evander Holyfield-John Ruiz August 12 bout for its vacant heavyweight belt.

All-Time Heavyweight Upsets

Buster Douglas was a 42-1 underdog when he defeated previously-unbeaten heavyweight champion Mike Tyson on Feb. 10, 1990. That 10th-round knockout ranks as the biggest upset in boxing history. By comparison, 45-year-old George Foreman was only a 3-1 underdog before he unexpectedly won the title from Michael Moorer on Nov. 5, 1994.

Here are the best-known upsets in the annals of the heavyweight division. All fights were for the world championship except the Max Schmeling-Joe Louis bout.

Date	Winner	Loser	Result	KO Time	Location
9/7/1892	James J. Corbett	John L. Sullivan	KO 21	1:30	Olympic Club, New Orleans
4/5/1915	Jess Willard	Jack Johnson	KO 26	1:26	Mariano Race Track, Havana
9/23/26	Gene Tunney	Jack Dempsey	Wu 10	–	Sesquicentennial Stadium, Phila.
6/13/35	James J. Braddock	Max Baer	Wu 15	–	Mad.Sq.Garden Bowl, L.I. City
6/19/36	Max Schmeling	Joe Louis	KO 12	2:29	Yankee Stadium, New York
7/18/51	Jersey Joe Walcott	Ezzard Charles	KO 7	0:55	Forbes Field, Pittsburgh
6/26/59	Ingemar Johansson	Floyd Patterson	TKO 3	2:03	Yankee Stadium, New York
2/25/64	Cassius Clay	Sonny Liston	TKO 7	*	Convention Hall, Miami Beach
10/30/74	Muhammad Ali	George Foreman	KO 8	2:58	20th of May Stadium, Zaire
2/15/78	Leon Spinks	Muhammad Ali	Ws 15	–	Hilton Pavilion, Las Vegas
9/21/85	Michael Spinks	Larry Holmes	Wu 15	–	Riviera Hotel, Las Vegas
2/10/90	Buster Douglas	Mike Tyson	KO 10	1:23	Tokyo Dome, Tokyo
11/5/94	George Foreman	Michael Moorer	KO 10	2:03	MGM Grand, Las Vegas
11/9/96	Evander Holyfield	Mike Tyson	TKO 11	0:37	MGM Grand, Las Vegas
4/22/01	Hasim Rahman	Lennox Lewis	KO 5	2:32	Johannesburg, South Africa

*Liston failed to answer bell for Round 7.

Muhammad Ali's Career Pro Record

Born Cassius Marcellus Clay, Jr. on Jan. 17, 1942, in Louisville; Amateur record of 100-5; won light-heavyweight gold medal at 1960 Olympic Games; Pro record of 56-5 with 37 KOs in 61 fights.

1960

Date	Opponent (location)	Result
Oct. 29	Tunney Hunsaker, Louisville	Wu 6
Dec. 27	Herb Siler, Miami Beach	TKO 4

1961

Date	Opponent (location)	Result
Jan. 17	Tony Esperti, Miami Beach	TKO 3
Feb. 7	Jim Robinson, Miami Beach	TKO 1
Feb. 21	Donnie Fleeman, Miami Beach	TKO 7
Apr. 19	Lamar Clark, Louisville	KO 2
June 26	Duke Sabedong, Las Vegas	Wu 10
July 22	Alonzo Johnson, Louisville	Wu 10
Oct. 7	Alex Miteff, Louisville	TKO 6
Nov. 29	Willi Besmanoff, Louisville	TKO 7

1962

Date	Opponent (location)	Result
Feb. 10	Sonny Banks, New York	TKO 4
Feb. 28	Don Warner, Miami Beach	TKO 4
Apr. 23	George Logan, Los Angeles	TKO 4
May 19	Billy Daniels, Los Angeles	TKO 7
July 20	Alejandro Lavorante, Los Angeles	KO 5
Nov. 15	Archie Moore, Los Angeles	KO 4

1963

Date	Opponent (location)	Result
Jan. 24	Charlie Powell, Pittsburgh	KO 3
Mar. 13	Doug Jones, New York	Wu 10
June 18	Henry Cooper, London	TKO 5

1964

Date	Opponent (location)	Result
Feb. 25	Sonny Liston, Miami Beach	TKO 7

(won World Heavyweight title)

After the fight, Clay announces he is a member of the Black Muslim religious sect and has changed his name to Muhammad Ali.

1965

Date	Opponent (location)	Result
May 25	Sonny Liston, Lewiston, Me	KO 1
Nov. 22	Floyd Patterson, Las Vegas	TKO 12

1966

Date	Opponent (location)	Result
Mar. 29	George Chuvalo, Toronto	Wu 15
May 21	Henry Cooper, London	TKO 6
Aug. 6	Brian London, London	KO 3
Sept. 10	Karl Mildenberger, Frankfurt	TKO 12
Nov. 14	Cleveland Williams, Houston	TKO 3

1967

Date	Opponent (location)	Result
Feb. 6	Ernie Terrell, Houston	Wu 15
Mar. 22	Zora Folley, New York	KO 7
Apr. 28	Refuses induction into U.S. Army and is stripped of world title by WBA and most state commissions the next day.	
June 20	Found guilty of draft evasion in Houston; fined $10,000 and sentenced to 5 years; remains free pending appeals, but is barred from the ring.	

1968-69 (Inactive)

1970

Date	Opponent (location)	Result
Feb. 3	Announces retirement.	
Oct. 26	Jerry Quarry, Atlanta	TKO 3
Dec. 7	Oscar Bonavena, New York	TKO 15

1971

Date	Opponent (location)	Result
Mar. 8	Joe Frazier, New York	Lu 15

(for World Heavyweight title)

June 28	U.S. Supreme Court reverses Ali's 1967 conviction saying he had been drafted improperly.	
July 26	Jimmy Ellis, Houston	TKO 12

(won vacant NABF Heavyweight title)

Nov. 17	Buster Mathis, Houston	Wu 12
Dec. 26	Jurgen Blin, Zurich	KO 7

1972

Date	Opponent (location)	Result
Apr. 1	Mac Foster, Tokyo	Wu 15
May 1	George Chuvalo, Vancouver	Wu 12
June 27	Jerry Quarry, Las Vegas	TKO 7
July 19	Al (Blue) Lewis, Dublin, Ire	TKO 11
Sept. 20	Floyd Patterson, New York	TKO 7
Nov. 21	Bob Foster, Stateline, Nev	TKO 8

1973

Date	Opponent (location)	Result
Feb. 14	Joe Bugner, Las Vegas	Wu 12
Mar. 31	Ken Norton, San Diego	Ls 12

(lost NABF Heavyweight title)

Sept. 10	Ken Norton, Inglewood, Calif.	Ws 12

(regained NABF Heavyweight title)

Oct. 20	Rudi Lubbers, Jakarta, Indonesia	Wu 12

1974

Date	Opponent (location)	Result
Jan. 28	Joe Frazier, New York	Wu 12
Oct. 30	George Foreman, Kinshasa, Zaire	KO 8

(regained World Heavyweight title)

1975

Date	Opponent (location)	Result
Mar. 24	Chuck Wepner, Cleveland	TKO 15
May 16	Ron Lyle, Las Vegas	TKO 11
June 30	Joe Bugner, Kuala Lumpur, Malaysia	Wu 15
Oct. 1	Joe Frazier, Manila, Philippines	TKO 14

1976

Date	Opponent (location)	Result
Feb. 20	Jean Pierre Coopman, San Juan	KO 5
Apr. 30	Jimmy Young, Landover, Md	Wu 15
May 24	Richard Dunn, Munich	TKO 5
Sept. 28	Ken Norton, New York	Wu 15

1977

Date	Opponent (location)	Result
May 16	Alfredo Evangelista, Landover	Wu 15
Sept. 29	Earnie Shavers, New York	Wu 15

1978

Date	Opponent (location)	Result
Feb. 15	Leon Spinks, Las Vegas	Ls 15

(lost World Heavyweight title)

Sept. 15	Leon Spinks, New Orleans	Wu 15

(regained World Heavyweight title)

1979

Date		
June 27	Announces retirement.	

1980

Date	Opponent (location)	Result
Oct. 2	Larry Holmes, Las Vegas	TKO by 11

1981

Date	Opponent (location)	Result
Dec. 11	Trevor Berbick, Nassau	Lu 10

(retires after fight)

Major Titleholders

Note the following sanctioning body abbreviations: NBA (National Boxing Association), WBA (World Boxing Association), WBC (World Boxing Council), GBR (Great Britain), IBF (International Boxing Federation), plus other national and state commissions. Fighters who retired as champion are indicated by (*) and champions who abandoned or relinquished their titles are indicated by (†).

Heavyweights

Widely accepted champions in CAPITAL letters. Current champions in **bold** type (as of Oct. 23, 2001).

Note: Muhammad Ali was stripped of his world title in 1967 after refusing induction into the Army (see Muhammad Ali's Career Pro Record). George Foreman was stripped of his WBA and IBF titles in 1995, but remained active as linear champion (see Boxing: Major Bouts 1998-99).

Champion	Held Title	Champion	Held Title
JOHN L. SULLIVAN	1885–92	Mike Weaver (WBA)	1980–82
JAMES J. CORBETT	1892–97	LARRY HOLMES	1980–85
BOB FITZSIMMONS	1897–99	Michael Dokes (WBA)	1982–83
JAMES J. JEFFRIES	1899–1905*	Gerrie Coetzee (WBA)	1983–84
MARVIN HART	1905–06	Tim Witherspoon (WBC)	1984
TOMMY BURNS	1906–08	Pinklon Thomas (WBC)	1984–86
JACK JOHNSON	1908–15	Greg Page (WBA)	1984–85
JESS WILLARD	1915–19	MICHAEL SPINKS	1985–87
JACK DEMPSEY	1919–26	Tim Witherspoon (WBA)	1986
GENE TUNNEY	1926–28*	Trevor Berbick (WBC)	1986
MAX SCHMELING	1930–32	Mike Tyson (WBC)	1986–87
JACK SHARKEY	1932–33	James (Bonecrusher) Smith (WBA)	1986–87
PRIMO CARNERA	1933–34	Tony Tucker (IBF)	1987
MAX BAER	1934–35	MIKE TYSON (WBC, WBA, IBF)	1987–90
JAMES J. BRADDOCK	1935–37	BUSTER DOUGLAS (WBC, WBA, IBF)	1990
JOE LOUIS	1937–49*	EVANDER HOLYFIELD (WBC, WBA, IBF)	1990–92
EZZARD CHARLES	1949–51	RIDDICK BOWE (WBA, IBF)	1992–93
JERSEY JOE WALCOTT	1951–52	Lennox Lewis (WBC)	1992–94
ROCKY MARCIANO	1952–56*	EVANDER HOLYFIELD (WBA, IBF)	1993–94
FLOYD PATTERSON	1956–59	MICHAEL MOORER (WBA, IBF)	1994
INGEMAR JOHANSSON	1959–60	Oliver McCall (WBC)	1994–95
FLOYD PATTERSON	1960–62	GEORGE FOREMAN (WBA, IBF)	1994–95
SONNY LISTON	1962–64	Bruce Seldon (WBA)	1995–96
CASSIUS CLAY (MUHAMMAD ALI)	1964–67	GEORGE FOREMAN	1995–96
Ernie Terrell (WBA)	1965–67	Frank Bruno (WBC)	1995–96
Joe Frazier (NY)	1968–70	Mike Tyson (WBC)	1996†
Jimmy Ellis (WBA)	1968–70	Mike Tyson (WBA)	1996
JOE FRAZIER	1970–73	Michael Moorer (IBF)	1996–1997
GEORGE FOREMAN	1973–74	Evander Holyfield (WBA, IBF)	1996–2000
MUHAMMAD ALI	1974–78	Lennox Lewis (WBC)	1997–2000
LEON SPINKS	1978	LENNOX LEWIS (WBA, WBC, IBF)	2000
Ken Norton (WBC)	1978	Evander Holyfield (WBA)	2000–01
Larry Holmes (WBC)	1978–80	LENNOX LEWIS (WBC, IBF)	2000–01
MUHAMMAD ALI	1978–79*	**John Ruiz** (WBA)	2001–
John Tate (WBA)	1979–80	**Hasim Rahman** (WBC, IBF)	2001–

Note: John L. Sullivan held the Bare Knuckle championship from 1882-85.

Cruiserweights

Current champions in **bold** type.

Champion	Held Title	Champion	Held Title
Marvin Camel (WBC)	1980	Glenn McCrory (IBF)	1989–90
Carlos De Leon (WBC)	1980–82	Jeff Lampkin (IBF)	1990
Ossie Ocasio (WBA)	1982–84	Massimiliano Duran (WBC)	1990–91
S.T. Gordon (WBC)	1982–83	Bobby Czyz (WBA)	1991–92†
Carlos De Leon (WBC)	1983–85	Anaclet Wamba (WBC)	1991–95
Marvin Camel (IBF)	1983–84	James Pritchard (IBF)	1991
Lee Roy Murphy (IBF)	1984–86	James Warring (IBF)	1991–92
Piet Crous (WBA)	1984–85	Alfred Cole (IBF)	1992–96
Alfonso Ratliff (WBC)	1985	Orlin Norris (WBA)	1993–95
Dwight Braxton (WBA)	1985–86	Nate Miller (WBA)	1995–97
Bernard Benton (WBC)	1985–86	Marcelo Dominguez (WBC)	1996–98
Carlos De Leon (WBC)	1986–88	Adolpho Washington (IBF)	1996–97
Evander Holyfield (WBA)	1986–88	Uriah Grant (IBF)	1997
Ricky Parkey (IBF)	1986–87	Imamu Mayfield (IBF)	1997–98
Evander Holyfield (WBA/IBF)	1987–88	Arthur Williams (IBF)	1998–99
Evander Holyfield	1988†	Fabrice Tiozzo (WBA)	1997–2000
Toufik Belbouli (WBA)	1989	**Juan Carlos Gomez** (WBC)	1998–
Robert Daniels (WBA)	1989–91	**Vassiliy Jirov** (IBF)	1999–
Carlos De Leon (WBC)	1989–90	**Virgil Hill** (WBA)	2000–

Major Titleholders (Cont.)
Light Heavyweights
Widely accepted champions in CAPITAL letters. Current champions in **bold** type.

Champion	Held Title	Champion	Held Title
JACK ROOT	1903	Mike Rossman (WBA)	1978–79
GEORGE GARDNER	1903	Marvin Johnson (WBC)	1978–79
BOB FITZSIMMONS	1903–05	Matthew (Franklin) Saad Muhammad (WBC)	1979–81
PHILADELPHIA JACK O'BRIEN	1905–12*	Marvin Johnson (WBA)	1979–80
JACK DILLON	1914–16	Eddie (Gregory)	
BATTLING LEVINSKY	1916–20	Mustapha Muhammad (WBA)	1980–81
GEORGES CARPENTIER	1920–22	Michael Spinks (WBA)	1981–83
BATTLING SIKI	1922–23	Dwight (Braxton) Muhammad Qawi (WBC)	1981–83
MIKE McTIGUE	1923–25	MICHAEL SPINKS	1983–85†
PAUL BERLENBACH	1925–26	J.B. Williamson (WBC)	1985–86
JACK DELANEY	1926–27†	Slobodan Kacar (IBF)	1985–86
Jimmy Slattery (NBA)	1927	Marvin Johnson (WBA)	1986–87
TOMMY LOUGHRAN	1927-29	Dennis Andries (WBC)	1986–87
JIMMY SLATTERY	1930	Bobby Czyz (IBF)	1986–87
MAXIE ROSENBLOOM	1930–34	Leslie Stewart (WBA)	1987
George Nichols (NBA)	1932	Virgil Hill (WBA)	1987–91
Bob Godwin (NBA)	1933	Prince Charles Williams (IBF)	1987–93
BOB OLIN	1934–35	Thomas Hearns (WBC)	1987
JOHN HENRY LEWIS	1935–38	Donny Lalonde (WBC)	1987–88
MELIO BETTINA (NY)	1939	Sugar Ray Leonard (WBC)	1988
Len Harvey (GBR)	1939–42	Dennis Andries (WBC)	1989
BILLY CONN	1939–40†	Jeff Harding (WBC)	1989–90
ANTON CHRISTOFORIDIS (NBA)	1941	Dennis Andries (WBC)	1990–91
GUS LESNEVICH	1941–48	Jeff Harding (WBC)	1991–94
Freddie Mills (GBR)	1942–46	Thomas Hearns (WBA)	1991–92
FREDDIE MILLS	1948–50	Iran Barkley (WBA)	1992†
JOEY MAXIM	1950–52	Virgil Hill (WBA)	1992–97
ARCHIE MOORE	1952–62	Henry Maske (IBF)	1993–96
Harold Johnson (NBA)	1961	Virgil Hill (WBA/IBF)	1996–97
HAROLD JOHNSON	1962–63	Mike McCallum (WBC)	1994–95
WILLIE PASTRANO	1963–65	Fabrice Tiozzo (WBC)	1995–96
Eddie Cotton (Mich.)	1963–64	Roy Jones Jr. (WBC)	1996
JOSE TORRES	1965–66	Montell Griffin (WBC)	1996
DICK TIGER	1966–68	D. Michaelczewski (WBA/IBF)	1997†
BOB FOSTER	1968–74*	William Guthrie (IBF)	1997–98
Vicente Rondon (WBA)	1971–72	Lou Del Valle (WBA)	1997–98
John Conteh (WBC)	1974–77	**ROY JONES JR.** (WBA/WBC)	1997–
Victor Galindez (WBA)	1974–77	Reggie Johnson (IBF)	1998–99
Miguel A. Cuello (WBC)	1977–78	**ROY JONES JR.** (WBA/WBC/IBF)	1999–
Mate Parlov (WBC)	1978		

Super Middleweights
Current champions in **bold** type.

Champion	Held Title	Champion	Held Title
Murray Sutherland (IBF)	1984	Frank Liles (WBA)	1994–99
Chong-Pal Park (IBF)	1984–87	Roy Jones (WBA)	1994–96
Chong-Pal Park (WBA)	1987–88	Thulane Malinga (WBC)	1996
Graziano Rocchigiani (IBF)	1988–89	Vincenzo Nardiello (WBC)	1996
Fugencio Obelmejias (WBA)	1988–89	Robin Reid (WBC)	1996–97
Ray Leonard (WBC)	1988–90†	Charles Brewer (IBF)	1997–98
In-Chut Baek (WBA)	1989–90	**Sven Ottke** (IBF)	1998–
Lindell Holmes (IBF)	1990–91	Thulane Malinga (WBC)	1997–98
Christophe Tiozzo (WBA)	1990–91	Richie Woodhall (WBC)	1998–99
Mauro Galvano (WBC)	1990–92	Byron Mitchell (WBA)	1999–2000
Victor Cordova (WBA)	1991	Markus Beyer (WBC)	1999–2000
Darrin Van Horn (IBF)	1991–92	Glenn Gatley (WBC)	2000
Iran Barkley (WBA)	1992	Dingaan Thobela (WBC)	2000
Nigel Benn (WBC)	1992–96	Bruno Girard (WBA)	2000–01†
James Toney (IBF)	1992–94	Dave Hilton (WBC)	2000†
Michael Nunn (WBA)	1992–94	**Byron Mitchell** (WBA)	2001–
Steve Little (WBA)	1994	**Eric Lucas** (WBC)	2001–

Middleweights
Widely accepted champions in CAPITAL letters. Current champions in **bold** type.

Champion	Held Title	Champion	Held Title
JACK (NONPAREIL) DEMPSEY	1884–91	TOMMY RYAN	1898–1907
BOB FITZSIMMONS	1891–97	STANLEY KETCHEL	1908
CHARLES (KID) McCOY	1897–98	BILLY PAPKE	1908

Champion	Held Title
STANLEY KETCHEL	1908–10
FRANK KLAUS	1913
GEORGE CHIP	1913–14
AL McCOY	1914–17
Jeff Smith (AUS)	1914
Mick King (AUS)	1914
Jeff Smith (AUS)	1914–15
Lee Darcy (AUS)	1915–17
MIKE O'DOWD	1917–20
JOHNNY WILSON	1920–23
Wm. Bryan Downey (Ohio)	1921–22
Dave Rosenberg (NY)	1922
Jock Malone (Ohio)	1922–23
Mike O'Dowd (NY)	1922
Lou Bogash (NY)	1923
HARRY GREB	1923–26
TIGER FLOWERS	1926
MICKEY WALKER	1926–31†
GORILLA JONES	1931–32
MARCEL THIL	1932–37
Ben Jeby (NY)	1932–33
Lou Brouillard (NBA, NY)	1933
Vince Dundee (NBA, NY)	1933–34
Teddy Yarosz (NBA, NY)	1934–35
Babe Risko (NBA, NY)	1935–36
Freddie Steele (NBA, NY)	1936–38
FRED APOSTOLI	1937–39
Al Hostak (NBA)	1938
Solly Krieger (NBA)	1938–39
Al Hostak (NBA)	1939–40
CEFERINO GARCIA	1939–40
KEN OVERLIN	1940–41
Tony Zale (NBA)	1940–41
BILLY SOOSE	1941
TONY ZALE	1941–47
ROCKY GRAZIANO	1947–48
TONY ZALE	1948
MARCEL CERDAN	1948–49
JAKE La MOTTA	1949–51
SUGAR RAY ROBINSON	1951
RANDY TURPIN	1951
SUGAR RAY ROBINSON	1951–52*
CARL (BOBO) OLSON	1953–55
SUGAR RAY ROBINSON	1955–57
GENE FULLMER	1957
SUGAR RAY ROBINSON	1957
CARMEN BASILIO	1957–58
SUGAR RAY ROBINSON	1958–60

Champion	Held Title
Gene Fullmer (NBA)	1959–62
PAUL PENDER	1960–61
TERRY DOWNES	1961–62
PAUL PENDER	1962–63
Dick Tiger (WBA)	1962–63
DICK TIGER	1963
JOEY GIARDELLO	1963–65
DICK TIGER	1965–66
EMILE GRIFFITH	1966–67
NINO BENVENUTI	1967
EMILE GRIFFITH	1967–68
NINO BENVENUTI	1968–70
CARLOS MONZON	1970–77*
Rodrigo Valdez (WBC)	1974–76
RODRIGO VALDEZ	1977–78
HUGO CORRO	1978–79
VITO ANTUOFERMO	1979–80
ALAN MINTER	1980
MARVELOUS MARVIN HAGLER	1980–87
SUGAR RAY LEONARD	1987
Frank Tate (IBF)	1987–88
Sumbu Kalambay (WBA)	1987–89
Thomas Hearns (WBC)	1987–88
Iran Barkley (WBC)	1988–89
Michael Nunn (IBF)	1988–91
Roberto Duran (WBC)	1989–90*
Mike McCallum (WBA)	1989–91
Julian Jackson (WBC)	1990–93
James Toney (IBF)	1991–93†
Reggie Johnson (WBA)	1992–93
Roy Jones Jr. (IBF)	1993–94†
Gerald McClellan (WBC)	1993–95†
John David Jackson (WBA)	1993–94
Jorge Castro (WBA)	1994–97
Julian Jackson (WBC)	1995
Bernard Hopkins (IBF)	1995–
Quincy Taylor (WBC)	1995–96
Shinji Takehara (WBA)	1995–96
William Joppy (WBA)	1996–97
Keith Holmes (WBC)	1996–98
Julio Cesar Green (WBA)	1997–98
William Joppy (WBA)	1998–2001
Hassine Cherifi (WBC)	1998–99
Keith Holmes (WBC)	1999–2001
Bernard Hopkins (IBF/WBC)	2001–
Felix Trinidad (WBA)	2001
BERNARD HOPKINS (IBF/WBA/WBC)	2001–

Junior Middleweights

Widely accepted champions in CAPITAL letters. Current champions in **bold** type.

Champion	Held Title
ERNILE GRIFFITH (EBU)	1962–63
DENNIS MOYER	1962–63
RALPH DUPAS	1963
SANDRO MAZZINGHI	1963–65
NINO BENVENUTI	1965–66
KI-SOO KIM	1966–68
SANDRO MAZZINGHI	1968
FREDDLIE LITTLE	1969–70
CARMELO BOSSI	1970–71
KOICHI WAJIMA	1971–74
OSCAR ALBARADO	1974–75
KOICHI WAJIMA	1975
Miguel de Oliveira (WBC)	1975–76
JAE-DO YUH	1975–76
Elisha Obed (WBC)	1975–76
KOICHI WAJIMA	1976
JOSE DURAN	1976
Eckhard Dagge (WBC)	1976–77
MIGUEL ANGEL CASTELLINI	1976–77

Champion	Held Title
EDDIE GAZO	1977–78
Rocky Mattioli (WBC)	1977–79
MASASHI KUDO	1978–79
Maurice Hope (WBC)	1979–81
AYUB KALULE	1979–81
Wilfred Benitez (WBC)	1981–82
SUGAR RAY LEONARD	1981–82
Tadashi Mihara (WBA)	1981–82
Davey Moore (WBA)	1982–83
Thomas Hearns (WBC)	1982–84
Roberto Duran (WBA)	1983–84
Mark Medal (IBF)	1984
THOMAS HEARNS	1984–86
Mike McCallum (WBA)	1984–87
Carlos Santos (IBF)	1984–86
Buster Drayton (IBF)	1986–87
Duane Thomas (WBC)	1986–87
Matthew Hilton (IBF)	1987–88
Lupe Aquino (WBC)	1987

Major Titleholders (Cont.)

Champion	Held Title	Champion	Held Title
Gianfranco Rosi (WBC)	1987–88	Paul Vaden (IBF)	1995
Julian Jackson (WBA)	1987–90	Carl Daniels (WBA)	1995
Donald Curry (WBC)	1988–89	Terry Norris (WBC)	1995–97
Robert Hines (IBF)	1988–89	Terry Norris (IBF)	1995–96
Darrin Van Horn (IBF)	1989	Laurent Boudouani (WBA)	1996–99
Rene Jacquote (WBC)	1989	Raul Marquez (IBF)	1997
John Mugabi (WBC)	1989–90	Keith Mullings (WBC)	1997–99
Gianfranco Rosi (IBF)	1989–94	Yori Boy Campas (IBF)	1997–98
Terry Norris (WBC)	1990–94	Fernando Vargas (IBF)	1998–2000
Gilbert Dele (WBA)	1991	Javier Castillejo (WBC)	1999–2001
Vinny Pazienza (WBA)	1991–92	David Reid (WBA)	1999–00
Julio Cesar Vasquez (WBA)	1992–95	Felix Trinidad (WBA/IBF)	2000–01†
Simon Brown (WBC)	1994	**Oscar De La Hoya** (WBC)	2001–
Terry Norris (WBC)	1994–	**Fernando Vargas** (WBA)	2001–
Vincent Pettway (IBF)	1994–95	**Ronald Wright** (IBF)	2001–

Welterweights

Widely accepted champions in CAPITAL letters. Current champions in **bold** type.

Champion	Held Title	Champion	Held Title
PADDY DUFFY	1888–90	VIRGIL AKINS	1958
MYSTERIOUS BILLY SMITH	1892–94	DON JORDAN	1958–60
TOMMY RYAN	1894–98	BENNY (KID) PARET	1960–61
MYSTERIOUS BILLY SMITH	1898–1900	EMILE GRIFFITH	1961
MATTY MATTHEWS	1900	BENNY (KID) PARET	1961–62
EDDIE CONNOLLY	1900	EMILE GRIFFITH	1962–63
JAMES (RUBE) FERNS	1900	LUIS RODRIGUEZ	1963
MATTY MATHEWS	1900–01	EMILE GRIFFITH	1963–66†
JAMES (RUBE) FERNS	1901	Charlie Shipes (Calif.)	1966–67
JOE WALCOTT	1901–04	CURTIS COKES	1966–69
THE DIXIE KID	1904–05	JOSE NAPOLES	1969–70
HONEY MELLODY	1906–07	BILLY BACKUS	1970–71
Mike (Twin) Sullivan	1907–08†	JOSE NAPOLES	1971–75
Harry Lewis	1908–1.1	Hedgemon Lewis (NY)	1972–73
Jimmy Gardner	1908	Angel Espada (WBA)	1975–76
Jimmy Clabby	1910–11	JOHN H. STRACEY	1975–76
WALDEMAR HOLBERG	1914	CARLOS PALOMINO	1976–79
TOM McCORMICK	1914	Pipino Cuevas (WBA)	1976–80
MATT WELLS	1914–15	WILFREDO BENITEZ	1979
MIKE GLOVER	1915	SUGAR RAY LEONARD	1979–80
JACK BRITTON	1915	ROBERTO DURAN	1980
TED (KID) LEWIS	1915–16	Thomas Hearns (WBA)	1980–81
JACK BRITTON	1916–17	SUGAR RAY LEONARD	1980–82
TED (KID) LEWIS	1917–19	Donald Curry (WBA)	1983–85
JACK BRITTON	1919–22	Milton McCrory (WBC)	1983–85
MICKEY WALKER	1922–26	DONALD CURRY	1985–86
PETE LATZO	1926–27	LLOYD HONEYGHAN	1986–87
JOE DUNDEE	1927–29	JORGE VACA (WBC)	1987–88
JACKIE FIELDS	1929–30	LLOYD HONEYGHAN (WBC)	1988–89
YOUNG JACK THOMPSON	1930	Mark Breland (WBA)	1987
TOMMY FREEMAN	1930–31	Marlon Starling (WBA)	1987–88
YOUNG JACK THOMPSON	1931	Tomas Molinares (WBA)	1988–89
LOU BROUILLARD	1931–32	Simon Brown (IBF)	1988–91
JACKIE FIELDS	1932–33	Mark Breland (WBA)	1989–90
YOUNG CORBETT III	1933	MARLON STARLING (WBC)	1989–90
JIMMY McLARNIN	1933–34	Aaron Davis (WBA)	1990–91
BARNEY ROSS	1934	Maurice Blocker (WBC)	1990–91
JIMMY McLARNIN	1934–35	Meldrick Taylor (WBA)	1991–92
BARNEY ROSS	1935–38	Simon Brown (WBC)	1991
HENRY ARMSTRONG	1938–40	Maurice Blocker (IBF)	1991–93
FRITZIE ZIVIC	1940–41	Buddy McGirt (WBC)	1991–93
Izzy Jannazzo (Md.)	1940–41	Crisanto Espana (WBA)	1992–94
Freddie (Red) Cochrane	1941–46	Pernell Whitaker (WBC)	1993–97
MARTY SERVO	1946*	Felix Trinidad (IBF)	1993–99
SUGAR RAY ROBINSON	1946–51†	Ike Quartey (WBA)	1994–98†
Johnny Bratton	1951	James Page (WBA)	1998–2000†
KID GAVILAN	1951–54	Oscar De La Hoya (WBC)	1997–99
JOHNNY SAXTON	1954–55	Felix Trinidad (WBC/IBF)	1999–2000†
TONY DeMARCO	1955	Oscar De La Hoya (WBC)	2000
CARMEN BASILIO	1955–56	**Shane Mosley** (WBC)	2000–
JOHNNY SAXTON	1956	**Andrew Lewis** (WBA)	2001–
CARMEN BASILIO	1956–57†	**Vernon Forrest** (IBF)	2001–

Junior Welterweights

Widely accepted champions in CAPITAL letters. Current champions in **bold** type.

Champion	Held Title	Champion	Held Title
PINKEY MITCHELL	1922–25	Gene Hatcher (WBA)	1984–85
RED HERRING	1925	Ubaldo Sacco (WBA)	1985–86
MUSHY CALLAHAN	1926–30	Lonnie Smith (WBC)	1985–86
JACK (KID) BERG	1930–31	Patrizio Oliva (WBA)	1986–87
TONY CANZONERI	1931–32	Gary Hinton (IBF)	1986
JOHNNY JADICK	1932–33	Rene Arredondo (WBC)	1986
Sammy Fuller	1932–33	Tsuyoshi Hamada (WBC)	1986–87
BATTLING SHAW	1933	Joe Louis Manley (IBF)	1986–87
TONY CANZONERI	1933	Terry Marsh (IBF)	1987
BARNEY ROSS	1933–35	Juan Coggi (WBA)	1987–90
TIPPY LARKIN	1946	Rene Arredondo (WBC)	1987
CARLOS ORTIZ	1959–60	Roger Mayweather (WBC)	1987–89
DUILIO LOI	1960–62	James McGirt (IBF)	1988
EDDIE PERKINS	1962	Meldrick Taylor (IBF)	1988–90
DUILIO LOI	1962–63	Julio Cesar Chavez (WBC)	1989–94
Roberto Cruz	1963	Julio Cesar Chavez (IBF)	1990–91
EDDIE PERKINS	1963–65	Loreto Garza (WBA)	1990–91
CARLOS HERNANDEZ	1965–66	Juan Coggi (WBA)	1991
SANDRO LOPOPOLO	1966–67	Edwin Rosario (WBA)	1991–92
PAUL FUJII	1967–68	Rafael Pineda (IBF)	1991–92
NICOLINO LOCHE	1968–72	Akinobu Hiranaka (WBA)	1992
Pedro Adigue (WBC)	1968–70	Pernell Whitaker (IBF)	1992–93†
Bruno Arcari (WBC)	1970–74	Charles Murray (IBF)	1993–94
ALFONSO FRAZER	1972	Jake Rodriguez (IBF)	1994–95
ANTONIO CERVANTES	1972–76	Juan Coggi (WBA)	1993–94
Perico Fernandez (WBC)	1974–75	Frankie Randall (WBC)	1994
Saensak Muangsurin (WBC)	1975–76	Frankie Randall (WBA)	1994–96
WILFRED BENITEZ (WBC)	1976–79	Juan Coggi (WBA)	1996
Miguel Velasquez (WBC)	1976	Julio Cesar Chavez (WBC)	1994–96
Saensak Muangsurin (WBC)	1976–78	Kostya Tszyu (IBF)	1995–97
Antonio Cervantes (WBA)	1977–80	Frankie Randall (WBC)	1996–97
Sang-Hyun Kim (WBC)	1978–80	Oscar De La Hoya (WBC)	1996–97†
Saoul Mamby (WBC)	1980–82	Khalid Rahilou (WBA)	1997–98
Aaron Pryor (WBA)	1980–83	Sharmba Mitchell (WBA)	1998–2001
Leroy Haley (WBC)	1982–83	Vincent Phillips (IBF)	1997–99
Aaron Pryor (IBF)	1983–85	Terronn Millet (IBF)	1999–00†
Bruce Curry (WBC)	1983–84	**Kostya Tszyu** (WBC)	1999–
Johnny Bumphus (WBA)	1984	**Zab Judah** (IBF)	2000–
Bill Costello (WBC)	1984–85	**Kostya Tszyu** (WBC/WBA)	2001–

Lightweights

Widely accepted champions in CAPITAL letters. Current champions in **bold** type.

Champion	Held Title	Champion	Held Title
JACK McAULIFFE	1886–94	Slugger White (Md.)	1943
GEORGE (KID) LAVIGNE	1896–99	Bob Montgomery (NY)	1943
FRANK ERNE	1899–02	Sammy Angott (NBA)	1943–44
JOE GANS	1902–04	Beau Jack (NY)	1943–44
JIMMY BRITT	1904–05	Bob Montgomery (NY)	1944–47
BATTLING NELSON	1905–06	Juan Zurita (NBA)	1944–45
JOE GANS	1906–08	IKE WILLIAMS	1947–51
BATTLING NELSON	1908–10	JAMES CARTER	1951–52
AD WOLGAST	1910–12	LAURO SALAS	1952
WILLIE RITCHIE	1912–14	JAMES CARTER	1952–54
FREDDIE WELSH	1915–17	PADDY DeMARCO	1954
BENNY LEONARD	1917–25*	JAMES CARTER	1954–55
JIMMY GOODRICH	1925	WALLACE (BUD) SMITH	1955–56
ROCKY KANSAS	1925–26	JOE BROWN	1956–62
SAMMY MANDELL	1926–30	CARLOS ORTIZ	1962–65
AL SINGER	1930	Kenny Lane (Mich.)	1963–64
TONY CANZONERI	1930–33	ISMAEL LAGUNA	1965
BARNEY ROSS	1933–35†	CARLOS ORTIZ	1965–68
TONY CANZONERI	1935–36	CARLOS TEO CRUZ	1968–69
LOU AMBERS	1936–38	MANDO RAMOS	1969–70
HENRY ARMSTRONG	1938–39	ISMAEL LAGUNA	1970
LOU AMBERS	1939–40	KEN BUCHANAN	1970–72
Sammy Angott (NBA)	1940–41	Pedro Carrasco (WBC)	1971–72
LEW JENKINS	1940–41	Mando Ramos (WBC)	1972
SAMMY ANGOTT	1941–42	ROBERTO DURAN	1972–79†
Beau Jack (NY)	1942–43	Chango Carmona (WBC)	1972

Major Titleholders (Cont.)

Champion	Held Title
Rodolfo Gonzalez (WBC)	1972–74
Ishimatsu Suzuki (WBC)	1974–76
Esteban De Jesus (WBC)	1976–78
Jim Watt (WBC)	1979–81
Ernesto Espana (WBA)	1979–80
Hilmer Kenty (WBA)	1980–81
Sean O'Grady (WBA, WAA)	1981
Alexis Arguello (WBC)	1981–82
Claude Noel (WBA)	1981
Andrew Ganigan (WAA)	1981–82
Arturo Frias (WBA)	1981–82
Ray Mancini (WBA)	1982–84
ALEXIS ARGUELLO	1982–83
Edwin Rosario (WBC)	1983–84
Choo Choo Brown (IBF)	1984
Livingstone Bramble (WBA)	1984–86
Harry Arroyo (IBF)	1984–85
Jose Luis Ramirez (WBC)	1984–85
Jimmy Paul (IBF)	1985–86
Hector Camacho (WBC)	1985–86
Edwin Rosario (WBA)	1986–87
Greg Haugen (IBF)	1986–87
Julio Cesar Chavez (WBA)	1987–88
Jose Luis Ramirez (WBC)	1987–88
JULIO CESAR CHAVEZ (WBC, WBA)	1988–89
Vinny Pazienza (IBF)	1987–88
Greg Haugen (IBF)	1988–89
Pernell Whitaker (IBF, WBC)	1989–90

Champion	Held Title
Edwin Rosario (WBA)	1989–90
Juan Nazario (WBA)	1990
PERNELL WHITAKER (IBF, WBC, WBA)	1990–92†
Joey Gamache (WBA)	1992
Miguel A. Gonzalez (WBC)	1992–96
Tony Lopez (WBA)	1992–93
Dingaan Thobela (WBA)	1993
Fred Pendleton (IBF)	1993–94
Orzubek Nazarov (WBA)	1993–98
Rafael Ruelas (IBF)	1994–95
Oscar De La Hoya (IBF)	1995†
Phillip Holiday (IBF)	1995–97
Jean-Baptiste Mendy (WBC)	1996–97
Stevie Johnston (WBC)	1997–98
Shane Mosley (IBF)	1997–99†
Cesar Bazan (WBC)	1998–99
Jean-Baptiste Mendy (WBA)	1998–99
Julien Lorcy (WBA)	1999
Stevie Johnston (WBC)	1999–00
Stefano Zoff (WBA)	1999
Israel Cardona (IBF)	1999
Paul Spadafora (IBF)	1999–
Gilberto Serrano (WBA)	1999–00
Takanori Hatakeyama (WBA)	2000–01
Jose Luis Castillo (WBC)	2000–
Julien Lorcy (WBA)	2001
Raul Balbi (WBA)	2001–

Junior Lightweights

Widely accepted champions in CAPITAL letters. Current champions in **bold** type.

Champion	Held Title
JOHNNY DUNDEE	1921–23
JACK BERNSTEIN	1923
JOHNNY DUNDEE	1923–24
STEVE (KID) SULLIVAN	1924–25
MIKE BALLERINO	1925
TOD MORGAN	1925–29
BENNY BASS	1929–31
KID CHOCOLATE	1931–33
FRANKIE KLICK	1933–34
SANDY SADDLER	1949–50
HAROLD GOMES	1959–60
GABRIEL (FLASH) ELORDE	1960–67
YOSHIAKI NUMATA	1967
HIROSHI KOBAYASHI	1967–71
Rene Barrientos (WBC)	1969–70
Yoshiaki Numata (WBC)	1970–71
ALFREDO MARCANO	1971–72
Ricardo Arredondo (WBC)	1971–74
BEN VILLAFLOR	1972–73
KUNIAKI SHIBATA	1973
BEN VILLAFLOR	1973–76
Kuniaki Shibata (WBC)	1974–75
Alfredo Escalera (WBC)	1975–78
SAMUEL SERRANO	1976–80
Alexis Arguello (WBC)	1978–80
YASUTSUNE UEHARA	1980–81
Rafael Limon (WBC)	1980–81
Cornelius Boza-Edwards (WBC)	1981
SAMUEL SERRANO	1981–83
Rolando Navarrete (WBC)	1981–82
Rafael Limon (WBC)	1982
Bobby Chacon (WBC)	1982–83
ROGER MAYWEATHER	1983–84
Hector Camacho (WBC)	1983–84

Champion	Held Title
ROCKY LOCKRIDGE	1984–85
Hwan-Kil Yuh (IBF)	1984–85
Julio Cesar Chavez (WBC)	1984–87
Lester Ellis (IBF)	1985
WILFREDO GOMEZ	1985–86
Barry Michael (IBF)	1985–87
ALFREDO LAYNE	1986
BRIAN MITCHELL	1986–91
Rocky Lockridge (IBF)	1987–88
Azumah Nelson (WBC)	1988–94
Tony Lopez (IBF)	1988–89
Juan Molina (IBF)	1989–90
Tony Lopez (IBF)	1990–91
Joey Gamache (WBA)	1991
Brian Mitchell (IBF)	1991
Genaro Hernandez (WBA)	1991–95
James Leija (WBC)	1994
Juan Molina (IBF)	1991–95
Gabriel Ruelas (WBC)	1994–95
Eddie Hopson (IBF)	1995
Tracy Patterson (IBF)	1995
Azumah Nelson (WBC)	1995–97
Choi Yong-Soo (WBA)	1995–98
Arturo Gatti (IBF)	1995–98†
Genaro Hernandez (WBC)	1997–98
Floyd Mayweather Jr. (WBC)	1998–
Takanori Hatakeyama (WBA)	1998–99
Roberto Garcia (IBF)	1998–99
Lavka Sim (WBA)	1999
Diego Corrales (IBF)	1999–2001
Baek Jong-Kwon (WBA)	1999–2000
Joel Casamayor (WBA)	2000–
Steve Forbes (IBF)	2001–

Featherweights

Widely accepted champions in CAPITAL letters. Current champions in **bold** type.

Champion	Held Title	Champion	Held Title
TORPEDO BILLY MURPHY	1890	JOHNNY FAMECHON (WBC)	1969–70
YOUNG GRIFFO	1890–92	VICENTE SALDIVAR (WBC)	1970
GEORGE DIXON	1892–97	KUNIAKI SHIBATA (WBC)	1970–72
SOLLY SMITH	1897–98	Antonio Gomez (WBA)	1971–72
Ben Jordan (GBR)	1898–99	CLEMENTE SANCHEZ (WBC)	1972
Eddie Santry (GBR)	1899–1900	Ernesto Marcel (WBA)	1972–74
DAVE SULLIVAN	1898	JOSE LEGRA (WBC)	1972–73
GEORGE DIXON	1898–1900	EDER JOFRE (WBC)	1973–74
TERRY McGOVERN	1900–01	Ruben Olivares (WBA)	1974
YOUNG CORBETT II	1901–04	Bobby Chacon (WBC)	1974–75
JIMMY BRITT	1904	ALEXIS ARGUELLO (WBA)	1974–76†
ABE ATTELL	1904	Ruben Olivares (WBC)	1975
BROOKLYN TOMMY SULLIVAN	1904–05	David (Poison) Kotey (WBC)	1975–76
ABE ATTELL	1906–12	DANNY (LITTLE RED) LOPEZ (WBC)	1976–80
JOHNNY KILBANE	1912–23	Rafael Ortega (WBA)	1977
Jem Driscoll (GBR)	1912–13	Cecilio Lastra (WBA)	1977–78
EUGENE CRIQUI	1923	Eusebio Pedroza (WBA)	1978–85
JOHNNY DUNDEE	1923–24†	SALVADOR SANCHEZ (WBC)	1980–82
LOUIS (KID) KAPLAN	1925–26†	Juan LaPorte (WBC)	1982–84
Dick Finnegan (Mass.)	1926–27	Wilfredo Gomez (WBC)	1984
BENNY BASS	1927–28	Min-Keun Oh (IBF)	1984–85
TONY CANZONERI	1928	Azumah Nelson (WBC)	1984–88
ANDRE ROUTIS	1928–29	Barry McGuigan (WBA)	1985–86
BATTLING BATTALINO	1929–32†	Ki-Young Chung (IBF)	1985–86
Tommy Paul (NBA)	1932–33	Steve Cruz (WBA)	1986–87
Kid Chocolate (NY)	1932–33	Antonio Rivera (IBF)	1986–88
Freddie Miller (NBA)	1933–36	Antonio Esparragoza (WBA)	1987–91
Baby Arizmendi (MEX)	1935–36	Calvin Grove (IBF)	1988
Mike Belloise (NY)	1936–37	Jorge Paez (IBF)	1988–91†
Petey Sarron (NBA)	1936–37	Jeff Fenech (WBC)	1988–90†
HENRY ARMSTRONG	1937–38†	Marcos Villasana (WBC)	1990–91
Joey Archibald (NY)	1938–39	Yung-Kyun Park (WBA)	1991–93
Leo Rodak (NBA)	1938–39	Troy Dorsey (IBF)	1991
JOEY ARCHIBALD	1939–40	Manuel Medina (IBF)	1991–93
Petey Scalzo (NBA)	1940–41	Paul Hodkinson (WBC)	1991–93
Jimmy Perrin (La.)	1940–41	Tom Johnson (IBF)	1993–97
HARRY JEFFRA	1940–41	Goyo Vargas (WBC)	1993
JOEY ARCHIBALD	1941	Kevin Kelley (WBC)	1993–95
Richie Lemos (NBA)	1941	Eloy Rojas (WBA)	1993–96
CHALKY WRIGHT	1941–42	Alejandro Gonzalez (WBC)	1995
Jackie Wilson (NBA)	1941–43	Manuel Medina (WBC)	1995–96
WILLIE PEP	1942–48	Wilfredo Vasquez (WBA)	1996–98†
Jackie Callura (NBA)	1943	Luisito Espinosa (WBC)	1995–99
Phil Terranova (NBA)	1943–44	Naseem Hamed (IBF)	1997†
Sal Bartolo (NBA)	1944–46	Hector Lizarraga (IBF)	1997–98
SANDY SADDLER	1948–49	Freddie Norwood (WBA)	1998
WILLIE PEP	1949–50	Manuel Medina (IBF)	1998–99
SANDY SADDLER	1950–57*	Antonio Cermeno (WBA)	1998–99
HOGAN (KID) BASSEY	1957–59	Cesar Soto (WBC)	1999–00
DAVEY MOORE	1959–63	Paul Ingle (IBF)	1999–2000
ULTIMINIO (SUGAR) RAMOS	1963–64	Mbuelo Botile (IBF)	2000–01
VICENTE SALDIVAR	1964–67*	Guty Espadas (WBC)	2000–01
Howard Winstone (GBR)	1968	Freddie Norwood (WBA)	1999–00
Raul Rojas (WBA)	1968	**Derrick Gainer** (WBA)	2000–
Jose Legra (WBC)	1968–69	**Erik Morales** (WBC)	2001–
Shozo Saijyo (WBA)	1968–71	**Frankie Toledo** (IBF)	2001–

Junior Featherweights

Current champions in **bold** type.

Champion	Held Title	Champion	Held Title
Jack (Kid) Wolfe	1922–23	Jaime Garza (WBC)	1983
Carl Duane	1923–24	Bobby Berna (IBF)	1983–84
Rigoberto Riasco (WBC)	1976	Loris Stecca (WBA)	1984
Royal Kobayashi (WBC)	1976	Seung-Il Suh (IBF)	1984–85
Dong-Kyun Yum (WBC)	1976–77	Victor Callejas (WBA)	1984–85
Wilfredo Gomez (WBC)	1977–83	Juan (Kid) Meza (WBC)	1984–85
Soo-Hwan Hong (WBA)	1977–78	Ji-Woo Kim (IBF)	1985–86
Ricardo Cardona (WBA)	1978–80	Lupe Pintor (WBC)	1985–86
Leo Randolph (WBA)	1980	Samart Payakaroon (WBC)	1986–87
Sergio Palma (WBA)	1980–82	Seung-Hoon Lee (IBF)	1987–88
Leonardo Cruz (WBA)	1982–84	Louie Espinoza (WBA)	1987

Major Titleholders (Cont.)

Champion	Held Title
Jeff French (WBC)	1987
Julio Gervacio (WBA)	1987–88
Daniel Zaragoza (WBC)	1988–90
Jose Sanabria (IBF)	1988–90
Bernardo Pinango (WBA)	1988
Juan Jose Estrada (WBA)	1988–89
Fabrice Benichou (IBF)	1989–90
Jesus Salud (WBA)	1989–90
Welcome Ncita (IBF)	1990–92
Paul Banke (WBC)	1990
Luis Mendoza (WBA)	1990–91
Raul Perez (WBA)	1992
Pedro Decima (WBC)	1990–91
Kiyoshi Hatanaka (WBC)	1991
Daniel Zaragoza (WBC)	1991–92

Champion	Held Title
Tracy Patterson (WBC)	1992–94
Kennedy McKinney (IBF)	1993–94
Wilfredo Vasquez (WBA)	1992–95
Vuyani Bungu (IBF)	1994–99†
Hector Acero Sanchez (WBC)	1994–95
Antonio Cermeno (WBA)	1995–98†
Daniel Zaragoza (WBC)	1995–97
Erik Morales (WBC)	1997–00†
Enrique Sanchez (WBA)	1998
Nestor Garza (WBA)	1998–00
Lehlohonolo Ledwaba (IBF)	1999–2001
Clarence Adams (WBA)	2000–01
Willie Jorrin (WBC)	2000–
Manny Pacquiao (IBF)	2001–

Bantamweights

Widely accepted champions in CAPITAL letters. Current champions in **bold** type.

Champion	Held Title
TOMMY (SPIDER) KELLY	1887
HUGHEY BOYLE	1887–88
TOMMY (SPIDER) KELLY	1889
CHAPPIE MORAN	1889–90
Tommy (Spider) Kelly	1890–92
GEORGE DIXON	1890–91
Billy Plummer	1892–95
JIMMY BARRY	1894–99
Pedlar Palmer	1895–99
TERRY McGOVERN	1899–1900
HARRY HARRIS	1901–02
DANNY DOUGHERTY	1900–01
HARRY FORBES	1901–03
FRANKIE NEIL	1903–04
JOE BOWKER	1904–05
JIMMY WALSH	1905–06†
OWEN MORAN	1907–08
MONTE ATTELL	1909–10
FRANKIE CONLEY	1910–11
JOHNNY COULON	1911–14
Digger Stanley (GBR)	1910–12
Charles Ledoux (GBR)	1912–13
Eddie Campi (GBR)	1913–14
KID WILLIAMS	1914–17
Johnny Ertle	1915–18
PETE HERMAN	1917–20
Memphis Pal Moore	1918–19
JOE LYNCH	1920–21
PETE HERMAN	1921
JOHNNY BUFF	1921–22
JOE LYNCH	1922–24
ABE GOLDSTEIN	1924
CANNONBALL EDDIE MARTIN	1924–25
PHIL ROSENBERG	1925–27
Teddy Baldock (GBR)	1927
BUD TAYLOR (NBA)	1927–28†
Willie Smith (GBR)	1927–28
Bushy Graham (NY)	1928–29
PANAMA AL BROWN	1929–35
Sixto Escobar (NBA)	1934–35
BALTAZAR SANGCHILLI	1935–36
Lou Salica (NBA)	1935
Sixto Escobar (NBA)	1935–36
TONY MARINO	1936
SIXTO ESCOBAR	1936–37
HARRY JEFFRA	1937–38
SIXTO ESCOBAR	1938–39*
Georgie Pace (NBA)	1939–40
LOU SALICA	1940–42
MANUEL ORTIZ	1942–47
HAROLD DADE	1947
MANUEL ORTIZ	1947–50
VIC TOWEEL	1950–52

Champion	Held Title
JIMMY CARRUTHERS	1952–54*
ROBERT COHEN	1954–56
Raul Macias (NBA)	1955–57
MARIO D'AGATA	1956–57
ALPHONSE HALIMI	1957–59
JOE BECERRA	1959–60*
Johnny Caldwell (EBU)	1961–62
EDER JOFRE	1961–65
MASAHIKO FIGHTING HARADA	1965–68
LIONEL ROSE	1968–69
RUBEN OLIVARES	1969–70
CHUCHO CASTILLO	1970–71
RUBEN OLIVARES	1971–72
RAFAEL HERRERA	1972
ENRIQUE PINDER	1972–73
ROMEO ANAYA	1973
Rafael Herrera (WBC)	1973–74
ARNOLD TAYLOR	1973–74
SOO-HWAN HONG	1974–75
Rodolfo Martinez (WBC)	1974–76
ALFONSO ZAMORA	1975–77
Carlos Zarate (WBC)	1976–79
JORGE LUJAN	1977–80
Lupe Pintor (WBC)	1979–83
JULIAN SOLIS	1980
JEFF CHANDLER	1980–84
Albert Davila (WBC)	1983–85
RICHARD SANDOVAL	1984–86
Satoshi Shingaki (IBF)	1984–85
Jeff Fenech (IBF)	1985
Daniel Zaragoza (WBC)	1985
Miguel (Happy) Lora (WBC)	1985–88
GABY CANIZALES	1986
BERNARDO PINANGO	1986–87
Wilfredo Vasquez (WBA)	1987–88
Kevin Seabrooks (IBF)	1987–88
Kaokor Galaxy (WBA)	1988
Moon Sung-Kil (WBA)	1988–89
Kaokor Galaxy (WBA)	1989
Raul Perez (WBC)	1988–91
Orlando Canizales (IBF)	1988–94†
Luisito Espinosa (WBA)	1989–91
Greg Richardson	1991
Joichiro Tatsuyoshi (WBC)	1991–92
Israel Contreras (WBA)	1991–92
Eddie Cook (WBA)	1992
Victor Rabanales (WBC)	1992–93
Jorge Julio (WBA)	1992–93
Jung-Il Byun (WBC)	1993
Junior Jones (WBA)	1993–94
Yasuei Yakushiji (WBC)	1993–95
John M. Johnson (WBA)	1994
Daorung Chuvatana (WBA)	1994–95

Champion	Held Title
Harold Mestre (IBF)	1995
Mbuelo Botile (IBF)	1995–97
Wayne McCullough (WBC)	1995–96
Veeraphol Sahaprom (WBA)	1995–96
Nana Yaw Konadu (WBA)	1996
Daorung Chuvatana (WBA)	1996–97
Nana Yaw Konadu (WBA)	1997–98

Champion	Held Title
Sirimongkol Singmanassak (WBC)	1996–97
Tim Austin (IBF)	1997–
Joichiro Tatsuyoshi (WBC)	1997–98
Johnny Tapia (WBC)	1998–99
Veerapol Sahaprom (WBC)	1998–
Paulie Ayala (WBA)	1999–2001
Eidy Moya (WBA)	2001–

Junior Bantamweights

Widely accepted champions in CAPITAL letters. Current champions in **bold** type.

Champion	Held Title
Rafael Orono (WBC)	1980–81
Chul-Ho Kim (WBC)	1981–82
Gustavo Ballas (WBA)	1981
Rafael Pedroza (WBA)	1981–82
Jiro Watanabe (WBA)	1982–84
Rafael Orono (WBC)	1982–83
Payao Poontarat (WBC)	1983–84
Joo-Do Chun (IBF)	1983–85
JIRO WATANABE	1984–86
Kaosai Galaxy (WBA)	1984
Ellyas Pical (IBF)	1985–86
Cesar Polanco (IBF)	1986
GILBERTO ROMAN	1986–87
Ellyas Pical (IBF)	1986
Santos Laciar (WBC)	1987
Tae-Il Chang (IBF)	1987
Sugar Rojas (WBC)	1987–88
Ellyas Pical (IBF)	1987–89
Gilberto Roman (WBC)	1988–89
Juan Polo Perez (IBF)	1989–90
Nana Konadu (WBC)	1989–90
Sung-Kil Moon (WBC)	1990–93
Robert Quiroga (IBF)	1990–93

Champion	Held Title
Julio Borboa (IBF)	1993–94
Katsuya Onizuka (WBA)	1993–94
Lee Hyung-Chul (WBA)	1994–95
Jose Luis Bueno (WBC)	1993–94
Hiroshi Kawashima (WBC)	1994–97
Harold Grey (IBF)	1994–95
Alimi Goitia (WBA)	1995–96
Yokthai Sith-Oar (WBA)	1996–97
Carlos Salazar (WBA)	1995–96
Harold Grey (IBF)	1996
Danny Romero (IBF)	1996–97
Gerry Penalosa (WBC)	1997–98
Johnny Tapia (IBF)	1997–98†
Satoshi Iida (WBA)	1997–98
Cho In-Joo (WBC)	1998–00
Jesus Rojas (WBA)	1998–99
Mark Johnson (IBF)	1999–00†
Hideki Todaka (WBA)	1999–2000
Masanori Tokuyama (WBC)	2000–
Felix Machado (IBF)	2000–
Leo Gamez (WBA)	2000–01
Celes Kobayashi (WBA)	2001–

Flyweights

Widely accepted champions in CAPITAL letters. Current champions in **bold** type.

Champion	Held Title
Sid Smith (GBR)	1913
Bill Ladbury (GBR)	1913–14
Percy Jones (GBR)	1914
Joe Symonds (GBR)	1914–16
JIMMY WILDE	1916–23
PANCHO VILLA	1923–25
FIDEL LaBARBA	1925–27*
FRENCHY BELANGER (NBA,IBU)	1927–28
Izzy Schwartz (NY)	1927–29
Johnny McCoy (Calif.)	1927–28
Newsboy Brown (Calif.)	1928
FRANKIE GENARO (NBA,IBU)	1928–29
Johnny Hill (GBR)	1928–29
SPIDER PLADNER (NBA,IBU)	1929
FRANKIE GENARO (NBA,IBU)	1929–31
Willie LaMorte (NY)	1929–30
Midget Wolgast (NY)	1930–35
YOUNG PEREZ (NBA,IBU)	1931–32
JACKIE BROWN (NBA,IBU)	1932–35
BENNY LYNCH	1935–38†
Small Montana (NY,Calif.)	1935–37
PETER KANE	1938–43
Little Dado (NBA,Calif.)	1938–40
JACKIE PATERSON	1943–48
RINTY MONAGHAN	1948–50*
TERRY ALLEN	1950
SALVADOR (DADO) MARINO	1950–52
YOSHIO SHIRAI	1953–54
PASCUAL PEREZ	1954–60
PONE KINGPETCH	1960–62
MASAHIKO (FIGHTING) HARADA	1962–63
PONE KINGPETCH	1963
HIROYUKI EBIHARA	1963–64
PONE KINGPETCH	1964–65

Champion	Held Title
SALVATORE BURRINI	1965–66
Horacio Accavallo (WBA)	1966–68
WALTER McGOWAN	1966
CHARTCHAI CHIONOI	1966–69
EFREN TORRES	1969–70
Hiroyuki Ebihara (WBA)	1969
Bernabe Villacampo (WBA)	1969–70
CHARTCHAI CHIONOI	1970
Berkrerk Chartvanchai (WBA)	1970
Masao Ohba (WBA)	1970–73
ERBITO SALAVARRIA	1970–73
Betulio Gonzalez (WBC)	1972
Venice Borkorsor (WBC)	1972–73
VENICE BORKORSOR	1973
Chartchai Chionoi (WBA)	1973–74
Betulio Gonzalez (WBA)	1973–74
Shoji Oguma (WBC)	1974–75
Susumu Hanagata (WBA)	1974–75
Miguel Canto (WBC)	1975–79
Erbito Salavarria (WBA)	1975–76
Alfonso Lopez (WBA)	1976
Guty Espadas (WBA)	1976–78
Betulio Gonzalez (WBA)	1978–79
Chan-Hee Park (WBC)	1979–80
Luis Ibarra (WBA)	1979–80
Tae-Shik Kim (WBA)	1980
Shoji Oguma (WBC)	1980–81
Peter Mathebula (WBA)	1980–81
Santos Laciar (WBA)	1981
Antonio Avelar (WBC)	1981–82
Luis Ibarra (WBA)	1981
Juan Herrera (WBA)	1981–82
Prudencio Cardona (WBC)	1982
Santos Laciar (WBA)	1982–85

Major Titleholders (Cont.)

Champion	Held Title	Champion	Held Title
Freddie Castillo (WBC)	1982	Muangchai Kittikasem (WBC)	1991–92
Eleoncio Mercedes (WBC)	1982–83	Yong-Kang Kim (WBA)	1991–92
Charlie Magri (WBC)	1983	Rodolfo Blanco (IBF)	1992
Frank Cedeno (WBC)	1983–84	Yuri Arbachakov (WBC)	1992–97
Soon-Chun Kwon (IBF)	1983–85	Aquiles Guzman (WBA)	1992
Koji Kobayashi (WBC)	1984	Phichit Sithbangprachan (IBF)	1992–94†
Gabriel Bernal (WBC)	1984	David Griman (WBA)	1992–94
Sot Chitalada (WBC)	1984–88	Saen Sor Ploenchit (WBA)	1994–96
Hilario Zapate (WBA)	1985–87	Francisco Tejedor (IBF)	1995
Chong-Kwan Chung (IBF)	1985–86	Danny Romero (IBF)	1995–96
Bi-Won Chung (IBF)	1986	Mark Johnson (IBF)	1996–99†
Hi-Sup Shin (IBF)	1986–87	Jose Bonilla (WBA)	1996–97
Dodie Penalosa (IBF)	1987	Chatchai Sasakul (WBC)	1997–98
Fidel Bassa (WBA)	1987–89	Hugo Soto (WBA)	1998–99
Choi Chang-Ho (IBF)	1987–88	Manny Pacquiao (WBC)	1998–99
Rolando Bohol (IBF)	1988	**Irene Pacheco** (IBF)	1999–
Yong-Gang Kim (WBC)	1988–89	Leo Gamez (WBA)	1999
Duke McKenzie (IBF)	1988–89	Medgoen Lukchaopormasak (WBC)	1999–00
Dave McAuley (IBF)	1989–92	Sornpichai Kratindaenggym (WBA)	1999–00
Sot Chitalada (WBC)	1989–91	**Eric Morel** (WBA)	2000–
Jesus Rojas (WBA)	1989–90	Malcolm Tunacao (WBC)	2000–01
Yul-Woo Lee (WBA)	1990	**Pongsaklek Wonjongkam** (WBC)	2001–
Leopard Tamakuma (WBA)	1990–91		

Junior Flyweights

Current champions in **bold** type.

Champion	Held Title	Champion	Held Title
Franco Udella (WBC)	1975	Yul-Woo Lee (WBC)	1989
Jaime Rios (WBA)	1975–76	Muangchai Kittikasem (IBF)	1989–90
Luis Estaba (WBC)	1975–78	Humberto Gonzalez (WBC)	1989–90
Juan Guzman (WBA)	1976	Michael Carbajal (IBF)	1990–94
Yoko Gushiken (WBA)	1976–81	Rolando Pascua (WBC)	1990
Freddy Castillo (WBC)	1978	Melchor Cob Castro (WBC)	1991
Netrnoi Vorasingh (WBC)	1978	Humberto Gonzalez (WBC)	1991–93
Sung-Jun Kim (WBC)	1978–80	Hirokia Ioka (WBA)	1991–92
Shigeo Nakajima (WBC)	1980	Michael Carbajal (WBC)	1993–94
Hilario Zapata (WBC)	1980–82	Myung-Woo Yuh (WBA)	1993
Pedro Flores (WBA)	1981	Leo Gamez (WBA)	1993–95
Hwan-Jin Kim (WBA)	1981	Humberto Gonzalez (WBC/IBF)	1994–95
Katsuo Tokashiki (WBA)	1981–83	Choi Hi-Yong (WBA)	1995–96
Amado Urzua (WBC)	1982	Saman Sor Jaturong (WBC/IBF)	1995–96
Tadashi Tomori (WBC)	1982	Carlos Murillo (WBA)	1996
Hilario Zapata (WBC)	1982–83	Keiji Yamaguchi (WBA)	1996
Jung-Koo Chang (WBC)	1983–88	Michael Carbajal (IBF)	1996–97
Lupe Madera (WBA)	1983–84	Saman Sor Jaturong (WBC)	1995–99
Dodie Penalosa (IBF)	1983–86	Phichit Chor Siriwat (WBC)	1996–00†
Francisco Quiroz (WBA)	1984–85	Mauricio Pastrana (IBF)	1997–98†
Joey Olivo (WBA)	1985	Will Grigsby (IBF)	1999
Myung-Woo Yuh (WBA)	1985–91	**Choi Yo-Sam** (WBC)	1999–
Jum-Hwan Choi (IBF)	1986–88	**Ricardo Lopez** (IBF)	1999–
Tacy Macalos (IBF)	1988–89	Beibis Mendoza (WBA)	2000–01
German Torres (WBC)	1988–89	**Rosendo Alvarez** (WBA)	2001–

Strawweights

Current champions in **bold** type.

Champion	Held Title	Champion	Held Title
Franco Udella (WBC)	1975	Hilario Zapata (WBC)	1982–83
Jaime Rios (WBA)	1975–76	Jung-Koo Chang (WBC)	1983–88
Luis Estraba (WBC)	1975–78	Lupe Madera (WBA)	1983–84
Juan Guzman (WBA)	1976	Dodie Penalosa (IBF)	1983–86
Yoko Gushiken (WBA)	1976–81	Francisco Quiroz (WBA)	1984–85
Freddy Castillo (WBC)	1978	Joey Olivo (WBA)	1985
Netrnoi Vorasingh (WBC)	1978	Myung-Woo Yuh (WBA)	1985–93
Sung-Jun Kim (WBC)	1978–80	Jum-Hwan Choi (IBF)	1986–88
Shigeo Nakajima (WBC)	1980	Tacy Macalos (IBF)	1988–89
Hilario Zapata (WBC)	1980–82	German Torres (WBC)	1988–89
Pedro Flores (WBA)	1981	Yul-Woo Lee (WBC)	1989
Hwan-Jin Kim (WBA)	1981	Muangchai Kittikasem (IBF)	1989–90
Katsuo Tokashiki (WBA)	1981–83	Humberto Gonzalez (WBC)	1989–90
Amado Urzua (WBC)	1982	Michael Carbajal (IBF)	1990
Tadashi Tomori (WBC)	1982	Rolando Pascua (WBC)	1990

Champion	Held Title	Champion	Held Title
Melchor Cob Castro (WBC)	1991	Noel Arambulet (WBA)	1999-00†
Ricardo Lopez (WBC)	1990-98	Joma Gamboa (WBA)	2000
Ratanapol Voraphin (IBF)	1992-97	Keitaro Hoshino (WBA)	2000-01
Chana Porpaoin (WBA)	1993-95	**Jose Antonio Aguirre** (WBC)	2000-
Rosendo Alvarez (WBA)	1995-98	Chana Porpaoin (WBA)	2001
Ricardo Lopez (WBA/WBC)	1998-99†	**Robert Leyva** (IBF)	2001-
Zolani Petelo (IBF)	1997-2001†	Yutaka Niida (WBA)	2001-
Wandee Chor Chareon (WBC)	1999-00		

Annual Awards
Ring Magazine Fight of the Year

First presented in 1945 by Nat Fleischer, who started *The Ring* magazine in 1922.

Multiple matchups: Muhammad Ali vs. Joe Frazier, Carmen Basilio vs. Sugar Ray Robinson and Rocky Graziano vs. Tony Zale (2).

Multiple fights: Muhammad Ali (6); Carmen Basilio (5); George Foreman and Joe Frazier (4); Rocky Graziano, Rocky Marciano and Tony Zale (3); Nino Benvenuti, Bobby Chacon, Ezzard Charles, Arturo Gatti, Marvin Hagler, Thomas Hearns, Evander Holyfield, Sugar Ray Leonard, Floyd Patterson, Sugar Ray Robinson and Jersey Joe Walcott (2).

Year	Winner	Loser	Result		Year	Winner	Loser	Result	
1945	Rocky Graziano	Red Cochrane	KO	10	1974	Muhammad Ali	George Foreman	KO	8
1946	Tony Zale	Rocky Graziano	KO	6	1975	Muhammad Ali	Joe Frazier	KO	14
1947	Rocky Graziano	Tony Zale	KO	6	1976	George Foreman	Ron Lyle	KO	4
1948	Marcel Cerdan	Tony Zale	KO	12	1977	Jimmy Young	George Foreman	W	12
1949	Willie Pep	Sandy Saddler	W	15	1978	Leon Spinks	Muhammad Ali	W	15
1950	Jake LaMotta	Laurent Dauthuille	KO	15	1979	Danny Lopez	Mike Ayala	KO	15
1951	Jersey Joe Walcott	Ezzard Charles	KO	7	1980	Saad Muhammad	Yaqui Lopez	KO	14
1952	Rocky Marciano	Jersey Joe Walcott	KO	13	1981	Sugar Ray Leonard	Thomas Hearns	KO	14
1953	Rocky Marciano	Roland LaStarza	KO	11	1982	Bobby Chacon	Rafael Limon	W	15
1954	Rocky Marciano	Ezzard Charles	KO	8	1983	Bobby Chacon	C. Boza-Edwards	W	12
1955	Carmen Basilio	Tony DeMarco	KO	12	1984	Jose Luis Ramirez	Edwin Rosario	KO	4
1956	Carmen Basilio	Johnny Saxton	KO	9	1985	Marvin Hagler	Thomas Hearns	KO	3
1957	Carmen Basilio	Sugar Ray Robinson	W	15	1986	Stevie Cruz	Barry McGuigan	W	15
1958	Sugar Ray Robinson	Carmen Basilio	W	15	1987	Sugar Ray Leonard	Marvin Hagler	W	12
1959	Gene Fullmer	Carmen Basilio	KO	14	1988	Tony Lopez	Rocky Lockridge	W	12
					1989	Roberto Duran	Iran Barkley	W	12
1960	Floyd Patterson	Ingemar Johansson	KO	5	1990	Julio Cesar Chavez	Meldrick Taylor	KO	12
1961	Joe Brown	Dave Charnley	W	15	1991	Robert Quiroga	Akeem Anifowoshe	W	12
1962	Joey Giardello	Henry Hank	W	10	1992	Riddick Bowe	Evander Holyfield	W	12
1963	Cassius Clay	Doug Jones	W	10	1993	Michael Carbajal	Humberto Gonzalez	KO	7
1964	Cassius Clay	Sonny Liston	KO	7	1994	Jorge Castro	John David Jackson	TKO	9
1965	Floyd Patterson	George Chuvalo	W	12	1995	Saman Sorjaturong	Chiquita Gonzalez	KO	7
1966	Jose Torres	Eddie Cotton	W	15	1996	Evander Holyfield	Mike Tyson	TKO	11
1967	Nino Benvenuti	Emile Griffith	W	15	1997	Arturo Gatti	Gabriel Ruelas	KO	5
1968	Dick Tiger	Frank DePaula	W	10	1998	Ivan Robinson	Arturo Gatti	W	10
1969	Joe Frazier	Jerry Quarry	KO	7	1999	Paulie Ayala	Johnny Tapia	W	12
1970	Carlos Monzon	Nino Benvenuti	KO	12	2000	Erik Morales	Marco Antonio Barrera	W	12
1971	Joe Frazier	Muhammad Ali	W	15					
1972	Bob Foster	Chris Finnegan	KO	14					
1973	George Foreman	Joe Frazier	KO	2					

Ring Magazine Fighter of the Year

First presented in 1928 by Nat Fleischer, who started *The Ring* magazine in 1922.

Multiple winners: Muhammad Ali (5); Joe Louis (4); Joe Frazier, Evander Holyfield and Rocky Marciano (3); Ezzard Charles, George Foreman, Marvin Hagler, Thomas Hearns, Ingemar Johansson, Sugar Ray Leonard, Tommy Loughran, Floyd Patterson, Sugar Ray Robinson, Barney Ross, Dick Tiger and Mike Tyson (2)

Year		Year		Year		Year	
1928	Gene Tunney	1943	Fred Apostoli	1959	Ingemar Johansson	1974	Muhammad Ali
1929	Tommy Loughran	1944	Beau Jack			1975	Muhammad Ali
1930	Max Schmeling	1945	Willie Pep	1960	Floyd Patterson	1976	George Foreman
1931	Tommy Loughran	1946	Tony Zale	1961	Joe Brown	1977	Carlos Zarate
1932	Jack Sharkey	1947	Gus Lesnevich	1962	Dick Tiger	1978	Muhammad Ali
1933	No award	1948	Ike Williams	1963	Cassius Clay	1979	Sugar Ray Leonard
1934	Tony Canzoneri	1949	Ezzard Charles	1964	Emile Griffith		
	& Barney Ross			1965	Dick Tiger	1980	Thomas Hearns
1935	Barney Ross	1950	Ezzard Charles	1966	No award	1981	Sugar Ray Leonard
1936	Joe Louis	1951	Sugar Ray Robinson	1967	Joe Frazier		& Salvador Sanchez
1937	Henry Armstrong	1952	Rocky Marciano	1968	Nino Benvenuti	1982	Larry Holmes
1938	Joe Louis	1953	Carl (Bobo) Olson	1969	Jose Napoles	1983	Marvin Hagler
1939	Joe Louis	1954	Rocky Marciano			1984	Thomas Hearns
		1955	Rocky Marciano	1970	Joe Frazier	1985	Donald Curry
1940	Billy Conn	1956	Floyd Patterson	1971	Joe Frazier		& Marvin Hagler
1941	Joe Louis	1957	Carmen Basilio	1972	Muhammad Ali	1986	Mike Tyson
1942	Sugar Ray Robinson	1958	Ingemar Johansson		& Carlos Monzon	1987	Evander Holyfield
				1973	George Foreman		

Year		Year		Year		Year	
1988	Mike Tyson	1992	Riddick Bowe	1996	Evander Holyfield	2000	Felix Trinidad
1989	Pernell Whitaker	1993	Michael Carbajal	1997	Evander Holyfield		
1990	Julio Cesar Chavez	1994	Roy Jones Jr.	1998	Floyd Mayweather Jr.		
1991	James Toney	1995	Oscar De La Hoya	1999	Paulie Ayala		

Note: Cassius Clay changed his name to Muhammad Ali after winning the heavyweight title in 1964.

All-Time Leaders

As compiled by *The Ring Record Book and Encyclopedia.*

Knockouts

	Division		Career	No
1	Archie Moore	Lt. Heavy	1936–63	130
2	Young Stribling	Heavy	1921–33	126
3	Billy Bird	Welter	1920–48	125
4	George Odwel	Welter	1930–45	114
5	Sugar Ray Robinson	Middle	1940–65	110
6	Sandy Saddler	Feather	1944–56	103
7	Sam Langford	Middle	1902–26	102
8	Henry Armstrong	Welter	1931–45	100
9	Jimmy Wilde	Fly	1911–23	98
10	Len Wickwar	Lt. Heavy	1928–47	93

Total Bouts

	Division		Career	No
1	Len Wickwar	Lt. Heavy	1928–47	463
2	Jack Britton	Welter	1905–30	350
3	Johnny Dundee	Feather	1910–32	333
4	Billy Bird	Welter	1920–48	318
5	George Marsden	n/a	1928–46	311
6	Maxie Rosenbloom	Lt. Heavy	1923–39	299
7	Harry Greb	Middle	1913–26	298
8	Young Stribling	Lt. Heavy	1921–33	286
9	Battling Levinsky	Lt. Heavy	1910–29	282
10	Ted (Kid) Lewis	Welter	1909–29	279

Former Champions Who Have Won Back Heavyweight Title

Only 11 times since 1892 has the heavyweight championship been lost by a fighter who was able to win it back. Eight men have done it, Evander Holyfield has done it three times and Muhammad Ali twice.

	Lost To	Won Back From		Lost To	Won Back From
Floyd Patterson	Johansson (1959)	Johansson (1960)	Mike Tyson	Douglas (1990)	Bruno (1996)
Muhammad Ali	Frazier (1971)	Foreman (1974)	Evander Holyfield	Moorer (1994)	Tyson (1996)
Muhammad Ali	L Spinks (1978)	L Spinks (1978)	Lennox Lewis	McCall (1994)	McCall (1997)
Tim Witherspoon	Thomas (1984)	Tubbs (1986)	Evander Holyfield	Lewis (1999)	Ruiz (2000)*
Evander Holyfield	Bowe (1992)	Bowe (1993)			
George Foreman	Ali (1974)	Moorer (1994)	*Moorer won the vacant IBF title in a fight with Axel		
Michael Moorer	Foreman (1994)	Schulz (1996)*	Schulz. Holyfield won the vacant WBA title in a fight with John Ruiz.		

Triple Champions

Fighters who have won widely-accepted world titles in more than two divisions. Henry Armstrong is the only fighter listed to hold three titles simultaneously. Note that (*) indicates title claimant.

Sugar Ray Leonard (5) WBC Welterweight (1979-80,80-82); WBA Jr. Middleweight (1981); WBC Middleweight (1987); WBC Super Middleweight (1988-90); WBC Light Heavyweight (1988).

Oscar De La Hoya (4) IBF Lightweight (1995-96); WBC Super Lightweight (1996-97); WBC Welterweight (1997-99); WBC Jr. Middleweight (2001–).

Roberto Duran (4) Lightweight (1972-79); WBC Welterweight (1980); WBA Jr. Middleweight (1983-84); WBC Middleweight (1989-90).

Leo Gamez (4) WBA Strawweight (1988-90); WBA Jr. Flyweight (1993-95); WBA Flyweight (1999); WBA Junior Bantamweight (2000-01).

Thomas Hearns (4) WBA Welterweight (1980-81); WBC Jr. Middleweight (1982-84); WBC Light Heavyweight (1987); WBA Light Heavyweight (1991); WBC Middleweight (1987-88).

Pernell Whitaker (4) IBF/WBC/WBA Lightweight (1989-92); IBF Jr. Welterweight (1992-93); WBC Welterweight (1993-97); WBC Jr. Middleweight (1995).

Alexis Arguello (3) WBA Featherweight (1974-77); WBC Jr. Lightweight (1978-80); WBC Lightweight (1981-83).

Henry Armstrong (3) Featherweight (1937-38); Welterweight (1938-40); Lightweight (1938-39).

Iran Barkley (3) WBC Middleweight (1988-89); IBF Super Middleweight (1992-93); WBA Light Heavyweight (1992).

Wilfredo Benitez (3) Jr. Welterweight (1976-79); Welterweight (1979); WBC Jr. Middleweight (1981-82).

Tony Canzoneri (3) Featherweight (1928); Lightweight (1930-33); Jr. Welterweight (1931-32,33).

Julio Cesar Chavez (3) WBC Jr. Lightweight (1984-87); WBA/WBC Lightweight (1987-89); WBC/IBF Jr. Welterweight (1989-91); WBC Jr. Welterweight (1991-94, 1994).

Jeff Fenech (3) IBF Bantamweight (1985); WBC Jr. Featherweight (1986-88); WBC Featherweight (1988-90).

Bob Fitzsimmons (3) Middleweight (1891-97); Light Heavyweight (1903-05); Heavyweight (1897-99).

Wilfredo Gomez (3) WBC Super Bantamweight (1977-83); WBC Featherweight (1984); WBA Jr. Lightweight (1985-86).

Emile Griffith (3) Welterweight (1961,62-63,63-66); Jr. Middleweight (1962-63); Middleweight (1966-67,67-68).

Roy Jones Jr. (3) IBF Middleweight (1993-94); IBF Super Middleweight (1994-96); WBC Light Heavyweight (1996, 1997–); WBA Light Heavyweight (1998–); IBF Light Heavyweight (1999–).

Mike McCallum (3) WBA Jr. Middleweight (1984-88); WBA Middleweight (1989-91); WBC Light Heavyweight (1994-95).

Terry McGovern (3) Bantamweight (1899-1900); Featherweight (1900-01); Lightweight* (1900-01).

Barney Ross (3) Lightweight (1933-35); Jr. Welterweight (1933-35); Welterweight (1934, 35-38).

Felix Trinidad (3) IBF/WBC Welterweight (1993-2000); WBA/IBF Jr. Middleweight (2000-01); WBA Middleweight (2001).

Wilfredo Vazquez (3) WBA Bantamweight (1987-88); WBA Jr. Featherweight (1992-95); WBA Featherweight (1996-98).

Miscellaneous Sports

Doug Swingley drives his team across the frozen Golovin Bay on their way to a victory at the 2001 Iditarod Trail Sled Dog Race.

AP/Wide World Photos

Too Good to be True

The Little League World Series was sadly tarnished by the Danny Almonte age scandal.

Dave Ryan *is a broadcaster for ESPN's Little League World Series coverage.*

When trying to tell just how old a little leaguer is, size isn't everything.

Last year, Julian Vandervelde from Davenport (Iowa) East Little League stood at 6-foot-2, 230 pounds. The 12-year-old was the biggest player in Little League World Series history.

This year, Peter Leslie of Bainbridge Island, Washington stood about 4-foot-5 and weighed 90 pounds. The vast disparity of kids' appearances at 11 or 12 years old can be stunning. Some are shaving every day, some are still waiting for their voices to change.

At this year's event, I interviewed Danny Almonte several times. With his manager Alberto Gonzalez translating, I simply could not tell how old Almonte was. He stood about 5-foot-7 and weighed about 125 pounds. His voice was half changed and he didn't have a five o'clock shadow. On the Little League grounds, when his team wasn't playing, his broken English improved dramatically when his young female fans approached for pictures and autographs. To me, he

seemed like any other little leaguer in Williamsport—enjoying the time of his life. For most players at the Little League World Series, Williamsport is the most fun they've ever had.

And did Almonte ever have fun. After his perfect game against Apopka, Fla., the Almonte bandwagon really began to roll.

It was an irresistible story: Kids growing up in the shadows of Yankee Stadium in the Bronx making it all the way to Williamsport. The "Baby Bombers," led by Almonte, were in every headline, every TV news show.

Almost overnight, Almonte became a national star. He thrived under the spotlight. He and his Rolando Paulino Little League teammates were permanently accessible. No matter how many times Gonzalez was asked about interviewing Almonte, the answer was always yes.

Orel Hershiser presented Almonte with an autographed photo and letter from big leaguer and fellow flame-thrower Randy Johnson. Harold Reynolds arranged a phone conversation with Ken Griffey Jr. We reported every move Almonte and

Danny Almonte *dominated the competition at the Little League World Series, throwing a perfect game, a one-hitter and a two-hitter in Williamsport, Penn.*

the Baby Bombers made. It was a golden story that floated into the U.S. championship game, before Apopka got revenge and beat the Bronx team without Almonte on the mound (Apopka later lost, 2-1, to Tokyo in the title game).

Saying Almonte was dominant on the mound is the understatement of this or last century. I called the play-by-play of his perfect game and was in the stands as a reporter watching his one-hitter over Oceanside, Calif. Very good hitters couldn't come close to catching up to his pitches.

His command of pitches, his poise on the mound and happy-go-lucky demeanor were the perfect combination. Almonte, who throws 75 mph (from a mound just 45 feet from home plate),

allowed a total of three hits in his three starts and struck out 46. The run he allowed in the last inning of his last game was the only run he gave up all summer. He seemed too good to be true. Sadly, he was.

After much debate, two birth certificates and vocal protests from his parents, it was ruled that Almonte was 14 years old and ineligible to compete. The Baby Bombers were disqualified.

The purity of the Little League World Series is tarnished for now. Still, I can't wait to return next August. There is one place that can bring back our belief that baseball is a wholesome game, a place where kids from all over the world come together.

That place is Williamsport, Penn.

CHESS

World Champions

Garry Kasparov became the youngest man to win the world chess championship when he beat fellow Russian Anatoly Karpov in 1985 at age 22. In 1993, Kasparov and then-#1 challenger Nigel Short of England broke away from the established International Chess Federation (FIDE) to form the Professional Chess Association (the PCA was disbanded in 1998). FIDE retaliated by stripping Kasparov of the world title and arranging a playoff that was won by Karpov, the former title-holder. Karpov successfully defended the FIDE title several times before failing to show up for the 1999 FIDE World Championship Tournament that was won by Alexander Khalifman. Indian Viswanathan Anand, who won the 2000 FIDE World Championship, is currently the FIDE World Champion.

In his first title defense in five years, Kasparov faced world #2 Vladimir Kramnik for 16 matches in the unofficial (though more widely recognized) world championship from Oct. 8–Nov. 4, 2000 in London. The 25-year-old Kramnik defeated the longtime world champion 8½–6½ in a stunning result. Kasparov failed to win a single game, but despite the loss is still the top-ranked player in the world. Kramnik is scheduled to defend his title as world champion in October 2002.

Years		Years		Years	
1866-94	Wilhelm Steinitz, Austria	1957-58	Vassily Smyslov, USSR	1975-85	Anatoly Karpov, USSR
1894-1921	Emanuel Lasker, Germany	1958-59	Mikhail Botvinnik, USSR	1985-2000	Garry Kasparov, RUS
1921-27	Jose Capablanca, Cuba	1960-61	Mikhail Tal, USSR	2000–	Vladimir Kramnik, RUS
1927-35	Alexander Alekhine, France	1961-63	Mikhail Botvinnik, USSR	*Fischer defaulted the championship
1935-37	Max Euwe, Holland	1963-69	Tigran Petrosian, USSR	in 1975.	
1937-46	Alexander Alekhine, France	1969-72	Boris Spassky, USSR		
1948-57	Mikhail Botvinnik, USSR	1972-75	Bobby Fischer, USA*		

U.S. Champions

The 2001 United States chess champion will be crowned in Seattle when the tournament takes place on January 5-13, 2002.

Years		Years		Years	
1857-71	Paul Morphy	1954-57	Arthur Bisguier	1986	Yasser Seirawan
1871-76	George Mackenzie	1957-61	Bobby Fischer	1987	Joel Benjamin
1876-80	James Mason	1961-62	Larry Evans		& Nick DeFirmian
1880-89	George Mackenzie	1962-68	Bobby Fischer	1988	Michael Wilder
1889-90	Samuel Lipschutz	1968-69	Larry Evans	1989	Roman Dzindzichashvili,
1890	Jackson Showalter	1969-72	Samuel Reshevsky		Stuart Rachels
1890-91	Max Judd	1972-73	Robert Byrne		& Yasser Seirawan
1891-92	Jackson Showalter	1973-74	Lubomir Kavalek	1990	Lev Alburt
1892-94	Samuel Lipschutz		& John Grefe	1991	Gata Kamsky
1894	Jackson Showalter	1974-77	Walter Browne	1992	Patrick Wolff
1894-95	Albert Hodges	1978-80	Lubomir Kabalek	1993	Alexander Shabalov
1895-97	Jackson Showalter	1980-81	Larry Evans,		& Alex Yermolinsky
1897-1906	Harry Pillsbury		& Walter Browne	1994	Boris Gulko
1906-09	Vacant		Larry Christiansen	1995	Alexander Ivanov
1909-36	Frank Marshall	1981-83	Walter Browne	1996	Alexander Yermolinsky
1936-44	Samuel Reshevsky		& Yasser Seirawan	1997	Joel Benjamin
1944-46	Arnold Denker	1983	Roman Dzindzichashvili,	1998	Nick de Firmian
1946-48	Samuel Reshevsky		Larry Christiansen	1999	Boris Gulko
1948-51	Herman Steiner		& Walter Browne	2000	Joel Benjamin, Yasser Seirawan & Alex Shabalov
1951-54	Larry Evans	1984-85	Lev Alburt		

DOGS

Iditarod Trail Sled Dog Race

In 2001, Doug Swingley became only the second back-to-back-to-back Iditarod Champion in history, cruising to victory in nine days, 19 hours, 55 minutes and 50 seconds. When Swingley crossed the burled arch marking the finish line on Front Street in Nome, Alaska he tied Susan Butcher at second place on the list of most Iditarod titles with four. Besting runner-up Linwood Fielder by over eight hours, Swingley earned $63,000 and the keys to a new $39,000 pick-up truck.

Seventy-nine teams began the race on March 3 in Anchorage, 57 would finish. Swingley credited good dog breeding and a serious training regimen for his success.

In even-numbered years the trail follows the 1,151-mile Northern Route, while in odd-numbered years, it takes a slightly different 1,161-mile Southern Route.

Multiple winners: Rick Swenson (5); Susan Butcher and Doug Swingley (4); Martin Buser and Jeff King (3).

Year		Elapsed Time	Year		Elapsed Time
1973	Dick Wilmarth	20 days, 00:49:41	1985	Libby Riddles	18 days, 00:20:17
1974	Carl Huntington	20 days, 15:02:07	1986	Susan Butcher	11 days, 15:06:00
1975	Emmitt Peters	14 days, 14:43:45	1987	Susan Butcher	11 days, 02:05:13
1976	Gerald Riley	18 days, 22:58:17	1988	Susan Butcher	11 days, 11:41:40
1977	Rick Swenson	16 days, 16:27:13	1989	Joe Runyan	11 days, 05:24:34
1978	Dick Mackey	14 days, 18:52:24	1990	Susan Butcher	11 days, 01:53:23
1979	Rick Swenson	15 days, 10:37:47	1991	Rick Swenson	12 days, 16:34:39
1980	Joe May	14 days, 07:11:51	1992	Martin Buser	10 days, 19:17:00
1981	Rick Swenson	12 days, 08:45:02	1993	Jeff King	10 days, 15:38:15
1982	Rick Swenson	16 days, 04:40:10	1994	Martin Buser	10 days, 13:02:39
1983	Rick Mackey	12 days, 14:10:44	1995	Doug Swingley	9 days, 02:42:19
1984	Dean Osmar	12 days, 15:07:33	1996	Jeff King	9 days, 05:43:13

Year		Elapsed Time	Year		Elapsed Time
1997	Martin Buser	9 days, 08:31:45	2000	Doug Swingley	9 days, 00:58:06*
1998	Jeff King	9 days, 05:52:26	2001	Doug Swingley	9 days, 19:55:50
1999	Doug Swingley	9 days, 14:31:07	*Race record.		

Westminster Kennel Club

Best in Show

Best in Show at the 125th annual All-Breed Dog Show of the Westminster Kennel Club held February 12-13, 2001, was the Bichon Frise Ch. Special Times Just Right. Known at home as J.R., the winner of the non-sporting group is an all white beauty shown by Scott Sommer of Houston, Texas, and owned by Mrs. Cecelia Ruggles of Ridgefield, Conn. The 3-year-old male, who was selected among 2,500 dogs in 158 breeds, was bred by Eleanor A. McDonald and Flavio Werneck of Brazil. After winning best-in-show honors J.R. waved to the horde of photographers with both front legs.

The Westminster show is the most prestigious dog show in the country, and one of America's oldest annual sporting events.

Multiple winners: Ch. Warren Remedy (3); Ch. Chinoe's Adamant James, Ch. Comejo Wycollar Boy, Ch. Flornell Spicy Piece of Halleston; Ch. Matford Vic, Ch. My Own Brucie, Ch. Pendley Calling of Blarney, Ch. Rancho Dobe's Storm (2).

Year		Breed	Year		Breed
1907	Warren Remedy	Fox Terrier	1955	Kippax Fearnought	Bulldog
1908	Warren Remedy	Fox Terrier	1956	Wilber White Swan	Toy Poodle
1909	Warren Remedy	Fox Terrier	1957	Shirkhan of Grandeur	Afghan Hound
1910	Sabine Rarebit	Fox Terrier	1958	Puttencove Promise	Standard Poodle
1911	Tickle Em Jock	Scottish Terrier	1959	Fontclair Festoon	Miniature Poodle
1912	Kenmore Sorceress	Airedale	1960	Chick T'Sun of Caversham	Pekingese
1913	Strathway Prince Albert	Bulldog	1961	Cappoquin Little Sister	Toy Poodle
1914	Brentwood Hero	Old English Sheepdog	1962	Elfinbrook Simon	W. Highland Terrier
1915	Matford Vic	Old English Sheepdog	1963	Wakefield's Black Knight	English Springer Spaniel
1916	Matford Vic	Old English Sheepdog	1964	Courtenay Fleetfoot of Pennyworth	Whippet
1917	Comejo Wycollar Boy	Fox Terrier	1965	Carmichaels Fanfare	Scottish Terrier
1918	Haymarket Faultless	Bull Terrier	1966	Zeloy Mooremaides Magic	Fox Terrier
1919	Briergate Bright Beauty	Airedale	1967	Bardene Bingo	Scottish Terrier
1920	Comejo Wycollar Boy	Fox Terrier	1968	Stingray of Derryabah	Lakeland Terrier
1921	Midkiff Seductive	Cocker Spaniel	1969	Glamoor Good News	Skye Terrier
1922	Boxwood Barkentine	Airedale	1970	Arriba's Prima Donna	Boxer
1923	No best-in-show award		1971	Chinoe's Adamant James	E.S. Spaniel
1924	Barberryhill Bootlegger	Sealyham	1972	Chinoe's Adamant James	E.S. Spaniel
1925	Governor Moscow	Pointer	1973	Acadia Command Performance	Standard Poodle
1926	Signal Circuit	Fox Terrier	1974	Gretchenhof Columbia River	German SH Pointer
1927	Pinegrade Perfection	Sealyham	1975	Sir Lancelot of Barvan	Old Eng. Sheepdog
1928	Talavera Margaret	Fox Terrier	1976	Jo Ni's Red Baron of Crofton	Lakeland Terrier
1929	Land Loyalty of Bellhaven	Collie	1977	Dersade Bobby's Girl	Sealyham
1930	Pendley Calling of Blarney	Fox Terrier	1978	Cede Higgens	Yorkshire Terrier
1931	Pendley Calling of Blarney	Fox Terrier	1979	Oak Tree's Irishtocrat	Irish Water Spaniel
1932	Nancolleth Markable	Pointer	1980	Sierra Cinnar	Siberian Husky
1933	Warland Protector of Shelterock	Airedale	1981	Dhandy Favorite Woodchuck	Pug
1934	Flornell Spicy Bit of Halleston	Fox Terrier	1982	St. Aubrey Dragonora of Elsdon	Pekingese
1935	Nunsoe Duc de la Terrace of Blakeen	Stan. Poodle	1983	Kabik's The Challenger	Afghan Hound
1936	St. Margaret Magnificent of Clairedale	Sealyham	1984	Seaward's Blackbeard	Newfoundland
1937	Flornell Spicy Bit of Halleston	Fox Terrier	1985	Braeburn's Close Encounter	Scottish Terrier
1938	Daro of Maridor	English Setter	1986	Marjetta National Acclaim	Pointer
1939	Ferry v.Rauhfelsen of Giralda	Doberman	1987	Covy Tucker Hill's Manhattan	German Shepherd
1940	My Own Brucie	Cocker Spaniel	1988	Great Elms Prince Charming II	Pomeranian
1941	My Own Brucie	Cocker Spaniel	1989	Royal Tudor's Wild As The Wind	Doberman
1942	Wolvey Pattern of Edgerstoune	W. Highland Terrier	1990	Wendessa Crown Prince	Pekingese
1943	Pitter Patter of Piperscroft	Miniature Poodle	1991	Whisperwind on a Carousel	Stan. Poodle
1944	Flornell Rarebit of Twin Ponds	Welsh Terrier	1992	Lonesome Dove	Fox Terrier
1945	Shieling's Signature	Scottish Terrier	1993	Salilyn's Condor	E.S. Spaniel
1946	Hetherington Model Rhythm	Fox Terrier	1994	Chidley Willum	Norwich Terrier
1947	Warlord of Mazelaine	Boxer	1995	Gaelforce Post Script	Scottish Terrier
1948	Rock Ridge Night Rocket	Bedling. Terrier	1996	Clussex Country Sunrise	Clumber Spaniel
1949	Mazelaine's Zazarac Brandy	Boxer	1997	Parsifal di Casa Netzer	Standard Schnauzer
1950	Walsing Winning Trick of Edgerstoune	Scot. Terrier	1998	Fairewood Frolic	Norwich Terrier
1951	Bang Away of Sirrah Crest	Boxer	1999	Loteki's Supernatural Being	Papillon
1952	Rancho Dobe's Storm	Doberman	2000	Salilyn 'N Erin's Shameless	E.S. Spaniel
1953	Rancho Dobe's Storm	Doberman	2001	Special Times Just Right	Bichon Frise
1954	Carmor's Rise and Shine	Cocker Spaniel			

FISHING

IGFA All-Tackle World Records

All-tackle records are maintained for the heaviest fish of any species caught on any line up to 130-lb (60 kg) class and certified by the International Game Fish Association. Records logged through Aug. 20, 2001. **Address:** 300 Gulf Stream Way, Dania Beach, Fla. 33004. **Telephone:** (954) 927-2628.

FRESHWATER FISH

Species	Lbs-Oz	Where Caught	Date	Angler
Barramundi	83-7	N. Queensland, Australia	Sept. 23, 1999	David Powell
Bass, Guadalupe	3-11	Lake Travis, TX	Sept. 25, 1983	Allen Christenson Jr.
Bass, largemouth	22-4	Montgomery Lake, GA	June 2, 1932	George W. Perry
Bass, redeye	8-12	Apalachicola River, FL	Jan. 28, 1995	Carl W. Davis
Bass, Roanoke	1-5	Nottoway River, VA	Nov. 11, 1991	Tom Elkins
Bass, rock	3-0	York River, Ontario	Aug. 1, 1974	Peter Gulgin
Bass, smallmouth	10-14	Dale Hollow, TN	Apr. 24, 1969	John T. Gorman
Bass, spotted	9-9	Pine Flat Lake, CA	Oct. 12, 1996	Kirk Sakamoto
Bass, striped (landlocked)	67-8	O'Neill Forebay, San Luis, CA	May 7, 1992	Hank Ferguson
Bass, Suwannee	3-14	Suwannee River, FL	Mar. 2, 1985	Ronnie Everett
Bass, white	6-13	Lake Orange, VA	July 31, 1989	Ronald L. Sprouse
Bass, whiterock	27-5	Greers Ferry Lake, AR	Apr. 24, 1997	Jerald C. Shaum
Bass, yellow	2-9	Duck River, TN	Feb. 27, 1998	John T. Chappell
Bass, yellow (hybrid)	3-5	Big Cypress Bayou, TX	Mar. 27, 1991	Patrick Collin Myers
Bluegill	4-12	Ketona Lake, AL	Apr. 9, 1950	T.S. Hudson
Bowfin	21-8	Florence, SC	Jan. 29, 1980	Robert L. Harmon
Buffalo, bigmouth	70-5	Bussey Brake, Bastrop, LA	Apr. 21, 1980	Delbert Sisk
Buffalo, black	63-6	Mississippi River, IA	Aug. 14, 1999	Jim Winters
Buffalo, smallmouth	82-3	Athens Lake, AL	June 6, 1993	Randy Collins
Bullhead, black	7-7	Mill Pond, NY	Aug. 25, 1993	Kevin Kelly
Bullhead, brown	6-1	Waterford, NY	Apr. 26, 1998	Bobby Triplett
Bullhead, yellow	4-4	Mormon Lake, AZ	May 11, 1984	Emily Williams
Burbot	18-11	Angenmanelren, Sweden	Oct. 22, 1996	Margit Agren
Carp, bighead	20-0	Mentro, MO	July 26, 1999	Rick Hayden
Carp, black	40-12	Chiba, Japan	Apr. 1, 2000	Kenichi Hosoi
Carp, common	75-11	St. Cassien, France	May 21, 1987	Leo van der Gugten
Carp, crucian	5-1	Kaltersee, Italy	July 16, 1997	Jorg Marquand
Catfish, blue	111-0	Wheeler's Reservoir, TN	July 5, 1996	William McKinley
Catfish, channel	58-0	Santee-Cooper Res., SC	July 7, 1964	W.B. Whaley
Catfish, flathead	123-9	Elk City Reservoir, KS	Mar. 14, 1998	Ken Paulie
Catfish, flatwhiskered	9-4	Rio Paraquai, Brazil	Sept. 11, 1996	Cavour Pieranti
Catfish, gilded	85-8	Amazon River, Brazil	Nov. 15, 1986	Gilberto Fernandes
Catfish, redtail	97-7	Amazon River, Brazil	July 16, 1988	Gilberto Fernandes
Catfish, sharptoothed	79-5	Orange River, South Africa	Dec. 5, 1992	Hennie Moller
Catfish, white	21-8	East Lyme, CT	Apr. 22, 2001	Thomas Urquahart
Char, Arctic	32-9	Tree River, Canada	July 30, 1981	Jeffery Ward
Crappie, black	4-8	Kerr Lake, VA	Mar. 1, 1981	L. Carl Herring Jr.
Crappie, white	5-3	Enid Dam, MS	July 31, 1957	Fred L. Bright
Dolly Varden	19-4	Unnamed River, AK	Sept. 4, 1998	Gary D. Ordway
Dorado	51-5	Corrientes, Argentina	Sept. 27, 1984	Armando Giudice
Drum, freshwater	54-8	Nickajack Lake, TN	Apr. 20, 1972	Benny E. Hull
Gar, alligator	279-0	Rio Grande, TX	Dec. 2, 1951	Bill Valverde
Gar, Florida	15-14	Flagler Beach, FL	Oct. 3, 1999	Randy Michael Carmean
Gar, longnose	50-5	Trinity River, TX	July 30, 1954	Townsend Miller
Gar, shortnose	5-12	Rend Lake, IL	July 16, 1995	Donna K. Willmart
Gar, spotted	9-12	Lake Mexia, TX	Apr. 7, 1994	Rick Rivard
Goldfish	6-10	Lake Hodges, CA	Apr. 17, 1996	Florentino M. Abena
Grayling, Arctic	5-15	Katseyedie River, N.W.T.	Aug. 16, 1967	Jeanne P. Branson
Inconnu	53-0	Pah River, AK	Aug. 20, 1986	Lawrence E. Hudnall
Kokanee	9-6	Okanagan Lake, Brit. Columbia	June 18, 1988	Norm Kuhn
Muskellunge	67-8	Hayward, WI	July 24, 1949	Cal Johnson
Muskellunge, tiger	51-3	Lac Vieux-Desert, WI-MI	July 16, 1919	John A. Knobla
Peacock, butterfly	10-8	Bolivar State, Brazil	Jan. 6, 2000	Antonio Campa G.
Peacock, speckled	27-0	Rio Negro, Brazil	Dec. 4, 1994	Gerald (Doc) Lawson
Perch, Nile	230-0	Lake Nasser, Egypt	Dec. 20, 2000	William Toth
Perch, white	4-12	Messalonskee Lake, ME	June 4, 1949	Mrs. Earl Small
Perch, yellow	4-3	Bordentown, NJ	May, 1865	Dr. C.C. Abbot
Pickerel, chain	9-6	Homerville, GA	Feb. 17, 1961	Baxley McQuaig Jr.
Pickerel, grass	1-0	Dewart Lake, IN	June 9, 1990	Mike Berg
Pickerel, redfin	2-4	St. Pauls, NC	June 27, 1997	Edward C. Davis
Pike, northern	55-1	Lake of Grefeern, Germany	Oct. 16, 1986	Lothar Louis
Redhorse, greater	9-3	Salmon River, Pulaski, NY	May 11, 1985	Jason Wilson

Species	Lbs-Oz	Where Caught	Date	Angler
Redhorse, silver	11-7	Plum Creek, WI	May 29, 1985	Neal D.G. Long
Salmon, Atlantic	79-2	Tana River, Norway	1928	Henrik Henriksen
Salmon, chinook	97-4	Kenai River, AK	May 17, 1985	Les Anderson
Salmon, chum	35-0	Edye Pass, Brit. Columbia	July 11, 1995	Todd Johansson
Salmon, coho	33-4	Salmon River, Pulaski, NY	Sept. 27, 1989	Jerry Lifton
Salmon, pink	13-1	St. Mary's River, Ontario	Sept. 23, 1992	Ray Higaki
Salmon, sockeye	15-3	Kenai River, AK	Aug. 9, 1987	Stan Roach
Sauger	8-12	Lake Sakakawea, ND	Oct. 6, 1971	Mike Fischer
Shad, American	11-4	Conn. River, S. Hadley, MA	May 19, 1986	Bob Thibodo
Shad, gizzard	4-6	Lake Michigan, IN	Mar. 2, 1996	Mike Berg
Sturgeon, lake	168-0	Georgian Bay, Canada	May 29, 1982	Edward Paszkowski
Sturgeon, white	468-0	Benicia, CA	July 9, 1983	Joey Pallotta 3rd
Tigerfish, giant	97-0	Zaire River, Kinshasa, Zaire	July 9, 1988	Raymond Houtmans
Tilapia	6-5	Lake Arsenal, Costa Rica	Feb. 10, 1995	Marvin C. Smith
Trout, Apache	5-3	White Mountain, AZ	May 29, 1991	John Baldwin
Trout, brook	14-8	Nipigon River, Ontario	July, 1916	Dr. W.J. Cook
Trout, brown	40-4	Little Red River, AR	May 9, 1992	Rip Collins
Trout, bull	32-0	Lake Pond Orielle, ID	Oct. 27, 1949	N.L. Higgins
Trout, cutthroat	41-0	Pyramid Lake, NV	Dec., 1925	John Skimmerhorn
Trout, golden	11-0	Cooks Lake, WY	Aug. 5, 1948	Charles S. Reed
Trout, lake	72-0	Great Bear Lake, N.W.T.	Aug. 19, 1995	Lloyd E. Bull
Trout, rainbow	42-2	Bell Island, AK	June 22, 1970	David Robert White
Trout, tiger	20-13	Lake Michigan, WI	Aug. 12, 1978	Peter M. Friedland
Walleye	25-0	Old Hickory Lake, TN	Aug. 2, 1960	Mabry Harper
Warmouth	2-7	Guess Lake, Holt, FL	Oct. 19, 1985	Tony D. Dempsey
Whitefish, lake	14-6	Meaford, Ontario	May 21, 1984	Dennis M. Laycock
Whitefish, mountain	5-8	Elbow River, Manitoba	Aug. 1, 1995	Randy G. Woo
Whitefish, round	6-0	Putahow River, Manitoba	June 14, 1984	Allan J. Ristori
Zander	25-2	Trosa, Sweden	June 12, 1986	Harry Lee Tennison

SALTWATER FISH

Species	Lbs-Oz	Where Caught	Date	Angler
Albacore	88-2	Gran Canaria, Canary Islands	Nov. 19, 1977	Siegfried Dickemann
Amberjack, greater	155-12	Challenger Bank, Bermuda	Aug. 16, 1992	Larry Trott
Angelfish, gray	4-0	S.Beach Jetty, Miami, FL	July 12, 1999	Rene G. de Dios
Barracuda, great	85-0	Christmas Is., Rep. of Kiribati	Apr. 11, 1992	John W. Helfrich
Barracuda, Mexican	21-0	Phantom Island, Costa Rica	Mar. 27, 1987	E. Greg Kent
Barracuda, pickhandle	25-5	Scottburgh, South Africa	July 3, 1996	Demetrios Stamatis
Bass, barred sand	13-3	Huntington Beach, CA	Aug. 29, 1988	Robert Halul
Bass, black sea	10-4	Virginia Beach, VA	Jan. 1, 2000	Allan P. Paschall
Bass, European	20-14	Cap d'Agde, France	Sept. 8, 1999	Robert Mari
Bass, giant sea	563-8	Anacapa Island, CA	Aug. 20, 1968	J.D. McAdam Jr.
Bass, striped	78-8	Atlantic City, NJ	Sept. 21, 1982	Albert R. McReynolds
Bluefish	31-12	Hatteras, NC	Jan. 30, 1972	James M. Hussey
Bonefish	19-0	Zululand, South Africa	May 26, 1962	Brian W. Batchelor
Bonito, Atlantic	18-4	Faial Island, Azores	July 8, 1953	D. Gama Higgs
Bonito, Pacific	21-3	Malibu, CA	July 30, 1978	Gino M. Picciolo
Cabezon	23-0	Juan de Fuca Strait, WA	Aug. 4, 1990	Wesley Hunter
Cobia	135-9	Shark Bay, W. Australia	July 9, 1985	Peter W. Goulding
Cod, Atlantic	98-12	Isle of Shoals, NH	June 8, 1969	Alphonse Bielevich
Cod, Pacific	35-0	Unalaska Bay, AK	June 16, 1999	Jim Johnson
Conger	133-4	South Devon, England	June 5, 1995	Vic Evans
Dolphinfish	88-0	Highbourne Cay, Bahamas	May 5, 1998	Richard D. Evans
Drum, black	113-1	Lewes, DE	Sept. 15, 1975	Gerald M. Townsend
Drum, red	94-2	Avon, NC	Nov. 7, 1984	David G. Deuel
Eel, American	9-4	Cape May, NJ	Nov. 9, 1995	Jeff Pennick
Eel, marbled	36-1	Durban, South Africa	June 10, 1984	Ferdie van Nooten
Flounder, southern	20-9	Nassau Sound, FL	Dec. 23, 1983	Larenza Mungin
Flounder, summer	22-7	Montauk, NY	Sept. 15, 1975	Charles Nappi
Grouper, Warsaw	436-12	Gulf of Mexico, Destin, FL	Dec. 22, 1985	Steve Haeusler
Haddock	14-15	Saltraumen, Germany	Aug. 15, 1997	Heike Neblinger
Halibut, Atlantic	355-6	Valevag, Norway	Oct. 20, 1997	Odd Arve Gunderstad
Halibut, California	58-9	Santa Rosa Island, CA	June 26, 1999	Roger W. Borrell
Halibut, Pacific	459-0	Dutch Harbor, AK	June 11, 1996	Jack Tragis
Jack, almaco (Pacific)	132-0	La Paz, Baja Calif., Mexico	July 21, 1964	Howard H. Hahn
Jack, crevalle	57-14	Southwest Pass, LA	Aug. 15, 1997	Leon D. Richard
Jack, horse-eye	29-8	Ascencion Island, South Atlantic	May 28, 1993	Mike Hanson
Jewfish	680-0	Fernandina Beach, FL	May 20, 1961	Lynn Joyner
Kawakawa	29-0	Clarion Island, Mexico	Dec. 17, 1986	Ronald Nakamura
Lingcod	69-0	Langara Is., Brit. Columbia	June 16, 1992	Murray M. Romer
Mackerel, cero	17-2	Islamorada, FL	Apr. 5, 1986	G. Michael Mills

FISHING (Cont.)

Species	Lbs-Oz	Where Caught	Date	Angler
Mackerel, king	.93-0	San Juan, Puerto Rico	Apr. 18, 1999	Steve Perez Graulau
Mackerel, Spanish	.13-0	Ocracoke Inlet, NC	Nov. 4, 1987	Robert Cranton
Marlin, Atlantic blue	1402-2	Vitoria, Brazil	Feb. 29, 1992	Paulo R.A. Amorim
Marlin, black	1560-0	Cabo Blanco, Peru	Aug. 4, 1953	A.C. Glassell Jr.
Marlin, Pacific blue	1376-0	Kaaiwi Point, Kona, HI	May 31, 1982	Jay W. deBeaubien
Marlin, striped	494-0	Tutakaka, New Zealand	Jan. 16, 1986	Bill Boniface
Marlin, white	181-14	Vitoria, Brazil	Dec. 8, 1979	Evandro Luiz Coser
Permit	.56-2	Ft. Lauderdale, FL	June 30, 1997	Thomas Sebestyen
Pollock	.50-0	Salstraumen, Norway	Nov. 30, 1996	Thor-Magnus Ukang
Pollack, European	.27-6	Salcombe, Devon, England	Jan. 16, 1986	Robert S. Milkins
Pompano, African	.50-8	Daytona Beach, FL	Apr. 21, 1990	Tom Sargent
Roosterfish	114-0	La Paz, Baja Calif., Mexico	June 1, 1960	Abe Sackheim
Runner, blue	.11-2	Dauphin Island, AL	June 28, 1997	Stacey M. Moiren
Runner, rainbow	.37-9	Clarion Island, Mexico	Nov. 21, 1991	Tom Pfleger
Sailfish, Atlantic	141-1	Luanda, Angola	Feb. 19, 1994	Alfredo de Sousa Neves
Sailfish, Pacific	221-0	Santa Cruz,Is., Ecuador	Feb. 12, 1947	C.W. Stewart
Seabass, white	.83-12	San Felipe, Mexico	Mar. 31, 1953	L.C. Baumgardner
Seatrout, spotted	.17-7	Ft. Pierce, FL	May 11, 1995	Craig F. Carson
Shark, blue	454-0	Martha's Vineyard, MA	July 19, 1996	Pete Bergin
Shark, great white	2664-0	Ceduna, S. Australia	Apr. 21, 1959	Alfred Dean
Shark, Greenland	1708-9	Trondheimsfjord, Norway	Oct. 18, 1987	Terje Nordtvedt
Shark, hammerhead	991-0	Sarasota, FL	May 30, 1982	Allen Ogle
Shark, shortfin mako	1115-0	Black River, Mauritius	Nov. 16, 1988	Patrick Guillanton
Shark, porbeagle	507-0	Pentland Firth, Scotland	Mar. 9, 1993	Christopher Bennet
Shark, bigeye thresher	802-0	Tutukaka, New Zealand	Feb. 8, 1981	Dianne North
Shark, tiger	1780-0	Cherry Grove, SC	June 14, 1964	Walter Maxwell
Snapper, cubera	121-8	Cameron, LA	July 5, 1982	Mike Hebert
Snapper, red	.50-4	Gulf of Mexico, LA	June 23, 1996	Capt. Doc Kennedy
Snook	.57-12	Rio Naranjo, Quepos, Costa Rica	Aug. 23, 1991	George Beck
Spearfish, Mediterranean	.90-13	Madeira Island, Portugal	June 2, 1980	Joseph Larkin
Swordfish	1182-0	Iquique, Chile	May 7, 1953	Louis Marron
Tarpon	283-4	Sherbro Is., Sierra Leone	Apr. 16, 1991	Yvon Victor Sebag
Tautog	.25-0	Ocean City, NJ	Jan. 20, 1998	Anthony R. Monica
Tuna, Atlantic bigeye	392-6	Gran Canaria, Puerto Rico	July 25, 1996	Dieter Vogel
Tuna, blackfin	.45-8	Key West, FL	May 4, 1996	Sam J. Burnett
Tuna, bluefin	1496-0	Aulds Cove, Nova Scotia	Oct. 26, 1979	Ken Fraser
Tuna, longtail	.79-2	Montague Is., NSW, Australia	Apr. 12, 1982	Tim Simpson
Tuna, Pacific bigeye	435-0	Cabo Blanco, Peru	Apr. 17, 1957	Dr. Russell Lee
Tuna, skipjack	.45-4	Flathead Bank, Mexico	Nov. 16, 1996	Brian Evans
Tuna, southern bluefin	348-5	Whakatane, New Zealand	Jan. 16, 1981	Rex Wood
Tuna, yellowfin	388-12	San Benedicto Island, Mexico	Apr. 1, 1977	Curt Wiesenhutter
Tunny, little	.35-2	Cape de Garde, Algeria	Dec. 14, 1988	Jean Yves Chatard
Wahoo	158-8	Loreto, Baja Calif., Mexico	June 10, 1996	Keith Winter
Weakfish	.19-2	Jones Beach, Long Island, NY	Oct. 11, 1984	Dennis R. Rooney
	19-2	Delaware Bay, DE	May 20, 1989	William E. Thomas

B.A.S.S. Masters Classic

Kevin Van Dam of Kalamazoo, Mich., became the 31st annual B.A.S.S. Masters Classic champion on the waters of the Louisiana Delta in New Orleans. The three-time B.A.S.S. Angler of the Year won the 2001 title by weighing in 15 fish for a total of 32 pounds, five ounces. Van Dam earned the $100,000 top prize using a half-black, blue and purple Strike King Premier Elite jig and a Wild Thing soft-plastic creative-type lure, both on a 25 pound test. Van Dam, who bested Scott Rook of Arkansas by one pound, one ounce, exclaimed, "This is so awesome. Except for when my kids were born, this is probably the happiest moment of my life."

The B.A.S.S. Masters Classic is fishing's version of the Masters golf tournament. Invitees to the three-day event include the 25 top-ranked pros on the B.A.S.S. tour and the five top-ranked anglers from each BASSMASTER Invitational circuit. Anglers may weigh only seven bass per day and each bass must be at least 12 inches long. Competitors are allowed only seven rods and reels and are limited to the tackle they can pack into two tournament-approved tackleboxes. Only artificial lures are permitted. The first Classic, held at Lake Mead, Nev. in 1971, was a $10,000 winner-take-all event.

Multiple winners: Rick Clunn (4); George Cochran, Bobby Murray and Hank Parker (2).

Year		Weight	Year		Weight
1971	Bobby Murray, Hot Springs, Ark	.43-11	1981	Stanley Mitchell, Fitzgerald, Ga	.35-2
1972	Don Butler, Tulsa, Okla	.38-11	1982	Paul Elias, Laurel, Miss	.32-8
1973	Rayo Breckenridge, Paragould, Ark	.52-8	1983	Larry Nixon, Hemphill, Tex	.18-1
1974	Tommy Martin, Hemphill, Tex	.33-7	1984	Rick Clunn, Montgomery, Tex	.75-9
1975	Jack Hains, Rayne, La	.45-4	1985	Jack Chancellor, Phenix City, Ala	.45-0
1976	Rick Clunn, Montgomery, Tex	.59-15	1986	Charlie Reed, Broken Bow, Okla	.23-9
1977	Rick Clunn, Montgomery, Tex	.27-7	1987	George Cochran, N. Little Rock, Ark	.15-5
1978	Bobby Murray, Nashville, Tenn	.37-9	1988	Guido Hibdon, Gravois Mills, Mo	.28-8
1979	Hank Parker, Clover, S.C	.31-0	1989	Hank Parker, Denver, N.C	.31-6
1980	Bo Dowden, Natchitoches, La	.54-10	1990	Rick Clunn, Montgomery, Tex	.34-5

Year		Weight	Year		Weight
1991	Ken Cook, Meers, Okla 33-2		1997	Dion Hibdon, Stover, Mo. 34-13	
1992	Robert Hamilton Jr., Brandon, Miss..........59-6		1998	Denny Brauer, Camdenton, Mo. 46-3	
1993	David Fritts, Lexington, N.C. 48-6		1999	Davy Hite, Prosperity, S.C................55-10	
1994	Bryan Kerchal, Newtown, Conn 36-7		2000	Woo Daves, Spring Grove, Va.............27-13	
1995	Mark Davis, Mount Ida, Ark...............47-14		2001	Kevin Van Dam, Kalamazoo, Mich. 32-5	
1996	George Cochran, Hot Springs, Ark.........31-14				

LITTLE LEAGUE BASEBALL

World Series

Played annually in late August in Williamsport, Penn. at Original Field in Williamsport, Penn. from 1947-1958 and at Howard J. Lamade Stadium since 1959 and also at newly constructed Volunteer Stadium starting in 2001.

Multiple winners: Taiwan (16); California and Japan (5); Connecticut, New Jersey and Pennsylvania (4); Mexico (3); New York, South Korea, Texas and Venezuela (2).

Year	Winner	Score	Loser	Year	Winner	Score	Loser
1947	Williamsport, PA	16-7	Lock Haven, PA	1975	Lakewood, NJ	4-3	*Tampa, FL
1948	Lock Haven, PA	6-5	St. Petersburg, FL	1976	Tokyo, Japan	10-3	Campbell, CA
1949	Hammonton, NJ	5-0	Pensacola, FL	1977	Li-Teh, Taiwan	7-2	El Cajon, CA
1950	Houston, TX	2-1	Bridgeport, CT	1978	Pin-Tung, Taiwan	11-1	Danville, CA
1951	Stamford, CT	3-0	Austin, TX	1979	Hsien, Taiwan	2-1	Campbell, CA
1952	Norwalk, CT	4-3	Monongahela, PA	1980	Hua Lian, Taiwan	4-3	Tampa, FL
1953	Birmingham, AL	1-0	Schenectady, NY	1981	Tai-Chung, Taiwan	4-2	Tampa, FL
1954	Schenectady, NY	7-5	Colton, CA	1982	Kirkland, WA	6-0	Hsien, Taiwan
1955	Morrisville, PA	4-3	Merchantville, NJ	1983	Marietta, GA	3-1	Barahona, D. Rep.
1956	Roswell, NM	3-1	Merchantville, NJ	1984	Seoul, S. Korea	6-2	Altamonte, FL
1957	Monterrey, Mexico	4-0	La Mesa, CA	1985	Seoul, S. Korea	7-1	Mexicali, Mex.
1958	Monterrey, Mexico	10-1	Kankakee, IL	1986	Tainan Park, Taiwan	12-0	Tucson, AZ
1959	Hamtramck, MI	12-0	Auburn, CA	1987	Hua Lian, Taiwan	21-1	Irvine, CA
1960	Levittown, PA	5-0	Ft. Worth, TX	1988	Tai Ping, Taiwan	10-0	Pearl City, HI
1961	El Cajon, CA	4-2	El Campo, TX	1989	Trumbull, CT	5-2	Kaohsiung, Taiwan
1962	San Jose, CA	3-0	Kankakee, IL	1990	Taipei, Taiwan	9-0	Shippensburg, PA
1963	Granada Hills, CA	2-1	Stratford, CT	1991	Taichung, Taiwan	11-0	Danville, CA
1964	Staten Island, NY	4-0	Monterrey, Mex.	1992	Long Beach, CA	6-0	Zamboanga, Phil.
1965	Windsor Locks, CT	3-1	Stoney Creek, Can.	1993	Long Beach, CA	3-2	Panama
1966	Houston, TX	8-2	W. New York, NJ	1994	Maracaibo, Venezuela	4-3	Northridge, CA
1967	West Tokyo, Japan	4-1	Chicago, IL	1995	Tainan, Taiwan	17-3	Spring, TX
1968	Osaka, Japan	1-0	Richmond, VA	1996	Taipei, Taiwan	13-3	Cranston, RI
1969	Taipei, Taiwan	5-0	Santa Clara, CA				(called after 5th inn.)
1970	Wayne, NJ	2-0	Campbell, CA	1997	Guadalupe, Mexico	5-4	Mission Viejo, CA
1971	Tainan, Taiwan	12-3	Gary, IN	1998	Toms River, NJ	12-9	Kashima, Japan
1972	Taipei, Taiwan	6-0	Hammond, IN	1999	Osaka, Japan	5-0	Phenix City, AL
1973	Tainan City, Taiwan	12-0	Tucson, AZ	2000	Maracaibo, Venezuela	3-2	Bellaire, TX
1974	Kao Hsiung, Taiwan	12-1	Red Bluff, CA	2001	Tokyo, Japan	2-1	Apopka, FL

*Foreign teams were banned from the tournament in 1975, but allowed back in the following year.

Note: In 1992, Zamboanga City of the Philippines beat Long Beach, 15-4, but was stripped of the title a month later when it was discovered that the team had used several players from outside the city limits. Long Beach was then awarded the title by forfeit, 6-0 (one run for each inning of the game).

POWER BOAT RACING

APBA Gold Cup

Bonney Lake, Wash., native Mike Hanson earned his third career hydroplane victory by winning the 2001 Gold Cup in Detroit, Mich. Hanson, who obtained his first victory with new team owners Lori and Mike Jones, finished just ahead of runners-up Greg Hopp, Steve David and local favorite Mark Weber.

The American Power Boat Association Gold Cup for unlimited hydroplane racing is the oldest active motorsports trophy in North America. The first Gold Cup was competed for on the Hudson River in New York in June and September of 1904. Since then several cities have hosted the race, led by Detroit (32 times) and Seattle (14). Note that (*) indicates driver was also owner of the winning boat.

Drivers with multiple wins: Chip Hanauer (11); Bill Muncey (8); Gar Wood (5); Dean Chenoweth and Dave Villwock (4); Caleb Bragg, Tom D'Eath, Lou Fageol, Ron Musson, George Reis and J.M. Wainwright (3); Danny Foster, George Henley, Vic Kliesrath, E.J. Schroeder, Bill Schumacher, Zalmon G. Simmons Jr., Joe Taggart, Mark Tate and George Townsend (2).

Year	Boat	Driver	Avg. MPH	Year	Boat	Driver	Avg. MPH
1904	Standard (June)	Carl Riotte*	23.160	1910	Dixie III	F.K. Burnham*	32.473
1904	Vingt-Et-Un II	W. Sharpe Kilmer*	24.900	1911	MIT II	J.H. Hayden*	37.000
	(Sept.)			1912	P.D.Q. II	A.G. Miles*	39.462
1905	Chip I	J.M. Wainwright*	15.000	1913	Ankle Deep	C.S. Mankowski*	42.779
1906	Chip II	J.M. Wainwright*	25.000	1914	Baby Speed	Jim Blackton	48.458
1907	Chip II	J.M. Wainwright*	23.903		Demon II	& Bob Edgren	
1908	Dixie II	E.J. Schroeder*	29.938	1915	Miss Detroit	Johnny Milot	37.656
1909	Dixie II	E.J. Schroeder*	29.590			& Jack Beebe	

Power Boat Racing (Cont.)

Year	Boat	Driver	Avg. MPH	Year	Boat	Driver	Avg. MPH
1916	Miss Minneapolis	Bernard Smith	48.860	1961	Miss Century 21	Bill Muncey	99.678
1917	Miss Detroit II	Gar Wood*	54.410	1962	Miss Century 21	Bill Muncey	100.710
1918	Miss Detroit II	Gar Wood	51.619	1963	Miss Bardahl	Ron Musson	105.124
1919	Miss Detroit III	Gar Wood*	42.748	1964	Miss Bardahl	Ron Musson	103.433
				1965	Miss Bardahl	Ron Musson	103.132
1920	Miss America I	Gar Wood*	62.022	1966	Tahoe Miss	Mira Slovak	93.019
1921	Miss America I	Gar Wood*	52.825	1967	Miss Bardahl	Bill Shumacher	101.484
1922	Packard Chriscraft	J.G. Vincent*	40.253	1968	Miss Bardahl	Bill Shumacher	108.173
1923	Packard Chriscraft	Caleb Bragg	43.867	1969	Miss Budweiser	Bill Sterett	98.504
1924	Baby Bootlegger	Caleb Bragg*	45.302	1970	Miss Budweiser	Dean Chenoweth	99.562
1925	Baby Bootlegger	Caleb Bragg*	47.240	1971	Miss Madison	Jim McCormick	98.043
1926	Greenwich Folly	George Townsend*	47.984	1972	Atlas Van Lines	Bill Muncey	104.277
				1973	Miss Budweiser	Dean Chenoweth	99.043
1927	Greenwich Folly	George Townsend*	47.662	1974	Pay 'n Pak	George Henley	104.428
				1975	Pay 'n Pak	George Henley	108.921
1928	Not held			1976	Miss U.S.	Tom D'Eath	100.412
1929	Imp	Richard Hoyt*	48.662	1977	Atlas Van Lines	Bill Muncey*	111.822
				1978	Atlas Van Lines	Bill Muncey*	100.412
1930	Hotsy Totsy	Vic Kliesrath*	52.673	1979	Atlas Van Lines	Bill Muncey*	100.765
1931	Hotsy Totsy	Vic Kliesrath*	53.602				
1932	Delphine IV	Bill Horn	57.775	1980	Miss Budweiser	Dean Chenoweth	106.932
1933	El Lagarto	George Reis*	56.260	1981	Miss Budweiser	Dean Chenoweth	116.387
1934	El Lagarto	George Reis*	55.000	1982	Atlas Van Lines	Chip Hanauer	120.050
1935	El Lagarto	George Reis*	55.056	1983	Atlas Van Lines	Chip Hanauer	118.507
1936	Impshi	Kaye Don	45.735	1984	Atlas Van Lines	Chip Hanauer	130.175
1937	Notre Dame	Clell Perry	63.675	1985	Miller American	Chip Hanauer	120.643
1938	Alagi	Theo Rossi*	64.340	1986	Miller American	Chip Hanauer	116.523
1939	My Sin	Z.G. Simmons Jr.*	66.133	1987	Miller American	Chip Hanauer	127.620
1940	Hotsy Totsy III	Sidney Allen*	48.295	1988	Miss Circus Circus	Chip Hanauer & Jim Prevost	123.756
1941	My Sin	Z.G. Simmons Jr.*	52.509				
1942-45	Not held			1989	Miss Budweiser	Tom D'Eath	131.209
1946	Tempo VI	Guy Lombardo*	68.132	1990	Miss Budweiser	Tom D'Eath	143.176
1947	Miss Peps V	Danny Foster	57.000	1991	Winston Eagle	Mark Tate	137.771
1948	Miss Great Lakes	Danny Foster	46.845	1992	Miss Budweiser	Chip Hanauer	136.282
1949	My Sweetie	Bill Cantrell	73.612	1993	Miss Budweiser	Chip Hanauer	141.296
1950	Slo-Mo-Shun IV	Ted Jones	78.216	1994	Smokin' Joe's	Mark Tate	145.532
1951	Slo-Mo-Shun V	Lou Fageol	90.871	1995	Miss Budweiser	Chip Hanauer	149.160
1952	Slo-Mo-Shun IV	Stan Dollar	79.923	1996	Pico/American Dream	Dave Villwock	149.328
1953	Slo-Mo-Shun IV	Joe Taggart & Lou Fageol	99.108				
				1997	Miss Budweiser	Dave Villwock	129.366
1954	Slo-Mo-Shun V	Lou Fageol	92.613	1998	Miss Budweiser	Dave Villwock	140.704
1955	Gale V	Lee Schoenith	99.552	1999	Miss Pico	Chip Hanauer	152.591
1956	Miss Thriftway	Bill Muncey	96.552	2000	Miss Budweiser	Dave Villwock	139.416
1957	Miss Thriftway	Bill Muncey	101.787	2001	Tubby's Subs	Mike Hanson	140.519
1958	Hawaii Kai III	Jack Regas	103.000				
1959	Maverick	Bill Stead	104.481				
1960	Not held						

PRO RODEO

All-Around Champion Cowboy

Joe Beaver of Huntsville, Texas, won the all-around cowboy title at the 2000 National Finals Rodeo in grand fashion, finishing with a total of $225,396. Beaver began the 42nd annual championship at the Thomas & Mack Center in Las Vegas, Nev., seemingly out of the running in the all-around and ended the week with his third all-around title.

The Professional Rodeo Cowboys Association (PRCA) title of all-around world champion cowboy goes to the rodeo athlete who wins the most prize money in a single year in two or more events, earning a minimum of $2,000 in each event. Only prize money earned in sanctioned PRCA rodeos is counted. From 1929-44, all-around champions were named by the Rodeo Association of America (earnings for those years are not available).

Multiple winners: Ty Murray (7); Tom Ferguson and Larry Mahan (6); Jim Shoulders (5); Joe Beaver, Lewis Feild and Dean Oliver (3); Everett Bowman, Louis Brooks, Clay Carr, Bill Linderman, Phil Lyne, Gerald Roberts, Casey Tibbs and Harry Tompkins (2).

Year		Year		Year		Year	
1929	Earl Thode	1934	Leonard Ward	1939	Paul Carney	1944	Louis Brooks
1930	Clay Carr	1935	Everett Bowman	1940	Fritz Truan	1945-46	No award
1931	John Schneider	1936	John Bowman	1941	Homer Pettigrew		
1932	Donald Nesbit	1937	Everett Bowman	1942	Gerald Roberts		
1933	Clay Carr	1938	Burel Mulkey	1943	Louis Brooks		

Year		Earnings	Year		Earnings	Year		Earnings
1947	Todd Whatley	$18,642	1965	Dean Oliver	$33,163	1983	Roy Cooper	$153,391
1948	Gerald Roberts	21,766	1966	Larry Mahan	40,358	1984	Dee Pickett	122,618
1949	Jim Shoulders	21,495	1967	Larry Mahan	51,996	1985	Lewis Feild	130,347
1950	Bill Linderman	30,715	1968	Larry Mahan	49,129	1986	Lewis Feild	166,042
1951	Casey Tibbs	29,104	1969	Larry Mahan	57,726	1987	Lewis Feild	144,335
1952	Harry Tompkins	30,934				1988	Dave Appleton	121,546
1953	Bill Linderman	33,674	1970	Larry Mahan	41,493	1989	Ty Murray	134,806
1954	Buck Rutherford	40,404	1971	Phil Lyne	49,245			
1955	Casey Tibbs	42,065	1972	Phil Lyne	60,852	1990	Ty Murray	213,772
1956	Jim Shoulders	43,381	1973	Larry Mahan	64,447	1991	Ty Murray	244,231
1957	Jim Shoulders	33,299	1974	Tom Ferguson	66,929	1992	Ty Murray	225,992
1958	Jim Shoulders	32,212	1975	Tom Ferguson	50,300	1993	Ty Murray	297,896
1959	Jim Shoulders	32,905	1976	Tom Ferguson	87,908	1994	Ty Murray	246,170
			1977	Tom Ferguson	65,981	1995	Joe Beaver	141,753
1960	Harry Tompkins	32,522	1978	Tom Ferguson	83,734	1996	Joe Beaver	166,103
1961	Benny Reynolds	31,309	1979	Tom Ferguson	96,272	1997	Dan Mortensen	184,559
1962	Tom Nesmith	32,611				1998	Ty Murray	264,673
1963	Dean Oliver	31,329	1980	Paul Tierney	105,568	1999	Fred Whitfield	217,819
1964	Dean Oliver	31,150	1981	Jimmie Cooper	105,861			
			1982	Chris Lybbert	123,709	2000	Joe Beaver	225,396

SOAP BOX DERBY

All-American Soap Box Derby

The 64th annual Soap Box Derby in Akron, OH, produced three champions from opposite ends of the nation. Michael Flynn, age 12 of Harrison Township, Mich., rolled to the Masters title while 15-year-old James Rogers of Hilton, N.Y., raced to a win in the Super Stock division. Altaloma, Calif. native, Chad Eyerly, 11, cruised to victory in the Stock division. Unfortunately, participants' times were not recorded due to a technological malfunction.

There are three competitive divisions: 1. Stock (ages 9-16) — made up of generic, prefab racers that come from Derby-approved kits, can be assembled in four hours and don't exceed 200 pounds when driver, car and wheels are weighed together; 2. Super Stock (ages 10-16) — the same as Stock only with a weight limit of 220 pounds; 3. Masters (ages 11-16) — made up of racers designed by the drivers, but constructed with Derby-approved hardware. The racing ramp at Derby Downs is 953.75 feet with an 11 percent grade.

One champion reigned at the All-American Soap Box Derby each year from 1934-75; Junior and Senior division champions from 1976-87; Kit and Masters champions from 1988-91; Stock, Kit and Masters champions from 1992-94; Stock, Super Stock and Masters champions starting in 1995.

Year		Hometown	Age	Year		Hometown	Age
1934	Robert Turner	Muncie, IN	11	1970	Samuel Gupton	Durham, NC	13
1935	Maurice Bale Jr.	Anderson, IN	13	1971	Larry Blair	Oroville, CA	13
1936	Herbert Muench Jr.	St. Louis	14	1972	Robert Lange Jr.	Boulder, CO	14
1937	Robert Ballard	White Plains, NY	12	1973	Bret Yarborough	Elk Grove, CA	11
1938	Robert Berger	Omaha, NE	14	1974	Curt Yarborough	Elk Grove, CA	11
1939	Clifton Hardesty	White Plains, NY	11	1975	Karren Stead	Lower Bucks, PA	11
1940	Thomas Fisher	Detroit	12	1976	JR: Phil Raber	Sugarcreek, OH	11
1941	Claude Smith	Akron, OH	14		SR: Joan Ferdinand	Canton, OH	14
1942-45	Not held			1977	JR: Mark Ferdinand	Canton, OH	10
1946	Gilbert Klecan	San Diego	14		SR: Steve Washburn	Bristol, CT	15
1947	Kenneth Holmboe	Charleston, WV	14	1978	JR: Darren Hart	Salem, OR	11
1948	Donald Strub	Akron, OH	13		SR: Greg Cardinal	Flint, MI	13
1949	Fred Derks	Akron, OH	15	1979	JR: Russell Yurk	Flint, MI	10
					SR: Craig Kitchen	Akron, OH	14
1950	Harold Williamson	Charleston, WV	15	1980	JR: Chris Fulton	Indianapolis	11
1951	Darwin Cooper	Williamsport, PA	15		SR: Dan Porul	Sherman Oaks, CA	12
1952	Joe Lunn	Columbus, GA	11	1981	JR: Howie Fraley	Portsmouth, OH	11
1953	Fred Mohler	Muncie, IN	14		SR: Tonia Schlegel	Hamilton, OH	13
1954	Richard Kemp	Los Angeles	14	1982	JR: Carol A. Sullivan	Rochester, NH	10
1955	Richard Rohrer	Rochester, NY	14		SR: Matt Wolfgang	Lehigh Val., PA	12
1956	Norman Westfall	Rochester, NY	14	1983	JR: Tony Carlini	Del Mar, CA	10
1957	Terry Townsend	Anderson, IN	14		SR: Mike Burdgick	Flint, MI	14
1958	James Miley	Muncie, IN	15	1984	JR: Chris Hess	Hamilton, OH	11
1959	Barney Townsend	Anderson, IN	13		SR: Anita Jackson	St. Louis	15
1960	Fredric Lake	South Bend, IN	11	1985	JR: Michael Gallo	Danbury, CT	12
1961	Dick Dawson	Wichita, KS	13		SR: Matt Sheffer	York, PA	14
1962	David Mann	Gary, IN	14	1986	JR: Marc Behan	Dover, NH	9
1963	Harold Conrad	Duluth, MN	12		SR: Tami Jo Sullivan	Lancaster, OH	13
1964	Gregory Schumacher	Tacoma, WA	14	1987	JR: Matt Margules	Danbury, CT	11
1965	Robert Logan	Santa Ana, CA	12		SR: Brian Drinkwater	Bristol, CT	14
1966	David Krussow	Tacoma, WA	12	1988	KIT: Jason Lamb	Des Moines, IA	13
1967	Kenneth Cline	Lincoln, NE	13		MAS: David Duffield	Kansas City	13
1968	Branch Lew	Muncie, IN	11	1989	KIT: David Schiller	Dayton, OH	12
1969	Steve Souter	Midland, TX	12		MAS: Faith Chavarria	Ventura, CA	12

Soap Box Derby (Cont.)

Year		Hometown	Age
1990	MAS: Sami Jones	Salem, OR	13
	KIT: Mark Mihal	Valparaiso, IN	12
1991	MAS: Danny Garland	San Diego, CA	14
	KIT: Paul Greenwald	Saginaw, MI	13
1992	MAS: Bonnie Thornton	Redding, CA	12
	KIT: Carolyn Fox	Sublimity, OR	11
	STK: Loren Hurst	Hudson, OH	10
1993	MAS: Dean Lutton	Delta, OH	14
	KIT: D.M. Del Ferraro	Stow, OH	12
	STK: Owen Yuda	Boiling Springs, PA	10
1994	MAS: D.M. Del Ferraro	Akron, OH	13
	KIT: Joel Endres	Akron, OH	14
	STK: Kristina Damond	Jamestown, NY	13
1995	MAS: J. Fensterbush	Kingman, AZ	11
	SS: Darcie Davisson	Kingman, AZ	11
	STK: Karen Thomas	Jamestown, NY	11
1996	MAS: Tim Scrofano	Conneaut, OH	12
	SS: Jeremy Phillips	Charlestown, WV	14
	STK: Matt Perez	No. Canton, OH	12

Year		Hometown	Age
1997	MAS: Wade Wallace	Elk Hart, IN	11
	SS: Dolline Vance	Salem, OR	13
	STK: Mark Stephens	Waynesboro, VA	13
1998	MAS: James Marsh	Cleveland, OH	12
	SS: Stacy Sharp	Kingman, AZ	14
	STK: Hailey Simpson	Salem, OR	10
1999	MAS: Allan Endres	Barberton, OH	14
	SS: Alisha Ebner	Salem, OR	15
	STK: Justin Pillow	Deland, FL	12
2000	MAS: Cody Butler	Anderson, IN	12
	SS: Derek Etherington	Anderson, IN	11
	STK: Rachel Curran	Medina, OH	13
2001	MAS: Michael Flynn	Harrison Township, MI	12
	SS: James Rogers	Hilton, NY	15
	STK: Chad Eyerly	Altaloma, CA	11

SOFTBALL

Men's and women's national champions since 1933 in Major Fast Pitch, Major Slow Pitch and Super Slow Pitch (men only). Sanctioned by the Amateur Softball Association of America.

MEN
Major Fast Pitch

Multiple winners: Clearwater Bombers (10); Raybestos Cardinals (5); Sealmasters (4); Briggs Beautyware, Decatur Pride, Pay'n Pak and Zollner Pistons (3); Billard Barbell, Hammer Air Field, Kodak Park, Meierhoffer, National Health Care, Penn Corp and Peterbilt Western (2).

Year		Year		Year	
1933	J.L. Gill Boosters, Chicago	1959	Sealmasters, Aurora, IL	1982	Peterbilt Western
1934	Ke-Nash-A, Kenosha, WI	1960	Clearwater Bombers	1983	Franklin Cardinals, Stratford, CA
1935	Crimson Coaches, Toledo, OH	1961	Sealmasters	1984	California Kings, Merced, CA
1936	Kodak Park, Rochester, NY	1962	Clearwater Bombers	1985	Pay'n Pak, Seattle
1937	Briggs Body Team, Detroit	1963	Clearwater Bombers	1986	Pay'n Pak
1938	The Pohlers, Cincinnati	1964	Burch Tool, Detroit	1987	Pay'n Pak
1939	Carr's Boosters, Covington, KY	1965	Sealmasters	1988	TransAire, Elkhart, IN
1940	Kodak Park	1966	Clearwater Bombers	1989	Penn Corp, Sioux City, IA
1941	Bendix Brakes, South Bend, IN	1967	Sealmasters	1990	Penn Corp
1942	Deep Rock Oilers, Tulsa, OK	1968	Clearwater Bombers	1991	Gianella Bros., Rohnert Park, CA
1943	Hammer Air Field, Fresno, CA	1969	Raybestos Cardinals	1992	National Health Care, Sioux City, IA
1944	Hammer Air Field	1970	Raybestos Cardinals	1993	National Health Care
1945	Zollner Pistons, Ft. Wayne, IN	1971	Welty Way, Cedar Rapids, IA	1994	Decatur (IL) Pride
1946	Zollner Pistons	1972	Raybestos Cardinals	1995	Decatur Pride
1947	Zollner Pistons	1973	Clearwater Bombers	1996	Green Bay All-Car, Green Bay, WI
1948	Briggs Beautyware, Detroit	1974	Gianella Bros., Santa Rosa, CA	1997	Tampa Bay Smokers, Tampa Bay, FL
1949	Tip Top Tailors, Toronto	1975	Rising Sun Hotel, Reading, PA	1998	Meierhoffer-Fleeman, St. Joseph, MO
1950	Clearwater (FL) Bombers	1976	Raybestos Cardinals	1999	Decatur Pride
1951	Dow Chemical, Midland, MI	1977	Billard Barbell, Reading, PA	2000	Meierhoffer
1952	Briggs Beautyware	1978	Billard Barbell	2001	Frontier Players Casino, St. Joseph, MO
1953	Briggs Beautyware	1979	McArdle Pontiac/Cadillac, Midland, MI		
1954	Clearwater Bombers				
1955	Raybestos Cardinals	1980	Peterbilt Western, Seattle		
1956	Clearwater Bombers	1981	Archer Daniels Midland, Decatur, IL		
1957	Clearwater Bombers				
1958	Raybestos Cardinals				

Super Slow Pitch

Multiple winners: Ritch's/Superior (4); Howard's/Western Steer and Steele's Sports (3); Lighthouse/Worth (2).

Year		Year		Year	
1981	Howard's/Western Steer, Denver, NC	1988	Starpath, Monticello, KY	1995	Lighthouse/Worth, Stone Mt., GA
1982	Jerry's Catering, Miami	1989	Ritch's Salvage, Harrisburg, NC	1996	Ritch's/Superior
1983	Howard's/Western Steer	1990	Steele's Silver Bullets	1997	Ritch's/Superior
1984	Howard's/Western Steer	1991	Sun Belt/Worth, Atlanta	1998	Lighthouse/Worth
1985	Steele's Sports, Grafton, OH	1992	Ritch's/Superior, Windsor Locks, CT	1999	Team Easton, California
1986	Steele's Sports	1993	Ritch's/Superior	2000	Team TPS, Louisville, KY
1987	Steele's Sports	1994	Bellcorp., Tampa	2001	Long Haul, Albertville, MN

Major Slow Pitch

Multiple winners: Gatliff Auto Sales, Riverside Paving and Skip Hogan A.C. (3); Campbell Carpets, Hamilton Tailoring, Howard's Furniture, Long Haul TPS and New Construction (2).

Year	Year	Year
1953 Shields Construction, Newport, KY	1971 Pile Drivers, Va. Beach, VA	1988 Bell Corp/FAF, Tampa, FL
1954 Waldneck's Tavern, Cincinnati	1972 Jiffy Club, Louisville, KY	1989 Ritch's Salvage, Harrisburg, NC
1955 Lang Pet Shop, Covington, KY	1973 Howard's Furniture, Denver, NC	1990 New Construction, Shelbyville, IN
1956 Gatliff Auto Sales, Newport, KY	1974 Howard's Furniture	1991 Riverside Paving, Louisville
1957 Gatliff Auto Sales	1975 Pyramid Cafe, Lakewood, OH	1992 Vernon's, Jacksonville, FL
1958 East Side Sports, Detroit	1976 Warren Motors, J'ville, FL	1993 Back Porch/Destin (FL) Roofing
1959 Yorkshire Restaurant, Newport, KY	1977 Nelson Painting, Okla. City	1994 Riverside Paving, Louisville
1960 Hamilton Tailoring, Cincinnati	1978 Campbell Carpets, Concord, CA	1995 Riverside Paving
1961 Hamilton Tailoring	1979 Nelco Mfg. Co., Okla. City	1996 Bell II, Orlando, FL
1962 Skip Hogan A.C., Pittsburgh	1980 Campbell Carpets	1997 Long Haul TPS, Albertville, MN
1963 Gatliff Auto Sales	1981 Elite Coating, Gordon, CA	1998 Chase Mortgage/Easton,
1964 Skip Hogan A.C.	1982 Triangle Sports, Minneapolis	Wilmington, NC
1965 Skip Hogan A.C.	1983 No.1 Electric & Heating,	1999 Gasoline Heaven/Worth,
1966 Michael's Lounge, Detroit	Gastonia, NC	Commack, NY
1967 Jim's Sport Shop, Pittsburgh	1984 Lilly Air Systems, Chicago	2000 Long Haul TPS
1968 County Sports, Levittown, NY	1985 Blanton's Fayetteville, NC	2001 New Construction
1969 Copper Hearth, Milwaukee	1986 Non-Ferrous Metals, Cleveland	
1970 Little Caesar's, Southgate, MI	1987 Stapath, Monticello, KY	

WOMEN

Major Fast Pitch

Multiple winners: Raybestos Brakettes (21); Orange Lionettes (9); Jax Maids (5); California Commotion (4); Arizona Ramblers and Redding Rebels (3); Hi-Ho Brakettes, J.J. Krieg's, National Screw & Manufacturing and Phoenix Storm (2).

Year	Year	Year
1933 Great Northerns, Chicago	1953 Betsy Ross Rockets, Fresno, CA	1971 Raybestos Brakettes
1934 Hart Motors, Chicago	1954 Leach Motor Rockets, Fresno, CA	1972 Raybestos Brakettes
1935 Bloomer Girls, Cleveland	1955 Orange Lionettes	1973 Raybestos Brakettes
1936 Nat'l Screw & Mfg., Cleveland	1956 Orange Lionettes	1974 Raybestos Brakettes
1937 Nat'l Screw & Mfg.	1957 Hacienda Rockets, Fresno, CA	1975 Raybestos Brakettes
1938 J.J. Krieg's, Alameda, CA	1958 Raybestos Brakettes,	1976 Raybestos Brakettes
1939 J.J. Krieg's	Stratford, CT	1977 Raybestos Brakettes
1940 Arizona Ramblers, Phoenix	1959 Raybestos Brakettes	1978 Raybestos Brakettes
1941 Higgins Midgets, Tulsa, OK	1960 Raybestos Brakettes	1979 Sun City (AZ) Saints
1942 Jax Maids, New Orleans	1961 Gold Sox, Whittier, CA	1980 Raybestos Brakettes
1943 Jax Maids	1962 Orange Lionettes	1981 Orlando (FL) Rebels
1944 Lind & Pomeroy, Portland, OR	1963 Raybestos Brakettes	1982 Raybestos Brakettes
1945 Jax Maids	1964 Erv Lind Florists, Portland, OR	1983 Raybestos Brakettes
1946 Jax Maids	1965 Orange Lionettes	1984 Los Angeles Diamonds
1947 Jax Maids	1966 Raybestos Brakettes	1985 Hi-Ho Brakettes, Stratford, CT
1948 Arizona Ramblers	1967 Raybestos Brakettes	1986 So. California Invasion
1949 Arizona Ramblers	1968 Raybestos Brakettes	1987 Orange County Majestics,
1950 Orange (CA) Lionettes	1969 Orange Lionettes	Anaheim, CA
1951 Orange Lionettes	1970 Orange Lionettes	1988 Hi-Ho Brakettes
1952 Orange Lionettes		

Other 2001 Champions

Slow Pitch

MEN

East Class A—Creative Stucco/Easton, Columbus, Ohio
West Class A—T's 13, Omaha, Neb.
Major Industrial—Sikorsky Aircraft, Stratford, Conn.
Class A Industrial—C&W Cable, Annville, N.Y.
35-Over—Four Star, Cleveland, Ohio
40-Over—7-7 Tires, Evansville, Ind.
45-Over—Frankenstein/Maroadi Mifflin, Pittsburgh, Penn.
50-Over Major—Fergies, Annapolis, Md.
55-Over Major—Thomas Engineering, Mannassas, Va.
60-Over—Florida Crush Legends, Fort Myers, Fla.
Church—Evangel Temple, Jacksonville, Fla.

WOMEN

Class A—Armed Forces, Ft. Indiantown Gap, Penn.
Church—Ben Hill United Methodist, Atlanta, Ga.

COED

Major—CSC/Hardliners, Euless, Tex.
Class A—4J Boys, Bowie, Md.

Fast Pitch

MEN

Class B—Coors Light, Ashland, Ohio
Class C—Home Federal, Grand Island, Neb.
40-Over—Maryland Masters, Forrestville, Md.
45-Over—California Painters, Stockton, Calif.
23-Under—Munger Bulldogs, Munger, Mich.

WOMEN

Class A—Carterville Cougars, Carterville, Ill.
Class B—Yuengling Brewery, Ocala, Penn.
Class C—Frederick Express, Smithsburg, Md.

Modified Pitch

Women's Major—Renegades, Hookset, N.H.
Men's (9) Major—Matarazzo Seadogs, Boston, Mass.
Men's (10) Major—Bonnell's, Erie, Penn
Men's (9) Class A—Skyliner's, Pompton, NJ

Softball (Cont.)

Year		Year		Year	
1989	Whittier (CA) Raiders	1994	Redding Rebels	1998	California Commotion
1990	Raybestos Brakettes	1995	Redding Rebels	1999	California Commotion
1991	Raybestos Brakettes	1996	California Commotion,	2000	Phoenix Storm, Phoenix, AZ
1992	Raybestos Brakettes		Woodland Hills	2001	Phoenix Storm
1993	Redding (CA) Rebels	1997	California Commotion		

Major Slow Pitch

Multiple winners: Spooks (5); Dana Gardens (4); Universal Plastics (3); Cannan's Illusions, Bob Hoffman's Dots, Key Ford Mustangs and Marks Brothers Dots (2).

Year		Year		Year	
1959	Pearl Laundry, Richmond, VA	1975	Marks Brothers Dots	1988	Spooks
1960	Carolina Rockets, High Pt., NC	1976	Sorrento's Pizza, Cincinnati	1989	Cannan's Illusions, Houston
1961	Dairy Cottage, Covington, KY	1977	Fox Valley Lassies,	1990	Spooks
1962	Dana Gardens, Cincinnati		St. Charles, IL	1991	Cannan's Illusions, San Antonio
1963	Dana Gardens	1978	Bob Hoffman's Dots, Miami	1992	Universal Plastics, Cookeville, TN
1964	Dana Gardens	1979	Bob Hoffman's Dots	1993	Universal Plastics
1965	Art's Acres, Omaha, NE	1980	Howard's Rubi-Otts,	1994	Universal Plastics
1966	Dana Gardens		Graham, NC	1995	Armed Forces, Sacramento
1967	Ridge Maintenance, Cleveland	1981	Tifton (GA) Tomboys	1996	Spooks
1968	Escue Pontiac, Cincinnati	1982	Richmond (VA) Stompers	1997	Taylor's, Glendale, MD
1969	Converse Dots, Hialeah, FL	1983	Spooks, Anoka, MN	1998	not held
1970	Rutenschruder Floral, Cincinnati	1984	Spooks	1999	Lakerettes, Conneaut Lake, PA
1971	Gators, Ft. Lauderdale, FL	1985	Key Ford Mustangs,		
1972	Riverside Ford, Cincinnati		Pensacola, FL	2000	Premier Sports, Pittsboro, NC
1973	Sweeney Chevrolet, Cincinnati	1986	Sur-Way Tomboys, Tifton, GA	2001	Shooters/Nike, Orlando, FL
1974	Marks Brothers Dots, Miami	1987	Key Ford Mustangs		

TRIATHLON

World Championship

Contested since 1989, the Triathlon World Championship consists of a 1.5-kilometer swim, a 40-kilometer bike ride and a 10-kilometer run. The 2001 championship took place on July 22 in Edmonton, Alberta, Canada.

Multiple winners: MEN—Simon Lessing (4); Spencer Smith (2). WOMEN—Emma Carney, Michelle Jones and Karen Smyers (2).

MEN

Year		Time
1989	Mark Allen, United States	1:58:46
1990	Greg Welch, Australia	1:51:37
1991	Miles Stewart, Australia	1:48:20
1992	Simon Lessing, Great Britain	1:49:04
1993	Spencer Smith, Great Britain	1:51:20
1994	Spencer Smith, Great Britain	1:51:04
1995	Simon Lessing, Great Britain	1:48:29
1996	Simon Lessing, Great Britain	1:39:50
1997	Chris McCormack, Great Britain	1:48:29
1998	Simon Lessing, Great Britain	1:55:31
1999	Dimitry Gaag, Kazakhstan	1:45:25
2000	Oliver Marceau, France	1:51:41
2001	Peter Robertson, Australia	1:48:01

WOMEN

Year		Time
1989	Erin Baker, New Zealand	2:10:01
1990	Karen Smyers, United States	2:03:33
1991	Joanne Ritchie, Canada	2:02:04
1992	Michellie Jones, Australia	2:02:08
1993	Michellie Jones, Australia	2:07:41
1994	Emma Carney, Australia	2:03:19
1995	Karen Smyers, USA	2:04:58
1996	Jackie Gallagher, Australia	1:50:52
1997	Emma Carney, Australia	1:59:22
1998	Joanne King, Australia	2:07:25
1999	Loretta Harrop, Australia	1:55:28
2000	Nicole Hackett, Australia	1:54:43
2001	Siri Lindley, United States	1:58:51

Ironman Championship

Contested in Hawaii since 1978, the Ironman Triathlon Championship consists of a 2.4-mile swim, a 112-mile bike ride and 26.2-mile run. The race begins at 7 a.m. and continues all day until the course is closed at midnight.

MEN

Multiple winners: Mark Allen and Dave Scott (6); Luc Van Lierde, Peter Reid and Scott Tinley (2).

Year	Date	Winner	Time	Runner-up	Margin	Start	Finish	Location
I	2/18/78	Gordon Haller	11:46	John Dunbar	34:00	15	12	Waikiki Beach
II	1/14/79	Tom Warren	11:15:56	John Dunbar	48:00	15	12	Waikiki Beach
III	1/10/80	Dave Scott	9:24:33	Chuck Neumann	1:08	108	95	Ala Moana Park
IV	2/14/81	John Howard	9:38:29	Tom Warren	26:00	326	299	Kailua-Kona
V	2/6/82	Scott Tinley	9:19:41	Dave Scott	17:16	580	541	Kailua-Kona
VI	10/9/82	Dave Scott	9:08:23	Scott Tinley	20:05	850	775	Kailua-Kona
VII	10/22/83	Dave Scott	9:05:57	Scott Tinley	0:33	964	835	Kailua-Kona
VIII	10/6/84	Dave Scott	8:54:20	Scott Tinley	24:25	1036	903	Kailua-Kona
IX	10/25/85	Scott Tinley	8:50:54	Chris Hinshaw	25:46	1018	965	Kailua-Kona
X	10/18/86	Dave Scott	8:28:37	Mark Allen	9:47	1039	951	Kailua-Kona
XI	10/10/87	Dave Scott	8:34:13	Mark Allen	11:06	1380	1284	Kailua-Kona
XII	10/22/88	Scott Molina	8:31:00	Mike Pigg	2:11	1277	1189	Kailua-Kona

Year	Date	Winner	Time	Runner-up	Margin	Start	Finish	Location
XIII	10/15/89	Mark Allen	8:09:15	Dave Scott	0:58	1285	1231	Kailua-Kona
XIV	10/6/90	Mark Allen	8:28:17	Scott Tinley	9:23	1386	1255	Kailua-Kona
XV	10/19/91	Mark Allen	8:18:32	Greg Welch	6:01	1386	1235	Kailua-Kona
XVI	10/10/92	Mark Allen	8:09:08	Cristian Bustos	7:21	1364	1298	Kailua-Kona
XVII	10/30/93	Mark Allen	8:07:45	Paulli Kiuru	6:37	1438	1353	Kailua-Kona
XVIII	10/15/94	Greg Welch	8:20:27	Dave Scott	4:05	1405	1290	Kailua-Kona
XIX	10/7/95	Mark Allen	8:20:34	Thomas Hellriegel	2:25	1487	1323	Kailua-Kona
XX	10/26/96	Luc Van Lierde	8:04:08	Thomas Hellriegel	1:59	1420	1288	Kailua-Kona
XXI	10/18/97	Thomas Hellriegel	8:33:01	Jurgen Zack	6:17	1534	1365	Kailua-Kona
XXII	10/3/98	Peter Reid	8:24:20	Luc Van Lierde	7:37	1487	1379	Kailua-Kona
XXIII	10/23/99	Luc Van Lierde	8:17:17	Peter Reid	5:37	1471	1419	Kailua-Kona
XXIV	10/14/00	Peter Reid	8:21:01	Tim DeBoom	2:09	1525	1426	Kailua-Kona
XXV	10/6/01	Tim DeBoom	8:31:18	Cameron Brown	14:52	1558	1364	Kailua-Kona

WOMEN

Multiple winners: Paula Newby-Fraser (8); Natascha Badmann (3); Erin Baker and Sylviane Puntous (2).

Year	Winner	Time	Runner-up	Year	Winner	Time	Runner-up
1978	No finishers			1990	Erin Baker	9:13:42	P. Newby-Fraser
1979	Lyn Lemaire	12:55.00	None	1991	Paula Newby-Fraser	9:07:52	Erin Baker
				1992	Paula Newby-Fraser	8:55:28	Julie Anne White
1980	Robin Beck	11:21:24	Eve Anderson	1993	Paula Newby-Fraser	8:58:23	Erin Baker
1981	Linda Sweeney	12:00:32	Sally Edwards	1994	Paula Newby-Fraser	9:20:14	Karen Smyers
1982	Kathleen McCartney	11:09:40	Julie Moss	1995	Karen Smyers	9:16:46	Isabelle Mouthon
1982	Julie Leach	10:54:08	Joann Dahlkoetter	1996	Paula Newby-Fraser	9:06:49	Natascha Badmann
1983	Sylviane Puntous	10:43:36	Patricia Puntous	1997	Heather Fuhr	9:31:43	Lori Bowden
1984	Sylviane Puntous	10:25:13	Patricia Puntous	1998	Natascha Badmann	9:24:16	Lori Bowden
1985	Joanne Ernst	10:25:22	Liz Bulman	1999	Lori Bowden	9:13:02	Karen Smyers
1986	Paula Newby-Fraser	9:49:14	Sylviane Puntous				
1987	Erin Baker	9:35:25	Sylviane Puntous	2000	Natascha Badmann	9:26:17	Lori Bowden
1988	Paula Newby-Fraser	9:01:01	Erin Baker	2001	Natascha Badmann	9:28:37	Lori Bowden
1989	Paula Newby-Fraser	9:00:56	Sylviane Puntous				

X GAMES

The ESPN Extreme Games, originally envisioned as a biannual showcase for "alternative" sports, were first held June 24-July 1, 1995 in Newport and Providence, R.I. and Mt. Snow, Vt. The success of the inaugural event prompted organizers to make it an annual competition. Newport would again serve as host for the redubbed X Games in 1996 before they moved to San Diego for 1997 and 1998. The X Games has evolved rapidly since its inception. New sports and events are added while others are dropped.

In 1997, the first Winter X Games were held at Snow Summit Mountain Resort in Big Bear Lake, Calif. before moving to Crested Butte, Colo. in 1998.

The 1999 and 2000 Summer X Games were held in San Francisco. The 1999 Winter X Games were again held in Crested Butte, Colo., Jan. 14-17. The Winter X Games took place at Mt. Snow, Vt. in 2000 and on Feb. 1-4 in 2001. The 2001 Summer X Games were held in Philadelphia and will take place there in 2002, as well.

Summer X Games
Bicycle Stunt

Year	Vert	Year	Dirt	Year	Street/Stunt Park	Year	Flatland
1995	Matt Hoffman	1995	Jay Miron	1996	Dave Mirra	1997	Trevor Meyer
1996	Matt Hoffman	1996	Joey Garcia	1997	Dave Mirra	1998	Trevor Meyer
1997	Dave Mirra	1997	T.J. Lavin	1998	Dave Mirra	1999	Trevor Meyer
1998	Dave Mirra	1998	Brian Foster	1999	Dave Mirra	2000	Martti Kuoppa
1999	Dave Mirra	1999	T.J. Lavin	2000	Dave Mirra	2001	Martti Kuoppa
2000	Jamie Bestwick	2000	Ryan Nyquist	2001	Bruce Crisman		
2001	Dave Mirra	2001	Stephen Murray				

Year	Downhill
2001	Brandon Meadows

Big-Air Snowboarding

Year	Men
1997	Peter Line
1998	Kevin Jones
1999	Peter Line
2000	not held

Year	Women
1997	Tina Dixon
1998	Janet Matthews
1999	Barrett Christy
2000	not held

Motocross

Year	Freestyle
1999	Travis Pastrana
2000	Travis Pastrana
2001	Travis Pastrana

Year	Step Up
2001	Tommy Clowers

Year	Big Air
2001	Kenny Bartram

Bungee Jumping

Year	
1995	Doug Anderson
1996	Peter Bihun
1997	event discontinued

X Games (Cont.)

Street Luge

Year	Dual
1995	Bob Pereyra
1996	Shawn Goular
1997	Biker Sherlock
1998	Biker Sherlock
1999	Dennis Derammelaere
2000	Bob Ozman
2001	not held

Year	Mass
1995	Shawn Gilbert
1996	Biker Sherlock
1997	Biker Sherlock
1998	Rat Sult
1999	event discontinued

Year	Super Mass
1997	Biker Sherlock
1998	Rat Sult
1999	David Rogers
2000	Bob Pereyra
2001	Brent DeKeyser

Year	King of the Hill
2001	Dennis Derammelaere

Skysurfing

Year	
1995	Fradet/Zipser
1996	Furrer/Scmid
1997	Hartman/Pappadato
1998	Rozov/Burch
1999	Fradet/Iodice
2000	Klaus/Rogers
2001	not held

Skateboard

Year	Vert Singles
1995	Tony Hawk
1996	Andy Macdonald
1997	Tony Hawk
1998	Andy Macdonald
1999	Bucky Lasek
2000	Bucky Lasek
2001	Bob Burnquist

Year	Vert Doubles
1997	Hawk/Macdonald
1998	Hawk/Macdonald
1999	Hawk/Macdonald
2000	Hawk/Macdonald
2001	Hawk/Macdonald

Year	Street/Park
1995	Chris Senn
1996	Rodil de Araujo Jr.
1997	Chris Senn
1998	Rodil de Araujo Jr.
1999	Chris Senn
2000	Eric Koston
2001	Kerry Getz

Year	Best Trick
2000	Bob Burnquist
2001	Matt Dove

Sportclimbing

Year	Men's Difficulty
1995	Ian Vickers
1996	Arnaud Petit
1997	Francois Legrand
1998	Christian Core
1999	Chris Sharma
2000	event discontinued

Year	Women's Difficulty
1995	Robyn Erbersfield
1996	Katie Brown
1997	Katie Brown
1998	Katie Brown
1999	Stephanie Bodet
2000	event discontinued

Year	Men's Speed
1995	Hans Florine
1996	Hans Florine
1997	Hans Florine
1998	Vladimir Netsvetaev
1999	Aaron Shamy
2000	Vladimir Zakharov
2001	Maxim Stenkovoy

Year	Women's Speed
1995	Elena Ovtchinnikova
1996	Cecile Le Flem
1997	Elena Ovtchinnikova
1998	Elena Ovtchinnikova
1999	Renata Piszczek
2000	Etti Hendrawati
2001	Elena Repko

In-Line Skating

Year	Men's Vert
1995	Tom Fry
1996	Rene Hulgreen
1997	Tim Ward
1998	Cesar Mora
1999	Eito Yasutoko
2000	Eito Yasutoko
2001	Taig Khris

Year	Women's Vert
1995	Tash Hodgeson
1996	Fabiola da Silva
1997	Fabiola da Silva
1998	Fabiola da Silva
1999	Ayumi Kawasaki
2000	Fabiola da Silva
2001	Fabiola da Silva

Year	Men's Street/Park
1995	Matt Salerno
1996	Arlo Eisenberg
1997	Arron Feinberg
1998	Jonathan Bergeron
1999	Nicky Adams
2000	Sven Boekhorst
2001	Jaren Grob

Year	Women's Street/Park
1997	Sayaka Yabe
1998	Jenny Curry
1999	Sayaka Yabe
2000	Fabiola da Silva
2001	Martina Svobodova

Year	Vert Triples
1998	Malina/Fogarty/Popa
1999	Khris/Bujanda/Boekhorst
2000	event discontinued

Year	Men's Downhill
1995	Derek Downing
1996	Dante Muse
1997	Derek Downing
1998	Patrick Naylor
1999	event discontinued

Year	Women's Downhill
1995	Julie Brandt
1996	Gypsy Tidwell
1997	Gypsy Tidwell
1998	Julie Brandt
1999	event discontinued

Watersports

Year	Barefoot Waterski Jumping
1995	Justin Seers
1996	Ron Scarpa
1997	Peter Fleck
1998	Peter Fleck
1999	event discontinued

Year	Men's Wakeboarding
1996	Parks Bonifay
1997	Jeremy Kovak
1998	Darin Shapiro
1999	Parks Bonifay
2000	Darin Shapiro
2001	Danny Harf

Year	Women's Wakeboarding
1997	Tara Hamilton
1998	Andrea Gaytan
1999	Meaghan Major
2000	Tara Hamilton
2001	Dallas Friday

X-Venture Race

Year	
1995	Team Threadbo*
1996	Team Kobeer
1997	Team Presidio
1998	event discontinued

*In 1995, Team Threadbo won the Eco-Challenge which was held in conjunction with the ESPN Extreme Games.

Winter X Games

CrossOver

Year	
1997	Brian Patch
1998	event discontinued

Free Skiing

Year	Men's Big Air
1999	J.F. Cusson
2000	Candide Thovex
2001	Tanner Hall

Year	Men's Skier X
1998	Dennis Rey
1999	Enak Gavaggio
2000	Shaun Palmer
2001	Zach Crist

Year	Women's Skier X
1999	Aleisha Cline
2000	Anik Demers
2001	Aleisha Cline

Ice Climbing

Year	Men's Difficulty
1997	Jaren Ogden
1998	Will Gadd
1999	Will Gadd
2000	event discontinued

Year	Women's Difficulty
1997	Bird Lew
1998	Kim Csizmazia
1999	Kim Csizmazia
2000	event discontinued

Year	Men's Speed
1997	Jared Ogden
1998	Will Gadd
1999	event discontinued

Year	Women's Speed
1997	Bird Lew
1998	Kim Csizmazia
1999	event discontinued

Skiboarding

Year	
1998	Mike Nick
1999	Chris Hawks
2000	Neal Lyons
2001	not held

Snowboarding

Year	Men's Big Air
1997	Jimmy Halopoff
1998	Jason Borgstede
1999	Kevin Sansalone

Year	Men's Big Air
2000	Peter Line
2001	Jussi Oksanen

Year	Women's Big Air
1997	Barrett Christy
1998	Tina Basich
1999	Barrett Christy
2000	Tara Dakides
2001	Tara Dakides

Year	Men's Boarder X
1997	Shaun Palmer
1998	Shaun Palmer
1999	Shaun Palmer
2000	Drew Neilson
2001	Scott Gaffney

Year	Women's Boarder X
1997	Jennie Waara
1998	Tina Dixon
1999	Maelle Ricker
2000	Leslee Olson
2001	Line Oestvold

Year	Men's Halfpipe
1997	Todd Richards
1998	Ross Powers
1999	Jimi Scott
2000	Todd Richards
2001	not held

Year	Women's Halfpipe
1997	Shannon Dunn
1998	Cara-Beth Burnside
1999	Michele Taggart
2000	S. Brun Kjeldaas
2001	not held

Year	Men's Superpipe
2001	Dan Kass

Year	Women's Superpipe
2001	Shannon Dunn

Year	Men's Slopestyle
1997	Daniel Franck
1998	Ross Powers
1999	Peter Line
2000	Kevin Jones
2001	Kevin Jones

Year	Women's Slopestyle
1997	Barrett Christy
1998	Jennie Waara
1999	Tara Dakides
2000	Tara Dakides
2001	Jaime MacLeod

Super-modified Shovel Racing

Year	
1997	Don Adkins
1998	event discontinued

Snow Mountain Bike Racing

Year	Men's Downhill
1997	Shaun Palmer
1998	Andrew Shandro
1999	event discontinued

Year	Women's Downhill
1997	Missy Giove
1998	Marla Streb
1999	event discontinued

Year	Men's Speed
1997	Phil Tintsman
1998	Jurgen Beneke
1999	event discontinued

Year	Women's Speed
1997	Cheri Elliott
1998	Elke Brutsaert
1999	event discontinued

Year	Men's Biker X
1999	Steve Peat
2000	Myles Rockwell
2001	not held

Year	Women's Biker X
1999	Tara Llanes
2000	Katrina Miller
2001	not held

Snomobiling

Year	Snocross
1998	Toni Haikonen
1999	Chris Vincent
2000	Tucker Hibbert
2001	Blair Morgan

Year	Hillcross
2001	Carl Kuster

Ultracross

Year	
2000	McLain/Lind
2001	Palmer/Takizawa

2001 Great Outdoors Games

Held July 12-15 in Lake Placid, N.Y. Winners of each event listed below.

Fishing

Flyfishing: Chuck Farneth, Little Rock, Ark.

Bass Fishing: Peter Thliveros, Jacksonville, Fla.

Sporting Dogs
(owners listed first)

Retriever Trials: Jerry Day & Super Sue, College Park, Ga.

Big Air: Mike Wallace & Jerry, Troy, N.Y.

Flyball: Rocket Relay, Hamilton, Ont.

Agility (large dogs): Julie Daniels & Spring

Agility (small dogs): Jean LaValley & Taz, Murfreesboro, Tenn.

Target Sports

Rifle Targets: Jerry Miculek, Princeton, La.

Shotgun Grid: Dustin Long, Antelope, Calif.

Archery: Randy Hendrix, Clemons, N.C.

Timber Events

Women's Endurance: Penny Halvorson, Alma Center, Wis.

Men's Endurance: Jason Wynyard, Auckland, NZE

Hot Saw: Mel Lentz, Dianna, W.V.

Springboard: Mitch Hewitt, Wamuran, Queensland, AUS

Men's Boom Run: J.R. Salzman, Rochester, Minn.

Women's Boom Run: Mandy Erdmann, LaCrosse, Wis.

Men's Log Rolling: J.R. Salzman, Rochester, Minn.

Women's Log Rolling: Tina Salzman, Lake Geneva, Wis.

Speed Climbing: Brian Bartow, Grants Pass, Ore.

Tree Topping: Gregg Hart, Maple Bridge, B.C.

Team Relay: Team Halvorson (P. Halvorson, C. Hughes, D. Bolstad, G. Duperre & J. Scutt), Alma Center, Wis.

YACHTING

The America's Cup

International yacht racing was launched in 1851 when England's Royal Yacht Squadron staged a 60-mile regatta around the Isle of Wight and offered a silver trophy to the winner. The 101-foot schooner *America*, sent over by the New York Yacht Club, won the race and the prize. Originally called the Hundred-Guinea Cup, the trophy was renamed The America's Cup after the winning boat's owners deeded it to the NYYC with instructions to defend it whenever challenged.

From 1870-1980, the NYYC successfully defended the Cup 25 straight times; first in large schooners and J-class boats that measured up to 140 feet in overall length, then in 12-meter boats. A foreign yacht finally won the Cup in 1983 when *Australia II* beat defender *Liberty* in the seventh and deciding race off Newport, R.I. Four years later, the San Diego Yacht Club's *Stars & Stripes* won the Cup back, sweeping the four races of the final series off Fremantle, Australia.

Then in 1988, New Zealand's Mercury Bay Boating Club, unwilling to wait the usual three- to four-year period between Cup defenses, challenged the SDYC to a match race, citing the Cup's 102-year-old Deed of Gift, which clearly stated that every challenge had to be honored. Mercury Bay announced it would race a 133-foot monohull. San Diego countered with a 60-foot catamaran. The resulting best-of-three series (Sept. 7-8) was a mismatch as the SDYC's catamaran *Stars & Stripes* won two straight by margins of better than 18 and 21 minutes. Mercury Bay syndicate leader Michael Fay protested the outcome and took the SDYC to court in New York State (where the Deed of Gift was first filed) claiming San Diego had violated the spirit of the deed by racing a catamaran instead of a monohull. N.Y. State Supreme Court judge Carmen Ciparick agreed and on March 28, 1989, ordered the SDYC to hand the Cup over to Mercury Bay. The SDYC refused, but did consent to the court's appointment of the New York Yacht Club as custodian of the Cup until an appeal was ruled on.

On Sept. 19, 1989, the Appellate Division of the N.Y. Supreme Court overturned Ciparick's decision and awarded the Cup back to the SDYC. An appeal by Mercury Bay was denied by the N.Y. Court of Appeals on April 26, 1990, ending three years of legal wrangling. To avoid the chaos of 1988-90, a new class of boat—75-foot monohulls with 110-foot masts—has been used by all competing countries since 1992. Note that (*) indicates skipper was also owner of the boat.

Challenger Series begins in October 2002 for the next America's Cup races scheduled for 2003.

Schooners And J-Class Boats

Year	Winner	Skipper	Series	Loser	Skipper
1851	America	Richard Brown	—	—	—
1870	Magic	Andrew Comstock	1-0	Cambria, GBR	J. Tannock
1871	Columbia (2-1) & Sappho (2-0)	Nelson Comstock Sam Greenwood	4-0	Livonia, GBR	J.R. Woods
1876	Madeleine	Josephus Williams	2-0	Countess of Dufferin, CAN	J.E. Ellsworth
1881	Mischief	Nathanael Clock	2-0	Atalanta, CAN	Alexander Cuthbert*
1885	Puritan	Aubrey Crocker	2-0	Genesta, GBR	John Carter
1886	Mayflower	Martin Stone	2-0	Galatea, GBR	Dan Bradford
1887	Volunteer	Henry Haff	2-0	Thistle, GBR	John Barr
1893	Vigilant	William Hansen	3-0	Valkyrie II, GBR	Wm. Granfield
1895	Defender	Henry Haff	3-0	Valkyrie III, GBR	Wm. Granfield
1899	Columbia	Charles Barr	3-0	Shamrock I, GBR	Archie Hogarth
1901	Columbia	Charles Barr	3-0	Shamrock II, GBR	E.A. Sycamore
1903	Reliance	Charles Barr	3-0	Shamrock III, GBR	Bob Wringe
1920	Resolute	Charles F. Adams	3-2	Shamrock IV, GBR	William Burton
1930	Enterprise	Harold Vanderbilt*	4-0	Shamrock V, GBR	Ned Heard
1934	Rainbow	Harold Vanderbilt*	4-2	Endeavour, GBR	T.O.M. Sopwith
1937	Ranger	Harold Vanderbilt*	4-0	Endeavour II, GBR	T.O.M. Sopwith

12-METER BOATS

Year	Winner	Skipper	Series	Loser	Skipper
1958	Columbia	Briggs Cunningham	4-0	Sceptre, GBR	Graham Mann
1962	Weatherly	Bus Mosbacher	4-1	Gretel, AUS	Jock Sturrock
1964	Constellation	Bob Bavier & Eric Ridder	4-0	Sovereign, AUS	Peter Scott
1967	Intrepid	Bus Mosbacher	4-0	Dame Pattie, AUS	Jock Sturrock
1970	Intrepid	Bill Ficker	4-1	Gretel II, AUS	Jim Hardy
1974	Courageous	Ted Hood	4-0	Southern Cross, AUS	John Cuneo
1977	Courageous	Ted Turner	4-0	Australia	Noel Robins
1980	Freedom	Dennis Conner	4-1	Australia	Jim Hardy
1983	Australia II	John Bertrand	4-3	Liberty, USA	Dennis Conner
1987	Stars & Stripes	Dennis Conner	4-0	Kookaburra III, AUS	Iain Murray

60-FT CATAMARAN VS 133-FT MONOHULL

Year	Winner	Skipper	Series	Loser	Skipper
1988	Stars & Stripes	Dennis Conner	2-0	New Zealand, NZE	David Barnes

75-FT INTERNATIONAL AMERICA'S CUP CLASS

Year	Winner	Skipper	Series	Loser	Skipper
1992	America[3]	Bill Koch* & Buddy Melges	4-1	Il Moro di Venezia, ITA	Paul Cayard
1995	Black Magic, NZE	Russell Coutts	5-0	Young America, USA	Dennis Conner & Paul Cayard
2000	Black Magic, NZE	Russell Coutts & Dean Barker	5-0	Luna Rossa, ITA	Francesco de Angelis

Deaths

The death of the irreplaceable **Dale Earnhardt** left auto racing fans across the country shocked and saddened in 2001.

Affirmed, 26; two-time Horse of the Year Award winner and last thoroughbred to win the Triple Crown (1978); won 22 of 29 career starts and earned $2,393,818; euthanized following months of leg problems; in Lexington, Ky., Jan. 12.

Tommie Agee, 58; N.Y. Mets center fielder best remembered for his two spectacular catches in Game 3 of the 1969 World Series to preserve a 5-0 victory en route to a 4-1 series upset of Baltimore; named A.L. Rookie of the Year in 1966 with Chicago; two-time All-Star; of cardiac arrest; in New York City, Jan. 22.

Michele Alboreto, 44; Italian Formula One driver, who found success on the endurance race circuit; won 1997 Le Mans 24 Hours with the TWR Porsche team; finished second in the F1 driver's championship in 1984; raced in the IRL from 1996-97; in a crash during a test drive; in Berlin, Germany, April 25.

Blaise Alexander, 25; Automobile Racing Club of America (ARCA) and NASCAR Busch Series driver killed in a crash on the 63rd lap of the EasyCare 100 at Lowe's Motor Speedway; ARCA rookie of the year in 1996; of injuries sustained in the crash; in Concord, N.C., Oct. 4.

Earl Anthony, 63; prolific bowling champion of the 1970s and 1980s, who became a fixture on the sport's national weekend telecasts; won more national tour titles (41) and major tournament titles (8) than any other bowler in history; reached the championship round (top-five) of a record 144 tournaments; first bowler to eclipse the $1 million mark in PBA earnings; named PBA Player of the Year six times (1974-76, 1981-83); become the PBA's all-time winningest player in 1976, surpassing Dick Weber with his 27th title; retired temporarily in 1984; returned to the national tour in 1987 with little success; joined the senior tour in 1988 and won seven more titles; worked as a commentator for PBA broadcasts into the 1990s; voted Bowler of the Decade for the 1970s; member of the PBA and American Bowling Congress halls of fame; of injuries sustained in a fall; in New Berlin, Wis., Aug. 14.

Chris Antley, 34; thoroughbred jockey whose career was interrupted by frequent bouts with alcohol, drugs and weight problems but seemed on the rebound after two Triple Crown victories aboard Charismatic in 1999; won first Kentucky Derby in 1991 (Strike the Gold); nation's leading rider in 1985 with 469 wins; finished career with 3,480 wins and his horses earned more than $92 million; lost his New York jockey's license in 1988 when he tested positive for cocaine and marijuana; of severe head trauma; in Pasadena, Calif., Dec. 3, 2000.

Eraste Autin, 18; incoming freshman fullback, who collapsed at a University of Florida preseason workout and died six days later; considered one of the country's top players at his position, he was expected to challenge for a spot in the starting lineup; of complications from heat stroke; in Gainesville, Fla., July 25.

Garnet (Ace) Bailey, 53; L.A. Kings director of pro scouting, who was a passenger on hijacked United Airlines Flight 175 that crashed into the World Trade Center; in his eighth season with the Kings; scouted for the Edmonton Oilers for 13 seasons, winning five Stanley Cups; played 11 seasons in the NHL with Boston, Detroit, St. Louis and Washington and one in the WHA (Edmonton); won two Stanley Cups with Boston; of injuries sustained in the crash; in New York City, Sept. 11.

Mark Bavis, 31; amateur scout with the L.A. Kings, who was a passenger on hijacked United Airlines Flight 175 that crashed into the World Trade Center; scouted college teams for the Kings and was instrumental in selecting two of the team's first three picks in the 2001 draft; former player at Boston University; his twin brother, Michael, is an assistant coach at Boston University; of injuries sustained in the crash; in New York City, Sept. 11.

Jim Benton, 84; Arkansas Razorbacks football star, NFL great and former coach at Arkansas A&M (now Ark.-Monticello); two-time All-Pro and member of the NFL All-Decade Team for the 1940s; won NFL championships with Chicago (1943) and Cleveland (1945); first NFL receiver to have 300 yards receiving in a game; earned All-America selection as a senior in 1937 when he led the nation in receiving with 48 catches for 814 yards; of cancer; in Pine Bluff, Ark., March 28.

Gary Bergman, 62; former Detroit Red Wings defenseman from 1964-1973; played 838 NHL games, totaling 68 goals and 299 assists; played in 1973 All-Star Game; of cancer; in Detroit, Dec. 8, 2000.

Curt Blefary, 57; named A.L. Rookie of the Year in 1965 as an outfielder with Baltimore; won World Series with the Orioles in 1966; also played for Houston, N.Y. Yankees, Oakland and San Diego over eight pro seasons; of pancreatitis; in Pompano Beach, Fla., Jan. 28.

Lou Boudreau, 84; wildly popular, athletic Cleveland Indians shortstop, who led A.L. shortstops in fielding percentage eight times; made history in 1942 when he was named Indians' player/manager at age 24, the youngest person to manage in major league history; led the league in batting (.327) in 1944; went 4-for-4 in Cleveland's one-game playoff with Boston in 1948, which clinched the pennant; won World Series title and A.L. MVP award in 1948 as well; seven-time All-Star; managed the Indians through 1950 then Boston (1952-54) and Kansas City (1955-57); won 1,162 games; credited with devising the Ted Williams Shift; became sports broadcaster in 1958; replaced Cubs skipper Charlie Grimm in May 1960; returned to broadcasting permanently in 1961; two-sport star (baseball, basketball) at the University of Illinois; captained his high school basketball team as a sophomore, a foreshadow of his future leadership abilities; elected to National Baseball Hall of Fame in 1970; cause of his death was not given; in Frankfort, Ill., Aug. 10.

Carl Brewer, 62; former NHL defenseman, who led a group of players in a lawsuit against the NHL Players' Association which resulted in a $40 million settlement in 1992; clubs were forced to reimburse surplus pension money the league had improperly used since 1982; won three Stanley Cups as a player with Toronto (1961-63); three-time NHL All-Star; led the league in penalty minutes twice; played in Detroit, St. Louis and the Toronto Toros (WHA); retired in 1974; a comeback with the Maple Leafs in 1980 lasted 20 games; cause of his death was not given; in Toronto, Canada, Aug. 25.

Diana Golden Brosnihan, 38; first disabled skier inducted into the U.S. National Ski Hall of Fame (1997); won 19 U.S. disabled championships before retiring after the 1990 season; lost her right leg to bone cancer when she was 12; of cancer; in Providence, R.I., Aug. 25.

Bob Buhl, 72; hard-throwing right-hander, who along with Warren Spahn and Lew Burdette, was a pitching star on the Milwaukee Braves' 1957 championship team; pitched in two All-Star Games; won 166 games with Milwaukee, Chicago and Philadelphia; earned a reputation for futility at the plate when he set a record for most at-bats in a season without a hit (0-for-70) in 1962; finished his career with a .089 average in 857 career plate appearances; cause of his death was not given; in Titusville, Fla., Feb. 16.

Ely Callaway, 82; golf visionary responsible for turning the Callaway Golf Co. into the world's biggest clubmaker and introducing the "Big Bertha" driver to weekend golfers; after a 30-year career in the textile industry, he bought a small golf company called Hickory Stick for $400,000 in 1984; through technological breakthroughs like his patented bore-through design and oversized irons, he increased Callaway sales from a modest $5 million in 1988 to $800 million a decade later; resigned as president and CEO on May 15; of pancreatic cancer; in Rancho Santa Fe, Calif., July 5.

AP/Wide World Photos
Earl Anthony

AP/Wide World Photos
Chris Antley

AP/Wide World Photos
Lou Boudreau

Lewis Chitengwa, 26; internationally renowned junior and amateur golfer, who turned pro in 1998 and was a rookie on the Canadian PGA Tour; first black man to win the South African men's amateur championship in 1993; native of Harare, Zimbabwe, he won his country's amateur championship three times; defeated Tiger Woods at the Orange Bowl International Junior Championship in 1992; played on the Buy.com Tour in 2000; became ill after second round of the Edmonton Open and died at the hospital later that afternoon; after being infected with meningococcal meningitis bacteria; in Edmonton, Alberta, Canada, June 30.

Charlie Coe, 77; remarkable amateur golfer who won U.S. amateur titles in 1949 and 1958; lost 1959 title defense to Jack Nicklaus after a 36-hole playoff; appeared in 19 Masters, finishing tied for second in 1961; appeared on seven Walker Cup teams and was named captain twice; cause of his death was not given; in Oklahoma City, Okla., May 16.

Jim Coleman, 89; colorful writer whose career as one of Canada's best-known sportswriters spanned nearly 70 years; most recently a columnist at the *Vancouver Province*; of heart failure after being treated for a broken hip; in Vancouver, B.C., Canada, Jan. 13.

Phil Collier, 75; San Diego-area baseball reporter for almost 40 years; broke the story that Sandy Koufax was retiring in 1966; became a national baseball writer in the 1980s and wrote a weekly column after his retirement in 1996 through 1999; inducted into the writer's wing of the Baseball Hall of Fame in 1990; of cancer; in San Diego, Feb. 24.

George Conner, 94; last surviving pre-World War II Indy 500 driver; started 14 races between 1935-52; finished third in 1949 and had five top-10 Indy 500 finishes; cause of his death was not given; in Indianapolis, March 30.

Neal Colzie, 48; former NFL defensive back and first round pick of the Oakland Raiders in 1975; played nine pro seasons with Oakland, Miami and Tampa Bay; second on the Raiders' career punt returns list; of a heart attack; in Miami, Aug. 19.

John Cooper, 77; British car designer responsible for the Mini Cooper and the introduction of rear-engine Formula One race cars; founded Cooper Car Co. with his father, Charles, in 1946; found success in the 1950s with a revolutionary car design that mounted the engine behind the driver, a standard concept today; a Cooper car, driven by Sterling Moss, won its first grand prix in 1958; won F1 constructors' titles in 1959 and 1960; his Mini Cooper acheived cult status in the 1960s thanks to celebrity owners like John Lennon and Paul McCartney; awarded a Commanders of the Order of the British Empire (CBE) in 1999 for his services to the motor industry; of cancer; in Worthing, England, Dec. 24, 2000.

Lord Colin Cowdrey, 67; former Kent and England captain considered one of the most gifted cricket batsmen of his generation; fourth highest scoring England player in test history with 7,264 runs in 114 tests (international matches); he was also a celebrated fielder and at one time held the English record with 120 test catches; past president of the Marylebone Cricket Club, the sport's ruling body in England, in 1987; chairman of the International Cricket Council 1989-93; knighted in 1992; appointed to the House of Lords in 1997 as Lord Cowdrey of Tonbridge; of a heart attack; in Angmering, England, Dec. 5, 2000.

József Csérmák, 68; first Olympic champion to break the 60-meter mark in the hammer throw (1952 Helsinki Olympics); won 1954 European championships; coached 1968 Olympic hammer champion, and fellow Hungarian, Gyula Zsivótzky; of a heart attack; in Tapolca, Hungary, Jan. 12.

Robert Damron, 36; professional motorcycle racer; named Dirt Motorcyclist of the Year in 2000 by the Oakland-based Motor Sports Press Association; in a crash while racing at the Perris Auto Speedway; in Perris, Calif., June 30.

Devaughn Darling, 18; Florida State freshman linebacker; registered 11 tackles in seven games on special teams in 2000; died after collapsing after an off-season workout; cause of his death was not given; in Tallahassee, Feb. 26.

Adhemar Ferreira da Silva, 73; Olympic triple jump champion in 1952 and 1956, and the only Brazilian athlete to win two Olympic gold medals; awarded the Olympic Merit award by the Brazilian Olympic Committee in 2000; of pneumonia; in Sao Paulo, Brazil, Jan. 12.

Lawrence (Crash) Davis, 82; minor league infielder made famous by the 1988 film "Bull Durham"; played for Raleigh, Reidsville and the Durham Bulls of the Carolina Leagues from 1946-51; hit a league-record 50 doubles and batted .318 for Durham in 1948; worked as a personnel executive for a North Carolina textile manufacturer for almost 30 years; retired in 1985; of cancer; in Greensboro, N.C., Aug. 31.

Eddie Donovan, 78; former GM and coach of the N.Y. Knicks; drafted Willis Reed in 1964 and dealt for Dave DeBusschere in 1968, two moves that helped New York win its first NBA title in 1970; was the opposing coach when Wilt Chamberlain scored 100 points in a game in 1962; coached St. Bonaventure to three postseason appearances; of complications from a stroke; in Bernardsville, N.J., Jan. 20.

Jaroslav Drobny, 79; Czech-born tennis Hall of Famer; won 133 career singles titles and was ranked in the world's top-10 for 10 consecutive years from 1946-55; won Grand Slam singles titles at Wimbledon (1954) and the French Open (1951-52); was 24-4 in Davis Cup singles matches from 1946-49; world class hockey player, who won a world amateur title with Czechoslovakia in 1947 and a silver medal at the 1948 St. Moritz Olympics; defected in 1959 and became a British citizen; cause of his death was not given; in London, England, Sept. 13.

Walter Dukes, 70; Seton Hall center who set the current NCAA single-season record for total rebounds (734) during the 1952-53 season; won NIT with Seton Hall in 1953 and was named tournament MVP; drafted by the Knicks, but, instead, signed a lucrative deal with the Harlem Globetrotters; played eight seasons in the NBA with New York, Minneapolis and Detroit; two-time NBA All-Star; cause of his death was not given; in Detroit, March 13.

Dale Earnhardt, 49; seven-time NASCAR Winston Cup champion and one of the most beloved drivers in auto racing history; considered the heart and soul of the sport by fans and sportswriters alike; best known for his dark sunglasses, push-broom mustache and his #3 black Chevrolet; nicknamed "The Intimidator" for his aggressive racing style; won more races at Atlanta Motor Speedway (nine) and Talladega Speedway (10) than any other driver; his 76 career victories placed him sixth on the all-time list at the time of his death; career leading money winner with $41,639,622; won at least one race each season from 1982-96; recorded a top-10 finish in 428 of his 676 career starts; won 22 career poles; won his first Daytona 500 in 1998, on his 20th attempt; first career victory: April 1, 1979 at Bristol Motor Speedway; won 1979 Rookie of the Year Award; won the National Motorsport Press Association's Driver of the Year Award four times and twice selected the American Driver of the Year; of injuries sustained in an accident on the final lap of the 2001 Daytona 500; in Daytona Beach, Fla., Feb. 18.

Jack Fleming, 77; former Pittsburgh Steelers announcer famous for his call of the "Immaculate Reception" in 1972; broadcast West Virginia basketball and football games for 42 years; cause of his death was not given; in Pittsburgh, Jan. 3.

Nate Fleming, 20; redshirt freshman guard on the Oklahoma State men's basketball team, who was killed when a team charter plane crashed near Denver while returning home from a game in Colorado; former walk-on; played in four games last season and was recovering this season from a broken nose; high school valedictorian; of injuries sustained in the crash; in Strasburg, Colo., Jan. 27.

Stan Fox, 48; race car driver whose career ended in a horrifying, first-lap accident at the Indianapolis 500 in 1995 where he was photographed with his legs dangling, unprotected, out of the wreckage of his car; started racing career in 1972 and made eight starts in nine years at the Indy 500; finished a career-best seventh in 1987; in an auto accident; in Auckland, New Zealand, Dec. 18, 2000.

Eddie Futch, 90; venerable boxing trainer, who worked with 20 world champions, including five heavyweight titleholders, during a career that spanned seven decades; trained heavyweight champions Joe Frazier, Larry Holmes, Trevor Berbick, Michael Spinks and Riddick Bowe; sparring partner of Joe Louis in Detroit in the 1930s; gained notoriety for refusing to allow Joe Frazier to go out for the final round of the "Thrilla in Manilla"; retired in 1997; inducted into International Boxing Hall of Fame in 1994; cause of death not given; in Las Vegas, Oct. 10.

Anders Gernandt, 80; Swedish Olympic equestrian competitor in 1956 and 1960; popular sportscaster and TV personality; of heart problems; in Stockholm, Sweden, Nov. 2, 2000.

Marty Glickman, 83; radio and television voice of New York sports for more than 55 years; became first N.Y. Knicks radio announcer in 1946; broadcast N.Y. Giants and Jets games as well as horse races at Yonkers Raceway; first voice of the NBA on television in 1954; accused the USOC of anti-Semitism at the 1936 Berlin Olympics for replacing him and the only other Jewish athlete on the track-and-field team in the 400-meter relay; member of the Basketball Hall of Fame, from complications after heart surgery; in New York City, Jan. 3.

Lou Groza, 76; Hall of Fame kicker and offensive lineman for the Cleveland Browns from 1946-67; nine-time Pro Bowler; NFL player of the year in 1954; scored a franchise record 1,349 career points; played in nine NFL title games and won four, including three in the 1950s and one in 1964; nicknamed "The Toe"; inducted into the Pro Football Hall of Fame in 1985; remained active with the Browns up until his death; the award given to the nation's top college kicker is named after him; cause of his death was not given; in Cleveland, Nov. 29, 2000.

Einar Gustafson, 65; baseball fan, whose battle with a rare form of non-Hodgkin's lymphoma as a child in 1948 inspired the Jimmy Fund, a cancer research organization and the official charity of the Boston Red Sox; given the nickname "Jimmy" by the foundation's founder, who wanted Gustafson to remain anonymous; his identity was a mystery until 1997 when his sister sent an explanatory letter with her annual donation; of cancer; in Caribou, Maine, Jan. 21.

Christl Haas, 57; Austrian skier, who won the gold medal in women's downhill at the 1964 Innsbruck Olympics; by drowning; in Manavgat, Turkey, July 8.

Harold (Happy) Hairston, 58; fierce rebounding forward, who played a key role on one of pro sports' greatest teams, the 1971 L.A. Lakers, set NBA record for rebounds in a quarter (13) against the 76ers in 1974; established the Happy Hairston Youth Foundation in Century City, Calif. after he retired; from complications of inoperable prostate cancer; in Los Angeles, May 1.

Lionel Hebert, 72; PGA and Senior PGA golfer who was half of the only brother combination to win PGA Championships; upset Dow Finsterwald to win 1957 PGA Championship, three years before his brother Jay won the major; Ryder Cup team member in 1957; two-time vice president of the PGA; cause of his death was not given; in Lafayette, La., Dec. 30, 2000.

Levi Jackson, 74; first black football player in Yale history and first to be elected captain (1949 team), a move that made local and national newspaper headlines; played fullback and punted; sixth-leading rusher in school history; joined Ford Motor Company in 1950 and held major executive positions in urban affairs and labor relations; received the Distinguished American Award from the Walter Camp Football Foundation in 1987; of congestive heart failure; in Detroit, Dec. 7, 2000.

Sam Jethroe, 83; one of the first black players in Major League Baseball history and the oldest player to ever win rookie of the year honors; nicknamed "The Jet" for his speed; debuted in 1950 with the Boston Braves, earning rookie honors at age 32; led the N.L. in stolen bases twice; played in the Negro Leagues and minor league baseball before and after his pro career; of a heart attack; in Erie, Penn., June 16.

Terry Johnson, 50; Los Angeles-area sportswriter and editor, who covered the L.A. Dodgers for 29 years; assistant sports editor at the *Antelope Valley Press* since 2000; in a car accident; in Los Angeles, July 4.

Horace A. (Jimmy) Jones, 94; Hall of Fame trainer who saddled Citation to the final two legs of the 1948 Triple Crown and two additional Kentucky Derby winners; won 54 stakes races and trained seven champion horses during his career from 1926-64; country's leading trainer five times (1947-49, 1957, 1961); first trainer to surpass the $1 million mark in earnings; son of Hall of Famer Ben Jones; cause of death not given; in Maryville, Mo., Sept. 2.

Henry Kaelarne, 88; Swedish runner who set two world records and won a bronze medal (5000m) at the 1936 Berlin Olympics; broke 2000m record in 1937 and the 3000m record in 1940; banned from competition in 1946 for violating his amateur status by accepting payments; originally Henry Jonsson, he changed his name in 1940; cause of his death was not given; in Stockholm, Sweden, March 17.

Dr. Robert Kerr, 65; controversial sports medicine specialist from California, who became known as the "steroid guru" for his well-documented support of performance-enhancing drugs during the 1980s; testified before the Canadian government in 1989 that he provided steroids for about 20 athletes who won medals at the 1984 Los Angeles Olympics; of a heart attack; in San Gabriel, Calif., Jan. 3.

Victor Kiam II, 74; former New England Patriots owner (1988-92) and part-owner of Remington Products Co., which specializes in electric razors; owned the Patriots when the team was sued by a female journalist who claimed a player exposed himself and made lewd comments, sparking a national debate in 1990 about women reporters in the locker room; of an unspecified heart condition; in Stamford, Conn., May 27.

David Kipiani, 50; star forward on the Soviet Union's national soccer team during the 1970s and 80s; coach of Georgia's national team since 1997; in a car crash; in Tbilisi, Georgia, Sept. 17.

Lou Kusserow, 73; record-setting tailback and safety at Columbia in the 1940s, who later became a producer for NBC Sports; scored two touchdowns in Columbia's 21-20 victory over Army in 1947 which snapped the Cadets' 30-game unbeaten streak; holds school records for career touchdowns and points; joined NBC as a business manager in 1957 and began producing six months later; produced six World Series, five Super Bowls, 15 years of golf and 12 years of baseball's "Game of the Week"; of complications from prostate cancer; in Rancho Mirage, Calif., June 30.

Daniel Lawson, 21; redshirt junior reserve guard on the Oklahoma State basketball team, who was killed when a team charter plane crashed near Denver while returning home from a game in Colorado; played in 17 games during the 2001 season and averaged 1.9 points-per-game; of injuries sustained in the crash; in Strasburg, Colo., Jan. 27.

Cawood Ledford, 75; voice of University of Kentucky football and basketball for nearly four decades; called UK games for various radio stations begining in 1953; retired after the 1991-92 basketball season; called 17 NCAA Final Fours; also a renowned horse racing broadcaster, calling the Kentucky Derby more than 15 times for CBS Radio; his thrilling call of Northern Dancer's 1964 Derby victory over Hill Rise is considered one of the sports' best; of cancer; in Harlan, Ky., Sept. 5.

Tony Leswick, 78; feisty Detroit Red Wings forward partly responsible for one of the most famous goals in NHL history; credited with the goal that was accidentally knocked into the Montreal net in OT of Game 7, claiming the 1954 Stanley Cup for Detroit; won titles with Detroit in 1952 and 1955 as well; compiled 868 penalty minutes, 165 goals and 159 assists in 740 regular-season games; of cancer; in British Columbia, Canada, July 1.

Carol Anne Letheren, 58; Canadian Olympic Association CEO and the official who took Ben Johnson's medal away at the 1988 Seoul Olympics; one of 14 women on the International Olympic Committee at the time of her death; member of the IOC co-ordinating committee for the 2002 Salt Lake City Olympics; former intercollegiate provincial badminton champion; officiated gymnastics at the 1976 and 1984 Olympics as well as five world championships; praised for her handling of the Johnson drug scandal, which was her springboard to an IOC seat in 1990; of a brain aneurysm; in Toronto, Feb. 2.

Raymond Lewis, 48; Los Angeles basketball legend, who left college early for the NBA but never played a minute of pro basketball due to a career path that took one tragic turn after another; a schoolyard and high school phenom, he averaged more than 30 points-per-game his first two years at Cal State Los Angeles (played varsity as a sophomore); drafted by Philadelphia in 1973, but held out over a contract dispute; lawsuits and frequent disappearances later kept him from playing with Utah of the ABA, Philadelphia again and the San Diego Clippers; from complications following the amputation of a leg; in Los Angeles, Feb. 11.

Woodley Lewis, 76; defensive back and kick returner, who led the NFL with 12 interceptions as a rookie in 1950; played with the Rams, Cardinals and Cowboys from 1950-61; of unspecified kidney and heart problems; in Los Angeles, Dec. 29, 2000.

Alois Lipburger, 44; Austria's ski jumping coach; silver medalist at the 1978 world championships; in a car accident on his way home from a world cup event; in Munich, Germany, Feb. 5.

John Lotz, 64; top assistant coach to Dean Smith at UNC from 1965-73 and head coach at Florida from 1973-80; named SEC Coach of the Year in 1977; ran UNC's community outreach program the last 20 years; after a short illness; in Chapel Hill, N.C., May 5.

Eddie Mathews, 69; left-handed slugging third baseman and 10-time All-Star, who has the distinction of being the only player to suit up for the Braves in Boston, Milwaukee and Atlanta; combined with Hank Aaron to form the most prolific home run tandem in major league history; the duo hit 863 homers from 1954-66, the highest total for teammates (Gehrig and Ruth had 859); hit 512 career home runs; hit 30-plus homers for nine straight years and posted five 100-plus RBI seasons; one of only five players to hit an extra-inning, game-winning home run in the World Series, as he did in Game 4 in 1957; won World Series titles with Milwaukee (1957) and Detroit (1968); twice led the N.L. in home runs (1953,1959); featured on the first cover of Sports Illustrated in August 1954; managed Atlanta during the mid-1970s; inducted into Baseball Hall of Fame in 1978; of complications from pneumonia; in La Jolla, Calif., Feb. 18.

Joey Maxim, 79; Hall of Fame boxer and former light heavyweight champion who outlasted Sugar Ray Robinson in a sweltering title fight at Yankee Stadium in 1952; won 175-pound world title in 1950 (Freddie Mills); lost heavyweight title fight in 1951 (Ezzard Charles); his defeat of Robinson in the 14th round in over 100-degree heat marked the only time Robinson did not answer the bell in his career; lost his title in 1952 (Archie Moore); retired in 1958 with a record of 82-29-4 and 21 KOs; suffered a stroke in February; cause of his death was not given; in West Palm Beach, Fla., June 2.

Stan (Chook) Maxwell, 66; pro hockey pioneer, who was one of the first black players to play professional hockey; starred in Canada's junior hockey ranks and signed with Punch Imlach's Quebec Aces of the Quebec Hockey League at age 20; played for the Montreal Royals and spent a number of seasons in the International Hockey League; retired in 1971; of cancer; in Turuo, Nova Scotia, Canada, Sept. 7.

AP/Wide World Photos
Eddie Mathews

AP/Wide World Photos
Willie Stargell

Minnesota Vikings
Korey Stringer

Al McGuire, 72; former Marquette men's college basketball coach and television commentator; coached Marquette from 1964-77 after seven seasons at Belmont (N.C.) Abby College; lead the Golden Eagles to 11 consecutive postseason appearances beginning in 1967; won NIT championship in 1970; won the school's only NCAA championship in his final game as a coach in 1977; won coach of the year honors in 1971 and 1974; compiled a 405-143 career record; his .739 winning percentage ranked him 18th all-time among Div. I coaches at the time of his death; elected to the Basketball Hall of Fame in 1992; spent 23 years as a broadcaster, first with NBC in 1977 and then CBS since 1992; retired March 2000; of a blood disorder; in Milwaukee, Jan. 26.

John McKay, 77; legendary USC football coach who popularized the "I" formation in the 1960s and later became the first head coach of the Tampa Bay Buccaneers franchise; remembered for his candor and sharp, witty one-liners when dealing with the press; once questioned about his team's execution, McKay quipped, "I think it's a good idea."; lost his first 26 games with Tampa Bay, an NFL record; led the Bucs to the 1979 NFC Championship Game and postseason appearances in 1981 and 1982; despite a 44-88-1 record in nine seasons (1976-84), he was the team's winningest coach until 1997; won four national titles at USC, only Bear Bryant has more (6); in 16 seasons was 127-40-8, had three undefeated seasons, and won nine Pac-8 titles; coached 40 first-team All-Americans and two Heisman Trophy winners; assistant coach at USC and Oregon before taking over the Trojans in 1960; three-year letterman at Oregon; inducted into College Football Hall of Fame in 1988; his son, Rich, is the Buccaneers' GM; of kidney failure due to complications from diabetes; in Tampa, June 10.

Ralph Miller, 82; Hall of Fame men's college basketball coach at Oregon State, Iowa and Wichita State; his 657 career victories places him 17th on the Div. I all-time list at the time of his death; had just three losing seasons during 38-year coaching career; won four Pac-10 titles at OSU and made eight NCAA tournament appearances in 19 seasons from 1971-89; his 1981 Beavers' team was ranked #1 for nine weeks; won two Big Ten titles in six seasons at Iowa; won one Missouri Valley Conference title in 13 seasons at Wichita State; two-time AP Coach of the Year; inducted into Basketball Hall of Fame in 1988; retired in 1989; court at Oregon State is named after him; cause of his death was not given; in Black Butte, Ore., May 15.

John Murray Murdoch, 96; was the oldest living Stanley Cup champion; speedy, defensive-minded forward who in 1926 was the first player signed by the N.Y. Rangers; helped New York win titles after the 1927-28 and 1932-33 seasons; played in 600 consecutive games, a record that stood for 30 years; scored 84 goals and had 108 assists, along with 197 penalty minutes, in 508 regular-season games; retired in 1937; coached Yale hockey for 27 years; cause of his death was not given; in Pawley's Island, S.C., May 17.

Dennis (Duke) Nalon, 87; two-time Indianapolis 500 pole-winner and fixture at the annual race since the 1950s; started 10 Indy 500s from 1938-53, finishing third in 1948; drove the pace car in 1981 and 1983; was one of the last two living pre-World War II Indy drivers, the other, George Connor, died on March 30; cause of his death was not given; in Indianapolis, Ind., Feb. 26.

Joe Norris, 93; organized the first American Bowling Congress "beer team" in 1933, which prompted the sport's most prolific bowling league and put Detroit at the center of the bowling map; captained the brewery-sponsored team that won the 1934 ABC title; nicknamed "Boy Wonder of Bowling"; bowled with a legendary team of American bowlers in an exhibition before the 1936 Berlin Olympics; in 1994, at age 86, became the oldest bowler in ABC history to roll a perfect 300 game, a record that has since been broken; was scheduled to play in a record 72nd ABC Championships Tournament in March; of pneumonia; in San Diego, Feb. 19.

Charley Pell, 60; Florida Gators football coach from 1979-84; resigned after the NCAA levied 59 sanctions against the program; compiled a 33-26-3 record and was 2-2 in bowl appearances; also coached at Clemson and Jacksonville State; former two-way lineman at Alabama; of cancer; in Gadsen, Ala., May 29.

Lowell Perry, 69; All-American receiver at the University of Michigan in the 1950s, who later became the NFL's first black coach in more than 40 years; won Rose Bowl over California in 1951; injured in his sixth NFL game with Pittsburgh in 1956 and retired; became the Steelers receivers coach a year later; hired by CBS to broadcast games in 1966; served as a lawyer with the National Labor Relations Board and the Chrysler management team after football; appointed by President Gerald Ford to head the Equal Employment Opportunity Commission in 1975; of cancer; in Southfield, Mich., Jan. 7.

Andy Phillip, 79; playmaking guard, who was the first NBA player to record 500 assists in a season (1952); five-time NBA All-Star; helped Boston win first of 16 NBA championships in 1957; All-American at Illinois where he ran the show for the "Whiz Kids" teams that won Big Ten titles in 1941 and 1942; inducted to Basketball Hall of Fame in 1961; cause of death was not given; in Rancho Mirage, Calif., April 28.

Cole Pittman, 21; Texas sophomore defensive end, who played in 23 games for the Longhorns, compiling 30 tackles and two sacks in two seasons; in a one-car accident; in Easterly, Texas, Feb. 26.

Hal Haig Prieste, 104; America's oldest Olympic medal winner; won a bronze medal in platform diving at 1920 Antwerp Olympics; played an original Keystone Kop in silent pictures, appearing in 25 movies and on Broadway; cause of his death was not given; in Camden, N.J., April 19.

Fred Raphael, 80; TV innovator whose work with the Emmy-winning "Shell's Wonderful World of Golf" and the Legends of Golf series in 1978 led to the creation of the Senior PGA Tour in 1980; of liver cancer; in Bridgehampton, N.Y., June 12.

Dick Rehbein, 45; New England Patriots quarterbacks coach; spent 23 seasons as an assistant coach in the NFL with Green Bay, Minnesota and the New York Giants; of cardiac arrest related to a previous heart condition; in Boston, Aug. 6.

Bill Rigney, 83; first manager of the San Francisco Giants after their move from Brooklyn in 1957, succeeding Leo Durocher a year earlier; won World Series as an infielder with the N.Y. Giants in 1951 and as a coach in 1954; managed the Giants, Angels and Twins in 18 seasons, compiled 1,239 career wins; after a brief stint as a scout he joined the Oakland A's front office in 1982; broadcast A's baseball in 1974 and again from 1983-84; of cancer; in Oakland, Feb. 20.

Gordon Ritz, 74; investor who helped found the Minnesota North Stars (now Dallas) and served as team president from 1976-78; of cancer; in Wayzata, Minn., Aug. 10.

Guy Rodgers, 65; four-time NBA All-Star guard and former Philadelphia "Big 5" star; led the NBA in assists twice; his 6,917 career assists put him 10th on the list of all-time leaders at the time of his death; recorded 20 assists in Chamberlain's 100-point game in 1962; averaged 11.7 points, 7.8 assists and 4.3 rebounds a game in 12 pro seasons; drafted by Philadelphia in 1958, also played for Chicago, Cincinnati and Milwaukee; two-time All-American at Temple; led the Owls to third place finishes in the 1956 and 1958 NCAA tournaments and the 1957 NIT; cause of his death was not given; in Los Angeles, Feb. 19.

Dean Roper, 62; Automobile Racing Club of America driver who died on the 17th lap of the Allen Crowe Memorial, 10 months after his son, Tony, was killed in a NASCAR truck series race; USAC Stock driving champion from 1981-83; winningest ARCA series driver on dirt with nine career victories; of a heart attack suffered during the race; in Springfield, Ill., Aug. 19.

Sandy Saddler, 75; former featherweight champion known for possessing an uncanny finishing punch for a man his size, which helped him earn a 144-16-2 record with 103 knockouts; had memorable four-fight series with Willie Pep during 1949-51, knocking Pep out in three of them; forced to retire as champion in 1957 after sustaining an eye injury when the taxi in which he was riding was involved in an accident; trained several pro boxers, including George Foreman in the 1970s; elected to the Boxing Hall of Fame in 1990; he had Alzheimer's disease; cause of his death was not given; in New York City, Sept. 18.

Hank Sauer, 84; two-time All-Star outfielder with the Chicago Cubs who won 1952 N.L. MVP honors despite the fact the Cubs finished fifth in the division; played 15 years with Cincinnati, Chicago-NL, St. Louis and the N.Y./San Francisco Giants; retired in 1959; stayed in baseball in several capacities, including scouting for the Giants until 1993; cause of his death was not given; in Burlingame, Calif., Aug. 24.

George Senesky, 78; member of the 1947 Philadelphia Warriors, the NBA's first championship team; coached the Warriors to another NBA title in 1956; led the nation in scoring and named an All-American his senior year at St. Joseph's (1943); cause of his death was not given; in Philadelphia, June 26.

Billy Ray Smith, 66; a 13-year NFL defensive lineman, who played in two Super Bowls with the Baltimore Colts; played for Los Angeles (1957) and Pittsburgh (1958-60) before being traded to the Colts; retired after 1971 Super Bowl; son, Billy Ray Jr., played linebacker with San Diego in the 1980s; of complications from cancer; in Little Rock, Ark., March 21.

Mark Smith, 41; former Illinois basketball standout, who along with teammate Eddie Johnson, led the Illini to their first NCAA tournament appearance in 18 years; fourth-leading scorer in Illinois basketball history; cause of his death was not given; in Peoria, Ill., June 27.

Mari-Rae Sopper, 35; gymnastics coach at UC-Santa Barbara who was one of the passengers aboard American Airlines Flight 77 which crashed into the Pentagon; on her way to California to take over the recently reinstated program; former assistant coach at the U.S. Naval Academy; of injuries sustained in the crash; in Washington D.C., Sept. 11.

Willie Stargell, 61; one of baseball's greatest home run hitters and the intimidating—but amicable—leader of the great Pittsburgh Pirates' teams of the 1970s; nicknamed "Pops" after inheriting his role as patriarch of the Pirates family after the death of teammate Roberto Clemente in 1972; 6-4, 225-pound outfielder and cleanup hitter often invoked in discussions of baseball's most prolific home-run hitters; hit 475 career home runs, and at one point in his career held the record for the longest homer in nearly half of the N.L. parks; most baseball historians agree the lefthanded hitter's HR total would have reached 600 if not for the fact that the Pirates played at Forbes Field (with its giant right-field power alley of 436 feet) for the first 8½ of his 21 seasons with the team; won N.L. pennants and World Series titles in 1971 and 1979; won six N.L. East titles from 1970-79; holds team records for home runs, extra-base hits and RBI; in 1979, at age 39, he had an unprecedented sweep of MVP awards (sharing regular season, playoffs, World Series); oldest player to be named MVP; led the N.L. in home runs twice and RBI once; retired in 1982; had coaching stints with the Pirates and Braves; inducted into Baseball Hall of Fame in 1988; a 12-foot bronze statue in his honor was unveiled in 2001 at PNC Park; suffered from a kidney disorder for several years; of a stroke; in Wilmington, N.C., April 9.

John Steadman, 73; Baltimore sportswriter and columnist; hired by the *Baltimore News-Post* in 1945; broke story of Baltimore's first return to the NFL in 1952; covered 719 straight Colts/Ravens games through Dec. 10, 2000; joined *The Evening Sun* in the 1980s, and the *Baltimore Sun* in 1995; authored seven books; won three Freedom Foundation medals; served on the selection committee for the Pro Football Hall of Fame; of cancer; in Baltimore, Jan. 1.

Cecilia Straub-Rubens, 83; co-owner and breeder of Tiznow, the 3-year-old thoroughbred, who won 2000 Breeders' Cup Classic; of a heart attack during surgery, three days after the race; in Newport Beach, Calif., Nov. 7, 2000.

Korey Stringer, 27; Minnesota Vikings Pro Bowl offensive tackle, who died of heat stroke during the team's preseason training camp; started the last 65 straight games at right tackle for the Vikings and played in 91 of a possible 93 regular season games in his six seasons; key blocker for RB Robert Smith, who rushed for a team-record 1,521 yards in 2000; first round draft pick (24th overall) out of Ohio State in 1995; voted Buckeye's team MVP and consensus All-American in 1994; Big Ten Offensive Lineman of the Year in 1993 and 1994; lost consciousness after a workout and was rushed to the hospital where his body temperature was measured at 108.8 degrees; believed to be the second training camp fatality in NFL history: J.V. Cain, a tight end for the St. Louis Cardinals, died of a heart attack on July 22, 1979; of complications from heat stroke; in Mankato, Minn., Aug. 1.

Eric Tipton, 86; star running back and punter at Duke in the mid-1930s; played seven seasons of Major League Baseball with Philadelphia and Cincinnati; assistant football coach at William & Mary and assistant football/baseball coach at Army; inducted into College Football Hall of Fame in 1965; cause of his death was not given; in Newport News, Va., Aug. 29.

Dan Towler, 73; one of three bruising fullbacks on the dynamic L.A. Rams teams of the 1950s and dedicated student of theology; one of three 200-pound-plus backs in the Rams' "Bull Elephants" backfield (Paul "Tank" Younger and Dick Hoerner); known as "Deacon Dan"; won NFL title with the Rams in 1951; named All-Pro from 1951-53; led the NFL in rushing once and touchdowns twice; gained 3,493 yards and scored 43 touchdowns in six pro seasons; remembered for missing several team meetings while pursuing a master's degree in religion at USC (which he received in 1955); retired from football in 1955 and was named pastor of the Lincoln Avenue Methodist Church in Pasadena, Calif.; longtime chaplain at Cal. State Los Angeles and president of the L.A. County Board of Education; cause of his death was not given; in Pasadena, Calif., Aug. 1.

Dan Turk, 38; half of the first brother-to-brother, long snapper-to-punter combination in NFL history; drafted by Pittsburgh in 1987; played 15 seasons at center with Tampa Bay, L.A./Oakland Raiders and Washington; teamed with his younger brother, Matt, a punter, in Washington (1997-99); his last career snap led to a botched fourth-quarter field goal attempt and resulted in a 14-13 loss to Tampa Bay in the playoffs on Jan 25, 2000; diagnosed with testicular cancer in April 2000; of cancer; in Ashburn, Va., Dec. 24, 2000.

Shawn Walsh, 46; University of Maine men's hockey coach, who turned a team that went 27-65 in the three seasons before he arrived into a two-time national champion; made 11 NCAA postseason appearances in 17 seasons at Maine from 1984-2001; won national titles after the 1992-93 and 1998-99 seasons; coached Hobey Baker recipients Scott Pellerin (1992) and Paul Kariya (1993), plus 26 other All-Americans while compiling a 399-215-44 record; ranked 11th in career victories among active coaches (and 19th all-time) at the time of his death; won national coach of the year honors in 1995; his use of an ineligible player during the 1991-92 season caused the team to forfeit games; served a one-year suspension after an NCAA investigation of the entire Maine athletic department in 1993-94; diagnosed with renal cell carcinoma, a rare form of cancer in June 2000; of cancer; in Bangor, Maine, Sept. 24.

Tim Weigel, 56; a 30-year veteran of Chicago's sports' airwaves; started his career at the defunct *Chicago Daily News* in 1971 and also worked for the *Chicago Sun Times*; after years at WLS-TV and WMAQ-TV, he was named sports director at WBBM-TV in 1995; Yale freshman-year roommate of longtime Chicago film critic Gene Siskel; diagnosed with a brain tumor in 2000; cause of his death was not given; in Evanston, Ill., June 17.

Rashidi Wheeler, 22; Northwestern University senior starting safety, who died following conditioning drills at the school; started all 12 games and had 88 tackles, a fumble recovery and three pass breakups for the Wildcats' team that tied for the Big Ten title in 2000; his death came two days after the death of Korey Stringer, the Vikings' lineman who suffered heat stroke at the team's training camp and died; of a fatal asthma attack; in Evanston, Ill., Aug. 3.

Diane Whipple, 33; women's lacrosse coach at St. Mary's College (Moraga, Calif.), who was the victim of a dog attack that made national headlines; former head coach at UC-San Diego; two-time first team All-American at Penn St. and NCAA National Player of the Year in 1990; of injuries sustained when she was attacked by a neighbor's two dogs while trying to get into her apartment; in San Francisco, Jan. 26.

Wyoming cross-country team; eight University of Wyoming cross-country runners killed in a head-on accident with a pickup truck driven by another student on U.S. 287; Nicholas Schabron, 20; Justin Lambert-Belanger, 20; Kyle Johnson, 20; Kevin Salverson, 19; Shane Shatto, 19; Joshua Jones, 22; Morgan McLeland, 21; and Cody Brown, 21; of injuries sustained in the crash; in Laramie, Wyo., Sept. 16.

Yushiro Yagi, 72; president of the Japan Olympic Committee; coached Japan's biathlon team at the 1972 Sapporo Olympics and skiers at the 1988 Calgary Olympics; led Japanese delegates at the opening ceremonies of the 1998 and 2000 Olympics; cause of his death was not given; in London, England, Sept. 13.

Paul (Tank) Younger, 73; first athlete from a predominantly black college (Grambling) to play in the NFL; member of the L.A. Rams' renowned "Bull Elephant" backfield (Dan Towler and Dick Hoerner) from 1949-57; sixth-leading rusher in Rams' history; front-office scout and executive with the Rams until 1975 and assistant GM with San Diego until 1987; returned to the Rams before retiring in 1995; inducted into College Football Hall of Fame in 2000; after a long illness; in Inglewood, Calif., Sept. 15.

Henry (Smokey) Yunick, 77; pioneer stock-car mechanic who worked for years out of the self-proclaimed "Best Damn Garage in Town" in Daytona Beach, Fla.; helped develop Chevrolet's original small-block engine; his cars won series titles in 1951 and 1953 and four of the first eight major stock car races run at Daytona, starting in 1959; inducted into International Motorsports Hall of Fame in 1990; of leukemia; in Daytona Beach, Fla., May 9.

Emil Zatopek, 78; legendary Czech-born track champion who won four Olympic gold medals and was a cult hero in his home country; held 18 world records; won gold medal at 1948 Olympics and his unprecedented three-gold performance in 1952 (5,000, 10,000 and marathon) in which he set Olympic records in three events, solidified his place in the highest class of track stars; first long distance runner to run a 10,000-meter race in under 29 minutes; his hunched shoulders and grimacing expression made him one of the sport's most recognizable runners; retired from running in 1958; continued to be a public figure after being stripped of his colonel's rank in Czechoslovakia's Communist army for supporting reform efforts in 1968; became first Czech athlete to be awarded the U.N.'s Pierre de Coubertin Prize for promoting fair play; suffered a stroke in Oct. 2000; cause of his death was not given; in Prague, Czech Republic, Nov. 22, 2000.

Mohamed Zerguini, 79; an IOC member since 1974, he was the eighth-longest serving delegate at the time of his death; one of 10 members reprimanded for his role in the Salt Lake City vote-buying scandal; Algerian Olympic Committee president from 1968-84; cause of his death was not given; in Algiers, Algeria, June 21.

RESEARCH MATERIAL

Many sources were used in the gathering of information for this almanac. Day-to-day material was almost always found in copies of *USA Today*, *The Boston Globe*, and *The New York Times* or online at various World Wide Web addresses (see below).

Several weekly and bi-weekly periodicals were also used in the past year's pursuit of facts and figures, among them— *Baseball America*, *Boxing Digest*, *ESPN the Magazine*, *FIFA News* (Soccer), *The Hockey News*, *The NCAA News*, *Soccer America*, *Sports Illustrated*, *The Sporting News*, *Street & Smith's Sports Business Journal*, *Track & Field News* and *USA Today Baseball Weekly*.

In addition, the following books provided background material for one or more chapters of the almanac.

Arenas & Ballparks

The Ballparks, by Bill Shannon and George Kalinsky; Hawthorn Books, Inc. (1975); New York.
Diamonds, by Michael Gershman; Houghton Mifflin Co. (1993); Boston.
Green Cathedrals (Revised Edition), by Philip Lowry; Addison-Wesley Publishing Co. (1992); Reading, Mass.
The NFL's Encyclopedic History of Professional Football, Macmillan Publishing Co. (1977); New York.
Take Me Out to the Ballpark, by Lowell Reidenbaugh; The Sporting News Publishing Co. (1983); St. Louis.
24 Seconds to Shoot (An Informal History of the NBA), by Leonard Koppett; Macmillan Publishing Co. (1968); New York.

Auto Racing

Indy: 75 Years of Racing's Greatest Spectacle, by Rich Taylor; St. Martin's Press (1991); New York.
2001 CART FedEx Championship Series Media Guide; Championship Auto Racing Teams; Troy, Mich.
2001 Pep Boys Indy Racing League Media Guide, by IMS Publications; Indianapolis.
2001 NASCAR Winston Cup Series Media Guide, compiled and edited by Sports Marketing Enterprises; NASCAR Winston Cup Series; Winston-Salem, N.C.
Marlboro Grand Prix Guide, 1950-2000 (2001 Edition), compiled by Jacques Deschenaux and Claude Michele Deschenaux; Charles Stewart & Company Ltd; Brentford, England.
NASCAR Online, produced by Turner Sports Interactive, http://www.nascar.com
CART Online, maintained by CART and VFX Digital Solutions, http://www.cart.com
Indy Racing Online, maintained by IRL, http://www.indyracingleague.com
NHRA Online, maintained by NHRA, http://www.nhra.com

Baseball

The All-Star Game (A Pictorial History, 1933 to Present), by Donald Honig; The Sporting News Publishing Co. (1987); St. Louis.
The Baseball Chronology, edited by James Charlton; Macmillan Publishing Co. (1991); New York.
The Baseball Encyclopedia (Ninth Edition), editorial director, Rick Wolff; Macmillan Publishing Co. (1993); New York.
The Complete 2001 Baseball Record Book, edited by Craig Carter; The Sporting News Publishing Co.; St. Louis.
The Scrapbook History of Baseball by Jordan Deutsch, Richard Cohen, Roland Johnson and David Neft; Bobbs-Merrill Company, Inc. (1975); Indianapolis/New York.
2001 Sporting News Official Baseball Guide, edited by Craig Carter and Dave Sloan; The Sporting News Publishing Co.; St. Louis.
2001 Sporting News Official Baseball Register, edited by Jeff Paur, David Walton, John Duxbury; The Sporting News Publishing Co.; St. Louis.
The Sports Encyclopedia: Baseball (1996 Edition), edited by David Neft and Richard Cohen; St. Martin's Press; New York.
Total Baseball (Seventh Edition), edited by John Thorn, Pete Palmer and Michael Gershman; Total Sports Publishing (2001); Kingston, NY.
The Official Site of Major League Baseball, produced by Major League Baseball Properties, Inc., http://www.mlb.com

College Basketball

All the Moves (A History of College Basketball), by Neil D. Issacs; J.B. Lippincott Company (1975); New York.
College Basketball, U.S.A. (Since 1892), by John D. McCallum; Stein and Day (1978); New York.
Collegiate Basketball: Facts and Figures on the Cage Sport, by Edwin C. Caudle; The Paragon Press (1960); Montgomery, Ala.
The Encyclopedia of the NCAA Basketball Tournament, written and compiled by Jim Savage; Dell Publishing (1990); New York.
The Final Four (Reliving America's Basketball Classic), compiled by Billy Reed; Host Communications, Inc. (1988); Lexington, Ky.
2000 NCAA Final Four Records Book, compiled by Gary Johnson; edited by Marty Benson; NCAA Books; Indianapolis, Ind.
The Modern Encyclopedia of Basketball (Second Revised Edition), edited by Zander Hollander; Dolphins Books (1979); Doubleday & Company, Inc.; Garden City, N.Y.
2000 NCAA Men's Records Book, compiled by Gary Johnson and Sean Straziscar; edited by Marty Benson; NCAA Books; Indianapolis, Ind.
2000 NCAA Women's Records Book, compiled by Richard M. Campbell and Jenifer L. Scheibler; edited by Vanessa L. Abell; NCAA Books; Indianapolis, Ind.
NCAA Online, produced by National Collegiate Athletic Association, http://www.ncaa.org
Plus many 2000-2001 NCAA Division I conference guides from America East to the WAC.

Pro Basketball

The Official NBA Basketball Encyclopedia (Third Edition), edited by Jan Hubbard; Doubleday (2000); New York.
2000-01 Sporting News Official NBA Guide; The Sporting News Publishing Co.; St. Louis.
2000-01 Sporting News Official NBA Register, edited by David Walton and John Hareas; The Sporting News Publishing Co.; St. Louis.
NBA Online, produced by NBA Media Ventures, LLC, ESPN Internet Ventures and/or Starwave Corporation, http://www.nba.com

Bowling

1995 Bowlers Journal Annual & Almanac; Luby Publishing; Chicago.
2001 PWBA Guide, Professional Women's Bowling Association; Rockford, Ill.
1999 PBA Media Guide; Professional Bowlers Association; Akron, Ohio.
PBA Online, produced by the Pro Bowlers Association, http://www.pba.com
PWBA Online, produced by Professional Women's Bowling Association, http://www.pwba.com

Boxing

The Boxing Record Book (1996), edited by Phill Marder; Fight Fax Inc.; Sicklerville, N.J.
The Ring 1985 Record Book & Boxing Encyclopedia, edited by Herbert G. Goldman; The Ring Publishing Corp.; New York.
The Ring: Boxing, The 20th Century, Steven Farhood, editor-in-chief; BDD Illustrated Books (1993); New York.

College Sports

1994-95 National Collegiate Championships, edited by Ted Breidenthal; NCAA Books; Overland Park, Kan.

1996-97 NAIA Championships History and Records Book; National Assn. of Intercollegiate Athletics; Tulsa, Okla.

1999-2000 National Directory of College Athletics, edited by Kevin Cleary; Collegiate Directories, Inc.; Cleveland.

NCAA Online, produced by National Collegiate Athletic Association, http://www.ncaa.org

College Football

Football: A College History, by Tom Perrin; McFarland & Company, Inc. (1987); Jefferson, N.C.

Football: Facts & Figures, by Dr. L.H. Baker; Farrar & Rinehart, Inc. (1945); New York.

Great College Football Coaches of the Twenties and Thirties, by Tim Cohane; Arlington House (1973); New Rochelle, N.Y.

2000 NCAA College Football Records Book, compiled by Richard M. Campbell, John Painter and Sean Straziscar; edited by Scott Deitch; NCAA Books; Indianapolis, Ind.

Saturday Afternoon, by Richard Whittingham; Workman Publishing Co., Inc. (1985); New York.

Saturday's America, by Dan Jenkins; Sports Illustrated Books; Little, Brown & Company (1970); Boston.

Tournament of Roses, The First 100 Years, by Joe Hendrickson; Knapp Press (1989); Los Angeles.

NCAA Online, produced by National Collegiate Athletic Association, http://www.ncaa.org

Plus numerous college football team and conference guides, especially the 2000 guides compiled by the Atlantic Coast Conference, Big Ten, Big 12 and Southeastern Conference.

Pro Football

2000 Canadian Football League Guide, compiled by the CFL Communications Dept.; Toronto.

The Football Encyclopedia (The Complete History of NFL Football from 1892 to the Present), compiled by David Neft and Richard Cohen; St. Martin's Press (1994); New York.

The Official NFL Encyclopedia, by Beau Riffenburgh; New American Library (1986); New York.

Official NFL 1999 Record and Fact Book, compiled by the NFL Communications Dept. and Seymour Siwoff, Elias Sports Bureau; edited by Chris McCloskey and Matt Marini; produced by NFL Properties, Inc.; Los Angeles.

The Scrapbook History of Pro Football, by Richard Cohen, Jordan Deutsch, Roland Johnson and David Neft; Bobbs-Merrill Company, Inc. (1976); Indianapolis/New York.

2000 Sporting News Football Guide, edited by Craig Carter, Terry Shea and Christen Sager; The Sporting News Publishing Co.; St. Louis.

2000 Sporting News Football Register, edited Brendan Roberts; The Sporting News Publishing Co.; St. Louis.

1995 Sporting News Super Bowl Book, edited by Tom Dienhart, Joe Hoppel and Dave Sloan; The Sporting News Publishing Co.; St. Louis.

Total Football II, edited by Bob Carroll, Michael Gershman, David Neft and John Thorn; HarperCollins; New York.

NFL.Com, produced by Starwave Corp., http://www.nfl.com

CFL Online, produced by SLAMI Sports, http://www.cfl.ca

Golf

The Encyclopedia of Golf (Revised Edition), compiled by Nevin H. Gibson; A.S. Barnes and Company (1964); New York.

Guinness Golf Records: Facts and Champions, by Donald Steel; Guinness Superlatives Ltd. (1987); Middlesex, England.

The History of the PGA Tour, by Al Barkow; Doubleday (1989); New York.

The Illustrated History of Women's Golf, by Rhonda Glenn, Taylor Publishing Co. (1991); Dallas.

2001 LPGA Player Guide, produced by LPGA Communications Dept.; Ladies Professional Golf Assn. Tour; Daytona Beach, Fla.

2000 PGA Tour Guide, written and edited by Chuck Adams, James Cramer, Nelson Luis and Lee Patterson; Professional Golfers Assn. Tour; Ponte Vedra, Fla.

Official Guide of the PGA Championships; Triumph Books (1994); Chicago.

The PGA World Golf Hall of Fame Book, by Gerald Astor, Prentice Hall Press (1991); New York.

2000 Senior PGA Tour Guide, written and edited by Dave Senko, Phil Stambaugh and Joan Von Thron-Alexander; Professional Golfers Assn. Tour; Ponte Vedra, Fla.

Pro-Golf 2000, PGA European Tour Media Guide, Virginia Water, Surrey, England.

The Random House International Encyclopedia of Golf, by Malcolm Campbell; Random House (1991); New York.

USGA Record Books (1895-1959, 1960-80 and 1981-90); U.S. Golf Association; Far Hills, N.J.

LPGA.com, produced by the LPGA and Ignite Sports Media LLC., http://www.lpga.com

PGA.com, produced by the PGA of America, http://www.pgaonline.com

PGATour.com, produced by PGA Tour Inc., http://www.pgatour.com

Hockey

Canada Cup '87: The Official History, No.1 Publications Ltd.; Toronto.

The Complete Encyclopedia of Hockey; edited by Zander Hollander; Visible Ink Press (1993); Detroit.

The Hockey Encyclopedia, by Stan Fischler and Shirley Walton Fischler; research editor, Bob Duff; Macmillan Publishing Co. (1983); New York.

Hockey Hall of Fame (The Official History of the Game and Its Greatest Stars), by Dan Diamond and Joseph Romain; Doubleday (1988); New York.

The National Hockey League, by Edward F. Dolan Jr.; W H Smith Publishers Inc. (1986); New York.

The Official National Hockey League 75th Anniversary Commemorative Book, edited by Dan Diamond; McClelland & Stewart, Inc. (1991); Toronto.

2000-01 Official NHL Guide & Record Book, compiled by the NHL Public Relations Dept.; New York/Montreal/Toronto.

2000-01 Sporting News Hockey Guide, edited by Craig Carter; The Sporting News Publishing Co.; St. Louis.

2000-01 Sporting News Hockey Register, edited by David Walton; The Sporting News Publishing Co.; St. Louis.

The Stanley Cup, by Joseph Romain and James Duplacey; Gallery Books (1989); New York.

The Trail of the Stanley Cup (Volumns I-III), by Charles L. Coleman; Progressive Publications Inc. (1969); Sherbrooke, Quebec.

Total Hockey (Second Edition), edited by Dan Diamond, et al.; Total Sports Publishing; Kingston, N.Y.

NHL.com, produced by the NHL Interactive Cyber Enterprises, http://www.nhl.com

Horse Racing

1999 NTRA Media Guide, compiled by the National Thoroughbred Racing Association; New York.

1997 American Racing Manual, compiled by the Daily Racing Form; Hightstown, N.J.

1997 Breeders' Cup Statistics; Breeders' Cup Limited; Lexington, Ky.

1996 Directory and Record Book, Thoroughbred Racing Associations of North America Inc.; Elkton, Md.

2000 Trotting and Pacing Guide, compiled and edited by John Pawlak; United States Trotting Association; Columbus, Ohio.

USTA online, produced by the USTA, http://www.ustrotting.com

NTRA online, hosted by Equibase, http://www.ntra.com

Equibase.com, hosted by Equibase, http://www.equibase.com

International Sports

Athletics: A History of Modern Track and Field (1860-1990, Men and Women), by Roberto Quercetani; Vallardi & Associati (1990); Milan, Italy.

1999 International Track & Field Annual, Association of Track & Field Statisticians; edited by Peter Matthews; SportsBooks Ltd.; Surrey, England.

Track & Field News' Little Blue Book; Metric conversion tables; From the editors of *Track & Field News* (1989); Los Altos, Calif.

US Ski Team online, produced by US Ski Team and SportsLine USA, http://www.usskiteam.com

Miscellaneous

The America's Cup 1851-1987 (Sailing for Supremacy), by Gary Lester and Richard Sleeman; Lester-Townsend Publishing (1986); Sydney, Australia.

The Encyclopedia of Sports (Fifth Revised Edition), by Frank G. Menke; revisions by Suzanne Treat; A.S. Barnes and Co., Inc. (1975); Cranbury, N.J.

ESPN SportsCentury, edited by Michael McCambridge; Hyperion (1999); New York.

The Great American Sports Book, by George Gipe; Doubleday & Company, Inc. (1978); Garden City, N.Y.

The 2001 Time/Information Please Almanac, edited by Borgna Brunner; Family Education Network; Boston.

1999 Official PRCA Media Guide, edited by Steve Fleming; Professional Rodeo Cowboys Association; Colorado Springs.

The Sail Magazine Book of Sailing, by Peter Johnson; Alfred A. Knopf (1989); New York.

Ten Years of the Ironman, Triathlete Magazine; October, 1988; Santa Monica, Calif.

The Ultimate Book of Sports Lists, by Mike Meserole; DK Publishing (1999); New York.

Iditarod online, produced by the Iditarod Trail Committtee and GCI, http://www.iditarod.com

PRCA online, produced by the Pro Rodeo Cowboys Association, http://www.prorodeo.com

Olympics

All That Glitters Is Not Gold (An Irreverent Look at the Olympic Games); by William O. Johnson, Jr.; G.P. Putnam's Sons (1972); New York.

Barcelona/Albertville 1992; edited by Lisa H. Albertson; for U.S. Olympic Committee by Commemorative Publications; Salt Lake City.

Chamonix to Lillehammer (The Glory of the Olympic Winter Games); edited by Lisa H. Albertson; for U.S. Olympic Committee by Commemorative Publication (1994); Salt Lake City.

The Complete Book of the Olympics (1992 Edition); by David Wallechinsky; Little, Brown and Co.; Boston.

The Games Must Go On (Avery Brundage and the Olympic Movement), by Allen Guttmann; Columbia University Press (1984); New York.

The Golden Book of the Olympic Games, edited by Erich Kamper and Bill Mallon; Vallardi & Associati (1992); Milan, Italy.

Hitler's Games (The 1936 Olympics), by Duff Hart-Davis; Harper & Row (1986); New York/London.

An Illustrated History of the Olympics (Third Edition); by Dick Schaap; Alfred A. Knopf (1975); New York.

The Nazi Olympics, by Richard D. Mandell; Souvenir Press (1972); London.

The Official USOC Book of the 1984 Olympic Games, by Dick Schaap; Random House/ABC Sports; New York.

The Olympics: A History of the Games, by William Oscar Johnson; Oxmoor House (1992); Birmingham, Ala.

Pursuit of Excellence (The Olympic Story), by The Associated Press and Grolier; Grolier Enterprises Inc. (1979); Danbury, Conn.

The Story of the Olympic Games (776 B.C. to 1948 A.D.), by John Kieran and Arthur Daley; J.B. Lippincott Company (1948); Philadelphia/New York.

United States Olympic Books (Seven Editions): 1936 and 1948-88; U.S. Olympic Association; New York.

The USA and the Olympic Movement, produced by the USOC Information Dept.; edited by Gayle Plant; U.S. Olympic Committee (1988); Colorado Springs.

Soccer

The American Encyclopedia of Soccer, edited by Zander Hollander; Everest House Publishers (1980); New York.

The European Football Yearbook (1994-95 Edition), edited by Mike Hammond; Sports Projects Ltd; West Midlands, England.

The Guinness Book of Soccer Facts & Feats, by Jack Rollin; Guinness Superlatives Ltd. (1978); Middlesex, England.

History of Soccer's World Cup, by Michael Archer; Chartwell Books, Inc. (1978); Secaucus, N.J.

The Simplest Game, by Paul Gardner; Collier Books (1994); New York.

The Story of the World Cup, by Brian Glanville; Faber and Faber Limited (1993); London/Boston.

2001 MLS Official Media Guide, edited by the MLS Communications staff; Los Angeles.

1991-92 MSL Official Guide, Major (Indoor) Soccer League; Overland Park, Kan.

FIFA online, produced by FIFA, http://www.fifa.com

MLSnet, produced by Major League Soccer, http://mlsnet.com

Tennis

Bud Collins' Modern Encyclopedia of Tennis, edited by Bud Collins and Zander Hollander; Visible Ink Press (1994); Detroit.

The Illustrated Encyclopedia of World Tennis, by John Haylett and Richard Evans; Exeter Books (1989); New York.

Official Encyclopedia of Tennis, edited by the staff of the U.S. Lawn Tennis Assn.; Harper & Row (1972); New York.

2000 ATP Tour Player Guide, edited by Greg Sharko; Association of Tennis Professionals Tour Publications; Ponte Vedra Beach, Fla.

2001 Sanex WTA Tour Media Guide, compiled by Sanex WTA Public Relations staff; Stamford, Conn.

ATP Tour online, produced by ATP Tour, Inc., http://www.atptour.com

WTA Tour Site, produced by the WTA Tour, http://www.wtatour.com

Who's Who

The Guinness International Who's Who of Sport, edited by Peter Mathews, Ian Buchanan and Bill Mallon; Guinness Publishing (1993); Middlesex, England.

101 Greatest Athletes of the Century, by Will Grimsley and the Associated Press Sports Staff; Bonanza Books (1987); Crown Publishers, Inc.; New York.

The New York Times Book of Sports Legends, edited by Joseph Vecchione; Simon & Schuster (1991); New York.

Superstars, by Frank Litsky; Vineyard Books, Inc. (1975); Secaucus, N.J.

A Who's Who of Sports Champions (Their Stories and Records), by Ralph Hickok, Houghton Mifflin Co. (1995); Boston.

Other Reference Books/Sites

Facts & Dates of American Sports, by Gorton Carruth & Eugene Ehrlich; Harper & Row, Publishers, Inc. (1988); New York.

Sports Market Place 1997 (January edition), edited by Kevin J. Myers; Franklin Quest Sports; Phoenix, Ariz.

The World Book Encyclopedia (1988 Edition); World Book, Inc.; Chicago.

The World Book Yearbook (Annual Supplements, 1954-95); World Book, Inc.; Chicago.

ESPN.com, produced by ESPN and Starwave Corp., http://espn.go.com

CBS SportsLine, produced by CBS and SportsLine USA, http://www.sportsline.com